Additional Content Online or on CD

Paragraph numbers in the main text marked with a "+", together with a 🖰 symbol in the margin, denote content available only on *White Book on Westlaw UK* and the *Civil Procedure CD*.

See page v and the list of content available online and on CD on page xiii for further details.

CIVIL PROCEDURE

Volume 2

The Civil Procedure Rules and Practice Directions contained in this volume are up-to-date to April 6, 2009. For further updates, see http://www.sweetandmaxwell.co.uk/whitebook.

Civil Procedure Rules Online and Forms Alerter—Password

To access the White Book Civil Procedure Rules website and to register for the Forms Alerter service you will need to enter the following password:

WB2009

LONDON

SWEET & MAXWELL

2009

Published in 2009 by Thomson Reuters (Legal) Limited
(Registered in England & Wales, Company No 1679046.
Registered Office and address for service:
100 Avenue Road, London, NW3 3PF) trading as Sweet & Maxwell.
Table of International and European Legislation and Additional Content Online and
On CD Contents typeset by Hobbs the Printers Ltd, Totton, Hampshire. All other
typesetting by Sweet & Maxwell electronic publishing system.
Printed by L.E.G.O. S.p.A., Lavis (TN), Italy.
For further information on our products and services, visit
www.sweetandmaxwell.co.uk.

*No natural forests were destroyed to make this product; only farmed timber was used
and replanted.*

British Library Cataloguing in Publication Data
A catalogue record for this book is available from the British Library

ISBN 978-1-84703-824-1

ADDITIONAL CONTENT ONLINE AND ON CD

A selection of existing content, together with brand new content, is available only on *White Book on Westlaw UK* and the *Civil Procedure CD*. This process has been started principally with Vol.2. We welcome any feedback—please email *whitebook@sweetandmaxwell.co.uk*

Please refer to the separate Additional Content Online and on CD list on page xiii for a detailed list of this material.

In order to assist navigation and to draw your attention to the relocated material, a ⌨ symbol is placed in the margin of the main text.

In tandem with the ⌨ symbol a system of cross-references is used. References to the relocated material are placed at the beginning of statutes or sections to flag that some or all of the content is online or and on CD only. References also appear within statutes or sections where a selection of material has been relocated. The latter alerts readers to relocated paragraph numbers and statutory sections (and relevant commentary).

Paragraph numbers marked with a "+" appear in the tables and index. The "+" denotes electronic content. Similar paragraph numbers appear in the cross-references mentioned above and within the statutory arrangement of sections.

On *White Book on Westlaw UK* and the *Civil Procedure CD*, the "+" paragraph numbers appear in their correct places, with the additional content remaining inline.

CONTENTS

See page xiii for a list of additional content online and on CD.

CONTENTS

See page xiii for a list of additional content online and on CD.

CONTENTS

See page xiii for a list of additional content online and on CD.

CONTENTS

See page xiii for a list of additional content online and on CD.

CONTENTS

See page xiii for a list of additional content online and on CD.

Contents

See page xiii for a list of additional content online and on CD

ADDITIONAL CONTENT ONLINE
AND ON CD

This is a list of content and associated commentary available **only** on **White Book on Westlaw UK** or the **Civil Procedure CD**. This list does not refer to print content (please see the previous print contents on page vii).

We welcome any feedback—please email whitebook@sweetandmaxwell.co.uk.

VOLUME ONE

VOLUME TWO

9B Other Statutes and Regulations

SERVICE INFORMATION

The White Book Service 2009

During 2008 we undertook a range of research with subscribers in order to help steer the continuing development of the White Book Service. As in previous years, we received a good response to our annual subscriber survey, which was followed up by a number of face-to-face interviews. Thank you to all who participated. A reminder that we welcome feedback from subscribers throughout the year—please email *whitebook@sweetandmaxwell.co.uk*.

Additional Content Online and on CD

A selection of existing content, together with brand new content, is available only on *White Book on Westlaw UK* and the *Civil Procedure CD*. We have started this process principally with Vol.2. Please refer to the Additional Content Online and on CD on page xiii for a detailed list.

In order to assist navigation and to draw your attention to the relocated material, a ⤸ symbol is placed in the margin of the text.

In tandem with the ⤸ symbol, a system of cross-references is used. References to relocated material are placed at the beginning of statutes or sections to flag that some or all of the content is online and on CD only. References also appear within statutes or sections where a selection of material has been relocated. The latter alerts readers to relocated paragraph numbers and statutory sections (and relevant commentary).

Paragraph numbers marked with a "+" symbol appear in the tables and index. The "+" symbol denotes electronic content. Similar paragraph numbers appear in the cross-references mentioned above and within the statutory arrangement of sections.

On *White Book on Westlaw UK* and the *Civil Procedure CD*, the "+" paragraph numbers appear in their correct places, with the additional content online and on CD remaining inline.

Up-to-date to April 6, 2009

Civil Procedure published on April 9, 2009. The Rules and Practice Directions have been updated to include changes introduced by the Civil Procedure (Amendment No.2) Rules 2008 (SI 2008/3085), in force on December 4, 2008 and TSO Update 48, and Civil Procedure (Amendment No.3) Rules 2008 (SI 2008/3327), in force April 6, 2009 and TSO Update 49. Amendments announced after April 6 will be published in the updating supplements in July and December. Notes have been included to indicate the in-force date of changes where necessary.

For further updates see **http://www.sweetandmaxwell.co.uk/ whitebook**. You will need to enter your subscriber password: **WB2009**. This site contains the latest Civil Procedure Rules and Practice Directions. Changes which have been introduced since *The White Book* published in April are highlighted in red.

Every effort has been made to ensure that the commentary and case law is as stated at April 6, 2009. *Civil Procedure News* and the two updating supplements will keep you abreast of developments through the subscription year.

Forms

The Forms Volume is no longer automatically included in the White Book Service (for new subscribers). New subscribers may order the Forms Volume separately. However, all subscribers will continue to be updated with the latest forms by way of receiving the Forms Release. We do ask that you keep your Forms Volume from one year to the next and update by way of filing the releases supplied, particularly as we cross-refer from the text of the CPR to forms in the Forms Volume and Forms CD in greater numbers this year. We avoid the duplication of forms in both the main volumes and the Forms Volume. This now includes Practice Direction forms, for which there is a new section in the Forms Volume and Forms CD.

The forms release is nominally published three times a year. In 2009, again in response to customer requests, we will not publish a paper forms release with the two supplements unless the number of new or amended forms released by the MOJ demands it (we will continue to release the Forms CD as normal). You will find a paper forms release released with the main volumes, which is the twenty-second release.

Electronic forms on the Forms and the White Book CDs are available in two formats—RTF/Word and PDF.

As a basic requirement, all 600-odd court forms and notes are available in RTF/Word format, just under 500 are also available as interactive PDFs, while 80 PDFs are able to be edited and saved using Adobe functionality.

Of course, you may wish to sign up to receive our Forms email alerter service. An email notice is sent to you when new court forms are published by the Court Service. You can also download forms from our website: **http://www.sweetandmaxwell.co.uk/whitebook**. You will need to enter the password: **WB2009**.

You may also wish to sign up to receive our email alerter service to notify you of changes to the Civil Procedure Rules as they are introduced by Statutory Instrument and as the changes come into force. This service is also available on **http:// www.sweetandmaxwell.co.uk/whitebook**.

Civil Procedure Forms CD and Adobe forms

Your 2009 subscription includes a CD-ROM containing all the forms provided in the Civil Procedure Forms Volume. We publish these forms as RTF/Word documents and PDFs. In addition, we have converted 80 PDFs of the most commonly used forms to allow edit and save functionality. See the accompanying Quick Reference Card for full details of this new service.

A reminder to register for the Forms Email Alerter Service—go to **http://www.sweetandmaxwell.co.uk/whitebook** to register to receive an email notice when new court forms are published by the Court Service. You can also download the forms from our website. You will need to enter the password: **WB2009**.

If you were a subscriber to the White Book Service in 2008, please remember to retain your *White Book Forms Volume*. This will continue to be updated during the 2009 subscription year. The twenty-second forms release is included with this new edition.

How to use Civil Procedure 2009

As ever, we have endeavoured to ensure that the content of *The White Book* is presented logically. The Civil Procedure Rules are reproduced in bold type to ensure they are easily distinguished from editorial comment and Practice Directions. Notes have been added to provide a full record of the changes to the Civil Procedure Rules. CPR Part numbers have been added to the thumb tabs at the side of each page.

Please refer to your User Guide which walks you through the navigational features and various components of *The White Book Service*, including the new cross-references to the additional content on-line and on CD.

Volume 1

The Civil Procedure Rules and Practice Directions (including Schs 1 and 2 containing those RSC and CCR still in force) are contained in Vol.1 with the following exceptions:

- *CPR on Specialist lists*—CPR Pts 58–63 (dealing with the Commercial Court, the Mercantile Courts, the Technology and Construction Court, Admiralty Claims and Arbitrations, and Patents and Other Intellectual Property Claims) are set out in Vol.2, Section 2.

- *CPR Pt 49—Specialist proceedings* —the proceedings dealt with under the Practice Direction to Pt 49 (Proceedings under the Companies Acts) are set out in Vol.2, Section 2.

Miscellaneous Practice Directions, Pre-Action Protocols, procedural guides and a guide to time limits are also reproduced in Vol.One.

Volume 2

The main elements of Vol.2 are the specialist areas of practice and procedure: the specialist lists dealt with by CPR Pts 58–63 and the specialist proceedings under CPR Pt 49, other specialist proceedings (e.g. Housing and Consumer) and procedural legislation. Volume 2 also includes Litigation and Procedural Topics such as Interim Remedies and Alternative Dispute Resolution.

A quick guide to finding key materials is set out below. See the separate User Guide for further information.

How to find ...

... CPR Rules and Supplementary Practice Directions (Vol.1, Section A)
The Civil Procedure Rules and Practice Directions are contained in Section A, which adopts the following paragraph system.

Part 3, r.1	para. **3.1**
Commentary to Part 3, r.1	para.3.1.**1**, (3.1.**2** etc.)
Practice Direction supplementing Part 3	para. 3**PD**.1
Second Practice Direction supplementing Part 3	para.3**BPD**.1

The paragraph numbers appear at the top outside corner of each page.

... Rules of the Supreme Court, County Court Rules and Supplementary Practice Directions
Section A also contains the re-enacted Rules of the Supreme Court and County Court Rules, with all supplementary Practice Directions. The following paragraph system is used:

RSC Order 52, r.1	para.**sc**52.1
Commentary to RSC Order 52.1	para.sc52.1.**1**, (sc52.1.**2** etc.)
Practice Direction supplementing Order 52	para.sc**pd**52.1
CCR Order 1, r.6	para.**cc**1.6
Commentary to CCR Order 1, r.6	para.cc1.6.**1**

... Miscellaneous Practice Direction (Vol.1, Section B)
Practice Directions which are not supplementary to a rule (e.g. the Practice Direction on Insolvency Proceedings) are contained in Section B, which adopts the following paragraph system.

Practice Direction Insolvency Proceedings, etc.	para.B1-001

... Pre-Action Protocols (Vol.1, Section C)
The Pre-Action Protocols are contained in Section C, which adopts the following paragraph system:

Practice Direction—Protocols	para.C0–001
Pre-Action Protocol for Personal Injury Claims	para.C1-001

... Chancery Guide
The Chancery Guide Appears in Section 1 of Vol.2 and is numbered para.1-1 onwards.

... Specialist Practice Directions under CPR Parts 58-63 and Specialist Court Guides, Applications under the Companies Act
Specialist Proceedings under CPR Parts 58-63 and Specialist Court Guides, Applications under the Companies Act appear in Section 2 of Vol.2 as follows:

CPR 58	Commercial Court
CPR 59	Mercantile Courts
CPR 60	Technology and Construction Courts

CPR 61	Admiralty Claims
CPR 62	Arbitration Claims
CPR 63	Patents and other Intellectual Property Claims
Practice Direction to CPR 49	Applications Under the Companies Act

... Forms
The forms are located in the Civil Procedure Forms Volume and on the Forms CD.

... Litigation and Procedural Topics...
These are located at the end of Vol.2 in Sections 11 to 15.

Service Elements

The White Book Service allows you to choose a customised product to suit your requirements.

Civil Procedure CD and Print Service
Annual subscription includes:
CD (includes all content in Vols 1 and 2 and the Forms Volume and additional research materials)
Civil Procedure 2009 Vol.1
Civil Procedure 2009 Vol.2
Civil Procedure Forms Updates
Civil Procedure Forms Volume (on request to new subscribers)
Two paper supplements
Civil Procedure News (10 issues a year)
Internet-based primary law updating
Forms email Alerter Service
Rules email Alerter Service
Subscription price: £499 plus VAT

Civil Procedure Volumes 1 and 2
Annual subscription includes:
Civil Procedure 2009 Vol.1
Civil Procedure 2009 Vol.2
Civil Procedure Forms CD
Civil Procedure Forms Updates
Civil Procedure Forms Volume (on request to new subscribers)
Two paper supplements
Civil Procedure News (10 issues a year)
Internet-based primary law updating
Forms email Alerter Service
Rules email Alerter Service
Subscription price: £429 plus VAT

Civil Procedure Volume 1
Annual subscription includes:
Civil Procedure 2009 Vol.1
Civil Procedure Forms CD
Civil Procedure Forms Updates
Civil Procedure Forms Volume (on request to new subscribers)

Two paper supplements
Civil Procedure News (10 issues a year)
Internet-based primary law updating
Forms email Alerter Service
Rules email Alerter Service
Subscription price: £329 plus VAT

Premium Online Service

Please contact our Westlaw UK helpdesk for further information on 0800 028 2200.

Customer Services

If you have a query relating to your subscription or you wish to purchase extra copies of Civil Procedure 2009, please call our Customer Services team on:

UK direct customers: 0845 600 9355

UK trade customers: 0845 082 1032

International customers: +44 (0) 1264 388560

Or you can write to:

Customer Services
Sweet & Maxwell
Freepost
PO Box 2000
Andover
SP10 9AH
United Kingdom
Website: *http://www.sweetandmaxwell.co.uk*
Email: *sweetandmaxwell.customer.services@thomson.com*

Comments and feedback

We are always pleased to receive comments and suggestions from customers. Address correspondence to: Publishing Editor, The White Book Service, Sweet & Maxwell, 100 Avenue Road, London, NW3 3PF or email *whitebook@sweetandmaxwell.co.uk*

The White Book Team
April 2009

CIVIL PROCEDURE RULES

SECTION 1

COURT GUIDES

1A   COURT GUIDES

1A   CHANCERY GUIDE

Editorial introduction

Litigants in the Chancery Division and in Chancery District Registries will need to   **1A–0**
make careful reference to the Chancery Guide. Particular attention is directed in the
Guide to administrative matters; separate parts deal with hearings before High Court
Judges, Masters and Registrars and the preparation for such hearings, including time
limits for filing bundles and skeleton arguments. Careful attention should be paid to
the need for accurate time estimates for hearings and the likely costs consequences of
inaccurate estimates.

An email protocol which is one of the appendices of the Guide was signed by the
Chancellor in April 2005. It permits the filing of skeleton arguments, chronologies and
draft orders by email but not authorities.

A new edition of the Guide was published in November 2005. As with previous editions it was issued after detailed consideration by the judges, Masters and Registrars of
the Division.

Practitioners should be aware that the Chancery Guide is from time to time updated
on the HMCS website. Such changes are reflected in the Chancery Guide as printed in
Civil Procedure.

Case Management Directions

Of particular value is Appendix 3 to the Guide. Parties preparing draft directions   **1A–0.1**
for attachment to allocation questionnaires for consideration at case management conferences in the Chancery Division or in District Registries of the Division should follow
the suggested form of directions. Parties should in every case discuss and seek to agree
procedural directions in the form set out in Appendix 3 and submit them with their
allocation questionnaires. This responsible practice assists the court in managing the
claim effectively and expeditiously. If an unusual or non-routine order is sought a
brief explanation for the court should be provided with the allocation questionnaire
and similarly if permission to adduce expert evidence is sought by the parties and if
the reason is not obvious an agreed explanation of the parties for use by the court is
appropriate.

Chancery Guide

October, 2005

Abbreviations used in this Guide: **1A–1**

Civil Procedure Rules	CPR
HM Courts Service	HMCS
Practice Direction supplementing a Civil Procedure Rule	PD
Rules of the Supreme Court 1965	RSC
Pre-trial review	PTR

Part 1 means CPR Part 1
rule 1.1 means CPR Part 1 rule 1.1

Paragraph numbers marked with a "+" can be found online and on CD.

5

PD 52 means the PD supplementing CPR Part 52

The Civil Procedure Rules (comprising Rules, Practice Directions, Pre-Action Protocols and Forms) are published by the Stationery Office. They are also published on the Department of Constitutional Affairs' website: www.dca.gov.uk. This Guide will also be found on the Chancery Division section of the Courts Service website: www.hmcourts-service.gov.uk.

As from October 2005, the effective head of the Chancery Division is the Chancellor of the High Court, formerly the Vice-Chancellor.

Preface

This is the fifth edition of the Chancery Guide. It is published ten years after the publication of the first. The changes made in the conduct of civil proceedings generally and in the Chancery Division in particular in the intervening period have been profound. The substitution of the old Rules of the Supreme Court with the Civil Procedure Rules is now virtually complete and amendments to the first editions of the Civil Procedure Rules are coming through.

As I wrote in the Preface to the fourth edition, the Chancery Guide is no substitute for the Civil Procedure Rules and associated Practice Directions. It seeks to give practical guidance on the conduct of cases in the Chancery Division within the framework of those rules and practice directions.

This edition has been produced under the supervision of Sir Lawrence Collins. I am very grateful to him for undertaking the task. The amount of work involved is considerable. It is additional to the normal workload of a judge of the Chancery Division and, in his case, to the editorial responsibility for Dicey and Morris on the Conflict of Laws. He has been assisted with regard to various topics by many others to whom I send my thanks too. It is always dangerous to mention them by name lest someone is inadvertently omitted; nevertheless I would like to pay particular tribute to: Chief Master Winegarten; Master Bragge; Registrar Derrett; Mrs V C Bell; Mr A D Parkinson; Miss R Warner; Mr J Smethurst; Mr S Adamyk.

The pattern of the last ten years has been for a new edition to appear every two to three years. The proposals for changes to civil litigation now under consideration suggest that this pattern, at least, will continue in the future. In the meantime I hope and believe that this edition will be of considerable use to all those who, in whatever capacity, have occasion to participate in litigation in the Chancery Division.

Andrew Morritt
Chancellor of the High Court
October 2005

CHAPTER 1

INTRODUCTORY

The overriding objective

1A–2 1.1 The aim of the Civil Procedure Rules and the Practice Directions which supplement them is to remove excessive delay and expense, and to improve access to justice through quicker, cheaper and more proportionate justice. As an integral part of the process, cases are closely monitored through to trial by the judiciary.

1.2 To achieve these aims, all procedural decisions under the CPR are guided by the overriding objective stated in rule 1.1. The court must deal with cases justly; dealing justly with a case includes, so far as practicable, ensuring that the parties are on an equal footing, saving expense, dealing with the case in ways which are proportionate to the sum at stake, to the importance of the case, to its complexity and to each party's financial position, ensuring expedition and fairness and allotting to each case an appropriate share of the court's resources.

About the Chancery Division

1A–3 1.3 The Chancery Division is one of the three parts, or Divisions, of the High Court of Justice, the other two being the Queen's Bench Division and the Family Division.

Paragraph numbers marked with a "+" can be found online and on CD.

The effective head of the Chancery Division is the Chancellor of the High Court ("the Chancellor"). There are currently seventeen High Court judges attached to the Division. In addition, in the Royal Courts of Justice in London, there are six judges who are referred to as Masters (one of whom is the Chief Master), and six judges who are referred to as Bankruptcy Registrars (one of whom is the Chief Registrar). In the District Registries (see Chapter 12) the work done by Masters in London is performed by District Judges. References in this Guide to a Master include, in the case of proceedings in a District Registry, references to a District Judge. Deputies sit on a regular basis for both judges and Masters. Any reference to a judge or Master in the Guide includes a reference to a person sitting as a deputy.

1.4 In general, trials of claims are heard by the judges, as are interim applications involving injunctions (including applications for freezing and search orders), while the majority of other work, including most procedural work and most post-trial work (eg accounts and inquiries) is conducted by the Masters. Masters may, however, direct that a matter be listed before a judge although they have jurisdiction, for example in the case of lengthy inquiries as to damages (see paragraphs 3.2 and 9.20 below).

1.5 The Chancery Division undertakes civil work of many kinds, including specialist work such as companies, patents and contentious probate. The range of cases heard in the Chancery Division is wide and varied. The major part of the case-load today involves business disputes of one kind or another. Often these are complex and involve substantial sums of money.

1.6 In many types of case (e.g. claims for professional negligence against solicitors, accountants, valuers or other professionals) the claimant has a choice whether to bring the claim in the Chancery Division or elsewhere in the High Court. But there are other types of case which, in the High Court, must be brought in the Chancery Division including claims (other than claims in the Commercial Court) relating to the application of Articles 81 and 82 of the EC Treaty and the equivalent provisions in the Competition Act 1998. The specialist work of the Chancery Division is dealt with in Section B of this Guide. There are also certain claims which must be started in the Chancery Division either in the High Court or in a District Registry where there is a Chancery District Registry or in the Central London Trial Centre (Chancery List).

About this Guide

1.7 The aim of this Guide is to provide additional practical information not already **1A–4** contained in the CPR or the Practice Directions supplementing them. Litigants and their advisers are expected to be familiar with the CPR. It is not the function of this Guide to summarise the CPR, nor should it be regarded as a substitute for them.

1.8 This Guide is published as part of a series of Guides to various civil courts. Where information is more readily available in another guide, this Guide may simply refer to it. A separate book contains Practice Forms for use in the Chancery Division and in the Queen's Bench Division. Some of the forms most commonly used in the Chancery Division are found in the Appendices to this Guide. Forms may also be downloaded from the HMCS website and may be found in the main procedural reference books.

1.9 Section A of this Guide is concerned with general civil work. Section B deals with specialist work. Some subjects are covered in more detail in the Appendices, and Appendix 1 sets out some contact details which may be useful.

1.10 Material which used to be contained in the Chancery Division Practice Directions and which remains relevant has been incorporated into either Section A or Section B of this Guide, as appropriate.

1.11 A reference in this Guide to a Part is to that Part of the CPR, to a rule is to the relevant rule in the CPR, unless otherwise stated, and to PD [number] is to the PD supplementing the Part so numbered, the title being given if necessary to distinguish one from another. The PD about costs, supplementing Parts 43 to 48, is called the Costs PD.

Paragraph numbers marked with a "+" can be found online and on CD.

1.12 This Guide states the position as at September 2005. During the currency of the Guide, and even in some cases before publication, there are likely to be changes in matters covered in the text, including room numbers and other contact details; these should be checked as necessary. The Guide will be kept under review in the light of practical experience and of changes to the rules and practice directions. Any comments on the text of the Guide are welcome and should be addressed to the clerk to the Chancellor.

1.13 The text of the Guide is also to be found, together with other Court Guides and other useful information concerning the administration of justice in the Chancery Division and elsewhere, on the HMCS website. Amendments will appear on the Guide on the website as appropriate: *www.hmcourts-service.gov.uk*. The Guide is also printed in the main procedural reference books.

SECTION A GENERAL CIVIL WORK

CHAPTER 2

STARTING PROCEEDINGS, SERVICE, ALLOCATION AND STATEMENTS OF CASE
Key Rules: CPR Parts 6, 7, 8, 9, 10, 15, 16, 18, 20 and 26 and CPR Schedule 1

How to start a claim

1A–5 2.1 Claims are issued out of the High Court of Justice, Chancery Division, either in the Royal Courts of Justice (Chancery Chambers) or in a District Registry. There is no Production Centre for Chancery claims.

2.2 The claim form must be issued either as a Part 7 claim under Part 7, or as a Part 8 claim under the alternative procedure for claims in Part 8.

2.3 When issuing proceedings, the general rule is that the title of the claim should contain only the names of the parties to the proceedings. To this there are four exceptions: (a) proceedings relating to the administration of an estate, which should be entitled "In the estate of AB deceased" (some cases relating to the estates of deceased Lloyd's names require additional wording: see paragraph 26.53 below); (b) contentious probate proceedings, which should be entitled "In the estate of AB deceased (probate)"; (c) proceedings under the Inheritance (Provision for Family and Dependants) Act 1975, which should be entitled "In the Matter of the Inheritance (Provision for Family and Dependants) Act 1975"; and (d) proceedings relating to pension schemes, which may be entitled "In the Matter of the [] Pension Scheme". In addition, proceedings in the Companies Court are entitled in the matter of the relevant company or other person and of the relevant legislation: see paragraph 20.5.

Service

1A–6 2.4 Part 6 applies to the service of documents, including claim forms. Unless the claimant notifies the court that he or she wishes to serve the claim form, or the court directs otherwise, it will be served by the court. Many solicitors, however, will prefer to serve the claim form themselves and will notify the court that they wish to do so.

Allocation

1A–7 2.5 The vast majority of claims issued, and all those retained, in the Chancery Division will be either expressly allocated to the multi-track or in the case of Part 8 claims, deemed allocated to that track. Chapter 13 deals with transfer to county courts.

Statements of case

1A–8 2.6 In addition to the matters which PD 16 requires to be set out specifically in the particulars of claim, a party must set out in any statement of case:

Paragraph numbers marked with a "+" can be found online and on CD.

(1) full particulars of any allegation of fraud, dishonesty, malice or illegality;

(2) where any inference of fraud or dishonesty is alleged, the facts on the basis of which the inference is alleged.

2.7 A party should not set out allegations of fraud or dishonesty unless there is material admissible in evidence to support the contentions made. Setting out such matters without such material being available may result in the particular allegations being struck out and may result in wasted costs orders being made against the legal advisers responsible.

2.8 Points of law may be set out in any statement of case, and any point to be taken under the Human Rights Act 1998 must be so set out.

2.9 In the preparation of statements of case, the guidelines in Appendix 2 should be followed.

2.10 The guidelines apply to: the claim form (unless no particulars are given in it); particulars of claim; defence; additional claims under Part 20; reply to a defence; and a response to a request for further information under Part 18.

2.11 Parties should not attach copies of documents or any expert's report to their statement of case if they are bulky.

2.12 Notwithstanding rule 15.8, claimants should if possible serve any reply before they file their allocation questionnaire. This will enable other parties to consider the reply before they file their allocation questionnaire.

Part 8 claims

2.13 This procedure is appropriate in particular where there is no substantial dispute **1A–9** of fact, such as where the case raises only questions of the construction of a document or a statute. Additionally, however, a large number of particular claims must be brought under Part 8 pursuant to PD 8. Of particular relevance will be applications to enforce charging orders by sale, contested applications with respect to funds in court, claims under the Inheritance (Provision for Family and Dependants) Act 1975 and proceedings relating to solicitors. Subject to jurisdiction, applications to enforce charging orders are now issued in the court in which the charging order was made. Proceedings to enforce charging orders made in any division of the High Court and the Court of Appeal are issued in the Chancery Division.

2.14 Provision is also made in Part 8 for a claim form to be issued without naming a defendant with the permission of the court. No separate application for permission is required where personal representatives seek permission to distribute the estate of a deceased Lloyd's name nor for applications under section 48 of the Administration of Justice Act 1985 (see further Chapter 26—Trusts). Where permission is needed, it is to be sought by application notice under Part 23.

2.15 Part 8 claims will generally be disposed of on written evidence. The features of the Part 8 procedure are:
(1) no particulars of claim
(2) no defence
(3) no allocation questionnaire
(4) no judgment in default
(5) normally no oral evidence.

2.16 Defendants who wish to contest a Part 8 claim or to take part in the proceedings should complete and file the acknowledgment of service in form N210 which accompanies the claim form. Alternatively the information required to be contained in the acknowledgment of service can be provided by letter. A party who does not wish to contest a claim should indicate that fact on the form acknowledging service or by letter.

Paragraph numbers marked with a "+" can be found online and on CD.

2.17 Claimants must file the written evidence, namely evidence by witness statement, on which they intend to rely with the claim form. Defendants are required to file and serve their evidence when they file their acknowledgment of service, namely within 14 days after service of the claim form (rule 8.5(3)). By paragraph 5.6 of PD 8, Alternative Procedure for Claims, a defendant's time for filing evidence may be extended by agreement for not more than 14 days from the filing of the acknowledgment of service. Any such agreement must be filed with the court by the defendant at the same time as he or she files an acknowledgment of service. The claimant has 14 days for filing evidence in reply but this period may be extended by agreement for not more than 28 days from service of the defendant's evidence. Again, any such agreement must be filed with the court. Any longer extension either for the defendant or the claimant requires an application to the court. It is recognised that in substantial matters the provisions in Part 8 may be burdensome upon defendants and in such matters the court will readily grant an extension. If the parties are in agreement that such an extension should be granted the application should be made in writing by letter. The parties should at all times act cooperatively.

2.18 Defendants who acknowledge service but do not intend to file evidence should notify the court in writing when they file their acknowledgment of service that they do not intend to file evidence. This enables the court to know what each defendant's intention is when it considers the file.

2.19 The general rule (exceptions include, for example, some claims under the Variation of Trusts Act 1958 or where a party has made a Part 24 application) is that the court file will be considered by the court after the time for acknowledgment of service has expired, or, if the time for serving the defendant's evidence has been extended, after the expiry of that period.

2.20 In some cases if the papers are in order the court will not require any oral hearing, but will be able to deal with the matter on paper by making a final order. In other cases the court will direct that the Part 8 claim is listed either for a disposal hearing or for a case management conference.

CHAPTER 3

THE COURT'S CASE MANAGEMENT POWERS
Key Rules: CPR rule 1.4, and Parts 3, 18, 19, 26, 29, 31, 39

1A–10 3.1 A key feature of the CPR is that cases are closely monitored by the court. Case management by the court includes: identifying disputed issues at an early stage; fixing timetables; dealing with as many aspects of the case as possible on the same occasion; controlling costs; disposing of cases summarily where they disclose no case or defence; dealing with the case without the parties having to attend court; and giving directions to ensure that the trial of a case proceeds quickly and efficiently. The court will expect the parties to co-operate with each other. Where appropriate the court will encourage the parties to use alternative dispute resolution (on which see Chapter 17) or otherwise help them settle the case. In particular, the court will readily grant a short stay at allocation or at any other stage to accommodate mediation or any other form of settlement negotiations. The court will not, however, normally, grant an open-ended stay for such purposes and if, for any reason, a lengthy stay is granted it will be on terms that the parties report to the court on a regular basis in respect of their negotiations.

3.2 In the Chancery Division case management is normally carried out by the Masters, but a judge may be nominated by the Chancellor to hear the case and to deal with the case management where it is appropriate due to the size or complexity of the case or for other reasons. A request by any or all parties for such a nomination should be addressed to the Chancellor.

Directions

1A–11 3.3 It is expected that parties and their advisers will endeavour to agree proposals for management of the case at the allocation stage in accordance with rule 29.4 and

Paragraph numbers marked with a "+" can be found online and on CD.

paragraphs 4.6 to 4.8 of PD 29. In particular, the parties should act co-operatively and seek to agree directions and a list of the issues to be tried. The court will approve the parties' proposals, if they are suitable, and give directions accordingly without a hearing. If it does not approve the agreed directions it may give modified directions or its own directions or, more usually, direct a case management conference. If the parties cannot agree directions then each party should put forward its own proposals for the future management of the case for consideration by the court. Draft orders commonly made by the Masters on allocation and at case management conferences are set out at Appendix 3, and parties drafting proposed directions for submission to a Master on allocation or at a case management conference should have regard to and make use, as appropriate, of those draft orders.

3.4 If parties do not, at the allocation stage, agree or attempt to agree directions and if, in consequence, the court is unable to give directions without ordering a case management conference, the parties should not expect to recover any costs in respect of such a case management conference.

3.5 In many claims the court will give directions without holding a case management conference.

3.6 Any party who considers that a case management conference should be held before any directions are given should so state in his or her allocation questionnaire (or, in the case of a Part 8 claim, inform the court in writing) and give reasons why he or she considers that a case management conference is required. The court when sending out allocation questionnaires will also send out a questionnaire inviting the parties to give their time estimate for any case management conference and to specify any dates or times inconvenient for the holding of a case management conference.

3.7 Wherever possible, the advocate(s) instructed or expected to be instructed to appear at the trial should attend any hearing at which case management directions are likely to be given. To this end the court when ordering a case management conference, otherwise than upon allocation, will normally send out questionnaires to the parties in respect of their availability. Parties must not, however, expect that a case management conference will be held in abeyance for a substantial length of time in order to accommodate the advocates' convenience.

3.8 Case management conferences are intended to deal with the general management of the case. They are not an opportunity to make controversial interim applications without appropriate notice to the opposing party. Accordingly, as provided by paragraph 5.8(1) of PD 29, where a party wishes to obtain an order not routinely made at a case management conference (such as an order for specific disclosure or summary disposal) such application should be made by separate Part 23 application to be heard at the case management conference and the case management conference should be listed for a sufficient period of time to allow the application to be heard. Where parties fail to comply with this paragraph it is highly unlikely that the court will entertain, other than by consent, an application which is not of a routine nature. It is the obligation of the parties to ensure that a realistic time estimate for hearings is given to the court.

3.9 Even where routine orders are sought (i.e. orders falling within the topics set out in paragraph 5.3 of PD 29) care should be taken to ensure that the opposing party is given notice of the orders intended to be sought.

Applications for information and disclosure

3.10 Before a party applies to the court for an order that another party provides him or her with any further information or specific disclosure of documents he or she must communicate directly with the other party in an attempt to reach agreement or narrow the issues before the matter is raised with the court. If not satisfied that the parties have taken steps to reach agreement or narrow the issues, the court will normally require such steps to be taken before hearing the application. **1A-12**

Paragraph numbers marked with a "+" can be found online and on CD.

Preliminary issues

1A–13 3.11 Costs can sometimes be saved by identifying decisive issues, or potentially decisive issues, and ordering that they are tried first. The decision of one issue, although not itself decisive in law of the whole case, may enable the parties to settle the remainder of the dispute. In such cases a preliminary issue may be appropriate.

3.12 At the allocation stage, at any case management conference and again at any PTR, consideration will be given to the possibility of the trial of preliminary issues the resolution of which is likely to shorten proceedings. The court may suggest the trial of a preliminary issue, but it will rarely make an order without the concurrence of at least one of the parties.

Group Litigation Orders

1A–14 3.13 Under rule 19.11, where there are likely to be a number of claims giving rise to common or related issues of fact, the court may make a Group Litigation Order ("GLO") for their case management. Such orders may be appropriate in chancery proceedings and there are a number in existence. A list of GLOs is published on the HMCS website. An application for a GLO is made under Part 23. The procedure is set out in PD 19 Group Litigation, which provides that the application should be made to the Chief Master, except for claims in a specialist list (such as the business of the Patents Court), when the application should be made to the senior judge of that list.

3.14 Claimants wishing to join in group litigation should issue proceedings in the normal way and should then apply (by letter) to be entered on the Group Register set up by a GLO. The details required for entry will be specified in the GLO. In the Chancery Division the Register is usually kept by the management court and is maintained either by the court or by the lead solicitors, as specified in the GLO. Where the Register is kept in the Chancery Division at the Royal Courts of Justice, it is kept by Mrs VC Bell, Chancery Lawyer (Room TM5.06, tel. 020 7947 6080). Any initial enquiries regarding GLOs may be addressed to her.

Trial timetable

1A–15 3.15 The judge at trial, or sometimes at the PTR, may determine the timetable for the trial. The advocates for the parties should be ready to assist the court in this respect if so required. The time estimate given for the trial should have been based on an approximate forecast of the trial timetable, and must be reviewed by each party at the stage of the PTR and as preparation for trial proceeds thereafter. If that review requires a change in the estimate the other parties' advocates and the court must be informed.

3.16 When a trial timetable is set by the court, it will ordinarily fix the time for the oral submissions and factual and expert evidence, and it may do so in greater or lesser detail. Trial timetables are always subject to any further order by the trial judge.

Pre-Trial Review

1A–16 3.17 In cases estimated to take more than 10 days and in other cases where the circumstances warrant it, the court may direct that a PTR be held (see rule 29.7).

3.18 Such a PTR will normally be heard by a judge. The date and time should be fixed with the Chancery Judges' Listing Officer. If the trial judge has already been nominated, the application will if possible be heard by that judge. The advocates' clerks must attend the Chancery Judges' Listing Officer in sufficient time so that the PTR can be fixed between four and eight weeks before the trial date.

3.19 A PTR should be attended by advocates who are to represent the parties at the trial.

Paragraph numbers marked with a "+" can be found online and on CD.

3.20 Not less than 7 days before the date fixed for the PTR the claimant, or another party if so directed by the court, must circulate a list of matters to be considered at the PTR, including proposals as to how the case should be tried, to the other parties, who must respond with their comments at least 2 days before the PTR.

3.21 The claimant, or another party if so directed by the court, should deliver a bundle containing the lists of matters to be considered and proposals served by the parties on each other and the trial timetable, together with the results of the discussions between the parties as to those matters, and any other documents the court is likely to need in order to deal with the PTR, to the Chancery Judges' Listing Office by 10am on the day before the day fixed for the hearing of the PTR.

3.22 At the PTR the court will review the state of preparation of the case, and deal with outstanding procedural matters, not limited to those apparent from the lists of matters lodged by the parties. The court may give directions as to how the case is to be tried, including directions as to the order in which witnesses are to be called (for example all witnesses of fact before all expert witnesses) or as to the time to be allowed for particular stages in the trial.

CHAPTER 4

DISCLOSURE OF DOCUMENTS AND EXPERT EVIDENCE

Key Rules: CPR Parts 18, 29, 31 and 35; PDs supplementing Parts 31 and 35

4.1 As part of its management of a case, the court will give directions about the disclosure of documents and any expert evidence. Attention is drawn to paragraphs 3.8 to 3.10 above. An application for specific disclosure should be made by a specific Part 3 application and is not to be regarded as a matter routinely dealt with at a case management conference. **1A–17**

Disclosure of Documents

4.2 Under the CPR, the normal order for disclosure is an order for standard disclosure, which requires disclosure of: **1A–18**

(1) *a party's own documents*—that is, the documents on which a party relies;

(2) *adverse documents*—that is, documents which adversely affect his or her own or another party's case or support another party's case; and

(3) *required documents*—that is, documents which a practice direction requires him or her to disclose.

4.3 The court may make an order for specific disclosure going beyond the limits of standard disclosure if it is satisfied that standard disclosure is inadequate.

4.4 The court will not make such an order readily. One of the clear principles underlying the CPR is that the burden and cost of disclosure should be reduced. The court will, therefore, seek to ensure that any specific disclosure ordered is proportionate in the sense that the cost of such disclosure does not outweigh the benefits to be obtained from such disclosure. The court will, accordingly, seek to tailor the order for disclosure to the requirements of the particular case. The financial position of the parties, the importance of the case and the complexity of the issues will be taken into account when considering whether more than standard disclosure should be ordered.

4.5 If specific disclosure is sought, the parties should give careful thought to the ways in which such disclosure can be limited, for example by requiring disclosure in stages or by requiring disclosure simply of sufficient documents to show a specified matter and so on. They should also consider whether the need for disclosure could be avoided by requiring a party to provide information under Part 18.

Expert Evidence

General

4.6 Part 35 contains particular provisions designed to limit the amount of expert **1A–19**

Paragraph numbers marked with a "+" can be found online and on CD.

evidence to be placed before the court and to reinforce the obligation of impartiality which is imposed upon an expert witness. The key question now in relation to expert evidence is the question as to what added value such evidence will provide to the court in its determination of a given case.

4.7 Fundamentally, Part 35 states that expert evidence must be restricted to what is reasonably required to resolve the proceedings and makes provision for the court to direct that expert evidence is given by a single joint expert. The parties should consider from the outset of the proceedings whether appointment of a single joint expert is appropriate.

Duties of an expert

1A-20 4.8 It is the duty of an expert to help the court on the matters within his or her expertise; this duty overrides any obligation to the person from whom the expert has received instructions or by whom he or she is paid (rule 35.3). Attention is drawn to PD 35.

4.9 In fulfilment of this duty, an expert must for instance make it clear if a particular question or issue falls outside his or her expertise or he or she considers that insufficient data are available on which to express an opinion. Any material change of view by an expert should be communicated in writing (through legal representatives) to the other parties without delay, and when appropriate to the court.

Single joint expert

1A-21 4.10 The introduction to PD 35 states that, where possible, matters requiring expert evidence should be dealt with by a single expert.

4.11 In very many cases it is possible for the question of expert evidence to be dealt with by a single expert. Single experts are, for example, often appropriate to deal with questions of quantum in cases where the primary issues are as to liability. Likewise, where expert evidence is required in order to acquaint the court with matters of expert fact, as opposed to opinion, a single expert will usually be appropriate. There remains, however, a substantial body of cases where liability will turn upon expert opinion evidence or where quantum is a primary issue and where it will be appropriate for the parties to instruct their own experts. For example, in cases where the issue for determination is as to whether a party acted in accordance with proper professional standards, it will often be of value to the court to hear the opinions of more than one expert as to the proper standard in order that the court becomes acquainted with the range of views existing upon the question and in order that the evidence can be tested in cross-examination.

4.12 It is not necessarily a sufficient objection to the making by the court of an order for a single joint expert that the parties have already appointed their own experts. An order for a single joint expert does not prevent a party from having his or her own expert to advise him or her, but he or she may well be unable to recover the cost of employing his or her own expert from the other party. The duty of an expert who is called to give evidence is to help the court.

4.13 When the use of a single joint expert is contemplated the court will expect the parties to co-operate in developing, and agreeing to the greatest possible extent, terms of reference for the expert. In most cases the terms of reference will (in particular) detail what the expert is asked to do, identify any documentary material he or she is asked to consider and specify any assumptions he or she is asked to make.

More than one expert—exchange of reports

1A-22 4.14 In an appropriate case the court will direct that experts' reports are delivered sequentially. Sequential reports may, for example, be appropriate if the service of the first expert's report would help to define and limit the issues on which such evidence may be relevant.

Paragraph numbers marked with a "+" can be found online and on CD.

Discussion between experts

4.15 The court will normally direct discussion between experts before trial. **1A–23**
Sometimes it may be useful for there to be further discussions during the trial itself.
The purpose of these discussions is to give the experts the opportunity:

(1) to discuss the expert issues; and

(2) to identify the expert issues on which they share the same opinion and those
on which there remains a difference of opinion between them (and what that
difference is).

4.16 Unless the court otherwise directs, the procedure to be adopted at these
discussions is a matter for the experts. It may be sufficient if the discussion takes place
by telephone.

4.17 Parties must not seek to restrict their expert's participation in any discussion
directed by the court, but they are not bound by any agreement on any issue reached
by their expert unless they expressly so agree.

Written questions to experts

4.18 It is emphasised that this procedure is only for the purpose (generally) of **1A–24**
seeking clarification of an expert's report where the other party is unable to
understand it. Written questions going beyond this can only be put with the
agreement of the parties or with the permission of the court. The procedure of
putting written questions to experts is not intended to interfere with the procedure
for an exchange of professional opinion in discussions between experts or to inhibit
that exchange of professional opinion. If questions that are oppressive in number or
content are put or questions are put without permission for any purpose other than
clarification of an expert's report, the court will not hesitate to disallow the questions
and to make an appropriate order for costs against the party putting them.

Request by an expert to the court for directions

4.19 An expert may file with the court a written request for directions to assist him or **1A–25**
her in carrying out his or her function as expert: rule 35.14. Copies of any such
request must be provided to the parties in accordance with rule 35.14(2) save where
the court orders otherwise. The expert should guard against accidentally informing
the court about, or about matters connected with, communications or potential
communications between the parties that are without prejudice or privileged. The
expert may properly be privy to the content of these communications because he or
she has been asked to assist the party instructing him or her to evaluate them.

Assessors

4.20 Under rule 35.15 the court may appoint an assessor to assist it in relation to any **1A–26**
matter in which the assessor has skill and experience. The report of the assessor is
made available to the parties. The remuneration of the assessor is determined by the
court and forms part of the costs of the proceedings.

CHAPTER 5

APPLICATIONS

Key Rules: CPR Parts 23 and 25, PDs 23 and 25

5.1 This Chapter deals with applications to a judge, including applications for interim **1A–27**
remedies, and applications to a Master. As regards the practical arrangements for
making, listing and adjourning applications, the Chapter is primarily concerned with
hearings at the Royal Courts of Justice. Hearings before Chancery judges outside
London are dealt with in Chapter 12.

5.2 It is most important that applications which need to be heard by a judge (e.g.

Paragraph numbers marked with a "+" can be found online and on CD.

most applications for an injunction) should be made to a judge. Any procedural application (e.g. for directions) should be made to a Master unless there is some special reason for making it to a judge. Otherwise the application may be dismissed with costs. If an application is to be made to a judge, the application notice should state that it is a judge's application.

5.3 Part 23 contains rules as to how an application may be made. In some circumstances it may be dealt with without a hearing, or by a telephone hearing.

Applications without notice

1A–28   5.4 Generally it is wrong to make an application without giving prior notice to the respondent. There are, however, two classes of exceptions.

   (1) First, there are cases where the giving of notice might frustrate the order (e.g. a search order) or where there is such urgency that there has not been time to give notice. Even in an urgent case, however, the applicant should notify the respondent informally of the application if possible, unless secrecy is essential.

   (2) Secondly, there are in the Chancery Division some procedural applications normally made without notice relating to such matters as service out of the jurisdiction, service, extension of the validity of claim forms, permission to issue writs of possession etc. All of these are properly made without notice but will be subjected by the rules to an express provision in any order made that the absent party will be entitled to apply to set aside or vary the order provided that application is so made within a given number of days of service of the order.

   (3) Thirdly, there are cases in which the defendant can only be identified by description and not by name: *Bloomsbury Publishing Group Ltd v News Group Newspapers Ltd* [2003] EWHC 1205 (Ch), [2003] 3 All ER 736. An application made without giving notice which does not fall within the classes of cases where absence of notice is justified may be dismissed or adjourned until proper notice has been given.

Applications without a hearing

1A–29   5.5 Part 23 makes provision for applications to be dealt with without a hearing. This is a useful provision in cases where the parties consent to the terms of the order sought or agree that a hearing is not necessary (often putting in written representations by letter or otherwise). It is also a useful provision in cases where, although the parties have not agreed to dispense with a hearing and the order is not consented to, the order sought by the application is, essentially, non-contentious. In such circumstances, the order made will, in any event, be treated as being made on the court's own initiative and will set out the right of any party affected by the application who has not been heard to apply to vary or set aside the order.

5.6 These provisions should not be used to deal with contentious matters without notice to the opposing party and without a hearing. Usually, this will result in delay since the court will simply order a hearing. It may also give rise to adverse costs orders. It will normally be wrong to seek an order which imposes sanctions in the event of non-compliance without notice and without a hearing. An application seeking such an order may well be dismissed.

Applications to a judge

1A–30   5.7 If an application is made to a judge in existing proceedings, e.g. for an injunction, it should be made by application notice. This is called an Interim Application. Normally three clear days' notice to the other party is required but in an emergency or for other good reason the application can be made without giving notice, or the full 3 days' notice, to the other side. Permission to serve on short notice may be obtained on application without notice to the Interim Applications judge. Such permission will not be given by the Master. Except in an emergency a party

Paragraph numbers marked with a "+" can be found online and on CD.

notifies the court of his or her wish to bring an application by delivering the requisite documents to the Chancery Judges' Listing Office (Room WG4) and paying the appropriate fee. He or she should at the same time deliver a completed "Judge's Application Information Form" in the form set out in Part 1 of Appendix 4. An application will only be listed if (1) two copies of the claim form and (2) two copies of the application notice (one stamped with the appropriate fee) are lodged in the Chancery Judges' Listing Office before 12 noon on the working day before the date for which notice of the application has been given.

5.8 The current practice is that one judge combines the functions of Interim Applications judge and Companies judge. His or her name will be found in the Daily Cause List and also in the Chancery Division Term List.

5.9 The Interim Applications judge is available to hear applications each day in term and an application notice can be served for any day in term except the last. If the volume of applications requires it, any other judge who is available to assist with Interim Applications will hear such applications as the Interim Applications judge may direct. Special arrangements are made for hearing applications out of hours and in vacation, for which see paragraphs 5.28 to 5.34 below.

5.10 At the beginning of each day's hearing the Interim Applications judge calls on each of the applications to be made that day in turn. This enables him or her to establish the identity of the parties, their state of readiness, their estimates of the duration of the hearing, and where relevant the degree of urgency of the case. On completion of this process, the judge decides the order in which he or she will hear applications and gives any other directions that may be necessary. Sometimes cases are released to other judges at this point. If cases are likely to take 2 hours or more (including pre-reading and oral delivery of judgment), the judge may order that they are given a subsequent fixed date for hearing (they are then called "Interim Applications by Order") and hears any application for a court order to last until the application is heard fully. Where on or before the day preceding the hearing it becomes likely that the time required for the application (including pre-reading and oral delivery of judgment) will exceed 2 hours, the Chancery Judges' Listing Officer (or, in appropriate cases, the clerk to the Applications Judge) must be notified immediately.

5.11 In such a case the solicitors or the clerks to counsel concerned should apply to the Chancery Judges' Listing Officer for a date for the hearing. Before so doing there must be lodged with the Chancery Judges' Listing Office a certificate signed by the advocate stating the estimated length of the hearing. Applications by order may be entered in the Interim Hearings List and, if not fixed by arrangement with the Chancery Judges' Listing Officer, will be liable to be listed for hearing in accordance with the timetable fixed by the judge.

5.12 Parties and their representatives should arrive at least ten minutes before the court sits. This will assist the usher to take a note of the names of those proposing to address the court and of their estimate of the hearing time. This information is given to the judge before he or she sits. Parties should also allow time before the court sits to agree any form of order with any other party if this has not already been done. If the form of the order is not agreed before the court sits, the parties may have to wait until there is a convenient break in the list before they can ask the court to make any agreed order. If an application, not being an Interim Application by Order, is adjourned the Associate in attendance will notify the Chancery Judges' Listing Office of the date to which it has been adjourned so that it may be relisted for the new date.

Agreed Adjournment of Interim Applications

5.13 If all parties to an Interim Application agree, it can be adjourned for not more **1A–31** than 14 days by counsel or solicitors attending the Chancery Judges' Listing Officer in Room WG4 at any time before 4pm on the day before the hearing of the application and producing consents signed by solicitors or counsel for all parties agreeing to the adjournment. A litigant in person must attend before the Chancery Judges' Listing

Paragraph numbers marked with a "+" can be found online and on CD.

Officer as well as signing a consent. This procedure may not be used for more than three successive adjournments and no adjournment may be made by this procedure to the last two days of any sitting.

Interim Applications by Order by agreement

1A–32 5.14 This procedure should also be used where the parties agree that the application will take two hours or more and that, in consequence, the application should be adjourned to be heard as an Interim Application by Order. In that event, the consents set out above should also contain an agreed timetable for the filing of evidence or confirmation that no further evidence is to be filed. Any application arising from the failure of a party to abide by the timetable and any application to extend the timetable must be made to the judge. Interim Applications by Order will, initially at least, enter the Interim Hearings warned list on the first Monday after close of evidence.

5.15 Undertakings given to the court may be continued unchanged over any adjournment. If, however, on an adjournment an undertaking is to be varied or a new undertaking given then that must be dealt with by the court.

The duty of disclosure

1A–33 5.16 On all applications made in the absence of the respondent the applicant and his or her legal representatives owe a duty to the court to disclose fully all matters relevant to the application, including matters, whether of fact or law, which are, or may be, adverse to it. If there is a failure to comply with this duty and an order is made, the court may subsequently set aside the order on that ground alone. The disclosure, if made orally, must be confirmed by witness statement or affidavit. The representatives for the applicant must specifically direct the court to passages in the evidence which disclose matters adverse to the application.

5.17 A party wishing to apply urgently to a judge for remedies without notice to the Respondent must notify the clerk to the Interim Applications judge by telephone (the number will be set out in the Daily Cause List). Where such an urgent application is made, two copies of the order sought and an electronic copy on disk (in Word for Windows) and a completed judge's Application Information Form in the form in Part 1 of Appendix 4 should, where possible, be included with the papers handed to the judge's clerk. Where an application is very urgent and the Interim Applications judge is unable to hear it promptly, it may be heard by any judge who is available, though the request for this must be made to the clerk to the Interim Applications judge, or, in default, to the Chancery Judges' Listing Officer. Every effort should be made to issue the claim form before the application is made. If this is not practicable, the party making the application must give an undertaking to the court to issue the claim form forthwith even if the court makes no order, unless the court orders otherwise. A party making an urgent application must ensure that all necessary fees are paid.

Freezing Injunctions and Search Orders

1A–34 5.18 The grant of freezing injunctions (both domestic and world-wide) and search orders is a staple feature of the work of the Interim Applications judge. Applications for such orders are invariably made without notice in the first instance; and in a proper case the court will sit in private in order to hear them. Where such an application is to be listed, two copies of the order sought, together with the application notice, should be lodged with the Chancery Judges' Listing Office. If the application is to be made in private, it will be listed as 'Application without notice' without naming the parties. The judge will consider, in each case, whether publicity might defeat the object of the hearing and, if so, may hear the application in private.

5.19 Freezing injunctions and search orders are never granted as a matter of course. A strong case must be made out, and applications need to be prepared with great care. The application should always be accompanied by a draft of the order which the court is to be invited to make.

Paragraph numbers marked with a "+" can be found online and on CD.

Period for which an injunction or an order appointing a receiver is granted if the application was without notice

5.20 When an application for an injunction is heard without notice, and the judge **1A–35** decides that an injunction should be granted, it will normally be granted for a limited period only—usually not more than seven days. The same applies to an interim order appointing a receiver. The applicant will be required to give the respondent notice of his or her intention to apply to the court at the expiration of that period for the order to be continued. In the meantime the respondent will be entitled to apply, though generally only after giving notice to the applicant, for the order to be varied or discharged.

Opposed applications without notice

5.21 These are applications of which proper notice has not been given to the **1A–36** respondents but which are made in the presence of both parties in advance of a full hearing of the application. The judge may impose time limits on the parties if, having regard to the pressure of business or for any other reason, he or she considers it appropriate to do so. On these applications, the judge may, in an appropriate case, make an order which will have effect until trial or further order as if proper notice had been given.

Implied cross-undertakings in damages where undertakings are given to the court

5.22 Often the party against whom an injunction is sought gives to the court an **1A–37** undertaking which avoids the need for the court to grant the injunction. In these cases, there is an implied undertaking in damages by the party applying for the injunction in favour of the other. The position is less clear where the party applying for the injunction also gives an undertaking to the court. The parties should consider and, if necessary, raise with the judge whether the party in whose favour the undertaking is given must give a cross-undertaking in damages in those circumstances.

Orders on applications

5.23 The judge may direct the parties to agree, sign and deliver to the court a **1A–38** statement of the terms of the order made by the court (commonly still referred to as a minute of order), particularly where complex undertakings are given.

Consents by parties not attending hearing

5.24 It is commonly the case that on an interim application the respondent does not **1A–39** appear either in person or by solicitors or counsel but the applicant seeks a consent order based upon a letter of consent from the respondent or his or her solicitors or a draft statement of agreed terms signed by the respondent's solicitors. This causes no difficulty where the agreed relief falls wholly within the relief claimed in the application notice.

5.25 If, however, the agreed relief goes outside that which is claimed in the application notice or even in the claim form or when undertakings are offered then difficulties can arise. A procedure has been established for this purpose to be applied to all applications in the Chancery Division.

5.26 Subject always to the discretion of the court, no order will be made in such cases **1A–40** unless a consent signed by or on behalf of the respondent to an application is put before the court in accordance with the following provisions:

   (1) Where there are solicitors on the record for the respondent the court will normally accept as sufficient a written consent signed by those solicitors on their headed notepaper.

   (2) Where there are solicitors for the respondent who are not on the record, the court will normally accept as sufficient a written consent signed by those solicitors on their headed notepaper only if in the consent (or some other

Paragraph numbers marked with a "+" can be found online and on CD.

document) the solicitors certify that they have fully explained to the respondent the effect of the order and that the respondent appeared to have understood the explanation.

(3) Where there is a written consent signed by a respondent acting in person the court will not normally accept it as sufficient unless the court is satisfied that the respondent understands the effect of the order either by reason of the circumstances (for example the respondent is himself a solicitor or barrister) or by means of other material (for example, the respondent's consent is given in reply to a letter explaining in simple terms the effect of the order).

(4) Where the respondent offers any undertaking to the court (a) the document containing the undertaking must be signed by the respondent personally, (b) solicitors must certify on their headed notepaper that the signature is that of the respondent and (c) if the case falls within (2) or (3) above, solicitors must certify that they have explained to the respondent the consequences of giving the undertaking and that the respondent appeared to understand the explanation.

Bundles and Skeleton Arguments

1A–41   5.27 See Chapter 7 below.

Out of hours emergency arrangements

1A–42   5.28 An application should not be made out of hours unless it is essential. An explanation will be required as to why it was not made or could not be made during normal court hours. Applications made during legal vacations must also constitute vacation business.

5.29 There is always a Duty Chancery Judge available to hear urgent out of hours applications. The following is a summary of the procedure:

(1) All requests for the Duty Chancery Judge to hear urgent matters are to be made through the judge's clerk. There may be occasions when the Duty Chancery Judge is not immediately available. The clerk will be able to inform the applicant of the judge's likely availability.

(2) Initial contact should be through the Security Office at the Royal Courts of Justice (tel: 020 7947 6260), who should be requested to contact the Duty Chancery Judge's clerk. The applicant must give a telephone number for the return call.

(3) When the clerk contacts the applicant, he or she will need to know:

   (a) the name of the party on whose behalf the application is to be made;

   (b) the name of the person who is to make the application and his or her status (counsel or solicitor);

   (c) the nature of the application;

   (d) the degree of urgency;

   (e) the contact telephone numbers.

(4) The Duty Judge will indicate to his or her clerk whether he or she is prepared to deal with the matter by telephone or whether it will be necessary for the matter to be dealt with by a hearing, in court or elsewhere. The clerk will inform the applicant and make the necessary arrangements.

(5) Applications for interim remedies will (normally) be heard by telephone only where the applicant is represented by counsel or solicitors (PD 25, Interim Injunctions, paragraph 4.5). If, however, an applicant not so represented indicates reasons why, exceptionally, the application should be heard by telephone, the judge may require that the applicant be attended by a responsible person who can confirm the identity of the applicant and the accuracy of what is said: see PD 23 paragraphs 6.3 and 8 . If satisfied that it is really necessary, the judge may grant an injunction on such an application, but it is likely to be granted for as short a time as possible pending a hearing on notice to the respondent.

Paragraph numbers marked with a "+" can be found online and on CD.

5.30 Which judge will, in appropriate cases, hear an out of hours application varies according to when the application is made.

(1) Weekdays. Out of hours duty, during term time, is the responsibility of the Applications Judge. He or she is normally available from 4.15pm until 10.15am Monday to Thursday.

(2) Weekends. A Duty Chancery Judge is nominated by rota for weekends, commencing 4.15pm Friday until 10.15am Monday.

(3) Vacation. The Vacation Judge also undertakes out of hours applications.

5.31 Sealing orders out of hours. In normal circumstances it is not possible to issue a sealed order out of hours. The judge may direct the applicant to lodge a draft of the order made at Chancery Chambers Registry by 10am on the following working day.

5.32 County court matters. Similar arrangements exist for making urgent applications out of hours in county court matters in certain parts of England and Wales. Contact with the Circuit judge on duty for the London County Courts can be made through the Security Office of the Royal Courts of Justice.

Vacation arrangements

5.33 There is a Chancery judge available to hear applications in vacation. **1A–43** Applications must generally constitute vacation business in that, in particular, they require to be immediately or promptly heard. Special arrangements exist, however, in the Companies Court for certain schemes of arrangement and reductions of capital to be heard in the Long Vacation (see paragraph 8 of PD 49—Applications under the Companies Act 1985).

5.34 In the Long Vacation, the Vacation judge sits each day to hear vacation business. In other vacations there are no regular sittings. Mondays and Thursdays are made available for urgent Interim Applications on notice. The judge is available on the remaining days for urgent business.

Applications to a Master

5.35 Applications to a Master should be made by application notice. Application **1A–44** notices are issued by the Masters' Appointments section in Room TM7.09. If the Master has already directed a case management conference the parties should ensure that all applications in the proceedings are properly issued and listed to be heard at the case management conference. If the available listed time is likely to be insufficient to give directions and hear any application the parties should co-operate and invite the court to arrange a longer appointment. It is the duty of the parties to seek to agree directions if possible and to provide a draft of the order for consideration by the Master.

5.36 Applications to a Master estimated to last in excess of two hours will require serious co-operation between the parties and will require the Master's directions before they are listed. The Master will normally give his permission to list such an application on condition that there is compliance with directions given by the Master.

5.37 Those directions are likely to require:

(1) that the applicant agrees the time estimate (see below) with his opponent;

(2) that, if the time allowed subsequently becomes insufficient, the court is informed and a new and longer appointment given;

(3) that the parties agree an appropriate timetable for filing evidence such that the hearing will be effective on the date listed;

(4) that positive confirmation is to be given to the Master five working days before the hearing date that the hearing remains effective; and

(5) that, in the event of settlement, the Master be informed of that fact.

5.38 The agreed time estimate must take into account not only the hearing time of

Paragraph numbers marked with a "+" can be found online and on CD.

the application but the time for the Master to give any judgment at the conclusion of the hearing. It should also take into account any further time that may be required for the Master to assess costs, and for any application for permission to appeal.

5.39 Failure to comply with the Master's directions given in respect of the listing of an appointment in excess of two hours may result, depending upon the circumstances, in the application not being heard or in adverse costs orders being made.

5.40 On any matter of substance, the Master is likely to require a bundle and skeleton arguments to be provided before the hearing, as detailed in paragraphs 7.40 to 7.50 below. Where directions are given in respect of an application to which paragraph 5.36 applies, the provision of a bundle and skeleton arguments should form part of the agreed timetable.

5.41 The Masters may also allow applications to be made to them informally. The Masters are normally listed to hear oral applications without notice between 2.15pm and 2.45pm (see paragraph 6.32 below). Such applications should not be used in place of a Part 23 application and care must be taken to notify in appropriate cases parties likely to be affected by any order made on the application. Letters should not be used in place of a Part 23 application, and parties should be particularly careful to keep any correspondence with the Masters to a minimum and to ensure that opposing parties receive copies of any correspondence. Failure in this regard will mean that the Master will refuse to deal with the correspondence. Correspondence should state that it has been copied to the other parties (or should state why it has not been copied). Unless the matter is one of urgency correspondence and any other documents should be sent by post. If, in a case of real urgency, a letter is sent by fax, it should not be followed by a hard copy, unless it contains an original document which needs to be filed. Further guidance is set out in the Chief Master's Practice Note reproduced at Appendix 5.

5.42 There is no distinction between term time and vacation so far as business before the Chancery Masters is concerned. They will deal with all types of business throughout the year. When a Master is on holiday, his or her list will normally be taken by a deputy Master.

Applications for payment out of court

1A–45   5.43 Applications for payment out of money held in court under paragraph 4.2 of PD 37 (for example, where money has been paid into court following compulsory purchase or repossession of property) must be made by Part 23 Application Notice (Form N244). The required documents should be sent to Room TM5.04. The following must be included:

(1) the reasons why the payment should be made (in Part C of the application notice)

(2) any relevant documents such as birth, marriage or death certificate, title deeds etc. (exhibited to the application notice)

(3) a statement whether or not anyone else has any claim to the money (in the Statement of Truth)

(4) bank details, ie the name and address of the relevant bank/building society branch, its Sort Code, and the Account Title and Number

(5) the Court fee of £50.

5.44 If there is a dispute as to entitlement to money in court, the Master may order the matter to proceed by Part 8 claim (see paragraph 2.13 above). In all other cases the Master will consider the file without a hearing and make an order for payment.

CHAPTER 6

LISTING ARRANGEMENTS

Key Rules: CPR Parts 29 and 39

6.1 This Chapter deals with listing arrangements for hearings before judges and **1A–46** Masters in the Royal Courts of Justice.

Hearings before Judges

Responsibility for listing

6.2 Subject to the direction of the Chancellor the Clerk of the Lists (Room WG3, **1A–47** Royal Courts of Justice) has overall responsibility for listing. Day by day management of Chancery listing is dealt with by the Chancery Judges' Listing Officer (Room WG4). All applications relating to listing should, in the first instance, be made to the Chancery Judges' Listing Officer, who will refer matters, as necessary, to the Clerk of the Lists. Any party dissatisfied with any decision of the Clerk of the Lists may, on one clear day's notice to all other parties, apply to the judge in charge of the list. Any such application should be made within seven days of the decision of the Clerk of the Lists and be arranged through the Chancery Judges' Listing Office.

6.3 There are three main lists in the Chancery Division: the Trial List, the General List and the Interim Hearings List. In addition there is a separate Patents List which is also controlled on a day-to-day basis by the Chancery Judges' Listing Officer in Room WG4 (see Chapter 23).

The Trial List

6.4 This comprises a list of all trials to be heard with witnesses. **1A–48**

The Interim Hearings List

6.5 This list comprises interim applications and appeals from Masters. **1A–49**

The General List

6.6 This list comprises other matters including revenue, bankruptcy and pension **1A–50** appeals, Part 8 proceedings, applications for judgment and all company matters.

6.7 The procedure for listing Chancery cases to be heard in the Royal Courts of Justice and listed in the Trial List is that at an early stage in the claim the court will give directions with a view to fixing the period during which the case will be heard. In a Part 7 claim that period (the Trial Window) will be determined by the court either when the case is allocated or subsequently at any case management conference or other directions hearing. In a Part 8 claim covered by this procedure, that is to say a Part 8 claim to be heard with witnesses, similar directions will be given when the Part 8 claim is listed for preliminary directions or for a case management conference. It is only in a small minority of Part 8 claims that the claim is tried by a judge in the Trial List and the Trial Window procedure applies. The bulk of Part 8 claims are heard on written evidence either by the Master or by the judge. Additionally, many Part 8 claims, even where oral evidence is to be called, will be heard by the Master pursuant to the jurisdiction set out in paragraph 4.1 of PD 2B—Allocation of Cases to Levels of Judiciary.

Allocation of Cases to Levels of Judiciary

6.8 In determining the Trial Window the court will have regard to the listing **1A–51** constraints created by the existing court list and will determine a Trial Window which provides the parties with enough time to complete their preparations for trial. A Trial Window, once fixed, will not be readily be altered. A list of current trial windows is published on the HMCS website. When determining the Trial Window the court will direct that one party, normally the claimant, makes an appointment to attend on the Chancery Judges' Listing Officer (Room WG4) to fix a trial date within the Trial Window, by such date as may be specified in the order and gives notice of that appointment to all other parties. It is to be understood that an order to attend on the Chancery Judges' Listing Officer imposes a strict obligation of compliance, without which the Trial Window that has been given will be lost.

Paragraph numbers marked with a "+" can be found online and on CD.

6.9 At the listing appointment, the Chancery Judges' Listing Officer will take account, insofar as it is practical to do so, of any difficulties the parties may have as to the availability of counsel, experts and witnesses. The Chancery Judges' Listing Officer will, nevertheless, try to ensure the speedy disposal of the trial by arranging a firm trial date as soon as possible within the Trial Window. If a Case Summary has been prepared (see PD 29 paragraphs 5.6 and 5.7) the claimant must produce a copy at the listing appointment together with a copy of the particulars of claim and any orders relevant to the fixing of the trial date. If, exceptionally, at the listing appointment, it appears to the Chancery Judges' Listing Officer that a trial date cannot be provided by the court within the trial window, he may fix the trial date outside the trial window at the first available date.

6.10 A party wishing to appeal a date allocated by the Chancery Judge's Listing Officer must, within 7 days of the allocation, make an application to the judge nominated to hear such applications. The application notice should be filed in the Chancery Judges' Listing Office and served, giving one clear day's notice to the other parties.

6.11 A trial date once fixed will, like a Trial Window, only rarely be altered or vacated. An application to adjourn a trial date will normally be made to the judge nominated to hear such applications (see further paragraph 7.38). Such an application will however be entertained by the Master if, for example, on the hearing of an interim application or case management conference it becomes clear that the trial date cannot stand without injustice to one or both parties.

Warned List—General and Interim Hearings Lists

1A–52 6.12 On each Friday of term and on such other days as may be appropriate, the Chancery Judges' Listing Officer will publish a Warned List, showing the matters that are liable to be heard in the following week. Any matters for which no date has been arranged will be liable to appear in the list for hearing with no warning save that given by the next day's list of cases, posted each afternoon outside Room WG4. Where a case is listed in the Warned List, the parties may agree to offer the case for a specified date, in accordance with the statement of Chancery Judges' Listing Office practice on offering cases issued by the Clerk of the Lists.

Estimate of duration

1A–53 6.13 If after a case is listed the estimated length of the hearing is varied, or if the case is settled, withdrawn or discontinued, the solicitors for the parties must forthwith inform the Chancery Judges' Listing Officer in writing. Failure so to do may result in an adverse costs order being made. If the case is settled but the parties wish the Master to make a consent order, the solicitor must notify the Chancery Judges' Listing Officer in writing, whereupon he or she will take the case out of the list and notify the Master. The Master may then make the consent order.

6.14 Seven days before the date for the hearing, the claimant's solicitors must inform the Chancery Judges' Listing Officer whether there is any variation in the estimate of duration, and, in particular, whether the case is likely to be disposed of in some summary way. If the claimant is a litigant in person, this must be done by the solicitor for the first-named defendant who has instructed a solicitor. If a summary disposal is likely, the solicitor must keep the Chancery Listing Officer informed of any developments as soon as they occur.

Applications after listing

1A–54 6.15 Where a case has been listed for hearing and because of the timing of the hearing an application is urgent, any application in the case may be made to the Interim Applications judge if the application cannot be heard by a Master without the hearing being delayed. Parties should not however list an application before the Interim Applications judge without first consulting the Masters' clerks (Room TM7.09) as to the availability of the assigned Master or, in an appropriate case,

Paragraph numbers marked with a "+" can be found online and on CD.

applying to the Master himself. Provision can be made for urgent applications to be dealt with by the Chief Master or a deputy (see further paragraph 6.29).

Appeals

6.16 All appeals for hearing by High Court judges in the Division are issued by the Clerk of the Lists, High Court Appeals Office (Room WG8). Enquiries relating to such appeals are to be made in the first instance to that office, except as provided by paragraph 6.18 below.

1A–55

Daily list of cases

6.17 This list, known as the Daily Cause List, is available on the Courts Service website: *www.hmcourts-service.gov.uk*.

1A–56

Listing of Particular Business

1A–57

6.18 **Appeals from Masters**

 (1) Appeals from Masters, where permission has been given, will appear in the Appeals Warned List. Such appeals (stamped with the appropriate fee) must be filed with the Clerk of the Lists' Office in Room WG7. When an appeal is filed an appeal number will be allocated and any future order will bear both the original claim number and the appeal number. On being satisfied that the case has been placed in the Warned List, solicitors should forthwith inform the Chancery Judges' Listing Officer whether they intend to instruct counsel and, if so, the name or names of counsel.

 (2) Any order made on appeal from a Master will be placed on the court file. However, practitioners should co-operate by ensuring that a copy of any relevant order is available to the Master at any subsequent hearing.

6.19 **Applications for permission to appeal from Masters**

Applications for permission to appeal from a decision of a Master (stamped with the appropriate fee) must be lodged in the clerk of the Lists' Office in Room WG7. If permission to appeal is granted the appeal will appear in the Interim Hearings List and the procedure set out above will apply.

6.20 **Bankruptcy Appeals**

Notice of appeal from the decision of a Registrar or of a county court should be lodged in the Clerk of the Lists' Office, Room WG7. The appeal will be entered in the Appeals Warned List, usually with a fixed date. The date of the hearing will be fixed by the Chancery Judges' Listing Officer in the usual way.

6.21 **Bankruptcy Applications**

All originating applications to the judge should be lodged with the Deputy Court Manager in Bankruptcy. Urgent applications without notice for (i) the committal of any person to prison for contempt or (ii) injunctions or the modification or discharge of injunctions will be passed directly to the clerk to the Interim Applications judge for hearing by that judge. All applications on notice for (i) and (ii) above, and applications referred to the judge by the Registrar, will be listed by the Chancery Judges' Listing Officer. Applications estimated not to exceed two hours will be heard by the Interim Applications judge. The Chancery Judges' Listing Officer is to give at least three clear days' notice of the hearing to the applicant and to any respondent who attended before the Registrar. Applications over two hours will be placed in the General List and listed accordingly.

6.22 **Companies Court**

Matters for hearing before the Companies judge, such as petitions for an administration order, petitions for approval by the court of schemes of arrangement

Paragraph numbers marked with a "+" can be found online and on CD.

and applications for the appointment of provisional liquidators, may be issued for hearing on any day of the week in term time (other than the last day of each term) and will be dealt with by the Interim Applications judge as Companies judge. Applications or petitions which are estimated to exceed two hours are liable to be stood over to a date to be fixed by the Chancery Judges' Listing Officer. Urgent applications will also be dealt with by the Interim Applications judge. Applications and petitions referred to the judge by the Registrar will be placed in the General List and listed accordingly.

6.23 Applications referred to the judge

Applications referred by the Master to the judge will be added to the Interim Hearings List. The power to refer applications made to the Master and in respect of which the Master has jurisdiction is now very sparingly exercised. The proper use of judicial resources dictates that where the Master has jurisdiction in respect of an interlocutory matter he should ordinarily exercise that jurisdiction.

6.24 Judge's Applications

Reference should be made to Chapter 5.

6.25 Revenue Appeals

Appeals will be entered in the Appeals Warned List, usually with fixed dates, and will be heard by such judges as are available. The dates for hearing are settled in the usual way on application to the Chancery Judges' Listing Officer. Where it would assist counsel and solicitor with their other commitments, the Chancery Listing Officer, if requested, will endeavour to fix two or more revenue appeals so that they will come on consecutively.

6.26 Short Applications

An application for judgment in default made to a judge (because the Master has no jurisdiction) should be made to the Interim Applications judge.

6.27 Summary Judgment

Where an application for summary judgment includes an application for an injunction, it usually has to be made to a judge because in most cases the Master cannot grant an injunction save in terms agreed by the parties. In such cases the application should be made returnable before the judge instead of the Master and will be listed in the General List. The return date to be inserted in the application notice should be a Monday at least 14 clear days after the application notice has been served. The application notice should be issued in the Chancery Judges' Listing Office (Room WG4) when there must be lodged two copies of the application notice and the witness statements or affidavits in support together with their exhibits. On the return date the application will normally be adjourned to a date to be fixed if the hearing is likely to take longer than thirty minutes. The adjourned date will be fixed in the usual way through the Chancery Judges' Listing Officer, and a certificate signed by an advocate as to the estimated length of the hearing must be lodged with the Chancery Judges' Listing Officer.

If the applicant informs the Chancery Judges' Listing Officer at the time of issue of an application notice for summary judgment returnable before a judge that directions have been agreed, or are not necessary, the application will be listed for a substantive hearing without being listed for directions.

If, subsequent to issue, the parties agree directions the Chancery Judges' Listing Officer will, on application, re-list the application for a substantive hearing and any directions hearing will be vacated. Time estimates should be agreed.

Paragraph numbers marked with a "+" can be found online and on CD.

6.28 Variation of Trusts: Application to a judge

Applications under the Variation of Trusts Act 1958 for a hearing before the judge may be listed for hearing in the General List without any direction by a Master on the lodgment in Room WG4 of a certificate signed by advocates for all the parties, stating (i) that the evidence is complete and has been filed; (ii) that the application is ready for hearing; and (iii) the estimated length of the hearing.

Hearings before Masters

Assignment of cases before Masters

6.29 The general rule is that cases are assigned to the Masters in accordance with the last digit of the claim number. At present cases are allocated as follows:

        0 and 1 Master Bragge
        2 and 3 Master Teverson
        4 and 5 Master Bowles
        6 and 7 Master Price
        8 and 9 Master Moncaster

1A–58

In view of administrative responsibilities, the Chief Master does not have assigned cases. He will take individual cases or classes of case in his own discretion and arrangements will be made accordingly through the Court Manager. Where an application is required to be heard at short notice or is urgent but the assigned Master's list cannot accommodate an early date for the length of hearing necessary, arrangements can often be made for it to be listed before the Chief Master. Application should first be made to the assigned Master, who will determine whether the case is one which it is appropriate to release to the Chief Master. In that event arrangements are made by the Court Manager (Room TM6.06)

Applications by the Official Solicitor under rule 21.12 to be appointed a guardian of a minor's estate are normally dealt with by the Chief Master. All applications for a Group Litigation Order in the Chancery Division have to be made to the Chief Master: see paragraph 3.13.

6.30 An important exception to the general rule is that all registered trade mark claims are assigned to Master Bragge. Practitioners must, therefore, ensure, both at the date of issue of proceedings and when any application is to be made, that the court staff are aware that the claim is a registered trade mark claim and that, irrespective of the claim number, the claim and any application in the claim is assigned to and should be listed before Master Bragge. Each month in term time a day or more is usually set aside in Master Bragge's list specifically for trade mark applications and practitioners should, if possible, seek to have applications listed on that day. If the provisions of this paragraph are ignored and an application in a registered trade mark claim is listed other than before Master Bragge, it is likely that the Master before whom it is listed will refuse to hear it. If Master Bragge is away it is to be expected that the claim will be heard by the Deputy sitting for him.

6.31 In addition, from time to time, the Chief Master assigns particular classes of case to particular Masters. This will normally relate to managed litigation where the particular parties will be aware that their cases have been specifically assigned.

Oral applications without notice to the Masters

6.32 Masters are normally available to hear short oral applications without notice at Applications without Notice time between 2.15pm and 2.45pm on working days. Notice should be given to the Master's Appointments section in Room TM7.09, or by telephone or fax, by 4.30pm on the previous working day (except in cases of real emergency when notice may be given at any time) so that the file will be before the Master. If this procedure is not followed the Master will be likely to refuse to deal with the application. The Master will expect notice of such an application to have been given in an appropriate case to the other party. Applications without Notice time must not be used as a substitute for cases where the issue and service of an Application Notice is appropriate. (See paragraph 5.41 above).

1A–59

Paragraph numbers marked with a "+" can be found online and on CD.

6.33 If the assigned Master is not available on any particular day, the applicant will be informed and (except in cases of emergency) asked to come when the assigned Master is next available. Applications will only be heard by another Master in cases of emergency or when the assigned Master is on vacation.

6.34 See also Chapter 5, paragraphs 5.35 to 42 (Applications to Masters).

CHAPTER 7

PREPARATION FOR HEARINGS
Key Rules: CPR Parts 29 and 39

1A–60 7.1 This Chapter contains guidance on the preparation of cases for hearings before judges and Masters. Guidelines about the conduct of trials are given in Chapter 8 of this Guide. When an affidavit or witness statement (or other document) is filed in Chancery Chambers in preparation for a hearing or for any other purpose, it should be accompanied by a written evidence lodgment form as set out in Part 2 of Appendix 4, unless it accompanies an application notice. The preparation of witness statements is covered in Chapter 8.

Hearings before Judges

1A–61 7.2 To ensure court time is used efficiently there must be adequate preparation of cases prior to the hearing. This covers, among other things, the preparation and exchange of skeleton arguments, compiling bundles of documents and dealing out of court with queries which need not concern the court. The parties should also use their best endeavours to agree before any hearing what are the issues or the main issues.

Estimates

1A–62 7.3 Realistic estimates of the length of time a hearing is expected to take must be given.

7.4 In estimating the length of a hearing, sufficient time must be allowed for reading any documents required to be read, the length of the speeches, the time required to examine witnesses (if any), and, if appropriate, an immediate judgment, together with the summary assessment of costs, in cases where that may arise, and any application for permission to appeal.

7.5 Except as mentioned below, a written estimate signed by the advocates for all the parties is required in the case of any hearing before a judge. This should be delivered to the Chancery Judges' Listing Officer:

(1) in the case of a trial, on the application to fix the trial date; and

(2) in any other case, as soon as possible after the application notice or case papers have been lodged withh the Chancery Judges' Listin Office.

7.6 If the estimate given in the application notice for an application to the Interim Applications judge (other than applications by order) or for an application listed before the Companies judge requires to be revised, the revised estimate should be given to the court orally when the application is called on.

Changes in Estimate

1A–63 7.7 The parties must inform the court immediately of any material change in a time estimate. They should keep each other informed of any such change. In any event a further time estimate signed by the advocates to the parties must be lodged when bundles are lodged (see paragraph 7.17 below).

Inaccurate estimates

1A–64 7.8 Where estimates prove inaccurate, a hearing may have to be adjourned to a later

Paragraph numbers marked with a "+" can be found online and on CD.

date and the party responsible for the adjournment is likely to be ordered to pay the costs thrown away.

Bundles

7.9 Bundles of documents for use in court will generally be required for all hearings **1A–65** if more than 25 pages are involved (and may be appropriate even if fewer pages are involved). The efficient preparation of bundles of documents is very important. Where bundles have been properly prepared, the case will be easier to understand and present, and time and costs are likely to be saved. Where documents are copied unnecessarily or bundled incompetently the cost may be disallowed.

7.10 Where the provisions of this Guide as to the preparation or delivery of bundles are not followed, the bundle may be rejected by the court or be made the subject of a special costs order.

7.11 The claimant or applicant (as the case may be) should begin his or her preparation of the bundles in sufficient time to enable:

(1) the bundles to be agreed with the other parties (so far as possible);

(2) references to the bundles to be used in skeleton arguments; and

(3) the bundles to be delivered to the court at the required time.

7.12 The representatives for all parties involved must co-operate in agreeing bundles for use in court. The court and the advocates should all have exactly the same bundles.

7.13 When agreeing bundles for trial, the parties should establish through their legal representatives, and record in correspondence, whether the agreement of bundles:

(1) extends no further than agreement of the composition and preparation of the bundles; or

(2) includes agreement that the documents in the bundles are authentic (see rule 32.19); or

(3) includes agreement that the documents may be treated as evidence of the facts stated in them.

The court will normally expect parties to agree that the documents, or at any rate the great majority of them, may be treated as evidence of the facts stated in them. A party not willing to agree should, when the trial bundles are lodged, write a letter to the court (with a copy to all other parties) stating that it is not willing to agree, and explaining why.

7.14 Documents disclosed are in general deemed to be admitted to be authentic under rule 32.19.

7.15 Detailed guidelines on the preparation of bundles are set out in Appendix 6, in addition to those in PD 39, Miscellaneous Provisions relating to Hearings, paragraph 3. These should always be followed unless there is good reason not to do so. Particular attention is drawn to the need to consider the preparation of a core bundle.

7.16 The general rule is that the claimant/applicant must ensure that one copy of a properly prepared bundle is delivered at the Chancery Judges' Listing Office not less than two clear days (and not more than seven days) before a trial or application by order. However, the court may direct the delivery of bundles earlier than this. Where oral evidence is to be given a second copy of the bundle must be available in court for the use of the witnesses. In the case of bundles to be used on judge's Applications (other than applications by order) the bundles must be delivered to the clerk to the Interim Applications judge by 10am on the morning preceding the day of the hearing unless the court directs otherwise. A bundle delivered to the court should always be in final form and parties should not make a request to alter the bundle after it has been delivered to the court save for good reason.

Paragraph numbers marked with a "+" can be found online and on CD.

7.17 When lodging the agreed bundles there should also be lodged a further agreed time estimate, together with an agreed reading list and an agreed time estimate in respect of that reading list. The time estimates and reading list must be signed by the advocates for the parties. Failing agreement as to the time estimates or reading list then separate reading lists and time estimates must be submitted signed by the appropriate advocate. See Appendix 7 as to reading lists.

7.18 If the case is one which does not require the preparation of a bundle, the advocate should check before the hearing starts that all the documents to which he or she wishes to refer and which ought to have been filed have been filed, and, if possible, indicate to the associate which they are.

7.19 Bundles provided for the use of the court should be removed promptly after the conclusion of the hearing unless the court directs otherwise.

Skeleton Arguments

1A–66 7.20 The general rule is that for the purpose of all hearings before a judge skeleton arguments should be prepared. The exceptions to this general rule are where the application does not warrant one, for example because it is likely to be short, or where the application is so urgent that preparation of a skeleton argument is impracticable or where an application is ineffective and the order is agreed by all parties (see also paragraphs 26.26 and 26.33).

Time for delivery of skeleton arguments

1A–67 7.21 **In the more substantial matters (e.g. trials and applications by order)—** not less than two clear days before the date or first date on which the application or trial is due to come on for hearing.

7.22 **On judge's applications without notice—** with the papers which the judge is asked to read on the application.

7.23 **On all other applications to a judge, including interim applications—** as soon as possible and not later than 10am on the day preceding the hearing.

7.24 Where a case is liable to be placed in the Warned List, consideration should be given to the preparation of skeleton arguments as soon as the case is placed in the Warned List, so that the skeleton arguments are ready to be delivered to the court on time. Preparation of skeleton arguments should not be left until notice is given that the case is to be heard. Notice may be given that the case is to be heard the next day.

Place to which skeleton arguments should be delivered

1A–68 7.25 If the name of the judge is not known, or the judge is a Deputy Judge, skeleton arguments should be delivered to the Chancery Judges' Listing Office (Room WG4).

7.26 If the name of the judge (other than a Deputy Judge) is known, skeleton arguments should be delivered to the judge's clerk.

Content of skeleton arguments

1A–69 7.27 Appendix 7 contains guidelines which should be followed on the content of skeleton arguments and chronologies, as well as indices and reading lists.

7.28 In most cases before a judge, a list of the persons involved in the facts of the case, a chronology and a list of issues will also be required. The chronology and list of issues should be agreed where possible. The claimant/applicant is responsible for preparing the list of persons involved and the chronology, and he or she should deliver these and his or her list of issues (if required) to the court with his or her skeleton argument.

7.29 Unless the court gives any other direction, the parties shall, as between

Paragraph numbers marked with a "+" can be found online and on CD.

themselves, arrange for the delivery, exchange, or sequential service of skeleton arguments and any list of persons involved, list of issues or chronology. Where there are no such arrangements, all such documents should, where possible, be given to the other parties (if any) in sufficient time before the hearing to enable them properly to consider them.

Failure to lodge bundles or skeleton arguments on time

7.30 Failure to lodge skeleton arguments and bundles in accordance with this Guide **1A–70** may result in:
    (1) the matter not being heard on the date in question;
    (2) the costs of preparation being disallowed; and
    (3) an adverse costs order being made.

7.31 In the Royal Courts of Justice, a log will be maintained of all late skeletons and bundles. The log will regularly be inspected by the Chancellor who will consider such further action as appropriate in relation to any recurrent failure by any chambers, barrister, or solicitors firm to comply with the requirements of the CPR and the Guide.

Authorities

7.32 Unless photocopies of authorities are provided, lists of authorities should be **1A–71** supplied to the usher by 9am on the first day of the hearing. Delivery of skeleton arguments does not relieve a party of his or her duty to deliver his or her list of authorities to the usher by the time stated.

7.33 Advocates should exchange lists of authorities by 4pm on the day before the hearing. Any failure in this regard which has the effect of increasing the length of a hearing or of giving rise to delay in the hearing of an application may give rise to an adverse costs order.

7.34 Excessive citation of authority should be avoided and practitioners must have full regard to the matters contained in *Practice Note (citation of cases: restrictions and rules)* [2001] 1 WLR 1001. In particular, the citation of authority should be restricted to the expression of legal principle rather than the application of such principle to particular facts. Practitioners must also, when citing authority, seek to ensure that their citations comply with *Practice Direction (Judgments: Neutral Citations)* [2002] 1 WLR 346.

Oral Argument

7.35 The court may indicate the issues on which it wishes to be addressed and those **1A–72** on which it wishes to be addressed only briefly.

Documents and Authorities

7.36 Only the key part of any document or authority should be read aloud in court. **1A–73**

7.37 At any hearing, handing in written material designed to reduce or remove the need for the court to take a manuscript note will assist the court and save time.

Adjournments

7.38 As a timetable for the case will have been fixed at an early stage, applications for **1A–74** adjournment of a trial should only be necessary where there has been a change of circumstances not known when the timetable was fixed.

<u>When to apply</u>
    (1) A party who seeks to have a hearing before a judge adjourned must inform the Chancery Judges' Listing Officer of his or her application as soon as possible.

Paragraph numbers marked with a "+" can be found online and on CD.

(2) Applications for an adjournment immediately before a hearing begins should be avoided as they take up valuable time which could be used for dealing with effective business and, if successful, they may result in a loss of court time altogether.

How to apply

(3) If the application is agreed, the parties should, in writing, apply to the Chancery Judges' Listing Officer. The Officer will consult the judge nominated for such matters. The judge may grant the application on conditions and give directions as to a new hearing date. But the judge may direct that the application be listed for a hearing and that all parties attend.

(4) If the adjournment is opposed the party asking for it should apply to the judge nominated for such matters or to the judge to whom the matter has been allocated. A hearing should be arranged, at the first opportunity, through the Chancery Judges' Listing Office.

(5) A short summary of the reasons for the adjournment should be delivered to the Chancery Judges' Listing Office, where possible by 12 noon on the day before the application is made. A witness statement or affidavit is not generally required.

(6) The party requesting an adjournment will, in general, be expected to show that he or she has conducted his or her own case diligently. Parties should take all reasonable steps to ensure that their cases are adequately prepared in sufficient time to enable a hearing before the court to proceed. Likewise, they should take reasonable steps to prepare and serve any document (including any written evidence) required to be served on any other party in sufficient time to enable the other party similarly to be adequately prepared.

(7) If a failure to take reasonable steps necessitates an adjournment, the court may disallow costs as between solicitor and client, or order the person responsible to pay the costs under rule 48.7, or dismiss the application, or make any other order (including an order for the payment of costs on an indemnity basis).

(8) A trial date may, on occasion, also be vacated by the Master in the circumstances envisaged in paragraph 6.11.

Hearings before Masters and Registrars

1A–75 7.39 As in the case of hearings before judges, there must be adequate preparation of cases prior to a hearing before the Masters and Registrars. Parties must ensure when issuing applications to be heard by the Masters and Registrars that time estimates are realistic and make proper allowance for the time taken to read any documents required to be read, give judgment and deal with the summary assessment of costs and any application for permission to appeal. The parties must inform the court and all other parties immediately of any material change in a time estimate. Where estimates prove inaccurate, the hearing may have to be adjourned to a later date and the party responsible for the adjournment is likely to be ordered to pay the costs thrown away.

7.40 In the case of a hearing before a Master or Registrar which is listed for one hour or more and in any other hearing before a Master or Registrar such as a case management conference, where a bundle would assist, a bundle should be provided.

7.41 Bundles must be provided for a trial or equivalent hearing (such as an account or inquiry or a Part 8 claim with oral evidence) which is listed before a Master or a Registrar. Such bundles must comply with Appendix 6 and contain or be accompanied by a reading list and an estimate of reading time as set out in paragraph 7.17 above.

7.42 Bundles provided for the use of the Master and Registrars should be removed promptly after the conclusion of the hearing unless the Master or Registrar directs otherwise.

Paragraph numbers marked with a "+" can be found online and on CD.

7.43 *Delivery of Bundles for hearings before Masters*

(1) Bundles should be delivered to Masters' Appointments, Room TM7.09, not less than 2 (and not more than 7) clear working days before the hearing. They should be clearly marked "For hearing on ..*[date]* before Master . . ..." They must not be taken to the Registry (Room TM5.04) or the Chancery Judges' Listing Office, and no document required for any hearing must be taken to the RCJ post room. Documents delivered to the wrong place are unlikely to reach the Master in time for the hearing, resulting in probable postponement and the party responsible for the adjournment is likely to be ordered to pay the costs thrown away.

(2) Detailed guidance on where to deliver documents in Chancery Chambers is at Appendix 8.

(3) Where no bundle is provided for the use of the Master, but a party intends to rely on the exhibits to a witness statement or affidavit, that party must ensure that those documents are filed with the court in sufficient time to be available to be read by the Master in advance of the hearing. Documents filed less than 10 days before a hearing must be taken to Masters' Appointments, Room TM7.09, for filing and marked "For hearing on..*[date]*before Master..." (Documents filed before that time should be filed in the Registry, Room TM5.04, in the normal way). Exhibits should not be placed in lever arch files but should be fastened securely, for example by treasury tags.

7.44 *Delivery of bundles for hearings before Bankruptcy Registrars*

Bundles should be delivered to Room TM1.10 not less than 2 (and not more than 7) clear working days before the hearing. The should be clearly marked "For hearing on ....*[date]* before Registrar ...."

7.45 *Delivery of bundles for hearings before Companies Court Registrars*

Bundles should be delivered to Room TM4.04 not less than 2 (and not more than 7) clear working days before the hearing. They should be clearly marked "For hearing on ....*[date]* before Registrar ...."

7.46 *Late delivery of bundles for hearings before Masters and Registrars*

Parties delivering bundles should note that a log will be kept recording the time of their delivery to Rooms TM1.10, TM4.04 and TM7.09. Any failure to comply with these requirements which results in the postponement of a hearing may render that party liable to pay the costs occasioned by the adjournment.

Note: Bundles for hearings before a Chancery judge must be delivered to the Chancery Judges' Listing Office (Room WG4).

Skeleton arguments

7.47 Skeleton arguments should normally be prepared in respect of any application **1A–76** before the Master or Registrar of one or more hours' duration and certainly for any trial or similar hearing. They are to be delivered to the same place and at the same time as bundles. The contents of the skeleton argument should be in accordance with Appendix 7.

7.48 Where a skeleton argument is required, photocopies of any authorities to be relied upon should be attached to the skeleton argument.

7.49 If pursuant to the e-mail protocol for communications with the Chancery Division (paragraph 14.8 below), a skeleton argument is sent electronically, then the provisions of the protocol as well as the time limits set out above must be followed. In particular, any authorities relied on should be delivered in hard form and, where it would assist, be accompanied by a copy of the skeleton argument in hard form.

7.50 Failure to deliver skeleton arguments or bundles in accordance with this Guide is likely to result in the matter not being heard on the date fixed, the costs of preparation being disallowed and an adverse costs order being made.

Paragraph numbers marked with a "+" can be found online and on CD.

Compromise or settlement of hearings

1A–77 7.51 When hearings before Masters are compromised or settled, Masters' Appointments (Room TM7.09) should be informed in writing immediately and in any event no later than 4pm on the day preceding the hearing. In the case of substantial hearings involving pre-reading Masters' Appointments should be informed immediately if it appears likely that a hearing will be ineffective, with a request that the Master is immediately notified. Written notification must be given to Room TM1.10 for Bankruptcy hearings and Room TM4.04 for Companies hearings. Failure to notify and consequent waste of court time may result in an adverse costs order being made.

CHAPTER 8

CONDUCT OF A TRIAL

Key Rules: CPR Parts 32 and 39

1A–78 8.1 An important aim of all concerned must be to ensure that at trial court time is used as efficiently as possible. Thorough preparation of the case prior to trial is the key to this.

8.2 Chapter 7 of this Guide applies to preparation for a trial as well as for other hearings in court. This Chapter contains matters which principally affect trials.

Time limits

1A–79 8.3 The court may, either at the outset of the trial or at any time thereafter, fix time limits for oral submissions, and the examination and cross-examination of witnesses. (See paragraphs 3.15 – 16.)

Oral submissions

1A–80 8.4 In general, and subject to any direction to the contrary by the trial judge, there should be a short opening statement on behalf of the claimant, at the conclusion of which the judge will invite short opening statements on behalf of the other parties.

8.5 Unless notified otherwise, advocates should assume that the judge will have read their skeleton arguments and the principal documents referred to in the reading list lodged in advance of the hearing (see paragraph 7.17). The judge will state at an early stage how much he or she has read and what arrangements are to be made about reading any documents not already read, for which an adjournment of the trial after opening speeches may be appropriate. If the judge needs to read any documents additional to those mentioned in the reading list lodged in advance of the hearing, a list should be provided during the opening.

8.6 It is normally convenient for any outstanding procedural matters to be dealt with in the course of, or immediately after, the opening statements.

8.7 After the evidence is concluded, and subject to any direction to the contrary by the trial judge, oral closing submissions will be made on behalf of the claimant first, followed by the defendant(s) in the order in which they appear on the claim form, followed by a reply on behalf of the claimant. In a lengthy and complex case each party should provide written summaries of their closing submissions.

8.8 The court may require the written summaries to set out the principal findings of fact for which a party contends.

Witness Statements

1A–81 8.9 In the preparation of witness statements for use at trial, the guidelines in Appendix 9 should be followed.

8.10 Unless the court orders otherwise, a witness statement will stand as the witness' evidence in chief if he or she is called and confirms that he or she believes the facts stated in the statement are true: rule 32.5.

Paragraph numbers marked with a "+" can be found online and on CD.

8.11 A witness may be allowed to supplement his or her witness statement orally at the trial before submitting to cross-examination, for example to deal with events occurring, or matters discovered, after his or her statement was served, or in response to matters dealt with by another party's witness, but a party seeking to examine in chief a witness who has provided a witness statement must satisfy the judge that there is good reason not to confine the evidence to the contents of his or her witness statement: see rule 32.5(3) and (4). Where practicable a supplementary witness statement should be prepared and served on the other parties, as soon as possible, to deal with matters not dealt with in the original witness statement. Permission is required to adduce a supplementary witness statement at trial if any other party objects to it. This need not be sought prior to service; it can be sought at a case management conference if convenient or, if need be, at trial.

8.12 Witnesses are expected to have re-read their witness statements shortly before they are called to give evidence.

8.13 Where a party decides not to call a witness whose witness statement has been served to give oral evidence at trial, prompt notice of this decision should be given to all other parties. The party should make plain when he or she gives this notice whether he or she proposes to put, or seek to put, the witness statement in as hearsay evidence. If he or she does not put the witness statement in as hearsay evidence, rule 32.5(5) allows any other party to put it in as hearsay evidence.

8.14 Facilities may be available to assist parties or witnesses with special needs, whether as regards access to the court, or audibility in court, or otherwise. The Chancery Judges' Listing Office should be notified of any such needs prior to the hearing. The Customer Service Officer (tel 020 7947 7731) can also assist with parking, access etc.

Cross-examination

8.15 The party cross-examining is not necessarily obliged to put his or her case to **1A–82** each witness even if they deal in chief with the same point. It may be sufficient if he or she puts it to one of the other side's witnesses. If that witness makes any admission or expresses any opinion or otherwise adds a qualification to his or her evidence, the party cross-examining can rely on it in argument but he or she cannot assume that other witnesses would have made the same admission or qualification and expressed the same opinion: see *Re Yarn Spinners' Agreement* [1959] 1 All ER 299 at 309 per Devlin J.

Expert Evidence

8.16 The trial judge may disallow expert evidence which either is not relevant for any **1A–83** reason, or which he or she regards as excessive and disproportionate in all the circumstances, even though permission for the evidence has been given.

8.17 The evidence of experts (or of the experts on a particular topic) is commonly taken together at the same time and after the factual evidence has been given. If this is to be done it should be agreed by the parties before the trial and should be raised with the judge at the PTR, if there is one, or otherwise at the start of the trial. Expert evidence should as far as possible be given by reference to the reports exchanged.

8.18 The evidence of experts must be impartial, complying with rule 35.3. If it is not it may be disregarded.

Physical exhibits

8.19 Some cases involve a number of physical exhibits. The parties should endeavour **1A–84** to agree the exhibits in advance and their system of labelling. Where it would be desirable, a scheme of display should be agreed (e.g. on a board with labels readable from a distance). Where witness statements refer to these, a note in the margin (which can be handwritten) of the exhibit number should be added.

Paragraph numbers marked with a "+" can be found online and on CD.

CHAPTER 9

JUDGMENTS, ORDERS AND PROCEEDINGS AFTER JUDGMENT

Key Rules: CPR Part 40, and PDs 40, 40B, 40D and 40E

Judgments

1A–85 9.1 Where judgment is reserved, the judge will normally deliver his or her judgment by handing down the written text without reading it out in open court. Where this course is adopted, the advocates will be supplied with the full text of the judgment in advance of delivery. In such cases, the advocates should familiarise themselves with the text of the judgment and be ready to deal with any points which may arise when judgment is delivered. The parties should seek to agree any consequential orders: see paragraph 3.1 of PD 40E.

9.2 The text may be shown, in confidence, to the parties, but only for the purpose of obtaining instructions and on the strict understanding that the judgment, or its effect, is not to be disclosed to any other person, or used in the public domain, and that no action is taken (other than internally) in response to the judgment. Advocates should notify the judge's clerk of any obvious errors or omissions.

9.3 The judgment does not take effect until formally delivered in court, when, if requested and so far as practicable, it will be made available to the law reporters and the press. The judge will normally direct that the written judgment may be used for all purposes as the text of the judgment, and that no transcript of the judgment need be made. Where such a direction is made, copies of the judgment may be obtained from the Mechanical Recording Department.

Orders

1A–86 9.4 It may often be possible for the court to prepare and seal an order more quickly if a draft of the order is handed in. Speed may be particularly important where the order involves the grant of an interim injunction or the appointment of a receiver without notice. In all but the most simple cases a draft order should be prepared and brought to the hearing.

9.5 The court may in any case direct the parties to agree and sign a statement of the terms of the order made by the court (still commonly called a minute of order). Where the proceedings are in the Royal Courts of Justice, the statement should, when agreed and signed, be delivered to Chancery Chambers Registry and Issue Section (Room TM5.04) unless otherwise requested. The statement must, under PD 40B, be filed no later than 7 days from the date of the order, unless the court directs otherwise. In the case of any dispute or difficulty as to the contents of the order, the parties should mention the matter to the judge or Master who heard the application.

9.6 Where a draft or an agreed statement of the terms of an order exists in electronic form, it is often helpful if the draft or agreed statement is provided to the court by e-mail or on disk as well as in hard copy, particularly if the order needs to be drawn quickly. Any disk supplied for this purpose must be new and newly-formatted before writing the material on it so as to minimise the risk of transferring a computer virus. The current word processing system used by the Chancery Associates is Word for Windows 2000. Enquiries regarding the provision of disks should be made of the associate responsible for drawing the order in question.

Drafting and Service of Orders

1A–87 9.7 Where a judge or Master directs that a statement of the terms of an order be agreed and signed, the agreed statement should be filed in Room TM5.04 as set out in paragraph 9.5 above. Agreed statements will normally be adopted as the order of the court.

9.8 Orders will be drawn up by the court, unless the judge or Master directs that no

Paragraph numbers marked with a "+" can be found online and on CD.

order be drawn. Unless a contrary order is made, or the party concerned has asked to serve the order, a sealed order will be sent by the court to each party.

9.9 Where a particular order is required to be served personally, the party concerned (see above) will be responsible for service.

9.10 If the order is to be drawn up by a party, three engrossments of the order proposed should be delivered or posted to:

Chancery Chambers Registry

Room TM5.04

Thomas More Building

Royal Courts of Justice

Strand

London WC2A 2LL

Forms of Order

9.11 Recitals will be kept to a minimum and the body of the order will be confined to **1A–88** setting out the decision of the court and the directions required to give effect to it. If upon receipt of an order any party is of the view that it is not drawn up in such a way as to give effect to the decision of the court, prompt notice must be given to the Chancery Chambers Registry in Room TM5.04 and to all other parties setting out the reasons for dissatisfaction. If the differences cannot be resolved, the objecting party may apply on notice for the order to be amended and should do so promptly

Copies of Orders

9.12 Copies of orders may be obtained from Room TM5.04 upon payment of the **1A–89** appropriate fee.

Consent Orders

9.13 All consent orders filed in Chancery Chambers and in respect of which a fee has **1A–90** been paid are referred to the Master for approval before the order is sealed.

Consent Orders under the Inheritance (Provision for Family and Dependants) Act 1975

9.14 Every final order embodying terms of compromise made in proceedings in the **1A–91** Chancery Division under the 1975 Act must under paragraph 18.2 of PD 57 contain a direction that a memorandum of the order shall be endorsed on or permanently annexed to the grant and a copy of the order shall be sent to the Principal Registry of the Family Division with the relevant grant of probate or letters of administration for endorsement notwithstanding that any particular order may not, strictly speaking, be an order under the 1975 Act.

Consents by parties not attending the hearing

9.15 This is covered in paragraphs 5.24–26 above. **1A–92**

Tomlin Orders

9.16 Where proceedings are to be stayed on agreed terms to be scheduled to the **1A–93** order, the draft order should be drawn so as to read, with any appropriate provision in respect of costs, as follows:
 "And the parties having agreed to the terms set out in the attached schedule
 IT IS BY CONSENT ORDERED

Paragraph numbers marked with a "+" can be found online and on CD.

That all further proceedings in this claim be stayed except for the purpose of carrying such terms into effect
AND for that purpose the parties have permission to apply".

This form of order is called a "TomlinOrder".

Proceedings after judgment

1A–94 9.17 Proceedings under judgments and orders in the Chancery Division are now regulated by PD 40 Accounts, Inquiries etc., PD 40B Judgments and Orders, and PD 40D Court's Powers in Relation to Land etc.

Directions

1A–95 9.18 Where a judgment or order directs further proceedings or steps, such as accounts or inquiries, it will often give directions as to how the accounts and inquiries are to be conducted, for example:

for accounts

    (1) who is to lodge the account and within what period;

    (2) within what period objection is to be made; and

    (3) arrangements for inspection of vouchers or other relevant documents;

for inquiries

    (4) whether the inquiry is to proceed on written evidence or with statements of case;

    (5) directions for service of such evidence or statements; and

    (6) directions as to disclosure.

9.19 If directions are not given in the judgment or order an application should be made to the assigned Master as soon as possible asking for such directions. The application notice should specify the directions sought. Before making the application, applicants should write to the other parties setting out the directions they seek and inviting their response within 14 days. The application to the court should not be made until after the expiry of that period unless there is some special urgency. The application must state that the other parties have been consulted and have attached to it copies of the applicant's letter to the other parties and of any response from them. The Master will then consider what directions are appropriate. In complex cases he or she may direct a case management conference.

9.20 If any inquiry is estimated to last more than two days and involves very large sums of money or strongly contested issues of fact or difficult points of law, the Master may direct that it be heard by a judge. The parties are under an obligation to consider whether in any particular case the inquiry is more suitable to be heard by a judge and should assist the Master in this. Accounts, however long they are estimated to take, will normally be heard by the Master. The Master is likely to want to give detailed directions in connection with the account and the form of it.

9.21 Under the Register of Judgments, Orders and Fines Regulations 2005, money judgments in claims commenced in the High Court after 6th April 2006 (unless exempt) are registered with the Registrar of Judgments, Orders and Fines. Returns are sent to the Registrar by the court. In non-contested cases (judgments in default or on admission) registration is immediate. In contested cases the judgment is not registered unless steps are taken to enforce it under Part 70 or Part 71.

9.22 Judgments which are the subject of an appeal under Part 52 are not registered until the appeal has been determined. The court officer responsible for returns (Malcolm Dann, Room TM 5.07, 020 7947 6531) should be informed if permission to appeal is granted after a judgment has been registered, and he should also be informed when an application is made under Part 70 or Part 71.

Paragraph numbers marked with a "+" can be found online and on CD.

9.23 If the judgment debt is satisfied, the judgment has been set aside or reversed, or the amount of the debt increases as a result of the issue of a final costs certificate or an increase in the amount of the debt as a consequence of enforcement proceedings, the court officer responsible for returns (as above) should be notified.

CHAPTER 10

APPEALS

Key Rules: CPR Part 52 and PD 52; PD Insolvency Proceedings, Part 4, paragraph 17: Appeals

General

10.1 This Chapter is concerned with the following appeals affecting the Chancery Division: **1A–96**

(1) Appeals within the ordinary work of the Division, from Masters to High Court judges;

(2) Insolvency appeals from High Court Registrars and from county courts to High Court judges;

(3) Appeals to High Court judges in the Chancery Division from orders in claims proceeding in a county court;

(4) Statutory appeals from tribunals and others to the Chancery Division.

Proceedings under the Companies Acts are specialist proceedings for the purposes of rule 49(2) and therefore as regards the destination of appeals. In those cases appeals from final decisions by a Registrar of the Companies Court go direct to the Court of Appeal. Such appeals are not covered in this Chapter.

10.2 This Chapter does not deal with appeals from High Court judges of the Division, except as regards permission to appeal, and as to giving notice to the court of an appeal in a contempt case. It does not deal with appeals in the course of the detailed assessment of costs.

10.3 The detailed procedure for appeals is set out in Part 52 and in PD 52, and in the PD relating to Insolvency Proceedings, to which reference should be made. This Chapter only refers to some of the salient points.

Permission to appeal

10.4 Permission to appeal is required in all cases except: (a) appeals against committal orders, (b) certain insolvency appeals and (c) certain statutory appeals. Permission to appeal will only be given where the court considers that the appeal would have a real prospect of success or there is some other compelling reason why the appeal should be heard (rule 52.3(6)). **1A–97**

10.5 An application for permission may be made to the lower court, but only if it is made at the hearing at which the decision to be appealed was made (rule 52.3(2)(a)). Permission may be granted, or refused, or granted in part (whether as to a part of the order, a ground of appeal or an issue) and refused as to the rest. It may be granted conditionally.

10.6 If the lower court refuses permission, or if permission is not applied for to the lower court at the original hearing, an application for permission may be made to the appeal court, by appeal notice.

10.7 An application to the appeal court for permission may be dealt with without a hearing, but if refused without a hearing the applicant may request that it be reconsidered at a hearing. Notice of the hearing is often given to the respondent; the respondent may submit written representations or attend the hearing but will not necessarily be awarded any costs of so doing even if permission to appeal is refused.

10.8 Guidance for litigants in relation to appeals to the High Court is available by way of a Practice Statement which may be obtained from the High Court Appeals Office at the Royal Courts of Justice (Room WG4).

Paragraph numbers marked with a "+" can be found online and on CD.

10.9 If a party who wishes to appeal cannot lodge all the documents which are required at the time when the appellant's notice is issued, the Appeals Office is able to allow some further time by way of an extension, but beyond this any further extension has to be allowed by a judge, who will consider the case on paper. If there is a delay in obtaining a transcript of the judgment to be appealed, the appellant should endeavour to obtain a note of the judgment, which the lawyers representing any party at the hearing below ought to be able to provide, at least as an interim measure before a transcript is obtained.

10.10 If the documents required for consideration of an application for permission to appeal have not been lodged, despite any extension which has been allowed, the case may be listed for oral hearing in the Dismissal List, for the appellant to show cause why the case should not be dismissed. The respondent will not normally be notified of such a hearing.

Time for appealing

1A–98 10.11 The time limit for an appeal notice to be filed at the appeal court is 21 days after the decision of the lower court to be appealed, unless the lower court fixes some other period, which may be longer or shorter. The lower court can only fix a different period if it does so at the time it makes the order to be appealed from. Otherwise only the appeal court can alter the time limits.

Stay

1A–99 10.12 Unless the lower court or the appeal court orders otherwise, an appeal does not operate as a stay of any order or decision of the lower court. A stay of execution may be applied for in the appellant's notice. If it is, it may be dealt with on paper. If the stay is required as a matter of great urgency, or before the appellant's notice can be filed, an application should be made to the Applications judge.

Appeals from Masters in cases proceeding in the Chancery Division

1A–100 10.13 If permitted, an appeal from a decision of a Master in a case proceeding in the Chancery Division usually lies to a High Court judge of the Division. An appeal from a final decision of a Master in a claim allocated to the multi-track lies direct to the Court of Appeal.

10.14 The appeal to the judge is limited to a review of the decision of the lower court, unless the court considers that, in the circumstances of the individual appeal, it would be in the interests of justice to hold a re-hearing. This principle applies to all appeals dealt with in this Chapter except where some other provision is made, as mentioned below. Unless the court does decide, exceptionally, to hold a re-hearing, the appeal will be allowed if the decision of the lower court was wrong or if it was unjust because of a serious procedural or other irregularity in the proceedings in the lower court.

Insolvency appeals

1A–101 10.15 An appeal lies from a county court (Circuit or District Judge) or a High Court Registrar in bankruptcy or company insolvency matters to a High Court judge of the Chancery Division, for which permission is not required.

10.16 Appeals in proceedings under the Company Directors Disqualification Act 1986 are treated as being in insolvency proceedings.

10.17 The time limit for such an appeal is the same as for ordinary Chancery appeals. An appeal is limited to a review of the decision of the lower court.

Appeals from orders made in county court claims

1A–102 10.18 An appeal against a decision of a circuit judge in a claim proceeding in a

Paragraph numbers marked with a "+" can be found online and on CD.

county court lies to the High Court, unless, either, the decision is a final decision in a claim allocated to the multi-track or in specialist proceedings to which rule 49(2) applies, or the decision is itself on an appeal; in either of these cases the appeal lies direct to the Court of Appeal. This does not apply, however, where the allocation to the multi-track is deemed, rather than the result of a specific order, so that in cases begun by a Part 8 claim form, even though they are deemed to be so allocated, appeals lie to the High Court. The general rules as to the requirement for permission described above apply to these appeals.

Statutory appeals

10.19 The Chancery Division hears a variety of appeals and cases stated under statute from decisions of tribunals and other persons. Some of these are listed or referred to in PD 52, but this is not exhaustive. Particular cases include appeals under the Taxes Management Act 1970 and the Inheritance Tax Act 1984, appeals from the Value Added Tax and Duties Tribunal, from the Pensions Ombudsman and the Occupational Pensions Regulatory Authority, from the Comptroller-General of Patents, Designs and Trade Marks, from the Chief Land Registrar, from the Commons Commissioners, and from the Charity Commissioners under the Charities Act 1993. **1A–103**

10.20 Tax and VAT appeals are dealt with in Chapter 25 below, and appeals in patent, design and trade mark matters in Chapter 23. For other appeals reference should be made to the relevant statute and to PD 52.

Appeals to the Court of Appeal: permission to appeal

10.21 An appeal lies from a judgment of a High Court judge of the Division to the Court of Appeal (unless an enactment makes it final and unappealable), but permission is required in all cases except where the order is for committal. Permission may be granted by the High Court judge, if applied to at the hearing at which the decision to be appealed was made, unless the order of the High Court judge was itself on an appeal, in which case permission may only be granted by the Court of Appeal. **1A–104**

Appeals in cases of contempt of court

10.22 Appellant's notices which by paragraph 21.4 of PD 52 are required to be served on "the court from whose order or decision the appeal is brought" may be served, in the case of appeals from the Chancery Division, on the Chief Master of the Chancery Division; service may be effected by leaving a copy of the notice of appeal with the clerk of the Lists in Room WG4, Royal Courts of Justice, Strand, London WC2A 2LL. **1A–105**

Dismissal by consent

10.23 The practice is as set out in paragraph 12 of PD 52, for all appeals except first appeals in insolvency matters. A document signed by solicitors for all parties must be lodged with the High Court Appeals Office (Room WG7), Royal Courts of Justice, Strand, London WC2A 2LL, requesting dismissal of the appeal. The appeal can be dismissed without any hearing by an order made in the name of the Chancellor. Any orders with directions as to costs will be drawn by the Chancery Associates. In the case of a first appeal in an insolvency matter, reference should be made to paragraph 17.22(8) of the PD Insolvency Proceedings. **1A–106**

CHAPTER 11

COSTS

Key Rules: CPR Parts 43 to 48 and the PD supplementing them

11.1 This Chapter does not set out to do more than refer to some salient points on costs relevant to proceedings in the Chancery Division. In particular it does not deal with the processes of detailed assessment or appeals in relation to such assessments. **1A–107**

Paragraph numbers marked with a "+" can be found online and on CD.

11.2 A number of provisions in respect of costs in the CPR and in the PD supplementing Parts 43 to 48 (Costs PD) are likely to be relevant to Chancery proceedings:

(1) *Informing the client of costs orders:* Solicitors have a duty to tell their clients, within 7 days, if an order for costs is made against them and they were not present at the hearing. Solicitors must also tell anyone else who has instructed them to act on the case or who is liable to pay their fees. They must inform these persons how the order came to be made (rule 44.2; Costs PD, paragraph 7.1).

(2) *Providing the court with estimates of costs:* The court can order a party to file an estimate of costs and to serve it on the other parties. (Costs PD, paragraph 6.3). This is to assist the court in deciding what case management orders to make and also to inform other parties as to their potential liability for costs. In addition parties must file estimates of costs when they file their allocation questionnaire or any listing questionnaire (Costs PD, paragraph 6.4).

(3) *Summary assessment of costs:* An outline of these provisions is given below. Their effect is that in the majority of contested hearings lasting no more than a day the court will decide, at the end of the hearing, not only who is to pay the costs but also how much those costs should be, and will order them to be paid, usually within 14 days. As a result the paying party will have to pay the costs at a much earlier stage than before.

(4) *Interim orders for costs:* Where the court decides immediately who is to pay particular costs, but does not assess the costs summarily, for example after a trial lasting more than a day, so that the final amount of costs payable has to be fixed by a detailed assessment, the court may order the paying party to pay a sum or sums on account of the ultimate liability for costs.

(5) *Interest on costs:* The court has power to award interest on costs from a date before the date of the order, so compensating the receiving party for the delay between incurring the costs and receiving a payment in respect of them from the paying party.

Summary Assessment

1A–108   11.3 The court will generally make a summary assessment of costs whenever the hearing lasts for less than one day. The judge or Master who heard the application or other hearing (which will include a trial, or the hearing of a Part 8 Claim, lasting less than a day) carries out the summary assessment. The court may decide not to assess costs summarily either because it orders the costs to be "costs in the case" or because it considers the case to be otherwise inappropriate for summary assessment, typically because substantial issues arise as to the amount of the costs claimed. Costs payable to a party funded by the Legal Services Commission cannot be assessed summarily.

11.4 In order that the court can assess costs summarily at the end of the hearing each party who intends to claim costs must, no later than 24 hours before the time fixed for the hearing, serve on the other party, and file with the court, his or her statement of costs. Paragraph 13.5 of the Costs PD contains requirements about the information to be included in this statement, and the form of the statement. Failure by a party to file and serve his or her statement of costs as required by paragraph 13.5 of the Costs PD will be taken into account by the court in deciding what order to make about costs and could result in a reduced assessment, in no order being made as to costs, or in the party being penalised in respect of the costs of any further hearing or detailed assessment hearing which may be required as a result of the party's failure.

11.5 Where the receiving party (the party to whom the costs are to be paid) is funded by the Legal Services Commission the court cannot assess costs summarily. It is not, however, prevented from assessing costs summarily by the fact that the paying party (the party by whom the costs are to be paid) is so funded. A summary assessment of costs payable by a person funded by the Legal Services Commission is not by itself a determination of the amount of those costs which the funded party is to pay (as to which see section 11 of the Access to Justice Act 1999 and regulation 10 of the Community Legal Services (Costs) Regulations 2000). Ordinarily, where costs are

Paragraph numbers marked with a "+" can be found online and on CD.

summarily assessed and ordered to be paid by a funded person the order will provide that the determination of any amount which the person who is or was in receipt of services funded by the Legal Services Commission is to pay shall be dealt with in accordance with regulation 10 of the Regulations.

11.6 The amount of costs to be paid by one person to another can be determined on the standard basis or the indemnity basis. The basis to be used is determined when the court decides that a person should pay the costs of another. The usual basis is the standard basis and this is the basis that will apply if the order does not specify the basis of assessment. Costs that are unreasonably incurred or are unreasonable in amount are not allowed on either basis.

11.7 On the standard basis the court only allows costs which are proportionate to the matters in issue. If it has any doubt as to whether the costs were reasonably incurred or reasonable and proportionate in amount, it resolves the doubt in favour of the paying party. The concept of proportionality will always require the court to consider whether the costs which have been incurred were warranted having regard to the issues involved. A successful party who incurs costs which are disproportionate to the issues involved and upon which he or she has succeeded will only recover an amount of costs which the court considers to have been proportionate to those issues.

11.8 On the indemnity basis the court resolves any doubt it may have as to whether the costs were reasonably incurred or were reasonable in amount in favour of the receiving party.

11.9 The court must take into account all the circumstances, including the parties' conduct and the other matters mentioned in rule 44.5. Indemnity costs are not confined to cases of improper or reprehensible conduct. They will not, however, usually be awarded unless there has been conduct by the paying party which the court regards as unreasonable or unless the case falls within rule 48.4 (see paragraph 11.13 below).

11.10 A party must normally pay costs which are awarded against him or her and summarily assessed within 14 days of the assessment. But the court can extend that time (rules 44.8, 3.1(2)(a)). The court may therefore direct payment by instalments, or defer the liability to pay costs until the end of the proceedings so that the costs can then be set against any costs or judgment to which the paying party then becomes entitled.

11.11 If the parties have agreed the amount of costs, they do not need to file a statement of the costs, and summary assessment is unnecessary. If the parties to an application are able to agree an order by consent without the parties attending they should also agree a figure for costs to be inserted in the order or agree that there should be no order as to costs. If the costs position cannot be agreed then the parties will have to attend on the appointment but unless good reason can be shown for the failure of the parties to deal with costs as set out above no costs will be allowed for that attendance. The court finds it most unsatisfactory if parties agree the terms of a consent order but not the provision for costs. Depending on the facts and circumstances, the court may not be able to decide on the question of costs without hearing the application fully, but it is not likely to be consistent with the overriding objective to allow the necessary amount of court time to the dispute on costs in such a case. The court may then have to decide the costs issue on a broad brush approach, making an order against one party or the other only if it is clear, without spending too much time on it, that such an order would be appropriate, and otherwise making no order as to the costs.

Conditional fee agreements

11.12 The court should be informed, on any application for the payment of costs, if **1A–109** any party has entered into a conditional fee agreement. The court can then consider whether, in the light of that agreement, to stay the payment of any costs which have been summarily assessed until the end of the action, or to decline to order the payment of costs on account under rule 44.3(8).

Paragraph numbers marked with a "+" can be found online and on CD.

Other provisions

1A–110 11.13 Parts 45 to 48, and the Costs PD, contain provisions regarding:

(1) special cases in which costs are payable;

(2) wasted costs;

(3) fixed costs (these are payable for instance if judgment for a sum of money is given in default); and

    (d) detailed assessment.

In the context of Chancery litigation attention is drawn to rule 48.2 (Costs orders in favour of or against non-parties); rule 48.3 (Amount of costs where costs are payable pursuant to a contract) (see further Costs PD paragraph 50 and see also Chapter 21—Mortgage Claims); and rule 48.4 and Costs PD paragraph 50A (Limitations on court's power to award costs in favour of trustee or personal representative). Reference may also be made to Chapter 26 as regards costs orders in trust litigation.

CHAPTER 12

DISTRICT REGISTRIES

General

1A–111 12.1 Many Chancery cases are heard outside London. There are eight Chancery District Registries: Birmingham, Bristol, Cardiff, Leeds, Liverpool, Manchester, Newcastle-upon-Tyne, and Preston. High Court or Circuit Chancery judges sit regularly at all of these centres.

12.2 Outside London, county courts have exclusive jurisdiction in bankruptcy, and proceedings in bankruptcy must therefore be brought in the relevant county court which has bankruptcy jurisdiction rather than in the District Registries.

Judges

1A–112 12.3 Two Chancery judges supervise the arrangements for the hearing of Chancery cases out of London. Mr Justice Hart is the Chancery Supervising judge for the Western, Wales and Chester, and Midland Circuits. Mr Justice Patten, as Vice-Chancellor of the County Palatine of Lancaster, is concerned with Chancery hearings on the Northern and North Eastern Circuits. Both these judges regularly take substantial Chancery matters for hearing outside London. Mr Justice Hart sits regularly in Birmingham, Bristol and Cardiff, but if appropriate will sit elsewhere on the relevant circuit, for example in Chester. Mr Justice Patten sits regularly in Manchester, Liverpool, Leeds and Newcastle, and may sit in Preston or in other court centres on either circuit (e.g. Carlisle or Sheffield) if business so requires.

12.4 There are also Specialist Circuit judges who have the authority to exercise the powers of a judge of the Chancery Division (under section 9 of the Supreme Court Act 1981, therefore known as section 9 judges) and who normally sit out of London. They exercise a general Chancery jurisdiction, subject to exceptions. Those exceptions are proceedings directly concerning revenue, and proceedings before the Patents Court constituted as part of the Chancery Division under section 96 of the Patents Act 1977.

12.5 Currently the Circuit judges who sit regularly in Chancery matters out of London are:

Judge Weeks QC (Bristol)
Judge Norris QC (Birmingham)
Judge Wyn Williams QC (Cardiff)
Judge Howarth (Manchester, Liverpool and Preston)
Judge Behrens (Leeds and Newcastle)
Judge Kaye QC (Leeds and Newcastle)

Paragraph numbers marked with a "+" can be found online and on CD.

Judge Hodge QC (Manchester, Liverpool and Preston)
Judge Gilliland QC (who normally sits in Salford hearing Technology and Construction cases), Judges Kershaw QC and Hegarty QC (who are the local Mercantile judges based in Manchester and Liverpool) and Judge Raynor QC also assist in the disposal of Chancery business on the Northern Circuit. So also, on the North-Eastern Circuit, does Judge Langan QC who is the Mercantile judge for Leeds and Newcastle. The Chancery, Mercantile and TCC judges assist each other in Birmingham, Bristol and Cardiff as well.

12.6 In addition certain other Circuit judges and some Queen's Counsel are authorised to take Chancery cases on the same basis.

Trials

12.7 If a Chancery case is proceeding in any District Registry other than a Chancery **1A–113** District Registry, the case should normally be transferred to the appropriate Chancery District Registry upon the first occasion the case comes before the court.

12.8 The venue of a Chancery trial out of London will normally be one of the centres mentioned above. However in appropriate circumstances (e.g. because of the number or age of local witnesses, the need for a site visit, or travel problems) arrangements can be made for a Chancery judge to sit elsewhere.

12.9 In cases of great difficulty or importance the trial may be by a High Court judge. Arrangements can also be made in exceptional circumstances for a High Court judge to deal with any of the matters excepted from the jurisdiction of an authorised Circuit judge. Such a judge may be one of the Chancery judges other than Hart or Patten JJ.

12.10 Where it is desired that a case be heard by a specialist Chancery judge outside one of the normal Chancery Centres, or be taken by a High Court judge, inquiries should normally be made in the first instance to the Listing Officer for the nearest Chancery District Registry on the relevant circuit. If the need arises, inquiries can also be made to the clerk to Mr Justice Hart or the clerk to Mr Justice Patten, as the case may be. If no relevant clerk is available, inquiries should be made to the Chancery Listing Officer at the Royal Courts of Justice in London. The clerks' contact numbers are in Appendix 1.

Applications

12.11 Subject to the following paragraphs any application should normally be made **1A–114** to a District Judge (unless it relates to a matter which a District Judge does not have power to hear).

12.12 A District Judge may of his or her own initiative (for instance because of the **1A–115** complexity of the matter or the need for specialist attention) direct that an application be referred to a High Court judge or an authorised Circuit Judge.

12.13 If all or any of the parties consider that the matter should be dealt with by a **1A–116** judge (High Court or Circuit), the parties or any of them may arrange that the matter be listed on one of the ordinary application days (see paragraph 12.14 below). The District Judges, who will consult where necessary with one of the Chancery judges (High Court or Circuit), are usually available by post or telephone to give guidance on procedural matters, for example the court before which the matter should come or whether the matter may be dealt with in writing.

Application Days before a judge

12.14 Applications days are listed regularly before a judge, when applications and **1A–117** short appeals, including all interim matters are heard. Normally all matters will be called into court at the commencement of the day in order to work out a running

Paragraph numbers marked with a "+" can be found online and on CD.

order. Matters will be heard without the court going into private session unless good reason is shown. Rights of audience are unaffected. Applications days in Newcastle are subject to the Newcastle telephone application pilot scheme (see PD 23B), and many applications there are dealt with by telephone hearings.

12.15 Applications days are: Monday in Birmingham, Thursday in Bristol and Friday in Cardiff. In Manchester and Liverpool application days are on Friday of each week alternating between Manchester and Liverpool. In Leeds and Newcastle Chancery and Mercantile application days are combined. In Leeds applications are heard most Fridays. In Newcastle there is at least one application day each month, on a Friday. An application which needs to be heard urgently may be made, by telephone or in person, on a day other than the regular applications day: the Listing Officer for the relevant centre should be approached as soon as possible when the need for an urgent hearing arises.

Applications out of hours and telephone applications

1A–118 12.16 These are governed by the general rules, save that in the case of applications out of hours, the party applying should contact the relevant court office. The main relevant contact numbers are set out in Appendix 1. In case of difficulty, contact the Royal Courts of Justice, on the number given in Appendix 1.

Agreed interim orders

1A–119 12.17 Normally a hearing will not be necessary. The procedure is as in the general rules.

12.18 A judge is unlikely to agree to more than two consent adjournments of an interim application. Applications to vacate a trial date will require substantial justification and a hearing, normally before the trial judge.

Local Listing Arrangements

1A–120 12.19 Listing arrangements may vary at different centres, depending on availability of judges and courtrooms. The current details are described below.

Birmingham: Shared Listing

1A–121 12.20 The Shared List

The shared list is primarily for use by the three specialised lists of the Birmingham District Registry—those operated by the Chancery, Mercantile and Technology and Construction Courts.

The shared list is in addition to the normal lists of those courts and allows better use to be made of judicial time. Given the settlement rate of trials in the three divisions, two additional cases, the fourth and fifth fixtures, will be listed at any one time, in addition to the three cases listed before the three specialist courts. Those two additional cases will be taken by any of the section 9 judges who become available. Cases are only entered into the shared list if there is a very strong expectation that they will be heard on the day fixed.

In order, therefore, for a case to enter the shared list it must be suitable for hearing before any of the section 9 specialist judges.

Suitability for listing a case in the shared list may be suggested by the District Judge at directions stage, or by the parties when applying for the case to be listed. It is likely that 4th and 5th fixtures will be allocated an earlier trial date than a case which has to be heard by the appropriate specialist judge.

The final decision to list a case in the shared list will lie with Judge Norris QC for Chancery cases, Judge Alton for Mercantile cases, and Judge Kirkham for Technology and Construction cases.

Paragraph numbers marked with a "+" can be found online and on CD.

Bristol: Reserve Listing

1A–122

12.21 In order to make available earlier hearing dates than would otherwise be possible, a reserve list is operated for Chancery cases listed to be heard in the Bristol District Registry. Cases in the reserve list are given a fixed date, usually as a second fixture. A second fixture will only be given when there is a very strong expectation of the case being heard on that date. Other judges are called upon in the event of both first and second fixtures being effective.

Cardiff: Reserve Listing

1A–123

12.22 Judge Wyn Williams QC sits both as a Chancery judge and a judge of the Technology and Construction Court. His list contains both categories of case. All cases are allocated a fixed starting date but some are first and some reserve fixtures. Other judges are called upon in the event of both first and reserve fixtures being effective. All the judges who sit at the Cardiff Civil Justice Centre (Judges Price QC, Masterman, Chambers QC and Hickinbottom) are authorised to sit as Chancery judges. Any discussions concerning listing should be with the Chancery Listing clerk in Cardiff.

Manchester, Liverpool and Preston

1A–124

12.23 The Shared List

When sitting at the same court centre, Judge Howarth and Judge Hodge QC will assist each other in the disposal of their respective daily lists. If necessary and if they are available at the relevant court centre, Judge Kershaw QC and Judge Hegarty QC (who are the local Mercantile judges), and other circuit judges will assist in the disposal of business. Listing for all Chancery matters in Manchester, Liverpool and Preston is dealt with from Manchester.

Second Fixtures

Given the very high settlement rate, most cases will be given a second fixture date as well as a first fixture date. Parties to second fixtures are notified in advance of the hearing date if the case will not be reached on that date. The amount of notice depends on the circumstances of the case. In some cases it may not be until the previous working day but it is usually farther ahead, and longer may be guaranteed in the case of particular difficulties.

Leeds and Newcastle

1A–125

12.24 When sitting at the same time in Leeds or Newcastle Judge Behrens, Judge Langan QC and Judge Kaye QC will assist each other in the disposal of their respective daily lists. The Chancery and Mercantile Court lists are run on a shared basis in both Leeds and Newcastle. Second fixtures are used in the same way as on the Northern Circuit, and on the same basis.

CHAPTER 13

COUNTY COURTS

Key Rules: CPR Part 30; PD 7, paragraph 2

Unified procedure

1A–126

13.1 A key feature of the civil justice reforms is the introduction of a unified procedure for the High Court and for county courts. The procedure to be followed in both courts is therefore the same.

Chancery cases brought in the county court

1A–127

13.2 Any county court has jurisdiction to hear a Chancery case, subject to two

Paragraph numbers marked with a "+" can be found online and on CD.

principal exceptions: (1) a probate claim in a county court must be brought in a county court where there is a Chancery District Registry: CPR part 57.2(3); (2) an intellectual property claim must be brought in any such county court or in the Patents County Court: CPR Part 63.13 and PD 63 paragraph 18.

13.3 If a case of a Chancery nature is brought in any county court, the claim form should be marked "Chancery business" in the top left hand corner: CPR Part 7, PD 2.5.

13.4 If a Chancery case is brought in a county court which does not coincide with a Chancery District Registry, consideration ought to be given at an early stage to whether it needs to have specialist case management or a specialist trial judge, because of the nature of the issues. If it needs either, then it may be necessary to transfer the case to a county court at a Chancery District Registry. If there are good reasons against such a transfer, for example because of the distance involved and the convenience of parties or witnesses, then it may be possible, with enough notice, to arrange that the trial is heard by a recorder with Chancery experience or even by a Chancery circuit judge. Guidance has been given to District Judges by the Chancery supervising judges as to the circumstances and types of case in respect of which either a transfer or a special arrangement for trial by a judge or recorder with specialist experience may be appropriate.

Transfer to a county court

1A–128 13.5 Any Chancery case which does not require to be heard by a High Court judge, and falls within the jurisdiction of the county courts, may be transferred to a county court. Where a case has been so transferred, the papers must be marked "Chancery Business" so as to ensure, so far as possible, suitable listing.

13.6 The jurisdiction of county courts is set out in the High Court and County Court Jurisdiction Order 1991 as amended, and in enactments amended by that Order.

13.7 The jurisdiction of the High Court to transfer cases to a county court is contained in the County Courts Act 1984, section 40, as substituted by the Courts and Legal Services Act 1990, section 2(1). Under that section, the court has jurisdiction in certain circumstances to strike out actions which ought to have been begun in a county court.

13.8 A claim with an estimated value of less than £50,000 will generally be transferred to a county court, if the county court has jurisdiction, unless it is either within a specialist list or is within the criteria in rule 30.3(2).

13.9 If the case is one of a specifically Chancery nature a transfer from the High Court will ordinarily be to the Central London County Court (Chancery List) ("the CLCC") where cases are heard by specialist Chancery Circuit judges or recorders and a continuous Chancery List is maintained, unless the parties prefer a transfer to a local county court.

13.10 Even where the estimated value of the claim is more than £50,000 transfer to the CLCC may still be ordered if the criteria in rule 30.3(2) point in that direction, in particular having regard to the criteria in rule 30.3(2)(d), namely the complexity of the facts, legal issues, remedies or procedures involved.

13.11 If a claim is transferred to a county court at the allocation stage no other directions will usually be given and all case management will be left to the county court.

13.12 The Chancery List at the CLCC is managed by the Business Chancery and Patents Section at 26 Park Crescent, London W1 4HT. The telephone number of the section manager is set out in Appendix 1. A guide to the Chancery List may be obtained from the section manager.

13.13 As an alternative to starting the case in the Chancery Division and transferring to the CLCC a case (if appropriate to be started there) may be started at the CLCC

Paragraph numbers marked with a "+" can be found online and on CD.

and a request made there for it to be transferred to the Chancery List. The request will receive judicial consideration and a transfer will be made if appropriate.

13.14 It should be noted that only in very limited circumstances may freezing orders or search orders be granted in the county court. If necessary, an application may be made in the High Court in aid of the county court proceedings if such an order is to be sought in a case where it cannot be granted in the county court.

13.15 Practitioners should continue to take care that Chancery cases requiring chancery expertise are dealt with in a county court with a Chancery District Registry.

Patents County Court

1A–129

13.16 See Chapter 23 below.

CHAPTER 14

USE OF INFORMATION TECHNOLOGY

Key Rules: CPR rule 1.4, Part 6;PD 6, PD 32, Annex 3

General

1A–130

14.1 The CPR contain certain provisions about the use of information technology in the conduct of cases. Apart from these provisions, no standard practice has evolved or been prescribed for the use of information technology in civil cases, but it is possible to identify certain areas in which electronic techniques may be used which should encourage the efficient and economical conduct of litigation.

14.2 It must be remembered, however, that it is unlikely that the number of litigants in person will diminish, and the number may well increase, in the future and that not all solicitors have available sophisticated IT facilities. Use of IT is acceptable only if no party to the case will be unfairly prejudiced and its use will save time or money.

14.3 A number of specific applications of information technology have been well developed in recent years. The use of fax, the provision of skeleton arguments on disk, and daily transcrripts on disk (with or withou appropriate software) have become commonplace. Short applications may be economically heard by a conference telephone call, provided that the parties ensure that the judge or Master has the relevant documents and a draft order. Taking evidence by video link has become more common, and the available technology has improved considerably. There is still little experience of the intensive use of information technology in the ordinary course of the trial by, for example, providing documents as images to be displayed.

14.4 In any case in which it is proposed to use information technology in the preparation, management and presentation of a case in a manner which is not provided for by the CPR, it may be necessary for directions to be given by the judge who is to hear the case. It is unlikely to be satisfactory for parties and their solicitors to agree to a particular application of information technology (for example, using imaging techniques to deal either with disclosure or with the preparation of documents for use in court, in effect by way of electronic bundles) without the agreement of the judge. Accordingly it is likely, particularly in heavy cases, that it will be desirable for a judge to be nominated to conduct the case. Where a nomination is desired, application should be made to the Chancellor in writing by letter addressed to his clerk for a judge to be nominated.

14.5 In every case in which it is proposed to use information technology, the first step will be for the solicitors for all parties to determine whether it is possible to establish a common protocol for the electronic exchange and management of information. It is recommended that the protocol provided by the Technology and Construction Solicitors' Association ("TeCSA") be used. The TeCSA protocol has enjoyed success and is available from TeCSA's website at *www.tecsa.org.uk/protocol/protocol.htm*. The CPR's underlying policy of co-operation and collaboration is particularly important in

Paragraph numbers marked with a "+" can be found online and on CD.

this context. In a large case the parties must facilitate the task of the judge by providing any additional help and IT know-how, including, for example, demonstrations, which he or she requires in order to control the case properly.

14.6 The judges of the Chancery Division and their clerks are equipped with IBM compatible computers running Windows (usually NT 4.0 but in some cases another version) and MS Office 97 or 2000. To avoid compatibility problems it is preferable that text files to be provided for use by a judge or clerk be provided in Rich Text Format (RTF).

Provision of information on disk: Skeleton arguments etc

1A–131 14.7 Skeleton arguments, chronologies, witness statements, experts' reports and other documents (if available in electronic form) should be provided on disk (or by e-mail) if the judge requests it. Enquiry should be made of the judge's clerk for this purpose. Where the complexity of the case justifies it, attention must be given to providing the judge with versions of the documents containing links to enable cross-references to be followed up in a convenient manner. Disks provided to judges must be checked for virus contamination and be clean.

E-mail communications with the Chancery Division

1A–132 14.8 A protocol for e-mail communications with the Chancery Division sets out how parties may communicate by e-mail on certain matters, and can be found at www.hmcourts-service.gov.uk. The protocol applies PD 5B on electronic communication and filing of documents in respect of specified documents: skeleton arguments, chronologies, reading lists, lists of issues, lists of authorities (but not the authorities themselves) and lists of *dramatis personae* sent in advance of a hearing. The protocol sets out the relevant email addresses, which are also to be found in Appendix 1. The clerk to the judge concerned should be contacted to find out whether the judge will accept other documents by e-mail and whether documents should be sent by e-mail direct to the judge's clerk's e-mail address.

Transcripts

1A–133 14.9 The various shorthand writers provide a number of different transcript services. These range from an immediately displayed transcript which follows the evidence as it is given (usually with about 10 seconds delay) to provision of transcripts of a day's proceedings one or two days in arrears. The use of transcripts is always of assistance if they can be justified on the ground of cost and in long cases they are a considerable advantage. If an instantaneous service is proposed, inquiries should be made of the judge's clerk, and sufficient time for the installation of the equipment necessary and for any familiarisation on the part of the judge with the system should be found. If special transcript-handling software is to be used by the parties, consideration should be given to making the software available to the judge.

14.10 If the shorthand writers make disks available (and nearly all do) the judge should be provided with disks as they appear if he or she requires them.

Fax communications

1A–134 14.11 The use of fax in the service of documents is now authorised by rule 6.2(1) and PD 6.

14.12 Each of the judges sitting in the Chancery Division may be reached by fax if the occasion warrants it. The respective judges' clerks' telephone and fax numbers are set out in Appendix 1. Where the name of the judge is not known, short documents may be sent to the Chancery Judges' Listing Office, whose fax number is also given in Appendix 1. Written evidence should not be sent by fax to this number. All fax messages should have a cover sheet setting out the name of the case, the case number and the judge's name, if known.

Telephone hearings

1A–135 14.13 Applications may be heard by telephone, if the court so orders, but normally

Paragraph numbers marked with a "+" can be found online and on CD.

15.10 Notice of hearing dates will be given by post to litigants at the address shown in the court file. A litigant in person will generally be given a fixed date for trial on application. A litigant in person who wishes to apply for a fixed date should ask the Chancery Judges' Listing Office for a copy of its Guidance Notes for Litigants in Person.

Assistance to litigants in person

15.11 A litigant who is acting in person may be assisted at a hearing by another person, often referred to as a McKenzie friend (see *McKenzie v. McKenzie* [1971] P 33). The litigant must be present at the hearing. If the hearing is in private, it is a matter of discretion for the court whether such an assistant is allowed to attend the hearing. That may depend, among other things, on the nature of the proceedings.

1A–138

15.12 The McKenzie friend is allowed to help by taking notes, quietly prompting the litigant and offering advice and suggestions to the litigant. The court can, and sometimes does, permit the McKenzie friend to address the court on behalf of the litigant, by making an order to that effect under section 27(2)(c) of the Courts and Legal Services Act 1990 (by reference to sections 17 and 18 of that Act), but this is an exceptional course. Some factors which may be relevant to whether this should be permitted have been discussed in reported judgments, including *Izzo v. Philip Ross & Co* [2002] B.P.I.R. 310 and *Paragon Finance v. Noueiri (Practice Note)* [2001] EWCA Civ 1402, [2001] 1 W.L.R. 2357.

15.13 The Personal Support Unit (Room M104) offers personal support for litigants in person, witnesses and others. The PSU will sometimes be able to accompany litigants into court to provide emotional support and give other guidance, but it does not give legal advice.

Representation on behalf of companies

15.14 Rule 39.6 allows a company or other corporation to be represented at trial by an employee if the employee has been authorised by the company or corporation to appear on its behalf and the court gives permission. Paragraph 5 of PD 39 describes what is needed to obtain permission from the court for this purpose and mentions some of the considerations relevant to the grant or refusal of permission.

1A–139

Robed and unrobed hearings

15.15 Advocates (and judges) wear robes at hearings by High Court judges of trials (including preliminary issues) and statutory appeals or cases stated. Robes are not worn for other hearings, including appeals from Masters, Bankruptcy Registrars and county courts. The Daily Cause List states, in relation to each judge's list, whether the matter is to be heard robed or unrobed. Robes are not worn at hearings before Masters. Robes are worn at the following hearings before Bankruptcy and Companies Court Registrars: public examinations of bankrupts and of directors or other officers of companies; applications for discharge from bankruptcy or for suspension of such discharge; all proceedings under the Company Directors Disqualification Act 1986; petitions to wind up companies; final hearings of petitions for the reduction of capital of companies.

1A–140

Solicitors' rights of audience

15.16 At hearings in chambers before 26 April 1999 solicitors had general rights of audience. The fact that a matter which would then have been heard in chambers is now heard in public under Part 39 does not affect rights of audience, so in such matters as would have been heard in chambers previously, the general right of audience for solicitors continues to apply. Such cases included appeals from Masters, applications for summary judgment, and those concerned with pleadings, security for costs and the like, pre-trial reviews, and applications concerned with the administration of a deceased person's estate, a trust or a charity. They did not include applications in what is now the Interim Applications List or the Companies Court, nor appeals from county courts or insolvency appeals. Solicitors do, however, have general rights of audience in personal insolvency matters; this is not affected by whether the hearing is in public or private.

1A–141

Paragraph numbers marked with a "+" can be found online and on CD.

15.17 If a solicitor who does not have the appropriate special right of audience wishes to be heard in a case which is not one which, before 26 April 1999, would have been heard in chambers nor a personal insolvency case, an application may be made for the grant of a special right of audience before the particular court and for the particular proceedings under the Courts and Legal Services Act 1990, section 27(2)(c).

Recording at hearings

1A–142 15.18 In the Royal Courts of Justice it is normal to record all oral evidence and any judgment delivered during a hearing before a judge. If any party wishes a recording to be made of any other part of the proceedings, this should be mentioned in advance or at the time of the hearing.

15.19 At hearings before Masters, it is not normally practicable to record anything other than any oral evidence and the judgment, but these will be recorded. No party or member of the public may use recording equipment without the court's permission.

CHAPTER 16

SUGGESTIONS FOR IMPROVEMENT AND COURT USERS' COMMITTEES

1A–143 16.1 Suggestions for improvements in this Guide or in the practice or procedure of the Chancery Division are welcome. Unless they fall within the remit of the committees mentioned at paras. 16.3 to 16.7 below, they should be sent to the clerk to the Chancellor.

Chancery Division Court Users' Committee

1A–144 16.2 The Chancery Division Court Users' Committee's function is to review, as may from time to time be required, the practice and procedure of all courts forming part of the Chancery Division, to ensure that they continue to provide a just, economical and expeditious system for the resolution of disputes. The Chancellor is the chairman. Its membership includes judges, a Master, barristers, solicitors and other representatives of court staff and users. Meetings are held three times a year, and more often if necessary. Suggestions for points to be considered by the Committee should be sent to the clerk to the Chancellor.

Insolvency Court Users' Committee

1A–145 16.3 Proposals for change in insolvency matters fall within the remit of the Insolvency Court Users' Committee unless they relate to the Insolvency Rules 1986. The members of the Insolvency Court Users' Committee include members of the Bar, the Law Society, the Insolvency Service and the Society of Practitioners of Insolvency. Meetings are held three times a year, and more often if necessary. Suggestions for points to be considered by the Committee should be sent to the clerk to the Chancellor.

Insolvency Rules Committee

1A–146 16.4 The Insolvency Rules Committee must be consulted before any changes to the Insolvency Rules 1986 are made. The Chairman of the Insolvency Rules Committee is Mr Justice David Richards. Proposals for changes in the Rules should be sent to The Insolvency Service, Room 502, PO Box 203, 21 Bloomsbury Street, London WC1B 3QW, with a copy to the clerk to Mr Justice David Richards.

Intellectual Property Court Users' Committee

1A–147 16.5 This considers the problems and concerns of intellectual property litigation generally. Membership of the committee includes the principal Patent judges, a Master, a representative of each of the Patent Bar Association, the Intellectual

Paragraph numbers marked with a "+" can be found online and on CD.

Property Lawyers Association, the Chartered Institute of Patent Agents, the Institute of Trade Mark Agents and the Trade Marks Designs and Patents Federation. It will also include one or more other Chancery judges. The Chairman is Mr Justice Pumfrey. Anyone having views concerning the improvement of intellectual property litigation is invited to make his or her views known to the committee, preferably through the relevant professional representative on the committee.

Pension Litigation Court Users' Committee

16.6 This consists of a judge and a Master, two barristers and two solicitors. Its **1A–148** Chairman is Mr Justice Etherton. Any suggestions for consideration by the committee should be sent to the clerk to Mr Justice Etherton.

Court Users' Committees outside London

16.7 There are several Court Users' Committees relating to Chancery work on circuit. **1A–149** They are as follows:

(1) *The Northern Circuit and the North-Eastern Circuit Court Users Committees*: the Northern Circuit Chancery Court Users' Committee, which meets in Manchester; the Leeds Chancery and Mercantile Court Users' Committee; and the Newcastle Joint Chancery Mercantile and TCC Court Users' Committee. Each of these meets two or three times a year, and has a membership including judges, court staff, barristers and solicitors. The Vice-Chancellor of the County Palatine of Lancaster chairs these three Committees, and the Vice-Chancellor's clerk acts as secretary to each Committee. All communications should be to the clerk.

(2) *The Western Circuit, Wales & Chester and Midland Circuits Court User Committees*: the circuit committees normally meet three or four times per year. They have a membership including judges, court staff, barristers and solicitors.

   (a) *Western Circuit*: Judge Weeks chairs the committee in Bristol (or Mr Justice Hart when there), Mrs Liz Bodman acts as secretary. All communications should be addressed to her at Chancery Listing Section, Bristol Crown Court, Small Street, Bristol.

   (b) *Wales & Chester Circuit*: Judge Williams chairs the committee in Cardiff (or Mr Justice Hart when there), the Diary Manager, Annette Parsons acts as secretary. All communications should be addressed to her at Cardiff Civil Justice Centre, 2 Park Street, Cardiff.

   (c) *Midland Circuit*: Judge Norris chairs the committee in Birmingham (or Mr Justice Hart when there), the Chancery Listing Officer, Amanda Lee acts as secretary. All communications should be addressed to her at Chancery Listing Section, Birmingham Civil Justice Centre, 33 Bull Street, Birmingham.

CHAPTER 17

ALTERNATIVE DISPUTE RESOLUTION

Key Rules: CPR rules 3.1 and 26.4

17.1 While emphasising the primary role of the court as a forum for deciding cases, **1A–150** the court encourages parties to consider the use of ADR (such as, but not confined to, mediation and conciliation) as a possible means of resolving disputes or particular issues.

17.2 The settlement of disputes by means of ADR can:

(1) significantly help litigants to save costs;

(2) save litigants the delay of litigation in reaching finality in their disputes;

(3) enable litigants to achieve settlement of their disputes while preserving their existing commercial relationships and market reputation;

(4) provide litigants with a wider range of solutions than those offered by litigation; and

Paragraph numbers marked with a "+" can be found online and on CD.

(5) make a substantial contribution to the more efficient use of judicial resources.

17.3 The court will in an appropriate case invite the parties to consider whether their dispute, or particular issues in it, could be resolved through ADR. In particular, it is to be expected that the judge or Master at any case management conference will inquire what steps can usefully be taken to resolve the dispute by settlement discussion, alternative dispute resolution or other means. The parties should be in a position to tell the court what steps have been taken or are proposed to be taken. The court may also adjourn the case for a specified period of time to encourage and enable the parties to use ADR and for this purpose extend the time for compliance by the parties or any of them with any requirement under the CPR or this Guide or any order of the court. The court may make such order as to the costs that the parties may incur by reason of the adjournment or their using or attempting to use ADR as may in all the circumstances seem appropriate.

17.4 Legal representatives in all cases should consider with their clients and the other parties concerned the possibility of attempting to resolve the dispute or particular issues by ADR and they should ensure that their clients are fully informed as to the most cost effective means of resolving their dispute.

17.5 Parties who consider that ADR might be an appropriate means of resolving their dispute, or particular issues in the dispute, may apply for directions at any stage.

17.6 The clerk to the Commercial Court keeps some published information as to individuals and bodies that offer ADR services. (The list also includes individuals and bodies that offer arbitration services.) If the parties are unable to agree upon a neutral individual, or panel of individuals, for ADR, they may refer to the judge for assistance, though the court will not recommend any particular body or individual to act as mediator or arbitrator.

SECTION B SPECIALIST WORK

CHAPTER 18

INTRODUCTION TO THE SPECIALIST WORK OF THE CHANCERY DIVISION

1A–151 18.1 As explained in Chapter 1 of this Guide, some proceedings in the High Court must be brought in the Chancery Division. These matters include:

(1) claims for the sale, exchange or partition of land, or the raising of charges on land;

(2) mortgage claims;

(3) claims relating to the execution of trusts;

(4) claims relating to the administration of the estates of deceased persons;

(5) bankruptcy matters;

(6) claims for the dissolution of partnerships or the taking of partnership or other accounts;

(7) claims for the rectification, setting aside or cancellation of deeds or other instruments in writing;

(8) contentious probate business;

(9) claims relating to patents, trade marks, registered designs, copyright or design right;

(10) claims for the appointment of a guardian of a minor's estate;

(11) jurisdiction under the Companies Acts 1985 and the Insolvency Act 1986 relating to companies;

(12) some revenue matters;

(13) claims relating to charities;

(14) some proceedings under the Solicitors Act 1974;

(15) proceedings under the Landlord and Tenant Acts 1927 (Part I), 1954 (Part II) and 1987 and the Leasehold Reform Act 1967;

Paragraph numbers marked with a "+" can be found online and on CD.

(16) proceedings (other than those in the Commercial Court) relating to the application of Articles 81 and 82 of the EC Treaty and the equivalent provisions of the Competition Act 1998.

(17) proceedings under other miscellaneous statutory jurisdictions.

18.2 There is concurrent jurisdiction with the Family Division under the Inheritance (Provision for Family and Dependants) Act 1975.

18.3 Certain appeals lie to the Chancery Division under statute. These are dealt with in paragraph 10.19. Intellectual property appeals and revenue appeals are also covered in Chapters 23 and 25 respectively.

18.4 The Chancery judges are the nominated judges of the Court of Protection but this Guide does not deal with the Court of Protection.

CHAPTER 19

THE BANKRUPTCY COURT

Key Rules: PD—Insolvency Proceedings; Insolvency Rules 1986

19.1 The Bankruptcy Court is part of the Chancery Division and disposes of **1A–152** proceedings relating to insolvent individuals arising under Parts VIII to XI of the Insolvency Act 1986 and related legislation. These include applications for interim orders to support an individual voluntary arrangement, applications to set aside a statutory demand, bankruptcy petitions and various applications concerned with the realisation and distribution of the assets of individuals who have been adjudged bankrupt, as well as proceedings concerning the administration in bankruptcy of the insolvent estate of a deceased person. The procedure in the Bankruptcy Court is governed by the Insolvency Rules and the PD—Insolvency Proceedings. Appeals in bankruptcy matters are covered in Chapter 10.

19.2 Proceedings in the Bankruptcy Court are issued in the Bankruptcy Issue and Search Room and are dealt with by the Registrars in Bankruptcy, not the Masters. Proceedings under Parts VIII to XI of the Insolvency Act 1986 should be entitled "IN BANKRUPTCY".

19.3 Certain matters, such as applications for injunctions or for committal for contempt, are heard by a judge. A judge is available to hear such matters each day in term time and applications may be listed for any such day. The judge will normally also be hearing the interim applications list for the day, but one or more other judges may be available to assist if necessary.

19.4 The Registrar may refer or adjourn proceedings to the judge, having regard to such matters as the complexity of the proceedings, whether the proceedings raise new or controversial points of law, the likely date and length of the hearing, public interest in the proceedings, and the availability of relevant specialist expertise. When proceedings have been referred or adjourned to the judge, interim applications and applications for directions or case management will be listed before a judge, except where liberty to apply to the Registrar has been given.

19.5 There are prescribed forms for use in connection with all types of statutory demand and of petitions for bankruptcy orders. Every other type of application is either an originating application in Form 7.1 (meaning an application to the court which is not an application in pending proceedings before the court) or an ordinary application in Form 7.2 (meaning any other application to the court).

Statutory demands

19.6 All applications to set aside a statutory demand are referred initially to a **1A–153** Registrar. The application may be dismissed by the court without a hearing if it fails to disclose sufficient grounds (see paragraph 12.4 of PD—Insolvency Proceedings and Insolvency Rules, r. 6.5(4). If it is not dismissed summarily, it will be allocated a

Paragraph numbers marked with a "+" can be found online and on CD.

hearing date when the Registrar may either dispose of it summarily or give directions for its disposal at a later date. Such directions will commonly include an order for the filing and service of written evidence and a listing certificate of compliance (see paragraph 19.13 below).

Bankruptcy petitions

1A–154 19.7 The court will not normally allow more than one bankruptcy petition to be presented against an individual at any one time.

19.8 In cases where the statutory demand relied on has not been personally served on the debtor or where execution of the debt has been returned unsatisfied in whole or in part, the permission of the Registrar is required before a petition may be presented to the court. For service of statutory demands see paragraphs 10–11 and 13 of PD—Insolvency Proceedings.

19.9 On presentation to the court a bankruptcy petition is given a distinctive number. The details of the name and address of the petitioner, of his solicitors and of the debtor are entered on a computerised record which may be searched by attendance at the Issue and Search Room. It will also be endorsed with a hearing date which may be extended on application without notice if the petitioner has been unable to serve the petition on the debtor before the hearing date (see paragraph 14 of PD—Insolvency Proceedings).

19.10 A debtor who intends to oppose the making of a bankruptcy order should file and serve a written notice in the prescribed form stating his grounds for opposing the petition not less than seven days before the hearing date. The court may give such further directions as to the filing of evidence and of listing certificates (see paragraph 19.13 below) as it considers appropriate to the disposal of the petition.

Other applications

1A–155 19.11 Many different types of application may be made to the court for the purpose of the administration of the estate and affairs of a bankrupt individual or insolvent person who is subject to an individual voluntary arrangement (IVA). These may involve such matters as the examination of the bankrupt or of persons having knowledge of his affairs, the realisation of assets in his estate and the determination of disputes regarding the validity of a creditor's claim to dividend or entitlement to vote at a creditors' meeting. Such applications will be given a hearing date when the Registrar will give such directions as are appropriate to the type of case, which may include directions for the filing and service of written evidence, for the cross-examination of witnesses and for the filing of certificates of compliance (see paragraph 19.13 below).

Orders without attendance

1A–156 19.12 In suitable cases the court will normally be prepared to make orders under Part VIII of the Act (interim orders for IVAs) and consent orders without attendance by the parties. Details of these types of order are set out in paragraph 16 of the PD—Insolvency Proceedings.

Listing certificates

1A–157 19.13 In order to prevent waste of the court's time each party to insolvency proceedings may be required by the court to file a listing certificate in which he will be required to certify whether the directions previously given by the court have been complied with, whether and by whom he will be represented at the final hearing, his estimate of the time required for such hearing and his and his representative's dates to avoid. On the filing of the certificates in any particular case the court will fix a date for the final hearing of the case and notify the parties.

Preparation for hearings before the Registrars

1A–158 19.14 Paragraphs 7.39 to 7.50 apply to hearings before the Bankruptcy Registrars. Skeleton arguments and bundles should be delivered to the Bankruptcy Registry.

Paragraph numbers marked with a "+" can be found online and on CD.

General information

19.15 Inspection of the court's record and court file in any insolvency proceedings is **1A–159** governed by Insolvency Rules, rr. 7.28 and 7.31.

19.16 The following publications regarding practice and procedure in the Bankruptcy Court are available free from the Bankruptcy Issue and Search Room and from Room TM1.10 Thomas More Building, Royal Courts of Justice:

   (1) Current Practice Direction and Practice Notes

   (2) A concise Guide to procedure in the Bankruptcy Court

   (3) *"I want to set aside my statutory demand—what do I do?"*

   (4) *"I have a petition against me—what do I do?"*

   (5) *"I want to appeal an order made by a District Judge or an order made by a Bankruptcy Registrar of the High Court—what can I do?"*

   (6) *"I wish to apply for my Certificate of Discharge from Bankruptcy—what do I do?"*

   (7) Dealing with debt—how to make someone bankrupt

   (8) Dealing with debt—how to petition for your own bankruptcy.

CHAPTER 20

THE COMPANIES COURT

Key Rules: PD 49—Applications under the Companies Act; PD—Insolvency; Insolvency Rules 1986; Insolvent Companies (Disqualification of Unfit Directors) Proceedings Rules 1987;PD—Directors Disqualification Proceedings

20.1 The Companies Court is a part of the Chancery Division. Applications in the **1A–160** High Court under the Companies Act 1985, the Insurance Companies Act 1982, the Financial Services and Markets Act 2002, the Insolvency Act 1986 in relation to companies registered in England and Wales, and the Company Directors Disqualification Act 1986, must be commenced in the Companies Court. Proceedings concerning insolvent partnerships, under the Insolvent Partnerships Order 1994, are also brought in the Companies Court (unlike proceedings against partners separately, which, if the partner is an individual, are brought in bankruptcy). Many other kinds of application are brought in the Companies Court. Appeals in Companies Court matters are dealt with in Chapter 10.

20.2 Applications, other than in insolvency, are governed by the Civil Procedure Rules and PD 49—Applications under the Companies Act 1985.

20.3 Applications in insolvency relating to companies (and to insolvent partnerships) are governed by the Insolvency Rules and PD—Insolvency Proceedings.

20.4 Proceedings under the Company Directors Disqualification Act 1986 are governed by the Insolvent Companies (Disqualification of Unfit Directors) Proceedings Rules 1987 and the PD—Directors Disqualification Proceedings.

20.5 Proceedings in the Companies Court under a particular statute should be entitled accordingly, thus:

   "In the matter of [name and registration number of the company] And in the matter of the Companies Act 1985 [and of any other statute as appropriate]"

   "In the matter of [name of the relevant company] And in the matter of the Company Directors Disqualification Act 1986"

   "In the matter of [name of the debtor] And in the matter of the Insolvency Act 1986 [and of any appropriate order, such as the Insolvent Partnerships Order 1994]"

20.6 The Companies Court has a separate administrative procedure. Proceedings are issued in the Companies Court General Office, and they are dealt with by the Registrars.

Paragraph numbers marked with a "+" can be found online and on CD.

20.7 Petitions for winding up, petitions for confirmation by the court of reduction of capital, and interim applications for directions in proceedings by shareholders are among the principal matters heard by the Registrars. A Registrar may direct that any case be heard by a judge even if it is a kind of application which would normally be heard by a Registrar.

20.8 Certain matters such as applications for an administration order under Part II of the Insolvency Act 1986, petitions for approval by the court of schemes of arrangement and applications for the appointment of provisional liquidators are heard by a judge. A judge is available to hear companies matters each day in term time, and applications to be heard by that judge may be listed for any such day. The judge will normally also be hearing the Interim Applications List for the day, but one or more other judges may be available to assist if necessary. The Registrar may refer or adjourn proceedings to the judge in accordance with the criteria set out in paragraph 19.4 above.

Preparation for hearings before the Registrars

1A–161 20.9 Paragraphs 7.39 to 7.50 apply to hearings before the Registrars of the Companies Court. Skeleton arguments and bundles should be delivered to the Companies Court Issue Section.

Administration Orders

1A–162 20.10 The statutory regime for administrations commencing on or after 15 September 2003, with certain exceptions, is found in the Insolvency Act 1986, schedule B1, which should be read with the new Part 2 of the Insolvency Rules 1986. Administrations commenced before 15 September 2003 and administrations of certain bodies (building societies, insolvent partnerships, limited liability partnerships, certain insurers, and public utility companies listed in section 249(1)(a)–(d) of the Enterprise Act 2002) continue to be governed by Part II of the Insolvency Act 1986 (or enacted before the introduction of Schedule B1) and the former Part 2 of the Insolvency Rules 1986. Administration creates a statutory moratorium and allows the affairs, business and property of the company to be managed by an administrator.

20.11 Administrators may be appointed by the court or out of court. By paragraph 3(i) of Schedule B1 the administrator must perform his duties with the objective of:

(1) rescuing the company as a going concern, or

(2) achieving a better result for the company's creditors as a whole than would be likely if the company were wound up (without first being in administration), or

(3) realising property in order to make a distribution to one or more secured or preferential creditors.

Court Order

1A–163 20.12 An application to the court must be commenced by the prescribed form of application (Form 2.1B under the new regime) and must be supported by an affidavit. The Act and Rules specify the information which must be included in the affidavit. The application may be made by the company, its directors, one or more creditors, the justices' chief executive for a magistrates' court (in relation to a fine) or any combination of the above. The application will be listed before a judge.

20.13 To make the order the court must be satisfied that the company is or is likely to become unable to pay its debts and that the administration order is likely to achieve the purpose of the administration.

Out of court

1A–164 20.14 Under the new regime, the holder of a qualifying floating charge, the company or its directors, may appoint an administrator without going through the court

Paragraph numbers marked with a "+" can be found online and on CD.

process. The appointment becomes effective when a notice of appointment in the prescribed form accompanied by the dministrators' consent to act and a statement by him that in his opinion the purpose of the administration is likely to be achieved has been filed with the court. Rule 2.19 makes special provision for filing notice of appointment by fax out of business hours. (Form 2.7B). The fax number for filing notice in the Royal Courts of Justice is 020 7947 6607.

Schemes of arrangement

20.15 A scheme under section 425 of the Companies Act 1985 can be proposed **1A–165** whether or not a company is in liquidation. It is necessary to obtain the sanction of the court to a scheme which has been approved by the requisite majority of members or creditors of each class at separately convened meetings directed by the court. If the company is insolvent the objective of the scheme may be more simply and economically achieved by a company voluntary arrangement under Part I of the Act. However, a scheme under section 425 has the advantage that the court may approve the distribution of assets otherwise than in accordance with creditors' strict legal rights.

20.16 The application for an order to convene meetings of members or creditors under section 425(1) is made by a CPR Part 8 claim form. The application will usually be heard by a Registrar, unless it is thought that issues of difficulty may arise, in which case it can be heard by a judge. The relevant practice is set out in *Practice Statement (Companies: Schemes of Arrangements)* [2002] 1 WLR 1345.

20.17 The application to sanction a scheme of arrangement, once approved by members or creditors by the statutory majority, is made by petition. The hearing of the petition at which the sanction of the court is sought will be before a judge. If the petition also seeks confirmation of a reduction of capital, there will first be an application to the Registrar for directions. In other cases the petition will go straight to a judge.

Winding up petitions

20.18 Proceedings to wind up a company are commenced by presenting a petition to **1A–166** the court. The presentation of a winding up petition can cause substantial damage to a company. A winding up petition should not be presented when it is known that there is a real dispute about the debt. Practitioners should make reasonable enquiries from their client as to the existence of any such dispute. The court may order a petitioner to pay the company's costs of a petition based on a disputed debt on the indemnity basis.

20.19 When a winding up petition is presented to either the Companies Court, a Chancery District Registry or a county court having jurisdiction, particulars including the name of the company and the petitioner's solicitors are entered in a computerised register. This is called the Central Registry of Winding Up Petitions. It may be searched by personal attendance at the Companies Court General Office, or by telephone on 020 7947 7328.

20.20 The requirement to advertise the petition (Insolvency Rules, r. 4.11(2)(b)) is mandatory, and designed to ensure that the class remedy of winding up by the court is made available to all creditors, and is not used simply as a means of putting pressure on the company to pay the petitioner's debt. Failure to comply with the rule, without good reason accepted by the court, may lead to the summary dismissal of the petition on the return date (Insolvency Rules, r. 4.11(5)). If the court, in its discretion, grants an adjournment, this will be on condition that the petition is advertised in due time for the adjourned hearing. No further adjournment for the purpose of advertisement will normally be granted.

20.21 If an order is made restraining advertisement while an application is made to the court to stop the proceedings, the case is listed in the Daily Cause List by number only so that the name of the company is not given.

Paragraph numbers marked with a "+" can be found online and on CD.

Proceedings for relief from unfairly prejudicial conduct under the Companies Act 1985, section 459

1A–167 20.22 Petitions under the Companies Act 1985, section 459, are liable to involve extensive factual enquiry and many of the measures summarised in Section A of this Guide which are designed to avoid unnecessary cost and delay are particularly relevant to them. Procedure is governed by the Companies (Unfair Prejudice Applications) Proceedings Rules 1986 (SI 1986/2000).

20.23 Where applications are brought in the Companies Court and in a related case in the Chancery Division at the same time, special arrangements can be made on request to the Chancery Judges' Listing Officer for the applications to be heard by the same judge.

Applications for leave to act as director of a company with a prohibited name

1A–168 20.24 Section 216 of the Insolvency Act 1986 restricts the use of a company name by any person who was a director or shadow director of the company in the 12 month period ending with the day upon which it went into insolvent liquidation—except with the leave of the court: section 216(3).

20.25 The application for leave is governed by the Insolvency Rules 1986, rr. 4.226 to 4.230. These rules provide for certain exceptions to the prohibition. The application for leave is by originating application supported by written evidence.

20.26 By r. 4.227 the court may call upon the liquidator for a report of the circumstances in which the company became insolvent and the extent of the applicant's apparent responsibility. However if the liquidator consents to the application it is helpful if his views are put before the court at the outset. The Registrar who then hears the application may be prepared to grant it at the first hearing.

20.27 Notice should be given to the Secretary of State and/or the Official Receiver.

General

1A–169 20.28 Inspection of the court's records and the court file in any insolvency proceedings is governed by Insolvency Rules, rr. 7.28 and 7.31.

20.29 The following leaflets are available from the Companies Court General Office:

    (1) Current Practice Directions and Practice Notes

    (2) *"I want to wind up a company which owes me money: what do I do?"*

    (3) Treasury Solicitors'—A Guide to company restoration

    (4) *"I want to apply to extend time for registration of a charge or to rectify a mis-statement or omission (in the registered particulars of a charge or of a memorandum of satisfaction): what do I do?"*

    (5) Dealing with debt. How to wind up your own company

CHAPTER 21

MORTGAGE CLAIMS

Key Rules: CPR Parts 55 and 73 and the PDs supplementing them

1A–170 21.1 Under Part 55 mortgage possession claims commenced since 15 October 2001, whether in respect of residential or commercial property, are generally heard in the county courts. The only exceptions to this are (a) a relatively small number of cases where either the county court has no jurisdiction or where the claimant can certify, verified by a statement of truth, the reasons for bringing the claim in the High Court and (b) any remaining transitional cases, i.e. mortgage possession claims commenced before 15 October 2001, and proceedings to enforce charging orders commenced prior to 25 March 2002, as to which directions should be sought from the assigned Master.

Paragraph numbers marked with a "+" can be found online and on CD.

21.2 PD 55 emphasises that High Court claims are to be regarded as exceptional and that while the value of the property and the size of the claim may well be relevant circumstances they will not, taken alone, normally justify the issue of proceedings in the High Court. High Court proceedings may, however, be justified where there are complicated disputes of fact or where a claim gives rise to points of law of general importance. Where a mortgage possession claim is issued in the High Court it is assigned to the Chancery Division. The provisions of Part 55 will apply to it.

21.3 The most common instance where, notwithstanding Part 55, the Chancery Division will retain jurisdiction in a mortgage possession case is where proceedings are brought seeking an order for sale under an equitable charge, ordinarily that created by a charging order, but where part of the relief claimed ancillary to the order for sale is an order for possession. Although rule 73.10 now provides that proceedings to enforce charging orders by sale should be made in the court in which the charging order was made, that provision is expressly subject to that court having jurisdiction. The jurisdiction of a county court to enforce a charge is confined to those cases where the amount secured by the charge falls within the relevant county court limit (currently £30,000) and it follows that in many cases where judgments have been obtained in county courts and charging orders made enforcement will nonetheless require proceedings in the High Court.

21.4 Such proceedings, as well as proceedings to enforce charging orders made in other divisions of the High Court, are assigned to the Chancery Division. The evidence required in support of such proceedings is that set out in paragraph 4.3 of PD 73.

21.5 There remains in the Chancery Division a number of mortgage possession proceedings issued prior to Part 55 coming into force (on 15 October 2001). Of those proceedings, some may never have been adjudicated upon and many will have given rise to suspended possession orders, in respect of which applications to issue execution may arise in reducing numbers.

21.6 Practitioners should also have regard to the fact that 'old' proceedings which have not been adjudicated upon and which were issued prior to 26 April 1999 will fall within the 'automatic stay' provisions of paragraph 19 of PD 51 so that a claimant wishing to proceed with such a claim will have to apply to lift the stay. Such an application may be made at the same time as the application for possession but the court will require sufficient evidence to allow it to determine properly whether it is appropriate to lift the stay. The application to lift the automatic stay should form one of the heads of relief in the Application Notice seeking possession. If the evidence in support exhibits a mortgage account sufficient to show what has happened on the account since the last time the claim was before the court (ex hypothesi from before 26 April 1999) no additional evidence will be likely to be necessary in support of the stay application.

21.7 The Chancery Division retains its jurisdiction in respect of redemption and foreclosure of mortgages and kindred matters.

21.8 Rule 48.3 and paragraph 50 of the Costs PD (Amount of costs where costs are payable under a contract) are of particular relevance to mortgage claims.

21.9 In summary, where under a mortgage a mortgagee has a contractual right to his or her costs, the court's discretion in respect of costs under section 51 of the Supreme Court Act 1981 should be exercised so as to reflect that contractual right. The power of the court to disallow a mortgagee's costs sought to be added to the security stems not from section 51 but from the power of the courts of equity to fix the terms upon which redemption will be allowed. A decision by the court to refuse costs to a mortgagee litigant may be a decision in the exercise of the court's discretion under section 51, or pursuant to its power to fix the terms upon which redemption will be allowed, or a decision as to the extent of the mortgagee's contractual right, in a given case, to add costs to his or her security, or any combination of these three things. A mortgagee is not to be deprived of a contractual or equitable right to add costs to his

Paragraph numbers marked with a "+" can be found online and on CD.

or her security without reference to the mortgagee's contractual or equitable rights to such costs and without a proper adjudication as to whether or not the mortgagee should be deprived of his or her costs.

CHAPTER 22

PARTNERSHIP CLAIMS AND RECEIVERS

Key Rules: RSC O.81 (in CPR, schedule 1); CPR Part 69, PDs 24 and 40

Partnership Claims

1A–171   22.1 In claims for or arising out of the dissolution of a partnership often the only matters in dispute between the partners are matters of accounting. In such cases there will be no trial. The court will, if appropriate, make a summary order under paragraph 6 of PD 24 for the taking of an account. This will be taken before the Master.

22.2 Only if there is a dispute as to the existence of a partnership (whether it is claimed that there never was a partnership or that the partnership is still continuing and has not been dissolved) or if there is a material dispute as to the terms of the partnership (e.g. as to the profit sharing ratios) will there be a trial, at which the judge will decide those issues. In such cases there will be a two stage procedure with the judge deciding these issues at the trial and ordering the winding up of the partnership which will involve the taking of the partnership accounts by the Master (see PD 40 Accounts, Inquiries etc.).

22.3 In some cases and in order to reduce costs, it may be appropriate for the parties to invite the Master to determine factual issues as a preliminary to the account, eg issues as to terms of the partnership or assets comprised in it. At any case management conference it will be particularly important to identify issues to be determined before an effective account or inquiry can be made. The court will not simply order accounts and inquiries without identifying the issues.

22.4 The expense of taking an account in court is usually wholly disproportionate to the amount at stake. Parties are strongly encouraged to refer disputes on accounts to a jointly instructed accountant for determination or mediation.

22.5 The functions of a receiver in a partnership action are limited. It is not his or her duty to wind up the partnership, like the liquidator of a company. His or her primary function is to get in the debts and preserve the assets pending winding up by the court and he or she has no power of sale without the permission of the court.

Receivers

1A–172   22.6 The procedure for the appointment of receivers by the court is comprehensively governed by Part 69 and its PD. A new Guide for receivers in the Chancery Division is available. Copies of the Guide can be obtained from an associate or from the Court Manager, Chancery Chambers. The Guide is also reproduced at Appendix 10. Particular attention should be paid to remuneration and the fact that it must be authorised on the basis specified in an order of the court.

CHAPTER 23

THE PATENTS COURT AND TRADE MARKS ETC.

Key Rules: CPR Part 63 and PD 63—Patents, etc

1A–173   23.1 The matters assigned to the Patents Court are essentially all those concerned with patents or registered designs. CPR Part 63 and PD 63 deal with its particular procedures. Appeals in patent, design and trade mark cases are governed by Part 52 (see CPR 63.17); reference should be made to Chapter 10 for the general procedure as regards such appeals.

Paragraph numbers marked with a "+" can be found online and on CD.

23.2 The principal Patent judges are Mr Justice Pumfrey and Mr Justice Kitchin. The other assigned Patents judges currently nominated are:

Mr Justice Patten
Mr Justice Lewison
Mr Justice Mann

Several senior practitioners have also been appointed to sit as Deputy High Court judges to hear Patent Court matters.

23.3 Mr Justice Pumfrey is the judge in charge of the Patents List.

23.4 In cases of great urgency, when a nominated judge or Deputy Judge is not available an application can be made to any other judge of the High Court, preferably a judge of the Chancery Division.

23.5 The procedure of the Patents Court is broadly that of the Chancery Division as a whole, but there are important differences.

23.6 The Patents Court has its own Court Guide which is available on the Patents Court website (*www.hmcourts-service.gov.uk*) and can also be found in para.2F–127 of Volume 2 of the White Book. That Guide must be consulted for guidance as to the procedure in the Patents Court.

23.7 The Court's diary can be accessed on its website. The Patents Court will endeavour, if the parties so desire and the case is urgent, to sit in September.

Patents County Court

23.8 Special provisions relate to the transfer of cases between the Patents Court and the Patents County Court. The Patents Court has no power to order the transfer to it of cases commenced in the Patents County Court which fall within the latter court's special jurisdiction (i.e. matters relating to patents and designs). On the other hand it does have the power to transfer cases commenced in the High Court to the Patents County Court.   **1A–174**

Registered trademarks and other intellectual property rights

23.9 CPR 63.13 to 63.15 and paragraphs 18 to 27 of PD 63 apply to claims relating to matters arising out of the Trade Marks Act 1994 and other intellectual property rights (such as copyright, passing off, design rights, etc.) as set out in paragraph 18 of PD 63. Claims under the Trade Marks Act 1994 must be brought in the Chancery Division. Among the Chancery Masters trade mark cases are assigned to Master Bragge.   **1A–175**

23.10 Appeals from decisions of the Registrar of Trade Marks are brought to the Chancery Division as a whole, not the Patents Court. Permission to appeal is not required.

CHAPTER 24

PROBATE AND INHERITANCE CLAIMS

Key Rules: CPR Part 57 and PD 57

Probate

24.1 In general, contentious probate proceedings follow the same pattern as an ordinary claim but there are important differences and Part 57 and PD 57 should be carefully studied. All probate claims are allocated to the multitrack. Particular regard should be had to the following: **1A–176**

(1) The claim form must be issued out of Chancery Chambers or out of the Chancery District Registries, or if the claim is suitable to be heard in the

Paragraph numbers marked with a "+" can be found online and on CD.

county court, a county court where there is also a Chancery District Registry, or the Central London County Court.

(2) A defendant must file an acknowledgment of service. An additional 14 days is provided for doing so.

(3) Save where the court orders otherwise, the parties must at the outset of proceedings lodge all testamentary documents in their possession and control with the court. At the same time parties must file written evidence describing any testamentary document of the deceased of which they have knowledge, stating, if any such document is not in the party's possession or control, the name and address, if known, of the person in whose possession or under whose control the document is. In the case of a claimant, these materials must be lodged at the time when the claim form is issued. In the case of a defendant, these materials must be lodged when service is acknowledged. If these requirements are not complied with it is likely that the claim will not be issued and, correspondingly, that the acknowledgment of service will not be permitted to be lodged.

(4) The court will generally ensure that all persons with any potential interest in the proceedings are joined as parties or served with notice under Part 19.8A.

(5) A default judgment cannot be obtained in a probate claim. Where, however, no defendant acknowledges service or files a defence, the claimant may apply for an order that the claim proceed to trial and seek a direction that the claim be tried on written evidence.

(6) If an order pronouncing for a will in solemn form is sought under Part 24, the evidence in support must include written evidence proving due execution of the will. In such a case, if a defendant has given notice under rule 57.7(5) that he raises no positive case but requires that the will be proved in solemn form and that, to that end, he wishes to cross examine the attesting witnesses, then the claimant's application for summary judgment is subject to the right of such a defendant to require the attesting witnesses to attend for cross examination.

(7) A defendant who wishes to do more than test the validity of the will by cross examining the attesting witnesses must set up by counterclaim his positive case in order to enable the court to make an appropriate finding or declaration as to which is the valid will, or whether a person died intestate or as the case may be.

(8) The proceedings may not be discontinued without permission. Even if they are compromised, it will usually be necessary to have an order stating to whom the grant is to be made, either under rule 57.11 (leading to a grant in common form), or after a trial on written evidence under paragraph 6.1(1) of PD 57 (leading to a grant in solemn form) or under section 49 of the Administration of Justice Act 1985 and paragraph 6.1(3) of PD 57 (again leading to a grant in solemn form). Practitioners should refer to PF38CH and adapt as appropriate.

24.2 When the court orders trial of a contentious probate claim on written evidence, or where the court is asked to pronounce in solemn form under Part 24, it is normally necessary for an attesting witness to sign a witness statement or swear an affidavit of due execution of any will or codicil sought to be admitted to probate. The will or codicil is at that stage in the court's possession and cannot be handed out of court for use as an exhibit to the witness statement or affidavit, so that the attesting witness has to attend at the Royal Courts of Justice.

24.3 Where an attesting witness is unable to attend the Royal Courts of Justice in order to sign his or her witness statement or swear his or her affidavit in the presence of an officer of the court, the solicitor concerned may request from Room TM7.09, a photographic copy of the will or codicil in question. This will be certified as authentic by the court and may be exhibited to the witness statement or affidavit of due execution in lieu of the original. The witness statement or affidavit must in that case state that the exhibited document is an authenticated copy of the document signed in the witness' presence.

Paragraph numbers marked with a "+" can be found online and on CD.

24.4 When a probate claim is listed for trial outside London, the solicitor for the party responsible for preparing the court bundle must write to Room TM7.09 and request that the testamentary documents be forwarded to the appropriate District Registry.

Inheritance (Provision For Family And Dependants) Act 1975

24.5 Claims under the Inheritance (Provision for Family and Dependants) Act 1975 **1A–177** in the Chancery Division will be allocated to the Multi-Track and are issued by way of a Part 8 claim. Ordinarily they will be tried by the Master unless an order is made transferring the claim to a county court for trial. They are governed by Part 57 and PD 57.

24.6 The written evidence filed by the claimant with the claim form must exhibit an official copy of the grant of probate or letters of administration together with every testamentary document in respect of which probate or letters of administration was granted.

24.7 A defendant must file and serve acknowledgment of service not later than 21 days after service of the Part 8 claim form. Any written evidence (subject to any extension agreed or directed) must likewise be served and filed no later than 21 days after service.

24.8 The personal representatives of the deceased are necessary defendants to a claim under the 1975 Act and the written evidence filed by a defendant who is a personal representative must comply with paragraph 16 of PD 57.

24.9 On the hearing of a claim under the 1975 Act, the personal representatives must produce the original grant of representation to the deceased's estate. If the court makes an order under the Act, the original grant together with a sealed copy of the order must, under paragraph 18.2 of PD 57, be sent to the Principal Registry of the Family Division, First Avenue House, 42–49 High Holborn, London WC1V 6NP for a memorandum of the order to be endorsed on or permanently annexed to the grant.

24.10 Where claims under the 1975 Act are compromised the consent order filed must comply with paragraph 9.14 of this Guide.

CHAPTER 25

REVENUE PROCEEDINGS

Key Rules: CPR Part 52, PD 52, paragraphs 23.2(11) to (16), 23.3 to 23.5, 23.8

25.1 Several kinds of revenue proceedings are heard in the Chancery Division. **1A–178** Usually the parties are HM Revenue and Customs on one side and a taxpayer on the other. The main examples are described below. Almost all of them are appeals against decisions made by lower level tribunals at first instance. The appeals are governed by Part 52. Reference should be made to Chapter 10 for the general procedure relating to such appeals.

Appeals from decisions of the General Commissioners relating to income tax, corporation tax or capital gains tax

25.2 The General Commissioners are a first instance appeal tribunal for cases **1A–179** concerning these three taxes. Appeals from their decisions, whether by the Revenue or by a taxpayer, are conducted on the basis of a case stated, drawn up by the General Commissioners, which sets out the facts, the arguments, and the General Commissioners' decision. The case stated is usually backed up by whatever documents were before the Commissioners. These appeals are limited to questions of law. The judge never hears evidence, and the appeal will almost certainly fail if the appellant's real complaint is that the General Commissioners got the facts wrong. The

Paragraph numbers marked with a "+" can be found online and on CD.

judge does have power to remit a case to the General Commissioners for them to hear further evidence and find further facts, but this is only rarely done.

25.3 The rules provide that, when the party who is appealing from the General Commissioners receives the case stated in its final form from the General Commissioners' clerk, the party has to transmit it to the High Court within 30 days. The court has no power to extend this time limit, which must be strictly observed if the court is to be able to hear the appeal: *New World Medical Ltd v Cormack* [2002] EWHC 124 5 (Ch), [2002] STC 1245.

Appeals from decisions of the Special Commissioners relating to income tax, corporation tax, capital gains tax or inheritance tax

1A–180 25.4 The Special Commissioners are the other first instance appeal tribunal for tax purposes, and hear cases relating to all four taxes mentioned above, known as the direct taxes. Appeals from their decisions, whether by the Revenue or by a taxpayer, are conducted, not on the basis of a case stated, but on the basis of the Special Commissioners' decision and the papers which they had before them. Those papers may include a transcript of the evidence or the Special Commissioners' notes of the evidence, but, as with appeals from General Commissioners, appeals to the Chancery Division are limited to questions of law. The judge never hears evidence. Again as with the General Commissioners, the judge has power to remit a case to the Special Commissioners for them to hear further evidence and find further facts, but this is only rarely done. There are time limits for filing an Appellant's Notice for an appeal from a decision of the Special Commissioners. In most cases the limit is 56 days from the date of the Commissioners' decision, but in some cases it is shorter. For details reference should be made to paragraph 23.5 of PD 52.

25.5 Exceptionally, appeals from the Special Commissioners in relation to the direct taxes may go directly to the Court of Appeal, so leapfrogging the Chancery Division.

25.6 Some inheritance tax appeals are exceptions to the normal procedure and do not start before the Special Commissioners, so that the Chancery Division is the court of first instance. These are limited to cases where the issues to be decided are wholly or mainly issues of law and there is no substantial dispute about the facts. Detailed procedural rules about appeals of this nature are to be found in paragraph 23.3 of PD 52.

Stamp duty appeals

1A–181 25.7 These are heard in the Chancery Division, and are conducted on the basis of a case stated drawn up by HM Revenue and Customs. Usually there is no oral evidence, but it has occasionally been heard.

25.8 Appeals relating to stamp duty reserve tax are also heard in the Chancery Division. Rules relating to such appeals have been made, but no such appeal has yet arisen.

Appeals from the Value Added Tax and Duties Tribunal

1A–182 25.9 Most of these appeals relate to VAT, but occasionally appeals on other duties, such as excise duty, arise. An appeal may be brought either by HM Revenue and Customs or by the taxpayer. As with appeals from the Special Commissioners relating to the direct taxes, exceptionally leapfrog appeals may lie direct to the Court of Appeal, but normally the appeal will be to the Chancery Division.

25.10 As with appeals from the Special Commissioners, VAT appeals are based on the Tribunal's decision and the documents in the case. The judge never hears evidence. The documents usually include a transcript of the evidence before the Tribunal or the Tribunal's notes of the evidence. Nevertheless, like appeals from the Special Commissioners concerning the direct taxes, an appeal lies only on a point of law. Usually the time limit for filing the appellant's notice is 56 days from the decision of the Tribunal.

Paragraph numbers marked with a "+" can be found online and on CD.

CHAPTER 26

TRUSTS

Key Rules: CPR Part 8; Part 19; Part 64 and PD 64

Introduction

26.1 This Chapter contains material about a number of aspects of proceedings **1A–183** concerning trusts, the estates of deceased persons (other than probate claims) and charities.

26.2 The topics covered in this Chapter are (a) applications by trustees for directions and related matters; (b) the Variation of Trusts Act 1958; (c) section 48 of the Administration of Justice Act 1985; (d) vesting orders as regards property in Scotland; (e) trustees under a disability; (f) lodgment of funds; (g) the estates of deceased Lloyd's Names; and (h) judicial trustees.

Trustees' applications for directions

26.3 Applications to the court by trustees for directions in relation to the **1A–184** administration of a trust or charity, or by personal representatives in relation to a deceased person's estate, are to be brought by Part 8 claim form, and are governed by Part 64, and its PDs; rule 8.2A is also relevant.

26.4 If confidentiality of the directions sought is important (for example, where the directions relate to actual or proposed litigation with a third party who could find out what directions the claimants are seeking through access to the claim form under rule 5.4) the statement of the remedy sought, for the purposes of rule 8.2(b), may be expressed in general terms. The trustees must, in that case, state specifically in the evidence what it is that they seek to be allowed to do.

26.5 The proceedings will normally be listed and heard in private: rule 39.2(3)(f) and paragraph 1.5 of PD 39. Accordingly the order made, and the other documents among the court records (apart from a claim form which has been served), will not be open to inspection by third parties without the court's permission: rule 5.4(2). If the matter is disposed of without a hearing, the order made will be expressed to have been made in private.

26.6 Part 64 deals with the joining of beneficiaries as defendants. Often, especially in the case of a private trust, it will be clear that some, and which, beneficiaries need to be joined as defendants. Sometimes, if there are only two views as to the appropriate course, and one is advocated by one beneficiary who will be joined, it may not be necessary for other beneficiaries to be joined since the trustees may be able to present the other arguments. Equally, in the case of a pension trust, it may not be necessary for a member of every possible different class of beneficiaries to be joined.

26.7 In some cases, it may be that the court will or might be able to assess whether or not to give the directions sought, or what directions to give, without hearing from any party other than the trustees. If the trustees consider that their case is in that category they may apply to the court under rule 8.2A for permission to issue the claim form without naming any defendants. They must apply to the court before the claim form is issued, and include a copy of the claim form that they propose to issue. Practitioners should note that this procedure may enable directions to be obtained about matters concerning the administration of a trust or estate in circumstances which would fall outside the relatively narrow confines of section 48 of the Administration of Justice Act 1985 where the expense and delay associated with an application naming defendants may not be in the interests of beneficiaries.

26.8 In other cases the trustees may know that beneficiaries need to be joined as defendants, or to be given notice, but may be in doubt as to which. Examples could include a case concerning a pension scheme with many beneficiaries and a number of

Paragraph numbers marked with a "+" can be found online and on CD.

different categories of interest, especially if they may be differently affected by the action for which directions are sought, or a private trust with a large class of discretionary beneficiaries. In those cases the trustees may apply for permission to issue the claim form without naming any defendants under rule 8.2A. The application may be combined with an application for directions as to which persons to join as parties or to give notice to under rule 19.8A.

26.9 In the case of a charitable trust the Attorney-General is always the appropriate defendant, and almost always the only one.

26.10 Applications for directions whether or not to take or defend or pursue litigation (see *Re Beddoe* [1893] 1 Ch 547) must be made by Part 8 claim, independently of the main litigation, to a Master not involved with the main case. They should be supported by evidence including the advice of an appropriately qualified lawyer as to the prospects of success and other matters relevant to be taken into account, including a cost estimate for the proceedings and any known facts concerning the means of the opposite party to the proceedings, and a draft of any proposed statement of case. There are cases in which it is likely to be so clear that the trustees ought to proceed as they wish that the costs of making the application, even on a simplified procedure without a hearing and perhaps without defendants, are not justified in comparison with the size of the fund or the matters at issue.

26.11 References to an appropriately qualified lawyer mean one whose qualifications and experience are appropriate to the circumstances of the case. The qualifications should be stated. If the advice is given on formal instructions, the instructions should always be put in evidence as well, so that the court can see the basis on which the advice was given. If it is not, the advice must state fully the basis on which it is given. If a hearing is necessary the lawyer whose opinion is relied on should if possible be the advocate at the hearing.

26.12 All applications for directions should be supported by evidence showing the value of the trust assets, the significance of the proposed litigation or other course of action for the trust, and why the court's directions are needed. In the case of a pension trust the evidence should include the latest actuarial valuation, and should describe the membership profile and, if a deficit on winding up is likely, the priority provisions and their likely effect.

26.13 On an application for directions about actual or possible litigation, the evidence should also state (i) whether any relevant Pre-Action Protocol has been followed, and (ii) whether the trustees have proposed or undertaken, or intend to propose, ADR, and (in each case) if not why not.

26.14 If a beneficiary of the trust is a party to the litigation about which directions are sought, with an interest opposed to that of the trustees, that beneficiary should be a defendant to the trustees' application, but any material which would be privileged as regards that beneficiary in the litigation should be put in evidence as exhibits to the trustees' witness statement, and should not be served on the beneficiary. However, if the claimant's representatives consider that no harm would be done by the disclosure of all or some part of the material then that material should be served on that defendant. That defendant may also be excluded from part of the hearing, including that which is devoted to discussion of the material withheld: see *Re Moritz* [1960] Ch 251; *Re Eaton* [1964] 1 W.L.R. 1269.

Case management directions

1A–185 26.15 The claim will be referred to the Master once a defendant has acknowledged service, or otherwise on expiry of the period for acknowledgment of service, (or, if no defendant is named, as soon as the claimant's evidence has been filed) to consider directions for the management of the case. Such directions may be given without a hearing in some cases; these might include directions as to parties or as to notice of proceedings, as mentioned in paragraph 26.8 above.

26.16 Case management directions will be given where the court grants an application to issue the claim form without naming a defendant under rule 8.2A.

Paragraph numbers marked with a "+" can be found online and on CD.

Proceeding without a hearing

26.17 The court will always consider whether it is possible to deal with the application **1A–186** on paper without a hearing. The trustees must always consider whether a hearing is needed for any reason. If they consider that it is they should say so and explain why in their evidence. If a defendant considers that a hearing is needed, this should be stated, and the reasons explained, in his evidence, if any, or otherwise in a letter to the court.

26.18 If the court would be minded to refuse to give the directions asked for on a consideration of the papers alone, the parties will be notified and given the opportunity, within a stated time, to ask for a hearing.

26.19 In charity cases, the Master may deal with the case without a hearing on the basis of a letter from or on behalf of the Attorney-General setting out his attitude to the application.

26.20 Cases in which the directions can be given without a hearing include those where personal representatives apply to be allowed to distribute the estate of a deceased Lloyd's name, following the decision in *Re Yorke* (deceased) [1997] 4 All ER 907 (see paragraphs 26.50–55 below), as well as applications under section 48 of the Administration of Justice Act 1985 (see paragraphs 26.37–42 below).

Evidence

26.21 The trustees' evidence should be given by witness statement. In order to **1A–187** ensure that, if directions are given, the trustees are properly protected by the order, they must ensure full disclosure of relevant matters, even if the case is to proceed with the participation of beneficiaries as defendants.

Consultation with beneficiaries

26.22 The evidence must explain what, if any, consultation there has been with **1A–188** beneficiaries, and with what result. In preparation for an application for directions in respect of litigation, the following guidance is to be followed.

(1) If the trust is a private trust where the beneficiaries principally concerned are not numerous and are all or mainly adult, identified and traceable, the trustees will be expected to have canvassed with all the adult beneficiaries the proposed or possible courses of action before applying for directions.

(2) If it is a private trust with a larger number of beneficiaries, including those not yet born or identified, or children, it is likely that there will nevertheless be some adult beneficiaries principally concerned, with whom the trustees must consult.

(3) In relation to a charitable trust the trustees must have consulted the Attorney-General, through the Treasury Solicitor, as well as the Charity Commissioners, whose consent to the application will have been needed under section 33 of the Charities Act 1993.

(4) In relation to a pension trust, unless the members are very few in number, no particular steps by way of consultation with beneficiaries (including, where relevant, employers) or their representatives are required in preparation for the application, though the trustees' evidence should describe any consultation that has in fact taken place. If no consultation has taken place, the court could in some cases direct that meetings of one or more classes of beneficiaries be held to consider the subject-matter of the application, possibly as a preliminary to deciding whether a member of a particular class ought to be joined as a defendant, though in a case concerning actual or proposed litigation, steps would need to be considered to protect privileged material from too wide disclosure.

26.23 If the court gives directions allowing the claimant to take, defend or pursue litigation it may do so up to a particular stage in the litigation, requiring the trustees,

Paragraph numbers marked with a "+" can be found online and on CD.

before they carry on beyond that point, to renew their application to the court. What stage that should be will depend on the likely management of the litigation under the CPR. If the application is to be renewed after disclosure of documents, and disclosed documents need to be shown to the court, it may be necessary to obtain permission to do this from the court in which the other litigation is proceeding. However, the implied undertaking limiting the use of documents disclosed by another party to the litigation does not preclude their use on an application by trustee parties for directions, since that is use for the purposes of the litigation: *White v. Biddulph*, Hart J, unreported, 22 May 1998.

26.24 In such a case the court may sometimes direct that the case be dealt with at that stage without a hearing if the beneficiaries obtain and lodge an opinion of an appropriately qualified lawyer supporting the continuation of the directions. Any such opinion will be considered by the court and, if thought fit, the trustees will be given a direction allowing them to continue pursuing the proceedings without a hearing.

26.25 In a case of urgency, such as where a limitation period or period for service of proceedings is about to expire, the court may give directions on a summary consideration of the evidence to cover the steps which need to be taken urgently, but limiting those directions so that the application needs to be renewed for fuller consideration at an early stage.

26.26 On any application for directions where a child is a defendant, the court will expect to have put before it the instructions to and advice of an appropriately qualified lawyer as to the benefits and disadvantages of the proposed, and any other relevant, course of action from the point of view of the child beneficiary. Where the matters to be drawn to the attention of the court are fully covered in the instructions and written opinion, it should not be necessary for a separate skeleton argument to be lodged, but the court needs to be informed that this is the case. The opinion should be given by the lawyer who is to be the advocate at the hearing.

Hearing

1A–189 26.27 The Master may give the directions sought though, if the directions relate to actual or proposed litigation, only if it is a plain case, and the Master may be prepared to proceed without a hearing: see PD 2 Allocation of Cases to Levels of Judiciary, paragraph 4.1 and paragraph 5.1(e), and see also paragraphs 26.17 to 26.20 above. Otherwise the case will be referred to the judge.

Representation Orders

1A–190 26.28 It is not necessary to make representation orders under rule 19.7 on an application for directions, and sometimes it would not be possible, for lack of separate representatives among the parties of all relevant classes of beneficiaries, but such orders can be useful in an appropriate case and they are sometimes made.

Costs

1A–191 26.29 Normally the trustees' costs of a proper application will be allowed out of the trust fund, on an indemnity basis, as will the assessed (or agreed) costs of beneficiaries joined as defendants, subject to their conduct of the proceedings having been proper and reasonable.

Prospective costs orders

1A–192 26.30 In proceedings brought by one or more beneficiaries against trustees, the court has power to direct that the beneficiaries be indemnified out of the trust fund in any event for any costs incurred by them and any costs which they may be ordered to pay to any other party, known as a prospective costs order: see *McDonald v. Horn* [1995] 1 All ER 961. Such an order may provide for payments out of the trust fund from time to time on account of the indemnity so that the beneficiaries' costs may be paid on an interim basis. Applications for prospective costs orders should be made on notice to

Paragraph numbers marked with a "+" can be found online and on CD.

the trustees. The court will require to be satisfied that there are matters which need to be investigated. How far the court will wish to go into that question, and in what way it should be done, will depend on the circumstances of the particular case. The order may be expressed to cover costs incurred only up to a particular stage in the proceedings, so that the application has to be renewed, if necessary, in the light of what has occurred in the proceedings in the meantime. See para. 6 of PD 64, to which is annexed a model form of order.

Charity trustees' applications for permission to bring proceedings

26.31 In the case of a charitable trust, if the Charity Commissioners refuse their **1A–193** consent to the trustees applying to the court for directions, under Charities Act 1993 section 33(2), and also refuse to give the trustees the directions under their own powers, under sections 26 or 29, the trustees may apply to the court under section 33(5). On such an application, which may be dealt with on paper, the judge may call for a statement from the Charity Commissioners of their reasons for refusing permission, if not already apparent from the papers. The court may require the trustees to attend before deciding whether to grant permission for the proceedings. It is possible to require notice of the hearing to be given to the Attorney- General, but this would not normally be appropriate.

Variation of Trusts Act 1958

26.32 An application under the Variation of Trusts Act 1958 should be made by a **1A–194** Part 8 claim form. As to listing of such applications see paragraph 6.27. The Master will not consider the file without an application.

26.33 Where any children or unborn beneficiaries will be affected by an arrangement under the Variation of Trusts Act 1958, evidence must normally be before the court which shows that their litigation friends or the trustees support the arrangements as being in the interests of the children or unborn beneficiaries, and exhibits a written opinion to this effect. In complicated cases a written opinion is usually essential to the understanding of the litigation friends and the trustees, and to the consideration by the court of the merits and fiscal consequences of the arrangement. If the written opinion was given on formal instructions, those instructions must be exhibited. Otherwise the opinion must state fully the basis on which it was given. The opinion must be given by the advocate who will appear on the hearing of the application. A skeleton argument may not be needed where a written opinion has been put in evidence and no matters not appearing from the instructions or the opinion are to be relied on: see paragraph 26.26 above.

26.34 Where the interests of two or more children, or two or more of the children and unborn beneficiaries, are similar, a single written opinion will suffice; and no written opinion is required in respect of those who fall within the proviso to section 1(1) of the Act (discretionary interests under protective trusts). Further, in proper cases the requirement of a written opinion may at any stage be dispensed with by the Master or the judge.

Stamp Duty

26.35 An undertaking by solicitors with regard to stamping is not required to be **1A–195** included in an order under the Variation of Trusts Act 1958 whether made by a judge or Master.

26.36 The Commissioners of Inland Revenue consider that the stamp duty position of duplicate orders is as follows:

    (1) Orders confined to the lifting of protective trusts. These orders are not liable for duty at all and should not be presented to a stamp office.

    (2) Orders effecting voluntary dispositions inter vivos. These orders may be certified under the Stamp Duty (Exempt Instruments) Regulations 1987 (S.I. 1987 No. 516), as within category L in the schedule to those regulations, in

Paragraph numbers marked with a "+" can be found online and on CD.

which case they should not be presented to a stamp office. Without such a certificate they attract 50p duty under the head "Conveyance or transfer of any kind not hereinbefore described."

(3) Orders outside those described at paragraphs (1) and (2) above that contain declarations of the trust, i.e. that effect no disposition of trust property. These orders attract 50p fixed duty under the head "Declaration of trust." They may be presented for stamping at any stamp office in the usual way, or sent for adjudication if preferred.

Applications under section 48 of the Administration of Justice Act 1985

1A–196 26.37 Applications under section 48 of the Administration of Justice Act 1985should be made by Part 8 Claim Form without naming a defendant, under rule 8.2A. No separate application for permission under rule 8.2A need be made. The claim should be supported by a witness statement or affidavit to which are exhibited: (a) copies of all relevant documents; (b) instructions to a person with a 10-year High Court qualification within the meaning of the Courts and Legal Services Act 1990 ("the qualified person"); (c) the qualified person's opinion; and (d) draft terms of the desired order.

26.38 The witness statement or affidavit (or exhibits thereto) should state: (a) the names of all persons who are, or may be, affected by the order sought; (b) all surrounding circumstances admissible and relevant in construing the document; (c) the date of qualification of the qualified person and his or her experience in the construction of trust documents; (d) the approximate value of the fund or property in question; and (e) whether it is known to the applicant that a dispute exists and, if so, details of such dispute.

26.39 When the file is placed before the Master he will consider whether the evidence is complete and if it is send the file to the judge.

26.40 The judge will consider the papers and, if necessary, direct service of notices under rule 19.8A or request such further information as he or she may desire. If the judge is satisfied that the order sought is appropriate, the order will be made and sent to the claimant.

26.41 If following service of notices under rule 19.8A any acknowledgment of service is received, the claimant must apply to the Master (on notice to the parties who have so acknowledged service) for directions. If the claimant desires to pursue the application to the court, in the ordinary case the Master will direct that the case proceeds as a Part 8 claim.

26.42 If on the hearing of the claim the judge is of the opinion that any party who entered an acknowledgment of service has no reasonably tenable argument contrary to the qualified person's opinion, in the exercise of his or her discretion he or she may order such party to pay any costs thrown away, or part thereof.

Vesting orders—property in Scotland

1A–197 26.43 In applications for vesting orders under the Trustee Act 1925 any investments or property situate in Scotland should be set out in a separate schedule to the claim form, and the claim form should ask that the trustees may have permission to apply for a vesting order in Scotland in respect thereto.

26.44 The form of the order to be made in such cases will (with any necessary variation) be as follows:

"It is ordered that the   [   ] as   Trustees   have permission to take all steps that may be necessary to obtain a vesting order in Scotland relating to [the securities] specified in the schedule herein."

Disability of Trustee

1A–198 26.45 There must be medical evidence showing incapacity to act as a trustee at the date of issue of the claim form and that the incapacity is continuing at the date of

Paragraph numbers marked with a "+" can be found online and on CD.

signing the witness statement or swearing the affidavit. The witness statement or affidavit should also show incapacity to execute transfers, where a vesting order of stocks and shares is asked for.

26.46 The trustee under disability should be made a defendant to the claim but need not be served unless he or she is sole trustee or has a beneficial interest.

Lodgment of Funds

26.47 Lodgment into the High Court of amounts of cash or securities of less than £500 under section 63 of the Trustee Act 1925, and rule 14(1) of the Court Funds Rules 1987 will not be accepted by the Accountant-General unless the Chief Master so signifies in writing. **1A–199**

26.48 The Accountant-General will refer the applicant to the Chief Master who will consider whether there is a more economical method of preserving the fund than lodging it in the High Court or, failing that, may suggest that the money be lodged in a county court (which has power to accept sums of up to £30,000 lodged under section 63 of the Trustee Act 1925).

26.49 If the Chief Master decides that a particular lodgment should be made in the High Court, he will so signify on the back of the request (in respect of applications under rule 14(1)(ii)(a)) or the office copy schedule to the affidavit (in respect of applications under rule 14(1)(ii)(b)).

Estates of Deceased Lloyd's Names

26.50 The procedure concerning the estates of deceased Lloyd's names is governed by a *Practice Statement* [2001] 3 All ER 765. **1A–200**

26.51 Personal representatives who wish to apply to the court for permission to distribute the estate of a deceased Lloyd's Name following *Re Yorke* (deceased) [1997] 4 All ER 907, or trustees who wish to administer any will trusts arising in such an estate, may, until further notice and if appropriate in the particular estate, adopt the following procedure.

26.52 The procedure will be appropriate where:

(1) the only, or only substantial, reason for delaying distribution of the estate is the possibility of personal liability to Lloyd's creditors; and

(2) all liabilities of the estate in respect of syndicates of which the Name was a member have for the years 1992 and earlier (if any) been reinsured (whether directly or indirectly) into the Equitas group; and

(3) all liabilities of the estate in respect of syndicates of which the Name was a member have for the years 1993 and later (if any) arise in respect of syndicates which have closed by reinsurance in the usual way or are protected by the terms of an Estate Protection Plan issued by Centrewrite Limited or are protected by the terms of EXEAT insurance cover provided by Centrewrite Limited.

26.53 In these circumstances personal representatives (and, if applicable, trustees) may apply by a Part 8 Claim Form headed "In the Matter of the Estate of [..........] deceased (a Lloyd's Estate) and In the Matter of the Practice Direction dated May 25 2001" for permission to distribute the estate (and, if applicable, to administer the will trusts) on the footing that no or no further provision need be made for Lloyd's creditors. Ordinarily, the claim form need not name any other party. It may be issued in this form without a separate application for permission under rule 8.2A.

26.54 The claim should be supported by a witness statement or an affidavit substantially in the form set out in Appendix 11 adapted as necessary to the particular circumstances and accompanied by a draft of the desired order substantially in the form also set out in Appendix 11. If the amount of costs has been

Paragraph numbers marked with a "+" can be found online and on CD.

agreed with the residuary beneficiaries (or, if the costs are not to be taken from residue, with the beneficiaries affected) their signed consent to those costs should also be submitted. If the Claimants are inviting the court to make a summary assessment they should submit a statement of costs in the form specified in the Costs PD. If in his discretion the Master (or outside London the District Judge) thinks fit, he will summarily assess the costs but with permission for the paying party to apply within 14 days of service of the order on him to vary or discharge the summary assessment. Subject to the foregoing, the order will provide for a detailed assessment unless subsequently agreed.

26.55 The application will be considered in the first instance by the Master who, if satisfied that the order should be made, may make the order without requiring the attendance of the applicants, and the court will send it to them. If not so satisfied, the Master may give directions for the further disposal of the application.

Judicial Trustees

1A–201   26.56 Judicial trustees are appointed by the court under the Judicial Trustees Act 1896, in accordance with the Judicial Trustee Rules 1983. An application for the appointment of a judicial trustee should be made by Part 8 claim (or, if in an existing claim, by an application notice in that claim) which must be served (subject to any directions by the court) on every existing trustee who is not an applicant and on such of the beneficiaries as the applicant thinks fit. Once appointed, a judicial trustee may obtain non-contentious directions from the assigned Master informally by letter, without the need for a Part 23 application (unless the court directs otherwise). Applications for directions can be sought from the court as to the trust or its administration by rule 8 of the Judicial Trustee Rules.

26.57 Where it is proposed to appoint the Official Solicitor as judicial trustee, inquiries must first be made to his office for confirmation that he is prepared to act if appointed. The Official Solicitor will not be required to give security.

26.58 A judicial trustee is entitled under rule 11 of the 1983 rules to such remuneration as is reasonable in respect of work reasonably performed. Applications for payment by the trustee must be by letter to the court, submitted with the accounts. A Practice Note issued by the Chief Chancery Master, with the authority of the Vice-Chancellor, on 1 July 2003 sets out the best practice to be followed in determining the amount of remuneration. The Practice Note mirrors the position regarding receivers' remuneration under CPR rule 69.7 and is reproduced at Appendix 12.

APPENDIX 1

ADDRESSES AND OTHER CONTACT DETAILS

1A–202   **1. Clerks to the Chancery Judges**

(all numbers to be preceded by 020 7947)

Clerk to:	telephone	fax
The Chancellor	6412	6572
Mr Justice Lindsay	6253	7185
Mr Justice Evans-Lombe	6657	6719
Mr Justice Blackburne	6589	7379
Mr Justice Lightman	6671	6291
Mr Justice Rimer	6418	6649
Mr Justice Park	6741	6196
Mr Justice Pumfrey	7482	6593
Mr Justice Hart	6419	6062
Mr Justice Lawrence Collins	7467	7298

Paragraph numbers marked with a "+" can be found online and on CD.

Clerk to:	telephone	fax
Mr Justice Patten	7617	6650
Mr Justice Etherton	6116	6165
Mr Justice Peter Smith	6183	6133
Mr Justice Lewison	6039	6894
Mr Justice David Richards	7419	6743
Mr Justice Mann	7964	6739
Mr Justice Warren	7260	7740
Mr Justice Kitchin	6518	6439

2. E-Mail Communications
1A–203

The e-mail protocol sets out how parties may communicate by e-mail on certain matters with the Chancery Division, and can be found at: *www.hmcourts-service.gov.uk*

The relevant e-mail addresses are:
   (a) For skeleton arguments, chronologies, reading lists, list of issues, lists of authorities (but not the authorities themselves) and lists of the persons involved in the facts of the case sent in advance of a hearing:

Judge:
rcjchancery.judgeslisting@hmcourts-service.gsi.gov.uk
[Note: The clerk to the judge concerned should be contacted to find out whether other documents will be accepted by e-mail, and whether documents should be sent direct to the judge's clerk's e-mail address.]

Chancery Master:
rcjchancery.mastersappointments@hmcourts-service.gsi.gov.uk

Bankruptcy Registrar:
rcjbankruptcy.registrarshearings@hmcourts-service.gsi.gov.uk

Companies Court Registrar:
rcjcompanies.orders@hmcourts-service.gsi.gov.uk

   (b) For the agreed terms of an Order which is ready to be sealed following the conclusion of a hearing:

Judge:
rcjchancery.ordersandaccounts@hmcourts-service.gsi.gov.uk

Chancery Master:
rcjchancery.ordersandaccounts@hmcourts-service.gsi.gov.uk

Bankruptcy Registrar:
rcjbankruptcy.registrarshearings@hmcourts-service.gsi.gov.uk

Companies Court Registrar:
rcjcompanies.orders@hmcourts-service.gsi.gov.uk

3. At the Royal Courts of Justice, Thomas More Building
1A–204

(All telephone extension numbers and fax numbers should be prefixed by 020 7947 unless otherwise specified)

1ST FLOOR

TM1.10	Bankruptcy Registrars' Clerks, applications without notice, Registrars' hearings and orders (6444) Bankruptcy Registrars' Chambers (6444/7387) Bankruptcy Court fax number (6378)

2ND FLOOR

TM2.04	Deputy Court Manager (6812)
TM2.07	Court Manager, Companies, Bankruptcy Courts (6870).

Paragraph numbers marked with a "+" can be found online and on CD.

TM2.09	Companies Court General Office: issue of all winding-up petitions and all other Companies Court applications; filing of documents (6294); Central Index (7328)
TM2.11	Bankruptcy Issue and Search Room; issue of all petitions presented by creditors and debtors and applications to set aside statutory demand and applications for interim orders; search room (6448); setting down appeals from Registrars and District and Circuit Judges (6863); Companies Court Fax number (6958)

3RD FLOOR

TM3.08	Bankruptcy and Companies Registry. Filing affidavits, witness statements and documents and requesting bankruptcy and company files for applications without notice to be made in Chambers; requests for office copies, lodging applications for certificates of discharge in bankruptcy (6441)

4TH FLOOR

TM4.04	Companies Schemes and reductions of capital (6727
TM4.05	Companies Orders Section: Winding up Court (6780); Registrars' Orders and disqualification of directors (6822)

5TH FLOOR

TM5.04	Chancery Chambers Registry and Issue Section: issue and amendment of all Chancery process, filing affidavits and witness statements (save those lodged within two days of a hearing before a Master which are to be filed in Room TM7.09); filing acknowledgements of service, searches of cause book; applications for office copy documents, including orders; transfers in and out (6148/6167)
TM5.05	Deputy Court Manager, Chancery Chambers. Certification of documents for use abroad (6754)
TM5.06	Lawyer, Chancery Chambers (6080).
TM5.07	Orders and Accounts Section. Associates: preparation of all Chancery Orders and Companies and Bankruptcy Court Orders; small payments; bills of costs for assessment; settlement of payment and lodgment schedules; accounts of receivers, judicial trustees, guardians and administrators; applications relating to security set by the court; matters arising out of accounts and inquiries ordered by the court (6855); Chancery Orders and Accounts Fax number: (7049)

6TH FLOOR

TM6.04	Chancery Masters' Library
TM6.05	Master Price
TM6.06	Court Manager, Chancery Chambers (6075)
TM6.07	Master Bowles
TM6.08	Secretary to Masters (6777)
TM6.09	Master Bragge

7TH FLOOR

TM7.05	Master Teverson
TM7.06	Master Moncaster
TM7.08	Chief Master Winegarten

Paragraph numbers marked with a "+" can be found online and on CD.

TM7.09   Masters' Appointments. Issue of Masters' applications, including
          applications without notice to Masters; filing affidavits and witness
          statements in proceedings before Masters (only if filed within two
          working days of hearing before the Master); applications to serve
          out of jurisdiction; filing stop notices; filing testamentary documents
          in contested probate cases; filing grants lodged under Part57; filing
          affidavits relating to funds paid into court under the Trustee Act
          1925, Compulsory Purchase Act 1965 and the Lands Clauses
          Consolidation Act 1845. Manager (6095); Clerks to Chancery
          Masters (6702/7391); Masters' Appointments Fax no: (7422)

4. At the Royal Courts of Justice but Outside Thomas More Building   1A–205

(Prefaced by 020 7947 unless otherwise specified).

RCJ Switchboard (6000)

RCJ Security Office (6260)

Fees Office (Room E01) (6527)

Clerk of the Lists, Room WG3 (6318)

Chancery Judges' Listing Office, Room WG4 (6778/6690)

High Court Appeals Office, Room WG7 (7518)

Chancery Judges' Listing Office Fax number*: (7345) *(*See* paragraph 14.12)

Officer in charge of mechanical recording (Room WB.14) (6154)

Head Usher (6356, fax 6668)

Customer Service Officer (7731)

Video-conferencing managers (6581, fax 6613)

RCJ Advice Bureau (0845 120 3715, or 020 7947 6880, fax 020 7947 7167)

Personal Support Unit (Room M104). (7701/7703 fax 7702)

5. London, Outside the Royal Courts of Justice   1A–206

Central London County Court

Civil Trial Centre, Chancery List, 26-29 Park Crescent, London W1N 4HT DX 97325
Regents Park 2

Business Chancery and Patents section (020 7917 7821/7887)

Fax 0207 917 7935/7940

6. Outside London   1A–207

The following are the Court addresses, telephone and fax numbers for the courts at
which there are regular Chancery sittings outside London:

Birmingham:	The Priory Courts, 33 Bull Street, Birmingham B4 6DS. Telephone: 0121-681-3033. Fax: 0121-681-3121
Bristol:	The Law Courts, Small Street, Bristol BS1 1DA. Telephone: 0117-976-3098. Fax: 0117-976-3074
Cardiff:	The Civil Justice Centre, 2 Park Street, Cardiff CF1 1ET. Telephone: 01222-376402. Fax: 01222-376470

Paragraph numbers marked with a "+" can be found online and on CD.

Leeds:	The Court House, 1 Oxford Row, Leeds LS1 3BG. Telephone: 0113-283-0040. Fax: 0113-244-8507.
Liverpool:	Queen Elizabeth II Law Courts, Derby Square, Liverpool L2 1XA. Telephone: 0151-473-7373. Fax: 0151-227-2806
Manchester:	The Courts of Justice, Crown Square, Manchester M3 3FL. Telephone: 0161-954-1800. Fax: 0161-832-5179
Newcastle:	The Law Courts, Quayside, Newcastle-upon-Tyne NE1 3LB. Telephone: 0191-201-2000. Fax: 0191-201-2001
Preston:	The Law Courts, Openshaw Place, Ringway, Preston PR1 2LL. Telephone: 01772-832300. Fax: 01772-832476.

In some centres resources do not permit the listing telephone numbers to be attended personally at all times. In cases of urgency, solicitors, counsel and counsel's clerks may come into the Chancery Court and leave messages with the member of staff sitting in Court.

Urgent Court business officer pager numbers for out of hours applications:

Birmingham (Midland Circuit):

	West Side:	07699-618079
	East Side:	07699-618078
Bristol:		07699-618088
Cardiff:		07699-618086
Manchester and Liverpool:		07699-618080
Preston		07699-618081
Newcastle		01399-618083
Leeds and Bradford		01399-618082

In case of difficulty out of hours, contact the Royal Courts of Justice on 020 7947 6260.

APPENDIX 2

GUIDELINES ON STATEMENTS OF CASE

1A–208 1. The document must be as brief and concise as possible.

2. The document must be set out in separate consecutively numbered paragraphs and sub-paragraphs.

3. So far as possible each paragraph or sub-paragraph should contain no more than one allegation.

4. The document should deal with the case on a point by point basis, to allow a point by point response.

5. Where the CPR require a party to give particulars of an allegation or reasons for a denial (see rule 16.5(2)), the allegation or denial should be stated first and then the particulars or reasons listed one by one in separate numbered sub-paragraphs.

6. A party wishing to advance a positive case must identify that case in the document; a simple denial is not sufficient.

7. Any matter which if not stated might take another party by surprise should be stated.

8. Where they will assist, headings, abbreviatiions and definitions should b used and a glossary annexed.

Paragraph numbers marked with a "+" can be found online and on CD.

9. Contentious headings, abbreviations, paraphrasing and definitions should not be used; every effort should be made to ensure that headings, abbreviations and definitions are in a form that will enable them to be adopted without issue by the other parties.

10. Particulars of primary allegations should be stated as particulars and not as primary allegations.

11. Schedules or appendices should be used if this would be helpful, for example where lengthy particulars are necessary.

12. The names of any witness to be called may be given, and necessary documents (including an expert's report) can be attached or served contemporaneously if not bulky (PD 16; Guide paragraph 2.11). Otherwise evidence should not be included.

13. A response to particulars stated in a schedule should be stated in a corresponding schedule.

14. A party should not set out lengthy extracts from a document in his or her statement of case. If an extract has to be included, it should be placed in a schedule.

15. The document must be signed by the individual person or persons who drafted it not, in the case of a solicitor, in the name of the firm only. It must be accompanied by a Statement of Truth.

APPENDIX 3

Case Management Directions

DRAFT ORDERS FOR USE ON ALLOCATION OR AT CASE MANAGEMENT **1A–209** CONFERENCES

Claim No.

IT IS ORDERED
1. Allocation to multi-track
(   ) that this claim is allocated to the multi-track.
2. Transfer of claims, including transfer from Part 8
(   ) that the claim be transferred to:
    (a) the   Division of the High Court;
    (b) the   District Registry;
    (c) the   [Central London] County Court [Chancery List].
(   ) that the issue(s)   *(define issue(s))* be transferred to   *(one of (a) to (c) above)* for determination.
(   ) that the   *(party)* apply by   *(date)* to a Judge of the Technology and Construction Court [*or other Specialist List*] for an Order to transfer the claim to that Court.
(   ) that the claim   *(title and claim number)* commenced in [the   County Court][the District Registry of], be transferred from that Court to the Chancery Division of the High Court.
(   ) that this claim shall continue as if commenced under Part 7 and shall be allocated to the multi-track.
3. Alternative dispute resolution
This claim be stayed until   [*one month*] for the parties to try to settle the dispute by alternative dispute resolution or other means. The parties shall notify the Court in writing at the end of that period whether settlement has been reached. The parties shall at the same time lodge *either*:
    (a) (if a settlement has been reached) a draft consent Order signed by all parties;
        or
    (b) (if no settlement has been reached) a statement of agreed directions signed

Paragraph numbers marked with a "+" can be found online and on CD.

by all parties or (in the absence of agreed directions) statements of the parties' respective proposed directions.

4. Probate cases only

(   ) that the   [*party*] file [his][her] witness statement or affidavit of testamentary scripts and lodge any testamentary script at Room TM7.09, Thomas More Building, Royal Courts of Justice, Strand, London WC2A 2LL [District Registry] by   (*date*).

5. Case summary

(   ) that [each party][the   (*party*)] by   (*date*) prepare and serve a case summary [not exceeding   words] on all other parties, to be agreed by   (*date*) and filed by   (*date*) and if it is not agreed by that date the parties shall file their own case summaries.

6. Trial date

(   ) that the trial of the claim/issue(s) take place between   (*date*) and (*date*) ('the trial window').

(   ) that the   (*party*) shall make an appointment to attend on the Listing Officer (Room WG4, Royal Courts of Justice, Strand, London WC2A 2LL; Tel. 020 7947 6816; Fax No. 020 7947 7352) to fix a trial date within the trial window, such appointment to be not later than   (*date*) and give notice of the appointment to all other parties.

(   ) that

(i) the claim be entered in the [Trial List][General List], with a listing category of   [A][B][C] (*to be decided by the Master with reference to the substance and difficulty of the case*), with a time estimate of   days/weeks

(ii) the trial take place in London (*or* identify venue).

7. Pre Trial Review

(   ) [the trial being estimated to last more than 10 days] that there be a Pre Trial Review on a date to be arranged by the Listing Officer [in conjunction with the parties] [to take place shortly before the trial and, if possible, in front of the Judge who will be conducting the trial] at which, except for urgent matters in the meantime, the Court will hear any further applications for Orders.

8. All directions agreed.

(   ) The parties having agreed directions it is by consent ordered:—
[Set out all the directions by reference to parties' draft Order on file].

9. Some directions agreed

(   ) The parties having agreed the following directions it is by consent ordered:
[Set out the agreed directions by reference to parties' draft Order on file as above,   and any further directions to be given at this stage].

10. Case management conference etc.

(   ) that there be a [further] case management conference before the Master in Room TM . ., Thomas More Building, Royal Courts of Justice, Strand, London WC2A 2LL on   (*date*) at   o'clock (of   hours/minutes duration).

(   ) that there shall be a case management conference (of   hours/ minutes duration). In order for the Court to fix a date the parties are to complete the accompanying questionnaire and file it by   (*date*).

(   ) that the   (*party*) apply for an appointment for a [further] case management conference by   (*date*).

(   ) At the case management conference, except for urgent matters in the meantime, the Court will hear any further applications for Orders and any party must file an Application Notice for any such Orders and serve it and supporting evidence (if any) by   (*date*).

11. Failure to file allocation questionnaire

(   ) that, ***no allocation questionnaire having been received from [the Claimant][the Defendant]***, if [the Claimant][the Defendant] [does not file [his][her] allocation questionnaire within 3 days after service of this Order upon [him][her], the [claim] [counterclaim] shall be struck out without further Order *[or as the case may be]*.

[Add Order as to costs].

12. Amendments to statement of case

Paragraph numbers marked with a "+" can be found online and on CD.

(   ) that the   (*party*) has permission to amend [his][her] statement of case as in the copy on the Court file [initialled by the Master].

(   ) that the amended statement of case be verified by a statement of truth.

(   ) that the amended statement of case be filed by   (*date*).

(   ) that [the amended statement of case be served by   (*date*).] [service of the amended statement of case be dispensed with].

(   ) that any consequential amendments to other statements of case be filed and served by   (*date*)

(   ) that the costs of and consequential to the amendment to the statement of case [shall be paid by   (*party*) in any event] [are assessed in the sum of £ and are to be paid by   (*party*)][within   (*time*)].

13. Addition of parties etc.

(   ) that the   (*party*) has permission:

(a) to [add][substitute][remove]   (*name of party*) as a   (*party*) and

(b) to amend [his][her] statement of case in accordance with the copy on the Court file [initialled by the Master].

and that the amended statement of case be verified by a statement of truth.

(   ) that the amended statement of case be:

(a) filed by   (*date*);

(b) served on   (*new party, existing parties or removed party, as appropriate*), by   (*date*).

(   ) that a copy of this Order be served on   (*new party, existing parties or removed party, as appropriate*), by   (*date*).

(   ) that any consequential amendments to other statements of case be filed and served by   (*date*).

(   ) that the costs of and consequential to the amendment to the statement of case [shall be paid by the   (*party*) in any event] [are assessed in the sum of £   and are to be paid by the   (*party*)].

14. Consolidation

(   ) that this claim be consolidated with claim number   (*number and title of claim*), the lead claim to be claim number   . [The title to the consolidated case shall be as set out in the Schedule to this Order].

15. Trial of issue

(   ) that the issue of   (*define issue*) be tried as follows:

(a) with the consent of the parties, before a Master

(i) on   (*date*) in Room TM   Thomas More Building, Royal Courts of Justice, Strand, London WC2A 2LL;

(ii) with a time estimate of   (hours),

(iii) with the filing of listing questionnaires dispensed with, *or*

(b) before a Judge

(i) with the trial of the issue to take place between   (*date*) and (*date*) ('the trial window')

(ii) with the   (*party*) to make an appointment to attend on the Listing Officer (Room WG4, Royal Courts of Justice, Strand, London WC2A 2LL; Tel. 020 7947 6778/6690; Fax No. 020 7947 7345) to fix a trial date within the trial window, such appointment to be not later than   (*date*) and to give notice of the appointment to all other parties.

(iii) with the issue to be entered in the [Trial List][General List],

with a listing category of [A][B][C] (*to be decided by the Master with reference to the substance and difficulty of the case*, and a time estimate of   days/ weeks and to take place in London (*or identify venue*).

16. Further information

(   ) that the   (*party*) provide by   (*date*) the [further information][clarification] sought in the request dated (*date*) [initialled by the Master].

Paragraph numbers marked with a "+" can be found online and on CD.

(   ) that any request for [further information][clarification] shall be served
by   [*date*].

17. Disclosure of documents

(   ) that each party give by   (*date*) standard disclosure to every other
party by list [by categories].

(   ) that the   (*party/parties*) give specific disclosure of documents [limited
to the issues of   ] described in the Schedule to this Order [initialled by the
Master] by list [by categories] by   (*date*).

(   ) that the   (*party*) give by   (*date*) standard disclosure by list [by categories] to   (*party*) of documents
limited to the issue(s) of   (*define issues*) by list.

18. Inspection of documents

(   ) that any requests for inspection or copies of disclosed documents shall be
made   within days after service of the list.

19. Preservation of property

(   ) that the   (*party*) preserve   (*give details of relevant
property*) until trial of the claim or further Order *or other remedy under* rule 25.1(1).

20. Witness statements

(   ) that each party serve on every other party the witness statement of the oral
evidence which the party serving the statement intends to rely on in relation to [any
issues of fact][the following issues of fact   (*define issues*)] to be
decided at the trial, those statements [and any notices of intention to rely on hearsay
evidence] to be

    (a) exchanged by   (*date*) or

    (b) served by   (*party*) by   (*date*) and   by-
        (*party*) by   (*date*)   pro-
        vided that before exchange the parties shall liaise with a view to agreeing
        a   method of identification of any documents referred to in any
        such witness statement.

(   ) that the   (*party*) has permission to serve a witness summary   relating   to   the   evidence   of   (*name*)
of   (*address*) [on every other party by][to be served
on   (*party*)/exchanged at the same time as exchange of witness
statements].

21. No expert evidence

(   ) no expert evidence being necessary, that [no party has permission to call or
rely on expert evidence][permission to call or rely on expert evidence is refused].

22. Single expert

(   ) that evidence be given by the report of a single expert in the field of-
        (*define field*) instructed jointly by the parties, on the issue of-
        (*define issue*) [and [his][her] fees shall be limited to £   ].

(   ) that if the parties are unable to agree [by   (*date*)] who that expert is
to be and about the payment of [his][her] fees any party may apply for
further   directions.

(   ) that unless the parties agree in writing or the Court orders otherwise, the
fees and expenses of the single expert shall be paid to [him][her] by the parties
equally.

(   ) that each party give [his][her] instructions to the single expert
by   (*date*).

(   ) that the report of the single expert be filed and served by [him][her] on the
parties by   (*date*).

(   ) that no party may recover from another party more than £   for the
fees and expenses of the expert.

(   ) that the evidence of the expert be given at the trial by [written report][ora-
l   evidence] of the expert.

23. Separate Experts

(   ) that each party has permission to adduce [oral] expert evidence in the field
of   (*specify*) [limited to   expert(s) [per party][on each side].

(   ) that the experts' reports shall be exchanged by   (*date*).

Paragraph numbers marked with a "+" can be found online and on CD.

84

(   ) that the experts shall hold a discussion for the purpose of:

    (a) identifying the issues, if any, between them; and

    (b) where possible, reaching agreement on those issues.

(   ) that the experts shall by   [*specify date after discussion*] prepare and file a statement for the Court showing:

    (a) those issues on which they are agreed; and

    (b) those issues on which they disagree and a summary of their reasons for disagreeing.

(   ) No party shall be entitled to recover by way of costs from any other party more than £   for the fees or expenses of an expert.

24. Definition and reduction of issues.

(   ) that by   (*date*) the parties list and discuss the issues in the claim- [including the experts' reports and statements] and attempt to define and narrow the   issues [including those issues the subject of discussion by the experts].

25. Trial bundle and skeleton arguments.

(   ) that not earlier than 7 days or later than 3 days before the date fixed for trial or of the claim entering the Warned List the Claimant shall file with the Chancery Listing Office a trial bundle for the use of the Judge in accordance with Appendix 6 of the Chancery Guide.

(   ) that skeleton arguments and chronologies shall be filed not less than 2 clear days before the date fixed for trial or of the claim entering the Warned List, in accordance with Appendix 7 of the Chancery Guide.

26. Settlement

(   ) that if the claim or part of the claim is settled the parties must immediately inform the Court, whether or not it is then possible to file a draft Consent Order to give   effect to the settlement.

27. Compliance with Directions

(   ) that the parties shall by   (*date*) notify the Court in writing that they have fully complied with all directions or state:

    (a) with which directions they have not complied;

    (b) why they have not complied; and

    (c) what steps they are taking to comply with the outstanding directions in time for the trial.

If the Court does not receive such notification or if the steps proposed to comply with outstanding directions are considered by the Court unsatisfactory, the Court   may order a hearing (and may make appropriate orders as to costs against a party in   default).

28. Costs

(   ) that the costs of this application be:

    (a) costs in the case;

    (b) summarily assessed at £   and paid by   (*party*); or

    (c) the [party/parties]'[s] in any event, to be subject to detailed assessment.

NOTE 1

The attention of the parties is drawn to the importance of seeking to agree at an early stage directions for the management of the case as emphasised in the Practice Direction to Part 29 of the Civil Procedure Rules.

NOTE 2

The parties may, subject to any agreement being in accordance with the provisions of the Civil Procedure Rules, agree to extend the time periods given in the directions above provided this <u>does not</u> affect the date given for any case management conference or pre-trial review or the date of the trial or trial period.

NOTE 3

If you fail to attend a hearing that has been ordered, the Court may order you to pay the costs of the other party, or parties, that do attend. Failure to pay those costs within the time stated may lead to your statement of case (claim or defence) being struck out.

Paragraph numbers marked with a "+" can be found online and on CD.

NOTE 4
If you do not comply with these directions, any other party to the claim will be entitled to apply to the Court for an order that your statement of case (claim or defence) be struck out.

APPENDIX 4

Part 1: Judge's Application Information Form

1A–210 Title as in claim form
Application Information

1.   [DATE APPLICATION TO BE HEARD]
2.   DETAILS OF SOLICITOR/PARTY LODGING THE APPLICATION
    a.   [Name]
    b.   [Address]
    c.   [Telephone No.]
    d.   [Reference]
    e.   [Acting for Claimant(s)/Defendant(s)]
3.   DETAILS OF COUNSEL/OR OTHER ADVOCATE
    a.   [Name]
    b.   [Address of Chambers/Firm]
    c.   [Telephone No.]
4.   DETAILS OF OTHER PART(Y'S)(IES') SOLICITORS
    a.   [Name]
    b.   [Address]
    c.   [Telephone No.]
    d.   [Reference]
[Acting for Claimant(s)/Defendant(s)]

Part 2: Written Evidence Lodgment Form

1A–211   **CHANCERY CHAMBERS**
TO FILING SECTION—ROOM TM5.04
CLAIM NO:
SHORT TITLE:
Herewith Affidavit or witness statement of . . . .
/or if other document specify. . . . .
filed in respect of:—

	Tick
1. Application before Judge on	
2. Application before Master on	
3. Charging Order	
4. Garnishee Order	
5. Permission to issue claim for possession	
6. Service by alternative method	
7. Service out of Jurisdiction	
8. Evidence	
9. Oral examination of debtor	
10. To enable a Master's order to be drawn	
11. Other (Specify)	

Signed
Solicitors for Claimant/Defendant
other (please specify)
Telephone No:
Ref:
Paragraph numbers marked with a "+" can be found online and on CD.

APPENDIX 5

CORRESPONDENCE WITH CHANCERY MASTERS—PRACTICE NOTE

1. One of the consequences of the new Rules and Practice Directions has been a **1A–212** significant increase in letters to the Court from parties and their solicitors. This imposes a heavy extra burden on the staff and Masters. It also means that court files have to be moved more often, which itself gives rise to problems. It would therefore be greatly appreciated if parties and solicitors involved in litigation before the Chancery Masters had regard to the following points.

2. When corresponding, please consider carefully (a) whether your letter is really necessary and (b) if it is who the correct addressee should be. Only address letters to the Master if the letter needs to be seen by him. If not address the letter to his clerk.

3. Letters and other documents should only be sent by fax if there is a real urgency, and should not be followed up with a hard copy. (If, exceptionally, a fax has contained a document the original of which needs to go on the court file, then the hard copy enclosing the original should be marked clearly "confirmation of fax").

4. As a general rule all correspondence, whether letter or fax, must be copied to the other parties. Correspondence should therefore state that it has been copied to the other parties (or else it should state that it has not and explain why).

5. Correspondence should not be used in place of a Part 23 application (which requires payment of a fee, a draft order and a statement of truth).

J Winegarten

Chief Chancery Master

July 2001

APPENDIX 6

GUIDELINES ON BUNDLES

Bundles of documents must comply with paragraph 3 of PD 39 Miscellaneous Pro- **1A–213** visions relating to Hearings. These guidelines are additional to those requirements, and they should be followed wherever possible.

1. The preparation of bundles requires co-operation between the legal representatives **1A–214** for all parties, and in many cases a high level of cooperation. It is the duty of all legal representatives to co-operate to the necessary level. Where a party is acting in person it is also that party's duty to co-operate as necessary with the other parties' legal representatives.

2. Bundles should be prepared in accordance with the following guidance.

Avoidance of duplication

3. No more than one copy of any one document should be included, unless there is **1A–215** good reason for doing otherwise. One such reason may be the use of a separate core bundle.

4. If the same document is included in the chronological bundles and is also an exhibit to an affidavit or witness statement, it should be included in the chronological bundle and where it would otherwise appear as an exhibit a sheet should instead be inserted. This sheet should state the page and bundle number in the chronological bundles where the document can be found.

5. Where the court considers that costs have been wasted by copying unnecessary

Paragraph numbers marked with a "+" can be found online and on CD.

documents, a special costs order may be made against the relevant person. In no circumstances should rival bundles be presented to the court.

Chronological order and organisation

1A–216 6. In general documents should be arranged in date order starting with the earliest document.

7. If a contract or other transactional document is central to the case it may be included in a separate place provided that a page is inserted in the chronological run of documents to indicate where it would have appeared chronologically and where it is to be found instead. Alternatively transactional documents may be placed in a separate bundle as a category.

Pagination

1A–217 8. This is covered by paragraph 3 of the PD, but it is permissible, instead of numbering the whole bundle, to number documents separately within tabs. An exception to consecutive page numbering arises in the case of the core bundle. For this it may be preferable to retain the original numbering with each bundle represented by a separate divider.

9. Page numbers should be inserted in bold figures, at the bottom of the page and in a form that can clearly be distinguished from any other pagination on the document.

Format and presentation

1A–218 10. Where possible, the documents should be in A4 format. Where a document has to be read across rather than down the page, it should so be placed in the bundle as to ensure that the top of the text starts nearest the spine.

11. Where any marking or writing in colour on a document is important, for example on a conveyancing plan, the document must be copied in colour or marked up correctly in colour.

12. Documents in manuscript, or not easily legible, should be transcribed; the transcription should be marked and placed adjacent to the document transcribed.

13. Documents in a foreign language should be translated; the translation should be marked and placed adjacent to the document translated; the translation should be agreed or, if it cannot be agreed, each party's proposed translation should be included.

14. The size of any bundle should be tailored to its contents. There is no point having a large lever-arch file with just a few pages inside. On the other hand bundles should not be overloaded as they tend to break. **No bundle should contain more than 300 pages.**

15. Binders and files must be strong enough to withstand heavy use.

16. Large documents, such as plans, should be placed in an easily accessible file. If they will need to be opened up often, it may be sensible for the file to be larger than A4 size.

Indices and labels

1A–219 17. Indices should, if possible, be on a single sheet. It is not necessary to waste space with the full heading of the action. Documents should be identified briefly but properly, e.g. "AGS3—Defendants Accounts".

18. Outer labels should use large lettering, e.g. "A. Pleadings." The full title of the action and solicitors' names and addresses should be omitted. A label should be used on the front as well as on the spine.

Paragraph numbers marked with a "+" can be found online and on CD.

19. A label should also be stuck on to the front inside cover of a file at the top left, in such a way that it can be seen even when the file is open.

Staples etc.

20. All staples, heavy metal clips etc. should be removed.

1A–220

Statements of case

21. Statements of case should be assembled in 'chapter' form, i.e. claim form followed by particulars of claim, followed by further information, irrespective of date.

1A–221

22. Redundant documents, e.g. particulars of claim overtaken by amendments, requests for further information recited in the answers given, should generally be excluded. Backsheets to statements of case should also be omitted.

Witness statements, affidavits and expert reports

23. Where there are witness statements, affidavits and/or expert reports from two or more parties, each party's witness statements etc. should, in large cases, be contained in separate bundles.

1A–222

24. The copies of the witness statements, affidavits and expert reports in the bundles should have written on them, next to the reference to any document, the reference to that document in the bundles. This can be done in manuscript.

25. Documents referred to in, or exhibited to, witness statements, affidavits and expert reports should be put in a separate bundle and not placed behind the statement concerned, so that the reader can see both the text of the statement and the document referred to at the same time.

26. Backsheets to affidavits and witness statements should be omitted.

New Documents

27. Before a new document is introduced into bundles which have already been delivered to the court—indeed before it is copied—steps should be taken to ensure that it carries an appropriate bundle/page number, so that it can be added to the court documents. It should not be stapled, and it should be prepared with punch holes for immediate inclusion in the binders in use.

1A–223

28. If it is expected that a large number of miscellaneous new documents will from time to time be introduced, there should be a special tabbed empty loose-leaf file for that purpose. An index should be produced for this file, updated as necessary.

Inter-Solicitor Correspondence

29. It is seldom that all inter-solicitor correspondence is required. Only those letters which are likely to be referred to should be copied. They should normally be placed in a separate bundle.

1A–224

Core bundle

30. Where the volume of documents needed to be included in the bundles, and the nature of the case, makes it sensible, a separate core bundle should be prepared for the trial, containing those documents likely to be referred to most frequently.

1A–225

Basis of agreement of bundles

31. See Chapter 7, paragraph 13.

1A–226

Photocopy authorities

32. If authorities, extracts from text-books etc. are photocopied for convenience for use in court, the photocopies should be placed in a separate bundle with an index

1A–227

Paragraph numbers marked with a "+" can be found online and on CD.

and dividers. Reduced size copies (i.e. 2 pages of original to each A4 sheet) should not be used. Where only a short passage from a long case is needed, the headnote and key pages only should be copied and the usher should be asked to have the full volume in court. Whenever possible the parties' advocates should liaise about these bundles in order to avoid duplication of copies.

APPENDIX 7

GUIDELINES ON SKELETON ARGUMENTS, CHRONOLOGIES, INDICES AND READING LISTS

Skeleton arguments

1A–228 1. A skeleton argument is intended to identify both for the parties and the court those points which are, and those that are not, in issue, and the nature of the argument in relation to those points which are in issue. It is not a substitute for oral argument.

2. Every skeleton argument should therefore:
    (1) identify concisely:
        (a) the nature of the case generally, and the background facts insofar as they are relevant to the matter before the court;
        (b) the propositions of law relied on with references to the relevant authorities;
        (c) the submissions of fact to be made with reference to the evidence;
    (2) be as brief as the nature of the issues allows—it should not normally exceed 20 pages of double-spaced A4 paper and in many cases it should be much shorter than this;
    (3) be in numbered paragraphs and state the name (and contact details) of the advocate(s) who prepared it;
    (4) avoid arguing the case at length;
    (5) avoid formality and make use of abbreviations, e.g. C for Claimant, A/345 for bundle A page 345, 1.1.95 for 1st January 1995 etc.

3. Paragraph 1 also applies to written summaries of opening speeches and final speeches. Even though in a large case these may necessarily be longer, they should still be as brief as the case allows.

Reading lists

1A–229 4. The documents which the Judge should if possible read before the hearing may be identified in a skeleton argument, but must in any event be listed in a separate reading list, if possible agreed between the advocates, which must be lodged with the agreed bundles, together with an estimate, if possible agreed, of the time required for the reading.

Chronologies and indices

1A–230 5. Chronologies and indices should be non-contentious and agreed with the other parties if possible. If there is a material dispute about any event stated in the chronology, that should be stated in neutral terms and the competing versions shortly stated.

6. If time and circumstances allow its preparation, a chronology or index to which all parties have contributed and agreed can be invaluable.

7. Chronologies and indices once prepared can be easily updated and may be of continuing usefulness throughout the case.

APPENDIX 8

DELIVERY OF DOCUMENTS IN CHANCERY CHAMBERS

1. Deliver of documents for Master's hearings

1A–231   (a) Deliver bundles and skeletons (if required) to Masters' Appointments, Room TM7.09, 2 clear working days (not more than 7) before the hearing.

Paragraph numbers marked with a "+" can be found online and on CD.

(b) Mark clearly "for hearing on ....(date) before Master ....

(c) Insert a reading list and estimate of reading time if appropriate.

(d) Bundles may be presented in ring binders or lever arch files, or as appropriate.

(e) Documents for Masters' hearings should not be taken direct to the Master's room unless in any particular case the Master has directed otherwise.

(f) Documents required for Masters' hearings should never be taken to (i) the Registry (Room TM5.04); (ii) the Chancery Judges' Listing Office (Room WG 4) or (iii) the RCJ Post Room)—if they are they may well not reach the Master in time.

Note:

Documents required for hearings before a Chancery judge must not be delivered to Chancery Chambers. They must be delivered to the Chancery Judges' Listing Office (Room WG 4).

2. Filing of documents

(a) Take or send documents required to be filed (i.e. placed on the Court file, either under the CPR or under an Order of the Court (e.g. statements of case, defences, allocation questionnaires, some witness statements)) to the Chancery Registry, Room TM5.04 for filing. **1A–232**

(b) But documents (e.g. witness statements, exhibits) required to be filed which are needed for a Masters' hearing within 10 working days must be delivered for filing to Masters' Appointments, Room 7.09 not the Registry.

(c) If bulky, use treasury tags, not files or ring binders.

APPENDIX 9

GUIDELINES ON WITNESS STATEMENTS

1. The function of a witness statement is to set out in writing the evidence in chief of the maker of the statement. Accordingly witness statements should, so far as possible, be expressed in the witness's own words. This guideline applies unless the perception or recollection of the witness of the events in question is not in issue. **1A–233**

2. Witness statements should be as concise as the circumstances of the case allow. They should be written in consecutively numbered paragraphs. They should present the evidence in an orderly and readily comprehensible manner. They must be signed by the witness, and contain a statement that he or she believes that the facts stated in his or her witness statement are true. They must indicate which of the statements made are made from the witness' own knowledge and which are made on information and belief, giving the source of the information or basis for the belief.

3. Inadmissible material should not be included. Irrelevant material should likewise not be included.

4. Any party on whom a witness statement is served who objects to the relevance or admissibility of material contained in a witness statement should notify the other party of his or her objection within 28 days after service of the witness statement in question and the parties concerned should attempt to resolve the matter as soon as possible. If it is not possible to resolve the matter, the party who objects should make an appropriate application, normally at the PTR, if there is one, or otherwise at trial.

5. It is incumbent on solicitors and counsel not to allow the costs of preparation of witness statements to be unnecessarily increased by overelaboration of the statements. Any unnecessary elaboration may be the subject of a special order as to costs.

6. Witness statements must contain the truth, the whole truth and nothing but the truth on the issues covered. Great care must be taken in the preparation of witness statements. No pressure of any kind should be placed on a witness to give other than

Paragraph numbers marked with a "+" can be found online and on CD.

a true and complete account of his or her evidence. It is improper to serve a witness statement which is known to be false or which the maker does not in all respects actually believe to be true. In addition, a professional adviser may be under an obligation to check where practicable the truth of facts stated in a witness statement if he or she is put on enquiry as to their truth. If a party discovers that a witness statement which he or she has served is incorrect he or she must inform the other parties immediately.

7. A witness statement should simply cover those issues, but only those issues, on which the party serving the statement wishes that witness to give evidence in chief. Thus it is not, for example, the function of a witness statement to provide a commentary on the documents in the trial bundle, nor to set out quotations from such documents, nor to engage in matters of argument. Witness statements should not deal with other matters merely because they may arise in the course of the trial.

8. Witness statements very often refer to documents. If there could be any doubt as to what document is being referred to, or if the document has not previously been made available on disclosure, it may be helpful for the document to be exhibited to the witness statement. If, to assist reference to the documents, the documents referred to are exhibited to the witness statement, they should nevertheless not be included in trial bundles in that form: see Appendix 6, paragraph 4. If (as is normally preferable) the documents referred to in the witness statement are not exhibited, care should be taken in identifying them, for example by reference to the lists of documents exchanged on disclosure. In preparation for trial, it will be necessary to insert cross-references to the trial bundles so as to identify the documents: see Appendix 6, paragraph 24.

9. If a witness is not sufficiently fluent in English to give his evidence in English, the witness statement should be in the witness' own language and a translation provided. If a witness is not fluent in English but can make himself understood in broken English and can understand written English, the statement need not be in his own words provided that these matters are indicated in the statement itself. It must however be written so as to express as accurately as possible the substance of his evidence.

APPENDIX 10

A GUIDE FOR RECEIVERS IN THE CHANCERY DIVISION

1A–234 1. This guide sets out brief notes on the procedure to be followed after an order has been made appointing a receiver in the Chancery Division. The procedure is now governed by CPR Part 69 and its PD.

2. Appendix C contains notes on the main powers and duties of a receiver and a copy should be passed to the receiver.

Action on the Appointment of a Receiver (Rule 69.6; PD 6&8)

1A–235 3. Where an order has been made appointing a receiver, it is generally necessary to apply for directions, by application notice under Part 23. Part 69 PD 6 lists the matters on which directions will usually be given. A draft order should normally be submitted with the Application Notice.

4. The application for directions should normally be made immediately after the making of the order appointing the receiver, especially where security has to be given within a limited time (see below). Only if the order appointing the receiver appoints him or her by name and gives full directions as to accounts and security will an application for directions not be necessary.

5. The receiver may of course apply to the Master at any time for other directions as necessary. Where the directions are unlikely to be contentious or important to the parties this may be done by letter (see Part 69 PD 8). *Giving Security* (Rule 69.5; PD 7).

Paragraph numbers marked with a "+" can be found online and on CD.

Giving Security (Rule 69.5; PD 7).

1A–236

6. The order appointing a receiver will normally include directions in relation to security, and will specify the date by which security is to be given. It is therefore important to obtain an early date for the directions hearing. If security is not completed within the time specified the receivership may be terminated and it will then be necessary for an application to be made to renew it. To avoid this, if it seems likely that security will not be given in time an application should be made at the directions hearing for an extension of time to give security.

7. When the amount of the security has been settled, a guarantee in Form PF 30 CH (Appendix A) must (unless the receiver is a licensed insolvency practitioner covered by bond, which has been extended to cover the appointment) be prepared and entered into with one of the four main clearing banks or the insurance company listed in Appendix B.

8. The guarantee must then be engrossed and executed, i.e. signed by the receiver and signed and sealed by the bank or insurance company. It should then be lodged in Chancery Chambers, Room TM7.09, Royal Courts of Justice, Strand London WC2A 2LL. It will then be signed by the Master and endorsed with a certificate of completion of security and placed on the court file. Where security is given by bond, written evidence of the extended bond and the sufficiency of its cover must be filed in Room 7.09 in accordance with the requirements of Part 69 PD 7.3(1).

9. If the amount of the security given is subsequently increased or decreased, an endorsement is made to the original guarantee.

Receiver's Remuneration (Rule 69.7; PD9)

1A–237

10. A receiver may only charge for his services if the court permits it and specifies the basis on which the receiver is to be remunerated. Unless the court directs the remuneration to be fixed by reference to some fixed scale, or percentage of rents collected, it will determine the amount in accordance with the criteria set out in rule 69.7(4).

Receiver's Accounts (Rule 69.8; PD 10).

1A–238

11. If directions as to the receiver's accounts have not been given in the order appointing the receiver, such directions must be obtained at the directions hearing.

12. Normally accounts are prepared half-yearly and must be delivered within a month of the end of the accounting period.

13. Generally accounts need only be presented to the court if any party receiving them serves notice on the receiver, under rule 69.8(3), that he objects to any item in the accounts.

Discharge of Receiver and Cancellation of Security (Rule 69.10&11)

1A–239

14. When a receiver has completed his duties, the receiver or any party should apply for an order discharging the receiver and cancelling the security.

15. When an order for cancellation of a receiver's security has been made, any guarantee and the duplicate order appointing the receiver are endorsed to that effect.

16. The endorsed guarantee and duplicate order should then be taken to the bank or insurance company by the solicitors for cancellation and return of any outstanding premium.

Paragraph numbers marked with a "+" can be found online and on CD.

Appendix A to Guide for Receivers

Guarantee for receiver's acts and defaults[1]

IN THE HIGH COURT OF JUSTICE

CHANCERY DIVISION

[TITLE]

I, ..(*Name*). of ..(*address*), the Receiver [and manager] appointed by Order dated ..(*date*) (*or* proposed to be appointed) in this claim hereby undertake to the Court duly to account for all money and property received by me as such Receiver [and manager] at such times and in such manner in all respects as the Court directs.

And we ..(*name* (*s*) *of surety or sureties*) hereby [jointly and severally[2]] undertake with the Court and guarantee to be answerable for any default by ......(*name*) as such Receiver [and manager] and upon such default to pay to any person or persons or otherwise as the Court directs any sum or sums not exceeding £ ..in total that may from time to time be certified by [a Master of the Supreme Court][a District Judge] to be due from ......(*name*) as Receiver [and manager] and we submit to the jurisdiction of the Court in this action to determine any claim made under this undertaking.

DATED this ....day of ....20 ....

Signed sealed and delivered by the above named..................in the presence of

or

The Common Seal of....................was hereunto affixed in the presence of:—

(*Signature of receiver*)

(*Seal of surety with appropriate signature or signatures*)

Appendix B to Guide for Receivers

Guarantees for Personal Applicants

The insurance company detailed below is willing to act as surety

Name of company	Address to be shown on and for correspondence
Zurich GSG Limited	Hawthorn Hall Hall Road Wilmslow Cheshire SK9 5BZ

Appendix C to Guide for Receivers

The Powers and Duties of a Receiver

1. The main function of a receiver appointed by the court is to protect the assets received by him pending the court proceedings. The following notes set out some of the more important powers and duties a receiver should be aware of.

---

[1] Adapted from Form PF 30CH.
[2] Omit these words in the case of a guarantee or other company.

Paragraph numbers marked with a "+" can be found online and on CD.

2. A receiver must obtain the permission of the court (which may be contained in the order appointing him) before he can:

    (a) bring, defend or compromise legal proceedings

    (b) *pay a debt (other than in a partnership claim)*

    (c) compromise a claim

    (d) purchase or sell assets other than in the normal course of business

    (e) grant obtain or surrender a lease or purchase or sell real property (even in the course of managing a business); since the appointment of a receiver is an equitable remedy it does not confer on him any title to land: unless the legal owner is prepared to join in the conveyance or lease the receiver would in any case have to obtain a vesting order under section 47 or section 50 of the Trustee Act 1925.

    (f) borrow money

    (h) carry on or close down or sell a business

    (i) employ additional staff in the course of managing a business

    (j) carry out repairs to property costing more than £1000 in any one accounting year

3. Receivers should ensure that they have insurance (if any) transferred into their own names and should consider the adequacy of the insurance cover.

4. Receivers are not entitled to instruct their own solicitors without the express permission of the court.

5. Receivers should seek the court's directions on any question of doubt which arises in the course of the receivership.

6. Receivers should bear in mind that their function as receiver does not include the preparation of partnership accounts and they cannot include fees for such work in their remuneration as receiver.

7. Unless expressly authorised by the court (whether in the Order appointing him or otherwise) the receiver must not part with assets in his hands, whether to the person appointing him or otherwise. If he has completed his functions as receiver before the disputes between the parties have been resolved in the proceedings, the receiver should normally apply to be discharged on lodging into court the money he is holding.

APPENDIX 11

LLOYD'S NAMES' ESTATE APPLICATIONS: FORMS

Form of Witness Statement

[Heading as in claim form]

1A–240

1A–241

1. We are the personal representatives of the estate of the above-named Deceased ("the Deceased") who died on [   ]. We obtained [a grant of probate][letters of administration] out of the [ ] Registry on [   ] and a copy of the grant [and the Deceased's will dated [   ]] is now produced and shown to us marked "   . 1". We make this witness statement in support of our application for permission to distribute the Deceased's estate [and to administer the will trusts of which we will be the Trustees following administration.]. This witness statement contains facts and matters which, unless otherwise stated, are within our own knowledge obtained in acting in the administration of the estate. We believe them to be true.

2. The Deceased was before his death an underwriting member of Lloyd's of London whose underwriting activities are treated as having ceased on [   ]. The estate was sworn for probate purposes at £[   ]. We are now in a position to complete the administration of the estate and to distribute it to the beneficiaries but we do not

Paragraph numbers marked with a "+" can be found online and on CD.

wish to do so [or to constitute the will trusts] without the authority of the Court because of the existence of possible contingent claims arising out of the Deceased's underwriting liabilities for which we might be liable.

3. The position concerning the Deceased's Lloyd's liabilities is as follows:

[3.1 The Deceased's liabilities in respect of the years of account 1992 and earlier were reinsured into Equitas as part of the Lloyd's settlement. There is now produced and shown to us marked "   .2" a copy of the certificate or statement of reinsurance into Equitas].

3.2 [The syndicates in which the Deceased participated in the years of account 1993 and later have [closed by reinsurance in the usual way] [are the subject of an Estate Protection Plan issued to the Deceased by Centrewrite Limited][are protected by an EXEAT policy obtained by the Claimants from Centrewrite Limited].

4. There is now produced and shown to us marked "   .3" a copy of a letter dated [   ] from the estate's Lloyd's agents confirming that [all] the syndicates have been reinsured to close [with the exception of [   ] which syndicate is protected by [the Estate Protection Plan][the EXEAT policy]] and confirming that in the case of failure of a reinsuring syndicate to honour its obligations, the primary liability to a creditor will fall on Lloyd's Central Fund. [A copy of the [Estate Protection Plan and Annual Certificate] [EXEAT policy] is now produced and shown to us marked "   .4".]

5. The Claimants believe that the interests of any Lloyd's claimant are reasonably secured by virtue of the fact that all the Lloyd's syndicates in which the Deceased participated have either been closed ultimately by reinsurance to close (in respect of any open years prior to 1992 into the Equitas group) or, in respect of subsequent years [have all closed by reinsurance] [are protected by the Estate Protection Plan][are protected by the EXEAT policy.] Equitas remains licensed to conduct insurance business and there is presently no reason to doubt its solvency. A copy of the latest report and accounts of Equitas Holdings Limited is now produced and shown to us marked "   .5". [The [Estate Protection Plan] [EXEAT policy] is provided by Centrewrite Limited which is a wholly-owned subsidiary of Lloyd's and the beneficiary of an undertaking by Lloyd's to maintain its solvency. We have no reason to doubt the solvency of Centrewrite. A copy of the latest report and accounts of Centrewrite Limited is now produced and shown to us marked "   . 6".]

6. As appears from the schedule now produced and shown to us marked ".7" in which we summarise the assets and liabilities of the estate, we have paid all the debts of the Deceased known to us (apart from the costs and expenses associated with the final administration of the estate) and we have also advertised for and dealt with all claimants in accordance with s.27 of the Trustee Act 1925 [or if not explain why].

7. We know of no special reason or circumstance which might give rise to doubt whether the provision described above can reasonably be regarded as adequate provision for potential claims against the estate and we ask for permission to distribute accordingly.

Form of Order

1A–242

[Heading as in claim form]

ON THE APPLICATION of the Claimants by Part 8 Claim Form dated [   ]
UPON READING the documents recorded on the Court file as having been read
IT IS ORDERED THAT:

1. the Claimants as [the personal representatives of the estate ("the Estate") of the above named deceased ("the Deceased")] [and] [the trustees of the trusts of the Deceased's will dated [   ]("the Will")] have permission to [distribute the Estate] [and] [administer the trusts of the Will and distribute capital and income in accordance with such trusts] without making any retention or further provision in respect of any contract of insurance or reinsurance under-written by the Deceased in the course of his business as an underwriting member of Lloyd's of London

Paragraph numbers marked with a "+" can be found online and on CD.

1B   QUEEN'S BENCH GUIDE

Editorial note

The coming into force of the Civil Procedure Rules 1998 highlighted the need for a   **1B–1**
Guide which would clarify the complexities of proceedings in the High Court in accordance with the new Rules. Here then is the first Queen's Bench Guide.

The Guide is intended to assist a litigant who wishes to bring a claim in the Queen's Bench Division at the Royal Courts of Justice by drawing his attention to the relevant Rules and Practice Directions, together with the procedures of the various offices within the Central office and of other related areas such as Listing.

The Guide will be updated at regular intervals as the need arises.
January 2007

SECTION 1

INTRODUCTION

1.1 The Guide

1.1.1 This Guide has been prepared by the Senior Master, acting under the authority   **1B–2**
of the President of the Queen's Bench Division and provides a general explanation of the work and practice of the Queen's Bench Division with particular regard to proceedings started in the Central Office, and is designed to make it easier for parties to use and proceed in the Queen's Bench Division.

1.1.2 The Guide must be read with the Civil Procedure Rules ("CPR") and the supporting Practice Directions. Litigants and their advisers are responsible for acquainting themselves with the CPR; it is not the task of this Guide to summarise the CPR, nor should anyone regard it as a substitute for the CPR. It is intended to bring the Guide up to date at regular intervals as necessary.

1.1.3 The Guide does not have the force of law, but parties using the Queen's Bench Division will be expected to act in accordance with this Guide. Further guidance as to the practice of the Queen's Bench Division may be obtained from the Practice Master (see paragraph 6.1 below).

1.1.4 It is assumed throughout the Guide that the litigant intends to proceed in the Royal Courts of Justice. For all essential purposes, though, the Guide is equally applicable to the work of the District Registries, which deal with the work of the Queen's Bench Division outside London, but it should be borne in mind that there are some differences.

1.1.5 The telephone numbers and room numbers quoted in the Guide are correct at the time of going to press. However, the room numbers quoted for the Clerk of the Lists and the Listing Office are effective as from 2nd October 2000.

1.2 The Civil Procedure Rules

1.2.1 The Overriding Objective set out in Part 1 of CPR is central to civil proceedings   **1B–3**
and enables the court to deal with cases justly. To further this aim the work is allocated to one of three tracks—the small claims track, the fast track and the multi-track—so as to dispose of the work in the most appropriate and effective way combined with active case management by the court.

1.2.2 The CPR are divided into Parts. A particular Part is referred to in the Guide as Part 7, etc., as the case may be. Any particular rule within a Part is referred to as Rule 6.4(2), and so on.

1.3 The Practice Directions

1.3.1 Each Part—or almost each Part—has an accompanying Practice Direction or   **1B–4**

Paragraph numbers marked with a "+" can be found online and on CD.

Directions, and other Practice Directions deal with matters such as the Pre-Action Protocols and some former Rules of the Supreme Court and the County Court Rules, which are still applicable, and scheduled to Part 50.

1.3.2 The Practice Directions are made pursuant to statute, and have the same authority as do the CPR themselves. However, in case of any conflict between a Rule and a Practice Direction, the Rule will prevail. Each Practice Direction is referred to in the Guide with the number of any Part that it supplements preceding it; for example, the Practice Direction supplementing Part 6 is referred to as the Part 6 Practice Direction. But where there is more than one Practice Direction supplementing a Part it will also be described either by topic, for example, Part 25 Practice Direction—Interim Payments, or where appropriate, the Part 40B Practice Direction.

1.4 The Forms

1B–5 1.4.1 The Practice Direction supplementing Part 4 (Forms) lists the practice forms that are generally required to be used by or referred to in the CPR, and also those referred to in such of the Rules of the Supreme Court and the County Court Rules as are still in force (see Part 50 of the CPR; Schedules 1 and 2).

1.4.2 Those listed in Table 1 with a number prefixed by the letter N are forms that are referred to in and generally required to be used by Rules or Practice Directions. Those listed in Table 2 are Practice Forms that may be used as precedents. The Civil Procedure Forms Volume contains a comprehensive set of forms for use in the High Court and the county courts; these are listed under the same numbers that previously identified them.

1.4.3 The forms may be modified as circumstances in individual cases require, but it is essential that a modified form contains at least as full information or guidance as would have been given if the original form had been used.

1.4.4 Where the Royal Arms appears on any listed form it must appear on any modification of that form. The same format for the Royal Arms as is used on the listed forms need not be used. All that is necessary is that there is a complete Royal Arms.

1.4.5 Forms are available from the Court Service website at www.hmcourts-service.gov.uk

1.5 The Queen's Bench Division

1B–6 1.5.1 The Queen's Bench Division is one of the three divisions of the High Court, together with the Chancery Division and Family Division. A Lord Justice of Appeal, currently Lord Justice Judge has been appointed by the Lord Chief Justice to be the President of the Queen's Bench Division and Lord Justice May has been appointed as Vice-President; a High Court Judge is appointed as Judge in charge of the Lists and is currently Mr Justice Eady.

1.5.2 Outside London, the work of the Queen's Bench Division is administered in provincial offices known as District Registries. In London, the work is administered in the Central Office at the Royal Courts of Justice. The work in the Central Office of the Queen's Bench Division is the responsibility of the Senior Master, acting under the authority of the President of the Queen's Bench Division.

1.5.3 The work of the Queen's Bench Division is (with certain exceptions) governed by the CPR. The Administrative Court, the Admiralty Court, the Commercial Court and the Technology and Construction Court are all part of the Queen's Bench Division. However, each does specialised work requiring a distinct procedure that to some extent modifies the CPR. For that reason each has an individual Part of the CPR, its own Practice Direction and (except for the Administrative Court) its own Guide, to which reference should be made by parties wishing to proceed in the specialist courts.

Paragraph numbers marked with a "+" can be found online and on CD.

1.5.4 The work of the Queen's Bench Division consists mainly of claims for;
- (1) damages in respect of
    - (a) personal injury,
    - (b) negligence,
    - (c) breach of contract, and
    - (d) libel and slander (defamation),
    - (e) other tortious acts
    - (f) breach of statutory duty
- (2) non-payment of a debt, and
- (3) possession of land or property.

Proceedings retained to be dealt with in the Central Office of the Queen's Bench Division will almost invariably be multi-track claims.

1.5.5 In many types of claim—for example claims in respect of negligence by solicitors, accountants, etc. or claims for possession of land—the claimant has a choice whether to bring the claim in the Queen's Bench Division or in the Chancery Division. However, there are certain matters that may be brought only in the Queen's Bench Division, namely:
- (1) High Court Enforcement Officer's interpleader proceedings,
- (2) applications for the enrolment of deeds,
- (3) registration of foreign judgments under the Civil Jurisdictions and Judgments Act 1982or the European Regulation,
- (4) applications for bail in criminal proceedings,
- (5) applications under the Administration of Justice Act 1920 and the Foreign Judgments (Reciprocal Enforcement) Act 1933 and European Regulations,
- (6) registration and satisfaction of Bills of Sale,
- (7) Election Petitions,
- (8) applications for orders to obtain evidence for foreign courts.

1.6 The Central Office

1.6.1 The information in this and the following paragraph is to be found in the Part **1B–7** 2 Practice Direction at paragraph 2; it is reproduced here for the convenience of litigants. The Central Office is open for business from 10 a.m. to 4.30 p.m. (except during August when it is open from 10 a.m. to 2.30 p.m.) on every day of the year except;
- (1) Saturdays and Sundays,
- (2) Good Friday and the day after Easter Monday,
- (3) Christmas Day and Boxing Day and, if these days are a Friday or Saturday, the Bank Holidays allotted in their place, then 28th December,
- (4) Bank Holidays in England and Wales (under the Banking and Financial Dealings Act 1971), and
- (5) such other days as the Lord Chancellor, with the concurrence or the Lord Chief Justice, the Master of the Rolls, the President of the Family Division and the Vice-Chancellor, may direct.

1.6.2 One of the Masters of the Queen's Bench Division is present on every day on which the Central Office is open for the purpose of superintending the business administered there and giving any directions that may be required on questions of practice and procedure. S/he is normally referred to as the "Practice Master". (See paragraph 6.1 below for information about the Practice Master and Masters in general.)

1.6.3 The Central Office consists of the Action Department, the Masters' Support Unit, the Foreign Process Section, the Masters' Secretary's Department, the Queen's Bench Associates' Department, the Clerk of the Lists, the Registry of the Technology and Construction Court and the Admiralty and Commercial Registry.

1.6.4 The Action Department deals with the issue of claims, responses to claims,

Paragraph numbers marked with a "+" can be found online and on CD.

admissions, undefended and summary judgments, enforcement, drawing up certain orders, public searches, provision of copies of court documents, enrolment of deeds, submission of references to the Court of Justice of the European Communities and registration of foreign judgments.

1.6.5 The Masters' Secretary's Department covers three discrete areas of work;
    (1) the Masters' Support Unit which provides support (a) to the Masters, including assisting with case-management, and (b) to the Senior Master,
    (2) Foreign Process, and
    (3) Investment of Children's Funds.

Also one of the staff acts as the Chief Clerk to the Prescribed Officer for Election Petitions (the Senior Master).

1.6.6 The Queen's Bench Associates sit in court with the Judges during trials and certain interim hearings. The Chief Associate manages the Queen's Bench Associates and also provides support to the Senior Master as the Queen's Remembrancer. The Associates draw up the orders made in court at trial and those interim orders that the parties do not wish to draw up themselves, or directed by a Master to be drawn by the Court.

1.6.7 The Clerk of the Lists lists all trials and matters before the Judges (see Section 8 below).

1.6.8 The Technology and Construction Court deals with claims which involve issues or questions which are technically complex or for which a trial by a Judge of that court is for any other reason desirable (see the Part 49C Practice Direction—Technology and Construction Court).

1.6.9 The Admiralty and Commercial Court deals mainly with shipping collision claims and claims concerning charters and insurance, and commercial arbitrations. See the Commercial Court Guide and the Part 49D Practice Direction—Commercial Court, the Part 49F Practice Direction—Admiralty and the Part 49G Practice Direction—Arbitrations.

1.7 The Judiciary

1B–8 1.7.1 The judiciary in the Queen's Bench Division consist of the High Court Judges (The Honourable Mr/Mrs Justice ... and addressed in court as my Lord/my Lady) and in the Royal Courts of Justice the Masters (Master ...); in the District Registries the work of the Masters is conducted by District Judges.

1.7.2 Trials normally takes place before a High Court Judge (or Deputy High Court Judge)who may also hear pre-trial reviews and other interim applications. Wherever possible the judge before whom a trial has been fixed will hear any pre-trial review. A High Court Judge will hear applications to commit for contempt of court, applications for injunctions and most appeals from Masters' orders. (See the Practice Direction to Part 2B Allocation of cases to levels of Judiciary, and see paragraphs 7.11 and 7.12 below for more information on hearings and applications.)

1.7.3 The Masters deal with interim and some pre-action applications, and manage the claims so that they proceed without delay. The Masters' rooms are situated in the East Block of the Royal Courts of Justice. Hearings take place in these rooms or (short hearings only) in the Bear Garden.

1.7.4 Cases are assigned on issue by a court officer in the Action Department to Masters on a rota basis, and that Master is then known as the assigned Master in relation to that case. (See paragraphs 6.2 and 6.3 below for more information about assignment and the Masters' lists.)

1.7.5 General enquiries about the business dealt with by the Masters should initially be made in writing to the Masters' Support Unit in Room E16.

Paragraph numbers marked with a "+" can be found online and on CD.

SECTION 2

GENERAL

2.1 Essential matters

2.1.1 Before bringing any proceedings, the intending claimant should think carefully **1B–9** about the implications of so doing. (See Section 3 below about steps to be taken before issuing a claim form.)

2.1.2 **A litigant who is acting in person faces a heavier burden in terms of time and effort than does a litigant who is legally represented, but all litigation calls for a high level of commitment from the parties. No intending claimant should underestimate this.**

2.1.3 The Overriding Objective of the CPR is to deal with cases justly, which means dealing with the claim in a way which is proportionate (amongst other things) to the amount of money involved. However, in all proceedings there are winners and losers; the loser is generally ordered to pay the costs of the winner and the costs of litigation can still be large. The risk of large costs is particularly acute in cases involving expert witnesses, barristers and solicitors. Also, the costs of an interim hearing are almost always summarily assessed and made payable by the unsuccessful party within 14 days after the order for costs is made. There may be a number of interim hearings before the trial itself is reached, so the costs must be paid as the claim progresses. (See also paragraph 2.5 Costs below.)

2.1.4 The intending claimant should also keep in mind that every claim must be proved, unless of course the defendant admits the allegations. There is little point in incurring the risks and expense of litigating if the claim cannot be proved. An intending claimant should therefore be taking steps to obtain statements from his/her prospective witnesses before starting the claim; if s/he delays until later, it may turn out that s/he is in fact unable to obtain the evidence that s/he needs to prove his/her claim. A defendant faces a similar task.

2.1.5 if s/he is to succeed, need an opinion from one or more expert witnesses, such as medical practitioners, engineers, accountants, or as the case may be. However s/he must remember that no expert evidence may be given at trial without the permission of the court. The services of such experts are in great demand, especially as, in some fields of expertise, there are few of them. It may take many months to obtain an opinion, and the cost may be high. (See paragraph 7.9 below for information about experts' evidence.) **If the claim is for compensation for personal injuries, the claimant must produce a medical report with his/her particulars of claim.**

2.1.6 The claimant must remember also not to allow the time limit for starting his/her claim to pass (see paragraph 2.3 below for information about time limits).

2.1.7 Any intending claimant should also have in mind that s/he will usually be required to give standard disclosure of the documents on which s/he relies. Although Rule 31.3(2) makes provision for a party not to be required to disclose documents if disclosure would be disproportionate to the value of the claim, in complex cases it may still be necessary to disclose relatively large quantities of documents, and this invariably involves much time, effort and expense. (See paragraph 7.8 below for information about disclosure.)

2.1.8 In many cases the parties will need legal assistance, whether by way of advice, drafting, representation at hearings or otherwise. It is not the function of court staff to give legal advice; however, subject to that, they will do their best to assist any litigant. Litigants in person who need assistance or funding should contact the Community Legal Service through their Information Points. The CLS are developing local networks of people giving legal assistance such as law centres, local solicitors or the Citizens Advice Bureaux. CLS Information Points are being set up in libraries and other public places. Litigants can telephone the CLS to find their nearest CLS

Paragraph numbers marked with a "+" can be found online and on CD.

Information Point on 0845 608 1122 or can log on to the CLS website at www.justask.org.uk for the CLS directory and for legal information.

2.1.9 The RCJ Advice Bureau off the Main Hall at the Royal Courts of Justice is open Monday to Friday from 10.00am to 1.00pm and from 2.00pm to 5.00pm. The Bureau is run by lawyers in conjunction with the Citizens Advice Bureau and is independent of the court. It is also a registered Charity No 1050358. The Bureau operates on a "first come first served" basis, or telephone advice is available on 0845 120 3715 Monday to Friday from 11.00am to 12.00pm and from 3.00pm to 4.00pm.

2.2 Inspection and Copies of Documents

1B–10 2.2.1 Intending claimants must not expect to be able to keep the details of a claim away from public scrutiny. In addition to the right of a party to obtain copies of documents in the proceedings to which s/he is a party from the court record (on payment of the prescribed fee), (see CPR 5.4B), any person may obtain from the court records a copy of a claim form when it has been served, and the particulars of claim but not documents attached to the particulars of claim. This applies to claims issued from 2 October 2006. For claims issued before that date particulars of claim may only be inspected or copied where they are included in or served with the claim form, on request and payment of the appropriate fee. Any judgment or order made in public (whether made at a hearing or without a hearing) may also be obtained from the records of the court on payment of the appropriate fee. Additionally, under CPR 5.4 other specified documents may be obtained with the permission of the court, upon making an application in accordance with Part 23.

2.2.2 Witness statements used at trial are open to inspection, at the time of the trial, unless the court directs otherwise. Considerations of publicity are often particularly important in deciding whether to commence proceedings in respect of an alleged libel or slander; such a claim may, by its attendant publicity, do more damage than was ever inflicted by the original publication. In such proceedings the claimant may decide to serve his/her particulars of claim separately from the claim form, in which case they are not open to inspection by non-parties, without the permission of the court.

2.2.3 CPR 5.4(7) gives details of where the court, on application by a party or person identified in the claim form, may restrict inspection and obtaining of copies.

2.3 Time Limits

1B–11 2.3.1 There are strict time limits that apply to every claim. First, there are time limits fixed by the Limitation Act 1980 [and some other Statutes, such as the Human Rights Act 1998 and the Defamation Act 1996] within which proceedings must be brought. There are circumstances in which the court may extend those time limits, but this should be regarded as exceptional. In all other cases, once the relevant time limit has expired, it is rarely possible to start a claim.

2.3.2 Secondly, in order to try and bring the proceedings to an early trial date, a timetable will be set with which all parties must comply. Unless the CPR or a Practice Direction provides otherwise, or the court orders otherwise, the timetable may be varied by the written agreement of the parties. However, there are certain "milestone" events in the timetable for which the parties may not vary the time limits. Examples of these are;

(1) return of the Allocation Questionnaire/Reply to Defence, which should be returned together with the Allocation Questionnaire
(2) date for the case management conference
(3) return of the Pre Trial Checklist
(4) date fixed for trial
(5) Defence when time has elapsed following the days from service of Particulars of Claim on the Defendant (CPR 15.5).

Where parties have extended a time limit by agreement, the party for whom the time has been extended must advise the Registry Section in writing of the appropriate

Paragraph numbers marked with a "+" can be found online and on CD.

event in the proceedings for which the time has been extended and the new date by which it must be done. For example, if an extension is agreed for the filing of the defence, it is for the defendant to inform the Registry Section.

2.3.3 The court has power to impose a sanction on any party who fails to comply with a time limit. If the court considers that a prior warning should be given before a sanction is imposed, it will make an 'unless' order; in other words, the court will order that, unless that party performs his/her obligation by the time specified, s/he will be penalised in the manner set out in the order. This may involve the party in default having his/her claim or statement of case struck out and judgment given against him. **An Order striking out a claim or statement of case must be applied for after the time specified has expired, as this is not automatic unless the Unless Order so provides.**

2.4 Legal Representation

2.4.1 A party may act in person or be represented by a lawyer. A party who is acting **1B–12** in person may be assisted at any hearing by another person (often referred to as a McKenzie friend) subject to the discretion of the Court. The McKenzie friend is allowed to help by taking notes, quietly prompting the litigant and offering advice and suggestions. The litigant however, must conduct his/her own case; the McKenzie friend may not represent him and may only in very exceptional circumstances be allowed to address the court on behalf of the litigant (see s.27(2)(c) of the Courts and Legal Services Act 1990).

2.4.2 A written statement should be provided to the court at any hearing concerning the representation of the parties in accordance with paragraph 5.1 of the Part 39 Practice Direction (the Court Record Form, found outside the Masters' Rooms or in the Bear Garden)..

2.4.3 At a trial, a company or corporation may be represented by an employee if the company or corporation authorises him to do so and the court gives permission. Where this is to be the case, the permission of the Judge who is to hear the case may be sought informally; paragraph 5 of the Part 39 Practice Direction describes what is needed to obtain permission from the court for this purpose and mentions some of the considerations relevant to the grant or refusal of permission. A further statement concerning representation should be provided in accordance with paragraph 5.2 of the Part 39 Practice Direction.

2.4.4 Experienced outdoor clerks from solicitors firms are permitted to appear before the Masters. Barristers' clerks may attend before a Master to fix a hearing date for Counsel.

The Personal Support Unit (PSU) is an independent charity, which supports litigants-in-person, witnesses, victims, their family members and other supporters attending the Royal Courts. There are now nearly 100 fully trained and experienced volunteers. Requests vary from the very simple to the complex. Some people just require directions or advice about procedures. Others need to unburden themselves, while others request the moral and emotional support of being accompanied in court. The PSU can be particularly helpful for clients with special needs.

The PSU

Room M104

Royal Courts of Justice

Strand

WC2A 2LL   Tel: 020 7947 7701/3   Fax: 020 7947 7702   email: rcj@thepsu.co.uk or: www.thepsu.co.uk

Paragraph numbers marked with a "+" can be found online and on CD.

2.5 Costs

1B–13 2.5.1 Costs are dealt with in Parts 43 to 48. There are important new provisions in the costs rules, particularly with respect to;
(1) informing the client of costs orders,
(2) providing the court with estimates of costs, and
(3) summary assessment of costs,
(4) interim orders for costs, and
(5) interest on costs.

2.5.2 Solicitors now have a duty under Rule 44.2 to notify their client within 7 days if an order for costs is made against him in his/her absence. Solicitors must also notify any other person who has instructed them to act in the proceedings or who is liable to pay their fees (such as an insurer, trade union or the Legal Services Commission (LSC)). They must also inform these persons how the order came to be made (paragraphs 7.1 and 7.2 of the Costs Practice Direction).

2.5.3 The court may at any stage order any party to file an estimate of base costs (substantially in the form of Precedent H in the Schedule of Costs Precedents annexed to the Costs Practice Direction) and serve copies on all the other parties (paragraph 6.3 of the Costs Practice Direction). This will both assist the court in deciding what case management directions to make and inform the other parties as to their potential liability for payment of costs.

2.5.4 If a party seeks an order for his/her costs, in order to assist the court in making a summary assessment, s/he must prepare a written statement of the costs s/he intends to claim in accordance with paragraph 13.5 of the Costs Practice Direction, following as closely as possible Form N260. In addition, when an Allocation Questionnaire or a Pre Trial Checklist is filed, the party filing it must file and serve an estimate of costs on all the other parties.

2.5.5 If the parties have agreed the amount of costs, they do not need to file a statement of the costs, and summary assessment is unnecessary. Or, where the parties agree a consent order without any party attending on the application, the parties should insert either an agreed figure for costs or that there should be no order for costs in the order (paragraph 13.4 of the Costs Practice Direction).

2.5.6 Unless the court decides not to order an assessment of costs where, for example, it orders costs to be "costs in the case", it may either make a summary assessment of costs or order a detailed assessment to take place. The court will generally make a summary assessment of costs at any hearing which lasts for less than one day;
(1) "summary assessment" is where the court, when making an order for costs, assesses those costs and orders payment of a sum of money in respect of them, and
(2) "detailed assessment" is the procedure by which the amount of costs is decided by a Costs Judge or Costs Officer at a later date in accordance with Part 47.

The provision of summary assessment means that the paying party is likely to be paying the costs at an earlier stage than s/he would have done under the previous rules (and see paragraph 2.5.15 below).

2.5.7 The court will not make a summary assessment of the costs of a receiving party (the party to whom the costs are to be paid) where s/he is;
(1) a child or patient within the meaning of Part 21 unless the solicitor acting for the child or patient has waived the right to further costs, or
(2) an assisted person or a person in receipt of funded services under sections 4-11 of the Access to Justice Act 1999.

The costs payable by a party who is an assisted person or a person in receipt of funded services may be summarily assessed as the assessment is not by itself a determination of the assisted person's ability to pay those costs.

2.5.8 Rule 44.3A prevents the court from assessing an additional liability in respect of a funding agreement before the conclusion of the proceedings. At an interim hearing

Paragraph numbers marked with a "+" can be found online and on CD.

therefore, the court will assess only the base costs. (See paragraph 14.9 of the Costs Practice Direction for assessing an additional liability and Section 19 for information about funding arrangements.)

2.5.9 Interim orders for costs; where the court decides immediately who is to pay particular costs, but does not assess the costs summarily, for example after a trial lasting more than a day, so that the final amount of costs payable has to be fixed at a detailed assessment, the court may order the paying party to pay a sum or sums on account of the ultimate liability for costs.

2.5.10 Interest on costs; the court has power to award interest on costs from a date before the date of the order, so compensating the receiving party for the delay between incurring costs and receiving a payment in respect of them.

2.5.11 Parties should note that where the court makes an order which does not mention costs, no party is entitled to costs in relation to that order.

2.5.12 Rule 44.3 describes the court's discretion as to costs and the circumstances to be taken into account when exercising its discretion. Rules 44.4 and 44.5 set out the basis of assessment and the factors to be taken into account in deciding the amount of costs.

2.5.13 The amount of costs to be paid by one party to another may be ordered to be assessed on the standard basis or on the indemnity basis. The basis to be used is decided when the court decides that a party should pay the costs of another. Costs that are unreasonably incurred or are unreasonable in amount are not allowed on either basis.

2.5.14 The standard basis is the usual basis for assessment where only costs which are proportionate to the matters in issue, are allowed, and any doubt as to whether the costs were reasonably incurred or reasonable and proportionate in amount is resolved in favour of the paying party. On the indemnity basis, any such doubts are resolved in favour of the receiving party.

2.5.15 A party must normally pay summarily assessed costs awarded against him within 14 days of the assessment, but the court can extend that time, direct payment by instalments, or defer the liability to pay the costs until the end of the proceedings so that they can then be set off against any costs or judgment to which the paying party becomes entitled.

2.5.16 Fixed costs relating to default judgments, certain judgments on admissions and summary judgments etc. are set out in Part 45. Part 46 relates to fast track costs.

2.5.17 Part 47 and Sections 28 to 49 of the Costs Practice Direction contain the procedure for detailed assessment together with the default provisions. Precedents A,B,C and D set out in the Schedule of Costs Precedents annexed to the Costs Practice Direction are model forms of bills of costs for detailed assessment. Section 43 deals with costs payable out of the Community Legal Service fund, Section 44 deals with costs payable out of a fund other than the CLS fund and Section 49 deals with costs payable by the LSC. Part 48 and Sections 50 to 56 of the Costs Practice Direction deal with Special Cases, in particular;
  (1) costs payable by or to a child or patient,
  (2) litigants in person, (see CPR 48.6 The costs allowed under this rule must not exceed, except in the case of a disbursement, two-thirds of the amount which would have been allowed if the litigant in person had been represented by a legal representative) and
  (3) wasted costs orders– personal liability of the legal representative.

2.5.18 Costs only proceedings are dealt with in Rule 44.12A and Section 17 of the Costs Practice Direction. They may be brought in the High Court only where the dispute was of such a value or type that had proceedings been brought they would have been commenced in the High Court. Proceedings are brought under Part 8 by

Paragraph numbers marked with a "+" can be found online and on CD.

the issue of a Claim Form in the Supreme Court Costs Office at Clifford's Inn, Fetter Lane, London EC4A 1DQ. (See also paragraphs 4.1.16 and 6.8.13 below.)

2.6 Court Fees

1B–14 2.6.1 The fees payable in the High Court as from 1 May 2008are set out in Schedule 1 to the Civil Proceedings Fees Order 2008 SI 2008/1053 .

2.6.2 In the Royal Courts of Justice fees are paid in the Fees Room E01 and by way of receipt for the fee, it is usually stamped on the document to which they relate.

2.7 Information Technology

1B–15 2.7.1 To support the work of the Central Office in operating the provisions of the CPR, and to facilitate effective case management there is a limited computerised system to provide a record of proceedings and to produce some court forms and orders.

2.7.2 A number of specific applications of information technology have been well developed in recent years; the use of fax, the provision of skeleton arguments on disk and daily transcripts on disk have become commonplace. Short applications may be dealt with more economically by a conference telephone call, and taking evidence by video link has become more common and the available technology has improved considerably. The CPR contains certain provisions about the use of information technology, for example, Part 6 and the Part 6 Practice Direction deal with service of documents by Fax or other electronic means, the Part 23 Practice Direction refers to telephone hearings and video conferencing, Rule 32.3 allows the use of evidence given by video link and the Part 5 Practice Direction refers to the filing of documents at court by Fax.

2.7.3 Parties may agree to use information technology in the preparation, management and presentation of a case; however the agreement of the Judge or Master should be sought before providing the court with material in electronic form. Where permission has been given by a specific Master, the material for use at a hearing or in support of an application can be provided on a CD-Rom or in some cases by e-mail. The parties should check with the court which word-processing format should be used. This will normally be Word 6 or in some cases in PDF format.

2.7.4 A protocol has been prepared as a guide to all persons who are involved in the use of video conferencing equipment in civil proceedings in the High Court. It covers its use in courtrooms where the equipment may be installed, and also the situation where the court assembles in a commercial studio or conference room containing video conferencing equipment. Copies of the Video- conferencing Protocol may be obtained from the Bar Council at a charge of £2.50 to cover expenses. A room has now been made available as an audio/video conferencing courtroom for applications to Masters, as a pilot measure. More information may be obtained from the Senior Master through the Masters' Secretary's Department.

SECTION 3

STEPS BEFORE ISSUE OF A CLAIM FORM

3.1 Settlement

1B–16 3.1.1 So far as reasonably possible, a claimant should try to resolve his/her claim without litigation. The court is increasingly taking the view that litigation should be a last resort and parties may wish to consider the use of Alternative Dispute Resolution ("ADR"). (See paragraph 6.6 below.)

3.1.2 There are codes of practice for preliminary negotiations in certain types of claim. These codes of practice are called "Protocols" and are set out in a schedule to the Protocols Practice Direction to the CPR. Even if there is no protocol that applies

Paragraph numbers marked with a "+" can be found online and on CD.

to the claim, the parties will nonetheless be expected to comply with the spirit of the Overriding Objective (see paragraph 4 of the Protocols Practice Direction).

3.1.3 An offer to settle a claim may be made by either party whether before or after a claim is brought. The court will take account of any offer to settle made before proceedings are started when making any order as to costs after proceedings have started.

3.2 Disclosure Before Proceedings Are Started

3.2.1 An intending claimant may need documents to which s/he does not yet have **1B–17** access. If the documents are not disclosed voluntarily, in accordance with the Pre Action Protocols, then Rule 31.16 sets out the provisions for making an application for disclosure of documents before proceedings have started. An Application Notice under Part 23 is required together with the appropriate fee. This may be issued in the Registry Section, Room E07 and will be assigned to a Master for hearing.

3.2.2 Essentially, the court must be satisfied that the applicant and respondent to the application are likely to be parties when proceedings are brought, that the required documents are those that the respondent would be required to disclose under Rule 31.6 when proceedings are brought and that their early disclosure might dispose of or assist the disposal of anticipated proceedings or save costs.

3.3 Defamation proceedings: Offer of Amends

3.3.1 Application may be made to the court before a claim is brought for the court's **1B–18** assistance in accepting an offer of amends under section 3 of the Defamation Act 1996. The application is made by Part 8 Claim Form. For more information see paragraph 4.1.15 Part 8 procedure and paragraph 8.1 defamation below.

SECTION 4

STARTING PROCEEDINGS IN THE CENTRAL OFFICE

4.1 Issuing The Claim Form

4.1.1 All claims must be started by issuing a Claim Form. The great majority of claims **1B–19** involve a dispute of fact, and the Claim Form should be issued in accordance with Part 7 of the CPR. The Part 8 procedure may be followed in the types of claim described in paragraphs 4.1.14 to 4.1.16 below.

4.1.2 The requirements for issuing a Claim Form are set out in Part 7 and the Part 7 Practice Direction, the main points of which are summarised in the following paragraphs.

4.1.3 The Practice Direction at paragraphs 2, 3 and 4 provides information as to;
   (1) where a claim should be started,
   (2) certain matters that must be included in the Claim Form, and
   (3) how the heading of the claim should be set out on the Claim Form.

In defamation cases, Part 53 and the Part 53 Practice Direction sets out matters that should be included in the Claim Form and particulars of claim. See also paragraph 12.7 below.

4.1.4 Proceedings are started when the court issues a Claim Form, and a Claim Form is issued on the date entered on the Claim Form by the court. However, where a Claim Form is received in the court office on an earlier date than the date of issue, then, for the purposes of the Limitation Act 1980, the claim is brought on the earlier date (see paragraphs 5.1 to 5.4 of the Part 7 Practice Direction).

4.1.5 To start proceedings in the Action Department, a claimant must use form N1 (or form N208 for a Part 8 claim) (or a form suitably modified as permitted by Part

Paragraph numbers marked with a "+" can be found online and on CD.

4), and should take or send the Claim Form to Room E07, Registry Section, Action Department, Central Office, Royal Courts of Justice, Strand, London WC2A 2LL. If the court is to serve the Claim Form, the claimant must provide sufficient copies for each defendant. The Claimant will be required to provide a Court copy, a Claimant's copy and one copy for each named Defendant. Copies of practice forms relevant to the work of the Action Department (including the Claim Form and Response Pack) are available from that office. Alternatively, claimants may produce their own forms, which may be modified as the circumstances require, provided that all essential information, especially any information or guidance that the form gives to the recipient, is included. (See Part 4 Forms.)

4.1.6 On issuing the Claim Form, the court will give or send the claimant a notice of issue endorsed with the date of issue of the Claim Form. If the claimant requires the court to serve the Claim Form, the date of posting and deemed date of service will also be endorsed on the notice of issue. Claimants and especially their solicitors who use the Action Department, are encouraged to serve their own documents but must inform the court when service has been effected (see paragraph 4.2.4 in relation to service by the claimant and the certificate of service). For certain types of claims, the notice of issue contains a request for judgment. (See paragraph 5 below for information about default judgments.)

4.1.7 A Claim Form must be served within 4 months after the date of issue (Rule 7.5) unless it is to be served out of the jurisdiction, when the period is 6 months; and Rule 7.6 and paragraph 7 of the Practice Direction set out how and on what grounds an extension of time for service of the Claim Form may be sought. (See Section 4.2 below about service.)

4.2 Particulars of Claim

1B–20 4.2.1 The particulars of claim may be;

(1) included in the Claim Form, (if served as part of the Claim Form they are available to be copied for any person under CPR 5.4—see para. 2.2 above)
(2) in a separate document served with the Claim Form, or
(3) in a separate document served within 14 days of service of the Claim Form provided that the particulars of claim are served within the latest time for serving the Claim Form.

4.2.2 A Claim Form that does not include particulars of claim must nonetheless contain a concise statement of the nature of the claim. Any Claim Form and/or Particulars of Claim that

(1) does not comply with the requirements of rule 16.2, or 16.4 or
(2) is garbled or abusive,

will be referred to a Master and is likely to be struck out by the court.

4.2.3 Where the particulars of claim are neither included in or served with the Claim Form;

(1) the Claim Form must contain a statement that particulars of claim will follow, and
(2) the particulars of claim must be served by the claimant and a copy then filed at the court together with a Certificate of Service (CPR 7.4(3))

However, where a Claim Form is to be served out of the jurisdiction, the particulars of claim, if not included in the claim form, must accompany it. (See paragraph 4.2.13 below.)

4.2.4 Certain forms must accompany the particulars of claim when they are served on the defendant. These forms are listed in Rule 7.8 and are included in a Response Pack, which is available from the Action Department.

4.2.5 A party who has entered into a funding arrangement and who wishes to claim

Paragraph numbers marked with a "+" can be found online and on CD.

an additional liability must give the Court and any other party information about that claim if s/he is to recover the additional liability. Where the funding arrangement has been entered into before proceedings are commenced, the claimant should file a notice of funding in form N251 when the Claim Form is issued.

4.2.6 Part 22 requires the Claim Form and particulars of claim to be verified by a statement of truth, and where the particulars of claim are not included in the Claim Form itself, these are to be separately verified by a statement of truth; see paragraph 6 of the Part 7 Practice Direction, and the Part 22 Practice Direction.

4.2.7 Part 16 and the Part 16 Practice Direction deal with statements of case, and in particular the contents of the Claim Form and the particulars of claim. Part 16 does not apply to claims in respect of which the Part 8 alternative procedure for claims is being used. See paragraph 5.6 below for more about statements of case. Note the requirements in relation to personal injury claims, fatal accident claims, hire purchase claims and recovery of land or goods.

4.3 Part 8 Procedure

4.3.1 A claimant may use the Part 8 procedure where;

1B–21

(1) s/he seeks the court's decision on a question that is unlikely to involve a substantial dispute of fact, or

(2) a Rule or Practice Direction requires or permits the use of the Part 8 procedure,

however, the court may at any stage order the claim to continue as if the claimant had not used the Part 8 procedure.

4.3.2 Certain matters that must be included on the Claim Form when the Part 8 procedure is being used are set out in Rule 8.2. The types of claim for which the Part 8 procedure may be used include;

(1) a claim by or against a child or patient that has been settled before the commencement of proceedings, the sole purpose of the claim being to obtain the approval of the court to the settlement,

(2) provided there is unlikely to be a substantial dispute of fact, a claim for a summary order for possession against named or unnamed defendants occupying land or premises without the licence or consent of the person claiming possession (Schedule 1- RSC O.113),

(3) a claim for provisional damages that has been settled before the commencement of proceedings, the sole purpose of the claim being to obtain a judgment by consent,

(4) a claim under s.3 of the Defamation Act 1996 (made other than in existing proceedings) and

(5) a claim under Rule 44.12A where the parties have agreed all issues before the commencement of proceedings except the amount of costs and an order for costs is required.

4.3.3 In addition to the provisions of Rule 8.1, attention is drawn also to the Part 8(B) Practice Direction which deals with proceedings brought under "the Schedule Rules".

See Paragraph 6.7 below for more information regarding the Part 8 procedure.

4.4 Service

4.4.1 Service of documents is dealt with in Part 6; Section I (Rules 6.1 to 6.11) contains provisions relating to service generally and Section II (Rules 6.12 to 6.16) contains special provisions relating to service of the Claim Form. Section III (Rules 6.17 to 6.31) deals with service out of the jurisdiction. Some of the more important provisions are described below.

1B–22

Within the Jurisdiction

4.4.2 The methods by which a document may be served are to be found in Rule 6.2. The court will serve a document that it has issued or prepared unless;

Paragraph numbers marked with a "+" can be found online and on CD.

(1) the party on whose behalf it is to be served notifies the court that s/he wishes to serve it himself,

(2) the court orders otherwise, or

(3) a Rule or Practice Direction provides otherwise.

It is anticipated that practitioners familiar with Central Office procedures will wish to continue to serve their own documents.

4.4.3 Where a party has entered into a funding agreement the notice of funding (form N251) must be served on all the other parties. If a claimant files his/her notice of funding when his/her Claim Form is issued, the Court will serve it on the other parties provided sufficient copies are provided. Otherwise the claimant must serve the notice of funding with the Claim Form. A defendant should file his/her notice of funding with his/her first document, i.e. his/her defence or acknowledgement of service etc. Sufficient copies of the notice should be provided for the Court to serve.

4.4.4 In all other circumstances a party must serve a notice of funding within 7 days of entering into the funding agreement.

4.4.5 Where the court has tried to serve a document but has been unable to serve it, the court will send a notice of non-service to the party on whose behalf it was to be served stating the method attempted. On receipt of this notice, the party should take steps to serve the document himself, as the court is under no further duty to effect service. The method of service used by the court will normally be first-class post.

4.4.6 Where a claimant has served a Claim Form, s/he must file a certificate of service that complies with the provisions of Rule 6.10. The certificate of service must be filed within 7 days of service of the Claim Form, and the claimant may not obtain judgment in default if it has not been filed .

4.4.7 Information as to how personal service is to be effected and as to service by electronic means is to be found in the Part 6 Practice Direction. Rule 6.6 deals with service on a child or patient.

4.4.8 A party must give an address for service within the jurisdiction. Rule 6.5 contains information as to the address for service.

4.2.9 A party may make an application for permission to serve a document by an alternative method to those set out in Rule 6.2. The application may be made without notice, and paragraph 9.1 of the Practice Direction sets out the evidence that will be required in support of the application. (Paragraph 7.12 below contains information in relation to applications.)

Out of the Jurisdiction

4.4.10 The provisions for service out of the jurisdiction are contained in Rules 6.17 to 6.31. Rule 6.19 sets out the provisions whereby a Claim Form may be served out of the jurisdiction without the permission of the court, and Rule 6.20 sets out the circumstances where the court's permission is required. Parties should also see the Practice Direction on service out of the jurisdiction.

4.4.11 A claimant may issue a Claim Form against defendants, one or some of whom appear to be out of the jurisdiction, without first having obtained permission for service out of the jurisdiction, provided that where the Claim Form is not one which may be served without the permission of the court under Rule 6.19, the Claim Form is endorsed by the court that it is "not for service out of jurisdiction".

4.4.12 Where a Claim Form is to be served in accordance with Rule 6.19 it must contain a statement of the grounds on which the claimant is entitled to serve it out of the jurisdiction. (See 6BPD.2). The statement should be as follows;

(1) *"I, (name) state that the High Court of England and Wales has power under the Civil Jurisdiction and Judgments Act 1982 to hear this claim and that no proceedings are*

Paragraph numbers marked with a "+" can be found online and on CD.

pending between the parties in Scotland, Northern Ireland or another Convention territory of any contracting state as defined by section 1(3) of the Act.", or

(2) where the proceedings are those to which Article 16 of Schedule 1, 3C or 4 to the Act refers,

"I, (name) state that the High Court of England and Wales has power under the Civil Jurisdiction and Judgments Act 1982, the claim having as its object rights in rem in immovable property or tenancies in immovable property (or otherwise in accordance with the provisions of Article 16 of Schedule 1, 3C or 4 to that Act) to which Article 16 of Schedule 1, 3C or 4 to that Act applies, to hear the claim and that no proceedings are pending between the parties in Scotland, Northern Ireland or another Convention territory of any contracting state as defined by section 1(3) of the Act.", or

(3) where the defendant is party to an agreement conferring jurisdiction to which Article 17 of Schedule 1, 3C or 4 to that Act applies,

"I, (name) state that the High Court of England and Wales has power under the Civil Jurisdiction and Judgments Act 1982, the defendant being a party to an agreement conferring jurisdiction to which Article 17 of Schedule 1, 3C or 4 to that Act applies, to hear the claim and that no proceedings are pending between the parties in Scotland, Northern Ireland or another Convention territory of any contracting state as defined by section 1(3) of the Act.".

(4) where the Judgments Regulation applies (except where Articles 22 or 23 of the Regulation, or Rule 6.19(2) applies),

"I, (name) state that the High Court of England and Wales has power under Council Regulation (EC) No 44/2001 of 22nd December 2000 (on jurisdiction and the recognition and enforcement of judgments in civil and commercial matters) to hear this claim and that no proceedings are pending between the parties in Scotland, Northern Ireland or any other Regulation state as defined by section 1(3) of the Civil Jurisdiction and Judgments Act 1982"

(5) where Article 22 of the Judgments Regulation applies,

"I, (name) state that the High Court of England and Wales has power under Council Regulation (EC) No 44/2001 of 22nd December 2000 (on jurisdiction and the recognition and enforcement of judgments in civil and commercial matters), the claim having as its object rights in rem in immovable property or tenancies in immovable property (or otherwise in accordance with the provisions of Article 22 of that Regulation) to which Article 22 of that Regulation applies, to hear this claim and that no proceedings are pending between the parties in Scotland, Northern Ireland or any other Regulation state as defined by section 1(3) of the Civil Jurisdiction and Judgments Act 1982"

(6) where Article 23 of the Judgments Regulation applies,

"I, (name) state that the High Court of England and Wales has power under Council Regulation (EC) No 44/2001 of 22nd December 2000 (on jurisdiction and the recognition and enforcement of judgments in civil and commercial matters), the defendant being party to an agreement conferring jurisdiction to which Article 23 of that Regulation applies, to hear this claim and that no proceedings are pending between the parties in Scotland, Northern Ireland or any other Regulation state as defined by section 1(3) of the Civil Jurisdiction and Judgments Act 1982"

(7) where Rule 6.19(2) applies,

"I, (name) state that the High Court of England and Wales has power to hear this claim under [state the provisions of the relevant enactment] which satisfies the requirements of rule 6.19(2), and that no proceedings are pending between the parties in Scotland, Northern Ireland, or in another Contracting State or Regulation State as defined by section 1(3) of the Civil Jurisdiction and Judgments Act 1982"

4.4.13 The statement should be signed and have set out the full name of the signatory. If a Claim Form as specified in paragraph 4.2.10 above does not bear the appropriate above statement, the Claim Form will be endorsed "not for service out of the jurisdiction".

4.4.14 An application for an order for permission to issue a Claim Form for service out of the jurisdiction or to serve the Claim Form out of the jurisdiction should be made in accordance with Part 23 (form PF 6(A) may be used). The application must be supported by written evidence, and may be made without notice. The written evidence should state the requirements set out in Rule 6.21(1) and (2).

Paragraph numbers marked with a "+" can be found online and on CD.

4.4.15 An order giving permission for service out of the jurisdiction should be in form PF 6(B) and will;

    (1) specify the country in which, or place at which, service is to be effected, and

    (2) specify the number of days within which the defendant may either

        (a) file an acknowledgement of service,

        (b) file or serve an admission, or

        (c) file a defence to

        the claim, and where an acknowledgement of service is filed, specify a further 14 days within which the defendant may file a defence. (This information can be found in the Table in the Practice Direction to Part 6 (6BPD.13))

4.4.16 Where service is to be effected in a country which requires a translation of the documents to be served, it is the claimant's responsibility to provide the translation of all the documents for each defendant. In every case, it is the claimant's duty to ensure that the Response Pack clearly states the appropriate period for responding to the Claim Form, and form N9, form N1C and other relevant forms must be modified accordingly. Every translation must be accompanied by a statement by the person making it;

    (1) that it is a correct translation, and

    (2) including the person's name, address and qualifications for making the translation.

4.4.17 The periods for acknowledging service of a Claim Form served out of the jurisdiction are set out in Rule 6.22 and in the Table contained in the Part 6 Section III Practice Direction, and the periods for serving a defence to a Claim Form served out of the jurisdiction are set out in Rule 6.23 and in the Table in the Practice Direction. Rule 6.24 describes the methods of service.

4.4.18 Where the Claim Form is to be served through;

    (1) the judicial authorities of the country where the Claim Form is to be served,

    (2) a British Consular authority in that country,

    (3) the authority designated under the Hague Convention in respect of that country, or

    (4) the Government of that country, or

    (5) where the court permits service on a State, the Foreign and Commonwealth Office,

    (6) the Receiving Agency designated under Regulation (EC) 1348/2000

the claimant should provide the Senior Master with the following documents by forwarding them to the Foreign Process section, Room E 10;

    (a) a request for service by the chosen method (in form **PF 7**),

    (b) a sealed copy and a duplicate copy of the Claim Form,

    (c) the Response Pack as referred to in paragraph 4.2.14,

    (d) a translation in duplicate, and the statement referred to in paragraph 4.2.13, and

    (e) any other relevant documents.

4.4.19 Where service has been requested in accordance with paragraph 4.2.16, the particulars of claim, if not included in the Claim Form, must accompany the Claim Form (in duplicate). Where the claimant is effecting service of the Claim Form direct (and not as in paragraph 4.2.16) and the Claim Form states that particulars of claim are to follow, the permission of the court is not required to serve the particulars of claim out of the jurisdiction.

4.4.20 Where an official certificate of service is received in a foreign language, it is the responsibility of the claimant to obtain a translation of the certificate. Where a defendant served out of the jurisdiction fails to attend a hearing, the official certificate of service is evidence of service. Otherwise the claimant may take no further steps

Paragraph numbers marked with a "+" can be found online and on CD.

against the defendant until written evidence showing that the Claim Form has been duly served is filed.

4.4.21 Further advice on service out of the jurisdiction may be obtained from the Foreign Process Section, Room E10.

SECTION 5

RESPONSE TO A PART 7 CLAIM

5.1 General

5.1.1 Responding to particulars of claim is dealt with in Part 9. A defendant may respond to the service of particulars of claim by; **1B–23**
   (1) filing or serving an admission in accordance with Part 14,
   (2) filing a defence in accordance with Part 15,
   (3) doing both if part only of the claim is admitted, or
   (4) filing an acknowledgement of service in accordance with Part 10.

5.1.2 Where a defendant receives a Claim Form that states that particulars of claim are to follow, s/he need not respond to the claim until the particulars of claim have been served on him.

5.1.3 If a defendant fails to;
   (1) file an acknowledgement of service within the time specified in rule 10.3, and
   (2) file a defence within the time specified in Rule 15.4, or
   (3) file or serve an admission in accordance with Part 14

the claimant may obtain default judgment if Part 12 allows it. (See paragraph 5.5 below for information about default judgments.)

5.2 Acknowledgement of Service

5.2.1 Acknowledgements of service are dealt with in Part 10. A defendant may file an acknowledgement of service if; **1B–24**
   (1) s/he is unable to file a defence within the period specified in Rule 15.4, or
   (2) s/he wishes to dispute the court's jurisdiction. (CPR 11.7).

Filing an acknowledgement of service extends the time for filing the defence by 14 days.

5.2.2 A defendant who wishes to acknowledge service of a Claim Form should do so by using form **N9**. Rule 10.5 states that the acknowledgement of service must;
   (1) be signed by the defendant or his/her legal representative, and
   (2) include the defendant's address for service which must be within the jurisdiction of the court (CPR 6.5).

The Part 10 Practice Direction contains information relating to the acknowledgement of service and how it may be signed.

5.3 Admissions

5.3.1 The manner in which a defendant may make an admission of a claim or part of a claim is set out in Rules 14.1 and 14.2, and Rules 14.3 to 14.7 set out how judgment may be obtained on a written admission. **1B–25**

5.3.2 Included in the Response Pack that will accompany the Claim Form when it is served on the defendant, is an admission form (form N9A for a specified amount and form N9C for an unspecified amount). If the defendant makes an admission and requests time to pay, s/he should complete as fully as possible the statement of means contained in the admission form, or otherwise give in writing the same details of his/her means as could have been given in the admission form.

Paragraph numbers marked with a "+" can be found online and on CD.

QB GUIDE

5.3.3 Where the defendant has;

(1) made an admission in respect of a specified sum and requested time to pay, or

(2) made an admission in respect of an unspecified sum, offered a sum in satisfaction (which is accepted) and requested time to pay,

and the claimant has not accepted the request for time to pay, on receipt of the claimant's notice the court will enter judgment for the amount admitted or offered (less any payments made) to be paid at the time and rate of payment determined by the court.

5.3.4 Where the defendant has;

(1) made an admission for an unspecified amount, or

(2) made an admission for an unspecified amount and offered in satisfaction a sum that the claimant has not accepted,

on receipt of the claimant's request for judgment the court will enter judgment for an amount to be decided by the court and costs.

5.3.5 The matters that the court will take into account when determining the time and rate of payment are set out in paragraph 5.1 of the Part 14 Practice Direction.

5.3.6 The court may determine the time and rate of payment with or without a hearing, but, where a hearing is to take place, the proceedings must, where the provisions of Rule 14.12(2) apply, be transferred to the defendant's home court. Where the Claim Form was issued in the Royal Courts of Justice the defendant's home court will be the district registry for the district in which the defendant's address given in the admission form is situated. If there is no such district registry the proceedings will remain in the Royal Courts of Justice.

5.3.7 The procedure for an application for re-determination of a decision determining the time and rate of payment is to be found in Rule 14.13 and paragraphs 5.3 to 5.6 of the Practice Direction.

5.3.8 Where judgment has been entered for an amount to be decided by the court and costs, the court will give any directions that it considers appropriate, which may include allocating the case to a track. (See paragraph 6.5 below about allocation.)

5.3.9 Judgment will not be entered on an admission where;

(1) the defendant is a child or patient, or

(2) the claimant is a child or patient and the admission is made in respect of

(a) a specified amount of money, or

(b) a sum offered in satisfaction of a claim for an unspecified amount of money.

See Part 21 and the Part 21 Practice Direction, and in particular Rule 21.10 which provides that, where a claim is made by or on behalf of a child or patient or against a child or patient, no settlement, compromise or payment shall be valid, so far as it relates to that person's claim, without the approval of the court.

5.4 Defence

1B-26 5.4.1 A defendant who wishes to defend all or part of a claim must file a defence, and if s/he fails to do so, the claimant may obtain default judgment if Part 12 allows it. The time for filing a defence is set out in Rule 15.4.

5.4.2 A form for defending the claim is included in the Response Pack. The form for defending the claim also contains provision for making a counterclaim. Part 22 requires a defence to be verified by a statement of truth (see the Part 15 Practice Direction, paragraph 2; and see also Part 22 and the Part 22 Practice Direction).

5.4.3 The parties may, by agreement, extend the period specified in Rule 15.4 for

Paragraph numbers marked with a "+" can be found online and on CD.

filing a defence by up to 28 days. If the parties do so, the defendant must notify the court in writing of the date by which the defence must be filed. If the Claimant will not agree to extend time for filing of the Defence, or if a Defendant seeks further time beyond 28 days for filing a defence, the Defendant must issue an application (see Part 23) to obtain a court order for further time. A Claimant may consent to such an application.

5.5 Default judgment

5.5.1 A party may obtain default judgment under Part 12 except in the circumstances **1B–27** set out in Rules 12.2 and 12.3(3) and paragraphs 1.2 and 1.3 of the Part 12 Practice Direction, which list the circumstances where default judgment may not be obtained.

5.5.2 To obtain default judgment under the circumstances set out in Rules 12.4(1) and 12.9(1), a party may do so by filing a request. A court officer deals with a request and provided s/he is satisfied that the provisions of paragraph 4.1 of the Part 12 Practice Direction have been complied with, s/he will enter the default judgment.

5.5.3 Default judgment in respect of claims specified in Rules 12.4(2)(a), 12.9 and 12.10 must be obtained by making an application to a Master. The following are some of the types of claim that require an application for default judgment;
  (1) against children and patients,
  (2) for costs (other than fixed costs) only,
  (3) for declaratory relief,
  (4) by one spouse against the other on a claim in tort,
  (5) for delivery up of goods where the defendant is not allowed the alternative of paying their value,
  (6) against the Crown, and
  (7) against a foreign State, diplomatic agents or persons or organisations who enjoy immunity from civil jurisdiction under the provisions of the International Organisations Acts 1968 and 1981.

Paragraph 4 of the Practice Direction provides information about the evidence required in support of an application for default judgment.

5.5.4 Where default judgment has been obtained for an amount to be decided by the court, the matter will be referred to a Master for directions to be given concerning the management of the case and any date to be fixed for a hearing.

5.6 Statements of case

5.6.1 Statements of case are defined in Rule 2.3(1) and comprise the particulars of **1B–28** claim and defence in the main proceedings and any further information given under Part 18 and also in any Part 20 proceedings, and any reply (which is optional); they are dealt with in Part 16. (Part 16 does not apply to claims proceeding under Part 8.)

5.6.2 The particulars of claim, whether contained in the Claim Form or served separately, should set out the claimant's claim clearly and fully. The same principle applies to the defence.

5.6.3 Part 16 sets out certain matters which must be included in a statement of case. Paragraphs 8 and 9 of the Part 16 Practice Direction contain matters which should be included in the particulars of claim in specific types of claim, and paragraph 10 lists matters which must be set out in the particulars of claim if relied on. In addition to the matters listed in paragraph 10, full particulars of any allegation of dishonesty or malice and, where any inference of fraud or dishonesty is alleged, the basis on which the inference is alleged should also be included. Points of law may be set out in any statement of case. For information in respect of statements of case in defamation claims see the Part 53 Practice Direction.

5.6.4 In addition to the information contained in Part 16 and the Part 16 Practice

Paragraph numbers marked with a "+" can be found online and on CD.

Direction, the following guidelines on preparing a statement of case should be followed;

    (1) a statement of case must be as brief and concise as possible and confined to setting out the bald facts and not the evidence of them,

    (2) a statement of case should be set out in separate consecutively numbered paragraphs and sub-paragraphs,

    (3) so far as possible each paragraph or sub-paragraph should contain no more than one allegation,

    (4) the facts and other matters alleged should be set out as far as reasonably possible in chronological order,

    (5) the statement of case should deal with the claim on a point-by-point basis, to allow a point-by-point response,

    (6) where a party is required to give reasons, the allegation should be stated first and then the reasons listed one by one in separate numbered sub-paragraphs,

    (7) a party wishing to advance a positive claim must identify that claim in the statement of case,

    (8) any matter which, if not stated, might take another party by surprise, should be stated,

    (9) where they will assist, headings, abbreviations and definitions should be used and a glossary annexed; contentious headings, abbreviations, paraphrasing and definitions should not be used and every effort should be made to ensure that they are in a form acceptable to the other parties,

    (10) particulars of primary allegations should be stated as particulars and not as primary allegations,

    (11) schedules or appendices should be used if this would be helpful, for example where lengthy particulars are necessary, and any response should also be stated in a schedule or appendix,

    (12) any lengthy extracts from documents should be placed in a schedule.

5.6.5 A statement of case should be verified by a statement of truth. If a party fails to verify his/her statement of case, it will remain effective unless struck out, but that party may not rely on the statement of case as evidence of any of the matters contained in it; a statement of case verified by a statement of truth is advisable as evidence only at hearings other than the trial (see Rule 32.6(2)). Any party may apply to the court for an order to strike out a statement of case, which has not been verified.

Section 6
Preliminary case management

6.1 The Practice Master

1B–29   6.1.1 On every working day, the Practice Master is available from 10.30a.m. to 1.00p.m. and from 2.00p.m. to 4.30p.m. to answer questions about the practice of the Queen's Bench Division. Usually, one Master takes the Morning Practice, and another Master takes the Afternoon Practice. This will be shown on the Daily Cause List and is also on the notice boards in the Masters' corridors, and on the Listing Notice board outside The Masters Support Unit, Room E16. Also, a board is placed on the door of the Master who is sitting as Practice Master.(NOTE: the Practice Master will finish at 12 noon on those days where the High Court Enforcement Officers Interpleader list is listed- this usually takes place on the first Monday in each month).

6.1.2 The Practice Master cannot give advice, whether about a given case or about the law generally, s/he is there simply to answer general questions about the CPR and practice governing the work of the Queen's Bench Division, and can deal with any consent order, notwithstanding that the claim in which it is to be made has been assigned to another Master. The Practice Master may grant stays of execution and deal with urgent applications, which do not require notice to be given to the respondent. It is unnecessary to make an appointment to see the Practice Master and litigants are generally seen in order of arrival.

Paragraph numbers marked with a "+" can be found online and on CD.

6.2 Assignment to Masters

6.2.1 A claim issued in the Central Office will normally be assigned upon issue to a particular Master as the procedural judge responsible for managing the claim. The Registry Section of the Action Department will endorse the name of the Assigned Master on the Claim Form. However, assignment may be triggered at an earlier stage, for example, by one of the following events;

    (1) an application for pre-action disclosure under Rule 31.16,

    (2) an application for an interim remedy before the commencement of a claim or where there is no relevant claim (Part 25).

It occasionally happens that a claim is assigned to a Master who may have an "interest" in the claim. In such cases the Senior Master will re-assign the claim to another Master.

6.2.2 Where either an application notice or Part 8 Claim Form is issued which requires a hearing date to be given immediately, the Registry will assign a Master and the Masters' Support Unit will give a hearing date.

6.2.3 The Senior Master may assign a particular Master to a class/group of claims or may re-assign work generally. At present Clinical negligence claims are assigned to Master Ungley and Master Yoxall. Claims for Mesothelioma are assigned to Master Whitaker. In the event of an assigned Master being on leave or for any other reason temporarily absent from the Royal Courts of Justice then the Masters' Support Unit may endorse on the appropriate document the name of another Master.

6.2.4 A court file will be opened when a Claim Form is issued. The name of the assigned Master will be endorsed on the Court File and entered on the Claim Forms. Any application notice in an assigned claim for hearing before a Master should have the name of the assigned Master entered on it by the solicitors/litigants making the application.

6.3 Listing before Masters

6.3.1 The Masters' lists consist of;

    (1) the Chambers List - short applications in Rooms E102 and E110 ("the Bear Garden lists"),

    (2) Private Room Appointments, (**using the prescribed PRA form**) and

    (3) the High Court Enforcement Officer's Interpleader applications (formerly Sheriffs' applications).

6.3.2 2 Parties attending on all applications before the Masters are requested to complete the Court Record Sheet (form PF 48), which will be used to record details of the claim, representation and the nature of the application. Copies of this form may be found in the writing desks in the Masters' corridors and the Bear Garden. The form will be placed on the file when the hearing is concluded.

6.3.3 Masters will sit each day at 10.30am in the Bear Garden, Rooms E102 and E110 to hear applications in the Chambers Lists (Bear Garden lists). Applications of up to 30 minutes duration are listed at 10.30am, 11.00am and 11.30am. Solicitors and Counsel may attend any application in these lists although the costs of being represented by Counsel may be disallowed if not fully justified. **If the Master considers that the application is likely to take longer than 30 minutes s/he may adjourn it to a private room appointment.** The applicant must then complete the PRA form giving details of the parties' availability as fully as possible. Failure to do so may result in the request form being returned for further information thereby delaying the hearing date. The PRA form is available in the Masters Support Unit, Room E16 and available from the Court Service Website.

6.3.4 **Hearing dates** for the Chambers Lists (Bear Garden lists) are given by the Masters' Support Unit. The assigned Master gives hearing dates for private room

1B–30

1B–31

Paragraph numbers marked with a "+" can be found online and on CD.

appointments personally. The parties or their legal representatives must inform the Masters' Support Unit of any settlements as soon as possible. All time estimates must be updated as necessary. Any Order made which as a consequence results in a hearing being not required must be notified to the Master by using the Notice of Cancellation form available from the Judgments & Orders Section Room E15 – E17. This should be completed by the parties, and will be sent to the Assigned Master to note in the Diary accordingly.

6.3.5 Applications in the Chambers Lists (Bear Garden list) may, by agreement or where the application notice has not been served, be transferred for a private room appointment on a date to be specified by the Master, or may be re-listed for another date in the Chambers List. In all other cases an application for a postponement of the hearing date must be made to the Master to whom the claim has been assigned. An application may be re-listed in the Chambers List (Bear Garden list) without permission of a Master if for any reason the application has not been heard or has not been fully disposed of.

6.3.6 When an application in the Bear Garden list is adjourned by a Master s/he will specify the date to which it is adjourned.

Adjournments

6.3.7 An application for the adjournment of a private room appointment must be made to the Master who gave the appointment unless the application is by agreement of all parties and the Master approves. The Master will usually require details of parties' availability. Any adjournment will normally be to a new hearing date.

6.3.8 If the application for an adjournment is opposed by any other party, the party seeking the adjournment must issue an application for an adjournment, if time permits, and must give the court, and all other parties as much notice as possible of such application. Where possible, it is preferable that such application is heard before the date for the hearing. **The Master will not grant an adjournment readily where it is opposed by any other party. Good reason will need to be shown, and if the reason is illness of a party, an original (not a photocopy) medical certificate signed and dated by a medical practitioner, setting out the reasons why attendance at court is not possible, will be required.**

6.3.9 If an adjournment of a hearing is granted, the Master will usually require details of parties' availability. Any adjournment will normally be to a new hearing date.

6.3.10 **Where an application for which a Master has given a private room appointment has been settled, it is the duty of the parties or their legal representatives, particularly those who obtained that appointment, to notify the Master immediately.**

6.3.11 If the Master hearing an application considers that the result might affect the date fixed for a trial, s/he may refer the application to the Judge in Charge of the List. This possibility should be considered when making an application and a request should be included in the application notice asking the Master to refer the application to the Judge.

6.3.12 If the Master considers that an application should more properly be heard by a Judge, s/he may either during the hearing or before it takes place refer the application to the Interim Applications Judge. Among the circumstances that may make this appropriate are;

    (1) that the time required for the hearing is longer than a Master could ordinarily make available,

    (2) that the application raises issues of unusual difficulty or importance, etc. or

    (3) that the outcome is likely to affect the trial date or window (in which case the referral will be to the Judge in Charge of the Lists).

Paragraph numbers marked with a "+" can be found online and on CD.

However, it is emphasised that no single factor or combination of factors is necessarily decisive, and the Master has a complete discretion.

6.3.13 The Sheriff's first return applications are interpleader applications (under RSC O.17 as set out in Schedule 1 to the CPR) and are listed at monthly intervals.

6.4 Automatic transfer

6.4.1 Part 26 requires certain claims to be transferred automatically. Where; **1B–32**
  (1) the claim is for a specified amount of money,
  (2) the claim has not been issued in a specialist list,
  (3) the defendant, or one of the defendants is an individual,
  (4) the claim has not been issued in the individual defendant's home court, and
  (5) the claim has not already been transferred to another individual defendant's home court,

the claim will, on receipt of the defence, be transferred to the individual defendant's home court.

6.4.2 Where the Claim Form was issued in the Royal Courts of Justice the defendant's home court will be the district registry or county court for the district in which the defendant's address for service as shown on the defence is situated. If there is no such district registry or county court the proceedings will remain in the Royal Courts of Justice. If the claim is against more than one individual defendant, the claim will be transferred to the home court of the defendant who first files his/her defence. (See Section 6.9 below about transfer following an order.)

6.5 Allocation

6.5.1 When a defence to a claim is received in the Action Department from all the **1B–33** defendants, or from one or more of the defendants and the time for filing a defence has expired, the Action Department Registry will send an Allocation Questionnaire to all parties to an action, unless it has been dispensed with. If an Allocation Questionnaire is dispensed with the appropriate fee is still payable (CPR 26.3.3).

6.5.2 The Allocation Questionnaire to be used in accordance with Part 26 is form N150. The Allocation Questionnaire will state the time within which it must be filed, which will normally be at least 14 days after the day on which it is deemed served. Where proceedings are automatically transferred to a defendant's home court, notwithstanding that the issuing court will send out the Allocation Questionnaire before transfer, the Allocation Questionnaire should nevertheless be returned to the receiving court, the address for which will be on the covering letter.

6.5.3 Each party should state in his/her Allocation Questionnaire if there is any reason why the claim should be managed and tried at a court other than the Royal Courts of Justice or the trial centre for a particular district registry. Paragraph 2.6 of the Part 29 Practice Direction sets out certain types of claim that are suitable for trial in the Royal Courts of Justice. Form PF 52will be sent out to parties with the Allocation Questionnaire. Parties are encouraged to agree directions for the management of the claim, in the form of PF 52 or similar as prescribed by the Master.

6.5.4 Where a party fails to file his/her Allocation Questionnaire within the specified time the court officer will refer the proceedings to the Master for his/her directions. The Master's directions may include "the standard unless order", that is that unless the defaulting party files his/her Allocation Questionnaire within 7 days, his/her statement of case will be struck out.

6.5.5 Where one but not all of the parties has filed an Allocation Questionnaire the Master may allocate the claim to the multi-track where s/he considers that s/he has sufficient information to do so. Alternatively, the Master may order that an allocation

Paragraph numbers marked with a "+" can be found online and on CD.

hearing take place and that all or any particular parties must attend. The court officer will then send out a Notice of Allocation Hearing (form N153) giving reasons for the hearing and any other directions.

6.5.6 Parties requesting a stay to settle the proceedings should do so in their Allocation Questionnaire or otherwise in writing. The court encourages parties to consider the use of ADR (see paragraph 6.6 below). The Master will normally direct the proceedings to be stayed for one month, but parties may by agreement seek an extension of the stay. Paragraph 3 of the Part 26 Practice Direction sets out the procedure for seeking an extension.

6.5.7 Parties are reminded that an estimate of costs should be filed and served when the Allocation Questionnaire is filed (see paragraph 6.4 of the Costs Practice Direction).

6.5.8 On receipt of the Allocation Questionnaires or on an allocation hearing the Master will allocate the claim to the multi-track or transfer the claim to the appropriate county court. Rule 26.6 sets out the scope of each track. By operation of para 2.1 of Part 7A Practice Direction and Rule 26.6(4), claims proceeding in the Royal Courts of Justice must be allocated to the multi-track.

6.6 Alternative Dispute Resolution ("ADR"):

1B–34 6.6.1 Parties are encouraged to use ADR (such as, but not confined to, mediation and conciliation) to try to resolve their disputes or particular issues. Legal representatives should consider with their clients and the other parties the possibility of attempting to resolve the dispute or particular issues by ADR and they should ensure that their clients are fully informed as to the most cost effective means of resolving their dispute.

6.6.2 The settlement of disputes by ADR can;
   (1) significantly reduce parties' costs,
   (2) save parties the delay of litigation in resolving their disputes,
   (3) assist parties to preserve their existing commercial relationships while resolving their disputes, and
   (4) provide a wider range of remedies than those available through litigation.

The Master will in an appropriate case invite the parties to consider whether their dispute, or particular issues in it, could be resolved by ADR. The Master may also either stay proceedings for a specified period of time or extend the time for compliance with an order, a Rule or Practice Direction to encourage and enable the parties to use ADR. Parties may apply for directions seeking a stay for ADR at any time.

6.6.3 Information concerning ADR may be obtained from the Admiralty and Commercial Court Registry.

6.7 Part 8—Alternative procedure for claims:

1B–35 6.7.1 Paragraphs 4.3.14 to 4.3.16 above deal with issuing a Part 8 Claim Form. The alternative procedure set out in Part 8 ("the Part 8 procedure") may not be used if a Practice Direction provides that it does not apply in respect of a particular type of claim. A Rule or Practice Direction may require or permit the use of the Pt 8 procedure and may disapply or modify any of the Pt 8 rules in respect of specified types of proceedings. The Part 8B Practice Direction deals with commencement of proceedings under the Rules of the Supreme Court and the County Court Rules the provisions of which remain in force in Schedules 1 and 2 to the CPR ("the Schedule rules"). The Schedule rules and the Practice Directions supporting them may require certain proceedings to be commenced by the issue of a Part 8 Claim Form with appropriate modifications to the Part 8 procedure.

6.7.2 The main features of the Part 8 procedure are;

Paragraph numbers marked with a "+" can be found online and on CD.

(1) Part 16 (statements of case) does not apply, but the claimant may be required to file Details of Claim when issuing,

(2) Part 15 (defence and reply) does not apply,

(3) judgment in default may not be obtained (Rule 12.2),

(4) Rules 14.4 to 14.7 (judgment by request on an admission) do not apply,

(5) a Part 8 claim shall be treated as being allocated to the multi-track.

6.7.3 All Part 8 Claim Forms will be referred to a Master for directions as soon as the Part 8 Claim Form is issued. These may include fixing a hearing date. Where a hearing date is fixed, notice of the hearing date must be served with the Claim Form. Where the Master does not fix a hearing date when the Claim Form is issued s/he will give directions for the disposal of the claim as soon as practicable after the receipt of the acknowledgement of service or as the case may be, the expiry of the period for acknowledging service.

6.7.4 Where a Part 8 Claim Form has been issued for the purpose of giving effect to a consent order for an award of damages to a child or patient or an award of provisional damages as in paragraph 4.1.15 (1) and (2) above, a draft of the order sought should be attached to the claim form. For more information see paragraphs 6.8.1 to 6.8.8 and 9.3.8 to 9.3.10 below about children and patients, and paragraphs 6.8.12, 9.3.11 and 9.3.12 below about provisional damages.

6.7.5 A defendant who wishes to respond to a Part 8 Claim Form should acknowledge service of it and may do so either by using form N210 or otherwise in writing giving the following information;

(1) whether s/he contests the claim, and

(2) where s/he is seeking a different remedy from that set out in the Claim Form, what that remedy is.

If a defendant does not acknowledge service of the Claim Form within the specified time, s/he may attend the hearing of the claim but may not take part in the hearing unless the court gives permission.

6.7.6 Rules 8.5 and 8.6 and paragraph 5 of the Part 8 Practice Direction (alternative procedure) deal with evidence to be relied on in Part 8 proceedings; **the claimant's evidence must be filed and served with the Claim Form, and the defendant's evidence (if any) must be filed with his/her acknowledgement of service.** If the defendant files written evidence s/he must at the same time serve it on the other parties. It is helpful to the court if, where the defendant does not intend to rely on written evidence, s/he notifies the court in writing to that effect.

6.7.7 Where a defendant contends that the Part 8 procedure should not be used, s/he should state the reasons for his/her contention on his/her acknowledgement of service. On receipt of the acknowledgement of service, the Master will give appropriate directions for the future management of the claim.

6.8 Specific matters which may be dealt with under the Part 8 procedure

Settlements on behalf of children and patients

6.8.1 Part 21 and the Part 21 Practice Direction set out the requirements for litigation by or against children and patients. References in Part 21, the Part 21 Practice Direction and in this guide to;

(1) "child" means a person under 18, and

(2) "patient" means a person who by reason of mental disorder within the meaning of the Mental Health Act 1983 is incapable of managing and administering his/her own property and affairs.

No settlement or compromise of a claim by or against a child or patient will be binding unless and until the court has approved it. In addition, a party may not obtain a default judgment against a child or patient without the permission of the court, and may not enter judgment on an admission against a child or patient.

1B–36

Paragraph numbers marked with a "+" can be found online and on CD.

6.8.2 A patient must have a litigation friend to conduct proceedings on his/her behalf, and so must a child unless the court makes an order permitting the child to act on his/her own behalf. A litigation friend is someone who can fairly and competently conduct proceedings on behalf of the child or patient. S/he must have no interest in the proceedings adverse to that of the child or patient, and all steps s/he takes in the proceedings must be taken for the benefit of the child or patient. Rules 21.5 to 21.8 and paragraphs 2 and 3 of the Practice Direction set out how a person may become a litigation friend.

6.8.3 Applications for the approval of settlements or compromises of claims by or against a child or patient proceeding in the Central Office are heard by a Master. If the purpose of starting the claim is for the approval of a settlement, a Part 8 Claim Form should be issued in accordance with form PF 170(A) which must contain a request for approval of the settlement (or compromise) and, in addition to the details of the claim, must set out the terms of the settlement (or compromise) or must have attached to it a draft consent order. The draft consent order should be in form N292, and should include the child's National Insurance Number, so that the child can be subsequently traced. See paragraph 6 of the Practice Direction for further information which the Master will require.

6.8.4 Where parties reach a settlement (or compromise) in proceedings started by the issue of a Part 7 Claim Form (where the trial has not started) an application must be made to the Master, or if the amount of the proposed settlement exceeds £750,000, to the Judge, in accordance with Part 23 for the approval of the settlement. The application notice should be in form PF170(B) and should have attached to it a draft consent order in form N292. (See CPR 21.10 PD 21 paras 6 & 7.) The application notice should be lodged in Room E16. (See Section 7.12 below for information about applications.) If the trial has started, oral application may be made to the trial judge. Applications for approval of a settlement on behalf of a child or patient will normally be heard in public unless the Judge or Master orders otherwise. If a settlement is approved in private, the terms of settlement will be announced in public.

6.8.5 Paragraph 8 of the Practice Direction gives information about control of money recovered by or on behalf of a child or patient. Paragraph 10 deals with investment of money on behalf of a child and paragraph 11 deals with investment on behalf of a patient. Enquiries concerning investment for a child are dealt with in Room E105.

6.8.6 In respect of investment on behalf of a child, the litigation friend or his/her legal representative should provide the Master or a Judge with a completed form PF 172 (request for investment) for completion by the Master. The child's birth certificate should also be provided. When investment directions have been given, the PF 172 will then be forwarded to the Court Funds Office for their investment managers to make the appropriate investment. The Court of Protection is responsible for the administration of patients' funds (unless they are small). Paragraph 11 of the Practice Direction gives full information about procedure for investment by the Court of Protection. These procedures may also be used for investment of money on behalf of a child or patient following an award of damages at trial.

6.8.7 Damages may also be paid to a child or patient by way of a structured settlement. A Judge or Master must approve a structured settlement on behalf of a child or patient. The Court of Protection must also approve a structured settlement on behalf of a patient. (For more information about structured settlements see the Part 40C Practice Direction—Structured Settlements.)

6.8.8 Control of a child's fund, provided s/he is not also a patient, passes to him when s/he reaches the age of 18 (see paragraph 12.2 of the Practice Direction).

Summary order for possession

6.8.9 In practice such claims are usually dealt with in the appropriate County Court. Paragraph 1 of Part 55 Practice direction gives details of the limited circumstances where a claim may be brought in the High Court. High Court claims for the possession of land subject to a mortgage will be assigned to the Chancery Division.

Paragraph numbers marked with a "+" can be found online and on CD.

Settlement of a provisional damages claim

6.8.12 A claim for provisional damages may proceed under Part 8 where the Claim Form is issued solely for the purpose of obtaining a consent judgment. The claimant must state in his/her Claim Form in addition to the matters set out in paragraph 4.4 of the Part 16 Practice Direction that the parties have reached agreement and request a consent judgment. A draft order in accordance with paragraph 4.2 of the Part 41 Practice Direction should be attached to the Claim Form. The claimant or his/her legal representative must lodge the case file documents (set out in the draft order) in Room E16. Once the Provisional damages claim has been approved the documents lodged will be compiled into a file and preserved by the Court. For more information about provisional damages claims and orders see Part 41 and the Part 41 Practice Direction, and section 9.3 below.

Costs only proceedings

6.8.13 Proceedings may be brought under Part 8 where the parties to a dispute have reached a written agreement before proceedings have been started but have been unable to agree an amount of costs. The costs only proceedings may be started by the issue of a Claim Form in the Supreme Court Costs Office at Clifford's Inn, Fetter Lane, London EC4A 1DQ. The Costs Practice Direction at Section 17 sets out in detail the provisions for issue and proceeding with the claim.

6.9 Transfer

6.9.1 Part 30 and the Part 30 Practice Direction deal with transfer of proceedings, within the High Court, from the High Court to the County Court and between County Courts. The jurisdiction of the High Court to transfer proceedings to the county courts is contained in s.40 of the County Courts Act 1984 as substituted by s.2(1) of the Courts and Legal Services Act 1990. Under that section the court has jurisdiction in certain circumstances to strike out claims that should have been started in a county court.

1B–37

6.9.2 Rule 30.2 sets out the provisions for the transfer of proceedings between;
   (1) county courts,
   (2) the Royal Courts of Justice and a district registry of the High Court, and
   (3) between district registries.

Rule 30.3 sets out the criteria to which the court will have regard when making an order for transfer. (See paragraph 6.4 above about automatic transfer.)

6.9.3 The High Court may order proceedings in any Division of the High Court to be transferred to another Division or to or from a specialist list. **An application for the transfer of proceedings to or from a specialist list must be made to a Judge dealing with claims in that list.**

6.9.4 A claim with an estimated value of less than £50,000 may generally be transferred to a county court, if the county court has jurisdiction, unless it is to proceed in the High Court under an enactment or in a specialist list

6.9.5 An order for transfer takes effect from the date it is made. When an order for transfer is sealed the court officer will immediately transfer the matter to the receiving court. At the same time, the court officer will also notify all parties of the transfer. An order for transfer to the High Court at the Royal Courts of Justice should state: "Transfer to the Central Office, Queen's Bench Division, [or as appropriate] at the Royal Courts of Justice."

6.9.6 Paragraph 5 of the Part 30 Practice Direction sets out the procedure for appealing an order for transfer. Where an order for transfer is made in the absence of notice given to a party, that party may apply to the court that made the order to have it set aside.

6.9.7 Where money has been paid into court before an order for transfer is made, the court may direct transfer of the money to the control of the receiving court.

Paragraph numbers marked with a "+" can be found online and on CD.

6.10 Part 20 proceedings:

1B–38 6.10.1 Part 20 deals with (a) counterclaims and (b) other additional claims, being claims for contribution or indemnity and what were formerly called "third party" claims. A Part 20 claim is treated as a claim for the purpose of the CPR with certain exceptions, for which see Rule 20.3.

6.10.2 A defendant may make a counterclaim by completing the defence and counterclaim form provided in the Response Pack. The fee for the Counterclaim will depend on the amount claimed, and will therefore be deemed the same as a fee for Issue of Claim (see Fees Annex 1). If the counterclaim is not filed with the defence, the permission of the court is required. Where a counterclaim brings in a new party, the defendant (Part 20 claimant) must apply to the court for an order in form PF 21A adding the new party as defendant.

6.10.3 A defendant claiming contribution or indemnity from another defendant may do so by filing a notice, in form PF 22, containing a statement of the nature and grounds of his/her claim and serving the notice on the other defendant.

6.10.4 Any other additional claim may be brought by the issue of a Part 20 Claim Form, N211. If the Part 20 Claim Form is issued at a time other than when the defence is filed, the permission of the court is required. Rule 20.8 deals with service of a Part 20 Claim Form and Rule 20.12 sets out the forms which must accompany the Part 20 Claim Form.

6.11 Summary judgment

1B–39 6.11.1 The court may give summary judgment under Part 24 against a claimant or defendant;

   (1) if it considers that (a) the claimant has no real prospect of succeeding on the claim or issue, or (b) the defendant has no real prospect of successfully defending the claim, and

   (2) there is no other reason why the claim or issue should be disposed of at a trial.

6.11.2 The court may give summary judgment against a claimant in any type of proceedings, and against a defendant in any type of proceedings except (a) proceedings for possession of residential premises against a mortgagor, or a tenant or person holding over after the end of his/her tenancy where occupancy is protected within the meaning of the Rent Act 1977 or the Housing Act 1988, (b) proceedings for an Admiralty claim in Rem, and (c) contentious probate proceedings. For information about summary disposal of defamation claims see Part 53, the Part 53 Practice Direction and paragraph 12 7 below.

6.11.3 An application for summary judgment should be made in accordance with Part 23 and the application notice should contain the information set out in paragraph 2 of the Part 24 Practice Direction (parties may use forms PF 11 and PF 12 as precedents). The application notice should be filed and served on the respondent giving at least 14 days notice of the date fixed for the hearing and the issues to be decided at the hearing. Unless the application notice contains all the evidence on which the applicant relies, the application notice should identify that evidence.

6.11.4 In claims which include a claim for;

   (1) specific performance of an agreement,

   (2) rescission of such an agreement, or

   (3) forfeiture or return of a deposit made under such an agreement,

the application notice and any evidence in support must be served on the defendant not less than 4 days before the hearing. This replaces for such applications the 14 days notice usually required for summary judgment applications (Part 24 Practice Direction paragraph 7).

6.11.5 The application will normally be listed before a Master unless for example, an injunction is also sought. In that case the application notice should state that the application is intended to be made to a Judge.

Paragraph numbers marked with a "+" can be found online and on CD.

6.11.6 Where an order made on an application for summary judgment does not dispose of the claim or issue, the court will give case management directions in respect of the claim or issue.

6.12 Offers to settle and payments into and out of court:

6.12.1 A party may offer to settle a claim at any time. Part 36 deals with offers to settle and payments into court. An offer to settle made in accordance with Part 36 will have the costs and other consequences specified in that Part and may be made at any time after proceedings have started. Paragraph 1 of the Part 36 Practice Direction defines an offer made in accordance with Part 36. See also paragraph 5 of the Part 36 Practice Direction which contains general provisions concerning Part 36 offers and Part 36 payments. **1B–40**

6.12.2 A Part 36 offer may be made by any party, but to comply with Part 36 a defendant who makes an offer to settle for a specified sum must do so by way of a Part 36 payment into court. Paragraph 4.1(2) of the Part 36 Practice Direction sets out the requirements for making a Part 36 payment in respect of a claim proceeding in the Royal Courts of Justice. If a defendant has made a pre-action offer to settle and proceedings are then started, in order for the court to take account of his/her offer he/she must make a Part 36 payment of not less than the amount offered within 14 days of service of the Claim Form. See also paragraph 10 of the Part 36 Practice Direction which deals with compensation recovery in respect of Part 36 payments.

6.12.3 The times for accepting a Part 36 offer or Part 36 payment are set out in Rules 36.11 and 36.12; the general rule is that a Part 36 offer or Part 36 payment made more than 21 days before the start of the trial may be accepted without the permission of the court, within 21 days after it was made. Otherwise, the permission of the court must be obtained. A Part 36 offer is made when received by the offeree. A Part 36 payment is made when the Part 36 payment notice (form N242A) is served on the claimant.

6.12.4 A party may accept a Part 36 offer or Part 36 payment by serving on the offeror a notice of acceptance (form N243 may be used to accept a Part 36 payment) within the times set out in Rules 36.11 and 36.12. When a Part 36 offer or Part 36 payment is accepted within those times, the general rule is that the claimant will be entitled to his/her costs up to the date of service of the notice of acceptance.

6.12.5 To obtain money out of court on acceptance of a Part 36 payment, the claimant should file a request for payment (form N243/N201) in the Action Department of the Central Office, and file a copy in the Court Funds Office. See paragraph 8 of the Part 36 Practice Direction for full details of the procedure for obtaining payment out of court.

6.12.6 The court's permission is required for acceptance of a Part 36 offer or Part 36 payment;
  (1) which is not made or accepted within the times set out in Rules 36.11 and 36.12, or
  (2) where acceptance is by or on behalf of a child or patient, or
  (3) where a defence of tender has been put forward, or
  (4) otherwise as mentioned in Rule 36.17.

6.12.7 Where a Part 36 offer or Part 36 payment is not accepted and a trial of the claim takes place, Rule 36.20 sets out the costs consequences where a claimant fails to do better than the Part 36 offer or Part 36 payment, and Rule 36.21 sets out the costs and other consequences where a claimant does better than s/he proposed in his/her Part 36 offer.

6.12.8 In the Action Department a Part 36 offer or payment, if not accepted, will be kept in a separate file held by the Manager of the Registry Section and not made available to the trial judge until after determination.

Paragraph numbers marked with a "+" can be found online and on CD.

6.12.9 **It should be noted that there will be extensive changes to the Part 36 procedure, and to the provisions about payments into court, which will come into force on 6th April 2007. The above notes reflect the position before that date. For details of the changes please see the revised Parts 36 and 37 (Schedules 1 and 2 to The Civil Procedure (Amendment No. 3) Rules 2006).**

SECTION 7

CASE MANAGEMENT AND INTERIM REMEDIES

7.1 Case management—general:

1B–41 7.1.1 CPR requires the court to provide a high degree of case management. Case management includes; identifying disputed issues at an early stage; fixing timetables; dealing with as many aspects of the claim as possible on the same occasion; controlling costs; disposing of proceedings summarily where appropriate; dealing with the applications without a hearing where appropriate; and giving directions to ensure that the trial of a claim proceeds quickly and efficiently. The court will expect the parties to co-operate with each other, and where appropriate, will encourage the parties to use ADR or otherwise help them settle the case.

7.1.2 Parties and their legal representatives will be expected to do all that they can to agree proposals for the management of the claim in accordance with Rule 29.4 and paragraphs 4.6 to 4.8 of the Part 29 Practice Direction. There is provision in the Allocation Questionnaire for proposing certain directions to be made, otherwise parties may use form PF 50 for making the application (attaching to it the draft form of order in form PF 52) and file it for the Master's approval. If the Master approves the proposals s/he will give directions accordingly.

7.2 The Case Management Conference:

1B–42 7.2.1 Parties who are unable to agree proposals for the management of the case, should notify the Court of the matters which they are unable to agree.

7.2.2 Where;
   (1) the parties proposed directions are not approved, or
   (2) parties are unable to agree proposed directions, or
   (3) the Master wishes to make further directions,

the Master will generally either consult the parties or direct that a case management conference be held.

7.2.3 In relatively straightforward claims, the Court may give directions without holding a case management conference.

7.2.4 Any party who considers that a case management conference should be held before any directions are given should so state in his/her Allocation Questionnaire, (or in a Part 8 claim should notify the Master in writing), giving his/her reasons and supplying a realistic time estimate for the case management conference, with a list of any dates or times convenient to all parties, or most of them, in form PF 49.

7.2.5 Where a case management conference has been fixed, parties should ensure that any other applications are listed or made at that hearing. A party applying for directions at the case management conference should use form PF 50 for making their application and attach to it the draft order for directions (form PF 52).

7.2.6 Parties should consider whether a case summary would assist the Master at the Case Management Conference in dealing with the issues before him or her. Paragraph 5.7 of the Part 29 Practice Direction sets out the provisions for preparation of a case summary.

7.2.7 It may be appropriate for the advocates instructed or expected to be instructed

Paragraph numbers marked with a "+" can be found online and on CD.

to appear at the trial to attend any hearing at which case management directions are likely to be given. In any event, the legal representatives who attend the case management conference must be familiar with the case and have sufficient authority to deal with any issues which may arise. Where necessary, the court may order the attendance of a party.

7.3 Preliminary issues:

7.3.1 Costs can sometimes be saved by identifying decisive issues, or potentially **1B–43** decisive issues, and by the Court ordering that they be tried first. The decision of one issue, although not necessarily itself decisive of the claim as a whole, may enable the parties to settle the remainder of the dispute. In such a case, the trial of a preliminary issue may be appropriate.

7.3.2 At the allocation stage, at any case management conference and again at any pre-trial review, the court will consider whether the trial of a preliminary issue may be helpful. Where such an order is made, the parties and the court should consider whether the costs of the issue should be in the issue or in the claim as a whole.

7.3.3 Where there is an application for summary judgment, and issues of law or construction may be determined in the respondent's favour, it will usually be in the interests of the parties for such issues to be determined conclusively, rather than that the application should simply be dismissed.

7.4 Trial timetable:

7.4.1 To assist the court to set a trial timetable, a draft timetable should be prepared **1B–44** by the claimant's advocate(s) after consulting the other parties advocates. If there are differing views, those differences should be clearly indicated in the timetable. The draft timetable should be filed with the trial bundle.

7.4.2 The trial timetable will normally include times for giving evidence (whether of fact or opinion) and for oral submissions during the trial.

7.4.3 The trial timetable may be fixed at the case management conference, at any pre-trial review or at the beginning of the trial itself.

7.5 Listing Questionnaire (Pre Trial Check List):

7.5.1 The court will send out a Pre Trial Checklist (N170) to all parties for **1B–45** completion, specifying the date by which it must be returned.

7.5.2 Paragraph 6.4 of the Costs Practice Direction requires an estimate of costs to be filed and served with the Pre Trial Checklist.

7.6 Pre-trial review:

7.6.1 Where the trial of a claim is estimated to last more than 10 days, or where the **1B–46** circumstances require it, the Master may direct that a pre-trial review ("PTR") should be held. The PTR may be heard by a Master, but more usually is heard by a Judge.

7.6.2 Application should normally be made to the Queen's Bench Listing Officer for the PTR to be heard by the trial judge (if known), and the applicant should do all that s/he can to ensure that it is heard between 4 and 8 weeks before the trial date, and in any event long enough before the trial date to allow a realistic time in which to complete any outstanding matters.

7.6.3 The PTR should be attended by the advocates who are to represent the parties at the trial.

7.6.4 At least 7 days before the date fixed for the PTR, the applicant must serve the other parties with a list of matters to be considered at the PTR, and those other parties must serve their responses at least 2 days before the PTR. Account must be

Paragraph numbers marked with a "+" can be found online and on CD.

QB Guide

taken of the answers in any listing questionnaires filed. Realistic proposals must be put forward and if possible agreed as to the time likely to be required for each stage of the trial and as to the order in which witnesses are to be called.

7.6.5 The applicant should lodge a properly indexed bundle containing the listing questionnaires (if directed to be filed) and the lists of matters and the proposals, together with the results of discussions between the parties, and any other relevant material, in the Queen's Bench Listing Office, Room WG8, by no later than 10.30am on the day before the day fixed for the hearing of the PTR. If the PTR is to take place before a Master and he asks for the bundle in advance, it should be lodged in the Masters' Support Unit, Room E14. Otherwise it should be lodged at the hearing.

7.6.6 At the PTR, the court will review the parties' state of preparation, deal with any outstanding matters, and give any directions or further directions that may be necessary.

7.7 Requests for further information:

1B–47 7.7.1 A party seeking further information or clarification under Part 18 should serve a written request on the party from whom the information is sought before making an application to the court. Paragraph 1 of the Part 18 Practice Direction deals with how the request should be made, and paragraph 2 deals with the response. A statement of truth should verify a response. Parties may use form PF 56 for a combined request and reply, if they so wish.

7.7.2 If a party who has been asked to provide further information or clarification objects or is unable to do so, s/he must notify the party making the request in writing.

7.7.3 Where it is necessary to apply for an order for further information or clarification the party making the application should set out in or have attached to his/her application notice;
> (1) the text of the order sought specifying the matters on which further information or clarification is sought, and
>
> (2) whether a request has been made and, if so, the result of that request.

Applicants may use form PF 57 for their application notice.

7.8 Disclosure and Inspection of Documents:

1B–48   Disclosure and inspection of documents involves two stages. First, disclosure of the existence of documents and claiming privilege from inspection for such documents as may attract privilege (e.g. those to which 'legal advice' privilege applies); and secondly, offering facilities to the opposing party for inspection of certain of those documents.

7.8.1 Under Part 31, there is no longer any general duty to disclose documents. Instead, a party is prevented from relying on any document that s/he has not disclosed, and is required to give inspection of any document to which s/he refers in his/her statement of case or in any witness statement, etc.. The intention is that disclosure should be proportionate to the value of the claim.

7.8.2 If an order for disclosure is made, unless the contrary is stated, the Court will order standard disclosure, namely disclosure of only;
> (1) the documents on which a party relies,
>
> (2) the documents that adversely affect his/her own or another party's case,
>
> (3) the documents that support another party's case, and
>
> (4) the documents required to be disclosed by a relevant practice direction.

Parties should give standard disclosure by completing form N265 and may list the documents by category.

7.8.3 The court may either limit or dispense with disclosure (and the parties may agree to do likewise). The court may also order disclosure of specified documents or

Paragraph numbers marked with a "+" can be found online and on CD.

specified classes of documents. In deciding whether to make any such order for specific disclosure, the court will want to be satisfied that the disclosure is necessary, that the cost of disclosure will not outweigh the benefits of disclosure and that a party's ability to continue the litigation would not be impaired by any such order.

7.8.4 The court will therefore seek to ensure that any specific disclosure ordered is appropriate to the particular case, taking into account the financial position of the parties, the importance of the case and the complexity of the issues.

7.8.5 If specific disclosure is sought, a separate application for specific disclosure should be made in accordance with Part 23; it is not a matter that would be routinely dealt with at the CMC. The parties should give careful thought to ways of limiting the burdens of such disclosure, whether by giving disclosure in stages, by dispensing with the need to produce copies of the same document, by requiring disclosure of documents sufficient merely for a limited purpose, or otherwise. They should also consider whether the need for disclosure could be reduced or eliminated by a request for further information.

7.8.6 A party who has the right to inspect a document should give written notice of his/her wish to inspect to the party disclosing the document. That party must permit inspection not more than 7 days after receipt of the notice.

7.9 Experts and Assessors:

7.9.1 The parties in a claim must bear in mind that under Part 35 no party may call **1B–49** an expert or put in evidence an expert's report without the court's express permission, and the court is under a duty to restrict such evidence to what is reasonably required.

7.9.2 The duty of an expert called to give evidence is to assist the court. This duty overrides any obligation to the party instructing him or by whom s/he is being paid (see the Part 35 Practice Direction). In fulfilment of this duty, an expert must for instance make it clear if a particular question or issue falls outside his/her expertise or if s/he considers that insufficient information is available on which to express an opinion.

7.9.3 Before the Master gives permission, s/he must be told the field of expertise of the expert on whose evidence a party wishes to rely and where practicable the identity of the expert. Even then, s/he may, before giving permission, impose a limit on the extent to which the cost of such evidence may be recovered from the other parties in the claim.

7.9.4 Parties should always consider whether a single expert could be appointed in a particular claim or to deal with a particular issue. Before giving permission for the parties to call separate experts, the Master will always consider whether a single joint expert ought to be used, whether in relation to the issues as a whole or to a particular issue.

7.9.5 In many cases it is possible for the question of expert evidence or one or more of the areas of expert evidence to be dealt with by a single expert. Single experts are, for example, often appropriate to deal with questions of quantum in cases where primary issues are as to liability. Likewise, where expert evidence is required in order to acquaint the court with matters of expert fact, as opposed to opinion, a single expert will usually be appropriate. There remain, however, a body of cases where liability will turn upon expert opinion evidence and where it will be appropriate for the parties to instruct their own experts. For example, in cases where the issue for determination is as to whether a party acted in accordance with proper professional standards, it will often be of value to the court to hear the opinions of more than one expert as to the proper standard in order that the court becomes acquainted with the range of views existing upon the question and in order that the evidence can be tested in cross-examination.

7.9.6 It will not be a sufficient ground for objecting to an order for a single joint expert that the parties have already chosen their own experts. An order for a single

Paragraph numbers marked with a "+" can be found online and on CD.

joint expert does not prevent a party from having his/her own expert to advise him, though that is likely to be at his/her own cost, regardless of the outcome.

7.9.7 When the use of a single joint expert is being considered, the Master will expect the parties to co-operate in agreeing terms of reference for and instructions to the expert. In most cases, such terms of reference/instructions will include a statement of what the expert is asked to do, will identify any documents that s/he will be asked to consider and will specify any assumptions that s/he is asked to make.

7.9.8 The court will generally also order that experts in the same field confer on a 'without prejudice' basis, and then report in writing to the parties and the court on the extent of any agreement, giving reasons at least in summary for any continuing disagreement. A direction to 'confer' gives the experts the choice of discussing the matter by telephone or in any other convenient way, as an alternative to attending an actual meeting. Any material change of view of an expert should be communicated in writing to the other parties through their legal representatives, and when appropriate, to the court.

7.9.9 Written questions may be put to an expert within 28 days after service of his/her report, but must only be for purposes of clarification of the expert's report e.g. when the other party does not understand it. Questions going beyond this can only be put with the agreement of the parties or the Master's permission. The procedure of putting written questions to experts is not intended to interfere with the procedure for an exchange of professional opinion in discussions between experts or to inhibit that exchange of professional opinion. If questions that are oppressive in number or content are put without permission for any purpose other than clarification of the expert's report, the court is likely to disallow the questions and make an appropriate order for costs against the party putting them. (See paragraph 4.3 of the Part 35 Practice Direction with respect to payment of an expert's fees for answering questions under Rule 35.6.)

7.9.10 An expert may file with the court a written request for directions to assist him in carrying out his/her function as an expert. The expert should guard against accidentally informing the court about, or about matters connected with, communications or potential communications between the parties that are without prejudice or privileged. The expert may properly be asked to be privy to the content of these communications because s/he has been asked to assist the party instructing him to evaluate them.

7.9.11 Under Rule 35.15 the court may appoint an assessor to assist it in relation to any matter in which the assessor has skill and experience. The report of the assessor is made available to the parties. The remuneration of the assessor is decided by the court and forms part of the costs of the proceedings.

7.10 Evidence:

1B–50 7.10.1 Evidence is dealt with in the CPR in Parts 32, 33 and 34.

7.10.2 The most common form of written evidence is a witness statement. The Part 32 Practice Direction at paragraphs 17, 18 and 19 contains information about the heading, body (what it must contain) and format of a witness statement. The witness must sign a statement of truth to verify the witness statement; the wording of the statement of truth is set out in paragraph 20.2 of the Practice Direction.

7.10.3 A witness statement may be used as evidence in support of an interim application and, where it has been served on any other party to a claim, it may be relied on as a statement of the oral evidence of the witness at the trial. Part 33 contains provisions relating to the use of hearsay evidence in a witness statement.

7.10.4 In addition to the information and provisions for making a witness statement mentioned in paragraph 7.10.2, the following matters should be borne in mind;
  (1) a witness statement must contain the truth, the whole truth and nothing but the truth on the issues it covers,

Paragraph numbers marked with a "+" can be found online and on CD.

(2) those issues should consist only of the issues on which the party serving the witness statement wishes that witness to give evidence in chief and should not include commentary on the trial bundle or other matters which [may arise during the trial or] may have arisen during the proceedings,

(3) a witness statement should be as concise as the circumstances allow, inadmissible or irrelevant material should not be included,

(4) the cost of preparation of an over-elaborate witness statement may not be allowed,

(5) Rule 32.14 states that proceedings for contempt of court may be brought against a person if s/he makes, or causes to be made, a false statement in a document verified by a statement of truth without an honest belief in its truth,

(6) if a party discovers that a witness statement, which they have served, is incorrect they must inform the other parties immediately.

7.10.5 Evidence may also be given by affidavit but unless an affidavit is specifically required either in compliance with a court order, a Rule or Practice Direction, or an enactment, the party putting forward the affidavit may not recover from another party the cost of making an affidavit unless the court so orders.

7.10.6 The Part 32 Practice Direction at paragraphs 3 to 6 contains information about the heading, body, jurat (the sworn statement which authenticates the affidavit) and the format of an affidavit. The court will normally give directions as to whether a witness statement or, where appropriate, an affidavit is to be filed.

7.10.7 A statement of case, which has been verified by a statement of truth, and an application notice containing facts which have been verified by a statement of truth may also stand as evidence other than at the trial.

7.10.8 Evidence by deposition is dealt with in Part 34. A party may apply to a Master for an order for a person to be examined before a hearing takes place (Rule 34.8). Evidence obtained on an examination under that Rule is referred to as a deposition. The Master may order the person to be examined before either a Judge, an examiner of the court or such other person as the court appoints. The Part 34 Practice Direction at paragraph 4 sets out in detail how the examination should take place.

7.10.9 Provisions relating to applications for evidence by deposition to be taken either;

(1) in this country for use in a foreign court, or

(2) abroad for use in proceedings within the jurisdiction

are set out in detail in the Part 34 Practice Direction at paragraphs 5 and 6.

7.10.10 The procedure for issuing a witness summons is also dealt with in Part 34 and the Practice Direction. A witness summons may require a witness to;

(1) attend court, or

(2) produce documents to the court, or

(3) both,

on either a date fixed for the hearing or another date as the court may direct (but see also Rule 31.17 which may be used when there are areas of contention).

7.10.11 The court may also issue a witness summons in aid of a court or tribunal which does not have the power to issue a witness summons in relation to the proceedings before it (and see the Part 34 Practice Direction at paragraphs 1, 2 and 3).

7.10.12 To issue a witness summons, two copies should be filed in the Action Department, Room E07 for sealing; one copy will be retained on the court file.

7.10.13 A witness summons must be served at least 7 days before the date upon

Paragraph numbers marked with a "+" can be found online and on CD.

which the witness is required to attend. If this is not possible for any reason, an order must be sought from a Master that a witness summons is binding although it will be served less than 7 days before the date when the witness is required to attend. A Master will usually be prepared to deal with this in Practice, without notice.

7.10.14 A witness summons will be served by the court unless the party on whose behalf it is issued indicates in writing that s/he wishes to serve it himself. If time is a critical factor, it may be preferable for the party to serve the witness summons. For the method of service see the notes to Part 34 at paragraph 34.6.1.

7.10.15 At the time of service of the witness summons the witness must be offered "Conduct money" to defray his or her expenses of coming to, staying at, and returning from the place of the trial. Thus, where the court is to serve, the party on whose behalf it is issued must deposit the amount of conduct money in the court office. For the relevant amounts see the note at Part 34 paragraph 34.7.1.

7.11 Hearings:

Hearings generally

1B–51 **7.11.1 Hearings in public/private**

All hearings are in principle open to the public, even though in practice most of the hearings until the trial itself will be attended only by the parties and their representatives. However, in an appropriate case the court may decide to hold a hearing in private. Rule 39.2 lists the circumstances where it may be appropriate to hold a hearing in private. In addition, paragraph 1.5 of the Part 39 Practice Direction sets out certain types of hearings which may be listed in private.

7.11.2 The court also has the power under section 11 of the Contempt of Court Act 1981 to make an order forbidding publication of any details that might identify one or more of the parties. Such orders are granted only in exceptional cases.

7.11.3 References in the CPR and Practice Directions to hearings being in public or private do not restrict any existing rights of audience or confer any new rights of audience in respect of applications or proceedings which under the rules previously in force would have been heard in court or chambers respectively. Advocates (and judges) do not wear robes at interim hearings before High Court Judges. Robes are worn for trials and certain other proceedings such as preliminary issues, committals etc. It is not intended that the new routes of appeal should restrict the advocate's right of audience, in that, a solicitor who appeared in a county court matter which is the subject of an appeal to a High Court Judge would normally be allowed to appear at the appeal hearing.

7.11.4 Conduct of the parties

Parties are reminded that they are expected to act with courtesy and respect for the other parties present and for the proceedings of the court. Punctuality is particularly important; being late for hearings is unfair to the other parties and other court users, as well as being discourteous to them and to the court.

Preparation for hearings

7.11.5 To ensure court time is used efficiently there must be adequate preparation prior to the hearing. This includes the preparation and exchange of skeleton arguments, the compilation of bundles of documents and the giving of realistic time estimates. Where estimates prove inaccurate, a hearing may have to be adjourned to a later date, and the party responsible for the adjournment is likely to be ordered to pay the costs thrown away.

7.11.6 The parties should use their best endeavours to agree beforehand the issues, or main issues between them, and must co-operate with the court and each other to enable the court to deal with claims justly; parties may expect to be penalised for failing to do so.

Paragraph numbers marked with a "+" can be found online and on CD.

7.11.7 A bundle of documents must be compiled for the court's use at the trial, and also for hearings before the Interim Applications Judge or a Master where the documents to be referred to total 25 pages or more. The party lodging a trial or hearing bundle should supply identical bundles to all parties and for the use of witnesses. The efficient preparation of bundles is very important. Where bundles have been properly prepared, the claim will be easier to understand and present, and time and costs are likely to be saved. Where documents are copied unnecessarily or bundled incompetently, the costs may be disallowed. Paragraph 3 of the Part 39 Practice Direction sets out in full the requirements for compiling bundles of documents for hearings or trial.

7.11.8 The trial bundle must be filed not more than 7 and not less than 3 days before the start of the trial. Bundles for a Master's hearing should be brought to the hearing unless it is likely to assist the Master to read the bundle in advance in which case it should be lodged with the Masters' Support Unit or the Master directly 1–3 days in advance. The contents of the trial bundle should be agreed where possible, and it should be made clear whether in addition, they are agreeing that the documents in the bundle are authentic even if not previously disclosed and are evidence of the facts stated in them even if a notice under the Civil Evidence Act 1995 has not been served. If the trial/hearing bundles are extensive and either party wishes the judge to read certain documents in advance of the hearing, a reading list should be provided.

7.11.9 Lists of authorities for use at trial or at substantial hearings before a Judge should be provided to the usher by 9.00am on the first day of the hearing. For other applications before a Judge, or applications before a Master, copies of the authorities should be included in the bundle or in a separate bundle.

7.11.10 For trial and most hearings before a Judge, and substantial hearings before a Master, a chronology, a list of the persons involved and a list of the issues should be prepared and filed with the skeleton argument. A chronology should be non-contentious and agreed with the other parties if possible. If there is a material dispute about any event stated in the chronology, that should be stated.

7.11.11 Skeleton arguments should be prepared, filed and served;
   (1) for trials, not less than 2 days before the trial in the Listing Office, and
   (2) for substantial applications or appeals, not later than 1 day before the hearing in the Listing Office and, where the Master has requested papers in advance of the hearing, in the Masters' Support Unit Room E16 or directly with the Master. Parties should avoid handing skeleton arguments to the other party at the door of the court even for less substantial hearings, so that each party has time to consider the other party's case.

7.11.12 A skeleton argument should;
   (1) concisely summarise the party's submissions in relation to each of the issues,
   (2) cite the main authorities relied on, which may be attached,
   (3) contain a reading list and an estimate of the time it will take the Judge to read,
   (4) be as brief as the issues allow and not normally be longer than 20 pages of double-spaced A4 paper,
   (5) be divided into numbered paragraphs and paged consecutively,
   (6) avoid formality and use understandable abbreviations, and
   (7) identify any core documents which it would be helpful to read beforehand.

7.11.13 Where a party decides not to call a witness whose witness statement has been served, to give oral evidence at trial, prompt notice of this decision should be given to all other parties. The party should also indicate whether s/he proposes to put, or seek to put, the witness statement in as hearsay evidence. If s/he does not, any other party may do so.

Recording of proceedings

7.11.14 At any hearing, including the trial, any oral evidence, the judgment or

Paragraph numbers marked with a "+" can be found online and on CD.

decision (including reasons) and any summing up to a jury will be recorded. At hearings before Masters, it is not normally practicable to record anything other than oral evidence and any judgment, but these will be recorded. If a party wishes the whole proceedings to be recorded that party should inform the Master at the start of the hearing. A party to the proceedings may obtain a transcript of the proceedings on payment of the appropriate charge, from the Courts Recording and Transcription Unit, Room WB14. A person who is not a party to the proceedings may not obtain a transcript of a hearing which took place in private without the permission of the court.

7.11.15 No person or party may use unofficial recording equipment at a hearing without the permission of the court; to do so constitutes a contempt of court.

7.12 Applications:

1B–52 7.12.1 Applications for court orders are governed by Part 23 and the Part 23 Practice Direction. Rule 23.6 and paragraph 2 of the Part 23 Practice Direction set out the matters an application notice must include. The Part 23 Practice Direction states that form N244 may be used, however, parties may prefer to use form PF 244 which is available for use in the Royal Courts of Justice only. To make an application the applicant must file an application notice unless a Rule or Practice Direction permits otherwise or the court dispenses with the requirement for an application notice. Except in cases of extreme urgency, or where giving notice might frustrate the order (as with a search order), an application notice must be served on every party unless a Rule or Practice Direction or a court order dispenses with service (see paragraph 7.12.3 below).A Master will not normally make an order on the basis of correspondence alone.

7.12.2 Applications for remedies which a Master has jurisdiction to grant should ordinarily be made to a Master. The Part 2 Practice Direction (Allocation of cases to levels of Judiciary) contains information about the types of applications which may be dealt with by Masters and Judges. An application notice for hearing by;
    (1) a Judge should be issued in the Listing Office, Room WG8, and
    (2) a Master should be issued in the Masters' Support Unit, Room E16,

and wherever possible should be accompanied by a draft in double spacing of the order sought.

7.12.3 The following are examples of applications which may be heard by a Master where service of the application notice is not required;
    (1) service by an alternative method (Rule 6.8),
    (2) service of a claim form out of the jurisdiction (section III of Part 6),
    (3) default judgment under Rule 12.11(4) or (5),
    (4) substituting a party under Rule 19.1(4),
    (5) permission to issue a witness summons under Rule 34.3(2),
    (6) deposition for use in a foreign court (CPR Part 34 Section II),
    (7) Interim Charging Order (CPR Part 73)), and
    (8) Interim Third Party Debt Order (CPR Part 72).

7.12.4 Paragraph 3 of the Part 23 Practice Direction states in addition that an application may be made without serving an application notice;
    (1) where there is exceptional urgency,
    (2) where the overriding objective is best furthered by doing so,
    (3) by consent of all parties, and
    (4) where a date for a hearing has been fixed and a party wishes to make an application at that hearing but does not have sufficient time to serve an application notice.

With the court's permission an application may also be made without serving an application notice where secrecy is essential.

Paragraph numbers marked with a "+" can be found online and on CD.

7.12.5 Where an application is heard in the absence of one or more of the parties, it is the duty of the party attending to disclose fully all matters relevant to the application, even those matters adverse to the applicant. Failure to do so may result in the order being set aside. In addition any party who has not had notice of a hearing may apply to have the order set aside within 7 days of service of the order made at the hearing.

7.12.6 Where notice of an application is to be given, the application notice should be served as soon as practicable after issue and, if there is to be a hearing, at least 3 clear days before the hearing date, unless the CPR provides a longer period or for permission for shorter service is obtained from a Master. Where there is insufficient time to serve an application notice, informal notice of the application should be given unless the circumstances of the application require secrecy.

7.12.7 The court may deal with an application without a hearing if;
    (1) the parties agree the terms of the order sought,
    (2) the parties agree that the application should be dealt with without a hearing, or
    (3) the court does not consider that a hearing would be appropriate.

7.12.8 The court may deal with an application or part of an application by telephone where it is convenient to do so or in matters of extreme urgency. Applications where there are a number of contested issues or where the hearing is likely to take longer than 45 minutes are not usually suitable for telephone hearings. The hearings most appropriate for a telephone hearing are Case Management Conferences and short applications for, e.g. extensions of time. See paragraph 6 of the Part 23 Practice Direction for the procedure to be followed.

7.12.9 Urgent applications

Applications of extreme urgency may be made out of hours and will be dealt with by the duty judge. An explanation will be required as to why it was not made or could not be made during normal court hours.

7.12.10 Initial contact should be made through the Security Office on 020 7947 6260 who will require the applicant's phone number. The clerk to the duty judge will then contact the applicant and will require the following information;
    (1) the name of the party on whose behalf the application is to be made,
    (2) the name and status of the person making the application,
    (3) the nature of the application,
    (4) the degree of urgency, and
    (5) the contact telephone number(s).

7.12.11 The duty judge will indicate to his/her clerk if s/he thinks it appropriate for the application to be dealt with by telephone or in court. The clerk will inform the applicant and make the necessary arrangements. Where the duty judge decides to deal with the application by telephone, and the facility is available, it is likely that the judge will require a draft order to be faxed to him. An application for an injunction will be dealt with by telephone only where counsel or solicitors represent the applicant.

7.12.12 It is not normally possible to seal an order out of hours. The judge is likely to order the applicant to file the application notice and evidence in support on the same or next working day, together with two copies of the order for sealing.

7.13 Interim remedies:

7.13.1 Interim remedies which the court may grant are listed in Rule 25.1. An order **1B–53** for an interim remedy may be made at any time including before proceedings are started and after judgment has been given. Some of the most commonly sought remedies are injunctions, many of which are heard by the Interim Applications Judge.

Paragraph numbers marked with a "+" can be found online and on CD.

QB GUIDE

7.13.2 Where a Claim has been started, an application on notice for an injunction should be filed in the Listing Office, Room WG8 for a hearing to be listed. If the application is to be made without giving notice to the other parties in the first instance, the Application Notice stamped with the appropriate fee should be brought to the Interim Applications Court, Court 37, together with the evidence in support, a skeleton argument (where appropriate) and two copies of the Order sought. Applications without notice are heard in Court 37 at 10.00am and 2.00pm, and at such other times as the urgency of the application dictates.

7.13.3 Where an injunction is granted without the other party being present it will normally be for a limited period; a return date 1 to 2 weeks ahead. If the injunction order contains an undertaking to issue a Claim Form, this should be issued before the Application Notice for the return date is filed in Room WG8 prior to service.

7.13.4 The Part 25 (Interim Injunctions) Practice Direction at paragraph 4 deals fully with making urgent applications and those without notice, and paragraphs 6, 7 and 8 deal specifically with search orders and freezing injunctions, examples of which are annexed to the Practice Direction.

7.13.5 Certain applications may be heard in private if the judge thinks it appropriate to do so (Rule 39.2(3)). An application to go into private should be made at the outset of the hearing. Certain applications for search orders and freezing injunctions might be appropriate for hearing in private.

7.13.6 Applications for interim payments are heard by a Master. The application notice should be filed in the Masters' Support Unit, Room E14. The requirements for obtaining an order for an interim payment are fully dealt with in the Part 25 (Interim Payments) Practice Direction.

7.14 Interlocutory Orders

1B–54 **7.14.1 Orders made by the Masters**

In the majority of cases Orders by Masters in the Queen's Bench Division are drawn up by one of the parties, who must then arrange to have this sealed by the Judgment & Orders Section (Room E17) and effect service on all other parties. In a limited number of circumstances, e.g. where an order is made of the court's own initiative, the court will draw up, seal and serve an order.

7.14.2 Where an application notice has been issued, and there has been a hearing, the Master will endorse the order in handwriting upon the original application notice. (If the original is not at the hearing, the party drawing up the order will have to ask the Master's permission to treat a photocopy as an original). If the parties have provided a draft order, will endorse this, with or without amendment. The application notice would then be endorsed "Order in the form initialled". If the hearing is one where there is no application notice, for example a Case Management Conference, then the Master will endorse the order on any Notice of the hearing sent by the court, or will use a draft order provided by one of the parties to endorse the order.

7.14.3 The Master will usually direct which party should be responsible for drawing up the Order. In the absence of such direction, this will be the party who issued the application to which the order relates, or the Claimant where the order was made in a case management conference. The Master will also direct a date by which the order should be drawn up, sealed and served. If no date is specified, the order must be served within 14 days of the date it was made.

7.14.4 The party responsible for drawing up the order should lodge with the Judgments & Orders Section:
   (i) The application notice (or other document) endorsed by the Master;
   (ii) Clean copies for sealing, one for each party and one for the court file;
   (iii) Evidence of payment of the court fee

Paragraph numbers marked with a "+" can be found online and on CD.

(2) give judgment for the claimant and grant him summary relief.

8.3.2 Summary relief includes the following;
  (1) a declaration that the statement was false and defamatory of the claimant,
  (2) an order that the defendant publish or cause to be published a suitable correction and apology,
  (3) damages not exceeding £10,000,
  (4) an order restraining the defendant from publishing or further publishing the matter complained of.

8.3.3 Applications for summary disposal are dealt with in Rule 53.2 and paragraphs 5.1 to 5.3 of the Part 53 Practice Direction. Substantial claims and those involving the Police authorities or the Media or those seeking an order restraining publication will be dealt with by the Judge in charge of the Jury list or another designated Judge, and the application notice should be filed in the Listing Office, Room WG8. Applications for summary disposal in other defamation claims may be made at first instance to a Master.

8.3.4 An application notice for summary disposal must state;
  (1) that it is an application for summary disposal made in accordance with section 8 of the Act,
  (2) the matters set out in paragraph 2(3) of the Part 24 Practice Direction, and
  (3) whether or not the defendant has made an offer to make amends under section 2 of the Act, and whether or not it has been withdrawn.

The application may be made at any time after service of the particulars of claim and the provisions of Rule 24.4(1)(a) and (b) do not apply.

8.3.5 Where the court has made an order for summary relief as in 12.7.9(2) above (specifying the date by which the parties should agree the content, time, manner, form and place of publication of the correction and apology) and the parties are unable to comply within the specified time, the claimant must prepare a summary of the court's judgment and serve it on the other parties within 3 days following the date specified in the order for the content to be agreed by the parties.

8.3.6 If the parties are unable to agree the summary, they must within 3 days of its receipt, apply to the court by;
  (1) filing an application notice, and
  (2) and serving on all the other parties a copy of the summary showing the revisions they wish to make to it.

The court (normally the Judge who delivered the judgment) will then settle the summary.

8.4 Statements read in Court

8.4.1 Paragraph 6 of the Practice Direction only applies where a party wishes to accept a Part 36 offer, Part 36 payment or other offer of settlement.

1B–59

8.4.2 An application for permission to make the statement before a Judge in Court may be made before or after acceptance of the Part 36 offer, Part 36 payment or other offer to settle, and should be made in accordance with Part 23 to the Senior Master, or if s/he is not available, to the Practice Master. The application notice, together with a copy of the statement, should be filed in the Masters' Support Unit, Room E16.

8.4.3 Where permission has been given, the parties may take a copy of the order to the Listing Office, Room WG8 for the matter to be listed before the Judge in charge of the Jury List for mention. Otherwise, the Action Department will send the court file to the Listing Office for the matter to be listed.

Paragraph numbers marked with a "+" can be found online and on CD.

QB Guide

SECTION 9

LISTING BEFORE JUDGES

9.1 Responsibility for Listing:

1B–60 9.1.1 At the Case Management Conference hearing the Master will give a period of between one and three months within which the Clerk of the Lists is to arrange the trial. This is known as the "trial window". It should normally start on a Monday. The parties (usually counsel's clerks) attend before the Queen's Bench Listing Officer to agree a "trial period", usually a 3 day period, within which the trial will commence. A Master will not generally order a trial fixture without first consulting the Listing Officer.

9.1.2 The Clerk of the Lists (Room WG3, Royal Courts of Justice) is in general responsible for listing. All applications relating to listing should in the first instance be made to him. Any party dissatisfied with any decision of the Clerk of the Lists may, on one day's notice to all other parties, apply to the Judge in charge of the List.

9.1.3 The application should be made within 7 days of the decision of the Clerk of the Lists and should be arranged through the Queen's Bench Listing Office, Room WG5.

9.2 The Lists:

1B–61 9.2 There are three Lists, namely;
    (1) the Jury List
    (2) the Trial List, and
    (3) the Interim Hearings List.

The Lists are described below.

9.3 The Jury List:

1B–62 9.3.1 Claims for damages for libel and slander (defamation), fraud, malicious prosecution and false imprisonment will be tried by a Judge and jury unless the court orders trial by a Judge alone.

9.3.2 Where a claim is being tried by a Judge and jury it is vitally important that the jury should not suffer hardship and inconvenience by having been misled by an incorrect time estimate. It is therefore essential that time estimates given to the court are accurate and realistic.

9.3.3 Dates for the trial of substantial claims will be fixed by the Listing Office within the trial window after consideration of the parties' views. In such cases the Listing Office may, in addition, impose an alternative reserve date several weeks or months in advance of the trial date, in an endeavour to dispose of claims more quickly and to fill gaps in the List created by frequent settlements. When a reserve date is so allocated a "cut off" date will be stated by the Clerk of the Lists again, after consideration of any views expressed by the parties and having regard to the complexity of the claim and the commitments of counsel and expert witnesses. On the cut off date a decision will be made by the Clerk of the Lists to break or confirm the reserved date for trial.

9.3.4 If a party considers that s/he will suffer significant prejudice as the result of the decision of the Clerk of the Lists relating to either a reserved date or the cut off date s/he may apply to the Judge in charge of the Jury List for reversal or variation of the decision, as set out in paragraph 9.1.2 above.

9.3.5 Jury applications will enter the Interim Warned List not less than two weeks from the date the application notice is filed. Parties may "offer" a date for hearing the application within the week for which they are warned. Subject to court availability,

Paragraph numbers marked with a "+" can be found online and on CD.

the application will be listed on the offered date. Any application not reached on the offered date will return to the current Warned List and will be taken from that List as and when required.

9.3.6 Applications in defamation claims in respect of "meaning" (for an explanation of "meaning" see paragraph 4.1 of the Part 53 Practice Direction) may be listed in private on a specific day allocated for such matters.

9.3.7 Jury applications of length and/or complexity may be fixed by the same manner as set out in paragraph 8.3.6 above. (See the section below on The Trial List for general information about fixing trials).

9.3.8 Applications for directions and other applications within the Master's jurisdiction should firstly be made to a Master unless;
    (1) a direction has been given for the arranging of a trial date, or
    (2) a date has been fixed or a window given for the trial.

Interim applications made after (1) or (2) above should be made to the Judge. The Master will use his/her discretion to refer a matter to the Judge if s/he thinks it right to do so.

9.3.9 If a party believes that the Master is very likely to refer the application to the Judge, for example where there is a substantial application to strike out, the matter should first be referred to the Master or Practice Master on notice to the other parties without waiting for a private room appointment. The Master will then decide whether the application should be referred to the Judge.

9.4 The Trial List:

9.4.1 This List consists of trials (other than Jury trials), preliminary questions or issues ordered to be tried and proceedings to commit for contempt of court. **1B–63**

9.4.2 The Royal Courts of Justice presents unique problems in terms of fixing trial dates. The number of Judges and Masters involved and their geographical location has caused, for the time being at least, a different approach to the fixing of trials in the Chancery and Queen's Bench Divisions.

9.4.3 The requirement of Judges to go on Circuit, sit in the Criminal Division of the Court of Appeal, deal with cases in the Administrative Court and other lists make it difficult to fix dates for trials before particular Judges. Accordingly the following will only apply to the Listing Offices in the Royal Courts of Justice.

9.4.4 At as early an interim stage as practicable, the court will give directions with a view to fixing the trial date or period within which the trial is to begin (the trial window).

9.4.5 For that purpose the court may;
    (1) direct that the trial do not begin earlier than a specified date calculated to provide enough time for the parties to complete any necessary preparations for trial, and/or
    (2) direct that the trial date be within a specified period, and/or
    (3) specify the trial date or window.

9.4.6 If directions under 8.4.5(1) or (2) are given the court will direct the parties to attend upon the Clerk of the Lists in Room W11 at such time and place as may be specified in order to fix the trial date or trial window.

9.4.7 The claimant must, unless some other party agrees to do so, take out an appointment with the Clerk of the Lists within 7 days of obtaining the direction in paragraph 8.4.6 above and give notice of the appointment to all other parties. If an appointment is not taken out within the 7 days, the Listing Office will appoint a date for a listing hearing and give notice of the date to all parties.

Paragraph numbers marked with a "+" can be found online and on CD.

9.4.8 At the listing hearing the Clerk of the Lists will take account, in so far as it is practical to do so, of any difficulties the parties may have as to availability of counsel, experts and witnesses. The Clerk of the Lists will, nevertheless, try to ensure the speedy disposal of the trial by arranging a firm trial date as soon as possible within the trial window or, as the case may be, after the "not before" date directed by the court under paragraph 8.4.5 above. If exceptionally it appears to the Clerk of the Lists at the listing hearing that a trial date cannot be provided within a trial window, s/he may fix the trial date outside the trial period at the first available date. (If a case summary has been prepared (see the Part 29 Practice Direction The Multi-track, paragraphs 5.6 and 5.7) the claimant must produce a copy at the listing hearing together with a copy of particulars of claim and any orders relevant to the fixing of the trial date.)

9.4.9 The Listing Office will notify the Masters' Support Unit of any trial date or trial window given. In accordance with Rule 29.2(3) notice will also be given to all the parties.

9.4.10 A party who wishes to appeal a date or window allocated by the Listing Officer must, within 7 days of the notification, make an application to the Judge nominated by each Division to hear such applications. The application notice should be filed in the Listing Office and served, giving one days notice, on the other parties.

9.5 The Interim Hearings List:

1B–64 9.5.1 This List consists of interim applications, appeals and applications for judgment.

9.5.2 On each Thursday of Term and on such other days as may be appropriate, the Clerk of the Lists will publish a Warned List showing the matters in the Interim Hearings List that are liable to be heard in the following week. Any matters for which no date has been arranged will be liable to appear in the List for hearing with no warning save that given by the Cause List for the following day, posted each afternoon outside Room WG5.

9.5.3 Fixtures will only be given in exceptional circumstances. The parties may by agreement "offer" preferred dates for their matter to be heard, to be taken from the List on designated days, within the week following entry into the Warned List in accordance with Listing Office practice. Matters lasting less than a day are usually offered for two preferred consecutive days and matters lasting more than a day are usually offered for three preferred consecutive days.

9.6 General:

1B–65 9.6.1 In addition to the matters listed to be heard by individual Judges, the Daily Cause List for each day may list "unassigned cases". These are matters from the two Lists to be heard that day but not assigned to a particular Judge. If on any day a matter assigned to a particular Judge proves to be ineffective, s/he will hear an unassigned case. It is hoped that the great majority of unassigned cases will be heard on the day that they are listed but this cannot be absolutely guaranteed. Parties engaged in matters listed as unassigned should attend outside the court where the matter is listed. The Clerk of the Lists will notify them as soon as possible, which Judge is to hear the matter. It is not the practice to list cases as unassigned unless the parties consent and there are no witnesses.

9.6.2 Appeals from Masters' decisions will appear in the Interim Hearings List. The notices of appeal (stamped with the appropriate fee) must be filed in Room WG7. On being notified that the appeal has been set down the solicitors should immediately inform the Clerk of the Lists whether they intend to instruct counsel and, if so, the names of counsel.

9.7 Listing before the Interim Applications Judge:

1B–66 9.7.1 All interim applications on notice to the Interim Applications Judge will initially

Paragraph numbers marked with a "+" can be found online and on CD.

be entered in a List for hearing. They will be listed for hearing in Room E101 or some other nominated venue on any day of the week. Any matter which cannot be disposed of with within one hour will not be taken on the date given for the listed hearing.

9.7.2 If the parties agree that a matter cannot be disposed of within one hour, the applicant/appellant;

    (1) may, on filing the application notice/notice of appeal, seek to have the matter placed directly into the Interim Hearings Warned List, or

    (2) must as soon as practicable and in any event not later than 24 hours before the hearing date transfer the matter into the Interim Hearings List.

If the parties do not so agree, or agree less than 24 hours before the hearing date, the parties must attend on that date.

9.7.3 Matters in the Interim Hearings List will be listed by the Clerk of the Lists in Room WG3, and the parties will be notified by the Listing Office (Room WG5) of the date on which the matter will enter the Warned List. Matters in the Warned List may be listed for hearing at any time on or after that date.

9.7.4 In order to ensure that a complete set of papers in proper order is available for the Judge to read before the hearing, the parties must in advance of the hearing lodge in room WG4 a bundle, properly paginated in date order, and indexed, containing copies of the following documents;

    (1) the application notice or notice of appeal,

    (2) any statements of case,

    (3) copies of all written evidence (together with copy exhibits) on which any party intends to rely, and

    (4) any relevant order made in the proceedings.

9.7.5 The bundle should be agreed if possible. In all but simple cases a skeleton argument and, where that would be helpful, a chronology should also be lodged. (See paragraph 8.9.1 and 8.9.2 below in respect of skeleton arguments.)

9.7.6 Where a date for the hearing has been arranged the bundle must be lodged not later than 3 clear days before the fixed date. For application or appeals where there is no fixed date for hearing, the bundle must be lodged not later than 48 hours after the parties have been notified that the matter is to appear in the Warned List. (For information concerning trial bundles see the Part 39 Practice Direction.)

9.7.7 Except with the permission of the Judge no document may be used in evidence or relied on unless a copy of it has been included in the bundle referred to in paragraph 8.7.6 above. If any party seeks to rely on written evidence which has not been included in the bundle, that party should lodge the original (with copy exhibits) in Room WG5 in advance of the hearing, or otherwise with the Court Associate before the hearing commences.

9.7.8 In appeals from District Judges the provisions of paragraphs 8.7.4, 8.7.5, 8.7.6 and 8.7.7 should be complied with. In addition, the notes (if any) of reasons given by the District Judge, prepared by the District Judge, counsel or solicitors should be lodged.

9.7.9 Subject to the discretion of the Judge, any application or appeal normally made to the Interim Applications Judge may be made in the month of September. In the month of August, except with the permission of a Judge, only appeals in respect of orders;

    (1) to set aside a claim form, or service of a claim form,

    (2) to set aside judgment,

    (3) for stay of execution,

    (4) for any order by consent,

    (5) for permission to enter judgment,

Paragraph numbers marked with a "+" can be found online and on CD.

   (6) for approval of settlements or for interim payment,

   (7) for relief from forfeiture,

   (8) for a Third Party Debt Order,

   (9) for a garnishee order,

   (10) for relief by way of High Court Enforcement Officer's interpleader,

   (11) for relief by way of sheriff's interpleader,

   (12) for transfer to a county court or for trial by Master, or

   (13) for time where time is running in the month of August,

may be heard, and only applications of real urgency will be dealt with, for example, urgent applications in respect of injunctions, or for possession (under RSC O.113 in Schedule 1 to Part 50).

9.7.10 It is desirable, where this is practical, that application notices or notices of appeal are submitted to the Practice Master or a Judge prior to the hearing of the application or appeal so that they can be marked "fit for August" or "fit for vacation". If they are so marked, then normally the Judge will be prepared to hear the application or appeal in August, if marked "fit for August" or in September if marked "fit for vacation". The application to a Judge to have the papers so marked should normally be made in writing, the application shortly setting out the nature of the application or appeal and the reasons why it should be dealt with in August or in September, as the case may be.

9.8 The Lists generally:

1B–67   9.8.1 Where a fixed date has been given it is the duty of the parties to keep the Clerk of the Lists fully informed as to the current position of the matter with regard to negotiations for settlement, whether all aspects of the claim are being proceeded with, an estimate of the length of the hearing, and so on.

9.8.2 Applications for adjournments will not be granted except for the most cogent reasons. If an application is made because solicitors were unaware of the state of the List they may be ordered personally to pay the costs of the application.

9.8.3 A party who seeks to have a hearing before a Judge adjourned must inform the Clerk of the Lists of his/her application as soon as possible. Applications for an adjournment immediately before a hearing begins should be avoided as they take up valuable time which could be used for dealing with effective matters and, if successful, may result in court time being wasted.

9.8.4 If the application is made by agreement, the parties should, in writing, apply to the Clerk of the Lists who will consult the Judge nominated to deal with such matters. The Judge may grant the application on conditions that may include giving directions for a new hearing date.

9.8.5 If the application is opposed the applicant should apply to either the nominated Judge or the Judge to whom the matter has been allocated. A hearing should then be arranged through the Clerk of the Lists. A short summary of the reasons for the adjournment should be lodged with the Listing Office where possible by 10.30am on the day before the application is to be made. Formal written evidence is not normally required.

9.8.6 The applicant will be expected to show that s/he has conducted his/her own case diligently. Any party should take all reasonable steps;

   (1) to ensure his/her case is adequately prepared in sufficient time to enable the hearing to proceed, and

   (2) to prepare and serve any document (including any evidence) required to be served on any other party in sufficient time to enable that party also to be prepared.

9.8.7 If a party or his/her solicitor's failure to take reasonable steps necessitates an

Paragraph numbers marked with a "+" can be found online and on CD.

adjournment, the court may dismiss the application or make any other order including an order penalising the defaulting party in costs.

9.9 Listing Office—general matters:

9.9.1 To facilitate the efficient listing of proceedings, parties are reminded that **1B–68** skeleton arguments concisely summarising each party's submissions must be prepared and filed with the Listing Office;

(1) for trials, not less than 3 days before the trial, and

(2) for substantial applications or appeals, not later than 1 day before the hearing.

9.9.2 If it is anticipated that a Skeleton Argument will be filed late, a letter of explanation should accompany it which will be shown to the Judge before whom the trial or hearing is to take place.

9.9.3 For parties' information, the following targets for the disposal of matters in the Lists have been agreed as set out below:

Interim Hearings Warned List within 4 weeks

From date of fixing;

Trials under 5 days within 4 months

Trials over 5 but under 10 days within 6 months

Trials over 10 but under 20 days within 9 months

Trials over 20 days within 12 months.

SECTION 10

TRIAL, JUDGMENTS AND ORDERS

10.1 General:

10.1.1 The trial of a claim in the Royal Courts of Justice normally takes place before **1B–69** a High Court Judge or a Deputy sitting as a High Court Judge. A Master may assess the damages or sum due to a party under a judgment and, subject to any Practice Direction, may try a claim which is

(1) treated as being allocated to the multi-track because it is proceeding under Part 8, or

(2) with the consent of the parties, allocated to the multi-track under Part 26.

10.1.2 Claims for defamation, malicious prosecution or false imprisonment will be tried by a Judge sitting with a Jury unless the court orders otherwise.

10.2 The Trial:

10.2.1 See paragraph 2.4 above about representation at the trial, and paragraphs **1B–70** 7.11.14 and 7.11.15 above about recording of proceedings.

10.2.2 Rule 39.3 sets out the consequences of a party's failure to attend the trial and see also paragraph 2 of the Part 39 Practice Direction.

10.2.3 The Judge may fix a timetable for evidence and submissions if it has not already been fixed. The claimant's advocate will normally begin the trial with a short opening speech, and the Judge may then allow the other party to make a short speech. Each party should provide written summaries of their opening speeches if the points are not covered in their skeleton arguments.

10.2.4 It is normally convenient for any outstanding procedural matters or applications to be dealt with in the course of, or immediately after, the opening

Paragraph numbers marked with a "+" can be found online and on CD.

speech. In a jury trial such matters would normally be dealt with before the jury is sworn in.

10.2.5 Unless the court orders otherwise, a witness statement will stand as the evidence in chief of the witness, provided s/he is called to give oral evidence. With the court's permission, a witness may amplify his/her witness statement or give evidence in relation to new matters which have arisen since the witness statement was served on the other parties.

10.2.6 The Court Associate will be responsible for any exhibits produced as evidence during the trial. After the trial, the exhibits are the responsibility of the party who produced them. Where a number of physical exhibits are involved, it is desirable, if possible, for the parties to agree a system of labelling and the manner of display, beforehand. The Associate will normally draw the Judgment or order made at the trial.

10.2.7 At a jury trial, it is the parties' responsibility to provide sufficient bundles of documents for the use of the jury.

10.2.8 Facilities are available to assist parties or witnesses with special needs. The Listing Office should be notified of any needs or requirements prior to the trial.

10.3 Judgments and orders:

1B–71 10.3.1 Part 40 deals with judgments and orders. Rule 40.2 contains the standard requirements of a judgment or order and Rule 40.3 contains provisions about drawing them up, see also paragraph 1 of the Part 40B Practice Direction for more information.

10.3.2 Provisions concerning consent orders are contained in Rule 40.6 which sets out in paragraph (3) the types of consent judgments and orders that may be sealed and entered by a court officer, provided;

(1) that none of the parties is a litigant in person, and

(2) the approval of the court is not required by a Rule, a Practice Direction or an enactment.

Other types of consent order require an application to be made to a Master or Judge for approval. It is common for a respondent to a consent order not to attend the hearing but to provide a written consent. The consent may either be written on the document or contained in a letter, and must be signed by the respondent, or where there are solicitors on record as acting for him, by his/her solicitors. Paragraph 3 of the Part 40B Practice Direction contains further information about consent orders.

10.3.3 Rule 40.11 sets out the time for complying with a judgment or order, which is 14 days unless the judgment or order specifies otherwise (for example by instalments), or a Rule specifies a different time, or the judgment or proceedings have been stayed.

10.3.4 The Part 40B Practice Direction contains further information about the effect of non-compliance with a judgment or order (and sets out the penal notice), adjustment of the final judgment sum in respect of interim payments and compensation recovery, and refers to various precedents for types of judgments and orders. See also;

(1) the Part 40 Practice Direction- Accounts and Enquiries, and

(2) the Part 40C Practice Direction- Structured Settlements which sets out the procedure to be followed both on settlement and after trial. Precedents for structured settlement orders, Parts 1 and 2, are annexed to the Practice Direction.

10.3.5 Where judgment is reserved, the Judge may deliver his/her judgment by handing down the written text without reading it out in open court. Where this is the case, the advocates will be supplied with the full text of the judgment in advance of

Paragraph numbers marked with a "+" can be found online and on CD.

delivery. The advocates should then familiarise themselves with the contents and be ready to deal with any points which may arise when the judgment is delivered. Any direction or requirement as to confidentiality must be complied with.

10.3.6 The judgment does not take effect until formally delivered in court. If the judgment is to be handed down in writing copies will then be made available to the parties and, if requested and so far as practicable, to the law reporters and the press.

10.3.7 The Judge will usually direct that the written judgment may be used for all purposes as the text of the judgment, and that no transcript need be made. Where such a direction is made, a copy will be provided to the court's Recording and Transcription Unit, Room WB14, from where further copies may be obtained (and see paragraph 7.11.14 above).

Judgment or order for payment of money on behalf of a child or patient

10.3.8 The usual order made at trial will make provision for any immediate payment to the litigation friend or his/her legal representative and for the balance of the award to be placed to a special investment account pending application to a Master or District Judge (in the case of a child) or the Court of Protection (in the case of a patient) for investment directions. The order will specify the time within which the application should be made. It should also deal with any interest accrued to the date of Judgment, and or any interest which accrues in the future. An Order should also refer to Majority directions, and decisions on investment of the fund in Court.

10.3.9 The litigation friend or his/her legal representative should then write to or make an appointment with;
(1) in the case of a child, the Master or District Judge in accordance with paragraph 6.8.6 above and the Part 21 Practice Direction, or
(2) in the case of a patient, the Court of Protection in accordance with paragraph 11 of the Part 21 Practice Direction.

10.3.10 10.3.10 Where after trial the Judge has found in favour of a child or patient, instead of judgment being given, the proposed award of damages may be paid by way of a structured settlement. The structure must be approved by the Judge, and in the case of a patient must also be approved by the Court of Protection. (See also the Part 40C Practice Direction—Structured Settlements.)

Provisional damages

10.3.11 Rule 41.1 defines an award of provisional damages. Where there is a chance that a claimant may in the future develop a particular disease or deterioration as a result of the event giving rise to the claim, s/he can seek an award of damages for personal injury on the assumption that s/he will not develop the disease or deterioration, with provision for him to make a further application within the time specified in the order, if s/he does so develop the disease or deterioration.

10.3.12 The Part 41 Practice Direction gives further information about provisional damages awards and, in particular, about the preservation of the case file for the time specified in the order for making a further application, and the documents to be included in the case file. A precedent for a provisional damages judgment is annexed to the Practice Direction.

SECTION 11

APPEALS

11.1 General:

11.1.1 Appeals are governed by Part 52 and the Part 52 Practice Direction. The **1B–72** contents of Part 52 are divided into three sections; I—General Rules about Appeals, II—Special Provisions applying to the Court of Appeal, and III—Provisions about reopening Appeals.

Paragraph numbers marked with a "+" can be found online and on CD.

11.1.2 The Practice Direction is divided into four sections; I—General Provisions about Appeals, II—General Provisions about Statutory Appeals and Appeals by way of Case Stated, III—Provisions about Specific Appeals and IV—Provisions about Reopening Appeals.

11.1.3 The following paragraphs apply to orders made after 2nd May 2000 and are intended only to draw parties' attention to the basic provisions for bringing an appeal in or from the Queen's Bench Division. For further information about these procedures and about other specific types of appeal, parties should refer to Part 52, the Practice Direction and the Civil Appeals Guide.

For the purposes of Part 52 and the Part 52 Practice Direction, except where the meaning indicates otherwise, the term "Judge" includes a Master or District Judge.

11.1.4 Routes of Appeal—An appeal will lie from the decision of:

A District Judge of a county court; to a Circuit Judge
A Master or a District Judge of a District Registry of the High Court; to a High Court Judge
A Circuit Judge; to a High Court Judge
A High Court Judge; to the Court of Appeal,

unless the decision to be appealed is a final decision in a claim allocated to the multi-track or in specialist proceedings (under the Companies Acts 1985 or 1989 or to which Sections I, II or III of Part 57 or any of Parts 58 to 63 apply), in which case the appeal will lie to the Court of Appeal.

11.1.5 Unless the lower court or the appeal court orders otherwise, filing an Appellant's Notice does not operate as a stay of any order or decision of the lower court. A stay must be specifically sought either in the Appellant's Notice or separately in accordance with Part 23.

11.2 Permission to appeal:

1B–73 11.2.1 Permission to appeal is required to appeal from a decision of a Judge in a county court or the High Court, except where the appeal is in respect of;

(1) a committal order,
(2) a refusal to grant habeas corpus,
(3) a secure accommodation order made under s.25 of The Children Act 1989,
(4) certain statutory appeals, or
(5) where a Practice Direction so provides.

11.2.2 Applicants are encouraged to seek permission at the hearing at which the decision to be appealed against is made. If it is not, or if it is sought and refused, permission should be sought from the court appealed to ("the appeal court"). Where permission is sought from the appeal court it must be requested in the Appellant's Notice. Permission may be granted, or refused, or granted in part (whether as to a part of the order, a ground of appeal or an issue) and refused as to the rest. (See paragraphs 4.1 to 4.24 of the Practice Direction in respect of permission to appeal.)

11.2.3 Refusal of permission at a hearing is, effectively, the end of the road (s.54(4) of the Access to Justice Act 1999 and paragraph 4.8 of the Practice Direction), save in extremely rare cases where the Court of Appeal or the High Court may reopen a final appeal or refusal of permission (52.17).

11.2.4 Where the decision sought to be appealed to the Court of Appeal was itself made on appeal to a county court or the High Court, permission must be sought from the Court of Appeal (52.13(1)). The Court of Appeal will not grant permission unless an important point of principle or practice is involved, or there is some other compelling reason.

11.2.5 Court Appeals Listing Office, Room WG7. An application for permission to

Paragraph numbers marked with a "+" can be found online and on CD.

appeal to the Court of Appeal is made by filing an Appellant's Notice in the Civil Appeals Office Registry, Room E307.

11.2.6 Before an application for permission can be considered, whether on the papers or at a hearing, the documents in support of the appeal must be lodged. The documents listed at section 11 of the Appellant's Notice should be lodged when the Appellant's Notice is filed. If the appellant needs more time to lodge the documents he/she must complete section 11 to obtain an extension of up to 14 days. This extension may be granted by a court officer. If the appellant is still unable to obtain the documents he/she may apply in writing for a further extension. This may also be granted by a court officer but any subsequent application for an extension must be made to a Judge.

11.2.7 Where the documents are not lodged in accordance with the extended time period and no further application for an extension is made, the matter will be placed in a Dismissal list before the Judge in charge of the List on notice to the appellant.

11.2.8 Where permission to appeal is being sought from the Court of Appeal, the Appellant must file the documents set out in paragraph 5.6, 5.6A, 5.9 and 5.12 of the Part 52 practice direction.

11.2.9 An application for permission is normally first considered on the papers without a hearing, although the application may be listed for a hearing at the outset, if the appellant requests it (52.3.5). Where permission is refused on the papers, the applicant may request that it be reconsidered at a hearing. The request should be made within 7 days of service of the notice of refusal.

11.2.10 The court will give notice of the permission hearing to the parties. A respondent who volunteers written submissions or attends the permission hearing will not normally be allowed his/her costs. If the court requests submissions from or the attendance of a Respondent, he/she will normally be allowed his/her costs if permission is refused (paragraphs 4.22–4.24 of the Part 52 practice direction).

11.3 Notices:

11.3.1 Rule 52.4 and paragraph 5 of the Practice Direction deal with the Appellant's **1B–74** Notice. The appellant must file 3 copies of his/her notice at the appeal court either within a period specified by the court appealed from ("the lower court") or, if no such period is specified, within 21 days of the date of the decision appealed from. The notice must be served on each respondent as soon as practicable, and in any event not later than 7 days after it is filed.

11.3.2 A respondent must file a notice where;
    (1) he/she also wishes to appeal the lower court's decision,
    (2) he/she wishes to uphold the decision of the lower court for different or additional reasons to those given by the lower court, or
    (3) he/she is seeking permission to appeal from the appeal court.

11.3.3 The Respondent's Notice must be filed either within a period specified by the lower court or, if no such period is specified, within 14 days of;
    (1) the date the respondent is served with the appellant's notice where
        (a) permission to appeal was given by the lower court or
        (b) permission to appeal is not required,
    (2) the date the respondent is served with notification that the appeal court has given the appellant permission to appeal, or
    (3) the date the respondent is served with notification that the application for permission to appeal and the appeal itself are to be heard together.

(Paragraph 7 of the Part 52 practice direction deals with the Respondent's Notice.)

11.3.4 The notices to be used are as follows;

Paragraph numbers marked with a "+" can be found online and on CD.

(1) the Appellant's Notice—form N161, and

(2) the Respondent's Notice—form N162.

There is a leaflet available from the Listing Office, Room WG7 entitled "I want to appeal", which provides information about High Court appeals.

11.4 Procedure where permission is obtained:

1B–75 11.4.1 Where permission to appeal has been granted by the appeal court, the appellant must serve the appeal bundle on each respondent within 7 days of receiving the order giving permission to appeal.

11.4.2 The Appellant must include in the appeal bundle the Respondent's Notice and a skeleton argument (if any), any relevant transcripts of evidence, any documents which the parties have agreed are relevant and the order granting permission. If the order granting permission was made at an oral hearing, a transcript or note of the judgment should also be lodged. Where permission was refused in respect of a particular issue, any papers relating solely to that issue should be removed from the bundle. See paragraph 15.4 for more information on preparing the appeal bundle.

11.4.3 The High Court Appeals Office will notify the parties of either the hearing date or of the "listing window" during which the appeal is likely to be heard. Where the appeal is in the Court of Appeal, the Civil Appeals Office Registry will notify the parties of the "hear by" date and will send the appellant an Appeal Questionnaire. Paragraph 15.7 contains more information about listing in the Court of Appeal.

11.4.4 The Appeal Questionnaire must be completed and returned within 14 days of the date of the notification letter. The Appeal Questionnaire must contain the matters set out in paragraphs 6.5 and 6.6 of the Part 52 practice direction.

11.4.5 In the Court of Appeal, all the papers required for the hearing must be filed at least 7 days before the hearing. For an appeal to the High Court, all papers should be lodged not later than [2 days] before the hearing

11.5 Disposing of applications for permission and appeals where the Appellant does not wish to proceed:

1B–76 11.5.1 The following does not apply where any party to the proceedings is a child or patient.

11.5.2 The appellant may request that his/her application or appeal be dismissed. The request must state that the appellant is not a child or patient. If the request includes a statement from the respondent that he/she is not a child or patient and consents to the dismissal order being made without costs, the order will be so made. Otherwise the dismissal order will be made on the basis that the appellant pays the costs of the application or appeal.

11.6 Appeals in cases of contempt of court:

1B–77 11.6.1 Appellant's Notices which by paragraph 21.4 of the Part 52 Practice Direction (appeals in cases of contempt of court (s.13 of the Administration of Justice Act 1960)) are required to be served on "the court from whose order or decision the appeal is brought". In the case of appeals from the Queen's Bench Division, the Senior Master of the Queen's Bench Division should be served but service may be effected by leaving a copy of the Appellant's Notice with the High Court Appeals Office in Room WG7, Royal Courts of Justice, Strand, London WC2A 2LL.

Paragraph numbers marked with a "+" can be found online and on CD.

SECTION 12

ENFORCEMENT

12.1 General:

12.1.1 Enforcement in the High Court is governed by CPR Parts 70 and 74 together **1B–78** with RSC Orders 17, 45 to 47 and 52 as in Schedule 1 to the CPR.

12.1.2 RSC O. 45 deals with enforcement generally. A judgment or order for payment of money (other than into court) may be enforced by a writ of Fieri Facias, Third Party Debt Order Third Party Debt Order, a Charging Order or the appointment of a receiver. A judgment or order to do or abstain from doing an act may be enforced by a writ of sequestration (with the permission of the court) or an order of committal. A judgment or order for possession of land may be enforced by a writ of possession, and a judgment or order for delivery of goods without the alternative of paying their value by a writ of specific delivery. In each case, where RSC O.45 r.5 applies enforcement may also be by a writ of sequestration or an order of committal.

12.2 Writs of execution:

12.2.1 RSC O.46 deals with writs of execution generally. Rules 2 and 3 set out the **1B–79** circumstances when permission to issue a writ is necessary. Rule 4 contains provisions for making an application for permission. Rule 5 deals with applications for permission to issue a writ of sequestration. RSC O. 47 contains provisions concerning writs of Fieri Facias. Forms of writs of execution may be used as follows:

(1) writs of fieri facias in form Nos. 53 to 63,
(2) writs of delivery in form Nos. 64 and 65,
(3) writs of possession in form Nos. 66 and 66A,
(4) writ of sequestration in form No 67,
(5) writ of restitution in form No 68,
(6) writ of assistance in form No 69.

12.2.2 With certain exceptions, writs of execution issued in the Royal Courts of Justice are executed by the High Court Enforcement Officer. RSC O.46 r.6 sets out the provisions for issue of writs of execution. In the Queen's Bench Division writs of execution are issued in the Central Office in Room E15–E17. Before the Writ can be sealed for issue, a signed praecipe for its issue must be filed in one of forms PF 86 to 90, as appropriate, stamped with the appropriate fee. A copy of the judgment or order requiring enforcement should also be provided.

12.2.3 On an application for permission to issue a writ of possession under RSC O.45 r.3(2), if the property consists of a house of which various parts are sublet to, or in the occupation of, different persons, the evidence in support should show the nature and length of the notice which has been given to the various occupiers. Where the defendant or any other persons are in actual possession of the premises of which possession is sought, the evidence must contain the following information:

(1) whether the premises or any part of it is residential,
(2) if so,
   (a) what is the rateable value of the residential premises, and
   (b) whether it is let furnished or unfurnished and, if furnished, the amount of furniture it contains, and
(3) any other matters that will assist the Master in deciding whether any occupier is protected by the Rent Acts.

12.2.4 Where a party wishes to enforce a judgment or order expressed in a foreign currency by the issue of a writ of fieri facias, the praecipe must be endorsed with the following certificate:

"I/We certify that the rate current in London for the purchase of (state the unit

Paragraph numbers marked with a "+" can be found online and on CD.

of foreign currency in which the judgment is expressed) at the close of business on (state the nearest preceding date to the date of issue of the writ of fieri facias) was ( ) to the £ sterling and at this rate the sum of (state amount of the judgment debt in the foreign currency) amounts to £ ."

The schedule to the writ of fieri facias should be amended;

(1) showing the amount of the judgment or order in the foreign currency at paragraph 1.

(2) inserting a new paragraph 2. as follows: "2. Amount of the sterling equivalent as appears from the certificate endorsed on the praecipe for issue of the writ £ "

(3) renumbering the remaining paragraphs accordingly.

The writ of fieri facias will then be issued for the sterling equivalent of the judgment expressed in foreign currency as appears from the certificate.

12.2.5 County Court judgments or orders to which Article 8(1) of the High Court and County Courts Jurisdiction Order 1991 applies may be enforced in the High Court, and since 26th April 1999, any County Court judgment for over £600 may be transferred to the High Court for enforcement by a High Court Enforcement Officer (except where it is a judgment arising from a regulated agreement under the Consumer Credit Act).

12.2.6 The party seeking enforcement should obtain from the appropriate county court a certificate of the judgment of the county court in compliance with CCR O. 22 r.8(1A) (in Schedule 2 to the CPR), setting out details of the judgment or order to be enforced, sealed with the seal of that court and dated and signed by an officer of that court and stating on its face that it is granted for the purpose of enforcing the judgment or order by execution against goods in the High Court. Form N293A is a "Combined Certificate of Judgment and Request for Writ of Fieri Facias" and should be used.

12.2.7 A correctly completed form N293A together with a copy should be filed in Room E15–E17 where the court officer will;

(1) allocate a reference number,

(2) date seal the Certificate and copy, returning the original to the party and retaining the copy, and

(3) enter the proceedings in a register kept for that purpose.

The certificate shall be treated for enforcement purposes as a High Court judgment and interest at the appropriate rate shall run from the date of the Certificate.

12.2.8 The title of all subsequent documents shall be set out as follows:

"
                                        IN THE HIGH COURT OF JUSTICE
                                        QUEEN'S BENCH DIVISION
                                        High Court Claim No.
                                        County Court Claim No.

(Sent from the [   ] County Court by Certificate dated (*date*))

Claimant

Defendant   "

When the writ of fieri facias is issued, the Certificate of judgment retained by the

Paragraph numbers marked with a "+" can be found online and on CD.

party shall be date sealed by the court officer on the bottom left hand corner and endorsed with the designation of the Sheriff to whom the writ is directed.

12.2.9 The Sheriffs Lodgement Centre at 20–21 Tooks Court, London EC4A 1LB provides a service for arranging transfer up of county court judgments. (A helpline is provided on 020 7205 2555)

12.2.10 It is important to remember in these cases that although any application for a stay of execution may be made to a Master in the High Court by application notice filed in accordance with Part 23, all other applications for enforcement or other relief must be made to the issuing county court. This practice is followed in the district registries with such variations as circumstances require.

12.2.11 When a writ of execution has been issued in the Royal Courts of Justice it may then be delivered to the Sheriffs Lodgement Centre. Value Added Tax is payable in addition to the High Court Enforcement Officer's fee on the services for which the fee is payable, and must be paid at the time of delivery of the writ. If the goods, chattels and property to be seized in execution are not within Greater London, the High Court Enforcement Officer will direct the writ to a High Court Enforcement Officer who is authorised to act in the appropriate district. Goods, which may not be seized in execution of a writ, are set out in s.138(3A) of the Supreme Court Act 1981 as follows:

(1) such tools, books, vehicles and other items of equipment as are necessary to that person for use personally by him in his/her employment, business or vocation,

(2) such clothing, bedding, furniture, household equipment and provisions as are necessary for satisfying the basic domestic needs of that person and his/her family,

(3) any money, bank notes, bills of exchange, promissory notes, bonds, specialties or securities for money belonging to that person.

12.2.12 When first executing a writ of fieri facias the High Court Enforcement Officer will deliver to the debtor or leave at each place where execution is levied a notice of seizure in form No 55. This is commonly known as "walking possession" and the notice explains to the debtor the situation with regard to the goods seized and what s/he then has to do.

12.2.13 After execution of a writ of execution, the High Court Enforcement Officer will endorse on the writ a statement of the manner in which s/he has executed it and will send a copy of the statement to the party issuing the writ.

12.3 Interpleader proceedings (RSC O.17):

12.3.1 Where a person is under liability in respect of a debt or property and has **1B–80** been, or expects to be claimed against by two or more persons claiming the same debt or property, if the person under liability does not dispute the debt or claim the property, s/he may apply to the court for relief by way of interpleader, i.e. for the entitlement of the persons claiming the same debt or property to be established in separate proceedings between them.

12.3.2 Where the High Court Enforcement Officer has seized goods in execution and a person other than the person against whom the writ of execution was issued wishes to claim the goods seized, s/he must give notice of his/her claim to the High Court Enforcement Officer, including in his/her notice a statement of his/her address which will be his/her address for service. The High Court Enforcement Officer will then give notice of that claim to the judgment creditor on whose behalf the goods were seized, in form PF 23. The notice requires the judgment creditor to state whether s/he admits or disputes the claim. The claimant must do so within 7 days of receipt of the High Court Enforcement Officer's notice and may use form PF 24 to do so.

12.3.3 Where the judgment creditor admits the claim, the High Court Enforcement Officer will withdraw from possession of the goods and may apply under RSC O.17

Paragraph numbers marked with a "+" can be found online and on CD.

r.2(4) for an order to restrain a claim being brought against him for having taken possession of the goods. Where the claimant disputes the claim, the High Court Enforcement Officer may apply for interpleader relief. An application for interpleader relief if made in existing proceedings is made by an application in accordance with Part 23, otherwise it is made by the issue of a Part 8 claim form.

12.3.4 The Master may deal with the claims summarily, or may direct an issue to be tried between the parties in dispute (see RSC O.17 r.5) or make such other order as is appropriate.

12.4 Examination of judgment debtor (Part 71):

1B–81 12.4.1 Where a person ("the judgment creditor") has obtained a judgment or order for payment of a sum of money against a person ("the judgment debtor"), the judgment creditor may apply for an order requiring the judgment debtor to attend to be orally examined concerning his assets and means. If the judgment debtor is a company or corporation, the court will order a named officer of the company or corporation to attend for examination. In the case of a judgment or order which is not for payment of a sum of money, the court may make an order for the attendance of the party liable for his examination on such questions as may be specified in the order.

12.4.2 An application for an order under Part 71 should be made in accordance with Part 23 without notice to any other party. The application must be supported by evidence giving details of the judgment or order, including the amount still owing, and showing that the judgment creditor is entitled to enforce the judgment or order. Where the judgment debtor is a company or corporation the evidence must give details of the officer to be examined. Form PF 98 may be used as a precedent for the evidence in support. Where a judgment creditor has obtained judgments in several different proceedings against the same judgment debtor, only one application need be made, setting out in the body of the application details of all the judgments on which examination is sought.

12.4.3 The examination will take place before a Master, Registrar, district judge or nominated officer, as may be ordered, and will normally be at the court where the least expense will be incurred, usually the county court for the area where the judgment debtor lives. If a different court is requested by the applicant the reason why should be given in the application notice.

12.4.4 The application notice/evidence should be filed in the Masters' Support Unit Room E16 for consideration by a Master who will, if satisfied, make the order sought. Where the examination is to take place in a county court, the judgment creditor should lodge a copy of the order with the county court and obtain an appointment for the examination. If the examination is to take place in the Royal Courts of Justice, the order should be taken to Room E17 where the appointment will be endorsed on the order. In the Central Office the officers are nominated at the discretion of the Senior Master and their names may be obtained from Room E17.

12.4.5 The order (endorsed with the penal notice as set out in paragraph 9.1 of the Part 40B Practice Direction) together with details of the appointment must be served personally on the judgment debtor or on the officer of the judgment debtor company or corporation to be examined. A judgment debtor should be offered his/her conduct money, *i.e.* expenses of travelling to and from the examination and of attending to give evidence.

12.4.6 The officer conducting the examination will take down, or arrange to have taken down in writing the judgment debtor's statement. The officer will read the statement to the judgment debtor and will ask him or her to sign it. If he or she refuses to do so the officer will sign the statement. If the judgment debtor refuses to answer any question or if any other difficulties arise, the matter will be referred to the Interim Applications Judge in Court 37.

Paragraph numbers marked with a "+" can be found online and on CD.

s/he will make an order in form No 83 for a hearing to take place in respect of the application for the appointment of the receiver and granting an injunction meanwhile.

12.7.5 If the judgment creditor does not seek an injunction, the application notice should be filed and served together with the evidence in support (as in paragraph 11.7.3 above but without paragraph (6)).

12.7.6 At the hearing of the application to appoint the receiver, the Master will, if s/he thinks fit, make an order in form No 84. A copy of the order appointing the receiver shall be served by the judgment creditor on the receiver and all other parties to the proceedings.

12.7.7 Where a receiver has been ordered to give security under RSC O.30 r.2, the judgment creditor should obtain an appointment before the Master who made the order appointing the receiver, to settle the form and amount of the security. Unless otherwise ordered, the security will be in the form of a guarantee. The judgment creditor should have prepared a draft form of guarantee for the Master to approve at the appointment. Form PF 30CH may be used as a precedent for the guarantee.

12.7.8 RSC O.30 r.3 deals with the remuneration of the receiver which may either be assessed by the Master or referred to a costs judge. RSC O.30 r.5 contains the provisions for submitting the receiver's accounts.

12.8 Committals, etc. (RSC O.52):

12.8.1 The court has power to punish contempt of court by an order of committal to prison or by other means. These may be by ordering the payment of a fine, by the issue of a writ of sequestration, or by making a hospital or guardianship order under certain provisions of the Mental Health Act 1983. Committal applications under RSC O.52 r.4 are always dealt with by a High Court Judge. The following provisions apply to applications made under RSC O.52 r.4.

1B–85

12.8.2 The application should be made in existing proceedings by filing an application notice. If not in existing proceedings, a Part 8 Claim Form should be issued (see paragraphs 2.1 and 2.2 of the practice direction - Committal Applications). The Claim Form or application notice must contain a prominent notice stating the possible consequences of the court making a committal order. The notice is annexed at the end of the practice direction.

12.8.3 Evidence in support of a committal application must be by affidavit and, together with the Part 8 Claim Form or application notice, must be served personally on the person sought to be committed giving 14 days notice unless otherwise directed by the court (paragraph 4.2 of the practice direction). A date for the hearing must be obtained from the Listing Office, Room WG8 and endorsed on or served with the Claim Form or application notice.

12.8.4 Committal proceedings will normally be heard in public, but see RSC O.52 r.6 which sets out certain types of cases which may be heard in private, and see paragraph 9 of the Practice Direction.

12.8.5 Committal proceedings will normally be heard in public, but see RSC O.52 r.6 which sets out certain types of cases which may be heard in private (although brief details of the case must be read out in public) and see paragraph 9 of the Practice Direction.

12.8.6 Where the court makes a finding of contempt, details of the contempt and of the order or undertaking breached (where appropriate) must be set out in the order. The term of any period of committal must be stated in the order and must not exceed two years. A fine must be expressed as payable to Her Majesty the Queen and the order must state the amount of the fine and the date and time within which it must be paid. A contemnor and his solicitors will be notified separately as to how the

Paragraph numbers marked with a "+" can be found online and on CD.

fine should be paid. A precedent of the order is in form No. 85 and will normally be drawn by the court.

12.8.7 When an order for committal to prison is made, the court will issue a warrant to the Tipstaff authorising him to convey the contemnor to the appropriate prison. A copy of the order should be served on the prison governor and the Official Solicitor. RSC O.52 r.8 deals with the discharge of a person committed.

12.9 Execution against property of Foreign or Commonwealth States:

1B–86   12.9.1 In cases where judgment has been obtained against a foreign or Commonwealth State and it is sought to execute the judgment by a writ of fieri facias, a charging order or a Third Party Debt Order, the following provisions apply:

(1) Before the writ of fieri facias is issued, the Master must be informed in writing and his/her direction sought. In cases where an application is to be made for a charging order to show cause or a Third Party to show cause, the evidence in support of the application must include a statement that the execution sought is against a foreign or Commonwealth State.

(2) The Master, having been so informed will, as soon as practicable, inform the Foreign and Commonwealth Office ("FCO") of the application and will not permit the issue of a writ of fieri facias, nor grant an order to show cause until the FCO has been so informed. The Protocol Division of the Head of Diplomatic Missions and International Organisations Unit of the FCO may be contacted by telephone on 020 7008 0991 or by Fax on 020 7008 0978.

(3) Having regard to all the circumstances of the case, the Master may postpone the decision whether to issue the writ or grant the order to show cause for so long as s/he considers reasonable for the purpose of enabling the FCO to furnish further information relevant to his/her decision, but not for longer than 3 days from the time of his/her contacting the FCO. In the event that no further information is received from the FCO within 24 hours of its being informed, then the writ of fieri facias may be issued or the order to show cause may be sealed without further delay.

12.10 Recovery of enforcement costs:

1B–87   12.10.1 Subsection (3) of section 15 of the Courts and Legal Services Act 1990 enables a person taking steps to enforce a money judgment in the High Court to recover the costs of any previous attempt to enforce that judgment. Subsection (4) of section 15 excludes costs that the court considers to have been unreasonably incurred.

12.10.2 The application for an enforcement costs order is made to a Master and should be made in accordance with Part 23 but the application notice need not be served on the judgment debtor. The application will normally be dealt with without a hearing and must be supported by evidence substantially as set out in form PF 205. The deponent should exhibit sufficient vouchers, receipts or other documents as are reasonably necessary to verify the amount of the costs of previous attempts to enforce the judgment.

12.10.3 If the Master is satisfied that such an order is appropriate, s/he will make an order for payment of the amount of such costs as s/he considers may be recoverable under subsection (3) of section 15. If the amount of such costs is less than that claimed by the judgment creditor, the Master may either disallow the balance or give directions for a detailed assessment or other determination of the balance. If after assessment or other determination it appears that the judgment creditor is entitled to further costs beyond those originally allowed, s/he may issue a further writ of fieri facias or take other lawful steps to enforce those costs. Interest on the costs runs either from the date the Master made the enforcement costs order or from the date of the costs certificate.

12.11 Enforcement of Magistrates' Courts' orders:

1B–88   12.11.1 The Magistrates' Courts Act 1980, s.87 provides that payment of a sum ordered to be paid on a conviction of a magistrates' court may be enforced by the

Paragraph numbers marked with a "+" can be found online and on CD.

High Court or a county court (otherwise than by the issue of a writ of fieri facias or other process against goods or by imprisonment or attachment of earnings) as if the sum were due to the clerk of the magistrates' court under a judgment of the High Court or county court, as the case may be.

12.11.2 In the Central Office, the application is made to a Master and should be made in accordance with Part 23. Where enforcement is sought by a Third Party Debt Order or charging order to show cause, the application will normally be dealt with without a hearing. Otherwise the application notice and evidence in support should be served on the defendant.

12.11.3 The application must be supported by a witness statement or affidavit in a form appropriate to the type of execution sought and must have exhibited to it the authority of the magistrates' court to take the proceedings which will recite the conviction, the amount outstanding and the nature of the proceedings authorised to be taken (Magistrates Courts Forms Rules 1981, Form 63).

12.11.4 The application notice and evidence in support together with an additional copy of the exhibit should be filed in Room E15 where it will be assigned a reference number from the register kept for that purpose. The Master according to the type of enforcement sought will then deal with the matter.

12.11.5 This practice will also be followed in the District Registries with such variations as circumstances may render necessary.

12.12 Enforcement of Foreign Judgments and Enforcement of High Court Judgments Abroad

12.12.1 CPR 74 deals with enforcement of judgments in different jurisdictions. **1B–89** Section 1 covers enforcement in England & Wales of judgments of foreign courts.

12.12.2 If a foreign court is not a party to an agreement with this country on mutual recognition and enforcement of judgments, then a fresh action will need to be brought based on that foreign judgment. Such an action can usually be made by a Part 8 claim.

12.12.3 Section 1 of the rule covers enforcement of judgments of foreign courts covered by the Administration of Justice Act 1933 ("the 1933 Act"), the Foreign Judgments (Reciprocal Enforcement) Act 1933 ("the 1933 Act"), the Civil Jurisdiction and Judgments Act 1982 ("the 1982 Act") and the Council Regulation (EC) No. 44/2001 of 22nd December 2000 ("the Judgments Regulation").

12.12.4 A list of the countries that are covered by each of the various Acts and the Judgments Regulation is set out in Her Majesty's Court Service 'Notes for Guidance' on the above Acts and Regulation, which can be obtained from the Judgments & Orders Section of the Action Department of the Central Office (Room E17). This also contains the standard forms used and sets out the procedure for applications for registration.

Reciprocal enforcement; the Administration of Justice Act 1920 the Foreign Judgments (Reciprocal Enforcement) Act 1933, the Civil Jurisdiction and Judgments Act 1982 and the Judgments Regulation.

12.12.5 CPR 74.4 sets out how an application for registration of a foreign judgment in the High Court under the 1920, 1933 or 1982 Acts under the Judgments Regulation may be made. The application should be made without notice being served on any other party, but the Master may direct that a Part 8 Claim Form should be issued and served.

12.12.6 CPR 74.4 (2)–(6) sets out what the evidence in support of the application should contain or have exhibited to it. The foreign judgment will be registered in the foreign currency in which it is expressed and must not be converted into Sterling in

Paragraph numbers marked with a "+" can be found online and on CD.

the evidence in support. When it comes to enforcing the foreign judgment, the amount should then be converted in accordance with the instructions set out above in paragraph 11 in respect of the type of enforcement sought.

12.12.7 The order giving permission to register the judgment must be drawn up by, or on behalf of the judgment creditor and will be entered in the Register of Judgments kept in the Action Department Room E17 of the Central Office for that purpose. The order will usually contain a direction that the costs of and caused by the application and the registration be assessed and added to the judgment as registered. The Order for registration of the judgment must state the matters set out in CPR 74.6 (3) including the right of the judgment debtor to apply, and the time within which s/he may do so, to have the registration set aside. The notice must be served on the judgment debtor in accordance with CPR 74.6 (1).

12.12.8 An application to set aside the registration of a judgment under CPR 74.7 (1) must be made in accordance with Part 23 and be supported by a witness statement or affidavit.

12.12.9 Section 2 of CPR 74 covers enforcement in foreign countries of judgments of the High Court and County Court of England & Wales. A judgment creditor who wishes to enforce such a judgment abroad must apply for a certified copy of the judgment.

12.12.10 Section 3 of CPR 74 deals with enforcement of UK Judgments in other parts of the UK. A person who wishes to enforce a judgment of the High Court or County Court of England & Wales in another part of the UK may apply for a certified copy of the judgment.

12.12.11 An application for a certified copy of a judgment entered in the High Court may be made without notice and must be supported by evidence, in accordance with CPR 74.13 for enforcement of High Court and County judgments in foreign countries, and in accordance with CPR 74.17 or 18 for enforcement of High Court and County judgments in other parts of the UK. The certified copy will be endorsed with a certificate signed by the Master. The forms of certificate are included in the 'Notes for Guidance' referred to in paragraph 11.12.4 above. Where the application was made under s. 10 of the Foreign Judgments (Reciprocal Enforcement) Act 1933, an additional certificate will be issued and signed by the Master [as in form PF 155.] Judgment creditors who intend to seek enforcement abroad should ensure that their judgment is endorsed as follows:

"This judgment carries interest from (date) at the rate of 8% per annum in accordance with the provisions of the Judgments Act 1838".

12.12.12 An application may also be made for registration in the High Court of a judgment given by a court in another part of the UK.

12.12.13 The certificate must be filed for registration in Room E15–E17 in the Action Department within 6 months from the date of its issue. Under paragraph 9 of schedule 6 to the Act of 1982 an application may be made to stay the enforcement of the certificate. The application may be made without notice being served on any other party supported by a witness statement or affidavit stating that the applicant is entitled and intends to apply to the judgment court to set aside or stay the judgment.

Applications under s.18 of the Act of 1982; judgment containing non-money provisions: The procedure is set out in CPR 74.16(3).

12.12.14 The certificates will be entered in the register of certificates in respect of judgments ordered to be registered under CPR 74 PD 3 kept in the Central Office for that purpose.

Enforcement of European Community judgments

12.12.15 Section 4 of CPR deals with enforcement of European Community judgments in England and Wales, that is, judgments not of the national courts of

Paragraph numbers marked with a "+" can be found online and on CD.

Member States but rather the judgments of the courts and institutes of the community itself.

12.12.16 CPR 74.19 An application for registration may be made without notice being served on any other party and must be supported by written evidence containing or having exhibited to it the matters referred to in CPR 74.21 (1).

12.12.17 The order for registration must contain the information and exhibit the documents required by CPR 74.22. The order for registration will be entered in the register of the Judgments and Orders kept in the Action Department Room E17, Central Office for that purpose. The registration order must be served on every person against whom judgment was given.

12.12.18 An application to vary or cancel a registration under the provisions of CPR 74.23 shall be made by application notice in accordance with Part 23, supported by written evidence, and must be made within 28 days of service of the registration order.

Enforcement of recommendations etc. under the Merchant Shipping (Liner Conferences) Act 1982

12.12.19 Applications under s. 9 of the Act of 1982 for registration of a recommendation, determination or award, are dealt with by a Commercial Judge and shall be made by the issue of a Part 8 Claim Form. The application should be supported by evidence in accordance with CPR 74 PD 12.

12.12.20 The order giving permission to register the recommendation, determination or award must be drawn up by or on behalf of the party making the application, and entered in the register of the recommendations, determinations and awards ordered to be registered under s. 9 of the Act of 1982, directed by the Senior Master to be kept in the Admiralty and Commercial Registry.

Regulation (EC) No. 805/2004 of the European Parliament and of the Council of 21 April 2004 ("the European Enforcement Order")

12.12.21 The European Enforcement Order (EEO) creates a simplified method of enforcement for uncontested claims throughout the EU member states (except Denmark). Details of the procedure are contained in Section V of Part 74.

12.12.22 An application for an EEO certificate must be made by Form N219 or N219A depending upon whether the Judgment was by agreement/admission/settlement or in default of defence or objection. The application may be made without notice and will be dealt with without a hearing, unless the Master orders a hearing.

12.12.23 An application under Article 6(2) of the EEO Regulation for a certificate indicating the lack or limitation of enforceability of an EEO certificate must be made to the court of origin by application in accordance with Part 23.

12.12.24 An application under Article 10 of the EEO Regulation for rectification or withdrawal of an EEO certificate must be made to the court of origin and may be made by application in accordance with Part 23.

12.12.25 A person seeking to enforce an EEO in England and Wales must lodge at the court in which enforcement proceedings are to be brought the documents required by Article 20 of the EEO Regulation.

12.12.26 Where an EEO certificate has been lodged and the judgment debtor applies to stay or limit the enforcement proceedings under Article 23 of the EEO Regulation, such application must be made by application in accordance with Part 23 to the court in which the EEO is being enforced.

Paragraph numbers marked with a "+" can be found online and on CD.

12.12.27 An application under Article 21 of the EEO Regulation that the court should refuse to enforce an EEO must be made by application in accordance with Part 23 to the court in which the EEO is being enforced.

Section 13

Miscellaneous

13.1 Service of foreign process (RSC O.69):

1B–90 13.1.1 RSC O.69 applies to the service on a person in England or Wales of any process in connection with civil or commercial proceedings in a foreign court or tribunal. A request for service is made to the Senior Master from either Her Majesty's Principal Secretary of State for Foreign and Commonwealth Affairs, or where the foreign court or tribunal is in a convention country, from a consular or other authority of that country.

13.1.2 Where the foreign court or tribunal certifies that the person to be served understands the language of the process, it is not necessary to provide a translation. RSC O.69 r.3 deals with the manner of service; the process may be served through the machinery of the county court and the usual practice is for the Senior Master to provide a certificate for the bailiff or county court officer to use. The Senior Master may make an order for service by an alternative method based on the bailiff's certificate.

13.1.3 When service has been effected, the Senior Master will send a certificate, together with a copy of the process served, to the authority who requested service, stating how service was effected, or why service could not be effected. There is a discretion to charge for the costs of service or attempted service, but recovery is usually sought only where the country requesting service does not provide a reciprocal free service.

13.1.4 Council Regulation (EC) No 1348/2000 ('the Service Regulation') applies to service on a person in England & Wales of proceedings in from courts in other European Union Member States, and provides a complete code for service of proceedings between member states. The Senior Master is the central body designated under Article 3 of the Regulation. The Regulation can be found at CPR Practice Direction 6.36.

13.2 Rectification of register of deeds of arrangement (RSC O.94 r.4)

1B–91 13.2.1 Deeds of arrangement must be registered. The registration office is at the Department of Trade.

13.2.2 An application for an order as set out in RSC O.94 r.4(1)(a) or (b) must be made to a Master of the Queen's Bench Division. Notice need not be served on any other party and a witness statement must support the application or affidavit as described in rule 4(2).

13.3 Exercise of jurisdiction under the Representation of the People Acts (RSC O.94 r.5):

1B–92 13.3.1 RSC O.94 r.5 describes the jurisdiction of the High Court under the above Acts. The practice is governed by the Election Petition Rules 1960 (as amended). The Senior Master is the Prescribed Officer.

13.3.2 Under Part III of the Representation of the People Act 1983, the result of a parliamentary or local government election may be questioned on the grounds of some irregularity either before or during the election. The provisions of Part III have also been applied to European Parliamentary elections.

13.3.3 The challenge is made by the issue of an Election Petition
(1) in respect of a Parliamentary election by one or more electors or

Paragraph numbers marked with a "+" can be found online and on CD.

(2) in respect of a local government election by four or more electors,

or by an unsuccessful or alleged candidate.

The member/councillor whose election is complained of is a Respondent to the petition as is the Returning Officer if his/her conduct is complained of. The petition is issued in the Election Petitions Office, Room E08, normally within 21 days of the election (although this may be extended in certain circumstances).

13.3.4 The petition is tried by two High Court Judges of the Queen's Bench Division in respect of Parliamentary elections or by a Commissioner in respect of Local Government elections. The Commissioner must be a lawyer of not less than 10 years standing who neither resides nor practices in the area concerned. The trial usually takes place in the constituency/local government area for which the Election Petition has been issued, although preliminary matters are usually dealt with at the Royal Courts of Justice.

13.3.5 The election court may confirm the result of the election, or substitute another candidate as the member/councillor, or may order the election to be re-run.

13.3.6 Applications for remedies under various sections of the Representation of the People Act 1983 are also issued in the Election Petitions Office, and are usually heard by an Election Rota Judge.

13.3.7 Outside the court offices' opening times, but while the building is still open to the public, election petitions and applications may be left in the letterbox located outside Room E08. When the building is closed, Election Petitions and applications may be left with Security at the Main Entrance, up until midnight on the last day for service.

13.4 Bills of Sale Acts 1878 and 1882 and the Industrial and Provident Societies Act 1967 (RSC O.95):

13.4.1 Every bill of sale and absolute bill of sale to which the Act of 1878 applies must **1B–93** be registered under s.8 of that Act, within 7 clear days of its making, and, under s.11 of the Act of 1878, the registration of a bill of sale must be renewed at least once every 5 years. The register for the purpose of the Bills of Sale Acts contains the particulars of registered bills of sale and an alphabetical index of the names of the grantors, and is kept in the Action Department in Room E15–E17.

13.4.2 An application to register a bill of sale which is made within the prescribed time should be made by filing in Room E15–E17 the original bill of sale and any document annexed to it together with a witness statement or affidavit in form PF 179 or PF 180. An application to re-register a bill of sale which is made within the prescribed time should be made by filing in Room E15–E17 a witness statement or affidavit in form PF 181.

13.4.3 An application to rectify;
   (1) an omission to register, by extending the time for registration, or
   (2) an omission or mis-statement of the name, residence or occupation of a person in the register, by correcting the registration,

must be made by witness statement or affidavit to a Master of the Queen's Bench Division. In addition to the matters set out in forms PF 179 or PF 180, the evidence in support must also set out the particulars of the omission and state the grounds on which the application is made.

13.4.4 Where the residence of the grantor of the bill of sale or the person against whom the process is issued is outside the London bankruptcy district, or where the bill of sale describes the goods as being in a place outside that district, the Central Office will send copies of the bill of sale to the appropriate county court district judge.

Paragraph numbers marked with a "+" can be found online and on CD.

13.4.5 The Master, on being satisfied that the omission or mis-statement of name, residence or occupation of a person in the register was accidental or due to inadvertence, may order the omission or mis-statement to be rectified by the insertion in the register of the correct name, residence or occupation of the person.

13.4.6 Where the Master is satisfied that the omission to register a bill of sale or a witness statement or affidavit of renewal within the prescribed time was accidental or due to inadvertence, s/he may extend the time for registration on such terms as s/he thinks fit. In order to protect any creditors who have accrued rights of property in the assets in respect of which the bill of sale was granted between the date of the bill and its actual registration, any order to extend the time for registration will normally be made "without prejudice" to those creditors. The order will be drawn up in form PF 182.

13.4.7 An application for an order that a memorandum of satisfaction be written on a registered copy of a bill of sale, made without the consent of the person entitled to the benefit of the bill of sale, must be made by the issue of a Part 8 Claim Form. Where the consent of the person entitled to the benefit of the bill of sale has been obtained, the application may be made by a witness statement or affidavit containing that consent and verifying the signature on it. Form PF 183 contains precedents for the evidence and forms of consent. Where the application is made with consent, the evidence need not be served on any other person. If the Master is satisfied on the evidence, s/he will endorse his/her approval on the witness statement or affidavit (an order is not normally drawn up) and send it to Room E17 for a memorandum of satisfaction to be entered on the copy of the Bill in the Registry. If a copy of the bill of sale has been sent to a county court district judge, a notice of satisfaction will be sent to that district judge.

13.4.8 Where the consent has not been obtained, the Claim Form must be served on the person entitled to the benefit of the bill of sale and must be supported by evidence that the debt (if any) for which the bill of sale was made has been satisfied or discharged.

13.4.9 An application to restrain removal on sale of goods seized in accordance with RSC O.95 r.3 and under the proviso to s.7 of the Bills of Sale Act (1878) Amendment Act 1882 must be made by the issue of a Part 8 Claim Form for hearing before the Interim Applications Judge.

13.4.10 Under the Industrial and Provident Societies Act 1967 an application to record an instrument creating a fixed or floating charge on the assets of a registered society or to rectify any omission or mis-statement in it must be made within 14 days beginning with the date of its execution.

13.4.11 Under RSC O.95 r.5 and in accordance with s.1(5) of the Act of 1967 the court may order;

    (1) that the period for making an application for recording a charge be extended, or

    (2) an omission or mis-statement in such an application be rectified.

The procedure for obtaining an order as in (1) or (2) above is similar to that under s.14 of the Bills of Sale Act 1878 and must be made by witness statement or affidavit to a Master of the Queen's Bench Division as in paragraph 12.4.3 above and must exhibit a copy of the instrument duly authenticated in the prescribed manner together with any other particulars relating to the charge.

13.4.12 RSC O.95 r.3 refers to the assignment of book debts; the register of assignments of book debts is kept in Room E15–E17 in the Central Office. An application for registration under s.344 of the Insolvency Act 1986 should be made in accordance with RSC O.95 r.6(2). Parties may use form PF 186 for their evidence in support. It is helpful if the original assignment is also produced.

13.5 Enrolment of deeds and other documents:

Paragraph numbers marked with a "+" can be found online and on CD.

13.5.1 Any deed or document which by virtue of any enactment is required or authorised to be enrolled in the Supreme Court may be enrolled in the Central Office. See the Part 5 Practice Direction at paragraph 6 which fully sets out the procedure for enrolment and contains in an appendix the Enrolment of Deeds (Change of Name) Regulations 1994.

1B–94

13.6 Bail (RSC O.79 r.9):

13.6.1 With the coming into force on 5th April 2004 of section 17of the Criminal Justice Act 2003, the Queen's Bench Division of the High Court no longer has the power to grant bail in criminal proceedings to a defendant in custody who has been refused bail, or to vary the arrangements for bail of an inferior court.

1B–95

13.6.2 The limited remaining right of the High Court to grant bail in specific circumstances is exercised by the Administrative Court.

13.7 References to the Court of Justice of the European Communities:

13.7.1 A party wishing to apply for an order under CPR 68 may do so by application before or at the trial or hearing. An application made before the trial or hearing should be made in accordance with Part 23.

1B–96

13.7.2 Before making an order for reference, the Court will pay close attention to the terms of Part 68 of the CPR, to form PF 109 and to the "Guidance of the Court of Justice of the European Communities on References by National Courts for Preliminary Rulings" which may be found in the *Practice Direction (ECJ References: Procedure)* (1999) 1 WLR 260.

13.7.3 It is the responsibility of the Court, rather than the parties, to settle the terms of the reference. This should identify as clearly, succinctly and simply as the nature of the case permits the question to which the Court of England & Wales seeks an answer and it is very desirable that language should be used which lends itself readily to translation.

13.7.4 The referring court should, in a single document scheduled to the order (in form PF 109);

 (1) identify the parties and summarise the nature and history of the proceedings,
 (2) summarise the salient facts, indicating whether these are proved or admitted or assumed,
 (3) make reference to the rules of national law (substantive and procedural) relevant to the dispute,
 (4) summarise the contentions of the parties as far as relevant,
 (5) explain why a ruling of the European Court is sought, identifying the EC provisions whose effect is in issue, and
 (6) formulate, without avoidable complexity, the question(s) to which an answer is requested.

13.7.5 Where the document is in the form of a judgment, passages, which are not relevant to the reference, should be omitted from the text scheduled to the order. Incorporation of appendices, annexes or enclosures as part of the document should be avoided, unless the relevant passages lend themselves readily to translation and are clearly identified.

13.7.6 When the order of reference has been approved by the Judge and sealed by the court, the order, together with any other necessary documents should be promptly passed to Room E.209 where the Clerk will process the reference for the attention of the Senior Master of the Queen's Bench Division, for transmission to Luxembourg without avoidable delay.

13.8 Group Litigation Orders "GLOs":

13.8.1 Section III of Part 19 and the Practice Direction - Group Litigation deal with claims where multiple parties are claimants.

1B–97

Paragraph numbers marked with a "+" can be found online and on CD.

QB Guide

13.8.2 When considering applying for a GLO, the applicant should contact the Law Society at 113 Chancery Lane, London WC2A 1PL, who may be able to assist in putting the applicant in contact with other parties who may also be interested in applying for a GLO in the same matter.

13.8.3 The consent of either the Lord Chief Justice or the Vice-Chancellor to the GLO is required. In the Queen's Bench Division the application should be made to the Senior Master in accordance with Part 23. If the Senior Master is minded to make the GLO s/he will forward a copy of the application notice and any written evidence to the Lord Chief Justice. The application notice should include the information set out in paragraph 3.2 of the Practice Direction.

13.8.4 A group register will be set up and maintained by a party to the GLO of all the parties to the group of claims to be managed under the GLO. In order to publicise the GLO when it has been made, a copy should be supplied to the Law Society and to the Senior Master. A record of each GLO made will be maintained in the Central Office in a Nationwide Register of all GLO's notified to the Senior Master.

13.8.5 The Practice Direction sets out how the group litigation will be managed. In particular, a managing judge will be appointed. The case management directions are likely to direct;

(1) that a "Group Particulars of Claim" containing the various claims of the claimants on the group register are served,

(2) that one claim proceed as a "test" claim, and

(3) a cut-off date after which no additions may be made to the group register.

(4) that all documents in the GLO be headed in the name of the Group Litigation name

Guide to Civil Proceedings Fees from 6 April 2006

1B–98   Annex 1

Editorial note —Annex 1 to the Guide contains the text of the Civil Proceedings Fees Order 2004 (SI 2004/3121),as amended to April 6, 2006. That Order has been replaced entirely (with effect from May 1, 2008) by the Civil Proceedings Fees Order 2008 (SI 2008/1053). For the complete text of that order, see Section 10 below.

1B–99   Annex 2

The following is a list of abbreviations commonly used by Masters on endorsements of orders, though there may be some variation as between individual Masters	
A.D.R	Alternative Dispute Resolution
Aff.	Affidavit
A.M-T	Allocate to Multi Track
A.N.	Appointment Notice
App.	Application
A.Q.	Allocation Questionnaire
A.S.	Assessed summarily
B.N.L.T.	By no later than
C.C.	County Court
C.I.A.	Costs in the application
C.I.A.E.	Costs in any event
C.I.C.	Costs in the case
Cl.	Claimant
Col.	Certificate for Counsel
C.M.C.	Case Management Conference

Paragraph numbers marked with a "+" can be found online and on CD.

C.O.A.	Charging order absolute
C.O.C.B.	Costs of and caused by
C.O.S.C.	Charging order to show cause
C.R.	Costs reserved
C.T.R.	Costs of today reserved
D./Def.	Defendant/Defence
D.A.I/N.A.	Detailed assessment if not agreed
Disc.	Disclosure
Dism.	Dismissed
Disp. C/S.	Dispense with requirement of certificate of service
F.C.	Fixed costs
F.C.O.	Final Charging Order
F.I.	Further information
F.O.	Further order
F.O.D.	First open date
I.A.E.	In any event
I.B.	Indemnity basis
Insp.	Inspection
I.T.P.D.O.	Interim Third Party Debt Order
J.	Judgment
L.A.	Legal Aid
L.A.A.	Legal Aid assessment
L.Q.	Listing Questionnaire
O.	Order
On C.Serv.	On producing Certificate of Service
O. Exam.	Oral examination
P/C.	Particulars of claim
P.D.	Practice direction
Pm.	Permission
Pm. A.	Permission to apply/appeal
Pm. R.	Permission to restore
Pm. R.F.D.	Permission to restore for further directions
Pt.	Part
P.R.A.	Private Room Appointment
R.	Rule
S.A.	Set aside/Special allowance
S.O.J.	Service out of the jurisdiction
S/C	Statement of Case
S.B.	Standard basis
S/T	Statement of truth
Tfr.	Transfer
T.P.D.O	Third Party Debt Order
W.N.	Without notice
W.C.O.	Wasted Costs Order
W.N.	Without notice
W.S.	Witness Statement

Paragraph numbers marked with a "+" can be found online and on CD.

1C THE SUPREME COURT COSTS OFFICE GUIDE 2006

TABLE OF CONTENTS

1C–1

SCCO Guide

Paragraph numbers marked with a "+" can be found online and on CD.

Paragraph numbers marked with a "+" can be found online and on CD.

8.8 Obtaining files from other courts

Paragraph numbers marked with a "+" can be found online and on CD.

SCCO Guide

Paragraph numbers marked with a "+" can be found online and on CD.

SCCO GUIDE

Paragraph numbers marked with a "+" can be found online and on CD.

Paragraph numbers marked with a "+" can be found online and on CD.

Paragraph numbers marked with a "+" can be found online and on CD.

LIST OF COSTS JUDGES AND COSTS OFFICERS

1C–2

Costs Judge	Room	
Chief Master Hurst (*Senior Costs Judge*)	2.08	**SCCO postal address**
Master Wright	2.12	Clifford's Inn
Master Rogers	2.24	Fetter Lane

Paragraph numbers marked with a "+" can be found online and on CD.

Master Rogers	2.24
Master O'Hare	2.17
Master Campbell	2.23
Master Simons	2.22
Master Simons	2.22
Master Gordon-Saker	2.03
Master Haworth	2.02

London EC4A 1DQ
(DX 44454 Strand)

Costs Officer	Room
Mr D P O'Riordan	2.07
(Senior Costs Officer)	
Mr J Lambert	1.05
(Principal Costs Officer)	
Mr C J Baker	1.09
Mr J Martin	1.17
Mr F Edwards	1.12
Miss C Bowstead	2.18
(Acting Court Manager)	
Mr P Emery	1.07
Miss M Myers	1.19
Mrs I Sainthouse	2.25
Mrs A Alese	1.13
Mrs V Campbell	1.15

Telephone numbers

PA to Senior Costs Judge	020 7947 6618
Costs Judges Section	020 7947 7124
Costs Officers Section	020 7947 7121
Court of Protection	020 7947 6469
Issue Section	020 7947 6163

Certificates

Costs Judges'	020 7947 7124
Costs Officers'	020 7947 7121

Fax Numbers

Costs Judges Section	020 7947 6247
Costs Officers Section	020 7947 6344
General Office	020 7947 6344

LIST OF REGIONAL COSTS JUDGES

Northern Circuit
District Judge Duerden
Bury County Court
Tenterden Street
Bury, Lancs BL9 0HJ
DX 702615 BURY 2
Tel Number: 0161 7641344
Fax Number: 0161 7634995

Bury

Wales and Chester Circuit
District Judge Davies
Carmarthen County Court
The Old Vicarage
Picton Terrace
Carmarthen
Wales SA31 1BJ
DX 99570 CARMARTHEN 2
Tel Number: 01267 228010
Fax Number: 01267 221844

Carmarthen

1C-3

Paragraph numbers marked with a "+" can be found online and on CD.

District Judge Heyworth   Liverpool
Liverpool County Court
35 Vernon Street
Liverpool L2 1BX
DX 702600 LIVER-
POOL 5
Tel Number: 0151 296
2200
Fax Number: 0151 296
2201

District Judge Park   Carlisle
Carlisle County Court
Courts of Justice
Earl Street
Carlisle, Cumbria CA1
1DJ
DX 65331 CARLISLE 2
Tel Number: 01228
520619
Fax Number: 590588

District Judge Smedley   Liverpool
Liverpool County Court
Queen Elizabeth II Law
Courts
Derby Square
Liverpool L2 1XA
DX 702600 LIVER-
POOL 5
Tel Number: 0151
4737373
Fax Number: 0151
2581587

District Judge Turner   Blackpool
Blackpool County Court
The Law Courts
Chapel Street
Blackpool
Lancs FY1 5RJ
DX 724900 BLACK-
POOL 10
Tel Number: 01253
754020
Fax Number: 01253
295255

District Judge Evans   Newport
Newport County Court
Olympia House, 3rd
Floor
Upper Dock Street
Newport
Gwent NP20 1PQ
DX 99480
NEWPORT (SOUTH
WALES) 4
Tel Number: 01633
227150
Fax Number: 01633
263820

District Judge Wallace   Maccles-
Macclesfield County   field
Court
2nd Floor, Silk House
Park Green
Macclesfield
Cheshire SK11 7NA
DX 702498 MACCLES-
FIELD 3
Tel Number: 01625
412800
Fax Number: 01625
501262

Western Circuit   Bournemouth
District Judge Dancey
Bournemouth County
Court
The Courts of Justice
Deansleigh Road
Bournemouth BH7 7DS
DX 98420
BOURNEMOUTH 4
Tel Number: 01202
502800
Fax Number: 01202
502801

District Judge James   Aldershot
Aldershot & Farnham   & Farn-
County Court   ham
78/82 Victoria Road
Aldershot
Hants GU11 1SS
DX 98530 ALDERSHOT
2
Tel Number: 01252
796800
Fax Number: 01252
345705

Paragraph numbers marked with a "+" can be found online and on CD.

North-Eastern Circuit District Judge Besford Kingston-upon-Hull County Court Lowgate Kingston-upon-Hull Hull HU1 2EZ DX 703010 HULL 5 Tel Number: 01482 586161 Fax Number: 01482 588527	Hull	District Judge Wainwright Exeter County Court The Castle Exeter Devon EX4 3PS DX 98440 EXETER 2 Tel Number: 01392 210655 Fax Number: 01392 433546	Exeter
District Judge Hill Scarborough County Court Pavilion House Valley Bridge Road Scarborough North Yorkshire YO11 2JS DX 65140 SCARBOR- OUGH 2 Tel Number: 01723 366361 Fax Number: 01723 501992	Scarbor- ough	**South-Eastern (North)** **Circuit** District Judge Bazley- White Ipswich County Court 8 Arcade Street Ipswich, Suffolk IP1 1EJ DX 97730 IPSWICH 3 Tel Number: 01473 214256 Fax Number: 01473 251797	Ipswich
District Judge Spencer Leeds County Court The Courthouse 1 Oxford Row Leeds LS1 3BG DX 703016 LEEDS 6 Tel Number: 0113 2830040 Fax Number: 0113 2452305	Leeds	District Judge Sparrow Norwich County Court The Law Courts Bishopgate Norwich NR3 1UR DX 97385 NORWICH 5 Tel Number: 01603 728200 Fax Number: 01603 760863	Norwich
Midland Circuit District Judge Mackenzie Worcester County Court The Shirehall Foregate Street Worcester WR1 1EQ DX 721120 WORCESTER 11 Tel Number: 01905 730800 Fax Number: 01905 730801	Worcester	**South-East (South)** **Circuit** District Judge Lethem Tunbridge Wells County Court Merevale House 42/46 London Road Tunbridge Wells Kent TN1 1DP DX 98220 TUNBRIDGE WELLS 3 Tel Number: 01892 515515 Fax Number: 01892 513676	Tunbridge Wells
District Judge Middleton Birmingham County Court The Priory Courts 33 Bull Street Birmingham B4 6DS DX 701987 Tel Number: 0121 6814441 Fax Number: 0121 681 3001/2	Birming- ham	District Judge Matthews Oxford County Court St Aldates Oxford OX1 1TL DX 964500 OXFORD 4 Tel Number: 01865 264200 Fax Number: 01865 790773	Oxford

SCCO Guide

Paragraph numbers marked with a "+" can be found online and on CD.

District Judge Millard
Nottingham County
Court
60 Canal Street
Nottingham NG1 7EJ
DX 702381 NOTTING-
HAM 7
Tel Number: 0115
9103500
Fax Number: 0115
9103510

Notting-
ham

1C–4

FOREWORD

Dealing with the costs of a case can often be just as complicated as the substantive issues themselves. This, the third (and largest) edition of the Supreme Court Costs Office Guide has been written by the Masters and Officers of the Supreme Court Costs Office who deal with the many complexities of costs issues on a daily basis. It does not seek to replace the rules set out in the Civil Procedure Rules and Practice Directions, but gives practical information and guidance for dealing with this area of law. As ever, like its predecessors, it will be an invaluable friend to anyone who uses it – whether they are lawyers or litigants.

THE RIGHT HONOURABLE SIR ANTHONY CLARKE MASTER OF THE ROLLS, HEAD OF CIVIL JUSTICE

July 2006

GLOSSARY

1C–5

Additional liability	Items of costs which are recoverable in certain circumstances: that part of a success fee (defined below) under a conditional fee agreement (also defined below) which is recoverable from a paying party (defined below) and/or a reasonable sum in respect of a relevant insurance premium (also defined below) and/or an additional amount which is sometimes recoverable in respect of "self insurance" notionally incurred by a litigant whose case is funded by a trade union or similar body. These three forms of additional liability are the items about which the paying party should have received a notice of funding (defined below).
Applications clerk	The clerk to whom all papers and enquiries should be directed concerning the issue of claim forms and application notices: the applications clerk's office is currently located in Room 2.13.
Appropriate office	The office in which a request for a detailed assessment hearing should be filed: it is the County Court Office or District Registry for the court in which the order for costs was made or, in all other cases, the Supreme Court Costs Office (SCCO). Where the SCCO is the appropriate office for the request, it is also the appropriate office for any request or application made earlier in the detailed assessment proceedings, eg, a request for a default costs certificate, a request or application to set aside such a certificate and applications for extension of time and sanctions for delay.
Central Funds	Money provided by Parliament out of which may be paid the costs of defendants in criminal cases in respect of which a "defendants costs order" has been made.

Paragraph numbers marked with a "+" can be found online and on CD.

Clerk of Appeals	The clerk to whom all papers and enquiries should be directed which relate to SCCO work concerning criminal fee appeals. The Clerk of Appeal's office is currently located in Room 2.13.
Conditional fee agreement	An agreement with a legal representative which provides for the payment of fees or part of them only in specified circumstances. A party who wishes to recover a success fee payable under the agreement from his opponent should serve a notice of funding on the opponent at the outset of the claim.
Costs between the parties	Costs payable by one litigant to another litigant under the terms of an order made by the court. The expression is used in order to distinguish these costs from "solicitor and client costs" (costs payable by a client to a solicitor under the terms of a contract made between them) and "LSC only costs" (costs payable by the Legal Services Commission to a solicitor or barrister).
Costs Judges	Judges sitting in the SCCO (also known as Taxing Masters and as Masters of the SCCO). Costs Judges also act as District Judges of the Principal Registry of the Family Division, and as District Judges of the County Court when assessing costs from those courts. When assessing costs under an order of the Adjudicator to HM Land Registry they sit as his Deputy Adjudicators.
Costs Officers	Authorised court officers who assess most bills for sums not exceeding certain amounts specified from time to time. From their decisions, appeals lie as of right to the Costs Judges.
Costs-only proceedings	The procedure to be followed where, before court proceedings are commenced, the parties to a dispute reach an agreement on all issues, including which party is to pay costs, but are unable to agree the amount of those costs.
Counsel	One or more advocates acting for a litigant. Very senior advocates are awarded the title "Queen's Counsel".
CPD	The Costs Practice Direction, supplementing the CPR (defined below).
CPR	The Civil Procedure Rules which, supplemented by the CPD (defined above) govern the procedure to be followed in most civil cases brought in the SCCO. The text of the CPR and the CPD are set out in practitioner's books such as the White Book Service and the Civil Court Practice. Most of the relevant texts are also included on the SCCO page of the Court Service website (as to which, see para. 1.10, below).
Detailed assessment	The judicial process under which bills of costs are checked as to their reasonableness; the court may allow or disallow any items claimed in a bill or may vary any figures claimed in respect of them.
Determining officer	The court officer in criminal cases (only) who first assesses the costs payable to a defendant out of Central Funds (defined above) or payable by the LSC to solicitors and counsel under criminal legal aid orders. Costs Judges have jurisdiction to hear appeals from the decisions of Determining Officers.

Paragraph numbers marked with a "+" can be found online and on CD.

Disbursements	Sums of money, e.g., court fees, counsel's fees and witness expenses which are paid or payable by a "receiving party" (defined below) which cannot and do not include any element of profit for that party or for the solicitor acting for him. A special meaning is given to this term in the case of litigants in person (see para. 22.2, below).
Form N252 and other N forms	Court forms which are referred to in the CPD (defined above). Copies of the forms for use in the SCCO can be obtained from the SCCO itself or from the SCCO page of the Court Service Website (as to which, see para. 1.10, below).
Funding arrangement	An arrangement made by a litigant which gives rise to an additional liability (defined above).
Insurance premium	The sum paid or payable by a litigant who has taken out an "after the event" insurance policy taken out in respect of particular litigation and covering against the risk of losing that litigation.
Litigant in person	A party to any proceedings who does not have a solicitor or other legal representative duly authorised to represent him or her in those proceedings.
LSC	The Legal Services Commission, which is the body set up by Parliament to provide financial help as to the costs of legal services provided to litigants in civil claims and defendants in criminal cases who come within certain eligibility criteria.
LSC funded client	A litigant who has been granted financial help by the Legal Services Commission.
Notice of Funding	A notice (usually in Form N251) by which one party warns another of any additional liability (defined above) which may later be recoverable.
Offer to settle	An offer in writing made by one party to another in detailed assessment proceedings proposing the payment of a specific sum of money thereby avoiding the need for any further delay or expense. If the offer is not accepted and the costs in question are later subject to detailed assessment, neither party is allowed to reveal the existence of the offer to the Costs Judge or Costs Officer until the detailed assessment has been completed. The letter containing the offer should include the words "without prejudice save as to the costs of the detailed assessment" or words to that effect.
Part 23 application	Applications made by any party which relate to existing or intended detailed assessment proceedings. The notice of application should be in Form N244 (as to which, see above).
Part 36 offer or payment	An offer in writing made by one litigant to another during the proceedings preceding the detailed assessment proceedings, proposing to settle those proceedings on specified terms. After proceedings have started an offer by a defendant to settle a money claim should be supported by a payment into court of the specific sum offered.
Paying party	The party to detailed assessment proceedings who is liable to pay the costs which are the subject of the assessment. The opposing party is referred to as the "receiving party" which is defined below.

Paragraph numbers marked with a "+" can be found online and on CD.

Points of dispute	A written statement made by the paying party identifying the areas of disagreement as to the costs to be assessed. In respect of each item of costs which is disputed the statement should outline the reason for disputing it and, where a reduction is sought, should suggest the reduced figure.
Profit costs	Costs paid or payable in respect of work done by a solicitor which are not "disbursements" (defined above).
Provisional assessment	An assessment of costs made without a hearing. Subsequently the court notifies the receiving party of the sum proposed to be allowed and requires the receiving party to so inform the court office within 14 days if he wishes a hearing to be convened.
RCJ	The Royal Courts of Justice the postal address of which is Strand, London, WC2A 2LL.
Receiving party	A party to detailed assessment proceedings who is entitled to recover from another party the costs which are the subject of the assessment. In the case of "costs between the parties" (defined above) the receiving party is the person in whose favour the court's order for costs was made or the solicitor or other legal representative acting for such a person. In the case of "solicitor and client costs" (which is defined below) the receiving party is the solicitor.
SCCO	The Supreme Court Costs Office the postal address of which is Clifford's Inn, Fetter Lane, London, EC4A 1DQ.
Sitting Master	Each day the Master so nominated for that day deals with any applications in matters not yet assigned to other Masters and is also available to give guidance on points of practice to the Judges of the Supreme Court and other courts throughout the country and (via his clerk) to any litigants or lawyers seeking his help.
Solicitor and client costs	See "costs between the parties" above.
Statement of truth	A statement to be included in any claim form, application notice or witness statement which confirms that the facts stated therein are true. The statement of truth must be signed by the litigant, or his litigation friend or legal representative or witness as the case may be.
Success fees	An additional fee which is payable in certain circumstances under the terms of a conditional fee agreement. The success fee must be expressed as a percentage of the other profit costs payable under the agreement.
Summary assessment	The procedure by which the court, when making an award of costs, immediately calculates and specifies the sum of costs it allows.
Wasted costs order	An order against a legal representative which disallows, or, as the case may be, orders the legal representative to meet, the whole or any part of costs found to have been incurred as a result of improper, unreasonable or negligent acts or omissions on the part of the legal representative or any consequential costs.

Paragraph numbers marked with a "+" can be found online and on CD.

Section 1

Introduction

1C-6 **1.1 The work of the SCCO**

(a) The Supreme Court Costs Office (SCCO) is a distinct part of the High Court, separate from the Queens Bench Division, Chancery Division and Family Division. It has two ranks of judicial officer: Costs Judges (also known as Taxing Masters and as Masters of the SCCO) and costs officers (senior civil servants from whose decisions appeals lie as of right to a Costs Judge).

(b) The primary function of the SCCO is the assessment of costs which are recoverable from a litigant by another litigant or by a lawyer. In the past, assessments (then called "taxations") were conducted by specialist Judges appointed to each court. In 1842 the office of Taxing Master was created and Taxing Masters were appointed to each Division of the High Court. The Supreme Court Taxing Office was originally one of the Departments which made up the Central Office. At the start of the 20th century it took over the work of the Chancery Taxing Masters. In 1999 the Civil Procedure Rules ("CPR") adopted the term "detailed assessment" in place of "taxation" at which time the SCCO was created. It now has jurisdiction to assess costs awarded by any Judge of the Court of Appeal, High Court or County Court. Since 2000 it has had the jurisdiction to assess orders for costs made in the Family Division of the High Court and in the Principal Registry.

(c) Regional Costs Judges

Regional Costs Judges have been appointed on all circuits outside London. They are District Judges who have been appointed to hear detailed assessment of bills of costs that fall within the criteria of the scheme at a venue which is convenient to the parties and their legal representatives.

The criteria for a detailed assessment to be referred to a Regional Costs Judge, rather than the local District Judge, are as follows: the time estimate for the detailed assessment exceeds one day; and/or the sum claimed exceeds £50,000; and/or complex arguments on points of law, or an issue affecting a group of similar cases, are identified in the points of dispute or the reply or are referred to in argument at a detailed assessment hearing.

Once a request for detailed assessment in Form **N258** has been filed at court the bill will be referred to a District Judge who will consider whether it falls within the criteria for reference to a Regional Costs Judge. If it does, the bill will be referred to the appropriate Regional Costs Judge who will then decide whether to accept it and will give any directions required, including directions as to listing.

If a party wishes to make submissions as to whether any particular detailed assessment fulfils the criteria for reference to a Regional Costs Judge, or as to the most convenient court for any hearing before a Regional Costs Judge, they should first consult the other parties or their legal representatives before making submissions to the court. It is helpful if such submissions are filed with the court when the request for detailed assessment is lodged. If possible the parties should attempt to agree the reference to the Regional Costs Judge, any directions and the most convenient venue.

A list of the names and court addresses of the District Judges who were appointed Regional Costs Judges in 2005 is set out on pages 12 and 13 [para.1C-3], above.

1.2 Representation

1C-7 (a) Solicitors

In most cases parties will be represented by the solicitors who have acted for them in the litigation in which the order for costs has been made. The name, address, telephone and fax numbers and reference of each such solicitor is set out on the Statement of Parties which is lodged when a request for a detailed assessment hearing is made (see further, Section 8, below).

Where proceedings are brought by claim form under Part III of the Solicitors Act 1974, the name and other details of each party's solicitor are set out in the claim form or in the acknowledgment of service, as the case may be.

Paragraph numbers marked with a "+" can be found online and on CD.

Solicitors remain on the record of the court until they obtain an order for their removal, or until another firm or the litigant in person files and serves a notice of acting. Notices of acting should be filed in the SCCO and also in the court office of the court in which the relevant order for costs was made if proceedings are still continuing in that court.

The firm on the record may be represented by a fee earner, for example, a partner, an assistant solicitor, a legal executive, a trainee solicitor or a paralegal or other clerk employed by the firm. Alternatively, firms outside London sometimes instruct a firm of solicitors in London to act on their behalf as an agent at any hearing.

(b) Bankrupt Party

A bankrupt has no right to be heard unless an order under Section 303 of the Insolvency Act 1986 has been made. It is normally for the trustee in bankruptcy to decide what steps to take on behalf of the bankrupt's estate in relation to any proceedings in the SCCO.

(c) Company

Under the CPR, companies are not required to act by a solicitor when starting proceedings or defending them. Thus, they may act by any duly authorised agent. Where a document is to be verified on behalf of a company a statement of truth as to that document may be signed by any person holding a senior position in the company. However, once a matter proceeds to a hearing, the company, by its officers or employees or otherwise, has no personal right of audience. CPR 39.6 permits the representation of a company "at trial" by an employee but this is not as of right; the rule states that the person wishing to speak for the company must obtain the court's permission. The Practice Direction to that rule sets out the information to be given to the court in such circumstances, states that such permission should be sought in advance and states that such permission may be obtained informally and without notice to the other parties. Although CPR 39.6 concerns representation at trial, the Practice Direction provisions concern representations at any hearing.

(d) Costs draftsmen

At present independent costs draftsmen have no rights of audience as such but, by concession, are treated as if they are in the employ of the firm of solicitors instructing them. They have no rights of audience on behalf of a litigant in person (but see McKenzie Friend below). In the near future the Association of Law Costs Draftsmen will be authorised to grant rights of audience and rights to conduct litigation to certain of its members when participating in detailed assessments.

(e) Patents agents, trademark agents and claims consultants

In any patent action conducted by a patent agent, the patent agent may have a right to appear. Similar rights have now been granted to trademark agents in respect of trademark cases. In certain cases (such as arbitrations and planning matters) surveyors and other persons acting as claims consultants who have conducted the proceedings may be permitted to appear.

(f) Counsel and counsel's clerks

Counsel properly briefed by solicitors or by the litigant have full rights of audience. However, if they appear on their own behalf without a brief they are not entitled to a fee. Counsel's clerks attending as such do not have any right of audience. However, in an exceptional case, counsel's clerk may be allowed a hearing on behalf of counsel if counsel so requests in writing and if the Costs Judge or costs officer so allows.

(g) McKenzie Friend

As a general rule, a litigant in person will be allowed to receive the assistance of a friend at the hearing to give advice and to take notes (but not to act as advocate).However, in a particular case, the court may refuse to allow such assistance to be given, or to be continued, if there are strong and compelling reasons for believing that such assistance will impede the efficient administration of justice.

1.3 Sitting Master

1C–8

Costs Judges act from time to time on a rota basis as Sitting Master to hear applications, in detailed assessment proceedings which have not been assigned to a particular Costs Judge or costs officer, to hear applications under the Solicitors Act 1974 and to deal with enquiries relating to practice and law arising out of

Paragraph numbers marked with a "+" can be found online and on CD.

assessments. Such enquiries may be made indirectly, via his clerk, or, in the case of Judges of the Supreme Court or other courts throughout the country, directly.

1C–9 **1.4 Office hours**

In common with other civil courts the SCCO is open from 10 am until 4.30 pm from Mondays to Fridays. It is closed on public holidays and on the Tuesday after Easter Monday.

1C–10 **1.5 SCCO Support Sections**

Once proceedings have been commenced in the SCCO further work done in preparation for hearings is dealt with by the clerks of the Costs Judges Section for hearings before a Master and by clerks of the Costs Officers Section for hearings before a costs officer. When an assessment has been completed and the appropriate fees paid these Sections will also deal with the issue of the final costs certificates. The clerks in these Sections deal with appointments, correspondence and telephone enquiries. They do not give legal advice to parties. However, assistance and guidance will be given in appropriate circumstances as to general office practice.

Assistance and guidance on technical matters which are complex and difficult may be referred to the Principal Costs Officer or to a designated senior clerk who will endeavour to help, possibly after consultation with the Costs Judge or costs officer to whom the case has been allocated.

1C–11 **1.6 The SCCO file**

On receiving the appropriate documents and court fees in respect of each application or request the court clerks will open a file and allocate to it a distinct file number. Subsequently further documents may be added to that file, eg, correspondence, witness statements, notes of hearings and the orders made thereon. Unless the court otherwise orders, any party to the proceedings is entitled, without permission, to obtain a copy of any document filed in the SCCO in respect of those proceedings if he pays any prescribed fee and files a written request for the document. Persons other than parties have much more limited rights of obtaining documents from the court file (CPR 5.4).

1C–12 **1.7 Referrals to the RCJ Citizens Advice Bureau**

(a) The Citizens Advice Bureau is able to give general legal advice to litigants in person and, for this purpose, maintains an office in the Royal Courts of Justice near the Main Hall.

(b) The Bureau operates on a "first come first served" basis. Clients will be seen first by a receptionist who will assess their eligibility for assistance by the Bureau. If they are eligible and the advice and assistance sought falls within the Bureau's remit they will be referred to a lawyer who will endeavour to provide the advice or assistance sought. Problems which can be resolved quickly will normally be dealt with there and then. If matters need more time, for example those involving a difficult point of law or procedure, or those requiring more information, research or the drafting of documents, the client will be asked to come back and an appointment made.

(c) Further information about the RCJ Citizens Advice Bureau and its referral scheme can be obtained from the SCCO Support Sections.

1C–13 **1.8 Contacting the SCCO by letter or fax**

(a) Although, during office hours, applications and other documents may be delivered by hand to the Costs Office, in practice most are delivered by letter or by fax. All such documentation should be sent with a covering letter stating any SCCO references relevant to the documentation. If a fee is payable the documentation should include a cheque or bankers draft made in favour of HM Paymaster General or HMPG. Parties who wish to pay court fees in cash must hand deliver the payment to Room E01 in the Royal Courts of Justice.

(b) Letters and documentation may be sent by post to:

The Court Manager
Supreme Court Costs Office

Paragraph numbers marked with a "+" can be found online and on CD.

Cliffords Inn
Fetter Lane
London EC4A 1DQ

Or by document exchange (DX) to DX 44454 Strand.

(c) In an emergency urgent documents may be sent to the Costs Office by fax on number 020 7947 6247 or 020 7947 6344. If the fax relates to a hearing, the date and time of the hearing should be prominently displayed as well as the relevant SCCO reference number. Examples of urgent documents it is appropriate to send by fax are: documents required by the court at short notice before the hearing and letters informing the court of a settlement which obviates the need for some or all parties to attend a hearing. A fax should not be used to send letters or documents of a routine or non urgent nature, bills of costs, papers supporting bills or skeleton arguments.

(d) Where a document is filed by fax, the party filing it is not required in addition to send to the SCCO any further copy of that document, eg by post or document exchange. Documents sent by fax are not to be regarded as filed at court unless and until they are delivered by the court's fax machine. If a fax is delivered after 4 pm, or at any time on a day when the court office is closed, it will be treated as filed on the next day the court office is open.

1.9 Contacting the SCCO by telephone

1C–14

(a) The SCCO can be contacted via the telephone numbers set out in the List of Costs Judges and Costs Officers (see page 11, [para.1C–2] above) or via the switchboard at the Royal Courts of Justice, the number of which is 020 7947 6000. Also once a file has been opened and the SCCO has entered into correspondence thereon the SCCO notepaper and compliments slips will show the telephone number of the relevant clerk. Parties should use this number when contact by letter or fax is not possible or not appropriate.

(b) In some cases the hearing of a detailed assessment may be conducted by telephone. If it is a hearing at which more than one party may be represented, the court will give directions as to who must arrange the conference call and the Costs Office number which should be used on that call. Most telephone hearings concern cases in which only one party wishes to attend. In those cases the court will give directions stating the Costs Office telephone number to be used, the date and time of the appointment and stating whether it should be by way of a conference call or an ordinary telephone call.

1.10 SCCO page on the Court Service Website

1C–15

The SCCO page on the Court Service Website comprises a miscellany of information including the text of various guides and guideline figures published by the SCCO and the text of the Civil Procedure Rules and Practice Directions on Costs and summaries of recent costs appeals which contain important points of principle. The address of the SCCO page is www.hmcourts-service.gov.uk/infoabout/scco/index.htm.

SECTION 2

ENTITLEMENT TO COSTS

2.1 The meaning of "Costs"

1C–16

(a) The word "costs" is defined in CPR 43.2. Costs normally fall into two categories:

(i) expenses of a type which solicitors frequently incur when acting on behalf of clients (such as counsel's fees, court fees, witness expenses etc). These are known as "disbursements".

(ii) The fees which a solicitor charges to his client. These are known as "solicitors' charges" or "profit costs".

(b) Costs payable by one party to another can, in appropriate circumstances, include costs incurred before the issue of proceedings (*In re Gibson's Settlement Trusts* [1981] Ch 179).

2.2 Liability to pay costs

1C–17

(a) In litigation, no party has a right to costs. Costs are in the discretion of the court. If, however, the court sees fit to make an order as to the costs of the litigation,

Paragraph numbers marked with a "+" can be found online and on CD.

the general rule is that the unsuccessful party will be ordered to pay the costs of the successful party (CPR 44.3(2)(a)). The court may make an order for costs which reflects the extent to which each party has been successful in relation to different issues.

(b) Costs as between solicitor and client are payable to the solicitor according to the terms of any contract he has made with the client or, alternatively, in the case of an LSC funded client, according to the Regulations made under the Legal Aid Act 1988 and the Access to Justice Act 1999.

1C–18 **2.3 Orders which the Court may make**

(a) In deciding what order to make about costs the court is required to have regard to all the circumstances including the conduct of all the parties; whether a party has succeeded on part of his case, even if not wholly successful; and whether or not there has been a payment into court or an offer of settlement: (CPR 44.3(4)).

(b) The court has complete discretion as to what order for costs to make but those orders may include an order that a party must pay:

  (i) a proportion of another party's costs;
  (ii) a stated amount in respect of another party's costs;
  (iii) costs from or until a certain date;
  (iv) costs incurred before proceedings have begun;
  (v) costs relating to particular steps in the proceedings;
  (vi) costs relating only to a distinct part of the proceedings; and
  (vii) interest on costs from or until a certain date.

(c) The court has, in addition, the power to order a party to pay an amount on account of costs before the costs are assessed (CPR 44.3(8)).

(d) Paragraph 8.5 of the Costs Practice Direction ("CPD") lists the more common costs orders which the court may make in proceedings before trial and explains their effect.

1C–19 **2.4 Bases of assessment**

(a) The court may order costs between the parties to be assessed on either the *standard basis* or the *indemnity basis*. The court will not allow costs which have been unreasonably incurred or which are unreasonable in amount.

(b) On the *standard basis*, the court will only allow costs which are proportionate to the matters in issue and will resolve any doubt which it may have as to whether costs were reasonably incurred or reasonable and proportionate in amount in favour of the paying party: (CPR 44.4(2)).

(c) Where the court assesses costs on the *indemnity basis* it will resolve any doubt which it may have as to whether costs were reasonably incurred or were reasonable in amount in favour of the receiving party (CPR 44.4(3)).

(d) In LSC funded cases, costs are payable to solicitors and counsel on the *standard basis* subject to Regulations which prescribe the amounts to be allowed in certain cases.

(e) In respect of costs payable to a solicitor by his client, the basis of assessment is the indemnity basis to which certain presumptions and limitations apply (see CPR 48.8 and CPD Section 54).

1C–20 **2.5 Methods of assessment of costs**

(a) When the court makes an order about costs, it may carry out a summary assessment then and there and order the payment of a sum of money in respect of costs, or it may order a detailed assessment of the costs. If a detailed assessment is ordered the receiving party must, amongst other things, prepare a bill setting out the work done and, ultimately, the court will go through that bill, hearing argument from both sides as to what items and amounts should and should not be allowed.

(b) The general rule is that the court will make a summary assessment of the costs at the conclusion of the trial of a case which has been dealt with on the fast track and at the conclusion of any other hearing which has lasted for not more than one day. In certain cases the Court of Appeal will also carry out a summary assessment. Summary assessment will be carried out unless there is good reason for not doing so, for example where the paying party shows substantial grounds for disputing the sum claimed for costs that cannot be dealt with summarily, or there is insufficient time to carry out a summary assessment (CPR 44.7; CPD Sections 12, 13 and 14).

Paragraph numbers marked with a "+" can be found online and on CD.

2.6 The Indemnity Principle   1C–21

The principle is that a successful party cannot recover from an unsuccessful party more by way of costs than the successful party is liable to pay his or her legal representatives. There are several exceptions to the principle including the statutory exceptions concerning legal aid and conditional fee agreements. There have been calls for the total abolition of the principle. Unless and until that occurs the following three propositions continue to apply:

(i) A party in whose favour an order for costs has been made may not recover more than he is liable to pay his own solicitors: *Harold v Smith* [1860] 5 Hurl. &N. 381 at 385 and *Gundry v Sainsbury* [1910] 1KB 645 CA.

(ii) Where a party puts a statement of costs before the court for summary assessment that statement must be signed by the party or a legal representative. The form states: "The costs estimated above do not exceed the costs which the [*party*] is liable to pay in respect of the work which this estimate covers."

(iii) The signature of a statement of costs or a bill for detailed assessment by a solicitor is in normal circumstances sufficient to enable the court to be satisfied that the indemnity principle has not been breached: *Bailey v IBC Vehicles Ltd* [1998] 3 All ER 570 CA.

2.7 Duty to notify clients of adverse costs orders   1C–22

Where the court makes an order for costs against a person who is legally represented but is not present when the order is made, that party's solicitor must notify the client in writing of the costs order no later than seven days after the solicitor receives notice of the order (CPR 44.2).

2.8 Some special cases   1C–23

(a) In certain cases a right to costs on the *standard basis* arises even though the court does not make a specific order for costs. The occasions when this happens are under:

(i) CPR 3.7(4) (defendant's right to costs where claim struck out for non payment of fees);

(ii) CPR 36.13(1) (claimant's right to costs where he accepts defendants' Part 36 offer or Part 36 payment);

(iii) CPR 36.14 (claimant's right to costs where defendant accepts the claimant's Part 36 offer); or

(iv) CPR 38.6 (defendant's right to costs where claimant discontinues).

(b) In any other case, where the court makes an order but does not mention costs, no party is entitled to costs in relation to that order (CPR 44.13(1)).

(c) An appeal court may, unless it dismisses the appeal, make orders about costs of the proceedings in the lower court as well as the costs of the appeal (CPR 44.13(2)).

(d) Where proceedings are transferred from one court to another, the court to which they are transferred may (subject to any order made by the transferring court) deal with all the costs, including the costs before the transfer (CPR 44.13(3)).

(e) In a probate claim where a defendant has in his defence given notice that he requires the will to be proved in solemn form (as to which see CPR 57.7(5)), the court will not make an order for costs against the defendant unless it appears that there was no reasonable ground for opposing the will. The term "probate claim" is defined in CPR 57.1.

2.9 Costs where money is payable by or to a child or patient   1C–24

(a) Where a child or patient is ordered to pay money to another party the court may make a summary assessment of those costs or may order a detailed assessment.

(b) Where a child or patient is liable to pay money to his or her solicitor the court must order a detailed assessment of those costs (CPR 48.5) unless the case falls within one of those circumstances described in CPD Section 51 (eg another party has agreed to pay a specified sum in respect of costs and the solicitor acting for the child or patient has waived the right to claim further costs).

2.10 Costs of trustees and personal representatives   1C–25

Trustees and personal representatives who are parties to litigation are generally entitled to their costs, so far as not recovered from any other party, out of any fund

Paragraph numbers marked with a "+" can be found online and on CD.

SCCO Guide

which they hold as trustee or personal representative. The costs are assessed on the indemnity basis. If a trustee or personal representative has acted for a benefit other than that of the fund the court may make a different order (CPR 48.4).

1C–26 **2.11 Mortgagees' costs**

Depending on the terms of the mortgage, a mortgage lender is likely to be able to recover any costs incurred in litigation (except for costs which are unreasonably incurred or which are unreasonable in amount) as a matter of contract between the lender and the borrower. CPD Section 50 sets out the principles which apply to litigation costs relating to a mortgage (CPR 48.3).

1C–27 **2.12 Group Litigation Orders**

CPR Part 19 deals with Group Litigation Orders. CPR 48.6A provides that unless the court otherwise orders group litigants are severally (not jointly) liable for an equal proportion of the "common costs". ("Common costs" are defined in CPR 48.6A(2).) In addition, a group litigant is liable for the individual costs of his or her own claim. A group litigant coming late to the group register may be ordered to be liable for a proportion of the costs incurred before that litigant's name is entered on the register (CPR 48.6A(6)). Paragraph 16 of the Practice Direction Supplementing Part 19 provides that the Costs Judge will apportion the amounts of common costs and individual costs, if the court has not already done so.

1C–28 **2.13 Costs in the Companies Court**

In the Companies Court "the usual compulsory order" made on a winding-up petition includes provision for the payment of the petitioner's costs and one set of costs for the supporting creditors out of the assets of the company. Thus in a simple case if the usual compulsory order is made it will not generally be necessary to ask for a separate order for costs. If however there are opposing creditors and the petition succeeds, the costs of the opposing creditors are not paid out of the company's assets unless they are expressly allowed by the court.

1C–29 **2.14 Costs in family proceedings**

In family proceedings CPR Parts 43, 44 (except CPR 44.9 to 44.12), 47 and 48 apply to the assessment of costs; CPR 44.3(2) (costs follow the event) does not apply (Family Proceedings (Miscellaneous Amendments) Rules 1999 SI 1999 No.1012). The Costs Practice Direction applies to the extent that the CPR apply and references in the Direction to "claimant" and "defendant" should be read as references to the equivalent terms used in family proceedings.

1C–30 **2.15 Success fees and insurance premiums**

In certain cases the Access to Justice Act 1999 permits the recovery of costs under a conditional fee agreement which provides for a success fee and permits the recovery of sums paid or payable in respect of after the event insurance. Further information about these items of costs is given in Section 19 (below) and the procedures to be followed to deal with possible success fee disputes between legal representatives and clients are given in Section 20, below. It should be noted that, although family proceedings cannot be the subject of an enforceable conditional fee agreement (with or without a success fee) the reasonable cost of after the event insurance premiums in such proceedings may be recoverable.

1C–31 **2.16 Costs in relation to pre commencement disclosure and orders for disclosure against a non party**

Sections 33 and 34 of the Supreme Court Act 1981 and Sections 52 and 53 of the County Courts Act 1984 give the court powers, exercisable before commencement of proceedings, in relation to disclosure, and the power to make an order against a non party for disclosure of documents and inspection of property. The general rule is that the court will award the person against whom the order is sought, his costs of the application and of complying with any order which is made. If however that party

Paragraph numbers marked with a "+" can be found online and on CD.

has unreasonably opposed the application or failed to comply with any relevant pre-action protocol the court may well make a different order (CPR 48.1).

2.17 Costs orders in favour of or against non parties

1C–32

(a) The court may order costs to be paid to or by a person who is not a party to the proceedings in which those costs have been incurred. Such an order is likely to be made only in exceptional circumstances. Where the court is considering making such an order, that person must be added as a party to the proceedings and must be given a reasonable opportunity to attend the hearing at which the court will consider the matter further (CPR 48.2 and see CPR Part 19 as to adding a person as a party). When the court makes such an order, the costs awarded can only be those incurred in the proceedings before it.

(b) The Court of Appeal has recently given guidance about the liabilities of professional funders, who have financed part of a Claimant's costs of litigation, to pay a contribution towards the costs of a successful defendant (see *Arkin v Borchard Lines Ltd* [2005] 1 WLR 3055; [2005] 3 All ER 613).

2.18 Costs following acceptance of an offer to settle

1C–33

(a) CPR Part 36 deals with offers to settle and payments into court. Where a defendant's Part 36 offer or Part 36 payment is accepted without needing the permission of the court, the claimant is entitled to the costs of the proceedings up to the date of serving notice of acceptance (CPR 36.13(1)). Where a claimant's Part 36 offer is accepted without needing the permission of the court, the claimant is entitled to the costs of the proceedings up to the date upon which the defendant serves notice of acceptance (CPR 36.14). In these cases an order for costs is deemed to be made (see para 2.8 above).

(b) Where a claimant fails to do better than the defendant's Part 36 offer or Part 36 payment, the court will, unless it considers it unjust to do so, order the claimant to pay any costs incurred by the defendant after the latest date on which the payment or offer could have been accepted without needing the permission of the court (CPR 36.20).

(c) Where a claimant does better than was proposed in the claimant's Part 36 offer, the court may order interest at a rate not exceeding 10% above base rate, on the whole or part of the sum of money awarded to the claimant, for some or all of the periods starting with the latest date on which the defendant could have accepted the offer without needing the permission of the court. The court also has the power to order that the claimant is entitled to costs on the indemnity basis (as to which, see para 2.4, above) and to award interest on those costs at a rate not exceeding 10% above base rate (as to which, see Section 15, below). The court will make an order in such terms unless it considers it unjust to do so (CPR 36.21(4)).

(d) In deciding whether or not it would be unjust to make such an order, the court will take into account all the circumstances including the terms of the Part 36 offer, the stage in the proceedings when the offer was made, the information available to the parties at the time when the offer was made and the conduct of the parties with regard to the giving or refusing to give information for the purpose of enabling the offer to be made or evaluated (CPR 36.21(5)).

2.19 Costs in small claims

1C–34

(a) In a case which has been allocated to the small claims track, the court may not order a party to pay costs to another party except in the limited circumstances set out in CPR 27.14(2). These include the fixed costs attributable to issuing the claim payable under CPR Part 45, and any costs which the court summarily assesses and orders to be paid by a party who has behaved unreasonably.

(b) The court also has the power to order a party to pay court fees paid by another party and expenses which a party or a witness has reasonably incurred in attending court. Paragraphs 7.2 and 7.3 of the Practice Direction Supplementing CPR Part 27 set out the maximum amount which the court may allow.

(c) The limits on costs also apply to any fee or reward for acting on behalf of a party to the proceedings, charged by a lay representative exercising a right of audience (CPR 27.14(4)).

(d) Where the parties consent to a claim being allocated to the small claims track, even though the amount of the claim exceeds the financial limit for small claims, the

Paragraph numbers marked with a "+" can be found online and on CD.

SCCO GUIDE

claim is treated for the purpose of costs as if it were proceeding on the fast track. In those circumstances the trial costs are in the discretion of the court but will not exceed the appropriate amount (having regard to the size of the claim) of fast track trial costs (CPR 27.14(5)).

(e) The effect on costs on allocation and reallocation to the small claims track is described in para 2.21, below.

1C–35 **2.20 Costs in fast track cases**

(a) In fast track cases the court's power to award trial costs is limited in accordance with CPR Part 46. Where the value of the claim does not exceed £3,000 the trial costs which the court may award will be £350. Where the value of the claim is more than £3,000 but not more than £10,000 the trial costs are £500 and where the value of the claim is more than £10,000 the trial costs are £750. The court may not award more or less than those amounts unless it decides not to award any trial costs or the circumstances set out in CPR 46.3 apply. The court has the power to apportion the amount awarded between the parties to reflect their respective degrees of success on the issues at trial (CPR 46.2(2)).

(b) The exceptional cases in which higher costs may be ordered are set out in CPR 46.3. These cover additional legal representatives, an additional liability in respect of a funding arrangement (see Section 19 below), separate trials, litigants in person, counterclaims and unreasonable and improper behaviour.

(c) Where a fast track case settles before the start of the trial and the court is assessing the amount of costs to be allowed in respect of a party's advocate for preparing for trial, it may not allow an amount exceeding the amount of fast track trial costs which would have been payable had the trial taken place (CPR 44.10).

1C–36 **2.21 Costs following allocation and reallocation**

The special rules which apply to small claims and fast track trial costs do not apply until the claim is allocated to a particular track. Once the claim is allocated to a particular track those special rules apply to the period before as well as after allocation except where the court or a Practice Direction provides otherwise (CPR 44.9). Any costs orders made before a claim is allocated to the small claims or fast track will not be affected by the allocation (CPR 44.11(1)). Where a claim is allocated to one track and subsequently re-allocated to a different track then, unless the court orders otherwise, any special rules about costs applying to the first track will apply to the claim up to the date of reallocation, and the rules applying to the second track will apply from the date of reallocation (CPR 44.11(2)).

1C–37 **2.22 Time for complying with orders for costs**

When the court makes an order for the payment of costs the paying party must make the payment within 14 days of the date of the order specifying the amount payable (CPR 44.8). The court may extend the time for payment, but if it does not do so and the costs are not paid within the 14 day period, the receiving party may take steps to enforce the order.

1C–38 **2.23 VAT**

(a) On an assessment of costs between the parties the receiving party must ensure that no claim for VAT is made in the bill if that party is able to recover it as input tax. Disputes as to the recoverability of VAT in bills between the parties are usually resolved by the making of a certificate as to the VAT position by the solicitors or auditors of the party receiving costs or by H M Revenue & Customs.

(b) Cases in which the receiving party cannot recover VAT on the costs payable by the paying party include the following:

   (i) the receiving party is a VAT registered taxable person and the supply of legal services was obtained for the purpose of his business;

   (ii) the receiving party is domiciled outside the European Union;

   (iii) the receiving party is domiciled outside the UK but is domiciled in the European Union and received the supply of legal services for the purposes of his business; or

   (iv) the receiving party is a legal representative representing himself (the "self supply" exception to VAT).

Paragraph numbers marked with a "+" can be found online and on CD.

(c) CPD Section 5 sets out some special provisions relating to VAT.

SECTION 3

FORM AND LAYOUT OF BILLS

3.1 Essential ingredients

1C–39

(a) Each bill should start with the full title of the proceedings, the name of the party whose bill it is and a description of the order for costs or other document giving the right to detailed assessment (as to which, see CPD 40.4).

(b) The bill should then give some background information about the case including a brief description of the proceedings, a statement of the status of the fee earners in respect of whom costs are claimed, the rates claimed for each such person and a brief explanation of any agreement or arrangement between the receiving party and his legal representatives which affects the costs claimed in the bill. There may also be a further matter to deal with if the party whose bill it is previously filed an estimate of costs in these proceedings. If there is a difference of 20% or more between the costs in the estimate and the costs (excluding the amount of any additional liability) claimed in the bill, the background information should state the reasons for that difference. See further as to differences between estimates and bills in paragraph 9.3 below.

(c) After the title and background information, it is convenient to divide the paper into several columns headed as follows: item number, date and description of work done, VAT, disbursements, profit costs.

(d) The bill should conclude with a summary showing the total costs claimed and with such of the certificates made by the receiving party or his legal representatives which are relevant (see further, paragraph 3.5 below).

3.2 Dividing bills of costs into separate parts

1C–40

Sometimes it is necessary or convenient to divide the section of the bill containing the actual items of costs into separate parts, numbered consecutively. For example, division into parts is necessary where there has been a change of solicitor, or where there has been some other change in the funding arrangements (eg to show costs incurred before, during and after the currency of LSC funding) to show costs claimed under different orders against different paying parties and to show costs before and after a change in the rate of VAT.

3.3 Dividing each part into separate items

1C–41

(a) In each part of a bill all the items claimed must be consecutively numbered and must be divided under such of the following heads as may be appropriate:

(1) Attendances on the court and counsel, in chronological order, up to the date of the notice of commencement.

(2) Attendances on and communications with the receiving party.

(3) Attendances on and communications with witnesses, including any expert witness.

(4) Attendances to inspect any property or place for the purposes of the proceedings.

(5) Attendances on and communications with other persons including officers of public records.

(6) Communications with the court and with counsel.

(7) Work done on documents: preparing and considering documentation, including documentation relating to pre action protocols where appropriate, work done in connection with arithmetical calculations of compensation and/or interest and time spent collating documents.

(8) Work done in connection with negotiations with a view to settlement if not already covered in the heads listed above.

(9) Attendances on and communications with London and other agents and work done by them.

(10) Other work done which was of or incidental to the proceedings which is not already covered in any of the heads listed above.

(b) In the list of items just given, the word "attendances" includes interviews and

Paragraph numbers marked with a "+" can be found online and on CD.

meetings and the word "communications" covers letters and e-mails sent and telephone calls.

(c) In each part of a bill which claims items under head 1 (attendances on court and counsel) a note should be made setting out, in chronological order with dates, all the relevant events in the proceedings including events which do not constitute chargeable items and including all orders for costs which the court has made (whether or not a claim is made in respect of those costs in this bill). Note that head 1 covers only attendances on the court and counsel. Communications with the court and counsel fall within head 6.

(d) Under heads 2 to 10, claims in respect of routine communications should be claimed as a single amount at the end of each head (*e.g.* "29 routine letters out at £x each and 8 routine telephone calls at £y each...£z"). If the number of attendances and non routine communications under a head is less than 20, each of them should be set out, in chronological order with dates. However, if under any head the number of attendances and non routine communications amount to 20 or more, the claim for the cost of those items in that part of the bill should be for the total only and should refer to a schedule in which the full record of dates and details is set out. Where bills contain more than one schedule each schedule should be numbered consecutively.

1C–42 3.4 Model forms of bills of costs

The CPD contains several model forms of bill of costs. The use of these model forms is not compulsory but is recommended and, when a different form is used, a short explanation of why it has been adopted should appear in the narrative towards the beginning. Precedent A is the one which is most frequently used in practice: it is illustrated in the Appendix, below, para A-1.

1C–43 3.5 Certificates in bills of costs

The final part of the bill of costs should contain such one or more of the prescribed certificates as are appropriate to the case and then the signature of the receiving party or his legal representative. These certificates give information on matters such as any rulings made as to entitlement to interest on costs, any payments made by the paying party on account of costs included in the bill and as to the receiving party's entitlement to recover from the paying party the VAT he is or has been liable to pay on the costs claimed. The text of the certificates is set out in the Appendix, below, para A-2.

1C–44 3.6 Disk copies of bills

If the bill of costs is capable of being copied onto a computer disk, the paying party is entitled to demand a disk copy free of charge (CPD para 32.11).

SECTION 4

COMMENCEMENT OF DETAILED ASSESSMENT PROCEEDINGS

1C–45 4.1 Earliest time for commencement

(a) Except where a summary assessment is carried out by the court, costs payable between the parties are not assessed until the conclusion of the proceedings out of which the order for costs arises, unless the court expressly orders an earlier detailed assessment (CPR 47.1). A Costs Judge or District Judge may make an order allowing detailed assessment proceedings to be commenced where there is no realistic prospect of the claim continuing (CPD para 28.1).

(b) Similarly where costs are payable out of the Community Legal Services Fund, detailed assessment should not be sought until the conclusion of the proceedings or until the discharge of the LSC certificate.

(c) Costs payable to a solicitor by his client are assessed if and when an order for detailed assessment is made (see further section 26 below).

(d) An appeal against an order for costs or an order for detailed assessment does not by itself operate as a stay of those proceedings unless the court so orders (CPR 47.2). An application for such a stay may be made either to the court whose order is being appealed or to the appeal court.

Paragraph numbers marked with a "+" can be found online and on CD.

4.2 Latest time for commencement

(a) Detailed assessment proceedings must be commenced within three months after the judgment, order or event giving rise to the right to costs (CPR 47.7); in civil recovery proceedings under the Proceeds of Crime Act 2002 the time limit is reduced to two months, see further Section 32, below. The parties may agree between themselves to extend or shorten the time specified by the rule for commencing detailed assessment proceedings. A party may apply to the appropriate office (as to which, see para 8.1, below) for an order to extend or shorten the period of three months, but permission is not required to commence detailed assessment proceedings out of time.

(b) If the receiving party fails to commence detailed assessment proceedings within the period specified by the rule, or by order of the court, the paying party may apply for an order under CPR 47.8(1) requiring the receiving party to commence the proceedings within a specified time. The court may direct that unless the receiving party does commence the detailed assessment proceedings within the time specified by the court, all or part of the costs will be disallowed.

(c) Where the receiving party commences proceedings for detailed assessment out of time but the paying party has not made an application under CPR 47.8(1), the court may disallow all or part of the interest otherwise payable to the receiving party but the court will not impose any other sanction unless there has been misconduct (CPR 47.8(3)).

4.3 Serving a notice of commencement

(a) Detailed assessment proceedings in respect of an order for costs between the parties are commenced by the receiving party serving on the paying party a notice of commencement in Form **N252** and a copy of the bill of costs. The notice of commencement must be completed to show the total amount of costs claimed in the bill and the extra sum which will be payable by way of fixed costs and court fees if a default costs certificate is obtained (CPR 47.6).

(b) The notice of commencement must be served on the paying party and on any other relevant persons, ie,

- (i) any person who has taken part in the proceedings which gave rise to the assessment and who is directly liable under an order for costs made against him;
- (ii) any person who has given to the receiving party notice in writing that he has a financial interest in the outcome of the assessment and wishes to be a party accordingly;
- (iii) any other person whom the court orders to be treated as a relevant person (CPD para. 32.8).

4.4 Documents to accompany the notice of commencement

(a) The list of documents to be served together with a notice of commencement depends upon whether or not the receiving party is seeking to recover an "additional liability", as to which see Section 19, below.

(b) If the detailed assessment is in respect of costs without any additional liability, the receiving party must serve, in addition to the notice of commencement and the bill of costs, copies of the fee notes of counsel and of any expert, in respect of fees claimed in the bill and written evidence as to any other disbursement claimed which exceeds £250, and a statement of parties giving the name and address for service of any person upon whom the receiving party intends to serve the notice of commencement (CPD para 32.3).

(c) If the detailed assessment is in respect of an additional liability only, the receiving party must serve, in addition to the notice of commencement and bill of costs, the relevant details of the additional liability and a statement of parties (CPD para 32.4). (Paragraph 19.6 below sets out the relevant details of additional liability which must be given.)

(d) If the detailed assessment is in respect of both costs and an additional liability, the receiving party must serve all the documents set out in (b) and (c) above.

4.5 Procedure where costs are agreed

If the paying party and the receiving party agree the amount of costs, either may apply for a costs certificate (either interim or final) in the amount agreed (CPR 47.10 and, see further, para 17.9, below).

Paragraph numbers marked with a "+" can be found online and on CD.

1C–50 **4.6 Cases in which notices of commencement are unnecessary**

(a) In the following cases detailed assessment proceedings are commenced by the filing in court of a request for a detailed assessment hearing:

(i) costs of a LSC funded client which are payable only out of the Community Legal Service Fund (CPR 47.17 and see Form **N258A**).

(ii) Costs payable out of a fund other than the Community Legal Service Fund (CPR 47.17A and see Form **N258B**).

(iii) Costs to be assessed pursuant to an order under Part III of the Solicitors Act 1974 (CPR 48.8 and see Form **N258C**).

(b) In these cases there is no requirement to serve a notice of commencement on any party and there is no entitlement to the issue of a default costs certificate in respect of the assessment.

Section 5
Points of Dispute and Reply

1C–51 **5.1 Time for Points of Dispute and consequences of not serving**

(a) Any party served with notice of commencement and the bill of costs may dispute any item in the bill by serving points of dispute on the receiving party and every other party to the detailed assessment proceedings. This must be done within 21 days after the date of service of the notice of commencement (CPR 47.9(2)), unless the parties agree to extend or shorten the time specified by the rule. A party may apply to the court for the time to be extended or shortened.

(b) Where a notice of commencement is served on a party outside England and Wales the period within which that party should serve points of dispute is to be calculated by reference to CPR Part 6 Section III (special provisions about service out of the jurisdiction) as if the notice of commencement was a claim form and as if the period for serving points of dispute were the period for filing a defence.

(c) If the receiving party is not served with any points of dispute and the period for doing so has expired, he may apply for a default costs certificate, as to which, see Section 6, below: (CPR 47.9(4)).

1C–52 **5.2 Form and contents of Points of Dispute**

(a) Points of dispute should be short and to the point and should follow as closely as possible Precedent G of the Schedule of Costs Precedents (see Appendix, para. A-3).

(b) The points of dispute should identify each item in the bill of costs which is disputed, state concisely the nature and grounds of the dispute and, where practicable, suggest a figure to be allowed instead of the figure which has been claimed. As a general rule, where details of an item are given in a schedule to the bill (eg, the Documents Item) it is not necessary for the Points of Dispute to deal separately with each individual entry in that schedule.

(c) A paying party may dispute a bill on the basis that the costs claimed therein exceed the amount of costs shown in an estimate of costs which the receiving party previously filed in the proceedings. In order to raise this dispute the paying party should include in his Points of Dispute a statement setting out his case if he:

(i) claims that he reasonably relied on the estimate of costs filed by the receiving party; or

(ii) wishes to rely upon the costs shown in the estimate in order to dispute the reasonable or proportionality of the costs claimed in the bill.

(N.B. the consequences of raising such a point of dispute are considered further in paragraph 9.3, below.)

(d) Where the receiving party claims an additional liability, a party serving points of dispute may include a request for information about other methods of financing costs which were available to the receiving party (CPD para 35.7(1)).

(e) The points of dispute should be signed by the party or his solicitor. If the points of dispute are capable of being copied onto a computer disk, the receiving party is entitled to demand a disk copy free of charge (CPD para 35.6).

1C–53 **5.3 Time limit for replies and their format**

(a) Where points of dispute are served the receiving party may serve a reply on the other parties to the assessment proceedings. The time limit for a reply is 21 days after service on him of the points of dispute (CPR 47.13).

Paragraph numbers marked with a "+" can be found online and on CD.

(b) There is no obligation upon a receiving party to serve a reply. Before doing so the receiving party should consider whether the expense of a reply can be justified: it probably cannot if the reply will merely deny the points in dispute.

(c) The reply may take the form of an annotation to the points of dispute (see para 5.2(d) above) or may be set out on a separate document. Serving a reply on a separate document does not avoid the obligation to file points of dispute annotated as necessary in order to show which items have been agreed and their value and which items remain in dispute and their value (see further para 8.2, below).

5.4 Where points of dispute challenge success fees

1C–54

If a paying party challenges the amount of a success fee claimed on behalf of counsel or a solicitor, it may become necessary for the court to rule not only upon that point of dispute, but also upon the liability of the receiving party to pay to his legal representatives any disallowed amount. The procedure to be followed in such cases is set out in Section 20, below.

SECTION 6

OBTAINING A DEFAULT COSTS CERTIFICATE

6.1 When and how to apply

1C–55

(a) The deadline for serving points of dispute is 21 days after the date of service of notice of commencement (see para 5.1, above). A receiving party who is not served with points of dispute on or before that deadline can request the issue of a default costs certificate (CPR 47.9(4)) unless the case is one of those described in para 6.2, below.

(b) A request for a default costs certificate must be made in Form **N254** and must be accompanied by a copy of the order for costs or other document giving the right to detailed assessment (as to which, see CPD para 40.4). The form must be signed by the receiving party or his solicitor. A court fee is payable (see further, Section 27, below).

(c) The request in Form **N254** must be filed in the District Registry or County Court in which the case was being dealt with when the judgment or order for costs was made or when the event occurred which gave rise to the right to assessment, or to which it has subsequently been transferred; in all other cases the request must be filed in the SCCO.

6.2 Cases in which the default costs certificate procedure does not apply

1C–56

(a) If there is more than one paying party, the receiving party has no right to a default costs certificate if one or more of the paying parties serves points of dispute. However, paying parties who serve points of dispute late or who fail to serve them at all have no right to be heard at the subsequent detailed assessment unless the court gives permission (CPR 47.9 and 47.14).

(b) The default costs certificate procedure does not apply to costs of a LSC funded client which are payable out of the Community Legal Service Fund, costs payable out of a fund other than the Community Legal Service Fund, or costs to be assessed pursuant to an order under Part III of the Solicitors Act 1974. Further information concerning these cases is given in paras 4.6 and 8.1 of this Guide.

6.3 Form of default costs certificate

1C–57

(a) A default costs certificate will be in Form **N255**. It will include an order to pay the costs to which it relates, the fixed costs payable in respect of solicitor's charges on the issue of a default costs certificate and the fee paid on the request for the issue of a default costs certificate.

(b) The receiving party may either draw up a default costs certificate and deliver it to the court together with the request, or may leave it to the court to draw it up.

6.4 Effect of a default costs certificate

1C–58

(a) The amount certified in the default costs certificate must be paid within 14 days of the date of the certificate unless, upon an application made by either party, whether before or after the issue of the certificate, the court has specified some other date (CPR 44.8).

Paragraph numbers marked with a "+" can be found online and on CD.

(b) An application to stay enforcement of a default costs certificate issued by the SCCO may be made to a Costs Judge or to a court which has jurisdiction to enforce the certificate (see further Section 17, below). Proceedings for enforcement of a default costs certificate may not be issued in the SCCO (CPD para 37.7).

(c) Default costs certificates are addressed to the paying party. Where the receiving party is funded by the LSC, the issue of a default costs certificate does not prohibit, govern, or affect any detailed assessment of the same costs which may have to be made to determine the sum payable out of the Community Legal Service Fund (CPD para 37.5, and see further Section 24, below).

SECTION 7

APPLYING TO SET ASIDE A DEFAULT COSTS CERTIFICATE

1C–59 **7.1 Application by receiving party**

(a) Where (i) the receiving party has purported to serve the notice of commencement on the paying party; (ii) a default costs certificate has been issued; and (iii) the receiving party subsequently discovers that the notice of commencement did not reach the paying party at least 21 days before the default costs certificate was issued, the receiving party must file a request for the default costs certificate to be set aside (which can be done by a court clerk without any hearing) or apply to the court for directions. The receiving party may take no further steps in the detailed assessment proceedings or the enforcement of the default costs certificate until the certificate has been set aside or the court has given directions (CPR 47.12(4)).

(b) A receiving party who has obtained a default costs certificate for the wrong amount (whether for too much or for too little) may apply to the court for an order varying the certificate (as to applications generally, see Section 17, below).

1C–60 **7.2 Application by paying party**

(a) To obtain an order setting aside a default costs certificate a paying party should apply on notice in Form **N244** together with a copy of the bill of costs, a copy of the default costs certificate and a draft of the points of dispute he proposes to serve if his application is granted, and any other evidence supporting his application.

(b) In deciding whether to grant the application the court will consider, amongst other things, whether the application was made promptly and whether the applicant has shown some good reason why the order should be made. Where appropriate the court may make an order subject to conditions (such as a condition requiring the applicant to make a payment on account of the costs in question), or may instead of setting aside the certificate vary it (eg, to specify some other sum payable or some other date for payment).

1C–61 **7.3 Orders and directions on set aside applications**

(a) If a default costs certificate is set aside the court will give directions for the management of the detailed assessment proceedings.

(b) The Appendix, below, contains standard forms of order commonly made on set aside applications in the SCCO; a conditional order, an unconditional order, an order adjourning the application and an order dismissing the application (see para A-4).

SECTION 8

REQUESTS FOR A DETAILED ASSESSMENT HEARING

1C–62 **8.1 Forms of request**

(a) There are four forms of request:

  (i) **N258**: request for detailed assessment hearing (general form).

  (ii) **N258A**: request for detailed assessment (legal aid/LSC only).

  (iii) **N258B**: request for detailed assessment (costs payable out of a fund other than the Community Legal Service Fund).

  (iv) **N258C**: request for detailed assessment hearing pursuant to an order under Part 3 of the Solicitors Act 1974.

(b) The request should be filed in the District Registry or County Court in which the case was being dealt with when the judgment or order for costs was made or when

Paragraph numbers marked with a "+" can be found online and on CD.

the event occurred which gave rise to the right to assessment, or to which it has subsequently been transferred; in all other cases the request must be filed in the SCCO (CPR 47.4). Special provisions apply to cases proceeding in the London County Courts: see para 8.2, below.

(c) In cases in which Form **N258** is appropriate, the request should be filed within six months after the judgment, order or event giving rise to the right to costs. In cases in which any of the other three forms of request is appropriate, the request should be filed within three months after the judgment, order or event giving rise to the right to costs. As to the making of agreements or applications for an extension of this time limit, see para 17.5, below.

8.2 Detailed assessment by the SCCO of costs of civil proceedings in London County Courts

1C–63

Where there is an order or judgment for costs in civil proceedings in the courts listed below, the receiving party must file the request for detailed assessment in the SCCO. All applications and requests must be made there. The relevant courts: Barnet, Bow, Brentford, Bromley, Central London, Clerkenwell, Croydon, Edmonton, Ilford, Lambeth, Mayors and City of London, Romford, Shoreditch, Uxbridge, Wandsworth, West London, Willesden and Woolwich.

8.3 Documents to accompany the request

1C–64

(a) Each form of request contains a series of tick boxes which give guidance as to the documents which should accompany the request. In cases of difficulty or uncertainty litigants and their representatives should also refer to the full list of documents which is set out in the Costs Practice Direction at para. 40.2.

(b) As to the fee which may be payable when filing a request, further details are given in Section 27, below.

8.4 Allocation to a Costs Officer or Costs Judge

1C–65

(a) As a general rule bills not exceeding £35,000, excluding VAT, will be allocated to a costs officer and larger bills will be allocated to a Costs Judge. Costs Judges also assess bills with a value below £35,000, excluding VAT, where they are linked to other bills which exceed that sum, or involve an assessment under the Solicitors Act 1974.

(b) On receipt of a form of request for a detailed assessment hearing, duly completed, the court clerk will enter the case on the computer, give it a reference number and then allocate the case by ballot to a particular costs officer or Costs Judge. The court clerk will then prepare an acknowledgement of the request which gives details of the reference number and the initials of the costs officer or Costs Judge to whom it has been assigned.

(c) Where the parties are agreed that the detailed assessment should not be made by a costs officer the receiving party should so inform the court clerk when filing the request. The court clerk will then allocate the case to a Costs Judge.

(d) If, after a case has been allocated to a costs officer, a party who objects to the detailed assessment being made by a costs officer must apply to a Costs Judge setting out the reasons for the objection. If sufficient reason is shown the court will direct that the bill should be assessed by a Costs Judge.

8.5 Obtaining the date for the hearing

1C–66

(a) On receipt of the request for a detailed assessment hearing the court will fix a date for the hearing, or, if the costs officer or Costs Judge so decides, will give directions or fix a date for a preliminary appointment.

(b) The court will give at least 14 days notice of the time and place of the detailed assessment hearing to every person whose name and address appears on the statement of persons to who notice should be given which accompanies the request. When giving such notice the court will also distribute the annotated points of dispute lodged by the receiving party together with the request.

(c) Cases assigned to a costs officer are usually given a date for hearing not more than 12 weeks later than the date the request for a hearing was filed. Cases assigned to a Costs Judge are usually given a date for hearing not more than six months later than the date upon which the request for a hearing was filed. When filing the request the

Paragraph numbers marked with a "+" can be found online and on CD.

SCCO GUIDE

receiving party should also file a note of any dates upon which, to his knowledge, a detailed assessment hearing would be inconvenient for any party likely to attend.

(d) One or two cases every day will be listed before the Principal Costs Officer in Room 2.07 each day. The cases will be allocated on the day to a Costs Judge or costs officer who becomes available.

(e) As to the making of an application to change the date for hearing once fixed, see para. 17.6.

1C–67   8.6 Application for an interim costs certificate

(a) At any time after the receiving party has filed the request for a detailed assessment hearing, the receiving party may apply for the issue of an interim costs certificate. Further details about making applications are given in Section 17, below. The application should be listed before the costs officer or Costs Judge to whom the case has been allocated. If the detailed assessment has been allocated to a Deputy Costs Judge the application will be heard by the Sitting Master (see para 1.3).

(b) In determining what, if any, interim certificate to make, the court will consider, amongst other things, the bill of costs, points of dispute thereon and any reply thereto and the certificate in the bill as to any payments on account which have already been made.

(c) The form of interim costs certificate, **N257**, specifies the amount which must be paid, the time within which payment must be made and specifies whether the payment should be made to the receiving party or into court to await the issue of a final costs certificate. Payment into court is made at The Court Office, Kingsway, WC2B 6LE (DX 44455 Strand). Cheques must be made payable to the "Accountant General of the Supreme Court". The general form is the Form 100 Requests for Lodgment which must be accompanied by the relevant request for lodgment and proof that court proceedings exist.

(d) An application to amend, cancel or stay enforcement of an interim costs certificate may be made to a Costs Judge (but not to a costs officer) and applications to stay enforcement may also be made to any court which has jurisdiction to enforce the certificate. Proceedings for enforcement of an interim costs certificate may not be issued in the SCCO.

1C–68   8.7 Lodging papers in support of the bill

(a) Unless the court otherwise directs the receiving party must file with the court the papers in support of the bill not less than seven days before the date for the detailed assessment hearing and not more than 14 days before that date.

(b) Save as mentioned below the papers to be filed and the order in which they are to be arranged is as follows:

(i) instructions and briefs to counsel arranged in chronological order together with all advices, opinions and drafts received and response to such instructions. Instructions are now frequently given by letter or email. These instructions should be separated or copied from the file if the original instructions sent to counsel are not available;

(ii) reports and opinions of medical and other experts;

(iii) any other relevant papers;

(iv) a full set of any relevant pleadings to the extent that they have not already been filed in court;

(v) correspondence, files and attendance notes;

(vi) where the claim also includes a claim in respect of an additional liability (as to which, see Section 19, below) any paper relevant to the issues raised by the claim for additional liability.

(c) Where a claim is in respect of an additional liability only, the papers to be filed are such of those papers listed at (b) above as are relevant to the issues raised by the claim for additional liability.

(d) Further information about lodging documents and about orders for the production of documents is given in Section 10, below.

1C–69   8.8 Obtaining files from other courts

Where a District Registry or a County Court has directed that the detailed assessment hearing shall be at the SCCO, the District Registry or County Court will send their

Paragraph numbers marked with a "+" can be found online and on CD.

court file to the SCCO. The receiving party is responsible for filing all other papers at the SCCO. If, in cases in which the order for costs was made in the Royal Courts of Justice, the parties consider that the court file is required for the assessment proceedings, they should so notify the SCCO in sufficient time to enable the SCCO to obtain it.

SECTION 9

THE DETAILED ASSESSMENT HEARING

9.1 The conduct of the hearing

1C–70

(a) The general rule is that all hearings are in public (CPR 39.2). However, the court is not required to make special arrangements for accommodating members of the public who wish to attend and, therefore, members of the public have no right to admission if their admission is impracticable. The court may, if appropriate, adjourn the proceedings to a larger room or court in order to make their admission practicable.

(b) A hearing or any part of it may be private, for example if it involves confidential information (including information relating to personal financial matters) and publicity would damage that confidentiality. Other examples are set out in the Practice Direction to CPR 39. At the start of a public hearing, or during it, either party may request the court to rule that, thereafter, the hearing should be conducted in private. Any judgment or order given or made in private must, when drawn up, be clearly marked that the court was "sitting in private" (CPR 39 Practice Direction para 1.13).

(c) No person other than the receiving party, the paying party and any party who has served points of dispute may be heard at the detailed assessment hearing unless the court gives permission (CPR 47.14). As to the rights of audience of persons claiming to represent such parties, see para 1.2, above.

(d) No person other than the receiving party, the paying party and any party who has served points of dispute may be heard at the detailed assessment hearing unless the court gives permission (CPR 47.14). As to the rights of audience of persons claiming to represent such parties, see para 1.2, above.

9.2 The decisions made at the hearing

1C–71

(a) A hearing that takes place at a court will usually be tape recorded by the court. A party may obtain a transcript of such a recording on payment of the proper transcribing charges (Practice Direction para 5 to CPD 27). It is still important that the parties and/or their representatives keep a careful note of the submissions and the decisions which are given as the hearing proceeds.

(b) Having considered the evidence, both oral and written, and having heard argument, the court will normally give a decision orally in respect of each item as and when it deals with it. On any complicated matter that may arise, the costs officer or Costs Judge may reserve his decision and, if he does so, his decision on that matter may be delivered either at a subsequent hearing or in writing.

(c) The adverse rulings that may be made if a receiving party fails to abide by any estimate of costs he previously gave in the proceedings is considered in paragraph 9.3, below.

(d) Often, the final matter dealt with at the hearing is the award of the costs of the detailed assessment proceedings. As to this see further, Section 11, below.

(e) Some information about the possibility of bringing an appeal against any decision made, and the time limit in which to do so, is given in Section 13, below.

9.3 Relevance of estimates of costs previously given

1C–72

(a) On an assessment of the costs of a party, the court may have regard to any estimate previously filed by that party, or by any other party in the same proceedings. Such an estimate may be taken into account as a factor, among others, when assessing the reasonableness and proportionality of any costs claimed.

(b) If there is a difference of 20% or more between the costs claimed by a receiving party (excluding the amount of any additional liability claimed) and the costs shown in an estimate of costs filed by that party, the court may regard the difference as evidence that the costs claimed are unreasonable or disproportionate if—

    (i) the receiving party has not provided a satisfactory explanation for that difference; or

Paragraph numbers marked with a "+" can be found online and on CD.

SCCO Guide

(ii) the court is satisfied that the paying party reasonably relied on the estimate of costs.

1C–73 **9.4 Removing the papers in support**

Once the detailed assessment hearing has ended it is the responsibility of the receiving party and of any legal representative appearing for him to remove the papers filed in support of the bill. If it is not possible to remove the papers immediately after the hearing they may, by permission of the court be left with a court clerk for collection at a later date, within the next seven days.

1C–74 **9.5 Hearing outside London**

If it is appropriate to do so, arrangements can be made for a Costs Judge to hear a detailed assessment in a court room outside London.

SECTION 10

PRODUCTION OF CONFIDENTIAL DOCUMENTS IN DETAILED ASSESSMENT HEARINGS

1C–75 **10.1 Receiving party's duty to lodge documents**

(a) Unless the court directs otherwise, the receiving party must file with the court the papers in support of the bill not less than seven days before the date of a detailed assessment hearing and not more than 14 days before that date.

(b) The CPD gives further details about "the papers in support of the bill" (see para. 8.6, above). In respect of each item of costs claimed in the bill the papers in support include all of the papers relevant to that item, whether they are favourable to the receiving party's case or unfavourable, or whether or not they are confidential or privileged. The lodging of documents as required by the CPD does not amount to a waiver of any privilege in those documents.

1C–76 **10.2 Court's power to order production of documents**

(a) The court may direct the receiving party to produce any document which, in the opinion of the court, is necessary to enable it to reach its decision. These documents will in the first instance be produced to the court, but the court may ask the receiving party to elect whether to disclose the particular document to the paying party in order to rely on the contents of that document, or whether to decline disclosure and instead rely on other evidence (CPD 40.14).

(b) The court's power to order production to the court of documents which the receiving party does not wish to produce will not be used to require production of those documents to the paying party. Because many of the documents in support of a bill are confidential and/or privileged there is no disclosure stage in detailed assessment hearings as there is in other civil proceedings.

1C–77 **10.3 Deciding points of dispute in favour of the paying party**

If, having examined papers lodged with or produced to the court, the court makes a decision based on those documents wholly in favour of the paying party, the court will so inform the parties and give brief reasons therefor if necessary. The paying party has no right to see the documents relied on by the court in reaching a decision which is wholly favourable to the paying party.

1C–78 **10.4 Deciding points of dispute in favour of the receiving party**

(a) If, having examined documents lodged with or produced to the court, the court is minded to determine a point of dispute wholly or partly in favour of the receiving party it does not automatically follow that the paying party will have a right to see all the documents relied on by the court in reaching that decision. The court should enquire of the paying party whether the paying party is content to accept that ruling (subject to appeal) or whether the paying party wishes to see the documents relied on by the court in making the ruling. In many cases the paying party will be content to agree that the court alone should see those documents. The alternatives (see below) may lead to additional delay and an increase in costs.

Paragraph numbers marked with a "+" can be found online and on CD.

(b) If the paying party declines to accept the court's ruling without inspecting documents, then, save as explained in paras (f) to (h) below, the court will put the receiving party to his election between showing the documents in question to the paying party or not relying upon them and offering to prove the fact of which the document is evidence by some other means. Alternatively the receiving party may decide to withdraw the claim for the costs of it. The court may give directions enabling the receiving party to have a fair opportunity to provide other evidence. In reaching its final decision on the issue the court will not take account of documents which the receiving party has elected not to show to the paying party.

(c) If the receiving party elects to show the documents in question to the paying party, the court may give directions to ensure that this is done fairly and that the paying party is given a reasonable opportunity to consider the documents and to make observations thereon. When showing documents to the paying party it is permissible to blank out parts of the disclosed documents on the ground that they are irrelevant to the issue of costs.

(d) It is standard practice for the client care letter (redacted where appropriate) to be shown to the paying party. The Court of Appeal has held that it should become usual practice for a conditional fee agreement (redacted where appropriate) to be disclosed for the purpose of costs proceedings in which a success fee is claimed. If a conditional fee agreement with a success fee relates to court proceedings the Conditional Fee Agreements Regulations 2000 state that the agreement must provide for disclosure of the reasons for setting the percentage increase at the level stated in the agreement.

(e) No production of documents is appropriate where the court determines that the point of dispute raised is spurious or vexatious only.

(f) No production is appropriate in respect of documents which the court did not rely upon in reaching its decision and which the receiving party did not deploy.

(g) The court will not compel production of any documents where it is unnecessary or disproportionate to do so.

(h) The court will exercise its discretion to put the receiving party to his election having regard to the requirements of fairness and justice. In particular it may consider whether the production could be made to the paying party's legal representatives only, and whether any confidential matter which is irrelevant can be excluded from the production.

(i) If, in respect of any privileged documents, the receiving party elects to waive its privilege by showing them to the paying party, that waiver is for the purposes of the detailed assessment only and the privilege can be re-asserted in any subsequent context.

10.5 Avoiding or minimising the expense and delay of production

1C–79

The production of documents at a detailed assessment hearing may well cause substantial delay to that hearing and may prejudice or embarrass any appeal made in the proceedings in which the costs were awarded or in any similar proceedings between the same parties. Receiving parties should therefore consider in advance what voluntary disclosure to their opponents they are willing to make and, how such disclosure can be achieved before the detailed assessment hearing without substantially damaging any privilege they wish to retain. If necessary, directions can be made by consent. Directions can also be made providing split hearing dates or times so as to facilitate the orderly disposal of the points in dispute. If production of documents may substantially prejudice or embarrass any appeal or linked proceedings, orders can be made adjourning the detailed assessment proceedings pending the determination of the other proceedings and directing the payment of interim costs certificates in the meantime.

SECTION 11

COSTS OF DETAILED ASSESSMENT PROCEEDINGS

11.1 Entitlement

1C–80

(a) As a general rule the receiving party is entitled to the costs of the detailed assessment proceedings (CPR 47.18). For exceptions concerning non acceptance of offers to

Paragraph numbers marked with a "+" can be found online and on CD.

settle, findings of delay or misconduct and the special rules applicable to assessments under the Solicitors Act 1974, see below, para. 11.4 and Sections 16 and 26 respectively.

(b) In deciding whether to depart from the general rule, where it applies, the court must have regard to all the circumstances including the conduct of the parties, the amounts, if any by which the bill of costs has been reduced and whether it was reasonable for a party to claim or dispute any item.

(c) The costs of the detailed assessment proceedings are usually assessed at the end of the hearing, but, in an exceptional case, may be assessed at a subsequent hearing. It is not necessary to provide details of those costs in advance unless the court makes an order to that effect.

1C–81 11.2 Offers to settle: general provisions

(a) Either party may make an offer to settle the claim for costs which is expressed to be "without prejudice, save as to the costs of the detailed assessment proceedings." Such an offer may relate to any issue in dispute between the parties. Its main purpose is to enable the parties to explore the possibility of negotiating a compromise which will not damage the subsequent presentation of their case if no compromise is reached.

(b) Paying parties should usually make their offers within 14 days after service of the notice of commencement. Receiving parties should usually make their offers within 14 days after service of the points of dispute. Offers made after these periods are likely to be given less weight unless there is good reason for the offer not having been made until the later time.

(c) The terms of the offer must be clear. There is no obligation to give details or a breakdown showing how the sum specified was arrived at, but unless the offer states otherwise, it will be treated as including the costs of the preparation of the bill, interest and VAT. A subsequent increased offer may be made.

1C–82 11.3 Where an offer to settle is accepted

If an offer to settle is accepted an application may be made for an agreed costs certificate (as to which, see para 17.9, below). If, because of acceptance, the whole of the detailed assessment proceedings are now settled, the receiving party must give notice of that fact to the court immediately, preferably by fax. The current fax numbers are: 020 7947 6247 (Room 2.13) or 6344 (General Office).

1C–83 11.4 Where an offer to settle is not accepted

(a) The existence of an offer to settle must not be communicated to the costs officer or Costs Judge conducting the hearing until the question of costs of the detailed assessment proceedings falls to be decided (CPR 47.19).

(b) When an offer to settle is properly brought to the attention of the court, the court may take it into account when deciding what, if any, order for costs to make. For example, if the court decides that an offer to settle made by the paying party ought reasonably to have been accepted by the receiving party, the court may:

(i) disallow the receiving party, wholly or in part, any costs of the detailed assessment, and/or

(ii) award costs in the detailed assessment to the paying party who made the offer.

SECTION 12

FINAL COSTS CERTIFICATES

1C–84 12.1 Completing the bill of costs

(a) At the detailed assessment hearing, the court will note on the bill of costs all items allowed, disallowed or reduced. The receiving party must, after the hearing, make clear the correct figures agreed or allowed in respect of each item and re-calculate the summary of the bill.

(b) The receiving party must file the completed bill of costs at the SCCO no later than 14 days after the detailed assessment hearing. When filing the bill of costs, the receiving party must lodge receipted fee notes and accounts in respect of all disbursements. However, there is no obligation to produce receipted fee notes or accounts in respect of disbursements (other than those relating to counsel's fees) which

Paragraph numbers marked with a "+" can be found online and on CD.

individually do not exceed £500 if the bill includes a certificate that such disbursements have been duly discharged (see Precedent F(5) which is illustrated in the Appendix, below, para A-2). Also, the court may have given a direction at the detailed assessment hearing which dispenses with the need for the production of some or all the fee notes and accounts in question. For example, the bill may be marked "vouching of [all disbursements] [expert's fees] is dispensed with.

12.2 Failure to file completed bill of costs

1C–85

If the receiving party fails to file the completed bill of costs within 14 days of the detailed assessment hearing, the paying party may make an application for such directions as may be appropriate under the court's general powers of management. As to applications generally, see Section 17, below.

12.3 Effect of final costs certificate

1C–86

(a) A final costs certificate will include an order to pay the costs to which it relates, unless the court orders otherwise (CPR 47.16)

(b) If the receiving party has failed to comply with the obligation to produce receipted fee notes and receipted accounts in respect of disbursements which have been allowed, the final costs certificate will be for an amount not exceeding the amount (if any) allowed in respect of profit costs and the amount of allowed disbursements in respect of which receipted fee notes or receipted accounts have been produced to the court but only to the extent indicated by those receipts.

(c) As a general rule the amount shown as payable in a final costs certificate will be the amount payable after taking into account the amount payable under any interim certificate already given and/or the amount payable under any order to pay costs on account. However, if the court is satisfied that no payments have been made in respect of previous certificates or orders, the certificate may include an order to pay the gross amount of costs payable. The text of such a certificate should, after stating the amount of the total costs, contain an endorsement such as:

"and, no sums having been paid under the order of Mr Justice X dated…,or under the interim certificate issued herein dated…

(d) The paying party must comply with the order for the payment of costs within 14 days of the date of the certificate or within such later date as the court may specify (CPR 44.8).

12.4 Order to stay enforcement

1C–87

Any application to stay enforcement of an interim or final costs certificate issued by the SCCO must be made to a Costs Judge or to a court which has jurisdiction to enforce the certificate.

12.5 Enforcement of certificate

1C–88

Proceedings for enforcement of an interim or final costs certificate may not be issued in the SCCO.

SECTION 13

APPEALS AGAINST DECISIONS IN DETAILED ASSESSMENT PROCEEDINGS

13.1 Routes of appeal

1C–89

(a) From a decision of a costs officer in a High Court case there is a right of appeal (in other words, no permission to appeal is needed) to a Costs Judge with a further appeal (for which permission is required) to a High Court Judge.

(b) From a decision of a Costs Judge in a High Court matter parties may, if permission is granted, bring an appeal to a High Court Judge with a further appeal to the Court of Appeal.

(c) The route of an appeal from a decision of a Costs Judge in a County Court matter depends upon whether the Costs Judge heard the matter whilst sitting as a Deputy District Judge of the County Court. If he did so the parties may, if permission is granted, bring an appeal to a Circuit Judge in the County Court with a further appeal to the Court of Appeal.

Paragraph numbers marked with a "+" can be found online and on CD.

SCCO Guide

(d) In London County Court cases which are not transferred to the SCCO so as to become High Court cases, the appeal from a Costs Judge lies, if permission is granted, to the London Designated Civil Judge, sitting at the Central London County Court.

1C–90 **13.2 Seeking permission to appeal**

(a) No permission to appeal is required from any decision made by a costs officer.

(b) From any decision of a Costs Judge (including decisions made on an appeal from a costs officer) permission to appeal is required. The general test for permission is whether the appeal has any real prospect of success. The permission should normally be sought orally at the time of the hearing. If refused, or if not sought then, the intending appellant must include an application for permission in his appellant's notice (as to which, see para. 13.4, below).

(c) In order to bring a further appeal to the Court of Appeal from the decision of a High Court Judge permission is required from the Court of Appeal (CPR 52.13). The general test for permission in such a case is whether the appeal would raise an important point of principle or practice or whether there is some other compelling reason for the Court of Appeal to hear it.

(d) A permission to appeal may limit the issues which may be raised on the appeal and may be made subject to conditions.

1C–91 **13.3 Time limits for appeals**

(a) An intending appellant must file an appeal notice within 14 days after the date of the decision he wishes to appeal against (CPR 47.22 and 52.4). If a party has good reason for seeking a longer period in which to appeal he should apply for an extension of time, either on the occasion when the decision is made, or by including such an application in his appeal notice.

(b) The time for appeal runs from the date of the decision to be appealed against, not from the end of the detailed assessment. However, a costs officer or Costs Judge may make a direction that the time for appeal will not begin to run until the detailed assessment has been concluded.

1C–92 **13.4 Documentation on appeals**

(a) Form **N161** is the prescribed form of notice for all costs appeals. On an appeal from a costs officer the notice, once filed, will be served on other parties by the court office. On an appeal from a Costs Judge the appellant must arrange service of a copy of the notice on each respondent as soon as practicable and, in any event, within seven days after filing.

(b) Form **N161** summarises the documents which should be prepared in support of the appeal. In particular, the appellant must supply a suitable record of the judgment being appealed, ie, an approved transcript, alternatively a written judgment signed by the costs officer or Costs Judge, or alternatively in the case of a costs officer, the officer's comments written on the bill, or, in the case of a Costs Judge, a note of the judgment which is agreed by the respondent and/or approved by the Costs Judge.

(c) Form **N162** is the prescribed form of respondent's notice for all costs appeals. However, a respondent is not required to serve a respondent's notice if he intends to rely solely upon the judgment of the court below for the reasons given by that court.

1C–93 **13.5 Conduct of the appeal**

(a) On an appeal from a costs officer, the Costs Judge will rehear the proceedings which gave rise to the decision appealed against and may make any order and give any directions which he considers appropriate.

(b) An appeal from the decision of a Costs Judge is limited to a review of that decision, unless the court considers that it would be in the interests of justice to hold a rehearing.

(c) On an appeal from a decision of a Costs Judge it is customary for the court to sit with two assessors, one of whom will be a Costs Judge and the other will be a practising barrister or solicitor.

SECTION 14

CORRECTING ACCIDENTAL SLIPS OR OMISSIONS IN FINAL COSTS CERTIFICATES

1C–94 **14.1 The Slip Rule**

The court may at any time correct an accidental slip or omission in any certificate issued by the court and may vary any certificate in order to make the meaning and

Paragraph numbers marked with a "+" can be found online and on CD.

intention of the court clear: see CPR 40.12 (often known as the "slip rule") and the Practice Direction supplementing it. Although it is mainly used to correct typographical or arithmetical mistakes, the slip rule can also be used to correct other more substantial errors and omissions in expressing the manifest intention of the court.

14.2 Applications for amendment

1C–95

An application under the slip rule may be made informally (eg, by letter) or formally, by application under Part 23 (as to which see Section 17, below). The application may be dealt with without a hearing if the applicant so requests, or with the consent of all parties, or where the court does not consider that a hearing would be appropriate. However, if the application is, or is likely to be, opposed, it should be listed for hearing before a Costs Judge.

SECTION 15

INTEREST ON COSTS

15.1 Entitlement to interest on costs

1C–96

(a) In respect of costs payable by order and included in a bill of costs for detailed assessment the receiving party may be entitled to interest under Section 17 of the Judgments Act 1838 or Section 74 of the County Courts Act 1984. If so the entitlement to interest begins on the date upon which the order for costs was made (not the date upon which the costs were assessed) unless the court otherwise orders (CPR 40.8 and 44.3(6)(g)). However,

(i) In respect of the costs of the detailed assessment proceedings, the interest begins to run from the date of the default, interim or final costs certificate, as the case may be; and

(ii) Under CPR 44.3(6)g the court has power to order interest on costs to run from a date other than the date of judgment.

(b) In respect of costs payable by contract (eg, costs payable to a solicitor by his client or former client) the entitlement to interest normally depends upon the terms of that contract. However a statutory right to interest may arise under the Solicitors (Non Contentious Business) Remuneration Order 1994 or the Late Payment of Commercial Debts (Interest) Act 1998.

15.2 Effect on final costs certificates

1C–97

(a) If the amount of costs payable under an order for costs proceeds to a detailed assessment, the final costs certificate issued will record the date of entitlement to interest and the effect of any rulings which the court has made as to interest. Where a bill of costs covers costs payable under an order or orders in respect of which the receiving party wishes to claim interest from different dates, the bill should be divided into separate parts so as to enable such interest to be calculated. If not so divided the date of entitlement to interest recorded in the certificate will be the latest of the relevant dates.

(b) Only in an exceptional case (eg where enforcement proceedings on a final costs certificate are to be taken abroad) will a final costs certificate record the amount of interest accrued up to the date of the certificate and/or the daily rate of interest accruing thereafter. In order to obtain such a certificate the receiving party should apply, on notice to the paying party, justifying the rate of interest claimed and, where payments on account have been made, explaining the effect which such payments have had on the calculation of interest.

(c) In respect of costs payable to a solicitor by his client or former client the final costs certificate will record neither the date of entitlement to any interest nor the amount of any interest accrued or accruing.

SECTION 16

APPLICATIONS CONCERNING DELAY, MISCONDUCT OR WASTED COSTS

16.1 Sanction for delay in commencing detailed assessment proceedings

1C–98

(a) Under CPR 47.7 detailed assessment proceedings must be commenced within three months of the date of the order for costs or other event under which the right to

Paragraph numbers marked with a "+" can be found online and on CD.

costs arose by the receiving party serving on the paying party the documents referred to in CPR 47.6(1) (see Section 4 above).

(b) Permission to commence detailed assessment proceedings out of time is not required (CPD 33.4) but if the receiving party has failed to commence detailed assessment proceedings within the deadline the paying party may apply for an order under CPR 47.8(1) disallowing all the costs to which the receiving party would otherwise be entitled unless the detailed assessment proceedings are commenced within such further time as the court may specify.

(c) An application for an order under Rule 47.8(1) must be made in writing, issued in the appropriate court office and served at least seven days before the hearing.

(d) If the receiving party commences proceedings for detailed assessment late but before the paying party makes an application under CPR 47.8(1) the court may disallow all or part of the interest on costs that would otherwise be payable but must not impose any other sanction except in accordance with CPR 44.14 (powers in relation to misconduct, see below).

1C–99   16.2 Misconduct by litigants or legal representatives

(a) The court may make an order under CPR 44.14 where—

   (i) a litigant or his legal representative, in connection with a summary or detailed assessment, fails to comply with a rule, practice direction or court order; or

   (ii) it appears to the court that the conduct of a party or his legal representative, before or during the proceedings which gave rise to the assessment proceedings, was unreasonable or improper.

(b) Examples of conduct which is unreasonable or improper includes steps which are calculated to prevent or inhibit the court from furthering its overriding objective which is to deal with cases justly.

(c) The sanctions which the Court can impose are:

   (i) disallowance of all or part of the costs which are beng assessed; or

   (ii) ordering the party at fault or his legal representative to pay the costs which the misconduct has caused any other party to incur.

(d) Before making such an order the Court must give the party or the legal representative in question a reasonable opportunity to attend a hearing to give reasons why such an order should not be made.

(e) Where the court makes an order under CPR 44.14 against a legally represented party and that party is not present when the order is made, that party's solicitor must notify his client in writing of the order no later than seven days after the solicitor receives notice of the order.

1C–100   16.3 Personal liability of legal representatives for costs—wasted costs orders

(a) In addition to the court's powers under CPR 44.14 the court can also order a *legal representative* to pay a specified sum of costs to a party or disallow a specific sum where costs have been wasted (CPR 48.7).

(b) The court may make a wasted costs order only if:—

   (i) The legal representative has acted improperly, unreasonably or negligently;

   (ii) his conduct has caused a party to incur unnecessary costs; and

   (iii) it is just in all the circumstances to order him to compensate that party for the whole or part of those costs.

(c) Before making a wasted costs order a Court may direct a Costs Judge to inquire into the matter and report back to the Court. It may also refer the matter to a Costs Judge to deal with outright.

1C–101   16.4 Principles on which wasted costs orders are made

(a) The Court of Appeal laid down guidelines in *Ridehalgh v Horsefield* [1994] Ch 205, CA to assist the court in deciding whether a legal representative has acted improperly, unreasonably or negligently:

   (i) acting "improperly" covers but is not confined to conduct which would ordinarily be held to justify disbarrment of barristers, striking off from the roll of solicitors, suspension from practice or other serious professional penalty;

   (ii) acting "unreasonably" describes conduct which is vexatious, designed to harass the other side rather than advance the resolution of the case;

Paragraph numbers marked with a "+" can be found online and on CD.

(iii) acting "negligently" denotes, in an untechnical way, failure to act with the competence reasonably expected of ordinary members of the legal profession.

(b) In general, wasted costs applications should be left until after the end of the trial. It is usual for the aggrieved party rather than the Court to raise the issue of wasted costs, but the Court can make a wasted costs order against a legal representative of its own initiative.

16.5 Procedural steps on applications for a wasted costs order

1C–102

(a) A party may apply for a wasted costs order by filing an application notice in accordance with Part 23 (as to which, see Section 17, below) or by making an application orally in the course of any hearing (CPD 53.3).

(b) A Part 23 application must be supported by evidence (CPD 53.8) which:

(i) sets out what the legal representative has done or failed to do; and,

(ii) identifies the costs that he may be ordered to pay or which are sought against him.

(c) The court will then give directions about the procedure to be followed in order to ensure that the issues are dealt with in a way which is as fair, simple and summary as the circumstances permit.

16.6 Deciding whether to make a wasted costs order

1C–103

(a) As a general rule the court will consider whether to make a wasted costs order in two stages (CPD paragraph 53.6):

> *Stage One*—The Court must be satisfied that it has before it evidence or material, which, if unanswered, would be likely to lead to a wasted costs order being made, and that the wasted costs proceedings are justified notwithstanding the likely costs involved. If not so satisfied the Court will decide that further proceedings are not justified.
>
> *Stage Two*—The Court will give the legal representative an opportunity to give reasons why a wasted costs order should not be made before deciding whether to do so.

(b) If an application is made under Part 23 the Court can proceed direct to Stage Two if it is satisfied that the legal representative has already had a reasonable opportunity to give his reasons.

Section 17

Other Applications in Detailed Assessment Proceedings

17.1 Applications generally

1C–104

(a) Detailed assessment proceedings are commenced by the receiving party serving on the paying party a notice of commencement, a copy of the bill of costs and certain other documents. After that date, and sometimes even before that date, applications relating to the proceedings or intended proceedings can be made by any party.

(b) An application can be made in the Supreme Court Costs Office if that is the "appropriate office" for the purposes of CPR 47.4 (and see para. 8.1, above). In order to make an application, the party must file in court a notice of application, copies of any documents relied on in support and the appropriate court fee, or a fee exemption certificate (see Section 27, below).

(c) The notice of application should be in Form **N244**. Note that the use of such a form and the requirement to pay a court fee may be avoided in some cases; if the SCCO has previously made an order or given directions in the detailed assessment proceedings, that order may include a "liberty to apply" which entitles the parties seeking a further order or directions to write to the court requesting it to restore the previous application rather than issuing a new one.

17.2 Evidence in support of applications

1C–105

(a) All evidence relied on in support of an application must be filed in court, ideally at the same time the application notice is filed.

(b) Part C of Form **N244** enables the applicant to identify the evidence relied on in support of his application. The applicant can rely upon written evidence set out in the notice or in a separate witness statement. In either case such evidence must contain a statement of truth, ie, a statement in the following form:

Paragraph numbers marked with a "+" can be found online and on CD.

[I believe] [the (claimant or as may be) believes] that the facts stated in this application notice (or witness statement as may be)] are true.

The statement of truth must be signed by the litigant, or his litigation friend, or legal representative or witness, as may be.

(c) Other documents, not especially prepared for the purpose of the application, may also be relied on as evidence, eg, copies of letters received and letters sent.

1C–106 17.3 Extension of time for commencing detailed assessment proceedings

The time limit for commencing detailed assessment proceedings is summarised in para 4.2, above. The parties may agree to extend this time. Alternatively, the receiving party can make an application for an order extending the time limit. Note that permission to commence detailed assessment proceedings out of time is not required.

1C–107 17.4 Extensions of time for service of points of dispute

The time limit for service of points of dispute is summarised in para 5.1, above. Failure to serve points of dispute in time may lead to the receiving party obtaining a default costs certificate (as to which see Section 6, above). The parties may agree to extend the time for service of points of dispute, alternatively the paying party may apply to the appropriate office for an order extending the time limit.

1C–108 17.5 Extension of other time limits

The time limit for serving a reply to points of dispute is summarised in para 5.1 above and the time limit for filing a request for a detailed assessment hearing is summarised in para 8.1, above. In any case directions of the court may impose further time limits for the taking of certain steps, eg the service of witness statements. All these time limits may be extended by the agreement of the parties or, alternatively, by an order made upon an application.

1C–109 17.6 Changing the date fixed for a detailed assessment hearing

A date fixed for the hearing of a detailed assessment cannot be changed or cancelled merely by the agreement of the parties unless the parties agree a compromise and the detailed assessment proceedings are settled. If detailed assessment proceedings are settled the receiving party must give notice of that fact to the court immediately, preferably by fax. The current fax numbers are: 020 7947 6247 or 6344. In other cases, if one or all parties wishes to vary a date fixed, he or they must make an application in N244 or request the court to restore a previous application for hearing, if a "liberty to apply" has previously been given.

1C–110 17.7 Amending bills of costs, points of dispute or replies

If a party wishes to vary his bill of costs, points of dispute or reply, an amended or supplementary document must be filed with the court and copies of it must be served on all other relevant parties. Note that permission is not required but the court may later disallow the variation or permit it only upon conditions, including conditions as to the payment of any costs caused or wasted by the variation.

1C–111 17.8 Case management directions

Where appropriate any party can apply for case management directions, such as timetable directions for the exchange of witness statements and facilitating cross examination, or timetable directions concerning the detailed assessment of "linked bills", ie other bills of costs made in the same proceedings. Especially in the case of larger bills of costs, ie, bills exceeding £200,000, timetable directions may be given fixing a series of dates for the detailed assessment hearing. For example, if the estimated hearing time is five days, a one day appointment may be given for particular points of dispute (perhaps relating to VAT entitlement, solicitor's hourly rates, and all fees claimed in respect of the trial) with a four day appointment for the remaining points of dispute to take place some four weeks later. Splitting the hearing into two appointments usually enables the court to give an earlier appointment than it otherwise could. Also, by determining selected issues at the first appointment, the

Paragraph numbers marked with a "+" can be found online and on CD.

parties may be able to agree the remaining points so obviating the need for the later appointment.

17.9 Agreed costs certificates
1C–112

(a) Parties may agree all or part of the costs before or after the court has become involved in the detailed assessment proceedings. An interim or a final certificate can be issued.

(b) In the course of proceedings a receiving party may claim that the paying party has agreed to pay costs but will neither pay those costs nor join in a consent application. The receiving party may apply under Part 23 for an interim or final certificate to be issued. The application must be supported by evidence and will be heard by a Costs Judge.

17.10 Change of solicitor
1C–113

(a) Where a solicitor's business address has been properly given as the address for service of a party that solicitor is said to be "on the record" as acting for that party and, as such, will continue to be served with documents and will be expected to attend court hearings until such time as he is "off the record". That will not occur until a notice of change of solicitor is filed by or on behalf of the party, or, in a LSC funded case, until the solicitor files a notice of discharge of revocation of the funding certificate, or until the solicitor obtains an order for the removal of his name from the record.

(b) In practice, when a solicitor and client fall out and the client is not intending to instruct another solicitor, the former solicitor will often prepare a notice of change and either obtain the client's signature to it and then file it or will send it to the former client for him to sign and file. The former solicitor will no doubt warn the client that, if he refuses or unreasonably fails to serve and/or file the notice the solicitor may apply for an order that the solicitor has ceased to act together with an order for the costs of the application.

(c) An application for an order declaring that a solicitor has ceased to be the solicitor acting for a party should be made under Part 23 and should be supported by evidence. The notice of application and evidence should not be served on other parties to the proceedings but should be served on the former client unless the court directs otherwise.

(d) An applicant for an order declaring that he has ceased to be the solicitor acting for a party should consider whether he wishes the application to be dealt with without a hearing. As a general rule the court will make an order without a hearing (adding liberty to apply to stay, set aside or vary the order) if satisfied that the application is made by consent, is unopposed or appears overwhelmingly strong.

17.11 Stay of detailed assessment proceedings
1C–114

The bringing of an appeal against an order for costs does not stay the detailed assessment of those costs unless the court so orders (CPR 47.2). An application to stay the detailed assessment pending an appeal may be made either to the court whose order is being appealed or to the court who will hear the appeal. The application should not normally be made to the SCCO.

17.11 Stay of enforcement of costs certificates
1C–115

(a) Applications for an order staying enforcement of a default costs certificate, an interim costs certificate or a final costs certificate issued by the SCCO may be made either to the SCCO or to a court which has general jurisdiction to enforce the certificate. In the SCCO the application will be heard by the Costs Judge who assessed the costs in question or, if the costs were assessed by a costs officer, by the Sitting Master. The application should usually be accompanied by evidence of the paying party's income, assets, other liabilities and proposals for payment. The usual form of order granting a stay is on terms requiring the paying party to pay off the certified costs by specified instalments.

(b) If the certificate relates to the costs of a County Court case sent to the SCCO for assessment which nevertheless remains a County Court case, the paying party may, as an alternative to applying for a stay of enforcement, apply to the SCCO or the County Court for an order varying the certificate into an order for payment by instalments.

17.13 Other applications
1C–116

The paragraphs mentioned below contain notes on the following applications in detailed assessment proceedings:

Paragraph numbers marked with a "+" can be found online and on CD.

- for assessment before conclusion of main proceedings (para. 4.1),
- for an order setting aside a default costs certificate (paras 7.1 and 7.2),
- for assignment from a costs officer to a Costs Judge (para. 8.3),
- for an interim costs certificate (para. 8.5),
- for permission to appeal (para. 13.2),
- for correcting accidental slips or omissions in certificates (para. 14.2),
- for sanctions for failure to commence in time (para. 16.1), and
- for a wasted costs order (para. 16.3).

SECTION 18

CASES TRANSFERRED FROM OTHER COURTS

1C–117 **18.1 Assessment of costs awarded in the High Court and the County Courts**

(a) Bills of costs in proceedings in the District Registries of the High Court and County Courts are frequently transferred to the SCCO either at the request of the parties or of the Court's own initiative. This is likely to occur when the District Judge considers the size and complexity of the bill warrants such a transfer.

(b) When bills are transferred from a District Registry or a County Court by an order of that Court, the parties will be served with a copy of that order. Sometimes such an order is made immediately prior to the date fixed for detailed assessment at that Court, which itself may be some time after the parties first requested a hearing date. Every effort is made by the SCCO to list the transferred case at the earliest opportunity. When, however, the parties have already waited for a significant time for their bill to be assessed by the local Court, they should notify the SCCO of this fact immediately after the order transferring the case is made, so that as early a hearing date as possible can be given. If this is not done, the parties may find themselves at the end of the queue of cases awaiting a hearing date at the SCCO.

(c) If it is appropriate to do so, arrangements can be made for a Costs Judge to hear a detailed assessment in a court room outside London. Receiving parties seeking such arrangements should request them by letter lodged with the Judge's clerk when the request for detailed assessment is lodged or when the matter has been transferred to the SCCO.

1C–118 **18.2 Assessment of costs awarded by other tribunals and bodies**

Various statutes give the SCCO jurisdiction to assess costs in litigation including the following:

(i) Election petitions

(ii) Proceedings under the Arbitration Acts

(iii) Proceedings before National Health Service Committees, Tribunals and other similar bodies

(iv) Proceedings before the Employment Appeal Tribunal

(v) Proceedings before VAT tribunals

(vi) Determinations by the Secretary of State for Environment or his appointed local planning inspectors as a result of local planning inquiries

(vii) Proceedings before the Solicitor's disciplinary tribunal

(viii) Proceedings before the Copyright Tribunal.

(ix) Competition appeals.

(x) Proceedings before the Financial Services and Markets Tribunal.

(xi) Proceedings under the Justices and Justices' Clerks (Costs) Regulations 2001

(xii) Proceedings under the General Commissioners of Income Tax (Costs) Regulations 2001.

SECTION 19

FUNDING ARRANGEMENTS

1C–119 **19.1 Introduction**

(a) The Access to Justice Act 1999 permits the recovery of costs under a conditional fee agreement which provides for a success fee. The Act also provides for recovery of

Paragraph numbers marked with a "+" can be found online and on CD.

after the event insurance premiums by way of costs, and recovery of an additional amount where a membership organisation undertakes to meet liabilities which members of the organisation, or other persons who are party to the proceedings may incur, to pay the costs of other parties to the proceedings (see Sections 27, 29 and 30 Access to Justice Act 1999). These arrangements are known as "funding arrangements" (CPR 43.2) and the percentage increase, insurance premium or additional amount in respect of provision made by a membership organisation is known as an "additional liability". Premiums in respect of before the event insurance polices (such as household and motor insurance policies) are not recoverable.

(b) The court will not assess any additional liability until the conclusion of the proceedings, or that part of the proceedings to which the funding arrangement relates. At the conclusion of the proceedings the court may make a summary assessment of all the costs, including any additional liability; make an order for detailed assessment of the additional liability but make a summary assessment of the other costs; or make an order for detailed assessment of all the costs (CPR 44.3A).

19.2 Providing information about funding arrangements 1C–120

(a) A party who wishes to claim an additional liability from a paying party must give any other party information about the funding arrangement and must also provide similar information when the funding arrangement changes. Information is given on Form **N251**. The party must state whether he has entered into a conditional fee agreement which provides for a success fee; taken out an insurance policy to which Section 29 of the Access to Justice Act 1999 applies; or made an arrangement with a membership organisation for the purpose of Section 30 of the Access to Justice Act 1999 (CPR 44.15). CPD Section 19 gives further details about the information to be given.

(b) When giving notice of funding in respect of a conditional fee agreement with a success fee, the party must state the date of the agreement and identify the claim or claims to which it relates.

(c) Where the funding arrangement is an after the event insurance policy, the party must state, when giving notice of funding, the name of the insurer, the date of the policy and must identify the claim or claims to which it relates.

(d) To be recoverable the insurance premium must have been paid or must be payable for insurance against the risk of incurring a costs liability in the proceedings, which was taken out *after* the event that is the subject matter of the claim (CPR 43.2(1)(m)).

(e) Where the funding arrangement is with a membership organisation, the party must state when giving notice of funding, the name of the body and must set out the date and terms of the undertaking it has given and must identify the claim or claims to which it relates.

(f) Where a party has entered into more than one funding arrangement in respect of a claim, for example a conditional fee agreement and an insurance policy, a single notice containing the information set out in Form **N251** may contain the required information about both or all of them.

SECTION 20

ASSESSMENT OF SUCCESS FEES AND AFTER THE EVENT INSURANCE PREMIUMS

20.1 Compliance with Conditional Fee Agreement and Collective Conditional Fee Agreement Regulations 1C–121

(a) The indemnity principle provides that a successful party cannot recover from an unsuccessful party more by way of costs than the successful party is liable to pay to his or her legal representatives (see Section 2.6). However the Access to Justice Act 1999 provides that a conditional fee agreement can now be made whereby the fees and expenses of the successful party's legal representatives will be payable even though the indemnity principle would otherwise prevent it.

(b) Until their revocation (see below) the Regulations which governed conditional fee agreements were the Conditional Fee Agreements Regulations 2000, the Access to Justice (Membership Organisations) Regulations 2000 and the Collective Conditional Fee Agreements Regulations 2000. With effect from 1 November 2005 the Access to

Paragraph numbers marked with a "+" can be found online and on CD.

SCCO GUIDE

Justice (Membership Organisations) Regulations 2000 are replaced by new Regulations and the Conditional Fee Agreements Regulations 2000 and the Collective Conditional Fee Agreements Regulations 2000 have been replaced by the Solicitors Practice (Client Care) Amendment Rules 2005 and a new Law Society's Model CFA Agreement (for use in personal injury and clinical negligence cases).

(c) A conditional fee agreement is unenforceable unless it satisfies all the conditions imposed by Section 58 of the Courts and Legal Services Act 1990 (as amended by the Access to Justice Act 1999) and the Regulations made under it (where the CFA or CCFA was entered into before 1 November 2005).

(d) However the court will not declare a conditional fee agreement unenforceable unless the failure to satisfy those conditions has a materially adverse effect on the protection of the interests of the client or the proper administration of justice.

(e) If the court rules that a conditional fee agreement is unenforceable, the client under that agreement will not be liable to pay any fees or disbursements under it. Similarly, because of the indemnity principle, he will not be able to recover any of those fees and disbursements from any other litigant. However, the client may be able to recover any disbursements which he has already paid.

1C-122 **20.2 Documents to accompany the bill**

Where a party seeks the detailed assessment of an additional liability the details which he must give together with the bill and notice of commencement are as follows:

(a) In the case of a conditional fee agreement with a success fee:
   (i) a statement showing the amount of costs which have been summarily assessed or agreed and the percentage increase which has been claimed in respect of those costs; and
   (ii) a statement of the reasons for the percentage increase (where the CFA or CCFA was entered into before 1 November 2005).

(b) If the additional liability is an after the event insurance premium a copy of the insurance certificate showing whether the policy covers:
   (i) the receiving party's own costs;
   (ii) his opponent's costs; or
   (iii) his own costs and his opponent's costs; and
   (iv) the maximum extent of that cover and the amount of the premium paid or payable.

(c) If the receiving party claims an additional amount under Section 30 of the Access to Justice Act 1999 (Membership Organisations) a statement setting out the basis upon which the receiving party's liability for the additional amount is calculated.

1C-123 **20.3 Factors to be taken into account during assessment**

(a) A party may not recover as an additional liability—
   (i) any proportion of a success fee which is to compensate the legal representative for the fact that he will have to wait to be paid his fees and expenses; or
   (ii) any amount (when the agreement is made with a membership organisation) which exceeds the likely cost of taking out after the event insurance to cover another party's costs; or
   (iii) any additional liability during a period in which he (or she) failed to provide to the other party the information required by the court or by the Rules and Practice Directions about the funding arrangements or the reasons for setting the level of a success fee.

(b) Where a success fee is irrecoverable for the reasons given in (a)(iii) above, the court may consider granting relief from the sanctions. CPR 3.9 sets out the circumstances in which the court may grant relief.

(c) The court will consider the amount of any additional liability separately from the base costs and a success fee will not be reduced simply because, when added to the base costs, it appears to be disproportionate.

(d) In deciding whether the base costs are reasonable the court will consider the factors set out in CPR 44.5.

(e) When considering the amount of an additional liability the court will have

Paragraph numbers marked with a "+" can be found online and on CD.

regard to the facts and circumstances as they reasonably appeared when the agreement was made (or varied).

(f) Factors to be taken into account in deciding whether a success fee is reasonable include:

(i) the risk that fees or expenses might not become payable;

(ii) the legal representative's liability to fund disbursements;

(iii) what other methods of funding the costs were available.

(g) In costs only proceedings (see Section 21) the court will have regard to the time when and the extent to which the claim had been settled without the need to commence proceedings.

(h) Factors to be taken into account in deciding whether an after the event insurance premium is reasonable include:

(i) how its cost compares with the likely cost of funding the case with a conditional fee agreement with a success fee and supporting insurance (if it is not already so funded);

(ii) the level and extent of the insurance cover provided;

(iii) the availability of pre-existing insurance cover;

(iv) whether any part of the premium would be rebated in the event of early settlement;

(v) the amount of commission payable to the receiving party or his legal representatives or agents.

(i) The additional amount recoverable in respect of the membership organisation must not exceed the likely cost of the premium of an insurance policy against the risk of incurring a liability to pay the costs of other parties to the proceedings.

20.4 Fixed success fees

1C–124

CPR Part 45 provides for fixed success fees in certain road traffic accident disputes and certain Employers Liability claims.

20.5 Disputes between legal representatives and their clients

1C–125

(a) The following notes in this section apply only to cases in which the relevant CFA or CCFA was entered into before 1 November 2005. The Regulations which continue to govern such agreements (see above) provide that, in certain circumstances, if a success fee allowed on assessment is lower than the contractual success fee, the disallowed amount ceases to be payable under the agreement unless the court is satisfied that it should continue to be so payable. CPR 44.16 and CPD Section 20 set out the procedure, summarised below, by which a ruling can be obtained as to whether the disallowed amount should continue to be payable by the client.

(b) If the points of dispute served by the paying party challenge a success fee claimed in respect of counsel's fees, the solicitor must so inform counsel within three days and counsel must reply within ten days or be taken to accept the reduction (unless the court otherwise orders).

(c) If points of dispute served by the paying party challenge the success fee of the solicitor or counsel, the solicitor must write to the client within three days giving a clear written explanation of the dispute and the effect it will have if it is upheld in whole or in part. The letter must also explain the client's right to attend any subsequent hearing at court when the matter is raised and should invite the client to inform the solicitors whether or not the client wishes to attend any subsequent hearings.

(d) When requesting a hearing date (see Section 8.1) the solicitor must certify:

(i) the existence of any dispute as to the success fee,

(ii) the intention (if it be the case) to apply for any disallowed amount to continue to be payable by the client,

(iii) that he has given a written explanation to the client, and

(iv) whether the client wishes to attend any subsequent hearing.

(e) On receipt of notice from the court of the date for an assessment hearing, the solicitor must, within the next seven days, give written notice to the client and, if appropriate, to counsel, stating the date, time and place of the hearing.

Paragraph numbers marked with a "+" can be found online and on CD.

(f) At the hearing attended by the paying party the receiving party, the solicitor and counsel may attend or may be separately represented and may make oral or written submissions.

(g) If a success fee payable by the paying party is assessed at a figure lower than the contractually agreed figure and the legal representative still wishes to recover the contractually agreed figure he may apply for an order that the disallowed amount should continue to be payable by his client and the court may adjourn the hearing to enable the client to be notified of the order sought and, if necessary to be separately represented (CPR 44.16). The order sought does not affect the paying party and, therefore, the paying party need not attend the adjourned hearing.

(h) The court may decide the issue, whether the disallowed amount should continue to be payable, without an adjournment if the receiving party and all relevant legal representatives consent to the court doing so, and if the receiving party (or if corporate, an officer thereof) is present in court and if the court is satisfied that the issue can be fairly decided without an adjournment. In any other case the court will give directions and fix the date for the hearing of the application.

Section 21

Costs Only Proceedings

1C–126 21.1 Introduction

(a) CPR 44.12A sets out the procedure to be followed where, before court proceedings are commenced, the parties to a dispute reach agreement on all issues, including which party is to pay costs, but are unable to agree the amount of those costs.

(b) Two distinct steps are required: firstly an application under CPR Part 8 seeking an order for costs; and secondly detailed assessment of those costs.

(c) It is not appropriate for either party to take the first step unless:

    (i) the parties must have reached an agreement on all the issues, including which party is to pay the costs;

    (ii) that agreement has been made or confirmed in writing; and

    (iii) no proceedings must have been started and the parties (*after a proper attempt at agreement*) must have failed to agree the amount of the costs.

1C–127 21.2 The application under CPR Part 8

(a) Either party may start costs only proceedings. The claim should be issued in the court in which the main proceedings would have been heard if that had been necessary.

(b) The Part 8 claim form (form **N208**) must: (i) identify the claim or dispute to which the agreement to pay costs relates; (ii) state the date and terms of the agreement on which the claimant relies; (iii) set out a draft of the order sought; (iv) state the amount of the costs claimed; and (v) state whether costs are claimed on the standard or the indemnity basis.

(c) The evidence filed in support of the claim must include copies of the documents relied upon to prove the agreement to pay costs.

1C–128 21.3 Obtaining the order for costs

(a) The court may make an order in the terms of the claim without the necessity of a hearing if:

    (i) the defendant fails to file an acknowledgment of service within the time allowed to do so and the claimant has written to the court requesting an order; or

    (ii) if the defendant files an acknowledgment of service stating that he does not contest the making of an order in the terms of the claim; or

    (iii) if a consent order under CPR 40.6 is filed which is signed by or on behalf of all parties and none of them is a litigant in person and the approval of the court is not required by any other rule.

(b) In costs only proceedings to which CPR 45 Section II applies (ie certain road traffic accident claims where the total amount of agreed damages does not exceed £10,000) the court must assess the costs in the manner set out in that section (ie it should allow certain fixed recoverable costs plus success fee and disbursements: ap-

Paragraph numbers marked with a "+" can be found online and on CD.

plications for greater amounts will be entertained only if the court considers that exceptional circumstances make it appropriate to do so).

(c) In cases in which CPR 45 Section II does not apply, the court will dismiss the claim without a hearing if it is opposed, ie, if the defendant files an acknowledgment of service stating that he intends to contest the proceedings or to seek a different remedy. A claim will not be treated as opposed and therefore dismissed merely because the defendant states in an acknowledgment of service that he disputes the amount of the claim for costs.

(d) Standard forms of order commonly made in the SCCO under CPR 44.12A are illustrated in the Appendix, below, para A-5.

(e) Unless all parties consent the order for costs will not include an order for a payment of costs on account. In costs only proceedings, the only issue to be decided by the court when making the order is whether or not there should be an assessment.

21.4 Conducting the detailed assessment proceedings

1C–129

(a) An order for costs made under CPR 44.12A will be treated as an order for the amount of costs to be decided by a detailed assessment to which Part 47 applies, as to which, see Sections 3 to 17, above.

(b) As to the receiving party's entitlement to apply for an interim costs certificate once a request for a detailed assessment hearing has been made, see para. 8.5 above.

(c) In cases in which an additional liability is claimed (as to which, see Section 19, above) the court will have regard to the time when and the extent to which the claim has been settled and to the fact that the claim has been settled without the need to commence proceedings.

(d) CPR 45.13 and 45.14 provides that a costs penalty will be imposed upon any claimant in proceedings governed by CPR 45 Section II who claims costs greater than the fixed recoverable costs plus success fee and disbursements but fails to achieve an increase greater than 20% of the amount in respect of fixed recoverable costs: the claimant will be awarded only the fixed recoverable costs (unless in fact a lower sum has been assessed), plus success fee, plus disbursements and will be ordered to pay the defendant's costs of the proceedings.

SECTION 22

LITIGANTS IN PERSON

22.1 Introduction

1C–130

(a) A person is a "litigant in person" during any stage of proceedings in court in which he or she is not represented by a solicitor or firm of solicitors. For this purpose the term "litigant in person" may include a company or other corporation, a barrister, a solicitor, a solicitor's employee or other authorised litigator who is acting for himself. However, the term does not include a solicitor who, instead of acting for himself, is represented in proceedings by his firm or by himself in his firm's name (CPD 52.5).

(b) Litigants in person have rights of audience in all detailed assessment proceedings. As to their entitlement to have a MacKenzie Friend present, see Section 1 para 1.2, above.

(c) The costs recoverable by parties in respect of periods when they are or were litigants in person are governed by the Litigants in Person (Costs and Expenses) Act 1975 and by CPR 48.6. This section of the Guide is intend to help parties understand the position. Reference must be made to the Act and the CPR if there is any doubt.

(d) The staff of the SCCO are not permitted to give rulings or legal advice on the Act or on the CPR nor to enter into any lengthy or technical advice as to the meaning of this Guide nor to recommend any individual solicitors or costs draftsmen who may be willing to give advice or assistance.

(e) Advice and assistance may be available from the Citizen's Advice Bureau in the Royal Courts of Justice. Further information as to this is given in Section 1 para 1.7, above.

(f) A litigant in person who is unable to obtain copies of any prescribed form needed may ask the Costs Office for help (see Section 1 paras 1.5, 1.8 and 1.9). Most of the "N" forms mentioned in this Guide can be supplied free of charge.

Paragraph numbers marked with a "+" can be found online and on CD.

SCCO GUIDE

1C–131 **22.2 Costs recoverable by litigants in person**

(a) The costs of litigants in person can be divided into four categories:

(i) out of pocket expenses (such as court fees, fares travelling to court, witness fees, etc) if they relate to work or disbursements which would have been done or made by a solicitor had a solicitor acted for the litigant in person.

(ii) Payments made to obtain expert assistance in connection with assessing the claim for costs. For this purpose a person is an expert if he is a barrister, solicitor, Fellow of the Institute of Legal Executives, Fellow of the Association of Law Costs Draftsmen, or a law costs draftsman who is a member of the Academy of Experts or the Expert Witness Institute. However, a litigant in person cannot recover any costs in respect of a person or entity whose services he retains to provide general assistance in litigation unless that person or entity has a right to conduct litigation within the meaning of s 28 Courts and Legal Services Act 1990 (see *Agassi v HM Inspector of Taxes*) [2005] EWCA Civ 1507. (Such a right is conferred by the Law Society, the Bar Council, the Institute of Legal Executives or an appropriate professional body.)

(iii) Costs for work done by the litigant in person which caused him or her pecuniary loss (for example, a litigant in person who is employed losing a day's pay through attending a court hearing or through going on a long journey to interview an essential witness).

(iv) Costs for work done by a litigant in person which did not cause him or her any pecuniary loss (eg, the examples just given if the work was done during leisure time).

1C–132 **22.3 Procedure on detailed assessment**

(a) The procedure by which a litigant in person seeks to obtain costs from another party is as set out in Sections 3 to 17 of this Guide (briefly, service of a bill plus notice of commencement and certain other documents, obtaining a default costs certificate or, if points of dispute are served, serving a reply and/or filing a request for a detailed assessment hearing).

(b) Where a litigant in person wishes to prove that he has suffered financial loss he should produce to the court any written evidence he relies on to support that claim and must serve a copy of that evidence on the paying party at the same time as serving the notice of commencement.

1C–133 **22.4 Calculation of charges for time spent by a litigant in person preparing the case**

(a) In order to determine charges for time spent, the costs officer or Costs Judge must decide four questions:

(i) What items of work were done and what time was actually spent on those items?

(ii) In respect of each item, how long was it reasonable for the litigant in person to spend? The time allowed may be less than the time actually spent by the litigant in person and more than the time that would have been spent by a solicitor, had a solicitor been employed to undertake that item.

(iii) What hourly rate or other rate is it reasonable to apply in respect of time reasonably spent by the litigant in person? Unless financial loss can be shown the rate allowed is £9.25 per hour under CPD Section 52.4 (£25 per hour in the Employment Appeal Tribunal).

(iv) If all the items of work for which costs are recoverable had been undertaken by a solicitor, what would a solicitor's reasonable charges have been for doing such work?

(b) The evidence to be served in support of a claim to prove financial loss should include what work a litigant carried out during the case, what employment the litigant may have taken up but for the case and what job offers were received and/or refused on account of the case (see *Mainwaring v Goldtech Investments Ltd*) [1997] 1 Costs LR 143 at page 156).

(c) There is an overall limit on charges for time spent preparing the case which can never be exceeded. The cost officer or Costs Judge cannot allow more than two thirds of the sum which a solicitor could reasonably have charged for doing the work (CPR Section 46(2)).

Paragraph numbers marked with a "+" can be found online and on CD.

22.5 Calculation of disbursements

1C–134

(a) The litigant in person will be allowed all his reasonable disbursements (such as court fees, out of pocket expenses) in full if the costs officer or Costs Judge decides all of the following questions in his or her favour:

(i) were these disbursements actually incurred?

(ii) If so, at the time they were incurred, did it then appear necessary or at least reasonable to incur them?

(iii) Are the sums claimed for each disbursement reasonable in amount?

(b) If, in respect of any disbursement the answers to questions (i) or (ii) is no, the amount claimed for that disbursement will be wholly disallowed.

(c) If, in respect of any disbursement, the answers to questions (i) and (ii) are yes but the answer to question (iii) is no, the costs officer or Costs Judge may allow a reduced amount for that disbursement.

(d) There is an overall limit on charges for time spent which can never be exceeded. The cost officer or Costs Judge cannot allow more than two thirds of the sum determined in answer to question (iv) above.

Section 23

Court of Protection Cases

23.1 Introduction

1C–135

(a) The Court of Protection is an office of the Supreme Court and exercises jurisdiction in respect of the protection and management of the property and affairs of persons of who, by reason of mental disorder, are incapable of managing their own affairs ("patients").

(b) The relevant statutes and rules include the Mental Health Act 1983, the Enduring Powers of Attorney Act 1985 and the Court of Protection Rules 2001, relevant passages of all of which are set out and annotated in Volume 2 of the Supreme Court Practice.

(c) The Judges of the Court of Protection include the Master and his Deputies, from whom an appeal lies to the Judges of the Chancery and Family Divisions. A judge, the Master, or any nominated officer authorised under section 94 of the Mental Health Act 1983, may exercise the functions of the court.

(d) This Section of the Guide is published with the assistance and approval of the Master of the Court of Protection.

23.2 Orders and directions as to costs

1C–136

(a) All orders as to costs are at the discretion of the court and nothing in this guidance should be interpreted as removing or restricting the Court's discretion in any way.

(b) There are three methods of quantifying costs:

- Agreed costs,
- Fixed costs,
- Detailed assessment of costs.

23.3 Agreed costs

1C–137

(a) Agreed costs are not generally available. The procedure is now governed by the Practice Note of 11 October 2004. As a general principle, all bills of costs must be assessed, except where fixed costs are available. The procedure to assess bills below £3,000 should be used for all bills where professionals used to seek agreement.

(b) The Court of Protection recognises that in certain circumstances it would not be in the client's best interests to request an assessment, for example where the cost of assessment is disproportionate to the amount of the bill. The court may agree costs in such circumstances, as long as the fixed costs provisions do not cover the work. If solicitors consider that a costs assessment would not be appropriate, they should apply to the court setting out the reasons and requesting the court to agree the bill. Any request must be accompanied by a narrative bill setting out the hours spent and the level and status of the fee earner concerned, together with fee notes and vouchers for any disbursements. The court may also exercise its discretion to agree costs at any time whether or not it is in the context of a formal application.

Paragraph numbers marked with a "+" can be found online and on CD.

1C-138 **23.4 Fixed costs**

(a) The Master of the Court of Protection specifies the amounts allowed under the categories of fixed costs in consultation with the Law Society. The rates are published annually in practice notes issued by the Master. The amounts allowed under each category are maximum amounts. Where there are reasonable grounds for thinking that costs will not exceed the maximum amount allowed, solicitors may take a lower figure without further reference to the Court or the PGO. For example if the professional reasonably believes the general management costs for the year will not exceed £400, then they may take that figure without drawing a bill.

(b) Solicitors may also take fixed costs for general management pro-rata if the period covered by the bill is less than one year, for example where the patient dies or the receiver retires before the anniversary date.

(c) Although fixed costs are set in consultation with the Law Society and apply mainly to the work of solicitors, accountants may elect to take an amount not exceeding fixed costs for any work covered in categories II III and VII below. The court may also apply the fixed costs procedure to any other non-solicitor if it is appropriate to do so, and it is open to any other professional to apply to the court for authority to receive fixed costs at any time.

(d) The categories of fixed costs are:

Category I	Work up to and including the date upon which the First General Order or Short Order is entered
Category II	(a) Preparation and lodgment of a receivership account
	(b) Preparation and lodgment of a receivership account which has been certified by a solicitor under the provisions of the Practice Notes dated 13 September 1984 and 5 March 1985 reported at [1984] 3 All ER 320 and [1985] 1 All ER 884 respectively
Category III	General management costs in the first year
	(a) where there are lay receivers and the court has authorised the receiver to employ solicitors to carry out work not usually requiring professional assistance under rule 87 of the Court of Protection Rules 2001
	(b) where there are professional receivers
	General management work in the second and subsequent years
	(c) where there are lay receivers and the court has authorised the receiver to employ solicitors to carry out work not usually requiring professional assistance under rule 87 of the Court of Protection Rules 2001
	(d) where there are professional receivers
	(e) Where a professional is dealing with the affairs of an individual under an order of the court, and the assets of the individual are less than £16,000, then the professional may take a general management fee of 2.5% of the patient's assets on the anniversary of the order appointing the professional to act (plus VAT).
Category IV	Applications under s.36 (9) or 54 of the Trustee Act 1925 or section 20 of the Trusts of Land and Appointment of Trustees Act 1996 for the appointment of a new trustee in the place of the patient and applications under section 96(1)(k) of the Mental Health Act 1983 for the authority to exercise any power vested in the patient whether beneficially, or as guardian or trustee, or otherwise.
Category V	Conveyancing costs, except where the sale or purchase is made by trustees.

Paragraph numbers marked with a "+" can be found online and on CD.

Category VI	Work up to and including the date upon which an order appointing a replacement receiver is entered.
Category VII	Preparation of an Inland Revenue income tax return on behalf of a patient.

(e) In most straightforward or routine receivership cases, solicitors will usually opt to take fixed costs because they can be paid quickly and easily. However, the court recognises that in some cases this will not be appropriate, therefore, in all categories of work, solicitors may, if they prefer, apply for an assessment of their costs.

23.5 Commencing detailed assessment

1C–139

(a) The detailed assessment of costs under orders or directions of the Court of Protection is dealt with in accordance with the CPR. Solicitors should lodge a request for a detailed assessment at the Supreme Court Costs Office (not the Court of Protection or the PGO), using Form **N258B** if payable out of a fund, or Form **N258** if payable by one party to another, together with the authority for assessment, the bill of costs, all supporting papers and a lodgment fee (currently £200, or £100 for bills below £3,000 fee 4 COP Rules as amended).

(b) The authority for assessing a Court of Protection bill of costs must derive from an order or direction of the Court of Protection. The general rule is "one order-one bill" so the request should not consolidate two or more orders in one bill. The exception is a bill for the preparation of a receivership account, which may be included in a bill for general management.

23.6 Bill format

1C–140

(a) The bill of costs should be prepared in accordance with the model forms set out in the CPD (see para 3.4, above) except where the short form bill (described below) is appropriate. The bill should state correct title of the matter, the name and address, telephone number and reference of the solicitor. The bill should list each chargeable item of work in chronological order with dates. It should also show any relevant events even if it does not constitute a chargeable item. If the bill is for general management it should state the year covered (e.g. from 21 December 2004 to 20 December 2005).

(b) Where the amount of the bill does not exceed £3,000, excluding VAT and disbursements the solicitor may request the Costs Office to assess the costs using the short form bill. The procedure is the same as that for an application for detailed assessment, except that solicitors may use a simplified form of bill, which will not require the services of a costs draftsman. The cost of drawing a long form of bill will not usually be recoverable in cases where a short form bill is appropriate. A copy of the model short form bill is set out in the Appendix, below, para A-10.

23.7 Authorities to assess costs

1C–141

(a) The First General Order is the authority to assess the costs of the application to appoint the receiver. The Costs Office will treat costs of the application as ending on the issue date of the First General Order (which may be some time after the actual date of the order). The costs officer will treat any costs incurred after the issue of the order as general management costs.

(b) If the order provides for fixed costs, but solicitors elect for assessment, it is not necessary to apply to the Court of Protection for an amended direction. Instead, under a general direction issued by the Court of Protection and dated the 25 July 1990, solicitors may elect for assessment simply by lodging a bill with the Costs Office. The bill should contain a certificate stating that fixed costs have not been taken.

(c) If the application is for the assessment of general management costs, the costs officer will need to know that the court has agreed that the professional receiver is to be paid general management costs. When lodging the first year's general management bill, the receiver should send a copy of the First General Order authorising him or her to be paid professional costs. The Costs Office will keep a record so it is not necessary to send a copy of the First General Order in subsequent years. Unless there are any special circumstances, general management costs should be claimed annually, usually after passing the annual account.

(d) Any other solicitor in the matter will need to send the direction of the court, usually a letter, authorising the receiver to employ a solicitor to do work not usually requiring professional assistance (see para 23.9, below). They should also lodge a copy

Paragraph numbers marked with a "+" can be found online and on CD.

of the First General Order so that the Costs Office can record who is receiver and note any specific directions.

(e) Costs for preparing the receiver's annual account are assessed after passing the receiver's account. Solicitors should enclose with their bill a copy of the letter from the PGO sent out when the account has been passed.

(f) In all cases, where fixed costs are available, solicitors should confirm, when lodging their bill for assessment, that they have not taken fixed costs for the work. The simplest way of doing this is to add an endorsement to the bill.

1C–142 23.8 The detailed assessment

(a) The Costs Office will deal with most assessments on a provisional basis by post. If the solicitor is not satisfied with the assessment he must inform the costs officer within 14 days of receipt of the provisional assessment. The Costs Office will then fix a date for hearing. In practice the costs officer will deal with any enquiries by telephone or letter.

(b) If the order provides for costs to be paid other than from the patient's estate, the solicitor must provide a statement of parties and Notice of Commencement. The Costs Office will send an appointment for the hearing to all parties. Rule 47.17A of the Civil Procedure Rules 1998 provides that a trustee, receiver or any other party managing the patient's fund or litigation, is a person who will be treated as having a financial interest in the outcome of a detailed assessment, therefore solicitors must provide their name, address and reference, in case the costs officer decides they should be sent the bill of costs or notice of assessment. As a matter of good practice, solicitors must serve a copy of the bill on the receiver prior to lodgement, as this will help to allay disputes where the receiver is unaware that costs have been claimed from the patient's estate until receipt of the final costs certificate.

(c) After completion of the assessment, the solicitor must complete the summary on the bill certifying the castings as correct, and return the original bill to the Costs Office for the issue of the costs certificate. There is no fee for sealing the certificate.

1C–143 23.9 Solicitors and other professional persons carrying out the receiver's work

(a) Rule 87(1) of the Court of Protection Rules 2001 states that no receiver for a patient, other than the Official Solicitor, shall, unless authorised by the Court of Protection, be entitled at the expense of the patient's estate to employ a solicitor or other professional person to do any work not usually requiring professional assistance.

(b) The court may authorise professionals to be paid costs formally by way of an order or informally for example by letter. Although this guide describes the procedure in relation to solicitors' costs, the Court of Protection and the Costs Office will treat other professionals in a similar way.

(c) The Court of Protection has discretion to order assessment on either the standard or indemnity basis (rule 43 (remuneration) and rules 84 – 89 (costs) COP Rules). Definitions of standard and indemnity bases of costs are set out in para 2.4, above.

(d) As a general principle, the court will require assessment of costs on the standard basis. This is because the legal definition of the standard basis will only allow costs that are proportionate to the matters in issue. There is no test of proportionality in the definition of the indemnity basis, which precludes the costs officer from taking into account the amount of money involved, the financial position of the client and the complexity of the case.

(e) Following the Practice Direction issued by the Master of the Court of Protection on 2 March 2005, all orders providing for costs made on or after 1 April 2005 will, unless the court specifically directs otherwise, provide for assessment on the standard basis. This includes orders issued on or after that date providing for fixed costs, where the professional elects to seek an assessment pursuant to the general direction dated the 25 July 1990.

(f) The Court of Protection retains the discretion to order costs on the indemnity basis. Solicitors may apply to the court for an order for costs on the indemnity basis, if they feel the circumstances of the case justify it. However, solicitors undertaking work in expectation of receiving costs on the indemnity basis do so at their own risk that such an order may not be made.

(g) It is not possible to define exactly what circumstances might persuade the court to agree to assessment on the indemnity rather than standard basis. There are an infi-

Paragraph numbers marked with a "+" can be found online and on CD.

nite variety of situations that might justify the making of such an order and the judge has wide discretion in relation to the ordering of costs. The onus is therefore on the solicitors to persuade the court that costs should be paid on the indemnity basis.

23.10 Non-professional receivers

1C–144

(a) In cases where the receiver is not a professional person, he or she is required to carry out the full range of receivership duties. These duties are set out in the Receiver's Handbook published by the Public Guardianship Office and the Receiver's Declaration that applicants submit on applying for appointment as receiver.

(b) On occasions, the receiver may wish to employ at the client's expense a solicitor or other professional person to do work not usually requiring professional assistance. If a receiver engages a solicitor to assist in this way, the receiver or solicitor must apply to the court for authorisation under rule 87 of the COP Rules.

(c) Where an authorisation under rule 87 has been granted the solicitor must provide a copy of it to the Costs Office when submitting a bill for assessment. If no such authority has been obtained, the costs officer will disallow the claim, although they may still apply 'out of time' to the Court of Protection, for directions under rule 87. The court will usually provide retrospective authorisation where the professional has acted in good faith, for example in cases of emergency or where urgent action is required to protect the client's property. In most cases the court would expect the professional to seek advance authorisation.

(e) The court considers the completion of annual accounts to be work that sometimes requires professional assistance and therefore solicitors do not need to apply for directions under rule 87 if they are instructed by a receiver to prepare annual accounts.

23.11 General management work

1C–145

(a) The Court of Protection's jurisdiction extends only to the management and administration of the client's financial affairs. The court cannot give directions concerning aspects of clients' affairs that are not financial. It follows that solicitors will only be allowed costs for work relating to the client's financial affairs.

(b) If the costs officer disallows an item in a bill that the solicitor feels is properly chargeable as work relating to financial affairs, they should raise this upon review of the provisional assessment and if that is unsuccessful, take the question to appeal. Neither the court nor the PGO can intervene in the assessment process since this function is reserved to the Supreme Court Costs Office by reason of rule 86 COP Rules.

(c) If the receiver is a solicitor or other professional person then, subject to the terms of the order appointing them as receiver, they may be paid costs for the whole of the receivership duties, as long as those duties relate to the management of the client's financial affairs. The interpretation of those duties may cause difficulties for professional receivers, as some of the duties listed in the Receiver's Handbook (published by the PGO) and the Receiver's Declaration do not relate directly to financial affairs. As a general rule the court would not expect professional receivers to undertake the non-financial duties of a receiver, but would expect the receiver to take reasonable steps to ensure that, wherever possible those duties were undertaken by someone else.

(d) On occasions some non-financial activities, such as visits to clients or attendance at case conferences, may be necessary in order to safeguard a client's financial affairs. In such cases, the costs officer may accept well-founded arguments that such general management costs should be allowed on assessment. If the circumstances of the case are unusual and require the receiver to be actively involved in the management of the client's day-to-day affairs, then the receiver should draw this to the costs officer's attention in a covering letter submitted with the bill. The costs officer would also expect that any receivership work, be it legal or non-legal, be undertaken by an appropriate fee earner in the firm, which may not necessarily be the appointed receiver.

23.12 Cost of sale or purchase of property

1C–146

(a) The assessment of costs of sale or purchase of a property will normally take place at the conclusion of the transaction unless the court has made other directions. The estate agent's charges should appear in the completion statement and not as a disbursement on the bill.

Paragraph numbers marked with a "+" can be found online and on CD.

SCCO GUIDE

(b) If the sale was by trustees of a jointly owned property, the Costs Office will assess the costs of the application to appoint new trustees; but the conveyancing costs can only be approved by the trustees.

1C–147 **23.13 Deceased patients**

If the patient dies when the assessment of costs are pending, the solicitor should inform the Costs Office, who will suspend the assessment until after the court gives final directions. The solicitor must serve a copy of his bill upon the patient's personal representative upon resumption of the assessment process.

SECTION 24

LEGAL AID/LSC CASES

1C–148 **24.1 Introduction**

(a) Because of changes made by the Administration of Justice Act 1999 the old legal aid scheme, the Legal Aid Board and the Legal Aid Fund have all been replaced by a new funding scheme, the Legal Services Commission ("LSC") and the Community Legal Service Fund. Cases started under the old scheme continue largely as before but, on conclusion, will be paid for out of the Community Legal Service Fund.

(b) Under the old scheme legal aid paid for legal services supplied to "assisted persons". Under the new scheme legal aid provides legal services for "clients". In this Guide the term "LSC funded client" is used to cover both assisted persons and "clients".

(c) The modern form of order for what used to be called "legal aid taxation" is now "detailed assessment of the costs of the [party] which are payable out of the Community Legal Service Fund".

1C–149 **24.2 Costs payable by another person as well as out of the Fund**

(a) Where the costs are payable by another person as well as out of the Community Legal Service Fund, the rules governing commencement of detailed assessment proceedings, points of dispute and replies are the same as those which apply to between the parties cases generally (see Sections 3 and 17 above). The Schedule of Costs Precedents includes model forms of bills for use in such cases (Precedents C and D).

(b) The request for detailed assessment hearing must (in addition to the items set out in Section 8 above) be accompanied by:

  (i) the legal aid certificate, the LSC certificate and relevant amendment certificate, any authorities and any certificates of discharge or revocation;

  (ii) a certificate in Precedent F(3) and where appropriate a certificate in Precedent F(4) of the Schedule of Costs Precedents (as to which, see Appendix para A-2);

  (iii) if the LSC funded client has a financial interest in the detailed assessment hearing and wishes to attend, the postal address of that person to which the court will send notice of any hearing;

  (iv) if the rates payable out of the Community Legal Service Fund are prescribed rates (ie if the Civil Legal Aid (Remuneration) Regulations 1994 apply), a schedule (the "Legal Aid /LSC Schedule") setting out all the items in the bill which are claimed against other parties calculated at the legal aid prescribed rates. Precedent E of the Schedule of Costs Precedents should be followed as closely as possible;

  (v) a copy of any default costs certificate in respect of the costs claimed in the bill.

(c) The LSC funded client should not be served with a copy of the notice of commencement and should only be served with a copy of the bill if he or she has a financial interest in the detailed assessment.

24.3 Procedure where costs are payable by another person as well as out of the
1C–150 **Fund**

(a) Unless the legal aid/LSC only sections of the bill are comparatively small or otherwise easy to deal with, the detailed assessment will be conducted in two stages.

  (i) In the first stage the court will consider only the between the parties sections of the bill, the points of dispute thereon and any replies made.

Paragraph numbers marked with a "+" can be found online and on CD.

(ii) In the second stage the court will consider the legal aid/LSC only sections of the bill and the Legal Aid/LSC Schedule.

(b) The Legal Aid/LSC Schedule is of no concern to the party against whom costs have been awarded between the parties and indeed that person should not normally attend the second stage of the detailed assessment.

(c) The LSC funded client's solicitor will have prepared the Legal Aid/LSC Schedule in advance of the detailed assessment. It may therefore be necessary to begin the second stage of the detailed assessment by altering the Schedule so as to update it, taking account of the decisions made during the first stage of the detailed assessment.

(d) In respect of any item appearing in the Legal Aid/LSC only sections of the bill, the court will consider what sum, if any, it is reasonable to allow in respect of that item.

(e) In respect of any item deleted or reduced in the Legal Aid/LSC Schedule so as to take into account decisions made during the first stage of the detailed assessment, the court may be requested to consider whether any part of that item can be restored via an appropriate alteration to the Legal Aid/LSC only sections of the bill.

24.4 The cost of detailed assessment proceedings
1C–151

(a) Costs incurred on behalf of a LSC funded client in respect of a detailed assessment between the parties are treated in the same way as other costs incurred on his behalf, and whether or not they are payable by the other party, may also be claimed against the Community Legal Service Fund. In general the party whose bill is the subject of detailed assessment is entitled to the costs of the detailed assessment proceedings. However the court may make some other order in relation to all or part of the costs of the detailed assessment proceedings. (See Section 11 above.)

(b) The LSC funded client will not be required to make any contribution to the Community Legal Service Fund on account of the costs of the detailed assessment proceedings and the statutory charge does not apply in relation to any resulting increase in the net liability of the Fund arising from the costs of the detailed assessment proceedings. The cost of drawing up a bill of costs is however not included as part of the costs of the detailed assessment proceedings (Civil Legal Aid (General) Regulations 1989, Regulation 119 as amended).

24.5 Costs payable only out of the Community Service Legal Fund
1C–152

(a) Where costs are payable only out of the Community Legal Service Fund, the solicitor representing the LSC funded client may request a detailed assessment of costs within 3 months after the date upon which the right to detailed assessment arose. The request must be in Form **N258A** and must be accompanied by a copy of the bill of costs and the other documents listed in paragraph 43.3 of the Costs Practice Direction.

(b) Where the solicitor has certified that the LSC funded client has a financial interest and wishes to attend, the court will, on receipt of the request for detailed assessment, fix a date for the detailed assessment hearing.

(c) Where the solicitor has certified that the LSC funded client has no financial interest or does not wish to attend the detailed assessment, the court will provisionally assess the costs without the attendance of the solicitor, unless it considers that a hearing is necessary. After the court has provisionally assessed the bill, it will return it to the solicitor. If the solicitor informs the court within 14 days after he receives the provisionally assessed bill that he wants the court to hold a detailed assessment hearing, the court will fix a date for such hearing.

24.6 Duty to inform counsel
1C–153

It is the duty of the LSC funded client's solicitor to notify counsel in writing within 7 days after the detailed or provisional assessment where the fees claimed on his behalf have been reduced or disallowed on assessment and the solicitor must endorse the bill with the date on which such notice was given or that no such notice is necessary. If the bill is endorsed with the date upon which notice was given to counsel the court may not issue the certificate until 14 days have elapsed from the date so endorsed (see Civil Legal Aid (General) Regulations 1989, Regulation 112 and Precedent F(4) of the Schedule of Costs Precedents in Appendix 1, below, para A-2).

24.7 Completing the bill and the legal aid assessment certificate
1C–154

It is the responsibility of the legal representative to complete the bill by entering in the bill the correct figures allowed in respect of each item, recalculating the summary

Paragraph numbers marked with a "+" can be found online and on CD.

of the bill appropriately and completing the Legal Aid Assessment certificate in Form **EX 80A**.

1C–155 **24.8 Agreement of between the parties costs**

(a) Where the Civil Legal Aid (Remuneration) Regulations 1994 do not apply to the detailed assessment (which is generally the case where the legal aid certificate was issued before 25 February 1994) the Civil Legal Aid (General) Regulations 1989, Regulation 106 remains applicable and an agreement of between the parties costs is not possible unless the agreement is accepted in full and final settlement of the costs ie with no further claim against the Fund. Therefore where in such cases the receiving party wishes to make a claim against the Fund, the parties will be informed that there will have to be a detailed assessment of the whole bill. However, because of the measure of agreement which has been reached, the detailed assessment of the between the parties sections of the bill may not take very long to complete.

(b) In cases where the Civil Legal Aid (Remuneration) Regulations do apply the Civil Legal Aid (General) Regulations 1989, Regulation 106A permits the LSC funded client's solicitor to apply for an assessment limited to legal aid/LSC only costs provided the between the parties costs have been both agreed and paid.

1C–156 **24.9 Costs appeals**

The solicitor for a LSC funded client may appeal against a decision of a Costs Judge or District Judge in detailed assessment proceedings in accordance with Rules of Court (ie CPR Part 52) and if counsel acting for the LSC funded client notifies the solicitor that he is dissatisfied with the decision the solicitor must appeal on counsel's behalf. The costs of any such appeal will only be payable out of the Community Legal Services Fund to the extent that the court hearing the appeal so orders. For the detailed Regulations relating to appeals involving LSC funded clients see Civil Legal Aid (General) Regulations 1989, Regulation 113 as amended and CPR 47.20(2).

Section 25

Costs Orders Against LSC Funded Clients and/or the LSC

1C–157 **25.1 The Access to Justice Act 1999 and the Regulations**

(a) Any costs ordered to be paid by a LSC funded client must not exceed the amount which is a reasonable one for him to pay having regard to all the circumstances including the financial resources of all the parties to the proceedings and their conduct in connection with the dispute to which the proceedings relate (Access to Justice Act 1999, Section 11).

(b) The Community Legal Service (Costs) Regulations 2000 ("the Costs Regulations") and the Community Legal Service (Costs Protection) Regulations 2000 ("the Costs Protection Regulations") are Regulations made under the Access to Justice Act 1999 and provide a code governing orders for costs against assisted persons/ LSC funded clients and against the LSC.

(c) The ordinary rules governing the assessment of costs (Parts 44 to 48 of the CPR) do not apply to the assessment of such costs. The procedure to be followed in such cases is set out in Sections 21–23 of the Costs Practice Direction.

1C–158 **25.2 Orders which the court awarding costs may make**

(a) If the court decides to make an order for costs against a LSC funded client it may either make an order that the amount of the costs payable by the LSC funded client is to be determined by a Costs Judge or District Judge or make an order which specifies the amount which the LSC funded client is to pay.

(b) If the court decides to make an order that the amount payable by the LSC funded client is to be determined by a Costs Judge or District Judge it may also state the amount which that person would, had costs protection not applied, have been ordered to pay ie the full costs which would be determined by summary assessment. Alternatively the court may make findings of facts eg about the conduct of all the parties which must be taken into account by the Costs Judge or District Judge in the subsequent determination proceedings.

(c) The court will not make an order which specifies the amount which the LSC

Paragraph numbers marked with a "+" can be found online and on CD.

funded client is to pay unless it considers that it has sufficient information before it to decide what amount is reasonable and either the order also states the amount of the full costs (ie the amount which that person would, had costs protection not applied, have been ordered to pay) or the court is satisfied that the full costs would exceed the amount which it has specified that the LSC funded client must pay.

(d) If the LSC funded client does not have costs protection in respect of all of the costs (eg the certificate was not in force during the whole of the proceeding) the order must also identify the sum payable in respect of which the LSC funded client had costs protection and the sum payable in respect of which he did not have costs protection. (See Section 22 of the Costs Practice Direction.)

(e) A specimen order for costs against a claimant who is a LSC funded client is set out in the Appendix, below, para. A-6.

25.3 Costs against the LSC

1C–159

(a) If an application for an order for costs against the LSC is made the criteria set out in Regulation 5 of the Costs Protection Regulations will apply. Before the LSC can be ordered to pay the whole or any part of the costs incurred by a non-funded party all of several conditions must be satisfied:

   (i) the costs ordered to be paid by the LSC funded client must be less than the full costs (ie the amount which that person would, had costs protection not applied, have been ordered to pay);

   (ii) the proceedings must have been finally decided in favour of the non-funded party;

   (iii) the non funded party must provide written notice of intention to seek an order against the LSC within 3 months of the making of the order for costs against the LSC funded client;

   (iv) the court must be satisfied that it is just and equitable in the circumstances that provision for the costs should be made out of public funds; and,

   (v) where the costs are incurred in a court of first instance, the proceedings must have been instituted by the LSC funded client and, the court must be satisfied that the non-funded party will suffer severe financial hardship unless the order is made.

(b) Where the application for funded services was made on or after 3 December 2001 the three months time limit referred to in (iii) above may be extended if there is a good reason for the delay; and in (v) above only a non funded party who is an individual may apply but the court will not have to be satisfied that the financial hardship he or she will suffer will be severe.

25.4 Orders which a Costs Judge or District Judge may subsequently make

1C–160

(a) An order for costs to which Section 11(1) of the Access to Justice Act 1999 applies may specify the amount of full costs and may specify the amount payable by the LSC funded client. Where appropriate an application may be made to the District Judge or Costs Judge of the relevant court to determine:

   (i) the amount of full costs;

   (ii) the amount payable by the LSC funded client;

   (iii) the amount payable by the LSC itself.

(b) The procedure for determination is set out in Section 23 of the Costs Practice Direction which is summarised below.

25.5 Form of application

1C–161

Applications for such orders must be made in the appropriate court office on an application in Form **N244** accompanied by:

   (i) the receiving party's bill of costs (unless the full costs have already been determined);

   (ii) the receiving party's statement of resources (defined below); and

   (iii) if the receiving party intends to seek costs against the LSC, written notice to that effect.

25.6 The response by the LSC funded client

1C–162

(a) Within 21 days of being served with the application, the LSC funded client must respond by filing a statement of resources (defined below) and serving a copy of it on

Paragraph numbers marked with a "+" can be found online and on CD.

SCCO GUIDE

the receiving party and, where relevant, on the Regional Director. The LSC funded client may also, within the same time limit, file and serve written points disputing the bill of costs.

(b) The 21 day time limit mentioned above may be extended by agreement between the parties or by order of the court.

1C–163 **25.7 Effect of non compliance by the LSC funded client**

If the LSC funded client fails to file a statement of resources without good reason, the court will determine his liability (and the amount of full costs if relevant) and need not hold an oral hearing for any such determination.

1C–164 **25.8 Further procedure where a statement of resources by the LSC funded client is filed or is not required**

(a) When the LSC funded client files a statement of resources the court will fix a hearing date and give the relevant parties at least 14 days notice. If the application is made only against the LSC the court may fix a hearing date at the time of issue of the application.

(b) Applications which proceed to a hearing to determine the liability of the LSC funded client will, in the first instance, be listed as a hearing to be held in private. At the start of the hearing, or during it, any party may request the court to rule that, thereafter, the hearing should be conducted in public.

1C–165 **25.9 Response by the Regional Director of the LSC**

The Regional Director of the LSC may appear at any hearing at which a costs order may be made against the LSC or may file a written statement as described in para. 23.10 of the Costs Practice Direction.

1C–166 **25.10 Costs of application**

When dealing with the application the court has a discretion as to whether the costs of the application are payable by one party to another, the amount of those costs, and (if relevant) when they are to be paid.

1C–167 **25.11 Statements of resources**

(a) A "statement of resources" should set out details of the financial resources and expectations of the maker of the statement and of his "partner" (a person with whom he or she lives as a couple). The resources of a partner are not treated as the LSC client's resources if the partner has a contrary interest in the proceedings.

(b) A full definition of "statement of resources" is given in para. 22.1 of the Costs Practice Direction. In order to comply with that paragraph the party making a statement of resources may be able to adapt the text of Form **N9A** a copy of which is obtainable from the court office or from a Citizens Advice Bureau.

(c) The Costs Regulations provide for the filing of statements of resources not only by the LSC funded client but also by the receiving party. As regards costs incurred in appeal proceedings, applications are often made by large commercial companies or litigants who are insured or who are publicly funded. In such cases a statement of resources stating merely that the applicant is "able to pay its costs out of its own resources" or "is insured" or "is a publicly funded body" will suffice. In such cases the court will assume that the applicant will not suffer any severe financial hardship if the application fails.

(d) Where the court is determining an application for a costs order against the LSC and the costs were not incurred in a court of first instance, a statement of resources does not have to filed by the receiving party.

1C–168 **25.12 Specimen forms of order**

Para A-6 of the Appendix, below, sets out a specimen order for costs against a claimant who is an LSC funded client and also a specimen order for use by a Costs Judge or District Judge when determining the amount of costs payable by an LSC funded client.

SECTION 26
APPLICATIONS UNDER THE SOLICITORS ACT 1974

1C–169 **26.1 Introduction**

(a) Application may be made under Section 70 of the Solicitors Act 1974 for an order for the detailed assessment of a solicitor's bill of costs. The application can relate to

Paragraph numbers marked with a "+" can be found online and on CD.

the whole bill, or can be limited to the profit costs only or to the disbursements only. Most such applications are made by the client or former client of the solicitor who delivered the bill. In practice solicitors make the application against their client or former client only where they wish to escape the consequences of a remuneration certificate issued by the Law Society. Although, in other cases, the solicitors may have a right to apply under Section 70 they almost invariably bring simple debt proceedings instead and, if prevented from obtaining a default judgment, seek summary judgment for an amount "to be assessed" (see High Court Practice Form 15).

(b) Application may also be made under Section 71 of the 1974 Act where a bill of costs is payable by a party who is not the client of the solicitors. For example beneficiaries under a will or a borrower whose mortgage or charge obliges him to pay the legal costs of the lender (usually a bank or a building society).

(c) The application is heard by a Costs Judge. If an order for detailed assessment is made, that detailed assessment will also be heard by a Costs Judge.

26.2 Detailed assessment as of right or on terms

1C–170

(a) If the application is made within one calendar month of receipt of the bill, the Costs Judge must order detailed assessment.

(b) If the application is made more than one calendar month, but less than a year from receipt of the bill, the Costs Judge may impose conditions, for example, that the amount of the bill should be paid into court to abide the event.

(c) No order will be made, except in special circumstances, if:
  (i) 12 months have elapsed from the delivery of the bill or
  (ii) Judgment has been obtained for the recovery of the costs covered by the bill or
  (iii) The bill has been paid less than 12 months before the date upon which the application was issued.

(d) If the bill has been paid more than 12 months before the date upon which the application was issued the Costs Judge has no power to order that bill be assessed.

26.3 The forms to use

1C–171

(a) Application for the detailed assessment of a solicitor's bill of costs is made by a claim form to which CPR Part 8 applies. The specimen form is set out in the Appendix, below, para. A-7. This form is also used for other applications under the Act.

(b) If an order for detailed assessment is made there are two standard forms of order: precedents L and M in the Schedule of Costs Precedents included in the Costs Practice Direction (see further, para. 26.5, below)

26.4 Commencing the application

1C–172

(a) Applicants must send or bring to the SCCO
  (i) Three copies of the claim form with draft order sought.
  (ii) A cheque for the fee made payable to H M Paymaster General (as to which, see para. 27.1, below).
  (iii) The original bill(s) or copies of the original(s) which are certified by or on behalf of the applicants as being true and complete copies.

(b) Once the payment of the fee has been processed, the application will be passed to the application clerk in Room 2.13, who will list it for hearing before a Costs Judge. The court will serve the application unless there are particular reasons why the applicant should serve it. The application will usually be listed for a short appointment (15 minutes). If the hearing is likely to exceed the allotted time it may be necessary to adjourn it to a new date with a realistic time estimate. This step may become due, for example, when evidence is filed in reply to the application.

(c) In most cases, witness statement evidence is not required unless the application becomes contested, a certificate of special circumstances under Section 70(3) of the Act is sought or the Costs Judge so directs.

26.5 The hearing of the application

1C–173

(a) Where an application is made by a litigant in person, an order will not be made in the absence of the parties. The litigant in person must attend in order that the Costs Judge may explain the effect of Section 70(9) of the Act ("the one-fifth rule", as to which, see para. 26.6 below).

Paragraph numbers marked with a "+" can be found online and on CD.

(b) If no-one attends on behalf of the respondent, the Costs Judge may make the order sought, conditional upon adequate proof of service of the application.

(c) It is now common practice for a time-table to be incorporated into the order, based upon Rule 48.10 dealing with service of a breakdown of the bill, service of points of dispute, any reply and the request for a hearing date. A specimen order is included in the Appendix, below, para. A-8.

(d) The costs of the application will usually be treated as part of the costs of the detailed assessment and dealt with at the conclusion of the detailed assessment hearing.

(e) The order is usually drawn up by the court, and a copy served on all parties. The Costs Judge may direct that the order be drawn up by the successful party. In that event, three copies of the order must be lodged with the clerk to the Costs Judge. Copies will then be served on the parties.

1C–174 26.6 The costs of the assessment

(a) Statutory provisions apply where costs are assessed under Sections 70 or 71 of the Solicitors Act 1974. If the bill or bills are reduced by more than one fifth (excluding VAT) the solicitors will be ordered to pay the costs of the detailed assessment. If the bill or bills are reduced by less than one fifth the other party will be ordered to pay the costs of the detailed assessment. The Costs Judge may order otherwise if there are special circumstances.

(b) If on a detailed assessment of non-contentious costs, the costs allowed are less than one half of the costs claimed, the Costs Judge will report those facts to the Council of the Law Society. The report will be addressed to The Law Society Consumer Complaints Service, Victoria Court, 8 Dormer Place, Royal Leamington Spa, Warwickshire CV32 5AE.

SECTION 27

COURT FEES PAYABLE IN THE SCCO

1C–175 27.1 Introductory

(a) The fees payable for proceedings within the SCCO are set out in the Supreme Court (Review of Taxation in Criminal Cases) Fees Order 1984 (1994 No.340) as amended, the Civil Proceedings Fees Order 2004 and the Family Proceedings Fees Order 2004. Certain fees are prescribed by the Court of Protection Rules 2001 as amended. All of these orders and rules, except the first mentioned, are set out in practitioners' books such as the White Book and the Green Book. In cases of difficulty enquiry may be made at the Costs Office (see paras 1.5, 1.8 and 1.9, above).

(b) The following list, while not exhaustive, includes the fees most commonly encountered in matters before the Supreme Court Costs Office, and are valid at the time of publication. The County Court fees and fees in Family Proceedings appear in brackets:

	High Court	County Court	Family Proceedings
(i) Request for a default costs certificate:	£50	(£45)	(£60)
(ii) Request or application to set aside a default costs certificate:	£100	(£65)	(£65)
(iii) On filing request for a detailed assessment where the applicant is legally aided or publicly funded and no other party is ordered to pay the costs of the proceedings:	£120	(£105)	(£140)
(iv) On filing request for a detailed assessment other than (iii) above (including assessment of costs payable to a solicitor by his client):	£600	(£300)	(£250)

Paragraph numbers marked with a "+" can be found online and on CD.

(v) On applying for the court's approval of a certificate of costs payable from the Community Service Fund:	£50	(£35)	(£35)
(vi) On any appeal against decisions in detailed assessment proceedings:	£200	(£105)	(£105)
(vii) On an application for an order under Part III of the Solicitors Act 1974 for the assessment of costs payable to a solicitor by his client or on the commencement of costs only proceedings:	£50	(£35)	(£35)

The above fees apply to all cases where the order or authority for assessment of costs was made on or after 10 January 2006.

27.2 Time for payment

1C–176

Normally a request, an application or an appeal will not be accepted by the court office unless the appropriate fee is first paid. This should be in the form of a cheque payable to HM Paymaster General. In exceptional circumstances a costs officer may allow an application to be issued on an undertaking by the applicant or his solicitors that the appropriate fee will be paid within a limited period thereafter.

27.3 Exemptions

1C–177

(a) No fee is payable by a party who, at the time when the fee would otherwise be payable, is in receipt of a qualifying benefit and is not in receipt of legal aid or LSC funding for the purposes of the proceedings.

(b) "Qualifying benefits" referred to above are as follows:

(i) income support;

(ii) working tax credit provided that:

(a) child tax credit is being paid to the party or otherwise following a claim for child tax credit made jointly by members of a married couple or an unmarried couple as defined in Sections 3(5) and (6) of the Tax Credits Act 2002, which includes the party; or

(b) there is a disability element or severe disability element (or both) to the tax credit received by the party—

AND that the gross annual income taken into account for the calculations of the working tax credit is £14,600 or less;

(c) income based job seeker's allowance

(d) guarantee credit under the State Pension Credit Act, 2002.

(c) The Lord Chancellor may, where it appears that the payment of any fee would, owing to the exceptional circumstances of the particular case, involve undue financial hardship, reduce or remit the fee in the particular case.

(d) Where a fee has been paid which was not payable under the above provisions, or which has been reduced because of undue financial hardship, the fee will be refunded provided the party who paid the fee applies within six months of payment. The six month time limit may be extended if there is good reason for the application being made after the end of the six month period.

(e) In family proceedings no fee is payable by a person under 18 or in respect of whom an order for financial relief (under paragraph 2 of Schedule 1 to the Children Act 1989) is in force or is being applied for, provided that that person is not a beneficiary of a trust fund in court of a value of more than £50,000.

27.4 Appeal fee

1C–178

An appeal, whether from a Costs Judge to a High Court Judge, or from a costs officer to a Costs Judge, attracts a fee (currently £200). It is to be noted that informal

Paragraph numbers marked with a "+" can be found online and on CD.

appeals from costs officers to Costs Judges by letter are not permissible. The appropriate appeal notice must be used and the fee paid.

1C–179 **27.5 Fee for transcripts**

Although proceedings in the SCCO are recorded no transcripts of the recordings are made unless and until a party applies for a transcript and pays the fee. Application must be made by letter or telephone call to the Mechanical Recording Department at the RCJ, who will release the tapes only to one of the official tape transcribers (a list of whom is available from the Mechanical Recording Department). The amount of the fee payable for transcription will depend on the nature and length of the hearing.

1C–180 **27.6 Fee for providing copies**

In certain circumstances parties and other persons can inspect the SCCO file of a case and obtain copies of any document thereon (see para 1.6, above). The court fee charged is £1 for the first page and 20p for each subsequent page. For electronic copies the charge is £3 per disk.

SECTION 28

REMUNERATION OF COURT APPOINTED OFFICE HOLDERS

1C–181 **28.1 Introduction**

(a) Trustees in Bankruptcy, Joint Provisional Receivers and Liquidators are frequently appointed by Judges of the Companies Court to manage or wind up bankrupt estates or insolvent companies. The remuneration of such Court appointed Office Holders is generally met out of the assets of the insolvent estate in question. The amount which they are entitled to charge is fixed by the Court taking into account factors set out in the Insolvency Rules 1986 (see rule 4.30 and 6.138). These include the complexity of the case and the value and nature of the property the Trustee, the Receiver or Liquidator has to deal with.

(b) Guidance about the evidence required to support claims by Office Holders for remuneration is given in *Mirror Group Newspapers v Maxwell* [1998] BCC 324, Ferris J. Assistance can also be found in the report of Mr Justice Ferris' Working Party on the Remuneration of Office Holders dated July 1998 (in particular paragraph 4.3, and Section 8). The Statement of Insolvency Practice 9 (SIP9) issued by the Society of Insolvency Practitioners (now called 3R) gives additional guidance, in particular paragraph 3. Costs are now likely to be assessed on the indemnity if requested following BAI (Run Off) Ltd (Neuberger LJ, July 5, 2004, unrep.). Attention is also drawn to the Insolvency Practice Statement – "The fixing and approval of the remuneration of appointees" (2004).

1C–182 **28.2 Reference to a Costs Judge for report**

(a) The costs involved in receiverships and liquidations can be large, sometimes exceeding £1,000,000. In cases where substantial sums are involved, Judges and Registrars of the Companies Court may refer any request for remuneration made by a Court Appointed Office Holder to a Costs Judge for a report.

(b) The Companies Court order will direct the Court Appointed Office Holder to lodge a duplicate bundle of the documents presented to the Judge or Registrar at the Costs Office. It will also require him to apply to the Costs Judge assigned to the matter for a directions hearing. At that hearing the Costs Judge will give directions for the filing of any further evidence or documents.

(c) When all relevant material has been lodged, the Costs Judge will prepare a report for the use of the Companies Court Judge or Registrar. This report contains recommendations about the level of remuneration to allow. These are not binding and the ultimate decision as to the amount of the Office Holders' remuneration is taken by the Judge or Registrar.

1C–183 **28.3 Applications for interim payments**

In long running liquidations and receiverships, Office Holders frequently apply for interim payments of remuneration. Such applications can be made informally to the Costs Judge to whom the matter has been assigned. He will then make a

Paragraph numbers marked with a "+" can be found online and on CD.

recommendation to the Companies Court about the level of interim remuneration to allow.

SECTION 29

JUSTICES OF THE PEACE, JUSTICES' CLERKS AND GENERAL COMMISSIONERS OF INCOME TAX

29.1 Introduction

(a) This Section of the Guide deals with the determination of costs where the court has made an order that the Lord Chancellor pay the costs of proceedings under Section 53A of the Justices of the Peace Act 1997 ("Section 53A") or under Section 2A of the Taxes Management Act 1970 ("Section 2A"). The amount of costs payable by the Lord Chancellor will be determined in accordance with the Justices and Justices Clerks (Costs) Regulations 2001 (SI 2001 No.1296) or the General Commissioners of Income Tax (Costs) Regulations 2001 (SI 2001 No.1304), and not in accordance with the CPR 47.

(b) The costs payable by the Lord Chancellor under an order under Section 53A are the costs of proceedings in respect of any act or omission of a Justice of the Peace or a Justices' Clerk in the execution (or purported execution) of his duty—

    (i) as a single Justice; or

    (ii) as a Justices' Clerk exercising, by virtue of any statutory provision, any of the functions of a single Justice.

(c) The costs payable by the Lord Chancellor under an order made under Section 2A are the costs of proceedings in respect of any act or omission of a General Commissioner in the execution (or purported execution) of his duty as a General Commissioner.

(d) The court will normally, when making the order for costs, determine the amount it considers sufficient reasonably to compensate the receiving party for any costs properly incurred by him in the proceedings and specify that amount in the order.

(e) The court may direct that the amount of costs be determined by a Costs Judge, where the hearing has lasted more than one day, or there is insufficient time for the court to determine the costs on the day of the hearing, or the court considers that there is other good reason for the Costs Judge to determine the amount of the costs.

(f) A court which makes an order under Section 53A or Section 2A which determines the amount payable by the Lord Chancellor or which directs that the amount be determined by a Costs Judge, must serve that order on the receiving party and on the Lord Chancellor.

29.2 Time limit for proceedings in the SCCO

(a) Where the court orders the costs to be determined by a Costs Judge the receiving party is required by the Regulations to file a claim for costs and a copy of the order in the Supreme Court Costs Office and to serve a copy of the claim on the Lord Chancellor.

(b) The time for filing and serving such a claim is no later than three months from (but excluding) the date on which the order was made. The Costs Judge may on the application of the receiving party, in exceptional circumstances, extend the period of three months.

29.3 Form of application

(a) A claim for costs to be determined by a Costs Judge following an order under Section 53A or Section 2A is made by a claim form to which CPR Part 8 applies (Form **N208**) accompanied by copies of:

    (i) the order of the court giving the right to costs;

    (ii) a statement signed by the receiving party or his solicitor giving the name, address for service, reference and telephone number and fax number, if any, of (a) the receiving party and (b) the Lord Chancellor;

    (iii) copies of any orders made by the court relating to the costs of the proceedings which are to be determined;

    (iv) any fee notes of counsel;

    (v) receipts or accounts for other disbursements relating to items claimed; and,

1C–184

1C–185

1C–186

Paragraph numbers marked with a "+" can be found online and on CD.

(vi) the relevant papers in support of the costs claimed.

(b) In respect of the costs claimed, the receiving party may either:
 (i) file with the claim form a bill of costs, the form and layout of which is similar to the bills referred to in Section 3 above; or
 (ii) set out in the claim form a summary of the items of work done by a legal representative, or the receiving party as a litigant in person, as appropriate; the dates on which items of work were done; the time taken; and the sums claimed. The claims form must specify any disbursements claimed, including counsel's fees; the circumstances in which they were incurred and the amounts claimed in respect of them.

(c) If the receiving party wishes to draw any special circumstances to the attention of the Costs Judge those circumstances must be specified in the bill or in the claim form.

(d) The current court fee payable in respect of determinations under these Regulations is £120.

1C–187 **29.4 Service on the Lord Chancellor**

(a) Within three months from the date on which the order under Section 53A or Section 2A was made, the receiving party must serve a sealed copy of the claim form together with copies of:
 (i) the order of the court giving the right to costs;
 (ii) any bill of costs filed;
 (iii) any fee notes of counsel;
 (iv) receipts or accounts for other disbursements relating to items claimed.

(b) The procedure for service of the claim form is governed by RSC Order 77 rule 4 which is scheduled to the CPR.

1C–188 **29.5 Written representations and replies**

(a) The Lord Chancellor may, if so advised, no later than one month from (but excluding) the date on which he received the claim from the receiving party, file written representations in respect of the claim, at the Supreme Court Costs Office and at the same time serve a copy of them on the receiving party.

(b) Where the Lord Chancellor makes written representations the receiving party may, if so advised, file a reply at the Supreme Court Costs Office within 21 days after service of the written representations on the receiving party. A copy of the reply must be served on the Lord Chancellor at the same time.

1C–189 **29.6 Case management directions**

The Costs Judge may give directions in respect of:
 (i) the claim;
 (ii) any written representations or reply;
 (iii) the filing and serving of any further particulars or documents; and,
 (iv) to ensure that the determination of costs is dealt with justly.

1C–190 **29.7 The determination**

(a) After receiving points of dispute and/or a reply, or after the time for filing such documents has expired, if earlier, the Costs Judge will provisionally determine the amount of costs without the attendance of either party unless—
 (i) either party has required the court to fix a date for a hearing; or
 (ii) the court considers that a hearing is necessary.

(b) After a provisional determination, the court will give both parties notice of the amount which the court proposes to allow.

(c) The court will fix a date for hearing if either party informs the court, within 14 days after receipt of notice of provisional determination, that he wants the court to hold a hearing.

(d) Where the court fixes a date for a determination hearing, it will give at least 14 days notice to each party of the place, date and time of the hearing.

1C–191 **29.8 Costs of proceedings in the SCCO**

In respect of costs incurred in the SCCO CPR 44.3 gives the court a discretion as to whether the costs of the application are payable by one party to another, the amount of those costs and when they are to be paid.

Paragraph numbers marked with a "+" can be found online and on CD.

29.9 Result of the determination
1C–192

(a) On a provisional determination, or at a determination hearing, the court will note on the bill of costs or claim form all items allowed, disallowed or reduced.

(b) Once the determination has been concluded—

  (i) if the receiving party is legally represented, the legal representative should within the next 14 days make clear to the court the correct figures agreed or allowed in respect of each item and should recalculate the amount to be allowed; or

  (ii) if the receiving party is not legally represented, the Lord Chancellor should, within the next 14 days make clear to the court the correct figures agreed or allowed in respect of each item and should recalculate the amount to be allowed.

(c) On the completion of the determination the court will draw up an order specifying the amount payable by the Lord Chancellor under the order made under Section 53A or Section 2A and specify what if any order for the costs of the proceedings in the SCCO was made and (if appropriate) the amount of those costs.

29.10 Appeals
1C–193

CPR Part 52 applies to any appeal brought in respect of proceedings to which this section applies. Information about appeals and the time limits which apply is given in Section 13, above.

SECTION 30

THE FINANCIAL SERVICES AND MARKETS ACT 2000

30.1 Orders for costs between the parties
1C–194

(a) The Financial Services and Markets Act 2000, Section 132 provides for the establishment of the Financial Services and Markets Tribunal as part of the scheme for the regulation of financial services and markets. Schedule 13 to the Act empowers the Tribunal to order payment of costs in certain circumstances by one party to another in proceedings before the Tribunal.

(b) The Financial Services and Markets Tribunal Rules 2001 (S.I. 2001 No.2476) provide that where the Tribunal makes a costs order it may order that an amount fixed by the Tribunal shall be paid by one party to another, or that the costs shall be assessed on such basis as it may specify "by a costs official" (Rule 21(3)).

(c) Where an order for costs to be assessed is made by the Tribunal the costs will be assessed in the SCCO in accordance with the procedure set out in Sections 3 to 17 of this Guide (briefly, service of a bill plus notice of commencement and certain other documents, obtaining a default costs certificate, or, if points of dispute are served, serving a reply and/or filing a request for a detailed assessment hearing).

30.2 Costs under the Financial Services and Markets Tribunal Legal Assistance Scheme
1C–195

(a) The Financial Services and Markets Tribunal (Legal Assistance) Regulations 2001 (S.I. 2001 No. 3632) and the Financial Services and Markets Tribunal (Legal Assistance) Scheme (Costs) Regulations 2001 (S.I. 2001 No. 3633) are long and detailed. The provisions are similar to but not the same as those governing the assessment of costs in criminal proceedings. This Guide contains the barest outline and should not be relied upon as a comprehensive version of the Regulations. Reference should therefore be made to the Regulations themselves.

(b) The Legal Assistance Regulations govern the provision of legal assistance in respect of matters which are referred to the Tribunal by individuals against whom the Financial Services Authority has decided to take action in respect of alleged market abuse. The Costs Regulations make provision for the remuneration of work done under a legal assistance order in respect of cases before the Tribunal. They make provision for interim and staged payments in long cases and also for hardship payments. The two Schedules to the Costs Regulations set out details of the fees in respect of solicitors and advocates which are payable.

30.3 Claims for costs by solicitors
1C–196

(a) Solicitors are required to submit their claims for costs within three months of the conclusion of the proceedings to which the claim relates. The costs will be determined

Paragraph numbers marked with a "+" can be found online and on CD.

by a costs officer of the Supreme Court Costs Office. The claim should be documented in the same way, as far as possible, as a claim to a Crown Court determining officer would be, in respect of costs payable under a criminal legal aid order.

(b) The classes of work in respect of which a claim for costs may be made are:

(i) preparation, including taking instructions, advising, interviewing witnesses, ascertaining the Authority's case, preparing and perusing documents, dealing with letters and telephone calls which are not routine, preparing the advocacy, instructing an advocate and expert witnesses, conferences and consultations;

(ii) advocacy;

(iii) attending at court where an advocate is assigned, including conferences with the advocate at court;

(iv) travelling and waiting; and

(v) dealing with routine letters written and routine telephone calls (Regulation 13(1)).

(c) Fees will be allowed, as appropriate, to the following grades of fee earner:

(i) senior solicitor;

(ii) solicitor, legal executive or fee earner of equivalent experience;

(iii) trainee or fee earner of equivalent experience (Regulation 13(6)).

1C–197 30.4 Claims for fees by an advocate

(a) An advocate wishing to claim fees in respect of work done under a legal assistance order must submit the claim within three months of the conclusion of the proceedings to which it relates. The costs claimed will be detemined by a costs officer of the Supreme Court Costs Office. The claim should be documented in the same way, as far as possible, as a claim to a Crown Court determining officer would be, in respect of costs payable under a criminal legal aid order.

(b) The classes of fee which may be allowed are as follows:

(i) a basic fee for preparation, including preparation for any hearing before the main hearing, and, where appropriate, the first day of the main hearing including where they took place on that day, short conferences, consultations, applications and appearances and any other preparation;

(ii) a refresher fee for any day or part of a day during which a hearing continued, including, where it took place on that day, short conferences, consultations, applications and appearances, and any other preparation;

(iii) subsidiary fees for:

(a) attendance at conferences and consultations not covered by (a) or (b) above;

(b) written advices or other written work; and

(c) attendance at hearings before the main hearing, applications and appearances not covered by (a) or (b) above (Regulation 16(2)).

1C–198 30.5 Interim payments, staged payments and hardship payments

(a) The Financial Services and Markets Tribunal (Legal Assistance) Scheme (Costs) Regulations 2001, Regs 6, 8, 9 and 10 permit the making of applications to a costs officer in respect of the interim payment of disbursements already made, staged payments in long cases, interim payments in respect of attendances already made before the Tribunal and hardship payments in certain other circumstances. The application should be made in writing addressed to the principal costs officer and should be in a form similar to that used in similar applications to Crown Court determining officers.

(b) The procedures for redetermination, appeal and further appeal (see below) do not apply to decisions made by a costs officer concerning interim payments or staged payments.

(c) At the conclusion of a case in which an interim payment, staged payment or hardship payment has been allowed:

(i) the representative must submit a claim for the determination of his overall remuneration whether or not such a claim will result in any payment additional to those already made; and

(ii) the costs officer will take into account any payments already made when determining what, if any, further sum is payable to the representative, or, as the case may be, what, if any, sum should be repaid by him.

Paragraph numbers marked with a "+" can be found online and on CD.

30.6 Redetermination of costs

1C–199

(a) Where a representative is dissatisfied with the costs which have been determined, application may be made for redetermination of the costs. The application must be made within 21 days of the receipt of notification of the costs payable. The application should be made in writing to the costs officer specifying the matters in respect of which the application is made and the grounds of objection.

(b) The form of application should be similar to the form of application for redetermination used in the Crown Courts and should be accompanied by the particulars, information and documents supplied in connection with the original claim and must also state whether the applicant wishes to appear or be represented. If the applicant does wish to appear or be represented the costs officer will notify the applicant of the time and date of hearing.

(c) Having considered the applicant's submissions the costs officer will redetermine the costs, whether by way of increase or decrease, and will notify the applicant of the decision. The applicant may then request in writing that the appropriate officer give reasons for his decision. Such a request must be made within 21 days of the receipt of the notification of the decision on redetermination (Regulation 19).

30.7 Appeals to a Costs Judge

1C–200

(a) Where a costs officer has given reasons for the decision on determination and redetermination a representative who is dissatisfied with the decision may appeal to a Costs Judge. The appeal must be brought within 21 days of the receipt of the costs officer's reasons. The appeal is by notice in writing to the Senior Costs Judge in a similar form to that used in criminal fee appeals (see Appendix, para. A-9).

(b) The notice of appeal must specify separately:

  (i) each item appealed against, showing, where appropriate, the amount claimed for the item;

 (ii) the amount determined and the grounds of the objection to the determination; and

(iii) state whether the appellant wishes to appear or to be represented, or whether he will accept a decision given in his absence.

(c) The notice of appeal must be accompanied by:

  (i) a copy of the written representations made to the costs officer on the application for redetermination;

 (ii) the costs officer's reasons for his decision on redetermination; and

(iii) the particulars, information and documents supplied to the costs officer on redetermination.

(d) If so directed by the Lord Chancellor, or in any other case where it appears appropriate to do so, the Senior Costs Judge will send to the Lord Chancellor a copy of the notice of appeal together with the supporting documents. The Lord Chancellor may arrange for written or oral representations to be made on his behalf and if he intends to do so he will inform the Senior Costs Judge and the appellant. The appellant will be permitted a reasonable opportunity to make representations in reply.

30.8 Conduct of the appeal

1C–201

(a) The Costs Judge will inform the interested parties of the date of any hearing and may give directions as to the conduct of the appeal.

(b) The Costs Judge may consult the Tribunal or the costs officer and may require the appellant to provide any further information which is required for the purpose of the appeal.

(c) Unless the Costs Judge otherwise directs no further evidence will be received on the hearing of the appeal and no ground of objection will be valid which was not raised on the application for redetermination.

(d) The Costs Judge has the same powers as the costs officer and may alter the redetermination of the costs officer in respect of any sum allowed, whether by increase or decrease as he thinks fit.

(e) The decision of the Costs Judge will be given to the interested parties and the costs officer in writing. Except where he confirms or decreases sums redetermined, the Costs Judge may allow the appellant a sum in respect of part or all of any reasonable costs incurred in connection with the appeal.

Paragraph numbers marked with a "+" can be found online and on CD.

1C–202 **30.9 Further appeals to a High Court Judge**

(a) The decision of the Costs Judge on appeal is final unless the Costs Judge certifies a point of principle of general importance. A representative who is dissatisfied with the decision of the Costs Judge on appeal may apply for such a certificate. That application must be made within 21 days of the notification of the Costs Judge's decision on appeal. Where the Costs Judge certifies a point of principle of general importance the representative may appeal to the High Court against the decision of the Costs Judge and the Lord Chancellor must be made a respondent to such an appeal. The appeal must be brought within 21 days of receipt of the Costs Judges certificate.

(b) If the Lord Chancellor is dissatisfied with the decision of the Costs Judge on appeal he may, if no appeal has been made by the representative, appeal to the High Court against that decision.

(c) An appeal to the High Court must be brought in the Queen's Bench Division and follow the procedure set out in CPR Part 8. The appeal will be heard and determined by a Single Judge whose decision is final. The Judge has the same powers as the costs officer and the Costs Judge and may reverse, affirm or amend the decision appealed against or make such other order as he thinks fit.

1C–203 **30.10 Extension of time limits**

(a) All the time limits referred to may for good reason be extended by the costs officer, the Costs Judge or the High Court as appropriate.

(b) Where a representative, without good reason has failed to comply with the time limit, time may be extended in exceptional circumstances and in such circumstances the costs officer, Costs Judge or High Court Judge will consider whether it is reasonable in the circumstances to reduce the costs. The representative will be allowed a reasonable opportunity to show cause orally or in writing why the costs should not be reduced. A representative may appeal to a Costs Judge against a decision under these provisions made by a costs officer under the procedure described in para. 30.8, above.

SECTION 31

CRIMINAL FEE APPEALS

1C–204 **31.1 Introductory**

(a) Costs Judges have jurisdiction to hear appeals from the decisions of Determining Officers of the Crown Court, the Divisional Court of the Queen's Bench Division and the Court of Appeal (Criminal Division) in each of the following cases:

(i) Appeals by parties awarded costs out of Central Funds (as to which see the Costs in Criminal Cases (General) Regulations 1986.

(ii) Appeals by solicitors and counsel entitled to remuneration under the Legal Aid Act 1988 (as to which see the Legal Aid in Criminal and Care Proceedings (Costs) Regulations 1989).

(iii) Appeals by solicitors and counsel entitled to remuneration under the Access to Justice Act, 1999 and the Criminal Defence Service (Funding) Order 2001.

(iv) Appeals by solicitors and advocates entitled to remuneration under the Criminal Procedure Rules 2005 (formerly the Crown Court Rules 1982 Part IV).

(v) Appeals by litigants in person having the benefit of costs orders under any of the above enactments.

(b) All Costs Judges have been appointed Deputy Adjudicators to HM Land Registry for the purpose of assessing such costs.

1C–205 **31.2 The Criminal Costs Practice Direction**

Detailed guidance as to the SCCO practice on criminal fee appeals and the procedure on further appeals to a High Court Judge is set out in the *Practice Direction (Criminal Proceedings: Costs)* [2004] 1 WLR 2657; [2004] 2 All ER 1070; [2004] 2 Cr App R395 (the "Criminal Costs Practice Direction).

1C–206 **31.3 Nominated masters**

At present there are five Costs Judges who deal with criminal fee appeals, namely Chief Master Hurst (Senior Costs Judge), Master Rogers, Master Campbell, Master Simons and Master Gordon-Saker.

Paragraph numbers marked with a "+" can be found online and on CD.

31.4 The Notice of Appeal

1C–207

(a) The Notice of Appeal must be in writing and must be lodged with the Clerk of Appeals, together with the fee (currently £100) and the additional material referred to in the Criminal Costs Practice Direction within 21 days of receipt of the reasons given for the decision or within such longer time as the Costs Judge may direct; (under the Criminal Procedure Rules 2005 the period is 14 days). Papers are lodged with the Clerk of Appeals in Room 2.14.

(b) The Notice of Appeal should follow the Form A in Schedule 3 to the Criminal Costs Practice Direction and illustrated in the Appendix (para A-9, below). It is important that the Notice of Appeal should clearly identify (i) the matters which are being appealed to the Costs Judge and (ii) the amount in dispute in relation to each item.

(c) Notices of Appeal must be signed by advocates personally or by a partner in the appellant firm of Solicitors.

(d) It occasionally happens that appellants fail to serve the Determining Officer with a copy of the Notice of Appeal. The Regulations are mandatory in this respect and failure to do so may result in the appeal being dismissed without the merits being considered.

31.5 The Grounds of Appeal

1C–208

(a) The Grounds of Appeal should correspond with the Notice of Appeal. Points raised in the Notice of Appeal which are not supported by grounds may be dismissed and conversely matters included in the Grounds of Appeal which are not mentioned in the Notice of Appeal may not be separately decided.

(b) The Grounds of Appeal are an integral part of the Notice of Appeal and should be submitted at the same time. If for some reason the Grounds of Appeal cannot be prepared within the time allowed for lodging Notice of Appeal an application for an extension of time should be made.

(c) It is important to be both concise and specific in the Grounds of Appeal. Particular attention should be paid to the provisions of the Criminal Costs Practice Direction.

(d) Uncertified decisions of Costs Judges are not binding on Costs Judges or Determining Officers and will rarely if ever be of any assistance.

(e) Only in exceptional cases will a Costs Judge consider material not before the Determining Officer (leave is required in Schedule 1 to the 2001 Funding Order para 21(11) of Reg. 15(11) of the 1989 Regs; Reg. 9(11) of the 1986 Regs) or Reg 78.5(5) of the Criminal Procedure Rules 2005. Requests to consider such material should always be included in the Notice of Appeal.

31.6 Supplementary Grounds of Appeal

1C–209

Occasionally the Determining Officer does not give written Reasons in respect of all matters upon which the appellant wishes to bring before the Costs Judge. In that situation, provided the appellant has raised them at the re-determination stage, and in his/her request for written Reasons, the appellant should ask the Determining Officer for supplementary written Reasons and may then lodge supplementary Grounds of Appeal.

31.7 Lodging of documents in support of appeal

1C–210

(a) It frequently happens that far more material is lodged in support of the appeal than is either necessary or desirable. For instance in a case of a multi-handed appeal by a number of Counsel it is not normally necessary to lodge more than one set of depositions etc. Liaison between appellants is important.

(b) Before lodging substantial volumes of papers it is advisable to contact the Clerk of Appeals who will if necessary liaise with the Costs Judge as to what documents are required.

(c) The relevant documents should be lodged no more than 10 days prior to an oral hearing. In the case of appeals to be dealt with on paper only and without an attendance, all relevant papers should be lodged with the Notice and Grounds of Appeal.

31.8 Appeals on paper only

1C–211

(a) Appeals made on paper only and without an attendance may be dealt with more quickly than appeals dealt with by way of a hearing. All appellants should give careful

Paragraph numbers marked with a "+" can be found online and on CD.

SCCO GUIDE

consideration, at the stage of lodging their appeals, to the question of whether or not they consider it necessary to attend.

(b) An appellant seeking the costs of an appeal to be dealt with on paper only, should specify the particular sum claimed in a document accompanying the Grounds of Appeal or in a covering letter. If no sum is claimed, the Master will normally only order refund of the appeal fee paid.

1C–212 31.9 The hearing of an appeal

All hearings may be attended by the counsel or representatives of the solicitors concerned in the matter or a duly authorised agent on their behalf, who may include another solicitor, another counsel or a costs draftsperson. Such oral hearings are informal and conducted in private. They are seldom of lengthy duration but where an appellant considers that an unusually lengthy hearing is necessary this should be indicated in a covering letter with the Notice and Grounds of Appeal.

1C–213 31.10 Multi-handed appeals

Wherever possible appeals in relation to the same case by all or many of the advocates and/or solicitors concerned are listed together or at short consecutive intervals on the same day. Where this presents problems to individual appellants, representations should be made to the Clerk of Appeals who will consult the Costs Judge as to whether an exception can be made to this general rule. It may however be possible to hear all the appeals of advocates in one particular case on the same day and all the appeals of solicitors in relation to the same case on another day.

1C–214 31.11 Appeals by same advocate

Where counsel, particularly from out of London, have a number of separate appeals every effort will be made to list these together to avoid unnecessary journeys.

1C–215 31.12 Appeals by telephone or video link

All Costs Judges are prepared to hear criminal appeals by telephone or video link, especially where the sums involved are small or disproportionate to the costs of travel to London. Requests for any such hearing should be made to the Clerk of Appeals when lodging the appeal. Telephone appeals can usually be listed quite quickly but video appeals take longer because of pressure on the limited video facilities in the RCJ.

1C–216 31.13 Procedure subsequent to the appeal

(a) In every case the Regulations require that the Master should give his reasons in writing. There is inevitably a time lag between the oral hearing and the despatch of the written Reasons. Only rarely will the Costs Judge consider material submitted after the hearing.

(b) A successful appellant is entitled to ask for his costs which are normally assessed by the Costs Judge at the end of the hearing. It is important that any appellant should submit details to the Costs Judge at the hearing of travelling expenses or any unusual expenditure in relation to the appeal.

(c) In all cases where an appeal is successful the court fee paid (currently £100) is added to the sums allowed, unless the Costs Judge otherwise directs.

1C–217 31.14 Further appeal

(a) The Department of Constitutional Affairs has an independent right of appeal against any decisions adverse to the LSC Fund or Central Funds and in those cases no leave from the Costs Judge is required.

(b) In other cases, whether Central Funds or LSC funded cases, a further, and final, appeal is possible where the Costs Judge has certified that a point of principle of general importance is involved. It is necessary to apply within 21 days of receipt of the Master's written Reasons (14 days in the case of proposed appeals under the Criminal Procedure Rules 2005) for a certificate to be granted by the Costs Judge and, in accordance with the Criminal Costs Practice Direction, the form of certificate sought should wherever possible be submitted with the application.

Paragraph numbers marked with a "+" can be found online and on CD.

(c) If the Costs Judge grants a certificate, the appeal lies to a Judge of the High Court, Queen's Bench Division who will normally sit with two assessors one of whom will be another Costs Judge.

(d) If the Costs Judge refuses a certificate no further appeal is possible.

(e) The decision of the High Court Judge is final, and no further appeal is permitted.

31.15 Time limits
1C–218

(a) The time limits laid down by the Regulations and the Practice Direction should always be complied with. It is not a sufficient reason for granting an extension of time that the Determining Officer has taken many months to produce his or her Written Reasons which are being appealed to the Costs Judge. Further it is not sufficient to justify an extension of time that all the papers needed to support the appeal are not immediately available.

(b) It not infrequently happens particularly at Christmas, Easter and holiday times that it is difficult to comply with the strict 21 day time limit (14 days in the case of Criminal Procedure Rules 2005 appeals) laid down in the Regulations. In those situations, an appellant should always apply before the relevant time limit expires seeking a short extension and giving grounds in support of that application.

(c) Where the 21/14 day time limit has expired an application for leave to appeal out of time should be mounted at the first possible opportunity thereafter and should initially be submitted in writing. The letter should always be signed by the appellant, not by his clerk, or another solicitor within his office. It should give a full explanation for the delay and justification advanced for granting leave out of time.

(d) Such applications are in the first instance dealt with by one of the Costs Judges on the papers. Where such an application is refused the appellant may renew his application by asking for an oral hearing before the Costs Judge. Permission is sometimes granted subject to a percentage penalty reducing the amount of any increase in costs which would otherwise have been obtained on the appeal.

(e) Where such oral hearings take place the Costs Judge will try to dispose of the substantive appeal immediately after the leave application. Those attending such applications should come prepared to address the merits of the substantive appeal, having lodged all the relevant papers. An additional fee of £100 is payable, where such leave is granted.

31.16 Divisional Court/Administrative Court central funds assessments
1C–219

All such determinations are currently dealt with by Costs Judge Rogers. He is treated as the Determining Officer in accordance with the 1986 Regulations. A dissatisfied party may ask him to redetermine those costs and thereafter to give his written reasons. Any party still dissatisfied may then appeal to the Senior Costs Judge who will follow the same procedure as in an appeal from a Determining Officer in the Crown Court or Court of Appeal.

SECTION 32

CIVIL RECOVERY PROCEEDINGS UNDER THE PROCEEDS OF CRIME ACT 2002

32.1 Introductory
1C–220

(a) The Proceeds of Crime Act 2002 makes provision for the confiscation of the assets of persons convicted of criminal offences and, in certain circumstances, of those "tainted" by criminality. Where the Director of the Assets Recovery Agency is empowered to bring proceedings for a recovery order under the Act he may also apply to the High Court for a property freezing order or an interim receiving order which prohibits any person, to whose property the order applies, from dealing with that property. The court may make exclusions from that prohibition for certain purposes including the meeting of reasonable legal expenses.

(b) The Proceeds of Crime Act 2002 and the Regulations made thereunder make special provision for two types of proceedings in the Supreme Court Costs Office:—

  (i) during civil recovery proceedings, referrals to determine the amount which exclusions should allow for reasonable legal costs; and

Paragraph numbers marked with a "+" can be found online and on CD.

SCCO GUIDE

(ii) at the conclusion of civil recovery proceedings, the assessment of any person's reasonable legal expenses in those proceedings where the court has made a recovery order which provides for the payment of those expenses.

(c) The Proceeds of Crime Act 2002 (Legal Expenses in Civil Recovery Proceedings) Regulations 2005 (SI 2005/3382) specify the hourly rates of remuneration which may be allowed in respect of work done by legal representatives. Higher rates may be allowed for cases involving substantial, novel or complex issues of law or fact and the rates are increase for legal representatives whose offices are situated in certain London post code areas and districts.

1C–221 **32.2 Exclusions to meet reasonable legal expenses**

(a) Where the court makes a property freezing order, or an interim receiving order, on an application without notice it will normally make an exclusion from the order to enable the respondent to meet his reasonable legal costs of taking advice in relation to the order, preparing a statement of assets and, if so advised, apply for the order to be set aside or varied. The initial exclusion will not normally exceed £3,000.

(b) When the court makes a property freezing order or an interim receiving order before a claim for a recovery order has been commenced, the court may also make an exclusion to enable the respondent to meet his reasonable legal costs, so that, when the claim is commenced, he may file an acknowledgment of service and any written evidence on which he intends to rely, or may apply for a further exclusion for the purpose of enabling him to meet his reasonable costs of the proceedings.

(c) Save as mentioned below, when the court makes an order or gives directions in civil recovery proceedings it will at the same time consider whether it is appropriate to make or vary an exclusion for the purpose of enabling any person affected by the order or directions to meet his reasonable legal costs. However, in order to obtain an exclusion going beyond the preliminary steps mentioned in sub paragraphs (a) and (b) above the person whose costs are to be provided for must make and file a statement of assets.

(d) The court will normally refer to a Costs Judge any question relating to the amount which an exclusion should allow for reasonable legal costs in respect of proceedings or a stage in the proceedings.

(e) An exclusion made for the purpose of enabling a person to meet his reasonable legal costs will specify:

(i) the stage or stages of civil recovery proceedings to which it relates;
(ii) the maximum amount which may be released in respect of legal costs for each specified stage; and
(iii) the total amount which may be released in respect of legal costs pursuant to the exclusion.

(f) Once expenses provided for by an exclusion have been incurred a person may seek the Director's agreement to the release of an interim payment in respect of those expenses. The amount which may be released is the amount which the Director agrees, or 65% of the amount claimed, whichever is the greater.

(g) If a person becomes aware that his legal costs have exceeded or will exceed the maximum amount allowed for a specified stage, or the total amount allowed for all stages, he should apply for a further exclusion or for a variation in the existing exclusion as soon as reasonably practicable.

1C–222 **32.3 Procedure on referrals relating to exclusions**

(a) Where a matter has been referred to a Costs Judge, either party may make an application to the SCCO on Form N244 accompanied by a copy of the relevant order, copies of any evidence relied on in support and a statement of parties.

(b) If the application is made by the person whose reasonable legal costs are to be provided for:

(i) the evidence in support should include an estimate of costs substantially in the form illustrated in Precedent H in the Schedule of Costs Precedents annexed to the Costs Practice Direction; and
(ii) when fixing the date for hearing the Costs Judge will also give a direction as to the filing and service of any points of dispute on the estimated costs.

(c) A specimen form of order for directions on applications made by a person whose costs are to be provided for is included in the Appendix, below, para A-11.

Paragraph numbers marked with a "+" can be found online and on CD.

(d) On receipt of an application the SCCO will endeavour to list it for a date for hearing not less than 14 days after nor more than 42 days after the date of issue. The party making the application should specify his preferred dates for hearing in that period. Ideally, he should specify at least one day in each week of that period.

32.4 Assessment of costs following a recovery order

1C–223

(a) The Regulations set out the procedure for determining the amount payable in respect of legal expenses once the High Court has made a recovery order which vests property in the trustee for civil recovery and provides for the payment of those expenses out of that property. The Regulations also specify the hourly rates of remuneration which may be allowed in respect of work done by legal representatives.

(b) The amount of costs provided for by a recovery order may be agreed with the Director of the Assets Recovery Agency. In such a case the Director will give notice of the agreed sum to the person seeking costs and to the trustee for civil recovery.

(c) If the legal expenses are not agreed with the Director, the person seeking them must commence detailed assessment proceedings in accordance with CPR Part 47. Generally speaking the procedure is as set out in Sections 3 to 17 of this Guide (briefly, service of a bill plus notice of commencement and certain other documents, obtaining a default costs certificate or, if points of dispute are served, serving a reply and/or filing a request for a detailed assessment hearing).

(d) The notice of commencement plus other documents must be served not later than two months after the date of the recovery order.

(e) Unless the costs are subsequently agreed or unless a default costs certificate is obtained, a request for a detailed assessment hearing must be filed in the Supreme Court Costs Office not later than two months after the expiration of the period for commencing the detailed assessment proceedings.

(f) Further details of the procedure to be followed are set out in Section 49A of the Costs Practice Direction. Notice in particular:

    (i) the paying party is the trustee for civil recovery;

    (ii) the notice of commencement must also be served on the Director of the Assets Recovery Agency;

    (iii) in addition to the documents usually served with a notice of commencement (as to which, see para 4.4(b) of this Guide) the receiving party must also serve a statement giving the date, amount and source of all interim payments which have been released in respect of the costs in question;

    (iv) in addition to the documents usually filed with a request for a detailed assessment hearing (as to which, see para 8.2(a) of this Guide) the receiving party must also file copies of all exclusions from property freezing orders or interim receiving orders which relate to the costs to be assessed and copies of every estimate of costs filed by the receiving party in support of an application for such an exclusion; and

    (v) the costs will be assessed on the standard basis, subject to the Regulations specifying the hourly rates which may be allowed.

(g) If the sum payable in respect of a person's legal expenses exceeds the total amount which has been released in respect of those expenses, the trustee for civil recovery must pay the balance out of the assets recovered.

(h) The trustee for civil recovery may only make a payment in respect of a person's legal expenses to the solicitor who is instructed to act for that person or, where appropriate, to the solicitor who was so instructed when the legal expenses to which the sum relates were incurred.

(i) If the sum payable in respect of a person's legal expenses is less than the total amount which has been released in respect of those expenses, the person to whose expenses the sum relates must repay the balance to the trustee.

SECTION 33

COSTS ORDERS MADE BY THE ADJUDICATOR TO HM LAND REGISTRY

33.1 Introductory

1C–224

(a) The Adjudicator to HM Land Registry (Practice and Procedure Rules) 2003 SI No.2003/2171 contains provisions about the making of orders for costs and the basis of

Paragraph numbers marked with a "+" can be found online and on CD.

SCCO GUIDE

assessment (standard or indemnity) and provides that the order may specify the amount of costs or, alternatively, may award "costs to be assessed".

(b) All Costs Judges have been appointed Deputy Adjudicators to HM Land Registry.

1C–225 33.2 Assessments referred to the SCCO

(a) The remaining paragraphs of this section set out the procedure to be followed where a party is awarded costs by an order of the Adjudicator to HM Land Registry and the order directs that that party may apply to the Supreme Court Costs Office for assessment.

(b) On receiving the file from HM Land Registry the Costs Judge will issue standard directions with regard to the service and filing of Points of Dispute and the consequences of failing to do so.

(c) Either party may apply to the Costs Judge for further direction. If points of dispute have already been served (whether by order or voluntarily) the receiving party may file a *request for a detailed assessment hearing*. Such applications or requests are not governed by the CPR and, at present, no court fees are payable.

1C–226 33.3 Applications for directions

(a) The form of application should be similar to the form used in applications governed by the CPR, ie, Form **N244**, and should be accompanied by:

   (i) a copy of the order for costs made by the Adjudicator,

   (ii) a copy of the bill served pursuant to that order, and

   (iii) a statement of parties.

(b) The application will normally be dealt with without a hearing.

(c) Two standards forms of order are illustrated in the appendix below, para A-12:—

   (i) an order giving the defendant notice to show cause why the bill of costs should not be assessed as drawn because of his failure to comply with a direction by the Adjudicator to serve points of dispute;

  (ii) directions for the service of points of dispute and (if the claimant so wishes) for the service of a reply. This form will also state the provisional date for a hearing if points of dispute are served and, if they are not, states that the claimant will be entitled to obtain an assessment of his bill as drawn.

1C–227 33.4 Request for a detailed assessment hearing

(a) The form of request should be similar to the form used in most cases governed by the CPR, ie, Form **N258**. This form contains a series of tick boxes which give guidance as to the documents which should accompany the request.

(b) On receipt of the request the court will fix a date for the hearing or, if the Costs Judge so decides, will give directions or fix a date a date for a preliminary appointment.

(c) The court will give at least 14 days notice of the time and place of the detailed assessment hearing to every person whose name and address appears on the statement of parties.

(d) On completion of the detailed assessment, the form of Order made is shown on A-13.

SECTION 34

SCCO CONSULTATION GROUPS

1C–228 34.1 Costs Practitioners Group

(a) This advisory group (formerly known as the Taxation Users Group) is run under the auspices of the Supreme Court Costs Office. Two Costs Judges are members, one of whom acts as Chairman. The current Chairman is Master O'Hare. The Senior Costs Judge sometimes attends as does the Principal Costs Officer. The Council of Circuit Judges, The District Judges Association, the Bar Council, The Law Society, The London Solicitors Litigation Association, The Association of Personal Injury Lawyers (APIL), The Forum of Insurance Lawyers (FOIL) and the Association of Law Costs Draftsmen are all represented.

(b) The group generally meets twice a year in the Supreme Court Costs Office, its function being to comment upon and make recommendations for the improvement of

Paragraph numbers marked with a "+" can be found online and on CD.

the current and evolving practice of assessment of costs. Although it is an advisory group, as it consists of representatives of all the principal "users" it is intended to be influential and to afford a regular opportunity for informal exchanges of views on existing practice and how the same can be improved. Minutes are taken and circulated.

(c) Organisations and bodies wishing to apply for membership of the Costs Practitioners Group should write to its Chairman, c/o the SCCO.

34.2 SCCO Users Group

1C–229

(a) This Group, which is organised by the SCCO Court Manager, is open to any court user who wishes to attend. Meetings are held about three times each year, the dates of meetings being shown on the Customer Services Notice Board in Room 1.02. Persons stating their intention to attend the next meeting will later receive an invitation to contribute agenda items for that meeting.

(b) The main objective of the Group is to enable the SCCO to explain the services it provides and the standards of service it seeks to achieve. Commonly arising issues include statistics about waiting lists for hearings and turn around times for the issue of certificates.

(c) Meetings are usually attended by the Principal Costs Officer, the Court Manager, the Customer Services Manager and representatives from the Association of Law Costs Draftsmen, the Citizens Advice Bureau, the Law Society and the Legal Services Commission plus several members of the public. Minutes are taken and circulated.

SCCO GUIDE

Paragraph numbers marked with a "+" can be found online and on CD.

APPENDIX

SOME STANDARD FORMS AND PRECEDENTS

1C–230

SCHEDULE OF COSTS PRECEDENTS
PRECEDENT A

IN THE HIGH COURT OF JUSTICE   2000 - B - 9999

QUEEN'S BENCH DIVISION

BRIGHTON DISTRICT REGISTRY

BETWEEN

AB   Claimant

- and -

CD   Defendant

**CLAIMANT'S BILL OF COSTS TO BE ASSESSED PURSUANT
TO THE ORDER DATED 26th JULY 2000**

V.A.T. No. 33 4404 90

In these proceedings the claimant sought compensation for personal injuries and other losses suffered in a road accident which occurred on Friday 1st January 1999 near the junction between Bolingbroke Lane and Regency Road, Brighton, East Sussex. The claimant had been travelling as a front seat passenger in a car driven by the defendant. The claimant suffered severe injuries when, because of the defendant's negligence, the car left the road and collided with a brick wall.

The defendant was later convicted of various offences arising out of the accident including careless driving and driving under the influence of drink or drugs.

In the civil action the defendant alleged that immediately before the car journey began the claimant had known that the defendant was under the influence of alcohol and therefore consented to the risk of injury or was contributorily negligent as to it. It was also alleged that, immediately before the accident occurred, the claimant wrongfully took control of the steering wheel so causing the accident to occur.

The claimant first instructed solicitors, E F & Co, in this matter in July 2000. The claim form was issued in October 2000 and in February 2001 the proceedings were listed for a two day trial commencing 25th July 2001. At the trial the defendant was found liable but the compensation was reduced by 25% to take account of contributory negligence by the claimant. The claimant was awarded a total of £78,256.83 plus £1,207.16 interest plus costs.

The claimant instructed E F & Co under a conditional fee agreement dated 8th July 2000 which specifies the following base fees and success fees.

     Partner - £180 per hour plus VAT
     Assistant Solicitor - £140 per hour plus VAT
     Other fee earners - £85 per hour plus VAT
     Success fees exclusive of disbursement funding costs: 40%
     Success fee in respect of disbursement funding costs: 7.5% (not claimed in this bill)

Paragraph numbers marked with a "+" can be found online and on CD.

Except where the contrary is stated the proceedings were conducted on behalf of the claimant by an assistant solicitor, admitted November 1999.

E F & Co instructed Counsel (Miss GH, called 1992) under a conditional fee agreement dated 5th June 2001 which specifies a success fee of 75% and base fees, payable in various circumstances, of which the following are relevant

Fees for interim hearing whose estimated duration is up to 2 hours: £600
Brief for trial whose estimated duration is 2 days: £2,000
Fee for second and subsequent days: £650 per day

Paragraph numbers marked with a "+" can be found online and on CD.

SCCO GUIDE

Item No.	Description of work done	V.A.T.	Disburse-ments	Profit Costs
	8th July 2000 - EF & Co instructed			
	22nd July 2000 - AEI with Eastbird Legal Protection Ltd			
1	Premium for policy		£ 120.00	
	7th October 2000 - Claim issued			
2	Issue fee	-	£ 400.00	
	21st October 2000 - Particulars of claim served			
	25th November 2000 - Time for service of defence extended by agreement to 14th January 2001			
3	Fee on allocation	-	£ 80.00	
	20th January 2001 - case allocated to multi-track			
	9th February 2001 - Case management conference at which costs were awarded to the claimant and the base costs were summarily assessed at £400 (paid on 24th February 2001)			
	23rd February 2001 - Claimant's list of documents			
	12th April 2001 - Payment into court of £25,126.33			
	13th April 2001 - Filing pre-trial checklist			
4	Fee on listing	-	£ 400.00	
	28th June 2001 - Pre trial review: costs in case Engaged 1.5 hours £210.00 Travel and waiting 2.00 hours £280.00			
5	Total solicitor's base fee for attending			£ 490.00
6	Counsel's base fee for pre trial review (Miss GH)		£ 600.00	
	25th July 2001 - Attending first day of trial; adjourned part heard Engaged in Court 5.00 hours £700.00 Engaged in conference 0.75 hours £105.00 Travel and waiting 1.5 hours £210.00			
7	Total solicitor's base fee for attending			£1,015.00
8	Counsel's base fee for trial (Miss GH)		£2,000.00	
9	Fee of expert witness (Dr. IJ)	-	£ 850.00	
10	Expenses of witnesses of fact	-	£ 84.00	
	26th July 2001 - Attending second day of trial when judgment was given for the claimant in the sum of £78,256.53 plus £1207.16 interest plus costs Engaged in Court 3.00 hours £420.00 Engaged in conference 1.5 hours £210.00 Travel and waiting 1.5 hours £210.00			
11	Total solicitor's base fee for attending			£ 840.00
12	Counsel's base fee for second day (Miss GH)		£ 650.00	
	To Summary	£ -	£5,184.00	£2,345.00

Item No.	Description of work done	V.A.T.	Disburse-ments	Profit Costs
13	**Claimant** 8th July 2000 - First instructions: 0.75 hours by Partner: base fee			£ 135.00
14	Other timed attendances in person and by telephone - See Schedule 1 Total base fee for Schedule 1 - 7.5 hours			£1,050.00
15	Routine letters out and telephone calls - 29 (17 + 12) total base fee			£ 406.00
16	**Witnesses of Fact** Timed attendances in person, by letter out and by telephone - See Schedule 2 Total base fee for Schedule 2 - 5.2 hours			£ 728.00
17	Routine letters out, e mails and telephone calls - 8 (4 + 2 + 2)total base fee			£ 112.00
18	Paid travelling on 9th October 2000	£ 4.02	£ 22.96	
19	**Medical expert (Dr. IJ)** 11th September 2000 - long letter out 0.33 hours: base fee			£ 46.20
20	30th January 2001 - long letter out 0.25 hours base fee			£ 35.00
21	23rd May 2001 - telephone call 0.2 hours base fee			£ 28.00
22	Routine letters out and telephone calls - 10 (6 + 4) total base fee			£ 140.00
23	Dr. IJ's fee for report	-	£ 350.00	
24	**Defendant and his solicitor** 8th July 2000 - timed letter sent 0.5 hours: base fee			£ 70.00
25	19th February 2001 - telephone call 0.25 hours: base fee			£ 35.00
26	Routine letters out and telephone calls - 24 (18 + 6) total base fee			£ 336.00
27	**Communications with the court** Routine letters out and telephone calls - 9 (8 + 1) total base fee			£ 126.00
28	**Communications with Counsel** Routine letters out, e mails and telephone calls - 19 (4 + 7 + 8) total base fee			£ 266.00
29	**Work done on documents** Timed attendances - See Schedule 3 Total base fees for Schedule 3 - 0.75 hours at £180, 44.5 hours at £140, 12 hours at £85			£7,385.00
30	**Work done on negotiations** 23rd March 2001 - meeting at offices of Solicitors for the Defendant Engaged - 1.5 hours £210.00 Travel and waiting - 1.25 hours £175.00 Total base fee for meeting			£ 385.00
31	**Other work done** Preparing and checking bill Engaged: Solicitor - 1 hour £140.00 Engaged: Costs Draftsman - 4 hours £340.00 Total base fee on other work done			£ 480.00
	To Summary	£ 4.02	£ 372.96	£11,763.20

Paragraph numbers marked with a "+" can be found online and on CD.

Item No.	Description of work done	V.A.T.	Disburse -ments	Profit Costs
32	Success fee on solicitor's base fee on interim orders which were summarily assessed (40% of £400) plus VAT at 17.5%	£ 28.00		£ 160.00
33	VAT on solicitor's other base fees (17.5% of £14,108.20)	£ 2,468.94		
34	Success fee on solicitor's other base fees (40% of £14,108.20) plus VAT at 17.5%	£ 987.58		£ 5,643.28
35	VAT on Counsel's base fees (17.5% of £3,250)'	£ 568.75		
36	Success fee on Counsel's base fee (75% of £3,250) plus VAT at 17.5%'	£ 426.57	£ 2,437.50	
	To Summary	£ 4,479.84	£ 2,437.50	£ 5,803.28
	SUMMARY			
	Page 3 £	-	£ 5,184.00	£ 2,345.00
	Page 4 £	4.02	£ 372.96	£ 11,763.20
	Page 5 £	4,479.84	£2,437.50	£ 5,803.28
	Totals:	£ 4,483.86	£ 7,994.46	£ 19,911.48
	Grand total:			£ 32,389.80

A-2 Certificates in bills : Schedule of Costs Precedents, Precedent F

- Appropriate certificates under headings (1) and (2) are required in all cases. The appropriate certificate under (3) is required in all cases in which the receiving party is an assisted person or a LSC funded client. Certificates (4), (5) and (6) are optional. Certificate (6) may be included in the bill, or, if the dispute as to VAT recoverability arises after service of the bill, may be filed and served as a supplementary document amending the bill under paragraph 39.10 of this Practice Direction.

- All certificates must be signed by the receiving party or by his solicitor. Where the bill claims costs in respect of work done by more than one firm of solicitors, certificate (1), appropriately completed, should be signed on behalf of each firm.

(1)   CERTIFICATE AS TO ACCURACY

I certify that this bill is both accurate and complete [and]

(where the receiving party was funded by legal aid/LSC)
☐ [in respect of Part(s) ..... of the bill] all the work claimed was done pursuant to a certificate issued by the Legal Aid Board/ Legal Services Commission granted to [the assisted person] [the LSC funded client].

(where costs are claimed for work done by an employed solicitor)
☐ [in respect of Part(s) .... of the bill] the case was conducted by a solicitor who is an employee of the receiving party.

(other cases where costs are claimed for work done by a solicitor)
☐ [in respect of Part(s) ..... of the bill] the costs claimed herein do not exceed the costs which the receiving party is required to pay me/my firm.

SCCO Guide

(2)   CERTIFICATE AS TO INTEREST AND PAYMENTS

I certify that:

☐   No rulings have been made in this case which affects my/the receiving party's entitlement (if any) to interest on costs.

or

☐   The only rulings made in this case as to interest are as follows:
[give brief details as to the date of each ruling, the name of the Judge who made it and the text of the ruling]

and

☐   No payments have been made by any paying party on account of costs included in this bill of costs.

or

☐   The following payments have been made on account of costs included in this bill of costs:
[give brief details of the amounts, the dates of payment and the name of the person by or on whose behalf they were paid]

(3)   CERTIFICATE AS TO INTEREST OF ASSISTED PERSON/ LSC FUNDED CLIENT PURSUANT TO REGULATION 119 OF THE CIVIL LEGAL AID (GENERAL) REGULATIONS 1989

I certify that the assisted person/ LSC funded client has no financial interest in the detailed assessment.

or

I certify that a copy of this bill has been sent to the assisted person/ LSC funded client pursuant to Regulation 119 of the Civil Legal Aid General Regulations 1989 with an explanation of his/her interest in the detailed assessment and the steps which can be taken to safeguard that interest in the assessment.   He/she has/has not requested that the costs officer be informed of his/her interest and has/has not requested that notice of the detailed assessment hearing be sent to him/her.

(4)   CONSENT TO THE SIGNING OF THE CERTIFICATE WITHIN 21 DAYS OF DETAILED ASSESSMENT PURSUANT TO REGULATION 112 AND 121 OF THE CIVIL LEGAL AID (GENERAL) REGULATIONS 1989

I certify that notice of the fees reduced or disallowed on detailed assessment has been given in writing to counsel on [date].

or

I certify that: there having been no reduction or disallowance of counsel's fees it is not necessary to give notice to counsel.

I/we consent to the final costs certificate being issued immediately.

(5)   CERTIFICATE IN RESPECT OF DISBURSEMENTS NOT EXCEEDING £500

I hereby certify that all disbursements listed in this bill which individually do not exceed £500 (other than those relating to counsel's fees) have been duly discharged.

(6)   CERTIFICATE AS TO RECOVERY OF VAT

With reference to the pending assessment of the [claimant's/defendant's] costs and disbursements herein which are payable by the [claimant/defendant] we the undersigned [solicitors to] [auditors of] the [claimant/defendant] hereby certify that the [claimant/defendant] on the basis of its last completed VAT return [would/would not be entitled to recover would/be entitled to recover only percent of the] Value Added Tax on such costs and disbursements, as input tax pursuant to Section 14 of the Value Added Tax Act 1983.

Paragraph numbers marked with a "+" can be found online and on CD.

A-3 Points of dispute : Schedule of Costs Precedents, Precedent G

IN THE HIGH COURT OF JUSTICE   2000 B 9999

QUEEN'S BENCH DIVISION

BRIGHTON DISTRICT REGISTRY

B E T W E E N

AB

- and -

CD

Claimant

Defendant

POINTS OF DISPUTE SERVED BY THE DEFENDANT

Item	Dispute	Claimant's Comments
General point	Base rates claimed for the assistant solicitor and other fee earners are excessive. Reduce to £100 and £70 respectively plus VAT. Each item in which these rates are claimed should be recalculated at the reduced rates.	
(1)	The premium claimed is excessive. Reduce to £95.	

Item	Dispute	Claimant's Comments
(14)	The claim for timed attendances on claimant (schedule 1) is excessive. Reduce to 4 hours ie. £400 at reduced rates.	

Paragraph numbers marked with a "+" can be found online and on CD.

(32)   The total claim for work done on documents
        by the assistant solicitor is excessive. A
        reasonable allowance in respect of documents
        concerning court and counsel is 8 hours, for
        documents concerning witnesses and the
        expert witness, 6.5 hours, for other documents,
        5.5 hours. Reduce to 20 hours ie. £2,000 at
        reduced rates (£3,155 in total).

(34)   The time claimed is excessive. Reduce
        solicitors time to 0.5 hours ie. to £50 at
        reduced rates and reduce the costs draftsman's
        time to three hours ie. £210 (£260 in total).

(35)   The success fee claimed is excessive. Reduce
        to 25% ie. £100 plus VAT of £17.50.

(36)   The total base fees when recalculated on the
        basis of the above points amount to £7,788,
        upon which VAT is £1,362.90.

(37)   The success fee claimed is excessive. Reduce
        to 25% of £7,788 ie £1,947.50 plus VAT of
        £340.73.

(39)   The success fee claimed is excessive. Reduce
        to 50% ie £1,625 plus VAT of £284.38.

Served on ....[date] by .... [name][solicitors for] the Defendant.

SCCO GUIDE

Paragraph numbers marked with a "+" can be found online and on CD.

A-4 Standard orders made on applications to set aside default costs certificates

(a)   Conditional order

ORDER

To Claimant's Solicitor	**In the High Court of Justice** **Supreme Court Costs Office**
	SCCO Ref:
To Defendant's Solicitor	Claimant (include Ref)
	Defendants (include Ref)
	Date

MASTER [   ] Costs Judge

UPON THE APPLICATION of the [   ]

AND UPON HEARING the

AND UPON READING the documents on the court file.

IT IS ORDERED as follows:

(1)   On or before 4 pm on [   ] the [   ] must pay to the
[   ] [into court] the sum of [£   ] on account of the costs claimed by the
[   ] herein and must forthwith give notice of any payment into court to the
[   ].

(2)   If and when the [   ] complies with paragraph (1) the default costs
certificate issued herein will be automatically set aside and, on receiving notice of the
payment, the [   ] must forthwith return the original certificate to the Supreme
Court Costs Office to be so marked.

(3)   If the default costs certificate issued herein is automatically set aside the following
directions shall apply:

Paragraph numbers marked with a "+" can be found online and on CD.

(a)   Within [14 days] of the payment referred to in paragraph (1) the [   ]
must serve Points of Dispute on the [   ] [and on the other parties
hereto].   Points of Dispute should not be filed in court at that stage.

(b)   Within [28] days of receipt of the Points of Dispute the [   ] must
file a request for a detailed assessment hearing in Form N258.

(a)   The [   ] having already served Points of Dispute, the
[   ] must on or before 4 pm on [   ] file a request for a
detailed assessment hearing in Form N258.

( )   The Form N258 to be filed by the [   ] must be duly
completed and must specify the SCCO reference for this application.

( )   The [   ] has permission to serve a reply to the Points of Dispute if
he does so before filing the request in Form N258.

(4)   Enforcement of the default costs certificate is stayed until [   ] upon
which date if it has not by then been automatically set aside, the [   ] can
proceed to enforce it.

(5)   The costs of and thrown away by this application are awarded to the [   ]
and are summarily assessed at £   [including VAT] [VAT not recoverable] which
sum is payable on or before [   ]

(6)   There shall be a detailed assessment of the costs of the [   ] which are
payable out of the Community Service Fund.

( )   Any party hereto may request a further hearing of this application in order to obtain
further or other directions.

(b)   Unconditional order

[Heading and opening words as in A-4(a) above]

IT IS ORDERED as follows:

(1)   The default costs certificate issued herein dated [   ] is hereby
set aside and the [   ] must forthwith return the original certificate to the Supreme
Court Costs Office to be so marked.

(2)   On or before 4 pm on [   ] the [   ] must serve Points
of Dispute on the [   ] [and on the other parties hereto].   Points of Dispute
should not be filed in court at that stage.

(3)   Within [28] days of receipt of the Points of Dispute the [   ] must file a
request for a detailed assessment hearing in Form N258.

( )   The [   ] having already served Points of Dispute, the [   ]
must on or before 4 pm on [   ] file a request for a detailed assessment
hearing in Form N258.

( )   The Form N258 to be filed by the [   ] must be duly completed and
must specify the SCCO reference for this application.

( )   The [   ] has permission to serve a reply to the Points of Dispute if he does
so before filing the request in Form N258.

( )   The costs of and thrown away by this application are awarded to the [   ]
and are summarily assessed at £   (including VAT) (VAT not recoverable) which
sum [may be set off against any costs payable by the [   ] to the [   ]]
[is payable on or before [   ]].

( )   There shall be a detailed assessment of the costs of the [   ] which are
payable out of the Community Service Fund.

( )   Any party hereto may request a further hearing of this application in order to obtain
further or other directions.

(c) Dismissal of application

[Heading and opening words as in A-4(a) above]

IT IS ORDERED as follows:

(1)   The application to set aside the default costs certificate herein is dismissed

(2)   Enforcement of the default costs certificate issued herein is stayed

(3)   The costs of this application are awarded to the [   ] and are summarily assessed at £   (including VAT) (VAT not recoverable) which sum is payable on or before [   ].

(4)   The costs of the application are awarded to [   ] to be assessed if not agreed.

(5)   There shall be a detailed assessment of the costs of the [   ] which are payable out of the Community Service Fund.

(d)   Adjournment of application

[Heading and opening words as in A-4(a) above]

IT IS ORDERED as follows:

(1)   This application is adjourned to [   ] [a date to be fixed].

(2)   Enforcement of the default costs certificate issued herein is stayed until the conclusion of this application or further order.

A-5 Standard orders made in costs-only proceedings

(a) Order for detailed assessment

[Heading as in A-4(a) above]

UPON THE APPLICATION of the Claimant.

AND UPON READING the documents on the Court file.

IT IS ORDERED:

(1)   The Defendant must pay the Claimants costs of the claim relating to [the accident on   ] in respect of which terms of settlement have been agreed.

(2)   The Claimant must commence detailed assessment proceedings in accordance with CPR, Rule 47.6 for assessment on the Standard basis. (Rule 47.6 provides for the service of a Notice of Commencement and other documents).

(3)   The costs of this application are costs in the assessment.

(b) Dismissal of application

[Heading and opening words as in A-5(a) above]

IT IS ORDERED:

(1)   Application dismissed.

(2)   Liberty to both parties to apply to stay, set aside or vary this order.

(3)   Liberty to both parties to apply for their costs of this application if such application is made within 28 days of any determination of the Claimant's entitlement to the costs of the claim relating to [the accident on   ] which costs are the subject matter of this application.

A-6 Standard orders made against Legal Services Commission funded clients

(a)   Award of costs against a Claimant who is a Legal Services Commission funded client

[Heading and opening words as in A-4(a) above]

IT IS ORDERED THAT:

1.   The claim is dismissed.

2.   The full costs of this claim which have been incurred by the defendant are [summarily assessed at £   ] [to be determined by a Costs Judge or District Judge].

3.   The claimant (a party who was in receipt of services funded by the Legal Services Commission) do pay to the Defendant [nil] [£   ] [an amount to be determined by a Costs Judge or District Judge]. [When determining such costs the Costs Judge or District Judge should take into account the following facts:

[Here list any findings as to the party's conduct in the proceedings or otherwise which are relevant to the determination of the costs payable by the LSC funded client]

4.   On or before (date) the claimant must pay into court £   on account of the costs payable under paragraph 2, above.

5.   There be a detailed assessment of the costs of the claimant which are payable out of the Community Legal Service Fund.

(b)   Order specifying the amounts payable, for use by a costs judge

[Heading and opening words as in A-4(a) above with (if relevant) the addition of the words "sitting in private"]

IT IS ORDERED THAT:

Paragraph numbers marked with a "+" can be found online and on CD.

SCCO Guide

1.   The full costs of the [defendant] herein, [including the costs of this application] are assessed at £

2.   The amount of costs which it is reasonable for the [claimant] to pay to the [defendant] is [nil] [£   which sum is payable to the [defendant] on or before (date)].

3.   The sum of £   paid into court on account of the costs specified in paragraph 2 above and any interest accruing thereon shall be paid out to the [defendant in part satisfaction] [claimant] as specified in the payment schedule to this Order.

4.   The amount of costs payable by the Legal Services Commission to the [defendant] [including the costs of this application] is £   which sum is payable to the [defendant] on or before (date).

[Schedule in Form 200 (see Court Funds Rules 1987)]

Paragraph numbers marked with a "+" can be found online and on CD.

A-7 Claim form for remedies under Solicitors Act 1974:
Schedule of Costs Precedents, Precedent J
ROYAL ARMS

IN THE HIGH COURT OF JUSTICE   Claim No.

SUPREME COURT COSTS OFFICE

IN THE MATTER OF [name of solicitor or solicitors' firm]

Claimant
                        SEAL

Defendant(s)

CLAIM FORM (CPR Part 8)

Details of claim (see also overleaf)

The following orders are applied for:

( )   An order in standard form for the delivery of a bill of costs in [all causes and matters] [the following causes and matters
....
....
] in which the Defendant has acted for the Claimant(s).

( )   An order in standard form for the detailed assessment of the bill(s) dated
....[and] [bearing the invoice numbers
.... delivered by the [claimant/Defendant] to the
[Defendant/Claimant/person named ....]

( )   An order dealing with the costs of this application

Defendant's name and address   £

                        Court fee
                        Solicitor's costs
                        Issue date

The court office at the Supreme Court Costs Office, Cliffords Inn, Fetter Lane, London EC4A 1DQ is open between 10.00 am and 4.30 pm, Monday to Friday. When corresponding with the court, please address forms or letters to the Court Manager and quote the claim number.

Paragraph numbers marked with a "+" can be found online and on CD.

Claim No.

Details of claim (continued)

Statement of Truth

*(I believe) (The Claimant believes) that the facts stated in these particulars of claim are true.

*I am duly authorised by the Claimant to sign this statement.

Full name ....

Name of Claimant's solicitor's firm

Signed .... position or office held ....

*(Claimant) (Litigation friend) (Claimant's solicitor) (if signing on behalf of firm or

company)

*delete as appropriate

Claimant's or claimant's solicitor's address to
which documents should be sent if different from
overleaf. If you are prepared to accept service
by DX, fax or e-mail, please add details.

A-8 Standard order in claim under Solicitors Act 1974: order on client's application

[Heading and opening words as in A-4(a) above]

IT IS ORDERED that:

(1)   A detailed assessment must be made of the bill dated [   ] delivered to the Claimant by the Defendants.

(2)   On making the detailed assessment, the court must also assess the costs of these proceedings and certify what is due to or from either party in respect of the bill and the costs of these proceedings.

(3)   Until these proceedings are concluded the Defendants must not commence or continue any proceedings against the Claimant in respect of the bill mentioned above.

(4)   Upon payment by the Claimant of any sum certified as due to the Defendants in these proceedings the Defendants must deliver to the Claimant all the documentation in the Defendant's possession or control which belong to the Claimant.

(5)   CPR 48.9 applies, varied as follows:

(a)   on or before   the Defendants must serve a breakdown of costs (including a cash account);
(b)   within 28 days of service of the breakdown of costs the Claimant must serve Points of Dispute thereon (ie, a brief statement identifying each item in the breakdown which is disputed, summarising the nature and grounds of dispute in respect of that item and, where practicable, suggesting a figure to be allowed for each item in respect of which a reduction is sought);
(c)   if the Defendants wish to serve a reply, they must do so within 14 days of service on them of the Points of Dispute;
(d)   either party may file a request for a hearing date upon payment of the appropriate fee and the filing of a time estimate –
        (i) after Points of Dispute have been served, but;
        (ii) no later than   ;
(e)   if a request for a hearing date is filed the matter is reserved to Master [   ] who has provisionally appointed it for hearing on   .

(6)   The costs of this application shall be treated as costs of the detailed assessment.

Paragraph numbers marked with a "+" can be found online and on CD.

A-9 Notice of appeal prescribed for criminal costs appeals

FORM "A"

Form of Notice of Appeal

Appeal Pursuant to the Costs in Criminal Cases (General) Regulations 1986/ The Legal Aid in Criminal and Care Proceedings (Costs) Regulations 1989/ The Crown Court Rules, 1982, the Criminal Defence Service (Funding) Order 2001

Crown Court/ Divisional

Court/ Court of Appeal Criminal Division

Regina v ....

Appeal of ....

Case No ....

To: A Costs Judge and to the appropriate authority of the

....

Crown Court/ Divisional Court/ Court of Appeal Criminal Division.

The Appellant .... appeals to a Costs Judge against the redetermination of the costs in the above matter.

The following are the items in respect of which the Applicant appeals:

Item	Description	Amount Claimed	Amount Allowed	Total Amount in Dispute After Redetermination
1.				
2.				
3. etc				£ ....

Grounds of Objection (To Be Set Out in Full)
We confirm that a copy of this notice has been served upon the appropriate authority.

The Appellant should attach to this Notice of Appeal his/her Grounds of Objection and in so doing provide the Costs Judge with a detailed response to the written reasons provided by the Determining Officer.

Do you wish to attend the hearing of your Appeal: Yes/ No

Dated the   day of

(Signed   ....

            ....

            Appellant

Address   ....

            ....

            ....

            ....

Tel No.   ....

Ref.   ....

Fax No.   ....

DX No.   ....

E-Mail   ....

Form A-10

IN THE COURT OF PROTECTION

Case No:- ....

SCCO reference ....

(to be completed by the court)

IN THE MATTER OF

.... (A patient)

Short form bill of costs of the Receiver of *(e.g.) General Management for the period............ ...... to be assessed pursuant to the First General Order dated .... and General Direction dated 19/11/82*

One paragraph summary of work carried out

Fee earner category .... Rate claimed ....

Work done:-   **Charge:-**

Time spent in personal attendances
22/9/02   45mins   Upon patient   ....
Time spent in travel ....
Letters Sent ....
Telephone Calls ....
Time spent on documents ....
Other work *(give details)*
....
....
                              Sub Total   ....
                              V.A.T.   ....
Disbursements (list below)
....
....   Disbursements   ....
                              V.A.T.   .   ...
                              Grand Total   ....

I certify that this bill is both accurate and complete.

....
Partner

Short form bill of costs for use in Court of Protection assessments where the total costs claimed, excluding vat, do not exceed £3000

Name, address and reference of solicitor filing bill

A-11 Standard order for directions on a referral made in Civil Recovery Proceedings

[Heading as in A-4(a) above]

UPON THE APPLICATION of the Defendant AND UPON READING the documents on the court file IT IS ORDERED as follows:

1   This matter now stands adjourned to a hearing before Master [　] in Room [　] in the Supreme Court Costs Office on [*date to be fixed*] (2 hours allowed) for the Claimant to show cause why the exclusion in respect of the Defendant's reasonable legal costs should not specify:-

(1) the stage or stages in the civil recovery proceedings;
(2) the maximum amount which may be released in respect of legal costs for each specified stage; and
(3) the total amount which may be released in respect of legal costs pursuant to the exclusion

in the manner, and in the amounts, set out in the Defendant's estimate of costs which is referred to in the application notice herein.

2   On or before [*date to be fixed*] the Claimant must file in court and serve on the Defendant Points of Dispute on the estimate (i.e., a brief statement identifying each item in the estimate which is disputed, summarising the nature and grounds of dispute in respect of that item and, where practicable, suggesting a figure to be allowed for each item in respect of which a reduction is sought).

3   Liberty to [both] [all] parties to apply by letter to the Court requesting the Court to stay, set aside or vary this Order.

A-12 Standard orders and directions in respect of costs awarded by the Adjudicator of HM Land Registry

(a)   Order for paying party to show cause following a failure to comply with an order to serve Points of Dispute

[Heading as in A-4(a) above]

UPON THE APPLICATION of the Claimant AND UPON READING the documents on the court file IT IS ORDERED as follows:

1. This application now stands listed for hearing on [*date to be fixed*] in Room [ ] in the Supreme Court Costs Office (30 minutes allowed) for the Defendant to show cause why the Claimant's bill of costs served pursuant to the Order of the Adjudicator to HM Land Registry dated [   ] should not be assessed as drawn because of the Defendant's failure to serve Points of Dispute in compliance with that Order.

2. The costs of and incidental to this Order are reserved.

3. Liberty to all parties to apply by letter to the Court requesting the Court to stay, set aside or vary this Order.

(b)   Timetable directions for Points of Dispute and detailed assessment hearing

[Heading and opening words as in A-12(a) above]

1. Within 21 days of service of this Order the Defendant must serve Points of Dispute on the Claimant's bill of costs served upon the Defendant pursuant to the Order of the Adjudicator to HM Land Registry dated [ ].

2. If the Defendant fails to serve Points of Dispute in compliance with this Order the Claimant may by letter, and without further notice to the Defendant, request Master [ ] to assess the Claimant's bill of costs as drawn.

3. The Claimant may file a request for a hearing date after Points of Dispute have been served, but no later than [*date to be fixed*].

4. If a request for a hearing date is filed the matter is reserved to Master [ ] who has provisionally appointed it for hearing on [*date to be fixed*].

5. If the Claimant wishes to serve a reply, he must do so before filing a request for a hearing date.

6. The costs of and incidental to this Order are reserved.

Liberty to all parties to apply by letter to the Court requesting the Court to stay, set aside or vary this Order.

Paragraph numbers marked with a "+" can be found online and on CD.

A-13 Costs certificate in respect of costs assessed on behalf of the Adjudicator of HM Land Registry

ORDER

**ADJUDICATOR TO HER MAJESTY'S LAND REGISTRY
LAND REGISTRATION ACT 2002**

IN THE MATTER OF A REFERENCE FROM H.M. LAND REGISTRY

To Applicant's Solicitor

To Respondent's Solicitor

SUPREME COURT COSTS OFFICE	
SCCO Ref.	
Case No.	
Applicant	
Respondent	
Date	2006

**MASTER   COSTS JUDGE
SITTING AS A DEPUTY ADJUDICATOR**

PURSUANT TO THE ORDER of the Adjudicator dated

I have assessed the costs of the   in the sum of £ inclusive of the costs of assessment

The   must pay the sum of £   to the by the   day of   2006

The court office at Clifford's Inn, Fetter Lane, London, EC4A 1DQ is open between 10 am and 4.30 pm Monday to Friday.   Address all communications to the Court Manager quoting the SCCO reference number.

Paragraph numbers marked with a "+" can be found online and on CD.

SECTION 2

SPECIALIST PROCEEDINGS

SECTION 2

SPECIALIST PROCEEDINGS

2A   COMMERCIAL COURT

PART 58—COMMERCIAL COURT

Contents

Editorial introduction

Part 58 was added to the CPR by Civil Procedure (Amendment No.5) Rules 2001 **2A–2** (SI 2001/4015), and came into force on March 25, 2002.

Related sources

- Part 62—Arbitration Claims (see para.2E–7 *et seq*.)   **2A–3**
- The Admiralty and Commercial Courts Guide (see para.2A–39 *et seq*).
- Practice Direction—Arbitrations (see para.2E–46 *et seq*.)
- Arbitration Act 1950 Pt II (see para.2E–57 *et seq*.)
- Arbitration Act 1996 (see para.2E–83 *et seq*.)
- Civil Procedure Rules including CPR 1, 2, 6, 7, 8, 9, 10, 11, 12, 14, 15, 16, 17, 18, 20, 22, 23, 24, 25, 32, 34, 35, 43–48, 70, 71,72, 73 and 74
- Heavy and Complex Cases—Checklist (see para. 2A–18.1)

Forms

- **N1(CC)** Claim form   **2A–4**
- **N1C(CC)** Notes for defendant
- **N9(CC)** Acknowledgment of service
- **N208(CC)** Claim form (Part 8)
- **N208C(CC)** Notes for defendant
- **N210(CC)** Acknowledgment of service (Part 8)
- **N211(CC)** Claim form (Part 20)
- **N211C(CC)** Notes for Part 20 defendant
- **N213(CC)** Acknowledgment of service (Part 20)
- **N244(CC)** Application Notice
- **N265(CC)** List of documents: standard disclosure

Paragraph numbers marked with a "+" can be found online and on CD.

Scope of this Part and interpretation[1]

2A–5   **58.1—(1) This Part applies to claims in the Commercial Court of the Queen's Bench Division.**

(2) In this Part and its practice direction, "commercial claim" means any claim arising out of the transaction of trade and commerce and includes any claim relating to—

     (a) a business document or contract;

     (b) the export or import of goods;

     (c) the carriage of goods by land, sea, air or pipeline;

     (d) the exploitation of oil and gas reserves or other natural resources;

     (e) insurance and re-insurance;

     (f) banking and financial services;

     (g) the operation of markets and exchanges;

     (h) the purchase and sale of commodities;

     (i) the construction of ships;

     (j) business agency; and

     (k) arbitration.

2A–6   *Note* —The Commercial Court may continue to hear a banking case notwithstanding that the debt is secured by a mortgage and that High Court claims for possession of land subject to mortgage are assigned to the Chancery Division by Practice Direction—Possession Claims, supplementing CPR Pt 55 (*Midland Bank Ltd v Stamps* [1978] 1 W.L.R. 627; [1978] 3 All E.R. 1, a case under the pre-October 1, 2001 law).

Specialist list[2]

2A–7   **58.2—(1) The commercial list is a specialist list for claims proceeding in the Commercial Court.**

(2) One of the judges of the Commercial Court shall be in charge of the commercial list.

Application of the Civil Procedure Rules[3]

2A–8   **58.3 These Rules and their practice directions apply to claims in the commercial list unless this Part or a practice direction provides otherwise.**

Proceedings in the commercial list[4]

2A–9   **58.4—(1) A commercial claim may be started in the commercial list.**

(2) Rule 30.5 applies to claims in the commercial list, except that a Commercial Court judge may order a claim to be transferred to any other specialist list.

---

[1] Introduced by the Civil Procedure (Amendment No.5) Rules 2001 (SI 2001/4015).
[2] Introduced by the Civil Procedure (Amendment No.5) Rules 2001 (SI 2001/4015).
[3] Introduced by the Civil Procedure (Amendment No.5) Rules 2001 (SI 2001/4015).
[4] Introduced by the Civil Procedure (Amendment No.5) Rules 2001 (SI 2001/4015) and amended by the Civil Procedure (Amendment No.4) Rules 2005 (SI 2005/3515).

Paragraph numbers marked with a "+" can be found online and on CD.

(Rule 30.5(3) provides that an application for the transfer of proceedings to or from a specialist list must be made to a judge dealing with claims in that list).

Claim form and particulars of claim[1]

2A–10 58.5—(1) If, in a Part 7 claim, particulars of claim are not contained in or served with the claim form—

- (a) the claim form must state that, if an acknowledgment of service is filed which indicates an intention to defend the claim, particulars of claim will follow;
- (b) when the claim form is served, it must be accompanied by the documents specified in rule 7.8(1);
- (c) the claimant must serve particulars of claim within 28 days of the filing of an acknowledgment of service which indicates an intention to defend; and
- (d) rule 7.4(2) does not apply.

(2) A statement of value is not required to be included in the claim form.

(3) If the claimant is claiming interest, he must—

- (a) include a statement to that effect; and
- (b) give the details set out in rule 16.4(2),

in both the claim form and the particulars of claim.

Acknowledgment of service[2]

2A–11 58.6—(1) A defendant must file an acknowledgment of service in every case.

(2) Unless paragraph (3) applies, the period for filing an acknowledgment of service is 14 days after service of the claim form.

(3) Where the claim form is served out of the jurisdiction, or on the agent of a defendant who is overseas, the time periods provided by rules 6.12(3), 6.35 and 6.37(5) apply after service of the claim form.

Disputing the court's jurisdiction[3]

2A–12 58.7—(1) Part 11 applies to claims in the commercial list with the modifications set out in this rule.

(2) An application under rule 11(1) must be made within 28 days after filing an acknowledgment of service.

(3) If the defendant files an acknowledgment of service indicating an intention to dispute the court's jurisdiction, the claimant need not serve particulars of claim before the hearing of the application.

Paragraph numbers marked with a "+" can be found online and on CD.

Default judgment[1]

2A–13   58.8—(1) If, in a Part 7 claim in the commercial list, a defendant fails to file an acknowledgment of service, the claimant need not serve particulars of claim before he may obtain or apply for default judgment in accordance with Part 12.

(2) Rule 12.6(1) applies with the modification that paragraph (a) shall be read as if it referred to the claim form instead of the particulars of claim.

Admissions[2]

2A–14   58.9—(1) Rule 14.5 does not apply to claims in the commercial list.

(2) If the defendant admits part of a claim for a specified amount of money, the claimant may apply under rule 14.3 for judgment on the admission.

(3) Rule 14.14(1) applies with the modification that paragraph (a) shall be read as if it referred to the claim form instead of the particulars of claim.

Defence and Reply[3]

2A–15   58.10—(1) Part 15 (defence and reply) applies to claims in the commercial list with the modification to rule 15.8 that the claimant must—

(a) file any reply to a defence; and
(b) serve it on all other parties,

within 21 days after service of the defence.

(2) Rule 6.35 (in relation to the period for filing a defence where the claim form is served out of the jurisdiction) applies to claims in the commercial list, except that if the particulars of claim are served after the defendant has filed an acknowledgment of service the period for filing a defence is 28 days from service of the particulars of claim.

Statements of case[4]

2A–16   58.11 The court may at any time before or after the issue of the claim form order a claim in the commercial list to proceed without the filing or service of statements of case.

Part 8 claims[5]

2A–17   58.12 Part 8 applies to claims in the commercial list, with the modification that a defendant to a Part 8 claim who wishes to rely

---

[1] Introduced by the Civil Procedure (Amendment No.5) Rules 2001 (SI 2001/4015).
[2] Introduced by the Civil Procedure (Amendment No.5) Rules 2001 (SI 2001/4015).
[3] Introduced by the Civil Procedure (Amendment No.5) Rules 2001 (SI 2001/4015) and amended by the Civil Procedure (Amendment) Rules 2008 (SI 2008/2178).
[4] Introduced by the Civil Procedure (Amendment No.5) Rules 2001 (SI 2001/4015).
[5] Introduced by the Civil Procedure (Amendment No.5) Rules 2001 (SI 2001/4015).

Paragraph numbers marked with a "+" can be found online and on CD.

on written evidence must file and serve it within 28 days after filing an acknowledgment of service.

Case management[1]

2A–18

58.13—(1) All proceedings in the commercial list are treated as being allocated to the multi-track and Part 26 does not apply.

(2) The following parts only of Part 29 apply—

    (a) rule 29.3(2) (legal representative to attend case management conferences and pre-trial reviews);

    (b) rule 29.5 (variation of case management timetable) with the exception of rule 29.5(1)(c).

(3) As soon as practicable the court will hold a case management conference which must be fixed in accordance with the practice direction.

(4) At the case management conference or at any hearing at which the parties are represented the court may give such directions for the management of the case as it considers appropriate.

Heavy and Complex Cases

2A–18.1

A checklist for Commercial Court Judges and any deputies on the implementation of the Commercial Court Long Trials Working Party (CCLTWP) has been produced. It identifies matters which the Commercial Court judges and deputies should consider with the parties during the pilot scheme implementing the CCLTWP which started on February 1, 2008. A copy of the checklist can be obtained from the Admiralty and Commercial Courts Registry at EB13 RCJ. See too *http://www.judiciary.gov.uk/docs/ rep_comm_wrkg_party_long_trials.pdf* [Accessed September 10, 2008]. The Working Parties Committee is due to reconvene in 2009, at which time they will be reviewing all items included in the Checklist. All Commercial Court publications can be found on the HMCS website (*http://www.hmcourts-service.gov.uk* [Accessed February 4, 2009]).

Disclosure—ships papers[2]

2A–19

58.14—(1) If, in proceedings relating to a marine insurance policy, the underwriters apply for specific disclosure under rule 31.12, the court may—

    (a) order a party to produce all the ships papers; and

    (b) require that party to use his best endeavours to obtain and disclose documents which are not or have not been in his control.

(2) An order under this rule may be made at any stage of the proceedings and on such terms, if any, as to staying the proceedings or otherwise, as the court thinks fit.

The Order

2A–20

(a) Although the insurer applying for an order is usually the defendant, the procedure is available to an insurer who is suing as claimant, e.g. to recover overpayments inducted by deception or mistake (*Boulton v Houlder Bros.* [1904] 1 K.B. 784, CA).

(b) *Persons to whom the order is directed.* The order is usually directed to the claimant himself and to all persons interested in the proceeding and in the insurance (*China*

---

[1] Introduced by the Civil Procedure (Amendment No.5) Rules 2001 (SI 2001/4015).
[2] Introduced by the Civil Procedure (Amendment No.5) Rules 2001 (SI 2001/4015).

Paragraph numbers marked with a "+" can be found online and on CD.

COMMERCIAL COURTS

Steamship Co v Commercial Union Assurance Co (1881) 8 QBD 142); "persons interested" means those interested on the claimant's side, not the underwriters themselves (*ibid.*). See also, as to the person to whom the order is to be directed, *China Traders Co v Royal Exchange Assurance* [1898] 2 Q.B. 187 at 189; *London Insurance Co v Chambers* (1900) 5 Com.Cas. 241. The affidavit or witness statement in answer must show the interest of the deponent or may be rejected as defective (*Avon v Miall*, November 27, 1925, unrep., Branson J. in Chambers) and must account for all documents in the possession and control of those to whom the order is addressed (*Graham etc. Co v Motor Union Co* [1922] 1 K.B. 563); if a particular "interested person" is thought to have relevant documents the order may expressly require an affidavit from him (*ibid.*).

(c) *Documents to be disclosed.* All material documents may be ordered to be disclosed and it is not a reason for refusing to make disclosure that they are not in the possession of the person to whom the order is directed: he must, in such a case, use all reasonable endeavors to obtain the documents and will only be excused on showing that these have been unavailing; thus a mortgagee must, if he can, obtain disclosure of the documents in possession of the mortgagor who operated the ship (*West of England Bank v Canton Insurance Co* (1877) 2 Ex.D. 472) and cargo owners suing as claimants must, if they can, obtain disclosure of the papers in possession of the shipowners or their servants (*Teneria Moderna Franco Espanola v New Zealand Insurance Co* [1924] 1 K.B. 79, CA).

(d) *Order staying proceedings.* The purpose of a stay may be to postpone the time for delivery of a defence or to ensure compliance with the order. It is a matter of discretion whether, and at what stage, a stay will be granted (*Probatina Shipping Co v Sun Insurance Office* [1974] Q.B. 635; [1974] 2 All E.R. 478, CA). It will be removed on compliance with the order or on showing to the Court that all reasonable endeavours have been made to comply (see cases cited in sub-paragraphs (b) and (c)).

A stay does not preclude the defendant from applying for a further and better information (*Abdela v Mutual Property Investment Ltd* [1921] W.N. 23, CA) nor prevent a party from recovering costs for the reasonable preparation of his case while the stay is in force (*Pecheries Ostendaises v Merchants' Marine Insurance Co* [1928] 1 K.B. 750, CA).

Judgments and orders[1]

2A–21 **58.15—(1) Except for orders made by the court on its own initiative and unless the court orders otherwise, every judgment or order will be drawn up by the parties, and rule 40.3 is modified accordingly.**

(2) An application for a consent order must include a draft of the proposed order signed on behalf of all the parties to whom it relates.

(3) Rule 40.6 (consent judgments and orders) does not apply.

---

[1] Introduced by the Civil Procedure (Amendment No.5) Rules 2001 (SI 2001/4015).

Paragraph numbers marked with a "+" can be found online and on CD.

PRACTICE DIRECTION—COMMERCIAL COURT
This Practice Direction supplements CPR Part 58

General

1.1 This practice direction applies to commercial claims proceed- **2A–22** ing in the commercial list of the Queen's Bench Division. It supersedes all previous practice directions and practice statements in the Commercial Court.

1.2 All proceedings in the commercial list, including any appeal from a judgment, order or decision of a master or district judge before the proceedings were transferred to the Commercial Court, will be heard or determined by a Commercial Court judge, except that—

   (1)   another judge of the Queen's Bench Division or Chancery Division may hear urgent applications if no Commercial Court judge is available; and

   (2)   unless the court otherwise orders, any application relating to the enforcement of a Commercial Court judgment or order for the payment of money will be dealt with by a master of the Queen's Bench Division or a district judge.

1.3 Provisions in other practice directions which refer to a master or district judge are to be read, in relation to claims in the commercial list, as if they referred to a Commercial Court judge.

1.4 The Admiralty and Commercial Registry in the Royal Courts of Justice is the administrative office of the court for all proceedings in the commercial list.

Starting proceedings in the Commercial Court

2.1 Claims in the Commercial Court must be issued in the **2A–23** Admiralty and Commercial Registry.

2.2 When the Registry is closed, a request to issue a claim form may be made by fax, using the procedure set out in Appendix A to this practice direction. If a request is made which complies with that procedure, the claim form is issued when the fax is received by the Registry.

2.3 The claim form must be marked in the top right hand corner "Queen's Bench Division, Commercial Court".

2.4 A claimant starting proceedings in the commercial list, other than an arbitration claim, must use practice form **N1(CC)** for Part 7 claims or practice form **N208(CC)** for Part 8 claims.

Applications before proceedings are issued

3.1 A party who intends to bring a claim in the commercial list **2A–24** must make any application before the claim form is issued to a Commercial Court judge.

3.2 The written evidence in support of such an application must state that the claimant intends to bring proceedings in the commercial list.

3.3 If the Commercial Court judge hearing the application considers that the proceedings should not be brought in the commercial

Paragraph numbers marked with a "+" can be found online and on CD.

list, he may adjourn the application to be heard by a master or by a judge who is not a Commercial Court judge.

Transferring proceedings to or from the Commercial Court

2A–25   **4.1** If an application is made to a court other than the Commercial Court to transfer proceedings to the commercial list, the other court may—

    (1)   adjourn the application to be heard by a Commercial Court judge; or

    (2)   dismiss the application.

4.2 If the Commercial Court orders proceedings to be transferred to the commercial list—

    (1)   it will order them to be transferred to the Royal Courts of Justice; and

    (2)   it may give case management directions.

4.3 An application by a defendant, including a Part 20 defendant, for an order transferring proceedings from the commercial list should be made promptly and normally not later than the first case management conference.

4.4 A party applying to the Commercial Court to transfer a claim to the commercial list must give notice of the application to the court in which the claim is proceeding, and the Commercial Court will not make an order for transfer until it is satisfied that such notice has been given.

Acknowledgment of service

2A–26   **5.1** For Part 7 claims, a defendant must file an acknowledgment of service using practice form **N9(CC)**.

5.2 For Part 8 claims, a defendant must file an acknowledgment of service using practice form **N210(CC)**.

Default judgment and admissions

2A–27   **6.** The practice directions supplementing Parts 12 and 14 apply with the following modifications—

    (1)   paragraph 4.1(1) of the practice direction supplementing Part 12 is to be read as referring to the service of the claim form; and

    (2)   the references to "particulars of claim" in paragraphs 2.1, 3.1 and 3.2 of the practice direction supplementing Part 14 are to be read as referring to the claim form.

Variation of time limits

2A–28   **7.1** If the parties, in accordance with rule 2.11, agree in writing to vary a time limit, the claimant must notify the court in writing, giving brief written reasons for the agreed variation.

7.2 The court may make an order overriding an agreement by the parties varying a time limit.

Amendments

2A–29   **8.** Paragraph 2.2 of the practice direction supplementing Part 17 is

Paragraph numbers marked with a "+" can be found online and on CD.

modified so that amendments to a statement of case must show the original text, unless the court orders otherwise.

Service of documents

9. Unless the court orders otherwise, the Commercial Court will 2A–30 not serve documents or orders and service must be effected by the parties.

Case management

10.1 The following parts only of the practice direction supplement- 2A–31 ing Part 29 apply—

(1)   paragraph 5 (case management conferences), excluding paragraph 5.9 and modified so far as is made necessary by other specific provisions of this practice direction; and

(2)   paragraph 7 (failure to comply with case management directions).

10.2 If the proceedings are started in the commercial list, the claimant must apply for a case management conference—

(a)   for a Part 7 claim, within 14 days of the date when all defendants who intend to file and serve a defence have done so; and

(b)   for a Part 8 claim, within 14 days of the date when all defendants who intend to serve evidence have done so.

10.3 If the proceedings are transferred to the commercial list, the claimant must apply for a case management conference within 14 days of the date of the order transferring them, unless the judge held, or gave directions for, a case management conference when he made the order transferring the proceedings.

10.4 Any party may, at a time earlier than that provided in paragraphs 10.2 or 10.3, apply in writing to the court to fix a case management conference.

10.5 If the claimant does not make an application in accordance with paragraphs 10.2 or 10.3, any other party may apply for a case management conference.

10.6 The court may fix a case management conference at any time on its own initiative. If it does so, the court will give at least 7 days notice to the parties, unless there are compelling reasons for a shorter period of notice.

10.7 Not less than 7 days before a case management conference, each party must file and serve—

(1)   a completed case management information sheet; and

(2)   an application notice for any order which that party intends to seek at the case management conference, other than directions referred to in the case management information sheet.

10.8 Unless the court orders otherwise, the claimant, in consultation with the other parties, must prepare—

(1)   a case memorandum, containing a short and uncontroversial summary of what the case is about and of its material case history;

Paragraph numbers marked with a "+" can be found online and on CD.

(2)   a list of issues, with a section listing important matters which are not in dispute; and

(3)   a case management bundle containing—
   (a) the claim form;
   (b) all statements of case (excluding schedules), except that, if a summary of a statement of case has been filed, the bundle should contain the summary, and not the full statement of case;
   (c) the case memorandum;
   (d) the list of issues;
   (e) the case management information sheets and, if a pre-trial timetable has been agreed or ordered, that timetable;
   (f) the principal orders of the court; and
   (g) any agreement in writing made by the parties as to disclosure,

   and provide copies of the case management bundle for the court and the other parties at least 7 days before the first case management conference or any earlier hearing at which the court may give case management directions.

10.9 The claimant, in consultation with the other parties, must revise and update the documents referred to in paragraph 10.8 appropriately as the case proceeds. This must include making all necessary revisions and additions at least 7 days before any subsequent hearing at which the court may give case management directions.

Pre-trial review

2A–32   **11.1** At any pre-trial review or case management hearing, the court will ensure that case management directions have been complied with and give any further directions for the trial that are necessary.

11.2 Advocates who are to represent the parties at the trial should represent them at the pre-trial review and any case management hearing at which arrangements for the trial are to be discussed.

11.3 Before the pre-trial review, the parties must discuss and, if possible, agree a draft written timetable for the trial.

11.4 The claimant must file a copy of the draft timetable for the trial at least two days before the hearing of the pre-trial review. Any parts of the timetable which are not agreed must be identified and short explanations of the disagreement must be given.

11.5 At the pre-trial review, the court will set a timetable for the trial, unless a timetable has already been fixed or the court considers that it would be inappropriate to do so or appropriate to do so at a later time.

2A–31.1   *Editorial note*—See Heavy and Complex Cases at para. 2A–18.1 above.

Case management where there is a Part 20 claim

2A–33   **12.** Paragraph 5 of the practice direction supplementing Part 20 applies, except that, unless the court otherwise orders, the court will give case management directions for Part 20 claims at the same case management conferences as it gives directions for the main claim.

Paragraph numbers marked with a "+" can be found online and on CD.

Evidence for applications

13.1 The general requirement is that, unless the court orders **2A–34** otherwise—

(1)   evidence in support of an application must be filed and served with the application (see rule 23.7(3));

(2)   evidence in answer must be filed and served within 14 days after the application is served; and

(3)   evidence in reply must be filed and served within 7 days of the service of evidence in answer.

13.2 In any case in which the application is likely to require an oral hearing of more than half a day the periods set out in paragraphs 13.1(2) and (3) will be 28 days and 14 days respectively.

13.3 If the date fixed for the hearing of an application means that the times in paragraphs 13.1(2) and (3) cannot both be achieved, the evidence must be filed and served—

(1)   as soon as possible; and

(2)   in sufficient time to ensure that the application may fairly proceed on the date fixed.

13.4 The parties may, in accordance with rule 2.11, agree different periods from those in paragraphs 13.1(2) and (3) provided that the agreement does not affect the date fixed for the hearing of the application.

Judgments and orders

14.1 An application for a consent order must include a draft of the **2A–35** proposed order signed on behalf of all parties to whom it relates (see paragraph 10.4 of the practice direction supplementing Part 23).

14.2 Judgments and orders are generally drawn up by the parties (see rule 58.15). The parties are not therefore required to supply draft orders on disk (see paragraph 12.1 of the practice direction supplementing Part 23).

APPENDIX A

Procedure for issue of claim form when Registry is closed— paragraph 2.2

1. A request to issue a claim form may be made by fax when the **2A–36** Registry is closed, provided that—

(a)   the claim form is signed by a solicitor acting on behalf of the claimant; and

(b)   it does not require the permission of the court for its issue (unless such permission has already been given).

2. The solicitor requesting the issue of the claim form ("the issuing solicitor") must—

(a)   endorse on the claim form and sign the endorsement set out below;

(b)   send a copy of the claim form so endorsed to the Registry by fax for issue under paragraph 2.2 of this practice direction; and

Paragraph numbers marked with a "+" can be found online and on CD.

(c)   complete and sign a certificate in the form set out below, certifying that he has received a transmission report confirming that the fax has been transmitted in full, and stating the time and date of transmission.

3. When the Registry is next open to the public after the issue of a claim form in accordance with this procedure, the issuing solicitor or his agent must attend and deliver to the Registry—

(a)   the original of the claim form which was sent by fax (including the endorsement and the certificate) or, if the claim form has been served, a true and certified copy of it;

(b)   as many copies of the claim form as the Registry requires; and

(c)   the transmission report.

4. When a court officer at the Registry has checked that—

(a)   the claim form delivered under paragraph 3 matches the claim form received by fax; and

(b)   the correct issue fee has been paid,

he will allocate a number to the case, and seal, mark as "original" and date the claim form with the date of issue (being the date when the fax is recorded at the Registry as having been received).

5. If the issuing solicitor has served the unsealed claim form on any person, that solicitor must as soon as practicable—

(a)   inform that person of the case number; and

(b)   if requested, serve him with a copy of the sealed and dated claim form at any address in the United Kingdom, unless the court orders otherwise.

6. Any person served with a claim form issued under this procedure may, without paying a fee, inspect and take copies of the documents lodged at the Registry under paragraphs 2 and 3 above.

7. The issue of a claim form in accordance with this procedure takes place when the fax is recorded at the Registry as having been received, and the claim form has the same effect for all purposes as a claim form issued under Part 7 or 8. Unless the court otherwise orders, the sealed version of the claim form retained by the Registry is conclusive proof that the claim form was issued at the time and on the date stated.

8. If the procedure set out in this Appendix is not complied with, the court may declare that a claim form shall be treated as not having been issued.

Endorsement

2A–37   A claim form issued pursuant to a request by fax must be endorsed as follows:

"1. This claim form is issued under paragraph 2.2 of the Commercial Court practice direction and may be served notwithstanding that it does not bear the seal of the Court.

2. A true copy of this claim form and endorsement has been sent to the Admiralty and Commercial Registry, Royal Courts of Justice, Strand, London WC2A 2LL, at the time and date

Paragraph numbers marked with a "+" can be found online and on CD.

certified below by the solicitor whose name appears below ("the issuing solicitor").

3. It is the duty of the issuing solicitor or his agent to attend at the Registry when it is next open to the public for the claim form to be sealed.

4. Any person served with this unsealed claim form—

   (a) will be notified by the issuing solicitor of the case number;

   (b) may require the issuing solicitor to serve that person with a copy of the sealed claim form at an address in the United Kingdom, unless the court orders otherwise.

   (c) may inspect without charge the documents lodged at the Registry by the issuing solicitor.

5. I, the issuing solicitor, undertake [to the Court, to the defendants named in this claim form, and to any other person served with this claim form]—

   (a) that the statement in paragraph 2 above is correct;

   (b) that the time and date given in the certificate with this endorsement are correct;

   (c) that this claim form is a claim form which may be issued under paragraph 2.2 and Appendix A of the Commercial Court practice direction;

   (d) that I will comply in all respects with the requirements of Appendix A of the Commercial Court practice direction; and

   (e) that I will indemnify any person served with the claim form before it is sealed against any loss suffered as a result of the claim form being or becoming invalid as a result of any failure to comply with Appendix A of the Commercial Court practice direction.

   (Signed)

   Solicitor for the claimant"

   [**Note**: the endorsement may be signed in the name of the firm of solicitors rather than an individual solicitor, or by solicitors' agents in their capacity as agents acting on behalf of their professional clients.]

Certificate

The issuing solicitor must sign a certificate in the following form— **2A–38**

   "I certify that I have received a transmission report confirming that the transmission of a copy of this claim form to the Registry by fax was fully completed and that the time and date of transmission to the Registry were *[enter the time and date shown on the transmission report]*.

   Dated

   (Signed)

   Solicitor for the claimant"

   [**Note**: the certificate must be signed in the name of the firm

Paragraph numbers marked with a "+" can be found online and on CD.

of solicitors rather than an individual solicitor, or by solicitors' agents in their capacity as agents acting on behalf of their professional clients.]

THE ADMIRALTY AND COMMERCIAL COURTS GUIDE

Paragraph numbers marked with a "+" can be found online and on CD.

7th Edition: 2006

COMMERCIAL COURTS

INTRODUCTION

It is now nearly five years since the last edition of the Admiralty & Commercial Court Guide. During that time there have been many amendments to the Civil Procedure Rules and the court has received numerous suggestions from practitioners for improvements to the Guide. This new edition reflects an enormous amount of work by my colleagues to revise the Guide to reflect those amendments and to take on board the suggestions. I am particularly grateful to Mr Justice Anthony Colman who has undertaken the role of editor in chief.

As before, the Guide is not intended to provide a blueprint for litigation to which practitioners and the court must unthinkingly conform. The interests of efficiency and justice are paramount and the Guide must be treated as a flexible instrument so as to enable the Court to continue to provide a service to the international business community of the highest quality.

Comments about the new edition are always welcome. A working group under the chairmanship of Mr Justice Richard Aikens is to be set up to consider ways of further improving the service which the Court provides. The next edition may thus not be so long in gestation.

The Hon. Mr. Justice David Steel
Judge in Charge of the Commercial and Admiralty Courts

Paragraph numbers marked with a "+" can be found online and on CD.

December 2006

A.

PRELIMINARY

A1 The procedural framework

2A–40 A1.1 Proceedings in the Commercial Court are governed by the Civil Procedure Rules ("CPR") and Practice Directions. CPR Part 58 and its associated practice direction deal specifically with the Commercial Court. Part 61 deals with the Admiralty Court and Part 62 deals with arbitration applications. Parts 58 and 61 and their associated practice directions are set out in Appendix 1; Rule 62 and its associated practice direction is set out in Appendix 2.

A1.2 The Admiralty & Commercial Courts Guide is published with the approval of the Lord Chief Justice and the Head of Civil Justice in consultation with the Judges of the Admiralty and Commercial Courts and with the advice and support of the Admiralty Court and Commercial Court Committees. It is intended to provide guidance about the conduct of proceedings in the Admiralty and Commercial Courts and, within the framework of the Civil Procedure Rules and Practice Directions, to establish the practice to be followed in those courts.

A1.3 In matters for which specific provision is not made by the Guide, the parties, their solicitors and counsel will be expected to act reasonably and in accordance with the spirit of the Guide.

A1.4 The requirements of the Guide are designed to ensure effective management of proceedings in the Admiralty and Commercial Courts. If parties fail to comply with these requirements the court may impose sanctions including orders for costs and (where appropriate) wasted costs orders.

A1.5 Pre-trial matters in the Admiralty and Commercial Courts are dealt with by the judges of those Courts: **58PD § 1.2**.

A1.6 The Court expects a high level of co-operation and realism from the legal representatives of the parties. This applies to dealings (including correspondence) between legal representatives as well as to dealings with the Court.

A1.7 In order to avoid excessive repetition, the Guide has been written by reference to proceedings in the Commercial Court. Practitioners should treat the guidance as applicable to proceedings in the Admiralty Court unless the content of Part 61 or Section N of this Guide ("Admiralty") specifically requires otherwise.

A1.8 Parties may communicate with by e-mail with the Commercial and Admiralty Courts on certain matters:
  - a. to communicate the Case Management Unit, including the lodging of progress monitoring information sheets;
  - b. to communicate with the Registry in relation to the approval by the Judge of draft Order following a hearing before that Judge, queries on Orders made, requests to transfer a case into or out of the Commercial Court and general correspondence, including questions on practice;

  Note: Orders submitted for sealing must be submitted on paper.
  - c. to communicate with the Listing Office in matters relating to listing (including the lodging of pre-trial checklists) and to lodge skeleton arguments with the listing office;
  - d. to communicate with the Admiralty Marshal (except for out of hours business).

Note: The Court cannot accept any other documents by e-mail at present. In particular e-mail cannot be used to lodge pleadings, affidavits, witness statements,

Paragraph numbers marked with a "+" can be found online and on CD.

the case shall proceed without the filing or service of particulars of claim or defence or of any other statement of case. This facility is to be used with caution. It is unlikely to be appropriate unless all the issues have already been clearly defined in previous exchanges between the parties either in the course of a pre-claim form application or in previous correspondence and then only when the issues are of law or construction.

Interest

B3.9 The claim form (and not only the particulars of claim) must comply with the requirements of rules 16.4(1)(b) and 16.4(2) concerning interest: rule 58.5(3).

B3.10 References to particulars of claim in rule 12.6(1)(a) (referring to claims for interest where there is a default judgment) and rule 14.14(1)(a) (referring to claims for interest where there is a judgment on admissions) may be treated as references to the claim form: rules 58.8(2) and 58.9(3).

Issue of a claim form when the Registry is closed

B3.11 A request for the issue of a Part 7 claim form may be made by fax at certain times when the Registry is closed to the public: **PD58 § 2.2**. The procedure is set out in Appendix 3. Any further details may be obtained from the Registry. The fax number is 020 7947 6667.

B4 Part 8 claims

Form

B4.1 A claimant who wishes to commence a claim under CPR Part 8 must use **2A–47** practice form **N208(CC)**: **PD58 § 2.4**. A copy of this practice form is included at the end of this Guide.

B4.2 Attention is drawn to the requirement in rule 8.2(a) that where a claimant uses the Part 8 procedure his claim form must state that Part 8 applies. Similarly, PD7 § 3.3 requires that the claim form state (if it be the case) that the claimant wishes his claim to proceed under Part 8 or that the claim is required to proceed under Part 8.

Marking and statement of truth

B4.3 Sections B3.2 (marking) and B3.7 (statement of truth) also apply to a claim form issued under Part 8.

Issue of a claim form when the Registry is closed

B4.4 A request for the issue of a Part 8 claim form may be made by fax at certain times when the Registry is closed to the public: **PD58 § 2.2**. The procedure is set out in Appendix 3.

Time for filing evidence in opposition to a Part 8 claim

B4.5 A defendant to a Part 8 claim who wishes to rely on written evidence must file and serve it within 28 days after filing an acknowledgment of service: rule 58.12.

B5 Part 20 claims

Form

B5.1 Adapted versions of the Part 20 claim form and acknowledgment of service **2A–48** (Practice Forms no. **N211** and **N213**) and of the related Notes to Part 20 claimant and Part 20 defendant have been approved for use in the Commercial Court. Copies of the practice forms are included at the end of the Guide.

Paragraph numbers marked with a "+" can be found online and on CD.

COMMERCIAL COURTS

B6 Service of the claim form

Service by the parties

2A–49 B6.1 Claim forms issued in the Commercial List are to be served by the parties, not by the Registry: **PD58 § 9**.

Methods of service

B6.2 Methods of service are set out in CPR Part 6, which is supplemented by a Practice Direction.

B6.3 PD6 § § 2.1 and 3.1 concern service by document exchange and by fax. Service of the claim form on the legal representative of the defendant by document exchange or fax will not be effective unless that legal representative has authority to accept service. It is desirable to obtain confirmation from the legal representative in writing that he has instructions to accept service of a claim form on behalf of the defendant.

Applications for extension of time

B6.4 Applications for an extension of time in which to serve a claim form are governed by rule 7.6. Rule 7.6(3)(a), which refers to service of the claim form by the court, does not apply in the Commercial Court.

B6.5 The evidence required on an application for an extension of time is set out in PD7 § 8.2.

Certificate of service

B6.6 When the claimant has served the claim form he must file a certificate of service: rule 6.14(2). Satisfaction of this requirement is relevant, in particular, to the claimant's ability to obtain judgment in default (see Part 12) and to the right of a non-party to search for, inspect and take a copy of the claim form under rule 5.4(2)(a).

B7 Service of the claim form out of the jurisdiction

2A–50 B7.1 Applications for permission to serve a claim form out of the jurisdiction are governed by rules 6.19 to 6.31. A guide to the appropriate practice is set out in Appendix 15.

B7.2 Service of process in some foreign countries may take a long time to complete; it is therefore important that solicitors take prompt steps to effect service.

B8 Acknowledgment of service

2A–51 *Part 7 claims*

B8.1

(a) A defendant must file an acknowledgment of service in every case: rule 58.6(1). An adapted version of practice form **N9** (which includes the acknowledgment of service) has been approved for use in the Commercial Court. A copy of this practice form (Form **N9(CC)**) is included at the end of the Guide, together with adapted versions of the notes for claimants and defendants on completing and replying to a Part 7 claim form.

(b) The period for filing an acknowledgment of service is calculated from the service of the claim form, whether or not particulars of claim are contained in or accompany the claim form or are to follow service of the claim form. Rule 9.1(2), which provides that in certain circumstances the defendant need not respond to the claim until particulars of claim have been served on him, does not apply: rule 58.6(1).

Paragraph numbers marked with a "+" can be found online and on CD.

Part 8 claims

B8.2

(a) A defendant must file an acknowledgment of service in every case: rule 58.6(1). An adapted version of practice form **N210** (acknowledgment of service of a Part 8 claim form) has been approved for use in the Commercial Court. A copy of this practice form (Form **N210(CC)**) is included at the end of the Guide, together with adapted versions of the notes for claimants and defendants on completing and replying to a Part 8 claim form.

(b) The time for filing an acknowledgment of service is calculated from the service of the claim form.

Acknowledgment of service in a claim against a firm

B8.3

(a) PD10 § 4.4 allows an acknowledgment of service to be signed on behalf of a partnership by any of the partners or a person having the control or management of the partnership business, whether he be a partner or not.

(b) However, attention is drawn to Schedule 1 to the CPR which includes, with modifications, provisions previously contained in RSC Order 81 concerning acknowledgment of service by a person served as a partner who denies his liability as such. (see also the note at the end of CPR Part 10).

Time for filing acknowledgment of service

B8.4

(a) Except in the circumstances described in section B8.4(b) and B8.4(c), or is otherwise ordered by the court, the period for filing an acknowledgment of service is 14 days after service of the claim form.

(b) If the claim form has been served out of the jurisdiction without the permission of the court under rule 6.19, the time for filing an acknowledgment of service is governed by rule 6.22, save that in all cases time runs from the service of the claim form: rule 58.6(3).

(c) If the claim form has been served out of the jurisdiction with the permission of the court under rule 6.20 the time for filing an acknowledgment of service is governed by rule 6.21(4)(a), the second practice direction supplementing rule 6 and the table to which it refers, save that in all cases time runs from the service of the claim form: rule 58.6(3).

B9 Disputing the court's jurisdiction

Part 7 claims

B9.1

(a) If the defendant intends to dispute the court's jurisdiction or contend that the court should not exercise its jurisdiction he must

    (i) file an acknowledgment of service — rule 11(2); and

    (ii) issue an application notice seeking the appropriate relief.

(b) An application to dispute the court's jurisdiction must be made within 28 days of filing an acknowledgment of service: rule 58.7(2).

(c) If the defendant wishes to rely on written evidence in support of that application, he must file and serve that evidence when he issues the application.

(d) The parties to that application should consider at the time of the application and as soon as possible thereafter whether the application is a 'heavy application' within Section F6.1 likely to last more than half a day but for which the automatic timetable provisions in PD 58 para 13.2 and F6.3 – F6.5 will not for any reason be appropriate. If any party considers that special timetabling is required otherwise than in accordance with those automatic provisions it should at once so inform all other parties and the Listing Office. Unless a timetable covering those matters covered by Section F6.3 to F6.5 can be agreed forthwith, the applicant must without delay inform the Listing Office that a directions hearing will be required. For the purposes of such a hearing all

2A–52

Paragraph numbers marked with a "+" can be found online and on CD.

parties must by 1pm on the day before that hearing lodge with the Listing Office a brief summary of the issues of fact and law likely to arise on the application, a list of witnesses of fact whose witness statements or affidavits are likely to be adduced by that party, a list of expert witnesses on whose report that party intends to reply, an estimate of how long the hearing will take and a proposed pre-hearing timetable.

(e) If the defendant makes an application under rule 11(1), the claimant is not bound to serve particulars of claim until that application has been disposed of: rule 58.7(3).

Part 8 claims

B9.2

(a) The provisions of section B9.1(a)–(c) also apply in the case of Part 8 claims.

(b) If the defendant makes an application under rule 11(1), he is not bound to serve any written evidence on which he wishes to rely in opposition to the substantive claim until that application has been disposed of: rule 11.9.

Effect of an application challenging the jurisdiction

B9.3 An acknowledgment of service of a Part 7 or Part 8 claim form which is followed by an application challenging the jurisdiction under Part 11 does not constitute a submission by the defendant to the jurisdiction: rules 11(3) and 11(7).

B9.4 If an application under Part 11 is unsuccessful, and the court then considers giving directions for filing and serving statements of case (in the case of a Part 7 claim) or evidence (in the case of a Part 8 claim), a defendant does not submit to the jurisdiction merely by asking for time to serve and file his statement of case or evidence, as the case may be.

B10 Default judgment

2A–53 B10 Default judgment is governed by Part 12 and PD12. However, because in the Commercial Court the period for filing the acknowledgment of service is calculated from service of the claim form, the reference to "particulars of claim" in PD12 § 4.1(1) should be read as referring to the claim form: **PD58 § 6(1)**.

2A–54 ### B11 Admissions

B11

(a) Admissions are governed by CPR Part 14, and PD14, except that the references to "particulars of claim" in PD14 § § 2.1, 3.1 and 3.2 should be read as referring to the claim form: **PD58 § 6(2)**.

(b) Adapted versions of the practice forms of admission (practice forms no. **N9A** and no. **N9C**) have been approved for use in the Commercial Court. Copies of these practice forms (Forms **N9A(CC)** and **N9C(CC)**) are included at the end of the Guide.

B12 Transfer of cases into and out of the Commercial List

2A–55 B12.1 The procedure for transfer and removal is set out in **PD58 § 4**. All such applications must be made to the Commercial Court: rule 30.5(3).

B12.2 Although an order to transfer a case to the Commercial List may be made at any stage, any application for such an order should normally be made at an early stage in the proceedings.

B12.3 Transfer to the Commercial List may be ordered for limited purposes only, but a transferred case will normally remain in the Commercial List until its conclusion.

B12.4 An order transferring a case out of the Commercial List may be made at any stage, but will not usually be made after a pre-trial timetable has been fixed at the case management conference (see section D8).

Paragraph numbers marked with a "+" can be found online and on CD.

B12.5 Some commercial cases may more suitably, or as suitably, be dealt with in one of the Mercantile Courts or the London Mercantile Court. Parties should consider whether it would be more appropriate to begin proceedings in one of those courts and the Commercial Judge may on his own initiative order the case to be transferred there. Guidance on practical steps for transferring cases to the London Mercantile Court and to the Mercantile Courts is contained in a Guidance Note at Appendix 18.

C.

PARTICULARS OF CLAIM, DEFENCE AND REPLY

C1 Form, content, serving and filing   2A–56

C1.1

(a) Particulars of claim, the defence and any reply must be set out in separate consecutively numbered paragraphs and be as brief and concise as possible.

(b) If it is necessary for the proper understanding of the statement of case to include substantial parts of a lengthy document the passages in question should be set out in a schedule rather than in the body of the case.

(c) The document must be signed by the individual person or persons who drafted it, not, in the case of a solicitor, in the name of the firm alone.

C1.2

(a) Particulars of claim, the defence and also any reply must comply with the provisions of rules 16.4 and 16.5, save that rules 16.5(6) and 16.5(8) do not apply.

(b) The requirements of PD16 § 8.4–9.1 (which relate to claims based upon oral agreements, agreements by conduct and Consumer Credit Agreements and to reliance upon evidence of certain matters under the Civil Evidence Act 1968) should be treated as applying to the defence and reply as well as to the particulars of claim.

    (i) full and specific details must be given of any allegation of fraud, dishonesty, malice or illegality; and

    (ii) where an inference of fraud or dishonesty is alleged, the facts on the basis of which the inference is alleged must be fully set out.

(d) Any legislative provision upon which an allegation is based must be clearly identified and the basis of its application explained.

(e) Any provision of The Human Rights Act 1998 (including the Convention) on which a party relies in support of its case must be clearly identified and the basis of its application explained.

(f) Any principle of foreign law or foreign legislative provision upon which a party's case is based must be clearly identified and the basis of its application explained.

(g) It is important that if a defendant or Part 20 defendant wishes to advance by way of defence or defence to counterclaim a positive case on causation or quantification of damages, full details of that case should be included in the defence or Part 20 defence at the outset or, if not then available, as early as possible thereafter.

C1.3

(a) PD16 § 7.3 relating to a claim based upon a written agreement should be treated as also applying to the defence, unless the claim and the defence are based on the same agreement.

(b) In most cases attaching documents to or serving documents with a statement of case does not promote the efficient conduct of the proceedings and should be avoided.

(c) If documents are to be served at the same time as a statement of case they should normally be served separately from rather than attached to the statement of case.

(d) Only those documents which are obviously of critical importance and necessary for a proper understanding of the statement of case should be attached to or served with it. The statement of case must itself refer to the fact that documents are attached to or served with it.

Paragraph numbers marked with a "+" can be found online and on CD.

(e) An expert's report should not be attached to the statement of case and should not be filed with the statement of case at the Registry. A party must obtain permission from the court in order to adduce expert evidence at trial and therefore any party which serves an expert's report without obtaining such permission does so at his own risk as to costs.

(f) Notwithstanding PD16 § 7.3(1), a true copy of the complete written agreement may be made available at any hearing unless the court orders otherwise.

Adapted versions of the practice forms of defence and counterclaim have been approved for use in the Commercial Court. Copies of these practice forms are included at the end of this Guide.

Summaries

C1.4 If a statement of case exceeds 25 pages (excluding schedules), a summary, not exceeding 4 pages, must also be filed and served. The summary should cross-refer to the paragraph numbering of the full statement of case. The summary is to be included in the case management bundle: **section D7.2(ii)**.

Length

C1.5 Parties serving statements of case should bear in mind that the court will take into account the length of the document served when considering any application by another party for further time within which to respond.

Statement of truth

C1.6 Particulars of claim, a defence and any reply must be verified by a statement of truth: rule 22.1. So too must any amendment, unless the court otherwise orders: rule 22.1(2); see also **section C5.4**.

C1.7 The required form of statement of truth is as follows:

(i) for particulars of claim, as set out in **PD7 § 7.2** or **PD16 § 3.4**;

(ii) for a defence, as set out in **PD15 § 2.2** or **PD16 § 12.2**;

(iii) for a reply the statement of truth should follow the form for the particulars of claim, but substituting the word "reply" for the words "particulars of claim" (see **PD22 § 2.1**).

C1.8 A party may apply to the court for permission that a statement of truth be signed by a person other than one of those required by rule 22.1(6) .

C1.9 If insurers are conducting proceedings on behalf of many claimants or defendants a statement of truth may be signed by a senior person responsible for the case at a lead insurer, but

(i) the person signing must specify the capacity in which he signs;

(ii) the statement of truth must be a statement that the lead insurer believes that the facts stated in the document are true; and

(iii) the court may order that a statement of truth also be signed by one or more of the parties.

See **PD22 § 3.6B**.

C1.10 A statement of case remains effective (although it may not be relied on as evidence) even where it is not verified by a statement of truth, unless it is struck out: **PD22 § § 4.1–4.3**.

Service

C1.11 All statements of case are served by the parties, not by the court: **PD58 § 9**.

Filing

C1.12 The statements of case filed with the court form part of the permanent record of the court.

Paragraph numbers marked with a "+" can be found online and on CD.

C2 Serving and filing particulars of claim

C2.1 Subject to any contrary order of the court and unless particulars of claim are **2A–57** contained in or accompany the claim form

(i) the period for serving particulars of claim is 28 days after filing an acknowledgment of service: rule 58.5(1)(c);

(ii) the parties may agree extensions of the period for serving the particulars of claim. However, any such agreement must be evidenced in writing and notified to the court, addressed to the Case Management Unit: **PD58 § 7.1**;

(iii) any notification of an agreed extension exceeding 6 weeks, or which when taken together with preceding extensions exceeds 6 weeks in total, must be accompanied by a brief statement of the reasons for the extension.

C2.2 The court may make an order overriding any agreement by the parties varying a time limit: **PD58 § 7.2**.

C2.3 The claimant must serve the particulars of claim on all other parties. A copy of the claim form will be filed at the Registry on issue. If the claimant serves particulars of claim separately from the claim form he must file a copy within 7 days of service together with a certificate of service: rule 7.4(3).

C3 Serving and filing a defence

C3.1 The defendant must serve the defence on all other parties and must at the same **2A–58** time file a copy with the court.

C3.2

(a) If the defendant files an acknowledgment of service which indicates an intention to defend the period for serving and filing a defence is 28 days after service of the particulars of claim, subject to the provisions of rule 15.4(2). (See also Appendix 15 for cases where the claim form has been served out of the jurisdiction).

(b) The defendant and the claimant may agree that the period for serving and filing a defence shall be extended by up to 28 days: rule 15.5(1).

(c) An application to the court is required for any further extension. If the parties are able to agree that a further extension should be granted, a draft consent order should be provided together with a brief explanation of the reasons for the extension.

C3.3 The general power to agree variations to time limits contained in rule 2.11 and PD58 § 7.1 enables parties to agree extensions of the period for serving and filing a defence that exceed 28 days. The length of extension must in all cases be specified. Any such agreement must be evidenced in writing and comply with the requirements of section C2.1.

C3.4

(a) Where an extension is agreed the defendant must, in accordance with rule 15.5(2), notify the court in writing; the notification should be addressed to the Case Management Unit.

(b) Any notification of an agreed extension exceeding 6 weeks, or which when taken together with preceding extensions exceeds 6 weeks in total, must be accompanied by a brief statement (agreed by the claimant and the defendant) of the reasons for the extension. The reasons will be brought to the attention of the Judge in Charge of the Commercial List.

C3.5 The claimant must notify the Case Management Unit by letter when all defendants who intend to serve a defence have done so. This information is material to the fixing of the case management conference (see section D3.1).

C4 Serving and filing a reply

C4.1 Subject to section C4.3, the period for serving and filing a reply is 21 days after **2A–59** service of the defence: rule 58.10(1).

Paragraph numbers marked with a "+" can be found online and on CD.

COMMERCIAL COURTS

C4.2

(a) A reply must be filed at the same time as it is served: rule 15.8(b); rule 15.8(a) does not apply in proceedings in the Commercial List.

(b) The reply should be served before case management information sheets are provided to the court (see section D8.5). In the normal case, this will allow the parties to consider any reply before completing the case management information sheet, and allow time for the preparation of the case memorandum and the list of issues each of which is required for the case management conference (see sections D4–D7).

C4.3 In some cases, more than 21 days may be needed for the preparation, service and filing of a reply. In such cases an application should be made on paper for an extension of time and for a postponement of the case management conference. The procedure to be followed when making an application on paper is set out in section F4.

C4.4 Any reply must be served by the claimant on all other parties: rule 58.10(1).

2A–60 C5 Amendment

C5.1

(a) Amendments to a statement of case must show the original text, unless the court orders otherwise: **PD58 § 8**.

(b) Amendments may be shown by using footnotes or marginal notes, provided they identify precisely where and when an amendment has been made.

(c) Unless the court so orders, there is no need to show amendments by colour-coding.

(d) If there have been extensive amendments it may be desirable to prepare a fresh copy of the statement of case. However, a copy of the statement of case showing where and when amendments have been made must also be made available.

C5.2 All amendments to any statement of case must be verified by a statement of truth unless the court orders otherwise: rule 22.1(2).

C5.3 Questions of amendment, and consequential amendment, should wherever possible be dealt with by consent. A party should consent to a proposed amendment unless he has substantial grounds for objecting to it.

C5.4 Late amendments should be avoided and may be disallowed.

D.

CASE MANAGEMENT IN THE COMMERCIAL COURT

D1 Generally

2A–61 D1.1 All proceedings in the Commercial List will be subject to management by the court.

D1.2 All proceedings in the Commercial List are automatically allocated to the multi-track and consequently Part 26 and the rules relating to allocation do not apply: rule 58.13(1).

D1.3 Except for rule 29.3(2) (legal representatives to attend case management conferences and pre-trial reviews) and rule 29.5 (variation of case management timetable), Part 29 does not apply to proceedings in the Commercial List: rule 58.13(2).

Editorial note

2A–61.1   See Heavy and Complex Cases at para. 2A–18.1 , above.

Paragraph numbers marked with a "+" can be found online and on CD.

D2 Key features of case management in the Commercial Court

D2 Case management is governed by rule 58.13 and PD58 § 10. In a normal **2A–62** commercial case commenced by a Part 7 claim form, case management will include the following 10 key features:

(1) statements of case will be exchanged within fixed or monitored time periods;

(2) a case memorandum, a list of issues and a case management bundle will be produced at an early point in the case;

(3) the case memorandum, list of issues and case management bundle will be amended and updated or revised on a running basis throughout the life of the case and will be used by the court at every stage of the case;

(4) a mandatory case management conference will be held shortly after statements of case have been served, if not before (and preceded by the parties lodging case management information sheets identifying their views on the requirements of the case);

(5) at the case management conference the court will (as necessary) discuss the issues in the case and the requirements of the case with the advocates retained in the case. The court will set a pre-trial timetable and give any other directions as may be appropriate;

(6) before the progress monitoring date the parties will report to the court, using a progress monitoring information sheet, the extent of their compliance with the pre-trial timetable;

(7) on or shortly after the progress monitoring date a judge will (without a hearing) consider progress and give such further directions as he thinks appropriate;

(8) if at the progress monitoring date all parties have indicated that they will be ready for trial, all parties will complete a pre-trial checklist;

(9) in many cases there will be a pre-trial review; in such cases the parties will be required to prepare a trial timetable for consideration by the court;

(10) throughout the case there will be regular reviews of the estimated length of trial.

D3 Fixing a case management conference

D3.1 A mandatory case management conference will normally take place on the first **2A–63** available date 6 weeks after all defendants who intend to serve a defence have done so. This will normally allow time for the preparation and service of any reply (see section C4).

D3.2

(a) If proceedings have been started by service of a Part 7 claim form, the claimant must take steps to fix the date for the case management conference with the Listing Office in co-operation with the other parties within 14 days of the date when all defendants who intend to file and serve a defence have done so: **PD58 § 10.2(a)**. The parties should bear in mind the need to allow time for the preparation and service of any reply.

(b) If proceedings have been begun by service of a Part 8 claim form, the claimant must take steps to fix a date for the case management conference with the Listing Office in co-operation with the other parties within 14 days of the date when all defendants who wish to serve evidence have done so: **PD58 § 10.2(b)**.

D3.3

(a) In accordance with section C3 the Registry will expect a defence to be served and filed by the latest of

  (i) 28 days after service of particulars of claim (as certified by the certificate of service); or

  (ii) any extended date for serving and filing a defence as notified to the court in writing following agreement between the parties; or

  (iii) any extended date for serving and filing a defence as ordered by the court on an application.

Paragraph numbers marked with a "+" can be found online and on CD.

(b) If within 28 days after the latest of these dates has passed for each defendant, the parties have not taken steps to fix the date for the case management conference, the Case Management Unit will inform the Judge in Charge of the List, and at his direction will take steps to fix a date for the case management conference without further reference to the parties.

D3.4 If the proceedings have been transferred to the Commercial List, the claimant must apply for a case management conference within 14 days of the date of the order transferring them, unless the judge held, or gave directions for, a case management conference when he made the order transferring the proceedings: **PD58 § 10.3**.

D3.5 If the claimant fails to make an application as required by the rules, any other party may apply for a case management conference: **PD58 § 10.5**.

D3.6

(a) In some cases it may be appropriate for a case management conference to take place at an earlier date.
(b) Any party may apply to the court in writing at an earlier time for a case management conference: **PD58 § 10.4**. A request by any party for an early case management conference should be made in writing to the Judge in Charge of the List, on notice to all other parties, at the earliest possible opportunity.

D3.7 If before the date on which the case management conference would be held in accordance with section D3 there is a hearing in the case at which the parties are represented, the business of the case management conference will normally be transacted at that hearing and there will be no separate case management conference.

D3.8 The court may fix a case management conference at any time on its own initiative. If it does so, the court will normally give at least 7 days notice to the parties: **PD58 § 10.6**.

D3.9 A case management conference may not be postponed or adjourned without an order of the court.

2A–64 **D4 Two-Judge team system**

D4.1

(a) Cases which are exceptional in size or complexity or in having a propensity to give rise to numerous pre-trial applications may be allocated to a management team of two designated judges.
(b) An application for the appointment of a two-judge management team should be made in writing to the Judge in Charge of the List at the time of fixing the case management conference.
(c) If an order is made for allocation to a two-judge team, one of the designated judges will preside at all subsequent pre-trial case management conferences and other hearings.

D4.2 Except for an application for an interim payment, all applications in the case, and the trial itself, will be heard by one or other of the designated judges.

D5 Case memorandum

2A–65 D5.1 In order that the judge conducting the case management conference may be informed of the general nature of the case and the issues which are expected to arise, after service of the defence and any reply the solicitors and counsel for each party shall draft an agreed case memorandum.

D5.2 The case memorandum should contain:
    (i) a short and uncontroversial description of what the case is about; and

Paragraph numbers marked with a "+" can be found online and on CD.

(ii) a very short and uncontroversial summary of the material procedural history of the case.

D5.3 Unless otherwise ordered, the solicitors for the claimant are to be responsible for producing and filing the case memorandum.

D5.4 The case memorandum should not refer to any application for an interim payment, to any order for an interim payment, to any voluntary interim payment, or to any payment or offer under CPR Part 36 or Part 37.

D5.5

(a) It should be clearly understood that the only purpose of the case memorandum is to help the judge understand broadly what the case is about. The case memorandum does not play any part in the trial. It is unnecessary, therefore, for parties to be unduly concerned about the precise terms in which it is drafted, provided it contains a reasonably fair and balanced description of the case. Above all the parties must do their best to spend as little time as practicable in drafting and negotiating the wording of the memorandum and keep clearly in mind the need to limit costs.

(b) Accordingly, in all but the most exceptional cases it should be possible for the parties to draft an agreed case memorandum. However, if it proves impossible to do so, the claimant must draft the case memorandum and send a copy to the defendant. The defendant may provide its comments to the court (with a copy to the claimant) separately.

(c) The failure of the parties to agree a case memorandum is a matter which the court may wish to take into account when dealing with the costs of the case management conference.

D6 List of issues

D6.1 After service of the defence (and any reply), the solicitors and counsel for each party shall produce an agreed list of the important issues in the case. The list should include both issues of fact and issue of law. A separate section of the document should list what is common ground between the parties (or any of them, specifying which).   **2A–66**

D6.2 Unless otherwise ordered, the solicitors and counsel for the claimant are to have responsibility for the production and revision of the list of issues.

D7 Case management bundle

Preparation

D7.1 Before the case management conference (see sections D3 and D8), a case management bundle should be prepared by the solicitors for the claimant: **PD58 § 10.8**.   **2A–67**

Contents

D7.2 The case management bundle should only contain the documents listed below (where the documents have been created by the relevant time):

(i) the claim form;

(ii) all statements of case (excluding schedules), except that, if a summary has been prepared, the bundle should contain the summary, not the full statement of case;

(iii) the case memorandum (see section D5);

(iv) the list of issues (see section D6);

(v) the case management information sheets and the pre-trial timetable if one has already been established (see sections D8.5 and D8.9);

(vi) the principal orders in the case; and

(vii) any agreement in writing made by the parties to disclose documents without

Paragraph numbers marked with a "+" can be found online and on CD.

COMMERCIAL COURTS

making a list or any agreement in writing that disclosure (or inspection or both) shall take place in stages.

See generally **PD58 § 10.8**.

D7.3 The case management bundle must not include a copy of any order for an interim payment.

Lodging the case management bundle

D7.4 The case management bundle should be lodged with the Listing Office at least 7 days before the (first) case management conference (or earlier hearing at which the parties are represented and at which the business of the case management conference may be transacted: see section D3.7).

Preparation and upkeep

D7.5 The claimant (or other party responsible for the preparation and upkeep of the case management bundle), in consultation with the other parties, must revise and update the case management bundle as the case proceeds: **PD58 § 10.9**. The claimant should attend at the Case Management Unit for this purpose at the following stages:

   (i) within 10 days of the case management conference, in order to add the pre-trial timetable (or any other order made at the case management conference) and an updated case memorandum;

   (ii) within 10 days of an order being made on an application, if in the light of the order or the application it is necessary to add a copy of the order made (as a principal order in the case) or an updated case memorandum;

   (iii) within 14 days of the service of any amended statement of case (or summary), in order to substitute a copy of the amended statement of case (or summary) for that which it replaces and to incorporate an updated case memorandum and (if appropriate) a revised list of issues;

   (iv) within 10 days of any other revision to the case memorandum or list of issues, in order to incorporate the revised document.

D8 Case Management Conference

2A–68 *Application to postpone the case management conference*

D8.1

(a) An application to postpone the case management conference must be made within 21 days after all defendants who intend to serve a defence have done so.
(b) The application will be dealt with on paper unless the court considers it appropriate to direct an oral hearing.

Attendance at the case management conference

D8.2 Clients need not attend a case management conference unless the court otherwise orders. A representative who has conduct of the case must attend from each firm of solicitors instructed in the case. At least one of the advocates retained in the case on behalf of each party should also attend.

D8.3

(a) The case management conference is a very significant stage in the case. It is not simply a substitute for the summons for directions under the former Rules of the Supreme Court and although parties are encouraged to agree proposals for directions for the consideration of the court, directions will not normally be made by consent without the need for attendance.

(b) The general rule in the Commercial Court, as the Commercial and Admiralty Courts Guide makes clear, is that there must be an oral Case Management Conference (CMC) at court.

Paragraph numbers marked with a "+" can be found online and on CD.

(c) However, there are cases which are out of the ordinary where it may be possible to dispense with an oral hearing if the issues are straightforward and the costs of an oral hearing cannot be justified.

(d) In such a case, if the parties wish to ask the Court to consider holding the CMC on paper, they must lodge all the appropriate documents by no later than 12 noon on the Tuesday of the week in which the CMC is fixed for the Friday. That timing will be strictly enforced. If all the papers are not provided by that time, the CMC must be expected to go forward to an oral hearing. If the failure to lodge the papers is due to the fault of one party and it is for that reason an oral CMC takes place, that party will be at risk as to costs.

(e) With the papers (which will include the Case Management bundle with the information sheets fully completed by each party), the parties must lodge a draft Order (agreed by the parties) for consideration by the Judge and a statement signed by each advocate:

  (i) confirming that the parties have considered and discussed all the relevant issues and brought to the Court's attention anything that was unusual; and

  (ii) setting out information about any steps that had been taken to resolve the dispute by ADR, any future plans for ADR or an explanation as to why ADR would not be appropriate.

(f) In the ordinary course of things it would be unlikely that any case involving expert evidence or preliminary issues would be suitable for a CMC on paper. In cases involving expert evidence, the Court is anxious to give particular scrutiny to that evidence, given the cost such evidence usually involves and the need to focus that evidence. In cases where preliminary issues are sought, the Court will need to examine the formulation of those issues and discuss whether they are really appropriate.

Applications

D8.4

(a) If by the time of the case management conference a party wishes to apply for an order in respect of a matter not covered by Questions (1)–(16) in the case management information sheet, he should make that application at the case management conference.

(b) In some cases notice of such an application may be given in the case management information sheet itself: see section D8.5(c).

(c) In all other cases the applicant should ensure that an application notice and any supporting evidence is filed and served in time to enable the application to be heard at the case management conference.

Materials: case management information sheet and case management bundle

D8.5

(a) All parties attending a case management conference must complete a case management information sheet: **PD58 § 10.7**. A standard form of case management information sheet is set out in Appendix 6. The information sheet is intended to include reference to all applications which the parties would wish to make at a case management conference.

(b) A completed case management information sheet must be provided by each party to the court (and copied to all other parties) at least 7 days before the case management conference.

(c) Applications not covered by the standard questions raised in the case management information sheet should be entered under Question (17). No other application notice is necessary if written evidence will not be involved and the 7 day notice given by entering the application on the information sheet will in all the circumstances be sufficient to enable all other parties to deal with the application.

D8.6 The case management bundle must be provided to the court at least 7 days before the case management conference: **PD58 § 10.8**. Only where it is essential for

Paragraph numbers marked with a "+" can be found online and on CD.

the court on the case management conference to see the full version of a statement of case that has been summarised in accordance with section C1.4 above should a copy of that statement of case be lodged for the case management conference.

The hearing

D8.7 The court's power to give directions at the case management conference is to be found in rules 3.1 and 58.13(4). At the case management conference the judge will:

(i) discuss the issues in the case, and the requirements of the case, with the advocates retained in the case;

(ii) fix the entire pre-trial timetable, or, if that is not practicable, fix as much of the pre-trial timetable as possible; and

(iii) in appropriate cases make an ADR order.

D8.8 At the Case Management Conference, and again at the Pre-Trial Review, consideration will be given to the possibility of the trial of a preliminary issue or issues the resolution of which is likely to shorten the proceedings. An example is a relatively short question of law which can be tried without significant delay (though the implications of a possible appeal for the remainder of the case cannot be lost sight of). The court may suggest the trial of a preliminary issues, but it will rarely make an order without the concurrence of at least one of the parties.

D8.9

(a) Rules 3.1(2) and 58.13(4) enable the court at the case management conference to stay the proceedings while the parties try to settle the case by alternative means. The case management information sheet requires the parties to indicate whether a stay for such purposes is sought.

(b) In an appropriate case an ADR order may be made without a stay of proceedings. The parties should consider carefully whether it may be possible to provide for ADR in the pre-trial timetable without affecting the date of trial.

(c) Where a stay has been granted for a fixed period for the purposes of ADR the court has power to extend it. If an extension of the stay is desired by all parties, a judge will normally be prepared to deal with an application for such an extension if it is made before the expiry of the stay by letter from the legal representatives of one of the parties. The letter should confirm that all parties consent to the application.

(d) An extension will not normally be granted for more than four weeks unless clear reasons are given to justify a longer period, but more than one extension may be granted.

The pre-trial timetable

D8.10 The pre-trial timetable will normally include:

(i) a progress monitoring date (see section D12 below); and

(ii) a direction that the parties attend upon the Clerk to the Commercial Court to obtain a fixed date for trial.

Variations to the pre-trial timetable

D8.11 The parties may agree minor variations to the time periods set out in the pre-trial timetable without the case needing to be brought back to the court provided that the variation

(i) will not jeopardise the date fixed for trial;

(ii) does not relate to the progress monitoring date; and

(iii) does not provide for the completion after the progress monitoring date of any step which was previously scheduled to have been completed by that date.

D8.12 If in any case it becomes apparent that variations to the pre-trial timetable are required which do not fall within section D8.10 above, the parties should apply to have the case management conference reconvened immediately. The parties should not wait until the progress monitoring date.

Paragraph numbers marked with a "+" can be found online and on CD.

D9 Case management conference: Part 8 claims

D9 In a case commenced by the issue of a Part 8 claim form, a case management **2A–69** conference will normally take place on the first available date 6 weeks after service and filing of the defendant's evidence. At that case management conference the Court will make such pre-trial directions as are necessary, adapting (where useful in the context of the particular claim) those of the case management procedures used for a claim commenced by the issue of a Part 7 claim form.

D10 Case management conference: Part 20 claims

D10.1 Wherever possible, any party who intends to make a Part 20 claim should do **2A–70** so before the hearing of the case management conference dealing with the main claim.

D10.2 Where permission to make a Part 20 claim is required it should be sought at the case management conference in the main claim.

D10.3 If the Part 20 claim is confined to a counterclaim by a defendant against a claimant alone, the court will give directions in the Part 20 claim at the case management conference in the main claim.

D10.4 If the Part 20 claim is not confined to a counterclaim by a defendant against a claimant alone, the case management conference in the main claim will be reconvened on the first available date 6 weeks after service by the defendant of the new party of parties to the proceedings.

D10.5 All parties to the proceedings (i.e. the parties to the main claim and the parties to the Part 20 claim) must attend the reconvened case management conference. There will not be a separate case management conference for the Part 20 claim alone.

D10.6 In any case involving a Part 20 claim the court will give case management directions at the same case management conferences as it gives directions for the main claim: **PD58 § 12**. The court will therefore normally only give case management directions at hearings attended by all parties to the proceedings.

D10.7 The provisions of D10.4, D10.5 and D10.6 apply equally to Part 20 claims brought by parties who are not also parties to the main claim.

D11 Management throughout the case

D11 The court will continue to take an active role in the management of the case **2A–71** throughout its progress to trial. Parties should be ready at all times to provide the court with such information and assistance as it may require for that purpose.

D12 Progress monitoring

Fixing the progress monitoring date

D12.1 The progress monitoring date will be fixed at the case management conference **2A–72** and will normally be after the date in the pre-trial timetable for exchange of witness statements and expert reports.

Progress monitoring information sheet

D12.2 At least 3 days (i.e. three clear days) before the progress monitoring date the parties must each send to the Case Management Unit (with a copy to all other parties) a progress monitoring information sheet to inform the court:

(i) whether they have complied with the pre-trial timetable, and if they have not, the respects in which they have not; and

(ii) whether they will be ready for a trial commencing on the fixed date specified in the pre-trial timetable, and if they will not be ready, why they will not be ready.

Paragraph numbers marked with a "+" can be found online and on CD.

D12.3 A standard form of progress monitoring information sheet is set out in Appendix 12.

D13 Reconvening the case management conference

2A-73 D13.1 If in the view of the court the information given in the progress monitoring sheets justifies this course, the court may direct that the case management conference be reconvened.

D13.2 At a reconvened hearing of the case management conference the court may make such orders and give such directions as it considers appropriate. If the court is of the view that due to the failure of the parties or any of them to comply with the case management timetable the trial cannot be fairly and efficiently conducted on the date fixed, it may vacate the trial date and make such order for costs as is appropriate.

D14 Pre-trial checklist

2A-74 D14 Not later than three weeks before the date fixed for trial each party must send to the Listing Office (with a copy to all other parties) a completed checklist confirming final details for trial (a "pre-trial checklist") in the form set out in Appendix 13.

2A-75 ### D15 Further information

D15.1

(a) If a party declines to provide further information requested under Part 18, the solicitors or counsel who are to appear at the application for the parties concerned must communicate directly with each other in an attempt to reach agreement before any application is made to the court.

(b) No application for an order that a party provide further information will normally be listed for hearing without prior written confirmation from the applicant that the requirements of this section D15.1(a) have been complied with.

D15.2 Because it falls within the definition of a statement of case (see rule 2.3(1)) a response providing further information under CPR Part 18 must be verified by a statement of truth.

D16 Fixed trial dates

2A-76 D16.1 Most cases will be given fixed trial dates immediately after the pre-trial timetable has been set at the case management conference.

D16.2 A fixed date for trial is given on the understanding that if previous fixtures have been substantially underestimated or other urgent matters need to be heard, the trial may be delayed. Where such delay might cause particular inconvenience to witnesses or others involved in the trial, the Clerk to the Commercial Court should be informed well in advance of the fixed date.

D17 Estimates of length of trial

2A-77 D17.1 At the case management conference an estimate will be made of the minimum and maximum lengths of the trial. The estimate will appear in the pre-trial timetable and will be the basis on which a date for trial will be fixed.

D17.2 If a party subsequently instructs new advocate(s) to appear on its behalf at the trial, the Listing Office should be notified of that fact within 14 days. Advocates newly instructed should review the estimate of the minimum and maximum lengths of the trial, and submit to the Listing Office a signed note revising or confirming the estimate as appropriate.

D17.3 A confirmed estimate of the minimum and maximum lengths of the trial,

Paragraph numbers marked with a "+" can be found online and on CD.

signed by the advocates who are to appear at the trial, should be attached to the pre-trial checklist.

D17.4 It is the duty of all advocates who are to appear at the trial to seek agreement, if possible, on the estimated minimum and maximum lengths of trial.

D17.5 The provisional estimate and (after it is given) the confirmed estimate must be kept under review by the advocates who are to appear at the trial. If at any stage an estimate needs to be revised, a signed revised estimate (whether agreed or not) must be submitted by the advocates to the Clerk to the Commercial Court.

D17.6 Accurate estimation of trial length is of great importance to the efficient functioning of the court. The court will be guided by, but will not necessarily accept, the estimates given by the parties

D18 Pre-Trial Review and trial timetable

D18.1 The court will order a pre-trial review in any case in which it considers it appropriate to do so. **2A–78**

D18.2 A pre-trial review will normally take place between 8 and 4 weeks before the date fixed for trial.

D18.3 Whenever possible the pre-trial review will be conducted by the trial judge. It should be attended by the advocates who are to appear at the trial: **PD58 § 11.2**.

D18.4 Before the pre-trial review or, if there is not to be one, not later than 7 days before the trial is due to commence, the parties must attempt to agree a timetable for the trial providing for oral submissions, witnesses of fact and expert evidence: **PD58 § 11.3**. The claimant must file a copy of the draft timetable at least two days before the date fixed for the pre-trial review; any differences of view should be clearly identified: **PD58 § 11.4**. At the pre-trial review the judge may set a timetable for the trial and give such other directions for the conduct of the trial as he considers appropriate.

D19 Orders **2A–79**

D19.1

(a) Except for orders made by the court on its own initiative under rule 3.3, and unless the court otherwise orders, every judgment or order will be drawn up by the parties and rule 40.3 is modified accordingly: rule 58.15(1).
(b) Consent orders are to be drawn up in accordance with the procedure described in section F9.
(c) All other orders are to be drawn up in draft by the parties and dated in the draft with the date of the judge's decision. The claimant is to have responsibility for drafting the order, unless it was made on the application of another party in which case that other party is to have the responsibility.
(d) Two copies of the draft, signed by the parties themselves, or by their solicitors or counsel, must be lodged with the Registry **within five days** of the decision of the court reflected in the draft.

D19.2 If the court orders that an act be done by a certain date without specifying a time for compliance, the latest time for compliance is 4.30 p.m. on the day in question.

D19.3 Orders that are required to be served must be served by the parties, unless the court otherwise directs.

Paragraph numbers marked with a "+" can be found online and on CD.

E.

Disclosure

E1 Generally

2A–80 E1.1 The court will seek to ensure that disclosure is no wider than appropriate. Anything wider than standard disclosure (see section E3) will need to be justified.

E2 Procedure

2A–81 E2.1 At the case management conference the court will normally wish to consider one or more of the following:

(i) ordering standard disclosure: rule 31.5(1);

(ii) dispensing with or limiting standard disclosure: rule 31.5(2);

(iii) ordering sample disclosure;

(iv) ordering disclosure in stages;

(v) ordering disclosure otherwise than by service of a list of documents, for example, by service of copy documents; and

(vi) ordering specific disclosure: rule 31.12.

E2.2 The obligations imposed by an order for disclosure continue until the proceedings come to an end. If, after a list of documents has been prepared and served, the existence (present or past) of further documents to which the order applies comes to the attention of the disclosing party, that party must prepare and serve a supplemental list.

E3 Standard disclosure

2A–82 E3.1 Standard disclosure is defined by rule 31.6. Where standard disclosure is ordered a party is required to disclose only:

(i) the documents on which he relies; and

(ii) documents which—

— adversely affect his own case;

— adversely affect another party's case; or

— support another party's case; and

(iii) documents which he is required to disclose by any relevant practice direction.

E3.1A All parties should have regard to issues which may specifically arise concerning electronic data and documents:

(1) Rule 31.4 contains a broad definition of a document. This extends to electronic documents, including e-mail and other electronic communications, word processed documents and databases. In addition to documents that are readily accessible from computer systems and other electronic devices and media, the definition covers those documents that are stored on servers and back-up systems and electronic documents that have been "deleted". It also extends to additional information stored and associated with electronic documents known as metadata. In most cases metadata is unlikely to be relevant.

(2) The parties should, prior to the first Case Management Conference, discuss any issues that may arise regarding searches for and the preservation of electronic documents. This may involve the parties providing information about the categories of electronic documents within their control, the computer systems, electronic devices and mediaon which any relevant documents may be held, the storage systems maintained by the parties and their document retention policies. In the case of difficulty or disagreement, the matter should be referred to a judge for directions at the earliest practical date, if possible at the first Case Management Conference.

(3) The parties should co-operate at an early stage as to the format in which electronic copy documents are to be provided on inspection. In the case of difficulty or disagreement, the matter should be referred to a Judge for directions at the earliest practical date, if possible at the first Case Management Conference.

(4) The existence of electronic documents impacts upon the extent of the reasonable search required by Rule 31.7 for the purposes of standard disclosure. The factors that may be relevant in deciding the reasonableness of a search for electronic documents include (but are not limited to) the following—

(a) The number of documents involved.

Paragraph numbers marked with a "+" can be found online and on CD.

(b) The nature and complexity of the procedings.

(c) The ease and expense of retrieval of any particular document.

This includes:

(i) The accessibility of electonic documents or data including email communications on computer systems, servers, back-up systems and other electronic devices or media that may contain such documents taking into account alterations or developments in hardware or software systems used by the disclosing party and/or available to enable access to such documents.

(ii) The location of relevant electronic documents, data, computer systems, servers, back-up systems and other electronic devices or media that may contain such documents.

(iii) The likelihood of locating relevant data.

(iv) The cost of recovering any electronic documents.

(v) The cost of disclosing and providing inspection of any relevant electronic documents.

(vi) The likelihood that electronic documents will be materially altered in the course of recovery, disclosure or inspection.

(d) The significance of any document which is likely to be located during the search.

It may be reasonable to search some or all of the parties' electronic storage systems. In some circumstances, it may be reasonable to search for electronic documents by means of keyword searches (agreed as far as possible between the parties) even where a full review of each and every document would be unreasonable. There may be other forms of electronic search that may be appropriate in particular circumstances.

E3.2 A party who contends that to search for a category or class of document under rule 31.6(b) would be unreasonable must indicate this in his case management information sheet (see Appendix 6).

E3.3 In order to comply with rule 31.10(3) (which requires the list to identify the documents in a convenient order and manner and as concisely as possible) it will normally be necessary to list the documents in date order, to number them consecutively and to give each a concise description. However, where there is a large number of documents all falling within a particular category the disclosing party may (unless otherwise ordered) list those documents as a category rather than individually.

E3.4 Each party to the proceedings must serve a separate list of documents. This applies even if two or more parties are represented by the same firm of solicitors.

E3.5 If the physical structure of a file may be of evidential value (e.g. a placing or chartering file) solicitors should make one complete copy of the file in the form in which they received it before any documents are removed for the purpose of giving disclosure or inspection.

E3.6 Unless the Court directs otherwise, the disclosure statement must comply with the requirements of rules 31.7(3) and 31.10(6). In particular, it should

(i) expressly state that the disclosing party believes the extent of the search to have been reasonable in all the circumstances; and

(ii) draw attention to any particular limitations on the extent of the search adopted for reasons of proportionality and give the reasons why they were adopted.

E3.7 The disclosure statement for standard disclosure should begin with the following words:

"[I/we], [name(s)] state that [I/we] have carried out a reasonable and proportionate search to locate all the documents which [I am/*here name the party* is] required to disclose under [the order made by the Court or the agreement in writing made between the parties] on the [] day of [] 20[]."

Paragraph numbers marked with a "+" can be found online and on CD.

COMMERCIAL COURTS

E3.8 The disclosure statement for standard disclosure should end with the following certificate:

> "[I/we] certify that [I/we] understand the duty of disclosure and to the best of [my/our] knowledge [I have/*here name the party* has] carried out that duty. [I/we] certify that the list above is a complete list of all documents which are or have been in [my/*here name the party's*] control and which [I am/*here name the party* is] obliged under [the said order or the said agreement in writing] to disclose."

E3.9 An adapted version of practice form **N265** (list of documents: standard disclosure) has been approved for use in the Commercial Court. A copy of this practice form (Form **N265(CC)**) is included at the end of the Guide. The court may at any stage order that a disclosure statement be verified by affidavit.

E3.10

(a) For the purposes of PD31 § 4.3 the court will normally regard as an appropriate person any person who is in a position responsibly and authoritatively to search for the documents required to be disclosed by that party and to make the statements contained in the disclosure statement concerning the documents which must be disclosed by that party

(b) A legal representative may in certain cases be an appropriate person.

(c) An explanation why the person is considered an appropriate person must still be given in the disclosure statement.

(d) A person holding an office or position in the disclosing party but who is not in a position responsibly and authoritatively to make the statements contained in the disclosure statement will not be regarded as an appropriate person to make the disclosure statement of the party.

(e) The court may of its own initiative or on application require that a disclosure statement also be signed by another appropriate person.

E3.11 All parties should have regard to issues which may specifically arise concerning electronic data and documents:

(a) Rule 31.4 contains a broad definition of a document. This extends to electronic documents, including e-mail and other electronic communications, word processed documents and databases. In addition to documents that are readily accessible from computer systems and other electronic devices and media, the definition covers those documents that are stored on servers and back-up systems and electronic documents that have been "deleted". It also extends to additional information stored and associated with electronic documents known as metadata. In most cases metadata is unlikely to be relevant.

(b) The parties should, prior to the first Case Management Conference, discuss any issues that may arise regarding searches for and the preservation of electronic documents. This may involve the parties providing information about the categories of electronic documents within their control, the computer systems, electronic devices and media on which any relevant documents may be held, the storage systems maintained by the parties and their document retention policies. In the case of difficulty or disagreement, the matter should be referred to a judge for directions at the earliest practical date, if possible at the first Case Management Conference. For this purpose the parties should before any such hearing co-operate to provide the court with an explicit account of the issues as to retrieval and disclosure of electronic documents which have arisen and where proportionality is in issue each party should provide the court with an informed estimate of the volume of documents involved and the cost of their retrieval and disclosure.

(c) The parties should co-operate at an early stage as to the format in which electronic copy documents are to be provided on inspection. In the case of difficulty or disagreement, the matter should be referred to a Judge for directions at the earliest practical date, if possible at the first Case Management Conference.

(d) The existence of electronic documents impacts upon the extent of the reasonable search required by Rule 31.7 for the purposes of standard disclosure. The factors that may be relevant in deciding the reasonableness of a search for electronic documents include (but are not limited to) the following:—

Paragraph numbers marked with a "+" can be found online and on CD.

   (i) The number of documents involved.

   (ii) The nature and complexity of the proceedings.

   (iii) The ease and expense of retrieval of any particular document. This includes

    (1) The accessibility of electronic documents or data including e-mail communications on computer systems, servers, back-up systems and other electronic devices or media that may contain such documents taking into account alterations or developments in hardware or software systems used by the disclosing party and/or available to enable access to such documents.

    (2) The location of relevant electronic documents, data, computer systems, servers, back-up systems and other electronic devices or media that may contain such documents.

    (3) The likelihood of locating relevant data.

    (4) The cost of recovering any electronic documents.

    (5) The cost of disclosing and providing inspection of any relevant electronic documents.

    (6) The likelihood that electronic documents will be materially altered in the course of recovery, disclosure or inspection.

   (iv) The significance of any document which is likely to be located during the search.

(e) It may be reasonable to search some or all of the parties' electronic storage systems. In some circumstances, it may be reasonable to search for electronic documents by means of keyword searches (agreed as far as possible between the parties) even where a full review of each and every document would be unreasonable. There may be other forms of electronic search that may be appropriate in particular circumstances.

E4 Specific disclosure

E4.1 Specific disclosure is defined by rule 31.12(2). **2A–83**

E4.2 An order for specific disclosure under rule 31.12 may in an appropriate case direct a party to carry out a thorough search for any documents which it is reasonable to suppose may adversely affect his own case or support the case of the party applying for disclosure or which may lead to a train of enquiry which has either of these consequences and to disclose any documents located as a result of that search: **PD31 § 5.5.**

E4.3 Where an application is made for specific disclosure the party from whom disclosure is sought should provide to the applicant and to the Court information as to the factors listed in E3.11(d) above and its documents retention policy, to the extent such information is relevant to the application. At the hearing of the application, the Court may take into account the factors listed in E3.11(d) as well as the width of the request and the conduct of the parties.

E4.4 The court may at any stage order that specific disclosure be verified by affidavit or witness statement.

E4.5 Applications for ship's papers are provided for in rule 58.14.

E5 Authenticity **2A–84**

E5.1

(a) Where the authenticity of any document disclosed to a party is not admitted, that party must serve notice that the document must be proved at trial in accordance with CPR 32.19. Such notice must be served by the latest date for serving witness statements or within 7 days of disclosure of the document, whichever is later.

(b) Where, apart from the authenticity of the document itself, the date upon which a document or an entry in it is stated to have been made or the person by whom the document states that it or any entry in it was made or any other feature of the docu-

Paragraph numbers marked with a "+" can be found online and on CD.

ment is to be challenged at the trial on grounds which may require a witness to be called at the trial to support the contents of the document, such challenge

(i) must be raised in good time in advance of the trial to enable such witness or witnesses to be called;

(ii) the grounds of challenge must be explicitly identified in the skeleton argument or outline submissions in advance of the trial.

(c) Where, due to the late disclosure of a document it or its contents or character cannot practicably be challenged within the time limits prescribed in (a) or (b), the challenge may only be raised with the permission of the court and having regard to the Overriding Objective (CPR 1.1).

F.

APPLICATIONS

2A–85 **F1 Generally**

F1.1

(a) Applications are governed by CPR Part 23 and PD23 as modified by rule 58 and PD58. As a result

(i) PD23 § § 1 and 2.3–2.6 do not apply;

(ii) PD23 § § 2.8 and 2.10 apply only if the proposed (additional) application will not increase the time estimate already given for the hearing for which a date has been fixed; and

(iii) PD23 § 3 is subject in all cases to the judge's agreeing that the application may proceed without an application notice being served.

(b) An adapted version of practice form **N244** (application notice) has been approved for use in the Commercial Court. A copy of this practice form (Form **N244(CC)**) is included at the end of the Guide.

F1.2 An application for a consent order must include a draft of the proposed order signed on behalf of all parties to whom it relates: **PD58 § 14.1**.

F1.3 The requirement in PD23 § 12.1 that a draft order be supplied on disk does not apply in the Commercial Court since orders are generally drawn up by the parties: **PD58 § 14.2**.

Service

F1.4 Application notices are served by the parties, not by the court: **PD58 § 9**.

Evidence

F1.5

(a) Particular attention is drawn to PD23 § 9.1 which points out that even where no specific requirement for evidence is set out in the Rules or Practice Directions the court will in practice often need to be satisfied by evidence of the facts that are relied on in support of, or in opposition to, the application.

(b) Where convenient the written evidence relied on in support of an application may be included in the application notice, which may be lengthened for this purpose.

Time for service of evidence

F1.6 The time allowed for the service of evidence in relation to applications is governed by PD58 § 13.

Paragraph numbers marked with a "+" can be found online and on CD.

Hearings

F1.7

(a) Applications (other than arbitration applications) will be heard in public in accordance with rule 39.2, save where otherwise ordered.

(b) With certain exceptions, arbitration applications will normally be heard in private: rule 62.10(3). See section O.

(c) An application without notice for a freezing order or a search order will normally be heard in private.

F1.8 Parties should pay particular attention to PD23 § 2.9 which warns of the need to anticipate the court's wish to review the conduct of the case and give further management directions. The parties should be ready to give the court their assistance and should be able to answer any questions that the court may ask for this purpose.

F1.9 PD23 § § 6.1–6.5 and § 7 deal with the hearing of applications by telephone (other than an urgent applications out of court hours) and the hearing of applications using video-conferencing facilities. These methods may be considered when an application needs to be made before a particular Commercial Judge who is currently on circuit. In most other cases applications are more conveniently dealt with in person.

F2 Applications without notice

F2.1 All applications should be made on notice, even if that notice has to be short, unless **2A–86**

(i) any rule or Practice Direction provides that the application may be made without notice; or

(ii) there are good reasons for making the application without notice, for example, because notice would or might defeat the object of the application.

F2.2 Where an application without notice does not involve the giving of undertakings to the court, it will normally be made and dealt with on paper, as, for example, applications for permission to serve a claim form out of the jurisdiction, and applications for an extension of time in which to serve a claim form.

F2.3 Any application for an interim injunction or similar remedy will require an oral hearing.

F2.4

(a) A party wishing to make an application without notice which requires an oral hearing before a judge should contact the Clerk to the Commercial Court at the earliest opportunity.

(b) If a party wishes to make an application without notice at a time when no commercial judge is available he should apply to the Queen's Bench Judge in Chambers (see section P1.1).

F2.5 On all applications without notice it is the duty of the applicant and those representing him to make full and frank disclosure of all matters relevant to the application.

F2.6 The papers lodged for the application should include two copies of a draft of the order sought. Save in exceptional circumstances where time does not permit, all the evidence relied upon in support of the application and any other relevant documents must be lodged in advance with the Clerk to the Commercial Court. If the application is urgent, the Clerk to the Commercial Court should be informed of the fact and of the reasons for the urgency. Counsel's estimate of reading time likely to be required by the court should also be provided.

F3 Expedited applications

F3.1 The Court will expedite the hearing of an application on notice in cases of **2A–87** sufficient urgency and importance.

Paragraph numbers marked with a "+" can be found online and on CD.

F3.2 Where a party wishes to make an expedited application a request should be made to the Clerk to the Commercial Court on notice to all other parties.

2A–88 **F4 Paper applications**

F4.1

(a) Although contested applications are usually best determined at an oral hearing, some applications may be suitable for determination on paper.

(b) Attention is drawn to the provisions of rule 23.8 and PD23 § 11. If the applicant considers that the application is suitable for determination on paper, he should ensure before lodging the papers with the court

> (i) that the application notice together with any supporting evidence has been served on the respondent;
>
> (ii) that the respondent has been allowed the appropriate period of time in which to serve evidence in opposition;
>
> (iii) that any evidence in reply has been served on the respondent; and
>
> (iv) that there is included in the papers
>
>> (A) the written consent of the respondent to the disposal of the application without a hearing; or
>>
>> (B) a statement by the applicant of the grounds on which he seeks to have the application disposed of without a hearing, together with confirmation that a copy has been served on the respondent.

(c) Only in exceptional cases will the court dispose of an application without a hearing in the absence of the respondent's consent.

F4.2

(a) Certain applications relating to the management of proceedings may conveniently be made in correspondence without issuing an application notice.

(b) It must be clearly understood that such applications are not applications without notice and the applicant must therefore ensure that a copy of the letter making the application is sent to all other parties to the proceedings.

(c) Accordingly, the following procedure should be followed when making an application of this kind:

> (i) the applicant should first ascertain whether the application is opposed by the other parties;
>
> (ii) if it is, the applicant should apply to the court by letter stating the nature of the order which it seeks and the grounds on which the application is made;
>
> (iii) a copy the letter should be sent (by fax, where possible) to all other parties at the same time as it is sent to the court;
>
> (iv) any other party wishing to make representations should do so by letter within two days (i.e. two clear days) of the date of the applicant's letter of application. The representations should be sent (by fax, where possible) to the applicant and all other parties at the same time as they are sent to the court;
>
> (v) the court will advise its decision by letter to the applicant. The applicant must forthwith copy the court's letter to all other parties, by fax where possible.

F5 Ordinary applications

2A–89 F5.1 Applications likely to require an oral hearing lasting half a day or less are regarded as "ordinary" applications.

F5.2 Ordinary applications will generally be heard on Fridays, but may be heard on other days. Where possible, the Listing Office will have regard to the availability of advocates when fixing hearing dates.

F5.3 Many ordinary applications, especially those in the non-Counsel list on Fridays,

Paragraph numbers marked with a "+" can be found online and on CD.

are very short indeed (e.g. applications to extend time). As in the past, it is likely that many, if not most, of such applications can be heard without evidence and on short (i.e. a few days) notice. The parties should however have in mind what is said in section F1.5(a) above.

F5.4

(a) The timetable for ordinary applications is set out in PD58 § 13.1 and is as follows:
  (i) evidence in support must be filed and served with the application;
  (ii) evidence in answer must be filed and served within 14 days thereafter;
  (iii) evidence in reply (if any) must be filed and served within 7 days thereafter.
(b) This timetable may be abridged or extended by agreement between the parties provided that any date fixed for the hearing of the application is not affected: **PD58 § 13.4**. In appropriate cases, this timetable may be abridged by the Court.

F5.5 An application bundle (see section F11) must be lodged with the Listing Office by 1 p.m. one clear day before the date fixed for the hearing. The case management bundle will also be required on the hearing; this file will be passed by the Listing Office to the judge. Only where it is essential for the court on the hearing of the ordinary application to see the full version of a statement of case that has been summarised in accordance with section C1.4 above should a copy of that statement of case be lodged for the ordinary application.

F5.6 Save in very short and simple cases, skeleton arguments must be provided by all parties. These must be lodged with the Listing Office and served on the advocates for all other parties to the application by 1 p.m. on the day before the date fixed for the hearing (i.e. the immediately preceding day) together with an estimate of the reading time likely to be required by the court. Guidelines on the preparation of skeleton arguments are set out in Part 1 of Appendix 9.

F5.7 Thus, for an application estimated for a half day or less and due to be heard on a Friday:
  (i) the application bundle must be lodged by 1 p.m. on Wednesday; and
  (ii) skeleton arguments must be lodged by 1 p.m. on Thursday.
  If, for reasons outside the reasonable control of the advocate a skeleton argument cannot be delivered to the Listing Office by 1pm, it should be delivered direct to the clerk of the judge listed to hear the application and in any event not later than 4pm the day before the hearing.

F5.8 The applicant should, as a matter of course, provide all other parties to the application with a copy of the application bundle at the cost of the receiving party. Further copies should be supplied on request, again at the cost of the receiving party.

F5.9 Problems with the lodging of bundles or skeleton arguments should be notified to the Clerk to the Commercial Court as far in advance as possible. **If the application bundle or skeleton argument is not lodged by the time specified, the application may be stood out of the list without further warning**.

F6 Heavy applications

F6.1 Applications likely to require an oral hearing lasting more than half a day are **2A–90** regarded as "heavy" applications.

F6.2 Heavy applications normally involve a greater volume of evidence and other documents and more extensive issues. They accordingly require a longer lead-time for preparation and exchange of evidence. Where possible the Listing Office will have regard to the availability of advocates when fixing hearing dates.

F6.3 The timetable for heavy applications is set out in PD58 § 13.2 and is as follows:
  (i) evidence in support must be filed and served with the application;
  (ii) evidence in answer must be filed and served within 28 days thereafter;

Paragraph numbers marked with a "+" can be found online and on CD.

(iii) evidence in reply (if any) must be filed and served as soon as possible, and in any event within 14 days of service of the evidence in answer.

F6.4

(a) An application bundle (see section F11 must be lodged with the Listing Office by 4 p.m. two days (i.e. two clear days) before the date fixed for the hearing together with a reading list and an estimate for the reading time likely to be required by the court as agreed between the counsel or other advocates to appear on the application. The case management bundle will also be required on the hearing; this file will be passed by the Listing Office to the judge.

(b) Only where it is essential for the court on the hearing of the application to see the full version of a statement of case that has been summarised in accordance with section C1.4 above should a copy of that statement of case be lodged for the application.

F6.5 Skeleton arguments must be lodged with the Listing Office and served on the advocates for all other parties to the application as follows:–

(i) applicant's skeleton argument (with chronology unless one is unnecessary, and with a dramatis personae if one is warranted), by 4 p.m. two days (i.e. two clear days) before the hearing;

(ii) respondent's skeleton argument, by 4 p.m. one day (i.e. one clear day) before the hearing.

Guidelines on the preparation of skeleton arguments are set out in Part 1 of Appendix 9.

F6.6 Thus, for an application estimated for more than half a day and due to be heard on a Thursday:

(i) the application bundle and the applicant's skeleton argument must be lodged by 4 p.m. on Monday;

(ii) the respondent's skeleton argument must be lodged by 4 p.m. on Tuesday.

F6.7 The applicant must, as a matter of course, provide all other parties to the application with a copy of the application bundle at the cost of the receiving party. Further copies must be supplied on request, again at the cost of the receiving party.

F6.8 Problems with the lodging of bundles or skeleton arguments should be notified to the Clerk to the Commercial Court as far in advance as possible. **If the application bundle or skeleton argument is not lodged by the time specified, the application may be stood out of the list without further warning.**

F7 Evidence

2A–91 F7.1 Although evidence may be given by affidavit, it should generally be given by witness statement, except where PD32 requires evidence to be given on affidavit (as, for example, in the case of an application for a freezing order or a search order: **PD32 § 1.4**). In other cases the Court may order that evidence be given by affidavit: **PD32 § 1.4(1) and 1.6.**

F7.2 Witness statements and affidavits must comply with the requirements of PD32, save that photocopy documents should be used unless the court orders otherwise.

F7.3

(a) Witness statements must be verified by a statement of truth signed by the maker of the statement: rule 22.1.

(b) At hearings other than trial an applicant may rely on the application notice itself, and a party may rely on his statement of case, if the application notice or statement of case (as the case may be) is verified by a statement of truth: rule 32.6(2).

(c) A statement of truth in an application notice may also be signed as indicated in sections C1.8 and C1.9 above.

Paragraph numbers marked with a "+" can be found online and on CD.

F7.4 Proceedings for contempt of court may be brought against a person who makes, or causes to be made, a false statement in a witness statement (or any other document verified by a statement of truth) without an honest belief in its truth: rule 32.14(1).

F8 Reading time

2A-92

F8

(a) It is essential for the efficient conduct of the court's business that the parties inform the court of the reading required in order to enable the judge to dispose of the application within the time allowed for the hearing and of the time likely to be required for that purpose. Accordingly

  (i) in the case of all heavy applications and in the case of other applications, if any advocate considers that the time required for reading is likely to exceed two hours, each party must lodge with the Listing Office not later than 1pm two clear days before the hearing of the application a reading list with an estimate of the time likely to be required by the court for reading;

  (ii) in the case of all other applications each party must lodge with the Listing Office by 1pm on the day before the date fixed for the hearing of an application (ie the immediately preceding day) a reading list with an estimate of the time required to complete the reading;

  (iii) each party's reading list should identify the material on both sides which the court needs to read.

(b) **Failure to comply with these requirements may result in the adjournment of the hearing.**

F9 Applications disposed of by consent

2A-93

F9.1

(a) Consent orders may be submitted to the court in draft for approval and initialling without the need for attendance.

(b) Two copies of the draft, one of which (or a counterpart) must be signed on behalf of all parties to whom it relates, should be lodged at the Registry. The copies should be undated. The order will be dated with the date on which the judge initials it, but that does not prevent the parties acting on their agreement immediately if they wish.

(c) The parties should act promptly in lodging the copies at the Registry. If it is important that the orders are made by a particular date, that fact (and the reasons for it) should be notified in writing to the Registry.

F9.2 For the avoidance of doubt, this procedure is not normally available in relation to a case management conference or a pre-trial review. Whether or not the parties are agreed as between themselves on the directions that the court should be asked to consider giving at a case management conference or a pre-trial review, attendance will normally be required. See section D8.3.

F9.3 Where an order provides a time by which something is to be done the order should wherever possible state the particular date by which the thing is to be done rather than specify a period of time from a particular date or event: rule 2.9.

F10 Hearing dates, time estimates and time limits

F10.1 Dates for the hearing of applications to be attended by advocates are normally fixed after discussion with the counsel's clerks or with the solicitor concerned. **2A-94**

F10.2 The efficient working of the court depends on accurate estimates of the time needed for the oral hearing of an application. Over-estimating can be as wasteful as under-estimating.

F10.3 Subject to section F10.4, the Clerk to the Commercial Court will not accept or act on time estimates for the oral hearing of applications where those estimates

Paragraph numbers marked with a "+" can be found online and on CD.

exceed the following maxima:

Application to set aside service:	4 hours
Application for summary judgment:	4 hours
Application to set aside or vary interim remedy:	4 hours
Application to set aside or vary default judgment:	2 hours
Application to amend statement of case:	1 hour
Application for specific disclosure:	1 hour
Application for security for costs:	1 hour

F10.4 A longer listing time will only be granted upon application in writing specifying the additional time required and giving reasons why it is required. A copy of the written application should be sent to the advocates for all other parties in the case at the same time as it is sent to the Listing Office.

F10.5

(a) Not later than five days before the date fixed for the hearing the applicant must provide the Listing Office with his current estimate of the time required to dispose of the application.

(b) If at any time either party considers that there is a material risk that the hearing of the application will exceed the time currently allowed it must inform the Listing Office immediately.

F10.6

(a) All time estimates should be given on the assumption that the judge will have read in advance the skeleton arguments and the documents identified in the reading list. In this connection attention is drawn to section F8.

(b) A time estimate for an ordinary application should allow time for judgment and consequential matters; a time estimate for a heavy application should not.

F10.7 Save in the situation referred to at section F10.8, a separate estimate must be given for each application, including any application issued after, but to be heard at the same time as, another application.

F10.8 A separate estimate need not be given for any application issued after, but to be heard at the same time as, another application where the advocate in the case certifies in writing that

(i) the determination of the application first issued will necessarily determine the application issued subsequently; or

(ii) the matters raised in the application issued subsequently are not contested.

F10.9 If it is found at the hearing that the time required for the hearing has been significantly underestimated, the judge hearing the application may adjourn the matter and may make any special costs orders (including orders for the immediate payment of costs and wasted costs orders) as may be appropriate.

F10.10 Failure to comply with the requirements for lodging bundles for the application will normally result in the application not being heard on the date fixed at the expense of the party in default (see further sections F5.9 and F6.8 above). An order for immediate payment of costs may be made.

2A–95 F11 Application bundles

F11.1

(a) Bundles for use on applications may be compiled in any convenient manner but must contain the following documents (preferably in separate sections in the following order):

Paragraph numbers marked with a "+" can be found online and on CD.

322

(i) a copy of the application notice;

(ii) a draft of the order which the applicant seeks;

(iii) a copy of the statements of case;

(iv) copies of any previous orders which are relevant to the application;

(v) copies of the witness statements and affidavits filed in support of, or in opposition to, the application, together with any exhibits.

(b) Copies of the statements of case and of previous orders in the action should be provided in a separate section of the bundle. They should not be exhibited to witness statements.

(c) Witness statements and affidavits previously filed in the same proceedings should be included in the bundle at a convenient location. They should not be exhibited to witness statements.

(d) Where for the purpose of the application it is likely to be necessary for the court to read in chronological order correspondence or other documents located as exhibits to different affidavits or witness statements, copies of such documents should be filed and paged in chronological order in a separate composite bundle or bundles which should be agreed between the parties. If time does not permit agreement on the contents of the composite bundle, it is the responsibility of the applicant to prepare the composite bundle and to lodge it with the Listing Office by 4pm two clear days before the hearing in the case of heavy applications and one clear day before the hearing in the case of all other applications.

F12 Chronologies, indices and dramatis personae

F12.1 For most applications it is of assistance for the applicant to provide a **2A–96** chronology which should be cross-referenced to the documents. Dramatis personae are often useful as well.

F12.2 Guidelines on the preparation of chronologies and indices are set out in Part 2 of Appendix 9.

F13 Authorities

F13.1 On some applications there will be key authorities that it would be useful for **2A–97** the judge to read before the oral hearing of the application. Copies of these authorities should be provided with the skeleton arguments.

F13.2 It is also desirable for bundles of the authorities on which the parties wish to rely to be provided to the judge hearing the application as soon as possible after skeleton arguments have been exchanged.

F13.3 Authorities should only be cited when they contain some principle of law relevant to an issue arising on the application and where their substance is not to be found in the decision of a court of higher authority.

F14 Costs

F14.1 Costs are dealt with generally at section J13. **2A–98**

F14.2 Reference should be also be made to the rules governng the summary assessment of costs for shorter hearings contained in Parts 43 and 44.

F14.3 In carrying out a summary assessment of costs, the court may have regard amongst other matters to:

(i) advice from a Commercial Costs Judge or from the Chief Costs Judge on costs of specialist solicitors and counsel;

(ii) any survey published by the London Solicitors Litigation Association showing the average hourly expense rate for solicitors in London;

(iii) any information provided to the court at its request by one or more of the specialist associations (referred to at section A4.2) on average charges by specialist solicitors and counsel.

Paragraph numbers marked with a "+" can be found online and on CD.

F15 Interim injunctions

2A–99 *Generally*

F15.1

(a) Applications for interim injunctions are governed by CPR Part 25.

(b) Applications must be made on notice in accordance with the procedure set out in CPR Part 23 unless there are good reasons for proceeding without notice.

F15.2 A party who wishes to make an application for an interim injunction must give the Clerk to the Commercial Court as much notice as possible.

F15.3

(a) Except when the application is so urgent that there has not been any opportunity to do so, the applicant must issue his claim form and obtain the evidence on which he wishes to rely in support of the application before making the application.

(b) On applications of any weight, and unless the urgency means that this is not possible, the applicant should provide the court at the earliest opportunity with a skeleton argument.

(c) An affidavit, and not a witness statement, is required on an application for a freezing order or a search order: **PD25 § 3.1.**

Fortification of undertakings

F15.4

(a) Where the applicant for an interim remedy is not able to show sufficient assets within the jurisdiction of the Court to provide substance to the undertakings given, particularly the undertaking in damages, he may be required to reinforce his undertakings by providing security.

(b) Security will be ordered in such form as the judge decides is appropriate but may, for example, take the form of a payment into court, a bond issued by an insurance company or a first demand guarantee or standby credit issued by a first-class bank.

(c) In an appropriate case the judge may order a payment to be made to the applicant's solicitors to be held by them as officers of the court pending further order. Sometimes the undertaking of a parent company may be acceptable.

Form of order

F15.5 Standard forms of wording for orders for freezing orders and search orders are set out in Appendix 5. The forms should be used save to the extent that the judge hearing a particular application considers there is good reason for adopting a different form.

F15.6 A phrase indicating that an interim remedy is to remain in force until judgment or further order means that it remains in force until the delivery of a final judgment. If an interim remedy continuing after judgment is required, say until judgment has been satisfied, an application to that effect must be made (see further section K1).

F15.7 It is good practice to draft an order for an interim remedy so that it includes a proviso which permits acts which would otherwise be a breach of the order to be done with the written consent of the claimant's solicitors. This enables the parties to agree in effect to variations (or the discharge) of the order without the necessity of coming back to the court.

Paragraph numbers marked with a "+" can be found online and on CD.

of dispute resolution, how far the prospects of a successful mediation or other means of dispute resolution are likely to be enhanced by completion of pleadings, disclosure of documents, provision of further information under CPR 18, exchange of factual witness statements or exchange of experts' reports.

G1.8 The Judge may further consider in an appropriate case making an ADR Order in the terms set out in Appendix 7.

G1.9

(a) The Clerk to the Commercial Court keeps some published information on individuals and bodies that offer ADR and arbitration services. If the parties are unable to agree upon a neutral individual or panel of individuals to act as a mediator or give an early neutral evaluation, the normal form of ADR order set out in Appendix 7 contains at paragraph 3 a mandatory requirement that the case management conference should be restored to enable the court to facilitate agreement on a neutral or panel of neutrals. In order to avoid the cost of a restored case management hearing, the parties may agree to send to the court their respective list of available neutrals, so as to enable the judge to suggest a name from those lists. In any other case the parties may by consent refer to the judge for assistance in reaching such agreement.
(b) The court will not recommend any individual or body to act as a mediator or arbitrator.

G1.10 At the case management conference or at any other hearing in the course of which the judge makes an order providing for ADR he may make such order as to the costs that the parties may incur by reason of their using or attempting to use ADR as may in all the circumstances seem appropriate. The orders for costs are normally costs in the case, meaning that if the claim is not settled, the costs of the ADR procedures will follow the ultimate event, or that each side shall bear its own costs of those procedures if the case is not settled.

G1.11 In some cases it may be appropriate that an ADR order should be made following judgment if application is made for permission to appeal. In such cases the court may adjourn the application for permission to appeal while making an ADR order providing for ADR procedures to be completed within a specified time and, failing settlement with that period, for the application for permission to appeal to be restored.

G1.12 At the case management conference the court may consider that an order directed to encouraging bilateral negotiations between the parties' respective legal representatives is likely to be a more cost-effective and productive route to settlement then can be offered by a formal ADR or ENE Order. In such a case the court will set a date by which there is to be a meeting between respective solicitors and their respective clients' officials responsible for decision-taking in relation to the case in question.

G2 Early neutral evaluation

G2.1 In appropriate cases and with the agreement of all parties the court will provide **2A–102** a without-prejudice, non-binding, early neutral evaluation ("ENE") of a dispute or of particular issues.

G2.2 The approval of the Judge in Charge of the List must be obtained before any ENE is undertaken.

G2.3 If, after discussion with the advocates representing the parties, it appears to a judge that an ENE is likely to assist in the resolution of the dispute or of particular issues, he will, with the agreement of the parties, refer the matter to the Judge in Charge of the List.

Paragraph numbers marked with a "+" can be found online and on CD.

G2.4

(a) The Judge in Charge of the List will nominate a judge to conduct the ENE.
(b) The judge who is to conduct the ENE will give such directions for its preparation and conduct as he considers appropriate.

G2.5 The judge who conducts the ENE will take no further part in the case, either for the purpose of the hearing of applications or as the judge at trial, unless the parties agree otherwise.

H.

EVIDENCE FOR TRIAL

H1 Witnesses of fact

Preparation and form of witness statements

2A–103 H1.1 Witness statements must comply with the requirements of PD32. The following points are also emphasised:

(i) the function of a witness statement is to set out in writing the evidence in chief of the witness; as far as possible, therefore, the statement should be in the witness's own words;

(ii) it should be as concise as the circumstances of the case allow without omitting any significant matters;

(iii) it should not contain lengthy quotations from documents;

(iv) it should not engage in argument;

(v) it must indicate which of the statements made in it are made from the witness's own knowledge and which are made on information or belief, giving the source for any statement made on information or belief;

(vi) it must contain a statement by the witness that he believes the matters stated in it are true; proceedings for contempt of court may be brought against a person if he makes, or causes to be made, a false statement in a witness statement without an honest belief in its truth: rule 32.14(1).

H1.2 It is improper to put pressure of any kind on a witness to give anything other than his own account of the matters with which his statement deals. It is also improper to serve a witness statement which is known to be false or which it is known the maker does not in all respects actually believe to be true.

Fluency of witnesses

H1.3 If a witness is not sufficiently fluent in English to give his evidence in English, the witness statement should be in the witness's own language and a translation provided.

H1.4 If a witness is not fluent in English but can make himself understood in broken English and can understand written English, the statement need not be in his own words provided that these matters are indicated in the statement itself. It must however be written so as to express as accurately as possible the substance of his evidence.

Witness statement as evidence in chief

H1.5

(a) Where a witness is called to give oral evidence, his witness statement is to stand as his evidence in chief unless the Court orders otherwise: rule 32.5(2).
(b) In an appropriate case the trial judge may direct that the whole or any part of a witness's evidence in chief is to be given orally. Any application for such an order should be made at the beginning of the trial.

Paragraph numbers marked with a "+" can be found online and on CD.

Additional evidence from a witness

H1.6

(a) A witness giving oral evidence at trial may with the permission of the court amplify his witness statement and give evidence in relation to new matters which have arisen since the witness statement was served: rule 32.5(3). Permission will be given only if the Court considers that there is good reason not to confine the evidence of the witness to the contents of his witness statement: rule 32.5(4).

(b) A supplemental witness statement should normally be served where the witness proposes materially to add to, alter, correct or retract from what is in his original statement. Permission will be required for the service of a supplemental statement. Such application should be made at the pre-trial review or, if there is no pre-trial review, as early as possible before the start of the trial. If application is made at any later stage, the applicant must provide compelling evidence explaining its delay in adducing such evidence.

(c) It is the duty of all parties to ensure that the statements of all factual witnesses intended to be called or whose statements are to be tendered as hearsay statements should be exchanged simultaneously unless the court has otherwise ordered. Witnesses additional to those whose statements have been initially exchanged may only be called with the permission of the court which will not normally be given unless prompt application is made supported by compelling evidence explaining the late introduction of that witness's evidence.

Notice of decision not to call a witness

H1.7

(a) A party who has decided not to call to give oral evidence at trial a witness whose statement has been served must give prompt notice of this decision to all other parties. He must at the same time state whether he proposes to put the statement in as hearsay evidence.

(b) If the party who has served the statement does not put it in as hearsay evidence, any other party may do so: rule 32.5(5).

Witness summonses

H1.8

(a) Rules 34.2–34.8 deal with witness summonses, including a summons for a witness to attend court or to produce documents in advance of the date fixed for trial.

(b) Witness summonses are served by the parties, not the court.

H2 Expert witnesses

Application for permission to call an expert witness

H2.1 Any application for permission to call an expert witness or serve an expert's report should normally be made at the case management conference. **2A–104**

H2.2 Parties should bear in mind that expert evidence can lead to unnecessary expense and they should be prepared to consider the use of single joint experts in appropriate cases. In many cases the use of single joint experts is not appropriate and each party will generally be given permission to call one expert in each field requiring expert evidence. These are referred to in the Guide as "separate experts".

H2.3 When the use of a single joint expert is contemplated, the court will expect the parties to co-operate in developing, and agreeing to the greatest possible extent, terms of reference for that expert. In most cases the terms of reference will (in particular) identify in detail what the expert is asked to do, identify any documentary materials he is asked to consider and specify any assumptions he is asked to make.

Provisions of general application in relation to expert evidence

H2.4 The provisions set out in Appendix 11 to the Guide apply to all aspects of expert evidence (including expert reports, meetings of experts and expert evidence

Paragraph numbers marked with a "+" can be found online and on CD.

given orally) unless the court orders otherwise. Parties should ensure that they are drawn to the attention of any experts they instruct at the earliest opportunity.

Form and content of expert's reports

H2.5 Expert's reports must comply with the requirements of PD35 § § 1 and 2.

H2.6

(a) In stating the substance of all material instructions on the basis of which his report is written as required by rule 35.10(3) and PD35 § 1.2(8) an expert witness should state the facts or assumptions upon which his opinion is based.
(b) The expert must make it clear which, if any, of the facts stated are within his own direct knowledge.
(c) If a stated assumption is, in the opinion of the expert witness, unreasonable or unlikely he should state that clearly.

H2.7 It is useful if a report contains a glossary of significant technical terms.

H2.8 Where the evidence of an expert, such as a surveyor, assessor, adjuster, or other investigator is to be relied upon for the purpose of establishing primary facts, such as the condition of a ship or other property as found by him at a particular time, as well as for the purpose of deploying his expertise to express an opinion on any matter related to or in connection with the primary facts, that part of his evidence which is to be relied upon to establish the primary facts, is to be treated as factual evidence to be incorporated into a factual witness statement to be exchanged in accordance with the order for the exchange of factual witness statements. The purpose of this practice is to avoid postponing disclosure of a party's factual evidence until service of expert reports.

Statement of truth

H2.9

(a) The report must be signed by the expert and must contain a statement of truth in accordance with Part 35.
(b) Proceedings for contempt of court may be brought against a person if he makes, or causes to be made, without an honest belief in its truth, a false statement in an expert's report verified in the manner set out in this section.

Request by an expert to the court for directions

H2.10 An expert may file with the court a written request for directions to assist him in carrying out his function as expert, but

(i) at least 7 days before he does so (or such shorter period as the court may direct) he should provide a copy of his proposed request to the party instructing him; and
(ii) at least 4 days before he does so (or such shorter period as the court may direct) he should provide a copy of his proposed request to all other parties.

Exchange of reports

H2.11 In appropriate cases the court will direct that the reports of expert witnesses be exchanged sequentially rather than simultaneously. The sequential exchange of expert reports may in many cases save time and costs by helping to focus the contents of responsive reports upon true rather than assumed issues of expert evidence and by avoiding repetition of detailed factual material as to which there is no real issue. Sequential exchange is likely to be particularly effective where experts are giving evidence of foreign law or are forensic accountants.This is an issue that the court will normally wish to consider at the case management conference.

Meetings of expert witnesses

H2.12 The court will normally direct a meeting or meetings of expert witnesses before trial. Sometimes it may be useful for there to be further meetings during the trial itself.

Paragraph numbers marked with a "+" can be found online and on CD.

H2.13 The purposes of a meeting of experts are to give the experts the opportunity
   (i) to discuss the expert issues;
   (ii) to decide, with the benefit of that discussion, on which expert issues they share or can come to share the same expert opinion and on which expert issues there remains a difference of expert opinion between them (and what that difference is).

H2.14 Subject to section H2.16 below, the content of the discussion between the experts at or in connection with a meeting is without prejudice and shall not be referred to at the trial unless the parties so agree: rule 35.12(4).

H2.15 Subject to any directions of the court, the procedure to be adopted at a meeting of experts is a matter for the experts themselves, not the parties or their legal representatives.

H2.16 Neither the parties nor their legal representatives should seek to restrict the freedom of experts to identify and acknowledge the expert issues on which they agree at, or following further consideration after, meetings of experts.

H2.17 Unless the court orders otherwise, at or following any meeting the experts should prepare a joint memorandum for the court recording:
   (i) the fact that they have met and discussed the expert issues;
   (ii) the issues on which they agree;
   (iii) the issues on which they disagree; and
   (iv) a brief summary of the reasons for their disagreement.

H2.18 If experts reach agreement on an issue that agreement shall not bind the parties unless they expressly agree to be bound by it.

Written questions to experts

H2.19

(a) Under rule 35.6 a party may, without the permission of the court, put written questions to an expert instructed by another party (or to a single joint expert) about his report. Unless the court gives permission or the other party agrees, such questions must be for the purpose only of clarifying the report.
(b) The court will pay close attention to the use of this procedure (especially where separate experts are instructed) to ensure that it remains an instrument for the helpful exchange of information. The court will not allow it to interfere with the procedure for an exchange of professional opinion at a meeting of experts, or to inhibit that exchange of professional opinion. In cases where (for example) questions that are oppressive in number or content are put, or questions are put for any purpose other than clarification of the report, the court will not hesitate to disallow the questions and to make an appropriate order for costs against the party putting them.

Documents referred to in experts' reports

H2.20 Unless they have already been provided on inspection of documents at the stage of disclosure, copies of any photographs, plans, analyses, measurements, survey reports or other similar documents relied on by an expert witness as well as copies of any unpublished sources must be provided to all parties at the same time as his report.

H2.21

(a) Rule 31.14(e) provides that (subject to rule 35.10(4)) a party may inspect a document mentioned in an expert's report. In a commercial case an expert's report will frequently, and helpfully, list all or many of the relevant previous papers (published or unpublished) or books written by the expert or to which the expert has contributed. Requiring inspection of this material may often be unrealistic, and the collating and copying burden could be huge.

Paragraph numbers marked with a "+" can be found online and on CD.

(b) Accordingly, a party wishing to inspect a document in an expert report should (failing agreement) make an application to the court. The court will not permit inspection unless it is satisfied that it is necessary for the just disposal of the case and that the document is not reasonably available to the party making the application from an alternative source.

Trial

H2.22 At trial the evidence of expert witnesses is usually taken as a block, after the evidence of witnesses of fact has been given. The introduction of additional expert evidence after the commencement of the trial can have a severely disruptive effect. Not only is it likely to make necessary additional expert evidence in response, but it may also lead to applications for further disclosure of documents and also to applications to call further factual evidence from witnesses whose statements have not previously been exchanged. Accordingly, experts' supplementary reports must be completed and exchanged not later than the progress monitoring date and the introduction of additional expert evidence after that date will only be permitted upon application to the trial judge and if there are very strong grounds for admitting it.

H3 Evidence by video link

2A–105 H3.1 In an appropriate case permission may be given for the evidence of a witness to be given by video link. If permission is given the court will give directions for the conduct of this part of the trial.

H3.2 The party seeking permission to call evidence by video link should prepare and serve on all parties and lodge with the Court a memorandum dealing with the matters outlined in the Video-conferencing Protocol (Appendix 14) and setting out precisely what arrangements are proposed. Where the proposal involves transmission from a location with no existing video-link facility, experience shows that questions of feasibility, timing and cost will require particularly close investigation.

H3.3 An application for permission to call evidence by video link should be made, if possible, at the case management conference or, at the latest, at any pre-trial review. However, an application may be made at an even later stage if necessary. Particular attention should be given to the taking of evidence by video link whenever a proposed witness will have to travel from a substantial distance abroad and his evidence is likely to last no more than half a day.

H3.4 In considering whether to give permission for evidence to be given in this way the court will be concerned in particular to balance any potential savings of costs against the inability to observe the witness at first hand when giving evidence.

H4 Taking evidence abroad

2A–106 H4.1 In an appropriate case permission may be given for the evidence of a witness to be taken abroad. CPR Part 34 contains provisions for the taking of evidence by deposition, and the issue of letters of request.

H4.2 In a very exceptional case, and subject in particular to all necessary approvals being obtained and diplomatic requirements being satisfied, the court may be willing to conduct part of the proceedings abroad. However, if there is any reasonable opportunity for the witness to give evidence by video link, the court is unlikely to take that course.

J.

TRIAL

J1 Expedited trial

2A–107 J1.1 The Commercial Court is able to provide an expedited trial in cases of sufficient urgency and importance.

Paragraph numbers marked with a "+" can be found online and on CD.

J1.2 A party seeking an expedited trial should apply to the Judge in Charge of the Commercial List on notice to all parties at the earliest possible opportunity. The application should normally be made after issue and service of the claim form but before service of particulars of claim.

J2 Split trials

J2.1 It will sometimes be advantageous to try liability first. Assessment of damages can be referred to a judge of the Technology and Construction Court or to a Master, or the parties may choose to ask an arbitrator to decide them. The same approach can be applied to other factual questions. **2A–108**

J3 Documents for trial

J3.1 Bundles of documents for the trial must be prepared in accordance with Appendix 10. **2A–109**

J3.2 The number, content and organisation of the trial bundles must be approved by the advocates with the conduct of the trial.

J3.3 Consideration must always be given to what documents are and are not relevant and necessary. Where the court is of the opinion that costs have been wasted by the copying of unnecessary documents it will have no hesitation in making a special order for costs against the person responsible.

J3.4 The number content and organisation of the trial bundles should be agreed in accordance with the following procedure:

(i) the claimant must submit proposals to all other parties at least 6 weeks before the date fixed for trial; and

(ii) the other parties must submit details of additions they require and any suggestions for revision of the claimant's proposals to the claimant at least 4 weeks before the date fixed for trial.

This information must be supplied in a form that will be most convenient for the recipient to understand and respond to. The form to be used should be discussed between the parties before the details are supplied.

J3.5

(a) It is the claimant's responsibility to prepare and lodge the agreed trial bundles.

(b) If another party wishes to put before the court a bundle that the claimant regards as unnecessary he must prepare and lodge it himself.

J3.6

(a) Preparation of the trial bundles must be completed not later than 2 weeks before the date fixed for trial unless the court orders otherwise.

(b) Any party preparing a trial bundle should, as a matter of course, provide all other parties who are to take part in the trial with a copy, at the cost of the receiving party. Further copies should be supplied on request, again at the cost of the receiving party.

J3.7 Unless the court orders otherwise, a full set of the trial bundles must be lodged with the Listing Office at least 7 days before the date fixed for trial.

J3.8 Failure to comply with the requirements for lodging bundles for the trial may result in the trial not commencing on the date fixed, at the expense of the party in default. An order for immediate payment of costs may be made.

J3.9 If oral evidence is to be given at trial, the claimant must provide a clean unmarked set of all relevant trial bundles for use in the witness box. The claimant is responsible for ensuring that these bundles are kept up to date throughout the trial.

Paragraph numbers marked with a "+" can be found online and on CD.

COMMERCIAL COURTS

J4 Information technology at trial

2A–110 J4.1 The use of information technology at trial is encouraged where it is likely substantially to save time and cost or to increase accuracy.

J4.2 If any party considers that it might be advantageous to make use of information technology in preparation for, or at, trial, the matter should be raised at the case management conference. This is particularly important if it is considered that document handling systems would assist disclosure and inspection of documents or the use of documents at trial.

J4.3 Where information technology is to be used for the purposes of presenting the case at trial the same system must be used by all parties and must be made available to the court. In deciding whether and to what extent information technology should be used at the trial the court will have regard to the financial resources of the parties and will consider whether it is appropriate that, having regard to the parties' unequal financial resources, it is appropriate that the party applying for the use of such information technology should initially bear the cost subject to the court's ultimate order as to the overall costs following judgment.

J5 Reading lists, authorities and trial timetable

2A–111 J5.1 Unless the court orders otherwise, a single reading list approved by all advocates must be lodged with the Listing Office not later than 1 p.m. two days (i.e. two clear days) before the date fixed for trial together with an estimate of the time required for reading.

J5.2

(a) If any party objects to the judge reading any document in advance of the trial, the objection and its grounds should be clearly stated in a letter accompanying the trial bundles and in the skeleton argument of that party.
(b) Parties should consider in particular whether they have any objection to the judge's reading the witness statements before the trial.
(c) In the absence of objection, the judge will be free to read the witness statements and documents in advance.

J5.3

(a) A composite bundle of the authorities referred to in the skeleton arguments should be lodged with the Listing Office as soon as possible after skeleton arguments have been exchanged.
(b) Unless otherwise agreed, the preparation of the bundle of authorities is the responsibility of the claimant, who should provide copies to all other parties. Advocates should liaise in relation to the production of bundles of authorities to ensure that the same authority does not appear in more than one bundle.

J5.4 Cases which are unreported and which are also not included in the index of Judgments of the Commercial Court and Admiralty Court of England and Wales should normally only be cited where the advocate is ready to give an assurance that the transcript contains a statement of some relevant principle of law of which the substance, as distinct from some mere choice of phraseology, is not to be found in any judgment that has appeared in one of the general or specialised series of law reports. The index of Judgments of the Commercial Court and Admiralty Court of England and Wales can be found www.hmcourt-service.gov.uk/infoabout/admiralcomm/index.htm via the link to "Searchable index of court cases" (at bottom of the box on right hand side of Commercial Court and Admiralty Court), and is also available at the BAILII website where it can be found at www.bailii.org/cgi-bin/summaries.cgi?index=comm.

Paragraph numbers marked with a "+" can be found online and on CD.

J5.5

(a) When lodging the reading list the claimant should also lodge a trial timetable.

(b) A trial timetable may have been fixed by the judge at the pre-trial review (section D18.4 above). If it has not, a trial timetable should be prepared by the advocate(s) for the claimant after consultation with the advocate(s) for all other parties.

(c) If there are differences of view between the advocate(s) for the claimant and the advocate(s) for other parties, these should be shown.

(d) The trial timetable will provide for oral submissions, witness evidence and expert evidence over the course of the trial. On the first day of the trial the judge may fix the trial timetable, subject to any further order.

J6 Skeleton arguments etc. at trial

J6.1 Written skeleton arguments should be prepared by each party. Guidelines on the preparation of skeleton arguments are set out in Part 1 of Appendix 9. **2A–112**

J6.2 Unless otherwise ordered, the skeleton arguments should be served on all other parties and lodged with the court as follows:

(i) by the claimant, not later than 1 p.m. two days (i.e. two clear days) before the start of the trial;

(ii) by each of the defendants, not later than 1 p.m. one day (i.e. one clear day) before the start of the trial.

J6.3 In heavier cases it will often be appropriate for skeleton arguments to be served and lodged at earlier times than indicated at section J6.2. The timetable should be discussed between the advocates and may be the subject of a direction in the pre-trial timetable or at any pre-trial review.

J6.4 The claimant should provide a chronology with his skeleton argument. Indices (i.e. documents that collate key references on particular points, or a substantive list of the contents of a particular bundle or bundles) and dramatics personae should also be provided where these are likely to be useful. Guidelines on the preparation of chronologies and indices are set out in Part 2 of Appendix 9.

J7 Trial sitting days and hearing trials in public

J7.1 Trial sitting days will not normally include Fridays. **2A–113**

J7.2 Where it is necessary in order to accommodate hearing evidence from certain witnesses or types of witness, the court may agree to sit outside normal hours.

J7.3 The general rule is that a hearing is to be in public: rule 39.2(1).

J8 Oral opening statements at trial

J8.1 Oral opening statements should as far as possible be uncontroversial and in any event no longer than the circumstances require. Even in a very heavy case, oral opening statements may be very short. There remains some confusion amongst advocates as to what is necessary to adduce a document other than a witness statement or expert report in evidence. Whereas there can be no doubt that any disclosed document can be relied on as evidence of the facts contained in it or as evidence of its existence or the use to which it was put, see Civil Evidence Act 1995 S.2(4) and CPR 32.19 the mere inclusion of a document in the agreed trial bundles does not in itself mean that it is being adduced in evidence by either party see Appendix 10. For this to happen either the parties must agree that the document in question is to be treated as put in evidence by one or other of them and the judge so informed or they must actively adduce the document in evidence by some other means. This might be done by counsel inviting the judge to read the document relied upon before the calling of oral evidence. It may however be more efficient for the document or part of it to be read to the court in the course of opening. That will be a matter for the judgment of the advocates in each case. However, whichever course is adopted, it will not normally be appropriate for reliance to be placed in final **2A–114**

Paragraph numbers marked with a "+" can be found online and on CD.

speeches on any document, not already specifically adduced in evidence by one of the means described.

J8.2 At the conclusion of the opening statement for the claimant the advocates for each of the other parties will usually each be invited to make a short opening statement.

J9 Applications in the course of trial

2A–115 J9.1 It will not normally be necessary for an application notice to be issued for an application which is to be made during the course of the trial, but all other parties should be given adequate notice of the intention to apply.

J9.2 Unless the judge directs otherwise the parties should prepare skeleton arguments for the hearing of the application

J10 Oral closing submissions at trial

2A–116 J10.1 All parties will be expected to make oral closing submissions, whether or not closing submissions have been made in writing. It is a matter for the advocate to consider how in all the circumstances these oral submissions should be presented.

J10.2 Unless the trial judge directs otherwise, the claimant will make his oral closing submissions first, followed by the defendant(s) in the order in which they appear on the claim form with the claimant having a right of reply.

2A–117 ### J11 Written closing submissions at trial

J11.1

(a) In a more substantial trial, the court will normally also require closing submissions in writing before oral closing submissions.

(b) In such a case the court will normally allow an appropriate period of time after the conclusion of the evidence to allow the preparation of these submissions.

(c) Even in a less substantial trial the court will normally require a skeleton argument on matters of law.

2A–118 ### J12 Judgment

J12.1

(a) When judgment is reserved the judge may deliver judgment orally or by handing down a written judgment.

(b) If the judge intends to hand down a written judgment a copy of the draft text marked
  "Draft Judgment"
and bearing the rubric:
  *"This is a judgment to which the new Practice Direction — Reserved Judgments (which supplements CPR Part 40 with effect from 1st October 2005) applies. It will be handed down on   at   in Court No
  . This Judgment is confidential to Counsel and Solicitors, but a copy may be shown, in confidence, to the parties provided that neither the Judgment nor its substance is disclosed to any other person or used in the public domain, and no action is taken (other than internally) in response to the Judgment, before the Judgment is handed down. Any breach of this obligation of confidentiality may be treated as a contempt of court. The official version of the judgment will be available from the Mechanical Recording Department of the Royal Courts of Justice once it has been approved by the judge.
  The court is likely to wish to hand down its judgment in an approved final form. Counsel should therefore submit any list of typing corrections and other obvious errors in writing (Nil returns are required) to the clerk to   , by fax to 020 7947
                    or   via   email   at   ,   by*

Paragraph numbers marked with a "+" can be found online and on CD.

on _____ , *so that changes can be incorporated, if the judge accepts them, in the handed down judgment."*

will normally be supplied to the advocates one clear day before the judgment is to be delivered.

(c) Advocates should inform the judge's clerk not later than noon on the day before judgment is to be handed down of any typographical or other errors of a similar nature which the judge might wish to correct. This facility is confined to the correction of textual mistakes and is not to be used as the occasion for attempting to persuade the judge to change the decision on matters of substance.

(d) The requirement to treat the text as confidential must be strictly observed. Failure to do so amounts to a contempt of court.

J12.2

(a) Judgment is not delivered until it is formally pronounced in open court.

(b) Copies of the approved judgment will be made available to the parties, to law reporters and to any other person wanting a copy.

(c) The judge may direct that the written judgment stand as the definitive record and that no transcript need be made. Any editorial corrections made at the time of handing down will be incorporated in an approved official text as soon as possible, and the approved official text, so marked, will be available from the Mechanical Recording Department.

J12.3 If at the time of pronouncement of the judgment any party wishes to apply for permission to appeal to the Court of Appeal, that application should be supported by written draft grounds of appeal.

J13 Costs

J13.1 The rules governing the award and assessment of costs are contained in CPR **2A–119** Parts 43 to 48.

J13.2 The summary assessment procedure provided for in Parts 43 and 44 also applies to trials lasting one day or less.

K.

AFTER TRIAL

K1 Continuation, variation and discharge of interim remedies and undertakings **2A–120**

K1.1

(a) Applications to continue, vary or discharge interim remedies or undertakings should be made to a Commercial Judge, even after trial.

(b) If a party wishes to continue a freezing order after trial or judgment, care should be taken to ensure that the application is made before the existing freezing order has expired.

K2 Accounts and enquiries

K2.1 The court may order that accounts and inquiries be referred to a judge of the **2A–121** Technology and Construction Court or to a Master. Alternatively, the parties may choose to refer the matter to arbitration.

K3 Enforcement

K3.1 Unless the court orders otherwise, all proceedings for the enforcement of any **2A–122** judgment or order for the payment of money given or made in the Commercial Court will be referred automatically to a master of the Queen's Bench Division or a district judge: **PD58 § 1.2(2)**.

Paragraph numbers marked with a "+" can be found online and on CD.

K3.2 Applications in connection with the enforcement of a judgment or order for the payment of money should accordingly be directed to the Registry which will allocate them to the Admiralty Registrar or to one of the Queen's Bench masters as appropriate.

K4 Assessment of damages or interest after a default judgment

2A–123 K4.1 Unless the court orders otherwise, the assessment of damages or interest following the entry of a default judgment for damages or interest to be assessed will be carried out by the Admiralty Registrar or one of the Queen's Bench masters to whom the case is allocated by the Registry.

L.

MULTI-PARTY DISPUTES

L1 Early consideration

2A–124 L1.1 Cases which involve, or are expected to involve, a large number of claimants or defendants require close case management from the earliest point. The same is true where there are, or are likely to be, a large number of separate cases involving the same or similar issues. Both classes of case are referred to as "multi-party" disputes.

L1.2

(a) The Judge in Charge of the List should be informed as soon as it becomes apparent that a multi-party dispute exists or is likely to exist and an early application for directions should be made.

(b) In an appropriate case an application for directions may be made before issue of a claim form. In some cases it may be appropriate for an application to be made without notice in the first instance.

L2 Available procedures

2A–125 L2.1 In some cases it may be appropriate for the court to make a Group Litigation Order under Part 19 of the Rules. In other cases it may be more convenient for the court to exercise its general powers of management. These include powers

(i) to dispense with statements of case;

(ii) to direct parties to serve outline statements of case;

(iii) to direct that cases be consolidated or managed and tried together;

(iv) to direct that certain cases or issues be determined before others and to stay other proceedings in the meantime;

(v) to advance or put back the usual time for pre-trial steps to be taken (for example the disclosure of documents by one or more parties or a payment into court).

L2.2 Attention is drawn to the provisions of Section III of Part 19, rules 19.10–19.15 and the practice direction supplementing Section III of Part 19. Practitioners should note that the provisions of Section III of Part 19 give the court additional powers to manage disputes involving multiple claimants or defendants. They should also note that a Group Litigation Order may not be made without the consent of the Lord Chief Justice: **PD19B § 3.3(1)**.

L2.3 An application for a Group Litigation Order should be made in the first instance to the Judge in Charge of the List: **PD19B § 3.5**.

M.

LITIGANTS IN PERSON

M1 The litigant in person

2A–126 M1.1 Litigants in person appear less often in the Commercial Court than in some other courts. Their position requires special consideration.

Paragraph numbers marked with a "+" can be found online and on CD.

M2 Represented parties

M2.1 Where a litigant in person is involved in a case the court will expect solicitors and counsel for other parties to do what they reasonably can to ensure that he has a fair opportunity to prepare and put his case.   **2A–127**

M2.2 The duty of an advocate to ensure that the court is informed of all relevant decisions and legislative provisions of which he is aware (whether favourable to his case or not) and to bring any procedural irregularity to the attention of the court during the hearing is of particular importance in a case where a litigant in person is involved.

M2.3 Further, the court will expect solicitors and counsel appearing for other parties to ensure that the case memorandum, the list of issues and all necessary bundles are prepared and provided to the court in accordance with the Guide, even where the litigant in person is unwilling or unable to participate.

M2.4 If the claimant is a litigant in person the judge at the case management conference will normally direct which of the parties is to have responsibility for the preparation and upkeep of the case management bundle.

M2.5 At the case management conference the court may give directions relating to the costs of providing application bundles and trial bundles to the litigant in person.

M3 Companies without representation

M3.1 Although rule 39.6 allows a company or other corporation with the permission of the court to be represented at trial by an employee, the complexity of most cases in the Commercial Court makes that unsuitable. Accordingly, permission is likely to be given only in unusual circumstances.   **2A–128**

N.

ADMIRALTY

N1 General

N1.1 Proceedings in the Admiralty Court are dealt with in Part 61 and its associated practice direction.   **2A–129**

N1.2 The Admiralty & Commercial Courts Guide has been prepared in consultation with the Admiralty Judge. It has been adopted to provide guidance about the conduct of proceedings in the Admiralty Court. The Guide must be followed in the Admiralty Court unless the content of Part 61, its associated practice direction or the terms of this section N require otherwise.

N1.3 One significant area of difference between practice in the Commercial Court and practice in the Admiralty Court is that many interlocutory applications are heard by the Admiralty Registrar who has all the powers of the Admiralty judge save as provided otherwise: rule 61.1(4).

N2 The Admiralty Court Committee

N2.1 The Admiralty Court Committee provides a specific forum for contact and consultation between the Admiralty Court and its users. Its meetings are usually held in conjunction with the Commercial Court Users Committee. Any correspondence should be addressed to the Deputy Admiralty Marshal, Royal Courts of Justice, Strand, WC2A 2LL.   **2A–130**

N3 Commencement of proceedings, service of Statements of Case and associated matters

N3.1 Sections B and C of this guide apply to all Admiralty claims except: **2A–131**

Paragraph numbers marked with a "+" can be found online and on CD.

(i) a claim in rem;

(ii) a collision claim; and

(iii) a limitation claim.

N4 Commencement and early stages of a claim in rem

2A-132 N4.1 The early stages of an in rem claim differ from those of other claims.

The procedure is governed generally by rule 61.3 and PD61 § § 3.1–3.11.

N4.2 In addition, the following sections of the Guide apply to claims in rem: B3.3, B3.7–B3.11, B6.4–B6.6, C1.1–C1.9, C1.11 and C2.1 (ii)–C5.4.

N4.3 Subject to PD61 § 3.7, section C1.10 of the Guide also applies to claims in rem.

N4.4 After an acknowledgement of service has been filed a claim in rem follows the procedure applicable to a claim proceeding in the Commercial List, save that the Claimant is allowed 75 days in which to serve his particulars of claim: **PD61 § 3.10**.

N5 The early stages of a Collision Claim

2A-133 N5.1 Where a collision claim is commenced in rem, the general procedure applicable to claims in rem applies subject to rule 61.4 and PD61 § § 4.1–4.5.

N5.2 Where a collision claim is not commenced in rem the general procedure applicable to claims proceeding in the Commercial List applies subject to rule 61.4 and PD61 § § 4.1–4.5.

N5.3 Service of a claim form out of the jurisdiction in a collision claim (other than a claim in rem) is permitted in the circumstances identified in rule 61.4(7) only and the procedure set out in Appendix 15 of the Guide should be adapted accordingly.

N5.4 One particular feature of a collision action is that the parties must prepare and file a Collision Statement of Case. Prior to the coming into force of Part 61, a Collision Statement of Case was known as a Preliminary Act and the law relating to Preliminary Acts continues to apply to Collision Statements of Case: **PD61 § 4.5**.

N5.5 The provisions of Appendix 4 apply to part 2 of a Collision Statement of Case (but not to part 1).

N5.6 Every party is required, so far as it is able, to provide full and complete answers to the questions contained in part 1 of the Collision Statement of Case. The answers should descend to a reasonable level of particularity.

N5.7 The answers to the questions contained in part 1 are treated as admissions made by the party answering the questions and leave to amend such answers will be granted only in exceptional circumstances. As to the principles applicable to the amendment of particulars of claim in a collision claim reference should be made to the judgment of Gross J. in The Topaz [2003] 2 Lloyd's Rep 19.

N6 The early stages of a Limitation Claim

2A-134 N6.1 The procedure governing the early stages of a limitation claim differs significantly from the procedure relating to other claims and is contained in rule 61.11 and PD61 § 10.1.

N6.2 Service of a limitation claim form out of the jurisdiction is permitted in the circumstances identified in rule 61.11 (5) only and the procedure set out in Appendix 15 of the Guide should be adapted accordingly.

N7 Issue of documents when the Registry is closed.

2A-135 N7.1 When the Registry is closed (and only when it is closed) an Admiralty claim

Paragraph numbers marked with a "+" can be found online and on CD.

form may be issued on the following designated fax machine: 020 7947 6245 and only on that machine.

N7.2 The procedure to be followed is set out in Appendix 3 of the Guide.

N7.3 The issue of an Admiralty claim form in accordance with the procedure set out in Appendix 3 shall have the same effect for all purposes as a claim form issued in accordance with the relevant provisions of rule 61 and PD61.

N7.4 When the Registry is closed (and only when it is closed) a notice requesting a caution against release may be filed on the following designated fax machine: 020 7947 6245 and only on that machine. This machine is manned 24 hours a day by court security staff (telephone 020 7947 6260).

N7.5 The notice requesting the caution should be transmitted with a note in the following form for ease of identification by security staff:
   "CAUTION AGAINST RELEASE
   Please find notice requesting caution against release of the ... (*name ship/identify cargo*) ... for filing in the Admiralty & Commercial Registry."

N7.6 The notice must be in Admiralty Form No. **ADM11** and signed by a solicitor acting on behalf of the applicant.

N7.7 Subject to the provisions of sections N7.9 and N7.10 below, the filing of the notice takes place when the fax is recorded as having been received.

N7.8 When the Registry is next open to the public, the filing solicitor or his agent shall attend and deliver to the Registry the document which was transmitted by fax together with the transmission report. Upon satisfying himself that the document delivered fully accords with the document received by the Registry, the court officer shall stamp the document delivered with the time and date on which the notice was received, enter the same in the caution register and retain the same with the faxed copy.

N7.9 Unless otherwise ordered by the court, the stamped notice shall be conclusive proof that the notice was filed at the time and on the date stated.

N7.10 If the filing solicitor does not comply with the foregoing procedure, or if the notice is not stamped, the notice shall be deemed never to have been filed.

N8 Case Management

N8.1 The case management provisions of the Guide apply to Admiralty claims save **2A–136** that:
   (i) In Admiralty claims the case management provisions of the Guide are supplemented by PD61 § § 2.1–2.3 which make provision for the early classification and streaming of cases;
   (ii) In a collision case the claimant should apply for a case management conference within 7 days after the last Collision Statement of Case is filed;
   (iii) In a limitation claim where the right to limit is not admitted and the claimant seeks a general limitation decree, the claimant must, within 7 days after the date of the filing of the defence of the defendant last served or the expiry of the time for doing so, apply to the Admiralty Registrar for a case management conference: **PD61 § 10.7**;
   (iv) In a collision claim or a limitation claim a mandatory case management conference will normally take place on the first available date 5 weeks after the date when the claimant is required to take steps to fix a date for the case management conference;
   (v) In a limitation claim, case management directions are initially given by the Registrar: **PD61 § 10.8**;
   (vi) In the Admiralty Court, the Case Management Information Sheet should be in the form in Appendix 6 of this Guide but should also include the following questions:–

Paragraph numbers marked with a "+" can be found online and on CD.

COMMERCIAL COURTS

   1. Do any of the issues contained in the List of Issues involve questions of navigation or other particular matters of an essentially Admiralty nature which require the trial to be before the Admiralty Judge?
   2. Is the case suitable to be tried before a Deputy Judge nominated by the Admiralty Judge?
   3. Do you consider that the court should sit with nautical or other assessors? If you intend to ask that the court sit with one or more assessors who is not a Trinity Master, please state the reasons for such an application.

N8.2 The two judge team system referred to in section D.4 of the Guide does not apply to Admiralty claims.

N9 Evidence

2A–137 N9.1 In collision claims, section H1.5 and Appendix 8 are subject to the proviso that experience has shown that it is usually desirable for the main elements of a witness' evidence in chief to be adduced orally.

Authenticity

N9.2

(a) Where the authenticity of any document disclosed to a party is not admitted, that party must serve notice that the document must be proved at trial in accordance with CPR 32.19. Such notice must be served by the latest date for serving witness statements or within 7 days of disclosure of the document, whichever is later.

(b) Where, apart from the authenticity of the document itself, the date upon which a document or an entry in it is stated to have been made or the person by whom the document states that it or any entry in it was made or any other feature of the document is to be challenged at the trial on grounds which may require a witness to be called at the trial to support the contents of the document, such challenge

   (i) must be raised in good time in advance of the trial to enable such witness or witnesses to be called;
   (ii) the grounds of challenge must be explicitly identified in the skeleton argument or outline submissions in advance of the trial.

(c) Where, due to the late disclosure of a document it or its contents or character cannot practicably be challenged within the time limits prescribed in (a) or (b), the challenge may only be raised with the permission of the court and having regard to the Overriding Objective (CPR 1.1).

Skeleton arguments in Collision Claims

N9.3 In collision claims the skeleton argument of each party must be accompanied by a plot or plots of that party's case or alternative cases as to the navigation of vessels during and leading to the collision. All plots must contain a sufficient indication of the assumptions used in the preparation of the plot.

N10 Split trials, accounts, enquiries and enforcement

2A–138 N10.1 In collision claims it is usual for liability to be tried first and for the assessment of damages and interest to be referred to the Admiralty Registrar.

N10.2 Where the Admiralty Court refers an account, enquiry or enforcement, it will usually refer the matter to the Admiralty Registrar.

N11 Release of vessels out of hours

2A–139 N11.1 This section makes provision for release from arrest when the Registry is closed.

N11.2 An application for release under rule 61.8(4)(c) or (d) may, when the Registry is closed, be made in, and only in, the following manner:

Paragraph numbers marked with a "+" can be found online and on CD.

(i) The solicitor for the arrestor or the other party applying must telephone the security staff at the Royal Courts of Justice (020 7947 6260) and ask to be contacted by the Admiralty Marshal, who will then respond as soon as practicably possible;

(ii) Upon being contacted by the Admiralty Marshal the solicitor must give oral instructions for the release and an oral undertaking to pay the fees and expenses of the Admiralty Marshal as required in Form No. **ADM12**;

(iii) The arrestor or other party applying must then send a written request and undertaking on Form No. **ADM12** by fax to a number given by the Admiralty Marshal;

(iv) The solicitor must provide written consent to the release from all persons who have entered cautions against release (and from the arrestor if the arrestor is not the party applying) by sending such consents by fax to the number supplied by the Admiralty Marshal;

(v) Upon the Admiralty Marshal being satisfied that no cautions against release are in force, or that all persons who have entered cautions against release, and if necessary the arrestor, have given their written consent to the release, the Admiralty Marshal shall effect the release as soon as practicable.

N11.3 Practitioners should note that the Admiralty Marshal is not formally on call and therefore at times may not be available to assist. Similarly the practicalities of releasing a ship in some localities may involve the services of others who may not be available outside court hours.

N11.4 This service is offered to practitioners for use during reasonable hours and on the basis that if the Admiralty Marshal is available and can be contacted he will use his best endeavours to effect instructions to release but without guarantee as to their success.

N12 Use of postal facilities in the Registry

N12.1 Applications together with the requisite documents may be posted to:

2A–140

The Admiralty and Commercial Registry,

Room EB15,

Royal Courts of Justice,

Strand,

London WC2A 2LL.

N12.2 In addition to the classes of business for which the use of postal facilities is permitted by the CPR or the Commercial Court Guide, the filing of the following classes of documents is also permitted in Admiralty matters:

(i) Requests for cautions;

(ii) Collision Statements of Case.

N12.3

(a) Documents sent by post for filing must be accompanied by two copies of a list of the documents sent and an envelope properly addressed to the sender.

(b) On receipt of the documents in the Registry, the court officer will, if the circumstances are such that had the documents been presented personally they would have been filed, cause them to be filed and will, by post, notify the sender that this has been done. If the documents would not have been accepted if presented personally the court officer will not file them but will retain them in the Registry for collection by the sender and will, by post, so inform the sender.

(c) When documents received through the post are filed by the court officer they will be sealed and entered as filed on the date on which they were received in the Registry.

Paragraph numbers marked with a "+" can be found online and on CD.

COMMERCIAL COURTS

N13 Insurance of arrested property

2A–141 N13.1 The Marshal will not insure any arrested property for the benefit of parties at any time during the period of arrest (whether before or after the lodging of an application for sale, if any).

N13.2 The Marshal will use his best endeavours (but without any legal liability for failure to do so) to advise all parties known to him as being on the record in actions in rem against the arrested property, including those who have filed cautions against release of that property, before any such property moves or is moved beyond the area covered by the usual port risks policy.

N13.3 In these circumstances, practitioners' attention is drawn to the necessity of considering the questions of insuring against port risks for the amount of their clients' interest in any property arrested in an Admiralty action and the inclusion in any policy of a "Held Covered" clause in case the ship moves or is moved outside the area covered by the usual port risks policy. The usual port risks policy provides, among other things, for a ship to be moved or towed from one berth to another up to a distance of five miles within the port where she is lying.

N14 Assessors

2A–142 14.1 In collision claims and other cases involving issues of navigation and seamanship, the Admiralty Court usually sits with assessors. The parties are not permitted to call expert evidence on such matters without the leave of the court: rule 61.13.

14.2 Parties are reminded of the practice with regard to the disclosure of any answers to the court's questions and the opportunity for comment on them as set out in the Judgment of Gross J. in The Global Mariner [2005] 1 Lloyd's Rep 699 at p702.

14.3 Provision is made in rule 35.15 for assessors' remuneration. The usual practice is for the court to seek an undertaking from the claimant to pay the remuneration on demand after the case has concluded.

O.

ARBITRATION

2A–143 ### O1 Arbitration claims

O1.1

(a) Applications to the court under the Arbitration Acts 1950–1996 and other applications relating to arbitrations are known as "arbitration claims".
(b) The procedure applicable to arbitration claims is to be found in Part 62 and its associated practice direction. Separate provision is made

  (i) by Section I for claims relating to arbitrations to which the Arbitration Act 1996 applies;
  (ii) by Section II for claims relating to arbitrations to which the Arbitration Acts 1950–1979 ("the old law") apply; and
  (iii) by Section III for enforcement proceedings.

(c) For a full definition of the expression "arbitration claim" see rule 62.2(1) (claims under the 1996 Act) and rule 62.11(2) (claims under the old law).
(d) Part 58 applies to arbitration claims in the Commercial Court insofar as no specific provision is made by Part 62: rule 62.1(3).

Claims under the Arbitration Act 1996

O2 Starting an arbitration claim

2A–144 O2.1 Subject to section O2.3 an arbitration claim must be started by the issue of an arbitration claim form in accordance with the Part 8 procedure: rule 62.3(1).

Paragraph numbers marked with a "+" can be found online and on CD.

O2.2 The claim form must be substantially in the form set out in Appendix A to practice direction 62: **PD62 § 2.2**.

O2.3 An application to stay proceedings under section 9 of the Arbitration Act 1996 must be made by application notice in the proceedings: rule 62.3(2).

O2.4 Where a question arises as to whether an arbitration agreement is null and void, inoperative or incapable of being performed the court may deal with it in the same way as provided by rule 62.8(3) which applies where a question arises as to whether an arbitration agreement has been concluded or the dispute which is the subject matter of the proceedings falls within the terms of such an agreement.

O3 The arbitration claim form

O3.1 The arbitration claim form must contain, among other things, a concise statement of the remedy claimed and, if an award is challenged, the grounds for that challenge: rule 62.4(1).

O3.2 Reference in the arbitration claim form to a witness statement or affidavit filed in support of the claim is not sufficient to comply with the requirements of rule 62.4(1).

O4 Service of the arbitration claim form

O4.1 An arbitration claim form issued in the Admiralty & Commercial Registry must be served by the claimant.

O4.2

(a) The rules governing service of the claim form are set out in Part 6 of the Civil Procedure Rules.
(b) Unless the court orders otherwise an arbitration claim form must be served on the defendant within 1 month from the date of issue: rule 62.4(2).

O4.3

(a) An arbitration claim form may be served out of the jurisdiction with the permission of the court: rule 62.5(1).
(b) Rules 6.24–6.29 apply to the service of an arbitration claim form out of the jurisdiction: rule 62.5(3).

O4.4 The court may exercise its powers under rule 6.8 to permit service of an arbitration claim form on a party at the address of the solicitor or other representative acting for him in the arbitration: **PD62 § 3.1**.

O4.5 The claimant must file a certificate of service within 7 days of serving the arbitration claim form: **PD62 § 3.2**.

O5 Acknowledgment of service

O5.1

(a) A defendant must file an acknowledgment of service of the arbitration claim form in every case: rule 58.6(1).
(b) An adapted version of practice form **N210** (acknowledgment of service of a Part 8 claim form) has been approved for use in the Commercial Court. A copy of this practice form (Form **N210(CC)**) is included at the end of the Guide, together with adapted versions of the notes for claimants and defendants on completing and replying to an arbitration claim form.

O5.2 The time for filing an acknowledgment of service is calculated from the service of the arbitration claim form.

Paragraph numbers marked with a "+" can be found online and on CD.

O6 *Standard directions*

O6.1 The directions set out in **PD62** **§ 6.2–6.7** apply unless the court orders otherwise.

O6.2 The claimant should apply for a hearing date as soon as possible after issuing an arbitration claim form or (in the case of an appeal) obtaining permission to appeal.

O6.3 A defendant who wishes to rely on evidence in opposition to the claim must file and serve his evidence within 21 days after the date by which he was required to acknowledge service: **PD62 § 6.2**.

O6.4 A claimant who wishes to rely on evidence in response to evidence served by the defendant must file and serve his evidence within 7 days after the service of the defendant's evidence: **PD62 § 6.3**.

O6.5 An application for directions in a pending arbitration claim should be made by application notice under Part 23. Where an arbitration application involves recognition and/or enforcement of an agreement to arbitrate and that application is challenged on the grounds that the parties to the application were not bound by an agreement to arbitrate, it will usually be necessary for the court to resolve that issue in order to determine the application. For this purpose it may be necessary for there to be disclosure of documents and/or factual and/or expert evidence. In that event, it is the responsibility of those advising the applicant to liaise with the other party and to arrange with the Listing Office for a case management conference to be listed as early as possible to enable the court to give directions as to the steps to be taken before the hearing of the application.

O7 *Interim remedies*

O7.1 An application for an interim remedy under section 44 of the Arbitration Act 1996 must be made in an arbitration claim form: **PD62 § 8.1**.

O8 Challenging the award

Challenge by way of appeal

2A–145 O8.1 A party wishing to appeal against the award of an arbitrator or umpire must set out in the arbitration claim form

    (i) the question of law on which the appeal is based; and

    (ii) a succinct statement of the grounds of appeal,

identifying the relevant part(s) of the award and reasons.

O8.2 If the appeal is brought with the agreement of the other parties to the proceedings, a copy of their agreement in writing must be filed with the arbitration claim form.

O8.3 A party seeking permission to appeal must

    (i) state in his arbitration claim form the grounds on which he contends that permission to appeal should be given **PD62 § 12.1**; and

    (ii) file and serve with the arbitration claim form any written evidence on which he wishes to rely for the purposes of satisfying the court of the matters referred to in section 69(3) of the 1996 Act: **PD62 § 12.2**.

O8.4

(a) If the defendant wishes to oppose the claimant's application for permission to appeal he must file a witness statement setting out

    (i) the grounds on which he opposes the grant of permission; and

Paragraph numbers marked with a "+" can be found online and on CD.

    (ii) any evidence on which he relies in relation to the matters mentioned in section 69(3) of the 1996 Act: **PD62 § § 12.3(1) & (2)**.

(b) If the defendant wishes to contend that the award should be upheld for reasons other than those expressed in the award, he must set out those reasons in his witness statement: **PD62 § 12.3(3)**.

O8.5 The court will normally determine applications for permission to appeal without an oral hearing. If the court considers that an oral hearing is required, it will give further directions as appropriate.

Challenging an award for serious irregularity

O8.6

(a) An arbitration claim challenging an award on the ground of serious irregularity under section 68 of the 1996 Act is appropriate only in cases where there are grounds for thinking

    (i) that an irregularity has occurred which

    (ii) has caused or will cause **substantial** injustice to the party making the challenge.

(b) An application challenging an award on the ground of serious irregularity should therefore not be regarded as an alternative to, or a means of supporting, an application for permission to appeal.

O8.7 The challenge to the award must be supported by evidence of the circumstances on which the claimant relies as giving rise to the irregularity complained of and the nature of the injustice which has been or will be caused to him.

O8.8 If the nature of the challenge itself or the evidence filed in support of it leads the court to consider that the claim has no real prospect of success, the court may exercise its powers under rule 3.3(4) to dismiss the application summarily. In such cases the applicant will have the right to apply to the court to set aside the order and to seek directions for the hearing of the application.

Multiple claims

O8.9 If the arbitration claim form includes both a challenge to an award by way of appeal and a challenge on the ground of serious irregularity, the applications should be set out in separate sections of the arbitration claim form and the grounds on which they are made separately identified.

O8.10 In such cases the papers will be placed before a judge to consider how the applications may most appropriately be disposed of. It is usually more appropriate to dispose of the application to set aside or remit the award before considering the application for permission to appeal.

O9 Time limits

O9.1 An application to challenge an award under sections 67 or 68 of the 1996 Act or **2A–146** to appeal under section 69 of the Act must be brought within 28 days of the date of the award: **see** section 70(3).

O9.2 The court has power to vary the period of 28 days fixed by section 70(3) of the 1996 Act: rule 62.9(1). However, it is important that any challenge to an award be pursued without delay and the court will require cogent reasons for extending time.

O9.3 An application to extend time made **before** the expiry of the period of 28 days must be made in a Part 23 application notice, but the application notice need not be served on any other party: rule 62.9(2) and **PD62 § 11.1(1)**.

O9.4 An application to extend time made **after** the expiry of the period of 28 days

Paragraph numbers marked with a "+" can be found online and on CD.

must be made in the arbitration claim form in which the applicant is seeking substantive relief: rule 62.9(3)(a).

O9.5 An application to vary the period of 28 days will normally be determined without a hearing and prior to the consideration of the substantive application: **PD62 § 10.2**.

Claims under the Arbitration Acts 1950–1979

O10 Starting an arbitration claim

2A-147
O10.1 Subject to section O10.2 an arbitration claim must be started by the issue of an arbitration claim form in accordance with the Part 8 procedure: rule 62.13(1).

O10.2 The claim form must be substantially in the form set out in Appendix A to PD62 § 2.2.

O10.3 An application to stay proceedings on the grounds of an arbitration agreement must be made by application notice in the proceedings: rule 62.13(2).

O11 The arbitration claim form

O11.1 An arbitration claim form must state the grounds of the claim or appeal: rule 62.15(5)(a).

O11.2 Reference in the arbitration claim form to the witness statement or affidavit filed in support of the claim is not sufficient to comply with the requirements of rule 62.15(5)(a).

O12 Service of the arbitration claim form

O12.1 An arbitration claim form issued in the Admiralty & Commercial Registry must be served by the claimant.

O12.2 The rules governing service of the claim form are set out in Part 6 of the Civil Procedure Rules.

O12.3

(a) An arbitration claim form may be served out of the jurisdiction with the permission of the court: rule 62.16(1).
(b) Rules 6.24–6.29 apply to the service of an arbitration claim form out of the jurisdiction: rule 62.16(4).

O12.4 Although not expressly covered by PD62, the court may in an appropriate case exercise its powers under rule 6.8 to permit service of an arbitration claim form on a party at the address of the solicitor or other representative acting for him in the arbitration.

O12.5 The claimant must file a certificate of service within 7 days of serving the claim form.

2A-148 Acknowledgment of service

O13.1

(a) A defendant must file an acknowledgment of service in every case: rule 58.6(1).
(b) An adapted version of practice form **N210** (acknowledgment of service of a Part 8 claim form) has been approved for use in the Commercial Court. A copy of this practice form (Form **N210(CC)**) is included at the end of the Guide, together with adapted versions of the notes for claimants and defendants on completing and replying to an arbitration claim form.

Paragraph numbers marked with a "+" can be found online and on CD.

O13.2 The time for filing an acknowledgment of service is calculated from the service of the arbitration claim form.

O14 Standard directions

O14.1 Where the claim or appeal is based on written evidence, a copy of that evidence must be served with the arbitration claim form: rule 62.15(5)(b).

O14.2 Where the claim or appeal is made with the consent of the arbitrator or umpire or other parties, a copy of every written consent must be served with the arbitration claim form: rule 62.15(5)(c).

O14.3 An application for directions in a pending arbitration claim should be made by application notice under Part 23.

O15 Interim remedies

O15.1 An application for an interim remedy under section 12(6) of the 1950 Act must be made in accordance with Part 25.

O15.2 The application must be made by arbitration claim form.

O15.3 A claim under section 12(4) of the 1950 Act for an order for the issue of a witness summons to compel the attendance of a witness before an arbitrator or umpire where the attendance of the witness is required within the district of a District Registry may be started in that Registry: rule 62.14.

O16 Challenging the award

Challenge by way of appeal

O16.1 A party wishing to appeal against the award of an arbitrator or umpire must **2A-149** file and serve with the arbitration claim form a statement of the grounds for the appeal, specifying the relevant part(s) of the award and reasons: rule 62.15(6).

O16.2 A party seeking permission to appeal must also file and serve with the arbitration claim form any written evidence in support of the contention that the question of law concerns a term of the contract or an event which is not "one off": rule 62.15(6).

O16.3 Any written evidence in reply must be filed and served not less than 2 days before the hearing of the application for permission to appeal: rule 62.15(7).

O16.4 A party who wishes to contend that the award should be upheld for reasons other than those set out in the award and reasons must file and serve on the claimant a notice specifying the grounds of his contention not less than 2 days before the hearing of the application for permission to appeal: rule 62.15(8).

O16.5 Applications for permission to appeal will be heard orally, but will not normally be listed for longer than half an hour. Skeleton arguments should be lodged.

Claims to set aside or remit the award

O16.6 A claim to set aside or remit an award on the grounds of misconduct should not be regarded as an alternative to, or a means of supporting, an application for permission to appeal.

O16.7 The directions set out in PD62 § § 6.2–6.7 should be followed unless the court orders otherwise.

Multiple claims

O16.8 If the arbitration claim form includes both an appeal and an application to set aside or remit the award, the applications should be set out in separate sections of the arbitration claim form and the grounds on which they are made separately identified.

Paragraph numbers marked with a "+" can be found online and on CD.

COMMERCIAL COURTS

O16.9 The court may direct that one application be heard before the other or may direct that they be heard together, as may be appropriate. It is usually more appropriate to dispose of the application to set aside or remit the award before considering the application for permission to appeal.

2A–150 **O17 Time limits**

O17.1

(a) Time limits governing claims under the 1950 and 1979 Acts are set out in rule 62.15.

(b) Different time limits apply to different claims. **It is important to consult** rule 62.15 **to ensure that applications are made within the time prescribed.**

(c) The court has power under rule 3.1(2) to vary the time limits prescribed by rule 62.15, but will require cogent reasons for doing so.

Provisions applicable to all arbitrations

Enforcement of awards

2A–151 O18.1 All applications for permission to enforce awards are governed by Section III of Part 62, rule 62.17.

O18.2 An application for permission to enforce an award in the same manner as a judgment may be made without notice, but the court may direct that the arbitration claim form be served, in which case the application will continue as an arbitration claim in accordance with the procedure set out in Section I: rule 62.18(1)–(3).

O18.3 An application for permission to enforce an award in the same manner as a judgment must be supported written evidence in accordance with rule 62.18(6).

O18.4

(a) Two copies of the draft order must accompany the application.

(b) If the claimant wishes to enter judgment, the form of the judgment must correspond to the terms of the award.

(c) The defendant has the right to apply to the court to set aside an order made without notice giving permission to enforce the award and the order itself must state in terms

    (i) that the defendant may apply to set it aside within 14 days after service of the order or, if the order is to be served out of the jurisdiction, within such other period as the court may set; and

    (ii) that it may not be enforced until after the end of that period or any application by the defendant to set it aside has been finally disposed of: rule 62.18(9) & (10).

Matters of general application

O19 Transfer of arbitration claims

2A–152 O19.1 An arbitration claim which raises no significant point of arbitration law or practice will normally be transferred

    (i) if a rent-review arbitration, to the Chancery Division;

    (ii) if a construction or engineering arbitration, to the Technology and Construction Court;

    (iii) if an employment arbitration, to the Central London County Court Mercantile List.

O19.2 Salvage arbitrations will normally be transferred to the Admiralty Court.

O20 Appointment of a Commercial Judge as sole arbitrator or umpire

O20.1 Section 93 of the Arbitration Act 1996 provides for the appointment of a

Paragraph numbers marked with a "+" can be found online and on CD.

Commercial Judge as sole arbitrator or umpire. The Act limits the circumstances in which a Judge may accept such an appointment.

O20.2 Enquiries should be directed to the Judge in charge of the Commercial List or the Clerk to the Commercial Court.

P.

MISCELLANEOUS

P1 Out of hours emergency arrangements

P1.1

(a) When the Listing Office is closed, solicitors or counsel's clerks should in an emergency contact the Clerk to the Queen's Bench Judge in Chambers by telephone through the security desk at the Royal Courts of Justice: **PD58 § 2.2**.
(b) The telephone number of the security desk is included in the list of addresses and contact details at the end of the Guide.

P1.2 When the Listing Office is closed an urgent hearing will initially be dealt with by the Queen's Bench Judge in Chambers who may dispose of the application himself or make orders allowing the matter to come before a Commercial Judge at the first available opportunity.

P2 Index of decisions of the Commercial and Admiralty Courts

P2.1 An Index has been prepared on a subject-matter basis of unreported Commercial Court and Admiralty Court judgments from 1995 onwards. The Index is updated regularly.

P2.2 The Index is provided as a service to litigants and to the legal profession, and to assist the Commercial Court and the Admiralty Court to maintain reasonable consistency of approach in those areas of law and procedure most frequently before them.

P2.3 The index of Judgments of Commercial Court and Admiralty Court of England and Wales is available to all Internet users and can be found at: www.hmcourts-service.gov.uk/infoabout/admiralcomm/index.htm via the link to "Searchable index of court cases" (at bottom of the box on right hand side of Commercial Court and Admiralty Court). The Index is also available at the BAILII website and can be found at www.bailii.org/cgi-bin/summaries.cgi?index=comm

P2.4 The judgments referred to in the Index are kept in the Registry. They may be consulted there.

P2.5 Copies of the judgments referred to in the Index may be obtained from the Registry (or where there is difficulty, from the clerk to the judge) unless the judgment is in the form of a transcript, in which case copies should be obtained from the shorthand writers or other transcript agency.

APPENDIX 1

Part 58 (Commercial Court)—reproduced at paras 2A–1 *et seq.*
Part 61 (Admiralty Court)—reproduced at paras 2D–1 *et seq.*
Practice Direction to Part 58—reproduced at paras 2A–22 *et seq.*
Practice Direction to Part 61—reproduced at paras 2D–86 *et seq.*

APPENDIX 2

Part 62 (Arbitration)—reproduced at paras 2E–1 *et seq.*
Practice Direction to Part 62—reproduced at paras 2E–46 *et seq.*

APPENDIX 3

PROCEDURE FOR ISSUE OF CLAIM FORM WHEN REGISTRY CLOSED

(See generally sections B3.11 and B4.4 of the Guide.)

Paragraph numbers marked with a "+" can be found online and on CD.

2A–153

2A–154

2A–155

2A–156

2A–157

Procedure

The procedure is as follows:

1. The claim form must be signed by a solicitor acting on behalf of the claimant, and must not require the permission of the Court for its issue (unless such permission has already been given).

2. The solicitor causing the claim form to be issued ("the issuing solicitor") must

(i) endorse on the claim form the endorsement shown below and sign that endorsement;

(ii) send a copy of the claim form so endorsed to the Registry by fax for issue under this section; and

(iii) when he has received a transmission report stating that the transmission of the claim form to the Registry was completed in full and the time and the date of the transmission, complete and sign the certificate shown below.

3. When the Registry is next open to the public after the issue of a claim form in accordance with this procedure the issuing solicitor or his agent shall attend and deliver to the Registry the document which was transmitted by fax (including the endorsement and the certificate), or if that document has been served, a true and certified copy of it, together with as many copies as the Registry shall require and the transmission report.

4. When the proper officer at the Registry has checked and is satisfied that the document delivered under paragraph 3 fully accords with the document received under paragraph 2, and that all proper fees for issue have been paid, he shall allocate a number to the case, and seal, mark as "original" and date the claim form with the date on which it was issued (being, as indicated below, the date when the fax is recorded at the Registry as having been received).

5. As soon as practicable thereafter the issuing solicitor shall inform any person served with the unsealed claim form of the case number, and (on request) shall serve any such person with a copy of the claim form sealed and dated under paragraph 4 above (at such address in England and Wales as the person may request) and the person may, without paying a fee, inspect and take copies of the documents lodged at the Registry under paragraphs 2 and 3 above.

Effect of issue following request by fax

2A–158   The issue of a claim form in accordance with this procedure takes place when the fax is recorded at the Registry as having been received, and the claim form bearing the endorsement shall have the same effect for all purposes as a claim form issued under CPR Part 7 [or 8, as the case may be]. Unless otherwise ordered the sealed version of the claim form retained by the Registry shall be conclusive proof that the claim form was issued at the time and on the date stated. If the procedure set out in this Appendix is not complied with, the court may declare (on its own initiative or on application) that the claim form shall be treated as not having been issued.

Endorsement

2A–159   A claim form issued pursuant to a request by fax must be endorsed as follows:

"1. This claim form is issued under section B3.11/B4.4 of the Commercial Court Guide and may be served notwithstanding that it does not bear the seal of the Court.

2. A true copy of this claim form and endorsement has been transmitted to the Admiralty and Commercial Registry, Royal Courts of Justice, Strand, London WC2A 2LL, at the time and date certified below by the undersigned solicitor.

3. It is the duty of the undersigned solicitor or his agent to attend at the Registry when it is next open to the public for the claim form to be sealed.

4. Any person upon whom this unsealed claim form is served will be notified by the undersigned solicitor of the number of the case and may require the undersigned solicitor to serve a copy of the sealed claim form at an address in

Paragraph numbers marked with a "+" can be found online and on CD.

England and Wales and may inspect without charge the documents which have been lodged at the Registry by the undersigned solicitor.

5. I, the undersigned solicitor, undertake to the Court, to the defendants named in this claim form, and to any other person upon whom this claim form may be served:

(i) that the statement in paragraph 2 above is correct;

(ii) that the time and date given in the certificate at the foot of this endorsement are correct;

(iii) that this claim form is a claim form which may be issued under section B3.11 (or B4.4, as the case may be) of the Commercial Court Guide;

(iv) that I will comply in all respects with the requirements of section B3.11/B4.4 of the Commercial Court Guide;

(v) that I will indemnify any person served with the claim form before it is sealed against any loss suffered as a result of the claim form being or becoming invalid in accordance with section B3.11/B4.4 of the Commercial Court Guide.

(Signed)

Solicitor for the claimant"

[**Note**: the endorsement may be signed in the name of the firm of solicitors rather than an individual solicitor, or by solicitors' agents in their capacity as agents acting on behalf of their professional clients.]

Certificate

A solicitor who causes a claim form to be issued pursuant to a request sent by fax **2A–160** must sign a certificate in the following form:

"I, the undersigned solicitor, certify that I have received a transmission report confirming that the transmission of a copy of this claim form to the Registry by fax was fully completed and that the time and date of transmission to the Registry were *[enter the time and date shown on the transmission report]*.

Dated

(Signed)

Solicitor for the claimant."

[**Note**: the certificate may be signed in the name of the firm of solicitors rather than an individual solicitor, or by solicitors' agents in their capacity as agents acting on behalf of their professional clients]

APPENDIX 4

STATEMENTS OF CASE

The following principles apply to all statements of case and should, as far as pos- **2A–161** sible, also be observed when drafting a Part 8 claim form, which will not contain, or be followed by, particulars of claim:

1. The document must be as brief and concise as possible.

2. The document must be set out in separate consecutively numbered paragraphs and sub-paragraphs.

3. So far as possible each paragraph or sub-paragraph should contain no more than one allegation.

4. The document must deal with the case on a point by point basis to allow a point by point response.

5. Where particulars are given of any allegation or reasons given for a denial, the allegation or denial should be stated first and the particulars or reasons for it listed one by one in separate numbered sub-paragraphs.

6. A party wishing to advance a positive case should set that case out in the document; a simple denial is not sufficient.

7. Any matter which, if not stated, might take another party by surprise should be stated.

Paragraph numbers marked with a "+" can be found online and on CD.

8. Where they will assist:

    (i) headings should be used; and

    (ii) abbreviations and definitions should be established and used, and a glossary annexed.

9. Contentious headings, abbreviations and definitions should not be used. Every effort should be made to ensure that headings, abbreviations and definitions are in a form that will enable them to be adopted without issue by the other parties.

10. Particulars of primary allegations should be stated as particulars and not as primary allegations.

11. If it is necessary to rely upon a substantial amount of detailed factual information or lengthy particulars in support of an allegation, these should be set out in schedules or appendices.

12. Particular care should be taken to set out only those factual allegations which are necessary to support the case. Evidence should not be included.

13. A response to particulars set out in a schedule should be set out in a corresponding schedule.

14. If it is necessary for the proper understanding of the statement of case to include substantial parts of a lengthy document the passages in question should be set out in a schedule rather than in the body of the case.

15. Contentious paraphrasing should be avoided.

16. The document must be signed by the individual person or persons who drafted it, not, in the case of a solicitor, in the name of the firm alone.

APPENDIX 5

FORMS OF SEARCH ORDER AND FREEZING INJUNCTION

2A-162 Note that the most up-to-date version of these forms can be found in the Civil Procedure Forms Volume.

APPENDIX 6

CASE MANAGEMENT INFORMATION SHEET

2A-163 Party lodging information sheet:

Name of solicitors:

Name(s) of advocates for trial:

[Note: This Sheet should normally be completed with the involvement of the advocate(s) instructed for trial. If the claimant is a litigant in person this fact should be noted at the foot of the sheet and proposals made as to which party is to have responsibility for the preparation and upkeep of the case management bundle.]

(1) By what date can you give standard disclosure?

(2) In relation to standard disclosure, do you contend in relation to any category or class of document under rule 31.6(b) that to search for that category or class would be unreasonable? If so, what is the category or class and on what grounds do you so contend?

(3) Is specific disclosure required on any issue? If so, please specify.

(4) By what dates can you (a) give specific disclosure or (b) comply with a special disclosure order?

Paragraph numbers marked with a "+" can be found online and on CD.

(5) May the time periods for inspection at rule 31.15 require adjustment, and if so by how much?

(6) Are amendments to or is information about any statement of case required? If yes, please give brief details of what is required.

(7) Can you make any additional admissions? If yes, please give brief details of the additional admissions.

(8) Are any of the issues in the case suitable for trial as preliminary issues?

(9) (a) On the evidence of how many witnesses of fact do you intend to rely at trial (subject to the directions of the Court)? Please give their names, or explain why this is not being done.

(b) By what date can you serve signed witness statements?

(c) How many of these witnesses of fact do you intend to call to give oral evidence at trial (subject to the directions of the Court)? Please give their names, or explain why this is not being done.

(d) Will interpreters be required for any witness?

(e) Do you wish any witness to give oral evidence by video link? Please give his or her name, or explain why this is not being done. Please state the country and city from which the witness will be asked to give evidence by video link.

(10) (a) On what issues may expert evidence be required?

(b) Is this a case in which the use of a single joint expert might be suitable (see rule 35.7)?

(c) On the evidence of how many expert witnesses do you intend to rely at trial (subject to the directions of the Court)? Please give their names, or explain why this is not being done. Please identify each expert's field of expertise.

(d) By what date can you serve signed expert reports?

(e) When will the experts be available for a meeting or meetings of experts?

(f) How many of these expert witnesses do you intend to call to give oral evidence at trial (subject to the directions of the Court)? Please give their names, or explain why this is not being done.

(g) Will interpreters be required for any expert witness?

(h) Do you wish any expert witness to give oral evidence by video link? Please give his or her name, or explain why this is not being done. Please state the country and city from which the witness will be asked to give evidence by video link.

(11) What are the advocates' present provisional estimates of the minimum and maximum lengths of the trial?

(12) What is the earliest date by which you believe you can be ready for trial?

(13) Is this a case in which a pre-trial review is likely to be useful?

(14) Is there any way in which the Court can assist the parties to resolve their dispute or particular issues in it without the need for a trial or a full trial?

(15) (a) Might some form of Alternative Dispute Resolution procedure assist to resolve or narrow the dispute or particular issues in it?

Paragraph numbers marked with a "+" can be found online and on CD.

(b) Has the question at (a) been considered between the client and legal representatives (including the advocate(s) retained)?

(c) Has the question at (a) been explored with the other parties in the case?

(d) Do you request that the case is adjourned while the parties try to settle the case by Alternative Dispute Resolution or other means?

(e) Would an ADR order in the form of Appendix 7 to the Commercial Court Guide be appropriate?

(f) Are any other special directions needed to allow for Alternative Dispute Resolution?

(16) What other applications will you wish to make at the Case Management Conference?

(17) Does provision need to be made in the pre-trial timetable for any application or procedural step not otherwise dealt with above? If yes, please specify the application or procedural step.

(18) Are there, or are there likely in due course to be, any related proceedings (e.g. a Part 20 claim)? Please give brief details.

[Signature of solicitors]

Note: This information sheet must be lodged with the Clerk to the Commercial Court at least 7 days before the Case Management Conference (with a copy to all other parties): see section D8.5 of the Commercial Court Guide.

APPENDIX 7

DRAFT ADR ORDER

2A–164 1. On or before [*] the parties shall exchange lists of 3 neutral individuals who are available to conduct ADR procedures in this case prior to [*]. Each party may [in addition] [in the alternative] provide a list identifying the constitution of one or more panels of neutral individuals who are available to conduct ADR procedures in this case prior to [*].

2. On or before [*] the parties shall in good faith endeavour to agree a neutral individual or panel from the lists so exchanged and provided.

3. Failing such agreement by [*] the Case Management Conference will be restored to enable the Court to facilitate agreement on a neutral individual or panel:

4. The parties shall take such serious steps as they may be advised to resolve their disputes by ADR procedures before the neutral individual or panel so chosen by no later than [*].

5. If the case is not finally settled, the parties shall inform the Court by letter prior to [disclosure of documents/exchange of witness statements/exchange of experts' reports] what steps towards ADR have been taken and (without prejudice to matters of privilege) why such steps have failed. If the parties have failed to initiate ADR procedures the Case Management Conference is to be restored for further consideration of the case.

6. [Costs].

Note: The term "ADR procedures" is deliberately used in the draft ADR order. This is in order to emphasise that (save where otherwise provided) the parties are free to use the ADR procedure that they regard as most suitable, be it mediation, early neutral evaluation, non-binding arbitration etc.

Paragraph numbers marked with a "+" can be found online and on CD.

APPENDIX 8

STANDARD PRE-TRIAL TIMETABLE

1. [Standard disclosure is to be made by [*], with inspection [*] days after notice.]   **2A–165**

2. Signed statements of witnesses of fact, and hearsay notices where required by rule 33.2, are to be exchanged not later than [*].

3. Unless otherwise ordered, witness statements are to stand as the evidence in chief of the witness at trial.

4. Signed reports of experts
   (i) are to be confined to one expert for each party from each of the following fields of expertise: [*];
   (ii) are to be confined to the following issues: [*];
   (iii) are to be exchanged [sequentially/simultaneously];
   (iv) are to be exchanged not later than [date or dates for each report in each field of expertise].

5. Meeting of experts
   (i) The meeting of experts is to be by [*];
   (ii) The joint memorandum of the experts is to be completed by [*];
   (iii) Any short supplemental expert reports are to be exchanged [sequentially/simultaneously] by not later than [date or dates for each supplemental report].

6. [If the experts' reports cannot be agreed, the parties are to be at liberty to call expert witnesses at the trial, limited to those experts whose reports have been exchanged pursuant to 4. above.]

[Or: The parties are to be at liberty to apply to call as expert witnesses at the trial those experts whose reports they have exchanged pursuant to 4. above, such application to be made not earlier than [*] and not later than [*].]

7. Preparation of trial bundles to be completed in accordance with Appendix 10 to the Commercial Court Guide by not later than [*].

8. The provisional estimated length of the trial is [*].

9. Within [*] days the parties are to attend on the Clerk to the Commercial Court to fix the date for trial which shall be not before [*].

10. The progress monitoring date is [*]. Each party is to lodge a completed progress monitoring information sheet with the Clerk to the Commercial Court at least 3 days before the progress monitoring date (with a copy to all other parties).

11. Each party is to lodge a completed pre-trial checklist not later than 3 weeks before the date fixed for trial.

12. [There is to be a pre-trial review not earlier than [*] and not later than [*]].

13. Save as varied by this order or further order, the practice and procedures set out in the Admiralty & Commercial Courts Guide are to be followed.

14. Costs in the case.

15. Liberty to restore the Case Management Conference.

Paragraph numbers marked with a "+" can be found online and on CD.

APPENDIX 9

SKELETON ARGUMENTS, CHRONOLOGIES AND INDICES

Part 1 Skeleton arguments

2A–166   1. A skeleton argument is intended to identify both for the parties and the court those points which are, and are not, in issue and the nature of the argument in relation to those points that are in issue. It is not a substitute for oral argument.

2. Skeleton arguments must therefore
     (a) identify concisely:
         (i) the nature of the case generally and the background facts insofar as they are relevant to the matter before the court;
         (ii) the propositions of law relied on with references to the relevant authorities;
         (iii) the submissions of fact to be made with references to the evidence;
     (b) be in numbered paragraphs and state the name of the advocate(s) who prepared them; and
     (c) should avoid arguing the case at length.

Part 2 Chronologies and indices

2A–167   3. As far as possible chronologies and indices should not be prepared in a tendentious form. The ideal is that the court and the parties should have a single point of reference that all find useful and are happy to work with.

4. Where there is disagreement about a particular event or description, it is useful if that fact is indicated in neutral terms and the competing versions shortly stated.

5. If time and circumstances allow its preparation, a chronology or index to which all parties have contributed and agreed can be invaluable.

6. Chronologies and indices once prepared can be easily updated and are of continuing usefulness throughout the life of the case.

APPENDIX 10

PREPARATION OF BUNDLES

2A–168   1. The preparation of bundles requires a high level of co-operation between legal representatives for all parties. It is the duty of all legal representatives to co-operate to this high level.

2. Bundles should be prepared as follows:
     (i) No more than one copy of any one document should be included, unless there is good reason for doing otherwise;
     (ii) Contemporaneous documents, and correspondence, should be included in chronological order;
     (iii) Where a contract or similar document is central to the case it may be included in a separate place provided that a page is inserted in the chronological run of documents to indicate
         (A) the place the contract or similar document would have appeared had it appeared chronologically and
         (B) where it may be found instead;
     (iv) Documents in manuscript, or not fully legible, should be transcribed; the transcription should be marked and placed adjacent to the document transcribed;
     (v) Documents in a foreign language should be translated; the translation should be marked and placed adjacent to the document transcribed; the translation should be agreed, or, if it cannot be agreed, each party's proposed translation should be included;
     (vi) If a document has to be read across rather than down the page, it should be so placed in the bundle as to ensure that the top of the text is nearest the spine;
     (vii) **No bundle should contain more than 300 pages;**
     (viii) Bundles should not be overfilled, and should allow sufficient room for later insertions. Subject to this, the size of file used should not be a size that is larger than necessary for the present and anticipated contents;

Paragraph numbers marked with a "+" can be found online and on CD.

(ix) Bundles should be paginated, in the bottom right hand corner and in a form that can clearly be distinguished from any existing pagination on the document;

(x) Bundles should be indexed, save that a chronological bundle of contemporaneous documents need not be indexed if an index is unlikely to be useful;

(xi) Bundles should be numbered and named on the outside and on the inside front cover, the label to include the short title of the case, and a description of the bundle (including its number, where relevant).

3. Documents within bundles should be marked as follows:

(i) When copy documents from exhibits have been included in the bundle(s), then unless clearly unnecessary, the copy of the affidavit or witness statement to which the documents were exhibited should be marked in the right hand margin (in manuscript if need be) to show where the document referred to may be found in the bundle(s).

(ii) Unless clearly unnecessary, where copy documents in a bundle are taken from the disclosure of more than one party the documents should be marked in the top right hand corner (in manuscript if need be) to show from which party's disclosure the copy document has been taken;

(iii) Where there is a reference in a statement of case or witness statement to a document which is contained in the trial bundles a note should be made in the margin (if necessary in manuscript) identifying the place where that document is to be found. Unless otherwise agreed this is the responsibility of the party tendering the statement of case or witness statement.

4. For the trial a handy-sized core bundle should normally be provided containing the really important documents in the case. The documents in this bundle should be paginated, but each page should also bear its bundle and page number reference in the main bundles. It is particularly important to allow sufficient room for later insertions (see paragraph 2(viii) above).

5. Large documents, such as plans, should be placed in an easily accessible file.

6.

(a) When agreeing bundles for trial, legal representatives should bear in mind the effect of the Civil Evidence Act 1995 and of rules 33.2(3) (notice requiring proof of authenticity) and 32.19 (hearsay notices).

(b) Pursuant to those provisions, documents which have not been the subject of a notice served in accordance with rule 32.19(2) (requiring proof of authenticity) will be admissible as evidence of the truth of their contents even if there has been non-compliance with the notice requirements of s. 2(1) of the 1995 Act and rule 33.2 (see s. 2(4) of the Act). Accordingly, save for documents in respect of which there has been a timely notice to prove authenticity, all documents in the trial bundle will be admissible in evidence without more.

(c) The fact that documents in the trial bundle are admissible in evidence does not mean that all such documents form part of the evidence in the trial. It is the trial advocate's responsibility to indicate clearly to the court before closing his or her case the written evidence which forms part of that case. This should be done in the written opening statement or in the oral opening statement if the document is then available. Documents which have not previously been put in evidence before the closure of the parties' cases should not normally be referred to as evidence in the course of final speeches.

APPENDIX 11

EXPERT EVIDENCE—REQUIREMENTS OF GENERAL APPLICATION

1. It is the duty of an expert to help the court on the matters within his expertise: **2A–169** rule 35.3(1). This duty is paramount and overrides any obligation to the person from whom the expert has received instructions or by whom he is paid: rule 35.3(2).

2. Expert evidence presented to the court should be, and should be seen to be, the independent product of the expert uninfluenced by the pressures of litigation.

Paragraph numbers marked with a "+" can be found online and on CD.

3. An expert witness should provide independent assistance to the court by way of objective unbiased opinion in relation to matters within his expertise. An expert witness should never assume the role of an advocate.

4. An expert witness should not omit to consider material facts which could detract from his concluded opinion.

5. An expert witness should make it clear when a particular question or issue falls outside his expertise.

6. If an expert's opinion is not properly researched because he considers that insufficient data is available, this must be stated in his report with an indication that the opinion is no more than a provisional one.

7. In a case where an expert witness who has prepared a report is unable to confirm that the report contains the truth, the whole truth and nothing but the truth without some qualification, that qualification must be stated in the report.

8. If, after exchange of reports, an expert witness changes his view on a material matter having read another expert's report or for any other reason, such change of view should be communicated in writing (through the party's legal representatives) to the other side without delay, and when appropriate to the court.

Appendix 12

Progress Monitoring Information Sheet

2A–170   **The information supplied should be printed in bold characters**

[SHORT TITLE OF CASE and FOLIO NUMBER]
Fixed trial date/provisional range of dates for trial specified in the pre-trial timetable:
Party lodging information sheet:
Name of solicitors:
Name(s) of advocates for trial:
[Note: this information sheet should normally be completed with the involvement of the advocate(s) instructed for trial]
    (1) Have you complied with the pre-trial timetable in all respects?
    (2) If you have not complied, in what respects have you not complied?
    (3) Will you be ready for a trial commencing on the fixed date (or, where applicable, within the provisional range of dates) specified in the pre-trial timetable?
    (4) If you will not be ready, why will you not be ready?
    [*Signature of solicitors*]
Note: This information sheet must be lodged with the Case Management Unit at least 3 days before the progress monitoring date (with a copy to all other parties): see section D12.2 of the Guide.

Appendix 13

Pre-Trial Checklist

2A–171   **The information supplied should be printed in bold characters**

[SHORT TITLE OF CASE and FOLIO NUMBER]
a. Trial date:
b. Party lodging checklist:
c. Name of solicitors:
d. Name(s) of advocates for trial:
[**Note**: this checklist should normally be completed with the involvement of the advocate(s) instructed for trial]
    1. Have you completed preparation of trial bundles in accordance with Appendix 10 to the Commercial Court Guide?

Paragraph numbers marked with a "+" can be found online and on CD.

2. If not, when will the preparation of the trial bundles be completed?

3. Which witnesses of fact do you intend to call?

4. Which expert witness(es) do you intend to call (if directions for expert evidence have been given)?

5. Will an interpreter be required for any witness and if so, have any necessary directions already been given?

6. Have directions been given for any witness to give evidence by video link? If so, have all necessary arrangements been made?

7. What are the advocates' confirmed estimates of the minimum and maximum lengths of the trial? (A confirmed estimate of length signed by the advocates should be attached).

8. What is your estimate of costs already incurred and to be incurred at trial for the purposes of section 46 of the Practice Direction supplementing CPR Part 43? (If the trial is not expected to last more than **one day** the estimate should be substantially in the form of a statement of costs as illustrated in Form H of the Schedule of Costs Forms annexed to the Practice Direction).

[Signature of solicitors]

APPENDIX 14

VIDEO CONFERENCING GUIDANCE

This guidance is for the use of video conferencing (VCF) in civil proceedings. It is **2A–172** in part based, with permission, upon the protocol of the Federal Court of Australia. It is intended to provide a guide to all persons involved in the use of VCF, although it does not attempt to cover all the practical questions which might arise.

Video conferencing generally

1. The guidance covers the use of VCF equipment both (a) in a courtroom, whether via equipment which is permanently placed there or via a mobile unit, and (b) in a separate studio or conference room. In either case, the location at which the judge sits is referred to as the "local site". The other site or sites to and from which transmission is made are referred to as "the remote site" and in any particular case any such site may be another courtroom. The guidance applies to cases where VCF is used for the taking of evidence and also to its use for other parts of any legal proceedings (for example, interim applications, case management conferences, pre-trial reviews).

2. VCF may be a convenient way of dealing with any part of proceedings: it can involve considerable savings in time and cost. Its use for the taking of evidence from overseas witnesses will, in particular, be likely to achieve a material saving of costs, and such savings may also be achieved by its use for taking domestic evidence. It is, however, inevitably not as ideal as having the witness physically present in court. Its convenience should not therefore be allowed to dictate its use. A judgment must be made in every case in which the use of VCF is being considered not only as to whether it will achieve an overall cost saving but as to whether its use will be likely to be beneficial to the efficient, fair and economic disposal of the litigation. In particular, it needs to be recognised that the degree of control a court can exercise over a witness at the remote site is or may be more limited than it can exercise over a witness physically before it.

3. When used for the taking of evidence, the objective should be to make the VCF session as close as possible to the usual practice in a trial court where evidence is taken in open court. To gain the maximum benefit, several differences have to be taken into account. Some matters, which are taken for granted when evidence is taken in the conventional way, take on a different dimension when it is taken by VCF: for example, the administration of the oath, ensuring that the witness understands who is at the local site and what their various roles are, the raising of any objections to the evidence and the use of documents.

4. It should not be presumed that all foreign governments are willing to allow their nationals or others within their jurisdiction to be examined before a court in England

Paragraph numbers marked with a "+" can be found online and on CD.

or Wales by means of VCF. If there is any doubt about this, enquiries should be directed to the Foreign and Commonwealth Office (International Legal Matters Unit, Consular Division) with a view to ensuring that the country from which the evidence is to be taken raises no objection to it at diplomatic level. The party who is directed to be responsible for arranging the VCF (see paragraph 8 below) will be required to make all necessary inquiries about this well in advance of the VCF and must be able to inform the court what those inquiries were and of their outcome.

5. Time zone differences need to be considered when a witness abroad is to be examined in England or Wales by VCF. The convenience of the witness, the parties, their representatives and the court must all be taken into account. The cost of the use of a commercial studio is usually greater outside normal business hours.

6. Those involved with VCF need to be aware that, even with the most advanced systems currently available, there are the briefest of delays between the receipt of the picture and that of the accompanying sound. If due allowance is not made for this, there will be a tendency to "speak over" the witness, whose voice will continue to be heard for a millisecond or so after he or she appears on the screen to have finished speaking.

7. With current technology, picture quality is good, but not as good as a television picture. The quality of the picture is enhanced if those appearing on VCF monitors keep their movements to a minimum.

Preliminary arrangements

2A–173 8. The court's permission is required for any part of any proceedings to be dealt with by means of VCF. Before seeking a direction, the applicant should notify the listing officer, diary manager or other appropriate court officer of the intention to seek it, and should enquire as to the availability of court VCF equipment for the day or days of the proposed VCF. The application for a direction should be made to the Master, District Judge or Judge, as may be appropriate. If all parties consent to a direction, permission can be sought by letter, fax or e-mail, although the court may still require an oral hearing. All parties are entitled to be heard on whether or not such a direction should be given and as to its terms. If a witness at a remote site is to give evidence by an interpreter, consideration should be given at this stage as to whether the interpreter should be at the local site or the remote site. If a VCF direction is given, arrangements for the transmission will then need to be made. The court will ordinarily direct that the party seeking permission to use VCF is to be responsible for this. That party is hereafter referred to as "the VCF arranging party".

9. Subject to any order to the contrary, all costs of the transmission, including the costs of hiring equipment and technical personnel to operate it, will initially be the responsibility of, and must be met by, the VCF arranging party. All reasonable efforts should be made to keep the transmission to a minimum and so keep the costs down. All such costs will be considered to be part of the costs of the proceedings and the court will determine at such subsequent time as is convenient or appropriate who, as between the parties, should be responsible for them and (if appropriate) in what proportions.

10. The local site will, if practicable, be a courtroom but it may instead be an appropriate studio or conference room. The VCF arranging party must contact the listing officer, diary manager or other appropriate officer of the court which made the VCF direction and make arrangements for the VCF transmission. Details of the remote site, and of the equipment to be used both at the local site (if not being supplied by the court) and the remote site (including the number of ISDN lines and connection speed), together with all necessary contact names and telephone numbers, will have to be provided to the listing officer, diary manager or other court officer. The court will need to be satisfied that any equipment provided by the parties for use at the local site and also that at the remote site is of sufficient quality for a satisfactory transmission. The VCF arranging party must ensure that an appropriate person will be present at the local site to supervise the operation of the VCF throughout the

Paragraph numbers marked with a "+" can be found online and on CD.

transmission in order to deal with any technical problems. That party must also arrange for a technical assistant to be similarly present at the remote site for like purposes.

11. It is recommended that the judge, practitioners and witness should arrive at their respective VCF sites about 20 minutes prior to the scheduled commencement of the transmission.

12. If the local site is not a courtroom, but a conference room or studio, the judge will need to determine who is to sit where. The VCF arranging party must take care to ensure that the number of microphones is adequate for the speakers and that the panning of the camera for the practitioners' table encompasses all legal representatives so that the viewer can see everyone seated there.

13. The proceedings, wherever they may take place, form part of a trial to which the public is entitled to have access (unless the court has determined that they should be heard in private). If the local site is to be a studio or conference room, the VCF arranging party must ensure that it provides sufficient accommodation to enable a reasonable number of members of the public to attend.

14. In cases where the local site is a studio or conference room, the VCF arranging party should make arrangements, if practicable, for the royal coat of arms to be placed above the judge's seat.

15. In cases in which the VCF is to be used for the taking of evidence, the VCF arranging party must arrange for recording equipment to be provided by the court which made the VCF direction so that the evidence can be recorded. An associate will normally be present to operate the recording equipment when the local site is a courtroom. The VCF arranging party should take steps to ensure that an associate is present to do likewise when it is a studio or conference room. The equipment should be set up and tested before the VCF transmission. It will often be a valuable safeguard for the VCF arranging party also to arrange for the provision of recording equipment at the remote site. This will provide a useful back-up if there is any reduction in sound quality during the transmission. A direction from the court for the making of such a back-up recording must, however, be obtained first. This is because the proceedings are court proceedings and, save as directed by the court, no other recording of them must be made. The court will direct what is to happen to the back-up recording.

16. Some countries may require that any oath or affirmation to be taken by a witness accord with local custom rather than the usual form of oath or affirmation used in England and Wales. The VCF arranging party must make all appropriate prior inquiries and put in place all arrangements necessary to enable the oath or affirmation to be taken in accordance with any local custom. That party must be in a position to inform the court what those inquiries were, what their outcome was and what arrangements have been made. If the oath or affirmation can be administered in the manner normal in England and Wales, the VCF arranging party must arrange in advance to have the appropriate holy book at the remote site. The associate will normally administer the oath.

17. Consideration will need to be given in advance to the documents to which the witness is likely to be referred. The parties should endeavour to agree on this. It will usually be most convenient for a bundle of the copy documents to be prepared in advance, which the VCF arranging party should then send to the remote site.

18. Additional documents are sometimes quite properly introduced during the course of a witness's evidence. To cater for this, the VCF arranging party should ensure that equipment is available to enable documents to be transmitted between sites during the course of the VCF transmission. Consideration should be given to whether to use a document camera. If it is decided to use one, arrangements for its use will need to be established in advance. The panel operator will need to know the number and size of documents or objects if their images are to be sent by document camera. In many

Paragraph numbers marked with a "+" can be found online and on CD.

cases, a simpler and sufficient alternative will be to ensure that there are fax transmission and reception facilities at the participating sites.

The hearing

2A–174 19. The procedure for conducting the transmission will be determined by the judge. He will determine who is to control the cameras. In cases where the VCF is being used for an application in the course of the proceedings, the judge will ordinarily not enter the local site until both sites are on line. Similarly, at the conclusion of the hearing, he will ordinarily leave the local site while both sites are still on line. The following paragraphs apply primarily to cases where the VCF is being used for the taking of the evidence of a witness at a remote site. In all cases, the judge will need to decide whether court dress is appropriate when using VCF facilities. It might be appropriate when transmitting from courtroom to courtroom. It might not be when a commercial facility is being used.

20. At the beginning of the transmission, the judge will probably wish to introduce himself and the advocates to the witness. He will probably want to know who is at the remote site and will invite the witness to introduce himself and anyone else who is with him. He may wish to give directions as to the seating arrangements at the remote site so that those present are visible at the local site during the taking of the evidence. He will probably wish to explain to the witness the method of taking the oath or of affirming, the manner in which the evidence will be taken, and who will be conducting the examination and cross-examination. He will probably also wish to inform the witness of the matters referred to in paragraphs 6 and 7 above (co-ordination of picture with sound, and picture quality).

21. The examination of the witness at the remote site should follow as closely as possible the practice adopted when a witness is in the courtroom. During examination, cross-examination and re-examination, the witness must be able to see the legal representative asking the question and also any other person (whether another legal representative or the judge) making any statements in regard to the witness's evidence. It will in practice be most convenient if everyone remains seated throughout the transmission.

APPENDIX 15

SERVICE OUT OF THE JURISDICTION: RELATED PRACTICE

Service out of the jurisdiction without permission

2A–175 1. Before issuing a claim form or seeking permission to serve out of the jurisdiction, it is necessary to consider whether the jurisdiction of the English courts is affected by the Civil Jurisdiction and Judgments Act 1982. Where each claim in the claim form is a claim which the Court has by virtue of the Civil Jurisdiction and Judgments Act 1982 power to hear and determine, service of the claim form out of the jurisdiction may be effected without permission provided that the requirements of rule 6.19 are satisfied and the claim form is endorsed before issue with a statement that the court has power under the Act to hear and determine the claim against the defendant, and that no proceedings involving the same claim are pending between the parties in Scotland, Northern Ireland or another convention country. Care must be taken to see that the endorsement is not made unless the statement is accurate.

2A–176 Application for permission: affidavit or witness statement

2.

(a) On applications for permission under rule 6.20 the written evidence must, amongst other things:

  (i) identify the paragraph or paragraphs of rule 6.20 relied on as giving the court jurisdiction to order service out, together with a summary of the facts relied on as bringing the case within each such paragraph;

Paragraph numbers marked with a "+" can be found online and on CD.

(ii) state the belief of the deponent that there is a good claim and state in what place or country the defendant is or probably may be found;

(iii) summarise the considerations relied upon as showing that the case is a proper one in which to subject a party outside the jurisdiction to proceedings within it;

(iv) draw attention to any features which might reasonably be thought to weigh against the making of the order sought;

(v) state the deponent's grounds of belief and sources of information;

(vi) exhibit copies of the documents referred to and any other significant documents.

(b) Where convenient the written evidence should be included in the form of application notice, rather than in a separate witness statement. The form of application notice may be extended for this purpose.

Application for permission: copies of draft order

3. The documents submitted with the application must include two copies of a draft **2A–177** of the order sought which must state the time allowed for acknowledgment of service in accordance with any applicable practice direction and paragraphs 6 and 7 below.

Application for permission: copy or draft of claim form

4. A copy or draft of the claim form which the applicant intends to issue and serve **2A–178** must be provided for the judge to initial. If the endorsement to the claim form includes causes of action or claims not covered by the grounds on which permission to serve out of the jurisdiction can properly be granted, permission will be refused unless the draft is amended to restrict it to proper claims. Where the application is for the issue of a concurrent claim form, the documents submitted must also include a copy of the original claim form.

Arbitration matters

5. Service out of the jurisdiction in arbitration matters is governed by Part 62. As to **2A–179** the 1968 Convention on Jurisdiction in the context of arbitration, see Article 1(4).

Practice under rules 6.19 and 6.20

2A–180

6.

(a) Although a Part 7 claim form may contain or be accompanied by particulars of claim, there is no need for it to do so and in many cases particulars of claim will be served after the claim form: rule 58.5.

(b) A defendant should acknowledge service in every case: rule 58.6(1).

(c) The period for filing acknowledgment of service will be calculated from the service of the claim form, whether or not particulars of claim are to follow: rule 58.6.

(d) The period for serving, and filing, particulars of claim (where they were not contained in the claim form and did not accompany the claim form) will be calculated from acknowledgment of service: rule 58.5(1)(c).

(e) The period for serving and filing the defence will be calculated from service of the particulars of claim: rule 58.10(2).

7. Time for serving and filing a defence is calculated as follows:

(i) where particulars of claim were included in or accompanied the claim form the period for serving and filing a defence is 21 or 31 days as prescribed by rule 6.23, or the number of days shown in the table in practice direction 6BPD, in either case plus an additional 14 days;

(ii) where particulars of claim were not included in and did not accompany the claim form, the period for serving and filing a defence is 28 days from the service of the particulars of claim.

APPENDIX 16

SECURITY FOR COSTS: RELATED PRACTICE

First applications

1. First applications for security for costs should not be made later than at the Case **2A–181**

Paragraph numbers marked with a "+" can be found online and on CD.

Management Conference and in any event any application should not be left until close to the trial date. Delay to the prejudice of the other party or the administration of justice will probably cause the application to fail, as will any use of the application to harass the other party. Where it is intended to make an application for security at the Case Management Conference the procedure, and timetable for evidence, for an ordinary application must be followed (see section F5 of the Guide).

Successive applications

2A–182 2. Successive applications for security can be granted where the circumstances warrant. If a claimant wishes to seek to preclude any further application it is incumbent on him to make that clear.

Evidence

2A–183 3. An affidavit or witness statement in support of an application for security for costs should deal not only with the residence of the claimant (or other respondent to the application) and the location of his assets but also with the practical difficulties (if any) of enforcing an order for costs against him.

Investigation of the merits of the case

2A–184 4. Investigation of the merits of the case on an application for security is strongly discouraged. Only in those cases where it can be shown without detailed investigation of evidence or law that the claim is certain or almost certain to succeed or fail will the merits be taken into consideration.

Undertaking by the applicant

2A–185 5. In appropriate cases an order for security for costs may only be made on terms that the applicant gives an undertaking to comply with any order that the court may make if the court later finds that the order for security for costs has caused loss to the claimant and that the claimant should be compensated for such loss. Such undertakings are intended to compensate claimants in cases where no order for costs is ultimately made in favour of the applicant.

Stay of proceedings

2A–186 6. It is not usually convenient or appropriate to order an automatic stay of the proceedings pending the provision of the security. It leads to delay and may disrupt the preparation of the case for trial, or other hearing. Experience has shown that it is usually better to give the claimant (or other relevant party) a reasonable time within which to provide the security and the other party liberty to apply to the court in the event of default. This enables the court to put the claimant to his election and then, if appropriate, to dismiss the case.

Amount of security

2A–187 7. Where the dispute on an application for security for costs relates to the correct evaluation of the amount of costs likely to be allowed to a successful defendant on an assessment of costs, parties should consider whether it would be advantageous for the judge hearing the application to sit with a Costs Judge as an informal assessor. The judge himself may take such an initiative.

APPENDIX 17

COMMERCIAL COURT USER E-MAIL GUIDANCE

Introduction

2A–188 1. This guidance sets out how parties may communicate by e-mail with the Commercial and Admiralty Courts on certain matters with effect from 17 March 2003.

Paragraph numbers marked with a "+" can be found online and on CD.

Initial period of application

2. This guidance will apply for an initial period of 6 months. Towards the end of that period, the guidance will be reviewed in the light of the experience gained. It may then be revised as necessary.

2A–189

Documents for which e-mail may be used

3. E-mail may be used:

2A–190

   a. to communicate with the Case Management Unit, including the lodging of progress monitoring information sheets;

   b. to communicate with the Registry in relation to the approval by the Judge of draft Order following a hearing before that Judge, queries on Orders made, requests to transfer a case into or out of the Commercial Court and general correspondence, including questions on practice;

   Note: Orders submitted for sealing must be submitted on paper.

   c. to communicate with the Listing Office in matters relating to listing (including the lodging of pre-trial checklists) and to lodge skeleton arguments with the listing office;

   d. to communicate with the Admiralty Marshal (except for out of hours business).

   Note: The Court cannot accept any other documents by e-mail at present. In particular e-mail cannot be used to lodge pleadings, affidavits, witness statements, case memoranda and lists of issues.

Restrictions

4. A party should not use e-mail to take any step in a claim which requires a fee to be paid for that step. If a party sends by e-mail a document for which a fee is payable upon filing, the document will be treated as not having been filed.

2A–191

5. Where a party sends or lodges a document by e-mail he should still comply with any rule or practice direction requiring the document to be served on any other person.

6. Nothing in this guidance requires any person to accept service of a document by e-mail.

Sending e-mails to the Court: addresses

7. For Listing matters, the e-mail addresses are:

2A–192

   a. For all matters relating to listing (except Friday applications), for the lodging of pre-trial check lists and for all skeleton arguments:

E-mail Commercial Court Listing

   b. For matters relating to Friday applications (except skeleton arguments)

E-mail Friday applications

8. For matters relating to case management and the Case Management Unit (including the lodging of progress monitoring sheets), the address is:

2A–193

E-mail Case Management

9. For all correspondence for the Registry the address is:

2A–194

E-mail Registry

10. For all matters for the Admiralty Marshal or the business of the Admiralty Marshal, the address is:

2A–195

Paragraph numbers marked with a "+" can be found online and on CD.

E-mail Admiralty Marshal

2A–196

The subject line

11. The subject line of the e-mail should contain only the following information which should be in the following order:

    a. First, the proper title of the claim (abbreviated as necessary) with the claimant named first and the defendant named second; unless the action is an Admiralty action, the name of the ship should not be used:

    b. Second, the claim number.

Form and content of the e-mail

2A–197 12. Correspondence and documents may be sent either as text or attachments, except that documents required to be in a practice form should be sent in that form as attachments using one of the formats specified in paragraph 17.

13. Parties must not use e-mail to send any document which exceeds 40 pages in the aggregate of normal typescript in length or 2 MB whichever is the smaller. Documents may not be subdivided to comply with this requirement.

14. Where a party files a document by e-mail, he should not send a hard copy in addition, unless there are good reasons for so doing or the Court requires.

15. Parties are advised to bear in mind when sending correspondence or documents of a confidential or sensitive nature that the security of e-mails cannot be guaranteed.

16. Where a time limit applies, it remains the responsibility of the party to ensure that the document is filed in time. Parties are advised to allow for delays or downtime on their server or the servers used by the Court.

Attachments

2A–198 17. Attachments should be in one of the following formats:

    a. Microsoft Word viewer/reader (.doc) in Word 1997 or later format

    b. Rich Text Format as (.rtf) files

    c. Plain/Formatted Text as (.txt) files

    d. Hypertext documents as (.htm) files

    e. Adobe Acrobat as (.pdf) files minimum viewer version 4

Receipt of e-mail by the Court

2A–199 18. A document is not filed until the e-mail is received by the court at the addressee's computer terminal, whatever time it is shown to have been sent.

19. The time of receipt of an e-mail at the addressee's computer terminal will be recorded.

20. If an e-mail is received after 4 p.m. it will be treated as having been received on the next day the court office is open.

21. No automatic acknowledgment of the receipt of an e-mail will be sent; the subject matter of the e-mail will be considered in the ordinary way. If a response to the subject matter of the e-mail is not received within a reasonable period, the sender should assume that the court has not received it and should send the e-mail again, or file the document by another means.

22. Parties should not telephone to enquire as to the receipt of an e-mail. They should observe the procedure set out in paragraph 21.

Replies to e-mails snt to the court

2A–200 23. The court will normally send any reply by e-mail to documents or correspondence sent by e-mail.

Paragraph numbers marked with a "+" can be found online and on CD.

a. All replies will be sent to the e-mail address from which the e-mail has been sent. If the sender wishes the reply to be copied to other parties or to another e-mail address used by the sender of the message, such e-mail addresses must be specified in the copy line.

b. The Court will not send copies to clients or others not on the record; the copy line must therefore not contain the addresses of such persons.

c. The e-mail should also contain in the body of the e-mail the name and telephone number of the sender.

Note: It is important that each firm or set of chambers considers putting in place a system to deal with the absence of the individual who has sent the e-mail and to whom the Court will ordinarily reply. Two possible solutions are:

a. A central mail box within each firm, either from which the e-mail is sent to the Court (and which will therefore receive the reply) or to which it is copied by the individual sender who sends it direct to the Court (and who will receive a copy of the reply);

b. a second individual e-mail address within the firm to which the reply will be copied so that any reply can be monitored.

It must be for each firm and set of chambers to devise its own system.

Communication with the Clerk to a Commercial Judge

24. No documents or correspondence should be sent by e-mail to the Clerk to a **2A–201** Commercial Judge dealing with a case, unless:

a. an arrangement is made with the Clerk in each specific instance in which e-mail is to be used;

b. if such an arrangement is made, the e-mail must be copied to the appropriate Listing Office Address, the Case Management Unit Address, The Registry Address, or the Admiralty Marshal Address, as the case may be.

Note: Draft Orders for the approval of the Judge must be submitted through the Registry.

11 March 2003

APPENDIX 18

GUIDANCE ON PRACTICAL STEPS FOR TRANSFERRING CASES TO THE MERCANTILE COURTS

1. If a case is suitable for transfer to a Mercantile Court, either party can apply to the **2A–202** Commercial Judge prior to the CMC for transfer or, if no such application is made, the Commercial Judge will normally consider this with the parties at the CMC. He will expect the parties to have considered this issue prior to the CMC. Among the factors that the parties should consider are the size and complexity of the claim, the location of the parties and their legal advisers and the convenience of the witnesses. If transfer is contemplated, the parties should also contact the appropriate listing officer (at the telephone numbers set out at paragraph 10) to ascertain likely trial dates.

2. If the case is one that is suitable for transfer and a decision is made to transfer prior to the CMC, the Commercial Judge will order that the case be transferred to a Mercantile Court and the CMC will take place at the Mercantile Court.

3. If the case is one that is suitable for transfer and a decision is made to transfer at the CMC, the Commercial Judge will, in order to save the costs of a further hearing in the Mercantile Court, usually make all the directions with the appropriate timetable down to trial in the same way as if the case were to remain in the

Paragraph numbers marked with a "+" can be found online and on CD.

COMMERCIAL COURTS

Commercial Court, including a direction to fix the trial date through the appropriate listing officer (see paragraph 10 below) within a specified period of time. If, as is usually the case, it is thought desirable to give the parties time to try and settle the case through direct negotiation or ADR, this will be built into the timetable.

4. The Commercial Judge will consider the time at which transfer is to take place and this must be specified in the Order

5. The Commercial Judge will decide whether he considers a PTR or further CMC appears necessary at that stage; normally a further PTR or CMC (through a hearing at Court) will not be necessary as in the type of case transferred such a PTR or further CMC would not normally take place in the Commercial Court and would add to the costs. Therefore, unless the Order otherwise provides or the Judge of the Mercantile Court otherwise directs, the next hearing in court will usually be the trial.

6. The Order must be drawn up in the usual way and lodged with the Commercial Registry Room EB13 in the RCJ.
- If the draft Order was not initialled in court by the Judge, the Order will then be sent to the Judge who made the Order to be approved. That normally takes 3–4 days
- If the draft Order was initialled in court by the Judge at the hearing, the Order can be brought straight up to the Registry to be sealed.

7. Once the Order comes back, the Registry will put the Order in the various out trays for the solicitors clerks to collect. If the Order was sent in via the post, then the Registry will return it via the post or, if the firm of solicitors are not one of the regular users, the Registry will inform them of the procedure as to how to collect the Order.

8. Once the Order is sealed, the transfer from the Commercial Court is during normal circumstances effected by the Registry within one week; the transfer is effected by the Registry sending the court file and the Order to the Mercantile Court as the case may be. The Registry will also inform all parties on record once the case has been transferred.

9. The Mercantile Court will then receive all the papers which were on the Commercial Court file and they will give the case one of their own numbers and inform the parties.

10. The case will then continue in exactly the same way as if at the Commercial Court save that the hearing date must be fixed with the listing office at the Mercantile Court within the time limit specified in the Order. The parties must contact the specialist listing officer at the Court to which the case has been transferred. The telephone and fax numbers of the listing officers for the specialist list are:

London

020 7947 6826

Fax 020 7947 7670

Birmingham:

0121 681 3035

Fax 0121 681 3121

Paragraph numbers marked with a "+" can be found online and on CD.

Bristol:

0117 976 3098

Fax 0117 976 3074

Leeds:

0113 254 2607

Fax 0113 242 6380

Newcastle:

0191 201 2047

Fax 0191 201 252

Liverpool/Manchester:

0161 954 1779

Fax 0161 954 1705

Wales and Chester:

02920 376476

Fax 02920 376475

Parties are asked to speak to the specialist listing officers who will tell them of the facilities available at other Courts.

11. The Commercial Court monitors compliance with its Orders through the case management unit and the provision of progress monitoring information sheets which have to be provided by the Progress Monitoring Date specified in the Order. The standard directions for the Mercantile Courts provide for a Progress Monitoring Date; such a date should therefore be provided for in any Order. The Mercantile Courts monitor progress in accordance with paragraph 8 of the Mercantile Courts Practice Direction supplemental to Part 59. A PTR (either in court or by telephone conference) may be held in the Mercantile Courts if the parties make a request or the Mercantile Judge so directs.

12. The parties are expected to keep the listing officer of the Court to which the case is transferred apprised of any settlement of the case. In an unusual case where the Commercial Judge has not made all the directions or the parties need to make an application either orally or in writing, then the appropriate directions will be considered and made by the Mercantile Judge.

ADDRESSES AND CONTACT DETAILS

The Admiralty Marshal: 2A–203
Room EB12
Royal Courts of Justice

Paragraph numbers marked with a "+" can be found online and on CD.

Strand

London WC2A 2LL

Tel: 020 7947 6111

Fax: 020 7947 7671

The Admiralty & Commercial Registry:

Room EB13

Royal Courts of Justice

Strand,

London WC2A 2LL

Tel: 020 7947 6112

Fax: 020 7947 6245

DX 44450 STRAND

The Admiralty & Commercial Court Listing Office:

Room EB09

Royal Courts of Justice

Strand,

London WC2A 2LL

Tel: 020 7947 6826

Fax: 020 7947 7670

DX 44450 STRAND

The Secretary to the Commercial Court Committee:

Mrs Angela Hodgson

Room EB09

Royal Courts of Justice

Strand

London WC2A 2LL

Tel: 020 7947 6826

Fax: 020 7947 7670

DX 44450 STRAND

Out of hours emergency number: (Security Office at Royal Courts of Justice): 020 7947 6000.

Fax number for the procedure under sections B3.11 and B4.4 of the Guide for the issue of claim forms when the Registry is closed: 020 7947 6667.

FORMS

2A–204   [These are not available at present in Word or HTML, but are available on the Commercial Court website in PDF format.]

2A–205   *Note* —For numbered Court forms, see also the *Civil Procedure Forms Volume.*

Paragraph numbers marked with a "+" can be found online and on CD.

2B   MERCANTILE COURTS

PART 59—MERCANTILE COURTS

Contents

Editorial introduction

Part 59 is added to the CPR by the Civil Procedure (Amendment No.5) Rules 2001 **2B–2**
(SI 2001/4015) and came into force on March 25, 2002.

Related sources

- For Individual Mercantile Court Guides see *http://www.hmcourts-service.gov.uk/* **2B–2.1**
  publications/guidance/admiralcomm/index.htm [Accessed May 9, 2008].
- For the Mercantile Courts Directions Template, see para.2B–14.1, below.
- For the Admiralty and Commercial Court Guide see para.2A–39 and following, above.

Scope of this Part and interpretation[1]

59.1—(1) This Part applies to claims in Mercantile Courts.   **2B–3**

(2) A claim may only be started in a Mercantile Court if it—

    **(a) relates to a commercial or business matter in a broad
sense; and**

    **(b) is not required to proceed in the Chancery Division or
in another specialist list.**

(3) In this Part and its practice direction—

    **(a) "Mercantile Court" means a specialist list established
within the courts listed in the Practice Direction;**

    **(b) "mercantile claim" means a claim proceeding in a
Mercantile Court; and**

    **(c) "Mercantile judge" means a judge authorised to sit in a
Mercantile Court.**

MERCANTILE COURTS

---

[1] Introduced by the Civil Procedure (Amendment No.5) Rules 2001 (SI 2001/4015)
and amended by the Civil Procedure (Amendment) Rules 2006 (SI 2006/1689).

Paragraph numbers marked with a "+" can be found online and on CD.

Note

2B–4   *The London Mercantile Court* —The new London Mercantile Court has opened its doors in the Royal Courts of Justice at the Strand. The Mercantile Court operates a separate list within the Commercial Court following rule changes that came into effect on October 1, 2006.

The new court seeks to resolve business cases that do not require trial by High Court Judges in the full Commercial Court. This will mean less complex cases can be dealt with faster and at proportionate cost. In addition parties will be able to use the Central London Mediation Scheme for alternative dispute resolution.

Judge David Mackie Q.C. is the judge in charge of the new London Mercantile Court. He will work closely with the Commercial Court regarding assignment of cases. The court is also part of the south eastern circuit and will hear mercantile cases outside London.

The mercantile court used to operate under the jurisdiction of the London Civil Justice Centre. The new court under the Commercial Court brings all of London's business cases under one roof.

Notes

1. Hearings of the London Mercantile Court take place at the Royal Courts of Justice. All enquires about Listing should be made to Room EB09, The Commercial Court Listing Office, Royal Courts of Justice, Strand—020 7947 6826 or by email to ComCt.Listing@hmcourts-service.gsi.gov.uk. All other enquiries should be made to Room EB13, The Registry, Royal Courts of Justice, Strand—020 7947 6112 or by email to ComCt.Registry@hmcourts-service.gsi.gov.uk.

2. Judge Mackie is a solicitor and was for 15 years Head of Litigation at a large City firm. In 2003 he was made CBE for services to pro bono work. He became a Judge in July 2004 and is based at The Royal Courts of Justice.

3. Judge Brian Knight Q.C. is also a Mercantile Judge for the South Eastern Circuit and will sit in the new Court when his other commitments permit. Some Circuit judges and Queens Counsel with wide business experience are authorised to sit as Deputy judges of the Court.

4. Further enquiries, email to the Listing Office referred to above and Judge Mackie will call you back.

Application of the Civil Procedure Rules[1]

2B–5   **59.2 These Rules and their practice directions apply to mercantile claims unless this Part or a practice direction provides otherwise.**

Transfer of proceedings[2]

2B–6   **59.3 Rule 30.5 applies with the modifications that—**

    (a) a Mercantile judge may transfer a mercantile claim to another Mercantile Court; and

    (b) a Commercial Court judge may transfer a claim from the Commercial Court to a Mercantile Court.

(Rule 30.5(3) provides that an application for the transfer of proceedings to or from a specialist list must be made to a judge dealing with claims in that list).

---

[1] Introduced by the Civil Procedure (Amendment No.5) Rules 2001 (SI 2001/4015).
[2] Introduced by the Civil Procedure (Amendment No.5) Rules 2001 (SI 2001/4015) and amended by the Civil Procedure (Amendment No.4) Rules 2005 (SI 2005/3515).

Paragraph numbers marked with a "+" can be found online and on CD.

Claim form and particulars of claim[1]

59.4—(1) If particulars of claim are not contained in or served **2B-7**
with the claim form—

      (a) the claim form must state that, if an acknowledgment of
           service is filed which indicates an intention to defend
           the claim, particulars of claim will follow;

      (b) when the claim form is served, it must be accompanied
           by the documents specified in rule 7.8(1);

      (c) the claimant must serve particulars of claim within 28
           days of the filing of an acknowledgment of service
           which indicates an intention to defend; and

      (d) rule 7.4(2) does not apply.

  (2) If the claimant is claiming interest, he must—

      (a) include a statement to that effect; and

      (b) give the details set out in rule 16.4(2),

in both the claim form and the particulars of claim.

  (3) Rules 12.6(1)(a) and 14.14(1)(a) apply with the modification
that references to the particulars of claim shall be read as if they
referred to the claim form.

Acknowledgment of service[2]

59.5—(1) A defendant must file an acknowledgment of service in **2B-8**
every case.

  (2) Unless paragraph (3) applies, the period for filing an
acknowledgment of service is 14 days after service of the claim
form.

  (3) Where the claim form is served out of the jurisdiction, or on
the agent of a defendant who is overseas, the time periods provided
by rules 6.12(3), 6.35 and 6.37(5)apply after service of the claim
form.

Disputing the court's jurisdiction[3]

59.6—(1) Part 11 applies to mercantile claims with the modifica- **2B-9**
tions set out in this rule.

  (2) An application under rule 11(1) must be made within 28
days after filing an acknowledgment of service.

  (3) If the defendant files an acknowledgment of service indicating an intention to dispute the court's jurisdiction, the claimant
need not serve particulars of claim before the hearing of the
application.

Default judgment[4]

59.7—(1) Part 12 applies to mercantile claims, except that rules **2B-10**

MERCANTILE COURTS

---

[1] Introduced by the Civil Procedure (Amendment No.5) Rules 2001 (SI 2001/4015).
[2] Introduced by the Civil Procedure (Amendment No.5) Rules 2001 (SI 2001/4015)
and amended by the Civil Procedure (Amendment) Rules 2008 (SI 2008/2178).
[3] Introduced by the Civil Procedure (Amendment No.5) Rules 2001 (SI 2001/4015).
[4] Introduced by the Civil Procedure (Amendment No.5) Rules 2001 (SI 2001/4015).

Paragraph numbers marked with a "+" can be found online and on CD.

12.10 and 12.11 apply as modified by paragraphs (2) and (3) of this rule.

(2) If, in am Part 7 claim—

(a) the claim form has been served but no particulars of claim have been served; and

(b) the defendant has failed to file an acknowledgment of service,

the claimant must make an application if he wishes to obtain a default judgment.

(3) The application may be made without notice, but the court may direct it to be served on the defendant.

Admissions[1]

2B–11   59.8—(1) Rule 14.5 does not apply to mercantile claims.

(2) If the defendant admits part of a claim for a specified amount of money, the claimant may apply under rule 14.3 for judgment on the admission.

Defence and Reply[2]

2B–12   59.9—(1) Part 15 (Defence and Reply) applies to mercantile claims with the modification to rule 15.8 that the claimant must—

(a) file any reply to a defence; and

(b) serve it on all other parties,

within 21 days after service of the defence.

(2) Rule 6.35 (in relation to theperiod for filing a defence where the claim form is served out of the jurisdiction) applies to mercantile claims, except that if the particulars of claim are served after the defendant has filed an acknowledgment of service the period for filing a defence is 28 days from service of the particulars of claim.

Statements of case[3]

2B–13   59.10 The court may at any time before or after issue of the claim form order a mercantile claim to proceed without the filing or service of statements of case.

Case management[4]

2B–14   59.11—(1) All mercantile claims are treated as being allocated to the multi-track, and Part 26 does not apply.

(2) The following parts only of Part 29 apply—

(a) rule 29.3(2) (appropriate legal representative to attend

---

[1] Introduced by the Civil Procedure (Amendment No.5) Rules 2001 (SI 2001/4015).
[2] Introduced by the Civil Procedure (Amendment No.5) Rules 2001 (SI 2001/4015) and amended by the Civil Procedure (Amendment) Rules 2008 (SI 2008/2178).
[3] Introduced by the Civil Procedure (Amendment No.5) Rules 2001 (SI 2001/4015).
[4] Introduced by the Civil Procedure (Amendment No.5) Rules 2001 (SI 2001/4015).

Paragraph numbers marked with a "+" can be found online and on CD.

**case management conferences and pre-trial reviews);
and**

(b) **rule 29.5 (variation of case management timetable) with
the exception of rule 29.5(1)(c).**

(3) **As soon as practicable the court will hold a case management conference which must be fixed in accordance with the
practice direction.**

(4) **At the case management conference or at any hearing at
which the parties are represented the court may give such directions for the management of the case as it considers appropriate.**

Directions

A Mercantile Courts Directions template has been produced and approved for use   **2B–14.1**
by all Mercantile Courts in the country though it is the responsibility of each court to
determine the appropriate directions for each case. It is intended to be sent out
electronically as a Word attachment to regular users and to parties on the filing of the
defence and in due course to have it available via the webguide for the Mercantile
Courts currently being devised. Meanwhile contact with the Mercantile Clerk at the
Mercantile Court Birmingham may help.

Judgments and orders[1]

59.12—(1) **Except for orders made by the court of its own initia-   2B–15
tive and unless the court otherwise orders every judgment or order
will be drawn up by the parties, and rule 40.3 is modified
accordingly.**

(2) **An application for a consent order must include a draft of
the proposed order signed on behalf of all the parties to whom it
relates.**

(3) **Rule 40.6 (consent judgments and orders) does not apply.**

[1] Introduced by the Civil Procedure (Amendment No.5) Rules 2001 (SI 2001/4015).

Paragraph numbers marked with a "+" can be found online and on CD.

PRACTICE DIRECTION—MERCANTILE COURTS
This Practice Direction supplements Part 59

General

2B–16   **1.1** This practice direction applies to mercantile claims.

1.2 Mercantile Courts are established in—

(1)   the following district registries of the High Court—Birmingham, Bristol, Cardiff, Chester, Leeds, Liverpool, Manchester, Mold and Newcastle upon Tyne; and

(2)   the Commercial Court of the Queen's Bench Division at the Royal Courts of Justice (called 'The London Mercantile Court').

1.3 All mercantile claims will be heard or determined by a Mercantile judge, except that—

(1)   an application may be heard and determined by any other judge who, if the claim were not a mercantile claim, would have jurisdiction to determine it, if—

(a)   the application is urgent and no Mercantile judge is available to hear it; or

(b)   a Mercantile judge directs it to be heard by another judge; and

(2)   unless the court otherwise orders, all proceedings for the enforcement of a Mercantile Court judgment or order for the payment of money will be dealt with by a district judge.

1.4 Provisions in other practice directions which refer to a master or district judge are to be read, in relation to mercantile claims, as if they referred to a Mercantile judge.

Starting proceedings in a Mercantile Court

2.1 A claim should only be started in a Mercantile Court if it will benefit from the expertise of a Mercantile judge.

2.2 The claim form must be marked in the top right hand corner 'Queen's Bench Division, ... District Registry, Mercantile Court' or 'Queen's Bench Division, the London Mercantile Court' as appropriate.

Applications before proceedings are issued

3.1 A party who intends to bring a claim in a Mercantile Court must make any application before the claim form is issued to a judge of that court.

3.2 The written evidence in support of such an application should show why the claim is suitable to proceed as a mercantile claim.

Transfer of proceedings to or from a Mercantile Court

4.1 If a claim which has not been issued in a Mercantile Court is suitable to continue as a mercantile claim—

(1)   any party wishing the claim to be transferred to a Mercantile Court may make an application for transfer to the court to which transfer is sought;

(2)   if all parties consent to the transfer, the application may be

Paragraph numbers marked with a "+" can be found online and on CD.

made by letter to the mercantile listing officer of the court to which transfer is sought, stating why the case is suitable to be transferred to that court and enclosing the written consents of the parties, the claim form and statements of case.

4.2 If an application for transfer is made to a court which does not have power to make the order, that court may—

(1)   adjourn the application to be heard by a Mercantile judge; or

(2)   dismiss the application.

4.3 A Mercantile judge may make an order under rule 59.3 of his own initiative.

Default judgment and admissions

5. The practice directions supplementing Parts 12 and 14 apply with the following modifications—

(1)   paragraph 4.1(1) of the practice direction supplementing Part 12 is to be read as referring to the service of the claim form; and

(2)   the references to "particulars of claim" in paragraphs 2.1, 3.1 and 3.2 of the practice direction supplementing Part 14 are to be read as referring to the claim form.

Variation of time limits by agreement

6.1 If the parties, in accordance with rule 2.11, agree in writing to vary a time limit, the claimant must notify the court in writing, giving brief written reasons for the agreed variation.

6.2 The court may make an order overriding an agreement by the parties varying a time limit.

Case management

7.1 The following parts only of the practice direction supplementing Part 29 apply—

(1)   paragraph 5 (case management conferences), excluding paragraph 5.9 and modified so far as is made necessary by other specific provisions of this practice direction; and

(2)   paragraph 7 (failure to comply with case management directions).

7.2 If proceedings are started in a Mercantile Court, the claimant must apply for a case management conference—

(1)   for a Part 7 claim, within 14 days of the date when all defendants who intend to file and serve a defence have done so; and

(2)   for a Part 8 claim, within 14 days of the date when all defendants who intend to serve evidence have done so.

7.3 If proceedings are transferred to a Mercantile Court, the claimant must apply for a case management conference within 14 days of receiving an acknowledgment of the transfer from the receiving court, unless the judge held, or gave directions for, a case manage-

Paragraph numbers marked with a "+" can be found online and on CD.

ment conference when he made the order transferring the proceedings.

7.4 Any party may, at a time earlier than that provided in paragraphs 7.2 or 7.3, apply in writing to the court to fix a case management conference.

7.5 If the claimant does not make an application in accordance with paragraphs 7.2 or 7.3, any other party may apply for a case management conference.

7.6 The court may fix a case management conference at any time on its own initiative. If it does so, the court will give at least seven days' notice to the parties, unless there are compelling reasons for a shorter period of notice.

7.7 Not less than seven days before a case management conference—

   (1)   each party shall file and serve—

      (a) a case management information sheet substantially in the form set out at Appendix A to this practice direction; and

      (b) an application notice for any order which that party intends to seek at the case management conference, other than directions referred to in the case management information sheet; and

   (2)   the claimant (or other party applying for the conference) shall in addition file and serve—

      (a) a case management file containing—

      — the claim form;

      — the statements of case (excluding schedules of more than 15 pages);

      — any orders already made;

      — the case management information sheets; and

      — a short list of the principal issues to be prepared by the claimant; and

      (b) a draft order substantially in the form set out at Appendix B to this practice direction, setting out the directions which that party thinks appropriate.

7.8 In appropriate cases—

   (1)   the parties may, not less than 7 days before the date fixed for the case management conference, submit agreed directions for the approval of the judge;

   (2)   the judge will then either—

      (a) make the directions proposed; or

      (b) make them with alterations; or

      (c) require the case management conference to proceed; but

   (3)   the parties must assume that the conference will proceed until informed to the contrary.

7.9 If the parties submit agreed directions and the judge makes them with alterations, any party objecting to the alterations may, within 7 days of receiving the order containing the directions, apply to the court for the directions to be varied.

7.10 The directions given at the case management conference—

(1)   will normally cover all steps in the case through to trial, including the fixing of a trial date or window, or directions for the taking of steps to fix the trial date or window; and

(2)   may include the fixing of a progress monitoring date or dates, and make provision for the court to be informed as to the progress of the case at the date or dates fixed.

7.11 If the court fixes a progress monitoring date, it may after that date fix a further case management conference or a pre-trial review on its own initiative if—

(1)   no or insufficient information is provided by the parties; or

(2)   it is appropriate in view of the information provided.

Pre-trial review and questionnaire

8.1 The court may order a pre-trial review at any time.

8.2 Each party must file and serve a completed pre-trial check list substantially in the form set out in Appendix C to this practice direction—

(1)   if a pre-trial review has been ordered, not less than 7 days before the date of the review; or

(2)   if no pre-trial review has been ordered, not less than 6 weeks before the trial date.

8.3 When pre-trial check lists are filed under paragraph 8.2(2)–

(1)   the judge will consider them and decide whether to order a pre-trial review; and

(2)   if he does not order a pre-trial review, he may on his own initiative give directions for the further preparation of the case or as to the conduct of the trial.

8.4 At a pre-trial review—

(1)   the parties should if possible be represented by the advocates who will be appearing at the trial;

(2)   any representatives appearing must be fully informed and authorised for the purposes of the review; and

(3)   the court will give such directions for the conduct of the trial as it sees fit.

Evidence for applications

9.1 The general requirement is that, unless the court orders otherwise—

(1)   evidence in support of an application must be filed and served with the application: see rule 23.7(3);

(2)   evidence in answer must be filed and served within 14 days after the application is served;

(3)   evidence in reply must be filed and served within 7 days of the service of the evidence in answer.

9.2 In any case in which the application is likely to require an oral hearing of more than half a day the periods set out in paragraphs 9.1(2) and (3) will be 28 days and 14 days respectively.

9.3 If the date fixed for the hearing of the application means that the times in paragraphs 9.1(2) and (3) cannot both be achieved, the evidence must be filed and served—

(1) as soon as possible; and

(2) in sufficient time to ensure that the application may fairly proceed on the date fixed.

9.4 The parties may, in accordance with rule 2.11, agree different periods from those provided above, provided that the agreement does not affect the ability to proceed on the date fixed for the hearing of the application.

Files for applications

10. Before the hearing of any application, the applicant must—

(1) provide to the court and each other party an appropriate indexed file for the application with consecutively numbered pages; and

(2) attach to the file an estimate of the reading time required by the judge.

Judgments and orders

11.1 After any hearing the claimant must draw up a draft order, unless the decision was made on the application of another party in which case that party must do so.

11.2 A draft order must be submitted by the party responsible for drawing it up within 3 clear days of the decision, with sufficient copies for each party and for one to be retained by the court.

11.3 The sealed orders will be returned to the party submitting them, who will be responsible for serving the order on the other parties.

11.4 Orders must be dated with the date of the decision, except for consent orders submitted for approval, which must be left undated.

Editorial note

2B–16.1   See para.2B–14.1 Directions, above.

Paragraph numbers marked with a "+" can be found online and on CD.

Annex A

Case Management Information Sheet - Mercantile Courts

[Title of Case]

This information sheet must be filed with Mercantile Listing at least 7 days before the Case Management Conference, and copies served on all other parties: see paragraph 7.7 of the Mercantile Courts Practice Direction.

Party filing:
Solicitors:
Advocate(s) for trial:
Date:

Substance of case
1.   What in about 20 words maximum is the case about?
        Please provide a separate concise list of issues in a complex case.

Parties
2.   Are all parties still effective?
3.   Do you intend to add any further party?

Statements of case
4.   Do you intend to amend your statement of case?
5.   Do you require any "further information" - see CPR 18?

Disclosure
6.   By what date can you give standard disclosure?
7.   Do you contend that to search for any type of document falling within CPR 31.6(b) would be
        unreasonable within CPR 31.7(2); if so, what type and on what grounds?
8.   Is any specific disclosure required - CPR 31.12?
9.   Is a full disclosure order appropriate?
10.   By what dates could you give:
        (i)   any specific disclosure referred to at 8; and
        (ii)   full disclosure?

Admissions
11.   Can you make any additional admissions?

Preliminary issues
12.   Are any issues suitable for trial as preliminary issues? If yes, which?

Witnesses of fact
13.   On how many witnesses of fact do you intend to rely at the trial (subject to the court's
        direction)?
14.   Please name them, or explain why you do not.
15.   Which of them will be called to give oral evidence?
16.   When can you serve their witness statements?
17.   Will any require an interpreter?

Expert evidence
18.   Are there issues requiring expert evidence?
19.   If yes, what issues?
20.   Might a single joint expert be suitable on any issues (see CPR 35.7)?
21.   What experts do you intend (subject to the court's direction) to call? Please give the number,
        their names and expertise.
22.   By what date can you serve signed expert reports?
23.   Should there be meetings of experts of like disciplines, of all disciplines? By when?
24.   Which experts, if any, do you intend not to call at the trial?

Paragraph numbers marked with a "+" can be found online and on CD.

25. Will any require an interpreter?

Trial
26. What are the advocates' present estimates of the length of the trial?
27. What is the earliest date that you think the case can be ready for trial?
28. Where should the trial be held?
29. Is a Pre-Trial Review advisable?

A.D.R.
30. Might some form of Alternative Dispute Resolution assist to resolve the dispute or some part of it?
31. Has this been considered with the client?
32. Has this been considered with the other parties?
33. Do you want the case to be stayed pending A.D.R. or other means of settlement - CPR 26.4; or any other directions relating to A.D.R.?

Other applications
34. What applications, if any, not covered above, will you be making at the conference?

Costs
35. What, do you estimate, are your costs to date?
36. What, do you estimate, will be your costs to end of trial?

[Signature of party/solicitor]

Paragraph numbers marked with a "+" can be found online and on CD.

Annex B

Standard Directions in Mercantile Courts

[Title of case with Judge's name]

Order for Directions
made on [   ]

1. Standard disclosure is to be made by [   ].
    Inspection on 48 hours notice to be completed by [   ].

2. Signed statements of witnesses of fact, and hearsay notices when required by CPR 33.2, are to be exchanged not later than [   ].

    Unless otherwise ordered, the witness statements are to stand as the evidence in chief of the witnesses at trial.

3. Each party has permission to call at the trial expert witnesses as follows:

Number	Expertise	Issue(s) to be covered

    whose reports are to be exchanged by [   ].

4. Experts of like disciplines are to:

    (i) meet without prejudice by [   ] to identify the issues between them and to attempt to reach agreement on such issues, and

    (ii) prepare a joint statement pursuant to CPR 35.12(3), by [   ].

or

3. Expert evidence in the following field(s) of expertise is limited to a written report by a single expert jointly instructed by the parties:

Expertise	Issue(s) to be covered

4. (i) The report of the single joint expert is to be produced by [   ].

    (ii) Any questions to the expert are to be presented to him by [   ] and answered by [   ].

    (iii) Any party may apply not later than [   ] for an order that the expert witness shall give oral evidence at the trial.

5. The case will be tried in [   ] by judge alone, estimated length of trial [   ] days, [commencing on   ] [not before   ].
    [The claimant is to apply to the mercantile listing officer to fix a date for the trial, not later than [   ], specifying dates which any party wishes to avoid.]

Paragraph numbers marked with a "+" can be found online and on CD.

[6 .   The progress monitoring date is [   ]. Each party is to notify the court in writing
by that date (with a copy to all other parties) of the progress of the case, including -

(i)   whether the directions have been complied with in all respects;

(ii)   if any directions are outstanding, which of them and why; and

(iii)   whether a further case management conference or a pre-trial review is required.]

7.   There will be a pre-trial review on [   ].
[In the event of both parties notifying the court in writing not less than [   ] days before the
pre-trial review that it is not required, then it will be vacated.]

8.   Signed pre-trial check lists are to be filed and served by [   ] [not less than 7 days
before the pre-trial review] [not less than 6 weeks before the trial date].

9.   Trial bundles must be agreed, prepared and delivered to counsel not less than [   ]
days before the trial date, and to the court not less than [   ] days before the trial
date.

10.   Costs in the case.

DATED

Editorial note
2B–18.1   See para.2B–14.1 above.

Paragraph numbers marked with a "+" can be found online and on CD.

Annex C

Pre-trial Check List - Mercantile Courts

[Title of Case]

Where a Pre-trial Review has been ordered, this check list must be filed with Mercantile Listing not less than 7 days before the Pre-trial Review, and copies served on all other parties.
Where a Pre-trial Review has not been ordered, it must be filed and served not less than 6 weeks before the trial date .
See paragraph 8.2 of the Mercantile Courts Practice Direction.

a.   Trial Date:
b.   Whether Pre-trial Review ordered:
c.   Date of Review:
d.   Party lodging:
e.   Solicitors:
f.   Advocate(s) for trial:
g.   Date lodged:

[Note: this checklist should normally be completed with the involvement of the advocate(s) instructed for trial.]

1.   Have all the directions made to date been carried out?
2.   If not, what remains to be carried out? When will it be carried out?
3.   Do you intend to take any further steps regarding:
     (i)   statements of case?
     (ii)   disclosure?
     (iii)   witnesses and witness statements?
     (iv)   experts and expert reports?
     If yes in any case, what and by when?
4.   Will the preparation of trial bundles be completed not later than 3 weeks before the date fixed for trial? If not, what is the position?
5.   What witnesses of fact do you intend to call?
6.   (Where directions for expert evidence have been given) what experts do you intend to call?
7.   Is any interpreter needed: for whom?
8.   If a Pre-trial Review has not been ordered, do you think one would be useful?
9.   What are the advocate(s)' confirmed estimates of the minimum and maximum lengths of the trial? A confirmed estimate signed by the advocate(s) and dated must be attached.
10   (i)   Might some form of alternative dispute resolution now assist?
     (ii)   Has the question been considered with the client?
     (iii)   Has the question been explored with the other parties to the case?

[Signature of party/solicitor]

Note

Each of the Mercantile Courts now has its own guide, and these are available on the **2B–20** Court Service website or in hard copy from the individual courts concerned. For more information see *http://www.hmcourts-service.gov.uk* [Accessed July 24, 2007].

Paragraph numbers marked with a "+" can be found online and on CD.

2C PROCEEDINGS IN THE TECHNOLOGY AND CONSTRUCTION COURT

PART 60—TECHNOLOGY AND CONSTRUCTION COURT CLAIMS

Contents

Editorial introduction

Part 60 is added to the CPR by Civil Procedure (Amendment No.5) Rules 2001 (SI **2C-2** 2001/4015) and came into force on March 25, 2002.

The Technology and Construction Court

This court is the successor in title to the Official Referees Courts. The first Official **2C-3** Referees of the Supreme Court of Justice were appointed in 1876 under the Judicature Acts.1873–75. Any question could be referred for trial with or without consent of the parties if it involved the prolonged investigation of documents or accounts or of any scientific or local investigation. The report of an Official Referee on a trial had to be accepted as if it were the verdict of a jury but he could not give judgment or make any order as to costs. By the Judicature Act 1884 power was given for an Official Referee to give a judgment, make orders for costs and exercise the powers of a High Court judge in a case referred to him. The Arbitration Act of 1889 enabled parties to an arbitration agreement to require an Official Referee to sit as an arbitrator. From the outset much of the Official Referee's work was concerned with the construction industry in all its aspects. The Courts Act 1971 provided that in future "Official Referees business" should be dealt with by such Circuit Judges as the Lord Chancellor should determine. Although the title "Official Referee" was not legally preserved it continued to be used universally. By 1998 references were a rarity and most of the work tried in the court was commenced in the Official Referees Registry or transferred from the Chancery Division or the Queen's Bench Division. The description of the court was considered to be inaccurate and anachronistic and in October of 1998 the Lord Chancellor with the concurrence of the Lord Chief Justice directed that the court should be renamed the Technology and Construction Court of the High Court of Justice. The Technology and Construction Court (TCC) was opened by the Lord Chancellor on October 9, 1998. From that time the mode of address of all judges has been "my Lord". On April 26, 1999 the Civil Procedure Rules came into force incorporating many of the case management practices pioneered by the Official Referees during the 1980s and 1990s and reflecting the interventionist ethos of the court.

The Technology and Construction Courts in London —There are eight courts situated on the second to sixth floors of St Dunstans House, 133–137 Fetter Lane, London EC4A 1HD. The Registry is on the 3rd floor.

The constitution of the courts in London and elsewhere and assignment of cases is described in the Technology and Construction Court Guide (2nd edn) (see para.2C–37), and the Technology and Construction Court: Statement by the Lord Chief Justice of England and Wales, June 7, 2005 (LCJ Statement), (see para.2C–35) which deals with the interim arrangements pending a final determination as to the

Paragraph numbers marked with a "+" can be found online and on CD.

future of the TCC (para.5 of the LCJ Statement). The current position in London is that the judge in charge of the TCC, Ramsey J., sits as a full-time TCC judge. There are two further High Court judges (Akenhead and Coulson JJ.) who each sit in the TCC for at least half of each term, depending on the caseload and their other commitments. In addition, there are three Senior Circuit judges who are full-time TCC judges in London.

General[1]

2C-4   **60.1—(1) This Part applies to Technology and Construction Court claims ("TCC claims").**

> **(2) In this Part and its practice direction—**
>> **(a) "TCC claim" means a claim which—**
>>> **(i) satisfies the requirements of paragraph (3); and**
>>> **(ii) has been issued in or transferred into the specialist list for such claims;**
>> **(b) "Technology and Construction Court" means any court in which TCC claims are dealt with in accordance with this Part or its practice direction; and**
>> **(c) "TCC judge" means any judge authorised to hear TCC claims.**

> **(3) A claim may be brought as a TCC claim if—**
>> **(a) it involves issues or questions which are technically complex; or**
>> **(b) a trial by a TCC judge is desirable.**

> **(The practice direction gives examples of types of claims which it may be appropriate to bring as TCC claims).**

> **(4) TCC claims include all official referees' business referred to in section 68(1)(a) of the Supreme Court Act 1981[2].**

> **(5) TCC claims will be dealt with—**
>> **(a) in a Technology and Construction Court; and**
>> **(b) by a TCC judge, unless—**
>>> **(i) this Part or its practice direction permits otherwise; or**
>>> **(ii) a TCC judge directs otherwise.**

Comment

2C-5   A non-exhaustive list of the types of claim which are commonly dealt with in the TCC is set out at para.2.1 of the Pt 60 Practice Direction (para.2C–16 below). There is also a discussion of the wide variety of claims appropriate for the TCC at s.1.3.1 of the TCC Guide (2nd edn) at para.2C–41 below.

Specialist list[3]

2C-6   **60.2—(1) TCC claims form a specialist list.**

> **(2) A judge will be appointed to be the judge in charge of the TCC specialist list.**

---

[1] Introduced by the Civil Procedure (Amendment No.5) Rules 2001 (SI 2001/4015).
[2] 1981 c.54.
[3] Introduced by the Civil Procedure (Amendment No.5) Rules 2001 (SI 2001/4015).

Paragraph numbers marked with a "+" can be found online and on CD.

Application of the Civil Procedure Rules[1]

60.3 **These Rules and their practice directions apply to TCC** 2C–7
claims unless this Part or a practice direction provides otherwise.

Issuing a TCC claim[2]

60.4 **A TCC claim must be issued in—** 2C–8
    (a) **the High Court in London;**
    (b) **a district registry of the High Court; or**
    (c) **a county court specified in the practice direction.**

Comment

Paragraph 3.1 of the Pt 60 Practice Direction sets out the correct way of starting a 2C–9
TCC claim (see para.2C–18 below). Detailed guidance as to the correct procedure on
commencement in the TCC is set out in ss.3.1 to 3.4 of the TCC Guide (2nd edn), at
paras 2C–51 to 2C–54 below. Guidance on the procedure for transferring a case
started elsewhere into the TCC is set out in s.3.6 of the TCC Guide (para.2C–56
below).

Reply[3]

60.5 **Part 15 (Defence and Reply) applies to TCC claims with the** 2C–10
modification to rule 15.8 that the claimant must—
    (a) **file any reply to a defence; and**
    (b) **serve it on all other parties,**
within 21 days after service of the defence.

Case management[4]

60.6—**(1) All TCC claims are treated as being allocated to the** 2C–11
multi-track and Part 26 does not apply.

**(2) Part 29 and its practice direction apply to the case manage-
ment of TCC claims, except where they are varied by or inconsistent with the practice direction to this Part.**

Comment

Case management is an extremely important part of the work of the TCC. In a 2C–12
complex case, the parties can expect to attend at least one case management conference at the outset of proceedings, one review case management conference, which will
usually be heard after disclosure of documents and before the exchange of evidence,
and a pre-trial review (PTR), listed to be heard about 4–6 weeks before the trial itself.
Once a TCC claim has been issued or a claim has been transferred into the TCC
specialist list, then the claim will be assigned to a named TCC judge who will have the
primary responsibility for the case management of the claim (see para.6 of the Pt 60
Practice Direction at para.2C–23 below, and s.3.7 of the TCC Guide, at para.2C–57
below). The first case management conference will take place early, often before
defences have been served (see para.8.1 of the Practice Direction at para.2C–27 below
and s.5 of the TCC Guide at para.2C–66 below). Thereafter, in addition to any review
CMCs and the PTR, noted above, the assigned TCC judge will also deal with any
specific applications made by any party to the proceedings (see para.7 of the Pt 60

---

[1] Introduced by the Civil Procedure (Amendment No.5) Rules 2001 (SI 2001/4015).
[2] Introduced by the Civil Procedure (Amendment No.5) Rules 2001 (SI 2001/4015).
[3] Introduced by the Civil Procedure (Amendment No.5) Rules 2001 (SI 2001/4015).
[4] Introduced by the Civil Procedure (Amendment No.5) Rules 2001 (SI 2001/4015).

Paragraph numbers marked with a "+" can be found online and on CD.

Practice Direction at para.2C–25 below, and s.6 of the TCC Guide at para.2C–76 below).

Judgments and Orders[1]

2C–13   **60.7—(1) Except for orders made by the court of its own initiative and unless the court otherwise orders, every judgment or order made in claims proceeding in the Technology and Construction Court will be drawn up by the parties, and rule 40.3 is modified accordingly.**

(2) An application for a consent order must include a draft of the proposed order signed on behalf of all the parties to whom it relates.

(3) Rule 40.6 (consent judgments and orders) does not apply.

Comment

2C–14   At the first CMC, the court will almost always direct the claimant to draw up the relevant order within a specified time so that it can be approved by the court: see s.5.8.1 of the TCC Guide at para.2C–73 below. Similarly, at the conclusion of any application hearing, the court will usually require the applicant to draw up the necessary order: see s.6.6.4 of the TCC Guide at para.2C–81 below. Where the parties indicate to the court that they have agreed the terms of an order, the TCC judge will endeavour to endorse the terms which have been agreed, unless he or she considers that the agreed terms fail to take into account important features of the case as a whole, or the principles of the CPR. At the very least, the agreed terms will form the starting-point of the judge's consideration of the orders to be made: see s.5.7.1 of the TCC Guide at para.2C–72 below.

---

[1] Introduced by the Civil Procedure (Amendment No.3) Rules 2005 (SI 2005/2292).

Paragraph numbers marked with a "+" can be found online and on CD.

PRACTICE DIRECTION—TECHNOLOGY AND CONSTRUCTION COURT CLAIMS

This Practice Direction supplements CPR Part 60   **2C–15**

General

1. This practice direction applies to Technology and Construction Court claims ('TCC claims').

TCC claims

2.1 The following are examples of the types of claim which it may **2C–16** be appropriate to bring as TCC claims—

(a)   building or other construction disputes, including claims for the enforcement of the decisions of adjudicators under the Housing Grants, Construction and Regeneration Act 1996;

(b)   engineering disputes;

(c)   claims by and against engineers, architects, surveyors, accountants and other specialised advisers relating to the services they provide;

(d)   claims by and against local authorities relating to their statutory duties concerning the development of land or the construction of buildings;

(e)   claims relating to the design, supply and installation of computers, computer software and related network systems;

(f)   claims relating to the quality of goods sold or hired, and work done, materials supplied or services rendered;

(g)   claims between landlord and tenant for breach of a repairing covenant;

(h)   claims between neighbours, owners and occupiers of land in trespass, nuisance etc.;

(i)   claims relating to the environment (for example, pollution cases);

(j)   claims arising out of fires;

(k)   claims involving taking of accounts where these are complicated; and

(l)   challenges to decisions of arbitrators in construction and engineering disputes including applications for permission to appeal and appeals.

2.2 A claim given as an example in paragraph 2.1 will not be suitable for this specialist list unless it demonstrates the characteristics in rule 60.1(3). Similarly, the examples are not exhaustive and other types of claim may be appropriate to this specialist list.

Comment

A TCC claim in rule 60.1(3) is one which involves issues or questions which are **2C–17** technically complex or for which a trial by a judge of a TCC is for any other reason desirable. The effect of the rule is that a TCC judge may try any case within the business of the Chancery and Queen's Bench divisions. The new rule is widely framed because the court has historically adapted itself to deal with new problems arising out of technical advances and customarily deals with cases involving multi-parties and cases which may occupy a great deal of time. See also section 1.3.1 of the TCC Guide, 2nd edition (see para.2C–41 below).

Paragraph numbers marked with a "+" can be found online and on CD.

2C–17.1 Most TCC claims are commenced under CPR Pt 7. However, where the point at issue is a matter of construction of the contract, or some other clearly identifiable point of law, then the claimant may choose to start proceedings under CPR Pt 8. The advantage of this procedure in the TCC is that a hearing for the final disposition of the Pt 8 claim can usually be arranged within a matter of weeks. In such circumstances, it is necessary for the court to ensure that the claim is properly brought under Pt 8. It is anticipated that current economic difficulties will lead to an increase in the use of Pt 8 in the TCC: see *Walter Lilly and Co Ltd v DMW Developments Ltd* [2008] EWHC 3139 (TCC).

How to start a TCC claim

2C–18 **3.1** TCC claims must be issued in the High Court or in a county court specified in this practice direction.

3.2 The claim form must be marked in the top right-hand corner 'Technology and Construction Court' below the words 'The High Court, Queen's Bench Division' or 'The _____ County Court'.

3.3 TCC claims brought in the High Court outside London may be issued in any District Registry, but it is preferable that wherever possible they should be issued in one of the following District Registries, in which a TCC judge will usually be available—Birmingham, Bristol, Cardiff, Chester, Exeter, Leeds, Liverpool, Manchester, Mold, Newcastle upon Tyne and Nottingham.

3.4 The county courts in which a TCC claim may be issued are the following—Birmingham, Bristol, Cardiff, Central London, Chester, Exeter, Leeds, Liverpool, Manchester, Mold, Newcastle upon Tyne and Nottingham.

Comment

2C–19 TCC claims may be dealt with in the High Court or County Court. Hitherto TCC business (formerly O.R. business) fell only within the jurisdiction of the High Court. A claim with a value under the County Court limit can be issued in any of the County Courts named in 3.4.

A case of complexity or involving matters of public importance may be considered appropriate for transfer to the London Technology and Construction Court by way of example where a point on a contract is involved which may affect similar contracts commonly used in the construction industry. Otherwise such a case would proceed to trial in the appropriate County Court.

2C–19.1 Larger TCC claims may be appropriate for trial by a High Court Judge, but it may also be convenient for the parties for the litigation to be managed, and the trial to take place, in one of the TCC's regional centres. This potential problem was addressed by Ramsey J. in *Neath Port Talbot County BC v Currie and Brown Project Management Ltd* [2008] EWHC 1508 (TCC). He concluded that the case in question was suitable for trial by a High Court Judge but he refused to transfer the case from Bristol to London because Bristol formed a convenient location for the trial. He ruled that the case management would continue to be undertaken by the principal TCC judge in Bristol, and that the trial would be conducted by a High Court Judge, also in Bristol.

Applications before proceedings are issued

2C–20 **4.1** A party who intends to issue a TCC claim must make any application before the claim form is issued to a TCC judge.

4.2 The written evidence in support of such an application must state that the proposed claim is a TCC claim.

Comment

2C–21 It is important to note that a party who intends to issue a TCC claim must comply with the Pre-Action Protocol for Construction and Engineering Disputes, which is set

Paragraph numbers marked with a "+" can be found online and on CD.

out at Section C5 of Vol.1 of Civil Procedure. The principal ingredients of this process are set out in s.2 of the TCC Guide, starting at para.2C–44 below. Unlike any other pre-action protocol, the Protocol for Construction and Engineering Disputes requires a pre-action meeting between the parties, which can often lead to an early resolution of the dispute. Failure to comply with the Pre-Action Protocol may well result in the TCC proceedings being stayed until such compliance has been achieved (see *Cundall Johnson & Partners LLP v Whipps Cross University Hospital NHS Trust* [2007] EWHC 2178 (TCC)).

Comment

Recent decisions have demonstrated that the TCC will adopt a pragmatic approach **2C–21.1** in circumstances where a party has failed to comply with the precise procedure set out in the Pre-action Protocol. What matters is compliance with the substance of the Protocol and, in particular, ensuring that each side has a clear understanding of the position of the other: see *Orange Personal Communications Services Ltd v Hoare Lea (A firm)* [2008] EWHC 223 (TCC). Depending on the circumstances, it will be unusual for seperate proceedings commenced subsequently against another defendant, or Pt 20 proceedings, to be made the subject of the Protocol; see *Alfred McAlpine Capital Projects Ltd v Siac Construction (UK) Ltd* [2006] B.L.R. 139.

The importance of considering the claimant's pre-action conduct in the round was **2C–21.2** stressed by Akenhead J. in *TJ Brent Ltd v Black and Veatch Consulting Ltd* [2008] EWHC 1497 (TCC) when he said that:

"what the court should do in considering the Pre-action Protocol is to look at the matters in substance, not as a matter of semantics ... it is the court's job in reviewing this matter to look at matters in substance and not for technical non-compliances with the ... requirements in the Pre-action Protocol."

In that case he concluded that there had been substantial compliance with the Protocol.

Pre-Action Mediation

There will be cases in which, prior to the commencement of proceedings, the par- **2C–21.3** ties will engage in a mediation, either as part of the Protocol process or as a separate attempt at dispute resolution. The costs of such mediations can be significant. In *Lobster Group Ltd v Heidelberg Graphic Equipment* [2008] EWHC 413 (TCC) Coulson J. found that, as a general rule, the costs of a pre-action mediation were not recoverable in subsequent proceedings. He therefore concluded that such costs should be left out of account in any consideration of a subsequent application for security for costs under CPR Pt 23.

Pre-Action Disclosure

Given the volume of documents involved in many TCC disputes, it is common for **2C–21.4** prospective claimants to seek pre-action disclosure against prospective defendants pursuant to CPR 31.16. The relevant principles to be applied on such applications are set out by the Court of Appeal in *Black v Sumitomo Corporation* [2002] 1 W.L.R. 1562. One of the matters to be considered on such an application is the nature of the prospective claim and its prospects of success. In *Gwelhayl Ltd v Midas Construction Ltd* [2008] EWHC 2316, the application for pre-action disclosure failed because, on the facts, the judge was unable to conclude there would be any claim at all, let alone a claim with a real prospect of success.

Transfer of proceedings

5.1 Where no TCC judge is available to deal with a claim which **2C–22** has been issued in a High Court District Registry or one of the county courts listed in paragraph 3.4 above, the claim may be transferred—

(1) if it has been issued in a District Registry, to another District Registry or to the High Court in London; or

(2) if it has been issued in a county court, to another county court where a TCC judge would be available.

5.2 Paragraph 5.1 is without prejudice to the court's general powers to transfer proceedings under Part 30.

Paragraph numbers marked with a "+" can be found online and on CD.

(Rule 30.5(3) provides that an application for the transfer of proceedings to or from a special list must be made to a judge dealing with claims in that list).

5.3 A party applying to a TCC judge to transfer a claim to the TCC specialist list must give notice of the application to the court in which the claim is proceeding, and a TCC judge will not make an order for transfer until he is satisfied that such notice has been given.

Comment
2C–22.1 There have been three recent cases in which proceedings have been transferred into the TCC from other divisions of the High Court or courts outside London. They are *Fosse Me Ltd v Conde Nast* [2007] EWHC 2614 (TCC), a fire case; *Corby Group Litigation v Corby BC* [2007] EWHC 3174 (TCC), a personal injury case arising from reclamation and decontamination work at a former steel works complex; and *Brynley Collins v Raymond J Drumgold* [2008] EWHC 584 (TCC) a claim for some £300,000 arising out of allegedly defective foundations, transferred from the county court. In the last case the judge said that on applications to transfer in, the TCC would first consider whether the dispute in question was one of the types of claim which para.2.1 of the Pt 60 Practice Direction identified as being a claim suitable for the TCC. If so, the court would go on to ask whether the financial value of the claim and/or its complexity meant that, in accordance with the overriding objective, the case should be transferred to the TCC. He noted that what will often be critical is the view that the court takes of the complexity of the issues in the action itself. In addition, the court would consider broader questions of convenience to the parties.

As set out in App.D of the Technology and Construction Court Guide (para. 2C–151 below onwards) there are a number of district registries, civil justice centres, and county courts where there is at least one TCC judge. Accordingly, any application to transfer a case to the TCC in London from a provincial county court or district registry may depend, at least in part, upon the availability in that county court or district registry of a TCC judge. In *Brynley Collins v Raymond J Drumgold*, the absence of a TCC judge at the county court in question was a factor in the judge's decision to transfer the case to London.

Assignment of claim to a TCC judge
2C–23 **6.1** When a TCC claim is issued or an order is made transferring a claim to the TCC specialist list, the court will assign the claim to a named TCC judge ('the assigned TCC judge') who will have the primary responsibility for the case management of that claim.

6.2 All documents relating to the claim must be marked in similar manner to the claim form with the words 'Technology and Construction Court' and the name of the assigned TCC judge.

Comment
2C–24 As to assignment see section 3.7 of the TCC Guide, 2nd edition (see para.2C–57 below), and LCJ Statement (para.2C–35).

Applications
2C–25 **7.1** An application should normally be made to the assigned TCC judge. If the assigned TCC judge is not available, or the court gives permission, the application may be made to another TCC judge.

7.2 If an application is urgent and there is no TCC judge available to deal with it, the application may be made to any judge who, if the claim were not a TCC claim, would be authorised to deal with the application.

Paragraph numbers marked with a "+" can be found online and on CD.

Comment

In all vacations a TCC judge sits as a vacation judge on Wednesdays to deal with in-   **2C–26** terlocutory matters of all kinds and at other times by arrangement with his clerk or the registry, to deal with applications for injunctions, charging applications and any other urgent matter.

Applications to the assigned judge will cover a wide variety of topics. They will include applications for summary judgment or an interim payment; an interlocutory or permanent injunction; specific disclosure; or particular orders relating to delays in the provision of (or defects within) another party's pleadings and evidence. In addition, a party who has complied with the timetable or order of the court must make a specific application to the assigned judge if another party has failed to comply with that same timetable or order. It is important that, if one party is in significant delay, such default is brought to the attention of the assigned judge at the earliest opportunity, particularly if the delay threatens the feasibility of the trial date. The procedure to be followed in making and responding to applications is set out in s.6 of the TCC Guide (starting at para.2C–76 below).

Given the complexity of many TCC cases, it is not uncommon for parties to seek the trial of preliminary issues. The principles which the assigned judge will apply when considering an application for the hearing of preliminary issues are set out in some detail in s.8 of the TCC Guide (starting at para.2C–90 below). Whilst preliminary issues can often be a superficially attractive method of saving time, and therefore costs, it is important to note that, all too often, the hearing of preliminary issues does not lead to any such saving. For a recent warning as to the dangers of ordering preliminary issues in a TCC case, see para.61 of the judgment of Sir John Chadwick in *Perrin v Northampton BC* [2007] EWCA Civ 1353. For a TCC case in which, on the facts, the judge concluded that the ordering of preliminary issues would not substantially save time or money and would not significantly improve the possibility of a settlement, see *Leading Rule v Phoenix Interiors Ltd* [2007] EWHC 2293 (TCC).

Comment

One of the most common kind of applications in the TCC relates to specific   **2C–26.1** disclosure and/or redacted documents. It is not uncommon for parties in TCC litigation to withhold numerous documents or to disclose them with parts redacted, and for the other side then to seek disclosure of the documents or to have the redactions removed. In *Atos Consultant Ltd v Avis PLC* [2007] EWHC 323 (TCC) the court had to consider whether the material being redacted was either privileged or relevant. The judge said that the right approach was, firstly, to consider the evidence produced on the application; secondly, if the court was satisfied that the right to withhold inspection (of all or part of the document) was established by the evidence and there were no sufficient for challenging the correctness of that asserted right, the court would uphold the right; thirdly, if court was not satisfied that the right to withhold inspection was established (because, for instance, the evidence did not establish a legal right to withhold inspection), then the court would order inspection of the documents; fourthly, if sufficient grounds were shown for challenging the correctness of the asserted right then the court might order further evidence to be produced on oath or, if there was no other appropriate method of properly deciding whether the right to withhold inspection should be upheld, it might decide to inspect the documents; fifthly, if the court decided to inspect the documents then, having undertaken such an inspection, it might invite further representations from the parties.

Without prejudice material

Another difficulty can arise out of the parties' attempts to compromise their disputes   **2C–26.2** at the time, or shortly after, they first arose. During such attempts, one party may say something which, subsequently, the other party wishes to rely on. This can lead to arguments as to whether such statements were made as part of "without prejudice" negotiations (in which case the material will generally be inadmissible) or whether one of the exceptions to that general rule might apply (if, say, the communication did not unequivocally indicate the maker's intention to negotiate). The various authorities were summarised in *Galliford Try Construction Ltd v Mott MacDonald Ltd* [2008] EWHC 6030 (TCC) in which, on the facts, the judge concluded that the evidence in question arose out of genuine negotiations and was therefore the subject of the general "without prejudice" exclusion. He also found that the relevant privilege or admissibility had not

Paragraph numbers marked with a "+" can be found online and on CD.

TCC

been waived. The question of waiver also arose in *Farm Assist Ltd v The Secretary of State for Environment, Food and Rural Affairs* [2008] EWHC 3079 (TCC) in which Ramsey J. held that the documents in question were subject to legal advice privilege which had not been waived, notwithstanding the fact that the state of mind of the recipient of that legal advice was very much in issue in the case.

Applications under CPR Parts 24 and 25

2C–26.3   A claimant with a large claim will often seek summary judgment pursuant to CPR Pt 24, or an interim payment pursuant to CPR Pt 25, in an attempt to recover a significant sum promptly. Such applications can lead the responding party to flood the court with paper in the hope that the judge will conclude that the matter is inappropriate for summary judgment. In *Jacobs UK Ltd v Skidmore Owings and Merrill LLP* [2008] EWHC 2847 (TCC) Coulson J. said:

> "In commercial cases, it is all too easy for a party who wishes to avoid summary judgment under CPR Part 24 to put in lengthy statements, and exhibit numerous documents, in the hope that the court will conclude that the issues will have to be dealt with at a trial, and that summary judgment is inappropriate. That risk is particularly acute in the TCC, where the parties often need no invitation to swamp the court with extraneous documentation. It is therefore incumbent on the court to consider the parties' submissions on the material provided and to see whether, no matter how detailed the documentation, the necessary tests have been made out."

He emphasised that, without undertaking this task, whatever the level of detail provided, it was not possible for the court to say whether there was a defence at all or, if there was, whether it had a "real prospect of success" and, even if it did, whether the defence raised could only be described as "possible", with the result that a conditional order might be appropriate under r.24.6.

Unless Orders

2C–26.4   Where one party persistently fails to comply with court orders, it may be appropriate for the court to make an unless order, which will spell out in detail the consequences of any further non-compliance. In *E Group Ltd v Baker [t/a 'Hello']* [2008] EWHC 2349 (TCC) the defendant failed to comply with the number of orders of the court. An unless order was made against her with which she also failed to comply. The court was satisfied that the unless order was entirely justified, and that the automatic and draconian consequences of the defendant's non-compliance were therefore triggered. The defendant's defence was thus struck out.

Case management conference

2C–27   **8.1** The court will fix a case management conference within 14 days of the earliest of these events—

    (1)   the filing of an acknowledgment of service;

    (2)   the filing of a defence; or

    (3)   the date of an order transferring the claim to a TCC.

8.2 When the court notifies the parties of the date and time of the case management conference, it will at the same time send each party a case management information sheet and a case management directions form.

(The case management information sheet and the case management directions form are in the form set out in Appendixes A and B to this practice direction).

8.3 Not less than two days before the case management conference, each party must file and serve on all other parties—

    (1)   completed copies of the case management information sheet and case management directions form; and

    (2)   an application notice for any order which that party intends

Paragraph numbers marked with a "+" can be found online and on CD.

to seek at the case management conference, other than directions referred to in the case management directions form.

8.4 The parties are encouraged to agree directions to propose to the court by reference to the case management directions form.

8.5 If any party fails to file or serve the case management information sheet and the case management directions form by the date specified, the court may—

(1) impose such sanction as it sees fit; and

(2) either proceed with or adjourn the case management conference.

8.6 The directions given at the case management conference will normally include the fixing of dates for—

(1) any further case management conferences;

(2) a pre-trial review;

(3) the trial of any preliminary issues that it orders to be tried; and

(4) the trial.

Comment

Note that 8.3 gives a minimum time for exchange and return of the case management questionnaire and case management directions form. In substantial and complex cases it is desirable to exchange and serve at least four clear days before the hearing to assist the judge. An early exchange and return also gives the parties further opportunity to consider each other's proposals and agree matters before the hearing. 8.5 provides for sanctions and underlines the philosophy behind the rules and reflected in 4.3 (above) there should be no slippage and the time and resource of the court should not be wasted.

Paragraph 8.6—the Agenda for the first case conference will be based upon the form at Appendix B of the Practice Direction. Each case coming before the TCC varies as to its length, complexity and parties, and tailor made directions may be given or agreed to suit the case. For example, where a view is appropriate the timing of the view having regard to the changing state of the matter in dispute as when remedial work is being carried out. Directions may be given that a building or structure must not be altered before experts have had the proper opportunity to examine it fully; for the joint making of trial pits, bore holes, laboratory tests, or analyses; where a Scott schedule has been ordered, that the parties should select representative items for trial; arrangements for video displays, demonstrations and the like. It is at this stage that the court may consider whether an ADR direction may be given (see Pt 1.4(2)(E)) and whether it is necessary to extend time compliance requirements of the CPR to enable the parties to investigate ADR. Consideration may also be given at this stage as to whether an early neutral evaluation (ENE) would be appropriate by a judge of the court. It is open for the parties, should they so wish, in an appropriate case, to make an application that a judge of the court can be appointed to act as mediator. Note, that a judge acting as mediator thereafter ceases to take any part in the trial in, of the action. In the event of it proceeding it would be tried before another judge. In relation to resolution by trial, consideration will be given to the trial of an issue, or split trials of liability/damages.

Paragraph 8.6 contains provision that at the first case management conference, the court will usually fix the date for the trial of the case. This is so, but the direction will normally be in the following form:

Trial: Week beginning ...   *For fees' purposes only this is not notice by the court of the trial date.*

Estimated length ... days   (see Supreme Court Fees Order 1999, para.2.2, Schedule 1, column 2).

2C–28

Paragraph numbers marked with a "+" can be found online and on CD.

399

See also the guidance given in s.5 of the TCC Guide (2nd edn) (see para.2C–66 below). Paragraph 8.6(3) preliminary issues, see s.8 of the TCC Guide (2nd edn) (see para.2C–90 below).

It may be that, in the lead-up to or at the commencement of the first case management conference, the parties will be able to agree the orders to be made by the court. The assigned judge will take the agreed terms as the starting-point for his consideration of the orders to be made and, if appropriate, may often make the order in the precise terms that have been agreed: see s.5.7.1 of the TCC Guide at para.2C–72 below. If the terms have been agreed by the parties and approved by the judge well in advance of the case management conference, then it may be that there will be no need for a hearing at all. However, the assigned judge will usually want to see the parties at this early stage to identify any matters of potential concern; to explore the possibility of ADR; and to emphasise any particular aspects of the trial preparation which he or she considers to be of importance.

Cost Capping

2C–28.1 At or shortly after the first case management conference, the parties may need to consider whether or not it would be appropriate to apply for costs capping orders pursuant to s.51(3) of the Supreme Court Act 1981 and CPR 3.1(2)(m). These can be particularly important in group litigation. The appropriate principles were set out by Akenhead J. in *Claimants v Corby BC* [2008] EWHC 619 (TCC). He concluded that he should fix an overall costs cap but that, in so doing, he had to have regard to the constituent elements of each party's submitted cost estimates. He reiterated that an overall costs cap had to allow an element of flexibility because, in practice, some of the costs would go down as well as up.

Assessors

2C–28.2 Given the technical nature of most TCC work, it might be thought surprising that TCC judges do not sit more often with assessors appointed pursuant to CPR 35.15. The principles applicable to the appointment of assessors were recently set out in *Balcombe Group PLC v London Development Agency* [2008] EWHC 1392 (TCC). On the facts of that case, the judge refused one party's application for the appointment of assessors, concluding that it would not be proportionate to make such an order on the facts of that case. He also said that:

> "the evaluation of a lengthy list of individual items of claim, and the consideration of their reasonableness or (otherwise), is one of the principal functions of the TCC and there is no reason to distinguish this case from the ordinary run of quantum disputes arising out of property development and building work."

He concluded that, generally, such disputes were not suitable for assessors.

Pre-trial review

2C–29 **9.1** When the court fixes the date for a pre-trial review it will send each party a pre-trial review questionnaire.

(The pre-trial review questionnaire is in the form set out in Appendix C to this practice direction).

9.2 Each party must file and serve on all other parties completed copies of the questionnaire not less than two days before the date fixed for the pre-trial review.

9.3 The parties are encouraged to agree directions to propose to the court.

9.4 If any party fails to return or exchange the questionnaire by the date specified the court may—

(1) impose such sanction as it sees fit; and

(2) either proceed with or adjourn the pre-trial review.

9.5 At the pre-trial review, the court will give such directions for the conduct of the trial as it sees fit.

Paragraph numbers marked with a "+" can be found online and on CD.

Comment

The parties will be reminded by a letter from the court of the date and time of the **2C–30** pre-trial review. That letter will contain the following text.

"For the purposes of the fees order notice is now given that the trial has been fixed for (date) accordingly a fee of £600 must be paid within 14 days of the date of this notice, i.e. by (date 14 days from the date of dispatch of the letter) by the claimant or claimants, if the action is proceeding on the counter claim alone by the defendant. Payment is to be made (preferably by cheque) at the Registry of this Court or to the Fees Room in the Main Building (i.e. at the Royal Courts of Justice). The PTR questionnaire (see below) must be presented when payment is made as the receipt of payment of the fee is stamped on it.

If the fee is not paid by the date specified rule 3.7(4) states that the claim (or counterclaim) will be struck out automatically and that the claimant (or the defendant, as the case may be) will be liable for the costs incurred by the other party(ies) unless the Court orders otherwise.

You are reminded that as well as the completed Pre-Trial Reviews Questionnaires all proposed directions (which should be agreed wherever possible) be lodged by all parties with me not later than two clear days before the date of the PTR. Copies of the Questionnaire and the PTR Direction Form are obtainable from the Registry. Any questions relating to the fee should be addressed to the Registry but all other questions about the PTR must be addressed to me. Signed Clerk to the Judge."

Paragraph 9.2—see note to 8.3 above.

Paragraph 9.5—the court will take stock and ensure that there has been no unjustifiable slippage of the timetable. Where there has, directions will be given to ensure timely compliance. Since witness statements and experts may well have been exchanged this may be an appropriate time for parties to further consider ADR. In relation to conduct of the trial, further directions may be given to ensure that the proper issues are tried. The parties in the light of the pleadings, expert reports exchanged and witness statements served, may well have been required to provide a list of issues for trial to be considered at the PTR. If not already given, leave to call expert witnesses may be considered in the light of the exchange of expert reports and the identification of issues on which they are or are not agreed (see Pt 35.12(3)). Consideration will be given as to the necessity of supplemental witness/expert reports, and leave may be given. A trial timetable should be agreed by the parties and, failing such agreement, will be determined by the trial judge. Consideration will be given to such matters as the order of witnesses, e.g. the hearing of all witnesses' fact on both sides followed by the expert evidence, and to the organisation of trial bundles, i.e. indexing, time and service of index and proposed bundles, and the preparation of a core bundle(s) with cross references to the full trial bundles, where appropriate. Directions may be given at this as to whether the pleadings the claimant or defendant will open the trial and as to the service of written openings for the court/opposing party(ies) and written responses, if appropriate, and the provision of a chronology and cast list. A direction may be given as to the filing of disks (if obtainable) of the statements of case, witness statements, experts' reports, trial bundles and opening notes.

See also s.14 of the TCC Guid (2nd edn) (see para.2C–122).

Experience shows that the listing and hearing of a pre-trial review some weeks before the commencement date of the trial has two specific benefits. First, it provides a mechanism by which any minor slippage in the original timetable can be made good without endangering the trial date. In cases of significant default, however, it is critically important that the parties do not allow the fact that there is a forthcoming PTR to absolve them from making an earlier application to the court seeking compliance by the defaulting party. One party's failure to take a significant step (such as the service of witness statements or expert's reports) cannot be left to be resolved at the pre-trial review because, by that late stage, the delay in taking such a step, and the failure of any other party to bring that delay to the attention of the court, will leave the judge with the unpalatable choice between either adjourning the trial, or allowing the trial to go ahead with at least one party at a significant disadvantage.

Secondly, the PTR allows the assigned judge and the parties to resolve in some detail precisely how the trial will be conducted. This might even extend to resolving any questions of the admissibility of the evidence contained within the witness statements or expert's reports. Thus, because of the work that has been done at the PTR,

Paragraph numbers marked with a "+" can be found online and on CD.

the first day of a trial in the TCC will usually involve short oral openings and then, by mid-morning, the commencement of oral evidence. The PTR should ensure that valuable trial time is not lost in dealing with interlocutory and preliminary matters which should have been resolved weeks before.

Listing

2C–31   **10** The provisions about listing questionnaires and listing in Part 29 and its practice direction do not apply to TCC claims.

Trial

2C–32   **11.1** Whenever possible the trial of a claim will be heard by the assigned TCC judge.

11.2 A TCC claim may be tried at any place where there is a TCC judge available to try the claim.

Comment

2C–33   The procedure to be followed where judgment is reserved is set out in sections 15.9.2 and 15.9.3 of the TCC Guide (see para.2C–135 below). In more complex cases, the judge will normally reserve judgment and hand down a written judgment as soon as possible thereafter. A draft copy of this judgment may be circulated in advance of the formal handing down, in order that the parties can notify the judge of any clerical errors or slips which they note in the judgment. The circulation of such a draft is not to be taken as an opportunity to re-argue the issues in the case. If the assigned judge wants further assistance on a particular point he will either request that assistance before circulating the draft, or will identify the particular paragraph or paragraphs in the draft which he requires the parties to check and/or comment upon, together with an explanation of the specific point on which their further assistance is being sought. Often in multi-party litigation, some of the claims and cross-claims will have been compromised immediately prior to the trial. This can give rise to an issue as to whether one party can utilise the expert's reports served by another party who, by then, is no longer part of the trial. In *Gurney Consulting Engineers v Gleeds Health and Safety Ltd* [2006] EWHC 43 (TCC) the court concluded that, where one party has disclosed an expert's report, any other party in the litigation may use that report as evidence at the trial, whether or not the party who originally commissioned the report was still a party to the proceedings. Precisely the same conclusion was reached in *Shepherd & Neame v EDF Energy Networks [SPN] Plc* [2008] EWHC 123 (TCC).

Appendices

Editorial note

2C–34   The following forms which are annexed to this PD as Appendices A, B and C can be found in the *Civil Procedure Forms Volume*:

- TCC/CM1
- TCC/CMCDIR
- TCC/PTR1

Paragraph numbers marked with a "+" can be found online and on CD.

TECHNOLOGY AND CONSTRUCTION COURT: STATEMENT BY THE LORD CHIEF JUSTICE OF ENGLAND & WALES

1. This announcement is made on behalf of myself and the Lord **2C–35** Chancellor. It reflects the importance which both the Lord Chancellor and I attach to the work of the Technology and Construction Court ("TCC").

2. The TCC is a specialist court, which operates at eleven court centres across the country. It comprises one High Court judge (who devotes about half of his working time to the business of the TCC) and 41 senior circuit and circuit judges. Of these circuit judges eight are full time TCC judges and the remainder spend only part of their time hearing TCC cases. Of the eight full time TCC judges, five are based at St Dunstan's House in London ("the London TCC"), one in Birmingham, one in Manchester and one in Liverpool. There are also 23 recorders who, because of their experience of the relevant classes of work, are specifically authorised to hear TCC cases when required. Most of the full time TCC judges (and all of those at the London TCC) are senior circuit judges.

3. The construction sector accounts for about 10% of the UK's GDP. The IT sector also accounts for a significant and growing proportion of GDP. Disputes within these industries or between providers and end users are often of considerable complexity. The sums at issue are huge. Some of the disputes arise from construction projects overseas or involve international parties. These disputes are of comparable size and importance to general commercial litigation. TCC judges try some of the most arduous and complex cases which come before the civil courts.

4. The existing TCC judges have a high degree of expertise in the management and trial of complex construction and IT cases. I pay tribute to the excellent work, which those judges are doing and have done for many years. Nevertheless the lack of involvement of High Court judges in the work of the TCC has been a source of concern within the IT and construction industries and within the profession. Hitherto the TCC has only had the services of one High Court judge for approximately half of his working time. It is now desirable for High Court judges to play a larger role in the management and trial of IT and construction litigation.

5. Arrangements for the longer term future of the TCC are currently under consideration by the Lord Chancellor, the Lord Chief Justice and the Master of the Rolls. In the meantime, however, we have decided that interim arrangements must be put in place, in order to ensure that all TCC cases are tried by appropriate judges. The interim arrangements, which will come into effect today, are as follows:

(i) The High Court judge in charge of the TCC (currently Jackson J) will no longer be required to spend half of each term away from the TCC. Instead he will be principally based at the TCC and will only sit in other courts when there is no TCC work requiring the immediate involvement of a High Court judge.

Paragraph numbers marked with a "+" can be found online and on CD.

(ii) The judge in charge of the TCC will (with the assistance of the registry manager) consider every new case which is started in or transferred into the London TCC. He will classify each new case as "HCJ" or "SCJ". The most complex and heavy cases will be classified "HCJ". These will be managed and tried either by the judge in charge of the TCC or by another suitable High Court judge. The majority of cases, however, will be classified as "SCJ". These cases may be allocated to a named senior circuit judge by the judge in charge of the TCC; alternatively, they will be so allocated by operation of the rota.

(iii) It is neither practicable nor necessary for the judge in charge of the TCC to consider TCC cases which are commenced in, or transferred to, court centres outside London. Nevertheless, if any TCC case started outside London appears to require management and trial by a High Court judge, then the full time or principal TCC judge at that court centre should refer the case to the judge in charge of the TCC for a decision as to its future management and trial.

(iv) When proceedings are commenced in, or transferred to, the London TCC, any party to those proceedings may make brief representations by letter as to the appropriate classification.

6. Work is currently in progress on the preparation of a new edition of the TCC Guide. There has been widespread consultation with judges, court users and the profession about the contents of the Guide. The new edition of the Guide will set out the criteria which the judge in charge of the TCC will apply, when allocating cases to the appropriate level of judge. It will also provide that the judge in charge may change the classification of cases from "HCJ" to "SCJ", or vice versa, as appropriate.

7. I am confident that the TCC will continue, as it has done in the past, constantly seeking to improve the service which it provides to court users.

The Right Honourable The Lord Woolf
Lord Chief Justice of England and Wales
7th June 2005

Comment

2C–36   The 2nd edition of the Technology and Construction Court Guide is set out below. As to allocation of cases in the London TCC, see Guide at ss.3.7.1–3.7.4 inclusive (see para.2C–57).

Paragraph numbers marked with a "+" can be found online and on CD.

Technology and Construction Court Guide

Second Edition

(issued 3 October 2005, revised with effect from 1 October 2007)

2C–37

EXPLANATORY NOTE: This First Revision of the Second Edition of the TCC Guide makes **2C–38**
the following changes:

- *The contact details in Appendix D have been updated.*
- *Some minor inconsistencies in the provisions re time limits have been corrected.*
- *Paragraphs 2.1.3 and 2.4.2 have been revised to reflect amendments to the Pre-Action Protocol.*
- *Paragraphs 3.7.3 and 5.7.1 have been amended in the light of comments made by court users.*
- *Reference to the new Protocol re Provisional Bookings has been added to paragraph 3.7.4.*
- *Paragraph 4.5.5 has been deleted and paragraph 4.8.1 has been added in relation to lodging of documents.*
- *A sentence has been added to paragraph 5.2.1 to deal with the problem of fixing the first case management conference in multi-party cases.*
- *Paragraph 10.4.1 has been amended to reflect a recent decision.*

2C–39

Paragraph numbers marked with a "+" can be found online and on CD.

TCC

SECTION 1.

INTRODUCTION

1.1 Purpose of Guide

1.1.1 This new edition of the Technology and Construction Court ("TCC") Guide is intended to provide straightforward, practical guidance to the conduct of litigation in the TCC. Whilst it is intended to be comprehensive, it naturally concentrates on the most important aspects of such litigation. It therefore cannot cover all the procedural points that may arise. It does, however, describe the main elements of the practice that is likely to be followed in most TCC cases.

1.1.2 The Guide reflects the flexible framework within which litigation in the TCC is habitually conducted. The requirements set out in the Guide are designed to ensure effective management of proceedings in the TCC. It must always be remembered that, if parties fail to comply with these requirements, the court may impose sanctions including orders for costs.

1.1.3 In respect of those procedural areas for which specific provision is not made in this Guide, the parties, together with their advisors, will be expected to act reasonably and in accordance with both the spirit of the Guide and the overriding objective at CPR Rule 1.1

1.1.4 It is not the function of the Guide to summarise the Civil Procedure Rules ("the CPR"), and it should not be regarded as a substitute for the CPR. The parties and their advisors are expected to familiarise themselves with the CPR and, in particular, to understand the importance of the "overriding objective" of the CPR. The TCC endeavours to ensure that all its cases are dealt with justly and with proper proportionality. This includes ensuring that the parties are on an equal footing; taking all practicable steps to save expenditure; dealing with the dispute in ways which are proportionate to the size of the claim and cross-claim and the importance of the case to the parties; and managing the case throughout in a way that takes proper account of its complexity and the different financial positions of the parties. The court will also endeavour to ensure expedition, and to allot to each case an appropriate share of the court's resources.

1.1.5 This new edition of the TCC Guide has been prepared in consultation with the judges of the TCC in London, Cardiff, Birmingham, Manchester and Leeds, and with the advice and support of TECBAR, TeCSA, the Society for Computers and Law and the TCC Users' Committees in London, Cardiff, Birmingham, Manchester, Liverpool and Leeds. The TCC Guide is published with the approval of the Head of Civil Justice and the deputy Head of Civil Justice.

1.2 The CPR

2C-40 1.2.1 Proceedings in the TCC are governed by the CPR and the supplementary Practice Directions. CPR Part 60 and its associated Practice Direction deal specifically with the practice and procedure of the TCC.

1.2.2 Other parts of the CPR that frequently arise in TCC cases include Part 8 (Alternative Procedure for Claims); Parts 12 and 13 (Default Judgment and Setting Aside); Part 17 (Amendments); Part 20 (Counterclaims and Other Additional Claims); Part 24 (Summary Judgment); Part 25 (Interim Remedies and Security for Costs); Part 26 (Case Management); Part 32 (Evidence); Part 35 (Experts and Assessors) and Part 62 (Arbitration Claims).

1.3 The TCC

2C-41 1.3.1 <u>What are TCC Claims?</u> CPR Rules 60.1 (2) and (3) provide that a TCC claim is a claim which (i) involves technically complex issues or questions (or for which trial by a TCC judge is desirable) and (ii) has been issued in or transferred into the TCC

Paragraph numbers marked with a "+" can be found online and on CD.

specialist list. Paragraph 2.1 of the TCC Practice Direction identifies the following as examples of the types of claim which it may be appropriate to bring as TCC claims—

(a) building or other construction disputes, including claims for the enforcement of the decisions of adjudicators under the Housing Grants, Construction and Regeneration Act 1996;

(b) engineering disputes;

(c) claims by and against engineers, architects, surveyors, accountants and other specialised advisors relating to the services they provide;

(d) claims by and against local authorities relating to their statutory duties concerning the development of land or the construction of buildings;

(e) claims relating to the design, supply and installation of computers, computer software and related network systems;

(f) claims relating to the quality of goods sold or hired, and work done, materials supplied or services rendered;

(g) claims between landlord and tenant for breach of a repairing covenant;

(h) claims between neighbours, owners and occupiers of land in trespass, nuisance, etc.

(i) claims relating to the environment (for example, pollution cases);

(j) claims arising out of fires;

(k) claims involving taking of accounts where these are complicated; and

(l) challenges to decisions of arbitrators in construction and engineering disputes including applications for permission to appeal and appeals.

It should be noted that this list is not exhaustive and other types of claim may well be appropriate for the TCC.

1.3.2 The Court. Both the High Court and the county courts deal with TCC business. Circuit judges and recorders only have jurisdiction to manage and try TCC cases if they have been nominated by the Lord Chancellor pursuant to section 68 (1) (a) of the Supreme Court Act 1981. It should be noted that those circuit judges who have been nominated pursuant to section 68(1) of the Supreme Court Act 1981 fall into two categories: "full time" TCC judges and "part time" TCC judges. "Full time" TCC judges spend most of their time dealing with TCC business, although they will do other work when there is no TCC business requiring their immediate attention. "Part time" TCC judges are circuit judges who are only available to sit in the TCC for part of their time. They have substantial responsibilities outside the TCC.

In respect of a court centre where there is no full time TCC judge, the term "principal TCC judge" is used in this Guide to denote the circuit judge who has principal responsibility for TCC work.

The phrase "Technology and Construction Court" or "TCC" or "the court" is used in this Guide to denote any court which deals with TCC claims. All of the courts which deal with TCC claims form a composite group of courts. When those courts are dealing with TCC business, CPR Part 60, its accompanying Practice Direction and this Guide govern the procedures of those courts. The High Court judge in charge of the TCC ("the Judge in Charge"), although based principally in London, has overall responsibility for the judicial supervision of TCC business in those courts.

1.3.3 The TCC in London. The principal centre for TCC work is the High Court in London at St Dunstan's House, 133-137 Fetter Lane, London, EC4A 1HD. The Judge in Charge of the TCC sits principally at St Dunstan's House together with five full time TCC judges. Subject to paragraph 3.7.1 below, any communication or enquiry concerning a TCC case, which is proceeding at St Dunstan's House, should be directed to the clerk of the judge who is assigned to that case. The various contact details for the judges' clerks are set out in Appendix D.

The TCC judges who are based at St Dunstan's House will, when appropriate, sit at court centres outside London.

TCC county court cases in London are brought in (or transferred to) the Central London Civil Justice Centre, 13-14 Park Crescent, London W1N 4HT.

Paragraph numbers marked with a "+" can be found online and on CD.

1.3.4 District Registries. TCC claims can be brought in the High Court outside London in any District Registry, although the Practice Direction states that it is preferable that, wherever possible, such claims should be issued in one of the following District Registries: Birmingham, Bristol, Cardiff, Chester, Exeter, Leeds, Liverpool, Newcastle, Nottingham and Salford (Manchester). There are full-time TCC Judges in Birmingham, Liverpool and Salford (Manchester). Contact details are again set out in Appendix D. There are part time TCC judges and/or recorders nominated to deal with TCC business available at most court centres throughout England and Wales.

In a number of regions a "TCC liaison district judge" has been appointed. It is the function of the TCC liaison district judge:

(a) To keep other district judges in that region well informed about the role and remit of the TCC (in order that appropriate cases may be transferred to the TCC at an early, rather than late, stage).

(b) To deal with any queries from colleagues concerning the TCC or cases which might merit transfer to the TCC.

(c) To deal with any subsidiary matter which a TCC judge directs should be determined by a district judge pursuant to rule 60.1(5)(b)(ii).

(d) To deal with urgent applications in TCC cases pursuant to paragraph 7.2 of the Practice Direction (i.e. no TCC judge is available and the matter is of a kind that falls within the district judge's jurisdiction).

1.3.5 County Courts outside London. TCC claims may also be brought in those county courts which are specified in the Part 60 Practice Direction. The specified county courts are: Birmingham, Bristol, Cardiff, Chester, Exeter, Leeds, Liverpool, Newcastle, Nottingham and Salford (Manchester). Contact details are again set out in Appendix D.

Where TCC proceedings are brought in a county court, statements of case and applications should be headed:

"In the ... County Court
Technology and Construction Court"

This heading is important because in TCC cases (subject to the limited exceptions mentioned in paragraph 1.3.4 above) district judges do not have jurisdiction to hear applications or make orders.

1.3.6 The division between High Court and county court TCC cases. As a general rule TCC claims for more than £50,000 are brought in the High Court, whilst claims for lower sums are brought in the county court. However, this is not a rigid dividing line. The monetary threshold for High Court TCC claims tends to be higher in London than in the regions. Regard must also be had to the complexity of the case and all other circumstances. Arbitration claims and claims to enforce or challenge adjudicators' awards are generally (but not invariably) brought in the High Court. The scale of fees differs in the High Court and the county court. This is a factor which should be borne in mind in borderline cases.

1.4 The TCC Users' Committees

2C-42 1.4.1 The continuing ability of the TCC to meet the changing needs of all those involved in TCC litigation depends in large part upon a close working relationship between the TCC and its users.

1.4.2 London. The Judge in Charge chairs two meetings a year of the London TCC Users' Committee. The judge's clerk acts as secretary to the Committee and takes the minutes of meetings. That Committee is made up of representatives of the London TCC judges, the barristers and solicitors who regularly use the Court, the professional bodies, such as architects, engineers and arbitrators, whose members are affected by the decisions of the Court, and representatives of both employers and contractors' groups.

Paragraph numbers marked with a "+" can be found online and on CD.

1.4.3 <u>Outside London.</u> There are similar meetings of TCC Users' Committees in Birmingham, Salford (Manchester), Liverpool, Cardiff and Leeds. Each Users' Committee is chaired by the full time TCC judge or the principal TCC judge in that location.

1.4.4 The TCC regards these channels of communication as extremely important and all those who are concerned with the work of the Court are encouraged to make full use of these meetings. Any suggestions or other correspondence raising matters for consideration by the Users' Committee should, in the first instance, be addressed to the clerk to the Judge in Charge at St. Dunstan's House or to the clerk to the appropriate TCC judge outside London.

1.5 Specialist Associations

1.5.1 There are a number of associations of legal representatives which are represented on the Users' Committees and which also liaise closely with the Court. These contacts ensure that the Court remains responsive to the opinions and requirements of the professional users of the Court.

1.5.2 The relevant professional organisations are the TCC Bar Association ("TECBAR") and the TCC Solicitors Association ("TeCSA"). Details of the relevant contacts at these organisations are set out on their respective websites, namely www.tecbar.org and www.tecsa.org.

2C–43

SECTION 2.

PRE-ACTION PROTOCOL

2.1 Introduction

2.1.1 There is a Pre-Action Protocol for Construction and Engineering Disputes. Where the dispute involves a claim against architects, engineers or quantity surveyors, this Protocol prevails over the Professional Negligence Pre-Action Protocol: see paragraph 1.1 of the Protocol for Construction and Engineering Disputes and paragraph A.1 of the Professional Negligence Pre-Action Protocol. The current version of the Construction and Engineering Pre-Action Protocol ("the Protocol") is set out in volume 1 of the White Book at section C.

2C–44

2.1.2 The purpose of the Protocol is to encourage the frank and early exchange of information about the prospective claim and any defence to it; to enable parties to avoid litigation by agreeing a settlement of the claim before the commencement of proceedings; and to support the efficient management of proceedings where litigation cannot be avoided.

2.1.3 <u>Proportionality.</u> The overriding objective (CPR rule 1.1) applies to the pre-action period. The Protocol must not be used as a tactical device to secure advantage for one party or to generate unnecessary costs. In lower value TCC claims (such as those likely to proceed in the county court), the letter of claim and the response should be simple and the costs of both sides should be kept to a modest level. In all cases the costs incurred at the Protocol stage should be proportionate to the complexity of the case and the amount of money which is at stake. The Protocol does not impose a requirement on the parties to marshal and disclose all the supporting details and evidence that may ultimately be required if the case proceeds to litigation.

2.2 To Which Claims Does The Protocol Apply?

2.2.1 The court will expect all parties to have complied in substance with the provisions of the Protocol in all construction and engineering disputes. The only exceptions to this are identified in paragraph 2.3 below.

2C–45

2.2.2 The court regards the Protocol as setting out normal and reasonable pre-action conduct. Accordingly, whilst the Protocol is not mandatory for a number of the claims

Paragraph numbers marked with a "+" can be found online and on CD.

noted by way of example in paragraph 1.3.1 above, such as computer cases or dilapidations claims, the court would, in the absence of a specific reason to the contrary, expect the Protocol generally to be followed in such cases prior to the commencement of proceedings in the TCC.

2.3 What Are The Exceptions?

2C–46 2.3.1 A claimant does not have to comply with the Protocol if his claim:

(a) is to enforce the decision of an adjudicator;

(b) includes a claim for interim injunctive relief;

(c) will be the subject of a claim for summary judgment pursuant to Part 24 of the CPR; or

(d) relates to the same or substantially the same issues as have been the subject of a recent adjudication or some other formal alternative dispute resolution procedure.

2.3.2 In addition, a claimant need not comply with any part of the Protocol if, by so doing, his claim may become time-barred under the Limitation Act 1980. In those circumstances, a claimant should commence proceedings without complying with the Protocol and must, at the same time, apply for specific directions as to the timetable and form of procedure to be adopted. The court may order a stay of those proceedings pending completion of the steps set out in the Protocol.

2.4 What Are The Essential Ingredients Of The Protocol?

2C–47 2.4.1 The Letter of Claim. The letter of claim must comply with Section 3 of the Protocol. Amongst other things, it must contain a clear summary of the facts on which each claim is based; the basis on which each claim is made; and details of the relief claimed, including a breakdown showing how any damages have been quantified. The claimant must also provide the names of experts already instructed and on whom he intends to rely.

2.4.2 The Defendant's Response. The defendant has 14 days to acknowledge the letter of claim and 28 days (from receipt of the letter of claim) either to take any jurisdiction objection or to respond in substance to the letter of claim. Paragraph 4.3.1 of the Protocol enables the parties to agree an extension of the 28 day period up to a maximum of 3 months. In any case of substance it is quite usual for an extension of time to be agreed for the defendant's response. The letter of response must comply with section 4 of the Protocol. Amongst other things, it must state which claims are accepted, which claims are rejected and on what basis. It must set out any counterclaim to be advanced by the defendant. The defendant should also provide the names of experts who have been instructed and on whom he intends to rely. If the defendant fails either to acknowledge or to respond to the letter of claim in time, the claimant is entitled to commence proceedings.

2.4.3 Pre-action Meeting. The Construction and Engineering Protocol is the only Protocol under the CPR that generally requires the parties to meet, without prejudice, at least once, in order to identify the main issues and the root causes of their disagreement on those issues. The purpose of the meeting is to see whether, and if so how, those issues might be resolved without recourse to litigation or, if litigation is unavoidable, what steps should be taken to ensure that it is conducted in accordance with the overriding objective. At or as a result of the meeting, the parties should consider whether some form of alternative dispute resolution ("ADR") would be more suitable than litigation and if so, they should endeavour to agree which form of ADR to adopt. Although the meeting is "without prejudice", any party who attended the meeting is at liberty to disclose to the Court at a later stage that the meeting took place; who attended and who refused to attend, together with the grounds for their refusal; and any agreements concluded between the parties.

2.5 What Happens To The Material Generated By The Protocol?

2C–48 2.5.1 The letter of claim, the defendant's response, and the information relating to attendance (or otherwise) at the meeting are not confidential or 'without prejudice'

Paragraph numbers marked with a "+" can be found online and on CD.

and can therefore be referred to by the parties in any subsequent litigation. The detail of any discussion at the meeting(s) and/or any note of the meeting cannot be referred to the court unless all parties agree.

2.5.2 Normally the parties should include in the bundle for the first case management conference: (a) the letter of claim, (b) the response, and (c) any agreed note of the pre-action meeting: see Section 5 below. The documents attached to or enclosed with the letter and the response should not be included in the bundle.

2.6 What If One Party Has Not Complied With The Protocol?

2.6.1 There can often be a complaint that one or other party has not complied with the Protocol. The court will consider any such complaints once proceedings have been commenced. If the court finds that the claimant has not complied with one part of the Protocol, then the court may stay the proceedings until the steps set out in the Protocol have been taken.   **2C–49**

2.6.2 Paragraph 2.3 of the Practice Direction in respect of Protocols (section C of volume 1 of the White Book) makes plain that the court may make adverse costs orders against a party who has failed to comply with the Protocol. The court will exercise any sanctions available with the object of placing the innocent party in no worse a position than he would have been if the Protocol had been complied with.

2.6.3 The court is unlikely to be concerned with minor infringements of the Protocol or to engage in lengthy debates as to the precise quality of the information provided by one party to the other during the Protocol stages. The court will principally be concerned to ensure that, as a result of the Protocol stage, each party to any subsequent litigation has a clear understanding of the nature of the case that it has to meet at the commencement of those proceedings.

2.7 Costs of compliance with the Protocol

2.7.1 If compliance with the Protocol results in settlement, the costs incurred will not be recoverable from the paying party, unless this is specifically agreed.   **2C–50**

2.7.2 If compliance with the Protocol does not result in settlement, then the costs of the exercise cannot be recovered as costs, unless:
- those costs fall within the principles stated by Sir Robert Megarry V-C in *Re Gibson's Settlement Trusts* [1981] Ch 179; or
- the steps taken in compliance with the Protocol can properly be attributable to the conduct of the action.

SECTION 3.
COMMENCEMENT AND TRANSFER

3.1 Claim Forms

3.1.1 All proceedings must be started using a claim form under CPR Part 7 or CPR Part 8. All claims allocated to the TCC are assigned to the Multi-Track: see CPR Rule 60.6(1).   **2C–51**

3.2 Part 7 Claims

3.2.1 The Part 7 claim form must be marked "Technology and Construction Court" in the appropriate place on the form.   **2C–52**

3.2.2. Particulars of Claim may be served with the claim form, but this is not a mandatory requirement. If the Particulars of Claim are not contained in or served with the claim form, they must be served within **14 days** after service of the claim form.

Paragraph numbers marked with a "+" can be found online and on CD.

3.2.3 A claim form must be verified by a statement of truth, and this includes any amendment to a claim form, unless the court otherwise orders.

3.3 Part 8 Claims

2C–53   3.3.1 The Part 8 claim form must be marked "Technology and Construction Court" in the appropriate place on the form.

3.3.2 A Part 8 claim form will normally be used where there is no substantial dispute of fact, such as the situation where the dispute turns on the construction of the contract or the interpretation of statute. For example, claims challenging the jurisdiction of an adjudicator or the validity of his decision are sometimes brought under Part 8. In those cases the relevant primary facts are often not in dispute. Part 8 claims will generally be disposed of on written evidence and oral submissions.

3.3.3 It is important that, where a claimant uses the Part 8 procedure, his claim form states that Part 8 applies and that the claimant wishes the claim to proceed under Part 8.

3.3.4 A statement of truth is again required on a Part 8 claim form.

3.4 Service

2C–54   3.4.1 Claim forms issued in the TCC at St Dunstan's House in London are to be served by the claimant, not by the Registry. In some other court centres claim forms are served by the court, unless the claimant specifically requests otherwise.

3.4.2 The different methods of service are set out in CPR Part 6 and the accompanying Practice Direction.

3.4.3 Applications for an extension of time in which to serve a claim form are governed by CPR Rule 7.6. The evidence required on an application for an extension of time is set out in paragraph 8.2 of Practice Direction A supplementing CPR Part 7.

3.4.4 When the claimant has served the claim form, he must file a certificate of service: Rule 6.14(2). This is necessary if, for instance, the claimant wishes to obtain judgment in default (CPR Part 12).

3.4.5 Applications for permission to serve a claim form out of the jurisdiction are subject to Rules 6.19–6.31 inclusive.

3.5 Acknowledgement of Service

2C–55   3.5.1 A defendant must file an acknowledgment of service in response to both Part 7 and Part 8 claims. Save in the special circumstances that arise when the claim form has been served out of the jurisdiction, the period for filing an acknowledgment of service is 14 days after service of the claim form.

3.6 Transfer

2C–56   3.6.1 Proceedings may be transferred from any Division of the High Court or from any specialist list to the TCC pursuant to CPR rule 30.5. The order made by the transferring court should be expressed as being subject to the approval of a TCC judge. The decision whether to accept such a transfer must be made by a TCC judge: see rule 30.5(3). Many of these applications are uncontested, and may conveniently be dealt with on paper. Transfers from the TCC to other Divisions of the High Court or other specialist lists are also governed by CPR rule 30.5. In London there are quite often transfers between the Commercial Court and the TCC, in order to ensure that cases are dealt with by the most appropriate judge. Outside London there are quite often transfers between the TCC and the mercantile courts.

3.6.2 A TCC claim may be transferred from the High Court to one of the county courts noted above, and from any county court to the High Court, if the criteria

Paragraph numbers marked with a "+" can be found online and on CD.

stated in CPR Rule 30.3 are satisfied. In ordinary circumstances, proceedings will be transferred from the TCC in the High Court to the TCC in an appropriate county court if the amount of the claim does not exceed £50,000.

3.6.3 Where no TCC judge is available to deal with a TCC claim which has been issued in a district registry or one of the county courts noted above, the claim may be transferred to another district registry or county court or to the High Court TCC in London (depending upon which court is appropriate).

3.7 Assignment

3.7.1 Where a claim has been issued at or transferred to the TCC at St Dunstan's **2C–57** House in London, the Judge in Charge of the TCC ("the Judge in Charge") shall with the assistance of court staff classify the case either "HCJ" or "SCJ".

   (i) If the case is classified "HCJ", it shall be managed and tried either by the Judge in Charge or by another High Court judge, who will be identified after consultation between the Judge in Charge and the Vice-President of the Queen's Bench Division. The clerical administration of "HCJ" cases will be carried out by the Case Administration Unit ("CAU") of the TCC at St Dunstan's House. The CAU will also deal with the listing of all applications and trials in such cases.
  (ii) If the case is classified "SCJ", it shall be managed and tried by one of the senior circuit judges, who is a full time TCC judge in London. Cases in the latter category will either (a) be assigned by the Judge in Charge to a specific senior circuit judge or (b) be assigned to a senior circuit judge by operation of the rota. The assigned judge will have primary responsibility for the management of that case.
 (iii) Although continuity of judge is regarded as important, it will sometimes be necessary for there to be a change of assigned judge. If no judge is available during the period fixed for trial, then the case may be tried by one of the deputy judges or recorders who has been nominated by the Lord Chancellor under section 68(1)(a) of the Supreme Court Act 1981.

3.7.2 When classifying a case "HCJ" or "SCJ", the Judge in Charge will take into account the following matters, as well as all the circumstances of the case:

   1. The size and complexity of the case.
   2. The nature and importance of any points of law arising.
   3. The amount of money which is at stake.
   4. Whether the case is one of public importance.
   5. Whether the case has an international element or involves overseas parties.
   6. The limited number of High Court judges and the needs of other court users, both civil and criminal.

Most TCC cases in London will be classified "SCJ". The Judge in Charge may change the classification of any case from "HCJ" to "SCJ" or from "SCJ" to "HCJ", if it becomes appropriate to do so. There will be a band of cases near the borderline between "HCJ" and "SCJ", where the classification will be liable to change depending upon the settlement rate of other cases and the availability of judges.

3.7.3 When proceedings are commenced in, or transferred to, the TCC at St Dunstan's House in London, any party to those proceedings may write to the court setting out matters relevant to classification. Any such letter should be clear and concise and should be copied to all other parties. A defendant who wishes to send such a letter should do so as soon as he becomes aware of the proceedings. Any party who believes that a case has been wrongly classified (whether "HCJ" or "SCJ") should write to the court promptly setting out his grounds for that belief. All letters referred to in this paragraph are referred to the judge in charge of the TCC or (in his absence) to the other TCC High Court judge for consideration.

3.7.4 When a case has been assigned to a named senior circuit judge in the TCC at St Dunstan's House, all communications to the court about the case (save for

Paragraph numbers marked with a "+" can be found online and on CD.

communications in respect of fees) shall be made to that judge's clerk. When a TCC case has been assigned to a named High Court judge, all such communications shall be made to the CAU or to the judge's clerk as appropriate. A Protocol on HMCS website sets out the procedure which will be followed when the CAU accepts a "provisional booking" for a High Court judge. All communications in respect of fees, however, should be sent to the Registry. All statements of case and applications should be marked with the name of the assigned judge.

3.7.5 There are full time TCC judges at Birmingham, Liverpool and Salford (Manchester). There are principal TCC judges at other court centres outside London. TCC cases at these court centres are assigned to judges either (a) by direction of the full time or principal TCC judge or (b) by operation of a rota. It will not generally be appropriate for the Judge in Charge (who is based in London) to consider TCC cases which are commenced in, or transferred to, court centres outside London. Nevertheless, if any TCC case brought in a court centre outside London appears to require management and trial by a High Court judge, then the full time or principal TCC judge at that court centre should refer the case to the Judge in Charge for a decision as to its future management and trial.

3.7.6 When a TCC case has been assigned to a named circuit judge at a court centre other than St Dunstan's House, all communications to the court about the case (save for communications in respect of fees) shall be made to that judge's clerk. All communications in respect of fees should be sent to the relevant registry. All statements of case and applications should be marked with the name of the assigned judge.

SECTION 4.

ACCESS TO THE COURT

4.1 General Approach

2C–58 4.1.1 There may be a number of stages during the case management phase when the parties will make applications to the court for particular orders: see Section 6 below. There will also be the need for the court to give or vary directions, so as to enable the case to progress to trial.

4.1.2 The court is acutely aware of the costs that may be incurred when both parties prepare for an oral hearing in respect of such interlocutory matters and is always prepared to consider alternative, and less expensive, ways in which the parties may seek the court's assistance.

4.1.3 There are certain stages in the case management phase when it will generally be better for the parties to appear before the assigned judge. Those are identified at Section 4.2 below. But there are other stages, and/or particular applications which a party may wish to make, which could conveniently be dealt with by way of a telephone hearing (Section 4.3 below) or by way of a paper application (Section 4.4 below).

4.2 Hearings in Court

2C–59 4.2.1 First Case Management Conference. The court will normally require the parties to attend an oral hearing for the purposes of the first Case Management Conference. This is because there may be matters which the judge would wish to raise with the parties arising out of the answers to the case management information sheets and the parties' proposed directions: see section 5.4 below. Even in circumstances where the directions and the case management timetable may be capable of being agreed by the parties and the court, the assigned judge may still wish to consider a range of case management matters face-to-face with the parties, including the possibility of ADR. See paragraphs 7.2.3, 7.3.2, 8.1.3, 11.1, 13.3, 13.4 and 16.3.2 below.

4.2.2 Whilst the previous paragraph sets out the ideal position, it is recognised that in low value cases the benefits of personal attendance might be outweighed by the costs involved. This is particularly so at court centres outside London, where the parties may have to travel substantial distances to court. Ultimately, the question whether personal attendance should be dispensed with at any particular case management conference must be decided by the judge, after considering any representations made and the circumstances of that particular case.

4.2.3 Pre-trial Review. It will normally be helpful for the parties to attend before the judge on a Pre-trial Review ("PTR"). It is always preferable for Counsel or other advocates who will be appearing at the trial to attend the PTR. Again, even if the parties can agree beforehand any outstanding directions and the detailed requirements for the management of the trial, it is still of assistance for the judge to raise matters of detailed trial management with the parties at an oral hearing. In appropriate cases, e.g. where the amount in issue is disproportionate to the costs of a full trial, the judge may wish to consider with the parties whether there are other ways in which the dispute might be resolved.

4.2.4 Whether or not other interlocutory applications require to be determined at an oral hearing will depend on the nature and effect of the application being made. Disputed applications for interim payments, summary judgment and security for costs will almost always require an oral hearing. Likewise, the resolution of a contested application to enforce an adjudicator's decision will normally be heard orally. At the other end of the scale, applications for extensions of time for the service of pleadings or to comply with other orders of the court can almost always be dealt with by way of a telephone hearing or in writing.

4.3 Telephone Hearings

4.3.1 Depending on the nature of the application and the extent of any dispute **2C–60** between the parties, the Court is content to deal with many case management matters and other interlocutory applications by way of a telephone conference.

4.3.2 Whilst it is not possible to lay down mandatory rules as to what applications should be dealt with in this way (rather than by way of an oral hearing in court), it may be helpful to identify certain situations which commonly arise and which can conveniently be dealt with by way of a telephone conference.

  (a) If the location of the court is inconvenient for one or more of the parties, or the value of the claim is low, then the CMC and the PTR could, in the alternative to the procedure set out in Section 4.2 above, take place by way of a telephone conference. The judge's permission for such a procedure would have to be sought in advance.
  (b) If the parties are broadly agreed on the orders to be made by the court, but they are in dispute in respect of one or two particular matters, then a telephone hearing is a convenient way in which those outstanding matters can be dealt with by the parties and the assigned judge.
  (c) Similarly, specific arguments about costs, once a substantive application has been disposed of, or arguments consequential on a particular judgment or order having been handed down, may also conveniently be dealt with by way of telephone hearing.
  (d) Other applications which, depending on their size and importance, may conveniently be dealt with by way of a telephone hearing include limited applications in respect of disclosure and specific applications as to the scope and content of factual or expert evidence exchanged by the parties.

4.3.3 Telephone hearings are not generally suitable for matters which are likely to last for more than an hour, although the judge may be prepared, in an appropriate case, to list a longer application for a telephone hearing.

4.3.4 Practical matters. Telephone hearings can be listed at any time between 8.30 a.m. and 5.30 p.m., subject to the convenience of the parties and the availability of the judge. Any party, who wishes to have an application dealt with by telephone, should make such request by letter or e-mail to the judge's clerk, sending copies to all other

Paragraph numbers marked with a "+" can be found online and on CD.

TCC

parties. Except in cases of urgency, the judge will allow a period of three days for the other parties to comment upon that request before deciding whether to deal with the application by telephone.

4.3.5 If permission is given for a telephone hearing, the court will normally indicate which party is to make all the necessary arrangements. In most cases, it will be the applicant. The procedure to be followed in setting up and holding a telephone hearing is that set out in section 6 of the Practice Direction supplementing CPR Part 23. The party making arrangements for the telephone hearing must ensure that all parties and the judge have a bundle for that hearing with identical pagination.

It is vital that the judge has all the necessary papers, in good time before the telephone conference, in order that it can be conducted efficiently and effectively.

4.4 Paper Applications

2C–61 4.4.1 CPR rule 23.8 and section 11 of the accompanying Practice Direction enable certain applications to be dealt with in writing. Parties in a TCC case are encouraged to deal with applications in writing, whenever practicable. Applications for both abridgments of time and extensions of time can generally be dealt with in writing, as well as all other variations to existing directions which are wholly or largely agreed. Disputes over particular aspects of disclosure and evidence may also be capable of being resolved in this way.

4.4.2 If a party wishes to make an application to the court, it should ask itself the question: "Can this application be conveniently dealt with in writing?" If it can, then the party should issue the application and make its (short) written submissions both in support of its application and why it should be dealt with on paper. The application, any supporting evidence and the written submissions should be provided to all parties, as well as the court. These must include a draft of the precise order sought.

4.4.3 The party against whom the application is made, and any other interested party, should respond within 3 days dealing both with the substantive application and the request for it to be dealt with in writing.

4.4.4 The court can then decide whether or not to deal with the application in writing. If the parties are agreed that the court should deal with it in writing, it will be rare for the court to take a different view. If the parties disagree as to whether or not the application should be dealt with in writing, the court can decide that issue and, if it decides to deal with it in writing can go on to resolve the substantive point on the basis of the parties' written submissions.

4.4.5 Further guidance in respect of paper applications is set out in Section 6.7 below.

4.4.6 It is important for the parties to ensure that all documents provided to the court are also provided to all the other parties, so as to ensure that both the court and the parties are working on the basis of the same documentation. The pagination of any bundle which is provided to the court and the parties must be identical.

4.5 E-mail Communications

2C–62 4.5.1 The general rules relating to communication and filing of documents by e-mail are set out in CPR Part 5, Practice Direction B.

4.5.2 The judges' clerks all have e-mail addresses identified in Appendix D. They welcome communication from the parties electronically. By agreement with the judge's clerk, it may also be possible to provide documents to the Court in this way. However, it should be noted that HM Court Service has imposed a blanket restriction of 2MB on the length of any e-mail, including its attachments. This equates to approximately 40 pages of normal typescript.

Paragraph numbers marked with a "+" can be found online and on CD.

4.5.3 Depending on the particular circumstances of an individual trial, the assigned judge may ask for an e-mail contact address for each of the parties and may send e-mail communications to that address. In addition, the judge may provide a direct contact email address so that the parties can communicate directly with him out of court hours. In such circumstances, the judge and the parties should agree the times at which the respective e-mail addresses can be used.

4.5.4 Every e-mail communication to and from the judge must be simultaneously copied to all the other parties.

4.6 Video Conferencing

4.6.1 In appropriate cases, particularly where there are important matters in dispute **2C–63** and the parties' representatives are a long distance from one another and/or the court, the hearing may be conducted by way of a Video Conference ("VC"). Prior arrangements will be necessary for any such hearing.

4.6.2 In London, a VC can be arranged through the VC suite at the Royal Courts of Justice. However, this facility is popular and will need to be booked well in advance of the hearing. Alternatively, there are a number of other VC suites in the Strand/Fleet Street area which would be suitable. Details of these facilities are available from the judges' clerks.

4.6.3 Outside London, a VC can be arranged at the following TCC courts with the requisite facilities: Birmingham, Bristol, Cardiff, Central London, Chester, Exeter, Leeds, Liverpool, Newcastle-upon-Tyne, Nottingham, Salford (Manchester) and Winchester.

4.7 Contacting the court out of hours

4.7.1 Occasionally it is necessary to contact a TCC judge out of hours. For example, it **2C–64** may be necessary to apply for an injunction to prevent the commencement of building works which will damage adjoining property; or for an order to preserve evidence. A case may have settled and it may be necessary to inform the judge, before he/she spends an evening or a weekend reading the papers.

4.7.2 <u>At St Dunstan's House</u>. RCJ Security has been provided with the telephone numbers and other contact information of all the TCC judges based at St Dunstan's House and of the court manager. If contact is required with a judge out of hours, the initial approach should be to RCJ Security on 0207-947-6000. Security will then contact the judge and/or the court manager and pass on the message or other information. If direct contact with the judge or court manager is required, RCJ Security must be provided with an appropriate contact number. This number will then be passed to the judge and/or the court manager, who will decide whether it is appropriate for him or her to speak directly to the contacting party.

4.7.3 <u>At other court centres</u>. At the Central London Civil Justice Centre and at all court centres outside London there is a court officer who deals with out of hours applications.

4.8 Lodging documents

4.8.1 In general documents should be lodged in hard copy and not sent by email or **2C–65** fax. This causes unnecessary duplication as well as additional work for hard-pressed court staff. Only if matters are urgent may documents be sent by either email or fax, with a hard copy sent by way of confirmation and marked as such. In certain cases, the court may ask for documents to be submitted in electronic form by email or otherwise, where that is appropriate.

Paragraph numbers marked with a "+" can be found online and on CD.

TCC

SECTION 5.

CASE MANAGEMENT AND THE FIRST CMC

5.1 General

2C-66 5.1.1 The general approach of the TCC to case management is to give directions at the outset and then throughout the proceedings to serve the overriding objective of dealing with cases justly. The judge to whom the case has been assigned has wide case management powers, which will be exercised to ensure that:

- the real issues are identified early on and remain the focus of the ongoing proceedings;
- a realistic timetable is ordered which will allow for the fair and prompt resolution of the action;
- costs are properly controlled and reflect the value of the issues to the parties and their respective financial positions.

5.1.2 In order to assist the judge in the exercise of his case management functions, the parties will be expected to co-operate with one another at all times. See CPR rule 1.3. Costs sanctions may be applied, if the judge concludes that one party is not reasonably co-operating with the other parties.

5.1.3 A hearing at which the judge gives general procedural directions is a case management conference ("CMC"). CMCs are relatively informal and business-like occasions. Counsel are not robed. Representatives sit when addressing the judge.

5.1.4 The following procedures apply in order to facilitate effective case management:

- Upon commencement of a case in the TCC, it is allocated automatically to the multitrack. The provisions of CPR Part 29 apply to all TCC cases.
- The TCC encourages a structured exchange of proposals and submissions for CMCs in advance of the hearing, so as to enable the parties to respond on an informed basis to proposals made.
- The judges of the TCC operate pro-active case management. In order to avoid the parties being taken by surprise by any judicial initiative, the judge will consider giving prior notification of specific or unusual case management proposals to be raised at a case management conference.

5.1.5 The TCC's aim is to ensure that the trial of each case takes place before the judge who has managed the case since the first CMC. Whilst continuity of judge is not always possible, because of the need to double- or triple-book judges, or because cases can sometimes overrun their estimated length through no fault of the parties, this remains an aspiration of case management within the TCC.

5.2 The Fixing of the First CMC

2C-67 5.2.1 Where a claim has been started in the TCC, or where it has been transferred into the TCC, paragraph 8.1 of the Part 60 Practice Direction requires the court to fix the first CMC within 14 days of the earliest of

- the filing by the defendant of an acknowledgement of service or
- the filing by the defendant of the defence or
- the date of the order transferring the case to the TCC.

If some defendants but not others are served with proceedings, the claimant's solicitors should so inform the court and liaise about the fixing of the first CMC.

5.2.2 This means that the first CMC takes place relatively early, sometimes before the defendant has filed a defence. However, if, as will usually be the case, the parties have complied with the protocol (Section 2 above) they will have a good idea of each other's respective positions, and an effective CMC can take place. If, on the other hand, there has been a failure to comply with the protocol, or there are other reasons why the issues are not clearly defined at the outset, then it may be important for the judge to be involved at an early stage.

5.2.3 Despite the foregoing considerations, it is sometimes apparent to the parties that it will be more cost effective to postpone the first CMC until after service of the defence or the defences. If any of the parties wishes to delay the first CMC until then, they can write to the judge's clerk explaining why a delayed CMC is appropriate. If

Paragraph numbers marked with a "+" can be found online and on CD.

such a request is agreed by the other party or parties, it is likely that the judge will grant the request.

5.3 The Case Management Information Sheet and Other Documents

5.3.1 All parties are expected to complete a detailed response to the case management information sheet sent out by the Registry when the case is commenced/transferred. A copy of a blank case management information sheet is attached as Appendix A. It is important that all parts of the form are completed, particularly those sections (e.g. concerned with estimated costs) that enable the judge to give directions in accordance with the overriding objective.

2C–68

5.3.2 The Registry will also send out a blank standard directions form to each party. A copy is attached at Appendix B. This sets out the usual directions made on the first CMC. The parties should fill them in, indicating the directions and timetable sought. The parties should return both the questionnaire and the directions form to the court, so that the areas (if any) of potential debate at the CMC can be identified. The parties are encouraged to exchange proposals for directions and the timetable sought, with a view to agreeing the same before the CMC for consideration by the court.

5.3.3 If the case is large or complex, it is helpful for the advocates to prepare a Note to be provided to the judge the day before the CMC which can address the issues in the case, the suggested directions, and the principal areas of dispute between the parties. If such a Note is provided, it is unnecessary for the claimant also to prepare a Case Summary as well.

5.3.4 In smaller cases, a Case Summary for the CMC, explaining briefly the likely issues, can be helpful. Such Case Summaries should be non-contentious and should (if this is possible without incurring disproportionate cost) be agreed between the parties in advance of the hearing.

5.4 Checklist of Matters likely to be considered at the first CMC

5.4.1 The following checklist identifies the matters which the judge is likely to want to consider at the first CMC, although it is not exhaustive:

2C–69

- The need for, and content of, any further pleadings. This is dealt with in Section 5.5 below.
- The outcome of the Protocol process, and the possible further need for ADR. ADR is dealt with in Section 7 below.
- The desirability of dealing with particular disputes by way of a Preliminary Issue hearing. This is dealt with in Section 8 below.
- Whether the trial should be in stages (e.g. stage 1 liability and causation, stage 2 quantum). In very heavy cases this may be necessary in order to make the trial manageable. In more modest cases, where the quantum evidence will be extensive, a staged trial may be in the interest of all parties.
- The appropriate orders in respect of the disclosure of documents. This is dealt with in Section 11 below.
- The appropriate orders as to the exchange of written witness statements. This is dealt with in Section 12 below. It should be noted that, although it is normal for evidence-in-chief to be given by way of the written statements in the TCC, the judge may direct that evidence about particular disputes (such as what was said at an important meeting) should be given orally without reference to such statements.
- Whether it is appropriate for the parties to rely on expert evidence and, if so, what disciplines of experts should give evidence, and on what issues. This may be coupled with an order relating to the carrying out of inspections, the obtaining of samples, the conducting of experiments, or the performance of calculations. Considerations relating to expert evidence are dealt with in Section 13 below. The parties must be aware that, in accordance with the overriding objective, the judge will only give the parties permission to rely on expert evidence if it is both necessary and appropriate, and, even then, will wish to ensure that the scope of any such evidence is limited as far as possible.

Paragraph numbers marked with a "+" can be found online and on CD.

- In certain cases the possibility of making a costs cap order. See section 16.3 below.
- The appropriate timetable for the taking of the various interlocutory steps noted above, and the fixing of dates for both the PTR and the trial itself (subject to paragraph 5.4.2 below). The parties will therefore need to provide the judge with an estimate for the length of the trial, assuming all issues remain in dispute. Unless there is good reason not to, the trial date will generally be fixed at the first CMC (although this may be more difficult at court centres with only one TCC judge). Therefore, to the extent that there are any relevant concerns as to availability of either witnesses or legal representatives, they need to be brought to the attention of the court on that occasion. The length of time fixed for the trial will depend on the parties' estimates, and also the judge's own view.

If the parties' estimate of trial length subsequently changes, they should inform the clerk of the assigned judge immediately.

5.4.2 The fixing of the trial date at the CMC is usually as a provisional fixture. Therefore no trial fee is payable at this stage. The court should at the same time specify a date upon which the fixture will cease to be "provisional" and, therefore, the trial fee will become payable. This should ordinarily be two months before the trial date. It should be noted that:

- if the trial fee is not paid within 14 days of the due date, then the whole claim will be struck out: see CPR rule 3.7(1)(a) and (4);
- if the court is notified at least 14 days before the trial date that the case is settled or discontinued, then the trial fee, which has been paid, shall be refunded: see fee 2.2 in Schedule 1 to the Civil Proceedings Fees Order 2004.

For all other purposes other than payment of the trial fee, the provisional date fixed at the CMC shall be regarded as a firm date.

5.4.3 Essentially, the judge's aim at the first CMC is to set down a detailed timetable which, in the majority of cases, will ensure that the parties need not return to court until the PTR.

5.5 Further Pleadings

2C–70 5.5.1 Defence. If no defence has been served prior to the first CMC, then (except in cases where judgment in default is appropriate) the court will usually make an order for service of the defence within a specified period. The defendant must plead its positive case. Bare denials and non-admissions are, save in exceptional circumstances, unacceptable.

5.5.2 Further Information. If the defendant wants to request further information of the Particulars of Claim, the request should, if possible, be formulated prior to the first CMC, so that it can be considered on that occasion. All requests for further information should be kept within reasonable limits, and concentrate on the important parts of the case.

5.5.3 Reply. A reply to the defence is not always necessary. However, where the defendant has raised a positive defence on a particular issue, it may be appropriate for the claimant to set out in a reply how it answers such a defence. If the defendant makes a counterclaim, the claimant's defence to counterclaim and its reply (if any) should be in the same document.

5.5.4 Part 20 Claims. The defendant should, at the first CMC, indicate (so far as possible) any Part 20 claims that it is proposing to make, whether against the claimant or any other party. Part 20 claims are required to be pleaded in the same detail as the original claim. They are a very common feature of TCC cases, because the widespread use of sub-contractors in the UK construction industry often makes it necessary to pass claims down a contractual chain. Defendants are encouraged to start any necessary Part 20 proceedings as soon as possible. It is undesirable for applications to join Part 20 defendants, to be made late in the proceedings.

Paragraph numbers marked with a "+" can be found online and on CD.

5.6 Scott Schedules

5.6.1 It can sometimes be appropriate for elements of the claim, or any Part 20 claim, **2C–71** to be set out by way of a Scott Schedule. For example, claims involving a final account or numerous alleged defects or items of disrepair, may be best formulated in this way, which then allows for a detailed response from the defendant. Sometimes, even where all the damage has been caused by one event, such as a fire, it can be helpful for the individual items of loss and damage to be set out in a Scott Schedule. The secret of an effective Scott Schedule lies in the information that is to be provided. This is defined by the column headings. The judge may give directions for the relevant column headings for any Schedule ordered by the court. It is important that the defendant's responses to any such Schedule are as detailed as possible. Each party's entries on a Scott Schedule should be supported by a statement of truth.

5.6.2 Nevertheless, before any order is made or agreement is reached for the preparation of a Scott Schedule, both the parties and the court should consider whether this course (a) will genuinely lead to a saving of cost and time or (b) will lead to a wastage of costs and effort (because the Scott Schedule will simply duplicating earlier schedules, pleadings or expert reports). A Scott Schedule should only be ordered by the court, or agreed by the parties, in those cases where it is appropriate and proportionate.

5.6.3 When a Scott Schedule is ordered by the court or agreed by the parties, the format must always be specified. The parties must co-operate in the physical task of preparation. Electronic transfer between the parties of their respective entries in the columns will enable a clear and user-friendly Scott Schedule to be prepared, for the benefit of all involved in the trial.

5.7 Agreement Between the Parties

5.7.1 Many, perhaps most, of the required directions at the first CMC may be agreed **2C–72** by the parties. If so, the judge will endeavour to make orders in the terms which have been agreed, unless he considers that the agreed terms fail to take into account important features of the case as a whole, or the principles of the CPR. The agreed terms will always, at the very least, form the starting-point of the judge's consideration of the orders to be made at the CMC. If the agreed terms are submitted to the judge 3 days in advance of the hearing date, it may be possible to avoid the need for a hearing altogether.

5.7.2 The approach outlined in paragraph 5.7.1 above is equally applicable to all other occasions when the parties come before the court with a draft order that is wholly or partly agreed.

5.8 Drawing Up of Orders

5.8.1 Unless the court itself draws up the order, it will direct one party (usually the **2C–73** claimant or applicant) to do so within a specified time. That party must draw up the order and lodge it with the court for approval. Once approved, the order will be stamped by the court and returned to that party for service upon all other parties.

5.9 Further CMC

5.9.1 In an appropriate case, the judge will fix a review CMC, to take place part way **2C–74** through the timetable that has been set down, in order to allow the court to review progress, and to allow the parties to raise any matters arising out of the steps that have been taken up to that point. This will not, however, be ordered automatically.

5.9.2 Each party will be required to give notice in writing to the other parties and the court of any order which it will be seeking at the review CMC, two days in advance of the hearing..

Paragraph numbers marked with a "+" can be found online and on CD.

TCC

5.10 The Permanent Case Management Bundle

2C–75   5.10.1 In conjunction with the judge's clerk, the claimant's solicitor is responsible for ensuring that, for the first CMC and at all times thereafter, there is a permanent bundle of copy documents available to the judge, which contains:

- any relevant documents resulting from the Pre-Action Protocol;
- the claim form and all statements of case;
- all orders;
- all completed case management information sheets.

5.10.2 The permanent case management bundle can then be supplemented by the specific documents relevant to any particular application that may be made. Whether these supplementary documents should (a) become a permanent addition to the case management bundle or (b) be set on one side, will depend upon their nature. The permanent case management bundle may remain at court and be marked up by the judge; alternatively, the judge may direct that the permanent case management bundle be maintained at the offices of the claimant's solicitors and provided to the court when required.

Section 6.

Applications after the First CMC

6.1 Relevant parts of the CPR

2C–76   6.1.1 The basic rules relating to all applications that any party may wish to make are set out in CPR Part 23 and its accompanying Practice Directions.

6.1.2 Part 7 of the Practice Direction accompanying CPR Part 60 is also of particular relevance.

6.2 Application Notice

2C–77   6.2.1 As a general rule, any party to proceedings in the TCC wishing to make an application of any sort must file an application notice (rule 23.3) and serve that application notice on all relevant parties as soon as practicable after it has been filed (rule 23.4). Application notices should be served by the parties, unless (as happens in some court centres outside London) service is undertaken by the court.

6.2.2 The application notice must set out in clear terms what order is sought and, more briefly, the reasons for seeking that order: see rule 23.6.

6.2.3 The application notice must be served at least 3 days before the hearing at which the Court deals with the application: rule 23.7 (1). Such a short notice period is only appropriate for the most straight-forward type of application.

6.2.4 Most applications, in particular applications for summary judgment under CPR Part 24 or to strike out a statement of case under CPR rule 3.4, will necessitate a much longer notice period than 3 days. In such cases, it is imperative that the applicant obtain a suitable date and time for the hearing of the application from the assigned judge's clerk before the application notice is issued. The applicant must then serve his application notice and evidence in support sufficiently far ahead of the date fixed for the hearing of the application for there to be time to enable the respondent to serve evidence in response. Save in exceptional circumstances, there should be a minimum period of 10 working days between the service of the notice (and supporting evidence) and the hearing date. If any party considers that there is insufficient time before the hearing of the application or if the time estimate for the application itself is too short, that party must notify the Judge's clerk and the hearing may then be refixed by agreement.

6.2.5 When considering the application notice, the judge may give directions in writing as to the dates for the provision or exchange of evidence and any written submissions or skeleton arguments for the hearing.

Paragraph numbers marked with a "+" can be found online and on CD.

6.3 Evidence in Support

6.3.1 The application notice when it is served must be accompanied by all evidence in support: rule 23.7 (2). **2C–78**

6.3.2 Unless the CPR expressly requires otherwise, evidence will be given by way of witness statements. Such statements must be verified by a statement of truth signed by the maker of the statement: rule 22.1.

6.4 Evidence in opposition and Evidence in reply

6.4.1 Likewise, any evidence in opposition to the application should, unless the rules expressly provide otherwise, be given by way of witness statement verified by a statement of truth. **2C–79**

6.4.2 It is important to ensure that the evidence in opposition to the application is served in good time before the hearing so as to enable:

- the court to read and note up the evidence;
- the applicant to put in any further evidence in reply that may be considered necessary.

Such evidence should be served at least 5 working days before the hearing.

6.4.3 Any evidence in reply should be served not less than 3 working days before the hearing. Again, if there are disputes as to the time taken or to be taken for the preparation of evidence prior to a hearing, or any other matters in respect of a suitable timetable for that hearing, the court will consider the written positions of both parties and decide such disputes on paper. It will not normally be necessary for either a separate application to be issued or a hearing to be held for such a purpose.

6.4.4 If the hearing of an application has to be adjourned because of delays by one or other of the parties in serving evidence, the court is likely to order that party to pay the costs straight away, and to make a summary assessment of those costs.

6.5 Application Bundle

6.5.1 The bundle for the hearing of anything other than the most simple and straightforward application should consist of: **2C–80**

- the permanent case management bundle (see Section 5.8 above);
- the witness statements provided in support of the application, together with any exhibits;
- the witness statements provided in opposition to the application together with exhibits;
- any witness statements in reply, together with exhibits.

6.5.2 The permanent case management bundle will either be with the court or with the claimant's solicitors, depending on the order made at the first CMC: see paragraph 5.9 above. If it is with the claimant's solicitors, it should be provided to the court not less than **2 working days** before the hearing. In any event, a paginated bundle (see paragraph 6.5.4 below) containing any material specific to the application should also be provided to the court not less than 2 working days before the hearing, unless otherwise directed by the judge. A failure to comply with this deadline may result in the adjournment of the hearing, and the costs thrown away being paid by the defaulting party.

6.5.3 In all but the simplest applications, the court will expect the parties to provide skeleton arguments and copies of any authorities to be relied on. The form and content of the skeleton argument is principally a matter for the author, although the judge will expect it to identify the issues that arise on the application, the important parts of the evidence relied on, and the applicable legal principles. For detailed guidance as to the form, content and length of skeleton arguments, please see

Paragraph numbers marked with a "+" can be found online and on CD.

paragraph 7.11.12 of the Queen's Bench Guide; Appendix 3 of the Chancery Guide; and Appendix 9 of the Commercial Court Guide.

6.5.4 For an application that is estimated to last ½ day or less, the skeleton should be provided no later than 1 pm on the last working day before the hearing. It should be accompanied by photocopies of the authorities relied on.

6.5.5 For an application that is estimated to last more than ½ day, the skeleton should be provided no later than 4 pm one clear working day before the hearing. It should be accompanied by photocopies of the authorities relied on.

6.5.6 The time limits at paragraphs 6.5.4 and 6.5.5 above will be regarded as the latest times by which such skeletons should be provided to the court. Save in exceptional circumstances, no extension to these periods will be permitted.

6.5.7 Pagination. It is generally necessary for there to be a paginated bundle for the hearing. Where the parties have produced skeleton arguments, these should be crossreferred to the bundle page numbers.

6.6 Hearings

2C–81 6.6.1 Arbitration applications may be heard in private: see CPR rule 62.10. All other applications will be heard in public in accordance with CPR rule 39.2, save where otherwise ordered.

6.6.2 Provided that the application bundle and the skeletons have been lodged in accordance with the time limits set out above, the parties can assume that the court will have a good understanding of the points in issue. However, the court will expect to be taken to particular documents relied on by the parties and will also expect to be addressed on any important legal principles that arise.

6.6.3 It is important that the parties ensure that every application is dealt with in the estimated time period. Since many applications are dealt with on Fridays, it causes major disruption if application hearings are not disposed of within the estimated period. If the parties take too long in making their submissions, the application may be adjourned, part heard, and the Court may impose appropriate costs sanctions.

6.6.4 At the conclusion of the hearing, unless the court itself draws up the order, it will direct the applicant's solicitor to do so within a specified period.

6.7 Paper Applications

2C–82 6.7.1 Contested applications are usually best disposed of at an oral hearing (either in court or by telephone). However, as noted in Section 4 above, some applications may be suitable for determination on paper. The procedure for dealing with paper applications is outlined in paragraph 4.4 above.

6.7.2 In addition, certain simple applications (particularly in lower value cases) arising out of the management of the proceedings may be capable of being dealt with by correspondence without the need for any formal application or order of the court. This is particularly true of applications to vary procedural orders, which variations are wholly or largely agreed, or proposals to vary the estimated length of the trial. In such cases, the applicant should write to the other parties indicating the nature of its application and to seek their agreement to it. If, however, it emerges that there is an issue to be resolved by the court, then a formal application must be issued and dealt with in the normal manner.

6.8 Consent Orders

2C–83 6.8.1 Consent Orders may be submitted to the Court in draft for approval and initialling without the need for attendance.

6.8.2 Two copies of the draft order should be lodged, at least one of which should be signed. The copies should be undated.

Paragraph numbers marked with a "+" can be found online and on CD.

6.8.3 As noted above, whilst the parties can agree between themselves the orders to be made either at the Case Management Conference or the Pre-Trial Review, it is normally necessary for the Court to consider the case with the parties (either at an oral hearing or by way of a telephone conference) on those occasions in any event.

6.8.4 Generally, when giving directions, the court will endeavour to identify the date by which the relevant step must be taken, and will not simply provide a period during which that task should be performed. The parties should therefore ensure that any proposed consent order also identifies particular dates, rather then periods, by which the relevant steps must be taken.

6.9 Costs

6.9.1 Costs are dealt with generally at Section 16 below.   **2C–84**

6.9.2 The costs of any application which took a day or less to be heard and disposed of will be dealt with summarily, unless there is a good reason for the court not to exercise its powers as to the summary assessment of costs.

6.9.3 Accordingly, it is necessary for parties to provide to the court and to one another their draft statements of costs no later than 24 hours before the start of the application hearing. Any costs which are incurred after these draft statements have been prepared, but which have not been allowed for (e.g. because the hearing has exceeded its anticipated length), can be mentioned at the hearing.

SECTION 7.

ADR

7.1 General

7.1.1 The court will provide encouragement to the parties to use alternative dispute **2C–85** resolution ("ADR") and will, whenever appropriate, facilitate the use of such a procedure. In this Guide, ADR is taken to mean any process through which the parties attempt to resolve their dispute, which is voluntary. In most cases, ADR takes the form of mediation conducted by a neutral mediator. Alternative forms of ADR include formal inter-party negotiations or (occasionally) early neutral evaluations. In an early neutral evaluation either a judge or some other neutral person receives a concise presentation from each party and then states his own evaluation of the case.

7.1.2 Although the TCC is an appropriate forum for the resolution of all IT and construction/engineering disputes, the use of ADR can lead to a significant saving of costs and may result in a settlement which is satisfactory to all parties.

7.1.3 Legal representatives in all TCC cases should ensure that their clients are fully aware of the benefits of ADR and that the use of ADR has been carefully considered prior to the first CMC.

7.2 Timing

7.2.1 ADR may be appropriate before the proceedings have begun or at any **2C–86** subsequent stage.

7.2.2 The TCC Pre-Action Protocol (Section 2 above) itself provides for a type of ADR, because it requires there to be at least one face-to-face meeting between the parties before the commencement of proceedings. At this meeting, there should be sufficient time to discuss and resolve the dispute. As a result of this procedure having taken place, the court will not necessarily grant a stay of proceedings upon demand and it will always need to be satisfied that an adjournment is actually necessary to enable ADR to take place.

7.2.3 However, at the first CMC, the court will want to be addressed on the parties' views as to the likely efficacy of ADR, the appropriate timing of ADR, and the

Paragraph numbers marked with a "+" can be found online and on CD.

TCC

advantages and disadvantages of a short stay of proceedings to allow ADR to take place. Having considered the representations of the parties, the court may order a short stay to facilitate ADR at that stage. Alternatively, the court may simply encourage the parties to seek ADR and allow for it to occur within the timetable for the resolution of the proceedings set down by the court.

7.2.4 At any stage after the first CMC and prior to the commencement of the trial, the court, will, either on its own initiative or if requested to do so by one or both of the parties, consider afresh the likely efficacy of ADR and whether or not a short stay of the proceedings should be granted, in order to facilitate ADR.

7.3 Procedure

2C–87 7.3.1 In an appropriate case, the court may indicate the type of ADR that it considers suitable, but the decision in this regard must be made by the parties. In most cases, the appropriate ADR procedure will be mediation.

7.3.2 If at any stage in the proceedings the court considers it appropriate, an ADR order in the terms of Appendix E may be made. If such an order is made at the first CMC, the court may go on to give directions for the conduct of the action up to trial (in the event that the ADR fails). Such directions may include provision for a review CMC.

7.3.3 The court will not ordinarily recommend any individual or body to act as mediator or to perform any other ADR procedure. In the event that the parties fail to agree the identity of a mediator or other neutral person pursuant to an order in the terms of Appendix E, the court may select such a person from the lists provided by the parties. To facilitate this process, the court would also need to be furnished with the C.V's of each of the individuals on the lists.

7.3.4 Information as to the types of ADR procedures available and the individuals able to undertake such procedures is available from TeCSA, TECBAR, the Civil Mediation Council, and from some TCC court centres outside London.

7.4 Non-Cooperation

2C–88 7.4.1 _Generally._ At the end of the trial, there may be costs arguments on the basis that one or more parties unreasonably refused to take part in ADR. The court will determine such issues having regard to all the circumstances of the particular case. In _Halsey v Milton Keynes General NHS Trust_ [2004] EWCA Civ 576; [2004] 1 WLR 3002, the Court of Appeal identified six factors that may be relevant to any such consideration:

  a) the nature of the dispute;
  b) the merits of the case;
  c) the extent to which other settlement methods have been attempted;
  d) whether the costs of the ADR would be disproportionately high;
  e) whether any delay in setting up and attending the ADR would have been prejudicial;
  f) whether the ADR had a reasonable prospect of success.

7.4.2 _If an ADR Order Has Been Made._ The court will expect each party to co-operate fully with any ADR which takes place following an order of the court. If any other party considers that there has not been proper co-operation in relation to arrangements for the mediation, the complaint will be considered by the court and cost orders and/or other sanctions may be ordered against the defaulting party in consequence. However, nothing in this paragraph should be understood as modifying the rights of all parties to a mediation to keep confidential all that is said or done in the course of that mediation.

7.5 Early Neutral Evaluation

2C–89 7.5.1 An early neutral evaluation ("ENE") may be carried out by any appropriately qualified person, whose opinion is likely to be respected by the parties. In an

Paragraph numbers marked with a "+" can be found online and on CD.

appropriate case, and with the consent of all parties, a TCC judge may provide an early neutral evaluation either in respect of the full case or of particular issues arising within it. Such an ENE will not, save with the agreement of the parties, be binding on the parties.

7.5.2 If the parties would like an ENE to be carried out by the court, then they can seek an appropriate order from the assigned judge either at the first CMC or at any time prior to the commencement of the trial.

7.5.3 The assigned judge may choose to do the ENE himself. In such instance, the judge will take no further part in the proceedings once he has produced the ENE, unless the parties expressly agree otherwise. Alternatively, the assigned judge will select another available TCC judge to undertake the ENE.

7.5.4 The judge undertaking the ENE will give appropriate directions for the preparation and conduct of the ENE. This may include a stay of the substantive proceedings whilst the ENE is carried out. The ENE may be carried out entirely on paper. Alternatively, there may be an oral hearing (either with or without evidence). The parties should agree whether the entire ENE procedure is to be without prejudice, or whether it can be referred to at any subsequent trial or hearing.

SECTION 8.

PRELIMINARY ISSUES

8.1 General

8.1.1 The hearing of Preliminary Issues ("PI"), at which the court considers and **2C–90** delivers a binding judgment on particular issues in advance of the main trial, can be an extremely cost-effective and efficient way of narrowing the issues between the parties and, in certain cases, of resolving disputes altogether.

8.1.2 Some cases listed in the TCC lend themselves particularly well to this procedure. A PI hearing can address particular points which may be decisive of the whole proceedings; even if that is not the position, it is often possible for a PI hearing to cut down significantly on the scope (and therefore the costs) of the main trial.

8.1.3 At the first CMC the court will expect to be addressed on whether or not there are matters which should be taken by way of Preliminary Issues in advance of the main trial. Subject to paragraph 8.5 below, it is not generally appropriate for the court to make an order for the trial of preliminary issues until after the defence has been served. After the first CMC, and at any time during the litigation, any party is at liberty to raise with any other party the possibility of a PI hearing and the court will consider any application for the hearing of such Preliminary Issues. In many cases, although not invariably, a PI order will be made with the support of all parties.

8.1.4 Whilst, for obvious reasons, it is not possible to set out hard and fast rules for what is and what is not suitable for a PI hearing, the criteria set out in Section 8.2 below should assist the parties in deciding whether or not some or all of the disputes between them will be suitable for a PI hearing.

8.1.5 Drawbacks of preliminary issues in inappropriate cases. If preliminary issues are ordered inappropriately, they can have adverse effect. Evidence may be duplicated. The same witnesses may give evidence before different judges, in the event that there is a switch of assigned judge. Findings may be made at the PI hearing, which are affected by evidence called at the main hearing. The prospect of a PI hearing may delay the commencement of ADR or settlement negotiations. Also two trials are more expensive than one. For all these reasons, any proposal for preliminary issues needs to be examined carefully, so that the benefits and drawbacks can be evaluated. Also the court should give due weight to the views of the parties when deciding whether a PI hearing would be beneficial.

Paragraph numbers marked with a "+" can be found online and on CD.

8.1.6 Staged trials. The breaking down of a long trial into stages should be differentiated from the trial of preliminary issues. Sometimes it is sensible for liability (including causation) to be tried before quantum of damages. Occasionally the subject matter of the litigation is so extensive that for reasons of case management the trial needs to be broken down into separate stages.

8.2 Guidelines

2C–91 8.2.1 The Significance of the Preliminary Issues. The court would expect that any issue proposed as a suitable PI would, if decided in a particular way, be capable of:

- resolving the whole proceedings or a significant element of the proceedings; or
- significantly reducing the scope, and therefore the costs, of the main trial; or
- significantly improving the possibility of a settlement of the whole proceedings.

8.2.2 Oral Evidence. The court would ordinarily expect that, if issues are to be dealt with by way of a PI hearing, there would be either no or relatively limited oral evidence. If extensive oral evidence was required on any proposed PI, then it may not be suitable for a PI hearing. Although it is difficult to give specific guidance on this point, it is generally considered that a PI hearing in a smaller case should not take more than about 2 days, and in a larger and more complex case, should not take more than about 4 days.

8.3 Common Types of Preliminary Issue

2C–92 The following are commonly resolved by way of a PI hearing:

(a) Disputes as to whether or not there was a binding contract between the parties.

(b) Disputes as to what documents make up or are incorporated within the contract between the parties and disputes as to the contents or relevance of any conversations relied on as having contractual status or effect.

(c) Disputes as to the proper construction of the contract documents or the effect of an exclusion or similar clause.

(d) Disputes as to the correct application of a statute or binding authority to a situation where there is little or no factual dispute.

(e) Disputes as to the existence and/or scope of a statutory duty.

(f) Disputes as to the existence and/or scope of a duty of care at common law in circumstances where there is no or little dispute about the relevant facts.

8.4 Other Possible Preliminary Issues

2C–93 The following can sometimes be resolved by way of a preliminary issue hearing, although a decision as to whether or not to have such a hearing will always depend on the facts of the individual case:

8.4.1 A Limitation Defence. It is often tempting to have limitation issues resolved in advance of the main trial. This can be a good idea because, if a complex claim is statutebarred, a decision to that effect will lead to a significant saving of costs. However, there is also a risk that extensive evidence relevant to the limitation defence (relating to matters such as when the damage occurred or whether or not there has been deliberate concealment) may also be relevant to the liability issues within the main trial. In such a case, a preliminary issue hearing may lead to a) extensive duplication of evidence and therefore costs and b) give rise to difficulty if the main trial is heard by a different judge.

8.4.2 Causation and 'No Loss' Points. Causation and 'No Loss' points may be suitable for a PI hearing, but again their suitability will diminish if it is necessary for the court to resolve numerous factual disputes as part of the proposed PI hearing. The most appropriate disputes of this type for a PI hearing are those where the defendant contends that, even accepting all the facts alleged by the claimant, the claim must fail by reason of causation or the absence of recoverable loss.

8.4.3 'One-Off' Issues. Issues which do not fall into any obvious category, like economic duress, or misrepresentation, may be suitable for resolution by way of a PI hearing, particularly if the whole case can be shown to turn on them.

Paragraph numbers marked with a "+" can be found online and on CD.

8.5 Use of PI as an adjunct to ADR

8.5.1 Sometimes parties wish to resolve their dispute by ADR, but there is one major **2C–94** issue which is a sticking point in any negotiation or mediation. The parties may wish to obtain the court's decision on that single issue, in the expectation that after that they can resolve their differences without further litigation.

8.5.2 In such a situation the parties may wish to bring proceedings under CPR Part 8, in order to obtain the court's decision on that issue. Such proceedings can be rapidly progressed. Alternatively, if the issue is not suitable for Part 8 proceedings, the parties may bring proceedings under Part 7 and then seek determination of the critical question as a preliminary issue. At the first CMC the position can be explained and the judge can be asked to order early trial of the proposed preliminary issue, possibly without the need for a defence or any further pleadings.

8.6 Precise Wording of PI

8.6.1 If a party wishes to seek a PI hearing, either at the first CMC or thereafter, that **2C–95** party must circulate a precise draft of the proposed preliminary issues to the other parties and to the court well in advance of the relevant hearing.

8.6.2 If the court orders a PI hearing, it is likely to make such an order only by reference to specific and formulated issues, in order to avoid later debate as to the precise scope of the issues that have been ordered. Of course, the parties are at liberty to propose amendments to the issues before the PI hearing itself, but if such later amendments are not agreed by all parties, they are unlikely to be ordered.

8.7 Appeals

8.7.1 When considering whether or not to order a PI hearing, the court will take into **2C–96** account the effect of any possible appeal against the PI judgment, and the concomitant delay caused.

8.7.2 At the time of ordering preliminary issues, both the parties and the court should specifically consider whether, in the event of an appeal against the PI judgment, it is desirable that the trial of the main action should (a) precede or (b) follow such appeal. It should be noted, however, that the first instance court has no power to control the timetable for an appeal. A first instance court's power to extend time under CPR rule 52.4(2)(a) for filing an appellant's notice is effectively limited to 14 days (see paragraph 5.19 of the Practice direction supplementing Part 52). The question whether an appeal should be (a) expedited or (b) stayed is entirely a matter for the Court of Appeal. Nevertheless, the Court of Appeal will take notice of any "indication" given by the lower court in this regard.

SECTION 9.

ADJUDICATION BUSINESS

9.1 Introduction

9.1.1 The TCC is ordinarily the court in which the enforcement of an adjudicator's **2C–97** decision and any other business connected with adjudication is undertaken. Adjudicators' decisions predominantly arise out of adjudications which are governed by the mandatory provisions of the Housing Grants, Construction and Regeneration Act 1996 ("HGCRA"). These provisions apply automatically to any construction contract as defined in the legislation. Some Adjudicators' decisions arise out of standard form contracts which contain adjudication provisions, and others arise from ad-hoc agreements to adjudicate. The TCC enforcement procedure is the same for all three kinds of adjudication.

9.1.2 In addition to enforcement applications, declaratory relief is sometimes sought

Paragraph numbers marked with a "+" can be found online and on CD.

TCC

in the TCC at the outset of an adjudication in respect of matters such as the jurisdiction of the adjudicator or the validity of the adjudication. This kind of application is dealt with in Paragraph 9.4 below.

9.1.3 The HGCRA provides for a mandatory 28-day period within which the entire adjudication process must be completed, unless a) the referring party agrees to an additional 14 days, or b) both parties agree to a longer period. In consequence, the TCC has moulded a rapid procedure for enforcing an adjudication decision that has not been honoured. Other adjudication proceedings are ordinarily subject to similar rapidity.

9.2 Procedure In Enforcement Proceedings

2C–98 9.2.1 Unlike arbitration business, there is neither a practice direction nor a claim form concerned with adjudication business. The enforcement proceedings normally seek a monetary judgment so that CPR Part 7 proceedings are usually appropriate. However, if the enforcement proceedings are known to raise a question which is unlikely to involve a substantial dispute of fact and no monetary judgment is sought, CPR Part 8 proceedings may be used instead.

9.2.2 The TCC has fashioned a procedure whereby enforcement applications are dealt with promptly. The details of this procedure are set out below.

9.2.3 The claim form should identify the construction contract, the jurisdiction of the adjudicator, the procedural rules under which the adjudication was conducted, the adjudicator's decision, the relief sought and the grounds for seeking that relief.

9.2.4 The claim form should be accompanied by an application notice that sets out the procedural directions that are sought. Commonly, the claimant's application will seek an abridgement of time for the various procedural steps, and summary judgment under CPR Part 24. The claim form and the application should be accompanied by a witness statement or statements setting out the evidence relied on in support of both the adjudication enforcement claim and the associated procedural application. This evidence should ordinarily include a copy of the adjudicator's decision.

9.2.5 The claim form, application notice and accompanying documents should be lodged in the appropriate registry or court centre clearly marked as being a "paper without notice adjudication enforcement claim and application for the urgent attention of a TCC judge". The parties will be informed that the enforcement proceedings will be assigned to a named judge. That judge will then manage the proceedings up to and including any hearing. He will ordinarily provide his directions made in connection with the procedural application within 3 working days of the receipt of the application notice at the courts.

9.2.6 The procedural application is dealt with by a TCC judge on paper, without notice. The paper application and the consequent directions should deal with:

    (a) the abridged period of time in which the defendant is to file an acknowledgement of service;

    (b) the time for service by the defendant of any witness statement in opposition to the relief being sought;

    (c) an early return date for the hearing of the summary judgment application and a note of the time required or allowed for that hearing; and

    (d) identification of the judgment, order or other relief being sought at the hearing of the adjudication claim.

The order made at this stage will always give the defendant liberty to apply.

9.2.7 A direction providing for a date by which the claim form, supporting evidence and court order providing for the hearing are to be served on the defendant should ordinarily also be given when the judge deals with the paper procedural application.

Paragraph numbers marked with a "+" can be found online and on CD.

9.2.8 The directions will ordinarily provide for an enforcement hearing within 28 days of the directions being made and for the defendant to be given at least 14 days from the date of service for the serving of any evidence in opposition to the adjudication application. In more straightforward cases, the abridged periods may be less.

9.2.9 Draft standard directions of the kind commonly made by the court on a procedural application by the claimant in an action to enforce the decision of an adjudicator are attached as Appendix F.

9.2.10 The claimant should, with the application, provide an estimate of the time needed for the hearing of the application. This estimate will be taken into account by the judge when fixing the date and length of the hearing. The parties should, if possible jointly, communicate any revised time estimate to the court promptly and the judge to whom the case has been allocated will consider whether to refix the hearing date or alter the time period that has been allocated for the hearing.

9.2.11 If the parties cannot agree on the date or time fixed for the hearing, a paper application must be made to the judge to whom the hearing has been allocated for directions.

9.3 The Enforcement Hearing

9.3.1 Where there is any dispute to be resolved at the hearing, the judge should be **2C–99** provided with copies of the relevant sections of the HGCRA, the adjudication procedural rules under which the adjudication was conducted, the adjudicator's decision and copies of any adjudication provisions in the contract underlying the adjudication.

9.3.2 Subject to any more specific directions given by the court, the parties should lodge, by 4.00 p.m. one clear working day before the hearing, a bundle containing the documents that will be required at the hearing and copies of any authorities which are to be relied on. The parties should also file and serve short skeleton arguments, summarising their respective contentions as to why the adjudicator's decision is or is not enforceable or as to any other relief being sought. For a hearing that is expected to last half a day or less, the skeletons should be provided no later than 1 p.m. on the last working day before the hearing. For a hearing that is estimated to last more than half a day, the skeletons should be provided no later than 4 p.m. one clear working day before the hearing.

9.3.3 The parties should be ready to address the court on the limited grounds on which a defendant may resist an application seeking to enforce an adjudicator's decision or on which a court may provide any other relief to any party in relation to an adjudication or an adjudicator's decision.

9.4 Other Proceedings Arising Out Of Adjudication

9.4.1 As noted above, the TCC will also hear any applications for declaratory relief **2C–100** arising out of the commencement of a disputed adjudication. Commonly, these will concern:
   a) Disputes over the jurisdiction of an adjudicator. It can sometimes be appropriate to seek a declaration as to jurisdiction at the outset of an adjudication, rather than both parties incurring considerable costs in the adjudication itself, only for the jurisdiction point to emerge again at the enforcement hearing.
   b) Disputes over whether there is a written contract between the parties or, in appropriate cases, whether there is a construction contract within the meaning of the Act.
   c) Disputes over the permissible scope of the adjudication, and, in particular, whether the matters which the claimant seeks to raise in the adjudication are the subject of a pre-existing dispute between the parties.

9.4.2 Any such application will be immediately assigned to a named judge. In such

Paragraph numbers marked with a "+" can be found online and on CD.

TCC

circumstances, given the probable urgency of the application, the judge will usually require the parties to attend a CMC within 2 working days of the assignment of the case to him, and he will then give the necessary directions to ensure the speedy resolution of the dispute.

9.4.3 It sometimes happens that one party to an adjudication commences enforcement proceedings, whilst the other commences proceedings under Part 8, in order to challenge the validity of the adjudicator's award. This duplication of effort is unnecessary and it involves the parties in extra costs, especially if the two actions are commenced at different court centres. Accordingly there should be sensible discussions between the parties or their lawyers, in order to agree the appropriate venue and also to agree who shall be claimant and who defendant. All the issues raised by each party can and should be raised in a single action.

SECTION 10.

ARBITRATION

10.1 Arbitration Claims in the TCC

2C–101 10.1.1 "Arbitration claims" are any application to the court under the Arbitration Act 1996 and any other claim concerned with an arbitration that is referred to in CPR 62.2(1). Common examples of arbitration claims are challenges to an award on grounds of jurisdiction under section 67, challenges to an award for serious irregularity under section 68 or appeals on points of law under section 69 of the Arbitration Act 1996. Arbitration claims may be started in the TCC, as is provided for in paragraph 2.3 of the Practice Direction—Arbitration which supplements CPR Part 62.

10.1.2 In practice, arbitration claims arising out of or connected with a construction or engineering arbitration (or any other arbitration where the subject matter involved one or more of the categories of work set out in paragraph 1.3.1 above) should be started in the TCC. The only arbitration claims that must be started in the Commercial Court are those (increasingly rare) claims to which the old law (i.e. the pre-1996 Act provisions) apply: see CPR rule 62.12.

10.1.3 The TCC follows the practice and procedure for arbitration claims established by CPR Part 62 and (broadly) the practice of the Commercial Court as summarised by Section O of the *Admiralty and Commercial Courts Guide*. In the absence of any specific directions given by the court, the automatic directions set out in section 6 of the Practice Direction supplementing CPR Part 62 govern the procedures to be followed in any arbitration claim from the date of service up to the substantive hearing.

10.2 Leave to appeal

2C–102 10.2.1 Where a party is seeking to appeal a question of law arising out of an award pursuant to section 69 of the Arbitration Act 1996 and the parties have not in their underlying contract agreed that such an appeal may be brought, the party seeking to appeal must apply for leave to appeal pursuant to sections 69(2), 69(3) and 69(4) of that Act. That application must be included in the arbitration claim form as explained in paragraph 12 of the Practice Direction.

10.2.2 In conformity with the practice of the Commercial Court, the TCC will normally consider any application for permission to appeal on paper after the defendant has had an appropriate opportunity to answer in writing the application being raised.

10.2.3 The claimant must include within the claim form an application for permission to appeal. No separate application notice is required.

10.2.4 The claim form and supporting documents must be served on the defendant. The judge will not consider the application for permission to appeal until (a) a

Paragraph numbers marked with a "+" can be found online and on CD.

certificate of service has been filed at the appropriate TCC registry or court centre and (b) a further 28 days have elapsed, so as to enable the defendant to file written evidence in opposition. Save in exceptional circumstances, the only material admissible on an application for permission to appeal is (a) the award itself and any documents annexed to the award and (b) evidence relevant to the issue whether any identified question of law is of general public importance.

10.2.5 If necessary, the judge dealing with the application will direct an oral hearing with a date for the hearing. That hearing will, ordinarily, consist of brief submissions by each party. The judge dealing with the application will announce his decision in writing or, if a hearing has been directed, at the conclusion of the hearing with brief reasons if the application is refused.

10.2.6 Where the permission has been allowed in part and refused in part:

(a) Only those questions for which permission has been granted may be raised at the hearing of the appeal.

(b) Brief reasons will be given for refusing permission in respect of the other questions.

10.2.7 If the application is granted, the judge will fix the date for the appeal, and direct whether the same judge or a different judge shall hear the appeal.

10.3 Appeals where leave to appeal is not required

10.3.1 Parties to a construction contract should check whether they have agreed in the underlying contract that an appeal may be brought without leave, since some construction and engineering standard forms of contract so provide. If that is the case, the appeal may be set down for a substantive hearing without leave being sought. The arbitration claim form should set out the clause or provision which it is contended provides for such agreement and the claim form should be marked "Arbitration Appeal—Leave not required".

2C–103

10.3.2 Where leave is not required, the claimant should identify each question of law that it is contended arises out of the award and which it seeks to raise in an appeal under section 69. If the defendant does not accept that the questions thus identified are questions of law or maintains that they do not arise out of the award or that the appeal on those questions may not be brought for any other reason, then the defendant should notify the claimant and the court of its contentions and apply for a directions hearing before the judge nominated to hear the appeal on a date prior to the date fixed for the hearing of the appeal. Unless the judge hearing the appeal otherwise directs, the appeal will be confined to the questions of law identified in the arbitration claim form.

10.3.3 In an appropriate case, the judge may direct that the question of law to be raised and decided on the appeal should be reworded, so as to identify more accurately the real legal issue between the parties.

10.4 The hearing of the appeal

10.4.1 Parties should ensure that the court is provided only with material that is relevant and admissible to the point of law. This will usually be limited to the award and any documents annexed to the award: see *Hok Sport Ltd v Aintree Racecourse Ltd* [2003] BLR 155 at 160. However, the court should also receive any document referred to in the award, which the court needs to read in order to determine a question of law arising out of the award: see *Kershaw Mechanical Services Ltd v Kendrick Construction Ltd* [2006] EWHC 727 (TCC).

2C–104

10.4.2 On receiving notice of permission being granted, or on issuing an arbitration claim form in a case where leave to appeal is not required, the parties should notify the court of their joint estimate or differing estimates of the time needed for the hearing of the appeal.

10.4.3 The hearing of the appeal is to be in open court unless an application (with

Paragraph numbers marked with a "+" can be found online and on CD.

TCC

notice) has previously been made that the hearing should be wholly or in part held in private and the court has directed that this course should be followed.

10.5 Section 68 applications—Serious Irregularity

2C-105 10.5.1 In some arbitration claims arising out of construction and engineering arbitrations, a party will seek to appeal a question of law and, at the same time, seek to challenge the award under section 68 of the Arbitration Act 1996 on the grounds of serious irregularity. This raises questions of procedure, since material may be admissible in a section 68 application which is inadmissible on an application or appeal under section 69. Similarly, it may not be appropriate for all applications to be heard together. A decision is needed as to the order in which the applications should be heard, whether there should be one or more separate hearings to deal with them and whether or not the same judge should deal with all applications. Where a party intends to raise applications under both sections of the Arbitration Act 1996, they should be issued in the same arbitration claim form or in separate claim forms issued together. The court should be informed that separate applications are intended and asked for directions as to how to proceed.

10.5.2 The court will give directions as to how the section 68 and section 69 applications will be dealt with before hearing or determining any application. These directions will normally be given in writing but, where necessary or if such is applied for by a party, the court will hold a directions hearing at which directions will be given. The directions will be given following the service of any documentation by the defendant in answer to all applications raised by the claimant.

10.6 Successive awards and successive applications

2C-106 10.6.1 Some construction and engineering arbitrations give rise to two or more separate awards issued at different times. Where arbitration applications arise under more than one of these awards, any second or subsequent application, whether arising from the same or a different award, should be referred to the same judge who has heard previous applications. Where more than one judge has heard previous applications, the court should be asked to direct to which judge any subsequent application is to be referred.

10.7 Other applications and Enforcement

2C-107 10.7.1 All other arbitration claims, and any other matter arising in an appeal or an application concerning alleged serious irregularity, will be dealt with by the TCC in the same manner as is provided for in CPR Part 62, Practice Direction—Arbitration and Section O of *The Admiralty and Commercial Courts Guide*.

10.7.2 All applications for permission to enforce arbitration awards are governed by Section III of Part 62 (rules 62.17–62.19).

10.7.3 An application for permission to enforce an award in the same manner as a judgment or order of the court may be made in an arbitration claim form without notice and must be supported by written evidence in accordance with rule 62.18(6). Two copies of the draft order must accompany the application, and the form of the order sought must correspond to the terms of the award.

10.7.4 An order made without notice giving permission to enforce the award:
  (a) must give the defendant 14 days after service of the order (or longer, if the order is to be served outside the jurisdiction) to apply to set it aside;
  (b) must state that it may not be enforced until after the expiry of the 14 days (or any longer period specified) or until any application to set aside the order has been finally disposed of: rule 62.18(9) and (10).

10.7.5 On considering an application to enforce without notice, the judge may direct that, instead, the arbitration claim form must be served on specified parties, with the result that the application will then continue as an arbitration claim in accordance with the procedure set out in Section I of Part 62: see rule 62.18(1)–(3).

Paragraph numbers marked with a "+" can be found online and on CD.

SECTION 11.

DISCLOSURE

11.1 Standard Disclosure

11.1.1 The appropriate disclosure and inspection orders to be made will normally be **2C–108** considered and made at the first case management conference. This is governed by CPR Part 31 and the Practice Direction supplementing it. This procedure provides for standard disclosure, being disclosure and inspection in accordance with CPR Part 31 of:

(a) the documents upon which a party relies;
(b) the documents which adversely affect his or another party's case or support another party's case; and
(c) the documents which a party is required to disclose by any relevant practice direction.

11.2 Limiting disclosure and the cost of disclosure

11.2.1 In many cases being conducted in the TCC, standard disclosure will not be **2C–109** appropriate. This may for any one or more of the following reasons:

(a) The amount of documentation may be considerable, given the complexity of the dispute and the underlying contract or contracts, and the process of giving standard disclosure may consequently be disproportionate to the issues and sums in dispute.
(b) The parties may have many of the documents in common from their previous dealings so that disclosure is not necessary or desirable.
(c) The parties may have provided informal disclosure and inspection of the majority of these documents, for example when complying with the pre-action Protocol.
(d) The cost of providing standard disclosure may be disproportionate.

In such cases, the parties should seek to agree upon a more limited form of disclosure or to dispense with formal disclosure altogether. Such an agreement could limit disclosure to specified categories of documents or to such documents as may be specifically applied for.

11.2.2 Where disclosure is to be provided, the parties should consider whether it is necessary for lists of documents to be prepared or whether special arrangements should be agreed as to the form of listing and identifying disclosable documents, the method, timing and location of inspection and the manner of copying or providing copies of documents. Where documents are scattered over several locations, or are located overseas or are in a foreign language, special arrangements will also need to be considered. Thought should also be given to providing disclosure in stages or to reducing the scope of disclosure by providing the relevant material in other forms.

11.2.3 Electronic data and documents give rise to particular problems as to searching, preserving, listing, inspecting and other aspects of discovery and inspection. These problems should be considered and, if necessary made the subject of special directions. Furthermore, in appropriate cases, disclosure, inspection and the provision of copies of hard copies may be undertaken using information technology. Attention is drawn to the relevant provisions in CPR Part 31, to *the Admiralty and Commercial Courts Guide* concerned with Electronic Disclosure, and to the TeCSA IT Protocol which provide guidance in relation to these matters. In appropriate cases the TCC will order that the provisions concerning electronic disclosure contained in section E of *the Admiralty and Commercial Courts Guide* shall apply.

11.2.4 All these matters should be agreed between the parties. If it is necessary to raise any of these matters with the court they should be raised, if possible, at the first

Paragraph numbers marked with a "+" can be found online and on CD.

CMC. If points arise on disclosure after the first CMC, they may well be capable of being dealt with by the court on paper.

11.3 Service using information technology

2C-110 11.3.1 The parties should consult with each other before the first CMC with a view to arranging the service and (where required) filing of pleadings, schedules, witness statements, experts' reports, disclosure lists and other documents in computer readable form as well as in hard copy. The parties should also consider whether to maintain a common running index, so that every document which has been exchanged between the parties has a unique reference number. Any agreement reached on these matters should be recorded and made the subject of an order for directions. Where agreement is not possible, the parties should raise these matters for decision at a CMC.

SECTION 12.

WITNESS STATEMENTS AND FACTUAL EVIDENCE FOR USE AT TRIAL

12.1 Witness statements

2C-111 12.1.1 Witness statements should be prepared generally in accordance with CPR Part 22.1 (documents verified by a statement of truth) and CPR Part 32 (provisions governing the evidence of witnesses) and their practice directions, particularly paragraphs 17 to 22 of the Practice Direction supplementing CPR Part 32.

12.1.2 Unless otherwise directed by the court, witness statements should <u>not</u> have annexed to them copies of other documents and should <u>not</u> reproduce or paraphrase at length passages from other documents. The only exception arises where a specific document needs to be annexed to the statement in order to make that statement reasonably intelligible.

12.1.3 When preparing witness statements, attention should be paid to the following matters:

(a) Even when prepared by a legal representative or other professional, the witness statement should be, so far as practicable, in the witness's own words.

(b) The witness statement should indicate which matters are within the witness's own knowledge and which are matters of information and belief. Where the witness is stating matters of hearsay or of either information or belief, the source of that evidence should also be stated.

(c) The witness statement must include a statement by the witness that he believes the facts stated to be true.

(d) A witness statement should be no longer than necessary and should not be argumentative.

12.2 Other matters concerned with witness statements

2C-112 12.2.1 <u>Foreign language.</u> If a witness is not sufficiently fluent in English to give his evidence in English, the witness statement should be in his or her own language and an authenticated translation provided. Where the witness has a broken command of English, the statement may be drafted by others so as to express the witness's evidence as accurately as possible. In that situation, however, the witness statement should indicate that this process of interpolation has occurred and also should explain the extent of the witness's command of English and how and to what parts of the witness statement the process of interpolation has occurred.

12.2.2 <u>Reluctant witness.</u> Sometimes a witness is unwilling or not permitted or is unavailable to provide a witness statement before the trial. The party seeking to adduce this evidence should comply with the provisions of CPR rule 32.9 concerned with the provision of witness summaries.

12.2.3 <u>Hearsay.</u> Parties should keep in mind the need to give appropriate notice of their intention to rely on hearsay evidence or the contents of documents without

Paragraph numbers marked with a "+" can be found online and on CD.

serving a witness statement from their maker or from the originator of the evidence contained in those documents. The appropriate procedure is contained in CPR rules 33.1–33.5.

12.3 Cross-referencing

2C–113

12.3.1 Where a substantial number of documents will be adduced in evidence or contained in the trial bundles, it is of considerable assistance to the court and to all concerned if the relevant page references are annotated in the margins of the copy witness statements. It is accepted that this is a time-consuming exercise, the need for which will be considered at the PTR, and it will only be ordered where it is both appropriate and proportionate to do so. See further paragraphs 14.5.1 and 15.2.3 below.

12.4 Video link

2C–114

12.4.1 If any witness (whose witness statement has been served and who is required to give oral evidence) is located outside England and Wales or would find a journey to court inconvenient or impracticable, his evidence might be given via a video link. Thought should be given before the PTR to the question whether this course would be appropriate and proportionate. Such evidence is regularly received by the TCC and facilities for its reception, whether in appropriate court premises or at a convenient venue outside the court building, are now readily available.

12.4.2 Any application for a video link direction and any question relating to the manner in which such evidence is to be given should be dealt with at the PTR. Attention is drawn to the Video-conferencing Protocol set out at Annex 3 to the Practice Direction—Witness Evidence. The procedure described in Annex 3 is followed by the TCC.

SECTION 13.

EXPERT EVIDENCE

13.1 Nature of expert evidence

2C–115

13.1.1 Expert evidence is evidence as to matters of a technical or scientific nature and will generally include the opinions of the expert. The quality and reliability of expert evidence will depend upon (a) the experience and the technical or scientific qualifications of the expert and (b) the accuracy of the factual material that is used by the expert for his assessment. Expert evidence is dealt with in detail in CPR Part 35 ("Experts and Assessors") and in the Practice Direction supplementing Part 35. Particular attention should be paid to all these provisions, given the detailed reliance on expert evidence in most TCC actions. Particular attention should also be paid to the "Protocol for the instruction of experts to give evidence in civil claims" published by the Civil Justice Council in June 2005. This protocol has been approved by the Master of the Rolls.

13.1.2 The provisions in CPR Part 35 are concerned with the terms upon which the court may receive expert evidence. These provisions are principally applicable to independently instructed expert witnesses. In cases where a party is a professional or a professional has played a significant part in the subject matter of the action, opinion evidence will almost inevitably be included in the witness statements. Any points arising from such evidence (if they cannot be resolved by agreement) can be dealt with by the judge on an application or at the PTR.

13.2 Control of expert evidence

2C–116

13.2.1 Expert evidence is frequently needed and used in TCC cases. Experts are often appointed at an early stage. Most types of case heard in the TCC involve more than one expertise and some, even when the dispute is concerned with relatively

Paragraph numbers marked with a "+" can be found online and on CD.

TCC

small sums, involve several different experts. Such disputes include those concerned with building failures and defects, delay and disruption, dilapidations, subsidence caused by tree roots and the supply of software systems. However, given the cost of preparing such evidence, the parties and the court must, from the earliest pre-action phase of a dispute until the conclusion of the trial, seek to make effective and proportionate use of experts. The scope of any expert evidence must be limited to what is necessary for the requirements of the particular case.

13.2.2 At the first CMC, or thereafter, the court may be asked to determine whether the cost of instructing experts is proportionate to the amount at issue in the proceedings, and the importance of the case to the parties. In dealing with any issues of proportionality, the court should be provided with estimates of the experts' costs.

13.2.3 The parties should also be aware that the court has the power to limit the amount of the expert's fees that a party may recover pursuant to CPR 35.4(4).

13.3 Prior to and at the first CMC

2C–117 13.3.1 There is an unresolved tension arising from the need for parties to instruct and rely on expert opinions from an early pre-action stage and the need for the court to seek, wherever possible, to reduce the cost of expert evidence by dispensing with it altogether or by encouraging the appointment of jointly instructed experts. This tension arises because the court can only consider directing joint appointments or limiting expert evidence long after a party may have incurred the cost of obtaining expert evidence and have already relied on it. Parties should be aware of this tension. So far as possible, the parties should avoid incurring the costs of expert evidence on uncontroversial matters or matters of the kind referred to in paragraph 13.4.3 below, before the first CMC has been held.

13.3.2 In cases where it is not appropriate for the court to order a single joint expert, it is imperative that, wherever possible, the parties' experts co-operate fully with one another. This is particularly important where tests, surveys, investigations, sample gathering or other technical methods of obtaining primary factual evidence are needed. It is often critical to ensure that any laboratory testing or experiments are carried out by the experts together, pursuant to an agreed procedure. Alternatively, the respective experts may agree that a particular firm or laboratory shall carry out specified tests or analyses on behalf of all parties.

13.3.3 Parties should, where possible, disclose initial or preliminary reports to opposing parties prior to any pre-action protocol meeting, if only on a without prejudice basis. Such early disclosure will assist in early settlement or mediation discussions and in helping the parties to define and confine the issues in dispute with a corresponding saving in costs.

13.3.4 Before and at the first CMC and at each subsequent pre-trial stage of the action, the parties should give careful thought to the following matters:

    (a) The number, disciplines and identity of the expert witnesses they are considering instructing as their own experts or as single joint experts.

    (b) The precise issues which each expert is to address in his/her reports, to discuss without prejudice with opposing parties' experts and give evidence about at the trial.

    (c) The timing of any meeting, agreed statement or report.

    (d) Any appropriate or necessary tests, inspections, sampling or investigations that could be undertaken jointly or in collaboration with other experts. Any such measures should be preceded by a meeting of relevant experts at which an appropriate testing or other protocol is devised. This would cover (i) all matters connected with the process in question and its recording and (ii) the sharing and agreement of any resulting data or evidence.

    (e) Any common method of analysis, investigation or reporting where it is appropriate or proportionate that such should be adopted by all relevant experts. An example of this would be an agreement as to the method to be used to ana-

Paragraph numbers marked with a "+" can be found online and on CD.

lyse the cause and extent of any relevant period of delay in a construction project, where such is in issue in the case.

(f) The availability and length of time that experts will realistically require to complete the tasks assigned to them.

13.3.5 In so far as the matters set out in the previous paragraph cannot be agreed, the court will give appropriate directions. In giving permission for the reception of any expert evidence, the court will ordinarily order the exchange of such evidence, with a definition of the expert's area of expertise and a clear description of the issues about which that expert is permitted to give evidence. It is preferable that, at the first CMC or as soon as possible thereafter, the parties should provide the court with the name(s) of their expert(s).

13.4 Single joint experts

13.4.1 An order may be made, at the first CMC or thereafter, that a single joint **2C–118** expert should address particular issues between the parties. Such an order would be made pursuant to CPR Parts 35.7 and 35.8.

13.4.2 Single joint experts are not usually appropriate for the principal liability disputes in a large case, or in a case where considerable sums have been spent on an expert in the pre-action stage. They are generally inappropriate where the issue involves questions of risk assessment or professional competence.

13.4.3 On the other hand, single joint experts can often be appropriate:

(a) in low value cases, where technical evidence is required but the cost of adversarial expert evidence may be prohibitive;

(b) where the topic with which the single joint expert's report deals is a separate and self-contained part of the case, such as the valuation of particular heads of claim;

(c) where there is a subsidiary issue, which requires particular expertise of a relatively uncontroversial nature to resolve;

(d) where testing or analysis is required, and this can conveniently be done by one laboratory or firm on behalf of all parties.

13.4.4 Where a single joint expert is to be appointed or is to be directed by the court, the parties should attempt to devise a protocol covering all relevant aspects of the appointment (save for those matters specifically provided for by CPR rules 35.6, 35.7 and 35.8).

13.4.5 The matters to be considered should include: any ceiling on fees and disbursements that are to be charged and payable by the parties; how, when and by whom fees will be paid to the expert on an interim basis pending any costs order in the proceedings; how the expert's fees will be secured; how the terms of reference are to be agreed; what is to happen if terms of reference cannot be agreed; how and to whom the jointly appointed expert may address further enquiries and from whom he should seek further information and documents; the timetable for preparing any report or for undertaking any other preparatory step; the possible effect on such timetable of any supplementary or further instructions. Where these matters cannot be agreed, an application to the court, which may often be capable of being dealt with as a paper application, will be necessary.

13.4.6 The usual procedure for a single joint expert will involve:

(a) The preparation of the expert's instructions. These instructions should clearly identify those issues or matters where the parties are in conflict, whether on the facts or on matters of opinion. If the parties can agree joint instructions, then a single set of instructions should be delivered to the expert. However, rule 35.8 expressly permits separate instructions and these are necessary where joint instructions cannot be agreed

(b) The preparation of the agreed bundle, which is to be provided to the expert. This bundle must include CPR Part 35, the Practice Direction supplementing Part 35 and the section 13 of the TCC Guide.

Paragraph numbers marked with a "+" can be found online and on CD.

(c) The preparation and production of the expert's report.

(d) The provision to the expert of any written questions from the parties, which the expert must answer in writing.

13.4.7 In most cases the single joint expert's report, supplemented by any written answers to questions from the parties, will be sufficient for the purposes of the trial. Sometimes, however, it is necessary for a single joint expert to be called to give oral evidence. In those circumstances, the usual practice is for the judge to call the expert and then allow each party the opportunity to cross-examine. Such cross-examination should be conducted with appropriate restraint, since the witness has been instructed by the parties. Where the expert's report is strongly in favour of one party's position, it may be appropriate to allow only the other party to cross-examine.

13.5 Meetings of experts

2C–119 13.5.1 The desirability of holding without prejudice meetings between experts at all stages of the pre-trial preparation should be kept in mind. The desired outcome of such meetings is to produce a document whose contents are agreed and which defines common positions or each expert's differing position. The purpose of such meetings includes the following:

(a) to define a party's technical case and to inform opposing parties of the details of that case;

(b) to clear up confusion and to remedy any lack of information or understanding of a party's technical case in the minds of opposing experts;

(c) to identify the issues about which any expert is to give evidence;

(d) to narrow differences and to reach agreement on as many "expert" issues as possible; and

(e) to assist in providing an agenda for the trial and for cross examination of expert witnesses, and to limit the scope and length of the trial as much as possible.

13.5.2 In many cases it will be helpful for the parties' respective legal advisors to provide assistance as to the agenda and topics to be discussed at an experts' meeting. However, (save in exceptional circumstances and with the permission of the judge) the legal advisors must not attend the meeting. They must not attempt to dictate what the experts say at the meeting.

13.5.3 Experts' meetings can sometimes usefully take place at the site of the dispute. Thought is needed as to who is to make the necessary arrangements for access, particularly where the site is occupied or in the control of a non-party. Expert meetings are often more productive, if (a) the expert of one party (usually the claimant) is appointed as chairman and (b) the experts exchange in advance agendas listing the topics each wishes to raise and identifying any relevant material which they intend to introduce or rely on during the meeting.

13.5.4 It is generally sensible for the experts to meet at least once before they exchange their reports.

13.6 Experts' Joint Statements

2C–120 13.6.1 Following the experts' meetings, and pursuant to CPR 35.12 (3), the judge will almost always require the experts to produce a signed statement setting out the issues which have been agreed, and those issues which have not been agreed, together with a short summary of the reasons for their disagreement. In any TCC case in which expert evidence has an important role to play, this statement is a critical document and it must be as clear as possible.

13.6.2 It should be noted that, even where experts have been unable to agree very much, it is of considerable importance that the statement sets out their disagreements and the reasons for them. Such disagreements as formulated in the joint statement are likely to form an important element of the agenda for the trial of the action.

Paragraph numbers marked with a "+" can be found online and on CD.

13.6.3 Whilst the parties' legal advisors may assist in identifying issues which the statement should address, those legal advisors must not be involved in either negotiating or drafting the experts' joint statement.

13.7 Experts' Reports

13.7.1 It is the duty of an expert to help the court on matters within his expertise. This duty overrides any duty to his client: CPR rule 35.3. Each expert's report must be independent and unbiased. **2C–121**

13.7.2 The parties must identify the issues with which each expert should deal in his report. Thereafter, it is for the expert to draft and decide upon the detailed contents and format of his report, so as to conform with section 2 of the Part 35 Practice Direction. It is appropriate, however, for the party instructing an expert to indicate that the report (a) should be as short as is reasonably possible; (b) should not set out copious extracts from other documents; (c) should identify the source of any opinion or data relied upon; and (d) should not annex or exhibit more than is reasonably necessary to support the opinions expressed in the report.

SECTION 14.

THE PRE-TRIAL REVIEW

14.1 Timing and Attendance

14.1.1 The Pre-Trial Review ("PTR") will usually be fixed for a date that is 4–6 weeks in advance of the commencement of the trial itself. It is vital that the advocates, who are going to conduct the trial, should attend the PTR and every effort should be made to achieve this. It is usually appropriate for the PTR to be conducted by way of an oral hearing or, at the very least, a telephone conference. **2C–122**

14.2 Documents

14.2.1 The parties must complete the PTR Questionnaire (a copy of which is at Appendix C attached) and return it in good time to the court. In addition, the judge may order the parties to provide other documents for the particular purposes of the PTR. **2C–123**

14.2.2 In an appropriate case, the advocates for each party should prepare a Note for the PTR, which addresses:
- any outstanding directions or interlocutory steps still to be taken;
- the issues for determination at the trial;
- the most efficient way in which those issues might be dealt with at the trial, including all questions of timetabling of witnesses.

These Notes should be provided to the court by 4 p.m. one clear day before the PTR.

14.2.3 The parties should also ensure that, for the PTR, the court has an up-to-date permanent case management bundle, together with a bundle of the evidence (factual and expert) that has been exchanged. This Bundle should also be made available to the court by 4 p.m. one clear day before the PTR.

14.3 Outstanding Directions

14.3.1 It can sometimes be the case that there are still outstanding interlocutory steps to be taken at the time of the PTR. That will usually mean that one, or more, of the parties has not complied with an earlier direction of the court. In that event, the court is likely to require prompt compliance, and may make costs orders to reflect the delays. **2C–124**

14.3.2 Sometimes a party will wish to make an application to be heard at the same

Paragraph numbers marked with a "+" can be found online and on CD.

time as the PTR. Such a practice is unsatisfactory, because it uses up time allocated for the PTR, and it gives rise to potential uncertainty close to the trial date. It is always better for a party, if it possibly can, to make all necessary applications well in advance of the PTR. If that is not practicable, the court should be asked to allocate additional time for the PTR, in order to accommodate specific applications. If additional time is not available, such applications will not generally be entertained.

14.4 Issues

2C–125   14.4.1 The parties should, if possible, provide the judge at the PTR with an agreed list of the Issues for the forthcoming trial (including, where appropriate, a separate list of technical issues to be covered by the experts).

14.4.2 If the parties are unable to agree the precise formulation of the issues, they should provide to the court their respective contentions as to what the issues are, and why.

14.4.3 In order to determine the best way to deal with the trial, it is necessary for the issues to be identified. If the precise formulation of the issues is a matter of dispute between the parties, the judge will note the parties' respective contentions, but is unlikely to give a ruling on this matter at the PTR.

14.5 Timetabling and Trial Logistics

2C–126   14.5.1 Much of the PTR will be devoted to a consideration of the appropriate timetable for the trial, and other logistical matters. These will commonly include:

- Directions in respect of oral and written openings.
- Sequence of oral evidence; for example, whether all the factual evidence should be called before the expert evidence.
- Timetabling of oral evidence. (To facilitate this exercise, the advocates should tell the judge which witnesses need to be cross-examined and which evidence can be agreed.)
- Whether any form of time limits should be imposed. (Since the purpose of time limits is to ensure that that the costs incurred and the resources devoted to the trial are proportionate, this is for the benefit of the parties. The judge will endeavour to secure agreement to any time limits imposed.)
- Directions in respect of the trial bundle: when it should be agreed and lodged; the contents and structure of the bundle; avoidance of duplication; whether witness statements and/or expert reports should be annotated with cross references to page numbers in the main bundle (see paragraph 12.3 above); and similar matters.
- Whether there should be a core bundle; if so how it should be prepared and what it should contain. (The court will order a core bundle in any case where (a) there is substantial documentation and (b) having regard to the issues it is appropriate and proportionate to put the parties to cost of preparing a core bundle).
- Rules governing any email communication during trial between the parties and the court.
- Any directions relating to the use of simultaneous transcription at trial (this subject to agreement between the parties).

14.5.2 The topics identified in paragraph 14.5.1 are discussed in greater detail in section 15 below.

SECTION 15.

THE TRIAL

15.1 Arrangements prior to the trial—witnesses

2C–127   15.1.1 Prior to the trial the parties' legal representatives should seek to agree on the following matters, in so far as they have not been resolved at the PTR: the order in

Paragraph numbers marked with a "+" can be found online and on CD.

which witnesses are to be called to give evidence; which witnesses are not required for cross examination and whose evidence in consequence may be adduced entirely from their witness statements; the timetable for the trial and the length of time each advocate is to be allowed for a brief opening speech. When planning the timetable, it should be noted that trials normally take place on Mondays to Thursdays, since Fridays are reserved for applications.

15.1.2 The witnesses should be notified in advance of the trial as to: (a) when each is required to attend court and (b) the approximate period of time for which he or she will be required to attend.

15.1.3 It is the parties' responsibility to ensure that their respective witnesses are ready to attend court at the appropriate time. It is never satisfactory for witnesses to be interposed, out of their proper place. It would require exceptional circumstances for the trial to be adjourned for any period of time because of the unavailability of a witness.

15.2 Opening notes, trial bundle and oral openings

15.2.1 Opening notes. Unless the court has ordered otherwise, each party's advocate **2C–128** should provide an opening note, which outlines that party's case in relation to each of the issues identified at the PTR. Each opening note should indicate which documents (giving their page numbers in the trial bundle) that party considers that the judge should pre-read. The claimant's opening note should include a neutral summary of the background facts, as well as a chronology and cast list. The other parties' opening notes should be shorter and should assume familiarity with the factual background. In general terms, all opening notes should be of modest length and proportionate to the size and complexity of the case. Subject to any specific directions at the PTR, the claimant's opening note should be served two clear working days before the start of the trial; the other parties opening notes should be served by 1 p.m. on the last working day before the trial.

15.2.2 Trial bundles. Subject to any specific directions at the PTR, the trial bundles should be delivered to court at least three working days before the hearing. It is helpful for the party delivering the trial bundles to liaise in advance with the judge's clerk, in order to discuss practical arrangements, particularly when a large number of bundles are to be delivered. The parties should provide for the court an agreed index of all trial bundles. There should also be an index at the front of each bundle. This should be a helpful guide to the contents of that bundle. (An interminable list, itemising every letter or sheet of paper is not a helpful guide. Nor are bland descriptions, such as "exhibit 'JT3', of much help to the bundle user.) The spines of bundles should be clearly labelled.

15.2.3 As a general rule the trial bundles should be clearly divided between statements of case, orders, contracts, witness statements, expert reports and correspondence/ minutes of meetings. The correspondence/ minutes of meetings should be in a separate bundle or bundles and in chronological order. Documents should only be included, if they are relevant to the issues in the case or helpful as background material. Documents should not be duplicated. Exhibits to witness statements should generally be omitted, since the documents to which the witnesses are referring will be found elsewhere in the bundles. The bundles of contract documents and correspondence/ minutes of meetings should be paginated, so that every page has a discrete number. The other bundles could be dealt with in one of two ways:

- The statements of case, witness statements and expert reports could be placed in bundles and continuously paginated.
- Alternatively, the statements of case, witness statements and expert reports could be placed behind tabbed divider cards, and then the internal numbering of each such document can be used at trial. If the latter course is adopted, it is vital that the internal page numbering of each expert report continues sequentially through the appendices to that report.

The ultimate objective is to create trial bundles, which are user friendly and in which

Paragraph numbers marked with a "+" can be found online and on CD.

any page can be identified with clarity and brevity (e.g. "bundle G page 273" or "defence page 3" or "Dr Smith page 12"). The core bundle, if there is one (as to which see paragraph 14.5.1 above), will be a separate bundle with its own pagination

15.2.4 Opening speeches. Subject to any directions made at the PTR, each party will be permitted to make an opening speech. These speeches should be prepared and presented on the basis that the judge will have pre-read the opening notes and the documents identified by the parties for pre-reading. The claimant's advocate may wish to highlight the main features of the claimant's case and/or to deal with matters raised in the other parties' opening notes. The other parties' advocates will then make shorter opening speeches, emphasising the main features of their own cases and/or responding to matters raised in the claimant's opening speech.

15.2.5 It is not usually necessary or desirable to embark upon legal argument during opening speeches. It is, however, helpful to foreshadow those legal arguments which (a) explain the relevance of particular parts of the evidence or (b) will assist the judge in following a party's case that is to be presented during the trial.

15.2.6 Narrowing of issues. Experience shows that often that the issues between the parties progressively narrow as the trial advances. Sometimes this process begins during the course of opening speeches. Weaker contentions may be abandoned and responses to those contentions may become irrelevant. The advocates will co-operate in focussing their submissions and the evidence on the true issues between the parties, as those issues are thrown into sharper relief by the adversarial process.

15.3 Simultaneous transcription

2C-129 15.3.1 Many trials in the TCC, including the great majority of the longer trials, are conducted with simultaneous transcripts of the evidence being provided. There are a number of transcribing systems available. It is now common for a system to be used involving simultaneous transcription onto screens situated in court. However, systems involving the production of the transcript in hard or electronic form at the end of the day or even after a longer period of time are also used. The parties must make the necessary arrangements with one of the companies who provide this service. The court can provide a list, on request, of all companies who offer such a service.

15.3.2 In long trials or those which involve any significant amount of detailed or technical evidence, simultaneous transcripts are helpful. Furthermore, they enable all but the shortest trials to be conducted so as to reduce the overall length of the trial appreciably, since the judge does not have to note the evidence or submissions in longhand as the trial proceeds. Finally, a simultaneous transcript makes the task of summarising a case in closing submissions and preparing the judgment somewhat easier. It reduces both the risk of error or omission and the amount of time needed to prepare a reserved judgment.

15.3.3 If possible, the parties should have agreed at or before the PTR whether a simultaneous transcript is to be employed. It is usual for parties to agree to share the cost of a simultaneous transcript as an interim measure pending the assessment or agreement of costs, when this cost is assessable and payable as part of the costs in the case. Sometimes, a party cannot or will not agree to an interim cost sharing arrangement. If so, it is permissible for one party to bear the cost, but the court cannot be provided with a transcript unless all parties have equal access to the transcript. Unlike transcripts for use during an appeal, there is no available means of obtaining from public funds the cost of a transcript for use at the trial.

15.4 Time limits

2C-130 15.4.1 Generally trials in the TCC are conducted under some form of time limit arrangement. Several variants of time limit arrangements are available, but the TCC has developed the practice of imposing flexible guidelines in the form of directions as to the sharing of the time allotted for the trial. These are not mandatory but an advocate should ordinarily be expected to comply with them.

Paragraph numbers marked with a "+" can be found online and on CD.

15.4.2 The practice is, in the usual case, for the court to fix, or for the parties to agree, at the PTR or before trial an overall length of time for the trial and overall lengths of time within that period for the evidence and submissions. The part of those overall lengths of time that will be allocated to each party must then be agreed or directed.

15.4.3 The amount of time to be allotted to each party will not usually be the same. The guide is that each party should have as much time as is reasonably needed for it to present its case and to test and cross examine any opposing case, but no longer.

15.4.4 Before the trial, the parties should agree a running order of the witnesses and the approximate length of time required for each witness. A trial timetable should be provided to the court when the trial starts and, in long trials, regularly updated.

15.4.5 The practice of imposing a strict guillotine on the examination or cross examination of witnesses, is not normally appropriate. Flexibility is encouraged, but the agreed or directed time limits should not ordinarily be exceeded without good reason. It is unfair on a party, if that party's advocate has confined cross-examination to the agreed time limits, but an opposing party then greatly exceeds the corresponding time limits that it has been allocated.

15.4.6 An alternative form of time limit, which is sometimes agreed between the parties and approved by the court, is the "chess clock arrangement". The available time is divided equally between the parties, to be used by the parties as they see fit. Thus each side has X hours. One representative on each side operates the chess clock. The judge has discretion "to stop the clock" in exceptional circumstances. A chess clock arrangement is only practicable in a two-party case.

15.5 Oral evidence

15.5.1 Evidence in chief is ordinarily adduced by the witness confirming on oath the **2C–131** truth and accuracy of the previously served witness statement or statements. A limited number of supplementary oral questions will usually be allowed (a) to give the witness an opportunity to become familiar with the procedure and (b) to cover points omitted by mistake from the witness statement or which have arisen subsequent to its preparation.

15.5.2 In some cases, particularly those involving allegations of dishonest, disreputable or culpable conduct or where significant disputes of fact are not documented or evidenced in writing, it is desirable that the core elements of a witness's evidence-in-chief are given orally. The giving of such evidence orally will often assist the court in assessing the credibility or reliability of a witness.

15.5.3 If any party wishes such evidence to be given orally, a direction should be sought either at the PTR or during the openings to that effect. Where evidence in chief is given orally, the rules relating to the use of witness statements in cross-examination and to the adducing of the statement in evidence at any subsequent stage of the trial remain in force and may be relied on by any party.

15.5.4 It is usual for all evidence of fact from all parties to be adduced before expert evidence and for the experts to give evidence in groups with all experts in a particular discipline giving their evidence in sequence. Usually, but not invariably, the order of witnesses will be such that the claimant's witnesses give their evidence first, followed by all the witnesses for each of the other parties in turn. If a party wishes a different order of witnesses to that normally followed, the agreement of the parties or a direction from the judge must be obtained in advance.

15.5.5 In a multi-party case, attention should be given (when the timetable is being discussed) to the order of cross-examination and to the extent to which particular topics will be covered by particular cross-examiners. Where these matters cannot be agreed, the order of cross-examination will (subject to any direction of the judge) follow the order in which the parties are set out in the pleadings. The judge will seek

Paragraph numbers marked with a "+" can be found online and on CD.

to limit cross examination on a topic which has been covered in detail by a preceding cross examination.

15.5.6 The coaching of witnesses or the suggestion of answers that may be given, before that witness starts to give evidence, is not permitted. Any prior discussion between the lawyers and the witness about the giving of evidence should be confined to factual information about the evidence-giving process. In short, witness familiarisation is permissible, but witness coaching is not. The boundary between witness familiarisation and witness coaching is discussed by the Court of Appeal in *R v Momodou* [2005] EWCA Crim 177 at [61]–[62]. Once a witness has started giving evidence, he cannot discuss the case or his evidence either with the lawyers or with anyone else until he has finally left the witness box. Occasionally a dispensation is needed (for example, an expert may need to participate in an experts' meeting about some new development). In those circumstances the necessary dispensation will either be agreed between the advocates or ordered by the judge.

15.6 Submissions during the trial

2C–132   15.6.1 Submissions and legal argument should be kept to a minimum during the course of the trial. Where these are necessary, (a) they should, where possible, take place when a witness is not giving evidence and (b) the judge should be given forewarning of the need for submissions or legal argument. Where possible, the judge will fix a time for these submissions outside the agreed timetable for the evidence.

15.7 Closing submissions

2C–133   15.7.1 The appropriate form of closing submissions can be determined during the course of the trial. Those submissions may take the form of (a) oral closing speeches or (b) written submission alone or (c) written submissions supplemented by oral closing speeches. In shorter or lower value cases, oral closing speeches immediately after the evidence may be the most cost effective way to proceed. Alternatively, if the evidence finishes in the late afternoon, a direction for written closing submissions to be delivered by specified (early) dates may avoid the cost of a further day's court hearing. In longer and heavier cases the judge may (in consultation with the advocates) set a timetable for the delivery of sequential written submissions (alternatively, an exchange of written submissions) followed by an oral hearing. In giving directions for oral and/or written closing submissions, the judge will have regard to the circumstances of the case and the overriding objective.

15.7.2 It is helpful if, in advance of preparing closing submissions, the parties can agree on the principal topics or issues that are to be covered. It is also helpful for the written and oral submissions of each party to be structured so as to cover those topics in the same order.

15.7.3 It is both customary and helpful for the judge to be provided with a photocopy of each authority and statutory provision that is to be cited in closing submissions.

15.8 Views

2C–134   15.8.1 It is sometimes necessary or desirable for the judge to be taken to view the subjectmatter of the case. In normal circumstances, such a view is best arranged to take place immediately after the openings and before the evidence is called. However, if the subject matter of the case is going to be covered up or altered prior to the trial, the view must be arranged earlier. In that event, it becomes particularly important to avoid a change of judge. Accordingly, the court staff will note on the trial diary the fact that the assigned judge has attended a view. In all subsequent communications between the parties and court concerning trial date, the need to avoid a change of judge must be borne firmly in mind.

15.8.2 The matters viewed by the judge form part of the evidence that is received

Paragraph numbers marked with a "+" can be found online and on CD.

and may be relied on in deciding the case. However, nothing said during the view to (or in the earshot of) the judge, has any evidential status, unless there has been an agreement or order to that effect.

15.8.3 The parties should agree the arrangements for the view and then make those arrangements themselves. The judge will ordinarily travel to the view unaccompanied and, save in exceptional circumstances when the cost will be shared by all parties, will not require any travelling costs to be met by the parties.

15.9 Judgments

2C–135

15.9.1 Depending on the length and complexity of the trial, the judge may (a) give judgment orally immediately after closing speeches; (b) give judgment orally on the following day or soon afterwards; or (c) deliver a reserved judgment in writing at a later date.

15.9.2 Where judgment is reserved. The judge will normally indicate at the conclusion of the trial what arrangements will be followed in relation to (a) the making available of any draft reserved judgment and (b) the handing down of the reserved judgment in open court. If a judgment is reserved, it will be handed down as soon as possible. Save in exceptional circumstances, any reserved judgment will be handed down within 3 months of the conclusion of the trial. Any enquiries as to the progress of a reserved judgment should be addressed in the first instance to the judge's clerk, with notice of that enquiry being given to other parties. If concerns remain following the judge's response to the parties, further enquiries or communication should be addressed to the judge in charge of the TCC.

15.9.3 If the judge decides to release a draft judgment in advance of the formal hand down, this draft judgment will be confidential to the parties and their legal advisers. Solicitors and counsel on each side should send to the judge a note (if possible, agreed) of any clerical errors or slips which they note in the judgment. However, this is not to be taken as an opportunity to re-argue the issues in the case.

15.10 Disposal of judge's bundle after conclusion of the case

2C–136

15.10.1 The judge will have made notes and annotations on the bundle during the course of the trial. Accordingly, the normal practice is that the entire contents of the judge's bundle are disposed of as confidential waste. The empty ring files can be recovered by arrangement with the judge's clerk.

15.10.2 If any party wishes to retrieve from the judge's bundle any particular items of value which it has supplied (e.g. plans or photographs), a request for these items should be made to the judge's clerk promptly at the conclusion of the case. If the judge has not made annotations on those particular items, they will be released to the requesting party.

SECTION 16.
COSTS

16.1 General

2C–137

16.1.1 All disputes as to costs will be resolved in accordance with CPR Part 44, and in particular CPR rule 44.3.

16.1.2 The judge's usual approach will be to determine which party can be properly described as 'the successful party', and then to investigate whether there are any good reasons why that party should be deprived of some or all of their costs.

16.1.3 It should be noted that, in view of the complex nature of TCC cases, a consideration of the outcome on particular issues or areas of dispute can sometimes be an appropriate starting point for any decision on costs.

Paragraph numbers marked with a "+" can be found online and on CD.

16.2 Summary Assessment of Costs

2C-138   16.2.1 Interlocutory hearings that last one day or less will usually be the subject of a summary assessment of costs in accordance with CPR 44.7 and section 13 of the Costs Practice Direction. The parties must ensure that their statements of costs, on which the summary assessment will be based, are provided to each other party, and the Court, no later than 24 hours before the hearing in question: see paragraph 6.9.3 above.

16.2.2 The *Supreme Court Costs Office Guide to the Summary Assessment of Costs* sets out clear advice and guidance as to the principles to be followed in any summary assessment. Generally summary assessment proceeds on the standard basis. In making an assessment on the standard basis, the court will only allow a reasonable amount in respect of costs reasonably incurred and any doubts must be resolved in favour of the paying party.

16.2.3 In arguments about the hourly rates claimed, the judge will have regard to the principles set out by the Court of Appeal in *Wraith v Sheffield Forgemasters Ltd* [1998] 1 WLR 132: i.e. the judge will consider whether the successful party acted reasonably in employing the solicitors who had been instructed and whether the costs they charged were reasonable compared with the broad average of charges made by similar firms practising in the same area.

16.2.4 In addition, when considering hourly rates, the judge in the TCC may have regard to the guideline rates published from time to time by TecSA.

16.2.5 The court will also consider whether unnecessary work was done or an unnecessary amount of time was spent on the work.

16.2.6 It may be that, because of pressures of time, and/or the nature and extent of the disputes about the level of costs incurred, the court is unable to carry out a satisfactory summary assessment of the costs. In those circumstances, the court will direct that costs be assessed on the standard (or indemnity) basis and will order an amount to be paid on account of costs under CPR Rule 44.3(8).

16.3 Costs Cap Orders

2C-139   16.3.1 In exercising case management powers, the judge may make costs cap orders which, in normal circumstances, will be prospective only. He should only do so, however, where there is a real and substantial risk that, without such an order:
- (a) costs will be disproportionately or unreasonably incurred and
- (b) such costs cannot be controlled by conventional case management and a detailed assessment of costs after a trial, and
- (c) it is just to make such an order.

See CPR rule 3.1 and the notes to that rule in the White Book headed "Prospective costs cap orders".

16.3.2 The possibility of a costs cap order should be considered at the first CMC. The later such an order is sought, the more difficult it may be to impose an effective costs cap.

16.4 Costs: Miscellaneous

2C-140   16.4.1 The court may at any stage order any party to file and serve on the other parties an estimate of costs: see CPR rule 3.1(2)(ii) and section 6 of the Costs Practice Direction. The case management information sheet for the first CMC requires such costs information. This information allows the court properly to exercise its case management functions. In appropriate cases (and where it is proportionate to do so) the judge will exercise his power under paragraph 3 of the Costs Practice Direction to direct the parties to file estimates of costs prepared in such a way as to demonstrate the likely effects of giving or not giving or not giving a particular case management direction.

Paragraph numbers marked with a "+" can be found online and on CD.

APPENDIX D

CONTACT DETAILS FOR TECHNOLOGY AND CONSTRUCTION COURT

The High Court of Justice, Queen's Bench Division　　　　　　**2C–151**
Technology and Construction Court
St Dunstan's House
133-137 Fetter Lane
London EC4A 1HD

Comment

Since Appendix D contains contact details, the information within it requires regu- **2C–152**
lar updating. The version of Appendix D above has been modified to bring it up to
date.

(a) Management

Court Manager: Mr Wilf Lusty　　　　　　　　　　　　　　　　　　**2C–153**
Case Administration Unit Manager/Registry Manager: Mr Steven Gibbon
(steven.gibbon@hmcourts-service.gsi.gov.uk)

Registry: Tel: 020 7947 6022
Fax: 020 7947 7428

Case Administration Unit: Tel: 020 7947 7156
Fax: 020 7947 6465

(b) TCC Judges

Mr Justice Ramsey　　　　　　　　　　　　　　　　　　　　　　　**2C–154**
Clerk: Mr David Hamilton (david.hamilton5@hmcourts-service.gsi.gov.uk)
Tel: 0207 947 6331
Fax: 0207 073 4701

Mr Justice Akenhead
Clerk: Mr Sam Taylor (Sam.Taylor1@hmcourts-service.gsi.gov.uk)
Tel: 0207 947 7445

Mr Justice Coulson
TBA
Tel: 0207 947 6547

His Honour Judge Anthony Thornton QC
Clerk: Ms Anne Farrelly (anne.farrelly@hmcourts-service.gsi.gov.uk)
Tel: 020 7947 6457

His Honour Judge David Wilcox
Clerk: Ms Pam Gilham (pamela.gilham@hmcourts-service.gsi.gov.uk)
Tel: 020 7947 6450

His Honour Judge John Toulmin CMG QC
Clerk: Steven Gibbon (steven.gibbon@hmcourts-service.gsi.gov.uk)
Tel: 020 7947 6498

- The following seven High Court Judges will be available, when necessary and
  by arrangement with the Vice-President of the Queen's Bench Division, to sit
  in the TCC:
      Mr Justice Burton
      Mr Justice Elias
      Mr Justice Field

Paragraph numbers marked with a "+" can be found online and on CD.

451

TCC

Mr Justice Ouseley
Mr Justice Simon
Mr Justice Christopher Clarke
Mr Justice Teare

- The Case Administration Unit, headed by Steven Gibbon, administers cases classified as "HCJ" (see section 3.7 of guide).

Birmingham District Registry: Birmingham County Court
33 Bull Street
Birmingham B4 6DS
TCC listing and clerk to HH Judge Kirkham: Peter Duke (Peter.Duke@hmcourts-service.gsi.gov.uk)
Tel: 0121 681 3181
Fax: 0121 681 3121

TCC Judges
Her Honour Judge Frances Kirkham (full time TCC Judge)
Her Honour Judge Simon Brown QC (Mercantile Judge)
Her Honour Judge Caroline Alton (Mercantile Judge)
His Honour Judge Charles Purle QC (Chancery Judge)

Other judges in Birmingham who have been nominated to deal with TCC business are: His Honour Judge MacDuff Q.C.

Bristol District Registry: Bristol County Court
TCC Listing Office
The Law Courts
Small Street
Bristol BS1 1DA
TCC Listing officers: Dan Cuthbertson and Priya Patel
Email: bristolcclisting@hmcourts-service.gsi.gov.uk
Tel: 0117 910 6700
Fax: 0117 910 6727

TCC Judges
His Honour Judge Mark Havelock-Allan QC (principal TCC judge)
His Honour Judge Patrick McCahill QC

Cardiff District Registry: Cardiff County Court
Cardiff Civil Justice Centre
2 Park Street
Cardiff CF10 1 ET
Main switchboard: 02920 376 400
Fax: 02920 376 475
Listing office: 02920 376 412
Circuit Judges Listing Manager: Graham Driver
Tel: 02920 376483, graham.driver@hmcourts-service.gsi.gov.uk
Specialist Listing Officer: Tracey Davies
Tel: 02920 376412, tracey.davies@hmcourts-service.gsi.gov.uk

TCC Judges
His Honour Judge Gary Hickinbottom (principal TCC judge)
His Honour Judge Nicholas Chambers QC

Central London Civil Justice Centre
26 Park Crescent,

Paragraph numbers marked with a "+" can be found online and on CD.

London WIN 4HT
Listing office for TCC, Chancery and Mercantile Courts
Tel: 0207 917 7932 / 7933
Chancery and Specialist Section Manager: Ms Kathlyn Antoine
Tel: 0207 917 7889/ 7821
Fax: 0207 917 7935

TCC Judges
His Honour Judge Brian Knight QC (principal TCC judge)
His Honour Judge Paul Collins CBE
His Honour Judge Edward Bailey

Chester District Registry: Chester County Court
The Chester Civil Justice Centre
Trident House
Little St John Street
Chester CH1 1SN
Diary Manager: Julie Burgess
Email: Julie.burgess@hmcourts-service.gsi.gov.uk
Tel: 01244 404200
Fax: 01244 404300

TCC Judge
His Honour Judge Derek Halbert

Exeter District Registry: Exeter County Court
Southernhay Gardens
Exeter
Devon
EX1 1UH
Tel: 01392 415350
Fax: 01392 415645

TCC Judge
His Honour Judge Jeremy Griggs

Leeds Combined Court Centre
The Courthouse
1 Oxford Row
Leeds LS1 3BG

High Court Civil Listing Officers: David Eaton and Terence Pendlebury
Tel: 0113 306 2440/2441
Fax: 0113 242 6380
Email: david.eaton@hmcourts-service.gsi.gov.uk

TCC Judges
His Honour Judge John Cockroft (principal TCC judge)
His Honour Judge John Behrens
His Honour Judge Peter Langan QC
His Honour Judge Simon Grenfell
His Honour Judge Simon Hawkesworth QC
His Honour Judge Kaye QC

Leicester District Registry: Leicester County Court
90 Wellington Street

Paragraph numbers marked with a "+" can be found online and on CD.

Leicester LE1 6ZZ
Tel: 0116 222 5700
Fax: 0116 222 5763

TCC Judge
His Honour Judge David Brunning

Liverpool District Registry: Liverpool Combined Court Centre
Liverpool Civil & Family Courts
35 Vernon Street
Liverpool L2 2BX
TCC listing officer: Jackie Jones
Tel: 0151 296 2444
Fax: 0151 295 2201

TCC Judges
His Honour Judge David Mackay (full time TCC judge)
His Honour Judge Stephen Stewart QC
His Honour Judge Graham Platt

Mold County Court
Law Courts
Civic Centre
Mold Flintshire
Wales CH7 1AE
TCC listing officer: Selina Wilkes
Tel: 01352 707405
Fax: 01352 753874

TCC Judges
Will attend from Cardiff when required

Newcastle upon Tyne Combined Court Centre
The Law Courts
Quayside
Newcastle upon Tyne NE1 3LA
Tel: 0191 201 2029
Listing Officer: Mrs Carol Gallagher—carol.gallagher@hmcourts-service.gsi.gov.uk
Tel: 0191 201 2047
Fax: 0191 201 2001

TCC Judge
His Honour Judge Christopher Walton
District Judge Atherton

Nottingham District Registry: Nottingham County Court
60 Canal Street
Nottingham NG1 7EJ
Tel 0115 910 3500
Fax: 0115 910 3510

TCC Judge
His Honour Judge Richard Inglis

Salford District Registry: Salford County Court
Prince William House

Paragraph numbers marked with a "+" can be found online and on CD.

Peel Cross Road
Salford M5 4RR
TCC clerks: Isobel Rich and David Fernandez
Tel: 0161 745 7511
Fax: 0161 745 7202
Email: Hearings@salford.countycourt.gsi.gov.uk

TCC Judges
His Honour Judge Phillip Raynor QC (full time TCC judge)
His Honour Judge Stephen Davies (full time TCC judge)

The following judges at Manchester are nominated to deal with TCC business: His Honour Judge Brendan Hegarty QC, His Honour Judge David Hodge QC, His Honour Judge Mark Pelling QC and His Honour Judge David Waksman QC.

Sheffield Combined Court Centre
The Law Courts
50 West Bar
Sheffield S3 8PH
Tel: 0114 281 2419
Fax: 0114 281 2585

TCC Judge
His Honour Judge John Bullimore

Winchester Combined Court Centre
The Law Courts
Winchester
Hampshire
SO23 9EL
Diary Manager: Mr Wayne Hacking—email wayne.hacking@hmcourts-service.gsi.gov.uk
Tel: 023 8021 3254
Civil Listing Officer: Mrs Karen Hart—email karen.hart@hmcourts-serviec.gsi.gov.uk
Tel: 01962 814 113
Switchboard: 01962 814100
Fax: 01962 814260

TCC Judge
His Honour Judge Iain Hughes QC

APPENDIX E

DRAFT ADR ORDER

1. By [   ] the parties shall exchange lists of three neutral individuals who **2C–155** have indicated their availability to conduct a mediation/ENE in this case prior to [   ].

2. By [   ] the parties shall agree an individual from the exchanged lists to conduct the mediation/ENE by [   ]. If the parties are unable to agree on the neutral individual, they will apply to the Court in writing by [   ] and the Court will choose one of the listed individuals to conduct the mediation/ENE.

3. There will be a stay of the proceedings until [   ] to allow the mediation/ENE to take place. On or before that date, the Court shall be informed as to whether or not the case has been finally settled. If it has not been finally settled, the parties will:

Paragraph numbers marked with a "+" can be found online and on CD.

455

a) comply with all outstanding directions made by the Court;

b) attend for a review CMC on [   ].

Appendix F

Draft Directions in Adjudication Enforcement Proceedings

2C-156   Upon reading the Claim Form, Particulars of Claim, the Claimant's without notice application dated the   day of   200   and the evidence in support thereof

IT IS ORDERED THAT:

1. The Claimant's solicitor shall [as soon as practicable after receipt of this Order/ by 4pm on   day of   ] serve upon the Defendant

a. The Claim Form and Response Pack

b. This Order

c. The Claimant's Application Pursuant to Part 24 and the Claimant's evidence in support.

2. The time for the Defendant to file its acknowledgement of service is abridged to [   ] days.

3. The Claimant hereby has permission to issue an application pursuant to CPR Part 24 without an acknowledgement of service or Defence having been filed.

4. The Part 24 application will be heard on the   day of   at   am/pm at   . Estimated Length of Hearing   hours]

5. Any further evidence in relation to the Part 24 Application shall be served and filed

a. By the Defendant, [14 days after the service of the documents in Paragraph 1 above/ at least 5 working days before the date fixed for the hearing of the Application] [on the   day of   ]

b. By the Claimant, in response to that of the Defendant, [at least 3 working days before the date fixed for the hearing of the Application] [on the   day of   200   ]

and in either case no later than 4.00pm upon that day.

6. The Claimant's solicitor shall file a paginated bundle comprising

a. The witness statements provided in support of the application, together with any exhibits;

b. The witness statements provided in opposition to the application together with exhibits;

c. Any witness statements in reply, together with exhibits;

d. Photocopies of relevant authorities.

This bundle is to be provided no later than [2 working days before the hearing of the Application] [on day   of   ].

7. The parties shall file and serve skeleton arguments by no later than [4.00pm one clear working day before the hearing/ 1pm the last working day before the hearing]* [on the day   of   ]

8. The costs of and incidental to these directions are reserved to the Part 24 hearing. Permission to apply in respect of such costs in the absence of such hearing.

9. The parties have permission to apply to the court on 48 hours written notice to the other to seek to set aside or vary these directions.

* Depending whether the hearing is estimated to last in excess of 1/2 day or not

Paragraph numbers marked with a "+" can be found online and on CD.

2D ADMIRALTY JURISDICTION AND PROCEEDINGS

PART 61—ADMIRALTY CLAIMS

Contents

Editorial introduction

This Part and its supplementing Practice Direction do not provide a complete code **2D–2** for these proceedings but have to be read in conjunction with the other Civil Procedure Rules. The application of the Civil Procedure Rules and the Practice Directions which supplement them is in Admiralty proceedings subject to the provisions of this Practice Direction. Part 61 also assigns certain claims to the QBD and provides that they are to be taken by the Admiralty court.

The following points are of importance:

— There is now no jurisdiction in the County Court in Admiralty matters (see Civil Courts (Amendment) (No.2) Order 1999 (SI 1999/1011).

— All Admiralty claims *in rem* or *in personam* should be commenced in the Admiralty and Commercial Registry at the RCJ. In cases of urgency out of London reference should be made to the Admiralty and Commercial Registry at the RCJ.

— All arrests will be dealt with by the Admiralty Marshal at the Admiralty and Commercial Registry in London.

— As a general rule in cases where there is an arrest, the file and matter will be retained in the Admiralty and Commercial Registry for all purposes save as may be otherwise specifically ordered.

— All arrests are to be supported by a Solicitor's undertaking to pay the Marshal's arrest expenses or disbursements or by a payment in in respect thereof.

— The caveat system is preserved, but caveats are now termed cautions.

— An acknowledgment of service must be filed in every Admiralty claim *in rem* and in every other Admiralty claim formerly called claims *in personam* unless liability is admitted on **ADM16** in a limitation claim. Such acknowledgment must be filed within 14 days of service of the claim form irrespective of whether or not particulars of claim are served with it.

— An Admiralty other claim (see the Practice Direction—Admiralty Claims, para.12.1) is subject to the same rules as an ordinary claim where service is to be affected out of the jurisdiction save for the special rules set out in CPR r.6.20(17A) and as regards a limitation claim form only in r.61.11(5) and a collision claim form in r.61.4.

Paragraph numbers marked with a "+" can be found online and on CD.

— There are special rules as to times for service of a claim *in rem*.

(a) The validity for service of an *in rem* claim form is 12 months, see r.61.3(5)(b).

(b) The time for service of particulars of claim in an *in rem* claim if not served with the *in rem* claim form is 75 days after service of the *in rem* claim form, see r.61.3(3)(b).

Collision and limitation claims have their own special procedures see rr.61.4 and 6.11 respectively. The Preliminary Act procedure still applies in collision claims but Preliminary Acts are now termed Collision Statements of Case.

Related sources

2D-3
- Supreme Court Act 1981 ss.20–24, s.27 and s.150 (see paras 2D–145 *et seq.*)
- Hovercraft Act 1968 ss.2–4 (see paras 2D–203+ *et seq.*)
- Merchant Shipping Act 1995 ss.92–93, ss.185–189, ss.190, 192, 224 and 229–230 (see paras 2D–208 *et seq.*)
- The Admiralty and Commercial Courts Guide (see paras 2A–39 *et seq.*).

Forms

2D-4
- **ADM1** Claim form (Admiralty claim form *in rem*)
- **ADM1A** Claim form (Admiralty claim form for other claims)
- **ADM1C** Notes for defendant on replying to an *in rem* claim form
- **ADM2** Acknowledgment of service/response pack (Admiralty claim *in rem*)
- **ADM3** Collision Statement of Case
- **ADM4** Application and undertaking for arrest and custody
- **ADM5** Outline form of declaration in support of application for warrant of arrest
- **ADM6** Notice to consular officer of intention to apply for warrant of arrest
- **ADM7** Request for caution against arrest
- **ADM9** Warrant of arrest
- **ADM10** Standard directions to the admiralty marshal
- **ADM11** Request for caution against release
- **ADM12** Application and undertaking for release
- **ADM12A** Request for withdrawal of caution against release
- **ADM13** Application for judgment in default of filing an acknowledgment of service and/or defence or collision statement of case
- **ADM14** Order for sale of a ship
- **ADM15** Claim form (Admiralty limitation claim)
- **ADM15B** Notes for defendant (Admiralty limitation claim)
- **ADM16** Notice of admission of right of claimant to limit liability
- **ADM16A** Defence to admiralty limitation claim
- **ADM16B** Acknowledgment of service/response pack (Admiralty limitation claim)
- **ADM17** Application for restricted decree of limitation
- **ADM17A** Application for general limitation decree
- **ADM18** Restricted decree of limitation
- **ADM19** Decree of limitation
- **ADM20** Defendant's claim in a limitation claim
- **ADM21** Outline form of declaration as to inability of a defendant to file and serve statement of case under a decree of limitation

2D-5 *Note* —**ADM1A**—An Admiralty Claim *in personam* shall be commenced on a Pt 7 claim form as adapted for a Commercial Court claim, save for taking into consideration any logical or textual modifications made to the "Notes for Claimant on completing a claim form" in the Commercial Court, in order to accord with the practice of the Admiralty Court.

The formats for Pt 7 and Pt 8 claim forms for Commercial Court claims, the notes and response packs thereto together with certain other forms as adapted shall apply to

Paragraph numbers marked with a "+" can be found online and on CD.

an Admiralty action *in personam* (or *in rem*, if applicable) with the appropriate alterations.

Scope and interpretation[1]

61.1—(1) This Part applies to admiralty claims.

2D–6

(2) **In this Part—**

(a) **"admiralty claim" means a claim within the Admiralty jurisdiction of the High Court as set out in section 20 of the Supreme Court Act 1981[2];**

(b) **"the Admiralty Court" means the Admiralty Court of the Queen's Bench Division of the High Court of Justice;**

(c) **"claim in rem" means a claim in an admiralty action in rem;**

(d) **"collision claim" means a claim within section 20(3)(b) of the Supreme Court Act 1981;**

(e) **"limitation claim" means a claim under the Merchant Shipping Act 1995[3] for the limitation of liability in connection with a ship or other property;**

(f) **"salvage claim" means a claim—**

(i) **for or in the nature of salvage;**

(ii) **for special compensation under; Article 14 of Schedule 11 to the Merchant Shipping Act 1995**

(iii) **for the apportionment of salvage; and**

(iv) **arising out of or connected with any contract for salvage services;**

(g) **"caution against arrest" means a caution entered in the Register under rule 61.7;**

(h) **"caution against release" means a caution entered in the Register under rule 61.8;**

(i) **"the Register" means the Register of cautions against arrest and release which is open to inspection as provided by the practice direction;**

(j) **"the Marshal" means the Admiralty Marshal;**

(k) **"ship" includes any vessel used in navigation; and**

(l) **"the Registrar" means the Queen's Bench Master with responsibility for Admiralty claims.**

(3) **Part 58 (Commercial Court) applies to claims in the Admiralty Court except where this Part provides otherwise.**

(4) **The Registrar has all the powers of the Admiralty judge except where a rule or practice direction provides otherwise.**

Admiralty jurisdiction

---

[1] Amended by the Civil Procedure (Amendment No.5) Rules 2001 (SI 2001/4015).

[2] 1981 c.54; s.20 was amended by the Merchant Shipping (Salvage and Pollution) Act 1994 (c.28) s.1(6) and Sch. 2, para.6; the Merchant Shipping Act 1995 (c.21) s.314(2) and Sch.13, para.59 and by the Merchant Shipping and Maritime Security Act 1997 (c.28) s.29(1) and Sch. 6, para.2.

[3] 1995 c.21.

Paragraph numbers marked with a "+" can be found online and on CD.

2D–7   As to the Admiralty jurisdiction of the High Court see SCA 1981 ss.20 to 24 (paras 2D–145 *et seq.* below), the Hovercraft Act 1968 as amended by SCA 1981 (paras 2D–203+ *et seq.*), the Merchant Shipping Act 1995 s.166.

The court is seised of a claim *in rem* from the moment of service of the claim form or of arrest of a ship (whichever is the earlier). Where, however, proceedings are brought against a ship already under arrest in High Court proceedings, the court will be seised of jurisdiction from the moment the claim form is issued. The court cannot have jurisdiction over a ship which does not come within the jurisdiction (*The Freccia del Nord* [1989] 1 Lloyd's Rep. 388). The court is seised of a claim *in personam* (see Practice Direction—Admiralty Claims, para.12, Other Claims) when the defendant is served with the claim form (*Neste Chemicals SA v D.K. Line SA The Sargasso* [1993] 1 Lloyd's Rep. 424, affirmed [1994] 3 All E.R. 180; [1994] 2 Lloyd's Rep. 6, CA). This is so whether service is to be effected within or without the jurisdiction and in the latter case may have first involved an application for permission to serve out of the jurisdiction. This is a matter of importance when considering Arts 21 and 22 of the Convention on Jurisdiction and the Enforcement of Judgments in Civil and Commercial Matters 1968.

Further, for cases subject to EC law, Council Regulation 44/2001 on jurisdiction and the recognition and enforcement of judgments in civil and commercial matters, effective from March 1, 2002, Section 9, *Lis pendens*—related actions, art.30 provides:

For the purposes of this Section, a court shall be deemed to be seised:

1. at the time when the document instituting the proceedings or an equivalent document is lodged with the court, provided that the plaintiff has not subsequently failed to take the steps he was required to take to have service effected on the defendant, or

2. if the document has to be served before being lodged with the court, at the time when it is received by the authority responsible for service, provided that the plaintiff has not subsequently failed to take the steps he was required to take to have the document lodged with the court.

Article 2 of the 1968 Brussels Convention on Jurisdiction and the Enforcement of Judgments in Civil and Commercial Matters covers all forms of proceedings in civil and commercial matters whether *in rem* or *in personam* and the word "sued" in Arts 2 and 3 of the Convention should be construed accordingly (*The Deichland* [1989] 2 Lloyd's Rep. 113, CA). Where an arrest within art.1(2) of the 1952 Arrest Convention is effected, the claimant is entitled to rely upon art.57 of the 1968 Convention as excluding the exclusive jurisdiction of another convention country which would otherwise apply under art.2 of the 1968 Convention in the absence of some exempting factor under art.5 of the 1968 Convention, see *The Anna H* [1994] 1 Lloyd's Rep. 287, affirmed [1995] 1 Lloyd's Rep. 11, CA. The Court of Appeal further held that the Arrest Convention required only that the legal consequences of judicial detention of the ship should be that it became security for a maritime claim not that the claimant's commercial motive must be to obtain security.

In *Canada Trust Co v Stolzenberg* [2000] 4 All E.R. 481, the House of Lords held that on the true construction of Articles 2 and 6 of the Lugano Convention on Jurisdiction and the Enforcement of Judgments in Civil and Commercial Matters 1988 (identical for present purposes to the terms of the 1968 Brussels Convention referred to above), the word "sued" referred to the initiation of proceedings, and accordingly the English court took jurisdiction over a defendant, for the purposes of those provisions, on the date that the writ [claim form] was issued. Such a conclusion was supported by the language of the convention which used the concepts "sued", "bring proceedings" and "instituted proceedings" interchangeably.

Admiralty Court

2D–8   This is part of the QBD. It has jurisdiction in all causes and matters assigned by SCA 1981 to that division which involve the exercise of the High Court's Admiralty jurisdiction or its jurisdiction as a prize court. See SCA 1981 ss.5, 6, 61 and 62 and Sch.1.

Claim in rem

2D–9   Admiralty claims may be either *in rem* or *in personam*. (now known as other Admiralty Claims).

Paragraph numbers marked with a "+" can be found online and on CD.

An Admiralty claim *in rem* is in effect a claim against a *res*. (*The Longford* (1888) 14 P.D. 34, *per* Lord Esher M.R. at 37; *The City of Mecca* (1879) 5 P.D. 28 at 33; 6 P.D. 106; *The Burns* [1907] P. 137; SCA 1981 s.21 (para.2D–178 below). A *res* is usually a ship but may in some cases be cargo or freight, an aircraft or hovercraft. In such a claim the claimant may cause the *res* to be arrested if it is within the jurisdiction (see rules 61.5 *et seq.*). If the *res* is arrested and the claimant's claim is successful then unless the *res* has been released (as to which see rr.61.8 *et seq.*) judgment may be given against the *res* and an order made for its appraisement and sale. The proceeds of sale will be paid into court and will, after deduction of the fees and expenses of the Admiralty Marshal in connection with the arrest, custody, appraisement and the sale of the *res*, be available in or towards satisfaction of the claimant's judgment. If, as is frequently the case, there is more than one claim against the *res*, payment out of the proceeds of sale will be ordered in accordance with the Admiralty rules as to the priorities of claims, claims of the same priority ranking *pari passu*. As to proceedings for the determination of priority of claims (see r.61.10).

A claim *in rem* may also be instituted against the proceeds of sale by the court of a *res*.

If in a claim *in rem* issue or service of the claim form has been acknowledged and the claim form is not set aside, the personal liability of the defendant who has appeared is added and judgment may be given against him as well as against the *res*. See *The Gemma* [1899] P.285, CA and *The August 8* [1983] 2 A.C. 450; [1983] 1 Lloyd's Rep. 351, PC.

In *Republic of India v India Steamship Co Ltd* [1997] 3 W.L.R. 818; [1998] 1 Lloyd's Rep. 1 HL(E) it was held that for the purposes of s.34 of the Civil Jurisdiction and Judgments Act 1982:

"a [claim] *in rem* is an action against the owners from the moment that the Admiralty Court is seised with jurisdiction. The jurisdiction of the Admiralty Court is invoked by the service of a [claim form], or, where a [claim form] is deemed to be served, as a result of the acknowledgment of the issue of the [claim form] by the defendant before service (*The Banco* [1971] P.137). From that moment the owners are parties *in rem*".

Dicta of Lord Brandon in *The August 8* [1983] 2 A.C. 450; [1983] 2 W.L.R. 419 at 456, PC, and *The Deichland* [1990] 1 Q.B. 361, CA, applied and *The Nordglimt* [1988] Q.B. 183 overruled. The case reviews claims *in rem* generally and states that the idea that a ship can be a defendant in legal proceedings was always a legal fiction which can now be discarded holding that in reality a claim *in rem* is an action against the owners. *Quaere* the extent and effect of the reasoning in this case in claims *in rem* generally. The position in respect of cases involving a maritime lien was expressly reserved as requiring separate consideration. See too *The Irina Zharkikh* [2001] 2 Lloyd's Rep. 319 (N.Z. Ct.).

A defendant who has acknowledged issue or service of the claim form may provide security in order to avoid the arrest of the *res* or to obtain its release if it has been arrested.

Sale by the court in a claim *in rem* is a sale of the whole property and it is sold free of all claims, encumbrances, liens, etc., with a clean title (see, e.g. *The Acrux* [1962] 1 Lloyd's Rep. 405) all existing claims, etc., being transferred to the proceeds of sale, against which claims begun after the sale must be brought. See also *The Blitz* [1992] 2 Lloyd's Rep. 441—sale of vessel by a local authority pursuant to its powers under s.44 of the Harbours, Docks and Piers Clauses Act 1847 is a sale free from mortgages. The position regarding maritime liens is unclear.

In *The Cerro Colorado* [1993] 1 Lloyd's Rep. 58, the court declared that any conduct which impedes or is likely to impede the ability of the Admiralty Marshal to achieve a fair market value upon the sale of the vessel (including but not limited to published statements that the vessel will, after sale by the Admiralty Marshal, remain encumbered with existing claims) is an interference with the administration of justice. Such conduct may expose anyone responsible to proceedings for contempt of court.

The following are the main matters of procedure peculiar to a claim *in rem*:

(a) a special form of claim form is used. See PD 61 para.3.1;

(b) service of the claim form must be in a manner prescribed by PD 61 para.3.6;

(c) judgment in default of acknowledgment of service, defence, defence to

Paragraph numbers marked with a "+" can be found online and on CD.

counterclaim or the filing of a collision statement of case must be applied for by application under rule 61.9;

(d) a claim form *in rem* cannot be served outside the jursidiction;

Claims against two or more "sister" ships

2D–10   When the AJA 1956 came into force it became possible in many cases for a claimant to proceed *in rem* against any one of a number of ships in the same beneficial ownership, see s.3(4). The practice soon became established in such cases of issuing one claim form against some or all of the ships against which the claimant was entitled to proceed and later amending the claim form by striking out the names of all ships save the one in respect of which the claim form had been served or against which a warrant of arrest had been issued. The claim form should be amended immediately after service by deleting all but one of the ship's names upon it (*The Freccia del Nord* [1989] 1 Lloyd's Rep. 388 at 391).

In *The Banco* [1971] P. 137; [1971] 1 Lloyd's Rep. 49, CA, in which it was held that only one ship could be served with a claim form *in rem* or arrested in respect of one cause of action, the practice described above was, by a majority, approved. See now SCA 1981 s.21(8) (paras 2D–178 and 2D–190 below).

Claims in rem and other claims

2D–11   If it is desired to commence proceedings both *in rem* and *in personam* separate claim forms must be issued. See para.2D–143.

Cautions

2D–12   See rr.61.7 and 61.8.

Limitation Claim

2D–13   See para.1.4, *British Shipping Laws*, Vols 1 and 11 (but note the change of onus of proof introduced since last publication of Vols 1 and 11). Limitation actions must be assigned to the Queen's Bench Division and taken by the Admiralty Court (r.61.2(i)(c)). For special rules relating to limitation actions see r.61.11 below.

Ship

2D–14   Compare the definition of ship in SCA 1981 s.24 and see note "Ship" at para.2D–153 below.

A ship is equipment within the meaning of s.1 of the Employers'Liability (Defective Equipment) Act 1969 (*The Derbyshire* [1988] A.C. 276; [1988] 1 Lloyd's Rep. 109, HL).

Limitation of claims

2D–15   There are special periods, subject to the court's discretion, in collision and salvage: Merchant Shipping Act 1995 ss.190 and 195.

Admiralty claims[1]

2D–16   **61.2—(1) The following claims must be started in the Admiralty Court—**

      (a) a claim—

            (i) in rem;

            (ii) for damage done by a ship;

            (iii) concerning the ownership of a ship;

            (iv) under the Merchant Shipping Act 1995;

            (v) for loss of life or personal injury specified in section 20(2)(f) of the Supreme Court Act 1981;

---

[1] Amended by the Civil Procedure (Amendment No.5) Rules 2001 (SI 2001/4015) and the Civil Procedure (Amendment No.4) Rules 2005 (SI 2005/3515).

Paragraph numbers marked with a "+" can be found online and on CD.

        (vi) by a master or member of a crew for wages;

        (vii) in the nature of towage; or

        (viii) in the nature of pilotage;

    (b) a collision claim;

    (c) a limitation claim; or

    (d) a salvage claim.

(2) Any other admiralty claim may be started in the Admiralty Court.

(3) Rule 30.5 applies to claims in the Admiralty Court except that the Admiralty Court may order the transfer of a claim to—

    (a) the Commercial list;

    (b) a Mercantile Court;

    (c) the Mercantile list at the Central London County Court; or

    (d) any other appropriate court.

Restrictions on Admiralty jurisdiction

(1) Collision and similar actions if in personam —See SCA 1981 s.22 (para.2D–191).   **2D–17**

(2) Wages actions —Section 4 of the Consular Relations Act 1968, provides that **2D–18** Orders in Council may be made to exclude or limit the jurisdiction to entertain proceedings relating to the pay or conditions of service of the master or crew of any ship or aircraft belonging to a state specified in the Order unless the Consul has first been notifed of the intention to invoke the jurisdiction of the court and has not objected. Orders have been made in respect of Austria, Belgium, Bulgaria, Denmark, Federal Republic of Germany, Greece, Hungary, Italy, Japan, Mexico, Norway, Poland, Romania, Spain, Sweden, Yugoslavia, Czechoslovakia and Egypt. (See Statutory Instruments 1970 Nos. 1903–1905, 1907–1914, 1917, 1918 and 1920, 1971 No. 1846 1978 No. 275 1976/768 and 1986/217.) Each of these orders provides for a period of two weeks for objection. Following the dissolution of Yugoslavia the position in respect of the individual former constituent member states is uncertain. It is suggested that the Consul of the individual state concerned is notified.

The above-mentioned Orders in Council additionally require a statement to the effect that the consular officer of the state concerned has been notified of the intention to invoke the jurisdiction of the court and has not objected within a period of two weeks from the date of such notification to be included among the details on which the claim is based at the time when the proceedings are commenced.

Further Orders in Council may be issued from time to time.

In *The Andrea Ursula* [1971] Fo. 61 and 81, it was held that proceedings were a nullity for non-compliance with the above mentioned statutory requirements.

(3) Crown —No claim *in rem* lies against the Crown, but in certain circumstances **2D–19** such a claim may be allowed to continue as if *in personam*: Crown Proceedings Act 1947 s.29 (Vol.2, Section 21L).

(4) Foreign sovereign states, etc. —As to claims against foreign sovereigns, foreign **2D–20** sovereign states, ambassadors and diplomatic agents, members of their suites and certain international organisations generally, see CPR r.12.10. As to claims *in rem* against state owned ships and cargoes see also the State Immunity Act 1978 ss.10, 12 and 13.

A ship, belonging to private owners, requisitioned by the Crown, cannot be arrested while in Government service though if a maritime lien attaches it may be enforced after derequisitioning (*The Broadmayne* [1916] P. 64) and though a claim lies against the owners of the ship if the crew remain their servants (*The Messicano* (1916) 32 T.L.R. 519; *The Crindon* (1918) 35 T.L.R. 81; *The Eolo* [1918] 2 Ir.R. 78).

Paragraph numbers marked with a "+" can be found online and on CD.

2D–21   *(5) Rhine Navigation Convention 1868* —No court in England or Wales has jurisdiction in cases falling to be determined in accordance with the provisions of this convention. See SCA 1981 s.23 (para.2D–194).

2D–22   *(6) Nuclear Installations Act 1965* —This Act consolidates and repeals the Nuclear Installations (Licensing and Insurance) Act 1959, and (with one exception relating to the Electricity (Amendment) Act 1961) the Nuclear Installations (Amendment) Act 1965. In the event of an occurrence involving nuclear matter, reference should be made to the Act; in particular, s.14 (protection for ships and aircraft) makes claims *in rem* against ships or aircraft and limitation of liability under the Merchant Shipping Act 1995 unavailable: the Act substitutes a new approach. This Act was amended by the Nuclear Installations Act 1969.

2D–23   *(7) Liquidation and bankruptcy* —As to liquidation see the Insolvency Act 1986 s.130. See also *The Constellation* [1966] 1 W.L.R. 272; [1965] 2 Lloyd's Rep. 538; *Re Aro Co Ltd* [1980] Ch. 196; [1980] 1 All E.R. 1067, CA.

Claims in rem[1]
2D–24   **61.3—(1) This rule applies to claims in rem.**

(2) A claim in rem is started by the issue of an in rem claim form as set out in the practice direction.

(3) Subject to rule 61.4, the particulars of claim must—

> **(a) be contained in or served with the claim form; or**

> **(b) be served on the defendant by the claimant within 75 days after service of the claim form.**

(4) An acknowledgment of service must be filed within 14 days after service of the claim form.

(5) The claim form must be served—

> **(a) in accordance with the practice direction; and**

> **(b) within 12 months after the date of issue and rules 7.5 and 7.6 are modified accordingly.**

(6) If a claim form has been issued (whether served or not), any person who wishes to defend the claim may file an acknowledgment of service.

Claim in rem
2D–25   A claim *in rem* may properly be issued only when the jurisdiction can be invoked by proceedings *in rem* under ss.21(2), (3), (4) or (5) of SCA 1981 (paras 2D–178 and 2D–179 to 2D–189). See too note "Claim in rem" under r.61.1.3 above.

Renewal of claim form
2D–26   As to renewal of a claim form *in rem* on grounds of impossibility of service on the ship see *The Berny* [1979] Q.B. 80; [1978] 1 All E.R. 1065; [1977] 2 Lloyd's Rep. 533. As to renewal of claim form generally see CPR r.7.6 and notes thereto.

Acknowledgment of service before actual service
2D–27   In a claim *in rem* or limitation claim *issue* of the claim form may be acknowledged, see r.61.3(6) above.

Methods of service
2D–28   For methods of service of a claim form *in rem* see PD 61 para.3.6 which includes

---

[1] Amended by the Civil Procedure (Amendment No.5) Rules 2001 (SI 2001/4015).

Paragraph numbers marked with a "+" can be found online and on CD.

service by an alternative method under CPR r.6.8 so long as *res* is within the jurisdiction.

Special provisions relating to collision claims[1]

61.4—(1) This rule applies to collision claims.   **2D–29**

(2) A claim form need not contain or be followed by particulars of claim and rule 7.4 does not apply.

(3) An acknowledgment of service must be filed.

(4) A party who wishes to dispute the court's jurisdiction must make an application under Part 11 within 2 months after filing his acknowledgment of service.

(5) Every party must—

    (a) within 2 months after the defendant files the acknowledgment of service; or

    (b) where the defendant applies under Part 11 within 2 months after the defendant files the further acknowledgment of service,

file at the court a completed collision statement of case in the form specified in the practice direction.

(6) A collision statement of case must be—

    (a) in the form set out in the practice direction; and

    (b) verified by a statement of truth.

(7) A claim form in a collision claim may not be served out of the jurisdiction unless—

    (a) the case falls within section 22(2)(a), (b) or (c) of the Supreme Court Act 1981[2]; or

    (b) the defendant has submitted to or agreed to submit to the jurisdiction; and

the court gives permission in accordance with Section IV of Part 6.

(8) Where permission to serve a claim form out of the jurisdiction is given, the court will specify the period within which the defendant may file an acknowledgment of service and, where appropriate, a collision statement of case.

(9) Where, in a collision claim in rem ("the original claim")—

    (a) (i) a Part 20 claim; or

        (ii) a cross-claim in rem

arising out of the same collision or occurrence is made; and

    (b) (i) the party bringing the original claim has caused the arrest of a ship or has obtained security in order to prevent such arrest; and

        (ii) the party bringing the Part 20 claim or cross-

---

[1] Amended by the Civil Procedure (Amendment No.5) Rules 2001 (SI 2001/4015) and the Civil Procedure (Amendment) Rules 2008 (SI 2008/2178).
[2] 1981 c.54.

Paragraph numbers marked with a "+" can be found online and on CD.

claim is unable to arrest a ship or otherwise obtain security,

the party bringing the Part 20 claim or cross claim may apply to the court to stay the original claim until sufficient security is given to satisfy any judgment that may be given in favour of that party.

(10) The consequences set out in paragraph (11) apply where a party to a claim to establish liability for a collision claim (other than a claim for loss of life or personal injury)—

(a) makes an offer to settle in the form set out in paragraph (12) not less than 21 days before the start of the trial;

(b) that offer is not accepted; and

(c) the maker of the offer obtains at trial an apportionment equal to or more favourable than his offer.

(11) Where paragraph (10) applies the parties will, unless the court considers it unjust, be entitled to the following costs—

(a) the maker of the offer will be entitled to—

(i) all his costs from 21 days after the offer was made; and

(ii) his costs before then in the percentage to which he would have been entitled had the offer been accepted; and

(b) all other parties to whom the offer was made—

(i) will be entitled to their costs up to 21 days after the offer was made in the percentage to which they would have been entitled had the offer been accepted; but

(ii) will not be entitled to their costs thereafter.

(12) An offer under paragraph (10) must be in writing and must contain—

(a) an offer to settle liability at stated percentages;

(b) an offer to pay costs in accordance with the same percentages;

(c) a term that the offer remain open for 21 days after the date it is made; and

(d) a term that, unless the court orders otherwise, on expiry of that period the offer remains open on the same terms except that the offeree should pay all the costs from that date until acceptance.

Collision statement of case, formerly called preliminary act

2D–30 "The object of the collision statement of case is to obtain from the parties statements of the facts at a time when they are fresh in their recollection" (per Sir Robert Phillimore, in *The Frankland* (1872) L.R. 3 A. & E. 511). The other main purpose is to force the parties to "plead blind" (*The Vortigern* (1859) Sw. 518). A statement of fact in a collision statement of case is a formal admission, binding the party making it, and can only be departed from by special permission (per Fletcher Moulton L.J. in *The Seacombe, The Devonshire* [1912] P.21, 59, *The Devonshire* [1912] P. 21, 59; see *The Ladybell* (1933) 49 T.L.R. 595; 46 Ll.L.Rep. 342). As a rule, therefore, the court will not allow either party subsequently to alter anything in his collision statement of case, not even to correct a clerical error (*The Miranda* (1882) 7 P.D. 185). But in *The Esso Brussels* (1968) Fo. 373, unrep., on this point, permission was given during the trial to amend

Paragraph numbers marked with a "+" can be found online and on CD.

Articles xii and xiv. Permission, however, is sometimes asked for and given to lead evidence not in accordance with the party's collision statement of case; if witnesses give evidence not in accordance with the collision statement of case and no leave is asked for, the court may hold the party to what is in the collision statement of case (see *The Semiramis* [1952] 2 Lloyd's Rep. 86 at 93). The court is not bound by the admissions in any collision statement of case (see, e.g. *The Vanessa* [1960] 1 Lloyd's Rep. 82; *The Geo. W. McKnight* (1947) 80 Ll.L.R. 419, HL). A party who has filed a defective collision statement of case, which does not give the information required by the rule, may be ordered on application by the other party to amend it (*The Godiva* (1886) 11 P.D. 20) or to give particulars.

Note that the present and previous rules are wider than the rule which they replaced. The old rule referred to "actions for damage by collision between vessels..."; *The El Oso* (1925) 21 Ll.L.Rep. 340; *Armstrong v Gaselee* (1889) 22 QBD 250; *Secretary of State for India v Hewitt & Co* (1888) 6 Asp. 384; *The John Boyne* (1877) 36 L.T. 29; 3 Asp. M.L.C. 346, are cases decided under that rule. Each party is required in his collision statement of case to state the material facts upon which he founds his case and the court may order the costs of a collision statement of case which differs widely from the facts proved at the trial to be disallowed on taxation (*The Pelican I* (1926) 25 Ll.L.Rep. 150). The information must be given fully; any concealment will be viewed by the court with suspicion and, as stated, on the application of the other party, the court may order amendment (*The Godiva,* above) or particulars so that all the questions are answered properly. When a ship in a river is on a fixed course as opposed to a course which is constantly changed, either the magnetic or the true course should be stated (*The Rievaulx Abbey* (1910) 11 Asp. 437). In a collision case in which one ship is, or both ships are, at anchor, the collision statement of case or collision statements of case filed on behalf of the owners of the anchored ship or both anchored ships should state in art.vii the heading of the ship at anchor (*The Macroom* (1927) 17 Asp. 288 (one ship at anchor, the other under way): *The Erna* (1927) 27 Ll.L.Rep. 170 (a dragging case; both ships at anchor)). In *The Judith M.* (1968) 112 S.J. 859, a statement in the claimant's collision statement of case (art.(ix)(b)) and elsewhere that the defendants' ship was heading "across the bows" of the claimant's ship "from port to starboard" was criticised by Brandon J.; it was desirable to state such heading with greater particularity. A defendant is not entitled to demand of another defendant whom he blames in his defence that he shall file a collision statement of case, unless he issues a claim form against him (*The Carlston and the Balcombe* [1926] P. 82).

Section 20(3)(b)(i) SCA 1981 "... collision between ships ..."

A floating landing stage is not a ship, therefore no collision statements of case are required in an action arising from a collision between a steamship and it (*The Craighall* [1910] P. 207). On the other hand, where claimants whose ship, A, was in collision with another, B, blamed the owners of B and also the dock authority which had some measure of control over B it was held that all three parties must file collision statements of case; the dock authority were obliged to do the best they could to answer the questions in the collision statement of case (*The Beaverford* [1961] 1 W.L.R. 793; [1960] 3 All E.R. 612; [1960] 2 Lloyd's Rep. 216). This case was followed in *British Oil & Cake Mills Ltd v John H. Whitaker (Tankers) Ltd (The Grainger's No.4)* [1964] 1 W.L.R. 1474; [1964] 3 All E.R. 705; [1964] 2 Lloyd's Rep. 415. A collision statement of case is required of a widow whose husband has been killed in a collision (see *Webster v M. S. & L. Ry.* [1884] W.N. 1). This is so even where the ship has been sunk in the collision with the loss of all hands. See as to further information concerning information contained in collision statements of case: (*The Isle of Cyprus* (1890) 15 P.D. 134; *The Bernard* [1905] W.N. 73; *The Biola* (1876) 34 L.T. 185; *The Radnorshire* (1880) 5 P.D. 172).

2D–31

Dispensing with or limiting collision statement of case

It is considered that the court retains power to order dispensing with or limiting the requirement under this paragraph of collision statements of case under its general CPR powers or inherent jurisdiction in appropriate though rare cases. An order to dispense with or limit the filing of collision statements of case will not be made on a consent application; the court will always require the parties to attend and explain the reasons for the application. Application is made by application notice before the Registrar.

2D–32

Paragraph numbers marked with a "+" can be found online and on CD.

Expert Witnesses etc

2D–33   For guidance in use of expert witnesses, illustrative plotting and computer stimulation, see *Owners of the Pelopidas v Owners of the TRSL Concord* [1999] 2 All E.R. (Comm) 737.

Damages

2D–33.1   In *Owners of the Front Ace v Owners of the Vicky 1 ("The Front Ace")* [2008] EWCA Civ 101; [2008] 2 All E.R. (Comm) 42; [2008] 2 Lloyd's Rep. 45; [2008] 1 C.L.C. 229, the Court of Appeal held that the ballast/laden or loss of use/loss of profit basis was not the appropriate methodology to be adopted in all cases where a shipowner lost a fixture as a result of a collision. On the question of whether a percentage deduction for loss of a chance was appropriate in the assessment of the quantum of damages in respect of a collision at sea, it held that where the expert witnesses had agreed the appropriate market rate for use of the vessel, in assessing the damages the Admiralty Registrar had been wrong to make a deduction of 20 per cent for "loss of a chance" from that agreed figure.

Costs

2D–33.2   In *"KRYSIA" Maritime Inc v Intership Ltd* [2008] EWHC 1880 (Admlty); [2008] WL 2976625, Aikens J. held that the general rule in CPR 44.3(2)(a) applies to claims where liability is apportioned, unless there was a good reason why it should not do so. He held that no rule or principle had been established in the Admiralty Court, where there is no counterclaim, that a claimant who is found at fault under section 187(1) and (2) of the Merchant Shipping Act 1995 should recover its costs in proportion to the percentage of liability of the defendant.

Arrest[1]

2D–34   **61.5—(1) In a claim in rem—**

    (a) a claimant; and

    (b) a judgment creditor

may apply to have the property proceeded against arrested.

(2) The practice direction sets out the procedure for applying for arrest.

(3) A party making an application for arrest must—

    (a) request a search to be made in the Register before the warrant is issued to determine whether there is a caution against arrest in force with respect to that property; and

    (b) file a declaration in the form set out in the practice direction.

(4) A warrant of arrest may not be issued as of right in the case of property in respect of which the beneficial ownership, as a result of a sale or disposal by any court in any jurisdiction exercising admiralty jurisdiction in rem, has changed since the claim form was issued.

(5) A warrant of arrest may not be issued against a ship owned by a State where by any convention or treaty, the United Kingdom has undertaken to minimise the possibility of arrest of ships of that State until—

    (a) notice in the form set out in the practice direction has been served on a consular officer at the consular office

---

[1] Amended by the Civil Procedure (Amendment No.5) Rules 2001 (SI 2001/4015).

Paragraph numbers marked with a "+" can be found online and on CD.

of that State in London or the port at which it is intended to arrest the ship; and

(b) a copy of that notice is attached to any declaration under paragraph (3)(b).

(6) Except—

(a) with the permission of the court; or

(b) where notice has been given under paragraph (5),

a warrant of arrest may not be issued in a claim in rem against a foreign ship belonging to a port of a State in respect of which an order in council has been made under section 4 of the Consular Relations Act 1968,[1] until the expiration of 2 weeks from appropriate notice to the consul.

(7) A warrant of arrest is valid for 12 months but may only be executed if the claim form—

(a) has been served; or

(b) remains valid for service at the date of execution.

(8) Property may only be arrested by the Marshal or his substitute.

(9) Property under arrest—

(a) may not be moved unless the court orders otherwise; and

(b) may be immobilised or prevented from sailing in such manner as the Marshal may consider appropriate.

(10) Where an in rem claim form has been issued and security sought, any person who has filed an acknowledgment of service may apply for an order specifying the amount and form of security to be provided.

General note

Where the Admiralty jurisdiction of the High Court may be and is invoked by a **2D–35** claim *in rem* the *res* proceeded against may be arrested if it is within the territorial jurisdiction of the court. For the circumstances in which the jurisdiction *in rem* may be invoked see SCA 1981 s.21 (para.2D–178). It will be observed that in some cases only the property concerned may be proceeded against *in rem* (s.21(2) *ibid.*) and that if a maritime lien has attached, a claim *in rem* may be brought against the ship or property in question regardless of any change of ownership since the cause of action arose other than by a judicial sale. In all other cases it is necessary to look at the person, if any, who was liable *in personam* at the time the cause of action arose; a claim *in rem* may be brought against ships of which he is the beneficial owner or demise charterer at the time of the issue of the claim provided he was the owner or charterer or in possession or control of the ship in connection with which the claim arose at the time when the claim arose. The expression "claim is brought" means "when the claim form is issued" (*The Carmania II* [1963] 2 Lloyd's Rep. 152). Once a claim is brought against a ship by issue of a claim form a sale of the ship by her owner will not deprive the claimant of any rights he may have (*The Monica S* [1968] P. 741; [1967] 3 All E.R. 740; [1967] 2 Lloyd's Rep. 113). But *quaere* the effect of *The Blitz* [1992] 2 Lloyd's Rep. 441. As to the requirements regarding personal liability in actions *in rem* generally and where there is a maritime lien in particular, see *The Father Thames* [1979] 2 Lloyd's Rep. 364.

Until the Civil Jurisdiction and Judgments Act 1982 the sole purpose of an action *in rem* was to obtain security in respect of a judgment of the court (or a sum due under a settlement) in that claim, the court had no jurisdiction to arrest ships or to keep ships

---

[1] 1968 c.18.

Paragraph numbers marked with a "+" can be found online and on CD.

under arrest for other purposes, see *The Cap Bon* [1967] 1 Lloyd's Rep. 543. Now s.26 of the 1982 Act enables the Admiralty Court to retain the security of the *res* or the security for the purpose of arbitration or other proceedings in a United Kingdom or overseas court. See also *The Jalamatsyr* [1987] 2 Lloyd's Rep. 164.

The issue of a warrant of arrest is not a discretionary remedy. If the statutory requirements set out in PD 61, para.61.5.3 are complied with the claimant is entitled to issue the warrant of arrest and if there is such compliance there is no further scope for the application of any duty of full and frank disclosure, *The Varna* [1993] 2 Lloyd's Rep. 253.

A vessel cannot remain in the custody of the Admiralty Marshal and yet be allowed to trade outside the jurisdiction (*The Bazias 3, The Bazias 4* [1993] Q.B. 673; [1993] 2 W.L.R. 854; [1993] 2 All E.R. 964; [1993] 1 Lloyd's Rep. 101, CA).

The Admiralty Marshal may pursuant to the undertaking in **ADM4** call for money on account of the expenses of an arrest as occasion demands.

Merchant Shipping Act 1995

2D–36   Where a state has enacted legislation giving effect to the provisions of the International Convention Relating to the Limitation of the Liability of Owners of Sea-Going Ships 1957, but not the International Convention on Limitation of Liability for Maritime Claims 1976, the setting up of a limitation fund in such a state will not prevent the arrest of a ship in another state which has enacted legislation giving effect to the 1976 Convention.

Crown: foreign sovereign states, etc.

2D–37   See notes under paras 2D–19 and 2D–20 above. Since the termination of the 1968 Treaty and Protocols between the UK and the USSR there is no longer any treaty or convention within 61.5(5) in force.

Delay in prosecution of claim

2D–38   The Marshal is not a shipkeeper and parties should not delay in prosecuting an action in which a vessel is under arrest (*The Italy II* [1987] 2 Lloyd's Rep. 162).

Wrongful arrest

2D–39   Whether a caution has been entered or not, if property is arrested by reason of *mala fides* or *crassa negligentia*, damages may be recovered in Admiralty or, indeed, at common law (*The Walter D. Wallett* [1893] P. 202; *The Evangelismos* (1858) 12 Moo. P.C. 352; Swa. 378; *The Strathnaver* (1875) 1 App. Cas. 58; *The Cathcart* (1867) L.R. 1 A. & E. 314; *The Eudora* (1879) 4 P.D. 208). Damages may also be recovered where an arrest has been unduly continued (*The Cheshire Witch* (1858) Br. & Lush. 362; *The Margaret and Jane* (1869) L.R. 2 A. & E. 345). As to claims for damages where release has been delayed owing to a caution against release and payment having been entered without good and sufficient reason, see r.61.8(5). See also r.61.7(5)(b).

Rule 61.5(8)

2D–40   The warrant may only be executed by being served by the Marshal or his substitute upon the ship or property concerned in accordance with PD 61, para.61.5.5. The Marshal's officer acts as his substitute in London; elsewhere Customs officers and County Court bailiffs do so. See too *The Berny* [1977] 2 Lloyd's Rep. 533 at 548.

> "The court has to bear in mind that the duty of arresting a ship, and often at the time of serving a [claim form] on her, falls on the Admiralty Marshal or his deputies, and it should not adopt an approach to the matter which would or might expose these persons to unreasonable difficulties or dangers."

The claim form and warrant are frequently served at approximately the same time, but either may be served first. As to effect of failure to comply with the requirements as to service, see *The Prins Bernhard* [1964] P. 117; [1963] 3 All E.R. 735; [1963] 2 Lloyd's Rep. 236. As to the non-fatal character of a minor failure, see *The Sullivar* [1965] 2 Lloyd's Rep. 350.

Freight, being incorporeal, cannot be arrested nor can a claim form be served upon it, but where a claim is brought against freight, or cargo and freight, or ship, cargo and freight, the claim form can as against freight, be served on the cargo concerned or the ship in which it was carried, see PD 61 para.3.6(1) and a warrant can be executed against the cargo or ship or both (PD 61 para.5.5) in the manner prescribed.

Paragraph numbers marked with a "+" can be found online and on CD.

Contempt of court

To move a ship from where she is lying with knowledge of the fact that a warrant **2D–41** has been issued, is contempt of court (*The Seraglio* (1885) 10 P.D. 120) and *a fortiori* after the warrant has been served. As to various acts amounting to contempt see *The Petrel* (1836) 3 Hagg. 299; *The Bure* (1850) 14 Jur. Pt 1, 1123; *The Armenian* (Sh.Gaz. March 1874); *The Rhenania* (Sh.Gaz. November 1909); *The Selina Stanford Times*, November 17, 1908. For modern examples see *The Jarlinn* [1965] 1 W.L.R. 1098; [1965] 2 All E.R. 886; [1965] 2 Lloyd's Rep. 191; *The Jarvis Brake* [1976] 2 All E.R. 886; [1976] 2 Lloyd's Rep. 320; *The Merdeka* [1982] 1 Lloyd's Rep. 401.

It is contempt to attempt to sell a ship in respect of which an order for sale by the court is in force (*The Jarvis Brake* [1976] 2 All E.R. 886. See also *Cerro Colorado* [1993] 1 Lloyd's Rep. 58).

Security in claim in rem[1]

61.6—(1) This rule applies if, in a claim in rem, security has 2D–42 been given to—

    (a) obtain the release of property under arrest; or

    (b) prevent the arrest of property.

(2) The court may order that the—

    (a) amount of security be reduced and may stay the claim until the order is complied with; or

    (b) claimant may arrest or re-arrest the property proceeded against to obtain further security.

(3) The court may not make an order under paragraph (2)(b) if the total security to be provided would exceed the value of the property at the time—

    (a) of the original arrest; or

    (b) security was first given (if the property was not arrested).

Rule 61.6.2(b)

In *The Prinsengracht* [1993] 1 Lloyd's Rep. 41, applying *The Arctic Star, The Times*, **2D–43** February 5, 1985; it was held that arrest or re-arrest after security is given and before judgment is to be viewed in the light of whether the arrest or re-arrest is oppressive and vexatious in the circumstances of the particular case.

Cautions against arrest[2]

61.7—(1) Any person may file a request for a caution against 2D–44 arrest.

(2) When a request under paragraph (1) is filed the court will enter the caution in the Register if the request is in the form set out in the practice direction and—

    (a) the person filing the request undertakes—

        (i) to file an acknowledgment of service; and

        (ii) to give sufficient security to satisfy the claim with interest and costs; or

    (b) where the person filing the request has constituted a limitation fund in accordance with Article 11 of the

---

[1] Amended by the Civil Procedure (Amendment No.5) Rules 2001 (SI 2001/4015).
[2] Amended by the Civil Procedure (Amendment No.5) Rules 2001 (SI 2001/4015).

Paragraph numbers marked with a "+" can be found online and on CD.

Convention on Limitation of Liability for Maritime Claims 1976[1] he—

    (i) states that such a fund has been constituted; and

    (ii) undertakes that the claimant will acknowledge service of the claim form by which any claim may be begun against the property described in the request.

(3) A caution against arrest—

    (a) is valid for 12 months after the date it is entered in the Register; but

    (b) may be renewed for a further 12 months by filing a further request.

(4) Paragraphs (1) and (2) apply to a further request under paragraph (3)(b).

(5) Property may be arrested if a caution against arrest has been entered in the Register but the court may order that—

    (a) the arrest be discharged; and

    (b) the party procuring the arrest pays compensation to the owner of or other persons interested in the arrested property.

Rule 61.7(2)(b)

2D–45   The 1976 Convention is now to be found in Sch.7 to the Merchant Shipping Act 1995.

Entry of caution against arrest

2D–46   The entry of a caution does not in fact prevent the issue or execution of a warrant of arrest but a person who causes property to be arrested despite the existence of a caution and without good and sufficient reason may be ordered to pay damages. See r.61.7(5).

Withdrawal of caution against arrest

2D–47   If a cautioner wishes to withdraw a current caution against arrest, application for such withdrawal must be made to the court, *The Iberian Ocean*, October 25, 2002, Admiralty Court.

Release and cautions against release[2]

2D–48   61.8—(1) Where property is under arrest—

    (a) an in rem claim form may be served upon it; and

    (b) it may be arrested by any other person claiming to have an in rem claim against it.

(2) Any person who—

    (a) claims to have an in rem right against any property under arrest; and

    (b) wishes to be given notice of any application in respect of that property or its proceeds of sale,

---

[1] The text of the Convention is set out in Sch.7 to the Merchant Shipping Act 1995 (c.21).

[2] Amended by the Civil Procedure (Amendment No.5) Rules 2001 (SI 2001/4015).

Paragraph numbers marked with a "+" can be found online and on CD.

the value of the *res*. See *The Charlotte* [1920] P. 78. Where there is a dispute as to the amount of security to be provided, an application can be made to the court to determine the amount. See, for example, *The Moscanthy* [1971] 1 Lloyd's Rep. 37. The application should normally be made to the Admiralty Registrar by application notice in the claim asking for the release of the property upon provision of security for a stated amount. Where security has been provided in an excessive amount e.g., in order to obtain the prompt release of the property, an application may be made to the court for reduction of the amount of security.

It is, of course, always open to a party not to provide security and to allow his property to remain under arrest.

A party demanding excessive security may have to pay (1) the costs of a successful application to reduce the amount of that security and (2) the expense of providing the excess. Further as to security and release see British Shipping Laws, Vol. 1. The power to exact security must not be used oppressively; where there is a genuine dispute or discussion about the appropriate amount, the party seeking security ought to put his cards on the table and explain to the other party or his solicitors the grounds on which he claims to exercise this strong power: (*The Moscanthy* [1971] 1 Lloyd's Rep. 37 at 46–47).

Letters of undertaking

See *C Itoh & Co Ltd v Campanhia De Navegaçao Lloyd Brasileiro and Steamship Mutual Underwriting Association (Bermuda) Ltd* [1999] 1 Lloyd's Rep. 115; *Same v Republic Federativa Do Brasil (The Rio Assu) (No.2)* [1999] 1 Lloyd's Rep. 115, CA held *inter alia* that on the true construction of the letter of undertaking the liability of the demise charterers' P & I Club under the letter of undertaking survived the demise of the demise charterer of the vessel. **2D–51**

See too *Galaxy Energy International Ltd v Assuranceforeningen Skuld (The Oakwell)* [1999] 1 Lloyd's Rep. 249 held *inter alia* that on a true construction of the letter of undertaking the obligation to instruct solicitors to accept service of the claim was unaffected by the fact that the vessel had been sold post provision of the letter and before proceedings issued.

Release when claim stayed

In *The Bazias 3, The Bazias 4* [1993] Q.B. 673; [1993] 2 W.L.R. 854; [1993] 1 Lloyd's Rep. 101, the Court of Appeal held that the effect of s.26 of the Civil Jurisdiction and Judgments Act 1982 was to assimilate *in rem* proceedings in the Admiralty Court with arbitration claims so that the discretion to release an arrested vessel was the same in both cases. Accordingly on an application to release a vessel held as security for a claim in arbitration the court would in accordance with the usual practice only exercise its discretion to release on provision of sufficient security to cover the claim, plus interest and costs on the basis of the claimant's reasonably arguable best case. Inconvenience and difficulty in finding sufficient liquid financial resources were not sufficient grounds for departing from the usual practice. There would be no cross-undertaking as to damages under s.26(2). The court granted a stay of action under s.1 of the Arbitration Act 1975 and ordered both vessels to remain under arrest pending further order. **2D–52**

Release by setting aside warrant of arrest

E.g. where the declaration leading to warrant of arrest contains material inaccuracies relating to the statutory requirements set out in PD 61 para.5.3 and arrest cannot be validly maintained: in *The Varna* [1993] 2 Lloyd's Rep. 253, CA, the court held that beyond the establishment of the facts then required by O.75, r.5(9) and now by PD 61 para.61.5.3 there was no further scope for an attack upon the issue not being a discretionary remedy. The Court of Appeal, however, stated that a warrant might be set aside as a result of the claim *in rem* being struck out or the proceedings stayed and that there might be a general discretionary power on a with notice application to set aside the warrant on the basis that its continuance was in all the circumstances unjust. **2D–53**

Release pursuant to Merchant Shipping Act 1995

Section 185 and Sch.7 provide that the court may, and in certain circumstances must, order the release of a ship or other property which has been arrested, or the security given to prevent, or obtain release from, arrest. See also *The Putbus* [1969] P. 136; [1969] 2 All E.R. 676; [1969] 1 Lloyd's Rep. 253, CA). **2D–54**

Paragraph numbers marked with a "+" can be found online and on CD.

Rule 61.8(5)

2D–55   For cases see *The Cormer* (1863) Br. & L. 161; *The Don Ricardo* (1880) 5 P.D. 121; 4 Asp. M.L.C. 225.

Rule 61.8(7)

2D–56   The object of this provision is to enable a person who has a substantial interest in the *res* to intervene, if this interest may be injuriously affected by the claim against the *res* and to protect his interests (*The Dowthorpe* (1843) 2 W.Rob. 73, 77). The rights of an intervener are limited to the protection of his interest in the *res*, and he has no *locus standi* to raise issues which are not material to his purpose (*The Lord Strathcona* [1925] P. 143; see also *The Byzantion* (1922) 127 L.T. 756; 16 Asp. M.L.C. 19, as to defences which an intervener may and those which he may not set up). Application is to the Admiralty Registrar.

Inherent jurisdiction

2D–57   The court has inherent jurisdiction to allow a person who has no interest in the property under arrest to intervene, if the effect of the arrest is to cause him serious hardship, difficulty or danger (*The Mardina Merchant* [1975] 1 W.L.R. 147; [1974] 3 All E.R. 749; [1974] 2 Lloyd's Rep. 424, in which the interests of a harbour authority were adversely affected by the presence of the arrested ship at one of their quays).

As to intervention for the purpose of applying to be added as a defendant or for other purposes see CPR r.19.

Judgment in default[1]

2D–58   **61.9—(1) In a claim in rem (other than a collision claim) the claimant may obtain judgment in default of—**

    (a) an acknowledgment of service only if—

        (i) the defendant has not filed an acknowledgment of service; and

        (ii) the time for doing so set out in rule 61.3(4) has expired; and

    (b) defence only if—

        (i) a defence has not been filed; and

        (ii) the relevant time limit for doing so has expired.

(2) In a collision claim, a party who has filed a collision statement of case within the time specified by rule 61.4(5) may obtain judgment in default of a collision statement of case only if—

    (a) the party against whom judgment is sought has not filed a collision statement of case; and

    (b) the time for doing so set out in rule 61.4(5) has expired.

(3) An application for judgment in default—

    (a) under paragraph (1) or paragraph (2) in an in rem claim must be made by filing—

        (i) an application notice as set out in the practice direction;

        (ii) a certificate proving service of the claim form; and

        (iii) evidence proving the claim to the satisfaction of the court; and

---

[1] Amended by the Civil Procedure (Amendment No.5) Rules 2001 (SI 2001/4015).

Paragraph numbers marked with a "+" can be found online and on CD.

Rule 61.10(3)

An application under this paragraph should be made in the claim brought by the **2D–68** applicant. Notice of application must be served on all persons who have obtained judgment against the ship and on all cautioners. The names and addresses for service of these persons can be obtained from the Admiralty and Commercial Registry.

Note

As to priorities, see *British Shipping Laws, McGuffie: Admiralty Practice* and Halsbury's **2D–69** *Laws of England*; and Meeson, *Admiralty Jurisdiction and Practice*. See also as to variation of order determining priorities, *The Fairport (No.4)* [1967] 1 W.L.R. 964; [1967] 2 All E.R. 914n; [1967] 1 Lloyd's Rep. 602. For examples of subrogation of mortgagees to the rights and priorities of master and crew upon payment, *with permission of the court*, by the mortgagees of the master's and crew's wages, see *The Berostar* [1970] 2 Lloyd's Rep. 403 and *The Vasilia* [1972] 1 Lloyd's Rep. 51.

In *The Ruta* [2000] 1 W.L.R. 2068; [2001] 1 All E.R. 450, it was held that questions of priority were not capable of being compartmentalised in the form of strict rules of ranking, since the courts had adopted a broad discretionary approach, rival claims being ranked by reference to considerations of equity, public policy and commercial expediency, with the ultimate aim of doing that which was just in the circumstances of each case; and that, since the wage claimants had no alternative form of redress against the vessel owners and the only remedy open to them was to recover their unpaid wages from the proceeds of sale of the vessel, considerations of public policy justified according them a very high level of priority, giving them precedence over the damage claims and the contractual claim of the caveator.

Payment out from proceeds of sale under rule 61.10(3) and (4)

The court has no jurisdiction to order payment out from the proceeds of a sale by **2D–70** order of the court, to persons other than judgment holders or, in the case of the residue after all claims have been satisfied, the defendant (*The Saxon King* 1975 Fo. 253 unrep.). Exceptionally, payment out may be ordered to any person where the defendants and all other parties interested in the proceeds of sale (judgment holders, interveners and caveators) consent (*The Valiant* 1977 Fo. 446 unrep.). A payment out on account may be ordered where all parties consent, or where the priorities are such that it is clear the claimant will ultimately be entitled to at least the amount ordered. See *The Reina (No.2)* [1963] 2 Lloyd's Rep. 513.

Charging and stop orders

Payment out from proceeds of sale may be affected by a charging order or stop or- **2D–71** der pursuant to CPR Pt 74 or an application or order under CPR r.72.10.

Note

As to apportionment of a payment in a salvage action, see *The Talamba and the Troll* **2D–72** [1965] P. 433; [1965] 2 All E.R. 775; [1965] 2 Lloyd's Rep. 128.

In particular, note the observations of Sheen J. in *The Vasili Shelgunov* [1988] 2 Lloyd's Rep. 34, at 38 in relation to Admiralty claims *in personam*. Approved by Court of Appeal [1989] 1 Lloyd's Rep. 542, CA.

Limitation claims[1]

61.11—(1) This rule applies to limitation claims. **2D–73**

(2) A claim is started by the issue of a limitation claim form as set out in the practice direction.

(3) The—

    (a) claimant; and

    (b) at least one defendant

---

[1] Amended by the Civil Procedure (Amendment No.5) Rules 2001 (SI 2001/4015) and the Civil Procedure (Amendment) Rules 2008 (SI 2008/2178).

Paragraph numbers marked with a "+" can be found online and on CD.

must be named in the claim form, but all other defendants may be described.

(4) The claim form—

    (a) must be served on all named defendants and any other defendant who requests service upon him; and

    (b) may be served on any other defendant.

(5) The claim form may not be served out of the jurisdiction unless—

    (a) the claim falls within section 22(2)(a), (b) or (c) of the Supreme Court Act 1981[1];

    (b) the defendant has submitted to or agreed to submit to the jurisdiction of the court; or

    (c) the Admiralty Court has jurisdiction over the claim under any applicable Convention; and

the court grants permission in accordance with Section IV of Part 6.

(6) An acknowledgment of service is not required.

(7) Every defendant upon whom a claim form is served must—

    (a) within 28 days of service file—

        (i) a defence; or

        (ii) a notice that the defendant admits the right of the claimant to limit liability; or

    (b) if the defendant wishes to—

        (i) dispute the jurisdiction of the court; or

        (ii) argue that the court should not exercise its jurisdiction,

file within 14 days of service (or where the claim form is served out of the jurisdiction, within the time specified in rule 6.35) an acknowledgment of service as set out in the practice direction.

(8) If a defendant files an acknowledgment of service under paragraph (7)(b) he will be treated as having accepted that the court has jurisdiction to hear the claim unless he applies under Part 11 within 14 days after filing the acknowledgment of service.

(9) Where one or more named defendants admits the right to limit—

    (a) the claimant may apply for a restricted limitation decree in the form set out in the practice direction; and

    (b) the court will issue a decree in the form set out in the practice direction limiting liability only against those named defendants who have admitted the claimant's right to limit liability.

(10) A restricted limitation decree—

    (a) may be obtained against any named defendant who fails to file a defence within the time specified for doing so; and

---

[1] 1981 c.54.

Paragraph numbers marked with a "+" can be found online and on CD.

ADMIRALTY

    (b) need not be advertised, but a copy must be served on the defendants to whom it applies.

(11) Where all the defendants upon whom the claim form has been served admit the claimant's right to limit liability—

    (a) the claimant may apply to the Admiralty Registrar for a general limitation decree in the form set out in the practice direction; and

    (b) the court will issue a limitation decree.

(12) Where one or more of the defendants upon whom the claim form has been served do not admit the claimant's right to limit, the claimant may apply for a general limitation decree in the form set out in the practice direction.

(13) When a limitation decree is granted the court—

    (a) may—

        (i) order that any proceedings relating to any claim arising out of the occurrence be stayed;

        (ii) order the claimant to establish a limitation fund if one has not been established or make such other arrangements for payment of claims against which liability is limited; or

        (iii) if the decree is a restricted limitation decree, distribute the limitation fund; and

    (b) will, if the decree is a general limitation decree, give directions as to advertisement of the decree and set a time within which notice of claims against the fund must be filed or an application made to set aside the decree.

(14) When the court grants a general limitation decree the claimant must—

    (a) advertise it in such manner and within such time as the court directs; and

    (b) file—

        (i) a declaration that the decree has been advertised in accordance with paragraph (a); and

        (ii) copies of the advertisements.

(15) No later than the time set in the decree for filing claims, each of the defendants who wishes to assert a claim must file and serve his statement of case on—

    (a) the limiting party; and

    (b) all other defendants except where the court orders otherwise.

(16) Any person other than a defendant upon whom the claim form has been served may apply to the court within the time fixed in the decree to have a general limitation decree set aside.

(17) An application under paragraph (16) must be supported by a declaration—

    (a) stating that the applicant has a claim against the claimant arising out of the occurrence; and

Paragraph numbers marked with a "+" can be found online and on CD.

> (b) setting out grounds for contending that the claimant is not entitled to the decree, either in the amount of limitation or at all.
>
> (18) The claimant may constitute a limitation fund by making a payment into court.
>
> (19) A limitation fund may be established before or after a limitation claim has been started.
>
> (20) If a limitation claim is not commenced within 75 days after the date the fund was established—
>
> > (a) the fund will lapse; and
> >
> > (b) all money in court (including interest) will be repaid to the person who made the payment into court.
>
> (21) Money paid into court under paragraph (18) will not be paid out except under an order of the court.
>
> (22) A limitation claim for—
>
> > (a) a restricted decree may be brought by counterclaim; and
> >
> > (b) a general decree may only be brought by counterclaim with the permission of the court.

Limitation claim

2D-74 For definition see r.61.1(2)(e). These claims are assigned to the Queen's Bench Division and taken by the Admiralty Court, see r.61.2(1)(c). See also SCA 1981 s.20(1)(b) and (3)(c). Limitation of liability may be relied on by way of defence to a claim or counterclaim.

A limitation decree or declaration can be granted before liability is established. The establishment of liability either by trial or agreement is not a precondition to the seeking and granting of a limitation decree or declaration, see *Bouygues Offshore SA. v Caspian Shipping Co* [1998] 2 Lloyd's Rep. 461. See further *The "Western Regent"* [2005] EWHC 240 (Admlty); [2005] 2 Lloyd's Rep 54 at para.20:

> "...an ability to constitute a limitation fund under Article 11.1 of the 1976 Convention is neither a pre-condition of the jurisdiction to hear and determine a limitation claim nor of the power given to the Court in an appropriate case to grant a limitation decree." (Affirmed [2005] EWCA Civ 985; [2005] 2 Lloyd's Rep 359, CA)

In *Herceg Novi (Owners) v Ming Galaxy (Owners)* [1998] 4 All E.R. 238; [1998] 2 Lloyd's Rep. 454, CA, the court held that the 1976 Convention was not an internationally sanctioned and objective view of where substantial justice was viewed as lying, but was simply the view of some 30 states. Moreover, the preference for the 1976 Convention had no greater justification than for the 1957 regime and, in terms of abstract justice, neither convention was objectively more just than the other. Accordingly, since substantial justice would be done in Singapore, the appeal would be allowed and an unconditional stay of the English action would be granted.

In *MSC Mediterranean Shipping Co SA v Delmur BVBA (The Rosa M)* [2000] 2 All E.R. (Comm) 458, the court held that for it to be established that the claimant's liability was not limited under art.4 of the Convention, it was necessary for the defendant to prove that the casualty was caused by the personal act or omission of the charterers, that those personal acts or omissions were committed recklessly and at the time of those acts or omissions the *alter ego* of the charterers actually knew that the casualty would probably result. In the absence of any allegation of intent, the authorities made it clear that a person challenging the right to limit had to establish both reckless conduct and knowledge that the relevant loss would probably result, and "shut-eye" knowledge did not constitute "knowledge" for the purposes of art.4, which required actual knowledge. This approach has been affirmed by the Court of Appeal in *The Leerort* [2001] 2 Lloyd's Rep. 291, the court holding that it is only the personal act or omission of a shipowner which defeats the right to limit. A shipowner is defined in art 1 as the owner, charterer, manager or operator of a seagoing ship. Thus, to defeat the right to limit, it is necessary to identify the causative act or omission on the part of such a person that caused the loss. Furthermore, it is only conduct committed with intent to cause such loss, or recklessly with knowledge that such loss would probably result, that defeats the right to limit. It seems that person challenging the right to limit must establish both reckless conduct *and* knowledge that the relevant loss would probably result. In considering the relevant loss the court continued that it seems that where the loss in respect of which a claim is made resulted from a collision between ship A and ship B, the owners of ship A, or cargo in ship A, will only defeat the right to limit liability on the owner of ship B if they can prove that the owner of ship B intended that it should collide with ship A, or acted recklessly with the knowledge that it was likely to do so (para.13).

The alternative, which is perhaps arguable, is that the claimant merely has to prove that the owner of ship B intended that his ship should collide with another ship, or acted recklessly with the knowledge that it was likely to do so (*ibid.*, para.17).

On the facts of this case it is not necessary to decide which alternative is correct. In either event the reality is that when damage results from a collision the shipowner will only lose his right to limit if it can be proved that he deliberately or recklessly acted in way which he knew was likely to result in the loss of or damage to the property of another in circumstances where, inevitably, the same consequences would be likely to flow to his own vessel (*ibid.*, para.18).

Article 2.1(a) of the 1976 Convention does not extend the right to limit to a claim for damage to the vessel by reference to the tonnage of which limitation is to be calculated, see *CMA CGM SA v Classica Shipping Co Ltd (The CMA Djakarta)* [2004] EWCA Civ 114; [2004] 1 Lloyd's Rep. 460, CA. Nor does the Convention provide for a limitation on liablity for the costs of litigation, see *Thompson v Masterton* [2004] 1 Lloyd's Rep 304 [Roy. Ct. Guernsey]. See too *Newcastle Port Corp v Pevitt (The Robert Whitmore)* [2004] 2 Lloyd's Rep. 47 (NSWSC), fund is exclusive of costs.

Claim form

Special Admiralty Forms, Admiralty Limitation claim form, see the *Civil Procedure Forms Volume*. **2D–75**

Service

The claim form must be served on all named defendants in the claim form and not merely described. As to service out of the jurisdiction see r.61.11(5). **2D–76**

In the *ICL Shipping Ltd v Chin Tai Steel Enterprise Co Ltd (The ICL Vikraman)* [2003] EWHC 2320; [2004] 1 W.L.R. 2254; [2004] 1 Lloyd's Rep. 21 the court held that in CPR r.61.11(5)(c) the "claim" referred to is the claim to limit rather than any underlying claim and the words "any applicable convention" should be construed as covering the 1976 Convention. This case also concerns the construction and scope of Arts 11 and 13 of the 1976 Convention.

Restricted decree

When a claimant in a limitation claim is satisfied that there will be no claims upon the fund other than the claims of the defendants who have acknowledged issue or service of the claim form the claimant may not want a decree which is good against the world. The claimant may apply to the Admiralty Registrar to amend the claim form by deleting reference to any defendants other than those named. The application should be accompanied by a letter signed by all consenting parties stating that in their view it is not anticipated that any further claims will emerge. The Registrar may then order payment out of the limitation fund in court. **2D–77**

If further claimants do emerge after payment out the claimant will be obliged to constitute a new fund should they wish to limit their liability against the new claimants. This practice arises from a decision of Sheen J. in an unreported case (*The Rena* [1979] Fo. 138).

Owner-master

As to the right of an owner-master to limit his liability, see *The Annie Hay* [1968] P. 341; [1968] 1 All E.R. 657; [1968] 1 Lloyd's Rep. 141. **2D–78**

Paragraph numbers marked with a "+" can be found online and on CD.

Charterers

2D–79   Charterers cannot limit their liability under the 1976 Convention in respect of claims brought by owners against them: see *Aegean Sea Traders Corp v Repsol Petroleo SA* [1998] 2 Lloyd's Rep. 39. See further *CMA CGM SA v Classica Shipping Co Ltd (The CMA Djakarta)* [2004] EWCA Civ 114; [2004] 1 Lloyd's Rep. 460, CA. The term charterers is to be given its ordinary meaning. Accordingly, the charterer's ability to limit will depend on the type of claim brought against him and not the capacity (e.g. qua owner) in which he was acting when his liability was incurred.

In *Metvale Ltd v Monsanto International SARL* [2008] EWHC 3002 (Admiralty Court), on the hearing of a preliminary issue, it was held that a slot charterer is within the definition of "shipowner" for the purposes of Art 1 of the 1976 Convention and were entitled to limit their liability under the Convention and under the Merchant Shipping Act 1995.

Costs of application

2D–80   The costs of an application for a decree of limitation under the former s.17 of the Merchant Shipping Act 1979, now s.185 of the Merchant Shipping Act 1995, should normally follow the event, see *The Capitan San Luis* [1994] Q.B. 465; [1994] 2 W.L.R. 465; [1994] 2 W.L.R. 299; [1994] 1 All E.R. 1016; [1993] 2 Lloyd's Rep. 573. In this case it was held that the shipowners should pay the costs of proving the matters which he had to establish in order to obtain the decree and that the claimant should pay the costs of investigating and determining the facts which the Convention provided he must prove, if at the end of the day he failed to establish those facts.

Rule 61.11.13(a)(iii)

2D–81   It seems that in a distribution pursuant to this paragraph, the court would order interest accrued on the limitation fund in court to be apportioned *pro rata* to the distribution.

Stay of proceedings[1]

2D–82   **61.12 Where the court orders a stay of any claim in rem—**

> **(a) any property under arrest in the claim remains under arrest; and**
>
> **(b) any security representing the property remains in force,**

unless the court orders otherwise.

Assessors[2]

2D–83   **61.13 The court may sit with assessors when hearing—**

> **(a) collision claims; or**
>
> **(b) other claims involving issues of navigation or seamanship, and**

the parties will not be permitted to call expert witnesses unless the court orders otherwise.

Assessors

2D–84   In the specified cases, nautical assessors usually advise the Court of Appeal and the Judge of the Admiralty Court upon questions of navigation and seamanship if such questions arise. In some cases only one nautical assessor is called in and occasionally their attendance is dispensed with altogether. In the Admiralty Court, the assessors are usually two of the Elder Brethren of Trinity House neither of whom should have been in the service of any party to the claim (*The Bremen* (1931) 47 T.L.R. 505) save where an Elder Brother is a retired officer of the Royal Navy and one of H.M. ships is

---

[1] Amended by the Civil Procedure (Amendment No.5) Rules 2001 (SI 2001/4015).
[2] Amended by the Civil Procedure (Amendment No. 5) Rules 2001 (SI 2001/4015).

Paragraph numbers marked with a "+" can be found online and on CD.

involved. If Trinity House is a party, one or two of such Court of Appeal assessors as are not Elder Brethren may be called on. Where nautical assessors are present, evidence in the nature of expert opinion on matters of nautical skill and practice, and as to the deductions to be drawn from nautical facts, is usually inadmissible (*The Gazelle* (1842) 1 W.Rob. 471). In *The St Chad* [1965] 2 Lloyd's Rep. 1, affirming; [1965] 1 Lloyd's Rep. 107, however, an order made provided for a fishery assessor to assist the court and also for each side to be at liberty to call an experienced trawler skipper to give general evidence on the system of work in trawlers of the relevant type, as the system was said to have changed so recently that the new developments might be outside the practical experience of a fishery assessor. A comparable order was made in *The Bedford Earl* 1954 Fo. 218 unrep., but this case never came to trial. As to the Court of Appeal, see para.9A–213 below.

See generally CPR r.35.15 and Practice Direction—Experts and Assessors para.6.1 at 35–006 and the Admiralty and Commercial Courts Guide, Section N.14 and para. 2D–142 below.

Assessors may be called in to assist the Registrar at a reference, see PD 61 para.13.3. The function of nautical assessors is to advise the court upon nautical matters (*The City of Berlin* [1908] P. 110; see *The New Pelton* [1891] P. 258; *The River Derwent* (1891) 7 Asp. 467). There is no right of cross-examination. The decision of the case rests entirely with the judge (*The Gannet* [1900] A.C. 234; *Owners of SS. Australia v Owners of SS. Nautilus* [1927] A.C. 145; *San Onofre, The v Melanie, The (No.1)* [1925] A.C. 246; *Owners of the Artemisia v Owners of the Douglas* [1927] A.C. 164); this equally applies in the Court of Appeal (*The Llanelly* (1926) 25 Ll.L.Rep. 37, p.39, HL) and House of Lords (*The Marinegra* [1960] 2 Lloyd's Rep. 1). Even in purely nautical matters the judge is not bound to follow the advice of his assessors, if it does not agree with his own opinion (see *The Magna Charta* (1872) 1 Asp. 153; *Aid, The* (1881) L.R. 6 P.D. 84; *Beryl, The* (1884) L.R. 9 P.D. 137, 141; *Swanland, The* (1855) 2 Sp. 107; *Fred, The* (1895) 7 Asp. 550; *Owners of SS. Melanie v Owners of SS. San Onofre (No.1)* [1925] A.C. 246; *Owners of SS. Australia v Owners of Cargo of SS. Nautilus*, above; *Spero, The* (1947-48) 81 Ll. L. Rep. 350 at 354 see *The British Resource* (1941) 70 Ll.L.Rep. 93 at 102, per du Parcq L.J., and *Carrick Coast, The* (1947-48) 81 Ll. L. Rep. 447 at 451, per Willmer J.) as to judging ordinary navigating officers by the exceptionally high standard of knowledge and experience of the Elder Brethren. The assessors should not be asked any question that is tantamount to asking them whether they would find for the claimant or the defendant (see *The Ausomia* (1920) 2 L.L.Rep. 123 at 124, HL). The assessors in an appeal court are not substituted for those previously consulted. They are additional but not to be preferred to them unless the advice given is such as in itself is more acceptable to the appellate court (*Sobieski, The* [1949] P. 313 at 379). There is no question of appeal from one set of assessors to another set (*Owners of SS. Australia v Owners of Cargo of SS. Nautilus*. See also *The Fina Canada* [1962] 2 Lloyd's Rep. 445). In *The St Chad* [1965] 2 Lloyd's Rep. 1, CA, Willmer L.J. pointed out that nautical assessors in the Court of Appeal and the court below were of equal standing. He also said that it was their function to advise on nautical questions put to them by the court whether or not such question had been canvassed by counsel. If there is a difference of opinion between assessors and a judge cannot decide which advice is sound he must regard the point as not proven (see *The Dageld* (1947) 80 Ll.L.Rep. 517, reversing (1947) 80 Ll.L.Rep. 225 at 230; *Owners of S.S. Australiav Owners of Cargo of SS. Nautilus*) but he may reach a decision by rejecting the advice of one assessor and accepting that of the other (see *The Taiwan* (1947) 80 Ll.L.Rep. 580 at 586).

In order to comply with art.6(1) of the European Convention for the Protection of Human Rights and Fundamental Freedoms when a court has received evidence from an assessor it is appropriate, except in cases where such discussion is unnecessary in the light of submissions made earlier, that the preferable modern practice of putting questions to the assessors after discussion with counsel should be complemented by a practice of disclosing their answers to counsel, either orally or in writing—in order that any inappropriate submission can be made as to whether the judge should accept this advice, *Owners of the Bow Spring v Owners of the Manzanillo* [2004] EWCA Civ 1007; [2005] 1 W.L.R. 144; [2004] 4 All E.R. 899; [2005] 1 Lloyd's Rep 1, CA.

The Court of Appeal has been known to adopt the advice of Elder Brethren in the lower court, rejecting that of their own assessors (*The Sobieski*, above; see also *The Miraflores and The Abadesa* [1966] P. 18; [1966] 1 All E.R. 553; [1966] 1 Lloyd's Rep. 97 at

Paragraph numbers marked with a "+" can be found online and on CD.

108, per Willmer L.J. A judge will not infrequently state in his judgment that he has sought advice on certain points, giving the results of having done so without detail, and saying whether he accepts or rejects the advice tendered (contrast *The Aurelian* [1957] 2 Lloyd's Rep. 417 at 422, where Willmer J. set out verbatim in his judgment the questions put to the Elder Brother). Questions and answers are in writing in the Court of Appeal.

As to assessors' fees, see para.2D–142 below; *mutatis mutandis* the fees in the High Court and Court of Appeal are the same.

PRACTICE DIRECTION—ADMIRALTY CLAIMS
This Practice Direction supplements CPR Part 61

2D–85

61.1 Scope

1.1 The Practice Direction supplementing Part 58 (Commercial Claims) also applies to Admiralty claims except where it is inconsistent with Part 61 or this practice direction.

Admiralty and Commercial Registry

RCJ Room EB13 (Tel. 020 7947 6112). Hours: 10.00–16.30. See PD to CPR Pt 2, at 2PD.2.

2D–86

Inquiries as to practice may be made in person or by telephone. The Admiralty and Commercial Registry was initially established by *Practice Direction* [1987] 3 All E.R. 616 issued by the Lord Chief Justice with the concurrence of the Admiralty judge and the judge in charge of the Commercial List. In relation to Admiralty and Commercial matters it replaces and carries out all the functions of the Central Office including the issuing of processes. Fees are paid to the Supreme Court Accounts Office, but the Registry may accept payment of a fee for a single item by way of a Solicitor's cheque.

Issue of claim form by fax

See Practice Direction—Commercial Court, para.2.2 and Appendix A thereto.

2D–87

Use of postal facilities in the Registry

Section N12 of the Admiralty and Commercial Courts Guide provides as follows:

2D–88

N12.1 Applications together with the requisite documents may be posted to:

> The Admiralty and Commercial Registry,
> Room EB13,
> Royal Courts of Justice,
> Strand,
> London WC2 2LL.

N12.2 In addition to the classes of business for which the use of postal facilities is permitted by the CPR or the Commercial Court Guide, the filing of the following classes of documents is also permitted in Admiralty matters:

   (i) Requests for cautions;

   (ii) Collision Statements of Case

N12.3

   (a) Documents sent by post for filing must be accompanied by two copies of a list of the documents sent and an envelope properly addressed to the sender.

   (b) On receipt of the documents in the Registry, the court officer will, if the circumstances are such that had the documents been presented personally they would have been filed, cause them to be filed and will, by post, notify the sender that this has been done. If the documents would not have been accepted if presented personally the court officer will not file them but will retain them in the Registry for collection by the sender and will, by post, so inform the sender.

   (c) When documents received through the post are filed by the court officer they will be sealed and entered as filed on the date on which they were received in the Registry.

Issuance of Admiralty Claim Forms and Warrants of Arrest out of High Court District Registries post March 25, 2002

It is not intended that the facility to issue Admiralty Claim Forms and Warrants of Arrest from District Registries of the High Court be removed under the new Part 61 and its associated Practice Direction. This facility should be continued. There must however be prior consultation with the Admiralty Marshal before any Warrant of Arrest is issued as has happened hitherto and the court file must be sent immediately

2D–89

Paragraph numbers marked with a "+" can be found online and on CD.

upon the issue of the Claim Form and any Warrant of Arrest to the Admiralty and Commercial Registry at the Royal Courts of Justice as before in order that the Admiralty Registrar may issue case management directions as required by the new Admiralty Practice Direction.

In so far as the new rule and Practice Direction read in conjunction with Part 58 and its Practice Direction provide that such facilities are to be provided out of the Admiralty and Commercial Registry the issuing District Registry will be deemed as providing the same on behalf of the Admiralty and Commercial Registry so long as the procedure outlined above is followed. District Registry numbering will continue to be used in the first place on issue. (Admiralty Registrar, March 18, 2002).

Case management

2D–90   **2.1** After a claim form is issued the Registrar will issue a direction in writing stating—

(1) whether the claim will remain in the Admiralty Court or be transferred to another court; and

(2) if the claim remains in the Admiralty Court–

    (a) whether it will be dealt with by–

        (i) the Admiralty judge; or

        (ii) the Registrar; and

    (b) whether the trial will be in London or elsewhere.

2.2 In making these directions the Registrar will have regard to–

(1) the nature of the issues and the sums in dispute; and

(2) the criteria set in rule 26.8 so far as they are applicable.

2.3 Where the Registrar directs that the claim will be dealt with by the Admiralty judge, case management directions will be given and any case management conference or pre-trial review will be heard by the Admiralty judge.

Application to Judge and to Admiralty Registrar

2D–91   Any party wishing to make an application to an Admiralty Judge should apply to the Admiralty and Commercial Registry (Listing Office) where all necessary arrangements will be made. Applications to the Admiralty Registrar should be applied for in the Admiralty and Commercial Registry (General Office).

61.3 Claims in rem

2D–92   **3.1** A claim form in rem must be in Form **ADM1**.

3.2 The claimant in a claim in rem may be named or may be described, but if not named in the claim form must identify himself by name if requested to do so by any other party.

3.3 The defendant must be described in the claim form.

3.4 The acknowledgment of service must be in Form **ADM2**. The person who acknowledges service must identify himself by name.

3.5 The period for acknowledging service under rule 61.3(4) applies irrespective of whether the claim form contains particulars of claim.

3.6 A claim form in rem may be served in the following ways:

(1) on the property against which the claim is brought by fixing a copy of the claim form–

    (a) on the outside of the property in a position which may reasonably be expected to be seen; or

    (b) where the property is freight, either–

Paragraph numbers marked with a "+" can be found online and on CD.

(i) on the cargo in respect of which the freight was earned; or

(ii) on the ship on which the cargo was carried;

(2) if the property to be served is in the custody of a person who will not permit access to it, by leaving a copy of the claim form with that person;

(3) where the property has been sold by the Marshal, by filing the claim form at the court;

(4) where there is a notice against arrest, on the person named in the notice as being authorised to accept service;

(5) on any solicitor authorised to accept service;

(6) in accordance with any agreement providing for service of proceedings; or

(7) in any other manner as the court may direct under rule 6.15 provided that the property against which the claim is brought or part of it is within the jurisdiction of the court.

3.7 In claims where the property—

(1) is to be arrested; or

(2) is already under arrest in current proceedings,

the Marshal will serve the in rem claim form if the claimant requests the court to do so.

3.8 In all other cases in rem claim forms must be served by the claimant.

3.9 Where the defendants are described and not named on the claim form (for example as "the Owners of the Ship X"), any acknowledgment of service in addition to stating that description must also state the full names of the persons acknowledging service and the nature of their ownership.

3.10 After the acknowledgment of service has been filed, the claim will follow the procedure applicable to a claim proceeding in the Commercial list except that the claimant is allowed 75 days to serve the particulars of claim.

3.11 A defendant who files an acknowledgment of service to an in rem claim does not lose any right he may have to dispute the jurisdiction of the court (see rule 10.1(3)(b) and Part 11).

3.12 Any person who pays the prescribed fee may, during office hours, search for, inspect and take a copy of any claim form in rem whether or not it has been served.

Amendment of claim form

Where after the issue of a claim in an action *in rem* the defendants' vessel is sold, the title of the defendants should be amended to read "The Owners of the ship X, now named Y" (*The Mawan* [1988] 2 Lloyd's Rep. 459 at 460.) **2D–93**

Paragraph 61.3.6(3)

The property must have been sold by the court and part of the proceeds of sale must still be in court. Where property has been sold by an agent who retains the proceeds, a claim form cannot be served on those proceeds (*The Optima* (1905) 74 L.T.P. 94; *The Fornjot* (1907) 24 T.L.R. 26). In *The Eva* (1950) 84 Ll.L.R. 20 wartime compensation money was held not to be a *res* or represent a *res*. **2D–94**

Paragraph numbers marked with a "+" can be found online and on CD.

61.4 Collision claims

2D–95   **4.1** A collision statement of case must be in Form **ADM3**.

4.2 A collision statement of case must contain—

(1) in Part 1 of the form, answers to the questions set out in that Part; and

(2) in Part 2 of the form, a statement—

(a) of any other facts and matters on which the party filing the collision statement of case relies;

(b) of all allegations of negligence or other fault which the party filing the collision statement of case makes; and

(c) of the remedy which the party filing the collision statement of case claims.

4.3 When he files his collision statement of case each party must give notice to every other party that he has done so.

4.4 Within 14 days after the last collision statement of case is filed each party must serve a copy of his collision statement of case on every other party.

4.5 Before the coming into force of Part 61, a collision statement of case was known as a Preliminary Act and the law relating to Preliminary Acts will continue to apply to collision statements of case.

61.5 Arrest

2D–96   **5.1** An application for arrest must be—

(1) in Form **ADM4** (which must also contain an undertaking); and

(2) accompanied by a declaration in Form **ADM5**.

5.2 When it receives an application for arrest that complies with the rules and the practice direction the court will issue an arrest warrant.

5.3 The declaration required by rule 61.5(3)(b) must be verified by a statement of truth and must state—

(1) in every claim–

(a) the nature of the claim or counterclaim and that it has not been satisfied and if it arises in connection with a ship, the name of that ship;

(b) the nature of the property to be arrested and, if the property is a ship, the name of the ship and her port of registry; and

(c) the amount of the security sought, if any.

(2) in a claim against a ship by virtue of section 21(4) of the Supreme Court Act 1981—

(a) the name of the person who would be liable on the claim if it were not commenced in rem;

(b) that the person referred to in sub-paragraph (a) was, when the right to bring the claim arose

(i) the owner or charterer of; or

(ii) in possession or in control of,

the ship in connection with which the claim arose; and

(c) that at the time the claim form was issued the person referred to in sub-paragraph (a) was either—

Paragraph numbers marked with a "+" can be found online and on CD.

(i) the beneficial owner of all the shares in the ship in respect of which the warrant is required; or

(ii) the charterer of it under a charter by demise;

(3) in the cases set out in rules 61.5(5) and (6) that the relevant notice has been sent or served, as appropriate; and

(4) in the case of a claim in respect of liability incurred under section 153 of the Merchant Shipping Act 1995, the facts relied on as establishing that the court is not prevented from considering the claim by reason of section 166(2) of that Act.

5.4 The notice required by rule 61.5(5)(a) must be in Form **ADM6**.

5.5 Property is arrested—

(1) by service on it of an arrest warrant in Form **ADM9** in the manner set out at paragraph 3.6(1); or

(2) where it is not reasonably practicable to serve the warrant, by service of a notice of the issue of the warrant—

(a) in the manner set out in paragraph 3.6(1) on the property; or

(b) by giving notice to those in charge of the property.

5.6 When property is arrested the Registrar will issue standard directions in Form **ADM10**.

5.7 The Marshal does not insure property under arrest.

Specific Applications

An application to move a vessel under arrest (see r.61.5(9)) or to sell the same below the appraised value are made to the Admiralty Registrar or as he may direct. **2D–97**

As to the practice to be followed by the Marshal when a ship is under arrest and a harbour or dock authority claims or purports to exercise a statutory power of detention or sale in respect of unpaid dock dues, see *The Queen of the South* [1968] P. 449; [1968] 1 All E.R. 1163; [1968] 1 Lloyd's Rep. 182 and *The Freightline One* [1986] 1 Lloyd's Rep. 266. In *The Girl Irene* [1991] Fo. 774, the court directed that the Marshal was to follow the same practice in respect of a claim by Trinity House for unpaid light dues. Where some doubt arises as to the right of a harbour or dock authority to detain a ship, that authority should seek a declaration from the court (*The Baltico* (1982) H. No. 140. Hartlepool District Registry).

Mooring charges do not constitute "ship dues" within the meaning of s.26(3) of the Harbours Act 1964 and as defined by s.57(1) of the 1964 Act. Accordingly there is no power to distrain for non-payment of mooring charges under s.44 of the Harbours, Docks and Piers Clauses Act 1847: see *R. v Carrick DC Ex p. Prankerd (The Winnie Rigg)* [1998] 2 Lloyd's Rep. 675; [1999] Q.B. 1119.

As to applications to discharge cargo where ship or cargo is under arrest, see r.61.8(8) and (9).

Applications under r.61.5(4) and (6) are made without notice to the Admiralty Registrar.

Insurance premiums

Premiums paid by claimants to insure their interest in arrested property were held in *The Fairport* [1965] 2 Lloyd's Rep. 183 at 186, to be recoverable as costs but not to constitute a head of claim under AJA 1956 s.1 (see now SCA 1981 s.20). **2D–98**

Insurance of arrested property

Section N13 of the Admiralty and Commercial Courts Guide provides as follows: **2D–99**

N13.1 The Marshal will not insure any arrested property for the benefit of parties at any time during the period of arrest (whether before or after the lodging of an application for sale, if any).

N13.2 The Marshal will use his best endeavours (but without any legal liability for

Paragraph numbers marked with a "+" can be found online and on CD.

failure to do so) to advise all parties known to him as being on the record in actions in rem against the arrested property, including those who have filed cautions against release of that property, before any such property moves or is moved beyond the area covered by the usual port risks policy.

N13.3 In these circumstances, practitioners' attention is drawn to the necessity of considering the questions of insuring against port risks for the amount of their clients' interest in any property arrested in an Admiralty action and the inclusion in any policy of a "Held Covered "clause in case the ship moves or is moved outside the area covered by the usual port risks policy. The usual port risks policy provides, among other things, for a ship to be moved or towed from one berth to another up to a distance of five miles within the port where she is lying.

Declarations

2D–100   As to the contents of these declarations see PD 61 para.61.5.3 above.

Para.61.5.3 "... her port of registry ..."

2D–101   The object of this requirement is to minimise the risk of the arrest of a different ship bearing the same name as the ship intended to be arrested. If the port of registry is not known this should be stated in the declaration.

Practice

2D–102   The declaration, warrant and a copy of it are taken to or transmitted to the Admiralty and Commercial Registry and a search of the Register requested. A clerk in the Registry will search the Register and inform the applicant whether a caution against arrest of the property is in force. If there is no caution against arrest in force or if it is desired to issue a warrant despite the existence of a caution, the declaration is filed and the warrant and copy lodged. The proper officer, if he is satisfied that the declaration complies with the requirements of this rule (or if permission to issue despite non-compliance has been given) will issue the warrant. The warrant and copy are retained in the Registry.

False or inaccurate statement in declaration to lead warrant of arrest

2D–103   If the statutory requirements set out in para.61.5.3 are complied with then there is no further scope for the application of any duty of full and frank disclosure see *The Varna* [1993] 2 Lloyd's Rep. 253 but as to such statutory requirements it is the duty of a declarant to correct promptly and frankly any false or inaccurate statement that he finds he has made in his declaration (*The Nordglimt* [1988] Q.B. 183; [1987] 2 Lloyd's Rep. 470).

61.7 Cautions against arrest

2D–104   **6.1** The entry of a caution against arrest is not treated as a submission to the jurisdiction of the court.

6.2 The request for a caution against arrest must be in form **ADM7**.

6.3 On the filing of such a request, a caution against arrest will be entered in the Register.

6.4 The Register is open for inspection when the Admiralty and Commercial Registry is open.

Para.61.6.2 and 3 "... the Register..."

2D–105   There is only one book in which all cautions in Admiralty are entered; it is kept in the Admiralty and Commercial Registry at the Royal Courts of Justice in London where all cautions must be entered. As to cautions against arrest see r.61.7 and against release see r.61.8. As to searches see r.61.5 and PD 61 para.6.4.

61.8 Release and cautions against release

2D–106   **7.1** The request for a caution against release must be in Form **ADM11**.

7.2 On the filing of such a request, a caution against release will be entered in the Register.

Paragraph numbers marked with a "+" can be found online and on CD.

7.3 The Register is open for inspection when the Admiralty and Commercial Registry is open.

7.4 A request for release under rule 61.8(4)(c) and (d) must be in Form **ADM12**.

7.5 A withdrawal of a caution against release must be in form **ADM12A**.

Application to secure release

In cases where an applicant wishes to secure release of his property whether held at the instance of the arrestor or any person who has entered a caution, the procedure in the Admiralty and Commercial Registry will be as set out below. The purpose of this procedure is to arrange that such an application is dealt with by the tribunal likely to be able to dispose of it most expeditiously and cheaply.   **2D–107**

(1) The application notice should be issued normally before the Registrar with the date left blank.

(2) The applicant should attend at the Admiralty and Commercial Registry upon the issue of the application notice for the purpose of obtaining a direction by the Registrar as to whether the application will be heard before the Registrar or before the judge. Unless there is attendance at the Registry the application will be issued before the Registrar.

(3) The applicant attending upon the issue of the application notice should, if it is desired that the application be heard initially by the judge, be prepared to indicate orally why the application is more suitable for the judge than the Registrar (e.g. substantial savings in costs or time would normally be reasons militating in favour of initial hearing by the judge).

(4) A direction as to the hearing will normally be given forthwith and date and time set for the hearing.

Release of vessels out of hours

Section N11 of the Admiralty and Commercial Courts Guide provides as follows: **2D–108**

N11.1 This section makes provision for release from arrest when the Registry is closed.

N11.2 An application for release under rule 61.8(4)(c) or (d) may, when the Registry is closed, be made in, and only in, the following manner:

(i) The solicitor for the arrestor or the other party applying must telephone the security staff at the Royal Courts of Justice (020 7947 6260) and ask to be contacted by the Admiralty Marshal, who will then respond as soon as practicably possible;

(ii) Upon being contacted by the Admiralty Marshal the solicitor must give oral instructions for the release and an oral undertaking to pay the fees and expenses of the Admiralty Marshal as required in Form **ADM12**;

(iii) The arrestor or other party applying must then send a written request and undertaking on Form **ADM12** by fax to a number given by the Admiralty Marshal;

(iv) The solicitor must provide written consent to the release from all persons who have entered cautions against release (and from the arrestor if the arrestor is not the party applying) by sending such consents by fax to the number supplied by the Admiralty Marshal;

(v) Upon the Admiralty Marshal being satisfied that no cautions against release are in force, or that all persons who have entered cautions against release, and if necessary the arrestor, have given their written consent to the release, the Admiralty Marshal shall effect the release as soon as practicable.

N11.3 Practitioners should note that the Admiralty Marshal is not formally on call and therefore at times may not be available to assist. Similarly the practicalities of releasing a ship in some localities may involve the services of others who may not be available outside court hours.

N11.4 This service is offered to practitioners for use during reasonable hours and on the basis that if the Admiralty Marshal is available and can be contacted he will use his best endeavours to effect instructions to release but without guarantee as to their success.

Paragraph numbers marked with a "+" can be found online and on CD.

Withdrawal of cautions

2D–109   A caution against release may be withdrawn by lodging a written request in Form **ADM12A** (see para.7.5 above). Where a solicitor acts for more than one cautioner and wishes to withdraw some or all of their cautions, this may be done by a single request, adapted as necessary.

"... the Register..."

2D–110   See under para. 2D–105 above.

61.9 Judgment in default

2D–111   **8.1** An application notice for judgment in default must be in form **ADM13**.

61.10 Sale by the court and priorities

2D–112   **9.1** Any application to the court concerning–

(1) the sale of the property under arrest; or

(2) the proceeds of sale of property sold by the court

will be heard in public and the application notice served on–

(a) all parties to the claim;

(b) all persons who have requested cautions against release with regard to the property or the proceeds of sale; and

(c) the Marshal.

9.2 Unless the court orders otherwise an order for sale will be in form **ADM14**.

9.3 An order for sale before judgment may only be made by the Admiralty judge.

9.4 Unless the Admiralty judge orders otherwise, a determination of priorities may only be made by the Admiralty judge.

9.5 When—

(1) proceeds of sale are paid into court by the Marshal; and

(2) such proceeds are in a foreign currency,

the funds will be placed on one day call interest bearing account unless the court orders otherwise.

9.6 Unless made at the same time as an application for sale, or other prior application, an application to place foreign currency on longer term deposit may be made to the Registrar.

9.7 Notice of the placement of foreign currency in an interest bearing account must be given to all parties interested in the fund by the party who made the application under paragraph 9.6.

9.8 Any interested party who wishes to object to the mode of investment of foreign currency paid into court may apply to the Registrar for directions.

Court Fees on Sale

2D–113   On the sale of a ship or goods —

Subject to a minimum fee of £200,

(a) for every £100 or fraction of £100 of the price up to £100,000..   £1

(b) for every £100 or fraction of £100 of the price exceeding £100,000..   50p

Paragraph numbers marked with a "+" can be found online and on CD.

Where there is sufficient proceeds of sale in court, fee 5.2 shall be taken by transfer from the proceeds of sale in court.

(See item 5.2 of Supreme Court Fees Order 1999, as amended). For other related charges see paras 2D–140 and 2D–141 below.

61.11 Limitation claims

10.1 The claim form in a limitation claim must be—   **2D–114**

(1) in form **ADM15**; and

(2) accompanied by a declaration—

    (a) setting out the facts upon which the claimant relies; and

    (b) stating the names and addresses (if known) of all persons who, to the knowledge of the claimant, have claims against him in respect of the occurrence to which the claim relates (other than named defendants),

    verified by a statement of truth.

10.2 A defence to a limitation claim must be in form **ADM16A**.

10.3 A notice admitting the right of the claimant to limit liability in a limitation claim must be in form **ADM16**.

10.4 An acknowledgment of service in a limitation claim must be in form **ADM16B**.

10.5 An application for a restricted limitation decree must be in form **ADM17** and the decree issued by the court on such an application must be in form **ADM18**.

10.6 An application for a general limitation decree must be in form **ADM17A**.

10.7 Where—

(1) the right to limit is not admitted; and

(2) the claimant seeks a general limitation decree in form **ADM17A**,

the claimant must, within 7 days after the date of the filing of the defence of the defendant last served or the expiry of the time for doing so, apply for an appointment before the Registrar for a case management conference.

10.8 On an application under rule 61.11(12) the Registrar may—

(1) grant a general limitation decree; or

(2) if he does not grant a decree—

    (a) order service of a defence;

    (b) order disclosure by the claimant; or

    (c) make such other case management directions as may be appropriate.

10.9 The fact that a limitation fund has lapsed under rule 61.11(20)(a) does not prevent the establishment of a new fund.

10.10 Where a limitation fund is established, it must be—

(1) the sterling equivalent of the number of special drawing rights to which [the claimant] claims to be entitled to limit his liability under the Merchant Shipping Act 1995; together with

(2) interest from the date of the occurrence giving rise to his liability to the date of payment into court.

Paragraph numbers marked with a "+" can be found online and on CD.

10.11 Where the claimant does not know the sterling equivalent referred to in paragraph 10.10(1) on the date of payment into court he may—

(1) calculate it on the basis of the latest available published sterling equivalent of a special drawing right as fixed by the International Monetary Fund; and

(2) in the event of the sterling equivalent of a special drawing right on the date of payment into court being different from that used for calculating the amount of that payment into court the claimant may—

(a) make up any deficiency by making a further payment into court which, if made within 14 days after the payment into court, will be treated, except for the purpose of the rules relating to the accrual of interest on money paid into court, as if made on the date of that payment into court; or

(b) apply to the court for payment out of any excess amount (together with any interest accrued) paid into court.

10.12 An application under paragraph 10.11(2)(b)—

(1) may be made without notice to any party; and

(2) must be supported by evidence proving, to the satisfaction of the court, the sterling equivalent of the appropriate number of special drawing rights on the date of payment into court.

10.13 The claimant must give notice in writing to every named defendant of—

(1) any payment into court specifying—

(a) the date of the payment in;

(b) the amount paid in;

(c) the amount and rate of interest included; and

(d) the period to which it relates; and

(2) any excess amount (and interest) paid out to him under paragraph 10.11(2)(b).

10.14 A claim against the fund must be in form **ADM20**.

10.15 A defendant's statement of case filed and served in accordance with rule 61.11(15) must contain particulars of the defendant's claim.

10.16 Any defendant who is unable to file and serve a statement of case in accordance with rule 61.11(15) and paragraph 10.15 must file a declaration, verified by a statement of truth, in form **ADM21** stating the reason for his inability.

10.17 No later than 7 days after the time for filing claims [or declarations], the Registrar will fix a date for a case management conference at which directions will be given for the further conduct of the proceedings.

10.18 Nothing in rule 61.11 prevents limitation being relied on by way of defence.

Limitation fund and interest

2D–115   Any person wishing to constitute a limitation fund must pay into court a fund con-

Paragraph numbers marked with a "+" can be found online and on CD.

stituted in accordance with s.185 and Sch.7 to the Merchant Shipping Act 1995, together with interest thereon from the date of the occurrence giving rise to his liability until the date of the constitution of the limitation fund pursuant to para.8(1) of Pt II of Sch.7 to the Act. The rate of interest is now fixed by the Merchant Shipping (Liability of Shipowners and Others) (Rate of Interest) Order 1999 (SI 1999/1922), effective September 1, 1999; by the Merchant Shipping (Liability of Shipowners and Others) (Rate of Interest) (Amendment) Order 2003 (SI 2003/3136) effective December 31, 2003 and the Merchant Shipping (Liability of Shipowners and Others) (New Rate of Interest) Order 2004 (SI 2004/931) effective April 28, 2004.

The rate of interest is:
  (a) where the occurrence takes place before September 1, 1999 but the fund is constituted on or after that date:
     (i) 12 per cent from the date of the occurrence until December 31, 1994;
     (ii) 6.75 per cent on and after January 1, 1995 until August 31, 1998;
     (iii) 8.5 per cent on and after September 1, 1998 until August 31, 1999, and
     (iv) the prescribed rate on and after September 1, 1999, until December 30, 2003; or
  (b) where the occurrence takes place on or after September 1, 1999, but before December 31, 2003 the prescribed rate.

Further, art.2 of SI 2003/3136 provides as follows:
"2. The rate of interest for the purposes of article 11(1) of the Convention on Limitation of Liability for Maritime Claims 1976 (b) shall be the prescribed rate—
     (a) where the occurrence takes place before 31st December 2003, but the fund is constituted on or after that date; and
     (b) where the occurrence takes place on or after 31st December 2003".

The prescribed rate is defined as one per cent more than the base rate quoted from time to time by the Bank of England or the rate of interest set by any body which may supersede it and, where there is for the time being more than one such rate, the lowest of them (art.2 of the SI 2004/931).

Tonnage

2D–116

The limitation tonnage is usually proved in the case of a British registered ship by a certified copy of the Tonnage Certificate. As to the tonnage of ships of a foreign country which has adopted the British tonnage regulations, see Merchant Shipping Act 1995 s.12. For a list of these countries see *British Shipping Laws*, Vol.11, under s.84 of the Merchant Shipping Act 1894, now s.12 of the 1995 Act. See too the Merchant Shipping (Liability of Shipowners and Others) (Calculation of Tonnage) Order 1986 (SI 1986/1040); the Merchant Shipping (Tonnage) Regulations 1997 (SI 1997/1510) and the Merchant Shipping (Tonnage) (Fishing Vessels) Amendment Regulations 1998 (SI 1998/1916).

Sterling equivalents

2D–117

For ascertainment of sterling equivalents, see Sch.7, Pt II, para.7 to the Merchant Shipping Act 1995.

Paras 10.8 and 10.17 "... directions ..."

2D–118

An order will usually be made providing for statements of case, disclosure, and any other directions deemed necessary and the imposition of a set timetable for expeditious disposal of the matter.

Proceeding against or concerning the International Oil Pollution Compensation Fund 1992 and the International Oil Pollution Supplementary Fund

2D–119

11.1 For the purposes of section 177 of the Merchant Shipping Act 1995 ('the Act'), the Fund may be given notice of proceedings by any party to a claim against an owner or guarantor in respect of liability under section 153 of the Act by that person serving a notice in writ-

Paragraph numbers marked with a "+" can be found online and on CD.

ing on the Fund together with copies of the claim form and any statements of case served in the claim.

11.2 Notice given to the Fund under paragraph 11.1 shall be deemed to have been given to the Supplementary Fund.

11.3 The Fund or the Supplementary Fund may intervene in any claim to which paragraph 11.1 applies, (whether or not served with the notice), by serving notice of intervention on the—

(1) owner;

(2) guarantor; and

(3) court.

11.4 Where a judgment is given against—

(1) the Fund in any claim under section 175 of the Act;

(2) the Supplementary Fund in any claim under section 176A of the Act,

the Registrar will arrange for a stamped copy of the judgment to be sent by post to—

(a) the Fund (where paragraph (1) applies);

(b) the Supplementary Fund (where paragraph (2) applies).

11.5 Notice to the Registrar of the matters set out in—

(1) section 176(3)(b) of the Act in proceedings under section 175; or

(2) section 176B(2)(b) of the Act in proceedings under section 176A, must be given in writing and sent to the court by—

(a) the Fund (where paragraph (1) applies);

(b) the Supplementary Fund (where paragraph (2) applies).

Pollution damage

2D–120   A claim by fish processors for the loss of profitable sales of processed whelks held to be secondary, derivative, relational and/or indirect, lacking in proximity and thus too remote. The "Sea Empress", [2002] EWHC 1095 (Admiralty); [2002] 2 All E.R. (Comm) 416; [2003] 1 Lloyd's Rep. 123, applying *Landcatch Ltd v The International Oil Pollution Compensation Fund* [1999] 2 Lloyd's Rep. 316; affirmed [2003] EWCA Civ 65 [2003] 2 All E.R. (Comm.) 1; [2003] 1 Lloyd's Rep 327, CA.

Other claims

2D–121   **12.1** This section applies to admiralty claims which, before the coming into force of Part 61, would have been called claims in personam. Subject to the provisions of Part 61 and this practice direction relating to limitation claims and to collision claims, the following provisions apply to such claims.

12.2 All such claims will proceed in accordance with Part 58 (Commercial Court).

12.3 The claim form must be in Form **ADM1A** and must be served by the claimant.

12.4 The claimant may be named or may be described, but if not named in the claim form must identify himself by name if requested to do so by any other party.

12.5 The defendant must be named in the claim form.

12.6 Any person who files a defence must identify himself by name in the defence.

Paragraph numbers marked with a "+" can be found online and on CD.

Claims in personam (now called other claims)

An Admiralty action *in personam* is like an action in tort or contract in the QBD. It **2D–122** differs from such an action however in that it is subject to the rules of this order which modify those applicable to an ordinary QB action, e.g. collision cases, r.61.4 and the application of Pt 58 thereto unless inconsistent with Pt 61 and this practice direction.

Duration of Admiralty Claim in personam (other claims) for service out of the jurisdiction

The period of validity of a claim form *in personam* in admiralty proceedings for ser- **2D–123** vice out of the jurisdiction is six months.

References to the Registrar

13.1 The court may at any stage in the claim refer any question or **2D–124** issue for determination by the Registrar (a "reference").

13.2 Unless the court orders otherwise, where a reference has been ordered—

(1) if particulars of claim have not already been served, the claim- ant must file and serve particulars of claim on all other parties within 14 days after the date of the order; and

(2) any party opposing the claim must file a defence to the claim within 14 days after service of the particulars of claim on him.

13.3 Within 7 days after the defence is filed, the claimant must ap- ply for an appointment before the Registrar for a case management conference.

General note

It is the long-established practice of the Admiralty Court after liability has been **2D–125** determined, to refer to the Admiralty Registrar the matter of the assessment of the amount of the claimant's claim and of the counterclaim if there be one. There is, however, no rule that the assessment of damages must be referred (*The Fremantle* [1954] 2 Lloyd's Rep. 20) and in personal injury and Fatal Accidents Acts cases it is not unusual for the judge to assess damages. See, e.g. *Connell v Hellyer Brothers Ltd* [1963] 2 Lloyd's Rep. 249; *The St Chad (No.2)* [1965] 2 Lloyd's Rep. 347.

Questions of amount have occasionally been referred before trial. See, e.g. *The Happy Return* (1828) 2 Hagg. 198 at 207 but this has not been done for many years. In *The Lathara* (1930) 37 Ll.L.Rep. 160, it seems that all issues in the claim were referred to the Registrar.

Where the assessment of damages involves a question of causation this is in some cases decided by the judge at the trial or thereafter. See, e.g. *The Maid of Kent* (1881) 6 P.D. 178, *The Guildford* [1956] 2 Lloyd's Rep. 74; *The Lucile Bloomfield* [1967] 2 Lloyd's Rep. 308. If it is desired to have such questions decided by the judge at the trial this matter should be raised on the case management conference. In exercising its discre- tion the court will be guided by the consideration whether the matter is one which can better be dealt with by the court at the trial, or later at the reference (*The Maid of Kent* (1881) 6 P.D. 178, *ibid.*).

Assessors

In modern practice the Registrar decides questions without the assistance of **2D–126** merchants. Nautical and other assessors, however, are sometimes appointed. If the parties agree in desiring the Registrar to sit with a merchant (the full title is "merchant assessor") or other assessor, they should apply by letter to the Admiralty and Com- mercial Registry. In the event of disagreement between the parties an application should be made on notice.

How references may rise

A reference may arise out of the judgment or decree made on the trial or the hear- **2D–127** ing of an application; out of the decree in a limitation claim made on the hearing of an application under r.61.11, or an order on a consent application.

Paragraph numbers marked with a "+" can be found online and on CD.

Where in an action *in personam* (other claim) judgment in default is entered "for an amount of money to be decided by the court" there can be no reference and the assessment is governed by CPR r.12.7.

Claim in reference. See para.13.2 above

2D–128   The claim referred to in this provision should in the first place state in a few words how the claim arises; thus in a collision claim it would begin with a short statement giving the date of the collision, the voyage on which the vessel was engaged, and, if she was repaired, the place and date and duration of such repair. In every case the several heads of claim should then be set out and numbered consecutively. It is not correct and is confusing, to call the claim a statement of case. It is a claim in a reference. For content and format of forms of claim see *Atkin's Encyclopaedia of Court Forms in Civil Proceedings*, Vol.3, Form 181 (2003 Issue).

Limitation references

2D–129   In references in limitation claim a claimant need not serve a copy of his claim on any other party. Any claimant may, however, on the payment of the proper fee, inspect and obtain a copy of the claim and any other documents filed by any other claimant against the fund. See CPR r.5.4(1). In practice copies of these documents are supplied on request by the solicitors concerned on payment of the usual copying charges.

If any claimant wishes to dispute the claim of another he should so inform the Admiralty and Commercial Registry by letter in order that he can be given notice of the appointment fixed for the hearing of that other's claim.

In a claim arising out of a collision between ships A and B if there are cross claims and both ships have been held to blame (or the matter has been settled on a both to blame basis) and the owners of A obtain a limitation decree it may be necessary to assess their claim in order to arrive at the amount which the owners of B are entitled to claim against the fund. It will be necessary to do this if there are other claimants against the fund. See *The Stoom vart Maatschappf Nederland v The Peninsular and Oriental Steam Navigation Co* (1882) 7 App. Cas. 795. In this event the practice is for the owners of B to put forward in their claim a deduction in respect of the appropriate proportion of the damages of the owners of A as agreed or, failing agreement, estimated. This figure may be disputed by any other claimant.

Filing amended claims

2D–130   A claimant should not amend his filed claim but should file another claim in amended form. No leave is required. If, however, the alterations are of such a character and are made at such a late stage as to embarrass the paying party at the reference, the Registrar may, in his discretion, adjourn the reference or take some other course as he thinks fit.

Evidence

2D–131   The ordinary rules of evidence apply on the hearing of a reference but are, by agreement between the parties, frequently relaxed in order to save time and expense.

Proved recoverable amount

2D–132   The convention of awarding one per cent of proved recoverable amount to compensate for disruption to business and expenditure of management available to shipowners does not extend to cargo owners (*Owners of the Ship Kumanovo v Owners of the Ship Massira* [1998] 2 Lloyd's Rep. 301). The convention itself was re-affirmed in *"The Charlotte C"* [2005] 2 Lloyd's Rep. 626.

Hearing; general note

2D–133   A party to a reference may be represented by counsel, solicitor, legal executive or solicitor's clerk.

If a sum has been paid into court and the award is less than the amount paid in, the party who made the payment in is entitled to an order enabling him to take the balance out of court (*The Mona* [1894] P. 265).

Inquiry regarding a shorthand record at references may be made of the Registry.

Paragraph numbers marked with a "+" can be found online and on CD.

Delay; interest

See *The Nassau* [1965] 1 Lloyd's Rep. 236 and cases cited. **2D–134**

Interest: date for addition

On compromising an Admiralty claim for collision damages interest should be **2D–135** added to each claim before striking the balance, such balance to be struck on the date of assessment or of agreement of claims; see *The Lu Shan* [1993] 2 Lloyd's Rep. 259.

Interest in personal injury and fatal accident cases

See SCA 1981 s.35A (see para.9A–122 below). **2D–136**

Costs of reference

The costs of the reference are in the Registrar's discretion. Where two vessels are **2D–137** held to blame in a collision claim the costs in the reference of each claimant are dealt with on the basis of the reference being a separate proceeding from the claim (*The Consett* (1880) 5 P.D. 77). As to the effect of failure to give notice of survey, see *The Solace (No.2)* (1936) 55 Ll.L.Rep. 201. Usually where the claimant recovers a substantial proportion of the sum claimed he is given the costs of the reference, and where an offer has been made and the amount awarded in the reference is less, the offeror will usually be entitled to the costs after the offer was made (see *The Norseman* [1957] 1 Lloyd's Rep. 503; *The Reading* [1908] P. 162). If one claimant in a reference in a limitation claim puts forward a claim which is contested successfully by another, the former may be condemned to pay the costs of the successful claimant in contesting the claim, i.e. the costs over and above those of proving his own claim (*The Clan Canning* [1906] Fo. 206).

Undertakings

14.1 Where, in [Part 61] or this practice direction, any undertak- **2D–138** ing to the Marshal is required it must be given—

(1) in writing and to his satisfaction; or

(2) in accordance with such other arrangements as he may require.

14.2 Where any party is dissatisfied with a direction given by the Marshal in this respect he may apply to the Registrar for a ruling.

Note

The personal undertaking of the party's solicitor is normally given. Where the ex- **2D–139** penses of effecting or maintaining the arrest are more than minimal, successive demands are likely to be made by the Marshal beginning soon after the arrest.

As to recovery from the proceeds of sale of sums paid to the Marshal by an arresting party, see *The Falcon* [1981] 1 Lloyd's Rep. 13. The Marshal's expenses of maintaining the arrest from the time of the order for appraisement and sale and the expenses of the sale are payable in the first instance by the party applying therefor. *The Falcon* [1981] 1 Lloyd's Rep. 13, above at 17. As to liability for the expenses of a second and subsequent arrests see *ibid*. As to recovery from the proceeds of sale of sums paid to the Marshal, insurance premiums, solicitors' costs of arrest, etc., crew's wages, interveners' costs and interest, see *The World Star* [1987] 1 Lloyd's Rep. 452.

For priorities and the method of determining the same see *British Shipping Laws*, Vol.1, para.1574, *The Falcon* [1981] 1 Lloyd's Rep. 13, above. *The World Star* [1987] 1 Lloyd's Rep. 452, above, and *The Rubi Sea* [1992] 1 Lloyd's Rep. 634.

The fees and commission paid by the Marshal to Brokers in addition to their reasonable expenses for carrying out a Judicial sale of a vessel are as follows:

Scale of valuation fees as from May 25, 1998

Not exceeding £20,000: £200 **2D–140**

Exceeding £20,000: £400

Where the condition of the ship and/or the state of the market make it advisable that there should be a dual valuation for both trading and demolition purposes the full fee will apply in respect of the valuation for trading and in addition a fee at half the above rates will apply in respect of the valuation for demolition.

Paragraph numbers marked with a "+" can be found online and on CD.

Scale of Commission as from May 25, 1998

2D–141

6 per cent on the first £5,000

5 per cent on the next £10,000 up to £15,000

3 per cent on the next £15,000 up to £30,000

1 per cent on the balance over £30,000.

OTHER ADMIRALTY PRACTICE DIRECTIONS AND STATEMENTS

REMUNERATION OF NAUTICAL AND OTHER ASSESSORS PRACTICE DIRECTION [1994] 1 W.L.R. 599

2D–142 See now CPR, r.35.13. The *Remuneration of Nautical and Other Assessors Practice Direction* [1994] 1 W.L.R. 599 has been revoked by Practice Direction (Admiralty: Assessors' Renumeration) QBD, [2007] 1 W.L.R. 2508. The following guidance has been given as to the level of renumeration which should normally be paid:

(1) Full day's attendance at hearing: £600

(2) Half-day's attendance at hearing: £300

(3) Attendance at court when case is not heard: £80 per hour

(4) Consultation with the court on a day when there is no hearing: £300

(5) Attendance to hear reserved judgment (including any consultation with the court on the same day): £150

(6) If notice of attendance is countermanded less than 2 days before the hearing: £300

and as before:

(1) Assessors should receive reasonable sums for their travelling expenses and subsistence.

(2) Where there is a cross appeal, or where appeals are heard together, or where actions are consolidated or tried together, the proceedings should be treated as one appeal or action as the case may be.

(3) In the absence of special directions given in a particular case, the remuneration and expenses should be paid by the appellant or the party setting down the action as the case may be without prejudice to any right to recover from any other party the amount so paid on taxation.

Paragraph numbers marked with a "+" can be found online and on CD.

USE OF CLAIM FORMS IN REM AND IN PERSONAM/OTHER CLAIMS

If it is desired to commence proceedings both *in rem* and *in personam* **2D–143** separate claim forms must be issued.

See Practice Direction (Admiralty: [Claim Form]) [1979] 1 W.L.R. 426; [1979] 2 All E.R. 155.

TAXATION OF COSTS

At the request of the Admiralty Registrar, all costs [other than **2D–144** those summarily assessed] in Admiralty matters will be taxed in the Supreme Court Taxing Office.

Practice Direction (Admiralty Taxation of Costs) [1986] 1 W.L.R. 1310.

Supreme Court Act 1981

(1981 c.54)   **2D–145**

ARRANGEMENT OF SECTIONS

PART II

JURISDICTION

ADMIRALTY JURISDICTION

Introductory note

Sections 20–24 of this Act replace with amendments AJA 1956 ss.1 and 3–8 as **2D–146** amended. These sections were repealed by s.152 of and Sch.7 to this Act. Section 2 had been repealed by the Courts Act 1971 Sch.11. Amendments to ss.20–24 have been made from time to time and latterly by and consequent upon the Merchant Shipping Act 1995 which came into force on January 1, 1996.

The 1956 Act had replaced s.22 of the Judicature Act 1925 and extended the Admiralty jurisdiction to give effect to much of the International Convention Relating to the Arrest of Seagoing Ships and the International Convention on Certain Rules concerning Civil Jurisdiction in Matters of Collision both of which were signed at Brussels on May 10, 1952. See British Shipping Laws (Singh, International Maritime Law Conventions (1983)) for the texts of these conventions.

Paragraph numbers marked with a "+" can be found online and on CD.

Part II

Jurisdiction

Admiralty jurisdiction

Admiralty jurisdiction of High Court

2D–147   **20.**—(1) The Admiralty jurisdiction of the High Court shall be as follows, that is to say—

(a) jurisdiction to hear and determine any of the questions and claims mentioned in subsection (2);

(b) jurisdiction in relation to any of the proceedings mentioned in subsection (3);

(c) any other Admiralty jurisdiction which it had immediately before the commencement of this Act; and

(d) any jurisdiction connected with ships or aircraft which is vested in the High Court apart from this section and is for the time being by rules of court made or coming into force after the commencement of this Act assigned to the Queen's Bench Division and directed by the rules to be exercised by the Admiralty Court.

(2) The questions and claims referred to in subsection (1)(a) are—

(a) any claim to the possession or ownership of a ship or to the ownership of any share therein;

(b) any question arising between the co-owners of a ship as to possession, employment or earnings of that ship;

(c) any claim in respect of a mortgage of or charge on a ship or any share therein;

(d) any claim for damage received by a ship;

(e) any claim for damage done by a ship;

(f) any claim for loss of life or personal injury sustained in consequence of any defect in a ship or in her apparel or equipment, or in consequence of the wrongful act, neglect or default of—

(i) the owners, charterers or persons in possession or control of a ship; or

(ii) the master or crew of a ship, or any other person for whose wrongful acts, neglects or defaults the owners, charterers or persons in possession or control of a ship are responsible.

being an act, neglect or default in the navigation or management of a ship, in the loading, carriage or discharge of goods on, in or from the ship, or in the embarkation, carriage or disembarkation of persons on, in or from the ship;

(g) any claim for loss of or damage to goods carried in a ship;

(h) any claim arising out of any agreement relating to the

Paragraph numbers marked with a "+" can be found online and on CD.

carriage of goods in a ship or to the use or hire of a ship;

(j) any claim—

   (i) under the Salvage Convention 1989;

   (ii) under any contract for or in relation to salvage services; or

   (iii) in the nature of salvage not falling within (i) or (ii) above;

or any corresponding claim in connection with an aircraft.

(k) any claim in the nature of towage in respect of a ship or an aircraft;

(l) any claim in the nature of pilotage in respect of a ship or an aircraft;

(m) any claim in respect of goods or materials supplied to a ship for her operation or maintenance;

(n) any claim in respect of the construction, repair or equipment of a ship or dock charges or dues;

(o) any claim by a master or member of the crew of a ship for wages (including any sum allotted out of wages or adjudged by a superintendent to be due by way of wages);

(p) any claim by a master, shipper, charterer or agent in respect of disbursements made on account of a ship;

(q) any claim arising out of an act which is or is claimed to be a general average act;

(r) any claim arising out of bottomry;

(s) any claim for the forfeiture or condemnation of a ship or of goods which are being or have been carried, or have been attempted to be carried, in a ship, or for the restoration of a ship or any such goods after seizure, or for droits of Admiralty.

(3) The proceedings referred to in subsection (1)(b) are—

(a) any application to the High Court under the Merchant Shipping Act 1995.

(b) any action to enforce a claim for damage, loss of life or personal injury arising out of—

   (i) a collision between ships; or

   (ii) the carrying out of or omission to carry out a manoeuvre in the case of one or more of two or more ships; or

   (iii) non-compliance, on the part of one or more of two or more ships, with the collision regulations;

(c) any action by shipowners or other persons under the Merchant Shipping Act 1995 for the limitation of the amount of their liability in connection with a ship or other property.

(4) The jurisdiction of the High Court under subsection (2)(b) includes power to settle any account outstanding and unsettled be-

Paragraph numbers marked with a "+" can be found online and on CD.

tween the parties in relation to the ship, and to direct that the ship, or any share thereof, shall be sold, and to make such other order as the court thinks fit.

(5) Subsection (2)(e) extends to—

    (a) any claim in respect of a liability incurred under Chapter III of Part VI of the Merchant Shipping Act 1995; and

    (b) any claim in respect of a liability falling on the International Oil Pollution Compensation Fund, or on the International Oil Pollution Compensation Fund 1992 or on the International Oil Pollution Compensation Supplementary Fund 2003, under Chapter IV of Part VI of the Merchant Shipping Act 1995.

(6) In subsection 2(j)—

    (a) the "Salvage Convention 1989" means the International Convention on Salvage, 1989 as it has effect under section 224 of the Merchant Shipping Act 1995;

    (b) the reference to salvage services includes services rendered in saving life from a ship and the reference to any claim under any contract for or in relation to salvage services includes any claim arising out of such a contract whether or not arising during the provision of the services;

    (c) the reference to a corresponding claim in connection with an aircraft is a reference to any claim corresponding to any claim mentioned in sub-paragraph (i) or (ii) of paragraph (j) which is available under section 87 of the Civil Aviation Act 1982.

(7) The preceding provisions of this section apply—

    (a) in relation to all ships or aircraft, whether British or not and whether registered or not and wherever the residence or domicile of their owners may be;

    (b) in relation to all claims, wherever arising (including, in the case of cargo or wreck salvage, claims in respect of cargo or wreck found on land); and

    (c) so far as they relate to mortgages and charges, to all mortgages or charges, whether registered or not and whether legal or equitable, including mortgages and charges created under foreign law;

Provided that nothing in this subsection shall be construed as extending the cases in which money or property is recoverable under any of the provisions of the Merchant Shipping Act 1995.

2D–148   *Note*—Amended by SI 2006/1265, art.13, with effect from September 8, 2006, being the date on which the Supplementary Fund Protocol comes into force (London, Edinburgh and Belfast Gazettes, July 21, 2006).

Admiralty jurisdiction generally

2D–149   The Admiralty Court can entertain a claim transferred to it, though it could not have been properly instituted in that court (*The Montrosa* [1917] P. 1).

The jurisdiction *in personam* is, in collision and similar cases, restricted (see s.22 and

Paragraph numbers marked with a "+" can be found online and on CD.

r.61.4(7) and r.61.11(5) and see r.6.20(17A). For other restrictions on the jurisdiction see paras 2D–17 *et seq.*.

As to the jurisdiction to restrain by injunction an act on the high seas, see *The Tubantia* [1924] P. 78.

Specific performance may be ordered in an Admiralty claim *in rem* (or *in personam*) (*The Conoco Britannia* [1972] 2 Q.B. 543; [1972] 2 All E.R. 283; [1972] 1 Lloyd's Rep. 342).

It is now possible for a judgment creditor in a claim *in rem* to arrest both in respect of a national judgment *in rem* as well as a foreign judgment *in rem*. See r.61.5(1) above at para.2D–34. Formerly it was only possible to arrest to enforce a foreign judgment *in rem*, see *The Despina G.K.* [1982] 3 W.L.R. 950; [1982] 2 Lloyd's Rep. 555.

The existence of an unsatisfied judgment *in personam* or arbitration award does not prevent the bringing of a claim *in rem* on the same cause of action. See *The Rena K* [1978] 1 Lloyd's Rep. 545 at 560 and cases there cited. See also *The Saint Anna* [1983] 1 Lloyd's Rep. 637. But see *The Bumbesti* noted at para.2D–164 below.

Admiralty claims *in personam* are now termed "other claims". See Practice Direction—Admiralty Claims, para.61.12.

s.20(1)(c)

Paragraph (c) of this subsection replaces the "sweeping up" provisions at the end of **2D–150**
s.1(1) of the AJA 1956. In *The Queen of the South* [1968] P. 449; [1968] 1 All E.R. 1163; [1968] 1 Lloyd's Rep. 182, Brandon J., while expressing no concluded opinion, said that it appeared that the effect of this "sweeping up" provision in the AJA s.1(1) was to preserve to the court the jurisdiction over, *inter alia*, claims for what were known, before the coming into force of that Act, as "necessaries," a term not reproduced in it.

Construction of paras (a)–(s)

Where any provision of this Act which appears to be intended to give effect to the **2D–151**
Arrest Convention of 1952 is capable of more than one meaning the court may look at the Convention in order to gain assistance in deciding which meaning is to be preferred. See *The Eschersheim* [1975] 1 W.L.R. 83 at 89; [1974] 3 All E.R. 307 at 314; [1974] 2 Lloyd's Rep. 188 at 192 and cases there cited. See also [1976] 1 W.L.R. 430 at 434; [1976] 1 All E.R. 920 at 924; [1976] 2 Lloyd's Rep. 1 at 6, HL(E).

As to resort to the *travaux préparatoires* of the Convention as an aid to interpretation, see *Gatoil International Inc v Arkwright-Boston Manufacturers Mutual Insurance Co* [1985] A.C. 255; [1985] 1 All E.R. 129, HL(Sc).

Paragraph "(2)(a) any claim to the possession or ownership of a ship or to the ownership of any share therein ..."—Jurisdiction

Jurisdiction to hear a claim for a declaration that the plaintiff is entitled to be **2D–152**
registered as the owner of a British ship is given by this paragraph (*The Bineta* [1966] 2 Lloyd's Rep. 419).

"Ship"

See s.24(1), para.2D–195. See too s.313 of the Merchant Shipping Act 1995 which **2D–153**
replaces s.742 of the Merchant Shipping Act 1894 and the cases cited in British Shipping Laws, (Temperley, *Merchant Shipping Acts*, 7th edn (1976)) under s.742 of the Merchant Shipping Act 1894. A sailing dinghy used on a reservoir for pleasure was held not to be a "vessel in navigation" within s.742 aforesaid, see *Curtis v Wild* [1991] 4 All E.R. 172; and a jet-ski was held not to be "a ship", see *Steedman v Scofield* [1992] 2 Lloyd's Rep. 163. See too *R. v Goodwin* [2005] EWCA Crim 3184; [2006] 1 W.L.R. 546; [2006] 2 All E.R. 519; [2006] 1 Lloyd's Rep. 432, CA, (a s.58(2)(b) and s.313(1) of the Merchant Shipping Act 1995 case) in which the Court of Appeal held that though it was not possible to conclude on the basis of its construction that the particular jet-ski involved was not a "vessel", the words "used in navigation" excluded craft such as a jet-ski which were used simply for having fun on the water without the object of going somewhere. See also the Hovercraft Act 1968 s.2(1), para.2D–203+.

Foreigners

The court has jurisdiction to entertain a claim between foreigners as to possession **2D–154**
of a ship within the jurisdiction, see subs.(7)(a). But it seems it may refuse to adjudicate (*The Jupiter (No.2)* [1925] P. 69, CA).

Paragraph numbers marked with a "+" can be found online and on CD.

Paragraph "(2)(b) any question arising between the co-owners of a ship as to possession, employment or earnings of that ship"

2D–155   *Note* —This paragraph must be read with subs.(4) of this section.

Paragraph "(2)(c) any claim in respect of a mortgage of or charge on a ship or any share therein"

2D–156   *Note* —See also subs.(7)(c), which provides that this paragraph shall apply to all mortgages and charges on ships. As to the meaning of "charge" see the note to s.21, paras 2D–179 to 2D–190.

As to the circumstances in which a mortgagee can recover payments made by him for insurance of the mortgaged ship, see *The Basildon* [1967] 2 Lloyd's Rep. 134.

Paragraph "(2)(d) any claim for damage received by a ship"

2D–157   *Note* —This includes damage done by something other than a ship; see *Mersey Docks and Harbour Board v Turner, The Zeta* [1893] A.C. 469 (collision with pierhead); *The Upcerne* [1912] P. 160 (collision with gas buoy).

Section 21, which provides for the mode of exercise of Admiralty jurisdiction, makes no provision for proceedings *in rem* in respect of claims falling within this paragraph. In practice, many such claims will fall within para.(2)(e) also.

Paragraph "(2)(e) any claim for damage done by a ship"

2D–158   *Note* —This paragraph must be read with subs.(5), which extends it to certain claims in connection with oil pollution.

Damage done by a ship carries a maritime lien in the usual case; this is subject, however, to exceptions, e.g. no lien attaches under present law to a government ship.

"Done by a ship"

2D–159   "The figurative phrase 'damage done by a ship' is a term of art in maritime law whose meaning is well settled by authority (*The Vera Cruz (No. 2)* (1884) 9 P. D. 96; *Currie v M'Knight* [1897] A.C. 97). To fall within the phrase not only must the damage be the direct result or natural consequence of something done by those engaged in the navigation of the ship but the ship itself must be the actual instrument by which the damage was done. The commonest case is that of collision, which is specifically mentioned in the Convention: but physical contact between the ship and whatever object sustains the damage is not essential—a ship may negligently cause a wash by which some other vessel or some property on shore is damaged"

per Lord Diplock, *The Eschersheim* [1976] 1 W.L.R. 430 at 438; [1976] 1 All E.R. 920 at 926; [1976] 2 Lloyd's Rep. 1 at 8. See also the judgments in the Court of Appeal [1976] 1 W.L.R. 339; [1976] 1 All E.R. 441; [1976] 1 Lloyd's Rep. 81. See also *The Minerva* [1933] P. 224; 46 Ll.L.Rep. 212 (part of a ship's derrick fell damaging a barge alongside); *The Chr. Knudsen* [1932] P. 153; 43 Ll.L.Rep. 423 (damage to dock by barge being sunk in it) and *The Dagmara and Ama Antxine* [1988] 1 Lloyd's Rep. 431(claimant's vessel forced to leave fishing grounds due to alleged dangerous navigation of defendant's vessel).

See too *The Rama* [1996] 2 Lloyd's Rep. 281; damages for deceit and/or for negligent misrepresentation in relation to a charterparty where the ship was not the active cause of the damage or the noxious instrument or the instrument in the physical sense of the loss was not damage done by a ship within s.20(2)(e) so as to give rise to a maritime lien.

Paragraph "(2)(f) any claim for loss of life or personal injury"

2D–160   *Note* —This paragraph should be read together with subs.(1)(b) and subs.(3)(b).

Paragraph numbers marked with a "+" can be found online and on CD.

Paragraph "(2)(g) any claim for loss of or damage to goods carried in a ship"—"Loss"

It is arguable that "loss" is wide enough to include a claim for conversion against a carrier (*The Wildgans*, 1976, Fo. 947).

2D–161

"Goods"

"Goods" includes baggage, see s.24(1), para.2D–195. The term "baggage," however, covers the baggage of passengers or travellers only. The belongings of those on board a ship as employees of the shipowners in order to man and operate her are not baggage nor are they goods under this paragraph. (*The Eschersheim* [1975] 1 W.L.R. 83; [1974] 3 All E.R. 307; [1974] 2 Lloyd's Rep. 188).

The claims of crew members for lost or damaged belongings will in many cases come within para.(2)(e).

2D–162

Paragraph "(2)(h) any claim arising out of any agreement relating to the carriage of goods in a ship or to the use or hire of a ship"

Note —Although this paragraph is in different terms from s.22(1)(a) (xii) of the JA 1925, which it replaces, it is wide enough to cover claims, whether in contract or in tort, arising out of any agreement relating to the carriage of goods in a ship (*The St Elefterio* [1957] P. 179; [1957] 2 All E.R. 374; [1957] 1 Lloyd's Rep. 283). This case was followed in *The Moscanthy* [1971] 1 Lloyd's Rep. 37.

An agreement for the payment of premiums on an insurance policy over goods to be carried by sea is not connected with the carriage of goods in a ship in a sufficiently direct sense to be capable of coming within this paragraph. See *Gatoil International Inc v Arkwright-Boston Manufacturers Mutual Insurance Co* [1985] A.C. 255; [1985] 1 All E.R. 129, HL(Sc.). See also *The Sea Friends* [1991] 2 Lloyd's Rep. 322.

An agreement for the hire by shipowners of containers to be carried in a ship is not within this paragraph (*ibid.*, at pp.263, 271 and 131, 137 of the respective reports). (See also the note to para.(m)). Nor is a claim on a salvage agreement for damages for breach of an undertaking to obtain security from cargo owners. (*The Tesaba* [1982] 1 Lloyd's Rep. 397, which is referred to in *Gatoil* above at pp.263, 268 and 131, 135 of the respective reports).

2D–163

"Arising out of"

These words are to be given the wider meaning of "connected with" and not the narrower meaning of "arising under" (*The Antonis P. Lemos* [1985] A.C. 711; [1985] 1 All E.R. 695; [1985] 1 Lloyd's Rep. 283, HL). In *The Hamburg Star* [1994] 1 Lloyd's Rep. 399 claims for indemnity and contribution under the Civil Liability (Contribution) Act 1978 were held to be claims arising out of an agreement for carriage of containers and their contents.

In *The Bumbesti* [2000] Q.B. 559; [1999] 2 Lloyd's Rep. 481, the court held (inter alia) that the claim was an action on an arbitration award and arose out of an agreement to refer disputes which had arisen under a bare-boat charterparty and that such agreement to refer was not "an agreement in relation to the use and hire of a ship" but one distinct from the principal contract, i.e. the bare-boat charterparty. Accordingly the claim did not fall within subs.(h).

2D–164

"Goods"

See note to para.(2)(g).

2D–165

"Use or hire"

In deciding whether a particular agreement is an agreement relating to the use of a ship or not the court will look at the substances of the matter. See *The Eschersheim*, para.2D–151 in which it was held that a salvage agreement on Lloyd's form was, on the facts of that case, an agreement for the use of a ship.

In *The Stella Nora*, 1981, Com.L.R. 200 it was held that a management agreement, which provided that the managers would be solely entitled to enter into charterparties for the owners of the ship they were to manage, was an agreement relating to the use or hire of that ship.

To come within this paragraph the claim need not have its origin in an agreement between the claimant and the defendant (*The Antonis P. Lemos* [1985] A.C. 711; [1985] 1 All E.R. 695; [1985] 1 Lloyd's Rep. 283, HL).

2D–166

Paragraph numbers marked with a "+" can be found online and on CD.

Paragraph "(2)(j) any claim ... Salvage Convention 1989 ..."

2D–167   *Note* —Derivation—s.1(6) and Sch.2 of the Merchant Shipping (Salvage and Pollution) Act 1994. The 1994 Act was repealed by the Merchant Shipping Act 1995 with saving and amendment of this provision and providing by s.224 the enactment of the Salvage Convention 1989 with a commencement date of January 1, 1995.

This paragraph must be read together with subss.(6) and (7)(b).

See, generally, British Shipping Laws (Kennedy, *Law of Salvage* , 7th edn (2002)); *Halsbury's Laws of England*, 4th edn (2001 Reissue).

This paragraph does not cover a claim by the owners of property salved against salvors for negligence in the salvage operations. *The Eschersheim* [1976] 1 W.L.R. 339 at 346, 353 and 359; [1976] 1 All E.R. 441 at 446, 452 and 458; [1976] 1 Lloyd's Rep. 81 at 89, 90 and 95.

The court has power to award interest on a salvage award (*The Aldora* [1975] Q.B. 748; [1975] 2 All E.R. 69; [1975] 1 Lloyd's Rep. 617).

Salvage services rendered in non-tidal waters do not give rise to a claim for salvage reward (*The Goring* [1988] 1 Lloyd's Rep. 397, HL).

In *The Sava Star* [1995] 2 Lloyd's Rep. 134; the court held that there was no reason in principle why cargo owners could not issue a salvage claim against an owner where services of a salvage nature were rendered voluntarily in the sense that they were not rendered pursuant to a duty owed to the ship owners and were not part of what might ordinarily be expected of a cargo owner such as providing advice about the characteristics of the cargo.

Paragraph "(2)(k) any claim in the nature of towage in respect of a ship or an aircraft"

2D–168   *Note* —A "claim in the nature of towage" may include escorting without actually making fast: *The Leoborg* [1962] 2 Lloyd's Rep. 146. "Towage" in relation to an aircraft means towage when it is waterborne. See s.24(1), para.2D–195.

Paragraph "(2)(l) any claim in the nature of pilotage in repsect of a ship or an aircraft"

2D–169   *Note* — "Pilotage" in relation to an aircraft means pilotage when it is waterborne. See s.24(1), para.2D–195.

Paragraph "(2)(m) any claim in respect of goods or materials supplied to a ship for her operation or maintenance"

2D–170   *Note* —In *The Fairport (No.5)* [1967] 2 Lloyd's Rep. 162 it was held that claims under this paragraph are certainly no narrower than claims which were formerly described as claims for necessaries in the Supreme Court of Judicature (Consolidation) Act 1925, and since there is authority that the word "necessaries" covers payment by way of advances to enable necessaries to be purchased then a similar construction should be given to this paragraph.

The words "in respect of" are wide words which should not be unduly restricted. They cover a claim for repayment of sums paid to sub-agents who had supplied goods to ships. *Centro Latino Americano de Commercio Exterior SA v Owners of the Ship Kommunar (No.1)* [1997] 1 Lloyd's Rep. 1.

Containers (in the sense in which that word is used in a commercial context) supplied whether by sale or lease to a shipowner to contain cargo loaded on board his ship or any sister ship available to him, are not supplied to that ship for her operation or maintenance within the meaning of this paragraph (*The River Rima* [1987] 2 Lloyd's Rep. 106, CA. Approved by HL [1988] 2 Lloyd's Rep. 193).

In *The Edinburgh Castle* [1999] 2 Lloyd's Rep. 362 the following were held to fall within s.20(2)(m) namely food, drink and other consumables supplied for use of the officers and crew; food, drink and other consumables supplied for the use or consumption of the passengers on the vessel; the provision of services, in particular, the provision of officers and crew of suitable calibre for the operation and manning of the vessel

Paragraph numbers marked with a "+" can be found online and on CD.

and a wide range of equipment supplied to the vessel. See too *"Nore Challenger"* and *"Nore Commander"* [2001] 2 Lloyd's Rep. 103.

Paragraph "(2)(n) any claim in respect of the construction, repair or equipment of a ship or dock charges or dues"

2D–171

Note —In the *Stinne Peter* 1986 Fo. 171, Sheen J., on an ex parte motion, held that a classification certificate was part of the equipment of a ship and the classification society's claim for issuing it fell within this paragraph.

Paragraph "(2)(o) any claim by a master or member of the crew of a ship for wages"

2D–172

Note —The jurisdiction in respect of wages is in relation to the ships of some foreign countries restricted by Orders in Council made under s.4 of the Consular Relations Act 1968, see para.2D–18. Furthermore, the court may refuse to entertain a claim for wages by the master or a member of the crew of a ship which is not a British ship, see s.24(2).

As to the recovery as wages of or other emoluments and sums payable but not paid by an employer in respect of, e.g. taxes, insurance and pension contributions, see *The Halcyon Skies* [1977] Q.B. 14; [1976] 1 All E.R. 856; [1976] 1 Lloyd's Rep. 461 and cases cited therein.

In *The Fairport* [1967] P. 167; [1966] 2 Lloyd's Rep. 7, it was held that *The Carolina* (1875) 3 Asp.M.C. 141 was wrongly decided and that accordingly the institution of a wages claim did not terminate a contract of service; wages thereafter accruing might be recovered as such in the action.

It is well settled that there is a maritime lien for wages. See *The Halcyon Skies* [1977] Q.B. 14; [1976] 1 All E.R. 856; [1976] 1 Lloyd's Rep. 461 at 26, 864 and 467 of the respective reports. See too *The Ever Success* [1999] 1 Lloyd's Rep. 824. This maritime lien applies only to the ship aboard which the wages were earned (*The El Hussein* 1982 Fo. 693). There is a right *in rem* in respect of wages earned aboard a sister ship. Thus, where a claim is brought against ship A for wages earned aboard her and aboard a sister ship B, on payment out of proceeds of sale, wages earned in A will rank before, and wages earned in B after, any mortgage. This should be considered together with s.21(8), at para.2D–178, before joining a claim for wages earned aboard a sister ship to a claim for wages earned aboard the ship proceeded against.

A master's claim for wages ranks *pari passu* with the claims of seamen (*The Royal Wells* [1984] 2 Lloyd's Rep. 255, not following earlier cases).

Severence pay is not wages within this sub-section and as opposed to wages does not give rise to a maritime lien (*The Tacoma City* [1991] 1 Lloyd's Rep. 330).

In *The Turiddu* [1999] 2 Lloyd's Rep. 401, CA, it was held that foreign members of a ship's crew requesting an allotted part of their wages to be paid through an agency to an identified person in their home country retained the benefit of a maritime lien over the vessel for unpaid wages in relation to that alloted part.

Paragraph "(2)(p) any claim by a master, shipper, charterer or agent in respect of disbursements made on account of a ship"

2D–173

Note —A master has a maritime lien for his wages and for all disbursements or liabilities properly made or incurred by him on account of the ship. See the Merchant Shipping Act 1995 s.41 replacing the Merchant Shipping Act 1970 s.18 and the notes to that section in *British Shipping Laws* (Temperley, *Merchant Shipping Acts*, 7th edn (1976)). See also *The Fairport (No.3)* [1966] 2 Lloyd's Rep. 253.

"Agent"

2D–174

It is arguable that the term agent in this paragraph is not restricted to a person carrying on a business as a ship's agent in the usually accepted sense but is wide enough to include a manager of a ship (*The Corona Energy* 1977 Fo. 174). However, the term agent does not extend to an insurance broker seeking to recover premiums paid out on behalf of ship's owners (*The Sea Friends* [1991] 2 Lloyd's Rep. 322).

Fees charged by agents for their services may be "disbursements" (*The Westport (No.3)* [1966] 1 Lloyd's Rep. 342).

Paragraph numbers marked with a "+" can be found online and on CD.

Paragraph "(2)(q) ... general average act ..." Paragraph "(2)(r) ... bottomry ..." Paragraph "(2)(s) ... forfeiture or condemnation of a ship or of goods"

2D–175   Note.—In *The Skylark* [1965] P. 474; [1965] 2 Lloyd's Rep. 250, it was held that the Commissioners of Customs and Excise had a right to proceed *in rem* under the equivalent paragraph of the AJA 1956 for forfeiture of a ship under the Temporary Importation (Private Vehicles, Vessels and Aircraft) Regulations 1961.

"Arising out of"

2D–176   See the first note at para.2D–164 above.

Subsection (7)

2D–177   This paragraph applies only to aircraft referred to in s.20(2)(j), (k) and (l). The Admiralty jurisdiction does not extend, therefore, to a claim in respect of a mortgage of an aircraft (*The Glider Standard Austria S.H.* [1965] P. 463; [1965] 2 All E.R. 1022; [1965] 2 Lloyd's Rep. 189).

Mode of exercise of Admiralty jurisdiction

2D–178   **21.**—(1) Subject to section 22, an action in personam may be brought in the High Court in all cases within the Admiralty jurisdiction of that court.

(2) In the case of any such claim as is mentioned in section 20(2)(a), (c) or (s) or any such question as is mentioned in section 20(2)(b), an action in rem may be brought in the High Court against the ship or property in connection with which the claim or question arises.

(3) In any case in which there is a maritime lien or other charge on any ship, aircraft or other property for the amount claimed, an action in rem may be brought in the High Court against that ship, aircraft or property.

(4) In the case of any such claim as is mentioned in section 20(2)(e) to (r), where—

(a) the claim arises in connection with a ship; and

(b) the person who would be liable on the claim in an action in personam ("the relevant person") was, when the cause of action arose, the owner or charterer of, or in possession or in control of, the ship,

an action in rem may (whether or not the claim gives rise to a maritime lien on that ship) be brought in the High Court against—

(i) that ship, if at the time when the action is brought the relevant person is either the beneficial owner of that ship as respects all the shares in it or the charterer of it under a charter by demise; or

(ii) any other ship of which, at the time when the action is brought, the relevant person is the beneficial owner as respects all the shares in it.

(5) In the case of a claim in the nature of towage or pilotage in respect of an aircraft, an action in rem may be brought in the High Court against that aircraft if, at the time when the action is brought, it is beneficially owned by the person who would be liable on the claim in an action *in personam*.

(6) Where, in the exercise of its Admiralty jurisdiction, the High Court orders any ship, aircraft or other property to be sold, the

Paragraph numbers marked with a "+" can be found online and on CD.

court shall have jurisdiction to hear and determine any question arising as to the title to the proceeds of sale.

(7) In determining for the purposes of subsections (4) and (5)whether a person would be liable on a claim in an action in personam it shall be assumed that he has his habitual residence or a place of business within England or Wales.

(8) Where, as regards any such claim as is mentioned in section 20(2)(e) to (r), a ship has been served with a writ or arrested in an action in rem brought to enforce that claim, no other ship may be served with a writ or arrested in that or any other action in rem brought to enforce that claim: but this subsection does not prevent the issue, in respect of any one such claim, of a writ naming more than one ship or of two or more writs each naming a different ship.

Note —Generally as to claims *in rem*, see CPR r.61.3 and notes thereunder and *British Shipping Laws*, Vol.1, *Admiralty Practice*. **2D–179**

subs.(3) "... maritime lien ..."

It is well settled that there is a maritime lien in respect of the following claims: damage done by a ship, salvage, wages, master's disbursements and bottomry. It is doubtful whether there is a maritime lien for pilotage. This question was left open in *The Ambatielos*; *The Cephalonia* [1923] P. 68. As to maritime liens generally see *The Tolten* [1946] P. 135 at 144 and 145 and cases there cited by Scott L.J. See also *The Father Thames* [1979] 2 Lloyd's Rep. 364. **2D–180**

subs.(3) "... other charge ..."

See *The St. Merriel* [1963] P. 247; [1963] 1 Lloyd's Rep. 63; *The Acrux* [1965] P. 391 at 403; [1965] 1 Lloyd's Rep. 565 at 572. **2D–181**

subs.(4) "... in connection with a ship ..."

As to the effect of these words in s.3(4) of the 1956 Act, see the passage in the speech of Lord Diplock in *The Eschersheim* [1976] 1 W.L.R. 430 at 436H; [1976] 1 All E.R. 920 at 925d; [1976] 2 Lloyd's Rep. 1, HL(E), in the respective reports. In *The Span Terza* [1982] 1 Lloyd's Rep. 225, the Court of Appeal held that this passage was *obiter* and by a majority allowed the arrest of the ship "X" where the claimant (owner of the ship "Y") was claiming for charter hire in a claim *in rem* against the ship "X" which was owned by the person to whom the "Y" had been chartered by the claimant. **2D–182**

subs.(4) "... liable ... in personam ..."

The purpose of the words "the person who would be liable on the claim in an action *in personam*" is to identify the person or persons whose ship or ships may be arrested (*The St Elefterio* [1957] P. 179 at 186; [1957] 2 All E.R. 374 at 377; [1957] 1 Lloyd's Rep. 283 at 287). But only one ship may be arrested, see subs.(8). **2D–183**

subs.(4) "... beneficial owner ..."

For the meaning of beneficial owner in this subsection see *The Andrea Ursula* [1973] Q.B. 265; [1971] 1 All E.R. 821; [1971] 1 Lloyd's Rep. 145 and *The I Congreso del Partido* [1981] 1 Lloyd's Rep. 536 at 560 *et seq.* in which *The Andrea Ursula* was not followed. See also *The Father Thames* [1979] 2 Lloyd's Rep. 364 at 366 and 367. **2D–184**

subs.(4)(b)(i) "... charterer ..."

The effect of these words in sub-para.(i) is to enable a claim *in rem* to be brought against a ship on demise charter if the demise charterer of it when the claim form is issued is the person who would be liable *in personam*, and was when the cause of action arose the owner, charterer or in possession or in control of the ship in connection with which the claim arose. **2D–185**

The "relevant person" can be a demise charterer within this subsection even in the absence of a consensual agreement between the parties in the nature of a demise

Paragraph numbers marked with a "+" can be found online and on CD.

charter if the legal relationship between the parties invests the "relevant person" with the right of a demise character against the owner of the vessel. See *Bridge Oil Ltd v Owners and/or Demise Charterers of the Ship Giuseppe di Vittorio* [1998] 1 Lloyd's Rep. 136, CA.

A slot charterer of spaces on a container ship for the carriage of goods is capable of coming within the definition of a charterer in s.21(4)(b) of the Supreme Court Act 1981 despite the fact that a slot charter gave control of only part of the vessel to the charterer, *MSC Mediterranean Shipping Company SA v Polish Ocean Lines (The Tychy)* [1999] 2 Lloyd's Rep. 11, CA.

subs.(4) "... when the action is brought ..."

2D–186   This means when the claim form is issued (*The Carmania 11* [1963] 2 Lloyd's Rep. 152).

subs.(4) "... owner ..."

2D–187   Section 21 does not confer a right to arrest a ship owned by a sister company of the owners of the ship giving rise to the cause of action (*The Evpo Agnic* [1988] 2 Lloyd's Rep. 411, CA). See too *The Nazym Khikmet and Other Ships* [1996] 2 Lloyd's Rep. 362, CA.

subs.(4)(b)

2D–188   It is not sufficient that the cause of action, being one falling within s.20(2)(e) to (r), should arise probably, but not necessarily, in connection with a ship owned by or demise chartered to or in the possession or control of the relevant person as defined by s.21(4)(b) (*The River Rima* [1987] 2 Lloyd's Rep. 106, CA. Approved by HL [1988] 2 Lloyd's Rep. 193). See too *The Lloyd Pacifico* [1995] 1 Lloyd's Rep. 54.

Change of ownership after issue of claim form

2D–189   This does not affect the claimant's right of claim *in rem* against the ship or prevent her arrest in the claim (*The Monica S* [1968] P. 741; [1967] 3 All E.R. 740; [1967] 2 Lloyd's Rep. 113 and see *The Andria*, renamed *The Vasso* (1984) 81 L.S.Gaz. 592).

subs.(8)

2D–190   Subsection (8) gives statutory effect to the decision of the Court of Appeal in *The Banco* [1971] P. 137; [1971] 1 All E.R. 524; [1971] 1 Lloyd's Rep. 49.

Where the claim form includes claims in respect of more than one ship, e.g. claims in respect of repairs to two or more ships in the same ownership, service of the claim form on or the arrest of any of the ships named in it will normally prevent valid service of that claim form on or the arrest of, any other ship named in it. Furthermore, after such service or arrest no other claim form *in rem* may be served or ship arrested in respect of any of the claims specified in the first claim form.

It seems however that in a case such as this if the claim form clearly shows what claims are made against each ship and there is no overlapping, all the ships against which claims are made in the claim form may be arrested and/or served with the claim form.

This subsection does not prevent the arrest of a ship where another has previously been arrested in the mistaken belief that she was a sister ship. The affidavit in support of the application for the second arrest should refer to the previous mistaken arrest and the reasons for it (*The Stephan J.* [1985] 2 Lloyd's Rep. 344).

Restrictions on entertainment of actions in personam in collision and other similar cases

2D–191   22.—(1) This section applies to any claim for damage, loss of life or personal injury arising out of—

> (a) a collision between ships; or
> (b) the carrying out of, or omission to carry out, a manoeuvre in the case of one or more of two or more ships; or
> (c) non-compliance, on the part of one or more of two or more ships, with the collision regulations.

Paragraph numbers marked with a "+" can be found online and on CD.

ADMIRALTY

(2) The High Court shall not entertain any action in personam to enforce a claim to which this section applies unless—

   (a) the defendant has his habitual residence or a place of business within England or Wales; or

   (b) the cause of action arose within inland waters of England or Wales or within the limits of a port of England or Wales; or

   (c) an action arising out of the same incident or series of incidents is proceeding in the court or has been heard and determined in the court.

In this subsection—

"inland waters" includes any part of the sea adjacent to the coast of the United Kingdom certified by the Secretary of State to be waters falling by international law to be treated as within the territorial sovereignty of Her Majesty apart from the operation of that law in relation to territorial waters;

"port" means any port, harbour, river, estuary, haven, dock, canal or other place so long as a person or body of persons is empowered by or under an Act to make charges in respect of ships entering it or using the facilities therein, and "limits of a port" means the limits thereof as fixed by or under the Act in question or, as the case may be, by the relevant charter or custom;

"charges" means any charges with the exception of light dues, local light dues and any other charges in respect of lighthouses, buoys or beacons and of charges in respect of pilotage.

(3) The High Court shall not entertain any action in personam to enforce a claim to which this section applies until any proceedings previously brought by the plaintiff in any court outside England and Wales against the same defendant in respect of the same incident or series of incidents have been discontinued or otherwise come to an end.

(4) Subsections (2) and (3) shall apply to counterclaims (except counterclaims in proceedings arising out of the same incident or series of incidents) as they apply to actions, the references to the plaintiff and the defendant being for this purpose read as references to the plaintiff on the counterclaim and the defendant to the counterclaim respectively.

(5) Subsections (2) and (3) shall not apply to any action or counterclaim if the defendant thereto submits or has agreed to submit to the jurisdiction of the court.

(6) Subject to the provisions of subsection (3), the High Court shall have jurisdiction to entertain an action in personam to enforce a claim to which this section applies whenever any of the conditions specified in subsections (2)(a) to (c) is satisfied, and the rules of court relating to the service of process outside the jurisdiction shall make such provision as may appear to the rule-making authority to be appropriate having regard to the provisions of this subsection.

Paragraph numbers marked with a "+" can be found online and on CD.

(7) Nothing in this section shall prevent an action which is brought in accordance with the provisions of this section in the High Court being transferred, in accordance with the enactments in that behalf, to some other court.

(8) For the avoidance of doubt it is hereby declared that this section applies in relation to the jurisdiction of the High Court not being Admiralty jurisdiction, as well as in relation to its Admiralty jurisdiction.

subs.(2)(c)

2D–192   In *The World Harmony* [1967] P. 341; [1965] 2 All E.R. 139; [1965] 1 Lloyd's Rep. 244, it was held that the critical date under the equivalent provision in the AJA 1956(s.4(1)(c)), was the date when the claim form was issued and that when two claims are begun in two places on the same day, neither is previous or subsequent to the other.

subs.(6) "... rules of court ..."

2D–193   See CPR r.61.4(7) and r.6.20(17A).

High Court not to have jurisdiction in cases within Rhine Convention

2D–194   **23.** The High Court shall not have jurisdiction to determine any claim or question certified by the Secretary of State to be a claim or question which, under the Rhine Navigation Convention, falls to be determined in accordance with the provisions of that Convention; and any proceedings to enforce such a claim which are commenced in the High Court shall be set aside.

Supplementary provisions as to Admiralty jurisdiction

2D–195   **24.**—(1) In sections 20 to 23 and this section, unless the context otherwise requires—

"collision regulations" means safety regulations under section 85 of the Merchant Shipping Act 1995;

"goods" includes baggage;

"master" has the same meaning as in the Merchant Shipping Act 1995, and accordingly includes every person (except a pilot) having command or charge of a ship;

"the Rhine Navigation Convention" means the Convention of the 7th October 1868 as revised by any subsequent Convention;

"ship" includes any description of vessel used in navigation and (except in the definition of "port" in section 22(2)and in subsection (2)(c) of this section) includes, subject to section 2(3)of the Hovercraft Act 1968, a hovercraft;

"towage" and "pilotage", in relation to an aircraft, mean towage and pilotage while the aircraft is waterborne.

(2) Nothing in sections 20 to 23 shall—

(a) be construed as limiting the jurisdiction of the High Court to refuse to entertain an action for wages by the master or a member of the crew of a ship, not being a British ship;

Paragraph numbers marked with a "+" can be found online and on CD.

(b) affect the provisions of section 226 of the Merchant Shipping Act 1995 (power of a receiver of wreck to detain a ship in respect of a salvage claim); or

(c) authorise proceedings in rem in respect of any claim against the Crown, or the arrest, detention or sale of any of Her Majesty's ships or Her Majesty's aircraft, or, subject to section 2(3)of the Hovercraft Act 1968, Her Majesty's hovercraft, or of any cargo or other property belonging to the Crown.

(3) In this section—

"Her Majesty's ships" and "Her Majesty's aircraft" have the meanings given by section 38(2) of the Crown Proceedings Act 1947;

"Her Majesty's hovercraft" means hovercraft belonging to the Crown in right of Her Majesty's Government in the United Kingdom or Her Majesty's Government in Northern Ireland.

Note —Amended by the Merchant Shipping Act 1995 Sch.13. **2D–196**

Ship
See further as to the meaning of ship, para.2D–153. **2D–197**

OTHER PARTICULAR FIELDS OF JURISDICTION

* * * *

Prize jurisdiction of High Court

27. The High Court shall, in accordance with section19(2), have as **2D–198** a prize court—

(a) all such jurisdiction as is conferred on it by the Prize Acts 1864 to 1944 (in which references to the High Court of Admiralty are by virtue of paragraph 1 of Schedule 4 to this Act to be construed as references to the High Court); and

(b) all such other jurisdiction on the high seas and elsewhere as it has as a prize court immediately before the commencement of this Act.

Note —Derived from the JA 1925 s.23. **2D–199**

PART VI

MISCELLANEOUS AND SUPPLEMENTARY

SUPPLEMENTARY

* * * *

Admiralty jurisdiction: provisions as to Channel Islands, Isle of Man, colonies, etc.

150.—(1) Her Majesty may by Order in Council— **2D–200**

Paragraph numbers marked with a "+" can be found online and on CD.

(a) direct that any of the provisions of sections 20 to 24 specified in the Order shall extend, with such exceptions, adaptations and modifications as may be so specified, to any of the Channel Islands or the Isle of Man; or

(b) make, for any of the Channel Islands or the Isle of Man, provision for any purposes corresponding to the purposes of any of the provisions of those sections.

(2) Her Majesty may by Order in Council direct, either generally or in relation to particular courts or territories, that the Colonial Courts of Admiralty Act 1890 shall have effect as if for the reference in section 2(2) of that Act to the Admiralty jurisdiction of the High Court in England there were substituted a reference to the Admiralty jurisdiction of that court as defined by section 20 of this Act, subject, however, to such adaptations and modifications of section 20 as may be specified in the Order.

(3) Her Majesty may by Order in Council direct that any of the provisions of sections 21 to 24 shall extend, with such exceptions, adaptations and modifications as may be specified in the Order, to any colony or to any country outside Her Majesty's dominions in which Her Majesty has jurisdiction in right of the government of the United Kingdom.

(4) Subsections (1) and (3) shall each have effect as if the provisions there mentioned included section 2(2) of the Hovercraft Act 1968 (application of the law relating to maritime liens in relation to hovercraft and property connected with them).

2D–201   *Note* —Derived from the AJA 1956 s.56.

Hovercraft Act 1968

2D–202

(1968 c.59)

Paragraph numbers marked with a "+"denote content that is available on White Book on Westlaw UK or the Civil Procedure CD.

Merchant Shipping Act 1995

2D–208

(1995 c.21)

Paragraph numbers marked with a "+" can be found online and on CD.

PART IV

SAFETY

ASSISTANCE AT SEA

Duty of ship to assist the other in case of collision

92.—(1) In every case of collision between two ships, it shall be the
duty of the master of each ship, if and so far as he can do so without
danger to his own ship, crew and passengers (if any)— **2D–209**

(a) to render to the other ship, its master, crew and passengers (if any) such assistance as may be practicable,
and may be necessary to save them from any danger
caused by the collision, and to stay by the other ship
until he has ascertained that it has no need of further assistance; and

(b) to give to the master of the other ship the name of his
own ship and also the names of the ports from which it
comes and to which it is bound.

(2) The duties imposed on the master of a ship by subsection (1)
above apply to the masters of United Kingdom ships and to the
masters of foreign ships when in United Kingdom waters.

(3) The failure of the master of a ship to comply with the provisions of this section shall not raise any presumption of law that the
collision was caused by his wrongful act, neglect, or default.

Paragraph numbers marked with a "+" can be found online and on CD.

(4) [*Penalties for non compliance*].

2D–210   *Note* —Derivation—Merchant Shipping Act 1894 s.422(1); the Merchant Shipping (Registration) Act 1993 Sch.4, para.6(2); and the Maritime Conventions Act 1911 s.4(2).

Duty to assist aircraft in distress

2D–211   **93.**—(1) The master of a ship, on receiving at sea a signal of distress from an aircraft or information from any source that an aircraft is in distress, shall proceed with all speed to the assistance of the persons in distress (informing them if possible that he is doing so) unless he is unable, or in the special circumstances of the case considers it unreasonable or unnecessary, to do so, or unless he is released from this duty under subsection (4) or (5) below.

(2) [...]

(3) The duties imposed on the master of a ship by subsection (1) above apply to the masters of United Kingdom ships and to the masters of foreign ships when in United Kingdom waters.

(4) [...]

(5) A master shall be released from the duty imposed by subsection (1) above, if he is informed by the persons in distress, or by the master of any ship that has reached the persons in distress, that assistance is no longer required.

(6) [*Penalties for non compliance*].

(7) Compliance by the master of a ship with the provisions of this section shall not affect his right, or the right of any other person, to salvage.

2D–212   *Note* —Derivation—Merchant Shipping (Safety Convention) Act 1949 s.22(1) and (2); the Merchant Shipping (Registration, etc.) Act 1993 Sch.4, para.6(2); and the Merchant Shipping (Safety Convention) Act 1949 s.22(3), (4), (5) and (8) and s.37(3).

Section 93 has been amended by The Merchant Shipping (Distress Messages) Regulation 1998 (SI 1998/1691) reg.2.

subs.(1)

2D–213   A vessel which puts herself into unusual peril by reason of rendering assistance under this section is not to be regarded as negligent on that account. The principles of the common law as laid down in *Haynes v Harwood* [1935] 1 K.B. 146, apply (*The Gusty and the Daniel M.* [1940] P. 159, a case on the former s.6 of the Maritime Conventions Act 1911, see para.2D–221, below).

subs.(7)

2D–214   *The Tower Bridge* [1936] P. 30 is a case in which salvage is awarded in such circumstances.

PART VII

LIABILITY OF SHIPOWNERS AND OTHERS

*   *   *   *

LIMITATION OF LIABILITY OF SHIPOWNERS, ETC., AND SALVORS FOR

MARITIME CLAIMS

Limitation of liability for maritime claims

2D–215   **185.**—(1) The provisions of the Convention on Limitation of Li-

Paragraph numbers marked with a "+" can be found online and on CD.

ability for Maritime Claims 1976 as set out in Part I of Schedule 7 (in this section and Part II of that Schedule referred to as "the Convention") shall have the force of law in the United Kingdom.

(2) The provisions of Part II of that Schedule shall have effect in connection with the Convention, and subsection (1) above shall have effect subject to the provisions of that Part.

(2A) Her Majesty may by Order in Council make such modifications of Parts I and II of Schedule 7 as She considers appropriate in consequence of the revision of the Convention by the Protocol of 1996 amending the Convention (in this section referred to as "the 1996 Protocol").

(2B) If it appears to Her Majesty in Council that the Government of the United Kingdom has agreed to any further revision of the Convention or to any revision of article 8 of the 1996 Protocol, She may by Order in Council make such modifications of Parts I and II of Schedule 7 and subsections (2C) and (2D) below as She considers appropriate in consequence of the revision.

(2C) The Secretary of State may by order make such amendments of Parts I and II of Schedule 7 as appear to him to be appropriate for the purpose of giving effect to any amendment of a relevant limit which is adopted in accordance with article 8 of the 1996 Protocol.

(2D) In subsection (2C) above "a relevant limit" means any of the limits for the time being specified in either of the following provisions of the Convention—

    (a) article 6, paragraph 1, and

    (b) article 7, paragraph 1.

(2E) No modification made by virtue of subsection (2A), (2B) or (2C) above shall affect any rights or liabilities arising out of an occurrence which took place before the day on which the modification comes into force.

(3) The provisions having the force of law under this section shall apply in relation to Her Majesty's ships as they apply in relation to other ships.

(4) The provisions having the force of law under this section shall not apply to any liability in respect of loss of life or personal injury caused to, or loss of or damage to any property of, a person who is on board the ship in question or employed in connection with that ship or with the salvage operations in question if—

    (a) he is so on board or employed under a contract of service governed by the law of any part of the United Kingdom; and

    (b) the liability arises from an occurrence which took place after the commencement of this Act.

In this subsection, "ship" and "salvage operations" have the same meaning as in the Convention.

(5) A draft of an Order in Council proposed to be made by virtue of subsection (2A) or (2B) above shall not be submitted to Her Maj-

Paragraph numbers marked with a "+" can be found online and on CD.

esty in Council unless it has been approved by a resolution of each House of Parliament.

2D–216   *Note* —Derivation—Merchant Shipping Act 1979 s.17, s.35(2) and Sch.5, para.3. Subsections (2A) to (2E) inserted by the Merchant Shipping and Maritime Security Act 1997 s.15. These subsections are now in force. As at December 2002 see only under s.185(2A), the Merchant Shipping (Convention on Limitation of Liability for Maritime Claims) (Amendment) Order 1998 (SI 1998/1258)—not in force until the 1996 Protocol amending the 1976 Convention on Liability for Maritime Claims comes into force internationally.

Exclusion of liability

2D–217   **186.**—(1) Subject to subsection (3) below, the owner of a United Kingdom ship shall not be liable for any loss or damage in the following cases, namely—

> (a) where any property on board the ship is lost or damaged by reason of fire on board the ship; or
> (b) where any gold, silver, watches, jewels or precious stones on board the ship are lost or damaged by reason of theft, robbery or other dishonest conduct and their nature and value were not at the time of shipment declared by their owner or shipper to the owner or master of the ship in the bill of lading or otherwise in writing.

(2) Subject to subsection (3) below, where the loss or damage arises from anything done or omitted by any person in his capacity of master or member of the crew or (otherwise than in that capacity) in the course of his employment as a servant of the owner of the ship, subsection (1) above shall also exclude the liability of—

> (a) the master, member of the crew or servant; and
> (b) in a case where the master or member of the crew is the servant of a person whose liability would not be excluded by that subsection apart from this paragraph, the person whose servant he is.

(3) This section does not exclude the liability of any person for any loss or damage resulting from any such personal act or omission of his as is mentioned in Article 4 of the Convention set out in Part I of Schedule 7.

(4) This section shall apply in relation to Her Majesty's ships as it applies in relation to other ships.

(5) In this section "owner", in relation to a ship, includes any part owner and any charterer, manager or operator of the ship.

2D–218   *Note* —Derivation—Merchant Shipping Act 1979 s.18; and the Merchant Shipping (Registration, etc.) Act 1993 Sch.4, para.6(1).

MULTIPLE FAULT, APPORTIONMENT, LIABILITY AND CONTRIBUTION

Damage or loss: apportionment of liability

2D–219   **187.**—(1) Where, by the fault of two or more ships, damage or loss is caused to one or more of those ships, to their cargoes or freight, or to any property on board, the liability to make good the damage or

Paragraph numbers marked with a "+" can be found online and on CD.

loss shall be in proportion to the degree in which each ship was in fault.

(2) If, in any such case, having regard to all the circumstances, it is not possible to establish different degrees of fault, the liability shall be apportioned equally.

(3) This section applies to persons other than the owners of a ship who are responsible for the fault of the ships, as well as to the owners of a ship and where, by virtue of any charter or demise, or for any other reason, the owners are not responsible for the navigation and management of the ship, this section applies to the charterers or other persons for the time being so responsible instead of the owners.

(4) Nothing in this section shall operate so as to render any ship liable for any loss or damage to which the fault of the ship has not contributed.

(5) Nothing in this section shall affect the liability of any person under a contract of carriage or any contract, or shall be construed as imposing any liability upon any person from which he is exempted by any contract or by any provision of law, or as affecting the right of any person to limit his liability in the manner provided by law.

(6) In this section "freight" includes passage money and hire.

(7) In this section references to damage or loss caused by the fault of a ship include references to any salvage or other expenses, consequent upon that fault, recoverable at law by way of damages.

Note —Derivation—Maritime Conventions Act 1911 s.1(1), s.1(1) proviso (a), (b) and (c), s.1(2) and s.9(4).   **2D–220**

General note

The Merchant Shipping Act 1995 came into force on January 1, 1996, see s.315 of   **2D–221**
the 1995 Act. The 1995 Act is described as an act to consolidate the Merchant Shipping Acts 1894 to 1994 and other enactments relating to merchant shipping. Among those other enactments was the Maritime Conventions Act 1911 the text of which is to be found in the 1995 edition and earlier editions of this publication. In relation to s.1 of the 1911 Act (now s.187 of the 1995 Act set out above), s.3(1) of the Law Reform (Contributory Negligence) Act 1945 provided that the 1945 Act should not apply to any claim to which s.1 of the 1911 Act applied and that the 1911 Act should have effect as if the 1945 had not been passed. The intention of the 1911 Act and now of the provisions of the 1995 Act derived therefrom and of the 1945 Act is the same so that similar principles should be applied by the common law courts and the admiralty courts in the same way. See *Davies v Swan Motor Co (Swansea Corp Ltd and James, Third Parties)* [1949] 2 K.B. 291 at 319, per Evershed L.J. See also *The Miraflores and the Abadesa* [1966] P. 18 at 33; [1966] 1 Lloyd's Rep. 97 at 110, per Willmer L.J. Section 185 now applies in the case of ships belonging to Her Majesty as it applies in the case of other ships, see s.192(1) and (2) of the Merchant Shipping Act 1995. On the basis that the 1995 Act is a consolidating act case law previously appearing in the notes to the provisions of the 1911 Act has been retained.

"Fault of two or more ships"

For definition of "ship", see the Merchant Shipping Act 1995 s.313. See too the   **2D–222**
definitions of "vessel" and "ship" in the Merchant Shipping Act 1894 s.742 and the cases cited in the notes to that section in *British Shipping Laws* (Temperley, *Merchant Shipping Acts* 7th edn (1976)). A sailing dinghy used on a reservoir for pleasure has been held not to be a "vessel in navigation" within s.742 aforesaid, see *Curtis v Wild* [1991] 4 All E.R. 172; and a jet-ski not to be a "ship", see *Steedman v Scofield* [1992] 2 Lloyd's Rep. 163. See too *R. v Goodwin* noted at para.2D–153.

Paragraph numbers marked with a "+" can be found online and on CD.

Of the Maritime Conventions Act 1911 (see under General Note above) it was said: "The ... Act personifies the vessel, treating it at one time as the actor, at another as suffering damage or loss, and at another as liable to make good such damage or loss. The truth is, of course, that for the purpose of ascertaining the legal effect, the word in one context connotes those responsible for the navigation of the vessel; in another, those who are interested in her, her cargo or freight; and in another, those who are in law answerable for the conduct of those in charge.", *per* Warrington J. in *The Cairnbahn* [1914] P. 25 at 34, CA.

The words "by the fault of two or more ships", and the words of s.190 "by the fault of that ship", are entirely general, and are wide enough to include not only faults of navigation but other faults as well. See *The Norwhale* [1975] Q.B. 589; [1975] 2 All E.R. 501; [1975] 1 Lloyd's Rep. 610, a case decided under ss.1(1) and 8 of the Maritime Conventions Act 1911.

As to the proof of "fault," the rule is the same as in common law cases, namely, that the onus is on the party setting up a case of negligence to prove both the breach of duty and the consequent damage (*SS. Heranger (Owners) v SS. Diamond (Owners)* [1939] A.C. 94). However, in *The Minosa* (1944) 77 L.R. 218 at 219, the judge said: "The fact that one ship does not allege any fault against the other seems to me to be quite immaterial if the court after inquiring into all the facts finds that such fault exists. I think, therefore, that this is a case in which liability should be apportioned." See also *The Shelbrit IV* (1945) 78 Ll.L.Rep. 50.

It should be noted, however, that the negligence of an officer on board a ship is not always to be treated as "the fault of the ship"; see *The Sobieski* [1949] P. 313, and *The Glaucus and the City of Florence* [1948] P. 95. In the former case a collision occurred between two ships, the S and the E, as the result of the negligence of each of them and as the result, also, of the negligence of a senior escort officer, L, on board a naval ship, the L A, which was escorting the S. L's negligence consisted of his failure to transmit information of the approach, detected by radar, of the E. It was held that L's negligence was not the negligence of his ship, the L A. Therefore, the court held, the Maritime Conventions Act (see under General Note above) had no application to the claim of the S against L, and that claim failed also at common law because of the contributory negligence of the S, the collision having occurred before the coming into force of the Law Reform (Contributory Negligence) Act 1945.

"Damage or loss"

2D–223   As to what may be recovered under the head of damages in a collision action, see *British Shipping Laws* (Marsden, Collisions at Sea).

"The word 'loss' is wide enough to include that form of pecuniary prejudice which consists in compensating third parties for wrong done to them by the fault of persons for whose conduct the party prejudiced must answer," *per* Lord Sumner in *The Cairnbahn* [1914] P. 25 at 33, CA. In *The Abadesa* [1966] 1 Lloyd's Rep. 118, a case under the Maritime Conventions Act 1911, however, it was decided that " Sect.1 deals with material claims, claims for material damage; Sects. 2 and 3 with personal injuries and loss of life." The corresponding sections are now ss.187, 188 and 189.

"One or more of those ships"

2D–224   An innocent third ship, not being one of "those ships" who were "at fault," can, it seems, still recover the whole of her damages from either of the vessels by the fault of which damage to her has been caused, leaving the ship which has paid to recover a proportionate share from the other ship at fault; see *The Cairnbahn* [1914] P. 25, where a collision occurred between a steamship and a barge in tow of and controlled by a tug. The tug-owners had no interest in the barge. The steamship and tug were found equally to blame for the collision. The owners of the innocent barge recovered the full amount of their damage from the steamship. In a subsequent claim against the tug the steamship was held entitled to include in her claim for damages half the amount of damages which she had paid to the barge. To bring the case within the section it is not necessary that the two ships on whom lies the liability to make good the damage should themselves have been in collision.

With this should be contrasted the decision in *The Umona* [1914] P. 141, where a collision occurred between a steamship and a dumb-barge in tow of and controlled by a tug whose owners also owned the barge. The fault was apportioned as to three-

Paragraph numbers marked with a "+" can be found online and on CD.

fourths to the steamship and one-fourth to the tug. The owners of cargo laden on the barge were held only entitled to recover from the steamship three-quarters of their damage in accordance with the doctrine enunciated in *The Milan* (1860) Lush. 388; 31 L.J.Ad. 105; followed in *The Drumlanrig* [1911] A.C. 16.

Only damage or loss to ships is within the section; so that, in *Manchester Ship Canal Co (Alpha) v Helgoy* (1924) 18 Ll.L.Rep. 191, a jetty belonging to the owners of ship A was damaged in collision between ships A and B, for which both A and B were equally to blame. Though a moiety of the damage to A and B was recoverable from the owners of B and A respectively, no part of the damage to the jetty was recoverable from the owners of B for the claim in respect of the damage to the jetty is a common law claim and, as the collision causing the damage occurred before the coming into force of the Law Reform (Contributory Negligence) Act 1945, was defeated by the defence based on the contributory negligence of the servants of the owners of A. *Quaere*, however, whether this decision is consistent with certain passages in the judgment in *The Cairnbahn* [1914] P. 25, which suggests that all forms of pecuniary loss suffered by owners of ships involved in a collision are within the section. See, too, as to collision with wreck, *The Manorbier Castle* (1922) 129 L.T. 31; 16 Asp.M.L.C. 151.

"Cargoes"

2D–225

The innocent owner of cargo on board either of the colliding ships could, prior to the JA 1873, recover in a common law action in tort the whole of his damages from either of the wrong-doing ships unless defeated as regards the carrying ship by the terms of the contract of carriage. In Admiralty, he could only recover half his damages against the other ship if both were found to blame for the collision (*The Milan* (1860) Lush. 388; 31 L.J.Adm. 105). From 1873 until 1911 this Admiralty rule prevailed in all courts. Since the Maritime Conventions Act 1911 and now, under this Act, he can recover from the other ship a share of his damages proportionate to the degree in which such ship was in fault (*The Umona* [1914] P. 141). Nothing in this rule or the Act prevents the cargo owner from recovering his damages in full from the carrying ship should the terms of the contract of carriage permit (*The Bushire* (1886) 5 Asp.M.L.C. 416; 52 L.T. 740).

"Liability to make good the damage or loss"

2D–226

These words are equivalent to "the burden of the damage or loss"; per Warrington J. in *The Cairnbahn* [1914] P. 25 at 37. Further as to liability, see para.2D–227.

Of s.1 of the Maritime Conventions Act 1911 (see under General Note above) it was said: Section 1 "is mandatory. It does not say that the liability shall be apportioned equally unless different degrees of fault are shown. It is the other way round. It says that the court must apportion the liability in proportion to the degree in which each vessel was at fault unless it is impossible to do so" (per Davies L.J., *The Anneliese* [1970] 1 Lloyd's Rep. 355 at 362, CA; see cases cited therein).

Application of rule of division of loss when liability is limited

2D–227

In *Stoomvaart Maatschapfy Nederland v Peninsular and Oriental S N Co (The Voorwaarts; The Khedive)* (1882) 7 App. Cas. 795, the House of Lords, following the rule laid down in *The Woodrop-Sims* (1815) 2 Dods. Ad. 83; *The Lord Melville* (1815) 5 Shaws Sc. App. Cas. 395; *The Petersfield and the Judith Randolph* (1789) Marsd. Ad. Cas. 332, decided that upon a finding of both to blame only one liability arose, namely, a liability upon the part of the owners of the ship that had done the greater damage to pay to the owners of the other ship the difference between the moieties of the losses suffered by the two ships, and that where the former limited their liability under the Merchant Shipping Acts (now the Merchant Shipping Act) the latter were only entitled to prove against the fund in court for this difference.

It is submitted that there is nothing in the present section to affect this rule as to unity of liability; but its application where both ships are held to blame with unequal degrees of fault may give rise to anomalous results even more striking than those which occurred under the old rule. It may happen that the ship which has been found to be at fault in the greater degree will, nevertheless, if she has also received the greater damage be entitled to some payment. Thus, for example, where the damage done to A amounts to £10,000 and to B £30,000, and the degree of fault in A is found to be $1/3$ and in B $2/3$, A, though only $1/3$ to blame, will have to pay B £3,333, i.e. the

Paragraph numbers marked with a "+" can be found online and on CD.

difference between £10,000 (⅓ of B's damage) and £6,666 (⅔ of A's damage). If A limits her liability, B can prove against the fund for £3,333.

Three ships involved

2D–228   Where A, being towed by B, collides with C, and the court finds A and B one-half to blame and C one-half to blame, there is no obligation on the court to apportion the blame as between A and B. There is a joint and several liability in A and B to reimburse C in respect of a moiety of C's damage and a single liability in C to reimburse A and B in respect of a moiety of the damage, if any, sustained by them respectively (*The Socrates and the Champion* [1923] P. 76).

Where A collides with B while B is towing C, and the court finds that B and C are separately and distinctly at fault, the court will apportion blame as between B and C; see *The M.S.C. Panther and the Ericbank* [1957] P. 143 (distinguishing *The Socrates and the Champion* [1923] P. 76).

Where A goes aground negligently in avoiding B and C which have negligently collided, "the liability of each ship involved shall be assessed by comparison of her fault with the fault of each of the other ships involved individually, separately and in no way conjunctively." See *Miraflores v Owners of the George Livanos (The Miraflores, The Abadesa and The Livanos)* [1966] P. 18, per Winn L.J., affirmed by the House of Lords [1967] 1 A.C. 826; [1967] 1 All E.R. 672; [1967] 1 Lloyd's Rep. 191.

No collision

2D–229   The section is not confined to cases where two ships have actually been in collision. For example, where A, by her wash due to her excessive speed caused B, which was improperly moored, to break adrift and suffer damage, the loss was found to be due to the fault of both A and B, and was accordingly apportioned. *The Batavier III* (1925) 134 L.T. 155; 42 T.L.R. 8. See too, *The Cairnbahn* [1914] P. 25.

"Fault"

2D–230   No definition of "fault" is given in the Act or the Convention (see Sch.7, Parts I & II). The basis of liability in a claim of damage by collision under the old Admiralty rule, and also, under the present section, is negligence causing or contributing to the *loss*. See, for example, *The Margaret* (1881) 6 P.D. 76, where, in a collision between a schooner at anchor and a dumb barge, the schooner, whose only fault consisted in having an anchor improperly suspended in such a position that it holed and sank the barge was held liable to pay for half the loss suffered by the barge, whose sole negligence caused the collision. See, too, *The Monte Rosa* [1893] P. 23, and presumably the same principle would be applied to cases under the present section. It is true that in *The Peter Benoit* (1915) 84 L.J.P. 197; 31 T.L.R. 227, CA; 85 L.J.P. 12; 32 T.L.R. 124, H.L.R. the Court of Appeal and the House of Lords held that the fault for which the liability is to be apportioned under this section must be "fault causing or contributing to the collision." But this decision must be read *secundum subjectam materiam*. The court was considering the effect of a breach of a local by-law (which, in fact, contributed neither to the collision nor to the loss) and must not be taken to have questioned the proposition of law illustrated above by *The Margaret* (1881) 6 P.D. 76, namely, that liability attaches to acts of negligence causing or contributing to the loss; see *The Kaiser Wilhelm II* (1916) 85. L.J.P. 34; 31 T.L.R. 615.

It is now well established that in assessing degrees of fault and apportioning blame, regard must be had both to the blameworthiness or culpability of the conduct and also its causative potency as a factor contributing to the collision and damage. See *Stapley v Gypsum Mines Ltd* [1953] A.C. 663 and *The British Aviator* [1965] 1 Lloyd's Rep. 271 at 277.

Costs

2D–231   Until the case of *The Modica* [1926] P. 72, the regular practice from the commencement of the Maritime Conventions Act in 1911 was that, where in a collision action it was found that each ship had been to blame, although in different degrees, the court would apply in cases under this Act the old rule of making each ship pay her own costs. This practice was based upon the rulings of Bargrave Deane J. in *The Rosalia* [1912] P. 109, and of Sir Samuel Evans P. in *The Bravo* (1912) 29 T.L.R. 122. In *The Modica*, however, Hill J., after reviewing the authorities, laid down the principle that

Paragraph numbers marked with a "+" can be found online and on CD.

Crown ships

This section now applies in the case of ships belonging to Her Majesty as it applied **2D–246** in the case of other vessels; see the Merchant Shipping Act 1995 s.192(1) and (2).

General Note

If an innocent passenger on board ship A receives personal injuries in a collision **2D–247** between A and B, for which both ships are equally to blame, and recovers damages against A, A can recover a moiety from B subject to B's right to limit his liability in appropriate cases, for the passenger could have recovered against B in the first place.

An illustration of the working of subs.(3) formerly the proviso to s.3 of the Maritime Conventions Act 1911 is afforded by *The Cedric* [1920] P. 193. The representatives of the crew of a French sailing ship lost in collision with a British ship, for which both were equally to blame, had recovered in full the amount of the claims from the British ship. The owners of the latter were unable to recover a moiety of their damages in respect of these life claims in contribution from the French owners, on proof that by French law the representatives of the crew would have had no valid claim against the French ship.

"Fault"

As to the personification of the ship, see s.187 at paras 2D–219, 2D–222. See too **2D–248** para.2D–230.

Costs

Costs incurred in unreasonably disputing liability cannot be made the subject of **2D–249** contribution (*The Cairnbahn (No.2)* (1914) 30 T.L.R. 309, CA).

"Recover by way of contribution"

It seems that this right of contribution can be enforced by the third party proce- **2D–250** dure provided for by CPR Pt 20.

Proceedings to endorce contribution must be commenced within one year of the date of payment (see s.190, below).

"Statutory ... limitation"

As to limitation of liability see s.185 of and Sch.7 to the Merchant Shipping Act **2D–251** 1995 which came into force on January 1, 1996 replacing s.17 and Pts I and IIof Sch.4 to the Merchant Shipping Act 1979.

"The same rights and powers"

i.e. a person claiming contribution can proceed *in rem* or *in personam*. See the SCA **2D–252** 1981 s.20(1)(f), para.2D–147.

TIME LIMIT FOR PROCEEDINGS AGAINST OWNERS OR SHIP

Time limit for proceedings against owners or ship

190.—(1) This section applies to any proceedings to enforce any **2D–253** claim or lien against a ship or her owners—

    (a) in respect of damage or loss caused by the fault of that ship to another ship, its cargo or freight or any property on board it; or

    (b) for damages for loss of life or personal injury caused by the fault of that ship to any person on board another ship.

(2) The extent of the fault is immaterial for the purposes of this section.

(3) Subject to subsections (5) and (6) below, no proceedings to which this section applies shall be brought after the period of two years from the date when—

Paragraph numbers marked with a "+" can be found online and on CD.

    (a) the damage or loss was caused; or

    (b) the loss of life or injury was suffered.

(4) Subject to subsections (5) and (6) below, no proceedings under any of sections 187 to 189 to enforce any contribution in respect of any overpaid proportion of any damages for loss of life or personal injury shall be brought after the period of one year from the date of payment.

(5) Any court having jurisdiction in such proceedings may, in accordance with rules of court, extend the period allowed for bringing proceedings to such extent and on such conditions as it thinks fit.

(6) Any such court, if satisfied that there has not been during any period allowed for bringing proceedings any reasonable opportunity of arresting the defendant ship within—

    (a) the jurisdiction of the court, or

    (b) the territorial sea of the country to which the plaintiff's ship belongs or in which the plaintiff resides or has his principal place of business,

shall extend the period allowed for bringing proceedings to an extent sufficient to give a reasonable opportunity of so arresting the ship.

2D–254   *Note* —Derivation—Maritime Conventions Act 1911 s.8 and s.8 proviso.

General note

2D–255   This section applies to claims against a ship or her owners for (1) damage sustained by a ship (2) damage sustained by cargo or goods aboard a ship (3) loss of life or personal injury of persons aboard a ship (4) contribution under s.189 of the Act. Further, in relation to the second and third types of claim it applies only to claims made against a ship (or the owners of a ship) other than the ship in which the cargo or goods or persons killed or injured were carried. See *The Niceto de Larrinaga* [1966] P. 80; [1965] 2 All E.R. 930; [1965] 2 Lloyd's Rep. 134.

H.M. Ships

2D–256   With the exception of subs.(6) this section applies to H.M. ships, see the Merchant Shipping Act 1995 s.192(1).

"...shall be brought"

2D–257   The effect of this section, like that of most of statutes of limitation, is not to extinguish the cause of action, but merely to bar the right to maintain the claim. See *The P.L.M. 8* [1920] P. 236; *The Dorie S.S. Co v Kamanetz Podolsk* (1923) 14 Ll.L.Rep. 512(Sc.).

The defence must be specifically pleaded; see CPR Pt 16 and Practice Direction—Statements of Case. As to the effect of omitting to plead, see *Re Robinson's Settlement* [1912] 1 Ch. 717 at 728, per Buckley L.J.

An entry of an acknowledgment of service to a claim form does not prevent the defendant from raising this defence (*The Llandovery Castle* [1920] P. 119).

If the defendant desires to raise any defence based on this section, he should raise it as a preliminary objection by way of application whether the claim is *in personam* or *in rem*. See *The Niceto de Larrinaga* [1965] 2 Lloyd's Rep. 134. On the hearing of such application the claimant may apply to the court for the exercise of its discretion in extending the time. If the objection is upheld the proper order is not that the claim form should be set aside, but that the claim is not maintainable; see *The P.L.M. 8* [1920] P. 236.

Section 190(3)(b) envisaged that there might be cases where time did not run from the date of collision and provided for cases where the date of loss of life or injury was not the same as the date of collision, see *Sweet v Owners of Blyth Lifeboat*, *The Times*, February 22, 2002 where time began to run from the date on which the claimant first developed a recognised psychiatric injury rather than from the date of collision between the vessels.

"Owners"

For the meaning of "owners," see s.187(3) and para.2D–233.   **2D–258**

"Damages for loss of life"

In *The Alnwick sub nom. Robinson v Owners of the Motor Tug Alnwick* [1965] P. 357, CA,   **2D–259**
it was held that s.8 the precursor of this section was not affected by s.3 of the Law Reform (Limitation of Actions, etc.) Act 1954 and that the relevant period of limitation for an action in respect of loss of life which fell within s.8 was therefore two years. See the Limitation Act 1980 ss.31 *et seq.*

"... caused by the fault of that ship ..."

See para.2D–230.   **2D–260**

"... No proceedings ... shall be brought after the period of two years [or as appropriate, one year] ... "   **2D–261**

In *The Espanoleto* [1920] P. 223; 36 T.L.R. 554, it was held that inasmuch as the period of limitation provided by the precursor (s.8 of the Maritime Conventions Act) of this section was not absolute, the court should consider an application to renew on its merits and inquire whether the circumstances were such that the court would have given permission to *issue* the claim form notwithstanding that the time had expired, on the ground that the claimant had exercised due diligence in prosecuting his claim. If permission to issue the claim form would have been given, *a fortiori* a renewal of a claim form taken out within the prescribed time should be granted. See also *The World Harmony* [1965] 1 Lloyd's Rep. 244; [1967] P. 341; [1965] 2 All E.R. 139.

Where liability for damage has been proved or admitted, and the party liable has obtained a decree entitling him to limit his liability, claimants against the limitation fund may challenge the right of proof of other claimants who have not commenced proceedings within the periods prescribed by this section, for they are entitled to raise any defence which would have been open to the limiting person. But in such a case the court will generally consider the fact that limitation proceedings have been instituted as a sufficient ground for extending the time for commencing proceedings: *The Dispenser* [1920] P. 228. *Secus*, if the non-issue of the claim form resulted from the deliberate election of the claimant not to sue in this country (*The Nedenes* (1925) 23 Lloyd's Rep. 57).

"May ... extend"

Substantial grounds must be shown before the court will exercise its discretion to   **2D–262**
deprive the defendant of the limitation which he prima facie enjoys; and the Court of Appeal will not interfere with the exercise of this discretion unless it is shown that a wrong principle has been applied (*The Kashmir* [1923] P. 85, CA); *The James Westoll* [1923] P. 94n., CA, or, *semble*, unless the Court of Appeal considers that there were special circumstances or substantial reasons calling for an extension of the limitation period: *Robinson v Alnwick (Owners)*, *The Alnwick* [1965] P. 357; [1965] 3 W.L.R. 118, CA; *sub nom. The Alnwick* [1965] 1 Lloyd's Rep. 69, reversed *ibid.*, 320, CA. See also *The Hesselmoor and the Sergeant* [1951] 1 Lloyd's Rep. 146 (where Willmer J. reviewed some of the earlier authorities) *The Sauria and the Trent* [1957] 1 Lloyd's Rep. 396, CA (where it was successfully contended that an informal admission of liability amounted to a contractual undertaking not to plead the defence of limitation of action) and three later decisions illustrating the application of the proviso to the Maritime Conventions Act 1911 s.8 from which this section is derived, *Bartlett v Admiralty (The Vadne)* [1959] 2 Lloyd's Rep. 480 (discretion exercised) and *The Vadne* [1960] 1 Lloyd's Rep. 260; and *The Sunpak* [1960] 2 Lloyd's Rep. 213 (exercise of discretion refused)). For a case in which the court exercised its discretion in favour of a counterclaiming defendant, see *The Fairplay XIV* [1939] P. 57. See also *The World Harmony* (exercise of discretion refused). In *The Al Tahith* [1995] 2 Lloyd's Rep. 336 a case under the former s.8, M.C.A. 1911, it was said that the test to be applied is the same as under the former

Paragraph numbers marked with a "+" can be found online and on CD.

RSC O.6, r.8 but note that CPR r.7.6 which replaces O.6, r.8 introduces a new approach.

There is no antithesis between subs.(5) and subs.(6). Thus, even in cases where there has been reasonable opportunity of arresting, the court may extend the period if satisfied that there were reasonable grounds for not issuing the claim form earlier, *The Arraiz* (1924) 19 Lloyd's Rep. 382; 132 L.T. 715, a case on the proviso to the former s.8 from which both present subss.(5)and (6)are derived.

"And shall ... extend"

2D–263   Subsection (6) does not extend to Her Majesty's ships, see s.192(1) below.

"Reasonable opportunity"

2D–264   The fact that the vessel has been within the jurisdiction for a few days within the period does not necessarily disprove lack of reasonable opportunity to arrest (*The Largo Law* (1920) 123 L.T. 560; 15 Asp.M.L.C. 104). See also *The Berny* [1977] 2 Lloyd's Rep. 533 at 547–549, where the question of reasonable opportunity to serve the claim form arose in connection with renewal of a claim form *in rem*.

* * * *

APPLICATION TO CROWN AND ITS SHIPS

Application to Crown and its ships

2D–265   **192.**—(1) Sections 185, 186, 187, 188, 189 and 190 (except subsection (6)) apply in the case of Her Majesty's ships as they apply in relation to other ships and section 191 applies to the Crown in its capacity as an authority or person specified in subsection (1).

(2) In this section "Her Majesty's ships" means—

(a) ships of which the beneficial interest is vested in Her Majesty;

(b) ships which are registered as Government ships;

(c) ships which are for the time being demised or sub-demised to or in the exclusive possession of the Crown;

except that it does not include any ship in which Her Majesty is interested otherwise than in right of Her Government in the United Kingdom unless that ship is for the time being demised or sub-demised to Her Majesty in right of Her Government in the United Kingdom or in the exclusive possession of Her Majesty in that right.

(3) In the application of subsection (2) above to Northern Ireland, any reference to Her Majesty's Government in the United Kingdom includes a reference to Her Government in Northern Ireland.

2D–266   *Note* —Derivation—The Crown Proceedings Act 1947 ss.5, 6 , 7, 30(1) and 38(2); the Merchant Shipping Act 1979 Sch.5, para.3; and the Crown Proceedings Order 1981 (SI 1981/233) art.30(1).

Compulsory insurance or security

2D–267   **192A.**—(1) Subject to subsections (2) and (3) below, the Secretary of State may make regulations requiring that, in such cases as may be prescribed by the regulations, while a ship is in United Kingdom waters, there must be in force in respect of the ship—

(a) a contract of insurance insuring such person or persons

Paragraph numbers marked with a "+" can be found online and on CD.

2E ARBITRATION PROCEEDINGS

PART 62—ARBITRATION CLAIMS

Contents

Editorial introduction

Part I of Pt 62 is concerned with applications to which the Arbitration Act 1996 ap- **2E–2** plies, Pt II is concerned with matters to which the old law applies, and Pt III with common enforcement procedures.

"The old law" means the enactments specified in s.107 of the Arbitration Act 1996 as they stood before their amendment or repeal by the 1996 Act, namely the Arbitration Act 1950 (see SCP 1999, Vol.2, Section 21A, paras 21A–1 *et seq.*); the Arbitration Act 1975 (see SCP 1999, Vol.2, Section 21B, paras 21B–1 *et seq.*) and the Arbitration Act 1979 (see SCP 1999, Vol.2, Section 21C, paras 21C–1 *et seq.*).

The old law is preserved as a result of the provisions of s.109(2) of the Arbitration Act 1996 which provided that any order bringing the Act into force might contain any

Paragraph numbers marked with a "+" can be found online and on CD.

transitional provisions as might appear necessary and the provisions of the Arbitration Act 1996 (Commencement No.1) Order 1996, made on December 16, 1996, by way of transitional provision, provide that:

2. The old law shall continue to apply to:

(a) arbitral proceedings commenced before the appointed day [January 31, 1997];

(b) arbitration applications commenced or made before the appointed day;

(c) arbitration applications commenced or made on or after the appointed day relating to arbitral proceedings commenced before the appointed day;

and the provisions of the Act which would otherwise be applicable shall not apply.

Note

2E-3   With the passage of time since the coming into force of the 1996 Act (January 31, 1997) the transitional concept of the "old law" is now (July 2005 onwards) considered to be for all practical purposes in a state of desuetude if not without any effect. See further at 2E-22.

Part II of the 1950 Act together with the First Schedule thereto were not repealed by the 1996 Act and survive in their own right independently of the transitional concept of "the old law" but are now rarely relied upon.

The Application

2E-4   Arbitration applications under the 1996 Act (see Sect.I of Part 62) save for application under s.9, are made by use of an arbitration claim form (see rule 62.3, the Practice Direction—Arbitration and the reference to the form set out at Appendix A to the practice direction). Applications under s.9 are made by ordinary application process in the existing proceedings. The courts where the arbitration claim form may be issued are set out in the Practice Direction—Arbitration, para.62.2.3.

Applications under "the old law" see (Sect.II of Part 62) save for s.4 of the 1950 Act applications are made by the use of an arbitration claim form and must be stated in the Commercial Court and issued out of the Admiralty and Commercial Registry at the RCJ London and where required to be heard by a judge must be heard by a judge of that court unless he otherwise directs, see rule 62.12 and Practice Direction—Arbitration, para.62.14.1. Claims for the attendance of witnesses within the area of a district registry may be started within the relevant district registry, see r.62.14 and see the Practice Direction, para.7.2.

Applications for enforcement should be made using an arbitration claim form and may be considered by a Judge, Master, Admiralty Registrar or District Judge.

Related sources

2E-5
- Arbitration Act 1950 Pt II (see paras 2E-57 *et seq.*).
- Arbitration Act 1996 (see paras 2E-83 *et seq.*).
- The preserved "old law"
  — Arbitration Act 1950 Pt I (see SCP 1999, Vol.2, Section 21A).
  — Arbitration Acts 1975 and 1979 (see SCP 1999, Vol.2, Sections 21B and 21C).
- High Court and County Court (Allocation of Arbitration Proceedings) Order 1996 (SI 1996/3215), as amended.
- CPR Pt 6.
- CPR Pt 8.
- CPR Pt 11
- CPR Pt 25.
- CPR Pt 34.
- CPR Pts 58 and 59.
- CPR Pt 74.
- The Admiralty and Commercial Courts Guide, Section O.
- The Technology and Construction Court Guide, Section 10.

Forms

2E-6
- **N8** Claim form (arbitration)
- **N8A** Notes for claimant

Paragraph numbers marked with a "+" can be found online and on CD.

- **N8B** Notes for defendant
- **N15** Acknowledgment of service (arbitration claims)

Scope of this Part and interpretation[1]

62.1—(1) This Part contains rules about arbitration claims.   2E–7

(2) In this Part—

    (a) "the 1950 Act" means the Arbitration Act 1950;

    (b) "the 1975 Act" means the Arbitration Act 1975;

    (c) "the 1979 Act" means the Arbitration Act 1979;

    (d) "the 1996 Act" means the Arbitration Act 1996;

    (e) references to—

        (i) the 1996 Act; or

        (ii) any particular section of that Act

include references to that Act or to the particular section of that Act as applied with modifications by the ACAS Arbitration Scheme (England and Wales) Order 2001; and

    (f) "arbitration claim form" means a claim form in the form set out in the practice direction.

(3) Part 58 (Commercial Court) applies to arbitration claims in the Commercial Court, Part 59 (Mercantile Court) applies to arbitration claims in the Mercantile Court and Part 60 (Technology and Construction Court claims) applies to arbitration claims in the Technology and Construction Court, except where this Part provides otherwise.

I. Claims under the 1996 Act

Interpretation[2]

62.2—(1) In this Section of this Part "arbitration claim"   2E–8
means—

    (a) any application to the court under the 1996 Act;

    (b) a claim to determine—

        (i) whether there is a valid arbitration agreement;

        (ii) whether an arbitration tribunal is properly constituted; or what matters have been submitted to arbitration in accordance with an arbitration agreement;

    (c) a claim to declare that an award by an arbitral tribunal is not binding on a party; and

    (d) any other application affecting—

        (i) arbitration proceedings (whether started or not); or

        (ii) an arbitration agreement.

(2) This Section of this Part does not apply to an arbitration claim to which Sections II or III of this Part apply.

---

[1] Amended by the Civil Procedure (Amendment No.5) Rules 2001 (SI 2001/4015).
[2] Amended by the Civil Procedure (Amendment No.5) Rules 2001 (SI 2001/4015).

Paragraph numbers marked with a "+" can be found online and on CD.

Starting the claim[1]

2E–9   **62.3—(1) Except where paragraph (2) applies an arbitration claim must be started by the issue of an arbitration claim form in accordance with the Part 8 procedure.**

(2) **An application under section 9 of the 1996 Act to stay legal proceedings must be made by application notice to the court dealing with those proceedings.**

(3) **The courts in which an arbitration claim may be started are set out in the practice direction.**

(4) **Rule 30.5 applies with the modification that a judge of the Technology and Construction Court may transfer the claim to any other court or specialist list.**

Note

2E–10   This rule is supplemented by Practice Direction—Arbitration para.2 (see para.2E–46 below). See too the High Court and County Courts (Allocation of Arbitration Proceedings) Order 1996 at paras 2E–375 *et seq.*

Arbitration claim form[2]

2E–11   **62.4—(1) An arbitration claim form must—**

(a) **include a concise statement of—**

(i) **the remedy claimed; and**

(ii) **any questions on which the claimant seeks the decision of the court;**

(b) **give details of any arbitration award challenged by the claimant, identifying which part or parts of the award are challenged and specifying the grounds for the challenge;**

(c) **show that any statutory requirements have been met;**

(d) **specify under which section of the 1996 Act the claim is made;**

(e) **identify against which (if any) defendants a costs order is sought; and**

(f) **specify either—**

(i) **the persons on whom the arbitration claim form is to be served, stating their role in the arbitration and whether they are defendants; or**

(ii) **that the claim is made without notice under section 44(3) of the 1996 Act and the grounds relied on.**

(2) **Unless the court orders otherwise an arbitration claim form must be served on the defendant within 1 month from the date of issue and rules 7.5 and 7.6 are modified accordingly.**

(3) **Where the claimant applies for an order under section 12 of the 1996 Act (extension of time for beginning arbitral proceedings**

---

[1] Amended by the Civil Procedure (Amendment No.5) Rules 2001 (SI 2001/4015) and the Civil Procedure (Amendment No.4) Rules 2005 (SI 2005/3515).

[2] Amended by the Civil Procedure (Amendment No.5) Rules 2001 (SI 2001/4015).

Paragraph numbers marked with a "+" can be found online and on CD.

(3) After the period of 28 days has expired—

    (a) an application for an order extending time under paragraph (1) must—

        (i) be made in the arbitration claim form; and

        (ii) state the grounds on which the application is made;

    (b) any defendant may file written evidence opposing the extension of time within 7 days after service of the arbitration claim form; and

    (c) if the court extends the period of 28 days, each defendant's time for acknowledging service and serving evidence shall start to run as if the arbitration claim form had been served on the date when the court's order is served on that defendant.

Hearings[1]

62.10—(1) The court may order that an arbitration claim be heard either in public or in private.   **2E–18**

(2) Rule 39.2 does not apply.

(3) Subject to any order made under paragraph (1)—

    (a) the determination of—

        (i) a preliminary point of law under section 45 of the 1996 Act; or

        (ii) an appeal under section 69 of the 1996 Act on a question of law arising out of an award,

will be heard in public; and

    (b) all other arbitration claims will be heard in private.

(4) Paragraph (3)(a) does not apply to—

    (a) the preliminary question of whether the court is satisfied of the matters set out in section 45(2)(b); or

    (b) an application for permission to appeal under section 69(2)(b).

Application for variation of time

This rule is supplemented by Practice Direction—Arbitration para.11.1 (see para.2E–50 below).   **2E–18.1**

Note

In *Moscow City Council v Bankers Trust Co* [2004] EWCA Civ 314; [2005] Q.B. 207; [2004] 3 W.L.R. 533; [2004] 4 All E.R. 746; [2004] 2 Lloyd's Rep. 179, the Court of Appeal reviewed the several considerations material to deciding whether the hearing of an arbitration claim should be in public or in private and whether publication of any judgment given or order made should be restricted or not. At para.34, Mance L.J. said: **2E–19**

    "The consideration that parties have elected to arbitrate confidentially and privately cannot dictate the position is respect of arbitration claims brought to court under CPR 62.10. CPR 62.10 therefore only represents a starting point. Such proceedings are no longer consensual. The possibility of pursuing them ex-

---

[1] Amended by the Civil Procedure (Amendment No.5) Rules 2001 (SI 2001/4015).

Paragraph numbers marked with a "+" can be found online and on CD.

ists in the public interest. The courts, when called upon to exercise the supervisory role assigned to them under the Arbitration Act 1996, are acting as a branch of the state, not as a mere extension of the consensual arbitral process. Nevertheless, they are acting in the public interest to facilitate the fairness and well-being of a consensual method of dispute resolution, and both the Rule Committee and the courts can still take into account the parties' expectations regarding privacy and confidentiality when agreeing to arbitrate."

And at paras 38 and 39:

"...In arbitration claims relating to such arbitrations, the starting point may easily give way to a public hearing. In every case, while it will be appropriate to start the hearing in private as contemplated by CPR 62.10, the court should be ready to hear representations from one or other party that the hearing should be continued in public, and should anyway if appropriate raise this possibility with the parties, as Lord Woolf stressed in *Ex p. Kaim Todner*.

Further, even though the hearing may have been in private, the court should, when preparing and giving judgment, bear in mind that any judgment should be given in public, where this can be done without disclosing significant confidential information."

And at para.42:

"...It is, I think, better to describe CPR 62.10 and indeed 39.2 as establishing starting points, rather than as presumptions. If neither the parties nor the judge of his or her own motion raises any question about the appropriateness of private hearing, where that is the starting position, then the hearing will remain private. But, once the question of publication is raised, the judge's task is to weigh all relevant circumstances; and even where it is not raised by the parties, he or she may if appropriate raise it of his own motion."

See too *Emmott v Michael Wilson & Partners* [2008] EWCA Civ 184, [2008] 1 Lloyd's Rep. 616, CA, where the paramountcy of privacy in arbitration and the associated obligation of confidentiality and the exceptions thereto are reviewed. See also para. 31.22.1, above.

II. Other Arbitration Claims

Scope of this Section[1]

2E-20   **62.11—(1) This Section of this Part contains rules about arbitration claims to which the old law applies.**

(2) In this Section—

> **(a) "the old law" means the enactments specified in Schedules 3 and 4 of the 1996 Act as they were in force before their amendment or repeal by that Act; and**

> **(b) "arbitration claim" means any application to the court under the old law and includes an appeal (or application for permission to appeal) to the High Court under section 1(2) of the 1979 Act[2].**

(3) This Section does not apply to—

> **(a) a claim to which Section III of this Part applies; or**

> **(b) a claim on the award.**

Note

---

[1] Amended by the Civil Procedure (Amendment No.5) Rules 2001 (SI 2001/4015).

[2] 1979 c.42; repealed by the Arbitration Act 1996 (c.23), s.107(2) and Sch.4 but continues to apply to claims commenced before January 31, 1997 by virtue of the Arbitration Act 1996 (Commencement No.1) Order 1996 (SI 1996/3146) art.4 and Sch.2.

Paragraph numbers marked with a "+" can be found online and on CD.

"The old law" namely the Arbitration Act 1950; the Arbitration Act 1975; and the **2E–21** Arbitration Act 1979, the texts of which are set out in SCP 1999, Vol.2, Section 21 at paras 21A-1 *et seq.*, 21B–1 *et seq.*, and 21C–1 *et seq.* respectively. See too under Note at 2E–3 above.

Other Arbitration Claims—Section II

It is important to note that the provisions of Sect.II of Part 62 and Sect.II of its as- **2E–22** sociated Practice Direction apply only to arbitration claims under "the old law". Such provisions should not be applied by analogy or otherwise to claims under the 1996 Act for which a more flexible regime consistent with the modern approach to arbitration is provided. In particular for 1996 Act claims a more flexible point of entry and jurisdiction is provided (see PD 62.2.3) allowing an arbitration claim to be issued and considered as appropriate to its subject matter in the Chancery Division, the Technology and Construction Court, the Mercantile lists (where established) and TCC lists of the High Court District Registries as well as the Commercial Court as hitherto. Applications for a stay under s.4 of the 1950 Act or under s.9 of the 1996 Act were and are in any event made in whatever court is dealing with the proceedings concerned.

Applications to Judge[1]

62.12 A claim— **2E–23**

    (a) **seeking permission to appeal under section 1(2) of the 1979 Act;**

    (b) **under section 1(5) of that Act (including any claim seeking permission); or**

    (c) **under section 5 of that Act,**

must be made in the High Court and will be heard by a judge of the Commercial Court unless any such judge directs otherwise.

Effect of rule

In connection with the following commentary it is suggested that reference be made **2E–24** first to the Note at 2E–3 and the Note at 2E–22 above.

Applications under s.1(5) of the 1979 Act must be made to a judge. These are applications to order the arbitrator or umpire concerned to state the reasons for his award in sufficient detail to enable the court, should an appeal be brought under s.1 of the 1979 Act, to consider any questions of law arising out of the award. The reason for this requirement is because of the likely complexity and importance of the questions which will probably arise in considering whether the award does or does not sufficiently set out the reasons for the award. An application under s.1(5) of the 1979 Act, including any application for permission is made by an arbitration form in accordance with Pt 8, which must be served on the arbitrator or umpire, as the case may be, and on all the parties to the reference (see r.62.13(3)).

Applications under s.5 of the 1979 Act must be made to a judge. These are applications to empower the arbitrator or umpire to continue with the reference in default of acknowledgment of service by any party or of non-compliance by a party with an order made by the arbitrator or umpire in the same manner as a Judge of the High Court might continue with proceedings where a party fails to comply with an order of the court or a requirement of the rules of court.

Applications for permission to appeal to the court under s.1(2) of the 1979 Act must be made to a judge. Section 1(2) provides that an appeal shall lie to the court on any question of law arising out of an award made on an arbitration agreement and in s.1(3) it is stated that an appeal may be brought by any of the parties to the reference (a) with the consent of all the other parties or (b) with the permission of the court.

Applications under this rule must be made, where a claim is pending by application notice in the claim, and in any other case by a Pt 8 arbitration claim form (see r.62.13(1) and (2).

---

[1] Amended by the Civil Procedure (Amendment No.5) Rules 2001 (SI 2001/4015).

Paragraph numbers marked with a "+" can be found online and on CD.

It should further be noted that applications under this rule which are required to be heard by a Judge must be heard by a Commercial judge, unless he directs otherwise (see r.62.12, and Practice Direction—Arbitration para.14.1).

Apart from the matters specified in this rule, all other applications arising under the Arbitration Act 1950, may be made in chambers and heard by the judge, Master or Admiralty Registrar. They include applications to stay proceedings under s.4, to appoint an arbitrator or umpire under s.10, for the issue of a witness summons, and all other matters included in s.12(6) of the Arbitration Act 1950. The effect of this rule is to negative the decisions in *Raymond and Reid v Granger* [1952] 2 All E.R. 1952, and *Kruger Townwear Ltd v Northern Assurance Co* [1953] 1 W.L.R. 1049; [1953] 2 All E.R. 727n.

Without notice applications for injunctions

2E–25 CPR r.25.2, which permits applications for injunctive relief in cases in urgency, before the issue of a Pt 7 claim form or a Pt 8 claim form. Where injunctive relief is granted in such circumstances, however, the claim form should be issued promptly thereafter. It is unacceptable that a *Mareva* injunction, for example, granted in aid of an arbitration, should remain in force for two months after its grant without any originating process to sustain it; accordingly such an injunction will be discharged (*Siporex Trade SA v Comdel Commodities Ltd* [1986] 2 Lloyd's Rep. 428; (1986) 136 N.L.J. 538).

Starting the claim[1]

2E–26 **62.13—(1) Except where paragraph (2) applies an arbitration claim must be started by the issue of an arbitration claim form in accordance with the Part 8 procedure.**

(2) Where an arbitration claim is to be made in existing proceedings—

    (a) it must be made by way of application notice; and

    (b) any reference in this Section of this Part to an arbitration claim form includes a reference to an application notice.

(3) The arbitration claim form in an arbitration claim under section 1(5) of the 1979 Act (including any claim seeking permission) must be served on—

    (a) the arbitrator or umpire; and

    (b) any other party to the reference.

Claims in District Registries[2]

2E–27 **62.14 If—**

    (a) a claim is to be made under section 12(4) of the 1950 Act[3] for an order for the issue of a witness summons to compel the attendance of the witness before an arbitrator or umpire; and

    (b) the attendance of the witness is required within the district of a District Registry,

---

[1] Amended by the Civil Procedure (Amendment No.5) Rules 2001 (SI 2001/4015).
[2] Amended by the Civil Procedure (Amendment No.5) Rules 2001 (SI 2001/4015).
[3] 1950 c.27; s.12(4) was repealed by the Arbitration Act 1996 (c.23), s.107(2) and Sch. 4 but continues to apply to claims commenced before January 31, 1997 by virtue of the Arbitration Act 1996 (Commencement No.1) Order 1996 (SI 1996/3146) art.4 and Sch.2.

Paragraph numbers marked with a "+" can be found online and on CD.

the claim may be started in that Registry.

Time limits and other special provisions about arbitration claims[1]

62.15—(1) An arbitration claim to—

    (a) remit an award under section 22 of the 1950 Act[2];

    (b) set aside an award under section 23(2) of that Act[3] or otherwise; or

    (c) direct an arbitrator or umpire to state the reasons for an award under section 1(5) of the 1979 Act,

must be made, and the arbitration claim form served, within 21 days after the award has been made and published to the parties.

(2) An arbitration claim to determine any question of law arising in the course of a reference under section 2(1) of the Arbitration Act 1979 must be made, and the arbitration claim form served, within 14 days after—

    (a) the arbitrator or umpire gave his consent in writing to the claim being made; or

    (b) the other parties so consented.

(3) An appeal under section 1(2) of the 1979 Act must be filed, and the arbitration claim form served, within 21 days after the award has been made and published to the parties.

(4) Where reasons material to an appeal under section 1(2) of the 1979 Act are given on a date subsequent to the publication of the award, the period of 21 days referred to in paragraph (3) will run from the date on which reasons are given.

(5) In every arbitration claim to which this rule applies—

    (a) the arbitration claim form must state the grounds of the claim or appeal;

    (b) where the claim or appeal is based on written evidence, a copy of that evidence must be served with the arbitration claim form; and

    (c) where the claim or appeal is made with the consent of the arbitrator, the umpire or the other parties, a copy of every written consent must be served with the arbitration claim form.

(6) In an appeal under section 1(2) of the 1979 Act—

    (a) a statement of the grounds for the appeal specifying the relevant parts of the award and reasons; and

    (b) where permission is required, any written evidence in

2E–28

ARBITRATION

---

[1] Amended by the Civil Procedure (Amendment No.5) Rules 2001 (SI 2001/4015).

[2] 1950 c.27; s.22 was repealed by the Arbitration Act 1996 (c.23), s.107(2) and Sch.4 but continues to apply to claims commenced before January 31, 1997 by virtue of the Arbitration Act 1996 (Commencement No.1) Order 1996 (SI 1996/3146) art.4 and Sch.2.

[3] 1950 c.27; s.23(2) was repealed by the Arbitration Act 1996 (c.23), s.107(2) and Sch. 4 but continues to apply to claims commenced before January 31, 1997 by virtue of the Arbitration Act 1996 (Commencement No.1) Order 1996 (SI 1996/3146) art.4 and Sch.2.

Paragraph numbers marked with a "+" can be found online and on CD.

support of the contention that the question of law concerns—

(i) a term of a contract; or

(ii) an event,

which is not a "one-off" term or event,

must be filed and served with the arbitration claim form.

(7) Any written evidence in reply to written evidence under paragraph (6)(b) must be filed and served on the claimant not less than 2 days before the hearing.

(8) A party to a claim seeking permission to appeal under section 1(2) of the 1979 Act who wishes to contend that the award should be upheld for reasons not expressed or fully expressed in the award and reasons must file and serve on the claimant, a notice specifying the grounds of his contention not less than 2 days before the hearing.

General Note to 2E–30 and 2E–32 to 2E–36

2E–29   In connection with the above mentioned commentaries reference should be made first to the Note at 2E–3 and the Note at 2E–22.

Time for applying

2E–30   The 21–day time limit imposed by r.62.15(1) applies both to an application to set aside an award under s.23(2) of the Arbitration Act 1950 and to an application at common law for a declaration that an award is void on the grounds of the arbitrator's conduct. The time–limit cannot be circumvented simply by avoiding the use of the term "misconduct" in the application (*Cook International Inc v BV Handelsmaatschappij Jean Delvaux* [1985] 2 Lloyd's Rep. 225 at 233). The 21 day–time limit is not mandatory. The court has jurisdiction to extend time, see *Nagusina Naviera v Allied Maritime Inc* [2002] C.L.C. 385 (a case under s.1(2) of the Arbitration Act 1979 and concerning the relevance of CPR r.7.6).

"Made and published"

2E–31   An award is made and published when the arbitrator gives notice to the parties that it is ready. Delay in taking up the award does not extend the time for appealing or applying (*The Archipelagos* [1979] Lloyd's Rep. 289; *Selous Street Properties Ltd v Oronel Fabrics Ltd* (1984) 270 E.G. 643).

Appeal under s.1(2) of the Arbitration Act 1979—practice

2E–32   The practice is regulated by the provisions of r.62.15, and, in particular, by subrules (3) to (8) thereof inclusive. See too Section O of the Admiralty and Commercial Courts Guide and in particular paras O.16.1 *et seq.* at paras 2A–149 *et seq.* above.

Service out of the jurisdiction[1]

2E–33   62.16—(1) Subject to paragraph (2)—

(a) any arbitration claim form in an arbitration claim under the 1950 Act or the 1979 Act; or

(b) any order made in such a claim,

may be served out of the jurisdiction with the permission of the court if the arbitration to which the claim relates—

(i) is governed by the law of England and Wales; or

---

[1] Amended by the Civil Procedure (Amendment No.5) Rules 2001 (SI 2001/4015) and the Civil Procedure (Amendment) Rules 2008 (SI 2008/2178).

Paragraph numbers marked with a "+" can be found online and on CD.

(ii) has been, is being, or will be, held within the jurisdiction.

(2) An arbitration claim form seeking permission to enforce an award may be served out of the jurisdiction with the permission of the court whether or not the arbitration is governed by the law of England and Wales.

(3) An application for permission to serve an arbitration claim form out of the jurisdiction must be supported by written evidence—

> **(a) stating the grounds on which the application is made; and**
>
> **(b) showing in what place or country the person to be served is, or probably may be found.**

(4) Rules 6.40 to 6.46 apply to the service of an arbitration claim form under paragraph (1).

(5) An order giving permission to serve an arbitration claim form out of the jursidiction must specify the period within which the defendant may file an acknowledgment of service.

Note

This rule is really an extension of CPR r.6.36, and an additional case in which service out of the jurisdiction is permissible with the permission of the court. For observations on the differences between service out of jurisdiction under the former RSC O.11 the forerunner of this rule and under this rule, see *Mayer Newman Co Ltd v Al Ferro Commodities Corp SA* [1990] 2 Lloyd's Rep. 290 at 293, CA, *per* Bingham L.J. The basis of the jurisdiction under this rule is that the "arbitration is to be or has been held within the jurisdiction". The practice under this rule is the same in all respects as under CPR r.6.36, including the requirement under CPR r.6.45 that translations be provided of documents for service on a foreign state in arbitration proceedings unless the official language or an official language of that State is English.   **2E–34**

Civil Jurisdiction and Judgments Acts 1982

Article 1 of the Brussels Convention, which forms the first Schedule to the Act, provides that the convention shall not apply to arbitration. The word "arbitration" in art.1 covers all matters connected with arbitration, including the question whether there is a valid arbitration agreement (*Marc Rich & Co AG v Societa Italiana Impianti pA (The Atlantic Emperor) (No.1)*, [1989] 1 Lloyd's Rep. 548). Thus where a claimant issues a Pt 8 arbitration claim form seeking the appointment of an arbitrator under s.10(3) of the Arbitration Act 1950, the Italian defendant having denied the existence of the alleged arbitration agreement, the claimant may properly seek permission to serve the Pt 8 arbitration claim form out of the jurisdiction under this rule, and should not attempt to serve without leave in Italy under the convention (*ibid.*).   **2E–35**

Application

This rule is concerned only with applications by and against parties to an arbitration which relate to the arbitration to which they are parties. Thus the natural meaning of the para.is that the application must be against the other party to the reference and not a non-party (as case under the pre-1997 RSC O.73, r.7 being *The Cienvik* [1996] 2 Lloyd's Rep. 395). The reasoning of the court in *The Cienvik* was adopted by the Court of Appeal in *Tate and Lyle Industries Ltd v CIA Usina Bulhoes and Cargill Inc* [1997] 1 Lloyd's Rep. 355, when holding that there is no jurisdiction to issue a without notice injunction against a proposed defendant not a party to the arbitration under s.12 of the 1950 Act.   **2E–36**

Paragraph numbers marked with a "+" can be found online and on CD.

III. Enforcement

Scope of this Section[1]

2E-37   **62.17 This Section of this Part applies to all arbitration enforcement proceedings other than by a claim on the award.**

Enforcement of awards[2]

2E-38   **62.18—(1) An application for permission under—**
    (a) **section 66 of the 1996 Act[3];**
    (b) **section 101 of the 1996 Act;**
    (c) **section 26 of the 1950 Act[4]; or**
    (d) **section 3(1)(a) of the 1975 Act,[5]**
to enforce an award in the same manner as a judgment or order may be made without notice in an arbitration claim form.

(2) The court may specify parties to the arbitration on whom the arbitration claim form must be served.

(3) The parties on whom the arbitration claim form is served must acknowledge service and the enforcement proceedings will continue as if they were an arbitration claim under Section I of this Part.

(4) With the permission of the court the arbitration claim form may be served out of the jurisdiction irrespective of where the award is, or is treated as, made.

(5) Where the applicant applies to enforce an agreed award within the meaning of section 51(2) of the 1996 Act—
    (a) **the arbitration claim form must state that the award is an agreed award; and**
    (b) **any order made by the court must also contain such a statement.**

(6) An application for permission must be supported by written evidence—
    (a) **exhibiting—**
        (i) **where the application is made under section 66 of the 1996 Act or under section 26 of the 1950 Act, the arbitration agreement and the original award (or copies);**
        (ii) **where the application is under section 101 of the**

---

[1] Amended by the Civil Procedure (Amendment No.5) Rules 2001 (SI 2001/4015).
[2] Amended by the Civil Procedure (Amendment No.5) Rules 2001 (SI 2001/4015) and the Civil Procedure (Amendment) Rules 2008 (SI 2008/2178).
[3] 1996 c.23.
[4] 1950 c.27; s.26 was repealed by the Arbitration Act 1996 (c. 23), s.107(2) and Sch. 4 but continues to apply to claims commenced before January 31, 1997 by virtue of the Arbitration Act 1996 (Commencement No.1) Order 1996 (SI 1996/3146) art.4 and Sch.2.
[5] 1975 c.3; repealed by the Arbitration Act 1996 (c.23), s.107(2) and Sch.4 but continues to apply to claims commenced before January 31, 1997 by virtue of the Arbitration Act 1996 (Commencement No.1) Order 1996 (SI 1996/3146) art.4 and Sch.2.

Paragraph numbers marked with a "+" can be found online and on CD.

> > 1996 Act, the documents required to be produced by section 102 of that Act; or
> >
> > (iii) where the application is under section 3(1)(a) of the 1975 Act, the documents required to be produced by section 4 of that Act;
> >
> > (b) stating the name and the usual or last known place of residence or business of the claimant and of the person against whom it is sought to enforce the award; and
> >
> > (c) stating either—
> >
> > > (i) that the award has not been complied with; or
> > >
> > > (ii) the extent to which it has not been complied with at the date of the application.

(7) An order giving permission must—

> (a) be drawn up by the claimant; and
>
> (b) be served on the defendant by—
>
> > (i) delivering a copy to him personally; or
> >
> > (ii) sending a copy to him at his usual or last known place of residence or business.

(8) An order giving permission may be served out of the jurisdiction—

> (a) without permission; and
>
> (b) in accordance with rules 6.40 to 6.46 as if the order were an arbitration claim form.

(9) Within 14 days after service of the order or, if the order is to be served out of the jurisdiction, within such other period as the court may set—

> (a) the defendant may apply to set aside the order; and
>
> (b) the award must not be enforced until after—
>
> > (i) the end of that period; or
> >
> > (ii) any application made by the defendant within that period has been finally disposed of.

(10) The order must contain a statement of—

> (a) the right to make an application to set the order aside; and
>
> (b) the restrictions on enforcement under rule 62.18(9)(b).

(11) Where a body corporate is a party any reference in this rule to place of residence or business shall have effect as if the reference were to the registered or principal address of the body corporate.

Written evidence in support of application

As to the importance of full and frank disclosure in any affidavit and by like token **2E-39** in any witness statement in support of application which in the first instance is made without notice, and the relevant considerations where non-disclosure is established (see *Curacao Trading Co BV v Harkisandas & Co* [1992] 21 Lloyd's Rep. 186).

Copies of draft order/Contents of affidavit/Witness statement in support

In addition to any written evidence Section O of the the Admiralty and Commercial **2E-40** Courts Guide, para.O18.4(a) requires two copies of a draft order to be provided and

Paragraph numbers marked with a "+" can be found online and on CD.

requires that care be taken to see that the affidavit or witness statement and the draft order meet the requirements of this provision.

Interest on awards[1]

2E–41   **62.19—(1) Where an applicant seeks to enforce an award of interest the whole or any part of which relates to a period after the date of the award, he must file a statement giving the following particulars—**

(a) **whether simple or compound interest was awarded;**

(b) **the date from which interest was awarded;**

(c) **where rests were provided for, specifying them;**

(d) **the rate of interest awarded; and**

(e) **a calculation showing—**

(i) **the total amount claimed up to the date of the statement; and**

(ii) **any sum which will become due on a daily basis.**

(2) A statement under paragraph (1) must be filed whenever the amount of interest has to be quantified for the purpose of—

(a) **obtaining a judgment or order under section 66 of the 1996 Act (enforcement of the award); or**

(b) **enforcing such a judgment or order.**

Registration in High Court of foreign awards[2]

2E–42   **62.20—(1) Where—**

(a) **an award is made in proceedings on an arbitration in any part of a British overseas territory or other territory to which Part I of the Foreign Judgments (Reciprocal Enforcement) Act 1933[3] ("the 1933 Act") extends;**

(b) **Part II of the Administration of Justice Act 1920[4] extended to that part immediately before Part I of the 1933 Act was extended to that part; and**

(c) **an award has, under the law in force in the place where it was made, become enforceable in the same manner as a judgment given by a court in that place,**

rules 74.1 to 74.7 and 74.9 apply in relation to the award as they apply in relation to a judgment given by the court subject to the modifications in paragraph (2).

(2) The modifications referred to in paragraph (1) are as follows—

(a) **for references to the State of origin are substituted references to the place where the award was made; and**

---

[1] Amended by the Civil Procedure (Amendment No.5) Rules 2001 (SI 2001/4015).

[2] Amended by the Civil Procedure (Amendment No.5) Rules 2001 (SI 2001/4015), the Civil Procedure (Amendment) Rules 2002 (SI 2002/2058) and the Civil Procedure (Amendment) Rules 2008 (SI 2008/2178).

[3] 1933 c.13 (23 & 24 Geo. 5).

[4] 1920 c.81 (10 & 11 Geo. 5); s.10 of Pt II was substituted by the Civil Jurisdiction and Judgments Act 1982 (c.27), s.35(2) and s.14 of Pt II was amended by the Civil Jurisdiction and Judgments Act 1982 (c.27), s.35(3).

Paragraph numbers marked with a "+" can be found online and on CD.

(b) the written evidence required by rule 74.4 must state (in addition to the matters required by that rule) that to the best of the information or belief of the maker of the statement the award has, under the law in force in the place where it was made, become enforceable in the same manner as a judgment given by a court in that place.

Note

A foreign award expressed in a foreign currency must not be converted into sterling for the purposes of registration, see Rate of Exchange, para.74.11.9 in Vol.1 of *The White Book*.

2E–43

Registration of awards under the Arbitration (International Investment Disputes) Act 1966[1]

62.21—(1) In this rule—

2E–44

(a) "the 1966 Act" means the Arbitration (International Investment Disputes) Act 1966[2];

(b) "award" means an award under the Convention;

(c) "the Convention" means the Convention on the settlement of investment disputes between States and nationals of other States which was opened for signature in Washington on 18th March 1965[3];

(d) "judgment creditor" means the person seeking recognition or enforcement of an award; and

(e) "judgment debtor" means the other party to the award.

(2) Subject to the provisions of this rule, the following provisions of Part 74 apply with such modifications as may be necessary in relation to an award as they apply in relation to a judgment to which Part I of the Foreign Judgments (Reciprocal Enforcement) Act 1933 applies—

(a) rule 74.1;

(b) rule 74.3;

(c) rule 74.4(1) , (2)(a) to (d) , and (4);

(d) rule 74.6 (except paragraph (3)(c) to (e)); and

(e) rule 74.9(2).

(3) An application to have an award registered in the High Court under section 1 of the 1966 Act[4] must be made in accordance with the Part 8 procedure.

(4) The written evidence required by rule 74.4 in support of an application for registration must—

---

[1] Amended by the Civil Procedure (Amendment No.5) Rules 2001 (SI 2001/4015) and the Civil Procedure (Amendment) Rules 2002 (SI 2002/2058).
[2] 1966 c.41.
[3] The text of the Convention is set out in the Schedule to the Arbitration (International Investment Disputes) Act 1966 (c.41).
[4] 1966 c.41; s.1 was amended by the Administration of Justice Act 1977 (c.38), ss.4 and 32(4) and Sch. 5, Pt I and by the Supreme Court Act 1981 (c.54), s.152(1) and Sch.5.

Paragraph numbers marked with a "+" can be found online and on CD.

ARBITRATION

(a) **exhibit the award certified under the Convention instead of the judgment (or a copy of it); and**

(b) **in addition to stating the matters referred to in rule 74.4(2)(a) to (d), state whether—**

    (i) **at the date of the application the enforcement of the award has been stayed (provisionally or otherwise) under the Convention; and**

    (ii) **any, and if so what, application has been made under the Convention, which, if granted, might result in a stay of the enforcement of the award.**

(5) Where, on granting permission to register an award or an application made by the judgment debtor after an award has been registered, the court considers—

(a) **that the enforcement of the award has been stayed (whether provisionally or otherwise) under the Convention; or**

(b) **that an application has been made under the Convention which, if granted, might result in a stay of the enforcement of the award,**

the court may stay the enforcement of the award for such time as it considers appropriate.

Scope of rule

2E–45   This rule provides the machinery for the registration of an award rendered pursuant to the Convention set out in the Schedule to the Arbitration (International Investment Disputes) Act 1966. The procedure follows, in large measure, but with the necessary modifications, the provisions of CPR r.74, since this Act is in many respects similar to the Foreign Judgments (Reciprocal Enforcement) Act 1933.

Rule 62.21(2) makes it unecessary to convert an award under this Act expressed in foreign currency into sterling for the purposes of its registration.

Paragraph numbers marked with a "+" can be found online and on CD.

PRACTICE DIRECTION—ARBITRATION

This Practice Direction supplements CPR Part 62   **2E–46**

Section I

1.1 This Section of this Practice Direction applies to arbitration claims to which Section I of Part 62 applies.

1.2 In this Section "the 1996 Act" means the Arbitration Act 1996.

1.3 Where a rule provides for a document to be sent, it may be sent—

(1)   by first class post—

(2)   through a document exchange; or

(3)   fax, electronic mail or other means of electronic communication.

62.3 Starting the claim

2.1 An arbitration claim under the 1996 Act (other than under section 9) must be started in accordance with the High Court and County Courts (Allocation of Arbitration Proceedings) Order 1996 by the issue of an arbitration claim form.

2.2 An arbitration claim form must be substantially in the form set out in Appendix A to this practice direction.

2.3 Subject to paragraph 2.1, an arbitration claim form—

(1)   may be issued at the courts set out in column 1 of the table below and will be entered in the list set out against that court in column 2;

(2)   relating to a landlord and tenant or partnership dispute must be issued in the Chancery Division of the High Court.

Court	List
Admiralty and Commercial Registry at the Royal Courts of Justice, London	Commercial list
Technology and Construction Court Registry, St. Dunstan's House, London	TCC list
District Registry of the High Court (where mercantile court established)	Mercantile list
District Registry of the High Court (where arbitration claim form marked 'Technology and Construction Court' in top right hand corner)	TCC list

2.3A An arbitration claim form must, in the case of an appeal, or application for permission to appeal, from a judge-adjudicator, be issued in the Civil Division of the Court of Appeal. The judge hearing the application may adjourn the matter for oral argument before two judges of that court.

Paragraph numbers marked with a "+" can be found online and on CD.

Note

2E-47   The High Court and County Courts (Allocation of Arbitration Proceedings) Order 1996 is SI 1996/3215 and came into force on January 31, 1997. It has been amended by SI 1999/1010.

Appendix A

2E-48   The Forms **N8,N8A**, **N8B** and **N15** can be found in the *Civil Procedure Forms Volume*.

Fees

2E-49   See the Supreme Court Fees Order 1999 (SI 1999/687) and, in particular, items 1.2, 2.4 and 2.5, and 4.4 and 4.5.

Arbitration claim form

Service

2E-50   **3.1** The court may exercise its powers under rule 6.15 to permit service of an arbitration claim form at an address of a party's solicitor or representative acting for that party in the arbitration.

3.2 Where the arbitration claim form is served by the claimant he must file a certificate of service within 7 days of service of the arbitration claim form.

(Rule 6.17 specifies what a certificate of service must show).

Acknowledgment of service or making representations by arbitrator or ACAS

4.1 Where—

(1)   an arbitrator; or

(2)   ACAS (in a claim under the 1996 Act as applied with modifications by the ACAS Arbitration Scheme (England and Wales) Order 2001)

is sent a copy of an arbitration claim form (including an arbitration claim form sent under rule 62.6(2)), that arbitrator or ACAS (as the case may be) may—

(a) apply to be made a defendant; or

(b) make representations to the court under paragraph 4.3.

4.2 An application under paragraph 4.1(2)(a) to be made a defendant—

(1)   must be served on the claimant; but

(2)   need not be served on any other party.

4.3 An arbitrator or ACAS may make representations by filing written evidence or in writing to the court.

Supply of documents from court records

5.1 An arbitration claim form may only be inspected with the permission of the court.

62.7 Case management

6.1 The following directions apply unless the court orders otherwise.

6.2 A defendant who wishes to rely on evidence before the court must file and serve his written evidence—

(1)   within 21 days after the date by which he was required to acknowledge service; or,

Paragraph numbers marked with a "+" can be found online and on CD.

(2) where a defendant is not required to file an acknowledgement of service, within 21 days after service of the arbitration claim form.

6.3 A claimant who wishes to rely on evidence in reply to written evidence filed under paragraph 6.2 must file and serve his written evidence within 7 days after service of the defendant's evidence.

6.4 Agreed indexed and paginated bundles of all the evidence and other documents to be used at the hearing must be prepared by the claimant.

6.5 Not later than 5 days before the hearing date estimates for the length of the hearing must be filed together with a complete set of the documents to be used.

6.6 Not later than 2 days before the hearing date the claimant must file and serve—

(1) a chronology of the relevant events cross-referenced to the bundle of documents;

(2) (where necessary) a list of the persons involved; and

(3) a skeleton argument which lists succinctly—

   (a) the issues which arise for decision;

   (b) the grounds of relief (or opposing relief) to be relied upon;

   (c) the submissions of fact to be made with the references to the evidence; and

   (d) the submissions of law with references to the relevant authorities.

6.7 Not later than the day before the hearing date the defendant must file and serve a skeleton argument which lists succinctly—

(1) the issues which arise for decision;

(2) the grounds of relief (or opposing relief) to be relied upon;

(3) the submissions of fact to be made with the references to the evidence; and

(4) the submissions of law with references to the relevant authorities.

Securing the attendance of witnesses

7.1 A party to arbitral proceedings being conducted in England or Wales who wishes to rely on section 43 of the 1996 Act to secure the attendance of a witness must apply for a witness summons in accordance with Part 34.

7.2 If the attendance of the witness is required within the district of a district registry, the application may be made at that registry.

7.3 A witness summons will not be issued until the applicant files written evidence showing that the application is made with—

(1) the permission of the tribunal; or

(2) the agreement of the other parties.

Interim remedies

8.1 An application for an interim remedy under section 44 of the 1996 Act must be made in an arbitration claim form.

Paragraph numbers marked with a "+" can be found online and on CD.

Applications under sections 32 and 45 of the 1996 Act

9.1 This paragraph applies to arbitration claims for the determination of—

(1) a question as to the substantive jurisdiction of the arbitral tribunal under section 32 of the 1996 Act; and

(2) a preliminary point of law under section 45 of the 1996 Act.

9.2 Where an arbitration claim is made without the agreement in writing of all the other parties to the arbitral proceedings but with the permission of the arbitral tribunal, the written evidence or witness statements filed by the parties must set out any evidence relied on by the parties in support of their contention that the court should, or should not, consider the claim.

9.3 As soon as practicable after the written evidence is filed, the court will decide whether or not it should consider the claim and, unless the court otherwise directs, will so decide without a hearing.

Decisions without a hearing

10.1 Having regard to the overriding objective the court may decide particular issues without a hearing. For example, as set out in paragraph 9.3, the question whether the court is satisfied as to the matters set out in section 32(2)(b) or section 45(2)(b) of the 1996 Act.

10.2 The court will generally decide whether to extend the time limit under section 70(3) of the 1996 Act without a hearing. Where the court makes an order extending the time limit, the defendant must file his written evidence within 21 days from service of the order.

62.9 Variation of time

11.1 An application for an order under rule 62.9(1)—

(1) before the period of 28 days has expired, must be made in a Part 23 application notice; and

(2) after the period of 28 days has expired, must be set out in a separately identified part in the arbitration claim form.

Applications for permission to appeal

12.1 Where a party seeks permission to appeal to the court on a question of law arising out of an arbitration award, the arbitration claim form must—

(1) identify the question of law; and

(2) state the grounds
on which the party alleges that permission should be given.

12.2 The written evidence in support of the application must set out any evidence relied on by the party for the purpose of satisfying the court—

(1) of the matters referred to in section 69(3) of the 1996 Act; and

(2) that permission should be given.

12.3 The written evidence filed by the respondent to the application must—

Paragraph numbers marked with a "+" can be found online and on CD.

(1)   state the grounds on which the respondent opposes the grant of permission;

(2)   set out any evidence relied on by him relating to the matters mentioned in section 69(3) of the 1996 Act; and

(3)   specify whether the respondent wishes to contend that the award should be upheld for reasons not expressed (or not fully expressed) in the award and, if so, state those reasons.

12.4 The court will normally determine applications for permission to appeal without an oral hearing.

12.5 Where the court refuses an application for permission to appeal without an oral hearing, it must provide brief reasons.

12.6 Where the court considers that an oral hearing is required, it may give such further directions as are necessary.

Section II

13.1 This Section of this Practice Direction applies to arbitration claims to which Section II of Part 62 applies.

62.13 Starting the claim

14.1 An arbitration claim must be started in the Commercial Court and, where required to be heard by a judge, be heard by a judge of that court unless he otherwise directs.

Effect of rule

The commentary which follows together with that at 2E–52 and 2E–53 should be read subject to the Note at 2E–3 and the Note at 2E–22 to which reference should be made. It is important to note that the requirement to channel arbitration applications through the Commercial Court as is necessary for Sect.II claims has been replaced in the case of 1996 Act claims by a more flexible regime. See further at 2E–22 and PD 62.2.3.

This rule has the effect of channelling all applications under Sect.II of Pt 62 in the first instance to the Commercial Court. The rule thus recognises that in practice the subject of arbitration is substantially a commercial matter and should be dealt with by a Commercial Judge both as a matter of convenience and the proper distribution of business in the High Court and also to enable uniformity of practice and procedure to be fostered and encouraged.

On the other hand, of course, there is a great volume of important arbitrations which may be described as "non-commercial" in the sense that the subject matter does not fall within the definition of a "commercial claim" and applications relating to such arbitrations which require to be heard by a judge under r.62.12, will no doubt be directed by a Commercial Judge to be heard by another judge of the High Court.

The normal practice should be that all applications for permission to appeal to the High Court are to be heard by a Commercial Judge unless any such judge otherwise directs, and if permission is granted, consideration could then be given to whether there should be a direction that the appeal itself should be heard by a judge who is not a Commercial Judge (*per* Donaldson L.J. in *F. G. Whitley & Sons Co Ltd v Clwyd CC, The Times*, August 6, 1982).

In *Ashbank Property Co Ltd v Department of Transport, The Times*, July 25, 1994; *Independent*, October 3, 1994; held that where a notice of application to set aside an arbitration award had been incorrectly issued in the Chancery Division it was inappropriate to transfer the same to the Commercial Court as that would be to grant an inappropriate extension of time for an appeal.

It is the practice in the Commercial Court for one Judge to hear the application for permission to appeal under s.1(2) of the 1979 Act and for another judge to hear the appeal itself but there are exceptional cases where it would be quite right that the same judge should hear the appeal; ultimately, it must be a matter for the judge's discretion (*Hiscox v Outhwaite (No.2)* [1991] 1 W.L.R. 545, CA).

2E–51

Paragraph numbers marked with a "+" can be found online and on CD.

Application

2E–52   By arbitration claim form in accordance with Pt 8 procedure, unless claim made in existing proceedings by way of application notice. Matters referred to in r.62.12 and application in respect of matters referred to in r.62.15(1) and (2) are to be made by issuing an arbitration claim form and will be heard by a judge of the Commercial Court unless such judge otherwise directs.

Where permission to appeal is required, it should be applied for to a judge in private by an application in existing proceedings or by a Pt 8 claim if no existing proceedings issued in the Admiralty and Commercial Registry. Such permission is required under s.1(3) of the Act of 1979, unless all parties to the reference consent.

2E–53   For ss.22 and 23 of the Arbitration Act 1950 and ss.1 and 2 of the Arbitration Act 1979, see SCP 1999, Vol.2, Section 21.

Section III

2E–54   **15.1** This Section of this Practice Direction applies to enforcement proceedings to which Section III of Part 62 applies.

62.21 Registration of awards under the Arbitration (International Investment Disputes) Act 1966

16.1 Awards ordered to be registered under the 1966 Act and particulars will be entered in the Register kept for that purpose at the Admiralty and Commercial Registry.

Editorial note

2E–55   With the exception of ss.35 to 42 and the First and Second Schedule to the Arbitration Act 1950, the texts of the Arbitration Act 1950, of the Arbitration Act 1975 and of the Arbitration Act 1979 (the "old law") are not printed in this publication. Such texts and related annotations are to be found in SCP 1999, Vol.2 at Section 21A, paras 21A–1 *et seq.*, (the 1950 Act), paras 21B–1 *et seq.* (the 1975 Act) and paras 21C–1 *et seq.* (the 1979 Act) to which reference should be made as necessary.

Appendix A

2E–56   The following form which is contained in Appendix A to this PD can be found in the Civil Procedure Forms Volume:

- N8

Arbitration Act 1950

2E–57   (14 GEO. 6 C.27)

ARRANGEMENT OF SECTIONS

PART II

Paragraph numbers marked with a "+" can be found online and on CD.

Paragraph numbers marked with a "+" denote content that is available on White Book on Westlaw UK or the Civil Procedure CD.

Arbitration Act 1996

(1996 c.23)

ARRANGEMENT OF SECTIONS

PART I

ARBITRATION PURSUANT TO AN ARBITRATION AGREEMENT

INTRODUCTORY

Paragraph numbers marked with a "+" can be found online and on CD.

Paragraph numbers marked with a "+" can be found online and on CD.

**Paragraph numbers marked with a "+" denote content that is available on White
Book on Westlaw UK or the Civil Procedure CD.**

Introductory note

The provisions of the Arbitration Act 1996 save for a few exceptions were brought **2E–84**
into force on January 31, 1997 by the Arbitration Act 1996 (Commencement No.1)
Order 1996, made December 16, 1996. That Order also provides that "the old law"
shall continue to apply to:

(a) arbitral proceedings commenced before the appointed day (i.e. January 31,
1997);

(b) arbitration applications commenced or made before the appointed day;

(c) arbitration applications commenced or made on or after the appointed day relating to arbitral proceedings commenced before the appointed day;
and that the provisions of the Act which would otherwise be applicable shall not apply.

The Order also provides that the provisions of the Act which it brings into force
shall apply to any other legal proceedings even though arbitral proceedings have not
been commenced.

Accordingly as from January 31, 1997 there are two alternative regimes though the
enforcement provisions of Pt II of the Arbitration Act 1950 are common to both. It
will be necessary therefore to determine according to the above application provisions
which regime is appropriate. These application provisions are reflected in CPR Pt
62—Arbitration Claims and the Practice Direction—Arbitration supplementing CPR Pt
62.

Paragraph numbers marked with a "+" can be found online and on CD.

The "old law" is defined in the said Order as the enactments mentioned in s.107 of the Act (the Consequential amendments and repeals provision). Included and now preserved in respect of the arbitral and legal proceedings referred to under (a), (b) and (c) above are the Arbitration Act 1950, the Arbitration Act 1975, and the Arbitration Act 1979.

General note

2E–85
The preamble to the 1996 Act states that it is "An act to restate and improve the law relating to arbitration pursuant to an arbitration agreement; to make other provision relating to arbitration and arbitration awards; and for connected purposes".

The 1996 Act applies to all arbitrations commenced after January 31, 1997 and to all applications made to the court on or after January 31, 1997, in respect of arbitrations yet to be commenced at the time of the application.

The Act enlarges the extent to which the principles of arbitration law are expressed in statutory form. It uses language that is "user friendly". It increases the authority of the parties to arbitral proceedings to regulate the proceedings themselves and restricts the role of the court to supporting the arbitral process save where court intervention is required to achieve justice between the parties.

Thus, for example access to the court to intervene is denied where the agreement provides a mechanism for resolving the question unless that mechanism has been tried and failed. The circumstances in which an award can be challenged are now more precisely defined as are the circumstances in which leave can be given for appealing against an award. There is statutory expression of an arbitral tribunal's powers to rule on matters affecting its own jurisdiction and of the guidelines developed by the court since 1979 on the circumstances in which leave to appeal against an award may be granted. The Act further specifies the grounds on which an award may be set aside or remitted or an arbitration removed thus removing the general discretion available under "the old law".

The court

2E–86
This is defined by s.105 of the Arbitration Act 1996 as meaning the High Court or a county court subject to powers vested in the Lord Chancellor by order to allocate and to impose restrictions in terms of specified proceedings and court.

By the High Court and County Courts (Allocation of Arbitration Proceedings) Order 1996 (SI 1996/3215) set out in full at paras 2E–375 *et seq.*, which came into force on January 31, 1997, it was inter alia provided:

> "2. Subject to articles 3 to 5, proceedings under the Act shall be commenced and taken in the High Court.
>
> 3. Proceedings under section 9 of the Act (stay of legal proceedings) shall be commenced in the court in which the legal proceedings are pending.
>
> 4. Proceedings under sections 66 and 101(2) (enforcement of awards) of the Act may be commenced in any county court.
>
> 5. Proceedings under the Act may be commenced and taken in the Central London County Court Mercantile List." [Now without effect.]

The Application

2E–87
Arbitration applications under the 1996 Act (see Sect.I of Pt 62) save for application under s.9, are made by use of an arbitration claim form (see r.62.3, the Practice Direction—Arbitration and the reference to the form set out at Appendix A to the practice direction). Applications under s.9 are made by ordinary application process in the existing proceedings. The courts where the arbitration claim form may be issued are set ou in the Practice Direction—Arbitration.

Applications under "the old law" see (Sect.II of Pt 62) save for s.4 of the 1950 Act applications are made by the use of an arbitration claim form and must be stated in the Commercial Court and issued out of the Admiralty and Commercial Registry at the R.C.J. London and where required to be heard by a judge must be heard by a judge of that court unless he otherwise directs, see r.62.12 and Practice Direction—Arbitration, para.14.1. Claims for the attendance of witnesses within the aread of a district registry may be started within the relevant district registry, see r.62.14.

Applications for enforcement should be made using an arbitration claim form and may be considered by a Judge, Master, Admiralty Regular or District Judge.

Paragraph numbers marked with a "+" can be found online and on CD.

regard to the parties' agreement and all the relevant circumstances.

"the juridical seat of the arbitration"

For factors relevant to the determination of the juridical seat of the arbitration, see **2E–93** *Dubai Islamic Bank PJSC v Paymentech Merchant Services Inc* [2001] 1 Lloyd's Rep. 65.

Choice of the seat of the arbitration will invariably (that is subject to agreement otherwise) coincide with the choice of procedural law; further agreement as to the seat of arbitration was akin to an exclusive jurisdiction clause and subject to an agreement otherwise determined the court having supervisory jurisdiction to the exclusion of the court of some other jurisdiction; *C v D* [2007] EWHC 1541(Comm); [2007] 2 Lloyd's Rep. 367 , affirmed on appeal [2007] EWCA Civ 1282; [2008] 1 Lloyd's Rep 239, CA . See for an instance of agreement to the contrary *Braes of Doune Wind Farm (Scotland) Ltd v Alfred McAlpine Business Services Ltd* [2008] EWHC 426 (TCC); [2008] 1 Lloyd's Rep. 608 (seat of arbitration Scotland, governing law English).

Mandatory and non-mandatory provisions

4.—(1) The mandatory provisions of this Part are listed in Sched-   **2E–94** ule 1 and have effect notwithstanding any agreement to the contrary.

(2) The other provisions of this Part (the "non-mandatory provisions") allow the parties to make their own arrangements by agreement but provide rules which apply in the absence of such agreement.

(3) The parties may make such arrangements by agreeing to the application of institutional rules or providing any other means by which a matter may be decided.

(4) It is immaterial whether or not the law applicable to the parties' agreement is the law of England and Wales or, as the case may be, Northern Ireland.

(5) The choice of a law other than the law of England and Wales or Northern Ireland as the applicable law in respect of a matter provided for by a non-mandatory provision of this Part is equivalent to an agreement making provision about that matter.

For this purpose an applicable law determined in accordance with the parties' agreement, or which is objectively determined in the absence of any express or implied choice, shall be treated as chosen by the parties.

Agreements to be in writing

5.—(1) The provisions of this Part apply only where the arbitra-   **2E–95** tion agreement is in writing, and any other agreement between the parties as to any matter is effective for the purposes of this Part only if in writing. The expressions "agreement", "agree" and "agreed" shall be construed accordingly.

(2) There is an agreement in writing—

    (a) if the agreement is made in writing (whether or not it is signed by the parties),

    (b) if the agreement is made by exchange of communications in writing, or

    (c) if the agreement is evidenced in writing.

(3) Where parties agree otherwise than in writing by reference to terms which are in writing, they make an agreement in writing.

Paragraph numbers marked with a "+" can be found online and on CD.

(4) An agreement is evidenced in writing if an agreement made otherwise than in writing is recorded by one of the parties, or by a third party, with the authority of the parties to the agreement.

(5) An exchange of written submissions in arbitral or legal proceedings in which the existence of an agreement otherwise than in writing is alleged by one party against another party and not denied by the other party in his response constitutes as between those parties an agreement in writing to the effect alleged.

(6) References in this Part to anything being written or in writing include its being recorded by any means.

2E–96   *Note* —Compare s.32 of the 1950 Act and s.7(1) of the 1975 Act.

THE ARBITRATION AGREEMENT

Definition of arbitration agreement

2E–97   **6.**—(1) In this Part an "arbitration agreement" means an agreement to submit to arbitration present or future disputes (whether they are contractual or not).

(2) The reference in an agreement to a written form of arbitration clause or to a document containing an arbitration clause constitutes an arbitration agreement if the reference is such as to make that clause part of the agreement.

2E–98   *Note* —Compare s.32 of the 1950 Act and s.7(1) of the 1975 Act.

Agreement to submit to arbitration

2E–99   An agreement which gives one party alone the right to refer a dispute to arbitration was held to be a valid agreement to refer future disputes to arbitration within s.32 of the 1950 Act (*Pittalis v Sherefettin* [1986] 2 W.L.R. 1003; [1986] 2 All E.R. 227, CA). See too *Three Shipping Ltd v Harebell Shipping Ltd* [2004] EWHC 2001 (Comm); [2005] 1 Lloyd's Rep. 509 (a 1996 Act case).

The fact that a contractual agreement to refer disputes to arbitration depended upon the exercise of an option, even by the party claiming arbitration, does not prevent it from being "an agreement to refer future disputes" within s.27 of the 1950 Act (*Navigazione Alta Italia SpA v Concordia Maritime Chartering AB* [1990] 2 Lloyd's Rep. 234).

Where a bill of lading directs the reader to the charterparty which contains a clause providing for arbitration of disputes "arising ... out of his contract" the bill of lading incorporates the arbitration clause and the parties are bound by its terms (*Astro Valiente Compania Naviera SA v Pakistan Ministry of Food and Agriculture (No.2), The Emanuel Colocotronis* [1982] 1 W.L.R. 1096; [1982] 1 All E.R. 823).

A clause in a charterparty providing that "either party may elect to have the dispute referred to arbitration" is merely an agreement to agree to arbitrate, but once a valid election is made no further agreement is needed or contemplated for the arbitration to take place, and therefore once the election is duly made and the option to arbitrate exercised, and both the agreement and the option are expressed in writing, a binding written arbitration agreement comes into existence and there is no want of mutuality since either party could make election (*Westfal-Larsen & Co A/S v Ikerigi Compania Naviera SA, The Messiaki Bergen* [1983] 1 All E.R. 382; [1983] 1 Lloyd's Rep. 424).

The words in sub-clause (2) "if the reference is such as to make that clause part of the agreement" were held in *Trygg Hansa Insurance Co v Equitas Ltd* [1998] 2 Lloyd's Rep. 439, to preserve the pre-existing law that general words of incorporation in an agreement were not appropriate to incorporate an arbitration clause. See too *Cigna Life Insurance v Intercaser SA* [2001] Lloyd's Rep. I.R. 821.

Paragraph numbers marked with a "+" can be found online and on CD.

Separability of arbitration agreement

7. Unless otherwise agreed by the parties, an arbitration agreement which forms or was intended to form part of another agreement (whether or not in writing) shall not be regarded as invalid, non-existent or ineffective because that other agreement is invalid, or did not come into existence or has become ineffective, and it shall for that purpose be treated as a distinct agreement.

2E–100

Note —In *Fiona Trust and Holdings Corp v Privalov* [2007] UKHL 40; [2007] Bus L.R. 1719, HL the House of Lords held that s.7 of the 1996 Act was to be interpreted so that the main agreement and the arbitration agreement had to be treated as having been separately concluded and the arbitration agreement could be invalidated only on a ground which related to the arbitration agreement and was not merely a consequence of the invalidity of the main agreement. The doctrine of separability required direct impeachment of the arbitration agreement before it could be set aside. Further in construing the relevant clause the presumption should be in the absence of clear language to the contrary that all disputes including as to the validity of the contract were to be decided by the same arbitral tribunal.

2E–101

For s.8 of the Arbitration Act 1996 (see Arrangement) plus any related commentary see paragraphs 2E–102+ to 2E–103+ on White Book on Westlaw UK or the Civil Procedure CD.

STAY OF LEGAL PROCEEDINGS

Stay of legal proceedings

9.—(1) A party to an arbitration agreement against whom legal proceedings are brought (whether by way of claim or counterclaim) in respect of a matter which under the agreement is to be referred to arbitration may (upon notice to the other parties to the proceedings) apply to the court in which the proceedings have been brought to stay the proceedings so far as they concern that matter.

2E–104

(2) An application may be made notwithstanding that the matter is to be referred to arbitration only after the exhaustion of other dispute resolution procedures.

(3) An application may not be made by a person before taking the appropriate procedural step (if any) to acknowledge the legal proceedings against him or after he has taken any step in those proceedings to answer the substantive claim.

(4) On an application under this section the court shall grant a stay unless satisfied that the arbitration agreement is null and void, inoperative, or incapable of being performed.

(5) If the court refuses to stay the legal proceedings, any provision that an award is a condition precedent to the bringing of legal proceedings in respect of any matter is of no effect in relation to those proceedings.

Note —Compare s.4(1) of the 1950 Act and s.1 of the 1975 Act. This is a mandatory provision (see s.4) and applies even though the seat of arbitration is outside England and Wales or where no seat of arbitration has been designated (see s.2). Section 9(5) does not apply to statutory arbitrations. See further, para.9A–178.1 below.

2E–105

Paragraph numbers marked with a "+" can be found online and on CD.

Appeal

2E–106   There is a right of appeal to the Court of Appeal, see *INCO Europe Ltd v First Choice Distribution* [1999] 1 W.L.R. 270; [1999] 1 All E.R. 820; [1999] C.L.C. 165, CA. The court held that the general terms of s.107 and Sch.3 of the 1996 Act (*q.v.*) were not to be construed as removing the right of appeal which had existed under earlier legislation (affirmed by HL(E) [2000] 1 W.L.R. 586; [2000] 2 All E.R. 109; [2000] 1 Lloyd's Rep 467.

A Party to an arbitration agreement

2E–107   It is "a party" to an arbitration agreement against whom "legal proceedings are brought ......in respect of a matter which under the agreement is to be referred to arbitration" who may apply under s.9(1) for a stay of such legal proceedings. In this context, "a party" includes "any person claiming under or through a party to the agreement" (s.82(2)). Section 9 cannot apply if the parties to the court proceedings are not the parties (or persons claiming through or under a party) to the abitration agreement, as it would be wholly inconsistent with the purpose and structure of the 1996 Act, and of s.9 in particular, if a stay could be obtained against a claimant who was not a party to the agreement (*City of London v Sancheti* [2008] EWCA Civ 1283; *The Times* December 1, 2008, CA (where held that a mere legal or commercial relationship between the applicant for a stay and the claimant was not sufficient)).

Who may apply

2E–108   It is not necessary that all parties to the submission, other than the claimant in the claim, should join in application to stay (see *Willesford v Watson* (1873) 8 Ch.App. 473).

The Application

2E–109   This is in by ordinary application notice and is made to the court in which the legal proceedings are pending (see r.62.3(2)).

Form of Order

2E–110   See Queen's Bench Masters' Practice Forms, Form **PF 167** (see *Civil Procedure Forms Volume*).

"... or after he has taken any step in those proceedings to answer the substantive claim"

2E–111   Though the application cannot precede the taking of the appropriate step if any to acknowledge the legal proceedings, the application must be made before taking any step to answer the substantive claim. So an application for security for costs was held to bar the defendant from obtaining a stay hereunder (*Adams v Cattley* (1892) 66 L.T. 687); so also the issue of an application for disclosure, see *Chappell v North* [1891] 2 Q.B. 252, cited above; so also attending an application for directions issued by the claimant and agreeing to or obtaining an order thereon (*County Theatres, etc. Ltd v Knowles* [1902] 1 K.B. 480; *Richardson v Le Maitre* [1903] 2 Ch. 222; *Stein v Buncle* [1902] W.N. 44; *Cohen v Arthur* (1912) 56 S.J. 344); or without an order being made, but an undertaking given to furnish an account (*Ochs v Ochs Bros.* [1909] 2 Ch. 121). After defence it is too late (*West London, etc. Co v Abbott* (1881) 29 W.R. 584). Also after defendant has obtained time to plead and agreed to take short notice of trial (*Smith v British Marine* [1883] W.N. 176). Opposition to an application for final judgment may constitute a step in the action; but no "step" is taken by a defendant opposing an application who not merely raises the matter of the arbitration clause in his affidavit (or witness statement), but also at the same time takes out an application to stay the claim (*Pitchers Ltd v Plaza (Queensbury) Ltd* [1940] 1 All E.R. 151, CA). *Cf.* also *Parker, Gaines & Co Ltd v Turpin* [1918] 1 K.B. 358.

     The defendant must, however, act timeously. Thus if a defendant resists summary judgment proceedings by serving an affidavit or witness statement in opposition, but omits to issue an application to stay the claim until after a first hearing of the claimant's application which is merely adjourned for a further and fuller hearing, he will be deemed to have taken a step in the claim (*Turner & Goudy v McConnell* [1985] 1 W.L.R. 898; [1985] 2 All E.R. 34, CA; *Rumput (Panama) SA v Islamic Republic of Iran Shipping Lines, The League* [1984] 2 Lloyd's Rep. 259). A party who initiates an application for a stay pending an arbitration does not take a "step" in the proceedings within the meaning of s.9(3) of the 1996 Act if he, either simultaneously or subsequently, invokes or ac-

Paragraph numbers marked with a "+" can be found online and on CD.

cepts the court's jurisdiction provided he does so only conditionally on his stay application failing (*Capital Trust Investments Ltd v Radio Design TJ AB* [2001] 3 All E.R. 756, affirmed [2002] 2 All E.R. 159, CA).

Similarly, if a defendant issues an application for an extension of time for defence, but omits to issue an application to stay until after the application for has been dealt with, he will be held to have taken a step in the proceedings (*Ford's Hotel Co Ltd v Bartlett* [1896] A.C. 1, HL). If, on the other hand, a defendant issues an application to stay, and, at the same time, issues an application for an extension of time for defence until after the hearing of the application to stay, he is unlikely to be held to have taken a step in the proceedings by the issue of the further time application (*London Sack & Bag Co Ltd v Dixon & Lugton Ltd* [1943] 2 All E.R. 763, CA).

Where defendant gave notice demanding particulars of case, that was held to be no step in the claim (*Ives v Willans* [1894] 1 Ch. 68; affirmed [1894] 2 Ch. 478; and *cf. Patteson v Northern Accident Ins. Soc.* [1901] 2 Ir.R. 262) and the same where the defendant before defence wrote to claimant under the former O.3, r.5 for further time to plead and obtained it (*Brighton Marine, etc. Co v Woodhouse* [1893] 2 Ch. 486); and where the defendant filed affidavits in the claim in answer to the claimant's affidavits in support of an application for a receiver, that was held to be no step in the claim (*Zalinoff v Hammond* [1898] 2 Ch. 92). The distinction seems to be that negotiation or correspondence between parties or their solicitors does not constitute a step in the claim, but an application, or the service of a pleading does. An application to strike out may be a step in the proceedings (*Leigh v English Property* [1976] 2 Lloyd's Rep. 298; *Eagle Star Insurance Co Ltd v Yuval Insurance Ltd* [1978] 1 Lloyd's Rep. 357).

A defendant did not take any step to answer the substantive claim so as to lose his right to apply for a stay by applying for relief which was otiose to the relief he needed in addition to the relief he did need; see *Patel v Patel* [2000] Q.B. 551, CA. In this case the defendant asked for the default judgment to be set aside (the relief he needed) but in addition and unnecessarily for leave to defend and counterclaim which he was entitled to do once default judgment was set aside.

The institution of an action within the time limit in a competent court in the United States between the same parties which was subsequently stayed because it was brought in breach of a London arbitration clause would not be regarded as steps having been taken under s.9 of the Arbitration Act 1996 when considering an application subsequently made out of time to appoint an arbitrator (*Thyssen Inc v Calypso Shipping Corp SA* [2000] 2 Lloyd's Rep. 243).

Whether additional matters sought to be raised by way of amendment to existing proceedings attract the stay provisions of s.9 of the 1996 Act depends on whether such additional matters "were part and parcel of the dispute of which the court was already seised or whether they were discrete matters in respect of which s.9 entitled the defendant to insist that they be arbitrated" (*Ahad v S Uddin* [2005] EWCA Civ 883).

Onus of showing that claim should proceed

It rests on the claimant to show that the dispute ought not to be referred to arbitration (*Hodgson v Ry. Passengers Assn. Co* (1882) 9 QBD 188; and see *Vawdrey v Simpson* [1896] 1 Ch. 166). The rule is now mandatory if the matters within subs.(4) are established. It is to be noted that the words "or that there was not in fact any dispute between the parties with regard to the matter agreed to be referred" (see s.1(1) of the 1975 Act) have not been re-enacted in s.9. Accordingly, where an amount due under an agreement was either disputed or simply not paid there was a dispute as to the amount due even though no answer to the claim existed in law or in fact. Such dispute was within the arbitration clause and proceedings at law brought to recover it had to be stayed (see *Halki Shipping Corp v Sopex Oils Ltd* [1997] 1 W.L.R. 1268; [1997] 3 All E.R. 833; [1998] 1 Lloyd's Rep. 49; affirmed by CA by a majority of 2:1, [1998] 1 W.L.R. 726; [1998] 2 All E.R. 23; [1998] 1 Lloyd's Rep. 465).

In *Wealands v C.L.C. Contractors Ltd* [1998] C.L.C. 808, the court held on an application by a sub-contractor for third party proceedings against it by the contractor to be stayed under s.9 of the Arbitration Act 1996 that despite the disadvantages of the claim against the third party going to arbitration (if the plaintiff did not join the third party as a defendant) the 1996 Act gave priority to party autonomy and entitled the third party as of right to the stay which is sought (affirmed [1999] 2 Lloyd's Rep. 739, CA).

2E–112

Paragraph numbers marked with a "+" can be found online and on CD.

In *Prekons Insaat Sanayi AS v Rowlands Castle Contracting Group Ltd* [2006] EWHC 1367 (Comm); [2007] 1 Lloyd's Rep. 98 the court held that the only relevant ground upon which a stay under s.9 of the Arbitration Act 1996 can in these circumstances be resisted is if the claim under the agreement containing an arbitration clause, if made out, operates in partial or total extinction or defeasance of the claim under the contract/s not containing an arbitration agreement, relying on *Aectra Refining and Marketing Inc v Exmar NV* [1995] 1 Lloyd's Rep. 191 at 199–202 *per* Hoffmann L.J.

Where a party objected under s.9 of the 1996 Act to a matter being considered other than by arbitrators then a dispute as to whether or not an arbitration agreement was time barred by limitation should be considered by the arbitrators even though the claimant might if he failed on such issue need to seek the exercise of the court's discretion under s.12 of the 1996 Act; *Grimaldi Compagnia di Navigazione SpA v Sekihyo Line Ltd* [1999] 1 W.L.R. 708; [1998] 3 All E.R. 943.

In *Ahmad Al-Naimi (T/A Buildmaster Construction Services) v Islamic Press Agency Inc* [2000] 1 Lloyd's Rep. 522, CA the court held that—

(1) If the court decided that it was the court which should determine whether the matters the subject of the action were the subject of an arbitration clause, unless the parties were agreed that the matter should be resolved on affidavit, then, if there was a triable issue directions should be given for trying that issue: under the CPR the court had a wider discretion to rule what evidence it needed to decide any particular point; and

(2) On a proper construction of s.9 it could be said with force that a court should be satisfied (a) that that there was an arbitration clause and (b) that the subject of the action was within that clause before the court could grant a stay under that section; but a stay under the inherent jurisdiction might in fact be sensible in a situation where the court could not be sure of these matters but could see that good sense and litigation management made it desirable for an arbitrator to consider the whole matter first.

See too note at para. 2E–101.

In *Sonatrach Petroleum Corp (BVI) v Ferrell International Ltd* [2002] 1 All E.R. (Comm) 627 (head-charter provided for arbitration in Japan but sub-charter gave jurisdiction to English courts) held that the unenforceability of method of proper law selection in sub-charter did not mean the choice of forum was also void as the latter was free-standing and a stay was granted in respect of a claim brought under the sub-charter.

Section 9 does not apply to petitions under s.459 of the Companies Act 1985 as the shareholders statutory right to petition is inalienable and cannot be diminished by a contact for arbitration, *Exeter City AFC Ltd v Football Conference Ltd* [2004] EWHC 831(Ch); [2004] 1 W.L.R. 2910; [2004] 4 All E.R. 1179.

An agreement to arbitrate pursuant to the Football Association Rules did not infringe a party's right to a fair trial guaranteed by art.6 of the ECHR: *Stretford v Football Association Ltd* [2007] EWCA Civ 238; [2007] 2 All E.R. (Comm) 1; [2007] 2 Lloyd's Rep. 31, CA.

The court has no jurisdiction to order a stay under s.9(1) of the 1996 Act (as opposed to under its inherent jurisdiction if appropriate) unless it is satisfied: (a) that there was a concluded arbitration agreement; and (b) the issue was a matter which under the arbitration clause was to be referred to arbitration: see *Albon v Naza Motor Trading Sdn Bhd (No.3)* [2007] EWHC 665 (Ch); [2007] 2 All E.R. 1075; [2007] 2 Lloyd's Rep. 1 . The court also held that s.9(4) assumed that there was a concluded agreement but that the same was devoid of legal effect, e.g. for duress, mistake, fraud or waiver and that s.30 of the 1996 Act did not preclude the court itself from determining whether the arbitration agreement had been concluded. See too CPR r.62.8(3).

Inoperative

2E–113   An arbitration agreement is inoperative where a defendant had shown an intention not to be bound by the agreement to refer and the other party (the claimant) had accepted such repudiation, *Downing v Al Tameer Establishment* [2002] EWCA Civ 721; [2002] 2 All E.R. (Comm) 545, CA.

"Incapable of being performed"

2E–114   The words in s.1(1) of the 1979 Act "incapable of being performed" were held to refer only to the question whether an arbitration agreement is capable of being

Paragraph numbers marked with a "+" can be found online and on CD.

performed up to the point when it results in an award and should not be construed as extending to the question whether, once an award has been made, the party against whom it is made will be incapable of satisfying it, for the impecuniosity of the loser rendering him unable to pay the amount of the award does not make the arbitration incapable of being performed (*The Rena K* [1979] Q.B. 377; [1979] 1 All E.R. 397; [1978] 1 Lloyd's Rep. 545). Nor was an arbitration agreement incapable of being performed within the meaning of s.1(1) of the Act merely because one party cannot afford the arbitration (*Paczy v Haendler & Natermann GmbH* [1981] F.S.R. 250).

Reference of interpleader issue to arbitration

10.—(1) Where in legal proceedings relief by way of interpleader is granted and any issue between the claimants is one in respect of which there is an arbitration agreement between them, the court granting the relief shall direct that the issue be determined in accordance with the agreement unless the circumstances are such that proceedings brought by a claimant in respect of the matter would not be stayed. **2E–115**

(2) Where subsection (1) applies but the court does not direct that the issue be determined in accordance with the arbitration agreement, any provision that an award is a condition precedent to the bringing of legal proceedings in respect of any matter shall not affect the determination of that issue by the court.

Note—Compare s.5 of the 1950 Act. This is a mandatory provision (see s.4) and applies even though the seat of arbitration is outside England and Wales or where no seat of arbitration has been designated. Subsection (2) does not apply to statutory arbitrations. **2E–116**

Retention of security where Admiralty proceedings stayed

11.—(1) Where Admiralty proceedings are stayed on the ground that the dispute in question should be submitted to arbitration, the court granting the stay may, if in those proceedings property has been arrested or bail or other security has been given to prevent or obtain release from arrest— **2E–117**

    (a) order that the property arrested be retained as security for the satisfaction of any award given in the arbitration in respect of that dispute, or

    (b) order that the stay of those proceedings be conditional on the provision of equivalent security for the satisfaction of any such award.

(2) Subject to any provision made by rules of court and to any necessary modifications, the same law and practice shall apply in relation to property retained in pursuance of an order as would apply if it were held for the purposes of proceedings in the court making the order.

Note—See s.26 of the Civil Jurisdiction and Judgments Act 1982. This is a mandatory provision (see s.4). **2E–118**

COMMENCEMENT OF ARBITRAL PROCEEDINGS

Power of court to extend time for beginning arbitral proceedings, etc.

12.—(1) Where an arbitration agreement to refer future disputes **2E–119**

Paragraph numbers marked with a "+" can be found online and on CD.

to arbitration provides that a claim shall be barred, or the claimant's right extinguished, unless the claimant takes within a time fixed by the agreement some step—

> (a) to begin arbitral proceedings, or
>
> (b) to begin other dispute resolution procedures which must be exhausted before arbitral proceedings can be begun,

the court may by order extend the time for taking that step.

(2) Any party to the arbitration agreement may apply for such an order (upon notice to the other parties), but only after a claim has arisen and after exhausting any available arbitral process for obtaining an extension of time.

(3) The court shall make an order only if satisfied—

> (a) that the circumstances are such as were outside the reasonable contemplation of the parties when they agreed the provision in question, and that it would be just to extend the time, or
>
> (b) that the conduct of one party makes it unjust to hold the other party to the strict terms of the provision in question.

(4) The court may extend the time for such period and on such terms as it thinks fit, and may do so whether or not the time previously fixed (by agreement or by a previous order) has expired.

(5) An order under this section does not affect the operation of the Limitation Acts (see section 13).

(6) The leave of the court is required for any appeal from a decision of the court under this section.

2E–120 *Note* —Compare s.27 of the 1950 Act. This is a mandatory provision (see s.4). This section does not apply to statutory arbitrations.

"Claim"

2E–121 Under s.27 of the 1950 Act, it was held that the word claims therein was not to be construed as meaning "causes of action", but should be given a wide and liberal interpretation and it will thus extend to any claim to have determined by arbitration a matter in issue between the parties, e.g. a claim for arbitration so as to assess the proper amount of a salvage award (*Sioux Inc v China Salvage Co Kwangchow Branch* [1980] 1 W.L.R. 996; [1980] 3 All E.R. 154, CA).

"... the Court may by order extend the time for taking that step"

2E–122 The court's powers hereunder are only in respect of provisions laying down time limits for commencing proceedings. Thus in *Crown Estate Commissioners v John Mowlem & Co Ltd* 70 B.L.R. 1 the Court of Appeal, disapproving *McLaughlin & Harvey Plc v P&O Developments Ltd* 55 B.L.R. 101, held that the court does not have power under this section to extend the time for commencing arbitration proceedings under clause 30.9.3. of the JCT Standard Form of Building Contract (1980 PwQ) since on its true construction that clause does not lay down any time limit for commencing proceedings but is concerned solely with the evidential effect of a final certificate in any proceedings which may be *commenced* and accordingly there was nothing for the court to extend (a case under s.27 of the 1950 Act).

Section 12 of the 1996 Act is markedly more restricted than its predecessor, s.27 of the 1950 Act. See in particular subs.3. It is now not possible to extend time because the court concludes in general terms that it would be just to do so (*Cathiship SA v Allanasons Ltd, The Catherine Helen* [1998] 3 All E.R. 714).

A party's failure properly to read a contractual provision relating to the time limit

Paragraph numbers marked with a "+" can be found online and on CD.

for commencing an arbitration was not a circumstance which triggered the court's power under s.12(3)(a) of the Arbitration Act 1996, to permit an extension of time for bringing arbitral proceedings. The aim of s.12(3) was to allow the court to consider an extension in relation to circumstances where the parties would not reasonably have contemplated them as being ones where the time-bar would apply (*Harbour and General Works Ltd v Environment Agency* [2000] 1 W.L.R. 950; [1999] 2 All E.R. (Comm) 686; [2000] 1 All E.R. 50; [2001] 1 Lloyd's Rep. 65, CA).

For ss.13 to 23 of the Arbitration Act 1996 (see Arrangement) plus any related commentary see paragraphs 2E–123+ to 2E–145+ on White Book on Westlaw UK or the Civil Procedure CD.

Power of court to remove arbitrator

24.—(1) A party to arbitral proceedings may (upon notice to the other parties, to the arbitrator concerned and to any other arbitrator) apply to the court to remove an arbitrator on any of the following grounds— **2E–146**

    (a) that circumstances exist that give rise to justifiable doubts as to his impartiality;

    (b) that he does not possess the qualifications required by the arbitration agreement;

    (c) that he is physically or mentally incapable of conducting the proceedings or there are justifiable doubts as to his capacity to do so;

    (d) that he has refused or failed—

        (i) properly to conduct the proceedings, or

        (ii) to use all reasonable despatch in conducting the proceedings or making an award,

and that substantial injustice has been or will be caused to the applicant.

(2) If there is an arbitral or other institution or person vested by the parties with power to remove an arbitrator, the court shall not exercise its power of removal unless satisfied that the applicant has first exhausted any available recourse to that institution or person.

(3) The arbitral tribunal may continue the arbitral proceedings and make an award while an application to the court under this section is pending.

(4) Where the court removes an arbitrator, it may make such order as it thinks fit with respect to his entitlement (if any) to fees or expenses, or the repayment of any fees or expenses already paid.

(5) The arbitrator concerned is entitled to appear and be heard by the court before it makes any order under this section.

(6) The leave of the court is required for any appeal from a decision of the court under this section.

Note—Compare ss.13(3), 23 and 24(1) of the 1950 Act. This is a mandatory provision (see s.4). **2E–147**

"(a) circumstances exist that give rise to justifiable doubts as to his impartiality", etc.

In *Petroships Pte Ltd of Singapore v Petec Trading & Investment Corp of Vietnam (The Petro Ranger)* [2001] 2 Lloyd's Rep. 348 the court stated that careful regard should be **2E–148**

Paragraph numbers marked with a "+" can be found online and on CD.

had to paras 105 and 106 of the report on the Arbitration Bill by the Departmental Advisory Commitee on Arbitration Law, which provide as follows:

> "105. We have included, as grounds for removal, the refusal or failure of an arbitrator properly to conduct the proceedings, as well as failing to use all reasonable despatch in conducting the proceedings or making an award, where the result has caused or will cause substantial injustices to the applicant. We trust that the courts will not allow the first of these matters to be abused by those intent on disrupting the arbitral process. To this end we have included a provision allowing the tribunal to continue while an application is made. There is also Clause 73 which effectively requires a party to 'put up or shut up' if a challenge is to be made.

> 106. We have every confidence that the courts will carry through the intent of this part of the Bill, which is that it should only be available where the conduct of the arbitrator is such as to go so beyond anything that could reasonably be defended that substantial injustice has resulted or will result. The provision is not intended to allow the Court to substitute its own view as to how the arbitral proceedings should be conducted. Thus the choice by an arbitrator of a particular proceedure, unless it breaches the duty laid on arbitrators by Clause 33, should on no view justify the removal of an arbitrator, even if the court would not itself have adopted that procedure. In short, this ground only exists to cover what we hope will be the very rare case where an arbitrator so conducts the proceedings that it can fairly be said that instead of carrying through the object of arbitration as stated in the Bill, he is in effect frustrating that object. Only if the Court confines itself in this way can this power of removal be justified as a measure supporting rather than subverting the arbitral process."

Where circumstances have made the arbitrator an interested party (e.g. litigation between the arbitrator and one of the parties) leave to revoke will be given (*Re Baring Bros. & Co and Doulton & Co* (1892) 61 L.J.Q. 704). But the mere fact that one of the parties has issued a claim form against the arbitrator is not sufficient to disqualify the latter from acting where he has taken no positive step in retaliation (*Belcher v Roedean School Site, etc. Ltd* (1901) 85 L.T. 468). The test is the same as that which applied to all who made judicial decisions, namely whether there was any real danger that the arbitrator was biased.

> "...when deciding whether bias has been established, the Court personifies the reasonable man. The Court considers on all the material which is placed before it whether there is any real danger of unconscious bias on the part of the decision maker. This is the case irrespective of whether it is a Judge or an arbitrator who is the subject of the allegation of bias".

See *AT&T Construction v Saudi Cable Co* [2000] CLC 220; [2000] 2 Lloyd's Rep 127, CA at 136.

In *Laker Airways Inc v FLS Aerospace Ltd* [1999] 2 Lloyd's Rep. 45 (Barristers from the same Chambers appointed applicants' and respondents' arbitrators) the court stated at p.48:

> "The test is an objective one—whether circumstances exist that give rise to justifiable doubts as to an arbitrator's impartiality. The test is thus objective in at least two respects: the Court must find that circumstances exist, and are not merely believed to exist (although I suppose that a belief may itself be a circumstance); and secondly, those circumstances must justifiable or perhaps unreasonable doubt is not sufficient: it is not enough honestly to say that one has lost confidence in the arbitrator's impartiality. On the other hand, doubts, if justifiable, are sufficient: it is not necessary to prove actual bias."

The test for bias under s.24(1) is the same as that irregularity under s.68 where the application is made on the grounds of bias, see *Rustal Trading Ltd v Gill & Duffus SA* [2000] 1 Lloyd's Rep. 14.

In *ASM v HARRIS* [2007] EWHC 1513; [2008] 1 Lloyd's Rep. 61 it was held that bias of one arbitrator is not bias of all.

Abortive arbitration

2E–149

> "When an arbitration for any reason becomes abortive it is the duty of a court of law, in working out a contract of which such arbitration is part of the practical machinery, to supply the defect which has occurred. It is the duty of a court in

Paragraph numbers marked with a "+" can be found online and on CD.

such circumstances to come to the assistance of parties by removal of the impasse and the extrication of their rights" (*Cameron v Caddy* [1914] A.C. 651 at 656).

So in *Neal v Richardson* [1938] 1 All E.R. 753, CA, where an architect being appointed to act as arbitrator, refused to grant certificates or to arbitrate, the court refused to stay a claim in which the builder sought relief *aliunde*. On the other hand apart from the specific agreement the architect does not act as an arbitrator between the parties in issuing interim certificates (*Sutcliffe v Thackrah* [1974] A.C. 727; [1974] 1 All E.R. 859, overruling *Chambers v Goldthorpe* [1901] 1 K.B. 624, CA).

For ss.25 to 29 of the Arbitration Act 1996 (see Arrangement) plus any related commentary see paragraphs 2E–150+ to 2E–159+ on White Book on Westlaw UK or the Civil Procedure CD.

JURISDICTION OF THE ARBITRAL TRIBUNAL

Competence of tribunal to rule on its own jurisdiction

30.—(1) Unless otherwise agreed by the parties, the arbitral tribunal may rule on its own substantive jurisdiction, that is, as to—

    (a) whether there is a valid arbitration agreement,

    (b) whether the tribunal is properly constituted, and

    (c) what matters have been submitted to arbitration in accordance with the arbitration agreement.

2E–160

(2) Any such ruling may be challenged by any available arbitral process of appeal or review or in accordance with the provisions of this Part.

Note—This is a mandatory provision (see s.4). For adaptation of s.30(1)(a) in case of statutory arbitration see s.96 below.

2E–161

Counterclaims

Factors determining whether arbitrators may entertain a counterclaim are the true construction of the agreement to refer and whether the counterclaim is a transaction set-off or other true defence as opposed to a completely independent set-off, see *Metal Distributors (UK) Ltd v ZCCM Investment Holdings PLC* [2005] EWHC 156 (Comm); [2005] 2 Lloyd's Rep.37. However an arbitral tribunal's jurisdiction to determine and give effect to a transaction set-off depends upon the true construction of the arbitration agreement, see *Econet Satellite Services Ltd v Vee Networks Ltd* [2006] EWHC 1664 (Comm); [2006] 2 All E.R. (Comm) 989; [2006] 2 Lloyd's Rep. 423.

2E–162

Objection to substantive jurisdiction of tribunal

31.—(1) An objection that the arbitral tribunal lacks substantive jurisdiction at the outset of the proceedings must be raised by a party not later than the time he takes the first step in the proceedings to contest the merits of any matter in relation to which he challenges the tribunal's jurisdiction. A party is not precluded from raising such an objection by the fact that he has appointed or participated in the appointment of an arbitrator.

2E–163

(2) Any objection during the course of the arbitral proceedings that the arbitral tribunal is exceeding its substantive jurisdiction must be made as soon as possible after the matter alleged to be beyond its jurisdiction is raised.

(3) The arbitral tribunal may admit an objection later than the time specified in subsection (1) or (2) if it considers the delay justified.

Paragraph numbers marked with a "+" can be found online and on CD.

(4) Where an objection is duly taken to the tribunal's substantive jurisdiction and the tribunal has power to rule on its own jurisdiction, it may—

      (a) rule on the matter in an award as to jurisdiction, or

      (b) deal with the objection in its award on the merits.

If the parties agree which of these courses the tribunal should take, the tribunal shall proceed accordingly.

(5) The tribunal may in any case, and shall if the parties so agree, stay proceedings whilst an application is made to the court under section 32 (determination of preliminary point of jurisdiction).

2E–164   *Note* —This is a mandatory provision (see s.4). The prescribed circumstances without which the application will not be considered are to be noted.

Determination of preliminary point of jurisdiction

2E–165   **32.**—(1) The court may, on the application of a party to arbitral proceedings (upon notice to the other parties), determine any question as to the substantive jurisdiction of the tribunal. A party may lose the right to object (see section 73).

(2) An application under this section shall not be considered unless—

      (a) it is made with the agreement in writing of all the other parties to the proceedings, or

      (b) it is made with the permission of the tribunal and the court is satisfied—

            (i) that the determination of the question is likely to produce substantial savings in costs,

            (ii) that the application was made without delay, and

            (iii) that there is good reason why the matter should be decided by the court.

(3) An application under this section, unless made with the agreement of all the other parties to the proceedings, shall state the grounds on which it is said that the matter should be decided by the court.

(4) Unless otherwise agreed by the parties, the arbitral tribunal may continue the arbitral proceedings and make an award while an application to the court under this section is pending.

(5) Unless the court gives leave, no appeal lies from a decision of the court whether the conditions specified in subsection (2) are met.

(6) The decision of the court on the question of jurisdiction shall be treated as a judgment of the court for the purposes of an appeal.

But no appeal lies without the leave of the court which shall not be given unless the court considers that the question involves a point of law which is one of general importance or is one which for some other special reason should be considered by the Court of Appeal.

2E–166   *Note* —This is a mandatory provision (see s.4).

Paragraph numbers marked with a "+" can be found online and on CD.

Application of section

Guidance on the circumstances in which the court can entertain an application under s.32 by a party to arbitral proceedings is contained in *Vale do Rio doce Navegacao SA v Shanghai Bao Steel Ocean Shipping Co Ltd* [2000] 2 Lloyd's Rep. 1. The court should not intervene except in the limited circumstances specified. Where the other alleged party to an arbitration agreement denies he is a party thereto the court stated at para.54:

2E–167

> "The Act sets out in very clear terms the steps that a party who contends that there is another party to an arbitration agreement should take. First he should appoint an arbitrator. If the other party appoints an arbitrator, then s.31(1) makes it clear that his appointment of an arbitrator does not prevent him challenging the substantive jurisdiction of the tribunal. If the other party does not appoint an arbitrator, then the default provisions (s.17) or failure to appoint procedures (s.18) apply. Once the arbitral tribunal is constituted, then in accordance with the policy of the Act it is for that tribunal to rule on its own jurisdiction, save in the circumstances specified in s.32. Any award made can then be changed under s.67. The rights of the party who challenges the existence of the arbitration agreement and takes no part are protected by s.72; he is given the right to recourse to the Courts in the circumstances set out."

There is no jurisdiction under s.32 as regards non-parties to the arbitration (e.g. brokers). See further para.2E–13 above.

THE ARBITRAL PROCEEDINGS

General duty of the tribunal

33.—(1) The tribunal shall—

2E–168

    (a) act fairly and impartially as between the parties, giving each party a reasonable opportunity of putting his case and dealing with that of his opponent, and

    (b) adopt procedures suitable to the circumstances of the particular case, avoiding unnecessary delay or expense, so as to provide a fair means for the resolution of the matters falling to be determined.

(2) The tribunal shall comply with that general duty in conducting the arbitral proceedings, in its decisions on matters of procedure and evidence and in the exercise of all other powers conferred on it.

Note —This is a mandatory provision (see s.4).

2E–169

For ss.34 to 41 of the Arbitration Act 1996 (see Arrangement) plus any related commentary see 2E–170+ to 2E–185+ on White Book on Westlaw UK or the Civil Procedure CD.

POWERS OF COURT IN RELATION TO ARBITRAL PROCEEDINGS

Enforcement of peremptory orders of tribunal

42.—(1) Unless otherwise agreed by the parties, the court may make an order requiring a party to comply with a peremptory order made by the tribunal.

2E–186

(2) An application for an order under this section may be made—

    (a) by the tribunal (upon notice to the parties),

    (b) by a party to the arbitral proceedings with the permission of the tribunal (and upon notice to the other parties), or

Paragraph numbers marked with a "+" can be found online and on CD.

(c) where the parties have agreed that the powers of the court under this section shall be available.

(3) The court shall not act unless it is satisfied that the applicant has exhausted any available arbitral process in respect of failure to comply with the tribunal's order.

(4) No order shall be made under this section unless the court is satisfied that the person to whom the tribunal's order was directed has failed to comply with it within the time prescribed in the order or, if no time was prescribed, within a reasonable time.

(5) The leave of the court is required for any appeal from a decision of the court under this section.

2E–187   *Note* —Compare s.5 of the 1979 Act. This section was amended by Scheme for Construction Contracts (England and Wales) Regulations 1998 (SI 1998/649) so far as construction contracts are concerned in that art.24 thereof provides as follows:

"**24.** Section 42 of the Arbitration Act 1996 shall apply to this Scheme subject to the following modifications—

(a) in subsection (2) for the word "tribunal" wherever it appears there shall be substituted the word "adjudicator",

(b) in subparagraph (b) of subsection (2) for the words "arbitral proceedings" there shall be substituted the word "adjudication",

(c) subparagraph (c) of subsection (2) shall be deleted, and

(d) subsection (3) shall be deleted."

Securing the attendance of witnesses

2E–188   **43.**—(1) A party to arbitral proceedings may use the same court procedures as are available in relation to legal proceedings to secure the attendance before the tribunal of a witness in order to give oral testimony or to produce documents or other material evidence.

(2) This may only be done with the permission of the tribunal or the agreement of the other parties.

(3) The court procedures may only be used if—

(a) the witness is in the United Kingdom, and

(b) the arbitral proceedings are being conducted in England and Wales or, as the case may be, Northern Ireland.

(4) A person shall not be compelled by virtue of this section to produce any document or other material evidence which he could not be compelled to produce in legal proceedings.

2E–189   *Note* —Compare s.12(4) and (5) of the 1950 Act. This is a mandatory provision (see s.4).

"A witness summons"

2E–190   Normally issues at the Admiralty and Commercial Registry at the Royal Courts of Justice, Strand, London WC2A 2LL, or a district registry where attendance of witness required within the district of the district registry (see Practice Direction—Arbitration, paras 7.1 to 7.3).

Perjury

2E–191   It was held that perjury committed in an arbitration under the Workmen's Compensation Act was perjury at Common Law and punishable as such (*R. v Crossley* (1909) 100 L.T. 463, CA). See the Perjury Act 1911.

2E–192   *Note* —There is no power under s.43 for a court to order disclosure against a third party as opposed to issuing a witness summons for the production in evidence of

Paragraph numbers marked with a "+" can be found online and on CD.

specific documents. Nor are the court's powers under CPR r.31.17 to be translated into the context of arbitration, see *BNP Paribas v Deloitte & Touche LLP* [2003] EWHC 2874 (Comm).

Court powers exercisable in support of arbitral proceedings

44.—(1) Unless otherwise agreed by the parties, the court has for the purposes of and in relation to arbitral proceedings the same power of making orders about the matters listed below as it has for the purposes of and in relation to legal proceedings.

    2E–193

(2) Those matters are—

  (a) the taking of the evidence of witnesses;

  (b) the preservation of evidence;

  (c) making orders relating to property which is the subject of the proceedings or as to which any question arises in the proceedings—

    (i) for the inspection, photographing, preservation, custody or detention of the property, or

    (ii) ordering that samples be taken from, or any observation be made of or experiment conducted upon, the property;

and for that purpose authorising any person to enter any premises in the possession or control of a party to the arbitration;

  (d) the sale of any goods the subject of the proceedings;

  (e) the granting of an interim injunction or the appointment of a receiver.

(3) If the case is one of urgency, the court may, on the application of a party or proposed party to the arbitral proceedings, make such orders as it thinks necessary for the purpose of preserving evidence or assets.

(4) If the case is not one of urgency, the court shall act only on the application of a party to the arbitral proceedings (upon notice to the other parties and to the tribunal) made with the permission of the tribunal or the agreement in writing of the other parties.

(5) In any case the court shall act only if or to the extent that the arbitral tribunal, and any arbitral or other institution or person vested by the parties with power in that regard, has no power or is unable for the time being to act effectively.

(6) If the court so orders, an order made by it under this section shall cease to have effect in whole or in part on the order of the tribunal or of any such arbitral or other institution or person having power to act in relation to the subject-matter of the order.

(7) The leave of the court is required for any appeal from a decision of the court under this section.

Note —Compare s.12(6) of the 1950 Act.

    2E–194

Examination of Witness Order

    2E–195

In *Commerce & Industry Co of Canada v Certain Underwriters at Lloyd's of London* [2002] 1 W.L.R. 1323; [2002] 2 All E.R. (Comm) 204; [2002] 1 Lloyd's Rep. 219, the court (a) declined a letter of request from New York arbitrators on the basis the reference in s.1

Paragraph numbers marked with a "+" can be found online and on CD.

of the Evidence (Proceedings in Other Jurisdictions) Act 1975 to a "tribunal" did not include a private arbitral tribunal and (b) declined to exercise its power under s.44 in respect of ordering the taking of the evidence of witnesses which may be exercised even where the seat arbitration is outside England and Wales or Northern Ireland on the basis that it was inappropriate to do (see s.2(3) of the 1996 Act above) because of differences in procedure, namely the discovery of information by witness testimony under the curial law of New York which had never been part of English procedure.

Preservation of Evidence etc

2E–196   Whilst s.44(2) did not provide for an order for disclosure by a non-party it permitted an order for the inspection, photocopying and preservation of documents in the hands of third parties for the purpose of resolving an issue in the arbitration, (a feasibility study for deepening harbour in a breach of safe berth warranty claim) *Assimina Maritime Ltd v Pakistan National Shipping; The Tasmin Spirit* [2004] EWHC 3005 (Comm); [2005] 1 All E.R. (Comm) 460; [2005] 1 Lloyd's Rep. 525.

Interim Injunctions

2E–197   In *Channel Tunnel Group Ltd v Balfour Beatty Construction Ltd* [1993] A.C. 334; [1993] 2 W.L.R. 262; [1993] 1 All E.R. 664; [1993] 1 Lloyd's Rep. 291, the House of Lords held that on the true construction of s.12(6)(h) of the Arbitration Act 1950 there was no power to grant an interim injunction in respect of a foreign arbitration but that an interim injunction pursuant to s.37(1) of the Supreme Court Act 1981 could be granted to assist or reinforce a foreign arbitration if circumstances so required even though a stay of English proceedings was ordered. In the cited case an interim injunction was refused as to grant the same would have pre-empted the very decision the support of which formed the raison d'être of the injunction. The House of Lords also held that the court had an inherent power to stay proceedings brought before it in breach of agreement to decide disputes by an alternative method whether or not the procedure agreed amounted to an arbitration agreement within s.1 of the Arbitration Act 1975.

In *Cetelem SA v Roust Holdings Ltd* [2005] EWCA Civ 618; [2005] 1 W.L.R. 3555; [2005] 4 All E.R. 52; [2005] 2 Lloyd's Rep. 494 (an interim injunction case) the Court of Appeal held that:

> "on the true construction of s.44(3) of the 1996 Act if the case is one of urgency the court only has jurisdiction to make such orders as it thinks necessary for the purpose of preserving evidence or assets"

not following the wider approach of *Hiscox Underwriting Ltd v Dickson* [2004] EWHC 479; [2004] 1 All E.R. (Comm) 753; [2004] 2 Lloyd's Rep. 438 that s.44(3) was permissive and not restrictive of the powers conferred by s.44(1) and (2) and further holding that a contractual right could be an asset for the purposes of s.44(3).

Time when powers exercisable

2E–198   It is doubtful that there is jurisdiction under this provision to order pre-delivery tests and inspection of a vessel before a cause of action had arisen for defective condition upon delivery or circumstances giving rise to an injunction under (formerly) RSC O.29, r.1; see *Tsakos Shipping & Trading SA v Orizon Tanker Co Ltd (The Centaurus Mar)* [1998] C.L.C. 1003.

Sub-section (7)

2E–199   For the purposes of s.44(7) "the court" means the court of first instance but "...a decision of a judge which the court had no jurisdiction to make is not a decision 'under the section' within the meaning of s.44(7) of the 1996 Act", see *Cetelem SA* at para.2E–197, above.

Determination of preliminary point of law

2E–200   **45.**—(1) Unless otherwise agreed by the parties, the court may on the application of a party to arbitral proceedings (upon notice to the other parties) determine any question of law arising in the course of the proceedings which the court is satisfied substantially affects the rights of one or more of the parties. An agreement to dispense with

Paragraph numbers marked with a "+" can be found online and on CD.

reasons for the tribunal's award shall be considered an agreement to exclude the court's jurisdiction under this section.

(2) An application under this section shall not be considered unless—

    (a) it is made with the agreement of all the other parties to the proceedings, or

    (b) it is made with the permission of the tribunal and the court is satisfied—

        (i) that the determination of the question is likely to produce substantial savings in costs, and

        (ii) that the application was made without delay.

(3) The application shall identify the question of law to be determined and, unless made with the agreement of all the other parties to the proceedings, shall state the grounds on which it is said that the question should be decided by the court.

(4) Unless otherwise agreed by the parties, the arbitral tribunal may continue the arbitral proceedings and make an award while an application to the court under this section is pending.

(5) Unless the court gives leave, no appeal lies from a decision of the court whether the conditions specified in subsection (2) are met.

(6) The decision of the court on the question of law shall be treated as a judgment of the court for the purposes of an appeal.

But no appeal lies without the leave of the court which shall not be given unless the court considers that the question is one of general importance, or is one which for some other special reason should be considered by the Court of Appeal.

Note —Compare s.2 of the 1979 Act. **2E-201**

Determination of preliminary point of law **2E-202**

    The Act has a procedure under which an application may be made to the court to determine any question of law arising in the course of the reference, but restrictions are imposed on the making of such applications and the right to make an application may in specified circumstances also be excluded by agreement between the parties.

    It should, however, be emphasised that s.45 provides for an essentially speedy procedure designed to interrupt the arbitration to the minimum possible extent and it is an exception to the general rule that the courts do not intervene in the course of an arbitration, and therefore, save in wholly exceptional cases, e.g. where the preliminary question of law would determine the whole dispute between the parties it is not to be used to obtain definitive decisions from the Court of Appeal or the House of Lords (*per* Donaldson L.J. in *Babanaft International Co SA v Avant Petroleum Inc* [1982] 1 W.L.R. 871 at 882; [1982] 3 All E.R. 244 at 252) a case on s.2 of the 1979 Act.

For ss.46 to 65 of the Arbitration Act 1996 (see Arrangement) plus any related commentary see paragraphs 2E-203+ to 2E-240+ on White Book on Westlaw UK or the Civil Procedure CD.

POWERS OF THE COURT IN RELATION TO AWARD

Enforcement of the award

66.—(1) An award made by the tribunal pursuant to an arbitration agreement may, by leave of the court, be enforced in the same manner as a judgment or order of the court to the same effect. **2E-241**

Paragraph numbers marked with a "+" can be found online and on CD.

(2) Where leave is so given, judgment may be entered in terms of the award.

(3) Leave to enforce an award shall not be given where, or to the extent that, the person against whom it is sought to be enforced shows that the tribunal lacked substantive jurisdiction to make the award.

The right to raise such an objection may have been lost (see section 73).

(4) Nothing in this section affects the recognition or enforcement of an award under any other enactment or rule of law, in particular under Part II of the [1950 c. 27.] Arbitration Act 1950 (enforcement of awards under Geneva Convention) or the provisions of Part III of this Act relating to the recognition and enforcement of awards under the New York Convention or by an action on the award.

2E–242   *Note* —Compare s.26(1) of the 1950 Act. This is a mandatory provision (see s.4).

"By leave of the Court"

2E–243   Where the court is of opinion that the award is legally invalid, it may refuse permission to enforce it. *Cf. Re Stone and Hastie Arb.* [1903] 2 K.B. 463, CA. Permission should be given in nearly all cases to enforce an award as a judgment unless there is real ground for doubting the validity of the award, and the ambit of this section should not be circumscribed (*Middlemiss & Gould v Hartlepool Corp* [1972] 1 W.L.R. 1643; [1973] 1 All E.R. 172, CA, and see *Curacac Trading Co BV v Harkisandas & Co* [1992] 2 Lloyd's Rep. 186 at 192 approving statement in Mustill and Boyd, *Commercial Arbitration*, 2nd edn, p.419 to the effect that the court would probably now only refuse the application where the objection cannot properly be disposed of without trial.

"Be enforced"

2E–244   This may be done by permission at any time, though the time for setting the award aside has not expired.

A person who obtains permission under this section to enforce an award is not thereby prevented from bringing a claim on the award (*China Steam Navigation Co v Van Laun* (1905) 22 T.L.R. 26). It is an implied term of an arbitration agreement that an award for the payment of money should be in a form which is capable of being enforced in the same manner as a judgment, and the court has power to remit such an award so that it may be amended to put it in such a form (*Margulies Ltd v Dafnis Thomaides Ltd* [1958] 1 W.L.R. 398; [1958] 1 All E.R. 777).

A confidentiality or non-disclosure agreement in respect of an arbitration should not be construed so as to prevent in terms of enforcement a party relying on an award in respect of rights declared in his favour by the award, *Associated Electric and Gas Insurance Services Ltd v European Reinsurance Co of Zurich* [2003] UKPC 11; [2003] 1 W.L.R. 1041.

In *Michael Carter v Harold Simpson Associates (Architects) Ltd*; [2004] UKPC 29; [2005] 1 W.L.R. 919; [2004] 2 Lloyd's Rep. 512, PC, (a case concerning Jamaican law) the Privy Council held that the unremitted parts of an award remain valid and can properly form the subject matter of enforcement. Effect of *Johnson v Latham* (1851) 20 L.J. Q.B. 236 considered.

Claim on the award

2E–245   "It is well settled that procedure by [claim] upon an award is one that ought to be pursued where the objections raised are such as to render the validity of the award a matter of doubt. Where there are matters which may gravely affect the validity of the award, no order should be made giving [permission] to proceed summarily under the award." *Per* Swinfen Eady, M.R., *Re Boks & Co and Peters, Rushton & Co Arbn.* [1919] 1 K.B. 491. In this case Lush J. in Chambers refused permission to enforce the award as the contract between the parties was an illegal one. In *May v Mills* (1914) 30 T.L.R.

Paragraph numbers marked with a "+" can be found online and on CD.

287, there was a doubt on the face of the proceedings whether there had been a valid arbitration. The Master refused leave to enforce the award. The Judge in Chambers reversed this decision, which was restored by the CA, who left the claimant to bring a claim on the award. The defendant had refused throughout to take any part in the arbitration. In the claim judgment was given for the defendant with costs of all the proceedings.

An application under s.66 is not a suitable procedure in a case where an objection is taken to the award which cannot properly be disposed of without a trial (*Allied Vision Ltd v VPS Film Entertainment GmbH* [1991] 1 Lloyd's Rep. 392), a case under s.26 of the 1950 Act.

When confronted with a clause which purports to provide that the rights of the parties shall be governed by a system of law which is neither English law nor the law of any other state, or which is a serious modification of such law, the court has to decide (a) whether the parties intend to create legally enforceable rights and obligations (b) whether the resulting agreement is sufficiently certain to constitute a legally enforceable contract, and (c) whether it will be contrary to public policy to enforce the award because there is some illegality present, or because enforcement will clearly be injurious to the public good (*Deutsche Schachtbau- und Tiefbohr GmbH v Ras Al Khaimah National Oil Co* [1987] 3 W.L.R. 1023; [1987] 2 All E.R. 796, CA reversed on another point *sub nom. Deutsche Schachtbau- und Tiefbohr GmbH v Shell International Petroleum Co Ltd* [1988] 3 W.L.R. 230; [1988] 2 All E.R. 833, HL). An award made by I.C.C. arbitrators in Geneva, applying a system of law which represented a common denominator of the principles underlying the laws of contract of various nations was held to be enforceable on application of these tests (*ibid.*).

Counterclaim

2E-246

In a claim on an award the defendant is not estopped from counterclaiming for rectification of the agreement to refer (*Crane v Hegeman-Harris Co Inc* [1939] 1 All E.R. 662).

Appeal from order to enforce award

2E-247

The principles applicable to obtaining permission to appeal out of time (see *C.M. Van Stillevoldt BV v E.L. Carviers Inc* [1983] 1 W.L.R. 207; and *Norwich and Peterborough Building Society v Steed* [1991] 1 W.L.R. 449) provided an appropriate guide to the court in exercising its discretion whether to extend time for permission to appeal where permission had been granted to enforce an award as a judgment and judgment had been entered (*Soinco Savi v Novokuznetsk Aluminium Plant* [1998] 2 Lloyd's Rep. 337, CA).

Limitation

2E-248

On a claim to enforce or an application for permission to enforce an arbitration award in the same way as a judgment, the cause of action accrues when the party against whom the award has been made fails to honour the award, not when the breach of contract to which the award relates occurs (*Agromet Motoimport v Maulden Engineering Co (Beds) Ltd* [1985] 1 W.L.R. 762; [1985] 2 All E.R. 436).

Practice—Methods of enforcement

2E-249

There are two methods of enforcement of an award which are open to the applicant namely:

1. By application directly to enforce the award (see para.2E-250 below) and if permission is granted.
2. By entering judgment in terms of the award and so to enforce the judgment by one or more of the usual forms of execution award.

These methods are not alternative, but successive. The applicant may apply for permission to enforce the award in the same manner as a judgment or order to the same effect, and if such permission is given, he may then proceed to enter judgment in the terms of the award. There is no need for a further application for permission to enter such a judgment, but it should be noted that there may be advantages in proceeding to the second stage of entering judgment instead of being content with an order granting leave to permission the award as a judgment, e.g. by suing upon the judgment or otherwise proceeding by execution or registration or other method of

Paragraph numbers marked with a "+" can be found online and on CD.

enforcement in a foreign court or by obtaining the recognition of the judgment in a foreign court or by relying on the judgment as *res judicata*.

Application

2E–250   (See generally CPR Pt 62—Arbitration Claims, r.62.18) In the light of the wider point of entry for enforcement matters application for permission to enforce an award under this section should be made in the first instance without notice to a Master, Admiralty Registrar or district judge of the district registry. The application should be made upon an arbitration claim form supported by written evidence such as an affidavit or witness statement which, in the QBD in London, should be left with the Admiralty and Commercial Registry in Room EB 13. The affidavit or witness statement should exhibit the arbitration agreement and the original award or copies thereof, and should state the name and the usual or last known place of abode or business of the applicant and the person against whom it is sought to enforce the award, and either that the award has not been complied with or the extent to which it has not been complied with at the date of the application (see Pt 62, r.62.18(6)). Where the application is under s.101 of the 1996 Act or s.3(1)(a) of the 1975 Act, different documents must be exhibited as specified in subss.6(a)(ii) and (iii). The Master may either grant the application on a without notice basis or direct the application to be issued. It should ask for "permission to enforce the award dated—in the above arbitration in the same manner as a judgment or order to the same effect"; and "that the respondent do pay the costs of this application to be taxed". The applicant must produce before the Master the original award (or a duplicate) and a copy thereof, together with an affidavit or witness statement intituled as above, verifying both the original, the copy award, and the arbitration agreement. On issuing execution without entering judgment, the copy award must be filed (no fee) at the Admiralty and Commercial Registry, together with the order for permission to enforce it. But if a judgment is to be signed, the award should first be filed and an office copy produced on signing judgment. In the QBD a reference number will be given on signing judgment or issuing execution as on the commencement of a claim. The award will be marked with a seal to indicate that execution has issued on it. All subsequent proceedings should bear the reference number. In the Chancery Division the papers are lodged in Chancery Chambers and a similar practice followed.

Costs

2E–251   The costs of the application for permission to enforce the award should be included in the order, no matter how small the amount awarded and the certificate for such costs produced on issuing execution.

Taxation of costs under the award may be obtained on production of the award either before or after permission to enforce it has been obtained. And this applies to taxation of the charges of the arbitrator, provided he has not himself taxed and fixed the amount of the costs of the reference and award by, and as part of, his award.

Costs where judgment may be entered

2E–252   If it is desired to enter judgment for the amount awarded, the application should be so framed as to provide for "the costs of any judgment which may be entered hereunder". If this precaution is not taken, it may be impossible to secure an order for the costs incurred in signing judgment.

Service out of the jurisdiction

2E–253   The application may, with permission, be served out of the jurisdiction, see r.62.18(4). Service out of the jurisdiction of an order giving permission to enforce does not require permission, see r.62.18(8).

"Judgment ... in terms of the award"

2E–254   A judgment so entered may be enforced in the usual way. But it is important to notice that no provision is made for the costs which may be incurred in making the necessary application under this section. The incidence of such costs will no doubt be settled, in the ordinary course, by the Master who hears that application, and his order can be enforced as if it were a judgment; but if it is proposed to enforce the award as a judgment—e.g. by suing upon it in a foreign court—no terms other than those to

Paragraph numbers marked with a "+" can be found online and on CD.

be found in the award can be included in the judgment. See for instance *Walker v Rowe* [2000] 1 Lloyd's Rep. 116—there is no power to add s.35 Supreme Court Act 1981 interest to an award which made no provision for post award interest because to do so would be to alter the terms of the award rather than entering judgment in terms of the award.

However by analogy with the decision in *Gater Assets Ltd v NAK Naftogaz Ukrainiy* [2008] EWHC 1108 (Comm); [2008] 1 Lloyd's Rep. 295 (Beatson J.), a New York Convention case, interest under the Judgments Act 1838 as amended is payable from the date of entry of the judgment even where no interest was awarded by the arbitrators.

Challenging the award: substantive jurisdiction

67.—(1) A party to arbitral proceedings may (upon notice to the other parties and to the tribunal) apply to the court—   **2E–255**

    (a) challenging any award of the arbitral tribunal as to its substantive jurisdiction; or

    (b) for an order declaring an award made by the tribunal on the merits to be of no effect, in whole or in part, because the tribunal did not have substantive jurisdiction.

A party may lose the right to object (see section 73) and the right to apply is subject to the restrictions in section 70(2) and (3).

(2) The arbitral tribunal may continue the arbitral proceedings and make a further award while an application to the court under this section is pending in relation to an award as to jurisdiction.

(3) On an application under this section challenging an award of the arbitral tribunal as to its substantive jurisdiction, the court may by order—

    (a) confirm the award,

    (b) vary the award, or

    (c) set aside the award in whole or in part.

(4) The leave of the court is required for any appeal from a decision of the court under this section.

Note —Compare ss.22 and 23 of the 1950 Act. This is a mandatory provision (see   **2E–256**
s.4). A challenge under this section involves a re-hearing rather than a review, see *Azov Shipping Co v Baltic Shipping Co (No.1)* [1999] 1 All E.R. 476; [1999] 1 Lloyd's Rep. 68; *Peterson Farms Inc v C&M Farming Ltd* [2004] EWHC 121 (Comm); [2004] 1 Lloyd's Rep. 603.

The identification of parties to an arbitration agreement is a matter of substantive not procedural law, see *Peterson Farms Inc v C&M Farming Ltd* above in which award in favour of non-parties which were within the same group of companies as the company named in the arbitration agreement held to have been made without jurisdiction.

Arbitrators have to be appointed in compliance with any applicable procedure for appointment. Any irregularity in appointment invalidates the arbitration. There is no room in arbitration for for the common law doctrine which can sometimes validate the acts of an apparent or reputed judge. See *Sumukan Ltd v Commonwealth Secretariat* [2007] EWCA Civ 1148; [2008] Bus L.R. 858; [2008] 1 Lloyd's Rep. 40, CA.

Section 67(1)(b)
See *Mohsin v Commonwealth Secretariat* [2002] EWHC 377 (Comm); March 1, 2002   **2E–257**
for interplay of this section and s.73 of the 1996 Act (loss of right to object).

The leave of the court is required
Only the trial judge can grant permission to appeal against a decision under s.67.   **2E–258**
There is no jurisdiction in the Court of Appeal to do so: *Athletic Union of Constantinople*

Paragraph numbers marked with a "+" can be found online and on CD.

v National Basketball Association [2002] 1 W.L.R. 2863; [2002] 3 All E.R. 897, CA (see similarly *Henry Boot Construction v Malmaison Hotel* at para.2E–268 below).

Effect of an order pursuant to s.67(3)(c)

2E–259   Upon an order setting aside the award or a declaration that the award was of no effect, the arbitration reverted to the position it was in before the arbitrator published his award so that the arbitrator was not *functus officio, Hussman (Europe) Ltd v Pharaon* [2003] EWCA Civ 266; [2003] 1 All E.R. (Comm) 879, CA.

Section 67(4)

2E–259.1   It is not incompatible with the European Convention on Human Rights for Parliament to seek to further restrict second appeals as provided in subs.4, *Republic of Kazakhstan v Istil Group Ltd* [2007] EWCA Civ 471; [2007] 2 Lloyd's Rep. 548.

Challenging the award: serious irregularity

2E–260   **68.**—(1) A party to arbitral proceedings may (upon notice to the other parties and to the tribunal) apply to the court challenging an award in the proceedings on the ground of serious irregularity affecting the tribunal, the proceedings or the award. A party may lose the right to object (see section 73) and the right to apply is subject to the restrictions in section 70(2) and (3).

(2) Serious irregularity means an irregularity of one or more of the following kinds which the court considers has caused or will cause substantial injustice to the applicant—

  (a) failure by the tribunal to comply with section 33 (general duty of tribunal);

  (b) the tribunal exceeding its powers (otherwise than by exceeding its substantive jurisdiction: see section 67);

  (c) failure by the tribunal to conduct the proceedings in accordance with the procedure agreed by the parties;

  (d) failure by the tribunal to deal with all the issues that were put to it;

  (e) any arbitral or other institution or person vested by the parties with powers in relation to the proceedings or the award exceeding its powers;

  (f) uncertainty or ambiguity as to the effect of the award;

  (g) the award being obtained by fraud or the award or the way in which it was procured being contrary to public policy;

  (h) failure to comply with the requirements as to the form of the award; or

  (i) any irregularity in the conduct of the proceedings or in the award which is admitted by the tribunal or by any arbitral or other institution or person vested by the parties with powers in relation to the proceedings or the award.

(3) If there is shown to be serious irregularity affecting the tribunal, the proceedings or the award, the court may—

  (a) remit the award to the tribunal, in whole or in part, for reconsideration,

  (b) set the award aside in whole or in part, or

  (c) declare the award to be of no effect, in whole or in part.

Paragraph numbers marked with a "+" can be found online and on CD.

The court shall not exercise its power to set aside or to declare an award to be of no effect, in whole or in part, unless it is satisfied that it would be inappropriate to remit the matters in question to the tribunal for reconsideration.

(4) The leave of the court is required for any appeal from a decision of the court under this section.

Note —Compare ss.22 and 23 of the 1950 Act. This is a mandatory provision (see s.4).   **2E–261**

"On the ground of serious irregularity"

This means irregularity of one or more of the kinds set out in sub-para.(2) which   **2E–262** the court considers has or will cause substantial injustice to the applicant. In *Petroships Pte Ltd v Petec Trading and Investment Corp (The "Petro Ranger")* [2001] 2 Lloyd's Rep. 348, the following commentary on this section appears at p.351:

1. Section 68 sets out a closed list of irregularities (which it is not open to the court to extent).
2. Section 68 reflects the internationally accepted view that the court should be able to correct serious failure to comply with the "due process" of arbitral proceedings: *cf*. art.34 of the Model Law.
3. A serious irregularity has to pass the test of causing "substantial injustice" before the court can act (s.68(2)).
4. The test of "substantial injustice" is intended to be applied by way of support for the arbitral process, not by way of interference with that process. Thus it is only in those cases where it can be said that what has happened is so far removed from what could reasonably be expected of the arbitral process, that the court will take action.
5. The test is not what would have happened had the matter been litigated. To apply such a test wouls be to ignore the fact that the parties have agreed to arbitrate not litigate.
6. Having chosen arbitration, the parties cannot complain of substantial injustice, unless what has happened cannot on any view be defended as an acceptable consequence of that choice.
7. Section 68 is designed as a longstop, only available in extreme cases, where the tribunal has gone so wrong in its conduct of the arbitration in one of the respects listed in s.68, that justice calls out for it to be corrected.
8. Section 68 must not be used as a means of circumventing the restrictions upon the court's power to intervene in arbitral proceedings. Further, the distinction between s.68 and s.69 must be maintained. In addition, the court's powers under s.70(4) should be borne in mind (see below).
9. Section 68(2)(d) ("failure by the tribunal to deal with all issues which were put to it") does not require a tribunal to set out each step by which they reached their conclusion or to deal with each point made by a party. There is a distinction between criticism of the reasoning and a failure to deal with an issue (Mr Justice Thomas in *Hussmann (Europe) Ltd v Al Ameen Development & Trade Co* [2000] 2 Lloyd's Rep. 83, at p.97, col. 1).

In *Lesotho Highlands Development Authority v Impregilo SpA* [2005] UKHL 43 a case where "the issue was whether the tribunal had exceeded its powers within the meaning of s.68(2)(b)" and concerned ss.48(4) and 49(3) of the 1996 Act, Lord Steyn said:

"**28** ... This is a mandatory provision. The policy in favour of party autonomy does not permit derogation from the provisions of section 68. A number of preliminary observations about section 68 are pertinent. First, unlike the position under the old law, intervention under section 68 is only permissible *after* an award has been made. Secondly, the requirement is a serious irregularity. It is a new concept in English arbitration law. Plainly a high threshold must be satisfied. Thirdly, it must be established that the irregularity caused or will cause substantial injustice to the applicant. This is designed to eliminate technical and unmeritorious challenges. It is also a new requirement in English arbitration law. Fourthly, the irregularity must fall within the closed list of categories set out in paragraphs (a) to (i).

Paragraph numbers marked with a "+" can be found online and on CD.

29 It will be observed that the list of irregularities under section 68 may be divided into those which affect the arbitral procedure, and those which affect the award. But nowhere in section 68 is there any hint that a failure by the tribunal to arrive at the "correct decision" could afford a ground for challenge under section 68. On the other hand, section 68 has a meaningful role to play...

31 By its very terms section 68(2)(b) assumes that the tribunal acted within its substantive jurisdiction. It is aimed at the tribunal *exceeding its powers* under the arbitration agreement, terms of reference or the 1996 Act. Section 68(2)(b) does not permit a challenge on the ground that the tribunal arrived at a wrong conclusion as a matter of law or fact. It is not apt to cover a mere error of law. The view is reinforced if one takes into account that a mistake in interpreting the contract is the paradigm of a "question of law" which may in the circumstances specified in section 69 be appealed unless the parties have excluded that right by agreement. In cases where the right of appeal has by agreement, sanctioned by the Act, has been excluded, it would be curious to allow a challenge under section 68(2)(b) to be based on a mistaken interpretation of the underlying contract. Moreover, it would be strange where there is no exclusion agreement, to allow parallel challenges under section 68(2)(b) and section 69.

32 In order to decide whether section 68(2)(b) is engaged it will be necessary to focus intensely on the particular power under an arbitration agreement, the terms of reference, or the 1996 Act which is involved, judged in all the circumstances of the case. In making this general observation it must always be borne in mind that the erroneous exercise of an available power cannot by itself amount to an excess of power. A mere error of law will not amount to an excess of power under section 68(2)(b)."

See too *Profilati Italia SRL v Painewebber Inc* [2001] 1 Lloyd's Rep. 715 (a case of innocent failure to disclosure) the court held that even where a successful party was said to have procured the award in a way which was contrary to public policy it would normally be necessary to satisfy the court that some form of reprehensible or unconscionable conduct on his part had contributed in a substantial way to obtaining an award in his favour; and the court should not be quick to interfere under s.68. Applied in *The Mariana* [2005] EWHC 219 (Comm); [2005] 1 Lloyd's Rep. 640.

See too *Cuflet Chartering v Carousel Shipping Co Ltd (The "Marie H")* [2001] 1 Lloyd's Rep. 707 (conduct alleged to have induced other party into believing that steps to obtaining an award would not be taken while negotiations were current), held that nothing short of unconscionable conduct (of which there had to be cogent evidence) would justify setting aside the award. Inadvertent conduct, however, careless would would not suffice.

In *Hussmann (Europe) Ltd v Al Ameen Development & Trade Co* (see above) it was also held that a meeting between the tribunal and an expert witness in the absence of the parties and without their knowledge which was subsequently brought to the attention of the parties during oral examination of the expert with opportunity to cross-examine him, did not constitute a serious irregularity within the section.

The removal of one of three arbitrators for apparent bias did not without more result in a requirement that the remaining two should recuse themselves. *ASM Shipping Ltd v Harris* [2007] EWHC 1513 (Comm); *The Times* August 6, 2007.

A failure to address central issue by GAFA constituted a serious irregularity within s.68(2)(d), see *Ascot Commodities NV v Olam International Ltd* [2002] C.L.C 277.

For the interplay of s.73 (loss of right to object) of the 1996 Act upon s.68 see *Moshin v The Commonwealth Secretariat* [2002] EWHC 377 (Comm), March 1, 2002.

The court has a discretion to allow an arbitrator's confidential reasons to be adduced in evidence despite any agreement to treat the same as confidential. Indeed in the light of the issues raised by s.68 the court would allow confidential reasons to be adduced unless it was unnecessary to do so, or the allegations made were clearly groundless or there was some other exceptional reason not to do so, *Tame Shipping Ltd v Easy Navigation Ltd* [2004] EWHC 1862 (Comm); [2004] 2 All E.R. (Comm) 521; [2004] 2 Lloyd's Rep. 626, para.27.

For the extent to which and the circumstances in which an arbitrator may rely upon his own experience/knowledge without breaching his obligation under s.33 or so as to commit a serious irregularity under s.68 of the 1996 Act, see *Checkpoint Ltd v Strathclyde Pension Fund* [2003] EWCA Civ 84; [2003] UKPC D1, citing *Fox v P.G. Wellfair Ltd* [1981] 2 Lloyd's Rep 514, CA.

Paragraph numbers marked with a "+" can be found online and on CD.

The following pre-1996 Act cases may still provide examples of irregularity:

(1) If the arbitrator, without proper notice to both parties, gave audience to one of the parties in the absence of the other, that is a good reason for setting aside the award (*Re Gregson and Armstrong Arbn.* (1894) 70 L.T. 106; and see *The Warwick* (1890) 15 PD 189). Where the arbitrator heard the evidence of each party in the absence of the other, the award was set aside, although the party moving to set the award aside had made no objection at the time (*Ramsden & Co Ltd v Jacobs* [1922] 1 K.B. 640) but where a charterparty contained a clause that in the event of a dispute arising it should be referred to arbitration, each party to nominate an arbitrator, who was to be a commercial man, and that if the arbitrators differed they should appoint an umpire, and the umpire so appointed made his award after hearing the arbitrators, but without giving notice to or hearing the parties, it was held that, in view of the practice in commercial arbitrations, the award must stand (*French Government v Owners of S.S. Tsurushima Maru* (1921) 37 T.L.R. 961, CA).

(2) If the arbitrator wrongly rejects relevant evidence, his award will be set aside (*Trayfoot v Lock* [1957] 1 All E.R. 423). It is a settled principle that arbitrators must not take evidence in secret and therefore where an arbitrator who is an expert having special knowledge of the particular subject-matter is minded to use his special knowledge to form a different view of the facts from that given in evidence by expert witnesses called by the parties he should not do so without giving them an opportunity of dealing with it, and especially so where one party only appears before him (*Fisher v P.G. Wellfair Ltd* [1981] Com.L.R. 140; [1981] 2 Lloyd's Rep. 514, CA).

An arbitrator should use his special expertise to evaluate evidence, not to supply it. Furthermore he should not receive evidence in the absence of one of the parties or use any particular factual knowledge acquired by him in other proceedings (*Top Shop Estates Ltd v Danino* (1985) 273 E.G. 197).

Jurisdiction of arbitrator on remission

Where an award was remitted under s.22 of the Arbitration Act 1950 the arbitrator's jurisdiction was held to be limited to consideration of matters previously raised, together with any additional matters specified by the court in its order; he was not empowered to consider other issues (*Interbulk Ltd v Aiden Shipping Co Ltd*; *The Vimiera (No.3)* [1986] 2 Lloyd's Rep. 75). **2E–263**

Appeal on point of law

69.—(1) Unless otherwise agreed by the parties, a party to arbitral proceedings may (upon notice to the other parties and to the tribunal) appeal to the court on a question of law arising out of an award made in the proceedings. An agreement to dispense with reasons for the tribunal's award shall be considered an agreement to exclude the court's jurisdiction under this section. **2E–264**

(2) An appeal shall not be brought under this section except—

    (a) with the agreement of all the other parties to the proceedings, or

    (b) with the leave of the court.

The right to appeal is also subject to the restrictions in section 70(2) and (3).

(3) Leave to appeal shall be given only if the court is satisfied—

    (a) that the determination of the question will substantially affect the rights of one or more of the parties,

    (b) that the question is one which the tribunal was asked to determine,

    (c) that, on the basis of the findings of fact in the award—

        (i) the decision of the tribunal on the question is obviously wrong, or

Paragraph numbers marked with a "+" can be found online and on CD.

> > > (ii) the question is one of general public importance and the decision of the tribunal is at least open to serious doubt, and
> >
> > (d) that, despite the agreement of the parties to resolve the matter by arbitration, it is just and proper in all the circumstances for the court to determine the question.
>
> (4) An application for leave to appeal under this section shall identify the question of law to be determined and state the grounds on which it is alleged that leave to appeal should be granted.
>
> (5) The court shall determine an application for leave to appeal under this section without a hearing unless it appears to the court that a hearing is required.
>
> (6) The leave of the court is required for any appeal from a decision of the court under this section to grant or refuse leave to appeal.
>
> (7) On an appeal under this section the court may by order—
>
> > (a) confirm the award,
> >
> > (b) vary the award,
> >
> > (c) remit the award to the tribunal, in whole or in part, for reconsideration in the light of the court's determination, or
> >
> > (d) set aside the award in whole or in part.
>
> The court shall not exercise its power to set aside an award, in whole or in part, unless it is satisfied that it would be inappropriate to remit the matters in question to the tribunal for reconsideration.
>
> (8) The decision of the court on an appeal under this section shall be treated as a judgment of the court for the purposes of a further appeal.
>
> But no such appeal lies without the leave of the court which shall not be given unless the court considers that the question is one of general importance or is one which for some other special reason should be considered by the Court of Appeal.

2E–265   *Note* —Compare ss.1 and 3 of the 1979 Act.

Appeal to the High Court

2E–266   The rules in Pt 62, s.II apply to appeals to the court under this section. Express provisions relating to applications for permission to appeal are found in Practice Direction—Arbitration para.12 (see para.2E–50 above).

The purpose and function of the restrictions on appeals on points of law imposed by s.69 and related provisions were examined in *Royal and Sun Alliance Insurance Plc v BAE Systems (Operations) Ltd* [2008] EWHC 743 (Comm); [2008] 1 Lloyd's Rep. 712 (Walker J.). In that case it was noted (at para.11) that, in relation to appeals under s.69, by s.4(2) of the 1996 Act parties are permitted to make their own arrangements by agreement with particular provisions of that section (including that requiring leave to appeal) and s.70 applying only in the absence of such agreement.

If no question of English law arises, there is no power in the English court to grant leave to appeal under s.69(1) interpolating the wording of s.82 of the Act, see *Reliance Industries Ltd v Enron Oil & Gas India Ltd* [2002] 1 Lloyd's Rep. 645 (arbitrators applying Indian law in construing contract). Case also emphasised importance under s.69 to establish that, despite the agreement of the parties to resolve the matter by arbitration, it is just and proper in all the circumstances for the court to determine the question.

A judge should give sufficient reason for his decision so as to enable a party to

Paragraph numbers marked with a "+" can be found online and on CD.

understand why he had won or lost. What is sufficient will depend upon the issues involved in a particular case. The *Antaios* [1985] A.C. 191 guidance no longer holds good, see *North Range Shipping Ltd v Seatrans Shipping Corp (The Western Triumph)* [2002] EWCA Civ 405; [2002] 1 W.L.R. 2397; [2002] 4 All E.R. 390; [2002] 2 Lloyd's Rep. 1. The court said:

"Section 69(3) contains a variety of threshold tests. At the very least we think an unsuccessful applicant for leave should be told which of those tests he has failed ... But does the judge need to go further and explain in every case why the relevant threshold test has been failed? We think the answer to this question is "No". If the question is not one of law, does not substantially affect the rights of one or more of the parties or is not one which the tribunal was asked to determine, an adequate reason for the judge's decision will in almost all cases have been given simply by identifying the test or tests which the applicant has failed without the need to say more. The same applies we think to the question of general public importance. However, when one gets to whether the tribunal's decision was obviously wrong or not open to serious doubt, we do not think that it is possible to give an unqualified answer to the question we have posed. It may be enough simply to refer to the statutory test, but we do not think it is possible to say that this will always be so. It would be enough to say "For the reasons given by the arbitrators" if that was the judge's reason. Otherwise it may be necessary to go further. But any further reasons need only be brief so as to show the losing party why he has lost. Such reasons will of course be given against a background of a full hearing, a reasoned award and detailed submissions as to why leave to appeal should be granted. In other words, the judge's brief reasons are directed to a fully informed applicant."

See too the penumltimate and last paragraph of 2E–268 below.

In *The Agios Dimitrios* [2004] EWHC 2232 (Comm); [2005] 1 Lloyd's Rep. 23 the court at paras 5, 6 and 7 stated:

"5. The philosophy and purpose underlying the s.69 procedure requires the achievement of finality of awards consistently with the on-going judicial development of English commercial law. The s.69(3) tests are designed to reflect this philosophy and purpose. Section 69(3)(c) therefore distinguishes between cases where the material question of law is one of general public interest and cases where it is not. A different threshold test is to be applied in the former case (the serious doubt test) from the latter (the obviously wrong test), but in both cases the test is to be applied to the question of law strictly 'on the basis of the findings of facts in the award'. In other words the Court takes the findings of fact as an immutable basis for testing the correctness of the arbitrators' decision on the question of law unless the Court takes the view that the award does not contain reasons or 'does not set out the tribunal's reasons in sufficient detail to enable the Court properly to consider the application or appeal', in which case it can order the arbitrators to give reasons in sufficient detail under s.70(3).

6. The Court's function under s.69 is thus to look exclusively at the award for the purpose of ascertaining whether the threshold tests under s.69(3) have been satisfied. Above all, it does not go behind what appears on the face of the award and it is not concerned with the circumstances in which the award came to be made and in particular with whether those circumstances were such as to amount to serious irregularity which has caused or will cause substantial injustice to either of the parties. The Act provides, by s.68, an entirely self-contained procedural regime for dealing with such circumstances.

7. Consequently, the combination in one hearing of applications under both sections involves two quite distinct processes of judicial analysis. In many cases determination of the s.69 application for leave to appeal before that of the s.68 application may be logically preferable. This is because the determination by the Court of the question whether there has obviously been an error of law on such facts as have been found or whether there is serious doubt as to that, will often have a direct bearing on the question whether if there has been the serious irregularity complained of for the purposes of the s.68 application such irregularity has given rise to substantial injustice. In each case, however, it is a matter for the Court whether the application for leave to appeal should be tried first. There may be cases where the procedural irregularity complained of is of such a kind

Paragraph numbers marked with a "+" can be found online and on CD.

that it would be logically preferable for the s.68 application to be determined first so that, if it succeeds, the award can be set aside or remitted to the arbitrators before leave to appeal is considered. After all, following remission, the issue of law in question might not eventually arise."

It is not contrary to art.6 of the European Convention on Human Rights by agreement to restrict or exclude the supervisory regime of s.69; see *Sukuman Ltd v Commonwealth Secretariat* [2006] EWHC 304 (Comm); [2006] Lloyd's Rep. 53.

The words "final and binding" did not of themselves amount to an exclusion of the right to appeal but may together with other factors amount thereto; *Essex CC v Premier Recycling Ltd* [2007] B.L.R. 233, QBD (TCC).

Amongst other things, para.12 of Practice Direction—Arbitration (see para.2E–50 above) provides that the written evidence filed by a respondent to an application for permission to appeal under s.69 must specify whether that party wishes to contend that the award should be upheld for reasons not expressed in the award. In these circumstances, the grounds upon which the respondent relies (and as to which, inevitably, the court must come to its own conclusions) must be based on a point of law or points of law (*CTI Group Inc v Transclear SA (The "Mary Nour") (No.2)* [2008] EWHC 2340 (Comm); [2008] 1 Lloyd's Rep. 250 (Field J.)).

Question of general public importance

2E–267 The requirement that the decision of the arbitrators is at least open to serious doubt is broader than that propounded by Lord Diplock in *"The Nema"* [1982] A.C. 724 (at p.743D) that there was a strong prima facie case that the arbitrator's decision was wrong, see *CMA CGM SA v Beteiligungs-Kommanditgesellscaft MS "Northern Pioneer" Schiffahrtgesellschaft MBH* [2002] EWCA Civ 1878; [2003] 1 W.L.R. 1015; [2003] 1 Lloyd's Rep 212; [2003] 3 All E.R. 330; [2003] 1 All E.R. (Comm) 204, CA.

Appeals to the Court of Appeal

2E–268 In furtherance of the policy of injecting speed and finality in relation to arbitration awards, the Act re-enacts the far-reaching limitations on the right of appeal from decisions or orders of the High Court to the Court of Appeal.

Thus, it is provided that no appeal shall be to the Court of Appeal from a decision of the High Court on an appeal against an arbitration award under s.69 of the Act or from a decision determining a preliminary question of law (s.45) unless two conditions are satisfied, namely,

(a) the High Court or the Court of Appeal gives permission, and

(b) it is considered by the High Court that the question of law to which its decision relates, is either one of general public importance or is one which for some other special reason should be considered by the Court of Appeal under ss.69(8) and 45(6) of the Act,

Restrictions on the right of appeal to the Court of Appeal are contained in the Supreme Court Act 1981 s.18.

The mere fact that a High Court judge reaches a different conclusion from that of arbitrators he considers very experienced does not constitute a "special reason" justifying the granting of permission to appeal to the Court of Appeal (*Pera Shipping Corp v Petroship SA*, [1985] 2 Lloyd's Rep. 103, CA).

In *Henry Boot Construction (UK) Ltd v Malmaison Hotel (Manchester) Ltd* [2000] 2 Lloyd's Rep. 625 [2001] Q.B. 388; [2001] 1 All E.R. 257 CA, the court held (1) that on the true construction of s.69(8) of the Arbitration Act 1996 a party who wished to appeal from a decision of the High Court or a county court on appeal from an arbitration award required the permission of the High Court or the county court, as the case might be; and that the Court of Appeal had no jurisdiction either to grant permission itself or to review a refusal of the High Court or a county court to grant permission and (2) that s.55 of the Access to Justice Act 1999, which limited the right of appeal where there had already been one appeal, did not impliedly repeal s.69(8) of the Arbitration Act 1996; and that, accordingly (by a 2:1 majority), since s.55 of the Act of 1999 had no effect on s.69(8) of the Act of 1996, where the court which heard an appeal from an arbitrator gave permission to the Court of Appeal, there was no additional requirement to obtain the permission of the Court of Appeal.

In *CGU International Insurance plc v Astra Zeneca Insurance Co Ltd* [2006] EWCA Civ

Paragraph numbers marked with a "+" can be found online and on CD.

1340; [2007] 1 Lloyd's Rep. 142, the court held that there was a residual discretion to permit an appeal despite the judge's refusal of leave where the refusal could be challenged on the ground of unfairness under art.6 of the European Convention on Human Rights. Courts would however not allow such power which existed to ensure that injustice was avoided to become itself an unfair instrument for subverting statute and undermining the process of arbitration. See too *ASM Shipping Ltd of India v TTMI Ltd of England* [2006] EWCA Civ 1341; [2007] 1 Lloyd's Rep. 136 (residual discretion not involved; no overarching principle in Human Rights Convention that an award tainted by apparent bias must be set aside: application of margin of appreciation in domestic court).

The exclusion of a right of appeal was not a matter of domestic law to be regarded as an onerous or unusual provision which had to be specifically drawn to the attention of the other party in order to be incorporated into the arbitration agreement nor did such exclusion infringe the other party's rights under art.6 of the ECHR: *Sumukan Ltd v The Commonwealth Secretariat* [2007] EWCA Civ 243; [2007] 3 All E.R. 342; [2007] 2 Lloyd's Rep. 87, CA.

Challenge or appeal: supplementary provisions

70.—(1) The following provisions apply to an application or appeal under section 67, 68 or 69.

(2) An application or appeal may not be brought if the applicant or appellant has not first exhausted—

    (a) any available arbitral process of appeal or review, and

    (b) any available recourse under section 57 (correction of award or additional award).

(3) Any application or appeal must be brought within 28 days of the date of the award or, if there has been any arbitral process of appeal or review, of the date when the applicant or appellant was notified of the result of that process.

(4) If on an application or appeal it appears to the court that the award—

    (a) does not contain the tribunal's reasons, or

    (b) does not set out the tribunal's reasons in sufficient detail to enable the court properly to consider the application or appeal,

the court may order the tribunal to state the reasons for its award in sufficient detail for that purpose.

(5) Where the court makes an order under subsection (4), it may make such further order as it thinks fit with respect to any additional costs of the arbitration resulting from its order.

(6) The court may order the applicant or appellant to provide security for the costs of the application or appeal, and may direct that the application or appeal be dismissed if the order is not complied with.

The power to order security for costs shall not be exercised on the ground that the applicant or appellant is—

    (a) an individual ordinarily resident outside the United Kingdom, or

    (b) a corporation or association incorporated or formed under the law of a country outside the United Kingdom, or whose central management and control is exercised outside the United Kingdom.

2E–269

Paragraph numbers marked with a "+" can be found online and on CD.

(7) The court may order that any money payable under the award shall be brought into court or otherwise secured pending the determination of the application or appeal, and may direct that the application or appeal be dismissed if the order is not complied with.

(8) The court may grant leave to appeal subject to conditions to the same or similar effect as an order under subsection (6) or (7).

This does not affect the general discretion of the court to grant leave subject to conditions.

2E-270   *Note* —Compare s.23(3) of the 1950 Act, and s.1(5) and (6) of the 1979 Act. This is a mandatory provision (see s.4).

Time for appeal/Exhaustion of Specified Remedies s.70(2)

2E-271   There is a 28 day time limit and the appellant must first have exhausted any available arbitral process of appeal or review or any available recourse under s.57.

This time limit may be extended, see s.80(5) below. For factors relevant to an application to extend time, see *Aoot Kalmneft v Glencore International AG* [2001] 2 All E.R. (Comm) 577.

For a case on exhaustion of any available recourse under s.57 see *Torch Offshore LLC v Cable Shipping Inc* [2004] EWHC 787 (Comm); [2004] 2 All E.R. (Comm) 365.

Reasons for awards

2E-272   By s.52(4) of the 1996 Act an award must contain reasons for the award unless it is an agreed award or the parties have agreed to dispense with reasons. Section 70(4) extends the power of the court to order reasons to applications under ss.67 and 68 as well as to applications under s.69. For an example of the existence of this power see *Petroships Pte Ltd v Petec Trading & Investment Corp* [2001] 2 Lloyd's Rep. 348.

Terms

2E-273   In granting permission to appeal, the High Court may impose such conditions as it considers reasonable (*ibid.*) as for example, that the minimum sum due to the successful party should be paid over to him or that the sum in dispute should be in some way secured, e.g. by payment into court or otherwise.

Section 70(7)

2E-274   In *Peterson Farms Inc v C&M Farming Ltd* [2003] EWHC 2298; [2004] 1 Lloyd's Rep. 614 the court considered factors material to the exercise of its discretion under s.70(7) holding inter alia that in most cases, it is likely that demonstration by the party against whom the jurisdictional challenge is made that the challenge is flimsy or otherwise lacks substance is likely to be regarded as a threshold requirement for the court's consideration whether in all the circumstances it is appropriate to require, as a condition of proceeding under s.67, that money payable under the award shall be brought into court or otherwise secured pending the determination of the application.

Challenge or appeal: effect of order of court

2E-275   **71.**—(1) The following provisions have effect where the court makes an order under section 67, 68 or 69 with respect to an award.

(2) Where the award is varied, the variation has effect as part of the tribunal's award.

(3) Where the award is remitted to the tribunal, in whole or in part, for reconsideration, the tribunal shall make a fresh award in respect of the matters remitted within three months of the date of the order for remission or such longer or shorter period as the court may direct.

Paragraph numbers marked with a "+" can be found online and on CD.

(4) Where the award is set aside or declared to be of no effect, in whole or in part, the court may also order that any provision that an award is a condition precedent to the bringing of legal proceedings in respect of a matter to which the arbitration agreement applies, is of no effect as regards the subject matter of the award or, as the case may be, the relevant part of the award.

Note —Compare s.22(2) of the 1950 Act, and s.1(8) of the 1979 Act. This is a mandatory provision (see s.4). Section 71(4) does not apply to statutory arbitrations.   **2E–276**

For s.72 of the Arbitration Act 1996 (see Arrangement) plus any related commentary see paragraphs 2E–277+ to 2E–278+ on White Book on Westlaw UK or the Civil Procedure CD.

Loss of right to object

73.—(1) If a party to arbitral proceedings takes part, or continues   **2E–279**
to take part, in the proceedings without making, either forthwith or within such time as is allowed by the arbitration agreement or the tribunal or by any provision of this Part, any objection—

    (a) that the tribunal lacks substantive jurisdiction,

    (b) that the proceedings have been improperly conducted,

    (c) that there has been a failure to comply with the arbitration agreement or with any provision of this Part, or

    (d) that there has been any other irregularity affecting the tribunal or the proceedings,

he may not raise that objection later, before the tribunal or the court, unless he shows that, at the time he took part or continued to take part in the proceedings, he did not know and could not with reasonable diligence have discovered the grounds for the objection.

(2) Where the arbitral tribunal rules that it has substantive jurisdiction and a party to arbitral proceedings who could have questioned that ruling—

    (a) by any available arbitral process of appeal or review, or

    (b) by challenging the award,

does not do so, or does not do so within the time allowed by the arbitration agreement or any provision of this Part, he may not object later to the tribunal's substantive jurisdiction on any ground which was the subject of that ruling.

Note —This is a mandatory provison (see s.4). See too *Rustal Trading Ltd v Gill &*   **2E–280**
Duffus SA [2002] 1 Lloyd's Rep. 14.

Examples:

See *Rustal Trading Ltd v Gill & Duffus SA* [2000] 1 Lloyd's Rep. 14 and *Moshin v The*   **2E–281**
Commonwealth Secretariat [2002] EWHC 377 (Comm), March 1, 2002 (both cases of continuing to participate in the arbitral proceedings without objection with full knowledge and/a means of knowledge). See too *VEE Networks Ltd v Econet Wireless International Ltd* [2004] EWHC 2909; [2005] 1 All E.R. (Comm) 303; [2005] 1 Lloyd's Rep. 192.

The words "any objection" and "that objection" mean any ground of objection and   **2E–282**
that ground of objection, see *Primetrade AG v Ythan Ltd* [2005] EWHC 2399 (Comm); [2006] 1 All E.R. 367; [2006] 1 Lloyd's Rep. 457. The ground should be looked at broadly. Case also considered the extent to which new evidence should be admitted in support of a new or different argument within an existing ground of objection.

Paragraph numbers marked with a "+" can be found online and on CD.

For ss.74 to 78 of the Arbitration Act 1996 (see Arrangement) plus any related commentary see paragraphs 2E–283+ to 2E–289+ on White Book on Westlaw UK or the Civil Procedure CD.

Power of court to extend time limits relating to arbitral proceedings

2E–290   79.—(1) Unless the parties otherwise agree, the court may by order extend any time limit agreed by them in relation to any matter relating to the arbitral proceedings or specified in any provision of this Part having effect in default of such agreement. This section does not apply to a time limit to which section 12 applies (power of court to extend time for beginning arbitral proceedings, etc.).

(2) An application for an order may be made—

    (a) by any party to the arbitral proceedings (upon notice to the other parties and to the tribunal), or

    (b) by the arbitral tribunal (upon notice to the parties).

(3) The court shall not exercise its power to extend a time limit unless it is satisfied—

    (a) that any available recourse to the tribunal, or to any arbitral or other institution or person vested by the parties with power in that regard, has first been exhausted, and

    (b) that a substantial injustice would otherwise be done.

(4) The court's power under this section may be exercised whether or not the time has already expired.

(5) An order under this section may be made on such terms as the court thinks fit.

(6) The leave of the court is required for any appeal from a decision of the court under this section.

For ss.80 to 81 of the Arbitration Act 1996 (see Arrangement) plus any related commentary see paragraphs 2E–291+ to 2E–293+ on White Book on Westlaw UK or the Civil Procedure CD.

Minor definitions

2E–294   82.—(1) In this Part—

"arbitrator", unless the context otherwise requires, includes an umpire;

"available arbitral process", in relation to any matter, includes any process of appeal to or review by an arbitral or other institution or person vested by the parties with powers in relation to that matter;

"claimant", unless the context otherwise requires, includes a counterclaimant, and related expressions shall be construed accordingly;

"dispute" includes any difference;

"enactment" includes an enactment contained in Northern Ireland legislation;

"legal proceedings" means civil proceedings in the High Court or a county court;

Paragraph numbers marked with a "+" can be found online and on CD.

"peremptory order" means an order made under section 41(5) or made in exercise of any corresponding power conferred by the parties;

"premises" includes land, buildings, moveable structures, vehicles, vessels, aircraft and hovercraft;

"question of law" means—

(a) for a court in England and Wales, a question of the law of England and Wales, and

(b) for a court in Northern Ireland, a question of the law of Northern Ireland;

"substantive jurisdiction", in relation to an arbitral tribunal, refers to the matters specified in section 30(1)(a) to (c), and references to the tribunal exceeding its substantive jurisdiction shall be construed accordingly.

(2) References in this Part to a party to an arbitration agreement include any person claiming under or through a party to the agreement.

For ss.83 to 98 of the Arbitration Act 1996 (see Arrangement) plus any related commentary see paragraphs 2E–295+ to 2E–343+ on White Book on Westlaw UK or the Civil Procedure CD.

PART III

RECOGNITION AND ENFORCEMENT OF CERTAIN FOREIGN AWARDS

ENFORCEMENT OF GENEVA CONVENTION AWARDS

Continuation of Part II of the Arbitration Act 1950

99. Part II of the [1950 c. 27.] Arbitration Act 1950 (enforcement of certain foreign awards) continues to apply in relation to foreign awards within the meaning of that Part which are not also New York Convention awards.   2E–344

Note —Compare ss.35 to 42 of the 1950 Act, and s.2 of the 1975 Act.   2E–345

Geneva Convention Countries

Section 99 does not apply to countries which are also New York Convention States   2E–346
and the list below should be checked against the list at para.2E–350, below.

List of Territories to which the Geneva Convention applies:

The United Kingdom of Great Britain and Northern Ireland

Anguilla	India
British Virgin Islands	Republic of Ireland
Cayman Islands	Israel
Falkland Islands	Italy
Falkland Islands Dependencies	Japan
Gibraltar	Kenya
Montserrat	Luxembourg

Paragraph numbers marked with a "+" can be found online and on CD.

Turks and Caicos Islands	Malta
Antigua and Barbuda	Mauritius
Austria	Netherlands (including Curacao)
Bahamas	New Zealand
Bangladesh	Pakistan
Belgium	Portugal
Belize	Romania
†Czechoslovakia	Saint Christopher and Nevis
Denmark	St. Lucia
Dominica	Spain
Finland	Sweden
Federal Republic of Germany	Switzerland
France	Tanzania
*German Democratic Republic	Thailand
Greece	Western Samoa
Grenada	†Yugoslavia
Guyana	Zambia

*The German Democratic Republic is now part of the Federal Republic of Germany.

† For the position of the former constituent states of Yugoslavia and of Czechoslovakia under this convention see *http://untreaty.un.org* but in any event such position is overshadowed where a state has acceded to the New York Convention (see below).

RECOGNITION AND ENFORCEMENT OF NEW YORK CONVENTION AWARDS

New York Convention awards

2E–347   **100.**—(1) In this Part a "New York Convention award" means an award made, in pursuance of an arbitration agreement, in the territory of a state (other than the United Kingdom) which is a party to the New York Convention.

(2) For the purposes of subsection (1) and of the provisions of this Part relating to such awards—

   (a) "arbitration agreement" means an arbitration agreement in writing, and

   (b) an award shall be treated as made at the seat of the arbitration, regardless of where it was signed, despatched or delivered to any of the parties.

In this subsection "agreement in writing" and "seat of the arbitration" have the same meaning as in Part I.

(3) If Her Majesty by Order in Council declares that a state specified in the Order is a party to the New York Convention, or is a party in respect of any territory so specified, the Order shall, while in force, be conclusive evidence of that fact.

(4) In this section "the New York Convention" means the Convention on the Recognition and Enforcement of Foreign Arbitral Awards adopted by the United Nations Conference on International Commercial Arbitration on 10th June 1958.

2E–348   *Note* —Compare s.7 of the 1975 Act.

Paragraph numbers marked with a "+" can be found online and on CD.

New York Convention States

The following states have been specified by Order in Council (as amended from time to time by the Arbitration (Foreign Awards) (Orders) as being parties to the New York Convention, namely:

2E–349

ARBITRATION

Algeria	Indonesia
Antigua and Barbuda	Republic of Ireland
Argentina	Israel
Australia (including all the external territories for the international relations of which Australia is responsible)	Italy
Austria	Japan
Bahrain	Jordan
Belgium	Kenya
Belize	Korea
Benin	Kuwait
Botswana	Luxembourg
Bulgaria	Madagascar
Burkina Faso	Malaysia
Byelorussian Soviet Socialist Republic	Mexico
Cambodia	Monaco
Cameroon	Morocco
Canada	Netherlands (including the Netherlands Antilles)
Central African Republic	New Zealand
Chile	Niger
China	Nigeria
Colombia	Norway
Costa Rica	Panama
Cuba	Peru
Cyprus	Philippines
Czechoslovakia‡	Poland
Denmark (including Greenland and the Faroe Islands)	Romania
Djibouti	San Marino
Dominica	Singapore
Ecuador	South Africa
Egypt	Spain
Finland	Sri Lanka
France (including all the territories of the French Republic)	Sweden
Federal Republic of Germany	Switzerland
German Democratic Republic*	Syria
Ghana	Tanzania
Greece	Thailand
Guatemala	Trinidad and Tobago
Haiti	Tunisia
Holy See	Ukrainian Soviet Socialist Republic**
Hungary	Uruguay
India	

Paragraph numbers marked with a "+" can be found online and on CD.

† The Union of Soviet Socialist Republics is now dissolved. In many respects the Russian Federation has succeeded to its international obligations but the precise position is uncertain. For the position of the countries which previously formed part of the Union of Soviet Socialist Republics but are not within the Russian Federation see the websites referred to under 2E–346 above.

United States of America (including all the territories for the international relations of which the United States of America is responsible)

‡ For the signatory position of the former constituent states of Yugoslavia and Czechoslovakia consult the websites referred to under 2E–346 above.

*The German Democratic Republic is now part of the Federal Republic of Germany.

** The Ukrainian Soviet Socialist Republic is now the Ukraine.

2E–350 *Note* —The list at para.2E–349, above, identifies those signatories to the New York Convention in respect of whom an Order in Council envisaged under subs.(3) has been made. Not all signatories to the Convention are the subject of such an Order in Council. For a complete list of signatories recourse should be had to the website of the International Chamber of Commerce—Arbitration, or the website of the United Nations Commission on International Trade Law.

Recognition and enforcement of awards

2E–351   **101.**—(1) A New York Convention award shall be recognised as binding on the persons as between whom it was made, and may accordingly be relied on by those persons by way of defence, set-off or otherwise in any legal proceedings in England and Wales or Northern Ireland.

(2) A New York Convention award may, by leave of the court, be enforced in the same manner as a judgment or order of the court to the same effect.

As to the meaning of "the court" see section 105.

(3) Where leave is so given, judgment may be entered in terms of the award.

2E–352   *Note* —Compare s.3 of the 1975 Act.

"… be enforced …as a judgment" s.101(2)

2E–353   A foreign state which has agreed in writing to submit a dispute to arbitration cannot claim state immunity in respect of English proceedings to enforce the award: *Svenska Petroleum Exploration AB v Government of the Republic of Lithuania (No.2)* [2006] EWCA Civ 1529; [2007] Q.B. 886; [2007] 1 Lloyd's Rep. 193 applying s.9(1) of the State Immunity Act 1978.

Interest under the Judgments Act 1838 as amended is payable from the date of entry of the judgment even where interest was not ordered in the arbitral award. See *Gater Assets Ltd v NAK Naftogaz Ukrainiy* [2008] EWHC 1108 (Comm); [2008] 2 Lloyd's Rep. 295 (Beatson J.).

There is no objection in principle to enforcement of part only of an award, provided the part to be enforced could be ascertained from the face of the award and judgment could be given in the same terms as those in the award (*IPCO (Nigeria) Ltd v Nigerian National Petroleum Corp* [2008] EWCA Civ 1157; *The Times* November 11, 2008, CA.

Security for costs

2E–354   For opposing views as to whether there is or there is not jurisdiction to order security for costs in respect of an application to enforce the New York Convention award under this section, see *Gater Assets Ltd v NAK Naftogaz Ukrainiy* [2007] EWCA Civ 988; [2007] 2 Lloyd's Rep. 588, CA.

Paragraph numbers marked with a "+" can be found online and on CD.

Evidence to be produced by party seeking recognition or enforcement

102.—(1) A party seeking the recognition or enforcement of a
New York Convention award must produce—   **2E–355**

    (a) the duly authenticated original award or a duly certified copy of it, and

    (b) the original arbitration agreement or a duly certified copy of it.

(2) If the award or agreement is in a foreign language, the party
must also produce a translation of it certified by an official or sworn
translator or by a diplomatic or consular agent.

Note—Compare s.4 of the 1975 Act.   **2E–356**

Refusal of recognition or enforcement

103.—(1) Recognition or enforcement of a New York Convention   **2E–357**
award shall not be refused except in the following cases.

(2) Recognition or enforcement of the award may be refused if
the person against whom it is invoked proves—

    (a) that a party to the arbitration agreement was (under the law applicable to him) under some incapacity;

    (b) that the arbitration agreement was not valid under the law to which the parties subjected it or, failing any indication thereon, under the law of the country where the award was made;

    (c) that he was not given proper notice of the appointment of the arbitrator or of the arbitration proceedings or was otherwise unable to present his case;

    (d) that the award deals with a difference not contemplated by or not falling within the terms of the submission to arbitration or contains decisions on matters beyond the scope of the submission to arbitration (but see subsection (4);

    (e) that the composition of the arbitral tribunal or the arbitral procedure was not in accordance with the agreement of the parties or, failing such agreement, with the law of the country in which the arbitration took place;

    (f) that the award has not yet become binding on the parties, or has been set aside or suspended by a competent authority of the country in which, or under the law of which, it was made.

(3) Recognition or enforcement of the award may also be refused
if the award is in respect of a matter which is not capable of settlement by arbitration, or if it would be contrary to public policy to
recognise or enforce the award.

(4) An award which contains decisions on matters not submitted
to arbitration may be recognised or enforced to the extent that it
contains decisions on matters submitted to arbitration which can be
separated from those on matters not so submitted.

Paragraph numbers marked with a "+" can be found online and on CD.

(5) Where an application for the setting aside or suspension of the award has been made to such a competent authority as is mentioned in subsection (2)(f), the court before which the award is sought to be relied upon may, if it considers it proper, adjourn the decision on the recognition or enforcement of the award.

It may also on the application of the party claiming recognition or enforcement of the award order the other party to give suitable security.

2E-358   *Note* —Compare s.5 of the 1975 Act.

Enforcing court and curial court the same

2E-359   Where the enforcing court and the court of the country whose law governs the award (the curial court) are the same, and application is made to that court to set aside or suspend a Convention award, that court may exercise both the curial court's power to set aside or suspend the award and, at the same time, the enforcing court's discretion to permit the pending supervisory process to continue and to refuse enforcement of the award if that process will result in the award being set aside or suspended by itself as the curial court, since, where the application is made to itself, as the curial court, to set aside or suspend the award it has as the enforcing court power under s.5(2) (now s.103(2)) to refuse enforcement of or reliance on the award and power under s.5(5) (now s.103(5)) to adjourn the proceedings, notwithstanding that the only proceedings consist of the application to itself as the curial court to set aside the award in which necessarily the award upon by the party seeking to have it set aside (*Hiscox v Outhwaite (No.1)* [1991] 3 All E.R. 641, HL).

In *Minmetals Germany GmbH v Ferco Steel Ltd* [1999] 1 All E.R. (Comm) 315; *The Times*, March 1, 1999 it was held that by agreeing the place of a foreign arbitration, a party not only agreed to submit all contractual disputes to arbitration but also agreed that the conduct of the arbitration should be subject to the supervisory jurisdiction of the courts of that place. Further the court stated that in a case where a party against whom enforcement was sought alleged that a New York Convention award should not be enforced on the ground that such enforcement would lead to substantial injustice and therefore be contrary to English public policy the following must normally be included among the relevant considerations:

1. The nature of the procedural injustice.
2. Whether that party had invoked the supervisory jurisdiction of the seat of the arbitration.
3. Whether a remedy was available under that jurisdiction.
4. Whether the courts of that jurisdiction had conclusively determined the enforcee's complaint in favour of upholding the award.
5. If that party had failed to invoke that remedial jurisdiction, what reason had he and, in particular, whether he was acting, unreasonably in failing to do so.

Grounds of refusal

2E-360   In *Roseel NV v Oriental Commercial & Shipping Co (UK) Ltd* [1991] 2 Lloyd's Rep. 625, held that an agreement in parallel New York legal proceedings prior to award that any proceedings to confirm or vacate arbitration will be brought in New York did not constitute a ground within s.5(2)(f) of the Arbitration Act 1975 (now s.103(2)(f)) to refuse enforcement nor was it a precondition to enforcement that there should be assets within the jurisdiction.

In *Omnium de Traitement et de Valorisation SA v Hilmarton Ltd* [1999] 2 Lloyd's Rep. 222 (ICC arbitration where proper law of contract was Swiss law and curial seat of arbitration was the Canton of Geneva in a matter involving a business practice unlawful under Algerian law but involving no bribery or corruption and lawful under Swiss law) the court said that it was not adjudicating upon the underlying contract but deciding whether or not an arbitration award should be enforced in England and that in such context it seemed:

"that (absent a finding of fact of corrupt practices which would give rise to obvious public policy considerations) the fact that English law would or might have

Paragraph numbers marked with a "+" can be found online and on CD.

arrived at a different result is nothing to the point. Indeed the reason for the different result is that Swiss law is different from English law, and the parties chose Swiss law and Swiss arbitration. If anything, this consideration dictates (as a matter of policy of the upholding of international arbitral awards) that the award should be enforced."

In *Kanoria v Guinness* [2006] EWCA Civ 222; [2006] 1 Lloyd's Rep. 701 the Court of Appeal upheld the refusal of enforcement where the enforcee had been unable to present his case because he had never been notified of the case made against him, approving the statement of Colman J. in the Minmetals case referred to at 2E–359 above at p.326 thereof that

"the inability to present a case to arbitrators within s.103(2)(c) contemplates at least that the enforcee has been prevented from presenting his case by matters outside his control. This will normally cover the case where the procedure adopted has been operated in a manner contrary to the rules of natural justice."

Subsection (5)

On an application to adjourn an application for leave to enforce a foreign arbitration award because of a legal challenge to the validity of the award in a foreign jurisdiction, the court should consider the strength or otherwise of the argument for setting aside the award and the ease or difficulty of enforcing the award if an order for security was not made, together with any other relevant considerations (*Soleh Boneh International Ltd v Government of the Republic of Uganda* [1993] 2 Lloyd's Rep. 208).

2E–361

Saving for other bases of recognition or enforcement

104. Nothing in the preceding provisions of this Part affects any right to rely upon or enforce a New York Convention award at common law or under section 66.

2E–362

Note —Compare s.6 of the 1975 Act.

2E–363

PART IV

GENERAL PROVISIONS

Meaning of "the court": jurisdiction of High Court and county court

105.—(1) In this Act "the court" means the High Court or a county court, subject to the following provisions.

2E–364

(2) The Lord Chancellor may by order make provision—

    (a) allocating proceedings under this Act to the High Court or to county courts; or

    (b) specifying proceedings under this Act which may be commenced or taken only in the High Court or in a county court.

(3) The Lord Chancellor may by order make provision requiring proceedings of any specified description under this Act in relation to which a county court has jurisdiction to be commenced or taken in one or more specified county courts.

Any jurisdiction so exercisable by a specified county court is exercisable throughout England and Wales or, as the case may be, Northern Ireland.

[(3A) The Lord Chancellor must consult the Lord Chief Justice of

Paragraph numbers marked with a "+" can be found online and on CD.

England and Wales or the Lord Chief Justice of Northern Ireland (as the case may be) before making an order under this section.

(3B) The Lord Chief Justice of England and Wales may nominate a judicial office holder (as defined in section 109(4) of the Constitutional Reform Act 2005) to exercise his functions under this section.

(3C) The Lord Chief Justice of Northern Ireland may nominate any of the following to exercise his functions under this section–

    (a) the holder of one of the offices listed in Schedule 1 to the Justice (Northern Ireland) Act 2002;

    (b) a Lord Justice of Appeal (as defined in section 88 of that Act).]

(4) An order under this section—

    (a) may differentiate between categories of proceedings by reference to such criteria as the Lord Chancellor sees fit to specify, and

    (b) may make such incidental or transitional provision as the Lord Chancellor considers necessary or expedient.

(5) An order under this section for England and Wales shall be made by statutory instrument which shall be subject to annulment in pursuance of a resolution of either House of Parliament.

(6) An order under this section for Northern Ireland shall be a statutory rule for the purposes of the [S.I. 1979/1573 (N.I. 12).] Statutory Rules (Northern Ireland) Order 1979 which shall be subject to annulment in pursuance of a resolution of either House of Parliament in like manner as a statutory instrument and section 5 of the [1946 c. 36.] Statutory Instruments Act 1946 shall apply accordingly.

2E–365   Note —Subsections (3A)–(3C) inserted by the Constitutional Reform Act 2005 s.15(1), Sch.4, Pt 1, para.250, with effect from April 3, 2006 (SI 2006/1014).

2E–366   Note —The proceedings under the Act have been allocated by the High Court and County Courts (Allocation of Arbitration Proceedings) Order 1996 (SI 1996/3215) at para.2E–375. Subsections (3A)–(3C) inserted by the Constitutional Reform Act 2005 , s.15(1), Sch.4, para.250,

Crown application

2E–367   **106.**—(1) Part I of this Act applies to any arbitration agreement to which Her Majesty, either in right of the Crown or of the Duchy of Lancaster or otherwise, or the Duke of Cornwall, is a party.

(2) Where Her Majesty is party to an arbitration agreement otherwise than in right of the Crown, Her Majesty shall be represented for the purposes of any arbitral proceedings—

    (a) where the agreement was entered into by Her Majesty in right of the Duchy of Lancaster, by the Chancellor of the Duchy or such person as he may appoint, and

    (b) in any other case, by such person as Her Majesty may appoint in writing under the Royal Sign Manual.

(3) Where the Duke of Cornwall is party to an arbitration agreement, he shall be represented for the purposes of any arbitral proceedings by such person as he may appoint.

Paragraph numbers marked with a "+" can be found online and on CD.

(4) References in Part I to a party or the parties to the arbitration agreement or to arbitral proceedings shall be construed, where subsection (2) or (3) applies, as references to the person representing Her Majesty or the Duke of Cornwall.

Note —Compare s.30 of the 1950 Act.

2E–368

For ss.107 to 110 of the Arbitration Act 1996 (see Arrangement) plus any related commentary see paragraphs 2E–369+ to 2E–373+ on White Book on Westlaw UK or the Civil Procedure CD.

SECTION 4(1). **SCHEDULE 1**

MANDATORY PROVISIONS OF PART I

2E–374

sections 9 to 11 (stay of legal proceedings);
section 12 (power of court to extend agreed time limits);
section 13 (application of Limitation Acts);
section 24 (power of court to remove arbitrator);
section 26(1) (effect of death of arbitrator);
section 28 (liability of parties for fees and expenses of arbitrators);
section 29 (immunity of arbitrator);
section 31 (objection to substantive jurisdiction of tribunal);
section 32 (determination of preliminary point of jurisdiction);
section 33 (general duty of tribunal);
section 37(2) (items to be treated as expenses of arbitrators);
section 40 (general duty of parties);
section 43 (securing the attendance of witnesses);
section 56 (power to withhold award in case of non-payment);
section 60 (effectiveness of agreement for payment of costs in any event);
section 66 (enforcement of award);
sections 67 and 68 (challenging the award; substantive jurisdiction and serious irregularity), and sections 70 and 71 (supplementary provisions; effect of order of court) so far as relating to those sections;
section 72 (saving for rights of person who takes no part in proceedings);
section 73 (loss of right to object);
section 74 (immunity of arbitral institutions, etc.);
section 75 (charge to secure payment of solicitors' costs).

High Court and County Courts (Allocation of Arbitration Proceedings) Order 1996

(S.I. 1996 No. 3215)

1.—(1) This Order may be cited as the High Court and County **2E–375** Courts (Allocation of Arbitration Proceedings) Order 1996 and shall come into force on 31st January 1997.

(2) In this Order, "the Act" means the Arbitration Act 1996.

2. Subject to articles 3 to 5, proceedings under the Act shall be **2E–376** commenced and taken in the High Court.

3. Proceedings under section 9 of the Act (stay of legal proceed- **2E–377** ings) shall be commenced in the court in which the legal proceedings are pending.

4. Proceedings under sections 66 and 101(2) (enforcement of **2E–378** awards) of the Act may be commenced in any county court.

5.—(1) Proceedings under the Act may be commenced and taken **2E–379** in the Central London County Court Mercantile List.

Paragraph numbers marked with a "+" can be found online and on CD.

(2) Where, in exercise of the powers conferred by sections 41 and 42 of the County Courts Act 1984(b) the High Court or the judge in charge of the Central London County Court Mercantile List orders the transfer of proceedings under the Act which were commenced in the Central London County Court Mercantile List to the High Court, those proceedings shall be taken in the High Court.

(3) Where, in exercise of its powers under section 40(2) of the County Courts Act 1984(c) the High Court orders the transfer of proceedings under the Act which were commenced in the High Court to the Central London County Court Mercantile List, those proceedings shall be taken in the Central London County Court Mercantile List.

(4) In exercising the powers referred to in paragraphs (2) and (3) regard shall be had to the following criteria—

    (a) the financial substance of the dispute referred to arbitration, including the value of any claim or counterclaim;

    (b) the nature of the dispute referred to arbitration (for example, whether it arises out of a commercial or business transaction or relates to engineering, building or other construction work);

    (c) whether the proceedings are otherwise important and, in particular, whether they raise questions of importance to persons who are not parties and

    (d) the balance of convenience points to having the proceedings taken in the Central London County Court Mercantile List,

and, where the financial substance of the dispute exceeds £200,000, the proceedings shall be taken in the High Court unless the proceedings do not raise questions of general importance to persons who are not parties.

(5) The value of any claim or counterclaim shall be calculated in accordance with rule 16.3(6) of the Civil Procedure Rules 1998.

(6) In this article "the Central London County Court Mercantile List" means the Mercantile Court established at the Central London County Court pursuant to Part 59 of the Civil Procedure Rules 1998.

2E–380   **6.** Nothing in this Order shall prevent the judge in charge of the commercial list (within the meaning of section 62(3) of the Supreme Court Act 1981) from transferring proceedings under the Act to another list, court or Division of the High Court to which he has power to transfer proceedings and, where such an order is made, the proceedings may be taken in that list, court or Division as the case may be.

2E–381   *Note* —As amended by the High Court and County Courts (Allocation of Arbitration Proceedings) (Amendment) Order 1999 (SI 1999/1010) and the Civil Procedure (Modification of Enactments) Order 2002.

    Throughout the Arbitration Act 1996, references to "the court" mean the High Court or a county court, but the jurisdiction of the two levels of court is not concurrent. By this Order, by exercise of powers under s.105, "proceedings under the Act" are allocated to the High Court and the county courts and proceedings which may be commenced or taken only in the High Court or in a county court are specified. The gen-

Paragraph numbers marked with a "+" can be found online and on CD.

2F INTELLECTUAL PROPERTY PROCEEDINGS

PART 63—PATENTS AND OTHER INTELLECTUAL PROPERTY CLAIMS

Contents

Editorial introduction

These rules insert into the Civil Procedure Rules 1998, as Part 63, new rules govern- **2F–2** ing the procedure for intellectual property rights, in particular patents, registered designs and registered trade marks. They also apply to unregistered intellectual property rights, and in particular copyright, design right and passing off cases. They supersede the rules in Practice Direction 49E. This part and its supplementing Practice Direction do not provide a complete guide for intellectual property proceedings. They should be read in conjunction with other Civil Procedure Rules. The application of the other Civil Procedure Rules and their practice directions is subject to the provisions of this practice direction.

Paragraph numbers marked with a "+" can be found online and on CD.

Related sources

2F-3
- The Patents Court Guide, available on the Court Service website along with the Patents Court Diary: *http://www.hmcourts-service.gov.uk* [Accessed August 20, 2007] and at para.2F–127 below.

Scope of this Part and interpretation[1]

2F-4   **63.1—(1) This Part applies to all intellectual property claims including—**

    (a) registered intellectual property rights such as—

        (i) patents;

        (ii) registered designs; and

        (iii) registered trade marks; and

    (b) unregistered intellectual property rights such as—

        (i) copyright;

        (ii) design right;

        (iii) the right to prevent passing off; and

        (iv) the other rights set out in the practice direction.

  (2) In this Part—

    (a) "the 1977 Act" means the Patents Act 1977[2];

    (b) "the 1988 Act" means the Copyright, Designs and Patents Act 1988[3];

    (c) "the 1994 Act" means the the Trade Marks Act 1994[4];

    (d) "the Comptroller" means the Comptroller General of Patents, Designs and Trade Marks;

    (e) "patent" means a patent under the 1977 Act and includes any application for a patent or supplementary protection certificate granted under—

        (i) the Patents (Supplementary Protection Certificates) Rules 1997[5];

        (ii) the Patents (Supplementary Protection Certificate for Medicinal Products) Regulations 1992[6]; and

        (iii) the Patents (Supplementary Protection Certificate for Plant Protection Products) Regulations 1996[7];

    (f) "Patents Court" means the Patents Court of the High Court constituted as part of the Chancery Division by section 6(1) of the Supreme Court Act 1981[8];

    (g) "Patents County Court" means a county court designated as a Patents County Court under section 287(1) of the 1988 Act;

    (gg) "patents judge" means a person nominated under sec-

[1] Amended by the Civil Procedure (Amendment No.4) Rules 2005 (SI 2005/3515).
[2] 1977 c.37.
[3] 1988 c.48.
[4] 1994 c.26.
[5] SI 1997/64.
[6] SI 1992/3091.
[7] SI 1996/3120.
[8] 1981 c.54.

Paragraph numbers marked with a "+" can be found online and on CD.

tion 291(1) of the 1988 Act as the patents judge of a patents county court[1];

(h) "the register" means whichever of the following registers is appropriate—

(i) patents maintained by the Comptroller under section 32 of the 1977 Act;

(ii) designs maintained by the registrar under section 17 of the Registered Designs Act 1949[2];

(iii) trade marks maintained by the registrar under section 63 of the 1994 Act;

(iv) Community trade marks maintained by the Office for Harmonisation in the Internal Market under Article 83 of Council Regulation (EC) 40/94[3]; and

(v) Community designs maintained by the Office for Harmonisation in the Internal Market under Article 72 of Council Regulation (EC) 6/2002[4]; and

(i) "the registrar" means—

(i) the registrar of trade marks; or

(ii) the registrar of registered designs,

whichever is appropriate.

(3) Claims to which this Part applies are allocated to the multi-track.

Application of the Civil Procedure Rules

63.2 These Rules and their practice directions apply to intellectual property claims unless this Part or a practice direction provides otherwise.   **2F–5**

Effect of rule

See *SmithKline Beecham Plc v Apotex Europe Ltd (Costs) (No.2)* [2004] EWCA Civ 1703.   **2F–6**
In respect of all intellectual property matters the general rule is now that the Civil Procedure Rules apply unless a rule in Pt 63 provides otherwise.

I. Patents and registered designs

Scope of Section I

63.3—(1) This Section of this Part applies to claims in—   **2F–7**

(a) the Patents Court; and

(b) a Patents County Court.

(2) Claims in the court include any claim relating to matters arising out of—

(a) the 1977 Act;

(b) the Registered Designs Act 1949; and

---

[1] SI 2005/2292.
[2] 1949 c.88.
[3] OJ No.L11, 14.1.1994, p.1.
[4] OJ No.L3, 5.1.2002, p.1.

Paragraph numbers marked with a "+" can be found online and on CD.

(c) the Defence Contracts Act 1958[1].

Specialist list

2F–8   63.4 Claims in the Patents Court and a Patents County Court form specialist lists for the purpose of rule 30.5.

Patents Judge

2F–9   63.4A—(1) Subject to paragraph (2), proceedings in the patents county court shall be dealt with by the patents judge.[2]

(2) When a matter needs to be dealt with urgently and it is not practicable or appropriate for the patents judge to deal with such matter, the matter may be dealt with by another judge with appropriate specialist experience who shall be nominated by the Vice-Chancellor.

Transfer between Divisions and to and from a specialist list

2F–10   Rule 30.5 provides that the High Court may order proceedings in any Division of the High Court to be transferred to another Division and order proceedings to be transferred to or from a specialist list. Applications for the transfer of proceedings must be made to a judge dealing with claims in that list.

In order to ensure access to justice for parties with limited financial resources, s.289 of the Copyright, Designs and Patents Act 1988 contains special provisions concerning transfer of proceedings between the High Court and a patents county court.

Actions within the special jurisdiction of a patents county court may be ordered to be transferred to such a court by the High Court either of its own motion or on the application of any party to the proceedings. In considering whether to make such an order, the High Court shall have regard to the financial position of the parties and may order transfer notwithstanding that the proceedings are likely to raise an important question of law or fact.

Such actions may also be ordered to be transferred from a patents county court to the High Court by the county court either of its own motion or on the application of any party to the proceedings. The county court is required to have regard to the financial position of the parties and may refrain from ordering transfer notwithstanding that the proceedings are likely to raise an important question of law or fact.

The High Court does not have the power to order proceedings within the special jurisdiction of a patents county court to be transferred from the Patents County Court.

When an action is transferred to the Patents County Court, the court will, after consultation with the parties, give any directions deemed appropriate for the purpose of bringing the pleadings and any other documents in the case and outstanding procedural steps into conformity with its own procedures.

Role of a Patent County Court

2F–11   It is the role of a Patent County Court to make litigation cheaper and more accessible in the more straightforward disputes. In *Warheit v Olympia Tools Ltd (Costs)*, unrep., there was further argument on costs following an appeal from a two-day trial in Patents County Court in which the costs claimed were in excess of £250,000. It was held that the costs should be subject to detailed assessment, and it was made clear that these costs were far in excess of what Lord Chancellor envisaged when setting up Patents County Court. In future, efforts should be made to keep costs in proportion with the complexity of the proceedings. See e.g. *Unilin Beheer BV v Berry Floor NV* [2004] F.S.R. 14 on the wisdom of conducting experiments in the Patents County

---

[1] 1958, c.38.

[2] Note the title of the former Vice-Chancellor is now "The Chancellor of the High Court".

Paragraph numbers marked with a "+" can be found online and on CD.

Court. It was not appropriate to start proceedings in the Patents County Court where the subject matter of the patents was complex and the ultimate time estimate of 15 days for the trial was amply justified—*Halliburton Energy Services Inc v Smith International (North Sea) Ltd* [2005] EWHC 1623 (Pat).

Starting the claim

63.5 Claims to which this Section of this Part applies must be started— 2F–12

(a) **by issuing a Part 7 claim form; or**

(b) **in existing proceedings under Part 20.**

Without Notice Applications

As the court is only being presented with one side of the story when a without no- 2F–13 tice application is made, there must be *complete disclosure of all material facts*. Failure to make disclosure of matters which are or may be adverse to the party making the application may result in any order made being subsequently set aside on the ground of non-disclosure. It may also have serious consequences for any person who has made an affidavit in support of the application and any professional person representing the applicant. See *Elvee Ltd v Taylor* [2001] EWCA Civ 1943—search and seizure orders; *The Gadget Shop Ltd v The Bug.com Ltd* [2001] F.S.R. 26—search orders, Part 25, CPR proper execution; *Memory Corp v Sidhu* [2000] F.S.R. 921—freezing orders.

Where allegations of copying made, search and seizure orders should be made in the Chancery Division; see *Elvee Ltd v Taylor* [2001] EWCA Civ 1943.

Except in the case of a "search and seizure" (old Anton Piller) order or a "freezing" (old Mareva) injunction, the court may require notice to be given to any person affected by the application.

See also *Cinpres Gas Injection Ltd v Melea Ltd*, *The Times*, December 21, 2005— allegations should be set out fully in a witness statement served as soon as is practicable, counsel and solicitors have responsibility for taking full notes of what was said at a without notice hearing. Without notice applications should only be made where to give notice would frustrate the purpose of the order—where notice is not given it is necessary to explain that failure to the Judge.

Security for costs

The general principle is that parties to proceedings are not required to give secu- 2F–14 rity for the costs of other parties. However, a claimant or a counterclaiming defendant (except a defendant in a patent or design action whose counterclaim raises only the invalidity of the patent or design) may be ordered to give such security if ordinarily resident out of England and Wales or if it is a limited company and there is credible evidence that there is reason to believe that it will be unable to pay the other side's costs.

Affidavit evidence in support of an application for security of costs should deal inter alia with any alleged practical difficulties of enforcing an order for costs.

Successive applications for security can be made. However, applications should always be made at the earliest possible moment: delay is a ground for refusal. The assistance of the registrar may be sought in assessing the amount of costs likely to be awarded on taxation.

Pleadings

In a claim for infringement of a patent, the claim form must show which of the 2F–15 claims in the specification of the patent are alleged to be infringed and give at least one example of each type of infringement alleged, and a copy of each document referred to in the claim form (with translation if necessary) must be served with the claim form (See PD 63 para.11.1).

The statement of case should be full but concise. It must set out all facts, matters and arguments relied on as establishing the allegations made and justifying the relief sought. It is the duty of the claimant to plead case on liability and relief (e.g. springboard relief) in advance (*Kirin-Amgen Inc v Transkaryotic Therapies Inc (No.2)* [2002] R.P.C. 3). That case sets out the factors that should be taken into account in considering whether it is just to permit the claimant to subsequently broaden relief.

Paragraph numbers marked with a "+" can be found online and on CD.

Amendment to particulars of claim

2F–16   Patent actions are subject to the general provisions of CPR Pt 17 and the overriding
objective that cases should be dealt with fairly. In general therefore amendments
ought to be allowed so that the real dispute between the parties can be adjudicated
upon. Although the requirements of the Civil Procedure Rules are mandatory there is
an element of discretion as to when the mandatory conditions need to be satisfied—see
Dendron GmbH v University of California (Amendment of Claim) [2003] EWHC 2771.

There is no special rule in patent cases that permits a patentee to amend its pleaded
claim after judgment—see *Nikken Kosakusho Works v Pioneer Trading Co* [2005] EWCA
Civ 906.

Particulars of infringements

2F–17   The onus always rests on the claimant to prove infringement (*Whatmough v Morris
Motors* (1940) 57 R.P.C. 177).

The patentee need not give his construction of his patent, the function of particulars
of infringements being merely to point out to the defendant what specific act on his
part is complained of so as to prevent surprise at the trial (*Wenham Co Ltd v Champion
Gas Lamp Co* (1891) 8 R.P.C. 22; *Marsden v Albrecht* (1910) 27 R.P.C. 785). See also *Lux
Traffic Controls Ltd v Staffordshire Public Works Company Ltd* [1991] R.P.C. 73.

If the particulars allege as an instance a sale to A., and the defendants admit the
sale of an exactly similar article to B., this will be admissible (*Sykes v Howarth* (1879) 12
Ch D 826 at 829).

Each type of infringement alleged constitutes a separate cause of action and must
be separately particularised (*Sorata Ltd v Gardex Ltd* [1984] R.P.C. 317, CA) however
see also *Building Product Design Ltd v Sandtoft Roof Tiles Ltd* [2004] F.S.R. 40 where
products of a different material to those complained of in the particulars of infringement were also held to infringe, and *Building Product Design Ltd v Sandtoft Roof Tiles Ltd
(No.2)* [2004] F.S.R. 41 —the requirements of the Civil Procedure Rules 1998 Pt 63
that each type of infringement had to be specifically pleaded in a patent infringement
action recognised the importance of economy with regard to costs as well as in relation
to the court's resources, the implementation of public policy regarding the finality of
litigation and practical good sense.

As to particulars of acts alleged to have been performed by directors of a company
personally joined as defendants in an action against the company, see *British Thomson
Houston Co Ltd v Irradiant LampWorks Ltd* (1924) 41 R.P.C. 338.

CPR, r.63.9 requires that the statement of case in a patent action must contain
particulars as set out in the CPR, PD 63 para.11, which provides that the statement of
case has to show both which of the claims in the specification of the patent had been
infringed and at least one example of each type of alleged infringement. A claimant
should therefore plead specific facts in relation to each potential way in which a patent
is alleged to have been infringed and provide examples. See *Cranway Ltd v Playtech Ltd*
[2007] EWHC 182 (Pat).

Amendment of particulars of infringements

2F–18   If the claimant wants to recover relief for infringement of a claim of a patent, it
must amend the pleadings to plead infringement of that claim. The request for further and other relief is not wide enough to encompass such an allegation. Moreover, a
claimant seeking to so amend cannot require that the defendant shows it would have
run its case differently in the light of such an amendment. A serious possibility that it
would have done so was enough. See *Kirin-Amgen Inc v Transkaryotic Therapies Inc
(No.2)* [2002] EWCA Civ 1096.

Sandvik Aktiebolag v K. R. Pfiffner (UK) Limited [2000] F.S.R. 17—"holding pleadings"; there is no automatic right to amend even if the other side could be compensated
by costs; although the jurisdiction to strike out pleadings should be sparingly used.

In *Godfrey L. Cabot Inc v Philblack Ltd* [1961] R.P.C. 19, leave was given in a summons of the claimant to amend its own particulars of breaches to delete therefrom one
instance of infringement and replace it by two others, even though the defendant
objected that the two remaining instances of infringement were not sufficiently
particularised. It was stated that the defendant's right to apply for fuller particulars of
these two instances was not prejudiced by the amendment allowed.

Abandonment of specific particulars was held not to be a discontinuance, in relation

Paragraph numbers marked with a "+" can be found online and on CD.

to subject-matter thereof, in *Anxionnaz v Rolls-Royce Ltd* [1963] R.P.C. 81. In *General Tire and Rubber Co v International Synthetic Rubber Co* [1968] R.P.C. 161, re-amendment of the statement of claim to allege a joint infringement was allowed.

In *Dow Chemical AG v Spence Bryson and Co Ltd* [1982] F.S.R. 397, where the original particulars clearly complained of an infringement by manufacture, and all parties knew that manufacture had only taken place in Northern Ireland by the first defendant who operated there, an amendment to extend the particulars so as to more securely found an application for disclosure relating to Northern Ireland was allowable as involving no new cause of action.

Whilst the practice in patent actions is that if one act of infringement is proved, a claimant will generally be granted an injunction in general terms to restrain infringement, and an inquiry as to damages suffered from infringing acts is not limited to the particular infringing act which has been pleaded and proved, it does not follow in the least that the particulars of infringement are no part of the cause of action, and that a claim in respect of a different manufactured product is necessarily part of the same cause of action as the original claim. The form of order for the inquiry as to damages, and the form of injunction, are matters of relief only, rather than indicating the cause of action for which relief is granted; *Sorata Ltd v Gardex Ltd* [1984] R.P.C. 317. For the appropriate scope of patent injunctions, see *Coflexip SA v Stolt Comex Seaway MS Ltd* [2001] R.P.C. 9, CA.

A proposed amendment to make a conditional allegation of infringement, on the basis that the claimant would only allege infringement of a second patent if unsuccessful in relation to an earlier, different patent is not a proper alternative plea and should not be allowed (*Beloit Technologies Inc v Valmet Paper Machinery Inc* [1994] R.P.C. 664).

The court has a complete discretion to impose terms where a claimant seeks to withdraw an allegation of infringement, and it is the practice of the Patents Court to require some kind of undertaking from the claimant in relation to future claims (*Albright & Wilson Ltd v SB Chemicals* [1994] R.P.C. 608).

Terms of amendment

The imposition of terms is in the discretion of the court, and save in the strongest case the CA will not interfere (*Wilson v Wilson* (1899) 16 R.P.C. 315). **2F–19**

Further and better particulars

If the defendant is unable to ascertain from the particulars with sufficient precision what type of machine or process is complained of, the onus will lie on him to apply for further and better particulars, and to give some evidence to show that the information given is insufficient (*Haslam & Co v Hall* (1887) 4 R.P.C. 203); he should not wait until the trial to complain, but in appropriate cases further particulars will not be ordered until after disclosure and inspection (*Mullard Radio Valve Co Ltd v Tungsram Electric Lamp Works (Great Britain) Ltd* (1932) 49 R.P.C. 279). **2F–20**

The exchange of witness statements may make the ordering of burdensome particulars undesirable (*Lux Traffic Controls Ltd v Staffordshire Public Works Company Ltd* [1991] R.P.C. 73).

Action by exclusive licensee under patent

By s.67 of the 1977 Act an exclusive licensee may take proceedings in respect of infringements committed after the date of his licence. The patentee must be either joined as claimant or added as defendant (subs.(2)). An interim injunction may be refused if the defendants did not know of the fact that the claimants were exclusive licensees (*Christian Salvesen (Oil Services) Ltd v Odfjell Drilling and Consulting Co (UK) Ltd* [1985] R.P.C. 569). **2F–21**

Parties

For proper parties and amendments to add parties see *PLG Research Ltd v Ardon International Ltd* [1992] F.S.R. 59. An equitable owner of a patent is entitled to commence proceedings without joining the assignor provided that at a later date the legal owner is made a party to proceedings; see *Baxter International Inc v Nederlands Produktielaboratorium voor Bloedtransusiapparatuur BV* [1998] R.P.C. 250. Exclusive licensees may sue for damages, but their licence must be registered; whilst a mere record of an older licence will justify damages from the date of the older licence, registration of a **2F–22**

Paragraph numbers marked with a "+" can be found online and on CD.

INTELLECTUAL PROPERTY

modification will not (*M.M.M. v Rennicks (UK) Ltd* [1992] F.S.R. 118). A director who merely facilitates infringement does not necessarily procure it: he will not be liable unless his involvement would be such as to render him liable as a joint tortfeasor if the company had not existed (*PLG Research Ltd v Ardon International Ltd* [1993] F.S.R. 197).

Threats in patent proceedings

2F-23   Section 70 of the 1977 Act provides a remedy for groundless threats of patent infringement proceedings. Section 70 permits threats to bring proceedings for an infringement alleged to consist of making or importing a product for disposal or of using a process. Section 70(4) allows threats to be made against primary infringers only in respect of acts of primary infringement, and does not allow threats against a primary infringer in relation to secondary acts of infringement, which remain actionable (*Cavity Trays Ltd v RMC Panel Products Ltd* [1996] R.P.C. 361).

Mere notification of the existence of a patent does not constitute a threat.

The threats may be direct or indirect, and the action may be brought by any person aggrieved thereby. Threats in respect of acts done while a patent application is pending are actionable within s.70(1) of the Patents Act 1977, as are threats to sue once the patent is granted. An individual intimately connected with the management of a company against which threats are directed is a person aggrieved and able to sue for threats. See *Brain v Ingledew Brown Bennison and Garret* [1995] F.S.R. 552 (partially reversed on appeal, but not as to the legal findings). The threats must have been made within the jurisdiction (*Egg Fillers and Containers (Aust.) Proprietary Ltd v Holed-Tite Packing Corp and Packing Products Corp* (1934) 51 R.P.C. 9). The remedies are a declaration, injunction and damages unless the defendant proves that the act the subject of the threats would constitute an infringement of a patent or of rights arising from publication of a complete specification, in respect of a claim not shown by the claimant to be invalid. A defendant who pleads that any threat was justifiable must give particulars identifying the acts relied on as being infringing acts of the claimant in respect of which proceedings were threatened (*Reymes-Cole v Elite Hosiery Co Ltd* [1961] R.P.C. 277). The claimant is not entitled to relief even though some of the patents to which the threats related are invalid or uninfringed, if other such patents are valid and infringed. The defendant may counterclaim in respect of infringement, under the ordinary rules relating to counterclaims. Where the threats are admitted, the onus of proof shifts to the defendant who alleges infringement, and the defendant should then open the case (*Lewis Faulk v Jacobwitz* [1944] Ch. 64). A claim for threats may be made by way of counterclaim in an action for infringement (see, e.g. *Norton & Gregory Ltd v Jacobs* (1937) 54 R.P.C. 271). The fact that threats are malicious does not entitle the claimant to increased damages (*Berkeley & Young Ltd v Stillwell* (1940) 57 R.P.C. 291). An interlocutory injunction to restrain threats may be granted, even where threats are made only in solicitors' letters before action (*H.V.E. (Electric) Ltd v Cuffin Holdings Ltd* [1964] 1 W.L.R. 378; [1964] 1 All E.R. 674; [1964] R.P.C. 149, CA).

Threats in registered design right proceedings

2F-24   Section 26 of the 1949 Act provides a remedy for groundless threats of registered design right infringement proceedings. Section 26 permits threats to bring proceedings for an infringement alleged to consist of the making or importing of anything.

A mere notification that a design is registered does not constitute a threat.

Discontinuance

2F-25   The normal rule in the event of a claimant discontinuing a claim is that the claimant has to pay the defendant's costs. The CPR gives the court a discretion however— see *Coca-Cola Company, The v Mabe* [2002] F.S.R. 47.

Defence and reply

2F-26   **63.6 Part 15 applies with the modification—**

(a) to rule 15.4 that in a claim for infringement under rule 63.9, the defence must be filed within 42 days of service of the claim form; and

(b) to rule 15.8 that the claimant must—

Paragraph numbers marked with a "+" can be found online and on CD.

> **(i) file any reply to a defence; and**
> **(ii) serve it on all other parties,**
> within 21 days of service of the defence.

Time for defence

The general rule is that a defence must be served 14 days after service of a **2F-27**
particulars of claim or, if the defendant files an acknowledgment of service, 28 days after service of the particulars of claim. Where the claim is a claim for infringement
under r.63.9 however, the defendant has 42 days from the service of the *claim form* to
serve a defence. Rule 63.9(1) sets out that in a claim for infringement or an application in which validity is challenged, the statement of case must particularise that
challenge. Rule 63.9(2) sets out that in a claim for infringement the extended time period of 42 days applies. In the past it was this extended time period applied only to
those infringement cases in which the validity of a patent or registered design was
challenged. It would now appear that in accordance with r.63.9(2) the extended time
for serving a defence now applies to all claims for infringement, and not just those
where the validity is challenged. This may simply reflect the fact that in the vast majority of infringement actions validity is in issue. This reading of the rules does make the
words "under rule 93.9" otiose however.

Separate representation

Bristol Myers Squibb Co v Baker Norton Pharmaceuticals Inc [2001] R.P.C. 1—separately **2F-28**
defended. Defendants will only fail to recover costs if it was unreasonable to have
sought separate representation.

Defence that the patentee has granted licences with prohibited conditions

This defence, given by the Patents Act 1977, s.44 exists where the patentee has **2F-29**
imposed on licensees or purchasers or hirers certain conditions in restraint of trade attaching to the sale or use of the invention.

If the prohibited contract has effect in the UK it is irrelevant that it is governed by a
foreign law which does not have a provision similar to that in the UK (*Chiron Corp v
Organon Teknika Ltd (No.2)* [1992] 3 C.M.L.R. 813; [1993] F.S.R. 324).

Where a defendant succeeds on a s.44 defence there is jurisdiction to allow the
claimant to alter the offending agreement after judgment and amend his pleadings after which the successful defence disappears; but leave to amend was refused in *Chiron
Corp v Organon Teknika Ltd (No.4)* [1994] F.S.R. 252.

A s.44 defence which is good against a claim by the patentee may fail against an
exclusive licensee who was not a party to, and did not consent to, the offending agreement (*Chiron Corp v Organon Tekuka Ltd (No.12)* [1995] F.S.R. 153).

Defence that use is for service of the Crown

An action against the Crown for infringement of patent will be struck out: *Dory v* **2F-30**
Sheffield Health Authority [1991] F.S.R. 221.

Striking out defences

For an example of striking out Euro defences judged incapable of success see *Chiron* **2F-31**
Corp v Organon Teknika Ltd (No.2) [1992] 3 C.M.L.R. 813; [1993] F.S.R. 324, upheld on
appeal: [1994] F.S.R. 187.

Where the defendants had been guilty of a number of significant breaches of court
orders such that a fair trial was no longer possible it was appropriate to make a finding
of contumacious default and strike out the defence see *Nutrinova Nutrition Specialties &
Food Ingredients* [2002] EWHC 1729; (2002) 25(9) I.P.D. 25065.

It was not appropriate to strike out aspects of a defence detailing the claimant's
tactical motives in bringing a claim for declaratory relief in a patent action because the
conduct and motives of a claimant could be taken into account. See *Interdigital Technology Corporation v Nokia Corporation and Nokia Siemens Network Oy* [2008] EWHC 504
(Pat). The judge held in that case that it was concerned with a developing area of jurisprudence and so the court needed to exercise special caution when striking out
claims.

See also *Football Association Premier League Ltd v LCD Publishing Ltd* [2007] EWHC
3171, in which it was also inappropriate to strike out a competition defence raised by a

Paragraph numbers marked with a "+" can be found online and on CD.

defendant in response to claims for breach of copyright, infringement of trade mark and various economic torts, but it was appropriate to make an unless order requiring the company to provide particulars of its competition defence.

Challenge of validity

2F–32   A patentee is required to particularise its positive case even though the burden of proof is on the claimant seeking a declaration of non-infringement. See *Baxter Healthcare Corporation v Abbott Laboratories* [2005] EWHC 2878 (Pat). See also notes below on counterclaims for invalidity.

Time for reply

2F–33   Rule 15.8 stipulates that a claimant must file any reply to the defence at the same time as serving his allocation questionnaire and serve his reply on the other parties at the same time as he files it. Since r.26.3(6) which sets out the period for filing the allocation questionnaire is deemed not to apply by r.63.7(2) below, the period for filing any reply is set at within 21 days of service of the defence.

Case management[1]

2F–34   **63.7—(1)** [...]

(2) **Part 26 and any other rule that requires a party to file an allocation questionnaire do not apply.**

(3) **The following provisions only of Part 29 apply—**

(a) **rule 29.3(2) (legal representatives to attend case management conferences);**

(b) **rule 29.4 (the court's approval of agreed proposals for the management of proceedings); and**

(c) **rule 29.5 (variation of case management timetable) with the exception of paragraph (1)(b) and (c).**

(4) **As soon as practicable the court will hold a case management conference which must be fixed in accordance with the practice direction.**

Case management

2F–35   The usual provisions relating to case management at the preliminary stage, i.e. those set out in r.26, do not apply to patent and registered design proceedings. The court will hold a case management conference as soon as practicable. Paragraphs 4.1–4.12 of the Practice Direction supplementing Pt 63 (see para.63PD.4 below) deal generally with the procedure to be adopted in relation to case management. Paragraph 5 (except subpara.5.9) and para.7 of the Practice Direction supplementing Pt 29 still apply, but only insofar as the provisions in that Practice Direction are consistent with the provisions of the Practice Direction supplementing Pt 63.

2F–35.1   *Jurisdiction of Masters* —Masters' jurisdiction is set out in the Practice Direction 63.8 (8.1). In relation to 8.1(5), note the Direction, dated July 16, 2008, from Mr Justice Kitchin, the Senior Judge of the Patents Court, that a Master or a Deputy Master may deal with an application by a non-party under CPR r.5.4C for a copy of the Grounds of Invalidity annexed to a Statement of Case in which challenge is made to the validity of a patent or registered design.

Legal representation at case management conferences

2F–36   The first provision that still applies is r.29.3(2), which stipulates that parties legal representatives at a case management conference should be familiar with the case and

---

[1] Amended by the Civil Procedure (Amendment No.5) Rules 2003 (SI 2003/3361) and the Civil Procedure (Amendment No.4) Rules 2005 (SI 2005/3515).

Paragraph numbers marked with a "+" can be found online and on CD.

should have sufficient authority to deal with any issues that are likely to arise. As with r.29.3(2), if non-compliance with this rule leads to an adjournment the court will expect to make a wasted costs order (for which seer.48.7).

Conduct of parties and practitioners

The Court was entitled to expect that parties and their representatives acted in a professional and sensible manner and did not bring disputes which were unnecessary before the court. See *Dr Reddy's Laboratories (UK) Ltd v Eli Lilly* [2007] EWHC 1872 (Pat). **2F–36.1**

Stays

Where the likelihood was that validity proceedings in the Patents Court would more quickly resolve commercial uncertainty than proceedings in the EPO, it would normally be a proper exercise of discretion to decline to stay the Patents Court proceedings. See *Glaxo Group Ltd v Genentech Inc and Biogen Idec Inc* [2008] EWCA Civ 23. **2F–36.2**

In trade mark cases the situation is not analogous. Where proceedings relating to a trade mark were pending both in the English courts and in the Office for Harmonisation in the Internal Market, there was no presumption that the English proceedings would be stayed. See *Kitfix Swallow Group Ltd v Great Gizmos Ltd* [2007] EWHC 2668 (Ch) (2008) 31(1) I.P.D. 31003 *The Times*, December 19, 2007.

Agreed directions/case management

If the parties can agree proposals for the management of the case they should notify the court and inform the court what the agreed proposals are. If the court thinks the agreed proposals suitable, a hearing may be unnecessary. Even if not all the proposals are suitable, those which are will be taken into account by the court when setting down directions. This is obviously beneficial in terms of time and cost. The parties should therefore attempt to come to some agreement about directions wherever possible in order to help the court to further the overriding objective (r.1.3). Parties who do so will be rewarded in costs. Parties who are combative are liable to be penalised in costs whether or not their case succeeds at trial. **2F–37**

Variation of case management timetable

Rule 29.5 still applies with the exception of r.29.5(1)(c), which relates to listing questionnaires (r.29.6 relating to listing questionnaires (previously called pre-trial check lists) does not apply to patent and registered design right cases). Paragraphs 6.1 to 6.5 of the Practice Direction supplementing Pt 29 deal generally with the procedure to be adopted in order to obtain a variation in the directions given, however in accordance with the Practice Direction to Pt 63 these provisions no longer apply to patents and registered design cases. **2F–38**

Experiments

Where a party seeks to establish any fact by experimental proof conducted for the purpose of litigation he must, at least 21 days before service of the application notice for directions under para.9.3 of the practice direction, or within such other time as the court may direct, serve on all parties a notice stating the facts which he seeks to establish and giving full particulars of the experiments proposed to establish them. A party served with notice under para.9.1 of the practice direction must within 21 days after such service, serve on the other party a notice stating whether or not he admits each fact and may request the opportunity to inspect a repetition of all or a number of the experiments identified in the notice served under para.9.1. Where any fact which a party seeks to establish by experimental proof is not admitted, he must apply to the court for permission and directions by application notice (see practice direction paras 9.1 to 9.3). However, no automatic provisions for experiments should be made during the course of case management, and no permission at all should be granted for experiments that are directed at the issue of construction—see *Merck & Co Inc v Generics (UK) Ltd* [2003] EWHC 2842 (Pat). **2F–39**

Although experiments were not necessarily inappropriate in Patents County Court litigation, their appropriateness should be considered at the case management stage and adverse cost consequences may flow from any failure to take account of the reali-

Paragraph numbers marked with a "+" can be found online and on CD.

ties of the case—see *Unilin Beheer BV v Berry Floor NV* [2004] F.S.R. 14 (overturned on appeal though no adverse comment made in relation to the above).

Where a party fails to permit the other party to see a repetition of an experiment, it is possible for that other party to apply to have the notice of experiments struck out. Whether this will be done depends on the circumstances (*American Cyanamid Co v Ethicon Ltd* [1978] R.P.C. 667, experiment not repeated because trial would be delayed and party wanting inspection partly to blame).

Late applications to introduce experiments or like matter which may result in further delay and expense are likely to be refused (*H. & R. Johnson Tiles Ltd v Candy Tiles Ltd* [1985] F.S.R. 253 (late photographs relating to infringement refused)).

The regime for managing experimental evidence provided by the CPR should not be undermined. Poorly documented, unrepeated experiments coming into proceedings at a late stage should be strenuously avoided. Experimental evidence should be kept to a minimum, and that minimum should consist of inspected experiments. See *Monsanto Technology LLC v Cargill International SA* [2008] F.S.R. 7, where late experiments sought to be introduced by way of witness statements were excluded.

To prove that a skilled man carrying out a recipe would be able to do so using his ordinary skills, the recipe should ideally be given to a scientist of ordinary skills to try. There is a benefit if the experiment is carried out by a single court appointed expert, which the parties ought to consider when they apply for leave to adduce such evidence. See *Apotex Europe Ltd v SmithKline Beecham Plc* [2004] EWCA Civ 1568.

A party was entitled to disclosure of documents relating to "work up experiments" that had been carried out for the purpose of litigation in which revocation of patents had been sought—*Mayne Pharma Pty Ltd v Debiopharm SA* [2006] EWHC 164.

As to disclosure in relation to work-up experiments see para.2F–52 below.

Use of models

2F–40 Where a party intends to rely on any model or apparatus, he must apply to the court for directions at the first case management conference (see practice direction 10.1).

Expert evidence

2F–41 A shipping case in the Commercial Court contains a discussion of the duties and responsibilities of expert witnesses which should be widely applicable (*The Ikarian Reefer* [1993] F.S.R. 563). See *Cantor Fitzgerald International v Tradition (UK) Ltd* [2000] R.P.C. 95 for the dangers of an expert acting as advocate or holding back relevant information. Expert witnesses are relied upon by the court to express a disinterested view. Any pressure, and any act which may have the effect of placing pressure, on a witness may be a contempt of court and dealt with accordingly. See *Glaxo Group Ltd's Patent* [2004] EWHC 477 (Ch).

In a patent case the role of an expert is principally to educate the court in the technology so that it can establish what the skilled man would have thought. However the court must be careful not to weigh an expert's ability to teach or give evidence over the reasons for his views. What ultimately matters is what the skilled man would have thought—see *Apotex Europe Ltd v SmithKline Beecham Plc* [2004] EWCA Civ 1568. See also *Kirin Amgen Inc v Hoechst Marion Roussel Ltd* [2004] UKHL 46, in which the appointment of a court expert to give the court a series of seminars in the material technology was approved of. It was suggested that such a course might usefully be adopted in future if the technology was "complex and undisputed" and the parties consented.

A party should not have more than one independent expert witness on each topic (*Gerber Garment Technology Inc v Lectra Systems Ltd* [1994] F.S.R. 471). Whilst sometimes it is of value for experts to tutor the Court as to the differences between works of the parties, evidence as to whether or not there has been copying in a copyright case is unlikely to be useful. See *IPC Media Ltd v Highbury Leisure Publishing Ltd* [2004] EWHC 2985 (Ch). Likewise the experts' views as to whether an article is commonplace are not helpful since this is a question for the court (even though such evidence is admissible under the Civil Evidence Act 1972). What matters are the reasons for any such opinion—see *Lambretta Clothing Co Ltd v Teddy Smith (UK) Ltd* [2004] EWCA (Civ) 886.

It is possible for an expert witness who lacks contemporaneous expertise to read himself into the state of the art. See *Inpro Licensing Sarl's Patent* [2006] EWHC 70 (Pat); [2006] R.P.C. 20.

Paragraph numbers marked with a "+" can be found online and on CD.

Survey Evidence

Survey evidence is often of little real value to the resolution of the issues, often **2F–41.1** because the wrong questions had been put. It was in the interests of saving costs and of shortening trials that any survey evidence which was called should be of value to the court. The prior leave of the court is usually required. An application with regard to adducing expert evidence in relation to that survey is also usually required. See *UK Channel Management Ltd v E! Entertainment Television Inc* [2007] EWHC 2339 (Ch); [2008] F.S.R. 5 (2007) and *O2 Ltd and O2 (UK) Ltd v Hutchison 3G Ltd* [2005] E.T.M.R. 61, Ch D.

Expert evidence in design right cases

Thermos Ltd v Alladdin Sales and Marketing Ltd [2000] F.S.R. 402—the calling of **2F–42** expert evidence served little purpose in registered design actions concerned with ordinary consumer articles. In accordance with the CPR the court would need to be informed precisely at what areas the expert evidence would be directed, and it would exercise caution before admitting expert evidence. See also *Oren (Isaac) v Red Box Toy Factory Ltd* [1999] F.S.R. 785.

Expert Evidence in trade mark cases

Confusion between trade marks was to be determined from the viewpoint of the **2F–42.1** average consumer in the light of all the relevant factors. Evidence of an expert as to his own opinion therefore added little when the tribunal could form its own view. There might, however, be a role for an expert witness where the markets in question were ones with which judges were unfamiliar. See *Esure Insurance Ltd v Direct Line Insurance Plc* [2008] EWCA Civ 842.

Similar fact evidence

See *Mattel Inc v Woolbro (Distributors) Ltd* [2003] EWHC 2412 (Ch) in which it was **2F–43** held that there was no automatic admission of "similar fact" evidence in cases involving copying—it would depend on the probative value of the evidence. The Court should be careful not to allow the introduction of evidence which was unfair or oppressive.

Agreed statements

In cases involving technical complexities, it has become the practice for the parties **2F–44** to prepare, where possible, an agreed statement of background technical facts (see, e.g. the "Phenothiazine Primer" used in *Olin Mathieson Chemical Corp v Biorex Laboratories Ltd* [1970] R.P.C. 157 at 197). In such cases the parties may also prepare written summaries of their submissions upon disputed matters. This was done, for example, in *Valensi v British Radio Corp Ltd* [1972] R.P.C. 373. In this case in the Court of Appeal, the defendants prepared a greatly extended explanatory document called a "Primer", and, although not an agreed document, it was greatly relied on by the court: [1973] R.P.C. 337 at 351, in *American Cyanamid Co's Patent* [1970] R.P.C. 306, the whole case was decided on agreed facts. See also *Evans Medical Ltd's Patent* [1998] R.P.C. 517 and *Hoechst Celanese Corp v BP Chemicals Ltd* [1998] F.S.R. 586 for duties of parties in relation to primers. This is reflected in the practice direction at para.4.10(2), which states that at the case management conference the court may direct that a document setting out basic undisputed technology should be prepared.

Scientific adviser

At the case management conference the court may direct that a scientific adviser **2F–45** under s.70(3) of the Supreme Court Act 1981 be appointed (it should be noted that r.35.15 applies to scientific advisers).

Disclosure and inspection

63.8 Part 31 is modified to the extent set out in the practice 2F–46
direction.

Paragraph numbers marked with a "+" can be found online and on CD.

Product descriptions

2F-47   Standard disclosure does not require the disclosure of documents relating to the infringement of a patent by a product or process if, before serving a list of documents, the defendant has served on the claimant and any other parties full particulars of the product or process alleged to infringe and any drawings or other illustrations explaining the product and process should they be necessary (See practice direction supplementing Pt 63, para.5.1(1)). As for the duties incumbent on those serving product descriptions, see *Alfred Taylor v Ishida (Europe) Ltd* [2000] F.S.R. 224; "...the function of a product description is in all respects equivalent to that of disclosure. The duties of all parties, both the professionals and of the parties themselves, in relation to a product description, are the same as they would be in relation to disclosure,...". See also *Consafe Engineering (UK) Ltd v Emtunga UK Ltd* [1999] R.P.C. 154—a description of the product in general terms or including tendentious assertions is not acceptable.

It was appropriate to grant an application by the claimants for disclosure, subject to appropriate safeguards, of the defendant's product description to technically qualified American attorneys in circumstances where, in the absence of such disclosure, it was impossible for the claimant's UK advisers to formulate any sensible request for further information—*Intel Corp v VIA Technologies Inc (Application; Disclosure)* [2002] EWHC 1434. *Rockwater Ltd v Coflexip SA* [2004] EWCA Civ 381—where an alleged infringer provides a description of a product or process under PD 63 para.5.1, it should be formally proved by a witness at trial if required by the other party.

Disclosure in relation to validity

2F-48   Standard disclosure does not require the disclosure of documents relating to any ground on which the validity of a patent is put in issue, except documents which fall in the period starting two years before the earliest claimed priority date and two years following that date (See practice direction supplementing Pt 63, para.5.1(2)). See *Nokia Corp v Interdigital Technology Corp* [2004] EWHC 2920.

The question of disclosure in relation to validity was considered by the Court of Appeal in *Nichia Corp v Argos* [2007] EWCA Civ 741; [2007] F.S.R. 38. Whilst it was arguable that where obviousness was being considered what the inventor actually did was irrelevant, nevertheless the evidence of the inventor was admissible. That evidence was secondary evidence, and thus no more than an aid to assessing the primary evidence. Prima facie, Pt 63 required disclosure of primary documents required by standard disclosure, i.e. those that adversely affected a party's own case or supported another party's case, limited to a period of two years on either side of the earliest priority date. A reasonable search for such documents was required. The parties could agree to dispense with such disclosure, as could the court. The extent to which searches for such documents was reasonable in a given case would depend on factors such as the difficulties and expense of such a search, and the likelihood that the exercise would result in documents of value or significance being disclosed. There is no blanket prima facie rule that disclosure would be dispensed with. In relation to potential limitations on disclosure in appropriate circumstances and the Court's discretion as to disclosure, see *Novartis AG v Johnson & Johnson Medical Ltd* [2008] EWHC 295 (Pat) ; *MMI Research Ltd v Cellxion Ltd* [2007] EWHC 2611 (Pat); [2008] F.S.R. 23 2007 and *Monsanto Technology LLC v Cargill International Plc* [2007] EWHC 1298 (Pat).

Disclosure in relation to commercial success

2F-49   Standard disclosure does not require the disclosure of documents relating to commercial success except as set out in the practice direction (See practice direction supplementing Pt 63, paras 5.1(3) and 5.2). This reflects the fact that virtually every commercial document produced relating to a product or process may be relevant to the success of that product or process. In order to rationalise the disclosure relating to the commercial success of a product therefore, the patentee must serve a schedule: identifying the article or product (for example by product code number) made in accordance with the claims of the patent; a summary by convenient periods of sales of any such articles; a summary by convenient periods of any equivalent prior article or product marketed before the article in question (if any); and a summary by convenient periods of any advertising or promotional expenditure on the article. In relation to a process, the patentee must serve a schedule: identifying the process made in accordance with the claims of the patent; a summary by convenient periods of revenue received by the use of the process; a summary by convenient periods of any equivalent

Paragraph numbers marked with a "+" can be found online and on CD.

perial Chemical Industries Plc [1989] R.P.C. 59, CA (disclosure to expert in France refused because of danger of leak). For further developments see *Roussel Uclaf v Imperial Chemical Industries Plc (No.2)* [1990] R.P.C. 45; [1990] F.S.R. 25; *British Thomson-Houston Co v Duram Ltd* (1915) 37 R.P.C. 121; *Coloured Asphalte Co Ltd v British Asphalt and Bitumen Ltd* (1936) 53 R.P.C. 89; *British Celanese Ltd v Courtaulds Ltd* (1932) 49 R.P.C. 345; *Helitune Ltd v Stewart Hughes Ltd* [1994] F.S.R. 422.

Even non-confidential documents discovered in English proceedings may not be authorised to be proffered in foreign proceedings in which it is impossible to protect confidence, lest confidential documents have to be produced to explain them (*Halcon International v Shell Transport and Trading Co* [1979] R.P.C. 97).

Documents containing commercial secrets

Extensive guidance was given by Whitford J. as to the circumstances in which documents filed in the Patent Office and subsequently in the Patents Court should be treated as confidential. (1) The fact that a document is said to contain "sensitive commercial information" does not necessarily mean that this material, which would otherwise become public property is to be excluded from public inspection; apart from generalities there must be some real indication as to why disclosure would be harmful. (2) Those requesting confidentiality should put in evidence. (3) Material which is going to form no part of the decision can remain confidential. (4) Material supplied by a third party on the basis of confidence which involves minimal excisions from a decision should be maintained as confidential unless there is some overwhelming public interest which makes it desirable that the public should have sight of it. (5) The appropriate procedure is for the matter to be dealt with before hearing so that if ruled against the person proffering the document can make up his mind whether he will go forward publicly, or have the material withdrawn (*Diamond Shamrock Technologies SA's Patent* [1987] R.P.C. 91). (See also *Lilly Icos Ltd v Pfizer Ltd (No.2)* [2002]1 All E.R. 842 in which it was said that the Court will only depart from normal rule of publicity of trials if very good reasons are given). **2F–58**

This position is somewhat different when a claimant wins a case and is then forced to disclose potentially confidential documents before the account of profits or assessment of damages can take place. Just such a situation arose in *Dyson Limited v Hoover Limited (No.3)* [2002] R.P.C. 42. In that case it was said that it is only in exceptional cases that a party can be prevented from having access to information which would play a substantial part in the case. The burden is on the party seeking to restrict disclosure to show that the case was sufficiently exceptional that significant restrictions on disclosure had to be maintained. It is for the party trying to restrict disclosure to justify it and to show why, in all the circumstances, notwithstanding onerous undertakings as to confidentiality and the like, documents should not be shown to the other party. See also *Smithkline Beecham Plc v Generics (UK) Ltd* [2003] EWCA Civ 1109 for discussion of the protection available to a party who discloses commercially sensitive documents in an action. See *Interdigital Technology Corporation v(1) Nokia Corporation (2) Nokia Siemens Networks Oy* [2008] EWHC 969 (Pat), in which the court considered the circumstances in which a party should be required to give disclosure of confidential business documents to representatives of the other party.

Inspection

In an action in which the validity of a patent is challenged, the court may order the inspection of machinery or apparatus where a party alleges such machinery or apparatus was used before the priority date of the claim (See PD 63 para.11.5(2)). **2F–59**

Privilege

Apart from the usual legal professional privilege, privilege for communications with patent agents has been established by the Copyright Designs and Patents Act 1988, s.280. For a case involving both heads see *Soc. Francaise Hoechst v Allied Colloids Ltd* [1992] F.S.R. 66. Privilege at common law may extend to foreign lawyers giving advice on English law (*IBM v Phoenix International Computers Ltd* [1995] F.S.R. 184). **2F–60**

See *David Instance v Denny Bros. Printing Ltd* [2000] F.S.R. 869 for discussion of privilege in documents created for the purposes of negotiating settlements and mediation and their use in subsequent litigation.

A defendant cannot rely on privilege against self-incrimination when he has ac-

INTELLECTUAL PROPERTY

cidentally handed over evidence of his own dishonesty; see *Bell Cablemedia Plc v Simmons* [2002] F.S.R. 34.

Claim for infringement and challenge to validity[1]

2F–61   **63.9—(1) In a claim for infringement or an application in which the validity of a patent or registered design is challenged, the statement of case must contain particulars as set out in the practice direction.**

(2) In a claim for infringement, the period for service of the defence or Part 20 claim is 42 days after service of the claim form.

Claims for infringement in which validity is challenged

2F–62   The language used in r.63.9(1) does not make it entirely clear whether this rule applies to all claims for infringement *and* applications in which the validity of patents or designs is challenged, or only claims for infringement (and any other applications) in which validity is challenged. The practice direction only sets out stipulations for the statement of case in respect of claims in which validity is challenged, so it may be assumed that the latter interpretation is correct. There appears to be no such ambiguity in respect of r.63.9(2), which suggests that for all claims for infringement the period of service for the defence or Part 20 claim is 42 days after service of the claim form.

Counterclaims for invalidity

2F–63   *Stay against one of several defendants who does not challenge validity* —Where one of two defendants does not raise the issue of invalidity, the action may be stayed against that defendant until after the action against the other defendant has been determined (*McCreath v Mayor, etc., of South Shields* (1932) 49 R.P.C. 349). As to addition of defendant, see *Anxionnaz v Rolls-Royce Ltd* [1963] R.P.C. 81.

2F–64   *Grounds of invalidity: general* —The objections which may be taken against the validity of a patent, in an action for infringement or in revocation proceedings, are set out in s.72 of the Patents Act 1977 (including European Patents (UK)).

The statement of case must contain particulars of the relief sought and the issues except those relating to validity, which should be contained in a separate document annexed to it headed "Grounds of Invalidity". The "Grounds of Invalidity" must specify the grounds on which validity is challenged. Grounds of Invalidity were previously called "Particulars of Objections".

The separate grounds of invalidity must be stated, for, apart from granting leave to amend, the court will not consider objections not pleaded, even if they appear on the evidence. See Judgment of Lord Loreburn L.C. in *Alsop Flour Process Co v Flour Oxidising Co* (1908) 25 R.P.C. 490, and CA in *British United Shoe Machinery Co v Fussell & Co* (1908) 25 R.P.C. 631. Also, upon objection, the court may refuse to allow the admission of evidence or cross-examination relating to an insufficiently particularised plea of invalidity (*British Thomson-Houston Co Ltd v Tungstalite Ltd* (1940) 57 R.P.C. 271 at 275).

Particulars of objection to validity

2F–65   *(1) Want of novelty and want of any inventive step* —the particulars must specify such details of the matter in the state of the art relied on, namely—

   (1) in the case of matter made available to the public by written description—
       (a) the date on which and the means by which it was so made available, unless this is clear from the face of the matter; and
       (b) the identifying information allowing the public to access the matter; and
   (2) in the case of matter made available to the public by use—
       (a) the date or dates of such use;

---

[1] Amended by the Civil Procedure (Amendment No.5) Rules 2003 (SI 2003/3361).

Paragraph numbers marked with a "+" can be found online and on CD.

    (b) the name of all persons making such use;

    (c) any written material which identifies such use;

    (d) the existence and location of any apparatus employed in such use; and

    (e) all facts and matters relied on to establish that such matter was made available to the public.

See PD 63 paras 11.3 and 11.4.

If a defendant also decides to rely upon common general knowledge he should plead it distinctly (*Phillips v Ivel Cycle Co Ltd* (1890) 7 R.P.C. 77). Ordinarily a defendant need not give particulars of common general knowledge. However, particulars were in one case ordered of those portions of the specification relied upon by the defendant alleged to be common general knowledge (*Solaflex Signs Amalgamated Ltd v Allen Manufacturing Co Ltd* (1931) 48 R.P.C. 577). They were refused in *McCreath v Mayor, etc., of South Shields* (1932) 49 R.P.C. 349, but see *British Thomson-Houston Ltd v Tungstalite Ltd* (1940) 57 R.P.C. 271, where defendants failed to give particulars ordered.

(2) Insufficiency —the particulars must state, if appropriate, which examples of the **2F–66** invention cannot be made to work and in which respects they do not work or do not work as described in the specification (See practice direction paragraph 11.3(2)).

In response to a plea of insufficiency a patentee cannot be made to plead a positive case as against the whole world that his specification does sufficiently and fairly describe his invention and the manner of performing it. But in appropriate cases he can be made to give, in relation to each pleaded particular of insufficiency, particulars of the passage or passages in his complete specification alleged to contain a sufficient and fair description of that part of the invention and of the method by which it is to be performed, specifying in each case what it is alleged that a man skilled in the art would do in respect of that invention (*Polaroid Corp's Patent-Insufficiency Appeal* [1977] F.S.R. 233). However in most cases it seems that it will not be appropriate to order such particulars before experiments have been carried out (*Halcon International Inc v Shell Transport & Trading Co* [1977] F.S.R. 458).

Amendment of particulars of objections

    (a) Before trial

(1) The rule is that the patentee is to be placed in the same position as to **2F–67** discontinuing the action, or disclaiming a portion of his invention, as if the new particulars had formed a part of the old particulars. The form which has been consistently followed in the past is that in *Baird v Moule's Patent Earth Closet Co Ltd* (1881) L.R. 17 Ch. D. 139 (Note) set out in *Edison Telephone Co v India Rubber Co* (1881) L.R. 17 Ch. D. 137. In *See v Scott-Paine* (1933) 50 R.P.C. 56, where there was a counterclaim for revocation, the order provided that if the patentee elected to discontinue the action he should also consent to an order for revocation of his patent. However, see *Cil International Ltd v Vitrashop Ltd* [2002] F.S.R. 4 as to whether a *See v Scott-Paine* or *Earth Closet* order is necessarily appropriate. A *See v Scott-Paine* order is discretionary and the court must consider the merits in each case; its aim is not to penalise a defendant but to encourage the pleading of all the objections known to him. See also *Robert Hewitt v P. McCann Ltd* [1998] F.S.R. 688 where a *See v Scott-Paine* order was refused where no serious criticism could be levelled at the defendant.

In *Instance v Denny Bros. Printing Ltd* [1994] F.S.R. 396 the defendant sought a qualification on the usual *See v Scott-Paine* order that it be entitled to withdraw the amendments proposed at its election if the Claimant chose to discontinue. The qualification was rejected on the basis that amendment is an indulgence. A defendant must decide whether to amend.

    (b) Amendment at the trial—

will only be permitted if the new evidence could not by reasonable diligence have been found before: North P. in *Moss v Malings* (1886) L.R. 33 Ch D 603. Where on the evidence it appeared that the invention was insufficiently described (see note to r.21) and this was not alleged in the particulars, leave was given to

Paragraph numbers marked with a "+" can be found online and on CD.

amend, the patentees to have a fortnight to elect whether they would discontinue, the terms to be argued after election (*Badische Anilin and Soda Fabrik v La Societe Chimique* (1897) 14 R.P.C. 875).

The eminently sensible implication of *Helitune Ltd v Stewart Hughes Ltd* [1991] R.P.C. 78 is that if knowledge of a ground of invalidity (typically prior use by the patentee) comes to light only during cross examination, an amendment of the particulars of objections ought not to be subject to an Earth Closet order. Further a distinction may be drawn between prior documents and prior uses. In the case of the latter, the defendant may only be able to discover them by chance, and in such circumstances it may not be appropriate to grant a *See v Scott-Paine* order (*La Baigne Magiglo v Multiglow Fires* [1994] R.P.C. 295). For a case in which an *Earth Closet* Order was not made even though amendment was sought late and the party seeking revocation had been aware of the new prior art for some time, see *GEC Alsthom's Patent* [1996] F.S.R. 415. The purpose of Earth Closet Orders is to put the patentee in the position he would have been in from the point of view of costs and discontinuance if the particulars of objections had been fully and properly pleaded from the start. They are not to put the patentee in a "preferential" position (*Aumac Ltd's Patent* [1996] F.S.R. 843).

Amendment of pleadings, sought however late, ought to be allowed so as to determine the dispute between the parties (provided no injustice is caused) because it is the public interest that the validity of a patent should be fully tested (*Helitune* case, above).

Where a point is foreshadowed in witness statements, amendments of pleadings will be allowed if necessary; *Glaverbel SA v British Coal Corp (No.3)* [1993] F.S.R. 478.

Where the claimant in a patent infringement action opted following the making of a *See v Scott-Paine* order to discontinue, and then sought to designate the UK in relation to a similar European divisional patent, the Court would not re-open the *See v Scott Paine* order so as to prevent the claimant from suing on the European patent (*Aumac's Patent* [1995] F.S.R. 501).

Whilst the requirements of para.11 of the Practice Direction that particulars must be given in relation to an attack on novelty are mandatory, nonetheless the Court has a discretion whether to allow amendments before they have been properly particularised (*Dendron GmbH v University of California (Amendment of Claim)* [2003] EWHC 2771 (Ch), unrep., Ch D). The Court should exercise that discretion to prevent amendments being made with a view to obtaining documents to discover a cause of action or defence. The Court must judge whether the amendment is tantamount to a fishing expedition or not. (See *Visx Inc v Nidek Co Ltd (No.2)* [1999] F.S.R. 91).

Estoppel

2F–68   In *Chiron Corp v Organon Teknika Ltd (No.6)* [1994] F.S.R. 448, a defendant sued for a second time on the same patent, having unsuccessfully counterclaimed for its revocation in the first action, may not put the validity of the patent in issue in the second action (except possibly in exceptional circumstances). The matter was *res judicata* between the parties. *Chiron Corp v Organon Teknika Ltd (No.6)* has been reported in the Court of Appeal, where leave to appeal was obtained and then set aside (*Chiron Corp v Organon Teknika Ltd (No.14)* [1996] F.S.R. 701.

Whether and to what extent estoppel may arise from the findings of foreign Courts in parallel patent proceedings was considered in *Kirin Amgen Inc v Boehringer Mannheim GmbH* [1997] F.S.R. 289 and (regarding an unsuccessful opposition in the European Patent Office) *Buehler AG v Chronos Richardson Ltd* [1998] R.P.C. 609.

Commercial success

2F–69   In some cases a patentee may seek to rely upon the commercial success of his invention to rebut an allegation of obviousness. However such a case inherently involves a number of substantial questions, e.g. is the success due to what is claimed, or to other matters such as advertising, or good manufacture, or the later development of the details (whether further inventions or not) which make for commercial

Paragraph numbers marked with a "+" can be found online and on CD.

success? Whether there was a long-felt want met by the alleged invention is likewise often a question of significance. In *Raychem Corp's Patents* [1998] R.P.C. 31, Laddie J. went so far as to say that a plea of commercial success normally only added time and expense to the proceedings and served no useful purpose.

Paragraph 11.5(1) of the practice direction suggests that a patentee relying on commercial success must state the grounds on which he so relies on his claim form. This is plainly wrong. A patentee will not know (though he may fear) that a counterclaim for invalidity will be made at the time that he serves his claim form. It may be that for the words "claim form" one should read "statement of case".

For disclosure in relation to commercial success, see para.2F-49 above.

Foreign commercial success may be relevant (*Unilever v Gillette (UK) Ltd* [1989] R.P.C. 417).

Application to amend a patent specification in existing proceedings

63.10—(1) An application under section 75 of the 1977 Act for permission to amend the specification of a patent by the proprietor of the patent must be made by application notice. **2F-70**

(2) The application notice must—

    (a) give particulars of—

        (i) the proposed amendment sought; and

        (ii) the grounds upon which the amendment is sought;

    (b) state whether the applicant will contend that the claims prior to amendment are valid; and

    (c) be served by the applicant on all parties and the Comptroller within 7 days of its issue.

(3) The application notice must, if it is reasonably possible, be served on the Comptroller electronically.

(4) Unless the court otherwise orders, the Comptroller will forthwith advertise the application to amend in the journal.

(5) The advertisement will state that any person may apply to the Comptroller for a copy of the application notice.

(6) Within 14 days of the first appearance of the advertisement any person who wishes to oppose the application must file and serve on all parties and the Comptroller a notice opposing the application which must include the grounds relied on.

(7) Within 28 days of the first appearance of the advertisement the applicant must apply to the court for directions.

(8) Unless the court otherwise orders, the applicant must within 7 days serve on the Comptroller any order of the court on the application.

(9) In this rule, "the journal" means the journal published pursuant to rules made under section 123(6) of the 1977 Act.

Amendment

See *Oxford Gene Technology Ltd v Affymetrix Inc (No.2)* [2001] R.P.C. 18—privilege and disclosure in relation to amendment of patents. **2F-71**

Cause of action where amendment sought

A claim would not be struck out because the claimant alleged only that claims of a **2F-72**

Paragraph numbers marked with a "+" can be found online and on CD.

patent as sought to be amended were infringed. See *Zipher Ltd v Markem Systems Ltd* [2007] EWHC 154 (Pat).

Terms on which amendment allowed

2F-73   The form of the order will depend on the circumstances, and there is no form which is invariably to be followed in all cases (per Lindley L.J., in *Bray v Gardner* (1887) L.R. 34 Ch. D. 668 at 44). For terms on which liberty to apply to amend under the Act of 1883 was granted, see *Ludington Cigarette Machine Co v Baron Cigarette Machine Co* [1900] 1 Ch. 508; *Deeley v Perkes* [1896] A.C. 496; *Re Geipel's Patent* [1903] 2 Ch. 715; [1904] 1 Ch. 239; 20 R.P.C. 545; 21 R.P.C. 279. The form in the last-mentioned case was substantially followed in similar cirumstances in *Gillette Safety Razor Co v Luna Safety Razor Co* [1910] 2 Ch. 373, followed in *Rheinische Gummi and Celluloid Fabrik v British Xylonite Co Ltd* (1912) 29 R.P.C. 672, where the order is set out in full. This form of order was slightly varied in *NV Hollandsche Glas-en Metaalbank v Rockware Glass Syndicate Ltd* (1931) 48 R.P.C. 181; see also *Lilley v Artistic Novelties Ltd* (1913) 30 R.P.C. 18, *Rowland Edwards & C Ltd v Three Star Accumulators Ltd* (1934) 51 R.P.C. 370, and *White's Application* [1958] R.P.C. 287. The motion may be ordered to come on for hearing with the trial of the action (*British Celanese Ltd v Courtaulds Ltd* (1932) 49 R.P.C. 345; *Re Nier's Patent* (1938) 55 R.P.C. 1; *Astra A/B v Pharmaceutical Mfg Co* (1952) 69 R.P.C. 312) but this course may sometimes be inconvenient (*British Acoustic Films Ltd v Nettleford Productions* (1935) 52 R.P.C. 296; 53 R.P.C. 221, at 241; *Drysdale v Davey, Paxman & Co (Colchester) Ltd* (1938) 55 R.P.C. 95, at 108). The motion may be allowed on the terms that consequential amendments may be made in the pleadings, in which case the defendant (or petitioner) will usually be given the costs occasioned thereby. See *Haslam Foundry and Engineering Co v Goodfellow* (1888) 5 R.P.C. 28; *Re Chatwood's Patent* (1899) 16 R.P.C. 370; *NV Hollandsche Glas-en Metaalbank v Rockware Glass Syndicate Ltd* (1931) 48 R.P.C. 425; *Chrome-Alloying Co Ltd v Metal Diffusions Ltd* [1962] R.P.C. 33. Leave to amend was given in *Electrical & Musical Industries Ltd's Patent* [1963] R.P.C. 241, but the question of terms was deferred to the full hearing.

Where a perpetual injunction had been granted several years before the application to amend, the Court as a term of the permission to amend dissolved the injunction (*Re Kenrick and Jefferson's Patent* (1912) 29 R.P.C. 25).

In general it requires a special case before the Court imposes conditions when permitting amendment (*Wilkinson Sword Ltd v Gillette Industries Ltd* [1975] R.P.C. 101; *General Tire & Rubber Co (Frost's) Patent* [1974] F.S.R. 433).

After amendment, a patentee must start a fresh action rather than seek to enforce any relief he has obtained in a previous action. That practice is based upon the fact that there has been no judgment on infringement and validity in relation to the amended patent and upon the statutory provisions that an amendment dates back to the grant (*PLG Research Ltd v Ardon International Ltd (No.2)* [1993] F.S.R. 698).

Costs may be awarded to a successful patentee even though he later amends his specification and throws away all other relief obtained prior to amendment (*ibid.*).

Full disclosure of facts

2F-74   In amendment proceedings full disclosure is not always necessary since obligation primarily met by the statement of reasons; see *Intel Corp's Patent* [2002] R.P.C. 48.

Discretion to refuse amendment

2F-75   Amendment will not be allowed where the object is delay (*Re Stahlwerk, etc. Patent* (1918) 36 R.P.C. 13). However, amendment to validate an invalid claim is very different from amendment to delete an invalid claim. The latter kind of amendment is much easier to make (*Chiron Corp v Organon Teknika Ltd (No.7)* [1994] F.S.R. 458, and *Johnson Electric IndustrialManufactory Ltd v Mabuchi Motor KK (No.2)* [1996] F.S.R. 93). Even grave error is not the same as deliberately seeking an excessive monopoly (*Johnson v Mabuchi*, above). Where an error in the patent specification was brought to the patentee's attention by the defendants in their Particulars of Objection (now called "Grounds of Invalidity"), but where the patentee had to wait for further particulars of other objections, a delay of over two years in bringing the motion to amend was excused (*Alliance Flooring Co Ltd v Winsoflor Ltd* [1961] R.P.C. 95). It is not unreasonable to delay finalising amendments until the attack on the patent is pleaded (*Rediffusion Simulation Ltd v Link-Miles Ltd* [1993] F.S.R. 369). The conduct of the patentee in

Paragraph numbers marked with a "+" can be found online and on CD.

(3) Claims to which this Section of this Part applies must be brought in—

    (a) the Chancery Division;

    (b) a Patents County Court; or

    (c) a county court where there is also a Chancery district registry.

Clarity of Pleadings

Where a party seeks to revoke a trade mark from a date earlier than the date of the application for revocation, it should set out in the statement of grounds the date it contended for and explicitly allege that the grounds for revocation existed at an appropriate earlier date. See *Omega SA v Omega Engineering Inc* [2003] EWHC 1334.   **2F–79**

Discontinuance

The normal rule in the event of a claimant discontinuing a claim is that the claimant has to pay the defendant's costs. The CPR gives the court a discretion however— see *Coca-Cola Company, The v Mabe* [2002] F.S.R. 47.   **2F–80**

Claims under the 1994 Act

63.14 In a claim under the 1994 Act, the claim form or application notice must be served on the registrar where the relief sought would, if granted, affect an entry in the United Kingdom register.   **2F–81**

Claim for infringement of registered trade mark

63.15—(1) In a claim for infringement of a registered trade mark the defendant may—   **2F–82**

    (a) in his defence, challenge the validity of the registration of the trade mark; and

    (b) apply by Part 20 claim for—

        (i) revocation of the registration;

        (ii) a declaration that the registration is invalid; or

        (iii) rectification of the register.

(2) Where a defendant applies under paragraph (1)(b) and the relief sought would, if granted, affect an entry in the United Kingdom register, he must serve on the registrar a copy of his claim form.

Pleadings

Julian Higgins' Trade Mark Application [2000] R.P.C. 321 and *Club Europe Trade Mark* [2000] R.P.C. 329—trade mark notice of oppositions and statements of grounds are in effect pleadings—it is the function of pleadings to define the issues between the parties.   **2F–83**

The provision of material facts upon which an allegation was based is particularly important where an applicant for a declaration of invalidity relies upon s.5(4) of the 1994 Act. *Geobank Trade Mark* [1999] R.P.C. 682.

The provision that a defendant may challenge the validity of a registered trade mark in his defence must be read in the light of *Special Effects Limited v L'Oreal SA* [2006] EWHC 481 (Ch) in which it was held that a defendant whose opposition proceedings has been dismissed was estopped from challenging the validity in infringement proceedings.

Injunctive relief

Aktiebolaget Volvo v Heritage (Leicester) Ltd [2000] F.S.R. 253—trade marks; breadth of   **2F–84**

Paragraph numbers marked with a "+" can be found online and on CD.

injunction; wide injunction appropriate when evidence of behaviour not in accordance with honest business practices.

III. Service

Service[1]
2F–85   **63.16—(1) Subject to paragraph (2), Part 6 applies to service of a claim form and any document under this Part.**

(2) A claim form relating to a registered right may be served—

(a) **on a party who has registered the right at the address for service given for that right in the United Kingdom Intellectual Property Office register, provided the address is within the United Kingdom; or**

(b) **in accordance with rule 6.32(1), 6.33(1) or 6.33(2) on a party who has registered the right at the address for service given for that right in the appropriate register at—**

(i) **the United Kingdom Intellectual Property Office; or**

(ii) **the Office for Harmonisation in the Internal Market.**

Service out of the jurisdiction
2F–86   A foreign parent company and its UK subsidiary may have as good a common design to infringe a UK patent as any other joint tortfeasors, and if so, service outside the jurisdiction is proper (*Intel Corp v General Instrument Corp* [1991] R.P.C. 235). See also *Lubrizol v Esso (No.1)* [1992] R.P.C. 467, CA, where the parent company had not by taking procedural steps submitted to the jurisdiction, but was held to have admitted common design and the claimants had shown a good arguable case on infringement; but the joinder of the parent involved a new claim and relief against it would only run from six years previous to service upon it.

Molins v G.D SpA [2000] F.S.R. 893—service of proceedings.

IV. Appeals

Appeals from the Comptroller
2F–87   **63.17—(1) Part 52 applies to appeals from the Comptroller.**

(2) Patent appeals are to be made to the Patents Court, and other appeals to the Chancery Division.

(3) Where Part 52 requires a document to be served, it must also be served on the Comptroller or registrar, as appropriate.

Nature of Appeal from the Comptroller
2F–88   See *Ladney and Hendry's International Application* [1998] R.P.C. 319. Section 55 of the Access to Justice Act 1999 does not impliedly repeal or amend s.97(3) of the Patents Act 1977 or otherwise limit its scope: *Smith International Inc vSpecialised Petroleum Services Group Limited* [2005] EWCA Civ 1357.

2F–89   Section 97(3) of the Patents Act 1977 has not been impliedly repealed or amended

---

[1] Amended by the Civil Procedure (Amendment No.5) Rules 2003 (SI 2003/3361) and the Civil Procedure (Amendment) Rules 2008 (SI 2008/2178).

Paragraph numbers marked with a "+" can be found online and on CD.

by s.55 of the Access to Justice Act 1999, nor had it been limited in its scope. The appropriate test for second appeals under s.97(3) of the Patents Act 1977 is thus whether the proposed appeal has a real prospect of success. See *Smith International Inc's Patent* [2005] EWCA Civ 1357; [2006] F.S.R. 25.

The court will not refuse to entertain an appeal against a hearing officer's decision on an opinion given under the Patents Act 1977 s.74A on the basis that the procedure could only result in the production of non-binding opinions or decisions. The provision of non-binding opinions was potentially of great value to persons concerned with the validity or infringement of a patent, and as such did not involve a purely academic question but a living issue. The court should only decide that such an opinion was wrong if the hearing officer had failed to recognise that an examiner had made an error of principle or reached a conclusion that was clearly wrong. It was not the function of the court to express an opinion on the question that was the subject of the original request. See *In the matter of DLP Ltd* [2007] EWHC 2669 (Pat).

Costs on appeal

The normal rule in relation to appeals concerning matters arising under the 1977 Act is that the successful party is awarded his costs (*Extrude Hone Corp's Patent* [1982] R.P.C. 361, Whitford J.; *Omron's Patent* [1981] R.P.C. 125). This rule also applies to appeals to which the Comptroller is a party. If there is any further appeal the CA apply the usual rule of assessed costs (*Associated British Combustion Ltd's Patent* [1978] R.P.C. 581). Costs may be awarded on an application to the Court of Appeal for leave to appeal (*International Paint Co's Appn* [1982] R.P.C. 247). **2F–90**

Cross-examination on appeal

This will not normally be allowed. The proper time to ask for cross-examination is before the superintending examiner (*J. Sainsbury Ltd's Application* [1981] F.S.R. 406). **2F–91**

Trade mark appeals

For the principles on which new evidence should be allowed in an appeal from the Trade Marks Registry, see *Ministere de l'Agriculture de la Foret v Bernard Matthews Plc*, sub nom. *LABEL ROUGE Trade Mark* [2002] EWHC 190 and also *Joop v Canadelle Ltd Partnership of Canada* sub nom. *WUNDERKIND Trade Mark* [2002] R.P.C. 45; *Du Pont Trade Mark* [2003] EWCA Civ 1368, and *Omega Engineering Inc v Omega SA* [2004] EWHC 2315. **2F–92**

The specific provisions for patent and trade mark appeals in ss. 16 and 23 respectively of Practice Direction 49E no longer apply. By virtue of new r.63.17, all appeals to the court from the comptroller are governed by Pt 52 of the Civil Procedure Rules and (see rr 52.1(4) and 52.2) its supplementary Practice Direction 52. This affects the period to file the notice of appeal at the court; extension of that period; and the nature of the appeal. (*Nb*. The new Rules apply only to the courts in England and Wales.) See *Patent Office Practice Notice 1/2003 (Revised)* [2003] R.P.C. 46. For the role of the appellate court in trade mark appeals, see also *Harrison's Trade Mark Application* ("Chinawhite") [2002] EWHC 3009, *REEF Trade Mark* [2003] R.P.C. 5, CA, *POLICE Trade Mark* [2004] R.P.C. 35 and *Du Pont Trade Mark* [2003] EWCA Civ 1368

Period for appeal: Practice Direction 52 para.17.3

Notice of appeal must be filed at the court within 28 days after the date of the comptroller's decision. There is no discretion for the comptroller to direct a different period. **2F–93**

For trade mark appeals a period of 28 days already applied. However, the period prescribed by s.16.3 for patent appeals (14 days for matters of procedure and six weeks in other cases) is abolished, with the consequence that it is no longer necessary in patent proceedings for the hearing officer to determine whether the decision relates to a matter of procedure. In accordance with rr.52.4(3) and 63.17(3) and para.17.5 of PD 52, the appeal notice must be served on each respondent and on the comptroller as soon as practicable and in any event not later than seven days after it is filed. The period of 21 days prescribed by ss.16.8 and 23.4 of PD 49E is abolished.

Extension of the appeal period: CPR, r.52.6

Any application to extend the period for appeal must be made to the court. The **2F–94**

Paragraph numbers marked with a "+" can be found online and on CD.

Intellectual Property

parties cannot extend the period by agreement (r.52.6(2)). Further, it is no longer possible for the comptroller to extend the period at the request of a party.

An appellant who applies for an extension from the court must state the reasons for the delay and the steps taken prior to the application being made. The respondent has a right to be heard on the application.

The nature of the appeal: CPR, r.52.11

2F–95   In general, in accordance with r.52.11 the appeal will be limited to a review of the comptroller's decision. Section 16.15 of PD 49E, whereby patents appeals were by way of a rehearing rather than a review (although further evidence was prohibited on appeal except with the leave of the court) will no longer apply.

Appeals to the Appointed Person and the Registered Designs Appeal Tribunal

2F–96   *Appointed Person* —The period for appeal to the Appointed Person is 28 days under the Trade Marks Rules and the comptroller has sole jurisdiction to extend this period. In relation to the nature of the appeal, the Appointed Person is not bound by the Civil Procedure Rules but is generally guided by the court's approach to the distinction between review and rehearing.

Registered Designs Appeal Tribunal —The Registered Designs Appeal Tribunal Rules 1950 (as amended 1970) govern appeals to the Tribunal under s.28 of the Registered Designs Act 1949 (as amended by the Copyright, Designs and Patents Act 1988) and s.249 of the 1988 Act. Under these Rules the period for appeal is 14 days for a decision on a matter of procedure and six weeks for other decisions, and the comptroller may extend the period upon request made prior to its expiry.

Notices regulating European Patent Appeals

2F–97   **Notice from the Vice-President Directorate-General 3 dated 17 March 2008 concerning accelerated processing before the boards of appeal**

Parties with a legitimate interest may ask the boards of appeal to deal with their appeals rapidly. The boards can speed up an appeal as far as the procedural regulations allow.

Requests for accelerated processing must be submitted to the competent board either at the beginning of or during proceedings. They should contain reasons for the urgency together with relevant documents; no particular form is required.

This option is also available to the courts and competent authorities of the contracting states.

By way of example, the following circumstances could justify an appeal being dealt with particularly rapidly:

— where infringement proceedings have been brought or are envisaged
— where the decision of potential licensees of the patent in suit, that is the patent which is the subject of an appeal, hinges upon the outcome of the appeal proceedings
— where an opposition which is to be given accelerated processing (see Notice of the EPO dated 17 March 2008, OJ EPO 2008, 221) has been made the subject of an appeal.

By way of exception, the board may accelerate the procedure ex officio, for example in view of the disadvantages which could ensue from the suspensive effect of the appeal in the case in question.

Whether or not a particular case is regarded as urgent will depend on the nature of the case and not merely on whether accelerated processing is requested by the parties.

If, in view of the circumstances, the reasons given and the documents provided, the board decides to grant accelerated processing, this will involve in particular giving the appeal priority, and/or—with due respect for the parties' right to be heard and the fair administration of justice—adopting a strict framework for the procedure, for example concerning the time limits available before the final decision.

Article 99—OJ 1998, 361 Notice from the President of the European Patent Office dated 19 May 1998 concerning accelerated processing of oppositions where infringement proceedings have been instituted

Paragraph numbers marked with a "+" can be found online and on CD.

1. In cases where an infringement action in respect of a European patent is pending before a national court of a contracting state a party to the opposition proceedings may request accelerated processing. The request may be filed at any time. It must be filed in written reasoned form. The Office will then make every effort to issue the next procedural action (e.g. communication, summons to oral proceedings) within three months of receipt of the request or where the request is already filed within the opposition period, within three months after receipt of the patent proprietor's response to the notice of opposition (whichever is the later).

2. In addition, the EPO will also accelerate the processing of the opposition if it is informed by the national court or competent authority of a contracting state that infringement actions are pending.

3. However, the EPO has to rely on the co-operation of the parties to the proceedings who are expected in particular to make their submissions promptly and in full and in any case strictly to adhere to the time limits set by the EPO for replying to communications or commenting on written submissions from the other parties. Requests to extend time limits over and above the normal four-month period can only be granted in exceptional, duly substantiated cases.

Paragraph numbers marked with a "+" can be found online and on CD.

PRACTICE DIRECTION—PATENTS AND OTHER INTELLECTUAL PROPERTY CLAIMS

This Practice Direction supplements CPR Part 63

Contents of this Practice Direction

2F–98   **1.1** This practice direction is divided into three sections—
- Section I—Provisions about patents and registered designs;
- Section II—Provisions about registered trade marks and other intellectual property rights;
- Section III—Provisions about appeals.
- Section IV—Provisions about final orders

I. Provisions about Patents and Registered Designs

2F–99   **2.1** This Section of this practice direction applies to claims in the Patents Court and a Patents County Court.

2.2 The following claims must be dealt with in the court—

   (1)   any matter arising out of the 1977 Act, including—
      (a) infringement actions;
      (b) revocation actions;
      (c) threats under section 70 of the 1977 Act; and
      (d) disputes as to ownership;
   (2)   registered designs;
   (3)   Community registered designs; and
   (4)   semiconductor topography rights.

Starting the claim (rule 63.5)

2F–100   **3.1** A claim form to which this Section of this Part applies must be marked in the top right hand corner "Patents Court" below the title of the court in which it is issued.

Case management (rule 63.7)

2F–101   **4.1** The following parts only of the practice direction supplementing Part 29 apply—

   (1)   paragraph 5 (case management conferences)—
      (a) excluding paragraph 5.9; and
      (b) modified so far as is made necessary by other specific provisions of this practice direction; and
   (2)   paragraph 7 (failure to comply with case management directions).

4.2 Case management shall be dealt with by—

   (1)   a judge of the court; or
   (2)   a Master or district judge where a judge of the court so directs.

4.3 The claimant must apply for a case management conference within 14 days of the date when all defendants who intend to file and serve a defence have done so.

4.4 Where the claim has been transferred, the claimant must apply for a case management conference within 14 days of the date of the order transferring the claim, unless the court—

Paragraph numbers marked with a "+" can be found online and on CD.

(d) a summary by convenient periods of any expenditure which supported the use of the process in sub-paragraphs (a) and (c).

Short applications

6.1 Where any application is listed for a short hearing, the parties **2F–103** must file all necessary documents, skeleton arguments and drafts of any orders sought, by no later than 3.00 p.m. on the preceding working day.

6.2 A short hearing is any hearing which is listed for no more than 1 hour.

Timetable for trial

7.1 Not less than one week before the beginning of the trial, each **2F–104** party must inform the court in writing of the estimated length of its—

(1) oral submissions;

(2) examination in chief, if any, of its own witnesses; and

(3) cross-examination of witnesses of any other party.

7.2 At least four days before the date fixed for the trial, the claim- **2F–105** ant must file—

(1) the trial bundle; and

(2) a Reading Guide for the judge.

7.3 The Reading Guide filed under paragraph 7.2 must—

(1) be short and if possible, agreed;

(2) set out the issues, the parts of the documents that need to be read on each issue and the most convenient order that they should be read;

(3) identify the relevant passages in text books and cases, if appropriate; and

(4) not contain argument.

Jurisdiction of Masters

8.1 A Master may only deal with— **2F–105**

(1) orders by way of settlement, except settlement of procedural disputes;

(2) orders on applications for extension of time;

(3) applications for leave to serve out of the jurisdiction;

(4) applications for security for costs;

(5) other matters as directed by a judge of the court; and

(6) enforcement of money judgments.

Experiments

9.1 Where a party seeks to establish any fact by experimental proof **2F–106** conducted for the purpose of litigation he must, at least 21 days before service of the application notice for directions under paragraph 9.3, or within such other time as the court may direct, serve on all parties a notice—

(1) stating the facts which he seeks to establish; and

Paragraph numbers marked with a "+" can be found online and on CD.

(2)   giving full particulars of the experiments proposed to establish them.

9.2 A party served with notice under paragraph 9.1—

(1)   must within 21 days after such service, serve on the other party a notice stating whether or not he admits each fact; and

(2)   may request the opportunity to inspect a repetition of all or a number of the experiments identified in the notice served under paragraph 9.1.

9.3 Where any fact which a party seeks to establish by experimental proof is not admitted, he must apply to the court for permission and directions by application notice.

Use of models or apparatus
2F–107   **10.1** Where a party intends to rely on any model or apparatus, he must apply to the court for directions at the first case management conference.

Claim for infringement and challenge to validity (rule 63.9)
2F–108   **11.1** In a claim for infringement of a patent—

(1)   the statement of case must—
(a) show which of the claims in the specification of the patent are alleged to be infringed; and
(b) give at least one example of each type of infringement alleged; and

(2)   a copy of each document referred to in the statement of case, and where necessary a translation of the document, must be served with the statement of case.

11.2 Where the validity of a patent or registered design is challenged—

(1)   the statement of case must contain particulars of—
(a) the relief sought; and
(b) the issues except those relating to validity of the patent or registered design;

(2)   the statement of case must have a separate document annexed to it headed "Grounds of Invalidity" specifying the grounds on which validity of the patent is challenged;

(3)   a copy of each document referred to in the Grounds of Invalidity, and where necessary a translation of the document, must be served with the Grounds of Invalidity; and

(4)   the Comptroller must be sent a copy of the Grounds of Invalidity and where any such Grounds of Invalidity are amended, a copy of the amended document, at the same time as the Grounds of Invalidity are served or amended.

11.3 Where, in an application in which validity of a patent or a registered design is challenged, the Grounds of Invalidity include an allegation—

(1)   that the invention is not a patentable invention because it is not new or does not involve an inventive step, the particulars

Paragraph numbers marked with a "+" can be found online and on CD.

must specify such details of the matter in the state of art relied on, as set out in paragraph 11.4;

(2)   that the specification of the patent does not disclose the invention clearly enough and completely enough for it to be performed by a person skilled in the art, the particulars must state, if appropriate, which examples of the invention cannot be made to work and in which respects they do not work or do not work as described in the specification; or

(3)   that the registered design is not new, the particulars must specify such details of the matter in the state of art relied on, as set out in paragraph 11.4.

11.4 The details required under paragraphs 11.3(1) and 11.3(3) are—

(1)   in the case of matter or a design made available to the public by written description the date on which and the means by which it was so made available, unless this is clear from the face of the matter; and

(2)   in the case of matter or a design made available to the public by use—
(a) the date or dates of such use;
(b) the name of all persons making such use;
(c) any written material which identifies such use;
(d) the existence and location of any apparatus employed in such use; and
(e) all facts and matters relied on to establish that such matter was made available to the public.

11.5 In any proceedings in which the validity of a patent is challenged—

(1)   on the ground that the invention did not involve an inventive step, a party who wishes to rely on the commercial success of the patent must state the grounds on which he so relies in his statement of case; and

(2)   the court may order inspection of machinery or apparatus where a party alleges such machinery or apparatus was used before the priority date of the claim.

Application to amend a patent specification in existing proceedings (rule 63.10)

12.1 Not later than two days before the first hearing date the applicant, the Comptroller if he wishes to be heard, the parties to the proceedings and any other opponent, must file and serve a document stating the directions sought.   **2F–109**

12.2 Where the application notice is served on the Comptroller electronically under rule 63.10(3), it must comply with any requirements for the sending of electronic communications to the Comptroller.

Application by employee for compensation (rule 63.12)

13.1 Where an employee applies for compensation under section   **2F–110**

Paragraph numbers marked with a "+" can be found online and on CD.

40(1) or (2) of the 1977 Act, the court must at the case management conference give directions as to—

    (1) the manner in which the evidence, including any accounts of expenditure and receipts relating to the claim, is to be given at the hearing of the claim and if written evidence is to be given, specify the period within which witness statements or affidavits must be filed; and

    (2) the provision to the claimant by the defendant or a person deputed by him, of reasonable facilities for inspecting and taking extracts from the accounts by which the defendant proposes to verify the accounts in sub-paragraph (1) or from which those accounts have been derived.

Communication of information to the European Patent Office

2F–111   **14.1** The court may authorise the communication of any such information in the court files as the court thinks fit to—

    (1) the European Patent Office; or

    (2) the competent authority of any country which is a party to the European Patent convention.

14.2 Before authorising the disclosure of information under paragraph 14.1, the court shall permit any party who may be affected by the disclosure to make representations, in writing or otherwise, on the question of whether the information should be disclosed.

Order affecting entry in the register of patents or designs

2F–112   **15.1** Where any order of the court affects the validity of an entry in the register, the court and the party in whose favour the order is made, must serve a copy of such order on the Comptroller within 14 days.

15.2 Where the order is in favour of more than one party, a copy of the order must be served by such party as the court directs.

Claim for rectification of the register of patents or designs

2F–113   **16.1** Where a claim is made for the rectification of the register of patents or designs, the claimant must at the same time as serving the other parties, serve a copy of—

    (1) the claim form; and

    (2) accompanying documents

on the Comptroller or registrar, as appropriate.

16.2 Where documents under paragraph 16.1 are served on the Comptroller or registrar, he shall be entitled to take part in the proceedings.

European Community designs

2F–114   **17.1** The Patents Court and the Central London County Court are the designated Community design courts under Article 80(5) of Council Regulation (EC) 6/2002.

17.2 Where a counterclaim is filed at the Community design court, for a declaration of invalidity of a registered Community design, the

Paragraph numbers marked with a "+" can be found online and on CD.

Community design court shall inform the Office for Harmonisation in the Internal Market of the date on which the counterclaim was filed, in accordance with Article 86(2) of Council Regulation (EC) 6/2002.

17.3 On filing a counterclaim under paragraph 17.2, the party filing it must inform the court in writing that it is a counterclaim to which paragraph 17.2 applies and that the Office for Harmonisation in the Internal Market needs to be informed of the date on which the counterclaim was filed.

17.4 Where a Community design court has given a judgment which has become final on a counterclaim for a declaration of invalidity of a registered Community design, the Community design court shall send a copy of the judgment to the Office for Harmonisation in the Internal Market, in accordance with Article 86(4) of Council Regulation (EC) 6/2002.

17.5 The party in whose favour judgment is given under paragraph 17.4 must inform the Community design court at the time of judgment that paragraph 17.4 applies and that the Office for Harmonisation in the Internal Market needs to be sent a copy of the judgment.

II. Provisions about Registered Trade Marks and Other Intellectual Property Rights

Allocation (rule 63.13)

18.1 Any of the following claims must be brought in the Chancery Division, a Patents County Court or a county court where there is also a Chancery district registry—   **2F–115**

   (1)   copyright;

   (2)   rights in performances;

   (3)   rights conferred under Part VII of the 1988 Act;

   (4)   design right;

   (5)   Community design right;

   (6)   Olympic symbols;

   (7)   plant varieties;

   (8)   moral rights;

   (9)   database rights;

   (10)   unauthorised decryption rights;

   (11)   hallmarks;

   (12)   technical trade secrets litigation;

   (13)   passing off;

   (14)   geographical indications;

   (15)   registered trade marks; and

   (16)   Community registered trade marks.

18.2 There are Chancery district registries at Birmingham, Bristol, Caernarfon, Cardiff, Leeds, Liverpool, Manchester, Mold, Newcastle upon Tyne and Preston.

Starting the claim

19.1 A claim form to which this Section of this Part applies must be   **2F–116**

Paragraph numbers marked with a "+" can be found online and on CD.

marked in the top right hand corner "Chancery Division, Intellectual Property" below the title of the court in which it is issued.

Claims under the 1994 Act (rule 63.14)

2F–117   **20.1** Where the registrar refers to the court an application made to him under the 1994 Act, then unless within one month of receiving notification of the decision to refer, the applicant makes the application to the court, he shall be deemed to have abandoned it.

20.2 The period prescribed under paragraph 20.1 may be extended by—

    (1)   the registrar; or

    (2)   the court

where a party so applies, even if such application is not made until after the expiration of the period prescribed.

20.3 Where an application is made under section 19 of the 1994 Act, the applicant must serve his claim form or application notice on all identifiable persons having an interest in the goods, materials or articles within the meaning of section 19 of the 1994 Act.

Claim for infringement of registered trade mark (rule 63.15)

2F–118   **21.1** Where a document under rule 63.15(2) is served on the registrar, he—

    (1)   may take part in the proceedings; and

    (2)   need not serve a defence or other statement of case, unless the court otherwise orders.

Order affecting entry in the register of trade marks

2F–119   **22.1** Where any order of the court affects the validity of an entry in the register, the provisions of paragraphs 15.1 and 15.2 shall apply.

Claim for rectification of the register of trade marks

2F–120   **23.1** Where a claim is made for the rectification of the register of trade marks, the provisions of paragraphs 16.1 and 16.2 shall apply.

European Community trade marks

2F–121   **24.1** The Chancery Division of the High Court, a Patents County Court or a county court where there is also a Chancery district registry are designated Community trade mark courts under Article 91(1) of Council Regulation (EC) 40/94.

24.2 Where a counterclaim is filed at the Community trade mark court, for revocation or for a declaration of invalidity of a Community trade mark, the Community trade mark court shall inform the Office for Harmonisation in the Internal Market of the date on which the counterclaim was filed, in accordance with Article 96(4) of Council Regulation (EC) 40/94.

24.3 On filing a counterclaim under paragraph 24.2, the party filing it must inform the court in writing that it is a counterclaim to which paragraph 24.2 applies and that the Office for Harmonisation in the Internal Market needs to be informed of the date on which the counterclaim was filed.

Paragraph numbers marked with a "+" can be found online and on CD.

24.4 Where the Community trade mark court has given a judgment which has become final on a counterclaim for revocation or for a declaration of invalidity of a Community trade mark, the Community trade mark court shall send a copy of the judgment to the Office for Harmonisation in the Internal Market, in accordance with Article 96(6) of Council Regulation (EC) 40/94.

24.5 The party in whose favour judgment is given under paragraph 24.4 must inform the Community trade mark court at the time of judgment that paragraph 24.4 applies and that the Office for Harmonisation in the Internal Market needs to be sent a copy of the judgment.

Claim for additional damages under section 97(2) or section 229(3) of the 1988 Act

25.1 Where a claimant seeks to recover additional damages under **2F–122** section 97(2) or section 229(3) of the 1988 Act, the particulars of claim must include—

(1) a statement to that effect; and

(2) the grounds for claiming them.

Application for delivery up or forfeiture under the 1988 Act

26.1 Where a claimant applies under sections 99, 114, 195, 204, **2F–123** 230 or 231 of the 1988 Act for delivery up or forfeiture he must serve—

(1) the claim form; or

(2) application notice, where appropriate,

on all identifiable persons who have an interest in the goods, material or articles within the meaning of sections 114 or 204 of the 1988 Act.

Olympic symbols

27.1 In this practice direction "the Olympic Symbol Regulations" **2F–124** means the Olympic Association Right (Infringement Proceedings) Regulations 1995.

27.2 Where an application is made under regulation 5 of the Olympic Symbol Regulations, the applicant must serve his claim form or application notice on all identifiable persons having an interest in the goods, materials or articles within the meaning of regulation 5 of the Olympic Symbol Regulations.

III. Provisions about Appeals

Appeals and references from the Comptroller (rule 63.17)

28.1 Where— **2F–125**

(1) a person appointed by the Lord Chancellor to hear and decide appeals under section 77 of the 1994 Act, refers an appeal to the Chancery Division of the High Court under section 76(3) of the 1994 Act; or

(2) the Comptroller refers the whole proceedings or a question or issue to the Chancery Division of the High Court under section 251(1) of the 1988 Act,

Paragraph numbers marked with a "+" can be found online and on CD.

the appeal or reference must be brought within 14 days of the reference.

IV. Provisions about Final Orders

2F-126   **29.1** Where the court makes an order for delivery up or destruction of infringing goods, or articles designed or adapted to make such goods, the defendant will pay the costs of complying with that order unless the court orders otherwise.

29.2 Where the court finds that an intellectual property right has been infringed, the court may, at the request of the applicant, order appropriate measures for the dissemination and publication of the judgment to be taken at the defendant's expense.

The Patents Court and Patents County Court Guide

2F-127   Issued 7 July 2008
By authority of the Chancellor of the High Court

1. Introduction

This guide applies to both the Patents Court and the Patents County Court.

The general guidance applicable to matters in the Chancery Division, as set out in the Chancery Guide also applies to patent actions unless specifically mentioned below. "63PD" refers to the Practice Direction–Patents and Other Intellectual Property Claims which supplements CPR Part 63. Thus practitioners should consult this guide together with the Chancery Guide.

2. Allocation

2F-128   Actions proceeding in the Patents Court and the Patents County Court are allocated to the multi-track (Part 63.1(3)). Attention is drawn to Part 63.7 and 63PD.4 (case management).

3. The judges of the Patents Court

2F-129   The judges of the Patents Court and their clerks are set out below.

       Kitchin J (Clerk: Gillian Tarleton–tel 020 7947 6518, fax 020 7947 6439, (*Gillian.Tarleton@hmcourts-service.gsi.gov.uk*)–Senior Patents judge

       Patten J (Clerk: Anne Bateman–tel 020 7947 7617, fax 020 7947 6650, (*Anne.Bateman@hmcourts-service.gsi.gov.uk*)

       Lewison J (Clerk: Donald Bennett–tel 020 7947 6039, fax 020 7947 6894, (*Donald.Bennett@hmcourts-service.gsi.gov.uk*)

       Mann J (Clerk: Patricia Swales–tel 020 7947 7964, fax 020 7947 6739, (*Patricia.Swales@hmcourts-service.gsi.gov.uk*)

       Warren J (Clerk: Elizabeth Collum–tel 020 7947 7260, fax 020 7947 7740, (*Elizabeth.Collum2@hmcourts-service.gsi.gov.uk*)

       Floyd J (Clerk: Alison Hall–tel 020 70731740, fax 020 7947 6593, (*Alison.Hall@hmcourts-service.gsi.gov.uk*)

Trials of cases with a technical difficulty rating of 4 or 5 will normally be heard by Kitchin J. or Floyd J.

4. Patents County Court

2F-130   4.1 The Patents County Court judge is His Honour Judge Fysh QC (Clerk: Kav Rekhi—tel 020 7073 4251, fax 020 7073 4253 (*kav.rekhi@hmcourts-service.gsi.gov.uk*). The Patents County Court is situated at:

       Field House
       15-25 Breams Buildings
       London

Paragraph numbers marked with a "+" can be found online and on CD.

EC4A 1DZ

4.2 The issue of claim forms for the Patents County Court and general inquiries relating to procedure, may be addressed to:

The Specialist Section

Central London Civil Justice Centre ("CLCC")

26 Park Crescent

London

W1N 4HT

DX 97325 REGENTS PARK 2

Tel: 020 7917 7821

Fax: 020 7917 7935

Enquiries relating to listing and existing patent cases should be addressed to the Chancery Listing Office (see para.12 below)

4.3 The issue of all interlocutory processes will continue to be dealt with as at present by the clerk of HHJ Fysh QC at Field House either by post or personal attendance. The payment of the fee will continue to be made at the Fees Office Room E01 in the Royal Courts of Justice.

4.4 All proceedings when issued are sent by CLCC to the Clerk of HH Judge Fysh QC. Enquiries relating to an existing case in the Patents County Court after the claim form has been issued (except for enforcement) may be addressed to

The Clerk to His Honour Judge Fysh QC

Field House

15-25 Breams Buildings

London

EC4A 1DZ

Tel: 020 7073 4251

Fax: 020 7073 4253

4.5 Any document (other than a claim form or one relating to enforcement) on which a fee is payable should be sent to:

Room E01

Royal Courts of Justice

Strand

London

WC2A 2LL

DX 44450 STRAND

5. Judges able and willing to sit out of London

If the parties so desire, for the purpose of saving time or costs, the Patents Court **2F–131** and Patents County Court will sit out of London. Before any approach is made to the Chancery Listing Officer, the parties should discuss between themselves the desirability of such a course. If there is a dispute as to venue, the court will resolve the matter on an application. Where there is no dispute, the Chancery Listing Officer should be contacted as soon as possible so that arrangements can be put in place well before the date of the proposed hearing.

6. Intellectual Property Court Users' Committee

This committee (the "IPCUC") considers the problems and concerns of intellectual **2F–132** property litigators. Membership of the committee includes the judges of the Patents Court and the Patents County Court, a representative of each of the Intellectual Property Bar Association, the Intellectual Property Lawyers Association, the Chartered Institute of Patent Attorneys, the Institute of Trade Mark Attorneys and the Trade Marks Patents and Designs Federation. Anyone having views concerning the improvement of intellectual property litigation is invited to make his or her views known to the committee, preferably through the relevant professional representative on the committee. They may also be communicated to the secretary (Philip Westmacott, Bristows, 100 Victoria Embankment, London EC4Y ODH Tel: 020 7400 8000 Fax: 020 7400 8050).

Paragraph numbers marked with a "+" can be found online and on CD.

The Patents County Court also has a Users' Committee which has a membership and general remit similar to the IPCUC. Matters of specific interest to the Patents County Court do arise and are considered by this committee. Its secretary is Alan Johnson, Bristows (100 Victoria Embankment, London EC4Y ODH Tel: 020 7400 8000 Fax: 020 7400 8050).

Procedure in the Patents Court and Patents County Court

7. Statements of Case

2F-133

Time Limits

7.1 In general, the time limits set out in Part 15 apply to litigation of patents and registered designs. However, Part 63.6 and 63.9 modify Part 15 in respect of the time limits for filing defences and replies.

Content of statements of case

7.2 In general, statements of case (i.e. the pleadings of all parties) must comply with the requirements of Part 16. Furthermore, they should comply with Part 63.9 and 63PD.11. Copies of important documents referred to in a statement of case (e.g. an advertisement referred to in a claim of infringement form or documents cited in Grounds of Invalidity) should be served with the statement of case. Where any such document requires translation, a translation should be served at the same time.

Independent validity of claims

7.3 Where one party raises the issue of validity of a patent, the patentee (or other relevant party) should identify which of the claims of the patent are alleged to have independent validity as early as possible.

8. Active case management and streamlined procedure

2F-134

8.1 The claimants should apply for a case management conference ("CMC") within 14 days of the date when all defendants who intend to file and serve a defence have done so (63PD.4.3). If the claimants fail to do so, then any other party may apply for a CMC (63PD.4.6). Any party may apply in writing for a CMC prior to the above periods. Where a case has been transferred from another division or from another court, the claimants must file for a CMC within 14 days of the transfer (63PD.4.4).

8.2 Almost invariably CMCs in the Patents Court will be conducted by a judge. However, in the limited circumstances set out in 63PD.8.1 (see also para.16 below), a Master may conduct a CMC. Bundles in accordance with 63PD.4.9 should be filed with the court. In the Patents County Court, all CMCs are conducted by the judge of the Patents County Court and not by a district judge.

8.3 In general, parties should endeavour to agree directions prior to the date fixed for the CMC. Although the court has the right to amend directions which have been agreed, this will only happen where there is manifest reason for doing so.

8.4 In accordance with the overriding objective, the court will actively manage the case. In making any order for directions, the court will consider all relevant matters and have regard to the overriding objective with particular emphasis on proportionality, the financial position of the parties, the degree of complexity of the case, the importance of the case and the amount of money at stake.

8.5 The parties are reminded of their continuing obligation to assist the court to further the overriding objective. Moreover, it is the duty of the parties' advisors to remind litigants of the existence of mediation or other forms of alternative dispute resolution as a possible means to resolve disputes. In particular, the parties should consider:

(a) The need for and/or scope of any oral testimony from factual or expert witnesses. The court may confine cross-examination to particular issues and to time limits. The parties should consider whether oral testimony of witnesses should be given by video facility.

(b) The need for, and scope of, any disclosure of documents.

(c) The need for any experiments, process or product descriptions.

Paragraph numbers marked with a "+" can be found online and on CD.

    (d) The need for an oral hearing or whether a decision can be made on the papers. If an oral hearing is considered to be appropriate, the court may order that the hearing be of a fixed duration.

    (e) Whether there is a need for a document setting out the basic undisputed technology ("technical primer"), and if so, its scope and the steps to be taken to achieve agreement of it.

    (f) Whether a scientific adviser should be appointed.

    (g) Whether a costs-capping order should be made.

    (h) Whether there should be a stay of proceedings for mediation or other form of alternative dispute resolution.

8.6 *Streamlined procedure*

Any party may at any time apply to the court for a streamlined procedure in which:

    (a) all factual and expert evidence is in writing;

    (b) there is no requirement to give disclosure of documents;

    (c) there are no experiments;

    (d) cross-examination is only permitted on any topic or topics where it is necessary and is confined to those topics;

        or for any variant on the above.

8.7 Prior to applying for a streamlined procedure, the party seeking it should put its proposal to other parties in the proceedings and should endeavour to agree a form of order.

8.8 If the parties agree to a streamlined procedure, the proposed form of order should be put to the judge for approval as a paper application.

9. Admissions

9.1 With a view to early elimination of non-issues, practitioners are reminded of the necessity of making admissions as soon as possible. This should be done as early as possible, for instance, in a defence or reply. Thus, in a defence, a party may admit the acts complained of or that his article/process has certain of the features of a claim. In a reply a patentee may be able to admit prior publication of cited documents. For the effect of admissions, see Part 14.   **2F–135**

9.2 Parties should also consider serving a notice to admit facts in accordance with Part 32.18 for the purpose of identification of points not in dispute. By asking whether or not the defendant disputes that his article/process has certain features of the claim the real dispute can be narrowed. Thus the ambit of disclosure and of witness and expert statements will be narrowed.

9.3 Parties are reminded that when deciding the issue of costs, a court can take into account the conduct of the parties, including whether it was reasonable for a party to contest a particular issue – Part 44.3(5)(b).

9.4 The position should be kept under constant review. If there is any alteration in the admissions that can be made, the identity of the claims said to have independent validity, or the claims alleged to be infringed, that information should be communicated forthwith to the other parties.

10.2

10. Alternative Dispute Resolution ("ADR")

10.1 While emphasising its primary role as a forum for deciding patent and registered design cases, the Patents Court and Patents County Court encourage parties to consider the use of ADR (such as, but not confined to, mediation and conciliation) as an alternative means of resolving disputes or particular issues within disputes.   **2F–136**

10.2 Settlement of dispute by ADR has many advantages including significant saving of costs and providing parties with a wider range of solutions than can be offered by litigation. Legal representatives should consider and advise their clients as to the possibility of attempting to resolve the dispute via ADR. In an appropriate case, the Patents Court and Patents County Court may adjourn a case for a specified period of time to encourage and enable the parties to use ADR.

Paragraph numbers marked with a "+" can be found online and on CD.

10.3 The clerk to the Patents County Court judge has a list of mediation service providers which is available on request.

11. Disclosure

2F–137

11.1 Parties are obliged to provide disclosure in accordance with Part 31 as modified by Part 63.8 and 63PD.5

Process and Product Descriptions

11.2 Where appropriate, parties are encouraged to provide a Process and/or Product Description ("PPD") instead of standard disclosure relating to processes or products which are alleged to infringe or are otherwise relevant to proceedings.

11.3 PPDs must be adequate to deal with the nature of the allegation that has been advanced by the other party or parties. The parties have joint responsibility at an early stage to determine the nature of the case advanced so that the PPD is adequate to deal with that case.

11.4 Parties should bear in mind when preparing a PPD that they may be called on to prove it at trial. Any material omission or inaccuracy could result in a costly adjournment with consequential adverse orders, including as to costs.

Descriptions and drawings of processes or products

11.5 Parties are encouraged to agree descriptions and drawings of processes and/or products which are the subject of infringement proceedings or are alleged to constitute relevant prior art.

Models or apparatus of processes or products

11.6 If a party wishes to adduce a model or apparatus at trial, it should, if practicable, ensure that directions for such are given at the first CMC (63PD.10). Parties should endeavour to view and agree the accuracy of such models or apparatus where possible well in advance of the date of trial.

General matters relating to hearings of applications and Trials

12. Arrangements for listing

2F–138

12.1 The Chancery Listing Officer is responsible for the listing of all work of the Patents Court and the Patents County Court.

12.2 The Chancery Listing Officer and his staff are located in Room WG04 in the Royal Courts of Justice. The office is open to the public from 10.00 am to 4.30 pm each day. The telephone numbers are 020 7947 6778/6690 and the fax number is 020 7947 7345.

12.3 Appointments to fix trials and interim applications are dealt with on Tuesdays and Thursdays between 11.00 am and 12.00 noon. The applicant should first obtain an appointment from the Chancery Listing Officer and give 3 clear days' notice to all interested parties of the date and time fixed.

12.4 A party should not seek to list an application or cause the opposing advocate or counsel's clerk to "pencil in" a date for hearing prior to raising with the proposed respondent the subject-matter of the application so that, where possible, agreement may be reached on the subject-matter of the application. Applicants who fail properly to consult with the respondents prior to listing an application may be met with an adverse costs order.

Short applications

12.5 Short applications (i.e. those estimated to last no more than 1 hour) will usually be heard before the normal court day starts at 10.30 am e.g. 9.30 or 10 am. These can be issued and the hearing date arranged at any time by attendance at the Chancery Listing Office. Attention is drawn to 63PD.6 about the filing of documents and skeleton arguments.

Urgent applications and Without Notice applications

12.6 A party wishing to apply without notice to the respondent(s) should contact the Chancery Listing Office. In cases of emergency in vacation or out of normal court hours, the application should be made to the duty Chancery judge.

September sittings

12.7 The Patents Court and Patents County Court will endeavour, if the parties so desire and the case is urgent, to sit in September.

Paragraph numbers marked with a "+" can be found online and on CD.

Interim injunction hearings and expedited trials

12.8 Applicants for interim remedies (in particular, interim injunctions) and respondents are encouraged to consider whether an expedited (speedy) trial would better meet the interests of justice. Applications for expedited trials may be made at any time but should be made as soon as possible and notice given to all parties.

12.9 When an application for an interim injunction is made the applicant should, where practicable, make prior investigations with the Chancery Listing Officer about trial dates on an unexpedited and expedited basis having regard to the estimated length of trial.

13. Time estimates

13.1 In providing appropriate time estimates, parties must appreciate the need to **2F–139** give realistic and accurate time estimates and ensure that the time estimate includes a discrete reading time for the court to read the papers prior to the hearing of the application or trial. In general, the court will wish to read the skeleton arguments, the patent (where relevant), the prior art (where relevant), expert reports and other key documents (e.g. important witness statements). Advisors should bear in mind the technical difficulty of the case when considering the reading time estimate. The court will consider the imposition of guillotines where time estimates are exceeded.

Revised time estimates

13.2 Where parties and their legal advisors consider that a time estimate that has been provided (e.g. at the CMC) is unrealistic, they have a duty to notify the new time estimate to the Chancery Listing Office or, where appropriate, the judge's clerk as soon as possible.

14. Documents and timetable

14.1 Bundling for the hearing of applications and trials is of considerable **2F–140** importance and should be approached intelligently. The general guidance given in Appendix 6 of the Chancery Guide should be followed. Solicitors or patent attorneys who fail to do so may be required to explain why and may be penalised personally in costs.

14.2 If it is known which judge will be taking the hearing, papers for the hearing should be lodged directly with that judge's clerk. If there is insufficient time to lodge hard copies before the deadline, faxed documents of significance (and particularly skeleton arguments) should be supplied, followed up by clean hard copies. Alternatively to faxing documents, by agreement, documents may be sent by e-mail to the clerk of the judge concerned.

14.3 It is the responsibility of both parties to ensure that all relevant documents are lodged with the clerk of the judge who will be taking the hearing by noon two days before the date fixed for hearing unless some longer or shorter period has been ordered by the judge or is prescribed by this guide.

14.4 The judges request that all important documents also be supplied to them on disk or via e-mail in a format convenient for the judge's use (normally the current or a recent version of Microsoft Word 2003 for Windows or as a text searchable pdf). These will usually include skeleton arguments, important patents and drawings, the witness statements and expert reports.

14.5 Prior to trial, parties should ensure that they comply with the requirements of 63PD.7 concerning the provision of a trial timetable, trial bundle and reading guide for the judge. The trial timetable should be detailed and set out the times and dates that witnesses will be required to give evidence.

14.6 Where a technical primer has been produced, the parties should identify those parts which are agreed to form part of the common general knowledge. Usually, this should be done shortly after exchange of expert reports but a reasonable time prior to trial.

14.7 [0]11Skeleton arguments should be lodged in time for the judge to read them before an application or trial.

    (a) In the case of applications, this should normally be 10:30am the previous working day (or, in the case of short timetable applications, 3pm)

Paragraph numbers marked with a "+" can be found online and on CD.

(b) In the case of trials, this should normally be at least two working days before commencement of the trial. In substantial cases, a longer period (to be discussed with the clerk to the judge concerned) may be needed.

14.8 14.8[0]11Following the evidence in a substantial trial, a short adjournment may be granted to enable the parties to summarise their arguments in writing before oral argument.

Transcripts

14.9 In trials where a transcript of evidence is being made and supplied to the judge, the transcript should be supplied by e-mail and in hard copy.

15. Telephone applications

2F-141

15.1 For short (20 minutes or less) matters, the judges of the Patents Court and Patents County Court are willing to hear applications by telephone conference in accordance with the Practice Direction under Part 23. The party making the application is responsible for setting up the telephone application and informing the parties, Counsels' clerks and Chancery Listing of the time of the conference call.

15.2 It is possible for the application to be recorded, and if recording by the court rather than by British Telecom (or other service provider) is requested, arrangements should be made with the Chancery Listing Officer. The recording will not be transcribed. The tape will be kept by the clerk to the judge hearing the application for a period of six months. Arrangements for transcription, if needed, must be made by the parties.

15.3 This procedure should be used where it will save costs.

Miscellaneous

16. Jurisdiction of Masters

2F-142

16.1 Masters have only a limited jurisdiction in patent matters (see 63PD.8). Generally it is more convenient for consent orders (on paper or in court) to be made by a judge even where a Master has jurisdiction to do so.

16.2 Where a Master makes a consent order disposing of an action which has been fixed, it is the duty of all the parties' representatives to inform the Chancery Listing Officer that the case has settled. Where the validity of the patent was in issue, the United Kingdom Intellectual Property Office ("UKIPO") should also be informed.

16.3 In the Patents County Court, all matters go to the appointed judge and not to a district judge. In many cases, such matters may be dealt with on paper.

NB Direction, dated 16th July 2008, from Mr Justice Kitchin, the Senior Judge of the Patents Court:

"Pursuant to paragraph 8.1(5) of the Practice Direction to CPR Part 63, I hereby direct that a Master or a Deputy Master may deal with an application by a non-party under CPR rule 5.4C for a copy of the Grounds of Invalidity annexed to a Statement of Case in which challenge is made to the validity of a patent or registered design."

17. Consent orders

2F-143

17.1 The court is normally willing to make consent orders without the need for the attendance of any parties. A draft of the agreed order and the written consent of all the parties' respective solicitors or counsel should be supplied to the Chancery Listing Office. Unless the judge considers a hearing is needed, he will make the order in the agreed terms by initialling it. It will be drawn up accordingly and sent to the parties.

17.2 In the Patents County Court, consent orders should be sent to the judge's clerk or to the Chancery Listing Office.

18. Draft judgments

2F-144

18.1 Many judgments, particularly after a full trial, will be reserved and handed down at a later date, as advised by the Chancery Listing Office. Prior to that, the practice has arisen to provide the parties' legal representatives (or litigants

Paragraph numbers marked with a "+" can be found online and on CD.

in person) with a copy of the draft judgment for advocates to notify the court of typographical and obvious errors (if any). The text may be shown, in confidence, to the parties, but only for the purpose of obtaining instructions and on the strict understanding that the judgment, or its effect, is not to be disclosed to any other person, or used in the public domain, and that no action is taken (other than internally) in response to the judgment. Reference is invited to 40EPD.1.

19. Orders following judgment

19.1 Where a judgment is made available in draft before being given in open court **2F–145** the parties should, in advance of that occasion, exchange drafts of the desired consequential order. It is highly undesirable that one party should spring a proposal on the other for the first time when judgment is handed down. Where the parties are agreed as to the consequential order and have supplied to the judge a copy of the same signed by all parties or their representatives, attendance at the handing down of the judgment is not necessary.

20. Appeals from the Comptroller-General of Patents, Designs and Trade Marks ("the Comptroller")

Patents
2F–146

20.1 By virtue of statute, these lie only to the High Court and not the Patents County Court. They are now governed by Part 52 (see Part 63.17). Permission to appeal is not required. Note that the Comptroller must be served with a Notice of Appeal (Part 63.17(3)). The appellant has the conduct of the appeal and he or his representative should, within 2 weeks of lodging the appeal, contact the Chancery Listing Officer with a view to arranging a hearing date. The appellant must ensure that the appeal is set down as soon as is reasonably practicable after service of the notice of appeal. Parties are reminded that the provisions about the service of skeleton arguments apply to appeals from the Comptroller.

Registered Designs

20.2 Appeals in registered designs cases go to the Registered Designs Appeal Tribunal. This consists of one of the patent judges sitting as a tribunal. The CPR and PD do not apply to such appeals. Where such an appeal is desired, contact should be made direct with the Chancery Listing Officer.

Trade Marks

20.3 These are assigned to the Chancery Division as a whole, not the Patents Court (Part 63.17(2)). Permission to appeal is not required.

Appeals on paper only

20.4 The court will hear appeals on paper only if that is what the parties desire. If the appellant is willing for the appeal to be heard on paper only, he should contact the respondent and UKIPO at the earliest opportunity to discover whether such a way of proceeding is agreed. If it is, the Chancery Listing Office should be informed as soon as possible. The parties (and the Chancery Listing Officer if he/she desires) should liaise amongst themselves for early preparation of written submissions and bundles and provide the court with all necessary materials.

Specimen minute of order for directions

A draft order is annexed below covering most normal eventualities. The directions **2F–147** are intended only as a guide and are not "standard directions". Not all paragraphs will be applicable in every case.

Form of order for directions

AND UPON the parties' legal advisors having advised the litigants of the existence **2F–148** of mediation as a possible means of resolving this claim and counterclaim

Transfer

1. [This claim and counterclaim be transferred to the Patents County Court.] (If this order is made, no other order will generally be necessary, though it will generally be

Paragraph numbers marked with a "+" can be found online and on CD.

INTELLECTUAL PROPERTY

desirable for procedural orders to be made at this time to save the costs of a further conference in the Patents County Court.)

Amendments to statements of case

2. The claimants have permission to amend their claim form shown in red on the copy [annexed to the application notice/as signed by the solicitors for the parties/annexed hereto] and [to re-serve the same on or before [date]/and that re-service be dispensed with] and that the defendants have permission to serve a consequentially amended defence within [number] days [thereafter/hereafter] and that the claimants have permission to serve a consequentially amended reply (if so advised) within [number] days thereafter.

3. (a) The defendants have permission to amend their defence and counterclaim [and grounds of invalidity] as shown in red on the copy [annexed to the application notice/as signed by the solicitors for the parties/annexed hereto] and [to re-serve the same within [number] days/on or before[date]] [and that re-service be dispensed with] and that the claimants have permission to serve a consequentially amended reply (if so advised) within [number] days thereafter.

   [(b) The claimants do on or before [date] elect whether they will discontinue this claim and withdraw their defence to the amended counterclaim and consent to an order for the revocation of Patent No. . . . . . . ("the Patent") AND IF the claimants shall so elect and give notice thereof in the time aforesaid:

      (i) the Patent be revoked;

      (ii) the claimants shall pay the defendant's costs of the claim and counterclaim incurred up to and including [. . . . .] (date of service of original defence and counterclaim) which shall include the costs of obtaining and giving effect to the order for revocation; and

      (iii) the defendants shall pay the claimants' costs of the claim and counterclaim incurred thereafter.]

   (c) The defendants' [claimants'] costs of and caused by the amendments to the claim form [particulars of claim] [defence and counterclaim] [reply] be the defendants [claimants] in any event.

Further Information and Clarification

5. (a) The [claimants/defendants] do on or before [date] serve on the [defendants/claimants] the further information or clarification of the [specify statement of case] as requested by the [claimants/defendants] by their request served on the [defendants/claimants] on [date] [and/or]

   (b) The [claimants/defendants] do on or before [date] serve on the [defendants/claimants] [a response to their request for further information] [do answer the requests in their request for further information] or clarification of the [identify statement of case] served on the [defendants/claimants] on [date].

Admissions

6. The [claimants/defendants] do on or before [date] state in writing whether or not they admit the facts specified in the [defendants'/claimants'] notice to admit facts dated [date].

Security

7. The claimants/defendants do provide security for the defendants'/claimants' costs for its claim/counterclaim in the sum of £[state sum] by [paying such sums into court] [specify manner in which security to be given] and that:

      (i) in the meantime the claim [counterclaim] be stayed [and/or];

      (ii) unless security is given as ordered by the above date, the claim [counterclaim] be struck out without further order with the defendants'/claimants' costs of the claim [counterclaim] to be the subject of detailed assessment if not agreed.

Lists of Documents

8. (a) The claimants and the defendants respectively do on or before [state date] make and serve on the other of them a list in accordance with form N265 of

Paragraph numbers marked with a "+" can be found online and on CD.

the documents in their possession custody or control which they are required to disclose in accordance with the obligation of standard disclosure in accordance with Part 31 as modified by paragraph 5 of the Practice Direction - Patents etc. supplementing Part 63.

(b) In respect of those issues identified in Schedule [number] hereto disclosure shall be limited to those [documents/categories of documents] listed in Schedule [number].

Inspection

9. If any party wishes to inspect or have copies of such documents as are in another party's control, it shall give notice in writing that it wishes to do so and such inspection shall be allowed at all reasonable times upon reasonable notice and any copies shall be provided within [number] working days of the request upon the undertaking of the party requesting the copies to pay the reasonable copying charges.

Experiments

10. (a) Where a party desires to establish any fact by experimental proof, including an experiment conducted for the purposes of litigation or otherwise not being an experiment conducted in the normal course of research, that party shall on or before [date] serve on all the other parties a notice stating the facts which it desires to establish and giving full particulars of the experiments proposed to establish them.

(b) A party upon whom a notice is served under the preceding sub-paragraph shall within [number] days, serve on the party serving the notice a notice stating in respect of each fact whether or not that party admits it.

(c) Where any fact which a party wishes to establish by experimental proof is not admitted that party shall apply to the court for further directions in respect of such experiments.

[Or where paragraph 9 of the Practice Direction - Patents etc. supplementing CPR Part 63 has been complied with.]

11. (a) The claimants/defendants are to afford to the other parties an opportunity, if so requested, of inspecting a repetition of the experiments identified in paragraphs [specify them] of the notice[s] of experiments served on [date]. Any such inspection must be requested within [number] days of the date of this order and shall take place within [number] days of the date of the request.

(b) If any party shall wish to establish any fact in reply to experimental proof that party shall on or before [date] serve on all the other parties a notice stating the facts which it desires to establish and giving full particulars of the experiments proposed to establish them.

(c) A party upon whom a notice is served under the preceding sub-paragraph shall within [number] days serve on the party serving the notice a notice stating in respect of each fact whether or not that party admits it.

(d) Where any fact which a party wishes to establish by experimental proof in reply is not admitted the party may apply to the court for further directions in respect of such experiments.

Notice of Models, etc.

12. (a) If any party wishes to rely at the trial of this claim and counterclaim upon any model or apparatus, that party shall on or before [date] give notice thereof to all the other parties; shall afford the other parties an opportunity within [number] days of the service of such notice of inspecting the same and shall, if so requested, furnish the other party with copies or illustrations of such model or apparatus.

(b) No further or other model or apparatus shall be relied upon in evidence by either party save with consent or by permission of the court.

Product or Process Description

13. (a) The defendants/claimants do provide a written description together with relevant drawings of the following [product(s)] [process(es)] to the claimants/defendants by [. , ..].

i. [description of product or process];

Paragraph numbers marked with a "+" can be found online and on CD.

    ii. [description of product or process]; etc.

(b) The description served under paragraph (a) shall be accompanied by a signed written statement which shall:

    (i) state that the person making the statement is personally acquainted with the facts to which the description relates;

    (ii) verify that the description is a true and complete description of the product or process; and

    (iii) contain an acknowledgement by the person making the statement that he may be required to attend court in order to be cross-examined on the contents of the description.

Technical Primer

14. The parties shall use their best endeavours to agree on or before [date] a single technical primer setting out the basic undisputed technology and shall on or before [date] indicate which parts of the technical primer are agreed to form part of the common general knowledge.

Scientific Adviser

15. A.B is appointed a scientific adviser to assist the court in this claim and counterclaim, his/her costs to be met in the first instance in equal shares by the parties and to be costs in the claim and counterclaim, subject to any other order of the trial judge.

Written Evidence

16.(a) Each party shall on or before [date] serve on the other parties [signed] written statements of the oral evidence which the party intends to lead on any issues of fact to be decided at the trial, such statements to stand as the evidence in chief of the witness unless the court otherwise directs;

(b) Each party shall on or before [date] serve on the other parties [signed] written statements of the oral evidence which it intends to lead at trial in answer to facts and matters raised in the witness statements served on it under paragraph (a) and (b) above;

(c) Each party may call up to [number] expert witnesses in this claim and counterclaim provided that the said party:

    (i) supplies the name of such expert to the other parties and to the court on or before [date]; and

    (ii) no later than [date/[number days] before the date set for the hearing of this claim and counterclaim] serve upon the other parties a report of each such expert comprising the evidence which that expert intends to give at trial.

[(d) The claimant shall, with the cooperation of the other parties, arrange for the experts to meet on or before [date] to determine on what issues they agree and on what they disagree and the experts shall before [date] file a report stating where they agree and where they disagree and in the latter case, their reasons for disagreeing].

Admissibility of Evidence

17. A party who objects to any statements of any witness being read by the judge prior to the hearing of the trial, shall serve upon each other party a notice in writing to that effect setting out the grounds of the objection.

Non-Compliance

18. Where either party fails to comply with the directions relating to experiments and written evidence it shall not be entitled to adduce evidence to which such directions relate without the permission of the court.

Trial Bundles

19. Each party shall no later than [28] days before the date fixed for the trial of this claim and counterclaim serve upon the other parties a list of all the documents to be

Paragraph numbers marked with a "+" can be found online and on CD.

2G   COMPANIES ACT PROCEEDINGS

Companies Act 2006

(2006 c.46)

ARRANGEMENT OF SECTIONS

Derivative claims

260.—(1) This Chapter applies to proceedings in England and
Wales or Northern Ireland by a member of a company—

    (a) in respect of a cause of action vested in the company,
       and

    (b) seeking relief on behalf of the company. This is referred
       to in this Chapter as a "derivative claim".

(2) A derivative claim may only be brought—

    (a) under this Chapter, or

    (b) in pursuance of an order of the court in proceedings
       under section 994 (proceedings for protection of
       members against unfair prejudice).

(3) A derivative claim under this Chapter may be brought only in
respect of a cause of action arising from an actual or proposed act or
omission involving negligence, default, breach of duty or breach of
trust by a director of the company.

The cause of action may be against the director or another person
(or both).

(4) It is immaterial whether the cause of action arose before or after the person seeking to bring or continue the derivative claim
became a member of the company.

(5) For the purposes of this Chapter—

    (a) "director" includes a former director;

    (b) a shadow director is treated as a director; and

    (c) references to a member of a company include a person
       who is not a member but to whom shares in the company
       have been transferred or transmitted by operation of
       law.

Application for permission to continue derivative claim

261.—(1) A member of a company who brings a derivative claim
under this Chapter must apply to the court for permission (in
Northern Ireland, leave) to continue it.

(2) If it appears to the court that the application and the evidence

Paragraph numbers marked with a "+" can be found online and on CD.

filed by the applicant in support of it do not disclose a prima facie case for giving permission (or leave), the court—

    (a) must dismiss the application, and

    (b) may make any consequential order it considers appropriate.

(3) If the application is not dismissed under subsection (2), the court—

    (a) may give directions as to the evidence to be provided by the company, and

    (b) may adjourn the proceedings to enable the evidence to be obtained.

(4) On hearing the application, the court may—

    (a) give permission (or leave) to continue the claim on such terms as it thinks fit,

    (b) refuse permission (or leave) and dismiss the claim, or

    (c) adjourn the proceedings on the application and give such directions as it thinks fit.

Application for permission to continue claim as a derivative claim

2G–4   **262.**—(1) This section applies where—

    (a) a company has brought a claim, and

    (b) the cause of action on which the claim is based could be pursued as a derivative claim under this Chapter.

(2) A member of the company may apply to the court for permission (in Northern Ireland, leave) to continue the claim as a derivative claim on the ground that—

    (a) the manner in which the company commenced or continued the claim amounts to an abuse of the process of the court,

    (b) the company has failed to prosecute the claim diligently, and

    (c) it is appropriate for the member to continue the claim as a derivative claim.

(3) If it appears to the court that the application and the evidence filed by the applicant in support of it do not disclose a prima facie case for giving permission (or leave), the court—

    (a) must dismiss the application, and

    (b) may make any consequential order it considers appropriate.

(4) If the application is not dismissed under subsection (3), the court—

    (a) may give directions as to the evidence to be provided by the company, and

    (b) may adjourn the proceedings to enable the evidence to be obtained.

(5) On hearing the application, the court may—

    (a) give permission (or leave) to continue the claim as a derivative claim on such terms as it thinks fit,

Paragraph numbers marked with a "+" can be found online and on CD.

(b) refuse permission (or leave) and dismiss the application, or

(c) adjourn the proceedings on the application and give such directions as it thinks fit.

Whether permission to be given

263.—(1) The following provisions have effect where a member of a company applies for permission (in Northern Ireland, leave) under section 261 or 262.

2G–5

(2) Permission (or leave) must be refused if the court is satisfied—

(a) that a person acting in accordance with section 172 (duty to promote the success of the company) would not seek to continue the claim, or

(b) where the cause of action arises from an act or omission that is yet to occur, that the act or omission has been authorised by the company, or

(c) where the cause of action arises from an act or omission that has already occurred, that the act or omission—

(i) was authorised by the company before it occurred, or

(ii) has been ratified by the company since it occurred.

(3) In considering whether to give permission (or leave) the court must take into account, in particular—

(a) whether the member is acting in good faith in seeking to continue the claim;

(b) the importance that a person acting in accordance with section 172 (duty to promote the success of the company) would attach to continuing it;

(c) where the cause of action results from an act or omission that is yet to occur, whether the act or omission could be, and in the circumstances would be likely to be—

(i) authorised by the company before it occurs, or

(ii) ratified by the company after it occurs;

(d) where the cause of action arises from an act or omission that has already occurred, whether the act or omission could be, and in the circumstances would be likely to be, ratified by the company;

(e) whether the company has decided not to pursue the claim;

(f) whether the act or omission in respect of which the claim is brought gives rise to a cause of action that the member could pursue in his own right rather than on behalf of the company.

(4) In considering whether to give permission (or leave) the court shall have particular regard to any evidence before it as to the views of members of the company who have no personal interest, direct or indirect, in the matter.

(5) The Secretary of State may by regulations—

Paragraph numbers marked with a "+" can be found online and on CD.

    (a) amend subsection (2) so as to alter or add to the circumstances in which permission (or leave) is to be refused;

    (b) amend subsection (3) so as to alter or add to the matters that the court is required to take into account in considering whether to give permission (or leave).

(6) Before making any such regulations the Secretary of State shall consult such persons as he considers appropriate.

(7) Regulations under this section are subject to affirmative resolution procedure.

Application for permission to continue derivative claim brought by another member

2G–6   **264.**—(1) This section applies where a member of a company ("the claimant")—

    (a) has brought a derivative claim,

    (b) has continued as a derivative claim a claim brought by the company, or

    (c) has continued a derivative claim under this section.

(2) Another member of the company ("the applicant") may apply to the court for permission (in Northern Ireland, leave) to continue the claim on the ground that—

    (a) the manner in which the proceedings have been commenced or continued by the claimant amounts to an abuse of the process of the court,

    (b) the claimant has failed to prosecute the claim diligently, and

    (c) it is appropriate for the applicant to continue the claim as a derivative claim.

(3) If it appears to the court that the application and the evidence filed by the applicant in support of it do not disclose a prima facie case for giving permission (or leave), the court—

    (a) must dismiss the application, and

    (b) may make any consequential order it considers appropriate.

(4) If the application is not dismissed under subsection (3), the court—

    (a) may give directions as to the evidence to be provided by the company, and

    (b) may adjourn the proceedings to enable the evidence to be obtained.

(5) On hearing the application, the court may—

    (a) give permission (or leave) to continue the claim on such terms as it thinks fit,

    (b) refuse permission (or leave) and dismiss the application, or

    (c) adjourn the proceedings on the application and give such directions as it thinks fit.

Paragraph numbers marked with a "+" can be found online and on CD.

Note—The court procedure relating to the conduct of derivative claims is set out in **2G–6.1**
Pt 19.9 of the Civil Procedure Rules. A full commentary can be found in Vol.1 under
that rule.

PRACTICE DIRECTION—APPLICATIONS UNDER THE COMPANIES ACTS AND RELATED LEGISLATION

This Practice Direction supplements CPR Part 49   **2G–7**

Section I.

General

Definitions
  1. In this practice direction—
    'the 1985 Act' means the Companies Act 1985[1];
    'the 2006 Act' means the Companies Act 2006[2];
    'the CJPA' means the Criminal Justice and Police Act 2001[3];
    'the EC Regulation' means Council Regulation (EC) No. 2157/
        2001 of 8 October 2001 on the Statute for a European
        Company (SE);
    'Part VII FSMA' means Part VII of the Financial Services and
        Markets Act 2000[4];
    "the Cross-Border Mergers Regulations" means the Companies
        (Cross-Border Mergers) Regulations 2007.[5]

Application of this practice direction
  2. This practice direction applies to proceedings under—   **2G–8**
  (a)   the 1985 Act;
  (b)   the 2006 Act (except proceedings under Chapter 1 of Part
         11 or Part 30 of that Act);
  (c)   section 59 of the CJPA;
  (d)   Articles 22, 25 and 26 of the EC Regulation;
  (e)   Part VII FSMA; and
  (f)   the Cross-Border Mergers Regulations.

  (Part 19 and the practice direction supplementing Part 19 contain
provisions about proceedings under Chapter 1 of Part 11 of the 2006
Act (derivative claims)).

Application of this practice direction to certain proceedings in relation to limited liability partnerships
  3. This practice direction applies to proceedings under the 1985   **2G–9**
Act in relation to a limited liability partnership as if it were a
company.

Title of documents
  4.(1) The claim form in proceedings under the 1985 Act, the   **2G–10**

---

[1] 1985 c.6.
[2] 2006 c.46.
[3] 2001 c.16.
[4] 2000 c.8.
[5] S. 2007/2974.

Paragraph numbers marked with a "+" can be found online and on CD.

2006 Act, Part VII FSMA, the EC Regulation or the Cross-Border Mergers Regulations, and any application, affidavit, witness statement, notice or other document in such proceedings, must be entitled "In the matter of [*the name of the company in question*] and in the matter of [*the relevant law*]", where "[*the relevant law*]" means "the Companies Act 1985", "the Companies Act 2006", "Part VII of the Financial Services and Markets Act 2000", "Council Regulation (EC) No 2157/2001 of 8 October 2001 on the Statute for a European Company (SE)" or "the Companies (Cross-Border Mergers) Regulations 2007", as the case may be.

(2) Where a company changes its name in the course of proceedings, the title must be altered by—
(a) substituting the new name for the old; and
(b) inserting the old name in brackets at the end of the title.

(3) Where this practice direction requires a party to proceedings to notify another person of an application, such notification must be given by sending to that other person a copy of the claim form as soon as reasonably practicable after the claim form has been issued.

Starting proceedings and notification of application made

2G–11   **5.**(1) Proceedings to which this practice direction applies must be started by a Part 8 claim form—
(a) unless a provision of this or another practice direction provides otherwise, but
(b) subject to any modification of that procedure by this or any other practice direction.

(2) The claim form—
(a) will, where issued in the High Court, be issued out of the Companies Court or a Chancery district registry; or
(b) will, where issued in a county court, be issued out of a county court office.

(3) Where this practice direction requires a party to proceedings to notify another person of an application, such notification must, unless the court orders otherwise, be given by sending to that other person a copy of the claim form as soon as reasonably practicable after the claim form has been issued.

Section II.

Particular applications under the 1985 Act

Applications under section 721 of the 1985 Act (Production and inspection of books where offence suspected)

2G–12   **6.**(1) This paragraph applies to an application for an order under section 721 of the 1985 Act.

(2) No notice need be given to any person against whom the order is sought.

Paragraph numbers marked with a "+" can be found online and on CD.

Applications to sanction a compromise or arrangement

7.(1) This paragraph applies to an application for an order, under **2G–13** Part XIII of the 1985 Act, to sanction a compromise or arrangement.

(2) Where the application is made by the company concerned, or by a liquidator or administrator of the company, there need be no defendant to the claim unless the court so orders.

(3) The claim form must be supported by written evidence including—

(a) statutory information about the company; and

(b) the terms of the proposed compromise or arrangement.

(4) The claim form must seek—

(a) directions for convening a meeting of creditors or members or both, as the case requires;

(b) the sanction of the court to the compromise or arrangement, if it is approved at the meeting or meetings, and a direction for a further hearing for that purpose; and

(c) a direction that the claimant files a copy of a report to the court by the chairman of the meeting or of each meeting.

Section III.

Particular applications under the 2006 Act

References to provisions of the 2006 Act in this Section

8. In this Section, a reference to a section by number, not otherwise **2G–14** identified, is to the section so numbered in the 2006 Act.

Company generally to be made a party to a claim under the 2006 Act

9.(1) Where in a claim under the 2006 Act the company con- **2G–15** cerned is not the claimant, the company is to be made a defendant to the claim unless—

(a) any other enactment, the CPR or this or another practice direction makes a different provision; or

(b) the court orders otherwise.

(2) Where an application is made in the course of proceedings to which the company is or is required to be a defendant, the company must be made a respondent to the application unless—

(a) any other enactment, the CPR or this or another practice direction makes a different provision; or

(b) the court orders otherwise.

Applications under section 169 (Director's right to protest against removal)

10.(1) This paragraph applies to an application for an order under **2G–16** section 169(5).

Paragraph numbers marked with a "+" can be found online and on CD.

COMPANIES ACT

(2)   The claimant must notify the director concerned of the application.

Applications under section 295 (Application not to circulate members' statement) or section 317 (Application not to circulate members' statement)

2G–17   **11.**(1) This paragraph applies to an application for an order under section 295 or 317.

(2)   The claimant must notify each member who requested the circulation of the relevant statement of the application.

Proceedings under section 370 (Unauthorised donations—enforcement of directors' liabilities by shareholder action)

2G–18   **12.** Proceedings to enforce a director's liability under section 370 must be started by a Part 7 claim form.

Proceedings under section 456 (Application in respect of defective accounts or directors' report)

2G–19   **12A.**(1) This paragraph applies to an application for a declaration under section 456(1).

(2)   The claimant must notify any former director who was a director at the time of the approval of the annual accounts or directors' report of the application.

Proceedings under section 511, 514, 515, 518 or 520 (Representations or statements made by the auditor

2G–20   **12B.**(1) This paragraph applies to an application for an order under section 511(6), 514(7), 515(7), 518(9) or 520(2).

(2)   The claimant must notify the auditor of the application.

Proceedings under section 527 (Members' powers to require website publication of audit concerns)

2G–21   **12C.**(1) This paragraph applies to an application for an order under section 527(5).

(2)   The claimant must, unless the court orders otherwise, notify each member who requested a statement to be placed on the website of the application.

Proceedings under Parts 26 and 27 of the 2006 Act (Applications to sanction a compromise or arrangement)

2G–22   **12D.**(1) This paragraph applies to an application for an order under Parts 26 and 27 of the 2006 Act to sanction a compromise or arrangement.

(2)   Where the application is made by the company concerned, or by a liquidator or administrator of the company, there need be no defendant to the claim unless the court so orders.

(3)   The claim form must be supported by written evidence, including—

(a) statutory information about the company; and

Paragraph numbers marked with a "+" can be found online and on CD.

      (b) the terms of the proposed compromise or arrangement.

(4)   The claim form must seek—

      (a) directions for convening a meeting of creditors or members or both, as the case requires;

      (b) the sanction of the court to the compromise or arrangement, if it is approved at the meeting or meetings, and a direction for a further hearing for that purpose; and

      (c) a direction that the claimant files a copy of a report to the court by the chairman of the meeting or of each meeting.

Proceedings under section 955 (Takeovers—enforcement by the court)

13. Proceedings for an order under section 955 must be started by a Part 7 claim form.   **2G–23**

Proceedings under section 968 (Takeovers—effect on contractual restrictions)

14. Proceedings to recover compensation under section 968(6) must be started by a Part 7 claim form.   **2G–24**

Applications under section 1132 (Production and inspection of documents where offence suspected)

15.(1) This paragraph applies to an application for an order under section 1132.   **2G–25**

(2)   No notice need be given to any person against whom the order is sought.

Section IV.

Other applications

Applications under the EC Regulation—Article 25

16.(1) In this paragraph and paragraphs 16A and 17—   **2G–26**

      (a) a reference to an Article by number is a reference to the Article so numbered in the EC Regulation; and

      (b) 'SE' means a European public limited-liability company (Societas Europaea) within the meaning of the EC Regulation.

(1A)   Any document that is filed with the court must, if not in English, be accompanied by a translation of that document into English—

      (i) certified by a notary public or other qualified person; or

      (ii) accompanied by written evidence confirming that the translation is accurate.

(2)   An application for a certificate under Article 25(2)—

      (a) must set out the pre-merger acts and formalities applicable to the applicant company;

Paragraph numbers marked with a "+" can be found online and on CD.

(b) must be accompanied by evidence that those acts and formalities have been completed; and

(c) must be accompanied by copies of:

  (i) the draft terms of merger, as provided for in Article 20;

  (ii) the entry in the London Gazette containing the particulars specified in Article 21;

  (iii) a directors' report;

  (iv) an expert's report; and

  (v) the resolution of the applicant company approving the draft terms of merger in accordance with Article 23.

(3) In paragraph (2)(c)—

"directors' report" in relation to a company means a report by the directors of the company containing the information required by paragraph 4 of Schedule 15B to the 1985 Act or section 908 of the 2006 Act, as appropriate;;

"expert's report" in relation to a company means a report to the members of the company drawn up in accordance with—

  (a) paragraph 5 of Schedule 15B to the 1985 Act or section 909 of the 2006 Act, as appropriate; or

  (b) Article 22.

(4) There need be no defendant to the application.

Applications under the EC Regulation—Article 22 (appointment of an independent expert)

2G–27   16A.(1) An application under Article 22 for the appointment of an independent expert must be made—

  (a) where the application is made at the same time as or after the application under Article 25(2) for approval of the pre-merger acts and formalities has been filed with the court, by application notice pursuant to Part 23; or

  (b) where no application under Article 25(2) has been made, by a Part 8 claim form.

(2)   The application (whether by a claim form or application notice, as the case may be) must be accompanied by evidence in support of the application.

Applications under the EC Regulation—Article 26

2G–28   17.(1) Where under Article 26(2) a merging company is required to submit a certificate to the High Court, that company must, if no other merging company has begun proceedings under Article 26, begin such proceedings by issuing a Part 8 claim form.

(2)   There need be no defendant to the claim.

(3)   The claim form—

  (a) must name the SE and all of the merging companies;

Paragraph numbers marked with a "+" can be found online and on CD.

    (b) must be accompanied by the documents referred to in sub-paragraph (5); and

    (c) must be served on each of the other merging companies.

(4)   Where under Article 26(2) a merging company is required to submit a certificate to the High Court, and proceedings under Article 26 have already been begun, the company—

    (a) must, not more than 14 days after service on it of the claim form, file an acknowledgment of service and serve it on each of the other merging companies; and

    (b) must file the documents, in relation to each merging company, referred to in sub-paragraph (5) within the time limit specified in Article 26(2), and serve copies of them on each of the other merging companies.

(5)   The documents in relation to each merging company are—

    (a) the certificate issued under Article 25(2) in respect of the company;

    (b) a copy of the draft terms of merger approved by the company;

    (c) evidence that arrangements for employee involvement have been determined by the company pursuant to Council Directive 2001/86/EC of 8 October 2001 supplementing the Statute for a European company with regard to the involvement of employees; and

    (d) evidence that the SE has been formed in accordance with Article 26(4).

Applications under the Cross-Border Mergers Regulations

17A.(1) In this paragraph and paragraphs 17B to 17D a reference   **2G–29** to a regulation by number is a reference to the regulation so numbered in the Cross-Border Mergers Regulations.

(2)   Any document that is filed with the court must, if not in English, be accompanied by a translation of that document into English—

    (i) certified by a notary public or other qualified person; or

    (ii) accompanied by written evidence confirming that the translation is accurate.

Application for approval of pre-merger requirements

17B.(1) This paragraph applies to an application under regulation   **2G–30** 6.

(2)   There need be no defendant to the application.

(3)   The application must—

    (a) set out the pre-merger acts and formalities required by regulations 7 to 10 and 12 to 15 applicable to the applicant company; and

    (b) be accompanied by evidence that those acts and formalities have been completed properly.

(4)   Where an application under regulation 11 to summon a meeting of creditors has been made, the court will not

Paragraph numbers marked with a "+" can be found online and on CD.

determine the application under regulation 6 to approve the pre-merger requirements until the result of the meeting is known.

(5) Where the court makes an order certifying that all pre-merger acts and formalities have been completed properly, the applicant must draw up the order and file it no later than 7 days after the date on which the order was made so that it can be sealedGL by the court. The court will sealGL and return the order to the applicant within 15 days of receipt.

Application for appointment of independent expert or to summon a meeting of members or creditors

2G–31   17C.(1) This paragraph applies to—

(a) an application for the appointment of an independent expert under regulation 9;

(b) an application under regulation 11 for an order to summon a meeting of members or creditors or both.

(2) The application must be made—

(a) where the application is made at the same time as or after the application for approval of the pre-merger acts and formalities under regulation 6 has been filed with the court, by application notice pursuant to Part 23; or

(b) where no application under regulation 6 has been made, by a Part 8 claim form.

(3) The application (whether by a claim form or application notice, as the case may be) must be accompanied by evidence in support of the application.

Application for the approval of the completion of the merger

2G–32   17D.(1) This paragraph applies to an application under regulation 16.

(2) The application must be made by a Part 8 claim form.

(3) There need be no defendant to the application.

(4) The claim form must be accompanied by—

(a) the documents referred to in regulation 16(1)(b), (c) and (e);

(b) where appropriate, evidence that regulation 16(1)(f) has been complied with; and

(c) such other evidence as may be required to enable the court to decide the application.

(5) Where the court makes an order under regulation 16 approving the completion of the merger, it will fix a date on which the consequences of the merger are to take effect.

Applications under section 59 of the CJPA

2G–33   18.(1) In sub-paragraphs (2) to (8)—

(a) a reference to a section by number, not otherwise identi-

Paragraph numbers marked with a "+" can be found online and on CD.

fied, is a reference to the section so numbered in the CJPA; and

(b) references to a relevant interest in property have the same meaning as in section 59 of the CJPA.

(2) This paragraph applies to applications under section 59 in respect of property seized in exercise of the power conferred by section 448(3) of the 1985 Act (including any additional powers of seizure conferred by section 50 that are exercisable by reference to that power).

(3) The application must be supported by evidence—

(a) that the claimant has a relevant interest in the property to which the application relates; and

(b) in the case of an application under section 59(2), that one or more of the grounds set out in section 59(3) is satisfied in relation to the property.

(c) must be served on each of the other merging companies.

(4) Where the claimant has a relevant interest in the property, the defendants to the claim are to be—

(a) the person in possession of the property; and

(b) any other person who appears to have a relevant interest in the property.

(5) Where the claimant is in possession of the property, the defendants are to be—

(a) the person from whom the property was seized; and

(b) any other person who appears to have a relevant interest in the property.

(6) In the case of an application for the return of seized property, the claimant must serve a copy of the claim form and the claimant's evidence in support of it on the person specified, by the notice given under section 52 when the property was seized, as the person to whom notice of such an application should be given.

(7) If the claimant knows the identity of the person who seized the property, the claimant must also notify that person of the application.

(8) When the court issues the claim form it will fix a date for the hearing.

Section V.

Conduct of proceedings

Reduction of capital—evidence

19. In the case of an application to confirm a reduction in capital, **2G–34** if any shares were issued otherwise than for cash—

(a) for any shares so issued on or after 1st January 1901, it is sufficient to set out in the application the extent to which the shares are, or are treated as being, paid up; and

(b) for any shares so issued between 1st September 1867 and

Paragraph numbers marked with a "+" can be found online and on CD.

31st December 1900, the application must also show that the requirement as to the filing of the relevant contract with the Registrar of Joint Stock Companies in section 25 of the Companies Act 1867 [1] was complied with.

Section VI.

Miscellaneous

Service of documents

2G-35 **20.** The parties are responsible for service of documents in proceedings to which this practice direction applies.

Transitional provisions

2G-36 **21.** A claim started, or an application made, before 1st October 2007 may be continued in accordance with the practice direction in force on 30th September 2007 as if it had not been revoked.

Introduction

2G-37 The Practice Direction came into force on October 1, 2007.

Although not expressly stated to be the case (see para.2) it would appear that the Practice Direction supersedes all previous directions relating to applications under the Companies Acts and related legislation, the related legislation being that referred to in paras 1 and 2. Note, however, that para.5 explicitly refers to other Practice Directions and the transitional provisions made by para.21.

Companies Act 2006

2G-38 The Practice Direction appears to have been prompted by the Companies Act 2006 which received the royal assent on November 8, 2006 when a limited number of provisions came into force. Section 1300 of the Act provides for the remaining provisions to be brought into force by commencement orders.

Companies Court

2G-39 Applications under the legislation covered by the Practice Direction should be made to the Companies Court.

Companies Court is not a separate and distinct part of the High Court but is a descriptive term given to the part of the Chancery Division of the High Court which deals with cases which are generally commenced before the bankruptcy registrar sitting in Companies Court from time to time, or in the case of a District registry the district judge sitting in the equivalent capacity (*Re Shilena Hosiery Co Ltd* [1980] Ch. 219).

Commencing proceedings

2G-40 Proceedings should be commenced by Pt.8 claim form unless provision is made to the contrary (para.5). However, the use of petitions is still envisaged, e.g. in the case of proceedings under s.994 Companies Act 2006.

Issuing proceedings

2G-41 All applications and proceedings under the legislation covered by the Practice Direction are listed for directions or determination before the registrar (or district judge in a District Registry) save for applications for injunctions. The majority of cases are heard and finally determined by the registrar. The following are always heard and tried by the judge: final hearings of applications to sanction a scheme of arrangement under the Companies Acts or the Financial Services and Markets Act 2000; petitions under s.994 Companies Act 2006; applications for injunctions.

---

[1] 30 & 31 Vict. c.131.

Paragraph numbers marked with a "+" can be found online and on CD.

Urgent applications

Urgent applications estimated to last no more than 15 minutes may be listed by arrangement with the Companies Court clerks to be heard by the registrar at 10.15am. In addition, with effect from October 1, 2007 a duty registrar (covering both bankruptcy and companies work) will be available at 2pm each Wednesday during term to hear urgent applications or other applications of a time critical nature (e.g. applications for a debarring order where there is urgency). Parties asking for an application to be dealt with in the duty registrar's list should arrange for the court file and the application to be put before the duty registrar who will decide whether the application merits inclusion in the list. To enable the registrar to make that decision the application should be accompanied by a note signed by the solicitor with conduct of the application or counsel stating the nature of the application and why it is urgent or time critical. See para.3E–22.

2G–42

Schemes, reductions and similar proceedings

Arrangements for hearings of schemes and reductions (as well as those under the Financial Services and Markets Act 2000 and the Cross-Border Mergers Regulations 2007) in the Royal Courts of Justice should be made with the Companies Court case manager, Room TM 205 of the Thomas More Building, to whom inquiries may also be made by telephone (020 7947 6727). Papers should be lodged in TM 205 *at least* five working days before the hearing.

2G–43

A claim form must now be used in place of a petition. It should contain the information which would previously have been set out in a petition including the date of incorporation of the company, the company number, the name of the company and any change, the situation of the registered office, the objects, capital history, relevant provisions in the articles of association, relevant share rights, details of the necessary special resolution, the purpose of the reduction and the form of the minute. The relief sought should include an order dealing with any enquiry as to creditors and directions for the first advertisement (which is most conveniently put in the first paragraph of the relief sought).

On issue of the claim form the court will endorse it with the time and date of the first hearing before the registrar. At the first hearing the court will deal with any enquiry as to creditors and advertisement and adjourn the matter to be heard by the registrar in open court at a subsequent date which should have been agreed in advance with the court case manager.

No application notice is now required. The claim will be adjourned after each hearing until the final order is made.

Schemes of arrangement

A claim form must now be used in place of a petition. As not all the information required by the court for the final hearing will be available at the time of issue of the claim form a short form of claim will be accepted seeking an order convening the necessary meeting(s), directions in relation thereto, an order requiring the chairman to report the result of the meeting(s) to the court and sanction of the scheme at the final hearing before the judge. The claim form should also set out the directions sought as regards creditors where the scheme involves a reduction. A copy of the latest print of the scheme should be annexed to the claim form. The directions hearing is listed before the registrar.

2G–44

As the claim form will no longer contain all the matters which would otherwise have been contained in a petition (details of the company and its capital history and so on), those matters should be set out in the evidence. The evidence filed for the final hearing before the judge should explain any differences between the scheme annexed to the claim form and that in respect of which the final order is sought. The evidence must also include the chairman's report of the result of the meeting(s).

As in the case of reductions no application notice is now required. The claim will be adjourned after each hearing until the final order is made.

Applications to extend time for registering a charge or to rectify an omission or mis-statement (s.404)

The relevant provisions are to be found in s.404 of the Companies Act 1985 (s.873 of the Companies Act 2006).

2G–45

Paragraph numbers marked with a "+" can be found online and on CD.

COMPANIES ACT

Section 404 enables a party to apply for relief from the consequences of failing to register on time and omissions or misstatements in a memorandum of satisfaction to be rectified under s.403. The provisions as to registration are set out in ss.395–403 and 409.

The claim form should identify the charge in relation to which relief is sought and indicate the section of the Act under which the obligations to register arose (s.395 or s.400). The company will generally be the claimant in which case no other party need be joined in the proceedings or given notice. If the claimant is a party other than the company the company should be made a defendant and served with the proceedings.

The claim should be supported by evidence as to the circumstances under which the documents in question were not registered, setting out in detail the sequence of events surrounding the default. It must show that the omission to register (or misstatement of any particulars) was (a) accidental or (b) due to inadvertence (the nature of the inadvertence being set out) or (c) some other sufficient cause or (d) is not of a nature to prejudice the position of creditors or shareholders or (e) that there are other grounds on which it is just and equitable to grant relief. It should exhibit a copy of the document to be registered. Evidence of solvency should be filed confirming that no winding-up order has been made or resolution for winding-up passed, and that no winding up petition is pending, that no notice of a resolution to wind up has been given, that the company is continuing to carry on business, and that no judgment has been given against the company which remains unsatisfied (*Bootle Cold Storage, Re* [1901] WN 54; *Telomatic, Re* [1993] B.C.C. 404). Such evidence of solvency must be given by an officer of the company. Evidence of solvency is not, however, required where the application is to extend time for registration following the acquisition by the company of property subject to a charge registrable under s.400, or is of a kind which could not prejudice creditors (e.g. to reduce the amount of the secured debt).

The original document to be registered should be produced at the hearing.

In extending time the court will generally add to the order a provision that it is made without prejudice to the rights of any person acquired between the date of the creation of the charge and the date of its actual registration (*Re Joplin Brewery* [1902] 1 Ch 79; *Watson v Duff Morgan & Vermont (Holdings) Ltd* [1974] 1 All E.R. 794; *Re I. C. Johnson & Co* [1902] 2 Ch 101). For an exceptional case where the rights of intervening mortgagees were not preserved, see *Re Fablehill Ltd* [1991] B.C.L.C. 830.

The words in the order referred to above have been held not to put an unsecured creditor on the same footing as a debenture holder applying for an extension unless he has taken steps to enforce his debt or unless a winding up has intervened (*Re Ehrmann Bros.* [1906] 2 Ch 697) before actual registration (*Re Anglo Oriental Co* [1903] 1 Ch 914); but the court will not insert further words to protect unsecured creditors (*Re M. I. G. Trust Ltd* [1933] Ch 542, CA, affirmed in *Peat v Gresham Trust Ltd* [1934] A.C. 252).

As to the limits of the court's jurisdiction (e.g. to order the removal of unnecessary information) see *Re Calmex Ltd* [1989] 1 All E.R. 485; [1989] B.C.L.C. 299 ; *Igroup Ltd v Ocwen* [2003] EWHC 2431 (Ch); [2003] 4 All E.R. 1063 and in *Re Company (No.7466 of 2003)* [2004] EWHC 60. The court may, however, grant declaratory relief.

Where an order is sought for a declaration that a document wrongly filed on the register is of no effect the registrar of companies should be joined to and given notice of the proceedings.

2G–46   *Re Charles orders* —Where at the date of the making of the order a winding up is likely the order may reserve the right of the liquidator to apply to discharge the order within 21 days of commencement of the winding up if it occurred within a month of the making of the order (*Re L. H. Charles & Co* [1935] WN 15; *Exeter Trust Ltd v Screenways Ltd* [1991] B.C.L.C. 888). The order, if made, will extend time for registration (or rectification) but subject to a proviso "that the company, acting by any liquidator or administrator, or any unsecured creditor of the company shall be at liberty to apply to discharge or vary this order within [a period of time] after the commencement of any voluntary winding up of the company or any order for the winding up of the company" (or as the case may be). Such an order may be made where, exceptionally, there is no evidence of solvency (*Re Kris Cruisers Ltd* [1949] Ch 138). However, *Kris Cruisers Ltd* was not followed in *Re Ashpurton Estates Ltd* [1983] Ch 110; [1982] 3 All E.R. 665 in which it was held that imminent liquidation was a factor to be taken into account and

Paragraph numbers marked with a "+" can be found online and on CD.

that an order extending time should not be made after a company has gone into liquidation (see *Re Resinoid and Mica Products Ltd (Note)* [1983] Ch 132; [1982] 3 All ER 677, but *cf. R. M. Arnold & Co Ltd* [1984] B.C.L.C. 505 where the circumstances were exceptional; see also *Re Braemar Investments Ltd* [1988] 3 W.L.R. 596; [1988] B.C.L.C. 556, where the court ordered a motion by the liquidator to discharge the registrar's order extending time). In *Re Chantry House Developments plc* [1990] B.C.L.C. 813 the court made an order extending time, notwithstanding the company being in administrative receivership, but on an undertaking that the mortgagee would notify substantial unsecured creditors of the company within seven days of the making of the order and on terms that they could apply within 14 days to discharge the order and that the mortgagee would abide by any order made in such circumstances. Generally, however, where insolvent liquidation seems inevitable the court should decline to extend time (*Re Barrow Borough Transport Ltd* [1989] 3 W.L.R. 858 and *Re Telomatic Ltd* [1993] B.C.C. 404).

The court will only extend time in an application under s.404; it will not decide whether or not documents require registration (*Re Cunard Steamship Co* [1908] WN 160).

In *Exeter Trust Ltd v Screenways Ltd* [1991] B.C.L.C. 888 it was held that even if an order extending time was set aside the registrar of companies' certificate as to registration was conclusive evidence of the valid registration of the charge.

Following the decision in *Re Top Marques Car Rental Ltd* [2006] EWHC 109 (Ch), when making a *Re Charles* order the court will generally include the following provision:

"AND IT IS DIRECTED THAT the Registrar of Companies shall not issue a conclusive certificate of registration in respect of the [charge] until such time as the Registrar of Companies is satisfied that (1) no winding up or administration has commenced at the expiry of [28] days from the date of this order or (2) if a winding up or administration has commenced within [28] days from the date of this order no application has been made to vary or discharge this order by a liquidator or administrator within [56] days from the date of this order."

Paragraph numbers marked with a "+" can be found online and on CD.

PRACTICE DIRECTION—ORDER UNDER SECTION 127
INSOLVENCY ACT 1986

2G–47   *This Practice Direction supplements CPR Part 49*

1. Attention is drawn to the undesirability of asking as a matter of course for a winding up order as an alternative to an order under s.459 Companies Act 1985. The petition should not ask for a winding up order unless that is the remedy which the petitioner prefers or it is thought that it may be the only remedy to which the petitioner is entitled.

2G–48 **2.** Whenever a winding up order is asked for in a contributory's petition, the petition must state whether the petitioner consents or objects to an order under s.127 of the Insolvency Act 1986 ('a s.127 order') in the standard form. If he objects, the written evidence in support must contain a short statement of his reasons.

2G–49 **3.** If the petitioner objects to a s.127 order in the standard form but consents to such an order in a modified form, the petition must set out in the form of order to which he consents, and the written evidence in support must contain a short statement of his reasons for seeking the modification.

2G–50 **4.** If the petition contains a statement that the petitioner consents to a s.127 order, whether in the standard or a modified form, but the petitioner changes his mind before the first hearing of the petition, he must notify the respondents and may apply on notice to a Judge for an order directing that no s.127 order or a modified order only (as the case may be) shall be made by the Registrar, but validating dispositions made without notice of the order made by the Judge.

2G–51 **5.** If the petition contains a statement that the petitioner consents to a s.127 order, whether in the standard or a modified form, the Registrar shall without further enquiry make an order in such form at the first hearing unless an order to the contrary has been made by the Judge in the meantime.

2G–52 **6.** If the petition contains a statement that the petitioner objects to a s.127 order in the standard form, the company may apply (in the case of urgency, without notice) to the Judge for an order.

2G–53 **7.** Section 127 Order – Standard Form:

(Title etc.)

ORDER that notwithstanding the presentation of the said Petition
(1) payments made into or out of the bank accounts of the Company in the ordinary course of business of the Company and
(2) dispositions of the property of the Company made in the ordinary course of its business for proper value between the date of presentation of the Petition and the date of judgment on the Petition or further order in the meantime

shall not be void by virtue of the provisions of section 127 of the Insolvency Act 1986 in the event of an Order for the winding up of the Company being made on the said Petition provided that (the relevant bank) shall be under no obligation to verify for itself whether any transaction through the company's bank accounts is in the

Paragraph numbers marked with a "+" can be found online and on CD.

ordinary course of business, or that it represents full market value for the relevant transaction.

This form of Order may be departed from where the circumstances of the case require.

Companies Court—Practice Note 1 of 2003

Claims for an order restoring the name of a company to the Register or declaring the dissolution of a company void (ss.651 and 653 of the Companies Act 1985)

With effect from April 29, 2003 claims for order of this type issued in the High **2G–54** Court in London will be given a return date three months in advance of the date of issue. This is designed to enable the applicant(s) to have sufficient opportunity to complete the requirements of the Registrar of Companies. In this way it is intended to prevent repeated adjournments pending completion of those requirements and to save the expense of unnecessary and repeated attendance at court by the parties.

When the requirements of the Registrar of Companies have been met and the Treasury Solicitor is able to approve the application, a consent order may be filed for approval by the court without attendance. If an undertaking is required to be given to the court it must be given by the solicitor (partner) for the claimant(s) in Form **U1** (attached) or by the claimant in person in Form **U2** (attached).

In such circumstances the papers which must be filed at court by the claimant(s) with the consent order are:

1. A copy of the claim
2. A copy of the witness statement in support
3. Original evidence of service of the application on the company (where appropriate)
4. Original evidence of service of the application on the Registrar of Companies
5. Original evidence of service of the application on the Treasury Solicitor dealing with bona vacantia assets on behalf of the Crown, or on the solicitor for the Duchy of Lancaster or the Duke of Cornwall dealing with bona vacantia assets in those areas, exhibiting in either case the bona vacantia waiver letter received in reply
6. The original signed copy of any undertaking required to be given to the court
7. Four copies of the agreed consent order, one of which should be signed by or on behalf of each party by way of consent to the form of order

In the normal course the above documents will be seen by the Registrar within three working days of delivery to the court. If the papers are in order, the Registrar will make the agreed order and the court will send two sealed copies of the order to the applicant and one to the Treasury Solicitor. If the papers are not in order (or the court for some reason requires), the matter will be listed for the parties to attend at the earliest convenient date and notice of this appointment will be given by the court to the parties.

Chief Bankruptcy Registrar
Royal Courts of Justice, Strand, London, WC2A 2LL
April 2003

Editorial note

The following forms can be found in the *Civil Procedure Forms Volume*: **2G–55**

- U1
- U2

Companies Act 2006

The Practice Note came into force in relation to the provisions of the Companies **2G–56** Act 1985. New provisions are made by ss.1003ff. and 1029ff. of the Companies Act 2006.

Paragraph numbers marked with a "+" can be found online and on CD.

COMPANIES ACT

SECTION 3

OTHER PROCEEDINGS

3F	Personal Injury	
	Personal Injury	3F–1
	Access to Health Records Act 1990	3F–3
	Damages Act 1996	3F–33
	The Damages (Variation of Periodical Payments) Order 2005	3F–61
	Fatal Accidents Act 1976	3F–63
	Road Traffic Act 1988	3F–79
	Law Reform (Personal Injuries) Act 1948	3F–99
	The Untraced Drivers' Agreement Department of Transport Motor Insurers' Bureau (Compensation of Victims of Untraced Drivers)	3F–107.1
	Motor Insurers' Bureau (Compensation of Victims of Uninsured Drivers) Text of an Agreement dated the 13th August 1999	3F–143.1
	Compensation Act 2006	3F–182
	NHS Redress Act 2006	3F–221
3G	Data Protection Act 1998	
	Data Protection Act 1998	3G–1
3H	Consumer Credit and Consumer Law	
	Consumer Credit and Consumer Law	3H–1
	Consumer Credit Act 1974	3H–18
	Consumer Credit (Total Charge for Credit) Regulations 1980	3H–416
	The Consumer Credit (Agreements) Regulations 1983	3H–462
	Consumer Credit (Exempt Agreements) Order 1989	3H–498
	Misrepresentation Act 1967	3H–517
	Supply of Goods (Implied Terms) Act 1973	3H–526
	Unfair Contract Terms Act 1977	3H–546
	Sale of Goods Act 1979	3H–582
	Supply of Goods and Services Act 1982	3H–758
	The Package Travel, Package Holidays and Package Tours Regulations 1992	3H–836
	Contracts (Rights of Third Parties) Act 1999	3H–874
	Unfair Terms in Consumer Contracts Regulations 1999	3H–886
	The Consumer Protection (Distance Selling) Regulations 2000	3H–906
	Sale and Supply of Goods to Consumers Regulations 2002	3H–954
3I	Discrimination	
	Practice Direction—Proceedings Under Enactments Relating to Discrimination	3I–1
	Sex Discrimination Act 1975	3I–7
	Race Relations Act 1976	3I–26
	Disability Discrimination Act 1995	3I–47
	Equality Act 2006	3I–59
	The Equality Act (Sexual Orientation) Regulations 2007	3I–67

3A HOUSING

Common Law Procedure Act 1852

(15 & 16 VICT. c.76)

ARRANGEMENT OF SECTIONS

Paragraph numbers marked with a "+" denote content that is available on White Book on Westlaw UK or the Civil Procedure CD.

Law of Property Act 1925

(15 & 16 GEO. 5 c.20)

ARRANGEMENT OF SECTIONS

PART III

MORTGAGES, RENT CHARGES, AND POWERS OF ATTORNEY

MORTGAGES

PART V

LEASES AND TENANCIES

NOTICES

PART XII

Paragraph numbers marked with a "+" denote content that is available on White Book on Westlaw UK or the Civil Procedure CD.

PART III

MORTGAGES, RENT CHARGES, AND POWERS OF ATTORNEY

MORTGAGES

Sale of mortgaged property in action for redemption or foreclosure

91.—(1) Any person entitled to redeem mortgaged property may   3A–8
have a judgment or order for sale instead of for redemption in an action brought by him either for redemption alone, or for sale alone, or for sale or redemption in the alternative.

Paragraph numbers marked with a "+" can be found online and on CD.

HOUSING

(2) In any action, whether for foreclosure, or for redemption, or for sale, or for the raising and payment in any manner of mortgage money, the court, on the request of the mortgagee, or of any person interested either in the mortgage money or in the right of redemption, and, notwithstanding that—

(a) any other person dissents; or

(b) the mortgagee or any person so interested does not appear in the action;

and without allowing any time for redemption or for payment of any mortgage money, may direct a sale of the mortgaged property, on such terms as it thinks fit, including the deposit in court of a reasonable sum fixed by the court to meet the expenses of sale and to secure performance of the terms.

(3) But, in an action brought by a person interested in the right of redemption and seeking a sale, the court may, in the application of any defendant, direct the plaintiff to give such security for costs as the court thinks fit, and may give the conduct of the sale to any defendant, and may give such directions as it thinks fit respecting the costs of the defendants or any of them.

(4) In any case within this section the court may, if it thinks fit, direct a sale without previously determining the priorities of incumbrancers.

(5) This section applies to actions brought either before or after the commencement of this Act.

(6) In this section "mortgaged property" includes the estate or interest which a mortgagee would have had power to convey if the statutory power of sale were applicable.

(7) For the purposes of this section the court may, in favour of a purchaser, make a vesting order conveying the mortgaged property, or appoint a person to do so, subject or not to any incumbrance, as the court may think fit; or, in the case of an equitable mortgage, may create and vest a mortgage term in the mortgagee to enable him to carry out the sale as if the mortgage had been made by deed by way of legal mortgage.

[(8) The county court has jurisdiction under this section where the amount owing in respect of the mortgage or charge at the commencement of the proceedings does not exceed £30,000].

3A–9   Note —Amended by the County Courts Act 1984 s.148(1), Sch.2, Pt II, para.3(1); and the High Court and County Courts Jurisdiction Order 1991 (SI 1991/724) art.2(4) and (8).

"mortgage"
3A–10   See s.205(xvi).

"property"
3A–11   See s.205(xx).

"sale"
3A–12   See s.205(xxiv).

Paragraph numbers marked with a "+" can be found online and on CD.

"Sale of mortgaged property ..."

Under this section the court (which includes the county court if the amount owing **3A-13** in respect of the mortgage at the commencement of proceedings does not exceed £30,000) on the application of any person entitled to redeem the mortgaged property may direct the sale of the premises on such terms as it thinks fit. The court has a wide discretion and may order a sale of mortgaged property against the wishes of the lender where it would be unfair to the borrower to postpone sale, even if the mortgage would not be redeemed. In exercising that discretion, the court should have regard to the interests of all concerned and to what is just and equitable (see *Palk v Mortgage Funding Services* [1993] Ch. 330; [1993] 2 W.L.R. 415; [1993] 2 All E.R. 481, CA; and *Polonski v Lloyds Bank* (1999) 31 H.L.R. 721; *The Times*, May 6, 1997, Ch D).

In *Cheltenham and Gloucester Building Society v Krausz* [1997] 1 W.L.R. 1558; [1997] 1 All E.R. 21, CA, Phillips L.J. stated that he did not consider:

> "that the County Court, as part of its inherent jurisdiction, can properly suspend an order or warrant for possession in order to enable a mortgagor to apply to the High Court for an order under s.91. It [is] incumbent on the mortgagor to seek from the High Court any relief which the court is empowered to give before the warrant takes effect."

He noted that Administration of Justice Act 1970 s.36 (see below) makes it clear that parliament did not intend that the court should have power to curtail mortgagees' rights to possession unless the proceeds of sale were likely to discharge the mortgage debt. Millett L.J. expressed serious doubts as to whether *Barrett v Halifax Building Society* (1995) 28 H.L.R. 634, Ch D, where an order allowing the borrowers to sell even though the proceeds of sale would not discharge the mortgage debt, was correctly decided.

If the proceeds of sale are likely to be sufficient to redeem the mortgage, it is normal for the court to give conduct of the sale to the borrower since he or she has a greater incentive to achieve the best price. In *Cheltenham and Gloucester plc v Booker* [1997] 19 E.G. 155; (1997) 73 P. & C.R. 412; (1997) 29 H.L.R. 634, CA, where the proceeds of sale were not likely to be sufficient to redeem the mortgage and where the court was unable to exercise its discretion under Administration of Justice Act 1970 s.36 (see below) it was held that the court may give conduct of the sale of premises to the lender while postponing execution of a warrant for possession until completion of the sale, thus allowing the borrower to remain in occupation. There is no reason in principle for the court to accede to a lender's insistence upon immediate possession if:

(a) possession will only be required on completion;

(b) the presence of the borrowers pending completion will enhance, or at least not depress, the sale price;

(c) the borrowers will co-operate in the sale; and

(d) they will give possession to the purchasers on completion.

However, Millett L.J. stated these conditions are seldom likely to be satisfied and the circumstances in which such a course would be appropriate are hard to imagine. Such an order would "certainly be a rarity".

* * * *

PART V

LEASES AND TENANCIES

Restrictions on and relief against forfeiture of leases and underleases

146.—(1) A right of re-entry or forfeiture under any proviso or **3A-14** stipulation in a lease for a breach of any covenant or condition in the lease shall not be enforceable, by action or otherwise, unless and until the lessor serves on the lessee a notice—

(a) specifying the particular breach complained of; and

Paragraph numbers marked with a "+" can be found online and on CD.

(b) if the breach is capable of remedy, requiring the lessee to remedy the breach; and

(c) in any case, requiring the lessee to make compensation in money for the breach;

and the lessee fails, within a reasonable time thereafter, to remedy the breach, if it is capable of remedy, and to make reasonable compensation in money, to the satisfaction of the lessor, for the breach.

(2) Where a lessor is proceeding, by action by otherwise, to enforce such a right of re-entry or forfeiture, the lessee may, in the lessor's action, if any, or in any action brought by himself, apply to the court for relief; and the court may grant or refuse relief, as the court, having regard to the proceedings and conduct of the parties under the foregoing provisions of this section, and to all the other circumstances, thinks fit; and in case of relief may grant it on such terms, if any, as to costs, expenses, damages, compensation, penalty, or otherwise, including the granting of an injunction to restrain any like breach in the future, as the court, in the circumstances of each case, thinks fit.

(3) A lessor shall be entitled to recover as a debt due to him from a lessee, and in addition to damages (if any), all reasonable costs and expenses properly incurred by the lessor in the employment of a solicitor and surveyor or valuer, or otherwise, in reference to any breach giving rise to a right of re-entry or forfeiture which, at the request of the lessee, is waived by the lessor, or from which the lessee is relieved, under the provisions of this Act.

(4) Where a lessor is proceeding by action or otherwise to enforce a right of re-entry or forfeiture under any covenant, proviso, or stipulation in a lease, or for non-payment of rent, the court may, on application by any person claiming as under-lessee any estate or interest in the property comprised in the lease or any part thereof, either in the lessor's action (if any) or in any action brought by such person for that purpose, make an order vesting, for the whole term of the lease or any less term, the property comprised in the lease or any part thereof in any person entitled as under-lessee to any estate or interest in such property upon such conditions as to execution of any deed or other document, payment of rent, costs, expenses, damages, compensation, giving security, or otherwise, as the court in the circumstances of each case may think fit, but in no case shall any such under-lessee be entitled to require a lease to be granted to him for any longer term than he had under this original sub-lease.

(5) For the purposes of this section—

(a) "Lease" includes an original or derivative under-lease; also an agreement for a lease where the lessee has become entitled to have his lease granted; also a grant at a fee farm rent, or securing a rent by condition;

(b) "Lessee" includes an original or derivative under-lessee, and the persons deriving title under a lessee; also a grantee under any such grant as aforesaid and the persons deriving title under him;

Paragraph numbers marked with a "+" can be found online and on CD.

(c) "Lessor" includes an original or derivative under-lessor, and the persons deriving title under a lessor; also a person making such grant as aforesaid and the persons deriving title under him;

(d) "Under-lease" includes an agreement for an underlease where the underlessee has become entitled to have his underlease granted;

(e) "Underlessee" includes any person deriving title under an underlessee.

(6) This section applies although the proviso or stipulation under which the right of re-entry or forfeiture accrues is inserted in the lease in pursuance of the directions of any Act of Parliament.

(7) For the purposes of this section a lease limited to continue as long only as the lessee abstains from committing a breach of covenant shall be and take effect as a lease to continue for any longer term for which it could subsist, but determinable by a proviso for re-entry on such a breach.

(8) This section does not extend—

(i) To a covenant or condition against assigning, underletting, parting with the possession, or disposing of the land leased where the breach occurred before the commencement of this Act; or

(ii) In the case of a mining lease, to a covenant or condition for allowing the lessor to have access to or inspect books, accounts, records, weighing machines or other things, or to enter or inspect the mine or the working thereof.

(9) This section does not apply to a condition for forfeiture on the bankruptcy of the lessee or on taking in execution of the lessee's interest if contained in a lease of—

(a) Agricultural or pastoral land;

(b) Mines or minerals;

(c) A house used or intended to be used as a public-house or beershop;

(d) A house let as a dwelling-house, with the use of any furniture, books, works of art, or other chattels not being in the nature of fixtures;

(e) Any property with respect to which the personal qualifications of the tenant are of importance for the preservation of the value or character of the property, or on the ground of neighbourhood to the lessor, or to any person holding under him.

(10) Where a condition of forfeiture on the bankruptcy of the lessee or on taking in execution of the lessee's interest is contained in any lease, other than a lease of any of the classes mentioned in the last subsection, then—

(a) if the lessee's interest is sold within one year from the bankruptcy or taking in execution, this section applies to the forfeiture condition aforesaid;

Paragraph numbers marked with a "+" can be found online and on CD.

(b) if the lessee's interest is not sold before the expiration of that year, this section only applies to the forfeiture condition aforesaid during the first year from the date of the bankruptcy or taking in execution.

(11) This section does not, save as otherwise mentioned, affect the law relating to re-entry or forfeiture or relief in case of non-payment of rent.

(12) This section has affect notwithstanding any stipulation to the contrary.

(13) The county court has jurisdiction under this section.

3A–15   *Note* —Amended by the High Court and County Courts Jurisdiction Order (SI 1991/724) art.2(1)(a) and (8). Subsection (13) was added by the County Courts Act 1984 s.148(1), Sch.2 and then amended by High Court and County Courts Jurisdiction Order 1991 (SI 1991/724) art.2(1)(a) and (8). County courts now have unlimited jurisdiction.

No forfeiture notice before determination of breach.

3A–16   Commonhold and Leasehold Reform Act 2002 s.168 provides that a landlord under a long lease of a dwelling may not serve a notice under Law of Property Act 1925 s.146(1) unless it has been finally determined on an application under s.168(4) that the breach has occurred; or the tenant has admitted the breach; or a court in any proceedings, or an arbitral tribunal in proceedings pursuant to a post-dispute arbitration agreement, has finally determined that the breach has occurred. Section 168 is printed at para.3A–1593 below. Comonhold and Leasehold Reform Act 2002 s.76 provides that a lease is a long lease if it (a) is granted for a term of years certain exceeding 21 years; (b) is for a term fixed by law under a grant with a covenant or obligation for perpetual renewal (c) takes effect under Law of Property Act 1925 s.149(6) (leases terminable after a death or marriage); (d) was granted under the right to buy provisions of Housing Act 1985 Pt 5; (e) is a shared ownership lease; or (f) under Housing Act 1996 s.17 (the right to acquire). Section 77 contains certain exceptions.

"rent"

3A–17   See s.205(xxiii).

"lease", "lessee", "lessor", "under-lease" and "under-lessor"

3A–18   See s.146(5).

"Restrictions on and relief against forfeiture ..."

3A–19   Note that this section does not, save as is otherwise mentioned, affect the law relating to re-entry or forfeiture or relief in the case of non-payment of rent (s.146(11)). See the Common Law Procedure Act 1852 ss.210–212, above, the Supreme Court Act 1981 s.38, below, and the County Courts Act 1984 ss.138–140, below.

For the restriction on forfeiture or re-entry for arrears of service charges see the Housing Act 1996 s.81, below.

For a statement of the circumstances in which a tenant may apply for relief, see *Billson v Residential Apartments Ltd* [1992] 1 A.C. 494; [1992] 2 W.L.R. 15; [1992] 1 All E.R. 141, HL, where Lord Templeman said:

> "A tenant may apply for ... relief from forfeiture under section 146(2) after the issue of a section 146 notice but he is not prejudiced if he does not do so. A tenant cannot apply for relief after a landlord has forfeited a lease by issuing and serving a writ, has recovered judgment and has entered into possession pursuant to that judgment. If the judgment is set aside or succesfully appealed, the tenant will be able to apply for relief in the landlord's action but the court in deciding whether to grant relief will take into account any consequences of the original order and repossession and the delay of the tenant. A tenant may apply for relief after a landlord has forfeited by re-entry without first obtaining a court order for that purpose, but the court in deciding whether to grant relief will take into account all the circumstances including delay on the part of the tenant."

Paragraph numbers marked with a "+" can be found online and on CD.

Lord Templeman also indicated that he considered the practice of awarding indemnity costs as a condition of granting relief was ripe for reconsideration (but *cf. Church Commissioners v Ibrahim* [1997] 1 E.G.L.R. 13, CA and CPR r.48.3). See too *Fairview Investments Ltd v Sharma*, October 14, 1999, unrep. and *Gomba Holdings (UK) Ltd v Minories Finance Ltd (No.2)* [1993] Ch. 171 at p.194B, CA where the Court of Appeal stated that although costs are in the court's discretion, where there is a contractual right to costs, the discretion should ordinarily be exercised so as to reflect that contractual right. If a lessee is to be relieved from forfeiture, it should be on terms that reflect the lessee's breach of covenant and the lessor should not be left out of pocket by taking proper steps to protect his interests. Where a lessor has bargained for the protection afforded by a clause providing for payment of costs, a court should be slow to deprive him or her of that protection and should not do so without good reason.

Relief against notice to effect decorative repairs

147.—(1) After a notice is served on a lessee relating to the internal **3A–20** decorative repairs to a house or other building, he may apply to the court for relief, and if, having regard to all the circumstances of the case (including in particular the length of the lessee's term or interest remaining unexpired), the court is satisfied that the notice is unreasonable, it may, by order, wholly or partially relieve the lessee from liability for such repairs.

(2) This section does not apply—

    (i) where the liability arises under an express covenant or agreement to put the property in a decorative state of repair and the covenant or agreement has never been performed;

    (ii) to any matter necessary or proper—

        (a) for putting or keeping the property in a sanitary condition, or

        (b) for the maintenance or preservation of the structure;

    (iii) to any statutory liability to keep a house in all respects reasonably fit for human habitation;

    (iv) to any covenant or stipulation to yield up the house or other building in a specified state of repair at the end of the term.

(3) In this section "lease" includes an underlease and an agreement for a lease, and "lessee" has a corresponding meaning and includes any person liable to effect the repairs.

(4) This section applies whether the notice is served before or after the commencement of this Act, and has effect notwithstanding any stipulation to the contrary.

(5) The county court has jurisdiction under this section.

Note—Subsection (5) added by the County Courts Act 1984 s.148(1), Sch.2; re- **3A–21** pealed in part by the High Court and County Courts Jurisdiction Order 1991 (SI 1991/724) art.2(8), Sch. County courts now have unlimited jurisdiction.

* * * *

NOTICES

Regulations respecting notices

196.—(1) Any notice required or authorised to be served or given **3A–22** by this Act shall be in writing.

Paragraph numbers marked with a "+" can be found online and on CD.

HOUSING

(2) Any notice required or authorised by this Act to be served on a lessee or mortgagor shall be sufficient, although only addressed to the lessee or mortgagor by that designation, without his name, or generally to the persons interested, without any name, and notwithstanding that any person to be affected by the notice is absent, under disability, unborn, or unascertained.

(3) Any notice required or authorised by this Act to be served shall be sufficiently served if it is left at the last-known place of abode or business in the United Kingdom of the lessee, lessor, mortgagee, mortgagor, or other person to be served, in case of a notice required or authorised to be served on a lessee or mortgagor, is affixed or left for him on the land or any house or building comprised in the lease or mortgage, or, in case of a mining lease, is left for the lessee at the office or counting-house of the mine.

(4) Any notice required or authorised by this Act to be served shall also be sufficiently served, if it is sent by post in a registered letter addressed to the lessee, lessor, mortgagee, mortgagor, or other person to be served, by name, at the aforesaid place of abode or business, office, or counting-house, and if that letter is not returned by the postal operator (within the meaning of the Postal Services Act 2000) concerned undelivered; and that service shall be deemed to be made at the time at which the registered letter would in the ordinary course be delivered.

(5) The provisions of this section shall extend to notices required to be served by any instrument affecting property executed or coming into operation after the commencement of this Act unless a contrary intention appears.

(6) This section does not apply to notices served in proceedings in the court.

3A–23   *Note* —Amended by the Leasehold Property (Repairs) Act 1938 s.72; the Reserve and Auxiliary Forces (Protection of Civil Interests) Act 1951 s.29(b); the Recorded Delivery Service Act 1962 s.1, Sch.; and the Postal Services Act 2000 (Consequential Modifications No.1) Order (SI 2001/1149) Sch.1, para.7.

"notices"

3A–24   It is good practice for landlords by an express provision to incorporate this section into tenancy agreements. If they do not do so, it cannot be implied. In the absence of express incorporation, landlords must prove that notices to quit or notices of intention to seek possession have come to the attention of the tenant (see *Wandsworth LBC v Attwell* (1995) 27 H.L.R. 536; (1996) 01 E.G. 100; (1996) 94 L.G.R. 419, CA; and *Enfield LBC v Devonish* (1997) 29 H.L.R. 691; *The Times*, December 12, 1996, CA.

For s.205 of the Law of Property Act 1925 (see Arrangement) plus any related commentary see paragraphs 3A–25+ to 3A–26+ on White Book on Westlaw UK or the Civil Procedure CD.

National Assistance Act 1948

(11 & 12 GEO. 6 c.29)

ARRANGEMENT OF SECTIONS

PART III

LOCAL AUTHORITY SERVICES

PROVISION OF ACCOMMODATION

PART III

LOCAL AUTHORITY SERVICES

PROVISION OF ACCOMMODATION

Duty of local authorities to provide accommodation

21.—(1) Subject to and in accordance with the provisions of this 3A–27 Part of this Act, a local authority may with the approval of the Secretary of State, and to such extent as he may direct shall, make arrangements for providing—

    (a) residential accommodation for persons aged eighteen or over who by reason of age, illness, disability or any other circumstances are in need of care and attention which is not otherwise available to them; and

    (aa) residential accommodation for expectant and nursing mothers who are in need of care and attention which is not otherwise available to them.

    (b) [...]

(1A) A person to whom section 115 of the Immigration and Asylum Act 1999 (exclusion from benefits) applies may not be provided with residential accommodation under subsection (1)(a) if his need for care and attention has arisen solely—

    (a) because he is destitute; or

    (b) because of the physical effects, or anticipated physical effects, of his being destitute.

(1B) Subsections (3) and (5) to (8) of section 95, of the Immigration and Asylum Act 1999 and paragraph 2 of Schedule 8 to that Act, apply for the purposes of subsection (1A) as they apply for the purposes of that section, but for the references in subsections (5) and (7) of that section and in that paragraph to the Secretary of State substitute references to a local authority.

(2) In [making any such arrangements] a local authority shall have regard to the welfare of all persons for whom accommodation is provided, and in particular to the need for providing accommodation of different descriptions suited to different descriptions of such persons as are mentioned in the last foregoing subsection.

(2A) In determining for the purposes of paragraph (a) or (aa) of subsection (1) of this section whether care and attention are otherwise available to a person, a local authority shall disregard so much of the

Paragraph numbers marked with a "+" can be found online and on CD.

person's resources as may be specified in, or determined in accordance with, regulations made by the Secretary of State for the purposes of this subsection.

(2B) In subsection (2A) of this section the reference to a person's resources is a reference to his resources within the meaning of regulations made for the purposes of that subsection.

(3) [...]

(4) Subject to the provisions of section 26 of this Act. Accommodation provided by a local authority in the exercise of their functions under this section shall be provided in premises managed by the authority or, to such extent as may be determined in accordance with the arrangements under this section, in such premises managed by another local authority as may be agreed between the two authorities and on such terms, including terms as to the reimbursement of expenditure incurred by the said other authority, as may be so agreed.

(5) References in this Act to accommodation provided under this Part thereof shall be construed as references to accommodation provided in accordance with this and the five next following sections, and as including references to board and other services, amenities and requisites provided in connection with the accommodation except where in the opinion of the authority managing the premises their provision is unnecessary.

(6) References in this Act to a local authority providing accommodation shall be construed, in any case where a local authority agree with another local authority for the provision of accommodation in premises managed by the said other authority, as references to the first-mentioned local authority.

(7) Without prejudice to the generality of the foregoing provisions of this section, a local authority may—

(a) provide, in such cases as they may consider appropriate, for the conveyance of persons to and from premises in which accommodation is provided for them under this Part of the Act;

(b) make arrangements for the provision on the premises in which accommodation is being provided for such other services as appear to the authority to be required.

(8) [...] nothing in this section shall authorise or require a local authority to make any provision authorised or required to be made (whether by that or by any other authority) by or under any enactment not contained in this Part of this Act [or for authorised or required to be provided under the National Health Service Act 2006 or the National Health Service (Wales) Act 2006.]

3A–28   *Note* —Amended by the Local Government Act 1972 ss.195(6), 272(1), Sch.23, para.2(1), Sch.30; the National Health Service Reorganisation Act 1973 s.57(1), (2), Sch.4, para.44, Sch.5; the Housing (Homeless Persons) Act 1977 s.20(4), Sch.; the Children Act 1989 s.108(5), Sch.13, para.11(1); the National Health Service and Community Care Act 1990 s.42(1), 66, Sch.9, para.5(1)–(3), Sch.10; the Immigration and Asylum Act 1999 s.116; the Health and Social Care Act 2001 s.53; and by the National Health Service (Consequential Provisions) Act 2006 s.2 and Sch.1, para.2.

Paragraph numbers marked with a "+" can be found online and on CD.

Editorial introduction

The National Assistance Act 1948 s.21(1)(a) gives social services authorities power to **3A–29** make arrangements for the accommodation of adults who are in need of care and attention not otherwise available to them as a result of age, illness, disability or any other circumstances. The Secretary of State has directed that authorities shall make arrangements under s.21(1)(a) to provide accommodation for adults who are ordinarily resident in their areas or are in urgent need thereof and who, by reason of age, illness, disability or any other circumstance, are in need of care and attention not otherwise available to them. Note that s.21 was amended by Immigration and Asylum Act 1999 s.116 to exclude the provision of accommodation under s.21 to destitute asylum seekers.

Section 21 is not a safety net on which any person short of money can rely. The proper test is whether a person is "in need of care and attention" (*R. v Newham LBC Ex p. Plastin* (1997) 30 H.L.R. 261, QBD). In *R (M) v Slough BC* [2008] UKHL 52, [2008] 1 W.L.R. 1808; [2008] 4 All E.R. 831, the House of Lords held that a person who only needed provision of normal housing (with a fridge) was not necessarily in need of "care and attention". In order to be so, a person had to need "looking after".In *R. v Southwark Ex p. Hong Cui* (1999) 31 H.L.R. 639, QBD David Pannick QC sitting as a deputy judge held that: (1) an applicant must show that s/he is in desperate need of care and attention and that otherwise there is a risk that there would be damage to his/her health or for some other reason assistance is urgently required. It is not enough to be destitute; and (2) authorities must consider the circumstances of each individual case. A local authority's duty is to assess and meet applicants' needs, not to satisfy their preferences. (*R (Khana and Karim) v Southwark LBC* [2001] EWCA Civ 999; [2002] H.L.R. 31).

Children

There is no express provision that obliges a local authority to meet the needs of an **3A–29.1** individual child after assessment. National Assistance Act 1948 s.21 involves the notion of a target duty that becomes crystallised and enforceable after a needs assessment (see *R. v Kensington & Chelsea RLBC Ex p. Kujtim* [1999] 4 All E.R. 161). However, the language and structure of Children Act 1989 s.17 are entirely different from s.21. A child previously accommodated by s.21 is catered for by s.20 of the 1989 Act. Where a child requires accommodation of a particular kind and is in a family unit so that s.20 is not invoked, provision would generally be made through the housing legislation. Section 17 of the 1989 Act creates a general duty to safeguard and promote the welfare of children in need. However in *A and W v Lambeth LBC*; *G v Barnet LBC* (also reported as *R.(G) v Barnet LBC)* [2003] UKHL 57; [2004] 2 A.C. 208; [2003] 3 W.L.R. 1194; [2004] 1 All E.R. 97, the House of Lords rejected claims that Children Act 1989 s.17 gives rise to an enforceable duty to accommodate the children with their families. Social services departments are not statutorily required to arrange or provide accommodation for families with children who are not entitled to be housed through the usual channels, although they can do so. Section 17(1) is an overriding duty, a statement of general principle. It provides the broad aims which local authorities are to bear in mind when performing other duties set out in the Children Act and the specific duties for facilitating the discharge of those general duties which were set out in Pt I of Sch.2. A child in need within the meaning of s.17(10) is eligible for the provision of those services, but has no absolute right to them. Section 17(1) sets out duties of a general character which are intended to be for the benefit of children in need in the local social services authority's area in general. The other duties and the specific duties which follow have to be performed in each individual case by reference to the general duties which s.17(1) sets out. Section 17 refers to a range and level of services appropriate to the children's needs. It is broadly expressed, with a view to giving the greatest possible scope to the local social services authority as to what it chooses to do in the provision of those services. Although the services which the authority provide may include the provision of accommodation (see s.17(6)), the provision of residential accommodation to house a child in need so that he or she can live with the family is not the principal or primary purpose of the legislation. Housing is the function of the local housing authority. Detailed provisions for the acquisition and management of housing stock are contained in the Housing Acts. Provisions of that kind are entirely absent from the Children Act. The expenditure of limited resources on the provision

Paragraph numbers marked with a "+" can be found online and on CD.

of residential accommodation for housing children with their families would be bound to mean that there was less available for expenditure on other services designed for the performance of the general duty which s.17(1) identified. It would also sit uneasily with the legislation in the Housing Acts.

"local authority"

3A–30   See s.33 below.

"destitute"

3A–31   See the Immigration and Asylum Act 1999 s.95(3).

"resources"

3A–32   Where a local authority is satisfied that a person is in need of care and attention which is not otherwise available, lack of funds does not excuse it from performing its duty to make appropriate arrangements (*R. v Sefton MBC Ex p. Help the Aged* (1997-98) 1 C.C.L. Rep. 57, CA).

"accommodation"

3A–33   In *R. v Newham LBC Ex p. Medical Foundation of the Care of Victims of Torture* (1998) 30 H.L.R. 955, QBD, Moses J. held that the phrase "residential accommodation" means no more than where a person lives. It does not mean "accommodation with an institutional quality". See too *R. v Newham LBC Ex p. C* (1999) 31 H.L.R. 567, QBD.

Termination of duty

3A–34   See Immigration and Asylum Act 1999 Pt VI. The duty of central government to provide support to asylum seekers under Immigration and Asylum Act 1999 s.95 applies only where need arises solely from destitution rather than sickness, age or disability. Otherwise local authorities are obliged to provide accommodation under s.21. Regulation 6(4)of the Asylum Support Regulations 2000 (SI 2000/704) requires the secretary of state to take into account any other support available to an asylum seeker when determining whether that asylum seeker is destitute for the purposes of s.95(1). That regulation includes accomodation that the local authority is obliged to provide by s.21. See *R. (Westminster CC) v National Asylum Support Service* [2002] UKHL 38; [2002] 1 W.L.R. 2956.

Where a person's needs satisfy the criteria contained in the National Assistance Act 1948 s.21(1)(a), the authority has a continuing duty to provide accommodation while the person's needs remain the same. However an authority is entitled to treat its duty as discharged and to refuse to provide further accommodation if the person refuses accommodation offered or, following its provision manifests by his or her conduct a persistent and unequivocal refusal to observe the authority's reasonable requirements in relation to occupation of such accommodation. Before concluding that there has been such a refusal it is desirable that the authority write a final warning letter. Any decision by the authority to treat its duty as discharged by conduct requires a reassessment both of current need and careful consideration of the nature of that conduct, including any medical condition or infirmity known to the authority (*R. v Kensington and Chelsea RBC Ex p. Kutjim* [1999] 4 All E.R. 161, CA).

Asylum Seekers

3A–35   Asylum seekers are to be supported under the Immigration and Asylum Act 1999 Pt VI until the conclusion of any appeal. Thereafter, if they have a need for care and attention that does not arise solely because of destitution, they qualify under s.21. See *R v Wandsworth LBC Ex p. O*; *R v Leicester CC Ex p. Bhika* [2000] 1 W.L.R. 2539; [2000] 4 All E.R. 590 where Simon Brown L.J. accepted submissions that:

> "if an applicant's need for care and attention is to any material extent made more acute by some circumstances other than the mere lack of accommodation and funds, then, despite being subject to immigration control, he qualifies for assistance. Other relevant circumstances include, of course, age, illness and disability, all of which are expressly mentioned in section 21(1) itself. If, for example, an immigrant, as well as being destitute, is old, ill or disabled, he is likely to be yet more vulnerable and less well able to survive than if he were merely destitute."

Paragraph numbers marked with a "+" can be found online and on CD.

All other categories or persons from abroad, whether or not they have any pending immigration appeal qualify for assistance under s.21 if their need does not arise solely because of destitution. Where a destitute 'asylum-seeker' within the terms of Immigration and Asylum Act 1999 s.94(1) with children requires accommodation, a local authority's duty does not extend to accommodating the children. Responsibility for them falls on NASS rather than on the local authority and they are to be treated as "destitute" even though actually sheltered with their parent. In such circumstances, the appropriate practical solution is for the council to accommodate the whole family with NASS meeting the cost of accommodating the children (*R.(O) v Haringey LBC* [2004] EWCA Civ 535; [2004] H.L.R.44).

The fact that someone is unlawfully present in the United Kingdom does not preclude them from seeking accommodation under s.21 (*R. v Wandsworth LBC Ex p. O; R v Leicester CC Ex p. Bhika* [2000] 1 W.L.R. 2539; [2000] 4 All E.R. 590 where Simon Brown L.J. said:

"section 21(1) affords the very last possibility of relief, the final hope of keeping the needy off the streets. Not even illegality should to my mind bar an applicant who otherwise qualifies for support. For my part I would hold that the local authority has no business with the applicant's immigration status save only for the purpose of learning why the care and attention 'is not otherwise available to them' as section 21(1) requires—and indeed . . for reporting such applications to the immigration authorities if they conclude that the Home Office is unaware of their presence here.")

Under National Assistance Act 1948 s.21(1A) the responsibility for meeting the care and accommodation needs of disabled asylum-seekers falls upon the local authorities, not the NASS. For the purposes of National Assistance Act 1948 s.21(1A), local authorities have to decide whether applicants are in need of care and attention not otherwise available to them. They cannot take into account the provision of asylum support under the Immigration and Asylum Act 1999 because the Asylum Support Regulations 2000 required them to disregard the provision of asylum support when deciding whether a person was destitute (*Murua v Croydon LBC* (2002) 5 C.C.L. Rep. 51).

A local authority is not relieved of its duty to provide residential accomodation under s.21 even if the asylum seeker has applied to NASS and has been accepted for provision of support by them. (Asylum Support Regulations 2000 (SI 2000/704), reg.23 and *R. (on the application of Mani) v Lambeth LBC* [2003] EWCA Civ 836.

"discharge of duty"

See *Anufrijeva v Southwark LBC* [2003] EWCA Civ 1406; [2004] Q.B. 1124; [2004] 2 W.L.R. 603; [2004] 1 All E.R. 833 where the claimants unsuccessfully brought proceedings for damages under the Human Rights Act 1998 for breach of ECHR, art.8 claiming that the defendant council had failed to discharge its duty under s.21 because a property in which they had been housed was unsuitable. The Court of Appeal held that there is a stage at which the dictates of humanity require the state to intervene to prevent any person within its territory suffering dire consequences as a result of deprivation of sustenance. If support is necessary to prevent a person in this country reaching the point of art.3 degradation, then that support should be provided. If such a basic standard exists, it must require intervention by the state, whether the claimant is an asylum seeker who has not sought asylum promptly on entry or is a citizen entitled to all the benefits of our system. Article 8 is capable of imposing on a state a positive obligation to provide support (*R. (Bernard) v Enfield LBC* [2002] EWHC 2282 (Admin); [2003] U.K.H.R.R. 148). Those obligations are not however absolute. There must be some ground for criticising the failure to act—an element of culpability and knowledge that the claimant's private and family life are at risk. If there is delay, there is no infringement of art.8 unless substantial prejudice has been caused to the applicant. Maladministration does not infringe art.8 unless the consequences are serious. Isolated acts of even significant carelessness are unlikely to suffice. At first instance courts dealing with claims for maladministration should adopt a broad-brush approach, without a close examination of authorities or a prolonged examination of the facts. Remedies have to be just and appropriate and necessary to afford just satisfaction. Levels of damages awarded in tort, by the CICB and local government ombudsmen might all provide some rough guidance. Courts should look critically at any attempt to recover damages for maladministration under the Human Rights Act 1998 other than in the Administra-

3A–36

Paragraph numbers marked with a "+" can be found online and on CD.

tive Court. Before giving permission to apply for judicial review, the Administrative Court should require the claimant to explain why it is not more appropriate to use any internal complaints procedure.

* * * *

LOCAL AND CENTRAL AUTHORITIES

Local Authorities for purposes of Part III

3A-37   **33.**—(1) In this Part of this Act the expression "local authority" means a council which is a local authority for the purposes of the Local Authority Social Services Act 1970 in England or Wales, and a council constituted under section 2 of the Local Government, etc. (Scotland) Act 1994 in Scotland:

(2) [...]

Administration of Justice Act 1970

3A-38   (1970 c.31)

ARRANGEMENT OF SECTIONS

PART IV

ACTIONS BY MORTGAGEES FOR POSSESSION

SECT.

PART IV

ACTIONS BY MORTGAGEES FOR POSSESSION

Additional powers of court in action by mortgagee for possession of dwelling-house

3A-39   **36.**—(1) Where the mortgagee under a mortgage of land which consists of or includes a dwelling-house brings an action in which he claims possession of the mortgaged property, not being an action for foreclosure in which a claim for possession of the mortgaged property is also made, the court may exercise any of the powers conferred on it by subsection (2)below if it appears to the court that in the event of its exercising the power the mortgagor is likely to be able within a reasonable period to pay any sums due under the mortgage or to remedy a default consisting of a breach of any other obligation arising under or by virtue of the mortgage.

(2) The court—
    (a) may adjourn the proceedings, or
    (b) on giving judgment, or making an order, for delivery of possession of the mortgaged property, or at any time before the execution of such judgment or order, may—

Paragraph numbers marked with a "+" can be found online and on CD.

> (i) stay or suspend execution of the judgment or order, or
>
> (ii) postpone the date for delivery of possession,

for such period or periods as the court thinks reasonable.

(3) Any such adjournment, stay, suspension or postponement as is referred to in subsection (2) above may be made subject to such conditions with regard to payment by the mortgagor of any sum secured by the mortgage or the remedying of any default as the court thinks fit.

(4) The court may from time to time vary or revoke any condition imposed by virtue of this section.

(5) [...][1]

(6) In the application of this section to Northern Ireland, "the court" means a judge of the High Court in Northern Ireland, and in subsection (1) the words from "not being" to "made" shall be omitted.

"Additional powers of court ..."

For definitions of "dwelling-house", "mortgage", "mortgagee" and "mortgagor" see s.39 below. **3A–40**

See too the Administration of Justice Act 1973 s.8 (below).

At common law, where, under an instalment mortgage, by reason of default by the borrower, the whole money advanced has become payable, the lender is entitled to possession and the court has no jurisdiction to decline to make an order for possession or to adjourn the hearing, whether on terms of keeping up payments or paying arrears, if the mortgagee cannot be persuaded to agree to this course. To this the *sole exception* is that the application may be adjourned for a short time to afford the mortgagor a chance of paying off the mortgagee in full or otherwise satisfying him; but this should not be done if there is no reasonable prospect of this occurring (*Birmingham Citizens Permanent Building Society v Caunt* [1962] Ch. 883 at 912, Ch D). However, the Administration of Justice Act 1970 s.36 and the Administration of Justice Act 1973 s.8 (see below) give courts in mortgage possession proceedings power to adjourn, stay, suspend or postpone the date for the giving up of possession if it is likely that the arrears of instalments and interest can be repaid during a reasonable period. A bankrupt may make an application to the court for relief under Administration of Justice Acts 1970 and 1973 (*Nationwide BS v Purvis* [1998] B.P.I.R. 625, CA).

In *Royal Bank of Scotland v Miller* [2001] EWCA Civ 344; [2002] Q.B. 255; [2001] 3 W.L.R. 523, CA, it was held that (1) the relevant time for determining whether land consists of or includes a dwelling-house within the meaning of s.36 is the time when the mortgagee claims possession, not the date when the legal charge is entered into; and (2) breach of a term of the mortgage (e.g. occupation by a third party without consent) does not prevent s.36 from applying.

Section 8 does not apply to "all moneys" charges, since:

(a) the principal does not become due and cannot be sued upon until a written demand is made; and

(b) the charge does not provide for deferment after a written demand is made (*Habib Bank v Tailor* [1982] 1 W.L.R. 1218; [1982] 3 All E.R. 561, CA).

Accordingly a mortgagor with an all moneys charge against whom possession is sought can only rely upon s.36 if it is likely that all sums due (i.e. principal, interest and any other sums due under the mortgage) can be paid within a reasonable period.

An agreement to pay off outstanding sums drawn down from an overdraft facility secured by a charge by monthly instalments does not come within s.36 or s.8 either (*Rees Investments Ltd v Groves*, June 27, 2001, unrep., Ch D).

Administration of Justice Act 1970 s.36 has not abrogated the mortgagee's common

---

[1] Repealed by the Statute Law (Repeals) Act 2004 s.1(1), Sch.1, Pt 1.

Paragraph numbers marked with a "+" can be found online and on CD.

law right to take possession of property where court proceedings are not needed, e.g. where premises are unoccupied or where premises are sold by receivers in accordance with Law of Property Act 1925 s.101 (see *Western Bank Ltd v Schindler* [1977] Ch. 1, CA; *Ropaigealach v Barclays Bank Plc* [2000] 1 Q.B. 263; [1999] 3 W.L.R. 17; [1999] 4 All E.R. 235, CA and *Horsham Properties Group Ltd v Clark* [2008] EWHC 2327 (Ch); October 8, 2008, where it was held that LPA 1925 s.101 is not incompatible with ECHR Article I, Protocol 1). Parliament did not intend s.36 to give mortgagors protection from mortgagees who took possession without the assistance of the court (*cf.* Criminal Law Act 1977 s.6 and Consumer Credit Act 1974 s.126 where specific protection has been given to mortgagors from forcible re-entry).

Where the court exercises its power under s.36 to stay or suspend execution for such period as the court thinks reasonable, that period must be defined or rendered ascertainable. It is wrong to suspend in general terms without fixing any period for the length of the suspension (*Royal Trust Co of Canada v Markham* [1975] 3 All E.R. 433, CA).

The court cannot suspend an order for possession under s.36, however hard the circumstances, if there is no prospect of the borrower reducing the arrears (*Abbey National Mortgages v Bernard* (1995) 71 P. & C.R. 257, CA; see too *Abbey National Building Society v Mewton* [1995] 9 C.L. 346, CA).

Note also *Hyde Park Funding Ltd v Ioannou* [1999] 3 C.L.D. 428 (Barnet County Court) where mortgagees brought possession proceedings and a possession order was granted. Later they obtained a warrant. On the morning of the proposed eviction the borrower applied to a district judge to suspend the warrant. That application was dismissed and the borrower was evicted. The borrower appealed to a circuit judge. The lender contended that as the warrant had been executed, the court no longer had jurisdiction to suspend under Administration of Justice Act 1970 s.36. HHJ Connor allowed the appeal. On appeal from a district judge, a circuit judge can exercise all of the jurisdiction that the district judge had and can make any order that the district judge could have made. In view of new evidence adduced on the appeal, the correct order was to suspend on terms. The district judge's order was set aside and possession restored.

"a reasonable period"

3A–41   What is a reasonable period depends on the individual circumstances of each case, particularly the extent to which the mortgage and arrears are secured by the value of the property (*Bristol and West Building Society v Ellis* (1996) 73 P. & C.R. 158; (1996) 29 H.L.R. 282, CA). "The court should take as its starting point the full term of the mortgage and pose at the outset the question: would it be possible for the mortgagor to maintain payment-off of the arrears by instalments over that period?" (*Cheltenham and Gloucester Building Society v Norgan* [1996] 1 All E.R. 449 at 458; (1995) 28 H.L.R. 443; (1996) 72 P. & C.R. 46, CA, see too *First Middlesbrough Trading and Mortgage Co Ltd v Cunningham* (1974) 28 P. & C.R. 69, CA; and *Western Bank v Schindler* [1977] Ch. 1; [1976] 2 All E.R. 393, CA).

The court may exercise its discretion under s.36 without hearing formal sworn evidence on the basis of information given by defendants. "It must be possible for [judges] to act without evidence, especially where, as here, the mortgagor was present in court and available to be questioned and no objection to the reception of informal material is made by the mortgagee" (*Cheltenham and Gloucester Building Society v Grant* (1994) 26 H.L.R. 703 at 707, CA).

The court's powers under s.36 cease after a warrant has been executed (*Cheltenham and Gloucester Building Society v Obi* (1996) 28 H.L.R. 22, CA; and *National and Provincial Building Society v Ahmed* [1995] 38 E.G. 138, CA) unless the original order itself can be set aside, the warrant is obtained by fraud or there has been abuse of the process or oppression in its execution (*Hammersmith and Fulham LBC v Hill* [1994] 35 E.G. 124; (1995) 27 H.L.R. 368; [1994] 2 E.G.L.R. 51, CA).

See also *Mortgage Agency Services v Bal* (1998) 95(28) L.S.G. 31, CA (s.36 ceases to apply after execution of warrant).

Mortgage Pre-Action Protocol

3A–41.1   A new pre-action protocol for possession claims based on residential mortgage arrears came into force on November 19, 2008. See C12–001, the annotations thereto, CPR 55.10 and the commentary at 55.10.2.

Paragraph numbers marked with a "+" can be found online and on CD.

Forms of order

See County Court Forms **N29** (Order for possession (mortgaged property)) and **3A–42** **N31** (Order for possession of mortgaged land suspended under the Administration of Justice Act 1970 s.36 and the Administration of Justice Act 1973 s.8) as specified in the Practice Direction to CPR Pt 4, Table 3.

European Convention of Human Rights

There is no inconsistency between Administration of Justice Act 1970 s.36 and **3A–43** Convention rights under art.8 or art.1 of the First Protocol (*Barclays Bank v Alcorn* [2002] EWCA Civ 817; June 17, 2002).

* * * *

38A. This Part of this Act shall not apply to a mortgage securing **3A–44** an agreement which is a regulated agreement within the meaning of the Consumer Credit Act 1974.

Note —Inserted by the Consumer Credit Act 1974 s.192(3)(a), Sch.4, Pt 1, para.30. **3A–45**

Statutory protection

For the statutory protection given to borrowers under the Consumer Credit Act **3A–46** 1974, see below.

* * * * *

Interpretation of Part IV

39.—(1) In this Part of this Act— **3A–47**

"dwelling-house" includes any building or part thereof which is used as a dwelling;

"mortgage" includes a charge and "mortgagor" and "mortgagee" shall be construed accordingly;

"mortgagor" and "mortgagee" includes any person deriving title under the original mortgagor or mortgagee.

(2) The fact that part of the premises comprised in a dwelling-house is used as a shop or office or for business, trade or professional purposes shall not prevent the dwelling-house from being a dwelling-house for the purposes of this Part of this Act.

Defective Premises Act 1972

(1972 c.35) **3A–48**

ARRANGEMENT OF SECTIONS

Duty to build dwellings properly

1.—(1) A person taking on work for or in connection with the pro- **3A–49**

Paragraph numbers marked with a "+" can be found online and on CD.

HOUSING

vision of a dwelling (whether the dwelling is provided by the erection or by the conversion or enlargement of a building) owes a duty—

    (a) if the dwelling is provided to the order of any person, to that person; and

    (b) without prejudice to paragraph (a) above, to every person who acquires an interest (whether legal or equitable) in the dwelling;

to see that the work which he takes on is done in a workman-like or, as the case may be, professional manner, with proper materials and so that as regards that work the dwelling will be fit for habitation when completed.

(2) A person who takes on any such work for another on terms that he is to do it in accordance with instructions given by or on behalf of that other shall, to the extent to which he does it properly in accordance with those instructions, be treated for the purposes of this section as discharging the duty imposed on him by subsection (1) above except where he owes a duty to that other to warn him of any defects in the instructions and fails to discharge that duty.

(3) A person shall not be treated for the purposes of subsection (2) above as having given instructions for the doing of work merely because he has agreed to the work being done in a specified manner, with specified materials or to a specified design.

(4) A person who—

    (a) in the course of a business which consists of or includes providing or arranging for the provision of dwellings or installations in dwellings; or

    (b) in the exercise of a power of making such provision or arrangements conferred by or by virtue of any enactment;

arranges for another to take on work for or in connection with the provision of a dwelling shall be treated for the purposes of this section as included among the persons who have taken on the work.

(5) Any cause of action in respect of a breach of the duty imposed by this section shall be deemed, for the purposes of the Limitation Act 1939, the Law Reform (Limitation of Actions, &c.) Act 1954 and the Limitation Act 1963, to have accrued at the time when the dwelling was completed, but if after that time a person who has done work for or in connection with the provision of the dwelling does further work to rectify the work he has already done, any such cause of action in respect of that further work shall be deemed for those purposes to have accrued at the time when the further work was finished.

Duty to build dwellings properly

3A–50   This section imposes a duty to carry out work (whether by new building or conversion) for or in connection with the provision of a dwelling in a professional or workmanlike manner so that the premises are fit for habitation. It applies both to damage caused by the actual work and damage caused by failure to undertake necessary works (*Andrews v Schooling* [1991] 3 All E.R. 723; (1991) 23 H.L.R. 316, CA and *Mirza v Bhandal* August 1999, Legal Action 24, QBD).

Paragraph numbers marked with a "+" can be found online and on CD.

For cases excluded from s.1, see s.2, below.

The duty only applies to work carried out after January 1, 1974.

As to limitation, see s.1(5) and *Alderson v Beetham Organisation Ltd* [2003] EWCA Civ 408; [2003] H.L.R. 60.

Cases excluded from the remedy under section 1

2.—(1) Where—   3A–51

      (a) in connection with the provision of a dwelling or its first sale or letting for habitation any rights in respect of defects in the state of the dwelling are conferred by an approved scheme to which this section applies on a person having or acquiring an interest in the dwelling; and

      (b) it is stated in a document of a type approved for the purposes of this section that the requirements as to design or construction imposed by or under the scheme have, or appear to have, been substantially complied with in relation to the dwelling;

no action shall be brought by any person having or acquiring an interest in the dwelling for breach of the duty imposed by section 1 above in relation to the dwelling.

(2) A scheme to which this section applies—

      (a) may consist of any number of documents and any number of agreements or other transactions between any number of persons; but

      (b) must confer, by virtue of agreements entered into with persons having or acquiring an interest in the dwellings to which the scheme applies, rights on such persons in respect of defects in the state of the dwellings.

(3) In this section "approved" means approved by the Secretary of State, and the power of the Secretary of State to approve a scheme or document for the purposes of this section shall be exercisable by order, except that any requirements as to construction or design imposed under a scheme to which this section applies may be approved by him without making any order or, if he thinks fit, by order.

(4) The Secretary of State—

      (a) may approve a scheme or document for the purposes of this section with or without limiting the duration of his approval; and

      (b) may by order revoke or vary a previous order under this section or, without such an order, revoke or vary a previous approval under this section given otherwise than by order.

(5) The production of a document purporting to be a copy of an approval given by the Secretary of State otherwise than by order and certified by an officer of the Secretary of State to be a true copy of the approval shall be conclusive evidence of the approval, and without proof of the handwriting or official position of the person purporting to sign the certificate.

Paragraph numbers marked with a "+" can be found online and on CD.

HOUSING

(6) The power to make an order under this section shall be exercisable by statutory instrument which shall be subject to annulment in pursuance of a resolution by either House of Parliament.

(7) Where an interest in a dwelling is compulsorily acquired—

   (a) no action shall be brought by the acquiring authority for breach of the duty imposed by section 1 above in respect of the dwelling; and

   (b) if any work for or in connection with the provision of the dwelling was done otherwise than in the course of a business by the person in occupation of the dwelling at the time of the compulsory acquisition, the acquiring authority and not that person shall be treated as the person who took on the work and accordingly as owing that duty.

Duty of care with respect to work done on premises not abated by disposal of premises

3A–52   3.—(1) Where work of construction, repair, maintenance or demolition or any other work is done on or in relation to premises, any duty of care owed, because of the doing of the work, to persons who might reasonably be expected to be affected by the defects in the state of the premises created by the doing of the work shall not be abated by the subsequent disposal of the premises by the persons who owed the duty.

(2) This section does not apply—

   (a) in the case of premises which are let, where the relevant tenancy of the premises commenced, or the relevant tenancy agreement of the premises was entered into, before the commencement of this Act;

   (b) in the case of premises disposed of in any other way, when the disposal of the premises was completed, or a contract for their disposal was entered into, before the commencement of this Act; or

   (c) in either case, where the relevant transaction disposing of the premises is entered into in pursuance of an enforceable option by which the consideration for the disposal was fixed before the commencement of this Act.

"disposal"

3A–53   For the definition of "disposal", see s.6 below.

Landlord's duty of care in virtue of obligation or right to repair premises demised

3A–54   4.—(1) Where premises are let under a tenancy which puts on the landlord an obligation to the tenant for the maintenance or repair of the premises, the landlord owes to all persons who might reasonably be expected to be affected by defects in the state of the premises a duty to take such care as is reasonable in all the circumstances to see that they are reasonably safe from personal injury or from damage to their property caused by a relevant defect.

Paragraph numbers marked with a "+" can be found online and on CD.

(2) The said duty is owed if the landlord knows (whether as the result of being notified by the tenant or otherwise) or if he ought in all the circumstances to have known of the relevant defect.

(3) In this section "relevant defect" means a defect in the state of the premises existing at or after the material time and arising from, or continuing because of, an act or omission by the landlord which constitutes or would if he had had notice of the defect, have constituted a failure by him to carry out his obligation to the tenant for the maintenance or repair of the premises; and for the purposes of the foregoing provision "the material time" means—

    (a) where the tenancy commenced before this Act, the commencement of this Act; and

    (b) in all other cases, the earliest of the following times, that is to say—

        (i) the time when the tenancy commences;

        (ii) the time when the tenancy agreement is entered into;

        (iii) the time when possession is taken of the premises in contemplation of the letting.

(4) Where premises are let under a tenancy which expressly or impliedly gives the landlord the right to enter the premises to carry out any description of maintenance or repair of the premises, then, as from the time when he first is, or by notice or otherwise can put himself, in a position to exercise the right and so long as he is or can put himself in that position, he shall be treated for the purposes of subsections (1) to (3) above (but for no other purpose) as if he were under an obligation to the tenant for that description of maintenance or repair of the premises; but the landlord shall not owe the tenant any duty by virtue of this subsection in respect of any defect in the state of the premises arising from, or continuing because of, a failure to carry out an obligation expressly imposed on the tenant by the tenancy.

(5) For the purposes of this section obligations imposed or rights given by any enactment in virtue of a tenancy shall be treated as imposed or given by the tenancy.

(6) This section applies to a right of occupation given by contract or any enactment and not amounting to a tenancy as if the right were a tenancy, and "tenancy" and cognate expressions shall be construed accordingly.

"Landlord's duty of care ..."

Section 4 imposes on landlords a duty of care to all persons who might reasonably **3A–55** be affected by defects in the premises. The duty is to take such care as is reasonable in all the circumstances to see that they are reasonably safe from pesonal injury or from damage to their property (see, e.g. *Clarke v Taff Ely BC* (1983) 10 H.L.R. 44, QBD). The duty is owed if the landlord has the express or implied right under the agreement to enter the premises to carry out any description of maintenance or repair of the premises (e.g. *McAuley v Bristol City Council* [1992] 1 All E.R. 749; (1991) 23 H.L.R. 586; [1991] 46 E.G. 155, CA). See too the Rent Act 1977 ss.3(2) and 148 (below); and the Housing Act 1988 s.16 (below).

A tenant relying upon s.4 merely has to show a failure on the part of the landlord to take such care as is reasonable in the circumstances to see that the tenant is reason-

Paragraph numbers marked with a "+" can be found online and on CD.

ably safe from personal injury. That duty is owed if the landlord "ought in all circumstances" to have known of the relevant defect. That is a general test of negligence. There is no express or implied exclusion of the tenant from the category of persons who might be affected. The burden of a tenant in establishing a breach of duty under s.4 should not be equated with the need under Landlord and Tenant Act 1987 s.11 to demonstrate notice (actual or constructive) of the actual defect giving rise to injury (*Sykes v Harry* [2001] EWCA Civ 167; [2001] Q.B. 1014).

The word "premises" may include a paved area built by a previous tenant outside a house (*Smith v Bradford MDC* (1982) 4 H.L.R. 86; (1982) P. & C.R. 171, CA).

As to liability at common law, see *Targett v Torfaen BC* [1992] 3 All E.R. 27; (1992) 24 H.L.R. 164, CA.

Works required to remedy a defect in design are not works of "repair", giving that word the meaning that it has to bear in this context. In such circumstances s.4 is not engaged (*Lee v Leeds City Council* [2002] All E.R. 124; [2002] 1 W.L.R. 1488, CA).

Application to Crown

3A–56   **5.** This Act shall bind the Crown, but as regards the Crown's liability in tort shall not bind the Crown further than the Crown is made liable in tort by the Crown Proceedings Act 1947.

Supplemental

3A–57   **6.**—(1) In this Act—

"disposal", in relation to premises, includes a letting, and an assignment or surrender of a tenancy, of the premises and the creation by contract of any other right to occupy the premises, and "dispose" shall be construed accordingly;

"personal injury" includes any disease and any impairment of a person's physical or mental condition;

"tenancy" means—

(a) a tenancy created either immediately or derivatively out of the freehold, whether by a lease or underlease, by an agreement for a lease or underlease or by a tenancy agreement, but not including a mortgage term or any interest arising in favour of a mortgagor by his attorning tenant to his mortgagee; or

(b) a tenancy at will or a tenancy on sufferance; or

(c) a tenancy, whether or not constituting a tenancy at common law, created by or in pursuance of any enactment;

and cognate expressions shall be construed accordingly.

(2) Any duty imposed by or enforceable by virtue of any provision of this Act is in addition to any duty a person may owe apart from that provision.

(3) Any term of an agreement which purports to exclude or restrict, or has the effect of excluding or restricting, the operation of any of the provisions of this Act, or any liability arising by virtue of any such provision, shall be void.

(4) Section 4 of the Occupiers' Liability Act 1957 (repairing landlord's duty to visitors to premises) is hereby repealed.

Local Government Act 1972

(1972 c.70)

3A–57.1

PART XI

LEGAL PROCEEDINGS

Power of local authorities to prosecute or defend legal proceedings

222.—(1) Where a local authority consider it expedient for the promotion or protection of the interests of the inhabitants of their area— 3A–57.2

(a) they may prosecute or defend or appear in any legal proceedings and, in the case of civil proceedings, may institute them in their own name, and

(b) they may, in their own name, make representations in the interests of the inhabitants at any public inquiry held by or on behalf of any Minister or public body under any enactment.

(2) In this section "local authority" includes the Common Council and the London Fire and Emergency Planning Authority.

Amendment

Subsection (2): the words "and the London Fire and Emergency Planning Author- 3A–57.3 ity" in square brackets were inserted by the Greater London Authority Act 1999 s.328 and Sch.29, Pt I, para.20.

This section has effect as if a National Park authority were a principal council for the purposes of this Act and as if the relevant Park were the authority's area, by virtue of the Environment Act 1995 s.65, Sch.8, para.3(1).

See further the Local Government Reorganisation (Miscellaneous Provisions) Order 1990 (SI 1990/1765) art.4(3).

Editorial introduction

The purpose of s.222 is to enable local authorities to bring and defend proceedings 3A–57.4 in their own names without the involvement of the Attorney General. It does not give councils substantive powers. It is simply a procedural section which gives them powers formerly vested only in the Attorney General. The courts have considered the correct approach to the exercise of this power in the public interest in two principal contexts: the restraint of breaches of the criminal law and the suppression of public nuisances. Courts should be reluctant to grant injunctions in aid of the criminal law which, if disobeyed, may involve the infringer in sanctions far more onerous than the penalty imposed for the offence. See e.g. *Birmingham CC v Shafi* [2008] EWCA Civ 1186; October 30, 2008 where the terms of the injunction sought to restrain criminal behaviour were identical or almost identical to the terms of an ASBO. Sir Anthony Clarke M.R. and Rix L.J. stated that in such circumstances,

"where Parliament has legislated in detail to deal with a particular problem, the courts should in general leave the matter to be dealt with as Parliament intended and, save perhaps in exceptional circumstances, refuse to grant injunctive relief of the kind which can be obtained by an ASBO [44]. ... [the courts] should not now develop a separate but parallel jurisprudence in respect of identical orders." [61]

Where an injunction is sought under s.222 to restrain a public nuisance, the

Paragraph numbers marked with a "+" can be found online and on CD.

principles which the court should apply should be less restrictive than in the case where it is sought to restrain the commission of a crime. See e.g. *Nottingham CC v Zain (a minor)* [2001] EWCA Civ 1248; [2002] 1 W.L.R. 607 where the Court of Appeal held that a local authority had the power to institute proceedings in its own name for injunctive relief to restrain a public nuisance provided that it considered it expedient for the promotion and protection of the interests of the inhabitants of its area.

Administration of Justice Act 1973

3A–57.5

(1973 c.15)

ARRANGEMENT OF SECTIONS

PART II

MISCELLANEOUS

PART II

MISCELLANEOUS

Extension of powers of court in action by mortgagee of dwelling-house

3A–58   8.—(1) Where by a mortgage of land which consists of or includes a dwelling-house, or by any agreement between the mortgagee under such a mortgage and the mortgagor, the mortgagor is entitled or is to be permitted to pay the principal sum secured by instalments or otherwise to defer payment of it in whole or in part, but provision is also made for earlier payment in the event of any default by the mortgagor or of a demand by the mortgagee or otherwise, then for purposes of section 36 of the Administration of Justice Act 1970 (under which a court has power to delay giving a mortgagee possession of the mortgaged property so as to allow the mortgagor a reasonable time to pay any sums due under the mortgage) a court may treat as due under the mortgage on account of the principal sum secured and of interest on it only such amounts as the mortgagor would have expected to be required to pay if there had been no such provision for earlier payment.

(2) A court shall not exercise by virtue of subsection (1) above the powers conferred by section 36 of the Administration of Justice Act 1970 unless it appears to the court not only that the mortgagor is likely to be able within a reasonable period to pay any amounts regarded (in accordance with subsection (1) above) as due on account of the principal sum secured, together with the interest on those amounts, but also that he is likely to be able by the end of that period to pay any further amounts that he would have expected to be required to pay by then on account of that sum and of interest on it if there had been no such provision as is referred to in subsection (1)above for earlier payment.

(3) Where subsection (1) above would apply to an action in which a mortgagee only claimed possession of the mortgaged property, and

Paragraph numbers marked with a "+" can be found online and on CD.

the mortgagee brings an action for foreclosure (with or without also claiming possession of the property), then section 36 of the Administration of Justice Act 1970 together with subsections (1) and (2) above shall apply as they would apply if it were an action in which the mortgagee only claimed possession of the mortgaged property, except that—

    (a) section 36(2)(b) shall apply only in relation to any claim for possession; and

    (b) section 36(5) shall not apply.

(4) For purposes of this section the expressions "dwelling-house", "mortgage", "mortgagee" and "mortgagor" shall be construed in the same way as for the purposes of Part IV of the Administration of Justice Act 1970.

(5) [...]

(6) In the application of this section to Northern Ireland, subsection (3) shall be omitted.

Note —Repealed by the Statute Law (Repeals) Act 2004 s.1(1), Sch.1, Pt 1.   **3A–59**

"Extension of powers of court …"

See the Administration of Justice Act 1970 s.36, above and the commentary thereto. **3A–60**

The purpose of s.8 is to allow courts to exercise their powers to adjourn, stay, suspend or postpone the date for the giving up of possession in mortgage possession proceedings if it is likely that the arrears of instalments and interest can be repaid during a reasonable period, *cf. Halifax Building Society v Clark* [1973] Ch. 307; [1973] 2 All E.R. 33, where, prior to the passing of the 1973 Act, it was held that s.36 only applied where it was likely that all sums due (including the whole of the capital) could be paid during a reasonable period. Section 8 extends the possibility of relief under s.36 to mortgagors with endowment mortgages (*Bank of Scotland v Grimes* [1985] 2 All E.R. 254 and *Royal Bank of Scotland v Miller* [2001] EWCA Civ 344; [2002] Q.B. 255; [2001] 3 W.L.R. 523; see too *Habib Bank v Tailor* [1982] 1 W.L.R. 1218; [1982] 3 All E.R. 561).

Welsh Development Agency Act 1975

(1975 c.70)

    3A–60.1

For Sch.4 to the Welsh Development Agency Act 1975 plus any related commentary see paragraphs 3A–61+ to 3A–64+ on White Book on Westlaw UK or the Civil Procedure CD.

Protection from Eviction Act 1977

(1977 c.43)

    3A–65

ARRANGEMENT OF SECTIONS

PART I

UNLAWFUL EVICTION AND HARASSMENT

Paragraph numbers marked with a "+" can be found online and on CD.

HOUSING

PART I

UNLAWFUL EVICTION AND HARASSMENT

Restriction on re-entry without due process of law

3A–66   **2.** Where any premises are let as a dwelling on a lease which is subject to a right of re-entry or forfeiture it shall not be lawful to enforce that right otherwise than by proceedings in the court while any person is lawfully residing in the premises or part of them.

"court"

3A–67   See s.9.

"let"

3A–68   See s.8(2).

The purpose of this section is to prevent peaceable re-entry of premises "let as a dwelling" while there is "any person lawfully residing" in them or any part of them. In such circumstances possession proceedings must be brought in court. The phrase "let as a dwelling" in s.2 means "let wholly or partly as a dwelling". It therefore applies to premises which are let for mixed residential and business purposes (*Pirabakaran v Patel* [2006] EWCA Civ 685; [2006] 1 W.L.R. 3112).

For the restriction on forfeiture or re-entry for arrears of service charges see the Housing Act 1996 s.81, and, generally, Commonhold and Leasehold Reform Act 2002 ss.167–171, below.

Prohibition of eviction without due process of law

3A–69   **3.**—(1) Where any premises have been let as a dwelling under a tenancy which is neither a statutorily protected tenancy nor an excluded tenancy and—

  (a) the tenancy (in this section referred to as the former tenancy) has come to an end, but

  (b) the occupier continues to reside in the premises or part of them,

it shall not be lawful for the owner to enforce against the occupier, otherwise than by proceedings in the court, his right to recover possession of the premises.

(2) In this section "the occupier", in relation to any premises, means any person lawfully residing in the premises or part of them at the termination of the former tenancy.

(2A) Subsections (1) and (2) above apply in relation to any restricted contract (within the meaning of the Rent Act 1977) which—

  (a) creates a licence; and

  (b) is entered into after the commencement of section 69 of the Housing Act 1980;

as they apply in relation to a restricted contract which creates a tenancy.

Paragraph numbers marked with a "+" can be found online and on CD.

(2B) Subsections (1) and (2) above apply in relation to any premises occupied as a dwelling under a licence, other than an excluded licence, as they apply in relation to premises let as a dwelling under a tenancy, and in those subsections the expressions "let" and "tenancy" shall be construed accordingly.

(2C) References in the preceding provisions of this section and section 4(2A) below to an excluded tenancy do not apply to—

(a) a tenancy entered into before the date on which the Housing Act 1988 came into force, or

(b) a tenancy entered into on or after that date but pursuant to a contract made before that date,

but, subject to that, "excluded tenancy" and "excluded licence" shall be construed in accordance with section 3A below.

(3) This section shall, with the necessary modifications, apply where the owner's right to recover possession arises on the death of the tenant under a statutory tenancy within the meaning of the Rent Act 1977 or the Rent (Agriculture) Act 1976.

Note —Amended by the Housing Act 1980 s.69(1); and the Housing Act 1988 ss.30 and 40. **3A–70**

"tenancy" and "statutorily protected tenancy"
See s.8(1). **3A–71**

"excluded tenancy"
See s.3A. **3A–72**

"owner"
See s.8(3). **3A–73**

"court"
See s.9. **3A–74**

"let"
See s.8(2). **3A–75**

Prohibition of eviction without due process of law
This section prevents eviction without a court order. It applies to occupiers who are **3A–76** not statutorily protected (i.e. those who lack full security of tenure as defined in s.8(1), i.e. under Rent Act 1977, Rent (Agriculture) Act 1976, Landlord and Tenant Act 1954 Pt II, Agricultural Holdings Act 1986, Housing Act 1988 and Agricultural Tenancies Act 1995). Eviction of such tenants without a court order is unlawful.

It does not however apply to excluded tenants (see s.3A below). Excluded occupiers can be evicted without court orders.

Breach of s.3 is an actionable tort.

In *Mohamed v Manek and Kensington and Chelsea RLBC* (1995) 94 L.G.R. 211; (1995) 27 H.L.R. 439, CA, it was held that:

(a) the 1977 Act was not intended to apply to temporary housing provided by local authorities under the Housing Act 1985 s.63 (now Housing Act 1996 s.188; see too *Desnousse v Newham LBC* [2006] EWCA Civ 547; [2006] Q.B. 831— homeless person accommodated in self-contained accommodation owned by a private company, but managed by a housing association); and

(b) temporary accommodation in a hotel or hostel cannot be "premises occupied as a dwelling under a licence" for the purposes of s.3(2B).

Excluded tenancies and licences

3A.—(1) Any reference in this Act to an excluded tenancy or an **3A–77**

Paragraph numbers marked with a "+" can be found online and on CD.

excluded licence is a reference to a tenancy or licence which is excluded by virtue of any of the following provisions of this section.

(2) A tenancy or licence is excluded if—

    (a) under its terms the occupier shares any accommodation with the landlord or licensor; and

    (b) immediately before the tenancy or licence was granted and also at the time it comes to an end, the landlord or licensor occupied as his only or principal home premises of which the whole or part of the shared accommodation formed part.

(3) A tenancy or licence is also excluded if—

    (a) under its terms the occupier shares any accommodation with a member of the family of the landlord or licensor;

    (b) immediately before the tenancy or licence was granted and also at the time it comes to an end, the member of the family of the landlord or licensor occupied as his only or principal home premises of which the whole or part of the shared accommodation formed part; and

    (c) immediately before the tenancy or licence was granted and also at the time it comes to an end, the landlord or licensor occupied as his only or principal home premises in the same building as the shared accommodation and that building is not a purpose-built block of flats.

(4) For the purposes of subsections (2) and (3) above, an occupier shares accommodation with another person if he has the use of it in common with that person (whether or not also in common with others) and any reference in those subsections to shared accommodation shall be construed accordingly, and if, in relation to any tenancy or licence, there is at any time more than one person who is the landlord of licensor, any reference in those subsections to the landlord or licensor shall be construed as a reference to any one of those persons.

(5) In subsections (2) to (4) above—

    (a) "accommodation" includes neither an area used for storage nor a staircase, passage, corridor or other means of access;

    (b) "occupier" means, in relation to a tenancy, the tenant and, in relation to a licence, the licensee; and

    (c) "purpose-built block of flats" has the same meaning as in Part III of Schedule 1 to the Housing Act 1988;

and section 113 of the Housing Act 1985 shall apply to determine whether a person is for the purposes of subsection (3) above a member of another's family as it applies for the purposes of Part IV of that Act.

(6) A tenancy or licence is excluded if it was granted as a temporary expedient to a person who entered the premises in question or any other premises as a trespasser (whether or not, before the beginning of that tenancy or licence, another tenancy or licence to occupy the premises or any other premises had been granted to him).

Paragraph numbers marked with a "+" can be found online and on CD.

(7) A tenancy or licence is excluded if—

    (a) it confers on the tenant or licensee the right to occupy the premises for a holiday only; or

    (b) it is granted otherwise than for money or money's worth.

(7A) A tenancy or licence is excluded if it is granted in order to provide accommodation under section 4 or Part VI of the Immigration and Asylum Act 1999.

(7B) Section 32 of the Nationality, Immigration and Asylum Act 2002 (accommodation centre: tenure) provides for a resident's licence to occupy an accommodation centre to be an excluded licence.

(7C) A tenancy or licence is excluded if it is granted in order to provide accommodation under the Displaced Persons (Temporary Protection) Regulations 2005.

(8) A licence is excluded if it confers rights of occupation in a hostel, within the meaning of the Housing Act 1985, which is provided by—

    (a) the council of a county, county borough, district or London Borough, the Common Council of the City of London, the Council of the Isles of Scilly, the Inner London Education Authority, the London Fire and Emergency Planning Authority, a joint authority within the meaning of the Local Government Act 1985 or a residuary body within the meaning of that Act;

    (b) a development corporation within the meaning of the New Towns Act 1981;

    (c) the Commission for the New Towns;

    (d) an urban development corporation established by an order under section 135 of the Local Government, Planning and Land Act 1980;

    (e) a housing action trust established under Part III of the Housing Act 1988;

    (f) [...]

    (g) the Housing Corporation;

    (ga) the Secretary of State under section 89 of the Housing Associations Act 1985;

    (h) a housing trust (within the meaning of the Housing Associations Act 1985) which is a charity or a registered social landlord (within the meaning of the Housing Act 1985); or

    (i) any other person who is, or who belongs to a class of person which is, specified in an order made by the Secretary of State.

(9) The power to make an order under subsection (8)(i) above shall be exercisable by statutory instrument which shall be subject to annulment in pursuance of a resolution of either House of Parliament.

Note —Added by the Housing Act 1988 s.31. Amended by the Local Government **3A-78** (Wales) Act 1994 Sch.8, para.4(1); the Housing Act 1996 (Consequential Provisions) Order 1996 (SI 1996/2325) art.5, Sch.2, para.7; the Government of Wales Act 1998

Paragraph numbers marked with a "+" can be found online and on CD.

s.140 and Sch.16, para.2 and Sch.18, Pt IV the Immigration and Asylum Act 1996 Sch.14, para.73; Greater London Authority Act 1999 Sch.29, para.27; by the Nationality, Immigration and Asylum Act 2002 s.32(5); SI 2005/1379; and by the Immigration, Asylum and Nationality Act 2006 s.43(4)(a).

Excluded tenancies

3A–79   For a case in which the Court of Appeal considered s.3A(2) see *Sumeghova v McMahon* [2002] EWCA Civ 1581; [2003] H.L.R. 26, and for a case where Elias J. considered whether premises were "a hostel" (s.3A(8)), see *Rogerson v Wigan MBC* [2004] EWHC 1677 (QB); [2005] H.L.R. 10 (residents allocated bedrooms with their own locks in flat but shared the facilities with other residents, warden with master key and terms of occupation including a nightly curfew, a prohibition on alcohol and drugs. The premises met the statutory definition of a "hostel" in Housing Act 1985 s.622 in that they provided residential accommodation with facilities for preparation of food "otherwise than in separate or self contained accommodation"). See too *Mohamed v Manek and Kensington and Chelsea RLBC* (1995) 27 H.L.R. 439, CA and *Desnousse v Newham LBC* [2006] EWCA Civ 547; [2006] Q.B. 831.

For an example of a licence granted for money's worth (s.3A(7)), see *Polarpark Enterprises Inc v Allason* [2007] EWHC (Ch) 1088; [2008] L. & T.R. 6.

* * * *

PART II

NOTICE TO QUIT

* * * *

Validity of notices to quit

3A–80   **5.**—(1) Subject to subsection (1B) below no notice by a landlord or a tenant to quit any premises let (whether before or after the commencement of this Act) as a dwelling shall be valid unless—

> (a) it is in writing and contains such information as may be prescribed, and
>
> (b) it is given not less than 4 weeks before the date on which it is to take effect.

(1A) Subject to subsection (1B) below, no notice by a licensor or a licensee to determine a periodic licence to occupy premises as a dwelling (whether the licence was granted before or after the passing of this Act) shall be valid unless—

> (a) it is in writing and contains such information as may be prescribed, and
>
> (b) it is given not less than 4 weeks before the date on which it is to take effect.

(1B) Nothing in subsection (1) or subsection (1A) above applies to—

> (a) premises let on an excluded tenancy which is entered into on or after the date on which the Housing Act 1988 came into force unless it is entered into pursuant to a contract made before that date; or
>
> (b) premises occupied under an excluded licence.

(2) In this section "prescribed" means prescribed by regulations made by the Secretary of State by statutory instrument, and a statu-

Paragraph numbers marked with a "+" can be found online and on CD.

tory instrument containing any such regulations shall be subject to annulment in pursuance of a resolution of either House of Parliament.

(3) Regulations under this section may make different provision in relation to different descriptions of lettings and different circumstances.

Note —Amended by the Housing Act 1988 s.32.

3A–81

Excluded tenancies

Note that this section does not apply to excluded tenancies (see s.3A above, *Mohamed v Manek and Kensingson and Chelsea RLBC* (1995) 94 L.G.R. 211; (1995) 27 H.L.R. 439, CA and *Desnousse v Newham LBC* [2006] EWCA Civ 547; [2006] Q.B. 831).

3A–82

"let ... as a dwelling"

Premises let as an agricultural holding, even if there is a dwelling upon the holding, do not constitute "premises let as a dwelling" for the purposes of this section (see *National Trust for Places of Historic Interest v Knipe* [1997] 40 E.G. 151; *The Times*, June 21, 1997, CA).

3A–83

"not less than 4 weeks"

The statutory four-week period should be reckoned as a period which includes the first day of the notice but excludes the last day. The requirement for a minimum of four weeks' notice does not mean "28 clear days" (*Schnabel v Allard* [1967] 1 Q.B. 627; [1966] 3 All E.R. 816, CA). Note that the test generally applicable when interpreting a notice to quit is "Is the notice quite clear to a reasonable tenant reading it? Is it plain that he cannot be misled by it?" (*Carradine Properties Ltd v Aslam* [1976] 1 W.L.R. 442; [1976] 1 All E.R. 573, Ch D, where on September 6, 1974 landlords served a notice stating that they intended to terminate the lease on September 27, 1973. Their intention had been to determine it on September 27, 1975, but the reference to 1973 was a clerical error. The notice was held to be valid because the tenant reading the notice must have seen the mistake and realised that it was "obvious" that the landlord meant 1975. The decision in *Carradine Properties Ltd v Aslam* was approved by the House of Lords in *Mannai Investment Co Ltd v Eagle Star Life Assurance Co Ltd* [1997] A.C. 749; [1997] 2 W.L.R. 945; [1997] 3 All E.R. 352, HL.

It has been held that it is possible for a landlord and the tenant to waive the requirements of Protection from Eviction Act 1977 s.5 (*Hackney LBC v Snowden* (2001) 33 H.L.R. 49, CA; *Lewisham LBC v Lasisi-Agiri* [2003] EWHC 2392 (Ch); [2003] 45 E.G.C.S. 175).

3A–84

"such information as may be prescribed"

See the Notices to Quit (Prescribed Information) Regulations 1988 (SI 1988/2201) which apply to notices to quit served by landlords. It is as follows:

(1) If the tenant or licensee does not leave the dwelling, the landlord or licensor must get an order for possession from the court before the tenant or licensee can lawfully be evicted. The landlord or licensor cannot apply for such an order before the notice to quit or notice to determine has run out.

(2) A tenant or licensee who does not know if he has any right to remain in possession after a notice to quit or notice to determine runs out can obtain advice from a solicitor. Help with all or part of the cost of legal advice and assistance may be available under the Legal Aid Scheme. He should also be able to obtain information from a Citizens' Advice Bureau, a Housing Aid Centre or a Rent Officer.

There is no prescribed information for notices to quit served by tenants.

It is not necessary that the precise form of wording of the current regulations should be set out (see *Beckerman v Durling* (1983) 6 H.L.R. 87, CA; *Swansea CC v Hearn* (1991) 23 H.L.R. 284, CA, and *Tadema Holdings v Ferguson* [2000] 32 H.L.R. 866, cases where landlords used forms of notice to quit which complied with earlier regulations

3A–85

Paragraph numbers marked with a "+" can be found online and on CD.

which had been superseded and where in substance all the information required by the then current regulations was contained in the notice served).

As to service of notices to quit, see *Wandsworth LBC v Attwell* (1995) 27 H.L.R. 536; [1996] 01 E.G. 100; (1996) 94 L.G.R. 419, CA; and *Enfield LBC v Devonish* (1997) 29 H.L.R. 691, CA.

PART III

SUPPLEMENTAL PROVISIONS

* * * *

Interpretation

3A–86   8.—(1) In this Act "statutorily protected tenancy" means—

    (a) a protected tenancy within the meaning of the Rent Act 1977 or a tenancy to which Part I of the Landlord and Tenant Act 1954 applies;

    (b) a protected occupancy or statutory tenancy as defined in the Rent (Agriculture) Act 1976;

    (c) a tenancy to which Part II of the Landlord and Tenant Act 1954 applies;

    (d) a tenancy of an agricultural holding within the meaning of the Agricultural Holdings Act 1986 which is a tenancy in relation to which that Act applies.

    (e) an assured tenancy or assured agricultural occupancy under Part I of the Housing Act 1988;

    (f) a tenancy to which Schedule 10 to the Local Government and Housing Act 1989 applies;

    (g) a farm business tenancy within the meaning of the Agricultural Tenancies Act 1995.

(2) For the purposes of Part I of this Act a person who, under the terms of his employment, had exclusive possession of any premises other than as a tenant shall be deemed to have been a tenant and the expressions "let" and "tenancy" shall be construed accordingly.

(3) In Part I of this Act "the owner", in relation to any premises, means the person who, as against the occupier, is entitled to possession thereof.

(4) In this Act "excluded tenancy" and "excluded licence" have the meaning assigned by section 3A of this Act.

(5) If, on or after the date on which the Housing Act 1988 came into force, the terms of an excluded tenancy or excluded licence entered into before that date are varied, then—

    (a) if the variation affects the amount of the rent which is payable under the tenancy or licence, the tenancy or licence shall be treated for the purposes of sections 3(2C) and 5(1B) above as a new tenancy or licence entered into at the time of the variation; and

    (b) if the variation does not affect the amount of the rent which is so payable, nothing in this Act shall affect the

Paragraph numbers marked with a "+" can be found online and on CD.

determination of the question whether the variation is such as to give rise to a new tenancy or licence.

(6) Any reference in subsection (5) above to a variation affecting the amount of the rent which is payable under a tenancy or licence does not include a reference to—

(a) a reduction or increase effected under Part III or Part VI of the Rent Act 1977 (rents under regulated tenancies and housing association tenancies), section 78 of that Act (power of rent tribunal in relation to restricted contracts) or sections 11 to 14 of the Rent (Agriculture) Act 1976; or

(b) a variation which is made by the parties and has the effect of making the rent expressed to be payable under the tenancy or licence the same as a rent for the dwelling which is entered in the register under Part IV or section 79 of the Rent Act 1977.

Note —Amended by the Agricultural Holdings Act 1986 Sch.14, para.61; the Housing Act 1988 s.33; the Local Government and Housing Act 1989 Sch.11, para.54; and the Agricultural Tenancies Act 1995 Sch., para.29. **3A–87**

The court for purposes of Part I

9.—(1) The court for the purposes of Part I of this Act shall, subject **3A–88** to this section, be—

(a) the county court, in relation to premises with respect to which the county court has for the time being jurisdiction in actions for the recovery of land; and

(b) the High Court, in relation to other premises.

(2) Any powers of a county court in proceedings for the recovery of possession of any premises in the circumstances mentioned in section 3(1) of this Act may be exercised with the leave of the judge by any registrar of the court, except in so far as rules of court otherwise provide.

(3) Nothing in this Act shall affect the jurisdiction of the High Court in proceedings to enforce a lessor's right of re-entry or forfeiture or to enforce a mortgagee's right of possession in a case where the former tenancy was not binding on the mortgagee.

(4) Nothing in this Act shall affect the operation of—

(a) section 59 of the Pluralities Act 1838;

(b) section 19 of the Defence Act 1842;

(c) section 6 of the Lecturers and Parish Clerks Act 1844;

(d) paragraph 3 of Schedule 1 to the Sexual Offences Act 1956; or

(e) section 13 of the Compulsory Purchase Act 1965.

HOUSING

Paragraph numbers marked with a "+" can be found online and on CD.

Rent Act 1977

(1977 c.42)

Paragraph numbers marked with a "+" can be found online and on CD.

PART I

PRELIMINARY

PROTECTED AND STATUTORY TENANCIES

Protected tenants and tenancies

1. Subject to this Part of this Act, a tenancy under which a dwelling- **3A–90**
house (which may be a house or part of a house) is let as a separate
dwelling is a protected tenancy for the purposes of this Act. Any reference in this Act to a protected tenant shall be construed accordingly.

"let", "protected tenancy", "protected tenant" and "tenancy"
See s.152, below.   **3A–91**

Protected tenants and tenancies
The Rent Act 1977 provided security of tenure and rent regulation for many tenan- **3A–92**
cies created before January 15, 1989. The Housing Act 1988 s.34 (see below) lists three
circumstances in which tenancies created on or after January 15, 1989 may also be
within Rent Act protection. Otherwise private sector tenancies created after the
implementation of the Housing Act 1988 are either assured tenancies, assured shorthold tenancies or tenancies with no security of tenure.

There can be no Rent Act protection if the occupant has a licence, as opposed to a
tenancy (but see, e.g. *Street v Mountford* [1985] A.C. 809; [1985] 2 W.L.R. 877; [1985] 2
All E.R. 289, HL; *AG Securities v Vaughan* and *Antoniades v Villiers and Bridger* [1990] 1
A.C. 417; [1988] 3 W.L.R. 1205; [1988] 3 All E.R. 1058, HL; *Duke v Wynne* [1989] 3 All
E.R. 130, CA; *Hadjiloucas v Crean* [1988] 1 W.L.R. 1006; [1987] 3 All E.R. 1008, CA;
Nicolau v Pitt (1989) 21 H.L.R. 487; [1989] 21 E.G. 71, CA; *Aslan v Murphy* [1989] 3 All
E.R. 130, CA; and *Crancour Ltd v Da Silvaesa* (1986) 18 H.L.R. 265; (1986) 278 E.G.

Paragraph numbers marked with a "+" can be found online and on CD.

618, CA) or if any of the exceptions listed in Pt I of the Rent Act apply. Rent Act security of tenure operates by preventing landlords from recovering possession after termination of contractual tenancies unless they can prove a ground for possession and, when relying on certain grounds for possession, prove that it is reasonable to make a possession order (see the Rent Act 1977 s.98 and Sch.15, below).

See too *Gray v Taylor* [1998] 4 All E.R. 17, CA; and *Meynell Family Properties Ltd v Meynell*, June 1998, Legal Action 12, CA.

"as a separate dwelling"

3A–93   See *Goodrich v Paisner* [1957] A.C. 65; [1956] 2 All E.R. 176, HL; *Central London YMCA Housing Association Ltd v Goodman* (1992) 24 H.L.R. 109, CA; *Central London YMCA Housing Association Ltd v Saunders* (1991) 23 H.L.R. 212, CA; *Horford Investments v Lambert* [1976] Ch. 39; [1974] 1 All E.R. 131, CA; *Kavanagh v Lyroudias* [1985] 1 All E.R. 560, CA; *Mortgage Corp v Ubah* (1997) 73 P. & C.R. 500; (1997) 29 H.L.R. 48, CA; and *St Catherine's College v Dorling* [1980] 1 W.L.R. 66; [1979] 3 All E.R. 250, CA and *Mansfield DC v Langridge* [2008] EWCA Civ 264; [2008] H.L.R. 34.

The word "dwelling" is not a term of art with a specialised legal meaning. It is "the place where [an occupier] lives and to which he returns and which forms the centre of his existence ... No doubt he will sleep there and usually eat there; he will often prepare at least some of his meals there." However there is no legislative requirement that cooking facilities must be available for premises to qualify as a dwelling. In deciding whether an occupant has security of tenure:

> "The first step is to identify the subject-matter of the tenancy agreement. If this is a house or part of a house of which the tenant has exclusive possession with no element of sharing, the only question is whether, at the date when proceedings were brought, it was the tenant's home. If so, it was his dwelling ... The presence or absence of cooking facilities in the part of the premises of which the tenant has exclusive occupation is not relevant."

(See *Uratemp Ventures Ltd v Collins and Carrell* [2001] UKHL 43; [2002] 1 A.C. 301; [2001] 3 W.L.R. 806; [2002] 1 All E.R. 46.)

Statutory tenants and tenancies

3A–94   2.—(1) Subject to this Part of this Act—

(a) after the termination of a protected tenancy of a dwelling-house the person who, immediately before that termination, was the protected tenant of the dwelling-house shall, if and so long as he occupies the dwelling-house as his residence, be the statutory tenant of it; and

(b) Part I of Schedule 1 to this Act shall have effect for determining what person (if any) is the statutory tenant of a dwelling-house or, as the case may be, is entitled to an assured tenancy of a dwelling-house by succession at any time after the death of a person who, immediately before his death, was either a protected tenant of the dwelling-house or the statutory tenant of it by virtue of paragraph (a) above.

(2) In this Act a dwelling-house is referred to as subject to a statutory tenancy when there is a statutory tenant of it.

(3) In subsection (1)(a) above and in Part I of Schedule 1, the phrase "if and so long as he occupies the dwelling-house as his residence" shall be construed as it was immediately before the commencement of this Act (that is to say, in accordance with section 3(2) of the Rent Act 1968).

(4) A person who becomes a statutory tenant of a dwelling-house as mentioned in subsection (1)(a) above is, in this Act, referred to as a statutory tenant by virtue of his previous protected tenancy.

Paragraph numbers marked with a "+" can be found online and on CD.

(5) A person who becomes a statutory tenant as mentioned in subsection (1)(b) above is, in this Act, referred to as a statutory tenant by succession.

Note —Amended by the Housing Act 1988 s.39(1).   **3A–95**

"dwelling-house"
See ss.1 and 26.   **3A–96**

"let", "protected tenancy", "protected tenant" and "tenancy"
See s.152 below.   **3A–97**

Statutory tenants and tenancies
Section 2 provides that after termination of a contractual tenancy a statutory tenancy   **3A–98**
comes into existence if the tenant is still occupying the premises as a residence.

If two people are joint tenants under a protected tenancy, but one ceases to occupy the premises as a residence, the remaining tenant will become the statutory tenant on termination of the tenancy if s/he is still occupying them as a residence (*Lloyd v Sadler* [1978] Q.B. 774; [1978] 2 W.L.R. 721; [1978] 2 All E.R. 529, CA).

If tenants cease to occupy as a residence, there can be no statutory tenancy, and, if the contractual tenancy has been determined, tenants who cease to reside lose security of tenure (Rent Act 1977 s.2(1)(a)). Tenants who are temporarily absent may nevertheless still be occupying as a residence if they can show a de facto intention to return and some formal outward and visible sign of that intention—an *animus possidendi* and a *corpus possessionis*. A considerable body of case-law on this subject has built up over the years. See, e.g. *Hampstead Way Investments Ltd v Lewis-Weare* [1985] 1 W.L.R. 164; [1985] 1 All E.R. 564, HL; *Bevington v Crawford* (1974) 232 E.G. 191, CA; *Blanway Investments Ltd v Lynch* (1993) 25 H.L.R. 378, CA; *Brickfield Properties Ltd v Hughes* (1988) 20 H.L.R. 108; [1988] 24 E.G. 95, CA; *Brown v Brash* [1948] 2 K.B. 247; [1948] 1 All E.R. 922, CA; *DF Crocker Securities (Portsmouth) Ltd v Johal* (1989) 42 E.G. 103, CA; *Duke v Porter* (1986) 280 E.G. 633; (1987) 19 H.L.R. 1, CA; *Gofor Investments v Roberts* (1975) 29 P. & C.R. 366, CA; *Hall v King* (1987) 19 H.L.R. 440, CA; *Regalian Securities Ltd v Scheuer* (1982) 5 H.L.R. 48; (1982) 263 E.G. 973; (1982) 47 P. & C.R. 362, CA; *Richards v Green* (1984) 11 H.L.R. 1; (1983) 268 E.G. 443, CA; *Robert Thackray's Estate Ltd v Kaye* (1989) 21 H.L.R. 160, CA; *Tickner v Hearn* [1961] 1 All E.R. 65, CA; *Wigley v Leigh* [1950] 1 All E.R. 73, CA and *Prince v Robinson* (1999) 31 H.L.R. 89.

Terms and conditions of statutory tenancies

3.—(1) So long as he retains possession, a statutory tenant shall   **3A–99**
observe and be entitled to the benefit of all the terms and conditions of the original contract of tenancy, so far as they are consistent with the provisions of this Act.

(2) It shall be a condition of a statutory tenancy of a dwelling-house that the statutory tenant shall afford to the landlord access to the dwelling-house and all reasonable facilities for executing therein any repairs which the landlord is entitled to execute.

(3) Subject to section 5 of the Protection from Eviction Act 1977 (under which at least 4 weeks' notice to quit is required), a statutory tenant of a dwelling-house shall be entitled to give up possession of the dwelling-house if, and only if, he gives such notice as would have been required under the provisions of the original contract of tenancy, or, if no notice would have been so required, on giving not less than 3 months' notice.

(4) Notwithstanding anything in the contract of tenancy, a landlord who obtains an order for possession of a dwelling-house as

Paragraph numbers marked with a "+" can be found online and on CD.

against a statutory tenant shall not be required to give to the statutory tenant any notice to quit.

(5) Part II of Schedule 1 to this Act shall have effect in relation to the giving up of possession of statutory tenancies and the changing of statutory tenants by agreement.

"dwelling-house"
3A–100   See ss.1 and 26.

"statutory tenant"
3A–101   See ss.2 and 152.

"let", "protected tenancy", "protected tenant", and "tenancy"
3A–102   See ss.1 and 152.

EXCEPTIONS

Dwelling-houses above certain rateable values

3A–103   **4.**—(1) A tenancy which is entered into before April 1, 1990 or (where the dwelling-house had a rateable value on March 31, 1990) is entered into on or after April 1, 1990 in pursuance of a contract made before that date is not a protected tenancy if the dwelling-house falls within one of the Classes set out in subsection (2) below.

(2) Where alternative rateable values are mentioned in this subsection, the higher applies if the dwelling-house is in Greater London and the lower applies if it is elsewhere.

Class A

The appropriate day in relation to the dwelling-house falls or fell on or after April 1, 1973 and the dwelling-house on the appropriate day has or had a rateable value exceeding £1,500 or £750.

Class B

The appropriate day in relation to the dwelling-house fell on or after March 22, 1973, but before April 1, 1973, and the dwelling-house—

> (a) on the appropriate day had a rateable value exceeding £600 or £800, and
>
> (b) on April 1, 1973 had a rateable value exceeding £1,500 or £750.

Class C

The appropriate day in relation to the dwelling-house fell before March 22, 1973 and the dwelling-house—

> (a) on the appropriate day had a rateable value exceeding £400 or £200, and
>
> (b) on March 22, 1973 had a rateable value exceeding £600 or £300, and
>
> (c) on April 1, 1973 had a rateable value exceeding £1,500 or £750.

(3) If any question arises in any proceedings whether a dwelling-house falls within a Class in subsection (2) above, by virtue of its rate-

Paragraph numbers marked with a "+" can be found online and on CD.

able value at any time, it shall be deemed not to fall within that Class unless the contrary is shown.

(4) A tenancy is not a protected tenancy if—

    (a) it is entered into on or after April 1, 1990 (otherwise than, where the dwelling-house had a rateable value on March 31, 1990, in pursuance of a contract made before April 1, 1990), and

    (b) under it the rent payable for the time being is payable at a rate exceeding £25,000 a year.

(5) In subsection (4) above "rent" does not include any sum payable by the tenant as is expressed (in whatever terms) to be payable in respect of rates, council tax, services, repairs, maintenance or insurance, unless it could not have been regarded by the parties as a sum so payable.

(6) If any question arises in any proceedings whether a tenancy is precluded from being a protected tenancy by subsection (4) above, the tenancy shall be deemed to be a protected tenancy unless the contrary is shown.

(7) The Secretary of State may by order replace the amount referred to in subsection (4) above by an amount specified in the order; and such an order shall be made by statutory instrument which shall be subject to annulment in pursuance of a resolution of either House of Parliament.

Note —Amended by the References to Rating (Housing) Regulations 1990 (SI 1990/ 434) reg.2, Sch., paras 15 and 16; and (SI 1993/651), Sch.1, para.3. **3A–104**

Dwelling-houses above certain rateable values
The retrospective alteration of the rateable value does not bring a tenancy within protection (*Guest Heath plc v Mirza* (1990) 22 H.L.R. 399, QBD). **3A–105**

Tenancies at low rents
5.—(1) A tenancy which was entered into before April 1, 1990 or (where the dwelling-house under the tenancy had a rateable value on March 31, 1990) is entered into on or after April 1, 1990 in pursuance of a contract made before that date is not a protected tenancy if under the tenancy either no rent is payable or, the rent payable is less than two-thirds of the rateable value which is or was the rateable value of the dwelling-house on the appropriate day. **3A–106**

(2) Where—

    (a) the appropriate day in relation to a dwelling-house fell before March 22, 1973, and

    (b) the dwelling-house had on the appropriate day a rateable value exceeding, if it is in Greater London, £400 or, if it is elsewhere, £200.

subsection (1) above shall apply in relation to the dwelling-house as if the reference to the appropriate day were a reference to March 22, 1973.

(2A) A tenancy is not a protected tenancy if—

    (a) it is entered into on or after April 1, 1990 (otherwise

Paragraph numbers marked with a "+" can be found online and on CD.

HOUSING

than, where the dwelling-house had a rateable value on March 31, 1990, in pursuance of a contract made before April 1, 1990), and

(b) under the tenancy for the time being either no rent is payable or the rent is payable at a rate of, if the dwelling-house is in Greater London, £1,000 or less a year, and, if the dwelling-house is elsewhere, £250 or less a year.

(2B) Subsection (7) of section 4 above shall apply to any amount referred to in subsection (2A) above as it applies to the amount referred to in subsection (4) of that section.

(3) In this Act a tenancy falling within subsection (1) above is referred to as a "tenancy at a low rent".

(4) In determining whether a long tenancy is a tenancy at a low rent, there shall be disregarded such part (if any) of the sums payable by the tenant as is expressed (in whatever terms) to be payable in respect of rates, council tax, services, repairs, maintenance, or insurance, unless it could not have been regarded by the parties as a part so payable.

(5) In subsection (4) above "long tenancy" means a tenancy granted for a term certain exceeding 21 years, other than a tenancy which is, or may become, terminable before the end of that term by notice given to the tenant.

3A–107 *Note* —Amended by the Housing Act 1980 s.152 and Sch.26; the References to Rating (Housing) Regulations 1990 (SI 1990/434) paras 17 and 18; and the Local Government Finance (Housing) (Consequential Amendments) Order 1993 (SI 1993/651) Sch.1, para.4.

Tenancies at low rents

3A–108 The Court of Appeal in *Bostock v Bryant* (1990) 22 H.L.R. 449; [1990] 39 E.G. 64, CA, stated that "if parties to an agreement describe a payment ... as rent, the court will normally accept that it is properly so described", but in that case "the more natural inference to be drawn from the payments by the tenants of the gas and electricity bills was that it was simply a payment of their part of the expenses incurred and a sharing of the expenses of the house" ((1990) 22 H.L.R. at 452). In those circumstances the inference should not be drawn that the payments were rent.

Certain shared ownership leases

3A–109 5A.—(1) A tenancy is not a protected tenancy if it is a qualifying shared ownership lease, that is—

(a) a lease granted in pursuance of the right to be granted a shared ownership lease under Part V of the Housing Act 1985, or

(b) a lease granted by a housing association and which complies with the conditions set out in subsection (2) below.

(2) The conditions referred to in subsection (1)(b) above are that the lease—

(a) was granted for a term of 99 years or more and is not (and cannot become) terminable except in pursuance of a provision for re-entry or forfeiture;

Paragraph numbers marked with a "+" can be found online and on CD.

    (b) was granted at a premium, calculated by reference to the value of the dwelling-house or the cost of providing it, of not less than 25 per cent, or such other percentage as may be prescribed, of the figure by reference to which it was calculated;

    (c) provides for the tenant to acquire additional shares in the dwelling-house on terms specified in the lease and complying with such requirements as may be prescribed;

    (d) does not restrict the tenant's powers to assign, mortgage or charge his interest in the dwelling-house;

    (e) if it enables the landlord to require payment for outstanding shares in the dwelling-house, does so only in such circumstances as may be prescribed;

    (f) provides, in the case of a house, for the tenant to acquire the landlord's interest on terms specified in the lease and complying with such requirements as may be prescribed; and

    (g) states that the landlord's opinion that by virtue of this section the lease is excluded from the operation of this Act.

(3) The Secretary of State may by regulations prescribe anything requiring to be prescribed for the purposes of subsection (2) above.

(4) The regulations may—

    (a) make different provision for different cases or descriptions of case, including different provision for different areas, and

    (b) contain such incidental, supplementary or transitional provisions as the Secretary of State considers appropriate,

and shall be made by statutory instrument which shall be subject to annulment in pursuance of a resolution of either House of Parliament.

(5) In any proceedings the court may, if of opinion that it is just and equitable to do so, treat a lease as a qualifying shared ownership lease notwithstanding that the condition specified in subsection (2)(g) above is not satisfied.

(6) In this section—

"house" has the same meaning as in Part I of the Leasehold Reform Act 1967;

"housing association" has the same meaning as in the Housing Associations Act 1985; and

"lease" includes an agreement for a lease, and references to the grant of a lease shall be construed accordingly.

Note —Inserted by the Housing and Planning Act 1986 s.18 and Sch.4.   **3A–110**

Dwelling-houses let with other land

6. Subject to section 26 of this Act, a tenancy is not a protected   **3A–111** tenancy if the dwelling-house which is subject to the tenancy is let together with land other than the site of the dwelling-house.

Paragraph numbers marked with a "+" can be found online and on CD.

3A–112 **"dwelling-house"**
See ss.1 and 26.

3A–113 **"let", "protected tenancy", "protected tenant" and "tenancy"**
See ss.1 and 152.

Payments for board or attendance

3A–114 7.—(1) A tenancy is not a protected tenancy if under the tenancy the dwelling-house is bona fide let at a rent which includes payments in respect of board or attendance.

(2) For the purposes of subsection (1) above, a dwelling-house shall not be taken to be bona fide let at a rent which includes payments in respect of attendance unless the amount of rent which is fairly attributable to attendance, having regard to the value of the attendance to the tenant, forms a substantial part of the whole rent.

3A–115 **"dwelling-house"**
See ss.1 and 26.

3A–116 **"let", "protected tenancy", "protected tenant" and "tenancy"**
See ss.1 and 152.

3A–117 **Payments for board of attendance**
A tenancy cannot be a Rent Act protected tenancy if the rent includes "payment in respect of board or attendance ... [and] the value of the attendance to the tenant forms a substantial part of the whole rent".

In *Otter v Norman* [1989] A.C. 129; [1988] 3 W.L.R. 321; [1988] 2 All E.R. 897, HL, Lord Bridge approved *dicta* in *Wilkes v Goodwin* [1923] 2 K.B. 86 that any amount of board suffices, provided it is not *de minimis*, but stressed the need for the tenant's rent to include "not only the cost of the food and drink provided but also all the housekeeping chores which must be undertaken in shopping for provisions, preparation and service of meals on the premises and cleaning and washing up after meals" ([1988] 2 All E.R. at 901). It is clear that the provision of a box of uncooked and unprepared groceries once a week is not sufficient to constitute board, although this might amount to an "attendance". Lord Bridge also pointed out that the "courts have consistently set their face against artificial and contrived devices whereby landlords have sought to deny to tenants the protection intended to be conferred by the Rent Acts" (at 901). "Attendance" means "services personal to the tenant" and the question of "proportionality" is a question of fact for the trial judge (*Nelson Developments Ltd v Taboada* [1992] 34 E.G. 72; (1992) 24 H.L.R. 462, CA).

Lettings to students

3A–118 8.—(1) A tenancy is not a protected tenancy if it is granted to a person who is pursuing, or intends to pursue, a course of study provided by a specified educational institution and is so granted either by that institution or by another specified institution or body of persons.

(2) In subsection (1) above "specified" means specified, or of a class specified, for the purposes of this section by regulations made by the Secretary of State by statutory instrument.

(3) A statutory instrument containing any such regulations shall be subject to annulment in pursuance of a resolution of either House of Parliament.

Paragraph numbers marked with a "+" can be found online and on CD.

"protected tenancy", and "tenancy"
See ss.1 and 152.

3A–119

"specified educational institution"
See the Assured and Protected Tenancies (Lettings to Students) Regulations 1998 (SI 1998/1967) which define SEIs—basically any institution which provides higher or further education which is publicly funded and various other named institutions.

3A–120

Holiday lettings

9. A tenancy is not a protected tenancy if the purpose of the tenancy is to confer on the tenant the right to occupy the dwelling-house for a holiday.

3A–121

"dwelling-house"
See ss.1 and 26.

3A–122

"let", "protected tenancy", "protected tenant" and "tenancy"
See ss.1 and 152.

3A–123

Holiday lettings
In *Buchmann v May* [1978] 2 All E.R. 993, CA, the Court of Appeal held that the labels put on a transaction are not conclusive, but that where a tenancy agreement expressly states the purpose for which it is made, that statement is evidence of that purpose unless the tenant can establish that it does not correspond with the true purpose, either because the express label is a sham or because it is a false label. Although a court will be "astute to detect a sham where it appears that a provision has been inserted for the purpose of depriving the tenant of statutory protection under the Rent Acts" ([1978] 2 All E.R. 993 at 999), the burden of proof lies on the tenant. In that case there was no evidence which displaced the express purpose and accordingly there was no Rent Act protection. The court accepted the dictionary definition of a holiday as "a period of cessation of work, or period of recreation".

See too *R. v Rent Officer for Camden LBC Ex p. Plant* (1980) 257 E.G. 713; (1983) 7 H.L.R. 15, QBD, where there was "clear evidence that all the parties knew that [the applicants] were going to occupy it for the purpose of their work as students" and that that was "conclusive of the matter", and *McHale v Daneham* (1979) 249 E.G. 969, where H.H.J. Edwards, sitting at Bloomsbury and Marylebone County Court, held that there was "no reason why a working holiday should not fall within the provisions of s.9 of the Rent Act".

3A–124

Agricultural holdings

10.—(1) A tenancy is not a protected tenancy if—

(a) the dwelling-house is comprised in an agricultural holding and is occupied by the person responsible for the control (whether as tenant or as servant or agent of the tenant) of the farming of the holding, or

(b) the dwelling-house is comprised in the holding held under a farm business tenancy and is occupied by the person responsible for the control (whether as tenant or as servant or agent of the tenant) of the management of the holding.

(2) In subsection (1) above—

"agricultural holding" means any agricultural holding within the meaning of the Agricultural Holdings Act 1986 held under a tenancy in relation to which that Act applies, and

"farm business tenancy" and "holding" in relation to such a tenancy, have the same meaning as in the Agricultural Tenancies Act 1995.

3A–125

Paragraph numbers marked with a "+" can be found online and on CD.

HOUSING

3A-126 *Note* —Substituted by the Agricultural Tenancies Act 1995 Sch., para.27.

Licensed premises

3A-127 **11.** A tenancy of a dwelling-house which consists of or comprises premises which, by virtue of a premises licence under the Licensing Act 2003 may be used for the supply of alcohol (within the meaning of section 14 of that Act) for consumption on the premises shall not be a protected tenancy, nor shall such a dwelling-house be the subject of a statutory tenancy.

3A-128 *Note* —Amended by the Licensing Act 2003 s.198(1), Sch.6, para.67.

Resident landlords

3A-129 **12.**—(1) Subject to subsection (2) below, a tenancy of a dwelling-house granted on or after August 14, 1974 shall not be a protected tenancy at any time if—

    (a) the dwelling-house forms part only of a building and, except in a case where the dwelling-house also forms part of a flat, the building is not a purpose-built block of flats; and

    (b) the tenancy was granted by a person who, at the time when he granted it, occupied as his residence another dwelling-house which—

        (i) in the case mentioned in paragraph (a) above, also forms part of the flat; or

        (ii) in any other case, also forms part of the building; and

    (c) subject to paragraph 1 of Schedule 2 to this Act, at all times since the tenancy was granted the interest of the landlord under the tenancy has belonged to a person who, at the time he owned that interest, occupied as his residence another dwelling-house which—

        (i) in the case mentioned in paragraph (a) above, also formed part of the flat; or

        (ii) in any other case, also formed part of the building.

(2) This section does not apply to a tenancy of a dwelling-house which forms part of a building if the tenancy is granted to a person who, immediately before it was granted, was a protected or statutory tenant of that dwelling-house or of any other dwelling-house in that building.

(3) [...]

(4) Schedule 2 to this Act shall have effect for the purpose of supplementing this section.

3A-130 *Note* —Amended by the Housing Act 1980 ss.65(1) and 69(4).

"dwelling-house"
3A-131 See ss.1 and 26.

"statutory tenant"
3A-132 See ss.2 and 152.

Paragraph numbers marked with a "+" can be found online and on CD.

"let", "protected tenancy", "protected tenant" and "tenancy"
  See ss.1 and 152.

3A–133

"purpose-built block of flats"
  See Sch.2, para.4.

3A–134

Resident landlords
    In *Cooper v Tait* (1984) 15 H.L.R. 98; (1984) 271 E.G. 105, CA, the Court of Appeal held that the residence requirements may be fulfilled by just one out of several joint landlords.

3A–135

    When courts are considering whether a landlord is a resident landlord within the meaning of s.12 they should use the same test as when deciding whether a statutory tenant continues to occupy premises as a residence for the purposes of the Rent Act 1977 s.2 (see above). Landlords who are temporarily absent must leave in the premises some personal and visible sign of their intention to return (*Jackson v Pekic* [1989] 47 E.G. 141, CA).

    Questions as to whether or not premises are part of the same building are essentially a question of fact for the county court judge. In *Griffiths v English* (1981) 2 H.L.R. 134; (1982) 261 E.G. 257, CA; *Barnes v Gorsuch* (1982) 43 P. & C.R. 294; (1982) 263 E.G. 253; (1982) 43 P. & C.R. 294, CA; *Bardrick v Haycock* (1976) 1 P. & C.R. 420; (1981) 2 H.L.R. 118, CA; *Lewis-Graham v Conacher* [1992] 02 E.G. 171, CA, and *Wolff v Waddington* [1989] 47 E.G. 148, CA, the Court of Appeal declined to interfere with such findings.

Landlord's interest belonging to Crown

    13.—(1) Except as provided by subsection (2) below—

3A–136

      (a) a tenancy shall not be a protected tenancy at any time when the interest of the landlord under the tenancy belongs to Her Majesty in right of the Crown or to a government department or is held in trust for Her Majesty for the purposes of a government department; and

      (b) a person shall not at any time be a statutory tenant of a dwelling-house if the interest of his immediate landlord would at that time belong or be held as mentioned in paragraph (a) above.

    (2) An interest belonging to Her Majesty in right of the Crown shall not prevent a tenancy from being a protected tenancy or a person from being a statutory tenant if the interest is under the management of the Crown Estate Commissioners.

    Note—Substituted by the Housing Act 1980 s.73. See also the National Health Service and Community Care Act 1990 Sch.8, para.19.

3A–137

"dwelling-house"
  See ss.1 and 26.

3A–138

"statutory tenant"
  See ss.2 and 152.

3A–139

"protected tenancy" and "tenancy"
  See ss.1 and 152.

3A–140

"landlord"
  See s.152(1).

3A–141

Landlord's interest belonging to local authority, etc.

    14. A tenancy shall not be a protected tenancy at any time when the interest of the landlord under that tenancy belongs to—

3A–142

Paragraph numbers marked with a "+" can be found online and on CD.

HOUSING

(a) the council of a county or county borough;

(b) the council of a district or, in the application of this Act to the Isles of Scilly, the Council of the Isles of Scilly;

(bb) the Broads Authority;

(bc) a National Park Authority;

(c) the council of a London borough or the Common Council of the City of London;

(ca) [...]

(caa) a police authority established under section 3 of the Police Act 1996;

(caaa) [...];

(cba) an authority established for an area in England by an order under section 207 of the Local Government and Public Involvement in Health Act 2007 (joint waste authorities);

(cb) a joint authority established by Part IV of the Local Government Act 1985;

(d) the Commission for the New Towns;

(e) a development corporation established by an order made, or having effect as if made, under the New Towns Act 1981; or

(f) [...]

(g) an urban development corporation within the meaning of Part XVI of the Local Government, Planning and Land Act 1980;

(h) a housing action trust established under Part III of the Housing Act 1988;

(i) the Residuary Body of Wales (Corff Gweddilliol Cymru);

nor shall a person at any time be a statutory tenant of a dwelling-house if the interest of his immediate landlord would belong at that time to any of those bodies.

3A–143 Note —Amended by Local Government (Wales) Act 1994 Schs 8 and 13; the Police and Magistrates' Courts Act 1994 Sch.4; the Environment Act 1995 Sch.10; SI 1985/1884; the Local Government, Planning and Land Act 1980 s.155; the New Towns Act 1981 Sch.12; the Local Government Act 1985 Schs 14 and 17; the Norfolk and Suffolk Broads Act 1988 ss.21, 23, 27, Sch.6; the Housing Act 1988 s.62; the Education Reform Act 1988 s.237, Sch.13; the Police Act 1997 Sch.9, para.39; the Government of Wales Act 1998 Sch.18, Pt IV; the Criminal Justice and Police Act 2001 Sch.7, Pt 5 and the Local Government and Public Involvement in Health Act 2007, s.209, Sch.13, para.35 with effect from April 1, 2008 (SI 2008/917).

"dwelling-house"
3A–144 See ss.1 and 26.

"statutory tenant"
3A–145 See ss.2 and 152.

"protected tenancy", "protected tenant" and "tenancy"
3A–146 See ss.1 and 152.

"landlord"
3A–147 See s.152(1).

Paragraph numbers marked with a "+" can be found online and on CD.

Welsh Development Agency

Note that some tenants of the Welsh Development Agency do not enjoy security of tenure. See para.3A–60.1, The Welsh Development Agency Act 1975 Sch.4 as inserted by Government of Wales Act 1998 Sch.13.

3A–148

Landlord's interest belonging to housing association, etc.

15.—(1) A tenancy shall not be a protected tenancy at any time when the interest of the landlord under that tenancy belongs to a housing association falling within subsection (3) below; nor shall a person at any time be a statutory tenant of a dwelling-house if the interest of his immediate landlord would belong at that time to such a housing asociation.

3A–149

(2) A tenancy shall not be a protected tenancy at any time when the interest of the landlord under that tenancy belongs to—

(a) the Housing Corporation; or

(aa) [...]

(b) a housing trust which is a charity within the meaning of the Charities Act 1993; nor shall a person at any time be a statutory tenant of a dwelling-house if the interest of his immediate landlord would belong at that time to any of those bodies.

(3) A housing association falls within this subsection if—

(a) it is a registered social landlord within the meaning of the Housing Act 1985(see section 5(4) and (5) of that Act); or

(b) it is a co-operative housing association within the meaning of the Housing Associations Act 1985; or

(c) [...]

(d) [...]

(4) [...]

(5) In subsection (2) above "housing trust" means a corporation or body of persons which—

(a) is required by the terms of its constituent instrument to use the whole of its funds, including any surplus which may arise from its operations, for the purpose of providing housing accommodation; or

(b) is required by the terms of its constituent instrument to devote the whole, or substantially the whole, of its funds to charitable purposes and in fact uses the whole, or substantially the whole, of its funds for the purpose of providing housing accommodation.

(6) [...]

Note —Amended by the Housing Act 1980 ss.74 and 152 and Sch.26; the Housing (Consequential Provisions) Act 1985 s.4, Sch.2; the Housing Act 1988 s.140, Sch.17, para.99; the Charities Act 1993 s.98(1), Sch.6; and Order 1996 art.5, Sch.2, para.66 and the Government of Wales Act 1998 Sch.18, Pt IV.

3A–150

"dwelling-house"

See ss.1 and 26.

3A–151

Paragraph numbers marked with a "+" can be found online and on CD.

"statutory tenant"

3A–152   See ss.2 and 152.

"protected tenancy", "protected tenant" and "tenancy"

3A–153   See ss.1 and 152.

"landlord"

3A–154   See ss.152(1).

"registered social landlord"

3A–155   See the Housing Act 1996 ss.1–7.

"co-operative housing association"

3A–156   See the Housing Associations Act 1985 s.1, which defines a housing association as a "society, body of trustees or company (a) which is established for the purpose of, or amongst whose objects or powers are included those of, providing, constructing, improving or managing, or facilitating or encouraging the construction or improvement of, housing accommodation, and (b) which does not trade for profit or whose constitution or rules prohibit the issue of capital with interest or dividend exceeding such rate as may be prescribed by the treasury, whether with or without differentiation between share and loan capital" and a co-operative housing association as "a fully mutual housing association which is a friendly society registered under the Industrial and Provident Societies Act 1965 ..."

Landlord's interest belonging to housing co-operative

3A–157   **16.** A tenancy shall not be a protected tenancy at any time when the interest of the landlord under that tenancy belongs to a housing co-operative, within the meaning of section 27B of the Housing Act 1985 (agreements with housing co-operatives under certain superseded provisions) and the dwelling-house is comprised in a housing co-operative agreement within the meaning of that section.

3A–158   *Note* —Amended by the Housing and Planning Act 1986 s.24(1), (2), Sch.5, para.15.

"dwelling-house"

3A–159   See ss.1 and 26.

"protected tenancy" and "tenancy"

3A–160   See ss.1 and 152.

"housing co-operative"

3A–161   See the Housing Act 1985 s.5.

CONTROLLED AND REGULATED TENANCIES

* * * * *

Regulated tenancies

3A–162   **18.**—(1) Subject to sections 24(3) and 143 of this Act, a "regulated tenancy" is, for the purposes of this Act, a protected or statutory tenancy.

(2) Where a regulated tenancy is followed by a statutory tenancy of the same dwelling-house, the two shall be treated for the purposes of this Act as together constituting one regulated tenancy.

(3) [...]

Paragraph numbers marked with a "+" can be found online and on CD.

(4) [...]

Note—Amended by the Housing Act 1980 Schs 25, and 26. **3A–163**

"dwelling-house"
See ss.1 and 26. **3A–164**

"statuory tenant"
See ss.2 and 152. **3A–165**

"protected tenancy" and "tenancy"
See ss.1 and 152. **3A–166**

Modification of Act for controlled tenancies converted into regulated tenancies

18A. Schedule 17 to this Act applies for the purpose of modifying **3A–167**
the provisions of this Act in relation to a tenancy which, by virtue of
any of the following enactments, was converted from a controlled
tenancy into a regulated tenancy, that is to say—

(a) section 18(3) of this Act;

(b) paragraph 5 of Schedule 2 to the Rent Act 1968 (which was
superseded by section 18(3));

(c) Part VIII of this Act;

(d) Part III of the Housing Finance Act 1972 (which was
superseded by Part VIII);

(e) Part IV of the Act of 1972 (conversion by reference to rateable
values);

(f) section 64 of the Housing Act 1980 (conversion of remaining
controlled tenancies into regulated tenancies).

Note—Added by the Housing Act 1980 Sch.25. **3A–168**

* * * *

SHARED ACCOMMODATION

Tenant sharing accommodation with persons other than landlord

22.—(1) Where a tenant has the exclusive occupation of any ac- **3A–169**
commodation ("the separate accommodation") and—

(a) the terms as between the tenant and his landlord on
which he holds the separate accommodation include the
use of other accommodation ("the shared accommodation") in common with another person or other persons,
not being or including the landlord, and

(b) by reason only of the circumstances mentioned in
paragraph (a) above, the separate accommodation would
not, apart from this section, be a dwelling-house let on
or subject to a protected or statutory tenancy,

the separate accommodation shall be deemed to be a dwelling-
house let on a protected tenancy or, as the case may be, subject to a

Paragraph numbers marked with a "+" can be found online and on CD.

statutory tenancy and the following provisions of this section shall have effect.

(2) For the avoidance of doubt it is hereby declared that where, for the purpose of determining the rateable value of the separate accommodation, it is necessary to make an apportionment under this Act, regard is to be had to the circumstances mentioned in subsection (1)(a) above.

(3) While the tenant is in possession of the separate accommodation (whether as a protected or statutory tenant), any term or condition of the contract of tenancy terminating or modifying, or providing for the termination or modification of, his right to use any of the shared accommodation which is living accommodation shall be of no effect.

(4) Where the terms and conditions of the contract of tenancy are such that at any time during the tenancy the persons in common with whom the tenant is entitled to the use of the shared accommodation could be varied, or their number could be increased, nothing in subsection (3) above shall prevent those terms and conditions from having effect so far as they relate to any such variation or increase.

(5) Without prejudice to the enforcement of any order made under subsection (6) below, while the tenant is in possession of the separate accommodation, no order shall be made for possession of any of the shared accommodation, whether on the application of the immediate landlord of the tenant or on the application of any person under whom that landlord derives title, unless a like order has been made, or is made at the same time, in respect of the separate accommodation; and the provisions of section 98(1) of this Act shall apply accordingly.

(6) On the application of the landlord, the county court may make such order either—

    (a) terminating the right of the tenant to use the whole or any part of the shared accommodation other than living accommodation, or

    (b) modifying his right to use the whole or any part of the shared accommodation, whether by varying the persons or increasing the number of persons entitled to the use of that accommodation, or otherwise,

as the court thinks just.

(7) No order shall be made under subsection (6) above so as to effect any termination or modification of the rights of the tenant which, apart from subsection (3) above, could not be effected by or under the terms of the contract of tenancy.

(8) In this section "living accommodation" means accommodation of such a nature that the fact that it constitutes or is included in the shared accommodation is (or, if the tenancy has ended, was) sufficient, apart from this section, to prevent the tenancy from constituting a protected tenancy of a dwelling-house.

Paragraph numbers marked with a "+" can be found online and on CD.

"dwelling-house"
See ss.1 and 26.   **3A–170**

"statuory tenant"
See ss.2 and 152.   **3A–171**

"landlord", "protected tenancy" and "tenant"
See ss.1 and 152.   **3A–172**

SUBLETTINGS

Certain sublettings not to exclude any part of sub-lessor's premises from protection

23.—(1) Where the tenant of any premises, consisting of a house **3A–173** or part of a house, has sublet a part but not the whole of the premises, then, as against his landlord or any superior landlord, no part of the premises shall be treated as not being a dwelling-house let on or subject to a protected or statutory tenancy by reason only that—

(a) the terms on which any person claiming under the tenant holds any part of the premises include the use of accommodation in common with other persons; or

(b) part of the premises is let to any such person at a rent which includes payments in respect of board or attendance.

(2) Nothing in this section shall affect the rights against, and liabilities to, each other of the tenant and any person claiming under him, or of any two such persons.

"dwelling-house"
See ss.1 and 26.   **3A–174**

"statuory tenant"
See ss.2 and 152.   **3A–175**

"landlord" and "protected tenancy"
See ss.1 and 152.   **3A–176**

BUSINESS PREMISES

Premises with a business use

24.—(1) [...]   **3A–177**

(2) [...]

(3) A tenancy shall not be a regulated tenancy if it is a tenancy to which Part II of the Landlord and Tenant Act 1954 applies (but this provision is without prejudice to the application of any other provision of this Act to a sub-tenancy of any part of the premises comprised in such a tenancy).

Note—Amended by the Housing Act 1980 s.152 and Sch.26.   **3A–178**

Premises with business use
Section 24 provides that a tenancy cannot be a regulated tenancy if it is a business **3A–179** tenancy to which the Landlord and Tenant Act 1954 Pt II applies. The Landlord and

Paragraph numbers marked with a "+" can be found online and on CD.

Tenant Act 1954 s.23(2) provides that "'business' includes trade, profession or employment".

Premises are only occupied "for the purposes of a business" where the business activity on the premises is a significant purpose of the occupation or part of the reason for the occupation. Where, however, the business use is merely incidental to residential occupation, there is Rent Act protection (*Cheryl Investments Ltd v Saldanha* [1979] 1 All E.R. 5; [1978] 1 W.L.R. 1329, CA). This is essentially a question of fact for the trial judge—*Gurton v Parrott* (1991) 23 H.L.R. 418; [1991] 18 E.G. 161, CA; *Pulleng v Curran* (1982) 44 P. & C.R. 58, CA; and *Wright v Mortimer* (1996) 28 H.L.R. 719; [1996] E.G.C.S. 51, CA, where the Court of Appeal held that whether or not business user is a significant element of occupation is a question of fact and degree which is particularly within the trial judge's ability to decide. It is permissible for the judge to take into account the tenant's attachment to the flat and the fact that an informed or reasonable person would conclude that the tenant is not carrying on a business at the premises.

See too *Florent v Horez* (1983) 268 E.G. 807; (1984) 12 H.L.R. 1; (1984) 48 P. & C.R. 166, CA, where the Court of Appeal stated that the phrase "business user" has a broad meaning and approved a statement by Lindley L.J. in *Rolls v Miller* (1884) 27 Ch D 71 at 88, that business "means almost anything which is an occupation, as distinguished from a pleasure—anything which is an occupation or duty which requires attention is a business". These authorities were reviewed in *Tan v Sitkowski* [2007] EWCA Civ 30; [2007] 1 W.L.R. 1628 where it was held that the mere fact that business use of premises had ceased, and that landlords continued to accept rent, could not amount to positive consent to the change of use.

MISCELLANEOUS

Rateable value and meaning of "appropriate day"

3A–180   **25.**—(1) Except where this Act otherwise provides, the rateable value on any day of a dwelling-house shall be ascertained for the purposes of this Act as follows—

  (a) if the dwelling-house is a hereditament for which a rateable value is then shown in the valuation list, it shall be that rateable value;

  (b) if the dwelling-house forms part only of such a hereditament or consists of or forms part of more than one such hereditament, its rateable value shall be taken to be such value as is found by a proper apportionment or aggregation of the rateable value or values so shown.

(2) Any question arising under this section as to the proper apportionment or aggregation of any value or values shall be determined by the county court, and the decision of the county court shall be final.

(3) In this Act "the appropriate day"—

  (a) in relation to any dwelling-house which, on March 23, 1965, was or formed part of a hereditament for which a rateable value was shown in the valuation list then in force, or consisted or formed part of more than one such hereditament, means that date, and

  (b) in relation to any other dwelling-house, means the date on which such a value is or was first shown in the valuation list.

(4) Where, after the date which is the appropriate day in relation to any dwelling-house, the valuation list is altered so as to vary the

Paragraph numbers marked with a "+" can be found online and on CD.

rateable value of the hereditament of which the dwelling-house consists or forms part and the alteration has effect from a date not later than the appropriate day, the rateable value of the dwelling-house on the appropriate day shall be ascertained as if the value shown in the valuation list on the appropriate day had been the value shown in the list as altered.

(5) This section applies in relation to any other land as it applies in relation to a dwelling-house.

Land and premises let with dwelling-house

26.—(1) For the purposes of this Act, any land or premises let **3A–181** together with a dwelling-house shall, unless it consists of agricultural land exceeding two acres in extent, be treated as part of the dwelling-house.

(2) For the purposes of subsection (1) above "agricultural land" has the meaning set out in section 26(3)(a) of the General Rate Act 1967(exclusion of agricultural land and premises from liability for rating).

* * * *

PART VII

SECURITY OF TENURE

LIMITATIONS ON RECOVERY OF POSSESSION OF DWELLING-HOUSES LET ON PROTECTED TENANCIES OR SUBJECT TO STATUTORY TENANCIES

Grounds for possession of certain dwelling-houses

98.—(1) Subject to this Part of this Act, a court shall not make an **3A–182** order for possession of a dwelling-house which is for the time being let on a protected tenancy or subject to a statutory tenancy unless the court considers it reasonable to make such an order and either—

(a) the court is satisfied that suitable alternative accommodation is available for the tenant or will be available for him when the order in question takes effect, or

(b) the circumstances are as specified in any of the Cases in Part I of Schedule 15 to this Act.

(2) If, apart from subsection (1) above, the landlord would be entitled to recover possession of a dwelling-house which is for the time being let on or subject to a regulated tenancy, the court shall make an order for possession if the circumstances of the case are as specified in any of the Cases in Part II of Schedule 15.

(3) Part III of Schedule 15 shall have effect in relation to Case 9 in that Schedule and for determining the relevant date for the purposes of the Cases in Part II of that Schedule.

(4) Part IV of Schedule 15 shall have effect for determining

Paragraph numbers marked with a "+" can be found online and on CD.

whether, for the purposes of subsection (1)(a) above, suitable alternative accommodation is or will be available for a tenant.

(5) Part V of Schedule 15 shall have effect for the purpose of setting out conditions which are relevant to Cases 11 and 12 of that Schedule.

3A–183   *Note* —Amended by the Housing Act 1980 s.66.

Grounds for possession of certain dwelling-houses

3A–184   Section 98 contains the kernal of Rent Act security of tenure. In order to obtain possession a landlord must satisfy the court that a ground for possession (i.e. the availability of suitable alternative accommodation or one of the grounds in Sch.15) is made out, and, if the ground is a discretionary one, that it is reasonable to make an order for possession.

> "[I] f there is before the court a claim that the defendant is entitled to the benefit of the Rent Acts, the court may not make an order for possession unless it is satisfied, either by evidence or by admission by or on behalf of the defendant, that he is not entitled to that protection". (per Glidewell J. in *R. v Bloomsbury and Marylebone County Court, Ex p. Blackburne* (1984) 14 H.L.R. 56 at 67, QBD, approved by the Court of Appeal (1985) 275 E.G. 1273 at 1274). See also *Hounslow LBC v McBride* (1999) 31 H.L.R. 143, CA and *R. v Birmingham CC, Ex p. Foley*, March 2001, Legal Action 29, Queen's Bench Division.

Although not stated in s.98, landlords also have to ensure that any contractual tenancy has been determined.

"dwelling-house"

3A–185   See ss.1 and 26.

"statuory tenant"

3A–186   See ss.2 and 152.

"landlord" and "protected tenancy"

3A–187   See ss.1 and 152.

"regulated tenancy"

3A–188   See ss.18 and 152.

Suitable alternative accommodation

3A–189   See too Sch.15, Pt IV, below. Paragraph 5 provides that alternative accommodation must be reasonably suitable to the needs of the tenant and his family. In that context "needs" means "the needs for housing" or "need for accommodation for the purpose of habitation"—see *Hill v Rochard* [1983] 1 W.L.R. 478, CA and *Montross Associated Investments v Stone* March 2000, Legal Action 29, CA.

The court can properly take into account environmental matters (e.g. where the alternative accommodation offered had no garden, was on a busy thoroughfare, was next door to a fried-fish shop, near to a hospital, cinema and public house and with an open space to the rear which the local authority proposed to use as a transport depot), both when considering suitability to the tenant's needs and reasonableness (*Redspring v Francis* [1973] 1 W.L.R. 134; [1973] 1 All E.R. 640, CA), but only in so far as they relate to the property itself (not, e.g. matters such as the location of the tenant's friends, his mosque or cultural interests (*Siddiqui v Rashid* [1980] 1 W.L.R. 1018; [1980] 3 All E.R. 184, CA).

Part of a tenant's existing accommodation can amount to suitable alternative accommodation (see *Mykolyshyn v Noah* [1970] 1 W.L.R. 1271; [1971] 1 All E.R. 48, CA; *Thompson v Rolls* [1926] 2 K.B. 426; *Parmee v Mitchell* [1950] 1 All E.R. 872, CA; *McIntyre v Hardcastle* [1948] 1 All E.R. 696, CA; and *Scrace v Windust* [1955] 2 All E.R. 104, CA).

Paragraph numbers marked with a "+" can be found online and on CD.

Reasonable

See also commentary to the Housing Act 1985 s.84.

The question of reasonableness is an "overriding requirement" (*Smith v McGoldrick* (1976) 242 E.G. 1047) and gives the court a very wide discretion (*Bell London and Provincial Properties Ltd v Reuben* [1946] 2 All E.R. 547; and *Plaschkes v Jones* (1982) 9 H.L.R. 110). In *Cumming v Danson* [1942] 2 All E.R. 653 at 655, Lord Greene M.R. said:

"in considering reasonableness ... it is, in my opinion, perfectly clear that the duty of the Judge is to take into account all relevant circumstances as they exist at the date of the hearing. That he must do in what I venture to call a broad common-sense way as a man of the world, and come to his conclusion giving such weight as he thinks right to the various factors in the situation. Some factors may have little or no weight, others may be decisive, but it is quite wrong for him to exclude from his consideration matters which he ought to take into account."

In *Shrimpton v Rabbits*, 131 L.T. 478, KBD, Swift J. said that in considering the question of reasonableness the court "must consider all the circumstances affecting the holding of the premises by the person who holds them and as they relate to the landlord who wants to hold them". Acton J. said, "Because a [landlord's] wish is reasonable, it does not follow that it is reasonable in a court to gratify it."

In relation to rent arrears cases Denning L.J. (as he then was) has stated:

"It would be very unusual indeed for the tenant to be ordered out on the ground of non-payment of rent when the full amount was already paid into court. If the tenant is in arrear, in these cases under the Rent Restriction Acts the everyday practice is to make an order for possession, but to suspend it so long as the current weekly rent and a payment on account of the rent in arrear are paid." (*Hayman v Rowlands* [1957] 1 W.L.R. 317; [1957] 1 All E.R. 321, CA; but *cf. Dellenty v Pellow* [1951] 2 All E.R. 716, CA; and *Lee-Steere v Jennings* (1987) 20 H.L.R. 1, CA).

The first requirement for a judge who has found a ground for possession to be proved is to ask whether it is reasonable to make a possession order at all and then to ask whether the order should be stayed or suspended under s.100(2). The correct approach is to determine the extent of the rent arrears and how quickly those are likely to be paid. It is wrong to take into account matters which have not been pleaded.

"In considering whether it is reasonable to make an order ... the judge should consider all the relevant circumstances: but that is not a consideration at large. It is, or should be, a consideration in accordance with the pleadings. In my judgment, the matters proposed to be relied upon by the landlord in support of the contention that it would be reasonable to make an order for possession ... must be pleaded by the landlord." (per Sir Richard Scott V.-C. in *Raeuchle v Laimond Properties Ltd (Suspension of Possession Order)* (2001) 33 H.L.R. 10, CA); *cf. Taj v Ali* 97/17 L.S. Gaz., April 28, 2000, p.36, [2000] 43 E.G. 183; (2001) 33 H.L.R. 37, CA where it was said that a suspended possession order should not extend "into the mists of time" or where there were "no sensible terms on which the order could be suspended" (suspended possession order providing for payment of arrears over 55 years replaced with 28 day possession order).

Courts must consider whether it is reasonable to make an order for possession at the date of the hearing and not at an earlier stage (*Smith v McGoldrick* (1977) 242 E.G. 1047, CA). A judge's failure to consider reasonableness makes an order for possession a nullity (*Minchbourn Estates Ltd v Fernandez (No.2)* (1987) 19 H.L.R. 29; (1986) 280 E.G. 770, CA; and *Hounslow LBC v McBride* (1999) 31 H.L.R. 143, CA and *R. v Birmingham CC Ex p. Foley*, March 2001, Legal Action 29, QBD), even where an order is made "by consent"and money is paid to the tenant in return for the giving of vacant possession (*R. v Bloomsbury and Marylebone County Court Ex p. Blackburne* (1985) 275 E.G. 1273, CA). However, the Court of Appeal will "assume that the county court judge has taken all the relevant matters into account unless the contrary is clearly shown" and will only overrule a county court judge on the question of reasonableness "on very strong grounds" (*Dame Margaret Hungerford Charity Trustees v Beazeley* [1993] 29 E.G. 100, CA). See too *Battlespring Ltd v Gates* (1983) 268 E.G. 355, CA; *Dawncar Investments Ltd v Plews* [1993] 13 E.G. 110; (1993) 25 H.L.R. 639, CA; *Empson v Forde* [1990] 18 E.G. 99, CA and *Holloway v Povey* (1984) 15 H.L.R. 104; (1984) 271 E.G. 195, CA.

Paragraph numbers marked with a "+" can be found online and on CD.

Appeals on questions of reasonableness

3A–191   Although County Courts Act 1984 s.77(6) excludes appeals against judges' findings of fact, it does not exclude, in a proper case, the possibility of an appeal against a finding of reasonableness (*Castle Vale Housing Action Trust v Gallagher* [2001] EWCA Civ 944; (2001) 33 H.L.R. 810).

ECHR Art 8 and reasonableness

3A–192   The Court of Appeal has doubted whether Article 8 makes any difference to the way in which courts have approached questions of the reasonableness of making possessions order. Article 8 does, however, reinforce the importance of only making an order depriving someone of his or her home in circumstances where a clear case is made out (*Castle Vale Housing Action Trust v Gallagher* [2001] EWCA Civ 944; (2001) 33 H.L.R. 810, CA. See too *Newham LBC v Neal* [2003] EWCA Civ 541 February 25, 2003.). There is a need to find a fair balance and to protect the rights of the neighbours and other members of the public (*Lambeth LBC v Howard* [2001] EWCA Civ 468; (2001) 33 H.L.R. 636). See too *Harrow LBC v Qazi* [2003] UKHL 43; [2004] 1 A.C. 983; [2003] 3 W.L.R. 792, where Lord Hope and Lord Scott said that contractual and property rights cannot be defeated by a defence based on Article 8. See too *Newham LBC v Kibata* [2003] EWCA Civ 1785; [2004] H.L.R. 28 and *Bradney v Birmingham CC*; *Birmingham CC v McCann* [2003] EWCA Civ 1783; [2004] H.L.R. 27; *Lambeth LBC v Kay; Leeds CC v Price* [2006] UKHL 10; [2006] 2 A.C. 465; [2006] 2 W.L.R. 570 and *Birmingham City Council v Doherty* [2008] UKHL 57; [2008] 3 W.L.R. 636; but *cf. Mc-Cann v UK* App. No.19009/04, *The Times* May 13, 2008, where the ECtHR stated:

> "The loss of one's home is a most extreme form of interference with the right to respect for the home. Any person at risk of an interference of this magnitude should in principle be able to have the proportionality of the measure determined by an independent tribunal. . .(para.50)."

The "procedural safeguards" required by art.8 for the assessment of the proportionality of the interference are not met by the possibility of defendants in possession claims applying for judicial review. However, it would be only in very exceptional cases that occupiers would succeed in raising an arguable case which would require a court to examine the issue. In the great majority of cases, orders for possession could continue to be made "in summary proceedings".

* * * *

Extended discretion of court in claims for possession of certain dwelling-houses

3A–193   **100.**—(1) Subject to subsection (5) below, a court may adjourn, for such period or periods as it thinks fit, proceedings for possession of a dwelling-house which is let on a protected tenancy or subject to a statutory tenancy.

(2) On the making of an order for possession of such a dwelling-house, or at any time before the execution of such an order (whether made before or after the commencement of this Act), the court, subject to subsection (5) below, may—

(a) stay or suspend execution of the order, or

(b) postpone the date of possession.

for such period or periods as the court thinks fit.

(3) On any such adjournment as is referred to in subsection (1) above or any such stay, suspension or postponement as is referred to in subsection (2) above, the court shall, unless it considers that to do so would cause exceptional hardship to the tenant or would otherwise be unreasonable, impose conditions with regard to payment by the tenant of arrears of rent (if any) and rent or payments in respect of occupation after termination of the tenancy (mesne profits) and may impose such other conditions as it thinks fit.

Paragraph numbers marked with a "+" can be found online and on CD.

(4) If any such conditions as are referred to in subsection (3) above are complied with, the court may, if it thinks fit, discharge or rescind any such order as is referred to in subsection (2) above.

(4A) Subsection (4B) below applies in any case where—

(a) proceedings are brought for possession of a dwelling-house which is let on a protected tenancy or subject to a statutory tenancy;

(b) the tenant's spouse or former spouse, having rights of occupation under the Matrimonial Homes Act 1967, is then in occupation of the dwelling-house; and

(c) the tenancy is terminated as a result of those proceedings.

(4B) In any case to which this subsection applies, the spouse or former spouse shall, so long as he or she remains in occupation, have the same rights in relation to, or in connection with, any such adjournment as is referred to in subsection (1) above or any such stay, suspension or postponement as is referred to in subsection (2) above, as he or she would have if those rights of occupation were not affected by the termination of the tenancy.

(5) This section shall not apply if the circumstances are as specified in any of the Cases in Part II of Schedule 15.

Note —Amended by the Housing Act 1980 s.75.   **3A–194**

"dwelling-house"
See ss.1 and 26.   **3A–195**

"statuory tenant"
See ss.2 and 152.   **3A–196**

"protected tenancy"
See ss.1 and 152.   **3A–197**

"tenant"
See s.152.   **3A–198**

Extended discretion of court in claims for possession of certain dwelling-houses
See commentary to the Housing Act 1985 s.85 and the Housing Act 1988 s.9.   **3A–199**

Overcrowded dwelling-houses

101. At any time when a dwelling-house is overcrowded, within the meaning of Part X of the Housing Act 1985, in such circumstances as to render the occupier guilty of an offence, nothing in this Part of this Act shall prevent the immediate landlord of the occupier from obtaining possession of the dwelling-house.   **3A–200**

Note —Substituted by the Housing (Consequential Provisions) Act 1985 Sch.2, para.35.   **3A–201**

"overcrowding"
See the Housing Act 1985 ss.324–328.   **3A–202**

Overcrowded dwelling-houses
The Court of Appeal has held that where there is statutory overcrowding there is   **3A–203**

Paragraph numbers marked with a "+" can be found online and on CD.

HOUSING

no jurisdiction to make a suspended possession order (*Henry Smith's Charity v Bartosiak-Jentys* (1992) 24 H.L.R. 627, CA).

Compensation for misrepresentation or concealment in Cases 8 and 9

3A–204 **102.** Where, in such circumstances as are specified in Case 8 or Case 9 in Schedule 15 to this Act, a landlord obtains an order for possession of a dwelling-house let on a protected tenancy or subject to a statutory tenancy and it is subsequently made to appear to the court that the order was obtained by misrepresentation or concealment of material facts, the court may order the landlord to pay to the former tenant such sum as appears sufficient as compensation for damage or loss sustained by that tenant as a result of the order.

"dwelling-house"

3A–205 See ss.1 and 26.

"statuory tenant"

3A–206 See ss.2 and 152.

"protected tenancy"

3A–207 See ss.1 and 152.

"landlord" and "tenant"

3A–208 See s.152.

Compensation for misrepresentation or concealment in Cases 8 and 9

3A–209 See, e.g. *Thorne v Smith* [1947] K.B. 307, CA and *Clements v Simmonds* [2002] EWHC 1652 (QB); [2002] 41 E.G. 178. Note that the power of the court to award compensation under s.102 where possession has been obtained as a result of misrepresentation or concealment is limited to Case 8 (former employee) and Case 9 (dwelling reasonably required for occupation by landlord or landlord's family) (*cf.* Housing Act 1988 s.12). There is, however, no reason why a tenant should not bring proceedings based upon the common law tort of deceit (see, e.g. *Mafo v Adams* [1970] 1 Q.B. 548, CA).

* * * *

MISCELLANEOUS

Interpretation of Part VII

3A–210 **107.**—(1) In this Part of this Act, except where the context otherwise requires—

"dwelling" means a house or part of a house;

"lessee" means the person to whom is granted, under a restricted contract, the right to occupy the dwelling in question as a residence and any person directly or indirectly deriving title from the grantee; and

"lessor" means the person who, under a restricted contract, grants to another the right to occupy the dwelling in question as a residence and any person directly or indirectly deriving title from the grantor.

(2) References in this Part of this Act to a party to a contract include references to any person directly or indirectly deriving title from such a party.

Paragraph numbers marked with a "+" can be found online and on CD.

* * * *

PART XI

GENERAL

SUBLETTINGS

Effect on sub-tenancy of determination of superior tenancy

137.—(1) If a court makes an order for possession of a dwelling-house from— **3A–211**

   (a) a protected or statutory tenant, or
   (b) a protected occupier or statutory tenant as defined in the Rent (Agriculture) Act 1976,

and the order is made by virtue of section 98(1) or 99(2) of this Act or, as the case may be, under Part I of Schedule 4 to that Act, nothing in the order shall affect the right of any sub-tenant to whom the dwelling-house or any part of it has been lawfully sublet before the commencement of the proceedings to retain possession by virtue of this Act, nor shall the order operate to give a right to possession against any such sub-tenant.

(2) Where a statutorily protected tenancy of a dwelling-house is determined, either as a result of an order for possession or for any other reason, any sub-tenant to whom the dwelling-house or any part of it has been lawfully sublet shall, subject to this Act, be deemed to become the tenant of the landlord on the same terms as if the tenant's statutorily protected tenancy had continued.

(3) Where a dwelling-house—

   (a) forms part of premises which have been let as a whole on a superior tenancy but do not constitute a dwelling-house let on a statutorily protected tenancy; and
   (b) is itself subject to a protected or statutory tenancy,

then, from the coming to an end of the superior tenancy, this Act shall apply in relation to the dwelling-house as if, in lieu of the superior tenancy, there had been separate tenancies of the dwelling-house and of the remainder of the premises, for the like purposes as under the superior tenancy, and at rents equal to the just proportion of the rent under the superior tenancy.

In this subsection "premises" includes, if the sub-tenancy in question is a protected or statutory tenancy to which section 99 of this Act applies, an agricultural holding within the meaning of the Agricultural Holdings Act 1986 held under a tenancy to which that Act applies, and land comprised in a farm business tenancy within the meaning of the Agricultural Tenancies Act 1995.

(4) In subsections (2) and (3) above "statutorily protected tenancy" means—

   (a) a protected or statutory tenancy;
   (b) a protected occupancy or statutory tenancy as defined in the Rent (Agricultural) Act 1976; or

Paragraph numbers marked with a "+" can be found online and on CD.

    (c) if the sub-tenancy in question is a protected or statutory tenancy to which section 99 of this Act applies,

        (i) a tenancy of an agricultural holding within the meaning of the Agricultural Holdings Act 1986 which is a tenancy in relation to which that Act applies, or

        (ii) a farm business tenancy within the meaning of the Agricultural Tenancies Act 1995.

(5) Subject to subsection (6) below, a long tenancy of a dwelling-house which is also a tenancy at a low rent but which, had it not been a tenancy at a low rent, would have been a protected tenancy or an assured tenancy within the meaning of Part I of the Housing Act 1988, shall be treated for the purposes of subsection (2) above as a statutorily protected tenancy.

(6) Notwithstanding anything in subsection (5) above, subsection (2) above shall not have effect where the sub-tenancy in question was created (whether immediately or derivatively) out of a long tenancy falling within subsection (5) above and, at the time of the creation of the sub-tenancy—

    (a) a notice to terminate the long tenancy had been given under section 4(1) of the Landlord and Tenant Act 1954 or, as the case may be, served under paragraph 4(1) of Schedule 10 to the Local Government and Housing Act 1989; or

    (b) the long tenancy was being continued by section 3(1) of the said Act of 1954 or, as the case may be, paragraph 3 of the said Schedule 10;

unless the sub-tenancy was created with the consent in writing of the person who at the time when it was created was the landlord, within the meaning of Part I of the said Act of 1954 or, as the case may be, the said Schedule 10.

(7) This section shall apply equally where a protected occupier of a dwelling-house, or part of a dwelling-house, has a relevant licence as defined in the Rent (Agriculture) Act 1976, and in this section "tenancy" and all cognate expressions shall be construed accordingly.

3A–212   *Note* —Amended by the Agricultural Holdings Act 1986 Sch.14; the Housing Act 1988 s.140, Schs 17 and 18; the Local Government and Housing Act 1989 s.195, Sch.11, para.53; and the Agricultural Tenancies Act 1995 s.40, Sch.

Effect on sub-tenancy of determination of superior tenancy

3A–213   Section 137 provides that in some cases, on termination of a head tenancy, the sub-tenant of any dwelling house which has been lawfully sublet is deemed to become the tenant of the landlord and so gives some protection to sub-tenants when head tenancies come to an end.

    In three appeals heard together, reported as *Wellcome Trust v Hamad* [1998] Q.B. 638; [1998] 2 W.L.R. 156, CA, the Court of Appeal considered the construction of s.137(3) and the protection which it affords to sub-tenants. In each case buildings which comprised business premises (such as shops) on the ground floor and flats upstairs were let on long leases. These leases came within the provisions of the Landlord and Tenant Act 1954 Pt II. Subsequently Rent Act protected sub-tenancies of the residential parts of the buildings were granted. In all three cases county court judges relying on *Pittalis v Grant* [1989] Q.B. 605, CA, found that, after the termina-

Paragraph numbers marked with a "+" can be found online and on CD.

tion of the head leases, the sub-tenants fell outside Rent Act protection. The sub-tenants appealed, contending that *Pittalis v Grant* had been decided per incuriam. After giving detailed consideration to the Rent Acts from a historical perspective the Court of Appeal granted the tenants' appeals and in two cases set aside possession orders made against them. Rent Act 1977 s.137(3) "appears to contemplate that where there is a flat over a shop, and the flat is lawfully sublet for residential use, so as to afford the sub-tenant protection under the Rent Act as against the tenant, the sub-tenant should continue to enjoy the same protection against the head landlord when the superior letting comes to an end". *Pittalis v Grant* had been decided *per incuriam* because:

(1) the argument relied upon that if a tenancy is not regulated, the premises cannot be treated as a dwelling house, was fallacious. Premises may amount to a dwelling house without being let on a regulated tenancy; and

(2) the Court of Appeal had overlooked all of the authorities in which the accepted principles referred to by Lord Wilberforce in *Maunsell v Olins* [1975] A.C. 373, HL, were contained. In each of the three cases the premises concerned constituted a dwelling-house and accordingly s.137(3) did afford protection to the sub-tenants.

A statutory tenant cannot grant an effective sub-tenancy, at least so far as the landlord is concerned. If a statutory tenant moves out and purports to sub-let, the premises cannot be lawfully sub-let under s.137 (*Moreland Properties (UK) Ltd v Dhokia* [2003] EWCA Civ 1639; October 21, 2003).

Effect on furnished sub-tenancy of determination of superior unfurnished tenancy

138.—(1) If, in a case where section 137(2) of this Act applies, the conditions mentioned in subsection (2) below are fulfilled, the terms on which the sub-tenant is, by virtue of section 137(2), deemed to become the tenant of the landlord shall not include any terms as to the provision by the landlord of furniture or services. **3A–214**

(2) The conditions are—

(a) that the statutorily protected tenancy which is determined as mentioned in section 137(2) was neither a protected furnished tenancy nor a statutory furnished tenancy; and

(b) that, immediately before the determination of that statutorily protected tenancy, the sub-tenant referred to in section 137(2) was the tenant under a protected furnished tenancy or a statutory furnished tenancy; and

(c) that the landlord, within the period of six weeks beginning with the day on which the statutorily protected tenancy referred to in section 137(2) is determined, serves notice on the sub-tenant that this section is to apply to his tenancy or statutory tenancy.

(3) In this section "statutorily protected tenancy" has the same meaning as it has for the purposes of section 137(2) of this Act.

Note —Amended by the Housing Act 1980 s.152, Sch.25, para.51. **3A–215**

"statutory furnished tenancy"
See ss.2 and 152. **3A–216**

"protected tenancy"
See ss.1 and 152. **3A–217**

Paragraph numbers marked with a "+" can be found online and on CD.

"statutorily protected tenancy"

3A–218   See s.138(3).

"landlord" and "tenant"

3A–219   See s.152.

* * * *

JURISDICTION AND PROCEDURE

County court jurisdiction

3A–220   **141.**—(1) A county court shall have jurisdiction, either in the course of any proceedings relating to a dwelling or on an application made for the purpose by the landlord or the tenant, to determine any question—

(a) as to whether a tenancy is a protected tenancy or whether any person is a statutory tenant of a dwelling-house; or

(b) as to the rent limit; or

(c) [...]

(d) as to the application of Part V and sections 103 to 106 of this Act to a contract; or

(e) as to whether a protected, statutory or regulated tenancy is a protected, statutory or regulated furnished tenancy;

or as to any matter which is or may become material for determining any such question.

(2) [...]

(3) A county court shall have jurisdiction to deal with any claim or other proceedings arising out of any of the provisions of this Act specified in subsection (5) below, notwithstanding that by reason of the amount of the claim or otherwise the case would not, apart from this subsection, be within the jurisdiction of a county court.

(4) If, under any of the provisions of this Act specified in subsection (5) below, a person takes proceedings in the High Court which he could have taken in the county court, he shall not be entitled to recover any costs.

(5) The provisions referred to in subsections (3) and (4) above are—

(a) [...]

(b) in Part III, section 57;

(c) Part VII, except sections 98(2) and 101;

(d) in Part IX, sections 125 and 126;

(e) in Part X, sections 133(1), 134 and 135; and

(f) in this Part of this Act, sections 145 and 147.

3A–221   *Note*—Amended by the Housing Act 1980 s.152, Sch.26.

"dwelling-house"

3A–222   See ss.1 and 26.

Paragraph numbers marked with a "+" can be found online and on CD.

Rules as to procedure

142. [...]   **3A–228**

Note —Repealed by the Constitutional Reform Act 2005 ss.15(1), 146, Sch.4, para.94, **3A–229**
Sch.18.

* * * *

MISCELLANEOUS

Implied term in all protected tenancies

148. It shall be a condition of a protected tenancy of a dwelling- **3A–230**
house that the tenant shall afford to the landlord access to the
dwelling-house and all reasonable facilities for executing therein any
repairs which the landlord is entitled to execute.

* * * *

SUPPLEMENTAL

Interpretation

152.—(1) In this Act, except where the context otherwise requires— **3A–234**
   "the appropriate day" has the meaning assigned to it by section
        25(3) of this Act;
   "landlord" includes any person from time to time deriving title
        under the original landlord and also includes, in relation
        to any dwelling-house, any person other than the tenant
        who is, or but for Part VII of this Act would be, entitled to
        possession of the dwelling-house;
   "let" includes "sublet";

Paragraph numbers marked with a "+" can be found online and on CD.

HOUSING

"long tenancy" means a tenancy granted for a term of years certain exceeding 21 years, whether or not subsequently extended by act of the parties or by any enactment;

"protected furnished tenancy", "regulated furnished tenancy" and "statutory furnished tenancy" means a protected or, as the case may be, regulated or statutory tenancy—

(a) under which the dwelling-house concerned is bona fide let at a rent which includes payments in respect of furniture, and

(b) in respect of which the amount of rent which is fairly attributable to the use of furniture, having regard to the value of that use to the tenant, forms a substantial part of the whole rent;

"protected tenant" and "protected tenancy" shall be construed in accordance with section 1 of this Act;

"rates" includes water rates and charges but does not include an owner's drainage rate as defined in section 63(2)(a) of the Land Drainage Act 1976;

"rateable value" shall be construed in accordance with section 25 of this Act;

"regulated tenancy" shall be construed in accordance with section 18 of this Act;

"rent tribunal" has the meaning given by section 76(1) of this Act;

"rental period" means a period in respect of which a payment of rent falls to be made;

"restricted contract" shall be construed in accordance with section 19 of this Act;

"statutory tenant" and "statutory tenancy" shall be construed in accordance with section 2 of this Act;

"tenant" includes statutory tenant and also includes a sub-tenant and any person deriving title under the original tenant or sub-tenant;

"tenancy" includes "sub-tenancy";

"tenancy at a low rent" has the meaning assigned to it by section 5 of this Act.

(2) Except in so far as the context otherwise requires, any reference in this Act to any other enactment shall be taken as referring to that enactment as amended by or under any other enactment, including this Act.

3A–235 *Note* —Amended by the Housing Act 1980 s.152, Sch.26.

Paragraph numbers marked with a "+" can be found online and on CD.

SCHEDULES

SCHEDULE 1

STATUTORY TENANCIES

PART I

STATUTORY TENANTS BY SUCCESSION

1. Paragraph 2 below shall have effect, subject to section 2(3) of this Act, for the **3A–236** purpose of determining who is the statutory tenant of a dwelling-house by succession after the death of the person (in this Part of this Schedule referred to as "the original tenant") who, immediately before his death, was a protected tenant of the dwelling-house or the statutory tenant of it by virtue of his previous protected tenancy.

2.—(1) The surviving spouse, or civil partner, (if any) of the original tenant, if residing in the dwelling-house immediately before the death of the original tenant, shall after the death be the statutory tenant if and so long as he or she occupies the dwelling-house as his or her residence.

(2) For the purposes of this paragraph—

    (a) a person who was living with the original tenant as his or her wife or husband shall be treated as the spouse of the original tenant, and

    (b) a person who was living with the original tenant as if they were civil partners shall be treated as the civil partner of the original tenant.

(3) If, immediately after the death of the original tenant, there is, by virtue of sub-paragraph (2) above, more than one person who fulfils the conditions in sub-paragraph (1) above, such one of them as may be decided by agreement or, in default of agreement, by the county court shall for the purposes of this paragraph be treated (according to whether that one of them is of the opposite sex to, or of the same sex as, the original tenant) as the surviving spouse or the surviving civil partner.

3.—(1) Where paragraph 2 above does not apply, but a person was a member of the original tenant's family was residing with him in the dwelling-house at the time of and for the period of 2 years immediately before his death then, after his death, that person or if there is more than one such person such one of them as may be decided by agreement, or in default of agreement by the county court, shall be entitled to an assured tenancy of the dwelling-house by succession.

(2) If the original tenant died within the period of 18 months beginning on the operative date, then, for the purposes of this paragraph, a person who was residing in the dwelling-house with the original tenant at the time of his death and for the period which began 6 months before the operative date and ended at the time of his death shall be taken to have been residing with the original tenant for the period of 2 years immediately before his death.

4. A person who becomes the statutory tenant of a dwelling-house by virtue of paragraph 2 above is in this Part of this Schedule referred to as "the first successor".

5. If, immediately before his death, the first successor was still a statutory tenant, paragraph 6 below shall have effect for the purpose of determining who is entitled to an assured tenancy of the dwelling-house by succession after the death of the first successor.

6.—(1) Where a person who—

    (a) was a member of the original tenant's family immediately before that tenant's death, and

    (b) was a member of the first successor's family immediately before the first successor's death,

was residing in the dwelling-house with the first successor at the time of, and for the period of two years immediately before, the first successor's death, that person or, if there is more than one such person, such one of them as may be decided by

Paragraph numbers marked with a "+" can be found online and on CD.

agreement or, in default of agreement, by the county court shall be entitled to an assured tenancy of the dwelling-house by succession.

(2) If the first successor died within the period of 18 months beginning on the operative date, then, for the purposes of this paragraph, a person who was residing in the dwelling-house with the first successor at the time of his death and for the period which began six months before the operative date and ended at the time of his death shall be taken to have been residing with the first successor for the period of two years immediately before his death.

7. [...]

8. [...]

9. Paragraphs 5 to 8 above do not apply where the statutory tenancy of the original tenant arose by virtue of section 4 of the Requisitioned Houses and Housing (Amendment) Act 1955 or section 20 of the Rent Act 1965.

10.—(1) Where after a succession the successor becomes the tenant of the dwelling-house by the grant to him of another tenancy, "the original tenant" and "the first successor" in this Part of this Schedule shall, in relation to that other tenancy, mean the persons who were respectively the original tenant and the first successor at the time of the succession, and accordingly—

    (a) if the successor was the first successor, and, immediately before his death he was still the tenant (whether protected or statutory), paragraphs 6 and 7 above shall apply on his death,

    (b) if the successor was not the first successor; no person shall become a statutory tenant on his death by virtue of this Part of this Schedule.

(2) Sub-paragraph (1) above applies—

    (a) even if a successor enters into more than one other tenancy of the dwelling-house, and

    (b) even if both the first successor and the successor on his death enter into other tenancies of the dwelling-house.

(3) In this paragraph "succession" means the occasion on which a person becomes the statutory tenant of a dwelling-house by virtue of this Part of this Schedule and "successor" shall be construed accordingly.

(4) This paragraph shall apply as respects a succession which took place before August 27, 1972 if, and only if, the tenancy granted after the succession, or the first of those tenancies, was granted on or after that date, and where it does not apply as respects a succession, no account should be taken of that succession in applying this paragrpah as respects any later succession.

11.—(1) Paragraphs 5 to 8 above do not apply where—

    (a) the tenancy of the original tenant was granted on or after the operative date within the meaning of the Rent (Agriculture) Act 1976, and

    (b) both that tenancy and the statutory tenancy of the first successor were tenancies to which section 99 of this Act applies.

(2) If the tenants under both of the tenancies falling within sub-paragraph (1)(b) above were persons to whom paragraph 7 of Schedule 9 to the Rent (Agriculture) Act 1976 applies, the reference in sub-paragraph (1)(a) above to the operative date shall be taken as a reference to the date of operation for forestry workers within the meaning of that Act.

11A. In this Part of this Schedule "the operative date" means the date on which Part I of the Housing Act 1988 came into force.

3A–237   *Note* —Paragraph 2 amended by the Civil Partnership Act 2004 s.81, Sch.8, para.13.

PART II

RELINQUISHING TENANCIES AND CHANGING TENANTS

Payments demanded by statutory tenants as a condition of giving up possession

3A–238   12.—(1) A statutory tenant of a dwelling-house who, as a condition of giving up possession of the dwelling-house, asks for or receives the payment of any sum, or the giv-

Paragraph numbers marked with a "+" can be found online and on CD.

notifies the tenant in writing of his intention to occupy as his residence another dwelling-house in the building or, as the case may be, flat concerned, the
period beginning with the date on which the interest of the landlord under
the tenancy becomes vested in that individual as mentioned in that paragraph
and ending—

    (i) at the expiry of the period of six months beginning on that date, or

    (ii) on the date on which that interest ceases to be so vested, or

    (iii) on the date on which the condition in section 12(1)(c) again ap-
    plies,whichever is the earlier; and

(c) any period of not more than two years beginning with the date on which the
interest of the landlord under the tenancy becomes, and during which it
remains, vested—

    (i) [...]

    (ii) in trustees as such; or

    (iii) by virtue of section 9 of the Administration of Estates Act 1925, in the
    Probate Judge or the Public Trustee.

2. During any period when—

(a) the interest of the landlord under the tenancy referred to in section 12(1) is
vested in trustees as such, and

(b) that interest is held on trust for any person who occupies as his residence a
dwelling-house which forms part of the building or, as the case may be, flat
referred to in section 12(1)(a),the condition in section 12(1)(c) shall be deemed
to be fulfilled and, accordingly, no part of that period shall be disregarded by
virtue of paragraph 1 above.

2A.—(1) The tenancy referred to in section 12(1) falls within this paragraph if the
interest of the landlord under the tenancy becomes vested in the personal representatives of a deceased person acting in that capacity.

(2) If the tenancy falls within this paragraph, the condition in section 12(1)(c) shall
be deemed to be fulfilled for any period, beginning with the date on which the interest
becomes vested in the personal representatives and not exceeding two years, during
which the interest of the landlord remains so vested.

3. Throughout any period which, by virtue of paragraph 1 above, falls to be
disregarded for the purpose of determining whether the condition in section 12(1)(c)
is fulfilled with respect to a tenancy, no order shall be made for possession of the
dwelling-house subject to that tenancy, other than an order which might be made if
that tenancy were or, as the case may be, had been a regulated tenancy.

4. For the purposes of section 12, a building is a purpose-built block of flats if as
constructed it contained, and it contains, two or more flats; and for this purpose "flat"
means a dwelling-house which—

(a) forms part only of a building; and

(b) is separated horizontally from another dwelling-house which forms part of the
same building.

5. For the purposes of section 12, a person shall be treated as occupying a dwelling-
house as his residence if, so far as the nature of the case allows, he fulfils the same
conditions as, by virtue of section 2(3) of this Act, are required to be fulfilled by a
statutory tenant of a dwelling-house.

PART II

TENANCIES CEASING TO FALL WITHIN SECTION 12

6.—(1) In any case where—

3A–244

(a) a tenancy which, by virtue only of section 12, was precluded from being a
protected tenancy ceases to be so precluded and accordingly becomes a
protected tenancy, and

(b) before it became a protected tenancy a rent was registered for the dwelling
concerned under Part V of this Act,

    the amount which is so registered shall be deemed to be registered under Part
IV of this Act as the rent for the dwelling-house which is let on that tenancy,

Paragraph numbers marked with a "+" can be found online and on CD.

and that registration shall be deemed to take effect on the day the tenancy becomes a protected tenancy.

(2) Section 67(3) of this Act shall not apply to an application for the registration under Part IV of a rent different from that which is deemed to be registered as mentioned in sub-paragraph (1) above.

(3) [...]

(4) If, immediately before a tenancy became a protected tenancy as mentioned in sub-paragraph (1)(a) above, the rates in respect of the dwelling-house concerned were borne as mentioned in sub-section (3) of section 79 of this Act and the fact that they were so borne was noted as required by that sub-section then, in the application of Part IV in relation to the protected tenancy, section 71(2) of this Act shall be deemed to apply.

7. If, in a case where a tenancy becomes a protected tenancy as mentioned in sub-paragraph (1)(a) above—

(a) a notice to quit had been served in respect of the dwelling concerned before the date on which the tenancy became a protected tenancy, and

(b) the period at the end of which that notice to quit takes effect had, before that date, been extended under Part VII of this Act, and

(c) that period has not expired before that date,

the notice to quit shall take effect on the day following that date (whenever it would otherwise take effect) and, accordingly, on that day the protected tenancy shall become a statutory tenancy.

3A–245   *Note* —Amended by the Housing Act 1980 s.65, Sch.26; the Housing Act 1988 Sch.18; the Trusts of Land and Appointment of Trustees Act 1996 Sch.4; and the Law of Property (Miscellaneous Provisions) Act 1994 s.21(1), Sch.1.

Sch.2 should be read in conjunction with s.12 (see para.3A–129).

3A–246   * * * *

SECTION 98   SCHEDULE 15

GROUNDS FOR POSSESSION OF DWELLING-HOUSES LET ON OR SUBJECT TO PROTECTED OR STATUTORY TENANCIES

PART I

CASES IN WHICH COURT MAY ORDER POSSESSION

Case 1

Where any rent lawfully due from the tenant has not been paid, or any obligation of the protected or statutory tenancy which arises under this Act, or—

(a) in the case of a protected tenancy, any other obligation of the tenancy, in so far as is consistent with the provisions of Part VII of this Act, or

(b) in the case of a statutory tenancy, any other obligation of the previous protected tenancy which is applicable to the statutory tenancy,

has been broken or not performed.

Case 2

3A–247   Where the tenant or any person residing or lodging with him or any sub-tenant of his has been guilty of conduct which is a nuisance or annoyance to adjoining occupiers, or has been convicted of using the dwelling-house or allowing the dwelling-house to be used for immoral or illegal purposes.

Case 3

3A–248   Where the condition of the dwelling-house has, in the opinion of the court, deteriorated owing to acts of waste by, or the neglect or default of, the tenant or any person residing or lodging with him or any sub-tenant of his and, in the case of any act of waste by, or the neglect or default of, a person lodging with the tenant or sub-tenant

Paragraph numbers marked with a "+" can be found online and on CD.

of his, where the court is satisfied that the tenant has not, before the making of the order in question, taken such steps as he ought reasonably to have taken for the removal of the lodger or sub-tenant, as the case may be.

Case 4

Where the condition of any furniture provided for use under the tenancy has, in **3A–249** the opinion of the court, deteriorated owing to ill-treatment by the tenant or any person residing or lodging with him or any sub-tenant of his and, in the case of any ill-treatment by a person lodging with the tenant or a sub-tenant of his, where the court is satisfied that the tenant has not, before the making of the order in question, taken such steps as he ought reasonably to have taken for the removal of the lodger or sub-tenant, as the case may be.

Case 5

Where the tenant has given notice to quit and, in consequence of that notice, the **3A–250** landlord has contracted to sell or let the dwelling-house or has taken any other steps as the result of which he would, in the opinion of the court, be seriously prejudiced if he could not obtain possession.

Case 6

Where, without the consent of the landlord, the tenant has, at any time after— **3A–251**

(a) [...]

(b) 22nd March, 1973, in the case of a tenancy which became a regulated tenancy by virtue of section 14 of the Counter-Inflation Act 1973;

(bb) the commencement of section 73 of the Housing Act 1980, in the case of a tenancy which became a regulated tenancy by virtue of that section;

(c) 14th August, 1974, in the case of a regulated furnished tenancy; or

(d) 8th December, 1965, in the case of any other tenancy,

assigned or sublet the whole of the dwelling-house or sublet part of the dwelling-house, the remainder being already sublet.

Case 7

[...] **3A–252**

Case 8

Where the dwelling-house is reasonably required by the landlord for occupation as **3A–253** a residence for some person engaged in his whole-time employment, or in the whole-time employment of some tenant from him or with whom, conditional on housing being provided, a contract for such employment has been entered into, and the tenant was in the employment of the landlord or a former landlord, and the dwelling-house was let to him in consequence of that employment and he has ceased to be in that employment.

Case 9

Where the dwelling-house is reasonably required by the landlord for occupation as **3A–254** a residence for—

(a) himself, or

(b) any son or daughter of his over 18 years of age, or

(c) his father or mother, or

(d) if the dwelling-house is let on or subject to a regulated tenancy, the father or mother of his spouse or civil partner,

and the landlord did not become landlord by purchasing the dwelling-house or any interest therein after—

(i) 7th November, 1956, in the case of a tenancy which was then a controlled tenancy;

(ii) 8th March, 1973, in the case of a tenancy which became a regulated tenancy by virtue of section 14 of the Counter-Inflation Act 1973;

(iii) 24th May, 1974, in the case of a regulated furnished tenancy; or

Paragraph numbers marked with a "+" can be found online and on CD.

(iv) 23rd March, 1965, in the case of any other tenancy.

Case 10

3A-255 Where the court is satisfied that the rent charged by the tenant—

(a) for any sublet part of the dwelling-house which is a dwelling-house let on a protected tenancy or subject to a statutory tenancy is or was in excess of the maximum rent for the time being recoverable for that part, having regard to Part III of this Act, or

(b) for any sublet part of the dwelling-house which is subject to a restricted contract is or was in excess of the maximum (if any) which it is lawful for the lessor, within the meaning of Part V of this Act to require or receive having regard to the provisions of that Part.

3A-256 *Note* —Case 9 amended by the Civil Partnership Act 2004 s.81, Sch.8, para.14.

PART II

CASES IN WHICH COURT MUST ORDER POSSESSION WHERE DWELLIING-HOUSE SUBJECT TO REGULATED TENANCY

Case 11

3A-257 Where a person (in this case referred to as the "owner-occupier") who let the dwelling-house on a regulated tenancy had, at any time before the letting, occupied it as his residence and—

(a) not later than the relevant date the landlord gave notice, in writing to the tenant that possession might be recovered under this Case, and

(b) the dwelling-house has not, since—

(i) March 22, 1973, in the case of a tenancy which became a regulated tenancy by virtue of section 14 of the Counter-Inflation Act 1973;

(ii) August 14, 1974, in the case of a regulated furnished tenancy; or

(iii) December 8, 1965, in the case of any other tenancy,

been let by the owner-occupier on a protected tenancy with respect to which the condition mentioned in paragraph (a) above was not satisfied, and

(c) the court is of the opinion that of the conditions set out in Part V of this Schedule one of those in paragraphs (a) and (c) to (f) is satisfied.

If the court is of the opinion that, notwithstanding that the condition in paragraph (a) or (b) above is not complied with, it is just and equitable to make an order for possession of the dwelling-house, the court may dispense with the requirements of either or both of these paragraphs, as the case may require.

The giving of a notice before August 14, 1974 under section 79 of the Rent Act 1968 shall be treated, in the case of a regulated furnished tenancy, as compliance with paragraph (a) of this Case.

Where the dwelling-house has been let by the owner-occupier on a protected tenancy (in this paragraph referred to as "the earlier tenancy") granted on or after November 16, 1984 but not later than the end of he period of two months beginning with the commencement of the Rent (Amendment) Act 1985 and either—

(i) the earlier tenancy was granted for a term certain (whether or not to be followed by a further term or to continue thereafter from year to year or some other period) and was during that term a protected shorthold tenancy as defined in section 52 of the Housing Act 1980, or

(ii) the conditions mentioned in paragraphs (a) to (c) of Case 20 were satisfied with respect to the dwelling-house and the earlier tenancy,

then for the purposes of paragraph (b) above the condition in paragraph (a) above is to be treated as having been satisfied with respect to the earlier tenancy.

Case 12

3A-258 Where the landlord (in this Case referred to as "the owner") intends to occupy the dwelling-house as his residence at such time as he might retire from regular employment and has let it on a regulated tenancy before he has so retired and—

Paragraph numbers marked with a "+" can be found online and on CD.

(a) not later than the relevant date the landlord gave notice in writing to the tenant that possession might be recovered under this Case; and

(b) the dwelling-house has not, since August 14, 1974, been let by the owner paragraph (a) above was not satisfied; and

(c) the court is of the opinion that of the conditions set out in Part V of this Schedule one of those in paragraphs (b) to (e) is satisfied.

If the court is of the opinion that, notwithstanding that the condition in paragraph (a) or (b) above is not complied with, it is just and equitable to make an order for possession of the dwelling-house, the court may dispense with the requirements of either or both of those paragraphs, as the case may require.

Case 13

Where the dwelling-house is let under a tenancy for a term of years certain not **3A–259** exceeding eight months and—

(a) not later than the relevant date the landlord gave notice in writing to the tenant that possession might be recovered under this Case; and

(b) that dwelling-house was, at some time within the period of 12 months ending on the relevant date, occupied under a right to occupy it for a holiday.

For the purposes of this Case a tenancy shall be treated as being for a term of years certain notwithstanding that it is liable to determination by re-entry or on the happening of any event other than the giving of notice by the landlord to determine the term.

Case 14

Where the dwelling-house is let under a tenancy for a term of years certain not **3A–260** exceeding 12 months and—

(a) not later than the relevant date the landlord gave notice in writing to the tenant that possession might be recovered under this Case; and

(b) at some time within the period of 12 months ending on the relevant date, the dwelling-house was subject to such a tenancy as is referred to in section 8(1) of this Act.

For the purposes of this Case a tenancy shall be treated as being for a term of years certain notwithstanding that it is liable to determination by re-entry or on the happening of any event other than the giving of notice by the landlord to determine the term.

Case 15

Where the dwelling-house is held for the purpose of being available for occupation **3A–261** by a minister of religion as a residence from which to perform the duties of his office and—

(a) not later than the relevant date the tenant was given notice in writing that possession might be recovered under this Case, and

(b) the court is satisfied that the dwelling-house is required for occupation by a minister of religion as such a residence.

Case 16

Where the dwelling-house was at any time occupied by a person under the terms of **3A–262** his employment as a person employed in agriculture, and

(a) the tenant neither is nor at any time was so employed by the landlord and is not the widow of a person who was so employed, and

(b) not later than the relevant date, the tenant was given notice in writing that possession might be recovered under this Case, and

(c) the court is satisfied that the dwelling-house is required for occupation by a person employed, or to be employed, by the landlord in agriculture.

For the purposes of this Case "employed", "employment" and "agriculture" have the same meanings as in the Agricultural Wages Act 1948.

Case 17

Where proposals for amalgamation, approved for the purposes of a scheme under **3A–263** section 26 of the Agriculture Act 1967, have been carried out and, at the time when

Paragraph numbers marked with a "+" can be found online and on CD.

the proposals were submitted, the dwelling-house was occupied by a person responsible (whether as owner, tenant, or servant or agent of another) for the control of the farming of any part of the land comprised in the amalgamation and

(a) after the carrying out of the proposals, the dwelling-house was let on a regulated tenancy otherwise than to, or to the widow of, either a person ceasing to be so responsible as part of the amalgamation or a person who is, or at any time was, employed by the landlord in agriculture, and

(b) not later than the relevant date the tenant was given notice in writing that possession might be recovered under this Case, and

(c) the court is satisfied that the dwelling-house is required for occupation by a person employed, or to be employed, by the landlord in agriculture, and

(d) the proceedings for possession are commenced by the landlord at any time during the period of five years beginning with the date on which the proposals for the amalgamation were approved or, if occupation of the dwelling-house after the amalgamation continued in, or was first taken by, a person ceasing to be responsible as mentioned in paragraph (a) above or his widow, during a period expiring three years after the date on which the dwelling-house next became unoccupied.

For the purposes of this Case "employed" and "agriculture" have the same meanings as in the Agricultural Wages Act 1948 and "amalgamation" has the same meaning as in Part II of the Agriculture Act 1967.

Case 18

3A–264 Where—

(a) the last occupier of the dwelling-house before the relevant date was a person, or the widow of a person, who was at some time during his occupation responsible (whether as owner, tenant, or servant or agent of another) for the control of the farming of land which formed, together with the dwelling-house, an agricultural unit within the meaning of the Agriculture Act 1947, and

(b) the tenant is neither—

(i) a person, or the widow of a person, who is or has at any time been responsible for the control of the farming of any part of the said land, nor

(ii) a person, or the widow of a person, who is or at any time was employed by the landlord in agriculture, and

(c) the creation of the tenancy was not preceded by the carrying out in connection with any of the said land of an amalgamation approved for the purposes of a scheme under section 26 of the Agriculture Act 1967, and

(d) not later than the relevant date the tenant was given notice in writing that possession might be recovered under this Case, and

(e) the court is satisfied that the dwelling-house is required for occupation either by a person responsible or to be responsible (whether as owner, tenant, or servant or agent of another) for the control of the farming of any part of the said land or by a person employed or to be employed by the landlord in agriculture, and

(f) in a case where the relevant date was before August 9, 1972, the proceedings for possession are commenced by the landlord before the expiry of five years from the date on which the occupier referred to in paragraph (a) above went out of occupation.

For the purposes of this Case "employed" and "agriculture" have the same meanings as in the Agricultural Wages Act 1948 and "amalgamation" has the same meaning as in Part II of the Agriculture Act 1967.

Case 19

3A–265 Where the dwelling-house was let under a protected shorthold tenancy (or is treated under section 55 of the Housing Act 1980 as having been so let) and—

(a) there either has been no grant of a further tenancy of the dwelling-house since the end of the protected shorthold tenancy or, if there was such a grant, it was to a person the dwelling-house as a protected or statutory tenant; and

Paragraph numbers marked with a "+" can be found online and on CD.

(b) the proceedings for possession were commenced after appropriate notice by the landlord to the tenant and not later than three months after the expiry of the notice.

A notice is appropriate for this Case if—

(i) it is in writing and states that proceedings for possession under this Case may be brought after its expiry; and

(ii) it expires not earlier than three months after it is served nor, if, when it is served, the tenancy is a periodic tenancy, before that periodic tenancy could be brought to an end by a notice to quit served by the landlord on the same day;

(iii) it is served—

(a) in the period of three months immediately preceding the date on which the protected shorthold tenancy comes to an end; or

(b) if that date has passed, in the period of three months immediately preceding any anniversary of that date; and

(iv) in a case where a previous notice has been served by the landlord on the tenant in respect of the dwelling-house, and that notice was an appropriate notice, it is served not earlier than three months after the expiry of the previous notice.

Case 20

Where the dwelling-house was let by a person (in this Case referred to as "the owner")   **3A–266**
at any time after the commencement of section 67 of the Housing Act 1980 and—

(a) at the time when the owner acquired the dwelling-house he was a member of the regular armed forces of the Crown;

(b) at the relevant date the owner was a member of the regular armed forces of the Crown;

(c) not later than the relevant date the owner gave notice in writing to the tenant that possession might be recovered under this Case;

(d) the dwelling-house has not, since the commencement of section 67 of the Act of 1980 been let by the owner on a protected tenancy with respect to which the condition mentioned in paragraph (c) above was not satisfied; and

(e) the court is of the opinion that—

(i) the dwelling-house is required as a residence for the owner; or

(ii) of the conditions set out in Part V of this Schedule one of those in paragraphs (c) to (f) is satisfied.

If the court is of the opinion that, notwithstanding that the condition in paragraph (c) or (d) above is not complied with, it is just and equitable to make an order for possession of the dwelling-house, the court may dispense with the requirements of either or both of these paragraphs, as the case may require.

For the purposes of this Case "regular armed forces of the Crown" has the same meaning as in section 1 of the House of Commons Disqualification Act 1975.

Part III

Provisions Applicable to Case 9 and Part II of This Schedule

Provision for Case 9

1. A court shall not make an order for possession of a dwelling-house by reason only   **3A–267**
that the circumstances of the case fall within Case 9 in Part I of this Schedule if the court is satisfied that, having regard to all the circumstances of the case, including the question whether other accommodation is available for the landlord or the tenant, greater hardship would be caused by granting the order than by refusing to grant it.

Provision for Part II

2. Any reference in Part II of this Schedule to the relevant date shall be construed as   **3A–268**
follows—

(a) except in a case falling within paragraph (b) or (c) below, if the protected

Paragraph numbers marked with a "+" can be found online and on CD.

tenancy, or, in the case of a statutory tenancy, the previous contractual tenancy, was created before December 8, 1965, the relevant date means June 7, 1966; and

(b) except in a case falling within paragraph (c) below, if the tenancy became a regulated tenancy by virtue of section 14 of the Counter-Inflation Act 1973 and the tenancy or, in the case of a statutory tenancy, the previous contractual tenancy, was created before March 22, 1973, the relevant date means September 22, 1973; and

(c) in the case of a regulated furnished tenancy, if the tenancy, or, in the case of a statutory furnished tenancy, the previous contractual tenancy was created before August 14, 1974, the relevant date means February 13, 1975; and

(d) in any other case, the relevant date means the date of the commencement of the regulated tenancy in question.

PART IV

SUITABLE ALTERNATIVE ACCOMMODATION

3A-269 3. For the purposes of section 98(1)(a) of this Act, a certificate of the local housing authority for the district in which the dwelling-house in question is situated, certifying that the authority will provide suitable alternative accommodation for the tenant by a date specified in the certificate, shall be conclusive evidence that suitable alternative accommodation will be available for him by that date.

4.—(1) Where no such certificate as is mentioned in paragraph 3 above is produced to the court, accommodation shall be deemed to be suitable for the purposes of section 98(1)(a) of this Act if it consists of either—

(a) premises which are to be let as a separate dwelling such that they will then be let on a protected tenancy (other than one under which the landlord might recover possession of the dwelling-house under one of the cases in Part II of this Schedule), or

(b) premises to be let as a separate dwelling on terms which will, in the opinion of the court, afford to the tenant security of tenure reasonably equivalent to the security afforded by Part VII of this Act in the case of a protected tenancy of a kind mentioned in paragraph (a) above,

and, in the opinion of the court, the accommodation fulfils the relevant conditions as defined in paragraph 5 below.

(2) [...]

5.—(1) For the purposes of paragraph 4 above, the relevant conditions are that the accommodation is reasonably suitable to the needs of the tenant and his family as regards proximity to place of work, and either—

(a) similar as regards rental and extent to the accommodation afforded by dwelling-houses provided in the neighbourhood by any local housing authority for persons whose needs as regards extent are, in the opinion of the court, similar to those of the tenant and of his family; or

(b) reasonably suitable to the means of the tenant and to the needs of the tenant and his family as regards extent and character; and

that if any furniture was provided for use under the protected or statutory tenancy in question, furniture is provided for use in the accommodation which is either similar to that so provided or is reasonably suitable to the needs of the tenant and his family.

(2) For the purposes of sub-paragraph (1)(a) above, a certificate of a housing authority stating—

(a) the extent of the accommodation afforded by dwelling-houses provided by the authority to meet the needs of tenants with families of such number as may be specified in the certificate, and

(b) the amount of the rent charged by the authority for dwelling-houses affording accommodation of that extent,

shall be conclusive evidence of the facts so stated.

6. Accommodation shall not be deemed to be suitable to the needs of the tenant and his family if the result of their occupation of the accommodation would be that it

Paragraph numbers marked with a "+" can be found online and on CD.

would be an overcrowded dwelling-house for the purposes of Part X of the Housing Act 1985.

7. Any document purporting to be a certificate of a local housing authority named therein issued for the purposes of this Schedule and to be signed by the proper officer of that authority shall be received in evidence and, unless the contrary is shown, shall be deemed to be such a certificate without further proof.

8. In this Part "local housing authority" and "district" in relation to such an authority have the same meaning as in the Housing Act 1985.

PART V

PROVISIONS APPLYING TO CASES 11, 12 AND 20

1. In this Part of this Schedule— **3A–270**

"mortgage" includes a charge and "mortgagee" shall be construed accordingly;

"owner" means, in relation to Case 11, the owner-occupied; and

"successor in title" means any person deriving title from the owner, other than a purchaser for value or a person deriving title from a purchaser for value.

2. The conditions referred to in paragraph (c) in each of Cases 11 and 12 and in paragraph (e)(ii) of Case 20 are that—

(a) the dwelling-house is required as a residence for the owner or any member of his family who resided with the owner when he last occupied the dwelling-house as a residence;

(b) the owner has retired from regular employment and requires the dwelling-house as a residence;

(c) the owner has died and the dwelling-house is required as a residence for a member of his family who was residing with him at the time of his death;

(d) the owner has died and the dwelling-house is required by a successor in title as his residence or for the purpose of disposing of it with vacant possession;

(e) the dwelling-house is subject to a mortgage, made by deed and granted before the tenancy, and the mortgagee—

(i) is entitled to exercise a power of sale conferred on him by the mortgage or by section 101 of the Law of Property Act 1925; and

(ii) requires the dwelling-house for the purpose of disposing of it with vacant possession in exercise of that power; and

(f) the dwelling-house is not reasonably suitable to the needs of the owner, having regard to his place of work, and he requires it for the purpose of disposing of it with vacant possession and of using the proceeds of that disposal in acquiring, as his residence, a dwelling-house which is more suitable to those needs.

Note —Amended by the Housing Act 1980 ss.55, 66 and 67, Schs 7, 8 and 25; the **3A–271** Housing (Consequential Provisions) Act 1985 s.4, Sch.2, para.35; the Rent (Amendment) Act 1985 ss.1, 66; the Housing and Planning Act 1986 s.13; the Housing Act 1988 s.140, Sch.18; and the Civil Partnership Act 2004 s.81 and Sch.8, para.14.

Schedule 15 should be read in conjunction with s.98 (see para.3A–182).

Cases 1 to 10 are discretionary grounds

The court may only make a possession order if it considers it reasonable to do so **3A–272** and the court has discretion to suspend any order in accordance with s.100 (see above). Cases 11 to 19 are mandatory grounds—if the ground is proved, the court must make a possession order to take effect in 14 days, or if there is exceptional hardship, a maximum of 42 days (see the Housing Act 1980 s.89, below).

Case 1

A landlord must prove either that there are rent arrears or that there has been a **3A–273** breach of a term or other obligation of the tenancy.

Rent arrears —A landlord must prove two things, first that rent was lawfully due **3A–274**

Paragraph numbers marked with a "+" can be found online and on CD.

from the tenant and second that some rent remained unpaid, at the date of issue of the claim. This applies only to rent which is due from the actual tenant against whom possession is claimed and not to that due from a predecessor of the present tenant (*Tickner v Clifton* [1929] 1 K.B. 207). Rent becomes lawfully due at midnight on the day when it is payable (*Aspinall v Aspinall* [1961] Ch. 526). If rent is tendered after the due date, but before the commencement of proceedings, that prevents rent from being "lawfully due" unless time has been made the essence of the contract. The words "lawfully due" mean that the obligation to pay rent must have arisen and not been discharged (*Bird v Hildage* [1948] 1 K.B. 91; [1947] 2 All E.R. 7, CA). However, once a landlord shows that there were arrears of rent at the commencement of proceedings, the court has jurisdiction to make a possession order even if rent arrears are paid before the hearing (*Dellenty v Pellow* [1951] 2 K.B. 858; [1951] 2 All E.R. 716, CA). Prima facie it would not ordinarily be reasonable to make a possession order in such circumstances (see *Hayman v Rowlands* [1957] 1 W.L.R. 317; [1957] 1 All E.R. 321, CA) but where the tenant has frequently been in arrears and proceedings have been issued on a number of occasions, it may be reasonable to make a possession order (*Dellenty v Pellow*, above. See too *Lee-Steere v Jennings* (1987) 20 H.L.R. 1, CA). See also *Laimond Properties Ltd v Raeuchle*, also reported as *Raeuchle v Laimond Properties Ltd (Suspension of Possession Order)* (2001) 33 H.L.R. 10.

Failure to provide a rent book does not disentitle a landlord from recovering rent (*Shaw v Groom* [1970] 2 Q.B. 504; [1970] 2 W.L.R. 299; [1970] 1 All E.R. 702, CA).

3A–275   *Breach of any other tenancy obligation* —This limb of Case 1 is similar to the Housing Act 1988 Sch.2, Ground 12 (see below).

It should be noted that the original terms of the contractual tenancy continue to bind a statutory tenant in so far as they are consistent with the provisions of the Rent Act 1977 (see s.3(1) above).

A proviso in a contractual tenancy giving the landlord a right of re-entry if the tenant becomes bankrupt is an obligation under the subsequent statutory tenancy within the meaning of Case 1 *Cadogan Estates Ltd v McMahon* [2001] A.C. 378; [2000] 3 W.L.R. 1555; [2000] 4 All E.R. 897, HL.

Case 2

3A–276   *Nuisance or annoyance* —"Nuisance" and "annoyance" are both used in the natural sense of the words. This ground may be satisfied by drunkenness, abusive behaviour, noise, obstructive behaviour towards other occupiers or violence (per Wood J. in *Cobstone Investments Ltd v Maxim* [1984] 2 All E.R. 635). Unknown people coming to the premises at all hours of the day and night may amount to an annoyance (*Florent v Horez* (1984) 12 H.L.R. 1; (1983) 268 E.G. 807, CA).

It is not necessary for the premises of people complaining of nuisance or annoyance to be contiguous in the sense that they are physically joined to the dwelling-house rented by a defendant. The word "adjoining" is used in the wider sense of "neighbouring" (*Cobstone Investments Ltd v Maxim* [1985] Q.B. 140; [1983] 3 W.L.R. 563; [1984] 2 All E.R. 635, CA). See too *Northampton BC v Lovatt* (1998) 30 H.L.R. 875; (1998) 07 E.G. 142; *The Times*, January 3, 1998, CA.

3A–277   *Immoral of illegal purposes* —Where a landlord relies upon a conviction for using the dwelling-house or allowing the dwelling-house to be used for immoral or illegal purposes it is necessary to show that the crime has actually been committed on the premises and that the premises have been used for the purpose of committing the offence (*Abrahams v Wilson* [1971] 2 Q.B. 88; [1971] 2 W.L.R. 923; [1971] 2 All E.R. 114, CA). For example, there is a difference between drugs being in a defendant's immediate possession, on the one hand, and on the other hand the tenant using the premises to store drugs.

In a claim for possession based on nuisance or annoyance to adjoining occupiers, a judge may infer that adjoining occupiers have been affected, even if none of them gives evidence of actual nuisance (*Frederick Platts Co Ltd v Grigor* [1950] 1 All E.R. 941, CA).

Paragraph numbers marked with a "+" can be found online and on CD.

satisfied.. The most important of these is that the premises are "required as a residence". All that is required is that the landlord "bona fide wants" or "genuinely has the immediate intention" of occupying the premises (*Kennealy v Dunne* [1977] Q.B. 837, CA). The landlord need not require the premises as a permanent residence and fairly intermittent residence will be sufficient (*Naish v Curzon* (1984) 17 H.L.R. 220, CA; and *Davies v Peterson* (1989) 21 H.L.R. 63; (1989) 06 E.G. 130, CA). This is a question of fact in each case. It is sufficient if only one of two joint landlords requires the premises as a residence (*Tilling v Whiteman* [1979] 1 All E.R. 737, HL).

Case 13

"right to occupy it for a holiday" —See s.9 and commentary thereto, above.   3A–286

Case 14

See s.8 and annotations thereto, above.   3A–287

Case 16

The court cannot dispense with the requirement that notice must be served prior to   3A–288
the commencement of the tenancy. A term in a tenancy agreement that the tenant will vacate on 28 days' notice if the premises are required for another farm worker is not sufficient (*Fowler v Minchin* (1987) 19 H.L.R. 224, CA), but a certificate of fair rent which was handed to the tenant before the commencement of the tenancy and which stated that the tenancy was to be subject to Case 16 has been held to be sufficient (*Springfield Investments v Bell* (1990) 22 H.L.R. 440, CA).

Housing Act 1980

(1980 c.51)   3A–289

ARRANGEMENT OF SECTIONS

PART IV

JURISDICTION AND PROCEDURE

PART IV

JURISDICTION AND PROCEDURE

Discretion of court in certain proceedings for possession

88.—(1) Where, under the terms of a rental purchase agreement, a   3A–290
person has been let into possession of a dwelling-house and, on the termination of the agreement or of his right to possession under it, proceedings are brought for the possession of the dwelling-house, the court may—

(a) adjourn the proceedings; or

(b) on making an order for the possession of the dwelling-house, stay or suspend execution of the order or postpone the date of possession;

for such period or periods as the court thinks fit.

(2) On any such adjournment, stay, suspension or postponement the court may impose such conditions with regard to payments by

Paragraph numbers marked with a "+" can be found online and on CD.

the person in possession in respect of his continued occupation of the dwelling-house and such other conditions as the court thinks fit.

(3) The court may revoke or from time to time vary any condition imposed by virtue of this section.

(4) In this section "rental purchase agreement" means an agreement for the purchase of a dwelling-house (whether freehold or leasehold property) under which the whole or part of the purchase price is to be paid in three or more instalments and the completion of the purchase is deferred until the whole or a specified part of the purchase price has been paid.

(5) This section extends to proceedings for the possession of a dwelling-house which were begun before the commencement of this section unless an order for the possession of the dwelling-house was made in the proceedings and executed before the commencement of this section.

"rental purchase agreement"

3A–291   See s.88(4).

Restriction on discretion of court in making orders for possession of land

3A–292   **89.**—(1) Where a court makes an order for the possession of any land in a case not falling within the exceptions mentioned in subsection (2) below, the giving up of possession shall not be postponed (whether by the order or any variation, suspension or stay of execution) to a date later than fourteen days after the making of the order, unless it appears to the court that exceptional hardship would be caused by requiring possession to be given up by that date; and shall not in any event be postponed to a date later than six weeks after the making of the order.

(2) The restrictions in subsection (1) above do not apply if—

(a) the order is made in an action by a mortgagee for possession; or

(b) the order is made in an action for forfeiture of a lease; or

(c) the court had power to make the order only if it considered it reasonable to make it; or

(d) the order relates to a dwelling-house which is the subject of a restricted contract (within the meaning of section 19 of the 1977 Act); or

(e) the order is made in proceedings brought as mentioned in section 88(1) above.

Restriction on discretion of court in making orders for possession of land

3A–293   At common law judges had a discretion to allow occupiers a reasonable time before a possession order took effect even if they had no security of tenure (*Air Ministry v Harris* [1951] 2 All E.R. 862 (six months too long for licensees); *Sheffield Corp v Luxford* [1929] 2 K.B. 180 (one year too long); *Jones v Savery* [1951] 1 All E.R. 820 (one month reasonable)). However, this discretion was largely taken away by the Housing Act 1980. Apart from the exceptions contained in the section, orders for possession must now take effect not later than 14 days after the making of the order unless it would

Paragraph numbers marked with a "+" can be found online and on CD.

cause exceptional hardship, in which case the order can be postponed to a date which is not more than six weeks after the making of the order.

There are no reported decisions on the meaning of "exceptional hardship".

In *Hackney LBC v Side by Side (Kids) Ltd* [2003] EWHC 1813 (QBD); [2004] 1 W.L.R. 363, Stanley Burnton J. held that Housing Act 1980 s.89 applies as much to orders made in the High Court as to those made in the county court. The decision of Harman J. in *Bain & Co v Church Commissioners for England* [1989] 1 W.L.R. 24, Ch D, that "a court" meant "a county court" was clearly wrong. Further, Stanley Burnton J. held that the general words of s.89 "did not permit him to find that it did not apply to consent orders".

Section 89 does not restrict the power of the court to grant a stay pending appeal. (*Admiral Taverns (Cygnet) Limited v Daniel and Daly* [2008] EWCA Civ 1501, November 25, 2008.

Supreme Court Act 1981

(1981 c.54)

ARRANGEMENT OF SECTIONS

Relief against forfeiture for non-payment of rent

38.—(1) In any action in the High Court for the forfeiture of a **3A–294** lease for non-payment rent, the court shall have power to grant relief against forfeiture in a summary manner, and may do so subject to the same terms and conditions as to the payment of rent, costs or otherwise as could have been imposed by it in such an action immediately before the commencement of this Act.

(2) Where the lessee or a person deriving title under him is granted relief under this section, he shall hold the demised premises in accordance with the terms of the lease without the necessity for a new lease.

Relief against forfeiture for non-payment of rent

Relief from forfeiture for non-payment of rent may be obtained under the Com- **3A–295** mon Law Procedure Act 1852 ss.210 to 212, or in a summary way under s.38 of the 1981 Act.

"The Court, in exercising its jurisdiction to grant relief in cases of non-payment of rent is, of course, proceeding on the old principles of the Court of Equity which always regarded the condition of re-entry as being merely security for the payment of the rent and gave relief if the landlord could get his rent" (*Chandless-Chandless v Nicholson* [1942] 2 K.B. 321, CA, at 323 per Lord Greene M.R.).

Save in exceptional circumstances, therefore, the court grants relief where all the rent and costs have been paid or tendered (*Gill v Lewis* [1956] 2 Q.B. 1, CA).

Where an order is made giving relief in terms to be performed within a specified time, the court has power to extend the time, even though the original order did not expressly reserve "liberty to apply" (see *Chandless-Chandless v Nicholson*, above). Since the court can grant relief under this section in the exercise of the same powers as it could "immediately before the commencement of this Act," if relief from forfeiture is granted, the lessee will hold the demised premises according to the terms of the lease and without the necessity of any new lease (see s.46 of the Supreme Court of Judicature (Consolidation) Act 1925).

A statutory tenant under the Rent Act cannot claim relief under this section or s.146 of the LPA 1925 (see *Brewer v Jacobs* [1923] 1 K.B. 528).

As to relief against breaches of other covenants, see the LPA 1925 s.146.

Note also the County Courts Act 1984 s.138 (Provisions as to forfeiture for non-

HOUSING

Paragraph numbers marked with a "+" can be found online and on CD.

payment of rent), para.3A–297, below, and notes thereto, and, in particular, the explanation there of the effect of, and the legislative response to, *Di Palma v Victoria Square Property Co Ltd* [1986] Ch. 150; [1985] 2 All E.R. 676, CA.

County Courts Act 1984

3A–296

(1984 c.28)

FORFEITURE FOR NON-PAYMENT OF RENT

Provisions as to forfeiture for non-payment of rent

3A–297   **138.**—(1) This section has effect where a lessor is proceeding by action in a county court (being an action in which the county court has jurisdiction) to enforce against a lessee a right of re-entry or forfeiture in respect of any land for non-payment of rent.

(2) If the lessee pays into court or to the lessor not less than 5 clear days before the return day all the rent in arrear and the costs of the action, the action shall cease, and the lessee shall hold the land according to the lease without any new lease.

(3) If—

    (a) the action does not cease under subsection (2); and

    (b) the court at the trial is satisfied that the lessor is entitled to enforce the right of re-entry or forfeiture,

the court shall order possession of the land to be given to the lessor at the expiration of such period, not being less than 4 weeks from the date of the order, as the court thinks fit, unless within that period the lessee pays into court or to the lessor all the rent in arrear and the costs of the action.

(4) The court may extend the period specified under subsection (3) at any time before possession of the land is recovered in pursuance of the order under that subsection.

(5) [...] if—

    (a) within the period specified in the order; or

    (b) within that period as extended under subsection (4),

the lessee pays into court or to the lessor—

    (i) all the rent in arrear; and

    (ii) the costs of the action,

he shall hold the land acording to the lease without any new lease.

(6) Subsection (2) shall not apply where the lessor is proceeding in the same action to enforce a right of re-entry or forfeiture on any other ground as well as for non-payment of rent, or to enforce any other claim as well as the right of re-entry or forfeiture and the claim for arrears of rent.

Paragraph numbers marked with a "+" can be found online and on CD.

(7) If the lessee does not—

    (a) within the period specified in the order; or

    (b) with that period as extended under subsection (4), pay into court or to the lessor—

        (i) all the rent in arrear; and

        (ii) the costs of the action,

the order shall be enforceable in the prescribed manner and so long as the order remains unreversed the lessee shall, subject to subsections (8) and (9A), be barred from all relief.

(8) The extension under subsection (4) of a period fixed by a court shall not be treated as relief from which the lessee is barred by subsection (7) if he fails to pay into court or to the lessor all the rent in arrear and the costs of the action within that period.

(9) Where the court extends a period under subsection (4) at a time when—

    (a) that period has expired; and

    (b) a warrant has been issued for the possession of the land, the court shall suspend the warrant for the extended period; and, if before the expiration period, the lessee pays into court or to the lessor all the rent in arrear and all the costs of the action, the court shall cancel the warrant.

(9A) Where the lessor recovers possession of the land at any time after the making of the order under subsection (3) (whether as a result of the enforcement of the order or otherwise) the lessee may, at any time within six months from the date on which the lessor recovers possession, apply to the court for relief; and on any such application the court may, if it thinks fit, grant to the lessee such relief, subject to such terms and conditions, as it thinks fit.

(9B) Where the lessee is granted relief on an application under subsection (9A) he shall hold the land according to the lease without any new lease.

(9C) An application under subsection (9A) may be made by a person with an interest under a lease of the land derived (whether immediately or otherwise) from the lessee's interest therein in like manner as if he were the lessee; and on any such application the court may make an order which (subject to such terms and conditions as the court thinks fit) vests the land in such a person, as lessee of the lessor, for the remainder of the term of the lease under which he has any such interest as aforesaid, or for any lesser term.

In this subsection any reference to the land includes a reference to a part of the land.

(10) Nothing in this section or section 139 shall be taken to affect—

    (a) the power of the court to make any order which it would otherwise have power to make as respects a right of re-entry or forfeiture on any ground other than non-payment of rent; or

    (b) section 146(4) of the Law of Property Act 1925 (relief against forfeiture).

Paragraph numbers marked with a "+" can be found online and on CD.

3A-298   *Note* —Amended by the Administration of Justice Act 1985 ss.55 and 67(2), and Sch.8; and the Courts and Legal Services Act 1990 s.125(2), Sch.17, para.17.

See Form **N27** (*Civil Procedure Forms Volume*).

General note

3A-299   Forfeiture is a remedy which may be available to a lessor against a lessee prior to expiry of a fixed term lease; it has the effect of dispossessing the lessee. The remedy may be available, not only where the lessee fails to pay rent, but also in other circumstances (e.g. breach of any other covenant). This section has effect where a lessor is proceeding by action in a county court to enforce against a lessee a right of re-entry or forfeiture in respect of any land for non-payment of rent. Where proceedings to enforce a right of re-entry or forfeiture are brought for non-payment of rent and for some other reason, or for some other reason alone, the Law of Property Act 1925 s.146 is likely to apply. The 1925 Act may also apply where land has been forfeited, not by action, but by the lessor's re-entry without action; see also s.139(2), below.

Peaceable re-entry of premises "let as a dwelling" is unlawful while there is "any person lawfully residing in them or any part of them" (see the Protection from Eviction Act 1977 s.2, above). In such circumstances possession proceedings must be brought in court.

For the restriction on forfeiture or re-entry for arrears of service charges see the Housing Act 1996 s.81, below.

In relation to proceedings in the High Court, legislation dealing with forfeiture for non-payment of rent is found in the Common Law Procedure Act 1852 ss.210 to 212 (re-enacting provisions in the Landlord and Tenant Act 1730). But this legislation is not as elaborate as s.138; case law supplies the deficiencies. Note also the SCA 1981 s.38 (summary relief against forfeiture for non-payment of rent) (see para.3A–294 and commentary thereto).

In the CCA 1959, provisions as to the enforcement by action of a right of re-entry or forfeiture for non-payment of rent were found in s.191 (as amended by the Administration of Justice Act 1965 s.23). This section created certain difficulties, not all of which were remedied by the re-enactment of s.191, with some modifications, as s.138 of the 1984 Act. Consequently, the Administration of Justice Act 1985 s.55 added subss.(9A) to (9C) and made some minor amendments to subss.(5) and (7). The principal difficulty which had arisen was that the extent of the powers of the High Court, on the one hand, and of the county courts, on the other, differed and the relationship between the respective powers was a matter for doubt (see *Di Palma v Victoria Square Property Co Ltd* [1986] Ch. 150; [1985] 2 All E.R. 676, CA).

As a result of the Courts and Legal Services Act 1990 s.1 and Orders made under that section certain financial limits on the jurisdiction of county courts in relation to actions of the type referred to in subs.(1) of this section were removed and the jurisdictions of the High Court and the county courts became, in effect, co-terminous. At the same time, for the purpose of removing unnecessary distinctions between the two levels of jurisdiction, the words "or to the lessor" were added to subss.(2), (3), (5), (7), (8) and (9) by Sch.17, para.17 of the 1990 Act.

In effect, s.138 codifies an old equitable jurisdiction. The policy of the law stated in the section is to give lessees, against whom a right of re-entry or forfeiture may be enforced by a lessor for non-payment of rent, protections he would not otherwise enjoy, and which have the potential for enabling him to continue in occupation as lessee; where the protections apply, the lessee is relieved against forfeiture.

The section has no application to a case where there are arrears of service charges not deemed by the terms of the lease to be additional rent (*Escalus Properties Ltd v Robinson* [1996] Q.B. 231; [1995] 3 W.L.R. 524, CA).

Service by the lessor on the lessee of a notice under the Law of Property Act 1925 s.146, forfeiting a lease on grounds other than non-payment of rent, does not prevent the lessor subsequently claiming from the lessee under s.138 forfeiture for non-payment of rent due before service of the notice (*Church Commissioners for England v Nodjoumi* (1986) 51 P. & C.R. 155).

The broad scheme of s.138 is as follows. Subsection (2) states that, where a lessor brings an action to enforce a right of re-entry of forfeiture for non-payment of rent (but not for some other reason) and the action is not a mixed claim (see subs.(6)), then

Paragraph numbers marked with a "+" can be found online and on CD.

if the lessee pays arrears and costs within the time stipulated in that subsection he is relieved from forfeiture automatically; the action shall "cease" and the lease shall continue. Subss.(3) to (5) state that if the tenant does not so pay up and the court at trial is satisfied that the lessor is entitled to his remedy the court shall suspend the order for possession giving the lessee further time to pay. The time limit may be extended (and any warrant for possession suspended accordingly, see subs.(9)). If the tenant pays during the period of suspension, again he is relieved from forfeiture automatically (and any warrant is cancelled, see subs.(9)). If the tenant fails to pay, subs.(7) comes into play. This provision states that in these circumstances the order shall be enforceable in the prescribed manner and so long as the order remains unreversed the lessee shall "be barred from all relief", not only relief in any county court but also in the High Court. The lessor may proceed with a warrant for possession for the purpose of recovering possession. However, even in this event, from the tenant's point of view, all is not lost. At this late stage, if the lessor has not recovered possession (in pursuance of an order under subs.(3)), the tenant may still apply under subs.(4) for an extension (or a further extension) of the period for suspension of the order for possession fixed under subs.(3). It has been held in a county court that the divorced wife of a lessee, although not herself a lessee within the meaning of s.138, was a beneficial co-owner and so entitled to apply for an extension of time under s.138(4) and to pay the arrears on behalf of the lessee (*Bassett Road HA v Gough* [1998] 5 C.L.Y. 3653, Central London County Court). Further, if the lessor has recovered possession (whether as a result of the enforcement of the order or otherwise) the lessee may at any time within six months from the date on which the lessor recovered possession, apply to the court for relief (subs.(9A)). On such application relief is not automatic but discretionary; the court may grant relief as it thinks fit. (An application under subs.(9A) may be made by a person with an interest under a lease of land derived from the lessee's interest, subs.(9C), see further below.) In these two respects the lessee is not, in the terms of subs.(7), "barred from all relief" for his failure to pay within the period specified in the order for possession or as extended (as the case may be).

"lessor","lessee","lease"

For definitions, see s.140(1). "Lessee" includes mortgagee (*United Dominions Trust Ltd v Shellpoint Trustees Ltd* [1993] 4 All E.R. 310, CA). **3A–300**

Service of claim

If (a) one-half-year's rent is in arrear at the time of the commencement of the action, and (b) the lessor has a right to re-enter for non-payment of that rent, and (c) no sufficient distress is to be found on the premises countervailing the arrears then due, the service of the claim in the action shall stand in lieu of a demand and re-entry (s.139(1)). As to proof of insufficient distress, see *Rickett v Green* [1910] 1 K.B. 253. **3A–301**

"not less than 5 clear days before the return day" (subs.(2))

Section 147(1) states that "return day" means the day appointed in any summons or proceeding for the appearance of the defendant or any other day fixed for the hearing of any proceedings. In subs.(2) "return day" means the day so fixed, and not any later date upon which the action would fall actually to be tried in the absence of a payment under the subsection (*Swordheath Properties Ltd v Bolt* [1992] 2 E.G.L.R. 68; [1992] 38 E.G. 152, CA, following *R. v Registrar of the County Court at Leeds* (1886) 16 Q.B.D. 691, DC). **3A–302**

Lessee paying into court or to lessor (subss.(2), (3), (5), (7), (8) & (9))

Where payment into court or (semble) to the lessor of arrears of rent and costs is made by a person other than the lessee and that person does not make the payment on behalf of the lessee (e.g. an underlessee or mortgagee), the action does not "cease" by operation of subs.(2) as "lessee" in that subsection means the lessee against whom the action is brought as referred to in subs.(1) (*Matthews v Dobbins* [1963] 1 W.L.R. 227; [1963] 1 All E.R. 417, CA). **3A–303**

"the court shall order possession" (subs.(3))

Subsection (3) states that, if (a) the action does not cease under subs.(2), and (b) the court at the trial is satisfied that the lessor is entitled to enforce the right of re-entry or **3A–304**

Paragraph numbers marked with a "+" can be found online and on CD.

forfeiture, "the court shall order possession of the land". Where without doubt a lessor has established his claim he should be given judgment and the trial should not be adjourned against the wishes of the lessor except for good reason (*R. v Circuit Judge (sitting at Norwich Court) Ex p. Wathen* (1977) 33 P. & C.R. 423; (1976) 238 E.G. 45—in that case to give the lessee the opportunity to pay off the arrears).

Possession to be given at expiration of specified period

3A–305   An order for possession under subs.(3) must be suspended as provided by that subsection. Subsection (4) provides that the period may be extended at any time before possession of the land is recovered "in pursuance of the order" under subs.(3). There is some authority for the proposition that recovery of possession "in pursuance of the order" means recovery under a warrant for possession and not by other means (*Gadsby and Mitchell v Price and Harrison* [1985] C.L.Y. 1877).

"lessee pays...all the rent in arrear" (subss.(2), (3), (5), (7) & (9))

3A–306   The lease comes to an end when the claim is served. Rent is payable to the date of service and mesne profits thereafter. To facilitate the calculation of rent payable to date of service where rent is paid in arrears, the particulars of claim should state the daily rate at which the rent in arrear is to be calculated (PD 55 para.2.3(3)). Where the rent is payable in advance the lessor is entitled to be paid any rent due on a rent day which falls between issue and service (*Canas Property Co v KL Television Services* [1970] 2 Q.B. 433; [1970] 2 All E.R. 795, CA, see also *Capital and City Holdings Ltd v Dean Warburg Ltd* (1989) 58 P. & C.R. 346, CA).

In *Maryland Estates v Joseph* [1999] 1 W.L.R. 83; [1998] 3 All E.R. 193, CA, the Court of Appeal, held that the words used in County Courts Act 1984 s.138(3) ("the lessee pays into court ... all the rent in arrear") are not to be construed to mean that the court can order payment only of the rent in arrear at the date of the claim. It is to be assumed that leases continue after service of claims and that tenants remain under an obligation to pay sums reserved in leases as rent and that "all the rent in arrear" means the rent payable up to the date stated in the order.

Lessee's application for relief under subs.(9A)

3A–307   Where the lessor recovers possession at any time after the making of the order for possession under subs.(3), whether as a result of the enforcement of the order or otherwise (e.g. where the lessee left voluntarily) the lessee may at any time within six months from the date on which the lessor recovers possession apply to the court for relief. Upon such application, the court "may, if it thinks fit, grant to the lessee such relief, subject to such terms and conditions, as it thinks fit". Guidance on the exercise of the power to grant relief was given in *Chandless-Chandless v Nicholson* [1942] 2 K.B. 321; [1942] 2 All E.R. 315, CA, and *Gill v Lewis* [1956] 2 Q.B. 1; [1956] 2 W.L.R. 962, CA. See also *Silverman v AFCO (UK) Ltd* (1988) 56 P. & C.R. 185, CA (very late application made after a new lease to a third party had been executed properly refused); *Varndean Estates Ltd v Buckland and Buckland* (1967) 111 S.J. 684, CA (period of 18 months for the payment of the arrears of rent reasonable in the special circumstances, and arrears should include amount owing under earlier judgment in respect of arrears); *Brompton Securities Ltd (No.2), Re* [1988] 3 All E.R. 677 (save in exceptional circumstances, relief may be granted notwithstanding lessor has been bad payer in past); *Three Stars Property Holdings v Driscoll* [1986] CA Transcript 927; [1988] C.L.Y. 2795 (full payment of costs incurred by lessor may be imposed as a condition notwithstanding lessee legally aided with a nil contribution).

Application "by a person with an interest.... derived.... from the lessee's interest" (subs.(9C))

3A–308   PD 55 para.2.4 states that where the lessor knows of any person entitled to claim relief against forfeiture as underlessee (including a mortgagee) under subs.(9C) he shall give the name and address of that person in his particulars of claim and file a copy of the particulars for service on him. The holder of a charging order who has registered his interest is "a person with an interest under a lease" and may apply for relief from forfeiture under s.138(9C) (*Croydon (Unique) Ltd v Wright* [2001] Ch. 318; [2000] 2 W.L.R. 683; [1999] 4 All E.R. 257, CA).

An underlessee or mortgagee who fails to avail himself of the procedure for

Paragraph numbers marked with a "+" can be found online and on CD.

automatic relief provided for by subss.(2) and (5) may, by virtue of subs.(7), be barred from all relief, subject only to his right to apply for discretionary relief under subs.(9A) and (9C) within the specified six month period (*United Dominions Trust Ltd v Shellpoint Trustees Ltd* [1993] 4 All E.R. 310, CA; see also *Escalus Properties Ltd v Robinson* [1996] Q.B. 231; [1995] 3 W.L.R. 524, CA).

Law of Property Act 1925 s.146(4)

Section 138 has effect only where proceedings are brought for non-payment of **3A–309** rent. Subsection (10) states that nothing in this section (or in s.139) shall be taken to affect the power of the court to make any order which it would otherwise have power to make as respects a right of re-entry or forfeiture "on any ground other than non-payment of rent". Consequently, for example, the section does not affect the power of the court to grant relief from forfeiture to a lessee under s.146(2) of the 1925 Act, or to under-lessees claiming relief under s.146(4) of that Act. Relief from forfeiture may not be granted to a lessee under s.146(2) in proceedings based only on non-payment of rent (see s.146(11)). However, relief in proceedings based only on non-payment of rent, as well as proceedings based on other grounds (either additionally or alternatively), may be granted to an under-lessee under s.146(4). Because of this distinction between subss.(2) and (4) of s.146 of the 1925 Act subs.(10) of this section further provides that nothing in s.138 (or in s.139) shall be taken to affect s.146(4).

Service of summons and re-entry

139.—(1) In a case where section 138 has effect, if— **3A–310**

    (a) one-half-year's rent is in arrear at the time of the commencement of the action; and

    (b) the lessor has a right to re-enter for non-payment of that rent; and

    (c) no sufficient distress is to be found on the premises countervailing the arrears then due,

the service of the summons in the action in the prescribed manner shall stand in lieu of a demand and re-entry.

(2) Where a lessor has enforced against a lessee, by re-entry without action, a right of re-entry or forfeiture as respects any land for non-payment of rent, the lessee may ... at any time within six months from the date on which the lessor re-entered apply to the county court for relief, and on any such application the court may, if it thinks fit, grant to the lessee such relief as the High Court could have granted.

(3) Subsections (9B) and (C) of section 138 shall have effect in relation to an application under subsection (2) of this section as they have effect in relation to an application under subsection (9A) of that section.

Note —Amended by the Administration of Justice Act 1985 s.55; and the High **3A–311** Court and County Courts Jurisdiction Order 1991 (SI 1991/724) Sch., Pt I.

The county court has unlimited jurisdiction.

"lease", "lessee", "lessor", "under-lease", "under-lessee"

See s.140. **3A–312**

Interpretation of sections 138 and 139

140. For the purposes of sections 138 and 139— **3A–313**

    "lease" includes—

        (a) an original or derivative under-lease;

Paragraph numbers marked with a "+" can be found online and on CD.

(b) an agreement for a lease where the lessee has become entitled to have his lease granted; and

(c) a grant at a fee farm rent, or under a grant securing a rent by condition;

"lessee" includes—

(a) an original or derivative under-lessee;

(b) the persons deriving title under a lessee;

(c) a grantee under a grant at a fee farm rent, or under a grant securing a rent by condition; and

(d) the persons deriving title under such a grantee;

"lessor" includes—

(a) an original or derivative under-lessor;

(b) the persons deriving title under a lessor;

(c) a person making a grant at a fee farm rent, or a grant securing a rent by condition; and

(d) the persons deriving title under such a grantor;

"under-lease" includes an agreement for an under-lease where the under-lessee has become entitled to have his under-lease granted; and

"under-lessee" includes any person deriving title under an under-lessee.

Housing Act 1985

3A–314

(1985 c.68)

ARRANGEMENT OF SECTIONS

PART I

INTRODUCTORY PROVISIONS

LOCAL HOUSING AUTHORITIES

Paragraph numbers marked with a "+" can be found online and on CD.

PART I

INTRODUCTORY PROVISIONS

LOCAL HOUSING AUTHORITIES

Local housing authorities

1. In this Act "local housing authority" means a district council, a **3A–315** London borough council, the Common Council of the City of London, a Welsh county council or county borough council, or the Council of the Isles of Scilly.

Paragraph numbers marked with a "+" can be found online and on CD.

3A–316   *Note* —Amended by the Local Government (Wales) Act 1994 Sch.8, para.5(1).

* * * *

OTHER AUTHORITIES AND BODIES

Other descriptions of authority

3A–317   **4.** In this Act—

(a) "housing authority" means a local housing authority, or a new town corporation;

(b) "new town corporation" means a development corporation or the new towns residuary body;

(c) "development corporation" means a development corporation established by an order made, or having effect as if made, under the New Towns Act 1981;

(d) "urban development corporation" means an urban development corporation established under Part XVI of the Local Government, Planning and Land Act 1980;

(e) "local authority" means a county, county borough, district or London borough council, the Common Council of the City of London or the Council of the Isles of Scilly, in sections 43, 44 and 232 includes the Broads Authority, in sections 438, 441, 442, 443, and 458 includes the Broads Authority and a joint authority established by Part IV of the Local Government Act 1985 and the London Fire and Emergency Planning Authority, and in sections 45(2)(b), 50(2), 51(6), 80(1), 157(1), 171(2), 573(1), paragraph 2(1) of Schedule 1, grounds 7 and 12 in Schedule 2, ground 5 in Schedule 3, paragraph 7(1) of Schedule 4, paragraph 5(1)(b) of Schedule 5 and Schedule 16 includes the Broads Authority, a police authority established under section 3 of the Police Act 1996, [...] a joint authority established by Part IV of the Local Government Act 1985 and the London Fire and Emergency Planning Authority.

(f) "housing action trust" means a housing action established under Part III of the Housing Act 1988.

(g) "new towns residuary body" means—

(i) in relation to England, the Homes and Communities Agency so far as exercising functions in relation to anything transferred (or to be transferred) to it as mentioned in section 52(1)(a) to (d) of the Housing and Regeneration Act 2008; and

(ii) in relation to Wales, the Welsh Ministers so far as exercising functions in relation to anything transferred (or to be transferred) to them as mentioned in section 36(1)(a) (i) to (iii) of the New Towns Act 1981.

3A–318   *Note* —Amended by SI 1986/1; the Norfolk and Suffolk Broads Act 1988 s.21, Sch.6,

Paragraph numbers marked with a "+" can be found online and on CD.

para.25; the Education Reform Act 1988 s.237(2), Sch.13; the Housing Act 1988 s.62(7); the Local Government (Wales) Act 1994 s.22(2), Sch.8, para.5(3); the Police and Magistrates' Courts Act 1994 ss.43, 93, Schs 4 and 9; the Police Act 1996 s.103(1) Sch.7; the Police Act 1997 Sch.9, para.49; the Government of Wales Act 1998 Sch.15, para.7; the Greater London Authority Act 1999 Sch.29, para.42; the Criminal Justice and Police Act 2001 Sch.7, Pt 5; the Police Reform Act 2002 Sch.8, para.1 and the Housing and Regeneration Act 2008 (Consequential Provisions) Order 2008 (SI 2008/3002), para.3.

Housing associations

5.—(1) In this Act "housing association" means a society, body of **3A–319** trustees or company—

    (a) which is established for the purpose of, or amongst whose objects or powers are included those of, providing, constructing, improving or managing, or facilitating or encouraging the construction or improvement of, housing accommodation, and

    (b) which does not trade for profit or whose constitution or rules prohibit the issue of capital with interest or dividend exceeding such rate as may be prescribed by the Treasury, whether with or without differentiation as between share and loan capital.

(2) In this Act "fully mutual", in relation to a housing association, means that the rules of the association—

    (a) restrict membership to persons who are tenants or prospective tenants of the association, and

    (b) preclude the granting or assignment of tenancies to persons other than members;
    and "co-operative housing association" means a fully mutual housing association which is a society registered under the Industrial and Provident Societies Act 1965.

(3) In this Act "self-build society" means a housing association whose object is to provide, for sale to, or occupation by, its members, dwellings built or improved principally with the use of its members' own labour.

(4) In this Act "registered social landlord" means—

    (a) a housing association registered in the register maintained by the Housing Corporation under section 1 of the Housing Act 1996, or

    (b) a housing association registered in the register maintained by the Secretary of State under section 1 of the Housing Act 1996,
    subject as follows.

(5) References to registered social landlords include, where the context so permits, references to housing associations registered in the register maintained by Scottish Homes under section 3 of the Housing Associations Act 1985 (Scottish registered housing associations).

Note —Amended by the Housing Act 1996 (Consequential Provisions) Order 1996 **3A–320**

Paragraph numbers marked with a "+" can be found online and on CD.

HOUSING

(SI 1996/2325) art.5, Sch.2, para.14(1), (2); and the Government of Wales Act 1998 s.140 and Sch.16, para.6. See too *Qazi v Harrow LBC* [2003] UKHL 43; [2004] 1 A.C. 983; [2003] 3 W.L.R. 792 [2003] 4 All E.R. 461, where Lord Hope and Lord Scott said that contractual and property rights cannot be defeated by a defence based on art.8; *Lambeth LBC v Kay; Leeds CC v Price* [2006] UKHL 10; [2006] 2 A.C. 465; [2006] 2 W.L.R. 570 and *Birmingham City Council v Doherty* [2008] UKHL 57, July 30, 2008, [2008] 3 W.L.R. 636; *cf. McCann v UK App. No.19009/04, May 13, 2008, The Times*, May 23, 2008.

Housing associations and the Human Rights Act 1998

3A–321   Whilst the activities of a housing association need not involve the performance of public functions, in taking over the responsibilities of a local housing authority as landlord of a tenant who had been granted a non-secure tenancy pending the determination of her application as a homeless person and in deciding to bring possession proceedings, the functions of a housing association were so closely assimilated to the council that it was properly to be regarded as a functional public authority within the meaning of the Human Rights Act 1998 s.6(1) (*Poplar Housing & Regeneration Community Association Ltd v Donoghue* [2001] EWCA Civ 595, [2002] Q.B. 48; [2001] 3 W.L.R—although it should be noted that this decision was disapproved in *YL v Birmingham CC* [2007] UKHL 27; [2008] 1 A.C. 95 where Baroness Hale and Lord Mance both criticised the Court of Appeal's reasoning for relying too heavily upon the historical links between the local authority and the registered social landlord, rather than upon the nature of the function itself which was the provision of social housing. See too *R.. (Weaver) v London & Quadrant Housing Trust* [2008] EWHC 1377 (Admin), June 24, 2008 (the management and allocation of housing stock by a housing association was a function of a public nature and it was therefore to be regarded as a public authority within Human Rights Act 1998 s.6(3)(b) and so it was amenable to judicial review on conventional public law grounds in respect of its performance of that function).

Housing trusts

3A–322   **6.** In this Act "housing trust" means a corporation or body of persons which—

   (a) is required by the terms of its constituent instrument to use the whole of its funds, including any surplus which may arise from its operations, for the purpose of providing housing accommodation, or

   (b) is required by the terms of its constituent instrument to devote the whole, or substantially the whole, of its funds for charitable purposes and in fact uses the whole, or substantially the whole, of its funds for the purpose of providing housing accommodation.

Relevant Authority

3A–323   **6A.**—(1) In this Act "the Relevant Authority" means the Housing Corporation, the Secretary of State or Scottish Homes, subject as follows.

   (2) In relation to a housing association which is—

   (a) a registered charity which has its address for the purposes of registration by the Charity Commission in Wales,

   (b) a society registered under the Industrial and Provident Societies Act 1965 which has its registered office for the purposes of that Act in Wales, or

Paragraph numbers marked with a "+" can be found online and on CD.

(c) a company registered under the Companies Act 1985 which has its registered office for the purposes of that Act in Wales,

"the Relevant Authority" means the Secretary of State.

(3) In relation to a housing association which is a society registered under the Industrial and Provident Societies Act 1965 which has its registered office for the purposes of that Act in Scotland, "the Relevant Authority" means Scottish Homes.

(4) In relation to any other housing association which is a registered charity, a society registered under the Industrial and Provident Societies Act 1965 or a company registered under the Companies Act 1985, "the Relevant Authority" means the Housing Corporation.

(5) In this section "registered charity" means a charity which is registered under section 3 of the Charities Act 1993 and is not an exempt charity within the meaning of that Act.

3A–324

Note —Inserted by the Housing Act 1988 Sch.17; substituted by the Housing Act 1996 (Consequential Provisions) Order 1996 (SI 1996/2325) art.5, Sch.2, para.14(1), (3). Amended by the Government of Wales Act 1998 s.140 and Sch.16, paras 5 and 7; and the Charities Act 2006 s.75(1), Sch.8, para.77.

* * * *

PART IV

SECURE TENANCIES AND RIGHTS OF SECURE TENANTS

SECURITY OF TENURE

Secure tenancies

3A–325

79.—(1) A tenancy under which a dwelling-house is let as a separate dwelling is a secure tenancy at any time when the conditions described in sections 80 and 81 as the landlord condition and the tenant condition are satisfied.

(2) Subsection (1) has effect subject to—

(a) the exceptions in Schedule 1 (tenancies which are not secure tenancies),

(b) sections 89(3) and (4) and 90(3) and (4) (tenancies ceasing to be secure after death of tenant), and

(c) sections 91(2) and 93(2) (tenancies ceasing to be secure in consequence of assignment or subletting).

(3) The provisions of this Part apply in relation to a licence to occupy a dwelling-house (whether or not granted for a consideration) as they apply in relation to a tenancy.

(4) Subsection (3) does not apply to a licence granted as a temporary expedient to a person who entered the dwelling-house or any other land as a trespasser (whether or not, before the grant of

Paragraph numbers marked with a "+" can be found online and on CD.

HOUSING

that licence, another licence to occupy that or another dwelling-house had been granted to him).

"separate dwelling"

3A–326   See annotations to Rent Act 1977 s.1 above.

"dwelling-house"

3A–327   See s.112.

"landlord condition"

3A–328   See s.80.

"tenant condition"

3A–329   See s.81.

Secure tenancies

3A–330   This section provides the basic definition of a "secure tenancy" (or, in most circumstances, licence—see s.79(3) and (4)). The exceptions to security of tenure are set out in Sch.1, ss.89(3) and (4), 90(3) and (4), and 91(2) and (3). It is doubtful whether Parliament intended that a tenancy at will could be a secure tenancy, even where the conditions in ss.80 and s.81 are satisfied (*Banjo v Brent LBC* [2005] EWCA Civ 292; [2005] 1 W.L.R. 2520).

Sub-tenancies

3A–331   A secure tenancy for the purpose of s.79 is one in which there is a direct landlord and tenant relationship between a landlord, satisfying the landlord condition in s.80, and a tenant, satisfying the tenant condition in s.81. If a local housing authority grants a lease to a charitable housing trust which in turn grants a sub-tenancy to an individual who lives in the property, the occupier's secure sub-tenancy persists while the intermediate lease continues, so long as the parties continue to meet the landlord and tenant conditions. As soon as either of them ceases to do so or the sub-lease in respect of which s.79 provided security ceases to exist, so also does the secure sub-tenancy (*Lambeth LBC v Kay* [2004] EWCA Civ 926; [2004] H.L.R. 56 and *Bruton v London and Quadrant Housing Trust* [2000] 1 A.C. 406; [1999] 3 W.L.R. 150, HL).

The landlord condition

3A–332   **80.**—(1) The landlord condition is that the interest of the landlord belongs to one of the following authorities or bodies—

    a local authority,

    a development corporation,

    a housing action trust,

    an urban development corporation, in the case of a tenancy falling within subsections (2A) to (2E), the Homes and Communities Agency or the Welsh Ministers (as the case may be), or

    housing co-operative to which this section applies.

    (2) [...]

    (2A) A tenancy falls within this subsection if the interest of the landlord is transferred to—

        (a) the Homes and Communities Agency as mentioned in section 52(1)(a) to (d) of the Housing and Regeneration Act 2008, or

        (b) the Welsh Ministers as mentioned in section 36(1)(a)(i) to (iii) of the New Towns Act 1981.

    (2B) A tenancy falls within this subsection if it is entered into pur-

Paragraph numbers marked with a "+" can be found online and on CD.

suant to a contract under which the rights and liabilities of the prospective landlord are transferred to the Homes and Communities Agency or the Welsh Ministers as mentioned in subsection (2A)(a) or (b) (as the case may be).

(2C) A tenancy falls within this subsection if it is granted by the Homes and Communities Agency or the Welsh Ministers to a person (alone or jointly with others) who, immediately before it was entered into, was a secure tenant of the Homes and Communities Agency or the Welsh Ministers (as the case may be).

(2D) A tenancy falls within this subsection if—

    (a) it is granted by the Homes and Communities Agency or the Welsh Ministers to a person (alone or jointly with others),

    (b) before the grant of the tenancy, an order for possession of a dwelling-house let under a secure tenancy was made against the person (alone or jointly with others) and in favour of the Homes and Communities Agency or the Welsh Ministers (as the case may be) on the court being satisfied as mentioned in section 84(2)(b) or (c), and

    (c) the tenancy is of the premises which constitute the suitable accommodation as to which the court was so satisfied.

(2E) A tenancy falls within this subsection if it is granted by the Homes and Communities Agency or the Welsh Ministers pursuant to an obligation under section 554(2A).

(3) If a co-operative housing association ceases to be a registered social landlord, it shall, within the period of 21 days beginning with the date on which it ceases to be a registered social landlord, notify each of its tenants who thereby becomes a secure tenant, in writing, that he has become a secure tenant.

(4) This section applies to a housing co-operative within the meaning of section 27B (agreements under certain superseded provisions) where the dwelling-house is comprised in a housing co-operative agreement within the meaning of that section.

(5) In this Act and in any provision made under this Act, or made by or under any other enactment, a reference to—

    (a) a person within section 80 or 80(1) of this Act, or

    (b) a person who satisfies the landlord condition under this section,

includes a reference to the Homes and Communities Agency or to the Welsh Ministers so far as acting in their capacity as landlord (or, in the case of disposals, former landlord) in respect of a tenancy which falls within subsections (2A) to (2E) above but, subject to this, does not include the Homes and Communities Agency or the Welsh Ministers.

(6) Subsection (5)—

    (a) applies whether the person is described as an authority, body or landlord or in any other way and whether the reference is otherwise expressed in a different way, and

    (b) is subject to any provision to the contrary.

Paragraph numbers marked with a "+" can be found online and on CD.

3A–333   *Note* —Amended by the Housing Act 1996 (Consequential Provisions) Order 1996 (SI 1996/2325) art.5, Sch.2; the Housing Act 1988 Sch.18; the Housing and Planning Act 1986 Sch.5; Government of Wales Act 1998 Sch.18, Pt IV and the Housing and Regeneration Act 2008 (Consequential Provisions) Order 2008 (SI 2008/3002) para.10.

"local authority"

3A–334   See s.4.

"housing action trust"

3A–335   See s.4.

"an urban development corporation"

3A–336   See s.4.

"housing co-operative"

3A–337   See s.4.

"registered social landlord"

3A–338   See the Housing Act 1996 ss.1–7.

The landlord condition

3A–339   Note that if a housing association granted a tenancy before January 15, 1989, and all the other requirements of a secure tenancy exist, that tenancy remains a secure tenancy (see s.80(1) prior to amendment by the Housing Act 1988 and the Housing Act 1988 s.35). Tenancies granted by housing associations on or after January 15, 1989 are likely to be assured tenancies within the meaning of the Housing Act 1988.

The Court of Appeal has held that the landlord condition is not satisfied if there are joint landlords and only one of the joint landlords comes within the list of bodies specified in s.80(1) (see *R. v Council of City of Plymouth and Cornwall CC Ex p. Freeman* (1987) 19 H.L.R. 328, CA). See too *Knowsley Housing Trust v Revell*; *Helena Housing Ltd v Curtis* [2003] EWCA Civ 496; [2003] H.L.R. 63; *The Times*, April 17, 2003.

The tenant condition

3A–340   **81.** The tenant condition is that the tenant is an individual and occupies the dwelling-house as his only or principal home; or, where the tenancy is a joint tenancy, that each of the joint tenants is an individual and at least one of them occupies the dwelling-house as his only or principal home.

"dwelling-house"

3A–341   See s.112.

The tenant condition

3A–342   In order to gain or retain public sector security of tenure tenants must occupy premises as their "only or principal home"(*cf.* the Housing Act 1988 s.1(1)(b) ("as his only or principal home") the Leasehold Reform Act 1967 s.1 ("as his residence"), and the Rent Act 1977 s.2 ("as his residence")). Security of tenure and associated rights, such as the right to buy, are lost if secure tenants cease to occupy premises as their only or principal home (*Sutton LBC v Swann* (1986) 18 H.L.R. 140, CA) or if they sublet or part with possession of the whole (the Housing Act 1985 s.93). However, it is possible for tenants or licensees to have two or more homes in the public rented sector, but only the one which is the "principal" home can be secure.

In order to maintain a "home" a tenant need not be physically resident, so long as there is an intention to return after a temporary absence and some physical sign of continued occupation (e.g. furniture and possessions in the property). Two houses can be occupied as a home at the same time—*Crawley BC v Sawyer* (1988) 20 H.L.R. 98, CA, where a council tenant went to live with his "girlfriend" for a period of approximately one-and-a-half years during which time the gas and electricity supplies to the premises which he rented from the council were cut off. Held that the rented premises remained his principal home throughout the period.

Paragraph numbers marked with a "+" can be found online and on CD.

Temporary absence may be lengthy. In *Amoah v Barking and Dagenham LBC* (2001) 81 P. & C.R. D12; March 2001 Legal Action 27, Ch D a secure tenant was sentenced to 12 years' imprisonment. He left items of furniture in the property and appointed a relative to act as "caretaker" in his absence and intended to return on his release. Etherton J. held that he had retained his secure status.

The court should consider whether the tenant has an intention to return at the date of expiry of the notice to quit. It should focus on "the enduring intention" of the tenant and not on "fleeting changes of mind". This is particularly true of an elderly tenant in poor health whose intentions "may well have fluctuated from time to time and even from day to day". *Hammersmith and Fulham LBC v Clarke* (2001) 33 H.L.R. 77, CA.

It is possible for a tenant to lose security of tenure by reason of non-occupation but to regain it by re-occupying the property before service or a notice to quit—see *Hussey v Camden LBC* (1995) 27 H.L.R. 5, CA, where, as the tenant was occupying the property as his only or principal home at the time of service of the notice to quit, the Court of Appeal held that the earlier loss of security was irrelevant.

Subletting of the whole of premises means that any tenancy ceases to be secure (see *Jennings v Epping Forrest DC* (1993) 25 H.L.R. 241, CA; *Poland v Cadogan* [1980] 3 All E.R. 544, CA (the Leasehold Reform Act s.93(2)); *Muir Group Housing Association Ltd v Thornley* (1993) 25 H.L.R. 89, CA; *Brent LBC v Cronin* (1997) 30 H.L.R. 43, CA and *Ujima Housing Association v Asnah* (1998) 30 H.L.R. 831, CA (assured tenancy) *cf. Merton LBC v Salama* (1989) CAT No 89/169; June 1989 Legal Action 25, CA (parting with possession of part of premises)). Parting with possession is not to be inferred simply from the fact that another person has been allowed to use and occupy a tenant's home during his temporary absence (*Lam Kee Ying v Lam Shes Tong* [1975] A.C. 247, PC).

The Court of Appeal has held that (1) there is nothing in the Housing Act 1985 which renders it impossible or unlawful to grant a tenancy to a person not lawfully in this country; and (2) there is no public policy requirement that the word "lawfully" should be inserted into s.81 to limit security of tenure to those lawfully in occupation of their homes, see *Akinbolu v Hackney LBC* (1997) 29 H.L.R. 259, CA, where the council's claims that a tenancy was void because the tenant was an illegal overstayer and the council accordingly had no power to provide housing for him were rejected.

Security of tenure

82.—(1) A secure tenancy which is either—

    (a) a weekly or other periodic tenancy, or

    (b) a tenancy for a term certain but subject to termination by the landlord,

cannot be brought to an end by the landlord except by obtaining an order mentioned in subsection (1A);

(1A) These are the orders—

    (a) an order of the court for the possession of the dwelling-house;

    (b) an order under subsection (3);

    (c) a demotion order under section 82A.

(2) Where the landlord obtains an order for the possession of the dwelling-house, the tenancy ends on the date on which the tenant is to give up possession in pursuance of the order.

(3) Where a secure tenancy is a tenancy for a term certain but with a provision for re-entry or forfeiture, the court shall not order possession of the dwelling-house in pursuance of that provision, but in a case where the court would have made such an order it shall instead make an order terminating the tenancy on a date specified in the order and section 86 (periodic tenancy arising on termination of fixed term) shall apply.

3A–343

Paragraph numbers marked with a "+" can be found online and on CD.

HOUSING

(4) Section 146 of the Law of Property Act 1925 (restriction on and relief against forfeiture), except subsection (4) (vesting in under-lessee), and any other enactment or rule of law relating to forfeiture, shall apply in relation to proceedings for an order under subsection (3) of this section as if they were proceedings to enforce a right of re-entry or forfeiture.

3A–344   *Note* —Section 82 has been amended by Anti-Social Behaviour Act 2003 s.14(1). This amendment was brought into force in England on June 30, 2004 by the Anti-Social Behaviour Act 2003 (Commencement No.3 and Savings) Order 2004 (SI 2004/1502) (c.61). It does not have effect in relation to any proceedings for the possession of a dwelling-house begun before June 30, 2004. It was brought into force in Wales on April 30, 2005 by the Anti-Social Behaviour Act 2003 (Commencement No.4) (Wales) Order 2005 (SI 2005/1225) (w.83) (c.55). The amendment allows a secure tenancy to be brought to an end by a demotion order. This section has also been amended by Housing and Regeneration Act 2008 Sch.15, Pt I. The amendment relates to tolerated trespassers, but is not yet in force. The amendment is printed as part of the Housing and Regeneration Act 2008—see below.

Demotion order

3A–345   See s.82A.

"dwelling-house"

3A–346   See s.112.

"secure tenancy"

3A–347   See s.79.

Security of tenure

3A–348   This important section provides that a secure tenancy cannot be brought to an end by a *landlord* except by obtaining an order of the court. It does not apply where the tenancy has ceased to be secure (e.g. as a result of the tenant ceasing to occupy as his or her only or principal home—see s.81, but note the need for a court order under the Protection from Eviction Act 1977) or where the termination is brought about by the action of a tenant (see, e.g. *Hammersmith and Fulham LBC v Monk* [1992] 1 A.C. 478; [1991] 3 W.L.R. 1144; [1992] 1 All E.R. 1, HL; *Harrow LBC v Johnstone* [1997] 1 W.L.R. 459; [1997] 1 All E.R. 929, HL; and *Greenwich LBC v McGrady* (1982) 81 L.G.R. 288; (1982) 46 P. & C.R. 223; (1983) 6 H.L.R. 361; (1982) 267 E.G. 515, CA and *Notting Hill Housing Trust v Brackley* [2001] EWCA Civ 601; [2001] 35 E.G. 106; [2002] H.L.R. 212; [2001] L. & T.R. 467). The Court of Appeal has held that there was no breach of ECHR, art.8 where a local authority took possession proceedings against the wife of a sole tenant after the husband (the tenant) had served a valid notice to quit upon the council (*Kensington and Chelsea v O'Sullivan* [2003] EWCA Civ 371; *The Times*, March 27, 2003. See too *Harrow LBC v Qazi* [2003] UKHL 43; [2004] 1 A.C. 983; [2003] 3 W.L.R. 792).

For the prerequisites for a possession order, see s.83 (notice of intention to bring proceedings) s.84 and Sch.2 (grounds for possession).

The tenancy ends on the date specified by the court (see, e.g. *Thompson v Elmbridge BC* [1987] 1 W.L.R. 1425; (1987) 19 H.L.R. 526, CA; *Leicester City Council v Aldwinkle* (1992) 24 H.L.R. 40, CA; and *Brent LBC v Knightley* (1997) 29 H.L.R. 857; *The Times*, February 26, 1997)—but note Housing and Regeneration Act 2008 Sch.11 below which will provide that secure tenancies will continue until any warrant for possession is executed. This amendment is not yet in force.

Demotion because of anti-social behaviour

3A–349   **82A.**—(1) This section applies to a secure tenancy if the landlord is—

        (a) a local housing authority;

Paragraph numbers marked with a "+" can be found online and on CD.

        (b) a housing action trust;

        (c) a registered social landlord.

(2) The landlord may apply to a county court for a demotion order.

(3) A demotion order has the following effect—

        (a) the secure tenancy is terminated with effect from the date specified in the order;

        (b) if the tenant remains in occupation of the dwelling-house after that date a demoted tenancy is created with effect from that date;

        (c) it is a term of the demoted tenancy that any arrears of rent payable at the termination of the secure tenancy become payable under the demoted tenancy;

        (d) it is also a term of the demoted tenancy that any rent paid in advance or overpaid at the termination of the secure tenancy is credited to the tenant's liability to pay rent under the demoted tenancy.

(4) The court must not make a demotion order unless it is satisfied—

        (a) that the tenant or a person residing in or visiting the dwelling-house has engaged or has threatened to engage in—

            (i) housing-related anti-social conduct, or

            (ii) conduct to which section 153B of the Housing Act 1996 (use of premises for unlawful purposes) applies, and

        (b) that it is reasonable to make the order.

(5) Each of the following has effect in respect of a demoted tenancy at the time it is created by virtue of an order under this section as it has effect in relation to the secure tenancy at the time it is terminated by virtue of the order—

        (a) the parties to the tenancy;

        (b) the period of the tenancy;

        (c) the amount of the rent;

        (d) the dates on which the rent is payable.

(6) Subsection (5)(b) does not apply if the secure tenancy was for a fixed term and in such a case the demoted tenancy is a weekly periodic tenancy.

(7) If the landlord of the demoted tenancy serves on the tenant a statement of any other express terms of the secure tenancy which are to apply to the demoted tenancy such terms are also terms of the demoted tenancy.

(7A) In subsection (4)(a) 'housing-related anti-social conduct' has the same meaning as in section 153A of the Housing Act 1996.

(8) For the purposes of this section a demoted tenancy is—

        (a) a tenancy to which section 143A of the Housing Act 1996 applies if the landlord of the secure tenancy is a local housing authority or a housing action trust;

Paragraph numbers marked with a "+" can be found online and on CD.

(b) a tenancy to which section 20B of the Housing Act 1988 applies if the landlord of the secure tenancy is a registered social landlord.

3A–350   *Note* —Inserted by the Anti-Social Behaviour Act 2003 s.14(2) and brought into force in relation to England on June 30 (SI 2004/1502) and in relation to Wales on April 30, 2005 (SI 2005/1225); amended by the Police and Justice Act 2006 s.52, Sch.14, para.12.

Editorial note

3A–351   This section was inserted by Anti-Social Behaviour Act 2003 s.14(2). This amendment was brought into force in England on June 30, 2004 by the Anti-Social Behaviour Act 2003 (Commencement No.3 and Savings) Order 2004 (SI 2004/1502) (c.61). It was brought into force in Wales on April 30, 2005 by the Anti-Social Behaviour Act 2003 (Commencement No.4) (Wales) Order 2005 (SI 2005/1225) (w.83) (c.55).

Section 82A provides that a local authority, a housing action trust or a registered social landlord can apply for a demotion order. A demotion order ends the secure tenancy on a specified date. If the tenant remains in occupation, a new demoted tenancy begins on the same date. The court may only make the order if the tenant, another resident of or visitor to the tenant's home has behaved in a way which is capable of causing nuisance or annoyance or if such a person has used the premises for illegal purposes. In addition the court must be satisfied that it is reasonable to make the order. As to reasonableness in the context of anti-social behaviour by a tenant's children and the use of hearsay evidence, see *Washington Housing Company Ltd v Morson* [2005] EWHC 3407 (CHY); October 25, 2005.

Demoted tenancies lack security of tenure. If the landlord follows the procedure set out in Housing Act 1996 ss.143E and F, the court must make an order for possession (see Housing Act 1996 s.143D). Under a demoted tenancy, the parties, the period of the tenancy (unless it was for a fixed term) and rental terms remain the same, but a landlord may, apparently unilaterally, serve a statement of any other express terms of the secure tenancy which are to apply to the demoted tenancy. It was amended by the Police and Justice Act 2006 Sch.14, para.12.

Demoted tenancy

3A–352   See s.82A(8), Housing Act 1996 s.143A and Housing Act 1988 s.20B. Section 82A(3)(c) and (d) confirm that any rent owed or overpaid on the tenant's rent account under the secure tenancy should be transferred across to the demoted tenancy. Section 82A(5) sets out certain basic terms of the demoted tenancy at the point at which it is created.

Secure tenancy

3A–353   See s.79.

A local housing authority

3A–354   See Housing Act 1996 s.230 and Housing Act 1985 ss.1 and 2(2).

A housing action trust

3A–355   See Housing Act 1996 s.230 and Housing Act 1988 Pt III.

A registered social landlord

3A–356   See Housing Act 1996 Pt I, ss.1 to 3.

Anti-social behaviour or use of premises for unlawful purposes

3A–357   See Housing Act 1996 ss.153A and 153B.

Proceedings for possession or termination: notice requirements

3A–358   83.—(1) The court shall not entertain proceedings for an order mentioned in section 82(1A) unless—

Paragraph numbers marked with a "+" can be found online and on CD.

    (a) the landlord has served a notice on the tenant comply-
        ing with the provisions of this section, or

    (b) the court considers it just and equitable to dispense with
        the requirement of such a notice.

(2) A notice under this section shall—

    (a) be in a form prescribed by regulations made by the Sec-
        retary of State,

    (b) specify the ground on which the court will be asked to
        make the order, and

    (c) give particulars of that ground.

(3) Where the tenancy is a periodic tenancy and the ground or
one of the grounds specified in the notice is Ground 2 in Schedule 2
(nuisance or other anti-social behaviour), the notice—

    (a) shall also—

        (i) state that proceedings for the possession of the
           dwelling-house may be begun immediately, and

        (ii) specify the date sought by the landlord as the date
           on which the tenant is to give up possession of the
           dwelling-house, and

    (b) ceases to be in force twelve months after the date so
        specified.

(4) Where the tenancy is a periodic tenancy and Ground 2 in
Schedule 2 is not specified in the notice, the notice—

    (a) shall also specify the date after which proceedings for
        the possession of the dwelling-house may be begun, and

    (b) ceases to be in force twelve months after the date so
        specified.

(4A) If the proceedings are for a demotion order under section
82A the notice—

    (a) must specify the date after which the proceedings may
        be begun;

    (b) ceases to be in force twelve months after the date so
        specified.

(5) The date specified in accordance with subsection (3), (4) or
(4A) must not be earlier than the date on which the tenancy could,
apart from this Part, be brought to an end by notice to quit given by
the landlord on the same date as the notice under this section.

(6) Where a notice under this section is served with respect to a
secure tenancy for a term certain, it has effect also with respect to any
periodic tenancy arising on the termination of that tenancy by virtue
of section 86; and subsections (3) to (5) of this section do not apply to
the notice.

(7) Regulations under this section shall be made by statutory
instrument and may make different provision with respect to different cases or descriptions of case, including different provision for different areas.

Note —Substituted by the Housing Act 1996 s.147.   **3A–359**

Paragraph numbers marked with a "+" can be found online and on CD.

Section 83 has been amended by Anti-Social Behaviour Act 2003 s.14(3) and Sch.1. The amendments were brought into force in England on June 30, 2004 by the Anti-Social Behaviour Act 2003 (Commencement No.3 and Savings) Order 2004 (SI 2004/1502) (c.61). It was brought into force in Wales on April 30, 2005 by the Anti-Social Behaviour Act 2003 (Commencement No.4) (Wales) Order 2005 (SI 2005/1225) (w.83) (c.55).

Proceedings for possession or termination: notice requirements

3A–360   The Housing Act 1996 s.147 introduced completely new ss.83 and 83A which apply to notices served on or after February 12, 1997 (Housing Act 1996 (Commencement No.6) Order 1997 (SI 1997/66)). They are in similar form to the old s.83, but with two significant modifications, viz. the court may dispense with the requirement for a notice if it considers it just and equitable to do, and the notice may state that proceedings under new Ground 2 (nuisance or anti-social behaviour—see below) may be begun immediately.

For the prescribed forms of notice, see the Secure Tenancies (Notices) Regulations 1987 (SI 1987/775) (as amended by the Secure Tenancies (Notices) (Amendment) Regulations 1997 (SI 1997/71), the Secure Tenancies (Notices) (Amendment No.2) Regulations 1997 (SI 1997/377); the Secure Tenancies (Notices) (Amendment) (England) Regulations 2004 (SI 2004/1627) and the Secure Tenancies (Notices) (Amendment) (Wales) Regulations 2005 (SI 2005/1226) (w.84)). Paragraph 2(1) of the Regulations states that the notice should be "substantially to the same effect" as that contained in the Regulations. For cases where landlords used old versions of prescribed forms, see: *Beckerman v Durling* (1983) 6 H.L.R. 87, CA; *Swansea CC v Hearn* (1991) 23 H.L.R. 284, CA; and *Tadema Holdings v Ferguson* (2000) 32 H.L.R. 866, CA.

If the court does not consider it just and equitable to dispense with the notice requirement, s.83 precludes the court from granting an order for possession of a secure tenancy unless satisfied that a notice of intention to seek possession complying with the requirements of that section has been served. Such a notice must state the ground for possession and give "particulars" of the ground (s.83(2)(c)).

As to service see *Wandsworth LBC v Attwell* (1995) 27 H.L.R. 536; [1996] 01 E.G. 100; (1996) 94 L.G.R. 419, CA; *Enfield LBC v Devonish* (1997) 29 H.L.R. 691, CA and *Tadema Holdings v Ferguson* (2000) 32 H.L.R. 866, CA. If there are joint tenants, it should be addressed to all of them (*Newham LBC v Okotoro*, March 1993, Legal Action 11, Bow County Court).

Notices must specify a date which must not be earlier than the date on which the tenancy could otherwise be brought to an end by a notice to quit served by the landlord. (See also the Protection from Eviction Act 1977 s.5). However, a notice may state that proceedings under Ground 2 (nuisance or anti-social behaviour) may be begun immediately. In that case, the notice should state this and specify the date sought by the landlord as the date on which the tenant is to give up possession (s.83(3)).

Notices cease to be in force 12 months after the date specified in the notice. If that date passes, a new notice must be served (s.83(3)(b) and s.83A).

"particulars of the ground"

3A–361   In rent arrears cases the particulars given must at least show the amount claimed, and in all cases the notice must be sufficiently particularised to "tell the tenant what he had to do to put matters right before proceedings are commenced" (*Torridge DC v Jones* (1986) 18 H.L.R. 107 at 114; (1985) 276 E.G. 1253, CA). ("The reasons for taking this action are non-payment of rent" not sufficient—notice invalid). See too *East Devon DC v Williams and Mills*, December 1996, Legal Action 13, Exeter County Court (possession claimed under Sch.2, Ground 1 (breach of the terms of the tenancy). The notice set out the relevant terms but in the section marked "Particulars" merely repeated the terms in full, without indicating the conduct relied upon—possession claim struck out); *Slough BC v Robbins* [1996] 12 C.L. 353, Slough County Court (notice seeking possession giving as particulars: "Numerous complaints have been received over a period of time that annoyance and nuisance is being caused to your neighbours by noise and disruptive behaviour. This nuisance and annoyance has been investigated by my staff and I believe the complaints to be substantiated" held to be defective, proceedings struck out); and *South Buckinghamshire CC v Frances* [1985] 11 C.L. 152; [1985] C.L.Y. 1900, Slough County Court (where it was held that the Housing Act

Paragraph numbers marked with a "+" can be found online and on CD.

1980 s.33(2) (now the Housing Act 1985 s.83(2)(c)) required detailed particulars which should be similar to those required under the Law of Property Act 1925 s.146. It must be obvious to tenants what they must do. Although there was discretion to allow amendment of the notice (now contained in the Housing Act 1985 s.84(3)), the council would not be permitted "at a late stage" in the proceedings to amend the notice to include a schedule of dilapidations and particulars of nuisance which ought to have been included in the original notice).

However, in *Dudley MBC v Bailey* [1991] 10 E.G. 140; (1990) 22 H.L.R. 424, CA, Ralph Gibson L.J. stated that:

> "The question is whether, at the date of the notice, the landlord has in good faith stated the ground and given the particulars of that ground. The requirement of particulars is satisfied, in my judgment, if the landlord has stated in summary form the facts which he then intends to prove in support of the stated ground for possession. Error in the particulars does not, in my judgment, invalidate the notice, although it may well affect the decision of the court on the merits". ((1990) 22 H.L.R. 424 at 431).

See too *Marath v MacGillivray* (1996) 28 H.L.R. 484, CA, noted under the Housing Act 1988 s.8.

Section 83 expressly enables a court to give leave for a landlord to add to or alter the "grounds" on which possession is claimed (s.83(4)), but is silent about the addition or alteration of the "particulars" required by the notice. In *Camden LBC v Oppong* (1996) 28 H.L.R. 701, CA, the Court of Appeal held the s.83(4) power *ipso facto* extended to a power to add to or alter the particulars. The court stated that such leave would be granted only in circumstances where it would be just to do so and that the nature and extent of the addition or alteration would always be a critical factor.

The form of notice is prescribed by the Secure Tenancies (Notices) Regulations 1987 (SI 1987/775) (as amended by the Secure Tenancies (Notices) (Amendment) Regulations 1997 (SI 1997/71); the Secure Tenancies (Notices)(Amendment No.2) Regulations 1997 (SI 1997/377); the Secure Tenancies (Notices) (Amendment) (England) Regulations 2004 (SI 2004/1627); and the Secure Tenancies (Notices) (Amendment) (Wales) Regulations 2005 (SI 2005/1226) (w.84)). Paragraph 2(1) of the Regulations states that the notice should be "substantially to the same effect" as that contained in the Regulations. Minor variations are unlikely to invalidate a notice—see *Dudley MBC v Bailey* [1991] 10 E.G. 140; (1990) 22 H.L.R. 424, CA, where Ralph Gibson L.J. held that a notice, although not precisely in the prescribed form, was "substantially to the same effect". In *City of London v Devlin* (1995) 29 H.L.R. 58, CA, the Court of Appeal held that a notice seeking possession which had not been signed by the Director of Housing above that description which appeared on the printed form was "substantially to the same effect" as that prescribed and accordingly valid. Simon Brown L.J. stated that:

> "The reality here is that a series of aridly technical points raised by the applicant at trial were defeated by a series of creative, largely procedural rulings which were not even arguably impermissible."

"the court considers it just and equitable to do dispense with the requirement of such a notice" (s.83(1)(b))

This provision brings secure tenancies into line with assured tenancies (*cf.* the Housing Act 1988 s.8(1)(b)). It is "obviously only in relatively exceptional cases where the court should be prepared to dispense with a section 83 notice". (*Braintree DC v Vincent* [2004] EWCA Civ 415—a case where the Court of Appeal held that a judge was entitled to dispense with the notice on unusual facts. A s.83 notice would have been of no benefit to the tenant—indeed it would have been to her disadvantage because it would have postponed the date for possession and added to her liability for rent.) In *Kelsey HA v King* (1995) 28 H.L.R. 270, CA, it was held that it was just and equitable to dispense with the notice requirement where a notice served was found to be invalid because it had not given adequate particulars of the complaints of nuisance. The court had regard, inter alia, to:

(a) developments since the commencement of proceedings; and
(b) the late stage in the proceedings at which any point about the deficiency in the notice was taken.

See too *North British HA v Sheridan* [1999] 2 E.G.L.R. 138; [2000] L. & T.R. 115; (2000) 32 H.L.R. 346; (1999) 78 P. & C.R. D38.

3A–362

HOUSING

Paragraph numbers marked with a "+" can be found online and on CD.

Although the effect is different, the same wording is also used in the Rent Act 1977 Sch.15, Case 11, and the Housing Act 1988 Sch.2, Ground 1, where the court may dispense with the requirement that notice be served *before the grant* of certain tenancies. Those provisions have been considered by the Court of Appeal in *Fernandes v Parvardin* (1982) 5 H.L.R. 33; *Bradshaw v Baldwin-Wiseman* (1985) 17 H.L.R. 260; (1985) 49 P. & C.R. 382; and *Boyle v Verrall* (1996) 29 H.L.R. 436. The decisions in those cases indicate that although the power to dispense with notices is not limited to exceptional cases and may be exercised where oral notice has been given, it is unlikely to be exercised where no intimation of an intention to require possession has been given.

Additional requirements in relation to certain proceedings for possession

3A–363   **83A.**—(1) Where a notice under section 83 has been served on a tenant containing the information mentioned in subsection (3)(a) of that section, the court shall not entertain proceedings for the possession of the dwelling-house unless they are begun at a time when the notice is still in force.

(2) Where—

(a) a notice under section 83 has been served on a tenant, and

(b) a date after which proceedings may be begun has been specified in the notice in accordance with subsection (4)(a) of that section,

the court shall not entertain proceedings for the possession of the dwelling-house unless they are begun after the date so specified and at a time when the notice is still in force.

(3) Where—

(a) the ground or one of the grounds specified in a notice under section 83 is Ground 2A in Schedule 2 (domestic violence), and

(b) the partner who has left the dwelling-house as mentioned in that ground is not a tenant of the dwelling-house,

the court shall not entertain proceedings for the possession of the dwelling-house unless it is satisfied that the landlord has served a copy of the notice on the partner who has left or has taken all reasonable steps to serve a copy of the notice on that partner.

This subsection has effect subject to subsection (5).

(4) Where—

(a) Ground 2A in Schedule 2 is added to a notice under section 83 with the leave of the court after proceedings for possession are begun, and

(b) the partner who has left the dwelling-house as mentioned in that ground is not a party to the proceedings,

the court shall not continue to entertain the proceedings unless it is satisfied that the landlord has served a notice under subsection (6) on the partner who has left or has taken all reasonable steps to serve such a notice on that partner.

This subsection has effect subject to subsection (5).

(5) Where subsection (3) or (4) applies and Ground 2 in Schedule 2 (nuisance or other anti-social behaviour) is also specified in the notice under section 83, the court may dispense with the requirements

Paragraph numbers marked with a "+" can be found online and on CD.

as to service in relation to the partner who has left the dwelling-house if it considers it just and equitable to do so.

(6) A notice under this subsection shall—

(a) state that proceedings for the possession of the dwelling-house have begun,

(b) specify the ground or grounds on which possession is being sought, and

(c) give particulars of the ground or grounds.

Note —Added by the Housing Act 1996 s.147.   **3A–364**

Additional requirements in relation to certain proceedings for possession

This section contains special provisions concerning Ground 2A (domestic violence)   **3A–365**
(see Sch.2 below).

Grounds for orders for possession

84.—(1) The court shall not make an order for the possession of a   **3A–366**
dwelling-house let under a secure tenancy except on one or more of
the grounds set out in Schedule 2.

(2) The court shall not make an order for possession—

(a) on the grounds set out in Part I of that Schedule (grounds 1 to 8), unless it considers it reasonable to make the order,

(b) on the grounds set out in Part II of that Schedule (grounds 9 to 11), unless it is satisfied that suitable accommodation will be available for the tenant when the order takes effect,

(c) on the grounds set out in Part III of that Schedule (grounds 12 to 16), unless it both considers it reasonable to make the order and is satisfied that suitable accommodation will be available for the tenant when the order takes effect;

and Part IV of that Schedule has effect for determining whether suitable accommodation will be available for a tenant.

(3) Where a notice under section 83 has been served on the tenant, the court shall not make such an order on any of those grounds above unless the ground is specified in the notice; but the grounds so specified may be altered or added to with the leave of the court.

(4) Where a date is specified in a notice under section 83 in accordance with subsection (3) of that section, the court shall not make an order which requires the tenant to give up possession of the dwelling-house in question before the date so specified.

Note —Amended by the Housing Act 1996 s.147.   **3A–367**

"dwelling-house"

See s.112.   **3A–368**

"secure tenancy"

See s.79.   **3A–369**

Paragraph numbers marked with a "+" can be found online and on CD.

"notice"

3A–370   See s.83. As to the alteration of grounds in notices, see the commentary to s.83.

"suitable accommodation will be available"

3A–371   See Sch.2, Pt IV.

Grounds for orders for possession

3A–372   The court may not make an order for possession against a secure tenant unless satisfied that one of the grounds for possession listed in Sch.2 is proved and in addition that, depending upon the ground, it is reasonable to make an order for possession, or that suitable alternative accommodation will be available, or that it is both reasonable to make an order for possession and suitable alternative accommodation will be available.

The service of a notice exercising the right to buy (Housing Act 1985 Pt V) does not prevent a public sector landlord from seeking possession of the property on any of the grounds permitted by the Housing Act 1985 Sch.2. However, if the ground requires the court to consider "reasonableness", the fact that the tenant has exercised the right to buy is a circumstance to be taken into account (*Enfield LBC v McKeon* [1986] 1 W.L.R. 1007; [1986] 2 All E.R. 730, CA). See too *Bristol CC v Lovell* [1998] 1 W.L.R. 446; [1998] 1 All E.R. 775, HL and *Basildon DC v Wahlen* [2006] EWCA Civ 326; [2006] 1 W.L.R. 2744.

"reasonable"

3A–373   See too the commentary to the Rent Act 1977 s.98. It is for the landlord to satisfy the court that it is reasonable to make a possession order. Note too the Protocol for Possession Claims Based on Rent Arrears at C11–001 which aims to encourage more pre-action contact between landlords and tenants and to enable court time to be used more effectively. Courts should take into account whether this protocol has been followed when considering what orders to make. The first requirement for a judge who has found a ground for possession to be proved is to ask whether it is reasonable to make a possession order at all and then to ask whether the order should be stayed, suspended or postponed under s.100(2). The correct approach is to determine the extent of the rent arrears and how quickly those were likely to be paid. It is wrong to take into account matters which have not been pleaded.

> "In considering whether it is reasonable to make an order...the judge should consider all the relevant circumstances: but that is not a consideration at large. It is, or should be, a consideration in accordance with the pleadings. In my judgment, the matters proposed to be relied upon by the landlord in support of the contention that it would be reasonable to make an order for possession...must be pleaded by the landlord." (per Sir Richard Scott V.-C. in *Raeuchle v Laimond Properties Ltd (Suspension of Possession Order)* (2001) 33 H.L.R. 10, CA.

In view of the requirement that the appropriate grounds and conditions must be made out (e.g. as to reasonableness) "consent orders" have no place in public-sector proceedings. The court can have jurisdiction only if the necessary matters are proved by evidence or if there is express admission of the relevant facts (*Wandsworth LBC v Fadayomi* [1987] 3 All E.R. 474; (1987) 19 H.L.R. 512, CA; and *Hounslow LBC v McBride* (1999) 31 H.L.R. 143, CA, where after agreement between the parties in possession proceedings based upon Housing Act 1985 Grounds 1 and 2 a District Judge made a suspended possession order by consent without hearing evidence). Later the council alleged that Ms McBride had broken the conditions of the suspended order and applied for a warrant of possession. The Court of Appeal confirmed that both the possession order and the warrant should be set aside). See too *R. v Birmingham CC Ex p. Foley*, March 2001, Legal Action 29, Queen's Bench Division. A distinction has to be drawn between a form of order which contains an admission as to those matters on which the jurisdiction to make the order rests (e.g. reasonableness) and an order such as this one which did not.

"reasonable"—rent arrears

3A–374   In rent arrears cases, the importance of ascertaining the position in respect of welfare benefits was stressed by the Court of Appeal in *Second WRVS Housing Society v Blair* (1987) 19 H.L.R. 104, CA, where the tenant became affected by a psychiatric illness. His life "fell apart" and arrears mounted. He received supplementary benefit

Paragraph numbers marked with a "+" can be found online and on CD.

towards the housing costs but spent it on food. The county court judge, finding that there were arrears of £1,198 and that the tenant was still on supplementary benefit, ordered possession (suspended for two months in case the debt could be cleared in that time) and costs of £140. The Court of Appeal set aside the order, as the judge had failed to consider in detail the question of reasonableness and, in particular, the available welfare benefits. The case was sent back for reconsideration to ascertain "more fully the benefits which could be obtained from DHSS in relation to arrears and more generally in relation to [the tenant's] condition". Dillon L.J. stated "it is well known that arrangements can be made with the DHSS when housing benefit is payable to see that the rent is paid direct to the landlord and I feel that is a matter which should have been taken into account".

Also important are the tenant's past record and the reason for the arrears. See *Woodspring DC v Taylor* (1982) 4 H.L.R. 95, CA, where the defendants, who were in their mid-fifties, had been tenants of the council for 24 years. They had a good rent record. However, Mr Taylor was made redundant and received a large tax demand. His wife became ill. As a result rent arrears accrued. They owed £557 at the launch of possession proceedings and £700 at the date of the hearing. By this time they were receiving benefit and the DHSS was paying current rent plus £1 per week off the arrears. In the county court a registrar made an absolute possession order. The Court of Appeal set aside the order, finding that no reasonable registrar could have found that it was reasonable to make the order. Waller L.J. stated that it was "hard to understand a conclusion that it was reasonable to make an order turning them out of their house" (at 99).

See also *Brent LBC v Marks* (1999) 31 H.L.R. 343, CA: appeal by tenant against suspended possession on terms that the tenant pay current rent and £2.50 allowed. Following *Second WRVS Housing Society v Blair* (1987) 19 H.L.R. 104, the judge ought to have had more regard to the fact that current rent was being paid by deductions made by the DSS quarterly in arrears and that the benefit system was both causing and then dealing with the arrears. Looking at the overall position this was a responsible tenant whose position had stabilised. On a new exercise of the court's discretion, a possession order might not be made.

If a defendant counterclaims unsuccessfully for breach of repairing obligations, in ordinary circumstances, it is not reasonable to make a possession order, if the tenant has made arrangements, in the event of the failure of his counterclaim, for the early discharge of the arrears. However, in exceptional circumstances where there has been a bad history of persistent delay in paying rent, it may be reasonable to make an absolute order for possession (*Haringey LBC v Stewart* (1991) 23 H.L.R. 557; [1991] 2 E.G.L.R. 252, CA).

In *Drew-Morgan v Hamid-Zadeh* (2000) 32 H.L.R. 316, CA the Court of Appeal held that a judge was entitled to conclude that it was reasonable to make a possession order in the light of persistent non-payment which was inexcusable because the tenant had received housing benefit. The non-payment was plainly deliberate and avoidable. The fact that the tenant paid arrears during the hearing underlined the fact that she had been in a position to pay but had chosen not to do so until the last moment. The judge was also entitled to take into account false allegations made by the tenant.

"reasonable"—nuisance and annoyance

See too s.85A below.

3A–375

In *Brent LBC v Doughan* [2007] EWCA Civ 135, February 6, 2007, May L.J. stated "Eviction is likely to be a draconian step because the spectre of intentional homelessness under Pt 7 of the Housing Act 1996 looms over it. On the other hand the legislative policy is to enforce good behaviour between neighbours by court orders and thereby to protect others who may well be vulnerable from socially unacceptable behaviour." However, the proper approach in a case of the commission of "a most serious breach" of the tenancy agreement is that it will be reasonable to order possession in the absence of some exceptional circumstance—*Bristol CC v Mousah* (1997) 30 H.L.R. 32, CA (serious drug dealing). See too *Sandwell MBC v Hensley* [2007] EWCA 1425; [2008] H.L.R. 22, November 1, 2007 (outright possession order substituted on appeal for suspended possession order where tenant had pleaded guilty to a charge of being knowingly concerned with the cultivation of cannabis. It was said that where an individual commits a criminal offence, a possession order should only be suspended in

Paragraph numbers marked with a "+" can be found online and on CD.

exceptional circumstances where there is cogent evidence to demonstrate that the offender's particular conduct had ceased); *Glasgow DC v Heffron* [1997] October C.L.D. 618, Sheriff Court ("Any drug dealer would have to show genuine remorse and an intention not to return to old habits in order to avoid eviction"); and *Glasgow City Council v Lockhart*, 1997 Hous.L.R. 99; [1997] C.L.D. 633, Sheriff Court but *cf. North Devon Homes Ltd v Batchelor* [2008] EWCA Civ 840, July 22, 2008.

Similarly, where there is an admitted breach of covenant and an intention to continue with the breach a landlord should only be refused possession in a "very special case" (*Sheffield CC v Green* (1994) 26 H.L.R. 349, CA; *cf.*; *Accent Peerless Ltd (formerly Surrey Heath Housing Association Ltd) v Kingsdon* [2007] EWCA Civ 1314; December 12, 2007; *Bell London & Provincial Properties Ltd v Rueben* [1947] K.B. 157, CA). It is in the public interest that necessary and reasonable conditions in tenancy agreements are enforced fairly and effectively *Sheffield CC v Jepson* (1993) 25 H.L.R. 299, CA (tenant keeping a dog in breach of an express term of the tenancy agreement. Although there was little evidence about the defendant's dog in particular, reasonable to make suspended possession order). In a case involving the parking of a caravan in a front garden in breach of the terms of a tenancy agreement, the Court of Appeal held that the propriety of the council's policy was not a factor relevant to the exercise of discretion. The judge should not have been concerned with the propriety or impropriety of the policy rule. His concern should have been with the reasonableness in the particular case of ordering possession; *Barking and Dagenham LBC v Hyatt and Hyatt* (1992) 24 H.L.R. 406, CA, *cf. Wandsworth LBC v Hargreaves* (1994) 27 H.L.R. 142, CA (in breach of a term of the tenancy a visitor brought petrol into the flat to make petrol bombs, which were thrown from the window. A fire started in the flat from spilt petrol, causing £14,000 worth of damage. The Court of Appeal dismissed the council's appeal against a refusal of the county court judge to order possession); and *Greenwich LBC v Grogan* (2001) 33 H.L.R. 12, CA (17 year-old tenant pleaded guilty to handling stolen goods on the premises, sentenced to six months' youth custody. The Court of Appeal suspended the possession order for twelve months. In exercising its discretion, the court could take into account the wider public interest. The tenant was a young man trying to live a life free of crime and there was a serious possibility that that attempt would fail if he lost his flat. The council had a duty to consider its other tenants and people on its waiting list, but the balance was in favour of suspending the order). See too *Camden LBC v Gilsenan* (1999) 31 H.L.R. 81, CA: decision by circuit judge that it was reasonable to make a possession order upheld. The trial judge had differentiated between acts done by the defendant and acts done by her visitors; and *Newcastle Upon Tyne CC v Morrison* (2000) 32 H.L.R. 891, CA (single parent unable to control her "rampaging, destructive, intimidating and sometimes dangerous sons" with "quite appalling behaviour over a period of more than six years" involving "plain, repeated and grave breaches of the tenancy agreement, numerous offences affecting the neighbourhood and a dreadful catalogue of incidents". The Court of Appeal substituted a 28 day possession order for a suspended possession order). For a case in which a first instance judge dismissed a claim for possession but the Court of Appeal decided that it was reasonable to make a suspended possession order, see *Norwich City Council v Famuyiwa* [2004] EWCA Civ 1770; *The Times*, January 24, 2005. See too *Manchester City Council v Higgins* [2005] EWCA Civ 1423; [2006] H.L.R. 14 (suspended possession order replaced on appeal with outright possession order—misconduct so serious and persistent that it justified the making of an ASBO. This was strong but not conclusive evidence that the tenant would have forfeited any entitlement to retain possession).

An outright possession order may not be appropriate where the anti-social behaviour was not caused by the tenant, but by a member of the tenant's family who has since left the premises, with the result that the chances of recurrence are reduced. (*Castle Vale Housing Action Trust v Gallagher* [2001] EWCA Civ 944; (2001) 33 H.L.R. 810, CA). See too *Moat Housing Group South Ltd v Harris and Hartless* [2005] EWCA Civ 287; [2006] Q.B. 606; [2005] 3 W.L.R. 691; [2005] 4 All E.R. 1051, where having regard to good school reports, the absence of any criminal records or any serious record of police involvement with the tenant's family, and favourable testimonies given about the tenant, the Court of Appeal concluded that it would be right to suspend a possession order on the terms that there were no further breaches of the tenancy agreement. *Cf.* Kensington and *Chelsea RLBC v Simmonds* (1997) 29 H.L.R. 507, CA; *Northampton BC v Lovatt* (1998) 30 H.L.R. 875, CA; *Knowsley Housing Trust v McMullen*

Paragraph numbers marked with a "+" can be found online and on CD.

[2006] EWCA Civ 539; [2006] H.L.R. 43, CA and *Portsmouth City Council v Bryant* (2000) 32 H.L.R. 906; [2000] E.G.L.R. 287, CA.

In nuisance cases, the authority's obligations towards other tenants should be borne in mind; see s.85A and *Woking BC v Bystram* (1995) 27 H.L.R. 1; [1993] E.G.C.S. 208, CA (nuisance continuing—appropriate course was to make a suspended order for possession on terms that any further nuisance would lead to repossession in 28 days). See too *Solon South West Housing Association Ltd v James* [2004] EWCA Civ 1847; [2005] H.L.R. 24 (outright order confirmed by Court of Appeal).

A local authority's housing obligations towards the defendant if made homeless, and in particular the question of whether rehousing is likely to be refused as a result of intentional homelessness may have greater or lesser weight when considering reasonableness, depending on the circumstances—*cf. Rushcliffe BC v Watson* (1992) 24 H.L.R. 124, CA (the prospect that, if evicted, the tenant would probably be found to be intentionally homeless a very real consideration); *Bristol CC v Mousah* (1997) 30 H.L.R. 32, CA (whether the tenant would be rehoused as homeless was a matter for the council and not for the court); *Darlington BC v Sterling* (1996) 29 H.L.R. 309, CA (a decision by a Circuit Judge that as a District Judge had formed the view that the tenant ought not to be roofless he should not have ordered possession unless the council could show it would provide suitable alternative accommodation overturned by the Court of Appeal); and *Shrewsbury and Atcham BC v Evans* (1997) 30 H.L.R. 123, CA (the judge had not needed to consider how a tenant who had "flagrantly and deliberately lied about her circumstances" in order to obtain council housing would be rehoused).

See too *Lewisham LBC v Adeyemi* (2000) 32 H.L.R. 414, CA where the court dismissed a tenant's appeal against a possession order, where the tenant claimed that the judge, when considering reasonableness had failed to take into account whether the local authority would have a duty to rehouse under the Housing Act 1996 Pt VII. It is not for the court to make a pre-emptive decision on the possible outcome of an application that might or might not be made to the local authority. Entitlement to Pt VII accommodation is confined to the judgment of the local authority. It is not for the court to anticipate the outcome of that decision. The judge was well aware of the self-evident consequence of a possession order. The legal and practical consequences of homelessness however were not before the court, nor need they have been as they were for the local authority to determine; but *cf. North Devon Homes Ltd v Batchelor* [2008] EWCA Civ 840, July 22, 2008.

appeals on questions of reasonableness

Although County Courts Act 1984 s.77(6) excludes appeals against judges' findings **3A-376** of fact, it does not exclude, in a proper case, the possibility of an appeal against a finding of reasonableness (*Castle Vale Housing Action Trust v Gallagher* [2001] EWCA Civ 944; (2001) 33 H.L.R. 810). In *Brent LBC v Doughan* [2007] EWCA Civ 135; February 6, 2007, May L.J. stated:

> "The judgment as to reasonableness is intrinsically one of judicial balance akin to the exercise of a judicial discretion. It is the kind of judgment with which [the Court of Appeal] is likely to be slow to interfere for well trodden reasons."

See too *Ealing LBC v Jama* [2008] EWCA Civ 896, 25 June 2008.

ECHR Article 8 and reasonableness

The Court of Appeal has doubted whether art.8 makes any difference to the way in **3A-377** which courts have always approached questions of the reasonableness of making possessions order. Article 8 does, however, reinforce the importance of only making an order depriving someone of his or her home in circumstances where a clear case is made out (*Castle Vale Housing Action Trust v Gallagher* [2001] EWCA Civ 944; (2001) 33 H.L.R. 810). See too *Newham LBC v Neal* [2003] EWCA Civ 541; February 25, 2003. There is a need to find a fair balance and to protect the rights of the neighbours and other members of the public (*Lambeth LBC v Howard* [2001] EWCA Civ 468; (2001) 33 H.L.R. 636). See too *Harrow LBC v Qazi* [2003] UKHL 43; [2004] 1 A.C. 983; [2003] 3 W.L.R. 792, where Lord Hope and Lord Scott said that contractual and property rights cannot be defeated by a defence based on art.8. See too *Newham LBC v Kibata* [2003] EWCA Civ 1785; [2004] H.L.R. 28 and *Bradney v Birmingham CC*; *Birmingham CC v McCann* [2003] EWCA Civ 1783; [2004] H.L.R. 27; *Lambeth LBC v Kay; Leeds CC v Price* [2006] UKHL 10; [2006] 2 A.C. 465; [2006] 2 W.L.R. 570 and *Birmingham City*

Paragraph numbers marked with a "+" can be found online and on CD.

Council v Doherty [2008] UKHL 57, July 30, 2008, [2008] 3 W.L.R. 636 but *cf. McCann v UK* App. No.19009/04, May 13, 2008, *The Times* May 23, 2008, noted at para.3A–192.

Disability Discrimination Act 1995

3A–378   The effect of Disability Discrimination Act 1995 s.22(3)(c) is that it is unlawful to discriminate "by evicting [a] disabled person or subjecting him to any other detriment". Although unlawfulness under the Disability Discrimination Act is not a bar to a landlord seeking a possession order under the Housing Act, the fact that the eviction is unlawful and not justified is a highly relevant consideration for the s.7 discretion of whether or not to make a possession order. The Disability Discrimination Act contains its own code which requires a higher threshold than the Housing Act to justify an eviction (*North Devon Homes Ltd v Brazier* [2003] EWHC 574, QB). In *Manchester CC v Romano* [2004] EWCA (Civ) 834; [2005]1 W.L.R. 2775, the Court of Appeal, in a very thorough review of the legislation, stated that when a court considers the Disability Discrimination Act 1995 in the context of possession proceedings, the first matter which has to be determined is whether the person who complains about disability discrimination is a "disabled person" within the meaning of the Disability Discrimination (Meaning of Disability) Regulations 1996 (SI 1996/1455), Sch.1, ss.1–3, and the *Guidance on matters to be taking into account in determining questions relating to the definition of disability* issued by the Secretary of State. Secondly, the court should consider whether or not there has been discrimination—i.e. treating a disabled person less favourably for a reason which relates to the disabled person's disability. Thirdly, the court should consider whether the landlord's treatment of the tenant is justified. It is only justified if in the landlord's opinion the treatment (viz the decision to set in motion proceedings for possession) is necessary in order not to endanger the health or safety of any of the people living in neighbouring houses and it is reasonable, in all the circumstances, for the landlord to hold that opinion. The landlord must prove that if it does not take this action someone's health or safety would be endangered. It does not have to prove that that person's health or safety has actually been damaged. However, in view of the decision in *Lewisham LBC v Malcolm* [2008] UKHL 43; [2008] 4 All E.R. 525 it will now be rare for tenants to be able to rely successfully on the Disability Discrimination Act when defending possession claims. Lord Scott stated that if the physical or mental condition that constitutes the tenant's disability has played no motivating part in the decision of the alleged discriminator to inflict on the disabled person the treatment complained of (e.g. bringing a possession claim), the alleged discriminator's reason for that treatment cannot relate to the disability.

Forms of order

3A–379   Forms **N26** (Order for possession) and **N28** (Order for Possession (possession suspended) (rented property)) have been retained by the Practice Direction to CPR Pt 4, Table 3.

Extended discretion of court in certain proceedings for possession

3A–380   **85.**—(1) Where proceedings are brought for possession of a dwelling-house let under a secure tenancy on any of the grounds set out in Part I or Part III of Schedule 2 (grounds 1 to 8 and 12 to 16: cases in which the court must be satisfied that it is reasonable to make a possession order), the court may adjourn the proceedings for such period or periods as it thinks fit.

(2) On the making of an order for possession of such a dwelling-house on any of those grounds, or at any time before the execution of the order, the court may—

(a) stay or suspend the execution of the order, or

(b) postpone the date of possession,

for such period or periods as the court thinks fit.

(3) On such an adjournment, stay, suspension or postponement the court—

Paragraph numbers marked with a "+" can be found online and on CD.

    (a) shall impose conditions with respect to the payment by the tenant of arrears of rent (if any) and rent or payments in respect of occupation after the termination of the tenancy (mesne profits), unless it considers that to do so would cause exceptional hardship to the tenant or would otherwise be unreasonable, and

    (b) may impose such other conditions as it thinks fit.

(4) If the conditions are complied with, the court may, if it thinks fit, discharge or rescind the order for possession.

(5) Where proceedings are brought for possession of a dwelling-house which is let under a secure tenancy and—

    (a) the tenant's spouse or former spouse, or civil partner or former civil partner, having home rights under Part IV of the Family Law Act 1996 is then in occupation of the dwelling-house, and

    (b) the tenancy is terminated as a result of those proceedings,

the spouse or former spouse, or the civil partner or former civil partner, shall, so long as he or she remains in occupation, have the same rights in relation to, or in connection with, any adjournment, stay, suspension or postponement in pursuance of this section as he or she would have if those home rights were not affected by the termination of the tenancy.

(5A) If proceedings are brought for possession of a dwelling-house which let under a secure tenancy and—

    (a) an order is in force under section 35 of the Family Law Act 1996 conferring rights on the former spouse or former civil partner of the tenant or an order is in force under section 36 of that Act conferring rights on a cohabitant or former cohabitant (within the meaning of that Act) of the tenant,

    (b) the former spouse, former civil partner, cohabitant, or former cohabitant is then in occupation of the dwelling-house and

    (c) the tenancy is terminated as a result of those proceedings,

the former spouse, former civil partner, cohabitant or former cohabitant shall, so long as he or she remains in occupation, have the same rights in relation to, or in connection with any adjournment, stay, suspension or postponement in pursuance of this section as he or she would have if the rights conferred by the order referred to in paragraph (a) were not affected by the termination of the tenancy.

3A–381

Note —Amended by the Family Law Act 1996 Sch.8, para.53 and the Civil Partnership Act 2004 s.82, Sch.9, para.18. This section has also been amended by Housing and Regeneration Act 2008 Sch.15, Pt I. The amendment relates to tolerated trespassers, but is not yet in force. The amendment is printed as part of the Housing and Regeneration Act 2008—see below.

"dwelling-house"
  See s.112.

3A–382

Paragraph numbers marked with a "+" can be found online and on CD.

"secure tenancy"

3A-383   See s.79. See too Housing Act 1988 s.9.

Extended discretion of court in certain proceedings for possession

3A-384   The court's power to stay or suspend execution or postpone the date of possession may be exercised when making an order for possession or "at any time before the execution of the order" (s.85(2)).

A tenant against whom an outright order has been made under a discretionary ground is entitled to make a fresh application to a district judge to stay or suspend execution. Such an application:

> "is not in any way affected or fettered by the reasons given by [the district judge who heard the possession claim]...on such an application the district judge can take all relevant circumstances into account as they appear at the time of the application. Those will include any medical evidence which is before the court, any evidence as to the defendant's behaviour since the original order and the effect of an immediate order for possession which is not suspended upon the likelihood of the applicant being rehoused under the Housing Act 1996".

There is a continuing remedy in the county court (*Plymouth CC v Hoskin* [2002] EWCA Civ 684; May 1, 2002). See too *Ujima Housing Association v Smith*, April 2001 Legal Action 21; October 16, 2000, Ch D.

For the circumstances in which it is reasonable to suspend or postpone a possession order, see the commentary to s.84 above. Section 85(2) gives the court a wide discretion and expressly allows the court to suspend for such period as it thinks fit. The court practice is to be merciful to tenants and to give them a realistic opportunity to pay arrears. The question of whether it is appropriate for a tenant who owes substantial arrears to have the threat of losing her home hanging over her for years is a political question and does not go to the correctness of making an order (*Henry v Lambeth LBC* (2000) 32 H.L.R. 874, CA).

Where there is a substantial dispute about the amount claimed and the tenant's compliance with the order, the up-to-date position has to be clearly and accurately established before considering an application to suspend under s.85 (*Haringey LBC v Powell* (1996) 28 H.L.R. 798, CA).

When exercising its powers under s.85 the court shall impose conditions with respect to the repayment of arrears of rent and mesne profits unless it considers that to do so would cause exceptional hardship (s.85(3)). There have been no reported Court of Appeal decisions as to what might constitute "exceptional hardship".

Note that the form of suspended possession order in former County Court Form **N28** stated: "When you have paid the total amount mentioned, the plaintiff will not be able to take any steps to evict you as a result of this order"

If this Form of order was used, a suspended possession order becomes unenforceable at the moment that the balance of arrears is paid (see *Merton LBC v Hashmi CAT 94/1147*; September 1995, Legal Action 13, CA (former Form **N28**, cheque for arrears handed to council on morning of execution. The council's contention that the judgment had not been satisfied because the cheque for £300 had not cleared before execution was rejected, since the tenants had been told that the further payment would satisfy all that was owed)). There is nothing in s.85(2), or elsewhere in Housing Act 1985, which expressly or impliedly prevents a tenant, who has paid off all the arrears and costs, making an application to the court to exercise its powers under s.85(2). (*Porter v Shepherds Bush Housing Association* [2008] UKHL 70, December 10, 2008)—but note Housing and Regeneration Act 2008 Sch.11 below which will provide that secure tenancies will continue until any warrant for possession is executed. This amendment is not yet in force.

The right to apply for a postponement of an order for possession under s.85 is not an interest in land which is capable of being inherited. It is only available to the tenant, the tenant's spouse or former spouse in occupation (s.85(5), *Brent LBC v Knightley* (1997) 29 H.L.R. 857, CA and *Marshall v Bradford MBC* [2001] EWCA Civ 594; [2002] H.L.R. 22).

Procedure on breach of condition of postponed possession order

3A-384.1   In *Wandsworth LBC v Whibley* [2008] EWCA Civ 1259; November 14, 2008; [2008]

Paragraph numbers marked with a "+" can be found online and on CD.

The Times November 25, 2008 the Court of Appeal rejected the council's attempt to establish a general rule that applications to fix a date for possession following the making and breach of a postponed possession order should be dealt with summarily. Courts have an obligation to consider whether or not it is right to make an order and to examine the circumstances. Sedley L.J. said

"if, on being notified of the impending application [to fix a date for possession] and invited to respond, the defendant remains silent or puts in a plainly spurious or irrelevant response, an order may properly be made summarily. But if, as is more probable in nuisance cases, an issue is raised which is capable of affecting the court's decision, justice will require the defendant to be given an opportunity to put his or her case. The court will of course be astute not to let merely factitious [sic] or obstructive responses impede a summary disposal; but, inconvenient though it will be for the lessor and for a time nightmarish for the neighbours, it is not permissible for a tenant who has a possible tenable answer to lose his or her home unheard " [12].

He continued:

"What will not suffice to procure a hearing is an unsupported assertion that the tenant has an answer. Nor will a bare denial amount to an answer: save in exceptional cases the court will expect details, since a tenant who has already, by definition, breached the terms of the agreement has to have a cogent answer once there is prima facie evidence of repetition." [18]

At hearings to determine whether or not terms of a postponed possession order have been breached, the law permits the use of hearsay and enables most hearings to be conducted expeditiously. "Everything depends . . . on a judicial appraisal of how the issues can be fairly and economically determined."

Effect of breach of a suspended or postponed possession order

Until the implementation of the Housing and Regeneration Act 2008 Sch.11 (not **3A–385** yet in force, but printed below) the effect of suspended or postponed possession orders (e.g. with conditions that tenants pay current rent and a specified sum each week or month towards the arrears) depends on the type of tenancy and the wording of the order. As a result of recent case law, the position is complex and the wording of orders needs to be considered very carefully.

(a) *Orders made in Form N28 in use between 1993 and late 2001*

The form of **N28** introduced in 1993 and which commonly remained in use until late 2001, provided "The court has decided that unless you make the payments as set out in paragraph 3, you must give the plaintiff possession of [property] on [date]." These orders have always been described as "suspended possession orders" although the better view now is that they should be called "postponed possession orders" since the Housing Act 1985 s.85(2) provides that courts may " *postpone* the date of *possession*" and "*stay* or *suspend* the *execution*" of the order. However, in view of the fact that Form **N28** itself described such orders as "suspended" orders, and to avoid confusion, that term is still used in this paragraph. If a tenant has always complied with the terms of an order for possession in this form, any secure tenancy continues. (*cf. Sherrin v Brand* [1956] 1 Q.B. 403; [1956] 2 W.L.R. 131, CA) For example, a secure tenant continues to enjoy all the rights of a secure tenant, such as the right to buy, the right to mutual exchange etc.

However, breach of the terms of a suspended possession order made in this version of Form **N28** automatically brings a secure tenancy to an end. In *Thompson v Elmbridge BC* (1987) 19 H.L.R. 526, CA the local authority granted a secure tenancy to Mrs Thompson. She lived in the property with her husband. After arrears of rent had accrued, the council took possession proceedings and, in January 1985, obtained an order for possession in Form **N28** suspended on terms that the defendant paid current rent and a further £10 per week off the accrued arrears. In August 1985 Mrs Thompson left the premises, but her husband continued to live there. He was unemployed and although some rent was paid by the DHSS, further arrears accrued. Mr Thompson claimed that the tenancy was still continuing and that he accordingly had rights of occupation under the Matrimonial Homes Act 1983 s.1 (now the Family Law Act 1996 s.30). He applied to the court to suspend a war-

Paragraph numbers marked with a "+" can be found online and on CD.

rant of possession and for an order under the Matrimonial Homes Act 1983 Sch.1 (now the Family Law Act 1996 Sch.7) transferring the tenancy to him. The Court of Appeal, in dismissing Mr Thompson's appeal against the refusal of his application, held that on the true construction of the order, the tenancy had come to an end on the first occasion when Mrs Thompson breached the terms of the suspended order by failing to pay current rent or instalments towards the arrears on time. See too *Burrows v Brent LBC* [1996] 1 W.L.R. 1448; [1996] 4 All E.R. 577 HL, where the phrase "tolerated trespasser" was coined to describe such former tenants. In this "limbo" period, there is neither a tenancy nor a licence. Accordingly, there can be no breach of any express or implied obligations or duties relevant to tenancies or licences (e.g. to repair). See *Leicester City Council v Aldwinkle* (1992) 24 H.L.R. 40, CA; *Tower Hamlets LBC v Azad and Another* (1998) 30 H.L.R. 241, CA; *Brent LBC v Knightley* (1997) 29 H.L.R. 857, CA (no right to succeed under s.87 after death of tenant if breach of suspended possession order); *Hawkins v Newham LBC* [2005] EWCA Civ 451; [2005] H.L.R. 42 (right to succeed lost); *R..v Sheffield CC Ex p. Creaser and Jarvis,* September 1991, Legal Action 15, QBD (no right to internal review of decision to evict as required by the council's standard tenancy agreement after breach of suspended possession order); and *Marshall v Bradford MBC* [2001] EWCA Civ 594; [2002] H.L.R. 22 (claim for breach of repairing obligations struck out). However, a tolerated trespasser may bring proceedings in nuisance against the "landlord" (*Pemberton v Southwark LBC* [2000] 1 W.L.R. 1672; [2000] 3 All E.R. 924, CA (cockroach infestation from common parts)).

Suspended possession orders in this form provided "When you have paid the total amount mentioned the plaintiff will not be able to take any steps to evict you as a result of this order." Although that provision means that once the order has been complied with, new proceedings are necessary if there is a new breach, it does not have the effect of resurrecting or reviving the former tenancy when the total has been paid. (*Swindon BC v Aston* [2002] EWCA Civ 1850; [2003] H.L.R. 42).

(b) *Orders made in Form N28 in use between late 2001 and Spring 2006*

The form of **N28** introduced in late 2001 and which commonly remained in use until spring 2006, provided "the court orders that ... the defendant give the claimant possession of [property] on or before [date]." After further paragraphs ordering payment of rent and costs, it provided "This order is not to be enforced so long as the defendant pays the claimant the rent arrears and the amount for use and occupation [and costs] totalling £ by the payments set ut below in addition to the current rent." The Form **N28** itself described this as a "suspended" order and that was the general understanding until the decision in *Harlow DC v Hall* ([2006] EWCA Civ 156; [2006] 1 W.L.R. 2116). In that case, the Court of Appeal held that this form of order in fact terminated secure tenancies and converted occupants into tolerated trespassers *even if they complied with the terms of the order.*

(c) *Orders made in revised Form N28 in Spring and Summer 2006 and thereafter*

In view of *Harlow DC v Hall*, the Department for Constitutional Affairs advised courts to delete para.5 in Form **N28** and to substitute a new para.1 in Form **N28** in the following terms "1. The defendant give the claimant possession of (address of the property) on or before (date) provided that the date for possession will be postponed and the defendant's tenancy of the premises will continue, so long as the defendant pays the claimant the current rent and in addition the rent arrears and costs by the instalments set out below."

For secure tenants, the effect of this amendment is to revert to the pre-2001 position. Secure tenancies continue provided that tenants comply with the terms of the order, but immediately on breach such tenants become tolerated trespassers. A similar form of wording is used in new Form **N28A** provided for in the 42nd update.

(d) *Postponed orders made in Form N28A from Summer 2006*

In *Bristol CC v Hassan*; *Bristol CC v Glastonbury* [2006] EWCA Civ 656; [2006] 1 W.L.R. 2582, the Court of Appeal held that courts do not have to use Form **N28** and sanctioned a form of postponed order which allows secure tenancies

Paragraph numbers marked with a "+" can be found online and on CD.

to continue even after breach of the terms of the possession order. A modified version of the form of order propounded by the Court of Appeal has now been adopted as new Form **N28A** (see para.55.8.9). The importance of this form of postponed order is that as it does not state a date on which possession is to be given up it avoids the status of "tolerated trespasser" on breach. The Court of Appeal referred to the "very unsatisfactory position" of tolerated trespassers but went on to state: "What order the court will in fact make in any case will be a matter for the discretion of the judge on that occasion. ... If a tenant has a particularly bad record of payment, for instance, but is not yet deserving of an outright possession order, the court might wish to make an order along the lines of the current Form **N28**, although the use of the phrase "in addition to your current rent" would be inapposite since the contractual tenancy would have been brought to an end by the making of the order." (para.43)

Tolerated tenants who wrongfully remain in possession after the end of "ordinary"non-secure tenancies cease to be liable for mesne profits when possession is given up, irrespective of whether they give notice (*Merton LBC v Jones* [2008] EWCA Civ 660; [2008] 4 All E.R. 287).

Revival of secure tenancies

An agreement to forbear from evicting a former tenant after breach of a suspended **3A–386** possession order does not restore the old tenancy but simply means the occupier is in a legal limbo as a "tolerated trespasser" until either the agreement to forbear is broken (in which case the landlord can seek a warrant) or the former tenant applies successfully to the court to discharge, rescind or modify the order so as to revive the earlier tenancy (*Burrows v Brent LBC* [1996] 1 W.L.R. 1448; [1996] 4 All E.R. 577, HL; *Marshall v Bradford MBC* above and *Greenwich LBC v Regan* (1996) 28 H.L.R. 469; (1996) 72 P. & C.R. 507, CA, see too; *Hawkins v Newham LBC* [2005] EWCA Civ 451; [2005] H.L.R. 42; *Lambeth LBC v O'Kane*; *Helena Housing v Pinder* [2005] EWCA Civ 1010; [2006] H.L.R. 2 (sending notice of variation of tenancy conditions and four notices of revision of rent and water charges to tolerated trespasser did not create new tenancy); *cf. Swindon BC (formerly Thamesdown BC) v Aston* [2002] EWCA Civ 1850; [2003] H.L.R. 42; [2003] L. & T.R. 18 (conduct of both landlord and tenant after possession order, including the provision of a new tenancy agreement, was sensibly referable only to the existence of a new tenancy)). Occupiers are not, however, homeless because they continue in occupation by "rule of law" (Housing Act 1996 s.175(1)(c)).

If either party wishes to revive the old tenancy for the purpose of enforcing its express or implied terms, they can apply to the court for an order varying the date on which possession is to be given so that the old tenancy can be resurrected (s.85(2)). It is possible for a court to exercise the discretion to postpone the date for possession (Housing Act 1985 s.85(2)(a)) after the terms of a suspended possession order have been breached, with the effect that the tenancy and its obligations revive retrospectively (unless the court otherwise directs (s.85(3)(b)). See *Routh v Leeds CC* June 1998, Legal Action 11, CA; *Lambeth LBC v Rogers* (2000) 32 H.L.R. 361; [2000] 03 E.G. 127, CA; and *Islington LBC v Honeygan-Green* [2008] UKHL 70, December 10, 2008.

When considering an application to revive retrospectively a tenancy, the court should bear in mind: (i) the tenant's previous payment record; (ii) whether all parties were before the court; and (iii) whether the tenant was seeking merely the execution of works of repair or also damages for past disrepair (*Marshall v Bradford MBC* above).

Relevance of other conduct

(a) *on a landlord's application*—After a suspended possession order has been made, **3A–387** liberty to apply to the court by the landlord is implicit, without the need to start new proceedings for possession. If a landlord wishes to put new allegations before the court, the court can make a new order, even if the old order has not expired. Such a new order may provide for possession to be given up forthwith. The court has, on such an application, to bear in mind the guidance given in cases such as *Sheffield City Council v Hopkins* [2001] EWCA Civ 1023; [2002] H.L.R. 12; [2001] 26 E.G. 163, as to the exercise of its discretion in such a situation, and should be astute to ensure that tenants are not taken by surprise. However, that does not necessarily extend to insisting that the

Paragraph numbers marked with a "+" can be found online and on CD.

HOUSING

proceedings be delayed by the equivalent of the extra time that would have been taken had the landlord had to begin new proceedings (*Manchester City Council v Finn* [2002] EWCA Civ 1998; [2003] H.L.R. 41).

(b) *on a tenant's application*—The court, exercising its discretion on an application to suspend a warrant under s.85, may take account of matters (e.g. breaches of the terms of the tenancy agreement or anti-social behaviour) other than those relied upon as grounds for making the original possession order—although it is not always right to do so (*Sheffield City Council v Hopkins* [2001] EWCA Civ 1023; [2002] H.L.R. 12; [2001] 26 E.G. 163). Whilst not attempting to fetter the discretion of District Judges, the Court of Appeal stated that the following points are relevant: (1) The discretion should be used so as to further the policy of Housing Act 1985, Pt IV, reinforced by ECHR, art.8. The policy is only to evict after a serious breach of an obligation, where it is reasonable to do so and where the tenant is proved to have breached any condition of suspension; (2) The overriding objective of the Civil Procedure Rules, especially the need for applications to be dealt with in a summary and proportionate way, means that wider issues may not be able to be dealt with on an application to suspend or vary. They may need to be dealt with in some other way; (3) The tenant should have clear evidence of what is alleged, especially where the allegations were not contained in the original claim; (4) The fact that the landlord had or had not included the allegations as part of the original proceedings is relevant; (5) The discretion to consider other allegations should generally be exercised more readily in respect of matters occurring after commencement of the proceedings; (6) The court should also consider the practicalities of dealing with matters on the execution of a warrant; (7) The fact that the tenant is at the mercy of the court and the responsibilities of a public landlord to its other tenants. The list is not exhaustive. District Judges have to exercise the discretion bearing in mind the importance of the issue to the tenant, at risk of losing his home, and the responsibilities of social landlords to their other tenants. However it would appear that the court cannot take into account allegations which have not been proved or admitted by the tenant.

After execution of a warrant

3A–388   The court's power to stay or suspend execution or postpone the date of possession only applies before the execution of the order (*Hammersmith and Fulham LBC v Hill* (1995) 27 H.L.R. 368; [2001] L. & T.R. 423; [1994] 2 E.G.L.R. 51, CA and *Leicester CC v Aldwinkle* (1992) 24 H.L.R. 40, CA). After execution an occupier can only be restored to possession if either the possession order is set aside (see, e.g. *Governors of Peabody Donation Fund v Hay* (1987) 19 H.L.R. 145, CA; *Hackney LBC v White* (1996) 28 H.L.R. 219, CA; and *Tower Hamlets LBC v Abadie* (1990) 22 H.L.R. 264, CA) or the warrant has been obtained by fraud, abuse of process or oppression (*Hammersmith and Fulham LBC v Hill* (1995) 27 H.L.R. 368; [2001] L. & T.R. 423; [1994] 2 E.G.L.R. 51, CA (arguable that the council had behaved "oppressively" where the tenant claimed that after issue of the warrant, but before execution, council officers had said that the defendant would have no chance of having the warrant suspended unless she was able to pay £1,000 within 24 hours); *Saint v Barking and Dagenham LBC* (1999) 31 H.L.R. 620, CA (oppression where warrant executed without prior notification to tenant who was in prison and without inviting him to renew his application for housing benefit); and *William Sutton HT v Breen*, February 2000, Legal Action. See too *Islington LBC v Harridge*, *The Times*, June 30, 1993, CA.

In *Southwark LBC v Sarfo* (2000) 32 H.L.R. 602, CA, Roch L.J. said:

"Oppression may be very difficult if not impossible to define, but it is not difficult to recognise. It is the insistence by a public authority on its strict rights in circumstances which make that insistence manifestly unfair. The categories of oppression are not closed because no-one can envisage all the sets of circumstances which could make the execution of a warrant oppressive".

"Oppression" is not limited to acts by the landlord. Misleading information from a court office, depriving a tenant of taking steps to have execution of a warrant for possession stayed prior to execution, may amount to oppression (*Hammersmith and Fulham LBC v Lemeh* (2001) 33 H.L.R. 23; [2001] L & T R. 423, CA). See too *Lambeth LBC v Hughes* (2001) 33 H.L.R. 33, CA where the Court of Appeal held that:

Paragraph numbers marked with a "+" can be found online and on CD.

SUCCESSION ON DEATH OF TENANT

Persons qualified to succeed tenant

87. A person is qualified to succeed the tenant under a secure **3A–396**
tenancy if he occupies the dwelling-house as his only or principal
home at the time of the tenant's death and either—

    (a) he is the tenant's spouse or civil partner, or

    (b) he is another member of the tenant's family and has
          resided with the tenant throughout the period of twelve
          months ending with the tenant's death;

unless, in either case, the tenant was himself a successor, as
defined in section 88.

Note —Amended by the Civil Partnership Act 2004 s.81 and Sch.8, para.20.   **3A–397**

"dwelling-house"
  See s.112.   **3A–398**

"secure tenancy"
  See s.79.   **3A–399**

"member of the tenant's family"
  See s.113.   **3A–400**

"successor"
  See s.88.   **3A–401**

Persons qualified to succeed tenant

On the death of a secure tenant, another person living in the dwelling as his/her **3A–402**
only or principal home may succeed to the tenancy if s/he is either the spouse of the
tenant or a member of the tenant's family who has resided with the tenant throughout
the 12 months ending with the death. Co-habitees count as family members (s.113). In
"family member" succession cases, the burden of proof is on successors to show that
they are family members, that they have lived with the tenant for the 12 months and
that the dwelling is their only or principal home (*Peabody Donation Fund Governors v
Grant* (1983) 6 H.L.R. 41; (1982) 264 E.G. 925, CA). Section 87 is also relevant to the
question of assignment of secure tenancies, since one of the exceptions to the general
prohibition against assignment of secure tenancies (s.91) applies where the assignee is
"a person who would be qualified to succeed the tenant if the tenant died immediately
before the assignment".

Security of tenure is commonly lost when a tenant dies and there is no person
qualified to succeed to the tenancy. In such circumstances the tenancy passes to the
late tenant's executors or administrators. In the case of intestacy, the tenancy now passes to the Public Trustee (Law of Property (Miscellaneous Provisions) Act 1994 s.14). A
Practice Direction (Probate: Notice to Quit [1995] 1 W.L.R. 1120) indicates how a notice to quit may be served on the Public Trustee to bring the continuing tenancy to an
end. See too Sch.2, Ground 16 (ground for possession where dwelling more extensive
than reasonably required after succession).

It is not possible for there to be a joint succession to a secure tenancy (*Newham LBC
v Phillips* (1998) 30 H.L.R. 859; (1998) 96 L.G.R. 788, CA).

The twelve month residence requirement may be satisfied by residence with the
deceased council tenant in any premises or combination of premises (not necessarily
subject to secure tenancies for the whole period) for the one year ending with the date
of death (*Waltham Forest LBC v Thomas* [1992] 2 A.C. 198; [1992] 3 W.L.R. 131; [1992]
3 All E.R. 244, HL, overruling *South Northamptonshire DC v Power* [1987] 1 W.L.R.
1433, CA).

The term "residence" is interpreted in much the same way as in the Rent Act 1977

Paragraph numbers marked with a "+" can be found online and on CD.

HOUSING

s.2, the Housing Act 1985 s.81, and the Housing Act 1988 s.1. Periods of temporary absence (if there is an intention to return and a physical manifestation of that intention) or residence at other premises do not necessarily prevent "residence" continuing. See, e.g. *Peabody Donation Fund Governors v Grant* (1983) 6 H.L.R. 41; (1982) 264 E.G. 925, CA (daughter moved in to live with father who was ill for part of each week in order to look after him. She stayed in her father's flat four nights a week, kept her clothes and books there and regarded the flat as her home. She was entitled to succeed); *Camden LBC v Goldenberg* (1996) 28 H.L.R. 727; (1997) 73. P & C.R. 376, CA (grandson moved out after marriage, but he and his wife could not find alternative accommodation and as a result he moved back after ten weeks) and *Marsh v Lewisham LBC* December 1989, Legal Action 14, CA.

The Court of Appeal has held that the Housing Act 1985 s.87, when read together with the words "living together as husband and wife" in s.113, means that in order to be entitled to succeed a cohabitee must not only have lived with the deceased for a year but have lived as "husband or wife" for the whole year. Succession cannot be established where the cohabitation "as husband and wife" has been for only part of the 12 months of co-residence (*Westminster CC v Peart* (1992) 24 H.L.R. 389, CA).

Same sex couples may be treated in the same way as a husband and wife. The House of Lords has held that the words "as his or her wife or husband" in Rent Act 1977 Sch.1, para.2(2) must be read to mean "as if they were his or her wife or husband" in order to comply with the ECHR. Accordingly the survivor of a same sex couple who has been living in a loving and monogamous relationship with a tenant may be able to succeed to a secure tenancy (see *Ghaidan v Godin-Mendoza* [2004] UKHL 30; [2004] 2 A.C. 557; *cf. Harrogate BC v Simpson* (1985) 17 H.L.R. 205, CA and *Fitzpatrick v Sterling Housing Association* [2001] 1 A.C. 27; [1999] 3 W.L.R. 1113; [1999] 4 All E.R. 705, HL).

The term "member of the family" can only be satisfied by the relationships listed in Housing Act 1985 s.113. First cousins, even if thought of as brothers in African culture, cannot be within the section (*Brent LBC v Fofana* [2000] Ed. C.R. 425).

The right to succeed only applies where a secure tenancy is still in existence. It comes to an end if the terms of a suspended possession order have been breached (s.85(5), and *Brent LBC v Knightley* (1997) 29 H.L.R. 857, CA)—but note Housing and Regeneration Act 2008 Sch.11 below which will provide that secure tenancies will continue until any warrant for possession is executed. This amendment is not yet in force. A minor who satisfies the succession conditions may succeed to a secure tenancy. In that case a secure tenancy in equity vests in the minor. The Trusts of Land and Appointment of Trustees Act 1996 Sch.1 operates in such a way that the legal tenancy to which the minor succeeded is held on trust until the age of majority is reached (*Kingston upon Thames RLBC v Prince* [1999] 1 F.L.R. 593 and *Newham LBC v R (A Child)* [2004] EWCA Civ 41).

Cases where the tenant is a successor

3A–403   88.—(1) The tenant is himself a successor if—

(a) the tenancy vested in him by virtue of section 89 (succession to a periodic tenancy), or

(b) he was a joint tenant and has become the sole tenant, or

(c) the tenancy arose by virtue of section 86 (periodic tenancy arising on ending of term certain) and the first tenancy there mentioned was granted to another person or jointly to him and another person, or

(d) he became the tenant on the tenancy being assigned to him (but subject to subsections (2) to (3)), or

(e) he became the tenant on the tenancy being vested in him on the death of the previous tenant, or

(f) the tenancy was previously an introductory tenancy and he was a successor to the introductory tenancy.

(2) A tenant to whom the tenancy was assigned in pursuance of

Paragraph numbers marked with a "+" can be found online and on CD.

an order under section 23A or 24 of the Matrimonial Causes Act 1973 (property adjustment orders in connection with matrimonial proceedings) or section 17(1) of the Matrimonial and Family Proceedings Act 1984 (property adjustment orders after overseas divorce) is a successor only if the other party to the marriage was a successor.

(2A) A tenant to whom the tenancy was assigned in pursuance of an order under Part 2 of Schedule 5, or paragraph 9(2) or (3) of Schedule 7, to the Civil Partnership Act 2004 (property adjustment orders in connection with civil partnership proceedings or after overseas dissolution of civil partnership, etc.) is a successor only if the other civil partner was a successor.

(3) A tenant to whom the tenancy was assigned by virtue of section 92 (assignments by way of exchange) is a successor only if he was a successor in relation to the tenancy which he himself assigned by virtue of that section.

(4) Where within six months of the coming to an end of a secure tenancy which is a periodic tenancy ("the former tenancy") the tenant becomes a tenant under another secure tenancy which is a periodic tenancy, and—

    (a) the tenant was a successor in relation to the former tenancy, and

    (b) under the other tenancy either the dwelling-house or the landlord, or both, are the same as under the former tenancy,

the tenant is also a successor in relation to the other tenancy unless the agreement creating that tenancy otherwise provides.

Note —Amended by the Housing Act 1996 Sch.14, para.1, Sch.18, para.9; the Family Law Act 1996 Sch.8, para.34; and the Civil Partnership Act 2004 s.81 and Sch.8, para.21.   **3A–404**

"successor"
A person who was a joint tenant and became a sole tenant by right of survivorship before the implementation of the Housing Act 1980 is not "a successor" for the purposes of the Housing Act 1985 s.88 (*Birmingham City Council v Walker* [2007] UKHL 22; [2007] 2 A.C. 262; [2007] 2 W.L.R. 1057).   **3A–405**

"dwelling-house"
See s.112.   **3A–406**

"secure tenancy"
See s.79.   **3A–407**

"introductory tenancy"
See s.115A and the Housing Act 1996 s.124.   **3A–408**

Succession to periodic tenancy

89.—(1) This section applies where a secure tenant dies and the tenancy is a periodic tenancy.   **3A–409**

(2) Where there is a person qualified to succeed the tenant, the tenancy vests by virtue of this section in that person, or if there is more than one such person in the one to be preferred in accordance with the following rules—

Paragraph numbers marked with a "+" can be found online and on CD.

   (a) the tenant's spouse or civil partner is to be preferred to another member of the tenant's family;

   (b) of two or more other members of the tenant's family such of them is to be preferred as may be agreed between them or as may, where there is no such agreement, be selected by the landlord.

  (3) Where there is no person qualified to succeed the tenant, the tenancy ceases to be a secure tenancy—

   (a) where it is vested or otherwise disposed of in the course of the administration of the tenants' estate, unless the vesting or other disposal is in pursuance of an order made under—

    (i) section 23A or 24 of the Matrimonial Causes Act 1973 (property adjustment orders made in connection with matrimonial proceedings),

    (ii) section 17(1) of the Matrimonial and Family Proceedings Act 1984 (property adjustment orders after overseas divorce), or

    (iii) paragraph 1 of Schedule 1 to the Children Act 1989 (orders for financial relief against parents), or

    (iv) Part 2 of Schedule 5, or paragraph 9(2) or (3) of Schedule 7, to the Civil Partnership Act 2004 (property adjustment orders in connection with civil partnership proceedings or after overseas dissolution of civil partnership, etc.)

   (b) When it is known that when the tenancy is so vested or disposed of it will not be in pursuance of such an order.

  (4) A tenancy which ceases to be a secure tenancy by virtue of this section cannot subsequently become a secure tenancy.

3A–410 *Note*—Amended by the Housing Act 1996 Sch.18, para.10; the Family Law Act 1996 Sch.8, para.34; and the Civil Partnership Act 2004 ss.81, 261(4), Sch.8, para.22, Sch.30.

"secure tenancy"

3A–411 The right to succeed is lost if the terms of a suspended possession order in Form N28 are breached and the tenant becomes a tolerated trespasser before death (*Newham LBC v Hawkins* [2005] EWCA Civ 451; [2005] H.L.R. 42; and *Brent LBC v Knightley* (1997) 29 H.L.R. 857, CA). However the right to succeed may be retained if the order was made in Form **N28A**. See the commentary at 3A–385 above.

"member of the tenant's family"

3A–412 See s.113. Section 113 contains an exhaustive list of categories of family members eligible to succeed a secure tenant. Although that section is discriminatory in relation to a matter within the scope of ECHR, art.8 (the "home") and so art.14 is engaged, there is an objective justification for establishing a "closed" list in s.113, namely "certainty" in determining which members of a secure tenant's family are eligible to succeed and accordingly art.14 is not infringed. The fact that the Rent Acts contain no exhaustive definition of "member of the family" is not relevant to the construction of the section because the schemes of the Rent Act and the Housing Act tenancies are so different that a potential successor in one scheme has no "comparator" in the other scheme. On a claim for possession against a non-successor, the county court is not

Paragraph numbers marked with a "+" can be found online and on CD.

required to investigate the individual circumstances of the defendant in order to find the conditions of ECHR, art.8(2) made out. (*Michalak v Wandsworth LBC* [2002] EWCA Civ 271; [2003] 1 W.L.R. 617). See too *R. (Gangera) v Hounslow LBC* [2003] EWHC 794 Admin; [2003] H.L.R. 68 (where Moses J. held that the provisions prohibiting people in categories other than those listed in s.113 from succeeding to secure tenancies do not infringe ECHR, art.14 read with art.8) and *Harrow LBC v Qazi* [2003] UKHL 43; [2004] 1 A.C. 983; [2003] 3 W.L.R. 792; (where Lord Hope and Lord Scott approved these decisions and said that contractual and property rights cannot be defeated by a defence based on Article 8). See too *Newham LBC v Kibata* [2003] EWCA Civ 1785; [2004] H.L.R. 28 and *Bradney v Birmingham CC*; *Birmingham CC v McCann* [2003] EWCA Civ 1783; [2004] H.L.R. 27; *Lambeth LBC v Kay*; *Leeds CC v Price* [2006] UKHL 10; [2006] 2 A.C. 465; [2006] 2 W.L.R. 570 and *Birmingham City Council v Doherty* [2008] UKHL 57, July 30, 2008, [2008] 3 W.L.R. 636; but *cf. McCann v UK* App. No.19009/04, May 13, 2008, *The Times* May 23, 2008, noted at para.3A–192.

"qualified to succeed"

See s.87.   **3A–413**

It has been held that if a minor would be entitled to succeed, by operation of the Trusts of Land and Appointment of Trustees Act 1996 Sch.1, the tenancy should be held on trust for him or her: *Kingston upon Thames RLBC v Prince* (1999) 31 H.L.R. 794; [1999] L.G.R. 333, CA.

Devolution of term certain

90.—(1) This section applies where a secure tenant dies and the **3A–414** tenancy is a tenancy for a term certain.

(2) The tenancy remains a secure tenancy until—

(a) it vested or otherwise disposed of in the course of the administration of the tenant's estate, as mentioned in subsection (3), or

(b) it is known that when it is so vested or disposed of it will not be a secure tenancy.

(3) The tenancy ceases to be a secure tenancy on being vested or otherwise disposed of in the course of administration of the tenant's estate, unless—

(a) the vesting or other disposal is in pursuance of an order made under—

(i) section 23A or 24 of the Matrimonial Causes Act 1973 (property adjustment orders in connection with matrimonial proceedings),

(ii) section 17(1) of the Matrimonial and Family Proceedings Act 1984 (property adjustment orders after overseas divorce),

(iii) paragraph 1 of Schedule 1 to the Children Act 1989 (orders for financial relief against parents), or

(iv) Part 2 of Schedule 5, or paragraph 9(2) or (3) of Schedule 7, to the Civil Partnership Act 2004 (property adjustment orders in connection with civil partnership proceedings or after overseas dissolution of civil partnership, etc.), or

(b) the vesting or other disposal is to a person qualified to succeed the tenant.

Paragraph numbers marked with a "+" can be found online and on CD.

(4) A tenancy which ceases to be a secure tenancy by virtue of this section cannot subsequently become a secure tenancy.

3A–415   *Note* —Amended by the Housing Act 1996 Sch.18, para.11; the Family Law Act 1996; and the Civil Partnership Act 2004 ss.81, 261(4) and Sch.8, para.24, Sch.30.

"secure tenancy"
3A–416   See s.79.

"qualified to succeed"
3A–417   See s.87.

ASSIGNMENT, LODGERS AND SUBLETTING

3A–418   **91.**—(1) A secure tenancy which is—

    (a) a periodic tenancy, or

    (b) a tenancy for a term certain granted on or after 5th November 1982, is not capable of being assigned except in the cases mentioned in subsection (3).

(2) If a secure tenancy for a term certain granted before 5th November 1982 is assigned, then, except in the cases mentioned in subsection (3), it ceases to be a secure tenancy and cannot subsequently become a secure tenancy.

(3) The exceptions are—

    (a) an assignment in accordance with section 92 (assignment by way of exchange);

    (b) an assignment in pursuance of an order made under—

        (i) section 23A or 24 of the Matrimonial Causes Act 1973 (property adjustment orders in connection with matrimonial proceedings),

        (ii) section 17(1) of the Matrimonial and Family Proceedings Act 1984 (property adjustment orders after overseas divorce),

        (iii) paragraph 1 of Schedule 1 to the Children Act 1989 (orders for financial relief against parents), or

        (iv) Part 2 of Schedule 5, or paragraph 9(2) or (3) of Schedule 7, to the Civil Partnership Act 2004 (property adjustment orders in connection with civil partnership proceedings or after overseas dissolution of civil partnership, etc.)

    (c) an assignment to a person who would be qualified to succeed the tenant if the tenant died immediately before the assignment.

3A–419   *Note* —Amended by the Housing Act 1996 Sch.18, para.12; the Family Law Act 1996 Sch.8, para.34; and the Civil Partnership Act 2004 ss.81, 261(4), Sch.8, para.24, Sch.30.

"secure tenancy"
3A–420   See s.79.

Paragraph numbers marked with a "+" can be found online and on CD.

section 93(1)(b)(landlord's consent to subletting of part of dwelling-house).

(2) Consent shall not be unreasonably withheld (and if unreasonably withheld shall be treated as given), and if a question arises whether the withholding of consent was unreasonable it is for the landlord to show that it was not.

(3) In determining that question the following matters, if shown by the landlord, are among those to be taken into account—

    (a) that the consent would lead to overcrowding of the dwelling-house within the meaning of Part X (overcrowding);

    (b) that the landlord proposes to carry out works on the dwelling-house, or on the building of which it forms part, and that the proposed works will affect the accommodation likely to be used by the sub-tenant who would reside in the dwelling-house as a result of the consent.

(4) Consent may be validly given notwithstanding that it follows, instead of preceding, the action requiring it.

(5) Consent cannot be given subject to a condition (and if purporting to be given subject to a condition shall be treated as given unconditionally).

(6) Where the tenant has applied in writing for consent, then—

    (a) if the landlord refuses to give consent, it shall give the tenant a written statement of the reasons why consent was refused, and

    (b) if the landlord neither gives nor refuses to give consent within a reasonable time, consent shall be taken to have been withheld.

"dwelling-house"
  See s.112.

3A–436

"overcrowding"
  See s.324.

3A–437

Assignment or subletting where tenant condition not satisfied

3A–438

95.—(1) This section applies to a tenancy which is not a secure tenancy but would be if the tenant condition referred to in section 81 (occupation by the tenant) were satisfied.

(2) Sections 91 and 93(2) (restrictions on assignment or subletting of whole dwelling-house) apply to such a tenancy as they apply to a secure tenancy, except that—

    (a) section 91(3)(b) and (c) (assignments expected from restrictions) do not apply to such a tenancy for a term certain granted before 5th November 1982, and

    (b) references to the tenancy ceasing to be secure shall be disregarded, without prejudice to the application of the remainder of the provisions in which those references occur.

Paragraph numbers marked with a "+" can be found online and on CD.

3A–439   See s.79.

"tenant condition"
3A–440   See s.81.

* * * *

Acquisition of dwelling-house subject to statutory tenancy
3A–441   **109A.** Where an authority or body within section 80 (the landlord condition for secure tenancies) becomes the landlord of a dwelling-house subject to a statutory tenancy, the tenancy shall be treated for all purposes as if it were a contractual tenancy on the same terms, and the provisions of this Part apply accordingly.

3A–442   *Note* —Inserted by Housing and Planning Act 1986 s.24(1)(b), Sch.5, Pt 1, para.2.

SUPPLEMENTARY PROVISIONS

Jurisdiction of county court
3A–443   **110.**—(1) A county court has jurisdiction to determine questions arising under this Part and to entertain proceedings brought under this Part and claims, for whatever amount, in connection with a secure tenancy.

(2) That jurisdiction includes jurisdiction to entertain proceedings on the following questions—

(a) whether a consent required by section 92 (assignment by way of exchange) was withheld otherwise than on one or more of the grounds set out in Schedule 3,

(b) whether a consent required by section 93(1)(b) or 97(1) (landlord's consent to subletting of part of dwelling-house or to carrying out of improvements) was withheld or unreasonably withheld, or

(c) whether a statement supplied in pursuance of section 104(2)(b)(written statement of certain terms of tenancy) is accurate,

notwithstanding that no other relief is sought than a declaration.

(3) If a person takes proceedings in the High Court which, by virtue of this section, he could have taken in the county court, he is not entitled to recover any costs.

County court rules and directions
3A–444   **111.** [...]

3A–445   *Note* —Repealed by the Constitutional Reform Act 2005 ss.15(1), 146, Sch.4, paras 180, 181, Sch.18.

Introductory tenancies
3A–446   **111A.** Sections 102(1), (2) and (3)(a), 103 and 108 apply in relation to introductory tenancies as they apply in relation to secure tenancies.

Paragraph numbers marked with a "+" can be found online and on CD.

Note —Inserted by the Housing Act 1996 (Consequential Amendments) Order 1997 (SI 1997/74) art.2, Sch., para.3(a), (i).
3A–447
See also s.115A and the Housing Act 1996 s.124.

Meaning of "dwelling-house"
112.—(1) For the purposes of this Part a dwelling-house may be a **3A–448**
house or a part of a house.

(2) Land let together with a dwelling-house shall be treated for
the purposes of this Part as part of the dwelling-house unless the
land is agricultural land (as defined in section 26(3)(a) of the General
Rate Act 1967) exceeding two acres.

Members of a person's family
113.—(1) A person is a member of another's family within the **3A–449**
meaning of this Part if—
- (a) he is the spouse or civil partner of that person, or he
  and that person live together as husband and wife or as
  if they were civil partners, or
- (b) he is that person's parent, grandparent, child, grand-
  child, brother, sister, uncle, aunt, nephew or niece.

(2) For the purpose of subsection (1)(b)—
- (a) a relationship by marriage or civil partnership shall be
  treated as a relationship by blood,
- (b) a relationship of the half-blood shall be treated as a relationship of the whole blood,
- (c) the stepchild of a person shall be treated as his child,
  and
- (d) an illegitimate child shall be treated as the legitimate
  child of his mother and reputed father.

Note —Amended by the Civil Partnership Act 2004 s.81 and Sch.8, para.27. **3A–450**

Members of a person's family
See commentary to s.87. **3A–451**

Meaning of "landlord authority"
114.—(1) In this Part "landlord authority" means— **3A–452**
    a local housing authority,
    a registered social landlord other than a co-operative housing
      association,
    a housing trust which is a charity,
    a development corporation,
    a housing action trust, or
    an urban development corporation
    other than an authority in respect of which an exemption certif-
      icate has been issued.

(2) The Secretary of State may, on an application duly made by
the authority concerned, issue an exemption certificate to—
    a development corporation,
    a housing action trust, or

Paragraph numbers marked with a "+" can be found online and on CD.

an urban development corporation,

if he is satisfied that it has transferred, or otherwise disposed of, at least three-quarters of the dwellings which have at any time before the making of the application been vested in it.

(3) The application shall be in such form and shall be accompanied by such information as the Secretary of State may, either generally or in relation to a particular case, direct.

3A–453   *Note*—Amended by the Housing Act 1988 s.83; the Housing Act 1996 (Consequential Provisions) Order 1996 (SI 1996/2325) art.5, Sch.2, para.14 and the Government of Wales Act 1998 Sch.15, para.10 and Sch.18, Pt IV.

"local housing authority"
3A–454   See ss.1 and 2.

"housing action trust"
3A–455   See s.4.

"housing trust"
3A–456   See s.6.

"an urban development corporation"
3A–457   See s.4.

"development corporation"
3A–458   See s.4.

"registered social landlord"
3A–459   See the Housing Act 1996 ss.1–7.

Meaning of "long tenancy"

3A–460   **115.**—(1) The following are long tenancies for the purposes of this Part, subject to subsection (2)—

(a) a tenancy granted for a term certain exceeding 21 years, whether or not it is (or may become) terminable before the end of that term by notice given by the tenant or by re-entry or forfeiture;

(b) a tenancy for a term fixed by law under a grant with a covenant or obligation for perpetual renewal, other than a tenancy by sub-demise from one which is not a long tenancy;

(c) any tenancy granted in pursuance of Part V (the right to buy), including any tenancy granted in pursuance of that Part as it has effect by virtue of section 17 of the Housing Act 1996 (the right to acquire).

(2) A tenancy granted so as to become terminable by notice after a death is not a long tenancy for the purposes of this Part, unless—

(a) it is granted by a housing association which at the time of the grant is a registered social landlord

(b) it is granted at a premium calculated by reference to a percentage of the value of the dwelling-house or of the cost of providing it, and

Paragraph numbers marked with a "+" can be found online and on CD.

(c) at the time it is granted it complies with the requirements of the regulations then in force under section 140(4)(b) of the Housing Act 1980 or paragraph 4(2)(b) of Schedule 4A to the Leasehold Reform Act 1967 (conditions for exclusion of shared ownership leases from Part I of the Leasehold Reform Act 1967) or, in the case of a tenancy granted before any such regulations were brought into force, with the first such regulations to be in force.

Note —Amended by the Housing Act 1988 s.140, Sch.17, para.40; and the Housing Act 1996 (Consequential Provisions) Order 1996 (SI 1996/2325) art.5, Sch.2, para.14; and the Housing Act 1996 (Consequential Amendments No.2) Order 1997 (SI 1997/627) Sch.2, para.3. **3A–461**

Meaning of "introductory tenancy"

115A. In this Part "introductory tenancy" has the same meaning as in Chapter I of Part V of the Housing Act 1996. **3A–462**

Note —Inserted by the Housing Act 1996 s.141(1), Sch.14, para.3. See also the Housing Act 1996 s.124. **3A–463**

Minor definitions

116. In this Part— **3A–464**

"common parts", in relation to a dwelling-house let under a tenancy, means any part of a building comprising the dwelling-house and any other premises which the tenant is entitled under the terms of the tenancy to use in common with the occupiers of other dwelling-houses let by the landlord;

"housing purposes" means the purposes for which dwelling-houses are held by local housing authorities under Part II (provision of housing) or purposes corresponding to those purposes;

"rental period" means a period in respect of which a payment of rent falls to be made;

"term", in relation to a secure tenancy, includes a condition of the tenancy.

Index of defined expressions: Part IV

117. The following Table shows provisions defining or otherwise explaining expressions used in this Part (other than provisions defining or explaining an expression in the same section or paragraph)— **3A–465**

assured tenancy	section 622
cemetery	section 622
charity	section 622
common parts (in relation to a dwelling-house let under a tenancy)	section 116
consent	Schedule 3A, para.2(3)

Paragraph numbers marked with a "+" can be found online and on CD.

co-operative housing association	section 5(2)
development corporation	section 4(c)
dwelling-house	section 112
family (member of)	section 113
housing association	section 5(1)
housing authority	section 4(a)
housing purposes	section 116
housing trust	section 6
improvement	section 97(2)
introductory tenancy	section 115A
landlord	Schedule 2 Part V, para.7
landlord authority	section 114
local authority	section 4(e)
local housing authority	section 1, 2(2)
long tenancy	section 115
management agreement and manager	section 27(2) and 27B(4)
new town corporation	section 4(b)
qualified to succeed (on the death of a secure tenant)	section 87
registered social landlord	section 5(4) and (5)
relevant Authority	section 6A
rental period	section 116
secure tenancy	section 79
term (in relation to a secure tenancy)	section 116

3A-466   *Note* —Amended by the Housing and Planning Act 1986 s.24(1), (2), Sch.5; the Housing Act 1988 s.140, Sch.17; the Housing Act 1996 s.141(1), Sch.14, para.4; the Housing Act 1996 (Consequential Provisions) Order 1996 (SI 1996/2325) art.5, Sch.2, para.14 and the Government of Wales Act 1998 Sch.16, para.11 and Sch.18, Pt VI.

* * * *

DEMOLITION ORDERS

Demolition orders: recovery of possession of building to be demolished

3A-467   **270.**—(1) Where a demolition order has become operative with respect to any premises, the local housing authority shall serve on any occupier of the premises or any part of the premises a notice—

(a) stating the effect of the order,

(b) specifying the date by which the order requires the premises to be vacated, and

(c) requiring him to quit the premises before that date or before the expiration of 28 days from the service of the notice, whichever may be the later.

Paragraph numbers marked with a "+" can be found online and on CD.

(2) If any person is in occupation of the premises, or any part of them, at any time after the date on which the notice requires the premises to be vacated, the local housing authority or an owner of the premises may apply to the county court which shall thereupon order vacant possession of the premises or part to be given to the applicant within such period, of not less than two or more than four weeks, as the court may determine.

(3) Nothing in the Rent Acts or Part I of the Housing Act 1988 affects the provisions of this section relating to the obtaining possession of any premises.

(4) Expenses incurred by the local housing authority under this section in obtaining possession of any premises, or part of any premises, may be recovered by them by action from the owner, or from any of the owners, of the premises.

(5) A person who, knowing that a demolition order has become operative and applies to any premises—

> (a) enters into occupation of the premises, or a part of them, after the date by which the order requires them to be vacated, or
>
> (b) permits another person to enter into such occupation after that date,

commits a summary offence and is liable on conviction to a fine not exceeding level 5 on the standard scale and to a further fine not exceeding £5 for every day or part of a day on which the occupation continues after conviction.

Note —Amended by the Local Government and Housing Act 1989 Sch.9; and the Housing Act 1988 Sch.17.   **3A–468**

"demolition order"

Is defined by s.267 as "an order requiring that the premises—(a) be vacated within **3A–469** a specified period (of at least 28 days) from the date on which the order becomes operative, and (b) be demolished within six weeks after the end of that period, after the date on which it is vacated or, in either case, within such longer period as in the circumstances the local housing authority consider it reasonable to specify."

"local housing authority"

See ss.1 and 2.   **3A–470**

"owner"

Is defined by s.322:   **3A–471**

> "(a) ... a person (other than a mortgagee not in possession) who is for the time being entitled to dispose of the fee simple in premises, whether in possession or in the reversion, and
>
> (b) includes also a person holding or entitled to the rents and profits of the premises under a lease of which the unexpired term exceeds three years."

"premises"

Are defined by s.322 as "the dwelling-house, house in multiple occupation, building **3A–472** or part of building in respect of which the closing order or, as the case may be, demolition order is made." "Dwelling house" includes "any yard, garden outhouses and appurtenances belonging to it or usually enjoyed with it ..."

Paragraph numbers marked with a "+" can be found online and on CD.

HOUSING

"Rent Acts"

3A–473   Are defined by s.622 as the Rent Act 1977 and the Rent (Agriculture) Act 1976.

Demolition orders

3A–474   A tenant is not entitled to rely upon the protection of the Rent Act 1977 or the Housing Act 1988 when a demolition order is in force in relation to the premises (see *Marela v Machorowski* [1953] 1 Q.B. 565; and *Beaney v Branchett* (1987) 19 H.L.R. 471, CA). The effect of a demolition order is to remove security of tenure (*Johnson v Felton*; (1995) 27 H.L.R. 265, CA). However, any tenancy must still be terminated in the normal way (e.g. by notice to quit) (see *Aslan v Murphy (No.2)* [1990] 1 W.L.R. 766; [1989] 3 All E.R. 130, CA).

[THE NEXT PARAGRAPH IS 3A–482.]

SCHEDULES

SECTION 79   ## SCHEDULE 1

TENANCIES WHICH ARE NOT SECURE TENANCIES

Long leases

3A–482   1. A tenancy is not a secure tenancy if it is a long tenancy.

Introductory tenancies

3A–483   1A. A tenancy is not a secure tenancy if it is an introductory tenancy or a tenancy which has ceased to be an introductory tenancy—

(a) by virtue of section 133(3) of the Housing Act 1996 (disposal on death to non-qualifying person), or

(b) by virtue of the tenant, or in the case of a joint tenancy every tenant, ceasing to occupy the dwelling-house as his only or principal home.

Demoted tenancies

3A–484   1B. A tenancy is not a secure tenancy if it is a demoted tenancy within the meaning of section 143A of the Housing Act 1996.

Premises occupied in connection with employment

3A–485   2.—(1) Subject to sub-paragraph 4B, a tenancy is not a secure tenancy if the tenant is an employee of the landlord or of—

a local authority,
a development corporation,
a housing action trust,
an urban development corporation, or
the governors of an aided school,
and his contract of employment requires him to occupy the dwelling-house for the better performance of his duties.

(2) Subject to sub-paragraph 4B, a tenancy is not a secure tenancy if the tenant is a member of a police force and the dwelling-house is provided for him free of rent and rates in pursuance of regulations made under section 50 of the Police Act 1996(general regulations as to government, administration and conditions of service of police forces).

(3) Subject to sub-paragraph 4B, a tenancy is not a secure tenancy if the tenant is an employee of a fire and rescue authority and—

(a) his contract of employment requires him to live in close proximity to a particular fire station, and

(b) the dwelling-house was let to him by the authority in consequence of that requirement;

(4) Subject to sub-paragraph (4A) and (4B), a tenancy is not a secure tenancy if—

Paragraph numbers marked with a "+" can be found online and on CD.

(a) within the period of three years immediately preceding the grant the conditions mentioned in sub-paragraph (1), (2) or (3) have been satisfied with respect to a tenancy of the dwelling-house, and

(b) before the grant the landlord notified the tenant in writing of the circumstances in which this exception applies and that in its opinion the proposed tenancy would fall within this exception;

(4A) Except where the landlord is a local housing authority, a tenancy under sub-paragraph (4) shall become a secure tenancy when the periods during which the conditions mentioned in sub-paragraph (1), (2) or (3) are not satisfied with respect to the tenancy amount in aggregate to more than three years.

(4B) Where the landlord is a local housing authority, a tenancy under sub-paragraph (1), (2), (3) or (4) shall become a secure tenancy if the authority notify the tenant that the tenancy is to be regarded as a secure tenancy.

(5) In this paragraph "contract of employment" means a contract of service or apprenticeship, whether express or implied and (if express) whether oral or in writing.

Land acquired for development

3.—(1) A tenancy is not a secure tenancy if the dwelling-house is on land which **3A–486** has been acquired for development and the dwelling-house is used by the landlord, pending development of the land, as temporary housing accommodation.

(2) In this paragraph "development" has the meaning given by section 55 of the Town and Country Planning Act 1990 (general definition of development for purposes of that Act).

Accommodation for homeless persons

4. A tenancy granted in pursuance of any function under Part VII of the Hous- **3A–487** ing Act 1996 (homelessness) is not a secure tenancy unless the local housing authority concerned have notified the tenant that the tenancy is to be regarded as a secure tenancy.

Accommodation for Asylum Seekers

4A.—(1) A tenancy is not a secure tenancy if it is granted in order to provide ac- **3A–488** commodation under section 4 or Part VI of the Immigration and Asylum Act 1999.

(2) A tenancy mentioned in sub-paragraph (1) becomes a secure tenancy if the landlord notifies the tenant that it is to be regarded as a secure tenancy.

Temporary accommodation for persons taking up employment

5.—(1) Subject to sub-paragraphs (1A and 1B), a tenancy is not a secure tenancy **3A–489** if—

(a) the person to whom the tenancy was granted was not, immediately before the grant, resident in the district in which the dwelling-house is situated,

(b) before the grant of the tenancy, he obtained employment, or an offer of employment, in the district or its surrounding area,

(c) the tenancy was granted to him for the purpose of meeting his need for temporary accommodation in the district or its surrounding area in order to work there, and of enabling him to find permanent accommodation there, and

(d) the landlord notified him in writing of the circumstances in which this exception applies and that in its opinion the proposed tenancy would fall within this exception;

(1A) Except where the landlord is a local housing authority, a tenancy under sub-paragraph (1) shall become a secure tenancy on the expiry of one year from the grant or on earlier notification by the landlord to the tenant that the tenancy is to be regarded as a secure tenancy.

Paragraph numbers marked with a "+" can be found online and on CD.

(1B) Where the landlord is a local housing authority, a tenancy under sub-paragraph (1) shall become a secure tenancy is at any time the authority notify the tenant that the tenancy is to be regarded as a secure tenancy.

(2) In this paragraph—

"district" means district of a local housing authority; and

"surrounding area", in relation to a district, means the area consisting of each district that adjoins it.

Short-term arrangements

3A–490   6. A tenancy is not a secure tenancy if—

(a) the dwelling-house has been leased to the landlord with vacant possession for use as temporary housing accommodation,

(b) the terms on which it has been leased include provision for the lessor to obtain vacant possession from the landlord on the expiry of a specified period or when required by the lessor,

(c) the lessor is not a body which is capable of granting secure tenancies, and

(d) the landlord has no interest in the dwelling-house other than under the lease in question or as a mortgagee.

Temporary accommodation during works

3A–491   7. A tenancy is not a secure tenancy if—

(a) the dwelling-house has been made available for occupation by the tenant (or a predecessor in title of his) while works are carried out on the dwelling-house which he previously occupied as his home, and

(b) the tenant or predecessor was not a secure tenant of that other dwelling-house at the time when he ceased to occupy it as his home.

Agricultural holding etc.

3A–492   8.—(1) A tenancy is not secure if—

(a) the dwelling-house is comprised in an agricultural holding and is occupied by the person responsible for the control (whether as tenant or as servant or agent of the tenant) of the farming of the holding, or

(b) the dwelling-house is comprised in the holding held under a farm business tenancy and is occupied by the person responsible for the control (whether a tenant or as servant or agent of the tenant) of the management of the holding.

(2) In sub-paragraph (1) above—

"agricultural holding" means any agricultural holding within the meaning of the Agricultural Holdings Act 1986 held under a tenancy in relation to which that Act applies, and

"farm business tenancy" and

"holding" in relation to such a tenancy, have the same meaning as in the Agricultural Tenancies Act 1995.

Licensed premises

3A–493   9. A tenancy is not a secure tenancy if the dwelling-house consists of or includes premises which, by virtue of a premises licence under the Licensing Act 2003, may be used for the supply of alcohol (within the meaning of section 14 of that Act) for consumption on the premises.

Student lettings

3A–494   10.—(1) Subject to sub-paragraphs (2A) and (2B), a tenancy of a dwelling-house is not a secure tenancy if—

(a) it is granted for the purpose of enabling the tenant to attend a designated course at an educational establishment, and

(b) before the grant of the tenancy the landlord notified him in writing of the circumstances in which this exception applies and that in its opinion the proposed tenancy would fall within this exception.

Paragraph numbers marked with a "+" can be found online and on CD.

(2) A landlord's notice under sub-paragraph (1)(b) shall specify the educational establishment which the person concerned proposes to attend.

(2A) Except where the landlord is a local housing authority, a tenancy under sub-paragraph (1) shall become a secure tenancy on the expiry of the period specified in sub-paragraph (3) or on earlier notification by the landlord to the tenant that the tenancy is to be regarded as a secure tenancy.

(2B) Where the landlord is a local housing authority, a tenancy under sub-paragraph (1) shall become a secure tenancy if at any time the authority notify the tenant that the tenancy is to be regarded as a secure tenancy.

(3) The period referred to in sub-paragraph (2A) is—

    (a) in a case where the tenant attends a designated course at the educational establishment specified in the landlord's notice, the period ending six months after the tenant ceases to attend that (or any other) designated course at that establishment;

    (b) in any other case, the period ending six months after the grant of the tenancy.

(4) In this paragraph—

    "designated course" means a course of any kind designated by regulations made by the Secretary of State for the purposes of this paragraph;

    "educational establishment" means a university or institution which provides higher education or further education (or both); and for the purposes of this definition

    "higher education" and "further education" have the same meaning as in the Education Act 1996.

(5) Regulations under sub-paragraph (4) shall be made by statutory instrument and may make different provision with respect to different cases or descriptions of case, including different provision for different areas.

1954 Act tenancies

11. A tenancy is not a secure tenancy if it is one to which Part II of the Landlord and Tenant Act 1954 applies (tenancies of premises occupied for business purposes). **3A–495**

Almshouses

12. A licence to occupy a dwelling-house is not a secure tenancy of— **3A–496**

    (a) the dwelling-house is an almshouse, and

    (b) the licence was granted by or on behalf of a charity which—'

        (i) is authorised under its trusts to maintain the dwelling-house as an almshouse, and

        (ii) has no power under its trusts to grant a tenancy of the dwelling-house;

        and in this paragraph "almshouse" means any premises maintained as an almshouse, whether they are called an almshouse or not and "trusts" in relation to a charity, means the provisions establishing it as a charity and regulating its purposes and administration, whether those provisions take effect by way of trust or not.

Note —Amended by the Housing Act 1988 s.83; the Planning (Consequential Provisions) Act 1990, the Charities Act 1992; the Agricultural Holdings Act 1986 Sch.14; the Education Reform Act 1988 Sch.12; the Housing Act 1996 Schs 16 and 17; the Education Act 1996 Sch.7; the Agricultural Tenancies Act 1995 s.40, Sch.; the Police Act 1996 s.103, Sch.7, para.40 the Government of Wales Act 1998 Sch.18, Pt IV; the Immigration and Asylum Act 1999 Sch.14, para.81; the Anti-Social Behaviour Act 2003 s.14(5) and Sch.1; and by the Fire and Rescue Services Act 2004 s.53(1), Sch.1, para.62(1), (3); the Licensing Act 2003 Sch.6, paras 102, 104; the Fire and Rescue Services Act 2004 s.53(1), Sch.1, para.62(1), (3); theImmigration, Asylum and Nationality Act 2006 s.43(4) and the Housing and Regeneration Act 2008 (Consequential Provisions) Order 2008 (SI 2008/3002) para.28. The Schedule has also been amended by **3A–497**

Paragraph numbers marked with a "+" can be found online and on CD.

the Housing and Regeneration Act 2008 Sch.15 to introduce family intervention tenancies which cannot be secure tenancies. The amendment is printed as part of the Housing and Regeneration Act 2008—see below.

Sch.1 lists those types of tenancies and licences (see s.79) which cannot be secure.

Sch.1, para.1A—introductory tenancies

3A–498   See para.3A–1063.

Sch.1, para.1B—Demoted Tenancies

3A–499   This paragraph was inserted by the Anti-Social Behaviour Act 2003. See 3A–1117.

Sch.1, para.2—employees

3A–500   Schedule 1, para.2 excepts from security of tenure tenants who are employees of public sector landlords where their contract of employment requires occupation of the accommodation for the better performance of employment duties. The requirement may arise expressly or by implication from the contract of employment (para.2(5)). (Compare Sch.5, para.5 (5.13)—exception to right to buy where dwelling house is let in connection with employment *and* is within the curtilage of a building held for mainly non-housing purposes.)

In *Hughes v Greenwich LBC* [1994] 1 A.C. 170; [1993] 3 W.L.R. 821; [1993] 4 All E.R. 577, HL, the House of Lords rejected the council's assertion that a term which provided that a headmaster was required to occupy a house for the better performance of his duties should be implied into his contract in the absence of an express clause to that effect. This should be done only for a "compelling reason", i.e. if the council could prove that the employee could not perform his duties unless he occupied the particular accommodation.

The correct approach to be taken by a court in the light of *Hughes v Greenwich LBC* is to find out what duties the employee was required to perform. Having regard to the nature of these duties, the court should then ask itself the question whether or not it was practicable for those duties to be carried out if the employee did not live on the premises in question. Where there was a requirement to attend at the premises where the occupant was employed both in and out of hours and where it would not be practicable to carry out those duties without living at the provided premises, such occupation was "for the better performance of his duties". (See *Surrey CC v Lamond* (1999) 31 H.L.R. 1051; [1999] 12 E.G. 170, CA where it was held that there was a clear distinction between the position of a caretaker and that of a headmaster as in *Hughes v Greenwich LBC*). In *Wragg v Surrey CC* [2008] EWCA Civ 19; [2008] H.L.R. 30, Richards L.J. said:

> "[para.2(1)] is to be construed as laying down two distinct conditions: first, that 'his contract of employment requires him to occupy the dwelling-house'; secondly, that the requirement is 'for the better performance of his duties'. The first condition looks only to the terms of the contract: the question is simply whether the contract contains such a requirement or not. The second condition, however, raises an issue of fact outside the contract: the question is not whether the contract states that the requirement is for the better performance of his duties, but whether the requirement is in fact for the better performance of his duties ... [The second condition] should be construed as including an objective test: 'for' is to be read as 'to enable', the essential question being whether the required occupation of the property is intended to promote, and is reasonably capable of promoting, the better performance of the employee's duties."

The word "requires" means no more than that it is a term of the contract of employment with which the employee is required as a matter of fact to comply in order to perform his duty (*Brent LBC v Charles* (1997) 29 H.L.R. 876, CA). Retirement does not revive security (*South Glamorgan CC v Griffiths* (1992) 24 H.L.R. 334, CA). In determining whether an employee occupies for the "better performance of duties" the court is entitled to look beyond the written particulars of the contract of employment to the factual background leading to the tenant's occupation of the dwelling (*Campbell v City of Edinburgh DC* 1987 S.L.T. 51, Court of Session).

As Sch.1, para.2 uses the present tense "is" in setting out the conditions for exemption from security, the question is therefore whether the conditions are presently

Paragraph numbers marked with a "+" can be found online and on CD.

satisfied. In *Elvidge v Coventry CC* [1994] Q.B. 241; [1993] 3 W.L.R. 976; [1993] 4 All E.R. 903, CA, an employee/tenant lost his security of tenure by taking a new employment contract which expressly required him to occupy the cottage where he was already living for the better performance of his duties, even though the contractual tenancy itself had continued throughout. In contrast in *Greenfield v Berkshire CC* (1996) 28 H.L.R. 691; (1996) 73 P. & C.R. 280; (1996) 96 L.G.R. 327, CA a school caretaker who was granted a tenancy of a bungalow in school grounds for the better performance of his duties but was then made redundant acquired security of tenure when he found another job with the council at a different school and was allowed to stay in the bungalow until accommodation at the new school became available since by the date of the termination of the tenancy it was no longer a condition of his employment that he should occupy the particular property. As he had had new and different employment, his current occupation of the bungalow was not "referable" back to his last job (distinguishing *South Glamorgan CC v Griffiths* (1992) 24 H.L.R. 334, CA).

The phrase "the better performance of his duties" means that the tenant/employee's duties would not be so well performed if he or she lived elsewhere (*De Fontenay v Strathclyde Regional Council* 1990 S.L.T. (Ex. Div.) 605; *Fisher v Fife Regional Council* 1989 S.L.T. (Lands Tr.) 26; and *Stevenson v West Lothian DC* 1985 S.L.T. (Lands Tr.) 9). As to police officers, see *Holmes v South Yorkshire Police Authority* [2008] EWCA Civ 51; [2008] H.L.R. 33.

Sch.1, para.3—temporary use pending development

Schedule 1, para.3 provides that a tenancy of premises acquired for development **3A–501** and temporarily used as housing accommodation pending that or other development is not secure.

There are two distinct requirements, firstly, that the premises are on land acquired for development, and secondly, that they are used as temporary accommodation pending development. The immediate landlord need not be the body which acquired the land for development (*Hyde Housing Association Ltd v Harrison* (1991) 23 H.L.R. 57, CA.

In *Attley v Cherwell DC* (1989) 21 H.L.R. 613, CA, the Court of Appeal found development was intended and so the tenancy was not secure, even though the development might not be the same type of development as had originally been envisaged (*cf. Lillieshall Road Housing Co-operative Ltd v Brennan* (1992) 24 H.L.R. 193, CA).

Sch.1, para.4—accommodation for homeless persons

Article 8 does not entitle non-secure local authority tenants to have a county court **3A–502** judge (or the judicial review court) decide on the particular facts whether eviction was disproportionate to the council's aim of managing its housing stock properly. The effect of this would be to convert non-secure tenancies enjoyed by homeless persons into a form of secure tenancy. The balance of interests arising under Article 8(2) has in all its essentials been struck by the legislature when enacting the current scheme for the housing of homeless persons and their eviction (*Sheffield CC v Smart* [2002] EWCA Civ 4; [2002] H.L.R. 34).

See too *Harrow LBC v Qazi* [2003] UKHL 43; [2004] 1 A.C. 983; [2003] 3 W.L.R. 792, where Lord Hope and Lord Scott said that contractual and property rights cannot be defeated by a defence based on Article 8, although in exceptional cases where defendants believe that local authorities are acting unfairly or from improper notices, they can apply to the High Court for judicial review (per Lord Millett). Also *Newham LBC v Kibata* [2003] EWCA Civ 1785; [2004] H.L.R. 28 and *Bradney v Birmingham CC*; *Birmingham CC v McCann* [2003] EWCA Civ 1783; [2004] H.L.R. 27; *Lambeth LBC v Kay; Leeds CC v Price* [2006] UKHL 10; [2006] 2 A.C. 465; [2006] 2 W.L.R. 570 and *Birmingham City Council v Doherty* [2008] UKHL 57, July 30, 2008, [2008] 3 W.L.R. 636; but *cf. McCann v UK* App. No.19009/04, May 13, 2008, *The Times* May 23, 2008, noted at para.3A–192.

For the interrelationship between Sch.1, paras 4 and 6, see *City of Westminster v Boraliu* [2007] EWCA Civ 1339; [2008] 1 W.L.R. 2408.

Sch.1, para.6—private sector leasing

Schedule 1, para.6 excepts premises let under what are commonly called "private **3A–503** sector leasing" schemes. It applies when a private owner leases a property with vacant

Paragraph numbers marked with a "+" can be found online and on CD.

possession for use as temporary housing to a public landlord, which then sublets to an individual occupier. The sub-tenancy is excepted from secure status to ensure that vacant possession can be obtained at the expiry of the head lease.

See *Tower Hamlets LBC v Abdi* (1992) 91 L.G.R. 300; (1993) 25 H.L.R. 80, CA; *Hackney LBC v Lambourne* (1993) 25 H.L.R. 172, CA and *Haringey LBC v Hickey* [2006] EWCA 373; [2006] H.L.R. 36. For the interrelationship between Sch.1, paras 4 and 6, see *City of Westminster v Boraliu* [2007] EWCA Civ 1339; [2008] 1 W.L.R. 2408, November 2, 2007.

SECTION 84 SCHEDULE 2

GROUNDS FOR POSSESSION OF DWELLING-HOUSES LET UNDER SECURE TENAN-
CIES

PART I

GROUNDS ON WHICH COURT MAY ORDER POSSESSION IF IT CONSIDERS IT
REASONABLE

Ground 1

3A–504 Rent lawfully due from the tenant has not been paid or an obligation of the tenancy has been broken or not performed.

Ground 2

3A–505 The tenant or a person residing in or visiting the dwelling-house—
(a) has been guilty of conduct causing or likely to cause a nuisance or annoyance to a person residing, visiting or otherwise engaging in a lawful activity in the locality, or
(b) has been convicted of—
(i) using the dwelling-house of allowing it to be used for immoral or illegal purposes, or
(ii) an indictable offence committed in, or in the locality of, the dwelling-house.

Ground 2A

3A–506 The dwelling-house was occupied (whether alone or with others) by a married couple, a couple who are civil partners of each other, or a couple living together as husband and wife or a couple living together as if they were civil partners and—
(a) one or both of the partners is a tenant of the dwelling-house,
(b) one partner has left because of violence or threats of violence by the other towards—
(i) that partner, or
(ii) a member of the family of that partner who was residing with that partner im-mediately before the partner left, and
(c) the court is satisfied that the partner who has left is unlikely to return.

Ground 3

3A–507 The condition of the dwelling-house or of any of the common parts has deteriorated owing to acts of waste by, or the neglect or default of, the tenant or a person residing in the dwelling-house and, in the case of an act of waste by, or the neglect or default of, a person lodging with the tenant or a sub-tenant of his, the tenant has not taken such steps as he ought reasonably to have taken for the removal of the lodger or sub-tenant.

Ground 4

3A–508 The condition of furniture provided by the landlord for use under the tenancy, or for use in the common parts, has deteriorated owing to ill-treatment by the tenant or a person residing in the dwelling-house and, in the case of ill-treatment by a person lodging with the tenant or a sub-tenant of his, the tenant has not taken such steps as he ought reasonably to have taken for the removal of the lodger or sub-tenant.

Paragraph numbers marked with a "+" can be found online and on CD.

Ground 5

The tenant is the person, or one of the persons, to whom the tenancy was granted **3A–509** and the landlord was induced to grant the tenancy by a false statement made knowingly or recklessly by

(a) the tenant, or

(b) a person acting at the tenants instigation.

Ground 6

The tenancy was assigned to the tenant, or to a predecessor in title of his who is a **3A–510** member of his family and is residing in the dwelling-house, by an assignment made by virtue of section 92 (assignments by way of exchange) and a premium was paid either in connection with that assignment or the assignment which the tenant or predecessor himself made by virtue of that section.

In this paragraph "premium" means any fine or other like sum and any other pecuniary consideration in addition to rent.

Ground 7

The dwelling-house forms part of, or is within the curtilage of, a building which, or **3A–511** so much of it as is held by the landlord, is held mainly for purposes other than housing purposes and consists mainly of accommodation other than housing accommodation, and—

(a) the dwelling-house was let to the tenant or a predecessor in title of his in consequence of the tenant or predecessor being in the employment of the landlord, or of—

a local authority,

a development corporation,

a housing action trust,

an urban development corporation, or

the governors of an aided school,

and

(b) the tenant or a person residing in the dwelling-house has been guilty of conduct such that, having regard to the purpose for which the building is used, it would not be right for him to continue in occupation of the dwelling-house.

Ground 8

The dwelling-house was made available for occupation by the tenant (or a predecessor **3A–512** in title of his) while works were carried out on the dwelling-house which he previously occupied as his only or principal home and—

(a) the tenant (or predecessor) was a secure tenant of the other dwelling-house at the time when he ceased to occupy it as his home,

(b) the tenant (or predecessor) accepted the tenancy of the dwelling-house of which possession is sought on the understanding that he would give up occupation when, on completion of the works, the other dwelling-house was again available for occupation by him under a secure tenancy, and

(c) the works have been completed and the other dwelling-house is so available.

PART II

GROUNDS ON WHICH THE COURT MAY ORDER POSSESSION IF SUITABLE ALTERNATIVE ACCOMMODATION IS AVAILABLE

Ground 9

The dwelling-house is overcrowded, within the meaning of Part X, in such circum- **3A–513** stances as to render the occupier guilty of an offence.

Ground 10

The landlord intends, within a reasonable time of obtaining possession of the dwell- **3A–514** ing-house—

(a) to demolish or reconstruct the building or part of the building comprising the dwelling-house, or

Paragraph numbers marked with a "+" can be found online and on CD.

(b) to carry out work on that building or on land let together with, and thus treated as part of, the dwelling-house.

and cannot reasonably do so without obtaining possession of the dwelling-house.

Ground 10A

3A–515   The dwelling-house is in an area which is the subject of a redevelopment scheme approved by the Secretary of State or the Housing Corporation or Scottish Homes in accordance with Part V of this Schedule and the landlord intends a reasonable time of obtaining possession to dispose of the dwelling-house in accordance with the scheme.

or

Part of the dwelling-house is in such an area and the landlord intends within a reasonable time of obtaining possession to dispose of that part in accordance with the scheme and for that purpose reasonably requires possession of the dwelling-house.

Ground 11

3A–516   The landlord is a charity and the tenant's continued occupation of the dwelling-house would conflict with the objects of the charity.

PART III

GROUNDS ON WHICH THE COURT MAY ORDER POSSESSION IF IT CONSIDERS IT REASONABLE AND SUITABLE ALTERNATIVE ACCOMMODATION IS AVAILABLE

Ground 12

3A–517   The dwelling-house forms part of, or is within the curtilage of, a building which, or so much of it as is held by the landlord, is held mainly for purposes other than housing purposes and consists mainly of accommodation other than housing accommodation, or is situated in a cemetery, and—

(a) the dwelling-house was let to the tenant or a predecessor in title of his in consequence of the tenant or predecessor being in the employment of the landlord or of—

a local authority,

a development corporation,

a housing action trust,

an urban development corporation, or

the governors of an aided school,

and that employment has ceased, and

(b) the landlord reasonably requires the dwelling-house for occupation as a residence for some person either engaged in the employment of the landlord, or of such a body, or with whom a contract for such employment has been entered into conditional on housing being provided.

Ground 13

3A–518   The dwelling-house has features which are substantially different from those of ordinary dwelling-houses and which are designed to make it suitable for occupation by a physically disabled person who requires accommodation of a kind provided by the dwelling-house and—

(a) there is no longer such a person residing in the dwelling-house, and

(b) the landlord requires it for occupation (whether alone or with members of his family) by such a person.

Ground 14

3A–519   The landlord is a housing association or housing trust which lets dwelling-houses only for occupation (whether alone or with others) by persons whose circumstances (other than merely financial circumstances) make it especially difficult for them to satisfy their need for housing, and—

(a) either there is no longer such a person residing in the dwelling-house or the tenant has received from a local housing authority an offer of accommodation in premises which are to be let as a separate dwelling under a secure tenancy, and

(b) the landlord requires the dwelling-house for occupation (whether alone or with members of his family) by such a person.

Paragraph numbers marked with a "+" can be found online and on CD.

Ground 15

3A-520

The dwelling-house is one of a group of dwelling-houses which it is the practice of the landlord to let for occupation by persons with special needs and—

(a) a social service or special facility is provided in close proximity to the group of dwelling-houses in order to assist persons with those special needs,

(b) there is no longer a person with those special needs residing in the dwelling-house, and

(c) the landlord requires the dwelling-house for occupation (whether alone or with members of his family) by a person who had those special needs.

Ground 16

3A-521

The accommodation afforded by the dwelling-house is more extensive than is reasonably required by the tenant and—

(a) the tenancy vested in the tenant by virtue of section 89 (succession to periodic tenancy), the tenant being qualified to succeed by virtue of section 87(b)(members of family other than spouse), and

(b) notice of the proceedings for possession was served under section 83 or, where no such notice was served, the proceedings for possession were begun more than six months but less than twelve months after the date of the previous tenant's death.

The matters to be taken into account by the court in determining whether it is reasonable to make an order on this ground include—

(a) the age of the tenant,

(b) the period during which the tenant has occupied the dwelling-house as his only or principal home, and

(c) any financial or other support given by the tenant to the previous tenant.

PART IV

SUITABILITY OF ACCOMMODATION

3A-522

1. For the purposes of section 84(2)(b) and (c) (case in which court is not to make an order for possession unless satisfied that suitable accommodation will be available) accommodation is suitable if it consists of premises—

(a) which are to be let as a separate dwelling under a secure tenancy, or

(b) which are to be let as a separate dwelling under a protected tenancy, not being a tenancy under which the landlord might recover possession under one of the Cases in Part II of Schedule 15 to the Rent Act 1977 (cases where court must order possession),

(c) which are to be let as a separate dwelling under an assured tenancy which is neither an assured shorthold tenancy, within the meaning of Part I of the Housing Act 1988, nor a tenancy under which the landlord might recover possession under any of Grounds 1 to 5 in Schedule 2 to that Act,

and, in the opinion of the court, the accommodation is reasonably suitable to the needs of the tenant and his family.

2. In determining whether the accommodation is reasonably suitable to the needs of the tenant and his family, regard shall be had to—

(a) the nature of the accommodation which it is the practice of the landlord to allocate to persons with similar needs;

(b) the distance of the accommodation available from the place of work or education of the tenant and of any members of his family;

(c) its distance from the home of any member of the tenant's family if proximity to it is essential to that member's or the tenant's well-being;

(d) the needs (as regards extent of accommodation) and means of the tenant and his family;

(e) the terms on which the accommodation is available and the terms of the secure tenancy;

(f) if furniture was provided by the landlord for use under the secure tenancy, whether furniture is to be provided for use in the other accommodation, and if so the nature of the furniture to be provided.

Paragraph numbers marked with a "+" can be found online and on CD.

3. Where possession of a dwelling-house is sought on ground 9 (overcrowding such as to render occupier guilty of offence), other accommodation may be reasonably suitable to the needs of the tenant and his family notwithstanding that the permitted number of persons for that accommodation, as defined in section 326(3) (overcrowding: the space standard), is less than the number of persons living in the dwelling-house of which possession is sought.

4.—(1) A certificate of the appropriate local housing authority that they will provide suitable accommodation for the tenant by a date specified in the certificate is conclusive evidence that suitable accommodation will be available for him by that date.

(2) The appropriate local housing authority is the authority for the district in which the dwelling-house of which possession is sought is situated.

(3) This paragraph does not apply where the landlord is a local housing authority.

Part V

Approval of Redevelopment Schemes for Purposes of Ground 10A

3A–523   1.—(1) The Secretary of State may, on the application of the landlord, approve for the purposes of ground 10A in Part II of this Schedule a scheme for the disposal and redevelopment of an area of land consisting of or including the whole or part of one or more dwelling-houses.

(2) For this purpose—

    (a) "disposal" means a disposal of any interest in the land (including the grant of an option), and

    (b) "redevelopment" means the demolition or reconstruction of buildings or the carrying out of other works to buildings or land;

    and it is immaterial whether the disposal is to precede or follow the redevelopment.

(3) The Secretary of State may on the application of the landlord approve a variation of a scheme previously approved by him and may, in particular, approve a variation adding land to the area subject to the scheme.

2.—(1) Where a landlord proposes to apply to the Secretary of State for the approval of a scheme or variation it shall serve a notice in writing on any secure tenant of a dwelling-house affected by the proposal stating—

    (a) the main features of the proposed scheme or, as the case may be, the scheme as proposed to be varied,

    (b) that the landlord proposes to apply to the Secretary of State for approval of the scheme or variation, and

    (c) the effect of such approval, by virtue of section 84 and ground 10A in Part II of this Schedule, in relation to proceedings for possession of the dwelling-house,

    and informing the tenant that he may, within such period as the landlord may allow (which shall be at least 28 days from service of the notice), make representations to the landlord about the proposal.

(2) The landlord shall not apply to the Secretary of State until it has considered any representations made to it within that period.

(3) In the case of a landlord to which section 105 applies (consultation on matters of housing management) the provisions of this paragraph apply in place of the provisions of that section in relation to the approval or variation of a redevelopment scheme.

3.—(1) In considering whether to give his approval to a scheme or variation the Secretary of State shall take into account, in particular—

    (a) the effect of the scheme on the extent and character of housing accommodation in the neighbourhood,

    (b) over what period of time it is proposed that the disposal and redevelopment will take place in accordance with the scheme, and

    (c) to what extent the scheme includes provision for housing provided under the scheme to be sold or let to existing tenants or persons nominated by the landlord;

Paragraph numbers marked with a "+" can be found online and on CD.

and he shall take into account any representations made to him and, so far as they are brought to his notice, any representations made to the landlord.

(2) The landlord shall give to the Secretary of State such information as to the representations made to it, and other relevant matters, as the Secretary of State may require.

4. The Secretary of State shall not approve a scheme or variation so as to include in the area subject to the scheme—

(a) part only of one or more dwelling-houses, or

(b) one or more dwelling-houses not themselves affected by the works involved in redevelopment but which are proposed to be disposed of along with other land which is so affected,

unless he is satisfied that the inclusion is justified in the circumstances.

5.—(1) Approval may be given subject to conditions and may be expressed to expire after a specified period.

(2) The Secretary of State, on the application of the landlord or otherwise, may vary an approval so as to—

(a) add, remove or vary conditions to which the approval is subject; or

(b) extend or restrict the period after which the approval is to expire.

(3) Where approval is given subject to conditions, the landlord may serve a notice under section 83 (notice of proceedings for possession) specifying ground 10A notwithstanding that the conditions are not yet fulfilled but the court shall not make an order for possession on that ground unless satisfied that they are or will be fulfilled.

6. Where the landlord is a social landlord registered in the register maintained by the Housing Corporation under section 1 of the Housing Act 1996 or a housing association registered in the register maintained by Scottish Homes under section 3 of the Housing Associations Act 1985, the Housing Corporation, or Scottish Homes (and not the Secretary of State), has the functions conferred by this Part of this Schedule.

7. In this Part of this Schedule references to the landlord of a dwelling-house include any authority or body within section 80 (the landlord condition for secure tenancies) having an interest of any description in the dwelling-house.

Note—Schedule 2 amended by the Housing and Planning Act 1986 s.9; the Housing Act 1988 s.83 and Sch.17, para.65; the Housing Act 1996 ss.144–146; the Housing Act 1996 (Consequential Provisions) Order 1996 (SI 1996/2325), the Government of Wales Act 1998 s.140 and Sch.16, para.21 and Sch.18, Pt IV; the Civil Partnership Act 2004 s.81 and Sch.8, para.33, the Serious Organised Crime and Police Act 2005 s.111, Sch.7, para.45 and the Housing and Regeneration Act 2008 (Consequential Provisions) Order 2008 (SI 2008/3002) para.29.

3A–524

Sch.2, Ground 1—arrears or breach of obligation

See the commentary to the Rent Act 1977 Sch.15, Case 1.

As to reasonableness in claims for possession under "Ground 1", see commentary to s.84, above.

3A–525

Sch.2, Ground 2—nuisance or annoyance

As substituted by Housing Act 1996 s.144.

For the definition of "indictable offences", see the Interpretation Act 1978 Sch.1, which provides that "indictable offence" means an offence which, if committed by an adult, is triable on indictment, whether it is exclusively so triable or triable either way.

In *Kensington & Chelsea RLBC v Simmonds* (1997) 29 H.L.R. 507; *The Times*, July 15, 1996, CA, where conduct which was a nuisance or annoyance had persisted over a number of months, the Court of Appeal held that there was ample basis for the judge's findings that the tenant had allowed her son to abuse the neighbours. The Court also rejected the argument that it was necessary to show "fault" on the part of the tenant before a possession order could be made. The Court had to consider not only the interests of the tenant but also those of neighbours. It would be quite intolerable if neighbours were deprived of the possibility of relief because the tenant was incapable of controlling her son. See too *Portsmouth City Council v Bryant* (2000) 32 H.L.R. 906; [2000] E.H.L.R. 287, CA (claimant does not have to establish fault or even

3A–526

Paragraph numbers marked with a "+" can be found online and on CD.

knowledge on part of tenant, but the extent of personal fault is relevant when considering reasonableness.) In *Northampton BC v Lovatt* (1998) 30 H.L.R. 875; [1998] 07 E.G. 142; *The Times*, January 3, 1998, CA, the Court of Appeal confirmed that a tenant can be held responsible for acts of a minor child.

In relation to subpara.(b), indictable offences do not have to have been committed during the currency of the tenancy if a tenant pleads guilty or is convicted after the grant of the tenancy. See *Raglan Housing Association Ltd v Fairclough* [2007] EWCA Civ 1087; [2008] H.L.R. 21, where the defendant was arrested before the grant of his assured tenancy, but pleaded guilty after its grant. The Court of Appeal stated that a tenant who is convicted of supplying illegal drugs or of burgling his neighbours' houses poses no less a continuing threat if the offences were committed before he became a tenant than he would if they had been committed afterwards. The Court of Appeal was not agreed as to whether the ground could only be satisfied if the conviction itself (though not the facts on which it was based) occurred during the currency of the tenancy, but did not have to decide that point.

As to reasonableness in claims for possession under Ground 2, see commentary to s.84, above and s.85A.

Sch.2, Ground 2A—domestic violence

3A–527   As inserted by the Housing Act 1996 s.145 and amended by the Civil Partnership Act 2004 s.81, Sch.8, para.33.

The Housing Act 1996 s.145 introduced this ground for possession where there has been domestic violence. Ground 2A applies where one or both partners is a tenant and:

(a) one partner has left because of violence or threats of violence by the other towards that partner or a member of that partner's family; and

(b) the court is satisfied that the partner who has left is unlikely to return.

Landlords seeking to rely upon this ground must satisfy the court that notice of proceedings for possession has been served on the partner who has left the home or that they have taken reasonable steps to effect service (Housing Act 1996 s.147).

Where possession is sought under Ground 2A, it is not sufficient that the alleged violence or threats of violence were merely one of a range of causes of equal efficacy in the victim's departure from the property. For the ground to be made out it has to be established that the alleged violence or threat of violence was the dominant, principal and real cause of the departure (*Camden LBC v Mallett* (2001) 33 H.L.R. 20, CA).

Sched.2, Ground 5—tenancy obtained by false statement

3A–528   The Housing Act 1996 s.146 amended Ground 5 by widening it to include a statement made by "a person acting at the tenant's instigation". The word "instigate" means "to bring about or initiate". The Latin source of the word is *instigare*, to urge or incite. The Ground refers to "instigation" and not merely to someone "acting on behalf of the tenant". To come within Ground 5, the instigation must be of the false statement and not merely instigation of action in general on behalf of the tenant (*Merton LBC v Richards* [2005] EWCA Civ 639; May 11, 2005).

Ground 5 is only available where the defendant is the person to whom the tenancy was granted. The language of Ground 5 is clear and unambiguous and only refers to the current tenant—the person against whom possession is sought. The first seventeen words of Ground 5 make it clear that, if there has been an assignment, the word "tenant" does not include any predecessor in title who made the misrepresentation relied upon (*Islington LBC v Uckac* [2006] EWCA Civ 340; [2006] 1 W.L.R. 1303).

In *Rushcliffe BC v Watson* (1992) 24 H.L.R. 124, CA, Nourse L.J. approved comments made by the judge at first instance that the burden of proof in cases brought under Ground 5 was akin to the criminal standard because of the seriousness of the allegation. See too *Waltham Forest LBC v Roberts* [2004] EWCA Civ 940; [2005] H.L.R. 2.

In *Shrewsbury and Atcham BC v Evans* (1997) 30 H.L.R. 123, CA, where the tenant had "flagrantly and deliberately lied about her circumstances" in order to obtain council housing, Beldam L.J. said that:

"It would have been an affront to those who put forward their claims honestly, wait patiently and rely upon the local authority to deal fairly with their claims, if

Paragraph numbers marked with a "+" can be found online and on CD.

a judge had concluded that in the circumstances of this case it was not reasonable to make an order for possession."

As to reasonableness in claims for possession under Ground 5, see commentary to s.84, above and *Lewisham LBC v Adeyenni* (2000) 32 H.L.R. 414, CA.

Sch.2, Ground 10—property required for demolition or redevelopment

3A–529

This ground for possession may arise if a public landlord requires possession in order to carry out demolition or redevelopment work and cannot reasonably carry out the work without obtaining possession.

In *Wansbeck DC v Marley* (1988) 20 H.L.R. 247, CA, the Court of Appeal held that it was for the landlord to prove:

(a) that it intended to carry out works; and

(b) that such work could not reasonably be done without obtaining possession.

In this case there was no evidence on which the judge could have reached such conclusions. The tenant's appeal against a possession order was allowed.

Sch.2, Ground 10A—redevelopment

3A–530

As inserted by the Housing and Planning Act 1986 s.9.

Sch.2, Ground 16—dwelling more extensive than reasonably required after succession

3A–531

As amended by the Housing Act 1996 s.147(3). When considering whether or not to make a possession order under Ground 16, the court should consider family members living with the tenant. The correct date for establishing whether family members are residing with a tenant who has succeeded to a secure tenancy is the date of the hearing before the court, not the date of succession: *Wandsworth LBC v Randall* [2007] EWCA Civ 1126; *Wandsworth LBC v Randall* [2007] EWCA Civ 1126; [2008] 1 W.L.R. 359.

[THE NEXT PARAGRAPH IS 3A–545.]

Landlord and Tenant Act 1985

(1985 c.70)

3A–545

ARRANGEMENT OF SECTIONS

REPAIRING OBLIGATIONS

Paragraph numbers marked with a "+" can be found online and on CD.

Paragraph numbers marked with a "+" denote content that is available on White Book on Westlaw UK or the Civil Procedure CD.

REPAIRING OBLIGATIONS

Repairing obligations in short leases

3A–546 **11.**—(1) In a lease to which this section applies (as to which, see sections 13 and 14) there is implied a covenant by the lessor—

> (a) to keep in repair the structure and exterior of the dwelling-house (including drains, gutters and external pipes),
>
> (b) to keep in repair and proper working order the installations in the dwelling-house for the supply of water, gas and electricity and for sanitation (including basins, sinks, baths and sanitary conveniences, but not other fixtures, fittings and appliances for making use of the supply of water, gas or electricity), and
>
> (c) to keep in repair and proper working order the installations in the dwelling-house for space heating and heating water.

(1A) If a lease to which this section applies is a lease of a dwelling-house which forms part only of a building, then, subject to subsection (1B), the covenant implied by subsection (1) shall have effect as if—

> (a) the reference in paragraph (a) of that subsection to the dwelling-house included a reference to any part of the building in which the lessor has an estate or interest; and
>
> (b) any reference in paragraphs (b) and (c) of that subsection to an installation in the dwelling-house included a reference to an installation which, directly or indirectly, serves the dwelling-house and which either—
>
>> (i) forms part of any part of a building in which the lessor has an estate or interest; or
>>
>> (ii) is owned by the lessor or under his control.

(1B) Nothing in subsection (1A) shall be construed as requiring the lessor to carry out any works or repairs unless the disrepair (or failure to maintain in working order) is such as to affect the lessee's enjoyment of the dwelling-house or of any common parts, as defined

Paragraph numbers marked with a "+" can be found online and on CD.

in section 60(1) of the Landlord and Tenant Act 1987, which the lessee, as such, is entitled to use.

(2) The covenant implied by subsection (1) ("the lessor's repairing covenant") shall not be construed as requiring the lessor—

(a) to carry out works or repairs for which the lessee is liable by virtue of his duty to use the premises in a tenant-like manner, or would be so liable but for an express covenant on his part,

(b) to rebuild or reinstate the premises in the case of destruction or damage by fire, or by tempest, flood or other inevitable accident, or

(c) to keep in repair or maintain anything which the lessee is entitled to remove from the dwelling-house.

(3) In determining the standard of repair required by the lessor's repairing covenant, regard shall be had to the age, character and prospective life of the dwelling-house and the locality in which it is situated.

(3A) In any case where—

(a) the lessor's repairing covenant has effect as mentioned in subsection (1A), and

(b) in order to comply with the covenant the lessor needs to carry out works or repairs otherwise than in, or to an installation in, the dwelling-house, and

(c) the lessor does not have a sufficient right in the part of the building or the installation concerned to enable him to carry out the required works or repairs,

then, in any proceedings relating to a failure to comply with the lessor's repairing covenant, so far as it requires the lessor to carry out the works or repairs in question, it shall be a defence for the lessor to prove that he used all reasonable endeavours to obtain, but was unable to obtain, such rights as would be adequate to enable him to carry out the works or repairs.

(4) A covenant by the lessee for the repair of the premises is of no effect so far as it relates to the matters mentioned in subsection (1)(a) to (c), except so far as it imposes on the lessee any of the requirements mentioned in subsection (2)(a) or (c).

(5) The reference in subsection (4) to a covenant by the lessee for the repair of the premises includes a covenant—

(a) to put in repair or deliver up in repair,

(b) to paint, point or render,

(c) to pay money in lieu of repairs by the lessee, or

(d) to pay money on account of repairs by the lessor.

(6) In a lease in which the lessor's repairing covenant is implied there is also implied a covenant by the lessee that the lessor, or any person authorised by him in writing, may at reasonable times of the day and on giving 24 hours' notice in writing to the occupier, enter the premises comprised in the lease for the purpose of viewing their condition and state of repair.

Paragraph numbers marked with a "+" can be found online and on CD.

HOUSING

3A–547 *Note* —Amended by the Housing Act 1988 s.116.

"dwelling-house"

3A–548 See s.16.

"lease"

3A–549 See s.16.

"lessor"

3A–550 See s.16.

Protocol

3A–551 There is a Pre-action Protocol for Housing Disrepair Cases. See Vol.1, C10–001.

Repairing obligations in short leases

3A–552 The Landlord and Tenant Act 1985 s.11 (which re-enacts with some modifications the Housing Act 1961 s.32) implies into leases granted on or after October 24, 1961 (see s.13) for a term of less than seven years a covenant requiring landlords to keep in repair the structure and exterior of dwellings let to tenants. This includes drains, gutters and external pipes. Landlords are also obliged to keep in repair and proper working order installations in dwelling-houses for the supply of water, gas and electricity, for sanitation, for space heating and for heating hot water. To be in breach of this implied contractual duty landlords must:

(a) have knowledge of the defect; and

(b) then fail to carry out the repair within a reasonable period.

The repairing obligation cannot be transferred to tenants by express terms in the tenancy agreement (s.11(4), but see s.12 below). It does not apply to tenancies for a term of seven years or more.

Two important changes were made by the Housing Act 1988 s.116 to the landlord's obligations to repair found in s.11. First, the covenant to repair the "structure and exterior" was extended beyond the tenant's dwelling to cover "any part of the same building in which the lessor has an estate or interest". Secondly, the obligation to repair and maintain installations was extended from those in the dwelling to any installation which "directly or indirectly" serves the dwelling and is either part of the same building or owned by the landlord. Only tenancies granted after the commencement of the Housing Act 1988 (January 15, 1989) are affected by these changes. As to common parts, see though *Liverpool City Council v Irwin* [1977] A.C. 239; [1976] 2 All E.R. 39; (1984) 13 H.L.R. 38, HL.

Local authorities do not owe a higher repairing obligation under s.11 than other landlords (*Wainwright v Leeds City Council* (1984) 13 H.L.R. 117; (1984) 270 E.G. 1289, CA).

Section 11 does not apply where the Crown is the landlord (*Department of Transport v Egoroff* (1986) 278 E.G. 1361; (1986) 18 H.L.R. 326, CA) unless the lease is under the management of the Crown Estates Commissioners or a government department or a person holding in trust for Her Majesty for the purposes of a government department (s.14(5)).

Notice

3A–553 A landlord is not in breach of the implied covenant until a reasonable period has elapsed after the giving of notice of the defect (*O'Brien v Robinson* [1973] A.C. 912; [1973] 2 W.L.R. 393; [1973] 1 All E.R. 583, HL—collapse of bedroom ceiling due to a latent defect. Neither the tenant nor the landlord was aware of the defect until the collapse occurred. The House of Lords held that no liability under the Housing Act 1961 s.32 (now the Landlord and Tenant Act 1985 s.11) arose until the landlord had information about the existence of a defect in the premises which would put a reasonable person on enquiry as to whether works of repair were needed). See too *McGreal v Wake* (1984) 269 E.G. 1254; (1984) 13 H.L.R. 107, CA. The onus of proving that a reasonable period has passed is on the tenant (*Morris v Liverpool City Council* (1988) 14 E.G. 59; (1988) 20 H.L.R. 498, CA).

Notice of disrepair need not specify the precise nature or degree of want of repair.

Paragraph numbers marked with a "+" can be found online and on CD.

A letter from the solicitors which did not give details or enclose estimates or a report will normally be sufficient to put the landlord under an obligation to attend and inspect and thereafter carry out the repair (*Al Hassani v Merrigan* [1988] 03 E.G. 88; (1988) 20 H.L.R. 238, CA). The Court of Appeal has also held that a landlord local authority had notice of disrepair where an officer of the environmental health department had visited the property and seen the defects and the chief executive had received a report from the district valuer—prepared after a right to buy application— which drew attention to the defects, even though the tenancy agreement stated that notice of disrepair should be given direct to the architectural service of the council (*Dinefwr BC v Jones* (1987) 19 H.L.R. 445, CA). See too *Hall v Howard* (1988) 20 H.L.R. 566, CA (inspection report setting out items of disrepair taken into account in reaching a valuation of the property); and *Sheldon v West Bromwich Corp* (1984) 13 H.L.R. 23; (1984) 25 P. & C.R. 360, CA, where the Court of Appeal held that the state of discoloration of the water in a tank and the tank's age were sufficient to give the landlords actual knowledge of the need to repair. Information about the existence of such a defect which would put a reasonable person on inquiry as to whether works of repair are needed is sufficient for the landlord's repairing obligation to commence.

The requirement for notice to the landlord does not apply where reliance is placed upon the Defective Premises Act 1972 s.4 (see above) or where the disrepair is within part of a building retained by the landlord. See *British Telecommunications Plc v Sun Life Plc* [1995] 3 W.L.R. 622; [1995] 4 All E.R. 44; [1996] Ch. 69, CA, where Nourse L.J. stated:

"The general rule is that a covenant to keep premises in repair obliges the covenantor to keep them in repair at all times, so that there is breach of the obligation immediately a defect occurs. There is an exception where the obligation is the landlord's and the defect occurs in the demised premises themselves, in which case he is in breach of his obligation only when he has information about the existence of a defect such as would put a reasonable landlord on enquiry as to whether works of repair are needed and he has failed to carry out the works with reasonable expedition thereafter" ([1995] 4 All E.R. at 52).

In *Loria v Hammer* E.G.L.R. 249, Ch D, the cause of dampness was a failure to keep in repair the water tanks in the roof space and gutters around the roof. As these were in the common parts of a building, the landlord was held to be liable to repair irrespective of any notice.

"structure and exterior"

Outside walls of premises are part of the structure and so covered by the implied covenant, even if the lease expressly excludes them from the demise (*Campden Hill Towers Ltd v Gardner* [1977] Q.B. 823; [1977] 1 All E.R. 739; (1984) 13 H.L.R. 64, CA). The roof above a flat is capable of being part of the structure and exterior' of the dwelling comprising the flat within the meaning of the Housing Act 1961 s.32 (now the Landlord and the Tenant Act 1985 s.11), whether or not the roof is part of the demised premises (*Douglas-Scott v Scorgie* [1984] 1 W.L.R. 716; [1984] 1 All E.R. 1086, CA). See too *Ravenseft Properties Ltd v Davstone (Holdings) Ltd* [1980] Q.B. 12; [1979] 2 W.L.R. 897; [1979] 1 All E.R. 929, QBD.

However, in *Brown v Liverpool Corporation* [1969] 3 All E.R. 1345; (1984) 13 H.L.R. 1, CA, the Court of Appeal held that four shallow steps and a path made of flagstones between the house and the street were not part of the structure of the house and so not within the implied covenant. Similarly, in *Hopwood v Cannock Chase DC (formerly Rugeley UDC)* [1975] 1 W.L.R. 373; [1975] 1 All E.R. 796, CA, where the widow of the tenant tripped and fell on the edge of a paving slab in the yard behind the house, the Court of Appeal held that the yard did not form part of the essential means of access to the property and so was not part of the structure or exterior of the dwelling house for the purposes of the Housing Act 1961 s.32 (now the Landlord and Tenant Act 1985 s.11). See too *King v South Northamptonshire DC* [1992] 06 E.G. 152; (1992) 24 H.L.R. 284, CA.

In *Irvine v Morgan* (1992) 24 H.L.R. 1; [1991] 1 E.G.L.R. 261, QBD, Recorder Thayne Forbes, Q.C. held that the words "structure and exterior" do not mean that landlords are liable to repair the whole of the house. On the other hand, "structure" is not limited to the load-bearing parts. It consists of those elements of the overall dwelling-house which give it its essential stability and shape. The expression does not

3A–554

Paragraph numbers marked with a "+" can be found online and on CD.

extend to the many and various ways in which the dwelling-house will be fitted out, equipped, decorated and generally made habitable. Applying that test to the specific items, he held that:

- the separate garage and gates were not within the implied covenant;
- internal wall plaster and door furniture were decorative and therefore not part of the structure;
- external windows and doors and their constituent parts (including sashes) were either part of the structure or exterior;
- external painting was part of the obligation to repair the exterior;
- internal decorative painting of installations such as radiators was purely decorative and not part of the implied covenant.

See too *Quick v Taff Ely BC* [1986] 1 Q.B. 809; [1985] 3 W.L.R. 981; [1985] 3 All E.R. 321, CA (very severe condensation making house virtually unfit for human habitation not a breach of the s.11 covenant in the absence of evidence of disrepair to the structure or exterior) where Dillon L.J. stated:

"In the present case the liability of the council was to keep the structure and exterior of the house in repair—not the decorations. Though there is ample evidence of damage to the decorations and to bedding, clothing and other fabrics, evidence of damage to the subject-matter of the covenant, the structure and exterior of the house, is far too seek ... there is no evidence at all of physical damage to the walls—as opposed to the decorations—or the windows" ([1985] 3 All E.R. at 326).

Lawton L.J. stated:

"It follows that, on the evidence in this case, the trial judge should first have identified the parts of the exterior and structure of the house which were out of repair and then have gone on to decide whether, in order to remedy the defects, it was reasonably necessary to replace the concrete lintels over the windows, which caused 'cold bridging', and the single-glazed metal windows ..." (*ibid.*, at 328).

In *Lee v Leeds City Council* [2002] 1 W.L.R. 1488; [2002] All E.R. 124, CA the Court of Appeal held that: (1) *Quick* was not decided per incuriam because of a failure to consider the meaning given to "repair" in *Proudfoot v Hart* (1890) 25 QBD 42. Even if *Quick* was decided in ignorance of *Proudfoot*, both cases were before the court in *Post Office v Aquarius Properties Ltd* [1987] 1 All E.R. 1055 and the court did not regard them as inconsistent; and (2) In view of an express covenant to keep the structure in repair and the similar covenant which was otherwise implied under s.11, the court would not imply into local authority tenancies a term that the landlord was to keep the property "in good condition".

However, in *Staves v Leeds City Council* (1991) 23 H.L.R. 107; [1992] 29 E.G. 119, CA, where the condensation was so bad that the wall plaster had become saturated in places, the council conceded that the internal plasterwork was part of the structure. It argued, however, that, although the plaster was saturated, the patches concerned were minimal and the plaster was not in "disrepair". The Court of Appeal upheld H.H.J. Coles Q.C.'s finding that plaster when saturated is in disrepair and dismissed the *de minimis* argument. The plaster was in such poor condition that it required complete renewal. An award of £5,000 general damages (December 1990, Legal Action 17) was not disturbed. See too *Hussein v Mehman* [1992] 32 E.G. 59, Wood Green Trial Centre, where Assistant Recorder Sedley held that defective plaster on a bedroom ceiling was part of the "structure" for the purposes of s.11.

"age, character and prospective life of the dwelling-house"—(s.11(3))

3A–555   In *Dame Margaret Hungerford Charity Trustees v Beazeley* [1993] 29 E.G. 100, CA, the main allegation was that the landlords had failed to keep in repair a stone tile and wooden peg roof, probably 150 to 180 years old. The trial judge was satisfied that by 1989 the roof was in need of complete repair but that since that date the landlords had simply undertaken "running repairs" by replacing individual rotten pegs and slipped tiles. Preferring the evidence of the landlords' expert, and having regard to the age, character and prospective life of the dwelling, he held that the landlords were not in breach of the repairing covenant. Although replacing the roof would be ideal, it was no breach simply to keep patching up the old roof. The Court of Appeal dismissed

Paragraph numbers marked with a "+" can be found online and on CD.

the tenant's appeal, declining to interfere with the judge's findings of fact. See too *Newham LBC v Patel* (1984) 13 H.L.R. 77, CA; and *Murray v Birmingham City Council* (1988) 20 H.L.R. 39, CA, where the roof of a rented property built in 1908 had repeatedly failed, causing six incidents of rainwater penetration in six years. Although each had "sooner or later" been repaired by retiling or other minor work, the tenant pressed for complete replacement. The Court of Appeal dismissed the tenant's appeal against a county court finding in favour of the landlord. Slade L.J. said:

"I accept that in any case where a landlord or a tenant for that matter is under an obligation to keep in repair an old roof, the stage may come where the only practicable way of performing that covenant is to replace the roof altogether." (p.43)

However, dismissing the appeal, the Court of Appeal found that by the end of the tenancy in 1982 that stage had not been reached. If a tenant wanted to make good the assertion that the whole roof should be replaced, it would require evidence as to its general condition, its construction, the condition of battens and joists, the fixing of slates and expert evidence as to why piecemeal repair was no longer practicable.

On the other hand, a landlord was not entitled to rely upon s.11(3) where the property which was not near the end of its life, had been in disrepair for three years and would cost only £1,200 to repair (*McLean v Liverpool City Council* (1988) 20 H.L.R. 25; (1987) 283 E.G. 1395, CA).

"repair"

Section 11 obliges landlords to repair. The distinction between what is a repair and an improvement is therefore important. In *McDougall v Easington DC* (1989) 21 H.L.R. 310, CA (where the works involved reducing each property to its original concrete framework and then fitting new roofs, new windows and new internal fittings and retiling the floors), Mustill L.J. stated that:

3A–556

"... three different tests may be discerned, which may be applied separately or concurrently as the circumstances of the individual case may demand, but all are to be approached in the light of the nature and age of the premises, their condition when the tenant went into occupation, and the other express terms of the tenancy—

(i) whether the alterations went to the whole of the structure or only to a subsidiary part;

(ii) whether the effect of the alterations was to produce a building of a wholly different character than that which had been let;

(iii) what was the cost of the works in relation to the previous value of the building, and what was their effect on the value and lifespan of the building." (p.316)

See too *Wainwright v Leeds City Council* (1984) 13 H.L.R. 117; (1984) 270 E.G. 1289, CA, a case involving rising damp, where the Court of Appeal rejected the tenant's contention that the defendants were in breach of the Housing Act 1961 s.32 (now the Landlord and Tenant Act 1985 s.11) because they had failed to install a damp-proof course in a house which had originally been built without one. Landlords have no obligation to go beyond repairing the subject-matter of the demise (in that case a house with no damp-proof course); cf. *Elmcroft Developments Ltd v Tankersley-Sawyer* (1984) 15 H.L.R. 63; (1984) 270 E.G. 140, CA, where a landlord was obliged to repair a *defective* damp proof course.

In *Stent v Monmouth DC* (1987) 19 H.L.R. 269; (1987) 282 E.G. 705, CA, where the accumulation of water beneath the front door caused parts of the door to rot and required repeated replacement, the Court of Appeal held that the landlord was obliged to replace the existing door with a weatherproof door.

Proper working order

An installation for the supply of water is in proper working order if it is able to function under those conditions of supply that it is reasonable to anticipate will prevail. An unanticipated change in the nature of the supply of a utility may occur in a variety of circumstances. If a change is imposed deliberately because of some scientific or technical advance, the change is likely to be introduced in a manner and subject to conditions under which it is reasonable to expect customers to modify their installations to accomodate the change and business efficacy would suggest that the landlord's

3A–557

Paragraph numbers marked with a "+" can be found online and on CD.

HOUSING

duty to keep installations in proper working order would require him to make necessary modifications. In other circumstances, if the change is likely to be short-lived, the cost of modification might be disproportionate. Where the changed circumstances are likely to persist for a lengthy period it might seem wholly unreasonable for the landlord to leave his tenants deprived of a satisfactory supply of water for want of relatively modest expenditure on modifications. (*O'Connor v Old Etonians Housing Association Ltd* [2002] EWCA Civ 150; [2002] Ch. 295)—water pipes reduced from 1.25 inch diameter to 1 inch—unable to supply water during period when water pressure reduced).

The Court of Appeal has held that landlords were not obliged by the Housing Act 1961 s.32 (now the Landlord and Tenant Act 1985 s.11) to lag pipes which function satisfactorily in all but the most extreme weather conditions. Accordingly there was no liability on the part of landlords for damage caused by the bursting of an unlagged pipe in very severe cold (*Wycombe Health Authority v Barnett* (1982) 5 H.L.R. 84; (1982) 264 E.G. 619, CA).

The implied covenant to repair under s.11(1A)(b)(i) does not extend to installations located in parts of a building in which the lessor does not have an estate or interest, even if the lessor has an estate or interest in other parts of the same building (*Niazi Services Ltd v Van der Loo* [2004] EWCA Civ 53; [2004] 1 W.L.R. 1254—inadequate water pressure in top floor flat caused by works in ground floor/basement restaurant in which the mesne lessor of the top floor had no interest).

Specific performance

3A–558   See s.17, below.

Damages

3A–559   "The object of awarding damages against a landlord for breach of his covenant to repair is not to punish the landlord but, so far as money can, to restore the tenant to the position he would have been in had there been no breach. This object will not be acheived by applying one set of rules to all cases regardless of particular circumstances of the case. The facts of each case must be looked at carefully to see what damage the tenant has suffered and how he may be fairly compensated by a monetary award."

per Griffiths L.J. in *Calabar Properties Ltd v Stitcher* [1984] 1 W.L.R. 287; [1983] 3 All E.R. 759 at 768, CA).

In *Wallace v Manchester City Council* (1998) 30 H.L.R. 1111; *The Times*, July 23, 1998; [1998] 41 E.G. 223, CA, CA, Morritt L.J. said:

"First, the question in all cases of damages for breach of obligation to repair is what sum will, so far as money can, place the tenant in the position he would have been in if the obligation to repair had been duly performed by the landlord. Second, the answer to that question inevitably involves a comparison of the property as it was for the period when the landlord was in breach of his obligation with what it would have been if the obligation had been performed. Third, for the periods when the tenant remained in occupation of the property, notwithstanding the breach of the obligation to repair the loss to him requiring compensation is the loss of comfort and convenience which results from living in a property which was not in the state of repair it ought to have been if the landlord performed his obligation ... Fourth, if the tenant does not remain in occupation but, being entitled to do so, is forced by the landlord's failure to repair to sell or sublet the property he may diminution of the price or recoverable rent occasioned by the landlord's failure to perform his covenant to repair."

He continued:

"... the sum required to compensate the tenant for the distress and inconvenience ... may be ascertained in a number of different ways, including but not limited to a notional reduction in the rent. Some judges may prefer to use that method alone ... some may prefer a global award for discomfort and inconvenience ... and others may prefer a mixture of the two ... But, in my judgment, they are not bound to assess damages separately under heads of both diminution in value and discomfort because in cases within the third proposition those heads are alternative ways of expressing the same concept."

Morritt L.J. said that the source of the money with which to pay the rent (e.g. housing benefit) is irrelevant to the extent of the discomfort and inconvenience suffered by the tenant and what would be proper monetary compensation for it.

Paragraph numbers marked with a "+" can be found online and on CD.

In *Shine v English Churches Housing Group* [2004] EWCA Civ 434; [2004] H.L.R. 42, the Court of Appeal stated that although the guidelines in *Wallace* "are not to be applied in a mechanistic or dogmatic way", and that there are cases "where the level of distress or inconvenience experienced by a tenant may require an award in excess of the level of rent payable" if an award is made in excess of the rent payable, "clear reasons need to be given". The Court referred to "a basic rule of thumb that—all other things being equal—the maximum award of damages should be the rental value of the premises." Where a global award of damages is made, it should be cross-checked against the annual rent to ensure that damages are neither too high nor too low.

On the other hand, in *Earle v Charalambous* [2006] EWCA Civ 1090; [2007] H.L.R. 8; it was said:

"A long-lease of a residential property is not only a home, but is also a valuable property asset. Distress and inconvenience caused by disrepair are not free-standing heads of claim, but are symptomatic of interference with the lessee's enjoyment of that asset. If the lessor's breach of covenant has the effect of depriving the lessee of that enjoyment, wholly or partially, for a significant period, a notional judgment of the resulting reduction in rental value is likely to be the most appropriate starting point for assessment of damages. Generally, this reduction will not be capable of precise estimation; ... it will be a matter for the judgment for the court, rather than for expert valuation evidence."

The fact that offers of alternative accommodation have been made but not taken up "cannot ... affect the question of damages" (per Parker L.J. in *Lubren v Lambeth LBC* (1988) 20 H.L.R. 165, CA).

Even if a landlord is not at fault in carrying out its repairing obligations, there is an obligation to reinstate the property after completion of works to a reasonable standard, and that includes putting right damage done to decorations (*Bradley v Chorley BC* (1985) 17 H.L.R. 305, CA). See too *McGreal v Wake* (1984) 269 E.G. 1254; (1984) 13 H.L.R. 107, CA.

Damages may include loss of rent where it was foreseeable that the tenant might sub-let (*Mira v Aylmer Square Investments Ltd* [1990] 22 E.G. 61; (1990) 22 H.L.R. 182, CA).

Registration of a fair rent does not preclude recovery of damages for breach of repairing covenants (*Sturolson and Co v Mauroux* (1988) 20 H.L.R. 332, CA).

As to *quantum* generally, see *Brent LBC v Murphy (Carmel)* (1996) 28 H.L.R. 203, CA; *Chiodi v De Marney* [1988] 41 E.G. 80; (1989) 21 H.L.R. 6, CA; *Davies v Peterson* (1989) 21 H.L.R. 63, CA; *Dean v Ainley* [1987] 3 All E.R. 748, CA; *Elmcroft Developments Ltd v Tankersley-Sawyer* (1984) 15 H.L.R. 63, CA; *Taylor v Knowsley BC* (1985) 17 H.L.R. 376, CA; and *Televantos v McCulloch* [1991] 19 E.G. 18; (1991) 23 H.L.R. 412, CA.

Repairing obligations and the ECHR

In *Lee v Leeds City Council* [2002] EWCA Civ 6; [2002] 1 W.L.R. 1488; [2002] All E.R. 124, CA, the Court of Appeal held that Human Rights Act 1998 s.6 imposes an obligation on local authority landlords to take steps to ensure that the condition of dwelling houses which they let for social housing are such that the tenants' rights to respect for home and family life under art.8 are not infringed. However rights under art.8 are not unqualified (*Southwark LBC v Tanner* [2001] 1 A.C. 1) and there is nothing in the Strasbourg jurisprudence to support the proposition that s.6 and art.8 impose a general and unqualified obligation on local authorities in relation to the condition of their housing stock. There might though be cases where a local authority that had let a property that was unfit for human habitation or prejudicial to health would be in breach of the positive duty imposed by s.6 and art.8. In this case there was no such breach of duty. The conditions complained of did not seem to be sufficiently serious (*Lopez Ostra v Spain* (1994) 20 E.H.R.R. 277). **3A–560**

Restriction on contracting out of s.11

3A–561

12.—(1) A covenant or agreement, whether contained in a lease to which section 11 applies or in an agreement collateral to such a lease, is void in so far as it purports—

> (a) to exclude or limit the obligations of the lessor or the immunities of the lessee under that section, or

Paragraph numbers marked with a "+" can be found online and on CD.

HOUSING

(b) to authorise any forfeiture or impose on the lessee any penalty, disability or obligation in the event of his enforcing or relying upon those obligations or immunities,

unless the inclusion of the provision was authorised by the county court.

(2) The county court may, by order made with the consent of the parties, authorise the inclusion in a lease, or in an agreement collateral to a lease, of provisions excluding or modifying in relation to the lease, the provisions of section 11 with respect to the repairing obligations of the parties if it appears to the court that it is reasonable to do so, having regard to all the circumstances of the case, including the other terms and conditions of the lease.

"lease"

3A–562   See s.16.

"lessor"

3A–563   See s.16.

"lessee"

3A–564   See s.16.

Leases to which s.11 applies: general rule

3A–565   **13.**—(1) Section 11 (repairing obligations) applies to a lease of a dwelling-house granted on or after 24th October 1961 for a term of less than seven years.

(2) In determining whether a lease is one to which section 11 applies—

(a) any part of the term which falls before the grant shall be left out of account and the lease shall be treated as a lease for a term commencing with the grant,

(b) a lease which is determinable at the option of the lessor before the expiration of seven years from the commencement of the term shall be treated as a lease for a term of less than seven years, and

(c) a lease (other than a lease to which paragraph (b) applies) shall not be treated as a lease for a term of less than seven years if it confers on the lessee an option for renewal for a term which, together with the original term, amounts to seven years or more.

(3) This section has effect subject to—

section 14 (leases to which section 11 applies: exceptions), and

section 32(2) (provisions not applying to tenancies within Part II of the Landlord and Tenant Act 1954).

"dwelling-house"

3A–566   See s.16.

"lease"

3A–567   See s.16.

Paragraph numbers marked with a "+" can be found online and on CD.

"lessor"

See s.16.

3A–568

"lessee"

See s.16.

3A–569

"for a term of less than seven years"

In *Brikom Investments Ltd v Seaford* [1981] 1 W.L.R. 863; [1981] 2 All E.R. 783, CA, a **3A–570** tenant was allowed into possession in accordance with an agreement for a lease for a term of seven years on November 1. The lease was executed some days later but provided for a term of seven years commencing on November 1. The landlord contended that the Housing Act 1961 s.32 (now the Landlord and the Tenant Act 1985 s.11) did not apply because of the reference in s.32(1) to any lease "for a term of less than seven years". The Court of Appeal held that, in view of s.33(5) (now s.13(2)(a)), for the purposes of s.32 the commencement of the term was November 1 (*cf. Roberts v Church Commissioners* [1972] 1 Q.B. 278, CA). However, the landlord was estopped from denying that s.32 (now s.11) applied where the rent officer had registered a rent on the basis that the implied covenant applied, the rent registered had not been challenged or rectified and the landlord had been receiving the higher rent (*cf. Demetriou v Poolaction Ltd* [1991] 25 E.G. 113, CA). See too *Tomkins v Basildon DC* [2002] EWCA Civ 876; [2002] 43 E.G. 206.

Leases to which s.11 applies: exceptions

14.—(1) Section 11 (repairing obligations) does not apply to a new **3A–571** lease granted to an existing tenant, or to a former tenant still in possession, if the previous lease was not a lease to which section 11 applied (and, in the case of a lease granted before 24th October 1961, would not have been if it had been granted on or after that date).

(2) In subsection (1)—

"existing tenant" means a person who is when, or immediately before, the new lease is granted, the lessee under another lease of the dwelling-house;

"former tenant still in possession" means a person who—

(a) was the lessee under another lease of the dwelling-house which terminated at some time before the new lease was granted, and

(b) between the termination of that other lease and the grant of the new lease was continuously in possession of the dwelling-house or of the rents and profits of the dwelling-house; and

"the previous lease" means the other lease referred to in the above definitions.

(3) Section 11 does not apply to a lease of a dwelling-house which is a tenancy of an agricultural holding within the meaning of the Agricultural Holdings Act 1986 and in relation to which that Act applies or to a farm business tenancy within the meaning of the Agricultural Tenancies Act 1995.

(4) Section 11 does not apply to a lease granted on or after 3rd October 1980 to—

a local authority,

a National Park authority

a new town corporation,

an urban development corporation,

Paragraph numbers marked with a "+" can be found online and on CD.

the Development Board for Rural Wales,

a registered social landlord,

a co-operative housing association, or

an educational institution or other body specified, or of a class specified, by regulations under section 8 of the Rent Act 1977or paragraph 8 of Schedule I to the Housing Act 1988 (bodies making student lettings).

a housing action trust established under Part III of the Housing Act 1988.

(5) Section 11 does not apply to a lease granted on or after 3rd October 1980 to—

(a) Her Majesty in right of the Crown (unless the lease is under the management of the Crown Estate Commissioners), or

(b) a government department or a person holding in trust for Her Majesty for the purposes of a government department.

3A–572 Note —Amended by the Agricultural Holdings Act 1986 Sch.14, para.64; the Housing Act 1988 s.116; the Local Government and Housing Act 1989 Sch.11, para.89; the Housing Act 1996 (Consequential Provisions) Order 1996 (SI 1996/2325) Sch.2, para.16; and the Agricultural Tenancies Act 1995 Sch.

"dwelling-house"

3A–573 See s.16.

"lease"

3A–574 See s.16.

"lessor"

3A–575 See s.16.

"lessee"

3A–576 See s.16.

"local authority"

3A–577 See s.38.

"new town corporation"

3A–578 See s.38.

"registered social landlord"

3A–579 See s.38, the Housing Act 1985 s.5, and the Housing Act 1996 ss.1– 7.

"co-operative housing association"

3A–580 See s.38 and the Housing Associations Act 1985 s.1 which defines a housing association as a "society, body of trustees or company (a) which is established for the purpose of, or amongst whose objects or powers are included those of, providing, constructing, improving or managing, or facilitating or encouraging the construction or improvement of, housing accommodation, and (b) which does not trade for profit or whose constitution or rules prohibit the issue of capital with interest or dividend exceeding such rate as may be prescribed by the Treasury, whether with or without differentiation between share and loan capital" and a co-operative housing association as "a fully mutual housing association which is a friendly society registered under the Industrial and Provident Societies Act 1965..."

Jurisdiction of county court

3A–581 **15.** The county court has jurisdiction to make a declaration that

Paragraph numbers marked with a "+" can be found online and on CD.

section 11 (repairing obligations) applies, or does not apply, to a lease—

    (a) whatever the net annual value of the property in question, and

    (b) notwithstanding that no other relief is sought than a declaration.

Meaning of "lease" and related expressions

16. In sections 11 to 15 (repairing obligations in short leases)—   **3A–582**

    (a) "lease" does not include a mortgage term;

    (b) "lease of a dwelling-house" means a lease by which a building or part of a building is let wholly or mainly as a private residence, and "dwelling-house" means that building or part of a building;

    (c) "lessee" and "lessor" mean, respectively, the person for the time being entitled to the term of a lease and to the reversion expectant on it.

Specific performance of landlord's repairing obligations

17.—(1) In proceedings in which a tenant of a dwelling alleges a   **3A–583** breach on the part of his landlord of a repairing covenant relating to any part of the premises in which the dwelling is comprised, the court may order specific performance of the covenant whether or not the breach relates to a part of the premises let to the tenant and notwithstanding any equitable rule restricting the scope of the remedy, whether on the basis of a lack of mutuality or otherwise.

    (2) In this section—

    (a) "tenant" includes a statutory tenant,

    (b) in relation to a statutory tenant the reference to the premises let to him is to the premises of which he is a statutory tenant,

    (c) "landlord", in relation to a tenant, includes any person against whom the tenant has a right to enforce a repairing covenant, and

    (d) "repairing covenant" means a covenant to repair, maintain, renew, construct or replace any property.

"dwelling"
See s.38.   **3A–584**

"landlord"
See s.36.   **3A–585**

"statutory tenant"
See s.37 and the Rent Act 1977 s.2, and the Rent (Agriculture) Act 1976.   **3A–586**

"tenant"
See s.36.   **3A–587**
See too *Jeune v Queen's Cross Properties* [1974] Ch. 97; [1973] 3 W.L.R. 378; [1973] 3 All E.R. 97.

For ss.18 to 39 of the Landlord and Tenant Act 1985 (see Arrangement) plus any

Paragraph numbers marked with a "+" can be found online and on CD.

HOUSING

related commentary see paragraphs 3A–588+ to 3A–707+ on White Book on Westlaw UK or the Civil Procedure CD.

Landlord and Tenant Act 1987

3A–707.1

(1987 c.31)

 **Paragraph numbers marked with a "+" denote content that is available on White
Book on Westlaw UK or the Civil Procedure CD.**

Housing Act 1988

3A–722

(1988 c.50)

Paragraph numbers marked with a "+" can be found online and on CD.

PART I

RENTED ACCOMMODATION
CHAPTER I

ASSURED TENANCIES

MEANING OF ASSURED TENANCY ETC.

Assured tenancies

1.—(1) A tenancy under which a dwelling-house is let as a separate **3A–723**

Paragraph numbers marked with a "+" can be found online and on CD.

dwelling is for the purposes of this Act an assured tenancy if and so long as—

    (a) the tenant or, as the case may be, each of the joint tenants is an individual; and

    (b) the tenant or, as the case may be, at least one of the joint tenants occupies the dwelling-house as his only or principal home; and

    (c) the tenancy is not one which, by virtue of subsection (2) or subsection (6) below, cannot be an assured tenancy.

(2) Subject to subsection (3) below, if and so long as a tenancy falls within any paragraph in Part I of Schedule 1 to this Act, it cannot be an assured tenancy; and in that Schedule—

    (a) "tenancy" means a tenancy under which a dwelling-house is let as a separate dwelling;

    (b) Part II has effect for determining the rateable value of a dwelling-house for the purposes of Part I; and

    (c) Part III has effect for supplementing paragraph 10 in Part I.

(2A) The Secretary of State may by order replace any amount referred to in paragraphs 2 and 3A of Schedule 1 to this Act by such amount as is specified in the order; and such an order shall be made by statutory instrument which shall be subject to annulment in pursuance of a resolution of either House of Parliament.

(3) Except as provided in Chapter V below, at the commencement of this Act, a tenancy—

    (a) under which a dwelling-house was then let as a separate dwelling, and

    (b) which immediately before that commencement was an assured tenancy for the purposes of sections 56 to 58 of the Housing Act 1980 (tenancies granted by approved bodies),

shall become an assured tenancy for the purposes of this Act.

(4) In relation to an assured tenancy falling within subsection (3) above—

    (a) Part I of Schedule 1 to this Act shall have effect, subject to subsection (5) below, as if it consisted only of paragraphs 11 and 12; and

    (b) sections 56 to 58 of the Housing Act 1980 (and Schedule 5 to that Act) shall not apply after the commencement of this Act.

(5) In any case where—

    (a) immediately before the commencement of this Act the landlord under a tenancy is a fully mutual housing association, and

    (b) at the commencement of this Act the tenancy becomes an assured tenancy by virtue of subsection (3) above,

then, so long as that association remains the landlord under that tenancy (and under any statutory periodic tenancy which arises on the coming to an end of that tenancy), paragraph 12 of Schedule 1 to this Act shall have effect in relation to that tenancy with the omission of sub-paragraph (1)(h).

(6) [...]

(7) [...]

Note —Subsection (2A) added by the References to Rating (Housing) Regulations 1990 (SI 1990/434) para.27. Subsections (6) and (7) repealed by the Housing Act 1996 Sch.19, Pt VIII.

3A–724

"tenant"

See s.45.

3A–725

"dwelling-house"

See s.45.

3A–726

"let"

See s.45.

3A–727

"fully mutual housing association"

See the Housing Associations Act 1985 s.1, which defines a housing association as a "society, body of trustees or company (a) which is established for the purpose of, or amongst whose objects or powers are included those of, providing, constructing, improving or managing, or facilitating or encouraging the construction or improvement of, housing accommodation, and (b) which does not trade for profit or whose constitution or rules prohibit the issue of capital with interest or dividend exceeding such rate as may be prescribed by the treasury, whether with or without differentiation between share and loan capital".

3A–728

"A tenancy under which a dwelling-house is let"

Section 1 refers to: "A tenancy under which a dwelling-house is let ..." Therefore, there can only be an assured tenancy if there is a tenancy. There can be no such thing as an "assured licence". For the distinction between tenancies and licences see, e.g. *Street v Mountford* [1985] A.C. 809; [1985] 2 W.L.R. 877; [1985] 2 All E.R. 289, HL; *AG Securities v Vaughan* and *Antoniades v Villiers and Bridger* [1990] 1 A.C. 417; [1988] 3 W.L.R. 1205; [1988] 3 All E.R. 1058, HL; *Duke v Wynne* [1989] 3 All E.R. 130, CA; *Hadjiloucas v Crean* [1988] 1 W.L.R. 1006; [1987] 3 All E.R. 1008, CA; *Nicolau v Pitt* (1989) 21 H.L.R. 487; [1989] 21 E.G. 71, CA; *Aslan v Murphy* [1989] 3 All E.R. 130, CA; and *Crancour Ltd v Da Silvaesa* (1986) 18 H.L.R. 265; (1986) 78 E.G. 618, CA.

3A–729

Section 1 contains four pre-requisites for the creation of an assured tenancy: The dwelling-house must be let as a separate dwelling. This is the well known phrase which appears in the Rent Act 1977 s.1. If a tenancy comprises two or more separate units of accommodation which are let together to a tenant, there can be no assured tenancy (*St Catherine's College v Dorling* [1980] 1 W.L.R. 66; and *Kavanagh v Lyroudias* [1985] 1 All E.R. 560). See also *Central YMCA Housing Association v Goodman* (1992) 24 H.L.R. 109, CA, where Dillon L.J. referring to a furnished twin-bedded room in a hostel with a private bathroom and lavatory en suite, said that "... this room was no more a dwelling-house than a hotel room is a dwelling-house"); *Central YMCA Housing Association v Saunders* (1990) 23 H.L.R. 212, CA; *Parkins v Westminister CC* (1998) 30 H.L.R. 894, CA; and *R. v Rent Officer for Nottingham Ex p. Allen* (1985) 17 H.L.R. 481.

The word "dwelling" is not a term of art with a specialised legal meaning. It is: "the place where [an occupier] lives and to which he returns and which forms the centre of his existence...No doubt he will sleep there and usually eat there; he will often prepare at least some of his meals there".

However there is no legislative requirement that cooking facilities must be available for premises to qualify as a dwelling. In deciding whether an occupant has security of tenure: "The first step is to identify the subject-matter of the tenancy agreement. If this is a house or part of a house of which the tenant has exclusive possession with no element of sharing, the only question is whether, at the date when proceedings were brought, it was the tenant's

Paragraph numbers marked with a "+" can be found online and on CD.

home. If so, it was his dwelling ... The presence or absence of cooking facilities in the part of the premises of which the tenant has exclusive occupation is not relevant."

(See *Uratemp Ventures Ltd v Collins and Carrell* [2001] UKHL 43; [2002] 1 A.C. 301; [2001] 3 W.L.R. 806; [2002] 1 All E.R. 46, HL).

Section 3 provides that if a tenant enjoys exclusive occupation of some rented accommodation with a right to share other accommodation with other people, apart from the landlord, the mere fact that the other accommodation is shared, does not prevent the tenant from occupying the accommodation which is not shared as a separate dwelling (compare the Rent Act 1977 s.22 and the Housing Act 1985 s.79).

(b) The tenant, or if there are joint tenants, each of the joint tenants, must be individuals. A genuine letting to a company can never be an assured tenancy. See, e.g. *Hiller v United Dairies* [1934] 1 K.B. 57, CA; *Hilton v Plustitle Ltd* [1989] 1 W.L.R. 149; [1988] 3 All E.R. 1051, CA; *Kaye v Massbetter Ltd and Kanter* (1992) 24 H.L.R. 28, CA; and *Estavest Investments Ltd v Commercial Express Travel Ltd* (1989) 21 H.L.R. 106, CA and *Eaton Square Properties Ltd v O'Higgins* (2001) 33 H.L.R. 68, CA. In such cases, the tenancy is unprotected and may come to an end by effluxion of time or may be terminated by service of a notice to quit. If this occurs, a landlord who brings possession proceedings is automatically entitled to possession without having to prove any ground for possession.

(c) The tenant, or if there are joint tenants, at least one of them, must occupy the premises as his or her only or principal home (*cf.* the Housing Act 1985 s.81 ("as his only or principal home"), the Leasehold Reform Act 1967 s.1 ("as his residence") and the Rent Act 1977 s.2 ("as his residence"). It is not possible for assured tenants to maintain assured tenancies in more than one home at the same time, although there is no reason why an assured tenant should not be temporarily absent from the premises in question provided that they remain his or her only or main home. Tenancies cease to be assured if tenants cease to occupy premises as their only or principal home (*cf. Sutton LBC v Swann* (1986) 18 H.L.R. 140, CA).

In order to maintain a "home" a tenant need not be physically resident, so long as there is an intention to return after a temporary absence and some physical sign of continued occupation (e.g. furniture and possessions in the property). Two houses can be occupied as a home at the same time—*Crawley BC v Sawyer* (1988) 20 H.L.R. 98, CA, where a council tenant went to live with his "girlfriend" for a period of approximately one and a half years during which time the gas and electricity supplies to the premises which he rented from the council were cut off. Held that the rented premises remained his principal home throughout the period. However, if two houses are occupied, they cannot both be assured tenancies.

It is possible for a tenant to lose security of tenure by reason of non-occupation but to regain it by re-occupying the property before service of a notice to quit—see *Hussey v Camden LBC* (1995) 27 H.L.R. 5, CA, where, as the tenant was occupying the property as his only or principal home at the time of service of the notice to quit, the Court of Appeal held that the earlier loss of security was irrelevant.

Subletting of the whole of premises means that any tenancy cases to be assured—see *Ujima Housing v Ansah* (1998) 30 H.L.R. 831, CA; *Jennings v Epping Forest DC* (1993) 25 H.L.R. 241, CA; *Poland v Cadogan* [1980] 3 All E.R. 544, CA (Leasehold Reform Act 1993 s.93(2)); *Muir Group Housing Association Ltd v Thornley* (1993) 25 H.L.R. 89, CA; and *Brent LBC v Cronin* (1997) 30 H.L.R. 43, CA, *cf. Waltham Forest CBHA v Fanning* July 2001 Legal Action 33, (2001) March 12, QBD and *Merton LBC v Salama* (1989) CAT No.89/169; June 1989, *Legal Action 25*, CA (parting with possession of part of premises). Parting with possession is not to be inferred simply from the fact that another person has been allowed to use and occupy a tenant's home during his temporary absence (*Lam Kee Ying v Lam Shes Tong* [1975] A.C. 247, PC).

(d) A tenancy cannot be an assured tenancy if any of the exceptions listed in Sch.1 applies (see below). Many of these exceptions are similar to those set out in the Rent Act 1977 Pt I.

Paragraph numbers marked with a "+" can be found online and on CD.

Note also that a tenancy granted by a private landlord under arrangements made by a local housing authority in accordance with their functions under Housing Act 1996 ss.188, 190, 200 or 204 (interim duties towards the homeless) cannot be an assured tenancy within twelve months of the date of notification of the local authority's decision or the determination of any Housing Act 1996 s.202 review or s.204 appeal, unless the landlord notifies the tenant that the tenancy is to be an assured shorthold tenancy—see Housing Act 1996 s.209 as substituted by Homelessness Act 2002 Sch.1, para.19.

Letting of a dwelling-house together with other land

2.—(1) If, under a tenancy, a dwelling-house is let together with other land then, for the purposes of this Part of this Act— **3A–730**

(a) if and so long as the main purpose of the letting is the provision of a home for the tenant or, where there are joint tenants, at least one of them, the other land shall be treated as part of the dwelling-house; and

(b) if and so long as the main purpose of the letting is not as mentioned in paragraph (a) above, the tenancy shall be treated as not being one under which a dwelling-house is let as a separate dwelling.

(2) Nothing in subsection (1) above affects any question whether a tenancy is precluded from being an assured tenancy by virtue of any provision of Schedule 1 to this Act.

"tenancy"
See s.45.   **3A–731**

"tenant"
See s.45.   **3A–732**

"dwelling-house"
See s.45.   **3A–733**

"let"
See s.45.   **3A–734**

Tenant sharing accommodation with persons other than landlord

3.—(1) Where a tenant has the exclusive occupation of any accommodation (in this section referred to as "the separate accommodation") and— **3A–735**

(a) the terms as between the tenant and his landlord on which he holds the separate accommodation include the use of other accommodation (in this section referred to as "the shared accommodation") in common with another person or other persons, not being or including the landlord, and

(b) by reason only of the circumstances mentioned in paragraph (a) above, the separate accommodation would not, apart from this section, be a dwelling-house let on an assured tenancy,

the separate accommodation shall be deemed to be a dwelling-house let on an assured tenancy and the following provisions of this section shall have effect.

Paragraph numbers marked with a "+" can be found online and on CD.

(2) For the avoidance of doubt it is hereby declared that where, for the purpose of determining the rateable value of the separate accommodation, it is necessary to make an apportionment under Part II of Schedule 1 to this Act, regard is to be had to the circumstances mentioned in subsection (1)(a) above.

(3) While the tenant is in possession of the separate accommodation, any term of the tenancy terminating or modifying, or providing for the termination or modification of, his right to the use of any of the shared accommodation which is living accommodation shall be of no effect.

(4) Where the terms of the tenancy are such that, at any time during the tenancy, the persons in common with whom the tenant is entitled to the use of the shared accommodation could be varied or their number could be increased, nothing in subsection (3) above shall prevent those terms from having effect so far as they relate to any such variation or increase.

(5) In this section "living accommodation" means accommodation of such a nature that the fact that it constitutes or is included in the shared accommodation is sufficient, apart from this section, to prevent the tenancy from constituting an assured tenancy of a dwelling-house.

"assured tenancy"

3A–736   See s.1.

"tenancy"

3A–737   See s.45.

"tenant"

3A–738   See s.45.

"dwelling-house"

3A–739   See s.45.

"let"

3A–740   See s.45.

Sharing accommodation

3A–741   Note *Miller v Eyo* (1999) 31 H.L.R. 306, CA where the terms of the plaintiff's tenancy were that she had exclusive use of her bedroom with shared use of a living room, kitchen and bathroom/WC. Initially the only other bedroom in the flat was occupied by another tenant, but when she moved out the landlord and her family moved into the other bedroom and started to share the other parts of the flat with the plaintiff. Following *Gray v Brown* (1993) 25 H.L.R. 144, CA the Court of Appeal held that in the absence of an express term in the tenancy that the landlord had the right to re-enter and occupy, the tenancy came with s.3 and was assured. For a landlord to avoid this situation, a landlord's right to re-enter must be "clear and specific".

Certain sublettings not to exclude any part of sub-lessor's premises from assured tenancy

3A–742   **4.**—(1) Where the tenant of a dwelling-house has sub-let a part but not the whole of the dwelling-house, then, as against his landlord or any superior landlord, no part of the dwelling-house shall be treated as excluded from being a dwelling-house let on an assured tenancy by reason only that the terms on which any person claiming under

Paragraph numbers marked with a "+" can be found online and on CD.

the tenant holds any part of the dwelling-house include the use of accommodation in common with other persons.

(2) Nothing in this section affects the rights against, and liabilities to, each other of the tenant and any person claiming under him, or of any two such persons.

"assured tenancy"
See s.1.   **3A–743**

"tenancy"
See s.45.   **3A–744**

"tenant"
See s.45.   **3A–745**

"dwelling-house"
See s.45.   **3A–746**

"let"
See s.45.   **3A–747**

SECURITY OF TENURE

Security of tenure

5.—(1) An assured tenancy cannot be brought to an end by the   **3A–748**
landlord except by obtaining an order of the court in accordance
with the following provisions of this Chapter or Chapter II below or,
in the case of a fixed term tenancy which contains power for the
landlord to determine the tenancy in certain circumstances, by the
exercise of that power and, accordingly, the service by the landlord
of a notice to quit shall be of no effect in relation to a periodic assured tenancy.

(2) If an assured tenancy which is a fixed term tenancy comes to
an end otherwise than by virtue of—

(a) an order of the court, or

(b) a surrender or other action on the part of the tenant,

then, subject to section 7 and Chapter II below, the tenant shall
be entitled to remain in possession of the dwelling-house let under
that tenancy and, subject to subsection (4) below, his right to possession shall depend upon a periodic tenancy arising by virtue of this
section.

(3) The periodic tenancy referred to in subsection (2) above is
one—

(a) taking effect in possession immediately on the coming to
an end of the fixed term tenancy;

(b) deemed to have been granted by the person who was
the landlord under the fixed term tenancy immediately
before it came to an end to the person who was then the
tenant under that tenancy;

(c) under which the premises which are let are the same
dwelling-house as was let under the fixed term tenancy;

Paragraph numbers marked with a "+" can be found online and on CD.

(d) under which the periods of the tenancy are the same as those for which rent was last payable under the fixed term tenancy; and

(e) under which, subject to the following provisions of this Part of this Act, the other terms are the same as those of the fixed term tenancy immediately before it came to an end, except that any term which makes provision for determination by the landlord or the tenant shall not have effect while the tenancy remains an assured tenancy;

(4) The periodic tenancy referred to in subsection (2) above shall not arise if, on the coming to an end of the fixed term tenancy, the tenant is entitled, by virtue of the grant of another tenancy, to possession of the same or substantially the same dwelling-house as was let to him under the fixed term tenancy.

(5) If, on or before the date on which a tenancy is entered into or is deemed to have been granted as mentioned in subsection (3)(b) above, the person who is to be the tenant under that tenancy—

(a) enters into an obligation to do any act which (apart from this subsection) will cause the tenancy to come to an end at a time when it is an assured tenancy, or

(b) executes, signs or gives any surrender, notice to quit or other document which (apart from this subsection) has the effect of bringing the tenancy to an end at a time when it is an assured tenancy,

the obligation referred to in paragraph (a) above shall not be enforceable or, as the case may be, the surrender, notice to quit or other document referred to in paragraph (b) above shall be of no effect.

(5A) Nothing in subsection (5) affects any right of pre-emption—

(a) which is exercisable by the landlord under a tenancy in circumstances where the tenant indicates his intention to dispose of the whole of his interest under the tenancy, and

(b) in pursuance of which the landlord would be required to pay, in respect of the acquisition of that interest, an amount representing its market value.

"Dispose" means dispose by assignment or surrender, and "acquisition" has a corresponding meaning.

(6) If, by virtue of any provision of this Part of this Act, Part I of Schedule 1 to this Act has effect in relation to a fixed term tenancy as if it consisted only of paragraphs 11 and 12, that Part shall have the like effect in relation to any periodic tenancy which arises by virtue of this section on the coming to an end of the fixed term tenancy.

(7) Any reference in this Part of this Act to a statutory periodic tenancy is a reference to a periodic tenancy arising by virtue of this section.

3A-749 *Note* —Amended by the Housing Act 2004 s.222(1) and (2). This section has also been amended by Housing and Regeneration Act 2008 Sch.15, Pt I. The amendment

Paragraph numbers marked with a "+" can be found online and on CD.

> (b) the amount of the rent under the statutory periodic tenancy shall be altered to accord with any adjustment specified by the committee;

but for the purposes of paragraph (b) above the committee shall not direct a date earlier than the date specified, in accordance with subsection (3)(b) above, in the notice referred to them.

(8) Nothing in this section requires a rent assessment committee to continue with a determination under subsection (4) above if the landlord and tenant give notice in writing that they no longer require such a determination or if the tenancy has come to an end.

"tenancy"

See s.45.   **3A–758**

"tenant"

See s.45.   **3A–759**

"fixed term tenancy"

See s.45.   **3A–760**

"landlord"

See s.45.   **3A–761**

"statutory periodic tenancy"

See s.5(7).   **3A–762**

"prescribed"

See s.45 and the Assured Tenancies and Agricultural Occupancies (Forms) Regula- **3A–763** tions 1997 (SI 1997/194). Note that a notice conforms with the regulations if it is "substantially to the same effect" as that prescribed (para.2).

Fixing of terms of statutory periodic tenancy

Section 6 provides a mechanism by which landlords and tenants may propose new **3A–764** terms for a statutory period tenancy which has come into existence by virtue of s.5. At any time up to one year after the former tenancy has come to an end, either party may serve a notice proposing new terms. The notice must be in "the prescribed form" (see Assured Tenancies and Agricultural Occupancies (Forms) Regulations 1997 (SI 1997/194). If either party wishes to object to the proposed new terms, he or she may apply to the Rent Assessment Committee to determine whether they are terms which "might reasonably be expected to be found in an assured periodic tenancy of the dwelling-house concerned" granted by a willing landlord. The RAC may specify an adjustment of rent, even if none is sought, to take into account any new terms, if they consider it appropriate.

An application to a RAC must be made within three months of service of the notice proposing new terms. If no application is made to the RAC within the three-month time limit, the proposed new terms automatically take effect.

Demotion because of anti-social behaviour

6A.—(1) This section applies to an assured tenancy if the landlord **3A–765** is a registered social landlord.

(2) The landlord may apply to a county court for a demotion order.

(3) A demotion order has the following effect—

> (a) the assured tenancy is terminated with effect from the date specified in the order;

Paragraph numbers marked with a "+" can be found online and on CD.

HOUSING

    (b) if the tenant remains in occupation of the dwelling-house after that date a demoted tenancy is created with effect from that date;

    (c) it is a term of the demoted tenancy that any arrears of rent payable at the termination of the assured tenancy become payable under the demoted tenancy;

    (d) it is also a term of the demoted tenancy that any rent paid in advance or overpaid at the termination of the assured tenancy is credited to the tenant's liability to pay rent under the demoted tenancy.

(4) The court must not make a demotion order unless it is satisfied—

    (a) that the tenant or a person residing in or visiting the dwelling-house has engaged or has threatened to engage in—

        (i) housing-related anti-social conduct, or

        (ii) conduct to which section 153B of the Housing Act 1996 (use of premises for unlawful purposes) applies, and

    (b) that it is reasonable to make the order.

(5) The court must not entertain proceedings for a demotion order unless—

    (a) the landlord has served on the tenant a notice under subsection (6), or

    (b) the court thinks it is just and equitable to dispense with the requirement of the notice.

(6) The notice must—

    (a) give particulars of the conduct in respect of which the order is sought;

    (b) state that the proceedings will not begin before the date specified in the notice;

    (c) state that the proceedings will not begin after the end of the period of twelve months beginning with the date of service of the notice.

(7) The date specified for the purposes of subsection (6)(b) must not be before the end of the period of two weeks beginning with the date of service of the notice.

(8) Each of the following has effect in respect of a demoted tenancy at the time it is created by virtue of an order under this section as it has effect in relation to the assured tenancy at the time it is terminated by virtue of the order—

    (a) the parties to the tenancy;

    (b) the period of the tenancy;

    (c) the amount of the rent;

    (d) the dates on which the rent is payable.

(9) Subsection (8)(b) does not apply if the assured tenancy was for a fixed term and in such a case the demoted tenancy is a weekly periodic tenancy.

Paragraph numbers marked with a "+" can be found online and on CD.

(10) If the landlord of the demoted tenancy serves on the tenant a statement of any other express terms of the assured tenancy which are to apply to the demoted tenancy such terms are also terms of the demoted tenancy.

(10A) In subsection (4)(a) 'housing-related anti-social conduct' has the same meaning as in section 153A of the Housing Act 1996.

(11) For the purposes of this section a demoted tenancy is a tenancy to which section 20B of the Housing Act 1988 applies.

Editorial note

This section was inserted by Anti-Social Behaviour Act 2003 s.14(4). It was amended **3A–766** by the Police and Justice Act 2006 Sch.14, para.15. It was brought into force in England on June 30, 2004 by the Anti-Social Behaviour Act 2003 (Commencement No.3 and Savings) Order 2004 (SI 2004/1502) (c.61). It was brought into force in Wales on 30 April 2005 by the Anti-Social Behaviour Act 2003 (Commencement No.4) (Wales) Order 2005 (SI 2005/1225) (w.83) (c.55). Section 6A provides that a demotion order ends an assured tenancy on a specified date. If the tenant remains in occupation, a new demoted assured shorthold tenancy begins on the same date. The court may only make the order if the tenant, another resident of or visitor to the tenant's home has behaved in a way which is capable of causing nuisance or annoyance or if such a person has used the premises for illegal purposes. In addition the court must be satisfied that it is reasonable to make the order. Sections 6A(3)(c) and (d) confirm that any rent owed or overpaid on the tenant's rent account under the secure tenancy should be transferred across to the new demoted tenancy. Section 6A(5) requires landlords to serve notice on assured tenants before issuing demotion proceedings, and specify the information which the notice should contain. However the court may dispense with the requirement for notice if it thinks it is just and equitable to do so. For consideration of the words "just and equitable" in other contexts, see the commentary at paras 3A–362 and 3A–795.

Registered social landlord

See Housing Act 1996 s.230, subss.1 to 3. **3A–767**

Housing Act 1988, s.20B

See para.3A–884. **3A–768**

Orders for possession

7.—(1) The court shall not make an order for possession of a **3A–769** dwelling-house let on an assured tenancy except on one or more of the grounds set out in Schedule 2 to this Act; but nothing in this Part of this Act relates to proceedings for possession of such a dwelling-house which are brought by a mortgagee, within the meaning of the Law of Property Act 1925, who has lent money on the security of the assured tenancy.

(2) The following provisions of this section have effect, subject to section 8 below, in relation to proceedings for the recovery of possession of a dwelling-house let on an assured tenancy.

(3) If the court is satisfied that any of the grounds in Part I of Schedule 2 to this Act is established then, subject to subsections (5A) and (6) below, the court shall make an order for possession.

(4) If the court is satisfied that any of the grounds in Part II of Schedule 2 to this Act is established, then, subject to subsections (5A) and (6) below, the court may make an order for possession if it considers it reasonable to do so.

Paragraph numbers marked with a "+" can be found online and on CD.

HOUSING

(5) Part III of Schedule 2 to this Act shall have effect for supplementing Ground 9 in that Schedule and Part IV of that Schedule shall have effect in relation to notices given as mentioned in Grounds 1 to 5 of that Schedule.

(5A) The court shall not make an order for possession of a dwelling-house let on an assured periodic tenancy arising under Schedule 10 to the Local Government and Housing Act 1989 on any of the following grounds, that is to say,—

(a) Grounds 1, 2 and 5 in Part I of Schedule 2 to this Act;

(b) Ground 16 in Part II of that Schedule; and

(c) if the assured periodic tenancy arose on the termination of a former 1954 Act tenancy, within the meaning of the said Schedule 10, Ground 6 in Part I of Schedule 2 to this Act.

(6) The court shall not make an order for possession of a dwelling-house to take effect at a time when it is let on an assured fixed term tenancy unless—

(a) the ground for possession is Ground 2 or Ground 8 in Part I of Schedule 2 to this Act or any of the grounds in Part II of that Schedule, other than Ground 9 or Ground 16; and

(b) the terms of the tenancy make provision for it to be brought to an end on the ground in question (whether that provision takes the form of a provision for re-entry, for forfeiture, for determination by notice or otherwise).

(7) Subject to the preceding provisions of this section, the court may make an order for possession of a dwelling-house on grounds relating to a fixed term tenancy which has come to an end; and where an order is made in such circumstances, any statutory periodic tenancy which has arisen on the ending of the fixed term tenancy shall end (without any notice and regardless of the period) on the day on which the order takes effect.

3A–770 Note —Amended by the Local Government and Housing Act 1989 Sch.11. This section has also been amended by Housing and Regeneration Act 2008 Sch.15, Pt I. The amendment relates to tolerated trespassers, but is not yet in force. The amendment is printed as part of the Housing and Regeneration Act 2008—see below.

"assured tenancy"
3A–771 See s.1.

"tenancy"
3A–772 See s.45.

"dwelling-house"
3A–773 See s.45.

"let"
3A–774 See s.45.

"fixed term"
3A–775 See s.45.

Paragraph numbers marked with a "+" can be found online and on CD.

Orders for possession

Like the Rent Act 1977 s.98 and the Housing Act 1985 s.84, this section provides **3A–776** that a court may only make an order for possession against an assured tenant if a ground for possession is made out. The grounds are specified in Sch.2 (see below). In addition, depending upon the ground relied upon, the landlord may have to satisfy the court that it is reasonable to make an order for possession. For reasonableness, see the commentary to the Housing Act 1985 s.84, above. As to reasonableness (s.7(4)) see *West Kent Housing Association v Davis* (1991) 31 H.L.R. 415, CA; *New Charter Housing (North) Ltd v Ashcroft* [2004] EWCA Civ 310; [2004] H.L.R. 36 , *Knowsley Housing Trust v McMullen* [2006] EWCA Civ 539; [2006] H.L.R. 43 and *Moat Housing Group South Ltd v Harris and Hartless* [2005] EWCA Civ 287; [2006] Q.B. 606; [2005] 3 W.L.R. 691; [2005] 4 All E.R. 1051.

In relation to claims for possession where registered social landlords rely upon arrears of rent, see the Protocol for Possession Claims Based on Rent Arrears at C11–001 which aims to encourage more pre-action contact between landlords and tenants and to enable court time to be used more effectively. Courts should take into account whether this protocol has been followed when considering what orders to make.

A fixed term assured or assured shorthold tenancy can be terminated during the fixed term if the landlord can prove that any of Grounds 2 (premises required by mortgagee), 8 (two months' rent arrears), 10 (rent arrears), 11 (persistent rent arrears), 12 (breach of obligation), 13 (deterioration), 14 (nuisance or annoyance) or 15 (deterioration of furniture) (see Sch.2) exist and provided that the tenancy contains a provision entitling the landlord to do so (see s.7(6)).

Mandatory grounds for possession

Where a landlord is seeking possession under one of the mandatory grounds for **3A–777** possession (e.g. Ground 8) during the fixed term of a tenancy, the court has no power to grant relief from forfeiture under the County Courts Act 1984 s.138. In *Artesian Residential Investments Ltd v Beck* [2000] Q.B. 541; [2000] 2 W.L.R. 357; [1999] 3 All E.R. 113, CA a fixed term assured tenancy agreement included a proviso for re-entry and determination if the rent was at any stage 14 days in arrears. The defendant fell into rent arrears before the expiry of the term and, the landlord brought possession proceedings relying on the Housing Act 1988 Sch.2, Grounds 8 and 10. A possession order was made, but the defendant later paid all the arrears and applied for suspension of the possession order, relying upon the relief from forfeiture provisions of the County Courts Act 1984 s.138. H.H.J. Mitchell granted relief but the Court of Appeal held that the Housing Act 1988 s.5(1) sets out the only routes for bringing an assured tenancy to an end. There is no need for a parallel claim for forfeiture to prevent the contractual tenancy continuing after the granting of an order for possession under the Act. By its express words, s.5(1) makes it abundantly clear that an order for possession brings a tenancy to an end. This construction is also borne out by s.7(7) which provides that, when the court makes an order for possession on grounds relating to a fixed term tenancy which has come to an end, any ensuing statutory periodic tenancy which arises on the ending of the fixed term tenancy ends (without any notice or regardless of the period) on the day on which the order takes effect.

Furthermore, s.7(3) is explicit, obliging the court mandatorily to make an order for possession if satisfied that any of the grounds in Sch.2 is established subject, inter alia, to s.6. Section 7(6)(b) does no more than require provision for, e.g., forfeiture to be included in the terms of the tenancy, and does not set up forfeiture as an independent ground for terminating the tenancy. As a matter of principle there is no room for applying s.138. As there is no exercise of a right of re-entry or forfeiture for non-payment of rent, its requirements are not met.

Difficulties may arise where arrears are due to housing benefit problems. In *North British Housing Association Limited v Matthews* [2004] EWCA Civ 1736; [2005] 1 W.L.R. 3133; [2005] 2 All E.R. 667, when dismissing appeals by tenants who had been refused adjournments in order to attempt to resolve housing benefit problems, the Court of Appeal held that:

- The court cannot be satisfied that the landlord is entitled to possession before the date of the hearing. The date of the hearing is the date when the claim is heard. It is not the date fixed for the hearing if, on that date, an adjournment is granted without a hearing taking place at all.

Paragraph numbers marked with a "+" can be found online and on CD.

- There is no doubt that it is a perfectly proper exercise of the court's discretion to adjourn, if a case has to be taken out of the list because there is no judge available, or because there has been over-listing, or because the defendant is prevented by ill-health from attending court.
- The court retains jurisdiction to grant an adjournment before it is satisfied that the landlord is entitled to possession. It may be a proper exercise of discretion to adjourn the hearing before the court is satisfied that the landlord is entitled to possession—e.g. where there is an arguable claim for damages which can be set-off against arrears; where the tenant shows that there is an arguable defence based on accord and satisfaction or estoppel arising from an agreement whereby the landlord accepts an offer by the tenant to pay off the current rent and arrears at a certain rate in return for not pursuing the claim for possession; or where the court is satisfied that there is a real chance that the tenant would be given permission to apply for judicial review of the landlord's decision to claim possession because of abuse of power.
- However it is not legitimate to adjourn to enable the tenant to pay off arrears and so defeat the claim for possession, unless there are exceptional circumstances—e.g. if a tenant is robbed on the way to court, or if a computer failure prevents the housing benefit authority from being able to pay benefit due until the day after the hearing date. The fact that arrears are attributable to maladministration on the part of the housing benefit authority is not an exceptional circumstance.
- Once the court has expressed the conclusion that it is satisfied that the landlord is entitled to possession, there is no power to grant an adjournment in any circumstances (seess.7(3) and 9(6)). The court cannot be "satisfied" within the meaning of s.9(6) until the judge has given a judgment and effect is given to that judgment in a perfected order of the court.
- The Housing Corporation may consider it wise to expand its advice in Regulatory Circular 07/04 (see November 2004 Legal Action 23) about the need for effective liaison between landlords and housing benefit departments right up to the time when a possession claim for rent arrears is heard.

In a case where an outright order for possession was made under Ground 8, but the landlord subsequently accepted the tenant's offer to pay rent and £100 per month off arrears, the Court of Appeal held that the landlord had done nothing to affect the legal relations between the parties. No new or different terms were come to. The landlord had no intention to create a new tenancy. The legal relations between the parties were governed by the terms of the order until the landlord took a position inconsistent with the order (*Stirling v Leadenhall Residential 2 Ltd* [2001] EWCA Civ 1011; [2001] 3 All E.R. 645; [2002] 1 W.L.R. 499, CA).

Where an order for possession is made under one of the mandatory grounds in the Housing Act 1988 Sch.2, then that ground should be stated on the face of the order. It is not proper to return to the judge at a later date to find out the grounds on which he made the order to find out if it was made in exercise of his discretion. Accordingly, where an order for possession under those grounds failed to state the ground on the face of the order, it could be regarded as having been granted on uncertain grounds, and in those circumstances, a court could revisit the exercise of discretion by the previous judge (*Diab v Countrywide Rentals 1 Plc Independent*, November 5, 2001 (c.S)).

Disability Discrimination Act 1995

3A–778   The effect of Disability Discrimination Act 1995 s.22(3)(c) is that it is unlawful to discriminate "by evicting [a] disabled person or subjecting him to any other detriment". Although unlawfulness under the Disability Discrimination Act is not a bar to a landlord seeking a possession order under the Housing Act, the fact that the eviction is unlawful and not justified is a highly relevant consideration for the s.7 discretion of whether or not to make a possession order. The Disability Discrimination Act contains its own code which requires a higher threshold than the Housing Act to justify an eviction (*North Devon Homes Ltd v Brazier* [2003] EWHC 574 (QB); [2003] 22 EG 141). In *Manchester CC v Romano* [2004] EWCA Civ 834; [2005] 1 W.L.R. 2775, the Court of Appeal, in a very thorough review of the legislation, stated that when a court considers the Disability Discrimination Act 1995 in the context of possession proceedings, the first matter which has to be determined is whether the person who complains about

Paragraph numbers marked with a "+" can be found online and on CD.

disability discrimination is a "disabled person" within the meaning of the Disability Discrimination (Meaning of Disability) Regulations 1996 (SI 1996/1455), Sch.1, ss.1-3 and the *Guidance on matters to be taking into account in determining questions relating to the definition of disability* issued by the Secretary of State. Secondly, the court should consider whether or not there has been discrimination— i.e. treating a disabled person less favourably for a reason which relates to the disabled person's disability. Thirdly, the court should consider whether the landlord's treatment of the tenant is justified. It is only justified if in the landlord's opinion the treatment (viz. the decision to set in motion proceedings for possession) is necessary in order not to endanger the health or safety of any of the people living in neighbouring houses and it is reasonable, in all the circumstances, for the landlord to hold that opinion. The landlord must prove that if it does not take this action someone's health or safety would be endangered. It does not have to prove that that person's health or safety has actually been damaged. However, in view of the decision in *Lewisham LBC v Malcolm* [2008] UKHL 43; [2008] 4 All E.R. 525, it will now be rare for tenants to be able to rely successfully on the Disability Discrimination Act when defending possession claims. Lord Scott stated that if the physical or mental condition that constitutes the tenant's disability has played no motivating part in the decision of the alleged discriminator to inflict on the disabled person the treatment complained of (e.g. bringing a possession claim), the alleged discriminator's reason for that treatment cannot relate to the disability.

"consent orders"

The jurisdiction of the court to make an order for possession under s.7 is limited. If **3A–779** the court is not satisfied that a ground under Sch.2 has been established it does not have jurisdiction to make the order. A court is under a duty to determine whether the relevant ground has been established, whether or not it has been raised by the parties. Where a court lacks jurisdiction, it cannot be conferred merely by consent. To confer jurisdiction an admission that a ground is satisfied, either express or implied, has to be clearly shown. Any consent order should clearly spell out in express terms the admission made by the tenant, or the court should ask the tenant what admission was being made, so that there can be no room for confusion or doubt in the future (*Baygreen Properties Ltd v Gil* [2002] EWCA Civ 1340; [2003] H.L.R. 12; [2002] 49 EG 126— "possession order by consent" approved by circuit judge set aside).

appeals on questions of reasonableness

Although County Courts Act 1984 s.77(6) excludes appeals against judges' findings **3A–780** of fact, it does not exclude, in a proper case, the possibility of an appeal against a finding of reasonableness *Castle Vale Housing Action Trust v Gallagher* [2001] EWCA Civ 944; (2001) 33 H.L.R. 810, CA.

ECHR art 8 and reasonableness

The Court of Appeal has doubted whether art.8 makes any difference to the way in **3A–781** which courts have always approached questions of the reasonableness of making possessions order. Article 8 does, however, reinforce the importance of only making an order depriving someone of his or her home in circumstances where a clear case is made out (*Castle Vale Housing Action Trust v Gallagher* [2001] EWCA Civ 944; (2001) 33 H.L.R. 810. See too *Newham LBC v Neal* [2003] EWCA Civ 541, February 25, 2003.) There is a need to find a fair balance and to protect the rights of the neighbours and other members of the public. (*Lambeth LBC v Howard* [2001] EWCA Civ 468; (2001) 33 H.L.R. 636. See too *Harrow LBC v Qazi* [2003] UKHL 43; [2004] 1 A.C. 983; [2003] 3 W.L.R. 792, where Lord Hope and Lord Scott said that contractual and property rights cannot be defeated by a defence based on art.8. See too *Newham LBC v Kibata* [2003] EWCA Civ 1785; [2004] H.L.R. 28 and *Bradney v Birmingham CC*; *Birmingham CC v McCann* [2003] EWCA Civ 1783; [2004] H.L.R. 27; *Lambeth LBC v Kay; Leeds CC v Price* [2006] UKHL 10; [2006] 2 A.C. 465; [2006] 2 W.L.R. 570; and *Birmingham City Council v Doherty* [2008] UKHL 57, July 30, 2008, [2008] 3 W.L.R. 636 but *cf. McCann v UK* App. No.19009/04, May 13, 2008, *The Times* May 23, 2008, noted at para.3A–192).

Forms of order

See Forms **N26A** (Order that Claimant have possession (Assured tenancies)) and **3A–782** **N28** (Order for Possession (possession suspended) (rented property)) and **N28A** (Or-

Paragraph numbers marked with a "+" can be found online and on CD.

der for possession (rented premises)(postponed)) as specified in the Practice Direction to CPR Pt 4, Table 3.

Breach of suspended possession orders

3A–783 Breach of a suspended order does not convert an assured tenant into a tolerated trespasser—see *Knowsley Housing Trust v White* [2008] UKHL 70, December 10, 2008.

Notice of proceedings for possession

3A–784 8.—(1) The court shall not entertain proceedings for possession of dwelling-house let on an assured tenancy unless—

    (a) the landlord or, in the case of joint landlords, at least one of them has served on the tenant a notice in accordance with this section and the proceedings are begun within the time limits stated in the notice in accordance with subsections (3) to (4B) below, or

    (b) the court considers it just and equitable to dispense with the requirement of such a notice.

(2) The court shall not make an order for possession on any of the grounds in Schedule 2 to this Act unless that ground and particulars of it are specified in the notice under this section; but the grounds specified in such a notice may be altered or added to with the leave of the court.

(3) A notice under this section is one in the prescribed form informing the tenant that—

    (a) the landlord intends to begin proceedings for possession of the dwelling-house on one or more of the grounds specified in the notice; and

    (b) those proceedings will not begin earlier than a date specified in the notice in accordance with subsections (4) to (4B) below; and

    (c) those proceedings will not begin later than twelve months from the date of service of the notice.

(4) If a notice under this section specifies in accordance with subsection (3)(a) above Ground 14 in Schedule 2 to this Act (whether with or without other grounds), the date specified in the notice as mentioned in subsection (3)(b) above shall not be earlier than the date of the service of the notice.

(4A) If a notice under this section specifies in accordance with subsection (3)(a) above, any of Grounds 1, 2, 5 to 7, 9 and 16 in Schedule 2 to this Act (whether without other grounds or with any ground other than Ground 14), the date specified in the notice as mentioned in subsection (3)(b) above shall not be earlier than—

    (a) two months from the date of service of the notice; and

    (b) if the tenancy is a periodic tenancy, the earliest date on which, apart from section 5(1) above, the tenancy could be brought to an end by a notice to quit given by the landlord on the same date as the date of service of the notice under this section.

(4B) In any other case, the date specified in the notice as mentioned in subsection (3)(b) above shall not be earlier than the

Paragraph numbers marked with a "+" can be found online and on CD.

expiry of the period of two weeks from the date of the service of the notice.

(5) The court may not exercise the power conferred by subsection (1)(b) above if the landlord seeks to recover possession on Ground 8 in Schedule 2 to this Act.

(6) Where a notice under this section—

    (a) is served at a time when the dwelling-house is let on a fixed term tenancy, or

    (b) is served after a fixed term tenancy has come to an end but relates (in whole or in part) to events occurring during that tenancy,

the notice shall have effect notwithstanding that the tenant becomes or has become tenant under a statutory periodic tenancy arising on the coming to an end of the fixed term tenancy.

Note —Amended by the Housing Act 1996 s.151.　　　　　　　**3A–785**

"assured tenancy"
See s.1.　　　　　　　　　　　　　　　　　　　　　　　**3A–786**

"landlord", "tenancy" and "tenant"
See s.45.　　　　　　　　　　　　　　　　　　　　　　**3A–787**

"dwelling-house"
See s.45.　　　　　　　　　　　　　　　　　　　　　　**3A–788**

"fixed term"
See s.45.　　　　　　　　　　　　　　　　　　　　　　**3A–789**

"prescribed"
See s.45 and the Assured Tenancies and Agricultural Occupancies (Forms) Regula- **3A–790** tions 1997 (SI 1997/194). For cases where landlords used old versions of prescribed forms, see: *Beckerman v Durling* (1983) 6 H.L.R. 87, CA; *Swansea CC v Hearn* (1991) 23 H.L.R. 284, CA; and *Tadema Holdings v Ferguson*, (2000) 32 H.L.R. 866; *The Times*, November 25, 1999, CA.

Notice of proceedings for possession
Before bringing possession proceedings against assured tenants, landlords must ei- **3A–791** ther serve a "notice of proceedings for possession" in accordance with the Housing Act 1988 s.8, or (in cases other than Ground 8) persuade the court that it is just and equitable to dispense with that requirement. The relevant form is contained in the Assured Tenancies and Agricultural Occupancies (Forms) Regulations 1997 (SI 1997/194). Note that a notice conforms with the regulations if it is "substantially to the same effect" as that prescribed (para.2). The relevant form (Form 3) states that the landlord must, inter alia, "give the full text ... of each ground which is being relied upon". It is similar to the form of notice used in connection with public sector secure tenancies (Housing Act 1985 s.83). Particulars of the grounds relied upon have to be included, as well as the ground itself.

Normally notices of intention to bring possession proceedings against assured tenants only have to give two weeks notice, but in the case of Grounds 1 (landlord's occupation), 2 (mortgagee seeking to exercise power of sale), 5 (ministers of religion), 6 (housing association wishing to demolish or reconstruct), 7 (death of tenant), 9 (suitable alternative accommodation) and 16 (letting in consequence of employment) (all set out below) at least two months notice or notice equivalent to the contractual period of the tenancy, whichever is longer, has to be given. If the landlord relies upon Ground 14 (nuisance or annoyance) proceedings may be begun immediately after service (s.8(4)).

Paragraph numbers marked with a "+" can be found online and on CD.

Proceedings must be begun within 12 months of service of the notice, otherwise a new notice must be served. There is no need for a landlord of an assured tenant to serve a notice to quit as well as a notice of intention to bring proceedings (s.5(1)).

As to assured tenancy agreements that provide that (1) before bringing possession proceedings landlords will give four weeks notice and (2) that they will only rely upon certain grounds for possession, see *North British HA v Sheridan* (2000) 32 H.L.R. 346; [2000] L & T.R. 115, CA.

Service of section 8 notices

3A–792   The word "service" in ss.8 and 13 is an ordinary English word connoting delivery of a document to a particular person. It carries no implication that the document has to be read, understood or indeed known by the recipient to have been delivered as long as delivery is to the correct address. Such meaning does not change according to the capacity of the intended recipient. See *Tadema Holdings v Ferguson* (2000) 32 H.L.R. 866, CA.

"ground"

3A–793   Although the full text of the ground as set out in the Housing Act 1988 Sch.2 may not have to be repeated verbatim, "the words used [must] set out fully the substance of the ground so that the notice is adequate to achieve the legislative purpose of the provision. That purpose ... is to give ... information ... to enable the tenant to consider what she should do and, with or without advice, to do that which is in her power and which will best protect her against the loss of her home" (*Mountain v Hastings* [1993] 29 E.G. 96; (1993) 25 H.L.R. 427 at 433, CA, where the notice was held to be defective because it had omitted the words "both at the date of service of the Notice...and at the date of the hearing" and the explanation that " 'rent' means rent lawfully due from the tenant"). In *Mountain v Hastings* the Court of Appeal also held that the words in s.8(2) which allow a court to alter or add to the grounds specified in a notice assume that there is a valid notice and are solely directed to the possibility of adding to or deleting grounds.

particulars of the ground (s.8(2))

3A–794   See also the commentary to the Housing Act 1985 s.83.

The Court of Appeal has held that the particulars in a notice from a landlord to a tenant relying upon Ground 8 comply with the Housing Act 1988 s.8 provided that "it is made clear...that more than [two] months rent is at the date of that notice unpaid and due and provided also that in some way or other that notice makes it clear either how much, or how the tenant can ascertain how much, is alleged to be due". It is not necessary for the notice to contain a schedule of the arrears (*Marath v MacGillivray* (1996) 28 H.L.R. 484, CA, where the notice stated, as particulars of the arrears: "At a meeting between the landlord and tenant on July 24, 1994 the arrears were agreed at £103.29 ... Since that date no payments of rent have been made..." without giving a figure for the arrears as at the date of the notice was given). In *Marath* the Court of Appeal also indicated that under s.8(2) a court may allow particulars to be added if they have not been given earlier.

"the court considers it just and equitable to dispense with the requirement of such a notice" (s.8(1)(b))

3A–795   See the commentary to the Housing Act 1985 s.83(1)(b). Note that there is no power to dispense with service of a notice if Ground 8 (i.e. 8 weeks' arrears) is relied upon.

It is "obviously only in relatively exceptional cases where the court should be prepared to dispense with a...notice" (*Braintree DC v Vincent* [2004] EWCA Civ 415—a case where the Court of Appeal held that a judge was entitled to dispense with a statutory notice on unusual facts. A notice would have been of no benefit to the tenant—indeed it would have been to her disadvantage because it would have postponed the date for possession and added to her liability for rent). In *Kelsey HA v King* (1995) 28 H.L.R. 270, CA, it was held that in deciding whether it is just and equitable to dispense with service a court should "weigh all the factors before it" and "take all the circumstances into account, both from the view of the landlord and the tenant". In many cases, the fact that tenants have not been given "an opportunity to put right what it is

Paragraph numbers marked with a "+" can be found online and on CD.

the Family Law Act 1996 is in occupation of the dwelling-house, and

(b) the assured tenancy is terminated as a result of those proceedings,

the spouse or former spouse, or the civil partner or former civil partner, so long as he or she remains in occupation, shall have the same rights in relation to, or in connection with, any such adjournment as is referred to in subsection (1) above or any such stay, suspension or postponement as is referred to in subsection (2) above, as he or she would have if those home rights were not affected by the termination of the tenancy.

(5A) In any case where—

(a) at a time when proceedings are brought for possession of a dwelling-house let on an assured tenancy—

(i) an order is in force under section 35 of the Family Law Act 1996 conferring rights on the former spouse or former civil partner of the tenant, or

(ii) an order is in force under section 36 of that Act conferring rights on a cohabitant or former cohabitant (within the meaning of that Act) of the tenant,

(b) that former spouse, former civil partner, cohabitant or former cohabitant is then in occupation of the dwelling-house, and

(c) the assured tenancy is terminated as a result of those proceedings,

the former spouse, former civil partner, cohabitant or former cohabitant shall have the same rights in relation to, or in connection with, any such adjournment as is referred to in subsection (1) above or any such stay, suspension or postponement as is referred to in subsection (2) above as he or she would have if the rights conferred by the order referred to in paragraph (a) above were not affected by the termination of the tenancy.

(6) This section does not apply if the court is satisfied that the landlord is entitled to possession of the dwelling-house—

(a) on any of the grounds in Part I of Schedule 2 to this Act, or

(b) by virtue of subsection (1) or subsection (4) of section 21 below.

Note.—Amended by the Family Law Act 1996 Sch.8, para.59 and the Civil Partnership Act 2004 s.82, Sch.9, para.23. This section has also been amended by Housing and Regeneration Act 2008 Sch.15, Pt I. The amendment relates to tolerated trespassers, but is not yet in force. The amendment is printed as part of the Housing and Regeneration Act 2008—see below. **3A–803**

"assured tenancy"
See s.1. **3A–804**

"landlord", "tenancy" and "tenant"
See s.45. **3A–805**

Paragraph numbers marked with a "+" can be found online and on CD.

"dwelling-house"

3A–806   See s.45.

Extended discretion of court in possession claims

3A–807   See also commentary to the Housing Act 1985 s.85. This section gives the court a wide discretion, firstly at trial when considering the form of possession order to make and secondly after the making of a possession order at " *any time before the execution of such an order.*" See, e.g. *R. v Ilkeston County Court Ex p. Kruza* (1985) 17 H.L.R. 539, QBD, s.9 "gives a wide power to stay or suspend an order for possession which is applicable to all cases except those where it is expressly excluded by statute." The power may be exercised where circumstances have changed since the original hearing, even where an outright order was made by a different judge, (*Ujima HA v Smith* Legal Action 22, October 16, 2000, Ch D, April 2001, where the defendant was by the time of the application to suspend accepting her legal responsibility for serious damage to a shared kitchen and offering to pay £150 in compensation). See too *Plymouth CC v Hoskin* [2002] EWCA Civ 684; May 1, 2002 where the Court of Appeal said "There is a continuing remedy in the county court." However, the power only applies where there is a discretionary ground for possession (as opposed to a mandatory ground where the court's discretion is limited by the Housing Act 1980 s.89 (see above).

When exercising its powers under s.9 the court should impose conditions with respect to the repayment of arrears of rent and mesne profits unless it considers that to do so would cause exceptional hardship (s.9(3)). There have been no reported Court of Appeal decisions as to what might constitute "exceptional hardship".

Where there is a substantial dispute about the amount claimed and the tenant's compliance with the order, the up-to-date position has to be clearly and accurately established before considering an application to suspend under s.9 (*Haringey LBC v Powell* (1996) 28 H.L.R. 798, CA).

The court, exercising its discretion on an application to suspend a warrant under s.9, may take account of matters (*e.g.* breaches of the terms of the tenancy agreement or anti-social behaviour) other than those relied upon as grounds for making the original possession order—although it is not always be right to do so. (See *Sheffield City Council v Hopkins* [2001] EWCA Civ 1023; [2002] H.L.R. 12, CA) and the more detailed commentary at para.3A–387).

After execution an occupier can only be restored to possession if either the whole proceedings are set aside (see the commentary at 3A–388; *Leicester City Council v Aldwinkle* (1992) 24 H.L.R. 40, CA; *cf. Governors of Peabody Donation Fund v Hay* (1987) 19 H.L.R. 145, CA; and *Tower Hamlets LBC v Abadie* (1990) 22 H.L.R. 264, CA) or the warrant had been obtained by fraud, abuse of process or oppression (see *Hammersmith and Fulham LBC v Hill* (1995) 27 H.L.R. 368; [1994] 2 E.G.L.R. 51, CA; *Hackney LBC v White* (1995) 28 H.L.R. 219, CA; and *Tower Hamlets LBC v Azad* (1998) 30 H.L.R. 241, CA; but *cf. Islington LBC v Harridge, The Times*, 30 June, 1993, CA).

See also *Saint v Barking and Dagenham LBC* (1999) 31 H.L.R. 620, CA (oppression where warrant executed without prior notification to tenant who was in prison and without inviting him to renew his application for housing benefit).

On any of the grounds in Part I

3A–808   The extended discretion to stay or suspend does not apply where the landlord has satisfied one of the mandatory grounds for possession—s.9(6). See however *Capital Prime Plus Plc v Wills* (1999) 31 H.L.R. 926, CA where the landlord had consented to the suspension of the original possession order even though there were over two months' arrears. The Court of Appeal held that the order had not been made under Ground 8 and so, on subsequent default, the court did have power to suspend a warrant and *Diab v Countrywide Rentals 1 Plc, Independent*, November 5, 2001 (c.S) , noted at para.3A–777.

Proceedings for possession: anti-social behaviour

3A–809   **9A.**—(1) This section applies if the court is considering under section 7(4) whether it is reasonable to make an order for possession on ground 14 set out in Part 2 of Schedule 2 (conduct of tenant or other person).

Paragraph numbers marked with a "+" can be found online and on CD.

(2) The court must consider, in particular—

   (a) the effect that the nuisance or annoyance has had on persons other than the person against whom the order is sought;

   (b) any continuing effect the nuisance or annoyance is likely to have on such persons;

   (c) the effect that the nuisance or annoyance would be likely to have on such persons if the conduct is repeated.

Editorial note

This section was inserted by Anti-Social Behaviour Act 2003 s.14(6). It was brought into force in England on June 30, 2004 by the Anti-Social Behaviour Act 2003 (Commencement No.3 and Savings) Order 2004 (SI 2004/1502) (c.61). It was brought into force in Wales on April 30, 2005 by the Anti-Social Behaviour Act 2003 (Commencement No.4) (Wales) Order 2005SI No.1225 (w.83)(c.55).   **3A–810**

Reasonable

When considering whether or not to make a possession order and/or whether or not to make a suspended possession order under Sch.2, Ground 14, the court must consider whether it is reasonable to make such an order—see the commentary to s.7 at paras 3A–190 and 3A–373. Section 9A adds to that general consideration a requirement that the court must consider, in particular, the effect that the nuisance or annoyance has had and would be likely to have if continued on persons other than the defendant, e.g. neighbours.   **3A–811**

Special provisions applicable to shared accommodation

10.—(1) This section applies in a case falling within subsection (1) of section 3 above and expressions used in this section have the same meaning as in that section.   **3A–812**

(2) Without prejudice to the enforcement of any order made under subsection (3) below, while the tenant is in possession of the separate accommodation, no order shall be made for possession of any of the shared accommodation, whether on the application of the immediate landlord of the tenant or on the application of any person under whom that landlord derives title, unless a like order has been made, or is made at the same time, in respect of the separate accommodation; and the provisions of section 6 above shall have effect accordingly.

(3) On the application of the landlord, the court may make such order as it thinks just either—

   (a) terminating the right of the tenant to use the whole or any part of the shared accommodation other than living accommodation; or

   (b) modifying his right to use the whole or any part of the shared accommodation, whether by varying the persons or increasing the number of persons entitled to the use of that accommodation or otherwise.

(4) No order shall be made under subsection (3) above so as to effect any termination or modification of the rights of the tenant which, apart from section 3(3) above, could not be effected by or under the terms of the tenancy.

Paragraph numbers marked with a "+" can be found online and on CD.

"landlord", "tenancy" and "tenant"

3A–813   See s.45.

"separate accommodation"

3A–814   See s.3.

"shared accommodation"

3A–815   See s.3.

Payment of removal expenses in certain cases

3A–816   **11.**—(1) Where a court makes an order for possession of a dwelling-house let on an assured tenancy on Ground 6 or Ground 9 in Schedule 2 to this Act (but not on any other ground), the landlord shall pay to the tenant a sum equal to the reasonable expenses likely to be incurred by the tenant in removing from the dwelling-house.

(2) Any question as to the amount of the sum referred in subsection (1) above shall be determined by agreement between the landlord and the tenant or, in default of agreement, by the court.

(3) Any sum payable to a tenant by virtue of this section shall be recoverable as a civil debt due from the landlord.

"assured tenancy"

3A–817   See s.1.

"landlord", and "tenant"

3A–818   See s.45.

"dwelling-house"

3A–819   See s.45.

Payment of removal expenses in certain cases

3A–820   The court may only order a landlord to pay removal expenses if possession is claimed under Ground 6 (housing association wishing to demolish or reconstruct), or Ground 9 (suitable alternative accommodation).

Compensation for misrepresentation or concealment

3A–821   **12.** Where a landlord obtains an order for possession of a dwelling-house let on an assured tenancy on one or more of the grounds in Schedule 2 to this Act and it is subsequently made to appear to the court that the order was obtained by misrepresentation or concealment of material facts, the court may order the landlord to pay to the former tenant such sum as appears sufficient as compensation for damage or loss sustained by that tenant as a result of the order.

"assured tenancy"

3A–822   See s.1.

"landlord" and "tenant"

3A–823   See s.45.

"dwelling-house"

3A–824   See s.45.

Compensation for misrepresentation or concealment

3A–825   *cf.* the Rent Act 1977 s.102. See also *Mafo v Adams* [1970] 1 Q.B. 548, CA (proceedings based upon the common law tort of deceit).

Paragraph numbers marked with a "+" can be found online and on CD.

Increase of rent under assured periodic tenancies

13.—(1) This section applies to—   3A–826

    (a) a statutory periodic tenancy other than one which, by virtue of paragraph 11 or paragraph 12 in Part I of Schedule 1 to this Act, cannot for the time being be an assured tenancy; and

    (b) any other periodic tenancy which is an assured tenancy, other than one in relation to which there is a provision, for the time being binding on the tenant, under which the rent for a particular period of the tenancy will or may be greater than the rent for an earlier period.

(2) For the purpose of securing an increase in the rent under a tenancy to which this section applies, the landlord may serve on the tenant a notice in the prescribed form proposing a new rent to take effect at the beginning of a new period of the tenancy specified in the notice, being a period beginning not earlier than—

    (a) the minimum period after the date of the service of the notice; and

    (b) except in the case of a statutory tenancy—

        (i) in the case of an assured agricultural occupancy, the first anniversary of the date on which the first period of the tenancy began;

        (ii) in any other case, on the date that falls 52 weeks after the date on which the first period of the tenancy began; and;

    (c) if the rent under the tenancy has previously been increased by virtue of a notice under this subsection or a determination under section 14 below—

        (i) in the case of an assured agricultural occupancy, the first anniversary of the date on which the increased rent took effect;

        (ii) in any other case, the appropriate date.

(3) The minimum period referred to in subsection (2) above is—

    (a) in the case of a yearly tenancy, six months;

    (b) in the case of a tenancy where the period is less than a month, one month; and

    (c) in any other case, a period equal to the period of the tenancy,

(3A) The appropriate date referred to in subsection (2)(c)(ii) above is—

    (a) in a case to which subsection (3B) below applies, the date that falls 53 weeks after the date on which the increased rent took effect;

    (b) in any other case, the date that falls 52 weeks after the date on which the increased rent took effect.

(3B) This subsection applies where—

Paragraph numbers marked with a "+" can be found online and on CD.

    (a) the rent under the tenancy has been increased by virtue of a notice under this section or a determination under section 14 below on at least one occasion after the coming into force of the Regulatory Reform (Assured Periodic Tenancies) (Rent Increases) Order 2003; and

    (b) the fifty-third week after the date on which the last such increase took effect begins more than six days before the anniversary of the date on which the first such increase took effect.

(4) Where a notice is served under subsection (2) above, a new rent specified in the notice shall take effect as mentioned in the notice unless, before the beginning of the new period specified in the notice—

    (a) the tenant by an application in the prescribed form refers the notice to a rent assessment committee; or

    (b) the landlord and the tenant agree on a variation of the rent which is different from that proposed in the notice or agree that the rent should not be varied.

(5) Nothing in this section (or in section 14 below) affects the right of the landlord and the tenant under an assured tenancy to vary by agreement any term of the tenancy (including a term relating to rent).

3A–827   *Note* —Amended by the Regulatory Reform (Assured Periodic Tenancies) (Rent Increases) Order 2003 (SI 2003/259). The amendment was designed to overcome the argument that a strict interpretation of former s.13(2)(c) rendered many rent increases made by registered social landlords invalid because, although increases may have occurred annually, in some years they may have purported to take effect a few days earlier than "the first anniversary of the date" when the last increase took effect. The effect of the amendment is to enable landlords to set a fixed day (e.g. the first Monday in April) on which rent increases are to take effect. The first time that the rent is increased after the Order came into force on February 10, 2003, the increase may take effect not less than 52 weeks after the start of the tenancy or, if the rent has already been increased, not less than 52 weeks after the date of the last increase. On the second and subsequent occasions, the increase may take effect not less than 52 weeks after the last increase, unless that would result in the increase taking effect on a date falling a week or more before the anniversary of the first increase after the date on which the Order comes into force. In such a case the increase may not take effect until 53 weeks after the date of the last increase. As a result of this change the Assured Tenancies and Agricultural (Forms) (Amendment) (England) Regulations 2003 (SI 2003/260) prescribe new forms to be used by landlords when proposing new rents under s.13(2) from April 11, 2003. The Assured Tenancies and Agricultural Occupancies (Forms) (Amendment) (Wales) Regulations 2003 (SI 2003/307) (w.46) prescribe the new forms to be used in Wales.

"assured tenancy"
3A–828   See s.1.

"landlord", and "tenant"
3A–829   See s.45.

"dwelling-house"
3A–830   See s.45.

"statutory periodic tenancy"
3A–831   See s.5(7).

Paragraph numbers marked with a "+" can be found online and on CD.

(c) "category of dwellings" has the same meaning as in section 30(1) and (2) of that Act.

(4) In this section "rent" does not include any service charge, within the meaning of section 18 of the Landlord and Tenant Act 1985, but, subject to that, includes any sums payable by the tenant to the landlord on account of the use of furniture, in respect of council tax, or for any of the matters referred to in subsection (1)(a) of that section, whether or not those sums are separate from the sums payable for the occupation of the dwelling-house concerned or are payable under separate agreements.

(5) Where any rates in respect of the dwelling-house concerned are borne by the landlord or a superior landlord, the rent assessment committee shall make their determination under this section as if the rates were not so borne.

(6) In any case where—

(a) a rent assessment committee have before them at the same time the reference of a notice under section 6(2) above relating to a tenancy (in this subsection referred to as "the section 6 reference") and the reference of a notice under section 13(2) above relating to the same tenancy (in this subsection referred to as "the section 13 reference"), and

(b) the date specified in the notice under section 6(2) above is not later than the first day of the new period specified in the notice under section 13(2) above, and

(c) the committee propose to hear the two references together,

the committee shall make a determination in relation to the section 6 reference before making their determination in relation to the section 13 reference and, accordingly, in such a case the reference in subsection (1)(c) above to the terms of the tenancy to which the notice relates shall be construed as a reference to those terms as varied by virtue of the determination made in relation to the section 6 reference.

(7) Where a notice under section 13(2) above has been referred to a rent assessment committee, then, unless the landlord and the tenant otherwise agree, the rent determined by the committee (subject, in a case where subsection (5) above applies, to the addition of the appropriate amount in respect of rates) shall be the rent under the tenancy with effect from the beginning of the new period specified in the notice or, if it appears to the rent assessment committee that that would cause undue hardship to the tenant, with effect from such later date (not being later than the date the rent is determined) as the committee may direct.

(8) Nothing in this section requires a rent assessment committee to continue with their determination of a rent for a dwelling-house if the landlord and tenant give notice in writing that they no longer require such a determination or if the tenancy has come to an end.

(9) This section shall apply in relation to an assured shorthold

Paragraph numbers marked with a "+" can be found online and on CD.

tenancy as if in subsection (1)the reference to an assured tenancy were a reference to an assured shorthold tenancy.

3A-837   *Note* —Amended by the Local Government Finance (Housing) (Consequential Amendments) Order 1993 (SI 1993/651); and the Housing Act 1996 Sch.8, para.2(2).

"assured tenancy"

3A-838   See s.1.

"landlord", and "tenant"

3A-839   See s.45.

"dwelling-house"

3A-840   See s.45.

Determination of rent by rent assessment committee

3A-841   Section 14(1) requires RACs to assess the rent at which "the dwelling-house concerned might reasonably be expected to be let in the open market by a willing landlord under an assured tenancy" even if the rent assessed by the RAC is in excess of £25,000 and this means the tenancy ceases to be an assured tenancy. Parliament did not intend the References to Rating (Housing) Regulations 1990 (SI 1990/434) (para.29) (tenancies at a high rent cannot be assured tenancies) to introduce a rent cap (*R. v London RAP Ex p. Cadogan Estates* [1998] Q.B. 398; [1997] 3 W.L.R. 833, QBD).

In *N & D (London) Ltd v Gadson* (1992) 24 H.L.R. 64; [1992] 02 E.G. 176, QBD, Auld J. held that Housing Act 1988 s.14(2)(c), when stating that rent assessment committees should disregard "any reduction in the value of the dwelling-house attributable to a failure by the tenant to comply with any terms of the tenancy" only referred to default by the current tenant. They were obliged to take into account the current condition of the premises, even if that had been brought about by the default of the tenant's father before his death.

When applying the disregard for tenant's improvements (s.14(2)) the committee should not apply a de-capitalised discount based upon the cost of the works. They should simply take as the value of the property its current value less the improvements carried out (*Rowe v South West Rent Assessment Panel* [2001] EWHC 865 (Admin), October 23, 2001).

Note that ss.14A and 14B (inserted by the Local Government Finance (Housing) (Consequential Amendments) Order 1993 (SI 1993/651), provided for interim increases prior to April 1, 1994 where the landlord was liable for council tax.

Where a property is in disrepair, there is no requirement that the RAC should perform a two stage process of first calculating the open market rental of the property in good condition, and then indicating by a figure or percentage discount what allowance has been made for the actual condition of the property (*Ghani v London Rent Assessment Committee* [2002] EWHC 1167 (Admin); May 28, 2002).

Interim increase before 1st April 1994 of rent under assured periodic tenancies in certain cases where landlord liable for council tax

3A-842   **14A.**—(1) In any case where—

     (a) under Part I of the Local Government Finance Act 1992 the landlord of a dwelling-house let under an assured tenancy to which section 13 above applies or a superior landlord is liable to pay council tax in respect of a dwelling (within the meaning of that Part of that Act) which includes that dwelling-house,

     (b) under the terms of the tenancy (or an agreement collateral to the tenancy) the tenant is liable to make payments to the landlord in respect of council tax,

Paragraph numbers marked with a "+" can be found online and on CD.

    (c) the case falls within subsection (2) or subsection (3)
        below, and

    (d) no previous notice under this subsection has been served
        in relation to the dwelling-house,

the landlord may serve on the tenant a notice in the prescribed
form proposing an increased rent to take account of the tenant's liability to make payments to the landlord in respect of council tax,
such increased rent to take effect at the beginning of a new period of
the tenancy specified in the notice being a period beginning not
earlier than one month after the date on which the notice was served.

  (2) The case falls within this subsection if—

    (a) the rent under the tenancy has previously been increased
        by virtue of a notice under section 13(2) above or under
        a determination under section 14 above, and

    (b) the first anniversary of the date on which the increased
        rent took effect has not yet occurred.

  (3) The case falls within this subsection if a notice has been served
under section 13(2) above before 1st April 1993 but no increased
rent has taken effect before that date.

  (4) No notice may be served under subsection (1) above after 31st
March 1994.

  (5) Where a notice is served under subsection (1) above, the new
rent specified in the notice shall take effect as mentioned in the notice unless, before the beginning of the new period specified in the
notice—

    (a) the tenant by an application in the prescribed form refers
        the notice to a rent assessment committee, or

    (b) the landlord and the tenant agree on a variation of the
        rent which is different from that proposed in the notice
        or agree that the rent should not be varied.

  (6) Nothing in this section (or in section 14B below) affects the
right of the landlord and the tenant under an assured tenancy to
vary by agreement any term of the tenancy (including a term relating
to rent).

Note—Note that ss.14A and 14B (inserted by the Local Government Finance (Hous- **3A–843**
ing) (Consequential Amendments) Order 1993 (SI 1993/651), provided for interim
increases prior to April 1, 1994 where the landlord was liable for council tax.

Interim determination of rent by rent assessment committee

14B.—(1) Where, under subsection (5)(a) of section 14A above, a **3A–844**
tenant refers to a rent assessment committee a notice under subsection (1) of that section, the committee shall determine the amount by
which, having regard to the provisions of section 14(3A) above, the
existing rent might reasonably be increased to take account of the
tenant's liability to make payments to the landlord in respect of
council tax.

  (2) Where a notice under section 14A(1) above has been referred
to a rent assessment committee, then, unless the landlord and the

Paragraph numbers marked with a "+" can be found online and on CD.

tenant otherwise agree, the existing rent shall be increased by the amount determined by the committee with effect from the beginning of the new period specified in the notice or, if it appears to the committee that that would cause undue hardship to the tenant, with effect from such later date (not being later than the date the increase is determined) as the committee may direct.

(3) In any case where—

(a) a rent assessment committee have before them at the same time the reference of a notice under section 13(2) above relating to a tenancy (in this subsection referred to as "the section 13 reference") and the reference of a notice under section 14A(1) above relating to the same tenancy (in this subsection referred to as "the section 14A reference"); and

(b) the committee propose to hear the two references together,

the committee shall make a determination in relation to the section 13 reference before making their determination in relation to the section 14A reference, and if in such a case the date specified in the notice under section 13(2) above is later than the date specified in the notice under section 14A(1) above, the rent determined under the section 14A reference shall not take effect until the date specified in the notice under section 13(2).

(4) In this section "rent" has the same meaning as in section 14 above; and section 14(4) above applies to a determination under this section as it applies to a determination under that section.

3A–845   *Note* —Added by the Local Government Finance (Housing) (Consequential Amendments) Order 1993 (SI 1993/651) Sch.2.

Limited prohibition on assignment etc. without consent

3A–846   **15.**—(1) Subject to subsection (3) below, it shall be an implied term of every assured tenancy which is a periodic tenancy that, except with the consent of the landlord, the tenant shall not—

(a) assign the tenancy (in whole or in part); or

(b) sub-let or part with possession of the whole or any part of the dwelling-house let on the tenancy.

(2) Section 19 of the Landlord and Tenant Act 1927 (consents to assign not to be unreasonably withheld etc.) shall not apply to a term which is implied into an assured tenancy by subsection (1) above.

(3) In the case of a periodic tenancy which is not a statutory periodic tenancy or an assured periodic tenancy arising under Schedule 10 to the Local Government and Housing Act 1989, subsection (1) above does not apply if—

(a) there is a provision (whether contained in the tenancy or not) under which the tenant is prohibited (whether absolutely or conditionally) from assigning or sub-letting or parting with possession or is permitted (whether absolutely or conditionally) to assign, sub-let or part with possession; or

Paragraph numbers marked with a "+" can be found online and on CD.

(b) a premium is required to be paid on the grant or renewal of the tenancy.

(4) In subsection (3)(b) above "premium" includes—

(a) any fine or other like sum;

(b) any other pecuniary consideration in addition to rent;
and

(c) any sum paid by way of deposit, other than one which
does not exceed one-sixth of the annual rent payable
under the tenancy immediately after the grant or renewal in question.

Note—Amended by the Local Government and Housing Act 1989 Sch.11, para.102.　**3A–847**

"assured tenancy"
See s.1.　**3A–848**

"landlord", and "tenant"
See s.45.　**3A–849**

"dwelling-house"
See s.45　**3A–850**

"statutory periodic tenancy"
See s.5(7).　**3A–851**

Access for repairs

16. It shall be an implied term of every assured tenancy that the **3A–852**
tenant shall afford to the landlord access to the dwelling-house let on
the tenancy and all reasonable facilities for executing therein any
repairs which the landlord is entitled to execute.

"assured tenancy"
See s.1.　**3A–853**

"landlord", "tenancy" and "tenant"
See s.45.　**3A–854**

"dwelling-house"
See s.45.　**3A–855**

MISCELLANEOUS

Succession to assured periodic tenancy by spouse

17.—(1) In any case where—　**3A–856**

(a) the sole tenant under an assured periodic tenancy dies,
and

(b) immediately before the death, the tenant's spouse or
civil partner was occupying the dwelling-house as his or
her only or principal home, and

(c) the tenant was not himself a successor, as defined in
subsection (2) or subsection (3) below,

then, on the death, the tenancy vests by virtue of this section in

Paragraph numbers marked with a "+" can be found online and on CD.

the spouse or civil partner (and, accordingly, does not devolve under the tenant's will or intestacy).

(2) For the purposes of this section, a tenant is a successor in relation to a tenancy if—

(a) the tenancy became vested in him either by virtue of this section or under the will or intestacy of a previous tenant; or

(b) at some time before the tenant's death the tenancy was a joint tenancy held by himself and one or more other persons and, prior to his death, he became the sole tenant by survivorship; or

(c) he became entitled to the tenancy as mentioned in section 39(5) below.

(3) For the purposes of this section, a tenant is also a successor in relation to a tenancy (in this subsection referred to as "the new tenancy") which was granted to him (alone or jointly with others) if—

(a) at some time before the grant of the new tenancy, he was, by virtue of subsection (2) above, a successor in relation to an earlier tenancy of the same or substantially the same dwelling-house as is let under the new tenancy; and

(b) at all times since he became such a successor he has been a tenant (alone or jointly with others) of the dwelling-house which is let under the new tenancy or of a dwelling-house which is substantially the same as that dwelling-house.

(4) For the purposes of this section—

(a) a person who was living with the tenant as his or her wife or husband shall be treated as the tenant's spouse, and

(b) a person who was living with the tenant as if they were civil partners shall be treated as the tenant's civil partner.

(5) If, on the death of the tenant, there is, by virtue of subsection (4) above, more than one person who fulfils the condition in subsection (1)(b) above, such one of them as may be decided by agreement or, in default of agreement, by the county court shall for the purposes of this section be treated (according to whether that one of them is of the opposite sex to, or of the same sex as, the tenant) as the tenant's spouse or the tenant's civil partner.

3A–857 *Note*—Amended by the Civil Partnership Act 2004 s.81 and Sch.8, para.41.

"assured tenancy"

3A–858 See s.1.

"landlord", "tenancy" and "tenant"

3A–859 See s.45.

"dwelling-house"

3A–860 See s.45.

Paragraph numbers marked with a "+" can be found online and on CD.

force on February 28, 1997 which would otherwise have been assured tenancies are automatically *assured shorthold* tenancies lacking long term security of tenure. This applies whether the tenancy is granted orally or by a written agreement. In other words, the requirement of a s.20 notice (see below) informing the tenant that the tenancy will be an assured shorthold tenancy has been abolished. There are though several exceptions. The new rule does not apply where:

- the new tenancy is made pursuant to a contract made before the new provisions come into force (Housing Act 1996 s.96); or
- the landlord serves a notice before entering into the tenancy stating that the tenancy is not to be an assured shorthold tenancy (Housing Act 1996 Sch.7, para.1); or
- the landlord serves a notice after the grant of the tenancy stating that the tenancy is no longer an assured shorthold tenancy (Housing Act 1996 Sch.7, para.2); or
- there is a provision in the tenancy agreement stating that the tenancy is not an assured shorthold tenancy (Housing Act 1996 Sch.7, para.3); or
- the tenancy is an assured tenancy by succession—i.e. a spouse or member of the family of a statutory tenant under the Rent Act 1977 or the Rent (Agriculture) Act 1976 became an assured tenant after the death of the original tenant (Rent Act 1977 s.2(1)(b) and Sch.1; Housing Act 1988 s.39; and Housing Act 1996 Sch.7, para.4); or
- the tenancy was formerly a secure tenancy and became an assured tenancy, e.g. on transfer of housing stock from a local housing authority to a housing association or other landlord (Housing Act 1985 Pt IV; Housing Act 1988 s.38; and Housing Act 1996 Sch.7, para.5); or
- an assured tenancy came into existence on the ending of a long residential tenancy (Landlord and Tenant Act 1954 Pt I; Local Government and Housing Act 1989 s.186 and Sch.10; and Housing Act 1996 Sch.7, para.6); or
- the tenancy is granted to someone who immediately before its grant was an assured tenant (as opposed to an assured *shorthold* tenant) and is granted by someone who was the landlord under the old tenancy (Housing Act 1996 Sch.7, para.7); or
- in some cases the tenancy or licence is an assured agricultural occupancy (Rent (Agriculture) Act 1976; Housing Act 1988 s.24 and Sch.3; and Housing Act 1996 Sch.7, para.9).

Assured shorthold tenancies: pre-Housing Act 1996 tenancies

20.—(1) Subject to subsection (3) below, an assured tenancy which **3A–872** is not one to which section 19A above applies is an assured shorthold tenancy if—

    (a) it is a fixed term tenancy granted for a term certain of not less than six months,

    (b) there is no power for the landlord to determine the tenancy at any time earlier than six months from the beginning of the tenancy, and

    (c) a notice in respect of it is served as mentioned in subsection (2) below.

(2) The notice referred to in subsection (1)(c) above is one which—

    (a) is in such form as may be prescribed;

    (b) is served before the assured tenancy is entered into;

    (c) is served by the person who is to be the landlord under the assured tenancy on the person who is to be the tenant under that tenancy; and

Paragraph numbers marked with a "+" can be found online and on CD.

      (d) states that the assured tenancy to which it relates is to be a shorthold tenancy.

(3) Notwithstanding anything in subsection (1) above, where—

      (a) immediately before a tenancy (in this subsection referred to as "the new tenancy") is granted, the person to whom it is granted or, as the case may be, at least one of the persons to whom it is granted was a tenant under an assured tenancy which was not a shorthold tenancy, and

      (b) the new tenancy is granted by the person who, immediately before the beginning of the tenancy, was the landlord under the assured tenancy referred to in paragraph (a) above,

the new tenancy cannot be an assured shorthold tenancy.

(4) Subject to subsection (5) below, if, on the coming to an end of an assured shorthold tenancy (including a tenancy which was an assured shorthold but ceased to be assured before it came to an end), a new tenancy of the same or substantially the same premises comes into being under which the landlord and the tenant are the same as at the coming to an end of the earlier tenancy, then, if and so long as the new tenancy is an assured tenancy, it shall be an assured shorthold tenancy, whether or not it fulfils the conditions in paragraphs (a) to (c) of subsection (1) above.

(5) Subsection (4) above does not apply if, before the new tenancy is entered into (or, in the case of a statutory periodic tenancy, takes effect in possession), the landlord serves notice on the tenant that the new tenancy is not to be a shorthold tenancy.

(5A) Subsections (3) and (4) above do not apply where the new tenancy is one to which section 19A above applies.

(6) In the case of joint landlords—

      (a) the reference in subsection (2)(c) above to the person who is to be the landlord is a reference to at least one of the persons who are to be joint landlords; and

      (b) the reference in subsection (5) above to the landlord is a reference to at least one of the joint landlords.

3A–873   *Note* —Amended by the Housing Act 1996 Schs 8 and 19.

"assured tenancy"

3A–874   See s.1.

"landlord", and "tenant"

3A–875   See s.45.

"statutory periodic tenancy"

3A–876   See s.5(7).

"prescribed"

3A–877   See s.45 and the Assured Tenancies and Agricultural Occupancies (Forms) Regulations 1988 (SI 1988/2203). Note that a notice conforms with the regulations if it is "substantially to the same effect" as that prescribed (para.2).

Paragraph numbers marked with a "+" can be found online and on CD.

Assured shorthold tenancies: pre-Housing Act 1996 tenancies

This section now only applies to tenancies granted prior to February 28, 1997 (but **3A–878**
note the exceptions listed in s.19A). For tenancies granted after that date, see s.19A,
above.

Section 20 provides that for a tenancy granted before February 28, 1997 to be an
assured shorthold tenancy:

(a) there had to be a tenancy granted for a fixed term of not less than six months
(A tenancy granted for "a term certain of one year ... and ... thereafter from
month to month" is a tenancy granted for a term certain within the meaning
of s.20(1)(a) which was capable of being an assured shorthold tenancy. (*Goodman v Evely* [2001] EWCA Civ 104; [2002] H.L.R. 53; [2001] L.& T.R. 436,
CA)); and

(b) there could be no power enabling the landlord to determine the tenancy
within the first six months;
Section 45(4) provides that a power of re-entry or forfeiture for breach of a
condition does *not* count as a provision enabling the landlord to determine the
tenancy for this purpose; and

(c) a notice in the prescribed form had to be served on the prospective tenant
before the tenancy was entered into, stating that the tenancy was to be an assured shorthold tenancy.

This requirement was *mandatory*. There is no provision which allows the court to
dispense with the service of a notice before the initial grant of a pre-February 28, 1997
assured shorthold tenancy.

Service earlier on the day when the tenancy commenced was sufficient (*Bedding v Mc-
Carthy* [1994] 41 E.G. 151, CA). This is a pure question of fact. It was good practice,
although not a statutory requirement, for landlords to ensure that tenants endorsed a
note confirming receipt on a copy of the notice. A s.20 notice may be served upon a
prospective tenant's agent (*Yenula Properties Ltd v Naidu* [2002] EWCA Civ 719; [2003]
H.L.R. 18; [2002] 42 E.G.162).

Section 20 notices have been held to be invalid where the landlord inserted an incorrect date (*Panayi v Roberts* (1993) 25 H.L.R. 421, CA), where the dates in the notice
and the tenancy were "in complete conflict" (*Clickex Ltd v McCann* (2000) 32 H.L.R.
324; [1999] 30 EG 96, CA; where the four bullet points giving instructions and advice
to the tenant were omitted (*Manel v Memon* [2000] 33 E.G. 74, CA), where no date for
termination was inserted (*Mistry v Dave*, June 1995, Legal Action 20(cc)), where the
landlord's name, address and telephone number were missing (*Stephens v Lamb*, March
1996, Legal Action 12(cc)), and where the landlord's name was spelt incorrectly and
the notice was not signed (*Symons v Warren* [1995] C.L.W. 33/95(cc)).

However all these cases now have to be reconsidered in the light of cases such as
Ravenseft Proeprties Ltd v Hall and *B. Osborn & Co Ltd v Dior* [2003] H.L.R. 45 where
the Court of Appeal held that there is no statutory or common law doctrine of "obvious mistake" or any requirement to apply a two-stage test in which the court has first
to consider whether the error in the notice is obvious or evident before proceeding to
consider whether the notice read in context is sufficiently clear to leave a reasonable
recipient in no reasonable doubt as to the terms of the notice. There is only one statutory question, which is whether, notwithstanding any errors or omissions, the notice is
"substantially to the same effect" as a correct notice in accomplishing the purpose of
telling the proposed tenant of the special nature of an assured shorthold tenancy
(*Mannai Investment Co Ltd v Eagle Star Life Assurance Co Ltd* [1997] A.C. 749, HL). This
is a matter of fact and degree in each case. The resolution of that question is not a decision on a point of law that is binding on later courts (*White v Chubb; Kasseer v Freeman*
[2001] EWCA Civ 2034; *Ravenseft Properties Ltd v Hall* [2001] EWCA Civ 2034; [2002]
H.L.R. 33; [2002] 11 E.G. 156).

See too *York and Ross v Casey* (1999) 31 H.L.R. 209; [1998] 30 E.G. 110, CA where,
following *Mannai Investment Co Ltd v Eagle Star Life Assurance Co Ltd* [1997] A.C. 749;
[1997] 2 W.L.R. 945; [1997] 3 All E.R. 352, HL, the Court of Appeal held that a notice is valid even if it contains a minor misdescription if, in its contextual setting, it
informs a reasonably minded recipient how the notice is to operate. There is no material difference between contractual and statutory notices and accordingly the *Mannai* test is equally applicable to statutory notices. In this case where the section 20 notice gave a commencement date of September 28, 1996 but a date for termination of

Paragraph numbers marked with a "+" can be found online and on CD.

the tenancy of September 6, 1996, there was no doubt that the termination date was wrong. The real question was whether the correct termination date was sufficiently clear. In looking at a letter which accompanied the notice, there was no doubt that the termination date was understood to be March 27, 1997. See too *Garston v Scottish Widows* [1998] 1 W.L.R. 1583, CA.

See too *B. Osborn & Co Ltd v Dior* [2003] H.L.R. 45 where it was held that omission of landlords' particulars from a s.20 notice is not fatal. The question is whether the form is substantially to the same effect as the prescribed form.

Tenancy of same premises

3A–879   Note though that if a new tenancy of substantially the same premises was granted and at least one of the tenants was previously an assured shorthold tenant of the same landlord, the new tenancy automatically became an assured shorthold tenancy even if conditions (a) to (c) were not complied with (s.20(4)).

Post-Housing Act 1996 tenancies: duty of landlord to provide statement as to terms of tenancy

3A–880   **20A.**—(1) Subject to subsection (3) below, a tenant under an assured shorthold tenancy to which section 19A above applies may, by notice in writing, require the landlord under that tenancy to provide him with a written statement of any term of the tenancy which—

   (a) falls within subsection (2) below, and

   (b) is not evidenced in writing.

   (2) The following terms of a tenancy fall within this subsection, namely—

   (a) the date on which the tenancy began or, if it is a statutory periodic tenancy or a tenancy to which section 39(7) below applies, the date on which the tenancy came into being,

   (b) the rent payable under the tenancy and the dates on which that rent is payable,

   (c) any term providing for a review of the rent payable under the tenancy, and

   (d) in the case of a fixed term tenancy, the length of the fixed term.

   (3) No notice may be given under subsection (1) above in relation to a term of the tenancy if—

   (a) the landlord under the tenancy has provided a statement of that term in response to an earlier notice under that subsection given by the tenant under the tenancy, and

   (b) the term has not been varied since the provision of the statement referred to in paragraph (a) above.

   (4) A landlord who fails, without reasonable excuse, to comply with a notice under subsection (1) above within the period of 28 days beginning with the date on which he received the notice is liable on summary conviction to a fine not exceeding level 4 on the standard scale.

   (5) A statement provided for the purposes of subsection (1) above shall not be regarded as conclusive evidence of what was agreed by the parties to the tenancy in question.

Paragraph numbers marked with a "+" can be found online and on CD.

(6) Where—

   (a) a term of a statutory periodic tenancy is one which has
       effect by virtue of section 5(3)(e) above, or

   (b) a term of a tenancy to which subsection (7) of section 39
       below applies is one which has effect by virtue of subsec-
       tion (6)(e) of that section,

subsection (1) above shall have effect in relation to it as if
paragraph (b) related to the term of the tenancy from which it
derives.

(7) In subsections (1) and (3) above—

   (a) references to the tenant under the tenancy shall, in the
       case of joint tenants, be taken to be references to any of
       the tenants, and

   (b) references to the landlord under the tenancy shall, in
       the case of joint landlords, be taken to be references to
       any of the landlords.

Note —Added by the Housing Act 1996 s.97.　　　　　　　　　**3A–881**

"assured shorthold tenancy"
　See ss.19A and 20.　　　　　　　　　**3A–882**

"landlord", and "tenant"
　See s.45.　　　　　　　　　**3A–883**

Demoted assured shorthold tenancies

20B.—(1) An assured tenancy is an assured shorthold tenancy to **3A–884**
which this section applies (a demoted assured shorthold tenancy) if—

   (a) the tenancy is created by virtue of an order of the court
       under section 82A of the Housing Act 1985 or section 6A
       of this Act (a demotion order), and

   (b) the landlord is a registered social landlord.

(2) At the end of the period of one year starting with the day
when the demotion order takes effect a demoted assured shorthold
tenancy ceases to be an assured shorthold tenancy unless subsection
(3) applies.

(3) This subsection applies if before the end of the period
mentioned in subsection (2) the landlord gives notice of proceedings
for possession of the dwelling house.

(4) If subsection (3) applies the tenancy continues to be a demoted
assured shorthold tenancy until the end of the period mentioned in
subsection (2) or (if later) until one of the following occurs—

   (a) the notice of proceedings for possession is withdrawn;

   (b) the proceedings are determined in favour of the tenant;

   (c) the period of six months beginning with the date on
       which the notice is given ends and no proceedings for
       possession have been brought.

(5) Registered social landlord has the same meaning as in Part 1
of the Housing Act 1996.

Paragraph numbers marked with a "+" can be found online and on CD.

Editorial note

3A–885   This section was inserted by Anti-Social Behaviour Act 2003 s.15(1). It was brought into force in England on June 30, 2004 by the Anti-Social Behaviour Act 2003 (Commencement No.3 and Savings) Order 2004 (SI 2004/1502) (c.61). It was brought into force in Wales on April 30, 2005 by the Anti-Social Behaviour Act 2003 (Commencement No.4) (Wales) Order 2005 (SI 2005/1225) (w.83) (c.55).

Section 20B sets out the legal basis for the form of demoted tenancy that can be used by registered social landlords. A demoted assured shorthold tenancy is an assured shorthold tenancy during the demoted period but there is provision for the demoted assured shorthold tenancy automatically to turn into an assured tenancy after one year unless the landlord has issued a notice of proceedings for possession during that year. If a notice is issued, the tenancy remains a demoted assured shorthold tenancy beyond the first year until the notice is withdrawn or six months have passed and no proceedings have been issued; or, if proceedings have been issued, until they are determined in favour of the tenant. A demoted assured shorthold tenancy can be ended at any time during the demotion period. Unlike non-demoted assured shorthold tenancies a possession order granted on the basis that the landlord has given the required notice under s.21(4) of the Housing Act 1988 can take effect within the first six months of the tenancy.

Assured tenancy

3A–886   See s.1.

Assured shorthold tenancy

3A–887   See ss.19A and 20.

Registered social landlord

3A–888   See Housing Act 1996 Part I, ss.1 to 3.

Recovery of possession on expiry or termination of assured shorthold tenancy

3A–889   **21.**—(1) Without prejudice to any right of the landlord under an assured shorthold tenancy to recover possession of the dwelling-house let on the tenancy in accordance with Chapter I above, on or after the coming to an end of an assured shorthold tenancy which was a fixed term tenancy, a court shall make an order for possession of the dwelling-house if it is satisfied—

   (a) that the assured shorthold tenancy has come to an end and no further assured tenancy (whether shorthold or not) is for the time being in existence, other than an assured shorthold periodic tenancy (whether statutory or not); and

   (b) the landlord or, in the case of joint landlords, at least one of them has given to the tenant not less than two months' notice in writing stating that he requires possession of the dwelling-house.

   (2) A notice under paragraph (b) of subsection (1) above may be given before or on the day on which the tenancy comes to an end; and that subsection shall have effect notwithstanding that on the coming to an end of the fixed term tenancy a statutory periodic tenancy arises.

   (3) Where a court makes an order for possession of a dwelling-house by virtue of subsection (1) above, any statutory periodic tenancy which has arisen on the coming to an end of the assured shorthold tenancy shall end (without further notice and regardless of the period) on the day on which the order takes effect.

Paragraph numbers marked with a "+" can be found online and on CD.

(4) Without prejudice to any such right as is referred to in subsection (1) above, a court shall make an order for possession of a dwelling-house let on an assured shorthold tenancy which is a periodic tenancy if the court is satisfied—

(a) that the landlord or, in the case of joint landlords, at least one of them has given to the tenant a notice in writing stating that, after a date specified in the notice, being the last day of a period of the tenancy and not earlier than two months after the date the notice was given, possession of the dwelling-house is required by virtue of this section; and

(b) that the date specified in the notice under paragraph (a) above is not earlier than the earliest day on which, apart from section 5(1) above, the tenancy could be brought to an end by a notice to quit given by the landlord on the same date as the notice under paragraph (a) above.

(5) Where an order for possession under subsection (1) or (4) above is made in relation to a dwelling-house let on a tenancy to which section 19A above applies, the order may not be made so as to take effect earlier than—

(a) in the case of a tenancy which is not a replacement tenancy, six months after the beginning of the tenancy, and

(b) in the case of a replacement tenancy, six months after the beginning of the original tenancy.

(5A) Subsection (5) above does not apply to an assured shorthold tenancy to which section 20B (demoted assured shorthold tenancies) applies.

(6) In subsection (5)(b) above, the reference to the original tenancy is—

(a) where the replacement tenancy came into being on the coming to an end of a tenancy which was not a replacement tenancy, to the immediately preceding tenancy, and

(b) where there have been successive replacement tenancies, to the tenancy immediately preceding the first in the succession of replacement tenancies.

(7) For the purposes of this section, a replacement tenancy is a tenancy—

(a) which comes into being on the coming to an end of an assured short-hold tenancy, and

(b) under which, on its coming into being—

(i) the landlord and tenant are the same as under the earlier tenancy as at its coming to an end, and

(ii) the premises let are the same or substantially the same as those let under the earlier tenancy as at that time.

Note —Amended by the Local Government and Housing Act 1989 Sch.11, the **3A–890** Housing Act 1996 ss.98 and 99 and the Anti-Social Behaviour Act 2003 s.15(2).

Paragraph numbers marked with a "+" can be found online and on CD.

This section has also been amended by the Housing and Regeneration Act 2008 Sch.15, Pt I, but that amendment is not yet in force. The amendment is printed as part of the Housing and Regeneration Act 2008—see below.

"assured shorthold tenancy"

3A–891   See ss.19A and 20.

"landlord", and "tenant"

3A–892   See s.45.

"statutory periodic tenancy"

3A–893   See s.5(7).

Tenancy deposits and s.21 notices

3A–894   Housing Act 2004 s.215(1) provides that if a tenancy deposit (see Housing Act s.212(8)) has been paid in connection with an assured shorthold tenancy, no s.21 notice may be given in relation to the tenancy at any time when (a) the deposit is not being held in accordance with an authorised scheme (see Housing Act 2004 s.213(4)), or (b) the initial requirements of such a scheme (see s.213(4)) have not been complied with in relation to the deposit. These provisions were brought into force on April 6, 2007 by the Housing Act 2004 (Commencement No.7) (England) Order 2007 (SI 2007/1068) and the Housing Act 2004 (Commencement No.4) (Wales) Order 2007 (SI 2007/305). They apply to deposits paid on or after that date.

Houses in multiple occupation and s.21 notices

3A–895   Note that no s.21 notice may be given in relation to an assured shorthold tenancy in a house in multiple occupation if the house is not licensed in accordance with the provisions of the Housing Act 2004 Pt 2—see s.75.

Recovery of possession on expiry or termination of assured shorthold tenancy

3A–896   Assured shorthold tenancies lack long-term security of tenure. If the initial tenancy was for a fixed term and the tenant continues to occupy premises as his or her only or principal home, a statutory periodic tenancy arises, but all that a landlord need do to recover possession is to:

(a) prove that any fixed term tenancy has come to an end and that no new fixed term tenancy has been granted; and

(b) give at least two months notice to the tenant that the landlord requires possession. Such notice may be given before the fixed term expires.

There are no requirements as to the form of the notice, although it should be in writing (s.21(1)(b) and s.21(4)(a), as amended by the Housing Act 1996 s.98).

Although s.21(4)(a) refers to "a date specified in the notice", the Court of Appeal has held that no date need be specified in a s.21 notice provided that "the tenant knows or can easily ascertain the date referred to ... The word 'specified' ... means no more than 'made clear'" (*Lower Street Properties v Jones* (1996) 28 H.L.R. 877; [1996] 2 E.G.L.R. 67). Accordingly a notice which does not contain a date, but which provides a formula for calculating a date which complies with s.21(4)(a) (e.g. "at the end of the period of your tenancy which will end next after the expiration of two months from the service upon you of this notice") is valid.

If landlords comply with these requirements, they are automatically entitled to possession. The court has no power to suspend possession orders, apart from the Housing Act 1980 s.89(1) (see above). It has been held in the county court that a s.21 notice served before the commencement of the tenancy is not valid because at that stage there was no relationship of landlord and tenant, as required by s.21(1)(b)—see *Turpitt v Elizabeth*, August 1998, Legal Action 21, Edmonton County Court—although the better view is that such a notice is valid.

Uncertainty has been caused by the dichotomy between the Housing Act 1988 s.21(1)(b) and s.21(4)(a). Section 21(1)(b) merely provides that the landlord must give "the tenant not less than two months' notice stating that he requires possession of the dwelling-house". However, s.21(4)(a) provides that the date specified in a notice where there is "a periodic tenancy" shall be "the last day of a period of the tenancy". Al-

Paragraph numbers marked with a "+" can be found online and on CD.

though it has been argued that s.21(1) and s.21(4) are simply alternatives that may be used as landlords choose, the better view is that there is no need for the two months notice to expire on "the last day of a period of the tenancy" if the notice is served during a fixed term assured shorthold but this requirement has to be satisfied if the notice is served after the expiry of a fixed term (i.e. during a statutory periodic assured shorthold tenancy). The use of the words "without prejudice ... to ... subsection (1)" in s.21(4) clearly shows that the two subsections are alternatives and that s.21(4) is not an additional requirement for all s.21(1) notices. The words in s.21(2) ("A notice under paragraph (b) of subsection (1) above may be given before or on the day on which the tenancy comes to an end") indicate that a s.21(1) notice is one which can be served during a fixed term. In contrast, the use of the words "let on an assured shorthold tenancy which is a periodic tenancy" in s.21(4) indicate that the s.21(4)(b) requirement applies whenever a notice is served during a periodic tenancy—and that includes a statutory periodic tenancy (*cf.* s.13(1)(a) and (b) and s.15(3)). This approach is also supported by the Housing Act 1996 s.98 which refers to s.21(1) notices as being given "under a fixed term" and s.21(4) as the "corresponding provision for periodic tenancies".

In *Gracechurch SA v Tribhovan and Abdul* (2001) 33 H.L.R. 28, CA, Simon Brown L.J., while hearing an appeal on another issue, described the dismissal of possession proceedings, because a notice requiring possession from a periodic tenant did not expire on the last day of a period of the tenancy, as "clearly correct". This was confirmed by the Court of Appeal in *McDonald v Fernandez* [2003] EWCA Civ 1219; [2004] 1 W.L.R. 1027, when rejecting a landlord's contention that s.21 should be construed in the same way as the common law rules relating to notices to quit. It might be possible to give a notice to quit that expired on either the first day or the last day of a period of the tenancy, but that was not because there were two last days. It was because the last day ended at midnight and the first day of the new period would begin thereafter. A s.21 notice is not a notice to quit. The niceties of contractual notices to quit should not be imported into the plain words of the statute. Section 21(4)(a) requires the notice to specify the last date of the period. It is not a situation where the legislation permits the form to be substantially to the same effect. The subsection is clear and precise. Accordingly, a notice served during a periodic assured shorthold tenancy which does not expire "on the last day of a period of the tenancy" is unlikely to be valid.

In order to be valid, a notice served upon a periodic assured shorthold tenant—

(1) must specify a date after which possession is required—either by inserting a particular date or by using a formula, as in *Lower Street Properties v Jones* (above);

(2) give a date which is the last day of a period of the tenancy, and not any other day. The fact that the notice is too long does not save it from being defective. (*McDonald v Fernandez* [2003] EWCA Civ 1219 (above));

(3) make it clear that possession is required after that date. In *Notting Hill Housing Trust v Roomus* [2006] EWCA Civ 407; [2006] 1 W.L.R. 1375, the Court of Appeal found that a s.21 notice which stated "Possession is required of the premises which you hold as tenant(s) at the end of the period of your tenancy which will end after expiry of two months from the service upon you of this notice" was valid because the phrase "at the end of the ... tenancy" in the notice meant "after the end of the tenancy".

The Housing Act 1996 s.99, by inserting subss.(5) to (7), provides that possession orders made against tenants occupying under the Housing Act 1988 s.19A assured shorthold tenancies cannot take effect earlier than six months after the beginning of the tenancy. There is, however, no reason why a s.21(4) notice should not be served and proceedings commenced within six months of the grant of the tenancy.

A landlord relying upon s.21 may in most circumstances use the Accelerated Possession Procedure, using Form **N5A**, which if not defended, may result in a possession order without a hearing—(see CPR rr.55.11 to 55.19). In *Manel v Memon* [2000] 33 E.G. 74, CA, Holman J. said "[The accelerated possession procedure] is a robust machinery. It depends upon district judges rigorously considering the documents which have been filed. Some replies may be little more than a plea, however genuine, for mercy. But if, on the face of the reply, a matter has been raised which, if true, might arguably raise a defence; or if the documents filed by the claimant might arguably disclose a defect in his claim, then the district judge must necessarily be "not satis-

Paragraph numbers marked with a "+" can be found online and on CD.

fied" within the meaning of CCR O.49, r.6A(16) and a hearing on notice must be fixed."

The same applies to cases brought under CPR rr.55.11 to 55.19.

Section 21 and ECHR art.8

3A-897 Notwithstanding its mandatory terms, the right to possession contained in s.21(4) does not conflict with tenants' rights under ECHR art.8. The section is clearly necessary in a democratic society insofar as there has to be a procedure for recovering possession of property at the end of a tenancy. The court would defer to Parliament as to whether the restricted power of the court under that section was legitimate and proportionate (*Donoghue v Poplar HARCA* [2001] 3 W.L.R. 183, CA); also reported as *Poplar Housing & Regeneration Community Association Ltd v Donoghue* [2001] EWCA Civ 595 *Poplar Housing & Regeneration Community Association Ltd v Donoghue* [2001] EWCA Civ 595; [2002] Q.B. 48. (Note that in *Qazi v Harrow LBC* [2003] UKHL 43; [2004] 1 A.C. 983, Lord Scott stated that this case was correctly decided, but for the wrong reason.

Reference of excessive rents to rent assessment committee

3A-898 **22.**—(1) Subject to section 23 and subsection (2) below, the tenant under an assured shorthold tenancy may make an application in the prescribed form to a rent assessment committee for a determination of the rent which, in the committee's opinion, the landlord might reasonably be expected to obtain under the assured shorthold tenancy.

(2) No application may be made under this section if—

(a) the rent payable under the tenancy is a rent previously determined under this section;

(aa) the tenancy is one to which section 19A above applies and more than six months have elapsed since the beginning of the tenancy or, in the case of a replacement tenancy, since the beginning of the original tenancy; or

(b) the tenancy is an assured shorthold tenancy falling within subsection (4) of section 20 above (and, accordingly, is one in respect of which notice need not have been served as mentioned in subsection (2) of that section).

(3) Where an application is made to a rent assessment committee under subsection (1) above with respect to the rent under an assured shorthold tenancy, the committee shall not make such a determination as is referred to in that subsection unless they consider—

(a) that there is a sufficient number of similar dwelling-houses in the locality let on assured tenancies (whether shorthold or not); and

(b) that the rent payable under the assured shorthold tenancy in question is significantly higher than the rent which the landlord might reasonably be expected to be able to obtain under the tenancy, having regard to the level of rents payable under the tenancies referred to in paragraph (a) above.

(4) Where, on an application under this section, a rent assessment committee make a determination of a rent for an assured shorthold tenancy—

(a) the determination shall have effect from such date as the

Paragraph numbers marked with a "+" can be found online and on CD.

committee may direct, not being earlier than the date of the application;

(b) if, at any time on or after the determination takes effect, the rent which, apart from this paragraph, would be payable under the tenancy exceeds the rent so determined, the excess shall be irrecoverable from the tenant; and

(c) no notice may be served under section 13(2) above with respect to a tenancy of the dwelling-house in question until after the first anniversary of the date on which the determination takes effect.

(5) Subsections (4), (5) and (8) of section 14 above apply in relation to a determination of rent under this section as they apply in relation to a determination under that section and, accordingly, where subsection (5) of that section applies, any reference in subsection (4)(b) above to rent is a reference to rent exclusive of the amount attributable to rates.

(5A) Where—

(a) an assured tenancy ceases to be an assured shorthold tenancy by virtue of falling within paragraph 2 of Schedule 2A to this Act, and

(b) at the time when it so ceases to be an assured shorthold tenancy there is pending before a rent assessment committee an application in relation to it under this section, the fact that it so ceases to be an assured shorthold tenancy shall, in relation to that application, be disregarded for the purposes of this section.

(6) In subsection (2)(aa) above, the references to the original tenancy and to a replacement tenancy shall be construed in accordance with subsections (6) and (7) respectively of section 21 above.

Note —Amended by the Housing Act 1996 s.10, Sch.8, para.2, Sch.19, Pt IV.   **3A–899**

"assured shorthold tenancy"
See ss.19A and 20.   **3A–900**

"landlord", and "tenant"
See s.45.   **3A–901**

"statutory periodic tenancy"
See s.5(7).   **3A–902**

"dwelling-house"
See s.45.   **3A–903**

Reference of excessive rents to rent assessment committee
Assured shorthold tenants may apply to the rent assessment committee if they consider that the rent is excessive. This right cannot be exercised if more than six months have elapsed from the beginning of a s.19A tenancy.   **3A–904**

Termination of rent assessment committee's functions

23.—(1) If the Secretary of State by order made by statutory instrument so provides, section 22 above shall not apply in such cases or to   **3A–905**

Paragraph numbers marked with a "+" can be found online and on CD.

tenancies of dwelling-houses in such areas or in such other circumstances as may be specified in the order.

(2) An order under this section may contain such transitional, incidental and supplementary provisions as appear to the Secretary of State to be desirable.

(3) No order shall be made under this section unless a draft of the order has been laid before, and approved by a resolution of, each House of Parliament.

"dwelling-house"

3A–906   See s.45.

"tenancy"

3A–907   See s.45.

* * * *

CHAPTER IV

PROTECTION FROM EVICTION

Damages for unlawful eviction

3A–908   **27.**—(1) This section applies if, at any time after 9th June 1988, a landlord (in this section referred to as "the landlord in default") or any person acting on behalf of the landlord in default unlawfully deprives the residential occupier of any premises of his occupation of the whole or part of the premises.

(2) This section also applies if, at any time after 9th June 1988, a landlord (in this section referred to as "the landlord in default") or any person acting on behalf of the landlord in default—

(a) attempts unlawfully to deprive the residential occupier of any premises of his occupation of the whole or part of the premises, or

(b) knowing or having reasonable cause to believe that the conduct is likely to cause the residential occupier of any premises—

(i) to give up his occupation of the premises or any part thereof, or

(ii) to refrain from exercising any right or pursuing any remedy in respect of the premises or any part thereof,

does acts likely to interfere with the peace or comfort of the residential occupier or members of his household, or persistently withdraws or withholds services reasonably required for the occupation of the premises as a residence,

and, as a result, the residential occupier gives up his occupation of the premises as a residence.

(3) Subject to the following provisions of this section, where this section applies, the landlord in default shall, by virtue of this section, be liable to pay to the former residential occupier, in respect of his loss of the right to occupy the premises in question as his residence, damages assessed on the basis set out in section 28 below.

Paragraph numbers marked with a "+" can be found online and on CD.

(4) Any liability arising by virtue of subsection (3) above—

(a) shall be in the nature of a liability in tort; and

(b) subject to subsection (5) below, shall be in addition to any liability arising apart from this section (whether in tort, contract or otherwise).

(5) Nothing in this section affects the right of a residential occupier to enforce any liability which arises apart from this section in respect of his loss of the right to occupy premises as his residence; but damages shall not be awarded both in respect of such a liability and in respect of a liability arising by virtue of this section on account of the same loss.

(6) No liability shall arise by virtue of subsection (3) above if—

(a) before the date on which proceedings to enforce the liability are finally disposed of, the former residential occupier is reinstated in the premises in question in such circumstances that he becomes again the residential occupier of them; or

(b) at the request of the former residential occupier, a court makes an order (whether in the nature of an injunction or otherwise) as a result of which he is reinstated as mentioned in paragraph (a) above;

and, for the purposes of paragraph (a) above, proceedings to enforce a liability are finally disposed of on the earliest date by which the proceedings (including any proceedings on or in consequence of an appeal) have been determined and any time for appealing or further appealing has expired, except that if any appeal is abandoned, the proceedings shall be taken to be disposed of on the date of the abandonment.

(7) If, in proceedings to enforce a liability arising by virtue of subsection (3) above, it appears to the court—

(a) that, prior to the event which gave rise to the liability, the conduct of the former residential occupier or any person living with him in the premises concerned was such that it is reasonable to mitigate the damages for which the landlord in default would otherwise be liable, or

(b) that, before the proceedings were begun, the landlord in default offered to reinstate the former residential occupier in the premises in question and either it was unreasonable of the former residential occupier to refuse that offer or, if he had obtained alternative accommodation before the offer was made, it would have been unreasonable of him to refuse that offer if he had not obtained that accommodation,

the court may reduce the amount of damages which would otherwise be payable by such amount as it thinks appropriate.

(8) In proceedings to enforce a liability arising by virtue of subsection (3) above, it shall be a defence for the defendant to prove that he believed, and had reasonable cause to believe—

Paragraph numbers marked with a "+" can be found online and on CD.

(a) that the residential occupier had ceased to reside in the premises in question at the time when he was deprived of occupation as mentioned in subsection (1) above or, as the case may be, when the attempt was made or the acts were done as a result of which he gave up his occupation of those premises; or

(b) that, where the liability would otherwise arise by virtue only of the doing of acts or the withdrawal or withholding of services, he had reasonable grounds for doing the acts or withdrawing or withholding the services in question.

(9) In this section—

(a) "residential occupier", in relation to any premises, has the same meaning as in section 1 of the 1977 Act;

(b) "the right to occupy", in relation to a residential occupier, includes any restriction on the right of another person to recover possession of the premises in question;

(c) "landlord", in relation to a residential occupier, means the person who, but for the occupier's right to occupy, would be entitled to occupation of the premises and any superior landlord under whom that person derives title;

(d) "former residential occupier", in relation to any premises, means the person who was the residential occupier until he was deprived of or gave up his occupation as mentioned in subsection (1) or subsection (2) above (and, in relation to a former residential occupier, "the right to occupy" and "landlord" shall be construed accordingly).

"landlord"

3A–909   See subs.(9).

"residential occupier"

3A–910   See subs.(9) and the Protection from Eviction Act 1977 s.1 which defines "residential occupier" as "a person occupying the premises as a residence, whether under a contract or by virtue of any enactment or rule of law giving him the right to remain in occupation or restricting the right of any other person to recover possession of the premises."

"the 1977 Act"

3A–911   See s.33 which, for the purposes of this Chapter, states that this means the Protection from Eviction Act 1977.

Damages for unlawful eviction

3A–912   Section 27 provides a cause of action where a landlord or any person acting on behalf of the landlord:

(i) Unlawfully deprives a residential occupier of the whole or part of any premises which are occupied; or

(ii) Attempts unlawfully to deprive a residential occupier or the whole or part of any premises which are occupied; or

(iii) Causes a residential occupier to give up premises by either—

(a) Doing "acts likely to interfere with the peace or comfort of the residential occupier" or members of his or her household, or

(b) Persistently withdrawing or withholding services reasonably required for the occupation of premises as a residence, and

Paragraph numbers marked with a "+" can be found online and on CD.

(c) the landlord or person acting on behalf of the landlord knows or has reasonable cause to believe that this conduct is likely to cause the residential occupier to give up occupation of the premises or to refrain from exercising any right or pursuing any remedy in respect of the premises.

Much of the wording of the section is derived from the Protection from Eviction Act 1977.

It has been held by the Court of Session in Scotland, that the expression "acting on his behalf" in Housing (Scotland) Act 1988 s.36 (the Scottish equivalent to Housing Act 1988 s.27) is clear and unambiguous and encompasses anyone who is acting either as direct agent of the landlord, or as someone employed to do a particular act, or to undertake the management of the property with no particular fetter. It should not be read as imposing liability only where a landlord instigated or at least connived at his agent's illegitimate activities (*Scott v Thomson* 2003 S.L.T. 99, Court of Session, Ex Div.)

The word "unlawfully" means that the section applies not only to acts or omissions which are a trespass or a breach of contract, but also to acts which amount to breaches of the Protection from Eviction Act 1977 s.2 (Re-entry without court order), and s.3 (Eviction of former unprotected tenant or licensee without taking court proceedings).

Purchasers who are let into occupation as licensees before completion of the sale of premises may come within the definition of "landlord" in s.27(9)(c) (*Jones v Miah* (1992) 24 H.L.R. 578; [1992] 33 E.G. 59, CA). However, ss.27 and 28 impose liability on landlords alone to pay damages and accordingly no claim under these sections can lie against a landlord's agent as a joint tortfeasor (*Sampson v Wilson* [1996] Ch. 39; [1995] 3 W.L.R. 455, CA).

Landlords have a defence to proceedings if they can show that they "believed, or had reasonable cause to believe" that the occupier had ceased to occupy the premises, or that there were "reasonable grounds" for withdrawing or withholding services. It should also be noted that no damages are recoverable under ss.27 and 28 if the residential occupier is reinstated in the premises by the time at which any civil proceedings are disposed of or if a landlord has offered to reinstate the tenant and it was unreasonable of the tenant to refuse the offer of reinstatement (s.27(6) and (7)). In *Tagro v Cafane and Patel* [1991] 2 All E.R. 235, CA, the Court of Appeal held that, even though the tenant had obtained an injunction and even though the landlords had offered a key to a room which had been "wrecked", there had not been a reinstatement satisfying the Housing Act 1988 s.27(6)(b). See too *Wandsworth LBC v Osei-Bonsu* [1999] 1 All E.R. 265, CA.

A landlord's contention that s.27 only applies where "the seriousness of the landlord's conduct is established to a high degree and where he makes the tenant's position so intolerable that he is driven out of the property" was rejected by the Court of Appeal in *Abbott v Bayley* (2000) 32 H.L.R. 72, CA.

The real significance of s.27 is not the scope of the cause of action, which is narrower than the covenant for quiet enjoyment, but the way in which damages are to be assessed (see commentary to s.28 below).

The measure of damages

28.—(1) The basis for the assessment of damages referred to in **3A–913** section 27(3) above is the difference in value, determined as at the time immediately before the residential occupier ceased to occupy the premises in question as his residence, between—

(a) the value of the interest of the landlord in default determined on the assumption that the residential occupier continues to have the same right to occupy the premises as before that time; and

(b) the value of that interest determined on the assumption that the residential occupier has ceased to have that right.

(2) In relation to any premises, any reference in this section to

Paragraph numbers marked with a "+" can be found online and on CD.

HOUSING

the interest of the landlord in default is a reference to his interest in the building in which the premises in question are comprised (whether or not that building contains any other premises) together with its curtilage.

(3) For the purposes of the valuations referred to in subsection (1) above, it shall be assumed—

   (a) that the landlord in default is selling his interest on the open market to a willing buyer;

   (b) that neither the residential occupier nor any member of his family wishes to buy; and

   (c) that it is unlawful to carry out any substantial development of any of the land in which the landlord's interest subsists or to demolish the whole or part of any building on that land.

(4) In this section "the landlord in default" has the same meaning as in section 27 above and subsection (9) of that section applies in relation to this section as it applies in relation to that.

(5) Section 113 of the Housing Act 1985 (meaning of "members of a person's family") applies for the purposes of subsection (3)(b) above.

(6) The reference in subsection (3)(c) above to substantial development of any of the land in which the landlord's interest subsists is a reference to any development other than—

   (a) development for which planning permission is granted by a general development order for the time being in force and which is carried out so as to comply with any condition or limitation subject to which planning permission is so granted; or

   (b) a change of use resulting in the building referred to in subsection (2) above or any part of it being used as, or as part of, one or more dwelling-houses;

and in this subsection "general development order" has the meaning given in section 56(6) of the Town and Country Planning Act 1990 and other expressions have the same meaning as in that Act.

3A–914 *Note* —Amended by the Planning (Consequential Provisions) Act 1990 Sch.2, para.79(1).

"landlord"
3A–915 See s.27(9).

"residential occupier"
3A–916 See s.27(9) and the Protection from Eviction Act 1977 s.1, which defines "residential occupier" as "a person occupying the premises as a residence, whether under a contract or by virtue of any enactment or rule of law giving him the right to remain in occupation or restricting the right of any other person to recover possession of the premises."

"member of his family"
3A–917 See the Housing Act 1985 s.113.

The measure of damages
3A–918 Section 28 provides that damages are to be determined by subtracting the value of

Paragraph numbers marked with a "+" can be found online and on CD.

the premises if the tenant had remained in occupation from the value of the premises with vacant possession. In making such valuations, it is assumed that:

(i) The landlord is selling on the open market to a willing buyer; and

(ii) Neither the tenant nor any member of the tenant's family wishes to buy; and

(iii) No substantial development on the premises can be carried out unless planning permission has been granted by general development order within the meaning of the Town & County Planning Act 1990 s.56(6)).

Where a tenant is wrongfully evicted, but the eviction makes no difference to the value of the landlord's interest in the property, no damages can be awarded under the Housing Act 1988 ss.27 and 28 (*Melville v Bruton* (1997) 29 H.L.R. 319, CA).

In *Regalgrand Ltd v Dickerson* (1997) 29 H.L.R. 620; (1997) 75 P. & C.R. 313, CA, the judge reduced the tenants' damages from £12,000 to £1,500 pursuant to s.27(7)(a) because their conduct "was such that it [was] reasonable to mitigate the damages". The relevant conduct which she took into acount were:

(a) the withholding of rent without giving prior notice and without justification;

(b) the tenants' failure to inform the landlord that his installation of a new boiler had failed to cure the heating problems; and

(c) their intention to vacate in any event.

The tenants appealed on the grounds that the landlord had failed to plead mitigation, that the judge had failed to specify how she had arrived at the figure of £1,500, that their omissions were not "conduct" and that the judge had been wrong to take into account the arrears of rent. The Court of Appeal dismissed the appeal. Failure to pay rent was conduct. Although a mere intention (e.g. to leave) cannot amount to conduct, here the intention to leave has been partly acted upon because the tenants had moved their belongings and only very occasionally resided in the flat.

In view of s.27(5), damages awarded at common law for the loss of the right to occupy premises should be set off against damages awarded under ss.27 and 28 (*Mason v Nwokorie* (1994) 26 H.L.R. 60; [1994] 05 E.G. 155, CA). However, *Mason v Nwokorie* was distinguished in *Kaur (Kashmir) v Gill, The Times,* June 15, 1995, CA, where an award of general damages in addition to ss.27-28 damages was upheld because the damages had not been awarded for any loss of right to occupy, but rather for breaches of the covenant for quiet enjoyment. Note that:

"... where damages have been awarded to the tenant against the landlord under sections 27 and 28, there is no place for a further award of exemplary damages against either the landlord or against the person who assisted her in the eviction", but that principle does not prevent the award of aggravated damages" (per Sir Iain Glidewell in *Francis v Brown* (1997) 30 H.L.R. 143, CA).

In relation to damages, see also *Murray v Aslam* (1995) 27 H.L.R. 284, CA; *Francis v Brown* (1997) 30 H.L.R. 143, CA; *King v Jackson* (1998) 30 H.L.R. 541; [1998] 03 E.G. 138, CA and *Wandsworth LBC v Osei-Bonsu* [1999] 1 All E.R. 265, CA.

* * * *

CHAPTER V

PHASING OUT OF RENT ACTS AND OTHER TRANSITIONAL PROVISIONS

New protected tenancies and agricultural occupancies restricted to special cases

34.—(1) A tenancy which is entered into on or after the commencement of this Act cannot be a protected tenancy, unless—   **3A–919**

(a) it is entered into in pursuance of a contract made before the commencement of this Act; or

(b) it is granted to a person (alone or jointly with others) who, immediately before the tenancy was granted, was a protected or statutory tenant and is so granted by the person who at that time was the landlord (or one of the

Paragraph numbers marked with a "+" can be found online and on CD.

joint landlords) under the protected or statutory tenancy; or

(c) it is granted to a person (alone or jointly with others) in the following circumstances—

(i) prior to the grant of the tenancy, an order for possession of a dwelling-house was made against him (alone or jointly with others) on the court being satisfied as mentioned in section 98(1)(a) of, or Case 1 in Schedule 16 to the Rent Act 1977 or Case 1 in Schedule 4 to the Rent (Agriculture) Act 1976 (suitable alternative accommodation available); and

(ii) the tenancy is of the premises which constitute the suitable alternative accommodation as to which the court was so satisfied; and

(iii) in the proceedings for possession the court considered that, in the circumstances, the grant of an assured tenancy would not afford the required security and, accordingly, directed that the tenancy would be a protected tenancy; or

(d) it is a tenancy under which the interest of the landlord was at the time the tenancy was granted held by a the Commission for the New Towns or a development corporation, within the meaning of section 80 of the Housing Act 1985, and, before the date which has effect by virtue of paragraph (a) or paragraph (b) of subsection (4) of section 38 below, ceased to be so held by virtue of a disposal by the commission for the New Towns made pursuant to a direction under section 37 of the New Towns Act 1981.

(2) In subsection (1)(b) above "protected tenant" and "statutory tenant" do not include—

(a) a tenant under a protected shorthold tenancy;

(b) a protected or statutory tenant of a dwelling-house which was let under a protected shorthold tenancy which ended before the commencement of this Act and in respect of which at that commencement either there has been no grant of a further tenancy or any grant of a further tenancy has been to the person who, immediately before the grant, was in possession of the dwelling-house as a protected or statutory tenant;

and in this subsection "protected shorthold tenancy" includes a tenancy which, in proceedings for possession under Case 19 in Schedule 15 to the Rent Act 1977, is treated as a protected shorthold tenancy.

(3) In any case where—

(a) by virtue of subsections (1) and (2) above, a tenancy entered into on or after the commencement of this Act is an assured tenancy, but

Paragraph numbers marked with a "+" can be found online and on CD.

(b) apart from subsection (2) above, the effect of subsection (1)(b) above would be that the tenancy would be a protected tenancy, and

(c) the landlord and the tenant under the tenancy are the same as at the coming to an end of the protected or statutory tenancy which, apart from subsection (2) above, would fall within subsection (1)(b) above,

the tenancy shall be an assured shorthold tenancy (whether or not in the case of a tenancy to which the provision applies it fulfils the conditions in section 20(1) above) unless, before the tenancy is entered into, the landlord serves notice on the tenant that it is not to be a shorthold tenancy.

(4) A licence or tenancy which is entered into on or after the commencement of this Act cannot be a relevant licence or relevant tenancy for the purposes of the Rent (Agriculture) Act 1976 (in this subsection referred to as "the 1976 Act") unless—

(a) it is entered into in pursuance of a contract made before the commencement of this Act, or

(b) it is granted to a person (alone or jointly with others) who, immediately before the licence or tenancy was granted, was a protected occupier or statutory tenant, within the meaning of the 1976 Act, and is so granted by the person who at that time was the landlord or licensor (or one of the joint landlords or licensors) under the protected occupancy or statutory tenancy in question.

(5) Except as provided in subsection (4) above, expressions used in this section have the same meaning as in the Rent Act 1977.

Note —Amended by the Local Government and Housing Act 1989 s.195, Sch.11; **3A–920** Housing Act 1996 s.104, Sch.8, para.2 and the Housing and Regeneration Act 2008 (Consequential Provisions) Order 2008 (SI 2008/3002) para.37.

"commencement of this Act"
See s.141(2), which provides that Pt I shall come into force "at the expiry of the pe- **3A–921** riod of two months beginning on the day it is passed"—i.e. January 15, 1989.

"assured shorthold tenancy"
See ss.19A and 20. **3A–922**

"protected shorthold tenancy"
See the Housing Act 1980 s.52. **3A–923**

"landlord", and "tenancy"
See s.45. **3A–924**

New protected tenancies and agricultural occupancies restricted to special cases
Section 34 provides that no new Rent Act protected tenancies can be created after **3A–925** the Act came into force unless one of three exceptions applies. All new tenancies created on or after January 15, 1989 are assured or assured shorthold tenancies or totally unprotected tenancies unless:

(1) The tenancy was entered into in pursuance of a contract made before January 15, 1989, or

(2) The tenancy was granted to an existing 1977 Rent Act protected or statutory tenant by the same landlord. If there are joint tenants or joints landlords, it is

Paragraph numbers marked with a "+" can be found online and on CD.

sufficient for only one of the joint tenants to have been a protected tenant and for only one of the joint landlords to have been the landlord of the existing tenant or tenants. In *Secretarial Nominee Co Ltd v Thomas* [2005] EWCA Civ 1008; [2006] H.L.R. 5, the Court of Appeal held that s.34 "begins with the concept of a person who, after the commencement of the 1988 Act, is both a Rent Act tenant and has entered into a new tenancy. Such a person, moreover, has to have been a Rent Act tenant already before the new tenancy". The words "and prior to the commencement of this Act" in s.34 "have to be understood (in addition to the express requirement of "immediately before the tenancy was granted") as inherently qualifying the words "was a protected or statutory tenant". It is for the sake of such a tenant, and no other that the transitional protection of a protected tenancy is extended." The statutory language shows that the protection is for a particular person. Section 34 accordingly gave no rights to a person who had never been a joint tenant with a Rent Act tenant.

It is clear from *Hansard* (June 30, 1988, cols 75 and 87) that Parliament's intention was that this exception should apply even if the tenant was a protected tenant in other accommodation but has been granted a new post-January 15, 1989 tenancy in, say, a different building. This was confirmed by the Court of Appeal in *Laimond Properites Ltd v Al-Shakarchi* (1998) 30 H.L.R. 1099, CA, where the Court of Appeal held that s.34(1)(a), (b) and (c) deal with three separate situations. Section 34(1)(b) has no application in a case where the landlords have obtained an order for possession since the court "will have considered whether the new tenancy affords 'the required security' and whether the court should direct that the new tenancy be a protected tenancy". Roch L.J. also: (1) accepted submissions that s.34(1)(b) was mandatory, not permissive; and (2) approving *Gorringe v Twinsectra Ltd*, June 1994, Legal Action 11(cc), held that s.34(1)(b) protection applies both to new tenancies of the same premises and to tenancies of other premises granted by the same landlords. See too *Rajah v Arogol Co Ltd* [2001] EWCA Civ 454; [2002] H.L.R. 21, CA. It is the identity of the landlord and tenant that matters, not the identity of the premises. Further, the fact that the landlord has changed between the grant of the two tenancies does not affect the position. Section 34(1)(b) clearly refers to a grant at a later date by the person who was the landlord at the time of the later grant. Note too in *McAllister v Queens Cross Housing Association Ltd*, 2003 S.L.T. 971, a case involving a similar provision in Housing (Scotland) Act 1987 s.43(3)(c), where it was held that there is no requirement that the earlier tenancy should be of the same premises.

(3) Before the grant of the new tenancy an order for possession was made on the grounds of suitable alternative accommodation against a protected or statutory tenant (Rent Act 1977 s.98(1)(a) or Sched.16, Case 1) and in the possession proceedings relating to the earlier tenancy, the court directed that the tenancy of the suitable alternative accommodation shall be held on a protected tenancy. The court may make such a direction if an assured tenancy "would not afford the required security".

"restricted contracts"

3A–926   For the effect of Housing Act 1988 ss.34(1) and 36(2)(a) on restricted contracts, see *Rowe v Matthews* (2001) 33 H.L.R. 81, QBD.

Removal of special regimes for tenancies of housing associations etc.

3A–927   **35.**—(1) In this section "housing association tenancy" has the same meaning as in Part VI of the Rent Act 1977.

(2) A tenancy which is entered into on or after the commencement of this Act cannot be a housing association tenancy unless—

> (a) it is entered into in pursuance of a contract made before the commencement of this Act, or
>
> (b) it is granted to a person (alone or jointly with others) who, immediately before the tenancy was granted, was a

Paragraph numbers marked with a "+" can be found online and on CD.

tenant under a housing association tenancy and is so granted by the person who at that time was the landlord under that housing association tenancy; or

    (c) it is granted to a person (alone or jointly with others) in the following circumstances—

      (i) prior to the grant of the tenancy, an order for possession of a dwelling-house was made against him (alone or jointly with others) on the court being satisfied as mentioned in paragraph (b) or paragraph (c) of subsection (2) of section 84 of the Housing Act 1985; and

      (ii) the tenancy is of the premises which constitute the suitable accommodation as to which the court was so satisfied; and

      (iii) in the proceedings for possession the court directed that the tenancy would be a housing association tenancy; or

    (d) it is a tenancy under which the interest of the landlord was at the time the tenancy was granted held by the Commission for the New Towns or a development corporation, within the meaning of section 80 of the Housing Act 1985, and, before the date which has effect by virtue of paragraph (a) or paragraph (b) of subsection (4) of section 38 below, ceased to be so held by virtue of a disposal by the Commission for the New Towns made pursuant to a direction under section 37 of the New Towns Act 1981.

(3) Where, on or after the commencement of this Act, a registered social landlord, within the meaning of the Housing Act 1985 (see section 5(4) and (5) of that Act), grants a secure tenancy pursuant to an obligation under section 554(2A) of the Housing Act 1985 (as set out in Schedule 17 to this Act) then, in determining whether that tenancy is a housing association tenancy, it shall be assumed for the purposes only of section 86(2)(b) of the Rent Act 1977 (tenancy would be a protected tenancy but for section 15 or 16 of that Act) that the tenancy was granted before the commencement of this Act.

(4) Subject to section 38(4A) below a tenancy or licence which is entered into on or after the commencement of this Act cannot be a secure tenancy unless—

    (a) the interest of the landlord belongs to a local authority, a development corporation or an urban development corporation, all within the meaning of section 80 of the Housing Act 1985, or a housing action trust established under Part III of this Act; or

    (b) the interest of the landlord belongs to a housing co-operative within the meaning of section 27B of the Housing Act 1985 (agreements between local housing authorities and housing co-operatives) and the tenancy or licence is of a dwelling-house comprised in a housing co-operative agreement falling within that section, or

Paragraph numbers marked with a "+" can be found online and on CD.

(ba) the interest of the landlord belongs to the Homes and Communities Agency or the Welsh Ministers and the tenancy or licence falls within section 80(2A) to (2E) of the Housing Act 1985; or

(c) it is entered into in pursuance of a contract made before the commencement of this Act, or

(d) it is granted to a person (alone or jointly with others) who, immediately before it was entered into, was a secure tenant and is so granted by the body which at that time was the landlord or licensor under the secure tenancy, or

(e) it is granted to a person (alone or jointly with others) in the following circumstances—

   (i) prior to the grant of the tenancy or licence, an order for possession of a dwelling-house was made against him (alone or jointly with others) on the court being satisfied as mentioned in paragraph (b) or paragraph (c) of subsection (2) of section 84 of the Housing Act 1985; and

   (ii) the tenancy or licence is of the premises which constitute the suitable accommodation as to which the court was so satisfied; and

   (iii) in the proceedings for possession the court considered that, in the circumstances, the grant of an assured tenancy would not afford the required security and, accordingly, directed that the tenancy or licence would be a secure tenancy; or

(f) it is granted pursuant to an obligation under section 554(2A) of the Housing Act 1985 (as set out in Schedule 17 to this Act).

(5) If, on or after the commencement of this Act, the interest of the landlord under a protected or statutory tenancy becomes held by a housing association, a housing trust or the Housing Corporation or, where that interest becomes held by him as a result of the exercise by him of the functions under Part III of the Housing Associations Act 1985, the Secretary of State, nothing in the preceding provisions of this section shall prevent the tenancy from being a housing association tenancy or a secure tenancy and, accordingly, in such a case section 80 of the Housing Act 1985 (and any enactment which refers to that section) shall have effect without regard to the repeal of provisions of that section effected by this Act.

(6) In subsection (5) above "housing association" and "housing trust" have the same meaning as in the Housing Act 1985.

3A–928   *Note* —Amended by the Local Government and Housing Act 1989 s.195, Sch.11; the Housing Act 1996 (Consequential Provisions) Order 1996 (SI 1996/2325) art.5, Sch.2, para.18, Government of Wales Act 1998 Sch.15, para.15; Government of Wales Act 1998 (Housing) (Amendments) Order 1999 (SI 1999/61) and the Housing and Regeneration Act 2008 (Consequential Provisions) Order 2008 (SI 2008/3002) para.38.

Paragraph numbers marked with a "+" can be found online and on CD.

"fully mutual housing association" has the same meaning as in Part I of the Housing Associations Act 1985;

"landlord" includes any person from time to time deriving title under the original landlord and also includes, in relation to a dwelling-house, any person other than a tenant who is, or but for the existence of an assured tenancy would be, entitled to possession of the dwelling-house;

"let" includes "sub-let";

"prescribed" means prescribed by regulations made by the Secretary of State by statutory instrument;

"rates" includes water rates and charges but does not include an owner's drainage rate, as defined in section 63(2)(a) of the Land Drainage Act 1976;

"secure tenancy" has the meaning assigned by section 79 of the Housing Act 1985;

"statutory periodic tenancy" has the meaning assigned by section 5(7) above;

"tenancy" includes a sub-tenancy and an agreement for a tenancy or sub-tenancy; and

"tenant" includes a sub-tenant and any person deriving title under the original tenant or sub-tenant.

(2) Subject to paragraph 11 of Schedule 2 to this Act, any reference in this Part of this Act to the beginning of a tenancy is a reference to the day on which the tenancy is entered into or, if it is later, the day on which, under the terms of any lease, agreement or other document, the tenant is entitled to possession under the tenancy.

(3) Where two or more persons jointly constitute either the landlord or the tenant in relation to a tenancy, then, except where this Part of this Act otherwise provides, any reference to the landlord or to the tenant is a reference to all the persons who jointly constitute the landlord or the tenant, as the case may require.

(4) For the avoidance of doubt, it hereby declared that any reference in this Part of this Act (however expressed) to a power for a landlord to determine a tenancy does not include a reference to a power of re-entry or forfeiture for breach of any term or condition of the tenancy.

(5) Regulations under subsection (1) above may make different provision with respect to different cases or descriptions of case, including different provisions for different areas.

prescribed

See the Assured Tenancies and Agricultural Occupancies (Forms) Regulations (SI 1988/2203), amended by the Assured Tenancies and Agricultural Occupancies (Forms) (Amendment) Regulations (SI 1989/146); the Assured Tenancies and Agricultural Occupancies (Forms) (Amendment) Regulations 1990 (SI 1990/1532); the Assured Tenancies and Agricultural Occupancies (Forms) (Amendment) Regulations 1993 (SI 1993/654); the Assured Tenancies and Agricultural Occupancies (Forms) Regulations 1997 (SI 1997/194) and the Assured Tenancies and Agricultural (Forms) (Amendment) (England) Regulations 2003 (SI 2003/260).

3A–941

* * * *

3A–942

Paragraph numbers marked with a "+" can be found online and on CD.

SECTION 1

SCHEDULE 1

TENANCIES WHICH CANNOT BE ASSURED TENANCIES

PART I

THE TENANCIES

Tenancies entered into before commencement

1. A tenancy which is entered into before, or pursuant to a contract made before, the commencement of this Act.

Tenancies of dwelling-houses with high rateable values

3A–943 2.—(1) A tenancy—

(a) which is entered into on or after 1st April 1990 (otherwise than, where the dwelling-house had a rateable value on 31st March 1990, in pursuance of a contract made before 1st April 1990), and

(b) under which the rent payable for the time being is payable at a rate exceeding £25,000 a year.

(2) In sub-paragraph (1) "rent" does not include any sum payable by the tenant as is expressed (in whatever terms) to be payable in respect of rates, council tax, services, management, repairs, maintenance or insurance, unless it could not have been regarded by the parties to the tenancy as a sum so payable.

(2A.) A tenancy—

(a) which was entered into before the 1st April 1990, or on or after that date in pursuance of a contract made before that date, and

(b) under which the dwelling-house had a rateable value on 31st March 1990 which, if it is in Greater London, exceeded £1,500 and, if it is elsewhere, exceeded £750.

Tenancies at a low rent

3A–944 3. A tenancy under which for the time being no rent is payable.

(3A.) A tenancy—

(a) which is entered into on or after 1st April 1990 (otherwise than, where the dwelling-house had a rateable value on 31st March 1990, in pursuance of a contract made before 1st April 1990), and

(b) under which the rent payable for the time being is payable at a rate of, if the dwelling-house is in Greater London, £1,000 or less a year and, if it is elsewhere, £250 or less a year.

(3B.) A tenancy—

(a) which was entered into before 1st April 1990 or, where the dwelling-house had a rateable value on the 31st March 1990, on or after 1st April 1990 in pursuance of a contract made before that date, and

(b) under which the rent for the time being payable is less than two-thirds of the rateable value of the dwelling-house on 31st March 1990.

(3C.) Paragraph 2(2) above applies for the purposes of paragraphs 3, 3A and 3B as it applies for the purposes of paragraph 2(1).

Business tenancies

3A–945 4. A tenancy to which Part II of the Landlord and Tenant Act 1954 applies (business tenancies).

Licensed premises

3A–946 5. A tenancy under which the dwelling-house consists of or premises which, by virtue of a premises licence under the Licensing Act 2003 may be used for the supply of alcohol (within the meaning of section 14 of that Act) for consumption on the premises.

Paragraph numbers marked with a "+" can be found online and on CD.

912

Tenancies of agricultural land

3A-947

6.—(1) A tenancy under which agricultural land, exceeding two acres, is let together with the dwelling-house.

(2) In this paragraph "agricultural land" has the meaning set out in section 26(3)(a) of the General Rate Act 1967(exclusion of agricultural land and premises from liability for rating).

Tenancies of agricultural holdings etc

3A-948

7.—(1) A tenancy under which the dwelling-house—

(a) is comprised in an agricultural holding, and

(b) is occupied by the person responsible for the control (whether as tenant or as servant or agent of the tenant) of the farming of the holding.

(2) A tenancy under which the dwelling-house—

(a) is comprised in the holding held under a farm business tenancy, and

(b) is occupied by the person responsible for the control (whether as tenant or as servant or agent of the tenant) of the management of the holding.

(3) In this paragraph—

"agricultural holding" means any agricultural holding within the meaning of the Agricultural Holdings Act 1986 held under a tenancy in relation to which that Act applies, and

"farm business tenancy" and "holding", in relation to such a tenancy, have the same meaning as in the Agricultural Tenancies Act 1995.

Lettings to students

A-94

8.—(1) A tenancy which is granted to a person who is pursuing, or intends to pursue, a course of study provided by a specified educational institution and is so granted either by that institution or by another specified institution or body of person

(2) In sub-paragraph (1) above "specified" means specified, or of a class specific for the purposes of this paragraph by regulations made by the Secretary of Stat statutory instrument.

(3) A statutory instrument made in the exercise of the power conferred ub-paragraph (2) above shall be subject to annulment in pursuance of a resoluti ei ther House of Parliament.

Holiday lettings

3A-950

9. A tenancy the purpose of which is to confer on the tenant the right cup dwelling-house for a holiday.

Resident landlords

3A-951

10.—(1) A tenancy in respect of which the following conditions ar illed a case cep

(a) that the dwelling-house forms part only of a building arildi is not a where the dwelling-house also forms part of a flat, t purpose-built block of flats and ant by an indi-

(b) that, subject to Part III of this Schedule, the tenancy pie his only or vidual who, at the time when the tenancy was grante principal home another dwelling-house which,— so forms part of the

(i) in the case mentioned in paragraph (a) ab flat; or and

(ii) in any other case, also forms part of the b since the tenancy was

(c) that, subject to Part III of this Schedule, at y has belonged to an in-granted the interest of the landlord under th occupied as his only or dividual who, at the time he owned that principal home another dwelling-house wh ve, also formed part of the

(i) in the case mentioned in paragrap flat, or building; and

(ii) in any other case, also formed p om this sub-paragraph by sub-

(d) that the tenancy is not one which is e paragraph (3) below.

e found online and on CD.

Paragraph numbers marked with a

(2) If a tenancy was granted by two or more persons jointly, the reference in sub-paragraph (1)(b) above to an individual is a reference to any one of those persons and if the interest of the landlord is for the time being held by two or more persons jointly, the reference in sub-paragraph (1)(c) above to an individual is a reference to any one of those persons.

(3) A tenancy (in this sub-paragraph referred to as "the new tenancy") is excluded from sub-paragraph (1) above if—

(a) it is granted to a person (alone, or jointly with others) who, immediately before it was granted, was a tenant under an assured tenancy (in this sub-paragraph referred to as "the former tenancy") of the same dwelling-house or of another dwelling-house which forms part of the building in question; and

(b) the landlord under the new tenancy and under the former tenancy is the same person or, if either of those tenancies is or was granted by two or more persons jointly, the same person is the landlord or one of the landlords under each tenancy.

Crown tenancies

3A-952 11.—(1) A tenancy under which the interest of the landlord belongs to Her Majesty in right of the Crown or to a government department or is held in trust for Her Majesty for the purpose of a government department.

(2) The reference in sub-paragraph (1) above to the case where the interest of the landlord belongs to Her Majesty in right of the Crown does not include the case where that interest is under the management of the Crown Estate Commissioners or it is held by him as a result of the exercise by him of the functions under Part III 1985 of the Housing Associations Act 1985.

Local authority tenancies etc.

A-953 2.—(1) A tenancy under which the interest of the landlord belongs to—

(a) a local authority, as defined in sub-paragraph (2) below;

(b) the Homes and Communities Agency but only if the tenancy falls within subsections (2A) to (2E) of section 80 of the Housing Act 1985;

(c) the Welsh Ministers but only if the tenancy falls within subsections (2A) to (2E) of section 80 of the Housing Act 1985;

(d) an urban development corporation established by an order under section 135 of the Local Government, Planning and Land Act 1980;

(f) an authority established under section 10 of the Local Government Act 1985 (waste disposal authorities);

(f) the Lee Valley established for an area in England by an order under section 207 of the Local Government and Public Involvement in Health Act 2007 (joint waste authorities);

(g) a residuary body within the meaning of the Local Government Act 1985; or

(gg) the Residuary Body for Wales (Corff Gweddillol Cymru);

(h) a fully mutual housing association; or

(i) a housing action trust established under Part III of this Act.

(2) The following are local authorities for the purposes of sub-paragraph (1)(a) above—

(a) the council of a county;

(b) the Common Council, county borough, district or London borough;

(c) the Council of the Isles of Scilly;

(d) the City of London;

(da) the Broads Authority;

(e) a National Park authority;

(f) the Inner London Education Authority;

(g) a joint authority, within the meaning of the Local Government Act 1985; and

(h) a police authority established under section 3 of the Police Act 1964.

Accommodation for asylum-seekers

12A.—(1) A tenancy granted by a private landlord under arrangements for the pro- **3A–954**
vision of support for asylum-seekers or dependants or asylum-seekers made under
section 4 or Part VI of the Immigration and Asylum Act 1999.

(2) Private landlord means a landlord who is not within section 80(1) of the Housing Act 1985.

12B.—(1) A tenancy granted by a private landlord under arrangements for the provision of accommodation for persons with temporary protection made under the
Displaced Persons (Temporary Protection) Regulations 2005.

(2) "Private landlord" means a landlord who is not within section 80(1) of the Housing Act 1985.

Transitional cases

13.—(1) A protected tenancy, within the meaning of the Rent Act 1977. **3A–955**

(2) A housing association tenancy, within the meaning of Part VI of that Act.

(3) A secure tenancy.

(4) Where a person is a protected occupier of a dwelling-house, within the meaning
of the Rent (Agriculture) Act 1976, the relevant tenancy, within the meaning of that
Act, by virtue of which he occupies the dwelling-house.

PART II

RATEABLE VALUES

14.—(1) The rateable value of a dwelling-house at any time shall be ascertained for **3A–956**
the purposes of Part I of this Schedule as follows—

(a) if the dwelling-house is a hereditament for which a rateable value is then
shown in the valuation list, it shall be that rateable value;

(b) if the dwelling-house forms part only of such a hereditament or consists of or
forms part of more than one such hereditament, its rateable value shall be
taken to be such value as is found by a proper apportionment or aggregation
of the rateable value or values so shown.

(2) Any question arising under this Part of this Schedule as to the proper apportionment or aggregation of any value or values shall be determined by the county court
and the decision of that court shall be final.

15. Where, after the time at which the rateable value of a dwelling-house is material
for the purposes of any provision of Part I of this Schedule, the valuation list is altered
so as to vary the rateable value of the hereditament of which the dwelling-house
consists (in whole or in part) or forms part and the alteration has effect from that time
or from an earlier time, the rateable value of the dwelling-house at the material time
shall be ascertained as if the value shown in the valuation list at the material time had
been the value shown in the list as altered.

16. Paragraphs 14 and 15 above apply in relation to any other land which, under
section 2 of this Act, is treated as part of a dwelling-house as they apply in relation to
the dwelling-house itself.

PART III

PROVISIONS FOR DETERMINING APPLICATION OF PARAGRAPH 10 (RESIDENT LANDLORDS)

17.—(1) In determining whether the condition in paragraph 10(1)(c) above is at any **3A–957**
time fulfilled with respect to a tenancy, there shall be disregarded—

(a) any period of not more than twenty-eight days, beginning with the date on
which the interest of the landlord under the tenancy becomes vested at law
and in equity in an individual who, during that period, does not occupy as his
only or principal home another dwelling-house which forms part of the building or, as the case may be, flat concerned;

(b) if, within a period falling within paragraph (a) above, the individual concerned
notifies the tenant in writing of his intention to occupy as his only or principal

Paragraph numbers marked with a "+" can be found online and on CD.

home another dwelling-house in the building or, as the case may be, flat concerned, the period beginning with the date on which the interest of the landlord under the tenancy becomes vested in that individual as mentioned in that paragraph and ending—

    (i) at the expiry of the period of six months beginning on that date, or

    (ii) on the date on which that interest ceases to be so vested, or

    (iii) on the date on which that interest becomes again vested in such an individual as is mentioned in paragraph 10(1)(c) or the condition in that paragraph becomes deemed to be fulfilled by virtue of paragraph 18(1) or paragraph 20 below,

    whichever is the earlier; and

(c) any period of not more than two years beginning with the date on which the interest of the landlord under the tenancy becomes, and during which it remains, vested—

    (i) in trustees as such; or

    (ii) by virtue of section 9 of the Administration of Estates Act 1925, in the Probate Judge or the Public Trustee, within the meaning of that Act.

(2) Where the interest of the landlord under a tenancy becomes vested at law and in equity in two or more persons jointly, of whom at least one was an individual, sub-paragraph (1) above shall have effect subject to the following modifications—

(a) in paragraph (a) for the words from "an individual" to "occupy" there shall be substituted "the joint landlords if, during that period none of them occupies"; and

(b) in paragraph (b) for the words "the individual concerned" there shall be substituted "any of the joint landlords who is an individual"and for the words "that individual" there shall be substituted "the joint landlords".

18.—(1) During any period when—

(a) the interest of the landlord under the tenancy referred to in paragraph 10 above is vested in trustees as such, and

(b) that interest is held on trust for any person who or for two or more persons of whom at least one occupies as his only or principal home a dwelling-house which forms part of the building or, as the case may be, flat referred to in paragraph 10(1)(a),

the condition in paragraph 10(1)(c) shall be deemed to be fulfilled and accordingly, no part of that period shall be disregarded by virtue of paragraph 17 above.

(2) If a period during which the condition in paragraph 10(1)(c) is deemed to be fulfilled by virtue of sub-paragraph (1) above comes to an end on the death of a person who was in occupation of a dwelling-house as mentioned in paragraph (b) of that sub-paragraph, then, in determining whether that condition is at any time thereafter fulfilled, there shall be disregarded any period—

(a) which begins on the date of the death;

(b) during which the interest of the landlord remains vested as mentioned in sub-paragraph (1)(a) above; and

(c) which ends at the expiry of the period of two years beginning on the date of the death or on any earlier date on which the condition in paragraph 10(1)(c)becomes again deemed to be fulfilled by virtue of sub-paragraph (1) above.

19. In any case where—

(a) immediately before a tenancy comes to an end the condition in paragraph 10(1)(c) is deemed to be fulfilled by virtue of paragraph 18(1) above, and

(b) on the coming to an end of that tenancy the trustees in whom the interest of the landlord is vested grant a new tenancy of the same or substantially the same dwelling-house to a person (alone or jointly with others) who was the tenant or one of the tenants under the previous tenancy,

the condition in paragraph 10(1)(b) above shall be deemed to be fulfilled with respect to the new tenancy.

Paragraph numbers marked with a "+" can be found online and on CD.

20.—(1) The tenancy referred to in paragraph 10 above falls within this paragraph if the interest of the landlord under the tenancy becomes vested in the personal representatives of a deceased person acting in that capacity.

(2) If the tenancy falls within this paragraph, the condition in paragraph 10(1)(c) shall be deemed to be fulfilled for any period, beginning with the date on which the interest becomes vested in the personal representatives and not exceeding two years, during which the interest of the landlord remains so vested.

21. Throughout any period which, by virtue of paragraph 17 or paragraph 18(2) above, falls to be disregarded for the purpose of determining whether the condition in paragraph 10(1)(c) is fulfilled with respect to a tenancy, no order shall be made for possession of the dwelling-house subject to that tenancy, other than an order which might be made if that tenancy were or, as the case may be, had been an assured tenancy.

22. For the purposes of paragraph 10 above, a building is a purpose-built block of flats if as constructed it contained, and it contains, two or more flats; and for this purpose "flat" means a dwelling-house which—

(a) forms part only of a building; and

(b) is separated horizontally from another dwelling-house which forms part of the same building.

Note —Amended by the Reference to Rating (Housing) Regulations 1990 (SI 1990/ **3A–958** 434); the Local Government (Wales) Act 1994 Sch.9, para.9, and Sch.13, para.31; the Law of Property (Miscellaneous Provisions) Act 1994 Sch.1, para.11; the Local Government Finance (Housing) (Consequential Amendments) Order 1993 (SI 1993/651); and the Police and Magistrates' Court Act 1994 Sch.4, para.62; the Environmental Act 1995 s.78, Sch.10, para.28; the Agricultural Tenancies 1995 Sch., para.34; the Trusts of Land and Appointment of Trustees Act 1996 s.25(2), Sch.4; the Government of Wales Act 1998 Sch.18, Pt IV; the Government of Wales Act 1998 (Housing) (Amendments) Order 1999 (SI 1999/61); the Immigration and Asylum Act 1999 Sch.14, para.88; the Licensing Act 2003 s.198(1), Sch.6, para.108; SI 2005/1379; the Immigration, Nationality and Asylum Act 2006 s.43(4); the Local Government and Public Involvement in Health Act 2007 s.209(2), Sch.13, Pt.II, para.44 with effect from April 1, 2008 (SI 2008/917)and the Housing and Regeneration Act 2008 (Consequential Provisions) Order 2008 (SI 2008/3002) para.40. The Schedule has also been amended by Housing and Regeneration Act 2008 Sch.15 to introduce family intervention tenancies which cannot be assured tenancies. The amendment is printed as part of the Housing and Regeneration Act 2008—see below.

Schedule 1

This Schedule lists types of tenancies which cannot be assured **3A–959** tenancies:

Paragraph 1

A tenancy which is entered into before or pursuant to a contract made before Janu- **3A–960** ary 15, 1989.

"commencement of this Act"

See s.141(2) which provides that Pt I shall come into force "at the expiry of the pe- **3A–961** riod of two months beginning on the day it is passed"—i.e. January 15, 1989.

Paragraph 2

Tenancies of dwelling-houses with high rateable values—i.e. over £1,500 in Greater **3A–962** London, over £750 elsewhere (compare the Rent Act 1977 s.4). Note that the References to Rating (Housing) Regulations 1990 (SI 1990/434) provide that where tenancies are granted after April 1, 1990, they cannot be assured if the rent is more than £25,000 per annum. "Rent" does not include sums paid in respect of services, repairs, maintenance or insurance.

In *Bankway Properties v Dunsford* [2001] EWCA Civ 528; [2001] 1 W.L.R. 1369, CA the Court of Appeal found that a clause permitting a landlord to increase the rent of a tenant in receipt of housing benefit to £25,000 per annum was a mere device, which

Paragraph numbers marked with a "+" can be found online and on CD.

enabled the landlord, effectively when it chose, to recover possession. In those circumstances it was unenforceable and the landlord's claim for possession based upon arrears was dismissed.

Paragraph 3

3A–963   Tenancies at a low rent—either where no rent is payable or where the rent is less than two thirds of the rateable value. The date for determining whether a tenancy is a tenancy at a low rent is the date when the relevant issue arises (*Woozley v Woodall Smith* [1950] 1 K.B. 325). In effect a tenancy may drift in and out of being an assured tenancy, subject to fluctuating costs (compare the Rent Act 1977 s.5). Note that The References to Rating (Housing) Regulations provide that tenancies granted after April 1, 1990 cannot be assured if the *rent* is less than £1,000 per annum in London or less than £250 per annum outside London.

Paragraph 4

3A–964   Business tenancies—see Pt II of the Landlord & Tenant Act 1954 (compare the Rent Act 1977 ss.2 and 24 and see commentary thereto) and *Broadway Investments Hackney Ltd v Grant* [2006] EWCA Civ 1709; [2007] H.L.R. 23; where, Lloyd L.J., after considering the Landlord and Tenant Act 1954 s.23, said that the question posed by that section:

> "is a factual one. Does the tenant occupy all or part of the premises comprised in the tenancy, and if so does he occupy them, or part of them, for the purposes of a business carried on by him, or for those and other purposes?"

Paragraph 5

3A–965   Tenancies under which dwelling-houses consists of or comprise premises licensed for the sale of intoxicating liquors for consumption on the premises (compare the Rent Act 1977 s.11).

Paragraphs 6 and 7

3A–966   Tenancies under which agricultural land, exceeding two acres is let together with the dwelling-house and agricultural holdings within the meaning of the Agricultural Holdings Act 1986 (compare the Rent Act 1977 s.10).

Paragraph 8

3A–967   Lettings to students by a specified educational institution. See the Assured and Protected Tenancies (Lettings to Students) Regulations 1998 (SI 1998/1967) which define SEIs—basically any institution which provides higher or further education which is publicly funded and various other named institutions. Note also that lettings by registered housing associations to students cannot be assured tenancies (compare the Rent Act 1977 s.8).

Paragraph 9

3A–968   Holiday lettings—where the purpose of the tenancy is to confer on the tenant the right to occupy the dwelling-house for a holiday (see commentary to the Rent Act 1977 s.9). In *Buchmann v May* [1978] 2 All E.R. 993; (1976) 240 E.G. 49, CA, the Court of Appeal held that the labels put on a transaction are not conclusive, but that where a tenancy agreement expressly states the purpose for which it is made, that statement is evidence of that purpose, unless the tenant can establish that it does not correspond with the true purpose, either because the express label is a sham or because it is a false label. Although a court will be "astute to detect a sham where it appears that a provision has been inserted for the purpose of depriving the tenant of statutory protection under the Rent Acts" ([1978] 2 All E.R. at 999), the burden of proof lies on the tenant. In that case there was no evidence which displaced the express purpose and accordingly there was no Rent Act protection. The court accepted the dictionary definition of a holiday as "a period of cessation of work, or period of recreation". See also *R. v Rent Officer for Camden LBC Ex p. Plant* (1980) 257 E.G. 713; (1983) 7 H.L.R. 15, QBD, where there was "clear evidence that all the parties knew that [the applicants] were going to occupy it for the purpose of their work as students' and that that was "conclusive of the matter".

Paragraph numbers marked with a "+" can be found online and on CD.

Paragraph 10

Compare the Rent Act 1977 s.12 and the commentary to that section. **3A–969**

The provision of "Board" is *not* an exception (compare the Rent Act 1977 s.7).

Paragraph 12

Welsh Development Agency—Note that some tenants of the Welsh Development **3A–970** Agency do not enjoy security of tenure. See para.3A–60.1,the Welsh Development Agency Act 1975 Sch.4 as inserted by the Government of Wales Act 1998 Sch.13.

If one of the exceptions in Sch.1 applies, the tenant has no security of tenure. Once a notice to quit has been served and has expired the tenant has no statutory protection, except, in some cases, for the Protection from Eviction Act 1977 s.3 which provides that it is unlawful for a landlord to evict such a tenant without taking court proceedings. The landlord need only prove that the contractual tenancy has been terminated.

SECTION 7   SCHEDULE 2

GROUNDS FOR POSSESSION OF DWELLING-HOUSES LET ON ASSURED TENANCIES

PART I

GROUNDS ON WHICH COURT MUST ORDER POSSESSION

Ground 1

Not later than the beginning of the tenancy the landlord gave notice in writing to **3A–971** the tenant that possession might be recovered on this ground or the court is of the opinion that it is just and equitable to dispense with the requirement of notice and (in either case)—

(a) at some time before the beginning of the tenancy, the landlord who is seeking possession or, in the case of joint landlords seeking possession, at least one of them occupied the dwelling-house as his only or principal home; or

(b) the landlord who is seeking possession or, in the case of joint landlords seeking possession, at least one of them requires the dwelling-house as his, his spouse's or his civil partner's only or principal home and neither the landlord (or, in the case of joint landlords, any one of them) nor any other person who, as landlord, derived title under the landlord who gave the notice mentioned above acquired the reversion on the tenancy for money or money's worth.

Ground 2

The dwelling-house is subject to a mortgage granted before the beginning of the **3A–972** tenancy and—

(a) the mortgagee is entitled to exercise a power of sale conferred on him by the mortgage or by section 101 of the Law of Property Act 1925; and

(b) the mortgagee requires possession of the dwelling-house for the purpose of disposing of it with vacant possession in exercise of that power; and

(c) either notice was given as mentioned in Ground 1 above or the court is satisfied that it is just and equitable to dispense with the requirement of notice;

and for the purposes of this ground "mortgage" includes a charge and "mortgagee" shall be construed accordingly.

Ground 3

The tenancy is a fixed term tenancy for a term not exceeding eight months and— **3A–973**

(a) not later than the beginning of the tenancy the landlord gave notice in writing to the tenant that possession might be recovered on this ground; and

(b) at some time within the period of twelve months ending with the beginning of the tenancy, the dwelling-house was occupied under a right to occupy it for a holiday.

Ground 4

The tenancy is a fixed term tenancy for a term not exceeding twelve months and— **3A–974**

Paragraph numbers marked with a "+" can be found online and on CD.

(a) not later than the beginning of the tenancy the landlord gave notice in writing to the tenant that possession might be recovered on this ground, and

(b) at some time within the period of twelve months ending with the beginning of the tenancy, the dwelling-house was let on a tenancy falling within paragraph 8 of Schedule 1 to this Act.

Ground 5

3A-975 The dwelling-house is held for the purpose of being available for occupation by a minister of religion as a residence from which to perform the duties of his office and—

(a) not later than the beginning of the tenancy the landlord gave notice in writing to the tenant that possession might be recovered on this ground; and

(b) the court is satisfied that the dwelling-house is required for occupation by a minister of religion as such a residence.

Ground 6

3A-976 The landlord who is seeking possession or, if that landlord is a registered social landlord or charitable housing trust, a superior landlord intends to demolish or reconstruct the whole or a substantial part of the dwelling-house or to carry out substantial works on the dwelling-house or any part thereof or any building of which it forms part and the following conditions are fulfilled—

(a) the intended work cannot reasonably be carried out without the tenant giving up possession of the dwelling-house because—

(i) the tenant is not willing to agree to such a variation of the terms of the tenancy as would give such access and other facilities as would permit the intended work to be carried out, or

(ii) the nature of the intended work is such that no such variation is practicable, or

(iii) the tenant is not willing to accept an assured tenancy of such part only of the dwelling-house (in this sub-paragraph referred to as "the reduced part") as would leave in the possession of his landlord so much of the dwelling-house as would be reasonable to enable the intended work to be carried out and, where appropriate, as would give such access and other facilities over the reduced part as would permit the intended work to be carried out, or

(iv) the nature of the intended work is such that such a tenancy is not practicable; and

(b) either the landlord seeking possession acquired his interest in the dwelling-house before the grant of the tenancy or that interest was in existence at the time of that grant and neither that landlord (or, in the case of joint landlords, any of them) nor any other person who, alone or jointly with others, has acquired that interest since that time acquired it for money or money's worth; and

(c) the assured tenancy on which the dwelling-house is let did not come into being by virtue of any provision of Schedule 1 to the Rent Act 1977, as amended by Part I of Schedule 4 to this Act or, as the case may be, section 4 of the Rent (Agriculture) Act 1976, as amended by Part II of that Schedule.

For the purposes of this ground, if, immediately before the grant of the tenancy, the tenant to whom it was granted or, if it was granted to joint tenants, any of them was the tenant or one of the joint tenants of the dwelling-house concerned under an earlier assured tenancy or, as the case may be, under a tenancy to which Schedule 10 to the Local Government and Housing Act 1989 applied, any reference in paragraph (b) above to the grant of the tenancy is a reference to the grant of that or, as the case may be, to the grant of the tenancy to which the said Schedule 10 applied.

For the purposes of this ground "registered social landlord" has the same meaning as in the Housing Act 1985 (see section 5(4) and (5) of that Act) and "charitable housing trust" means a housing trust, within the meaning of the Housing Associations Act 1985, which is a charity, within the meaning of the Charities Act 1993.

For the purposes of this ground, every acquisition under Part IV of this Act shall be taken to be an acquisition for money or money's worth; and in any case where—

Paragraph numbers marked with a "+" can be found online and on CD.

    (i) the tenancy (in this paragraph referred to as "the current tenancy") was granted to a person (alone or jointly with others) who, immediately before it was granted, was a tenant under a tenancy of a different dwelling-house (in this paragraph referred to as "the earlier tenancy"), and

    (ii) the landlord under the current tenancy is the person who, immediately before that tenancy was granted, was the landlord under the earlier tenancy, and

    (iii) the condition in paragraph (b) above could not have been fulfilled with respect to the earlier tenancy by virtue of an acquisition under Part IV of this Act (including one taken to be such an acquisition by virtue of the previous operation of this paragraph),

the acquisition of the landlord's interest under the current tenancy shall be taken to have been under that Part and the landlord shall be taken to have acquired that interest after the grant of the current tenancy.

Ground 7

3A–977

The tenancy is a periodic tenancy (including a statutory periodic tenancy) which has devolved under the will or intestacy of the former tenant and the proceedings for the recovery of possession are begun not later than twelve months after the death of the former tenant or, if the court so directs, after the date on which, in the opinion of the court, the landlord or, in the case of joint landlords, any one of them became aware of the former tenant's death.

    For the purposes of this ground, the acceptance by the landlord of rent from a new tenant after the death of the former tenant shall not be regarded as creating a new periodic tenancy, unless the landlord agrees in writing to a change (as compared with the tenancy before the death) in the amount of the rent, the period of the tenancy, the premises which are let or any other term of the tenancy.

Ground 8

3A–978

Both at the date of the service of the notice under section 8 of this Act relating to the proceedings for possession and at the date of the hearing—

    (a) if rent is payable weekly or fortnightly, at least eight weeks rent is unpaid;

    (b) if rent is payable monthly, at least two months rent is unpaid;

    (c) if rent is payable quarterly, at least one quarter's rent is more than three months in arrears; and

    (d) if rent is payable yearly, at least three months' rent is more than three months in arrears;

and for the purpose of this ground "rent" means rent lawfully due from the tenant.

PART II

GROUNDS ON WHICH COURT MAY ORDER POSSESSION

Ground 9

3A–979

Suitable alternative accommodation is available for the tenant or will be available for him when the order for possession takes effect.

Ground 10

3A–980

Some rent lawfully due from the tenant—

    (a) is unpaid on the date on which the proceedings for possession are begun; and

    (b) except where subsection (1)(b) of section 8 of this Act applies, was in arrears at the date of the service of the notice under that section relating to those proceedings.

Ground 11

3A–981

Whether or not any rent is in arrears on the date on which proceedings for possession are begun, the tenant has persistently delayed paying rent which has become lawfully due.

Ground 12

3A–982

Any obligation of the tenancy (other than one related to the payment of rent) has been broken or not performed.

Paragraph numbers marked with a "+" can be found online and on CD.

HOUSING

Ground 13

3A–983   The condition of the dwelling-house or any of the common parts has deteriorated owing to acts of waste by, or the neglect or default of, the tenant or any other person residing in the dwelling-house and, in the case of an act of waste by, or the neglect or default of, a person lodging with the tenant or a sub-tenant of his, the tenant has not taken such steps as he ought reasonably to have taken for the removal of the lodger or sub-tenant.

For the purposes of this ground, "common parts" means any part of a building comprising the dwelling-house and any other premises which the tenant is entitled under the terms of the tenancy to use in common with the occupiers of other dwelling-houses in which the landlord has an estate or interest.

Ground 14

3A–984   The tenant or a person residing in or visiting the dwelling-house—

(a) has been guilty of conduct causing or likely to cause a nuisance or annoyance to a person residing, visiting or otherwise engaging in a lawful activity in the locality, or

(b) has been convicted of—

(i) using the dwelling-house or allowing it to be used immoral or illegal purposes, or

(ii) an indictable offence committed in, or in the locality of, the dwelling-house.

Ground 14A

3A–985   The dwelling-house was occupied (whether alone or with others) by a married couple, a couple who are civil partners of each other, or a couple living together as husband and wife or a couple living together as if they were civil partners and—

(a) one or both of the partners is a tenant of the dwelling-house,

(b) the landlord who is seeking possession is a registered social landlord or a charitable housing trust,

(c) one partner has left the dwelling-house because of violence or threats of violence by the other towards—

(i) that partner, or

(ii) children of the partnership.

(d) the court is satisfied that the partner who has left is unlikely to return.

For the purposes of this ground "registered social landlord" and "member of the family" have the same meaning as in Part I of the Housing Act 1996 and "charitable housing trust" means a housing trust, within the meaning of the Housing Associations Act 1985, which is a charity within the meaning of the Charities Act 1993.

Ground 15

3A–986   The condition of any furniture provided for use under the tenancy has, in the opinion of the court, deteriorated owing to ill-treatment by the tenant or any other person residing in the dwelling-house and, in the case of ill-treatment by a person lodging with the tenant or by a sub-tenant of his, the tenant has not taken such steps as he ought reasonably to have taken for the removal of the lodger or sub-tenant.

Ground 16

3A–987   The dwelling-house was let to the tenant in consequence of his employment by the landlord seeking possession or a previous landlord under the tenancy and the tenant has ceased to be in that employment.

For the purposes of this ground, at a time when the landlord is or was the Secretary of State, employment by a health service body, as defined in section 60(7) of the National Health Service and Community Care Act 1990, shall be regarded as employment by the Secretary of State.

Ground 17

3A–988   The tenant is the person, or one of the persons, to whom the tenancy was granted and the landlord was induced to grant the tenancy by a false statement made knowingly or recklessly by—

Paragraph numbers marked with a "+" can be found online and on CD.

(a) the tenant or,

(b) a person acting at the tenant's instigation.

PART III

SUITABLE ALTERNATIVE ACCOMMODATION

1. For the purposes of Ground 9 above, a certificate of the local housing authority for the district in which the dwelling-house in question is situated, certifying that the authority will provide suitable alternative accommodation for the tenant by a date specified in the certificate, shall be conclusive evidence that suitable alternative accommodation will be available for him by that date. **3A–989**

2. Where no such certificate as is mentioned in paragraph 1 above is produced to the court, accommodation shall be deemed to be suitable for the purposes of Ground 9 above if it consists of either—

(a) premises which are to be let as a separate dwelling such that they will then be let on an assured tenancy, other than—

    (i) a tenancy in respect of which notice is given not later than the beginning of the tenancy that possession might be recovered on any of Grounds 1 to 5 above, or

    (ii) an assured shorthold tenancy, within the meaning of Chapter II of Part I of this Act, or

(b) premises to be let as a separate dwelling on terms which will, in the opinion of the court, afford to the tenant security of tenure reasonably equivalent to the security afforded by Chapter I of Part I of this Act in the case of an assured tenancy of a kind mentioned in sub-paragraph (a) above,

and, in the opinion of the court, the accommodation fulfils the relevant conditions as defined in paragraph 3 below.

3.—(1) For the purposes of paragraph 2 above, the relevant conditions are that the accommodation is reasonably suitable to the needs of the tenant and his family as regards proximity to place of work, and either—

(a) similar as regards rental and extent to the accommodation afforded by dwelling-houses provided in the neighbourhood by any local housing authority for persons whose needs as regards extent are, in the opinion of the court, similar to those of the tenant and of his family; or

(b) reasonably suitable to the means of the tenant and to the needs of the tenant and his family as regards extent and character; and

that if any furniture was provided for use under the assured tenancy in question, furniture is provided for use in the accommodation which is either similar to that so provided or is reasonably suitable to the needs of the tenant and his family.

(2) For the purposes of sub-paragraph (1)(a) above, a certificate of a local housing authority stating—

(a) the extent of the accommodation afforded by dwelling-houses provided by the authority to meet the needs of tenants with families of such number as may be specified in the certificate, and

(b) the amount of the rent charged by the authority for dwelling-houses affording accommodation of that extent,

shall be conclusive evidence of the facts so stated.

4. Accommodation shall not be deemed to be suitable to the needs of the tenant and his family if the result of their occupation of the accommodation would be that it would be an overcrowded dwelling-house for the purposes of Part X of the Housing Act 1985.

5. Any document purporting to be a certificate of a local housing authority named therein issued for the purposes of this Part of this Schedule and to be signed by the proper officer of that authority shall be received in evidence and, unless the contrary is shown, shall be deemed to be such a certificate without further proof.

6. In this Part of this Schedule "local housing authority" and "district", in relation to such an authority, have the same meaning as in the Housing Act 1985.

Paragraph numbers marked with a "+" can be found online and on CD.

Part IV

Notices Relating to Recovery of Possession

3A–990   7. Any reference in Grounds 1 to 5 in Part I of this Schedule or in the following provisions of this Part to the landlord giving a notice in writing to the tenant is, in the case of joint landlords, a reference to at least one of the joint landlords giving such a notice.

8.—(1) If, not later than the beginning of a tenancy (in this paragraph referred to as "the earlier tenancy"), the landlord gives such a notice in writing to the tenant as is mentioned in any of Grounds 1 to 5 in Part I of this Schedule, then, for the purposes of the ground in question and any further application of this paragraph, that notice shall also have effect as if it had been given immediately before the beginning of any later tenancy falling within sub-paragraph (2) below.

(2) Subject to sub-paragraph (3) below, sub-paragraph (1) above applies to a later tenancy—

(a) which takes effect immediately on the coming to an end of the earlier tenancy; and

(b) which is granted (or deemed to be granted) to the person who was the tenant under the earlier tenancy immediately before it came to an end; and

(c) which is of substantially the same dwelling-house as the earlier tenancy.

(3) Sub-paragraph (1) above does not apply in relation to a later tenancy if, not later than the beginning of the tenancy, the landlord gave notice in writing to the tenant that the tenancy is not one in respect of which possession can be recovered on the ground in question.

9. Where paragraph 8(1) above has effect in relation to a notice given as mentioned in Ground 1 in Part I of this Schedule, the reference in paragraph (b) of that ground to the reversion on the tenancy is a reference to the reversion on the earlier tenancy and on any later tenancy falling within paragraph 8(2) above.

10. Where paragraph 8(1) above has effect in relation to a notice given as mentioned in Ground 3 or Ground 4 in Part I of this Schedule, any second or subsequent tenancy in relation to which the notice has effect shall be treated for the purpose of that ground as beginning at the beginning of the tenancy in respect of which the notice was actually given.

11. Any reference in Grounds 1 to 5 in Part I of this Schedule to a notice being given not later than the beginning of the tenancy is a reference to its being given not later than the day on which the tenancy is entered into and, accordingly, section 45(2) of this Act shall not apply to any such reference.

3A–991   *Note* —Amended by the Local Government and Housing Act 1989 s.195, Sch.11, paras 108 and 109; the NHS and Community Care Act 1990 Sch.8; the Charities Act 1993 s.98(1), Sch.6; the Housing Act 1996 ss.10, 101, 102, 148 and 149, Sch.19, Pt IX; the Housing Act 1996 (Consequential Provisions) Order 1996 (SI 1996/2325) art.5 and Sch.2, para.18; the Civil Partnership Act 2004 s.81 and Sch. 8, para.43 and the Serious Organised Crime and Police Act 2005 s.111, Sch.7, para.46.

Mandatory Grounds

Ground 1

3A–992   *Returning Owner Occupier:* This ground is similar to Case 11 in the Rent Act 1977 Sch.15, but more widely drafted. A landlord must prove that:

(a) At, or before, the grant of the tenancy the landlord gave notice in writing that possession might be recovered on this ground. The notice need not be in any particular form and may be included as a recital in any tenancy agreement provided that the agreement does not operate retrospectively. The court has power to dispense with such a notice if it considers it just and equitable.

AND EITHER

Paragraph numbers marked with a "+" can be found online and on CD.

defence to proceedings brought under Ground 8 (*Marath v MacGillivray* (1996) 28 H.L.R. 484, CA). As to the restrictions on the court's power to adjourn in such circumstances, see ss.7(3) and 9(6) and the commentary at 3A–777.

In *Day v Coltrane* [2003] EWCA Civ 342; [2003] 1 W.L.R. 1379 a tenant, facing a Ground 8 possession claim, handed the landlord a cheque for all the arrears on the day of the hearing. The landlord accepted the cheque and it was paid on first presentation. The Court of Appeal, allowing an appeal from a possession order, held that delivery of a cheque is a conditional payment. If the cheque is met, it is an actual payment from the date of delivery (*Homes v Smith* [2000] Lloyd's Rep. Bank. 139). That principle applies to Ground 8. If the cheque cleared, the debt was paid when the cheque was delivered. An uncleared cheque delivered to the landlord at or before the hearing and which was accepted by him, or which he was bound by an earlier agreement to accept, is to be treated as payment on the date of delivery provided it was subsequently paid on first presentation. At the date of the hearing there was jurisdiction to adjourn the claim to see whether the cheque would be paid.

Note that the court cannot dispense with the requirement for a s.8 notice when Ground 8 is relied upon (see s.8(5)).

Discretionary Grounds

Ground 9

Suitable Alternative Accommodation: As with the Rent Act 1977 s.98(1)(a), the availability of suitable alternative accommodation, either at the time of the hearing or when the order is to take effect, is a ground for possession. (See commentary to the Rent Act 1977 s.98). Pt III of Sch.2 gives further clarification as to the matters to be taken into account when determining whether or not accommodation is suitable. They are similar to those set out in the Rent Act 1977 Sch.15, Pt IV.

3A–1001

When a possession order is made under this ground, the landlord must pay a sum equal to the tenant's reasonable removal expenses (s.11(1)).

Ground 10

Rent Arrears: A landlord must prove that there were rent arrears both at the date when proceedings were begun and, unless the court considers it "just and equitable" to dispense with the need for service of a notice prior to issue, that there were arrears when the notice was served. This is the ground for possession which is most similar to Case 1 in Sch.15 to the Rent Act (see commentary thereto). A possession order may be made even if the arrears are paid off before the hearing, although in most circumstances there would be strong grounds for arguing that it would not be reasonable to make an order. See *Dellenty v Pellow* [1951] 2 All E.R. 716, CA; and *Lee-Steere v Jennings* (1987) 20 H.L.R. 1, CA.

3A–1002

Ground 11

Persistent Delay in Paying Rent: Even if there are no arrears on the date when possession proceedings are issued, persistent delay in paying rent which is due is a ground for possession. The phrase "persistent delay" is not defined, but is likely to have the same meaning as in the Landlord and Tenant Act 1954 s.30(1)(b)—i.e. one instalment of rent has been in arrears for a significant period of time or instalments have persistently been paid late, or both (see *Hopcutt v Carver* (1969) 209 E.G. 1069, CA; and *Horowitz v Ferand* [1956] C.L.Y. 4843). For an example of the court's exercise of its powers under Landlord and Tenant Act 1954 s.30(1)(b) (persistent delay in paying rent), see *Hazel v Akhtar* [2001] EWCA Civ 1883; [2002] 07 E.G. 124.

3A–1003

Ground 12

Breach of any obligation: This ground for possession is similar to the second limb of Case 1 in the Rent Act 1977 Sch.15 and applies if "any obligation of the tenancy (other than one related to the payment of rent) has been broken or not performed". See commentary to Case 1.

3A–1004

Ground 13

Waste or Neglect: This ground is similar to Case 3 in the Rent Act 1977 Sch.15, but slightly wider in that it applies not only to the premises let, but also to common parts.

3A–1005

Paragraph numbers marked with a "+" can be found online and on CD.

There is no need for a landlord to give advance warning of an intention to issue proceedings relying on this ground (*Lowe v Lendrum* (1950) 159 E.G. 423, CA) although failure to do so may be relevant when the court considers reasonableness and costs. See too *Holloway v Povey* (1984) 15 H.L.R. 104; (1984) 271 E.G. 195, CA.

Ground 14

3A–1006   *Nuisance or annoyance or conviction for illegal or immoral user:* The Housing Act 1996 s.148 introduced new Ground 14 which replaces the former "nuisance or annoyance" ground. For detailed commentary on Housing Act 1985 Sched 2, Ground 2, the comparable ground relating to secure tenants, see para.3A–505.

There is no requirement that any person visiting the premises and causing a nuisance should be there lawfully. The ground is wide enough, for example, to encompass behaviour by a former partner of a tenant who has been excluded, but returns contrary to the tenant's wishes. The widening of the ground from conduct which *is* a nuisance or annoyance to neighbours to conduct which *is likely to cause nuisance or annoyance* is designed to meet two problems. Firstly the new ground avoids the apparent need for landlords to produce neighbours as witnesses to whom nuisance or annoyance has been caused (but *cf. Frederick Platts Co v Grigor* [1950] 1 All E.R. 941, CA, where it was held that the court can infer that nuisance or annoyance has been caused without hearing evidence from anyone affected.) Secondly, the amended ground covers nuisance or annoyance to people who are not neighbours—e.g. housing officers (but *cf.* the wide definition of "neighbour" adopted by the Court of Appeal in *Northampton BC v Lovatt* (1998) 30 H.L.R. 875; 91 L.G.R. 548; [1998] 07 E.G. 142, CA. As to the meaning of locality in the context of Housing Act 1996 s.152, see *Manchester CC v Lawler* (1999) 31 H.L.R. 119, CA where it was said that it is a matter of fact for the judge in each case to determine whether the conduct complained of has occurred in the locality (held that an incident in a shopping centre three streets away from the property was "in the locality").

For the definition of indictable offences, see the Interpretation Act 1978 Sch.1, which provides "indictable offence" means an offence which, if committed by an adult, is triable on indictment, whether it is exclusively so triable or triable either way. Ground 14 is not restricted to offences committed during the currency of the tenancy. (*Raglan Housing Association Ltd v Fairclough* [2007] EWCA Civ 1087; (2007) *The Times* November 28, 2007; November 1, 2007 where the defendant was arrested before the grant of his tenancy, but pleaded guilty after its grant. The Court of Appeal stated that a tenant who is convicted of supplying illegal drugs or of burgling his neighbours' houses poses no less a continuing threat if the offences were committed before he became a tenant than he would if they had been committed afterwards. The Court of Appeal was not agreed as to whether the ground could only be satisfied if the conviction itself (though not the facts on which it was based) occurred during the currency of the tenancy, but did not have to decide that point.

Ground 14A

3A–1007   *Domestic Violence:*

"registered social landlord"

See the Housing Act 1996 ss.1– 7 and the Housing Act 1985 s.5.

The Housing Act 1996 s.149 introduced a new ground for possession against assured tenants of registered social landlords or charitable housing trusts where there has been domestic violence. Ground 14A applies where one partner is or both partners are tenants and:

    (a) one partner has left because of violence or threats of violence by the other towards that partner or a member of that partner's family; and

    (b) the court is satisfied that the partner who has left is unlikely to return.

Landlords seeking to rely upon this ground must satisfy the court that notice of proceedings for possession has been served on the partner who has left the home or that they have taken reasonable steps to effect service (Housing Act 1996 s.150, inserting new Housing Act 1988 s.8A).

Where possession is sought under Ground 14A, it is not sufficient that the alleged violence or threats of violence were merely one of a range of causes of equal efficacy in the victim's departure from the property. For the ground to be made out it has to be

Paragraph numbers marked with a "+" can be found online and on CD.

established that the alleged violence or threat of violence was the dominant, principal and real cause of the departure (*Camden LBC v Mallett* (2001) 33 H.L.R. 20, CA).

Ground 15

Deterioration of furniture: cf. the Rent Act 1977 Sch.15, Case 4.   **3A–1008**

Ground 16

Premises let to employees: An employer who has let accommodation to **3A–1009** an employee "in consequence" of employment may claim possession if the tenant has "ceased to be in that employment". This ground for possession is wider than Case 8, the comparable Rent Act ground. It applies whether or not the employer requires the premises for another employee.

Ground 17

See commentary to the Housing Act 1985 Sch.2, Ground 5.   **3A–1010**

SCHEDULE 2A

ASSURED TENANCIES: NON-SHORTHOLDS

Tenancies excluded by notice

1.—(1) An assured tenancy in respect of which a notice is served as mentioned in **3A–1011** sub-paragraph (2) below.

(2) The notice referred to in sub-paragraph (1) above is one which—

(a) is served before the assured tenancy is entered into,

(b) is served by the person who is to be the landlord under the assured tenancy on the person who is to be the tenant under that tenancy, and

(c) states that the assured tenancy to which it relates is not to be an assured shorthold tenancy.

2.—(1) An assured tenancy in respect of which a notice is served as mentioned in sub-paragraph (2) below.

(2) The notice referred to in sub-paragraph (1) above is one which—

(a) is served after the assured tenancy has been entered into,

(b) is served by the landlord under the assured tenancy on the tenant under that tenancy, and

(c) states that the assured tenancy to which it relates is no longer an assured shorthold tenancy.

Tenancies containing exclusionary provision

3. An assured tenancy which contains a provision to the effect that the tenancy is not **3A–1012** an assured shorthold tenancy.

Tenancies under section 39

4. An assured tenancy arising by virtue of section 39 above, other than one to which **3A–1013** subsection (7) of that section applies.

Former secure tenancies

5. An assured tenancy which became an assured tenancy on ceasing to be a secure **3A–1014** tenancy.

Former demoted tenancies

5A. An assured tenancy which ceases to be an assured shorthold tenancy by virtue of **3A–1015** section 20B(2) or (4).

Tenancies under Schedule 10 to the Local Government and Housing Act 1989

6. An assured tenancy arising by virtue of Schedule 10 to the Local Government and **3A–1016** Housing Act 1989 (security of tenure on ending of long residential tenancies).

Paragraph numbers marked with a "+" can be found online and on CD.

Tenancies replacing non-shortholds

3A–1017   7.—(1) An assured tenancy which—

(a) is granted to a person (alone or jointly with others) who, immediately before the tenancy was granted, was the tenant (or, in the case of joint tenants, one of the tenants) under an assured tenancy other than a shorthold tenancy ("the old tenancy"),

(b) is granted (alone or jointly with others) by a person who was at that time the landlord (or one of the joint landlords) under the old tenancy, and

(c) is not one in respect of which a notice is served as mentioned in sub-paragraph (2) below.

(2) The notice referred to in sub-paragraph (1)(c) above is one which—

(a) is in such form as may be prescribed,

(b) is served before the assured tenancy is entered into,

(c) is served by the person who is to be the tenant under the assured tenancy on the person who is to be the landlord under that tenancy (or, in the case of joint landlords, on at least one of the persons who are to be joint landlords), and

(d) states that the assured tenancy to which it relates is to be a shorthold tenancy.

8. An assured tenancy which comes into being by virtue of section 5 above on the coming to an end of an assured tenancy which is not a shorthold tenancy.

Assured agricultural occupancies

3A–1018   9.—(1) An assured tenancy—

(a) in the case of which the agricultural worker condition is, by virtue of any provision of Schedule 3 to this Act, for the time being fulfilled with respect to the dwelling-house subject to the tenancy, and

(b) which does not fall within sub-paragraph (2) or (4) below.

(2) An assured tenancy falls within this sub-paragraph if—

(a) before it is entered into, a notice—

(i) in such form as may be prescribed, and

(ii) stating that the tenancy is to be a shorthold tenancy,

is served by the person who is to be the landlord under the tenancy on the person who is to be the tenant under it, and

(b) it is not an excepted tenancy.

(3) For the purposes of sub-paragraph (2)(b) above, an assured tenancy is an excepted tenancy if—

(a) the person to whom it is granted or, as the case may be, at least one of the persons to whom it is granted was, immediately before it is granted, a tenant or licensee under an assured agricultural occupancy, and

(b) the person by whom it is granted or, as the case may be, at least one of the persons by whom it is granted was, immediately before it is granted, a landlord or licensor under the assured agricultural occupancy referred to in paragraph (a) above.

(4) An assured tenancy falls within this sub-paragraph if it comes into being by virtue of section 5 above on the coming to an end of a tenancy falling within sub-paragraph (2) above.

3A–1019   *Note* —Added by the Housing Act 1996 s.96, Sch.7.

Section 21 has been amended by Anti-Social Behaviour Act 2003 s.15(2) and para.5A has been inserted by Anti-Social Behaviour Act 2003 s.15(3). The amendment was brought into force in England on June 30, 2004 by the Anti-Social Behaviour Act 2003 (Commencement No.3 and Savings) Order 2004 (SI 2004/1502) (c.61). It was brought into force in Wales on 30 April 2005 by the Anti-Social Behaviour Act 2003 (Commencement No.4) (Wales) Order 2005 (SI 2005/1225) (w.83) (c.55). It has been held that the words 'assured tenancy' on the cover of a rent book were not a statement "that the assured tenancy to which it relates is not to be an assured shorthold tenancy" (para.1(2)(c)), because an assured shorthold tenancy is itself a type of assured tenancy. Further, the reference in para.1 to "a notice" being "served" is a reference to the ser-

Paragraph numbers marked with a "+" can be found online and on CD.

vice of a written notice. The rent book was clearly intended and used simply to record the payment of rent (*Andrews v Cunningham* [2007] EWCA Civ 762; [2008] H.L.R. 13; [2008] L. & T.R. 1).).

[THE NEXT PARAGRAPH IS 3A–1021.]

Criminal Justice and Public Order Act 1994

(1994 C.33)

3A–1021

ARRANGEMENT OF SECTIONS

Interim possession orders: false or misleading statements

75.—(1) A person commits an offence if, for the purpose of obtaining an interim possession order, he—   3A–1022

    (a) makes a statement which he knows to be false or misleading in a material particular; or

    (b) recklessly makes a statement which is false or misleading in a material particular.

(2) A person commits an offence if, for the purpose of resisting the making of an interim possession order, he—

    (a) makes a statement which he knows to be false or misleading in a material particular; or

    (b) recklessly makes a statement which is false or misleading in a material particular.

(3) A person guilty of an offence under this section shall be liable—

    (a) on conviction on indictment, to imprisonment for a term not exceeding two years or a fine or both;

    (b) on summary conviction, to imprisonment for a term not exceeding six months or a fine not exceeding the statutory maximum or both.

(4) In this section—

    "interim possession order" means an interim possession order (so entitled) made under rules of court for the bringing of summary proceedings for possession of premises which are occupied by trespassers;

    "premises" has the same meaning as in Part II of the Criminal Law Act 1977 (offences relating to entering and remaining on property); and

    "statement", in relation to an interim possession order, means any statement, in writing or oral and whether as to fact or belief, made in or for the purposes of the proceedings.

premises

See Criminal Law Act 1977 s.12(1) which states: 3A–1023

    "(a) 'premises' means any building, any part of a building under separate occupation, any land ancillary to a building, the site comprising any building or buildings together with any land ancillary thereto..."

Paragraph numbers marked with a "+" can be found online and on CD.

HOUSING

3A-1024 Section 12(2) provides that references to a building shall apply also to any structure other than a movable one, and to any movable structure, vehicle or vessel designed or adapted for use for residential purposes. Part of a building is under separate occupation if anyone is in occupation or entitled to occupation of that part as distinct from the whole. Land is ancillary to a building if it is adjacent to it and used (or intended for use) in connection with the occupation of that building or any part of it.

interim possession order

3A-1025 See s.75(4) and CPR rr.55.22 to 55.28.

Editorial note

3A-1026 Criminal Justice and Public Order Act 1994 ss.75 and 76 created interim possession orders (IPOs). They can only be granted against trespassers. Failure to comply with an IPO is a criminal offence. The IPO procedure can only be used if:

— the claimant is only seeking possession. A claimant cannot seek an IPO if there is a claim for another remedy (e.g. damages);
— the claimant has an immediate right to possession and has had such a right throughout the period of unlawful occupation;
— the defendants entered premises as trespassers. It cannot be used against former licensees, tenants or sub-tenants.

The procedure for obtaining an IPO is set out in CPR rr.55.22 to 55.28.

3A-1027 If an IPO has been made and served, any person who is present on the premises as a trespasser at any time during the currency of the order commits an offence unless he or she leaves the premises within 24 hours of service of the order (and does not return) or a copy of the order is not fixed to the premises. It is also an offence if a person who was on the premises when the order was served and who has left then re-enters or attempts to do so as a trespasser after the expiry of the order but within one year of the date of service of the order. Offences are triable summarily.

Interim possession orders: trespassing during currency of order

3A-1028 76.—(1) This section applies where an interim possession order has been made in respect of any premises and served in accordance with rules of court; and references to "the order" and "the premises" shall be construed accordingly.

(2) Subject to subsection (3), a person who is present on the premises as a trespasser at any time during the currency of the order commits an offence.

(3) No offence under subsection (2) is committed by a person if—

(a) he leaves the premises within 24 hours of the time of service of the order and does not return; or

(b) a copy of the order was not fixed to the premises in accordance with rules of court.

(4) A person who was in occupation of the premises at the time of service of the order but leaves them commits an offence if he re-enters the premises as a trespasser or attempts to do so after the expiry of the order but within the period of one year beginning with the day on which it was served.

(5) A person guilty of an offence under this section shall be liable on summary conviction to imprisonment for a term not exceeding six months or a fine not exceeding level 5 on the standard scale or both.

(6) A person who is in occupation of the premises at the time of

Paragraph numbers marked with a "+" can be found online and on CD.

service of the order shall be treated for the purposes of this section as being present as a trespasser.

(7) [...]

(8) In this section—

"interim possession order" has the same meaning as in section 75 above and "rules of court" is to be construed accordingly; and

"premises" has the same meaning as in that section that is to say the same meaning as in Part II of the Criminal Law Act 1977 (offences relating to entering and remaining on property).

Note —Amended by the Serious Organised Crime and Police Act 2005 s.111, Sch.7, para.31, Sch.17.   **3A–1029**

interim possession order
See s.75(4).   **3A–1030**

rules of court
See CPR rr.55.22 to 55.28.   **3A–1031**

premises
See commentary to s.75 and Criminal Law Act 1977 s.12.   **3A–1032**

[THE NEXT PARAGRAPH IS 3A–1045.]

Section 81—Restriction on termination of tenancy for failure to pay service charge

Housing Act 1996

(2006 c.52)   **3A–1045**

ARRANGEMENT OF SECTIONS

PART III

LANDLORD AND TENANT

CHAPTER I

TENANTS' RIGHTS

FORFEITURE

Paragraph numbers marked with a "+" can be found online and on CD.

Paragraph numbers marked with a "+" can be found online and on CD.

Paragraph numbers marked with a "+" can be found online and on CD.

HOUSING

PART III

LANDLORD AND TENANT
CHAPTER I

TENANTS' RIGHTS

FORFEITURE

Restriction on termination of tenancy for failure to pay service charge

81.—(1) A landlord may not, in relation to premises let as a dwelling, exercise a right of re-entry or forfeiture for failure by a tenant to pay a service charge or administartion charge unless—

    (a) it is finally determined by (or on appeal from) a leasehold valuation tribunal or by a court, or by an arbitral tribunal in proceedings pursuant to a post-dispute arbitration agreement, that the amount of the service charge or administration charge is payable by him, or

    (b) the tenant has admitted that it is so payable.

(2) The landlord may not exercise a right of re-entry or forfeiture by virtue of subsection (1)(a) until after the end of the period of 14 days beginning with the day after that on which the final determination is made.

(3) For the purposes of this section it is finally determined that the amount of a service charge or administration charge is payable—

    (a) if a decision that it is payable is not appealed against or otherwise challenged, at the end of the time for bringing an appeal or other challenge, or

    (b) if such a decision is appealed against or otherwise challenged and not set aside in consequence of the appeal or other challenge, at the time specified in subsection (3A).

(3A) The time referred to in subsection (3)(b) is the time when the appeal or other challenge is disposed of—

    (a) by the determination of the appeal or other challenge

Paragraph numbers marked with a "+" can be found online and on CD.

and the expiry of the time for bringing a subsequent appeal (if any), or

(b) by its being abandoned or otherwise ceasing to have effect.

(4) The reference in subsection (1) to premises let as a dwelling does not include premises let on—

(a) a tenancy to which Part II of the Landlord and Tenant Act 1954 applies (business tenancies),

(b) a tenancy of an agricultural holding within the meaning of the Agricultural Holdings Act 1986 in relation to which that Act applies, or

(c) a farm business tenancy within the meaning of the Agricultural Tenancies Act 1995.

(4A) References in this section to the exercise of a right of re-entry or forfeiture include the service of a notice under section 146(1) of the Law of Property Act 1925 (restriction on re-entry or forfeiture).

(5) In this section—

(a) "administration charge" has the meaning given by Part 1 of Schedule 11 to the Commonhold and Leasehold Reform Act 2002,

(b) "arbitration agreement" and "arbitral tribunal" have the same meaning as in Part 1 of the Arbitration Act 1996 (c.23) and "post-dispute arbitration agreement", in relation to any matter, means an arbitration agreement made after a dispute about the matter has arisen,

(c) "dwelling" has the same meaning as in the Landlord and Tenant Act 1985 (c.70), and (d).

(5A) Any order of a court to give effect to a determination of a leasehold valuation tribunal shall be treated as a determination by the court for the purposes of this section.

(6) Nothing in this section affects the exercise of a right of re-entry or forfeiture on other grounds.

Note —Amended by Commonhold and Leasehold Reform Act 2002 s.170.　　**3A–1046**

"Crown land"

Section 81 applies in relation to Crown land as in relation to other land (see the **3A–1047** Commonhold and Leasehold Reform Act 2002 s.172, which also defines "Crown land".

"service charge"

See the Landlord and Tenant Act 1985 s.18, above.　　**3A–1048**

"arbitral tribunal"

See the Arbitration Act 1996 Pt I.　　**3A–1049**

"dwelling"

See Landlord and Tenant Act 1985 s.38.　　**3A–1050**

"landlord, tenant, lease, tenancy"

See Landlord and Tenant Act 1985 s.36, para.3A–702+.　　**3A–1051**

"administration charge"

See Sch.11, Pt 1.　　**3A–1052**

Paragraph numbers marked with a "+" can be found online and on CD.

"post-dispute arbitration agreement"

3A–1053   See s.169(5). It means an arbitration agreement made after a breach has occurred (or is alleged to have occurred).

Restriction on termination of tenancy for failure to pay service charge

3A–1054   Section 81 prevents landlords from exercising a right of re-entry or forfeiture of premises let as a dwelling for failure to pay service charges unless the amount claimed is either agreed or admitted by the lessee or has been determined by a court or an arbitral tribunal in accordance with the Arbitration Act 1996 Pt I. If the service charge has been determined by a court or tribunal, the landlord cannot commence forfeiture proceedings until 14 days after the determination. Section 82 provides that the Law of Property Act 1925 s.146 notices relating to arrears of service charges must refer to s.81 and state that s.81 has been complied with. "Service charge" has the same meaning as in the Landlord and Tenant Act 1985 s.18(1)—i.e. sums payable "directly or indirectly, for services, repairs, maintenance, improvements or insurance or the landlord's costs of management" and which vary according to the relevant costs. The aim of this provision was to prevent freeholders from pressurising lessees who have genuine disputes about service charges (or their mortgagees) into paying up rather than face forfeiture proceedings. It came into force on September 24, 1996 (Housing Act 1996 s.232(2)).

   Courts are probably obliged to take s.81 into account even if it is not pleaded (*Mohammadi v Anston Investments Ltd* [2003] EWCA Civ 981; [2004] H.L.R. 8).

   In *Southwark LBC v Tornaritis* [1999] 7 C.L.D. 330, Lambeth County Court, H.H.J. Cox held that an earlier default judgment in respect of service charge arrears was a "determination" within the meaning of Housing Act 1996 s.81. The phrase "determination by a court" does not require a judicial determination.

   Section 81 has to be read in conjunction with the Landlord and Tenant Act 1985 s.19, as amended by the Housing Act 1996 s.83 which provides that lessors and lessees may apply to RACs sitting as Leasehold Valuation Tribunals (LVTs) to determine whether costs incurred for services, repairs, maintenance, etc. were reasonably incurred, whether such services or works were of a reasonable standard and whether sums payable by lessees before costs have been incurred are reasonable. There is a right of appeal to the Lands Tribunal, but only with the leave of the LVT or the Lands Tribunal (Housing Act 1996 s.83).

Notice under s.146 of the Law of Property Act 1925

3A–1055   82. [...]

3A–1056   *Note*—Repealed by the Commonhold and Leasehold Reform Act 2002 s.180, Sch.14.

* * * *

SERVICE CHARGES

Right to appoint surveyor to advise on matters relating to service charges

3A–1057   84.—(1) A recognised tenants' association may appoint a surveyor for the purposes of this section to advise on any matters relating to, or which may give rise to, service charges payable to a landlord by one or more members of the association. The provisions of Schedule 4 have effect for conferring on a surveyor so appointed rights of access to documents and premises.

   (2) A person shall not be so appointed unless he is a qualified surveyor.

   For this purpose "qualified surveyor" has the same meaning as in section 78(4)(a) of the Leasehold Reform, Housing and Urban

Paragraph numbers marked with a "+" can be found online and on CD.

Development Act 1993 (persons qualified for appointment to carry out management audit).

(3) The appointment shall take effect for the purposes of this section upon notice in writing being given to the landlord by the association stating the name and address of the surveyor, the duration of his appointment and the matters in respect of which he is appointed.

(4) An appointment shall cease to have effect for the purposes of this section if the association gives notice in writing to the landlord to that effect or if the association ceases to exist.

(5) A notice is duly given under this section to a landlord of any tenants if it is given to a person who receives on behalf of the landlord the rent payable by those tenants; and a person to whom such a notice is so given shall forward it as soon as may be to the landlord.

(6) In this section—

"recognised tenants' association" has the same meaning as in the provisions of the Landlord and Tenant Act 1985 relating to service charges (see section 29 of that Act); and

"service charge" means a service charge within the meaning of section 18(1) of that Act, other than one excluded from that section by section 27 of that Act (rent of dwelling registered and not entered as variable).

Application

Commonhold and Leasehold Reform Act 2002 s.172 provides that Housing Act 1996 s.84 applies in relation to Crown land as in relation to other land. The phrase "Crown land" is defined by Commonhold and Leasehold Reform Act 2002 s.172. That section was brought into force on September 30, 2003 by the Commonhold and Leasehold Reform Act (Commencement No.2 and Savings) (England) Order 2003 (SI 2003/1986) (c.82). **3A–1058**

"recognised tenants' association"

See the Landlord and Tenant Act 1985 s.29 which refers to an association of qualifying tenants being recognised "either—(a) by a notice in writing given by the landlord to the secretary of the association, or (b) by a certificate of a member of the local rent assessment committee panel." **3A–1059**

"service charge"

See commentary to s.81 and the Landlord and Tenant Act 1985 s.18. **3A–1060**

"qualified surveyor"

See the Leasehold Reform, Housing and Urban Development Act 1993 s.78(4)(a) which states that a person is a "qualified surveyor" if "(a) ... he is a qualified surveyor; (b) he is not disqualified from acting within the meaning of the Landlord and Tenant Act 1985 s.28(1); and (c) he is not the tenant of any premises contained in the relevant premises." See also the Leasehold Reform, Housing and Urban Development Act 1993 s.78(5). **3A–1061**

Schedule 4 gives such a surveyor the right to inspect documents and premises.

* * * * *

SUPPLEMENTARY

Jurisdiction of county courts

95.—(1) Any jurisdiction expressed by a provision to which this **3A–1062**

Paragraph numbers marked with a "+" can be found online and on CD.

section applies to be conferred on the court shall be exercised by a county court.

(2) There shall also be brought in a county court any proceedings for determining any question arising under or by virtue of any provision to which this section applies.

(3) Where, however, other proceedings are properly brought in the High Court, that court has jurisdiction to hear and determine proceedings to which subsection (1) or (2) applies which are joined with those proceedings.

(4) Where proceedings are brought in a county court by virtue of subsection (1) or (2), that court has jurisdiction to hear and determine other proceedings joined with those proceedings despite the fact that they would otherwise be outside its jurisdiction.

(5) The provisions to which this section applies are—

    (a) section 81 (restriction on termination of tenancy for failure to pay service charge), and

    (b) section 84 (right to appoint surveyor to advise on matters relating to service charges) and Schedule 4 (rights exercisable by surveyor appointed by tenants' association).

* * * *

PART V

CONDUCT OF TENANTS

CHAPTER I

INTRODUCTORY TENANCIES

GENERAL PROVISIONS

Introductory tenancies

3A-1063 **124.**—(1) A local housing authority or a housing action trust may elect to operate an introductory tenancy regime.

(2) When such an election is in force, every periodic tenancy of a dwelling-house entered into or adopted by the authority or trust shall, if it would otherwise be a secure tenancy, be an introductory tenancy, unless immediately before the tenancy was entered into or adopted the tenant or, in the case of joint tenants, one or more of them was—

    (a) a secure tenant of the same or another dwelling-house, or

    (b) an assured tenant of a registered social landlord (otherwise than under an assured shorthold tenancy) in respect of the same or another dwelling-house.

(3) Subsection (2) does not apply to a tenancy entered into or adopted in pursuance of a contract made before the election was made.

Paragraph numbers marked with a "+" can be found online and on CD.

(4) For the purposes of this Chapter a periodic tenancy is adopted by a person if that person becomes the landlord under the tenancy, whether on a disposal or surrender of the interest of the former landlord.

(5) An election under this section may be revoked at any time, without prejudice to the making of a further election.

"local housing authority"

See s.230 which refers to Housing Act 1985 (see the Housing Act 1985 ss.1 and 2 above). **3A–1064**

"housing action trust"

See s.230 which refers to the Housing Act 1988. See the Housing Act 1985 s.4 above. **3A–1065**

"dwelling house"

See s.139. **3A–1066**

"secure tenant"

See s.230 which refers to the Housing Act 1985 Pt IV. See the Housing Act 1985 s.79 above. **3A–1067**

"assured tenant"

See s.230 which refers to the Housing Act 1988 Pt I. See the Housing Act 1988 s.1 above. **3A–1068**

"assured shorthold tenancy"

See s.230 which refers to the Housing Act 1988 Pt I. See the Housing Act 1988 ss.19A and 20 above. **3A–1069**

Introductory tenancies

Introductory tenancies are a form of probationary tenancy granted by some local authorities lacking security of tenure within the first year of the tenancy. Housing Act 1985 Sch.1, para.1A provides that introductory tenancies cannot be secure tenancies (Housing Act 1996 Sch.14, para.5). **3A–1070**

Section 124 provides that "a local housing authority or housing action trust (HAT) may elect to operate an introductory tenancy regime". The Department of the Environment's Circular on Introductory Tenancies (2/97) suggests that local authorities should consult with existing tenants in accordance with the Housing Act 1985 s.105 before setting up an introductory tenancy regime (para.6). Where such an election is made, all new periodic tenancies and licences (Housing Act 1996 s.126) which would otherwise be secure tenancies will be introductory tenancies or licences unless immediately before the new tenancy, one or more of the tenants was either a secure tenant or an assured tenant of a registered social landlord. Tenancies remain introductory tenancies until the end of the "trial period" which lasts for one year after the date on which the tenancy was entered into, or the date on which the tenant was first entitled to possession, whichever is later. Note also that s.125A provides for the possible extension of the trial period by a further six months. Earlier periods when the tenant had another introductory tenancy or had an assured shorthold tenancy granted by a registered social landlord count towards the trial period provided that there is no gap between them.

Tenancies cease to be introductory tenancies if:

- the circumstances are such that the tenancy could not be secure; or
- a person or body other than a local housing authority or HAT becomes the landlord; or
- the election is revoked; or
- the tenant dies and there is no-one qualified to succeed (Housing Act 1996 ss.125 and 133(3)).

The Department of the Environment's Circular on Introductory Tenancies (2/97) suggests that landlords should ensure "that introductory tenancies can never be used

Paragraph numbers marked with a "+" can be found online and on CD.

HOUSING

as a weapon against vulnerable individuals and ensure that there are safeguards to protect such tenants...[They] must be vigilant to ensure that neighbours are not able to make a case for eviction against a vulnerable tenant whose behaviour may be different through no fault of their own (paras 9 and 11)". Where there are vulnerable tenants, they should liaise with social services and should have arrangements "for automatic notification to social services at an early stage once any problems arise (para.12)". The Circular also states that "eviction is not necessarily appropriate when problems arise between a vulnerable tenant and neighbours (para.14)" and that "landlords should have fair and rigorous procedures in place to investigate complaints against tenants (para.19)." The local authority associations have produced comprehensive good practice guidance on running an introductory regime which should be read in conjunction with the circular.

Landlords may only bring introductory tenancies to an end by obtaining a possession order in court (Housing Act 1996 s.127). Before bringing proceedings landlords must serve notices giving reasons for the decision to seek a possession order and specifying a date after which court proceedings may be begun. The notice given must be equivalent to that which would otherwise be needed to terminate the tenancy by notice to quit. It must also inform tenants of their right to "request a review of the landlord's decision" and that they may seek advice from a CAB, housing aid centre, law centre or solicitor (Housing Act 1996 s.128). The circular states:

"As good practice landlords should include a full statement of the reasons for seeking possession which could include a case history of the sequence of events (para.16)."

Where a landlord serves a Housing Act 1996 s.128 notice based upon the arrears, but then also relies upon allegations of nuisance, the correct procedure is normally for the landlord to serve an additional notice. However in a case where the tenant had not suffered any prejudice, and the same decision would have been reached, even without the allegations of nuisance, a tenant's challenge to the review process was dismissed (*R.(Laporte) v Newham LBC* [2004] EWHC 227 (Admin); [2004] 2 All E.R. 874).

"The precise way in which a landlord chooses to conduct...a review is for each landlord to determine" (DoE Circular: 2/97 para.22)." However, the Introductory Tenants (Review) Regulations 1997 (SI 1997/72) set out certain basic requirements to be followed on reviews. Reviews are not to be by way of a hearing unless tenants inform their landlords that they wish to have an oral hearing (para.2). A request for an oral hearing must be made within 14 days after receipt of the notice seeking possession. Reviews must be carried out by a person who was not involved in the original decision to seek possession (para.3). If the review is not to be conducted by an oral hearing, the tenant may make written representations (para.4). If there is an oral hearing, the tenant has a right to:

(a) be heard and accompanied or represented by another person;

(b) call persons to give evidence;

(c) put questions to anyone who gives evidence; and

(d) make representations in writing (para.5).

The tenant must be notified of the time, date and place of any hearing. It must take place not less than five days after the request for a hearing (para.6). The Regulations do not, however, specify a minimum period between notification of the date of the hearing and the hearing itself.

The review must be carried out and the tenant notified of the result before the date specified as the date after which proceedings may be begun.

If a landlord serves a notice which expires and then brings proceedings against an introductory tenant, the court must make a possession order. It is not necessary for the landlord to give evidence about the reason for seeking possession. All that is necessary is to prove that notice was served and that any review has been determined or that the period specified in the notice has expired (s.127). "Suspended possession orders ... are not appropriate for introductory tenancies. Applications to court for possession must lead to eviction" (DoE, para.20).

See too *Manchester City Council v Cochrane* [1999] 1 W.L.R. 809, CA where the Court of Appeal held that the word "shall" in s.127(2) means that once the requirements of s.128 have been complied with, the county court has no discretion but to make an order for possession.

Paragraph numbers marked with a "+" can be found online and on CD.

In a case where a landlord served a s.128 notice, but then told the tenant that proceedings would not be issued if she cleared the arrears at a rate of £3 per week, the Court of Appeal held that there was no requirement to give a further or second notice when the arrears started to increase again. Housing Act 1996 s.127 imposes a mandatory duty on the court to grant possession if "a" notice has been served in compliance with s.128. A requirement to serve a further notice would introduce unnecessary formality and might deter an authority from taking a humane "wait and see" approach before issuing proceedings. *Cardiff City Council v Stone* [2002] EWCA Civ 298; [2003] H.L.R. 47, CA. However, for a case where there was in reality a decision to reverse or quash the original decision, albeit with a warning about future conduct, see *Forbes v Lambeth LBC* [2003] EWHC 222 (Admin); [2003] H.L.R. 49. Crane J. stated that where the reasons for a decision have changed, the tenant ought at least to be given an opportunity to seek a review, not only to question the alleged facts, but also, crucially, to argue that it was not reasonable to require possession. If that were not done, the scheme of the Act would not be ECHR compliant.

The Act is silent as to the methods by which tenants may challenge review decisions. This is not dealt with in the Introductory Tenancies (Review) Regulations either and so tenants' only redress if they are dissatisfied with a review decision is to apply for judicial review. In view of the decisions in *Manchester CC v Cochrane* [1999] 1 W.L.R. 809, CA, and *Avon CC v Buscott* [1988] Q.B. 656; [1988] 1 All E.R. 841, CA, the traditional view was that county courts hearing subsequent possession proceedings could not consider public law defences based upon tenants' complaints about the review procedure or decisions. It was thought that the private law rights of tenants under introductory tenancies were no more than a right to remain in possession until an order for possession was made. The remedy for tenants in such cases, was to apply for the possession proceedings to be adjourned pending determination of their applications for judicial review. Whether or not that view still represents the law is arguable in view of the recognition by the House of Lords (albeit in a different scenario) in *Birmingham City Council v Doherty* [2008] UKHL 57, July 30, 2008, [2008] 3 W.L.R. 636; that judicial review-type scrutiny of the fairness and legality of a council's decision to bring proceedings may be presented by way of a defence to the possession claim.

In determining whether proceedings are started before the end of the trial period, proceedings are started by the issue of the claim form by the court (CPR r.7.2 and PD7, para.5.1), not when the claim form is received by the court (*Salford City Council v Garner* [2004] EWCA Civ 364; [2004] H.L.R. 35). If the "trial period" ends before determination of the possession proceedings, the tenancy will remain an introductory tenancy until the determination of proceedings or the date on which possession is to be given up, whichever is later (s.130(2)).

Although introductory tenants lack security of tenure, the Act gives them some rights which are equivalent to those of secure tenants, e.g. succession (Housing Act 1996 ss.131– 133 and 140) and information and consultation (ss.136– 137). The right to repair scheme (Housing Act 1985 s.96) has been extended to introductory tenancies by the Secure Tenancies (Right to Repair) (Amendment) Regulations 1997 (SI 1997/73). Assignment of introductory tenancies is in general prohibited although they may be transferred by orders made under the Matrimonial Causes Act 1973 s.24, the Matrimonial and Family Proceedings Act 1984, the Children Act 1989 Sch.1 and to a person who would be qualified to succeed the tenant if the tenant died immediately before the assignment (Housing Act 1996 s.134).

The provisions relating to introductory tenancies were brought into force on February 12, 1997 by the Housing Act 1996 (Commencement No.6 and Savings) Order 1997 (SI 1997/66).

Introductory tenants and the Human Rights Act 1998

In *R. (McLellan) v Bracknell Forest DC* [2001] EWCA Civ 1510; [2002] Q.B. 1129; **3A–1071**
[2002] 2 W.L.R. 1448; [2002] 1 All E.R. 899, the Court of Appeal held that:

(1) Eviction of an introductory tenant falls within ECHR art.8(1) (*Lambeth LBC v Howard* (2001) 33 HR 58, CA). Accordingly it is necessary to consider under art.8(2) whether an eviction is in accordance with the law and whether it is necessary for the protection of the rights of others. A tenant under an introductory tenancy has the right to raise the question whether it is reasonable in the particular case to insist on eviction, i.e. whether the eviction can be justified under art.8(2) (*Donoghue v Poplar*

Paragraph numbers marked with a "+" can be found online and on CD.

HARCA [2001] EWCA Civ 595 also reported as *Poplar HARCA v Donoghue* [2002] Q.B. 48, and Human Rights Act 1998 s.7(1)(b)). The review procedure taken together with the availability of judicial review provides adequate protection. Section 127 does not prevent tenants from relying on Convention rights if the procedure in *Manchester City Council v Cochrane* [1999] 1 W.L.R. 809 is followed. The fact that the tenant has failed to seek judicial review of the decision to seek possession does not deprive the county court of the power to consider whether there is arguably a breach of the Convention and to adjourn if necessary. Therefore the introductory tenancy scheme is not as such incompatible with Art 8 and there is no reason to think that individuals' rights will be infringed without remedy from the courts. If the pace of eviction is too fast the court may grant a limited extension of time under Housing Act 1980 s.89(1). Section 89 is not itself incompatible with art.8.

(2) The decision of the review panel involves the determination of an introductory tenant's civil rights and so ECHR art.6 is engaged. However the combination of the review panel plus judicial review is enough to meet the requirements of art.6. There is no requirement that a council must be satisfied that there has been a breach of the terms of the tenancy before serving notice—the question is whether, in the light of allegation and counter-allegation, it was reasonable for the council to take a decision to proceed with termination of the tenancy. There is no reason to believe that the review procedure will not be operated fairly, nor any reason to believe that judicial review will not provide an adequate safeguard to tenants enabling them to challenge any unfairness or infringement of their Convention rights, bearing in mind that the courts will "examine the decision maker's actions more rigorously" where a discretionary power is liable to interfere with fundamental human rights. Where a review has taken place it should be the norm for the council to set out in an affidavit before the county court how the review procedure was operated in each case so that the court has the necessary information to decide whether to adjourn pending an application for judicial review.

In *Merton LBC v Williams* [2002] EWCA Civ 980; [2003] H.L.R. 20, the Court of Appeal confirmed (following *McLellan*) that county courts hearing possession claims against introductory tenants have a general duty to consider the procedure that has been followed and to ensure that it complies both with the statutory procedure and the tenant's rights under the ECHR—although in the instant case a possession order should have been made because was no realistic prospect that any judicial review proceedings would succeed. See though *Harrow LBC v Qazi* [2003] UKHL 43; [2004] 1 A.C. 983; [2003] 3 W.L.R. 79 where Lord Hope and Lord Scott said that contractual and property rights cannot be defeated by a defence based on art.8; *Lambeth LBC v Kay; Leeds CC v Price* [2006] UKHL 10; [2006] 2 A.C. 465; [2006] 2 W.L.R. 570 and *Birmingham City Council v Doherty* [2008] UKHL 57, July 30, 2008, [2008] 3 W.L.R. 636. Note that in *Harrow LBC v Qazi* [2003] UKHL 43; [2004] 1 A.C. 983; [2003] 3 W.L.R. 79, Lord Scott also stated that *McLellan* was correctly decided, but for the wrong reason.

Duration of introductory tenancy

3A–1072　**125.**—(1) A tenancy remains an introductory tenancy until the end of the trial period, unless one of the events mentioned in subsection (5) occurs before the end of that period.

(2) The "trial period" is the period of one year beginning with—

(a) in the case of a tenancy which was entered into by a local housing authority or housing action trust—

(i) the date on which the tenancy was entered into, or

(ii) if later, the date on which a tenant was first entitled to possession under the tenancy; or

(b) in the case of a tenancy which was adopted by a local housing authority or housing action trust, the date of adoption;

but this is subject to subsections (3) and (4) and to section 125A (extension of trial period by 6 months).

Paragraph numbers marked with a "+" can be found online and on CD.

(3) Where the tenant under an introductory tenancy was formerly a tenant under another introductory tenancy, or held an assured shorthold tenancy from a registered social landlord, any period or periods during which he was such a tenant shall count towards the trial period, provided—

(a) if there was one such period, it ended immediately before the date specified in subsection (2), and

(b) if there was more than one such period, the most recent period ended immediately before that date and each period succeeded the other without interruption.

(4) Where there are joint tenants under an introductory tenancy, the reference in subsection (3) to the tenant shall be construed as referring to the joint tenant in whose case the application of that subsection produces the earliest starting date for the trial period.

(5) A tenancy ceases to be an introductory tenancy if, before the end of the trial period—

(a) the circumstances are such that the tenancy would not otherwise be a secure tenancy,

(b) a person or body other than a local housing authority or housing action trust becomes the landlord under the tenancy,

(c) the election in force when the tenancy was entered into or adopted is revoked, or

(d) the tenancy ceases to be an introductory tenancy by virtue of section 133(3)(succession).

(6) A tenancy does not come to an end merely because it ceases to be an introductory tenancy, but a tenancy which has once ceased to be an introductory tenancy cannot subsequently become an introductory tenancy.

(7) This section has effect subject to section 130 (effect of beginning proceedings for possession).

Amended by the Housing Act 2004 s.179.

3A–1073

Duration of introductory tenancy

See commentary to s.124.

3A–1074

"introductory tenancy"

See s.124.

3A–1075

"local housing authority"

See s.230 which refers to the Housing Act 1985 (see the Housing Act 1985 ss.1 and 2 above).

3A–1076

"housing action trust"

See s.230 which refers to the Housing Act 1988. See the Housing Act 1985 s.4 above.

3A–1077

"dwelling house"

See s.139.

3A–1078

"secure tenant"

See s.230 which refers to the Housing Act 1985 Pt IV. See the Housing Act 1985 s.79 above.

3A–1079

Paragraph numbers marked with a "+" can be found online and on CD.

"assured tenant"

3A-1080   See s.230 which refers to the Housing Act 1988 Pt I. See the Housing Act 1988 s.1 above.

"assured shorthold tenancy"

3A-1081   See s.230 which refers to the Housing Act 1988 Pt I. See the Housing Act 1988 ss.19A and 20 above.

"registered social landlord"

3A-1082   See s.1.

Extension of trial period by 6 months

3A-1083   **125A.**—(1) If both of the following conditions are met in relation to an introductory tenancy, the trial period is extended by 6 months.

(2) The first condition is that the landlord has served a notice of extension on the tenant at least 8 weeks before the original expiry date.

(3) The second condition is that either—

    (a) the tenant has not requested a review under section 125B in accordance with subsection (1) of that section, or

    (b) if he has, the decision on the review was to confirm the landlord's decision to extend the trial period.

(4) A notice of extension is a notice—

    (a) stating that the landlord has decided that the period for which the tenancy is to be an introductory tenancy should be extended by 6 months, and

    (b) complying with subsection (5).

(5) A notice of extension must—

    (a) set out the reasons for the landlord's decision, and

    (b) inform the tenant of his right to request a review of the landlord's decision and of the time within which such a request must be made.

(6) In this section and section 125B "the original expiry date" means the last day of the period of one year that would apply as the trial period apart from this section.

3A-1084   *Note* —Inserted by the Housing Act 2004 s.179.

trial period

3A-1085   See s.125(2).

review

3A-1086   See s.125B.

Review of decision to extend trial period

3A-1087   **125B.**—(1) A request for review of the landlord's decision that the trial period for an introductory tenancy should be extended under section 125A must be made before the end of the period of 14 days beginning with the day on which the notice of extension is served.

(2) On a request being duly made to it, the landlord shall review its decision.

Paragraph numbers marked with a "+" can be found online and on CD.

(3) The Secretary of State may make provision by regulations as to the procedure to be followed in connection with a review under this section.

Nothing in the following provisions affects the generality of this power.

(4) Provision may be made by regulations—

    (a) requiring the decision on review to be made by a person of appropriate seniority who was not involved in the original decision, and

    (b) as to the circumstances in which the person concerned is entitled to an oral hearing, and whether and by whom he may be represented at such a hearing.

(5) The landlord shall notify the tenant of the decision on the review.

If the decision is to confirm the original decision, the landlord shall also notify him of the reasons for the decision.

(6) The review shall be carried out and the tenant notified before the original expiry date.

Note—Inserted by the Housing Act 2004 s.179.   **3A–1088**

regulations

See the Introductory Tenancies (Review of Decisions to Extend a Trial Period) (England) Regulations 2006 (SI 2006/1077) and the Introductory Tenancies (Review of Decisions to Extend a Trial Period) (Wales) Regulations 2006 (SI 2006/2983) (w.274).   **3A–1089**

the original expiry date

See s.125A(6).   **3A–1090**

Licences

126.—(1) The provisions of this Chapter apply in relation to a licence to occupy a dwelling-house (whether or not granted for a consideration) as they apply in relation to a tenancy.   **3A–1091**

(2) Subsection (1) does not apply to a licence granted as a temporary expedient to a person who entered the dwelling-house or any other land as a trespasser (whether or not, before the grant of that licence, another licence to occupy that or another dwelling-house had been granted to him).

Licences

See commentary to s.124.   **3A–1092**

"dwelling house"

See s.139.   **3A–1093**

"temporary expedient"

cf. Housing Act 1985 s.79(4).   **3A–1094**

PROCEEDINGS FOR POSSESSION

Proceedings for possession

127.—(1) The landlord may only bring an introductory tenancy to   **3A–1095**

Paragraph numbers marked with a "+" can be found online and on CD.

an end by obtaining an order of the court for the possession of the dwelling-house.

(2) The court shall make such an order unless the provisions of section 128 apply.

(3) Where the court makes such an order, the tenancy comes to an end on the date on which the tenant is to give up possession in pursuance of the order.

Amendment

3A–1095.1   This section has also been amended by the Housing and Regeneration Act 2008 Sch.15, Pt I. The amendment is not yet in force. The amendment is printed as part of the Housing and Regeneration Act 2008—see below.

Proceedings for possession

3A–1096   See commentary to s.124 and *Manchester City Council v Cochrane* [1999] 1 W.L.R. 809, CA.

"dwelling house"

3A–1097   See s.139.

Notice of proceedings for possession

3A–1098   128.—(1) The court shall not entertain proceedings for the possession of a dwelling-house let under an introductory tenancy unless the landlord has served on the tenant a notice of proceedings complying with this section.

(2) The notice shall state that the court will be asked to make an order for the possession of the dwelling-house.

(3) The notice shall set out the reasons for the landlord's decision to apply for such an order.

(4) The notice shall specify a date after which proceedings for the possession of the dwelling-house may be begun.

The date so specified must not be earlier than the date on which the tenancy could, apart from this Chapter, be brought to an end by notice to quit given by the landlord on the same date as the notice of proceedings.

(5) The court shall not entertain any proceedings for possession of the dwelling-house unless they are begun after the date specified in the notice of proceedings.

(6) The notice shall inform the tenant of his right to request a review of the landlord's decision to seek an order for possession and of the time within which such a request must be made.

(7) The notice shall also inform the tenant that if he needs help or advice about the notice, and what to do about it, he should take it immediately to a Citizens' Advice Bureau, a housing aid centre, a law centre or a solicitor.

Notice of proceedings of possession

3A–1099   See commentary to s.124.

"dwelling house"

3A–1100   See s.139.

Paragraph numbers marked with a "+" can be found online and on CD.

"introductory tenancy"
See s.124.

3A–1101

Review of decision to seek possession

129.—(1) A request for review of the landlord's decision to seek an order for possession of a dwelling-house let under an introductory tenancy must be made before the end of the period of 14 days beginning with the day on which the notice of proceedings is served.

3A–1102

(2) On a request being duly made to it, the landlord shall review its decision.

(3) The Secretary of State may make provision by regulations as to the procedure to be followed in connection with a review under this section.

Nothing in the following provisions affects the generality of this power.

(4) Provision may be made by regulations—

    (a) requiring the decision on review to be made by a person of appropriate seniority who was not involved in the original decision, and

    (b) as to the circumstances in which the person concerned is entitled to an oral hearing, and whether and by whom he may be represented at such a hearing.

(5) The landlord shall notify the person concerned of the decision on the review.

If the decision is to confirm the original decision, the landlord shall also notify him of the reasons for the decision.

(6) The review shall be carried out and the tenant notified before the date specified in the notice of proceedings as the date after which proceedings for the possession of the dwelling-house may be begun.

Review of decision to seek possession
See commentary to s.124.

3A–1103

"dwelling house"
See s.139.

3A–1104

"introductory tenancy"
See s.124.

3A–1105

"regulations"
See the Introductory Tenants (Review) Regulations 1997 (SI 1997/72).

3A–1106

Effect of beginning proceedings for possession

130.—(1) This section applies where the landlord has begun proceedings for the possession of a dwelling-house let under an introductory tenancy and—

3A–1107

    (a) the trial period ends, or

    (b) any of the events specified in section 125(5) occurs (events on which a tenancy ceases to be an introductory tenancy).

Paragraph numbers marked with a "+" can be found online and on CD.

(2) Subject to the following provisions, the tenancy remains an introductory tenancy until—

    (a) the tenancy comes to an end in pursuance of section 127(3) (that is, on the date on which the tenant is to give up possession in pursuance of an order of the court), or

    (b) the proceedings are otherwise finally determined.

(3) If any of the events specified in section 125(5)(b) to (d) occurs, the tenancy shall thereupon cease to be an introductory tenancy but—

    (a) the landlord (or, as the case may be, the new landlord) may continue the proceedings, and

    (b) if he does so, section 127(2) and (3) (termination by landlord) apply as if the tenancy had remained an introductory tenancy.

(4) Where in accordance with subsection (3) a tenancy ceases to be an introductory tenancy and becomes a secure tenancy, the tenant is not entitled to exercise the right to buy under Part V of the Housing Act 1985 unless and until the proceedings are finally determined on terms such that he is not required to give up possession of the dwelling-house.

(5) For the purposes of this section proceedings shall be treated as finally determined if they are withdrawn or any appeal is abandoned or the time for appealing expires without an appeal being brought.

Amendment

3A–1107.1   This section has also been amended by the Housing and Regeneration Act 2008 Sch.15, Pt I. The amendment is not yet in force. The amendment is printed as part of the Housing and Regeneration Act 2008—see below.

Effect of beginning proceedings for possession

3A–1108   See commentary to s.124.

"dwelling house"

3A–1109   See s.139.

"introductory tenancy"

3A–1110   See s.124.

"trial period"

3A–1111   See s.125(2).

* * * *

SUPPLEMENTARY

Jurisdiction of county court

3A–1112   **138.**—(1) A county court has jurisdiction to determine questions arising under this Chapter and to entertain proceedings brought under this Chapter and claims, for whatever amount, in connection with an introductory tenancy.

Paragraph numbers marked with a "+" can be found online and on CD.

(2) That jurisdiction includes jurisdiction to entertain proceedings as to whether a statement supplied in pursuance of section 136(2)(b) (written statement of certain terms of tenancy) is accurate notwithstanding that no other relief is sought than a declaration.

(3) If a person takes proceedings in the High Court which, by virtue of this section, he could have taken in the county court, he is not entitled to recover any costs.

(4)—(6) [...]

Note —Amended by the Constitutional Reform Act 2005 ss.15(1), 146, Sch.4, para.256 and 257, Sch.18. **3A–1113**

Meaning of "dwelling-house"

139.—(1) For the purposes of this Chapter a dwelling-house may be a house or a part of a house. **3A–1114**

(2) Land let together with a dwelling-house shall be treated for the purposes of this Chapter as part of the dwelling-house unless the land is agricultural land which would not be treated as part of a dwelling-house for the purposes of Part IV of the Housing Act 1985 (see section 112(2) of that Act).

Members of a person's family: Chapter I

140.—(1) A person is a member of another's family within the meaning of this Chapter if— **3A–1115**

    (a) he is the spouse or civil partner of that person, or he and that person live together as husband and wife or as if they were civil partners, or

    (b) he is that person's parent, grandparent, child, grandchild, brother, sister, uncle, aunt, nephew or niece.

(2) For the purpose of subsection (1)(b)—

    (a) a relationship by marriage or civil partnership shall be treated as a relationship by blood,

    (b) a relationship of the half-blood shall be treated as a relationship of the whole blood, and

    (c) the stepchild of a person shall be treated as his child.

Note —This section has been amended by the Civil Partnership Act 2004 s.81 and Sch.8, para.51. **3A–1116**

* * * *

CHAPTER 1A

DEMOTED TENANCIES

GENERAL PROVISIONS

Demoted tenancies

143A.—(1) This section applies to a periodic tenancy of a dwelling-house if each of the following conditions is satisfied. **3A–1117**

Paragraph numbers marked with a "+" can be found online and on CD.

(2) The first condition is that the landlord is either a local housing authority or a housing action trust.

(3) The second condition is that the tenant condition in section 81 of the Housing Act 1985 is satisfied.

(4) The third condition is that the tenancy is created by virtue of a demotion order under section 82A of that Act.

(5) In this Chapter—
  (a) a tenancy to which this section applies is referred to as a demoted tenancy;
  (b) references to demoted tenants must be construed accordingly.

3A–1118   *Note* —This section was inserted by Anti-Social Behaviour Act 2003 s.14(5) and Sch.1, para.1.

Editorial note

3A–1119   Demoted tenancies lack security of tenure. If the landlord follows the procedure set out in the Housing Act 1996 s.143E and F, the court must make an order for possession (see the Housing Act 1996 s.143D).

"dwelling house"

3A–1120   See s.143O which provides that a dwelling house may be a house or a part of a house and that land let together with a dwelling-house must be treated for as part of the dwelling-house unless the land is agricultural land which would not be treated as part of a dwelling-house for the purposes of the Housing Act 1985 Pt 4.

Local housing authority

3A–1121   See the Housing Act 1996 s.230 and the Housing Act 1985 ss.1 and 2(2).

Housing action trust

3A–1122   See the Housing Act 1996 s.230 and the Housing Act 1988 Pt III.

Tenant condition

3A–1123   See the Housing Act 1985 s.81.

Duration of demoted tenancy

3A–1124   **143B.**—(1) A demoted tenancy becomes a secure tenancy at the end of the period of one year (the demotion period) starting with the day the demotion order takes effect; but this is subject to subsections (2) to (5).

(2) A tenancy ceases to be a demoted tenancy if any of the following paragraphs applies—
  (a) either of the first or second conditions in section 143A ceases to be satisfied;
  (b) the demotion order is quashed;
  (c) the tenant dies and no one is entitled to succeed to the tenancy.

(3) If at any time before the end of the demotion period the landlord serves a notice of proceedings for possession of the dwelling-house subsection (4) applies.

(4) The tenancy continues as a demoted tenancy until the end of the demotion period or (if later) until any of the following occurs—
  (a) the notice of proceedings is withdrawn by the landlord;

Paragraph numbers marked with a "+" can be found online and on CD.

(b) the proceedings are determined in favour of the tenant;

(c) the period of 6 months beginning with the date on which the notice is served ends and no proceedings for possession have been brought.

(5) A tenancy does not come to an end merely because it ceases to be a demoted tenancy.

Note —This section was inserted by Anti-Social Behaviour Act 2003 s.14(5), Sch.1, **3A–1125**
para.1.

Secure tenancy

See Housing Act 1985 s.79. **3A–1126**

Demoted tenancy

See Housing Act 1985 s.82A and s.143A, above. This section only applies to former **3A–1127**
secure tenancies while the tenant condition (see Housing Act 1985 s.81) continues to
apply. Demoted tenancies lack security of tenure. If the landlord follows the procedure set out in Housing Act 1996 ss.143E and F, the court must make an order for
possession (see Housing Act 1996 s.143D).

Change of landlord

143C.—(1) A tenancy continues to be a demoted tenancy for the **3A–1128**
duration of the demotion period if—

(a) at the time the demoted tenancy is created the interest of the landlord belongs to a local housing authority or a housing action trust, and

(b) during the demotion period the interest of the landlord transfers to another person who is a local housing authority or a housing action trust.

(2) Subsections (3) and (4) apply if—

(a) at the time the demoted tenancy is created the interest of the landlord belongs to a local housing authority or a housing action trust, and

(b) during the demotion period the interest of the landlord transfers to a person who is not such a body.

(3) If the new landlord is a registered social landlord or a person who does not satisfy the landlord condition the tenancy becomes an assured shorthold tenancy.

(4) If the new landlord is not a registered social landlord and does satisfy the landlord condition the tenancy becomes a secure tenancy.

(5) The landlord condition must be construed in accordance with section 80 of the Housing Act 1985.

Note —This section was inserted by Anti-Social Behaviour Act 2003 s.14(5), Sch.1, **3A–1129**
para.1.

Registered social landlord

See Housing Act 1996 s.230 referring back to Pt I (ss.1 to 3). **3A–1130**

Local housing authority

See Housing Act 1996 s.230 and Housing Act 1985 ss.1 and 2(2). **3A–1131**

Paragraph numbers marked with a "+" can be found online and on CD.

Housing action trust

3A–1132   See Housing Act 1996 s.230 and Housing Act 1988 Pt III.

Demoted tenancy

3A–1133   See Housing Act 1985 s.82A and s.143A, above. This section only applies to former secure tenancies while the tenant condition (see Housing Act 1985 s.81) continues to apply.

Secure tenancy

3A–1134   See Housing Act 1985 s.79.

Landlord condition

3A–1135   See Housing Act 1985 s.80 and the commentary at para.3A–332.

Assured shorthold tenancy

3A–1136   See Housing Act 1988 ss.19A and 20.

PROCEEDINGS FOR POSSESSION

Proceedings for possession

3A–1137   **143D.**—(1) The landlord may only bring a demoted tenancy to an end by obtaining an order of the court for possession of the dwelling-house.

(2) The court must make an order for possession unless it thinks that the procedure under sections 143E and 143F has not been followed.

(3) If the court makes such an order the tenancy comes to an end on the date on which the tenant is to give up possession in pursuance of the order.

Amendment

3A–1137.1   This section has also been amended by the Housing and Regeneration Act 2008 Sch.15, Pt I. The amendment is not yet in force. The amendment is printed as part of the Housing and Regeneration Act 2008—see below.

3A–1138   *Note*—This section was inserted by Anti-Social Behaviour Act 2003 s.14(5), Sch.1, para.1.

Demoted tenancy

3A–1139   See Housing Act 1985 s.82A and s.143A, above. This section only applies to former secure tenancies while the tenant condition (see Housing Act 1985 s.81) continues to apply.

Notice of proceedings for possession

3A–1140   **143E.**—(1) Proceedings for possession of a dwelling-house let under a demoted tenancy must not be brought unless the landlord has served on the tenant a notice of proceedings under this section.

(2) The notice must—

(a) state that the court will be asked to make an order for the possession of the dwelling-house;

(b) set out the reasons for the landlord's decision to apply for the order;

(c) specify the date after which proceedings for the possession of the dwelling-house may be begun;

Paragraph numbers marked with a "+" can be found online and on CD.

     (d) inform the tenant of his right to request a review of the landlord's decision and of the time within which the request must be made.

(3) The date specified under subsection (2)(c) must not be earlier than the date on which the tenancy could (apart from this Chapter) be brought to an end by notice to quit given by the landlord on the same date as the notice of proceedings.

(4) The court must not entertain proceedings begun on or before the date specified under subsection (2)(c).

(5) The notice must also inform the tenant that if he needs help or advice—

     (a) about the notice, or

     (b) about what to do about the notice,

he must take the notice immediately to a Citizen's Advice Bureau, a housing aid centre, a law centre or a solicitor.

Note —This section was inserted by Anti-Social Behaviour Act 2003 s.14(5), Sch.1, para.1. **3A–1141**

Editorial note

Demoted tenancies lack security of tenure. If a landlord follows the procedure set out in ss.143E and F, the court must make an order for possession (see Housing Act 1996 s.143D). **3A–1142**

Demoted tenancy

See Housing Act 1985 s.82A and s.143A, above. This section only applies to former secure tenancies while the tenant condition (see Housing Act 1985 s.81) continues to apply. **3A–1143**

Notice

A landlord must serve notice of proceedings on a demoted tenant before bringing possession proceedings. There is no prescribed form of notice. The notice must, among other things, set out the reasons for the landlord's decision to apply for a possession order and specify the date after which proceedings for possession may be begun. The date specified must not be earlier than the date on which the tenancy could be brought to an end by notice to quit—in most cases, in view of Protection from Eviction Act 1977 s.5, 28 days. Court proceedings should not be begun before that date. The notice must also inform the tenant of the right to request a review of the landlord's decision and of the time within which the request must be made—see s.143F. **3A–1144**

Review of decision to seek possession

143F.—(1) Before the end of the period of 14 days beginning with the date of service of a notice for possession of a dwelling-house let under a demoted tenancy the tenant may request the landlord to review its decision to seek an order for possession. **3A–1145**

(2) If a request is made in accordance with subsection (1) the landlord must review the decision.

(3) The Secretary of State may by regulations make provision as to the procedure to be followed in connection with a review under this section.

(4) The regulations may include provision—

     (a) requiring the decision on review to be made by a person

Paragraph numbers marked with a "+" can be found online and on CD.

of appropriate seniority who was not involved in the original decision;

(b) as to the circumstances in which the tenant is entitled to an oral hearing, and whether and by whom he may be represented at the hearing.

(5) The landlord must notify the tenant—

(a) of the decision on the review;

(b) of the reasons for the decision.

(6) The review must be carried out and notice given under subsection (5) before the date specified in the notice of proceedings as the date after which proceedings for possession of the dwelling-house may be begun.

3A-1146   *Note* —This section was inserted by Anti-Social Behaviour Act 2003 s.14(5), Sch.1, para.1.

Regulations

3A-1147   See the Demoted Tenancies (Review of Decisions) (England) Regulations 2004 (SI 2004/1679) and the Demoted Tenancies (Review of Decisions) (Wales) Regulations 2005 (SI 2005/1228) (w.86).

The provisions for an internal local authority review of the decision to seek possession conferred by the Demoted Tenancies (Review of Decisions) Regulations, when taken with the judicial review jurisdiction, satisfy the requirements of ECHR art.6 (*R (Gilboy) v Liverpool CC* [2008] EWCA Civ 751; [2008] 4 All E.R. 127).

Demoted tenancy

3A-1148   See Housing Act 1985 s.82A and s.143A, above. This section only applies to former secure tenancies while the tenant condition (see Housing Act 1985 s.81) continues to apply.

Request for review

3A-1149   A tenant who seeks to challenge a decision to bring proceedings may request that the landlord review its decision. However a request for a review must be made before the end of the period of 14 days beginning with the date of service of the notice for possession. The court has no power to grant an extension of time. The statutory framework is similar to that for introductory tenancies—see Housing Act 1996 s.129 and the commentary at para.3A-1102.

Effect of proceedings for possession

3A-1150   **143G.**—(1) This section applies if the landlord has begun proceedings for the possession of a dwelling-house let under a demoted tenancy and—

(a) the demotion period ends, or

(b) any of paragraphs (a) to (c) of section 143B(2) applies (circumstances in which a tenancy ceases to be a demoted tenancy).

(2) If any of paragraphs (a) to (c) of section 143B(2) applies the tenancy ceases to be a demoted tenancy but the landlord (or the new landlord as the case may be) may continue the proceedings.

(3) Subsection (4) applies if in accordance with subsection (2) a tenancy ceases to be a demoted tenancy and becomes a secure tenancy.

(4) The tenant is not entitled to exercise the right to buy unless—

Paragraph numbers marked with a "+" can be found online and on CD.

    (a) the proceedings are finally determined, and

    (b) he is not required to give up possession of the dwelling-house.

(5) The proceedings must be treated as finally determined if—

    (a) they are withdrawn;

    (b) any appeal is abandoned;

    (c) the time for appealing expires without an appeal being brought.

Note —This section was inserted by Anti-Social Behaviour Act 2003 s.14(5), Sch.1, para.1.   **3A–1151**

Demoted tenancy

   See Housing Act 1985 s.82A and s.143A, above. This section only applies to former secure tenancies while the tenant condition (see Housing Act 1985 s.81) continues to apply.   **3A–1152**

Secure tenancy

   See Housing Act 1985 s.79.   **3A–1153**

Right to buy

   See Housing Act 1985 Pt V.   **3A–1154**

SUCCESSION TO DEMOTED TENANCY

Succession to demoted tenancy

143H.—(1) This section applies if the tenant under a demoted tenancy dies   **3A–1155**

(2) If the tenant was a successor, the tenancy—

    (a) ceases to be a demoted tenancy, but

    (b) does not become a secure tenancy.

(3) In any other case a person is qualified to succeed the tenant if—

    (a) he occupies the dwelling-house as his only or principal home at the time of the tenant's death,

    (b) he is a member of the tenant's family, and

    (c) he has resided with the tenant throughout the period of 12 months ending with the tenant's death.

(4) If only one person is qualified to succeed under subsection (3) the tenancy vests in him by virtue of this section.

(5) If there is more than one such person the tenancy vests by virtue of this section in the person preferred in accordance with the following rules—

    (a) the tenant's spouse or civil partner (if the tenant has neither spouse or civil partner) the person mentioned in section 143P(1)(b) is to be preferred to another member of the tenant's family;

    (b) if there are two or more other members of the tenant's family the person preferred may be agreed between them or (if there is no such agreement) selected by the landlord.

Paragraph numbers marked with a "+" can be found online and on CD.

3A–1156   *Note* —This section was inserted by Anti-Social Behaviour Act 2003 s.14(5), Sch.1, para.1 and amended by the Civil Partnership Act 2004 s.81 Sch.8, para.55.

Editorial note

3A–1157   Section 143H provides for succession to demoted tenancies by members of a deceased tenant's family *cf*. Housing Act 1985 s.88 and the commentary at para.3A–402. There can only be one succession.

Demoted tenancy

3A–1158   See Housing Act 1985 s.82A and s.143A, above. This section only applies to former secure tenancies while the tenant condition (see Housing Act 1985 s.81) continues to apply.

Secure tenancy

3A–1159   See Housing Act 1985 s.79.

Only or principal home

3A–1160   This is the phrase which is used in the tenant condition for secure tenancies—see Housing Act 1985 s.81 and the commentary at para.3A–342.

Member of the tenant's family

3A–1161   See s.143P.

No successor tenant: termination

3A–1162   **143I.**—(1) This section applies if the demoted tenant dies and no person is qualified to succeed to the tenancy as mentioned in section 143H(3).

(2) The tenancy ceases to be a demoted tenancy if either subsection (3) or (4) applies.

(3) This subsection applies if the tenancy is vested or otherwise disposed of in the course of the administration of the tenant's estate unless the vesting or other disposal is in pursuance of an order under—

    (a) section 23A or 24 of the Matrimonial Causes Act 1973 (property adjustment orders in connection with matrimonial proceedings);

    (b) section 17(1) of the Matrimonial and Family Proceedings Act 1984 (property adjustment orders after overseas divorce, etc);

    (c) paragraph 1 of Schedule 1 to the Children Act 1989 (orders for financial relief against parents).

    (d) Part 2 of Schedule 5, or paragraph 9(2) or (3) of Schedule 7, to the Civil Partnership Act 2004 (property adjustment orders in connection with civil partnership proceedings or after overseas dissolution of civil partnership, etc).

(4) This subsection applies if it is known that when the tenancy is vested or otherwise disposed of in the course of the administration of the tenant's estate it will not be in pursuance of an order mentioned in subsection (3).

(5) A tenancy which ceases to be a demoted tenancy by virtue of this section cannot subsequently become a secure tenancy.

3A–1163   *Note* —This section was inserted by Anti-Social Behaviour Act 2003 s.14(5), Sch.1, para.1; amended by the Civil Partnership Act 2004 s.81, Sch.8, para.56.

Paragraph numbers marked with a "+" can be found online and on CD.

Demoted tenancy

    See Housing Act 1985 s.82A and s.143A, above. This section only applies to former **3A–1164** secure tenancies while the tenant condition (see Housing Act 1985 s.81) continues to apply.

Secure tenancy

    See Housing Act 1985 s.79. **3A–1165**

Person is qualified to succeed

    See ss.143H and 143P. **3A–1166**

Successor tenants

    143J.—(1) This section applies for the purpose of sections 143H **3A–1167** and 143I.

    (2) A person is a successor to a secure tenancy which is terminated by a demotion order if any of subsections (3) to (6) applies to him.

    (3) The tenancy vested in him—

        (a) by virtue of section 89 of the Housing Act 1985 or section 133 of this Act;

        (b) under the will or intestacy of the preceding tenant.

    (4) The tenancy arose by virtue of section 86 of the Housing Act 1985 and the original fixed term was granted—

        (a) to another person, or

        (b) to him jointly with another person.

    (5) He became the tenant on the tenancy being assigned to him unless—

        (a) the tenancy was assigned—

            (i) in proceedings under section 24 of the Matrimonial Causes Act 1973 (property adjustment orders in connection with matrimonial proceedings) or section 17(1) of the Matrimonial and Family Proceedings Act 1984 (property adjustment orders after overseas divorce, etc), or

            (ii) in proceedings under Part 2 of Schedule 5, or paragraph 9(2) or (3) of Schedule 7, to the Civil Partnership Act 2004 (property adjustment orders in connection with civil partnership proceedings or after overseas dissolution of civil partnership, etc),

        (b) where the tenancy was assigned as mentioned in paragraph (a)(i), neither he nor the other party to the marriage was a successor, and

        (c) where the tenancy was assigned as mentioned in paragraph (a)(ii), neither he nor the other civil partner was a successor.

    (6) He became the tenant on assignment under section 92 of the Housing Act 1985 if he himself was a successor to the tenancy which he assigned in exchange.

    (7) A person is the successor to a demoted tenancy if the tenancy vested in him by virtue of section 143H(4) or (5).

Paragraph numbers marked with a "+" can be found online and on CD.

(8) A person is the successor to a joint tenancy if he has become the sole tenant.

3A–1168 *Note* —This section was inserted by Anti-Social Behaviour Act 2003 s.14(5), Sch.1, para.1 and amended by the Civil Partnership Act 2004 s.81, Sch.8, para.57.

Demoted tenancy
3A–1169 See Housing Act 1985 s.82A and s.143A, above. This section only applies to former secure tenancies while the tenant condition (see Housing Act 1985 s.81) continues to apply.

Secure tenancy
3A–1170 See Housing Act 1985 s.79.

Successor
3A–1171 See ss.143H and 143P.

ASSIGNMENT

Restriction on assignment
3A–1172 **143K.**—(1) A demoted tenancy is not capable of being assigned except as mentioned in subsection (2).

(2) The exceptions are assignment in pursuance of an order made under—

(a) section 24 of the Matrimonial Causes Act 1973 (property adjustment orders in connection with matrimonial proceedings);

(b) section 17(1) of the Matrimonial and Family Proceedings Act 1984 (property adjustment orders after overseas divorce, etc.);

(c) paragraph 1 of Schedule 1 to the Children Act 1989 (orders for financial relief against parents).

(d) Part 2 of Schedule 5, or paragraph 9(2) or (3) of Schedule 7, to the Civil Partnership Act 2004 (property adjustment orders in connection with civil partnership proceedings or after overseas dissolution of civil partnership, etc).

3A–1173 *Note* —This section was inserted by Anti-Social Behaviour Act 2003 s.14(5), Sch.1, para.1 and amended by the Civil Partnership Act 2004 s.81, Sch.8, para.58.

Editorial note
3A–1174 Section 143K provides that a demoted tenancy cannot be assigned except in matrimonial proceedings or under Children Act 1989 *cf.* Housing Act 1985 s.91. There is no provision for mutual exchange *cf.* Housing Act 1985 s.92.

Demoted tenancy
3A–1175 See Housing Act 1985 s.82A and s.143A, above. This section only applies to former secure tenancies while the tenant condition (see Housing Act 1985 s.81) continues to apply.

REPAIRS

Right to carry out repairs
3A–1176 **143L.** The Secretary of State may by regulations under section 96 of the Housing Act 1985 (secure tenants: right to carry out repairs)

Paragraph numbers marked with a "+" can be found online and on CD.

apply to demoted tenants any provision made under that section in relation to secure tenants.

Note —This section was inserted by Anti-Social Behaviour Act 2003 s.14(5), Sch.1, para.1. **3A–1177**

Demoted tenancy
See Housing Act 1985 s.82A and s.143A, above. This section only applies to former secure tenancies while the tenant condition (see Housing Act 1985 s.81) continues to apply. **3A–1178**

Secure tenants: right to carry out repairs
See Housing Act 1985 s.96. **3A–1179**

Regulations
There are not yet any regulations. **3A–1180**

PROVISION OF INFORMATION

Provision of information

143M.—(1) This section applies to a local housing authority or a housing action trust if it is the landlord of a demoted tenancy. **3A–1181**

(2) The landlord must from time to time publish information about the demoted tenancy in such form as it thinks best suited to explain in simple terms and so far as it considers appropriate the effect of—

    (a) the express terms of the demoted tenancy;
    (b) the provisions of this Chapter;
    (c) the provisions of sections 11 to 16 of the Landlord and Tenant Act 1985 (landlord's repairing obligations).

(3) The landlord must ensure that information published under subsection (2) is, so far as is reasonably practicable, kept up to date.

(4) The landlord must supply the tenant with—

    (a) a copy of the information published under subsection (2);
    (b) a written statement of the terms of the tenancy, so far as they are neither expressed in the lease or written tenancy agreement (if any) nor implied by law.

(5) The statement required by subsection (4)(b) must be supplied on the grant of the tenancy or as soon as practicable afterwards.

Note —This section was inserted by Anti-Social Behaviour Act 2003 s.14(5), Sch.1, para.1. **3A–1182**

Demoted tenancy
See Housing Act 1985 s.82A and s.143A, above. This section only applies to former secure tenancies while the tenant condition (see Housing Act 1985 s.81) continues to apply. **3A–1183**

Sections 11 to 16 of the Landlord and Tenant Act 1985
See para.3A–546 *et seq.* **3A–1184**

SUPPLEMENTARY

Jurisdiction of county court

143N.—(1) A county court has jurisdiction— **3A–1185**

Paragraph numbers marked with a "+" can be found online and on CD.

      (a) to determine questions arising under this Chapter;

      (b) to determine questions arising under this Chapter;

      (c) to determine claims (for whatever amount) in connection with a demoted tenancy.

(2) The jurisdiction includes jurisdiction to entertain proceedings as to whether a statement supplied in pursuance of section 143M(4)(b) (written statement of certain terms of tenancy) is accurate.

(3) For the purposes of subsection (2) it is immaterial that no relief other than a declaration is sought.

(4) If a person takes proceedings in the High Court which, by virtue of this section, he could have taken in the county court he is not entitled to recover any costs.

(5) The Lord Chancellor may make such rules and give such directions as he thinks fit for the purposes of giving effect to this section.

(6) The rules and directions may provide—

      (a) for the exercise by a district judge of a county court of any jurisdiction exercisable under this section;

      (b) for the conduct of proceedings in private.

(7) The power to make rules must be exercised by statutory instrument subject to annulment in pursuance of a resolution of either House of Parliament.

3A–1186   *Note* —This section was inserted by Anti-Social Behaviour Act 2003 s.14(5), Sch.1, para.1.

Demoted tenancy

3A–1187   See Housing Act 1985 s.82A and s.143A, above. This section only applies to former secure tenancies while the tenant condition (see Housing Act 1985 s.81) continues to apply.

Rules and directions

3A–1188   See CPR Pt 65 and PD 65.

Meaning of dwelling house

3A–1189   **143O.**—(1) For the purposes of this Chapter a dwelling-house may be a house or a part of a house.

(2) Land let together with a dwelling-house must be treated for the purposes of this Chapter as part of the dwelling-house unless the land is agricultural land which would not be treated as part of a dwelling-house for the purposes of Part 4 of the Housing Act 1985.

3A–1190   *Note* —This section was inserted by Anti-Social Behaviour Act 2003 s.14(5), Sch.1, para.1.

Members of a person's family

3A–1191   **143P.**—(1) For the purposes of this Chapter a person is a member of another's family if—

      (a) he is the spouse or civil partner of that person;

      (b) he and that person live together as a couple in an endur-

Paragraph numbers marked with a "+" can be found online and on CD.

ing family relationship, but he does not fall within paragraph (c);

(c) he is that person's parent, grandparent, child, grand-child, brother, sister, uncle, aunt, nephew or niece.

(2) For the purposes of subsection (1)(b) it is immaterial that two persons living together in an enduring family relationship are of the same sex.

(3) For the purposes of subsection (1)(c)—

(a) a relationship by marriage or civil partnership must be treated as a relationship by blood;

(b) a relationship of the half-blood must be treated as a relationship of the whole blood;

(c) a stepchild of a person must be treated as his child.

Note —This section has been amended by the Anti-Social Behaviour Act 2003 s.14(5), Sch.1, para.1; amended by the Civil Partnership Act 2004 s.81, Sch.8, para.59.　**3A–1192**

Member of another's family

Cf. Housing Act 1985 s.113 and the commentary at para.3A–412. Section 143P(2)　**3A–1193** gives effect to the decision in *Ghaidan v Godin-Mendoza* [2004] UKHL 30; [2004] 2 A.C. 557; [2004] 3 W.L.R. 113.

Editorial note

This section was inserted by Anti-Social Behaviour Act 2003 s.14(5) and Sch.1. It　**3A–1194** was brought into force in England on June 30, 2004 by the Anti-Social Behaviour Act 2003 (Commencement No.3 and Savings) Order 2004 (SI 2004/1502) (c.61). It was brought into force in Wales on 30 April 2005 by the Anti-Social Behaviour Act 2003 (Commencement No.4) (Wales) Order 2005 (SI 2005/1225) (w.83) (c.55).

* * * *

CHAPTER III

INJUNCTIONS AGAINST ANTI-SOCIAL BEHAVIOUR

Power to grant injunctions against anti-social behaviour
152. [...]　**3A–1195**

Power of arrest for breach of other injunctions against anti-social behaviour
153. [...]　**3A–1196**

Note — Sections 152 and 153 were repealed by the Anti-Social Behaviour Act 2003,　**3A–1197** s.13 and replaced by new ss.153A—E below.

Anti-social behaviour injunction

153A.—(1) In this section— "anti-social behaviour injunction"　**3A–1198** means an injunction that prohibits the person in respect of whom it is granted from engaging in housing-related anti-social conduct of a kind specified in the injunction; "anti-social conduct" means conduct capable of causing nuisance or annoyance to some person (who need not be a particular identified person); "conduct" means conduct anywhere; "housing-related" means directly or indirectly relating to or affecting the housing management functions of a relevant landlord.

Paragraph numbers marked with a "+" can be found online and on CD.

(2) The court on the application of a relevant landlord may grant an anti-social behaviour injunction if the condition in subsection (3) is satisfied.

(3) The condition is that the person against whom the injunction is sought is engaging, has engaged or threatens to engage in housing-related conduct capable of causing a nuisance or annoyance to—

    (a) a person with a right (of whatever description) to reside in or occupy housing accommodation owned or managed by a relevant landlord,

    (b) a person with a right (of whatever description) to reside in or occupy other housing accommodation in the neighbourhood of housing accommodation mentioned in paragraph (a),

    (c) a person engaged in lawful activity in, or in the neighbourhood of, housing accommodation mentioned in paragraph (a), or

    (d) a person employed (whether or not by a relevant landlord) in connection with the exercise of a relevant landlord's housing management functions.

(4) Without prejudice to the generality of the court's power under subsection (2), a kind of conduct may be described in an anti-social behaviour injunction by reference to a person or persons and, if it is, may (in particular) be described by reference—

    (a) to persons generally,

    (b) to persons of a description specified in the injunction, or

    (c) to persons, or a person, specified in the injunction.

3A–1199   *Note* —Note: This section was inserted by the Police and Justice Act 2006 s.26. It was brought into force on April 6, 2007 by the Police and Justice Act 2006 (Commencement No.2, Transitional and Saving Provisions) Order 2007 (SI 2007/709) (c.30). It replaces an earlier version inserted by Anti-Social Behaviour Act 2003 s.13.

Editorial note

3A–1200   Section 153A(1) allows relevant landlords to obtain anti-social behaviour injunctions. It provides that the conduct to which that provision applies is conduct capable of causing nuisance or annoyance to some person (who need not be a particular identified person) even if no complaint has been made. The conduct must be "housing-related"— i.e. directly or indirectly relating to or affecting the housing management functions of a relevant landlord. The conduct may take place "anywhere"". Injunctions may be obtained against people who are engaging, have engaged or threaten to engage in housing-related conduct capable of causing a nuisance or annoyance to—

    (a) a person with a right to reside in or occupy housing accommodation owned or managed by a relevant landlord,

    (b) a person with a right to reside in or occupy other housing accommodation in the neighbourhood of housing accommodation mentioned in para.(a),

    (c) a person engaged in lawful activity in, or in the neighbourhood of, housing accommodation mentioned in para.(a), or

    (d) a person employed (whether or not by a relevant landlord) in connection with the exercise of a relevant landlord's housing management functions.

Relevant landlord

3A–1201   An application for an anti-social behaviour injunction may only be made by a relevant landlord. Section 153E(7) specifies bodies which may be relevant landlords. Housing action trusts (see the Housing Act 1996 s.230 and the Housing Act 1988 Part III),

Paragraph numbers marked with a "+" can be found online and on CD.

local authorities (see the Housing Act 1985 s.4(e)) and registered social landlords (see the Housing Act 1996 s.230 referring back to Part I (ss.1 to 3)) are all relevant landlords for the purposes of s.153A. A charitable housing trust which is not a registered social landlord is not a relevant landlord for the purposes of s.153A.

Court

This means either the High Court or a county court (s.153E(6)). In practice applications for anti-social behaviour injunctions should always be made to a county court. **3A–1202**

Housing accommodation

See s.153E(9). Housing accommodation includes flats, lodging-houses and hostels and any yard, garden, outhouses and appurtenances belonging to the accommodation or usually enjoyed with it. In relation to a neighbourhood, it includes the whole of the housing accommodation owned or managed by a relevant landlord in the neighbourhood and any common areas used in connection with the accommodation. Housing accommodation is owned (s.153A(4)) by a relevant landlord if either it is a person (other than a mortgagee not in possession) who is for the time being entitled to dispose of the fee simple in the premises, whether in possession or in reversion or holds or is entitled to the rents and profits of the premises under a lease which (when granted) was for a term of not less than three years. **3A–1203**

Housing management functions

See s.153E(11). The housing management functions of a relevant landlord include functions conferred by or under any enactment and the powers and duties of the landlord as the holder of an estate or interest in housing accommodation. **3A–1204**

Minors

In *Enfield LBC v B (A Minor)* [2000] 1 W.L.R. 2259, CA, the Court of Appeal doubted but left open the proposition that former s.152 could not apply to minors—but see *H v H (A Child) (Occupation Order: Power of Arrest)* [2001] 1 F.L.R. 641; [2001] 1 F.C.R. 370; [2001] Fam. Law 261, CA. (The court has the power to attach a power of arrest to an occupation order made under Family Law Act 1996 s.47(2) against a minor. By suggesting that such a power of arrest could not be made against a 17 year old, wording was implied upon the provisions of s.47(2) of the Act that just was not there) *Wookey v Wookey* [1991] Fam. 121; [1991] 3 W.L.R. 135, CA. But see *G v Harrow LBC* [2004] EWHC 17 (QB). (Complaints against 14 year old. The council obtained an injunction against him under Housing Act 1996 s.152 with a power of arrest. Roderick Evans J. granted the appeal. G was too young to be sent to prison for contempt. In the absence of evidence to the contrary, common sense and experience dictated that G would have no source of income or goods that could be sequestered. The injunction could not be properly or effectively enforced and so should not have been granted. Roderick Evans J. stated that if a council did seek an injunction against a minor, it should be in a position to place evidence before the judge of the minor's circumstances which would make enforcement by a way of a fine or sequestration of assets an effective sanction for breach). **3A–1205**

Procedure

The County Court (Amendment) Rules 1997 set out the procedure to be followed on applications for injunctions to restrain anti-social behaviour under Housing Act 1996 ss.152 and 153 by creating a new CCR O.49, r.6B, as amended by the Civil Procedure (Amendment No.4) Rules 2001. They have been replaced by a new CPR Pt 65 (Anti-social Behaviour and Harassment) and PD 65. CPR Pt 65 also contains provisions dealing with demoted tenancies, ASBOs and the Protection from Harassment Act 1997. The old procedure was also partly governed by a Practice Direction made by the Lord Chancellor on August 28, 1997. It has been revoked and not replaced. **3A–1206**

(i) *Applications for anti-social behaviour injunctions.* Applications for injunctions under ss.153A, 153B or 153D must be made in Form **N16A** and follow the Pt 8 procedure. They must be made in the court for the district in which the defendant resides or the conduct complained of occurred. (CPR r.65.3; PD 65 para.1; *cf.* CCR O.49, r.6B(1)).

(ii) All applications must state the terms of the injunction applied for and be sup-

Paragraph numbers marked with a "+" can be found online and on CD.

ported by written evidence. They must be made on two days notice unless the court otherwise directs. The defendant must be served personally. If the application is made without notice the affidavit should explain why notice has not been given. (CPR r.65.3; *cf*. CCR O.49, r.6B(2)–(4))

(iii) Unless otherwise directed applications made on notice should be heard in public. (CPR r.39.2; *cf*. PD to CCR O.49, r.6B(5)). In *Moat Housing Group South Ltd v Harris and Hartless* [2005] EWCA Civ 287; [2006] Q.B. 606; [2005] 3 W.L.R. 691; [2005] 4 All E.R. 1051, Brooke L.J., giving the judgment of the court, stressed that the grant of an injunction without notice is an exceptional remedy.

"It is hard to envisage a more intrusive 'without notice' order than one which requires a mother and her four young children to vacate their home immediately. .... As a matter of principle no order should be made in civil or family proceedings without notice to the other side unless there is a very good reason for departing from the general rule that notice must be given. Needless to say, the more intrusive the order, the stronger must be the reasons for the departure. It is one thing to restrain a defendant from what would in any event be anti-social behaviour for a short time until a hearing can be arranged at which both sides can be heard. It is quite another thing to make a 'without notice' order directing defendants to leave their home immediately and banning them from re-entering a large part of the area where they live."

After reviewing family law authorities on ouster injunctions, Brooke L.J. said that when deciding whether to exercise their discretion to make ASBIs without notice, judges should follow the guidance given in Family Law Act 1996 s.45(2)(a). Further, it is:

"inconceivable that a court would grant an ASBI without notice unless there was both violence (or a threat of violence) in the past and a risk of significant harm to one of the relevant persons during the short period between the time of service of the order and the time of the court hearing on notice."

(iv) Applications for injunctions must be made in Form **N16A** (PD65, para.1). Injunctions should be in Form **N16**. Wherever possible the claimant should file a draft of the order sought with the application and a disc with the draft order should be available to the court (PD 25 para.2.4). Injunctions must be "framed in terms appropriate and proportionate to the facts of the case". If there is a risk of significant harm to a particular person or persons it is usually appropriate for the injunction to identify that person or those persons. However, in order to justify granting a wider injunction, restraining someone from causing a nuisance or annoyance to, "a person of a similar description," it is normally necessary for the judge to make a finding that there has been use or threats of violence to persons of a similar description, and that there is a risk of significant harm to persons of a similar description if an injunction is not granted in respect of them. (*Manchester City Council v Lee* [2003] EWCA Civ 1256; [2004] 1 W.L.R. 349).

(v) If a power of arrest is sought, each provision which is to be subject to the power of arrest, must be set out in a separate clause of the injunction (CPR r.65.4). Powers of arrest may be sought in claim forms, acknowledgements of service or Pt 23 applications. They must be supported by written evidence. If made on notice, not less than two days notice must be given (CPR r.65.9) It is important to spell out in the injunction the specific activities which are forbidden and confine the power of arrest to those specific activities alone. Under ECHR law, citizens must be able, if necessary with appropriate advice, to foresee to a reasonable degree the consequences that a given action may produce (*Silver v United Kingdom* (1983) 5 E.H.R.R. 347, at paras 87–8). Summary arrest and detention are clearly an extremely serious interference with a person's private life, which can only be justified by an order which is "particularly precise" (*Kopp v Switzerland* (1999) 27 E.H.R.R. 91, at para.72). See too *Manchester City Council v Lee* [2003] EWCA Civ 1256; [2004] 1 W.L.R. 349 and, in a domestic violence context, *Hale v Tanner* [2000] 1 W.L.R. 2377, CA, which suggests a power of arrest be attached only to paragraphs prohibiting violence or physical proximity. This is confirmed by s.153C.

(vi) A without notice court order with a power of arrest attached deserves and demands early re-consideration, ideally within 14 days. There is nothing wrong in a without notice order being for a duration of six months, provided that it is of a non-intrusive type (such as a typical non-molestation or non-nuisance order) and the on

Paragraph numbers marked with a "+" can be found online and on CD.

notice hearing takes place timeously (*Moat Housing Group South Ltd v Harris and Hart-less* [2005] EWCA Civ 287; [2006] Q.B. 606; [2005] 3 W.L.R. 691; [2005] 4 All E.R. 1051).

(vii) The claimant must deliver a copy of an injunction with a Power of Arrest to any police station for the area where the conduct occurred—but if it was granted without notice, only after service on the defendant (CPR r.65.4 and Form **N110A**; *cf.* CCR O.49, r.6B(6)). The claimant must immediately inform the police station if an injunction containing a power of arrest is varied or discharged.

(viii) The question of jurisdiction has been dealt with by an amendment to PD2B. The former position was that the jurisdiction of the court under ss.152 and 153 could be exercised by district judges as well as circuit judges. The amendment to PD2B makes it clear that district and deputy district judges have jurisdiction to grant anti-social behaviour injunctions and to commit for contempt. There is no longer any requirement that district judges and deputy district judges have to have had appropriate training before exercising the jurisdiction (*cf.* the Practice Direction made by the Lord Chancellor on August 28, 1997 which has been revoked and not replaced). Notwithstanding the suggestion in some quarters that the former rule giving district judges jurisdiction was ultra vires, it is now accepted that this is not the case—see County Courts Act 1984 s.75(3)(d), repealed by Civil Procedure Act 1997 Sch.2, but Sch.1 of that Act provides that the Civil Procedure Rules may deal with the subjects contained in the former rules.

(ix) An application for a warrant of arrest under s.155(3) must be made in accordance with CPR Pt 23 and may be made without notice. A claimant seeking a warrant must file an affidavit setting out grounds for the application or give oral evidence. A warrant shall not be issued unless the application is substantiated on oath and the judge has reasonable grounds for believing the defendant has failed to comply with the injunction (CPR r.65.5).

(x) The judge before whom an arrested person is brought may deal with the matter or adjourn proceedings (CPR r.65.6). In such circumstances the arrested person may be remanded or released. If the person is released, the matter shall be dealt with by the same or another judge within 28 days of the date the arrested person appears in court. At least two days notice of the adjourned hearing must be given. (CPR r.65.6; *cf.* CCR O.49, r.6B(8B)).

(xi) Applications for bail. An application for bail made by a person arrested under a power of arrest attached to an injunction or a warrant of arrest issued under s.155(3) may be made either orally or in an application notice. An application notice seeking bail must contain (1) the full name of the person making the application; (2) the address of the place where the person making the application is detained; (3) the address where s/he would reside if bail were granted; (4) the amount of any proposed recognizance; and (5) the grounds for the application and, where a previous application has been refused, full details of any change in circumstances which has occurred since that refusal. A copy of the application notice must be served on the person who obtained the injunction. (PD 65 para.2; *cf.* PD to CCR O.49, r.6B)

(xii) If a person is bailed, subject to a recognizance, the recognizance may subsequently be taken by a judge, a justice of the peace, a justice's clerk, a senior police officer or the governor of a prison (CPR r.65.7; *cf.* CCR O.49, r.6B(11)).

Sentences for breach of s.153A injunctions

In *Tower Hamlets LBC v Long* (2000) 32 H.L.R. 219, CA, the Court of Appeal held that an immediate sentence of imprisonment was appropriate where a tenant had waged a personal vendetta against another tenant in breach of an injunction. However a prison sentence of three months was reduced to three weeks. In *Nottingham City Council v Cutts* (2001) 33 H.L.R. 7, CA, the Court of Appeal dismissed an appeal against an immediate sentence of twelve months imprisonment where there had been previous breaches and where the actual breaches consisted of attempts to punch, racist and other foul language, threats to kill and kicking and banging of doors. The judge "was undoubtedly right in the case to impose a substantial term of imprisonment". Although the sentence was "a stiff one" it was not "manifestly excessive". See too *Leicester City Council v Lewis* (2001) 33 H.L.R. 37, CA and *Leeds CC v MacDonald*, November 20, 2007, unrep.

In *Barnet LBC v Hurst* [2002] EWCA Civ 1009; [2003] 1 W.L.R. 722, the Court of

3A–1207

Appeal held that a sentence of nine months imprisonment for a defendant who had breached an undertaking not to assault, threaten, harass or cause nuisance to anyone residing in or visiting a block of flats where his father lived by being loud and noisy and disturbing the neighbours' sleep was manifestly too long. The sentence was reduced to three months. The maximum sentence of two years imprisonment should be reserved for the worst cases (*Turnbull v Middlesbrough BC* [2003] EWCA Civ 1327).

In *Longhurst Homes Ltd v Killen* [2008] EWCA Civ 402; March 11, 2008, a case of repeated, unpleasant and intimidating behaviour, but where no actual violence had been used, the Court of Appeal dismissed an appeal against nine months' imprisonment, stating that the judge was entitled to reach the conclusion that an immediate sentence of imprisonment was called for in the face of breaches of the injunction which had been deliberate and repeated. Although the overall sentence was stiff, and one which would not necessarily have been imposed by every judge, the judge had not stepped outside the bracket legitimately available to her.

In *Birmingham City Council v Flatt* [2008] EWCA Civ 739, June 12, 2008, the Court of Appeal stated that it does not follow that imprisonment is to be regarded as the automatic consequence of breach of an order and it is common practice to take some other course on the first occasion when someone breaches an injunction. However, in this case, the defendant had a history of violent and threatening conduct towards others. He had denied the breaches and shown no remorse. A sentence of imprisonment was not wrong in principle. Although the length of the sentence (four months' imprisonment for driving a vehicle at a neighbour, causing him injury and making false accusations about other neighbours) was at the top end of the range of sentences available for such a breach, it was not manifestly excessive and the judge had been entitled to take the view that this was not a case for a suspended sentence order.

Time spent in custody on remand is not deducted from the sentence imposed on a committal for contempt of court (*Delaney v Delaney* [1996] Q.B. 387, CA; *Sevketoglu v Sevketoglu* [2003] EWCA Civ 1570)—but it is important to note that pursuant to Criminal Justice Act 2003 s.258, a defendant can expect to serve half of the period of imprisonment imposed (see *Wear Valley DC v Robson* [2008] EWCA Civ 1470; November 14, 2008—six months' imprisonment for breaching an ASBI on five separate occasions by playing loud music, banging on residents' doors, using foul language, behaving in a drunken and abusive manner, allowing other alcoholics to visit his flat and threatening to smash up the flat evicted, described as a severe sentence, but wholly appropriate.).

Injunction against unlawful use of premises

3A–1208   **153B.**—(1) This section applies to conduct which consists of or involves using or threatening to use housing accommodation owned or managed by a relevant landlord for an unlawful purpose.

(2) The court on the application of the relevant landlord may grant an injunction prohibiting the person in respect of whom the injunction is granted from engaging in conduct to which this section applies.

3A–1209   *Note* —This section was inserted by Anti-Social Behaviour Act 2003 s.13.

Relevant landlord

3A–1210   An application for an anti-social behaviour injunction may only be made by a relevant landlord. Section 153E(7) specifies bodies which may be relevant landlords. Housing action trusts (see Housing Act 1996 s.230 and Housing Act 1988 Pt III), local authorities (see Housing Act 1985 s.4(e)) and registered social landlords (see Housing Act 1996 s.230 referring back to Part I (ss.1 to 3)) are all relevant landlords for the purposes of s.153A. A charitable housing trust which is not a registered social landlord is not a relevant landlord for the purposes of s.153B.

Court

3A–1211   This means either the High Court or a county court (s.153E(6)). In practice applications for anti-social behaviour injunctions should always be made to a county court.

Paragraph numbers marked with a "+" can be found online and on CD.

ing action trusts (see Housing Act 1996 s.230 and Housing Act 1988 Pt III), local authorities (see Housing Act 1985 s.4(e)) and registered social landlords (see Housing Act 1996 s.230 referring back to Pt I (ss.1 to 3)) are all relevant landlords for the purposes of s.153A. A charitable housing trust which is not a registered social landlord is not a relevant landlord for the purposes of s.153D (see s.153E(8)).

Court

This means either the High Court or a county court (s.153E(6)). In practice applications for injunctions to prevent a breach of a tenancy agreement should always be made to a county court. **3A–1225**

Power of arrest

See s.154 and the commentary to that section. **3A–1226**

Injunctions: supplementary

153E.—(1) This section applies for the purposes of sections 153A to 153D. **3A–1227**

(2) An injunction may—
- (a) be made for a specified period or until varied or discharged;
- (b) have the effect of excluding a person from his normal place of residence.

(3) An injunction may be varied or discharged by the court on an application by—
- (a) the person in respect of whom it is made;
- (b) the relevant landlord.

(4) If the court thinks it just and convenient it may grant or vary an injunction without the respondent having been given such notice as is otherwise required by rules of court.

(5) If the court acts under subsection (4) it must give the person against whom the injunction is made an opportunity to make representations in relation to the injunction as soon as it is practicable for him to do so.

(6) The court is the High Court or a county court.

(7) Each of the following is a relevant landlord—
- (a) a housing action trust;
- (b) a local authority (within the meaning of the Housing Act 1985);
- (c) a registered social landlord.

(8) A charitable housing trust which is not a registered social landlord is also a relevant landlord for the purposes of section 153D.

(9) Housing accommodation includes—
- (a) flats, lodging-houses and hostels;
- (b) any yard, garden, outhouses and appurtenances belonging to the accommodation or usually enjoyed with it;
- (c) in relation to a neighbourhood, the whole of the housing accommodation owned or managed by a relevant landlord in the neighbourhood and any common areas used in connection with the accommodation.

(10) A landlord owns housing accommodation if either of the following paragraphs applies to him—

Paragraph numbers marked with a "+" can be found online and on CD.

(a) he is a person (other than a mortgagee not in possession) who is for the time being entitled to dispose of the fee simple in the premises, whether in possession or in reversion;

(b) he is a person who holds or is entitled to the rents and profits of the premises under a lease which (when granted) was for a term of not less than three years.

(11) The housing management functions of a relevant landlord include—

(a) functions conferred by or under any enactment;

(b) the powers and duties of the landlord as the holder of an estate or interest in housing accommodation.

(12) Harm includes serious ill-treatment or abuse (whether physical or not).

3A–1228   *Note* —This section was inserted by Anti-Social Behaviour Act 2003 s.13.

Registered social landlord

3A–1229   See Housing Act 1996 s.230 referring back to Pt I, ss.1 to 3.

Powers of arrest: ex-parte applications for injunctions

3A–1230   **154.**—(1) In determining whether to exercise its power under section 153C(3) or 153D(4) to attach a power of arrest to an injunction which it intends to grant on an ex-parte application, the High Court or a county court shall have regard to all the circumstances including—

(a) whether it is likely that the applicant will be deterred or prevented from seeking the exercise of the power if the power is not exercised immediately, and

(b) whether there is reason to believe that the respondent is aware of the proceedings for the injunction but is deliberately evading service and that the applicant or any person of a description mentioned in any of paragraphs (a) to (d) of section 153A(3) (as the case may be) will be seriously prejudiced if the decision as to whether to exercise the power were delayed until substituted service is effected.

(2) Where the court exercises its power as mentioned in subsection (1), it shall afford the respondent an opportunity to make representations relating to the exercise of the power as soon as just and convenient at a hearing of which notice has been given to all the parties in accordance with rules of court.

3A–1231   *Note* —This section was amended by the Anti-Social Behaviour Act 2003 s.13(4). It was amended by the Police and Justice Act 2006 Sch.14, para.32, with effect from April 6, 2007 (SI 2007/709).

Powers of arrest: ex parte applications for injunctions

3A–1232   See commentary to ss.153A–E.

Arrest and remand

3A–1233   **155.**—(1) If a power of arrest is attached to certain provisions of an

Paragraph numbers marked with a "+" can be found online and on CD.

injunction by virtue of section 153C(3) or 153D(4), a constable may arrest without warrant a person whom he has reasonable cause for suspecting to be in breach of any such provision or otherwise in contempt of court in relation to a breach of any such provision. A constable shall after making any such arrest forthwith inform the person on whose application the injunction was granted.

(2) Where a person is arrested under subsection (1)—

    (a) he shall be brought before the relevant judge within the period of 24 hours beginning at the time of his arrest, and

    (b) if the matter is not then disposed of forthwith, the judge may remand him.

In reckoning for the purposes of this subsection any period of 24 hours no account shall be taken of Christmas Day, Good Friday or any Sunday.

(3) If the court has granted an injunction in circumstances such that a power of arrest could have been attached under section 153C(3) or 153D(4) but—

    (a) has not attached a power of arrest under the section in question to any provisions of the injunction, or

    (b) has attached that power only to certain provisions of the injunction,

then, if at any time the applicant considers that the respondent has failed to comply with the injunction, he may apply to the relevant judge for the issue of a warrant for the arrest of the respondent.

(4) The relevant judge shall not issue a warrant on an application under subsection (3) unless—

    (a) the application is substantiated on oath, and

    (b) he has reasonable grounds for believing that the respondent has failed to comply with the injunction.

(5) If a person is brought before a court by virtue of a warrant issued under subsection (4) and the court does not dispose of the matter forthwith, the court may remand him.

(6) Schedule 15 (which makes provision corresponding to that applying in magistrates' courts in civil cases under sections 128 and 129 of the Magistrates' Courts Act 1980) applies in relation to the powers of the High Court and a county court to remand a person under this section.

(7) If a person remanded under this section is granted bail by virtue of subsection (6), he may be required by the relevant judge to comply, before release on bail or later, with such requirements as appear to the judge to be necessary to secure that he does not interfere with witnesses or otherwise obstruct the course of justice.

Note —This section was amended by Anti-Social Behaviour Act 2003 s.13(5).   **3A–1234**

"relevant judge"

See s.158 and the commentary at 3A–1206, para.(viii)   **3A–1235**

Arrest and remand

See commentary to ss.152 and 153 and Form **N148**.   **3A–1236**

Paragraph numbers marked with a "+" can be found online and on CD.

Note that s.155(2)(b) and s.155(3)–(7) were implemented on October 15, 2001 by the Housing Act 1996 (Commencement No.13) Order 2001 (SI 2001/3164) (c.100). See too *Braintree DC v Clark* [1998] C.L.Y. 3724, CA. The county court has power to review a decision to grant bail or to remand in custody, especially when there has been a change in circumstance. Accordingly, the Court of Appeal's task on any appeal against a refusal to grant bail is one of review rather than rehearing. (*Newham LBC v Jones* [2002] EWCA Civ 1779 a case where an appeal was dismissed. Although the circuit judge did not specifically refer to the Bail Act 1976 when refusing bail, he did express concerns over the seriousness of the allegations and further breaches of the injunction).

Remand for medical examination and report

3A–1237   **156.**—(1) If the relevant judge has reason to consider that a medical report will be required, any power to remand a person under section 155 may be exercised for the purpose of enabling a medical examination and report to be made.

(2) If such a power is so exercised the adjournment shall not be for more than 4 weeks at a time unless the judge remands the accused in custody.

(3) If the judge so remands the accused, the adjournment shall not be for more than 3 weeks at a time.

(4) If there is reason to suspect that a person who has been arrested—

(a) under section 155(1), or

(b) under a warrant issued under section 155(4),

is suffering from mental disorder within the meaning of the Mental Health Act 1983, the relevant judge shall have the same power to make an order under that section (remand for report on accused's mental condition) as the Crown Court has under section 35 of that Act in the case of an accused person within the meaning of that section.

3A–1237.1   *Note* —Amended (subject to savings) by the Mental Health Act 2007 s.1(4), Sch.1, Pt.2, para.21 with effect from November 3 2008 (SI 2008/1900).

"relevant judge"

3A–1238   See s.158 and the commentary at 3A–1206, para.(vii).

Remand for medical examination and report

3A–1239   See commentary to ss.152 and 153.

Note that ss.155(2)(b) (remands in custody) and 155(3)–(7) (warrants for arrest), 156 (remand for medical examination), and Sch.15 (provisions corresponding with civil procedure in magistrates' courts) were implemented on October 15, 2001 by the Housing Act 1996 (Commencement No.13) Order 2001 (SI 2001/3164) (c.100).

Powers of arrest: supplementary provisions

3A–1240   **157.**—(1) If in exercise of its power under section 153C(3) or 153D(4) the High Court or a county court attaches a power of arrest to any provisions of an injunction, it may provide that the power of arrest is to have effect for a shorter period than the other provisions of the injunction.

(2) Any period specified for the purposes of subsection (1) may be extended by the court (on one or more occasions) on an application to vary or discharge the injunction.

Paragraph numbers marked with a "+" can be found online and on CD.

(3) If a power of arrest has been attached to certain provisions of an injunction by virtue of section 153C(3) or 153D(4), the court may vary or discharge the injunction in so far as it confers a power of arrest (whether or not any application has been made to vary or discharge any other provision of the injunction).

(4) An injunction may be varied or discharged under subsection (3) on an application by the respondent or the person on whose application the injunction was made.

Note —This section was amended by the Anti-Social Behaviour Act 2003 s.13(6).　**3A–1241**

Powers of arrest: supplementary provisions
See commentary at 3A–1206.　**3A–1242**

Interpretation: Chapter III

158.—(1) For the purposes of this Chapter—　**3A–1243**
　　　　"charitable housing trust" means a housing trust, within the meaning of the Housing Associations Act 1985, which is a charity within the meaning of the Charities Act 1993;
　　"child" means a person under the age of 18 years;
　　"harm"—
　　　　　　(a) in relation to a person who has reached the age of 18 years, means ill-treatment or the impairment of health, and
　　　　　　(b) in relation to a child, means ill-treatment or the impairment of health or development;
　　"health" includes physical or mental health;
　　"ill-treatment", in relation to a child, includes sexual abuse and forms of ill-treatment which are not physical;
　　"relevant judge", in relation to an injunction, means—
　　　　　　(a) where the injunction was granted by the High Court, a judge of that court,
　　　　　　(b) where the injunction was granted by a county court, a judge or district judge of that or any other county court;
　　"tenancy" includes a licence, and "tenant" and "landlord" shall be construed accordingly.

(2) Where the question of whether harm suffered by a child is significant turns on the child's health or development, his health or development shall be compared with that which could reasonably be expected of a similar child.

Note —This section was amended by the Anti-Social Behaviour Act 2003 s.13(7).　**3A–1244**

Interpretation: Chapter III
See commentary to ss.152 and 153.　**3A–1245**

"relevant judge"
See the commentary at para.3A–1206.　**3A–1246**

Paragraph numbers marked with a "+" can be found online and on CD.

* * * *

Part VII

Homelessness

Housing Act 1996—Pt VII

3A-1247   Pt VII completely replaced the homelessness provisions formerly found in the Housing Act 1985 Pt III (see the Housing Act 1996 Sch.19, Pt VIII) with a new statutory code contained in ss.175 to 218). Some of the old provisions were re-enacted without alteration (e.g. s.189 (priority need)) or with only minor amendments (e.g. ss.175–177 (definition of homelessness), s.188 (interim duty to accommodate), ss.198–199 (local connection), and ss.211–212 (protection of property)). However, other changes were far more significant. Significant amendments to the 1996 Act were also made by the Homelessness Act 2002.

When implementing the provisions of Pt VII authorities must have regard to the Guidance issued by the Department of the Environment (s.182). The current *Code of Guidance* was issued in July 2002 by the Office of the Deputy Prime Minister to reflect changes introduced by the Homelessness Act 2002. Copies are available from the Office of the Deputy Prime Minister, PO Box 236, Wetherby, West Yorkshire LS23 7NB. There is a separate Welsh Code of Guidance issued by the Welsh Assembly Government. Failure to consider the current edition of the *Code* may provide grounds for quashing a decision (*R. v Newham LBC Ex p. Bones* (1993) 25 H.L.R. 357, QBD). However the Code of Guidance is not a source of law. Although councils must take it into account and give reasons for departing from it, it is not binding on them (*Khatun v Newham LBC* [2004] EWCA Civ 55; [2005] Q.B. 37; [2004] 3 W.L.R. 417). Where the Code of Guidance is in conflict with the Act, the words of the Act prevail (*Griffin v Westminster City Council* [2004] EWCA Civ 108; [2004] H.L.R. 32).

See too Homelessness Act 2002 Pt I.

Homelessness and threatened homelessness

3A-1248   **175.**—(1) A person is homeless if he has no accommodation available for his occupation, in the United Kingdom or elsewhere, which he—

    (a) is entitled to occupy by virtue of an interest in it or by virtue of an order of a court,

    (b) has an express or implied licence to occupy, or

    (c) occupies as a residence by virtue of any enactment or rule of law giving him the right to remain in occupation or restricting the right of another person to recover possession.

(2) A person is also homeless if he has accommodation but—

    (a) he cannot secure entry to it, or

    (b) it consists of a moveable structure, vehicle or vessel designed or adapted for human habitation and there is no place where he is entitled or permitted both to place it and to reside in it.

(3) A person shall not be treated as having accommodation unless it is accommodation which it would be reasonable for him to continue to occupy.

(4) A person is threatened with homelessness if it is likely that he will become homeless within 28 days.

Paragraph numbers marked with a "+" can be found online and on CD.

"accommodation available for his occupation"

See s.176. Prison is not accommodation. It does not fall within s.175(a), (b) or (c). **3A–1249**
For accommodation to exist there has to be a right to occupy which is enforceable or
defensible in law. A prisoner cannot be said to have such a right of occupation. Detention is the antithesis of any such right. (*Stewart v Lambeth LBC* [2002] EWCA Civ 753;
[2002] H.L.R. 40 and *R. (B) v Southwark LBC* [2003] EWHC 1678 (Admin); [2004]
H.L.R. 3).

"any enactment or rule of law"

A person remaining in possession of premises after the date on which an order for **3A–1250**
possession has become effective but before the warrant for possession has been executed is occupying a residence by virtue of an enactment restricting the right of the
landlord to recover possession within s.175(1)(c). Enactment in that section includes
rules of court under which the warrant was obtained. That is the position under the
Protection from Eviction Act 1977 (*Haniff v Robinson* [1993] Q.B. 419; [1992] 3 W.L.R.
875; [1993] 1 All E.R. 185). Therefore a person only becomes homeless when the warrant for possession is executed (*R. (Sacupima) v Newham LBC* [2001] 1 W.L.R. 563,
QBD). See too *R. v Newham LBC Ex p. Khan* (2001) 33 H.L.R. 29, QBD. Tolerated trespassers are not homeless because they continue in occupation by "rule of law": (*Burrows v Brent LBC* [1996] 1 W.L.R. 1448; [1996] 4 All E.R. 577, HL, referring to the
Housing Act 1985 s.58(2)(c), now the Housing Act 1996 s.175(1)(c)).

"reasonable to continue to occupy"

See s.177. In assessing whether it is "reasonable to continue to occupy" existing ac- **3A–1251**
commodation, councils are entitled to take account of the existence of many families
even more severely overcrowded in their area (s.177(2)). It does not automatically follow that because a home is statutorily overcrowded, or that an offence is being committed by remaining in it, that it cannot be reasonable for a tenant to continue in
occupation. Furthermore, and in parallel to ss.175(3) and 177(2), s.210 (dealing with
suitability of accommodation) does not provide that overcrowded accommodation can
never be suitable, simply that the overcrowding provisions needed to be taken into account by the housing authority in deciding what to offer (*Harouki v RBK&C* [2007]
EWCA Civ 1000; [2008] 1 W.L.R. 797, although it should be noted that the judgment
contains the pre-2006 version of s.210).

Homelessness and threatened homelessness

Sections 175, 176 and 177 re-enact the provisions defining homelessness ("A person **3A–1252**
is homeless if he has no accommodation available for his occupation ...") and what is
accommodation which it is reasonable to occupy, formerly found in the Housing Act
1985 ss.58 and 75 with minor amendments. Section 177(3)provides that the Secretary
of State may specify other circumstances to be taken into account in determining
whether or not it is reasonable to continue in occupation. This has been done by the
Homelessness (Suitability of Accommodation) Order 1996 (SI 1996/3204) which states
that in considering whether it would have been reasonable for a person to continue to
occupy accommodation, authorities should take into account the applicant's financial
resources, including various specified forms of income, various specified costs relating
to accommodation and other reasonable living expenses. See *Odunsi v Brent LBC*,
unreported, 1999, Willesden County Court, where it was held that Homelessness
(Suitability of Accommodation) Order 1996 art.2 requires councils to consider whether
property is affordable. This is a mandatory obligation. The procedure is inquisitorial,
not adversarial.

Cannot secure entry

The condition in section 175(2)(a) requiring a person to be able to secure entry to **3A–1253**
accommodation refers to some kind of physical bar to gaining entry at the premises
themselves (e.g. displacement by unlawful eviction, squatting and the like) and not to
some difficulty, for whatever reason, of travelling to them (*Begum v Tower Hamlets LBC*;
[2000] Q.B. 133; [2000] 1 W.L.R. 306, CA).

reasonable to occupy

In *R. v Westminster City Council Ex p.Alouat* (1989) 21 H.L.R. 477, QBD, Schiemann **3A–1254**

Paragraph numbers marked with a "+" can be found online and on CD.

HOUSING

J. held that in the Housing Act 1985 s.58(2A)(now the Housing Act 1996 s.175(3)) "reasonableness" is not limited to statutory factors—non-statutory overcrowding, medical need and other matters should also be considered by local authorities. When determining whether it is reasonable to continue to occupy accommodation for the purposes of Pt 7, local authorities should have regard to the Housing Act 1985 Pt 10 (statutory overcrowding): *Elrify v Westminster City Council* [2007] EWCA Civ 332; [2007] H.L.R. 36. See too *Osei v Southwark LBC* [2007] EWCA Civ 787; [2008] H.L.R. 15 and *Waltham Forest LBC v Maloba* [2007] EWCA Civ 1281; [2008] H.L.R. 26.

Domestic violence

3A–1255   The provisions relating to homelessness as a result of domestic violence (Housing Act 1985 s.83(3)) have been re-enacted and broadened (Housing Act 1996 s.177(1)).

Even before the introduction of the specific reference to domestic violence in s.177(1), threats of violence were likely to be a relevant factor when considering whether or not it was reasonable for an applicant to continue to occupy premises. In *R. v Broxbourne BC Ex p. Willmoth* (1990) 22 H.L.R. 118, CA, the Court of Appeal (following and applying *R. v Kensington and Chelsea RBC Ex p. Hammell* [1989] 1 Q.B. 518; [1989] 2 W.L.R. 90; [1989] 1 All E.R. 1202, CA) held that s.58(2A) (now the Housing Act 1996 s.175(3)) required consideration of all matters related to continued occupation. Sir John Megaw said the reasonableness test is:

> "not necessarily or solely confined to looking at the actual quality of the accommodation within the four walls of the house or the room or flat which is the accommodation available. It may be the duty of the housing authority to consider also circumstances, matters and factors which may fall outside the limited consideration of the actual quality of physical accommodation itself ... Just as the difficulties created by a staircase or other approach to accommodation, to an applicant with physical infirmities, is relevant to reasonableness, so also are threats of violence, even though those threats come from one who is not resident in the accommodation (p.127)".

The Court of Appeal has held that the probability test in s.177(1), (namely whether it is probable that continued occupation would lead to domestic violence) is clear and unequivocal. It is a question of fact devoid of value judgments about what an applicant might or might not have done. Available measures that would probably prove effective in preventing actual or threatened violence might reduce the level of risk below one of probability. However, councils are not entitled to assume that such measures would be taken or would be effective if taken (*Bond v Leicester City Council* [2001] EWCA Civ 1544; [2002] H.L.R. 6).

The word "accommodation" in the Housing Act 1996 Pt 7 bears its ordinary meaning in the English language and includes accommodation in a women's refuge. Women in refuges are, therefore, only homeless if it is no longer "reasonable ... to continue to occupy" the accommodation (s.175(3)). In applying that test, local authorities should consider the matters of general and particular application referred to in *Manchester City Council v Moran; Richards v Ipswich BC* [2008] EWCA Civ 378; [2008] 1 W.L.R. 2387; [2008] 4 All E.R. 304.

Other Violence

3A–1256   Homelessness Act 2002 s.10 amended s.177 so as to provide that violence other than domestic violence may mean that it is not reasonable to continue to occupy existing accommodation. Violence includes threats of violence which are likely to be carried out. In England, this amendment was brought into force on July 31, 2002 by the Homelessness Act 2002 (Commencement No.1) (England) Order 2002 (SI 2002/1799) (c.56). In Wales, this amendment was brought into force on September 30, 2002 by the Homelessness Act 2002 (Commencement) (Wales) Order 2002 (SI 2002/1736) (w.166) (c.53).

Temporary accommodation

3A–1257   The amendment of the definition of homelessness in the Housing Act 1985 s.58 by the Housing and Planning Act 1986 s.14(2), which added a new s.58(2A)(now the Housing Act 1996 s.175(3)) which states that, "a person shall not be treated as having accommodation unless it is accommodation which it would be reasonable for him to continue to occupy", and a new s.58(2B)(now the Housing Act 1996 s.177(2)) which

Paragraph numbers marked with a "+" can be found online and on CD.

states that in determining whether it is reasonable to continue to occupy accommodation, regard may be had to the general circumstances prevailing in relation to housing in the district of the local housing authority to whom the applicant has applied for accommodation, have reversed the effect of the decision of the House of Lords in *R. v Hillingdon LBC Ex p. Puhlhofer* [1986] A.C. 484; [1986] 2 W.L.R. 259; [1986] 1 All E.R. 467, HL.

The mere fact that accommodation is temporary does not mean that a person is homeless. In *R. v Brent LBC Ex p. Awua* [1996] A.C. 55; [1995] 3 W.L.R. 215; [1995] 3 All E.R. 493, HL, Lord Hoffmann, giving the leading speech, observed that nothing in the Housing Act 1985 s.58 (now the Housing Act 1996 s.175) caused a person to be homeless simply because their accommodation was temporary, short-term or precarious until they were within 28 days of losing it (s.58(4)—now s.175(4)). He found it hard to imagine a case in which it could be said that it was not reasonable to continue to occupy accommodation simply on the basis it was temporary but he observed that:

> "On the other hand, the extent to which the accommodation is physically suitable, so that it would be reasonable for a person to continue to occupy it, must be related to the time for which he has been there and is expected to stay. A housing authority could take the view that a family like the Puhlhofers, put into a cramped and squalid bedroom, can be expected to make do for a temporary period. On the other hand, there will come a time at which it is no longer reasonable to expect them to continue to occupy such accommodation. At this point they come back within the definition of homelessness in section 58(1)" (now s.175(1)) ([1995] 3 All E.R. 498).

A council does not have to be satisfied that accommodation has some degree of permanence before it can conclude that a person is not homeless by reason of the availability of accommodation which it would be reasonable for him to occupy under s.175(3) (*Begum v Tower Hamlets LBC* [2000] Q.B. 133, CA).

Meaning of accommodation available for occupation

176. Accommodation shall be regarded as available for a person's occupation only if it is available for occupation by him together with—

(a) any other person who normally resides with him as a member of his family, or

(b) any other person who might reasonably be expected to reside with him.

References in this Part to securing that accommodation is available for a person's occupation shall be construed accordingly.

3A–1258

Meaning of accommodation available for occupation
See commentary to s.175.

3A–1259

Whether it is reasonable to continue to occupy accommodation

177.—(1) It is not reasonable for a person to continue to occupy accommodation if it is probable that this will lead to domestic violence or other violence against him, or against—

(a) a person who normally resides with him as a member of his family, or

(b) any other person who might reasonably be expected to reside with him.

(1A) For this purpose "violence" means—

(a) violence from another person; or

(b) threats of violence from another person which are likely to be carried out; and violence is "domestic violence" if it is from a person who is associated with the victim.

3A–1260

Paragraph numbers marked with a "+" can be found online and on CD.

(2) In determining whether it would be, or would have been, reasonable for a person to continue to occupy accommodation, regard may be had to the general circumstances prevailing in relation to housing in the district of the local housing authority to whom he has applied for accommodation or for assistance in obtaining accommodation.

(3) The Secretary of State may by order specify—

    (a) other circumstances in which it is to be regarded as reasonable or not reasonable for a person to continue to occupy accommodation, and

    (b) other matters to be taken into account or disregarded in determining whether it would be, or would have been, reasonable for a person to continue to occupy accommodation.

3A–1261   *Note* — Amended by Homelessness Act 2002 s.10. In England, this amendment was brought into force on July 31, 2002 by the Homelessness Act 2002 (Commencement No.1) (England) Order 2002 (SI 2002/1799) (c.56). In Wales, this amendment was brought into force on September 30, 2002 by the Homelessness Act 2002 (Commencement) (Wales) Order 2002 (SI 2002/1736) (w.166) (c.53).

Whether it is reasonable to continue to occupy accommodation

3A–1262   See commentary to s.175.

Meaning of associated person

3A–1263   **178.**—(1) For the purposes of this Part, a person is associated with another person if—

    (a) they are or have been married to each other;

    (aa) they are or have been civil partners of each other,

    (b) they are cohabitants or former cohabitants;

    (c) they live or have lived in the same household;

    (d) they are relatives;

    (e) they have agreed to marry one another (whether or not that agreement has been terminated);

    (ea) they have entered into a civil partnership agreement between them (whether or not that agreement has been terminated);

    (f) in relation to a child, each of them is a parent of the child or has, or has had, parental responsibility for the child.

(2) If a child has been adopted or falls within subsection (2A) two persons are also associated with each other for the purposes of this Part if—

    (a) one is a natural parent of the child or a parent of such a natural parent, and

    (b) the other is the child or a person—

        (i) who has become a parent of the child by virtue of an adoption order or who has applied for an adoption order, or

        (ii) with whom the child has at any time been placed for adoption.

Paragraph numbers marked with a "+" can be found online and on CD.

(2A) A child falls within this subsection if—

(a) an adoption agency, within the meaning of section 2 of the Adoption and Children Act 2002, is authorised to place him for adoption under section 19 of that Act (placing children with parental consent) or he has become the subject of an order under section 21 of that Act (placement orders), or

(b) he is freed for adoption by virtue of an order made—

(i) in England and Wales, under section 18 of the Adoption Act 1976,

(ii) in Scotland, under section 18 of the Adoption (Scotland) Act 1978, or

(iii) in Northern Ireland, under Article 17(1) or 18(1) of the Adoption (Northern Ireland) Order 1987.

(3) In this section—

"adoption order" means an adoption order within the meaning of section 72(1) of the Adoption Act 1976 or section 46(1) of the Adoption and Children Act 2002;

"child" means a person under the age of 18 years;

"civil partnership agreement" has the meaning given by section 73 of the Civil Partnership Act 2004;

"cohabitants" means —

(a) a man and a woman who, although not married to each other, are living together as husband and wife, or

(b) two people of the same sex who, although not civil partners of each other, are living together as if they were civil partners;, and "former cohabitants" shall be construed accordingly;

"parental responsibility" has the same meaning as in the Children Act 1989; and

"relative", in relation to a person, means—

(a) the father, mother, stepfather, stepmother, son, daughter, stepson, stepdaughter, grandmother, grandfather, grandson or granddaughter of that person or of that person's spouse, civil partner or former spouse or former civil partner, or

(b) the brother, sister, uncle, aunt, niece or nephew (whether of the full blood or of the half blood or by marriage or civil partnership) of that person or of that person's spouse, civil partner or former spouse or former civil partner, and includes, in relation to a person who is living or has lived with another person as husband and wife, a person who would fall within paragraph (a) or (b) if the parties were married to each other.

Note —This section has been amended by the Adoption and Children Act 2002 s.139(1), Sch.3, paras 89, 90, 91 and 92; and the Civil Partnership Act 2004 s.81 and Sch.8, para.61.

3A–1264

Paragraph numbers marked with a "+" can be found online and on CD.

HOUSING

Meaning of associated person

3A-1265   See commentary to s.175.

GENERAL FUNCTIONS IN RELATION TO HOMELESSNESS OR THREATENED

HOMELESSNESS

Duty of local housing authority to provide advisory services

3A-1266   **179.**—(1) Every local housing authority shall secure that advice and information about homelessness, and the prevention of homelessness, is available free of charge to any person in their district.

(2) The authority may give to any person by whom such advice and information is provided on behalf of the authority assistance by way of grant or loan.

(3) A local housing authority may also assist any such person—

(a) by permitting him to use premises belonging to the authority,

(b) by making available furniture or other goods, whether by way of gift, loan or otherwise, and

(c) by making available the services of staff employed by the authority.

"local housing authority"

3A-1267   See ss.217, 218, and 230 which refers to the Housing Act 1985—see the Housing Act 1985 ss.1 and 2 above.

Assistance for voluntary organisations

3A-1268   **180.**—(1) The Secretary of State or a local housing authority may give assistance by way of grant or loan to voluntary organisations concerned with homelessness or matters relating to homelessness.

(2) A local housing authority may also assist any such organisation—

(a) by permitting them to use premises belonging to the authority,

(b) by making available furniture or other goods, whether by way of gift, loan or otherwise, and

(c) by making available the services of staff employed by the authority.

(3) A "voluntary organisation" means a body (other than a public or local authority) whose activities are not carried on for profit.

"local housing authority"

3A-1269   See ss.217, 218 and 230 which refers to the Housing Act 1985—see the Housing Act 1985 ss.1 and 2 above.

Terms and conditions of assistance

3A-1270   **181.**—(1) This section has effect as to the terms and conditions on which assistance is given under section 179 or 180.

(2) Assistance shall be on such terms, and subject to such conditions, as the person giving the assistance may determine.

Paragraph numbers marked with a "+" can be found online and on CD.

(3) No assistance shall be given unless the person to whom it is given undertakes—

    (a) to use the money, furniture or other goods or premises for a specified purpose, and

    (b) to provide such information as may reasonably be required as to the manner in which the assistance is being used.

The person giving the assistance may require such information by notice in writing, which shall be complied with within 21 days beginning with the date on which the notice is served.

(4) The conditions subject to which assistance is given shall in all cases include conditions requiring the person to whom the assistance is given—

    (a) to keep proper books of account and have them audited in such manner as may be specified,

    (b) to keep records indicating how he has used the money, furniture or other goods or premises, and

    (c) to submit the books of account and records for inspection by the person giving the assistance.

(5) If it appears to the person giving the assistance that the person to whom it was given has failed to carry out his undertaking as to the purpose for which the assistance was to be used, he shall take all reasonable steps to recover from that person an amount equal to the amount of the assistance.

(6) He must first serve on the person to whom the assistance was given a notice specifying the amount which in his opinion is recoverable and the basis on which that amount has been calculated.

Guidance by the Secretary of State

182.—(1) In the exercise of their functions relating to homelessness and the prevention of homelessness, a local housing authority or social services authority shall have regard to such guidance as may from time to time be given by the Secretary of State. **3A–1271**

(2) The Secretary of State may give guidance either generally or to specified descriptions of authorities.

"local housing authority"

See ss.217, 218, and 230 which refers to the Housing Act 1985—see the Housing **3A–1272**
Act 1985 ss.1 and 2 above.

"social services authority"

See s.217. **3A–1273**

Guidance by the Secretary of State

When implementing the provisions of Pt VII authorities must have regard to the is- **3A–1274**
sued by the Department of the Environment (s.182). The current *Code of Guidance* was
issued in July 2002 by the Office of the Deputy Prime Minister to reflect changes
introduced by the Homelessness Act 2002. Copies are available from the Office of the
Deputy Prime Minister, PO Box 236, Wetherby, West Yorkshire LS23 7NB. There is a
separate Welsh Code of Guidance issued by the Welsh Assembly Government. The
Code of Guidance is not a source of law. Although councils must take it into account
and give reasons for departing from it, it is not binding on them (*R. (on the application*

Paragraph numbers marked with a "+" can be found online and on CD.

of Khatun) v Newham LBC [2004] EWCA Civ 55; [2005] Q.B. 37; [2004] 3 W.L.R. 417). Where the Code of Guidance is in conflict with the Act, the words of the Act prevail (*Griffin v Westminster City Council* [2004] EWCA Civ 108; [2004] H.L.R. 12.

APPLICATION FOR ASSISTANCE IN CASE OF HOMELESSNESS OR THREATENED HOMELESSNESS

Application for assistance

3A–1275   **183.**—(1) The following provisions of this Part apply where a person applies to a local housing authority for accommodation, or for assistance in obtaining accommodation, and the authority have reason to believe that he is or may be homeless or threatened with homelessness.

(2) In this Part—

"applicant" means a person making such an application,

"assistance under this Part" means the benefit of any function under the following provisions of this Part relating to accommodation or assistance in obtaining accommodation, and

"eligible for assistance" means not excluded from such assistance by section 185 (persons from abroad not eligible for housing assistance).

(3) Nothing in this section or the following provisions of this Part affects a person's entitlement to advice and information under section 179 (duty to provide advisory services).

3A–1276   *Note* —Amended by Immigration and Asylum Act 1999 Sch.14, para.116.

"homeless"

3A–1277   See s.175.

"threatened with homelessness"

3A–1278   See s.175.

"local housing authority"

3A–1279   See ss.217, 218, and 230 which refers to the Housing Act 1985—see the Housing Act 1985 ss.1 and 2, above.

"application"

3A–1280   The House of Lords has held that a child dependent on an adult cannot make an application for accommodation capable of triggering the duties under the Housing Act 1985 Pt III (now the Housing Act 1996 Pt VII). The Housing Act 1985 s.59(1)(b) (now s.189(1)(b)) plainly indicates that parliament intended dependent children to be the subject of applications by their carer (*R. v Oldham MBC Ex p. G* [1993] A.C. 509; [1993] 2 W.L.R. 609; [1993] 2 All E.R. 65 (also reported as *Garlick v Oldham MBC*, HL). Similarly, an adult lacking mental capacity was not owed duties under the Housing Act 1985 Pt III (now the Housing Act 1996 Pt VII). It is for local authorities to determine whether an applicant has sufficient mental capacity (i.e. the capacity to understand and deal with the concept of being offered accommodation) and their decisions can only be challenged if they are manifestly perverse or otherwise wrong on *Wednesbury* grounds (*R. v Tower Hamlets LBC Ex p. Begum (Ferdous)* [1993] A.C. 509; [1993] 2 W.L.R. 609; [1993] 2 All E.R. 65, HL).

Inquiry into cases of homelessness or threatened homelessness

3A–1281   **184.**—(1) If the local housing authority have reason to believe that

Paragraph numbers marked with a "+" can be found online and on CD.

an applicant may be homeless or threatened with homelessness, they shall make such inquiries as are necessary to satisfy themselves—

> (a) whether he is eligible for assistance, and
> (b) if so, whether any duty, and if so what duty, is owed to him under the following provisions of this Part.

(2) They may also make inquiries whether he has a local connection with the district of another local housing authority in England, Wales or Scotland.

(3) On completing their inquiries the authority shall notify the applicant of their decision and, so far as any issue is decided against his interests, inform him of the reasons for their decision.

(4) If the authority have notified or intend to notify another local housing authority under section 198 (referral of cases), they shall at the same time notify the applicant of that decision and inform him of the reasons for it.

(5) A notice under subsection (3) or (4) shall also inform the applicant of his right to request a review of the decision and of the time within which such a request must be made (see section 202).

(6) Notice required to be given to a person under this section shall be given in writing and, if not received by him, shall be treated as having been given to him if it is made available at the authority's office for a reasonable period for collection by him or on his behalf.

Amendment

Section 184 has been amended by Housing and Regeneration Act 2008 Sch.15. The amendment is not yet in force. The amendment is printed as part of the Housing and Regeneration Act 2008—see below. **3A–1281.1**

"homeless"

See s.175. **3A–1282**

"threatened with homelessness"

See s.175. **3A–1283**

"local housing authority"

See ss.217, 218, and 230 which refers to the Housing Act 1985—see the Housing Act 1985 ss.1 and 2 above. **3A–1284**

"applicant"

See s.183 and the commentary thereto. **3A–1285**

"eligible for assistance"

See s.185. **3A–1286**

"local connection"

See s.199. **3A–1287**

Inquiry into cases of homelessness or threatened homelessness

Section 184 sets out the matters into which a council must enquire on receiving an application from a potentially homeless applicant. These are such enquiries as are necessary to satisfy themselves as to: **3A–1288**

> (a) whether he or she is eligible for assistance; and
> (b) if so, whether any duty, and if so, what duty is owed.

Inadequate inquiries will leave a council decision (irrespective of its merit) open to challenge for failure to have regard to all relevant considerations.

Paragraph numbers marked with a "+" can be found online and on CD.

In *Cramp v Hastings LBC; Phillips v Camden LBC* [2005] EWCA Civ 1005; [2005] 4 All
E.R. 1014, the Court of Appeal stated that Parliament imposed the duty to make the
necessary inquiries upon housing officers, and, if there is a review, upon senior housing officers. It is for councils to judge what inquiries are necessary, and they are
susceptible to successful challenges on a point of law if and only if a judge in the
county court considers that no reasonable council could have failed to regard as necessary the further inquiries suggested by the appellant. As a matter of law a quashing order cannot be justified on the grounds "that it would have been helpful" if particular
inquiries had been made, or that "there might well have been additional information"
which further inquiries might have produced. Whether to make such inquiries is a
matter for the reviewing officer. The Court of Appeal stated that

> "these two cases evidence a worrying tendency in judges at [county court] level
> to overlook the fact that it will never be easy for a judge to say that an
> experienced senior housing officer on a homelessness review, who has considered
> all the reports readily available, and all the representations made by the ap-
> plicant's solicitors, has made an error of law when she considered that it was un-
> necessary to put in train further detailed inquiries, not suggested by the ap-
> plicant's solicitors, before she could properly make a decision on the review. The
> need to correct that tendency raises an important point of practice".

For other Court of Appeal decisions on the adequacy of inquiries under the 1985
Act, see *R. v Brent LBC Ex p. Grossett* (1996) 28 H.L.R. 9, CA; *R. v Exeter City Council Ex
p. Tranckle* (1994) 26 H.L.R. 244, CA; *R. v Kensington and Chelsea RBC Ex p. Bayani*
(1990) 22 H.L.R. 406, CA; *R. v Kensington and Chelsea RBC Ex p. Cunha* (1989) 21
H.L.R. 16, CA; *R. v Northavon DC Ex p. Palmer* (1995) 27 H.L.R. 576; (1995) 94 L.G.R.
568, CA; *R. v Sevenoaks DC Ex p. Reynolds* (1990) 22 H.L.R. 250, CA; *R. v Tower Hamlets
LBC Ex p. Shafia Khatun* (1995) 27 H.L.R. 465, CA and *Kacar v Enfield LBC* (2001) 33
H.L.R. 64, CA. Faced with an application based upon threatened homelessness, a
council has to take immediate steps under s.184 to determine whether the applicant is
eligible for assistance and what duty is owed. Where satisfied that the applicant is
threatened with homelessness, eligible for assistance and in priority need, the duty to
take steps to secure accommodation arises under section 195. The council cannot
remain inactive (*R. v Newham LBC Ex p. Khan* (2001) 33 H.L.R. 29, QBD).

ELIGIBILITY FOR ASSISTANCE

Persons from abroad not eligible for housing assistance

3A–1289   185.—(1) A person is not eligible for assistance under this Part if
he is a person from abroad who is ineligible for housing assistance.

(2) A person who is subject to immigration control within the
meaning of the Asylum and Immigration Act 1996 is not eligible for
housing assistance unless he is of a class prescribed by regulations
made by the Secretary of State.

(2A) No person who is excluded from entitlement to housing
benefit by section 115 of the Immigration and Asylum Act 1999
(exclusion from benefits) shall be included in any class prescribed
under subsection (2).

(3) The Secretary of State may make provision by regulations as
to other descriptions of persons who are to be treated for the
purposes of this Part as persons from abroad who are ineligible for
housing assistance.

(4) A person from abroad who is not eligible for housing assistance shall be disregarded in determining for the purposes of this
Part whether another person—

(a) is homeless or threatened with homelessness, or

(b) has a priority need for accommodation.

Paragraph numbers marked with a "+" can be found online and on CD.

Note—This section is amended by the Immigration and Asylum Act 1999 s.117 and the Homelessness Act 2002 Sch.1, para.7. Section 185 has been amended by Housing and Regeneration Act 2008 Sch.15. The amendment is not yet in force. The amendment is printed as part of the Housing and Regeneration Act 2008—see below.

3A–1290

"assistance"

See s.183.

3A–1291

"regulations"

See below.

3A–1292

"homeless"

See s.175.

3A–1293

"threatened with homelessness"

See s.175.

3A–1294

"priority need"

See s.189.

3A–1295

Persons from abroad not eligible for housing assistance

Section 185 provides that applicants *are not eligible* for assistance under Pt VII if—

3A–1296

(a) they are persons from abroad who are subject to immigration control under the Asylum and Immigration Act 1996. (Under the Immigration and Asylum Act 1999 Part VI, all people who applied for asylum after April 3, 2000 must rely upon the National Asylum Support Service, which, in some circumstances is obliged to provide accommodation); or

(b) they are persons who are not habitually resident in the Common Travel Area (s.185(2A) and Homelessness (England) Regulations 2000 No.701, para.4).

Both these provisions are subject to exceptions contained in the Allocation of Housing and Homelessness (Eligibility) (England) Regulations 2006 SI 2006/1294 and the Allocation of Housing and Homelessness (Miscellaneous Provisions) (England) Regulations 2006 SI 2006/2527, as amended by the Allocation of Housing and Homelessness (Eligibility) (England) (Amendment) (No.2) Regulations 2006 (SI 2006/3340) which apply to homelessness applications made on or after January 1, 2007 by Romanian and Bulgarian nationals. Note that an accession state national who is not working is prima facie not "eligible" under the Housing Act 1996 s.185. In such circumstances councils have no power to accommodate pending any appeal against that decision (save on human rights grounds) because of the prohibition in the Nationality, Immigration & Asylum Act 2002 Sch.3. (*Putans v Tower Hamlets LBC* [2006] EWHC 1634 (Ch); [2007] H.L.R. 10). (For Wales, see the Homelessness (Wales) Regulations 2006 SI 2006/2624 (w.227).)

First, the Allocation of Housing and Homelessness (Eligibility) (England) (Amendment) Regulations 2006 (SI 2006/1294), para.5 as amended by the Allocation of Housing and Homelessness (Miscellaneous Provisions) (England) Regulations 2006 SI 2006/2527 sets out five classes of persons who, although subject to immigration control, are eligible for housing assistance. (As indicated above, the intention of the government is that post-April 3, 2000 asylum seekers should seek accommodation through the National Asylum Support Service.) The classes eligible for housing assistance are:

- **Class A**—a person who is recorded by the Secretary of State as a refugee within the definition in Article 1 of the Refugee Convention and who has leave to enter or remain in the United Kingdom;
- **Class B**—a person—
  (i) who has exceptional leave to enter or remain in the United Kingdom granted outside the provisions of the Immigration Rules; and
  (ii) whose leave to enter or remain is not subject to a condition requiring him to maintain and accommodate himself, and any person who is dependent on him, without recourse to public funds;
- **Class C**—a person who is habitually resident in the United Kingdom, the Channel Islands, the Isle of Man or the Republic of Ireland and whose leave

Paragraph numbers marked with a "+" can be found online and on CD.

to enter or remain in the United Kingdom is not subject to any limitation or condition, other than a person—

(i) who has been given leave to enter or remain in the United Kingdom upon an undertaking given by his sponsor;

(ii) who has been resident in the United Kingdom, the Channel Islands, the Isle of Man or the Republic of Ireland for less than five years beginning on the date of entry or the date on which his sponsor gave the undertaking in respect of him, whichever date is the later; and

(iii) whose sponsor or, where there is more than one sponsor, at least one of whose sponsors, is still alive;

- **Class D**—a person who has humanitarian protection granted under the Immigration Rules; and

- **Class E**—a person who is an asylum-seeker whose claim for asylum is recorded by the Secretary of State as having been made before April 3, 2000 and in the circumstances mentioned in one of the following paragraphs—

(i) on arrival (other than on his re-entry) in the United Kingdom from a country outside the United Kingdom, the Channel Islands, the Isle of Man or the Republic of Ireland;

(ii) within three months from the day on which the Secretary of State made a relevant declaration, and the applicant was in Great Britain on the day on which the declaration was made; or

(iii) on or before February 4, 1996 by an applicant who was on February 4, 1996 entitled to benefit under reg.7A of the Housing Benefit (General) Regulations 1987 (persons from abroad).

The purpose of s.185(2A), an amendment brought about by the Homelessness Act 2002, (as of the subsection originally inserted by Immigration and Asylum Act 1999) is to limit the power of the Secretary of State to make regulations prescribing classes of persons subject to immigration control who may be eligible for assistance under Part VII. Section 185, as amended, excludes from the Housing Act 1996 Part VII people from abroad who are not entitled to housing benefit.

Local authorities may request information from the Secretary of State about a person's immigration status (Housing Act 1996 s.187). When considering an application for interim accommodation under s.188, local authorities have a duty to make enquiries, but where the Secretary of State has refused a non-EEA national's application for a resident's permit, a local authority is entitled to take such a refusal at face value. It is reasonable not to make further enquiries (*R. (on the application of Burns) v Southwark LBC* [2004] EWHC 1901 (Admin)).

Persons from abroad and priority need

3A–1297   Section 185(4) provides that persons from abroad who are not eligible for housing assistance are to be disregarded when determining whether or not an applicant has priority need. That sub-section is incompatible with art.14 of the ECHR to the extent that it requires a dependent child of a British citizen to be disregarded when determining whether the British citizen has a priority need for accommodation, when that child is subject to immigration control (*R. (Morris) v Westminster City Council* [2005] EWCA Civ 1184; [2006] H.L.R. 8).

Asylum-seekers and their dependents

3A–1298   **186.** [...]

Note

3A–1299   This section was repealed by Immigration and Asylum Act 1999 s.117(5) and Sch.16. Any accommodation which is to be made available for asylum seekers and their dependents should now be provided by via the National Asylum Support Service. See the Immigration and Asylum Act 1999 ss.94–100.

Provision of information by Secretary of State

3A–1300   **187.**—(1) The Secretary of State shall, at the request of a local

Paragraph numbers marked with a "+" can be found online and on CD.

housing authority, provide the authority with such information as they may require—

      (a) as to whether a person is a person to whom section 115 of the Immigration and Asylum Act 1999 (exclusion from benefits) applies, and

      (b) to enable them to determine whether such a person is eligible for assistance under this Part under section 185 (persons from abroad not eligible for housing assistance).

(2) Where that information is given otherwise than in writing, the Secretary of State shall confirm it in writing if a written request is made to him by the authority.

(3) If it appears to the Secretary of State that any application, decision or other change of circumstances has affected the status of a person about whom information was previously provided by him to a local housing authority under this section, he shall inform the authority in writing of that fact, the reason for it and the date on which the previous information became inaccurate.

Note —Amended by the Immigration and Asylum Act 1999 s.117(8).   **3A–1301**

"asylum seeker"
    See s.186.   **3A–1302**

"dependent of asylum seeker"
    See s.186.   **3A–1303**

"local housing authority"
    See ss.217, 218, and 230 which refers to the Housing Act 1985—see the Housing   **3A–1304**
Act 1985 ss.1 and 2, above.

Provision of information by Secretary of State
    See commentary to s.185.   **3A–1305**

Interim duty to accommodate in case of apparent priority need

188.—(1) If the local housing authority have reason to believe that **3A–1306** an applicant may be homeless, eligible for assistance and have a priority need, they shall secure that accommodation is available for his occupation pending a decision as to the duty (if any) owed to him under the following provisions of this Part.

(2) The duty under this section arises irrespective of any possibility of the referral of the applicant's case to another local housing authority (see sections 198 to 200).

(3) The duty ceases when the authority's decision is notified to the applicant, even if the applicant requests a review of the decision (see section 202).

The authority may secure that accommodation is available for the applicant's occupation pending a decision on a review.

Note —Amended by the Homelessness Act 2002 Sch.1, para.8.   **3A–1307**

Paragraph numbers marked with a "+" can be found online and on CD.

3A–1308 "eligible for assistance"

See s.185.

3A–1309 "assistance"

See s.183.

3A–1310 "local housing authority"

See ss.217, 218, and 230 which refer to the Housing Act 1985—see the Housing Act 1985 ss.1 and 2, above.

3A–1311 "homeless"

See s.175.

3A–1312 "threatened with homelessness"

See s.175.

3A–1313 "applicant"

See s.183 and the commentary thereto.

3A–1314 "priority need"

See s.189.

3A–1315 "available for his occupation"

See s.176.

3A–1316 Interim duty to accommodate

See *R. v Camden LBC Ex p. Mohammed* (1998) 30 H.L.R. 315, QBD (summarised at para.3A–1426); *R. v Newham LBC Ex p. Idowu*, August 1998, Legal Action 21, QBD; and *R. v Haringey LBC Ex p. Erdogan*, August 1998, Legal Action 23, QBD.

3A–1317 Suitability of interim accommodation

Accommodation provided under the interim duty to accommodate must be suitable. Lack of resources does not relieve councils from this mandatory duty. Section 188, when read with s.176, does not permit councils to split families in accommodation in separate dwellings (*Ealing LBC v Surdonja* (1999) 31 H.L.R. 686, QBD affirmed on appeal; [2001] Q.B. 97; [2000] 2 All E.R. 597, CA and [2001] UKHL 57; [2002] 1 A.C. 547; [2001] 3 W.L.R. 1339; [2001] 1 All E.R. 176, HL). When discharging their interim duties under s.188 local authorities should give individual consideration to the circumstances of particular applicants. The duty cannot be met by booking all applicants into bed and breakfast accommodation—*R. v Newham LBC Ex p. Ojuri (No.3)* (1999) 31 H.L.R. 452, CA, (Collins J.).

The question whether or not the accommodation is suitable requires an assessment of all the qualities of the accommodation in the light of the needs and requirements of the homeless person and his or her family. That means that the location of the accommodation may be relevant to an assessment of suitability. A council may act unlawfully in failing to have regard to the particular educational, employment and medical requirements of the family (*R.(Sacupima) v Newham LBC* [2001] 1 W.L.R. 563, CA, where a decision to provide bed and breakfast accommodation outside its area was quashed).

Priority need for accommodation

3A–1318 189.—(1) The following have a priority need for accommodation—

> (a) a pregnant woman or a person with whom she resides or might reasonably be expected to reside;
>
> (b) a person with whom dependent children reside or might reasonably be expected to reside;
>
> (c) a person who is vulnerable as a result of old age, mental illness or handicap or physical disability or other special

Paragraph numbers marked with a "+" can be found online and on CD.

reason, or with whom such a person resides or might reasonably be expected to reside;

(d) a person who is homeless or threatened with homelessness as a result of an emergency such as flood, fire or other disaster.

(2) The Secretary of State may by order—

(a) specify further descriptions of persons as having a priority need for accommodation, and

(b) amend or repeal any part of subsection (1).

(3) Before making such an order the Secretary of State shall consult such associations representing relevant authorities, and such other persons, as he considers appropriate.

(4) No such order shall be made unless a draft of it has been approved by resolution of each House of Parliament.

Priority need for accommodation

Categories of priority need are set out in Housing Act 1996 s.189, the Homelessness **3A–1319** (Priority Need for Accommodation) (England) Order 2002 (SI 2002/2051) and the Homeless Persons (Priority Need) (Wales) Order 2001 (SI 2001/607 (w.3)). Section 189(1), lists four categories of priority need, namely:

(a) She is pregnant or the applicant is a person with whom a pregnant woman resides or might reasonably be expected to reside.

(b) S/he has dependent children. There are two routes to priority need through dependent children (s.189(1)(b)). One is if dependent children are residing with the applicant. The other is if, although the children do not at present reside with the applicant, it is reasonable to expect them to do so in the future. The second route may apply if a parent who does not have day-to-day care and control of children but intends to have prolonged staying contact. The Act contains no definition of "dependent child" but the Homelessness Code of Guidance suggests that it should include "all children under 16, and all children aged 16 to 18 who are in, or are about to begin, full-time education or training" (para.14.2).

(c) S/he is vulnerable as a result of old age, mental illness or handicap or physical disability or other special reason, or is someone with whom such a person resides or might reasonably be expected to reside (s.189(1)(c)).

(d) S/he is homeless or threatened with homelessness as a result of an emergency such as a flood, fire or other disaster (s.189(1)(d)). If such a person is not intentionally homeless, the local authority must ensure that permanent alternative accommodation is made available.

The Homelessness (Priority Need for Accommodation) (England) Order 2002

In addition the Homelessness (Priority Need for Accommodation) (England) Order **3A–1320** 2002 (SI 2002/2051) provides that the following categories of people have a priority need for accommodation for the purposes of Pt 7 of the Housing Act 1996:

Children aged 16 or 17

3.—(1) A person (other than a person to whom paragraph (2) below applies) aged sixteen or seventeen who is not a relevant child for the purposes of section 23A of the Children Act 1989.

(2) This paragraph applies to a person to whom a local authority owe a duty to provide accommodation under section 20 of that Act (provision of accommodation for children in need).

Young people under 21

4.—(1) A person (other than a relevant student) who—

(a) is under twenty-one; and

Paragraph numbers marked with a "+" can be found online and on CD.

(b) at any time after reaching the age of sixteen, but while still under eighteen, was, but is no longer, looked after, accommodated or fostered.

Vulnerability: institutional backgrounds

5.—(1) A person (other than a relevant student) who has reached the age of twenty-one and who is vulnerable as a result of having been looked after, accommodated or fostered.

(2) A person who is vulnerable as a result of having been a member of Her Majesty's regular naval, military or air forces.

(3) A person who is vulnerable as a result of—

(a) having served a custodial sentence (within the meaning of section 76 of the Powers of Criminal Courts (Sentencing) Act 2000);

(b) having been committed for contempt of court or any other kindred offence;

(c) having been remanded in custody (within the meaning of paragraph (b), (c) or (d) of section 88(1) of that Act).

Vulnerability: fleeing violence or threats of violence

6. A person who is vulnerable as a result of ceasing to occupy accommodation by reason of violence from another person or threats of violence from another person which are likely to be carried out.

Priority need in Wales

3A–1321   The Homeless Persons (Priority Need) (Wales) Order 2001 (SI 2001/607 (w.3)) extended the priority need categories in s.189 to include anyone applying as a homeless person in Wales who is:

- aged 16 or 17;
- aged 18, 19 or 20 (who had been in local authority care and is at particular risk of sexual or financial exploitation);
- fleeing domestic violence or in fear of such violence if s/he returns home;
- homeless since leaving the regular armed forces; or
- homeless since leaving custody as a prisoner (and who has a local connection with the authority applied to).

It came into force on March 1, 2001.

Priority need and the ECHR

3A–1322   The provisions of s.189 do not breach ECHR art.8(1) in enacting a scheme of priorities whereby applications for accommodation by homeless persons are to be determined by local housing authorities. In assessing priorities, Parliament was entitled to take into account considerations such as vulnerability, which might or might not have an impact on family life, as well as those that inevitably did. Specifically art.8(1) does not require applicants with child spouses to be given priority over applicants with adult spouses or over other categories of applicant. (*Hackney LBC v Ekinci* [2001] EWCA Civ 776; [2002] H.L.R. 2).

Dependent children

3A–1323   The function of the priority need provisions relating to dependent children in Part VII is to keep families together. That brings them within the ambit of ECHR Art 8 dealing with the right to respect for "family life" (*R. (Morris) v Westminster City Council* [2005] EWCA Civ 1184; [2006] H.L.R. 8). The term "dependent child" in s.189(1) does not include a wife under the age of 18 who is in full-time education and depen-

Paragraph numbers marked with a "+" can be found online and on CD.

dent upon her husband (*Ekinci v Hackney LBC* [2001] EWCA Civ 1776, CA; [2002] H.L.R. 2).

A child in full-time employment cannot be dependent. However, there may be circumstances where 16 or 17-year-olds who are not financially dependent on their parents may be dependent on them in other ways, bringing them within s.189(1)(b). (*R. v Kensington and Chelsea RBC Ex p. Hammell* [1989] 1 Q.B. 518, CA—son aged 16, who was on a two-year YTS course at a training workshop, not dependent).

See also *R. v Kingswood BC Ex p. Smith-Morse* [1995] 2 F.L.R. 137, QBD; *R. v Lambeth LBC Ex p. Bodunrin* (1992) 24 H.L.R. 647, QBD.

It has been held that the test to be applied under Housing Act 1985 s.59(1)(b) (now Housing Act 1996 s.189(1)(b)) was whether dependent children resided with the applicant, not whether there was any "greater residency" with another adult (*R. v Leeds CC Ex p. Collier*, June 1998, Legal Action 14, QBD).

See too *Robinson v Hammersmith & Fulham LBC* [2006] EWCA Civ 1122; [2006] 1 W.L.R. 3295 where the applicant was about to turn 18 at the time of her application.

Vulnerable

Vulnerable means vulnerable in housing terms (*R. v Bath City Council Ex p. Sanger-* **3A–1324** *mano* (1985) 17 H.L.R. 94, QBD). See too *R. v Lambeth LBC Ex p. Carroll* (1988) 20 H.L.R. 142, QBD, where Webster J. confirmed that "vulnerable" means less able to fend for oneself when homeless or in finding and keeping accommodation.

Note that the Housing Act 1996 s.189(1)(c) draws a distinction between mental illness and mental handicap which is not concerned with illness but with either subnormality or severe subnormality (*R. v Bath City Council Ex p. Sangermano* (1985) 17 H.L.R. 94, QBD).

In *R. v Waveney DC Ex p. Bowers* [1983] Q.B. 238; [1982] 3 All E.R. 727, CA, the Court of Appeal held that although alcoholism does not normally give an applicant priority need, in this case Mr Bowers's brain injury, whether described as a mental handicap or other social reason, had increased his vulnerability to such an extent that he had priority need (*cf. R. v Westminster City Council Ex p. Ortiz* (1995) 27 H.L.R. 364, CA).

In relation to epilepsy, *cf. R. v Reigate and Banstead BC Ex p. Di Dominico* (1988) 20 H.L.R. 153, QBD; and *R. v Wandsworth BC Ex p. Banbury* (1987) 19 H.L.R. 76, QBD.

In *R. v Camden LBC Ex p. Pereira* (1999) 31 H.L.R. 317, CA, after reviewing recent authorities, the Court of Appeal stated that vulnerability involves not just the issue of whether applicants can find and keep accommodation, but also whether they are less able to fend for themselves in coping with the state of homelessness. The assessment required is a composite one and an individual is not homeless under the "coping with homelessness" approach unless s/he would suffer injury of detriment which an ordinary homeless person would not. See too *Thorne v Winchester CC*, April 2000, Legal Action 32, CA. Although the Code of Guidance (July 2002) para.8.13 states that the critical test in applying s.189(1)(c) is whether an applicant is less likely to be unable to fend for himself so that he is likely to suffer injury or detriment, the Court of Appeal has noted that the word "likelihood" does not appear in the relevant provisions of the Act. Although local authorities must have regard to the Code of Guidance when exercising their functions under the Act, where the Code of Guidance is in conflict with the Act, the words of the Act prevail. The correct test under s.189(1)(c) is whether homeless persons are less able to fend for themselves so that they will suffer injury or detriment, not whether they are likely to suffer injury or detriment. It is not necessary to put the gloss of likeliness into the statutory test (*Griffin v Westminster City Council* [2004] EWCA Civ 108; [2004] H.L.R. 32). See too *Chowdhoury v Islington LBC* [2004] EWCA Civ 08; *Osmani v Camden LBC* [2004] EWCA Civ 1706; [2005] H.L.R. 22; *Bellouti v Wandsworth LBC* [2005] EWCA Civ 602; *Aman v Camden LBC* [2006] EWCA Civ 750; May 11, 2006; *Tetteh v Kingston upon Thames RLBC* [2004] EWCA Civ 1775; [2005] H.L.R. 21 and *Allison v Wandsworth LBC* [2008] EWCA Civ 354, April 15, 2008.

As to the obligation of local authorities to make inquiries, see s.184 and (in relation to alleged vulnerability) *Cramp v Hastings LBC*; *Phillips v Camden LBC* [2005] EWCA Civ 1005; [2005] 4 All E.R. 1014.

Although it is proper for a local authority to consider medical opinion, the question of whether or not someone is vulnerable for "some other special reason" is to be answered by the authority itself, not by the medical adviser. Local authorities are

Paragraph numbers marked with a "+" can be found online and on CD.

HOUSING

therefore obliged to consider any other available evidence and make whatever appropriate enquiries are necessary beyond obtaining their own officers' opinions (*R. v Lambeth LBC Ex p. Carroll* (1988) 20 H.L.R. 142, QBD). In In *Shala v Birmingham CC* [2007] EWCA Civ 624; [2008] H.L.R. 8 the Court of Appeal gave extended guidance on the commissioning and use of medical advice by local housing authorities in deciding "priority need" cases. It stated that:

   (i) Although it is acceptable for local authorities to take specialist advice about medical evidence, care has to be taken not to appear to be using professional medical advisors simply to provide or shore up reasons for not accepting that an appellant is vulnerable.

   (ii) There is no harm and some good in medical advisers directly addressing those matters within their professional competence about which the local authority have to make a decision, so long as both they and the local authority recognise that it is for the latter to make their own appraisal of every opinion.

   (iii) Where an authority's medical expert is not a qualified psychiatrist, a local authority weighing his comments against the report of a qualified psychiatrist must not fall into the trap of thinking that it is comparing like with like; the authority's expert has the function of enabling the authority to understand the medical issues and to evaluate for themselves the expert evidence.

   (iv) Absent an examination of the patient, the authority's medical adviser's advice cannot itself constitute expert evidence of the applicant's condition.

   (v) Where an authority's medical adviser has not examined an applicant, he may, with consent, speak to the applicant's medical advisor on an informal basis about matters which need discussion.

There is no duty on authorities to refer every medical report to their medical advisors. (*Simms v Islington LBC* [2008] EWCA Civ 1083, October 16, 2008).

"emergency"

3A–1325   The phrase "emergency such as a flood, fire or other disaster" involves the sudden and wholly unexpected loss of a home in circumstances outside an applicant's control. It is not necessary to show that a home has been lost through some physical disaster. The disappearance of a caravan in unexplained circumstances may be an emergency under s.189(1)(d) (*Higgs v Brighton and Hove City Council* [2003] EWCA Civ 895; [2003] 1 W.L.R. 2241; [2003] 3 All E.R. 753). However a demolition order is not "an emergency such as a flood, fire or any other disaster" (*Noble v South Hertfordshire DC* (1985) 17 H.L.R. 80, CA). Similarly, the Court of Appeal has held that a person made homeless by an unlawful eviction is not homeless "as a result of an emergency" within the Housing Act 1985 s.59(1)(d)(now s.189(1)(d)) (*R. v Bristol City Council Ex p. Bradic* (1995) 94 L.G.R. 257; 27 H.L.R. 584, CA). The word "emergency" is qualified by the phrase "such as flood, fire or other disaster". However, emergencies giving rise to priority need are not limited to those with "natural" causes. Fires or floods caused by humans can give rise to priority need, but there must be physical damage which causes the accommodation to be uninhabitable.

DUTIES TO PERSONS FOUND TO BE HOMELESS OR THREATENED WITH HOMELESSNESS

Duties to persons becoming homeless intentionally

3A–1326   **190.**—(1) This section applies where the local housing authority are satisfied that an applicant is homeless and is eligible for assistance but are also satisfied that he became homeless intentionally.

(2) If the authority are satisfied that the applicant has a priority need, they shall—

      (a) secure that accommodation is available for his occupation for such period as they consider will give him a rea-

Paragraph numbers marked with a "+" can be found online and on CD.

sonable opportunity of securing accommodation for his occupation, and

(b) provide him with (or secure that he is provided with) advice and assistance in any attempts he may make to secure that accommodation becomes available for his occupation.

(3) If they are not satisfied that he has a priority need, they shall provide him with (or secure that he is provided with) advice and assistance in any attempts he may make to secure that accommodation becomes available for his occupation.

(4) The applicant's housing needs shall be assessed before advice and assistance is provided under subsection (2)(b) or (3).

(5) The advice and assistance provided under subsection (2)(b) or (3) must include information about the likely availability in the authority's district of types of accommodation appropriate to the applicant's housing needs (including, in particular, the location and sources of such types of accommodation).

Note —Amended by Homelessness Act 2002 Sch.1, paras 9 and 10.　　　**3A–1327**

"eligible for assistance"

See s.185.　　　**3A–1328**

"assistance"

See s.183.　　　**3A–1329**

"local housing authority"

See ss.217, 218, and 230 which refer to the Housing Act 1985—see the Housing Act **3A–1330** 1985 ss.1 and 2 above.

"homeless"

See s.175.　　　**3A–1331**

"applicant"

See s.183 and the commentary thereto.　　　**3A–1332**

"priority need"

See s.189.　　　**3A–1333**

"available for his occupation"

See s.176.　　　**3A–1334**

"homeless intentionally"

See s.191.　　　**3A–1335**

"a reasonable opportunity"

See *R. (Conville) v Richmond Upon Thames RLBC* [2006] EWCA Civ 718; [2006] 1 **3A–1336** W.L.R. 2808 and *R. (Nipyo) v Croydon LBC* [2008] EWHC 847 (Admin); [2008] H.L.R. 37.

Duties to persons becoming homeless intentionally

Local authorities only have minimal obligations to applicants who are intentionally **3A–1337** homeless. The definition of intentional homelessness in the Housing Act 1996 s.191(1) has five component parts. The homeless person must have:

(a) done a deliberate act,

Paragraph numbers marked with a "+" can be found online and on CD.

(b) which caused the loss of housing,

(c) which s/he ceased to occupy,

(d) which was available to him or her, and

(e) which it would have been reasonable to continue to occupy.

In addition a person is to be treated as becoming homeless intentionally if he or she enters "into an arrangement under which he is required to cease to occupy accommodation which it would be reasonable for him to continue to occupy, and ... the purpose of the arrangement is to enable him to become entitled to assistance" in accordance with Part VII of the Act "and there is no other good reason why he is homeless" (Housing Act 1996 s.191(3)).

A person is threatened with homelessness intentionally if homelessness is the "likely result" of his or her deliberate act or omission.

It is for each local authority to make its own enquiries and to form its own view as to whether homelessness is intentional or not (*R. v Slough BC Ex p. Ealing LBC* [1981] Q.B. 801; [1981] 1 All E.R. 601; [1981] 2 W.L.R. 399, CA; *Noh v Hammersmith and Fulham LBC* [2001] EWCA Civ 905; [2002] H.L.R. 54, and *R. v Basingstoke and Deane DC Ex p. Webb*; December 1989; Legal Action 15, QBD).

The material date for determining whether a person became homeless intentionally or unintentionally is the date on which s/he left the accommodation. What may have happened afterwards is irrelevant (*Din v Wandsworth LBC* [1983] 1 A.C. 657; [1981] 3 All E.R. 881, HL). See too *R. v Islington LBC Ex p. Hassan* (1995) 27 H.L.R. 485, QBD, where Deputy Judge Roger Toulson, QC quashed a finding of intentional homelessness because the council had erred in believing that it could take account of developments after the applicant became homeless but before his actual departure from the premises.

The burden is on local authorities to satisfy themselves that an applicant has become homeless intentionally. If there is doubt or uncertainty, the issue must be resolved in the applicant's favour (*R. v Gravesham BC Ex p. Winchester* (1986) 18 H.L.R. 207, QBD—finding upheld).

Note that a homeless person cannot be intentionally homeless for refusing an offer of permanent accommodation, as it has never been occupied (*R. v Brent LBC Ex p. Awua* [1996] A.C. 55; [1995] 3 W.L.R. 215; [1995] 3 All E.R. 493, HL, below). However, such a refusal may mean that a local authority has discharged its duty and owes no further obligations towards the homeless person.

There is no practical or policy reason why a woman who has been sent to prison for theft should not be regarded as having made herself intentionally homeless, even though she moved house between the commission of the offence and the start of her sentence (*Minchin v Sheffield City Council*, *The Times*, April 26, 2000, CA). See too *Stewart v Lambeth LBC* [2002] EWCA Civ 753; [2002] H.L.R. 40, noted above.

"deliberately does or fails to do ..."

3A-1338   In *Dyson v Kerrier DC* [1980] 1 W.L.R. 1205; [1980] 3 All E.R. 313, CA, the applicant had surrendered her tenancy of a council flat in Cambridgeshire and gone to Cornwall where she had relatives. She took an unprotected holiday let for about four-and-a-half months. Not long before the holiday let was due to expire she approached the council for accommodation. It decided that her impending homelessness had been caused "intentionally" by her giving up the flat in Cambridgeshire. The Court of Appeal held that the council was entitled to take into account the fact that if she had not surrendered the Cambridgeshire tenancy she would not have become homeless. See too *R. v Barking and Dagenham LBC Ex p. Okuneye* (1996) 28 H.L.R. 174, QBD and *R. v Tower Hamlets LBC Ex p. Abdul Jolil*, October 1998, Legal Action 22, QBD.

However, in *R. v Tower Hamlets LBC Ex p. Rouf* (1991) 23 H.L.R. 460, CA, the applicant who had been in Britain since 1963 returned to Bangladesh in 1985 for three years. During his absence, he allowed a friend to occupy his council flat. The friend did not pay the rent and the flat was repossessed. In 1988, after obtaining entry clearance for his family, the applicant returned to England with them. He found the flat boarded up and applied to the council as a homeless person. Following an interview during which the applicant gave details of the accommodation he had used in Bangladesh (two small rooms), the authority declared him intentionally homeless for leaving the family home in Bangladesh. The interviewing officer failed to raise with the

Paragraph numbers marked with a "+" can be found online and on CD.

applicant two of the crucial issues contained in the definition of intentional homelessness (Housing Act 1985 s.60(1)—now the Housing Act 1996 s.191(1))—first, was the accommodation available for his continued occupation, and secondly, was it reasonable for him to have continued in occupation? The interviewer "deduced" positive answers from the discussion with the applicant. The Court of Appeal quashed the decision. The applicant had returned to England unaware that his flat had been repossessed. He had accordingly acted in ignorance and his action could not be "deliberate" for the purposes of s.60(1), if he had acted in good faith (s.60(3)—now Housing Act 1996 s.191(2)). The council had not addressed the good faith point in either its enquiries or its decision letter. See too *Kacar v Enfield LBC* (2001) 33 H.L.R. 5, CA.

A family cannot become intentionally homeless simply because they choose to have additional children (*R. v Eastleigh BC Ex p. Beattie (No.1)* (1983) 10 H.L.R. 134, QBD).

Eviction following arrears

The key issue if arrears result in eviction and subsequent homelessness is whether **3A–1339** the accrual of arrears, or more commonly, the circumstances which led to the arrears, were "a deliberate act." Eviction as a result of rent arrears is not intentional if it is the result of spending assets on the necessities of life. The "necessities of life" may vary from family to family. It is for the authority to consider whether a failure to pay rent is deliberate or whether it is due to a tenant having insufficient money to pay for the necessities of life, not for the court. It is not for the authority to investigate every detail in an applicant's figures of income and expenditure and it is not necessary for them to put to applicants their opinion that certain items are not a necessity (*R. v Brent LBC Ex p. Baruwa* (1997) 29 H.L.R. 915, CA, where a finding of intentional homelessness was upheld). See too *R. v Brent LBC Ex p. Grossett* (1996) 28 H.L.R. 9, CA; *R. v Exeter City Council Ex p. Tranckle* (1994) 26 H.L.R. 244, CA; and *R. v Wandsworth LBC Ex p. Onwudiwe* (1994) 26 H.L.R. 302, CA. A finding of intentionality was also upheld in *Hobbs v Sutton LBC* (1994) 26 H.L.R. 132, CA (eviction following rent arrears but claims by the applicants that there had been confusion about the whereabouts of their landlord and their entitlement to housing benefit.) Similarly, in *R. v Barnet LBC Ex p. Rughooputh* (1993) 25 H.L.R. 607, CA, the applicant was made homeless following mortgage possession proceedings. The deliberate act which caused the loss of the home was the applicant's taking out a mortgage in 1987 beyond her means—she was unemployed, but had claimed to have an earned income of £18,000. The council's finding of intentional homelessness was upheld. The taking out of the mortgage was the act that caused the homelessness. It had been induced by fraudulent misrepresentation and so the Housing Act 1985 s.60(3) (now the Housing Act 1996 s.190(2)) could not apply to prevent the act from being "deliberate". See too *Watchman v Ipswich BC* [2007] EWCA Civ 348; [2007] H.L.R. 33 (council had been entitled to find that it was the taking out of a mortgage (and not the loss of a job) that had caused the homelessness).

On the other hand, in *R. v Wandsworth LBC Ex p. Hawthorne* [1995] 2 All E.R. 331; (1995) 27 H.L.R. 59, CA, a finding of intentional homelessness was quashed where the applicant had been evicted from her council home for rent arrears of over £3,000. She claimed that she had been unable to afford the rent, having had so low an income after her husband left her that she had been driven to choose between maintaining her children and paying the council. Nourse L.J. stated:

> "The purpose of Part III of the 1985 Act [now the Housing Act 1996 Part VII] is to house the homeless. Admittedly, it is no part of that purpose to house those whose homelessness has been brought upon them by their own fault. But equally it is no part of it to refuse housing to those whose homelessness has been brought upon them without fault on their part, for example by disability, sickness, poverty or even a simple inability to make ends meet."

The council had not considered the matters which had caused the applicant not to pay her rent. That was a fatal omission. It was no answer to assert that there had been a considered decision not to pay. The true question is: "What caused that decision?" See too *R. v Hillingdon LBC Ex p. Tinn* (1988) 20 H.L.R. 305, QBD, below; *R. v Shrewsbury and Atcham BC Ex p. Griffiths* (1993) 25 H.L.R. 613, QBD (decision of intentional homelessness after eviction for mortgage arrears quashed); *R. v Southwark LBC Ex p. Davies* (1994) 26 H.L.R. 677, QBD; and *R. v Camden LBC Ex p. Cosma* (1998) 30 H.L.R. 817, QBD (return to England following the failure of the applicant's restaurant enterprise in Cyprus. Finding of intentional homelessness quashed because of failure

Paragraph numbers marked with a "+" can be found online and on CD.

to make sufficient enquiries into the arrangements the applicant might (or might not) have been) able to make with lenders to stave off her eviction and accordingly whether it would have been reasonable for the applicant to have continued to occupy her home in Cyprus).

Eviction after anti-social behaviour

3A–1340   It is not necessary for authorities to show that the applicants have deliberately done something with the intention of being evicted. See *Devenport v Salford City Council* (1983) 8 H.L.R. 54, CA, where a finding of intentional homelessness was upheld after failure by parents to take any steps to control their children and the children's conduct resulted in the making of a possession order. Findings of intentional homelessness were also upheld in *R. v Rochester-upon-Medway City Council Ex p. Williams* (1994) 26 H.L.R. 588, QBD (failure to control children); *R. v Hammersmith and Fulham LBC Ex p. P* (1990) 22 H.L.R. 21, QBD (anti-social and criminal behaviour leading to the loss of homes); and *Denton v Southwark LBC* [2007] EWCA Civ 623; [2008] H.L.R. 11 ("deliberate act" of breaking mother's house rules led to be applicant being thrown out).

Acquiescence in conduct of partner

3A–1341   A woman who lives with a man who becomes intentionally homeless is not necessarily barred from relief by his conduct or by the fact that he may benefit undeservingly. However, depending on the facts, an authority may be entitled to assume that, in the absence of evidence to the contrary, she had acquiesced in his conduct and that accordingly she herself had become intentionally homeless (*R. v North Devon DC Ex p. Lewis* [1981] 1 W.L.R. 328; [1981] 1 All E.R. 27, QBD). See too *R. v Nottingham CC Ex p. Caine* (1995) 28 H.L.R. 374, CA (the applicant's partner had decided to withhold rent, for which housing benefit was being paid, because of the landlord's failure to carry out repairs. As a result of the arrears, the couple were evicted. Finding of intentional homelessness upheld because the applicant had acquiesced in the decision not to pay the rent and to use the housing benefit in the family budget); *R. v Tower Hamlets LBC Ex p. Khatun* (1995) 27 H.L.R. 344, CA (wife content in the marriage to leave decisions to her husband. The Court of Appeal held that she might properly be treated as having "joined" in her husband's decision to move accommodation); *R. v Barnet LBC Ex p. O'Connor* (1990) 22 H.L.R. 486, QBD; *R. v Ealing LBC Ex p. Salmons* (1991) 23 H.L.R. 272, QBD; *R. v East Herts DC Ex p. Bannon* (1986) 18 H.L.R. 515, QBD (acquiescence in nuisance); *R. v Swansea City Council Ex p. John* (1983) 9 H.L.R. 56, QBD (council entitled to reach conclusion that wife has acquiesced in husband's drunkenness which had led to eviction).

Cf. however, *R. v East Northamptonshire DC Ex p. Spruce* (1988) 20 H.L.R. 508, QBD (finding of intentional homelessness quashed because of insufficient inquiries into alleged acquiescence); *R. v Eastleigh BC Ex p. Beattie (No.2)* (1985) 17 H.L.R. 168, QBD (decision not to pay mortgage instalments based on legal advice; evidence that Mrs Beattie had protested about her husband not paying the mortgage. Finding of intentional homelessness quashed); *R. v Penwith DC Ex p. Trevena* (1985) 17 H.L.R. 526, QBD (no material on which the authority could conclude that Mr Trevena had been a party to the surrender of a tenancy by his wife or that it was a joint surrender or abandonment); *R.v Mole Valley DC Ex p. Burton* (1988) 20 H.L.R. 479, QBD; and *R. v Thanet DC Ex p. Groves* (1990) 22 H.L.R. 223, QBD (failure by council to have regard to wife's assertions that she did not know of, or participate in, the accumulation of arrears).

"act or omission in good faith"

3A–1342   An act or omission in good faith on the part of a person who was unaware of any relevant fact shall not be treated as deliberate (s.191(2)). When considering this question "there is a distinction between honest blundering and carelessness on the one hand, where a person can still act in good faith, and dishonesty on the other, where there can be no question of the person acting in good faith" (per Roch J. in *R. v Hammersmith and Fulham LBC Ex p. Lusi* (1991) 23 H.L.R. 260, QBD). See too *R. v Westminster CC Ex p. Obeid* (1996) 29 H.L.R. 389, QBD (ignorance about housing benefit); and *R. v Wandsworth LBC Ex p. Rose* (1984) 11 H.L.R. 107, QBD (applicant came to stay with her father but asked to leave because his accommodation was not satisfactory. The council was not entitled to assume, without making proper enquiries, that simply because the applicant had failed to ask her father about accommodation, she had acted other than in good faith about a relevant fact).

Paragraph numbers marked with a "+" can be found online and on CD.

In *R. v Westminster CC Ex p. N'Dormadingar*, *The Times*, November 20, 1997, QBD, Lightman J. enumerated the following principles which apply where someone gives up accommodation but claims not to be intentionally homeless because he or she is unaware of a material fact:

(1) An applicant must show that he or she is unaware of some relevant fact existing at the date that he or she gave up accommodation;

(2) Whether an applicant makes enquiries into the existence of the fact is relevant to his or her awareness of it;

(3) A fact is relevant where, had the applicant been aware of it, he or she would have taken it into account in deciding to give up accommodation;

(4) A fact must be sufficiently clear and definite for its existence to be objectively determined;

(5) Lack of, or deficiency in, foresight of the future does not constitute unawareness of an existing fact. To establish such unawareness it is necessary to show the existence at the relevant date of a factual state of affairs which falsifies the applicant's predictions.

In a case turning on whether ignorance was in good faith, the council should in interview tell an applicant if it believes that he or she is not acting in good faith (*R. v Westminster City Council Ex p. Moozary-Oraky* (1994) 26 H.L.R. 213, QBD).

"reasonable for him to continue to occupy"

In considering whether or not it is reasonable to continue to occupy accommodation, local authorities are not limited to housing issues and can have regard to things like employment prospects and loss of benefits in that locality (*per* Woolf J. in *R. v Hammersmith and Fulham LBC Ex p. Duro-Rama* (1983) 9 H.L.R. 71, QBD). See too *R. v Hillingdon LBC Ex p. Tinn* (1988) 20 H.L.R. 305, QBD, where Kennedy J. said:

"it cannot be reasonable [within the meaning of section 60 of the 1985 Act—(now Housing Act 1996 s.191)] for a person to continue to occupy accommodation when they can no longer discharge the fiscal obligations ... in relation to that accommodation without so straining their resources as to deprive themselves of the ordinary necessities of life, such as food, clothing, heat, transport and so forth" (p.308).

3A-1343

See too *R. v Camden LBC Ex p. Aranda* (1997) 30 H.L.R. 76, CA (surrender of London council flat under a scheme involving the receipt of a substantial sum to help them to buy privately followed by acquisition of a bungalow in Colombia. Applicant returned to London after failure to find work and being abandoned by her husband without financial support. Camden's finding of intentional homelessness was quashed. Any finding that the giving up of the Colombian home was intentional was impossible—no reasonable authority could have found, given the financial circumstances, that it would have been reasonable to continue in occupation); *R. v Basingstoke and Deane BC Ex p. Bassett* (1983) 10 H.L.R. 125, QBD (applicant not homeless as a result of leaving that accommodation, but rather as a result of the breakdown in the marriage and in particular her husband's conduct, which made it unreasonable for her to live with him); *R. v Islington LBC Ex p. Bibi* (1997) 29 H.L.R. 498, QBD (applicant left her home in Bangladesh because she had no access to sufficient monies to feed her family. Finding of intentional homelessness quashed); and *R. v Tower Hamlets LBC Ex p. Ojo* (1991) 23 H.L.R. 488, QBD (council gave "no proper consideration" to the question of whether, as a result of overcrowding of the applicant's home in Nigeria, it could be said that it was not reasonable to continue to occupy the accommodation).

See also *R. v Hillingdon LBC Ex p. Islam* [1983] 1 A.C. 688; [1981] 3 W.L.R. 109; [1981] 3 All E.R. 901, HL (husband, wife and several children evicted from shared room); *De Falco v Crawley BC* [1980] Q.B. 460; [1980] 2 W.L.R. 664; [1980] 1 All E.R. 913, CA (reasonable to have continued to occupy the accommodation in Italy); *cf. R. v Westminster City Council Ex p. Guilarte*, June 1994, Legal Action 13, QBD (applicant left accommodation in Venezuela because of the poor economy and high inflation in that country and because he thought he would find a better standard of living in Britain. Decision quashed because the council had failed to make enquiries as to (a) whether he could have remained in the specific accommodation he occupied in Venezuela, and, if so (b) why he chose to leave it).

In *R. v Wandsworth LBC Ex p. Henderson* (1986) 18 H.L.R. 522, QBD, there was acute disrepair and, as a result, the council served statutory notices. The tenants with-

Paragraph numbers marked with a "+" can be found online and on CD.

HOUSING

held rent and arrears accrued. The landlord began possession proceedings based on rent arrears. Even though the tenants counterclaimed and were represented by counsel, a possession order was made. The council decided that they had consented to the possession order and had become homeless intentionally. McNeill J. dismissed an application for judicial review. Even though the necessary repairs were very extensive and being carried out slowly, the local authority was entitled to decide that the tenants had "deliberately" left available accommodation. See too *R. v Waltham Forest LBC Ex p. Green* December 1997, Legal Action 15, QBD.

As to living conditions in shared accommodation, contrast *R. v Brent LBC Ex p. Yusuf* (1996) 29 H.L.R. 48, QBD; and *R. v Brent LBC Ex p. Bariise* (1999) 31 H.L.R. 50, CA.

Departure after violence

3A–1344 See *R. v Croydon LBC Ex p. Toth* (1988) 20 H.L.R. 576, CA (departure after threats by associates of applicant's husband, who had disappeared and was being sought in relation to an armed robbery. Finding of intentional homelessness upheld); *R. v Newham LBC Ex p. McIlroy* (1991) 23 H.L.R. 570, QBD (council was entitled to conclude that the family could have continued in their home or temporary accommodation in Belfast pending an urgent transfer application notwithstanding sectarian violence which had led to one of the applicants being shot at); *cf. R. v Brent LBC Ex p. McManus* (1993) 25 H.L.R. 643, CA (sectarian violence); *R. v Hillingdon LBC Ex p. H* (1988) 20 H.L.R. 554, QBD (intimidation and violence in Northern Ireland); *R. v Westminster City Council Ex p. Bishop* (1993) 25 H.L.R. 459, CA (departure of applicant's daughter from flat after she had been harassed and molested by drug-dealers followed by the applicant leaving as a result of violence and harassment from a former partner. Finding of intentional homelessness quashed); *R. v Westminster City Council Ex p. Ermakov* [1996] 2 All E.R. 302, CA; *R. v Barnet LBC Ex p. Babalola* (1996) 28 H.L.R. 196, QBD; *R. v Hillingdon LBC Ex p. McDowell*, December 1992, Legal Action 22, QBD (harassment from neighbours, culminating in the systematic wrecking of her car and ransacking of her flat. Finding of intentional homelessness quashed); *R. v Tynedale DC Ex p. McCabe* (1992) 24 H.L.R. 384, QBD (domestic violence); *R. v Northampton BC Ex p. Clarkson* (1992) 24 H.L.R. 529, QBD (sexual abuse) and *R. (McAuley and Stewart) v Highland Council*, Court of Session (Outer House), July 22, 2003 (harassment, threats and violence).

Affordability

3A–1345 The question of whether accommodation is affordable and accordingly whether it is reasonable to continue to occupy is not to be "judged on a Micawber test as to whether one's income exceeds, or fails to measure up to, the rent one is required to pay" (per Sir Thomas Bingham M.R. in *R. v Croydon LBC Ex p. Graham* (1994) 26 H.L.R. 286, CA, where the applicant had not acted unreasonably in moving (without prospect of homelessness) to cheaper suitable accommodation. See too *R. v Tower Hamlets LBC Ex p. Ullah* (1992) 24 H.L.R. 680, QBD (applicant sold house to repay loans. Finding of intentional homelessness quashed because council had failed to enquire into the loans, their terms and all the surrounding circumstances to determine where on the scale of necessity this situation fell). But *cf. R. v Leeds City Council Ex p. Adamiec* (1992) 24 H.L.R. 138, QBD, where although a home-owner fell into financial difficulties and mortgage arrears developed, no action was taken by the lender to enforce the loan and there was no threat of repossession proceedings. The owner sold the home, repaid the debt and applied to the council as a homeless person. The council decided that he was intentionally homeless. Webster J. dismissed an application for judicial review, but said "if [the family] had been threatened with repossession, then it would have been unreasonable for the council not to rehouse them". See also *R. v Westminster City Council Ex p. Ali* (1997) 29 H.L.R. 580, QBD.

Settled accommodation

3A–1346 Where someone applies to a local authority after leaving accommodation which is not settled, the council must first identify the last "settled" accommodation, the loss of which caused the present homelessness. For someone to remain intentionally homeless, there must be a causal link between past intentionality and present homelessness. Such a link may be broken if the applicant secures further "settled accommodation"

Paragraph numbers marked with a "+" can be found online and on CD.

after the original intentional homelessness. See, e.g. *R. v Brent LBC, Ex p. Awua* [1996] A.C. 55; [1995] 3 W.L.R. 215; [1995] 3 All E.R. 493, HL, where the applicant when originally homeless applied to Tower Hamlets LBC for accommodation. She accepted temporary accommodation pending enquiries. Subsequently, in discharge of the full housing duty, she was offered a housing association tenancy (Housing Act 1985 ss.65(2) and 69(1)(b)) but rejected it. Tower Hamlets accordingly terminated her right to occupy the temporary accommodation. The applicant then applied to Brent LBC, with which she also had a local connection. Brent declared her intentionally homeless due to her eviction from the temporary accommodation granted by Tower Hamlets. The House of Lords upheld Brent's decision. What Ms Awua had lost was plainly "accommodation". It did not matter whether that accommodation was temporary or otherwise. What mattered was whether by her act or omission she had lost it. On the facts, her failure to take up an offer of suitable permanent accommodation made through Tower Hamlets had caused the loss of the temporary accommodation and she was intentionally homeless. See too *R. v East Herts DC Ex p. Hunt* (1986) 18 H.L.R. 51, QBD (accommodation provided pending full discharge of council's duty was settled accommodation); but *cf. R. v Rushcliffe DC Ex p. Summerson and Buckley* (1993) 25 H.L.R. 577, QBD (a single hostel room without facilities intended for only very short-term occupation could not be regarded as settled); *Mohamed v Westminster CC* [2005] EWCA Civ 796;15 June 2005 (assured shorthold tenancy where housing benefit was capped at less than the rent due, resultant arrears of rent and an order for possession. Council decision that applicant had not had "settled" accommodation since her last application because the private sector accommodation had been unaffordable and overcrowded from the outset and the loss of it had been inevitable, upheld by Court of Appeal); and *Stewart v Lambeth LBC* [2002] EWCA Civ 753; [2002] H.L.R. 40, (tenant sentenced to imprisonment and then evicted for rent arrears. Held (1) the applicant had had no "settled accommodation" since the loss of his flat as prison could not be treated as a settled home. He had been detained against his will and so it was "incarceration" rather than a "home"; and (2) the causal connection between the offending and the homelessness had not been broken by an arrangement with the applicant's sister that she would pay the rent and her failure to perform it).

In *Lambert v Ealing LBC* [1982] 1 W.L.R. 550; [1982] 2 All E.R. 394, CA, a French widower left accommodation in Grenoble and came to England with three teenage daughters to occupy premises in Ealing on a holiday let. When the holiday let was terminated, he sought accommodation from the local authority. The Court of Appeal held that the accommodation which a person left "intentionally" did not have to be the same as the accommodation inhabited immediately before his/her ultimate homelessness. As Mr Lambert had not acquired any settled accommodation in the UK, he had become homeless intentionally when he left the home in Grenoble. See too *R. v Croydon LBC Ex p. Easom* (1993) 25 H.L.R. 262, QBD (series of tenancies in Australia where applicants were illegal immigrants not settled accommodation); *cf. R. v Camden LBC Ex p. Aranda* (1997) 30 H.L.R. 76, CA.

An assured shorthold tenancy may be settled accommodation. In *Knight v Vale Royal BC* [2003] EWCA Civ 1258; [2004] H.L.R. 9,the Court of Appeal stated that occupation under an assured shorthold tenancy is "likely to be settled rather than temporary" and that it is not right to assume that occupation for a period of as little as six months "is likely to be temporary rather than settled". However, it does not follow that occupation under an assured shorthold tenancy always constitutes settled accommodation. That remains a question of fact and degree "although the existence of an assured shorthold tenancy will normally be a significant pointer to the accommodation being settled". The question of whether or not such a tenancy is settled accommodation is a question of degree and judgment for the local authority (*R. v Christchurch BC Ex p. Conway* (1987) 19 H.L.R. 238, QBD (finding of intentional homelessness upheld); and *R. v Rochester-upon-Medway City Council Ex p. Williams* (1994) 26 H.L.R. 588, QBD (application for judicial review dismissed). See too *R. v Harrow LBC Ex p. Fahia* [1998] 1 W.L.R. 1396; [1998] 4 All E.R. 137, HL; *R. v Hackney LBC Ex p. Ajayi* [1997] August C.L.D. 306; June 1997, Legal Action 23, CA; and *R. v Merton LBC Ex p. Ruffle* (1989) 21 H.L.R. 361, QBD.

Becoming homeless intentionally

191.—(1) A person becomes homeless intentionally if he deliber- **3A–1347**

Paragraph numbers marked with a "+" can be found online and on CD.

ately does or fails to do anything in consequence of which he ceases to occupy accommodation which is available for his occupation and which it would have been reasonable for him to continue to occupy.

(2) For the purposes of subsection (1) an act or omission in good faith on the part of a person who was unaware of any relevant fact shall not be treated as deliberate.

(3) A person shall be treated as becoming homeless intentionally if—

> (a) he enters into an arrangement under which he is required to cease to occupy accommodation which it would have been reasonable for him to continue to oc- cupy, and
>
> (b) the purpose of the arrangement is to enable him to become entitled to assistance under this Part,

and there is no other good reason why he is homeless.

(4) [...]

3A–1348 *Note* —Amended by the Homelessness Act 2002 Sch.1, para.1.

"available for his occupation"
3A–1349 See s.176.

Becoming homeless intentionally
3A–1350 See commentary to s.190.

Duty to persons not in priority need who are not homeless intentionally

3A–1351 **192.**—(1) This section applies where the local housing authority—

> (a) are satisfied that an applicant is homeless and eligible for assistance, and
>
> (b) are not satisfied that he became homeless intentionally,

but are not satisfied that he has a priority need.

(2) The authority shall provide the applicant with (or secure that he is provided with) advice and assistance in any attempts he may make to secure that accommodation becomes available for his occupation.

(3) The authority may secure that accommodation is available for occupation by the applicant.

(4) The applicant's housing needs shall be assessed before advice and assistance is provided under subsection (2).

(5) The advice and assistance provided under subsection (2) must include information about the likely availability in the authority's district of types of accommodation appropriate to the applicant's housing needs (including, in particular, the location and sources of such types of accommodation).

3A–1352 *Note* —Amended by Homelessness Act 2002 Sch.1, paras 11 and 12.

"eligible for assistance"
3A–1353 See s.185.

Paragraph numbers marked with a "+" can be found online and on CD.

"assistance"
See s.183.   **3A–1354**

"local housing authority"
See ss.217, 218, and 230 which refer to the Housing Act 1985—see the Housing Act **3A–1355**
1985 ss.1 and 2, above.

"homeless"
See s.175.   **3A–1356**

"applicant"
See s.183 and the commentary thereto.   **3A–1357**

"priority need"
See s.189.   **3A–1358**

"homeless intentionally"
See s.191.   **3A–1359**

Duty and Power
   The only *duty* to persons not in priority need who are homeless unintentionally is to **3A–1360**
provide advice and assistance. However the amendment effected by Homelessness Act
2002 gives local housing authorities a *power* to secure that accommodation is made
available.

Duty to persons with priority need who are not homeless intentionally

   193.—(1) This section applies where the local housing authority **3A–1361**
are satisfied that an applicant is homeless, eligible for assistance and
has a priority need, and are not satisfied that he became homeless
intentionally.

   (2) Unless the authority refer the application to another local
housing authority (see section 198), they shall secure that accommodation is available for occupation by the applicant.

   (3) The authority are subject to the duty under this section until
it ceases by virtue of any of the following provisions of this section.

   (3A) The authority shall, on becoming subject to the duty under
this section, give the applicant a copy of the statement included in
their allocation scheme by virtue of section 167(1A) (policy on offering choice to people allocated housing accommodation under Part
6).

   (5) The local housing authority shall cease to be subject to the
duty under this section if the applicant, having been informed by the
authority of the possible consequence of refusal and of his right to
request a review of the suitability of the accommodation, refuses an
offer of accommodation which the authority are satisfied is suitable
for him and the authority notify him that they regard themselves as
having discharged their duty under this section.

   (6) The local housing authority shall cease to be subject to the
duty under this section if the applicant—

      (a) ceases to be eligible for assistance,
      (b) becomes homeless intentionally from the accommoda-
          tion made available for his occupation,

Paragraph numbers marked with a "+" can be found online and on CD.

    (c) accepts an offer of accommodation under Part VI (allocation of housing), or

    (cc) accepts an offer of an assured tenancy (other than an assured shorthold tenancy) from a private landlord,

    (d) otherwise voluntarily ceases to occupy as his only or principal home the accommodation made available for his occupation.

(7) The local housing authority shall also cease to be subject to the duty under this section if the applicant, having been informed of the possible consequence of refusal and of his right to request a review of the suitability of the accommodation, refuses a final offer of accommodation under Part 6.

(7A) An offer of accommodation under Part 6 is a final offer for the purposes of subsection (7) if it is made in writing and states that it is a final offer for the purposes of subsection (7).

(7B) The authority shall also cease to be subject to the duty under this section if the applicant accepts a qualifying offer of an assured shorthold tenancy which is made by a private landlord in relation to any accommodation which is, or may become, available for the applicant's occupation.

(7C) The applicant is free to reject a qualifying offer without affecting the duty owed to him under this section by the authority.

(7D) For the purposes of subsection (7B) an offer of an assured shorthold tenancy is a qualifying offer if—

    (a) it is made, with the approval of the authority, in pursuance of arrangements made by the authority with the landlord with a view to bringing the authority's duty under this section to an end;

    (b) the tenancy being offered is a fixed term tenancy (within the meaning of Part 1 of the Housing Act 1988 (c. 50)); and

    (c) it is accompanied by a statement in writing which states the term of the tenancy being offered and explains in ordinary language that—

        (i) there is no obligation to accept the offer, but

        (ii) if the offer is accepted the local housing authority will cease to be subject to the duty under this section in relation to the applicant.

(7E) An acceptance of a qualifying offer is only effective for the purposes of subsection (7B) if the applicant signs a statement acknowledging that he has understood the statement mentioned in subsection (7D).

(7F) The local housing authority shall not—

    (a) make a final offer of accommodation under Part 6 for the purposes of subsection (7); or

    (b) approve an offer of an assured shorthold tenancy for the purposes of subsection (7B), unless they are satisfied that the accommodation is suitable for the applicant and that it is reasonable for him to accept the offer.

Paragraph numbers marked with a "+" can be found online and on CD.

(8) For the purposes of subsection (7F) an applicant may reasonably be expected to accept an offer even though he is under contractual or other obligations in respect of his existing accommodation, provided he is able to bring those obligations to an end before he is required to take up the offer.

(9) A person who ceases to be owed the duty under this section may make a fresh application to the authority for accommodation or assistance in obtaining accommodation.

Note —Amended by Homelessness Act 2002 Sch.1, para.13. **3A–1362**

"assured tenancy"
See Housing Act 1988 s.1. **3A–1363**

"assured shorthold tenancy"
See Housing Act 1988 ss.19A and 20. **3A–1364**

"fixed term tenancy"
See Housing Act 1988 s.45. **3A–1365**

"eligible for assistance"
See s.185. **3A–1366**

"assistance"
See s.183. **3A–1367**

"local housing authority"
See ss.217, 218, and 230 which refer to the Housing Act 1985—see the Housing Act **3A–1368**
1985 ss.1 and 2 above.

"homeless"
See s.175. **3A–1369**

"applicant"
See s.183 and the commentary thereto. **3A–1370**

"priority need"
See s.189. **3A–1371**

"homeless intentionally"
See s.191. **3A–1372**

They are satisfied that the accommodation is suitable (s.193(7F))
See s.210 below and commentary at para.3A–1376, sub-paragraph (b). **3A–1373**

Duty to persons with priority need who are not homeless intentionally
If local housing authorities are satisfied that applicants are homeless, eligible for as- **3A–1374**
sistance, in priority need and not satisfied that they became homeless intentionally,
they have two possible courses of action:
 (a) to refer to another local authority. See Housing Act 1996 s.198 and the commentary at 3A–1402. Section 198 is almost exactly the same as the previous
  "local connection" provisions (Housing Act 1985 s.67), but it has been extended
  to include referral back to another authority where that other authority
  originally dealt with the applicant's homeless application and as a result placed
  the applicant in accommodation outside its boundaries; or
 (b) secure that suitable accommodation is made available for occupation (Housing
  Act 1996 ss.193(2) and 206). Once the conditions in s.193(1) are met, the duty

Paragraph numbers marked with a "+" can be found online and on CD.

to accommodate is triggered and it is unlawful to impose "any further hurdle or proviso before accepting that the duty arises". (e.g. service of notice to quit in relation to joint tenancy). See *R. (Hammia) v Wandsworth LBC* [2005] EWHC 1127; [2005] H.L.R. 45. In *Birmingham City Council v Aweys* [2008] EWCA Civ 48; [2008] 1 W.L.R. 2305, the Court of Appeal held that the s.193(2) duty arises immediately that a local authority decides that an applicant is unintentionally homeless and in priority need. Street homeless and the homeless at home are owed the same duty.

Under s.193, it is only in exceptional circumstances, if at all, that councils are allowed to "earmark" properties in advance because when a property actually becomes available it has to be offered to the family highest placed in the council's allocation scheme at that date (*R. (Amirun Begum) v Tower Hamlets LBC* [2002] EWHC 633 (Admin); [2003] H.L.R. 8).

No claim lies for damages in tort for breach of the statutory duties owed to the homeless (*O'Rourke v Camden LBC* [1998] A.C. 188; [1997] 3 W.L.R. 86; [1997] 3 All E.R. 23, HL).

Although ECHR art.8 does not impose on the state a duty to provide a home and the simple fact of "homelessness" does not therefore breach art.8, there may though be cases where it assists if homelessness causes interference with the claimant's family life or private life (*R. (Morris) v Newham LBC* [2002] EWHC 1262 (Admin); May 24, 2002—on the facts, claim dismissed).

"secure that accommodation is available for occupation"

3A–1375   The Housing Act 1996 s.176 requires that accommodation be secured not only for occupation by an applicant, but also for "any other person who normally resides with him as a member of his family". In *R. v Newham LBC Ex p. Khan* (2001) 33 H.L.R. 29, QBD Collins J. held that the decision to "split" a family who had lived together prior to homelessness was unlawful. *cf. R. v Westminster CC Ex p. Abo-Ragheed,* April 2001, Legal Action 22, November 27, 2001, QBD Admin Ct.

The s.193(2) duty cannot be performed by authorities leaving "homeless at home" applicants remaining in accommodation which is not "reasonable" for them to continue to occupy because s.175(3) prevents that amounting to "accommodation" at all (*Birmingham City Council v Aweys* [2008] EWCA Civ 48; [2008] 1 W.L.R. 2305).

Authorities must secure accommodation which is "suitable"—see the Housing Act 1996 s.206. See e.g. *R. v Newham LBC Ex p. Dada* [1996] Q.B. 507; [1995] 3 W.L.R. 540; [1995] 2 All E.R. 522. The requirement that accommodation is suitable means suitable for the persons to whom the duty is owed. It encompasses considerations of the range, nature and location of accommodation as well as its standard of condition, and likely duration of the applicant's occupancy (*Codona v Mid-Bedfordshire DC* [2004] EWCA Civ 925; [2005] H.L.R. 1). In considering whether accommodation is suitable authorities should have regard to the Housing Act 1985 Pts IX, X and XI (slum clearance, overcrowding and HMOs and the applicant's financial resources, including various specified forms of income, various specified costs relating to accommodation and other reasonable living expenses (Housing Act 1996 s.210 and the Homelessness (Suitability of Accommodation) Order 1996 (SI 1996/3204).

In addition, the Homelessness (Suitability of Accommodation) (England) Order 2003 (SI 2003/3326) prescribes the accommodation which is suitable for a person with family commitments—i.e. someone who is pregnant or with whom a pregnant woman or dependent children reside or might reasonably be expected to reside. Accommodation is not to be regarded as suitable if it is "B&B accommodation". B&B accommodation is accommodation which, whether or not breakfast is provided, is not self contained or which involves sharing certain amenities with another household. However there are exceptions. If there is no available accommodation, other than B&B accommodation, a local housing authority may house someone with family commitments in B&B accommodation, but only for a period or total of periods not exceeding six weeks.

An offer can only discharge the main housing duty under s.193(7F) if the authority is satisfied both that the accommodation is suitable and that it would be reasonable for the applicant to accept the offer. The particular needs of the applicant, for example to be protected from domestic violence and to be located near support networks, are relevant when considering suitability but that does not mean that those matters are mate-

Paragraph numbers marked with a "+" can be found online and on CD.

rial only to suitability. The submission that if premises were suitable it had to follow that it was reasonable to accept them was rejected in *Slater v Lewisham LBC* [2006] EWCA Civ 394; [2006] H.L.R. 37. There may be circumstances in which it is reasonable to refuse accommodation that is objectively suitable.

"cease to be subject to the duty"

Authorities cease to be under if a duty if the applicant: **3A–1376**

- after being informed about the possible consequences of refusal, refuses an offer of accommodation which the authority are satisfied is suitable (Housing Act 1996 s.193(5)); or
- ceases to be eligible for assistance (Housing Act 1996 s.193(6)(a)); or
- becomes homeless intentionally from the accommodation made available for occupation (Housing Act 1996 s.193(6)(b)); or
- accepts an offer of housing under the Housing Act 1996 Pt VI or otherwise ceases to occupy as his or her only or principal home the accommodation made available (Housing Act 1996 s.193(6)(c) and (d)); or
- after being informed of the possible consequences refuses an offer of Pt VI accommodation which the authority are satisfied was suitable (Housing Act 1996 s.193(7)(a)).
- the applicant accepts an offer of an assured tenancy from a private landlord (s.193(7B)).

The offer of an assured shorthold tenancy from a private landlord only ends the local housing authority's duty if it is a qualifying offer of a fixed term tenancy. The authority must be satisfied that it is suitable for the applicant and that it is reasonable for him or her to accept it. The landlord's offer must be accompanied by a written statement setting out the terms of the tenancy being offered and explaining that there is no obligation to accept the offer.

Under the Housing Act 1996 s.193(6), unless there is fraud, a local authority does not cease to be under a duty to accommodate simply because an applicant ceases to have priority need. (*R. v Brent LBC Ex p. Sadiq* (2001) 33 H.L.R. 47, CA). After a determination has been made, if a council considers that it was wrong, it may conduct a further "extra-statutory review". Decisions under the Housing Act 1996 as to whether applicants are in priority need or whether they are intentionally homeless are questions of public law. Accordingly once a decision has been taken the authority is permitted to revisit its conclusion (*Crawley BC v B* (2000) 32 H.L.R. 636, CA). See too *Porteous v West Dorset DC* [2004] EWCA Civ 244).

Refuses a final offer of accommodation (s.193(5) and (7))

Provided that an offer letter actually conveys the point that it is a "final" offer of **3A–1377** suitable accommodation and otherwise complies with s.193(7), the precise rubric need not be used (*Omar v Birmingham CC* [2007] EWCA Civ 610; [2007] H.L.R. 43).

The Court of Appeal considered the situation where an offer is refused, but a homeless person then makes a further application in *Tower Hamlets LBC v Rikha Begum* [2005] EWCA Civ 340; [2005] 1 W.L.R. 2103. It held that there was no test of "material change of circumstances" and that (applying *R. v Harrow LBC Ex p. Fahia* [1998] 1 W.L.R. 1396):

- an authority has to accept and consider a second application if it is not factually "identical" to the earlier one;
- this test of "exactly the same facts" was harder for an authority to use to refuse an application than the "material change of circumstances" approach;
- any new facts raised in the second approach to a council (provided not trivial or fanciful) require that it be treated as a fresh application;
- the question is whether the facts as presented are "new" and comparison has to be made by contrasting the material put forward on the new approach with the facts as they had stood when the earlier application was "disposed of" by an initial or review decision (as opposed to the date that the earlier application had been made);
- that question does not involve any "inquiries" by an authority, nor any investigation as to whether the asserted new facts are accurate (per Neuberger and Keene L.JJ.). The issue is simply whether, in the purported new applica-

Paragraph numbers marked with a "+" can be found online and on CD.

tion, the applicant has put forward facts which are different and the differences are neither fanciful nor trivial. A safeguard against applicants "inventing" new facts is the possibility of criminal prosecution. Pill L.J., however, considered that "some inquiry" might be necessary to establish (a) what matters are now relied upon and (b) whether they are the same matters or new matters.

Reviews

3A–1378   A decision as to suitability of s.193 accommodation is amenable to review under s.202(1)(f) and subsequent appeal to the county court under s.204. That is the appropriate route for any challenge. Would-be applicants should bear in mind that remedy and should not apply for judicial review (*R. v Merton LBC Ex p. Sembi* (2000) 32 H.L.R. 439, QBD). After a determination has been made, if a council considers that it was wrong, it may conduct a further "extra-statutory review". Decisions under Housing Act 1996 as to whether applicants are in priority need or whether they are intentionally homeless are questions of public law. Accordingly once a decision has been taken the authority is permitted to revisit its conclusion (*Crawley BC v B* (2000) 32 H.L.R. 636, CA. See too *Porteous v West Dorset DC* [2004] EWCA Civ 244; [2004] H.L.R. 30).

3A–1379   *Note* — Section 194 has been repealed by Homelessness Act 2002 s.6(4) which provides that Housing Act 1996 s.194 (power to continue to secure accommodation after minimum period of two years, formerly contained in s.193) shall cease to have effect. The section is unnecessary in the light of the abolition of the former provisions of s.193 limiting the duty to two years. In England, this amendment was brought into force on July 31, 2002 by the Homelessness Act 2002 (Commencement No.1) (England) Order 2002 (SI 2002/1799) (c.56). In Wales, this amendment was brought into force on September 30, 2002 by the Homelessness Act 2002 (Commencement) (Wales) Order 2002 (SI 2002/1736) (w.166) (c.53). Any person for whom a local housing authority was exercising their power under s.194 to continue to secure accommodation, immediately before implementation, is to be treated as a person to whom the authority owe the main duty under s.193 (Homelessness Act 2002 s.6(4)).

* * * *

Duties in case of threatened homelessness

3A–1380   **195.**—(1) This section applies where the local housing authority are satisfied that an applicant is threatened with homelessness and is eligible for assistance.

(2) If the authority—

(a) are satisfied that he has a priority need, and

(b) are not satisfied that he became threatened with homelessness intentionally,

they shall take reasonable steps to secure that accommodation does not cease to be available for his occupation.

(3) Subsection (2) does not affect any right of the authority, whether by virtue of a contract, enactment or rule of law, to secure vacant possession of any accommodation.

(3A) The authority shall, on becoming subject to the duty under this section, give the applicant a copy of the statement included in their allocation scheme by virtue of section 167(1A) (policy on offering choice to people allocated housing accommodation under Part 6).

(4) Where in pursuance of the duty under subsection (2) the authority secure that accommodation other than that occupied by the

Paragraph numbers marked with a "+" can be found online and on CD.

applicant when he made his application is available for occupation by him, the provisions of section 193(3) to (9) (period for which duty owed) apply, with any necessary modifications, in relation to the duty under this section as they apply in relation to the duty under section 193.

(5) If the authority—

(a) are not satisfied that the applicant has a priority need, or

(b) are satisfied that he has a priority need but are also satisfied that he became threatened with homelessness intentionally,

they shall provide him with (or secure that he is provided with) advice and assistance; in any attempts he may make to secure that accommodation does not cease to be available for his occupation.

(6) The applicant's housing needs shall be assessed before advice and assistance is provided under subsection (5).

(7) The advice and assistance provided under subsection (5) must include information about the likely availability in the authority's district of types of accommodation appropriate to the applicant's housing needs (including, in particular, the location and sources of such types of accommodation)."

(8) If the authority decide that they owe the applicant the duty under subsection (5) by virtue of paragraph (b) of that subsection, they may, pending a decision on a review of that decision—

(a) secure that accommodation does not cease to be available for his occupation; and

(b) if he becomes homeless, secure that accommodation is so available.

(9) If the authority—

(a) are not satisfied that the applicant has a priority need; and

(b) are not satisfied that he became threatened with homelessness intentionally,

the authority may take reasonable steps to secure that accommodation does not cease to be available for the applicant's occupation."

Note —Amended by the Homelessness Act 2002 Sch.1, para.14. Section 195 has also been amended by the Housing and Regeneration Act 2008 Sch.15. The amendment is not yet in force. The amendment is printed as part of the Housing and Regeneration Act 2008—see below. **3A–1381**

Duties in case of threatened homelessness
See commentary to s.193. **3A–1382**

"local housing authority"
See ss.217, 218, and 230 which refer to the Housing Act 1985—see the Housing Act 1985 ss.1 and 2 above. **3A–1383**

"available for his occupation"
See s.176. **3A–1384**

Paragraph numbers marked with a "+" can be found online and on CD.

3A-1385 **"priority need"**
See s.189.

3A-1386 **"eligible for assistance"**
See s.185.

Becoming threatened with homelessness intentionally

3A-1387 **196.**—(1) A person becomes threatened with homelessness intentionally if he deliberately does or fails to do anything the likely result of which is that he will be forced to leave accommodation which is available for his occupation and which it would have been reasonable for him to continue to occupy.

(2) For the purposes of subsection (1) an act or omission in good faith on the part of a person who was unaware of any relevant fact shall not be treated as deliberate.

(3) A person shall be treated as becoming threatened with homelessness intentionally if—

(a) he enters into an arrangement under which he is required to cease to occupy accommodation which it would have been reasonable for him to continue to occupy, and

(b) the purpose of the arrangement is to enable him to become entitled to assistance under this Part,

and there is no other good reason why he is threatened with homelessness.

(4) [...]

3A-1388 *Note*—Amended by the Homelessness Act 2002 s.5(1), Sch.2.

Becoming threatened with homelessness intentionally
3A-1389 See commentary to ss.190 and 193.

3A-1390 **"available for his occupation"**
See s.176.

3A-1391 **"threatened with homelessness intentionally"**
See s.195.

Duty where other suitable accommodation available
3A-1392 Homelessness Act s.9 provides that Housing Act 1996 s.197 (duty where other suitable accomodation available in their district) shall cease to have effect. In England, this amendment was brought into force on July 31, 2002 by the Homelessness Act 2002 (Commencement No.1) (England) Order 2002 (SI 2002/1799) (c.56). In Wales, this amendment was brought into force on September 30, 2002 by the Homelessness Act 2002 (Commencement) (Wales) Order 2002 (SI 2002/1736) (w.166) (c.56)). Any person for whom a local housing authority was exercising their power under s.197, immediately before implementation, is to be treated as a person to whom the authority owe the duty under s.193 (the main homelessness duty) (Homelessness Act 2002 s.6(4)).

3A-1393 **"local housing authority"**
See ss.217, 218, and 230 which refer to the Housing Act 1985—see the Housing Act 1985, ss.1 and 2, above.

3A-1394 **"available for his occupation"**
See s.176.

3A-1395 *Note*—Section 197 was repealed by the Homelessness Act 2002 ss.9(1), 18(2), Sch.2.

Paragraph numbers marked with a "+" can be found online and on CD.

* * * *

Referral of case to another local housing authority

198.—(1) If the local housing authority would be subject to the **3A–1396** duty under section 193 (accommodation for those with priority need who are not homeless intentionally) but consider that the conditions are met for referral of the case to another local housing authority, they may notify that other authority of their opinion.

(2) The conditions for referral of the case to another authority are met if—

    (a) neither the applicant nor any person who might reasonably be expected to reside with him has a local connection with the district of the authority to whom his application was made,

    (b) the applicant or a person who might reasonably be expected to reside with him has a local connection with the district of that other authority, and

    (c) neither the applicant nor any person who might reasonably be expected to reside with him will run the risk of domestic violence in that other district.

(2A) But the conditions for referral mentioned in subsection (2) are not met if—

    (a) the applicant or any person who might reasonably be expected to reside with him has suffered violence (other than domestic violence) in the district of the other authority; and

    (b) it is probable that the return to that district of the victim will lead to further violence of a similar kind against him.

(3) For the purposes of subsections (2) and (2A) "violence" means—

    (a) violence from another person; or

    (b) threats of violence from another person which are likely to be carried out; and violence is "domestic violence" if it is from a person who is associated with the victim.

(4) The conditions for referral of the case to another authority are also met if—

    (a) the applicant was on a previous application made to that other authority placed (in pursuance of their functions under this Part) in accommodation in the district of the authority to whom his application is now made, and

    (b) the previous application was within such period as may be prescribed of the present application.

(5) The question whether the conditions for referral of a case are satisfied shall be decided by agreement between the notifying authority and the notified authority or, in default of agreement, in accor-

Paragraph numbers marked with a "+" can be found online and on CD.

dance with such arrangements as the Secretary of State may direct by order.

(6) An order may direct that the arrangements shall be—

(a) those agreed by any relevant authorities or associations of relevant authorities, or

(b) in default of such agreement, such arrangements as appear to the Secretary of State to be suitable, after consultation with such associations representing relevant authorities, and such other persons, as he thinks appropriate.

(7) No such order shall be made unless a draft of the order has been approved by a resolution of each House of Parliament.

3A–1397   *Note* —Amended by Homelessness Act 2002 s.10.

Editorial note

3A–1398   The Allocation of Housing and Homelessness (Review Procedures) Regulations 1999 (SI 1999/71) include a specific provision for reviews of decisions made under s.198(5). See too the Homelessness (Decisions on Referrals) Order 1998 (SI 1998/1578).

"local housing authority"

3A–1399   See ss.217, 218, and 230 which refer to the Housing Act 1985—see the Housing Act 1985 ss.1 and 2 above.

"within such period as may be prescribed"

3A–1400   See the Allocation of Housing and Homelessness (Miscellaneous Provisions) (England) Regulations 2006 (SI 2006/2527).

"district"

3A–1401   See s.217(3).

Referral of case to another local housing authority

3A–1402   A local housing authority which finds itself subject to a duty under the Housing Act 1996 s.193 to an applicant who is unintentionally homeless and in priority need may, if the conditions in s.198 are fulfilled, refer the duty to another housing authority with which the applicant has a local connection. By s.199 an applicant can have a local connection with an area for one of four reasons:

(a) residence;

(b) employment;

(c) family; or

(d) special circumstances.

The onus of establishing a local connection rests on the applicant. Applicants must show that they have built up a real connection based on a period of residence, employment, family associations or other special circumstances. Where the claim is based on residence there is no reason why a local authority should not have guidelines that residence short of six months in the preceding year does not suffice (*R. v Eastleigh BC Ex p. Betts* [1983] 2 A.C. 613; [1983] 3 W.L.R. 397; [1983] 2 All E.R. 1111, HL).

The House of Lords has held that (1) on a statutory review of a decision to refer an application for accommodation to another authority on the basis that there is no local connection, any occupation by the applicant of interim accommodation within the first authority's district prior to the date of the review may constitute normal residence and so be taken into account as evidence of a local connection. So long as the place where someone eats and sleeps is voluntarily accepted by him, the reason why he is there rather than somewhere else does not prevent that place from being his normal residence; (2) the correct date to decide whether a person has a local connection is the

Paragraph numbers marked with a "+" can be found online and on CD.

date of the decision or, if there is a review, the date of the review—whether in the meantime the applicant has acquired or lost, by moving away, his local connection (*Mohamed v Hammersmith and Fulham LBC* [2001] UKHL 57; [2002] 1 A.C. 547; [2001] 3 W.L.R. 1339; [2002] 1 All E.R. 176.

For cases in the Court of Appeal on "local connection", see *R. v Greenwich LBC Ex p. Patterson* (1994) 26 H.L.R. 159, CA; *R. v Hammersmith & Fulham LBC Ex p.Duro-Rama* (1983) 9 H.L.R. 71, CA; *R. v Newham LBC Ex p. Tower Hamlets LBC* (1990) 23 H.L.R. 62, CA; *R. v Slough BC Ex p. Ealing LBC* [1981] Q.B. 801; [1981] 1 All E.R. 601; [1981] 2 W.L.R. 399, CA; *R. v Tower Hamlets LBC Ex p. Ali and Bibi* (1993) 25 H.L.R. 158, CA; *R. v Westminster CC Ex p. Benniche* (1996) 29 H.L.R. 230, *The Times*, April 15, 1996, CA. *R. v Ealing LBC Ex p. Fox*, (1998) 95(11) L.S.G. 35; *The Times*, March 9, 1998, QBD: voluntary work may be employment for the purposes of s.199(1)(b)) and *Ozbek v Ipswich BC* [2006] EWCA Civ 534; [2006] H.L.R. 41 (family associations too tenuous to amount to a "local connection").

The effect of the decision in *Al-Ameri v Kensington and Chelsea RLBC* [2004] UKHL 4; [2004] 2 A.C. 159; [2004] 2 W.L.R. 354 (that residence in a district in accommodation provided to a destitute asylum seeker under Immigration and Asylum Act 1999 was not capable of being regarded as residence in that district of the asylum seeker's own choice) has been reversed by Asylum and Immigration (Treatment of Claimants, etc) Act 2004 s.11 which added new ss.(6) and (7) to s.199. See 3A–1608+.

There is no statutory right to review of an authority's decision not to refer an application under s.198. Accordingly there is no right of appeal to a county court on that issue under s.204. The county court has no jurisdiction to consider on appeal whether local authorities have a duty to investigate the issue of local connection (*Sareen v Hackney LBC* [2003] EWCA Civ 351; [2003] H.L.R. 54).

Violence

Note that a referral to another authority may not be made if the applicant or a person who might reasonably be expected to live with the applicant runs the risk of violence in the other district. Since the amendment of s.198 by Homelessness Act 2002 s.10, "violence" is not limited to "domestic violence". "Violence" includes actual threats of physical violence which are likely to be carried out but not general racially motivated aggression and gestures (*Kensington & Chelsea RLBC v Danesh* [2006] EWCA Civ 1404; [2007] H.L.R. 17). **3A–1403**

Disputes

Homelessness (Decisions on Referrals) Order 1998 (SI 1998/1578) provides a mechanism for resolving disputes between housing authorities about whether or not the conditions of referral from one authority to another exist. Such questions are to be decided by a person to be appointed from a panel established by the Local Government Association. **3A–1404**

Local connection

199.—(1) A person has a local connection with the district of a local housing authority if he has a connection with it— **3A–1405**

    (a) because he is, or in the past was, normally resident there, and that residence is or was of his own choice,

    (b) because he is employed there,

    (c) because of family associations, or

    (d) because of special circumstances.

(2) ...

(3) Residence in a district is not of a person's own choice if—

    (a) ...

    (b) he, or a person who might reasonably be expected to reside with him, becomes resident there because he is detained under the authority of an Act of Parliament.

Paragraph numbers marked with a "+" can be found online and on CD.

HOUSING

(4) ...

(5) The Secretary of State may by order specify ... circumstances in which—

    (a) a person is not to be treated as employed in a district, or

    (b) residence in a district is not to be treated as of a person's own choice.

(6) A person has a local connection with the district of a local housing authority if he was (at any time) provided with accommodation in that district under section 95 of the Act 1999 (support for asylum seekers).

(7) But subsection (6) does not apply—

    (a) to the provision of accommodation for a person in a district of a local housing authority if he was subsequently provided with accommodation in the district of another local housing authority under section 95 of that Act, or

    (b) to the provision of accommodation in an accommodation centre by virtue of section 22 of the Nationality, Immigration and Asylum Act 2002 (c.41) (use of accommodation centres for section 95 support).

3A–1406   *Note* —Amended by the Asylum and Immigration (Treatment of Claimants, etc) Act 2004, s.11. The effect of the amendment is to reverse the effect of *Al-Ameri v Kensington and Chelsea RLBC* [2004] UKHL 4; [2004] 2 A.C. 159; [2004] 2 W.L.R. 354; [2004] 1 W.L.R. 1104. This section has also been amended by Housing and Regeneration Act 2008 s.315 so as to allow members of the armed forces to acquire a local connection. The amendment was brought into force on December 1, 2008 by the Housing and Regeneration Act 2008 (Commencement No.2 and Transitional, Saving and Transitory Provisions) Order 2008 SI 3068. The effect of the amendment is that a person in the armed forces is now able to establish a local connection with a district through residence or employment there, in the same way as a civilian.

Local connection

3A–1407   See commentary to s.198.

"local housing authority"

3A–1408   See ss.217, 218, and 230 which refer to the Housing Act 1985—see the Housing Act 1985 ss.1 and 2, above.

"district"

3A–1409   See s.217(3).

Duties to applicant whose case is considered for referral or referred

3A–1410   **200.**—(1) Where a local housing authority notify an applicant that they intend to notify or have notified another local housing authority of their opinion that the conditions are met for the referral of his case to that other authority—

    (a) they cease to be subject to any duty under section 188 (interim duty to accommodate in case of apparent priority need), and

    (b) they are not subject to any duty under section 193 (the main housing duty),

Paragraph numbers marked with a "+" can be found online and on CD.

but they shall secure that accommodation is available for occupation by the applicant until he is notified of the decision whether the conditions for referral of his case are met.

(2) When it has been decided whether the conditions for referral are met, the notifying authority shall notify the applicant of the decision and inform him of the reasons for it.

The notice shall also inform the applicant of his right to request a review of the decision and of the time within which such a request must be made.

(3) If it is decided that the conditions for referral are not met, the notifying authority are subject to the duty under section 193 (the main housing duty).

(4) If it is decided that those conditions are met, the notified authority are subject to the duty under section 193 (the main housing duty).

(5) The duty under subsection (1) ceases as provided in that subsection even if the applicant requests a review of the authority's decision (see section 202).

The authority may secure that accommodation is available for the applicant's occupation pending the decision on a review.

(6) Notice required to be given to an applicant under this section shall be given in writing and, if not received by him, shall be treated as having been given to him if it is made available at the authority's office for a reasonable period for collection by him or on his behalf.

Note —Amended by Homelessness Act 2002 s.5(1), Sch.1, para.15.　　**3A–1411**

Duties to applicant whose case is considered for referral or referred
See commentary to ss.193 and 198.　　**3A–1412**

"local housing authority"
See ss.217, 218, and 230 which refers to the Housing Act 1985—see the Housing Act 1985 ss.1 and 2 above.　　**3A–1413**

"district"
See s.217(3).　　**3A–1414**

"other suitable accommodation"
See s.197.　　**3A–1415**

Application of referral provisions to cases arising in Scotland

201. Sections 198 and 200 (referral of application to another local housing authority and duties to applicant whose case is considered for referral or referred) apply—　　**3A–1416**

    (a) to applications referred by a local authority in Scotland in pursuance of sections 33 and 34 of the Housing (Scotland) Act 1987, and

    (b) to persons whose applications are so transferred,

as they apply to cases arising under this Part (the reference in section 198 to this Part being construed as a reference to Part II of that Act).

Paragraph numbers marked with a "+" can be found online and on CD.

HOUSING

Right to request review of decision

3A-1417   **202.**—(1) An applicant has the right to request a review of—

(a) any decision of a local housing authority as to his eligibility for assistance,

(b) any decision of a local housing authority as to what duty (if any) is owed to him under sections 190 to 193 and 195 to 196 (duties to persons found to be homeless or threatened with homelessness),

(c) any decision of a local housing authority to notify another authority under section 198(1) (referral of cases),

(d) any decision under section 198(5) whether the conditions are met for the referral of his case,

(e) any decision under section 200(3) or (4) (decision as to duty owed to applicant whose case is considered for referral or referred), or

(f) any decision of a local housing authority as to the suitability of accommodation offered to him in discharge of their duty under any of the provisions mentioned in paragraph (b) or (e) or as to the suitability of accommodation offered to him as mentioned in section 193(7).

(1A) An applicant who is offered accommodation as mentioned in section 193(5) or (7) may under subsection (1)(f) request a review of the suitability of the accommodation offered to him whether or not he has accepted the offer.

(2) There is no right to request a review of the decision reached on an earlier review.

(3) A request for review must be made before the end of the period of 21 days beginning with the day on which he is notified of the authority's decision or such longer period as the authority may in writing allow.

(4) On a request being duly made to them, the authority or authorities concerned shall review their decision.

3A-1418   *Note* —Amended by the Homelessness Act 2002 s.5(1), Sch.1, para.16. Section 202 has also been amended by Housing and Regeneration Act 2008 Sch.15. The amendment is not yet in force. The amendment is printed as part of the Housing and Regeneration Act 2008—see below.

"available for his occupation"
3A-1419   See s.176.

"threatened with homelessness intentionally"
3A-1420   See s.195.

"assistance"
3A-1421   See s.183.

"local housing authority"
3A-1422   See ss.217, 218, and 230 which refer to the Housing Act 1985—see the Housing Act 1985 ss.1 and 2 above.

Paragraph numbers marked with a "+" can be found online and on CD.

"homeless"

See s.175.

"applicant"

See s.183 and the commentary thereto.

Reviews

On concluding their enquiries authorities, when they notify applicants of their deci- 3A–1425
sions and give their reasons, are also obliged to inform applicants of the right to
request a review of the decision in accordance with the Housing Act 1996 s.202 (Housing Act 1996 s.184(5)).

The *Code of Guidance* states that it is good practice to notify applicants of decisions
within three working days of the decision being made. Where possible decisions
should not only be provided in writing but also explained in person to the applicant
(para.17.3).

The Housing Act 1996 s.202 provides that applicants have a right to request a
review of any decision within 21 days of notification. The 21 day period may be
extended by the authority. The Allocation of Housing and Homelessness (Review
Procedures) Regulations 1999 (SI 1999/71) provide that:

- if the decision is to be reviewed by an officer of the authority, the review shall
  be carried out by a person who was not involved in the original decision and
  who is senior to the officer who made the original decision (*cf. Saunders v Hammersmith and Fulham LBC* [1999] 6 C.L.D. 347, West London County Court,
  where the officer who had made the original decision participated in the
  review with a more senior officer, Appeal allowed);
- the applicant should be notified that written representations may be made and
  shall be informed of the procedure to be followed;
- If the reviewer considers that there is deficiency or irregularity in the original
  decision or in the manner in which it was made but is minded nevertheless to
  make a decision which is against the interests of the applicant on one or more
  issues the reviewer shall notify the applicant (a) that the reviewer is so minded,
  and the reasons why; and (b) that the applicant, or someone acting on his
  behalf, may make representations to the reviewer orally or in writing or both
  orally and in writing (reg 8(2). In *Hall v Wandsworth LBC*; *Carter v Wandsworth
  LBC* [2004] EWCA Civ 1740, Carnwath L.J. said (para.30): "To summarise, the
  reviewing officer should treat regulation 8(2) as applicable, not merely when
  he finds some significant legal or procedural error in the decision, but whenever (looking at the matter broadly and untechnically) he considers that an
  important aspect of the case was either not addressed, or not addressed
  adequately, by the original decision-maker. In such a case, if he intends to
  confirm the decision, he must give notice of the grounds on which he intends
  to do so, and provide an opportunity for written and (if requested) oral
  representations."

  See too *Johnston v Lambeth LBC* [2008] EWCA Civ 690; *The Times* 30 June
  2008, June 19, 2008; where Rimer L.J. said: "...regulation 8(2) is not a
  discretionary option that the review officer can apply or disapply according to
  whether or not he or she considers that the service of a 'minded to find' notice
  would be of material benefit to the applicant. Regulation 8(2) imposes a dual,
  mandatory obligation upon the review officer. First, to 'consider' whether
  there was a deficiency or irregularity in the original decision or in the manner
  in which it was made. Secondly, if there was—and if the review officer is nonetheless minded to make a decision adverse to the applicant on one or more issues—to serve a 'minded to find' notice on the applicant explaining his reasons
  for his provisional views. In my judgment, there is no discretion on the review
  officer to give himself a dispensation from complying with either of those
  obligations."

  cf. *Gilby v Westminster CC* [2007] EWCA Civ 604; [2008] H.L.R. 7 (no shift in
  reasoning which required the reviewing officer to comply with the "minded-
  to"provisions of reg.8(2).
- decisions on reviews shall be notified to applicants within eight weeks of the

Paragraph numbers marked with a "+" can be found online and on CD.

day on which the request is made or such longer period as may be agreed by the applicant in writing.

With regards the adequacy of reasons given, courts would be slow to intervene and would only interfere where it was clear that the process of review was capable of being described as unfair.

An officer conducting a review must consider all the facts afresh, including information relevant to the period before the first decision, but only obtained thereafter, and to matters occurring after the initial decision, (*Mohamed v Hammersmith and Fulham LBC* [2001] UKHL 57; [2002] 1 A.C. 547; [2001] 3 W.L.R. 1339; [2002] 1 All E.R. 176, HL and *Sarahid v Camden LBC* [2004] EWCA Civ 1485; October 26, 2004). Reviewing officers acting under the Housing Act 1996 s.202 should consider the facts as at the date of the refusal. Although reviewing officers are entitled to take account of facts as at that date—even if previously unknown to the council—material dealing with what has occurred since then is irrelevant (*Omar v City of Westminster* [2008] EWCA Civ 421; [2008] H.L.R. 36).Where issues have been put to an applicant in interview, there is no reason why a review panel should offer an oral hearing (*Lomotey v Enfield LBC* [2004] EWCA Civ 627; [2004] H.L.R. 45. See too *Connors v Northampton BC* [2004] EWCA Civ 427).

There is no statutory right to a review of an authority's decision not to refer an application under s.198 (referral of case to another local housing authority). Accordingly there is no right of appeal to a county court on that issue under s.204 (*Sareen v Hackney LBC* [2003] EWCA Civ 351; [2003] H.L.R. 54).

Accommodation pending reviews and appeals

3A–1426 In *R.v Camden LBC Ex p. Mohammed* (1998) 30 H.L.R. 315, QBD, Latham J. considered the circumstances in which authorities should provide accommodation pursuant to s.188(3) pending a review. Camden's policy was that no interim accommodation was to be made available to an applicant pending a review of a refusal of an application for housing assistance under the Housing Act 1996 Pt.VII unless there were exceptional circumstances. Latham J. dismissed an application for a declaration that the policy was ultra vires. He considered the Housing Act 1996 ss.188(3), 202 and 204 and found that the council had a wide discretion. Use of the phrase "exceptional reasons" was a rational way of describing the approach to be adopted provided that the council carried out a balancing act and considered:

(1) the merits of the case itself and the extent to which it could properly be said that the decision was contrary to the merits of the case or was one which was finely balanced which could go either way;

(2) whether there was any new material which could have a real effect upon the decision under review; and

(3) the personal circumstances of the applicant and the consequence of an adverse decision.

Neither the statutory scheme nor any general principle of fairness nor the need to avoid the appearance of bias requires that a decision as to whether or not accommodation should be provided pending review should be taken by a different officer who was not involved in the initial decision on the homelessness application (*R (Abdi) v Lambeth LBC* [2007] EWHC 1565 (Admin); [2008] H.L.R. 5).

Section 204A, as inserted by Homelessness Act 2002 s.11, allows an applicant to appeal to the county court against a refusal by a local housing authority to exercise its powers to provide accommodation pending the hearing of a county court appeal, or against their decision to exercise the power for a limited period, or to cease from exercising that power. The county court should determine any such appeal on judicial review principles. There is however no right to appeal to the county court against a refusal to provide accommodation pending a review—any such challenge must still be brought by judicial review, as in *R. v Camden LBC Ex p. Mohammed* (above).

The effect of s.202(1A) is to reverse the effect of *Alghile v Westminster City Council* [2001] EWCA Civ 363; (2001) 33 H.L.R. 57 where it was held that an applicant could not accept accommodation *and* seek a review as to its suitability.

Failure to apply for review within 21 days

3A–1427 Councils have a discretion under s.202(3) to extend time to request a review, but that discretion has to be exercised in a principled way. This requires a consideration of the statutory scheme. Reasons for delay and the prospects of success are relevant but do not have to be balanced against each other. (*R. (C) v Lewisham LBC* [2003] EWCA Civ 927; [2003] 3 All E.R. 1277). See too *R.(Minhas) v Wandsworth LBC* [2004] EWHC 805).

Reconsideration of review

Councils are not precluded from reconsidering review decisions, but there is no requirement that they should do so. If a council fails to reconsider a review, the remedy for the applicant is to appeal the original review decision in the county court in accordance with s.204. The High Court should not entertain an application for judicial review in such circumstances because another remedy (i.e. appeal in the county court) is available—*R. v Westminster CC Ex p. Ellioua* (1999) 31 H.L.R. 440, CA. In *Demetri v Westminster CC* [2000] 1 W.L.R. 772, CA, the Court of Appeal held that: (1) while an applicant has no right to seek a review of a review decision (see s.202(2)) a council can agree to re-open its earlier decision (*R. v Westminster CC Ex p. Ellioua* (1999) 31 H.L.R. 440). If it does so, the council should make clear whether it is treating the earlier review decision as withdrawn and is conducting a new review or is simply "reconsidering" its earlier decision; (2) where an applicant is legally represented, the onus is on the advisers either to lodge an appeal within 21 days of the original review decision or to obtain clear agreement from the council that the review is being re-run and the earlier decision treated as non-existent. In the instant case no appeal had been lodged in time, no clear agreement to withdraw the earlier decision had been reached, and the council's agreement to "reconsider" the review decision did not have the effect of extending the time for appealing against it. Any judicial review challenge to a decision made on an extra-statutory reconsideration is unlikely to succeed (*R. (C) v Lewisham LBC* [2003] EWCA Civ 927; [2003] 3 All E.R. 1277 applying the test in *R. v Brighton and Hove BC Ex p. Nacion* (1999) 31 H.L.R. 1095, CA). **3A–1428**

The Court of Appeal has held that, in the absence of any exceptional circumstances, there is nothing objectionable in the same officer conducting a review and then (if it is agreed or ordered that there should be a further review) conducting a re-review or second review. This is because the reviewing officer does not review his or her own earlier decision but starts afresh to review a decision made by a more junior officer. There is nothing unfair about that. Further, as the Allocation of Housing and Homelessness (Review Procedures) Regulations 1999 (SI 1999/71) give no guidance as to who is to conduct a review the second time and there is nothing to suggest that it has to be someone who was not involved in the first decision, there is no breach of those regulations if the same officer conducts the further review (*Feld v Barnet LBC* [2004] EWCA Civ 1307; [2005] H.L.R. 9; *Pour v Westminster CC* [2004] EWCA Civ 1307; *The Times*, October 26, 2004).

Reasons

Section 203 requires local housing authorities to give reasons if the decision on review is to confirm the original decision. In *R. v Westminster CC Ex p. Ermakov* [1996] 2 All E.R. 302, a case involving Housing Act 1985, s.64 (now Housing Act 1996 s.184(3)), Hutchison L.J. said that the Act: **3A–1429**

> "requires a decision and at the same time reasons and if no reasons, which is the reality of the present case, or wholly deficient reasons are given, the applicant is prima facie entitled to have the decision quashed as unlawful".

He stated that the reasons given must be proper, adequate and intelligible and deal with the substantial points that have been raised. In *Hijazi v Kensington and Chelsea RLBC* [2003] EWCA Civ 692; [2003] H.L.R. 72, a case in which a circuit judge hearing a s.204 appeal had allowed further evidence from the reviewing officer that he had taken a doctor's report into account but had found that it did not take matters further, the Court of Appeal, dismissing a further appeal, held that while further evidence ought not to be considered where it added to, or supplemented, the reasons given in a review decision (see *R. v Westminster CC Ex p. Ermakov* [1996] 2 All E.R. 302), the statement in this case simply elucidated the reasons already given. For a case in which the Court of Appeal considered the adequacy of reasons given on review, see *Bernard v Enfield LBC* [2001] EWCA Civ 1831; [2002] H.L.R. 46.

Appeals

If the review results in confirmation of the original decision, reasons must be given. **3A–1430**

Paragraph numbers marked with a "+" can be found online and on CD.

SECTION 3A: HOUSING

The Act does not specify that they must be in writing. There is a right of appeal from a review decision to the county court on a point of law. Prior to amendment by Homelessness Act 2002 Sch.1, appeals to the court had to be brought within 21 days of "the date on which [the applicant] should have been notified" of the review decision (Housing Act 1996 s.204).

For the procedure for appeals, see CPR 52 and the commentary at 3A–1440.

In *Begum v Tower Hamlets LBC* [2000] Q.B. 133; [2000] 1 W.L.R. 306, CA it was held that the judge at first instance was right in construing the words "point of law" which qualify the right of appeal to the county court in s.204 as being wide enough to embrace any ground of challenge that would have been available in proceedings for judicial review (including *Wednesbury* irrationality). See too *Chief Adjudication Officer v Foster* [1993] A.C. 754, HL.

Where there is an appeal to a county court, the question for the court is whether the whole of the circumstances justify any relief in public law. A new ground for refusing accommodation should only be ignored if it can be faulted on public law grounds (*Crawley BC v B* (2000) 32 H.L.R. 636, CA). Where a court identifies procedural flaws in a local authority's decision making process, the decision may only be upheld if a court is satisfied that a properly directed local authority would inevitably have reached the same decision. The test of inevitability is a strict test. (*Ali and Nessa v Newham LBC* [2001] EWCA Civ 73; [2002] H.L.R. 20).

no duty owed

3A–1431 In *Warsame v Hounslow LBC* (2000) 32 H.L.R. 335; [2000] 1 W.L.R. 696, CA the council decided that a duty which it had owed to the applicants under the Housing Act 1996 s.193 ended upon the refusal by the applicants of an offer of a secure council tenancy made under the Housing Act Part VI, s.193(7). Reversing a circuit judge's decision that he had no jurisdiction to consider an appeal, the Court of Appeal held that a decision that "no duty was owed" was a decision as to "what duty (if any)" was owed by the council and accordingly was brought by Housing Act 1996 s.202(1)(b) within the statutory mechanism for review and appeal. It followed that the applicants could challenge the findings by the council which had led to the "no duty" decision (e.g. on the "suitability" and "acceptability" issues in s.193(7) itself). It would seem from the court's approach that a decision that "no (further) duty is owed" must be given in writing with reasons and must notify the right to review: Housing Act 1996 s.184.

Section 202 reviews, s.204 appeals and the ECHR

3A–1432 The House of Lords considered whether this procedure is ECHR compliant in *Begum (Runa) v Tower Hamlets LBC* [2003] UKHL 5; [2003] 2 A.C. 430; [2003] 2 W.L.R. 388; [2003] 1 All E.R. 731. (1) The House of Lords assumed, without deciding, that decisions made under Housing Act 1996 Pt VII do give rise to "civil rights" for the purposes of ECHR, art.6, although Lord Bingham stated that:

> "to hold that the right enjoyed by [a homeless person] is a 'civil right' for the purposes of article 6 would ... be to go further than the Strasbourg court has yet gone...".

(2) The s.202 review process does not comply with article 6 because the reviewing officer is not an "independent and impartial tribunal"—an employee cannot be independent of the authority. (3) However an appeal to the county court on a point of law (s.204) gives a right of access to a court of "full jurisdiction" for art.6 purposes. For reasons of good administration, the absence of a full fact finding jurisdiction in the court or tribunal to which an appeal lies from an administrative decision making body does not disqualify it for the purposes of art.6.

> "'Full jurisdiction' in this context does not necessarily mean full jurisdiction on fact or law, but ... 'jurisdiction to deal with the case as the nature of the decision requires'" (Lord Millett).

An authority's factual findings are "only staging posts on the way to much the broader judgments which the authority has to make." Lord Bingham stated that he:

> "would expect the county court judge to be alert to any indication that an applicant's case might not have been resolved by the authority in a fair, objective and even-handed way",

but could:

> "see no warrant for applying in this context notions of 'anxious scrutiny' ... or

Paragraph numbers marked with a "+" can be found online and on CD.

[an] enhanced approach to judicial review ... [or] 'a close and rigorous analysis' if by that is meant an analysis closer or more rigorous than would ordinarily be conducted by a careful and competent judge determining an application for judicial review."

Lord Hoffmann considered that the conventional principles of judicial review are sufficient.

The House of Lords declined to follow and apply dicta in *Adan v Newham LBC* [2001] EWCA Civ 1916; [2002] 1 All E.R. 931 that the limited right of appeal under s.204 means that the county court is not a court of full jurisdiction and that a local authority may use its contracting-out powers under the Local Authorities (Contracting Out of Allocation of Housing and Homelessness Functions) Order 1996 (SI 1996/3205) to appoint an independent and impartial tribunal to conduct the review in cases where a material dispute of primary fact has to be resolved.

Procedure on a review

203.—(1) The Secretary of State may make provision by regulations as to the procedure to be followed in connection with a review under section 202. Nothing in the following provisions affects the generality of this power.   **3A–1433**

(2) Provision may be made by regulations—

(a) requiring the decision on review to be made by a person of appropriate seniority who was not involved in the original decision, and

(b) as to the circumstances in which the applicant is entitled to an oral hearing, and whether and by whom he may be represented at such a hearing.

(3) The authority, or as the case may be either of the authorities, concerned shall notify the applicant of the decision on the review.

(4) If the decision is—

(a) to confirm the original decision on any issue against the interests of the applicant, or

(b) to confirm a previous decision—

(i) to notify another authority under section 198 (referral of cases), or

(ii) that the conditions are met for the referral of his case,

they shall also notify him of the reasons for the decision.

(5) In any case they shall inform the applicant of his right to appeal to a county court on a point of law, and of the period within which such an appeal must be made (see section 204).

(6) Notice of the decision shall not be treated as given unless and until subsection (5), and where applicable subsection (4), is complied with.

(7) Provision may be made by regulations as to the period within which the review must be carried out and notice given of the decision.

(8) Notice required to be given to a person under this section shall be given in writing and, if not received by him, shall be treated as having been given if it is made available at the authority's office for a reasonable period for collection by him or on his behalf.

Procedure on a review

See the commentary to s.202.   **3A–1434**

Paragraph numbers marked with a "+" can be found online and on CD.

"regulations"

3A–1435   See the Allocation of Housing and Homelessness (Review Procedures) Regulations 1999 (SI 1999/71).

Right of appeal to county court on point of law

3A–1436   **204.**—(1) If an applicant who has requested a review under section 202—

> (a) is dissatisfied with the decision on the review, or
>
> (b) is not notified of the decision on the review within the time prescribed under section 203,

he may appeal to the county court on any point of law arising from the decision or, as the case may be, the original decision.

(2) An appeal must be brought within 21 days of his being notified of the decision or, as the case may be, of the date on which he should have been notified of a decision on review.

(2A) The court may give permission for an appeal to be brought after the end of the period allowed by subsection (2), but only if it is satisfied—

> (a) where permission is sought before the end of that period, that there is a good reason for the applicant to be unable to bring the appeal in time; or
>
> (b) where permission is sought after that time, that there was a good reason for the applicant's failure to bring the appeal in time and for any delay in applying for permission.

(3) On appeal the court may make such order confirming, quashing or varying the decision as it thinks fit.

(4) Where the authority were under a duty under section 188, 190 or 200 to secure that accommodation is available for the applicant's occupation, or had the power under section 195(8) to do so, they may secure that accommodation is so available—

> (a) during the period for appealing under this section against the authority's decision, and
>
> (b) if an appeal is brought, until the appeal (and any further appeal) is finally determined.

3A–1437   *Note* —Amended by the Homelessness Act 2002 s.5(1), Sch.1, para.17.

Right of appeal to county court on point of law

3A–1438   See the commentary to s.202.

"review"

3A–1439   See ss.202 and 203.

Procedure for appeal

3A–1440   CPR Pt 52 (Appeals) applies to s.204 appeals. Appellants' notices in Form **N161** must be filed and served in all cases (PD 52 para.5.1). Appellants must also file bundles of documents with appellants' notices. Such bundles should include all documents which the appellant reasonably considers necessary to enable the court to reach its decision on the hearing of the appeal (para.5.6). If it is not possible to file all documents, the appellant must indicate which documents have not yet been filed and the reasons why they are not currently available (para.5.7).

Paragraph numbers marked with a "+" can be found online and on CD.

Appeals to the county court provided by s.204 are appeals for the purposes of the Access to Justice Act 1999 (Destination of Appeals) Order 2000 (SI 2000/1071). Accordingly appeals from the county court lie to the Court of Appeal and the more restrictive test for permission to appeal, as prescribed by Access to Justice Act 1999 s.55, applies (*Azimi v Newham LBC* (2001) 33 H.L.R. 51, CA).

District judges may not hear appeals pursuant to s.204 (PD 2B para.9A and *Crawley BC v B* (2000) 32 H.L.R. 636, CA).

Under CPR Pt 2.3 an appeal is brought by filing the notice of appeal. Filing means delivering by post or otherwise. Delivery of the appeal notice to the appropriate court is sufficient to constitute filing within the CPR, even if the court offices are closed. There is no need for a person to have received or authenticated it (*Van Aken v Camden LBC* [2002] EWCA Civ 1724; [2003] 1 W.L.R. 684; [2003] 1 All E.R. 552). See to *Aadan v Brent LBC* (2000) 32 H.L.R. 848, CA. Appeals must be brought within 21 days of applicants being notified of the decision or, as the case may be, of the date on which he should have been notified of a decision on review. Time to appeal does not run from the date of the review decision letter, but from the earliest date on which, on the facts, the review decision letter could have come to the applicant's attention (*Barrett v Southwark LBC* [2008] EWHC 1568 (QB)).

"extension of time for bringing appeal"

Section 204(2A) was inserted by Homelessness Act 2002, Sch.1. An extension of time may only be granted if permission is sought before the end of the period allowed by s.204(2) or there is a good reason for the applicant's failure to bring the appeal in time and for any delay in applying for permission. The word "only" in s.204(2A) provides a threshold which has to be passed before the merits can be considered. It is not open to a judge to have regard to the criteria in CPR r.3.9, or any other criteria, other than those specified in s.204(2A). If a judge is not satisfied that there are good reasons for a failure to bring an appeal in time, it is not possible to go on to consider the merits (*Short v Birmingham CC* [2004] EWHC 2112 (QB); [2005] H.L.R. 6). The concept of good reason was analogous to "good cause" used in social security provisions and explained by the social security commissioner in R(S) 2/63 (T) (*Barrett v Southwark LBC* [2008] EWHC 1538(QB)).

3A–1441

Judicial review

An application for judicial review is an abuse of the process, and not available, where a homeless person does not exhaust the right to a statutory review and appeal to the county court under ss.202 and 204 (*R. (on the application of Campbell) v Enfield LBC* [2001] EWHC Admin 354), but *cf. R. (Van der Stolk) v Camden LBC* [2002] EWHC 1261 (Admin); July 2002 Legal Action 26 (although judicial review would not normally lie where the claimant had not availed himself of a county court appeal, judicial review allowed in "an unusual case" where the claimant's health was poor and deteriorating and the medical report did add materially to what had been known about its effects on the claimant. His homelessness application should be reconsidered in the light of it).

3A–1442

New evidence on appeal

In *Cramp v Hastings LBC*; [2005] EWCA Civ 1005; [2005] 4 All E.R. 1014, the Court of Appeal stated that:

3A–1443

> "...judges in the county court need to be astute to ensure that evidential material over and above the contents of the housing file and the reviewing officer's decision is limited to that which is necessary to illuminate the points of law that are to be relied on in the appeal, or the issue of what, if any, relief ought to be granted. An undisciplined approach to the admission of new evidence may lead to the danger that the reviewing officer is found guilty of an error of law for not taking into account evidence that was never before her, notwithstanding the applicant's opportunity to make representations about the original decision."

Section 204(4): appeals

204A.—(1) This section applies where an applicant has the right to appeal to the county court against a local housing authority's decision on a review.

3A–1444

Paragraph numbers marked with a "+" can be found online and on CD.

(2) If the applicant is dissatisfied with a decision by the authority—

    (a) not to exercise their power under section 204(4) ("the section 204(4) power") in his case;

    (b) to exercise that power for a limited period ending before the final determination by the county court of his appeal under section 204(1) ("the main appeal"); or

    (c) to cease exercising that power before that time,

he may appeal to the county court against the decision.

(3) An appeal under this section may not be brought after the final determination by the county court of the main appeal.

(4) On an appeal under this section the court—

    (a) may order the authority to secure that accommodation is available for the applicant's occupation until the determination of the appeal (or such earlier time as the court may specify); and

    (b) shall confirm or quash the decision appealed against,

and in considering whether to confirm or quash the decision the court shall apply the principles applied by the High Court on an application for judicial review.

(5) If the court quashes the decision it may order the authority to exercise the section 204(4) power in the applicant's case for such period as may be specified in the order.

(6) An order under subsection (5)—

    (a) may only be made if the court is satisfied that failure to exercise the section 204(4) power in accordance with the order would substantially prejudice the applicant's ability to pursue the main appeal;

    (b) may not specify any period ending after the final determination by the county court of the main appeal.

3A–1445   *Note* —Inserted by Homelessness Act 2002 s.11. Note that PD 52 para.24.2 provides that

- an appeal under s.204A should be made in the same appellant's notice (Form **N161**) as a s.204 appeal or (if that is not possible) in separate appellant's notices;
- an application for an interim injunction in a s.204A appeal may be included in the appellant's notice; and
- where such an interim injunction is made without notice to the housing authority, that order will normally require that accommodation is secured only until a hearing date on which the authority can make representations.

PD2B, para.9 provides that appeals under s.204A may be not be heard by district judges.

When hearing a s.204A appeal, the county court should apply the same approach as directed in *R. v Brighton & Hove BC Ex p. Nacion* (1999) 31 H.L.R. 1095, CA unless the court decides that the local authority did not direct itself in accordance with *R. v London Borough of Camden Ex p. Mohammed* (1998) 30 H.L.R. 315, QBD. In that case it should quash the decision and decide whether it should itself exercise the s.204A(5) power to order the authority to provide temporary accommodation. There is no question of the county court embarking on an assessment of the merits of the appeal. That would be to go beyond the scope of the appeal as set out in *Nacion*. A challenge to the exercise of powers under s.188 of the Act still has to be brought by way of judicial

Paragraph numbers marked with a "+" can be found online and on CD.

1024

review (see *Francis v Kensington and Chelsea RLBC* [2003] EWCA Civ 443; [2003] 1 W.L.R. 2248; [2003] 2 All E.R. 1052).

Discharge of functions: introductory

205.—(1) The following sections have effect in relation to the dis- **3A–1446** charge by a local housing authority of their functions under this Part to secure that accommodation is available for the occupation of a person—

> section 206 (general provisions),
>
> section 208 (out-of-area placements),
>
> section 209 (arrangements with private landlord).

(2) In sections 206 and 208 those functions are referred to as the authority's "housing functions under this Part".

Note —Amended by the Homelessness Act 2002 s.5(1), Sch.1, para.18. **3A–1447**

Discharge of functions by local housing authorities

206.—(1) A local housing authority may discharge their housing **3A–1448** functions under this Part only in the following ways—

> (a) by securing that suitable accommodation provided by them is available,
>
> (b) by securing that he obtains suitable accommodation from some other person, or
>
> (c) by giving him such advice and assistance as will secure that suitable accommodation is available from some other person.

(2) A local housing authority may require a person in relation to whom they are discharging such functions—

> (a) to pay such reasonable charges as they may determine in respect of accommodation which they secure for his occupation (either by making it available themselves or otherwise), or
>
> (b) to pay such reasonable amount as they may determine in respect of sums payable by them for accommodation made available by another person.

Discharge of functions by local housing authorities
See the commentary to s.193. **3A–1449**

"local housing authority"
See ss.217, 218, and 230 which refer to the Housing Act 1985—see the Housing Act **3A–1450** 1985 ss.1 and 2, above.

Discharge of functions: provision of accommodation by the authority

207. [...] **3A–1451**

Note —This section was repealed by the Homelessness Act 2002, Sch.2. **3A–1452**

Paragraph numbers marked with a "+" can be found online and on CD.

Discharge of functions: out-of-area placements

3A-1453 **208.**—(1) So far as reasonably practicable a local housing authority shall in discharging their housing functions under this Part secure that accommodation is available for the occupation of the applicant in their district.

(2) If they secure that accommodation is available for the occupation of the applicant outside their district, they shall give notice to the local housing authority in whose district the accommodation is situated.

(3) The notice shall state—

    (a) the name of the applicant,

    (b) the number and description of other persons who normally reside with him as a member of his family or might reasonably be expected to reside with him,

    (c) the address of the accommodation,

    (d) the date on which the accommodation was made available to him, and

    (e) which function under this Part the authority was discharging in securing that the accommodation is available for his occupation.

(4) The notice must be in writing, and must be given before the end of the period of 14 days beginning with the day on which the accommodation was made available to the applicant.

Discharge of functions: out-of-area placements

3A-1454 See the commentary to s.193.

"local housing authority"

3A-1455 See ss.217, 218, and 230 which refer to the Housing Act 1985—see the Housing Act 1985 ss.1 and 2 above.

"district"

3A-1456 See s.217(3).

"available for his occupation"

3A-1457 See s.176.

Discharge of interim duties: arrangements with private landlord

3A-1458 **209.**—(1) This section applies where in pursuance of any of their housing functions under section 188, 190, 200 or 204(4) (interim duties) a local housing authority make arrangements with a private landlord to provide accommodation.

(2) A tenancy granted to the applicant in pursuance of the arrangements cannot be an assured tenancy before the end of the period of twelve months beginning with—

    (a) the date on which the applicant was notified of the authority's decision under section 184(3) or 198(5); or

    (b) if there is a review of that decision under section 202 or an appeal to the court under section 204, the date on

Paragraph numbers marked with a "+" can be found online and on CD.

which he is notified of the decision on review or the appeal is finally determined,

unless, before or during that period, the tenant is notified by the landlord (or in the case of joint landlords, at least one of them) that the tenancy is to be regarded as an assured shorthold tenancy or an assured tenancy other than an assured shorthold tenancy.

Note —Amended by Homelessness Act 2002 s.5(1), Sch.1, para.19.   **3A–1459**

private landlord
See s.217(1), as amended by Homelessness Act 2002 Sch.1, para.20.   **3A–1460**

assured shorthold tenancy
See Housing Act 1988 ss.19A and 20.   **3A–1461**

Discharge of functions: arrangements with private landlord
See the commentary to s.193.   **3A–1462**

"local housing authority"
See ss.217, 218, and 230 which refer to the Housing Act 1985—see the Housing Act   **3A–1463**
1985 ss.1 and 2 above.

"available for his occupation"
See s.176.   **3A–1464**

"assured tenancy"
See s.230 which refers to the Housing Act 1988 Pt I. See the Housing Act 1988 s.1   **3A–1465**
above.

"registered social landlord"
See s.1.   **3A–1466**

Suitability of accommodation

210.—(1) In determining for the purposes of this Part whether ac-   **3A–1467**
commodation is suitable for a person, the local housing authority
shall have regard to Parts 9 and 10 of the Housing Act 1985 (slum
clearance and overcrowding) and Parts 1 to 4 of the Housing Act
2004).

(2) The Secretary of State may by order specify—
    (a) circumstances in which accommodation is or is not to be
        regarded as suitable for a person, and
    (b) matters to be taken into account or disregarded in
        determining whether accommodation is suitable for a
        person.

Note —Amended by the Housing Act 2004 Sch.15, paras 40 and 43.   **3A–1468**

Suitability of accommodation
See the commentary to s.193, the Homelessness (Suitability of Accommodation   **3A–1469**
(England) Order 2003 (SI 2003/3326) and the Homelessness (Suitability of Accom-
modation) (Wales) Order 2006 (SI 2006/650 (w.71)).

"local housing authority"
See ss.217, 218, and 230 which refer to the Housing Act 1985—see the Housing Act   **3A–1470**
1985 ss.1 and 2 above.

Paragraph numbers marked with a "+" can be found online and on CD.

Protection of property of homeless persons and persons threatened with homelessness

3A–1471   **211.**—(1) This section applies where a local housing authority have reason to believe that—

    (a) there is danger of loss of, or damage to, any personal property of an applicant by reason of his inability to protect it or deal with it, and

    (b) no other suitable arrangements have been or are being made.

(2) If the authority have become subject to a duty towards the applicant under—

    section 188 (interim duty to accommodate),

    section 190, 193 or 195 (duties to persons found to be homeless or threatened with homelessness), or

    section 200 (duties to applicant whose case is considered for referral or referred),

then, whether or not they are still subject to such a duty, they shall take reasonable steps to prevent the loss of the property or prevent or mitigate damage to it.

(3) If they have not become subject to such a duty, they may take any steps they consider reasonable for that purpose.

(4) The authority may decline to take action under this section except upon such conditions as they consider appropriate in the particular case, which may include conditions as to—

    (a) the making and recovery by the authority of reasonable charges for the action taken, or

    (b) the disposal by the authority, in such circumstances as may be specified, of property in relation to which they have taken action.

(5) References in this section to personal property of the applicant include personal property of any person who might reasonably be expected to reside with him.

(6) Section 212 contains provisions supplementing this section.

"local housing authority"

3A–1472   See ss.217, 218, and 230 which refer to the Housing Act 1985—see the Housing Act 1985 ss.1 and 2 above.

3A–1473   For there to be a cause of action for a claim under s.211 the local authority must have reason to believe that: (a) there is a danger of loss or damage to property as a result of the owner being unable to protect it; and (b) no other suitable arrangements can be made (see ss.211(1)(a) and (b)). In view of the use of the word "danger", there has to be a likelihood of harm and not just the possibility of injury (*Deadman v Southwark LBC* (2001) 33 H.L.R. 865, CA).

Protection of property: supplementary provisions

3A–1474   **212.**—(1) The authority may for the purposes of section 211 (protection of property of homeless persons or persons threatened with homelessness)—

    (a) enter, at all reasonable times, any premises which are the usual place of residence of the applicant or which were his last usual place of residence, and

Paragraph numbers marked with a "+" can be found online and on CD.

(b) deal with any personal property of his in any way which is reasonably necessary, in particular by storing it or arranging for its storage.

(2) Where the applicant asks the authority to move his property to a particular location nominated by him, the authority—

(a) may, if it appears to them that his request is reasonable, discharge their responsibilities under section 211 by doing as he asks, and

(b) having done so, have no further duty or power to take action under that section in relation to that property.

If such a request is made, the authority shall before complying with it inform the applicant of the consequence of their doing so.

(3) If no such request is made (or, if made, is not acted upon) the authority cease to have any duty or power to take action under section 211 when, in their opinion, there is no longer any reason to believe that there is a danger of loss of or damage to a person's personal property by reason of his inability to protect it or deal with it.

But property stored by virtue of their having taken such action may be kept in store and any conditions upon which it was taken into store continue to have effect, with any necessary modifications.

(4) Where the authority—

(a) cease to be subject to a duty to take action under section 211 in respect of an applicant's property, or

(b) cease to have power to take such action, having previously taken such action,

they shall notify the applicant of that fact and of the reason for it.

(5) The notification shall be given to the applicant—

(a) by delivering it to him, or

(b) by leaving it, or sending it to him, at his last known address.

(6) References in this section to personal property of the applicant include personal property of any person who might reasonably be expected to reside with him.

Co-operation between relevant housing authorities and bodies

213.—(1) Where a local housing authority—   3A–1475

(a) request another relevant housing authority or body, in England, Wales or Scotland, to assist them in the discharge of their functions under this Part, or

(b) request a social services authority, in England, Wales or Scotland, to exercise any of their functions in relation to a case which the local housing authority are dealing with under this Part,

the authority or body to whom the request is made shall co-operate in rendering such assistance in the discharge of the functions to which the request relates as is reasonable in the circumstances.

Paragraph numbers marked with a "+" can be found online and on CD.

(2) In subsection (1)(a) "relevant housing authority or body" means—

    (a) in relation to England and Wales, a local housing authority, a new town corporation, a registered social landlord or a housing action trust;

    (b) in relation to Scotland, a local authority, a development corporation, a registered housing association or Scottish Homes.

    Expressions used in paragraph (a) have the same meaning as in the Housing Act 1985; and expressions used in paragraph (b) have the same meaning as in the Housing (Scotland) Act 1987.

(3) Subsection (1) above applies to a request by a local authority in Scotland under section 38 of the Housing (Scotland) Act 1987 as it applies to a request by a local housing authority in England and Wales (the references to this Part being construed, in relation to such a request, as references to Part II of that Act).

"local housing authority"

3A–1476   See ss.217, 218, and 230 which refer to the Housing Act 1985—see the Housing Act 1985 ss.1 and 2, above.

"social services authority"

3A–1477   See s.217.

Co-operation in certain cases involving children

3A–1478   **213A.**—(1) This section applies where a local housing authority have reason to believe that an applicant with whom a person under the age of 18 normally resides, or might reasonably be expected to reside—

    (a) may be ineligible for assistance;

    (b) may be homeless and may have become so intentionally; or

    (c) may be threatened with homelessness intentionally.

(2) A local housing authority shall make arrangements for ensuring that, where this section applies—

    (a) the applicant is invited to consent to the referral of the essential facts of his case to the social services authority for the district of the housing authority (where that is a different authority); and

    (b) if the applicant has given that consent, the social services authority are made aware of those facts and of the subsequent decision of the housing authority in respect of his case.

(3) Where the local housing authority and the social services authority for a district are the same authority (a "unitary authority"), that authority shall make arrangements for ensuring that, where this section applies—

    (a) the applicant is invited to consent to the referral to the social services department of the essential facts of his case; and

Paragraph numbers marked with a "+" can be found online and on CD.

(b) if the applicant has given that consent, the social services department is made aware of those facts and of the subsequent decision of the authority in respect of his case.

(4) Nothing in subsection (2) or (3) affects any power apart from this section to disclose information relating to the applicant's case to the social services authority or to the social services department (as the case may be) without the consent of the applicant.

(5) Where a social services authority—

(a) are aware of a decision of a local housing authority that the applicant is ineligible for assistance, became homeless intentionally or became threatened with homelessness intentionally, and

(b) request the local housing authority to provide them with advice and assistance in the exercise of their social services functions under Part 3 of the Children Act 1989, the local housing authority shall provide them with such advice and assistance as is reasonable in the circumstances.

(6) A unitary authority shall make arrangements for ensuring that, where they make a decision of a kind mentioned in subsection (5)(a), the housing department provide the social services department with such advice and assistance as the social services department may reasonably request.

(7) In this section, in relation to a unitary authority
"the housing department" means those persons responsible for the exercise of their housing functions; and
"the social services department" means those persons responsible for the exercise of their social services functions under Part 3 of the Children Act 1989.

Note —Amended by the Homelessness Act 2002 s.12.

3A–1479

Local housing authority—see Housing Act 1985 s.1.

Ineligible for assistance—see s.185.

Homeless intentionally—see s.191.

Threatened with homelessness intentionally—see s.191.

Unitary authority—see s.213A(3).

Social services authority—see s.213A(7) and the Children Act 1989 Pt III.

Co-operation with social services authority—If a local housing authority decide that an applicant, with whom a person under the age of 18 normally resides, may be ineligible for assistance, intentionally homeless, or threatened with homelessness intentionally, they must, subject to the consent of the applicant, make arrangements to ensure that the essential facts of the case are referred to the social services authority.

Children Act 1989—Local authorities have a power to provide assistance by way of accommodation under Children Act 1989 s.17. However s.17 does not impose an enforceable duty to provide assistance—see *A and W v Lambeth LBC*; *G v Barnet LBC* (also reported as *R.(on the application of G) v Barnet LBC*) [2003] UKHL 57; [2004] 2 A.C. 208; [2003] 3 W.L.R. 1194 and the commentary at 3A–29 above.

Paragraph numbers marked with a "+" can be found online and on CD.

HOUSING

False statements, withholding information and failure to disclose change of circumstances

3A–1480   **214.**—(1) It is an offence for a person, with intent to induce a local housing authority to believe in connection with the exercise of their functions under this Part that he or another person is entitled to accommodation or assistance in accordance with the provisions of this Part, or is entitled to accommodation or assistance of a particular description—

>   (a) knowingly or recklessly to make a statement which is false in a material particular, or
>
>   (b) knowingly to withhold information which the authority have reasonably required him to give in connection with the exercise of those functions.

(2) If before an applicant receives notification of the local housing authority's decision on his application there is any change of facts material to his case, he shall notify the authority as soon as possible.

The authority shall explain to every applicant, in ordinary language, the duty imposed on him by this subsection and the effect of subsection (3).

(3) A person who fails to comply with subsection (2) commits an offence unless he shows that he was not given the explanation required by that subsection or that he had some other reasonable excuse for non-compliance.

(4) A person guilty of an offence under this section is liable on summary conviction to a fine not exceeding level 5 on the standard scale.

"local housing authority"

3A–1481   See ss.217, 218 and 230 which refer to the Housing Act 1985—see the Housing Act 1985 ss.1 and 2 above.

See too the Housing Act 1985 Sch.2, Ground 5 above.

Regulations and orders

3A–1482   **215.**—(1) In this Part "prescribed" means prescribed by regulations of the Secretary of State.

(2) Regulations or an order under this Part may make different provision for different purposes, including different provision for different areas.

(3) Regulations or an order under this Part shall be made by statutory instrument.

(4) Unless required to be approved in draft, regulations or an order under this Part shall be subject to annulment in pursuance of a resolution of either House of Parliament.

Transitional and consequential matters

3A–1483   **216.**—(1) The provisions of this Part have effect in place of the provisions of Part III of the Housing Act 1985 (housing the homeless) and shall be construed as one with that Act.

Paragraph numbers marked with a "+" can be found online and on CD.

(2) Subject to any transitional provision contained in an order under section 232(4) (power to include transitional provision in commencement order), the provisions of this Part do not apply in relation to an applicant whose application for accommodation or assistance in obtaining accommodation was made before the commencement of this Part.

(3) The enactments mentioned in Schedule 17 have effect with the amendments specified there which are consequential on the provisions of this Part.

Minor definitions: Part VII

3A–1484

217.—(1) In this Part, subject to subsection (2)—

"private landlord" means a landlord who is not within section 80(1) of the Housing Act 1985 (c.68) (the landlord condition for secure tenancies); and

"relevant authority" means a local housing authority or a social services authority; and

"social services authority" means a local authority for the purposes of the Local Authority Social Services Act 1970, as defined in section 1 of that Act.

(2) In this Part, in relation to Scotland—

(a) "local housing authority" means a local authority within the meaning of the Housing (Scotland) Act 1988, and

(b) "social services authority" means a local authority for the purposes of the Social Work (Scotland) Act 1968.

(3) References in this Part to the district of a local housing authority—

(a) have the same meaning in relation to an authority in England or Wales as in the Housing Act 1985, and

(b) in relation to an authority in Scotland, mean the area of the local authority concerned.

Note —Amended by the Homelessness Act 2002 s.5(1) Sch.1, para.20.   **3A–1485**

Index of defined expressions: Part VII

3A–1486

218. The following Table shows provisions defining or otherwise explaining expressions used in this Part (other than provisions defining or explaining an expression used in the same section)—

accommodation available for occupation	section 176
applicant	section 183(2)
assistance under this Part	section 183(2)
associated (in relation to a person)	section 178
assured tenancy and assured shorthold tenancy	section 230
district (of local housing authority)	section 217(3)
eligible for assistance	section 183(2)

Paragraph numbers marked with a "+" can be found online and on CD.

homeless	section 175(1)
housing functions under this Part (in sections 206 and 208)	section 205(2)
intentionally homeless	section 191
intentionally threatened with homelessness	section 196
local connection	section 199
local housing authority—	
—in England and Wales	section 230
—in Scotland	section 217(2)(a)
minimum period (for purposes of section 193)	section 193(3) and (4)
prescribed	section 215(1)
priority need	section 189
private landlord	section 217(1)
reasonable to continue to occupy accommodation	section 177
registered social landlord	section 230
relevant authority	section 217(1)
social services authority	section 217(1) and (2)(b)
threatened with homelessness	section 175(4)

3A–1487   *Note* —Amended by Homelessness Act 2002 s.5(1), Sch.1, para.21. Section 218 has been amended by Housing and Regeneration Act 2008 Sch.15 to include reference to "restricted person" in amended s.184(7). The amendment is not yet in force. The amendment is printed as part of the Housing and Regeneration Act 2008—see below.

Anti-social behaviour: landlords' policies and procedures

3A–1488   **218A.**—(1) This section applies to the following landlords—

    (a) a local housing authority;

    (b) a housing action trust;

    (c) a registered social landlord.

(2) The landlord must prepare—

    (a) a policy in relation to anti-social behaviour;

    (b) procedures for dealing with occurrences of anti-social behaviour.

(3) The landlord must not later than 6 months after the commencement of section 12 of the Anti-Social Behaviour Act 2003 publish a statement of the policy and procedures prepared under subsection (2).

(4) The landlord must from time to time keep the policy and procedures under review and, when it thinks appropriate, publish a revised statement.

(5) A copy of a statement published under subsection (3) or (4)—

    (a) must be available for inspection at all reasonable hours at the landlord's principal office;

Paragraph numbers marked with a "+" can be found online and on CD.

(b) must be provided on payment of a reasonable fee to any person who requests it.

(6) The landlord must also—

(a) prepare a summary of its current policy and procedures;

(b) provide without charge a copy of the summary to any person who requests it.

(7) In preparing and reviewing the policy and procedures the landlord must have regard to guidance issued—

(a) by the Secretary of State in the case of a local housing authority or a housing action trust;

(b) by the Relevant Authority under section 36 in the case of a registered social landlord.

(8) Anti-social behaviour is—

(a) any housing-related anti-social conduct, or

(b) any conduct to which section 153B applies.

(8A) Housing-related anti-social conduct has the same meaning as in section 153A.

(9) Relevant Authority has the same meaning as in Part 1.

Note —This section was inserted by the Anti-Social Behaviour Act 2003 s.12. It was amended by the Police and Justice Act 2006 Sch.14, para.33, with effect from April 6, 2007 (SI 2007/709).　**3A–1489**

A local housing authority
See the Housing Act 1996 s.230 and Housing Act 1985 ss.1 and 2(2).　**3A–1490**

A housing action trust
See the Housing Act 1996 s.230 and Housing Act 1988 Pt III.　**3A–1491**

A registered social landlord
See the Housing Act 1996 s.230 referring back to Pt I (ss,1 to 3).　**3A–1492**

Anti-social behaviour
See the ss.153A and 153B above.　**3A–1493**

Relevant authority
See Housing Act 1996 s.56—i.e. the Housing Corporation or Housing for Wales.　**3A–1494**

Guidance
Guidance may be issued to local housing authorities or housing action trusts in England by the Secretary of State or, in Wales, by the National Assembly for Wales. Guidance to registered social landlords may be issued by the Housing Corporation in England or, in Wales, by the National Assembly for Wales. At present no guidance has been issued.　**3A–1495**

* * * *

PART VIII

MISCELLANEOUS AND GENERAL PROVISIONS

GENERAL

Meaning of "lease" and "tenancy" and related expressions

229.—(1) In this Act "lease" and "tenancy" have the same meaning.　**3A–1496**

Paragraph numbers marked with a "+" can be found online and on CD.

(2) Both expressions include—

    (a) a sub-lease or a sub-tenancy, and

    (b) an agreement for a lease or tenancy (or sub-lease or sub-tenancy).

(3) The expressions "lessor" and "lessee" and "landlord" and "tenant", and references to letting, to the grant of a lease or to covenants or terms, shall be construed accordingly.

*   *   *   *

SECTION 155(6)   SCHEDULE 15

ARREST FOR ANTI-SOCIAL BEHAVIOUR: POWERS OF HIGH COURT AND COUNTY COURT TO REMAND

Introductory

3A–1497   1.—(1) The provisions of this Schedule apply where the court has power to remand a person under section 155(2) or (5) (arrest for breach of injunction, &c.).

(2) In this Schedule "the court" means the High Court or a county court and includes—

    (a) in relation to the High Court, a judge of that court, and

    (b) in relation to a county court, a judge or district judge of that court.

Remand in custody or on bail

3A–1498   2.—(1) The court may—

    (a) remand him in custody, that is, commit him to custody to be brought before the court at the end of the period of remand or at such earlier time as the court may require, or

    (b) remand him on bail, in accordance with the following provisions.

(2) The court may remand him on bail—

    (a) by taking from him a recognizance, with or without sureties, conditioned as provided in paragraph 3, or

    (b) by fixing the amount of the recognizances with a view to their being taken subsequently, and in the meantime committing him to custody as mentioned in sub-paragraph (1)(a).

(3) Where a person is brought before the court after remand, the court may further remand him.

3.—(1) Where a person is remanded on bail, the court may direct that his recognizance be conditioned for his appearance—

    (a) before that court at the end of the period of remand, or

    (b) at every time and place to which during the course of the proceedings the hearing may from time to time be adjourned.

(2) Where a recognizance is conditioned for a person's appearance as mentioned in sub-paragraph (1)(b), the fixing of any time for him next to appear shall be deemed to be a remand.

(3) Nothing in this paragraph affects the power of the court at any subsequent hearing to remand him afresh.

4.—(1) The court shall not remand a person for a period exceeding 8 clear days, except that—

    (a) if the court remands him on bail, it may remand him for a longer period if he and the other party consent, and

    (b) if the court adjourns a case under section 156(1) (remand for medical examination and report), the court may remand him for the period of the adjournment.

(2) Where the court has power to remand a person in custody it may, if the remand is for a period not exceeding 3 clear days, commit him to the custody of a constable.

Paragraph numbers marked with a "+" can be found online and on CD.

Further remand

5.—(1) If the court is satisfied that a person who has been remanded is unable by **3A-1499** reason of illness or accident to appear or be brought before the court at the expiration of the period for which he was remanded, the court may, in his absence, remand him for a further time. This power may, in the case of a person who was remanded on bail, be exercised by enlarging his recognizance and those of any sureties for him to a later time.

(2) Where a person remanded on bail is bound to appear before the court at any time and the court has no power to remand him under sub-paragraph (1) the court may in his absence enlarge his recognizance and those of any sureties for him to a later time. The enlargement of his recognizance shall be deemed to be a further remand.

(3) Paragraph 4(1) (limit of period of remand) does not apply to the exercise of the powers conferred by this paragraph.

Postponement of taking of recognizance

6. Where under paragraph 2(2)(b) the court fixes the amount in which the principal **3A-1500** and his sureties, if any, are to be bound, the recognizance may afterwards be taken by such person as may be prescribed by rules of court, with the same consequences as if it had been entered into before the court.

Schedule 15

See the commentary to ss.153 to 155 above.. **3A-1501**

Note that ss.155(2)(b) (remands in custody), 155(3)–(7) (warrants for arrest), 156 (remand for medical examination), and Sch.15 (provisions corresponding with civil procedure in magistrate's courts) were implemented on October 15, 2001 by the Housing Act 1996 (Commencement No.13) Order 2001 (SI 2001/3164).

Crime and Disorder Act 1998

(1998 c.37) **3A-1502**

ARRANGEMENT OF SECTIONS

CRIME AND DISORDER: GENERAL

CRIME AND DISORDER: GENERAL

Anti-social behaviour orders

1.—(1) An application for an order under this section may be made **3A-1503** by a relevant authority if it appears to the authority that the following conditions are fulfilled with respect to any person aged 10 or over, namely—

> (a) that the person has acted, since the commencement date, in an anti-social manner, that is to say, in a manner that caused or was likely to cause harassment, alarm or distress to one or more persons not of the same household as himself; and

Paragraph numbers marked with a "+" can be found online and on CD.

HOUSING

(b) that such an order is necessary to protect relevant persons from further anti-social acts by him.

(1A) In this section and sections 1B, 1CA, 1E and 1F 'relevant authority' means —

(a) the council for a local government area;

(aa) in relation to England, a county council;

(b) the chief officer of police of any police force maintained for a police area;

(c) the chief constable of the British Transport Police Force;

(d) any person registered under section 1 of the Housing Act 1996 (c.52) as a social landlord who provides or manages any houses or hostel in a local government area; or

(e) a housing action trust established by order in pursuance of section 62 of the Housing Act 1988.

(1B) In this section 'relevant persons' means—

(a) in relation to a relevant authority falling within paragraph (a) of subsection (1A), persons within the local government area of that council;

(aa) in relation to a relevant authority falling within paragraph (aa) of subsection (1A), persons within the county of the county council;

(b) in relation to a relevant authority falling within paragraph (b) of that subsection, persons within the police area;

(c) in relation to a relevant authority falling within paragraph (c) of that subsection—

(i) persons who are within or likely to be within a place specified in section 31(1)(a) to (f) of the Railways and Transport Safety Act 2003 in a local government area; or

(ii) persons who are within or likely to be within such a place;

(d) in relation to a relevant authority falling within paragraph (d) or (e) of that subsection—

(i) persons who are residing in or who are otherwise on or likely to be on premises provided or managed by that authority; or

(ii) persons who are in the vicinity of or likely to be in the vicinity of such premises.

[...]

(3) Such an application shall be made by complaint to a magistrates' court.

(4) If, on such an application, it is proved that the conditions mentioned in subsection (1) above are fulfilled, the magistrates' court may make an order under this section (an "anti-social behaviour order") which prohibits the defendant from doing anything described in the order.

Paragraph numbers marked with a "+" can be found online and on CD.

(5) For the purpose of determining whether the condition mentioned in subsection (1)(a) above is fulfilled, the court shall disregard any act of the defendant which he shows was reasonable in the circumstances.

(5A) Nothing in this section affects the operation of section 127 of the Magistrates' Courts Act 1980 (limitation of time in respect of informations laid or complaints made in magistrates' court).

(6) The prohibitions that may be imposed by an anti-social behaviour order are those necessary for the purpose of protecting persons (whether relevant persons or persons elsewhere in England and Wales) from further anti-social acts by the defendant.

(7) An anti-social behaviour order shall have effect for a period (not less than two years) specified in the order or until further order.

(8) Subject to subsection (9) below, the applicant or the defendant may apply by complaint to the court which made an anti-social behaviour order for it to be varied or discharged by a further order.

(9) Except with the consent of both parties, no anti-social behaviour order shall be discharged before the end of the period of two years beginning with the date of service of the order.

(10) If without reasonable excuse a person does anything which he is prohibited from doing by an anti-social behaviour order, he is guilty of an offence and liable—

    (a) on summary conviction, to imprisonment for a term not exceeding six months or to a fine not exceeding the statutory maximum, or to both; or

    (b) on conviction on indictment, to imprisonment for a term not exceeding five years or to a fine, or to both.

(10A) The following may bring proceedings for an offence under subsection (10)—

    (a) a council which is a relevant authority;

    (b) the council for the local government area in which a person in respect of whom an anti-social behaviour order has been made resides or appears to reside.

    (c) Transport for London, where the anti-social behaviour order was made on an application by Transport for London.

(10B) If proceedings for an offence under subsection (10) are brought in a youth court section 47(2) of the Children and Young Persons Act 1933 (c. 12) has effect as if the persons entitled to be present at a sitting for the purposes of those proceedings include one person authorised to be present by a relevant authority.

(10C) In proceedings for an offence under subsection (10), a copy of the original anti-social behaviour order, certified as such by the proper officer of the court which made it, is admissible as evidence of its having been made and of its contents to the same extent that oral evidence of those things is admissible in those proceedings.

(10D) In relation to proceedings brought against a child or a young person for an offence under subsection (10)—

Paragraph numbers marked with a "+" can be found online and on CD.

(a) section 49 of the Children and Young Persons Act 1933 (restrictions on reports of proceedings in which children and young persons are concerned) does not apply in respect of the child or young person against whom the proceedings are brought;

(b) section 45 of the Youth Justice and Criminal Evidence Act 1999 (power to restrict reporting of criminal proceedings involving persons under 18) does so apply.

(10E) If, in relation to any such proceedings, the court does exercise its power to give a direction under section 45 of the Youth Justice and Criminal Evidence Act 1999, it shall give its reasons for doing so.

(11) Where a person is convicted of an offence under subsection (10) above, it shall not be open to the court by or before which he is so convicted to make an order under subsection (1)(b) (conditional discharge) of section 12 of the Powers of Criminal Courts (Sentencing) Act 2000 in respect of the offence.

(12) In this section—

"British Transport Police Force" means the force of constables appointed under section 53 of the British Transport Commission Act 1949 (c. xxix);

"child" and "young person" shall have the same meaning as in the Children and Young Persons Act 1933;

"the commencement date" means the date of the commencement of this section;

"local government area" means —

(a) in relation to England, a district or London borough, the City of London, the Isle of Wight and the Isles of Scilly;

(b) in relation to Wales, a county or county borough.

"policed premises" has the meaning given by section 53(3) of the British Transport Commission Act 1949.

3A–1504　*Note* —Amended by the Powers of the Court (Sentencing) Act 2000 s.165(1), Sch.9, para.192; the Police Reform Act 2002 s.61; the Anti-Social Behaviour Act 2003 s.85; SI 2004/1573; SI 2005/886; the Serious Organised Crime and Police Act 2005 ss.139(2), 140(2), 141(2), 142(2); the Violent Crime Reduction Act 2006 s.59(1) with effect from April 6, 2008 (SI 2008/791); and the Transport for London Act 2008 s.29(a) with effect from July 22, 2008.

Anti-social behaviour order

3A–1505　Such an order (an ASBO) may be granted if a person has acted in an anti-social manner, that is to say, in a manner that caused or was likely to cause harassment, alarm or distress to one or more persons not of the same household as himself and such an order is necessary to protect relevant persons from further anti-social acts (s.1(1)). When considering whether a person's conduct has caused or is likely to cause harassment, alarm or distress to others within the meaning of Crime and Disorder Act 1998 s.1(1)(a) "likely" means "more probable than not". The likelihood has to be proved to the criminal standard (see *Chief Constable of Lancashire v Potter* [2003] EWHC 2272 (Admin) and *R. (McCann) v Manchester Crown Court* [2002] UKHL 39; [2003] 1 A.C. 787; [2002] 3 W.L.R. 1313).. An ASBO may prohibit the defendant from doing anything described in the order. The prohibitions that may be imposed by an ASBO are "those necessary for the purpose of protecting persons (whether relevant persons

Paragraph numbers marked with a "+" can be found online and on CD.

or persons elsewhere in England and Wales) from further anti-social acts by the defendant" (s.1(4)and (6)). ASBOs have effect for the period (not less than two years) specified in the order or until further order (s.1(7)). Although ASBOs should be substantially and not just formally prohibitory, a restraint upon leaving or travelling between specified premises between particular times meets that test. Further there is nothing legally objectionable to a curfew provision in an ASBO if it is necessary for the protection of relevant people. Courts should however consider carefully the need for and duration of curfew provisions when making ASBOs. Just because ASBOs have to run for a minimum of two years, it does not follow that each and every prohibition within a particular ASBO has to endure for the life of the order (*R. (Lonergan) v Lewes Crown Court* [2005] EWHC 457 (Admin); [2005] 1 W.L.R. 2570).

Breach of an ASBO may be punished on summary conviction by imprisonment for a term not exceeding six months or a fine or both; or on conviction on indictment, by imprisonment for a term not exceeding five years or to a fine, or to both (s.1(10)).

In *Moat Housing Group South Ltd v Harris and Hartless* [2005] EWCA Civ 287; [2006] Q.B. 606; [2005] 3 W.L.R. 691; [2005] 4 All E.R. 1051, the Court of Appeal left open "the important question whether a failure to control one's children from being a nuisance, although it may constitute a breach of a tenancy agreement, is an 'act' of the type referred to in" Crime and Disorder Act 1998 s.1(1)(a).

As to the relationship between ASBOs and possession claims based upon anti-social behaviour, see e.g. *Knowsley Housing Trust v McMullen* [2006] EWCA Civ 539; [2006] H.L.R. 43.

A relevant authority

See s.1(1A), namely the council for a local government area, a county council, the **3A–1506** chief officer of police of any police force maintained for a police area, the chief constable of the British Transport Police Force, a social landlord who provides or manages any houses or hostel which is registered under Housing Act 1996 s.1 or a housing action trust (see Housing Act 1988 s.62). The Crime and Disorder Act 1998 (Relevant Authorities and Relevant Persons) Order 2006 (SI 2006/2137) added the Environment Agency and Transport for London to the list of organisations which may apply for ASBOs. Any person (or employee of that person) who exercises a local housing authority's management functions pursuant to an agreement under the Housing Act 1985 s.27, (such as an Arms Length Management Organisation—ALMO) may discharge the authority's functions under the Crime and Disorder Act 1998 ss.1– 1E (the Local Authorities (Contracting Out of Anti-Social Behaviour Order Functions) (England) Order 2007 SI 2007/1441).

Relevant persons

See s.1(1B). **3A–1507**

An application

Applications for ASBOs could originally only be made by complaint in the Magis- **3A–1508** trates Court, but see s.1B below (introduced by Police Reform Act 2002 s.63) which provides that ASBOs can be made in the county court if a relevant authority considers it is reasonable to make such an application. If the relevant authority or the person against whom the ASBO is sought is not already a party to the principal proceedings, an application can be made for him or her to be joined as a party. However a person may only be joined if his or her anti-social acts are material in relation to the principal proceedings (see s.1B(3C) below).

Power of Secretary of State to add to relevant authorities

1A.—(1) The Secretary of State may by order provide that the **3A–1509** chief officer of a body of constables maintained otherwise than by a police authority is, in such cases and circumstances as may be prescribed by the order, to be a relevant authority for the purposes of section 1 above.

(2) The Secretary of State may by order—

    (a) provide that a person or body of any other description

Paragraph numbers marked with a "+" can be found online and on CD.

specified in the order is, in such cases and circumstances as may be prescribed by the order, to be a relevant authority for the purposes of such of sections 1 above and 1B, 1CA, 1E and 1F below as are specified in the order; and

(b) prescribe the description of persons who are to be "relevant persons" in relation to that person or body.

3A–1510　*Note*—Inserted by the Police Reform Act 2002 s.62(1); amended by the Serious Organised Crime and Police Act 2005 s.139(3) s.142(2).

By order

3A–1511　See the Crime and Disorder Act 1998 (Relevant Authorities and Relevant Persons) Order 2006 (SI 2006/2137).

Orders in county court proceedings

3A–1512　**1B.**—(1) This section applies to any proceedings in a county court ('the principal proceedings').

(2) If a relevant authority—

(a) is a party to the principal proceedings, and

(b) considers that a party to those proceedings is a person in relation to whom it would be reasonable for it to make an application under section 1,

it may make an application in those proceedings for an order under subsection (4).

(3) If a relevant authority—

(a) is not a party to the principal proceedings, and

(b) considers that a party to those proceedings is a person in relation to whom it would be reasonable for it to make an application under section 1,

it may make an application to be joined to those proceedings to enable it to apply for an order under subsection (4) and, if it is so joined, may apply for such an order.

(3A) Subsection (3B) applies if a relevant authority is a party to the principal proceedings and considers—

(a) that a person who is not a party to the proceedings has acted in an anti-social manner, and

(b) that the person's anti-social acts are material in relation to the principal proceedings.

(3B) The relevant authority may—

(a) make an application for the person mentioned in subsection (3A)(a) to be joined to the principal proceedings to enable an order under subsection (4) to be made in relation to that person;

(b) if that person is so joined, apply for an order under subsection (4).

(3C) But a person must not be joined to proceedings in pursuance of subsection (3B) unless his anti-social acts are material in relation to the principal proceedings.

Paragraph numbers marked with a "+" can be found online and on CD.

(4) If, on an application for an order under this subsection, it is proved that the conditions mentioned in section 1(1) are fulfilled as respects that other party, the court may make an order which prohibits him from doing anything described in the order.

(5) Subject to subsection (6), the person against whom an order under this section has been made and the relevant authority on whose application that order was made may apply to the county court which made an order under this section for it to be varied or discharged by a further order.

(6) Except with the consent of the relevant authority and the person subject to the order, no order under this section shall be discharged before the end of the period of two years beginning with the date of service of the order.

(7) Subsections (5) to (7) and (10) to (12) of section 1 apply for the purposes of the making and effect of orders made under this section as they apply for the purposes of the making and effect of anti-social behaviour orders.

Note —Section 1B was inserted by the Police Reform Act 2002 s.63 and has been amended by the Anti-Social Behaviour Act 2003 s.85(5), (6). **3A–1513**

A relevant authority

See s.1(1A), namely the council for a local government area, a county council, the chief officer of police of any police force maintained for a police area, the chief constable of the British Transport Police Force, a social landlord who provides or manages any houses or hostel which is registered under Housing Act 1996 s.1 or a housing action trust (see Housing Act 1988 s.62). The Crime and Disorder Act 1998 (Relevant Authorities and Relevant Persons) Order 2006 (SI 2006/2137) added the Environment Agency and Transport for London to the list of organisations which may apply for ASBOs. Any person (or employee of that person) who exercises a local housing authority's management functions pursuant to an agreement under the Housing Act 1985 s.27, (such as an Arms Length Management Organisation—ALMO) may discharge the authority's functions under the Crime and Disorder Act 1998 ss.1– 1E (the Local Authorities (Contracting Out of Anti-social Behaviour Order Functions) (England) Order 2007 SI 2007/1441). **3A–1514**

Anti-social acts

See s.1(1)(a) which refers to behaviour that has caused or was likely to cause harassment, alarm or distress. **3A–1515**

Principal proceedings

See s.1B(1). **3A–1516**

Procedure

Applications for relevant authorities or persons against whom ASBOs are sought to be joined to the principal proceedings are made in accordance with CPR Pt 65. See CPR r.65.23 and the commentary thereto. Note that a person may only be joined if his or her "anti-social acts are material in relation to the principal proceedings" (s.1B(3C)). As ASBOs are civil and not criminal orders (*R. (McCann) v Manchester Crown Court* [2002] UKHL 39; [2003] 1 A.C. 787) it follows that hearsay evidence is admissible under the Civil Evidence Act 1995. See too *R. (on the application of W) v Acton Youth Court* [2005] EWHC 954 (Admin); May 19, 2005. However "the willingness of a civil court to admit hearsay evidence carries with it inherent dangers". Claimants should state, by convincing direct evidence, why it is not reasonable and practicable to produce the original makers of statements as witnesses. If statements involve multiple hearsay, the route by which the original statement came to the attention of the person attesting to it should be identified as far as practicable. When hearing such applica- **3A–1517**

HOUSING

Paragraph numbers marked with a "+" can be found online and on CD.

tions, it is better for judges to start their judgments with an analysis of the direct oral evidence received, and then to move onto the evidence of the absent named witnesses and anonymous witnesses. (See *Moat Housing Group South Ltd v Harris and Hartless* [2005] EWCA Civ 287; [2006] Q.B. 606; [2005] 3 W.L.R. 691; [2005] 4 All E.R. 1051.)

Children

3A–1518   County courts do not now have jurisdiction to make ASBOs against children. The pilot scheme provided for by Anti-Social Behaviour Act 2003 (Commencement No.4) Order 2004 (SI 2004/2168) has lapsed.

* * * *

Interim orders

3A–1519   **1D.**—(1) This section applies where—

(a) an application is made for an anti-social behaviour order;

(b) an application is made for an order under section 1B;

(c) a request is made by the prosecution for an order under section 1C; or

(d) the court is minded to make an order under section 1C of its own motion.

(2) If, before determining the application or request, or before deciding whether to make an order under section 1C of its own motion, the court considers that it is just to make an order under this section pending the determination of that application or request or before making that decision, it may make such an order.

(3) An order under this section is an order which prohibits the defendant from doing anything described in the order.

(4) An order under this section—

(a) shall be for a fixed period;

(b) may be varied, renewed or discharged;

(c) shall, if it has not previously ceased to have effect, cease to have effect on the determination of the application or request mentioned in subsection (1), or on the court's making a decision as to whether or not to make an order under section 1C of its own motion.

(5) In relation to cases to which this section applies by virtue of paragraph (a) or (b) of subsection (1), subsection (6), (8) and (10) to (12) of section 1 apply for the purposes of the making and effect of orders under this section as they apply for the purposes of the making and effect of anti-social behaviour orders.

(6) In relation to cases to which this section applies by virtue of paragraph (c) or (d) of subsection (1)—

(a) subsections (6) and (10) to (12) of section 1 apply for the purposes of the making and effect of orders under this section as they apply for the purposes of the making and effect of anti-social behaviour orders; and

(b) section 1CA applies for the purposes of the variation or discharge of an order under this section as it applies for the purposes of the variation or discharge of an order under section 1C.

Paragraph numbers marked with a "+" can be found online and on CD.

    (a) either less than 30 days or more than 60 days after the day on which the notice is given, or

    (b) before that on which he would have been liable to make it in accordance with the lease.

(4) If the date on which the tenant is liable to make the payment is after that on which he would have been liable to make it in accordance with the lease, any provisions of the lease relating to non-payment or late payment of rent have effect accordingly.

(5) The notice—

    (a) must be in the prescribed form, and

    (b) may be sent by post.

(6) If the notice is sent by post, it must be addressed to a tenant at the dwelling unless he has notified the landlord in writing of a different address in England and Wales at which he wishes to be given notices under this section (in which case it must be addressed to him there).

(7) In this section "rent" does not include—

    (a) a service charge (within the meaning of section 18(1) of the 1985 Act), or

    (b) an administration charge (within the meaning of Part 1 of Schedule 11 to this Act).

(8) In this section "long lease of a dwelling" does not include—

    (a) a tenancy to which Part 2 of the Landlord and Tenant Act 1954 (c.56) (business tenancies) applies,

    (b) a tenancy of an agricultural holding within the meaning of the Agricultural Holdings Act 1986 (c.5) in relation to which that Act applies, or

    (c) a farm business tenancy within the meaning of the Agricultural Tenancies Act 1995 (c.8).

(9) In this section—

"dwelling" has the same meaning as in the 1985 Act,

"landlord" and "tenant" have the same meanings as in Chapter 1 of this Part,

"long lease" has the meaning given by sections 76 and 77 of this Act, and

"prescribed" means prescribed by regulations made by the appropriate national authority.

Implementation

Section 166 was brought into force in so far as it confers power to make regulations **3A–1586** on July 26, 2002 in England and on January 1, 2003 in Wales by the Commonhold and Leasehold Reform Act 2002 (Commencement No.1, Savings and Transitional Provisions) (England) Order 2002 (SI 2002/1912) (c.58) and the Commonhold and Leasehold Reform Act 2002 (Commencement No.1, Savings and Transitional Provisions) (Wales) Order 2002 (SI 2002/3012) (w.284) (c.96). It was brought fully into force in England on February 28, 2005 by the Commonhold and Leasehold Reform Act 2002 (Commencement No.5 and Saving and Transitional Provision) Order 2004 (SI 2004/3056) (c.127) and in Wales on May 31, 2005 by the Commonhold and Leasehold Reform Act 2002 (Commencement No.3 and Saving and Transitional Provision) (Wales) Order 2005 (SI 2005/1353) (w.101) (c.59).

Paragraph numbers marked with a "+" can be found online and on CD.

3A–1587   Section 166(1) provides that a long lessee is not liable to make a payment of rent unless notice has been served. Section 166(2) provides that such a notice must specify the amount due, the date on which the lessee is liable to make the payment and, if different, the date on which the lessee would have been liable to make the payment in accordance with the lease. Section 166(2) is supplemented by the Landlord and Tenant (Notice of Rent) (England) Regulations 2004 (SI 2004/3096) and the Landlord and Tenant (Notice of Rent) (Wales) Regulations 2005 (SI 2005/1355) (w.103) which contain additional requirements, namely notes for both lessees and lessors. The content of the notes is set out in the Schedule to the Regulations, as part of the prescribed form of notice under s.166(1).

Dwelling

3A–1588   See Landlord and Tenant Act 1985 s.38.

landlord, tenant, lease, tenancy—see Landlord and Tenant Act 1985 s.36, para.3A–702+.

regulations—see the Landlord and Tenant (Notice of Rent) (England) Regulations 2004 (SI 2004/3096) and the Landlord and Tenant (Notice of Rent) (Wales) Regulations 2005 (SI 2005/1355) (w.103).

long lease—see s.76 which provides that a lease is a long lease if it (a) is granted for a term of years certain exceeding 21 years; (b) is for a term fixed by law under a grant with a covenant or obligation for perpetual renewal (c) takes effect under Law of Property Act 1925 s.149(6) (leases terminable after a death or marriage); (d) was granted under the right to buy provisions of Housing Act 1985 Pt 5; (e) is a shared ownership lease; or (f) under Housing Act 1996 s.17 (the right to acquire). Section 77 contains certain exceptions.

administration charge—see Sch.11, Pt 1.

FORFEITURE OF LEASES OF DWELLINGS

Failure to pay small amount for short period

3A–1589   **167.**—(1) A landlord under a long lease of a dwelling may not exercise a right of re-entry or forfeiture for failure by a tenant to pay an amount consisting of rent, service charges or administration charges (or a combination of them) ("the unpaid amount") unless the unpaid amount—

   (a) exceeds the prescribed sum, or
   (b) consists of or includes an amount which has been payable for more than a prescribed period.

(2) The sum prescribed under subsection (1)(a) must not exceed £500.

(3) If the unpaid amount includes a default charge, it is to be treated for the purposes of subsection (1)(a) as reduced by the amount of the charge; and for this purpose "default charge" means an administration charge payable in respect of the tenant's failure to pay any part of the unpaid amount.

(4) In this section "long lease of a dwelling" does not include—

   (a) a tenancy to which Part 2 of the Landlord and Tenant Act 1954 (c.56) (business tenancies) applies,
   (b) a tenancy of an agricultural holding within the meaning of the Agricultural Holdings Act 1986 (c.5) in relation to which that Act applies, or
   (c) a farm business tenancy within the meaning of the Agricultural Tenancies Act 1995 (c.8).

Paragraph numbers marked with a "+" can be found online and on CD.

(5) In this section—

"administration charge" has the same meaning as in Part 1 of
Schedule 11,

"dwelling" has the same meaning as in the 1985 Act,

"landlord" and "tenant" have the same meaning as in Chapter
1 of this Part,

"long lease" has the meaning given by sections 76 and 77 of this
Act, except that a shared ownership lease is a long lease
whatever the tenant's total share,

"prescribed" means prescribed by regulations made by the appropriate national authority, and

"service charge" has the meaning given by section 18(1) of the
1985 Act.

Implementation

Section 167 was brought into force in so far as it confers power to make regulations **3A–1590**
on July 26, 2002 in England and on January 1, 2003 in Wales by the Commonhold
and Leasehold Reform Act 2002 (Commencement No.1, Savings and Transitional Provisions) (England) Order 2002 (SI 2002/1912) (c.58) and the Commonhold and
Leasehold Reform Act 2002 (Commencement No.1, Savings and Transitional Provisions) (Wales) Order 2002 (SI 2002/3012) (w.284) (c.96). It was brought fully into force
in England on February 28, 2005 by the Commonhold and Leasehold Reform Act
2002 (Commencement No.5 and Saving and Transitional Provision) Order 2004 (SI
2004/3056) (c.127) and in Wales on May 31, 2005 by the Commonhold and Leasehold
Reform Act 2002 (Commencement No.3 and Saving and Transitional Provision)
(Wales) Order 2005 (SI 2005/1353) (w.101) (c.59).

Editorial introduction

Section 167(1) prevents a landlord under a long lease of a dwelling from exercising **3A–1591**
a right of re-entry or forfeiture for failure by a tenant to pay an amount consisting of
rent, service charges or administration charges (or a combination of them) unless the
unpaid amount exceeds the prescribed sum or consists of, or includes, an amount
which has been payable for more than a prescribed period. The Rights of Re-entry
and Forfeiture (Prescribed Sum and Period) (England) Regulations 2004 (SI 2004/
3086), and the Rights of Re-entry and Forfeiture (Prescribed Sum and Period) (Wales)
Regulations 2005 (SI 2005/1352) (w.100), which prescribe the sum of £350 and a period of three years.

"service charges"

See Landlord and Tenant Act 1985 s.18 as amended by Commonhold and **3A–1592**
Leasehold Reform Act 2002 Sch.9.

administration charge—see Sch.11, Pt 1.

dwelling—see Landlord and Tenant Act 1985 s.38.

landlord, tenant, lease, tenancy—see Landlord and Tenant Act 1985 s.36.

regulations—See the Rights of Re-entry and Forfeiture (Prescribed Sum and Period) (England) Regulations 2004 (SI 2004/3086) and the Rights of Re-entry and Forfeiture (Prescribed Sum and Period) (Wales) Regulations 2005 (SI 2005/1352) (w.100).

long lease—see s.76 which provides that a lease is a long lease if it (a) is granted for
a term of years certain exceeding 21 years; (b) is for a term fixed by law under a grant
with a covenant or obligation for perpetual renewal (c) takes effect under Law of Property Act 1925 s.149(6) (leases terminable after a death or marriage); (d) was granted
under the right to buy provisions of Housing Act 1985 Pt 5; (e) is a shared ownership
lease; or (f) under Housing Act 1996 s.17 (the right to acquire). Section 77 contains
certain exceptions.

No forfeiture notice before determination of breach

168.—(1) A landlord under a long lease of a dwelling may not **3A–1593**

Paragraph numbers marked with a "+" can be found online and on CD.

serve a notice under section 146(1) of the Law of Property Act 1925 (c.20) (restriction on forfeiture) in respect of a breach by a tenant of a covenant or condition in the lease unless subsection (2) is satisfied.

(2) This subsection is satisfied if—

    (a) it has been finally determined on an application under subsection (4) that the breach has occurred,

    (b) the tenant has admitted the breach, or

    (c) a court in any proceedings, or an arbitral tribunal in proceedings pursuant to a post-dispute arbitration agreement, has finally determined that the breach has occurred.

(3) But a notice may not be served by virtue of subsection (2)(a) or (c) until after the end of the period of 14 days beginning with the day after that on which the final determination is made.

(4) A landlord under a long lease of a dwelling may make an application to a leasehold valuation tribunal for a determination that a breach of a covenant or condition in the lease has occurred.

(5) But a landlord may not make an application under subsection (4) in respect of a matter which—

    (a) has been, or is to be, referred to arbitration pursuant to a post-dispute arbitration agreement to which the tenant is a party,

    (b) has been the subject of determination by a court, or

    (c) has been the subject of determination by an arbitral tribunal pursuant to a post-dispute arbitration agreement.

3A–1594   **implementation**—This section was brought into force in England on February 28, 2005 by the Commonhold and Leasehold Reform Act 2002 (Commencement No.5 and Saving and Transitional Provision) Order 2004 (SI 2004/3056) (c.127) and in Wales on May 31, 2005 by the Commonhold and Leasehold Reform Act 2002 (Commencement No.3 and Saving and Transitional Provision) (Wales) Order 2005 (SI 2005/1353) (w.101) (c.59).

    dwelling—see Landlord and Tenant Act 1985 s.38.

    landlord, tenant, lease, tenancy—see Landlord and Tenant Act 1985 s.36, para.3A–702+.

    long lease —see s.169 and s.76 which provides that a lease is a long lease if it (a) is granted for a term of years certain exceeding 21 years; (b) is for a term fixed by law under a grant with a covenant or obligation for perpetual renewal (c) takes effect under Law of Property Act 1925 s.149(6) (leases terminable after a death or marriage); (d) was granted under the right to buy provisions of Housing Act 1985 Pt 5; (e) is a shared ownership lease; or (f) under Housing Act 1996 s.17 (the right to acquire). Section 77 contains certain exceptions.

    arbitration agreement, arbitral tribunal—see s.169(5) and Arbitration Act 1996 Pt 1.

    post-dispute arbitration agreement —see s.169(5). It means an arbitration agreement made after a breach has occurred (or is alleged to have occurred).

Section 168: supplementary

3A–1595   **169.**—(1) An agreement by a tenant under a long lease of a dwelling (other than a post-dispute arbitration agreement) is void in so far as it purports to provide for a determination—

    (a) in a particular manner, or

Paragraph numbers marked with a "+" can be found online and on CD.

(b) on particular evidence,

of any question which may be the subject of an application under section 168(4).

(2) For the purposes of section 168 it is finally determined that a breach of a covenant or condition in a lease has occurred—

    (a) if a decision that it has occurred is not appealed against or otherwise challenged, at the end of the period for bringing an appeal or other challenge, or

    (b) if such a decision is appealed against or otherwise challenged and not set aside in consequence of the appeal or other challenge, at the time specified in subsection (3).

(3) The time referred to in subsection (2)(b) is the time when the appeal or other challenge is disposed of—

    (a) by the determination of the appeal or other challenge and the expiry of the time for bringing a subsequent appeal (if any), or

    (b) by its being abandoned or otherwise ceasing to have effect.

(4) In section 168 and this section "long lease of a dwelling" does not include—

    (a) a tenancy to which Part 2 of the Landlord and Tenant Act 1954 (c.56) (business tenancies) applies,

    (b) a tenancy of an agricultural holding within the meaning of the Agricultural Holdings Act 1986 (c.5) in relation to which that Act applies, or

    (c) a farm business tenancy within the meaning of the Agricultural Tenancies Act 1995 (c.8).

(5) In section 168 and this section—

"arbitration agreement" and "arbitral tribunal" have the same meaning as in Part 1 of the Arbitration Act 1996 (c.23) and "post-dispute arbitration agreement", in relation to any breach (or alleged breach), means an arbitration agreement made after the breach has occurred (or is alleged to have occurred),

"dwelling" has the same meaning as in the 1985 Act,

"landlord" and "tenant" have the same meaning as in Chapter 1 of this Part, and

"long lease" has the meaning given by sections 76 and 77 of this Act, except that a shared ownership lease is a long lease whatever the tenant's total share.

(6) Section 146(7) of the Law of Property Act 1925 (c.20) applies for the purposes of section 168 and this section.

(7) Nothing in section 168 affects the service of a notice under section 146(1) of the Law of Property Act 1925 in respect of a failure to pay—

    (a) a service charge (within the meaning of section 18(1) of the 1985 Act), or

    (b) an administration charge (within the meaning of Part 1 of Schedule 11 to this Act).

Paragraph numbers marked with a "+" can be found online and on CD.

HOUSING

3A-1596 **implementation**—This section was brought into force in England on February 28, 2005 by the Commonhold and Leasehold Reform Act 2002 (Commencement No.5 and Saving and Transitional Provision) Order 2004 (SI 2004/3056) (c.127) and in Wales on May 31, 2005 by the Commonhold and Leasehold Reform Act 2002 (Commencement No.3 and Saving and Transitional Provision) (Wales) Order 2005 (SI 2005/1353) (w.101) (c.59).

dwelling—see Landlord and Tenant Act 1985 s.38.

service charges—see Landlord and Tenant Act 1985 s.18 as amended by Commonhold and Leasehold Reform Act 2002 Sch.9.

landlord, tenant, lease, tenancy—see Landlord and Tenant Act 1985 s.36, para.3A-702+.

administration charge—see Sch.11, Pt 1.

* * * *

Power to prescribe additional or different requirements

3A-1597 **171.**—(1) The appropriate national authority may by regulations prescribe requirements which must be met before a right of re-entry or forfeiture may be exercised in relation to a breach of a covenant or condition in a long lease of an unmortgaged dwelling.

(2) The regulations may specify that the requirements are to be in addition to, or instead of, requirements imposed otherwise than by the regulations.

(3) In this section "long lease of a dwelling" does not include—

(a) a tenancy to which Part 2 of the Landlord and Tenant Act 1954 (c.56) (business tenancies) applies,

(b) a tenancy of an agricultural holding within the meaning of the Agricultural Holdings Act 1986 (c.5) in relation to which that Act applies, or

(c) a farm business tenancy within the meaning of the Agricultural Tenancies Act 1995 (c.8).

(4) For the purposes of this section a dwelling is unmortgaged if it is not subject to a mortgage, charge or lien.

(5) In this section—

"dwelling" has the same meaning as in the 1985 Act, and

"long lease" has the meaning given by sections 76 and 77 of this Act, except that a shared ownership lease is a long lease whatever the tenant's total share.

Implementation

3A-1598 Section 171 was brought into force in so far as it confers power to make regulations on July 26, 2002 in England and on January 1, 2003 in Wales by the Commonhold and Leasehold Reform Act 2002 (Commencement No.1, Savings and Transitional Provisions) (England) Order 2002 (SI 2002/1912) (c.58) and the Commonhold and Leasehold Reform Act 2002 (Commencement No.1, Savings and Transitional Provisions) (Wales) Order 2002 (SI 2002/3012) (w.284) (c.96). It was brought fully into force in England on February 28, 2005 by the Commonhold and Leasehold Reform Act 2002 (Commencement No.5 and Saving and Transitional Provision) Order 2004 (SI 2004/3056) (c.127).

"regulations"

3A-1599 At present, there are no regulations.

dwelling—see Landlord and Tenant Act 1985 s.38.

Paragraph numbers marked with a "+" can be found online and on CD.

long lease —see s.76 which provides that a lease is a long lease if it (a) is granted for a term of years certain exceeding 21 years; (b) is for a term fixed by law under a grant with a covenant or obligation for perpetual renewal (c) takes effect under Law of Property Act 1925 s.149(6) (leases terminable after a death or marriage); (d) was granted under the right to buy provisions of Housing Act 1985 Pt 5; (e) is a shared ownership lease; or (f) under Housing Act 1996 s.17 (the right to acquire). Section 77 contains certain exceptions.

CROWN APPLICATION

Application to Crown

172.—(1) The following provisions apply in relation to Crown land **3A–1600** (as in relation to other land)—

    (a) sections 18 to 30B of (and the Schedule to) the 1985 Act (service charges, insurance and managing agents),

    [...]

    (d) sections 46 to 49 of the 1987 Act (information to be furnished to tenants),

    [...]

    (f) section 81 of the Housing Act 1996 (c.52) (restriction on termination of tenancy for failure to pay service charge etc.),

    (g) section 84 of (and Schedule 4 to) that Act (right to appoint surveyor), and

    (h) in this Chapter, the provisions relating to any of the provisions within paragraphs (a) to (g), Part 1 of Schedule 11 and sections 164 to 171.

(2) Land is Crown land if there is or has at any time been an interest or estate in the land—

    (a) comprised in the Crown Estate,

    (b) belonging to Her Majesty in right of the Duchy of Lancaster,

    (c) belonging to the Duchy of Cornwall, or

    (d) belonging to a government department or held on behalf of Her Majesty for the purposes of a government department.

(3) No failure by the Crown to perform a duty imposed by or by virtue of any of sections 21 to 23A of, or any of paragraphs 2 to 4A of the Schedule to, the 1985 Act makes the Crown criminally liable; but the High Court may declare any such failure without reasonable excuse to be unlawful.

Implementation

Section 172 was partially brought into force, on 30 September 2003 in England and **3A–1601** on March 30, 2004 in Wales by the Commonhold and Leasehold Reform Act 2002 (Commencement No.2 and Savings) (England) Order 2003 (SI 2003/1986) (c.82) and the Commonhold and Leasehold Reform Act 2002 (Commencement No.2 and Savings) (Wales) Order 2004 (SI 2004/669) (w.62) (c.25). See too the Commonhold and Leasehold Reform Act 2002 (Commencement No.5 and Saving and Transitional Provision) Order 2004 (SI 2004/3056) (c.127).

HOUSING

Paragraph numbers marked with a "+" can be found online and on CD.

* * * *

SCHEDULE 11

ADMINISTRATION CHARGES PART 1 REASONABLENESS OF ADMINISTRATION CHARGES

Meaning of "administration charge"

3A-1602 1.—(1) In this Part of this Schedule "administration charge" means an amount payable by a tenant of a dwelling as part of or in addition to the rent which is payable, directly or indirectly—

(a) for or in connection with the grant of approvals under his lease, or applications for such approvals,

(b) for or in connection with the provision of information or documents by or on behalf of the landlord or a person who is party to his lease otherwise than as landlord or tenant,

(c) in respect of a failure by the tenant to make a payment by the due date to the landlord or a person who is party to his lease otherwise than as landlord or tenant, or

(d) in connection with a breach (or alleged breach) of a covenant or condition in his lease.

(2) But an amount payable by the tenant of a dwelling the rent of which is registered under Part 4 of the Rent Act 1977 (c.42) is not an administration charge, unless the amount registered is entered as a variable amount in pursuance of section 71(4) of that Act.

(3) In this Part of this Schedule "variable administration charge" means an administration charge payable by a tenant which is neither—

(a) specified in his lease, nor

(b) calculated in accordance with a formula specified in his lease.

(4) An order amending sub-paragraph (1) may be made by the appropriate national authority.

Reasonableness of administration charges

3A-1603 2. A variable administration charge is payable only to the extent that the amount of the charge is reasonable.

3A-1604 3.—(1) Any party to a lease of a dwelling may apply to a leasehold valuation tribunal for an order varying the lease in such manner as is specified in the application on the grounds that—

(a) any administration charge specified in the lease is unreasonable, or

(b) any formula specified in the lease in accordance with which any administration charge is calculated is unreasonable.

(2) If the grounds on which the application was made are established to the satisfaction of the tribunal, it may make an order varying the lease in such manner as is specified in the order.

(3) The variation specified in the order may be—

(a) the variation specified in the application, or

(b) such other variation as the tribunal thinks fit.

(4) The tribunal may, instead of making an order varying the lease in such manner as is specified in the order, make an order directing the parties to the lease to vary it in such manner as is so specified.

(5) The tribunal may by order direct that a memorandum of any variation of a lease effected by virtue of this paragraph be endorsed on such documents as are specified in the order.

(6) Any such variation of a lease shall be binding not only on the parties to the lease for the time being but also on other persons (including any predecessors in title), whether or not they were parties to the proceedings in which the order was made.

Notice in connection with demands for administration charges

3A-1605 4.—(1) A demand for the payment of an administration charge must be accompanied by a summary of the rights and obligations of tenants of dwellings in relation to administration charges.

Paragraph numbers marked with a "+" can be found online and on CD.

(2) The appropriate national authority may make regulations prescribing requirements as to the form and content of such summaries of rights and obligations.

(3) A tenant may withhold payment of an administration charge which has been demanded from him if sub-paragraph (1) is not complied with in relation to the demand.

(4) Where a tenant withholds an administration charge under this paragraph, any provisions of the lease relating to non-payment or late payment of administration charges do not have effect in relation to the period for which he so withholds it.

Liability to pay administration charges

5.—(1) An application may be made to a leasehold valuation tribunal for a determination whether an administration charge is payable and, if it is, as to—

    (a) the person by whom it is payable,

    (b) the person to whom it is payable,

    (c) the amount which is payable,

    (d) the date at or by which it is payable, and

    (e) the manner in which it is payable.

3A–1606

(2) Sub-paragraph (1) applies whether or not any payment has been made.

(3) The jurisdiction conferred on a leasehold valuation tribunal in respect of any matter by virtue of sub-paragraph (1) is in addition to any jurisdiction of a court in respect of the matter.

(4) No application under sub-paragraph (1) may be made in respect of a matter which—

    (a) has been agreed or admitted by the tenant,

    (b) has been, or is to be, referred to arbitration pursuant to a post-dispute arbitration agreement to which the tenant is a party,

    (c) has been the subject of determination by a court, or

    (d) has been the subject of determination by an arbitral tribunal pursuant to a post-dispute arbitration agreement.

(5) But the tenant is not to be taken to have agreed or admitted any matter by reason only of having made any payment.

(6) An agreement by the tenant of a dwelling (other than a post-dispute arbitration agreement) is void in so far as it purports to provide for a determination—

    (a) in a particular manner, or

    (b) on particular evidence,

    of any question which may be the subject matter of an application under sub-paragraph (1).

Interpretation

6.—(1) This paragraph applies for the purposes of this Part of this Schedule.

3A–1607

(2) "Tenant" includes a statutory tenant.

(3) "Dwelling" and "statutory tenant" (and "landlord" in relation to a statutory tenant) have the same meanings as in the 1985 Act.

(4) "Post-dispute arbitration agreement", in relation to any matter, means an arbitration agreement made after a dispute about the matter has arisen.

(5) "Arbitration agreement" and "arbitral tribunal" have the same meanings as in Part 1 of the Arbitration Act 1996 (c.23).

HOUSING

Paragraph numbers marked with a "+" can be found online and on CD.

Asylum and Immigration (Treatment of Claimants, etc.) Act 2004

3A–1607.1

(2004 c.19)

Paragraph numbers marked with a "+" denote content that is available on White Book on Westlaw UK or the Civil Procedure CD.

Housing Act 2004

3A–1611

(2004 c.34)

CHAPTER 4

TENANCY DEPOSIT SCHEMES

Tenancy deposit schemes

3A–1612 212.—(1) The appropriate national authority must make arrangements for securing that one or more tenancy deposit schemes are available for the purpose of safeguarding tenancy deposits paid in connection with shorthold tenancies.

(2) For the purposes of this Chapter a "tenancy deposit scheme" is a scheme which—

(a) is made for the purpose of safeguarding tenancy deposits paid in connection with shorthold tenancies and facilitating the resolution of disputes arising in connection with such deposits, and

(b) complies with the requirements of Schedule 10.

(3) Arrangements under subsection (1) must be arrangements made with any body or person under which the body or person ("the scheme administrator") undertakes to establish and maintain a tenancy deposit scheme of a description specified in the arrangements.

(4) The appropriate national authority may—

(a) give financial assistance to the scheme administrator;

(b) make payments to the scheme administrator (otherwise than as financial assistance) in pursuance of arrangements under subsection (1).

Paragraph numbers marked with a "+" can be found online and on CD.

(5) The appropriate national authority may, in such manner and on such terms as it thinks fit, guarantee the discharge of any financial obligation incurred by the scheme administrator in connection with arrangements under subsection (1).

(6) Arrangements under subsection (1) must require the scheme administrator to give the appropriate national authority, in such manner and at such times as it may specify, such information and facilities for obtaining information as it may specify.

(7) The appropriate national authority may make regulations conferring or imposing—

> (a) on scheme administrators, or
> (b) on scheme administrators of any description specified in the regulations,

such powers or duties in connection with arrangements under subsection (1) as are so specified.

(8) In this Chapter—

> "authorised", in relation to a tenancy deposit scheme, means that the scheme is in force in accordance with arrangements under subsection (1);
>
> "custodial scheme" and "insurance scheme" have the meaning given by paragraph 1(2) and (3) of Schedule 10);
>
> "money" means money in the form of cash or otherwise;
>
> "shorthold tenancy" means an assured shorthold tenancy within the meaning of Chapter 2 of Part 1 of the Housing Act 1988 (c. 50);
>
> "tenancy deposit", in relation to a shorthold tenancy, means any money intended to be held (by the landlord or otherwise) as security for—
>
>> (a) the performance of any obligations of the tenant, or
>>
>> (b) the discharge of any liability of his, arising under or in connection with the tenancy.

(9) In this Chapter—

> (a) references to a landlord or landlords in relation to any shorthold tenancy or tenancies include references to a person or persons acting on his or their behalf in relation to the tenancy or tenancies, and
> (b) references to a tenancy deposit being held in accordance with a scheme include, in the case of a custodial scheme, references to an amount representing the deposit being held in accordance with the scheme.

Note —Brought into force on April 6, 2007, in relation to England by SI 2007/1068 and in relation to Wales by SI 2007/305.   **3A–1613**

Editorial introduction

Tenancy deposit schemes have two main purposes. They aim to safeguard tenancy deposits paid in connection with assured shorthold tenancies and to facilitate the resolution of disputes arising in connection with such deposits. All authorised tenancy deposit schemes must comply with the requirements of Sch.10. Schemes are expected to   **3A–1614**

Paragraph numbers marked with a "+" can be found online and on CD.

be self-financing, but s.212(4) allows the appropriate national authority to give financial assistance. Tenancy deposit schemes must be either a custodial scheme or an insurance scheme (Sch.10, para.1(1)). Landlords may choose with which type of scheme to comply. A custodial scheme requires a landlord to pay any deposit money received to a scheme administrator, who is to keep the money in a separate account until the end of the tenancy when it will be returned to the landlord or the tenant, as appropriate. An insurance scheme allows a landlord to retain the deposit during the tenancy. At its end, if the tenant disputes any amount of the deposit that the landlord proposes to retain, the landlord must pay the disputed amount into an account held by the scheme administrator, who will hold it until the dispute is resolved. If the landlord has opted for this scheme, the scheme administrator is obliged to pay the tenant any sum that he is entitled to recover following the determination of the dispute, whether or not the landlord complies with his obligation to pay that amount into the scheme. Accordingly, the scheme administrator must maintain insurance to cover any failure by the landlord to do so, contributions towards the cost of which may be passed on to those landlords who opt for this approach as part of the administrators' costs (Sch.10, paras 5–8).

The primary sanction for non-compliance with the scheme is that landlords may not serve the Housing Act 1988 s.21 notices at any time where a deposit is not being safeguarded in accordance with an authorised scheme or where either the initial requirements of the scheme have not been met or the prescribed information regarding the safeguarding the deposit has not been given. See s.215 below. In addition tenants are entitled to claim a sum equivalent to three times the amount of the deposit from a defaulting landlord—see s.214 below.

tenancy deposit
3A–1615   See s.212(8).

shorthold tenancy
3A–1616   See s.212(8) and (9) and Housing Act 1988 s.19.

"regulations"
3A–1617   See Housing (Tenancy Deposit Schemes) Order 2007 (SI 2007/796), Housing (Tenancy Deposits) (Prescribed Information) Order 2007 (SI 2007/797) and Housing (Tenancy Deposits) (Specified Interest Rate) Order 2007 (SI 2007/798).

Requirements relating to tenancy deposits

3A–1618   **213.**—(1) Any tenancy deposit paid to a person in connection with a shorthold tenancy must, as from the time when it is received, be dealt with in accordance with an authorised scheme.

(2) No person may require the payment of a tenancy deposit in connection with a shorthold tenancy which is not to be subject to the requirement in subsection (1).

(3) Where a landlord receives a tenancy deposit in connection with a shorthold tenancy, the initial requirements of an authorised scheme must be complied with by the landlord in relation to the deposit within the period of 14 days beginning with the date on which it is received.

(4) For the purposes of this section "the initial requirements" of an authorised scheme are such requirements imposed by the scheme as fall to be complied with by a landlord on receiving such a tenancy deposit.

(5) A landlord who has received such a tenancy deposit must give the tenant and any relevant person such information relating to—

(a) the authorised scheme applying to the deposit,

Paragraph numbers marked with a "+" can be found online and on CD.

(b) compliance by the landlord with the initial requirements of the scheme in relation to the deposit, and

(c) the operation of provisions of this Chapter in relation to the deposit,

as may be prescribed.

(6) The information required by subsection (5) must be given to the tenant and any relevant person—

(a) in the prescribed form or in a form substantially to the same effect, and

(b) within the period of 14 days beginning with the date on which the deposit is received by the landlord.

(7) No person may, in connection with a shorthold tenancy, require a deposit which consists of property other than money.

(8) In subsection (7) "deposit" means a transfer of property intended to be held (by the landlord or otherwise) as security for—

(a) the performance of any obligations of the tenant, or

(b) the discharge of any liability of his, arising under or in connection with the tenancy.

(9) The provisions of this section apply despite any agreement to the contrary.

(10) In this section—

"prescribed" means prescribed by an order made by the appropriate national authority;

"property" means moveable property;

"relevant person" means any person who, in accordance with arrangements made with the tenant, paid the deposit on behalf of the tenant.

Note —Brought into force on April 6, 2007, in relation to England by SI 2007/1068 and in relation to Wales by SI 2007/305. **3A–1619**

"tenancy deposit"

See s.212(8). **3A–1620**

"authorised"

See s.212(8). **3A–1620.1**

"prescribed"

See s.213(10) and the Housing (Tenancy Deposits) (Prescribed Information) Order 2007 (SI 2007/797). **3A–1620.2**

"shorthold tenancy"

See s.212(8) and (9) and Housing Act 1988 s.19. **3A–1621**

Proceedings relating to tenancy deposits

214.—(1) Where a tenancy deposit has been paid in connection with a shorthold tenancy, the tenant or any relevant person (as defined by section 213(10)) may make an application to a county court on the grounds— **3A–1622**

(a) that the initial requirements of an authorised scheme (see section 213(4)) have not, or section 213(6)(a) has not, been complied with in relation to the deposit; or

Paragraph numbers marked with a "+" can be found online and on CD.

(b) that he has been notified by the landlord that a particular authorised scheme applies to the deposit but has been unable to obtain confirmation from the scheme administrator that the deposit is being held in accordance with the scheme.

(2) Subsections (3) and (4) apply if on such an application the court—

(a) is satisfied that those requirements have not, or section 213(6)(a) has not, been complied with in relation to the deposit, or

(b) is not satisfied that the deposit is being held in accordance with an authorised scheme,

as the case may be.

(3) The court must, as it thinks fit, either—

(a) order the person who appears to the court to be holding the deposit to repay it to the applicant, or

(b) order that person to pay the deposit into the designated account held by the scheme administrator under an authorised custodial scheme,

within the period of 14 days beginning with the date of the making of the order.

(4) The court must also order the landlord to pay to the applicant a sum of money equal to three times the amount of the deposit within the period of 14 days beginning with the date of the making of the order.

(5) Where any deposit given in connection with a shorthold tenancy could not be lawfully required as a result of section 213(7), the property in question is recoverable from the person holding it by the person by whom it was given as a deposit.

(6) In subsection (5) "deposit" has the meaning given by section 213(8).

3A-1623   *Note* —Brought into force on April 6, 2007, in relation to England by SI 2007/1068 and in relation to Wales by SI 2007/305.

"tenancy deposit"
3A-1624   See s.212(8).

"relevant person"
3A-1625   See s.213(10).

"shorthold tenancy"
3A-1626   See s.212(8) and (9) and Housing Act 1988 s.19.

"authorised scheme"
3A-1627   See s.213(4).

Procedure
3A-1627.1   Any application by a tenant for an order for repayment of the deposit, or an order for it to be paid into a designated account under a custodial scheme and for an order that the landlord pay a sum equivalent to three times the amount of the deposit should be started in the county court for the district in which the land is situated in accordance with CPR Pt 56. See s.214(1) and the commentary to CPR Pt 56.

Paragraph numbers marked with a "+" can be found online and on CD.

Proceedings relating to tenancy deposits

See in general the editorial introduction above. It appears that if landlords fail to comply with the requirements of s.213, courts have no discretion and must make orders sought under s.214. However, it has been held in the county court that provision of prescribed information outside the fourteen days required by s.213(5) and (6) does not trigger the right to a sum equivalent to three times the deposit, if the information is supplied before any application is made. (*Harvey v Bamforth* Sheffield County Court, August 8, 2008, November 2008 *Legal Action* 18).

3A–1627.2

Sanctions for non-compliance

215.—(1) If a tenancy deposit has been paid in connection with a shorthold tenancy, no section 21 notice may be given in relation to the tenancy at a time when—

3A–1628

    (a) the deposit is not being held in accordance with an authorised scheme, or

    (b) the initial requirements of such a scheme (see section 213(4)) have not been complied with in relation to the deposit.

(2) If section 213(6) is not complied with in relation to a deposit given in connection with a shorthold tenancy, no section 21 notice may be given in relation to the tenancy until such time as section 213(6)(a) is complied with.

(3) If any deposit given in connection with a shorthold tenancy could not be lawfully required as a result of section 213(7), no section 21 notice may be given in relation to the tenancy until such time as the property in question is returned to the person by whom it was given as a deposit.

(4) In subsection (3) "deposit" has the meaning given by section 213(8).

(5) In this section a "section 21 notice" means a notice under section 21(1)(b) or (4)(a) of the Housing Act 1988 (recovery of possession on termination of shorthold tenancy).

Note —Brought into force on April 6, 2007, in relation to England by SI 2007/1068 and in relation to Wales by SI 2007/305.

3A–1629

Landlords may not serve notices under Housing Act 1988 s.21 at any time where a deposit is not being safeguarded in accordance with an authorised scheme or where either the initial requirements of the scheme have not been met or the prescribed information regarding the safeguarding the deposit has not been given.

3A–1630

"tenancy deposit"

See s.212(8).

3A–1631

"shorthold tenancy"

See s.212(8) and (9) and Housing Act 1988 s.19.

3A–1632

"section 21 notice"

See Housing Act 1988 s.21 at 3A–889 and commentary at 3A–896.

3A–1632.1

"authorised scheme"

See s.213(4).

3A–1633

Paragraph numbers marked with a "+" can be found online and on CD.

* * * *

SECTION 212   SCHEDULE 10

PROVISIONS RELATING TO TENANCY DEPOSIT SCHEMES

Schemes to be custodial schemes or insurance schemes

3A–1634   1.—(1)A tenancy deposit scheme must be either—
   (a) a custodial scheme, or
   (b) an insurance scheme.

   (2) A "custodial scheme" is a scheme under which—
   (a) tenancy deposits in connection with shorthold tenancies are paid to the landlords under the tenancies,
   (b) amounts representing the deposits are then paid by the landlords into a designated account held by the scheme administrator, and
   (c) those amounts are kept by the scheme administrator in that account until such time as, in accordance with the scheme, they fall to be paid (wholly or in part) to the landlords or tenants under the tenancies.

   (3) An "insurance scheme" is a scheme under which—
   (a) tenancy deposits in connection with shorthold tenancies are paid to the landlords under the tenancies,
   (b) such deposits are retained by the landlords on the basis that, at the end of the tenancies—
      (i) such amounts in respect of the deposits as are agreed between the tenants and the landlords will be repaid to the tenants, and
      (ii) such amounts as the tenants request to be repaid to them and which are not so repaid will, in accordance with directions given by the scheme administrator, be paid into a designated account held by the scheme administrator,
   (c) amounts paid into that account are kept by the scheme administrator in the account until such time as, in accordance with the scheme, they fall to be paid (wholly or in part) to the landlords or tenants under the tenancies,
   (d) landlords undertake to reimburse the scheme administrator, in accordance with directions given by him, in respect of any amounts in respect of the deposits paid to the tenants by the scheme administrator (other than amounts paid to the tenants as mentioned in paragraph (c)), and
   (e) insurance is maintained by the scheme administrator in respect of failures by landlords to comply with such directions.

Provisions applying to custodial and insurance schemes

3A–1635   2.—(1)A custodial scheme must conform with the following provisions—
   paragraphs 3 to 4C, and
   paragraphs 9 to 10C.

   (2) An insurance scheme must conform with the following provisions—
   paragraphs 5 to 8, and
   paragraphs 9 and 10.

Custodial schemes: general

3A–1636   3.—(1)This paragraph applies to a custodial scheme.

   (2) The scheme must provide for any landlord who receives a tenancy deposit in connection with a shorthold tenancy to pay an amount equal to the deposit into a designated account held by the scheme administrator.

   (3) The designated account must not contain anything other than amounts paid into it as mentioned in sub-paragraph (2) and any interest accruing on such amounts.

   (4) Subject to sub-paragraph (5), the scheme administrator may retain any interest accruing on such amounts.

Paragraph numbers marked with a "+" can be found online and on CD.

(5) The relevant arrangements under section 212(1) may provide for any amount paid in accordance with paragraph 4 or 4C to be paid with interest—

(a) in respect of the period during which the relevant amount has remained in the designated account, and

(b) at such rate as the appropriate national authority may specify by order.

(6) With the exception of any interest retained in accordance with sub-paragraph (4), nothing contained in the designated account may be used to fund the administration of the scheme.

(7) In this paragraph "the relevant amount", in relation to a tenancy deposit, means the amount paid into the designated account in respect of the deposit.

Custodial schemes: termination of tenancies

4.—(1)A custodial scheme must make provision— **3A–1637**

(a) for enabling the tenant and the landlord under a shorthold tenancy in connection with which a tenancy deposit is held in accordance with the scheme to apply, at any time after the tenancy has ended, for the whole or part of the relevant amount to be paid to him, and

(b) for such an application to be dealt with by the scheme administrator in accordance with the following provisions of this paragraph.

(2) Sub-paragraph (3) applies where the tenant and the landlord notify the scheme administrator that they have agreed that the relevant amount should be paid—

(a) wholly to one of them, or

(b) partly to the one and partly to the other.

(3) If, having received such a notification, the scheme administrator is satisfied that the tenant and the landlord have so agreed, the scheme administrator must arrange for the relevant amount to be paid, in accordance with the agreement, within the period of 10 days beginning with the date on which the notification is received by the scheme administrator.

(4) Sub-paragraph (5) applies where the tenant or the landlord notifies the scheme administrator that—

(a) a court has decided that the relevant amount is payable either wholly to one of them or partly to the one and partly to the other, and

(b) that decision has become final.

(4A) Sub-paragraph (5) also applies where the tenant or the landlord notifies the scheme administrator that a person acting as an adjudicator under the provision made under paragraph 10 has made a binding decision that the relevant amount is payable either wholly to one of them or partly to one and partly to the other.

(5) If, having received a notification as mentioned in sub-paragraph (4) or (4A), the scheme administrator is satisfied as to the matters mentioned in that sub-paragraph, the scheme administrator must arrange for the relevant amount to be paid, in accordance with the decision, within the period of 10 days beginning with the date on which the notification is received by the scheme administrator.

(6) For the purposes of this Schedule a decision becomes final—

(a) if not appealed against, at the end of the period for bringing an appeal, or

(b) if appealed against, at the time when the appeal (or any further appeal) is disposed of.

(7) An appeal is disposed of—

(a) if it is determined and the period for bringing any further appeal has ended, or

(b) if it is abandoned or otherwise ceases to have effect.

(8) In this paragraph "the relevant amount" has the meaning given by paragraph 3(7).

Custodial schemes: termination of tenancies—absent or un-cooperative landlord or tenant

4A.—(1) The provision made by a custodial scheme for the purposes of paragraph **3A–1638**
4(1) in relation to the treatment of the relevant amount at the end of a tenancy must include provision—

(a) for enabling the landlord, if he considers that the conditions set out in sub-paragraph (2) are met, to apply to the scheme administrator for

Paragraph numbers marked with a "+" can be found online and on CD.

the whole or a specified part of the relevant amount ("the amount claimed") to be paid to him; and

(b) for such an application to be dealt with by the scheme administrator in accordance with the provisions of paragraph 4C.

(2) Such an application may be made if—

(a) at least 14 days have elapsed since the day on which the tenancy ended;

(b) the landlord and tenant have not reached an agreement under paragraph 4(2) with respect to the amount claimed;

(c) either sub-paragraph (3) or sub-paragraph (4) applies; and

(d) the landlord believes that he is entitled to be paid the amount claimed and that the amount claimed is referable to sums falling within sub-paragraph (5).

(3) This sub-paragraph applies if the landlord has no current address for, or other means of contacting, the tenant.

(4) This sub-paragraph applies if—

(a) the tenant has, since the tenancy ended, received from the landlord a written notice asking whether the tenant accepts that the landlord should be paid the whole or a specified part of the relevant amount; and

(b) the tenant has failed to respond to that notice within the period of 14 days beginning with the day on which he received the notice by indicating to the landlord whether he accepts that the landlord should be paid the relevant amount or the specified part of it (as the case may be).

(5) The amount claimed must be referable to—

(a) an amount of unpaid rent or any other sum due under the terms of the tenancy; or

(b) a liability of the tenant to the landlord arising under or in connection with the tenancy in respect of—

(i) damage to the premises subject to the tenancy, or

(ii) loss of or damage to property on those premises, other than damage caused by fair wear and tear.

(6) If sub-paragraph (4) applies and the notice specifies part of the relevant amount, the amount claimed in the application must not exceed the specified part.

(7) The application must be accompanied by a statutory declaration made by the landlord stating—

(a) the date on which the tenancy ended;

(b) that the landlord and the tenant have not reached any agreement under paragraph 4(2) with respect to the amount claimed, with details of any communications between them since that date (whether relating to the relevant amount or otherwise);

(c) the basis on which the amount claimed is calculated, with particulars of any facts relied on to justify claiming that amount;

(d) if the landlord relies on the condition in sub-paragraph (3), that he has no current address for, or other means of contacting, the tenant, giving particulars of any address (other than the premises subject to the tenancy) and other contact details (including telephone numbers or e mail addresses) which the landlord has had for the tenant;

(e) if the landlord relies on the condition in sub-paragraph (4), that the condition is met, with particulars of the facts relied on to demonstrate that it is met and attaching a copy of the notice given to the tenant;

(f) any information he has as to the whereabouts of the tenant;

(g) that he gives his consent, in the event of the tenant disputing that the landlord should be paid the amount claimed, for the dispute to be resolved through the use of the dispute resolution service;

(h) that he considers that he is entitled to be paid the amount claimed; and

(f) that he makes the statutory declaration knowing that if he knowingly and wilfully makes a false declaration he may be liable to prosecution under the Perjury Act 1911[2].

Paragraph numbers marked with a "+" can be found online and on CD.

4B.—(1) The provision made by a custodial scheme for the purposes of paragraph 4(1) in relation to the treatment of the relevant amount at the end of a tenancy must include provision—

    (a) for enabling the tenant, if he considers that the conditions set out in sub-paragraph (2) are met, to apply to the scheme administrator for the whole or a specified part of the relevant amount ("the amount claimed") to be paid to him; and

    (b) for such an application to be dealt with by the scheme administrator in accordance with the provisions of paragraph 4C.

(2) Such an application may be made if—

    (a) at least 14 days have elapsed since the day on which the tenancy ended;

    (b) the landlord and tenant have not reached an agreement under paragraph 4(2) with respect to the amount claimed;

    (c) either sub-paragraph (3) or sub-paragraph (4) applies; and

    (d) the tenant believes that he is entitled to be paid the amount claimed.

(3) This sub-paragraph applies if the tenant has no current address for, or other means of contacting, the landlord.

(4) This sub-paragraph applies if—

    (a) the landlord has, since the tenancy ended, received from the tenant a written notice asking whether the landlord accepts that the tenant should be paid the whole or a specified part of the relevant amount; and

    (b) the landlord has failed to respond to that notice within the period of 14 days beginning with the day on which he received the notice by indicating to the tenant whether he accepts that the tenant should be paid the relevant amount or the specified part of it (as the case may be).

(5) If sub-paragraph (4) applies and the notice specifies part of the relevant amount, the amount claimed in the application must not exceed the specified part.

(6) The application must be accompanied by a statutory declaration made by the tenant stating—

    (a) the date on which the tenancy ended;

    (b) that the landlord and the tenant have not reached any agreement under paragraph 4(2) with respect to the amount claimed, with details of any communications between them since that date (whether relating to the relevant amount or otherwise);

    (c) if the tenant relies on the condition in sub-paragraph (3), that he has no current address for, or other means of contacting, the landlord, giving particulars of any address and other contact details (including telephone numbers or e mail addresses) which the tenant has had for the landlord;

    (d) if the tenant relies on the condition in sub-paragraph (4), that the condition is met, with particulars of the facts relied on to demonstrate that it is met and attaching a copy of the notice given to the landlord;

    (e) any information he has as to the whereabouts of the landlord;

    (f) that he gives his consent, in the event of the landlord disputing that the tenant should be paid the amount claimed, for the dispute to be resolved through the use of the dispute resolution service;

    (g) that he considers that he is entitled to be paid the amount claimed; and

    (h) that he makes the statutory declaration knowing that if he knowingly and wilfully makes a false declaration he may be liable to prosecution under the Perjury Act 1911[3].

4C.—(1) Immediately upon receipt of—

    (a) a duly completed application from the landlord, accompanied by a statutory declaration which appears to meet the requirements of paragraph 4A(7), or

    (b) a duly completed application from the tenant, accompanied by a statutory declaration which appears to meet the requirements of paragraph 4B(6), the scheme administrator must give to the tenant or, as the case may be, the landlord ("the other party") a copy of the application and

Paragraph numbers marked with a "+" can be found online and on CD.

accompanying statutory declaration and a notice under sub-paragraph
(2).

(2) A notice under this sub-paragraph is a notice—
    (a) asking the other party to indicate—
        (i) whether he accepts that the applicant should be paid the whole
           or part of the amount claimed;
        (ii) if he accepts that part of the amount claimed should be paid,
           the amount he accepts should be paid; and
        (iii) if he does not accept that the applicant should be paid the
           whole of the amount claimed, whether he consents to the
           dispute being resolved through the use of the dispute resolu-
           tion service; and
    (b) warning the other party that—
        (i) the amount claimed will be paid to the applicant unless, within
           the relevant period, the other party informs the scheme
           administrator that he does not accept that the whole of the
           amount claimed should be paid to the applicant; and
        (ii) if the other party responds to the scheme administrator inform-
           ing him that he does not accept that the whole of the amount
           claimed should be paid to the applicant, but fails to respond
           within the relevant period to the question mentioned in
           paragraph (a)(iii), he will be treated as having given his consent
           for the dispute to be resolved through the use of the dispute
           resolution service.

(3) If within the relevant period the scheme administrator receives a response
from the other party to the effect that he accepts that the amount claimed should be
paid to the applicant—
    (a) the application must be granted; and
    (b) the scheme administrator must arrange for the amount claimed to be
        paid to the applicant within the period of 10 days beginning with the
        day on which the scheme administrator receives that response.

(4) If within the relevant period the scheme administrator receives a response
from the other party to the effect that he does not accept that the applicant should be
paid any of the amount claimed—
    (a) the application must be refused;
    (b) the scheme administrator must not pay the amount claimed to either
        party except in accordance with the relevant provisions of paragraph 4;
        and
    (c) the scheme administrator must inform the applicant of the other party's
        response to the questions asked in the notice under sub-paragraph (2).

(5) If within the relevant period the scheme administrator receives a response
from the other party to the effect that he accepts that part of the amount claimed
should be paid to the applicant—
    (a) sub-paragraph (3) applies in relation to that part of the amount
        claimed; and
    (b) sub-paragraph (4) applies to so much of the application as relates to
        the rest of the amount claimed.

(6) If the scheme administrator does not, within the relevant period, receive a response from the other party indicating whether he accepts that the whole or part of
the amount claimed should be paid to the applicant, the scheme administrator must
arrange for the amount claimed to be paid to the applicant within the period of 10
days beginning with the day after the last day of the relevant period.

(7) If within the relevant period the scheme administrator receives a response
from the other party to the effect that he does not accept that the applicant should be
paid the whole of the amount claimed but the other party fails within that period to
indicate whether he consents to the dispute being resolved through the use of the
dispute resolution service—
    (a) the other party is to be treated as having given his consent to the use of
        that service; and

(b) the scheme administrator must inform the applicant that such consent is treated as having been given.

(8) In this paragraph "the relevant period", in relation to the application, means the period of 14 days beginning with the day on which the notice mentioned in sub-paragraph (2) is received by the other party.

Insurance schemes: general

5.—(1)This paragraph applies to an insurance scheme.

3A–1639

[(1A) The scheme must make provision as to the requirements that fall to be complied with by the landlord or by the scheme administrator where—

(a) a landlord wishes to retain a tenancy deposit under the scheme; or

(b) a landlord retaining a tenancy deposit under the scheme (in relation to a tenancy that has not terminated) gives notice to the scheme administrator that he no longer wishes to retain the deposit under that scheme.]

(2) The scheme must provide that any landlord by whom a tenancy deposit is retained under the scheme must give the scheme administrator an undertaking that, if the scheme administrator directs the landlord to pay him any amount in respect of the deposit in accordance with paragraph 6(3) or (7), the landlord will comply with such a direction.

(3) The scheme must require the scheme administrator to effect, and maintain in force, adequate insurance in respect of failures by landlords by whom tenancy deposits are retained under the scheme to comply with such directions as are mentioned in sub-paragraph (2).

(3A) The scheme may make provision enabling the scheme administrator to determine that, by virtue of the landlord's failure to comply with a relevant obligation, a tenancy deposit which has previously been retained by a landlord under the scheme (and which relates to a tenancy which has not ended) is to cease to be retained under the scheme.

(3B) Provision under sub-paragraph (3A) must require the scheme administrator, before making a determination, to give a notice to the landlord stating that the scheme administrator proposes to make such a determination and the reasons for the proposal.

(4) If the scheme provides for landlords participating in the scheme to be members of the scheme, the scheme may provide for a landlord's membership to be terminated by the scheme administrator in the event of any failure by the landlord to comply with a relevant obligation.

(4A) Provision made under sub-paragraph (4) must require the scheme administrator, before determining that the landlord's membership be terminated, to give a notice to the landlord stating that the scheme administrator proposes to make such a determination and the reasons for the proposal.

(4B) On the termination of a landlord's membership under sub-paragraph (4)—

(a) any tenancy deposits previously retained by the landlord under the scheme (in relation to tenancies which had not ended before the termination) cease to be retained under the scheme; but

(b) the scheme continues to apply to a tenancy deposit retained by the landlord under the scheme in relation to a tenancy which ended before the termination as if the landlord were still a member.

(5) The scheme may provide for landlords participating in the scheme to pay to the scheme administrator—

(a) fees in respect of the administration of the scheme, and

(b) contributions in respect of the cost of the insurance referred to in sub-paragraph (3).

(6) Paragraph 5A makes further provision in relation to the procedure to be followed after a notice of the kind mentioned in sub-paragraph (1A)(b), (3B) or (4A) has been given in accordance with the scheme.

(7) In this paragraph "relevant obligation" means—

(a) the duty to comply with a direction mentioned in sub-paragraph (2); or

(b) any obligation under the scheme which is specified in the scheme as a relevant obligation for the purposes of this paragraph.

Requirements where deposit is to cease to be retained under an insurance scheme

Paragraph numbers marked with a "+" can be found online and on CD.

HOUSING

5A.—(1) This paragraph applies in relation to—

    (a) notice of the kind mentioned in paragraph 5(1A)(b) or (3B), or

    (b) a notice from the scheme administrator stating that he proposes to terminate a landlord's membership of the scheme under paragraph 5(4), given in accordance with an insurance scheme.

given in accordance with an insurance scheme.

(2) The scheme must make provision for the scheme administrator, in the case of a notice of the kind mentioned in paragraph 5(1A)(b) which has not been not withdrawn—

    (a) to determine the date on which the tenancy deposit is to cease to be retained under the scheme; and

    (b) to give a notice under sub-paragraph (4) to the landlord and to the tenant.

(3) The scheme must make provision for the scheme administrator, in the case of a notice of the kind mentioned in paragraph 5(3B), to take the following steps after the end of the period of 14 days beginning with the day on which that notice is received—

    (a) to determine whether the deposit should cease to be retained under the scheme and, if so, the date on which it is to cease to be so retained;

    (b) if the determination is that the deposit should continue to be retained under the scheme, to give a notice of the determination to the landlord;

    (c) if the determination is that the deposit should cease to be so retained, to give a notice under sub-paragraph (4) to the landlord and to the tenant.

(4) A notice under this sub-paragraph is a notice—

    (a) identifying the tenancy deposit in question;

    (b) informing the recipients of the notice of the determination made by the scheme administrator and stating the date when the deposit ceases to be retained under the scheme; and

    (c) giving a general explanation of the continuing effect of sections 213 to 215 of this Act in relation to the deposit (including in particular the effect of section 213 as modified by sub-paragraph (9)).

(5) The scheme must make provision for the scheme administrator, in the case of a notice of the kind mentioned in sub-paragraph (1)(b), to take the following steps after the end of the period of 14 days beginning with the day on which that notice is received—

    (a) to determine whether to terminate the landlord's membership and, if so, the date on which his membership is to terminate;

    (b) if the determination is that the landlord should continue as a member, to give a notice of the determination to the landlord; and

    (c) if the determination is that the membership should be terminated, to give a notice under sub-paragraph (6) to the landlord and to the tenant under any tenancy in relation to which a deposit affected by the determination is retained under the scheme.

(6) A notice under this sub-paragraph is a notice—

    (a) informing the recipients of the notice of the determination by the scheme administrator that the landlord's membership of the scheme is to be terminated and stating the date on which his membership terminates;

    (b) giving a general explanation of the effect of the termination on any tenancy deposits retained by the landlord under the scheme; and

    (c) giving a general explanation of the continuing effect of sections 213 to 215 of this Act in relation to any tenancy deposits that cease to be retained under the scheme as a result of the termination of membership (including in particular the effect of section 213 as modified by sub-paragraph (9)).

(7) The date determined under sub-paragraph (2)(a), (3)(a) or (5)(a) must not be within the period of three months beginning with the day on which the original notice mentioned in sub-paragraph (1) was received.

(8) A notice under sub-paragraph (4) or (6) must be given at least two months before the date on which the deposit ceases to be retained under the scheme or the landlord's membership terminates (as the case may be).

Paragraph numbers marked with a "+" can be found online and on CD.

(9) In the application of section 213 to a tenancy deposit which ceases to be retained under an insurance scheme ("the old scheme") by virtue of a determination mentioned in this paragraph—

  (a) references to receiving the deposit include a reference to ceasing to retain it under the terms of the old scheme;

  (b) subsection (3) has effect as if for the words "within the period of 14 days beginning with the date on which it is received" there were substituted "before the deposit ceases to be retained under the old scheme"; and

  (c) subsection (6)(b) has effect as if the reference to the date on which the landlord receives the deposit were a reference to the date on which the deposit ceases to be retained under the old scheme.

Insurance schemes: termination of tenancies

6.—(1) An insurance scheme must make provision in accordance with this paragraph **3A–1640** and paragraphs 6A to 8 in relation to the respective obligations of the landlord and the scheme administrator where—

  (a) a tenancy deposit has been retained by the landlord under the scheme, and

  (b) the tenancy has ended.

(2) Sub-paragraphs (3) to (9) apply where the tenant notifies the scheme administrator that—

  (a) the tenant has requested the landlord to repay to him the whole or any part of the deposit, and

  (b) the amount in question ("the outstanding amount") has not been repaid to him within the period of 10 days beginning with the date on which the request was made.

(2A) When a tenant gives notice under sub-paragraph (2) he must also indicate whether he consents to any dispute as to the amount to be repaid to him being resolved through the use of the dispute resolution service.

(3) On receiving a notification in accordance with sub-paragraph (2), the scheme administrator must direct the landlord—

  (a) to pay an amount equal to the outstanding amount into a designated account held by the scheme administrator, and

  (b) to do so within the period of 10 days beginning with the date on which the direction is received by the landlord.

(4) The following sub-paragraphs apply where the tenant or the landlord notifies the scheme administrator—

  (a) that a court has decided that the outstanding amount is payable either wholly to one of them or partly to the one and partly to the other and the decision has become final (see paragraph 4(6) and (7)),

  (b) that the tenant and landlord have agreed that such an amount is to be paid either wholly to one of them or partly to the one and partly to the other; or

  (c) that a person acting as an adjudicator under the provision made under paragraph 10 has made a binding decision that the outstanding amount is payable either wholly to one of them or partly to one and partly to the other.

(5) If the scheme administrator is satisfied as to the matters mentioned in sub-paragraph (4)(a), (b) or (c) (as the case may be), he must—

  (a) pay to the tenant any amount due to him in accordance with the decision or agreement (and, to the extent possible, pay that amount out of any amount held by him by virtue of sub-paragraph (3)), and

  (b) comply with sub-paragraph (6) or (7), as the case may be.

(6) Where any amount held by the scheme administrator by virtue of sub-paragraph (3) is more than any amount due to the tenant in accordance with the decision or agreement, the scheme administrator must pay the balance to the landlord.

(7) Where any amount so held by the scheme administrator is less than any amount so due to the tenant, the scheme administrator must direct the landlord to pay him the difference within the period of 10 days beginning with the date on which the direction is received by the landlord.

Paragraph numbers marked with a "+" can be found online and on CD.

(8) The scheme administrator must pay any amounts required to be paid to the tenant or the landlord as mentioned in sub-paragraph (5)(a) or (6) within 10 days beginning with the date on which the notification is received by the scheme administrator.

(9) The landlord must comply with any direction given in accordance with sub-paragraph (3) or (7).

Notice to be sent to landlord when a direction under paragraph 6(3) is given

3A–1641   6A.—(1) This paragraph applies where the scheme administrator of an insurance scheme gives a direction under paragraph 6(3) to a landlord.

(2) The scheme administrator must also send to the landlord a notice—

    (a) asking the landlord to indicate—

        (i) whether he accepts that the tenant should be repaid the whole or part of the outstanding amount;

        (ii) if he accepts that part of it should be repaid, the amount he accepts should be repaid; and

        (iii) if he does not accept that the tenant should be repaid the whole of the outstanding amount, whether he consents to the dispute being resolved through the use of the dispute resolution service; and

    (b) warning the landlord that if he does not accept that the tenant should be repaid the whole of the outstanding amount but fails to respond within the relevant period to the question mentioned in paragraph (a)(iii), he will be treated as having given his consent for the dispute to be resolved through the use of that service.

(3) If the scheme administrator does not, within the relevant period, receive a response from the landlord indicating whether he accepts that the whole or part of the outstanding amount should be paid to the tenant—

    (a) the scheme administrator must treat the lack of a response as an indication that the landlord does not accept that the tenant should be repaid any of the outstanding amount;

    (b) the scheme administrator must determine forthwith whether he is satisfied that the notice was received by the landlord;

    (c) if the scheme administrator determines that he is satisfied that it was so received, the landlord is to be treated as having given his consent for the dispute to be resolved through the use of the dispute resolution service; and

    (d) the scheme administrator must inform the tenant and the landlord whether or not such consent is to be treated as having been given.

(4) If within the relevant period the scheme administrator receives a response to the notice under sub-paragraph (2) to the effect that the landlord does not accept that the tenant should be repaid the whole of the outstanding amount but the landlord fails within that period to indicate whether he consents to the dispute being resolved through the dispute resolution service—

    (a) the landlord is to be treated as having given his consent for the dispute to be resolved through the use of that service; and

    (b) the scheme administrator must inform the tenant and the landlord that such consent is to be treated as given.

(5) In this paragraph—

    "the outstanding amount" has the same meaning as in paragraph 6;

    "the relevant period" means the period of 10 working days beginning with the day after that on which the notice referred to in sub-paragraph (2) is sent; and

    "working days" shall be taken to exclude Saturdays, Sundays, Christmas Day, Good Friday and any day which, under the Banking and Financial Dealings Act 1971, is a bank holiday in England and Wales.

Insurance schemes—supplementary provisions

3A–1642   7.—(1)The designated account held by the scheme administrator must not contain anything other than amounts paid into it as mentioned in paragraph 6(3) and any interest accruing on such amounts.

Paragraph numbers marked with a "+" can be found online and on CD.

(2) Subject to sub-paragraph (3), the scheme administrator may retain any interest accruing on such amounts.

(3) The relevant arrangements under section 212(1) may provide for any amount paid in accordance with paragraph 6(5)(a) or (6) to be paid with interest—

    (a) in respect of the period during which the relevant amount has remained in the designated account, and

    (b) at such rate as the appropriate national authority may specify for the purposes of paragraph 3(5)(b).

(4) With the exception of any interest retained in accordance with sub-paragraph (2), nothing contained in the designated account may be used to fund the administration of the scheme.

(5) In this paragraph "the relevant amount", in relation to a tenancy deposit, means the amount, in respect of the deposit, paid into the designated account by virtue of a direction given in accordance with paragraph 6(3).

8.—(1)The scheme must make provision for preventing double recovery by a tenant **3A–1643** in respect of the whole or part of the deposit, and may in that connection make provision—

    (a) for excluding or modifying any requirement imposed by the scheme in accordance with paragraph 6 or 7, and

    (b) for requiring the repayment of amounts paid to the tenant by the scheme administrator.

(2) In this paragraph "double recovery", in relation to an amount of a tenancy deposit, means recovering that amount both from the scheme administrator and from the landlord.

Notifications to tenants

9.—(1)Every custodial scheme or insurance scheme must provide for the scheme **3A–1644** administrator to respond as soon as is practicable to any request within sub-paragraph (2) made by the tenant under a shorthold tenancy.

(2) A request is within this sub-paragraph if it is a request by the tenant to receive confirmation that a deposit paid in connection with the tenancy is being held in accordance with the scheme.

Dispute resolution procedures

10.—(1)Every custodial scheme or insurance scheme must provide for facilities to be **3A–1645** available for enabling disputes relating to tenancy deposits subject to the scheme to be resolved without recourse to litigation.

(2) The scheme must not, however, make the use of such facilities compulsory in the event of such a dispute.

(3) The provision made under this paragraph may confer power on a person acting as an adjudicator in relation to such a dispute to decline to proceed, or continue to proceed, with the case.

(4) In this Schedule, in relation to a custodial scheme or an insurance scheme, "the dispute resolution service"means the facilities provided by the scheme in accordance with this paragraph.

Service of documents: general

10A. A tenancy deposit scheme may make provision as to the methods which may **3A–1646** be used for giving or sending any direction, notice or other document which falls to be given or sent under the scheme.

Service of documents by scheme administrator on landlords

10.B—(1) The provision made by a tenancy deposit scheme under paragraph 10A **3A–1647** may include provision for any direction, notice or other document mentioned in this Schedule which is to be given or sent to a landlord by the scheme administrator to be treated as having been received on the second day after the day on which it is sent by first class post to the landlord at the address last provided by him to the scheme administrator as the postal address to which correspondence may be sent.

(2) Sub-paragraph (1) does not apply to the notice mentioned in paragraph 6A(2).

Paragraph numbers marked with a "+" can be found online and on CD.

(3) Provision made under sub-paragraph (1) may require the scheme administrator—

(a) to send a document to an address other than that mentioned in that sub-paragraph; or

(b) to use or attempt to use any other available means of communication,

before sending a document which is to be treated as having been received as mentioned in that sub-paragraph.

Service of documents by scheme administrator on tenants

3A–1648 10C.—(1) The provision made by a tenancy deposit scheme under paragraph 10A may include provision for any notice or other document mentioned in this Schedule which is to be given or sent to a tenant by the scheme administrator to be treated as having been received on the second day after the day on which it is sent by first class post to the tenant at the proper address.

(2) In the case of a notice mentioned in paragraph 4C(2), the proper address is—

(a) the address (if any) last provided to the scheme administrator as the address to which correspondence may be sent; or

(b) if no such address has been provided, the address given in the landlord's statutory declaration as the tenant's last known address or, if the scheme administrator has a more recent address for the tenant, that address.

(3) In the case of a notice of the kind mentioned in paragraph 5A(4) or (6), the proper address is the address of the premises subject to the tenancy in question.

(4) Provision made under sub-paragraph (1) may require the scheme administrator—

(a) to send a document to an address other than the proper address, or

(b) to use or attempt to use any other available means of communication, before sending a document which is to be treated as having been received as mentioned in that sub-paragraph.

Power to amend

3A–1649 11. The appropriate national authority may by order make such amendments of this Schedule as it considers appropriate.

Interpretation

3A–1650 12. In this Schedule references to tenants under shorthold tenancies include references to persons who, in accordance with arrangements made with such tenants, have paid tenancy deposits on behalf of the tenants.

3A–1651 *Note* —Amended by the Housing (Tenancy Deposit Schemes) Order 2007 (SI 2007/796).

Housing and Regeneration Act 2008

3A–1652 (2008 c.17)

Paragraph numbers marked with a "+" can be found online and on CD.

* * * *

Family intervention tenancies: general

297—(1) In Schedule 1 to the Housing Act 1985 (c. 68) (tenancies   **3A–1653**
which are not secure tenancies) after paragraph 4 insert—

Family intervention tenancies

"4ZA—(1) A tenancy is not a secure tenancy if it is a family
intervention tenancy.

(2) But a tenancy mentioned in sub-paragraph (1) becomes a
secure tenancy if the landlord notifies the tenant that it is to be
regarded as a secure tenancy.

(3) In this paragraph "a family intervention tenancy" means,
subject to sub-paragraph (4), a tenancy granted by a local housing
authority in respect of a dwelling-house—

> (a) to a person ("the new tenant") against whom a pos-
> session order under section 84 in respect of an-
> other dwelling-house—
>> (i) has been made, in relation to a secure tenancy,
>> on ground 2 or 2A of Part 1 of Schedule 2;
>> (ii) could, in the opinion of the authority, have been
>> so made in relation to such a tenancy; or
>> (iii) could, in the opinion of the authority, have been
>> so made if the person had had such a tenancy;
>> and
> (b) for the purposes of the provision of behaviour sup-
> port services.

(4) A tenancy is not a family intervention tenancy for the
purposes of this paragraph if the local housing authority has failed
to serve a notice under sub-paragraph (5) on the new tenant
before the new tenant entered into the tenancy.

(5) A notice under this sub-paragraph is a notice stating—

> (a) the reasons for offering the tenancy to the new ten-
> ant;
> (b) the dwelling-house in respect of which the tenancy is
> to be granted;
> (c) the other main terms of the tenancy (including any
> requirements on the new tenant in respect of behav-
> iour support services);
> (d) the security of tenure available under the tenancy and
> any loss of security of tenure which is likely to result
> from the new tenant agreeing to enter into the
> tenancy;
> (e) that the new tenant is not obliged to enter into the
> tenancy or (unless otherwise required to do so) to sur-

Paragraph numbers marked with a "+" can be found online and on CD.

render any existing tenancy or possession of a dwelling-house;

(f) any likely action by the local housing authority if the new tenant does not enter into the tenancy or surrender any existing tenancy or possession of a dwelling-house.

(6) The appropriate national authority may by regulations made by statutory instrument amend sub-paragraph (5).

(7) A notice under sub-paragraph (5) must contain advice to the new tenant as to how the new tenant may be able to obtain assistance in relation to the notice.

(8) The appropriate national authority may by regulations made by statutory instrument make provision about the type of advice to be provided in such notices.

(9) Regulations under this paragraph may contain such transitional, transitory or saving provision as the appropriate national authority considers appropriate.

(10) A statutory instrument containing (whether alone or with other provision) regulations under this paragraph which amend or repeal any of paragraphs (a) to (f) of sub-paragraph (5) may not be made—

(a) by the Secretary of State unless a draft of the instrument has been laid before, and approved by a resolution of, each House of Parliament; and

(b) by the Welsh Ministers unless a draft of the instrument has been laid before, and approved by a resolution of, the National Assembly for Wales.

(11) Subject to this, a statutory instrument containing regulations made under this paragraph—

(a) by the Secretary of State is subject to annulment in pursuance of a resolution of either House of Parliament; and

(b) by the Welsh Ministers is subject to annulment in pursuance of a resolution of the National Assembly for Wales.

(12) In this paragraph—

"appropriate national authority" –

(a) in relation to England, means the Secretary of State; and

(b) in relation to Wales, means the Welsh Ministers;

"behaviour support agreement" means an agreement in writing about behaviour and the provision of support services made between the new tenant and the local housing authority concerned (or between persons who include those persons);

"behaviour support services" means relevant support services to be provided by any person to–

(a) the new tenant; or

Paragraph numbers marked with a "+" can be found online and on CD.

        (b) any person who is to reside with the new
tenant; for the purpose of addressing the kind of
behaviour which led to the new tenant falling
within sub-paragraph (3)(a);

"family intervention tenancy" has the meaning given by
sub-paragraph (3);

"the new tenant" has the meaning given by sub-paragraph
(3)(a);

"relevant support services" means support services of a
kind identified in a behaviour support agreement
and designed to meet such needs of the recipient as
are identified in the agreement."

(2) In Part 1 of Schedule 1 to the Housing Act 1988 (c. 50) (tenancies which cannot be assured tenancies) after paragraph 12 insert—

Family intervention tenancies

"12ZA—(1) A family intervention tenancy.

(2) But a family intervention tenancy becomes an assured
tenancy if the landlord notifies the tenant that it is to be regarded
as an assured tenancy.

(3) In this paragraph "a family intervention tenancy" means,
subject to sub-paragraph (4), a tenancy granted by a registered
provider of social housing or a registered social landlord ("the
landlord") in respect of a dwelling-house—

        (a) to a person ("the new tenant") against whom a possession order under section 7 in respect of another
dwelling-house—

           (i) has been made, in relation to an assured tenancy, on ground 14 or 14A of Part 2 of Schedule 2;

           (ii) could, in the opinion of the landlord, have been
so made in relation to such a tenancy; or

           (iii) could, in the opinion of the landlord, have been
so made if the person had had such a tenancy;
and

        (b) for the purposes of the provision of behaviour support services.

(4) A tenancy is not a family intervention tenancy for the
purposes of this paragraph if the landlord has failed to serve a
notice under sub-paragraph (5) on the new tenant before the new
tenant entered into the tenancy.

(5) A notice under this sub-paragraph is a notice stating—

        (a) the reasons for offering the tenancy to the new tenant;

        (b) the dwelling-house in respect of which the tenancy is
to be granted;

        (c) the other main terms of the tenancy (including any
requirements on the new tenant in respect of behaviour support services);

Paragraph numbers marked with a "+" can be found online and on CD.

(d) the security of tenure available under the tenancy and any loss of security of tenure which is likely to result from the new tenant agreeing to enter into the tenancy;

(e) that the new tenant is not obliged to enter into the tenancy or (unless otherwise required to do so) to surrender any existing tenancy or possession of a dwelling-house;

(f) any likely action by the landlord if the new tenant does not enter into the tenancy or surrender any existing tenancy or possession of a dwelling-house.

(6) The appropriate national authority may by regulations made by statutory instrument amend sub-paragraph (5).

(7) A notice under sub-paragraph (5) must contain advice to the new tenant as to how the new tenant may be able to obtain assistance in relation to the notice.

(8) The appropriate national authority may by regulations made by statutory instrument make provision about the type of advice to be provided in such notices.

(9) Regulations under this paragraph may contain such transitional, transitory or saving provision as the appropriate national authority considers appropriate.

(10) A statutory instrument containing (whether alone or with other provision) regulations under this paragraph which amend or repeal any of paragraphs (a) to (f) of sub-paragraph (5) may not be made—

(a) by the Secretary of State unless a draft of the instrument has been laid before, and approved by a resolution of, each House of Parliament; and

(b) by the Welsh Ministers unless a draft of the instrument has been laid before, and approved by a resolution of, the National Assembly for Wales.

(11) Subject to this, a statutory instrument containing regulations made under this paragraph—

(a) by the Secretary of State is subject to annulment in pursuance of a resolution of either House of Parliament; and

(b) by the Welsh Ministers is subject to annulment in pursuance of a resolution of the National Assembly for Wales.

(12) In this paragraph—

"appropriate national authority" –

(a) in relation to England, means the Secretary of State; and

(b) in relation to Wales, means the Welsh Ministers;

"behaviour support agreement" means an agreement in writing about behaviour and the provision of support services made between the new tenant, the landlord

Paragraph numbers marked with a "+" can be found online and on CD.

and the local housing authority for the district in which the dwelling-house which is to be subject to the new tenancy is situated (or between persons who include those persons);

"behaviour support services" means relevant support services to be provided by any person to–

(a) the new tenant; or

(b) any person who is to reside with the new tenant; for the purpose of addressing the kind of behaviour which led to the new tenant falling within sub-paragraph (3)(a);

"family intervention tenancy" has the meaning given by sub-paragraph (3);

"landlord" has the meaning given by sub-paragraph (3);

"local housing authority" (and the reference to its district) has the same meaning as in the Housing Act 1985 (see sections 1 and 2(1) of that Act);

"the new tenant" has the meaning given by sub-paragraph (3)(a);

"registered social landlord" has the same meaning as in Part 1 of the Housing Act 1996;

"relevant support services" means support services of a kind identified in a behaviour support agreement and designed to meet such needs of the recipient as are identified in the agreement."

(3) This section does not apply to any tenancy granted before the coming into force of this section.

Implementation

It was brought into force on January 1, 2009 by the Housing and Regeneration Act 2008 (Commencement No.2 and Transitional, Saving and Transitory Provisions) Order 2008 SI 3068.

3A–1654

Extent

This section applies to England and Wales.

3A–1655

secure tenancy

See Housing Act 1985 s.79 above.

3A–1656

Ground 2 or 2A

i.e. where the landlord has obtained a possession order based upon nuisance or annoyance or domestic violence.

3A–1657

registered social landlord

See Housing Act 1996 Pt 1. Registered charities which are housing associations are eligible for registration as social landlords under Housing Act 1996 s.2. In addition s.2 provides that societies registered under the Industrial and Provident Societies Act 1965 and companies registered under the Companies Act 1985 are eligible for registration if they are non-profit-making and established for the purpose of, or have among their objects or powers, the provision, construction, improvement or management of:

(a) houses to be kept available for letting;

(b) houses for occupation by members of the body, where the rules of the body restrict membership to persons entitled or prospectively entitled (as tenants or otherwise) to occupy a house provided or managed by the body; or

3A–1658

Paragraph numbers marked with a "+" can be found online and on CD.

(c) hostels.

behaviour support services

3A–1659   See para.4ZA (12)—i.e. those support services which are identified in a behaviour support agreement and are provided by any person to the new tenant or persons living with them for the purposes of addressing the anti-social behaviour which has led to the local authority taking possession action or of being of the opinion that such a possession claim could be made.

regulations

3A–1660   At present there are no regulations.

behaviour support agreement

3A–1661   See para.4ZA (12)—i.e. an agreement between the tenant and the local housing authority about behaviour and the provision of support services.

assured tenancy

3A–1662   See Housing Act 1988 s.1 above.

Ground 14 or 14A

3A–1663   i.e. where the landlord has obtained a possession order based upon nuisance or annoyance or domestic violence.

Family intervention tenancies

3A–1664   This section enables local housing authorities and registered providers of social housing (in England) and registered social landlords (in Wales) to offer tenancies which are not secure or assured to tenants who have lost or are potentially at risk of losing their secure or assured tenancy. These tenancies are offered to provide behavioural support services to tenants against whom a possession order for anti-social behaviour has been made or to tenants who could face possession proceedings on the grounds of anti-social behaviour. This is done by inserting new para.4ZA into Housing Act 1985 Sch.1 (tenancies which are not secure tenancies) and new para.12ZA into Housing Act 1988 Sch.1 to the (tenancies which cannot be assured tenancies).

Family intervention tenancies are voluntary. There is provision for the service of notices prior to the grant of family intervention tenancies. If no notice is served, the new tenancy cannot be a family intervention tenancy.

They can become secure or assured tenancies if the landlord so notifies the tenant.

Sub-paragraph (3) defines a family intervention tenancy for the purposes of this paragraph as a tenancy granted by a local authority to a person for the purposes of the provision of behaviour support services and against whom a possession order in respect of another dwelling-house:

- has been made in relation to a secure tenancy on the grounds of anti-social behaviour or;
- could have been so made in relation to a secure tenancy; or
- could have been so made if the tenant had had such a tenancy.

Sub-paragraph (4) provides the new tenancy will not be a family intervention tenancy unless the local housing authority has served a notice under sub-para.(5). Sub-paragraph (5) provides the information the notice must contain including that the tenant is under no obligation to enter into the tenancy or unless otherwise required to do so to surrender any existing tenancy or possession of a dwelling-house. Sub-paragraph (6) provides that the contents of the notice may be amended by regulations made by statutory instrument. In addition the notice must contain advice to the tenant as to how he or she may be able to obtain assistance in relation to the notice (sub-para.(7)). The type of advice to be included in notices may be provided for by regulations (sub-para.(8)) made by statutory instrument. Sub-paragraph (12) provides definitions for the terms used in the new paragraph 4ZA. Subsection (3) provides that the provisions in new para.4ZA of Schedule 1 to the Housing Act 1985 and para.12ZA of Pt 1 of Schedule 1 to the Housing Act 1988 will not apply to any tenancy granted before this section came into force—i.e. January 1, 2009.

Certain family intervention tenancies: termination

3A–1665   298—(1) A local housing authority must not serve a notice to quit on the tenant of a family intervention tenancy unless—

Paragraph numbers marked with a "+" can be found online and on CD.

(a) the authority has served a notice under subsection (2) on the tenant, and

(b) either—

(i) the tenant has not requested a review of the kind mentioned in subsection (2)(e) within the period of 14 days beginning with the service of the notice,

(ii) any such request has been withdrawn, or

(iii) the authority has served a notice on the tenant under subsection (4)(b).

(2) A notice under this subsection is a notice in writing stating—

(a) that the authority has decided to serve a notice to quit on the tenant,

(b) the effect of serving a notice to quit,

(c) the reasons for the authority's decision,

(d) when the authority is intending to serve the notice to quit, and

(e) that the tenant has the right to request, within the period of 14 days beginning with the service of the notice under this subsection, a review of the authority's decision.

(3) Subsection (4) applies if the tenant requests a review of the kind mentioned in subsection (2)(e) within the period of 14 days beginning with the service of the notice under subsection (2) and the request is not withdrawn.

(4) The local housing authority must—

(a) review its decision to serve a notice to quit on the tenant, and

(b) serve a notice on the tenant informing the tenant of the decision of the authority on the review and the reasons for it.

(5) The appropriate national authority may by regulations make provision about the procedure to be followed in connection with such a review.

(6) Regulations under subsection (5) may, in particular—

(a) specify the description of person who is to make the decision on a review,

(b) specify the circumstances in which the tenant is entitled to an oral hearing on a review,

(c) specify whether, and by whom, the tenant is entitled to be represented at such a hearing.

(7) A notice under subsection (2), and a notice to quit, served by a local housing authority in respect of a family intervention tenancy must contain advice to the tenant as to how the tenant may be able to obtain assistance in relation to the notice.

(8) The appropriate national authority may by regulations make provision about the type of advice to be provided in such notices.

(9) In this section—

"appropriate national authority" means –

(a) in relation to England, the Secretary of State, and

(b) in relation to Wales, the Welsh Ministers,

"family intervention tenancy" has the same meaning as in paragraph 4ZA of Schedule 1 to the Housing Act 1985 (c. 68),

and other expressions used in this section and in paragraph 4ZA of that Schedule have the same meaning as in that paragraph.

(10) This section does not apply to any tenancy granted before the coming into force of this section.

Implementation

3A–1666   It was brought into force on January 1, 2009 by the Housing and Regeneration Act 2008 (Commencement No.2 and Transitional, Saving and Transitory Provisions) Order 2008 SI 3068.

Extent

3A–1667   This section applies to England and Wales.

local housing authority

3A–1668   See Housing Act 1985 s.1 and 2(1)—i.e. a district council, a London borough council, the Common Council of the City of London, a Welsh county council or county borough council or the Council of the Isles of Scilly.

family intervention tenancy

3A–1669   See s.297.

appropriate national authority

3A–1670   See (9)—i.e. the Secretary of State in England and the Welsh Ministers in Wales.

regulations

3A–1671   See the Family Intervention Tenancies (Review of Local Authority Decisions) (England) Regulations 2008 SI No.3111.

review

3A–1672   In view of *R. (McLellan) v Bracknell Forest DC* [2001] EWCA 1510; [2002] QB 1129; and *R. (Gilboy) v Liverpool City Council* [2008] EWCA Civ 751, [2008] 4 All E.R. 127, the procedure for reviews does not appear to be incompatible with ECHR art.8 and there is no reason to think that individuals' rights will be infringed without remedy from the courts.

Editorial introduction

3A–1673   This section makes provision for the termination of local housing authority family intervention tenancies. Subsection (1) provides that local authorities should not serve notices to quit on tenants of family intervention tenancies unless notice under subs.(2) has been served on the tenant and either:

- the tenant has not requested a review of the kind specified in the notice (right to request, within 14 days of the service of the notice, a review of the authority's decision to evict);
- the tenant withdraws the request for a review; or
- a notice under subs.(4)(b) has been served on the tenant (notice of the reasoning and decision of the requested review).

Subsection (2) sets out the required contents of the notice. Subsections (3) and (4) explain what a local authority must do if a tenant requests a review of the local authority's decision within 14 days of the service of the notice under subs.(2). The local authority must carry out the review and serve notice of its decision and the reasons for it on the tenant. The procedure to be followed on review may be provided by regulations made by statutory instrument. The regulations may contain:

Paragraph numbers marked with a "+" can be found online and on CD.

- a description of the person who makes the review decision;
- the circumstances under which the tenant would be entitled to an oral review;
- whether or not and by whom the tenant can be represented during the review hearing.

Subsection (7) provides that any notice to quit or notice under subs.(2) served in respect of a family intervention tenancy, must also contain advice to the tenant about obtaining assistance in relation to the notice. Subsection (8) provides that the type of advice the notice to quit or notice under subs.(2) must include may be provided by regulations subject to the negative resolution procedure. Subsection (10) effectively applies the provisions of this section only to tenancies granted on or after the coming into force of this section.

Possession orders relating to certain tenancies

299 Schedule 11 (which makes provision about possession orders **3A–1674** and their effect on secure tenancies, assured tenancies, introductory tenancies and demoted tenancies including provision about the status of existing occupiers) has effect.

secure tenancies
See Housing Act 1985 s.79 above. **3A–1675**

assured tenancies
See Housing Act 1988 s.1 above. **3A–1676**

introductory tenancies
See Housing Act 1996 ss.124 above. **3A–1677**

demoted tenancies
See Housing Act 1985 s.82A, Housing Act 1988 ss.6A and 20B and Housing Act **3A–1678**
1996 s.143A, above.

Implementation
This section is not yet in force. It is due to be brought into force by commencement **3A–1679**
order. See s.325 (not reproduced in this work).

Extent
This section applies to England and Wales. **3A–1680**

Schedule 11—Possession orders relating to certain tenancies
Schedule 11 prevents the creation of tolerated trespassers in the future (by provid- **3A–1681**
ing that secure and assured tenancies continue until any warrant for possession is executed); and restores tenancy status to existing tolerated trespassers (by providing that a new "replacement tenancy" is deemed to arise provided that the former tenant continues to occupy the dwelling as his or her home). The amendments are the result of proposals originally set out in *Tolerated trespassers: A consultation paper*, published on August 20, 2007. The provisions for the abolition of tolerated trespasser status do not cover those who became trespassers before a stock transfer but the Act contains a regulation-making power to enable the Secretary of State to extend the provisions to that group.

Part 1 of Sch.11 amends the Housing Act 1985, the Housing Act 1988, and the Housing Act 1996 to provide that where a possession order is made against a secure, assured or demoted tenant, the tenancy will end on the date the tenant is evicted (unless the tenant ends the tenancy before that date). The provisions will prevent the creation in future of "tolerated trespassers" who remain in occupation in the property but without the tenancy agreement or the relevant statutory provisions applying.

Part 2 of the Schedule provides that where before commencement a tenant has already become a tolerated trespasser, a new tenancy will arise. Provision is made for the details of how this new tenancy will relate to the original tenancy.

Paragraphs 1 to 4 amend the Housing Act 1985. The amendments in para.2 to s.82

Paragraph numbers marked with a "+" can be found online and on CD.

HOUSING

ensure that where a possession order has been made in relation to a secure tenancy, the tenancy ends when the tenant is evicted. Paragraph 3 amends s.85 in relation to the discretion of the court in possession proceedings, gives the court wider powers to discharge or rescind a possession order, and repeals subss.(5) and (5A) which are now unnecessary since they relate only to tolerated trespassers.

Paragraphs 5 to 9 amend the Housing Act 1988. The amendments in para.6 to s.5 ensure that the tenancy will continue until the tenant is evicted. Paragraph 7 amends s.7(7) to the same effect with respect to fixed term tenancies which have ended. Paragraph 8 amends s.9 with regard to the discretion of the court in possession proceedings, giving the court wider powers to discharge or rescind a possession order, and repealing subsections (5) and (5A). Paragraph 9 amends s.21 with respect to when possession orders in respect of assured shorthold tenancies take effect. Where the court grants a possession order terminating a fixed term or periodic assured shorthold tenancy, including any statutory periodic tenancy arising on or after the end of the fixed term, the tenancy will end when the tenant is evicted.

Paragraphs 10 to 13 amend the Housing Act 1996. Paragraphs 11 and 12 amend ss.127 and 130 to provide that where a possession order has been made in relation to an introductory tenancy, the tenancy will end when the tenant is evicted, and para.13 makes similar provision for demoted tenancies by amending s.143D.

Paragraph 14 makes transitional provisions. The amended statutory provisions in Pt 1 of the Schedule about when tenancies end will not apply where a possession order has already been made, except in two circumstances. These exceptions are, firstly, that they will apply where the tenancy ended after a possession order was made but a new tenancy arises under Pt 2 of the Schedule; and secondly, that they will apply where a possession order was made before commencement and the tenancy has not yet ended (because commencement occurs before the date for possession specified in the possession order). Paragraph 14(3) ensures that the wider powers of the court to discharge or rescind possession orders apply to all possession orders whenever made. Paragraph 14(4) contains clarification of the reference to tenancies ending. Tenancies at present end on the date for possession specified in the possession order, but it is possible for the court subsequently to make an order varying the possession date to a date in the future. The effect of such an order is that the tenancy is restored without a break. Paragraph 14(4) clarifies that, where this has happened, the tenancy has not ended for the purposes of these provisions. The definition of "commencement date" in para.14(5) contains an exception to allow order making powers to come into effect earlier.

In Pt 2 of the Schedule, para.15 defines "an original tenancy" as a tenancy which ended as a result of a possession order (but not as a result of execution of the order— i.e. eviction). Paragraph 16(1) provides that a new tenancy of the dwelling-house let under the original tenancy is treated as arising on the commencement date, between the ex-landlord and the ex-tenant, if three conditions are satisfied. These conditions are, firstly, that the home condition is met; secondly, that the ex-landlord is entitled to let the dwelling-house (for instance, that there has not been a stock transfer to a new landlord); and thirdly, that the ex-landlord and ex-tenant have not in the meantime entered into a new tenancy. The remaining sub-paragraphs of para.16 set out details in relation to the home condition. Paragraph 16(2) provides that the dwelling-house must have been the only or principal home of the ex-tenant throughout the termination period, and still be so on the commencement date. Paragraph 16(3) defines the termination period. Subparagraphs (4) to (6) ensure that the home condition will be met where the ex-tenant has been evicted from the property, but the warrant of eviction is subsequently set aside (leaving the possession order still in force). Where this happens, if the ex-tenant returns to the property the new tenancy arises on the first day of resuming occupation. Paragraph 16(7) gives the appropriate national authority power by order to provide for other circumstances where the home condition is met.

Paragraph 17 specifies the nature in each case of the replacement tenancy. In all but one case, the replacement tenancy is of the same type as the original tenancy. The exception, in para.17(a)(ii), is where the original tenancy was an introductory tenancy but during the termination period the landlord revoked the introductory tenancy regime. In such circumstances the replacement tenancy will be secure. Paragraph 18 provides that the terms and conditions of the original tenancy immediately before it ended will apply to the new tenancy, subject to subparas.(2) to (6). Paragraph 18(2) enables changes made in the termination period in the amount of "rent" to apply to

Paragraph numbers marked with a "+" can be found online and on CD.

the new tenancy, and para.18(3) ensures that arrears of "rent" owed for the termination period will be owed in respect of the new tenancy. Paragraph 18(4) gives the appropriate national authority a power to provide by order for other modifications of the terms and conditions of the new tenancy. Paragraph 18(5) provides a safeguard by specifying that nothing in the preceding subparagraphs permits a term to be read into the new tenancy which could not have been applied to the original tenancy if it had not ended. For example, if the ex-landlord had been charging the ex-tenant higher "rent" during the termination period than would have been permissible had the tenancy been in force, the rent under the new tenancy will not be modified to take account of this. Paragraph 18(6) refers to the situation where an original introductory tenancy has to be replaced by a new secure tenancy, and requires the terms and conditions to be modified as necessary to reflect this.

Paragraph 19(1) provides that any statutory provisions relating to secure, assured, introductory or demoted tenancies apply to such a tenancy arising as a new tenancy under Pt 2 of the Schedule. Paragraph 19(2) and (3) provides that where the new tenancy is an introductory or demoted tenancy, the statutory provisions providing for the length of the tenancy are modified so as to secure that the new tenancy does not consist simply of the remainder of the one year period after taking into account the time spent under the original tenancy. Paragraph 19(4) gives the appropriate national authority power by order to modify any statutory provision as it applies to a new tenancy.

Paragraph 20 deals with the effect which court orders made in the course of the possession proceedings in respect of the original tenancy have on the new tenancy. The possession order itself is to be treated, so far as practicable, as applying to the new tenancy, and para.20(2) provides that any other court orders relating to occupation of the dwelling-house and made in contemplation of, in consequence of, or otherwise in connection with the possession order, and which are in force on the commencement date, must also be treated (so far as practicable) as applying to the new tenancy.

Paragraph 21 sets out circumstances in which the original tenancy and the new tenancy must be treated as the same and continuous tenancy, and deals with related matters. The two tenancies must be treated as the same and continuous for relevant purposes, which are listed in para.21(2). These are succession rights; calculation of qualification periods for the right to buy (which includes the preserved right to buy and the right to acquire); and enabling the landlord to rely on ground 8 of Sch.2 to the Housing Act 1985. In addition, the appropriate national authority may by order specify other relevant purposes. Paragraph 21(3) gives the court a power to order that the original tenancy and the new tenancy are to be treated as the same and continuous for the purpose of a relevant claim, so that the claim may apply to the termination period. A relevant claim is defined in para.21(4) as being a claim by either ex-landlord or ex-tenant against the other for breach of the tenancy agreement, or a claim by the ex-tenant against the ex-landlord for breach of statutory duty. Where a claim has already been made before the commencement date, it will only be a relevant claim if the proceedings have not yet been finally determined at that date. A power is given to the appropriate national authority to specify other types of claim as relevant for this purpose. Paragraph 21(5) defines when a claim is finally determined.

Paragraph 22 ensures that where tenants have been consulted pursuant to statutory requirements, the fact that occupants who were ex-tenants at the time were or were not allowed to vote does not mean that the consultation requirements were not complied with. The appropriate national authority is given a power to specify consultation requirements additional to those listed in para.22(2).

The effect of para.23 is that where there are ex-tenants who were formerly joint tenants, the occupation of the dwelling-house as only or principal home by at least one of them is sufficient for the home condition to be met. It also gives the appropriate national authority power by order to modify the way Pt 2 of the Schedule applies to joint tenancies.

Paragraph 24 gives the appropriate national authority power by order to provide that the provisions in Pt 2 of Schedule 11 apply to successor landlord cases, subject to any modifications specified in the order. Successor landlord cases are defined as cases where the original landlord's interest has been transferred to another person or any subsequent transferee.

Paragraph 25 repeats in relation to Pt 2 of the Schedule the provision in para.14(4),

Paragraph numbers marked with a "+" can be found online and on CD.

clarifying that where a tenancy which had formerly ended was restored (by the court varying the possession date in the order) such a tenancy then no longer counts as a tenancy which has ended for the purposes of these provisions.

Paragraph 26 contains definitions and interpretation of words and phrases used in the Schedule, or gives references to the paragraphs in which particular words and phrases are defined. It also makes provision for determining, where necessary, whether a dwelling-house is in England or Wales according to where council tax is paid.

Service charges: provision of information and designated accounts

3A–1682   303 Schedule 12 (which relates to the provision of information about service charges and to service charge funds) has effect.

Implementation
3A–1683   This section is not yet in force. It is due to be brought into force by commencement order. See s.325 (not reproduced in this work).

Schedule 12: provision of information and designated accounts
3A–1684   Schedule 12 makes changes to the requirements in the Landlord and Tenant Act 1985 and the Landlord and Tenant Act 1987 regarding the information that landlords must supply to service charge payers and how service charge monies are to be held. The changes were originally proposed in set out in *Commonhold and Leasehold Reform Act 2002: A Consultation Paper on Regular Statements of Account and Designated Client Accounts*, published on July 25, 2007.

The main amendments are to Landlord and Tenant Act 1985 s.21 (as substituted by the Commonhold and Leasehold Reform Act 2002) and Landlord and Tenant Act 1987 s.42A (as inserted by the 2002 Act). Section 21 and s.42A, as amended or introduced by the 2002 Act, have not been brought into force.

Paragraph 2 broadly replicates the effect of s.21. Subsection (1) provides the appropriate national authority (the Secretary of State in England, and the Welsh Ministers in Wales) with power to make regulations about the provision by landlords of dwellings of service charge information. Subsection (2) sets out the types of information that should be dealt with in those regulations. In particular, the regulations must, subject to exceptions, require a landlord to provide information about the service charges of the tenant and any "associated charges" (defined in subs.(10)); and the relevant costs relating to the service charges. Subsection (3) provides that the regulations must (subject to exceptions) require that a report by a qualified person be supplied with the information provided. Subsection (4) sets out the additional matters about which provision may be made in the regulations. In particular the regulations may make provision about the information and reports that need to be provided, the periods in relation to which information or reports are to be provided, the times at or by which they need to be provided, and the form and manner in which they may be provided. The regulations may also describe the persons who are "qualified persons" for the purposes of preparing the report that must accompany the information supplied by the landlord. Subsection (5) provides that the power under subs.(1) to make regulations is not limited in any way by the provisions of subss.(2) to (4). Subsection (6) allows regulations made under s.21 to make different provision for different cases, descriptions of case or different purposes and to make supplementary, incidental, consequential, transitional or saving provision that is considered to be appropriate. Subsection (7) provides that, subject to subss.(8) and (9), the regulations will be subject to the negative procedure. Subsections (8) and (9) provides that the first use of the regulation making powers by the appropriate national authority will be subject to the affirmative resolution procedure. Subsection (10) contains definitions.

Paragraphs 3 to 8 of the Schedule make amendments to Landlord and Tenant Act 1985 ss.21A, 22, 23, 26 and 27, which are consequential on the new terminology used in s.21.

Paragraph 9 repeals Landlord and Tenant Act 1985 s.28, which defines the meaning of "qualified accountant" for the purposes of providing a certificate supporting information supplied under the existing s.21. This is being replaced with the power to specify in regulations made under the new s.21(4) the persons who are qualified to provide a report on such information.

Paragraph numbers marked with a "+" can be found online and on CD.

Ineligible persons from abroad: statutory disregards

314 Schedule 15 (which amends Pts 6 and 7 of the Housing Act 1996 (c.52) in relation to certain ineligible persons from abroad and which makes related provision, including provision for Scotland and Northern Ireland) has effect.

3A–1685

Implementation

This section is not yet in force. It is due to be brought into force by commencement order. See s.325 (not reproduced in this work).

3A–1686

Ineligible persons from abroad: statutory disregards

Schedule 15 amends the Housing Act 1996 s.185(4) to remedy the declaration of incompatibility with the European Convention of Human Rights made in *R. (Morris) v Westminster CC* [2005] EWCA Civ 1184; [2006] H.L.R. 8. Section 185(4) formerly required local housing authorities in England and Wales to disregard ineligible household members when deciding whether an applicant for housing assistance was homeless or had a priority need for accommodation. The effect of Sch.15 is that the disregards no longer apply in the case of an applicant for housing assistance who is a British citizen, a Commonwealth citizen with a right of abode in the UK, or an EEA or Swiss national exercising an EU Treaty right to reside in the UK.

3A–1687

Schedule 15 also changes the way in which the duty owed to applicants who are found to be homeless and to have a priority need only by reliance on a household member who is a "restricted person" (a person who requires leave to enter or remain in the UK and does not have it, or a person who does have the required leave but that leave was granted on the condition that the person would have "no recourse to public funds") may be discharged. In such a case, local housing authorities are required, so far as possible, to bring their duty to secure accommodation to an end by ensuring that an offer of accommodation for a period of at least 12 months in the private rented sector is made to the applicant. If such an offer is made the duty is discharged whether or not the applicant accepts the offer.

Paragraph 3 amends Housing Act 1996 s.184 so that where a local housing authority decide that an applicant is owed a homelessness duty only by reliance on a restricted person, it must inform him or her of that fact, explain the reasons for the decision, and explain the nature of the duty owed to him as a result. Paragraph 3 also sets out the definition of "restricted person".

Paragraph 4 amends s.185 so that local housing authorities are required to disregard a housing applicant's ineligible household members only if the applicant is a person subject to immigration control who is not a national of an EEA State or Switzerland.

Paragraph 5 amends s.193 (duty owed to applicants who are eligible for assistance, unintentionally homeless and in priority need). It provides that, where the duty to secure that accommodation is available is owed only because the applicant has relied on a restricted person, the local housing authority must, so far as reasonably practicable, bring the duty to an end with a private accommodation offer. A "private accommodation offer" is an offer of an assured shorthold tenancy made by a private landlord for a fixed term of at least 12 months with the approval of, and by arrangement with, the local authority. The making of such an offer to the applicant brings the duty to an end regardless of whether the applicant accepts it.

Paragraph 6 amends s.195 (duty owed to applicants who are eligible for assistance, unintentionally threatened with homelessness and in priority need). It provides that where the duty to secure that accommodation does not cease to be available is owed only because the applicant has relied on a restricted person and the authority discharge the duty by securing alternative accommodation for the applicant, the local housing authority must, so far as reasonably practicable, bring the duty to an end with a private accommodation offer in the same way as for s.193 (see para.5 of the Schedule).

Paragraph 7 amends s.202 so that applicants have a right to ask for a review of the suitability of accommodation offered as a "private accommodation offer".

[THE NEXT PARAGRAPH IS 3A–1691.]

Paragraph numbers marked with a "+" can be found online and on CD.

SCHEDULE 11

Possession Orders Relating to Certain Tenancies

Part 1

Amendments to the Housing Acts of 1985, 1988 and 1996

Housing Act 1985 (c. 68)

3A–1691 1. The Housing Act 1985 is amended as follows.

3A–1692 2.—(1) Section 82 (security of tenure: date on which secure tenancy comes to an end as a result of a possession order etc.) is amended as follows.

(2) In subsection (1) for "by obtaining an order" substitute "as".

(3) For subsections (1A) and (2) substitute—

"(1A) The tenancy may be brought to an end by the landlord—
>(a) obtaining—
>>(i) an order of the court for the possession of the dwelling-house, and
>>(ii) the execution of the order,
>
>(b) obtaining an order under subsection (3), or
>
>(c) obtaining a demotion order under section 82A.

(2) In the case mentioned in subsection (1A)(a), the tenancy ends when the order is executed."

3A–1693 3.—(1) Section 85 (extended discretion of court in certain proceedings for possession) is amended as follows.

(2) In subsection (3)(a) omit the words from "or payments" to "profits),".

(3) For subsection (4) substitute—

"(4) The court may discharge or rescind the order for possession if it thinks it appropriate to do so having had regard to—
>(a) any conditions imposed under subsection (3), and
>(b) the conduct of the tenant in connection with those conditions."

(4) Omit subsections (5) and (5A).

* * * *

Housing Act 1988 (c. 50)

3A–1694 5. The Housing Act 1988 is amended as follows.

3A–1695 6.—(1) Section 5 (security of tenure) is amended as follows.

(2) For subsection (1) substitute—

"(1) An assured tenancy cannot be brought to an end by the landlord except by—
>(a) obtaining—
>>(i) an order of the court for possession of the dwelling-house under section 7 or 21, and
>>(ii) the execution of the order,
>
>(b) obtaining an order of the court under section 6A (demotion order), or
>
>(c) in the case of a fixed term tenancy which contains power for the landlord to determine the tenancy in certain circumstances, by the exercise of that power,
>
>and, accordingly, the service by the landlord of a notice to quit is of no effect in relation to a periodic assured tenancy.

(1A) Where an order of the court for possession of the dwelling-house is obtained, the tenancy ends when the order is executed."

(3) In subsection (2)(a) after "court" insert "of the kind mentioned in subsection (1)(a) or (b) or any other order of the court".

3A–1696 7. In section 7(7) (possession orders in cases of fixed term tenancies which have come to an end) for "on the day on which the order takes effect" substitute "in accordance with section 5(1A)".

Paragraph numbers marked with a "+" can be found online and on CD.

8.—(1)Section 9 (extended discretion of court in possession claims) is amended as **3A–1697** follows.

(2) In subsection (3) omit the words from "or payments" to "profits)".

(3) For subsection (4) substitute—

"(4) The court may discharge or rescind any such order as is referred to in subsection (2) if it thinks it appropriate to do so having had regard to—

(a) any conditions imposed under subsection (3), and

(b) the conduct of the tenant in connection with those conditions."

(4) Omit subsections (5) and (5A).

9.—(1)Section 21 (recovery of possession on expiry or termination of assured short- **3A–1698** hold tenancies) is amended as follows.

(2) In subsection (3) for "on the day on which the order takes effect" substitute "in accordance with section 5(1A)".

(3) After subsection (4) insert—

"(4A) Where a court makes an order for possession of a dwelling-house by virtue of subsection (4) above, the assured shorthold tenancy shall end in accordance with section 5(1A)."

Housing Act 1996 (c. 52)

10. The Housing Act 1996 is amended as follows. **3A–1699**

11.—(1)Section 127 (introductory tenancies: proceedings for possession) is amended **3A–1700** as follows.

(2) In subsection (1) for the words from "an order" to the end substitute

"—

(a) an order of the court for the possession of the dwelling-house, and

(b) the execution of the order."

(3) After subsection (1) insert—

"(1A) In such a case, the tenancy ends when the order is executed."

(4) In subsection (2) for "such an order" substitute "an order of the kind mentioned in subsection (1)(a)".

(5) Omit subsection (3).

12.—(1)Section 130 (introductory tenancies: effect of beginning proceedings for **3A–1701** possession) is amended as follows.

(2) In subsection (2)(a) for the words from "in pursuance of", where they first appear, to "of the court)" substitute "in accordance with section 127(1A)".

(3) In subsection (3)(b) for "127(2) and (3)" substitute "127(1A) and (2)".

13.—(1)Section 143D (demoted tenancies: proceedings for possession) is amended **3A–1702** as follows.

(2) In subsection (1) for the words from "an order" to the end substitute—

"—

(a) an order of the court for the possession of the dwelling-house, and

(b) the execution of the order."

(3) After subsection (1) insert—

"(1A) In such a case, the tenancy ends when the order is executed."

(4) Omit subsection (3).

Transitional provisions

14.—(1)Subject as follows, this Part of this Schedule does not apply to any posses- **3A–1703** sion order made before the commencement date.

Paragraph numbers marked with a "+" can be found online and on CD.

(2) This Part of this Schedule does apply to a possession order made before the commencement date if the order applies to—

    (a) a new tenancy by virtue of paragraph 20, or

    (b) a tenancy which has not ended pursuant to the order before that date.

(3) Paragraphs 3(3) and 8(3) apply to any possession order regardless of when it was made.

(4) In determining for the purposes of sub-paragraph (2) whether a tenancy has ended, any ending which was temporary because the tenancy was restored in consequence of a court order is to be ignored.

(5) In this paragraph "the commencement date" means the day on which section 299 comes into force for purposes other than the purposes of the Secretary of State or the Welsh Ministers making orders under Part 2 of this Schedule.

PART 2

REPLACEMENT OF CERTAIN TERMINATED TENANCIES

Circumstances in which replacement tenancies arise

3A-1704   15. In this Part of this Schedule "an original tenancy" means any secure tenancy, assured tenancy, introductory tenancy or demoted tenancy—

    (a) in respect of which a possession order was made before the commencement date, and

    (b) which ended before that date pursuant to the order but not on the execution of the order.

3A-1705   16.—(1)A new tenancy of the dwelling-house which was let under the original tenancy is treated as arising on the commencement date between the ex-landlord and the ex-tenant if—

    (a) on that date—

        (i) the home condition is met, and

        (ii) the ex-landlord is entitled to let the dwelling-house, and

    (b) the ex-landlord and the ex-tenant have not entered into another tenancy after the date on which the original tenancy ended but before the commencement date.

(2) The home condition is that the dwelling-house which was let under the original tenancy—

    (a) is, on the commencement date, the only or principal home of the ex-tenant, and

    (b) has been the only or principal home of the ex-tenant throughout the termination period.

(3) In this Part of this Schedule "the termination period" means the period—

    (a) beginning with the end of the original tenancy, and

    (b) ending with the commencement date.

(4) For the purposes of sub-paragraph (2)(a) the dwelling-house is the only or principal home of the ex-tenant on the commencement date even though the ex-tenant is then absent from the dwelling-house as a result of having been evicted in pursuance of a warrant if the warrant is subsequently set aside but the possession order under which it was granted remains in force.

(5) In that case, the new tenancy is treated as arising on the first day (if any) on which the ex-tenant resumes occupation of the dwelling-house as that person's only or principal home.

(6) For the purposes of sub-paragraph (2)(b) any period of time within the termination period is to be ignored if—

    (a) it is a period in which the ex-tenant was absent from the dwelling-house as a result of having been evicted in pursuance of a warrant which was then set aside although the possession order under which it was granted remained in force, and

    (b) the ex-tenant subsequently resumes occupation of the dwelling-house as the ex-tenant's only or principal home.

Paragraph numbers marked with a "+" can be found online and on CD.

(7) The appropriate national authority may by order provide for particular cases or descriptions of case, or particular circumstances, where the home condition is met where it would not otherwise be met.

Nature of replacement tenancies

17. The new tenancy is to be— **3A–1706**

    (a) a secure tenancy if—

        (i) the original tenancy was a secure tenancy, or

        (ii) the original tenancy was an introductory tenancy but no election by the ex-landlord under section 124 of the Housing Act 1996 (c. 52) is in force on the day on which the new tenancy arises,

    (b) an assured shorthold tenancy if the original tenancy was an assured shorthold tenancy,

    (c) an assured tenancy which is not an assured shorthold tenancy if the original tenancy was a tenancy of that kind,

    (d) an introductory tenancy if the original tenancy was an introductory tenancy and an election by the ex-landlord under section 124 of the Housing Act 1996 is in force on the day on which the new tenancy arises,

    (e) a demoted tenancy to which section 20B of the Housing Act 1988 (c. 50) applies if the original tenancy was a demoted tenancy of that kind, and

    (f) a demoted tenancy to which section 143A of the Housing Act 1996 applies if the original tenancy was a demoted tenancy of that kind.

18.—(1) The new tenancy is, subject as follows, to have effect on the same terms and **3A–1707** conditions as those applicable to the original tenancy immediately before it ended.

(2) The terms and conditions of the new tenancy are to be treated as modified so as to reflect, so far as applicable, any changes made during the termination period to the level of payments for the ex-tenant's occupation of the dwelling-house or to the other terms and conditions of the occupation.

(3) The terms and conditions of the new tenancy are to be treated as modified so that any outstanding liabilities owed by the ex-tenant to the ex-landlord in respect of payments for the ex-tenant's occupation of the dwelling-house during the termination period are liabilities in respect of rent under the new tenancy.

(4) The appropriate national authority may by order provide for other modifications of the terms and conditions of the new tenancy.

(5) Nothing in sub-paragraphs (2) to (4) is to be read as permitting modifications of the new tenancy which would not have been possible if the original tenancy had remained a tenancy throughout the termination period.

(6) The terms and conditions of a new secure tenancy which arises by virtue of paragraph 17(a)(ii) are to be treated as modified so far as necessary to reflect the fact that the new tenancy is a secure tenancy and not an introductory tenancy.

19.—(1) Any provision which is made by or under an enactment and relates to a **3A–1708** secure tenancy, assured tenancy, introductory tenancy or demoted tenancy applies, subject as follows, to a new tenancy of a corresponding kind.

(2) Any such provision which relates to an introductory tenancy applies to a new tenancy which is an introductory tenancy as if the trial period mentioned in section 125(2) of the Housing Act 1996 (c. 52) were the period of one year beginning with the day on which the new tenancy arises.

(3) Any such provision which relates to a demoted tenancy applies to a new tenancy which is a demoted tenancy as if the demotion period mentioned in section 20B(2) of the Housing Act 1988 (c. 50) or section 143B(1) of the Housing Act 1996 were the period of one year beginning with the day on which the new tenancy arises.

(4) The appropriate national authority may by order modify any provision made by or under an enactment in its application to a new tenancy.

Status of possession order and other court orders

20.—(1) The possession order in pursuance of which the original tenancy ended is to **3A–1709** be treated, so far as practicable, as if it applies to the new tenancy.

(2) Any court orders made before the commencement date which—

Paragraph numbers marked with a "+" can be found online and on CD.

HOUSING

(a) are in force on that date,

(b) relate to the occupation of the dwelling-house, and

(c) were made in contemplation of, in consequence of or otherwise in connection with the possession order,

are to be treated, so far as practicable, as if they apply to the new tenancy.

Continuity of tenancies

3A-1710   21.—(1)The new tenancy and the original tenancy are to be treated for the relevant purposes as—

(a) the same tenancy, and

(b) a tenancy which continued uninterrupted throughout the termination period.

(2) The relevant purposes are—

(a) determining whether the ex-tenant is a successor in relation to the new tenancy,

(b) calculating on or after the commencement date the period qualifying, or the aggregate of such periods, under Schedule 4 to the Housing Act 1985 (c. 68) (qualifying period for right to buy and discount),

(c) determining on or after the commencement date whether the condition set out in paragraph (b) of Ground 8 of Schedule 2 to that Act is met, and

(d) any other purposes specified by the appropriate national authority by order.

(3) In proceedings on a relevant claim the court concerned may order that the new tenancy and the original tenancy are to be treated for the purposes of the claim as—

(a) the same tenancy, and

(b) a tenancy which continued uninterrupted throughout the termination period.

(4) The following are relevant claims—

(a) a claim by the ex-tenant or the ex-landlord against the other for breach of a term or condition of the original tenancy—

(i) in respect of which proceedings are brought on or after the commencement date, or

(ii) in respect of which proceedings were brought, but were not finally determined, before that date,

(b) a claim by the ex-tenant against the ex-landlord for breach of statutory duty in respect of which proceedings are or were brought as mentioned in paragraph (a)(i) or (ii), and

(c) any other claim of a description specified by the appropriate national authority by order.

(5) For the purposes of sub-paragraph (4)(a) proceedings must be treated as finally determined if—

(a) they are withdrawn,

(b) any appeal is abandoned, or

(c) the time for appealing has expired without an appeal being brought.

Compliance with consultation requirements

3A-1711   22.—(1)The fact that—

(a) the views of the ex-tenant during the termination period were not sought or taken into account when they should have been sought or taken into account, or

(b) the views of the ex-tenant during that period were sought or taken into account when they should not have been sought or taken into account,

is not to be taken to mean that the consultation requirements were not complied with.

(2) The consultation requirements are—

(a) the requirements under—

(i) section 105(1) of the Housing Act 1985 (c. 68),

(ii) paragraphs 3 and 4 of Schedule 3A to that Act,

Paragraph numbers marked with a "+" can be found online and on CD.

(iii) regulations made under section 27AB of that Act which relate to arranging for ballots or polls with respect to a proposal to enter into a management agreement, and

(iv) section 137(2) of the Housing Act 1996 (c. 52), and

(b) any other requirements specified by the appropriate national authority by order.

Joint tenancies

23.—(1)In the application of this Part of this Schedule in relation to an original **3A–1712** tenancy which was a joint tenancy, a reference to the dwelling-house being the only or principal home of the ex-tenant is to be treated as a reference to the dwelling-house being the only or principal home of at least one of the extenants of the joint tenancy.

(2) The appropriate national authority may by order provide for this Part of this Schedule to apply in relation to an original tenancy which was a joint tenancy subject to such additional modifications as may be specified in the order.

Successor landlords

24.—(1)The appropriate national authority may by order provide for this Part of **3A–1713** this Schedule to apply, subject to such modifications as may be specified in the order, to successor landlord cases.

(2) For the purposes of sub-paragraph (1) a successor landlord case is a case, in relation to an original tenancy, where the interest of the ex-landlord in the dwelling-house—

(a) has been transferred to another person after the end of the original tenancy and before the commencement date, and

(b) on the commencement date, belongs to the person to whom it has been transferred or a subsequent transferee.

Supplementary

25. In determining for the purposes of this Part of this Schedule whether a tenancy **3A–1714** has ended, any ending which was temporary because the tenancy was restored in consequence of a court order is to be ignored.

26.—(1)In this Part of this Schedule— **3A–1715**

"appropriate national authority" means –

(a) in relation to a dwelling-house in England, the Secretary of State, and

(b) in relation to a dwelling-house in Wales, the Welsh Ministers,

"assured shorthold tenancy" and "assured tenancy" have the same meanings as in Part 1 of the Housing Act 1988 (c. 50) but do not include a demoted tenancy to which section 20B of that Act applies,

"the commencement date" means the day on which section 299 comes into force for purposes other than the purposes of the Secretary of State or the Welsh Ministers making orders under this Part of this Schedule,

"demoted tenancy" means a tenancy to which section 20B of the Act of 1988 or section 143A of the Housing Act 1996 (c. 52) applies,

"dwelling-house" –

(a) in relation to an assured tenancy, or a tenancy to which section 20B of the Act of 1988 applies, has the same meaning as in Part 1 of that Act,

(b) in relation to a tenancy to which section 143A of the Act of 1996 applies, has the same meaning as in Chapter 1A of Part 5 of that Act,

(c) in relation to an introductory tenancy, has the meaning given by section 139 of the Act of 1996, and

(d) in relation to a secure tenancy, has the meaning given by section 112 of the Housing Act 1985 (c. 68),

"ex-landlord" means the person who was the landlord under an original tenancy,

"ex-tenant" means the person who was the tenant under an original tenancy,

"introductory tenancy" has the same meaning as in Chapter 1 of Part 5 of the Act of 1996,

"modification" includes omission,

"new tenancy" means a tenancy which is treated as arising by virtue of paragraph

Paragraph numbers marked with a "+" can be found online and on CD.

HOUSING

16,

"original tenancy" has the meaning given by paragraph 15,

"possession order", in relation to a tenancy, means a court order for the possession of the dwelling-house,

"secure tenancy" has the same meaning as in Part 4 of the Act of 1985,

"successor" –

(a) in relation to a new tenancy which is an assured tenancy or which is a demoted tenancy to which section 20B of the Act of 1988 applies, has the same meaning as in section 17 of that Act,

(b) in relation to a new tenancy which is a demoted tenancy to which section 143A of the Act of 1996 applies, has the meaning given by section 143J of that Act,

(c) in relation to a new tenancy which is an introductory tenancy, has the same meaning as in section 132 of the Act of 1996, and

(d) in relation to a new tenancy which is a secure tenancy, has the same meaning as in section 88 of the Act of 1985.

"termination period" has the meaning given by paragraph 16(3).

(2) For the purposes of the definition of "appropriate national authority" in sub-paragraph (1) a dwelling-house which is partly in England and partly in Wales is to be treated—

(a) as being in England if it is treated as situated in the area of a billing authority in England by virtue of regulations under section 1(3) of the Local Government Finance Act 1992 (c. 14) (council tax in respect of dwellings), and

(b) as being in Wales if it is treated as situated in the area of a billing authority in Wales by virtue of regulations under that section.

SECTION 303   **SCHEDULE 12**

SERVICE CHARGES PROVISION OF INFORMATION AND DESIGNATED ACCOUNTS

Landlord and Tenant Act 1985 (c. 70)

3A–1716 1. The Landlord and Tenant Act 1985 is amended as follows.

3A–1717 2. For section 21 (as substituted by section 152 of the Commonhold and Leasehold Reform Act 2002 (c. 15)) (regular statements of account) substitute—

Service charge information

"21—(1) The appropriate national authority may make regulations about the provision, by landlords of dwellings to each tenant by whom service charges are payable, of information about service charges.

(2) The regulations must, subject to any exceptions provided for in the regulations, require the landlord to provide information about—

(a) the service charges of the tenant,

(b) any associated service charges, and

(c) relevant costs relating to service charges falling within paragraph (a) or (b).

(3) The regulations must, subject to any exceptions provided for in the regulations, require the landlord to provide the tenant with a report by a qualified person on information which the landlord is required to provide by virtue of this section.

(4) The regulations may make provision about—

(a) information to be provided by virtue of subsection (2),

(b) other information to be provided (whether in pursuance of a requirement or otherwise),

(c) reports of the kind mentioned in subsection (3),

(d) the period or periods in relation to which information or reports are to be provided,

(e) the times at or by which information or reports are to be provided,

Paragraph numbers marked with a "+" can be found online and on CD.

    (f) the form and manner in which information or reports are to be provided (including in particular whether information is to be contained in a statement of account),

    (g) the descriptions of persons who are to be qualified persons for the purposes of subsection (3).

(5) Subsections (2) to (4) do not limit the scope of the power conferred by subsection (1).

(6) Regulations under this section may—

    (a) make different provision for different cases or descriptions of case or for different purposes,

    (b) contain such supplementary, incidental, consequential, transitional, transitory or saving provision as the appropriate national authority considers appropriate.

(7) Regulations under this section are to be made by statutory instrument which, subject to subsections (8) and (9)—

    (a) in the case of regulations made by the Secretary of State, is to be subject to annulment in pursuance of a resolution of either House of Parliament, and

    (b) in the case of regulations made by the Welsh Ministers, is to be subject to annulment in pursuance of a resolution of the National Assembly for Wales.

(8) The Secretary of State may not make a statutory instrument containing the first regulations made by the Secretary of State under this section unless a draft of the instrument has been laid before, and approved by a resolution of, each House of Parliament.

(9) The Welsh Ministers may not make a statutory instrument containing the first regulations made by the Welsh Ministers under this section unless a draft of the instrument has been laid before, and approved by a resolution of, the National Assembly for Wales.

(10) In this section—

"the appropriate national authority" —

    (a) in relation to England, means the Secretary of State, and

    (b) in relation to Wales, means the Welsh Ministers,

"associated service charges", in relation to a tenant by whom a contribution to relevant costs is payable as a service charge, means service charges of other tenants so far as relating to the same costs."

3.—(1)Section 21A (withholding of service charges) is amended as follows.　　**3A–1718**

(2) For subsection (1) substitute—

"(1) A tenant may withhold payment of a service charge if—

    (a) the landlord has not provided him with information or a report—

        (i) at the time at which, or

        (ii) (as the case may be) by the time by which,

        he is required to provide it by virtue of section 21, or

    (b) the form or content of information or a report which the landlord has provided him with by virtue of that section (at any time) does not conform exactly or substantially with the requirements prescribed by regulations under that section."

(3) In subsection (2)—

    (a) in paragraph (a) for "accounting period to which the document" substitute "period to which the information or report", and

    (b) for paragraph (b) substitute—

"(b) amounts standing to the tenant's credit in relation to the service charges at the beginning of that period."

(4) In subsection (3)—

    (a) in paragraph (a) for "document concerned has been supplied" substitute "information or report concerned has been provided", and

    (b) for paragraph (b) substitute—

Paragraph numbers marked with a "+" can be found online and on CD.

HOUSING

"(b) in a case within paragraph (b) of that subsection, after information or a report conforming exactly or substantially with requirements prescribed by regulations under section 21 has been provided to the tenant by the landlord by way of replacement of that previously provided."

3A–1719 4.—(1)Section 22 (as substituted by section 154 of the Commonhold and Leasehold Reform Act 2002 (c. 15)) (inspection etc. of documents) is amended as follows.

(2) In subsection (1)(a) for the words from "the matters" to "under" substitute "information required to be provided to him by virtue of".

(3) In subsection (3) for "supplied with the statement of account under" substitute "provided with the information concerned by virtue of".

(4) In subsection (4)—
    (a) for "statement of account", wherever it appears, substitute "information",
    (b) for "supplied", wherever it appears, substitute "provided", and
    (c) in paragraph (b) for "21(4)" substitute "21".

3A–1720 5. In section 23(1) (as substituted by paragraph 1 of Schedule 10 to the Commonhold and Leasehold Reform Act 2002 (c. 15) (information held by superior landlord))—
    (a) for "a statement of account which the landlord is required to supply under" substitute "information which the landlord is required to provide by virtue of", and
    (b) after "of the relevant information" insert "which relates to those matters".

3A–1721 6. In section 23A(4) (effect of change of landlord)—
    (a) in paragraph (a) after "23" insert "and any regulations under section 21", and
    (b) after paragraph (b) insert
"and
    (c) any regulations under section 21 apply subject to any modifications contained in the regulations."

3A–1722 7. In section 26(1) (exception: tenants of certain public authorities) for "statements of account" substitute "service charge information, reports on such information".

3A–1723 8. In section 27 (exception: rent registered and not entered as variable) for "statements of account" substitute "service charge information, reports on such information".

3A–1724 9. Omit section 28 (meaning of "qualified accountant").

3A–1725 10. In section 39 (index of defined expressions) omit the entry in the Table for "qualified accountant". * * * *

SECTION 314   SCHEDULE 15

INELIGIBLE PERSONS FROM ABROAD: STATUTORY DISREGARDS

PART 1

ENGLAND AND WALES

Housing Act 1996 (c. 52)

3A–1726 1. The Housing Act 1996 is amended as follows.

* * * *

3A–1727 3.—(1)Section 184 (inquiry into cases of homelessness or threatened homelessness) is amended as follows.

(2) After subsection (3) insert—

"(3A) If the authority decide that a duty is owed to the applicant under section 193(2) or 195(2) but would not have done so without having had regard to a restricted person, the notice under subsection (3) must also—
    (a) inform the applicant that their decision was reached on that basis,

Paragraph numbers marked with a "+" can be found online and on CD.

3B   BUSINESS TENANCIES

Landlord and Tenant Act 1927

(17 & 18 GEO. 5 c.36)

ARRANGEMENT OF SECTIONS

PART I

COMPENSATION FOR IMPROVEMENTS AND GOODWILL ON THE TERMINATION OF TENANCIES OF BUSINESS PREMISES

PART I

COMPENSATION FOR IMPROVEMENTS AND GOODWILL ON THE TERMINATION OF TENANCIES OF BUSINESS PREMISES

Tenant's right to compensation for improvements

1.—(1) Subject to the provisions of this Part of this Act, a tenant of **3B–2**
a holding to which this Part of this Act applies shall, if a claim for the
purpose is made in the prescribed manner [and within the time
limited by section forty-seven of the Landlord and Tenant Act, 1954]
be entitled, at the termination of the tenancy, on quitting his holding, to be paid by his landlord compensation in respect of any

Paragraph numbers marked with a "+" can be found online and on CD.

improvement (including the erection of any building) on his holding made by him or his predecessors in title, not being a trade or other fixture which the tenant is by law entitled to remove, which at the termination of the tenancy adds to the letting value of the holding: Provided that the sum to be paid as compensation for any improvement shall not exceed—

(a) the net addition to the value of the holding as a whole which may be determined to be the direct result of the improvement; or

(b) the reasonable cost of carrying out the improvement at the termination of the tenancy, subject to a deduction of an amount equal to the cost (if any) of putting the works constituting the improvement into a reasonable state of repair, except so far as such cost is covered by the liability of the tenant under any covenant or agreement as to the repair of the premises.

(2) In determining the amount of such net addition as aforesaid, regard shall be had to the purposes for which it is intended that the premises shall be used after the termination of the tenancy, and if it is shown that it is intended to demolish or to make structural alterations in the premises or any part thereof or to use the premises for a different purpose, regard shall be had to the effect of such demolition, alteration or change of user on the additional value attributable to the improvement, and to the length of time likely to elapse between the termination of the tenancy and the demolition, alteration or change of user.

(3) In the absence of agreement between the parties, all questions as to the right to compensation under this section, or as to the amount thereof, shall be determined by the tribunal hereinafter mentioned, and if the tribunal determines that, on account of the intention to demolish or alter or to change the user of the premises, no compensation or a reduced amount of compensation shall be paid, the tribunal may authorise a further application for compensation to be made by the tenant if effect is not given to the intention within such time as may be fixed by the tribunal.

3B–3   *Note* —Section 1 was amended by Landlord and Tenant Act 1954 s.1(1)(a)(b) and s.47(5).

Editorial Note

3B–4   The Landlord and Tenant Act 1927 allows certain business tenants who carry out improvements to their holdings to claim compensation on quitting. This does not apply to tenants of mining leases (see s.25(1)) or tenancies of agricultural holdings (s.17(1)) or tenants who hold any office, appointment or employment from the landlord (s.17(2)). Tenants have to follow the strict procedures laid down in Pt I of this Act and comply with the time limit provided by Landlord and Tenant Act 1954 s.47—i.e. within the period of three months beginning on the date on which notice is given.

Sections 4 to 7 were repealed by Landlord and Tenant Act 1954 s.45 and Sch.7, Pt I.

holding

3B–5   i.e. premises held under a lease. See s.17.

Paragraph numbers marked with a "+" can be found online and on CD.

improvement

There is no definition of improvement in the Act, but s.1(1) provides that it must be **3B–6** something which at the termination of the tenancy adds to the letting value of the holding. Erection of a new building on unoccupied land may be an improvement within the Act (s.1(1) and *National Electric Theatres v Hudgell* [1939] Ch 553; [1939] 1 All E.R. 567). Section 2 provides that a tenant is not entitled to claim compensation in respect of certain types of improvements.

tenant

Any person entitled in possession to the holding under any contract of tenancy, **3B–7** whether the interest of such tenant was acquired by original contract, assignment, operation of law or otherwise (s.25). This includes sub-tenants. Note that the designation of landlord and tenant continues to apply to the parties until the conclusion of any proceedings taken under or in pursuance of this Act in respect of compensation (s.25(2)).

landlord

Any person who under a lease is, as between himself and the tenant or other lessee, **3B–8** for the time being entitled to the rents and profits of the demised premises payable under the lease (s.25).

trade or business

There is no definition of trade or business in the 1927 Act. It is generally accepted **3B–9** that the phrase is to be interpreted in a narrower sense than in the 1954 Act (see e.g. *Stuchbery v General Accident Fire and Life Assurance Corp* [1949] 2 K.B. 256; [1949] 1 All E.R. 1026, CA—solicitors carrying on profession, not trade or business, not entitled to compensation under the 1927 Act, but see s.17(3) and (4)).

procedural requirements

A tenant must serve on the landlord notice of intention to make improvements **3B–10** before carrying them out. The notice must be accompanied by a plan (s.3(1)). There is no prescribed form. Notice may be given in the form of a letter. See *Deerfield Travel Services v Wardens and Society of the Mistery or Art of the Leather Sellers* (1983) 46 P& C.R. 132, CA. The tenant may carry out the works if the landlord raises no objection within three months, even if a covenant in the lease provides otherwise. If the landlord objects, the tenant may apply to the court for a certificate that the improvement is a proper one (s.3(1)).

tribunal

i.e. a county court or the High Court. See s.21 and Landlord and Tenant Act 1954 **3B–11** s.63. For the procedure see Vol.1, PD 56 para.5.

the amount of compensation

See s.1(1). The landlord pays for the benefit received from the improvement. The **3B–12** sum to be paid shall not exceed the net addition to the value of the holding as a whole or the reasonable cost of carrying out the improvement at the termination of the tenancy.

Limitation on tenant's right to compensation in certain cases

2.—(1) A tenant shall not be entitled to compensation under this **3B–13** Part of this Act—

    (a) in respect of any improvement made before the commencement of this Act; or

    (b) in respect of any improvement made in pursuance of a statutory obligation, or of any improvement which the tenant or his predecessors in title were under an obligation to make in pursuance of a contract entered into, whether before or after the passing of this Act, for valuable consideration, including a building lease; or

Paragraph numbers marked with a "+" can be found online and on CD.

(c) in respect of any improvement made less than three years before the termination of the tenancy; or

(d) if within two months after the making of the claim under section one, subsection (1), of this Act the landlord serves on the tenant notice that he is willing and able to grant to the tenant, or obtain the grant to him of, a renewal of the tenancy at such rent and for such term as, failing agreement, the tribunal may consider reasonable; and, where such a notice is so served and the tenant does not within one month from the service of the notice send to the landlord an acceptance in writing of the offer, the tenant shall be deemed to have declined the offer.

(2) Where an offer of the renewal of a tenancy by the landlord under this section is accepted by the tenant, the rent fixed by the tribunal shall be the rent which in the opinion of the tribunal a willing lessee other than the tenant would agree to give and a willing lessor would agree to accept for the premises, having regard to the terms of the lease, but irrespective of the value attributable to the improvement in respect of which compensation would have been payable.

(3) The tribunal in determining the compensation for an improvement shall in reduction of the tenant's claim take into consideration any benefits which the tenant or his predecessors in title may have received from the landlord or his predecessors in title in consideration expressly or impliedly of the improvement.

3B–14   *Note* —The effect of s.2(1)(b) is restricted by Landlord and Tenant Act 1954 s.48(1).

tenant

3B–15   Any person entitled in possession to the holding under any contract of tenancy, whether the interest of such tenant was acquired by original contract, assignment, operation of law or otherwise (s.25). This includes sub-tenants. Note that the designation of landlord and tenant continues to apply to the parties until the conclusion of any proceedings taken under or in pursuance of this Act in respect of compensation (s.25(2)).

landlord

3B–16   Any person who under a lease is, as between himself and the tenant or other lessee, for the time being entitled to the rents and profits of the demised premises payable under the lease (s.25).

improvement

3B–17   See commentary to s.1.

tribunal

3B–18   i.e. a county court or the High Court. See s.21 and Landlord and Tenant Act 1954 s.63.

Landlord's right to object

3B–19   3.—(1) Where a tenant of a holding to which this Part of this Act applies proposes to make an improvement on his holding, he shall serve on his landlord notice of his intention to make such improvement, together with a specification and plan showing the proposed improvement and the part of the existing premises affected thereby,

Paragraph numbers marked with a "+" can be found online and on CD.

and if the landlord, within three months after the service of the notice, serves on the tenant notice of objection, the tenant may, in the prescribed manner, apply to the tribunal, and the tribunal may, after ascertaining that notice of such intention has been served upon any superior landlords interested and after giving such persons an opportunity of being heard, if satisfied that the improvement—

    (a) is of such a nature as to be calculated to add to the letting value of the holding at the termination of the tenancy; and

    (b) is reasonable and suitable to the character thereof; and

    (c) will not diminish the value of any other property belonging to the same landlord, or to any superior landlord from whom the immediate landlord of the tenant directly or indirectly holds;

and after making such modifications (if any) in the specification or plan as the tribunal thinks fit, or imposing such other conditions as the tribunal may think reasonable, certify in the prescribed manner that the improvement is a proper improvement.

Provided that, if the landlord proves that he has offered to execute the improvement himself in consideration of a reasonable increase of rent, or of such increase of rent as the tribunal may determine, the tribunal shall not give a certificate under this section unless it is subsequently shown to the satisfaction of the tribunal that the landlord has failed to carry out his undertaking.

(2) In considering whether the improvement is reasonable and suitable to the character of the holding, the tribunal shall have regard to any evidence brought before it by the landlord or any superior landlord (but not any other person) that the improvement is calculated to injure the amenity or convenience of the neighbourhood.

(3) The tenant shall, at the request of any superior landlord or at the request of the tribunal, supply such copies of the plans and specifications of the proposed improvement as may be required.

(4) Where no such notice of objection as aforesaid to a proposed improvement has been served within the time allowed by this section, or where the tribunal has certified an improvement to be a proper improvement, it shall be lawful for the tenant as against the immediate and any superior landlord to execute the improvement according to the plan and specification served on the landlord, or according to such plan and specification as modified by the tribunal or by agreement between the tenant and the landlord or landlords affected, anything in any lease of the premises to the contrary notwithstanding:

Provided that nothing in this subsection shall authorise a tenant to execute an improvement in contravention of any restriction created or imposed—

    (a) for naval, military or air force purposes;

    (b) for civil aviation purposes under the powers of the Air Navigation Act, 1920;

    (c) for securing any rights of the public over the foreshore or bed of the sea.

Paragraph numbers marked with a "+" can be found online and on CD.

(5) A tenant shall not be entitled to claim compensation under this Part of this Act in respect of any improvement unless he has, or his predecessors in title have, served notice of the proposal to make the improvement under this section, and (in case the landlord has served notice of objection thereto) the improvement has been certified by the tribunal to be a proper improvement and the tenant has complied with the conditions, if any, imposed by the tribunal, nor unless the improvement is completed within such time after the service on the landlord of the notice of the proposed improvement as may be agreed between the tenant and the landlord or may be fixed by the tribunal, and where proceedings have been taken before the tribunal, the tribunal may defer making any order as to costs until the expiration of the time so fixed for the completion of the improvement.

(6) Where a tenant has executed an improvement of which he has served notice in accordance with this section and with respect to which either no notice of objection has been served by the landlord or a certificate that it is a proper improvement has been obtained from the tribunal, the tenant may require the landlord to furnish to him a certificate that the improvement has been duly executed; and if the landlord refuses or fails within one month after the service of the requisition to do so, the tenant may apply to the tribunal who, if satisfied that the improvement has been duly executed, shall give a certificate to that effect.

Where the landlord furnishes such a certificate, the tenant shall be liable to pay any reasonable expenses incurred for the purpose by the landlord, and if any question arises as to the reasonableness of such expenses, it shall be determined by the tribunal.

3B-20 *Note* —Section 3 is restricted by Landlord and Tenant Act 1954 s.48(1).

holding

3B-21 i.e. premises held under a lease. See s.17.

tenant

3B-22 Any person entitled in possession to the holding under any contract of tenancy, whether the interest of such tenant was acquired by original contract, assignment, operation of law or otherwise (s.25). This includes sub-tenants. Note that the designation of landlord and tenant continues to apply to the parties until the conclusion of any proceedings taken under or in pursuance of this Act in respect of compensation (s.25(2)).

landlord

3B-23 Any person who under a lease is, as between himself and the tenant or other lessee, for the time being entitled to the rents and profits of the demised premises payable under the lease (s.25).

change of mind

3B-24 See commentary to s.1, above. Where a tenant serves a notice under s.3 stating an intention to carry out improvements, but then withdraws the notice after the landlord has served a counter notice, the landlord is not entitled to carry out the improvements (*Norfolk Capital Group Ltd v Cadogan Estates Ltd* [2004] EWHC 384 (ChD); [2004] 32 E.G. 64; [2004] 1 W.L.R. 1458).

improvement

3B-25 There is no definition of improvement in the Act, but s.1(1) provides that it must be something which at the termination of the tenancy adds to the letting value of the holding. See commentary to s.1, above.

Paragraph numbers marked with a "+" can be found online and on CD.

tribunal

    i.e. a county court or the High Court. See s.21 and Landlord and Tenant Act 1954   **3B–26**
s.63.

*   *   *   *

Rights of mesne landlords

    8.—(1) Where, in the case of any holding, there are several persons **3B–27**
standing in the relation to each other of lessor and lessee, the following provisions shall apply:— Any mesne landlord who has paid or is
liable to pay compensation under this Part of this Act, shall, at the
end of his term, be entitled to compensation from his immediate
landlord in like manner and on the same conditions as if he had
himself made the improvement [.] in question, except that it shall be
sufficient if the claim for compensation is made at least two months
before the expiration of his term: A mesne landlord shall not be
entitled to make a claim under this section unless he has, within the
time and in the manner prescribed, served on his immediate superior
landlord copies of all documents relating to proposed improvements
and claims which have been sent to him in pursuance of this Part of
this Act: Where such copies are so served, the said superior landlord
shall have, in addition to the mesne landlord, the powers conferred
by or in pursuance of this Part of this Act in like manner as if he
were the immediate landlord of the occupying tenant, and shall, in
the manner and to the extent prescribed, be at liberty to appear
before the tribunal and shall be bound by the proceedings:

    (2) In this section, references to a landlord shall include refer-
ences to his predecessors in title.

    Note —Section 8 was amended by Landlord and Tenant Act 1954, s.45 and Sch.7, **3B–28**
Pts I and II.

holding

    i.e. premises held under a lease. See s.17.   **3B–29**

tenant

    Any person entitled in possession to the holding under any contract of tenancy, **3B–30**
whether the interest of such tenant was acquired by original contract, assignment,
operation of law or otherwise (s.25). This includes sub-tenants. Note that the designation of landlord and tenant continues to apply to the parties until the conclusion of
any proceedings taken under or in pursuance of this Act in respect of compensation
(s.25(2)).

landlord

    Any person who under a lease is, as between himself and the tenant or other lessee, **3B–31**
for the time being entitled to the rents and profits of the demised premises payable
under the lease (s.25).

tribunal

    i.e. a county court or the High Court. See s.21 and Landlord and Tenant Act 1954 **3B–32**
s.63.

Restriction on contracting out

    9. This Part of this Act shall apply notwithstanding any contract to **3B–33**

Paragraph numbers marked with a "+" can be found online and on CD.

the contrary, being a contract made at any time after the eighth day of February, nineteen hundred and twenty-seven.

3B–34   *Note* —The former proviso to s.9 was repealed by Landlord and Tenant Act 1954 s.49.

Right of entry

3B–35   **10.** The landlord of a holding to which this Part of this Act applies, or any person authorised by him may at all reasonable times enter on the holding or any part of it, for the purpose of executing any improvement he has undertaken to execute and of making any inspection of the premises which may reasonably be required for the purposes of this Part of this Act.

landlord

3B–36   Any person who under a lease is, as between himself and the tenant or other lessee, for the time being entitled to the rents and profits of the demised premises payable under the lease (s.25).

holding

3B–37   i.e. premises held under a lease. See s.17.

Right to make deductions

3B–38   **11.**—(1) Out of any money payable to a tenant by way of compensation under this Part of this Act, the landlord shall be entitled to deduct any sum due to him from the tenant under or in respect of the tenancy.

(2) Out of any money due to the landlord from the tenant under or in respect of the tenancy, the tenant shall be entitled to deduct any sum payable to him by the landlord by way of compensation under this Part of this Act.

tenant

3B–39   Any person entitled in possession to the holding under any contract of tenancy, whether the interest of such tenant was acquired by original contract, assignment, operation of law or otherwise (s.25). This includes sub-tenants. Note that the designation of landlord and tenant continues to apply to the parties until the conclusion of any proceedings taken under or in pursuance of this Act in respect of compensation (s.25(2)).

landlord

3B–40   Any person who under a lease is, as between himself and the tenant or other lessee, for the time being entitled to the rents and profits of the demised premises payable under the lease (s.25).

Application of 13 & 14 Geo. 5. c.9. s.20

3B–41   **12.** Section twenty of the Agricultural Holdings Act, 1923 (which relates to charges in respect of money paid for compensation), as set out and modified in the First Schedule to this Act, shall apply to the case of money paid for compensation under this Part of this Act, including any proper costs, charges, or expenses incurred by a landlord in opposing any proposal by a tenant to execute an improvement, or in contesting a claim for compensation, and to money expended by a landlord in executing an improvement the notice of a

Paragraph numbers marked with a "+" can be found online and on CD.

proposal to execute which has been served on him by a tenant under this Part of this Act.

tenant

Any person entitled in possession to the holding under any contract of tenancy, **3B–42** whether the interest of such tenant was acquired by original contract, assignment, operation of law or otherwise (s.25). This includes sub-tenants. Note that the designation of landlord and tenant continues to apply to the parties until the conclusion of any proceedings taken under or in pursuance of this Act in respect of compensation (s.25(2)).

landlord

Any person who under a lease is, as between himself and the tenant or other lessee, **3B–43** for the time being entitled to the rents and profits of the demised premises payable under the lease (s.25).

Power to apply and raise capital money

13.—(1) Capital money arising under the Settled Land Act, 1925 **3B–44** [...] section twenty-eight of the Law of Property Act, 1925, or under the University and College Estates Act, 1925, may be applied—

    (a) in payment as for an improvement authorised by the Act of any money expended and costs incurred by a landlord under or in pursuance of this Part of this Act in or about the execution of any improvement;

    (b) in payment of any sum due to a tenant under this Part of this Act in respect of compensation for an improvement [...] and any costs, charges, and expenses incidental thereto;

    (c) in payment of the costs, charges, and expenses of opposing any proposal by a tenant to execute an improvement.

(2) The satisfaction of a claim for such compensation as aforesaid shall be included amongst the purposes for which a tenant for life, statutory owner, trustee for sale, or personal representative may raise money under section seventy-one of the Settled Land Act, 1925.

(3) Where the landlord liable to pay compensation for an improvement [...] is a tenant for life or in a fiduciary position, he may require the sum payable as compensation and any costs, charges, and expenses incidental thereto, to be paid out of any capital money held on the same trusts as the settled land.

In this subsection "capital money" includes any personal estate held on the same trusts as the land, and "settled land" includes land held on trust for sale or vested in a personal representative.

Note —Section 13 was amended by Trusts of Land and Appointment of Trustees Act **3B–45** 1925 Sch.4 and by Landlord and Tenant Act 1954 s.45, Sch.7, Pt I.

tenant

Any person entitled in possession to the holding under any contract of tenancy, **3B–46** whether the interest of such tenant was acquired by original contract, assignment, operation of law or otherwise (s.25). This includes sub-tenants. Note that the designation of landlord and tenant continues to apply to the parties until the conclusion of any proceedings taken under or in pursuance of this Act in respect of compensation (s.25(2)).

landlord

Any person who under a lease is, as between himself and the tenant or other lessee, **3B–47**

Paragraph numbers marked with a "+" can be found online and on CD.

for the time being entitled to the rents and profits of the demised premises payable under the lease (s.25).

Power to sell or grant leases notwithstanding restrictions

3B–48   **14.** Where the powers of a landlord to sell or grant leases are subject to any statutory or other restrictions, he shall, notwithstanding any such restrictions or any rule of law to the contrary, be entitled to offer to sell or grant any such reversion or lease as would under this Part of this Act relieve him from liability to pay compensation thereunder, and to convey and grant the same, and to execute any lease which he may be ordered to grant under this Part of this Act.

landlord

3B–49   Any person who under a lease is, as between himself and the tenant or other lessee, for the time being entitled to the rents and profits of the demised premises payable under the lease (s.25).

Provisions as to reversionary leases

3B–50   **15.**—(1) Where the amount which a landlord is liable to pay as compensation for an improvement under this Part of this Act has been determined by agreement or by an award of the tribunal, and the landlord had before the passing of this Act granted or agreed to grant a reversionary lease commencing on or after the termination of the then existing tenancy, the rent payable under the reversionary lease shall, if the tribunal so directs, be increased by such amount as, failing agreement, may be determined by the tribunal having regard to the addition to the letting value of the holding attributable to the improvement: Provided that no such increase shall be permissible unless the landlord has served or caused to be served on the reversionary lessee copies of all documents relating to the improvement when proposed which were sent to the landlord in pursuance of this Part of this Act.

(2) The reversionary lessee shall have the same right of objection to the proposed improvement and of appearing and being heard at any proceedings before the tribunal relative to the proposed improvement as if he were a superior landlord, and if the amount of compensation for the improvement is determined by the tribunal, any question as to the increase of rent under the reversionary lease shall, where practicable, be settled in the course of the same proceedings.

3B–51   *Note* —Section 15 was amended by Landlord and Tenant Act 1954 Sch.7, Pt II.

holding

3B–52   i.e. premises held under a lease. See s.17.

landlord

3B–53   Any person who under a lease is, as between himself and the tenant or other lessee, for the time being entitled to the rents and profits of the demised premises payable under the lease (s.25).

tribunal

3B–54   i.e. a county court or the High Court. See s.21 and Landlord and Tenant Act 1954 s.63.

Paragraph numbers marked with a "+" can be found online and on CD.

Landlord's right to reimbursement of increased taxes, rates or insurance premiums

16. Where the landlord is liable to pay any [...] rates (including **3B–55** water rate) in respect of any premises comprised in a holding, or has undertaken to pay the premiums on any fire insurance policy on any such premises, and in consequence of any improvement executed by the tenant on the premises under this Act the assessment of the premises or the rate of premium on the policy is increased, the tenant shall be liable to pay to the landlord sums equal to the amount by which—

      (a) the [...] rates payable by the landlord are increased by reason of the increase of such assessment;

      (b) the fire premium payable by the landlord is increased by reason of the increase in the rate of premium;

and the sums so payable by the tenant shall be deemed to be in the nature of rent and shall be recoverable as such from the tenant, [...].

Note —Section 16 was amended by Rent Act 1968 s.67(2); Finance Act 1963 Sch.13, **3B–56** Pt IV; and Housing Act 1980 s.152 and Sch.26.

tenant

    Any person entitled in possession to the holding under any contract of tenancy, **3B–57** whether the interest of such tenant was acquired by original contract, assignment, operation of law or otherwise (s.25). This includes sub-tenants. Note that the designation of landlord and tenant continues to apply to the parties until the conclusion of any proceedings taken under or in pursuance of this Act in respect of compensation (s.25(2)).

landlord

    Any person who under a lease is, as between himself and the tenant or other lessee, **3B–58** for the time being entitled to the rents and profits of the demised premises payable under the lease (s.25).

holding

    i.e. premises held under a lease. See s.17. **3B–59**

Holdings to which Part I. applies

17.—(1) The holdings to which this Part of this Act applies are any **3B–60** premises held under a lease, other than a mining lease, made whether before or after the commencement of this Act, and used wholly or partly for carrying on thereat any trade or business, and [not being—

      (a) agricultural holdings within the meaning of the Agricultural Holdings Act 1986 held under leases in relation to which that Act applies, or

      (b) holdings held under farm business tenancies within the meaning of the Agricultural Tenancies Act 1995]

(2) This Part of this Act shall not apply to any holding let to a tenant as the holder of any office, appointment or employment, from the landlord, and continuing so long as the tenant holds such office, appointment or employment, but in the case of a tenancy created after the commencement of this Act, only if the contract is in writing and expresses the purpose for which the tenancy is created.

Paragraph numbers marked with a "+" can be found online and on CD.

(3) For the purposes of this section, premises shall not be deemed to be premises used for carrying on thereat a trade or business—

    (a) by reason of their being used for the purpose of carrying on thereat any profession;

    (b) by reason that the tenant thereof carries on the business of subletting the premises as residential flats, whether or not the provision of meals or any other service for the occupants of the flats is undertaken by the tenant.

Provided that, so far as this Part of this Act relates to improvements, premises regularly used for carrying on a profession shall be deemed to be premises used for carrying on a trade or business.

(4) In the case of premises used partly for purposes of a trade or business and partly for other purposes, this Part of this Act shall apply to improvements only if and so far as they are improvements in relation to the trade or business.

3B–61   *Note* —Section 17 was amended by the Agricultural Tenancies Act 1995 Sch.1.

tenant

3B–62   Any person entitled in possession to the holding under any contract of tenancy, whether the interest of such tenant was acquired by original contract, assignment, operation of law or otherwise (s.25). This includes sub-tenants. Note that the designation of landlord and tenant continues to apply to the parties until the conclusion of any proceedings taken under or in pursuance of this Act in respect of compensation (s.25(2)).

landlord

3B–63   Any person who under a lease is, as between himself and the tenant or other lessee, for the time being entitled to the rents and profits of the demised premises payable under the lease (s.25).

mining lease

3B–64   A lease for any mining purpose or purposes connected therewith, and "mining purposes" include the sinking and searching for, winning, working, getting, making merchantable, smelting or otherwise converting or working for the purposes of any manufacture, carrying away, and disposing of mines and minerals, in or under land, and the erection of buildings, and the execution of engineering and other works suitable for those purposes (s.25)

trade or business

3B–65   There is no definition of trade or business in the 1927 Act. It is generally accepted that the phrase is to be interpreted in a narrower sense than in the 1954 Act (see e.g. *Stuchbery v General Accident Fire and Life Assurance Corp* [1949] 2 K.B. 256; [1949] 1 All E.R. 1026, CA—solicitors carrying on profession, not trade or business, not entitled to compensation under the 1927 Act, but see s.17(3) and (4)).

PART II

GENERAL AMENDMENTS OF THE LAW OF LANDLORD AND TENANT

Provisions as to covenants to repair

3B–66   **18.**—(1) Damages for a breach of a covenant or agreement to keep or put premises in repair during the currency of a lease, or to leave or put premises in repair at the termination of a lease, whether such covenant or agreement is expressed or implied, and whether general

Paragraph numbers marked with a "+" can be found online and on CD.

or specific, shall in no case exceed the amount (if any) by which the value of the reversion (whether immediate or not) in the premises is diminished owing to the breach of such covenant or agreement as aforesaid; and in particular no damage shall be recovered for a breach of any such covenant or agreement to leave or put premises in repair at the termination of a lease, if it is shown that the premises, in whatever state of repair they might be, would at or shortly after the termination of the tenancy have been or be pulled down, or such structural alterations made therein as would render valueless the repairs covered by the covenant or agreement.

(2) A right of re-entry or forfeiture for a breach of any such covenant or agreement as aforesaid shall not be enforceable, by action or otherwise, unless the lessor proves that the fact that such a notice as is required by section one hundred and forty-six of the Law of Property Act, 1925, had been served on the lessee was known either—

(a) to the lessee; or
(b) to an under-lessee holding under an under-lease which reserved a nominal reversion only to the lessee; or
(c) to the person who last paid the rent due under the lease either on his own behalf or as agent for the lessee or under-lessee;

and that a time reasonably sufficient to enable the repairs to be executed had elapsed since the time when the fact of the service of the notice came to the knowledge of any such person.

Where a notice has been sent by registered post addressed to a person at his last known place of abode in the United Kingdom, then, for the purposes of this subsection, that person shall be deemed, unless the contrary is proved, to have had knowledge of the fact that the notice had been served as from the time at which the letter would have been delivered in the ordinary course of post.

This subsection shall be construed as one with section one hundred and forty-six of the Law of Property Act, 1925.

(3) This section applies whether the lease was created before or after the commencement of this Act.

Note —Section 18 was amended by the Recorded Delivery Service Act 1962 s.1, Sch.   **3B–67**

re-entry or forfeiture
See the commentary to Law of Property Act 1925 s.146 at para.3A–16.   **3B–68**

deemed knowledge
See the commentary to s.23 below.   **3B–69**

Provisions as to covenants not to assign, &c. without licence or consent

19.—(1) In all leases whether made before or after the commence-   **3B–70**
ment of this Act containing a covenant condition or agreement against assigning, underletting, charging or parting with the possession of demised premises or any part thereof without licence or consent, such covenant condition or agreement shall, notwithstanding any express provision to the contrary, be deemed to be subject—

Paragraph numbers marked with a "+" can be found online and on CD.

(a) to a proviso to the effect that such licence or consent is not to be unreasonably withheld, but this proviso does not preclude the right of the landlord to require payment of a reasonable sum in respect of any legal or other expenses incurred in connection with such licence or, consent; and

(b) (if the lease is for more than forty years, and is made in consideration wholly or partially of the erection, or the substantial improvement, addition or alteration of buildings, and the lessor is not a Government department or local or public authority, or a statutory or public utility company) to a proviso to the effect that in the case of any assignment, under-letting, charging or parting with the possession (whether by the holders of the lease or any under-tenant whether immediate or not) effected more than seven years before the end of the term no consent or licence shall be required, if notice in writing of the transaction is given to the lessor within six months after the transaction is effected.

(1A) Where the landlord and the tenant under a qualifying lease have entered into an agreement specifying for the purposes of this subsection—

(a) any circumstances in which the landlord may withhold his licence or consent to an assignment of the demised premises or any part of them, or

(b) any conditions subject to which any such licence or consent may be granted,

then the landlord—

(i) shall not be regarded as unreasonably withholding his licence or consent to any such assignment if he withholds it on the ground (and it is the case) that any such circumstances exist, and

(ii) if he gives any such licence or consent subject to any such conditions, shall not be regarded as giving it subject to unreasonable conditions;

and section 1 of the Landlord and Tenant Act 1988 (qualified duty to consent to assignment etc.) shall have effect subject to the provisions of this subsection.

(1B) Subsection (1A) of this section applies to such an agreement as is mentioned in that subsection—

(a) whether it is contained in the lease or not, and

(b) whether it is made at the time when the lease is granted or at any other time falling before the application for the landlord's licence or consent is made.

(1C) Subsection (1A) shall not, however, apply to any such agreement to the extent that any circumstances or conditions specified in it are framed by reference to any matter falling to be determined by the landlord or by any other person for the purposes of the agreement, unless under the terms of the agreement—

Paragraph numbers marked with a "+" can be found online and on CD.

(a) that person's power to determine that matter is required to be exercised reasonably, or

(b) the tenant is given an unrestricted right to have any such determination reviewed by a person independent of both landlord and tenant whose identity is ascertainable by reference to the agreement,

and in the latter case the agreement provides for the determination made by any such independent person on the review to be conclusive as to the matter in question.

(1D) In its application to a qualifying lease, subsection (1)(b) of this section shall not have effect in relation to any assignment of the lease.

(1E) In subsection (1A) and (1D) of this section—

(a) "qualifying lease" means any lease which is a new tenancy for the purposes of section 1 of the Landlord and Tenant (Covenants) Act 1995 other than a residential lease, namely a lease by which a building or part of a building is let wholly or mainly as a single private residence; and

(b) references to assignment include parting with possession on assignment.

(2) In all leases whether made before or after the commencement of this Act containing a covenant condition or agreement against the making of improvements without a licence or consent, such covenant condition or agreement shall be deemed, notwithstanding any express provision to the contrary, to be subject to a proviso that such licence or consent is not to be unreasonably withheld; but this proviso does not preclude the right to require as a condition of such licence or consent the payment of a reasonable sum in respect of any damage to or diminution in the value of the premises or any neighbouring premises belonging to the landlord, and of any legal or other expenses properly incurred in connection with such licence or consent nor, in the case of an improvement which does not add to the letting value of the holding, does it preclude the right to require as a condition of such licence or consent, where such a requirement would be reasonable, an undertaking on the part of the tenant to reinstate the premises in the condition in which they were before the improvement was executed.

(3) In all leases whether made before or after the commencement of this Act containing a covenant condition or agreement against the alteration of the user of the demised premises, without licence or consent, such covenant condition or agreement shall, if the alteration does not involve any structural alteration of the premises, be deemed, notwithstanding any express provision to the contrary, to be subject to a proviso that no fine or sum of money in the nature of a fine, whether by way of increase of rent or otherwise, shall be payable for or in respect of such licence or consent; but this proviso does not preclude the right of the landlord to require payment of a reasonable sum in respect of any damage to or diminution in the value of the premises or any neighbouring premises belonging to him and of any legal or other expenses incurred in connection with such licence or consent.

Paragraph numbers marked with a "+" can be found online and on CD.

Where a dispute as to the reasonableness of any such sum has been determined by a court of competent jurisdiction, the landlord shall be bound to grant the licence or consent on payment of the sum so determined to be reasonable.

(4) This section shall not apply to leases of agricultural holdings within the meaning of the [Agricultural Holdings Act 1986], and paragraph (b) of subsection (1), subsection (2) and subsection (3) of this section shall not apply to mining leases.

3B–71 *Note* —Section 19 has been superseded in relation to secure tenancies by Housing Act 1985 s.97, s.109. It was amended by Agricultural Holdings Act 1986 ss.99 and 100, Sch.13, para.3 and Sch.14, para.15. See too Landlord and Tenant Act 1988.

tenant
3B–72 Any person entitled in possession to the holding under any contract of tenancy, whether the interest of such tenant was acquired by original contract, assignment, operation of law or otherwise (s.25). This includes sub-tenants. Note that the designation of landlord and tenant continues to apply to the parties until the conclusion of any proceedings taken under or in pursuance of this Act in respect of compensation (s.25(2)).

landlord
3B–73 Any person who under a lease is, as between himself and the tenant or other lessee, for the time being entitled to the rents and profits of the demised premises payable under the lease (s.25).

mining lease
3B–74 A lease for any mining purpose or purposes connected therewith, and "mining purposes" include the sinking and searching for, winning, working, getting, making merchantable, smelting or otherwise converting or working for the purposes of any manufacture, carrying away, and disposing of mines and minerals, in or under land, and the erection of buildings, and the execution of engineering and other works suitable for those purposes (s.25).

Reasonableness
3B–75 Section 19(1)(a) implies a proviso into leases that the "licence or consent is not to be unreasonably withheld". The leading case for determining whether or not the landlord has acted reasonably is *International Drilling Fluids Ltd v Louisville Investments (Uxbridge) Ltd* [1986] Ch 513; [1986] 2 W.L.R. 581; [1986] 1 All E.R. 321. The main principles as stated in that case are as follows (Balcombe J. at 325):

- The purpose of a covenant against assignment without the consent of the landlord, such consent not to be unreasonably withheld is to protect the lessor from having his premises used or occupied in an undesirable way or by an undesirable tenant or assignee.
- As a corollary a landlord is not entitled to refuse his consent to an assignment on grounds which have nothing to do with the relationship of landlord and tenant in regard to the subject matter of the lease.
- It is not necessary for the landlord to prove that the conclusions which led him to refuse consent were justified, if they were conclusions which might be reached by a reasonable man in the circumstances.
- If may be reasonable for the landlord to refuse his consent for an assignment on the ground of the purpose for which the proposed assignee intends to use the premises, even though that purpose is not forbidden by the lease.
- There is a divergence of authority on the question, in considering whether the landlord's refusal of consent is reasonable, whether it is permissible to have regard to the consequences to the tenant if consent to the proposed assignment is withheld. A proper reconciliation of the authorities can be achieved by saying that while a landlord need usually only consider his own relevant interest, there may be cases where there is such a disproportion between the benefit

Paragraph numbers marked with a "+" can be found online and on CD.

to the landlord and the detriment to the tenant if the landlord withholds his consent to an assignment, that it is unreasonable for the landlord to refuse consent.

- Subject to the propositions set out above, it is, in each case a question of fact, depending on all the circumstances, whether consent is being unreasonably withheld.

At the time of *International Drilling* the onus of proof was on the tenant, who had to prove that the consent had been unreasonably withheld. However, the position was reversed by s.1(6)(c) of the 1988 Act so that the burden is now on the landlord to prove that his refusal was reasonable (*Norwich v Shopmoor* [1998] 3 All E.R. 32).

Apportionment of rents

20.—(1) An order of apportionment of a rent reserved by a lease **3B–76** or any such other rent or payment as is mentioned in section ten of the Inclosure Act, 1854, may be made by the under sections ten to fourteen of that Act, on the application of any person interested in the rent or payment, or any part thereof, or in the land in respect of which such rent or payment is payable, without the concurrence of any other person: Provided that the Minister may in any such case, on the application of any person entitled to the rent or payment or any part thereof, require as a condition of making the order that any apportioned part of the rent or payment which does not exceed the yearly sum of [£5] shall be redeemed forthwith [in accordance with sections 8 to 10 of the Rentcharges Act 1977(which, for the purposes of this section, shall have effect with the necessary modifications)].

[(1A) An order of apportionment under sections 10 to 14 of the said Act of 1854 may provide for the amount apportioned to any part of the land in respect of which the rent or payment is payable to be nil.]

(2) Where the reason for the application was due to any action taken by a person other than the applicant, the Minister shall, notwithstanding anything in section fourteen of the Inclosure Act, 1854, have power to direct by whom and in what manner the expenses of the application or any part thereof are to be paid.

Note—Section 20 was amended by Housing Act 1980, s.143(1), the Rentcharges Act **3B–77** 1977 s.17(1) and Sch. 1, para.3 and by Housing Act 1980 s.143(3). The functions of the Minister of Agriculture and Fisheries under s.20 are now exercisable by the Secretary of State: see Transfer of Functions (Ministry of Food) Order 1955 (SI 1995/554); Minister of Land and Natural Resources Order 1965 (SI 1965/143); Ministry of Land and Natural Resources (Dissolution) Order 1967 (SI 1967/156) and Secretary of State for the Environment Order 1970 (SI 1970/1681).

PART III

GENERAL

The tribunal

21. The tribunal for the purposes of Part I of this Act shall be the **3B–78** court exercising jurisdiction in accordance with the provisions of section sixty-three of the Landlord and Tenant Act, 1954.

Note—The current s.21 was substituted by Landlord and Tenant Act 1954 s.63(10). **3B–79**

Paragraph numbers marked with a "+" can be found online and on CD.

* * * *

Service of notices

3B–80   **23.**—(1) Any notice, request, demand or other instrument under this Act shall be in writing and may be served on the person on whom it is to be served either personally, or by leaving it for him at his last known place of abode in England or Wales, or by sending it through the post in a registered letter addressed to him there, or, in the case of a local or public authority or a statutory or a public utility company, to the secretary or other proper officer at the principal office of such authority or company, and in the case of a notice to a landlord, the person on whom it is to be served shall include any agent of the landlord duly authorised in that behalf.

(1A) Occupation or the carrying on of a business—

    (a) by a company in which the tenant has a controlling interest; or

    (b) where the tenant is a company, by a person with a controlling interest in the company,

shall be treated for the purposes of this section as equivalent to occupation or, as the case may be, the carrying on of a business by the tenant.

(1B) Accordingly references (however expressed) in this Part of this Act to the business of, or to use, occupation or enjoyment by, the tenant shall be construed as including references to the business of, or to use, occupation or enjoyment by, a company falling within subsection (1A)(a) above or a person falling within subsection (1A)(b) above.

(2) Unless or until a tenant of a holding shall have received notice that the person theretofore entitled to the rents and profits of the holding (hereinafter referred to as "the original landlord") has ceased to be so entitled, and also notice of the name and address of the person who has become entitled to such rents and profits, any claim, notice, request, demand, or other instrument which the tenant shall serve upon or deliver to the original landlord shall be deemed to have been served upon or delivered to the landlord of such holding.

3B–81   *Note* —Section 23 was amended by the Recorded Delivery Service Act 1962 s.1.

tenant

3B–82   Any person entitled in possession to the holding under any contract of tenancy, whether the interest of such tenant was acquired by original contract, assignment, operation of law or otherwise (s.25). This includes sub-tenants. Note that the designation of landlord and tenant continues to apply to the parties until the conclusion of any proceedings taken under or in pursuance of this Act in respect of compensation (s.25(2)).

landlord

3B–83   Any person who under a lease is, as between himself and the tenant or other lessee, for the time being entitled to the rents and profits of the demised premises payable under the lease (s.25).

service of notices

3B–84   Section 23 provides that any notice, request, demand or other instrument can be

Paragraph numbers marked with a "+" can be found online and on CD.

served personally or left at the last known place of abode (which includes place of business—*Price v West London Investment Building Society Ltd* [1964] 1 W.L.R. 616; [1964] 2 All E.R. 318, CA; *cf. Arundel Corp v Khokher* [2003] EWCA Civ 1784; [2004 148 S.J.L.B. 25) of the person to be served or posted by registered or recorded delivery (s.1 of the Recorded Delivery Service Act 1962. (As to change of landlords, see s.23(2)). If one of these methods of service is adopted, service is deemed to be effected even if the document is not received by the intended recipient, if, for example, it is returned by the Post Office (*Blunden v Frogmore Investments Ltd* [2002] EWCA Civ 573; [2003] 2 P. & C.R. 6; [2003] 29 E.G. 153). If a notice is sent by recorded delivery, it is irrefutably deemed to have been served on the date that the notice was put in the post and not on the date of actual receipt (*Beanby Estates Ltd v Egg Stores (Stamford Hill) Ltd* [2003] EWHC 1252 (Ch); [2003] 1 W.L.R. 2064) and *CA Webber (Transport) Ltd v Network Rail Infrastructure Ltd (formerly Railtrack Plc)* [2003] EWCA Civ 1167; [2004] 1 W.L.R. 320; [2004] 3 All E.R. 202).

Application to Crown, Duchy, ecclesiastical and charity lands

24.—(1) This Act shall apply to land belonging to His Majesty in **3B–85** right of the Crown or the Duchy of Lancaster and to land belonging to the Duchy of Cornwall, and to land belonging to any Government department, and for that purpose the provisions of the Agricultural Holdings Act, 1923, relating to Crown and Duchy lands, as set out and adapted in Part I of the Second Schedule to this Act, shall have effect.

(2) The provisions of the Agricultural Holdings Act, 1923, with respect to the application of that Act to ecclesiastical and charity lands, as set out and adapted in Part II of the Second Schedule to this Act, shall apply for the purposes of this Act.

(3) [Repealed by Endowments and Glebe Measure 1976 (No. 4), s. 47(4), Sch. 8].

(4) Where any land is vested in the [official custodian for charities] in trust for any charity, the trustees of the charity and not the [custodian] shall be deemed to be the landlord for the purposes of this Act.

Note —Section 24 was amended by Charities Act 1960 Sch.6. The functions of the **3B–86** Ecclesiastical Commissioners are now exercisable by the Church Commissioners—see Church Commissioners Measure 1947 (No.2), s.2.

Interpretation

25.—(1) For the purposes of this Act, unless the context otherwise **3B–87** requires—

The expression "tenant" means any person entitled in possession to the holding under any contract of tenancy, whether the interest of such tenant was acquired by original contract, assignment, operation of law or otherwise;

The expression "landlord" means any person who under a lease is, as between himself and the tenant or other lessee, for the time being entitled to the rents and profits of the demised premises payable under the lease;

The expression "predecessor in title" in relation to a tenant or landlord means any person through whom the tenant or landlord has derived title, whether by assignment, by will, by intestacy, or by operation of law;

Paragraph numbers marked with a "+" can be found online and on CD.

The expression "lease" means a lease, under-lease or other tenancy, assignment operating as a lease or under-lease, or an agreement for such lease, under-lease tenancy, or assignment;

The expression "mining lease" means a lease for any mining purpose or purposes connected therewith, and

"mining purposes" include the sinking and searching for, winning, working, getting, making merchantable, smelting or otherwise converting or working for the purposes of any manufacture, carrying away, and disposing of mines and minerals, in or under land, and the erection of buildings, and the execution of engineering and other works suitable for those purposes;

The expression "term of years absolute" has the same meaning as in the Law of Property Act, 1925;

The expression "statutory company" means any company constituted by or under an Act of Parliament to construct, work or carry on any [.], tramway, hydraulic power, dock, canal or railway undertaking;

and the expression "public utility company" means any company within the meaning of the Companies (Consolidation) Act, 1908, or a society registered under the Industrial and Provident Societies Acts, 1893 to 1913, carrying on any such undertaking;

The expression "prescribed" means [prescribed by rules of court or by a practice direction].

(2) The designation of landlord and tenant shall continue to apply to the parties until the conclusion of any proceedings taken under or in pursuance of this Act in respect of compensation.

3B–88 *Note* —Section 25 was amended by the Gas Act 1986 s.67(3)(4), Sch.8, para.17, Sch.9, Pt 1, the Water Act 1989 s.190(3), Sch.27, Pt 1, the Electricity Act 1989 s.112(3)(4), Sch.17, para.35(1), Sch.18 and by SI 2001/2717, art.3.

Short title, commencement and extent

3B–89 **26.**—(1) This Act may be cited as the Landlord and Tenant Act 1927.

(2) [Repealed by Statute Law Revision Act 1950 (c. 6)]

(3) This Act shall extend to England and Wales only.

Landlord and Tenant Act 1954

3B–90 (2 & 3 ELIZ. 2 c.56)

ARRANGEMENT OF SECTIONS

PART II

SECURITY OF TENURE FOR BUSINESS, PROFESSIONAL AND OTHER TENANTS

Paragraph numbers marked with a "+" can be found online and on CD.

PART IV

MISCELLANEOUS AND SUPPLEMENTARY

SCHEDULES:

Paragraph numbers marked with a "+" can be found online and on CD.

PART II

SECURITY OF TENURE FOR BUSINESS, PROFESSIONAL AND OTHER TENANTS

Editorial note

3B–91   Part II of the Landlord and Tenant Act 1954 contains provisions regulating security of tenure as between landlords and tenants of business premises. Significant amendments were made by the Regulatory Reform (Business Tenancies) (England and Wales) Order 2003 (SI 2003/3096). These amendments apply to cases where the landlord gave a statutory notice of termination, or the tenant made a statutory request for a new tenancy on or after June 1, 2004—see the Regulatory Reform (Business Tenancies) (England and Wales) Order 2003 (SI 2003/3096) para.29(1). The full text of para.29 is as at 3B–93:

3B–92   Part II of the Act is reproduced as amended by the 2003 Reform Order. It will be necessary to refer to the Act in its unamended form where the transitional provisions apply.

The Order implemented most of the recommendations of the Law Commission contained in their 1992 paper Business Tenancies: A Periodic Review of the Landlord and Tenant Act Pt II (Law Com No.208).

In brief, the Order—

- changed the procedures to be followed to renew a tenancy or to terminate it without renewal. Both landlords and tenants are permitted to apply to the court for the terms of a new tenancy to be settled. Landlords are permitted to apply for an order that the tenancy be terminated without renewal if they can make out one of the statutory grounds for opposition. The requirement for a tenant to serve a counter-notice to a landlord's notice of termination is abolished.

- substituted new time limits for applications to the court to renew tenancies and enables the parties to agree to extend these.

- widened the circumstances in which landlord and tenant can operate the statutory procedures of Pt II. An individual and any company s/he controls should be treated as one and the same for the purposes of those procedures. Companies controlled by one individual should be treated as members of a group of companies.

- introduced several changes relating to interim rent. Tenants as well as landlords are allowed to apply to the court for interim rent. The date from which any interim rent determined by the court is payable becomes the earliest date for renewal of the tenancy which could have been specified in the statutory notice served by the landlord or tenant. A new method for the calculation of the amount of interim rent is introduced where the landlord does not oppose renewal. The interim rent is set at the same level as the rent for the new tenancy (i.e. usually, the open market rent), but subject to adjustment where market conditions or the occupational terms of the tenancy change significantly during the interim period. In other circumstances, the rules for calculation of interim rent formerly in s.24A(3), and now contained in s.24D(2), continue to apply although in a slightly modified form.

- amended the rules relating to the compensation that tenants may claim where their tenancies are not renewed. It changes the method of calculation of compensation where the tenant has occupied different parts of premises for different periods of time, and where different landlords control different parts. It also enables a tenant to claim compensation if induced not to apply to court, or to withdraw an application for renewal, because of a misrepresentation.

- replaced the requirement for both parties to apply to court for approval to an agreement to exclude security of tenure or to surrender a tenancy. The new procedure requires a landlord to serve a prescribed notice on the tenant at least 14 days before the parties enter into such an agreement. Tenants must sign a simple declaration that they have received and accepted the conse-

Paragraph numbers marked with a "+" can be found online and on CD.

quences of the notice. If the parties wish to waive the 14 day period, tenants have to sign a statutory declaration, rather than a simple declaration, that they have received and accepted the consequences of the notice. In the case of an agreement to exclude security of tenure, the declaration must be made before the tenant enters into the tenancy or becomes contractually bound to do so. In the case of an agreement to surrender, the declaration must be made before entering into the agreement. The forms of the notice, the simple declaration and the statutory declaration are set out in Scheds 1 to 4 to the Order.

- increased the categories of information which a landlord and tenant can require the other to provide towards the end of a tenancy term, in order to enable effective use of the statutory renewal or termination process. They also impose an obligation to keep such information up to date for six months, make provision for parties which transfer their interests and clarify the powers of the court where a party fails to comply with obligations to provide or update information.
- clarified what a tenant must do to terminate a tenancy to which Pt II applies. If a tenant has ceased to occupy the business premises at the expiry of the contractual term, no continuation tenancy arises. Where a tenancy has continued beyond the end of the fixed contractual term, the tenant must give three months notice, ending on any day. Where necessary, rent is apportioned.
- increased the length of the term of a new tenancy that the court may order from 14 to 15 years.

Transitional provisions

Paragraph 29 of the 2003 Reform Order contains transitional provisions. The most **3B–93** important of these for the purposes of proceedings is contained in para. 29(1). The effect of this paragraph is that Pt II of the 1954 Act as amended only applies where the s.25 notice or s.26 request was served on or after June 1, 2004 (when the 2003 Reform Order came into force). Where the notice or request was served before that date Pt II in its unamended form continues to apply. The full text of para.29 of the 2003 Reform Order is as follows:

(1) Where, before this Order came into force—

    (a) the landlord gave the tenant notice under section 25 of the Act; or

    (b) the tenant made a request for a new tenancy in accordance with section 26 of the Act,

nothing in this Order has effect in relation to the notice or request or anything done in consequence of it.

(2) Nothing in this Order has effect in relation—

    (a) to an agreement—

        (i) for the surrender of a tenancy which was made before this Order came into force and which fell within section 24(2)(b) of the Act; or

        (ii) which was authorised by the court under section 38(4) of the Act before this Order came into force; or

    (b) to a notice under section 27(2) of the Act which was given by the tenant to the immediate landlord before this Order came into force.

(3) Any provision in a tenancy which requires an order under section 38(4) of the Act to be obtained in respect of any subtenancy shall, so far as is necessary after the coming into force of this Order, be construed as if it required the procedure mentioned in section 38A of the Act to be followed, and any related requirement shall be construed accordingly.

Paragraph numbers marked with a "+" can be found online and on CD.

(4) If a person has, before the coming into force of this Order, entered into an agreement to take a tenancy, any provision in that agreement which requires an order under section 38(4) of the Act to be obtained in respect of the tenancy shall continue to be effective, notwithstanding the repeal of that provision by Article 21(2) of this Order, and the court shall retain jurisdiction to make such an order.

(5) Article 20 above does not have effect where the tenant quit the holding before this Order came into force.

(6) Nothing in Articles 23 and 24 above applies to a notice under section 40 of the Act served before this Order came into force.

Tenancies to which Part II applies

3B–94   **23.**—(1) Subject to the provisions of this Act, this Part of this Act applies to any tenancy where the property comprised in the tenancy is or includes premises which are occupied by the tenant and are so occupied for the purposes of a business carried on by him or for those and other purposes.

(1A) Occupation or the carrying on of a business—

(a) by a company in which the tenant has a controlling interest; or

(b) where the tenant is a company, by a person with a controlling interest in the company, shall be treated for the purposes of this section as equivalent to occupation or, as the case may be, the carrying on of a business by the tenant.

(1B) Accordingly references (however expressed) in this Part of this Act to the business of, or to use, occupation or enjoyment by, the tenant shall be construed as including references to the business of, or to use, occupation or enjoyment by, a company falling within subsection (1A)(a) above or a person falling within subsection (1A)(b) above.

(2) In this Part of this Act the expression "business" includes a trade, profession or employment and includes any activity carried on by a body of persons, whether corporate or unincorporate.

(3) In the following provisions of this Part of this Act the expression "the holding", in relation to a tenancy to which this Part of this Act applies, means the property comprised in the tenancy, there being excluded any part thereof which is occupied neither by the tenant nor by a person employed by the tenant and so employed for the purposes of a business by reason of which the tenancy is one to which this Part of this Act applies.

(4) Where the tenant is carrying on a business, in all or any part of the property comprised in a tenancy, in breach of a prohibition (however expressed) of use for business purposes which subsists under the terms of the tenancy and extends to the whole of that property, this Part of this Act shall not apply to the tenancy unless the immediate landlord or his predecessor in title has consented to the breach or the immediate landlord has acquiesced therein.

Paragraph numbers marked with a "+" can be found online and on CD.

In this subsection the reference to a prohibition of use for business purposes does not include a prohibition of use for the purposes of a specified business, or of use for purposes of any but a specified business, but save as aforesaid includes a prohibition of use for the purposes of some one or more only of the classes of business specified in the definition of that expression in subsection (2) of this section.

Note —Paragraphs (1A) and (1B) were added by para.13 of the Regulatory Reform **3B–95** (Business Tenancies)(England and Wales) Order 2003 (SI 2003/3096).

tenancy

See s.69(1). The definition includes an agreement for a lease or underlease, but **3B–96** does not include a mortgage. It also makes it clear that the Act applies to tenancies which have already been renewed under the provisions of the Act. Part II applies to sub tenancies. If a sub tenancy is granted in breach of a covenant, the superior landlord is not bound by the sub tenancy and may exercise rights of forfeiture, but the sub tenant, as against the mesne landlord may exercise the rights given by the Act (see s.69(1), *HL Bolton Engineering Co Ltd v TJ Graham & Sons Ltd* [1957] 1 Q.B. 159; [1956] 3 W.L.R. 804; [1956] 3 All E.R. 624, CA, and *D'Silva v Lister House Developments Ltd* [1971] Ch. 17; [1970] 2 W.L.R. 563; [1970] 1 All E.R. 858 (ChD)).

However, Landlord and Tenant Act 1954 Pt II does not apply to licences—see e.g. *Shell-Mex and BP v Manchester Garages* [1971] 1 W.L.R. 612; [1971] 1 All E.R. 841, CA (licence of petrol filling station) and *Dresden Estates v Collinson* (1988) 55 P. & C.R. 47, CA (licence of workshop and store) *National Car Parks Ltd v Trinity Development Co (Banbury) Ltd* [2001] L. & T.R. 33 (car park) and *Clear Channel UK Ltd v Manchester City Council* [2005] EWCA Civ 1304 ; [2006] L. & T.R. 7(advertising hoardings). *In Clear Channel*, in deciding that the agreement was a licence, the Court of Appeal had regard to a term that stated as follows: "This Agreement shall constitute a licence in respect of each Site and confers no tenancy on [the company] and possession of each Site is retained by [the Council] subject however to the rights and obligations created by this Agreement". Parker L.J. made it clear that he did not intend to cast any doubt on the principles of *Street v Mountford* but nonetheless stated: "On the other hand the fact remains that this was a contract negotiated between two substantial parties of equal bargaining power and with the benefit of full legal advice. Where the contract so negotiated contains not merely a label but a clause which sets out in unequivocal terms the parties' intention as to its legal effect, I would in any event have taken some persuading that its true effect was directly contrary to that expressed intention."

Tenancies at will are also excluded from statutory protection, although courts will look carefully at any agreements which are alleged to be tenancies at will (*Hagee (London) Ltd v AB Erikson and Larson* [1976] Q.B. 209; [1975] 3 W.L.R. 272; [1975] 3 All E.R. 234; (1975) 29 P. & C.R. 512, CA and *Manfield & Sons v Botchin* [1970] 2 Q.B. 612; [1970] 3 W.L.R 120; [1970] 3 All E.R. 143, QBD).

tenant

If there are joint tenants, for the purposes of the Act, "tenant" means all the joint **3B–97** tenants in whom the legal estate is vested (*Jacobs v Chaudhuri* [1968] 2 Q.B. 470; [1968] 2 W.L.R. 1098; [1968] 2 All E.R. 124, CA) As to partnerships, see s.41A below and for groups of companies, see s.42 below.

Premises

Parking spaces (and other incorporeal hereditaments) are "premises" that can be **3B–98** "occupied" for the purposes of s.23 (*Pointon York Group plc v Poulton* [2006] EWCA Civ 1001). Arden L.J.:

"That conclusion may in some cases lead to the conclusion that a tenancy may qualify under section 23 even though only the incorporeal hereditament is occupied for business purposes. But I do not see why in such a case that should not be possible if the incorporeal hereditament is capable of being occupied. It is possible to have a business use of the incorporeal hereditament alone, such as where a house is let with right to use garages or stables which are occupied used

Paragraph numbers marked with a "+" can be found online and on CD.

BUSINESS TENANCIES

for business purposes. It is difficult to see why this business use should not be protected even though the house is not used as part of the business. Section 23 expressly applies where only part of the premises is occupied for business use."

On the facts of this case, the judge had found that the tenant had occupied the parking spaces during business hours; and that was sufficient.

Occupation by tenant for purposes of a business

3B–99   See ss.23(1) and (2). Landlord and Tenant Act 1954 Pt II only applies where the property comprised in the tenancy is occupied by the tenant for the purposes of a business carried on by him. As to "business", see s.46 and s.23(2) which provides that "business" includes a trade, profession or employment and includes any activity carried on by a body of persons, whether corporate or unincorporate. Residential premises may be occupied for the purpose of a business if the business activity is "a significant purpose" (see e.g. *Cheryl Investments v Saldanha* [1978] 1 W.L.R. 1329; [1979] 1 All E.R. 5, CA; *Gurton v Parrott* (1991) 23 H.L.R. 418; [1991] 18 E.G. 161, CA; *Florent v Horez* (1984) 12 H.L.R. 1; *Lewis v Weldcrest* [1978] 1 W.L.R. 1107; [1978] 3 All E.R. 1226, CA; and *Wright v Mortimer* (1996) 28 H.L.R. 719, CA).

Premises are occupied if the tenant physically uses them and is able to control the day to day use of them by other persons (*Commissioner of Valuation for Northern Ireland v Fermanagh Protestant Board of Education* [1969] 1 W.L.R. 1708; [1969] 3 All E.R. 352, HL (a rating case). See too *Hancock & Willis v G.M.S. Syndicate* [1983] 1 E.G.L.R. 70, CA; *Graysim Holdings Ltd v P&O Property Holdings Ltd* [1994] 1 W.L.R. 992; [1994] 3 All E.R. 897, CA; [1996] A.C. 329; [1995] 3 W.L.R. 854; [1995] 4 All E.R. 831, HL). There can be no continuation tenancy if the tenant has ceased to occupy the premises for business purposes before the expiry of the contractual tenancy (*Esselte AB v Pearl Assurance Plc* [1997] 1 W.L.R. 891; [1997] 2 All E.R. 41, CA and see now s.27(1A) below). Occupation for the purposes of a business is a question of fact and degree. The mere fact that premises are empty does not take them outside Pt II—e.g. if structural repairs are needed (*I&H Caplan Ltd v Caplan (No.2)* [1963] 1 W.L.R. 1247; [1963] 2 All E.R. 930, Ch D—where the tenant closed down a general clothing and footwear business, sold off stock, but remained in occupation prior to re-opening solely selling ladies' garments). Premises may be occupied through employees, agents or managers (*Linden v Department of Health and Social Security* [1986] 1 W.L.R. 164; [1986] 1 All E.R. 691, ChD.) Protection is not lost if premises are shared but if the whole of premises are sub-let, it is the sub-tenant who is likely to be in occupation, not the mesne tenant (*Graysim Holdings Ltd v P&O Property Holdings Ltd* [1994] 1 W.L.R. 992; [1994] 3 All E.R. 897, CA; [1996] A.C. 329; [1995] 3 W.L.R. 854; [1995] 4 All E.R. 831, HL; *Bagettes Ltd v GP Estates Co Ltd* [1956] Ch. 290; [1956] 2 W.L.R. 773; [1956] 1 All E.R. 729, CA).

The county court has considered the question of shared occupation and its effect on security under Part II of the Act. In *Smith v Titanate Ltd* [2005] 2 E.G.L.R. 63 (HH Judge Roger Cooke at Central London County Court) the property was divided into six flats. The tenant ran a business of letting out the flats. The longer term lettings were on standard assured shorthold tenancies. Other lettings were on terms that included the provision of services but the judge held that these were tenancies. The question for the court was whether the tenant was in occupation of the individual flats for the purpose of a business. Held: No. The 1954 Act did not therefore apply (*Graysim Holdings Ltd v P&O Property Holdings Ltd* [1996] A.C. 329 applied). The judge analysed three different types of situation that might arise:

- Cases where flats are let on conventional terms, with the landlord doing no more than receiving the rents and performing the landlord's covenants. In those cases there is no business occupation of the flats.
- At the other end of the spectrum cases such as common lodging houses, or hostel/student halls of residence, where there is a high degree of control and the services are performed in circumstances in which the landlord has an unfettered access to the rooms for that purpose.
- Cases in the middle where there is some degree of control and/or less restricted access and/or a greater degree of intrusive service provision. Depending on the facts these may fall on either side of the line.

If a tenant voluntarily moves out after issuing a claim for a new tenancy, the claim may be struck out. On the other hand if events over which the tenant has no control

Paragraph numbers marked with a "+" can be found online and on CD.

(e.g. a fire) lead to absence from the premises, the tenant may continue to claim occupancy (*Morrison Holdings Ltd v Manders Property (Wolverhampton) Ltd* [1976] 1 W.L.R. 533; [1976] 2 All E.R. 205, CA and *Flairline Properties v Hassan* [1999] 1 EGLR 138 Anthony Hacking Q.C., Deputy High Court Judge).

Premises occupied for the purpose of a business in breach of a covenant against business or trade use in general are outside Pt II, unless the immediate landlord or his predecessor in title has consented to the breach or the immediate landlord has acquiesced therein. However a business carried out in breach of a covenant stipulated or prohibiting a particular type of business may come within Pt II (see s.23(4)). For government departments, see s.56(3).

The issue of a short gap between the tenant's physical occupation and the end of the lease was considered in the context of compensation in the case of *Bacciocchi v Academic Agency Ltd* [1998] 3 E.G.L.R. 157. *Pointon York Group plc v Poulton* [2006] EWCA Civ 1001 has confirmed that the principles in that case apply to occupation under s.23 so that "..a tenant need not be physically present in the premises if he is using them in some other way as an incident in the ordinary course or conduct of business life, provided that the premises are occupied by no other business occupier and are not used for any non-business purpose." (para.31). Prior to the end of the sublease, the subtenants employed contractors to decorate the offices and put in new carpets. While this work was being carried out the tenant's staff went to the premises to check on the progress of the work. The tenant intended to use the premises for its own business after expiry of the sublease and wanted to plan how the offices could be used in the future. The decorating and re-carpeting was finished the day after the sublease expired. On that day a director of the tenant went to the premises and spoke to the carpet layers. He confirmed that the works were suitable for the company's business occupation. It was also necessary to put in new wiring and computer systems but this could not be done in the few days between the end of the sublease and the end of the lease and were left to be carried out shortly afterwards. This was sufficient to constitute occupation and the landlord's action in evicting T the day after the expiry date in the headlease was unlawful. The lease had continued under Pt II of the 1954 Act.

excluded tenancies

Part II does *not* apply to—   **3B–100**

— agricultural holdings (see s.43(1)(a));
— farm business tenancies (see s.43(1)(aa));
— mining leases (see s.43(1)(b));
— most premises licensed for the sale of intoxicating liquor for consumption on the premises (see s.43(1)(d) below, but note the exceptions);
— most residential tenancies (see Rent Act 1977 s.24(3); Housing Act 1985 Sch.1, para.11 and Housing Act 1988 Sch.1, para.4)
— tenancies granted by reason of office, appointment or employment (see s.43(2));
— tenancies not exceeding six months (see s.43(3), but note the exceptions);
— where contracting out was authorised under the old s.38(4);

holding

See s.23(3) and s.32—i.e. prima facie the whole subject-matter of the tenancy (*Heath* **3B–101** *v Drown* [1973] A.C. 498; [1972] 2 W.L.R. 1306; [1976] 2 All E.R. 561, HL) except for those parts not occupied by the tenant or employees for business purposes.

the landlord

See s.44(1) which provides that "the landlord" means the person (whether or not he **3B–102** is the immediate landlord) who is the owner of that interest in the property comprised in the relevant tenancy which for the time being fulfils the conditions contained in ss.44(1)(a) and (b).

procedure

See CPR Pt 56, PD 56 and the commentary thereto.   **3B–103**

Continuation of tenancies to which Part II applies and grant of new tenancies

24.—(1) A tenancy to which this Part of this Act applies shall not **3B–104**

Paragraph numbers marked with a "+" can be found online and on CD.

come to an end unless terminated in accordance with the provisions of this Part of this Act; and, subject to the following provisions of this Act either the tenant or the landlord under such a tenancy may apply to the court for an order for the grant of a new tenancy—

(a) if the landlord has given notice under section 25 of this Act to terminate the tenancy, or

(b) if the tenant has made a request for a new tenancy in accordance with section 26 of this Act.

(2) The last foregoing subsection shall not prevent the coming to an end of a tenancy by notice to quit given by the tenant, by surrender or forfeiture, or by the forfeiture of a superior tenancy, unless—

(a) in the case of a notice to quit, the notice was given before the tenant had been in occupation in right of the tenancy for one month; or

(b) [...]

(2A) Neither the tenant nor the landlord may make an application under subsection (1) above if the other has made such an application and the application has been served.

(2B) Neither the tenant nor the landlord may make such an application if the landlord has made an application under section 29(2) of this Act and the application has been served.

(2C) The landlord may not withdraw an application under subsection (1) above unless the tenant consents to its withdrawal.

(3) Notwithstanding anything in subsection (1) of this section—

(a) where a tenancy to which this Part of this Act applies ceases to be such a tenancy, it shall not come to an end by reason only of the cesser, but if it was granted for a term of years certain and has been continued by subsection (1) of this section then (without prejudice to the termination thereof in accordance with any terms of the tenancy) it may be terminated by not less than three nor more than six months' notice in writing given by the landlord to the tenant;

(b) where, at a time when a tenancy is not one to which this Part of this Act applies, the landlord gives notice to quit, the operation of the notice shall not be affected by reason that the tenancy becomes one to which this Part of this Act applies after the giving of the notice.

3B–105   *Note* —The current s.24 was substituted by Law of Property Act 1969 s.15, Sch.1. It was amended by the Regulatory Reform (Business Tenancies) (England and Wales) Order 2003 (SI 2003/3096) art.3. Subsection (2)(b) was repealed by Sch.6. See too Landlord and Tenant (Licensed Premises) Act 1990 s.1(2); Leasehold Reform Act 1967 s.35(2); Rent Act 1977 s.108(3) and Opencast Coal Act 1958 s.37, Sch.7, para.22.

tenancy

3B–106   See s.69(1) and the commentary to s.23 above. The definition includes an agreement for a lease or underlease, but does not include a mortgage.

notice to quit

3B–107   Means a notice to quit given by the immediate landlord (see s.44(2)).

Paragraph numbers marked with a "+" can be found online and on CD.

the landlord

See s.44(1) which provides that "the landlord" means the person (whether or not he **3B–108** is the immediate landlord) who is the owner of that interest in the property comprised in the relevant tenancy which for the time being fulfils the conditions contained in ss.44(1)(a) and (b).

continuation

Business tenancies within the ambit of Pt II do not come to an end, notwithstand- **3B–109** ing effluxion of time, unless terminated in accordance with the provisions of the Act. On effluxion they are continued automatically by s.24(1) until terminated by notice in the prescribed form given either by the landlord (as defined in s.44) or tenant. All the terms and conditions of the contractual tenancy (apart from those relating to termination) continue to apply (see e.g. *Poster v Slough Estates Ltd* [1969] 1 Ch. 495; [1968] 1 W.L.R. 1515; [1968] 3 All E.R. 257, Ch D). The contractual rent continues to be payable, unless the landlord or the tenant applies to the court in accordance with s.24A for an interim rent. However, unless there is a clear and express provision in the contractual tenancy agreement, where the tenancy has been assigned, it is only the assignee who is liable for rent under the continuation tenancy (*City of London Corp v Fell* [1993] Q.B. 589; [1993] 3 W.L.R. 1164; [1993] 2 All E.R. 449, CA (affirmed in House of Lords, [1994] 1 A.C. 458; [1993] 2 W.L.R. 710; [1993] 4 All E.R. 968); *cf. GMS Syndicate Ltd v Gary Elliott Ltd* [1982] Ch. 1; [1981] 2 W.L.R. 478; [1981] 1 All E.R. 619, ChD). If the tenant vacates before the contractual expiry of the tenancy, he is not in occupation, and so no continuation tenancy can arise. In such circumstances there is no continuing liability for rent, even if an application has been made to the court for a new tenancy (*Surrey CC v Single Horse Properties Ltd* [2002] EWCA Civ 367; [2002] 1 W.L.R. 2106; [2002] 4 All E.R. 143).

termination

Business tenancies may be terminated by— **3B–110**
— a section 25 notice given by the landlord as defined by s.44, although, if agreement for a new tenancy is not reached, the tenant or the landlord may apply to the court for a new tenancy;
— a section 26 request by the tenant for a new tenancy. Again, if agreement is not reached, the tenant or the landlord may apply to the court for a new tenancy;
— a notice to quit, or notice exercising a break clause, given by the tenant (s.24(2), but note the exceptions);
— surrender (s.24(2) but see s.38 below); or
— forfeiture (s.24(2)).

application to the court

See s.29, CPR Pt 56 and PD 56. **3B–111**

Applications for determination of interim rent while tenancy continues

24A. **3B–112**

(1) Subject to subsection (2) below, if—

(a) the landlord of a tenancy to which this Part of this Act applies has given notice under section 25 of this Act to terminate the tenancy; or

(b) the tenant of such a tenancy has made a request for a new tenancy in accordance with section 26 of this Act,

either of them may make an application to the court to determine a rent (an "interim rent") which the tenant is to pay while the tenancy ("the relevant tenancy") continues by virtue of section 24 of this Act and the court may order payment of an interim rent in accordance with section 24C or 24D of this Act.

(2) Neither the tenant nor the landlord may make an application

Paragraph numbers marked with a "+" can be found online and on CD.

under subsection (1) above if the other has made such an application and has not withdrawn it.

(3) No application shall be entertained under subsection (1) above if it is made more than six months after the termination of the relevant tenancy.

3B–113   *Note* —New s.24A was inserted by the Regulatory Reform (Business Tenancies) (England and Wales) Order 2003 (SI 2003/3096).

tenancy

3B–114   See s.69(1) and the commentary to s.23 above. The definition includes an agreement for a lease or underlease, but does not include a mortgage.

the landlord

3B–115   See s.44(1) which provides that "the landlord" means the person (whether or not he is the immediate landlord) who is the owner of that interest in the property comprised in the relevant tenancy which for the time being fulfils the conditions contained in ss.44(1)(a) and (b).

Date from which interim rent is payable

3B–116   **24B.**—(1) The interim rent determined on an application under section 24A(1) of this Act shall be payable from the appropriate date.

(2) If an application under section 24A(1) of this Act is made in a case where the landlord has given a notice under section 25 of this Act, the appropriate date is the earliest date of termination that could have been specified in the landlord's notice.

(3) If an application under section 24A(1) of this Act is made in a case where the tenant has made a request for a new tenancy under section 26 of this Act, the appropriate date is the earliest date that could have been specified in the tenant's request as the date from which the new tenancy is to begin.

3B–117   *Note* —New s.24B was inserted by the Regulatory Reform (Business Tenancies) (England and Wales) Order 2003 (SI 2003/3096), art.18.

Amount of interim rent where new tenancy of whole premises granted and landlord not opposed

3B–118   **24C.**—(1) This section applies where—

(a) the landlord gave a notice under section 25 of this Act at a time when the tenant was in occupation of the whole of the property comprised in the relevant tenancy for purposes such as are mentioned in section 23(1) of this Act and stated in the notice that he was not opposed to the grant of a new tenancy; or

(b) the tenant made a request for a new tenancy under section 26 of this Act at a time when he was in occupation of the whole of that property for such purposes and the landlord did not give notice under subsection (6) of that section, and the landlord grants a new tenancy of the whole of the property comprised in the relevant tenancy to the tenant (whether as a result of an order for the grant of a new tenancy or otherwise).

(2) Subject to the following provisions of this section, the rent

Paragraph numbers marked with a "+" can be found online and on CD.

payable under and at the commencement of the new tenancy shall also be the interim rent.

(3) Subsection (2) above does not apply where—

    (a) the landlord or the tenant shows to the satisfaction of the court that the interim rent under that subsection differs substantially from the relevant rent; or

    (b) the landlord or the tenant shows to the satisfaction of the court that the terms of the new tenancy differ from the terms of the relevant tenancy to such an extent that the interim rent under that subsection is substantially different from the rent which (in default of such agreement) the court would have determined under section 34 of this Act to be payable under a tenancy which commenced on the same day as the new tenancy and whose other terms were the same as the relevant tenancy.

(4) In this section "the relevant rent" means the rent which (in default of agreement between the landlord and the tenant) the court would have determined under section 34 of this Act to be payable under the new tenancy if the new tenancy had commenced on the appropriate date (within the meaning of section 24B of this Act).

(5) The interim rent in a case where subsection (2) above does not apply by virtue only of subsection (3)(a) above is the relevant rent.

(6) The interim rent in a case where subsection (2) above does not apply by virtue only of subsection (3)(b) above, or by virtue of subsection (3)(a) and (b) above, is the rent which it is reasonable for the tenant to pay while the relevant tenancy continues by virtue of section 24 of this Act.

(7) In determining the interim rent under subsection (6) above the court shall have regard—

    (a) to the rent payable under the terms of the relevant tenancy; and

    (b) to the rent payable under any sub-tenancy of part of the property comprised in the relevant tenancy,

but otherwise subsections (1) and (2) of section 34 of this Act shall apply to the determination as they would apply to the determination of a rent under that section if a new tenancy of the whole of the property comprised in the relevant tenancy were granted to the tenant by order of the court and the duration of that new tenancy were the same as the duration of the new tenancy which is actually granted to the tenant.

(8) In this section and section 24D of this Act "the relevant tenancy" has the same meaning as in section 24A of this Act.

Note —New s.24C was inserted by the Regulatory Reform (Business Tenancies) **3B–119**
(England and Wales) Order 2003 (SI 2003/3096), art.18.

Amount of interim rent in any other case

24D.—(1) The interim rent in a case where section 24C of this Act **3B–120**
does not apply is the rent which it is reasonable for the tenant to pay

Paragraph numbers marked with a "+" can be found online and on CD.

while the relevant tenancy continues by virtue of section 24 of this Act.

(2) In determining the interim rent under subsection (1) above the court shall have regard—

      (a) to the rent payable under the terms of the relevant tenancy; and

      (b) to the rent payable under any sub-tenancy of part of the property comprised in the relevant tenancy,

but otherwise subsections (1) and (2) of section 34 of this Act shall apply to the determination as they would apply to the determination of a rent under that section if a new tenancy from year to year of the whole of the property comprised in the relevant tenancy were granted to the tenant by order of the court.

(3) If the court—

      (a) has made an order for the grant of a new tenancy and has ordered payment of interim rent in accordance with section 24C of this Act, but

      (b) either—

            (i) it subsequently revokes under section 36(2) of this Act the order for the grant of a new tenancy; or

            (ii) the landlord and tenant agree not to act on the order,

the court on the application of the landlord or the tenant shall determine a new interim rent in accordance with subsections (1) and (2) above without a further application under section 24A(1) of this Act.

3B–121   *Note* —New s.24D was inserted by the Regulatory Reform (Business Tenancies) (England and Wales) Order 2003 (SI 2003/3096), art.18.

Termination of tenancy by the landlord

3B–122   **25.**—(1) The landlord may terminate a tenancy to which this Part of this Act applies by a notice given to the tenant in the prescribed form specifying the date at which the tenancy is to come to an end (hereinafter referred to as "the date of termination"): Provided that this subsection has effect subject to the provisions of section 29B(4) of this Act and the provisions of Part IV of this Act as to the interim continuation of tenancies pending the disposal of applications to the court.

(2) Subject to the provisions of the next following subsection, a notice under this section shall not have effect unless it is given not more than twelve nor less than six months before the date of termination specified therein.

(3) In the case of a tenancy which apart from this Act could have been brought to an end by notice to quit given by the landlord—

      (a) the date of termination specified in a notice under this section shall not be earlier than the earliest date on which apart from this Part of this Act the tenancy could have been brought to an end by notice to quit given by the landlord on the date of the giving of the notice under this section; and

(b) where apart from this Part of this Act more than six months' notice to quit would have been required to bring the tenancy to an end, the last foregoing subsection shall have effect with the substitution for twelve months of a period six months longer than the length of notice to quit which would have been required as aforesaid.

(4) In the case of any other tenancy, a notice under this section shall not specify a date of termination earlier than the date on which apart from this Part of this Act the tenancy would have come to an end by effluxion of time.

(5) [...]

(6) A notice under this section shall not have effect unless it states whether the landlord is opposed to the grant of a new tenancy to the tenant.

(7) A notice under this section which states that the landlord is opposed to the grant of a new tenancy to the tenant shall not have effect unless it also specifies one or more of the grounds specified in section 30(1) of this Act as the ground or grounds for his opposition.

(8) A notice under this section which states that the landlord is not opposed to the grant of a new tenancy to the tenant shall not have effect unless it sets out the landlord's proposals as to—

(a) the property to be comprised in the new tenancy (being either the whole or part of the property comprised in the current tenancy);

(b) the rent to be payable under the new tenancy; and

(c) the other terms of the new tenancy.

Note —Subsection (5) was repealed by the Regulatory Reform (Business Tenancies) **3B–123** (England and Wales) Order 2003 (SI 2003/3096) which also inserted new subss. (6) to (8). Those amendments came into force June 1, 2004. They only apply where a landlord has given a tenant notice under s.25 or a tenant has made a request for a new tenancy in accordance with s.26 on or after that date.

tenancy

See s.69(1) and the commentary to s.23 above. The definition includes an agree- **3B–124** ment for a lease or underlease, but does not include a mortgage.

date of termination

See s.46 and s.25(1)—the date specified in the landlord's s.25 notice at which the **3B–125** tenancy is to come to an end.

termination

A s.25 notice is used to exercise a break clause, to terminate a tenancy which would **3B–126** have expired by effluxion of time at common law, to terminate a tenancy continuing under s.24 and to terminate a periodic tenancy.

notice to quit

Means a notice to quit given by the immediate landlord (see s.44(2)). A s.25 notice is **3B–127** not technically a notice to quit, although it has the effect of terminating the tenancy.

Requirements of a s.25 notice

A s.25 notice must: **3B–128**

(a) **be given by the landlord**—see s.44(1) which provides that "the landlord"

Paragraph numbers marked with a "+" can be found online and on CD.

means the person (whether or not he is the immediate landlord) who is the owner of that interest in the property comprised in the relevant tenancy which for the time being fulfils the conditions contained in s.44(1)(a) and (b). Notice may be served by an agent with the landlord's authority (*Tennant v London CC* (1957) 121 J.P. 428, CA; *London CC v Farren* [1956] 1 W.L.R. 1297; [1956] 3 All E.R. 401, CA) but the correct landlord must be named (*Morrow v Nadeem* [1986] 1 W.L.R. 1381; [1987] 1 All E.R. 237, CA). If there are joint landlords, all must join in giving the notice (*Dodson Bull Carpet Co Ltd v City of London Corp* [1975] 1 W.L.R. 781; [1975] 2 All E.R. 497, CA).

(b) **be given to the tenant.** If there are joint tenants, notice must be given to all of them (*Jacobs v Chaudhuri* [1968] 2 Q.B. 470; [1968] 2 W.L.R. 1098; [1968] 2 All E.R. 124, CA), but in the case of partners, see s.41A(4).

(c) **relate to the whole of the property comprised in the tenancy.** A notice which purports to apply to only part of the premises is ineffective (*Dodson Bull Carpet Co Ltd v City of London Corp.* [1975] 1 W.L.R. 781; [1975] 2 All E.R. 497, CA; *Kaiser Engineers & Contractors v Suibb (E.R.) & Sons* [1971] E.G.D. 553, CA).

(d) **specify a date for termination which complies with tenancy and the Act**—see ss.25(1) and (3). The date of termination specified in the notice cannot be earlier than the earliest date on which, contractually, the tenancy could be brought to an end by a notice to quit or break clause, or the date on which a fixed term tenancy would have expired by effluxion of time (*Crowhurst Park, Re* [1974] 1 W.L.R. 583; [1974] 1 All E.R. 991, Ch D). The notice must also be given not more than twelve nor less than six-months before the date of termination unless more than six months notice would have been required at common law. In calculating that period, the date on which the notice is given must be disregarded, with the result that the relevant period is the specified number of months which end on the corresponding day of the appropriate subsequent month (*Dodds v Walker* [1981] 1 W.L.R. 1027; [1981] 2 All E.R. 609, HL, a case on s.29). An obvious error as to the date may be corrected where it is clear that the tenant cannot be misled (*Carradine Properties Ltd v Aslam* [1976] 1 W.L.R. 442; [1976] 1 All E.R. 573, CA).

(e) **be in the prescribed form or substantially to the like effect.** There have been a number of new prescribed forms since June 1, 2004 (when the 2003 Reform Order amending Pt II of the 1954 Act came into effect) dealing with various different situations (the Landlord and Tenant Act 1954, Part 2 (Notices) (England and Wales) Regulations 2004 (SI 2004/1005). A full list is set out in Sch.1 to those regulations; and the forms themselves are in Sch.2. The two main forms that will be used in most cases are: (i) Form 1—to be used where the landlord is not opposed to the grant of a new tenancy; and (ii) Form 2—to be used where the landlord is opposed to the grant of a new tenancy. Where the landlord is not opposed to a new tenancy he must, in his s.25 notice, set out his proposals as to (i) the property to be comprised in the new tenancy, being either the whole or part of the property comprised in the tenancy; (ii) the rent to be payable under the new tenancy and (iii) the other terms of the new tenancy. The landlord must use the appropriate form listed in the schedule or "a form substantially to the same effect" (reg. 2(2)). The notes on the back of each form are part of the prescribed form and must be used. If they are omitted they will not be regarded as being in "a form substantially to same effect". These are important parts of the form and must be included. The fact that the tenant is not misled by their omission is irrelevant (*Sabella Ltd v Montgomery* [1998] 1 E.G.L.R. 65, CA).

service of notice

3B–129   See Landlord and Tenant Act 1927, s.23 which provides that any notice, request, demand or other instrument can be served personally or left at the last known place of abode (which includes place of business—*Price v West London Investment Building Society Ltd* [1964] 1 W.L.R. 616; [1964] 2 All E.R. 318, CA) of the person to be served or posted by registered or recorded delivery. (As to change of landlords, see Landlord and Tenant Act 1927 s.23(2)). If one of these methods of service is adopted, service is deemed to be effected even if the document is not received by the intended recipient, if, for example, it is returned by the Post Office (*Blunden v Frogmore Investments Ltd*

Paragraph numbers marked with a "+" can be found online and on CD.

[2002] EWCA Civ 573; [2003] 29 E.G. 153). If a notice is sent by recorded delivery it is irrefutably deemed to have been served on the date that the notice was put in the post and not on the date of actual receipt (*Beanby Estates Ltd v Egg Stores (Stamford Hill) Ltd* [2003] EWHC 1252 (Ch); [2003] 1 W.L.R. 2064 and *CA Webber (Transport) Ltd v Network Rail Infrastructure Ltd (formerly Railtrack Plc)* [2003] EWCA Civ 1167; [2004] 1 W.L.R. 320; [2004] 3All E.R. 202).

withdrawal of notice

For the limited circumstances in which a valid s.25 notice may be withdrawn, see Landlord and Tenant Act 1954 Sch.6, para.6. **3B–130**

more than one notice

For the position where a party serves more than one notice and the notices are contradictory, see *Barclays Bank Plc v Bee* [2001] EWCA Civ 1126; [2001] 37 E.G. 153. **3B–131**

Tenant's request for a new tenancy

26.—(1) A tenant's request for a new tenancy may be made where **3B–132** the current tenancy is a tenancy granted for a term of years certain exceeding one year, whether or not continued by section twenty-four of this Act, or granted for a term of years certain and thereafter from year to year.

(2) A tenant's request for a new tenancy shall be for a tenancy beginning with such date, not more than twelve nor less than six months after the making of the request, as may be specified therein:

Provided that the said date shall not be earlier than the date on which apart from this Act the current tenancy would come to an end by effluxion of time or could be brought to an end by notice to quit given by the tenant.

(3) A tenant's request for a new tenancy shall not have effect unless it is made by notice in the prescribed form given to the landlord and sets out the tenant's proposals as to the property to be comprised in the new tenancy (being either the whole or part of the property comprised in the current tenancy), as to the rent to be payable under the new tenancy and as to the other terms of the new tenancy.

(4) A tenant's request for a new tenancy shall not be made if the landlord has already given notice under the last foregoing section to terminate the current tenancy, or if the tenant has already given notice to quit or notice under the next following section; and no such notice shall be given by the landlord or the tenant after the making by the tenant of a request for a new tenancy.

(5) Where the tenant makes a request for a new tenancy in accordance with the foregoing provisions of this section, the current tenancy shall, subject to the provisions of sections 29B(4) and 36(2) of this Act and the provisions of Part IV of this Act as to the interim continuation of tenancies, terminate immediately before the date specified in the request for the beginning of the new tenancy.

(6) Within two months of the making of a tenant's request for a new tenancy the landlord may give notice to the tenant that he will oppose an application to the court for the grant of a new tenancy, and any such notice shall state on which of the grounds mentioned in section thirty of this Act the landlord will oppose the application.

Paragraph numbers marked with a "+" can be found online and on CD.

3B–133   *Note* —Section 26 is excluded by Leasehold Reform Act 1967 ss.17, 18, Sch.2, para.6(1). It was amended by the Regulatory Reform (Business Tenancies) (England and Wales) Order 2003 (SI 2003/3096). The amendment came into force June 1, 2004. It only applies where a landlord has given a tenant notice under s.25 or a tenant has made a request for a new tenancy in accordance with s.26 on or after that date.

tenancy

3B–134   See s.69(1) and the commentary to s.23 above. The definition includes an agreement for a lease or underlease, but does not include a mortgage.

current tenancy

3B–135   See s.46 and s.26(1)—the tenancy under which the tenant holds for the time being.

notice to quit

3B–136   Means a notice to quit given by the immediate landlord (see s.44(2)).

the landlord

3B–137   See s.44(1) which provides that "the landlord" means the person (whether or not he is the immediate landlord) who is the owner of that interest in the property comprised in the relevant tenancy which for the time being fulfils the conditions contained in ss.44(1)(a) and (b).

prescribed form

3B–138   See the Landlord and Tenant Act 1954, Part 2 (Notices) Regulations 2004 (SI 2004/1005). Regulation 2(2) allows a "form substantially to the like effect" of those contained in the regulations. See the commentary to s.25 above.

tenant's request

3B–139   Section 26 does not apply where (i) the landlord has already served a s.25 notice; (ii) the tenant has already given notice to quit; (iii) or the tenant has already given a s.27 notice to avoid continuance under the Act. If there are joint tenants, all must join in the request, unless they are partners (see s.41A). The request must be served upon the competent landlord or the landlord's authorised agent and set out the tenant's proposals as to the new tenancy. The request brings the existing tenancy to an end, but an interim continuation tenancy then comes into being (s.26(2)). Within two months of receipt the landlord may give a counter-notice stating that the grant of a new tenancy will be opposed on one of the s.30 grounds. Failure to give a counter-notice during the prescribed period prevents the landlord form opposing the grant of a new tenancy. There is no prescribed form for a landlord's counter-notice. As to contents, see *Marks (Morris) v British Waterways Board* [1963] 1 W.L.R. 1008; [1963] 3 All E.R. 28, CA.

A tenant's motive for requesting a new tenancy is irrelevant (*Sun Life Assurance Plc v Thales Tracs Ltd (formerly Racal Tracs Ltd)* [2001] EWCA Civ 704; [2001] 1 W.L.R. 1562; [2002] 1 All E.R. 64 notice served only to preserve compensation rights).

service

3B–140   See commentary to s.25.

Termination by tenant of tenancy for fixed term

3B–141   **27.**—(1) Where the tenant under a tenancy to which this Part of this Act applies, being a tenancy granted for a term of years certain, gives to the immediate landlord, not later than three months before the date on which apart from this Act the tenancy would come to an end by effluxion of time, a notice in writing that the tenant does not desire the tenancy to be continued, section 24 of this Act shall not have effect in relation to the tenancy, unless the notice is given before the tenant has been in occupation in right of the tenancy for one month.

(1A)   Section 24 of this Act shall not have effect in relation to a

Paragraph numbers marked with a "+" can be found online and on CD.

tenancy for a term of years certain where the tenant is not in occupation of the property comprised in the tenancy at the time when, apart from this Act, the tenancy would come to an end by effluxion of time.

(2) A tenancy granted for a term of years certain which is continuing by virtue of section 24 of this Act shall not come to an end by reason only of the tenant ceasing to occupy the property comprised in the tenancy but may be brought to an end on any day by not less than three months' notice in writing given by the tenant to the immediate landlord, whether the notice is given after the date on which apart from this Act the tenancy would have come to an end or before that date, but not before the tenant has been in occupation in right of the tenancy for one month.

(3) Where a tenancy is terminated under subsection (2) above, any rent payable in respect of a period which begins before, and ends after, the tenancy is terminated shall be apportioned, and any rent paid by the tenant in excess of the amount apportioned to the period before termination shall be recoverable by him.

Note —The current s.27 was substituted by Law of Property Act 1969 s.15, Sch.1 **3B–142** and amended by the Regulatory Reform (Business Tenancies) (England and Wales) Order 2003 (SI 2003/3096). The amendment came into force June 1, 2004. It does not have effect in relation to a notice given under s.27(2) prior to that date.

tenancy
See s.69(1) and the commentary to s.23 above. The definition includes an agree- **3B–143** ment for a lease or underlease, but does not include a mortgage.

the landlord
See s.44(1) which provides that "the landlord" means the person (whether or not he **3B–144** is the immediate landlord) who is the owner of that interest in the property comprised in the relevant tenancy which for the time being fulfils the conditions contained in ss.44(1)(a) and (b).

Renewal of tenancies by agreement
28. Where the landlord and tenant agree for the grant to the ten- **3B–145** ant of a future tenancy of the holding, or of the holding with other land, on terms and from a date specified in the agreement, the current tenancy shall continue until that date but no longer, and shall not be a tenancy to which this Part of this Act applies.

tenancy
See s.69(1) and the commentary to s.23 above. The definition includes an agree- **3B–146** ment for a lease or underlease, but does not include a mortgage.

current tenancy
See s.46 and s.26(1)—the tenancy under which the tenant holds for the time being. **3B–147**

holding
See s.46, s.32 and s.23(3) which provides that the expression "the holding" means **3B–148** the property comprised in the tenancy, there being excluded any part thereof which is occupied neither by the tenant nor by a person employed by the tenant ... for the purposes of a business by reason of which the tenancy is one to which this Part of this Act applies.

the landlord
See s.44(1) which provides that "the landlord" means the person (whether or not he **3B–149** is the immediate landlord) who is the owner of that interest in the property comprised

Paragraph numbers marked with a "+" can be found online and on CD.

in the relevant tenancy which for the time being fulfils the conditions contained in ss.44(1)(a) and (b).

agree

3B–150   Any agreement must be in writing (s.69(2)). Note too Law of Property (Miscellaneous Provisions) Act 1989 s.2.

Order by court for grant of new tenancy or termination of current tenancy

3B–151   29.—(1) Subject to the provisions of this Act, on an application under section 24(1) of this Act, the court shall make an order for the grant of a new tenancy and accordingly for the termination of the current tenancy immediately before the commencement of the new tenancy.

(2) Subject to the following provisions of this Act, a landlord may apply to the court for an order for the termination of a tenancy to which this Part of this Act applies without the grant of a new tenancy—

    (a) if he has given notice under section 25 of this Act that he is opposed to the grant of a new tenancy to the tenant; or

    (b) if the tenant has made a request for a new tenancy in accordance with section 26 of this Act and the landlord has given notice under subsection (6) of that section.

(3) The landlord may not make an application under subsection (2) above if either the tenant or the landlord has made an application under section 24(1) of this Act.

(4) Subject to the provisions of this Act, where the landlord makes an application under subsection (2) above—

    (a) if he establishes, to the satisfaction of the court, any of the grounds on which he is entitled to make the application in accordance with section 30 of this Act, the court shall make an order for the termination of the current tenancy in accordance with section 64 of this Act without the grant of a new tenancy; and

    (b) if not, it shall make an order for the grant of a new tenancy and accordingly for the termination of the current tenancy immediately before the commencement of the new tenancy.

(5) The court shall dismiss an application by the landlord under section 24(1) of this Act if the tenant informs the court that he does not want a new tenancy.

(6) The landlord may not withdraw an application under subsection (2) above unless the tenant consents to its withdrawal.

3B–152   *Note* —A new s.29 was substituted by the Regulatory Reform (Business Tenancies) (England and Wales) Order 2003 (SI 2003/3096), art.5. The amendment came into force June 1, 2004 but only applies where the s.25 notice or s.26 request was served on or after that date.

such property

3B–153   See s.32.

Paragraph numbers marked with a "+" can be found online and on CD.

such rent

See s.34.

3B–154

such other terms

See s.35.

3B–155

tenancy

See section 69(1) and the commentary to s.23 above. The definition includes an 3B–156
agreement for a lease or underlease, but does not include a mortgage.

date of termination

See s.46 and s.25(1)—the date specified in the landlord's s.25 notice at which the 3B–157
tenancy is to come to an end.

the landlord

See s.44(1) which provides that "the landlord" means the person (whether or not he 3B–158
is the immediate landlord) who is the owner of that interest in the property comprised
in the relevant tenancy which for the time being fulfils the conditions contained in
ss.44(1)(a) and (b).

procedure

See CPR Pt 56, Vol.1, para.56.0.1. Section 29 applications may be made to the 3B–159
county court (the norm—CPR r.56.2) in which the land is situated or the High Court.
They are Part 8 claims and Form **N208** should be used.

dismissing application

Since the changes to Pt II of the 1954 Act, the landlord as well as the tenant has 3B–160
been able to apply for an order that the court do grant the tenant a new lease. The
purpose of the change was to limit delay and to allow the landlord to start things off if
the tenant has not got on and applied for a new lease. This gives rise to the following
difficulty: What if the landlord applies for a new lease when the tenant does not want
one? To deal with this possibility a new s.29(5) states as follows:

"The court shall dismiss an application by the landlord under s.24(1) of this Act
if the tenant informs the court that he does not want a new tenancy".

However, neither the Act nor the rules provide for orders for costs if the tenant
does so inform the court. One can easily see factual situations where this might be
unfair to the landlord. *Trustees of the Portman Estate v Drexler* [2007] EWCA Civ 464 was
one of them. After some negotiations the landlord made an application for renewal.
Crucially, the tenant filed an acknowledgement of service agreeing to the grant of a
new lease but disputing the terms. Subsequently, the tenant found another property
and then informed the court, pursuant to s.29(5), that it did not want to take on the
new lease.

The judge at first instance made no order for costs because he treated the proceedings as having been compromised and felt that he was therefore required by guidance
given in *BCT Software Solutions Ltd v C Brewer & Sons Ltd* [2003] EWCA Civ 939 to
make no order for costs.

On appeal, the CA pointed out that the proceedings were not compromised. Rather,
the tenant had unilaterally decided not to proceed with the renewal. The CA
considered that service a notice under s.29(5) was equivalent to a discontinuance. The
tenant should therefore pay for the costs of the action. Evans-Lombe J. at paras 20 (ii)
and (ii):

"... by entering an acknowledgement of service assenting to such grant, the
defendants were, in effect, themselves launching proceedings for the granting of
a new tenancy but upon terms more favourable to them than the Claimants were
prepared to offer ... It seems to me that the service on the court by the
Defendants of notice under s.29(5) was the equivalent of a notice to discontinue
proceedings in which they had been seeking an order from the court awarding
them a new tenancy upon terms settled by the court. It follows that the judge
should have placed the burden of proof on the Defendants to establish facts
which would justify his departure from the normal order in these circumstances."

Paragraph numbers marked with a "+" can be found online and on CD.

Time limits for applications to court

3B–161   **29A.**—(1) Subject to section 29B of this Act, the court shall not entertain an application—

(a) by the tenant or the landlord under section 24(1) of this Act; or

(b) by the landlord under section 29(2) of this Act,

if it is made after the end of the statutory period.

(2) In this section and section 29B of this Act "the statutory period" means a period ending—

(a) where the landlord gave a notice under section 25 of this Act, on the date specified in his notice; and

(b) where the tenant made a request for a new tenancy under section 26 of this Act, immediately before the date specified in his request.

(3) Where the tenant has made a request for a new tenancy under section 26 of this Act, the court shall not entertain an application under section 24(1) of this Act which is made before the end of the period of two months beginning with the date of the making of the request, unless the application is made after the landlord has given a notice under section 26(6) of this Act.

3B–162   *Note* —New s.29A was substituted by the Regulatory Reform (Business Tenancies) (England and Wales) Order 2003 (SI 2003/3096). The amendment came into force June 1, 2004.

time limits

3B–163   Under the law prior to June 1, 2004 the tenant's application for a new tenancy had to be made "not less than two nor more than four months" after the giving of the landlord's s.25 or as the case may be the tenant's s.26 request. Many tenants missed this window of opportunity and lost their right to apply for a new tenancy. Since June 1, 2004 the deadline in respect of notices served on or after that date has been:

* the date specified in the s.25 notice; or
* the date immediately before the date specified in the s.26 request (s.29A(2)).

However, it should be noted (by tenants in particular) that where a s.26 request has been made by the tenant an application for a new tenancy cannot be made until the landlord has served a counter-notice or the time for so doing has passed (s.29A(3)). Thus, there still remains a potential trap that could invalidate applications.

no application shall be entertained

3B–164   The court has no power to extend time (*Hodgson v Armstrong* [1967] 2 Q.B. 299; [1967] 2 W.L.R. 311; [1967] 1 All E.R. 307, CA). Strict compliance with the timetable may be waived by the parties (*Kammins Ballrooms Co Ltd v Zenith Investments (Torquay) Ltd (No.1)* [1971] A.C. 850; [1970] 2 All E.R. 871, HL), but the landlord cannot agree to confer jurisdiction which the court does not have (e.g. because the application was made after the tenant ceased to be a tenant—*Meah v Sector Properties Ltd* [1974] 1 W.L.R. 547; [1974] 1 All E.R. 1074, CA). However note that the parties can agree to extend time before issue—see s.29B below.

If the tenant ceases to occupy for purposes of a business, the protection of Pt II is lost and the landlord may apply to have the claim dismissed or struck out (*I&H Caplan Ltd v Caplan (No.2)* [1963] 1 W.L.R. 1247; [1963] 2 All E.R. 930, Ch D).

Agreements extending time limits

3B–165   **29B.**—(1) After the landlord has given a notice under section 25 of this Act, or the tenant has made a request under section 26 of this Act, but before the end of the statutory period, the landlord and ten-

Paragraph numbers marked with a "+" can be found online and on CD.

ant may agree that an application such as is mentioned in section 29A(1) of this Act, may be made before the end of a period specified in the agreement which will expire after the end of the statutory period.

(2) The landlord and tenant may from time to time by agreement further extend the period for making such an application, but any such agreement must be made before the end of the period specified in the current agreement.

(3) Where an agreement is made under this section, the court may entertain an application such as is mentioned in section 29A(1) of this Act if it is made before the end of the period specified in the agreement.

(4) Where an agreement is made under this section, or two or more agreements are made under this section, the landlord's notice under section 25 of this Act or tenant's request under section 26 of this Act shall be treated as terminating the tenancy at the end of the period specified in the agreement or, as the case may be, at the end of the period specified in the last of those agreements.

Note —New s.29B was substituted by the Regulatory Reform (Business Tenancies) **3B–166** (England and Wales) Order 2003 (SI 2003/3096). The amendment came into force June 1, 2004 but only applies where the s.25 or s.26 notice was served on or after that date.

agreement in writing
The agreement to extend the time limit must be in writing (s.69(2)). Is an agree- **3B–167** ment by email in writing? Almost certainly yes. Section 5 and Sch.1 of the Interpretation Act 1978 provides that "writing" includes "typing, printing, lithography, photography and other modes of representing or reproducing words in a visible form, and expressions referring to writing are construed accordingly". However, any practitioner who has any doubt about this should insist upon an agreement in old fashioned correspondence. If the agreement is not forthcoming the application should be made before the time limit expires.

time of expiry
When agreeing a new deadline the parties should use whole days not specific mo- **3B–168** ments in time (e.g. 3.30pm on ...). Although the statute does not expressly forbid times it does seem to follow from the definition of "the statutory period" in s.29A(2) that only whole days are allowed. Indeed, generally speaking, the law does not recognise parts of days when dealing with notices.

agreement before time expires
If no application to the court is made before the expiry of the deadline or any **3B–169** agreed extension, the right to apply to the court will be lost and the tenancy will come to an end (s.29B(3)(4)).

Opposition by landlord to application for new tenancy

30.—(1) The grounds on which a landlord may oppose an applica- **3B–170** tion under section 24(1) of this Act, or make an application under section 29(2) of this Act, are such of the following grounds as may be stated in the landlord's notice under section 25 of this Act or, as the case may be, under subsection (6) of section 26 thereof, that is to say:—

　　　　(a) where under the current tenancy the tenant has any obligations as respects the repair and maintenance of the

Paragraph numbers marked with a "+" can be found online and on CD.

holding, that the tenant ought not to be granted a new tenancy in view of the state of repair of the holding, being a state resulting from the tenant's failure to comply with the said obligations;

(b) that the tenant ought not to be granted a new tenancy in view of his persistent delay in paying rent which has become due;

(c) that the tenant ought not to be granted a new tenancy in view of other substantial breaches by him of his obligations under the current tenancy, or for any other reason connected with the tenant's use or management of the holding;

(d) that the landlord has offered and is willing to provide or secure the provision of alternative accommodation for the tenant, that the terms on which the alternative accommodation is available are reasonable having regard to the terms of the current tenancy and to all other relevant circumstances, and that the accommodation and the time at which it will be available are suitable for the tenant's requirements (including the requirement to preserve goodwill) having regard to the nature and class of his business and to the situation and extent of, and facilities afforded by, the holding;

(e) where the current tenancy was created by the sub-letting of part only of the property comprised in a superior tenancy and the landlord is the owner of an interest in reversion expectant on the termination of that superior tenancy, that the aggregate of the rents reasonably obtainable on separate lettings of the holding and the remainder of that property would be substantially less than the rent reasonably obtainable on a letting of that property as a whole, that on the termination of the current tenancy the landlord requires possession of the holding for the purpose of letting or otherwise disposing of the said property as a whole, and that in view thereof the tenant ought not to be granted a new tenancy;

(f) that on the termination of the current tenancy the landlord intends to demolish or reconstruct the premises comprised in the holding or a substantial part of those premises or to carry out substantial work of construction on the holding or part thereof and that he could not reasonably do so without obtaining possession of the holding;

(g) subject as hereinafter provided, that on the termination of the current tenancy the landlord intends to occupy the holding for the purposes, or partly for the purposes, of a business to be carried on by him therein, or as his residence.

(1A) Where the landlord has a controlling interest in a company, the reference in subsection (1)(g) above to the landlord shall be construed as a reference to the landlord or that company.

Paragraph numbers marked with a "+" can be found online and on CD.

(1B) Subject to subsection (2A) below, where the landlord is a company and a person has a controlling interest in the company, the reference in subsection (1)(g) above to the landlord shall be construed as a reference to the landlord or that person.

(2) The landlord shall not be entitled to oppose an application under section 24(1) of this Act, or make an application under section 29(2) of this Act,on the ground specified in paragraph (g) of the last foregoing subsection if the interest of the landlord, or an interest which has merged in that interest and but for the merger would be the interest of the landlord, was purchased or created after the beginning of the period of five years which ends with the termination of the current tenancy, and at all times since the purchase or creation thereof the holding has been comprised in a tenancy or successive tenancies of the description specified in subsection (1) of section 23 of this Act.

(2A) Subsection (1B) above shall not apply if the controlling interest was acquired after the beginning of the period of five years which ends with the termination of the current tenancy, and at all times since the acquisition of the controlling interest the holding has been comprised in a tenancy or successive tenancies of the description specified in section 23(1) of this Act.

(3) [...]

Note —The current s.30 was substituted by the Law of Property Act 1969 s.15, Sch.1 **3B–171** and amended by the Regulatory Reform (Business Tenancies) (England and Wales) Order 2003 (SI 2003/3096) arts 6, 14 and subs.(3) was repealed by Sch.6, para.1. The amendments came into force June 1, 2004 but only apply where the s.25 notice or s.26 request was served after that date.

Business

See s.46 and s.23(2) which provides that "business" includes a trade, profession or **3B–172** employment and includes any activity carried on by a body of persons, whether corporate or unincorporate. See too the commentary to s.23 above.

current tenancy

See s.46 and s.26(1)—the tenancy under which the tenant holds for the time being. **3B–173**

holding

See s.46, s.32 and s.23(3) which provides that the expression "the holding" means **3B–174** the property comprised in the tenancy, there being excluded any part thereof which is occupied neither by the tenant nor by a person employed by the tenant ... for the purposes of a business by reason of which the tenancy is one to which this Part of this Act applies.

the landlord

See s.44(1) which provides that "the landlord" means the person (whether or not he **3B–175** is the immediate landlord) who is the owner of that interest in the property comprised in the relevant tenancy which for the time being fulfils the conditions contained in ss.44(1)(a) and (b).

grounds

Landlords may only rely upon grounds for opposing the grant of a new tenancy or **3B–176** termination under s.29(2) if they are specified in a s.25 notice or a counter-notice served in response to a tenant's s.26 notice.

s.30(1)(a) state of repair

The state of repair of the holding is only a ground for opposing the grant of a new **3B–177**

Paragraph numbers marked with a "+" can be found online and on CD.

tenancy if it results form the tenant's failure to comply with obligations. To be relied upon, the neglect to repair must be "substantial" (*Lyons v Central Commercial Properties* [1958] 1 W.L.R. 869; [1958] 2 All E.R. 767, CA). Even then, the court has a discretion and should have regard to the overall conduct of the tenant in relation to his obligations and the reason for any breach. There is no entitlement to compensation if this ground is established.

s.30(1)(b) persistent delay in paying rent

3B–178   There may be "persistent delay" if one instalment of rent has been in arrears for a significant period of time or instalments have persistently been paid late, or both (*Hopcutt v Carver* (1969) 209 E.G. 1069, CA; *Horowitz v Ferrand* [1956] C.L.Y. 4843. In exercising its discretion, the court may take into account both the conduct of the tenant and the landlord in relation to the late payments (*Hazel v Akhtar* [2001] EWCA Civ 1883; [2002] 07 E.G. 124—landlord who accepted late payment without complaint prevented form relying upon s.30(1)(b)). There is no entitlement to compensation if this ground is established.

s.30(1)(c) other substantial breaches of obligations, or any other reason connected with the tenant's use or management of the holding

3B–179   The court has a discretion and should have regard to the overall conduct of the tenant in relation to his obligations and the reason for any breach (*Eichner v Midland Bank Executor and Trustee Co* [1970] 1 W.L.R. 1120; [1970] 2 All E.R. 597, CA). There is no entitlement to compensation if this ground is established.

s.30(1)(d) offer of alternative accommodation for the tenant

3B–180   Alternative accommodation must be suitable for the tenant's requirements. For a case in which possession was refused because the alternative accommodation would have adversely affected the way in which the tenant's business was conducted, see *Singh v Malayan Theatres* [1953] A.C. 632; [1953] 3 W.L.R. 491, PC. The terms on which it is offered must be reasonable having regard to the terms of the current tenancy and all other circumstances. Accommodation must have been offered and still be available at the time of the court hearing. If this ground is established, the court has no discretion and must dismiss the application for a new tenancy. There is no entitlement to compensation if this ground is established.

s30(1)(e) aggregate of the rents reasonably obtainable on separate lettings less than the rent reasonably obtainable on a letting of that property as a whole

3B–181   This ground is rarely used in practice. It is designed to prevent a landlord from suffering prejudice as a result of sub-lettings created by a tenant. Even if the ground is established, the court has a discretion.

s.30(1)(f) intention of landlord to demolish or reconstruct

3B–182   See too s.31A. The landlord must show that the intention to demolish or reconstruct exists at the time of the hearing and will be fulfilled shortly after the date of the hearing. (*Betty's Cafes Ltd v Phillips Furnishing Stores Ltd (No.1)* [1959] A.C. 20; [1958] 2 W.L.R. 513; [1958] 1 All E.R. 607, HL). The intention must be genuine, firm, and settled, and unlikely to be changed (*Fleet Electrics v Jacey Investments* [1956] 1 W.L.R. 1027; [1956] 3 All E.R. 99, CA). There are two elements to the concept of intention: first, a genuine desire that the result will come about and, secondly, a reasonable prospect of bringing about that result. For example, in *Edwards v Thompson* (1990) 60 P. & C.R. 222, CA, a landlord failed to prevent the grant of a new tenancy because she had not found a developer at the time of the hearing and "there was a real possibility that [she] would not be in a position to carry out the entire development on the termination of the current tenancy ... She had failed to show that she had the means and ability; she had not established the necessary intention." (See too *Capocci v Goble* (1987) 284 E.G. 230, CA). A landlord's case is stronger if planning permission has been obtained in advance of the institution of court proceedings, but this is not essential if it can be shown that there is a reasonable prospect of getting consent (*Gregson v Cyril Lord Ltd* [1963] 1 W.L.R. 41; [1962] 3 All E.R. 907, CA).

It has been held that "reconstruction" means "a substantial interference with the structure of the premises and then a rebuilding, in probably a different form, of such

Paragraph numbers marked with a "+" can be found online and on CD.

part of the premises as has been demolished by reason of the interference with the structure" (*Joel v Swaddle* [1957] 1 W.L.R. 1094; [1957] 3 All E.R. 325 at p.329, CA—removal of internal walls and replacement with reinforced steel joists amounted to reconstruction of a substantial part). See too *Barth v Pritchard* [1990] 20 E.G. 65, CA and *Cook v Mott* (1961) 178 E.G. 637, CA). There is no requirement of demolition or construction of structural or load bearing features as a condition of applicability (*Ivorygrove Ltd v Global Grange Ltd* [2003] EWHC 1409 (Ch); [2003] 1 W.L.R. 2090).

The landlord must also show that the intended work cannot reasonably be carried out without the tenant giving up possession of the premises. "Possession" means "putting an end to legal rights of possession" and not merely access. For example, in *Heath v Drown* [1973] A.C. 498; [1972] 2 W.L.R. 1306; [1972] 2 All E.R. 561, HL a business tenant successfully defeated the landlord's claim even though the front wall of the premises had to be entirely rebuilt and it would not be possible to occupy the premises while such work was carried out. The landlord must show that the work cannot be carried out while the tenancy still exists.

If this ground is established, the court has no discretion and must dismiss the application for a new tenancy.

In *Wessex Reserve Forces and Cadets Association v White* [2005] EWCA Civ 1744(CA) the landlord relied upon s.30(1)(f) as a ground of opposition, stating that it intended to demolish some huts on the land. However, the huts were tenants' fixtures. These were the most substantial structures on the land and under the terms of the lease the tenant was required to remove them upon termination of its tenancy. The landlord could not therefore establish that it was going to demolish them.

In *Dogan v Semali Investments Ltd* [2005] EWCA Civ 1036 the issue was whether there was a reasonable prospect of obtaining planning permission for the landlord's proposals. The case reminds us that the burden on the landlord is not a high one and that (contrary to popular belief) it is not necessary (although as a matter of tactics highly desirable) to have planning permission at the date of the hearing. *Gatwick Parking Services Ltd v Sargent* [2000] 2 E.G.L.R. 45 applied.

s.30(1)(g) intention of landlord to occupy the holding for the purposes of a business or as his residence

For "intention" see the commentary to s.30(1)(f) above. The landlord need not **3B–183** intend to occupy personally. It is sufficient to intend to carry on the business through an agent or manager (*Hills (Patents) Ltd v University College Hospital Board of Governors* [1956] 1 Q.B. 90; [1955] 3 W.L.R. 523; [1955] 3 All E.R. 365, CA). An intention to sublet the whole is inconsistent with an intention to occupy (*Crowhurst Park, Re* [1974] 1 W.L.R. 583; [1974] 1 All E.R. 991, Ch D). As to trustees, see s.41(2) and groups of companies, s.42(3).

Note that this ground cannot be relied upon by a landlord who has purchased within the preceding five years if the premises have been let during the whole of that period (s.30(2)—see too *Northcote Laundry v Donnelly (Frederick)* [1968] 1 W.L.R. 562; [1968] 2 All E.R. 50, CA). The period of five years is calculated backwards from the date of determination of the current tenancy (see *Frederick Lawrence Ltd v Freeman Hardy & Willis Ltd (No.1)* [1959] Ch. 731; [1959] 3 W.L.R. 275; [1959] 3 All E.R. 77, CA). If this ground is established, the court has no discretion and must dismiss the application for a new tenancy.

application dismissed

Any continuation tenancy terminates on the expiry of three months beginning with **3B–184** the date on which the application is finally disposed of (Sch.6, para.4(3)).

misrepresentation or concealment

If the court refuses a new tenancy, and it later appears that the court was induced **3B–185** to refuse it by misrepresentation or concealment, the court may order compensation (s.37A).

Dismissal of application for new tenancy where landlord successfully opposes

31.—(1) If the landlord opposes an application under subsection **3B–186**

Paragraph numbers marked with a "+" can be found online and on CD.

(1) of section twenty-four of this Act on grounds on which he is entitled to oppose it in accordance with the last foregoing section and establishes any of those grounds to the satisfaction of the court, the court shall not make an order for the grant of a new tenancy.

(2) Where the landlord opposes an application under section 24(1) of this Act, or makes an application under section 29(2) of this Act, on one or more of the grounds specified in section 30(1)(d) to (f) of this Act but establishes none of those grounds, and none of the other grounds specified in section 30(1) of this Act, to the satisfaction of the court, then if the court would have been satisfied on any of the grounds specified in section 30(1)(d) to (f) of this Act, if the date of termination specified in the landlord's notice or, as the case may be, the date specified in the tenant's request for a new tenancy as the date from which the new tenancy is to begin, had been such later date as the court may determine, being a date not more than one year later than the date so specified—

(a) the court shall make a declaration to that effect, stating of which of the said grounds the court would have been satisfied as aforesaid and specifying the date determined by the court as aforesaid, but shall not make an order for the grant of a new tenancy;

(b) if, within fourteen days after the making of the declaration, the tenant so requires the court shall make an order substituting the said date for the date specified in the said landlord's notice or tenant's request, and thereupon that notice or request shall have effect accordingly.

3B–187   *Note* —Note s.31 was amended by the Regulatory Reform (Business Tenancies) (England and Wales) Order 2003 (SI 2003/3096), art.7. The amendments came into force June 1, 2004 but only applies where the s.25 notice or s.26 request was served on or after that date.

date of termination

3B–188   See s.46 and s.25(1)—the date specified in the landlord's s.25 notice at which the tenancy is to come to an end.

the landlord

3B–189   See s.44(1) which provides that "the landlord" means the person (whether or not he is the immediate landlord) who is the owner of that interest in the property comprised in the relevant tenancy which for the time being fulfils the conditions contained in ss.44(1)(a) and (b).

Grant of new tenancy in some cases where s. 30(1)(f) applies

3B–190   **31A.**—(1) Where the landlord opposes an application under section 24(1) of this Act on the ground specified in paragraph (f) of section 30(1) of this Act, or makes an application under section 29(2) of this Act on that ground,the court shall not hold that the landlord could not reasonably carry out the demolition, reconstruction or work of construction intended without obtaining possession of the holding if—

(a) the tenant agrees to the inclusion in the terms of the

Paragraph numbers marked with a "+" can be found online and on CD.

new tenancy of terms giving the landlord access and other facilities for carrying out the work intended and, given that access and those facilities, the landlord could reasonably carry out the work without obtaining possession of the holding and without interfering to a substantial extent or for a substantial time with the use of the holding for the purposes of the business carried on by the tenant; or

(b) the tenant is willing to accept a tenancy of an economically separable part of the holding and either paragraph (a) of this section is satisfied with respect to that part or possession of the remainder of the holding would be reasonably sufficient to enable the landlord to carry out the intended work.

(2) For the purposes of subsection (1)(b) of this section a part of a holding shall be deemed to be an economically separate part if, and only if, the aggregate of the rents which, after the completion of the intended work, would be reasonably obtainable on separate lettings of that part and the remainder of the premises affected by or resulting from the work would not be substantially less than the rent which would then be reasonably obtainable on a letting of those premises as a whole.

Note —Section 31A was inserted by Law of Property Act 1969 s.7(1) and amended **3B–191** by the Regulatory Reform (Business Tenancies) (England and Wales) Order 2003 (SI 2003/3096), art.8. The amendment came into force June 1, 2004.

business
See s.46 and s.23(2) which provides that "business" includes a trade, profession or **3B–192** employment and includes any activity carried on by a body of persons, whether corporate or unincorporate. See too the commentary to s.23 above.

holding
See s.46, s.32 and s.23(3) which provides that the expression "the holding" means **3B–193** the property comprised in the tenancy, there being excluded any part thereof which is occupied neither by the tenant nor by a person employed by the tenant ... for the purposes of a business by reason of which the tenancy is one to which this Part of this Act applies.

the landlord
See s.44(1) which provides that "the landlord" means the person (whether or not he **3B–194** is the immediate landlord) who is the owner of that interest in the property comprised in the relevant tenancy which for the time being fulfils the conditions contained in ss.44(1)(a) and (b).

Property to be comprised in new tenancy
32.—(1) Subject to the following provisions of this section, an or- **3B–195** der under section 29 of this Act for the grant of a new tenancy shall be an order for the grant of a new tenancy of the holding; and in the absence of agreement between the landlord and the tenant as to the property which constitutes the holding the court shall in the order designate that property by reference to the circumstances existing at the date of the order.

(1A) Where the court, by virtue of paragraph (b) of section 31A(1) of this Act, makes an order under section 29 of this Act for the grant

Paragraph numbers marked with a "+" can be found online and on CD.

of a new tenancy in a case where the tenant is willing to accept a tenancy of part of the holding, the order shall be an order for the grant of a new tenancy of that part only.

(2) The foregoing provisions of this section shall not apply in a case where the property comprised in the current tenancy includes other property besides the holding and the landlord requires any new tenancy ordered to be granted under section 29 of this Act to be a tenancy of the whole of the property comprised in the current tenancy; but in any such case—

(a) any order under the said section 29 for the grant of a new tenancy shall be an order for the grant of a new tenancy of the whole of the property comprised in the current tenancy, and

(b) references in the following provisions of this Part of this Act to the holding shall be construed as references to the whole of that property.

(3) Where the current tenancy includes rights enjoyed by the tenant in connection with the holding, those rights shall be included in a tenancy ordered to be granted under section 29 of this Act, except as otherwise agreed between the landlord and the tenant or, in default of such agreement, determined by the court.

3B–196   *Note* —The current s.32 was substituted by the Law of Property Act 1969 s.15, Sch.1.

holding

3B–197   The tenant is only entitled to require the grant of a new tenancy of his or her holding. For holdings, see s.46, s.32 and s.23(3) which provides that the expression "the holding" means the property comprised in the tenancy, there being excluded any part thereof which is occupied neither by the tenant nor by a person employed by the tenant ... for the purposes of a business by reason of which the tenancy is one to which this Part of this Act applies.

current tenancy

3B–198   See s.46 and s.26(1)—the tenancy under which the tenant holds for the time being.

the landlord

3B–199   See s.44(1) which provides that "the landlord" means the person (whether or not he is the immediate landlord) who is the owner of that interest in the property comprised in the relevant tenancy which for the time being fulfils the conditions contained in ss.44(1)(a) and (b).

parking previously under permission

3B–199.1   Facilities enjoyed by licence under the original lease are outside s.32(3). Thus, in *The Picture Warehouse Ltd v Cornhill Investments Ltd* [2008] EWHC 45 (QB) the tenant had the benefit of a licence from the landlord for its customers and delivery men to park on the forecourt outside the demised premises. However, there was no right under the lease to that effect. On renewing the lease the tenant was unable to obtain a term of the new lease giving it parking rights. Further, there is no jurisdiction under s.35(1) of the 1954 Act to enlarge the holding by ordering the grant of a right over the landlord's land that the tenant had not previously enjoyed.

Duration of new tenancy

3B–200   **33.** Where on an application under this Part of this Act the court makes an order for the grant of a new tenancy, the new tenancy shall be such tenancy as may be agreed between the landlord and the ten-

Paragraph numbers marked with a "+" can be found online and on CD.

ant, or, in default of such an agreement, shall be such a tenancy as may be determined by the court to be reasonable in all the circumstances, being, if it is a tenancy for a term of years certain, a tenancy for a term not exceeding fifteen years, and shall begin on the coming to an end of the current tenancy.

Note —Section 33 was amended by the Regulatory Reform (Business Tenancies) **3B–201** (England and Wales) Order 2003 (SI 2003/3096), art.26. The amendment came into force June 1, 2004 but only applies where the s.25 notice or s.26 request was served on or after that date.

duration

The norm is for the term of any new tenancy to be agreed between the landlord **3B–202** and the tenant. In the absence of agreement, the court determines a term which is "reasonable in all the circumstances". The court cannot order a tenancy for a term of more than fifteen years, but the parties are free to agree a longer term. The starting point is the length of the current term, but the court must strike a reasonable balance between conflicting considerations (*Edwards (J.H.) & Sons v Central London Commercial Estates* [1984] 2 E.G.L.R. 103, CA; *Upsons v Robins (E)* [1956] 1 Q.B. 131; [1955] 3 W.L.R. 584; [1955] 3 All E.R. 348, CA). For a list of the considerations that the court might take into account when deciding what term is "reasonable in all the circumstances", see *Woodfall*, para.23.146.

current tenancy

See s.46 and s.26(1)—the tenancy under which the tenant holds for the time being. **3B–203**

the landlord

See s.44(1) which provides that "the landlord" means the person (whether or not he **3B–204** is the immediate landlord) who is the owner of that interest in the property comprised in the relevant tenancy which for the time being fulfils the conditions contained in ss.44(1)(a) and (b).

Rent under new tenancy

34.—(1) The rent payable under a tenancy granted by order of the **3B–205** court under this Part of this Act shall be such as may be agreed between the landlord and the tenant or as, in default of such agreement, may be determined by the court to be that at which, having regard to the terms of the tenancy (other than those relating to rent), the holding might reasonably be expected to be let in the open market by a willing lessor, there being disregarded—

> (a) any effect on rent of the fact that the tenant has or his predecessors in title have been in occupation of the holding,
>
> (b) any goodwill attached to the holding by reason of the carrying on thereat of the business of the tenant (whether by him or by a predecessor of his in that business),
>
> (c) any effect on rent of an improvement to which this paragraph applies,
>
> (d) in the case of a holding comprising licensed premises, any addition to its value attributable to the licence, if it appears to the court that having regard to the terms of the current tenancy and any other relevant circumstances the benefit of the licence belongs to the tenant.

(2) Paragraph (c) of the foregoing subsection applies to any

Paragraph numbers marked with a "+" can be found online and on CD.

improvement carried out by a person who at the time it was carried out was the tenant, but only if it was carried out otherwise than in pursuance of an obligation to his immediate landlord and either it was carried out during the current tenancy or the following conditions are satisfied, that is to say,—

    (a) that it was completed not more than twenty-one years before the application to the court was made; and

    (b) that the holding or any part of it affected by the improvement has at all times since the completion of the improvement been comprised in tenancies of the description specified in section 23(1) of this Act; and

    (c) that at the termination of each of those tenancies the tenant did not quit.

(2A) If this Part of this Act applies by virtue of section 23(1A) of this Act, the reference in subsection (1)(d) above to the tenant shall be construed as including—

    (a) a company in which the tenant has a controlling interest, or

    (b) where the tenant is a company, a person with a controlling interest in the company.

(3) Where the rent is determined by the court the court may, if it thinks fit, further determine that the terms of the tenancy shall include such provision for varying the rent as may be specified in the determination.

(4) It is hereby declared that the matters which are to be taken into account by the court in determining the rent include any effect on rent of the operation of the provisions of the Landlord and Tenant (Covenants) Act 1995.

3B–206   *Note* —The current s.34 was substituted by the Law of Property Act 1969, s.15, Sch.1; s.34(4) was added by the Landlord and Tenant (Covenants) Act 1995 Sch.1 para.3. Section 34(2)(a) was amended and s.34(2A) inserted by the Regulatory Reform (Business Tenancies) (England and Wales) Order 2003 (SI 2003/3096), art.15.

rent

3B–207   In the absence of agreement between the parties, the court determines the rent at which, having regard to the terms of the tenancy, the holding might reasonably be expected to be let in the open market by a willing lessor, subject to a number of disregards. In view of the requirement to have regard to the terms of the tenancy, the court should determine any other disputed terms, before deciding the rent. (*O'May v City of London Real Property Co Ltd* [1983] 2 A.C. 726; [1982] 2 W.L.R. 407; [1982] 1 All E.R. 660, HL; *Cardshops v Davies* [1971] 1 W.L.R. 591; [1971] 2 All E.R. 721, CA) The best evidence of a reasonable open market rent is normally that of valuers relying upon comparables. The disregards in s.34(1) are principally matters related to the particular tenant—e.g. the effect of the tenant's occupation, any goodwill derived from the tenant's business and the effect of any improvements to which the section applies. It is possible for the court to fix a rent which increases by instalments (s.34(3), *Fawke v Viscount Chelsea* [1980] Q.B. 441; [1979] 3 W.L.R. 508; [1979] 3 All E.R. 568, CA and *88 High Road, Kilburn, Re* [1959] 1 W.L.R. 279; [1959] 1 All E.R. 527, Ch D—upwards only rent review).

    In *Trans-World Investments Ltd v Anita Dadarwalla* [2007] EWCA Civ 480 it was held that the trial judge was wrong to disregard the passing rent of the subject property under the lease. He was also wrong to disregard valuation evidence of a neighbouring property as a "rogue figure" on the basis that there was no evidence as to the circumstances in which the rent was calculated. Mummery L.J. at para.30:

Paragraph numbers marked with a "+" can be found online and on CD.

"In my judgment, the judge was wrong to disregard the passing rent and the rent of No 106 on the basis stated by him. The rents under the current lease and of the adjoining property at No 106 are relevant valuation evidence of market rent of the Property without the need for the court to require the party relying on those rents to produce positive evidence of the circumstances in which they were determined. Rather it is for the party who challenges the relevance of the passing rent and/or the rent of the adjoining property to adduce evidence of circumstances relied on to show that the rents are not relevant factors in the valuation exercise of determining the open market rent."

business

See s.46 and s.23(2) which provides that "business" includes a trade, profession or **3B–208** employment and includes any activity carried on by a body of persons, whether corporate or unincorporate. See too the commentary to s.23 above.

current tenancy

See s.46 and s.26(1)—the tenancy under which the tenant holds for the time being. **3B–209**

holding

See s.46, s.32 and s.23(3) which provides that the expression "the holding" means **3B–210** the property comprised in the tenancy, there being excluded any part thereof which is occupied neither by the tenant nor by a person employed by the tenant ... for the purposes of a business by reason of which the tenancy is one to which this Part of this Act applies.

the landlord

See s.44(1) which provides that "the landlord" means the person (whether or not he **3B–211** is the immediate landlord) who is the owner of that interest in the property comprised in the relevant tenancy which for the time being fulfils the conditions contained in ss.44(1)(a) and (b).

Other terms of new tenancy

35.—(1) The terms of a tenancy granted by order of the court **3B–212** under this Part of this Act (other than terms as to the duration thereof and as to the rent payable thereunder), including, where different persons own interests which fulfil the conditions specified in section 44(1) of this Act in different parts of it, terms as to the apportionment of the rent,shall be such as may be agreed between the landlord and the tenant or as, in default of such agreement, may be determined by the court; and in determining those terms the court shall have regard to the terms of the current tenancy and to all relevant circumstances.

(2) In subsection (1) of this section the reference to all relevant circumstances includes (without prejudice to the generality of that reference) a reference to the operation of the provisions of the Landlord and Tenant (Covenants) Act 1995.

Note —Subsections (1) and (2) were inserted by the Landlord and Tenant (Cove- **3B–213** nants) Act 1995 Sch.1, paras 4(1) and (2) and amended by the Regulatory Reform (Business Tenancies) (England and Wales) Order 2003 (SI 2003/3096), art.27(3). The amendment came into force June 1, 2004 but only applies where the s.25 notice or s.26 request was served on or after that date.

Other terms

In the absence of agreement between the parties, the court determines any other **3B–214** terms, having regard to the terms of the current tenancy, and all relevant circumstances. The court will normally follow the terms of the current tenancy—any

Paragraph numbers marked with a "+" can be found online and on CD.

party wishing to depart from them must give a reason (*O'May v City of London Real Property Co Ltd* [1983] 2 A.C. 726; [1982] 2 W.L.R. 407; [1982] 1 All E.R. 660, HL). Any change must be fair and reasonable and take into account the comparatively weak negotiating position of a sitting tenant seeking renewal (*Cardshops v Davies* [1971] 1 W.L.R. 591; [1971] 2 All E.R. 721, CA. See too *No.1 Albemarle Street, Re* [1959] Ch. 531; [1959] 1 All E.R. 250; Ch D). A facility enjoyed pursuant to a licence under the old lease cannot became a term of the new lease—see para. 3B–199A .

current tenancy

3B–215   See s.46 and s.26(1)—the tenancy under which the tenant holds for the time being.

the landlord

3B–216   See s.44(1) which provides that "the landlord" means the person (whether or not he is the immediate landlord) who is the owner of that interest in the property comprised in the relevant tenancy which for the time being fulfils the conditions contained in ss.44(1)(a) and (b).

Carrying out of order for new tenancy

3B–217   **36.**—(1) Where under this Part of this Act the court makes an order for the grant of a new tenancy, then, unless the order is revoked under the next following subsection or the landlord and the tenant agree not to act upon the order, the landlord shall be bound to execute or make in favour of the tenant, and the tenant shall be bound to accept, a lease or agreement for a tenancy of the holding embodying the terms agreed between the landlord and the tenant or determined by the court in accordance with the foregoing provisions of this Part of this Act; and where the landlord executes or makes such a lease or agreement the tenant shall be bound, if so required by the landlord, to execute a counterpart or duplicate thereof.

(2) If the tenant, within fourteen days after the making of an order under this Part of this Act for the grant of a new tenancy, applies to the court for the revocation of the order the court shall revoke the order; and where the order is so revoked, then, if it is so agreed between the landlord and the tenant or determined by the court, the current tenancy shall continue, beyond the date at which it would have come to an end apart from this subsection, for such period as may be so agreed or determined to be necessary to afford to the landlord a reasonable opportunity for reletting or otherwise disposing of the premises which would have been comprised in the new tenancy; and while the current tenancy continues by virtue of this subsection it shall not be a tenancy to which this Part of this Act applies.

(3) Where an order is revoked under the last foregoing subsection any provision thereof as to payment of costs shall not cease to have effect by reason only of the revocation; but the court may, if it thinks fit, revoke or vary any such provision or, where no costs have been awarded in the proceedings for the revoked order, award such costs.

(4) A lease executed or agreement made under this section, in a case where the interest of the lessor is subject to a mortgage, shall be deemed to be one authorised by section ninety-nine of the Law of Property Act 1925 (which confers certain powers of leasing on mortgagors in possession), and subsection (13) of that section (which

Paragraph numbers marked with a "+" can be found online and on CD.

allows those powers to be restricted or excluded by agreement) shall not have effect in relation to such a lease or agreement.

Carrying out of order for new tenancy

If the court orders the grant of a new tenancy, the landlord is bound to make and the tenant is bound to accept a new lease embodying the terms agreed or determined by the court, unless— **3B–218**

(a) the landlord and the tenant agree not to act on the order; or

(b) the tenant elects not to take the tenancy on the terms ordered. In such circumstances the tenant may apply to the court within 14 days of the making of the order for the revocation of the order. On such an application the court must revoke the order (s.36(2)).

See e.g. *88 High Road, Kilburn, Re* [1959] 1 W.L.R. 279; [1959] 1 All E.R. 527 where the order was revoked, but the tenant was ordered to pay the costs of the action and of the application to revoke.

current tenancy

See s.46 and s.26(1)—the tenancy under which the tenant holds for the time being. **3B–219**

holding

See s.46, s.32 and s.23(3) which provides that the expression "the holding" means the property comprised in the tenancy, there being excluded any part thereof which is occupied neither by the tenant nor by a person employed by the tenant ... for the purposes of a business by reason of which the tenancy is one to which this Part of this Act applies. **3B–220**

the landlord

See s.44(1) which provides that "the landlord" means the person (whether or not he is the immediate landlord) who is the owner of that interest in the property comprised in the relevant tenancy which for the time being fulfils the conditions contained in ss.44(1)(a) and (b). **3B–221**

Compensation where order for new tenancy precluded on certain grounds

37.—(1) Subject to the provisions of this Act, in a case specified in subsection (1A), (1B) or (1C) below (a "compensation case") the tenant shall be entitled on quitting the holding to recover from the landlord by way of compensation an amount determined in accordance with this section. **3B–222**

(1A) The first compensation case is where on the making of an application by the tenant under section 24(1) of this Act the court is precluded (whether by subsection (1) or subsection (2) of section 31 of this Act) from making an order for the grant of a new tenancy by reason of any of the grounds specified in paragraphs (e), (f) and (g) of section 30(1) of this Act (the "compensation grounds") and not of any grounds specified in any other paragraph of section 30(1).

(1B) The second compensation case is where on the making of an application under section 29(2) of this Act the court is precluded (whether by section 29(4)(a) or section 31(2) of this Act) from making an order for the grant of a new tenancy by reason of any of the compensation grounds and not of any other grounds specified in section 30(1) of this Act.

(1C) The third compensation case is where—

(a) the landlord's notice under section 25 of this Act or, as the case may be, under section 26(6) of this Act, states

Paragraph numbers marked with a "+" can be found online and on CD.

his opposition to the grant of a new tenancy on any of the compensation grounds and not on any other grounds specified in section 30(1) of this Act; and

(b) either—

    (i) no application is made by the tenant under section 24(1) of this Act or by the landlord under section 29(2) of this Act; or

    (ii) such an application is made but is subsequently withdrawn.

(2) Subject to the following provisions of this section, compensation under this section shall be as follows, that is to say—

(a) where the conditions specified in the next following subsection are satisfied in relation to the whole of the holding it shall be the product of the appropriate multiplier and twice the rateable value of the holding,

(b) in any other case it shall be [the product of the appropriate multiplier and] the rateable value of the holding.

(3) The said conditions are—

(a) that, during the whole of the fourteen years immediately preceding the termination of the current tenancy, premises being or comprised in the holding have been occupied for the purposes of a business carried on by the occupier or for those and other purposes;

(b) that, if during those fourteen years there was a change in the occupier of the premises, the person who was the occupier immediately after the change was the successor to the business carried on by the person who was the occupier immediately before the change.

(3A) If the conditions specified in subsection (3) above are satisfied in relation to part of the holding but not in relation to the other part, the amount of compensation shall be the aggregate of sums calculated separately as compensation in respect of each part, and accordingly, for the purpose of calculating compensation in respect of a part any reference in this section to the holding shall be construed as a reference to that part.

(3B) Where section 44(1A) of this Act applies, the compensation shall be determined separately for each part and compensation determined for any part shall be recoverable only from the person who is the owner of an interest in that part which fulfils the conditions specified in section 44(1) of this Act.

(4) Where the court is precluded from making an order for the grant of a new tenancy under this Part of this Act in a compensation case, the court shall on the application of the tenant certify that fact.

(5) For the purposes of subsection (2) of this section the rateable value of the holding shall be determined as follows:—

(a) where in the valuation list in force at the date on which the landlord's notice under section 25 or, as the case may be, subsection (6) of section 26 of this Act is given a value is then shown as the annual value (as hereinafter

Paragraph numbers marked with a "+" can be found online and on CD.

defined) of the holding, the rateable value of the holding shall be taken to be that value;

(b) where no such value is so shown with respect to the holding but such a value or such values is or are so shown with respect to premises comprised in or comprising the holding or part of it, the rateable value of the holding shall be taken to be such value as is found by a proper apportionment or aggregation of the value or values so shown;

(c) where the rateable value of the holding cannot be ascertained in accordance with the foregoing paragraphs of this subsection, it shall be taken to be the value which, apart from any exemption from assessment to rates, would on a proper assessment be the value to be entered in the said valuation list as the annual value of the holding;

and any dispute arising, whether in proceedings before the court or otherwise, as to the determination for those purposes of the rateable value of the holding shall be referred to the Commissioners of Inland Revenue for decision by a valuation officer.

An appeal shall lie to the Lands Tribunal from any decision of a valuation officer under this subsection, but subject thereto any such decision shall be final.

(5A) If part of the holding is domestic property, as defined in section 66 of the Local Government Finance Act 1988—

(a) the domestic property shall be disregarded in determining the rateable value of the holding under subsection (5) of this section; and

(b) if, on the date specified in subsection (5)(a) of this section, the tenant occupied the whole or any part of the domestic property, the amount of compensation to which he is entitled under subsection (1) of this section shall be increased by the addition of a sum equal to his reasonable expenses in removing from the domestic property.

(5B) Any question as to the amount of the sum referred to in paragraph (b) of subsection (5A) of this section shall be determined by agreement between the landlord and the tenant or, in default of agreement, by the court.

(5C) If the whole of the holding is domestic property, as defined in section 66 of the Local Government Finance Act 1988, for the purposes of subsection (2) of this section the rateable value of the holding shall be taken to be an amount equal to the rent at which it is estimated the holding might reasonably be expected to let from year to year if the tenant undertook to pay all usual tenant's rates and taxes and to bear the cost of the repairs and insurance and the other expenses (if any) necessary to maintain the holding in a state to command that rent.

(5D) The following provisions shall have effect as regards a determination of an amount mentioned in subsection (5C) of this section—

Paragraph numbers marked with a "+" can be found online and on CD.

> (a) the date by reference to which such a determination is to be made is the date on which the landlord's notice under section 25 or, as the case may be, subsection (6) of section 26 of this Act is given;
>
> (b) any dispute arising, whether in proceedings before the court or otherwise, as to such a determination shall be referred to the Commissioners of Inland Revenue for decision by a valuation officer;
>
> (c) an appeal shall lie to the Lands Tribunal from such a decision but, subject to that, such a decision shall be final.

(5E) Any deduction made under paragraph 2A of Schedule 6 to the Local Government Finance Act 1988 (deduction from valuation of hereditaments used for breeding horses etc.) shall be disregarded, to the extent that it relates to the holding, in determining the rateable value of the holding under subsection (5) of this section.

(6) The Commissioners of Inland Revenue may by statutory instrument make rules prescribing the procedure in connection with references under this section.

(7) In this section—

> the reference to the termination of the current tenancy is a reference to the date of termination specified in the landlord's notice under section 25 of this Act or, as the case may be, the date specified in the tenant's request for a new tenancy as the date from which the new tenancy is to begin;
>
> the expression "annual value" means rateable value except that where the rateable value differs from the net annual value the said expression means net annual value;
>
> the expression "valuation officer" means any officer of the Commissioners of Inland Revenue for the time being authorised by a certificate of the Commissioners to act in relation to a valuation list.

(8) In subsection (2) of this section "the appropriate multiplier" means such multiplier as the Secretary of State may by order made by statutory instrument prescribe and different multipliers may be so prescribed in relation to different cases.

(9) A statutory instrument containing an order under subsection (8) of this section shall be subject to annulment in pursuance of a resolution of either House of Parliament.

3B–223   *Note* —Section 37 was amended by the Local Government, Planning and Land Act 1980 Sch.33, paras 4(1) and 4(2); the Local Government and Housing Act 1989 s.149 and Sch.7, paras 2(2), 2(3), 2(4) and 4 and by the Local Government Finance (Miscellaneous Amendments and Repeal) Order 1990 (SI 1990/1285) art.2, Sch. Pt I, para.4(a) and by the Regulatory Reform (Business Tenancies) (England and Wales) Order 2003 (SI 2003/3096), art.19. The latter amendment came into force June 1, 2004 but only applies where the s.25 notice or s.26 request was served on or after that date.

business

3B–224   See s.46 and s.23(2) which provides that "business" includes a trade, profession or employment and includes any activity carried on by a body of persons, whether corporate or unincorporate. See too the commentary to s.23 above.

Paragraph numbers marked with a "+" can be found online and on CD.

current tenancy

See s.46 and s.26(1)—the tenancy under which the tenant holds for the time being. **3B–225**

date of termination

See s.46 and s.25(1)—the date specified in the landlord's s.25 notice at which the **3B–226** tenancy is to come to an end.

holding

See s.46, s.32 and s.23(3) which provides that the expression "the holding" means **3B–227** the property comprised in the tenancy, there being excluded any part thereof which is occupied neither by the tenant nor by a person employed by the tenant ... for the purposes of a business by reason of which the tenancy is one to which this Part of this Act applies.

the landlord

See s.44(1) which provides that "the landlord" means the person (whether or not he **3B–228** is the immediate landlord) who is the owner of that interest in the property comprised in the relevant tenancy which for the time being fulfils the conditions contained in ss.44(1)(a) and (b).

compensation

Put simply, a tenant is entitled to compensation if a landlord successfully relies **3B–229** upon s.30(1)(e) (aggregate of the rents reasonably obtainable on separate lettings less than the rent reasonably obtainable on a letting of that property as a whole), s.30(1)(f) (intention of landlord to demolish or reconstruct) or s.30(1)(g) (intention of landlord to occupy the holding for the purposes of a business or as his residence). If a court refuses the grant of a new tenancy on any these three grounds it must certify that fact (s.37(4)). The amount of compensation is either the product of the appropriate multiplier and the rateable value or the product of the appropriate multiplier and twice the rateable value. (See s.37 and the Landlord and Tenant Act 1954 (Appropriate Multiplier) Order 1990 (SI 1990/363)).

restriction on contracting out

See s.38(2). **3B–230**

Compensation for possession obtained by misrepresentation

37A.—(1) Where the court— **3B–231**

    (a) makes an order for the termination of the current tenancy but does not make an order for the grant of a new tenancy, or

    (b) refuses an order for the grant of a new tenancy,

and it subsequently made to appear to the court that the order was obtained, or the court was induced to refuse the grant, by misrepresentation or the concealment of material facts, the court may order the landlord to pay to the tenant such sum as appears sufficient as compensation for damage or loss sustained by the tenant as the result of the order or refusal.

    (2) Where—

        (a) the tenant has quit the holding—

            (i) after making but withdrawing an application under section 24(1) of this Act; or

            (ii) without making such an application; and

        (b) it is made to appear to the court that he did so by reason of misrepresentation or the concealment of material facts,

the court may order the landlord to pay to the tenant such sum

Paragraph numbers marked with a "+" can be found online and on CD.

as appears sufficient as compensation for damage or loss sustained by the tenant as the result of quitting the holding.

3B–232 *Note* —New s.37A was inserted by the Regulatory Reform (Business Tenancies) (England and Wales) Order 2003 (SI 2003/3096), art.20. The amendment came into force June 1, 2004 but only where the tenant quit the holding before that date (reg.29(5) of 2003 Order) but only where the tenant quit the holding before that date (reg.29(5) of 2003 Order; para.3B–93).

Restriction on agreements excluding provisions of Part II

3B–233 **38.**—(1) Any agreement relating to a tenancy to which this Part of this Act applies (whether contained in the instrument creating the tenancy or not) shall be void (except as provided by section 38A of this Act) in so far as it purports to preclude the tenant from making an application or request under this Part of this Act or provides for the termination or the surrender of the tenancy in the event of his making such an application or request or for the imposition of any penalty or disability on the tenant in that event.

(2) Where—

    (a) during the whole of the five years immediately preceding the date on which the tenant under a tenancy to which this Part of this Act applies is to quit the holding, premises being or comprised in the holding have been occupied for the purposes of a business carried on by the occupier or for those and other purposes, and

    (b) if during those five years there was a change in the occupier of the premises, the person who was the occupier immediately after the change was the successor to the business carried on by the person who was the occupier immediately before the change,

any agreement (whether contained in the instrument creating the tenancy or not and whether made before or after the termination of that tenancy) which purports to exclude or reduce compensation under section 37 of this Act shall to that extent be void, so however that this subsection shall not affect any agreement as to the amount of any such compensation which is made after the right to compensation has accrued.

(3) In a case not falling within the last foregoing subsection the right to compensation conferred by section 37 of this Act may be excluded or modified by agreement.

(4) [...]

3B–234 *Note* —The current s.38 was substituted by Law of Property Act 1969 s.15, Sch.I and was amended by the Regulatory Reform (Business Tenancies) (England and Wales) Order 2003 (SI 2003/3096), art.21 and Sch.5, para.4. Subsection (4) was repealed by Sch.6, para.1. The amendment came into force June 1, 2004. It does not apply to an agreement to contract out nor does it apply to an agreement for the surrender for a tenancy which was authorised by the court under s.38(4) before that date. (Regulation 29(2)(a)(ii) of the 2003 Order—for further transitional provisions see reg. 29(3) and (4); para.3B–93).

Agreements to exclude provisions of Part 2

3B–235 **38A.**—(1) The persons who will be the landlord and the tenant in

Paragraph numbers marked with a "+" can be found online and on CD.

relation to a tenancy to be granted for a term of years certain which will be a tenancy to which this Part of this Act applies may agree that the provisions of sections 24 to 28 of this Act shall be excluded in relation to that tenancy.

(2) The persons who are the landlord and the tenant in relation to a tenancy to which this Part of this Act applies may agree that the tenancy shall be surrendered on such date or in such circumstances as may be specified in the agreement and on such terms (if any) as may be so specified.

(3) An agreement under subsection (1) above shall be void unless—

    (a) the landlord has served on the tenant a notice in the form, or substantially in the form, set out in Schedule 1 to the Regulatory Reform (Business Tenancies) (England and Wales) Order 2003 ("the 2003 Order"); and

    (b) the requirements specified in Schedule 2 to that Order are met.

(4) An agreement under subsection (2) above shall be void unless—

    (a) the landlord has served on the tenant a notice in the form, or substantially in the form, set out in Schedule 3 to the 2003 Order; and

    (b) the requirements specified in Schedule 4 to that Order are met.

Note —New s.38A was inserted by the Regulatory Reform (Business Tenancies) **3B–236**
(England and Wales) Order 2003 (SI 2003/3096). The amendment came into force June 1, 2004. Section 38A sets out a completely new procedure for contracting out of the security provisions of Pt II of the 1954 Act and for agreements to surrender where Pt II of the Act applies. The procedure in each case is based upon three elements (i) notice in a prescribed form served upon the tenant by the landlord, (ii) a declaration from the tenant acknowledging receipt of the notice and (iii) a reference to the notice in the lease/agreement to surrender. The details are contained in Schs 1 to 4 of 2003 Reform Order—not set out in the *White Book*. Note that both under the old system of contracting out and the new it is necessary for the tenancy to be "for a term of years certain". In *London Borough of Newham v Thomas-Van Staden* [2008] EWCA Civ 1414 the term was not, on a proper construction of the lease, for a term of years certain. Thus, even though the court (under the old system) had a made court order approving the agreement to contract out the tenancy was in fact protected by the 1954 Act and the tenant was entitled to remain in possession.

Where a notice informing a prospective tenant that the lease is to be contracted out of Pt II of the 1954 Act is served more than 14 days before the lease is entered into, para.3 of Schedule 2 to the Regulatory Reform (Business Tenancies) (England and Wales) Order 2003 says that the tenant (or duly authorised person) "must" sign a simple declaration. However, if he in fact signs a statutory declaration that will still be effective (see *The Chiltern Railway Company Ltd v Patel* [2008] EWCA Civ 178 :

    "It would …be 'bordering on the absurd' if a statutory declaration was held to be ineffective on the grounds that it differed from the prescribed form because a) it was both expressly and in law in a more solemn form than that form; and b) although it stated that notice was served before the lease was entered into, it did not state that it was served more than fourteen days before the lease was entered into" (Lord Neuberger sitting in the Court of Appeal at para.11).

Saving for compulsory acquisitions

    39.—(1) […] **3B–237**

Paragraph numbers marked with a "+" can be found online and on CD.

(2) If the amount of the compensation which would have been payable under section thirty-seven of this Act if the tenancy had come to an end in circumstances giving rise to compensation under that section and the date at which the acquiring authority obtained possession had been the termination of the current tenancy exceeds the amount of [the compensation payable under section 121 of the Lands Clauses Consolidation Act 1845 or section 20 of the Compulsory Purchase Act 1965in the case of a tenancy to which this Part of this Act applies], that compensation shall be increased by the amount of the excess.

(3) Nothing in section twenty-four of this Act shall affect the operation of the said section one hundred and twenty-one.

3B–238   *Note* —Amended by Land Compensation Act 1973 s.47(3). Subsection (1) was repealed by Land Compensation Act 1973, Sch. 3.

current tenancy
3B–239   See s.46 and s.26(1)—the tenancy under which the tenant holds for the time being.

Duty of tenants and landlords of business premises to give information to each other

3B–240   **40.**—(1) Where a person who is an owner of an interest in reversion expectant (whether immediately or not) on a tenancy of any business premises has served on the tenant a notice in the prescribed form requiring him to do so, it shall be the duty of the tenant to give the appropriate person in writing the information specified in subsection (2) below.

(2) That information is—

  (a) whether the tenant occupies the premises or any part of them wholly or partly for the purposes of a business carried on by him;

  (b) whether his tenancy has effect subject to any sub-tenancy on which his tenancy is immediately expectant and, if so—

    (i) what premises are comprised in the sub-tenancy;

    (ii) for what term it has effect (or, if it is terminable by notice, by what notice it can be terminated);

    (iii) what is the rent payable under it;

    (iv) who is the sub-tenant;

    (v) (to the best of his knowledge and belief) whether the sub-tenant is in occupation of the premises or of part of the premises comprised in the sub-tenancy and, if not, what is the sub-tenant's address;

    (vi) whether an agreement is in force excluding in relation to the sub-tenancy the provisions of sections 24 to 28 of this Act; and

    (vii) whether a notice has been given under section 25 or 26(6) of this Act, or a request has been made under section 26 of this Act, in relation to the sub-

Paragraph numbers marked with a "+" can be found online and on CD.

tenancy and, if so, details of the notice or request; and

(c) (to the best of his knowledge and belief) the name and address of any other person who owns an interest in reversion in any part of the premises.

(3) Where the tenant of any business premises who is a tenant under such a tenancy as is mentioned in section 26(1) of this Act has served on a reversioner or a reversioner's mortgagee in possession a notice in the prescribed form requiring him to do so, it shall be the duty of the person on whom the notice is served to give the appropriate person in writing the information specified in subsection (4) below.

(4) That information is—

(a) whether he is the owner of the fee simple in respect of the premises or any part of them or the mortgagee in possession of such an owner,

(b) if he is not, then (to the best of his knowledge and belief)—

(i) the name and address of the person who is his or, as the case may be, his mortgagor's immediate landlord in respect of those premises or of the part in respect of which he or his mortgagor is not the owner in fee simple;

(ii) for what term his or his mortgagor's tenancy has effect and what is the earliest date (if any) at which that tenancy is terminable by notice to quit given by the landlord; and

(iii) whether a notice has been given under section 25 or 26(6) of this Act, or a request has been made under section 26 of this Act, in relation to the tenancy and, if so, details of the notice or request;

(c) (to the best of his knowledge and belief) the name and address of any other person who owns an interest in reversion in any part of the premises; and

(d) if he is a reversioner, whether there is a mortgagee in possession of his interest in the premises and, if so, (to the best of his knowledge and belief) what is the name and address of the mortgagee.

(5) A duty imposed on a person by this section is a duty—

(a) to give the information concerned within the period of one month beginning with the date of service of the notice; and

(b) if within the period of six months beginning with the date of service of the notice that person becomes aware that any information which has been given in pursuance of the notice is not, or is no longer, correct, to give the appropriate person correct information within the period of one month beginning with the date on which he becomes aware.

Paragraph numbers marked with a "+" can be found online and on CD.

(6) This section shall not apply to a notice served by or on the tenant more than two years before the date on which apart from this Act his tenancy would come to an end by effluxion of time or could be brought to an end by notice to quit given by the landlord.

(7) Except as provided by section 40A of this Act, the appropriate person for the purposes of this section and section 40A(1) of this Act is the person who served the notice under subsection (1) or (3) above.

(8) In this section—

"business premises" means premises used wholly or partly for the purposes of a business;

"mortgagee in possession" includes a receiver appointed by the mortgagee or by the court who is in receipt of the rents and profits, and "his mortgagor" shall be construed accordingly;

"reversioner" means any person having an interest in the premises, being an interest in reversion expectant (whether immediately or not) on the tenancy;

"reversioner's mortgagee in possession" means any person being a mortgagee in possession in respect of such an interest; and

"sub-tenant" includes a person retaining possession of any premises by virtue of the Rent (Agriculture) Act 1976 or the Rent Act 1977 after the coming to an end of a sub-tenancy, and "sub-tenancy" includes a right so to retain possession.

3B–241   *Note* —New s.40 was inserted by the Regulatory Reform (Business Tenancies) (England and Wales) Order 2003 (SI 2003/3096). The amendment came into force June 1, 2004. It does not apply to a notice under s.40 served before that date (reg. 29(6) of the 2003 Reform Order—see para.3B–93).

tenancy

3B–242   See s.69(1) and the commentary to s.23 above. The definition includes an agreement for a lease or underlease, but does not include a mortgage.

business

3B–243   See s.46 and s.23(2) which provides that "business" includes a trade, profession or employment and includes any activity carried on by a body of persons, whether corporate or unincorporate. See too the commentary to s.23 above.

prescribed form

3B–244   See the Landlord and Tenant Act 1954, Pt 2 (Notices) Regulations 2004 (SI 2004/1005). Regulation 2(2) allows a "form substantially to the like effect" of those contained in the regulations.

notice to quit

3B–245   Means a notice to quit given by the immediate landlord (see s.44(2)).

the landlord

3B–246   See s.44(1) which provides that "the landlord" means the person (whether or not he is the immediate landlord) who is the owner of that interest in the property comprised in the relevant tenancy which for the time being fulfils the conditions contained in ss.44(1)(a) and (b).

Duties in transfer cases

3B–247   **40A.**—(1) If a person on whom a notice under section 40(1) or (3)

Paragraph numbers marked with a "+" can be found online and on CD.

of this Act has been served has transferred his interest in the premises or any part of them to some other person and gives the appropriate person notice in writing—

      (a) of the transfer of his interest; and

      (b) of the name and address of the person to whom he transferred it,

on giving the notice he ceases in relation to the premises or (as the case may be) to that part to be under any duty imposed by section 40 of this Act.

  (2) If—

      (a) the person who served the notice under section 40(1) or (3) of this Act ("the transferor") has transferred his interest in the premises to some other person ("the transferee"); and

      (b) the transferor or the transferee has given the person required to give the information notice in writing—

          (i) of the transfer; and

          (ii) of the transferee's name and address,

the appropriate person for the purposes of section 40 of this Act and subsection (1) above is the transferee.

  (3) If—

      (a) a transfer such as is mentioned in paragraph (a) of subsection (2) above has taken place; but

      (b) neither the transferor nor the transferee has given a notice such as is mentioned in paragraph (b) of that subsection,

any duty imposed by section 40 of this Act may be performed by giving the information either to the transferor or to the transferee.

Note —New s.40A was inserted by the Regulatory Reform (Business Tenancies) (England and Wales) Order 2003 (SI 2003/3096). The amendment came into force June 1, 2004. It does not apply to a notice under s.40 served before that date.   **3B–248**

Proceedings for breach of duties to give information

40B. A claim that a person has broken any duty imposed by section 40 of this Act may be made the subject of civil proceedings for breach of statutory duty; and in any such proceedings a court may order that person to comply with that duty and may make an award of damages.   **3B–249**

Note —New s.40B was inserted by the Regulatory Reform (Business Tenancies) (England and Wales) Order 2003 (SI 2003/3096). The amendment came into force June 1, 2004. It does not apply to a notice under s.40 served before that date.   **3B–250**

Trusts

41.—(1) Where a tenancy is held on trust, occupation by all or any of the beneficiaries under the trust, and the carrying on of a business by all or any of the beneficiaries, shall be treated for the purposes of section twenty-three of this Act as equivalent to occupation or the carrying on of a business by the tenant; and in relation to a tenancy   **3B–251**

Paragraph numbers marked with a "+" can be found online and on CD.

to which this Part of this Act applies by virtue of the foregoing provisions of this subsection—

    (a) references (however expressed) in this Part of this Act and in the Ninth Schedule to this Act to the business of, or to carrying on of business, use, occupation or enjoyment by, the tenant shall be construed as including references to the business of, or to carrying on of business, use, occupation or enjoyment by, the beneficiaries or beneficiary;

    (b) the reference in paragraph (d) of [subsection (1) of] section thirty-four of this Act to the tenant shall be construed as including the beneficiaries or beneficiary; and

    (c) a change in the persons of the trustees shall not be treated as a change in the person of the tenant.

(2) Where the landlord's interest is held on trust the references in paragraph (g) of subsection (1) of section thirty of this Act to the landlord shall be construed as including references to the beneficiaries under the trust or any of them; but, except in the case of a trust arising under a will or on the intestacy of any person, the reference in subsection (2) of that section to the creation of the interest therein mentioned shall be construed as including the creation of the trust.

3B–252   *Note*—Amended by the Law of Property Act 1969 s.1(2).

tenancy

3B–253   See s.69(1) and the commentary to s.23 above. The definition includes an agreement for a lease or underlease, but does not include a mortgage.

business

3B–254   See s.46 and s.23(2) which provides that "business" includes a trade, profession or employment and includes any activity carried on by a body of persons, whether corporate or unincorporate. See too the commentary to s.23 above.

the landlord

3B–255   See s.44(1) which provides that "the landlord" means the person (whether or not he is the immediate landlord) who is the owner of that interest in the property comprised in the relevant tenancy which for the time being fulfils the conditions contained in ss.44(1)(a) and (b).

Partnerships

3B–256   **41A.**—(1) The following provisions of this section shall apply where—

    (a) a tenancy is held jointly by two or more persons (in this section referred to as the joint tenants); and

    (b) the property comprised in the tenancy is or includes premises occupied for the purposes of a business; and

    (c) the business (or some other business) was at some time during the existence of the tenancy carried on in partnership by all the persons who were then the joint tenants or by those and other persons and the joint tenants' interest in the premises was then partnership property; and

Paragraph numbers marked with a "+" can be found online and on CD.

      (d) the business is carried on (whether alone or in partner-
ship with other persons) by one or some only of the joint
tenants and no part of the property comprised in the
tenancy is occupied, in right of the tenancy, for the
purposes of a business carried on (whether alone or in
partnership with other persons) by the other or others.

(2) In the following provisions of this section those of the joint
tenants who for the time being carry on the business are referred to
as the business tenants and the others as the other joint tenants.

(3) Any notice given by the business tenants which, had it been
given by all the joint tenants, would have been—

      (a) a tenant's request for a new tenancy made in accordance
with section 26 of this Act; or

      (b) a notice under subsection (1) or subsection (2) of section
27 of this Act;

shall be treated as such if it states that it is given by virtue of this
section and sets out the facts by virtue of which the persons giving it
are the business tenants; and references in those sections and in section 24A of this Act to the tenant shall be construed accordingly.

(4) A notice given by the landlord to the business tenants which,
had it been given to all the joint tenants, would have been a notice
under section 25 of this Act shall be treated as such a notice, and references in that section to the tenant shall be construed accordingly.

(5) An application under section 24(1) of this Act for a new
tenancy may, instead of being made by all the joint tenants, be made
by the business tenants alone; and where it is so made—

      (a) this Part of this Act shall have effect, in relation to it, as if
the references therein to the tenant included references
to the business tenants alone; and

      (b) the business tenants shall be liable, to the exclusion of
the other joint tenants, for the payment of rent and the
discharge of any other obligation under the current
tenancy for any rental period beginning after the date
specified in the landlord's notice under section 25 of this
Act or, as the case may be, beginning on or after the
date specified in their request for a new tenancy.

(6) Where the court makes an order under section 29 of this Act
for the grant of a new tenancy it may order the grant to be made to
the business tenants or to them jointly with the persons carrying on
the business in partnership with them, and may order the grant to
be made subject to the satisfaction, within a time specified by the order, of such conditions as to guarantors, sureties or otherwise as appear to the court equitable, having regard to the omission of the
other joint tenants from the persons who will be the tenants under
the new tenancy.

(7) The business tenants shall be entitled to recover any amount
payable by way of compensation under section 37 or section 59 of
this Act.

Paragraph numbers marked with a "+" can be found online and on CD.

3B–257   *Note* —Section 41A was inserted by Law of Property Act 1969 s.9 and amended by by the Regulatory Reform (Business Tenancies) (England and Wales) Order 2003 (SI 2003/3096), Sch.5, para.5.

business

3B–258   See s.46 and s.23(2) which provides that "business" includes a trade, profession or employment and includes any activity carried on by a body of persons, whether corporate or unincorporate. See too the commentary to s.23 above.

current tenancy

3B–259   See s.46 and s.26(1)—the tenancy under which the tenant holds for the time being.

the landlord

3B–260   See s.44(1) which provides that "the landlord" means the person (whether or not he is the immediate landlord) who is the owner of that interest in the property comprised in the relevant tenancy which for the time being fulfils the conditions contained in ss.44(1)(a) and (b).

Groups of companies

3B–261   **42.**—(1) For the purposes of this section two bodies corporate shall be taken to be members of a group if and only if one is a subsidiary of the other or both are subsidiaries of a third body corporate or the same person has a controlling interest in both.

(2) Where a tenancy is held by a member of a group, occupation by another member of the group, and the carrying on of a business by another member of the group, shall be treated for the purposes of section 23 of this Act as equivalent to occupation or the carrying on of a business by the member of the group holding the tenancy; and in relation to a tenancy to which this Part of this Act applies by virtue of the foregoing provisions of this subsection—

(a) references (however expressed) in this Part of this Act and in the Ninth Schedule to this Act to the business of or to use occupation or enjoyment by the tenant shall be construed as including references to the business of or to use occupation or enjoyment by the said other member;

(b) the reference in paragraph (d) of subsection (1) of section 34 of this Act to the tenant shall be construed as including the said other member; and

(c) an assignment of the tenancy from one member of the group to another shall not be treated as a change in the person of the tenant.

(3) Where the landlord's interest is held by a member of a group—

(a) the reference in paragraph (g) of subsection (1) of section 30 of this Act to intended occupation by the landlord for the purposes of a business to be carried on by him shall be construed as including intended occupation by any member of the group for the purposes of a business to be carried on by that member; and

(b) the reference in subsection (2) of that section to the purchase or creation of any interest shall be construed as a reference to a purchase from or creation by a person other than a member of the group.

Paragraph numbers marked with a "+" can be found online and on CD.

3B–262

Note —The current s.42 was substituted by the Law of Property Act 1969 s.15, Sch.1 and amended by Companies Act 1989 s.144(4), s.213(2), s.215(2), Sch.18 para.3 and by the Regulatory Reform (Business Tenancies) (England and Wales) Order 2003 (SI 2003/3096) but only applies where the s.25 notice or s.26 request was served on or after that date.

business

3B–263

See s.46 and s.23(2) which provides that "business" includes a trade, profession or employment and includes any activity carried on by a body of persons, whether corporate or unincorporate.

the landlord

3B–264

See s.44(1) which provides that "the landlord" means the person (whether or not he is the immediate landlord) who is the owner of that interest in the property comprised in the relevant tenancy which for the time being fulfils the conditions contained in ss.44(1)(a) and (b).

Tenancies excluded from Part II

3B–265

43.—(1) This Part of this Act does not apply—

    (a) to a tenancy of an agricultural holding [[which is a tenancy in relation to which the Agricultural Holdings Act 1986 applies or a tenancy which would be a tenancy of an agricultural holding in relation to which that Act applied if subsection (3) of section 2 of that Act] did not have effect or, in a case where approval was given under subsection (1) of that section], if that approval had not been given;]

    (aa) [to a farm business tenancy;]

    (b) to a tenancy created by a mining lease;

    (c) [...]

    (d) [...]

(2) This Part of this Act does not apply to a tenancy granted by reason that the tenant was the holder of an office, appointment or employment from the grantor thereof and continuing only so long as the tenant holds the office, appointment or employment, or terminable by the grantor on the tenant's ceasing to hold it, or coming to an end at a time fixed by reference to the time at which the tenant ceases to hold it:

Provided that this subsection shall not have effect in relation to a tenancy granted after the commencement of this Act unless the tenancy was granted by an instrument in writing which expressed the purpose for which the tenancy was granted.

[(3) This Part of this Act does not apply to a tenancy granted for a term certain not exceeding six months unless—

    (a) the tenancy contains provision for renewing the term or for extending it beyond six months from its beginning; or

    (b) the tenant has been in occupation for a period which, together with any period during which any predecessor in the carrying on of the business carried on by the tenant was in occupation, exceeds twelve months.]

Paragraph numbers marked with a "+" can be found online and on CD.

3B–266   *Note* —Amended by Agricultural Tenancies Act 1995 Sch.1, para.10; Agricultural Holdings Act 1986 s.99, s.100, Sch.13, para.3, Sch.14, para.21; Agriculture Act 1958 Sch.1, Pt I, para.29; Housing Act 1980 Sch.26; Finance Act 1959 Sch.2, para.5; Landlord and Tenant (Licensed Premises) Act 1990 s.1(1)(2), s.2(2)(a); and Law of Property Act 1969 s.15, Sch.1.

tenancy

3B–267   See s.69(1) and the commentary to s.23 above. The definition includes an agreement for a lease or underlease, but does not include a mortgage.

mining lease

3B–268   See s.46 and Landlord and Tenant Act 1927, s.25 which defines "mining lease" as a lease for any mining purpose or purposes connected therewith, and "mining purposes" include the sinking and searching for, winning, working, getting, making merchantable, smelting or otherwise converting or working for the purposes of any manufacture, carrying away, and disposing of mines and minerals, in or under land, and the erection of buildings, and the execution of engineering and other works suitable for those purposes.

Jurisdiction of county court to make declaration

3B–269   **43A.** Where the rateable value of the holding is such that the jurisdiction conferred on the court by any other provision of this Part of this Act is, by virtue of section 63 of this Act, exercisable by the county court, the county court shall have jurisdiction (but without prejudice to the jurisdiction of the High Court) to make any declaration as to any matter arising under this Part of this Act, whether or not any other relief is sought in the proceedings.

3B–270   *Note* —Section 43A was inserted by the Law of Property Act 1969 s.13. Claims under Pt II should normally be brought in the county court. Only exceptional circumstances justify starting such a claim in the High Court (CPR r.56.2 and PD 56.2).

holding

3B–271   See s.46, s.32 and s.23(3) which provides that the expression "the holding" means the property comprised in the tenancy, there being excluded any part thereof which is occupied neither by the tenant nor by a person employed by the tenant … for the purposes of a business by reason of which the tenancy is one to which this Part of this Act applies.

Meaning of "the landlord" in Part II, and provisions as to mesne landlords, etc.

3B–272   **44.**—(1) Subject to subsections (1A) and (2) below, in this Part of this Act the expression "the landlord", in relation to a tenancy (in this section referred to as "the relevant tenancy"), means the person (whether or not he is the immediate landlord) who is the owner of that interest in the property comprised in the relevant tenancy which for the time being fulfils the following conditions, that is to say—

    (a) that it is an interest in reversion expectant (whether immediately or not) on the termination of the relevant tenancy, and

    (b) that it is either the fee simple or a tenancy which will not come to an end within fourteen months by effluxion of time and, if it is such a tenancy, that no notice has been given by virtue of which it will come to an end within fourteen months or any further time by which it may be continued under section 36(2) or section 64 of this Act,

Paragraph numbers marked with a "+" can be found online and on CD.

and is not itself in reversion expectant (whether immediately or not) on an interest which fulfils those conditions.

(1A) The reference in subsection (1) above to a person who is the owner of an interest such as is mentioned in that subsection is to be construed, where different persons own such interests in different parts of the property, as a reference to all those persons collectively.

(2) References in this Part of this Act to a notice to quit given by the landlord are references to a notice to quit given by the immediate landlord.

(3) The provisions of the Sixth Schedule to this Act shall have effect for the application of this Part of this Act to cases where the immediate landlord of the tenant is not the owner of the fee simple in respect of the holding.

Note —The current s.44 was substituted by the Law of Property Act 1969 s.15, Sch.1 **3B–273** and amended by the Regulatory Reform (Business Tenancies) (England and Wales) Order 2003 (SI 2003/3096), art.27(2). The latter amendment came into force June 1, 2004 but only applies where the s.25 notice or s.26 request was served on or after that date.

landlord

Only the competent landlord may give a s.25 notice or receive a s.26 request for a **3B–274** new tenancy. There can only be one competent landlord at any given time. Effectively it is the first person in the chain of landlords who has more than a nominal reversion. A mesne landlord, whose own tenancy is continuing under s.24 may be the landlord in relation to a sub-tenant of part of the premises, despite the uncertain duration of his own tenancy (*Bowes Lyon v Green* [1963] A.C. 420; [1961] 3 W.L.R. 1044; [1961] 3 All E.R. 843, HL). The landlord means the person with legal title to the land and so it is trustees rather than beneficiaries who are the competent landlord (*Biles v Caesar* [1957] 1 W.L.R. 156; [1957] 1 All E.R. 151, CA; *Morar v Chauhan* [1985] 1 W.L.R. 1263; [1985] 3 All E.R. 493, CA). Note s.40 which provides a mechanism allowing tenants to serve notices to obtain information as to the identity of the competent landlord.

holding

See s.46, s.32 and s.23(3) which provides that the expression "the holding" means **3B–275** the property comprised in the tenancy, there being excluded any part thereof which is occupied neither by the tenant nor by a person employed by the tenant … for the purposes of a business by reason of which the tenancy is one to which this Part of this Act applies.

45. […] **3B–276**

Note —Repealed by Statute Law (Repeals) Act 1974 (C.22), Pt XI. **3B–277**

Interpretation of Part II

46.—(1) In this Part of this Act:— **3B–278**

"business" has the meaning assigned to it by subsection (2) of section twenty-three of this Act;

"current tenancy" means the tenancy under which the tenant holds for the time being;

"date of termination" has the meaning assigned to it by subsection (1) of section twenty-five of this Act;

subject to the provisions of section thirty-two of this Act,

"the holding" has the meaning assigned to it by subsection (3) of section twenty-three of this Act;

Paragraph numbers marked with a "+" can be found online and on CD.

"interim rent" has the meaning given by section 24A(1) of this Act;

"mining lease" has the same meaning as in the Landlord and Tenant Act 1927.

(2) For the purposes of this Part of this Act, a person has a controlling interest in a company, if, had he been a company, the other company would have been its subsidiary; and in this Part—

"company" has the meaning given by section 735 of the Companies Act 1985; and

"subsidiary" has the meaning given by section 736 of that Act.

3B–279 *Note* — Section 46 was amended by the Regulatory Reform (Business Tenancies) (England and Wales) Order 2003 (SI 2003/3096). The amendment came into force June 1, 2004 but only applies where the s.25 notice or s.26 request was served on or after that date.

* * * *

PART IV

MISCELLANEOUS AND SUPPLEMENTARY

Jurisdiction of court for purposes of Parts I and II and of Part I of Landlord and Tenant Act 1927

3B–280 63.—(1) Any jurisdiction conferred on the court by any provision of Part I of this Act shall be exercised by the county court.

(2) Any jurisdiction conferred on the court by any provision of Part II of this Act or conferred on the tribunal by Part I of the Landlord and Tenant Act 1927, shall, subject to the provisions of this section, be exercised [by the High Court or a county court]

(3) [...]

(4) The following provisions shall have effect as respects transfer of proceedings from or to the High Court or the county court, that is to say—

(a) where an application is made to the one but by virtue of [an Order under section 1 of the Courts and Legal Services Act 1990] cannot be entertained except by the other, the application shall not be treated as improperly made but any proceedings thereon shall be transferred to the other court;

(b) any proceedings under the provisions of Part II of this Act or of Part I of the Landlord and Tenant Act 1927, which are pending before one of those courts may by order of that court made on the application of any person interested be transferred to the other court, if it appears to the court making the order that it is desirable that the proceedings and any proceedings before the other court should both be entertained by the other court.

(5) In any proceedings where in accordance with the foregoing

Paragraph numbers marked with a "+" can be found online and on CD.

* * * *

SECTION 44   SIXTH SCHEDULE

PROVISIONS FOR PURPOSES OF PART II WHERE IMMEDIATE LANDLORD IS NOT
THE FREEHOLDER   **3B–291**

Definitions

1. In this Schedule the following expressions have the meanings hereby assigned to **3B–292**
them in relation to a tenancy (in this Schedule referred to as "the relevant tenancy"),
that is to say:—

"the competent landlord" means the person who in relation to the tenancy is for
the time being the landlord (as defined by section 44) of this Act) for the
purposes of Part II of this Act;

"mesne landlord" means a tenant whose interest is intermediate between the relevant tenancy and the interest of the competent landlord; and

"superior landlord" means a person (whether the owner of the fee simple or a
tenant) whose interest is superior to the interest of the competent landlord.

Power of court to order reversionary tenancies

2. Where the period for which in accordance with the provisions of Part II of this **3B–293**
Act it is agreed or determined by the court that a new tenancy should be granted
thereunder will extend beyond the date on which the interest of the immediate
landlord will come to an end, the power of the court under Part II of this Act to order
such a grant shall include power to order the grant of a new tenancy until the expiration of that interest and also to order the grant of such a reversionary tenancy or reversionary tenancies as may be required to secure that the combined effects of those
grants will be equivalent to the grant of a tenancy for that period; and the provisions
of Part II of this Act shall, subject to the necessary modifications, apply in relation to
the grant of a tenancy together with one or more reversionary tenancies as they apply
in relation to the grant of one new tenancy.

Acts of competent landlord binding on other landlords

3.—(1) Any notice given by the competent landlord under Part II of this Act to **3B–294**
terminate the relevant tenancy, and any agreement made between that landlord and
the tenant as to the granting, duration, or terms of a future tenancy, being an agreement made for the purposes of the said Part II, shall bind the interest of any mesne
landlord notwithstanding that he has not consented to the giving of the notice or was
not a party to the agreement.

(2) The competent landlord shall have power for the purposes of Part II of this Act
to give effect to any agreement with the tenant for the grant of a new tenancy beginning with the coming to an end of the relevant tenancy, notwithstanding that the
competent landlord will not be the immediate landlord at the commencement of the
new tenancy, and any instrument made in the exercise of the power conferred by this
sub-paragraph shall have effect as if the mesne landlord had been a party thereto.

(3) Nothing in the foregoing provisions of this paragraph shall prejudice the provisions of the next following paragraph.

4.—(1) If the competent landlord, not being the immediate landlord, gives any such **3B–295**
notice or makes any such agreements as is mentioned in sub-paragraph (1) of the last
foregoing paragraph without the consent of every mesne landlord, any mesne landlord
whose consent has not been given thereto shall be entitled to compensation from the
competent landlord for any loss arising in consequence of the giving of the notice or
the making of the agreement.

(2) If the competent landlord applies to any mesne landlord for his consent to such
a notice or agreement, that consent shall not be unreasonably withheld, but may be
given subject to any conditions which may be reasonable (including conditions as to
the modification of the proposed notice or agreement or as to the payment of
compensation by the competent landlord).

(3) Any question arising under this paragraph whether consent has been unreason-

Paragraph numbers marked with a "+" can be found online and on CD.

ably withheld or whether any conditions imposed on the giving of consent are unreasonably shall be determined by the court.

3B–296   5. An agreement between the competent landlord and the tenant made for the purposes of Part II of this Act in a case where—

    (a) the competent landlord is himself a tenant, and

    (b) the agreement would apart from this paragraph operate as respects any period after the coming to an end of the interest of the competent landlord,

        shall not have effect unless every superior landlord who will be the immediate landlord of the tenant during any part of that period is a party to the agreement.

3B–297   6. Where the competent landlord has given a notice under section 25 of this Act to terminate the relevant tenancy and, within two months after the giving of the notice, a superior landlord—

    (a) becomes the competent landlord; and

    (b) gives to the tenant notice in the prescribed form that he withdraws the notice previously given;

        the notice under section 25 of this Act shall cease to have effect, but without prejudice to the giving of a further notice under that section by the competent landlord.

3B–298   7. If the competent landlord's interest in the property comprised in the relevant tenancy is a tenancy which will come or can be brought to an end within sixteen months (or any further time by which it may be continued under section 36(2) or section 64 of this Act) and he gives to the tenant under the relevant tenancy a notice under section 25 of this Act to terminate the tenancy or is given by him a notice under section 26(3) of this Act:—

    (a) the competent landlord shall forthwith send a copy of the notice to his immediate landlord; and

    (b) any superior landlord whose interest in the property is a tenancy shall forthwith send to his immediate landlord any copy which has been sent to him in pursuance of the preceding sub-paragraph or this sub-paragraph.

Landlord and Tenant Act 1988

3B–299

(1988 c.26)

ARRANGEMENT OF SECTIONS

Qualified duty to consent to assigning, underletting etc. of premises

3B–300   **1.**—(1) This section applies in any case where—

    (a) a tenancy includes a covenant on the part of the tenant not to enter into one or more of the following transactions, that is—

        (i) assigning,

        (ii) underletting,

        (iii) charging, or

        (iv) parting with the possession of,

the premises comprised in the tenancy or any part of the premises without the consent of the landlord or some other person, but

Paragraph numbers marked with a "+" can be found online and on CD.

(b) the covenant is subject to the qualification that the consent is not to be unreasonably withheld (whether or not it is also subject to any other qualification).

(2) In this section and section 2 of this Act—

(a) references to a proposed transaction are to any assignment, underletting, charging or parting with possession to which the covenant relates, and

(b) references to the person who may consent to such a transaction are to the person who under the covenant may consent to the tenant entering into the proposed transaction.

(3) Where there is served on the person who may consent to a proposed transaction a written application by the tenant for consent to the transaction, he owes a duty to the tenant within a reasonable time—

(a) to give consent, except in a case where it is reasonable not to give consent,

(b) to serve on the tenant written notice of his decision whether or not to give consent specifying in addition—

(i) if the consent is given subject to conditions, the conditions,

(ii) if the consent is withheld, the reasons for withholding it.

(4) Giving consent subject to any condition that is not a reasonable condition does not satisfy the duty under subsection (3)(a) above.

(5) For the purposes of this Act it is reasonable for a person not to give consent to a proposed transaction only in a case where, if he withheld consent and the tenant completed the transaction, the tenant would be in breach of a covenant.

(6) It is for the person who owed any duty under subsection (3) above—

(a) if he gave consent and the question arises whether he gave it within a reasonable time, to show that he did,

(b) if he gave consent subject to any condition and the question arises whether the condition was a reasonable condition, to show that it was,

(c) if he did not give consent and the question arises whether it was reasonable, for him not to do so, to show that it was reasonable,

and, if the question arises whether he served notice under that subsection within a reasonable time, to show that he did.

reasonable time

See e.g. *Blockbuster Entertainment Ltd v Barnsdale Properties Ltd* [2003] **3B–301** EWHC 2912, (Ch D); November 11, 2003 (landlord breached its statutory duty under s.1(3) by failing to consent to a proposed sublease within a reasonable time. There was a delay of two months and as a result the proposed sub-lessee withdrew its offer, leaving the premises empty for over a year. Lloyd J. held that there was no basis for withholding consent and the landlord should have consented

Paragraph numbers marked with a "+" can be found online and on CD.

within a week. Damages of over £70,000 were awarded to compensate the tenant for rent, contributions to insurance costs and rates).

In *NCR Ltd v Riverland Portfolio No.1 Ltd (No.2)* [2005] EWCA Civ 312; [2005] 22 EG 134 there was a covenant not to sublet without consent not to be unreasonably withheld. The landlord refused to consent to the tenant's proposed subletting. The tenant made two complaints: (i) that there had been an unreasonable delay and (ii) that the refusal was unreasonable. The judge found in favour of T but his decision was overturned in the CA. The case essentially turns upon its own facts and the evidence, including expert evidence, before the court but it does contain a useful summary of the law (paragraph 11 of the judgment). On the question of the reasonableness of the time taken to give a decision the judge considered that a period of two weeks was sufficient time for a decision once all the relevant information was available. This was criticised by Carnwarth LJ in the Court of Appeal, at para 21:

> "In my view, whatever earlier discussions there had been, Riverland was entitled to adequate time following receipt of the completed application to consider the serious financial and legal implications of a refusal with its advisers, and if necessary to report to the relevant Board. In the absence of special exceptional circumstances, a period of less than three weeks (particularly in the holiday period) cannot in my view be categorised as inherently unreasonable for that process.".

Conditions

3B–302   A landlord imposing a condition can only rely upon written reasons given within a reasonable time of receiving the tenant's application and within a reasonable time of imposing the condition. The question of reasonableness is determined by the information available to the landlord at the time he imposed the condition (*London & Argyll Developments Ltd v Mount Cook Land Ltd* [2002] 50 E.G.C.S. 111 (Ch D).)

"covenant", "consent", "tenancy" and "tenant"

3B–303   See s.5 and *Go West Ltd v Spigarolo* [2003] EWCA Civ 17; [2003] Q.B. 1140; [2003] 2 W.L.R. 986; [2003] 2 All E.R. 141; *The Times*, February 10, 2003, *Norwich Union Life Insurance Society v Shopmoor Ltd* [1999] 1 W.L.R. 531; *Footwear Corp Ltd v Amplight Properties Ltd* [1999] 1 W.L.R. 551 and *Mount Eden Land Ltd v Folia Ltd* [2003] EWHC 1815 (Ch); July 23, 2003 (minor breaches not a valid basis for refusing licence to under-let).

Once the landlord has given written notice with reasons refusing consent the period of reasonable time for giving consent has passed. The landlord cannot subsequently change his mind and say that the change has occurred within a reasonable time of the request. The fact that there were subsequent attempts to negotiate permission to assign did not deprive the tenant on the facts to its rights under the 1988 Act (*Go West Ltd v Spigarolo*, above).

Duty to pass on applications

3B–304   **2.**—(1) If, in a case where section 1 of this Act applies, any person receives a written application by the tenant for consent to a proposed transaction and that person—

>   (a) is a person who may consent to the transaction or (though not such a person) is the landlord, and
>   (b) believes that another person, other than a person who he believes has received that application or a copy of it, is a person who may consent to the transaction,

he owes a duty to the tenant (whether or not he owes him any duty under section 1 of this Act) to take such steps as are reasonable to secure the receipt within a reasonable time by the other person of a copy of the application.

(2) The reference in section 1(3) of this Act to the service of an application on a person who may consent to a proposed transaction includes a reference to the receipt by him of an application or a copy of an application (whether it is for his consent or that of another).

Paragraph numbers marked with a "+" can be found online and on CD.

"consent" and "tenancy"
  See s.5.
3B–305

"person who may consent"
  See s.1(2).
3B–306

"proposed transaction"
  See s.1(2).
3B–307

Qualified duty to approve consent by another

3.—(1) This section applies in any case where—
3B–308

  (a) a tenancy includes a covenant on the part of the tenant not without the approval of the landlord to consent to the sub-tenant—

   (i) assigning,

   (ii) underletting,

   (iii) charging, or

   (iv) parting with the possession of, the premises comprised in the sub-tenancy or any part of the premises, but

  (b) the covenant is subject to the qualification that the approval is not to be unreasonably withheld (whether or not it is also subject to any other qualification).

(2) Where there is served on the landlord a written application by the tenant for approval or a copy of a written application to the tenant by the sub-tenant for consent to a transaction to which the covenant relates the landlord owes a duty to the sub-tenant within a reasonable time—

  (a) to give approval, except in a case where it is reasonable not to give approval,

  (b) to serve on the tenant and the sub-tenant written notice of his decision whether or not to give approval specifying in addition—

   (i) if approval is given subject to conditions, the conditions,

   (ii) if approval is withheld, the reasons for withholding it.

(3) Giving approval subject to any condition that is not a reasonable condition does not satisfy the duty under subsection (2)(a) above.

(4) For the purposes of this section it is reasonable for the landlord not to give approval only in a case where, if he withheld approval and the tenant gave his consent, the tenant would be in breach of covenant.

(5) It is for a landlord who owed any duty under subsection (2) above—

  (a) if he gave approval and the question arises whether he gave it within a reasonable time, to show that he did,

  (b) if he gave approval subject to any condition and the question arises whether the condition was a reasonable condition, to show that it was,

Paragraph numbers marked with a "+" can be found online and on CD.

(c) if he did not give approval and the question arises
whether it was reasonable for him not to do so, to show
that it was reasonable,

and if the question arises whether he served notice under that
subsection within a reasonable time, to show that he did.

"covenant", "consent", "landlord", "tenancy" and "tenant"

3B–309   See s.5.

not to be unreasonably withheld

3B–310   Unless it can be shown that a trial judge has misdirected himself by erring in
principle or by reaching a conclusion that no reasonable judge could have reached,
the Court of Appeal will be slow to differ from his measurements of reasonableness
(*Arundel Corp v Khokher* [2003] EWCA Civ 1784; December 9, 2003).

"served"

3B–311   See s.5(2).

Breach of duty

3B–312   **4.** A claim that a person has broken any duty under this Act may
be made the subject of civil proceedings in like manner as any other
claim in tort for breach of statutory duty.

damages

3B–313   Where a landlord has all relevant information to enable it to make a decision under
s.1(3) as to whether or not to give licence to assign, but fails to respond and operates
in a cynical way designed to frustrate the assignment of premises, the court may mark
its disapproval by awarding a sum of exemplary damages that would cause the landlord
to consider seriously its future conduct (*Design Progression Ltd v ThurloeProperties Ltd*
[2004] EWHC 324, (Ch); *The Times*, March 2, 2004—award of £25,000 exemplary
damages plus £75,000 for loss of a premium and some other sums).

Interpretation

3B–314   **5.**—(1) In this Act—

"covenant" includes condition and agreement,

"consent" includes licence,

"landlord" includes any superior landlord from whom the
tenant's immediate landlord directly or indirectly holds,

"tenancy", subject to subsection (3) below, means any lease or
other tenancy (whether made before or after the coming
into force of this Act) and includes—

(a) a sub-tenancy, and

(b) an agreement for a tenancy and references in
this Act to the landlord and to the tenant are to be
interpreted accordingly, and

"tenant", where the tenancy is affected by a mortgage (within
the meaning of the Law of Property Act 1925) and the
mortgagee proposes to exercise his statutory or express
power of sale, includes the mortgagee.

(2) An application or notice is to be treated as served for the
purposes of this Act if—

(a) served in any manner provided in the tenancy, and

(b) in respect of any matter for which the tenancy makes no

Paragraph numbers marked with a "+" can be found online and on CD.

3C   CONTEMPT OF COURT ACT 1981

Contempt of Court Act 1981

(1981 c.49)   3C–1

ARRANGEMENT OF SECTIONS

STRICT LIABILITY

STRICT LIABILITY

The strict liability rule

1. In this Act "the strict liability rule" means the rule of law whereby **3C–2** conduct may be treated as a contempt of court as tending to interfere with the course of justice in particular legal proceedings regardless of intent to do so.

Limitation of scope of strict liability

2.—(1) The strict liability rule applies only in relation to publica- **3C–3** tions, and for this purpose "publication" includes any speech, writing, programme included in a cable programme service or other communication in whatever form, which is addressed to the public at large or any section of the public.

(2) The strict liability rule applies only to a publication which creates a substantial risk that the course of justice in the proceedings in question will be seriously impeded or prejudiced.

(3) The strict liability rule applies to a publication only if the

Paragraph numbers marked with a "+" can be found online and on CD.

proceedings in question are active within the meaning of this section at the time of publication.

(4) Schedule 1 applies for determining the times at which proceedings are to be treated as active within the meaning of this section.

(5) In this section "programme service" has the same meaning as in the Broadcasting Act 1990.

3C-4 *Note* —Amended by the Cable and Broadcasting Act 1984, Sch.5, para.39; and the Broadcasting Act 1990, s.203, Sch.20, para.31.

Meaning of "substantial risk" and "seriously impeded or prejudiced"

3C-5 "Substantial" describes the degree of risk; "seriously" describes the degree of impediment or prejudice to the course of justice; in combination the two words are intended to exclude a risk that is only remote (per Lord Diplock in *Attorney General v English* [1983] 1 A.C. 116; [1982] 2 All E.R. 903 at 919, HL). See also *Attorney General v Times Newspapers Ltd*; *The Times*, February 12, 1983, CA; and *Attorney General v BBC, Independent*, January 3, 1992.

"Substantial," as a qualification of "risk," does not have the meaning of "weighty," but rather "not insubstantial" or "not minimal"; the risk part of the test will usually be of importance in the context of the width of the publication, the court needing to consider whether there is an element of public interest in the publication which ought to be permitted and whether the proceedings sought to be protected are sufficiently proximate to the apprehended publication to require protection; proximity in time between the publication and the proceedings will probably have a greater bearing on the risk limb than on the seriousness limb, but may go to both (*Attorney General v News Group Newspapers Ltd* [1987] Q.B. 1, CA). Where the trial will not take place for at least ten months, the impact of the publication may be blunted (*ibid.*). Thus where nine months had elapsed between a single broadcast of an ephemeral nature and publication in a newspaper of limited circulation and the eventual trial, no contempt was held to have been committed (*Attorney General v Independent Television News Ltd* [1995] 2 All E.R. 370).

The publication of a statement that a defendant in criminal proceedings is awaiting trial on other charges does not, for the purposes of s.2(2) of the 1981 Act, necessarily create a substantial risk that the course of justice would be seriously impeded. The test is whether the statement created a substantial risk not whether it was the type of publication inherently liable to create such a risk. The risk has to be practical risk rather than a theoretical one (*Attorney General v Guardian Newspapers Ltd (No.3)* [1992] 1 W.L.R. 874.

Assessment of the risk will involve a consideration of the possible impact of the publication upon readers. Where an article appeared in an obscure weekly publication the possibility of any prospective juror having read the publication would be small and that small risk would be overwhelmed by a lengthy and complex trial. *Attorney General v Sunday Newspapers Ltd* [1999] C.O.D. 11.

On an application under s.2(2) it is not necessary to demonstrate the degree of prejudice which would justify an order by the trial judge for a stay of the criminal proceedings. It is a sufficient basis for a finding of contempt that the publication created a seriously arguable ground of appeal against conviction. *Attorney General v Birmingham Post and Mail Ltd* [1999] 1 W.L.R. 361 (Simon Brown L.J. and Thomas J.).

A distinction should be drawn between private pressure on a litigant, by an opposing litigant or a third party, and publication to a wide section of the public. As regards the latter, publication will not generally constitute contempt if it contains nothing more than fair and temperate criticism of a litigant; an article that goes beyond such criticism may create a substantial risk of prejudice (*Attorney General v Hislop* [1991] 2 W.L.R. 219; [1991] 1 Q.B. 514, CA).

Expressions of regret cannot excuse a breach of the strict liability rule although they might mitigate penalty. This is so even where the publishers did not intend such a consequence to ensue from the publication or foresee that it would or might have such an effect (*Attorney General v BBC, Independent*, January 3, 1992).

Paragraph numbers marked with a "+" can be found online and on CD.

A publication referring to particular legal proceedings is less likely to be held to create a substantial risk that the course of justice in those proceedings will be seriously impeded or prejudiced if the proceedings are to be heard by a judge rather than tried by a jury. The possibility that an appellate court will be influenced is even more remote. Hence a publication which prejudges appeal proceedings pending before the House of Lords, and which is unlikely to deter the parties from contesting the appeal, does not constitute a contempt of court (*Re Lonrho plc* [1989] 2 All E.R. 1100, HL). A litigant who seeks a judicial remedy to compel a particular course of action is not guilty of contempt of court under s.2(2) of the Act if he resorts to self-help to obtain the remedy without the assistance of the courts, since the fact that the litigant thereby pre-empts the decision of the courts does not amount to impeding or prejudicing the course of justice (*ibid.*).

Documents in a court file do not become available for inspection unless access to a particular document is granted by operation of the rules or by leave of the court in a particular case. Where a person inspects documents in the court file by deception or subterfuge and then publishes that which he discovers he interferes with the administration of justice and commits a contempt of court *Dobson v Hastings* (1991) 141 New L.J. 1625.

A stay of proceedings, which stops the continuance of proceedings before a court or tribunal, is not an order enforceable by proceedings for contempt because it is not capable of being breached by a party to the proceedings (*Minister of Foreign Affairs, Trade and Industry v Vehicle and Supplies Ltd* [1991] 1 W.L.R. 550, PC; [1990] 4 All E.R. 65).

The fact that words were spoken in a humorous, irreverent and often rude television programme ("Have I Got News for You") some six months before the trial did not diminish the risk of serious prejudice to the course of justice (*Attorney General v BBC* [1997] E.M.L.R. 76).

In determining the degree of risk the court will look at each publication separately, but the mere fact that by reason of earlier publications there is already some risk of prejudice does not prevent a finding that the latest publication has created a further risk. The crucial matter will be the residual impact of the publication on a notional juror at the time of the trial. It may be proper for a trial judge to stay proceedings on the ground of prejudice albeit that no individual is subsequently found to be guilty of contempt (*Attorney General v MGN Ltd* [1997] 1 All E.R. 456).

A third party will not be held liable for contempt in acting inconsistently with a court order unless that order is clear and precise both in its effect and scope. Moreover where it is sought to impose indirect liability on a third party it is not necessary to show that the relevant proceedings had been wholly frustrated or rendered utterly futile but rather some significant and adverse effect upon the administration of justice. Conduct by a third party which is inconsistent with a court order only in a trivial or technical way should not expose him to conviction for contempt (*Attorney General v Newspaper Publishing Plc* [1997] 1 W.L.R. 926).

"... If the proceedings in question are active"

The rules for determining the times at which proceedings are to be treated as active **3C–6** are set out in Sch.1 (see paras 3C–56 *et seq.* below). Proceedings in a Coroner's Court become active as soon as the inquest is opened, even where there has been an adjournment of all contentious matters after non-contentious matters have been dealt with (*Peacock v London Weekend Television Ltd, The Times*, November 27, 1985, CA).

Whether or not an action is in the High Court warned list, or is less than three months from the date fixed for trial, are not matters which can be substituted for the test of "activity" prescribed by paras 12 and 13 of Sch.1 (see para.3C–58, below) (*Attorney General v News Group Newspapers Ltd* [1987] Q.B. 1; [1986] 2 All E.R. 833, CA).

In cases where no active steps have been taken in any prosecution against a plaintiff (so that the strict liability rule under ss.1 and 2 of the Contempt of Court Act 1981 did not apply), but it is sought to restrain publication of material on the ground of contempt of court at common law, it is necessary for the court to be sure (a) that publication would create a risk of real prejudice if and when the prosecution proceeded, and (b) the material would be published with the specific intention of causing that risk (*Coe v Central Television, Cook and Thorne, Independent*, August 11, 1993).

Defence of innocent publication or distribution

3.—(1) A person is not guilty of contempt of court under the strict **3C–7**

Paragraph numbers marked with a "+" can be found online and on CD.

liability rule as the publisher of any matter to which that rule applies if at the time of publication (having taken all reasonable care) he does not know and has no reason to suspect that relevant proceedings are active.

(2) A person is not guilty of contempt of court under the strict liability rule as the distributor of a publication containing any such matter if at the time of distribution (having taken all reasonable care) he does not know that it contains such matter and has no reason to suspect that it is likely to do so.

(3) The burden of proof of any fact tending to establish a defence afforded by this section to any person lies upon that person.

(4) [...]

3C–8   *Note* —Subsection (4) repealed by the Statute Law (Repeals) Act 2004, s.1(1), Sch.1, Pt 1.

Contemporary reports of proceedings

3C–9   **4.**—(1) Subject to this section a person is not guilty of contempt of court under the strict liability rule in respect of a fair and accurate report of legal proceedings held in public, published contemporaneously and in good faith.

(2) In any such proceedings the court may, where it appears to be necessary for avoiding a substantial risk of prejudice to the administration of justice in those proceedings, or in any other proceedings pending or imminent, order that the publication of any report of the proceedings, or any part of the proceedings, be postponed for such period as the court thinks necessary for that purpose.

(2A) Where in proceedings for any offence which is an administration of justice offence for the purposes of section 54 of the Criminal Procedure and Investigations Act 1996 (acquittal tainted by an administration of justice offence) it appears to the court that there is a possibility that (by virtue of that section) proceedings may be taken against a person for an offence of which he has been acquitted, subsection (2) of this section shall apply as if those proceedings were pending or imminent.

(3) For the purposes of subsection (1) of this section a report of proceedings shall be treated as published contemporaneously—

    (a) in the case of a report of which publication is postponed pursuant to an order under subsection (2) of this section, if published as soon as practicable after that order expires;

    (b) in the case of a report of committal proceedings of which publication is permitted by virtue only of subsection (3) of section 8 of the Magistrates' Courts Act, if published as soon as practicable after publication is so permitted.

(4) [...]

3C–10   *Note* —Amended by the Criminal Justice and Public Order Act 1994, s.44, Sch.4, para.50; the Criminal Procedure and Investigations Act 1996, s.57; and the Defamation Act 1996, s.16, Sch.2; subs.(4) repealed by the Statute Law (Repeals) Act 2004, s.1(1), Sch.1, Pt 1.

Paragraph numbers marked with a "+" can be found online and on CD.

Legal proceedings held in public

The expression "legal proceedings held in public" refers to court proceedings, and **3C–11** not to events preceding them. Thus an arrest of a defendant is not a legal proceeding held in public and a film of the arrest cannot be the subject of an order under s.4(2); if the showing of the film is likely to prejudice the trial, the proper remedy is for the person affected to apply for an injunction in the High Court (*R. v Rhuddlan Justices Ex p. HTV Ltd* [1986] Crim.L.R. 329, DC).

Postponement of reports of proceedings

A magistrates' court in considering whether to make or continue a reporting re- **3C–12** striction order under s.4(2) of the Contempt of Court Act 1981 has, like the Crown Court, a discretionary power to hear representations from the press and it was to be expected that the power would ordinarily be exercised when the media asked to be heard (*R. v Clerkenwell Stipendiary Magistrates Ex p. The Telegraph plc* (1992) 142 New L.J. 1541; *Independent*, October 16, 1992) , indeed, members of the media should be asked whether they wish to make submissions, *Crawford v DPP The Times*, February 20, 2008 (Thomas L.J. and Dobbs J.)..

In relation to committal proceedings s.8 of the Magistrates' Courts Act 1980 already imposes restrictions on the reporting of such proceedings and, as a matter of general policy, justices should therefore be slow to make additional orders under s.4(2) of the 1981 Act (*R. v Beaconsfield Justices Ex p. Westminster Press Ltd*, *The Times*, June 28, 1994).

In considering whether to make an order under s.4(2) the court should seek to answer three questions: (i) was there a substantial risk of prejudice to the administration of justice? (ii) did it appear necessary for the avoidance of that prejudice that there should be some order made postponing publication of a report? (iii) if so, should the court, in its discretion, make an order and, if so, in what terms? *MGN Pensions Trustees Ltd v Bank of America National Trust and Savings Association* [1995] 2 All E.R. 355 (Lindsay J.). In determining whether publication of matter would cause a substantial risk of prejudice to a future trial, a court should credit the jury with the will and ability to abide by the judge's direction to decide the case only on the evidence before them. The court should also bear in mind that the staying power and detail of publicity, even in cases of notoriety, are limited and that the nature of a trial is to focus the jury's minds on the evidence put before them, rather than on matters outside the courtroom. The Court of Appeal's function on an appeal under s.159 of the Criminal Justice Act 1988 was to form its own view on the material before it. *Ex p. The Telegraph plc* [1993] 1 W.L.R. 980.

In considering whether it is "necessary" to make an order, both in the sense contemplated by s.4(2) and in the different sense contemplated by Art.10 of the European Convention on Human Rights, "restrictions ... as are prescribed by law and are necessary in a democratic society ..." the court should apply a three part test:

(1) Whether reporting would give rise to a "not unsubstantial" risk of prejudice to the administration of justice in the relevant proceedings. if not, that will be the end of the matter.

(2) If such a risk is perceived to exist, would a s.4(2) order eliminate it? If not there could be no necessity to impose such a ban and, again, that will be the end of the matter. If, however, an order would achieve the objective the judge must still consider whether the risk could be satisfactorily overcome by less restrictive means.

(3) If the judge concludes that there is indeed no other way of eliminating the risk of prejudice he must still ask whether the degree of risk contemplated should be regarded as tolerable in the sense of being "the lesser of two evils". At that stage value judgments may have to be made as to the priority between "competing public interests": *Ex p. The Telegraph Group PLC* [2001] 1 W.L.R. 1983 (Longmore L.J., Douglas Brown and Eady JJ.).

Since it is necessary to keep a permanent record of all orders made under s.4(2), all such orders must be formulated in precise terms, having regard to the decision in *R. v Horsham Justices Ex p. Farquharson* [1982] Q.B. 762; [1982] 2 All E.R. 269, and all orders under this section as well as under s.11 must be committed to writing either by the judge personally or by the clerk of the Court under the judges' direction. Such an order must state (a) its precise scope (b) the time at which it will cease to have effect if appropriate and (c) the specific purpose of making the order.

Paragraph numbers marked with a "+" can be found online and on CD.

Courts will normally give notice to the press in some form that an order has been made under either section of the Act and court staff should be prepared to answer any inquiry about a specific case, but it is, and will remain, the responsibility of those reporting cases, and their editors, to ensure that no breach of any order occurs and the onus rests with them to make inquiry in any case of doubt (Practice Direction (Contempt: Reporting Restrictions) [1982] 1 W.L.R. 1475; [1983] 1 All E.R. 64).

When making an order the courts should be diligent in accommodating and understanding the legitimate interests of the press and such an order should be drafted and made public in a way which makes it clear what may or may not be published, both as regards the proceedings themselves and the terms of the order. It is desirable that it be made in advance of the trial and the judge is at liberty to adjourn consideration of reporting restrictions until the press have been heard (*Attorney General v Guardian Newspapers Ltd (No.3)* [1992] 1 W.L.R. 874; [1992] 3 All E.R. 38).

Care should be taken over the wording of any notice pinned to the door of the court or given in some other form which may be read by jurors. Where the complete text of an order made under s.4(2), making it clear that the defendant faces further trials, is pinned to the door of the court and is seen to be read by a juror trying the case, there is a real possibility of prejudice to the defendant and the jury should be discharged (*R. v Hutton* [1990] Crim.L.R. 875, CA (Crim. Div)).

Where a jury has retired to spend a night at an hotel it is not necessary to postpone reports of the proceedings on television or radio for fear that members of the jury may watch television or listen to the radio while at the hotel; if it is considered necessary to insulate the members of the jury from the media, they can be deprived of access to television or radio, just as they can be denied access to newspapers, while at the hotel (*Re Central Independent Television plc* [1991] 1 All E.R. 347, CA (Crim. Div)).

A Judge's decision whether or not to order reporting restrictions under s.4(2) involves an exercise of discretion based on fact, and does not involve any question of law such as to entitle the Court of Appeal to interfere with the decision, unless it can be demonstrated that such discretion has been exercised on a fundamentally flawed basis (*Re Saunders, The Times,* February 8, 1990; *Independent,* February 8, 1990, CA).

It is important that there should be freedom of information unless some necessity is shown to prevent it. Thus where the managers of a company are alleged to have removed assets in breach of their duties, and where a receiver is appointed to ensure that certain funds should be secured until the Court can decide who is the true owner, there is no reason to restrict reporting of the judgment whereby the receiver is appointed. Nothing in such a judgment is likely to prejudice a fair trial of the managers involved, and any report that does not make it clear that, as yet, there are only unsubstantiated allegations, will not be fair and accurate, and itself will be a contempt of court by virtue of s.4 (*Barlow Clowes Gilt Managers Ltd v Clowes, The Times,* February 2, 1990).

Section 4(2) is designed to enable the court to prevent the publication of a report of proceedings, where the publication would prejudice the conduct of those proceedings or specific pending proceedings. The need for postponement cannot subsist beyond the end of the proceedings in question. In *Re Times Newspapers Ltd* [2008] 1 W.L.R. 234 (Lord Phillips of Worth Matravers C.J., Elias and Griffith Williams JJ.).

Discussion of public affairs

3C–13   5. A publication made as or as part of a discussion in good faith of public affairs or other matters of general public interest is not to be treated as a contempt of court under the strict liability rule if the risk of impediment or prejudice to particular legal proceedings is merely incidental to the discussion.

Incidental to the discussion

3C–14   The protection afforded by s.5 is intended to prevent the suppression of bona fide discussion in the media of controversial matters of public interest, merely by reason that contemporaneous legal proceedings exist in which some particular instance of such matters may be in issue, and the burden is on the Attorney General to prove that the publication does not fall within s.5 and that the risk of prejudice to a fair trial is

Paragraph numbers marked with a "+" can be found online and on CD.

not "merely incidental" to the discussion. Where a newspaper article forms part of a wider campaign and controversy as to the justiciability of mercy killing, it does not prejudice the fair trial of the doctor accused of the murder of a severely disabled baby, since it is no more than an incidental consequence of a discussion of a matter of general public interest, and is not a contempt of court (*Attorney General v English* [1983] A.C. 116; [1982] 2 All E.R. 903, HL. See also *Attorney General v Times Newspapers Ltd, The Times*, February 12, 1983, CA).

In considering whether a publication is a contempt of court by reason of prejudice to particular legal proceedings, or is merely incidental to discussion of matters of general public interest, it is appropriate to look at the subject matter of the discussion in the publication and to see how closely it relates to the particular legal proceedings; where the theme of the discussion is narrowly directed to the activities of a small group of identifiable persons, and where such activities are the subject matter of indictments charging one or more of those persons, it is impossible to categorise the discussion as no more than incidental to discussion of matters of general public interest (*Attorney General v TVS Television Ltd, The Times*, July 7, 1989; *Independent*, July 7, 1989).

Savings

6. Nothing in the foregoing provisions of this Act— 3C–15

(a) prejudices any defence available at common law to a charge of contempt of court under the strict liability rule;

(b) implies that any publication is punishable as contempt of court under that rule which would not be so punishable apart from those provisions;

(c) restricts liability for contempt of court in respect of conduct intended to impede or prejudice the administration of justice.

"Conduct intended to impede or prejudice the administration of justice"

A person not named in an interlocutory injunction may be in contempt of court by 3C–16
acting in a way contrary to the terms of that injunction. Such action may constitute "conduct intended to impede or prejudice the administration of justice", even though such intention is not the sole or principal intention of the contemnor (*Attorney General v Newspaper Publishing plc* [1987] 3 W.L.R. 942, CA. See also *Attorney General v Guardian Newspaper Publishing Ltd (No.2)*, *Independent*, October 17, 1987; *The Times*, October 20, 1987).

A person who is not a party to an action in which an injunction has been granted, commits a contempt of court if he knowingly does an act which is in breach of the injunction and which has the effect of destroying in whole or in part the subject matter of the action, so that the purpose of the trial of the action is wholly or partly nullified. (*Attorney General v Times Newspapers Ltd, The Times*, February 12, 1983, HL).

The purpose the Court seeks to achieve in granting an interlocutory injunction is to prevent the restrained acts from being done, pending a decision by the Court on the claims in the proceedings. Third parties will be in contempt if they wilfully interfere with the administration of justice by thwarting the achievement of *this* purpose in *those* proceedings. This is so, even if the injunction is drawn in seemingly over-wide terms. The remedy of the third party whose conduct is affected by the order is to apply to the court for the order to be varied. See *Attorney Generalv Punch Ltd* [2002] UKHL 50; [2003] 1 A.C. 1046; [2003] 2 W.L.R. 49, an appeal from [2001] EWCA Civ 403.

The Act makes extensive provision for what may be called statutory contempts, but the saving contained in s.6(c) indicates that something which falls short of contempt under the statute may still be contempt at common law. Hence a newspaper which publishes articles with specific intention of interfering with the course of justice in criminal proceedings which, though not pending, are virtually certain to be commenced in the near future may be guilty of contempt at a common law even if the articles do not come within the strict liability provisions of sections 1 and 2 (*Attorney General v News Group Newspapers Ltd* [1988] 3 W.L.R. 163; [1988] 2 All E.R. 907).

In *Attorney General v Sport Newspapers Ltd* [1991] 1 W.L.R. 1194; [1992] 1 All E.R.

Paragraph numbers marked with a "+" can be found online and on CD.

503, Bingham L.J. followed *Attorney General v News Group Newspapers plc* [1989] Q.B. 110, holding that, if publication creates a real risk of prejudice to the due administration of justice, and if the alleged contemnor publishes with the specific intent of causing such risk, contempt may be committed even though proceedings are neither in existence nor imminent. In the same case, however, Hogson J., disapproving *Attorney General v News Group Newspapers plc* (above), took the view that the time when the summary jurisdiction of judges over intentional publications contempts begins is when the relevant proceedings become pending, and that the ambit of such summary procedure should not be widened.

Consent required for institution of proceedings

3C–17   **7.** Proceedings for a contempt of court under the strict liability rule (other than Scottish proceedings) shall not be instituted except by or with the consent of the Attorney-General or on the motion of a court having jurisdiction to deal with it.

Consent of the Attorney General

3C–18   An application to commit a person for an alleged contempt which falls within the strict liability rule will be dismissed where the consent of the Attorney General has not been obtained (*Roger Bullivant Ltd v Ellis, Financial Times*, April 16, 1986).

Although a circuit judge has jurisdiction to deal with a contempt in the face of the court, he has no jurisdiction to deal with a contempt alleged to have been committed by the publication of a book, shortly before the commencement of criminal proceedings against a defendant, in which reference is made to the defendant being involved in serious organised crime, and which thereby tends, contrary to "the strict liability rule" prescribed by s.1, to interfere with the course of justice in those proceedings; except in the narrow range of cases where proceedings for contempt can be instituted under s.7 on the motion of the Court having jurisdiction to deal with the matter, proceedings for contempt under "the strict liability rule" can be commenced only by or with the consent of the Attorney General (*Taylor v Topping, The Times*, February 15, 1990; *Independent*, February 20, 1990). The decision of the law officers not to institute proceedings under s.7 cannot be challenged by way of an application for judicial review. *R. v Solicitor General Ex p. Taylor and Taylor* [1996] C.O.D. 61).

Other aspects of law and procedure

Confidentiality of jury's deliberations

3C–19   **8.**—(1) Subject to subsection (2) below, it is a contempt of court to obtain, disclose or solicit any particulars of statements made, opinions expressed, arguments advanced or votes cast by members of a jury in the course of their deliberations in any legal proceedings.

(2) This section does not apply to any disclosure of any particulars—

> (a) in the proceedings in question for the purpose of enabling the jury to arrive at their verdict, or in connection with the delivery of that verdict, or
>
> (b) in evidence in any subsequent proceedings for an offence alleged to have been committed in relation to the jury in the first mentioned proceedings,

or to the publication of any particulars so disclosed.

(3) Proceedings for a contempt of court under this section (other than Scottish proceedings) shall not be instituted except by or with the consent of the Attorney-General or on the motion of a court having jurisdiction to deal with it.

Paragraph numbers marked with a "+" can be found online and on CD.

Confidentiality of jury's deliberations

Any approach or attempt to take statements from jurors which might have the ef- **3C–20** fect of breaching s.8 is to run the risk of committing a contempt of court or even of an attempt to pervert the course of justice. In relation to enquiries concerning the jury the trial judge is *functus officio* after verdict and sentence and in such cases the proper course is to seek the consent of the Court of Appeal (*R. v Mickleburgh*, *The Times*, July 26, 1994).

The prohibitions contained in s.8 apply equally to the Court of Appeal as they do to others. It would therefore be a breach of s.8 for the court to enquire into the jury's deliberations in the retiring room. However, the section does not prevent the court from enquiring into what may have taken place at an hotel where the jury had stayed overnight before returning to court to resume its deliberations (*R. v Young (Stephen)*, [1995] Q.B. 324). In s.8(1) the word "disclose" is apt to include not only disclosure by a juror but also disclosure by some other, but not the republication of information already in the public domain (*Attorney General v Associated Newspapers* [1994] 2 W.L.R. 277; [1994] 1 All E.R. 556, HL).

A request by a judge for the names of jurors to which a note related was a breach of section 8(1), which applies to the court as it does to others, and of the long established principle that there is no right in anyone to enquire as to what occurred in the jury room, a principle reaffirmed in *Andrew Brown* (1907) 7 N.S.W. St.Rep. 291 and *R. v Thompson* [1962] 1 All E.R. 65 CA *R. v Schot and Barclay*, *The Times*, May 14, 1997).

Use of tape recorders

9.—(1) Subject to subsection (4) below, it is a contempt of court— **3C–21**

   (a) to use in court, or bring into court for use, any tape re-
       corder or other instrument for recording sound, except
       with the leave of the court;

   (b) to publish a recording of legal proceedings made by
       means of any such instrument, or any recording derived
       directly or indirectly from it, by playing it in the hearing
       of the public or any section of the public, or to dispose
       of it or any recording so derived, with a view to such
       publication;

   (c) to use any such recording in contravention of any condi-
       tions of leave granted under paragraph (a).

(2) Leave under paragraph (a) of subsection (1) may be granted or refused at the discretion of the court, and if granted may be granted subject to such conditions as the court thinks proper with respect to the use of any recording made pursuant to the leave; and where leave has been granted the court may at the like discretion withdraw or amend it either generally or in relation to any particular part of the proceedings.

(3) Without prejudice to any other power to deal with an act of contempt under paragraph (a) of subsection (1), the court may order the instrument, or any recording made with it, or both, to be forfeited; and any object so forfeited shall (unless the court otherwise determines on application by a person appearing to be the owner) be sold or otherwise disposed of in such manner as the court may direct.

(4) This section does not apply to the making or use of sound recordings for purposes of official transcripts of proceedings.

Use of tape recorders in court

The following Practice Direction was issued on November 19, 1981. See *Practice* **3C–22** *Direction (Tape Recorders)* [1981] 1 W.L.R. 1526; [1981] 3 All E.R. 848:

Paragraph numbers marked with a "+" can be found online and on CD.

1. Section 9 of the Contempt of Court Act 1981 contains provisions governing the unofficial use of tape recorders in court. Among other things it provides that it is a contempt of court to use in court, or bring into court for use, any tape recorder or other instrument for recording sound, except with the leave of the court; and it is also a contempt of court to publish a recording of legal proceedings or to use any such recording in contravention of any conditions which the court may have attached to the grant of permission to use the machine in court. These provisions do not apply to the making or use of sound recordings for purposes of official transcripts of proceedings, on which the Act imposes no restriction whatever.

2. The discretion given to the court to grant, withhold or withdraw leave to use tape recorders or to impose conditions as to the use of the recording is unlimited, but the following factors may be relevant to its exercise:

(a) the existence of any reasonable need on the part of the applicant for leave, whether a litigant or a person connected with the press or broadcasting, for the recording to be made;

(b) in a criminal case, or a civil case in which a direction has been given excluding one or more witnesses from the court, the risk that the recording could be used for the purpose of briefing witnesses out of court;

(c) any possibility that the use of a recorder would disturb the proceedings or distract or worry any witnesses or other participants.

3. Consideration should always be given whether conditions as to the use of a recording made pursuant to leave should be imposed. The identity and role of the applicant for leave and the nature of the subject matter of the proceedings may be relevant to this.

4. The particular restriction imposed by s.9(1)(b) of the 1981 Act applies in every case, but may not be present to the mind of every applicant to whom leave is given. It may, therefore, be desirable on occasion for this provision to be drawn to the attention of those to whom leave is given.

5. The transcript of a permitted recording is intended for the use of the person given leave to make it and is not intended to be used as, or to compete with, the official transcript mentioned in s.9(4) of the 1981 Act.

Sources of information

3C–23   **10.** No court may require a person to disclose, nor is any person guilty of contempt of court for refusing to disclose, the source of information contained in a publication for which he is responsible, unless it be established to the satisfaction of the court that disclosure is necessary in the interests of justice or national security or for the prevention of disorder or crime.

Application of section

3C–24   Section 10 is not directly applicable to a requirement made of a journalist by inspectors investigating possible offences under the Companies Acts, because such inspectors are not a court. The section, however, is indicative of the general policy prescribed by Parliament which should be applied by way of analogy on a reference arising out of such a requirement. If, therefore, the journalist is in a position to show that, if the inspectors were a court, he could rely on s.10 to support refusal to disclose his source of information, he has "reasonable excuse" for his refusal, within the meaning of s.178(2) of the Financial Services Act 1986, and will not be punishable as for a contempt of court under that section (*Re an Inquiry under the Company Securities (Insider Dealing) Act 1985* [1988] A.C. 660; [1988] 1 All E.R. 203, HL).

Interests of national security

3C–25   The prohibition in s.10 against the court making an order to disclose a source of information is of wide and general application, subject only to the four exceptions specified in the section, namely that disclosure is necessary in the interests of justice or national security or for the prevention of disorder or crime. Accordingly it is sufficient to attract the protection of s.10 if the order for disclosure might, but not necessarily

Paragraph numbers marked with a "+" can be found online and on CD.

would have the effect of disclosing a source of information. Moreover a publisher is not precluded from relying on s.10 in the face of a proprietary claim by an owner for the delivery up of his property. The onus of proving that the case falls within one of the four exceptions specified in the section lies on the party seeking the order, and the standard of proof required to satisfy the court that disclosure is necessary is the balance of probabilities. The interests of national security require that the identity of a person who discloses to a newspaper a memorandum of the Secretary of State for Defence classified as "secret" should be disclosed, where the risk to national security lies not in the publication of the particular document but in the possibility that the person who discloses it may in future disclose other classified documents, the disclosure of which would have more serious consequences for national security (*Secretary of State for Defence v Guardian Newspapers Ltd* [1985] A.C. 339; [1984] 3 All E.R. 601, HL).

Interests of justice

"The interests of justice" refer to the administration of justice in the course of legal **3C–26** proceedings in a court of law, a tribunal or a body exercising judicial power of the state, and not to the concept of justice in the abstract (*Secretary of State for Defence v Guardian Newspapers Ltd* (above)). The words "in the interests of justice" are to be construed in the technical sense of the administration of legal proceedings in a court of law; s.10 requires it to be established that disclosure is necessary for the administration of justice in that sense, and not merely that disclosure is expedient (*Maxwell v Pressdram Ltd* [1987] 1 W.L.R. 298; [1987] 1 All E.R. 656, CA). The public interest in the non-disclosure of journalists' sources may in a particular case outweigh the requirement that the sources be named in the interest of justice (*ibid.*).

To construe "justice" as the antonym of "injustice" is too wide but to confine it to the technical sense of the administration of justice in court of legal proceedings in a court of law is too narrow. It is in the interests of justice, within the meaning of the section, that persons should be enabled to exercise important legal rights and to protect themselves from serious legal wrongs, whether or not resort to legal proceedings in a court of law will be necessary to attain such objectives. It will not be sufficient, by itself, to establish the necessity of disclosure, for a party seeking disclosure of a source to show merely that he will be unable, without disclosure, to exercise the legal right or avert the threatened legal wrong on which he bases his claim. If the party seeking disclosure shows that his livelihood depends on it, that will put the case near one end of the spectrum. The greater the legitimate public interest in the information, the greater will be the importance of protecting the source: If the information is obtained illegally, that will diminish the importance of protecting the source unless, for example, the source has acted for the purpose of exposing iniquity (*X Ltd v Morgan Grampian (Publishers) Ltd* [1990] 2 All E.R. 1, HL). Hence disclosure of a journalist's source of confidential information about a company is necessary in the interests of justice, where the importance of protecting the source, whose complicity in obtaining the information is not counterbalanced by any legitimate public interest in publication of the information, is outweighed by the threat of severe damage to the company's business which can be avoided only if the information is recovered (*ibid.*). But now see the decision of the European Court of Human Rights that the order requiring the journalist to reveal his source of information, and the fine imposed on him for having refused to do so, constituted a violation of Art.10 of the European Convention of Human Rights (*Goodwin v UK, The Times*, March 28, 1996).

The question whether a publisher is to be required to disclose the source of information or return documents which would necessarily identify that source is to be determined in accordance with English law, as set out in s.10 and interpreted by the English courts in *X Ltd v Morgan-Grampian (Publishers) Ltd* [1991] 1 A.C. 1 (it being clear and unambiguous) and not therefore by the application of the decision of the European Court of Human Rights in *Goodwin v United Kingdom* (1996) 22 E.C.H.R. 123 (based on the same facts) and the interpretation of Art.10 of the ECHR (*Camelot Group plc v Centaur Communications Ltd, The Times*, July 15, 1997, per Kay J.).

Before the court will require journalists to break the important professional obligation to protect a source, the minimum requirement is that other avenues of enquiry should be explored in an attempt to identify the source. A single leak of counsel's draft advice was not sufficient to warrant an order for disclosure under s.10 of the Act. *John v Express Newspapers* [2000] 1 W.L.R.1931 (Lord Woolf M.R., Pill and May L.JJ.).

Paragraph numbers marked with a "+" can be found online and on CD.

An order for disclosure may be made, even if the information is not required for the purpose of bringing an action. The important protection which both s.10 and Art.10 provide for freedom of expression required however that the Court should scrutinise diligently any request for relief which would result in the Court interfering with freedom of expression including ordering the disclosure of journalists services. Both s.10 and Art.10 of the European Convention on Human Rights are one in making clear that the Court has to be sure that a sufficiently strong positive case has been made out in favour of disclosure before it will be ordered, *Ashworth Hospital Authority v MGN Ltd* [2002] 4 All E.R. 193 (House of Lords).

For the court to order a journalist to disclose the name of his source it must be established that it is both necessary, in the sense of there being an overriding interest, amounting to a pressing social need, and proportionate: *Mersey Care NHS Trust v Ackroyd* [2007] EWCA Civ 101; *The Times*, February 26, 2007, CA.

"Necessary for the prevention of crime"

3C–27 "Necessary" has a meaning that lies somewhere between "indispensable" on the one hand and "useful" or "convenient" on the other. It is a word which takes colour from its context. Whether a particular measure is necessary in a particular case involves an exercise of judgment on the established facts. "The prevention of crime" refers to the prevention of crime generally rather than to the prevention of a particular identifiable future crime. The court must be presented with sufficient material to enable it to exercise an independent judgment on the extent of the need for disclosure. It will pay proper regard to the views of those seeking disclosure, but must not act as a rubber stamp for those views (*Re an Inquiry under the Company Securities (Insider Dealing) Act 1985* [1988] A.C. 660; [1988] 1 All E.R. 203, HL). Disclosure by a defendant cannot be said to be necessary for the prevention of crime in circumstances where the prevention of crime is not the plaintiff's task, and where a criminal investigation would not be a likely consequence if the defendant's source were disclosed (*X (Health Authority) v Y.* [1988] 2 All E.R. 648). In considering whether it is "necessary" to require a journalist to reveal the source of a leaked document, the court will consider whether the applicant for the disclosure order has itself attempted to discover the source of the leak, otherwise than by applying to the Court (*Broadmoor Hospital v Hyde*, *The Times*, March 18, 1994; *Independent*, March 4, 1994).

Publication of matters exempted from disclosure in court

3C–28 **11.** In any case where a court (having power to do so) allows a name or other matter to be withheld from the public in proceedings before the court, the court may give such directions prohibiting the publication of that name or matter in connection with the proceedings as appear to the court to be necessary for the purpose for which it was so withheld.

Directions prohibiting publication

3C–29 The jurisdiction to order disclosure of the identity of a wrongdoer is one of general application, exisiting in equity. The "interests of justice" in s.10 means interests which were justifiable, and was not confined to the technical sense of the administration of justice in the course of legal proceedings in a court of law, *Ashworth Hospital Authority v MGN Ltd* [2001] 1 W.L.R. 515, (Lord Phillips of Worth Matravers M.R., May and Laws L.JJ.).

The Q.B. Divisional Court has no jurisdiction to entertain an application for judicial review of an order made under s.11 by a Crown Court in relation to a trial on indictment. The Divisional Court has noted, however, an increasing tendency to make orders under s.11, even where the name of a witness which it was forbidden to publish outside court had been referred to in the proceedings. It is doubtful whether s.11 has any application in such circumstances. It is of vital constitutional importance that criminal trials are held in public and freely reported. This consideration must outweigh the individual interests of particular persons who may feel embarrassment as a result of allegations made in the course of a trial (*R. v Central Criminal Court Ex p. Crook* (1985) 82 L.S.Gaz. 1408, DC; *The Times*, November 8, 1984).

Paragraph numbers marked with a "+" can be found online and on CD.

A court has no power under s.11 to prohibit the press from publishing the name of a defendant if, earlier in the proceedings, that name has not been withheld from the public (*R. v Arundel JJ. Ex p. Westminster Press Ltd* [1985] 1 W.L.R. 708; [1985] 2 All E.R. 390).

The general principle of law is that all evidence communicated to a court should be communicated publicly (*Attorney General v Leveller Magazine Ltd* [1979] A.C. 440, [1979] 2 All E.R. 745, HL). The general rule should not be departed from save where the nature of circumstances of the proceedings are such that its application would frustrate or render impracticable the administration of justice. Such circumstances are rare. It is a misuse of s.11 for magistrates to prohibit the publication of a defendant's address in order to protect him from possible harassment by his former wife (*R. v Evesham Justices Ex p. McDonagh* [1988] Q.B. 553; [1988] 1 All E.R. 371). A magistrate making an order under s.37 of the Public Health (Control of Disease) Act 1984 directing the removal to hospital of a person with a "notifiable disease" is a court for the purposes of s.11 of the Contempt of Court Act 1981 and has power to allow a patient's name to be withheld from the public. It is however a constrained power and exercisable only in so far as reasonably necessary to serve the ends of justice. While it would be unfair to allow publication of a patient's identity when subject to an ex parte order, once all reasonable opportunity to challenge that order had passed, no interest of justice was any longer involved. Any wish to protect privacy or avoid embarrassment is not a ground for the continuance of such a prohibition. *Birmingham Post & Mail Ltd v Birmingham City Council, Independent*, November 25, 1993). The power to make an order under s.11 must be exercised carefully and cannot be used simply to protect privacy or avoid embarrassment. In proceedings for judicial review any application for anonymity should usually be made at the same time as the application for leave to move. However, where the applicant's name alone might itself give rise to publicity, enquiry should first be made of the Crown Office, so that the application for an order under s.11 can be made as soon as the papers are lodged (*R. v Westminster City Council Ex p. Castelli and Garcia, The Times*, August 14, 1995).

The fact that publication of the summonses giving rise to the proceedings may have dire economic consequences leading to the closure of the defendant's business does not constitute an exceptional circumstances justifying magistrates making an order restricting publication under s.11 (*R. v Dover Justices Ex p. Dover DC, The Times*, October 21, 1991; *Independent*, October 21, 1991). It would be very rare indeed to find circumstances justifying departure from the general rule to prevent publication of material relating to a defendant's acquittal (*ibid.*).

Where, however, application is made to a court to hear proceedings *in camera* and for a direction under s.11 prohibiting publication of the proceedings, the court should accede to a request to hear the reasons for the application *in camera*, so that a decision may be made whether there is substance in the application without prejudicing the applicant (*R. v Tower Bridge Justices Ex p. Osborne* [1988] Crim.L.R. 382).

In relation to an application for judicial review it may sometimes be appropriate to make an interim order under s.11 of the Act at the ex parte leave stage so as to enable the applicant to provide more substantial evidence at the substantive hearing as to the damage which might be caused by disclosure. This case also contains an examination of the more recent authorities on s.11 (*R. v Somerset Health Authority Ex p. S* [1996] C.O.D. 244, per Brooke J.).

Offences of contempt of magistrates' courts

12.—(1) A magistrates' court has jurisdiction under this section to deal with any person who— **3C–30**

    (a) wilfully insults the justice or justices, any witness before or officer of the court or any solicitor or counsel having business in the court, during his or their sitting or attendance in court or in going to or returning from the court; or

    (b) wilfully interrupts the proceedings of the court or otherwise misbehaves in court.

Paragraph numbers marked with a "+" can be found online and on CD.

(2) In any such case the court may order any officer of the court, or any constable, to take the offender into custody and detain him until the rising of the court; and the court may, if it thinks fit, commit the offender to custody for a specified period not exceeding one month or impose on him a fine not exceeding £2,500, or both.

(2A) A fine imposed under subsection (2) above shall be deemed, for the purposes of any enactment, to be a sum adjudged to be paid by a conviction.

(3) [...]

(4) A magistrates' court may at any time revoke an order of committal made under subsection (2) and, if the offender is in custody, order his discharge.

(5) Section 135 of the Powers of Criminal Courts (Sentencing) Act 2000, Sched. 9, para. 83(a) and the following provisions of the Magistrates' Courts Act 1980 apply in relation to an order under this section as they apply in relation to a sentence on conviction or finding of guilty of an offence, namely: section 36 (restriction on fines in respect of young persons); sections 75 to 91 (enforcement); section 108 (appeal to Crown Court); section 136 (overnight detention in default of payment); and section 142(1) (power to rectify mistakes).

3C-31 *Note* —Amended by the Criminal Justice Act 1991, s.17(3), Sch.4; and the Criminal Justice Act 1993, s.65(3) (4) and Sch.3.

Jurisdiction of magistrates' courts

3C-32 A committal of a person to custody under s.12(2) for wilfully interrupting the proceedings of the Court does not amount to a summary conviction giving the person a right to legal representation before a sentence of imprisonment can be imposed. Nor does natural justice require the contemnor to be so represented (see *R. v Newbury Justices Ex p. du Pont* (1984) 148 J.P. 248; (1984) 78 Cr.App.R. 255).

By virtue of s.1(1) of the Criminal Justice Act 1982 a magistrates' court has no power to commit a person under the age of 17 for contempt; by virtue of s.9(1) of that Act and s.12 of this Act such a court does have power to commit for contempt a person between the ages of 17 and 21, but such power should be exercised only if the court is of opinion that no other method of dealing with the person is appropriate (*R. v Selby Justices Ex p. Frame* [1991] 2 All E.R. 344).

Where a defendant persisted in seeking to occupy that part of the court reserved for professional advocates, she was rightly held to be in contempt. The court should, however, never act in haste and should always give the alleged contemnor an opportunity to obtain legal advice and to apologise to the court (*R. v Pateley Bridge Justices Ex p. Percy* [1994] C.O.D. 453).

"Wilfully insults"

3C-33 "Insult" is to be given its ordinary meaning in the English language. Hence an alleged contemnor who threatens a witness does not thereby "wilfully insult" him as to confer jurisdiction on justices with the matter under s.12(1)(a) (*R. v Havant JJ. Ex p. Palmer* (1985) 149 J.P. 609; [1985] Crim.L.R. 658).

The provisions of s.12 of the Contempt of Court Act 1981 give a good indication of the type of behaviour which may amount to contempt in the face of the court at common law. Thus a wolf whistle directed at a juror returning into court was potentially insulting, offensive and a serious interference with the administration of justice and the courts. Jurors did not come to courts in order to have comments made about their personal appearance. The appropriate penalty was a moderate fine or detention until the end of the day or over the luncheon adjournment (*R. v Powell, The Times,* June 3, 1993).

Justices who peremptorily committed a solicitor to custody under s.12 of the Act for criticising the court's listing system had acted unreasonably. This was a classic case of a

Paragraph numbers marked with a "+" can be found online and on CD.

storm in a tea cup and like most storms so located no one had acted with entire good sense (*R. v Tamworth Justices Ex p. Walsh*, *The Times*, March 3, 1994; [1994] C.O.D. 277).

"Wilfully interrupts"

Magistrates have jurisdiction under s.12(1)(b) to deal with a person who "wilfully interrupts the proceedings of the court," whether the interruptions result from acts done inside or outside the court. In addition to the deliberate commission of the acts causing the interruptions, the mental element of intention that they should interrupt the proceedings must be established. Recklessness, in the sense that the interrupter knows that there is a risk that his acts will interrupt the proceedings but nevertheless goes on to do such acts, will be sufficient (*Bodden v Commissioner of Police for the Metropolis* [1990] 2 W.L.R. 76; [1989] 3 All E.R. 833, CA). **3C–34**

Appeal to Crown Court

An appeal from a conviction, or a sentence, for contempt of a Magistrates Court lies to the Crown Court under s.12(5) of the 1981 Act, but an appeal to the High Court by way of case stated or proceedings for judicial review may be brought where appropriate: *Haw v Westminster Magistrates Court* [2008] 3 W.L.R. 465 (Thomas L.J. and Gross J.). **3C–35**

Legal aid

13. [...]   **3C–36**

Note —Repealed by the Legal Aid Act 1988 s.45, Sch.6, and effectively replaced by s.29 of that Act.   **3C–37**

PENALTIES FOR CONTEMPT AND KINDRED OFFENCES

Proceedings in England and Wales

14.—(1) In any case where a court has power to commit a person to prison for contempt of court and (apart from this provision) no limitation applies to the period of committal, the committal shall (without prejudice to the power of the court to order his earlier discharge) be for a fixed term, and that term shall not on any occasion exceed two years in the case of committal by a superior court, or one month in the case of committal by an inferior court.   **3C–38**

(2) In any case where an inferior court has power to fine a person for contempt of court and (apart from this provision) no limit applies to the amount of the fine, the fine shall not on any occasion exceed £2,500.

(2A) In the exercise of jurisdiction to commit for contempt of court or any kindred offence the court shall not deal with the offender by making an order under section 60 of the Powers of Criminal Courts (Sentencing) Act 2000 (an attendance centre order) if it appears to the court, after considering any available evidence, that he is under 17 years of age.

(3) [...]

(4) Each of the superior courts shall have the like power to make a hospital order or guardianship order under section 37 of the Mental Health Act 1983 or an interim hospital order under section 38 of that Act in the case of a person suffering from mental disorder within the meaning of that Act who could otherwise be committed to prison for contempt of court as the Crown Court has under that section in the case of a person convicted of an offence.

Paragraph numbers marked with a "+" can be found online and on CD.

(4A) Each of the superior courts shall have the like power to make an order under section 35 of the said Act of 1983 (remand for report on accused's mental condition) where there is reason to suspect that a person who could be committed to prison for contempt of court is suffering from mental disorder within the meaning of that Act as the Crown Court has under that section in the case of an accused person within the meaning of that section.

(4A) For the purposes of the preceding provisions of this section a county court shall be treated as a superior court and not as an inferior court.

(5) The enactments specified in Part II of Schedule 2 shall have effect subject to the amendments set out in that Part, being amendments relating to the penalties and procedure in respect of certain offences of contempt in coroners' courts, county courts and magistrates' courts.

3C–39 *Note* —Amended by the Mental Health (Amendment) Act 1982 s.65(1), Sch.3; the Mental Health Act 1983 s.148, Sch.4; the County Courts (Penalties for Contempt) Act 1983 s.1; the Criminal Justice Act 1991 s.17(3), Sch.4; and the Criminal Justice Act 1993 s.65(3) (4), Sch.3. There are two subss.(2A) and (4A). The first subs.(2A) was inserted by the Criminal Justice Act 1982 s.77, Sch.14, para.60, Sch.16 and is amended by the Powers of Criminal Courts (Sentencing) Act 2000, Sch.9, para.84. Subsection (4) and the first subs.(4A) are amended by the Mental Health Act 2007 s.1(4), Sch.1, Pt.2, para.19 with effect from November 3, 2008 (SI 2008/1900).

"In any case where a court has power to commit a person to prison for contempt of court

3C–40 Section 14 applies to civil contempts (*Linnett v Coles* [1987] Q.B. 555; [1986] 3 All E.R. 652, CA). For guidance on sentencing where the contempt is constituted by a witness's refusal to give evidence see *R. v Montgomery (James)* [1995] 2 All E.R. 28. For general guidance on sentencing see *Hale v Tanner* [2000] 1 W.L.R. 2377. However this guidance was modified by *Lomas v Parle* [2002] EWCA Civ 1804 which pointed out that, if there are parallel criminal proceedings arising out of the same incident it is not for the first court to sentence to anticipate or allow for a likely further sentence. Rather it is for the second court to reflect the prior sentence to ensure that the defendant is not punished twice for the same act.

Mitigation

3C–41 Where an alleged contemnor is liable to imprisonment the court must afford him, whether or not he is legally represented, proper opportunity to mitigate, especially where the court has indicated that it was reluctant to consider any sentence other than one of immediate imprisonment (*Taylor v Persico*, *The Times*, February 12, 1992, CA).

A judge exercising the jurisdiction to punish for contempt will be well advised to invite, although he cannot require, the alleged contemnor to be legally represented. In this way he will obtain the assistance of counsel or solicitors in considering his powers and the circumstances of the case (*R. v Tyne Tees Television Ltd*, *The Times*, October 20, 1997, per Beldam L.J., Ognall and Buckley L.JJ.).

See further Practice Direction—Committal Applications at scpd52.1. This PD is distilled from a series of Court of Appeal decisions and should be treated as authoritive.

"A fixed term"

3C–42 The term, once imposed, may not be varied so as to increase its duration (*Westcott v Westcott* (1985) Fam.Law. 278, CA). An order committing a person to prison for contempt for an indefinite period, even if suspended for a fixed number of days, is not a committal for a fixed term and is ultra vires (*C (A Minor), Re*, *The Times*, July 22, 1985, CA).

Where, however, there has been no unfairness or material irregularity in the com-

Paragraph numbers marked with a "+" can be found online and on CD.

mittal proceedings, and where there has been nothing more than an irregularity in the drawing up of the committal order, the irregularity can be corrected on appeal by virtue of A.J.A. 1960, s.13(3), and the term varied so as to make the order lawful (*Linnett v Coles* [1987] Q.B. 555; [1986] 3 All E.R. 652, CA).

A Court dealing with a person for criminal contempt, whether at first instance or on appeal, has no power to make a probation order (*R. v Palmer* [1992] 1 W.L.R. 568).

S.14(1) does not enable the court on any one occasion to impose consecutive sentences which cumulatively exceed the two year maximum. Thus where a judge purported to give a contemnor credit for admitting breaches of an undertaking, but thereafter imposed consecutive sentences to a total of two years he could not be said to have made the reduction in sentence which he had promised (*Re R. (a Minor) (Contempt Sentence)* [1994] 1 W.L.R. 487; [1994] 2 All E.R. 144). The court cannot, moreover, on the same occasion both activate a suspended sentence and impose a new consecutive sentence which together exceed the two year maximum (*Villiers v Villiers* [1994] 2 All E.R. 149).

Where the contempt consists of a refusal to give evidence in a criminal trial the Court of Appeal, Criminal Division, has set out the principles to which a court should have regard in determining the appropriate sentence (*R. v Montgomery, The Times*, July 19, 1994).

A judge sitting in the county court who has found a party guilty of contempt, in breaching an order or undertaking, has no power to detain the contemnor in custody pending consideration of the sentence to be imposed (*Delaney v Delaney*, [1996] Q.B. 387). A High Court judge has only a very limited power (see *Wilkinson v S & anor* [2003] 1 W.L.R. 1254).

In considering what order to make against a local authority for its contempt in breaching its undertaking to perform its repairing obligations under a lease a judge was entitled to take judicial notice of numerous instances of past contempt in other claims against that authority by its tenants (*Hackney LBC v Mullen, Independent*, November 18, 1996).

Superior Court

For the meaning of superior court see s.19 below. The County Courts (Penalties for Contempt) Act 1983, which came into force on May 13, 1983, provides for county courts to be treated as superior courts for the purposes of this section (see subs.(4A) inserted by that Act), thus reversing the effect of the House of Lords' decision in *Peart v Stewart* [1983] 2 A.C. 109; [1983] 1 All E.R. 859.   **3C–43**

Inferior court

A coroner's court is an inferior court of record which has power to punish a person   **3C–44** for contempt of court committed in the face of the court, since it was necessary for the coroner to keep order in the proceedings which he has the duty of conducting (*R. v West Yorkshire Coroner Ex p. Smith* [1985] Q.B. 1096; [1985] 1 All E.R. 100). An industrial tribunal is also an inferior court and the Queen's Bench Divisional Court therefore has power to punish for contempt of that tribunal (*Peach Grey & Co (a firm) v Sommers* [1995] 2 All E.R. 513).

Suspension of order

A county court now has like power as the High Court to suspend a committal order   **3C–45** for contempt of court upon stated conditions, and to impose consecutive sentences for separate contempts (*Lee v Walker* [1985] Q.B. 1191; [1985] 1 All E.R. 781, CA).

* * * *

Enforcement of fines imposed by certain superior courts

16.—(1) Payment of a fine for contempt of court imposed by a   **3C–46** superior court, other than the Crown Court or one of the courts specified in subsection (4) below, may be enforced upon the order of the court—

> (a) in like manner as a judgment of the High Court for the payment of money; or

Paragraph numbers marked with a "+" can be found online and on CD.

(b) in like manner as a fine imposed by the Crown Court.

(2) Where payment of a fine imposed by any court falls to be enforced as mentioned in paragraph (a) of subsection (1)—

    (a) the court shall, if the fine is not paid in full forthwith or within such time as the court may allow, certify to Her Majesty's Remembrancer the sum payable;

    (b) Her Majesty's Remembrancer shall thereupon proceed to enforce payment of that sum as if it were due to him as a judgment debt;

    (c) [...].

(3) Where payment of a fine imposed by any court falls to be enforced as mentioned in paragraph (b) of subsection (1), the provisions of sections 139 and 140 of the Powers of Criminal Courts (Sentencing) Act 2000 shall apply as they apply to a fine imposed by the Crown Court.

(4) Subsection (1) of this section does not apply to fines imposed by the criminal division of the Court of Appeal or by the House of Lords [*Supreme Court*] on appeal from that division.

(5) The Fines Act 1833 shall not apply to a fine to which subsection (1) of this section applies.

(6) [...].

3C–47   *Note* —Amended by the Supreme Court Act 1981, s.152(4), Sch.7; the Industrial Tribunals Act 1996, s.45, Sch.3 and by the Powers of Criminal Courts (Sentencing) Act 2000, Sch.9, para.85; words underlined prospectively repealed and words in square brackets and italics prospectively substituted by the Constitutional Reform Act 2005, s.40, Sch.9, para.35(2), with effect from a date to be appointed.

Superior Court

3C–48   See s.19, para.3C–50 and note under s.14, para.3C–38.

Disobedience to certain orders of magistrates' courts

3C–49   **17.**—(1) The powers of a magistrates' court under subsection (3) of section 63 of the Magistrates' Court Act 1980 (punishment by fine or committal for disobeying an order to do anything other than the payment of money or to abstain from doing anything) may be exercised either of the court's own motion or by order on complaint.

(2) In relation to the exercise of those powers the provisions of the Magistrates'Court Act 1980 shall apply subject to the modifications set out in Schedule 3 to this Act.

* * * *

SUPPLEMENTAL

Interpretation

3C–50   **19.** In this Act—

    "court" includes any tribunal or body exercising the judicial power of the State, and "legal proceedings" shall be construed accordingly;

    "publication" has the meaning assigned by subsection (1) of sec-

Paragraph numbers marked with a "+" can be found online and on CD.

tion 2, and "publish" (except in section 9) shall be construed accordingly;

"Scottish proceedings" means proceedings before any court, including the Courts-Martial Appeal Court, the Restrictive Practices Court and Employment Appeal Tribunal, sitting in Scotland, and includes proceedings before the House of Lords [*Supreme Court*] in the exercise of any appellate jurisdiction over proceedings in such a court;

"the strict liability rule" has the meaning assigned by section 1;

"superior court" means [*Supreme Court*] the Court of Appeal, the High Court, the Crown Court, the Courts-Martial Appeal Court, the Restrictive Practices Court, the Employment Appeal Tribunal and any other court exercising in relation to its proceedings powers equivalent to those of the High Court, and includes the House of Lords in the exercise of its appellate jurisdiction.

Note —Amended by the Cable and Broadcasting Act 1984, Sch.5, para.39; and the **3C–51** Broadcasting Act 1990, Scheds 20 and 21; words underlined prospectively repealed and words in square brackets and italics prospectively substituted or inserted by the Constitutional Reform Act 2005, ss.40, 146, Sch.9, para.35(3), Sch.18, Pt II, with effect from a date to be appointed.

Court

A mental health review tribunal is a court for inter alia the purposes of s.19 (*Picker-* **3C–52** *ing v Liverpool Daily Post & Echo Newspapers plc* [1990] 2 W.L.R. 494; [1990] 1 All E.R. 335, CA; affd. on this ground (although reversed on others) [1991] 1 All E.R. 622, HL). The decision to the contrary in *Attorney General v Associated Newspapers Group plc* [1989] 1 W.L.R. 322; [1989] 1 All E.R. 604, is wrong (*ibid.*). See also generally the note at para.13A–45.

Superior Court

See n. "Superior court", para.3C–48. **3C–53**

Tribunals of Inquiry

20.—(1) In relation to any tribunal to which the Tribunals of In- **3C–54** quiry (Evidence) Act 1921 applies, and the proceedings of such a tribunal, the provisions of this Act (except subsection (3) of section 9) apply as they apply in relation to courts and legal proceedings; and references to the course of justice or the administration of justice in legal proceedings shall be construed accordingly.

(2) The proceedings of a tribunal established under the said Act shall be treated as active within the meaning of section 2 from the time when the tribunal is appointed until its report is presented to Parliament.

Short title, commencement and extent

21.—(1) This Act may be cited as the Contempt of Court Act 1981. **3C–55**

(2) The provisions of this Act relating to legal aid in England and Wales shall come into force on such day as the Lord Chancellor may appoint by order made by statutory instrument; and the provisions of this Act relating to legal aid in Scotland and Northern Ireland shall come into force on such day or days as the Secretary of State may so appoint.

Paragraph numbers marked with a "+" can be found online and on CD.

Different days may be appointed under this subsection in relation to different courts.

(3) Subject to subsection (2), this Act shall come into force at the expiration of the period of one month beginning with the day on which it is passed.

(4) Sections 7, 8(3), 12, 13(1) to (3), 14, 16, 17 and 18, Parts I and III of Schedule 2 and Schedules 3 and 4 of this Act do not extend to Scotland.

(5) This Act, except sections 15 and 17 and Schedules 2 and 3, extends to Northern Ireland.

SCHEDULE 1

TIMES WHEN PROCEEDINGS ARE ACTIVE FOR PURPOSES OF SECTION 2

Preliminary

3C–56 1. In this Schedule "criminal proceedings" means proceedings against a person in respect of an offence, not being appellate proceedings or proceedings commenced by motion for committal or attachment in England and Wales or Northern Ireland; and "appellate proceedings" means proceedings on appeal from or for the review of the decision of a court in any proceedings.

2. Criminal, appellate and other proceedings are active within the meaning of section 2 at the times respectively prescribed by the following paragraphs of this Schedule; and in relation to proceedings in which more than one of the steps described in any of those paragraphs is taken, the reference in that paragraph is a reference to the first of those steps.

Criminal proceedings

3C–57 3. Subject to the following provisions of this Schedule, criminal proceedings are active from the relevant initial step specified in paragraph 4 or 4A until concluded as described in paragraph 5.

4. The initial steps of criminal proceedings are—

(a) arrest without warrant;

(b) the issue, or in Scotland the grant, of a warrant for arrest;

(c) the issue of a summons to appear, or in Scotland the grant of a warrant to cite;

(d) the service of an indictment or other document specifying the charge;

(e) except in Scotland, oral charge.

4A. Where as a result of an order under section 54 of the Criminal Procedure and Investigations Act 1996 (acquittal tainted by an administration of justice offence) proceedings are brought against a person for an offence of which he has previously been acquitted, the initial step of the proceedings is a certification under subsection (2) of that section; and paragraph 4 has effect subject to this.

5. Criminal proceedings are concluded—

(a) by acquittal or, as the case may be, by sentence;

(b) by any other verdict, finding, order or decision which puts an end to the proceedings;

(c) by discontinuance or by operation of law.

6. The reference in paragraph 5(a) to sentence includes any order or decision consequent on conviction or finding of guilt which disposes of the case, either absolutely or subject to future events, and a deferment of sentence under section 1 of the Powers of Criminal Courts (Sentencing) Act 2000, s.219 or 432 of the Criminal Procedure (Scotland) Act 1975 or Article 14 of the Treatment of Offenders (Northern Ireland) Order 1976.

7. Proceedings are discontinued within the meaning of paragraph 5(c)—

(a) in England and Wales or Northern Ireland, if the charge or summons is withdrawn or a *nolle prosequi* entered;

Paragraph numbers marked with a "+" can be found online and on CD.

(aa) in England and Wales, if they are discontinued by virtue of section 23 of the Prosecution of Offences Act 1985;

(b) in Scotland, if the proceedings are expressly abandoned by the prosecutor or are deserted *simpliciter*;

(c) in the case of proceedings in England and Wales or Northern Ireland commenced by arrest without warrant, if the person arrested is released, otherwise than on bail, without having been charged.

8. Criminal proceedings before a court-martial or standing civilian court are not concluded until the completion of any review of finding or sentence.

9. Criminal proceedings in England and Wales or Northern Ireland cease to be active if an order is made for the charge to lie on the file, but become active again if leave is later given for the proceedings to continue.

9A. Where proceedings in England and Wales have been discontinued by virtue of section 23 of the Prosecution of Offences Act 1985, but notice is given by the accused under subsection (7) of that section to the effect that he wants the proceedings to continue, they become active again with the giving of that notice.

10. Without prejudice to paragraph 5(b) above, criminal proceedings against a person cease to be active—

(a) if the accused is found to be under a disability such as to render him unfit to be tried or unfit to plead or, in Scotland, is found to be insane in bar of trial; or

(b) if a hospital order is made in his case under section 51(5) of the Mental Health Act 1983 or Article 57(5) of the Mental Health (Northern Ireland) Order 1986 or, in Scotland, where an assessment order or a treatment order ceases to have effect by virtue of sections 52H or 52R respectively of the Criminal Procedure (Scotland) Act 1995

but become active again if they are later resumed.

11. Criminal proceedings against a person which become active on the issue or the grant of a warrant for his arrest cease to be active at the end of the period of twelve months beginning with the date of the warrant unless he has been arrested within that period, but become active again if he is subsequently arrested.

Other proceedings at first instance

12. Proceedings other than criminal proceedings and appellate proceedings are active from the time when arrangements for the hearing are made or, if no such arrangements are previously made, from the time the hearing begins, until the proceedings are disposed of or discontinued or withdrawn; and for the purposes of this paragraph any motion or application made in or for the purposes of any proceedings, and any pre-trial review in the county court, is to be treated as a distinct proceeding.

3C–58

13. In England and Wales or Northern Ireland arrangements for the hearing of proceedings to which paragraph 12 applies are made within the meaning of that paragraph—

(a) in the case of proceedings in the High Court for which provision is made by rules of court for setting down for trial, when the case is set down;

(b) in the case of any proceedings, when a date for the trial or hearing is fixed.

14. [*Proceedings in Scotland.*]

Appellate proceedings

15. Appellate proceedings are active from the time when they are commenced—

3C–59

(a) by application for leave to appeal or apply for review, or by notice of such an application;

(b) by notice of appeal or of application for review;

(c) by other originating process,

until disposed of or abandoned, discontinued or withdrawn.

16. Where, in appellate proceedings relating to criminal proceedings, the court—

(a) remits the case to the court below; or

(b) orders a new trial or a *venire de novo*, or in Scotland grants authority to bring a new prosecution,

Paragraph numbers marked with a "+" can be found online and on CD.

any further or new proceedings which result shall be treated as active from the conclusion of the appellate proceedings.

3C–60   *Note* —Amended by the Mental Health Act 1983, Sch.4, paras 57(c) and 59(c); the Prosecution of Offences Act 1985, s.31, Sch.1, paras 4 and 5; the Mental Health (Scotland) Act 1984, s.17, s.127(1), Sch.3, para.48; the Criminal Procedure and Investigations Act 1996, s.57 and by the Powers of Criminal Courts (Sentencing) Act 2000, Sch.9, para.86; and by SI 2005/465.

CROSS REFERENCE TO COUNTY COURTS ACT 1984

Power to commit for contempt

3C–61   For the power of a County Court to commit for contempt see s.118 of the County Courts Act 1984 (para.9A–654).

Paragraph numbers marked with a "+" can be found online and on CD.

3D PROCEEDINGS UNDER THE HUMAN RIGHTS ACT 1998

Human Rights Act 1998

(1998 c.42)

3D-1

INTRODUCTION

The Convention rights

1.—(1) In this Act, "the convention rights" means the rights and **3D-2** fundamental freedoms set out in—

Paragraph numbers marked with a "+" can be found online and on CD.

(a) Articles 2 to 12 and 14 of the Convention,

(b) Articles 1 to 3 of the First Protocol, and

(c) Article 1 of the Thirteenth Protocol.

as read with Articles 16 to 18 of the Convention.

(2) Those Articles are to have effect for the purposes of this Act subject to any designated derogation or reservation (as to which see sections 14 and 15).

(3) The Articles are set out in Schedule 1.

(4) The Secretary of State may by order make such amendments to this Act as he considers appropriate to reflect the effect, in relation to the United Kingdom, of a protocol.

(5) In subsection (4) "protocol" means a protocol to the Convention—

(a) which the United Kingdom has ratified; or

(b) which the United Kingdom has signed with a view to ratification.

(6) No amendment may be made by an order under subsection (4) so as to come into force before the protocol concerned is in force in relation to the United Kingdom.

Section 1(1)

3D–3   "The Convention" here means "the Convention ...as it has effect for the time being in relation to the United Kingdom", as defined in s.21(1). Thus if the effect of a provision of the Convention is limited or extinguished by some other, overriding provision of international law, such as a UN Security Council Resolution, that limitation affects the interpretation of the convention rights in the United Kingdom: *R (on the application of Al Jedda) v Secretary of State for Defence* [2007] UKHL 58; [2008] 1 A.C. 332; [2008] 2 W.L.R. 31. Also *R. (Quark Fishing Ltd) v Foreign Secretary* [2005] UKHL 57; [2005] 3 W.L.R. 837; [2005] 3 W.L.R. 837 at paras 25, 32, 56, 87 and 97 and *Al-Skeini v Secretary of State for Defence* [2007] UKHL 26; [2008] 1 A.C. 153; [2007] 3 W.L.R. 33; [2007] 3 All E.R. 685.

Section 1(1)(c)

3D–4   Substituted by the Human Rights Act 1998 (Amendment) Order 2004 (SI 2004/1574), art.2(1) to reflect the coming into force of Protocol 13 of the ECHR, concerning abolition of the death penalty.

Section 1(2)

3D–5   The United Kingdom entered a derogation to art.5 of the ECHR in order to enact Pt IV of the Anti-Terrorism Crime and Security Act 2001. This was contained in the Human Rights Act 1998 (Designated Derogation) Order 2001 (SI 2001/3644). However, that Order was quashed by the House of Lords in *A v Secretary of State for the Home Department* [2005] UKHL 71, [2006] 2 A.C. 221; [2005] 3 W.L.R. 1249; [2006] 1 All E.R. 575; [2006] H.R.L.R. 6; [2006] U.K.H.R.R. 225. Part IV of the Anti-Terrorism Crime and Security Act 2001 was repealed by the Prevention of Terrorism Act 2005, with effect from March 14, 2005, and the Human Rights Act 1998 (Amendment) Order 2005 (SI 2005/1071) of April 8, 2005, reflected the withdrawal of the derogation from art.5 in response to this.

Section 1(4)

3D–6   For procedure for making of an order under this section, see s.20(4).

Interpretation of Convention rights

3D–7   **2.**—(1) A court or tribunal determining a question which has arisen under this Act in connection with a Convention right must take into account any—

Paragraph numbers marked with a "+" can be found online and on CD.

(a) judgment, decision, declaration or advisory opinion of the European Court of Human Rights,

(b) opinion of the Commission given in a report adopted under Article 31 of the Convention,

(c) decision of the Commission in connection with Article 26 or 27(2) of the Convention, or

(d) decision of the Committee of Ministers taken under Article 46 of the Convention,

whenever made or given, so far as, in the opinion of the court or tribunal, it is relevant to the proceedings in which that question has arisen.

(2) Evidence of any judgment, decision, declaration or opinion of which account may have to be taken under this section is to be given in proceedings before any court or tribunal in such manner as may be provided by rules.

(3) In this section "rules" means rules of court or, in the case of proceedings before a tribunal, rules made for the purposes of this section—

(a) by the Lord Chancellor or the Secretary of State, in relation to any proceedings outside Scotland;

(b) by the Secretary of State, in relation to proceedings in Scotland; or

(c) by a Northern Ireland department, in relation to proceedings before a tribunal in Northern Ireland—

(i) which deals with transferred matters; and

(ii) for which no rules made under paragraph (a) are in force.

Note —Amended by SI 2003/1887 and SI 2005/3429.   **3D–8**

Section 2(1)

This requires any court or tribunal determining a question which has arisen under **3D–9** any Act in connection with a Convention right to "take into account" the decisions of the Strasbourg organs, whenever made or given so far as, in the opinion of the court or tribunal, it is relevant to the proceedings in which that question has arisen. The courts will not without good reason depart from the principles laid down in a carefully considered judgment of the ECHR sitting as a Grand Chamber: *R. (Anderson) v Secretary of State for the Home Department* [2002] UKHL 46; [2003] 1 A.C. 837; [2002] 3 W.L.R. 1800; [2002] 4 All E.R. 1089 per Lord Bingham at para.18. In the absence of some special circumstance, a court should follow any clear and consistent jurisprudence of the ECHR: *R. (on the application of Holding and Barnes plc) v Secretary of State for the Environment* [2001] UKHL 23, [2003] 2 A.C. 295, [2001] 2 W.L.R. 1389 HL, per Lord Slynn. This principle was interpreted in a limited way by the majority of the Court of Appeal in *Copsey v WWB Devon Clays Ltd* [2005] EWCA Civ 932; [2005] I.C.R. 1789; [2005] I.R.L.R. 811; 2005 H.R.L.R. 32. It may, however, be appropriate for a court to decline to follow the reasoning of the ECHR if it is unpersuasive: see *R. v Spear* [2002] UKHL 31, [2003] 1 A.C. 734 HL paras 12–13 and 65–66 and *R. v Lyons* [2002] UKHL 44, [2003] 1 A.C. 976, para.46.

The purpose of s.2 is to ensure that the same Convention rights are enforced under the HRA by courts within the United Kingdom as would be enforced by the ECHR in Strasbourg. It is not intended to provide Convention rights with a domestically autonomous meaning: *N v Secretary of State for the Home Department* [2005] UKHL 31; [2005] 2 A.C. 296; [2005] 2 W.L.R. 1124; [2005] 4 All E.R. 1017 per Lord Hope, para.25 and *R (on the application of Al Jedda) v Secretary of State for Defence* [2007] UKHL 58; [2008] 1

Paragraph numbers marked with a "+" can be found online and on CD.

A.C. 332; [2008] 2 W.L.R. 31. See too *R. (Quark Fishing Ltd) v Foreign Secretary* [2005] UKHL 57; [2005] 3 W.L.R. 837, *Aston Cantlow PCC v Wallbank* [2003] UKHL 37; [2004] 1 A.C. 546 at para 6 and *R. (Greenfield) v Home Secretary* [2005] UKHL 14; [2005] 1 W.L.R. 673; [2005] 2 All E.R. 240; [2005] H.R.L.R. 13; [2005] U.K.H.R.R. 323 at para.19. A national court should not, without strong reason, dilute or weaken the effect of Strasbourg case-law. Nor should the provision of more generous rights be the product of interpretation of the Convention by the national courts, since the meaning of the Convention should be uniform throughout the states party to it: *R. v Special Adjudicator Ex p. Ullah*, sub nom. *Doh v Secretary of State for the Home Department* [2004] UKHL 26, [2004] 2 A.C. 323; [2004] 3 W.L.R. 23 per Lord Bingham. See too *R. (SB) v Denbigh High School* [2006] UKHL 15; [2007] 1 A.C. 100; [2006] 2 W.L.R. 719 at para.29.

However (per Moses J at first instance in *Al-Jedda* [2005] EWHC 1809 (Admin); [2005] H.R.L.R. 39 at para.41), the "less than imperative terms" of the drafting were necessary to allow a distinction to be drawn between the ECHR approach and that of a domestic court, in that, for example, domestic courts may have a narrower area of discretion. Note s.11 of the Act: reliance on Convention rights does not restrict other wider rights available otherwise.

The principle of *stare decisis* compels domestic courts to follow the earlier decisions of higher courts, even if they conflict with later Strasbourg authority. See *Kay v Lambeth LBC* [2006] UKHL 10; [2006] 2 A.C. 465; [2006] 2 W.L.R. 570; [2006] U.K.R.R. 640. See too *R. (Animal Defenders International) v Secretary of State for Culture, Media & Sport* [2008] UKHL 15; [2008] 2 W.L.R. 781, and *R. (RJM) v Secretary of State for Work & Pensions* [2008] UKHL 63 at 59–67; *A v Hoare* [2006] EWCA Civ 395, *R (on the application of Gilboy) v Liverpool City Council* [2007] EWHC 2335; [2007] B.L.G.R. 837 and *Doherty v Birmingham CC* [2008] UKHL 57.

Section 2(1)(b)

3D–10   This refers to opinions given under art.31 of the Convention as it existed before amendment by the 11th Protocol. Article 31 dealt with the duty of the European Commission of Human Rights to report in the event that it did not secure a friendly settlement of an application which it had declared admissible. art.31(1) provided:

"If a solution is not reached, the Commission shall draw up a Report on the facts and state its opinion as to whether the facts found disclose a breach by the State concerned of its obligations under the Convention. The opinions of all the members of the Commission on this point may be stated in the Report."

Section 2(1)(c)

3D–11   This refers to art.26 of the Convention before it was amended by the 11th Protocol, which provided:

"The Commission may only deal with the matter [i.e. non-state applications] after all domestic remedies have been exhausted, according to the generally recognised rules of international law, and within a period of six months from the date on which the final decision was taken."

Article 27(2) of the unamended Convention provided:

"3. The Commission shall declare inadmissible any individual application submitted under art.25 which it considers incompatible with the provisions of the present Convention, manifestly ill-founded, or an abuse of the right of petition".

See now art.35 of the Convention as amended.

Section 2(1)(d)

3D–12   "Article 46—Binding force and execution of judgments

1. The High Contracting Parties undertake to abide by the final judgment of the Court in any case to which they are parties.

2. The final judgment of the Court shall be transmitted to the Committee of Ministers, which shall supervise its execution."

The reference to art.46 includes a reference to Arts 32 and 54 of the Convention before it was amended by the 11th Protocol: see s.21(3). Article 32(1) provided that if, after the Commission had adopted a Report under art.31, the case was not referred to the ECHR, "the Committee of Ministers [of the Council of Europe] shall decide by a

Paragraph numbers marked with a "+" can be found online and on CD.

majority of two-thirds of the members entitled to sit on the Committee whether there has been a violation of the Convention". Article 54 was virtually identical to the new art.46.

Section 2(2)

As to citation of Strasbourg authorities, see para.8 of the Practice Direction— **3D–13**
Miscellaneous Provisions Relating to Hearings: 39 PD.8. Excessive citation of authority is to be avoided. Decisions of the ECHR tend to repeat the same principles in successive cases in order to apply them to different situations. Citation of a single case may therefore be all that is required: *A v B Plc* [2002] EWCA Civ 337; [2003] Q.B. 195; [2002] 3 W.L.R. 542 paras 8–9.

Section 2(3)

The power to make rules under this subsection for England and Wales is exercis- **3D–14**
able by statutory instrument: see s.20(2). It can be annulled by resolution of either House of Parliament: see ss.20(5) and 20(7).

For citation of authorities concerning human rights see CPR Practice Direction supplementing r.39, para.8.1.

LEGISLATION

Interpretation of legislation

3.—(1) So far as it is possible to do so, primary legislation and sub- **3D–15** ordinate legislation must be read and given effect in a way which is compatible with the Convention rights.

(2) This section—
  (a) applies to primary legislation and subordinate legislation whenever enacted;
  (b) does not affect the validity, continuing operation or enforcement of any incompatible primary legislation; and
  (c) does not affect the validity, continuing operation or enforcement of any incompatible subordinate legislation if (disregarding any possibility of revocation) primary legislation prevents removal of the incompatibility.

Like the court's general free-standing jurisdiction to declare the meaning of legisla- **3D–16** tion, the interpretative obligation in s.3(1) is a general one. A claimant seeking a declaration as to the meaning of legislation under s.3(1) need not be a victim: it is sufficient that he or she has an interest and standing: see *R. (on the application of Rusbridger) v AG* [2003] UKHL 38; [2004] A.C. 357; [2003] 3 W.L.R. 232 para.21, per Lord Steyn. However, see para.3D–19 concerning declarations of incompatibility.

Section 3(1) introduced a new canon of construction, a "strong adjuration" to interpret legislation compatibly with the Convention, which may involve adopting a meaning other than the natural and ordinary meaning of the statutory words: see *R. v DPP Ex p. Kebilene* [2000] 2 A.C. 326; [1999] 3 W.L.R. 972; [1999] 4 All E.R. 801, per Lord Cooke of Thorndon. For a review of s.3 case-law, see the speech of Lord Steyn in *Ghaidan v Godin-Mendoza* [2004] UKHL 30; [2004] 2 A.C. 557; [2004] 3 W.L.R. 113. See also *R. v Holding* [2006] EWCA Crim 3185; [2006] 1 W.L.R. 1040; *Culnane v Morris* [2005] EWHC 2438; [2006] 2 All ER 149 (Admin) and *Secretary of State for the Home Department v MB* [2006] EWCA Civ 1140; [2008] 1 A.C. 440; [2006] 3 W.L.R. 831; [2006] H.R.L.R. 37, in which a declaration of incompatibility made by the High Court was reversed by the Court of Appeal, applying HRA s.3 so as to achieve an HRA-compatible construction of the Prevention of Terrorism Act 2005. See too the decision of the House of Lords: [2007] UKHL 46; [2008] 1 A.C. 440; [2007] 3 W.L.R. 681.

The particular statutory provision which is said to contravene Convention rights

Paragraph numbers marked with a "+" can be found online and on CD.

must be identified with precision by the claimant: see *R. v A (Complainant's Sexual History)* [2001] UKHL 25; [2001] 1 A.C. 45; [2001] 2 W.L.R. 1546, HL, per Lord Hope at 1582, 153 para.110; *R. v Lambert* [2001] 3 W.L.R. 206 at 234 para.8; *Re S (Care Order: Implementation of Care Plan)* [2002] UKHL 10; [2002] 2 A.C. 291; [2002] 2 W.L.R 720; [2002] 2 All E.R. 192 per Lord Nicholls at para.41.

The court must first ask whether, on ordinary construction, the statutory provision is compatible with Convention rights. If not, it must consider whether it is possible to read the provision in a manner which is compatible: *Brown v Stott* [2003] 1 A.C. 681; [2001] 2 All E.R. 97. These steps require the Court to identify the scope of the Convention right in question: *Brown*, per Lord Roger. As to what is "possible" see the case law on European Community law, e.g. *Marleasing SA v La Comercial Internacional de Alimentacion SA (C106/89)* [1990] E.C.R. I-4135 and *Litster v Forth Dry Dock & Engineering Company Limited* [1990] 1 A.C. 546. Techniques involved may be reading down of express language in a statute, or reading in. Section 3 may require a court to depart from the unambiguous meaning which the legislation would bear other than by reference to the purpose of compatibility with the Convention: see *Ghaidan v Godin-Mendoza* [2004] UKHL 30; [2004] 2 A.C. 557; [2004] 3 W.L.R. 113, per Lord Nicholls at para.30. This may involve departure from the intention of the Parliament which enacted the legislation. See also *R. v Holding* [2006] EWCA Crim 3185; [2006] 1 W.L.R. 1040, *Culnane v Morris* [2005] EWHC 2438; [2006] 2 All E.R. 149 and *R. (MB) v Secretary of State for the Home Department* [2006] EWHC (Admin), and [2006] EWCA Civ 1157, in which a declaration of incompatibility made by the High Court was reversed by the Court of Appeal, applying HRA s.3 so as to achieve an HRA-compatible construction of the Terrorism Act 2005. See too the decision of the House of Lords: [2007] UKHL 46; [2007] 3 WLR 681. Parliament's intention is normally to be deduced from the statutory language. It is seldom necessary to have regard to matters stated in Parliament by resort to Hansard: *Wilson v First County Trust Ltd (No.2)* [2003] UKHL 40; [2004] 1 A.C. 816; [2003] 3 W.L.R. 568; [2003] 4 All E.R. 97.

A compatible interpretation must be sought unless it is plainly impossible: the search is for a "possible" meaning, not one which is "reasonably possible": *R. v A (No 2)* [2001] UKHL 25; [2002] 1 A.C. 45; [2001] 2 W.L.R. 1546 HL; cf *R. (on the application of H) v Mental Health Review Tribunal for North and East London Region* [2001] EWCA Civ 415; [2002] Q.B. 1; [2001] 3 W.L.R. 512). See too *R (Hammond) v Secretary of State for the Home Department* [2005] UKHL 69; (2006) 1 A.C. 603 and *R. (MB) v Secretary of State for the Home Department* [2007] UKHL 46; [2007] 3 W.L.R. 681.

A s.3 interpretation is only invoked where it is necessary for it to be applied in order to arrive at a Convention compatible interpretation. Otherwise the court must afford the legislation its ordinary meaning. See *R. (Hurst) v Commissioner of Police for the Metropolis* [2007] UKHL 13; [2007] 2 A.C. 189; [2007] 2 W.L.R. 726; [2007] 2 All E.R. 1025.

The exercise is, however, one of interpretation not legislation. A Convention-compatible interpretation cannot be given to legislation if it is contrary to express statutory words or the necessary implication of the statute: *Poplar Housing & Regeneration Community Association Ltd v Donoghue* [2001] EWCA Civ 595; [2002] Q.B. 48; [2001] 3 W.L.R. 183, CA; *R (Anderson) v Secretary of State for the Home Department* [2002] UKHL 46; [2003] 1 A.C. 837; [2002] 3 W.L.R. 1800; [2002] 4 All E.R. 1089. There are two circumstances in which it would not be possible to use s.3 to achieve compatibility. First, a meaning which departs substantially from a fundamental feature of an Act of Parliament is likely to have crossed the boundary between interpretation and amendment: *Re S (Care Order: Implementation of Care Plan)* [2002] 2 A.C. 291; [2002] 2 W.L.R. 720; [2002] 2 All E.R. 192; [2002] 1 F.L.R. 815 per Lord Nicholls at para.40. Secondly, compatible interpretation would be impossible where the legislation in issue had wide ramifications, raising policy issues ill-suited for determination by the courts or court procedures, or would require the construction of a wide-ranging new extra-statutory scheme: *Re S (supra); Bellinger v Bellinger* [2003] UKHL 21; [2003] 2 A.C. 467; [2003] 2 W.L.R. 1174; [2003] 2 All E.R. 593.

Where a court does rely on s.3 it should limit the extent of the modified meaning to that necessary to achieve compatibility: see *Poplar Housing & Regeneration Community Association Ltd v Donoghue* [2001] EWCA Civ 595; *R. (on the application of Middleton) v HM Coroner for Western Somerset* [2004] UKHL 10; [2004] 2 A.C. 182; [2004] 2 W.L.R. 800; [2004] 2 All E.R. 465 (para 34).

Paragraph numbers marked with a "+" can be found online and on CD.

Declaration of incompatibility

4.—(1) Subsection (2) applies in any proceedings in which a court **3D–17** determines whether a provision of primary legislation is compatible with a Convention right.

(2) If the court is satisfied that the provision is incompatible with a Convention right, it may make a declaration of that incompatibility.

(3) Subsection (4) applies in any proceedings in which a court determines whether a provision of subordinate legislation, made in the exercise of a power conferred by primary legislation, is compatible with a Convention right.

(4) If the court is satisfied—

(a) that the provision is incompatible with a Convention right, and

(b) that (disregarding any possibility of revocation) the primary legislation concerned prevents removal of the incompatibility,

it may make a declaration of that incompatibility.

(5) In this section "court" means—

(a) the House of Lords;

(b) the Judicial Committee of the Privy Council;

(c) the Courts-Martial Appeal Court;

(d) in Scotland, the High Court of Justiciary sitting otherwise than as a trial court or the Court of Session;

(e) in England and Wales or Northern Ireland, the High Court or the Court of Appeal;

(f) the Court of Protection, in any matter being dealt with by the President of the Family Division, the Vice-Chancellor or a puisne judge of the High Court.

(6) A declaration under this section ("a declaration of incompatibility")—

(a) does not affect the validity, continuing operation or enforcement of the provision in respect of which it is given; and

(b) is not binding on the parties to the proceedings in which it is made.

Note —Amended by the Mental Capacity Act 2005 s.67 and Sch.6, para.43.　　**3D–18**

There is no strict requirement that a person who seeks a declaration of incompati- **3D–19** bility is a "victim" within s.7, provided he or she has a sufficient interest and standing: *R. (on the application of Rusbridger) v Att-Gen* [2003] UKHL 38; [2004] 1 A.C. 357; [2003] 3 W.L.R. 232 para.21, per Lord Steyn. Ordinarily, however, the court will only grant a declaration of incompatibility to a person who is a victim of an actual or proposed breach of a Convention right: *Re S (Care Order: Implementation of Care Plan)* [2002] 2 A.C. 291; [2002] 2 W.L.R. 720; [2002] 2 All E.R. 192; [2002] 1 F.L.R. 815 per Lord Nicholls; *Bellinger v Bellinger* [2003] UKHL 21; [2003] 2 A.C. 467; [2003] 2 W.L.R. 1174; [2003] 2 All E.R. 593. In any event, a person cannot apply for a declaration of incompatibility on the basis of a hypothetical argument, nor unless they are adversely affected by the impugned measure: *Joseph Taylor v Lancashire County Council and Secretary of State for the Environment, Food & Rural Affairs* [2005] EWCA Civ 284; [2005] 1 W.L.R. 2668; [2005] H.R.L.R. 17; [2005] U.K.H.R.R. 766, per Woolf, C.J.

Paragraph numbers marked with a "+" can be found online and on CD.

Unlike a claim under s.7, which can be considered by any court, only superior courts of record can make declarations of incompatibility (s.4(5)). When considering whether to make an order transferring proceedings from the County Court to the High Court, the court must have regard to the question of whether the making of a declaration of incompatibility has arisen or may arise: CPR r.30.3(2)(g). It is not, however, necessary to transfer the proceedings to the High Court merely because a breach of a Convention right is alleged, nor where an application for a declaration of incompatibility has been made which stands no chance of success: *V (A Child) (Care Proceedings: Human Rights Claims, Re* [2004] EWCA Civ 54; [2004] 1 W.L.R. 1433; [2004] 1 All E.R. 997; [2004] 1 F.W.L.R. 944.

A statutory lacuna is not the same as an incompatibility: see *S (Children) (Care Order: Implementation of Care Plan), Re* [2002] UKHL 10; [2002] 2 A.C. 291; [2002] 2 W.L.R. 720, per Lord Nicholls. See also s.6(3)(b) and s.6(6): failure to legislate does not amount to a breach of s.6(1).

A declaration of incompatibility is a remedy of last resort: it must be avoided unless it is plainly impossible to do so: *R. v A (No 2)* [2001] UKHL 25; [2002] 1 A.C. 45; [2001] 2 W.L.R. 1546 (see also commentary on s.3, above). Even where it is not possible to interpret a provision compatibly with the ECHR, the Court retains a discretion as to whether to grant a declaration, to be exercised according to the normal principles governing the grant of declarations. As to circumstances in which a declaration might be made, see *Wilson v First County Trust Ltd (No.2)* [2001] EWCA 633; [2002] Q.B. 74; [2001] 3 W.L.R. 42 (CA) (overruled on other grounds in *Wilson v first County Trust Ltd (No.2)* [2003] UKHL 40; [2004] 1 A.C. 816; [2003] 3 W.L.R. 568; [2003] 4 All E.R. 97).

Extrinsic evidence of legislative policy is admissible only in relation to a declaration of incompatibility: see also *Wilson v First County Trust Ltd (No.2)* [2003] UKHL 40; [2004] 1 A.C. 816; [2003] 3 W.L.R. 568; [2003] 4 All E.R. 97 at paras 61–67, per Lord Nicholls; *Evans v Amicus Healthcare Ltd* [2004] EWCA Civ 727, CA; [2005] Fam. 1; [2004] 3 W.L.R. 681; [2004] 3 All E.R. 1025, CA and *R. (on the application of Morris) v Westminster City Council (No.3)* [2005] EWCA Civ 1184; [2006] 1 W.L.R. 505; [2005] H.R.L.R. 43; [2006] U.K.H.R.R. 165, para.39, per Sedley L.J.

The fact that another power may achieve the same result as that which is prohibited by the operation of s.6(2), and which results in a declaration of incompatibility, does not mean that a statement of incompatibility is unnecessary if the impugned measure is incompatible with a Convention right. Other forms of statutory protection are immaterial. See *R. (on the application of Morris) v Westminster City Council (No.3)* [2005] EWCA Civ 1184; [2006] 1 W.L.R. 505; [2005] H.R.L.R. 43; [2006] U.K.H.R.R. 165, paras 53–55 and 82.

As to the procedure for making declarations of incompatibility, see s.5 post, and CPR, r.19.4A inserted by reg.3 of the Civil Procedure (Amendment No 4) Rules 2000 (SI 2000/2092).

3D–20   A request for a declaration of incompatibility should not be made on the basis of a hypothetical argument because a person cannot apply for a declaration under s.4(2) unless they are adversely affected by the legislation in question: *Joseph Taylor (Appellant) v Lancashire County Council (Respondent) & Secretary of State for Environment, Food and Rural Affairs (Intervener)* [2005] EWCA Civ 284; [2005] 1 W.L.R. 2668; [2005] H.R.L.R. 17; [2005] U.K.H.R.R. 766, para.43, per Woolf, C.J.

Right of Crown to intervene

3D–21   **5.**—(1) Where a court is considering whether to make a declaration of incompatibility, the Crown is entitled to notice in accordance with rules of court.

(2) In any case to which subsection (1) applies—

      (a) a Minister of the Crown (or a person nominated by him),

      (b) a member of the Scottish Executive,

      (c) a Northern Ireland Minister,

      (d) a Northern Ireland department,

is entitled, on giving notice in accordance with rules of court, to be joined as a party to the proceedings.

Paragraph numbers marked with a "+" can be found online and on CD.

(3) Notice under subsection (2) may be given at any time during the proceedings.

(4) A person who has been made a party to criminal proceedings (other than in Scotland) as the result of a notice under subsection (2) may, with leave, appeal to the House of Lords against any declaration of incompatibility made in the proceedings.

(5) In subsection (4)—

"criminal proceedings" includes all proceedings before the Courts-Martial Appeal Court; and

"leave" means leave granted by the court making the declaration of incompatibility or by the House of Lords.

As to the procedure for giving notice to the Crown, see CPR r.19.4A. **3D–22**

The parties should also give as much informal notice as possible to the Crown of the proceedings and the issues involved, and should copy this notice to the court: *Poplar Housing & Regeneration Community Association Ltd v Donoghue* [2001] EWCA Civ 595; [2002] Q.B. 48; [2001] 4 All E.R. 604; [2001] 3 W.L.R. 183, CA. "The Crown" means a person named in a list under the Crown Proceedings Act 1947 s.17, *ibid*. See e.g. *Wilkinson v Kitzinger & Attorney General (Lord Chancellor Intervening)* [2006] EWHC 2022 (Fam); [2007] 1 F.L.R. 295; [2007] 1 F.C.R. 183; [2006] H.R.L.R. 36.

PUBLIC AUTHORITIES

Acts of public authorities

6.—(1) It is unlawful for a public authority to act in a way which is **3D–23** incompatible with a Convention right.

(2) Subsection (1) does not apply to an act if—

(a) as the result of one or more provisions of primary legislation, the authority could not have acted differently; or

(b) in the case of one or more provisions of, or made under, primary legislation which cannot be read or given effect in a way which is compatible with the Convention rights, the authority was acting so as to give effect to or enforce those provisions.

(3) In this section "public authority" includes—

(a) a court or tribunal, and

(b) any person certain of whose functions are functions of a public nature,

but does not include either House of Parliament or a person exercising functions in connection with proceedings in Parliament.

(4) In subsection (3) "Parliament" does not include the House of Lords in its judicial capacity.

(5) In relation to a particular act, a person is not a public authority by virtue only of subsection (3)(b) if the nature of the act is private.

(6) "An act" includes a failure to act but does not include a failure to—

(a) introduce in, or lay before, Parliament a proposal for legislation; or

(b) make any primary legislation or remedial order.

Paragraph numbers marked with a "+" can be found online and on CD.

Section 6(1)

3D–24   Section 6(1) only applies to territory to which relevant provisions of the law have been extended by the United Kingdom: *R (on the application of Quark Fishing Limited) v Secretary of State for Foreign & Commonwealth Affairs* [2005] UKHL 57; [2005] 3 W.L.R. 837.

As to whether the Court should declare that a Defendant has acted in breach of s.6, compare the approaches of Simon Brown and Carnwarth L.JJ. in *R. (on the application of Purja) v Ministry of Defence* [2003] EWCA Civ 1345; [2004] 1 W.L.R. 289; [2004] U.K.H.R.R. 309; *The Times*, October 16, 2003. See also the decision of the House of Lords in *MB v Secretary of State for the Home Department* [2007] UKHL 46; [2008] 2 A.C. 440.

Section 6(1) and 6(3)

3D–25   As to the meaning of "public authority" see: *YL v Birmingham City Council* [2007] UKHL 27; [2007] 3 W.L.R. 112; [2007] 3 All E.R. 957; *The Times*, June 21, 2007. See too *Poplar Housing & Regeneration Community Association Limited v Donoghue* [2001] EWCA Civ 395; [2002] Q.B. 48; [2001] 3 W.L.R. 183 CA; *Austin Hall Building Ltd v Buckland Securities* [2001] B.L.R. 272; *R (on the application of A) v Partnerships in Care Ltd* [2002] EWHC 529; [2002] 1 W.L.R. 2610; *R. (on the application of Heather) v Leonard Cheshire Foundation* [2002] EWCA Civ 366; [2002] 2 All E.R. 936; [2002] H.R.L.R. 30; [2002] U.K.H.R.R. 883, *Aston Cantlow & Wilmcote with Billesley Parochial Church Council v Wallbank* [2003] UKHL 37; [2004] 1 A.C. 546; *Hampshire CC v Beer (t/a Hammer Trout Farm) sub nom. R. (on the application of Beer (t/a Hammer Trout Farm)) v Hampshire Farmers Markets Ltd* [2003] EWCA Civ 1056; [2004] 1 W.L.R. 233; [2004] U.K.H.R.R. 727; *Re Malcolm; Malcolm v Benedict Mackenzie (A Firm)* [2004] EWCA Civ 1748; [2005] 1 W.L.R. 1238 at [30]; *R. (on the application of West) v Lloyds of London* [2004] EWCA Civ 506; [2004] 3 All E.R. 251; [2004] 2 All E.R. (Comm) 1; *Cameron v Network Rail Infrastructure Ltd (formerly Railtrack Plc)* [2006] EWHC 1133; [2007] 1 W.L.R. 163 at [29].

Section 6(2)

3D–26   As to the extent and effect of s.6(2), see *Ghaidan v Ghodin-Mendoza* [2004] UKHL 30; [2004] 2 A.C. 557; [2004] 3 W.L.R. 113 at para.18; *Hooper v Department for Work & Pensions* [2005] UKHL 29 at paras 49–51.

Section 6(2) disapplies s.6(1) only if the public authority is acting so as to give effect to one or more provisions of primary legislation which cannot be read or given effect in a way which is compatible with Convention rights, having read the legislation, under s.3(1), in a way which is, if possible, compatible with the Convention: see *Brown v Stott* [2001] 2 W.L.R. 817, [2001] 2 All E.R. 97, per Lord Roger.

As to the effect of a finding that s.6(2) applies on the exercise of another power, see *R. (on the application of Morris) v Westminster City Council (No.3)* [2005] EWCA Civ 1184; [2006] 1 W.L.R. 505; [2005] H.R.L.R. 43; [2006] U.K.H.R.R. 165, paras 53–55 and 82.

The fact that a statute provides a specific scheme of enforcement by reference to specified public authorities does not confine any s.6(1) action to those bodies: *Marcic v Thames Water Utilities* [2003] UKHL 66; [2004] 2 A.C. 42; [2004] 1 All E.R. 135; [2003] 3 W.L.R. 1603, HL.

Section 6(3)

3D–27   The fact that courts are public authorities under s.6(1) may affect the approach they adopt in proceedings between two private bodies: for example, in the approach they take to determining whether to award an interim injunction to give effect to Arts 8 and 10 of the Convention: *A v B plc* [2002] EWCA Civ 337; [2003] Q.B. 195; [2002] 3 W.L.R. 542.

Proceedings

3D–28   **7.—(1) A person who claims that a public authority has acted (or proposes to act) in a way which is made unlawful by section 6(1) may—**

> **(a) bring proceedings against the authority under this Act in the appropriate court or tribunal, or**

Paragraph numbers marked with a "+" can be found online and on CD.

    (b) rely on the Convention right or rights concerned in any legal proceedings,

but only if he is (or would be) a victim of the unlawful act.

(2) In subsection (1)(a) "appropriate court or tribunal" means such court or tribunal as may be determined in accordance with rules; and proceedings against an authority include a counterclaim or similar proceeding.

(3) If the proceedings are brought on an application for judicial review, the applicant is to be taken to have a sufficient interest in relation to the unlawful act only if he is, or would be, a victim of that act.

(4) If the proceedings are made by way of a petition for judicial review in Scotland, the applicant shall be taken to have title and interest to sue in relation to the unlawful act only is he is, or would be, a victim of that act.

(5) Proceedings under subsection (1)(a) must be brought before the end of—

    (a) the period of one year beginning with the date on which the act complained of took place; or

    (b) such longer period as the court or tribunal considers equitable having regard to all the circumstances,

but that is subject to any rule imposing a stricter time limit in relation to the procedure in question.

(6) In subsection (1)(b) "legal proceedings" includes—

    (a) proceedings brought by or at the instigation of a public authority; and

    (b) an appeal against the decision of a court or tribunal.

(7) For the purposes of this section, a person is a victim of an unlawful act only if he would be a victim for the purposes of Article 34 of the Convention if proceedings were brought in the European Court of Human Rights in respect of that act.

(8) Nothing in this Act creates a criminal offence.

(9) In this section "rules" means—

    (a) in relation to proceedings before a court or tribunal outside Scotland, rules made by the Lord Chancellor or the Secretary of State for the purposes of this section or rules of court,

    (b) in relation to proceedings before a court or tribunal in Scotland, rules made by the Secretary of State for those purposes,

    (c) in relation to proceedings before a tribunal in Northern Ireland—

        (i) which deals with transferred matters; and

        (ii) for which no rules made under paragraph (a) are in force, rules made by a Northern Ireland department for those purposes,

and includes provision made by order under section 1 of the Courts and Legal Services Act 1990.

Paragraph numbers marked with a "+" can be found online and on CD.

(10) In making rules regard must be had to section 9.

(11) The Minister who has power to make rules in relation to a particular tribunal may, to the extent he considers it necessary to ensure that the tribunal can provide an appropriate remedy in relation to an act (or proposed act) of a public authority which is (or would be) unlawful as a result of section 6(1), by order add to—

(a) the relief or remedies which the tribunal may grant; or

(b) the grounds on which it may grant any of them.

(12) An order made under subsection (11) may contain such incidental, supplemental, consequential or transitional provision as the Minister making it considers appropriate.

(13) "The Minister" includes the Northern Ireland department concerned.

3D–29 *Note* —Amended by SI 2003/1887 and SI 2005/3429.

Sections 7(1) "public authority"
3D–30 As to meaning of public authority, see para.3D–25 above and *YL v Birmingham City Council* [2007] UKHL 27; [2008] 1 A.C. 95; [2007] 3 W.L.R. 112; [2007] 3 All E.R. 957.

Section 7(1), 7(3) and 7(7) "victim"
3D–31 As to the meaning of "victim" in art.34 (formerly art.25) of the Convention, see: Lester & Pannick, eds, *Human Rights Law & Practice* (2nd edn, Lexis Nexis, Butterworths, 2004) para.2.7.2; Wadham, Mountfield, Edmundson & Gallagher, *Blackstone's Guide to the Human Rights Act 1998* (4th edn, OUP, 2007), paras 5.3.1–5.3.3. See too *Director General of Fair Trading v Proprietary Association of Great Britain* [2001] EWCA Civ 1217; [2002] 1 W.L.R. 269 (CA) (association could not be a "victim" where its rights were not affected and where it had not been formally declared to be the representative of its members' interests). A person may continue to claim to be a victim where there is a continuing violation of a positive procedural obligation, even if he has received compensation for feelings of frustration, distress and anxiety from the ECHR: *Re McKerr* [2004] UKHL 12; [2004] 1 W.L.R. 807; [2004] 2 All E.R. 409; [2004] N.I. 212.

Section 7(1)(a) and 7(2) "appropriate court or tribunal"
3D–32 This is determined by the subject matter of the claim, and rules issued under the Act. See the Civil Procedure (Amendment No.4) Rules 2000 (SI 2000/2092) concerning procedure for treatment of human rights issues in the Administrative Court; the Family Proceedings (Amendment) Rules 2000 (SI 2000/2267) for family courts; Pt 33 CPR and Practice Direction 30 concerning transfer between courts; Criminal Appeals (Amendment) Rules 2000 (SI 2000/2036) concerning human rights issues in criminal courts; and the House of Lords: Practice Directions and Standing Orders Applicable to Civil Appeals and Practice Directions and Standing Orders Applicable to Criminal Appeals.

Practice Directions and Standard Orders Applicable to Civil Appeals and Practice Directions and Standing Orders Applicable to Criminal Appeals
3D–33 It is not necessary to transfer proceedings to the High Court merely because a breach of a Convention right is alleged, or where there is a claim for a declaration of incompatibility if it has no chance of success: *V (A Child) (Care Proceedings: Human Rights Claims, Re* [2004] EWCA Civ 54; [2004] 1 W.L.R. 1433; [2004] 1 All E.R. 997; [2004] 1 F.W.L.R. 944.

For employment claims where a declaration of incompatibility may be sought see *Whittaker v Watson (t/a P & M Watson Haulage)* [2002] I.C.R. 1244; [2002] 67 B.M.L.R. 28.

The Proscribed Organisation Appeals Commission is the appropriate tribunal in relation to matters related to proscription of a terrorist organisation under the Terrorism Act 2000: *R (Kurdistan Workers' Party) v Secretary of State for the Home Department* [2002] EWHC 644 (Admin); [2002] A.C.D. 99. See the Proscribed Organisations Appeal Commission (Human Rights Act Proceedings) Rules 2006 (SI 2006/2298).

Paragraph numbers marked with a "+" can be found online and on CD.

Section 7(2)

In *Anufrijeva v Southwark LBC* [2003] EWCA Civ 1406; [2004] Q.B. 1124; [2004] 2 **3D-34**
W.L.R. 613; [2004] 1 All E.R. 833, the Court of Appeal has given guidance as to the
approach in considering claims for damages for breaches of Convention rights involving maladministration. The Court also laid down the following procedural guidelines:

    (i) Courts should look critically at any attempt to recover HRA damages for mal-
       administration by any procedure other than judicial review.

    (ii) A claim for damages alone cannot be brought by judicial review (r.54.3(2)) but
       it should still be brought in the Administrative Court by an ordinary claim.
       (see also para.53). Note, however, that this refers only to an ordinary claim
       before the Administrative Court, that is to say a claim asserting breach of a
       public law duty (i.e. maladministration) which requires permission to enable it
       to proceed: *Andrews v Reading BC* [2004] EWHC 970; [2005] Env. L.R. 2;
       [2004]; [2004] U.K.H.R.R. 599, para.9 (Collins J).

    (iii) Before giving permission to apply for judicial review, the Administrative Court
       judge should require the claimant to explain why it would not be more ap-
       propriate to use any available internal complaint procedure or proceed by
       making a claim to the Parliamentary or Local Government Ombudsman at
       least in the first instance.

    (iv) If there is a legitimate claim for other relief, permission should if appropriate
       be limited to that relief and consideration given to deferring permission for
       the damages claim, adjourning or staying that claim until use has been made
       of ADR, whether by a reference to a mediator or an ombudsman or otherwise,
       or remitting that claim to a district judge or master if it cannot be dismissed
       summarily on grounds that in any event an award of damages is not required
       to achieve just satisfaction.

    (v) It is hoped that in future, claims that have to be determined by the courts can
       be determined by the appropriate level of judge in a summary manner by the
       judge reading the relevant evidence. The citing of more than three authorities
       should be justified and the hearing should be limited to half a day except in
       exceptional circumstances.

These guidelines may create certain practical difficulties and, it is suggested, may
not be appropriate outside the area to which the cases related, namely allegations of
breaches of positive obligations in the social welfare and immigration fields, arising out
of delay caused by maladministration.

Section 7(5)

See *Dunn v Parole Board* [2008] EWCA Civ 374; [2008] H.R.L.R. 32 and [2008] **3D-34.1**
U.K.H.R.R. 711.

Section 7(6)(b)

Proceedings brought by or at the instigation of a public authority include not only **3D-35**
the trial but also a victim's appeal in such proceedings: *R. v DPP Ex p. Kebilene* [2000]
2 A.C. 326; [1999] 3 W.L.R. 972; [1999] 4 All E.R. 801, per Lord Steyn.

As to the requirements of a statement of case relying on the Human Rights Act
1998 see PD 16, para.15.1 As to the requirements of an appellant's notice see PD 52,
paras 5.1A and 5.1B.

Applications for judicial review are not brought by or at the instigation of a public
authority: *R. v Haringey LBC Ex p. Ben-Abdelaziz* [2001] EWCA Civ 809; [2001] 1
W.L.R. 1485; [2001] A.C.D. 88.

Section 7(9)

The power to make rules under this subsection for England and Wales is exercis- **3D-36**
able by statutory instrument: see s.20(2). It can be annulled by resolution of either
House of Parliament: see ss.20(5) and 20(7).

Section 7(11)

For the procedure for making orders under this sub-section, see s.20(4). **3D-37**

Judicial remedies

8.—(1) In relation to any act (or proposed act) of a public author- **3D-38**

Paragraph numbers marked with a "+" can be found online and on CD.

ity which the court finds is (or would be) unlawful, it may grant such relief or remedy, or make such order, within its powers as it considers just and appropriate.

(2) But damages may be awarded only by a court which has power to award damages, or to order the payment of compensation, in civil proceedings.

(3) No award of damages is to be made unless, taking account of all the circumstances of the case, including—

    (a) any other relief or remedy granted, or order made, in relation to the act in question (by that or any other court), and

    (b) the consequences of any decision (of that or any other court) in respect of that act,

the court is satisfied that the award is necessary to afford just satisfaction to the person in whose favour it is made.

(4) In determining—

    (a) whether to award damages, or

    (b) the amount of an award,

the court must take into account the principles applied by the European Court of Human Rights in relation to the award of compensation under Article 41 of the Convention.

(5) A public authority against which damages are awarded is to be treated—

    (a) in Scotland, for the purposes of section 3 of the Law Reform (Miscellaneous Provisions) (Scotland) Act 1940 as if the award were made in an action of damages in which the authority has been found liable in respect of loss or damage to the person to whom the award is made;

    (b) for the purposes of the Civil Liability (Contribution) Act 1978 as liable in respect of damage suffered by the person to whom the award is made.

(6) In this section—

"court" includes a tribunal;

"damages" means damages for an unlawful act of a public authority; and

"unlawful" means unlawful under section 6(1).

3D–39   Remedies available under s.8 of the Act are all those within the court's powers, unconstrained by any new principles except in relation to damages, where ss.8(2)–8(4) apply.

Sections 8(3) and 8(4)

3D–40   As to the meaning of "just satisfaction", the principles applied by the ECHR must be taken into account (though they are not binding).

3D–41   A domestic court should not award damages under s.8 unless it is satisfied it is necessary to do so. A causal connection is required between the violation and the loss for which compensation is claimed (see *R. (on the application of Greenfield) v Secretary of State for the Home Department* [2005] UKHL 14; [2005] 1 W.L.R. 637; [2005] 2 All E.R. 240; [2005] H.R.L.R. 13, per Lord Bingham, para.11). The Court of Appeal gave guidelines as to the award of damages in *Anufrijeva v Southwark LBC* [2003] EWCA Civ 1406; [2004] Q.B. 1124; [2004] 2 W.L.R. 613; [2004] 1 All E.R. 833. The Court made clear

Paragraph numbers marked with a "+" can be found online and on CD.

its view that damages are not available as of right like damages for tort, but only as a discretionary remedy of last resort. The guiding remedial principle is *restitutio in integrum*, so that the claimant should, so far as possible, be put in the position in which he would have found himself if his Convention rights had not been infringed. But account must first be taken of the effect of any other remedies which the court has already been able to provide. Any remaining significant pecuniary loss caused by the breach should usually be assessed and awarded; but caution is to be exercised when deciding whether to award damages for non-pecuniary loss, and if so how much. The consequences of the breach must be serious, the damage must be more than distress and frustration, and the scale and manner of the violation can be taken into account. In cases of maladministration, awards by the Parliamentary or Local Government Ombudsman may be the only guide. The Court of Appeal also approved the approach of Sullivan J. in *R. (on the application of Bernard) v Enfield LBC* [2002] EWHC 2282; [2003] H.R.L.R. 4; [2003] U.K.H.R.R. 148 , where damages were awarded a severely disabled woman and her husband-carer, who had been left in unsuitable accommodation for 20 months in breach of art.8.

In *R. (on the application of H) v Secretary of State for the Home Department* [2003] UKHL 1; [2003] H.R.L.R. 570; [2003] 1 W.L.R. 411; [2003] 1 All E.R. 497, the House of Lords declined to award damages to a mental health patient since the violation had been publicly acknowledged and his right had been vindicated, the law had been amended in a way which should prevent similar violations in future, and he had not been the victim of unlawful detention, which art.5 is intended to avoid. For analysis of the principles applied in cases involving loss of opportunity or distress see *Re P* [2007] EWCA Civ 2; *The Times*, February 1, 2007.

Reported cases in which HRA damages have been awarded are *R. (Bernard) v Enfield LBC* (above); *R. (KB) v Mental Health Review Tribunal* [2003] EWHC 193; [2004] Q.B. 936; [2003] 3 W.L.R. 185; [2003] 2 All E.R. 209 and *Van Colle v Chief Constable of Hertfordshire* [2006] EWHC 360; [2006] 3 All E.R. 963; [2006] 1 F.C.R. 755; [2006] H.R.L.R. 25 and [2007] EWCA Civ 325 though the *Van Colle* decision on liability was overturned by the House of Lords: see [2008] UKHL 50; [2008] 3 W.L.R. 598; [2008] 3 All E.R. 977.

For authority on obligation of the courts to ensure effective protection of fundamental rights and to fashion new remedies where necessary see *Gairy v Attorney General of Grenada*, [2001] UKPC 30; [2001] 3 W.L.R. 779, PC. The limitation in s.21(1) read with s.38(2) of the Crown Proceedings Act 1947 must now be reading accordance with the provisions of the Human Rights Act.

Judicial acts

9.—(1) Proceedings under section 7(1)(a) in respect of a judicial act **3D–42** may be brought only—

    (a) by exercising a right of appeal;

    (b) on any application (in Scotland a petition) for judicial review; or

    (c) in such other forum as may be prescribed by rules.

(2) That does not affect any rule of law which prevents a court from being the subject of judicial review.

(3) In proceedings under this Act in respect of a judicial act done in good faith, damages may not be awarded otherwise than to compensate a person to the extent required by Article 5(5) of the Convention.

(4) An award of damages permitted by subsection (3) is to be made against the Crown, but no award may be made unless the appropriate person, if not a party to the proceedings, is joined.

(5) In this section—

    "appropriate person" means the Minister responsible for the court concerned, or a person or government department nominated by him;

Paragraph numbers marked with a "+" can be found online and on CD.

"court" includes a tribunal;

"judge" includes a member of a tribunal, a justice of the peace and a clerk or other officer entitled to exercise the jurisdiction of a court;

"judicial act" means a judicial act of a court and includes an act done on the instructions, or on behalf, of a judge; and

"rules" has the same meaning as in section 7(9).

3D–43 As to evidence in a claim in respect of a judicial act, see CPR r.33.9.

It is arguable that in *R. v Director General of Fair Trading v Proprietary Association of Great Britain* [2001] EWCA Civ. 1217; [2002] 1 W.L.R. 269, CA, the court should have found that there was a breach of ECHR art.6(1) arising out of the lack of independence of the first instance court, but refused the application for costs on the basis of s.9(3).

Section 9(2)

3D–44 See s.29(3) of the Supreme Court Act 1981. Considered in *R. v DPP Ex p. Kebilene* [2000] 2 A.C. 326; [1999] 3 W.L.R. 972; [1999] 4 All E.R. 801. See also *R. v Hertfordshire CC Ex p. Green Environmental Industries Ltd* [2000] 2 A.C. 412; [2000] 2 W.L.R. 373; [2000] 1 All E.R. 733, per Lord Cooke of Thorndon and Lord Hobhouse of Woodborough.

REMEDIAL ACTION

Power to take remedial action

3D–45 **10.**—(1) This section applies if—

    (a) a provision of legislation has been declared under section 4 to be incompatible with a Convention right and, if an appeal lies—

        (i) all persons who may appeal have stated in writing that they do not intended to do so;

        (ii) the time for bringing an appeal has expired and no appeal has been brought within that time; or

        (iii) an appeal brought within that time has been determined or abandoned; or

    (b) it appears to a Minister of the Crown or Her Majesty in Council that, having regard to a finding of the European Court of Human Rights made after the coming into force of this section in proceedings against the United Kingdom, a provision of legislation is incompatible with an obligation of the United Kingdom arising from the Convention.

(2) If a Minister of the Crown considers that there are compelling reasons for proceeding under this section, he may by order make such amendments to the legislation as he considers necessary to remove the incompatibility.

(3) If, in the case of subordinate legislation, a Minister of the Crown considers—

    (a) that it is necessary to amend the primary legislation under which the subordinate legislation in question was made, in order to enable the incompatibility to be removed; and

Paragraph numbers marked with a "+" can be found online and on CD.

(b) that there are compelling reasons for proceeding under this section,

he may by order make such amendments to the primary legislation as he considers necessary.

(4) This section also applies where the provision in question is in subordinate legislation and has been quashed, or declared invalid, by reason of incompatibility with a Convention right and the Minister proposes to proceed under paragraph 2(b) of Schedule 2.

(5) If the legislation is an Order in Council, the power conferred by subsection (2) or (3) is exercisable by Her Majesty in Council.

(6) In this section "legislation" does not include a Measure of the Church Assembly or of the General Synod of the Church of England.

(7) Schedule 2 makes further provision about remedial orders.

A declaration of incompatibility may serve a useful purpose even if the government **3D–45.1** has already indicated an intention to change the law. See *Bellinger v Bellinger* (2003) UKHL 21; [2003] 2 A.C. 467.

OTHER RIGHTS AND PROCEEDINGS

Safeguard for existing human rights

11. A person's reliance on a Convention right does not restrict— **3D–46**
    (a) any other right or freedom conferred on him by or under any law having effect in any part of the United Kingdom; or
    (b) his right to make any claim or bring any proceedings which he could make or bring apart from sections 7 to 9.

See *R. (Morgan Grenfell) v Special Commissioner of Income Tax* [2001] EWCA Civ 329; **3D–46.1** [2003] 1 A.C. 563; *R. (Wooder) v Feggetter* [2002] EWCA Civ 554; [2003] Q.B. 549, and *C plc v P* [2006] EWHC 1226 Ch; [2006] Ch. 549.

Freedom of expression

12.—(1) This section applies if a court is considering whether to **3D–47** grant any relief which, if granted might affect the exercise of the Convention right to freedom of expression.

(2) If the person against whom the application for relief is made ("the respondent") is neither present nor represented, no such relief is to be granted unless the court is satisfied—
    (a) that the applicant has taken all practicable steps to notify the respondent; or
    (b) that there are compelling reasons why the respondent should not be notified.

(3) No such relief is to be granted so as to restrain publication before trial unless the court is satisfied that the applicant is likely to establish that publication should not be allowed.

(4) The court must have particular regard to the importance of the Convention right to freedom of expression and, where the proceedings relate to material which the respondent claims, or which appears to the court, to be journalistic, literary or artistic material (or to conduct connected with such material), to—
    (a) the extent to which—

Paragraph numbers marked with a "+" can be found online and on CD.

(i) the material has, or is about to, become available to the public; or

(ii) it is, or would be, in the public interest for the material to be published;

(b) any relevant privacy code.

(5) In this section—

"court" includes a tribunal; and

"relief" includes any remedy or order (other than in criminal proceedings).

3D–48   The Court of Appeal gave guidance as to the application of s.12 in *A v B Plc* [2002] EWCA Civ 337; [2003] Q.B. 195; [2002] H.R.L.R. 25. See the approach of the Court of Appeal in *Clayton v Clayton* [2006] EWCA Civ 878. See too *Re Ward; BBC v CAFCASS Legal* [2007] EWHC 616 (Fam).

Section 12(3)

3D–49   In *Cream Holdings Ltd v Bannerjee* [2004] UKHL 44; [2005] 1 A.C. 253 it was held that, at this interlocutory stage, the test of likelihood was higher than the normal threshold for the grant of an interlocutory injunction in *American Cyanamid v Ethicon Ltd* [1975] A.C. 396 (whether the claim had a "real prospect" of success) but not so high as being that the claim was "more likely than not" to succeed, which standard was unworkable in practice. The standard is a flexible one: the degree of likelihood of success at trial needed to satisfy s.12(3) must depend on the circumstances. There is no automatic priority, or presumption that art.10 ECHR has greater weight than art.8, and the court should evaluate whether it is necessary in any given case to qualify the one right in order to protect the other: *Campbell v MGN Limited* [2004] UKHL 22; [2004] 2 A.C. 457; [2004] 2 W.L.R. 1232, para.55 (Lord Hoffmann) and para.141 (Baroness Hale). See also *Douglas v Hello! Ltd* [2001] Q.B. 967, para.150 per Keene L.J. and *Mahmud v Galloway & McKay* [2006] EWHC 1286; [2006] E.M.L.R. 26.See also *Boehringer Ingelheim Ltd v Vetplus Ltd* [2007] EWCA Civ 583; [2007] Bus. L.R. 1456; [2007] H.R.L.R. 33.

Section 12(4)

3D–50   The court cannot have "particular regard" to art.10 without having regard to the qualifications in art.10(2), such as the rights and freedoms of others: *Douglas v Hello! Ltd (No.1)* [2001] Q.B. 967, per Sedley L.J., para.133. Thus, the sub-section does not give either art.8 or 12 pre-eminence over the other: *S (A Child) (Identification: Restrictions on Publication), Re* [2004] UKHL 47; [2005] 1 A.C. 593; [2004] 3 W.L.R. 1129, Hale L.J. When the values of two rights are in conflict, it is necessary to focus intensely on their comparative importance. This includes consideration of the justifications for interfering with or restricting each right and the application of the proportionality test: *A Local Authority v PD* [2005] EWHC 1832; [2005] E.M.L.R. 35. See too *CC v AB* [2006] EWHC 3083.

The fact that an injunction will interfere with freedom of the press is of particular importance: *A v B Plc* [2002] EWCA Civ 337; [2003] Q.B. 195; [2002] 3 W.L.R. 542; [2002] All E.R. 545, para.11(iv). The reference to the "public interest" does not mean that the court is justified in interfering where there is no identifiable special public interest in any particular material to be published. Any interference with publication must be justified: *ibid.*, para.11(v). "Any relevant privacy code" includes the Press Complaints Commission Code of Practice, but this is only one factor. Courts should discourage advocates from seeking to rely on individual PCC decisions: *ibid.*, paras 11(xiv) and 11(xv). Where the balance does not clearly point in either direction, interim relief should be refused: *ibid.*, para.12. Note that although the lack of media challenge to an application does not in itself justify the grant of an order interfering with the rights of the press, it nevertheless demonstrates that the press does not believe that a significant inhibition of the exercise of its rights under art.10 exists: *Maxine Carr v News Group Newspapers Ltd* [2005] EWHC 971, QB. See also Anonymity Orders and Media Censorship in the "New Era of Human Rights" Paul Dougan, Ent. L.R. 2005, 16(6), 150–152

Paragraph numbers marked with a "+" can be found online and on CD.

Freedom of thought, conscience and religion

13.—(1) If a court's determination of any question arising under **3D–51** this Act might affect the exercise by a religious organisation (itself or its members collectively) of the Convention right to freedom of thought, conscience and religion, it must have particular regard to the importance of that right.

(2) In this section, "court" includes a tribunal.

See *R. (Williamson) v Secretary of State for Education* [2002] EWCA Civ 1926, [2003] **3D–51.1** Q.B. 1300 (also discussed in HL, but discussion of s.13 in CA); *R. (Amicus) v Secretary of State for Trade & Industry* [2004] EWHC 860 Admin, [2004] E.L.R. 311; *R. (Playfoot) v Governing Body of Millais School* [2007] EWHC 1698 Admin; [2007] 3 F.C.R. 754, [2007] E.L.R. 489 and *Surayanda v Welsh Ministers* [2007] EWCA Civ 893.

DEROGATIONS AND RESERVATIONS

Derogations

14.—(1) In this Act "designated derogation" means any derogation **3D–52** by the United Kingdom from an Article of the Convention, or of any protocol to the Convention, which is designated for the purposes of this Act in an order made by the Secretary of State.

(2) The derogation referred to in subsection (1)(a) is set out in Part I of Schedule 3.

(3) If a designated derogation is amended or replaced it ceases to be a designated derogation.

(4) But subsection (3) does not prevent the Secretary of State from exercising his power under subsection (1) to make a fresh designation order in respect of the Article concerned.

(5) The Secretary of State must by order make such amendments to Schedule 3 as he considers appropriate to reflect—

    (a) any designation order; or

    (b) the effect of subsection (3).

(6) A designation order may be made in anticipation of the making by the United Kingdom of a proposed derogation.

Note —The text of the UK's derogation is contained in Sch.3. **3D–53**

The power to make such an order is exercisable by statutory instrument: s.20(1). For procedure for making of an order under this section, see s.20(3).

Amended by the Secretary of State for Constitutional Affairs Order 2003 (SI 2003/1884) Sch.2, para.10.

The original derogation in Pt I of Sch.3 of the Act as enacted was deleted by the Human Rights Act (Amendment) Order 2001 (SI 2001/1216). A new derogation from ECHR art.5 was designated in order to enact Pt IV of the Anti-Terrorism Crime and Security Act 2001. This was contained in the Human Rights Act 1998 (Designated Derogation) Order 2001 (SI 2001/3644). However, that Order was quashed by the House of Lords in *A v Secretary of State for the Home Department* [2005] UKHL 71, [2006] 2 A.C. 221; [2005] 3 W.L.R. 1249; [2006] 1 All E.R. 575; [2006] H.R.L.R. 6; [2006] U.K.H.R.R. 225. Part IV of the Anti-Terrorism Crime and Security Act 2001 was repealed by the Prevention of Terrorism Act 2005, with effect from March 14, 2005, and the Human Rights Act 1998 (Amendment) Order 2005 (SI 2005/1071), of April 8, 2005, reflected the withdrawal of the derogation from art.5 in response to this.

Reservations

15.—(1) In this Act, "designated reservation" means— **3D–54**

Paragraph numbers marked with a "+" can be found online and on CD.

(a) the United Kingdom's reservation to Article 2 of the First Protocol to the Convention; and

(b) any other reservation by the United Kingdom to an Article of the Convention, or of any protocol to the Convention, which is designated for the purposes of this Act in an order made by the Secretary of State.

(2) The text of the reservation referred to in subsection (1)(a) is set out in Part II of Schedule 3.

(3) If a designated reservation is withdrawn wholly or in part it ceases to be a designated reservation.

(4) But subsection (3) does not prevent the Secretary of State from exercising his power under subsection (1)(b) to make a fresh designation order in respect of the Article concerned.

(5) The Secretary of State must by order make such amendments to this Act as he considers appropriate to reflect—

(a) any designation order; or

(b) the effect of subsection (3).

Note —The text of the UK's reservation is contained in Sch.3.

The power to make such an order is exercisable by statutory instrument: s.20(1). For procedure for making of an order under this section, see s.20(3).

Period for which designated derogations have effect

3D–55   16.—(1) If it has not already been withdrawn by the United Kingdom, a designated derogation ceases to have effect for the purposes of this Act, at the end of the period of five years beginning with the date on which the order designating it was made.

(2) At any time before the period—

(a) fixed by subsection (1), or

(b) extended by an order under this subsection,

comes to an end, the Secretary of State may by order extend it by a further period of five years.

(3) An order under section 14(1) ceases to have effect at the end of the period for consideration, unless a resolution has been passed by each House approving the order.

(4) Subsection (3) does not affect—

(a) anything done in reliance on the order; or

(b) the power to make a fresh order under section 14(1).

(5) In subsection (3) "period for consideration" means the period of forty days beginning with the day on which the order was made.

(6) In calculating the period for consideration, no account is to be taken of any time during which—

(a) Parliament is dissolved or prorogued; or

(b) both Houses are adjourned for more than four days.

(7) If a designated derogation is withdrawn by the United Kingdom, the Secretary of State must by order make such amendments to this Act as he considers are required to reflect that withdrawal.

3D–56   Note —Amended by the Secretary of State for Constitutional Affairs Order (SI 2003/1887), Sch.2, para.10.

Paragraph numbers marked with a "+" can be found online and on CD.

Section 16(2)

The power to make such an order is exercisable by statutory instrument: s.20(1). **3D–57**
For procedure for making an order under this sub-section, see s.20(4).

Section 16(7)

The power to make such an order is exercisable by statutory instrument: s.20(1). **3D–58**
For procedure for making an order under this sub-section, see s.20(3).

Periodic review of designated reservations

17.—(1) The appropriate Minister must review the designated **3D–59**
reservation referred to in section 15(1)(a)—

> (a) before the end of the period of five years beginning with
> the date on which section 1(2) came into force; and
> (b) if that designation is still in force, before the end of the
> period of five years beginning with the date on which
> the last report relating to it was laid under subsection
> (3).

(2) The appropriate Minister must review each of the other
designated reservations (if any)—

> (a) before the end of the period of five years beginning with
> the date on which the order designating the reservation
> first came into force; and
> (b) if the designation is still in force, before the end of the
> period of five years beginning with the date on which
> the last report relating to it was laid under subsection
> (3).

(3) The Minister conducting a review under this section must
prepare a report on the result of the review and lay a copy of it
before each House of Parliament.

JUDGES OF THE EUROPEAN COURT OF HUMAN RIGHTS

Appointment to European Court of Human Rights

18.—(1) In this section "judicial office" means the office of— **3D–60**

> (a) Lord Justice of Appeal, Justice of the High Court or
> Circuit judge, in England and Wales;
> (b) judge of the Court of Session or sheriff, in Scotland;
> (c) Lord Justice of Appeal, judge of the High Court or
> county court judge, in Northern Ireland.

(2) The holder of a judicial office may become a judge of the
European Court of Human Rights ("the Court") without being
required to relinquish his office.

(3) But he is not required to perform the duties of his judicial office while he is a judge of the Court.

(4) In respect of any period during which he is a judge of the
Court—

> (a) a Lord Justice of Appeal or Justice of the High Court is
> not to count as a judge of the relevant court for the
> purposes of section 2(1) or 4(1) of the Supreme Court
> Act 1981 (maximum number of judges) nor as a judge of

Paragraph numbers marked with a "+" can be found online and on CD.

the Supreme Court for the purposes of section 12(1) to (6) of that Act (salaries etc.);

(b) a judge of the Court of Session is not to count as a judge of that court for the purposes of section 1(1) of the Court of Session Act 1988 (maximum number of judges) or of section 9(1)(c) of the Administration of Justice Act 1973 ("the 1973 Act") (salaries etc.);

(c) a Lord Justice of Appeal or judge of the High Court in Northern Ireland is not to count as a judge of the relevant court for the purposes of section 2(1) or 3(1) of the Judicature (Northern Ireland) Act 1978 (maximum number of judges) nor as a judge of the Supreme Court of Northern Ireland for the purposes of section 9(1)(d) of the 1973 Act (salaries etc.);

(d) a Circuit judge is not to count as such for the purposes of section 18 of the Courts Act 1971 (salaries etc.);

(e) a sheriff is not to count as such for the purposes of section 14 of the Sheriff Courts (Scotland) Act 1907 (salaries etc.);

(f) a county court judge of Northern Ireland is not to count as such for the purposes of section 106 of the County Courts Act (Northern Ireland) 1959 (salaries etc.).

(5) If a sheriff principal is appointed a judge of the Court, section 11(1) of the Sheriff Courts (Scotland) Act 1971 (temporary appointment of sheriff principal) applies, while he holds that appointment, as if his office is vacant.

(6) Schedule 4 makes provision about judicial pensions in relation to the holder of a judicial office who serves as a judge of the Court.

(7) The Lord Chancellor or the Secretary of State may by order make such transitional provision (including, in particular, provision for a temporary increase in the maximum number of judges) as he considers appropriate in relation to any holder of a judicial office who has completed his service as a judge of the Court.

(7A) The following paragraphs apply to the making of an order under subsection (7) in relation to any holder of a judicial office listed in subsection (1)(a)—

(a) before deciding what transitional provision it is appropriate to make, the person making the order must consult the Lord Chief Justice of England and Wales;

(b) before making the order, that person must consult the Lord Chief Justice of England and Wales.

(7B) The following paragraphs apply to the making of an order under subsection (7) in relation to any holder of a judicial office listed in subsection (1)(c)—

(a) before deciding what transitional provision it is appropriate to make, the person making the order must consult the Lord Chief Justice of Northern Ireland;

(b) before making the order, that person must consult the Lord Chief Justice of Northern Ireland.

Paragraph numbers marked with a "+" can be found online and on CD.

(7C) The Lord Chief Justice of England and Wales may nominate a judicial office holder (within the meaning of section 109(4) of the Constitutional Reform Act 2005) to exercise his functions under this section.

(7D) The Lord Chief Justice of Northern Ireland may nominate any of the following to exercise his functions under this section—

    (a) the holder of one of the offices listed in Schedule 1 to the Justice (Northern Ireland) Act 2002;

    (b) a Lord Justice of Appeal (as defined in section 88 of that Act).

Note —Amended by the Constitutional Reform Act 2005 s.15(1), Sch.4, para.278.   **3D–61**
The power to make such an order is exercisable by statutory instrument: s.20(1). A statutory instrument made under this section can be annulled by resolution of either House of Parliament: see s.20(5).

PARLIAMENTARY PROCEDURE

Statements of compatibility

19.—(1) A Minister of the Crown in charge of a Bill in either House **3D–62** of Parliament must, before Second Reading of the Bill—

    (a) make a statement to the effect that in his view the provisions of the Bill are compatible with the Convention rights ("a statement of compatibility"); or

    (b) make a statement to the effect that although he is unable to make a statement of compatibility the government nevertheless wishes the House to proceed with the Bill.

(2) The statement must be in writing and be published in such manner as the Minister making it considers appropriate.

Note —This section came into force on November 24, 1998: The Human Rights Act **3D–63** 1998 (Commencement) Order 1998 (SI 1998/2882).
"The Convention" has been held to mean "The Convention as given effect by the **3D–64** Act for the time being in relation to the United Kingdom": that is, the Convention and rights of the same scope as would be perceived in Strasbourg: see *.R (on the application of Al Jedda) v Secretary of State for Defence* [2007] UKHL 58; [2008] 2 W.L.R. 31. See also *R. (Quark Shipping Ltd) v Foreign Secretary* [2005] UKHL 57; [2005] 3 W.L.R. 837 at paras 25, 32, 56, 87 and 97, paras 59–63 and 112.

SUPPLEMENTAL

Orders, etc., under this Act

20.—(1) Any power of a Minister of the Crown to make an order **3D–65** under this Act is exercisable by statutory instrument.

(2) The power of the Lord Chancellor or the Secretary of State to make rules (other than rules of court) under section 2(3) or 7(9) is exercisable by statutory instrument.

(3) Any statutory instrument made under section 14, 15 or 16(7) must be laid before Parliament.

(4) No order may be made by the Lord Chancellor or the Secretary of State under section 1(4), 7(11) or 16(2) unless a draft of the

Paragraph numbers marked with a "+" can be found online and on CD.

order has been laid before, and approved by, each House of Parliament.

(5) Any statutory instrument made under section 18(7) or Schedule 4, or to which subsection (2) applies, shall be subject to annulment in pursuance of a resolution of either House of Parliament.

(6) The power of a Northern Ireland department to make—
> (a) rules under section 2(3)(c) or 7(9)(c), or
>
> (b) an order under section 7(11),

is exercisable by statutory rule for the purposes of the Statutory Rules (Northern Ireland) Order 1979.

(7) Any rules made under section 2(3)(c) or 7(9)(c) shall be subject to negative resolution; and section 41(6) of the Interpretation Act (Northern Ireland) 1954 (meaning of "subject to negative resolution") shall apply as if the power to make the rules were conferred by an Act of the Northern Ireland Assembly.

(8) No order may be made by a Northern Ireland department under section 7(11) unless a draft of the order has been laid before, and approved by, the Northern Ireland Assembly.

3D–66   *Note*—Amended by SI 2003/1887 and SI 2005/3429.

Interpretation, etc.

3D–67   **21.**—(1) In this Act—

> "amend" includes repeal and apply (with or without modification);
>
> "the appropriate Minister" means the Minister of the Crown having charge of the appropriate authorised government department (within the meaning of the Crown Proceedings Act 1947);
>
> "the Commission" means the European Commission of Human Rights;
>
> "the Convention" means the Convention for the Protection of Human Rights and Fundamental Freedoms, agreed by the Council of Europe at Rome on November 4, 1950 as it has effect for the time being in relation to the United Kingdom;
>
> "declaration of incompatibility" means a declaration under section 4;
>
> "Minister of the Crown" has the same meaning as in the Ministers of the Crown Act 1975;
>
> "Northern Ireland Minister" includes the First Minister and the deputy First Minister in Northern Ireland;
>
> "primary legislation" means any—
>> (a) public general Act;
>>
>> (b) local and personal Act;
>>
>> (c) private Act;
>>
>> (d) Measure of the Church Assembly;
>>
>> (e) Measure of the General Synod of the Church of England;
>>
>> (f) Order in Council—

Paragraph numbers marked with a "+" can be found online and on CD.

>>> (i) made in exercise of Her Majesty's Royal Prerogative;
>>> (ii) made under section 38(1)(a) of the Northern Ireland Constitution Act 1973 of the corresponding provision of the Northern Ireland Act 1998; or
>>> (iii) amending an Act of a kind mentioned in paragraph (a), (b) or (c); and includes an order or other instrument made under primary legislation (otherwise than by the National Assembly for Wales, Welsh Ministers, the First Minister for Wales, the Counsel General to the Welsh Assembly Government, a member of the Scottish Executive, a Northern Ireland Minister or a Northern Ireland department) to the extent to which it operates to bring one or more provisions of that legislation into force or amends any primary legislation;

"the First Protocol" means the protocol to the Convention agreed at Paris on March 20, 1952;

"the Eleventh Protocol" means the protocol to the Convention (restructuring the control machinery established by the Convention) agreed at Strasbourg on May 11, 1994;

"the Thirteenth Protocol" means the protocol to the Convention (concerning the abolition of the death penalty in all circumstances) agreed at Vilnius on 3rd May 2002;

"remedial order" means an order under section 10;

"subordinate legislation" means any—

> (a) Order in Council other than one—
>> (i) made in exercise of Her Majesty's Royal Prerogative;
>> (ii) made under section 38(1)(a) of the Northern Ireland Constitution Act 1973 or the corresponding provision of the Northern Ireland Act 1998; or;
>> (iii) amending an Act of a kind mentioned in the definition of primary legislation;
> (b) Act of the Scottish Parliament;
> (ba) Measure of the National Assembly for Wales;
> (bb) Act of the National Assembly for Wales;
> (c) Act of the Parliament of Northern Ireland;
> (d) Measure of the Assembly established under section 1 of the Northern Ireland Assembly Act 1973;
> (e) Act of the Northern Ireland Assembly;
> (f) order, rules, regulations, scheme, warrant, byelaw or other instrument made under primary legislation (except to the extent to which it operates to bring one or more provisions of that legislation into force or amends any primary legislation);

Paragraph numbers marked with a "+" can be found online and on CD.

(g) order, rules, regulations, scheme, warrant, byelaw or other instrument made under legislation mentioned in paragraph (b), (c), (d) or (e) or made under an Order in Council applying only to Northern Ireland;

(h) order, rules, regulations, scheme, warrant, byelaw or other instrument made by a member of the Scottish Executive, Welsh Ministers, the First Minister for Wales, the Counsel General to the Welsh Assembly Government, a Northern Ireland Minister or Northern Ireland department in exercise of prerogative or other executive functions of Her Majesty which are exercisable by such a person on behalf of Her Majesty;

"transferred matters" has the same meaning as in the Northern Ireland Act 1998; and

"tribunal" means any tribunal in which legal proceedings may be brought.

(2) The references in paragraphs (b) and (c) of section 2(1) to Articles are to Articles of the Convention as they had effect immediately before the coming into force of the 11th Protocol.

(3) The reference in paragraph (d) of section 2(1) to Article 46 includes a reference to Articles 32 and 54 of the Convention as they had effect immediately before the coming into force of the Eleventh Protocol.

(4) The references in section 2(1) to a report or decision of the Commission or a decision of the Committee of Ministers include references to a report or decision made as provided by paragraphs 3, 4 and 6 of Article 5 of the 11th Protocol (transitional provisions).

(5) Any liability under the Army Act 1955, the Air Force Act 1955 or the Naval Discipline Act 1957 to suffer death for an offence is replaced by a liability to imprisonment for life or any less punishment authorised by those Acts; and those Acts shall accordingly have effect with the necessary modifications.

3D–68   *Note* —Amended by SI 2004/1574; and by the Government of Wales Act 2006 s.160(1), Sch.10, para.56, with effect immediately after the date of the 2007 ordinary election (see ss.3 and 161 of the 2006 Act).

Short title, commencement, application and extent

3D–69   **22.**—(1) This Act may be cited as the Human Rights Act 1998.

(2) Sections 18, 20 and 21(5) and this section come into force on the passing of this Act.

(3) The other provisions of this Act come into force on such day as the Secretary of State may by order appoint; and different days may be appointed for different purposes.

(4) Paragraph (b) of subsection (1) of section 7 applies to proceedings brought by or at the instigation of a public authority whenever the act in question took place; but otherwise that subsection does not apply to an act taking place before the coming into force of that section.

(5) This Act binds the Crown.

Paragraph numbers marked with a "+" can be found online and on CD.

(6) This Act extends to Northern Ireland.

(7) Section 21(5), so far as it relates to any provision contained in the Army Act 1955, the Air Force Act 1955 or the Naval Discipline Act 1957, extends to any place to which that provision extends.

Section 22(2) & 22(3)

The date on which the Act received Royal Assent was November 9, 1998. Section 19 came into force on November 24, 1998: The Human Rights Act 1998 (Commencement) Order 1998 (SI 1998/2882). The remainder of the Act came into force on October 2, 2000: The Human Rights Act 1998 (Commencement No 2) Order 2000 (SI 2000/1851). **3D–70**

Section 22(4)

As to what constitutes an act "brought by or at the instigation of a public authority", see commentary to s.7, and *R. v Haringey LBC, Ex p. Ben-Abdelaziz* [2001] EWCA Civ 809; [2001] 1 W.L.R. 1485; [2001] A.C.D. 88, *Advocate General for Scotland v Mac-Donald; Pearce v Governing Body of Mayfield School* [2003] UKHL 34; [2004] 1 All E.R. 339; *Malcolm v Mackenzie* [2004] EWHC 339; [2004] EWCA Civ 1748; [2005] 1 W.L.R. 1238 (Ch). **3D–71**

The object of s.22(4) is to protect defendants to proceedings brought by or at the instigation of a public authority: see *Wilson v First County Trust Ltd (No.2)* [2001] FWCA Civ 633; [2002] Q.B. 74; [2001] 3 W.L.R. 42; [2001] 3 All E.R. 229, CA, para 90.

Limited retrospective effect of s.3 may be permitted if no unfairness would be caused to any individual: *Commissioner of Police for the Metropolis v Hurst* [2005] EWCA Civ 890; [2005] 1 W.L.R. 3892; [2005] H.R.L.R. 31; [2005] U.K.H.R.R. 1259.

Acts of courts or tribunals which took place before October 2, 2000, which were required by primary legislation and which were done according to the meaning of the legislation which applied at the time are not affected by the provisions of the Act: *R. v Kansal* [2001] UKHL 62, [2002] 2 A.C. 69; [2001] 3 W.L.R. 1562 and *R. v Lyons* [2002] UKHL 44; [2003] H.R.L.R. 6. (Though *cf R. v DPPEx p Kebilene* [2000] 2 A.C. 326; [1999] 3 W.L.R. 972; [1999] 4 All E.R. 801 HL and *R. v Lambert* [2001] 3 All E.R. 577 HL).

The Act cannot be relied upon to make conduct which was lawful at the time when it took place retrospectively unlawful: see *Wainwright v Home Office* [2001] EWCA Civ 2081; [2002] Q.B. 1334, CA. However, a continuing failure to act dating from before the entry into force of the Act may become unlawful from the entry into force of the Act, though damages may only be claimed from the date of the coming into force of the Act: *Marcic v Thames Water Utilities* [2002] EWCA Civ 64 (overruled on other grounds by *Marcic v Thames Water Utilities Ltd* [2003] UKHL 66; [2004] 2 A.C. 42; [2003] 3 W.L.R. 1603; [2004] 1 All E.R. 135).

For continuing violation of positive obligations to investigate under art.2 or art.3 see *Re McKerr* [2004] UKHL 12; [2004] 1 W.L.R. 807; [2004] 2 All E.R. 409; [2004] N.I. 212.

SCHEDULE 1

THE ARTICLES

PART I

THE CONVENTION

RIGHTS AND FREEDOMS

Article 2—Right to life

1. Everyone's right to life shall be protected by law. No one shall be deprived of his life intentionally save in the execution of a sentence of a court following his conviction of a crime for which this penalty is provided by law. **3D–72**

Paragraph numbers marked with a "+" can be found online and on CD.

2. Deprivation of life shall not be regarded as inflicted in contravention of this Article when it results from the use of force which is no more than absolutely necessary:

(a) in defence of any person from unlawful violence;

(b) in order to effect a lawful arrest or to prevent the escape of a person lawfully detained;

(c) in action lawfully taken for the purpose of quelling a riot or insurrection.

Article 3—Prohibition of torture

3D–73   No one shall be subjected to torture or to inhuman or degrading treatment or punishment.

Article 4—Prohibition of slavery and forced labour

3D–74   1. No one shall be held in slavery or servitude.

2. No one shall be required to perform forced or compulsory labour.

3. For the purpose of this Article the term "forced or compulsory labour" shall not include:

(a) any work required to be done in the ordinary course of detention imposed according to the provisions of Article 5 of this Convention or during conditional release from such detention;

(b) any service of a military character or, in case of conscientious objectors in countries where they are recognised, service exacted instead of compulsory military service;

(c) any service exacted in case of an emergency or calamity threatening the life or well-being of the community;

(d) any work or service which forms part of normal civic obligations.

Article 5—Right to liberty and security

3D–75   1. Everyone has the right to liberty and security of person. No one shall be deprived of his liberty save in the following cases and in accordance with a procedure prescribed by law:

(a) the lawful detention of a person after conviction by a competent court;

(b) the lawful arrest or detention of a person for non-compliance with the lawful order of a court or in order to secure the fulfilment of any obligation prescribed by law;

(c) the lawful arrest or detention of a person effected for the purpose of bringing him before the competent legal authority on reasonable suspicion of having committed an offence or when it is reasonably considered necessary to prevent his committing an offence or fleeing after having done so;

(d) the detention of a minor by lawful order for the purpose of educational supervision or his lawful detention for the purpose of bringing him before the competent legal authority;

(e) the lawful detention of persons for the prevention of the spreading of infectious diseases, of persons of unsound mind, alcoholics or drug addicts or vagrants;

(f) the lawful arrest or detention of a person to prevent his effecting an unauthorised entry into the country or of a person against whom action is being taken with a view to deportation or extradition.

2. Everyone who is arrested shall be informed promptly, in a language which he understands, of the reasons for his arrest and of any charge against him.

3. Everyone arrested or detained in accordance with the provisions of paragraph 1(c) of this Article shall be brought promptly before a judge or other officer authorised by law to exercise judicial power and shall be entitled to trial within a reasonable time or to release pending trial. Release may be conditioned by guarantees to appear for trial.

4. Everyone who is deprived of his liberty by arrest or detention shall be entitled to take proceedings by which the lawfulness of his detention shall be decided speedily by a court and his release ordered if the detention is not lawful.

Paragraph numbers marked with a "+" can be found online and on CD.

5. Everyone who has been the victim of arrest or detention in contravention of the provisions of this Article shall have an enforceable right to compensation.

Article 6—Right to a fair trial

3D–76

1. In the determination of his civil rights and obligations or of any criminal charge against him, everyone is entitled to a fair and public hearing within a reasonable time by an independent and impartial tribunal established by law. Judgment shall be pronounced publicly but the press and public may be excluded from all or part of the trial in the interest of morals, public order or national security in a democratic society, where the interests of juveniles or the protection of the private life of the parties so require, or to the extent strictly necessary in the opinion of the court in special circumstances where publicity would prejudice the interests of justice.

2. Everyone charged with a criminal offence shall be presumed innocent until proved guilty according to law.

3. Everyone charged with a criminal offence has the following minimum rights:

   (a) to be informed promptly, in a language which he understands and in detail, of the nature and cause of the accusation against him;

   (b) to have adequate time and facilities for the preparation of his defence;

   (c) to defend himself in person or through legal assistance of his own choosing or, if he has not sufficient means to pay for legal assistance, to be given it free when the interest of justice so require;

   (d) to examine or have examined witnesses against him and to obtain the attendance and examination of witnesses on his behalf under the same conditions as witnesses against him;

   (e) to have the free assistance of an interpreter if he cannot understand or speak the language used in court.

Article 7—No punishment without law

3D–77

1. No one shall be held guilty of any criminal offence on account of any act or omission which did not constitute a criminal offence under national or international law at the time when it was committed. Nor shall a heavier penalty be imposed than the one that was applicable at the time the criminal offence was committed.

2. The Article shall not prejudice the trial and punishment of any person for any act or omission which, at the time when it was committed, was criminal according to the general principles of law recognised by civilised nations.

Article 8—Right to respect for private and family life

3D–78

1. Everyone has the right to respect for his private and family life, his home and his correspondence.

2. There shall be no interference by a public authority with the exercise of this right except such as is in accordance with the law and is necessary in a democratic society in the interests of national security, public safety or the economic well-being of the country, for the prevention of disorder or crime, for the protection of health or morals, or for the protection of the rights and freedoms of others.

Article 9—Freedom of thought, conscience and religion

3D–79

1. Everyone has the right to freedom of thought, conscience and religion; this right includes freedom to change his religion or belief and freedom, either alone or in community with others and in public or private, to manifest his religion or belief, in worship, teaching, practice and observance.

2. Freedom to manifest one's religion or beliefs shall be subject only to such limitations as are prescribed by law and are necessary in a democratic society in the interests of public safety, for the protection of public order, health or morals, or for the protection of the rights and freedoms of others.

Article 10—Freedom of expression

3D–80

1. Everyone has the right to freedom of expression. This right shall include freedom to hold opinions and to receive and impart information and ideas without interference by public authority and regardless of frontiers. This Article shall not prevent States from requiring the licensing of broadcasting, television or cinema enterprises.

Paragraph numbers marked with a "+" can be found online and on CD.

2. The exercise of these freedoms, since it carries with it duties and responsibilities, may be subject to such formalities, conditions, restrictions or penalties as are prescribed by law and are necessary in a democratic society, in the interests of national security, territorial integrity or public safety, for the prevention of disorder or crime, for the protection of health or morals, for the protection of the reputation or rights of others, for preventing the disclosure of information received in confidence, or for maintaining the authority and impartiality of the judiciary.

Article 11—Freedom of assembly and association

3D–81 1. Everyone has the right to freedom of peaceful assembly and to freedom of association with others, including the right to formand to join trade unions for the protection of his interests.

2. No restrictions shall be placed on the exercise of these rights other than such as are prescribed by law and are necessary in a democratic society in the interests of national security or public safety, for the prevention of disorder or crime, for the protection of health or morals or for the protection of the rights and freedoms of others. This Article shall not prevent the imposition of lawful restrictions on the exercise of these rights by members of the armed forces, of the police or of the administration of the State.

Article 12—Right to marry

3D–82 Men and women of marriageable age have the right to marry and to found a family, according to the national laws governing the exercise of this right.

Article 14—Prohibition of discrimination

3D–83 The enjoyment of the rights and freedoms set forth in this Convention shall be secured without discrimination on any ground such as sex, race, colour, language, religion, political or other opinion, national or social origin, association with a national minority, property, birth or other status.

Article 16—Restrictions on political activity of aliens

3D–84 Nothing in Articles 10, 11 and 14 shall be regarded as preventing the High Contracting Parties from imposing restrictions on the political activity of aliens.

Article 17—Prohibition of abuse of rights

3D–85 Nothing in this Convention may be interpreted as implying for any State, group or person any right to engage in any activity or perform any act aimed at the destruction of any of the rights and freedoms set forth herein or at their limitation to a greater extent than is provided for in the Convention.

Article 18—Limitation on use of restrictions on rights

3D–86 The restrictions permitted under this Convention to the said rights and freedoms shall not be applied for any purpose other than those for which they have been prescribed.

PART II

THE FIRST PROTOCOL

Article 1—Protection of property

3D–87 Every natural or legal person is entitled to the peaceful enjoyment of his possessions. No one shall be deprived of his possessions except in the public interest and subject to the conditions provided for by law and by the general principles of international law.

The preceding provisions shall not, however, in any way impair the right of a State to enforce such laws as it deems necessary to control the use of property in accordance with the general interest or to secure the payment of taxes or other contributions or penalties.

Article 2—Right to education

3D–88 No person shall be denied the right to education. In the exercise of any functions which it assumes in relation to education and to teaching, the State shall respect the

Paragraph numbers marked with a "+" can be found online and on CD.

right of parents to ensure such education and teaching in conformity with their own religious and philosophical convictions.

Article 3—Right to free elections

The High Contracting Parties undertake to hold free elections at reasonable intervals **3D–89** by secret ballot, under conditions which will ensure the free expression of the opinion of the people in the choice of the legislature.

PART III

THE THIRTEENTH PROTOCOL

Article 1—Abolition of the death penalty

The death penalty shall be abolished. No one shall be condemned to such penalty or **3D–90** executed.

Note —Substituted by the Human Rights Act 1998 (Amendment) Order 2004 (SI **3D–91** 2004/1574), art.2(3).

Article 2—Death penalty in time of war

A State may make provision in its law for the death penalty in respect of acts com- **3D–92** mitted in time of war or of imminent threat of war; such penalty shall be applied only in the instances laid down in the law and in accordance with its provisions. The State shall communicate to the Secretary General of the Council of Europe the relevant pro- visions of that law.

European Convention on Human Rights

ARTICLE 1

OBLIGATION TO RESPECT HUMAN RIGHTS

The High Contracting Parties shall secure to everyone within their jurisdiction the **3D–93** rights and freedoms defined in Section I of this Convention.

* * * *

ARTICLE 13

RIGHT TO AN EFFECTIVE REMEDY

Everyone whose rights and freedoms as set forth in this Convention are violated **3D–94** shall have an effective remedy before a national authority notwithstanding that the violation has been committed by persons acting in an official capacity.

Editorial note —Although not among the Convention rights to which s.1(2) of the **3D–95** Human Rights Act 1998 gives effect, Arts 1 and 13 of the Convention are also of significance. Their text is set out above.

Paragraph numbers marked with a "+" can be found online and on CD.

3E INSOLVENCY PROCEEDINGS

PRACTICE DIRECTION—INSOLVENCY PROCEEDINGS

Part One

1. General

1.1 In this Practice Direction:

(1) "The Act" means the Insolvency Act 1986 and includes the Act as applied to limited liability partnerships by the Limited Liability Partnerships Regulations 2001;

(2) "The Insolvency Rules" means the rules for the time being in force and made under s.411 and s.412 of the Act in relation to insolvency proceedings;

(3) "CPR" means the Civil Procedure Rules and "CPR" followed by a Part or rule by number means the Part or rule with that number in those Rules;

(4) "RSC" followed by an Order by number means the Order with that number set out in Schedule 1 to the CPR;

(5) "Insolvency proceedings" means any proceedings under the Act, the Insolvency Rules, the Administration of Insolvent Estates of Deceased Persons Order 1986 (SI 1986/1999), the Insolvent Partnership Order 1986 (SI 1986/2142), the Insolvent Partnerships Order 1994 (SI 1994/2421) or the Limited Liability Partnerships Regulations 2001.

(6) References to a 'company' shall include a limited liability partnership and references to a 'contributory' shall include a member of a limited liability partnership.

1.2 This Practice Direction shall come into effect on 26th April 1999 and shall replace all previous Practice Notes and Practice Directions relating to insolvency proceedings.

1.3 Except where the Insolvency Rules otherwise provide, service of documents in insolvency proceedings in the High Court will be the responsibility of the parties and will not be undertaken by the court.

1.4 Where CPR Part 2.4 provides for the court to perform any act, that act may be performed by a Registrar in Bankruptcy for the purpose of insolvency proceedings in the High Court.

1.5 A writ of execution to enforce any order made in insolvency proceedings in the High Court may be issued on the authority of a Registrar.

1.6(1) This paragraph applies where an insolvency practitioner ("the outgoing office holder") holds office as a liquidator, administrator, trustee or supervisor in more than one case and dies, retires from practice as an insolvency practitioner or is otherwise unable or unwilling to continue in office.

(2) A single application may be made to a Judge of the Chancery Division of the High Court by way of ordinary application in Form 7.2 for the appointment of a substitute office

Paragraph numbers marked with a "+" can be found online and on CD.

holder or office holders in all cases in which the outgoing office holder holds office, and for the transfer of each such case to the High Court for the purpose only of making such an order.

(3)   The application may be made by any of the following:

(i)   the outgoing office holder (if he is able and willing to do so);

(ii)   any person who holds office jointly with the outgoing office holder;

(iii)   any person who is proposed to be appointed as a substitute for the outgoing office holder; or

(iv)   any creditor in the cases where the substitution is proposed to be made.

(4)   The outgoing office holder (if he is not the applicant) and every person who holds office jointly with the office holder must be made a respondent to the application, but it is not necessary to join any other person as a respondent or to serve the application upon any other person unless the Judge or Registrar in the High Court so directs.

(5)   The application should contain schedules setting out the nature of the office held, the identity of the Court currently having jurisdiction over each case and its name and number.

(6)   The application must be supported by evidence setting out the circumstances which have given rise to the need to make a substitution and exhibiting the written consent to act of each person who is proposed to be appointed in place of the outgoing office holder.

(7)   The Judge will in the first instance consider the application on paper and make such order as he thinks fit. In particular he may do any of the following:

(i)   make an order directing the transfer to the High Court of those cases not already within its jurisdiction for the purpose only of the substantive application;

(ii)   if he considers that the papers are in order and that the matter is straightforward, make an order on the substantive application;

(iii)   give any directions which he considers to be necessary including (if appropriate) directions for the joinder of any additional respondents or requiring the service of the application on any person or requiring additional evidence to be provided;

(iv)   if he does not himself make an order on the substantive application when the matter is first before him, give directions for the further consideration of the substantive application by himself or another Judge of the Chancery Division or adjourn the substantive application to the Registrar for him to make such order upon it as is appropriate.

(8)   An order of the kind referred to in sub-paragraph (6)(i)

Paragraph numbers marked with a "+" can be found online and on CD.

shall follow the draft order in **Form PDIP 3** set out in the Schedule hereto and an order granting the substantive application shall follow the draft order in **Form PDIP 4** set out in the schedule hereto (subject in each case to such modifications as may be necessary or appropriate).

(9) It is the duty of the applicant to ensure that a sealed copy of every order transferring any case to the High Court and of every order which is made on a substantive application is lodged with the court having jurisdiction over each case affected by such order for filing on the court file relating to that case.

(10) It will not be necessary for the file relating to any case which is transferred to the High Court in accordance with this paragraph to be sent to the High Court unless a Judge or Registrar so directs.

Part Two

Companies

2. Advertisement of winding up petition

2.1 Insolvency Rule 4.11(2)(b) is mandatory, and designed to **3E–2** ensure that the class remedy of winding up by the court is made available to all creditors, and is not used as a means of putting pressure on the company to pay the petitioner's debt. Failure to comply with the rule, without good reason accepted by the court, may lead to the summary dismissal of the petition on the return date (Insolvency Rule 4.11(5)). If the court, in its discretion, grants an adjournment, this will be on condition that the petition is advertised in due time for the adjourned hearing. No further adjournment for the purpose of advertisement will normally be granted.

2.2 Copies of every advertisement published in connection with a winding up petition must be lodged with the Court as soon as possible after publication and in any event not later than the day specified in Insolvency Rule 4.14 of the Insolvency Rules 1986. This direction applies even if the advertisement is defective in any way (*e.g.* is published at a date not in accordance with the Insolvency Rules, or omits or misprints some important words) or if the petitioner decides not to pursue the petition (e.g. on receiving payment).

3. Certificate of compliance—time for filing

3.1 In the High Court in order to assist practitioners and the Court **3E–3** the time laid down by Insolvency Rule 4.14 of the Insolvency Rules 1986, for filing a certificate of compliance and a copy of the advertisement, is hereby extended to not later than 4.30 p.m. on the Friday preceding the day on which the petition is to be heard. Applications to file the certificate and the copy advertisement after 4.30 p.m. on the Friday will only be allowed if some good reason is shown for the delay.

Paragraph numbers marked with a "+" can be found online and on CD.

4. Errors in petitions

3E–4 **4.1** Applications for leave to amend errors in petitions which are discovered subsequent to a winding up order being made should be made to the Court Manager in the High Court and to the District Judge in the county court.

4.2 Where the error is an error in the name of the company, the Court Manager in the High Court and the District Judge in the county court may make any necessary amendments to ensure that the winding up order is drawn with the correct name of the company inserted. If there is any doubt, e.g. where there might be another company in existence which could be confused with the company to be wound up, the Court Manager will refer the application to the Registrar and the District Judge may refer it to the Judge.

4.3 Where an error is an error in the registered office of the company and any director or member of the company claims that the company was unaware of the petition by reason of it having been served at the wrong registered office, it will be open to them to apply to rescind the winding up order in the usual way.

4.4 Where it is discovered that the company had been struck off the Register of Companies prior to the winding up order being made, the matter must be restored to the list before the order is entered to enable an order for the restoration of the name to be made as well as the order to wind up.

5. Distribution of business

3E–5 **5.1** The following applications shall be made direct to the Judge and, unless otherwise ordered, shall be heard in public—

   (1) Applications to commit any person to prison for contempt;

   (2) Applications for urgent interim relief (e.g. applications pursuant to s.127 of the Act prior to any winding up order being made);

   (3) Applications to restrain the presentation or advertisement of a petition to wind up; or

   (4) Applications for the appointment of a provisional liquidator;

   (5) Petitions for administration orders or an interim order upon such a Petition;

   (6) Applications after an administration order has been made pursuant to s.14(3) of the Act (for directions) or s.18(3) of the Act (to vary or discharge the order);

   (7) Petitions to discharge administration orders and to wind up;

   (8) Applications pursuant to s.5(3) of the Act (to stay a winding up or discharge an administration order or for directions) where a voluntary arrangement has been approved;

   (9) Appeals from a decision made by a County Court or by a Registrar of the High Court.

5.2 Subject to paragraph 5.4 below all other applications shall be made to the Registrar or the District Judge in the first instance who may give any necessary directions and may, in the exercise of his discretion, either hear and determine it himself or refer it to the Judge.

Paragraph numbers marked with a "+" can be found online and on CD.

5.3 The following matters will also be heard in public—

(1) Petitions to wind up;

(2) Public examinations;

(3) All matters and applications heard by the Judge, except those referred by the Registrar or the District Judge to be heard in private or so directed by the Judge to be heard.

5.4 In accordance with directions given by the Lord Chancellor the Registrar has authorised certain applications in the High Court to be dealt with by the Court Manager of the Companies Court, pursuant to Insolvency Rule 13.2(2). The applications are:

(1) To extend or abridge time prescribed by the Insolvency Rules in connection with winding up (Insolvency Rule 4.3 and 12.9);

(2) For substituted service of winding up petitions (Insolvency Rule 4.8(6));

(3) To withdraw petitions (Insolvency Rule 4.15);

(4) For the substitution of a petitioner (Insolvency Rule 4.19);

(5) By the Official Receiver for limited disclosure of a statement of affairs (Insolvency Rule 4.35);

(6) By the Official Receiver for relief from duties imposed upon him by the rules (Insolvency Rule 4.47);

(7) By the Official Receiver for permission to give notice of a meeting by advertisement only (Insolvency Rule 4.59);

(8) To transfer proceedings from the High Court to a County Court (Insolvency Rule 7.11);

(9) For permission to amend any originating application.

[N.B. In District Registries all such applications must be made to the District Judge].

6. Drawing up of orders

6.1 The Court will draw up all orders except orders on the application of the Official Receiver or for which the Treasury Solicitor is responsible under the existing practice. **3E–6**

7. Rescission of a winding up order

7.1 Any application for the rescission of a winding up order shall be made within seven days after the date on which the order was made (Insolvency Rule 7.47(4)). Notice of any such application must be given to the Official Receiver. **3E–7**

7.2 Applications will only be entertained if made (a) by a creditor, or (b) by a contributory, or (c) by the company jointly with a creditor or with a contributory. The application must be supported by written evidence of assets and liabilities.

7.3 In the case of an unsuccessful application the costs of the petitioning creditor, the supporting creditors and of the Official Receiver will normally be ordered to be paid by the creditor or the contributory making or joining in the application. The reason for this is that if the costs of an unsuccessful application are made payable by the company, they fall unfairly on the general body of creditors.

Paragraph numbers marked with a "+" can be found online and on CD.

7.4 Cases in which the making of the winding up order has not been opposed may, if the application is made promptly, be dealt with on a statement by the applicant's legal representative of the circumstances; but apart from such cases, the court will normally require any application to be supported by written evidence.

7.5 There is no need to issue a form of application (Form 7.2) as the petition is restored before the Court.

8. Restraint of presentation of a winding-up petition

3E–8 **8.1** An application to restrain presentation of a Winding-up petition must be made to the Judge by the issue of an Originating Application (Form 7.1).

Part Three

Personal Insolvency—Bankruptcy

9. Distribution of business

3E–9 **9.1** The following applications shall be made direct to the Judge and unless otherwise ordered shall be heard in public:

   (1)   Applications for the committal of any person to prison for contempt;

   (2)   Application for injunctions or for the modification or discharge of injunctions;

   (3)   Applications for interlocutory relief or directions after the matter has been referred to the Judge.

9.2 All other applications shall be made to the Registrar or the District Judge in the first instance. He shall give any necessary directions and may, if the application is within his jurisdiction to determine, in his discretion either hear and determine it himself or refer it to the Judge.

9.3 The following matters shall be heard in public:

   (1)   The public examination of debtors;

   (2)   Opposed applications for discharge or for the suspension or lifting of the suspension of discharge;

   (3)   Opposed applications for permission to be a director;

   (4)   In any case where the petition was presented or the receiving order or order for adjudication was made before the appointed day, those matters and applications specified in Rule 8 of the Bankruptcy Rules 1952;

   (5)   All matters and applications heard by the Judge, except matters and applications referred by the Registrar or the District Judge to be heard by the Judge in private or directed by the Judge to be so heard.

9.4 All petitions presented will be listed under the name of the debtor.

9.5 In accordance with Directions given by the Lord Chancellor the Registrar has authorised certain applications in the High Court to be dealt with by the Court Manager of the Bankruptcy Court pursuant to Insolvency Rule 13.2(2). The applications are:

Paragraph numbers marked with a "+" can be found online and on CD.

(1)   by petitioning creditors: to extend time for hearing petitions (s.376 of the Act).

(2)   by the Official Receiver:

(a) To transfer proceedings from the High Court to a County Court (Insolvency Rule 7.13);

(b) to amend the full title of the proceedings (Insolvency Rule 6.35 and 6.47).

[N.B. In District Registries all such applications must be made to the District Judge].

10. Service abroad of statutory demand

10.1 A statutory demand is not a document issued by the Court. **3E–10** Leave to serve out of the jurisdiction is not, therefore, required.

10.2 Insolvency Rule 6.3(2) ("Requirements as to service") applies to service of the statutory demand whether outside or within the jurisdiction.

10.3 A creditor wishing to serve a statutory demand outside the jurisdiction in a foreign country with which a civil procedure convention has been made (including the Hague Convention) may and, if the assistance of a British Consul is desired, must adopt the procedure prescribed by rule 6.42. In the case of any doubt whether the country is a "convention country", enquiries should be made of the Queen's Bench Masters' Secretary Department, Room E216, Royal Courts of Justice.

10.4 In all other cases, service of the demand must be effected by private arrangement in accordance with Insolvency Rule 6.3(2) and local foreign law.

10.5 When a statutory demand is to be served out of the jurisdiction, the time limits of 21 days and 18 days respectively referred to in the demand must be amended. For this purpose reference should be made to the table set out in the practice direction supplementing Section III of Part 6.

10.6 A creditor should amend the statutory demand as follows:

(1)   For any reference to 18 days there must be substituted the appropriate number of days set out in the table plus 4 days, and

(2)   for any reference to 21 days there must be substituted the appropriate number of days in the table plus 7 days.

Attention is drawn to the fact that in all forms of the statutory demand the figure 18 and the figure 21 occurs in more than one place.

11. Substituted service

Statutory demands

11.1 The creditor is under an obligation to do all that is reasonable **3E–11** to bring the statutory demand to the debtor's attention and, if practicable, to cause personal service to be effected. Where it is not possible to effect prompt personal service, service may be effected by

Paragraph numbers marked with a "+" can be found online and on CD.

other means such as first class post or by insertion through a letter box.

11.2 Advertisement can only be used as a means of substituted service where:

(1)   The demand is based on a judgment or order of any Court;

(2)   The debtor has absconded or is keeping out of the way with a view to avoiding service and,

(3)   There is no real prospect of the sum due being recovered by execution or other process.

As there is no statutory form of advertisement, the Court will accept an advertisement in the following form:

STATUTORY DEMAND

(Debt for liquidated sum payable immediately following a judgment or order of the Court)

_____

To (Block letters)

of

TAKE NOTICE that a statutory demand has been issued by:

Name of Creditor:

Address:

The creditor demands payment of £   the amount now due on a judgment or order of the (High Court of Justice   Division) (.........County Court) dated the   day of 199   .

The statutory demand is an important document and it is deemed to have been served on you on the date of the first appearance of this advertisement. You must deal with this demand within 21 days of the service upon you or you could be made bankrupt and your property and goods taken away from you. If you are in any doubt as to your position, you should seek advice immediately from a solicitor or your nearest Citizens' Advice Bureau. The statutory demand can be obtained or is available for inspection and collection from:

Name:

Address:

(Solicitor for) the Creditor

Tel. No.   Reference:

You have only 21 days from the date of the first appearance of this advertisement before the creditor may present a Bankruptcy Petition. You have only 18 days within which to apply to the Court to set aside the demand.

11.3 In all cases where substituted service is effected, the creditor

Paragraph numbers marked with a "+" can be found online and on CD.

must have taken all those steps which would justify the Court making an order for substituted service of a petition. The steps to be taken to obtain an order for substituted service of a petition are set out below. Failure to comply with these requirements may result in the Court declining to file the petition: Insolvency Rule 6.11(9).

Petitions

11.4 In most cases, evidence of the following steps will suffice to justify an order for substituted service:

(1) One personal call at the residence and place of business of the debtor where both are known or at either of such places as is known. Where it is known that the debtor has more than one residential or business address, personal calls should be made at all the addresses.

(2) Should the creditor fail to effect service, a first class prepaid letter should be written to the debtor referring to the call(s), the purpose of the same and the failure to meet with the debtor, adding that a further call will be made for the same purpose on the   day of   19 at   hours at   (place). At least two business days notice should be given of the appointment and copies of the letter sent to all known addresses of the debtor. The appointment letter should also state that

    (a) in the event of the time and place not being convenient, the debtor is to name some other time and place reasonably convenient for the purpose;

    (b) (Statutory Demands) if the debtor fails to keep the appointment the creditor proposes to serve the debtor by [advertisement] [post] [insertion through a letter box] or as the case may be, and that, in the event of a bankruptcy petition being presented, the Court will be asked to treat such service as service of the demand on the debtor;

    (c) (Petitions) if the debtor fails to keep the appointment, application will be made to the Court for an order for substituted service either by advertisement, or in such other manner as the Court may think fit.

(3) In attending any appointment made by letter, inquiry should be made as to whether the debtor has received all letters left for him. If the debtor is away, inquiry should also be made as to whether or not letters are being forwarded to an address within the jurisdiction (England and Wales) or elsewhere.

(4) If the debtor is represented by a Solicitor, an attempt should be made to arrange an appointment for personal service through such Solicitor. The Insolvency Rules enable a Solicitor to accept service of a statutory demand on behalf of his client but there is no similar provision in respect of service of a bankruptcy petition.

(5) The written evidence filed pursuant to Insolvency Rule 6.11

Paragraph numbers marked with a "+" can be found online and on CD.

should deal with all the above matters including all relevant facts as to the debtor's whereabouts and whether the appointment letter(s) have been returned.

11.5 Where the Court makes an order for service by first class ordinary post, the order will normally provide that service be deemed to be effected on the seventh day after posting. The same method of calculating service may be applied to calculating the date of service of a statutory demand.

12. Setting aside a statutory demand

3E–12   **12.1** The application (Form 6.4) and written evidence in support (Form 6.5) exhibiting a copy of the statutory demand must be filed in Court within 18 days of service of the statutory demand on the debtor. Where service is effected by advertisement in a newspaper the period of 18 days is calculated from the date of the first appearance of the advertisement. Three copies of each document must be lodged with the application to enable the Court to serve notice of the hearing date on the applicant, the creditor and the person named in Part B of the statutory demand.

12.2 Where, to avoid expense, copies of the documents are not lodged with the application in the High Court, any order of the Registrar fixing a venue is conditional upon copies of the documents being lodged on the next business day after the Registrar's order otherwise the application will be deemed to have been dismissed.

12.3 Where the statutory demand is based on a judgment or order, the Court will not at this stage go behind the judgment or order and inquire into the validity of the debt nor, as a general rule, will it adjourn the application to await the result of an application to set aside the judgment or order.

12.4 Where the debtor (a) claims to have a counterclaim, set off or cross demand (whether or not he could have raised it in the action in which the judgment or order was obtained) which equals or exceeds the amount of the debt or debts specified in the statutory demand or (b) disputes the debt (not being a debt subject to a judgment or order) the Court will normally set aside the statutory demand if, in its opinion, on the evidence there is a genuine triable issue.

12.5 A debtor who wishes to apply to set aside a statutory demand after the expiration of 18 days from the date of service of the statutory demand must apply for an extension of time within which to apply. If the applicant wishes to apply for an injunction to restrain presentation of a petition the application must be made to the Judge. Paragraphs 1 and 2 of Form 6.5 (Affidavit in Support of Application to set Aside Statutory Demand) should be used in support of the application for an extension of time with the following additional paragraphs:

"3. That to the best of my knowledge and belief the creditor(s) named in the demand has/have not presented a petition against me.

4. That the reasons for my failure to apply to set aside the demand within 18 days after service are as follows: ... "

Paragraph numbers marked with a "+" can be found online and on CD.

If application is made to restrain presentation of a bankruptcy petition the following additional paragraph should be added:

"5. Unless restrained by injunction the creditor(s) may present a bankruptcy petition against me."

13. Proof of service of a statutory demand

13.1 Insolvency Rule 6.11(3) provides that, if the Statutory Demand   **3E–13** has been served personally, the written evidence must be provided by the person who effected that service. Insolvency Rule 6.11(4) provides that, if service of the demand (however effected) has been acknowledged in writing, the evidence of service must be provided by the creditor or by a person acting on his behalf. Insolvency Rule 6.11(5) provides that, if neither paragraphs (3) or (4) apply, the written evidence must be provided by a person having direct knowledge of the means adopted for serving the demand.

13.2 Form 6.11 (Evidence of personal service of the statutory demand): this form should only be used where the demand has been served personally and acknowledged in writing (see Insolvency Rule 6.11(4)). If the demand has not been acknowledged in writing, the written evidence should be provided by the Process Server and Paragraphs 2 and 3 (part of Form 6.11) should be omitted (See Insolvency Rule 6.11(3)).

13.3 Form 6.12 (Evidence of Substituted Service of the Statutory Demand): this form can be used whether or not service of the demand has been acknowledged in writing. Paragraphs 4 and 5 (part) provide for the alternatives. Practitioners are reminded, however, that the appropriate person to provide the written evidence may not be the same in both cases. If the demand has been acknowledged in writing, the appropriate person is the creditor or a person acting on his behalf. If the demand has not been acknowledged, that person must be someone having direct knowledge of the means adopted for serving the demand.

Practitioners may find it more convenient to allow process servers to carry out the necessary investigation whilst reserving to themselves the service of the demand. In these circumstances Paragraph 1 should be deleted and the following paragraph substituted:

"1. Attempts have been made to serve the demand, full details of which are set out in the accompanying affidavit of ..."

13.4 "Written evidence" means an affidavit or a witness statement.

14. Extension of hearing date of petition

14.1 Late applications for extension of hearing dates under   **3E–14** Insolvency Rule 6.28, and failure to attend on the listed hearing of a petition, will be dealt with as follows:

(1)   If an application is submitted less than two clear working days before the hearing date (for example, later than Monday for Thursday, or Wednesday for Monday) the costs of the application will not be allowed under Insolvency Rule 6.28(3).

(2)   If the petition has not been served and no extension has

Paragraph numbers marked with a "+" can be found online and on CD.

been granted by the time fixed for the hearing of the petition, and if no one attends for the hearing, the petition will be re-listed for hearing about 21 days later. The Court will notify the petitioning creditor's solicitors (or the petitioning creditor in person), and any known supporting or opposing creditors or their solicitors, of the new date and times. Written evidence should then be filed on behalf of the petitioning creditor explaining fully the reasons for the failure to apply for an extension or to appear at the hearing, and (if appropriate) giving reasons why the petition should not be dismissed.

(3) On the re-listed hearing the Court may dismiss the petition if not satisfied it should be adjourned or a further extension granted.

14.2 All applications for extension should include a statement of the date fixed for the hearing of the petition.

14.3 The petitioning creditor should attend (by solicitors or in person) on or before the hearing date to ascertain whether the application has reached the file and been dealt with. It should not be assumed that an extension will be granted.

15. Bankruptcy petition

3E–15   **15.** To help in the completion of the form of a creditor's bankruptcy petition, attention is drawn to the following points:

15.1 The petition does not require dating, signing or witnessing.

15.2 In the title it is only necessary to recite the debtor's name; *e.g.* Re John William Smith or Re J W Smith (Male). Any alias or trading name will appear in the body of the petition. This also applies to all other statutory forms other than those which require the "full title".

15.3 Where the petition is based on a statutory demand, only the debt claimed in the demand may be included in the petition.

15.4 In completing Paragraph 2 of the petition, attention is drawn to Insolvency Rule 6.8(1)(a) to (c), particularly where the "aggregate sum" is made up of a number of debts.

15.5 Date of service of the statutory demand (paragraph 4 of the petition):

(1) In the case of personal service, the date of service as set out in the affidavit of service should be recited and whether service is effected before/after 1700 hours on Monday to Friday or at any time on a Saturday or a Sunday: see CPR Part 6.7(2) and (3).

(2) In the case of substituted service (otherwise than by advertisement), the date alleged in the affidavit of service should be recited: see "11. Substituted Service" above.

(3) In the strictly limited case of service by advertisement under Insolvency Rule 6.3, the date to be alleged is the date of the advertisement's appearance or, as the case may be, its first appearance: see Insolvency Rules 6.3(3) and 6.11(8).

15.6 There is no need to include in the petition details of the person authorised to present it.

Paragraph numbers marked with a "+" can be found online and on CD.

15.7 Certificates at the end of the petition:

(1)   The period of search for prior petitions has been reduced to eighteen months.

(2)   Where a statutory demand is based wholly or in part on a County Court judgment, the following certificate is to be added:

"I/We certify that on the day of   19 I/We attended on the County Court and was/were informed by an officer of the Court that no money had been paid into Court in the action or matter   v   Claim No   pursuant to the statutory demand."

This certificate will not be required when the demand also requires payment of a separate debt, not based on a County Court judgment, the amount of which exceeds the bankruptcy level (at present £750).

15.8 Deposit on petition: the deposit will be taken by the Court and forwarded to the Official Receiver. In the High Court, the petition fee and deposit should be handed to the Supreme Court Accounts Office, Fee Stamping Room, who will record the receipt and will impress two entries on the original petition, one in respect of the Court fee and the other in respect of the deposit. In the County Court, the petition fee and deposit should be handed to the duly authorised officer of the Court's staff who will record its receipt.

In all cases cheque(s) for the whole amount should be made payable to "HM Paymaster General".

15.9 On the hearing of a petition for a bankruptcy order, in order to satisfy the Court that the debt on which the petition is founded has not been paid or secured or compounded the Court will normally accept as sufficient a certificate signed by the person representing the petitioning creditor in the following form:

"I certify that I have/my firm has made enquiries of the petitioning creditor(s) within the last business day prior to the hearing/adjourned hearing and to the best of my knowledge and belief the debt on which the petition is founded is still due and owing and has not been paid or secured or compounded save as to

Signed   Dated "

For convenience in the High Court this certificate will be incorporated in the attendance slip, which will be filed after the hearing. A fresh certificate will be required on each adjourned hearing.

15.10 On the occasion of the adjourned hearing of a petition for a bankruptcy order, in order to satisfy the Court that the petitioner has complied with Insolvency Rule 6.29, the petitioner will be required to file written evidence of the manner in which notice of the making of the order of adjournment and of the venue for the adjourned hearing has been sent to:

(i)   the debtor, and

(ii)   any creditor who has given notice under Insolvency Rule 6.23 but was not present at the hearing when the order for adjournment was made.

Paragraph numbers marked with a "+" can be found online and on CD.

16. Orders without attendance

3E–16   **16.1** In suitable cases the Court will normally be prepared to make orders under Part VIII of the Act (Individual Voluntary Arrangements), without the attendance of either party, provided there is no bankruptcy order in existence and (so far as is known) no pending petition. The orders are:

(1)   A fourteen day interim order with the application adjourned 14 days for consideration of the nominee's report, where the papers are in order, and the nominee's signed consent to act includes a waiver of notice of the application or a consent by the nominee to the making of an interim order without attendance.

(2)   A standard order on consideration of the nominee's report, extending the interim order to a date 7 weeks after the date of the proposed meeting, directing the meeting to be summoned and adjourning to a date about 3 weeks after the meeting. Such an Order may be made without attendance if the nominee's report has been delivered to the Court and complies with Section 256(1) of the Act and Insolvency Rule 5.10(2) and (3) and proposes a date for the meeting not less than 14 days from that on which the nominee's report is filed in Court under Insolvency Rule 5.10 nor more than 28 days from that on which that report is considered by the Court under Insolvency Rule 5.12.

(3)   A "concertina" Order, combining orders as under (1) and (2) above. Such an order may be made without attendance if the initial application for an interim order is accompanied by a report of the nominee and the conditions set out in (1) and (2) above are satisfied.

(4)   A final order on consideration of the Chairman's report. Such an order may be made without attendance if the Chairman's report has been filed and complies with Insolvency Rule 5.22(1). The order will record the effect of the Chairman's report and may discharge the interim order.

16.2 Provided that the conditions as under 16.1(2) and (4) above are satisfied and that the appropriate report has been lodged with the Court in due time the parties need not attend or be represented on the adjourned hearing for consideration of the Nominee's report or of the Chairman's report (as the case may be) unless they are notified by the Court that attendance is required. Sealed copies of the order made (in all four cases as above) will be posted by the Court to the applicant or his Solicitor and to the Nominee.

16.3 In suitable cases the Court may also make consent orders without attendance by the parties. The written consent of the parties will be required. Examples of such orders are as follows:

(1)   On applications to set aside a statutory demand, orders:

(a) dismissing the application, with or without an order for costs as may be agreed (permission will be given to present a petition on or after the seventh day after the date of the order, unless a different date is agreed);

Paragraph numbers marked with a "+" can be found online and on CD.

        (b) setting aside the demand, with or without an order for costs as may be agreed; or

        (c) giving permission to withdraw the application with or without an order for costs as may be agreed.

(2) On petitions: where there is a list of supporting or opposing creditors in Form 6.21, or a statement signed by or on behalf of the petitioning creditor that no notices have been received from supporting or opposing creditors, orders:

        (a) dismissing the petition, with or without an order for costs as may be agreed, or

        (b) if the petition has not been served, giving permission to withdraw the petition (with no order for costs).

(3) On other applications, orders:

        (a) for sale of property, possession of property, disposal of proceeds of sale

        (b) giving interim directions

        (c) dismissing the application, with or without an order for costs as may be agreed

        (d) giving permission to withdraw the application, with or without an order for costs as may be agreed.

If (as may often be the case with orders under subparagraphs (3)(a) or (b) above), an adjournment is required, whether generally with liberty to restore or to a fixed date, the order by consent may include an order for the adjournment. If adjournment to a date is requested, a time estimate should be given and the Court will fix the first available date and time on or after the date requested.

16.4 The above lists should not be regarded as exhaustive, nor should it be assumed that an order will be made without attendance as requested.

16.5 The procedure outlined above is designed to save time and costs but is not intended to discourage attendance.

16.6 Applications for consent orders without attendance should be lodged at least two clear working days (and preferably longer) before any fixed hearing date.

16.7 Whenever a document is lodged or a letter sent, the correct case number, code (if any) and year (for example 123/SD/99 or 234/99) should be quoted. A note should also be given of the date and time of the next hearing (if any).

16.8 Attention is drawn to Paragraph 4.4(4) of the Practice Direction relating to CPR Part 44.

16A. Bankruptcy Restrictions Orders

Making the application

16A.1 An application for a bankruptcy restrictions order is made **3E–17** as an ordinary application in the bankruptcy.

16A.2 The application must be made within one year beginning with the date of the bankruptcy order unless the court gives permis-

INSOLVENCY

Paragraph numbers marked with a "+" can be found online and on CD.

sion for the application to be made after that period. The one year period does not run while the bankrupt's discharge has been suspended under section 279(3) of the Insolvency Act 1986.

16A.3 An application for a bankruptcy restrictions order may be made by the Secretary of State or the Official Receiver ('the Applicant'). The application must be supported by a report which must include:

(a)   a statement of the conduct by reference to which it is alleged that it is appropriate for a bankruptcy restrictions order to be made; and

(b)   the evidence relied on in support of the application (r.6.241 Insolvency Rules 1986).

16A.4 The report is treated as if it were an affidavit (r.7.9(2) Insolvency Rules 1986) and is prima facie evidence of any matter contained in it (r.7.9(3)).

16A.5 The application may be supported by evidence from other witnesses which may be given by affidavit or (by reason of r.7.57(5) Insolvency Rules 1986) by witness statement verified by a statement of truth.

16A.6 The court will fix a first hearing which must be not less than 8 weeks from the date when the hearing is fixed (r.6.241(4) Insolvency Rules 1986).

16A.7 Notice of the application and the venue fixed by the court must be served by the Applicant on the bankrupt not more than 14 days after the application is made. Service of notice must be accompanied by a copy of the application together with the evidence in support and a form of acknowledgment of service.

16A.8 The bankrupt must file in court an acknowledgment of service not more than 14 days after service of the application on him, indicating whether or not he contests the application. If he fails to do so he may attend the hearing of the application but may not take part in the hearing unless the court gives permission.

Opposing the application

16A.9 If the bankrupt wishes to oppose the application, he must within 28 days of service on him of the application and the evidence in support (or such longer period as the court may allow) file in court and (within three days thereof) serve on the Applicant any evidence which he wishes the court to take into consideration. Such evidence should normally be in the form of an affidavit or a witness statement verified by a statement of truth.

16A.10 The Applicant must file any evidence in reply within 14 days of receiving the evidence of the bankrupt (or such longer period as the court may allow) and must serve it on the bankrupt as soon as reasonably practicable.

Hearings

16A.11 Any hearing of an application for a bankruptcy restrictions order must be in public (r.6.241(5) Insolvency Rules 1986). The hearing will generally be before the registrar or district judge in the first instance who may:

Paragraph numbers marked with a "+" can be found online and on CD.

(1)   adjourn the application and give directions;

(2)   make a bankruptcy restrictions order; or

(3)   adjourn the application to the judge.

Making a bankruptcy restrictions order

16A.12 When the court is considering whether to make a bankruptcy restrictions order, it must not take into account any conduct of the bankrupt prior to 1 April 2004 (art. 7 Enterprise Act (Commencement No. 4 and Transitional Provisions and Savings) Order 2003).

16A.13 The court may make a bankruptcy restrictions order in the absence of the bankrupt and whether or not he has filed evidence (r.6.244 Insolvency Rules 1986).

16A.14 When a bankruptcy restrictions order is made the court must send two sealed copies of the order to the Applicant (r.6.244(2) Insolvency Rules 1986), and as soon as reasonably practicable after receipt, the Applicant must send one sealed copy to the bankrupt (r.6.244(3)).

16A.15 A bankruptcy restrictions order comes into force when it is made and must specify the date on which it will cease to have effect, which must be between two and 15 years from the date on which it is made.

Interim bankruptcy restriction orders

16A.16 An application for an interim bankruptcy restrictions order may be made any time between the institution of an application for a bankruptcy restrictions order and the determination of that application (Sch 4A para. 5 Insolvency Act 1986). The application is made as an ordinary application in the bankruptcy.

16A.17 The application must be supported by a report as evidence in support of the application (r.6.246(1) Insolvency Rules 1986) which must include evidence of the bankrupt's conduct which is alleged to constitute the grounds for making an interim bankruptcy restrictions order and evidence of matters relating to the public interest in making the order.

16A.18 Notice of the application must be given to the bankrupt at least two business days before the date fixed for the hearing unless the court directs otherwise (r.6.245).

16A.19 Any hearing of the application must be in public (r.6.245).

16A.20 The court may make an interim bankruptcy restrictions order in the absence of the bankrupt and whether or not he has filed evidence (r.6.247).

16A.21 The bankrupt may apply to the court to set aside an interim bankruptcy restrictions order. The application is made by ordinary application in the bankruptcy and must be supported by an affidavit or witness statement verified by a statement of truth stating the grounds on which the application is made (r.6.248(2)).

16A.22 The bankrupt must send the Secretary of State, not less than 7 days before the hearing, notice of his application, notice of the venue, a copy of his application and a copy of the supporting affidavit.

Paragraph numbers marked with a "+" can be found online and on CD.

The Secretary of State may attend the hearing and call the attention of the court to any matters which seem to him to be relevant, and may himself give evidence or call witnesses.

16A.23 Where the court sets aside an interim bankruptcy restrictions order, two sealed copies of the order must be sent by the court, as soon as reasonably practicable, to the Secretary of State.

16A.24 As soon as reasonably practicable after receipt of sealed copies of the order, the Secretary of State must send a sealed copy to the bankrupt.

Bankruptcy restrictions undertakings

16A.25 Where a bankrupt has given a bankruptcy restrictions undertaking, the Secretary of State must file a copy in court and send a copy to the bankrupt as soon as reasonably practicable (r.6.250).

16A.26 The bankrupt may apply to annul a bankruptcy restrictions undertaking. The application is made as an ordinary application in the bankruptcy and must be supported by an affidavit or witness statement verified by a statement of truth stating the grounds on which it is made.

16A.27 The bankrupt must give notice of his application and the venue together with a copy of his affidavit in support to the Secretary of State at least 28 days before the date fixed for the hearing.

16A.28 The Secretary of State may attend the hearing and call the attention of the court to any matters which seem to him to be relevant and may himself give evidence or call witnesses.

16A.29 The court must send a sealed copy of any order annulling or varying the bankruptcy restrictions undertaking to the Secretary of State and the bankrupt.

Part Four

Appeals

17. Appeals in insolvency proceedings

3E–18   **17.1** This Part shall come into effect on 2nd May 2000 and shall replace and revoke Paragraph 17 of, and be read in conjunction with the Practice Direction—Insolvency Proceedings which came into effect on 26th April 1999 as amended.

    17.2(1) An appeal from a decision of a County Court (whether made by a District Judge or a Circuit Judge) or of a Registrar of the High Court in insolvency proceedings ("a first appeal") lies to a Judge of the High Court pursuant to s.375(2) of the Act and Insolvency Rules 7.47(2) and 7.48(2) (as amended by s.55 of the Access to Justice Act 1999).

    (2)   The procedure and practice for a first appeal are governed by Insolvency Rule 7.49 which imports the procedure and practice of the Court of Appeal. The procedure and practice of the Court of Appeal is governed by CPR Part

Paragraph numbers marked with a "+" can be found online and on CD.

52 and its Practice Direction, which are subject to the provisions of the Act, the Insolvency Rules and this Practice Direction: see CPR Part 52, rule 1(4).

(3)   A first appeal (as defined above) does not include an appeal from a decision of a Judge of the High Court.

17.3(1) Section 55 of the Access to Justice Act 1999 has amended s.375(2) of the Act and Insolvency Rules 7.47(2) and 7.48(2) so that an appeal from a decision of a Judge of the High Court made on a first appeal lies, with the permission of the Court of Appeal, to the Court of Appeal.

(2)   An appeal from a Judge of the High Court in insolvency proceedings which is not a decision on a first appeal lies, with the permission of the Judge or of the Court of Appeal, to the Court of Appeal (see CPR Part 52, rule 3);

(3)   The procedure and practice for appeals from a decision of a Judge of the High Court in insolvency proceedings (whether made on a first appeal or not) are also governed by Insolvency Rule 7.49 which imports the procedure and practice of the Court of Appeal as stated at Paragraph 17.2(2) above.

17.4 CPR Part 52 and its Practice Direction and Forms apply to appeals from a decision of a Judge of the High Court in insolvency proceedings.

17.5 An appeal from a decision of a judge of the High Court in insolvency proceedings requires permission set out in Paragraph 17.3(1) and (2) above.

17.6 A first appeal is subject to the permission requirement in CPR Part 52, rule 3.

17.7 Except as provided in this Part, CPR Part 52 and its Practice Direction and Forms do not apply to first appeals, but Paragraphs 17.8 to 17.23 inclusive of this Part apply only to first appeals.

17.8 Interpretation:

(a)   the expressions "appeal court", "lower court", "appellant", "respondent" and "appeal notice" have the meanings given in CPR Part 52.1(3);

(b)   'Registrar of Appeals' means—
   (i) in relation to an appeal filed at the Royal Courts of Justice in London, a registrar in bankruptcy; and
   (ii) in relation to an appeal filed in a district registry, a district judge of that district registry.

(c)   "appeal date" means the date fixed by the appeal court for the hearing of the appeal or the date fixed by the appeal court upon which the period within which the appeal will be heard commences.

17.9 An appellant's notice and a respondent's notice shall be in Form **PDIP 1** and **PDIP 2** set out in the Schedule hereto.

17.10(1)An appeal from a decision of a registrar in bankruptcy must be filed at the Royal Courts of Justice in London.

(2)   An appeal from a decision of a district judge sitting in a district registry may be filed—

Paragraph numbers marked with a "+" can be found online and on CD.

INSOLVENCY

        (a) at the Royal Courts of Justice in London; or

        (b) in that district registry.

(3)   An appeal from a decision made in a county court may be filed—

        (a) at the Royal Courts of Justice in London; or

        (b) in the Chancery district registry for the area within which the county court exercises jurisdiction.

(There are Chancery district registries of the High Court at Birmingham, Bristol, Caernarfon, Cardiff, Leeds, Liverpool, Manchester, Mold, Newcastle upon Tyne and Preston. The county court districts that each district registry covers are set out in Schedule 1 to the Civil Courts Order 1983.)

17.11(1) Where a party seeks an extension of time in which to file an appeal notice it must be requested in the appeal notice and the appeal notice should state the reason for the delay and the steps taken prior to the application being made; the court will fix a date for the hearing of the application and notify the parties of the date and place of hearing;

(2)   The appellant must file the appellant's notice at the appeal court within—

        (a) such period as may be directed by the lower court; or

        (b) where the court makes no such direction, 21 days after the date of the decision of the lower court which the appellant wishes to appeal.

(3)   Unless the appeal court orders otherwise, an appeal notice must be served by the appellant on each respondent—

        (a) as soon as practicable; and

        (b) in any event not later than 7 days, after it is filed.

17.12(1) A respondent may file and serve a respondent's notice.

(2)   A respondent who wishes to ask the appeal court to uphold the order of the lower court for reasons different from or additional to those given by the lower court must file a respondent's notice.

(3)   A respondent's notice must be filed within—

        (a) such period as may be directed by the lower court; or

        (b) where the court makes no such direction, 14 days after the date on which the respondent is served with the appellant's notice.

(4)   Unless the appeal court orders otherwise a respondent's notice must be served by the respondent on the appellant and any other respondent—

        (a) as soon as practicable; and

        (b) in any event not later than 7 days, after it is filed.

17.13(1) An application to vary the time limit for filing an appeal notice must be made to the appeal court.

(2)   The parties may not agree to extend any date or time limit set by—

        (a) this Practice Direction; or

(b) an order of the appeal court or the lower court.

17.14 Unless the appeal court or the lower court orders otherwise an appeal shall not operate as a stay of any order or decision of the lower court.

17.15 An appeal notice may not be amended without the permission of the appeal court.

17.16 A Judge of the appeal court may strike out the whole or part of an appeal notice where there is compelling reason for doing so.

17.17(1) In relation to an appeal the appeal court has all the powers of the lower court.

(2)   The appeal court has power to—

       (a) affirm, set aside or vary any order or judgment made or given by the lower court;

       (b) refer any claim or issue for determination by the lower court;

       (c) order a new trial or hearing;

       (d) make a costs order.

(3)   The appeal court may exercise its powers in relation to the whole or part of an order of the lower court.

17.18(1) Every appeal shall be limited to a review of the decision of the lower court.

(2)   Unless it orders otherwise, the appeal court will not receive—

       (a) oral evidence; or

       (b) evidence which was not before the lower court.

(3)   The appeal court will allow an appeal where the decision of the lower court was—

       (a) wrong; or

       (b) unjust because of a serious procedural or other irregularity in the proceedings in the lower court.

(4)   The appeal court may draw any inference of fact which it considers justified on the evidence.

(5)   At the hearing of the appeal a party may not rely on a matter not contained in his appeal notice unless the appeal court gives permission.

17.19 The following applications shall be made to a Judge of the appeal court:

(1)   for injunctions pending a substantive hearing of the appeal;

(2)   for expedition or vacation of the hearing date of an appeal;

(3)   for an order striking out the whole or part of an appeal notice pursuant to Paragraph 17.16 above;

(4)   for a final order on paper pursuant to Paragraph 17.22(8) below.

17.20(1) All other interim applications shall be made to the Registrar of Appeals in the first instance who may in his discre-

Paragraph numbers marked with a "+" can be found online and on CD.

INSOLVENCY

tion either hear and determine it himself or refer it to the Judge.

(2)   An appeal from a decision of a Registrar of Appeals lies to a Judge of the appeal court and does not require the permission of either the Registrar of Appeals or the Judge.

17.21 The procedure for interim applications is by way of ordinary application (see Insolvency Rule 12.7 and Schedule 4, Form 7.2).

17.22 The following practice applies to all first appeals to a Judge of the High Court whether filed at the Royal Courts of Justice in London, or filed at one of the other venues referred to in Paragraph 17.10 above:

(1)   on filing an appellant's notice in accordance with Paragraph 17.11(2) above, the appellant must file:

(a) two copies of the appeal notice for the use of the court, one of which must be stamped with the appropriate fee, and a number of additional copies equal to the number of persons who are to be served with it pursuant to Paragraph 17.22(4) below;

(aa) an approved transcript of the judgment of the lower court or, where there is no official record of the judgment, a document referred to in paragraph 5.12 of the Practice Direction supplementing CPR Part 52;

(b) a copy of the order under appeal; and

(c) an estimate of time for the hearing.

(2)   the above documents may be lodged personally or by post and shall be lodged at the address of the appropriate venue listed below:

(a) if the appeal is to be heard at the Royal Courts of Justice in London the documents must be lodged at Room 110, Thomas More Building, The Royal Courts of Justice, Strand, London WC2A 2LL;

(b) if the appeal is to be heard in Birmingham, the documents must be lodged at the District Registry of the Chancery Division of the High Court, 33 Bull Street, Birmingham B4 6DS;

(c) if the appeal is to be heard in Bristol the documents must be lodged at the District Registry of the Chancery Division of the High Court, Third Floor, Greyfriars, Lewins Mead, Bristol, BS1 2NR;

(ca) if the appeal is to be heard in Caernarfon the documents must be lodged at the District Registry of the Chancery Division of the High Court, Llanberis Road, Caernarfon, LL55 2DF;

(d) if the appeal is to be heard in Cardiff the documents must be lodged at the District Registry in the Chancery Division of the High Court, First Floor, 2 Park Street, Cardiff, CF10 1ET;

(e) if the appeal is to be heard in Leeds the documents must be lodged at the District Registry of the Chancery

Paragraph numbers marked with a "+" can be found online and on CD.

Division of the High Court, The Court House, 1 Oxford Row, Leeds LS1 3BG;

(f) if the appeal is to be heard in Liverpool the documents must be lodged at the District Registry of the Chancery Division of the High Court, Liverpool Combined Court Centre, Derby Square, Liverpool L2 1XA;

(g) if the appeal is to be heard in Manchester the documents must be lodged at the District Registry of the Chancery Division of the High Court, Courts of Justice, Crown Square, Manchester, M60 9DJ;

(ga) if the appeal is to be heard in Mold the documents must be lodged at the District Registry of the Chancery Division of the High Court, Law Courts, Civic Centre, Mold, CH7 1AE;

(h) if the appeal is to be heard at Newcastle upon Tyne the documents must be lodged at the District Registry of the Chancery Division of the High Court, The Law Courts, Quayside, Newcastle upon Tyne NE1 3LA;

(i) if the appeal is to be heard in Preston the documents must be lodged at the District Registry of the Chancery Division of the High Court, The Combined Court Centre, Ringway, Preston PR1 2LL.

(3)   if the documents are correct and in order the court at which the documents are filed will fix the appeal date and will also fix the place of hearing. That court will send letters to all the parties to the appeal informing them of the appeal date and of the place of hearing and indicating the time estimate given by the appellant. The parties will be invited to notify the court of any alternative or revised time estimates. In the absence of any such notification the estimate of the appellant will be taken as agreed. The court will also send to the appellant a document setting out the court's requirement concerning the form and content of the bundle of documents for the use of the Judge. Not later than 7 days before the appeal date the bundle of documents must be filed by the appellant at the address of the relevant venue as set out in sub-paragraph 17.22(2) above and a copy of it must be served by the appellant on each respondent.

(4)   the appeal notice must be served on all parties to the proceedings in the lower court who are directly affected by the appeal. This may include the Official Receiver, liquidator or trustee in bankruptcy.

(5)   the appeal notice must be served by the appellant or by the legal representative of the appellant and may be effected by:

(a) any of the methods referred to in CPR Part 6 rule 2; or

(b) with permission of the court, an alternative method pursuant to CPR Part 6 rule 8.

Paragraph numbers marked with a "+" can be found online and on CD.

(6)   service of an appeal notice shall be proved by a Certificate of Service in accordance with CPR Part 6, rule 10 (CPR Form **N215**) which must be filed at the relevant venue referred to at Paragraph 17.22(2) above immediately after service.

(7)   Subject to sub-paragraphs (7A) and (7B), the appellant's notice must be accompanied by a skeleton argument and a written chronology of events relevant to the appeal. Alternatively, the skeleton argument and chronology may be included in the appellant's notice. Where the skeleton argument and chronology are so included they do not form part of the notice for the purposes of rule 52.8.

(7A)   Where it is impracticable for the appellant's skeleton argument and chronology to accompany the appellant's notice they must be filed and served on all respondents within 14 days of filing the notice.

(7B)   An appellant who is not represented need not file a skeleton argument nor a written chronology but is encouraged to do so since these documents may be helpful to the court.

(8)   where an appeal has been settled or where an apellant does not wish to continue with the appeal, the appeal may be disposed of on paper without a hearing. It may be dismissed by consent but the appeal court will not make an order allowing an appeal unless it is satisfied that the decision of the lower court was wrong. Any consent order signed by each party or letters of consent from each party must be lodged not later than 24 hours before the date fixed for the hearing of the appeal at the address of the appropriate venue as set out in sub-paragraph 17.22(2) above and will be dealt with by the Judge of the appeal court. Attention is drawn to paragraph 4.4(4) of the Practice Direction to CPR Part 44 regarding costs where an order is made by consent without attendance.

17.23 Only the following paragraphs of the Practice Direction to CPR Part 52, with any necessary modifications, shall apply to first appeals: 5.10 to 5.20 inclusive.

17.24(1)Where, under the procedure relating to appeals in insolvency proceedings prior to the coming into effect of this Part of this Practice Direction, an appeal has been set down in the High Court or permission to appeal to the Court of Appeal has been granted before 2nd May 2000, the procedure and practice set out in this Part of this Practice Direction shall apply to such an appeal after that date.

(2)   Where, under the procedure relating to appeals in insolvency proceedings prior to the coming into effect of this Part of this Practice Direction, any person has failed before 2nd May 2000 either:

(a) in the case of a first appeal, to set down in the High Court an appeal which relates to an order made

Paragraph numbers marked with a "+" can be found online and on CD.

2000 (O.J. L160, 30.6.2000) came into force on May 31, 2002 and has direct application as domestic law. It applies to all the EU member states, except Denmark. It applies to "collective insolvency proceedings which entail the partial or total divestment of a debtor and the appointment of a liquidator" (Art.1(1)); see also *In re Eurofood IFSC Ltd* [2006] Ch. 508; [2007] 2 B.C.L.C. 151.Such proceedings are: winding up by the court, creditors' voluntary winding up with confirmation of the court (as to which see para.3E–88), administration, voluntary arrangements and bankruptcy (Art.2(a) and Annex A), and the term "liquidator" includes the relevant office holder in relation thereto (Art.2(b) and Annex C). The Regulation does not apply to insurance and certain other financial undertakings (Art.1(2)), nor does it apply to members' voluntary winding-up, schemes of arrangement, winding-up on the just and equitable ground or winding-up in the public interest (*Marann Brooks CSV Ltd, Re* [2003] B.P.I.R. 1159.

The Regulation provides for insolvency proceedings to be main proceedings or secondary (or territorial) proceedings (Art.3(1) and (2)). Jurisdiction is founded by reference to the debtor's centre of main interests, which in the case of a company is presumed (in the absence of proof to the contrary) to be its registered office (Art.3(1)) and in the case of an individual is likely to be the place of the debtor's business or his place of ordinary residence (in the absence of evidence to the contrary). Main proceedings are proceedings brought in the place of the debtor's centre of main interests and are universal in scope. Secondary or territorial proceedings may be brought in a country in which the debtor has an establishment, i.e. a "place of operations where the debtor carries out a non-transitory economic activity with human means and goods" (Arts.2(h) and 3(2)). Such proceedings are limited to assets within the territory. The court is thus obliged to consider whether it has jurisdiction before making an order, and when making an order, to state whether the Regulation applies and if so whether the proceedings are main, territorial or secondary. (For examples of the court's consideration of the jurisdictional issue see *A Company, Re (No.6394/2002)* [2002] All E.R. (D) 223 (Oct); *Marann Brooks CSV Ltd, Re* [2003] B.P.I.R. 1159; *BRAC Rent-A-Car Internaional Inc, Re* [2003] 2 All E.R. 201; [2003] 1 W.L.R. 1421; *Re Salvage Association* [2003] B.C.C. 504; *Skjevesland v Geveran Trading Co Ltd* [2003] B.P.I.R. 73; [2003] B.P.I.R. 924, *A Bankrupt, Re (No.136 of 2003)* [2003] All E.R. (D) 36 (Dec); *Shierson v Vlieland-Boddy* [2005] B.P.I.R. 1170; *Re Staubitz-Schreiber* (C-1/07) [2006] E.C.R. I-701; [2006] B.P.I.R. 510, ECJ; *Stojevic v Official Receiver* [2007] B.P.I.R. 141.)

The place where proceedings are opened (usually by the making of an order (Art.2(f)) determines the law applicable to the insolvency (Art.4(1)), but subject to various exceptions set out in detail in the Regulation.

The Regulation provides for automatic recognition of insolvency proceedings in member states (Arts.17 and 25). A creditors' voluntary liquidation requires "confirmation of the court" for such purposes (Annex A) (see para.3E–88).

The UNCITRAL model law

3E–27

The UNCITRAL model law on cross-border insolvency, implementing the model law and enabling representatives of foreign insolvency proceedings to seek recognition and other relief in Great Britain, came into force on April 4, 2006 (Insolvency Act 2000, s.14; the Cross-Border Insolvency Regulations 2006 (SI 2006/1030)).

Company

3E–28

"Company" means a company formed and registered under the Companies Act 1985 or under the former Companies Acts (i.e. the Joint Stock Companies Act, the Companies Act 1862, the Companies (Consolidation) Act 1908, the Companies Act 1929 and the Companies Act 1948 to 1983) but excluding those in what was Ireland (s.735(1) of the Companies Act 1985). As to jurisdiction in relation to a company incorporated by royal charter, see *Re Salvage Association* [2003] B.C.C. 504. As to the meaning of a UK-registered company see s.1158 of the Companies Act 2006.

Partnerships

3E–29

The insolvency of partnerships is dealt with largely by reference to the legislation on company insolvency (with appropriate modifications) Thus a partnership may propose a partnership voluntary arrangement under provisions set out in Sch.1 of the Insolvent Partnerships Order 1994 (as amended), seek an administration order or be wound up under Pt V of the Insolvency Act 1986.

Paragraph numbers marked with a "+" can be found online and on CD.

Limited liability partnerships

3E–30   The Limited Liability Partnerships Act 2000 created a new legal entity, the limited liability partnership and provided for the recognition of oversea limited liability partnerships. Pursuant to s.14 of the Limited Liability Partnerships Act 2000 and the Limited Liability Partnership Regulations 2001 (SI 2001/1090) Pts I, II, III, IV, VI and VII of the Insolvency Act 1986 apply with modifications to limited liability partnerships.

Company voluntary arrangements (Part I Insolvency Act 1986)

Company voluntary arrangements without moratorium

3E–31   The directors of a company, its administrator (where an administration order is in force) or its liquidator (where the company is being wound up) may propose to the creditors of the company a composition in satisfaction of its debts or a scheme of arrangement (a company voluntary arrangement) (s.1). The proposal must be made to all the company's creditors, and it must be for a composition of debts or a scheme of arrangement (as to which see *March Estates plc v Gunmark Ltd* [1996] 2 B.C.L.C. 1). Within 28 days (or any longer period the courts allows) the nominee must submit a report to the court stating whether a meeting of creditors and members of the company should be summoned to consider the proposal (s.2). The meetings must then be held at the time, date and place proposed (s.3(2)) The chairman of the meetings must report to the court the result of the meetings (s.4(6)). Members vote according to the rights attaching to their shares (r.1.18(1)) but are entitled to vote even where no voting rights attach to their shares (r.1.18(2)). A resolution to approve or modify the proposal must be passed by a majority in excess of three-quarters in value of creditors present in person or by proxy (r.1.19(1)).

Company voluntary arrangements with moratorium

3E–32   Under the provisions of the Insolvency Act 2000, which came into force on January 1, 2003, an "eligible company" (as defined by ss.2–4 of Sch.A1 of the Insolvency Act 1986), which must be a small company (as defined by s.247(3) of the Companies Act 1985), may obtain a moratorium without making an application for an administration order (s.1A). The moratorium commences when the directors file in court the company's proposal, a statement of affairs, a statement that the company is eligible for a moratorium and a statement from the nominee that he has consented to act and that in his opinion (a) the arrangement has a reasonable prospect of being approved and implemented, (b) the company is likely to have sufficient funds available during the moratorium to enable it to carry on its business, and (c) meetings of the company and its creditors should be summoned to consider the proposal. The moratorium lasts for 28 days but may be extended by resolution for up to two months after the date when the meetings were first held.

Filing of company voluntary arrangements

3E–33   In the High Court in London the proposal and accompanying documents should be filed in the issue room on the second floor, Thomas More Building, Royal Courts of Justice.

Partnership voluntary arrangements

3E–34   A partnership voluntary arrangement is made in much in the same way as a company voluntary arrangement (Insolvent Partnerships Order 1994 (as amended by the Insolvent Partnerships (Amendment) Order 2005). The moratorium provisions also apply to a partnership voluntary arrangement (Insolvent Partnerships (Amendment) (No.2) Order 2002 (SI 2002/2708)). A limited liability partnership may also propose a voluntary arrangement.

Challenges

3E–35   Within 28 days of the day on which the chairman's reports have been filed (as to which see *Re Bournemouth and Boscombe v AFC Co Ltd* [1998] B.P.I.R. 153) a person entitled to vote at a meeting or who would have been so entitled if he had notice of it, the nominee or his replacement, or (if applicable) the liquidator or administrator, may apply to challenge the approval of the arrangement on the ground of unfair prejudice

Paragraph numbers marked with a "+" can be found online and on CD.

in support setting out in detail why the petition should not be presented or advertised (usually because the petition debt is disputed). Since the application is for an injunction it is made direct to the judge. There is no provision to apply for a statutory demand to be set aside.

The court will not restrain a creditor from prosecuting a petition where the company can demonstrate solvency but has failed to pay a debt that is due (*Cornhill Insurance plc v Improvement Services Ltd* [1986] 1 W.L.R. 114).

Failure to advertise

Winding up is a class remedy. Accordingly the court attaches importance to the **3E–62** advertisement of a winding up petition. The petition should be advertised in the London Gazette (r.4.11(1)), but may be advertised elsewhere if the court so orders (r.4.11(3)). If a petition has not been advertised in accordance with r.4.11 the court may dismiss it (r.4.11(5) and para.2 of the Practice Direction). The court will not, as a general rule, dismiss the petition by reason only of a failure to advertise, at the first hearing of the petition. It will, however, do so as a general rule if the petition has not been advertised by any adjourned hearing unless there are exceptional circumstances for not complying with the general rule. It will almost certainly dismiss any petition that has not been advertised with a view to holding the unadvertised petition over the company's head for the purpose of obtaining costs from the company without an order of the court. If the court does adjourn the petition as a result of a failure to advertise it may do so on terms that the petitioner should have no costs in respect of the ineffective hearing.

Premature advertisement of the petition may result in dismissal if the breach of the rule appears to have been culpable, but will generally be waived if the petition is unopposed and no prejudice has been suffered by the company. The court may waive up to two days lateness in advertisement but will generally adjourn if the advertisement is more than two days late. The court may also waive minor errors in the advertisement (e.g. misspelling of the company's address) so long as the name and identity of the company in the advertisement are clear.

Certificate of compliance

The Petitioner must, at least five days before the hearing of the petition, file in **3E–63** court a certificate of compliance relating to service and advertisement of the petition (r.4.14(1)). It must show the date of presentation of the petition, the date fixed for the hearing, the dates of service and advertisement, and it must be accompanied by a copy of the advertisement of the petition. Failure to file a certificate of compliance may also result in dismissal of the petition (r.4.14(3)).

List of appearances

Any person who intends to appear on the hearing of the petition must give notice **3E–64** to the petitioner of his intention to do so, state whether he intends to support or oppose the petition and give details of the amount and nature of his debt (r.4.16). The petitioner must prepare a list of the persons who have given notice under r.4.16 and hand a copy of the list to the court before the hearing (r.4.17).

Hearing of the petition

In the High Court in London winding up petitions are heard on Wednesdays by **3E–65** the registrar.

At the hearing of the petition the petitioner may appear as may the company and any supporting or opposing creditor who has given notice under r.4.16 or has failed to give such notice but has been permitted by the court to appear (r.4.16(5)). The company may appear by a director or employee as well as by solicitors or counsel. However, the court will not generally allow accountants right of audience.

At the hearing, the court may dismiss the petition, adjourn it conditionally or unconditionally, or make an interim order or any other order it thinks fit (s.125(1)). It may also make an order that the company be wound up.

Petition contested —If the company opposes the making of a winding up order it **3E–66** should file in court and serve on the petitioner evidence in opposition not less than seven days before the date fixed for the hearing of the petition (r.4.18). In practice, if

Paragraph numbers marked with a "+" can be found online and on CD.

the company appears and indicates that it opposes the making of an order on grounds that appear to be substantial, the court will give directions for the filing and service of evidence in opposition and evidence in reply and order the petition to be heard at a later date, notwithstanding any failure to comply with the provisions of r.4.18.

3E–67 *Substitution of petitioner* —Where the petitioner is unable to proceed with his petition (e.g. because the petition debt is disputed) or is unable to seek a winding up order (e.g. because restrained by injunction from advertising, because he has failed to advertise or otherwise comply with the rules) or does not seek a winding up order for some other reason (e.g. because his debt has been paid), a creditor or contributory who would himself be entitled to present a petition may seek substitution. The application may be made informally at the hearing and without notice. If more than one creditor seeks substitution the court will generally substitute the creditor with the largest debt or the debt least likely to be disputed. The court will direct that the petition be amended and re-verified; it may order re-service but will generally dispense with re-advertisement if the petition has already been advertised. It will adjourn the petition so as to allow sufficient time for those steps to be taken.

3E–68 *Dismissal of the petition* —If the petitioner fails to appear, if the petitioner accepts that the petition debt is capable of dispute, or if the petition debt has been paid and no creditor or contributory seeks substitution, the court will generally dismiss the petition. It may also dismiss the petition for failure to advertise or for some other failure to comply with the Insolvency Rules 1986 (e.g. rr.4.11(5) and 4.14(3)).

The court must dismiss a petition for the winding up of a company in respect of which an administration order has been made (Sch.B1, para.40(1)(a)). It must suspend the petition where an administration has been appointed by the holder of a floating charge (Sch.B1, para.40(b). As to costs in such cases see para. 3E–72.

3E–69 *Usual compulsory order* —If the court is satisfied that the provisions of the Insolvency Act 1986 and the Insolvency Rules 1986 have been complied with and that the petition debt is not disputed on grounds which are substantial and that it is just and equitable to wind up the company it will make "the usual compulsory order", i.e. an order that the company be wound up by the court under the provisions of the Insolvency Act 1986. It will also make a declaration as to whether or not the EC Regulation on Insolvency Proceedings applies to the winding up and whether (if it does) the proceedings are main or secondary/territorial proceedings.

3E–70 *Double barrelled order* —Where a company has been struck off the register by the registrar of companies the court may order the company to be restored and wound up

3E–71 *After administration* — Where an administrator applies for the administration to cease and, with the approval of the creditors, petitions for the company to be wound up, the court will generally make the winding up order at the same time as the administrator seeks other relief, provided it is satisfied that all parties concerned, including the company, have had notice of his intention to do so. Where a petition has been suspended by virtue of para.40(1)(b) of Sch.B1 to the Act, the petition may be listed with the administrator's application for relief so that a winding up order may be made on the petition, provided that the petitioner appears and asks for the order to be made. The winding up order may be made whether or not the petition has been advertised and may be made at the first directions hearing without adjournment into the normal winding up list.

3E–72 *Costs and supervening insolvency* —Where after presentation of a petition a supervening insolvency event is initiated and then occurs (such as an administration order, voluntary arrangement or creditors' voluntary liquidation) the court will generally dismiss the petition and order that the costs be paid as an expense of the supervening insolvency (whether or not the petition has been advertised, but provided it has been served) and, where the insolvency practitioner in the supervening insolvency has not given consent to the payment of costs, give liberty to apply to vary or discharge the costs order provided it is exercised within 28 days of the making or service of the order. Where an administrator is appointed by the holder of a qualifying floating charge pursuant to para.14 of Sch.B1 after the presentation of the petition, the peti-

Paragraph numbers marked with a "+" can be found online and on CD.

Contributory's petition

A contributory's petition (unlike a creditor's petition) is not listed straight away for **3E–80** hearing but is given a first return date on which the petitioner and the company should attend before the registrar for directions to be given (r.4.22(2)). The petition must be served on the company at least 14 days before the hearing (r.4.22(4)). As to the range of directions which the court may give see r.4.23.

Supervisor's petition

A winding up petition presented by the supervisor of a voluntary arrangement **3E–81** under Part I of the Act must be presented to the court in which the nominee's report was filed (r.4.7(8)) and is treated as a petition presented by a contributory (r.4.7(9)). As to the appointment of the supervisor as liquidator see para.3E–73.

Applications for relief from the effects of s.127

Section 127 of the Insolvency Act 1986 renders certain transactions made after **3E–82** commencement of the winding up void. Thus, advertisement of a winding up petition will generally have the effect of freezing any bank accounts of the company. The company may apply for relief from the effects of the provisions of s.127 to the judge (if the application is urgent) or otherwise to the registrar. Any order made is commonly referred to as a validation order. For the form of the order see para. 7 of the Practice Direction Order under s.127 of the Insolvency Act 1986 (see para.2G–53). As to the principles governing such applications see *Re Gray's Inn Construction Co Ltd* [1980] 1 W.L.R. 711; [1980] 1 All E.R. 814; and *Re SA & D Wright Ltd, Denny v John Hudson & Co Ltd* [1992] B.C.C. 503

The application should generally be made to the registrar (see para.3E–125).

Applications for the appointment of a provisional liquidator

The court may appoint a provisional liquidator of a company at any time after pre- **3E–83** sentation of a winding up petition and before the making of a winding up order (s.135(1)). Such an appointment is generally made only where assets of the company are in jeopardy or in connection with a public interest petition. The application may be (and commonly is) made without notice to the company and is always made direct to the judge (see para. 3E–124.). It should be supported by full written evidence (as to the contents of which see r.4.25(2)).

Applications in the liquidation of companies

The winding up of a company (whether voluntary or by the court) does not bring **3E–84** the life of the company to an end. The company, acting by its liquidator, may bring proceedings in its own name even after it has been wound up. Thus, the company may by its liquidator and in its own name issue proceedings to collect a debt or to enforce any other right. Such proceedings should generally be issued in the court having the appropriate jurisdiction: the county court, for example, in the case of a debt action, the Chancery Division in the case of an action regarding intellectual property rights, and so on. However, the breadth of proceedings which the companies court may entertain is wide (*Re Shilena Hosiery Co Ltd* [1980] Ch. 219).

Applications to recover assets or relating to prior transactions

The Insolvency Act 1986 provides the administrator, administrative receiver or **3E–85** liquidator of a company with a wide range of remedies to enable him to recover assets of the company or undo the effects of prior transactions (see, for example in liquidations, s.127 (void transactions), ss.206–207 (fraud), s.212 (misfeasance etc.), ss.212–213 (fraudulent and wrongful trading), s.238 (transactions at an undervalue), s.239 (preferences), s.244 (extortionate credit transactions), s.245 (avoidance of floating charges) and s.246 (liens etc.)). Any application to enforce a right of the liquidator or to review or appeal against the conduct of a liquidator should be made to the court having jurisdiction in the winding up. The application should be made by originating or ordinary application (see para.3E–21) and be supported by written evidence. It will be listed for directions before the registrar and determined by him or the judge depending on the length and complexity of the case

Applications for directions in the winding up of a company

Section 112 of the Insolvency Act 1986 allows a liquidator, contributory or creditor **3E–86**

Paragraph numbers marked with a "+" can be found online and on CD.

to apply to the court to determine any question arising in the winding up of a company. The application should be made by originating or ordinary application (see para.3E–21) and supported by written evidence. It will be listed for directions before the registrar and determined by him or the judge depending on the length and complexity of the case.

Applications for private examinations

3E–87   Section 236 of the Insolvency Act 1986 enables an office holder to apply to the court for an order summoning to appear before it (a) any officer of the company, (b) any person known or suspected to have in his possession any property of the company or supposed to be indebted to the company, (c) any person whom the court thinks capable of giving information concerning the promotion, formation, business, dealings, affairs or property of the company (subs.2). Such person may be examined on oath (s.237(3) and (4)). Failure to attend may give rise to the issue of a warrant for the arrest of the person concerned (s.236(5)).

The case law relating to s.236 relief is voluminous and complex. The making of an order is a matter for the discretion of the court, but the discretion will generally be exercised in favour of an office holder (*Joint Liquidators of Sasea Finance Ltd v KPMG* [1998] B.C.C. 216) provided the application is made to enable him to carry out his proper functions (*British & Commonwealth Holdings plc v Spicer & Oppenheim (Re British & Commonwealth Holdings plc (No.2))* [1993] A.C. 426; [1992] B.C.C. 977). The formation of the liquidator of an intention to bring proceedings against the proposed examinee may be a factor weighing against the exercise of the discretion to make an order (*Re Castle New Homes Ltd* [1979] 1 W.L.R. 1075; [1979] 2 All E.R. 775 and *Re Cloverbay Ltd* [1991] Ch 90; [1990] B.C.C. 414; [1990] B.C.L.C. 449); an order will not be made to give the office holder a litigation advantage (*Re Atlantic Computers plc* [1998] B.C.C. 200); however an order may be made for the purpose of obtaining information other than for the administration of the liquidation (e.g. for the purposes of disqualification proceedings, *Re Pantmaenog Timber Co Ltd* [2003] UKHL 49; [2003] 3 W.L.R. 767; [2003] B.C.C. 659, HL). As to the use of compelled evidence in subsequent criminal proceedings see s.219(2A) of the Insolvency Act 1986.

Applications for confirmation by the court of a creditors' voluntary winding up

3E–88   The EC Regulation on Insolvency Proceedings (see para.3E–26) applies to creditors' voluntary winding up with confirmation by the court (Annex A). Article 19 of the Regulation provides that the appointment of a liquidator must be evidenced by a copy of the decision appointing him or by some other certificate issued by the court with jurisdiction. The procedure for applying for an order confirming a creditors' voluntary winding up is provided for by rr.7.62 *et seq.* of the Insolvency Rules 1986.

The application is made pursuant to r.7.62(1) and must be made by prescribed form 7.20 which incorporates the application, the evidence in support and the order to be made. The evidence must state the name of the applicant and of the company and its registered number, the date of the resolution to wind up the company, that the application is accompanied by the required documents and that the copies submitted are true copies, that the Regulation applies to the company, and whether the proceedings are main, territorial or secondary proceedings (r.7.62(2)). The application must be filed together with a copy and be accompanied by a copy of the resolution to wind up the company, evidence of the applicant's appointment as liquidator and the statement of affairs (r.7.62(3)). Whilst provision is made for the order to be made by a member of the court staff (r.7.62(7)), in the High Court the application should be made to the registrar who will make the order without a hearing provided that the papers are in order. The application need not be served on any other party (r.7.62(4)).

The order is made by the court completing and sealing the order section of the prescribed form and returning a completed and sealed copy to the applicant.

Applications to convert proceedings

3E–89   The EC Regulation on Insolvency Proceedings provides that the liquidator in main proceedings may request that proceedings listed in Annex A previously opened in another member state be converted into winding up proceedings if this is in the interests of creditors in the main proceedings (Art.37). The court may, on such an application, order that any such proceedings be converted into one of the proceedings listed in

Paragraph numbers marked with a "+" can be found online and on CD.

Annex B (i.e. winding up by or subject to the supervision of the court, creditors' voluntary winding up with confirmation by the court (see para.3E–88) or bankruptcy).

Individual Voluntary Arrangements (Part VIII Insolvency Act 1986)

Part VIII of the Insolvency Act 1986 allows a debtor to make a proposal to his creditors for what must be either a composition with his creditors or a scheme of arrangement of his affairs. A composition is effectively an agreement whereby creditors agree to accept a lesser sum in satisfaction of their debt; a scheme of arrangement may take any form which is acceptable to the parties but must provide for someone to act either as a trustee or otherwise for the purpose of supervising its implementation. As to compositions and schemes generally, see *Re Griffth* (1886) 3 Morr.111 and *Inland Revenue Commissioners v Adam & Partners Ltd* [2001] 1 B.C.L.C. 222. In practice the procedure to be followed in each case is the same and can be summarised as follows. A proposal is formulated, reviewed by the nominee who will then present it to the creditors at a meeting summoned for that purpose; if approved by a majority of in excess of three quarters of creditors in value it then becomes binding on the creditors. **3E–90**

The Insolvency Act 2000, ss.3 and 4 and Sch.3, and the Insolvency (Amendment) (No.2) Rules 2002 (SI 2712/2002) which came into force on January 1, 2003, enable the debtor to choose whether or not to apply for an interim order. If the debtor needs protection from his creditors, which now includes protection against peaceable re-entry by his landlord or distress (except with the permission of the court), then an interim order will be required and an application will need to be made to the court as before. The procedure has not changed and is set out in Pt 5 of the Insolvency Rules 1986. If protection is not required then the debtor may submit his proposal, which must comply with r.5.3 (as amended) and statement of affairs to the intended nominee who, if he is of the opinion that the debtor is an undischarged bankrupt or is able to petition for his own bankruptcy and is prepared to act, can call the meeting of creditors. The nominee must within 14 days (or such longer period as the court may allow) after receiving the proposal and statement of affairs submit a report to the court in which he must state whether in his opinion the voluntary arrangement has a reasonable prospect of being approved and implemented, whether a meeting of creditors should be summoned and if so the date, time and venue. This must be filed along with a copy of the proposal, the statement of affairs and form 5.5 (which contains the statement that it is not intended to apply for an interim order). The court will not read the report unless an application is made under the Act or Rules in relation to the proposal, for example to challenge the decision of the creditors' meeting under s.262 of the Insolvency Act 1986, (see r.5.14(1)). **3E–91**

The appropriate court in which to file is the court in which the debtor should file his own bankruptcy petition (r.6.40), or if an undischarged bankrupt the court with the conduct of the bankruptcy. Where the debtor is an undischarged bankrupt the nominee must send copies of his report, the proposal and the statement of affairs to the official receiver or trustee and to any petitioning creditor if a petition has been filed (r.5.5A(3)).

The nominee or supervisor appointed must either be a licensed insolvency practitioner or a member of a body recognised by the secretary of state for that purpose. To date no other body has been given such recognition. In either case he must have in force security for the proper performance of his functions. **3E–92**

In his report the nominee must state whether in his opinion the proposal has a reasonable prospect of being approved and implemented (ss.256 as amended by para.3 and para.5 of Sch.3 of the Insolvency Act 2000). An application may be made to the court for an order replacing a nominee where it is impractical or inappropriate for the nominee to continue to act. Section 260 of the Insolvency Act 1986 as amended by s.3 and para.10 of Sch.3 of the Insolvency Act 2000 provides that approval of a voluntary arrangement binds every person who in accordance with the rules was entitled to vote at the meeting (whether or not he was present or represented at it), or would have been so entitled had he had notice of it. The classes of person who may challenge the outcome of the meeting under s.262 of the Insolvency Act 1986 includes any person who was entitled, in accordance with the rules, to vote at the creditors' meeting or would have been so entitled had he had notice of it (r.5.3(2)). The content of the debtor's proposal must now state how it is proposed to deal with the claims of any person who is bound by the arrangement by virtue of this provision.

Paragraph numbers marked with a "+" can be found online and on CD.

Section 262A, Insolvency Act 1986, as enacted by s.3 and para.12 of Sch.3 of the Insolvency Act 2000, makes it an offence for a debtor to make any false representation or fraudulently to do, or omit to do, anything for the purpose of obtaining the approval of his creditors to a proposal, whether approved or not.

The Proposal

3E-93   The debtor must ensure that his proposal complies with the requirements of r.5.3 of the Insolvency Rules 1986 as amended. In particular it must deal with the EC Regulation on Insolvency Proceedings (see para.3E–26) and give details of the debtor's centre of main interests and/or his establishment (r.5.3(2)(q)). It is also necessary to set out not only the fees to be charged by the intended nominee but also to list the disbursements (r.5.3 (2)(g)).

Application for interim order

3E-94   If the debtor decides that he needs the protection of an interim order then the steps set out in Pt 5 of the Insolvency Rules must be followed. The debtor must give written notice of his proposal together with a copy of the proposal to the intended nominee (r.5.4(1)). If he is an undischarged bankrupt then he must also give notice to the or his trustee (r.5.4(5)). If the nominee is prepared to act he endorses his consent on the notice (r.5.4(3)) and returns it to the debtor. The debtor then has 7 days, or such longer period as the nominee may allow, to give the nominee his statement of affairs (r.5.8(2)).

The application may be made by the debtor where he is not bankrupt or by the debtor, the official receiver or his trustee where he is (s.253(3) of the Insolvency Act 1986). The application is by way of originating application accompanied by an affidavit or witness statement in support. The evidence must comply with r.5.1 of the Insolvency Rules 1986: it should give the reason for the application, details of any execution or other legal process, state whether the debtor is an undischarged bankrupt or able to file his own petition, confirm that there has been no other application within the last 12 months, name the nominee and confirm that he is qualified to act and is willing to act. A copy of the notice served upon the nominee endorsed with his consent to act must be exhibited to the written evidence (r.5.5(2)). If the nominee has completed his enquiries the application may be accompanied by his report.

Interim order

3E-95   Where it is not necessary to give any other party notice the court will often deal with the application in the absence of the parties and will only require a hearing if the papers are not in order. In the absence of a nominee's report the court will make an interim order for 14 days commencing the day following the making of the order and will fix a hearing date within the 14 day period to consider the nominee's report (r.5.6(3)). At the adjourned hearing if the nominee's report has not been filed the court may extend the 14 day period in certain circumstances, if appropriate. Where it has been filed and a date, time and venue have been given for the meeting of creditors (which is not less than 14 days from the date on which it was filed and not more than 28 days from the date on which it is considered by the court) the court will extend the interim order to a date 7 weeks after the proposed date of the meeting and adjourn the application to a date about 3 weeks after the date of the meeting for consideration of the chairman's report. The time scale allows for possible adjournment of the meeting. If the nominee's report accompanies the application the court may make a "concertina order" which combines the two orders set out above. The nominee must state in his report whether the debtor's proposal has a reasonable prospect of being approved (s.256 as amended). As to the obligations of a nominee in reporting to the court see *Greystoke v Hamilton-Smith* [1996] 2 B.C.L.C. 429; [1997] B.P.I.R. 24).

Where it has been necessary to give notice to other parties a hearing date will be fixed for consideration of the application when the parties will have the opportunity to make representations to the court about the proposal.

The court has a discretion as to whether or not to make an interim order. It will not make an order if the proposal is not viable (*Cooper v Fearnley* [1997] B.P.I.R. 20; *Hook v Jewson Ltd* [1997] B.C.C. 752) or cannot achieve the requisite majority (*Re Cove* [1990] 1 All E.R. 949). As to the importance of adhering to the statutory regime applicable to interim orders and individual voluntary arrangements see, for example,

Paragraph numbers marked with a "+" can be found online and on CD.

Greystoke v Hamilton-Smith [1996] 2 B.C.L.C. 429; [1997] B.P.I.R. 24; *Fletcher v Vooght* [2000] B.P.I.R. 435 and *Re N (a debtor)* [2002] B.P.I.R. 1024.

Chairman's report

The chairman's report must state whether the proposal was approved, with or **3E–96** without modifications, or rejected, set out the resolutions and the decision on each one, list the creditors who were present and how they voted, indicate whether it is governed by the E.C. Regulation on Insolvency Proceedings and if so whether the proceedings are main or territorial proceedings and include any other information he thinks should be made known to the court (r.5.22(2)). As to the chairman's obligations in conducting the meeting of creditors see *Re a Debtor (No.222 of 1990) Ex p. Bank of Ireland* [1992] B.C.L.C. 137; [1993] B.C.L.C. 233; as to his obligations in reporting to the court see *Re N (a debtor)* [2002] B.P.I.R. 1024.

Challenges

Within 28 days of the day on which the chairman's report was made to the court **3E–97** the debtor, a person entitled to vote at the creditors' meeting, the nominee, and, where the debtor is an undischarged bankrupt, the official receiver or trustee, may apply to challenge the approval of the arrangement on the ground of unfair prejudice or material irregularity at or in relation to the meeting (s.262 of the Insolvency Act 1986). The 28-day period may be extended (*Tager v Westpac Banking Corp* [1998] B.C.C. 73; [1997] 1 B.C.L.C. 313; [1997] B.P.I.R. 543.The application is made initially to the registrar and must be supported by written evidence detailing the matters complained of. As to creditors bound who did not receive notice, see para.3E–92, above.

Bankruptcy (Part IX Insolvency Act 1986)

Part IX of the Act enables a petition for a bankruptcy order to be presented by a **3E–98** creditor or creditors, the debtor, a temporary administrator within the meaning of Art.38 of the EC Regulation, a liquidator within the meaning of Art.2(b) appointed in proceedings by virtue of art.3(1) of the EC Regulation and the supervisor of a voluntary arrangement (s.264(1) of the Insolvency Act 1986).

Presentation of petition

A creditor's petition is normally presented to the court in whose insolvency district **3E–99** the debtor has carried on business; this may be different from the insolvency district in which the debtor resides.Petitions presented by government departments are always presented in the High Court. If the debtor is resident or carries on business in the London insolvency district or is not resident in England and Wales or his place of business or residence is not known the petition may also be presented in the High Court. See generally r.6.9 of the Insolvency Rules 1986.

Grounds of a creditor's petition

The grounds for a creditor's petition are set out in s.267(2) of the Insolvency Act **3E–100** 1986. A creditor may present a petition where the amount of the debt or debts is equal to or greater than the bankruptcy level, currently £750, the debt or debts are for a liquidated sum payable either immediately or at some future time and are unsecured and the debtor appears either to be unable to pay or to have no reasonable prospect of paying the debt or debts. Also there must be no outstanding application to set aside a statutory demand. It is possible for creditors to join in the presentation of a creditor's petition: the debts do not need to be interrelated but can be entirely separate. The creditor has a duty to disclose whether he holds any security though he may undertake in the petition to give it up for the benefit of all the creditors (s.269(1)(a)).

Inability to pay debts —The debtor is deemed to be unable to pay his debts if 3 weeks **3E–101** have elapsed since service of a statutory demand and the demand has not been complied with or set aside, or if execution of a judgment or court order in favour of the petitioner has been returned unsatisfied (s.268). As to the requirements in relation to unsatisfied execution see *Re a debtor (No.340 of 1992)* [1996] 2 All E.R. 211.

Statutory demand

The form of the statutory demand and the information it must contain is prescribed **3E–102** by rr.6.1 and 6.2. The form to be used will vary depending on the nature of the debt.

Paragraph numbers marked with a "+" can be found online and on CD.

The creditor is under an obligation to do all that is reasonable to bring the demand to the debtor's attention and, if practicable, to cause personal service to be effected (r.6.3(2)). The Practice Direction sets out in detail the steps to be taken to effect service. Where substituted service is effected the court will need to satisfied that the creditor has taken all steps which would justify the court making an order for substituted service of a petition

Application to set aside statutory demand

3E-103   The debtor may apply to the court to set aside the statutory demand within 18 days of its service upon him. The court will consider the application and will dismiss it summarily if it considers that it has no real prospect of success (r.6.5(1)); for example where the demand is based on a judgment, the court will not go behind it at this stage. In all other cases a date will be fixed for a directions hearing. As to the grounds on which the court will set aside a demand see r.6.5(4) of the Insolvency Rules 1986.

Paragraph 12 of the Practice Direction refers to the need to show a genuine triable issue. It would appear that the decision in *BPR Graphic Engineers (Yorks) Ltd* [2002] B.P.I.R. 544 to the effect that the test is lower than that applicable on an application for summary judgement no longer applies. The Court of Appeal has now held that there is no practical difference between a "genuine triable issue" and a "real prospect of success" for the purpose of an application to set aside a demand (*Ashworth v Newnote Ltd* [2007] EWCA Civ 793; [2007] B.P.I.R. 1012).

A petition (other than an expedited petition) may not be presented until the application is dealt with.

Expedited petition

3E-104   Although the prescribed period for compliance with a statutory demand is 3 weeks, if a creditor can establish that there is a serious possibility that before the end of the 3 week period the value of the debtor's property will be significantly diminished then the court may allow a petition to be presented before the expiry of the 3 weeks but no bankruptcy order can be made until 3 weeks have elapsed (s.270).

Petition

3E-105   The content of the petition (as to which see rr.6.6 – 6.11) must be verified (r.6.12(1)) and if it relies upon an unsatisfied statutory demand written evidence must be filed establishing service of the demand. The requirements to satisfy the court that service has been properly affected are set out in para.13 of the Practice Direction. If the petition relies upon a demand served more than 4 months before the filing of the petition the reason for the delay must be explained in the affidavit of verification, r.6.12(7).

The petition must be served personally. If this proves to be impossible then an application for substituted service may be made (see para.11 of the Practice Direction). The court may order service by post or other appropriate means, advertisement in a national newspaper or (rarely) the London Gazette. Again the Practice Direction sets out the criteria for this. The petition must comply with the EC Regulation and state whether it will apply and if so whether the proceedings will be main, territorial or secondary proceedings and the debtor's centre of main interests. Once presented the court fixes a date, time and place for the hearing and seals sufficient copies for service.

Service of the petition

3E-106   The petition must be served at least 14 days before the hearing date, but if service proves to be difficult an application may be made to the court on paper for an extension of the hearing date of the petition (r.6.28 of the Insolvency Rules 1986 and para.14 of the Practice Direction). The application should be made in advance of the hearing date; if made less than 2 days before the hearing costs will not be allowed.

A first extension will generally be granted without evidence, but where a further application is made by written evidence in support may be required.

Hearing of the petition

3E-107   The court will not make a bankruptcy order unless it is satisfied that the debt on which the petition is based is either (a) a debt which has not been paid, secured or compounded for or (b) a debt which the debtor has no reasonable prospect of being able to pay when it falls due (s.271(1)). Thus, at the hearing of the petition the court

Paragraph numbers marked with a "+" can be found online and on CD.

will need to satisfied that that the debt remains due and payable. The petitioner must complete a certificate of continuing debt so as to satisfy the court that the petition debt remains due (r.6.25). In the High Court in London this is incorporated in the attendance sheet. A fresh certificate is required for each adjourned hearing.

When a petition is adjourned the court will also need to be satisfied at the adjourned hearing that the petitioner has complied with r.6.29 and given written notice to the debtor of the adjourned hearing date and time, regardless of whether the debtor attended the previous hearing. The petitioner is also required to give notice to any creditor who has given notice under r.6.23 but was not present at the hearing when the adjournment was made.

At the hearing the petitioning creditor, the debtor, any supervisor under a voluntary arrangement and any other creditor who has given notice may be heard (r.6.18(3)). If the debtor intends to oppose the petition he must file with the court and serve the petitioning creditor with a notice setting out his grounds of opposition not less than 7 days before the hearing (r.6.21). The petitioning creditor must prepare a list of supporting/opposing creditors (r.6.24).

At the hearing the court, upon being satisfied that the papers are in order, may make a bankruptcy order noting in the record the time when the order was made. The court also has general power to dismiss stay or adjourn a petition for any reason and if stayed to impose conditions (s.266(3)). The court will not allow repeated adjournments to see if a debtor maintains payments by an instalment arrangement agreed with the petitioner.

Withdrawal, substitution and change of carriage of petition

Once issued a petition may not be withdrawn without the permission of the court **3E–108** (s.266(2)). Permission will only be given at a hearing.

At the hearing of the petition any creditor who has given notice and was in a position to issue his own petition at the date the petition was filed may apply to be substituted as petitioner (r.6.30). This will require amendment and possibly re-service of the petition.

Where a creditor who has given proper notice but was not in a position to file a petition at the time the petition was presented appears, and the petition debt remains unpaid, he may apply to the court for carriage of the petition (r.6.31). Amendment of the petition will not be necessary. As to change of carriage generally see *Re Purvis and another* [1997] 3 All E.R. 663.

Debtor's petition

The only ground upon which a debtor may present his own petition is that he is **3E–109** unable to pay his debts (s.272(1) and rr.6.37 to 6.50). The petition must contain sufficient information to establish that it is being brought in the right court and be accompanied by a statement of affairs detailing the debtor's assets and liabilities. The court will usually hear the petition immediately. Generally the High Court will make the order in the absence of the debtor. Where a bankruptcy order is made the court will notify the official receiver immediately.

Review, rescind or vary

Section 375(1) of the Insolvency Act gives the court power to review, rescind or **3E–110** vary any order made by it in the exercise of its jurisdiction. This provision is of very broad application but should not be used in place of an appeal. The fact that an appeal is pending does not prevent to court from rehearing a matter and reviewing any order made. The exercise of the power should be confined to cases in which there has been a change of circumstance since the making of the original order. The court may apply this provision to a bankruptcy order in circumstances where annulment is not possible (*Fitch v Official Receiver* [1996] 1 W.L.R. 242). For a detailed analysis of the jurisdiction see *Papanicola v Humphreys* [2005] EWHC 335 (Ch); [2005] 2 All E.R. 418.

Annulment

The jurisdiction to annul a bankruptcy order is found in ss.261 and 282 of the **3E–111** Insolvency Act. Section 261(1)(a) allows a bankrupt to apply for the annulment of the bankruptcy order if his creditors have at a meeting called for the purpose approved a proposal for a voluntary arrangement. The court cannot make the order before the

Paragraph numbers marked with a "+" can be found online and on CD.

INSOLVENCY

end of the period of 28 days beginning with the day on which the chairman's report was made to the court (s.261(2)). The official receiver and trustee (if appointed) are necessary parties and must be given notice of the application but they are not required to file any report. If the court feels that a relevant obligation under the arrangement has yet to be fulfilled, for example if a third party is to make a single lump sum payment, then the court may adjourn the annulment application until the payment has been received.

Section 282(1) gives the court power to annul a bankruptcy order on the basis that either (a) on grounds existing at the time the order was made it should not have been made or (b) the bankrupt has paid or secured his debts in full. Rules 6.206(1)(a), (2)–(4) as amended relate to ground (a) above. A report is required from the trustee or official receiver. The courts will generally be sympathetic if the debtor can provide a reasonable explanation for non-attendance in circumstances where his attendance would in all probability have led to the adjournment or dismissal of the petition. In such cases the annulment will be on terms that he pays the official receiver's fees, costs charges and expenses and the creditor's costs of the annulment application. Further, unless the creditor agrees to the petition being dismissed, it will be restored to the list for hearing. There is no point in annulling if the debtor is hopelessly insolvent or if the trustee's inquiries reveal that there is a strong case that the bankrupt has entered into antecedent transactions.

Annulment under s.282(1)(b) can only be granted where the official receiver or trustee confirms that he is satisfied it is appropriate and files with the court a detailed report to this effect (r.6.207). In the absence of such report the annulment cannot be granted. Note that before the court makes the order it must generally be satisfied that the debts and costs of the bankruptcy have been paid: the provisions relating to security for bankruptcy costs and debts relate only to those which are disputed or are claimed by creditors who cannot be traced (r.6.211).

The annulment of a bankruptcy order is a matter of discretion, and the court will not make an order where the bankrupt has not, for example, complied with his obligations to the official receiver or where there has been misconduct.

Where after the annulment has been granted a trustee wants an order for his release he must make a separate fee paid application.

Discharge

3E–112   Section 279 of the Insolvency Act 1986 provides for automatic discharge for the majority of bankrupts after one year (s.279(1)) or earlier if the official receiver files notice (see r.6.214A) that the affairs of the bankrupt do not require investigation or that such investigation has been concluded (s.279(2)) in which case the bankrupt is discharged when the notice is filed. The trustee (where one has been appointed) or a creditor may, within 28 days of receiving notice from the official receiver of his intention to file a notice under s.279(2), inform the official receiver that he objects to the proposed course of action (r.6.214A(5)). Reasons for objection must be given. The official receiver may reject the objection, he must also give reasons and the trustee or creditor may appeal (r.6.214A(5)(b) and r.7.50, Insolvency Rules 1986). Any appeal must be made within 14 days of the notification by the official receiver of his decision (r.7.50(2)). The official receiver may still apply to suspend discharge if a bankrupt fails to comply with his obligations. Section 279(3) provides that the official receiver may apply to suspend discharge until the end of a specified period or until the fulfilment of a specified condition (see also r.6.215).

The bankrupt's home

3E–113   Section 283A of the Insolvency Act 1986 introduces restrictions on the right of a trustee to realise the home of the bankrupt. Under this provision, where the bankrupt had an interest in a dwelling-house which was the sole or principal residence of the bankrupt, the bankrupt's spouse or former spouse at the date of the bankruptcy order, that interest ceases to be comprised in the bankrupt's estate at the end of three years beginning with the date of the bankruptcy and revests automatically in the bankrupt unless the trustee makes an application within the three year period or takes any of the other steps set out in the section. The three year period may be extended (s.283A(6)).

Bankruptcy Restrictions Order

3E–114   Section 281A and Sch.4A of the Insolvency Act 1986 set out post-discharge restrictions, the bankruptcy restrictions order and undertaking.

Paragraph numbers marked with a "+" can be found online and on CD.

The Secretary of State for Trade and Industry or the official receiver may make the application for a bankruptcy restrictions order (para.1, Sch.4A, Insolvency Act 1986). It is made as an ordinary application in the bankruptcy and must be supported by a report setting out the conduct relied on (r.6.241). The timing of the application is crucial and it must be made before the end of one year, beginning with the commencement of the bankruptcy (i.e. the making of the bankruptcy order) unless the discharge period has been suspended (para.3, Sch.4A). The application and supporting evidence must be served not more than 14 days after making the application (r.6.242(1)) and the defendant must file an acknowledgment of service indicating whether or not he contests the application not more than 14 days after service upon him (r.6.242(3)). Evidence in opposition must be filed within 28 days of service of the application and served on the Secretary of State within 3 days of filing it at the court (r.6.243(1)). The Secretary of State must file any evidence in reply within 14 days of receipt of the evidence in opposition and serve this on the bankrupt as soon as is reasonably practicable (r.6.243(2)).

A number of grounds of conduct likely to lead to the making of an order are set out in para.2(2) of Sch.4A but these are not exhaustive. The making of an order is obligatory if the court reaches the conclusion that it is appropriate to make one having regard to the bankrupt's conduct (para.2(1), Sch.4A). The order comes into force when it is made and may be for a period of between two and fifteen years (para.3, Sch.4A). The Act and the Rules also allow the court to make an interim bankruptcy restrictions order (see rr.6.245 to 6.248, Insolvency Rules 1986).

See generally *Randhawa v Official Receiver* [2006] EWHC 2946 (Ch); [2007] 1 W.L.R. 1700.

A bankrupt may enter into an undertaking, which has the same effect as an order (paras 7 to 9, Sch.4A; see also r.6.249, Insolvency Rules 1986). As to the circumstances in which it is appropriate to make an interim bankruptcy restrictions order see *Official Receiver v Merchant* [2006] B.P.I.R. 1525.

Appeal

Section 375(2) provides that an appeal from a decision of a County Court or a registrar of the High Court lies to a single judge of the High Court, and an appeal from the decision of that judge is to the Court of Appeal. Paragraph 17 of the Practice Direction sets out the procedure for first and second appeals. The appeal is a true appeal limited to a review of the decision of the lower court (*Vadher v Wesigard* [1997] B.C.C. 219) and will only be allowed if the decision was wrong or unjust because of a serious procedural irregularity or other irregularity in the proceedings. Permission is required for a second appeal and will only be given where either the appeal raises an important point of principle or practice or there is some other compelling reason. Where the first decision has been given by a judge of the High Court then either his permission is required or, if he refuses, the permission of the Court of Appeal is required before the appeal can proceed.

With effect from October 2, 2006 a first appeal in insolvency proceedings is subject to the permission requirement in CPR, r.52.3. The time in which to appeal is extended from 14 to 21 days. See also para.3E–123 below.

3E–115

Applications to fix an office holder's remuneration

The Insolvency Act 1986 and the Insolvency Rules 1986 allow an office holder to apply to the court for his remuneration to be fixed. An administrator may apply (rr.2.47(6) and 2.49(1)), as may a liquidator in relation to the remuneration of a receiver (s.36(1)) or in relation to his own remuneration (rr.4.130(1)) and 4.148A(6)). The court will not generally interfere in relation to the remuneration of a receiver unless it is excessive (*Potters Oils, Re (No.2)* [1986] 1 W.L.R. 201; [1985] 1 B.C.C. 99). The remuneration of a provisional liquidator must be fixed by the court (r.4.30(1)).

3E–116

Detailed guidance on office holders' remuneration is contained in the Report (July 1998), Statement of Insolvency Practice 9 (Recovery Professionals) and the Practice Statement—The Fixing and Approval of the Remuneration of Appointees (2004) the text of which can be found at para.3E–117 to 3E–123.

As to recent case law see *Barker v Bajjon* [2008] B.P.I.R. 771; *Cabletel Installations Ltd (In Liquidation), Re* [2005] B.P.I.R. 28, Ch D; *Independent Insurance Co Ltd (No.1), Re*

Paragraph numbers marked with a "+" can be found online and on CD.

[2002] EWHC 1577 (Ch); [2003] B.P.I.R. 562; [2002] 2 B.C.L.C. 709, Ch D; *Independent Insurance Co Ltd (No.2)*; Re [2003] EWHC 51 (Ch); [2003] B.P.I.R. 577; [2003] 1 B.C.L.C. 640, Ch D; *Mirror Group Newspapers plc v Maxwell (No.2)* [1998] 1 B.C.L.C. 638; [1998] B.C.C. 324; Ch D; *Simion v Brown* [2007] EWHC 511 (Ch); [2007] B.P.I.R. 412, *UIC Insurance Company Ltd (In Provisional Liquidation) (No.1)*, Re [2006] EWHC 2717 (Ch); [2007] B.P.I.R. 494, Ch D; *UIC Insurance Company Ltd (In Provisional Liquidation) (No.2), Re* [2007] B.P.I.R. 589 Ch D.

Practice Statement—The Fixing and Approval of the Remuneration of Appointees (2004)

3E–117

For "Practice Statement—The Fixing and Approval of the Remuneration of Appointees (2004)" see paragraphs 3E–118+ to 3E–123+ on White Book on Westlaw UK or the Civil Procedure CD.

Practice Note on the Hearing of Insolvency Proceedings

3E–124   1. The following statement was issued by the Vice-Chancellor.

2. This Practice Note supersedes all previous Practice Statements of the Bankruptcy Registrars dealing with jurisdiction and work distribution and the Guidelines issued by the Insolvency Court Users' Committee in November 1988.

3. As a general rule all petitions, claims and applications (except for those listed in paragraph 4 below) should be listed for initial hearing before a registrar or district judge in accordance with rule 7.6(2) Insolvency Rules 1986.

4. The following applications should always be listed before a judge:

Proceedings relating to insolvent companies

- applications for committal for contempt
- applications for an administration order
- applications for an injunction
- applications for the appointment of a provisional liquidator
- interim applications and applications for directions or case management after any proceedings have been referred or adjourned to the judge (except where liberty to apply to the registrar or district judge has been given);

Proceedings relating to insolvent individuals

- applications for committal for contempt
- applications for an injunction
- interim applications and applications for directions or case management after any proceedings have been referred or adjourned to the judge (except where liberty to apply to the registrar or district judge has been given).

5. When deciding whether to hear proceedings themselves or refer or adjourn them to the judge, the registrar or district judge should have regard to the following factors:

- the complexity of the proceedings
- whether the proceedings raise new or controversial points of law
- the likely date and length of the hearing

Paragraph numbers marked with a "+" can be found online and on CD.

- public interest in the proceedings
- the availability in the court which is likely to hear the proceedings of relevant specialist expertise.

6. Litigants and their advisors are reminded that paragraph 17 of the Practice Direction on Insolvency Proceedings applies to appeals and that an appeal from a registrar, district judge or County Court judge lies, in the first instance and without permission, to a single judge of the High Court.

23rd May 2005

Practice Note—Validation Orders (ss.127 and 284 Insolvency Act 1986)

The following Practice Note was issued by the Chancellor of the High Court. **3E–125.0**

Companies **3E–125**

1. Section 127(1) Insolvency Act 1986 provides,

"In a winding up by the court, any disposition of the company's property, and any transfer of shares, or alteration in the status of the company's members, made after the commencement of the winding up is, unless the court otherwise orders, void".

Section 129(2) Insolvency Act 1986 provides that,

"[T]he winding up of a company by the court is deemed to commence at the time of the presentation of the petition for winding up".

2. A company against which a winding up petition has been presented ("the company") may apply to the court after presentation of the petition for relief from the effects of the foregoing provisions by seeking an order that a disposition or dispositions of its property, including payments out of its bank account (whether such account is in credit or overdrawn), shall not be void in the event of a winding up order being made on the hearing of the petition (a "validation order").

3. In accordance with the *Practice Note on the Hearing of Insolvency Proceedings of 23 May 2005* [2005] BCC 456, [2005] B.P.I.R. 688 an application for a validation order should generally be made to the registrar or district judge. An application should be made to the judge only (a) where it is urgent and no registrar or district judge is available to hear it, or (b) where it is complex or raises new or controversial points of law, or (c) is estimated to last longer than 30 minutes.

4. Save in exceptional circumstances, notice of the making of the application should be given to (a) the petitioning creditor, (b) any person entitled to receive a copy of the petition pursuant to r. 4.10 Insolvency Rules 1986, (c) any creditor who has given notice to the petitioner of his intention to appear on the hearing of the petition pursuant to r. 4.16 Insolvency Rules 1986 and (d) any creditor who has been substituted as petitioner pursuant to r. 4.19 Insolvency Rules 1986.

5. The application should be supported by written evidence in the form of an affidavit or witness statement which, save in exceptional circumstances, should be made by a director or officer of the company who is intimately acquainted with the company's affairs and financial

Paragraph numbers marked with a "+" can be found online and on CD.

circumstances. If appropriate, supporting evidence in the form of an affidavit or witness statement from the company's accountant should also be produced.

6. The extent and contents of the evidence will vary according to the circumstances and the nature of the relief sought, but in the majority of cases it should include, as a minimum, the following information:

    (a) when and to whom notice has been given in accordance with paragraph 4 above;

    (b) the company's registered office;

    (c) company's nominal and paid up capital;

    (d) details of the circumstances leading to presentation of the petition;

    (e) how the company became aware of presentation of the petition;

    (f) whether the petition debt is admitted or disputed and, if the latter, brief details of the basis on which the debt is disputed;

    (g) full details of the company's financial position including details of its assets (including details of any security and the amount(s) secured) and liabilities, which should be supported, as far as possible, by documentary evidence, e.g. the latest filed accounts, any draft audited accounts, management accounts or estimated statement of affairs;

    (h) a cash flow forecast and profit and loss projection for the period for which the order is sought;

    (i) details of the dispositions or payments in respect of which an order is sought;

    (j) the reasons relied on in support of the need for such dispositions or payments to be made;

    (k) other information relevant to the exercise of the court's discretion;

    (l) details of any consents obtained from the persons mentioned in paragraph 4 above (supported by documentary evidence where appropriate).

7. Where an application is made urgently to enable payments to be made which are essential to continued trading (e.g. wages) and it is not possible to assemble all the evidence listed above, the court may consider granting limited relief for a short period, but there should be sufficient evidence to satisfy the court that the interests of creditors are unlikely to be prejudiced.

8. Where the application involves a disposition of property the court will need details of the property (including its title number if the property is land) and to be satisfied that any proposed disposal will be at a proper value. Accordingly an independent valuation should be obtained and exhibited to the evidence.

9. The court will need to be satisfied by credible evidence that the company is solvent and able to pay its debts as they fall due or that a particular transaction or series of transactions in respect of which the order is sought will be beneficial to or will not prejudice the interests

Paragraph numbers marked with a "+" can be found online and on CD.

of all the unsecured creditors as a class (*Denney v John Hudson & Co Ltd* [1992] B.C.L.C. 901, [1992] BCC 503, CA; *Re Fairway Graphics Ltd* [1991] B.C.L.C. 468).

10. A draft of the order sought should be attached to the application.

Individuals

11. Section 284 Insolvency Act 1986 provides, inter alia,

"(1) Where a person is adjudged bankrupt, any disposition of property made by that person in the period to which this section applies is void except to the extent that it is or was made with the consent of the court, or is or was subsequently ratified by the court.

"(2) Subsection (1) applies to a payment (whether in cash or otherwise) as it applies to a disposition of property and, accordingly, where any payment is void by virtue of that subsection, the person shall hold the sum paid for the bankrupt as part of his estate.

"(3) This section applies to the period beginning with the day of the presentation of the petition for the bankruptcy order and ending with the vesting, under Chapter IV of this Part [of the Act], of the bankrupt's estate in a trustee".

12. A person against whom a bankruptcy petition has been presented ("the debtor") may apply to the court after presentation of the petition for relief from the effects of the foregoing provisions by seeking an order that any disposition of his assets or payment made out of his funds, including any bank account (whether it is in credit or overdrawn), shall not be void in the event of a bankruptcy order being made on the petition (a "validation order").

13. In accordance with the *Practice Note on the Hearing of Insolvency Proceedings of 23 May 2005* [2005] BCC 456, [2005] BPIR 688 an application for a validation order should be made to the registrar or district judge.

14. Save in exceptional circumstances, notice of the making of the application should be given to (a) the petitioning creditor(s) or other petitioner, (b) any creditor who has given notice to the petitioner of his intention to appear on the hearing of the petition pursuant to r. 6.23 Insolvency Rules 1986, (c) any creditor who has been substituted as petitioner pursuant to r. 6.30 Insolvency Rules 1986 and (d) any creditor who has carriage of the petition pursuant to r. 6.3 1 Insolvency Rules 1986.

15. The application should be supported by written evidence in the form of an affidavit or witness statement which, save in exceptional circumstances, should be made by the debtor. If appropriate, supporting evidence in the form of an affidavit or witness statement from the debtor's accountant should also be produced.

16. The extent and contents of the evidence will vary according to the circumstances and the nature of the relief sought, but in a case where the debtor is trading or carrying on business it should include, as a minimum, the following information:

    (a) when and to whom notice has been given in accordance with paragraph 14 above;

Paragraph numbers marked with a "+" can be found online and on CD.

    (b) brief details of the circumstances leading to presentation of the petition;

    (c) how the debtor became aware of the presentation of the petition;

    (d) whether the petition debt is admitted or disputed and, if the latter, brief details of the basis on which the debt is disputed;

    (e) full details of the debtor's financial position including details of his assets (including details of any security and the amount(s) secured) and liabilities, which should be supported, as far as possible, by documentary evidence, e.g. accounts, draft accounts, management accounts or estimated statement of affairs;

    (f) a cash flow forecast and profit and loss projection for the period for which the order is sought;

    (g) details of the dispositions or payments in respect of which an order is sought;

    (h) the reasons relied on in support of the need for such dispositions or payments to be made;

    (i) any other information relevant to the exercise of the court's discretion;

    (j) details of any consents obtained from the persons mentioned in paragraph 14 above (supported by documentary evidence where appropriate).

17. Where an application is made urgently to enable payments to be made which are essential to continued trading (e.g. wages) and it is not possible to assemble all the evidence listed above, the court may consider granting limited relief for a short period, but there should be sufficient evidence to satisfy the court that the interests of creditors are unlikely to be prejudiced.

18. Where the debtor is not trading or carrying on business and the application relates only to a proposed sale, mortgage or re-mortgage of the debtor's home evidence of the following will generally suffice:

    (a) when and to whom notice has been given in accordance with paragraph 14 above;

    (b) whether the petition debt is admitted or disputed and, if the latter, brief details of the basis on which the debt is disputed;

    (c) details of the property to be sold, mortgaged or re-mortgaged (including its title number);

    (d) the value of the property and the proposed sale price, or details of the mortgage or re-mortgage;

    (e) details of any existing mortgages or charges on the property and redemption figures;

    (f) the costs of sale (e.g. solicitors' or agents' costs);

    (g) how and by whom any net proceeds of sale (or sums coming into the debtor's hands as a result of any mortgage or re-mortgage) are to be held pending the final hearing of the petition;

Paragraph numbers marked with a "+" can be found online and on CD.

(h) any other information relevant to the exercise of the court's discretion;

(i) details of any consents obtained from the persons mentioned in paragraph 14 above (supported by documentary evidence where appropriate).

19. Whether or not the debtor is trading or carrying on business, where the application involves a disposition of property the court will need to be satisfied that any proposed disposal will be at a proper value. Accordingly an independent valuation should be obtained and exhibited to the evidence.

20. The court will need to be satisfied by credible evidence that the debtor is solvent and able to pay his debts as they fall due or that a particular transaction or series of transactions in respect of which the order is sought will be beneficial to or will not prejudice the interests of all the unsecured creditors as a class (*Denney v John Hudson & Co Ltd* [1992] B.C.L.C. 901; [1992] BCC 503, CA; *Re Fairway Graphics Ltd* [1991] B.C.L.C. 468).

21. A draft of the order sought should be attached to the application.

Ratification of transactions

22. Similar considerations to those set out above are likely to apply to applications seeking ratification of a transaction or payment after the making of a winding up order or bankruptcy order.

11th January 2007

Insolvency Act 1986

1986 c. 45

3E–126

ARRANGEMENT OF SECTIONS

PART I

Paragraph numbers marked with a "+" can be found online and on CD.

Paragraph numbers marked with a "+" can be found online and on CD.

Paragraph numbers marked with a "+" can be found online and on CD.

Paragraph numbers marked with a "+" can be found online and on CD.

Paragraph numbers marked with a "+" can be found online and on CD.

Paragraph numbers marked with a "+" can be found online and on CD.

Paragraph numbers marked with a "+" can be found online and on CD.

INSOLVENCY

Paragraph numbers marked with a "+" can be found online and on CD.

Paragraph numbers marked with a "+" can be found online and on CD.

Paragraph numbers marked with a "+" can be found online and on CD.

**Paragraph numbers marked with a "+" denote content that is available on White
Book on Westlaw UK or the Civil Procedure CD.**

The Insolvency Rules 1986

1986/1925

3E–1365

ARRANGEMENT OF SECTIONS

Paragraph numbers marked with a "+" can be found online and on CD.

Paragraph numbers marked with a "+" can be found online and on CD.

Paragraph numbers marked with a "+" can be found online and on CD.

Paragraph numbers marked with a "+" can be found online and on CD.

Paragraph numbers marked with a "+" can be found online and on CD.

INSOLVENCY

Paragraph numbers marked with a "+" can be found online and on CD.

Paragraph numbers marked with a "+" can be found online and on CD.

Paragraph numbers marked with a "+" can be found online and on CD.

Paragraph numbers marked with a "+" can be found online and on CD.

INSOLVENCY

Paragraph numbers marked with a "+" can be found online and on CD.

Paragraph numbers marked with a "+" can be found online and on CD.

Paragraph numbers marked with a "+" can be found online and on CD.

Paragraph numbers marked with a "+" can be found online and on CD.

Paragraph numbers marked with a "+" can be found online and on CD.

Paragraph numbers marked with a "+" can be found online and on CD.

Paragraph numbers marked with a "+" can be found online and on CD.

Paragraph numbers marked with a "+" denote content that is available on the White Book on Westlaw UK Service or the Civil Procedure CD.

INSOLVENCY

Paragraph numbers marked with a "+" can be found online and on CD.

3F   PERSONAL INJURY

Introduction

Personal injury litigation forms a significant percentage of the work of the civil courts. This section includes materials which will be of special use to practitioners in this important area. Of course, the CPR apply to all types of litigation and this Section therefore supplements the rules and commentary in Vol.1. The CPR heralded a major change of direction for the adversarial system. Litigation is not the first option but is to be resorted to because there is no alternative. Thus the Pre-Action Protocol for Personal Injury Claims (C2–001) and the Pre-Action Protocol for Resolution of Clinical Disputes (C3–001) are the most widely used of the pre-action protocols.

A number of rules in the CPR make special provision for personal injury cases. These include:

r.2.3(1)—definition of "claim for personal injuries"

r.14.1A—Pre-action admissions

r.16.3(3)—pleading requirement for "statement of value"

PD 16 para.4—pleading requirements for PI claims, including the requirement to attach a medical report to the Particulars of Claim where the claimant is relying on the evidence of a medical practitioner

PD 16 para.5—pleading requirements for Fatal Accident Act cases

r.26.6—different financial values in PI cases for purpose of allocation to track

Pt 41—Provisional Damages

In addition the following rules, though not confined to PI cases, are often encountered:

Pt 25.1—Interim Remedies

PD 25B—Interim Payments

PD 26 para.12.4—Disposal Hearings

Part 28—The Fast Track (most fast track cases are PI cases)

r.31.6—standard disclosure

r.31.16—pre-action disclosure

Pt 35—Expert Evidence

Pt 36—Offers to Settle and Payments into Court

Pt 41, Sect.II—the courts powers to order periodical payments in PI cases

There are relatively few rules that have no application at all to PI cases. Thus Parts not specifically mentioned here should be referred to as the need arises.

In addition to statutes thought to be of particular use to PI practitioners this section includes the Rehabilitation Code of Practice. Rehabilitation is a welcome development and is something to be considered in all cases. It is of particular importance where the claimant has suffered serious injury. Rehabilitation concentrates on assessing the claimant's needs (including medical treatment) and for the defendant's insurers to meet the cost of providing them at an early stage. This marks a departure from thinking of claims solely in terms of money. Successful rehabilitation provides both a quicker and better outcome for the claimant and a lower cost for insurers. The Code provides a framework supported by all the main associations for insurers and PI lawyers in the UK. Note that the Rehabilitation Protocol now formally forms part of the Personal Injury Pre-Action protocol.

Material relevant to personal injury located elsewhere in this work

Paragraph numbers marked with a "+" can be found online and on CD.

Access to Health Records Act 1990

3F–3

(1990 c.23)

ARRANGEMENT OF SECTIONS

Paragraph numbers marked with a "+" denote content that is available on White Book on Westlaw UK or the Civil Procedure CD.

General note

3F–4 *The Access to Health Records Act 1990 came into force on 1st November 1991.*

The practical application of the parts of this Act included here, following the modifications introduced by the Data Protection Act 1998 is to enable the obtaining of the health records (as defined in s.1) of (in Scotland) persons who lack capacity, and more generally in relation to the medical records of deceased persons (where the application may be made by the Personal Representative of the Deceased or any person having a claim arising from the Deceased's death. The categories of persons entitled to apply under this Act were restricted in favour of the general personal data access regime contained in the Data Protection Act 1998, but use of the Access to Health Records Act 1990 may still be required for the two categories of application just referred to. Only the sections of direct relevance to personal injury claims are set out here.

Obtaining medical records: the 1990 Act and the Data Protection Act 1998

3F–5 In general patients (in the non-CPR sense of that term) have a right to have copies of their medical records, but in exceptional circumstances the law allows for records to be withheld. The Data Protection Act 1998 (most cases) and the Access to Health Records Act 1990 (in the two situations referred to in the preceding note) set out the legal code which applies, but in practice what is required in the first instance is to contact the medical professional concerned or to the Medical Records section or department in the case of larger institutions such as hospitals. The Clinical Disputes protocol at C3–001 in this work contains further information and pro-forma documents to assist. See also Health Service Circular HSC 2000/009 on the topic of patient information. A strictly limited fee may be charged for providing copies, under the provisions of the Data Protection Act 1998. (For a note on fees see the notes to section 4 below).

Disclosure of medical records under the 1990 Act may be refused on the basis set out in s.5.[1]

---

[1] Similarly under the Data Protection Act 1998 a record holder may refuse to supply records if he/she believes that disclosure of the contents may have an adverse affect on

Paragraph numbers marked with a "+" can be found online and on CD.

Medical Reports prepared for insurers/employers—Access to Medical Records Act 1988

For the law relating to access to medical reports prepared on behalf of insurers or employers, see s.1 of the Access to Medical Reports Act 1988 which states:

3F–6

> "It shall be the right of an individual to have access, in accordance with the provisions of this Act, to any medical report relating to the individual which is to be, or has been, supplied by a medical practitioner for employment purposes or insurance purposes".

That Act thus allows patients to obtain access to reports for insurers or employers and provides for the patient to ask for amendments. The patient can require that his/her own comments are appended if the report is not corrected. The Act also requires the patient's consent before any information is released to a third party in the context of reports requested by insurers or employers. The patient must be provided with the report before it is sent if the patient so wishes and the patient also has a right to refuse consent for the provision of a report.

Disclosure by doctor to own legal advisers

Note that there is some authority to the effect that a doctor who discloses a patient's medical records to his own solicitors, for the purpose of seeking legal advice as to whether the doctor is obliged to disclose the records in the course of litigation brought by the patient against him, does not thereby act in breach of the Data Protection legislation or the Access to Health Records Act 1990, or the general law of confidentiality (*Matthew Yeboah Mensah v Robert H Jones* [2004] EWHC 2699 (Ch D)). It was held that the disclosure was necessary to allow the doctor to obtain legal advice as to the extent of his obligation to make disclosure.

3F–7

Relevant Pre-action Protocols

See the Protocol for the Resolution of Clinical Disputes in Vol.1 of this work at C3–001 and the Protocol for Obtaining Hospital Records at C3–019.

3F–8

Definitions

"health record" "patient" "holder" see s.1
"health professional" see s.2
"care" "general practitoner" "Health Authority" "Health Board" "health service body" "information" "make" "Primary Care Trust" "Special Health Authority" "Strategic Health Authority" see s.11

3F–9

For ss.1 to 6 of the Access to Health Records Act 1990 (see Arrangement) plus any related commentary see paragraphs 3F–10+ to 3F–29+ on White Book on Westlaw UK or the Civil Procedure CD.

* * * *

Applications to the court

8.—(1) Subject to subsection (2) below, where the court is satisfied, on an application made by the person concerned within such period as may be prescribed by rules of court, that the holder of a health record has failed to comply with any requirement of this Act, the court may order the holder to comply with that requirement.

3F–30

(2) The court shall not entertain an application under subsection (1) above unless it is satisfied that the applicant has taken all such

the patient's health (Data Protection (Subject Access Modification) (Health) Order 2000 (SI 2000/413)), or may identify a third party (Data Protection Act 1998 s.7(4)). Under the 1998 Act refusal is permitted if copying requires "disproportionate effort" for which see the provisions of the Data Protection (Conditions under Paragraph 3 of Part II of Schedule 1) Order 2000, (SI 2000/185).

Paragraph numbers marked with a "+" can be found online and on CD.

steps to secure compliance with the requirement as may be prescribed by regulations made by the Secretary of State.

(3) For the purposes of subsection (2) above, the Secretary of State may by regulations require the holders of health records to make such arrangements for dealing with complaints that they have failed to comply with any requirements of this Act as may be prescribed by the regulations.

(4) For the purpose of determining any question whether an applicant is entitled to be given access under section 3(2) above to any health record, or any part of a health record, the court—

(a) may require the record or part to be made available for its own inspection; but

(b) shall not, pending determination of that question in the applicant's favour, require the record or part to be disclosed to him or his representatives whether by discovery (or, in Scotland, recovery) or otherwise.

For s.11 of the Access to Health Records Act 1990 (see Arrangement) plus any related commentary see paragraphs 3F–31+ to 3F–32+on White Book on Westlaw UK or the Civil Procedure CD.

Damages Act 1996

3F–33

(1996 c.48)

ARRANGEMENT OF SECTIONS

Paragraph numbers marked with a "+" denote content that is available on White Book on Westlaw UK or the Civil Procedure CD.

Note

3F–34 By s.8 (not reproduced in this work) this Act came into force two months after date of passage, i.e. in force from September 24, 1996.

The Courts Act 2003

3F–35 By s.100 and s.101 of the Courts Act 2003, which received Royal Assent on November 20, 2003, and which came into force on April 1, 2005 (SI 2005/910); ss.2, 2A, 2B and 4 were extensively substituted, and the text is shown here as amended by that Act.

Assumed rate of return on investment of damages

3F–36 1.—(1) In determining the return to be expected from the investment of a sum awarded as damages for future pecuniary loss in an action for personal injury the court shall, subject to and in accordance with rules of court made for the purposes of this section, take into account such rate of return (if any) as may from time to time be prescribed by an order made by the Lord Chancellor.

Paragraph numbers marked with a "+" can be found online and on CD.

(2) Subsection (1) above shall not however prevent the court taking a different rate of return into account if any party to the proceedings shows that it is more appropriate in the case in question.

(3) An order under subsection (1) above may prescribe different rates of return for different classes of case.

(4) Before making an order under subsection (1) above the Lord Chancellor shall consult the Government Actuary and the Treasury; and any order under that subsection shall be made by statutory instrument subject to annulment in pursuance of a resolution of either House of Parliament.

[(5) In the application of this section to Scotland—

(a) for the reference to the Lord Chancellor in subsections (1) and (4) there is substituted a reference to the Scottish Ministers; and

(b) in subsection (4)—

(i) "and the Treasury" is omitted; and

(ii) for "either House of Parliament" there is substituted "the Scottish Parliament".]

Note —Subsection (5) substituted by (Scotland Act 1998 (Consequential Modifications) (No.2) Order (SI 1999/1820) Sch.2(I), para.126(2).   **3F–37**

"personal injury"

By s.7 (not printed here), "personal injury" includes any disease and any impairment of a person's physical or mental condition and references to a claim or action for personal injury include references to such a claim or action brought by virtue of the Law Reform (Miscellaneous Provisions) Act 1934 and to a claim or action brought by virtue of the Fatal Accidents Act 1976.   **3F–38**

Orders and regulations under this section

The Damages (Personal Injury) Order 2001 (SI 2002/2301).   **3F–39**

Note

Section 10 of the Civil Evidence Act 1995 (see 9B–1080) provides that the H.M. Government Actuary's Department's tables known as the Ogden Tables are admissible in evidence when that section comes into force. In practice such tables are regularly used in court in any event: see *Wells v Wells* [1999] 1 A.C. 345 referred to more fully below, and *Longden v British Coal Corp* (1998) A.C. 653 at 671; [1997] 3 W.L.R. 1336 and in Scotland it has been held that the court can take judicial notice of the Ogden Tables at least for some purposes: *O'Brien's Curator Bonis v British Steel Plc* 1991 S.C. 315. In simple terms a claimant who receives a lump sum at trial representing future lost income is expected to be able to derive an investment income from that lump sum whilst also drawing down on the funds. An award of the full amount of the loss as a lump sum would overcompensate the claimant.   **3F–40**

Section 1 of the Damages Act 1996 provides that the Lord Chancellor may by order specify a particular assumed rate of annual return for the calculation of lump sum awards for future pecuniary loss, representing what is in effect the presumed rate of investment return available on the money without undue risk to the capital, on the footing that the capital is gradually drawn down and should be precisely exhausted by the end of the period of anticipated loss. The courts are enjoined by subs.(1) to "take into account" such a specified rate of return in accordance with court rules.

The Lord Chancellor's discount rate

By the Damages (Personal Injury) Order 2001 which came into force on June 28, 2001 the Lord Chancellor specified a rate of 2.5 per cent for this purpose, frequently referred to as the "discount rate".   **3F–41**

Paragraph numbers marked with a "+" can be found online and on CD.

In practice the manner in which practitioners approach the calculation of future pecuniary loss in a straightforward case making use of the 2.5 per cent rate is to consult the 2.5 per cent discount rate column within the Ogden tables, at the row representing the period of time over which the loss will occur. That provides a multiplier for the loss which takes into account normal likelihood of death (other than where there is a particular raised chance of death over and above normal mortality levels) and takes into account the accelerated recovery due to an estimated 2.5 per cent investment income on the lump sum whilst drawing down on the capital over the number of years specified as the loss period.

For general principles of calculation of lump sum damages see the judgment of Stephen J. in the High Court of Australia in *Todorovic v Waller* [1981] 56 A.L.J.R. 59 at 498 (approved in *Wells v Wells*; *Thomas v Brighton Health Authority*; [1999] 1 A.C. 345.) See also *Kemp and Kemp Quantum of Damages* vol.1, para.7–010), Judgment of Lord Pearson in *Taylor v O'Connor* [1971] A.C. 115, 140, and Lord Oliver of Aylmerton in *Hodgson v Trapp* [1989] A.C. 807, 826.

Prior to the announcement of the 2.5 per cent rate by the Lord Chancellor the prevailing rate was set by common law in the absence of any order under s.1. In *Wells v Wells*; *Thomas v Brighton Health Authority*; *Page v Sheerness Steel Co Plc* [1999] 1 A.C. 345 the House of Lords set a guideline rate of 3 per cent based on the average rate of return of Index Linked Government Securities, the House stressing that it was not in their view appropriate to assume a higher rate based on a premise that injured parties will invest in more hazardous forms of investment, per Lord Steyn:

"The premise that plaintiffs, who have perhaps been very seriously injured, are in the same position as ordinary investors is not one that I can accept. Such plaintiffs have not chosen to invest: the tort and its consequences compel them to do so. For plaintiffs an investment in equities is inherently risky, notably in regard to the timing of the investment...

Typically, by investing in equities an ordinary investor takes a calculated risk which he can bear in order to improve his financial position. On the other hand, the typical plaintiff requires the return from an award of damages to provide the necessities of life. For such a plaintiff it is not possible to cut back on medical and nursing care as well as other essential services. His objective must be to ensure that the damages awarded do not run out. It is money that he cannot afford to lose ... It is therefore unrealistic to treat such a plaintiff as an ordinary investor. It seems to me entirely reasonable for such a plaintiff to be cautious and conservative ... it seems to me difficult to say that an investment in index-linked securities by plaintiffs would be unreasonable."

The analysis of the underlying principles is informative notwithstanding the later decision of the Lord Chancellor to set a 2.5 per cent rather than 3 per cent rate and many of the reported cases between 1999 and 2001 refer to a 3 per cent rate in accordance with the *Wells v Wells* judgment.

The Damages (Personal Injury) Order 2001 (SI 2001/2301) sets the "discount rate" which the courts must take into account when awarding damages for future pecuniary loss in personal injury cases, under s.1 of the Damages Act 1996. Prior to the making of this Order the rate in use was fixed by Common Law at 3 per cent following the case of *Wells v Wells*; *Thomas v Brighton Health Authority*; *Page v Sheerness Steel Co Plc* [1999] 1 A.C. 345; [1998] 3 All E.R. 481 HL. The 2001 Order sets the rate at 2.5 per cent with effect from June 28, 2001

Basis for the Lord Chancellor's decision to set the rate

3F–42   The Lord Chancellor has a wide discretion to decide upon the most appropriate rate. His reasons for setting the 2.5 per cent were set out in his Reasons dated July 27, 2001 (*http://www.dca.gov.uk/civil/discount.htm#part3* [Accessed March 30, 2007]) at length, inter alia basing his decision on then current average gross redemption yield figures for Index linked Government Stock:

"it is highly desirable to exercise my powers under the Act so as to produce a situation in which claimants and defendants may have a reasonably clear idea about the impact of the discount rate upon their cases, so as to facilitate negotiation of settlements and the presentation of cases in court. In order to promote this objective, I have concluded that I should:

a. set a single rate to cover all cases.

Paragraph numbers marked with a "+" can be found online and on CD.

b. set a rate which is easy for all parties and their lawyers to apply in practice and which reflects the fact that the rate is bound to be applied in a range of different circumstances over a period of time. For this reason, I consider it appropriate to set the discount rate to the nearest half per cent...

c. set a rate which should obtain for the foreseeable future. I consider it would be very detrimental to the reasonable certainty which is necessary to promote the just and efficient resolution of disputes (by settlement as well as by hearing in court) to make frequent changes to the discount rate. Therefore, whilst I will remain ready to review the discount rate whenever I find there is a significant and established change in the relevant real rates of return to be expected, I do not propose to tinker with the rate frequently to take account of every transient shift in market conditions."

Court's discretion to depart from the 2.5 per cent rate

Whilst the court must take the rate set under this section "into account" the court is **3F–43** not bound to apply it. By s.1(2) the court may take into account a different rate if any party shows that a different rate is more appropriate, though on the strict wording it appears that a court may not decide to take into account a different rate merely of its own motion in the absence of submissions by a party. The courts will be prepared to depart from the rate, it seems, only with great reluctance for example if the Lord Chancellor's reasons for setting a particular rate were demonstrably wrong or omitted to take into account a significant factor. For two failed attempts to vary the former 3 per cent rate (decisions of the Court of Appeal in the period between judgment of the House of Lords in *Wells v Wells* and the announcement of the Lord Chancellor's rate of 2.5 per cent) see *Warriner v Warriner* [2002] 1 W.L.R. 1703 and *Warren v Northern General Hospital NHS Trust* [2000] 1 W.L.R. 1404.

Similarly, attempts to depart from the 2.5 per cent rate by the "back door", based on evidence that future care costs for the claimant would increase at a significantly steeper rate than general inflation, failed in three conjoined appeals to the Court of Appeal handed down on October 16, 2003 (*Cooke v United Bristol Healthcare NHS Trust* [2003] EWCA Civ 1370; *Sheppard v Stibbe* and another; *Page v Lee* [2003] EWCA Civ 1370) in which it was held that such would constitute an illegitimate attempt to subvert the "discount rate" set by the Lord Chancellor to be applied when assessing the multiplier for future loss.

In *Page v Plymouth Hospitals NHS Trust* [2004] EWHC 1154 All E.R. 367 (QB), the court rejected any argument that the Lord Chancellor when fixing the discount rate did so with the intention of abiding by the fudamental principle of full compensation, and had wished to achieve certainty and consistency. He was essentially prescribing the discount rate by reference to index-linked gilt-edged stock and not a mixed portfolio, and it was inherent in the Lord Chancellor's reasons for the 2001 Order that the costs of investment advice were taken into account in setting the discount rate. Accordingly predicted costs of investment advice and fund management charges incurred in the management of the claimant's award of damages could not be recovered as damages.

Periodical payments

2.—(1) A court awarding damages for future pecuniary loss in re- **3F–44** spect of personal injury—

(a) may order that the damages are wholly or partly to take the form of periodical payments, and

(b) shall consider whether to make that order.

(2) A court awarding other damages in respect of personal injury may, if the parties consent, order that the damages are wholly or partly to take the form of periodical payments.

(3) A court may not make an order for periodical payments unless satisfied that the continuity of payment under the order is reasonably secure.

Paragraph numbers marked with a "+" can be found online and on CD.

(4) For the purpose of subsection (3) the continuity of payment under an order is reasonably secure if—

(a) it is protected by a guarantee given under section 6 of or the Schedule to this Act,

(b) it is protected by a scheme under section 213 of theFinancial Services and Markets Act 2000 (compensation) (whether or not as modified by section 4 of this Act), or

(c) the source of payment is a government or health service body.

(5) An order for periodical payments may include provision—

(a) requiring the party responsible for the payments to use a method (selected or to be selected by him) under which the continuity of payment is reasonably secure by virtue of subsection (4);

(b) about how the payments are to be made, if not by a method under which the continuity of payment is reasonably secure by virtue of subsection (4);

(c) requiring the party responsible for the payments to take specified action to secure continuity of payment, where continuity is not reasonably secure by virtue of subsection (4);

(d) enabling a party to apply for a variation of provision included under paragraph (a), (b) or (c).

(6) Where a person has a right to receive payments under an order for periodical payments, or where an arrangement is entered into in satisfaction of an order which gives a person a right to receive periodical payments, that person's right under the order or arrangement may not be assigned or charged without the approval of the court which made the order; and—

(a) a court shall not approve an assignment or charge unless satisfied that special circumstances make it necessary, and

(b) a purported assignment or charge, or agreement to assign or charge, is void unless approved by the court.

(7) Where an order is made for periodical payments, an alteration of the method by which the payments are made shall be treated as a breach of the order (whether or not the method was specified under subsection (5)(b)) unless—

(a) the court which made the order declares its satisfaction that the continuity of payment under the new method is reasonably secure,

(b) the new method is protected by a guarantee given under section 6 of or the Schedule to this Act,

(c) the new method is protected by a scheme under section 213 of the Financial Services and Markets Act 2000 (compensation) (whether or not as modified by section 4 of this Act), or

(d) the source of payment under the new method is a government or health service body.

Paragraph numbers marked with a "+" can be found online and on CD.

(8) An order for periodical payments shall be treated as providing for the amount of payments to vary by reference to the retail prices index (within the meaning of section 833(2) of the Income and Corporation Taxes Act 1988) at such times, and in such a manner, as may be determined by or in accordance with Civil Procedure Rules.

(9) But an order for periodical payments may include provision—

(a) disapplying subsection (8), or

(b) modifying the effect of subsection (8).

Note —The above new text of s.2, and the text of ss.2A and 2B (below) were **3F-45** substituted for the old text of s.2 with effect from April 1, 2005 by SI 2005/901 by virtue of the Courts Act 2003 s.100. The Courts Act 2003 received Royal Assent on November 20, 2003. The 37th Update of the Civil Procedure Rules, published December 17, 2004, included provisions for periodical payments, and the amended rules appear in CPR, Pt 41, Sect.II. Those rules came into force on the date of entry into force of ss.100 and 101 of the Courts Act 2003 (namely April 1, 2005).

Note

For the court rules which relate to periodical payments, see CPR 41 Part II **3F-46** elsewhere in this work. The references to "government or health service body" in subs. (4)(c) and 7(d) are defined in section 2A below, and itemized in the Statutory Instrument which is referred to in the Note to that section below headed "Designated Government and Health Service Bodies".

The original text of s.2 did not provide the court with the power to impose a **3F-47** periodical payments order in a personal injury case, rather the court could make such an order only with the consent of the parties. The new sections 2, 2A and 2B reproduced here and below brought in a regime from April 1, 2005 where consent is not required for such an order where the damages are for future pecuniary loss for personal injury (and the court is now—under the new section 2(b)— required to consider whether such an order should be made. (Consent remains necessary for other forms of loss). This was in accordance with the recommendation of the Law Commission Report No.224 Cm. 2646 "Structured Settlements and Interim and Provisional Damages". The Law Commission recommended that in the absence of agreement there should be no judicial power to impose a structured settlement (paras 3.37–3.53 of the Report). Judicially however the power for the courts to order periodical payments was called for: See per Lord Steyn in *Wells v Wells*; *Thomas v Brighton Health Authority*; *Page v Sheerness Steel Co Plc* [1999] 1 A.C. 345 at 384B where s.2(1) was described as a "dead letter".

See also the Lord Chancellor's consultative document "Damages For Future Loss: Giving the Courts the Power to Order Periodical Payments for Future Loss and Care Costs in Personal Injury Cases", March 2002, which resulted in the Courts Act 2003 ss.100 and 101 to address the absence of a power to order periodical payments. The result was the scheme now set out in sections 2,2A and 2B reproduced below and which replaced this section from April 1, 2005 (SI 2005/910).

One of the potential problems with a periodical payment structured settlement, which can be over the course of the remainder of the claimant's life, is that the insurer or other source of funds for the payments may go into liquidation or otherwise cease to be able to pay at some date in the future, ss.4 to 6 provide a protective regime to deal with such eventualities.

Case law

For an example of s.2(1) in action, see *Peter Godbold v Rashid Mahmood* [2005] **3F-48** EWHC 1002 (QB). A periodical payments order under s.2(1)(a) was made for care and related costs which would recur over time. It was held that a periodical payments order eliminated uncertainty and risks of unfairness, and met the Claimant's needs having regard to factors in CPR PD41B. The order was also preferred because it facilitated budgeting by the Claimant because his income was secure.

As to the power provided under s.29(9), in *Lee Thompstone v Tameside and Glossop Acute Services NHS Trust* [2006] EWHC 2904 (QB) it was held the court was to

Paragraph numbers marked with a "+" can be found online and on CD.

PERSONAL INJURY

determine the way to meet the claimant's needs and that in applying ss.2(8) and 2(9) the claimant bore an evidential burden to adduce evidence sufficient to establish that the Retail Prices Index was inappropriate and that some other measure was appropriate. It was held that there was a probability that the expense of carers which the claimant needed would increase significantly more than the RPI would suggest. Indexation would therefore be insufficient. The court decided that on the facts of the case an indexation in payments linked to the 75th percentile of the annual survey of hours and earnings (ASHE) 6115 (the survey relating to occupational earnings for care assistants and home carers) was appropriate and would provide a reasonably accurate indicator of the growth of the earnings of carers of the type to be employed by the claimant. See also *Flora v Wakom (Heathrow)* [2005] EWHC 2822 (QB) and *A (A Child) v B Hospitals NHS Trust* [2006] EWHC 2833 (Admin), for the ASHE survey, visit *http:// www.statistics.gov.uk/StatBase/Product.asp?vlnk=13101* [Accessed March 30, 2007]

Flora v Wakom (Heathrow) Ltd was appealed unsuccessfully (at [2006] EWCA Civ 1103) where it was confirmed that there was nothing in the language of s.2(8) or (9) to suggest that the power to make provision disapplying or modifying the effect of s.2(8) could only be triggered in an exceptional case. A periodical payments order was not the same as a lump sum order and nothing in the Act suggested that Parliament had intended to provide compensation by periodical payments lower than would be awarded through the usual rule that that a victim of a tort was to be compensated as nearly as possible in full for pecuniary losses. It was noted that the courts should not consider questions of affordability when determining what order to make. Flora was applied, e.g. in *Sarwar v Kamran Ali* [2007] EWHC 1255 (QB). See also *RH v United Bristol Healthcare NHS Trust* [2007] EWHC 1441 (QB) where it was accepted on the facts that it was appropriate to index future periodic payments for the cost of care by reference to the earnings related index 6115 in the ASHE rather than the retail price index. *Thompstone v Tameside and Glossop Acute Services NHS Trust* was appealed, unsuccessfully, at [2008] EWCA Civ 5 and the Court of Appeal there rejected an argument that *Flora* was decided per incuriam.

Model orders

3F–48.1   In *Lee Carl Thompstone (A Minor, by his mother and litigation friend, Heather Brindley) v Thameside Hospital NHS Foundation Trust* [2008] EWHC 2948 the High Court extensively discussed the form of order under s.2 where the court makes provision as to the mechanics of indexation of periodical payments, and the judgment provides model forms of order. The model forms of order are available at para.48.60.2+.

For ss.2A and 2B of the Damages Act 1996 (see Arrangement) plus any related commentary see paragraphs 3F–49+ to 3F–53+ on White Book on Westlaw UK or the Civil Procedure CD.

Provisional damages and fatal accident claims

3F–54   3.—(1) This section applies where a person—

(a) is awarded provisional damages; and

(b) subsequently dies as a result of the act or omission which gave rise to the cause of action for which the damages were awarded.

(2) The award of the provisional damages shall not operate as a bar to an action in respect of that person's death under the Fatal Accidents Act 1976

(3) Such part (if any) of—

(a) the provisional damages; and

(b) any further damages awarded to the person in question before his death,

as was intended to compensate him for pecuniary loss in a period which in the event falls after his death shall be taken into account in assessing the amount of any loss of support suffered by the person or

Paragraph numbers marked with a "+" can be found online and on CD.

persons for whose benefit the action under the Fatal Accidents Act 1976 is brought.

(4) No award of further damages made in respect of that person after his death shall include any amount for loss of income in respect of any period after his death.

(5) In this section "provisional damages" means damages awarded by virtue of subsection (2)(a) of section 32A of the Supreme Court Act 1981 or section 51 of the County Courts Act 1984 and "further damages" means damages awarded by virtue of subsection (2)(b) of either of those sections.

(6) Subsection (2) above applies whether the award of provisional damages was before or after the coming into force of that subsection; and subsections (3) and (4) apply to any award of damages under the 1976 Act or, as the case may be, further damages after the coming into force of those subsections.

Note

3F–55

This section clarifies the linkage between provisional damages, the rights of the dependants of the deceased under the Inheritance (Provision for Family and Dependants) Act 1975, and damages under the Fatal Accidents Act 1976. The section applies where a person was awarded provisional damages—(damages awarded on the basis that there is a recognised specific risk of future development of a medical condition, or of further deterioration, which has not yet resulted in harm) but which will entitle the claimant to pursue a "further" damages claim in the event that the risk crystallises. For "provisional damages" see s.32A(2)(a) of the SCA 1981 and s.51 of the CCA 1984.

If the claimant in due course dies as a result of the tort which gave rise to the cause of action for which provisional damages were awarded, the fact that that award was made will not amount to a bar on the commencement of a claim by the deceased's dependants under the Fatal Accidents Act 1976 (see subs.(2)).

To extent that the award of damages was intended to be compensation for loss covering a period which in the event fell after the deceased died, then by subs.(3) the amount of the damages for that period must be taken into account by the court when it comes to assess damages for loss of support under the Fatal Accidents Act 1976. Relatedly subs.(4) provides that courts may not award amounts of "further damages" in respect loss of income under a provisional damages order after that persons' death. This avoids a risk of double recovery by relatives under both the Fatal Accidents Act 1976 and under the terms of the provisional order made within the deceased's original personal injury claim. For the meaning of "further damages" see s.32A(2)(b) of the SCA 1981 and s.51(2)(b) of the CCA 1984.

For ss.4 and 6 of the Damages Act 1996 (see Arrangement) and Periodical Payments Order—Model Schedule plus any related commentary see paragraphs 3F–56+ to 3F–60.2+ on White Book on Westlaw UK or the Civil Procedure CD.

The Damages (Variation of Periodical Payments) Order 2005

(S.I. 2005 No. 841)

Note —Section 2B(6) allows the Lord Chancellor to specify the circumstances in **3F–61** which a court may vary a periodical payments order. The Damages (Variation of Periodical Payments) Order 2005 (SI 2005/841) provides for such circumstances and the text of the body of the Order appears below.

Citation, commencement, interpretation and extent

1.—(1) This Order may be cited as the Damages (Variation of Periodical Payments) Order 2005 and shall come into force on the fourteenth day after the day on which it is made.

Paragraph numbers marked with a "+" can be found online and on CD.

(2) In this Order—

    (a) "the Act" means the Damages Act 1996;

    (b) "agreement" means an agreement by parties to a claim or action for damages which settles the claim or action and which provides for periodical payments;

    (c) "damages" means damages for future pecuniary loss in respect of personal injury;

    (d) "defence society" means the Medical Defence Union or the Medical Protection Society;

    (e) "variable agreement" means an agreement which contains a provision referred to in Article 9(1);

    (f) "variable order" means an order for periodical payments which contains a provision referred to in Article 2.

(3) In the application of this Order to Northern Ireland—

    (a) "claimant" means plaintiff;

    (b) "permission" means leave;

    (c) "statements of case" means, in the High Court, the writ and pleadings and, in the county court, the civil bill and any notice of intention to defend, defence, notice for particulars, replies and counterclaim.

(4) This Order extends to England and Wales and Northern Ireland.

(5) This Order applies to proceedings begun on or after the date on which it comes into force.

Power to make variable orders

2. If there is proved or admitted to be a chance that at some definite or indefinite time in the future the claimant will—

    (a) as a result of the act or omission which gave rise to the cause of action, develop some serious disease or suffer some serious deterioration, or

    (b) enjoy some significant improvement, in his physical or mental condition, where that condition had been adversely affected as a result of that act or omission,

        the court may, on the application of a party, with the agreement of all the parties, or of its own initiative, provide in an order for periodical payments that it may be varied.

Defendant's financial resources

3. Unless—

    (a) the defendant is insured in respect of the claim,

    (b) the source of payment under the order for periodical payments is a government or health service body within the meaning of section 2A(2) of the Act,

    (c) the payment is guaranteed under section 6 of or the Schedule to the Act, or

    (d) the order is made by consent and the claimant is neither a child, nor a person who lacks capacity within the meaning of the Mental Capacity Act 2005 (c.9) to administer and manage his property and affairs nor a patient within the meaning of Part VII of the Mental Health (Northern Ireland) Order 1986,

        the court will take into account the defendant's likely future financial resources in considering whether to make a variable order.

Award of provisional damages

4. The court may make a variable order in addition to an order for an award of provisional damages made by virtue of section 32A of the Supreme Court Act 1981 or section 51 of the County Courts Act 1984 or, in relation to Northern Ireland, paragraph 10(2)(a) of Schedule 6 to the Administration of Justice Act 1982.

Paragraph numbers marked with a "+" can be found online and on CD.

Contents of variable order

5. Where the court makes a variable order—

(a) the damages must be assessed or agreed on the assumption that the disease, deterioration or improvement will not occur;

(b) the order must specify the disease or type of deterioration or improvement;

(c) the order may specify a period within which an application for it to be varied may be made;

(d) the order may specify more than one disease or type of deterioration or improvement and may, in respect of each, specify a different period within which an application for it to be varied may be made;

(e) the order must provide that a party must obtain the court's permission to apply for it to be varied, unless the court otherwise orders.

Applications to extend period for applying for permission to vary

6. Where a period is specified under Article 5(c) or (d)—

(a) a party may make more than one application to extend the period, and such an application is not to be treated as an application to vary a variable order for the purposes of Article 7;

(b) a party may not make an application for the variable order to be varied after the end of the period specified or such period as extended by the court.

Limit on number of applications to vary

7. A party may make only one application to vary a variable order in respect of each specified disease or type of deterioration or improvement.

Case file

8.—(1) Where the court makes a variable order, the case file documents must be preserved by the court until the end of the period or periods specified under Article 5(c) or (d) or of any extension of them or, if no such period was specified, until the death of the claimant.

(2) The case file documents are, unless the court otherwise orders—

(a) the judgment as entered;

(b) the statements of case;

(c) the schedule of expenses and losses;

(d) a transcript of the judge's oral judgment;

(e) all medical reports relied on;

(f) a transcript of any parts of the claimant's own evidence which the judge considers necessary;

(g) any subsequent orders.

(3) A court officer must ensure that the case file documents are provided by the parties where necessary and filed on the court file.

(4) Where a variable order has been made, the legal representatives of the parties and, if the parties are insured, their insurers, must also preserve their own case file until the end of the period or periods specified under Article 5(c) or (d) or of any extension of them or, if no such period was specified, until the death of the claimant.

Variable agreements

9.—(1) If there is agreed to be a chance that at some definite or indefinite time in the future the claimant will—

(a) as a result of the act or omission which gave rise to the cause of action, develop some serious disease or suffer some serious deterioration, or

(b) enjoy some significant improvement, in his physical or mental condition, where that condition had been adversely affected as a result of that act or omission,

the parties to an agreement may agree that a party to it may apply to the court subsequently for its terms to be varied.

Paragraph numbers marked with a "+" can be found online and on CD.

(2) Where the parties agree to permit an application to vary the terms of an agreement, the agreement—

    (a) must expressly state that a party to it may apply to the court for its terms to be varied;

    (b) must specify the disease or type of deterioration or improvement;

    (c) may specify a period within which an application for it to be varied may be made;

    (d) may specify more than one disease or type of deterioration or improvement and may, in respect of each, specify a different period within which an application for it to be varied may be made.

(3) A party who is permitted by an agreement to apply for its terms to be varied must obtain the court's permission to apply for it to be varied.

Application for permission

10.—(1) An application for permission to apply for a variable order or a variable agreement to be varied must be accompanied by evidence—

    (a) that the disease, deterioration or improvement specified in the order or agreement has occurred, and

    (b) that it has caused or is likely to cause an increase or decrease in the pecuniary loss suffered by the claimant.

(2) Where the applicant is the claimant and he knows that the defendant is insured in respect of the claim and the identity of the defendant's insurers, he must serve the application notice on the insurers as well as on the defendant.

(3) Where the applicant is the claimant and he knows that the defendant is a member of a defence society and the identity of the defence society, he must serve the application notice on the defence society as well as on the defendant.

(4) The respondent to the application may, within 28 days after service of the application, serve written representations on the applicant and, if he does, must file them with the court.

(5) The court will deal with the application without a hearing.

Refusal of permission

11.—(1) Where permission is refused, the applicant may, within 14 days after service of the order, request the decision to be reconsidered at a hearing.

(2) No appeal lies from an order refusing permission after reconsideration.

Grant of permission

12.—(1) Where permission is granted, the court will also give directions as to the application for the variation of the variable order or the variable agreement.

(2) Directions must include directions as to—

    (a) the date by which the application for variation must be served and filed;

    (b) the service and filing of evidence.

(3) No appeal lies from an order granting permission.

Order for variation

13.—(1) On an application for the variation of a variable order or a variable agreement, if the court is satisfied—

    (a) that the disease, deterioration or improvement specified in the order or agreement has occurred, and

    (b) that it has caused or is likely to cause an increase or decrease in the pecuniary loss suffered by the claimant,

    it may order—

        (i) the amount of annual payments to be varied, either from the date of the application for permission or from the date of the application to vary if the order did not require the permission of the court for an application to vary, or from such later date as it may specify in the order;

Paragraph numbers marked with a "+" can be found online and on CD.

(ii) how each payment is to be made during the year and at what intervals;

(iii) a lump sum to be paid in addition to the existing periodical payments.

(2) Section 2(3) to (9) of the Act applies to orders under this Order as it applies to orders for periodical payments.

Application of rules of court

14. In England and Wales, the Civil Procedure Rules 1998 and in Northern Ireland, rules of court apply to applications under this Order, except where this Order makes provision inconsistent with Civil Procedure Rules or rules of court.

Note —Articles 5, 3(b), 3(c) and (3)(d) are amended by the Mental Capacity Act 2005 **3F–62** (Transitional and Consequential Provisions) Order 2007 (SI 2007/1898). Paragraph 3(d) was substituted by SI 2007/1898, art.6, Sch.1, para.37.

Fatal Accidents Act 1976

(1976 c.30)   **3F–63**

ARRANGEMENT OF SECTIONS

Note —The Act still retains its regnal year though it was virtually re-enacted by s.3 **3F–64** of the AJA 1982, subs.(1) substituting the following ss.1 to 4, and subs.(2) amending s.5.

Right of action for wrongful act causing death

1.—(1) If death is caused by any wrongful act, neglect or default **3F–65** which is such as would (if death had not ensued) have entitled the person injured to maintain an action and recover damages in respect thereof, the person who would have been liable if death had not ensued shall be liable to an action for damages, notwithstanding the death of the person injured.

(2) Subject to section 1A(2) below, every such action shall be for the benefit of the dependants of the person ("the deceased") whose death has been so caused.

(3) In this Act "dependant" means—

(a) the wife or husband or former wife or husband of the deceased;

(aa) the civil partner or former civil partner of the deceased;

(b) any person who—

(i) was living with the deceased in the same household immediately before the date of the death; and

(ii) had been living with the deceased in the same household for at least two years before that date; and

(iii) was living during the whole of that period as the husband or wife or civil partner of the deceased;

Paragraph numbers marked with a "+" can be found online and on CD.

PERSONAL INJURY

(c) any parent or other ascendant of the deceased;

(d) any person who was treated by the deceased as his parent;

(e) any child or other descendant of the deceased;

(f) any person (not being a child of the deceased) who, in the case of any marriage to which the deceased was at any time a party, was treated by the deceased as a child of the family in relation to that marriage;

(fa) any person (not being a child of the deceased) who, in the case of any civil partnership in which the deceased was at any time a civil partner, was treated by the deceased as a child of the family in relation to that civil partnership;

(g) any person who is, or is the issue of, a brother, sister, uncle or aunt of the deceased.

(4) The reference to the former wife or husband of the deceased in subsection (3)(a) above includes a reference to a person whose marriage to the deceased has been annulled or declared void as well as a person whose marriage to the deceased has been dissolved.

(4A) The reference to the former civil partner of the deceased in subsection (3)(aa) above includes a reference to a person whose civil partnership with the deceased has been annulled as well as a person whose civil partnership with the deceased has been dissolved.

(5) In deducing any relationship for the purposes of subsection (3) above—

(a) any relationship by marriage or civil partnership shall be treated as a relationship by consanguinity, any relationship of the half blood as a relationship of the whole blood, and the stepchild of any person as his child, and

(b) an illegitimate person shall be treated as the legitimate child of his mother and reputed father.

(6) Any reference in this Act to injury includes any disease and any impairment of a person's physical or mental condition.

3F–66 *Note* —Amended by the Civil Partnership Act 2004 s.83.

Note that in *Kotke v Saffarini* [2005] EWCA Civ 221 it was held that for the purposes of the "living together as husband and wife" test of subs.(3)(b)(iii) (and presumably therefore the "living together as civil partners" test, the trial judge had been correct to approach the test by drawing a distinction between wanting and intending to live in the same household, planning to do so and actually living in the same household. On the facts the deceased had retained his own home, leaving his clothes and belongings and keeping overnight bag at his partner's house. That lasted until he was able to dispose of his own house in order to purchase a new home with the Claimant. The mere sharing of shopping expenses was not the establishment of a joint household.

Bereavement

3F–67 **1A.**—(1) An action under this Act may consist of or include a claim for damages for bereavement.

(2) A claim for damages for bereavement shall only be for the benefit—

(a) of the wife or husband or civil partner of the deceased; and

Paragraph numbers marked with a "+" can be found online and on CD.

(b) where the deceased was a minor who was never married or a civil partner—

    (i) of his parents, if he was legitimate; and

    (ii) of his mother, if he was illegitimate.

(3) Subject to subsection (5) below, the sum to be awarded as damages under this section shall be £11,800.

(4) Where there is a claim for damages under this section for the benefit of both the parents of the deceased, the sum awarded shall be divided equally between them (subject to any deduction falling to be made in respect of costs not recovered from the defendant).

(5) The Lord Chancellor may by order made by statutory instrument, subject to annulment in pursuance of a resolution of either House of Parliament, amend this section by varying the sum of the time being specified in subsection (3) above.

Note —Amended (to insert the sum of £11,800 for causes of action which accrue on **3F–68** or after January 1, 2008) by the Damages for Bereavement (Variation of Sum) (England and Wales) Order 2007 (SI 2007/3489), art.2. Prior to January 1, 2008 the relevant sum was £10,000. The section was also amended by the Civil Partnership Act 2004 s.83.

Persons entitled to bring the action

2.—(1) The action shall be brought by and in the name of the **3F–69** executor or administrator of the deceased.

(2) If—

    (a) there is no executor or administrator of the deceased, or

    (b) no action is brought within six months after the death by and in the name of an executor or administrator of the deceased,

the action may be brought by and in the name of all or any of the persons for whose benefit an executor or administrator could have brought it.

(3) Not more than one action shall lie for and in respect of the same subject matter of complaint.

(4) The plaintiff in the action shall be required to deliver to the defendant or his solicitor full particulars of the persons for whom and on whose behalf the action is brought and of the nature of the claim in respect of which damages are sought to be recovered.

"more than one action"

Section 2(3) has to be construed compatibly with the ECHR (see Human Rights Act **3F–70** 1998 Sch.1), and "action" is to be interpreted as referring to "served process" (*Cachia v Faluyl* [2001] EWCA Civ 998; [2001] 1 W.L.R. 1966, CA).

In *Thompson v Arnold* [2007] EWHC 1875 (QB) it was held that statutory construction which prevented dependants from suing on the basis that the deceased had during her lifetime settled a claim in respect of the injuries, did not offend against Art.6 or Art.8 of the Convention. Not to permit a further claim where the defendant had already satisfied one claim during the deceased's lifetime did not show lack of respect for private or family life: *Reader v Molesworths Bright Clegg Solicitors* [2007] EWCA Civ 169 applied.

Assessment of damages

3.—(1) In the action such damages, other than damages for **3F–71**

Paragraph numbers marked with a "+" can be found online and on CD.

PERSONAL INJURY

bereavement, may be awarded as are proportioned to the injury resulting from the death to the dependants respectively.

(2) After deducting the costs not recovered from the defendant any amount recovered otherwise than as damages for bereavement shall be divided among the dependants in such shares as may be directed.

(3) In an action under this Act where there fall to be assessed damages payable to a widow in respect of the death of her husband there shall not be taken into account the re-marriage of the widow or her prospects of re-marriage.

(4) In an action under this Act where there fall to be assessed damages payable to a person who is a dependant by virtue of section 1(3)(b) above in respect of the death of the person with whom the dependant was living as husband or wife or civil partner there shall be taken into account (together with any other matter that appears to the court to be relevant to the action) the fact that the dependant had no enforceable right to financial support by the deceased as a result of their living together.

(5) If the dependants have incurred funeral expenses in respect of the deceased, damages may be awarded in respect of those expenses.

(6) Money paid into court in satisfaction of a cause of action under this Act may be in one sum without specifying any person's share.

3F–72   *Note* —Amended by the Civil Partnership Act 2004 s.83.

Assessment of damages

3F–73   Where the husband was in receipt of a retirement pension from his former employers' pension fund which constituted the whole or part of his income, the widow on his death suffered a loss of dependency and thus an "injury" under s.3(1) of the Act for which she was entitled to damages, and the allowances paid to her after her husband's death could be disregarded, since these were benefits which accrued to her as a result of his death under s.4 (*Pidduck v Eastern Scottish Omnibuses Ltd* [1990] 1 W.L.R. 993; [1990] 2 All E.R. 69, CA).

See also *Welsh Ambulance Services NHS Trust v Williams* [2008] EWCA Civ 81 (financial benefit that two children brought to the family subsequent to their father's death was irrelevant to the assessment of the dependency under s.3 of the Act. A dependant could not by their conduct after the death affect the value of the dependency).

Assessment of damages: disregard of benefits

3F–74   **4.** In assessing damages in respect of a person's death in an action under this Act, benefits which have accrued or will or may accrue to any person from his estate or otherwise as a result of his death shall be disregarded.

"Benefits"

3F–75   A pension and a widow's allowance received from an employer's pension fund are benefits for the purposes of s.4 and are to be disregarded in assessing damages for the deceased's death: *Pidduck v Eastern Scottish Omnibuses Ltd* [1989] 1 W.L.R. 317; [1989] 2 All E.R. 261. Monies awarded by virtue of the Pneumoconiosis etc. (Workers' Compensation) Act 1979 are not a 'benefit' within s.4 and must be taken into account when assessing damages under the Act: *Cameron v Vinters Defence Systems Ltd* [2007] EWHC 2267 (QB).

In *Arnup v MW White Ltd* [2008] EWCA Civ 447 the Court of Appeal held that the expression "or otherwise as a result of his death" in s.4 was wide enough to cover

Paragraph numbers marked with a "+" can be found online and on CD.

benefits in kind which accrued as a result of the death, and any other kind of benefit which might not yet have been identified.

Contributory negligence

5. Where any person dies as the result partly of his own fault and partly by the fault of any other person or persons, and accordingly if an action were brought for the benefit of the estate under the Law Reform (Miscellaneous Provisions) Act 1934 the damages recoverable could be reduced under section 1(1) of the Law Reform (Contributory Negligence) Act 1945, any damages recoverable in an action under this Act shall be reduced by a proportionate extent. **3F–76**

Note

Amended by the AJA 1982 s.3(2). **3F–77**

Premature action by dependants

An action by the dependants of the deceased claiming damages as dependants under the Fatal Accidents Act commenced within six months of the death of deceased, although premature and perhaps irregular, is nevertheless valid and sustainable where it appears that no executor or administrator of the deceased started proceedings against the defendant within six months of the death of the deceased and that the defendant has not suffered any prejudice by the action by the dependants (*Austin v Hart* [1983] 2 A.C. 640; [1983] 2 All E.R. 341, PC (decided on the provision in an Ordinance in Trinidad and Tobago substantially similar to the Fatal Accidents Act 1976 s.2)). **3F–78**

Road Traffic Act 1988

(1988 c.52) **3F–79**

ARRANGEMENT OF SECTIONS

Paragraph numbers marked with a "+" denote content that is available on White Book on Westlaw UK or the Civil Procedure CD.

Law Reform (Personal Injuries) Act 1948

(11 & 12 GEO. 6 c.41) **3F–99**

ARRANGEMENT OF SECTIONS

Paragraph 1—Common employment

Common employment

1.—(1) It shall not be a defence to an employer who is sued in re- **3F–100**

Paragraph numbers marked with a "+" can be found online and on CD.

spect of personal injuries caused by the negligence of a person employed by him, that that person was at the time the injuries were caused in common employment with the person injured.

(2) Accordingly the Employers'Liability Act 1880, shall cease to have effect, and is hereby repealed.

(3) Any provision contained in a contract of service or apprenticeship, or in an agreement collateral thereto (including a contract or agreement entered into before the commencement of this Act) shall be void in so far as it would have the effect of excluding or limiting any liability of the employer in respect of personal injuries caused to the person employed or apprenticed by the negligence of persons in common employment with him.

Measure of damages
3F–101   2.— [...]

(4) In an action for damages for personal injuries (including any such action arising out of a contract), there shall be disregarded, in determining the reasonableness of any expenses, the possibility of avoiding those expenses or part of them by taking advantage of facilities under the the National Health Service Act 2006 or the National Health Service (Wales) Act 2006 or the National Health Service (Scotland) Act 1978, or of any corresponding facilities in Northern Ireland.

[...]

3F–102   *Note* —Amended by the Fatal Accidents Act 1959; the Social Security (Consequential Provisions) Act 1975 s.1(3) and Sch.2. Social Security Pensions Act 1975 s.65(1) and Sch.4; the National Health Service Act 1977 s.129 and Sch.15; the Health and Social Security Act 1984 Sch.4, para.1; the Social Security Act 1989 Schs 4 and 9; and the Social Security Act 1990 Sch.1; subs. (1), (1A), (3), and (6) omitted by the Social Security (Recovery of Benefits) Act 1997 (1997 c.27), Sch.3 para.1; and the National Health Service (Consequential Provisions) Act 2006 s.2, Sch.1, paras 10, 11.

"Rights"—"value of rights"
3F–103   For the procedure in relation to Recoupment of Benefits from damages awards in personal injury cases see the Social Security (Recovery of Benefits) Act 1997 (1997 c.27) and regulations thereunder.

Definition of "personal injury"
3F–104   **3.** In this Act the expression "personal injury" includes any disease and any impairment of a person's physical or mental condition, and the expression "injured" shall be construed accordingly.

Application to Crown
3F–105   **4.** This Act shall bind the Crown.

* * * *

Short title and commencement
3F–106   **6.**—(1) This Act may be cited as the Law Reform (Personal Injuries) Act 1948.

(2) Section one and subsection (1) of section two of this Act shall

Paragraph numbers marked with a "+" can be found online and on CD.

apply only where the cause of action accrues on or after the day appointed for the National Insurance (Industrial Injuries) Act 1946, to take effect; but subsections (4) and (5) of the said section two shall apply whether the cause of action accrued or the action was commenced before or after the commencement of this Act.

The Untraced Drivers' Agreement Department of Transport Motor Insurers' Bureau (Compensation of Victims of Untraced Drivers)

3F–107.1

For "The Untraced Drivers' Agreement Department of Transport Motor Insurers' Bureau (Compensation of Victims of Untraced Drivers)" plus any related commentary see paragraphs 3F–107+ to 3F–143+ on White Book on Westlaw UK or the Civil Procedure CD.

Motor Insurers' Bureau (Compensation of Victims of Uninsured Drivers) Text of an Agreement dated the 13th August 1999 between the Secretary of State for the Environment, Transport and the Regions and Motor Insurers' Bureau together with some notes on its scope and purpose

3F–143.1

For "The Motor Insurers' Bureau (Compensation of Victims of Uninsured Drivers) Text of an Agreement" plus any related commentary see paragraphs 3F–144+ to 3F–167+ on White Book on Westlaw UK or the Civil Procedure CD.

Notes for the Guidance of Victims of Road Traffic Accidents

3F–167.1

For "Notes for the Guidance of Victims of Road Traffic Accidents" and the "Supplementary Uninsured Drivers Agreement 2008" plus any related commentary see paragraphs 3F–168+ to 3F–181.1+ on White Book on Westlaw UK or the Civil Procedure CD.

Compensation Act 2006

(2006 c.29)

3F–182

ARRANGEMENT OF SECTIONS

PART 1

STANDARD OF CARE

Paragraph numbers marked with a "+" can be found online and on CD.

PERSONAL INJURY

Paragraph numbers marked with a "+" denote content that is available on White Book on Westlaw UK or the Civil Procedure CD.

General note

3F–183   Part 1 of the Compensation Act 2006 reproduced here came into force on the date of Royal Assent (June 25, 2006) but s.16 of the Act makes special provision for s.3 which is discussed there and which has the effect of modifying the date from which s.3 takes effect. The Compensation Act as a whole contains provisions in relation to the law on negligence and breach of statutory duty, damages for mesothelioma, and in relation to the regulation of claims management services. The part reproduced here is that relating to negligence and breach of statutory duty, and damages for mesothelioma.

PART 1

STANDARD OF CARE

Deterrent effect of potential liability

3F–184   **1.** A court considering a claim in negligence or breach of statutory duty may, in determining whether the defendant should have taken particular steps to meet a standard of care (whether by taking precautions against a risk or otherwise), have regard to whether a requirement to take those steps might—

(a) prevent a desirable activity from being undertaken at all, to a particular extent or in a particular way, or

(b) discourage persons from undertaking functions in connection with a desirable activity.

Note

3F–185   Section 1 deals arises from the report of the "Better Regulation Task Force" in May 2004 entitled "Better Routes to Redress". A widespread misapprehension of the law relating to standard of care was perceived to lead to fear of litigation and, in consequence, risk averse behaviour which could be undesirable. The section seeks to clarify the law relating to what constitutes a breach of duty of care and addresses the issue of what amounts to 'reasonable care' when a court is deciding whether that standard has been met. What amounts to 'reasonable care in any particular case varies according to the circumstances. In some cases, what would be required to prevent injury of the kind suffered may be such that to demand it would be to demand more than is reasonable. Section 1 of the Act makes explicit the principle that a court may in determining whether the defendant should have taken particular steps to meet a standard of care take into account whether a requirement to take those steps might prevent a desirable activity from being undertaken, or discourage persons from undertaking functions in connection with a desirable activity. The section appears to be aimed at making explicit the net effects of judgments such as *Tomlinson v Congleton BC* [2003] UKHL 47 (and see *Ratcliff v McConnell* [1999] 1 W.L.R. 670 and *Donoghue v Folkestone Properties Ltd* [2003] 2 W.L.R. 1138). In *Tomlinson* a young man dived into a pool which had been formed from a flooded sand quarry, on a hot day. He had dived there before safely for much of his life but on this occasion struck his head on the sandy bottom and suffered catastrophic injury rendering him tetraplegic. He accepted that he had been a trespasser and relied on the common duty of care owed to him under s.1 of the Occupiers Liability Act 1984 namely to "take such care as is reasonable in all the circumstances of the case to see that he [did] not suffer injury on the premises by reason of the danger concerned". The defendant local authority had for many years prohibited swimming there and Notices had been erected saying "Dangerous Water. No Swimming". As Lord Hoffman noted in judgment, the policy had not been altogether effective because many people ignored the notices. The Claimant argued that the notices had been ineffectual and therefore it was necessary to take more drastic measures to prevent people from going into the water. Various schemes had been considered in the past for rendering the site safe and more attractive but none had been carried out, albeit a scheme had recently been approved and was pending implementation, following a council report which observed "To provide a facility that is open to the public and which contains beach and water areas is, [...] an open invitation and temptation to swim and engage in other water's edge activities despite the cautionary note that is struck by deterrent notices etc., and in that type of situation accidents become inevitable. We must therefore do everything that is reasonably possible to deter, discourage and prevent people from swimming or paddling in the lake or diving into the lake." Their Lordships conceded that there had been no breach, giving speeches in notably strong terms about interference with public freedom to take risk. Per Lord Hoffman at paras 34 and 46 with added italic emphasis indicating the foreshadowing of s.1 of the Compensation Act 2006:

> "34. My Lords, the majority of the Court of Appeal appear to have proceeded on the basis that if there was a foreseeable risk of serious injury, the Council was under a duty to do what was necessary to prevent it. But this in my opinion is an oversimplification. Even in the case of the duty owed to a lawful visitor under section 2(2) of the 1957 Act and even if the risk had been attributable to the state of the premises rather than the acts of Mr Tomlinson, the question of what amounts to "such care as in all the circumstances of the case is reasonable" depends upon assessing, as in the case of common law negligence, not only the likelihood that someone may be injured and the seriousness of the injury which may occur, but also the *social value of the activity which gives rise to the risk and the cost of preventative measures*. These factors have to be balanced against each other."

> "46 ... I think that there is an important question of freedom at stake. It is unjust that the harmless recreation of responsible parents and children with buckets and spades on the beaches should be prohibited in order to comply with what is thought to be a legal duty to safeguard irresponsible visitors against dangers which are perfectly obvious. The fact that such people take no notice of warnings cannot create a duty to take other steps to protect them. I find it difficult to express with appropriate moderation my disagreement with the proposition of Sedley LJ (at para. 45) that it is "only where the risk is so obvious that the occupier can safely assume that nobody will take it that there will be no liability". A duty to protect against obvious risks or self-inflicted harm exists only in cases in which there is no genuine and informed choice, as in the case of employees, or some lack of capacity, such as the inability of children to recognise danger (British Railways Board v Herrington [1972] AC 877) or the despair of prisoners which may lead them to inflict injury on themselves (Reeves v Commissioner of Police [2000] 1 AC 360)."

See also per Lord Hobhouse of Woodborough at 81:

> "81 ... it is not, and should never be, the policy of the law to require the protection of the foolhardy or reckless few to deprive, or interfere with, the enjoyment by the remainder of society of the liberties and amenities to which they are rightly entitled. Does the law require that all trees be cut down because some youths may climb them and fall? Does the law require the coast line and other beauty spots to be lined with warning notices? Does the law require that attractive water side picnic spots be destroyed because of a few foolhardy individuals who choose to ignore warning notices and indulge in activities dangerous only to themselves? The answer to all these questions is, of course, no. [...] In truth, the arguments for the claimant have involved an attack upon the liberties of the citi-

zen which should not be countenanced. They attack the liberty of the individual to engage in dangerous, but otherwise harmless, pastimes at his own risk and the liberty of citizens as a whole fully to enjoy the variety and quality of the landscape of this country. The pursuit of an unrestrained culture of blame and compensation has many evil consequences and one is certainly the interference with the liberty of the citizen. The discussion of social utility in the Illinois Supreme Court is to the same effect: Bucheleres v Chicago Park District 171 Ill 2d 435, at 457–8."

Apologies, offers of treatment or other redress

3F–186 **2.** An apology, an offer of treatment or other redress, shall not of itself amount to an admission of negligence or breach of statutory duty.

Note

3F–187 The section is self-explanatory and codifies existing law.

Mesothelioma: damages

3F–188 **3.**—(1) This section applies where—

    (a) a person ("the responsible person") has negligently or in breach of statutory duty caused or permitted another person ("the victim") to be exposed to asbestos,

    (b) the victim has contracted mesothelioma as a result of exposure to asbestos,

    (c) because of the nature of mesothelioma and the state of medical science, it is not possible to determine with certainty whether it was the exposure mentioned in paragraph (a) or another exposure which caused the victim to become ill, and

    (d) the responsible person is liable in tort, by virtue of the exposure mentioned in paragraph (a), in connection with damage caused to the victim by the disease (whether by reason of having materially increased a risk or for any other reason).

  (2) The responsible person shall be liable—

    (a) in respect of the whole of the damage caused to the victim by the disease (irrespective of whether the victim was also exposed to asbestos—

        (i) other than by the responsible person, whether or not in circumstances in which another person has liability in tort, or

        (ii) by the responsible person in circumstances in which he has no liability in tort), and

    (b) jointly and severally with any other responsible person.

  (3) Subsection (2) does not prevent—

    (a) one responsible person from claiming a contribution from another, or

    (b) a finding of contributory negligence.

  (4) In determining the extent of contributions of different responsible persons in accordance with subsection (3)(a), a court shall

Paragraph numbers marked with a "+" can be found online and on CD.

have regard to the relative lengths of the periods of exposure for which each was responsible; but this subsection shall not apply—

(a) if or to the extent that responsible persons agree to apportion responsibility amongst themselves on some other basis, or

(b) if or to the extent that the court thinks that another basis for determining contributions is more appropriate in the circumstances of a particular case.

(5) In subsection (1) the reference to causing or permitting a person to be exposed to asbestos includes a reference to failing to protect a person from exposure to asbestos.

(6) In the application of this section to Scotland—

(a) a reference to tort shall be taken as a reference to delict, and

(b) a reference to a court shall be taken to include a reference to a jury.

(7) The Treasury may make regulations about the provision of compensation to a responsible person where—

(a) he claims, or would claim, a contribution from another responsible person in accordance with subsection (3)(a), but

(b) he is unable or likely to be unable to obtain the contribution, because an insurer of the other responsible person is unable or likely to be unable to satisfy the claim for a contribution.

[Subsections (8)–(11) not reproduced]

Commencement

3F–189

Section 16 of the Act makes special provision for the commencement of s.3 in terms of the effect which it has, or may have, on settlements of compensation cases in relation to mesothelioma inasmuch as it is partially retrospective. The relevant part of s.16 states as follows

"16.—[...]

(3) Section 16 shall be treated as having always had effect.

(4) But the section shall have no effect in relation to—

(a) a claim which is settled before 3rd May 2006 (whether or not legal proceedings in relation to the claim have been instituted), or

(b) legal proceedings which are determined before that date.

(5) Where a claim is settled on or after that date and before the date on which this Act is passed, a party to the settlement may apply to a relevant court to have the settlement varied; and—

(a) a court is a relevant court for that purpose if it had, or would have had, jurisdiction to determine the claim by way of legal proceedings,

(b) an application shall be brought as an application in, or by way of, proceedings on the claim, and

(c) a court to which an application is made shall vary the settlement to such extent (if any) as appears appropriate to reflect the effect of section 16.

(6) Where legal proceedings are determined on or after that date and before the date on which this Act is passed, a party to the proceedings may apply to the court to vary the determination; and—

(a) "the court" means the court which determined the proceedings,

PERSONAL INJURY

(b) the application shall be treated as an application in the proceedings, and

(c) the court shall vary the determination to such extent (if any) as appears appropriate to reflect the effect of section 3."

Note

3F–189.1 *Regulations unders this section* —See the Compensation Act 2006 (Contribution for Mesothelioma Claims) Regulations 2006 (SI 2006/3259).

Note to s.3

3F–190 In *Fairchild v Glenhaven Funeral Services Ltd* [2002] UKHL 22, the House of Lords it was held that a claimant who contracted mesothelioma after exposure to asbestos at different times by several negligent defendants could sue any of them. Such applied even though he could not prove which exposure was the cause of the disease. Fairchild did not resolve whether liability should be joint and several. In the later case of *Barker v Corus UK Ltd* [2006] UKHL 20, the House of Lords decided that damages were to be apportioned according to the relative degree of contribution by the liable parties to the risk that the person would contract the disease. Section 3 of the Act endeavours to reverse *Barker* inasmuch as that decision meant that the risk of any of the defendants being insolvent and unable to pay the appropriate share would fall on the claimant such that the claimant would need to trace all defendants before liability could be apportioned, or commence multiple claims. Subsections (2) and (3) reverse the effects of the *Barker* judgment by allowing claimants to recover full compensation from any liable person, who in turn may seek a contribution from other liable persons. Subsection (3) also makes clear the existing law that if the victim is found to have negligently exposed himself to asbestos then damages may be reduced by way of contributory negligence. Subsection (4) provides guidance as to how the court should attribute liability, namely by having regard to the relative lengths of exposure to asbestos due to the negligence of each responsible person, though if the responsible persons agree otherwise or the court so decides then a different approach may be taken.

Subsections (7) onwards [not fully reproduced here] provide a power for HM Treasury to make provisions intended to accelerate the payment of damages to mesothelioma victims. Such provisions would enable responsible persons to claim money back from the Financial Services Compensation Scheme in circumstances in which previously only the claimant would have had such a right when another responsible person and their insurer are both insolvent.

For ss.4 to 18 of and Sch.1 to the Compensation Act 2006 (see Arrangement) plus any related commentary see paragraphs 3F–191+ to 3F–220+ on White Book on Westlaw UK or the Civil Procedure CD.

Editorial note

3F–191.1 For a case referring to s.4(2)(a) in the context of representatives at court see *D Miller v Community Links Trust Ltd* (2007) 29/10/2007 (EAT), LTL document No.AC0115268 (unrep.).

NHS Redress Act 2006

3F–221

(2006 c.44)

ARRANGEMENT OF SECTIONS

Paragraph numbers marked with a "+" can be found online and on CD.

Paragraph numbers marked with a "+" denote content that is available on White Book on Westlaw UK or the Civil Procedure CD.

3G   DATA PROTECTION ACT 1998

Introduction

3G–1 The Data Protection Act ("the Act" or "DPA") was passed to implement Directive 95/46 of October 24, 1995 on the protection of individuals with regard to the processing of personal data and the free movement of such data ("Directive 95/46"). It repealed the Data Protection Act 1984 which had been passed to enable the UK to ratify the Convention for the Protection of Individuals with regard to automatic processing of Personal Data ("Treaty 108"). The courts have referred to the Directive, Treaty 108 and the Convention Rights, particularly art.8, in interpreting cases on the Act. In case law since the Act came into force the courts have tended to consider the law of confidence and the emerging privacy rights under art.8 in conjunction with the Act. Further specific rights in relation to telecommunications services and electronic marketing are contained in the Privacy and Electronic Communications (EC Directive) Regulations 2003 (see para.3G–17). Retention of personal data derived from public telecommunications services is mandated by Directive 2006/24. In cases ECJ C–317/04 and C–317/05 the European Court of Justice held that Commission Decision 2004/535 on the transfer of Passenger Name Record on air passengers to the United States was outside the powers of the European Commission under Directive 95/46.

Data Protection Act 1998

(1998 c.29)

PART I

3G–2

PRELIMINARY

Basic interpretative provisions

3G–3 **1.**—(1) In this Act, unless the context otherwise requires—
"data" means information which—

> (a) is being processed by means of equipment operating automatically in response to instructions given for that purpose,
>
> (b) is recorded with the intention that it should be processed by means of such equipment,
>
> (c) is recorded as part of a relevant filing system or with the intention that it should form part of a relevant filing system,
>
> (d) does not fall within paragraph (a), (b) or (c) but forms part of an accessible record as defined by section 68;
>
> (e) is recorded information held by a public authority and does not fall within paragraphs (a) to (d).

"data controller" means, subject to subsection (4), a person who (either alone or jointly or in common with other persons) determines the purposes for which and the manner in which any personal data are, or are to be, processed;

"data processor", in relation to personal data, means any person (other than an employee of the data controller) who processes the data on behalf of the data controller;

"data subject" means an individual who is the subject of personal data;

Paragraph numbers marked with a "+" can be found online and on CD.

"personal data" means data which relate to a living individual who can be identified—

(a) from those data, or

(b) from those data and other information which is in the possession of, or is likely to come into the possession of, the data controller,

and includes any expression of opinion about the individual and any indication of the intentions of the data controller or any other person in respect of the individual;

"processing", in relation to information or data, means obtaining, recording or holding the information or data or carrying out any operation or set of operations on the information or data, including—

(a) organisation, adaptation or alteration of the information or data,

(b) retrieval, consultation or use of the information or data,

(c) disclosure of the information or data by transmission, dissemination or otherwise making available, or

(d) alignment, combination, blocking, erasure or destruction of the information or data;

"relevant filing system"means any set of information relating to individuals to the extent that, although the information is not processed by means of equipment operating automatically in response to instructions given for that purpose, the set is structured, either by reference to individuals or by reference to criteria relating to individuals, in such a way that specific information relating to a particular individual is readily accessible.

Notes

3G–4   "Data"—although the definition limits the scope of the Act by reference to the form in which information is held, material which would fall outside this definition may also be covered because it is the product of the processing of data. In *Campbell v Mirror Group Newspapers* [2003] 2 W.L.R. 80 it was held that the Act covered text and photographs printed in newspapers which were the immediate result of data processing. See para.3G–8 in relation to "processing". Confirmed (para.230) in *Michael Douglas, Catherine Zeta-Jones and Northern Shell Plc v Hello* [2003] EWHC 786. Conversely information held in machine readable form which can no longer be accessed because the technology is no longer available should fall outside the definition. In *Smith v Lloyds Bank Plc* [2005] EWHC 246 (Ch) the court rejected a contention that hard copy should be regarded as "data" because it could be scanned and become data or because it was produced from data within 1(1)(a).

Some types of manual filing systems are caught by this provision. See the definition of "relevant filing system" and para.3G–9.

"Accessible records" are manual records to which access was available under the Access to Health Records Act 1990 (health records) and the Access to Personal Files Act 1987 (personal information held for social work purposes by specified authorities and in relation to public sector tenancies). Accessible records are defined in s.68 and Scheds 11 and 12 of the Act. The rights of access are slightly modified in respect of such records. Such records are covered only by the rights of access and correction under the Act until October 2007, after which the Act applies in full.

Where information falls within the definition because it is intended to process it as data or include it in a relevant filing system s.1(3) provides that it is immaterial that the processing or inclusion should occur outside the EEA.

Paragraph numbers marked with a "+" can be found online and on CD.

Subsection (e) was added by s.68 of the Freedom of Information Act 2000. "Public authority" has the same meaning as in that Act. The effect of this, and further amendments made by ss.69–72 is to extend the right of subject access (see 3G–10), rectification etc. (see 3G–22) and compensation for inaccuracy (see 3G–20) to all types of information after January 1, 2005. The amendments impact only on public sector bodies (see also note 3G–9).

"Data controller"—this is a two part definition, the second part being in s.1(4). The **3G–5** terms "jointly" and "in common" are not defined.

The controller must determine both the manner and purpose of the processing. There may be two or more controllers sharing control in different ways. The Information Commissioner has suggested that:

"the determination of the purposes for which personal data are to be processed is paramount in deciding whether or not a person is a data controller"

Legal Guidance October 2001. The approach has not been tested by the courts and possibly should be treated with caution.

"Data processor"—a data controller who uses a data processor must ensure that the **3G–6** relationship is governed by a contract made or evidenced in writing covering security and control of the data. See Principle 7 Sch.1.

"Personal data" was considered in *Durant v Financial Services Authority* [2003] EWCA **3G–7** Civ 1746; [2004] F.S.R. 28; [2004] IP & T 814. Mr Durant had applied for access to information under s.7 of the Act. The court considered the meaning of the words "relate to" and the extent to which, if any, information must have the data subject as its focus, or main focus, before it is considered to relate to him. It held that the term has a narrow meaning:

"...not all information retrieved from a computer search against an individual's name is personal data within the Act. Mere mention of the data subject in a document held by a data controller does not necessarily amount to his personal data. Whether it does so in any particular instance depends on where it falls in a continuum of relevance or proximity to the data subject as distinct, say, from transactions or matters in which he may have been involved in a greater or lesser degree. It seems to me that there are two notions which may be of assistance. The first is whether the information is biographical in a significant sense, that is going beyond the recording of the putative data subject's involvement in a matter or an event that has no personal connotations, a life event in respect of which his privacy could not be said to be compromised. The second is one of focus. The information should have the putative data subject as its focus rather than some other person with whom he may have been involved or some other transaction or event in which he may have figured or had an interest, for example as in this case an investigation into some other person's or body's conduct that he may have instigated. In short it is information that affects his privacy, whether in his personal or family life, business or professional capacity."

per Auld L.J. at para.28. It should be noted that he went on to refer to the judgment of the European Court in the case of criminal proceedings against *Lindqvist* Case C-101/01 in which the court held that the term "personal data" covered name and identifying data such as a telephone number. Thus the name, and information immediately associated with the name, such as a statement in a report of a meeting that Mr X was present, will fall within the definition but the remainder of the report will not be personal data about Mr X merely by virtue of that one reference.

It is arguable that the definition has been narrowed in transposition from the definition in art.2 of the Directive in which it covers identifiable natural persons that is:

"one who can be identified, directly or indirectly, in particular by reference to an identification number or to one or more factors specific to his physical, physiological, mental, economic, cultural or social identity".

In *Lindqvist* the court held that the name of a person or identification of him by some other means, for instance by giving his telephone number, or information about his working conditions or hobbies, constituted personal data about the individual. *Durant* was applied in *Johnson v The Medical Defence Union Ltd* [2004] EWHC 2509.

In the Joined Cases C-465/00 *Rechnugshof and Osterreichischer Rundfunk* and C-139/01 *Joseph Lauermann and Osterreichischer Rundfunk*, an information request about the salaries paid to senior public servants was held to be information relating to

Paragraph numbers marked with a "+" can be found online and on CD.

identifiable natural persons and was therefore personal data. Activities of a professional nature should not be excluded from the ambit of personal data.

The EU Commission has reviewed the question of UK compliance with Directive 95/46 but no infrigement proceedings have yet been issued. The term has also been considered in a number of regulatory decisions under the FOIA and FOISA .

The House of Lords in *The Common Services Agency and The Scottish Information Commissioner* [2008] UKHL 47 held that the incidences of childhood leukaemia in Dumfries and Galloway were not personal data if the data was effectively anonymised because individual sufferers could not be identified.

In the consolidated appeals of *The Corporate Officer of the House of Commons v The Information Commissioner* EA/2006/0015 and 0016, an information request for the amount of expenses claimed by MPs did not contravene the DPA. Under Principle 1, fair processing notices were only required to be provided "so far as is practical" and failure to provide a notice should not prevent disclosure. Principle 2 was not contravened because the expenses of MPs are already published. The expenses of Scottish MPs have also been disclosed, following *Paul Hutcheon, The Sunday Herald and the Scottish Parliamentary Corporate Body* (Decision 033/2005).

As the definition covers only living individuals, the Act affords no protection for records relating to deceased persons. However in a decision of the Information Tribunal it was held that a form of confidentiality could endure after death to protect such information. See *Pauline Bluck v Information Commission* Appeal EA/2006/0090.

"Sensitive personal data" is defined in s.2 as information about racial or ethnic origin, political opinions, religious beliefs and a number of other specific categories set out in the section. Particular care should be taken when processing such types of data. Before processing such data the controller must ensure that he can rely on one or more of the grounds set out in Sch.3 as well as the normal grounds set out in Sch.2, SI 2000/417 or SI 2006/2068. Considered in *Lindqvist* where the court held that information that an individual had injured her foot and was working half-time on medical grounds was sensitive personal data.

Notes

3G–8   "Processing"—was considered by the Court of Appeal in *Campbell v MGN* [2003] 2 W.L.R. 80 per Lord Phillips MR at para.122 who held that the publication in hard copy, where data had previously been automatically processed, formed part of the processing and falls within the Act. The point was not specifically considered in the House of Lords but appears to have been accepted, per Lord Nicholls of Birkenhead at para.32: "It is not necessary for me to pursue the claim based on the Data Protection Act 1998. The parties were agreed that this claim stands or falls with the outcome of the main claim." If the House did not accept that publication in these circumstances fell under the Data Protection Act, the claim under that Act would have failed irrespective of the failure or success of the main claim. It was further considered in *Paul Johnson v Medical Defence Union* [2007] EWCA Civ 262 where the Court of Appeal held that the act of reading material, some from computerised and some from manual files and summarising the files was not within the definition of processing.

Information, as well as data, may be processed, thus the collection of information orally before it is captured as data may fall within the scope of the Act. This is made explicit in s.1(2).

Notes

3G–9   "Relevant filing system"—in *Durant* (see para.3G–7 above) the Court of Appeal considered three files and a sheaf of papers and agreed with the ruling in the High Court that in each case the material did not satisfy all the elements necessary to fall within the definition:

    — one file was not structured by reference to individuals at all;

    — one was referenced to the claimant but documents were filed in date order only; the other was referenced by issues and although it did contain a section on the claimant, there was no further internal structure of the material so that specific information could not be said to be readily accessible.

"I conclude....that a "relevant filing system" for the purpose of the Act is limited to a system:

        (1) in which the files forming part of it are structured or referenced in such

Paragraph numbers marked with a "+" can be found online and on CD.

a way as clearly to indicate at the outset of the search whether specific information capable of amounting to personal data of an individual requesting it under section 7 is held within the system, and, if so, in which file or files it is held; and

(2) which has, as part of its own structure or referencing mechanism, a sufficiently sophisticated and detailed means of readily indicating whether and where in an individual files or files specific criteria or information about the applicant can be located"

per Auld L.J. at para.50.

The definition is the starting point for the new exclusory definitions of "recorded" and "unstructured" manual information in s.68 and s.69 of the Freedom of Information Act 2000. Section 69 inserts a new s.9A in the DPA which applies to public authorities in England, Wales and Northern Ireland. Equivalent amendments have been made to impact in Scotland by the Freedom of Information (Scotland) Act 2002 (consequential modifications) Order 2004 (SI 2004/3089) made under the Scotland Act 2000 as the Freedom of Information (Scotland) Act 2002, being devolved legislation, could not be used to amend the Data Protection Act 1998. Thus the definition of a relevant filing system excludes material which would fall within these categories of information.

The term derives from "personal data filing system" in the Directive which provides that a data set may exist irrespective of whether the data set is: "centralised, decentralised or dispersed on a functional or geographic basis".

The Directive appears to allow Member States some margin of appreciation in how far they apply the Directive to manual files see art.4 and Recitals 15 and 27. The Government aimed at the narrowest possible coverage. Relevant material can be found in Hansard at Vol 587 No.95 col 467 Lords Rep March 16, 1998.

"Grounds for processing"—a data controller may only process personal data if he can rely on one or more of the six grounds set out in Sch.2. Where sensitive personal data (defined s.2) are to be processed the controller must rely on one or more of the further grounds set out in Sch.3, SI 2000/417 or SI 2006/2068. Where the term "necessary" is used in the Schedules, the word bears the same meaning as in the ECHRFF para.60: *Michael Stone v SE Coast Strategic Health Authority* [2006] EWHC 1668. Where a party has it within its power to comply with the requirements of the Act it cannot use a possible breach of the Data Protection Act as a reason for failure to meet a contractual obligation: *Grow with us v Green Thumb* [2006] EWHC 379.

"Personal or domestic"—data processed only for the personal, domestic or recreational purposes by an individual are exempt from most of the Act including the Principles and the individual rights. It follows that no remedies will be available whatever the use where the controller processes for such purposes s.36.

In *Lindqvist* the European Court had regard to the relevant preamble to the Directive in interpreting the equivalent exemption in the Swedish law. The court held a narrow interpretation applied so material posted on the internet would not fall within the exemption.

* * * *

Right of access to personal data

7.—(1) Subject to the following provisions of this section and to sections 8 and 9, an individual is entitled— **3G–10**

(a) to be informed by any data controller whether personal data of which that individual is the data subject are being processed by or on behalf of that data controller,

(b) if that is the case, to be given by the data controller a description of—

(i) the personal data of which that individual is the data subject,

(ii) the purposes for which they are being or are to be processed, and

Paragraph numbers marked with a "+" can be found online and on CD.

          (iii) the recipients or classes of recipients to whom they are or may be disclosed,

   (c) to have communicated to him in an intelligible form—

          (i) the information constituting any personal data of which that individual is the data subject, and

          (ii) any information available to the data controller as to the source of those data, and

   (d) where the processing by automatic means of personal data of which that individual is the data subject for the purpose of evaluating matters relating to him such as, for example, his performance at work, his credit worthiness, his reliability or his conduct, has constituted or is likely to constitute the sole basis for any decision significantly affecting him, to be informed by the data controller of the logic involved in that decision-taking.

(2) A data controller is not obliged to supply any information under subsection (1) unless he has received—

   (a) a request in writing, and

   (b) except in prescribed cases, such fee (not exceeding the prescribed maximum) as he may require.

(3) Where a data controller—

   (a) reasonably requires further information in order to satisfy himself as to the identity of the person making a request under this section and to locate the information which that person seeks, and

   (b) has informed him of that requirement,

the data controller is not obliged to comply with the request unless he is supplied with that further information.

(4) Where a data controller cannot comply with the request without disclosing information relating to another individual who can be identified from that information, he is not obliged to comply with the request unless—

   (a) the other individual has consented to the disclosure of the information to the person making the request, or

   (b) it is reasonable in all the circumstances to comply with the request without the consent of the other individual.

(5) In subsection (4) the reference to information relating to another individual includes a reference to information identifying that individual as the source of the information sought by the request; and that subsection is not to be construed as excusing a data controller from communicating so much of the information sought by the request as can be communicated without disclosing the identity of the other individual concerned, whether by the omission of names or other identifying particulars or otherwise.

(6) In determining for the purposes of subsection (4)(b) whether it is reasonable in all the circumstances to comply with the request without the consent of the other individual concerned, regard shall be had, in particular, to—

   (a) any duty of confidentiality owed to the other individual,

Paragraph numbers marked with a "+" can be found online and on CD.

(b) any steps taken by the data controller with a view to seeking the consent of the other individual,

(c) whether the other individual is capable of giving consent, and

(d) any express refusal of consent by the other individual.

(7) An individual making a request under this section may, in such cases as may be prescribed, specify that his request is limited to personal data of any prescribed description.

(8) Subject to subsection (4), a data controller shall comply with a request under this section promptly and in any event before the end of the prescribed period beginning with the relevant day.

(9) If a court is satisfied on the application of any person who has made a request under the foregoing provisions of this section that the data controller in question has failed to comply with the request in contravention of those provisions, the court may order him to comply with the request.

(10) In this section—

"prescribed" means prescribed by the Secretary of State by regulations:

"the prescribed maximum" means such amount as may be prescribed:

"the prescribed period" means forty days or such other period as may be prescribed:

"the relevant day", in relation to a request under this section, means the day on which the data controller receives the request or, if later, the first day on which the data controller has both the required fee and the information referred to in subsection (3).

(11) Different amounts or periods may be prescribed under this section in relation to different cases.

Notes

Subject access is one of the "rights of data subjects" under Principle 6 of Sch.1 (interpretation of the provision at para.8a of Pt II of Sch.1). Accordingly failure to comply with it may not only be the basis for an application to court by the data subject but also the subject of a request for assessment of processing by a data subject to the Information Commissioner under s.42. Failure to comply with a subject access request may give rise to the exercise of the Commissioner's supervisory jurisdiction. A data subject who has referred a failure to comply to the Commissioner is not bound to await the Commissioner's response before commencing action but may take independent action under s.7(9), *R. (Lord) v Secretary of State for the Home Department* [2003] EWHC 2073 (Admin). The appropriate procedure for handling an application to the court was considered in *Ezsias v Welsh Ministers* [2007] All E.R. (D) 65.

Since the Human Rights Act 1998 came into force a court must have regard to any relevant jurisprudence of the Court of Human Rights when interpreting legislation. Section 7(5) derives from the judgment of the ECtHR in *Gaskin v UK* [1990] 1 FLR 167; (1990) 12 E.H.R.R. 36 although the case was not referred to in *Lord* which considered (inter alia) this provision.

This section is one of the "subject information provisions" s.27(2). By virtue of s.27(5) the subject information provisions "shall have effect notwithstanding any enactment or rule of law prohibiting or restricting the disclosure or authorising the withholding of information" except as provided by Pt IV. Part IV sets out the exemptions. It follows that, if personal data are properly requested by a data subject from a data controller (see para.3G–5 above) in accordance with this section the data controller

3G–11

DATA PROTECTION

Paragraph numbers marked with a "+" can be found online and on CD.

must supply them unless one of the exemptions listed in Pt IV applies. Part IV incorporates the exemptions in Sch.7.

In a second case brought by Mr Johnson (see para.3G–7 above) *Johnson v The Medical Defence Union Ltd* [2004] EWHC 2509 the court held that the fact that documents did not contain personal data, and were therefore not available to him under a subject access request, did not preclude a claimant from seeking disclosure under CPR, Pt 31.

Rights of Access may also be founded on Convention rights. The European Court of Human Rights has ordered access be provided to information under art.8 rights in *Roche v UK (App.3255/96)* 20 BHRC 99; [2005] All E.R. (D.) 212 (Oct).

Exemptions

Class exemptions apply to personal data processed only for domestic and recreational purposes (s.36) (see para.3G–9 above), information available to the public by or under any enactment (s.34), references provided in confidence when in the hands of the giver only (para.1 Sch.7), judicial appointments and honours (para.3 Sch.7), certain Crown Offices exempt under Data Protection (Crown Appointments) Order 2000 (SI 2000/416), examination scripts (para.9 Sch.7) and where legal professional privilege or the equivalent privilege in Scotland, would apply (para.10 Sch.7).

Other exemptions are limited in extent: national security if "required for the purpose of safeguarding national security", s.28. A claim for exemption under s.28 must be supported by a Ministerial certificate. The breadth of a certificate issued by the Home Secretary was successfully challenged under s.28(6) before the National Security Panel of the Information Tribunal in the case of *Norman Baker MP v Secretary of State for the Home Department* [2001] U.K.H.R.R. 1275. The Panel concluded that the Minister was not justified in issuing a certificate which permitted the Security Service to issue a "neither confirm nor deny" response to a request made under s.7(1)(a) regardless of whether national security would be harmed in the particular case. Where the service of a s.43 notice by the Commissioner is met by the production of a s.28 certificate as a person "directly affected" under s.28(4). On the appeal the Tribunal may make appropriate determinations in those proceedings, including ordering that the Commissioner be given access to the material covered by the certificate. It followed that a certificate issued under s.28(2) which purported to wholly exclude the possible disclosure of information to which the certificate related to the Commissioner would be quashed: *R. (on the application of SSHD) v Information Tribunal*—Interested Party the Information Commissioner [2006] EWHC 2958.

Access to a number of classes of personal data is affected by modification orders which apply specific exemptions. These cover health information in accordance with the Data Protection (Subject Access Modification) (Health) Order 2000 (SI 2000/413), social work data in accordance with the Data Protection (Subject Access Modification) (Social Work) Order 2000 (SI 2000/415) and the Data Protection (Subject Access Modification) (Social Work) (Amendment) Order 2005, education information in accordance with the Data Protection (Subject Access Modification) (Education) Order 2000 (SI 2000/414) and a variety of additional special cases, such as material about embryos and adoption, covered by the Data Protection (Miscellaneous Subject Access Exemption) Order 2000 (SI 2000/419).

The remaining exemptions cover material held for the purposes of journalistic, literary or artistic work (s.32), information held for research purposes (s.33) (both exemptions only applicable where particular conditions apply), information which would be prejudicial to:

— the purposes of the detection of crime and related purposes (s.29);
— a range of regulatory activities (s.31);
— management forecasting or management planning (Sch.7 para.5);
— and negotiation (Sch.7 para.7).

In *R. (on the application of Alan Lord) v Secretary of State for the Home Department* [2003] EWHC 2073 the court held that s.29(1) requires the issue of whether disclosure is likely to prejudice the prevention or detection of crime to be determined in relation to each individual case (paras 122–127).

There are special provisions for access to examination marks to ensure that access rights cannot be used to obtain premature disclosure.

The remaining exemptions cover corporate finance under the Data Protection

Paragraph numbers marked with a "+" can be found online and on CD.

(Corporate Finance Exemption) Order 2000 (SI 2000/184) and preserve the privilege against self incrimination (Sch.7 para.11).

Information which is disclosed under a subject access obligation is not admissible against the disclosing data controller in proceedings for an offence under the Act, (Sch.7 para.11). Note however that the Act itself does not restrict the use of material disclosed as evidence in a prosecution for any other offence. Material disclosed can be used in civil proceedings and a subject access request is often a precursor of proceedings.

Two new exemptions are inserted by the Freedom of Information Act 2000 covering material which would infringe the privileges of the Houses of Parliament (Sch.6 paras 2–5) and information relating to personnel matters (s.33A inserted by s.70). The latter will only apply to manual data held in structured and unstructured files (see para.3G–9).

Note: the number and extent of exemptions has been criticised, as has the proliferation of class exemptions, as being open to challenge for being wider than those permissible under the Directive.

"Previous access rights"—access rights previously exercised by individuals under the Consumer Credit Act 1974, Access to Health Records Act 1990 and Access to Personal Files Act 1987 have been consolidated under the DPA although some of the detailed rules remain different.

For "data controller", "personal data" and "processed" see definitions above.

"Extent of obligations"—the controller must provide a description of the nature of the data and the purposes for which they are held as well as a copy of the information constituting the data. Note that the data subject has to be informed of the purposes for which the data are held and not the grounds for the processing relied on by the controller. Nevertheless the information provided may assist the data subject to determine whether he is entitled to exercise his right to object to processing under s.10 (see below). Where the information falls into the definition of unstructured personal data the data subject must describe the data requested and his request may be refused if it is estimated that the cost of compliance would exceed the appropriate limit (s.9A)

"Prescribed fee"—the fee is £10 for a subject access request, although different limits apply to applications for consumer credit files, medical data and unstructured personal data. Fees and time limits for response, which also differ with the type of application, are set out in the Data Protection (Subject Access) (Fees and Miscellaneous Provisions) Regulations 2000 (SI 2000/191). A request for information under one part of s.7 is taken to be a request for information under the first three sub-sections but is only to be taken as applying to s.7(1)(d) if the application shows an express intention to that effect.

In *R. v Chief Constable of B County Constabulary and the Director of the National Identification Service Ex p. R*, November 1997, unrep., a case under the equivalent provisions of the 1984 Act, it was held that the section establishes a simple duty to supply the data subject with all the information held upon him when he makes a request, with the implication that the data subject may not, as the claimant wished in that case, cherry pick particular material or omit some from the record. As a matter of practice it is common for data controllers to ask the data subject which material he wishes to receive and for data subjects to limit their request to particular files or types of data. It is submitted that this is not incompatible with the judgment in *Ex p. R* and the two issues can be distinguished. The mischief addressed by the decision in *R* was the desire of the data subject for the data controller to "doctor" the response to omit specific material for presentation to a third party.

"Personal data"—only "personal data" of which the applicant is the subject is available to him in response to an access request; the mere fact that a document may be retrievable by reference to an individual's name does not entitle him to a copy of it. The court considered the purpose of the right in *Durant* as being:

"to enable him to check whether the data controller's processing of it unlawfully infringes his privacy and, if so, to take such steps as the Act provides, for example in section 10 to 14, to protect it"

per Auld L.J. at para.27 (see para.3G–7).

"Third party data"—material may be omitted or "redacted" where the disclosure of

Paragraph numbers marked with a "+" can be found online and on CD.

such material would encroach upon the legitimate privacy or confidentiality of a third party but the controller must apply an appropriate balancing test to ensure that the interests of both the data subject and the third party are protected. This follows the ruling of the ECtHR in *Gaskin v UK* [1990]1 F.L.R. 167. The issue only arises where the personal data about the individual includes such third party material in such a manner that it is impossible to separate the two. If the "personal data" about the applicant can be provided by omitting material about others that course should be followed i.e. there should be no unnecessary or gratuitous disclosure of information about third parties.

In *R. (on the application of Alan Lord) v Secretary of State for the Home Department* [2003] EWHC 2073 held information about individuals in an employment capacity is personal data in which privacy interests subsist (para.46). A blanket policy of non-disclosure does not meet the balancing test required by 7(4); a selective and targeted approach to redaction of third party information is required (para.148).

The "data controller" must determine whether it is "reasonable in all the circumstances" to make the disclosure. The court when considering this will not review the entire sets of material but will proceed by examining the approach of the data controller to the decisions to omit material. It will ask what, if any, legitimate interest the data subject has in the disclosure of the identity of another individual named in or identifiable from personal data to which he is otherwise entitled (*Durant* para.61) The court will generally not substitute its own view for the view of the data controller as long as the data controller is shown to have approached the decision in a balanced and fair way, taking account of the relevant considerations.

"Jurisdiction"—exercisable by the High Court or a county court or, in Scotland Court of Session or the sheriff: s.15(1).

"Powers of the court"—applications for remedial orders may be made to the High Court or a county court. Section 7(9) provides that, where a court is satisfied on the application of a data subject that the data controller has failed to comply with a valid request, the court may order the controller to comply with the request. The judgments in the cases of *P v Wozencroft* [2002] EWHC 1724, *Durant* and *Lord* appear to regard this as affording the court a wide discretion. In *Durant* the judge in the High Court commented on the applicant's motives for making the access request as relevant to the nature of the judgment which he would have been prepared to make. On appeal it was argued that such an approach diverges from the requirements of the Directive or even the Act itself. The Directive provides in art.22 for Member States to provide for:

"the right of every person to a judicial remedy for any breach of the rights guaranteed him by the national law applicable to the processing in question,"

subject only to limited grounds of exemption. On appeal the court confirmed the breadth of judicial discretion. In the Act the considerations which are incorporated in s.8 are limited to whether the individual has made unreasonably frequent requests, whether the information would disclose a trade secret or whether the data relate to third parties, in addition the court may accept that the data should not be provided by means of a copy where to do so would involve disproportionate effort but the right may be satisfied by the adoption of another mechanism, for example inspection of the material. In *Lindqvist* the European Court addressed the issue of how prescriptive the terms of the Directive are where a private right may conflict with other rights or interests. It accepts that in some areas the State will have room to manoeuvre and must strike a balance between competing rights and interests (para.85). In *Lord*, the court commented that where the court has held that there are no grounds to withhold data, whether under an exemption, s.7(4) or8(2)(a) the Act:

"points powerfully in favour of the Court exercising its discretion in favour of the data subject ... at least where as here it is the data subjects' liberty interests that are at stake" (para.163).

A lower court does not appear to be able to order that an access request be complied with in part. In a case in which the court might be minded to seek to curtail the scope of an order it could deal with the problem by giving leave to amend the application for an order under its case management powers.

"Special purposes"—the special purposes are journalistic, literary and artistic purposes s.3. These are not further defined. Extensive exemptions are available to those who process personal data for the special purposes if publication would be in the

Paragraph numbers marked with a "+" can be found online and on CD.

public interest and compliance with the Act would be incompatible with the special purposes. In *Campbell v MGN (No.2)* the Court of Appeal overruled the High Court and held that the data controller has the benefit of s.32 **after** publication as well as before where the grounds are made out (para.130). It was suggested by the court that news media would usually be entitled to rely on the exemption.

Where personal data are processed for the special purposes with a view to the publication of material not previously published a court must stay proceedings brought under this section until a determination has been made by the Commissioner under s.45 or the claim is withdrawn s.32(4) and (5). The Information Commissioner may provide legal assistance to a claimant where a case involves the special purposes s.53 and Sch.10.

Where a controller has refused to respond to a repeated request he may be able to apply to strike out an action against him for failure to provide access under CPR, r.3.4 on the ground that the statement of claim discloses no reasonable ground for bringing a claim.

"Access to material to inspect"—a court considering an application under s.7(9) is entitled to inspect any relevant data or information as to the logic involved in any decision making in order to determine the case s.15(2). The court cannot permit disclosure to the claimant prior to the determination of the case. In the event that the court rules against the data controller the court must order access by the controller. It is not the role of the court itself to provide access.

"Position pending appeal"—under CPR, r.52.7 unless the Appeal Court or the lower Court orders otherwise an appeal does not operate as a stay of an order or decision. A "data controller" who intends to appeal against an order that he provide access to personal data should apply to the Information Tribunal for an appropriate order on the grounds of r.52.7.1.

"Compensation for breach"—if a failure to provide subject access has caused the data subject to suffer damage he may seek compensation under s.13. Where damage has been suffered the subject may also claim for any associated distress. There is a defence of due diligence against a compensation claim s.13(3).

Provisions supplementary to section 7

8.—(1) The Secretary of State may by regulations provide that, in such cases as may be prescribed, a request for information under any provision of subsection (1) of section 7 is to be treated as extending also to information under other provisions of that subsection. **3G–12**

(2) The obligation imposed by section 7(1)(c)(i) must be complied with by supplying the data subject with a copy of the information in permanent form unless—

    (a) the supply of such a copy is not possible or would involve disproportionate effort, or

    (b) the data subject agrees otherwise;

and where any of the information referred to in section 7(1)(c)(i) is expressed in terms which are not intelligible without explanation the copy must be accompanied by an explanation of those terms.

(3) Where a data controller has previously complied with a request made under section 7 by an individual, the data controller is not obliged to comply with a subsequent identical or similar request under that section by that individual unless a reasonable interval has elapsed between compliance with the previous request and the making of the current request.

(4) In determining for the purposes of subsection (3) whether requests under section 7 are made at reasonable intervals, regard shall be had to the nature of the data, the purposes for which the data are processed and the frequency with which the data are altered.

Paragraph numbers marked with a "+" can be found online and on CD.

DATA PROTECTION

(5) Section 7(1)(d) is not to be regarded as requiring the provision of information as to the logic involved in any decision-taking if, and to the extent that, the information constitutes a trade secret.

(6) The information to be supplied pursuant to a request under section 7 must be supplied by reference to the data in question at the time when the request is received, except that it may take account of any amendment or deletion made between that time and the time when the information is supplied, being an amendment or deletion that would have been made regardless of the receipt of the request.

(7) For the purposes of section 7(4) and (5) another individual can be identified from the information being disclosed if he can be identified from that information, or from that and any other information which, in the reasonable belief of the data controller, is likely to be in, or to come into, the possession of the data subject making the request.

Notes

3G–13   "Disproportionate effort"—*R. (Lord) v SSHD* held s.8(2)(a) cannot justify withholding information in the form in which the data subject would otherwise be entitled to receive it para.155.

* * * *

Right to prevent processing likely to cause damage or distress

3G–14   **10.**—(1) Subject to subsection (2), an individual is entitled at any time by notice in writing to a data controller to require the data controller at the end of such period as is reasonable in the circumstances to cease, or not to begin, processing, or processing for a specified purpose or in a specified manner, any personal data in respect of which he is the data subject, on the ground that, for specified reasons—

    (a) the processing of those data or their processing for that purpose or in that manner is causing or is likely to cause substantial damage or substantial distress to him or to another, and

    (b) that damage or distress is or would be unwarranted.

(2) Subsection (1) does not apply—

    (a) in a case where any of the conditions in paragraphs 1 to 4 of Schedule 2 is met, or

    (b) in such other cases as may be prescribed by the Secretary of State by order.

(3) The data controller must within twenty-one days of receiving a notice under subsection (1) ("the data subject notice") give the individual who gave it a written notice—

    (a) stating that he has complied or intends to comply with the data subject notice, or

    (b) stating his reasons for regarding the data subject notice as to any extent unjustified and the extent (if any) to which he has complied or intends to comply with it.

Paragraph numbers marked with a "+" can be found online and on CD.

came into force on June 25, 2004, implement the corporate telephone preference service.

Note: the Regulations do not provide for a specific right to apply to the court for breach of the special rules relating to electronic marketing. The general right under this section applies irrespective of how the marketing complained of is carried out. The Commissioner's powers of enforcement and individual rights for compensation for breach apply to electronic marketing under the Regulations (see para.3G–25 re appeals against enforcement notices and para.3G–20 re compensation).

"Powers of the court"—a court which is satisfied that a data subject has made an objection in accordance with the Act under s.11 which has not been complied with by the data controller may order the controller to take appropriate steps to comply.

"Compensation for breach"—if a failure to respond to a proper objection has caused the data subject to suffer damage he may seek compensation under s.13. Where damage has been suffered the subject may also claim for any associated distress. There is a defence of due diligence against a compensation claim: s.13(3).

"Jurisdiction"—exercisable by the High Court or a county court or, in Scotland Court of Session or the sheriff: s.15(1).

Rights in relation to automated decision-taking

12.—(1) An individual is entitled at any time, by notice in writing **3G–18** to any data controller, to require the data controller to ensure that no decision taken by or on behalf of the data controller which significantly affects that individual is based solely on the processing by automatic means of personal data in respect of which that individual is the data subject for the purpose of evaluating matters relating to him such as, for example, his performance at work, his credit worthiness, his reliability or his conduct.

(2) Where, in a case where no notice under subsection (1) has effect, a decision which significantly affects an individual is based solely on such processing as is mentioned in subsection (1)—

    (a) the data controller must as soon as reasonably practicable notify the individual that the decision was taken on that basis, and

    (b) the individual is entitled, within twenty-one days of receiving that notification from the data controller, by notice in writing to require the data controller to reconsider the decision or to take a new decision otherwise than on that basis.

(3) The data controller must, within twenty-one days of receiving a notice under subsection (2)(b) ("the data subject notice") give the individual a written notice specifying the steps that he intends to take to comply with the data subject notice.

(4) A notice under subsection (1) does not have effect in relation to an exempt decision; and nothing in subsection (2) applies to an exempt decision.

(5) In subsection (4) "exempt decision" means any decision—

    (a) in respect of which the condition in subsection (6) and the condition in subsection (7) are met, or

    (b) which is made in such other circumstances as may be prescribed by the Secretary of State by order.

(6) The condition in this subsection is that the decision—

    (a) is taken in the course of steps taken—

Paragraph numbers marked with a "+" can be found online and on CD.

(i) for the purpose of considering whether to enter into a contract with the data subject,

(ii) with a view to entering into such a contract, or

(iii) in the course of performing such a contract, or

(b) is authorised or required by or under any enactment.

(7) The condition in this subsection is that either—

(a) the effect of the decision is to grant a request of the data subject, or

(b) steps have been taken to safeguard the legitimate interests of the data subject (for example, by allowing him to make representations).

(8) If a court is satisfied on the application of a data subject that a person taking a decision in respect of him ("the responsible person") has failed to comply with subsection (1) or (2)(b), the court may order the responsible person to reconsider the decision, or to take a new decision which is not based solely on such processing as is mentioned in subsection (1).

(9) An order under subsection (8) shall not affect the rights of any person other than the data subject and the responsible person.

Notes

3G–19   There is no case law on this section. It is a complex provision. There are two aspects to the right:

(1) the right to stop a data controller from taking a relevant (non-exempt) decision by automated means; and

(2) the right to object to such a decision after the event and require it to be reviewed.

In order to ensure that individuals are aware of automated decisions data controllers must notify data subjects where such decisions are made, although there is no sanction if the controller fails to do so. **Note**: that the court may make an order against the "responsible person". It appears therefore that a person other than the relevant data controller for the personal data processed may be held responsible for the making of an automated decision.

"Exempt decisions"—may either be in relation to contractual situations or where the controller is processing on the basis of a statutory power. Either the effect of the decision must have been to grant the request of the individual or his interests must be protected in some other way e.g. by being entitled to make representations about the decision.

"Powers of the court"—a court which is satisfied that a data subject has served a notice in accordance with the Act under s.12 which has not been complied with by the data controller may order the controller to take appropriate steps to comply.

"Special purposes"—where personal data are processed for the special purposes with a view to the publication of material not previously published a court must stay proceedings brought under this section until a determination has been made by the Commissioner under s.45 or the claim is withdrawn s.32(4) and (5). The Information Commissioner may fund legal advice or assistance for a claimant where a case concerns the special purposes s.53 and Sch.10.

"Compensation for breach"—if a failure to respond to a proper objection has caused the data subject to suffer damage he may seek compensation under s.13. Where damage has been suffered the subject may also claim for any associated distress. There is a defence of due diligence against a compensation claim s.13(3).

"Jurisdiction"—exercisable by the High Court or a county court or, in Scotland Court of Session or the sheriff: s.15(1).

Compensation for failure to comply with certain requirements

3G–20   **13.**—(1) An individual who suffers damage by reason of any

Paragraph numbers marked with a "+" can be found online and on CD.

contravention by a data controller of any of the requirements of this Act is entitled to compensation from the data controller for that damage.

(2) An individual who suffers distress by reason of any contravention by a data controller of any of the requirements of this Act is entitled to compensation from the data controller for that distress if—

    (a) the individual also suffers damage by reason of the contravention, or

    (b) the contravention relates to the processing of personal data for the special purposes.

(3) In proceedings brought against a person by virtue of this section it is a defence to prove that he had taken such care as in all the circumstances was reasonably required to comply with the requirement concerned.

Notes

"Extent of right to compensation"—compensation is not only available for damage **3G–21** caused by failure to comply with the individual rights as noted above but for damage (and associated distress) caused by any contravention of the Act. The claimant need not be a data subject in order to bring proceedings, although it may be unlikely that damage will be caused to anyone who is not a data subject. The other provisions of the Act which might give rise to claims for damages are breach of the Principles, particularly Principle 7 which covers the requirements of adequate security for information. Under s.13(3) there is a defence of due diligence against a compensation claim.

In *Lord Ashcroft v Attorney General* [2002] EWHC 1122; [2002] All E.R. (D) 521, QBD Lord Ashcroft, having been unsuccessful in his claim for damages for breach of Principle under the 1984 Act, claimed damages under s.13 for the continued holding of irrelevant and inaccurate data post March 2000, when the 1998 Act came into force. The judge agreed that it was an arguable claim however it did not proceed to hearing.

In *Paul Johnson v Medical Defence Union* [2006] EWHC 321 the court held that compensation for distress may only be awarded for distress arising from the occurrence giving rise to the right to damages. Unlike defamation the damages for distress are not at large.

In *Abayomi Sofola v Lloyds TSB Bank* [2005] EWHC 1335 Tugendhat J., in a hearing in which he gave permission for a claimant to re-open an appeal so that claims under the Act could be considered, considered it arguable that the retention of material alleging a fraud on file for nine years without evidence could breach Principles 4 and 5.

"Compensation"—November 2003 it was reported that the Chief Constable of Greater Manchester had paid compensation of £2000 for psychiatric harm to a lady whose details had been accessed by a police officer neighbour; in *A v London Borough of Newham* it was reported that the Borough paid £5,000 to the parents of a child who was wrongly stigmatised as being HIV positive, the picture of the child having used on the front of a Council publication on HIV and Children. The Borough had continued to use the picture in that way even after the parents had complained. In *Douglas v Hello! Ltd (No.1)* [2001] Q.B. 967 Michael Douglas and his wife, Catherine Zeta Jones, received modest damages of £3750 each plus expenses of £50 each by way of nominal damages for breach of the Act in the High Court. However they received damages for a breach of confidence, described by the court as "abuse of private information", and the court stated that the DPA should not be seen as adding a separate route to recovery for damage or distress beyond the nominal amount, (para.239). The failure of the lower courts to grant the Douglases a permanent injunction and then to compensate for abuse of their private information was regretted by the Court of Appeal on appeal, *Douglas v Hello! Ltd (No.6)* [2005] EWCA Civ 595,which confirmed the award of damages was an appropriate level.The Court of Appeal took same view in *Ogle v Chief Constable of Thames Valley* [2001] EWCA Civ 598; [2001] All E.R. (D) 231, a claim for

Paragraph numbers marked with a "+" can be found online and on CD.

compensation arising from inaccurate data. The Claimant could not recover additional damages to those recovered on same facts for wrongful arrest.

"Special purposes"—where the processing is for those purposes but outside the scope of the exemptions the claimant can seek compensation for distress only, and need not show damage. In *Campbell v MGN* [2002] EWCA Civ 1373 the model who had been surreptitiously photographed by the Mirror newspaper attending a clinic was awarded £2,500 for damage and hurt feelings plus £1,000 for aggravated damages for a subsequent offensive article, although the judgment was overturned by Court of Appeal it was reinstated by the House of Lords which considered the case under the application of the law of confidence rather than as a Data Protection Act claim, see para.3G–8.

Where personal data are processed for the special purposes with a view to the publication of material not previously published a court must stay proceedings brought under this section until a determination has been made by the Commissioner under s.45 or the claim is withdrawn s.32(4) and (5). The Information Commissioner may fund legal advice or assistance for a claimant where a case concerns the special purposes s.53 and Sch.10.

"Injunction"—where the purpose of the claimant is to protect his privacy a claim may also lie in art.8 of the HRA 1998. There are difficulties for a claimant seeking to use the DPA in order to restrain the publication of material because of the provisions in ss.32 (4) which restrict the bringing of proceedings in relation to the special purposes until a determination has been made by the Commissioner under s.45.

"Jurisdiction"—exercisable by the High Court or a county court or, in Scotland Court of Session or the sheriff: s.15(1).

"Data Protection Principles"—s.4 and Sch.1. It is the duty of a data controller to comply with the data protection principles in relation to all personal data in respect of which he is the data controller. The eight principles require that personal data:

(1) are processed fairly and lawfully and in accordance with the fair processing rules set out in the Schedule;
(2) are processed for limited purposes and not in a manner incompatible with the notified purposes;
(3) are adequate relevant and not excessive in relation to those purposes;
(4) are accurate;
(5) are not kept for longer than is necessary;
(6) are processed in accordance with the rights of data subjects;
(7) are kept secure and
(8) are not transferred outside the EEA without adequate protection.

Information may be disclosed without breach of the principles in reliance on one or more of the non-disclosure exemptions s.27. In *Matthew Yeboah Mensah v Robert H Jones* [2004] EWHC 2699 (Ch) the data subject could not resist the disclosure of his medical records by his doctor for the purpose of seeking legal advice where the doctor had relied on the non-disclosure exemption in s.35(2).

In *Lindqvist* the European Court ruled that the posting of personal details on the internet where the site is hosted in the EEA does not amount to a transfer of the personal data.

In the Tribunal case of *S. Yorks v Information Commissioner Information Tribunal* (October 12, 2005) in 2005 the Tribunal held that the retention of records of criminal convictions did not breach Principle 5 as long as the records were retained for policing purposes.

The Privacy and Electronic Communications (EC Directive) Regulations 2003 include a mirror provision in reg.30 which entitles any person who has suffered damage (but not distress) by reason of a contravention of the Regulations by any other person to claim compensation for the damage, subject to a defence of due diligence. The damage would have to be specific to the electronic marketing and additional to damage suffered by reason of breach of the Act itself. An Internet service provider which suffers damage by its goodwill may bring proceedings under this provision against senders of unsolicited marketing emails. In an appropriate case the court will grant injunctive relief: *Microsoft Corp v McDonald*, December 12, 2006, unrep.

Rectification, blocking, erasure and destruction

3G–22   14.—(1) If a court is satisfied on the application of a data subject

Paragraph numbers marked with a "+" can be found online and on CD.

that personal data of which the applicant is the subject are inaccurate, the court may order the data controller to rectify, block, erase or destroy those data and any other personal data in respect of which he is the data controller and which contain an expression of opinion which appears to the court to be based on the inaccurate data.

(2) Subsection (1) applies whether or not the data accurately record information received or obtained by the data controller from the data subject or a third party but where the data accurately record such information, then—

    (a) if the requirements mentioned in paragraph 7 of Part II of Schedule 1 have been complied with, the court may, instead of making an order under subsection (1), make an order requiring the data to be supplemented by such statement of the true facts relating to the matters dealt with by the data as the court may approve, and

    (b) if all or any of those requirements have not been complied with, the court may, instead of making an order under that subsection, make such order as it thinks fit for securing compliance with those requirements with or without a further order requiring the data to be supplemented by such a statement as is mentioned in paragraph (a).

(3) Where the court—

    (a) makes an order under subsection (1), or

    (b) is satisfied on the application of a data subject that personal data of which he was the data subject and which have been rectified, blocked, erased or destroyed were inaccurate,

it may, where it considers it reasonably practicable, order the data controller to notify third parties to whom the data have been disclosed of the rectification, blocking, erasure or destruction.

(4) If a court is satisfied on the application of a data subject—

    (a) that he has suffered damage by reason of any contravention by a data controller of any of the requirements of this Act in respect of any personal data, in circumstances entitling him to compensation under section 13, and

    (b) that there is a substantial risk of further contravention in respect of those data in such circumstances,

the court may order the rectification, blocking, erasure or destruction of any of those data.

(5) Where the court makes an order under subsection (4) it may, where it considers it reasonably practicable, order the data controller to notify third parties to whom the data have been disclosed of the rectification, blocking, erasure or destruction.

(6) In determining whether it is reasonably practicable to require such notification as is mentioned in subsection (3) or (5) the court shall have regard, in particular, to the number of persons who would have to be notified.

Notes

"Accuracy"—personal data are inaccurate if they are "incorrect or misleading as to any matter of fact" s.70(2).

3G–23

Paragraph numbers marked with a "+" can be found online and on CD.

"Information received from a third party"—where data accurately reflect information received from the data subject or a third party and the controller has taken reasonable care to ensure accuracy, taking account of the purposes and, if the data subject notifies the controller that he regards the data as inaccurate, the controller marks the data to indicate that fact then there is no breach of the relevant Principle Sch.1, Pt II, para.7, nevertheless the data subject may ask the court to order deletion, blocking etc.

"Rectification, blocking, erasure and destruction"—are not defined terms. If rectification involves the alteration or removal of data it may conflict with requirements to maintain an audit trail for security purposes. Blocking appears to cover the case where the data remain on the record but access is forbidden either generally or to specific persons or for specific purposes. Erasure and destruction appear to import different meanings. It is suggested that erasure takes place where the media on which the data are held is not destroyed and destruction where the media are also destroyed.

In *P v Wozencroft* [2002] EWHC 1724, Fam the court considered an application under the DPA to amend an expert report which had been relied upon in family proceedings on the basis that the report was inaccurate. The judge ruled that it would be an abuse of process to seek to challenge an expert's report in satellite proceedings under the DPA and dismissed the case.

"Powers of the court"—a court which is satisfied that personal data are inaccurate may make any of the orders noted above as well as ordering enquiries to be made and data to be traced where it has been shown that inaccurate data have been disclosed to third parties.

"Special purposes"—where personal data are processed for the special purposes with a view to the publication of material not previously published a court must stay proceedings brought under this section until a determination has been made by the Commissioner under s.45 or the claim is withdrawn s.32(4) and (5). The Information Commissioner may fund legal advice or assistance for a claimant where a case concerns the special purposes s.53 and Sch.10.

"Compensation for breach"—if a failure to maintain accurate data or the dissemination of inaccurate data has caused the data subject to suffer damage he may seek compensation under s.13. Where damage has been suffered the subject may also claim for any associated distress. There is a defence of due diligence under s.13(3).

"Jurisdiction"—exercisable by the High Court or a county court or, in Scotland Court of Session or the sheriff: s.15(1).

Part V

3G–24   Appeals from that Tribunal may be made to the High Court.

* * * *

Rights of appeal

3G–25   **48.**—(1) A person on whom an enforcement notice, an information notice or a special information notice has been served may appeal to the Tribunal against the notice.

(2) A person on whom an enforcement notice has been served may appeal to the Tribunal against the refusal of an application under section 41(2) for cancellation or variation of the notice.

(3) Where an enforcement notice, an information notice or a special information notice contains a statement by the Commissioner in accordance with section 40(8), 43(5) or 44(6) then, whether or not the person appeals against the notice, he may appeal against—

    (a) the Commissioner's decision to include the statement in the notice, or

    (b) the effect of the inclusion of the statement as respects any part of the notice.

Paragraph numbers marked with a "+" can be found online and on CD.

(4) A data controller in respect of whom a determination has been made under section 45 may appeal to the Tribunal against the determination.

(5) Schedule 6 has effect in relation to appeals under this section and the proceedings of the Tribunal in respect of any such appeal.

Notes

"Information Tribunal Rules"—the Act continued the Data Protection Tribunal **3G–26** which became the Information Tribunal following the implementation of s.18(2) of the Freedom of Information Act 2000. The Tribunal operates under the Data Protection Tribunal (Enforcement Appeals) Rules 2000 (SI 2000/189), as amended by the Information Tribunal (Enforcement Appeal) (Amendment) Rules 2002 (SI 2002/2722). The amending Regulations were necessary to provide for cases under the Freedom of Information Act 2000 before January 2005. Further amendments have been made in the Information Tribunal (Enforcement appeals) Rules 2005 (SI 2005/14), The Information Tribunal (Enforcement Appeals) (Amendment) Rules 2005 (SI 2005/450) and the Information Tribunal (National Security Appeals) Rules 2005 (SI 2005/13). Separate rules of procedure, the Data Protection Tribunal (National Security Appeals) Rules 2000 (SI 2000/206), apply to hearings in relation to national security certificates under s.28(4).

"Appeals"—the Tribunal hears appeals against a range of orders which can be made by the Information Commissioner. Under the Data Protection Act 1998 it hears appeals against enforcement notices, information notices and special information notices, against the inclusion of urgency provisions in any of the notices, a determination that personal data are not held for the special purposes or the refusal to vary or cancel an enforcement notice. Sitting in special panel the Tribunal also hears appeals against the extent of national security certificates. Under the Freedom of Information Act 2000 it hears appeals against enforcement information notices, and decision notices under the Freedom of Information Act 2000 and the extent of national security certificates issued under that Act. Under the Privacy and Electronic Communications (EC Directive) Regulations 2003 it hears appeals against enforcement notices, information notices, against the inclusion of urgency provisions in a notice or the refusal to vary or cancel an enforcement notice.

In *R. v Ewing (Terence Patrick)* [1983] Q.B. 1039 held that the Information Tribunal was, for the purpose of hearing appeals against the issue of certificates on the grounds of national security, a court within the meaning of Supreme Court Act 1981, s.42 and a vexatious litigant requires leave to bring such proceedings.

Determination of appeals

49.—(1) If on an appeal under section 48(1) the Tribunal consid- **3G–27** ers—

    (a) that the notice against which the appeal is brought is not in accordance with the law, or

    (b) to the extent that the notice involved an exercise of discretion by the Commissioner, that he ought to have exercised his discretion differently,

the Tribunal shall allow the appeal or substitute such other notice or decision as could have been served or made by the Commissioner; and in any other case the Tribunal shall dismiss the appeal.

(2) On such an appeal, the Tribunal may review any determination of fact on which the notice in question was based.

(3) If on an appeal under section 48(2) the Tribunal considers that the enforcement notice ought to be cancelled or varied by reason of a change in circumstances, the Tribunal shall cancel or vary the notice.

(4) On an appeal under subsection (3) of section 48 the Tribunal may direct—

Paragraph numbers marked with a "+" can be found online and on CD.

(a) that the notice in question shall have effect as if it did not contain any such statement as is mentioned in that subsection, or

(b) that the inclusion of the statement shall not have effect in relation to any part of the notice,

and may make such modifications in the notice as may be required for giving effect to the direction.

(5) On an appeal under section 48(4), the Tribunal may cancel the determination of the Commissioner.

(6) Any party to an appeal to the Tribunal under section 48 may appeal from the decision of the Tribunal on a point of law to the appropriate court; and that court shall be—

(a) the High Court of Justice in England if the address of the person who was the appellant before the Tribunal is in England or Wales,

(b) the Court of Session if that address is in Scotland, and

(c) the High Court of Justice in Northern Ireland if that address is in Northern Ireland.

(7) For the purposes of subsection (6)—

(a) the address of a registered company is that of its registered office, and

(b) the address of a person (other than a registered company) carrying on a business is that of his principal place of business in the United Kingdom.

Notes

3G–28   A number of appeals have been heard by the FOIA since January 2005. In *S. Yorks v Information Commissioner Information Tribunal* (October 12, 2005) the Tribunal appears to have reserved a power to vary its order on subsequent application.

The powers of the Tribunal in dealing with appeals apply also to appeals under the Privacy and Electronic Communications (EU Directive) Regulations 2003 and the Freedom of Information Act 2000.

Powers of entry and inspection

3G–29   **50.** Schedule 9 (powers of entry and inspection) has effect.

* * * * *

SECTION 50   **SCHEDULE 9**

POWERS OF ENTRY AND INSPECTION

Issue of warrants

3G–30   1.—(1) If a circuit judge is satisfied by information on oath supplied by the Commissioner that there are reasonable grounds for suspecting—

(a) that a data controller has contravened or is contravening any of the data protection principles, or

(b) that an offence under this Act has been or is being committed,

and that evidence of the contravention or of the commission of the offence is to be found on any premises specified in the information, he may, subject to sub-paragraph (2) and paragraph 2, grant a warrant to the Commissioner.

(2) A judge shall not issue a warrant under this Schedule in respect of any personal

Paragraph numbers marked with a "+" can be found online and on CD.

data processed for the special purposes unless a determination by the Commissioner under section 45 with respect to those data has taken effect.

(3) A warrant issued under sub-paragraph (1) shall authorise the Commissioner or any of his officers or staff at any time within seven days of the date of the warrant to enter the premises, to search them, to inspect, examine, operate and test any equipment found there which is used or intended to be used for the processing of personal data and to inspect and seize any documents or other material found there which may be such evidence as is mentioned in that sub-paragraph.

2.—(1) A judge shall not issue a warrant under this Schedule unless he is satisfied— **3G–31**

(a) that the Commissioner has given seven days' notice in writing to the occupier of the premises in question demanding access to the premises, and

(b) that either—

    (i) access was demanded at a reasonable hour and was unreasonably refused, or

    (ii) although entry to the premises was granted, the occupier unreasonably refused to comply with a request by the Commissioner or any of the Commissioner's officers or staff to permit the Commissioner or the officer or member of staff to do any of the things referred to in paragraph 1(3), and

(c) that the occupier, has, after the refusal, been notified by the Commissioner of the application for the warrant and has had an opportunity of being heard by the judge on the question whether or not it should be issued.

(2) Sub-paragraph (1) shall not apply if the judge is satisfied that the case is one of urgency or that compliance with those provisions would defeat the object of the entry.

3. A judge who issues a warrant under this Schedule shall also issue two copies of it **3G–32** and certify them clearly as copies.

Execution of warrants

4. A person executing a warrant issued under this Schedule may use such reason- **3G–33** able force as may be necessary.

5. A warrant issued under this Schedule shall be executed at a reasonable hour un- **3G–34** less it appears to the person executing it that there are grounds for suspecting that the evidence in question would not be found if it were so executed.

6. If the person who occupies the premises in respect of which a warrant is issued **3G–35** under this Schedule is present when the warrant is executed, he shall be shown the warrant and supplied with a copy of it; and if that person is not present a copy of the warrant shall be left in a prominent place on the premises.

7.—(1) A person seizing anything in pursuance of a warrant under this Schedule **3G–36** shall give a receipt for it if asked to do so.

(2) Anything so seized may be retained for so long as is necessary in all the circumstances but the person in occupation of the premises in question shall be given a copy of anything that is seized if he so requests and the person executing the warrant considers that it can be done without undue delay.

Matters exempt from inspection and seizure

8. The powers of inspection and seizure conferred by a warrant issued under this **3G–37** Schedule shall not be exercisable in respect of personal data which by virtue of section 28 are exempt from any of the provisions of this Act.

9.—(1) Subject to the provisions of this paragraph, the powers of inspection and **3G–38** seizure conferred by a warrant issued under this Schedule shall not be exercisable in respect of—

(a) any communication between a professional legal adviser and his client in connection with the giving of legal advice to the client with respect to his obligations, liabilities or rights under this Act, or

(b) any communication between a professional legal adviser and his client, or between such an adviser or his client and any other person, made in connection with or in contemplation of proceedings under or arising out of this Act (including proceedings before the Tribunal) and for the purposes of such proceedings.

Paragraph numbers marked with a "+" can be found online and on CD.

(2) Sub-paragraph (1) applies also to—

(a) any copy or other record of any such communication as is there mentioned, and

(b) any document or article enclosed with or referred to in any such communication if made in connection with the giving of any advice or, as the case may be, in connection with or in contemplation of and for the purposes of such proceedings as are there mentioned.

(3) This paragraph does not apply to anything in the possession of any person other than the professional legal adviser or his client or to anything held with the intention of furthering a criminal purpose.

(4) In this paragraph references to the client of a professional legal adviser include references to any person representing such a client.

3G–39   10. If the person in occupation of any premises in respect of which a warrant is issued under this Schedule objects to the inspection or seizure under the warrant of any material on the grounds that it consists partly of matters in respect of which those powers are not exercisable, he shall, if the person executing the warrant so requests, furnish that person with a copy of so much of the material as is not exempt from those powers.

Return of warrants

3G–40   11. A warrant issued under this Schedule shall be returned to the court from which it was issued—

(a) after being executed, or

(b) if not executed within the time authorised for its execution;

and the person by whom any such warrant is executed shall make an endorsement on it stating what powers have been exercised by him under the warrant.

Offences

3G–41   12. Any person who—

(a) intentionally obstructs a person in the execution of a warrant issued under this Schedule, or

(b) fails without reasonable excuse to give any person executing such a warrant such assistance as he may reasonably require for the execution of the warrant, is guilty of an offence.

Vessels, vehicles etc.

3G–42   13. In this Schedule "premises" includes any vessel, vehicle, aircraft or hovercraft, and references to the occupier of any premises include references to the person in charge of any vessel, vehicle, aircraft or hovercraft.

Scotland and Northern Ireland

3G–43   14. In the application of this Schedule to Scotland—

(a) for any reference to a circuit judge there is substituted a reference to the sheriff,

(b) for any reference to information on oath there is substituted a reference to evidence on oath, and

(c) for the reference to the court from which the warrant was issued there is substituted a reference to the sheriff clerk.

3G–44   15. In the application of this Schedule to Northern Ireland—

(a) for any reference to a circuit judge there is substituted a reference to a county court judge, and

(b) for any reference to information on oath there is substituted a reference to a complaint on oath.

Notes

3G–45   Privacy and Electronic Communications (EC Directive) Regulations 2003 the power to apply for warrant of entry is extended to circumstances where a person has contravened or is contravening the requirements of those Regulations (para.10(a) Sch.1 PECR).

Paragraph numbers marked with a "+" can be found online and on CD.

"Without notice"—warrant may be granted without notice having been given to the occupier in limited circumstances where the matter is one of urgency or compliance would defeat the object of the entry. The burden of establishing that notice would defeat the object of the entry falls upon the applicant for the warrant. The provisions are silent as to the standard of proof required. The issue and execution of a warrant will amount to a breach of the art.8 rights of the occupier and therefore the requirement of proportionality will apply.

The Codes of Practices made pursuant to the Police and Criminal Evidence Act 1984 do not apply to warrants issued under this provision but it is thought that those executing warrants should ensure that equivalent standards are met.

"Seizure of property"—difficult questions may arise where the material which the investigator wishes to inspect appears to be held on computer. The officer executing the warrant is entitled to inspect, examine and test material on the premises and only to seize material which is evidence of breach of the Act. Therefore if the officer wishes to take a computer in order to carry out tests off site the consent of the occupier will be required to remove the computer or to take a forensic copy of the disk unless the inspection shows that the computer contains evidence of a breach.

"Copies"—the occupier must be provided with copies of material seized if he so requests. The Commissioner's office has in the past refused to provide copies if they were not requested at the execution of the warrant so anyone subject to a warrant is advised to require copies during the execution of the warrant.

"Legal privilege"—the investigator is not entitled to seize material which is subject to legal professional privilege. Note that this is an absolute provision and does not depend on the reasonable belief of the investigator that the material is not privileged.

Assistance by Commissioner in cases involving processing for the special purposes

53.—(1) An individual who is an actual or prospective party to any 3G–46 proceedings under section 7(9), 10(4), 12(8), 12A(3) or 14 or by virtue of section 13 which relate to personal data processed for the special purposes may apply to the Commissioner for assistance in relation to those proceedings.

(2) The Commissioner shall, as soon as reasonably practicable after receiving an application under subsection (1), consider it and decide whether and to what extent to grant it, but he shall not grant the application unless, in his opinion, the case involves a matter of substantial public importance.

(3) If the Commissioner decides to provide assistance, he shall, as soon as reasonably practicable after making the decision, notify the applicant, stating the extent of the assistance to be provided.

(4) If the Commissioner decides not to provide assistance, he shall, as soon as reasonably practicable after making the decision, notify the applicant of his decision and, if he thinks fit, the reasons for it.

(5) In this section—
    (a) references to "proceedings" include references to prospective proceedings, and
    (b) "applicant", in relation to assistance under this section, means an individual who applies for assistance.

(6) Schedule 10 has effect for supplementing this section.

SECTION 53(6)   SCHEDULE 10

FURTHER PROVISIONS RELATING TO ASSISTANCE UNDER SECTION 53

1. In this Schedule "applicant" and "proceedings" have the same meaning as in sec- 3G–47 tion 53.

Paragraph numbers marked with a "+" can be found online and on CD.

3G–48   2. The assistance provided under section 53 may include the making of arrangements for, or for the Commissioner to bear the costs of—

(a) the giving of advice or assistance by a solicitor or counsel, and

(b) the representation of the applicant, or the provision to him of such assistance as is usually given by a solicitor or counsel—

(i) in steps preliminary or incidental to the proceedings, or

(ii) in arriving at or giving effect to a compromise to avoid or bring an end to the proceedings.

3G–49   3. Where assistance is provided with respect to the conduct of proceedings—

(a) it shall include an agreement by the Commissioner to indemnify the applicant (subject only to any exceptions specified in the notification) in respect of any liability to pay costs or expenses arising by virtue of any judgment or order of the court in the proceedings,

(b) it may include an agreement by the Commissioner to indemnify the applicant in respect of any liability to pay costs or expenses arising by virtue of any compromise or settlement arrived at in order to avoid the proceedings or bring the proceedings to an end, and

(c) it may include an agreement by the Commissioner to indemnify the applicant in respect of any liability to pay damages pursuant to an undertaking given on the grant of interlocutory relief (in Scotland, an interim order) to the applicant.

3G–50   4. Where the Commissioner provides assistance in relation to any proceedings, he shall do so on such terms, or make such other arrangements, as will secure that a person against whom the proceedings have been or are commenced is informed that assistance has been or is being provided by the Commissioner in relation to them.

3G–51   5. In England and Wales or Northern Ireland, the recovery of expenses incurred by the Commissioner in providing an applicant with assistance (as taxed or assessed in such manner as may be prescribed by rules of court) shall constitute a first charge for the benefit of the Commissioner—

(a) on any costs which, by virtue of any judgment or order of the court, are payable to the applicant by any other person in respect of the matter in connection with which the assistance is provided, and

(b) on any sum payable to the applicant under a compromise or settlement arrived at in connection with that matter to avoid or bring to an end any proceedings.

3G–52   6. In Scotland, the recovery of such expenses (as taxed or assessed in such manner as may be prescribed by rules of court) shall be paid to the Commissioner, in priority to other debts—

(a) out of any expenses which, by virtue of any judgment or order of the court, are payable to the applicant by any other person in respect of the matter in connection with which the assistance is provided, and

(b) out of any sum payable to the applicant under a compromise or settlement arrived at in connection with that matter to avoid or bring to an end any proceedings.

Notes

3G–53   See para.3G–11 in relation to the actions in respect of which the data subject may wish to seek support from the Commissioner.

Notes

3G–54   "Provision"—gives the Tribunal power to deal with behaviour that might result in punishment for contempt of court were it to be perpetrated before a court.

Unlawful obtaining etc. of personal data

3G–55   55.—(1) A person must not knowingly or recklessly, without the consent of the data controller—

(a) obtain or disclose personal data or the information contained in personal data, or

Paragraph numbers marked with a "+" can be found online and on CD.

(b) procure the disclosure to another person of the information contained in personal data.

(2) Subsection (1) does not apply to a person who shows—

(a) that the obtaining, disclosing or procuring—

(i) was necessary for the purpose of preventing or detecting crime, or

(ii) was required or authorised by or under any enactment, by any rule of law or by the order of a court,

(b) that he acted in the reasonable belief that he had in law the right to obtain or disclose the data or information or, as the case may be, to procure the disclosure of the information to the other person,

(c) that he acted in the reasonable belief that he would have had the consent of the data controller if the data controller had known of the obtaining, disclosing or procuring and the circumstances of it, or

(ca) that he acted—

(i) for the special purposes,

(ii) with a view to the publication by any person of any journalistic, literary or artistic material, and

(iii) in the reasonable belief that in the particular circumstances the obtaining, disclosing or procuring was justified as being in the public interest,

(d) that in the particular circumstances the obtaining, disclosing or procuring was justified as being in the public interest.

(3) A person who contravenes subsection (1) is guilty of an offence.

(4) A person who sells personal data is guilty of an offence if he has obtained the data in contravention of subsection (1).

(5) A person who offers to sell personal data is guilty of an offence if—

(a) he has obtained the data in contravention of subsection (1), or

(b) he subsequently obtains the data in contravention of that subsection.

(6) For the purposes of subsection (5), an advertisement indicating that personal data are or may be for sale is an offer to sell the data.

(7) Section 1(2) does not apply for the purposes of this section; and for the purposes of subsections (4) to (6), "personal data" includes information extracted from personal data.

(8) References in this section to personal data do not include references to personal data which by virtue of section 28 are exempt from this section

Notes

In *R. v Rooney* [2006] EWCA Crim 1841 the court held that the disclosure that a couple had moved to "a new address in Tunstall" was a disclosure of information contained in personal data within s.55(1)(a) even though the identity of the individuals was not disclosed.

3G–56

Paragraph numbers marked with a "+" can be found online and on CD.

Section (ca) was added by s.78 of the Criminal Justice and Immigration Act 2008 and is not in force as at August 2008.

Pre-action disclosure may be granted under CPR, r.31.16 against a party which has unlawfully obtained personal data in breach of s.55: *Hughes v Carratu International Plc* [2006] EWHC 1791.

Monetary penalties

3G–57 Power of Commissioner to impose monetary penalty

55A.—(1) The Commissioner may serve a data controller with a monetary penalty notice if the Commissioner is satisfied that—

    (a) there has been a serious contravention of section 4(4) by the data controller,

    (b) the contravention was of a kind likely to cause substantial damage or substantial distress, and

    (c) subsection (2) or (3) applies.

(2) This subsection applies if the contravention was deliberate.

(3) This subsection applies if the data controller—

    (a) knew or ought to have known —

        (i) that there was a risk that the contravention would occur, and

        (ii) that such a contravention would be of a kind likely to cause substantial damage or substantial distress, but

    (b) failed to take reasonable steps to prevent the contravention.

(4) A monetary penalty notice is a notice requiring the data controller to pay to the Commissioner a monetary penalty of an amount determined by the Commissioner and specified in the notice.

(5) The amount determined by the Commissioner must not exceed the prescribed amount.

(6) The monetary penalty must be paid to the Commissioner within the period specified in the notice.

(7) The notice must contain such information as may be prescribed.

(8) Any sum received by the Commissioner by virtue of this section must be paid into the Consolidated Fund.

(9) In this section—

    "data controller" does not include the Crown Estate Commissioners or a person who is a data controller by virtue of section 63(3) ;

    "prescribed" means prescribed by regulations made by the Secretary of State.

Monetary penalty notices: procedural rights

3G–58 **55B.**—(1) Before serving a monetary penalty notice, the Commissioner must serve the data controller with a notice of intent.

(2) A notice of intent is a notice that the Commissioner proposes to serve a monetary penalty notice.

Paragraph numbers marked with a "+" can be found online and on CD.

(3) A notice of intent must—

    (a) inform the data controller that he may make written representations in relation to the Commissioner's proposal within a period specified in the notice, and

    (b) contain such other information as may be prescribed.

(4) The Commissioner may not serve a monetary penalty notice until the time within which the data controller may make representations has expired.

(5) A person on whom a monetary penalty notice is served may appeal to the Tribunal against—

    (a) the issue of the monetary penalty notice;

    (b) the amount of the penalty specified in the notice.

(6) In this section, "prescribed" means prescribed by regulations made by the Secretary of State.

Guidance about monetary penalty notices

55C.—(1) The Commissioner must prepare and issue guidance on how he proposes to exercise his functions under sections 55A and 55B. **3G–59**

(2) The guidance must, in particular, deal with—

    (a) the circumstances in which he would consider it appropriate to issue a monetary penalty notice, and

    (b) how he will determine the amount of the penalty.

(3) The Commissioner may alter or replace the guidance.

(4) If the guidance is altered or replaced, the Commissioner must issue the altered or replacement guidance.

(5) The Commissioner may not issue guidance under this section without the approval of the Secretary of State.

(6) The Commissioner must lay any guidance issued under this section before each House of Parliament.

(7) The Commissioner must arrange for the publication of any guidance issued under this section in such form and manner as he considers appropriate.

(8) In subsections (5) to (7), "guidance" includes altered or replacement guidance.

Monetary penalty notices: enforcement

55D.—(1) This section applies in relation to any penalty payable to the Commissioner by virtue of section 55A . **3G–60**

(2) In England and Wales, the penalty is recoverable—

    (a) if a county court so orders, as if it were payable under an order of that court;

    (b) if the High Court so orders, as if it were payable under an order of that court.

(3) In Scotland, the penalty may be enforced in the same manner as an extract registered decree arbitral bearing a warrant for execution issued by the sheriff court of any sheriffdom in Scotland.

(4) In Northern Ireland, the penalty is recoverable—

Paragraph numbers marked with a "+" can be found online and on CD.

    (a) if a county court so orders, as if it were payable under
        an order of that court;

    (b) if the High Court so orders, as if it were payable under
        an order of that court.

Notices under sections 55A and 55B: supplemental

3G–61   **55E.**—(1) The Secretary of State may by order make further provision in connection with monetary penalty notices and notices of intent.

    (2) An order under this section may in particular—

    (a) provide that a monetary penalty notice may not be served on a data controller with respect to the processing of personal data for the special purposes except in circumstances specified in the order;

    (b) make provision for the cancellation or variation of monetary penalty notices;

    (c) confer rights of appeal to the Tribunal against decisions of the Commissioner in relation to the cancellation or variation of such notices;

    (d) make provision for the proceedings of the Tribunal in respect of appeals under section 55B(5) or appeals made by virtue of paragraph (c);

    (e) make provision for the determination of such appeals;

    (f) confer rights of appeal against any decision of the Tribunal in relation to monetary penalty notices or their cancellation or variation.

    (3) An order under this section may apply any provision of this Act with such modifications as may be specified in the order.

    (4) An order under this section may amend this Act.

3G–62   *Note* —These provisions were inserted by s.144 of the Criminal Justice and Immigration Act 2008 but are not yet in force (as at January2008).

Criminal Justice and Immigration Act 1998

(2008 c.4)

Power to alter penalty for unlawfully obtaining etc. personal data

3G–63   **77.** (1)The Secretary of State may by order provide for a person who is guilty of an offence under section 55 of the Data Protection Act 1998 (c. 29) (unlawful obtaining etc. of personal data) to be liable—

    (a) on summary conviction, to imprisonment for a term not exceeding the specified period or to a fine not exceeding the statutory maximum or to both,

    (b) on conviction on indictment, to imprisonment for a term not exceeding the specified period or to a fine or to both.

    (2) In subsection (1)(a) and (b) "specified period" means a period provided for by the order but the period must not exceed—

Paragraph numbers marked with a "+" can be found online and on CD.

(a) in the case of summary conviction, 12 months (or, in Northern Ireland, 6 months), and

(b) in the case of conviction on indictment, two years.

(3) The Secretary of State must ensure that any specified period for England and Wales which, in the case of summary conviction, exceeds 6 months is to be read as a reference to 6 months so far as it relates to an offence committed before the commencement of section 282(1) of the Criminal Justice Act 2003 (c. 44) (increase in sentencing powers of magistrates' courts from 6 to 12 months for certain offences triable either way).

(4) Before making an order under this section, the Secretary of State must consult—

(a) the Information Commissioner,

(b) such media organisations as the Secretary of State considers appropriate, and

(c) such other persons as the Secretary of State considers appropriate.

(5) An order under this section may, in particular, amend the Data Protection Act 1998 .

Note —This provision came into force on May 8, 2008.   **3G–64**

DATA PROTECTION

Hearings —Proceedings brought under the Consumer Credit Act shall in the first **3H–12** instance be listed by the court as a hearing in private under CPR r.39.2(3)(c)—see para.39PD.1, para.1.5.

Costs —For claims for "fixed commencement costs" and for recovery of "fixed costs **3H–13** on entry of judgment" for delivery up of goods, see CPR Pt 45. In relation to such costs issues in the case of a summary judgment, see also para.24.6.7.

Enforcement of judgments —A County Court judgment which arose out of an agree- **3H–14** ment regulated by the Consumer Credit Act 1974 cannot be transferred to the High Court for enforcement: s.141 of the 1974 Act and art.8 of the High Court and County Courts Jurisdiction Order 1991 (para.9B–928). See also paras 70.3.2, sc.46.1.48, and cc25.13.1.

Bills of Sale —For registration of bills of sale, renewals of registration, entry of satis- **3H–15** faction, search of the register and related matters, see paras sc95.0.1 to sc95.4.1 and the Practice Direction supplementing RSC O.95 (at scpd95.1).

Exempt agreements (ss.16, 16A, 16B and 16C)

Section 16 of the Consumer Credit Act 1974 states that the Act does not regulate a **3H–16** consumer credit or consumer hire agreement if it falls into one of a series of categories. The matter is more finely regulated by an Order made under s.16, the Consumer Credit (Exempt Agreements) Order 1989 (as amended). Sections 16A, 16B and 16C provide for exemptions where the debtor or hirer is of high net worth (s.16A) or in business (s.16B) or takes buy-to-let credit (s.16C). For the terms of these four sections and detailed commentary, see para.3H–45+ *et seq.* available on the White Book on Westlaw UK Service or the Civil Procedure CD. Most exempt credit agreements are, however, subject to an order being made against the creditor under s.140B of the Act, if the court finds the relationship between the creditor and debtor to be unfair.

Consumer Credit Act 2006

The Consumer Credit Act 2006 has no substantive provisions but made significant **3H–17** amendments to the Consumer Credit Act 1974. The principal changes made by the 2006 Act (with the commencement dates shown in brackets) are the following:

- Removal of the financial limit in the definition of regulated agreement in ss.8 and 15 of the 1974 Act (as from April 6, 2008).
- Repeal of subss.(3) to (5) of s.127 of the 1974 Act, which in certain circum- stances made improperly executed agreements irredeemably unenforceable against the debtor or hirer (as from April 6, 2007).
- Replacement of the court's power to re-open an extortionate credit bargain (under ss.137–140) with similar powers (under new ss.140A–140D) where the court finds the relationship between creditor and debtor arising out of the agreement to be "unfair", a wider concept than that of an "extortionate credit bargain" (as from April 6, 2007).
- Expansion of the definition of ancillary credit business (in s.145 of the 1974 Act) to include "debt administration" and "credit information services" (as from October 1, 2008).
- Extension of the ombudsman scheme established under the Financial Services and Markets Act 2000, to include consumer credit jurisdiction thereby en- abling it to be used by an individual bringing a consumer credit complaint (as from April 6, 2007).
- Strengthening of the requirements to give notice and information to debtors and hirers in default/arrears (as from October 1, 2008).

The effect of transitional provisions is explained in commentary to the relevant sec- tions of the 1974 Act (below).

Paragraph numbers marked with a "+" can be found online and on CD.

Consumer Credit Act 1974

3H–18

(1974 c.39)

Paragraph numbers marked with a "+" can be found online and on CD.

Paragraph numbers marked with a "+" can be found online and on CD.

Paragraph numbers marked with a "+" can be found online and on CD.

Paragraph numbers marked with a "+" denote content that is available on White Book on Westlaw UK or the Civil Procedure CD.

[THE NEXT PARAGRAPH IS 3H–20.]

PART II

CREDIT AGREEMENTS, HIRE AGREEMENTS AND LINKED TRANSACTIONS

Consumer credit agreements

8.—(1) A consumer credit agreement is an agreement between an individual ("the debtor") and any other person ("the creditor") by which the creditor provides the debtor with credit of any amount.   3H–20

(2) [...]

(3) A consumer credit agreement is a regulated agreement within the meaning of this Act if it is not an agreement (an "exempt agreement") specified in or under section 16, 16A, 16B or 16C.

Note —Amended by the Consumer Credit (Increase of Monetary Limits) Order 1983 (SI 1983/1878); and the Consumer Credit (Increase of Monetary Limits) (Amendment) Order 1998 (SI 1998/996). Further amended and subs.(2) repealed by the Consumer Credit Act 2006 ss.2 and 70 and Sch.4 with effect from April 6, 2008 for certain purposes (SI 2007/3300 and SI 2008/831) and for remaining purposes October 31, 2008 (SI 2008/831 as amended by SI 2008/2444).   3H–21

Consumer credit agreements

As a general rule the Act and the regulations made under it apply only to "regulated" agreements. There are two kinds of regulated agreement: 3H–22

(i) those defined in this section, i.e. regulated consumer credit agreements; and

(ii) those defined in s.15, i.e. regulated consumer hire agreements.

"Exempt agreements"—An "exempt agreement" is not a "regulated agreement". There are, nevertheless, certain provisions in the Act which apply to most exempt agreements, namely the unfair relationships provisions in ss.140A to 140C and (in re-

Paragraph numbers marked with a "+" can be found online and on CD.

lation to certain agreements made before April 6, 2007) the extortionate credit bargain provisions in ss.137–140. See, further, the commentary to s.140A below.

"Individual"—No agreement is a consumer credit agreement or a regulated agreement unless the debtor is an "individual". A corporate body is not an individual. A partnership of up to three people is an "individual". Prior to April 6, 2007 a partnership of any number of people was an "individual"— see the definition of "individual" in s.189(1) and commentary to that section.

"Credit"—For the meaning of "credit" see s.9. "Credit" can be provided under an agreement—and that agreement can thus be a consumer credit agreement and a regulated agreement—even though the credit is never actually used. Thus a bank may agree to a customer having authority to go overdrawn to, say, a maximum of £10,000. Credit is provided even though the customer may subsequently choose not to use the overdraft facility. "Credit" is provided when the customer is granted the facility. Similarly, credit is provided when a credit card agreement is made and a credit card issued to the customer. A credit card agreement will normally be a regulated consumer credit agreement, i.e. unless the debtor is a company or other corporate body. A charge card agreement, however, will normally be an exempt agreement under s.16.

Financial limit

3H–23   Prior to amendments effected by the Consumer Credit Act 2006, the definition of "consumer credit agreement" included a financial limit. Thus any agreement which was made prior to April 6, 2008 and which provided an individual with credit exceeding a specified figure was not—and still is not—a consumer credit agreement. When the 1974 Act came into force, the specified figure was £5,000. From May 20, 1985 it became £15,000. In respect of any agreement made on or after May 1, 1998 the figure was £25,000. In relation to the specified figure there was an important distinction between fixed-sum credit and running-account credit, which terms are defined in s.10. When dealing with fixed-sum credit, the important question was whether the amount of the *credit* exceeded the specified figure. A loan of £25,000 was within the limit even though the repayments (i.e. including interest) would exceed £25,000. Similarly a hire-purchase or conditional sale agreement involving an initial down-payment of £2,000 and instalment payments totalling £27,000 was within the £25,000 figure provided that the instalment payments included a figure of at least £2,000 for interest (or credit charge). Neither the down payment nor the credit charges form part of the "credit". (For the rule that credit charges do not form part of the credit, see s.9(4).) As a rule of thumb, when dealing with a hire-purchase, conditional sale or credit sale agreement, one can ascertain the amount of the credit by deducting the down payment and any trade-in allowance from the cash price of the item being purchased; the resulting figure is the amount which, in common parlance, is being "borrowed", i.e. is the amount of "credit" (see also Sch.II, Pt II, Example 10). When dealing with running-account credit, e.g. a credit card agreement or an overdraft, the important question is whether the "credit-limit" (defined in s.10(2)) exceeded the figure specified, though there were anti-avoidance provisions in s.10(3).

3H–24   *Removal of financial limit—transitional provisions* —Article 4 of the Consumer Credit Act 2006 (Commencement No.4 and Transitional Provisions) Order 2008 (SI 2008/831), sets out transitional provisions. Article 4 prevents s.82(2) of the Consumer Credit Act 1974 applying in certain cases, with the following effect. An agreement made before April 6, 2008 under which the creditor provided the debtor with credit exceeding £25,000 will remain unregulated even if (a) it is varied or supplemented by a later agreement which does not provide for a cash loan, or (b) it is varied or supplemented by a later agreement which is an exempt agreement.

Subsection (2) was repealed and the financial limit was removed (subject to one exception) in relation to agreements made on or after April 6, 2008. The exception was buy-to-let credit agreements (defined and termed "relevant agreements" in Sch.1 to the Consumer Credit Act 2006 (Commencement No.4 and Transitional Provisions) Order 2008). In relation to these buy-to-let agreements, the relevant commencement date was October 1, 2008. Also on October 1, 2008, the Legislative Reform (Consumer Credit) Order 2008 (SI 2008/2826) came into effect. It ensured that buy-to-let credit agreements remained exempt by inserting a new s.16C into the Consumer Credit Act 1974 making certain agreements exempt—those agreements being defined exactly the same as "relevant agreements" had been defined in Sch.1 to SI 2008/831.

Paragraph numbers marked with a "+" can be found online and on CD.

Meaning of credit

9.—(1) In this Act "credit" includes a cash loan, and any other **3H–25** form of financial accommodation.

(2) Where credit is provided otherwise than in sterling it shall be treated for the purposes of this Act as provided in sterling of an equivalent amount.

(3) Without prejudice to the generality of subsection (1), the person by whom goods are bailed or (in Scotland) hired to an individual under a hire-purchase agreement shall be taken to provide him with fixed-sum credit to finance the transaction of an amount equal to the total price of the goods less the aggregate of the deposit (if any) and the total charge for credit.

(4) For the purposes of this Act, an item entering into the total charge for credit shall not be treated as credit even though time is allowed for its payment.

Meaning of credit

Subsection (1)—"Credit" appears intended to embrace the classic form of credit **3H–26** summed up in the phrase "Have now, pay later", or expressed as the deferment of an obligation to pay. An agreement for the provision of advertising services provided for payment to be made in full on the primary date (i.e. the signing of the agreement) or by instalments; this was held to be the provision of credit in that customers were permitted to defer payment beyond the primary date (*Stolink UK v Thomas* [1996] 1 C.L.Y. 1225). The term "credit hire agreement" is sometimes used to describe a hire agreement under which payment for the hire of goods is deferred for a period after the hire has come to an end. It involves the provision of credit because the duty to pay is contractually deferred for a significant period after payment has been earned: *Hatfield v Hiscock* [1998] C.C.L.R. 68 and *Dimond v Lovell* [2002] 1 A.C. 384, HL. (See further the notes to s.11.)

Whether a contract provides credit is to be determined as at the time the contract is made. Where at that time it is uncertain whether the arrangements between the parties will give rise to a debt at all, there is no "credit" merely because the contract postpones any obligation to pay until the possible indebtedness has crystallised: *Nejad v City Index Ltd* [2000] C.C.L.R. 7; *McMillan Williams (A Firm) v Range* [2004] C.C.L.R. 3; [2004] 1 W.L.R. 1858. A publishing contract, which provided for the author to be paid an advance on royalties coupled with a requirement for the author to repay after three years such amount of the advance as the sales in those three years had failed to earn, would not provide the author with credit. That conclusion might be different, however, if the amount of the advance was so great as to show that it was in reality a loan dressed up as an advance on royalties.

Professionally drafted contracts for the sale by J of a farm, for its lease-back to J and for J to have an option to re-purchase it later, were held not to amount to the provision of credit even though they were transactions made in order to enable J to cope with substantial financial problems: *Lavin v Johnson* [2002] EWCA Civ 1138.

After the event (ATE) insurance: a claimant in a personal injury claim action may well fund the proceedings by a conditional fee arrangement (CFA). If the claimant loses, the claimant will not have to pay legal fees but may well have costs awarded against her requiring her to pay the defendant's legal costs. The claimant therefore may, at the time of entering her CFA, take out an insurance policy to cover herself against that risk. Such a policy, known as "after the event" (ATE) insurance, may provide that the premium is not payable until the conclusion of the case. If so, does that amount to the provision of "credit", i.e. insurance cover now, pay later? In *Tilby v Perfect Pizza Ltd* [2003] C.C.L.R. 9 (also available on Court Service website), Senior Costs Judge Hurst held that there was no provision of "credit" unless payment of the premium was deferred for a significant period beyond the conclusion of the case. For the recoverability of an ATE insurance premium as part of a successful claimant's costs: see para.44.3A.3.

Paragraph numbers marked with a "+" can be found online and on CD.

3H–27   *Subsection(2)* —This is relevant to the various financial limits in the Act. Most of these are relevant at the time the agreement is made. For example an agreement made before April 6, 2008 and involving credit of more than £25,000 is not a regulated agreement (see s.8). Thus the relevant exchange rate to apply is that operative on the date of the making of the agreement. An agreement is either a regulated agreement or it is not; it cannot become one, or cease to be one, at some later date simply because the exchange rate has moved.

3H–28   *Subsection(3)* —This makes it clear that hire-purchase agreements are treated by the Act as consumer credit agreements and not as consumer hire agreements. Where the Act uses the terms "creditor or owner" and "debtor or hirer", in each case it is the former which is relevant to hire-purchase agreements. A hire-purchase agreement may itself use the terms "owner" and "hirer"; nevertheless, in the terminology employed in the Act, the parties are "creditor"and "debtor". The terms "owner" and "hirer", when used in the Act, refer only to the parties to consumer hire agreements.

3H–29   *Subsection(4)* —The "total charge for credit" is defined in the Consumer Credit (Total Charge for Credit) Regulations 1980, made under s.20. In determining whether a fixed-sum credit agreement (made before April 6, 2008) is within the financial limit to bring it within the definition of a regulated consumer credit agreement (see s.8(2)), any item which is part of the total charge for credit is to be ignored. In *Humberclyde Finance Ltd v Thompson* [1997] C.C.L.R. 23, CA, the debtor contracted to buy a car on conditional sale terms. The balance of the cash price (i.e. after deduction of the initial down payment which was paid by a part-exchange) was £14,497. However, the agreement contained also a payment waiver option which the debtor adopted and which provided that if the debtor (Mr Thompson) died within five years, Mrs Thompson would be relieved from having to pay any instalments which had not fallen due before his death. The fee for this option was £796. Despite the fact that, under the agreement, payment of this fee was a deferred obligation, it was held that the fee did not form part of the "credit", because it fell within the definition of the "total charge for credit". Thus the agreement involved "credit" of less than £15,000 (the then figure specified in s.8(2)) and was a regulated agreement. [*Query* whether the fee was *correctly* held to be within the definition of the total charge for credit—see Consumer Credit (Total Charge for Credit) Regulations 1980 below]. For further examples of the application of s.9(4), see *Huntpast Ltd v Leadbeater* [1993] C.C.L.R. 15, CA and *Watchtower Investments Ltd v Payne* [2001] EWCA Civ 1159; [2003] C.C.L.R. 10 and *McGinn v Grangewood Securities Ltd* [2002] EWCA Civ 522; [2003] C.C.L.R. 11 and *London North Securities Ltd v Meadows* [2005] EWCA Civ 956; [2005] C.C.L.R. 7—all explained at para.3H–432+. See also *Wilson v First County Trust (No.1)* [2001] Q.B. 407; [2003] C.C.L.R. 1—discussed in the commentary to s.127(3) below.

Running-account credit and fixed-sum credit

3H–30   **10.**—(1) For the purposes of this Act—

   (a) running-account credit is a facility under a consumer credit agreement whereby the debtor is enabled to receive from time to time (whether in his own person, or by another person) from the creditor or a third party cash, goods and services (or any of them) to an amount or value such that, taking into account payments made by or to the credit of the debtor, the credit limit (if any) is not at any time exceeded; and

   (b) fixed-sum credit is any other facility under a consumer credit agreement whereby the debtor is enabled to receive credit (whether in one amount or by instalments).

   (2) In relation to running-account credit, "credit limit" means, as respects any period, the maximum debit balance which, under the credit agreement, is allowed to stand on the account during that pe-

Paragraph numbers marked with a "+" can be found online and on CD.

riod, disregarding any term of the agreement allowing that maximum to be exceeded merely temporarily.

(3) For the purposes of paragraph (a) of section 16B(1), running-account credit shall be taken not to exceed the amount specified in that paragraph ("the specified amount") if—

    (a) the credit limit does not exceed the specified amount; or

    (b) whether or not there is a credit limit, and if there is, notwithstanding that it exceeds the specified amount,—

        (i) the debtor is not enabled to draw at any one time an amount which, so far as (having regard to section 9(4)) it represents credit, exceeds the specified amount, or

        (ii) the agreement provides that, if the debit balance rises above a given amount (not exceeding the specified amount), the rate of the total charge for credit increases or any other condition favouring the creditor or his associate comes into operation, or

        (iii) at the time the agreement is made it is probable, having regard to the terms of the agreement and any other relevant considerations, that the debit balance will not at any time rise above the specified amount.

Note—Amended by Consumer Credit Act 2006 s.5(2), with effect from April 6, 2008 **3H–31** (SI 2007/3300).

Running-account credit and fixed-sum credit

Typical examples of fixed-sum credits are: hire-purchase, conditional sale and **3H–32** credit sale agreements, bank loans (whether advanced as a lump sum or in instalments), pawnbrokers' loans, check trading credit (see also Sch.II, Pt II, Examples 9, 10, 17 and 23). A "credit hire" agreement has been held to be an example of fixed-sum credit (see notes to s.11). Typical examples of running-account credit are: credit card agreements, bank overdraft agreements, shop budget accounts (see also Sch.II, Pt II, Examples 15, 16, 18 and 23). Suppose a consumer applies to have a store credit card which is offered at the time the consumer decides to make a purchase and that both parties know and intend that the first debit to the account will be the price of the item being purchased. The fact that, when the credit agreement is made, the parties know that an exact sum is to be advanced under the credit agreement, is not enough to make the credit agreement one which is in part a fixed-sum credit agreement. That debit is merely the first drawing against a running-account facility: *Goshawk Dedicated (No.2) Ltd v The Governor and Company of the Bank of Scotland* [2005] EWHC 2906 (Ch); [2006] 2 All E.R. 610. The distinction between fixed-sum and running-account credit is important for the purposes of calculation of the "specified amount" in s.16B(1)(a). In relation to an agreement made before April 6, 2008, it is important for the purposes of the calculation of the specified figure which until that date was part of the definition (in s.8) of a consumer credit agreement. An agreement made prior to April 6, 2008 was not (and still is not) a consumer credit agreement if it provided credit exceeding £25,000—see commentary to s.8. As regards running-account agreements, the primary rule is that the credit limit is the determining factor. However, even if there is no credit limit or if the credit limit is higher than the specified amount (£25,000 prior to April 6, 2008), the agreement may nevertheless be taken, by virtue of s.10(3), to provide credit not exceeding that figure. Section 10(3) is an anti-avoidance provision to cope with the situation where an unrealistically high credit limit is agreed. A term that the interest rate increases if the debit balance rises above £25,000 (or any lower figure), would cause the application of s.10(3)(b)(ii)—(see also Sch.II, Pt II, Example

Paragraph numbers marked with a "+" can be found online and on CD.

6). If the agreement contains a term signifying that in the opinion of the parties s.10(3)(b)(iii) does not apply to the agreement, it (i.e. s.10(3)(b)(iii)) shall be taken not to apply unless the contrary is proved, see s.171(1)(see also Sch.II, Pt II, Example 6). By s.10(2) a term of the agreement allowing the debtor to exceed the credit limit merely temporarily is to be ignored (see also s.18(5) and Sch.II, Pt II, Examples 22 and 23).

Restricted-use credit and unrestricted-use credit

3H–33   **11.**—(1) A restricted-use credit agreement is a regulated consumer credit agreement—

> (a) to finance a transaction between the debtor and the creditor, whether forming part of that agreement or not, or
>
> (b) to finance a transaction between the debtor and a person (the "supplier") other than the creditor, or
>
> (c) to refinance any existing indebtedness of the debtor's, whether to the creditor or another person,

and "restricted-use credit" shall be construed accordingly.

(2) An unrestricted-use credit agreement is a regulated consumer credit agreement not falling within subsection (1), and "unrestricted-use credit" shall be construed accordingly.

(3) An agreement does not fall within subsection (1) if the credit is in fact provided in such a way as to leave the debtor free to use it as he chooses, even though certain uses would contravene that or any other agreement.

(4) An agreement may fall within subsection (1)(b) although the identity of the supplier is unknown at the time the agreement is made.

Restricted-use credit and unrestricted-use credit

3H–34   Credit is either restricted-use credit or unrestricted-use credit. These two definitions interrelate with those (in ss.12 and 13) of debtor-creditor agreement and debtor-creditor-supplier agreement. Also they are relevant to the definitions of some exempt agreements (see commentary to s.16). Where the credit is advanced in such a way that the debtor can spend it in any way he chooses (e.g. cash is put into the debtor's hands or into his current account), the credit is inevitably unrestricted-use credit (s.11(3)). That is so even if the debtor has agreed to use the credit only in a particular way. Where goods or services are supplied on credit, then the credit is tied to that particular purpose and the agreement will therefore fall within s.11(1)(a) or s.11(1)(b). It will be a s.11(1)(a) situation where the person providing the credit (the creditor) and the person contracting with the debtor to supply the goods or services (the supplier) are one and the same person, e.g. where a retailer supplies a fridge on terms that the debtor pays the retailer for it in instalments later. A s.11(1)(b) situation arises where the creditor and the supplier are two different persons, e.g. where the customer uses his regulated credit card to pay for goods or services. The credit card issuer (the creditor) provides credit to the customer to enable the customer to buy from the retailer. The customer's contract of purchase is with the retailer; his credit card agreement with the card issuer is a restricted-use credit agreement within s.11(1)(b). It is "restricted" use because, although the card can no doubt be used at many retail outlets, it is not available for use absolutely anywhere. If the card-holder (the debtor) is able to draw cash on his credit card account, he is, of course, free to use that cash as he chooses. In that case the credit card agreement is a "multiple agreement"(within s.18(1)(a)): when the debtor uses the card to pay for goods or services, the agreement is one for restricted-use credit within s.11(1)(b); when the debtor uses it to draw cash, it is an unrestricted-use credit agreement (see Sch.II, Pt II, Example 16).

Hatfield v Hiscock [1998] C.C.L.R. 68, involved a "credit hire" agreement for the hire of a motor vehicle for a period not exceeding three months and under which the pay-

Paragraph numbers marked with a "+" can be found online and on CD.

ment for the hire was deferred for a period after the hire had come to an end. This agreement was held to involve fixed-sum credit, albeit the amount of the credit was incapable of being quantified until some weeks or months after the agreement was made. In *Dimond v Lovell* [2000] Q.B. 216; [1999] 3 W.L.R. 561, the Court of Appeal held a similar "credit hire" agreement to be: a personal credit agreement within s.8(1); a consumer credit agreement within s.8(2); an agreement for fixed-sum credit within s.10(1)(b), and; a debtor-credit-supplier agreement within s.12(a). This analysis was apparently approved when a further appeal in *Dimond v Lovell* [2002] 1 A.C. 384 was dismissed by the House of Lords.

A hire-purchase agreement (or a conditional sale or credit sale agreement) entered into between the customer and a finance company to whom the customer has been introduced by a dealer for the purpose of enabling the customer to buy goods of the dealer on credit terms, may appear at first sight to be a s.11(1)(b) agreement. In fact it is not. In this scenario, the finance company buys the goods from the dealer and in turn contracts to supply them to the customer/debtor. The finance company is both creditor and supplier. It is the latter because under the hire-purchase contract the finance company contracts to supply the goods. It is to the finance company that the debtor can look if the goods are not delivered or if, say, there is a breach of the statutory implied terms (as to description, satisfactory quality, etc.). The credit in these cases is provided by the finance company to finance a transaction (i.e. for the supply of the goods) between the finance company and the debtor. Thus every regulated hire-purchase agreement, every regulated conditional sale agreement and every regulated credit sale agreement is a s.11(1)(a) agreement.

An agreement can be "to finance ..." or "to refinance ..." within s.11 only where it contains an express or implied term that the credit shall be used for that purpose. It is not enough that the parties had a common purpose or intention that the credit be used for that purpose, *National Westminster Bank v Story and Pallister* [1999] C.C.L.R. 70, CA.

Debtor-creditor-supplier agreements

12. A debtor-creditor-supplier agreement is a regulated consumer credit agreement being— **3H–35**

    (a) a restricted-use credit agreement which falls within section 11(1)(a), or

    (b) a restricted-use credit agreement which falls within section 11(1)(b)and is made by the creditor under pre-existing arrangements, or in contemplation of future arrangements, between himself and the supplier, or

    (c) an unrestricted-use credit agreement which is made by the creditor under pre-existing arrangements between himself and a person (the "supplier") other than the debtor in the knowledge that the credit is to be used to finance a transaction between the debtor and the supplier.

Debtor-creditor-supplier agreements

Every regulated agreement is either a debtor-creditor-supplier agreement (within s.12) or a debtor-creditor agreement (within s.13). The former identifies regulated consumer credit agreements: first where the creditor and the supplier are one and the same person (s.12(a)); and, secondly, where, though the creditor and supplier are separate persons, there is a business link between them such that the credit contract and the supply contract are linked in a business sense (s.12(b) and (c)). Later sections provide for the dealer to be deemed to be agent of the creditor in antecedent negotiations (s.56) and for the creditor to be jointly and severally liable for misrepresentations and breaches of contract committed by the supplier when the supplier is a different person from the creditor (s.75). These sections do not apply to debtor-creditor agreements. **3H–36**

Paragraph numbers marked with a "+" can be found online and on CD.

Every regulated hire-purchase agreement, every regulated conditional sale agreement and every regulated credit sale agreement is a debtor-creditor-supplier agreement within s.12(a) (see commentary to s.11 above). A regulated credit card agreement will be a debtor-creditor-supplier agreement within s.12(b) when the credit card is used to pay for goods or services and will be a debtor-creditor agreement within s.13(c) when used to withdraw cash (see commentary to s.11 above). A "credit hire" agreement is a debtor-creditor-supplier agreement within s.12(a)—see notes to s.11.

"Arrangements" is a key word intended to identify the link between the credit agreement and the supply agreement. The Crowther Report, which the Act was passed to implement, referred to the situation where the creditor and supplier were in effect in a "joint venture for mutual profit". For "arrangements", see s.187. An agreement for an individual to have an overdraft (with a credit limit of £25,000 or less) is a regulated consumer credit agreement; it is a debtor-creditor agreement. That is so irrespective of whether payment (for goods or services) out of that account is by means of either a cheque (whether or not backed by a cheque guarantee card) or an electronic debit card (e.g. Delta or Switch), see s.187(3) and (3A). It would be a debtor-creditor-supplier agreement (within s.12(b) or (c)) in the very unlikely event that the bank agreed to the overdraft pursuant to arrangements between the bank and a supplier whereby the bank agreed to grant credit to customers to enable them to make purchases from the supplier. Such a scenario would be more likely to occur, however, in the case of a bank loan (i.e. rather than an overdraft agreement). If that scenario did exist, the loan would be a debtor-creditor-supplier agreement even if the loan were advanced by means of unrestricted-use credit (e.g. if the bank advanced the credit, albeit under a separate loan agreement, by simply crediting it to the debtor's current account). In that case, if the loan was made under the arrangements between the bank and the supplier, and if the bank knew that it was to be used to finance a transaction between the debtor and the supplier, it would be a debtor-creditor-supplier agreement within s.12(c).

In relation to debtor-creditor-supplier and debtor-creditor agreements, see Sch.II, Pt II, Examples 8, 16, 17, 18 and 21.

Debtor-creditor agreements

3H–37   **13.** A debtor-creditor agreement is a regulated consumer credit agreement being—

(a) a restricted-use credit agreement which falls within section 11(1)(b) but is not made by the creditor under pre-existing arrangements, or in contemplation of future arrangements, between himself and the supplier, or

(b) a restricted-use credit agreement which falls within section 11(1)(c), or

(c) an unrestricted-use credit agreement which is not made by the creditor under pre-existing arrangements between himself and a person (the "supplier") other than the debtor in the knowledge that the credit is to be used to finance a transaction between the debtor and the supplier.

Debtor-creditor agreements

3H–38   See commentary to s.12.

Credit-token agreements

3H–39   **14.**—(1) A credit-token is a card, check, voucher, coupon, stamp, form, booklet or other document or thing given to an individual by a person carrying on a consumer credit business, who undertakes—

(a) that on the production of it (whether or not some other action is also required) he will supply cash, goods and services (or any of them) on credit, or

Paragraph numbers marked with a "+" can be found online and on CD.

(b) that where, on the production of it to a third party (whether or not any other action is also required), the third party supplies cash, goods and services (or any of them), he will pay the third party for them (whether or not deducting any discount or commission), in return for payment to him by the individual.

(2) A credit-token agreement is a regulated agreement for the provision of credit in connection with the use of a credit-token.

(3) Without prejudice to the generality of section 9(1), the person who gives to an individual an undertaking falling within subsection (1)(b) shall be taken to provide him with credit drawn on whenever a third party supplies him with cash, goods or services.

(4) For the purposes of subsection (1), use of an object to operate a machine provided by the person giving the object or a third party shall be treated as the production of the object to him.

Credit-token agreements

The basic concept of a credit-token is of an object on production of which cash, **3H–40** goods or services may be supplied on credit. The credit card is the typical case, but the term also covers trading vouchers, trading checks, and in some circumstances electronic debit (Delta or Swift) cards.

This section contains two definitions: "credit-token"; and "credit-token agreement". Only a regulated agreement can be a credit-token agreement. A credit-token can exist, on the other hand in relation to an agreement which is not a regulated agreement—though it can only be a credit-token if it is given by someone carrying on a "consumer credit business". *Query* whether a token issued in relation to an exempt agreement (e.g. an exempt charge card) by someone who also carries on a "consumer credit business" (e.g. issues regulated credit cards) can be a "credit-token"? See the definition of "consumer credit business" in s.189(1). It seems that an electronic debit card which can be used only to withdraw cash from machines operated by the bank which issued the card will be a credit-token only if the bank has agreed to the card holder having a debit balance on his account, since if the card is to be used simply to withdraw money from an account with a credit balance, the card does not fall within s.14(1)(a), there being no "credit" involved. If, on the other hand, the card can be used to withdraw money from a machine operated by a third party (e.g. another bank) the card appears capable of falling within s.14(1)(b). In that case it appears to be irrelevant (if it is the case) that the card is able to be used only in relation to a credit balance, since by s.14(3) the issuing bank is "taken" to provide the card holder with credit. Or does the reference in s.14(1)to the object being given by a person carrying on a consumer credit business imply that it is confined to objects issued in relation to regulated consumer credit agreements?

It is an offence to give an unsolicited credit-token, s.51(1). In that context, it has been held that the word "undertakes" in s.14(1) does not imply a requirement of a contract or of a binding undertaking, *Elliott v Director General of Fair Trading* [1980] 1 W.L.R. 977; [1980] C.C.L.R. 23. In that case a card having the appearance of a credit card was on its face stated to be a credit card available for immediate use. It was held that this was a credit-token even though a customer first presenting the card would have been required to enter a formal agreement and complete other formalities before getting credit.

Consumer hire agreements

15.—(1) A consumer hire agreement is an agreement made by a **3H–41** person with an individual (the "hirer") for the bailment or (in Scotland) the hiring of goods to the hirer, being an agreement which—

(a) is not a hire-purchase agreement, and

Paragraph numbers marked with a "+" can be found online and on CD.

CONSUMER

(b) is capable of subsisting for more than three months.

(c) [...]

(2) A consumer hire agreement is a regulated agreement if it is not an exempt agreement.

3H–42   *Note* —Amended by the Consumer Credit (Increase of Monetary Limits) Order 1983 (SI 1983/1878); and the Consumer Credit (Increase of Monetary Limits) (Amendment) Order 1988 (SI 1998/996). Subsection (1)(c) was repealed with effect from April 6, 2008 by the Consumer Credit Act 2006 ss.2(2), 70, Sch.4 (SI 2007/ 3300 and SI 2008/ 831).

Consumer hire agreements

3H–43   For "individual" see commentary to s.8. A hire-purchase agreement cannot be a consumer hire agreement. Hire-purchase agreements are credit agreements (see s.9(2)). The parties to a consumer hire agreement are referred to in the Act as "owner" and "hirer". An agreement is not a hire agreement if it does not provide for the bailee to pay (or provide some other reward) for the hire: *TRM Copy Centres (UK) Ltd v Lanwall Services Ltd* [2008] EWCA Civ 382; [2008] 4 All E.R. 608, (not hire when retailer agreed to have a photocopier on retailer's premises with no obligation to make any payment to the photocopier owner other than to account, less a commission, for payments made by members of the public for use of the machine). A hire agreement which is stated to have a duration of two months and which contains an option to renew the agreement for a further two months (whether exercisable by the hirer or the owner) is capable of subsisting for more than three months. Until April 6, 2008, subs.(1) contained a third paragraph—paragraph (c)—setting out a financial limit. Thus any hire agreement made before that date was not (and still is not) a consumer hire agreement if it required the hirer to make payments exceeding a specified figure. When the Act came into force, the figure in s.15(1)(c) was £5,000. On May 20, 1985, it was raised to £15,000. For agreements made on or after May 1, 1998 the figure was £25,000. An agreement, made before April 6, 2008, which was stated to last for seven years, which contained no clause entitling either party to terminate it before the expiry of the seven years, and which provided for quarterly rentals each of £1,000, was not a consumer hire agreement. This is because it required the debtor to make payments amounting to £28,000, i.e. exceeding £25,000. If, on the other hand, the agreement had contained a clause entitling the hirer to terminate the agreement at the end of three and a half years, it would have been a consumer hire agreement because it would then require the hirer to make payments of only £14,000, i.e. not exceeding £25,000. See also Sch.II, Pt II, Examples 20 and 24. The financial limit is no part of the definition in relation to agreements made after April 6, 2008. For "exempt" agreements, see ss.16, 16A and 16B.

Credit-hire agreements

3H–44   If the *bailment* is not capable of subsisting for more than three months, then the agreement is not a consumer hire agreement. That is so, even if the agreement is a "credit-hire" agreement and thus the period allowed for payment of the hire charges is much longer than three months: *Lagden v O'Connor* [2003] Q.B. 36; [2002] EWCA Civ 510. For whether a "credit-hire" agreement is a consumer credit agreement, see the commentaries to ss.8 and 11. For whether it is exempt, see commentary to s.16 (at the sixth bullet point).

For ss.16 to 16C of the Consumer Credit Act 1974 (see Arrangement) plus any related commentary see paragraphs 3H–45+ to 3H–54.0.2+ on White Book on Westlaw UK or the Civil Procedure CD.

Small agreements

3H–54   17.—(1) A small agreement is—

(a) a regulated consumer credit agreement for credit not exceeding £50, other than a hire-purchase or conditional sale agreement; or

Paragraph numbers marked with a "+" can be found online and on CD.

(b) a regulated consumer hire agreement which does not require the hirer to make payments exceeding £50,

being an agreement which is either unsecured or secured by a guarantee or indemnity only (whether or not the guarantee or indemnity is itself secured).

(2) Section 10(3)(a) applies for the purposes of subsection (1) as it applies for the purposes of section 16B(1)(a).

(3) Where—

(a) two or more small agreements are made at or about the same time between the same parties, and

(b) it appears probable that they would instead have been made as a single agreement but for the desire to avoid the operation of provisions of this Act which would have applied to that single agreement but, apart from this subsection, are not applicable to the small agreements,

this Act applies to the small agreements as if they were regulated agreements other than small agreements.

(4) If, apart from this subsection, subsection (3) does not apply to any agreements but would apply if, for any party or parties to any of the agreements, there were substituted an associate of that party, or associates of each of those parties, as the case may be, then subsection (3) shall apply to the agreements.

Note —Amended by the Consumer Credit (Increase of Monetary Limits) Order **3H–55** 1983 (SI 1983/1878). Also amended by s.5(3) of the Consumer Credit Act 2006 with effect from April 6, 2008 (SI 2007/3300).

Small agreements

This definition identifies agreements of low value and enables later sections to **3H–56** except some of them from some of the requirements of the Act, e.g. from the documentation requirements (see s.74). From the coming into force of the Act until January 1, 1984 the figure in s.17(1)(a) was £30. Since that date the figure has been £50. See Sch.II, Pt II, Examples 16, 17 and 22.

Multiple agreements

18.—(1) This section applies to an agreement (a "multiple agree- **3H–57** ment") if its terms are such as—

(a) to place a part of it within one category of agreement mentioned in this Act, and another part of it within a different category of agreement so mentioned, or within a category of agreement not so mentioned, or

(b) to place it, or a part of it, within two or more categories of agreement so mentioned.

(2) Where a part of an agreement falls within subsection (1), that part shall be treated for the purposes of this Act as a separate agreement.

(3) Where an agreement falls within subsection (1)(b), it shall be treated as an agreement in each of the categories in question, and this Act shall apply to it accordingly.

(4) Where under subsection (2) a part of a multiple agreement is to be treated as a separate agreement, the multiple agreement shall

Paragraph numbers marked with a "+" can be found online and on CD.

(with any necessary modifications) be construed accordingly; and any sum payable under the multiple agreement, if not apportioned by the parties, shall for the purposes of proceedings in any court relating to the multiple agreement be apportioned by the court as may be requisite.

(5) In the case of an agreement for running-account credit, a term of the agreement allowing the credit limit to be exceeded merely temporarily shall not be treated as a separate agreement or as providing fixed-sum credit in respect of the excess.

(6) This Act does not apply to a multiple agreement so far as the agreement relates to goods if under the agreement payments are to be made in respect of the goods in the form of rent (other than a rentcharge) issuing out of land.

Multiple agreements

3H–58   There is a controversy as to the proper interpretation of this section. Professor Goode in his *Consumer Credit Legislation* takes the view that an agreement can fall either within s.18(1)(a), or within s.18(1)(b), but not both. He takes the view that an agreement can fall within s.18(1)(a) only if it is a "multipart" agreement and not if it is a "unitary" agreement. (These terms are not to be found in the Act). This approach is inconsistent, however, with Examples 16 and 18 in Sch.II, Pt II. It is also inconsistent with s.18 operating, as it was surely meant to, as an anti-avoidance measure. Yet in *National Home Loans Corp v Hannah* [1997] C.C.L.R. 7, Professor Goode's thesis was followed apparently without any hesitation (or, indeed, acknowledgement). The case involved a loan agreement to lend over £52,000 which (a) was a refinancing of an existing loan of over £41,000, and also (b) provided extra spending of £10,915. It was held that even if the (a) part was for restricted-use credit and the (b) part was for unrestricted-use credit, it still did not fall within s.18(1)(a) and was not a multiple agreement. This was because it was a unitary agreement incapable of being split up without altering its essential character. The result was that something (i.e. part (b)) which, if looked at alone would have been a regulated agreement, escaped being designated as such by virtue of being included within an agreement outside the scope of the Act.

The opposing view to Professor Goode's is put by the draftsman of the Act, Francis Bennion, in *Multiple Agreements under the Consumer Credit Act 1974* [1999] C.I.C.C. 1. It is that an agreement, whether "unitary" or not, which falls into more than one category of agreement under the Act, is a multiple agreement and that those aspects of the agreement falling into any one such category are to be treated as a separate agreement—i.e. that part is to be treated as being, even though it is not in fact, a separate agreement. The difference between the two views can be vital because the effect of treating a part of an agreement as a separate agreement can be to cause that part to fall within the financial limits of the Act when otherwise it would not be a regulated agreement. When the matter surfaced in *National Westminster Bank v Story and Pallister* [1999] C.C.L.R. 70, Bennion's article was not referred to and the Court of Appeal avoided the issue by deciding that the two different parts, or aspects, of the agreement in that case were both within the same catetory of agreement within the Act, both involving unrestricted-use credit. The matter surfaced again in the House of Lords in *Dimond v Lovell* [2000] 1 A.C. 384. It was argued that by virtue of section 18 a "credit-hire" agreement was a multiple agreement, one part being for the hire of a car (non-regulated) and other part being for the allowing of credit to pay the hire charges (regulated). Lord Hoffman, giving the leading speech, simply said "Whatever a multiple agreement may be, one cannot divide up a contract in that way." The matter was fully argued for the first time in *Ocwen v Coxall and Coxall* [2004] C.C.L.R. 7, where H.H. Judge Holt held that Bennion's views were to be preferred to those of Professor Goode. In *London North Securities Ltd v Williams and Williams* (May 16, 2005, unrep., Reading Cty Ct) Recorder Gary Flather OBE QC entirely agreed with, and followed, that decision. In *London North Securities Ltd v Meadows* [2005] EWCA Civ 956; [2005] C.C.L.R. 7, the Court of Appeal set out the controversy but on the facts found it unnecessary to rule upon it. Francis Bennion's article and his addendum to it (written af-

Paragraph numbers marked with a "+" can be found online and on CD.

ter the decision in *National Westminster Bank v Story* [1999] Lloyd's Rep. Bank. 261; [1999] C.C.L.R. 70) can both be seen (as separate items) on Francis Bennion's website at *http://www.francisbennion.com* [Accessed December 5, 2007].

Linked transactions

19.—(1) A transaction entered into by the debtor or hirer, or a rel- **3H–59**
ative of his, with any other person ("the other party"), except one for the provision of security, is a linked transaction in relation to an actual or prospective regulated agreement (the "principal agreement") of which it does not form part if—

> (a) the transaction is entered into in compliance with a term of the principal agreement; or
> (b) the principal agreement is a debtor-creditor-supplier agreement and the transaction is financed, or to be financed, by the principal agreement, or
> (c) the other party is a person mentioned in subsection (2), and a person so mentioned initiated the transaction by suggesting it to the debtor or hirer, or his relative, who enters into it—
>> (i) to induce the creditor or owner to enter into the principal agreement, or
>> (ii) for another purpose related to the principal agreement, or
>> (iii) where the principal agreement is a restricted-use credit agreement, for a purpose related to a transaction financed, or to be financed, by the principal agreement.

(2) The persons referred to in subsection (1)(c) are—

> (a) the creditor or owner, or his associate;
> (b) a person who, in the negotiation of the transaction, is represented by a credit-broker who is also a negotiator in antecedent negotiations for the principal agreement;
> (c) a person who, at the time the transaction is initiated, knows that the principal agreement has been made or contemplates that it might be made.

(3) A linked transaction entered into before the making of the principal agreement has no effect until such time (if any) as that agreement is made.

(4) Regulations may exclude linked transactions of the prescribed description from the operation of subsection (3).

Linked transactions

For the meaning of the many technical terms in this section, see s.189(1). Three **3H–60**
provisions in particular have an impact upon linked transactions: ss.19(3), 69(1) and 96(1). If the debtor or hirer withdraws an offer to enter a regulated agreement or exercises his right to cancel a cancellable agreement, any linked transaction is automatically withdrawn from or cancelled (ss.19(3) and 69(1)). If for any reason the debtor's indebtedness is discharged early, the debtor is discharged from any further liability under any linked transaction (s.96(1)). However, by virtue of the Consumer Credit (Linked Transactions) (Exemptions) Regulations 1983 (SI 1983/1560), three types of linked transaction are exempted from the three provisions just mentioned which would otherwise have applied to them. Those three types of linked transaction are:

Paragraph numbers marked with a "+" can be found online and on CD.

(i) contracts of insurance;

(ii) written guarantees of goods; and

(iii) any transaction which is (or is made under) an agreement for the operation of a savings, deposit or current account.

For ss.20, 40 and 55 of the Consumer Credit Act 1974 (see Arrangement) plus any related commentary see paragraphs 3H–61+ to 3H–71+ on White Book on Westlaw UK or the Civil Procedure CD.

Antecedent negotiations

3H–72   **56.**—(1) In this Act "antecedent negotiations" means any negotiations with the debtor or hirer—

(a) conducted by the creditor or owner in relation to the making of any regulated agreement, or

(b) conducted by a credit-broker in relation to goods sold or proposed to be sold by the credit-broker to the creditor before forming the subject-matter of a debtor-creditor-supplier agreement within section 12(a), or

(c) conducted by the supplier in relation to a transaction financed or proposed to be financed by a debtor-creditor-supplier agreement within section 12(b) or (c),

and "negotiator" means the person by whom negotiations are so conducted with the debtor or hirer.

(2) Negotiations with the debtor in a case falling within subsection (1)(b) or (c) shall be deemed to be conducted by the negotiator in the capacity of agent of the creditor as well as in his actual capacity.

(3) An agreement is void if, and to the extent that, it purports in relation to an actual or prospective regulated agreement—

(a) to provided that a person acting as, or on behalf of, a negotiator is to be treated as the agent of the debtor or hirer, or

(b) to relieve a person from liability for acts or omissions of any person acting as, or on behalf of, a negotiator.

(4) For the purposes of this Act, antecedent negotiations shall be taken to begin when the negotiator and the debtor or hirer first enter into communication (including communication by advertisement), and to include any representations made by the negotiator to the debtor or hirer and any other dealings between them.

Antecedent negotiations

Subsection (1)

3H–73   The definition of antecedent negotiations is significant for two reasons:

(i) the agency provision in s.56(2);

(ii) no agreement will be cancellable under s.67 unless oral representations were made during "antecedent negotiations".

Section 56(1)(b) covers the triangular situation where the dealer sells the goods to a finance company which in turn contracts with the debtor to supply the goods to the debtor on hire-purchase, conditional sale or credit sale agreement terms. In that situation the dealer who introduces the debtor to the finance company is a "credit-broker" (s.189(1)). Section 56(1)(b) does not, however, cover the situation where the contract made by the finance company with the customer is a regulated consumer hire agree-

Paragraph numbers marked with a "+" can be found online and on CD.

ment (*Moorgate Mercantile Leasing Ltd v Gell and Ugolini* [1988] C.C.L.R. 1). Section 56(1)(c) covers the situation where, pursuant to arrangements between the creditor and the supplier, the creditor provides credit for the debtor to pay for goods or services supplied by the supplier, e.g. the debtor pays for the goods using his (regulated) credit card.

Deemed agency

Subsection (2) reverses the common law rule whereby the dealer (e.g. in the hire-purchase triangular situation) is not normally the agent of the finance company (*Branwhite v Worcester Works Finance* [1969] 1 A.C. 552). It means, inter alia, that statements, promises, etc., made to the debtor by the dealer are regarded as also made by the creditor who can accordingly be liable for misrepresentation or breach of a contractual promise. The deemed agency, in a s.56(1)(b) situation, relates only to statements and promises "in relation to" the goods being supplied to the debtor. This *does*, however, include, where the debtor has traded in a vehicle in part exchange for the new one (the "goods"), a promise by the dealer to use the part exchange allowance (or part of it) to discharge the debtor's indebtedness under the credit agreement by which the debtor acquired the traded in vehicle (*Forthright Finance Ltd v Ingate* [1997] 4 All E.R. 99; [1997] C.C.L.R. 95). Negotiations relating to the part-exchange and to the new vehicle were all part of the same transaction. *Forthright Finance Ltd v Ingate* was, however, distinguished in the situation where the dealer, having promised the debtor that he would pay off the debtor's indebtedness, used an intermediary credit broker to arrange the finance for the new vehicle: *Black Horse Ltd v Langford* [2007] EWHC 907; [2007] C.C.L.R. 5.

For a situation where at common law the dealer was held (contrary to the usual position) to have been expressly authorised by the finance company to accept the debtor's offer to enter a conditional sale agreement, thereby making the agreement by releasing the vehicle to the debtor upon the latter signing the finance company's proposal form, see *Carlyle Finance Ltd v Pallas Industrial Finance Ltd* [1999] C.C.L.R. 85, CA.

3H–74

Withdrawal from prospective agreement

57.—(1) The withdrawal of a party from a prospective regulated agreement shall operate to apply this Part to the agreement, any linked transaction and any other thing done in anticipation of the making of the agreement as it would apply if the agreement were made and then cancelled under section 69.

(2) The giving to a party of a written or oral notice which, however expressed, indicates the intention of the other party to withdraw from a prospective regulated agreement operates as a withdrawal from it.

(3) Each of the following shall be deemed to be the agent of the creditor or owner for the purpose of receiving a notice under subsection (2)—

   (a) a credit-broker or supplier who is the negotiator in antecedent negotiations, and

   (b) any person who, in the course of a business carried on by him, acts on behalf of the debtor or hirer in any negotiations for the agreement.

(4) Where the agreement, if made, would not be a cancellable agreement, subsection (1) shall nevertheless apply as if the contrary were the case.

3H–75

Withdrawal from prospective agreement

Deemed cancellation

By s.57(1) a prospective agreement which is withdrawn from, is deemed to have

3H–76

Paragraph numbers marked with a "+" can be found online and on CD.

been made, to have been a cancellable one and to have been cancelled, with the result that ss.67–73 below apply. For those linked transactions to which this provision does not apply, see commentary to s.19.

Deemed agency

3H–77   A wider range of persons than negotiator in antecedent negotiations is deemed agent of the creditor or owner for the purpose of receiving notice of the withdrawal. It could, for example, include the debtor's solicitor if he helped the debtor arrange the prospective agreement. A person deemed to receive a notice as agent of the creditor or owner is under a duty to transmit the notice to the creditor or owner forthwith (s.175).

Section 57 does not apply to agreements listed in ss.74 and 82(4).

For ss.58 and 59 of the Consumer Credit Act 1974 (see Arrangement) plus any related commentary see paragraphs 3H–78+ to 3H–81+ on White Book on Westlaw UK or the Civil Procedure CD.

MAKING THE AGREEMENT

Form and content of agreements

3H–82   **60.**—(1) The Secretary of State shall make regulations as to the form and content of documents embodying regulated agreements, and the regulations shall contain such provisions as appear to him appropriate with a view to ensuring that the debtor or hirer is made aware of—

(a) the rights and duties conferred or imposed on him by the agreement,

(b) the amount and rate of the total charge for credit (in the case of a consumer credit agreement),

(c) the protection and remedies available to him under this Act, and

(d) any other matters which, in the opinion of the Secretary of State, it is desirable for him to know about in connection with the agreement.

(2) Regulations under subsection (1) may in particular—

(a) require specified information to be included in the prescribed manner in documents, and other specified material to be excluded;

(b) contain requirements to ensure that specified information is clearly brought to the attention of the debtor or hirer, and that one part of a document is not given insufficient or excessive prominence compared with another.

(3) If, on an application made to the OFT by a person carrying on a consumer credit business or a consumer hire business, it appears to the OFT impracticable for the applicant to comply with any requirement of regulations under subsection (1) in a particular case, it may, by notice to the applicant direct that the requirement be waived or varied in relation to such agreements, and subject to such conditions (if any), as it may specify, and this Act and the regulations shall have effect accordingly.

(4) The OFT shall give a notice under subsection (3) only if it is satisfied that to do so would not prejudice the interests of debtors or hirers.

Paragraph numbers marked with a "+" can be found online and on CD.

Note —Amended by the Enterprise Act 2002 s.278 and Sch.25. **3H–83**

Form and content of agreements

The Consumer Credit (Agreements) Regulations 1983 (SI 1983/1553), as amended **3H–84**
with effect from May 31, 2005 by the Consumer Credit (Agreements)(Amendment)
Regulations 2004 (SI 2004/1482), lay down detailed requirements as to form and
content. Failure to comply with the regulations will result in the agreement being
improperly executed (see ss.61(1) and 65). These sections—and the regulations—do
not apply to agreements listed in ss.74 and 82(4).

Dispensations —Granted under subss.(3) and (4) by the Office of Fair Trading are **3H–85**
entered in the Consumer Credit Public Register.

**For ss.61 to 64 of the Consumer Credit Act 1974 (see Arrangement) plus any re-
lated commentary see paragraphs 3H–86+ to 3H–98+ on White Book on Westlaw
UK or the Civil Procedure CD.**

Consequences of improper execution

65.—(1) An improperly-executed regulated agreement is enforce- **3H–99**
able against the debtor or hirer on an order of the court only.

(2) A retaking of goods or land to which a regulated agreement
relates is an enforcement of the agreement.

Consequences of improper execution

An agreement is "improperly-executed" if the documentation requirements in **3H–100**
ss.57–63 are not complied with. The consequence is that the creditor will be unable to
enforce the agreement against the debtor or hirer without a court order. The court's
power to grant an order is restricted by s.127 (*q.v.*). For the effect of this on "security",
see s.113. Section 65(2) does not preclude the re-taking of goods or land where it is
done with the consent of the debtor or hirer given at the time of the re-possession (see
s.173(3)). If the debtor or hirer has disposed of the goods wrongfully to a third party,
then arguably recovery of them from that third party would not be prohibited since it
would not be an enforcement of the agreement "against the debtor or hirer". See the
case law on the rather different wording of s.90. Similarly, if say a hire purchase or
consumer hire agreement has terminated leaving the creditor with ownership, the
creditor has a right to recover the goods independently of the agreement, i.e. on the
basis of his ownership, and, arguably, in recovering the goods would not be enforcing
the agreement but relying on his ownership as the basis of the claim (see *Bowmaker v
Barnet Instruments Ltd* [1945] K.B. 65). Section 65(2) appears to deny such an argument.

There is no sanction provided for breach of s.65 but such a breach may be taken
into account by the Office of Fair Trading in determining if the creditor or owner is fit
to have a licence (see s.170(1) and (2)).

Section 65 does not apply to agreements listed in ss.74 and 82(4).

Procedure

For the relevant procedural rules see the notes to s.127 and the Introductory Note **3H–101**
About Procedure in Consumer Credit Cases, immediately before the start of this Act,
at para.3H–4 et seq. above.

**For s.66 of the Consumer Credit Act 1974 (see Arrangement) plus any related
commentary see paragraphs 3H–102+ to 3H–103+ on White Book on Westlaw UK
or the Civil Procedure CD.**

CANCELLATION OF CERTAIN AGREEMENTS WITHIN COOLING-OFF PERIOD

Cancellable agreements

67. A regulated agreement may be cancelled by the debtor or hirer **3H–104**

Paragraph numbers marked with a "+" can be found online and on CD.

in accordance with this Part if the antecedent negotiations included oral representations made when in the presence of the debtor or hirer by an individual acting as, or on behalf of, the negotiator, unless—

    (a) the agreement is secured on land, or is a restricted-use credit agreement to finance the purchase of land or is an agreement for a bridging loan in connection with the purchase of land, or

    (b) the unexecuted agreement is signed by the debtor or hirer at premises at which any of the following is carrying on any business (whether on a permanent or temporary basis)—

        (i) the creditor or owner;

        (ii) any party to a linked transaction (other than the debtor or hirer or a relative of his);

        (iii) the negotiator in any antecedent negotiations.

Cancellable agreements

3H–105   A statement is not a "representation" unless it:

    (a) is a statement of fact or opinion or an undertaking as to the future; and

    (b) is capable of inducing the proposed debtor or hirer to enter the regulated agreement (*Moorgate Services Ltd v Kabir* [1995] C.C.L.R. 74, CA).

A regulated agreement is cancellable if four conditions are satisfied:

    (i) antecedent negotiations included oral representations made in the presence of the debtor or hirer by or on behalf of the creditor or owner;

    (ii) the unexecuted agreement was signed by the debtor or hirer away from business premises identified in s.67(b);

    (iii) the agreement does not fall within s.67(a), s.74(1) or (2), or s.82(4) or (6);

    (iv) the agreement is not cancellable under the provisions of the Timeshare Act 1992.

Where negotiations are conducted by a dealer leading up to the common tripartite arrangement whereby the dealer sells the goods to a finance company which in turn contracts with the debtor to supply them to the debtor on hire-purchase terms, the first of these conditions will be satisfied. Where, however, the resultant agreement between the finance company is a consumer hire agreement, the negotiations between the dealer and the customer are not antecedent negotiations (*Lloyds Bowmaker Leasing Ltd v MacDonald* [1993] C.C.L.R. 65). For antecedent negotiations, see s.56. Note that an agreement may be cancellable if signed at the debtor's or hirer's own business premises. In relation to agreements within s.67(a), see ss.58 and 61(2) and (3). An agreement which is not cancellable (i.e. within the meaning of the Consumer Credit Act) may nevertheless be cancellable by virtue of other legislation, e.g. the Cancellation of Contracts made in a Consumer's Home or Place of Work, etc. Regulations 2008; or the Timeshare Act 1992. When an agreement appears to be cancellable under both the Consumer Credit Act 1974 and the 2008 Regulations just mentioned, the latter do not apply and it is cancellable only under the Consumer Credit Act. On the other hand where an agreement prima facie appears to be cancellable under both the Consumer Credit Act 1974 and the Timeshare Act 1992, it is in fact cancellable only under the Timeshare Act 1992. When the Timeshare Act 1992 was first enacted, the opposite solution was adopted (i.e. an agreement prima facie falling within the cancellation provisions of both enactments would in fact be cancellable only under the Consumer Credit Act). That position was reversed by s.1(6A) of the Timeshare Act 1992 which was inserted by the Timeshare Regulations 1997 (SI 1997/1081).

An agreement which is not cancellable under the Consumer Credit Act may be cancellable under the Consumer Protection (Distance Selling) Regulations 2000, which are set out at para.3H–906 below. An agreement is unlikely to be cancellable under both, since for an agreement to be cancellable under the former there have to be

Paragraph numbers marked with a "+" can be found online and on CD.

representations made in the presence of the debtor or hirer, whereas the latter apply only to "distance contracts", namely where the contract is concluded entirely by distance communication. Where a distance contract is cancellable under the regulations and is cancelled, that cancellation operates (reg.15) also to cancel any "related credit agreement".

Related to the concept of cancellation is that of canvassing off trade premises (defined in s.48). A regulated agreement made following canvassing off trade premises by someone whose licence did not specifically cover that activity may be unenforceable by virtue of s.40 (*q.v.*).

Distance credit contracts

A credit agreement made entirely by distance communication, though not cancel- **3H–106** lable under the Consumer Credit Act, may be cancellable under the Financial Services (Distance Marketing) Regulations 2004 (SI 2004/2095) which implemented the European Directive on the distance marketing of financial services (2002/65). Under these regulations a credit agreement concluded at a distance with a consumer (an individual acting outside any business of his) is cancellable by the consumer for a period of 14 days after the day on which the contract is made. This right of cancellation does not apply to: a "related credit agreement" cancelled under reg.15(1) of the Consumer Protection (Distance Selling) Regulations 2000; a credit agreement cancelled under reg.6A of the Timeshare Act 1992; a credit agreement where the consumer's obligation to repay is secured by a legal mortgage on land; a restricted-use credit agreement to finance the purchase of land or an existing building, or an agreement for a bridging loan in connection with the purchase of land or an existing building.

For ss.68 to 73 of the Consumer Credit Act 1974 (see Arrangement) plus any related commentary see paragraphs 3H–107+ to 3H–121+ on White Book on West-law UK or the Civil Procedure CD.

EXCLUSION OF CERTAIN AGREEMENTS FROM PART V

Exclusion of certain agreements from Part V

74.—(1) This part (except section 56) does not apply to— **3H–122**

    (a) a non-commercial agreement, or

    (b) a debtor-creditor agreement enabling the debtor to over-draw on a current account, or

    (c) a debtor-creditor agreement to finance the making of such payments arising on, or connected with, the death of a person as may be prescribed.

(2) This Part (except sections 55 and 56) does not apply to a small debtor-creditor-supplier agreement for restricted-use credit.

(2A) In the case of an agreement to which the Cancellation of Contracts made in a Consumer's Home or Place of Work etc. Regulations 2008 apply the reference in subsection (2) to a small agreement shall be construed as if in section 17(1)(a) and (b) "£35" were substituted for "£50".

(3) Subsection (1)(b) or (c) applies only where the OFT so determines, and such a determination—

    (a) may be made subject to such conditions as the OFT thinks fit, and

    (b) shall be made only if the OFT is of opinion that it is not against the interests of debtors.

(3A) Notwithstanding anything in subsection (3)(b) above, in relation to a debtor-creditor agreement under which the creditor is the

Paragraph numbers marked with a "+" can be found online and on CD.

CONSUMER

Bank of England or a bank within the meaning of the Bankers' Books Evidence Act 1879, the OFT shall make a determination that subsection (1)(b) above applies unless it considers that it would be against the public interest to do so.

(4) If any term of an agreement falling within subsection (1)(c) or (2) is expressed in writing, regulations under section 60(1) shall apply to that term (subject to section 60(3)) as if the agreement were a regulated agreement not falling within subsection (1)(c) or (2).

3H–123   *Note* —Amended by the Banking Act 1979 s.38 and SI 1987/2117 reg.9; the Enterprise Act 2002 s.278 and Sch.25 and by SI 2008/1816.

Exclusion of certain agreements from Part V

3H–124   For "non-commercial agreement" see s.189(1).

3H–125   *Subsection (1)(b)* —"current account" is not defined. The determination (dated December 21, 1989) of the Director General of Fair Trading (now the OFT) covers both formal and informal overdraft agreements where the creditor is a bank.

The determination contains conditions requiring the debtor to be given specified information as to the rate of interest and other credit charges incurred in relation to the overdraft. For interpretation of those conditions, see *Coutts & Co v Sebestyen* [2005] EWCA Civ 473, [2005] C.C.L.R. 4.

3H–126   *Subsection (1)(c)* —Covers only agreements financing payments prescribed by the Consumer Credit (Payments Arising on Death) Regulations 1983 (SI 1983/1554), namely: capital transfer tax; court fees for grant of probate or of letters of administration (or the resealing in the UK of a Commonwealth or colonial grant); payments to a surety in connection with a guarantee required as a condition of the grant of probate or of letters of administration. The determination (dated December 21, 1989) of the Director General of Fair Trading (now the OFT) limits the effect of subs.(1)(c) to credit granted by a bank to a debtor who is acting in the course of his trade or profession.

PART VI

MATTERS ARISING DURING CURRENCY OF CREDIT OR HIRE AGREEMENTS

Liability of creditor for breaches by supplier

3H–127   75.—(1) If the debtor under a debtor-creditor-supplier agreement falling within section 12(b) or (c) has, in relation to a transaction financed by the agreement, any claim against the supplier in respect of a misrepresentation or breach of contract, he shall have a like claim against the creditor, who, with the supplier, shall accordingly be jointly and severally liable to the debtor.

(2) Subject to any agreement between them, the creditor shall be entitled to be indemnified by the supplier for loss suffered by the creditor in satisfying his liability under subsection (1), including costs reasonably incurred by him in defending proceedings instituted by the debtor.

(3) Subsection (1) does not apply to a claim—

(a) under a non-commercial agreement, or

(b) so far as the claim relates to any single item to which the supplier has attached a cash price not exceeding £100 or more than £30,000.

Paragraph numbers marked with a "+" can be found online and on CD.

(4) This section applies notwithstanding that the debtor, in entering into the transaction, exceeded the credit limit or otherwise contravened any term of the agreement.

(5) In an action brought against the creditor under subsection (1) he shall be entitled, in accordance with rules of court, to have the supplier made a party to the proceedings.

Note —Amended by the Consumer Credit (Increase of Monetary Limits) Order 1983 (SI 1983/1878). **3H–128**

Liability of creditor for breaches by supplier

This section implements the recommendation of the Crowther Committee that there should be "connected lender liability" where the creditor and the supplier are two different persons and the creditor is, by arrangement with the supplier, providing credit to finance the debtor's purchase (of goods or services) from the supplier. The creditor is jointly and severally liable for the supplier's default but is entitled to an indemnity from the supplier. In the event of the supplier's insolvency the creditor will end up carrying the loss, unless the creditor can claim indemnity against anyone else, e.g. under the Civil Liability (Contribution) Act 1978. There is no doubt that s.75 applies where a (regulated) credit card is used by the debtor to pay for goods or services (within the limits in subs.(3)(b)). Credit card companies have variously maintained that s.75 does not apply: **3H–129**

- (i) to cards (including replacement cards) issued under agreements made before July 1, 1997 (the commencement date of s.75);
- (ii) where it is a second authorised card-holder on the debtor's account who used the card;
- (iii) to "four party" credit card transactions i.e. where it was not the creditor (the card issuer) who was the "merchant acquirer" who signed up the particular retailer to the credit-card payment system (e.g. VISA);
- (iv) where a British credit card is used to make a payment abroad.

The first two of these have not been determined in any reported decision. (i) is probably correct, but not in the case of an agreement which has been modified by agreement since July 1, 1977 (see s.82(2)); in any case the credit card companies have agreed "voluntarily" to accept s.75 liability (up to the amount of the credit used on the transaction in question) in relation to pre-July 1977 agreements. (ii) is arguable, but perhaps the second card holder *is* within the definition of "debtor" in s.189(1), see "credit" in s.9(1). (iii) and (iv) were considered in *Office of Fair Trading v Lloyds TSB Bank Plc* [2006] EWCA Civ 268; [2007] Q.B. 1, where it was held that s.75(1) does apply to "four party" credit card agreements and is not confined to applying only to transactions in the UK and hence does apply where a UK credit card is used in relation to transactions abroad. This decision was upheld in the House of Lords [2007] UKHL 48; [2007] 3 W.L.R.733. In *Bank of Scotland v Alfred Truman* [2005] EWHC 583, [2005] C.C.L.R.3, customers of a car dealer used their credit cards to pay deposits on cars to be supplied by the dealer. The dealer did not have credit card payment processing facilities. The defendant firm of solicitors had such facilities, having signed a merchant services agreement with the firm's bank. The defendant firm used its card processing facilities to process, on behalf of the dealer, the payments of deposits by the car dealer's customers. It was held that section 75 applied to these *five* party credit card transactions.

In *Jarrett v Barclays Bank and Royal Bank of Scotland* [1999] Q.B. 1; [1997] C.C.L.R. 32, CA, credit was advanced under a credit card agreement and under other regulated agreements to finance the purchase of timeshares in Portugal and Spain. Though in each case a claim by the debtor against the timeshare supplier was, by virtue of the Brussels Convention, subject to the exclusive jurisdiction of the Portuguese or Spanish court, it was held that that did not apply to actions under s.75 against the creditors, i.e. the British banks.

Where, relying on a breach of contract or misrepresentation, the debtor rescinds the supply agreement which was financed by a loan agreement within s.12(b) or (c), then a "like claim" under s.75 means a claim to rescind the loan agreement (*United Dominions Trust v Taylor* [1980] S.L.T. (Sh. Ct.) 28; [1980] C.C.L.R. 29, followed, despite academic criticism, in *Forward Trust Ltd v Hornsby* [1996] C.C.L.R. 18).

Paragraph numbers marked with a "+" can be found online and on CD.

3H–130   *Subsection (3)* —The original figures were increased to the current ones of £100 and £30,000 as from January 1, 1984 (SI 1983/1878). The limit refers to the cash price attached to the "item". This is arguably inconsistent with the Consumer Credit Directive (87/102) which allows a lower limit only where "the *transaction* in question is for an amount less than 200 ECU".

Duty to give notice before taking certain action

3H–131   **76.**—(1) The creditor or owner is not entitled to enforce a term of a regulated agreement by—

      (a) demanding earlier payment of any sum, or

      (b) recovering possession of any goods or land, or

      (c) treating any right conferred on the debtor or hirer by the agreement as terminated, restricted or deferred,

except by or after giving the debtor or hirer not less than seven days' notice of his intention to do so.

(2) Subsection (1) applies only where—

      (a) a period for the duration of the agreement is specified in the agreement, and

      (b) that period has not ended when the creditor or owner does an act mentioned in subsection (1),

but so applies notwithstanding that, under the agreement, any party is entitled to terminate it before the end of the period so specified.

(3) A notice under subsection (1) is ineffective if not in the prescribed form.

(4) Subsection (1) does not prevent a creditor from treating the right to draw on any credit as restricted or deferred and taking such steps as may be necessary to make the restriction or deferment effective.

(5) Regulations may provide that subsection (1) is not to apply to agreements described by the regulations.

(6) Subsection (1) does not apply to a right of enforcement arising by reason of any breach by the debtor or hirer of the regulated agreement.

Duty to give notice before taking certain action

3H–132   See commentary to s.98.

> **For ss.77 to 80 of the Consumer Credit Act 1974 (see Arrangement) plus any related commentary see paragraphs 3H–133+ to 3H–146+ on White Book on Westlaw UK or the Civil Procedure CD.**

Appropriation of payments

3H–147   **81.**—(1) Where a debtor or hirer is liable to make to the same person payments in respect of two or more regulated agreements, he shall be entitled, on making any payment in respect of the agreements which is not sufficient to discharge the total amount then due under all the agreements, to appropriate the sum so paid by him—

      (a) in or towards the satisfaction of the sum due under any one of the agreements, or

      (b) in or towards the satisfaction of the sums due under any

Paragraph numbers marked with a "+" can be found online and on CD.

two or more of the agreements in such proportions as he thinks fit.

(2) If the debtor or hirer fails to make any such appropriation where one or more of the agreements is—

(a) a hire-purchase agreement or conditional sale agreement, or

(b) a consumer hire agreement, or

(c) an agreement in relation to which any security is provided,

the payment shall be appropriated towards the satisfaction of the sums due under the several agreements respectively in the proportions which those sums bear to one another.

Appropriation of payments

3H–148

At common law, where the debtor owes two or more debts that have fallen due and they are payable by him to the same person (e.g. the debts are both owed to the same creditor, but under different contracts), then the debtor when he makes a payment can appropriate that payment as he chooses between the different debts. If when he pays he communicates no such appropriation to the payee (i.e. usually the creditor), the latter may appropriate the payments as the creditor chooses. No appropriation by the creditor is effective until it is communicated to the debtor. An unequivocal appropriation becomes both effective and irrevocable when communicated to the debtor (*Julian Hodge Bank Ltd v Hall* [1998] C.C.L.R. 14, CA). Where it applies, s.81(2) removes the creditor's common law right of appropriation and provides its own automatic appropriation. It appropriates the payment according to the sums that have fallen "due" under the different agreements. This then takes no account of instalments that have not fallen due at the time of the repayment. Where s.81(2) does not apply, e.g. when allocating a payment as between (a) instalments that have already fallen due, and (b) default interest that has accrued under the same agreement for failing to pay the instalments on time, the common law rules apply. In the case of a regulated hire purchase agreement this can have crucial significance in determining whether goods are "protected goods" within s.90 (*Julian Hodge Bank Ltd v Hall*, above).

Variation of agreements

3H–149

82.—(1) Where, under a power contained in a regulated agreement the creditor or owner varies the agreement, the variation shall not take effect before notice of it is given to the debtor or hirer in the prescribed manner.

(2) Where an agreement (a "modifying agreement") varies or supplements an earlier agreement, the modifying agreement shall for the purposes of this Act be treated as—

(a) revoking the earlier agreement, and

(b) containing provisions reproducing the combined effect of the two agreements,

and obligations outstanding in relation to the earlier agreement shall accordingly be treated as outstanding instead in relation to the modifying agreement.

(2A) Subsection (2) does not apply if the earlier agreement or the modifying agreement is an exempt agreement as a result of section 16(6C) or 16C.

(3) If the earlier agreement is a regulated agreement but (apart from this subsection) the modifying agreement is not then, unless the modifying agreement is—

Paragraph numbers marked with a "+" can be found online and on CD.

(a) for running account credit; or

(b) an exempt agreement as a result of section 16(6C) or 16C,

it shall be treated as a regulated agreement.

(4) If the earlier agreement is a regulated agreement for running-account credit, and by the modifying agreement the creditor allows the credit limit to be exceeded but intends the excess to be merely temporary, Part V (except section 56) shall not apply to the modifying agreement.

(5) If—

(a) the earlier agreement is a cancellable agreement, and

(b) the modifying agreement is made within the period applicable under section 68 to the earlier agreement,

then, whether or not the modifying agreement would, apart from this subsection, be a cancellable agreement, it shall be treated as a cancellable agreement in respect of which a notice may be served under section 68 not later than the end of the period applicable under that section to the earlier agreement.

(5A) Subsection (5) does not apply where the modifying agreement is an exempt agreement as a result of section 16(6C) or 16C.

(6) Except under subsection (5), a modifying agreement shall not be treated as a cancellable agreement.

(7) This section does not apply to a non-commercial agreement.

Note —Subsections (2A) and (5A) added and subs.(3) amended by the Financial Services and Markets Act 2000 (Consequential Amendments) Order 2005 (SI 2005/2967). Subsection (2A) amended by the Financial Services and Markets Act 2000 (Consequential Amendments) Order 2008 (SI 2008/733). References to s.16C added by the Legislative Reform (Consumer Credit) Order 2008 (SI 2008/2826).

Variation of agreements

3H–150   Subsection (1) deals with a variation which can be made unilaterally by the creditor or owner; i.e. because he has that power under the agreement. Subsections (2)–(5) deal with a variation which comes about by a subsequent agreement between the parties.

3H–151   *Unilateral variation* —The Consumer Credit (Notice of Variation of Agreements) Regulations 1977 (SI 1977/328), as amended, prescribe a general rule that the debtor or hirer must be given at least seven days' written notice of the change, but that changes in interest rate may normally be given by public notices placed in newspapers and in the creditor's business premises.

3H–152   *Modifying agreements* —An agreement varying an earlier agreement is a modifying agreement. Section 82(2)(b) means that an agreed variation could turn an unregulated agreement into a regulated one. A fixed-sum credit agreement made in 2006 providing the debtor with credit of £30,000 would not be a regulated agreement, because, prior to April 6, 2008 an agreement providing credit of more than £25,000 was not a consumer credit agreement. If in February 2009, the parties agreed to vary that agreement (e.g. by adding a further advance), that is regarded as a termination of the old agreement and the making of a new agreement. Unless it is an exempt agreement, the new agreement is a regulated agreement, the amount of the credit being irrelevant after April 6, 2008 when the financial limit was removed from the definition of a consumer credit agreement. A regulated modifying agreement will normally be subject to the documentation requirements in s.55 and ss.57–65, though not normally (see s.82(6)) to the cancellation provisions. The Consumer Credit (Agreements) Regulations

Paragraph numbers marked with a "+" can be found online and on CD.

1983 (SI 1983/1553) make provision for the form and contents of modifying agreements.

Liability for misuse of credit facilities

83.—(1) The debtor under a regulated consumer credit agreement   3H–153
shall not be liable to the creditor for any loss arising from use of the credit facility by another person not acting, or to be treated as acting, as the debtor's agent.

(2) This section does not apply to a non-commercial agreement, or to any loss in so far as it arises from misuse of an instrument to which section 4 of the Cheques Act 1957 applies.

Liability for misuse of credit facilities

Section 83(1) states a general rule which is subject to exceptions stated in s.84. The   3H–154
protection afforded does not, however, extend to the fraudulent use of payment cards (e.g. many charge cards) which are issued under exempt agreements (for "exempt agreements" see s.16 above). Similarly it does not apply to the unauthorised use of a cash withdrawal token to withdraw cash from an account, e.g. a current account, which has a credit balance—since the protection afforded by s.83 extends only to the unauthorised use of a "credit" facility. In the latter case the Banking Code of Practice (subscribed to by banks and building societies) offers a similar degree of protection to that afforded by ss.83 and 84 (taken together) in the case of misuse of a credit facility.

Fraudulent use of payment card in connection with distance contract

In the case of a distance contract, the Consumer Protection (Distance Selling)   3H–155
Regulations 2000 (SI 2000/2334) give protection to a consumer against the fraudulent use of any "payment card". A "payment card" includes credit cards, charge cards, debit cards and store cards. By reg.21, a consumer is entitled to cancel a payment where fraudulent (unauthorised) use has been made of his payment card in connection with a distance contract. Upon cancelling a payment, the consumer is entitled to be re-credited, or to have all sums returned by the card issuer. The regulations are set out at para.3H–906 below.

For ss.84 to 85 of the Consumer Credit Act 1974 (see Arrangement) plus any related commentary see paragraphs 3H–156+ to 3H–159+ on theWhite Book on Westlaw UK or the Civil Procedure CD.

Death of debtor or hirer

86.—(1) The creditor or owner under a regulated agreement is not   3H–160
entitled, by reason of the death of the debtor or hirer, to do an act specified in paragraphs (a) to (e) section 87(1) if at the death the agreement is fully secured.

(2) If at the death of the debtor or hirer a regulated agreement is only partly secured or is unsecured, the creditor or owner is entitled, by reason of the death of the debtor or hirer, to do an act specified in paragraphs (a) to (e) section 87(1) on an order of the court only.

(3) This section applies in relation to the termination of an agreement only where—

(a) a period for its duration is specified in the agreement, and

(b) that period has not ended when the creditor or owner purports to terminate the agreement,

but so applies notwithstanding that, under the agreement, any party is entitled to terminate it before the end of the period so specified.

Paragraph numbers marked with a "+" can be found online and on CD.

1403

(4) This section does not prevent the creditor from treating the right to draw on any credit as restricted or deferred, and taking such steps as may be necessary to make the restriction or deferment effective.

(5) This section does not affect the operation of any agreement providing for payment of sums—

    (a) due under the regulated agreement, or

    (b) becoming due under it on the death of the debtor or hirer,

out of the proceeds of a policy of assurance on his life.

(6) For the purposes of this section an act is done by reason of the death of the debtor or hirer if it is done under a power conferred by the agreement which is—

    (a) exercisable on his death, or

    (b) exercisable at will and exercised at any time after his death.

Death of debtor or hirer

3H–161   The object is to prevent the creditor or owner being entitled to terminate an agreement (other than in the sense of refusing to allow further drawings of credit, e.g. under a credit card agreement) simply because of the death of the debtor or hirer (or of any one of the debtors or hirers—s.185(4)). If the agreement is not "fully secured" then the creditor may be able to terminate the agreement by an order of the court, but only if he can satisfy the requirements in s.128. The same restrictions apply to prevent the creditor doing any of the other acts listed in s.87(1). Even though the debtor may have died, s.86 does not, however, prevent the creditor being entitled to do one of those things for some reason other than the death, e.g. by reason of a breach of the agreement (providing in that case that s.87 is complied with). "Fully secured" is not defined, but presumably means an agreement in relation to which there is security which if realised at the time of the debtor's or hirer's death would cover the whole of the outstanding debt under the agreement.

Procedure

3H–162   Where a court order is required under s.86(2) then the claim is governed by the Consumer Credit Act procedure in the Consumer Credit Practice Direction at para.7BPD.1, unless the claim relates to the recovery of land. If it is a mortgage repossesion action, the procedure set out in CPR Pt 55 should be used. See further, the Note About Procedure in Consumer Credit Cases, immediately before the start of this Act, at para.3H–4 *et seq.* above.

PART VII

DEFAULT AND TERMINATION

INFORMATION SHEETS

OFT to prepare information sheets on arrears and default

3H–163   **86A.**—(1) The OFT shall prepare, and give general notice of, an arrears information sheet and a default information sheet.

(2) The arrears information sheet shall include information to help debtors and hirers who receive notices under section 86B or 86C.

(3) The default information sheet shall include information to help debtors and hirers who receive default notices.

Paragraph numbers marked with a "+" can be found online and on CD.

(4) Regulations may make provision about the information to be included in an information sheet.

(5) An information sheet takes effect for the purposes of this Part at the end of the period of three months beginning with the day on which general notice of it is given.

(6) If the OFT revises an information sheet after general notice of it has been given, it shall give general notice of the information sheet as revised.

(7) A revised information sheet takes effect for the purposes of this Part at the end of the period of three months beginning with the day on which general notice of it is given.

Note —Inserted subject to transitional provisions by the Consumer Credit Act 2006 **3H–164** s.8 (for transitional provisions see Sch.3, para.5), with effect from January 31, 2007 (SI 2007/123). Sections 86B to 86F are inserted by the Consumer Credit Act 2006 ss.9–13. Subsections 86B(8), 86C(6) and 86E(2) and (7) were brought into force with effect from June 16, 2006 (SI 2006/1508); remaining subsections of ss.86B to 86F are in force with effect from October 1, 2008 (SI 2007/3300). For transitional provisions relating to ss.86A to 86F, see Consumer Credit Act 2006 Sch.3, paras 5– 9.

Arrears and default
  Sections 86A to 86F have been fully in force since October 1, 2008. They require **3H–165** the creditor to give notice of sums in arrears, including an arrears information sheet (prepared by the OFT), to the debtor. They require this to be done after the debtor has fallen into arrears by, broadly, more than two monthly (or four weekly) payments. The creditor is required to serve a notice (a notice of default sums) before becoming entitled to recover any "default sum" and is not entitled to any interest on a default sum in respect of the first 28 days after service of the notice. The creditor is not in any case entitled to recover any such interest at all unless it is simple interest. For "default sum", see s.187A.

SUMS IN ARREARS AND DEFAULT SUMS

Notice of sums in arrears under fixed-sum credit agreements etc

86B.—(1) This section applies where at any time the following **3H–166** conditions are satisfied—

  (a) that the debtor or hirer under an applicable agreement is required to have made at least two payments under the agreement before that time;

  (b) that the total sum paid under the agreement by him is less than the total sum which he is required to have paid before that time;

  (c) that the amount of the shortfall is no less than the sum of the last two payments which he is required to have made before that time;

  (d) that the creditor or owner is not already under a duty to give him notices under this section in relation to the agreement; and

  (e) if a judgment has been given in relation to the agreement before that time, that there is no sum still to be paid under the judgment by the debtor or hirer.

  (2) The creditor or owner—

Paragraph numbers marked with a "+" can be found online and on CD.

    (a) shall, within the period of 14 days beginning with the day on which the conditions mentioned in subsection (1) are satisfied, give the debtor or hirer a notice under this section; and

    (b) after the giving of that notice, shall give him further notices under this section at intervals of not more than six months.

(3) The duty of the creditor or owner to give the debtor or hirer notices under this section shall cease when either of the conditions mentioned in subsection (4) is satisfied; but if either of those conditions is satisfied before the notice required by subsection (2)(a) is given, the duty shall not cease until that notice is given.

(4) The conditions referred to in subsection (3) are—

    (a) that the debtor or hirer ceases to be in arrears;

    (b) that a judgment is given in relation to the agreement under which a sum is required to be paid by the debtor or hirer.

(5) For the purposes of subsection (4)(a) the debtor or hirer ceases to be in arrears when—

    (a) no payments, which he has ever failed to make under the agreement when required, are still owing;

    (b) no default sum, which has ever become payable under the agreement in connection with his failure to pay any sum under the agreement when required, is still owing;

    (c) no sum of interest, which has ever become payable under the agreement in connection with such a default sum, is still owing; and

    (d) no other sum of interest, which has ever become payable under the agreement in connection with his failure to pay any sum under the agreement when required, is still owing.

(6) A notice under this section shall include a copy of the current arrears information sheet under section 86A.

(7) The debtor or hirer shall have no liability to pay any sum in connection with the preparation or the giving to him of a notice under this section.

(8) Regulations may make provision about the form and content of notices under this section.

(9) In the case of an applicable agreement under which the debtor or hirer must make all payments he is required to make at intervals of one week or less, this section shall have effect as if in subsection (1)(a) and (c) for 'two' there were substituted 'four'.

(10) If an agreement mentioned in subsection (9) was made before the beginning of the relevant period, only amounts resulting from failures by the debtor or hirer to make payments he is required to have made during that period shall be taken into account in determining any shortfall for the purposes of subsection (1)(c).

(11) In subsection (10) "relevant period" means the period of 20 weeks ending with the day on which the debtor or hirer is required to have made the most recent payment under the agreement.

Paragraph numbers marked with a "+" can be found online and on CD.

(12) In this section "applicable agreement" means an agreement which

    (a) is a regulated agreement for fixed-sum credit or a regulated consumer hire agreement; and

    (b) is neither a non-commercial agreement nor a small agreement.

(13) In this section—

    (a) "payments" in relation to an applicable agreement which is a regulated agreement for fixed-sum credit means payments to be made at predetermined intervals provided for under the terms of the agreement; and

    (b) "payments" in relation to an applicable agreement which is a regulated consumer hire agreement means any payments to be made by the hirer in relation to any period in consideration of the bailment or hiring to him of goods under the agreement.

Note —Inserted by the Consumer Credit Act 2006 s.9. Subsection (8) was brought into force with effect from June 16, 2006 (SI 2006/1508); remaining subsections are in force with effect from October 1, 2008 (SI 2007/3300). Subsection (5) amended and subs.(13) added by the Legislative Reform (Consumer Credit) Order 2008 (SI 2008/2826).   **3H–167**

Subsection (8) —See the Consumer Credit (Information Requirements and Duration of Licences and Charges) Regulations 2007 (SI 2007/1167).   **3H–168**

Notice of sums in arrears under fixed-sum and consumer hire agreements
See the note to s.86A above and the comments there about arrears and default.   **3H–169**

Notice of sums in arrears under running-account credit agreements

86C.—(1) This section applies where at any time the following conditions are satisfied—   **3H–170**

    (a) that the debtor under an applicable agreement is required to have made at least two payments under the agreement before that time;

    (b) that the last two payments which he is required to have made before that time have not been made;

    (c) that the creditor has not already been required to give a notice under this section in relation to either of those payments; and

    (d) if a judgment has been given in relation to the agreement before that time, that there is no sum still to be paid under the judgment by the debtor.

(2) The creditor shall, no later than the end of the period within which he is next required to give a statement under section 78(4) in relation to the agreement, give the debtor a notice under this section.

(3) The notice shall include a copy of the current arrears information sheet under section 86A.

(4) The notice may be incorporated in a statement or other notice which the creditor gives the debtor in relation to the agreement by virtue of another provision of this Act.

Paragraph numbers marked with a "+" can be found online and on CD.

(5) The debtor shall have no liability to pay any sum in connection with the preparation or the giving to him of the notice.

(6) Regulations may make provision about the form and content of notices under this section.

(7) In this section 'applicable agreement' means an agreement which—

> (a) is a regulated agreement for running-account credit; and
>
> (b) is neither a non-commercial agreement nor a small agreement.

(8) In this section "payments" means payments to be made at predetermined intervals provided for under the terms of the agreement.

3H–171 *Note*—Inserted by the Consumer Credit Act 2006 s.10. Subsection (6) was brought into force with effect from June 16, 2006 (SI 2006/1508); remaining subsections are in force with effect from October 1, 2008 (SI 2007/3300). Subsection (8) added by the Legislative Reform (Consumer Credit) Order 2008 (SI 2008/2826).

3H–172 *Subsection (6)*—See the Consumer Credit (Information Requirements and Duration of Licences and Charges) Regulations 2007 (SI 2007/1167).

Notice of sums in arrears under running-account credit agreements

3H–173 See the note to s.86A above and the comments there about arrears and default.

Failure to give notice of sums in arrears

3H–174 **86D.**—(1) This section applies where the creditor or owner under an agreement is under a duty to give the debtor or hirer notices under section 86B but fails to give him such a notice—

> (a) within the period mentioned in subsection (2)(a) of that section; or
>
> (b) within the period of six months beginning with the day after the day on which such a notice was last given to him.

(2) This section also applies where the creditor under an agreement is under a duty to give the debtor a notice under section 86C but fails to do so before the end of the period mentioned in subsection (2) of that section.

(3) The creditor or owner shall not be entitled to enforce the agreement during the period of non-compliance.

(4) The debtor or hirer shall have no liability to pay—

> (a) any sum of interest to the extent calculated by reference to the period of non-compliance or to any part of it; or
>
> (b) any default sum which (apart from this paragraph)—
>
>> (i) would have become payable during the period of non-compliance; or
>>
>> (ii) would have become payable after the end of that period in connection with a breach of the agreement which occurs during that period (whether or not the breach continues after the end of that period).

Paragraph numbers marked with a "+" can be found online and on CD.

(5) In this section 'the period of non-compliance' means, in relation to a failure to give a notice under section 86B or 86C to the debtor or hirer, the period which—

    (a) begins immediately after the end of the period mentioned in (as the case may be) subsection (1)(a) or (b) or (2); and

    (b) ends at the end of the day mentioned in subsection (6).

(6) That day is—

    (a) in the case of a failure to give a notice under section 86B as mentioned in subsection (1)(a) of this section, the day on which the notice is given to the debtor or hirer;

    (b) in the case of a failure to give a notice under that section as mentioned in subsection (1)(b) of this section, the earlier of the following—

        (i) the day on which the notice is given to the debtor or hirer;

        (ii) the day on which the condition mentioned in subsection (4)(a) of that section is satisfied;

    (c) in the case of a failure to give a notice under section 86C, the day on which the notice is given to the debtor.

Note —Inserted by the Consumer Credit Act 2006 s.11, with effect from October 1, 2008 (SI 2007/3300). **3H–175**

Failure to give notice of sums in arrears

See the note to s.86A above and the comments there about arrears and default. **3H–176**

Notice of default sums

86E.—(1) This section applies where a default sum becomes payable under a regulated agreement by the debtor or hirer. **3H–177**

(2) The creditor or owner shall, within the prescribed period after the default sum becomes payable, give the debtor or hirer a notice under this section.

(3) The notice under this section may be incorporated in a statement or other notice which the creditor or owner gives the debtor or hirer in relation to the agreement by virtue of another provision of this Act.

(4) The debtor or hirer shall have no liability to pay interest in connection with the default sum to the extent that the interest is calculated by reference to a period occurring before the 29th day after the day on which the debtor or hirer is given the notice under this section.

(5) If the creditor or owner fails to give the debtor or hirer the notice under this section within the period mentioned in subsection (2), he shall not be entitled to enforce the agreement until the notice is given to the debtor or hirer.

(6) The debtor or hirer shall have no liability to pay any sum in connection with the preparation or the giving to him of the notice under this section.

(7) Regulations may—

Paragraph numbers marked with a "+" can be found online and on CD.

    (a) provide that this section does not apply in relation to a default sum which is less than a prescribed amount;

    (b) make provision about the form and content of notices under this section.

(8) This section does not apply in relation to a non-commercial agreement or to a small agreement.

3H–178   *Note* —Inserted by the Consumer Credit Act 2006 s.12. Subss.(2), (7) were brought into force with effect from June 16, 2006 (SI 2006/1508); remaining subsections are in force with effect from October 1, 2008 (SI 2007/3300).

3H–179   *Subsection (2) and (7)(b)* —For the prescribed period and the form and contents of notices, see the Consumer Credit (Information Requirements and Duration of Licences and Charges) Regulations 2007 (SI 2007/1167). The prescribed period is 35 days from a default sum becoming payable by the debtor or hirer.

Notice of default sums

3H–180   See the note to s.86A above and the comments there about arrears and default. For "default sum", see s.187A.

Interest on default sums

3H–181   **86F.**—(1) This section applies where a default sum becomes payable under a regulated agreement by the debtor or hirer.

(2) The debtor or hirer shall only be liable to pay interest in connection with the default sum if the interest is simple interest.

3H–182   *Note* —Inserted by the Consumer Credit Act 2006 s.13, with effect from October 1, 2008 (SI 2007/3300).

Interest on default sums

3H–183   For "default sum", see s.187A. See the note to s.86A above and the comments there about arrears and default.

DEFAULT NOTICES

Need for default notice

3H–184   **87.**—(1) Service of a notice on the debtor or hirer in accordance with section 88 (a "default notice") is necessary before the creditor or owner can become entitled, by reason of any breach by the debtor or hirer of a regulated agreement—

    (a) to terminate the agreement, or

    (b) to demand earlier payment of any sum, or

    (c) to recover possession of any goods or land, or

    (d) to treat any right conferred on the debtor or hirer by the agreement as terminated, restricted or deferred, or

    (e) to enforce any security.

(2) Subsection (1) does not prevent the creditor from treating the right to draw upon any credit as restricted or deferred, and taking such steps as may be necessary to make the restriction or deferment effective.

(3) The doing of an act by which a floating charge becomes fixed is not enforcement of a security.

Paragraph numbers marked with a "+" can be found online and on CD.

(4) Regulations may provide that subsection (1) is not to apply to agreements described by the regulations.

Need for default notice

Section 87 does not give the creditor or owner the right to take any of the actions listed in s.87(1). Its effect is that if he has that right, e.g. by virtue of a provision in the agreement or because of a repudiation by the debtor, he will not be entitled to exercise it until a default notice has been served (and has expired without the default having been rectified). This restriction applies only where the right to do one of those acts arises by reason of a breach of the agreement by the debtor or hirer. Where, however, it arises by some other reason (e.g. the agreement gives the creditor the right to terminate the agreement on the debtor becoming unemployed), then ss.76 and 98 may require prior service of a notice. The inclusion of s.87(1)(b) in the list means that an accelerated payments clause cannot be activated without service of a default notice (or a notice under s.76). Copies of any default notice must be served on each debtor or hirer (i.e. where there is more than one), s.185(1)(a) and on any surety (s.111). Notices served on the debtor or hirer under ss.76(1), 87(1) and 98(1) must be given in paper form: the Consumer Credit (Enforcement, Default and Termination Notices) Regulations 1983 (SI 1983/1561), as amended. The same regulations state that ss.76(1), 87(1) and 98(1) do not apply to non-commercial agreements in relation to which no security has been provided. For content and effect of default notice, see s.88. For default notice sent by post and never arriving, see s.176.

3H–185

Contents and effect of default notice

88.—(1) The default notice must be in the prescribed form and specify—

    (a) the nature of the alleged breach;

    (b) if the breach is capable of remedy, what action is required to remedy it and the date before which that action is to be taken;

    (c) if the breach is not capable of remedy, the sum (if any) required to be paid as compensation for the breach, and the date before which it is to be paid.

3H–186

(2) A date specified under subsection (1) must not be less than 14 days after the date of service of the default notice, and the creditor or owner shall not take action such as is mentioned in section 87(1) before the date so specified or (if no requirement is made under subsection (1)) before those 14 days have elapsed.

(3) The default notice must not treat as a breach failure to comply with a provision of the agreement which becomes operative only on breach of some other provision, but if the breach of that other provision is not duly remedied or compensation demanded under subsection (1) is not duly paid, or (where no requirement is made under subsection (1)) if the 14 days mentioned in subsection (2) have elapsed, the creditor or owner may treat the failure as a breach and section 87(1) shall not apply to it.

(4) The default notice must contain information in the prescribed terms about the consequences of failure to comply with it and any other prescribed matters relating to the agreement.

(4A) The default notice must also include a copy of the current default information sheet under section 86A.

(5) A default notice making a requirement under subsection (1) may include a provision for the taking of action such as is mentioned in section 87(1) at any time after the restriction imposed by subsec-

Paragraph numbers marked with a "+" can be found online and on CD.

tion (2) will cease, together with a statement that the provision will be ineffective if the breach is duly remedied or the compensation duly paid.

3H–187   *Note* —Amended by Consumer Credit Act 2006 s.14(1) and (2); subs.(4A) inserted by the Consumer Credit Act 2006 s.14(3), with effect from October 1, 2008 (SI 2007/3300).

Contents and effects of default notice

3H–188   For the prescribed form, see the Consumer Credit (Enforcement, Default and Termination Notices) Regulations 1983 (SI 1983/1561), as amended by the Consumer Credit (Information Requirements and Duration of Licences and Charges) Regulations 2007 (SI 2007/1167). The usual default is a failure to pay instalments. In that case, the action required to remedy the default, and which s.88(1)(b) requires the default notice to specify, is payment of the arrears together with any default interest owing on those arrears. If the default notice specifies a figure more than the giver of the notice is entitled to demand, then the default notice is invalid, *Woodchester Lease Management Services Ltd v Swain* [1999] 1 W.L.R. 263; [1999] C.C.L.R. 8, CA, although the court might overlook an error which was no more than de minimis. Besides complying with s.88 and with the regulations, the default notice must not put upon the debtor a repudiation when he has not committed one and must make clear when it expires (*Eshun v Moorgate Mercantile Co* [1971] 1 W.L.R. 722 (decided under the earlier provisions of the Hire Purchase Act 1965)). If the debtor or hirer rectifies the breach (i.e. by taking the action specified in s.88(1)(b) or (c)) the breach is taken not to have occurred (s.89). As soon as a default notice is served, the debtor or hirer is eligible to apply for a time order under s.129, under which the court could grant extra time for paying off arrears or remedying the breach. Even if the debtor does not apply for a time order and the breach is not rectified before the default notice expires, the creditor or owner may still face a restriction on enforcing the agreement. Thus he may not be entitled to recover goods or enter land without a court order (ss.90 and 92) and, if he brings proceedings to enforce the agreement, the debtor or hirer may in those proceedings apply for a time order.

Consumer Credit Act 2006

3H–189   Section 14(1) of the 2006 Act, which came into force on October 1, 2006 and applies to default notices served after that date even though the default may have occurred before that date, increased from seven to 14 days the period of notice specified in s.88(2) and (3). Subsection (4A) comes into force on October 1, 2008. It requires that the default notice includes a copy of a default information sheet (prepared by the OFT).

Compliance with default notice

3H–190   **89.** If before the date specified for that purpose in the default notice the debtor or hirer takes the action specified under section 88(1)(b) or (c) the breach shall be treated as not having occurred.

FURTHER RESTRICTION OF REMEDIES FOR DEFAULT

Retaking of protected hire-purchase, etc., goods

3H–191   **90.**—(1) At any time when—

    (a) the debtor is in breach of a regulated hire-purchase or a regulated conditional sale agreement relating to goods, and

    (b) the debtor has paid to the creditor one-third or more of the total price of the goods, and

    (c) the property in the goods remains in the creditor,

Paragraph numbers marked with a "+" can be found online and on CD.

the creditor is not entitled to recover possession of the goods from the debtor except on an order of the court.

(2) Where under a hire-purchase or conditional sale agreement the creditor is required to carry out any installation and the agreement specifies, as part of the total price, the amount to be paid in respect of the installation (the "installation charge") the reference in subsection (1)(b) to one-third of the total price shall be construed as a reference to the aggregate of the installation charge and one-third of the remainder of the total price.

(3) In a case where—

> (a) subsection (1)(a) is satisfied, but not subsection (1)(b), and
>
> (b) subsection (1)(b) was satisfied on a previous occasion in relation to an earlier agreement, being a regulated hire-purchase or regulated conditional sale agreement, between the same parties, and relating to any of the goods comprised in the later agreement (whether or not other goods were also included),

subsection (1) shall apply to the later agreement with the omission of paragraph (b).

(4) If the later agreement is a modifying agreement, subsection (3) shall apply with the substitution, for the second reference to the later agreement, of a reference to the modifying agreement.

(5) Subsection (1) shall not apply, or shall cease to apply, to an agreement if the debtor has terminated, or terminates, the agreement.

(6) Where subsection (1) applies to an agreement at the death of the debtor, it shall continue to apply (in relation to the possessor of the goods) until the grant of probate or administration, or (in Scotland) confirmation (on which the personal representative would fall to be treated as the debtor).

(7) Goods falling within this section are in this Act referred to as "protected goods".

Retaking of protected hire-purchase, etc., goods

Forcing the creditor to have to apply for a court order to recover possession of **3H–192** protected goods, makes it more likely that the debtor may apply for a time order (s.129), hoping thereby to prevent what would usually otherwise be for the debtor the rather disastrous financial consequences of termination of a hire-purchase or conditional sale agreement. Section 90 prevents the creditor being entitled, without a court order, to recover possession of protected goods "from the debtor". This does not prevent recovery of them from someone to whom the debtor has sold them or if the debtor has abandoned them but does prevent recovery from someone to whom the debtor has temporarily bailed them (e.g. lent them to a friend or left them at a garage for repair) (*Bentinck v Cromwell Engineering Ltd* [1971] 1 Q.B. 324). Nor does it prohibit recovery of the goods with the debtor's consent given at the time of the repossession (s.173(3)). For the consequences of recovering possession in contravention of s.90, see s.91.

Subsection (1)(b) —The term "payment" includes tender (s.189(1)). The "total price" **3H–193** (s.189(1)) does not include default interest that may accrue following lateness in paying off instalments. If after having fallen into arrears and after default interest has accrued, the debtor makes a further payment he can appropriate that payment as between applying it to paying off (a) instalments overdue, or (b) the accrued default interest. If he does not, the creditor has the right to make such appropriation. Apply-

Paragraph numbers marked with a "+" can be found online and on CD.

CONSUMER

ing it to (a) will, but applying it to (b) will not, increase the amount of the total price that has been paid and may make the crucial difference as to whether one third or more of the total price has been paid (*Julian Hodge Bank Ltd v Hall* [1998] C.C.L.R. 14, CA; and see s.81 as to appropriation of payments).

Procedure

3H–194   For a claim for a court order under s.90(1), the relevant procedure is the Consumer Credit procedure, set out in the Consumer Credit Practice Direction at para.7BPD.1. In a claim to which s.90(1) applies, the defendant may admit the claim and offer terms on which a return order should be suspended under s.135(1)(b)—see para.7BPD.8 for the relevant procedure. See also the Introductory Note About Procedure in Consumer Credit Cases, immediately before the start of this Act, at para.3H–4 *et seq.* above.

Consequences of breach of s.90

3H–195   **91.** If goods are recovered by the creditor in contravention of section 90—

> (a) the regulated agreement, if not previously terminated shall terminate, and
>
> (b) the debtor shall be released from all liability under the agreement, and shall be entitled to recover from the creditor all sums paid by the debtor under the agreement.

Recovery of possession of goods or land

3H–196   **92.**—(1) Except under an order of the court, the creditor or owner shall not be entitled to enter any premises to take possession of goods subject to a regulated hire-purchase agreement, regulated conditional sale agreement or regulated consumer hire agreement.

(2) At any time when the debtor is in breach of a regulated conditional sale agreement relating to land, the creditor is entitled to recover possession of the land from the debtor, or any person claiming under him, on an order of the court only.

(3) An entry in contravention of subsection (1) or (2) is actionable as a breach of statutory duty.

Recovery of possesion of goods or land

3H–197   Section 90 does not prevent recovery of the goods or land with consent of the relevant person(s) given at the time of the repossession (s.173(3)).

Procedure

3H–198   The relevant procedural rules are: (i) for a claim under subs.(1), the Consumer Credit Act procedure in the Consumer Credit Practice Direction at para.7BPD.1, and, (ii) for a claim under subs.(2), the procedure set out in CPR Pt 55. See further, the Introductory Note About Procedure at the start of this Act.

Interest not to be increased on default

3H–199   **93.** The debtor under a regulated consumer credit agreement shall not be obliged to pay interest on sums which, in breach of the agreement, are unpaid by him at a rate—

> (a) where the total charge for credit includes an item in respect of interest, exceeding the rate of that interest, or
>
> (b) in any other case, exceeding what would be the rate of the total charge for credit if any items included in the

Paragraph numbers marked with a "+" can be found online and on CD.

total charge for credit by virtue of section 20(2) were disregarded.

Interest not to be increased on default

Section 93 prevents the debtor being charged default interest at a rate in excess of **3H–200** the rate of the APR payable under the agreement. For the effect of a contract clause providing for interest (at the same APR as that payable under the agreement as whole) to be payable on arrears, including after judgment has been given for those arrears, see commentary to s.136 below and at 3H–891. With effect from October 1, 2008, only simple interest can be charged on a "default sum" (s.86F above). For "default sum", see s.187A.

For ss.93A to 125 of the Consumer Credit Act 1974 (see Arrangement) plus any related commentary see paragraphs 3H–201+ to 3H–279+ on White Book on West- law UK or the Civil Procedure CD.

LAND MORTGAGES

Enforcement of land mortgages

126. A land mortgage securing a regulated agreement is enforce- **3H–280** able (so far as provided in relation to the agreement) on an order of the court only.

Enforcement of land mortgages

This section also applies to a land mortgage which secures an agreement which is **3H–281** exempt by virtue of s.16(6C) and which would, but for s.16(6C), be a regulated agree- ment: see s.16(6D). Section 126 presumably prevents the creditor from retaking pos- session and from selling the property without a court order. It does not prevent anything, e.g. repossession, being done with the consent of the relevant person (the mortgagor?) given at the time of the repossession (s.173(3)). The relevant procedure for an application for an order under this section (being a claim for recovery of land) is the procedure set out in CPR Pt 55.

PART IX

JUDICIAL CONTROL

ENFORCEMENT OF CERTAIN REGULATED AGREEMENTS AND SECURITIES

Enforcement orders in cases of infringement

127.—(1) In the case of an application for an enforcement order **3H–282** under—

(a) section 65(1) (improperly executed agreements), or

(b) section 105(7)(a) or (b) (improperly executed security instruments), or

(c) section 111(2) (failure to serve copy of notice on surety), or

(d) section 124(1) or (2) (taking of negotiable instruments in contravention of section 123),

the court shall dismiss the application if, but only if, it considers it just to do so having regard to—

(i) prejudice caused to any person by the contravention in question, and the degree of culpability for it; and

Paragraph numbers marked with a "+" can be found online and on CD.

>   (ii) the powers conferred on the court by subsection (2) and sections 135 and 136.

  (2) If it appears to the court just to do so, it may in an enforcement order reduce or discharge any sum payable by the debtor or hirer, or any surety, so as to compensate him for prejudice suffered as a result of the contravention in question.

3H–283   *Note*—Subsections (3) to (5) were repealed with savings by the Consumer Credit Act 2006 ss.15 and 70, and Sch.4 (for savings see Sch.3, para.11), with effect from April 6, 2007 (SI 2007/123).

Enforcement orders in cases of infringement

No enforcement order possible before April 2007

3H–284   By virtue of subss.(3) to (5), certain agreements which had been improperly executed (e.g. where no agreement was signed or where the signed agreement did not contain certain basic minimum terms) were "irredeemably unenforceable": *Dimond v Lovell* [2000] Q.B. 216, confirmed in the House of Lords [2002] 1 A.C. 384. Subsection (3) to (5) ceased to have effect on April 6, 2007, except in relation to agreements made before that date (see the "savings" referred to in the note above). For their wording and the considerable case law to which they gave rise, see the *White Book 2006*.

Court's discretion

3H–285   Except where in relation to an agreement made before April 6, 2007 the court is prevented from granting an enforcement order by subss.(3)–(5), the court has a discretion whether to do so. It has a discretion to refuse to grant an enforcement order taking into account the factors spelt out in s.127(1)(i) and (ii). It might grant an enforcement order without any qualification if, despite the infringement, the debtor or hirer has suffered no prejudice (*Nissan Finance v Lockhart* [1993] C.C.L.R. 39, CA). It might refuse to grant an enforcement order, e.g. where the debtor or hirer would not have entered the agreement if it had been properly executed (*P.B. Leasing Ltd v Patel and Patel* [1995] C.C.L.R. 82). It might grant an enforcement order but (under ss.127(2) and 136) reduce the rate of interest where a failure to give the debtor an advance copy of the agreement and leave the debtor a pre-contract consideration period (under ss.58 and 61) has deprived the debtor of the opportunity of securing a loan elsewhere at a lower rate of interest (*National Guardian Mortgage Corp v Wilkes* [1993] C.C.L.R. 1). It might considerably reduce (under ss.127(2) and 136) the amount of an accelerated payment due after termination of a consumer hire agreement, where the documentation failed to include that information (*Rank Xerox v Hepple* [1994] C.C.L.R. 1). The Court of Appeal will not normally interfere with the exercise of the judge's discretion under s.127 unless it has not been exercised on the right principles (*Nissan Finance UK v Lockhart*, above).

Procedure

3H–286   In the case of an application under any of the sections referred to in s.127(1) the relevant procedural rules are as follows: (i) for a claim relating to the recovery of land, the procedure set out in CPR Pt 55; (ii) for any other claim, the Consumer Credit Act procedure in the Consumer Credit Practice Direction at para.7BPD.1. See further the Introductory Note About Procedure in Consumer Credit Cases, immediately before the start of this Act, at para.3H–4 *et seq.* above.

Enforcement orders on death of debtor or hirer

3H–287   **128.** The court shall make an order under section 86(2) if, but only if, the creditor or owner proves that he has been unable to satisfy himself that the present and future obligations of the debtor or hirer under the agreement are likely to be discharged.

Paragraph numbers marked with a "+" can be found online and on CD.

Time orders

129.—(1) Subject to subsection (3) below, if it appears to the court **3H–288**
just to do so—

    (a) on an application for an enforcement order; or

    (b) on an application made by a debtor or hirer under this
        paragraph after service on him of—

        (i) a default notice, or

        (ii) a notice under section 76(1) or 98(1); or

    (ba) on an application made by a debtor or hirer under this
        paragraph after he has been given a notice under sec-
        tion 86B or 86C; or

    (c) in an action brought by a creditor or owner to enforce a
        regulated agreement or any security, or recover posses-
        sion of any goods or land to which a regulated agree-
        ment relates,

the court may make an order under this section (a "time order").

(2) A time order shall provide for one or both of the following, as
the court considers just—

    (a) the payment by the debtor or hirer or any surety of any
        sum owed under a regulated agreement or a security by
        such instalments, payable at such times, as the court,
        having regard to the means of the debtor or hirer and
        any surety, considers reasonable;

    (b) the remedying by the debtor or hirer of any breach of a
        regulated agreement (other than non-payment of
        money) within such period as the court may specify.

(3) Where in Scotland a time to pay direction or a time to pay order has been made in relation to a debt, it shall not thereafter be
competent to make a time order in relation to the same debt.

Note—Amended by the Debtors (Scotland) Act 1987 Sch.6. Paragraph (ba) inserted **3H–289**
in subs.(1) by s.16 of the Consumer Credit Act 2006, with effect from October 1, 2008
(SI 2007/3300).

Time orders

The court's power under s.129(2)(a) to allow time for the payment is limited to "any **3H–290**
sum owed". This must mean, and is confined to, sums that have actually fallen due,
since otherwise there would be no need, in s.130(2), to extend the power, "in the case
of a hire-purchase and conditional sale agreement only", to allow the court to grant
the order in respect also of payments that have not yet fallen due. Where an accelerated payments clause has been activated (i.e. after expiry of a default notice under
s.87), then the whole outstanding balance will have fallen due by virtue of the clause;
in that case the court's power under s.129(2)(a) extends to the whole balance, irrespective of whether the agreement is a hire-purchase or conditional sale agreement. Where
a land mortgage has been granted as security for a loan and, after the debtor's default,
the creditor (no doubt after expiry of a default notice under s.87) commences repossession proceedings, that amounts to a "calling-in" of the loan entitling the creditor to
the whole of the outstanding balance; in that case, the court's power under s.127(2)(a)
extends to the whole debt including future instalments that would not otherwise have
fallen due yet (*Southern District Finance plc v Barnes* [1995] C.C.L.R. 62, CA). According
to this case, when a time order is made, it should normally be for a stipulated period

Paragraph numbers marked with a "+" can be found online and on CD.

on account of temporary financial difficulty; the correct judicial approach is first to consider whether it is just to make a time order, bearing in mind the positions of both parties. See also *First National Bank plc v Syed* [1991] 2 All E.R. 250; [1991] C.C.L.R. 37; there is no point making a time order involving payments that would be insufficient even to keep down the interest accruing on the account. If a time order is made, the court should suspend (see s.135) any possession order it also makes, for so long as the terms of the time order are complied with.

For supplementary matters see s.130 and for the court's power to vary the rate of interest or otherwise amend the agreement in consequence of a term of a time order, see s.136.

A time order is a final order (*Jenkins v Cedar Holdings Ltd* [1988] C.C.L.R. 34).

Procedure

3H–291   An application under s.129(1) will no doubt often be made by way of defence to an action begun by the creditor. In relation to mortgage possession claims, the Practice Direction supplementing CPR Pt 55 states at para.7.1 that the defendant may make an application for a time order under s.129 of the Consumer Credit Act 1974 either in his defence or by application notice in the proceedings (see 55PD.10).

An *originating* application for a time order (i.e. under s.129(1)(b) or (ba)), unless it "relates to the recovery of land", should be made using the Consumer Credit Act procedure, set out in the Consumer Credit Practice Direction at para.7BPD.1 and it should be made in the county court where the claimant resides or carries on business (para.4.3 of the Consumer Credit Act procedure). See further the Note About Procedure in Consumer Credit Cases, immediately before the start of this Act, at para.3H–4 *et seq.* above. An application under s.129(1)(ba) may be made only if the debtor or hirer has given notice of intent which complies with s.129A. An application under s.129(1)(ba) can be made regardless of when the agreement was made (Consumer Credit Act 2006 Sch.3, para.12).

For the evidentiary effect (for the purposes of s.129(2)(a)) of a defendant's admission and offer in a claim relating to "protected goods" under a regulated hire-purchase or conditional sale agreement, see 7BPD.8 and the commentary to s.90 above.

Debtor or hirer to give notice of intent etc. to creditor or owner

3H–292   **129A.**—(1) A debtor or hirer may make an application under section 129(1)(ba) in relation to a regulated agreement only if—

(a) following his being given the notice under section 86B or 86C, he gave a notice within subsection (2) to the creditor or owner; and

(b) a period of at least 14 days has elapsed after the day on which he gave that notice to the creditor or owner.

(2) A notice is within this subsection if it—

(a) indicates that the debtor or hirer intends to make the application;

(b) indicates that he wants to make a proposal to the creditor or owner in relation to his making of payments under the agreement; and

(c) gives details of that proposal.

3H–293   *Note* —Section 129A inserted by s.16 of the Consumer Credit Act 2006 with effect from October 1, 2008 (SI 2007/3300).

Notice of intent

3H–294   The purpose of s.129A is to encourage the parties to agree on a repayment arrangement without the need for the debtor to start proceedings for a time order.

Supplemental provisions about time orders

3H–295   **130.**—(1) Where in accordance with rules of court an offer to pay

---

Paragraph numbers marked with a "+" can be found online and on CD.

any sum by instalments is made by the debtor or hirer and accepted by the creditor or owner, the court may in accordance with rules of court make a time order under section 129(2)(a) giving effect to the offer without hearing evidence of means.

(2) In the case of a hire-purchase or conditional sale agreement only, a time order under section 129(2)(a) may deal with sums which, although not payable by the debtor at the time the order is made, would if the agreement continued in force become payable under it subsequently.

(3) A time order under section 129(2)(a) shall not be made where the regulated agreement is secured by a pledge if, by virtue of regulations made under section 76(5), 87(4) or 98(5), service of a notice is not necessary for enforcement of the pledge.

(4) Where, following the making of a time order in relation to a regulated hire-purchase or conditional sale agreement or a regulated consumer hire agreement, the debtor or hirer is in possession of the goods, he shall be treated (except in the case of a debtor to whom the creditor's title has passed) as a bailee or (in Scotland) a custodier of the goods under the terms of the agreement, notwithstanding that the agreement has been terminated.

(5) Without prejudice to anything done by the creditor or owner before the commencement of the period specified in a time order made under section 129(2)(b)("the relevant period"),—

    (a) he shall not while the relevant period subsists take in relation to the agreement any action such as is mentioned in section 87(1);

    (b) where—

        (i) a provision of the agreement ("the secondary provision") becomes operative only on breach of another provision of the agreement ("the primary provision"), and

        (ii) the time order provides for the remedying of such a breach of the primary provision within the relevant period,

he shall not treat the secondary provision as operative before the end of that period;

    (c) if while the relevant period subsists the breach to which the order relates is remedied it shall be treated as not having occurred.

(6) On the application of any person affected by a time order, the court may vary or revoke the order.

Supplemental provisions about time orders

See commentary to s.129.

3H–296

Interest payable on judgment debts etc.

130A.—(1) If the creditor or owner under a regulated agreement wants to be able to recover from the debtor or hirer post-judgment interest in connection with a sum that is required to be paid under a judgment given in relation to the agreement (the 'judgment sum'), he—

Paragraph numbers marked with a "+" can be found online and on CD.

3H–297

(a) after the giving of that judgment, shall give the debtor or hirer a notice under this section (the 'first required notice'); and

(b) after the giving of the first required notice, shall give the debtor or hirer further notices under this section at intervals of not more than six months.

(2) The debtor or hirer shall have no liability to pay post-judgment interest in connection with the judgment sum to the extent that the interest is calculated by reference to a period occurring before the day on which he is given the first required notice.

(3) If the creditor or owner fails to give the debtor or hirer a notice under this section within the period of six months beginning with the day after the day on which such a notice was last given to the debtor or hirer, the debtor or hirer shall have no liability to pay post-judgment interest in connection with the judgment sum to the extent that the interest is calculated by reference to the whole or to a part of the period which—

(a) begins immediately after the end of that period of six months; and

(b) ends at the end of the day on which the notice is given to the debtor or hirer.

(4) The debtor or hirer shall have no liability to pay any sum in connection with the preparation or the giving to him of a notice under this section.

(5) A notice under this section may be incorporated in a statement or other notice which the creditor or owner gives the debtor or hirer in relation to the agreement by virtue of another provision of this Act.

(6) Regulations may make provision about the form and content of notices under this section.

(7) This section does not apply in relation to post-judgment interest which is required to be paid by virtue of any of the following—

(a) section 4 of the Administration of Justice (Scotland) Act 1972;

(b) Article 127 of the Judgments Enforcement (Northern Ireland) Order 1981;

(c) section 74 of the County Courts Act 1984.

(8) This section does not apply in relation to a non-commercial agreement or to a small agreement.

(9) In this section 'post-judgment interest' means interest to the extent calculated by reference to a period occurring after the giving of the judgment under which the judgment sum is required to be paid.

3H–298 *Note* —Section 17 of the Consumer Credit Act 2006 provides for s.130A to be added. Subsections (6) and (9) inserted with effect from June 16, 2006 (SI 2006/1508); remaining subsections inserted with effect from October 1, 2008 (SI 2007/3300).

3H–299 *Subsection (6)* —See the Consumer Credit (Information Requirements and Duration of Licences and Charges) Regulations 2007 (SI 2007/1167).

Interest on judgment debts

3H–300 As from October 1, 2008, s.130A requires the creditor or owner to give notice to the

Paragraph numbers marked with a "+" can be found online and on CD.

debtor or hirer before being allowed to recover any post-judgment interest on any debts. It further requires the notice to be given at least every six months thereafter. Section 130A applies in relation to agreements whenever made but does not apply to sums payable under judgments given before October 1, 2008 (Consumer Credit Act 2006 Sch.3, para.13). See further para.40.8.16.

PROTECTION OF PROPERTY PENDING PROCEEDINGS

Protection orders

131. The court, on the application of the creditor or owner under a regulated agreement, may make such orders as it thinks just for protecting any property of the creditor or owner, or property subject to any security, from damage or depreciation pending the determination of any proceedings under this Act, including orders restricting or prohibiting use of the property or giving directions as to its custody.

3H–301

Protection orders

For powers to impose conditions or suspend the operation of the order or to vary agreements in consequence of the order, see ss.135 and 136. The Consumer Credit Act Practice Direction (para.7BPD.1) makes no reference to claims under this section, which appear from the wording of the section to be necessarily interim applications. Presumably an application under s.131 must comply with the rules about Applications for Court Orders (CPR Pt 23) and Interim Remedies (CPR Pt 25).

3H–302

HIRE AND HIRE-PURCHASE, ETC., AGREEMENTS

Financial relief for hirer

132.—(1) Where the owner under a regulated consumer hire agreement recovers possession of goods to which the agreement relates otherwise than by action, the hirer may apply to the court for an order that—

3H–303

    (a) the whole or part of any sum paid by the hirer to the owner in respect of the goods shall be repaid, and

    (b) the obligation to pay the whole or part of any sum owed by the hirer to the owner in respect of the goods shall cease,

and if it appears to the court just to do so, having regard to the extent of the enjoyment of the goods by the hirer, the court shall grant the application in full or in part.

(2) Where in proceedings relating to a regulated consumer hire agreement the court makes an order for the delivery to the owner of goods to which the agreement relates the court may include in the order the like provision as may be made in an order under subsection (1).

Financial relief for hirer

In *Automotive Financial Services v Henderson* [1993] C.C.L.R. 55; [1992] S.L.T. Sh.Ct. 63, the defenders suggested two different formulae for determining whether relief should be granted—one based on the interest and the administrative costs of the owner, the other based on the value of the goods supplied and their subsequent depreciation. The Sheriff Principal held that it would be wrong to control the application of s.132 by any formula not in the Act. Presumably, as with s.127 (see the com-

3H–304

Paragraph numbers marked with a "+" can be found online and on CD.

CONSUMER

mentary thereto), the Court of Appeal will not normally interfere with the exercise of the judge's discretion unless it has not been exercised on the right principles—or is patently unreasonable.

Where the owner claims under a liquidated damages clause (e.g. after an early termination of the agreement), the hirer may have alternative ways to challenge the claim by: (i) applying for relief under s.132; (ii) seeking relief at common law; (iii) challenging the validity of the clause on the ground that it is a penalty. For relief at common law, see *Starside Properties Ltd v Mustapha* [1974] 1 W.L.R. 816. The principles relating to penalties applicable in hire-purchase cases (see *Bridge v Campbell Discount Co Ltd* [1962] A.C. 600; [1962] 2 W.L.R. 439)are applicable also to consumer hire agreements: *Volkswagen Financial Services (UK) Ltd v Ramage* [2008] C.C.L.R. 3 (Cambridge Cty Ct) and see also *Robophone Facilities Ltd v Blank* [1966] 1 W.L.R. 1428.

Hire-purchase, etc., agreements: special powers of court

3H–305   133.—(1) If, in relation to a regulated hire-purchase or conditional sale agreement, it appears to the court just to do so—

(a) on an application for an enforcement order or time order; or

(b) in an action brought by the creditor to recover possession of goods to which the agreement relates,

the court may—

(i) make an order (a "return order") for the return to the creditor of goods to which the agreement relates;

(ii) make an order (a "transfer order") for the transfer to the debtor of the creditor's title to certain goods to which the agreement relates ("the transferred goods"), and the return to the creditor of the remainder of the goods.

(2) In determining for the purposes of this section how much of the total price has been paid ("the paid-up sum"), the court may—

(a) treat any sum paid by the debtor, or owed by the creditor, in relation to the goods as part of the paid-up sum;

(b) deduct any sum owed by the debtor in relation to the goods (otherwise than as part of the total price) from the paid-up sum,

and make corresponding reductions in amounts so owed.

(3) Where a transfer order is made, the transferred goods shall be such of the goods to which the agreement relates as the court thinks just; but a transfer order shall be made only where the paid-up sum exceeds the part of the total price referable to the transferred goods by an amount equal to at least one-third of the unpaid balance of the total price.

(4) Notwithstanding the making of a return order or transfer order, the debtor may at any time before the goods enter the possession of the creditor, on payment of the balance of the total price and the fulfilment of any other necessary conditions, claim the goods ordered to be returned to the creditor.

(5) When, in pursuance of a time order or under this section, the total price of goods under a regulated hire-purchase agreement or regulated conditional sale agreement is paid and any other necessary conditions are fulfilled, the creditor's title to the goods vests in the debtor.

Paragraph numbers marked with a "+" can be found online and on CD.

(6) If, in contravention of a return order or transfer order, any goods to which the order relates are not returned to the creditor, the court, on the application of the creditor, may—

    (a) revoke so much of the order as relates to those goods, and

    (b) order the debtor to pay the creditor the unpaid portion of so much of the total price as is referable to those goods,

(7) For the purposes of this section, the part of the total price referable to any goods is the part assigned to those goods by the agreement or (if no such assignment is made) the part determined by the court to be reasonable.

Hire-purchase, etc., agreements: special powers of court

    Section 133 provides for two possible orders in the case of a regulated hire-purchase **3H–306** or conditional sale agreement. A transfer order will be possible only where the goods subject to the agreement are divisible. Another way of expressing the formula, is that a transfer order is not possible unless the debtor has paid both (a) that part of the total price referable to the "transferred goods" and also (b) one quarter of the rest of the total price. This formula may need adjusting, however, by virtue of subs.(2). In the usual case, the choice before the court will be whether to make a return order or whether to make, if one is applied for, a time order (under s.129). If it decides to make a time order, it could make a return order, suspended, e.g. for so long as the debtor observes the terms of the time order, see s.135.

Evidence of adverse detention in hire purchase, etc., cases

134.—(1) Where goods are comprised in a regulated hire-purchase **3H–307** agreement, regulated conditional sale agreement or regulated consumer hire agreement, and the creditor or owner—

    (a) brings an action or makes an application to enforce a right to recover possession of the goods from the debtor or hirer, and

    (b) proves that a demand for the delivery of the goods was included in the default notice under section 88(5), or that, after the right to recover possession of the goods accrued but before the action was begun or the application was made, he made a request in writing to the debtor or hirer to surrender the goods,

then, for the purposes of the claim of the creditor or owner to recover possession of the goods, the possession of them by the debtor or hirer shall be deemed to be adverse to the creditor or owner.

(2) In subsection (1) "the debtor or hirer" includes a person in possession of the goods at any time between the debtor's or hirer's death and the grant of probate or administration, or (in Scotland) confirmation.

(3) Nothing in this section affects a claim for damages for conversion or (in Scotland) for delict.

SUPPLEMENTAL PROVISIONS AS TO ORDERS

Power to impose conditions, or suspend operation of order

135.—(1) If it considers it just to do so, the court may in an order **3H–308** made by it in relation to a regulated agreement include provisions—

Paragraph numbers marked with a "+" can be found online and on CD.

    (a) making the operation of any term of the order condi-
tional on the doing of specified acts by any party to the
proceedings;

    (b) suspending the operation of any term of the order ei-
ther—

        (i) until such time as the court subsequently directs,
or

        (ii) until the occurrence of a specified act or omission.

(2) The court shall not suspend the operation of a term requiring the delivery up of goods by any person unless satisfied that the goods are in his possession or control.

(3) In the case of a consumer hire agreement, the court shall not so use its powers under subsection (1)(b) as to extend the period for which, under the terms of the agreement, the hirer is entitled to possession of the goods to which the agreement relates.

(4) On the application of any person affected by a provision included under subsection (1), the court may vary the provision.

Power to impose conditions, or suspend operation of order

3H–309   These powers are relevant to ss.127(1)(ii), 129, 131, 132 and 133 (see commentaries to ss.127, 129 and 133). In a claim to which s.90(1) applies (protected goods under a hire-purchase or conditional sale agreement), the defendant may admit the claim and offer terms on which a return order should be suspended under s.135(1)(b)—see 7BPD.8 for the relevant procedure and for the evidentiary effect of such an admission in relation to s.135(2).

Power to vary agreements and securities

3H–310   **136.** The court may in an order made by it under this Act include such provision as it considers just for amending any agreement or security in consequence of a term of the order.

Power to vary agreements and securities

3H–311   When a time order is made, then unless the contemplated amendment under s.136 is truly a consequence of the time order, and the making of it is also just, there is no power to make it (*Southern & District Finance plc v Barnes* [1995] C.C.L.R. 62). When a time order is made in relation to future instalments that have not yet fallen due (i.e. in one of those limited types of case where that is possible), there will inevitably be consequences for the term of the loan or the rate of interest or both; in such a case the court has power to reduce the rate of interest in re-scheduling the debt (*ibid.*). The decision in *Southern & District Finance plc v Barnes* was, however, rather ambiguous since in that case the Court of Appeal having confirmed the above mentioned limitations on the court's power conferred by section 136, nevertheless then went on to confirm its use in an apparently very wide set of circumstances. In *Director General of Fair Trading v First National Bank* [2000] 1 W.L.R. 98; [2000] 1 All E.R. 240 Evans Lombe J. considered (obiter) that the court's powers under section 136 (as explained and applied in *Southern & District Finance v Barnes*) were ample to prevent the imposition on a borrower of post-judgment interest where it would not be just to impose such interest. [The case was brought under the Unfair Terms in Consumer Contracts Regulations 1994 and ultimately reached the House of Lords—see para.3H–891.] The court has wider powers to amend the agreement where it finds the parties' relationship to be unfair (ss.140A–140C). As regards interest on "default sums", see s.86F.

EXTORTIONATE CREDIT BARGAINS

Extortionate credit bargains

3H–312   **137.**—(1) If the court finds a credit bargain extortionate it may reopen the credit agreement so as to do justice between the parties.

Paragraph numbers marked with a "+" can be found online and on CD.

(2) In this section and sections 138 to 140,—

    (a) "credit agreement" means any agreement (other than an agreement which is an exempt agreement as a result of section 16(6C)) between an individual (the "debtor") and any other person (the "creditor") by which the creditor provides the debtor with credit of any amount, and

    (b) "credit bargain"—

        (i) where no transaction other than the credit agreement is to be taken into account in computing the total charge for credit, means the credit agreement, or

        (ii) where one or more other transactions are to be so taken into account, means the credit agreement and those other transactions, taken together.

3H–313   *Note*.—Repealed subject to savings and transitional provisions by the Consumer Credit Act 2006 ss.22(3) and 70, and Sch.4, (for savings and transitional provisions see Sch.3, para.15 and notes to s.140A below), with effect from April 6, 2007 (SI 2007/123). The original text was amended by the Financial Services and Markets Act 2000 (Regulated Activities) Order 2001 (SI 2001/544) (see notes to s.16).

Extortionate credit bargains

3H–314   Sections 137–140 deal with extortionate credit bargains. They apply not just to regulated consumer credit agreements, but to any "personal credit agreement", e.g. an exempt agreement or an agreement to provide an individual with credit of £30,000. Section 137 enables the court to re-open a "credit agreement" where a "credit bargain" is found to be extortionate. The definition of "credit agreement" (identical to that of "personal credit agreement" in s.8(1)), is not as wide as that of "credit bargain". For the definition of extortionate, see s.138. For court's powers on re-opening a credit agreement, see s.139. For applications to re-open the credit agreement and for possible rules as to limitation, see s.139 and commentary thereon.

Repeal of extortionate credit bargain provisions

3H–314.1   The extortionate credit bargain provisions (in ss.137–140) were replaced by the provisions on unfair creditor/debtor relationships (in ss.140A to 140D). In one respect, however, they remain relevant: a debtor can apply to the court to have an agreement re-opened under the extortionate credit bargain provisions, if the agreement was made before April 6, 2007 and was fully performed before April 6, 2008. Sections 140A to 140D do not apply, and ss.137–140 continue to apply, in relation to such agreements.

When bargains are extortionate

3H–315   **138.**—(1) A credit bargain is extortionate if it—

    (a) requires the debtor or a relative of his to make payments (whether unconditionally, or on certain contingencies) which are grossly exorbitant, or

    (b) otherwise grossly contravenes ordinary principles of fair dealing.

(2) In determining whether a credit bargain is extortionate, regard shall be had to such evidence as is adduced concerning—

    (a) interest rates prevailing at the time it was made,

    (b) the factors mentioned in subsections (3) to (5), and

    (c) any other relevant considerations.

(3) Factors applicable under subsection (2) in relation to the debtor include—

Paragraph numbers marked with a "+" can be found online and on CD.

(a) his age, experience, business capacity and state of health; and

(b) the degree to which, at the time of making the credit bargain, he was under financial pressure, and the nature of that pressure.

(4) Factors applicable under subsection (2) in relation to the creditor include—

(a) the degree of risk accepted by him, having regard to the value of any security provided;

(b) his relationship to the debtor; and

(c) whether or not a colourable cash price was quoted for any goods or services included in the credit bargain.

(5) Factors applicable under subsection (2) in relation to a linked transaction include the question how far the transaction was reasonably required for the protection of debtor or creditor, or was in the interest of the debtor.

3H–316 *Note* —Repealed subject to savings and transitional provisions by the Consumer Credit Act 2006 ss.22(3) and 70 and Sch.4 (for savings and transitional provisions see Sch.3, para.15 and notes to s.140A below), with effect from April 6, 2007 (SI 2007/123).

When bargains are extortionate

3H–317 *Burden of proof* —Rests upon the creditor (s.171(7)).

3H–318 *"Evidence ... adduced"* —The court will normally have regard to the "evidence adduced" about the factors listed. However, the court can take judicial notice, relying on its own general knowledge, e.g. of interest rates (*Castle Phillips Finance v Williams* [1986] C.C.L.R. 13).

3H–319 *Interest rates* —The court should consider rates for similar types of transaction prevailing at the time the agreement was made. It is essential to compare like with like. For example, a short term loan will not be exorbitant simply because the interest rate is higher than that obtainable for long term loans. A different approach might be possible if, say, an unworldly debtor has been talked into making an agreement in an expensive sector of the market when she could have equally well have obtained the credit via a less expensive type of agreement. In making comparison between the interest rate under the agreement and prevailing rates the APR should be used (*Davies v Direct Loans Ltd* [1986] 1 W.L.R. 823). Sometimes a credit agreement confers on the creditor a power to vary the rate of interest. In *Paragon Finance Plc v Nash* [2002] 1 W.L.R. 685; [2002] C.C.L.R. 2 the Court of Appeal declined to follow *Lombard Tricity Finance v Paton* [1989] 1 All E.R. 918, CA, and held: (i) post-contract variations to the rate of interest are irrelevant to whether the credit bargain is extortionate; (ii) the contractual power to vary the rate of interest is subject to an implied contractual term that the creditor will not exercise that power dishonestly, for an improper purpose, arbitrarily, capriciously or unreasonably. A creditor which raised its interest rate in an attempt to alleviate serious financial difficulties by passing on its increased costs to its borrowers, was held not to be in breach of that implied term—even though the variation increased the gap between the rate charged by the creditor and that charged by other lenders. A commercial lender is free to conduct its business in what it genuinely believes to be its best commercial interests: *Paragon Finance Ltd v Pender and Pender* [2005] EWCA Civ 760; [2005] 1 W.L.R. 3412; [2005] C.C.L.R. 5. The implied terms which in *Paragon* the Court of Appeal was prepared to imply are all negative and *Paragon* does not open the door to an implied term that a lender may have a positive obligation to reduce a rate of interest: *Sterling Credit v Rahman (No.2)* [2002] EWHC 3008 (Ch); [2003] C.C.L.R. 13.

Paragraph numbers marked with a "+" can be found online and on CD.

If a creditor has a policy of not exercising a contractual power to vary the interest rate (or the APR) even when market rates fall substantially, then failure to inform the debtor, at the time the agreement is made, about that policy is a relevant factor. If, however, the debtor would have entered the agreement even with that information, that factor is unlikely on its own to be sufficient to render the agreement extortionate: *Broadwick Financial Services Ltd v Spencer* [2002] EWCA Civ 35; [2002] 1 All E.R. (Comm) 446; [2002] C.C.L.R. 3. There were two further aspects of *Broadwick*. First, the debtor, a non-status borrower, was allowed to make payments based on a lower rate of interest than the contractual rate. This was by virtue of a "concession letter" given to the debtor at the time the agreement was made. The letter stated that it was "not intended to be legally binding" and that the lower rate was an *"ex gratia* concession". Secondly, the agreement provided for a rebate on early settlement calculated according to the "Rule of 78". Both these features of the case were irrelevant to the issue of whether the agreement was extortionate: the first because the concession was not intended to be legally binding and the concessionary rate was not substantially lower than the contractual interest rate; the second because calculating the rebate according to the "Rule of 78" was sanctioned by the Consumer Credit (Rebate on Early Settlement) Regulations 1983.

Alternative challenges —A debtor may be able to challenge terms of the agreement   **3H–320** (other than "core" terms, such as those which set the rate of interest payable under a loan agreement) as being "unfair" within the meaning of the Unfair Terms in Consumer Contracts Regulations 1994 (if the agreement was made after June 30, 1995 and before October 1, 1999) or the Unfair Terms in Consumer Contracts Regulations 1999 (if the agreement was made on or after October 1, 1999). For the 1999 regulations see para.3H–886 below. In *Falco Finance Ltd v Gough* [1999] C.C.L.R. 16 (Macclesfield County Court), the court considerd three features of a long term mortgage loan, namely: (i) its "dual rate" clause by which a lower ("concessionary") rate of interest was charged unless and until the debtor fell into arrears at any point; (ii) a clause providing for a rebate on redemption calculated on the "rule of 78" coupled with six months' notional deferral; and (iii) the charging of interest on a "flat rate" basis. The first was held to be extortionate within the meaning of s.138 while all three features were held to be unfair within the 1994 regulations. For an analysis of the application of the 1994 Regulations to a clause in a loan agreement imposing default interest at the contractual rate on outstanding arrears, including after judgment, see *Director General of Fair Trading v First National Bank plc* at para.3H–891 below.

Reopening of extortionate agreements

139.—(1) A credit agreement may, if the court thinks just, be   **3H–321** reopened on the ground that the credit bargain is extortionate—

    (a) on an application for the purpose made by the debtor or any surety to the High Court, county court or sheriff court; or

    (b) at the instance of the debtor or a surety in any proceedings to which the debtor and creditor are parties, being proceedings to enforce the credit agreement, any security relating to it, or any linked transaction; or

    (c) at the instance of the debtor or a surety in other proceedings in any court where the amount paid or payable under the credit agreement is relevant.

(2) In reopening the agreement, the court may, for the purpose of relieving the debtor or a surety from payment of any sum in excess of that fairly due and reasonable, by order—

    (a) direct accounts to be taken, or (in Scotland) an accounting to be made, between any persons,

    (b) set aside the whole or part of any obligation imposed on

Paragraph numbers marked with a "+" can be found online and on CD.

the debtor or a surety by the credit bargain or any related agreement,

(c) require the creditor to repay the whole or part of any sum paid under the credit bargain or any related agreement by the debtor or a surety, whether paid to the creditor or any other person,

(d) direct the return to the surety of any property provided for the purposes of the security, or

(e) alter the terms of the credit agreement or any security instrument.

(3) An order may be under subsection (2) notwithstanding that its effect is to place a burden on the creditor in respect of an advantage unfairly enjoyed by another person who is a party to a linked transaction.

(4) An order under subsection (2) shall not alter the effect of any judgment.

(5) In England and Wales an application under subsection (1)(a) shall be brought only in the county court in the case of—

(a) a regulated agreement, or

(b) an agreement (not being a regulated agreement) under which the creditor provides the debtor with fixed-sum credit or running-account credit.

(5A) [...]

(6) In Scotland an application under subsection (1)(a) may be brought in the sheriff court for the district in which the debtor or surety resides or carries on business.

(7) In Northern Ireland an application under subsection (1)(a) may be brought in the county court in the case of—

(a) a regulated agreement, or

(b) an agreement (not being a regulated agreement) under which the creditor provides the debtor with fixed-sum credit not exceeding £5,000 or running-account credit on which the credit limit does not exceed £5,000.

3H–322   *Note* —Repealed subject to savings and transitional provisions by the Consumer Credit Act 2006 ss.22(3) and 70, and Sch.4, (for savings and transitional provisions see Sch.3, para.15 and notes to s.140A below), with effect from April 6, 2007 (SI 2007/123).

Amended by the Debtors (Scotland) Act 1987 Sch.6; the Administration of Justice (Northern Ireland) Order 1975 (SI 1975/816) art.9(1), Sch.1; the County Courts Jurisdiction Order 1977 (SI 1977/600); the County Courts Jurisdiction Order 1981 (SI 1981/1123); the Administration of Justice Act 1982 Sch.3; the County Courts (Amendment) Rules (Northern Ireland) 1982 (SI 1982/120); the County Courts Act Sch.2; and the High Court and County Courts Jurisdiction Order 1991 (SI 1991/724).

Reopening of extortionate agreements

3H–323   *Restrictions on court's ability to re-open agreement* —An application under s.139(1) must be made within any relevant limitation period under the Limitation Act 1980. The proper approach, it is submitted, is that the Limitation Act has no application at all where the debtor makes the application to re-open the credit agreement (e.g. to be relieved of the obligation to pay a sum) as part of his *defence*, but that it may apply to a claim or counterclaim—see also *Extortionate Credit Bargain Claims and the Limitation Rules*

Paragraph numbers marked with a "+" can be found online and on CD.

(1998) 412 S.J. 274 and *Extortionate Loans: the Limitation Act revisited* (1999) 143 S.J. 646. Where an application under s.139 is for a remedy or remedies, other than for repayment of any sum, the claim is an action upon a specialty within s.8 of the Limitation Act 1980 and the relevant period limitation period expires 12 years after the agreement was made, *Rahman v Sterling Credit Ltd* [2001] 1 W.L.R. 496. The period is six years where the remedy claimed is repayment of any sum, Limitation Act 1980 s.9. The Court of Appeal in *Rahman* did not decide, but nevertheless appeared to imply, that the six year period under s.9 began when the agreement was made. This is surely wrong, because the period does not start until the cause of action accrues and the cause of action to recover a sum of money cannot accrue until that sum has first been paid—see the articles referred to above. *Rahman* did not deal with the situation where an extortionate credit bargain claim is made purely by way of defence. It involved a secure loan made in 1989 in respect of which a possession order had been made in 1990 but never executed. In 1998, the debtor wished to apply, by way of a counterclaim in the possession proceedings, to have the agreement re-opened as being extortionate. Holding that the 12 year limitation period had not expired, the Court of Appeal granted him permission under CPR 20.4 to file that counterclaim (which did not include a claim for repayment of any sum). The court declined to refuse permission on the grounds of issue stoppel, since the counterclaim was part of the same original action in which the possession order had been claimed. It was not a new action in which the defendant was seeking to raise an issue which should have been raised in an earlier action.

Procedure —An application under s.139(1) will no doubt often be made by the **3H–324** debtor (or surety) in an action begun by the creditor. Written notice of an intention to make such an application should be served on the court and all other parties within 14 days after the service of the claim form on the applicant: see para.7BPD.10. If such a notice is served, the applicant will be treated as having filed a defence. An originating application should be made using the Consumer Credit Act procedure, set out in the Consumer Credit Practice Direction at para.7BPD.1, unless it relates to the recovery of land. See further the Introductory Note About Procedure in Consumer Credit Cases, immediately before the start of this Act, at para.3H–4 *et seq.* above.

Interpretation of sections 137 to 139

140. Where the credit agreement is not a regulated agreement, **3H–325** expressions used in sections 137 to 139 which, apart from this section, apply only to regulated agreements, shall be construed as nearly as may be as if the credit agreement were a regulated agreement.

Note —Repealed subject to savings and transitional provisions by the Consumer **3H–326** Credit Act 2006 ss.22(3) and 70, and Sch.4, (for savings and transitional provisions see Sch.3, para.15 and notes to s.140A below), with effect from April 6, 2007 (SI 2007/123).

Unfair relationships between creditors and debtors

140A.—(1) The court may make an order under section 140B in **3H–327** connection with a credit agreement if it determines that the relationship between the creditor and the debtor arising out of the agreement (or the agreement taken with any related agreement) is unfair to the debtor because of one or more of the following—

    (a) any of the terms of the agreement or of any related agreement;

    (b) the way in which the creditor has exercised or enforced any of his rights under the agreement or any related agreement;

    (c) any other thing done (or not done) by, or on behalf of, the creditor (either before or after the making of the agreement or any related agreement).

Paragraph numbers marked with a "+" can be found online and on CD.

(2) In deciding whether to make a determination under this section the court shall have regard to all matters it thinks relevant (including matters relating to the creditor and matters relating to the debtor).

(3) For the purposes of this section the court shall (except to the extent that it is not appropriate to do so) treat anything done (or not done) by, or on behalf of, or in relation to, an associate or a former associate of the creditor as if done (or not done) by, or on behalf of, or in relation to, the creditor.

(4) A determination may be made under this section in relation to a relationship notwithstanding that the relationship may have ended.

(5) An order under section 140B shall not be made in connection with a credit agreement which is an exempt agreement by virtue of section 16(6C).

3H–328   *Note* —Inserted by the Consumer Credit Act 2006 s.19, with effect from April 6, 2007 (SI 2007/123).

Unfair relationships

3H–329   The powers available to the court under ss.140A to 140C effectively enable the court to remove any unfairness where the court determines that the relationship between creditor and debtor is unfair to the debtor.

Agreements to which unfair relationships provisions apply

3H–330   Sections 140A to 140C apply (see s.140C(1)) to agreements where credit is provided to an individual (which includes a partnership of up to three partners). Thus they apply not only to regulated credit agreements but also to exempt agreements. By way of exception, they do not apply (see s.140A(5)) to agreements which are exempt agreements by virtue of s.16(6C)(a). The latter are those subject to the regulatory regime under the Financial Services and Markets Act 2000 which are, broadly, any loan secured by a first legal mortgage on a dwelling in which the debtor or his family resides—see further the commentary to s.16 (at the third bullet point).

Limitation rules

3H–331   For the application of the limitation rules under ss.137–140, see *Rahman v Sterling Credit Ltd* [2001] I W.L.R. 496 and the commentary to s.139 above. In s.140B there is a clear distinction between the words "on an application made by" in s.140B(2)(a) and the words "at the instance of" in s.140B(2)(b) and (c). Thus, whereas the limitation rules will apply to an application under s.140B(2)(a), it is submitted that they have no application at all to the situation where the debtor or surety raises the issue of unfair relationship by way of defence. In relation to an application under s.140B(2) for a remedy or remedies other than for the repayment of money, the limitation period expires 12 years after the credit agreement was made, since such a claim is an action upon a specialty: *Rahman*, above. Where the remedy claimed in an application under s.140B(2)(a) is the repayment to the debtor or surety of money which he has paid, the limitation period is six years beginning with when the cause of action accrued: Limitation Act 1980 s.9. That period does not, it is submitted, begin until the date when the debtor or surety paid the money which is now being reclaimed, since the cause of action entitling the debtor or surety to reclaim that money cannot have accrued until he had first paid it. The latter limitation period will thus not finally expire until six years after the date of the debtor's final payment under the agreement. See further the articles cited in the notes to s.139.

Commencement and transitional provisions relating to unfair relationships

3H–332   Sections 140A to 140D were added by the Consumer Credit Act 2006, with effect from April 6, 2007: the Consumer Credit Act 2006 (Commencement No.2 and Transitional Provisions and Savings) Order 2007 (SI 2007/123). The transitional period, set out in paras 14 to 16 of Sch.3 to the Consumer Credit Act 2006 ended on

Paragraph numbers marked with a "+" can be found online and on CD.

April 5, 2008. After the transitional period (i.e. currently), ss.140A to 140C (and not ss.137–140) apply to agreements whenever made. There is one exception to that. The exception is that ss.137–140 (and not ss.140A to 140C) continue to apply to agreements which were made before April 6, 2007 and were fully performed before April 6, 2008. Thus, in the case of an agreement made before April 6, 2007 and fully performed before April 6, 2008, the debtor can seek to have the agreement re-opened under the extortionate credit bargain provisions but cannot challenge the agreement under the unfair relationship provisions.

Alternative challenges

For the possibility of a challenge that the terms of a credit agreement are "unfair" **3H–333** within the meaning of the Unfair Terms in Consumer Contracts Regulations 1999, see those Regulations at para.3H–886 below and also the commentary to s.138 above.

Powers of court in relation to unfair relationships

140B.—(1) An order under this section in connection with a credit **3H–334** agreement may do one or more of the following—

    (a) require the creditor, or any associate or former associate of his, to repay (in whole or in part) any sum paid by the debtor or by a surety by virtue of the agreement or any related agreement (whether paid to the creditor, the associate or the former associate or to any other person);

    (b) require the creditor, or any associate or former associate of his, to do or not to do (or to cease doing) anything specified in the order in connection with the agreement or any related agreement;

    (c) reduce or discharge any sum payable by the debtor or by a surety by virtue of the agreement or any related agreement;

    (d) direct the return to a surety of any property provided by him for the purposes of a security;

    (e) otherwise set aside (in whole or in part) any duty imposed on the debtor or on a surety by virtue of the agreement or any related agreement;

    (f) alter the terms of the agreement or of any related agreement;

    (g) direct accounts to be taken, or (in Scotland) an accounting to be made, between any persons.

(2) An order under this section may be made in connection with a credit agreement only—

    (a) on an application made by the debtor or by a surety;

    (b) at the instance of the debtor or a surety in any proceedings in any court to which the debtor and the creditor are parties, being proceedings to enforce the agreement or any related agreement; or

    (c) at the instance of the debtor or a surety in any other proceedings in any court where the amount paid or payable under the agreement or any related agreement is relevant.

(3) An order under this section may be made notwithstanding that its effect is to place on the creditor, or any associate or former

Paragraph numbers marked with a "+" can be found online and on CD.

associate of his, a burden in respect of an advantage enjoyed by another person.

(4) An application under subsection (2)(a) may only be made—

(a) in England and Wales, to the county court;

(b) in Scotland, to the sheriff court;

(c) in Northern Ireland, to the High Court (subject to subsection (6)).

(5) In Scotland such an application may be made in the sheriff court for the district in which the debtor or surety resides or carries on business.

(6) In Northern Ireland such an application may be made to the county court if the credit agreement is an agreement under which the creditor provides the debtor with—

(a) fixed-sum credit not exceeding £15,000; or

(b) running-account credit on which the credit limit does not exceed £15,000.

(7) Without prejudice to any provision which may be made by rules of court made in relation to county courts in Northern Ireland, such rules may provide that an application made by virtue of subsection (6) may be made in the county court for the division in which the debtor or surety resides or carries on business.

(8) A party to any proceedings mentioned in subsection (2) shall be entitled, in accordance with rules of court, to have any person who might be the subject of an order under this section made a party to the proceedings.

(9) If, in any such proceedings, the debtor or a surety alleges that the relationship between the creditor and the debtor is unfair to the debtor, it is for the creditor to prove to the contrary.

3H–335   *Note* —Inserted subject to transitional provisions by the Consumer Credit Act 2006 s.20 (for transitional provisions see Sch.3, paras 14 and 16), with effect from April 6, 2007 (SI 2007/123).

Powers of court in relation to unfair relationships

3H–336   See the commentary to s.140A.

3H–337   *Procedure* —An application under s.140B(2)(b) or (c) will no doubt often be made by the debtor (or surety) in an action begun by the creditor. Written notice of an intention to make such an application should be served on the court and all other parties within 14 days after the service of the claim form on the applicant: see para.7BPD.10. If such a notice is served, the applicant will be treated as having filed a defence.

Interpretation of ss.140A and 140B

3H–338   140C.—(1) In this section and in sections 140A and 140B 'credit agreement' means any agreement between an individual (the 'debtor') and any other person (the 'creditor') by which the creditor provides the debtor with credit of any amount.

(2) References in this section and in sections 140A and 140B to the creditor or to the debtor under a credit agreement include—

(a) references to the person to whom his rights and duties under the agreement have passed by assignment or operation of law;

Paragraph numbers marked with a "+" can be found online and on CD.

(b) where two or more persons are the creditor or the debtor, references to any one or more of those persons.

(3) The definition of 'court' in section 189(1) does not apply for the purposes of sections 140A and 140B.

(4) References in sections 140A and 140B to an agreement related to a credit agreement (the 'main agreement') are references to—

(a) a credit agreement consolidated by the main agreement;
(b) a linked transaction in relation to the main agreement or to a credit agreement within paragraph (a);
(c) a security provided in relation to the main agreement, to a credit agreement within paragraph (a) or to a linked transaction within paragraph (b).

(5) In the case of a credit agreement which is not a regulated consumer credit agreement, for the purposes of subsection (4) a transaction shall be treated as being a linked transaction in relation to that agreement if it would have been such a transaction had that agreement been a regulated consumer credit agreement.

(6) For the purposes of this section and section 140B the definitions of 'security' and 'surety' in section 189(1) apply (with any appropriate changes) in relation to—

(a) a credit agreement which is not a consumer credit agreement as if it were a consumer credit agreement; and
(b) a transaction which is a linked transaction by virtue of subsection (5).

(7) For the purposes of this section a credit agreement (the 'earlier agreement') is consolidated by another credit agreement (the 'later agreement') if—

(a) the later agreement is entered into by the debtor (in whole or in part) for purposes connected with debts owed by virtue of the earlier agreement; and
(b) at any time prior to the later agreement being entered into the parties to the earlier agreement included—

(i) the debtor under the later agreement; and
(ii) the creditor under the later agreement or an associate or a former associate of his.

(8) Further, if the later agreement is itself consolidated by another credit agreement (whether by virtue of this subsection or subsection (7)), then the earlier agreement is consolidated by that other agreement as well.

Note —Inserted subject to transitional provisions by the Consumer Credit Act 2006 s.21 (for transitional provisions see Sch.3, para.16), with effect from April 6, 2007 (SI 2007/123). **3H–339**

Interpretation of ss. 140A and 140B
See the commentary to s.140A. **3H–340**

Advice and information

140D. The advice and information published by the OFT under section 229 of the Enterprise Act 2002 shall indicate how the OFT **3H–341**

Paragraph numbers marked with a "+" can be found online and on CD.

expects sections 140A to 140C of this Act to interact with Part 8 of that Act.

3H–342 *Note* —Inserted by the Consumer Credit Act 2006 s.22, with effect from April 6, 2007 (SI 2007/123).

MISCELLANEOUS

Jurisdiction and parties

3H–343   **141.**—(1) In England and Wales the county court shall have jurisdiction to hear and determine—

   (a) any action by the creditor or owner to enforce a regulated agreement or any security relating to it;

   (b) any action to enforce any linked transaction against the debtor or hirer or his relative,

and such an action shall not be brought in any other court.

   (2) Where an action or application is brought in the High Court which, by virtue of this Act, ought to have been brought in the county court it shall not be treated as improperly brought, but shall be transferred to the county court.

   (3) In Scotland the sheriff court shall have jurisdiction to hear and determine any action referred to in subsection (1) and such an action shall not be brought in any other court.

   (3A) Subject to subsection (3B) an action which is brought in the sheriff court by virtue of subsection (3) shall be brought only in one of the following courts, namely—

   (a) the court for the place where the debtor of hirer is domiciled (within the meaning of section 41 or 42 of the Civil Jurisdiction and Judgments Act 1982);

   (b) the court for the place where the debtor of hirer carries on business; and

   (c) where the purpose of the action is to assert, declare or determine proprietary or possessory rights, or rights of security, in or over moveable property, or to obtain authority to dispose of moveable property, the court for the place the property is situated.

   (3B) Subsection (3A) shall not apply—

   (a) where Rule 3 of Schedule 8 to the said Act of 1982 applies; or

   (b) where the jurisdiction of another court has been prorogated by an agreement entered into after the dispute has arisen.

   (4) In Northern Ireland the county court shall have jurisdiction to hear and determine any action or application falling within subsection (1).

   (5) Except as may be provided by rules of court, all the parties to a regulated agreement, and any surety, shall be made parties to any proceedings relating to the agreement.

3H–344   *Note* —Amended by the Civil Jurisdiction and Judgments Act 1982 Sch.12.

Paragraph numbers marked with a "+" can be found online and on CD.

Jurisdiction and parties

The Consumer Credit Practice direction (which supplements CPR r.7.9) indicates in **3H–345** which county court a claim to recover goods, or an originating application for a time order (under s.129(1)(b)), may be started—generally the court in the district where the debtor or hirer resides or carries on business (para.7BPD.1, para.4). For the appropriate forum where the claim is between parties in different European states, see para.6.19.23.

Subsection (2) —Despite the words "which shall not be treated as improperly **3H–346** brought", the court now has, by virtue of the County Courts Act 1984 s.40(1)(b) (as substituted by the Courts and Legal Services Act 1990), discretion to strike out the proceedings if satisfied that the claimant knew or ought to have known that they should have been brought in the County Court (*Barclays Bank Plc v Brooks* [1997] C.C.L.R. 60). In any claim issued in the High Court in relation to a consumer credit agreement (e.g. a claim by the debtor or in relation to an exempt agreement), the particulars of claim must contain a statement that the action is not one to which s.141 applies (see para.7.6 of the Practice Direction supplementing CPR Pt 16 at para.16PD.7).

Subsection (5) —For additional requirements as to parties and for the court's power **3H–347** to dispense with the requirements of this subsection, see para.9 of the Consumer Credit Practice Direction (para.7BPD.1).

Procedure

A claim by a creditor or owner to enforce a regulated agreement will be subject to **3H–348** one of the following three sets of procedure:

- The procedure set out in CPR Pt 55, if it is a claim relating to recovery of land;
- The Consumer Credit Act procedure, set out in the Consumer Credit Practice Direction at para.7BPD.1, if either
  - (i) the agreement relates to goods, or
  - (ii) the agreement relates only to money and the claim involves an application for an order under any of ss.65(1), 86(2), 90, 92(1), 105(7)(a) or (b), 111(2), 124(1) or (2);
- A Pt 7 claim form (but not using the Consumer Credit Act procedure), if the agreement relates only to money and the claim does not involve an application under one of the above mentioned sections.

See further, the Note About Procedure in Consumer Credit Cases, immediately before the start of this Act, at para.3H–4 *et seq.* above.

Power to declare rights of parties

142.—(1) Where under any provision of this Act a thing can be **3H–349** done by a creditor or owner on an enforcement order only, and either—

 (a) the court dismisses (except on technical grounds only) an application for an enforcement order, or

 (b) where no such application has been made or such an application has been dismissed on technical grounds only, an interested party applies to the court for a declaration under this subsection,

the court may if it thinks just make a declaration that the creditor or owner is not entitled to do that thing, and thereafter no application for an enforcement order in respect of it shall be entertained.

 (2) Where—

 (a) a regulated agreement or linked transaction is cancelled under section 69(1), or becomes subject to section 69(2), or

Paragraph numbers marked with a "+" can be found online and on CD.

CONSUMER

(b) a regulated agreement is terminated under section 91,

and an interested party applies to the court for a declaration under this subsection, the court may make a declaration to that effect.

Power to declare rights of parties

3H–350   For the effect on security of a declaration under subs.(1), see s.113(3)(d) and (4).

> For ss.143 to 144 and ss.148 to 149 of the Consumer Credit Act 1974 (see Arrangement) plus any related commentary see paragraphs 3H–351+ to 3H–360+ on White Book on Westlaw UK or the Civil Procedure CD.

PART XI

ENFORCEMENT OF ACT

* * * *

No further sanctions for breach of Act

3H–361   **170.**—(1) A breach of any requirement made (otherwise than by any court) by or under this Act shall incur no civil or criminal sanction as being such a breach, except to the extent (if any) expressly provided by or under this Act.

(2) In exercising its functions under this Act the OFT may take account of any matter appearing to it to constitute a breach of a requirement made by or under this Act, whether or not any sanction for that breach is provided by or under this Act and, if it is so provided, whether or not proceedings have been brought in respect of the breach.

(3) Subsection (1) does not prevent the grant of an injunction, or the making of an order of certiorari, mandamus or prohibition or as respects Scotland the grant of an interdict or of an order under section 91 of the Court of Session Act 1868 (order for specific performance of statutory duty).

3H–362   *Note* —Amended by the Enterprise Act 2002 s.278 and Sch.25.

Onus of proof in various proceedings

3H–363   **171.**—(1) If an agreement contains a term signifying that in the opinion of the parties section 10(3)(b)(iii) does not apply to the agreement, it shall be taken not to apply unless the contrary is proved.

(2) It shall be assumed in any proceedings, unless the contrary is proved that when a person initiated a transaction as mentioned in section 19(1)(c) he knew the principal agreement had been made, or contemplated that it might be made.

(3) Regulations under section 44 or 52 may make provision as to the onus of proof in any proceedings to enforce the regulations.

(4) In proceedings brought by the creditor under a credit-token agreement—

(a) it is for the creditor to prove that the credit-token was lawfully supplied to the debtor, and was accepted by him, and

Paragraph numbers marked with a "+" can be found online and on CD.

(b) if the debtor alleges that any use made of the credit-token was not authorised by him, it is for the creditor to prove either—

    (i) that the use was so authorised, or

    (ii) that the use occurred before the creditor had been given notice under section 84(3).

(5) In proceedings under section 50(1) in respect of a document received by a minor at any school or other educational establishment for minors, it is for the person sending it to him at that establishment to prove that he did not know or suspect it to be such an establishment.

(6) In proceedings under section 119(1) it is for the pawnee to prove that he had reasonable cause to refuse to allow the pawn to be redeemed.

(7) ...

Note —Amended by the Consumer Credit Act 2006 s.70 and Sch 4, with effect from April 6, 2007 (SI 2007/123).   **3H–364**

Statements by creditor or owner to be binding

172.—(1) A statement by a creditor or owner is binding on him if given under—   **3H–365**

    section 77(1),

    section 78(1),

    section 79(1),

    section 97(1),

    section 107(1)(c),

    section 108(1)(c),

    section 109(1)(c).

(2) Where a trader—

    (a) gives a customer a notice in compliance with section 103(1)(b), or

    (b) gives a customer a notice under section 103(1) asserting that the customer is not indebted to him under an agreement,

the notice is binding on the trader.

(3) Where in proceedings before any court—

    (a) it is sought to rely on a statement or notice given as mentioned in subsection (1) or (2), and

    (b) the statement or notice is shown to be incorrect,

the court may direct such relief (if any) to be given to the creditor or owner from the operation of subsection (1) or (2) as appears to the court to be just.

Statements by creditor or owner to be binding

It would seem likely in exercising its discretion under subs.(3), the court will follow a very similar approach to that in estoppel cases. Indeed, a debtor may well seek to rely on s.172 and on estoppel as alternatives. For cases on estoppel see *United Overseas Bank v Jiwani* [1976] 1 W.L.R. 964 (bank, which had credited debtor's account erroneously, not estopped from reclaiming money from debtor as debtor had not altered his position on basis of the error), and *Lombard North Central v Stobart* [1990] C.C.L.R. 53,   **3H–366**

Paragraph numbers marked with a "+" can be found online and on CD.

CA (creditor issuing settlement statement in relation to unregulated conditional sale agreement for purchase of car—statement understating amount required to pay off outstanding debt—debtor selling the car in consequence of error—creditor estopped from making claim in contract or conversion).

Contracting-out forbidden

3H–367   **173.**—(1) A term contained in a regulated agreement or linked transaction, or in any other agreement relating to an actual or prospective regulated agreement or linked transaction, is void if, and to the extent that, it is inconsistent with a provision for the protection of the debtor or hirer or his relative or any surety contained in this Act or in any regulation made under this Act.

(2) Where a provision specified the duty or liability of the debtor or hirer or his relative or any surety in certain circumstances, a term is inconsistent with that provision if it purports to impose, directly or indirectly, an additional duty or liability on him in those circumstances.

(3) Notwithstanding subsection (1), a provision of this Act under which a thing may be done in relation to any person on an order of the court or the OFT only shall not be taken to prevent its being done at any time with that person's consent given at that time, but the refusal of such consent shall not give rise to any liability.

3H–368   *Note* —Amended by the Enterprise Act 2002 s.278 and Sch.25.

3H–369   *Consensual enforcement* —For apparently conflicting rulings on whether s.173(3) enables a debtor to give effective consent to enforcement of the agreement against himself where, without that consent, s.127(3) (now repealed) rendered the agreement unenforceable against him, see commentary to s.127 in the *White Book* 2006.

PART XII

SUPPLEMENTAL

GENERAL

* * * *

Service of documents

3H–370   **176.**—(1) A document to be served under this act by one person ("the server") on another person ("the subject") is to be treated as properly served on the subject if dealt with as mentioned in the following subsections.

(2) The document may be delivered or sent by an appropriate method to the subject, or addressed to him by name and left at his proper address.

(3) For the purposes of this Act, a document sent by post to, or left at, the address last known to the server as the address of a person shall be treated as sent by post to, or left at, his proper address.

(4) Where the document is to be served on the subject as being the person having any interest in land, and it is not practicable after

Paragraph numbers marked with a "+" can be found online and on CD.

reasonable inquiry to ascertain the subject's name or address, the document may be served by—

    (a) addressing it to the subject by the description of the person having that interest in the land (naming it), and

    (b) delivering the document to some responsible person on the land or affixing it, or a copy of it, in a conspicuous position on the land.

(5) Where a document to be served on the subject as being a debtor, hirer or surety, or as having any other capacity relevant for the purposes of this Act, is served at any time on another person who—

    (a) is the person last known to the server as having that capacity, but

    (b) before that time had ceased to have it,

the document shall be treated as having been served at that time on the subject.

(6) Anything done to a document in relation to a person who (whether to the knowledge of the server or not) has died shall be treated for the purposes of subsection (5) as service of the document on that person if it would have been so treated had he not died.

(7) The following enactments shall not be construed as authorising service on the Public Trustee (in England and Wales) or the Probate Judge (in Northern Ireland) of any document which is to be served under this Act—

    section 9 of the Administration of Estates Act 1925;

    section 3 of the Administration of Estates Act (Northern Ireland) 1955.

(8) References in the preceding subsections to the serving of a document on a person include the giving of the document to that person.

Note —Amended by the Law of Property (Miscellaneous Provisions) Act 1994 Sch.1 and by the Consumer Credit Act 1974 (Electronic Communications) Order 2004 (SI 2004/3236).   **3H–371**

Service of documents

    in *Lombard North Central v Power-Hines* [1995] C.C.L.R. 24, the debtor claimed in vain, that a default notice (under s.87) had not been received by him either because the postman was unreliable or because the debtor's young son had intercepted it. It was held that the fact that it did not come to the debtor's attention did not mean that he did not receive it. Section 176(2) was designed to apply where through no fault of the creditor the document does not come to the attention of the debtor. The court was entitled to assume that where the letter was not returned, it had been delivered.   **3H–372**

Electronic transmission of documents

    176A.—(1) A document is transmitted in accordance with this subsection if—   **3H–373**

    (a) the person to whom it is transmitted agrees that it may be delivered to him by being transmitted to a particular electronic address in a particular electronic form,

    (b) it is transmitted to that address in that form, and

    (c) the form in which the document is transmitted is such

Paragraph numbers marked with a "+" can be found online and on CD.

that any information in the document which is addressed to the person to whom the document is transmitted is capable of being stored for future reference for an appropriate period in a way which allows the information to be reproduced without change.

(2) A document transmitted in accordance with subsection (1) shall, unless the contrary is proved, be treated for the purposes of this Act, except section 69, as having been delivered on the working day immediately following the day on which it is transmitted.

(3) In this section, "electronic address" includes any number or address used for the purposes of receiving electronic communications.

3H–374 Note —Section 176A was added by the Consumer Credit Act 1974 (Electronic Communications) Order 2004 (SI 2004/3236).

INTERPRETATION

* * * *

Arrangements between creditor and supplier

3H–375 187.—(1) A consumer credit agreement shall be treated as entered into under pre-existing arrangements between a creditor and a supplier if it is entered into in accordance with, or in furtherance of, arrangements previously made between persons mentioned in subsection (4)(a), (b) or (c).

(2) A consumer credit agreement shall be treated as entered into in contemplation of future arrangements between a creditor and a supplier if it is entered into in the expectation that arrangements will subsequently be made between persons mentioned in subsection (4)(a), (b) or (c) for the supply of cash, goods and services (or any of them) to be financed by the consumer credit agreement.

(3) Arrangements shall be disregarded for the purposes of subsection (1) or (2) if—

    (a) they are arrangements for the making, in specified circumstances, of payments to the supplier by the creditor, and

    (b) the creditor holds himself out as willing to make, in such circumstances, payments of the kind to suppliers generally.

(3A) Subsections (1) and (2) do not apply to any disclosure of information by the Director to the Bank of England for the purpose of enabling or assisting the Bank to discharge its functions under the Banking Act 1987or the Director to discharge his functions under this Act.

(4) The persons referred to in subsections (1) and (2) are—

    (a) the creditor and the supplier;

    (b) one of them and an associate of the other's;

    (c) an associate of one and an associate of the other's.

(5) Where the creditor is an associate of the supplier's, the

Paragraph numbers marked with a "+" can be found online and on CD.

consumer credit agreement shall be treated, unless the contrary is proved, as entered into under pre-existing arrangements between the creditor and the supplier.

Note —Amended by the Banking Act 1987 s.89.   **3H–376**

Arrangements between creditor and supplier
See commentary to s.12.   **3H–377**

Subsection (1) —This does not define the only kind of arrangements that are capable of falling within s.12(b). The expression "treated as" was used to extend, rather than restrict, the scope of that section: *OFT v Lloyds Bank TSB* [2006] EWCA Civ 268; [2007] Q.B. 1, at para.65.

Definition of 'default sum'

187A.—(1) In this Act 'default sum' means, in relation to the debtor **3H–378** or hirer under a regulated agreement, a sum (other than a sum of interest) which is payable by him under the agreement in connection with a breach of the agreement by him.

(2) But a sum is not a default sum in relation to the debtor or hirer simply because, as a consequence of his breach of the agreement, he is required to pay it earlier than he would otherwise have had to.

Note —Inserted by the Consumer Credit Act 2006 s.18.   **3H–379**

Default sum
A repayment which the debtor has failed to pay under the agreement and in re- **3H–380** spect of which the debtor is thus in arrears is not a "default sum". A default sum is a sum which only becomes due because the debtor has defaulted, e.g. a fee payable by a debtor for late payment of an instalment or for exceeding his credit card limit.

See ss.86E and 86F above regarding (a) the notice required to be given when a default sum has become due and (b) interest on default sums.

Subsection (2) —A payment falling due earlier than it otherwise would have done, **3H–381** e.g. under an accelerated payments clause is not a default sum.

For ss.188 to 191 of and Sch.2 to the Consumer Credit Act 1974 (see Arrangement) plus any related commentary see paragraphs 3H–382+ to 3H–415+ on White Book on Westlaw UK or the Civil Procedure CD.

Consumer Credit (Total Charge for Credit) Regulations 1980

(S.I. 1980 No. 51)   **3H–416**

ARRANGEMENT OF REGULATIONS

PART I

Paragraph numbers marked with a "+" can be found online and on CD.

Paragraph numbers marked with a "+" denote content that is available on White Book on WestlawUK or the Civil Procedure CD.

Consumer Credit (Agreements) Regulations 1983

3H–462

(S.I. 1983 No, 1553)

ARRANGEMENT OF REGULATIONS

Paragraph numbers marked with a "+" denote content that is available on White Book on Westlaw UK or the Civil Procedure CD.

The Consumer Credit (Exempt Agreements) Order 1989

(S.I. 1989 No. 869)

3H–498

For The Consumer Credit (Exempt Agreements) Order 1989 see paragraphs 3H–499+ to 3H–516+ on White Book on Westlaw UK or the Civil Procedure CD.

Paragraph numbers marked with a "+" can be found online and on CD.

Misrepresentation Act 1967

(1967 C.7)

ARRANGEMENT OF SECTIONS

3H–517

Paragraph numbers marked with a "+" denote content that is available on White Book on Westlaw UK or the Civil Procedure CD.

Supply of Goods (Implied Terms) Act 1973

(1973 C.13)

ARRANGEMENT OF SECTIONS

3H–526

Paragraph numbers marked with a "+" denote content that is available on White Book on Westlaw UK or the Civil Procedure CD.

General note

3H–527

The only sections of this Act remaining unrepealed are s.14 and those sections relating to the terms as to title, description, satisfactory quality, fitness for purpose, and sample which are implied in hire-purchase contracts. The sections that imply these terms in hire-purchase agreements are s.8 (title), s.9 (description), s.10 (satisfactory quality and fitness for purpose) and s.11 (sample). These implied terms are word for word the same as the equivalent sections (12–15) of the Sale of Goods Act 1979 (*q.v.*) except for necessary changes of wording to adapt the provisions to apply to hire-purchase agreements. Thus, instead of "seller" and "buyer" the terms "creditor" and "debtor" are used to describe the parties. These are the same terms as used by the Consumer Credit Act 1974 to describe the parties to a hire-purchase agreement. The terms implied by the Supply of Goods (Implied Terms) Act 1973 are implied into all hire-purchase agreements, not just those which are regulated by the Consumer Credit Act 1974.

Exclusion of liability

3H–528

The statutory restrictions on excluding liability for breach of these terms are exactly the same as they are in relation to the implied terms in ss.12–15 of the Sale of Goods Act 1979 (see, in particular, the Unfair Contract Terms Act 1977 s.6).

Remedies

3H–529

The same terms are conditions as are the equivalent implied terms in ss.12–15 of the Sale of Goods Act 1979. As with a contract of sale of goods, a breach of one of these conditions entitles the debtor to reject the goods. In sale of goods a buyer who is not "dealing as a consumer" has no right to reject the goods for breach of the implied conditions if the breach is so slight that it would be unreasonable to reject the goods (Sale of Goods Act 1979 s.15A). The position is exactly the same under the Supply of Goods (Implied Terms) Act 1973 for a debtor who is not "dealing as a consumer" (s.11A). One small difference in the law, however, is that the sale of goods doctrine

Paragraph numbers marked with a "+" can be found online and on CD.

that the right of rejection is lost by "acceptance" (within the meaning of the Sale of Goods Act 1979 s.35) does not apply to hire-purchase agreements. The difference is small because the debtor under a hire-purchase agreement is subject to the doctrine of affirmation whereby he loses any right of rejection he may have when he affirms the contract (*U.C.B. Leasing Ltd v Holtom* [1987] C.C.L.R. 101; [1987] R.T.R. 82, CA). See also *Feldaroll Foundry Plc v Hermes Leasing (London) Ltd* [2004] EWCA Civ 747; [2004] C.C.L.R. 8.

In relation to remedies, the law relating to conditional sale agreements is exactly as just explained in relation to hire-purchase agreements. That is the effect of s.14, which, in relation to conditional sale agreements, disapplies s.11(4) of the Sale of Goods Act 1979.

For ss.8 to 11A and 14 to 15 of Supply of Goods (Implied Terms) Act 1973 (see Arrangement) plus any related commentary see paragraph 3H–530+ to 3H–545+ on White Book on Westlaw UK or the Civil Procedure CD.

Unfair Contract Terms Act 1977

3H–546

(1977 c.50)

ARRANGEMENT OF SECTIONS

PART I

INTRODUCTORY

Introductory Note

3H–547   This Act implemented, with some modifications, the recommendations in the Second Report on Exemption Clauses of the Law Commissions (Law. Com. No.69; Scot. Law Com. No.39). The Act does not apply to all contract terms, but only to those which purport to exempt or limit the liability of one of the parties to the contract. It restricts the ability of the parties to exclude or limit liability for: breach of contract, negligence or misrepresentation. It also restricts the exclusion of tortious liability by non-contractual notices. For legislation which applies to other contractual terms which are unfair: see the Unfair Terms in Consumer Contracts Regulations 1999 (below) and (in relation to unfair creditor/debtor relationships) the Consumer Credit Act 1974 ss.140A to 140C. Hitherto the privity of contract rule meant that generally speaking, a third party (X) could not rely upon a contractual exclusion clause in a contract between A and B, *Scruttons v Midland Silicones* [1962] A.C. 446. In such a case the provisions of the

Paragraph numbers marked with a "+" can be found online and on CD.

Unfair Contract Terms Act 1977 were irrelevant. The Contracts (Rights of Third Parties) Act 1999 has (subject to some exceptions) removed the inability of a third party to rely upon an exclusion clause where the clause was intended by the parties to benefit the third party and the third party was identified by name, class or description. In that case, the Unfair Contract Terms Act 1977 may then operate to restrict the effectiveness of the clause. A clause which is not affected by this Act may be rendered ineffective by the Unfair Terms in Consumer Contracts Regulations 1999 (see para.3H–886 below).

PART I

INTRODUCTORY

Scope of Part I

1.—(1) For the purposes of this Part of this Act, "negligence" means the breach— **3H–548**

 (a) of any obligation, arising from the express or implied terms of a contract, to take reasonable care or exercise reasonable skill in the performance of the contract;

 (b) of any common law duty to take reasonable care or exercise reasonable skill (but not any stricter duty);

 (c) of the common duty of care imposed by the Occupiers' Liability Act 1957 or the Occupiers' Liability Act (Northern Ireland) 1957.

(2) This Part of this Act is subject to Part III; and in relation to contracts, the operation of sections 2 to 4 and 7 is subject to the exceptions made by Schedule 1.

(3) In the case of both contract and tort, sections 2 to 7 apply (except where the contrary is stated in section 6(4)) only to business liability, that is liability for breach of obligations or duties arising—

 (a) from things done or to be done by a person in the course of a business (whether his own business or another's); or

 (b) from the occupation of premises used for business purposes of the occupier;

 and references to liability are to be read accordingly, but liability of an occupier of premises for breach of an obligation or duty towards a person obtaining access to the premises for recreational or educational purposes, being liability for loss or damage suffered by reason of the dangerous state of the premises, is not a business liability of the occupier unless granting that person such access for the purposes concerned falls within the business purposes of the occupier.

(4) In relation to any breach of duty or obligation, it is immaterial for any purpose of this Part of this Act whether the breach was inadvertent or intentional, or whether liability for it arises directly or vicariously.

Note —Amended by the Occupiers' Liability Act 1984 s.2. **3H–549**

Scope of Part I

Subsection (2) —The effect of Pt III is that the Act does not apply to: international **3H–550**

Paragraph numbers marked with a "+" can be found online and on CD.

supply contracts where possession or ownership of goods is to pass (s.26); foreign contracts where the parties have chosen English Law as the applicable law (s.27); exemption clauses allowed by UK legislation implementing international conventions (ss.28 and 29); and, contracts within Sch.1, para.1 of the Act. The latter include: insurance contracts; land transactions; formation and dissolution of companies; securities transactions. A contract of employment, which excluded the employer's liability for the employee's loss of share option rights in the event that the employee was wrongfully dismissed, related to the creation or transfer of securities (share option rights) and to that extent was outside the scope of the Act, *Micklefield v S.A.C. Technology Ltd* [1990] 1 W.L.R. 1002. Except in favour of a person dealing as a consumer, the Act, apart from s.2(1), does not apply to charterparties, marine salvage, contracts of carriage by ship or hovercraft (Sch.1, para.2).

3H–551   *Subsection (3)* —the expression "in the course of a business" has been held to have a restricted meaning in s.12. Even if that is correct in relation to s.12, it seems more likely that the expression here includes any transaction made by a business, whether or not such a transaction was the regular trade of that business. See the commentary to s.12.

AVOIDANCE OF LIABILITY FOR NEGLIGENCE, BREACH OF CONTRACTS, ETC.

Negligence liability

3H–552   **2.**—(1) A person cannot by reference to any contract term or to a notice given to persons generally or to particular persons exclude or restrict his liability for death or personal injury resulting from negligence.

(2) In the case of other loss or damage, a person cannot so exclude or restrict his liability for negligence except in so far as the term or notice satisfies the requirement of reasonableness.

(3) Where a contract term or notice purports to exclude or restrict liability for negligence a person's agreement to or awareness of it is not of itself to be taken as indicating his voluntary acceptance of any risk.

Negligence liability

3H–553   *Subsection (1)* —Two cases both concerned the same standard clause in a contract to hire a crane and driver. The clause provided that as between supplier and hirer, the driver would be regarded for all purposes as employee of the hirer. In *Phillips Products Ltd v Hyland* [1987] 1 W.L.R. 659 where the negligent driver drove the crane into a building belonging to the hirer, thereby damaging it, the hirer was the victim and claimed damages from the supplier for the negligence of the supplier's employee. The hirer succeeded in having the clause declared ineffective under subs.(2) as not satisfying the test of reasonableness. This case was distinguished in *Thomson v T. Lohan (Plant Hire) Ltd* [1987] 1 W.L.R. 649 where the driver brought a claim (successfully) against one employer (the hirer) for his injuries and the hirer sought to recover contribution from the supplier. The supplier was able to rely on the clause, since a clause which does not restrict the victim's ability to bring a claim but which merely apportions or allocates liability between potential defendants is not affected by s.2.

3H–554   *Subsection (2)* —For the requirement of reasonableness, see s.11. Even if a term satisfied the requirement of reasonableness, it would still be ineffective to exclude liability for negligence if either (a) it was not incorporated into the contract or (b) as a matter of construction, it does not operate to exclude liability for negligence or the loss in question. The language may not be sufficiently plain to exclude liability for negligence, *Hollier v Rambler Motors* [1972] 2 Q.B. 71. A disclaimer by a professional valuer giving a valuation of a house to a prospective lender and foreseeably relied

Paragraph numbers marked with a "+" can be found online and on CD.

upon by the borrower/buyer has been held invalid under this provision, *Smith v Eric S. Bush* [1990] 1 A.C. 381.

Liability arising in contract

3.—(1) This section applies as between contracting parties where **3H–555** one of them deals as consumer or on the other's written standard terms of business.

(2) As against that party, the other cannot by reference to any contract term—

    (a) when himself in breach of contract, exclude or restrict any liability of his in respect of the breach; or

    (b) claim to be entitled—

        (i) to render a contractual performance substantially different from that which was reasonably expected of him, or

        (ii) in respect of the whole or any part of his contractual obligation, to render no performance at all,

except in so far as (in any of the cases mentioned above in this subsection) the contract term satisfies the requirement of reasonableness.

Liability arising in contract

For the requirement of reasonableness, see s.11. For "deals as a consumer" see s.12. **3H–556** There is no definition of "standard terms of business". It certainly includes both (i) clauses prepared by a trade association or similar body for use generally in the trade and (ii) those prepared just by an individual contractor with no particular contract in mind.

Unreasonable indemnity clauses

4.—(1) A person dealing as consumer cannot by reference to any **3H–557** contract term be made to indemnify another person (whether a party to the contract or not) in respect of liability that may be incurred by the other for negligence or breach of contract, except in so far as the contract term satisfies the requirement of reasonableness.

(2) This section applies whether the liability in question—

    (a) is directly that of the person to be indemnified or is incurred by him vicariously:

    (b) is to the person dealing as consumer or to someone else.

LIABILITY ARISING FROM SALE OR SUPPLY OF GOODS

"Guarantee" of consumer goods

5.—(1) In the case of goods of a type ordinarily supplied for private **3H–558** use or consumption, where loss or damage—

    (a) arises from the goods proving defective while in consumer use; and

    (b) results from the negligence of a person concerned the manufacture or distribution of the goods,

liability for the loss or damage cannot be excluded or restricted by reference to any contract term or notice contained in or operating by reference to a guarantee of the goods.

Paragraph numbers marked with a "+" can be found online and on CD.

CONSUMER

(2) For these purposes—

    (a) goods are to be regarded as "in consumer use" when a person is using them, or has them in his possession for use, otherwise than exclusively for the purposes of a business; and

    (b) anything in writing is a guarantee if it contains or purports to contain some promise or assurance (however worded or presented) that defects will be made good by complete or partial replacement, or by repair, monetary compensation or otherwise.

(3) This section does not apply as between the parties to a contract under or in pursuance of which possession or ownership of the goods passed.

Sale and hire-purchase

3H–559   **6.**—(1) Liability for breach of the obligations arising from—

    (a) section 12 of the Sale of Goods Act 1979 (seller's implied undertakings as to title, etc.);

    (b) section 8 of the Supply of Goods (Implied Terms) Act 1973 (the corresponding thing in relation to hire-purchase),

cannot be excluded or restricted by reference to any contract term.

(2) As against *a* person dealing as consumer, liability for breach of the obligations arising from—

    (a) section 13, 14 or 15 of the 1979 Act (seller's implied undertakings as to conformity of goods with description or sample, or as to their quality or fitness for a particular purpose);

    (b) section 9, 10 or 11 of the 1973 Act (the corresponding things in relation to hire-purchase),

cannot be excluded or restricted by reference to any contract term.

(3) As against a person dealing otherwise than as consumer, the liability specified in subsection (2) above can be excluded or restricted by reference to a contract term, but only in so far as the term satisfies the requirement of reasonableness.

(4) The liabilities referred to in this section are not only the business liabilities defined by section 1(3), but include those arising under any contract of sale of goods or hire-purchase agreement.

3H–560   *Note* —Amended by the Sale of Goods Act 1979 s.63(2) and Sch.2.

Sale and hire-purchase

3H–561   This section restates provisions previously stated in the Sale of Goods Act 1893 s.55 as amended by the Supply of Goods (Implied Terms) Act 1973 and in the 1973 Act itself. For "dealing as a consumer", see s.12. For "requirement of reasonableness", see s.11 and Sch.2.

Miscellaneous contracts under which goods pass

3H–562   **7.**—(1) Where the possession or ownership of goods passes under

Paragraph numbers marked with a "+" can be found online and on CD.

or in pursuance of a contract not governed by the law of sale of goods or hire-purchase, subsections (2) to (4) below apply as regards the effect (if any) to be given to contract terms excluding or restricting liability for breach of obligation arising by implication of law from the nature of the contract.

(2) As against a person dealing as consumer, liability in respect of the goods' correspondence with description or sample, or their quality or fitness for any particular purpose, cannot be excluded or restricted by reference to any such term.

(3) As against a person dealing otherwise than as consumer, that liability can be excluded or restricted by reference to such a term, but only in so far as the term satisfies the requirement of reasonableness.

(3A) Liability for breach of the obligations arising under section 2 of the Supply of Goods and Services Act 1982 (implied terms about title etc. in certain contracts for the transfer of the property in goods) cannot be excluded or restricted by references to any such term.

(4) Liability in respect of—

    (a) the right to transfer ownership of the goods, or give possession; or

    (b) the assurance of quiet possession to a person taking goods in pursuance of the contract, cannot (in a case to which subsection (3A) above does not apply) be excluded or restricted by reference to any such term except in so far as the term satisfies the requirement of reasonableness.

3H–563

Note —Amended, and subs.(3A) added, by the Supply of Goods and Services Act 1982 s.17; subs.(5) repealed by The Regulatory Reform (Trading Stamps) Order 2005 (SI 2005/871).

Miscellaneous contracts

3H–564

The principal examples of contracts capable of falling within subs.(1) are: contracts of barter or exchange, contracts for services which involve the supply of goods; contracts of hire. See further, the commentary to the Sale of Goods Act 1979 s.2 (below).

OTHER PROVISIONS ABOUT CONTRACTS

Misrepresentation

3H–565

8.—(1) In the Misrepresentation Act 1967, the following is substituted for section 3— "Avoidance of provision excluding liability for misrepresentation

    3. If a contract contains a term which would exclude or restrict—

        (a) any liability to which a party to a contract may be subject by reason of any misrepresentation made by him before the contract was made; or

        (b) any remedy available to another party to the contract by reason of such a misrepresentation,

the term shall be of no effect except in so far as it satisfies the

Paragraph numbers marked with a "+" can be found online and on CD.

requirement of reasonableness as stated in section 11(1) of the Unfair Contract Terms Act 1977; and it is for those claiming that the term satisfies that requirement to show that it does"

(2) The same section is substituted for section 3 of the Misrepresentation Act (Northern Ireland) 1967.

Misrepresentation

3H–566   This section does not in any way qualify the right of a principal to limit the authority (actual or ostensible) of his agent, *Overbrooke Estates v Glencombe Park Properties* [1974] 1 W.L.R. 1335.

Effect of breach

3H–567   **9.**—(1) Where for reliance upon it a contract term has to satisfy the requirement of reasonableness, it may be found to do so and be given effect accordingly notwithstanding that the contract has been terminated either by breach or by a party electing to treat it as repudiated.

(2) Where on a breach the contract is nevertheless affirmed by a party entitled to treat it as repudiated, this does not of itself exclude the requirement of reasonableness in relation to any contract term.

Effect of breach

3H–568   If an exemption clause (a) is properly incorporated into the contract, (b), as a matter of construction, covers the breach in question and, (c) satisfies the requirement of reasonableness, then it may be relied upon notwithstanding the termination of the contract.

Evasion by means of secondary contract

3H–569   **10.** A person is not bound by any contract term prejudicing or taking away rights of his which arise under, or in connection with the performance of, another contract, so far as those rights extend to the enforcement of another's liability which this Part of this Act prevents that other from excluding or restricting.

Evasion by secondary contract

3H–570   This section applies only to clauses in a contract which seek to modify or exempt future liability and does not affect retrospective waivers of existing claims, *Tudor Grange Holdings Ltd v Citibank NA* [1992] Ch 53.

The "reasonableness" test

3H–571   **11.**—(1) In relation to a contract term, the requirement of reasonableness for the purposes of this Part of this Act, section 3 of the Misrepresentation Act 1967 and section 3 of the Misrepresentation Act (Northern Ireland) 1967 is that the term shall have been a fair and reasonable one to be included having regard to the circumstances which were, or ought reasonably to have been, known to or in the contemplation of the parties when the contract was made.

(2) In determining for the purposes of section 6 or 7 above whether a contract term satisfies the requirement of reasonableness, regard shall be had in particular to the matters specified in Schedule 2 to this Act; but this subsection does not prevent the court or arbitrator from holding, in accordance with any rule of law, that a term

Paragraph numbers marked with a "+" can be found online and on CD.

which purports to exclude or restrict any relevant liability is not a term of the contract.

(3) In relation to a notice (not being a notice having contractual effect), the requirement of reasonableness under this Act is that it should be fair and reasonable to allow reliance on it, having regard to all the circumstances obtaining when the liability arose or (but for the notice) would have arisen.

(4) Where by reference to a contract term or notice a person seeks to restrict liability to a specified sum of money, and the question arises (under this or any other Act) whether the term or notice satisfies the requirement of reasonableness, regard shall be had in particular (but without prejudice to subsection (2) above in the case of contract terms) to—

> (a) the resources which he could expect to be available to him for the purpose of meeting the liability should it arise; and
>
> (b) how far it was open to him to cover himself by insurance.

(5) It is for those claiming that a contract term or notice satisfies the requirement of reasonableness to show that it does.

The reasonableness test

In applying the test, the courts have to weigh relevant factors. When applying it for the purposes of ss.6 and 7 the court is given guidelines in Sch.2. These, however, are not exhaustive of the factors to be taken into account. The judge's task in weighing the various factors is akin to the exercise of a discretion and his decision on the issue of reasonableness will not be disturbed by an appellate court unless it proceeded on some erroneous principle or was plainly and obviously wrong, *Mitchell (George) v Finney Lock Seeds* [1983] 2 A.C. 803. In that case, a contract by which a farmer bought some seeds contained a clause limiting the liability of the sellers to no more than the purchase price of the seeds. The wrong seeds were supplied and the farmer's crop consequently failed. It was held in the House of Lords that the clause did not satisfy the test of reasonableness bearing in mind, inter alia, the following: (i) it had not been negotiated by any representative body; (ii) the buyers could not have discovered the error until after the crop had been sown; (iii) the buyers could not reasonably have been expected to cover the risk (of crop failure) by insurance whereas the sellers could easily, and at modest cost, have obtained liability insurance. An international computer firm's standard term limiting the firm's liability to a maximum of £100,000 has been held unreasonable, *St Albans DC v I.C.L. Ltd* [1996] 4 All E.R. 481, relevant factors including: (i) the parties were of unequal bargaining power; (ii) the limit of £100,000 was small in relation to the potential risk; (iii) the defendants held an aggregate of £50M of insurance cover world wide; (iv) the defendants were in a better position to insure. In assessing the reasonableness of a clause the court must consider the whole scope of the clause and not just that part upon which the defendant seeks to rely, *Stewart Gill Ltd v Horatio Myer & Co Ltd* [1992] Q.B. 600. In principle, a standard form clause which removes one party's right of set-off is subject to the requirement of reasonableness by virtue of s.3 as extended by s.13. Whether it will satisfy the requirement may depend upon whether the clause contains a further limitation of liability. In *Overland Shoes Ltd v Schenkers Ltd* [1998] 1 Lloyd's Rep. 498, a clause of the British International Freight Association which provided that customers must make prompt payment "without reduction or deferment on account of any claim, counterclaim or set-off" was held to satisfy the requirement. It had been drafted following wide consultation in the industry, was in common use, having been accepted by the trade as fair and reasonable and it merely defined the method of resolving competing claims, rather than seeking to limit liability. For more cases on the reasonableness test, see commentary to the Guidelines in Sch.2 below.

"Dealing as consumer"

12.—(1) A party to a contract "deals as consumer" in relation to another party if—

Paragraph numbers marked with a "+" can be found online and on CD.

3H–572

3H–573

    (a) he neither makes the contract in the course of a business nor holds himself out as doing so; and

    (b) the other party does make the contract in the course of a business; and

    (c) in the case of a contract governed by the law of sale of goods or hire-purchase, or by section 7 of this Act, the goods passing under or in pursuance of the contract are of a type ordinarily supplied for private use or consumption.

(1A) But if the first party mentioned in subsection (1) is an individual paragraph (c) of that subsection must be ignored.

(2) But the buyer is not in any circumstances to be regarded as dealing as consumer—

    (a) if he is an individual and the goods are second hand goods sold at public auction at which individuals have the opportunity of attending the sale in person;

    (b) if he is not an individual and the goods are sold by auction or by competitive tender.

3H–574   *Note*—Amended, and subs.(1A) added, by the Sale and Supply of Goods to Consumers Regulations 2002 (SI 2002/3045).

In the course of a business
3H–575   Where a business buys something in which it deals (e.g. a butcher buying meat) that is clearly a purchase in the course of a business. Where, however, a business buys something which is incidental to its business (e.g. the butcher buys a car for his business), then it has been held that the purchase is not "in the course of a business" unless the business makes such transactions regularly—two or three times in five years being insufficiently regular—*R & B Customs Brokers Co Ltd v United Dominions Trust* [1988] 1 W.L.R. 321. This decision seemed very doubtful in the light of the reasoning and the decision in *Stevenson v Rogers* [1999] 1 All E.R. 613, see commentary to Sale of Goods Act 1979 s.14. It was nevertheless followed and applied by the Court of Appeal in *Feldaroll Foundry Plc v Hermes Leasing (London) Ltd* [2004] EWCA Civ 747; [2004] C.C.L.R. 8. The amendments effected by the Sale and Supply of Goods to Consumers Regulations 2002 brought the definition of "dealing as a consumer" as it applies to non-corporate customers into line with the Directive on Certain Aspects of Sale of Goods and Consumer Guarantees (1999/3). See the Sale of Goods Act 1979 ss.14(2D) and 48A and commentaries, below.

Varieties of exemption clause
3H–576   **13.**—(1) To the extent that this Part of this Act prevents the exclusion or restriction of any liability it also prevents—

    (a) making the liability or its enforcement subject to restrictive or onerous conditions;

    (b) excluding or restricting any right or remedy in respect of the liability, or subjecting a person to any prejudice in consequence of his pursuing any such right or remedy;

    (c) excluding or restricting rules of evidence or procedure;

and (to that extent) sections 2 and 5 to 7 also prevent excluding or restricting liability by reference to terms and notices which exclude or restrict the relevant obligation or duty.

(2) But an agreement in writing to submit present or future dif-

Paragraph numbers marked with a "+" can be found online and on CD.

ferences to arbitration is not to be treated under this Part of this Act as excluding or restricting any liability.

Varieties of exemption clause

A clause which removes one party's right of set-off is a clause which excludes or restricts a right or remedy, see commentary to s.11 above.   **3H–577**

Interpretation of Part I

14. In this Part of this Act—   **3H–578**

"business" includes a profession and the activities of any government department or local or public authority;

"goods" has the same meaning as in the Sale of Goods Act 1979;

"hire-purchase agreement" has the same meaning as in the Consumer Credit Act 1974;

"negligence" had the meaning given by section 1(1);

"notice" includes an announcement, whether or not in writing, and any other communication or pretended communication; and

"personal injury" includes any disease and any impairment of physical or mental condition.

Note —Amended by the Sale of Goods Act 1979 s.63(2) and Sch.2.

* * * *

SCHEDULES   **3H–579**
SCHEDULE 2   **3H–580**

"GUIDELINES" FOR APPLICATION OF REASONABLENESS TEST

The matters to which regard is to be had in particular for the purposes of sections 6(3), 7(3) and (4), 20 and 21 are any of the following which appear to be relevant—

(a) the strength of the bargaining positions of the parties relative to each other, taking into account (among other things) alternative means by which the customer's requirements could have been met;

(b) whether the customer received an inducement to agree to the term, or in accepting it had an opportunity of entering into a similar contract with other persons, but without having to accept a similar term;

(c) whether the customer knew or ought reasonably to have known of the existence and extent of the term (having regard, among other things, to any custom of the trade and any previous course of dealing between the parties);

(d) where the term excludes or restricts any relevant liability if some condition is not complied with, whether it was reasonable at the time of the contract to expect that compliance with that condition would be practicable;

(e) whether the goods were manufactured, processed or adapted to the special order of the customer.

Guidelines for Application of Reasonableness Test

An exclusion clause may well be incorporated into the contract by virtue of being part of the small print on a standard form contract of one of the parties. The other party, typically a buyer, may not be aware of its existence or extent, e.g. may not have read the form or may not have understood it fully before signing it. Paragraph (c) of the Guidelines does not equate the position of a party who knows of the existence of an exclusion clause with a party who "ought to have known" of its existence: *Britvic Soft Drinks Ltd v Messer UK Ltd* [2002] 2 Lloyd's Rep. 368; [2002] EWCA Civ 548. A clause of which the buyer was unaware and which purported to exclude liability for lack of satisfactory quality or fitness for   **3H–581**

Paragraph numbers marked with a "+" can be found online and on CD.

purpose in a contract to sell an ingredient for use in making soft drinks failed the test in *Britvic*. Where, on the other hand, the buyer was aware of and had succeeded in getting amended (albeit not substantially) a clause excluding liability for consequential loss in a contract to supply software (which is notoriously liable to present problems), the clause was held to pass the test: *Watford Electronics Ltd v Sanderson CFL Ltd* [2001] 1 All E.R. (Comm) 696 and see also *SAM Business Systems Ltd v Hedley & Co* [2002] EWHC 2733; [2003] 1 All E.R.(Comm) 465.

Sale of Goods Act 1979

3H-582

(1979 c.54)

ARRANGEMENT OF SECTIONS

PART I

Paragraph numbers marked with a "+" can be found online and on CD.

Paragraph numbers marked with a "+" denote content that is available on White Book on Westlaw UK or the Civil Procedure CD.

Paragraph numbers marked with a "+" can be found online and on CD.

CONSUMER

For s.1 of the Sale of Goods Act 1979 (see Arrangement) plus any related commentary see paragraph 3H–583+ on White Book on Westlaw UK or the Civil Procedure CD.

Contract of sale

3H–584   **2.**—(1) A contract of sale of goods is a contract by which the seller transfers or agrees to transfer the property in goods to the buyer for a money consideration, called the price.

(2) There may be a contract of sale between one part owner and another.

(3) A contract of sale may be absolute or conditional.

(4) Where under a contract of sale the property in the goods is transferred from the seller to the buyer the contract is called a sale.

(5) Where under a contract of sale the transfer of the property in the goods is to take place at a future time or subject to some condition later to be fulfilled the contract is called an agreement to sell.

(6) An agreement to sell becomes a sale when the time elapses or the conditions are fulfilled subject to which the property in the goods is to be transferred.

Contracts of sale of goods

3H–585   Into contracts which are not contracts of sale of goods but which are analogous, terms are implied relating to goods supplied under the contract which terms are very similar to those implied in sale of goods contracts by ss.12–15 of the Sale of Goods Act. Those analogous contracts and the related implied terms provisions are as follows: hire-purchase agreements (Supply of Goods (Implied Terms) Act 1973 ss.8– 11); contracts of barter and contracts for services which involve the passing of property in goods (Supply of Goods and Services Act 1982 ss.2– 5A); contracts of hire (Supply of Goods and Services Act 1982 ss.6– 10A). Where under a contract no property in goods transfers and no goods are hired, it is possible that nevertheless goods are consumed in the course of providing a service to the customer—e.g. shampoo used in washing hair. In that case the common law may imply terms as to quality similar to those implied by statute in the above mentioned contracts, *Ingham v Emes* [1955] 2 Q.B. 366. A contract to supply computer software on disk is a sale of goods contract, whereas a contract to supply computer software in purely intangible form is not; in the latter case the court will be prepared to imply a term at common law that the software will be reasonably fit for its intended purpose, *St Albans DC v ICL* [1996] 4 All E.R. 481, CA.

For ss.3 to 10 of the Sale of Goods Act 1979 (see Arrangement) plus any related commentary see paragraphs 3H–586+ to 3H–596+ on White Book on Westlaw UK or the Civil Procedure CD.

When condition to be treated as warranty

3H–597   **11.**—(1) This section does not apply to Scotland.

(2) Where a contract of sale is subject to a condition to be fulfilled by the seller, the buyer may waive the condition, or may elect to treat the breach of the condition as a breach of warranty and not as a ground for treating the contract as repudiated.

(3) Whether a stipulation in a contract of sale is a condition, the breach of which may give rise to a right to treat the contract as

Paragraph numbers marked with a "+" can be found online and on CD.

repudiated, or a warranty, the breach of which may give rise to a claim for damages but not to a right to reject the goods and treat the contract as repudiated, depends in each case on the construction of the contract; and a stipulation may be a condition, though called a warranty in the contract.

(4) Subject to section 35A below where a contract of sale is not severable and the buyer has accepted the goods or part of them, the breach of a condition to be fulfilled by the seller can only be treated as a breach of warranty, and not as a ground for rejecting the goods and treating the contract as repudiated, unless there is an express or implied term of the contract to that effect.

(5) [...]

(6) Nothing in this section affects a condition or warranty whose fulfilment is excused by law by reason of impossibility or otherwise.

(7) Paragraph 2 of Schedule 1 below applies in relation to a contract made before 22 April 1967 or (in the application of this Act to Northern Ireland) 28 July 1967.

3H–598

Note —Subsection (1) substituted, subs.(4) amended and subs.(5) repealed by the Sale and Supply of Goods Act 1994 ss.3(2), 7, Sch.2, para.5(2), Sch.3.

For "acceptance" and the loss of right of rejection see ss.35 and 35A and commentaries, below.

Conditional sale agreements

3H–599

Subsection (4) does not—and thus the doctrine of "acceptance" does not—apply to a conditional sale agreement where the buyer deals as a consumer within s.12 of the Unfair Contract Terms Act 1977 (i.e. irrespective of whether the conditional sale agreement is regulated by the Consumer Credit Act 1974). In such a case the buyer's right to reject goods for breach of a condition is not lost by his "acceptance" but may be lost, as in the case of a hire-purchase agreement, by his affirmation of the contract. That is the effect of s.14 of the Supply of Goods (Implied Terms) Act 1973.

Implied terms about title, etc

3H–600

12.—(1) In a contract of sale, other than one to which subsection (3) below applies, there is an implied term on the part of the seller that in the case of a sale he has a right to sell the goods, and in the case of an agreement to sell he will have such a right at the time when the property is to pass.

(2) In a contract of sale, other than one to which subsection (3) below applies, there is also an implied term that—

   (a) the goods are free, and will remain free until the time when the property is to pass, from any charge or encumbrance not disclosed or known to the buyer before the contract is made, and

   (b) the buyer will enjoy quiet possession of the goods except so far as it may be disturbed by the owner or other person entitled to the benefit of any charge or encumbrance so disclosed or known.

(3) This subsection applies to a contract of sale in the case of which there appears from the contract or is to be inferred from its circumstances an intention that the seller should transfer only such title as he or a third person may have.

Paragraph numbers marked with a "+" can be found online and on CD.

CONSUMER

(4) In a contract to which subsection (3) above applies there is an implied term that all charges or encumbrances known to the seller and not known to the buyer have been disclosed to the buyer before the contract is made.

(5) In a contract to which subsection (3) above applies there is also an implied term that none of the following will disturb the buyer's quiet possession of the goods, namely—

    (a) the seller;

    (b) in a case where the parties to the contract intend that the seller should transfer only such title as a third person may have, that person;

    (c) anyone claiming through or under the seller or that third person otherwise than under a charge or encumbrance disclosed or known to the buyer before the contract is made.

(5A) As regards England and Wales and Northern Ireland, the term implied by subsection (1) above is a condition and the terms implied by subsections (2), (4) and (5) above are warranties.

(6) Paragraph 3 of Schedule 1below applies in relation to a contract made before 18 May 1973.

3H–601   *Note* —Subsections (1), (2), (4), (5) amended and subs.(5A) inserted by the Sale and Supply of Goods Act 1994 s.7, Sch.2, para.5(3).

Title to goods

3H–602   The classic example of a breach of the condition in s.12(1) is where the seller is not the owner and does not have the owner's authority to sell the goods. It makes no difference whether the seller knows that he is not the owner. He may honestly believe himself to be the owner (e.g. having in all innocence "bought" the goods from someone who had stolen them from the true owner). He is still in breach of this condition. It may be that the buyer does not discover until some months later that the seller was not the owner of the goods. If he then rejects the goods for breach of this condition, he is entitled to recover the whole of the purchase price as being money had and received on a total failure of consideration, *Rowland v Divall* [1923] 2 K.B. 500. This is so notwithstanding that the buyer has had the enjoyment of the goods for several months. The position is exactly the same where the contract is not a contract of sale of goods but one of hire-purchase, *Warman v Southern Counties Finance* [1949] 2 K.B. 576 (approved in *Barber v N.W.S. Bank* [1996] 1 W.L.R. 641, CA). For the corresponding condition as to title in contracts of hire-purchase, see Supply of Goods (Implied Terms) Act 1973 s.8.

The buyer's right to reject the goods for breach of the condition in s.12(1) is, apparently, not lost by his "acceptance" of the goods within the meaning of s.35. It will be lost, however, if the title is "fed" to him, *Butterworth v Kingsway Motors* [1954] 1 W.L.R. 1286. This typically occurs where the buyer buys goods from someone who acquired them on hire-purchase or conditional sale terms and who at the time of the sale has not become the owner (i.e. because he has not completed his instalment payments under the hire-purchase or conditional sale agreement). Here the seller is in breach of the implied condition as to title. If, however, at some later stage he completes his instalment payments, then the seller will at that moment acquire title which automatically and immediately will be fed to his buyer. If at that moment the buyer has not already rejected the goods, then he loses that right. He does, however, have a claim for damages (see s.53(1)) and the prima facie measure of damages will be the difference between the value of the goods at the time when the buyer should have acquired good title and their (lower) value at the time he did acquire good title, *Butterworth v Kingsway Motors* (above).

Normally, someone who sells goods which he does not own (and who does not have the owner's authority to sell) cannot transfer title to the buyer. *Nemo dat quod non*

Paragraph numbers marked with a "+" can be found online and on CD.

habet—a seller cannot give a good title which he does not himself have (Sale of Goods Act 1979 s.21(1)). There are, however, some exceptions to this principle, the main ones being: (i) where the true owner is estopped from asserting that the sale was unauthorised; (ii) where the seller is a mercantile agent in possession of the goods with the consent of the owner, is acting in the ordinary course of business of a mercantile agent and sells the goods to someone who takes in good faith and is unaware that the seller has no authority to make the sale (Factors Act 1889 s.2(1)); (iii) where the seller has a voidable title to the goods and that title has not been avoided at the time of the sale and the seller sells to someone buying in good faith without notice of the seller's defect of title (Sale of Goods Act 1979 s.23); (iv) where the seller is someone who has already sold the goods to someone else but who has retained the goods (or documents of title) and who then sells and delivers them to the buyer who receives them in good faith without notice of the earlier sale (Sale of Goods Act 1979 s.24); (v) where the seller is someone who had agreed to buy the goods and who has taken delivery of them but to whom property (title) has not yet passed and who sells and delivers them (or the documents of title) to a buyer who receives them in good faith and without notice of the rights of the original seller (Sale of Goods Act 1979 s.25). The latter exception (in s.25) does not apply where the contract under which the seller had acquired the goods was a hire-purchase agreement, because in that case the seller is not a "buyer", i.e. someone who has "bought or agreed to buy", *Helby v Matthews* [1895] A.C. 471, *Close Asset Finance v Care Graphics Machinery Ltd* [2000] C.C.L.R. 43. Nor does this exception apply where the contract under which the seller had acquired the goods is a conditional sale agreement which is a consumer credit agreement within the meaning of the Consumer Credit Act 1974 (Sale of Goods Act 1979 s.25(2)).

There is a further exception (in the Hire Purchase Act 1964 s.27) which applies only to the sale of motor vehicles. This applies where the seller is someone who is hiring the vehicle under a hire-purchase agreement or buying it under a conditional sale agreement and who, before he acquires title, sells the vehicle to a "private purchaser" who is bona fide and unaware of any relevant hire-purchase or conditional sale agreement. In that case the innocent private purchaser obtains good title to the vehicle (or, more accurately, such title as belonged to the person from whom the seller had acquired the vehicle on hire-purchase or conditional sale terms). A buyer who is aware only of a hire purchase agreement under which all the payments have been made is still an innocent purchaser (*Barker v Bell* 1 W.L.R. 983) as also is a buyer who originally had suspicions but whose suspicions had at the time he bought the car been laid to rest, *Dodds v Yorkshire Bank Finance Ltd* [1992] C.C.L.R. 92, CA. Someone who is carrying on business in the motor trade (whether as dealer or as finance house) is not a private purchaser—and that is so even if he is buying for his private (and not his business) purposes, *Stevenson v Beverley Bentinck* [1976] 1 W.L.R. 483 and see also *G.E. Capital Bank Ltd v Rushton and Jenking* [2005] EWCA Civ 1556; [2006] 1 W.L.R. 899. Where the purchaser is not a private purchaser and then himself sells the vehicle, then the first private purchaser who buys the vehicle thereafter will, providing he is bona fide and without notice, acquire title by virtue of the Hire Purchase Act 1964 s.27. Notwithstanding that an innocent private purchaser obtains good title to the vehicle by virtue of s.27, he still has the same right to reject the vehicle (and reclaim all money paid) as if s.27 did not apply (*Barber v NWS Bank* [1996] 1 W.L.R. 641). This is because nothing in s.27 exonerates the seller from any liability he would have been under apart from the section (s.27(3)).

Subsection (2) —Where the seller supplies goods which involve an infringement of the trade mark rights of a third party, that will amount to a breach of the condition in s.12(1) and also of the warranty of quiet possession, *Niblett Ltd v Confectioners' Materials Co* [1921] 3 K.B. 387. Where after the sale a third party obtained a patent and brought patent proceedings against the buyers to enforce the patent, the sellers were not in breach of the condition in s.12(1) which related to the time of the sale but were in breach of the warranty that "the buyer *will* enjoy quiet possession", *Microbeads v Vinhurst Road Markings* [1975] 1 W.L.R. 218.

Subsection (3) —A seller might, for example, acknowledge that he has only a limited title where he has found the goods which he is selling—a finder having only a limited, possessory, title.

Exclusion

It is not possible to contract out of liability for breach of the undertakings under **3H–603**

Paragraph numbers marked with a "+" can be found online and on CD.

s.12 where the liability is a business liability, see ss.1(3) and 6(1) of the Unfair Contract Terms Act 1977.

Sale by description

3H–604   **13.**—(1) Where there is a contract for the sale of goods by description, there is an implied term that the goods will correspond with the description.

(1A) As regards England and Wales and Northern Ireland, the term implied by subsection (1) above is a condition.

(2) If the sale is by sample as well as by description it is not sufficient that the bulk of the goods corresponds with the sample if the goods do not also correspond with the description.

(3) A sale of goods is not prevented from being a sale by description by reason only that, being exposed for sale or hire, they are selected by the buyer.

(4) Paragraph 4 of Schedule 1below applies in relation to a contract made before 18 May 1973.

3H–605   *Note* —Subsection (1) amended and subs.(1A) inserted by the Sale and Supply of Goods Act 1994 s.7, Sch.2, para.5(4).

By description

3H–606   It is a sale by description if the item is sold as corresponding to a description and the buyer placed some (but not necessarily exclusive) reliance upon the description, *Grant v Australian Knitting Mills* [1936] A.C. 85; *Beale v Taylor* [1967] 1 W.L.R. 1193. If it is not within the reasonable contemplation of the parties that the buyer is relying on the description, then it is not a sale by description, *Harlingdon & Leinster Enterprises Ltd v Christopher Hull Fine Art Ltd* [1991] 1 Q.B. 564 (painting attributed by seller to a painter of the German impressionist school when both seller and buyer knew that the buyer had, and the seller did not have, expertise and knowledge of the German expressionist school). If some of the goods supplied are outside the contract description, then that amounts to a breach of the condition, *Pinnock Bros. v Lewis & Peat* [1923] 1 K.B. 690 (castor oil included in goods supplied under contract to sell "copra cake"). The fact that the goods are of poor quality does not of itself indicate a failure to correspond with description. The key to the concept of description is "identification", not "quality", *Ashington Piggeries v Hill* [1972] A.C. 441. An expression in the contract which refers to quality (e.g. "fair average quality for the season"), though usually not part of the description and therefore not relevant to a claim under s.13, will nevertheless amount to an express term (albeit probably only a warranty and not a condition) of the contract.

Exclusion and remedies

3H–607   For the buyer's rights of rejection and to claim damages, see ss.11, 15A, 35, 35A and 53. For restrictions on the ability to exclude or limit the seller's liability, see Unfair Contract Terms Act 1977 ss.1– 6.

Implied terms about quality or fitness

3H–608   **14.**—(1) Except as provided by this section and section 15below and subject to any other enactment, there is no implied term about the quality or fitness for any particular purpose of goods supplied under a contract of sale.

(2) Where the seller sells goods in the course of a business, there is an implied term that the goods supplied under the contract are of satisfactory quality.

(2A) For the purposes of this Act, goods are of satisfactory quality

Paragraph numbers marked with a "+" can be found online and on CD.

if they meet the standard that a reasonable person would regard as satisfactory, taking account of any description of the goods, the price (if relevant) and all the other relevant circumstances.

(2B) For the purposes of this Act, the quality of goods includes their state and condition and the following (among others) are in appropriate cases aspects of the quality of goods—

(a) fitness for all the purposes for which goods of the kind in question are commonly supplied.

(b) appearance and finish,

(c) freedom from minor defects,

(d) safety, and

(e) durability.

(2C) The term implied by subsection (2) above does not extend to any matter making the quality of goods unsatisfactory—

(a) which is specifically drawn to the buyer's attention before the contract is made,

(b) where the buyer examines the goods before the contract is made, which that examination ought to reveal, or

(c) in the case of a contract for sale by sample, which would have been apparent on a reasonable examination of the sample.

(2D) If the buyer deals as consumer or, in Scotland, if a contract of sale is a consumer contract, the relevant circumstances mentioned in subsection (2A) above include any public statements on the specific characteristics of the goods made about them by the seller, the producer or his representative, particularly in advertising or on labelling.

(2E) A public statement is not by virtue of subsection (2D) above a relevant circumstance for the purposes of subsection (2A) above in the case of a contract of sale, if the seller shows that—

(a) at the time the contract was made, he was not, and could not reasonably have been, aware of the statement,

(b) before the contract was made, the statement had been withdrawn in public or, to the extent that it contained anything which was incorrect or misleading, it had been corrected in public, or

(c) the decision to buy the goods could not have been influenced by the statement.

(2F) Subsections (2D) and (2E) above do not prevent any public statement from being a relevant circumstance for the purposes of subsection (2A) above (whether or not the buyer deals as consumer or, in Scotland, whether or not the contract of sale is a consumer contract) if the statement would have been such a circumstance apart from those subsections.

(3) Where the seller sells goods in the course of a business and the buyer, expressly or by implication, makes known—

(a) to the seller, or

(b) where the purchase price or part of it is payable by instalments and the goods were previously sold by a credit-broker to the seller, to that credit-broker,

Paragraph numbers marked with a "+" can be found online and on CD.

CONSUMER

any particular purpose for which the goods are being bought, there is an implied term that the goods supplied under the contract are reasonably fit for that purpose, whether or not that is a purpose for which such goods are commonly supplied, except where the circumstances show that the buyer does not rely, or that it is unreasonable for him to rely, on the skill or judgment of the seller or credit-broker.

(4) An implied term about quality or fitness for a particular purpose may be annexed to a contract of sale by usage.

(5) The preceding provisions of this section apply to a sale by a person who in the course of a business is acting as agent for another as they apply to a sale by a principal in the course of a business, except where that other is not selling in the course of a business and either the buyer knows that fact or reasonable steps are taken to bring it to the notice of the buyer before the contract is made.

(6) As regards England and Wales and Northern Ireland, the terms implied by subsection (2) and (3) above are conditions.

(7) Paragraph 5 of Schedule 1 below applies in relation to a contract made on or after 18 May 1973 and before the appointed day, and paragraph 6 in relation to one made before 18 May 1973.

(8) In subsection (7) above and paragraph 5 of Schedule 1 below references to the appointed day are to the day appointed for the purposes of those provisions by an order of the Secretary of State made by statutory instrument.

3H–609   *Note* —Subsections (3) and (4) amended, subss.(2)–(2C) substituted for original subs.(2) and subs.(6) inserted by the Sale and Supply of Goods Act 1994 ss.1(1), 7, Sch.2, para.5(5); subss.(2D)–(2F) inserted by SI 2002/3045.

Goods supplied in the course of a business
3H–610   The implied terms apply to second hand as well as new goods. They apply also not only to the goods bought but also to other goods "supplied", e.g. a returnable bottle, even though the ownership in those goods is not to transfer to the buyer, *Geddling v Marsh* [1920] 1 K.B. 668. Apparently, in the case of a book or computer disk they apply not only to the tangible item but also to the information or program within it, *obiter* in *St Albans DC v ICL* [1996] 4 All E.R. 481, CA. The expression "in the course of a business" includes all sales of goods made by businesses, whether or not the sale of such goods was the regular trade of that business, *Stevenson v Rogers* [1999] Q.B. 1028; [1999] 2 W.L.R. 1064; [1999] 1 All E.R. 613 (distinguishing *R & B Customs Brokers Co Ltd v United Dominions Trust* [1988] 1 W.L.R. 321, a case decided under Unfair Contract Terms Act 1977 s.12).

Subsection (5) —where the (selling) agent is acting in the course of a business and the principal (seller) is not selling in the course of a business and the buyer is unaware of the latter fact and reasonable steps have not been taken to bring it to the buyer's attention, the buyer is entitled to rely on s.14 to bring proceedings against the principal (the seller), *Boyter v Thomson* [1995] 2 A.C. 628.

Satisfactory quality
3H–611   The Sale and Supply of Goods Act 1994 implemented recommendations in the Law Commission Final Report, *Sale and Supply of Goods* (1987), (Law Com. No.160 Cm. 137). Subsections 14(2) to (2C) replaced the previous subs.(2) thereby substituting "satisfactory quality" for the old expression "merchantable quality" and introducing the revised definition in subss.14(2A) and 14(2B). This refers to the goods' fitness for the purposes for which such goods are commonly supplied. In the case of a motor vehicle those purposes include not merely the purpose of driving it from place to place but of

Paragraph numbers marked with a "+" can be found online and on CD.

doing so with the appropriate degree of comfort, ease of handling and pride in the vehicle's outward and interior appearance: *Rogers v Parish (Scarborough) Ltd* [1987] Q.B. 933 (decided under the old definition of "merchantable quality" but still authoritative). The relative weight to be attached to the different characteristics of the vehicle depends on the market at which it is aimed. On a vehicle sold as new, the performance and finish to be expected are those of a model of average standard with no mileage—and no less is expected of a vehicle sold with a manufacturer's warranty. The same general approach is to be taken in the case of a second hand vehicle, though defects unacceptable on a new car, might be acceptable on a second hand model. It is a matter of degree, bearing in mind various factors including especially the price. Examples are: *Lee v York Coach and Marine* [1977] R.T.R. 35 (car unmerchantable when brakes were in such a state that they would have failed if driver had to perform an emergency stop); *Bartlett v Sydney Marcus* [1965] 1 W.L.R. 1013 (car not unmerchantable when one month after purchase it required new clutch—buyer had turned down seller's offer at time of sale to supply the car with new clutch fitted if buyer agreed to pay £25 extra); *Shine v General Guarantee Finance Co Ltd* [1988] 1 All E.R. 911 (20 month old Fiat held unmerchantable because, unknown to the buyer, it had been treated as a "write off" after being submerged in water for over 24 hours); *Crowther v Shannon* [1975] 1 W.L.R. 30 (eight year old Jaguar with 82,000 miles on clock, seized up after three weeks and 2,300 miles—held unfit for purpose under subs.14(3)); *Bramhill v Edwards* [2004] EWCA Civ 403, [2004] 2 Lloyd's Rep. 653 (American motorhome 102 inches wide sold for use on UK roads where it was illegal to use such a vehicle exceeding 100 inches in width, held to be of satisfactory quality in the light of evidence that the authorities turned a blind eye to such illegality and that such motorhomes were used by enthusiasts who knew of their non-compliance with the regulations). For an extended discussion of the requirement of satisfactory quality in relation to a contract to supply a computer system comprising hardware and software to a business, see *Anglo Group Plc v Winther Browne & Co Ltd* (2000) 144 S.J.L.B. 197; [2000] I.T.C.L.R. 559, available on the Court Service website.

Subsection (2C) —(a) where the defect is drawn to the buyer's attention but he is reasonably of the (erroneous) opinion that the defect can and will be rectified at no cost to himself, then the implied term may well not be excluded, per Neill L.J. in *R & B Customs Brokers Co Ltd v United Dominions Trust* [1988] 1 W.L.R. 321. (b) The buyer cannot complain of defects he should have discovered during any examination he made of the goods. Apparently, if the buyer made no examination, then this provision does not apply.

Subsections (2D) to (2F) —added by the Sale and Supply of Goods to Consumers Regulations 2002, these subsections implement art.2 of Directive on Certain Aspects of Sale of Goods and Consumer Guarantees (1999/44), which provides for the seller to be made liable for public statements made by the seller, the producer or his representative. Similar amendments were at the same time made to the Supply of Goods and Services Act 1982 ss.4 and 9 and to the Supply of Goods (Implied Terms) Act 1973 s.10. For the latter, see paras 3H–527 and 3H–536+ above.

Fitness for purpose

For the condition to be implied the buyer must make known to the seller the particular purpose for which the goods are required. The buyer may have made known a particular purpose (e.g. that he wants a garment to wear) but failed to indicate some particular idiosyncrasy of his intended use of them (e.g. that his skin is abnormally sensitive to contracting dermatitis). There is no breach of the term as to fitness for purpose where the failure of the goods to meet the intended purpose arises from an abnormal feature or idiosyncrasy, not made known to the seller, in the buyer or in the circumstances of the use of the goods by the buyer, *Slater v Finning* [1997] A.C. 473. That is so even if the buyer was himself unaware of the abnormal feature or idiosyncrasy.

Subsection (3)(b) applies to the situation where the buyer acquires the goods on conditional sale or credit sale terms in the typical triangular transaction, i.e. where the dealer (the credit broker) sells the goods to a finance company (the seller) which then contracts to supply them to the buyer on the aforesaid instalment terms; it is sufficient that the buyer has informed the dealer of the particular purpose. This is so irrespec-

3H–612

Paragraph numbers marked with a "+" can be found online and on CD.

CONSUMER

tive of whether the resulting contract is a consumer credit agreement regulated by the Consumer Credit Act 1974. If, however, the resulting contract is one of hire-purchase, then the Sale of Goods Act does not apply to it but it will instead contain virtually identical terms (similar to those in ss.12–15 of the Sale of Goods Act) implied by the Supply of Goods (Implied Terms) Act 1973 ss.8– 11.

Where goods are to be made to a specification supplied by the buyer, the buyer will still be placing reliance on the seller's skill and judgment in some respects (e.g. in regard to matters not covered by the specification). If the goods' subsequent unfitness for their intended purpose relates to the sphere of reliance placed upon the seller, the buyer will have a claim, *Cammell Laird & Co Ltd v Manganese Bronze & Brass Co Ltd* [1934] A.C. 402.

The implied term requires the goods to continue to be fit for the intended purpose for a reasonable period after delivery, so long as they remain in the same apparent state and condition as when they were delivered, apart from normal wear and tear, *Lambert v Lewis* [1982] A.C. 225. Often in practice, where goods are being put to a conventional use, there is little, if any, distinction between liability under s.14(3) and s.14(2), see e.g. *Crowther v Shannon*, above. Liability is strict and does not depend upon proof of negligence, *Frost v Aylesbury Dairy Co* [1905] 1 K.B. 608.

Exclusion and remedies

3H–613 For the buyer's rights of rejection and to claim damages, see ss.11, 15A, 35, 35A and 53. For restrictions on the ability to exclude or limit the seller's liability, see Unfair Contract Terms Act 1977 ss.1– 6.

SALE BY SAMPLE

Sale by sample

3H–614 **15.**—(1) A contract of sale is a contract for sale by sample where there is an express or implied term to that effect in the contract.

(2) In the case of a contract for sale by sample there is an implied term—

(a) that the bulk will correspond with the sample in quality;

(b) [...]

(c) that the goods will be free from any defect, making their quality unsatisfactory, which would not be apparent on reasonable examination of the sample.

(3) As regards England and Wales and Northern Ireland, the term implied by subsection (2) above is a condition.

(4) Paragraph 7 of Schedule 1below applies in relation to a contract made before 18 May 1973.

3H–615 *Note* —Subsection (2) amended and subs.(3) substituted by the Sale and Supply of Goods Act 1994 ss.1(2), 7, Sch.2, para.5(6), Sch.3.

[MISCELLANEOUS]

3H–616 *Note* —Inserted by the Sale and Supply of Goods Act 1994 s.4(1).

Modification of remedies for breach of condition in non-consumer cases

3H–617 15A.—(1) Where in the case of a contract of sale—

(a) the buyer would, apart from this subsection, have the right to reject goods by reason of a breach on the part of the seller of a term implied by section 13, 14or 15above, but

Paragraph numbers marked with a "+" can be found online and on CD.

> (b) the breach is so slight that it would be unreasonable for him to reject them,

then, if the buyer does not deal as consumer, the breach is not to be treated as a breach of condition but may be treated as a breach of warranty.

(2) This section applies unless a contrary intention appears in, or is to be implied from, the contract.

(3) It is for the seller to show that a breach fell within subsection (1)(b) above.

(4) This section does not apply to Scotland.

3H–618

Note —Section 15A was added with effect from January 3, 1995 by the Sale and Supply of Goods Act 1994, which implemented the recommendations in the Law Commission Final Report, *Sale and Supply of Goods* (1987), (Law Com. No.160 Cm. 137). "Dealing as a consumer" has the same meaning as in the Unfair Contract Terms Act 1977 s.12 (see s.61(5A) of the Sale of Goods Act 1979, as inserted by the Sale and Supply of Goods Act 1994). For s.12 of the 1977 Act see para.3H–573 above.

For ss.15B to 33 of the Sale of Goods Act 1979 (see Arrangement) plus any related commentary see paragraphs 3H–619+ to 3H–648+ on White Book on Westlaw UK or the Civil Procedure CD.

Buyer's right of examining goods

34.—(1) Unless otherwise agreed when the seller tenders delivery of the goods to the buyer, he is bound on request to afford the buyer a reasonable opportunity of examining the goods for the purpose of ascertaining whether they are in conformity with the contract and, in the case of a contract for sale by sample, of comparing the bulk with the sample.

3H–649

Note —Amended with effect from January 3, 1995 by the Sale and Supply of Goods Act 1994. See further the commentary to s.35.

3H–650

Acceptance

35.—(1) The buyer is deemed to have accepted the goods subject to subsection (2) below—

3H–651

> (a) when he intimates to the seller that he has accepted them, or
> (b) when the goods have been delivered to him and he does any act in relation to them which is inconsistent with the ownership of the seller.

(2) Where goods are delivered to the buyer, and he has not previously examined them, he is not deemed to have accepted them under subsection (1) above until he has had a reasonable opportunity of examining them for the purpose—

> (a) of ascertaining whether they are in conformity with the contract, and
> (b) in the case of a contract for sale by sample, of comparing the bulk with the sample.

(3) Where the buyer deals as consumer or (in Scotland) the contract of sale is a consumer contract, the buyer cannot lose his right to rely on subsection (2) above by agreement, waiver or otherwise.

(4) The buyer is also deemed to have accepted the goods when after the lapse of a reasonable time he retains the goods without intimating to the seller that he has rejected them.

Paragraph numbers marked with a "+" can be found online and on CD.

CONSUMER

(5) The questions that are material in determining for the purposes of subsection (4) above whether a reasonable time has elapsed include whether the buyer has had a reasonable opportunity of examining the goods for the purpose mentioned in subsection (2) above.

(6) The buyer is not by virtue of this section deemed to have accepted the goods merely because—(a) he asks for, or agrees to, their repair by or under an arrangement with the seller, or (b) the goods are delivered to another under a sub-sale or other disposition.

(7) Where the contract is for the sale of goods making one or more commercial units, a buyer accepting any goods included in a unit is deemed to have accepted all the goods making the unit; and in this subsection "commercial unit" means a unit division of which would materially impair the value of the goods or the character of the unit.

(8) Paragraph 10 of Schedule 1 below applies in relation to a contract made before 22 April 1967 or (in the application of this Act to Northern Ireland) 28 July 1967.

3H–652   *Note* —Amended, and subs.(7) added, with effect from January 3, 1995 by the Sale and Supply of Goods Act 1994.

Acceptance

3H–653   Acceptance of the goods (within the meaning of s.35) removes any right the buyer might have to reject the goods for breach of condition (see s.11(4) above). Loss of that right still leaves the buyer with a claim for damages, see s.53. In *Bernstein v Pamson Motors (Golders Green) Ltd* [1987] 2 All E.R. 220, it was held, at first instance, that acceptance occurred after lapse of a length of time which was reasonable for the buyer to try out the goods generally, which in that case was held to be less than three weeks after the buyer took delivery of a new car. That decision, however, no longer represents the law: *Clegg v Andersson* (below). One purpose of the amendments made by the 1994 Act was to allow the buyer an opportunity to check the goods to see if they conform to the contract, before the buyer is deemed to have lost his right to reject the goods for breach of condition. It is quite possible that long, perhaps months or years, after the buyer examined them for conformity and (let us assume) was unable to find any suggestion of non-conformity, the goods might prove not to have been of satisfactory quality. A reasonable period of time will not necessarily last years, however. An opportunity to examine the goods for conformity is not a guarantee that such an examination will necessarily be capable of discovering any non-conformity. Another purpose of the 1994 amendments was to encourage informal attempts at cure. Thus the buyer is now not taken to have accepted the goods simply because he asks for or agrees to their repair: s.35(6). Similarly he is entitled to a reasonable period to ascertain what would be required for modification or repair. In *Clegg v Andersson* [2003] EWCA Civ 320; [2003] 2 Lloyd's Rep. 32, the buyers had contracted to buy a new yacht costing £236,000, which when they took delivery had a keel which was dangerously overweight. The buyers returned the vessel to the seller after a few days and were not prepared to agree to repairs/modifications proposed by the seller until (a) the seller had first supplied them with details (with drawings and calculations) as to what was proposed and (b) the buyers had been able to take professional advice in the light of that information. When after approximately a further six months the seller supplied the information, the buyers took less than three weeks to reject the yacht. The Court held that the buyers had not accepted the yacht and had validly rejected it. A buyer is entitled to a reasonable period to ascertain what is required for modification or repair and in this case time had not begun to run until the buyers were given the requested information which was necessary for them to make a decision. There is, however, no general rule that acceptance cannot take place whilst the buyer is seeking information about possible alleged breaches of contract and possible cures for them: see *Jones v Callagher* [2004] EWCA Civ 10; [2004] 1 Lloyd's Rep.377, an ordinary case, where the

Paragraph numbers marked with a "+" can be found online and on CD.

defects in the goods (kitchen fitments) were obvious needing no expert to identify them and where a purported rejection five months after delivery was held to be too late. *Truk (UK) Ltd v Tokmakidis GmbH* [2000] 1 Lloyd's Rep. 543 involved a contract between two businesses for the sale and fitting of some lifting equipment to be paid for six months after delivery. The equipment was to be fitted to, and form part of, a towing vehicle which the buyer was then going to resell. Approximately six months after delivery the buyer was informed by a potential purchaser of the towing vehicle that the equipment was defective. The buyer immediately informed the seller and refused to pay the price pending investigation (by an appropriate company). About three months later, promptly upon receipt of the result of the investigation which confirmed the allegation, the buyer unequivocally rejected the goods. The judge held as follows. Where goods are sold for resale, a reasonable time in which to give notice of rejection should normally be the time actually taken to resell the goods, together with an additional period in which they can be inspected and tried out (by the sub-purchaser). Where the price is payable at a date after delivery, that reasonable period of time should normally last at least until the date for payment. The reasonable time had not expired when about six months after delivery, the buyer first questioned compliance. The buyer was entitled to a further period in which to investigate that issue. Accordingly the buyer had not accepted the goods when he validly rejected them nine months after delivery.

In *J & H Ritchie Ltd v Lloyd Ltd* [2007] 1 W.L.R. 670 (HL), s.35(6)(a) meant that the buyer's agreement to have faulty goods inspected and, if possible, repaired was not deemed an acceptance. It was an implied term of the inspection and repair agreement that during its currency the buyer would not exercise his right of rejection. It not being immediately obvious what was the nature of the defect or what could be done to correct it, it was a further implied term of the inspection and repair agreement that the seller would, if requested, provide information to enable the buyer to make an informed decision as to whether to accept the goods after they had been repaired. Failing provision of that information, the buyer was entitled to reject the goods.

Commercial Unit

Subsection (7) creates an exception to the rule in s.35A which rule allows the buyer to accept conforming goods without losing the right to reject non-conforming goods. For example, accepting volume A to M of a two volume dictionary would amount to acceptance of the other volume and thus prevent the buyer being able to reject either volume. Whether a three-piece suite amounts to a commercial unit would be a nice question of fact. **3H–654**

Right of partial rejection

35A.—(1) If the buyer— **3H–655**

    (a) has the right to reject the goods by reason of a breach on the part of the seller that affects some or all of them, but

    (b) accepts some of the goods, including, where there are any goods unaffected by the breach, all such goods,

he does not by accepting them lose his right to reject the rest.

(2) In the case of a buyer having the right to reject an instalment of goods, subsection (1) above applies as if references to the goods were references to the goods comprised in the instalment.

(3) For the purposes of subsection (1) above, goods are affected by a breach if by reason of the breach they are not in conformity with the contract.

(4) This section applies unless a contrary intention appears in, or is to be implied from, the contract.

Note —Inserted by the Sale and Supply of Goods Act 1994 ss.3(1), 8(2). **3H–656**

Right of partial rejection

The amendments made by the 1994 Act were designed, amongst other things, to **3H–657**

Paragraph numbers marked with a "+" can be found online and on CD.

CONSUMER

enable the buyer to accept conforming goods without thereby losing the right to reject goods which did not conform to the contract. Where the contract is not severable and the buyer accepts some *but not all* of the *conforming* goods, then subs.(1) will not apply, with the result that, applying s.11(4), the buyer will have lost the right to reject any of the goods whether conforming or not. Acceptance of part of a "commercial unit" amounts to acceptance of all of it, see s.35(7).

Buyer not bound to return rejected goods

3H–658 **36.** Unless otherwise agreed, where goods are delivered to the buyer, and he refuses to accept them, having the right to do so, he is not bound to return them to the seller, but it is sufficient if he intimates to the seller that he refuses to accept them.

3H–659 *Note*—The buyer is entitled to claim reasonably incurred storage expenses, if the seller fails to collect goods which the buyer has rightly rejected, *Kolfor Plant Ltd v Tilbury Plant Ltd* (1977) 121 S.J. 390. The buyer has no lien over rejected goods to enforce the return of the purchase price, *Lyons v May & Baker* [1923] 1 K.B. 695.

For ss.37 to 48 of the Sale of Goods Act 1979 (see Arrangement) plus any related commentary see paragraphs 3H–660+ to 3H–672+ on White Book on Westlaw UK or the Civil Procedure CD.

PART 5A

ADDITIONAL RIGHTS OF BUYER IN CONSUMER CASE

3H–673 *Note*—Inserted by SI 2002/3045.

Introductory

3H–674 **48A.**—(1) This section applies if—

(a) the buyer deals as consumer or, in Scotland, there is a consumer contract in which the buyer is a consumer, and

(b) the goods do not conform to the contract of sale at the time of delivery.

(2) If this section applies, the buyer has the right—

(a) under and in accordance with section 48B below, to require the seller to repair or replace the goods, or

(b) under and in accordance with section 48C below—

(i) to require the seller to reduce the purchase price of the goods to the buyer by an appropriate amount, or

(ii) to rescind the contract with regard to the goods in question.

(3) For the purposes of subsection (1)(b) above goods which do not conform to the contract of sale at any time within the period of six months starting with the date on which the goods were delivered to the buyer must be taken not to have so conformed at that date.

(4) Subsection (3) above does not apply if—

(a) it is established that the goods did so conform at that date;

Paragraph numbers marked with a "+" can be found online and on CD.

(b) its application is incompatible with the nature of the goods or the nature of the lack of conformity.

Note —Part 5A of the Act comprises ss.48A to 48F and was added with effect from **3H–675** March 31, 2003 by the Sale and Supply of Goods to Consumers Regulations 2002 (SI 2002/3045).

Consumer's additional rights for non-conformity

The Sale and Supply of Goods to Consumers Regulations 2002 implemented the **3H–676** Directive on Aspects of Sale of Goods and Consumer Guarantees (1999/44). They introduced additional remedies for a buyer dealing as a consumer where there has been any breach of an express term of the contract or of the statutory implied terms as to description, satisfactory quality, fitness for purpose and sample. Those additional remedies are set out in ss.48A to 48F. They include the right to require the goods to be repaired or replaced (if that is not a disproportionate remedy) and, failing that, to rescind the contract or obtain a reduction in the price. These rights are entirely additional and do not take away any right (e.g. to reject the goods for breach of condition and/or to claim damages for consequential loss) which the buyer has independently of ss.48A to 48F. If, however, the buyer chooses to require repair or replacement, he cannot reject the goods and terminate the contract without allowing the seller a reasonable time to comply with his request. Section 61(5A) of the Sale of Goods Act provides that "dealing as a consumer" has the same meaning as in s.12 of the Unfair Contract Terms Act 1977. For the latter, see para.3H–573 above. Similar provisions to those in ss.48A to 48F were added to the Supply of Goods and Services Act 1982 (s.11M to s.11S). Under the latter, the goods will also be non-conforming (and the buyer will thus be entitled to require repair or replacement) if, in installing the goods, the supplier has been in breach of the implied term that he will use reasonable care and skill. For the term as to reasonable care and skill, see Supply of Goods and Services Act 1982 s.13 at para.3H–818 below.

"The time of delivery" —is normally when the goods are physically handed over to the buyer. Where the buyer deals as a consumer and the seller is authorised or required to send the goods to the buyer, delivery of the goods to a carrier does not constitute delivery: s.32(4). In that case delivery will occur only when the carrier delivers to the buyer.

Repair or replacement of the goods

48B.—(1) If section 48A above applies, the buyer may require the **3H–677** seller—

(a) to repair the goods, or

(b) to replace the goods.

(2) If the buyer requires the seller to repair or replace the goods, the seller must—

(a) repair or, as the case may be, replace the goods within a reasonable time but without causing significant inconvenience to the buyer;

(b) bear any necessary costs incurred in doing so (including in particular the cost of any labour, materials or postage).

(3) The buyer must not require the seller to repair or, as the case may be, replace the goods if that remedy is—

(a) impossible, or

(b) disproportionate in comparison to the other of those remedies, or

(c) disproportionate in comparison to an appropriate reduction in the purchase price under paragraph (a), or rescission under paragraph (b), of section 48C(1) below.

Paragraph numbers marked with a "+" can be found online and on CD.

(4) One remedy is disproportionate in comparison to the other if the one imposes costs on the seller which, in comparison to those imposed on him by the other, are unreasonable, taking into account—

    (a) the value which the goods would have if they conformed to the contract of sale,

    (b) the significance of the lack of conformity, and

    (c) whether the other remedy could be effected without significant inconvenience to the buyer.

(5) Any question as to what is a reasonable time or significant inconvenience is to be determined by reference to—

    (a) the nature of the goods, and

    (b) the purpose for which the goods were acquired.

3H–678   *Note* —Inserted by SI 2002/3045.

Repair or replacement of the goods

3H–679   See note and commentary to s.48A above.

Reduction of purchase price or rescission of contract

3H–680   48C.—(1) If section 48A above applies, the buyer may—

    (a) require the seller to reduce the purchase price of the goods in question to the buyer by an appropriate amount, or

    (b) rescind the contract with regard to those goods,

if the condition in subsection (2) below is satisfied.

(2) The condition is that—

    (a) by virtue of section 48B(3) above the buyer may require neither repair nor replacement of the goods; or

    (b) the buyer has required the seller to repair or replace the goods, but the seller is in breach of the requirement of section 48B(2)(a) above to do so within a reasonable time and without significant inconvenience to the buyer.

(3) For the purposes of this Part, if the buyer rescinds the contract, any reimbursement to the buyer may be reduced to take account of the use he has had of the goods since they were delivered to him.

3H–681   *Note* —Inserted by SI 2002/3045.

Reduction of purchase price or rescission of contract

3H–682   See note and commentary to s.48A above

Relation to other remedies etc

3H–683   48D.—(1) If the buyer requires the seller to repair or replace the goods the buyer must not act under subsection (2) until he has given the seller a reasonable time in which to repair or replace (as the case may be) the goods.

(2) The buyer acts under this subsection if—

    (a) in England and Wales or Northern Ireland he rejects the goods and terminates the contract for breach of condition;

Paragraph numbers marked with a "+" can be found online and on CD.

(b) in Scotland he rejects any goods delivered under the contract and treats it as repudiated;

(c) he requires the goods to be replaced or repaired (as the case may be).

Note —Inserted by SI 2002/3045.   **3H–684**

Reasonable time for repair or replacement of goods
See note and commentary to s.48A above.   **3H–685**

Powers of the court

48E.—(1) In any proceedings in which a remedy is sought by   **3H–686**
virtue of this Part the court, in addition to any other power it has,
may act under this section.

(2) On the application of the buyer the court may make an order
requiring specific performance or, in Scotland, specific implement by
the seller of any obligation imposed on him by virtue of section 48B
above.

(3) Subsection (4) applies if—

(a) the buyer requires the seller to give effect to a remedy
under section 48B or 48C above or has claims to rescind
under section 48C, but

(b) the court decides that another remedy under section
48B or 48C is appropriate.

(4) The court may proceed—

(a) as if the buyer had required the seller to give effect to
the other remedy, or if the other remedy is rescission
under section 48C;

(b) as if the buyer had claimed to rescind the contract under
that section.

(5) If the buyer has claimed to rescind the contract the court may
order that any reimbursement to the buyer is reduced to take account of the use he has had of the goods since they were delivered to
him.

(6) The court may make an order under this section unconditionally or on such terms and conditions as to damages, payment of the
price and otherwise as it thinks just.

Note —Inserted by SI 2002/3045.   **3H–687**

Powers of the court
See note and commentary to s.48A above.   **3H–688**

Conformity with the contract

48F. For the purposes of this Part, goods do not conform to a   **3H–689**
contract of sale if there is, in relation to the goods, a breach of an
express term of the contract or a term implied by section 13, 14 or
15 above.

Note —Inserted by SI 2002/3045.   **3H–690**

Conformity with the contract
See note and commentary to s.48A above.   **3H–691**

Paragraph numbers marked with a "+" can be found online and on CD.

CONSUMER

For ss.49 to 52 of the Sale of Goods Act 1979 (see Arrangement) plus any related commentary see paragraphs 3H–692+ to 3H–695+ on White Book on Westlaw UK or the Civil Procedure CD.

Remedy for breach of warranty

3H–696   **53.**—(1) Where there is a breach of warranty by the seller, or where the buyer elects (or is compelled) to treat any breach of a condition on the part of the seller as a breach of warranty, the buyer is not by reason only of such breach of warranty entitled to reject the goods; but he may—

(a) set up against the seller the breach of warranty in diminution or extinction of the price, or

(b) maintain an action against the seller for damages for the breach of warranty.

(2) The measure of damages for breach of warranty is the estimated loss directly and naturally resulting, in the ordinary course of events, from the breach of warranty.

(3) In the case of breach of warranty of quality such loss is prima facie the difference between the value of the goods at the time of delivery to the buyer and the value they would have had if they had fulfilled the warranty.

(4) The fact that the buyer has set up the breach of warranty in diminution or extinction of the price does not prevent him from maintaining an action for the same breach of warranty if he has suffered further damage.

(5) This section does not apply to Scotland.

3H–697   *Note* —Subsection.(5) inserted by the Sale and Supply of Goods Act 1994 ss.7(1), 8(2), Sch.2, para.5.

For ss.53A to 64 of and Schs 1 to 4 to the Sale of Goods Act 1979 (see Arrangement) plus any related commentary see paragraphs 3H–698+ to 3H–757+ on White Book on Westlaw UK or the Civil Procedure CD.

Supply of Goods and Services Act 1982

3H–758   (S.I. 1982 c.29)

ARRANGEMENT OF SECTIONS

PART I

Paragraph numbers marked with a "+" can be found online and on CD.

Paragraph numbers marked with a "+" denote content that is available on White Book on Westlaw UK or the Civil Procedure CD.

For ss.1 to 11S of the Supply of Goods and Services Act 1982 (see Arrangement) plus any related commentary see paragraphs 3H–759+ to 3H–815+ on White Book on Westlaw UK or the Civil Procedure CD.

Implied terms as to description, quality and sample

Terms as to title, description, quality and sample are implied in contracts of sale of   **3H–816**
goods by the Sale of Goods Act 1979 ss.12– 15. Similar terms are implied by the Supply of Goods and Service Act 1982 in: contracts of barter or exchange, contracts whereby goods are exchanged for trading stamps and contracts for services under which the property is to pass (ss.1– 5A); contracts of hire (other than hire-purchase) (ss.6–11). These terms apply only to the goods supplied, not to the services. As with the terms implied by the Sale of Goods Act, any clause purporting to exclude or limit liability in respect of them is subject to the provisions of the Unfair Contract Terms Act 1977 (in this case, in particular, s.7 of that Act.) Sections 12–16 imply into contracts for the supply of services (whether or not the contract is one of sale of goods) terms which relate to the services provided—terms as to care and skill, time for performance and the remuneration.

Consumer's additional rights for non-conformity

Amendments to the Sale of Goods Act 1979 by the Sale and Supply of Goods to   **3H–817**

Paragraph numbers marked with a "+" can be found online and on CD.

Consumer Regulations 2002 (SI 2002/3045) are mirrored by similar amendments to the Supply of Goods and Services Act 1982. Sections 48A to 48F of the former Act give the buyer additional rights in relation to non-conforming goods (including the right to require repair or replacement of the goods), see para.3H–674 above. The Supply of Goods and Services Act 1982 contains, in ss.11M to 11S, provisions which are, with one exception, identical apart from necessary changes of wording. The exception is as follows. Whereas under both Acts the goods will be non-conforming if there is a breach of any of the statutory implied terms as to description, satisfactory quality, fitness for purpose or sample, under the Supply of Goods of Services Act the goods will also be non-conforming if, in installing the goods, the supplier has been in breach of the implied term in s.13 that he will use reasonable care and skill. For s.13 see below.

PART II

SUPPLY OF SERVICES

The contracts concerned

3H–818   **12.**—(1) In this Act a "contract for the supply of a service" means, subject to subsection (2) below, a contract under which a person, ("the supplier") agrees to carry out a service.

(2) For the purposes of this Act, a contract of service or apprenticeship is not a contract for the supply of a service.

(3) Subject to subsection (2) above, a contract is a contract for the supply of a service for the purposes of this Act whether or not goods are also—

(a) transferred or to be transferred, or

(b) bailed or to be bailed by way of hire,

under the contract, and whatever is the nature of the consideration for which the services is to be carried out.

(4) The Secretary of State may by order provide that one or more of sections 13 to 15 below shall not apply to services of a description specified in the order, and such an order may make different provision for different circumstances.

(5) The power to make an order under subsection (4) above shall be exercisable by statutory instrument subject to annulment in pursuance of a resolution of either House of Parliament.

"Contracts for the supply of a service"

3H–819   This concept will include not only contracts of which the substance is the provision of a service, but also a contract of sale of goods under which a service is also to be provided (e.g. the sale and installation of a washing machine).

Implied term about care and skill

3H–820   **13.** In a contract for the supply of a service where the supplier is acting in the course of a business, there is an implied term that the supplier will carry out the service with reasonable care and skill.

Implied term about care and skill

3H–821   For exclusion of liability see s.16. For case law on "in the course of a business", see commentary to Sale of Goods Act 1979 s.14. For the other party's right to require repair or replacement of goods where the supplier is in breach of the implied term as to care and skill in installing goods, see para.3H–817.

Implied term about time for performance

3H–822   **14.**—(1) Where, under a contract for the supply of a service by a

Paragraph numbers marked with a "+" can be found online and on CD.

supplier acting in the course of a business, the time for the service to be carried out is not fixed by the contracts, left to be fixed in a manner agreed by the contract or determined by the course of dealing between the parties, there is an implied term that the supplier will carry out the service within a reasonable time.

(2) What is a reasonable time is a question of fact.

Time for performance

A related requirement appears in the Consumer Protection (Distance Selling) Regulations 2000 (SI 2000/2334), which implemented the Distance Selling Directive (97/7) and are set out at para.3H–906. By reg.19(1), in the case of a "distance contract" which is not an "excepted contract", the supplier must, unless the parties agree otherwise, perform the contract within a period of 30 days, which period begins when the consumer forwarded his order to the supplier. Regulation 19(1) does not apply to any excepted contract, nor to timeshare agreements (within the meaning of the Timeshare Act 1992), nor to the following agreements: contracts for food, beverages or other goods used for everyday consumption supplied to the consumer at his residence or workplace by regular roundsmen; contracts for accommodation, catering, transport or leisure services where the supplier undertakes to supply the services on a specific date or within a specific period. Where reg.19(1) does apply and the supplier is unable to supply the goods or services ordered, reg.19(7) allows the supplier to supply substitute goods or services of equivalent price and quality, if the contract provided for that possibility. Apart from that possibility, if reg.19(1) applies and the supplier is unable, because the goods or services are not available, to perform the contract within the 30 days or such other period as the parties agree, reg.19(2) to (6) come into play. These contain consequential provisions: the supplier is required to reimburse any sum paid by or on behalf of the consumer, including any sum paid by a creditor under a personal credit agreement with the consumer; the contract shall be treated as if never made (except for any rights or remedies arising from the non-performance); any security provided in relation to the contract is to be treated as if never having had any effect.

3H–823

Implied term about consideration

15.—(1) Where, under a contract for the supply of a service, the consideration for the service is not determined by the contract, left to be determined in a manner agreed by the contract or determined by the course of dealing between the parties, there is an implied term that the party contracting with the supplier will pay a reasonable charge.

(2) What is a reasonable charge is a question of fact.

3H–824

Exclusion of implied terms, etc.

16.—(1) Where a right, duty or liability would arise under a contract for the supply of a service by virtue of this Part of this Act, it may (subject to subsection (2) below and the 1977 Act) be negatived or varied by express agreement, or by the course of dealing between the parties, or by such usage as binds both parties to the contract.

(2) An express term does not negative a term implied by this Part of this Act unless inconsistent with it.

(3) Nothing in this Part of this Act prejudices—

   (a) any rule of law which imposes on the supplier a duty stricter than that imposed by section 13 or 14 above; or

   (b) subject to paragraph (a) above, any rule of law whereby

3H–825

Paragraph numbers marked with a "+" can be found online and on CD.

any term not inconsistent with this Part of this Act is to be implied in a contract for the supply of a service.

(4) This Part of this Act has effect subject to any other enactment which defines or restricts the rights, duties or liabilities arising in connection with a service of any description.

Exclusion of implied terms

3H–826   The 1977 Act referred to in subs.(1) is the Unfair Contract Terms Act 1977. Liability for breach of the implied term as to care and skill in s.13 is negligence liability within the meaning of the 1977 Act and thus any attempt to exclude such liability is subject to s.2 of the 1977 Act. If the recipient of the services contracts as a consumer or the exclusion clause is a standard term of the service provider, s.3 of the 1977 Act will apply as well.

For ss.17–20 of and Sch.1 to the Supply of Goods and Services Act 1982 (see Arrangement) plus any related commentary see paragraphs 3H–827+ to 3H–835+ on White Book on Westlaw UK or the Civil Procedure CD.

The Package Travel, Package Holidays and Package Tours Regulations 1992

3H–836

(S.I. 1992 No. 3288)

ARRANGEMENT OF SECTIONS

General note

3H–837   These regulations implemented the EC Directive on Package Travel, Package Holidays and Package Tours 90/314. In various respects they enhance holiday makers' rights compared with what they would or might otherwise be. The ordinary law of contract and tort continues to apply to any holiday which is outside the regulations (i.e. if it is not a "package" within reg.2). Similarly, even where the holiday is a package within the regulations, the common law continues to apply in relation to matters not covered by the regulations. Thus, the regulations being silent on the matter, the assessment of damages is to be determined by decisions based on *Jarvis v Swans Tours Ltd* [1973] Q.B. 233.

As an alternative to court action, the ABTA (Association of British Travel Agents)

Paragraph numbers marked with a "+" can be found online and on CD.

arbitration scheme administered by the Chartered Institute of Arbitrators allows a claim for up to £5,000 (or £15,000 per booking) to be referred to arbitration if it is against an ABTA member.

For an authoritative account of this area of the law, see *Holiday Law* by Grant and Mason (3rd edn, Sweet and Maxwell, 2003).

Citation and commencement

1. These Regulations may be cited as the Package Travel, Package Holidays and Package Tours Regulations 1992 and shall come into force on the day after the day on which they are made.　　　　　　　　　**3H–838**

Interpretation

2.—(1) In these Regulations–　　　　　　　　　　　　　　　　　**3H–839**

"brochure" means any brochure in which packages are offered for sale;

"contract" means the agreement linking the consumer to the organiser or to the retailer, or to both, as the case may be;

"the Directive" means Council Directive 90/314/EEC on package travel, package holidays and package tours;

"member State" means a member State of the European Community or another State in the European Economic Area;

"offer" includes an invitation to treat whether by means of advertising or otherwise, and cognate expressions shall be construed accordingly;

"organiser" means the person who, otherwise than occasionally, organises packages and sells or offers them for sale, whether directly or through a retailer;

"the other party to the contract" means the party, other than the consumer, to the contract, that is, the organiser or the retailer, or both, as the case may be;

"package" means the pre-arranged combination of at least two of the following components when sold or offered for sale at an inclusive price and when the service covers a period of more than twenty-four hours or includes overnight accommodation:–

(a) transport;

(b) accommodation;

(c) other tourist services not ancillary to transport or accommodation and accounting for a significant proportion of the package, and

(i) the submission of separate accounts for different components shall not cause the arrangements to be other than a package;

(ii) the fact that a combination is arranged at the request of the consumer and in accordance with his specific instructions (whether modified or not) shall not of itself cause it to be treated as other than pre-arranged; and

"retailer" means the person who sells or offers for sale the package put together by the organiser.

Paragraph numbers marked with a "+" can be found online and on CD.

CONSUMER

(2) In the definition of "contract" in paragraph (1) above, "consumer" means the person who takes or agrees to take the package ("the principal contractor") and elsewhere in these Regulations "consumer" means, as the context requires, the principal contractor, any person on whose behalf the principal contractor agrees to purchase the package ("the other beneficiaries") or any person to whom the principal contractor or any of the other beneficiaries transfers the package ("the transferee").

3H–840   *Note* —Definition of "member state" added by the Package Travel, Package Holidays and Package Tours (Amendment) Regulations 1995 (SI 1995/1648).

"contract"

3H–841   This definition is taken from the Directive. It would appear that it is possible for an agreement to fall within this definition even though it is not what would at common law be recognised as a contract. Thus a travel agent might on a given occasion arrange for the consumer (a) flights with an airline and (b) accommodation with an hotel. That would constitute a "package" and the travel agent would be the "organiser", see para.3H–842 below. Yet the contracts for flights and accommodation may well have been between the consumer and, respectively, the airline and the hotel. In this situation, it can perhaps be said that there was an "agreement" between the travel agent and the consumer which was a "contract" within the meaning of the regulations, albeit it may not have been a contract at common law, the agreement being that the travel agent would make, or try to make, the arrangements which the consumer wanted.

"the other party to the contract"

3H–842   This expression is not derived from the Directive. In the usual situation the tour operator will be "the other party to the contract"", the travel agent having been merely an agent to bring about a contract between the consumer and tour operator. The definition clearly contemplates, however, that the travel agent (the retailer) can also, either alone or as well as the tour operator, be "the other party to the contract". The vagueness created by the words "as the case may be" leaves a great deal of scope for judicial interpretation. It allows the courts to determine who is (or are) the other party(ies) to the contract according to the facts of different cases. It also leaves open the possibility that the identity of "the other party to the contract" may vary according to which of the substantive regulations is in point. According to Goldring J. in *ABTA v Civil Aviation Authority* [2006] EWHC 13 (Admin), at para.161, "[T]he [regulations] do not exclude the application of the English law of contract . . .[W]hether the agreement links the consumer to the organiser or retailer or both depends upon the application of the English law of contract, in particular the law of agency. So too do decisions as to whether the organiser or retailer or both are parties to the contract or whether under regulation 15, the organiser or retailer or both are liable under it."

"Package"

3H–843   Only those holidays which are "packages" are affected by the regulations.

"Pre-arranged combination" —In *Club-Tour Viagens e Turismo SA v Lobo Goncalves Garrido (C400/00)* [2002] E.C.R. I-4051, the ECJ, in interpreting the Directive, determined two things: (i) arrangements put together by a travel agent at the request of, and according to the specifications of, a consumer (or defined group of consumers) can fall within the definition of a package; (ii) "pre-arranged combination" must be interpreted so as to include combinations of tourist services put together at the time when the contract is concluded between the travel agency and the consumer. Thus, where a travel agent had arranged both (a) a holiday at the destination resort and (b) the flights to reach the destination, that was a package within the regulations and, apparently, the travel agent was an "organiser" within the meaning of the regulations.

"Inclusive price" —The arrangement is not a package unless it is sold or offered "at an inclusive price". Thus an optional excursion which the consumer buys from the tour operator only after arrival at his holiday resort would not be part of the package.

Paragraph numbers marked with a "+" can be found online and on CD.

It would, however, be part of the package it if it was arranged (and the cost included) at the time the holiday was booked. In *Rechberger v Austria (C140/97)* [1999] E.C.R. I-3499; [2000] 2 C.M.L.R. 1, trips including travel and accommodation were offered (as part of an advertising campaign) to subscribers to a newspaper. The lucky travellers were to pay only airport taxes and, if they travelled alone, a single supplement. The price was held to be "inclusive", even though it did not equal the value of either the travel or the accommodation. Thus the trips were held to be "packages". According to Goldring J. in *ABTA v Civil Aviation Authority* [2006] EWHC 13 (Admin), at para.156:

> "[T]he words 'inclusive price' should be given their ordinary and natural meaning. If the substance of a transaction is the sale by the travel agent of separate and discrete components of ... a holiday, with no one part being connected with or dependent upon any other part (other than that they are sold together), ... the resultant price ... is no more an 'inclusive price' than is the total of goods at the checkout of a supermarket. For the sale of a package at an inclusive price the relationship between the component parts of the package must be such as to mean that the consumer is buying and paying for them as a whole; that the sale or offer for sale of one component part is in some way connected with or dependent on the sale or offer for sale of the others."

"Accommodation" —*Administrative Proceedings Concerning AFS Intercultural Programs Finland RY (C237/97)* [1999] E.C.R. I-825; [2000] 1 C.M.L.R. 845 involved a student exchange arrangement whereby students would be sent from Finland to study in another country for a period of six months or more, lodging with families which put them up free of charge. AFS Finland organised the exchange by: arranging transport, selecting the host family, arranging the school to be attended by students during their visit abroad, preparing documentation relating to the host country and organising a preparatory course for the students and their families. The ECJ held that the combination of all three of the following factors meant that the lodging with the families was not "accommodation" within the meaning of the Directive: (i) the lodging was free, (ii) it was not in a hotel or similar establishment, and (iii) it was for a long time.

"Other tourist services.." —In the *AFS Finland* case (see "Accommodation" above), it was held that AFS Finland did not organise "other tourist services" within the meaning of the Directive, because: (i) selecting the school for the exchange student to attend was not a tourist service, since its specific purpose was education of the student; (ii) selection of the host family, if it was a tourist service, was ancillary to accommodation; (iii) preparation of the documentation and the courses followed by the students and parents prior to departure, though within the definition of "tourist services", did not account for a significant proportion of the package.

"Organiser" and "retailer"

A tour operator, whether it markets its package holidays directly or via travel agents, is clearly an "organiser". A travel agent who sells such a package holiday will be a "retailer" but not normally an "organiser". However, in two situations a travel agent might be an "organiser". The first is where, in addition to selling the conventional package holiday and as part of that same transaction, the travel agent himself arranges transport to the hotel or the airport, *c.f.* the *Club-Tour* case at para.3H–841 above. Whilst the package travel company remains an "organiser" and the travel agent remains a "retailer" of the conventional package, the travel agent would appear to be "organiser" of the whole package, i.e. including the additional transport. The second situation is where in selling the package, the travel agent has acted as an undisclosed agent, i.e. held himself out, whether or not intentionally, as principal: *Hone v Going Places Leisure Travel Ltd* (QBD, Nov 16, 2000, confirmed in the Court of Appeal—see para.3H–866 below).

3H–844

Paragraph (2) —the definition of "consumer", coupled with the provisions of substantive regulations (including in particular reg.15), means that the common law rule of privity of contract is effectively abrogated. The consumer, whether that be the purchaser of the package or someone else in the party, can proceed against "the other party to the contract" in respect of any improper performance of the contract. Where the regulations apply, therefore, the consumer will not need to rely on the Contracts (Rights of Third Parties) Act 1999. Re "transferee", see reg.10 below.

Paragraph numbers marked with a "+" can be found online and on CD.

Application of Regulations

3H–845　**3.**—(1) These Regulations apply to packages sold or offered for sale in the territory of the United Kingdom.

(2) Regulations 4 to 15 apply to packages so sold or offered for sale on or after 31st December 1992.

(3) Regulations 16 to 22 apply to contracts which, in whole or part, remain to be performed on 31st December 1992.

Application of the regulations

3H–846　Subsection (3) is an example of very sloppy drafting. It is generally accepted that regs 16 to 22 apply to "contracts" sold after December 31, 1992 as well as to those which had been made previously and on that date still remained to be fully performed.

Descriptive matter relating to packages must not be misleading

3H–847　**4.**—(1) No organiser or retailer shall supply to a consumer any descriptive matter concerning a package, the price of a package or any other conditions applying to the contract which contains any misleading information.

(2) If an organiser or retailer is in breach of paragraph (1) he shall be liable to compensate the consumer for any loss which the consumer suffers in consequence.

Misleading information

3H–848　Where the only remedy claimed is damages, this regulation makes unnecessary any consideration of whether the misleading information amounted to either (a) an actionable misrepresentation or (b) a term of the contract. In *Mawdsley v Cosmosair Plc* [2002] EWCA Civ 587, the claimant and her husband booked a holiday for themselves and their two children. The defendant tour operator had advertised in its brochure that the hotel had "Lifts (in main building)". The restaurant, however, could be reached only via stairs because it was located on a mezzanine floor not served by the lifts. Whilst the claimant and her husband were descending the stairs carrying their baby daughter in a pushchair, the claimant lost her footing, fell and suffered injuries. It was held that "Lifts (in main building)" was a representation that all levels in the main building, including the restaurant, could be accessed by lift. That was "misleading information" for the purposes of Regulation 4, "with the result that [the defendant] is liable under that Regulation for all consequent damage", per Jonathan Parker L.J. at para.45. His Lordship continued: "Since Regulation 6 ... provides that particulars in the brochure are implied warranties in the contract, it follows that [the defendant] was also in breach of contract in that respect." There was a sufficient causal link between the misrepresentation that the restaurant could be accessed by lift and the accident which occurred on the stairs. There had been no novus actus interveniens since the claimant and her husband had behaved perfectly reasonably in taking their daughter in her pushchair in the way that they had (*Quinn v Burch Bros (Builders) Ltd* [1966] 2 Q.B. 370 distinguished).

Requirements as to brochures

3H–849　**5.** [Regulation 5 creates criminal offences in relation to brochures which do not include the price and information on the matters specified in Sch. 1 to the regulations.]

Circumstances in which particulars in brochure are to be binding

3H–850　**6.**—(1) Subject to paragraphs (2) and (3) of this regulation, the particulars in the brochure (whether or not they are required by regulation 5(1) above to be included in the brochure) shall constitute implied warranties (or, as regards Scotland, implied terms) for the purposes of any contract to which the particulars relate.

Paragraph numbers marked with a "+" can be found online and on CD.

(2) Paragraph (1) of this regulation does not apply–

    (a) in relation to information required to be included by virtue of paragraph 9 of Schedule 1 to these Regulations; or

    (b) where the brochure contains an express statement that changes may be made in the particulars contained in it before a contract is concluded and changes in the particulars so contained are clearly communicated to the consumer before a contract is concluded.

(3) Paragraph (1) of this regulation does not apply when the consumer and the other party to the contract agree after the contract has been made that the particulars in the brochure, or some of those particulars, should not form part of the contract.

Brochure contents as terms of the contract

    Mawdsley v Cosmosair Plc [2002] EWCA Civ 587 provides an example of the application of reg.6(1)—see para.3H–848 above.   **3H–851**

    The information "required to be included by virtue of paragraph 9 of Schedule 1" is information about "the arrangements for security for money paid over and for the repatriation of the consumer in the event of insolvency".

Information to be provided before contract is concluded

    7. [Regulation 7 creates criminal offences for a failure by "the   **3H–852** other party to the contract" to provide certain information to the intending consumer before the contract is made, namely information regarding: passport and visa requirements; health formalities; arrangements for security of money paid over and repatriation of the consumer in the event of insolvency.]

Information to be provided in good time

    8. [Regulation 8 creates criminal offences for a failure by "the   **3H–853** other party to the contract" to provide certain information to the consumer before the start of the journey, namely information regarding: transport arrangements, connections, accommodation en route, contact details of local representatives, holiday/travel insurance.]

Contents and form of contract

    9.—(1) The other party to the contract shall ensure that–   **3H–854**

    (a) depending on the nature of the package being purchased, the contract contains at least the elements specified in Schedule 2 to these Regulations;

    (b) subject to paragraph (2) below, all the terms of the contract are set out in writing or such other form as is comprehensible and accessible to the consumer and are communicated to the consumer before the contract is made; and

    (c) a written copy of these terms is supplied to the consumer.

(2) Paragraph (1)(b) above does not apply when the interval between the time when the consumer approaches the other party to the contract with a view to entering into a contract and the time of departure under the proposed contract is so short that it is impracticable to comply with the sub-paragraph.

Paragraph numbers marked with a "+" can be found online and on CD.

(3) It is an implied condition (or, as regards Scotland, an implied term) of the contract that the other party to the contract complies with the provisions of paragraph (1).

(4) In Scotland, any breach of the condition implied by paragraph (3) above shall be deemed to be a material breach justifying rescission of the contract.

Transfer of bookings

3H–855   **10.**—(1) In every contract there is an implied term that where the consumer is prevented from proceeding with the package the consumer may transfer his booking to a person who satisfies all the conditions applicable to the package, provided that the consumer gives reasonable notice to the other party to the contract of his intention to transfer before the date when departure is due to take place.

(2) Where a transfer is made in accordance with the implied term set out in paragraph (1) above, the transferor and the transferee shall be jointly and severally liable to the other party to the contract for payment of the price of the package (or, if part of the price has been paid, for payment of the balance) and for any additional costs arising from such transfer.

Transfer of bookings

3H–856   This regulation will sometimes enable a consumer to avoid having to pay cancellation charges by transferring his booking to someone else. It applies, however, only where the consumer is "prevented" from proceeding. It is not enough that the consumer has simply changed his mind.

Price revision

3H–857   **11.**—(1) Any term in a contract to the effect that the prices laid down in the contract may be revised shall be void and of no effect unless the contract provides for the possibility of upward or downward revision and satisfies the conditions laid down in paragraph (2) below.

(2) The conditions mentioned in paragraph (1) are that–

    (a) the contract states precisely how the revised price is to be calculated;

    (b) the contract provides that price revisions are to be made solely to allow for variations in:–

        (i) transportation costs, including the cost of fuel,

        (ii) dues, taxes or fees chargeable for services such as landing taxes or embarkation or disembarkation fees at ports and airports, or

        (iii) the exchange rates applied to the particular package; and

(3) Notwithstanding any terms of a contract,

        (i) no price increase may be made in a specified period which may not be less than 30 days before the departure date stipulated; and

        (ii) as against an individual consumer liable under the contract, no price increase may be made in re-

Paragraph numbers marked with a "+" can be found online and on CD.

spect of variations which would produce an increase of less than 2%, or such greater percentage as the contract may specify, ("non-eligible variations") and that the non-eligible variations shall be left out of account in the calculation.

Significant alterations to essential terms

12. In every contract there are implied terms to the effect that–   **3H–858**

   (a) where the organiser is constrained before the departure to alter significantly an essential term of the contract, such as the price (so far as regulation 11 permits him to do so), he will notify the consumer as quickly as possible in order to enable him to take appropriate decisions and in particular to withdraw from the contract without penalty or to accept a rider to the contract specifying the alterations made and their impact on the price; and

   (b) the consumer will inform the organiser or the retailer of his decision as soon as possible.

Withdrawal by consumer pursuant to regulation 12 and cancellation by organiser

13.—(1) The terms set out in paragraphs (2) and (3) below are **3H–859** implied in every contract and apply where the consumer withdraws from the contract pursuant to the term in it implied by virtue of regulation 12(a), or where the organiser, for any reason other than the fault of the consumer, cancels the package before the agreed date of departure.

(2) The consumer is entitled–

   (a) to take a substitute package of equivalent or superior quality if the other party to the contract is able to offer him such a substitute; or

   (b) to take a substitute package of lower quality if the other party to the contract is able to offer him one and to recover from the organiser the difference in price between the price of the package purchased and that of the substitute package; or

   (c) to have repaid to him as soon as possible all the monies paid by him under the contract.

(3) The consumer is entitled, if appropriate, to be compensated by the organiser for non-performance of the contract except where–

   (a) the package is cancelled because the number of persons who agree to take it is less than the minimum number required and the consumer is informed of the cancellation, in writing, within the period indicated in the description of the package; or

   (b) the package is cancelled by reason of unusual and unforeseeable circumstances beyond the control of the party by whom this exception is pleaded, the consequences of which could not have been avoided even if all due care had been exercised.

Paragraph numbers marked with a "+" can be found online and on CD.

(4) Overbooking shall not be regarded as a circumstance falling within the provisions of sub-paragraph (b) of paragraph (3) above.

Pre-departure cancellation

3H–860   The regulations are silent as to the position where the consumer cancels the contract other than in the situations covered in reg.12 (a price increase or other alteration to an essential term of the contract). Thus the consumer who cancels in any other situation will fall liable to pay the cancellation charges stated in the contract, unless they are challengeable under the Unfair Terms in Consumer Contracts Regulations 1999 (see para.3H–886) or are inconsistent with the terms of a code (e.g. ABTA) subscribed to by the tour organiser. For post-departure cancellation, see regulation 14.

Para.(3)(b) —The wording here follows exactly that of the Directive in its definition of "force majeure". Sometimes the "unusual and unforeseeable circumstances" will amount to what at common law would be a frustrating event (e.g. the destination resort is completed destroyed by fire). Nevertheless, it seems clear that the contract will not be frustrated but rather the consumer, though not entitled to compensation, will be entitled to the appropriate remedy under para.(2).

Significant proportion of services not provided

3H–861   **14.**—(1) The terms set out in paragraphs (2) and (3) below are implied in every contract and apply where, after departure, a significant proportion of the services contracted for is not provided or the organiser becomes aware that he will be unable to procure a significant proportion of the services to be provided.

(2) The organiser will make suitable alternative arrangements, at no extra cost to the consumer, for the continuation of the package and will, where appropriate, compensate the consumer for the difference between the services to be supplied under the contract and those supplied.

(3) If it is impossible to make arrangements as described in paragraph (2), or these are not accepted by the consumer for good reasons, the organiser will, where appropriate, provide the consumer with equivalent transport back to the place of departure or to another place to which the consumer has agreed and will, where appropriate, compensate the consumer.

Force majeure

3H–862   This regulation contains no exception for force majeure and thus it applies whatever may be the reason that a significant proportion of the services cannot be, or are not, provided. Thus it seems clear that a post-departure event which would otherwise have frustrated the contract at common law will not do so in the case of a package to which the regulations apply. For the position regarding a pre-departure event, see commentary to reg.13.

Compensation

3H–863   Paragraphs (2) and (3) state that compensation is to be paid "where appropriate". It is submitted that this regulation is to be read together with reg.15 and that payment of compensation under reg.14 will not be "appropriate" where the failure to provide the services falls within paras (a) to (c) of reg.15(2) and is not due to the fault of the organiser (or of another supplier of services). Similarly compensation would not be appropriate to the extent that liability to pay it is limited by an exclusion clause which is reasonable within the meaning of para.(4) of reg.15.

Liability of other party to the contract for proper performance of obligations under contract

3H–864   **15.**—(1) The other party to the contract is liable to the consumer

Paragraph numbers marked with a "+" can be found online and on CD.

for the proper performance of the obligations under the contract, irrespective of whether such obligations are to be performed by that other party or by other suppliers of services but this shall not affect any remedy or right of action which that other party may have against those other suppliers of services.

(2) The other party to the contract is liable to the consumer for any damage caused to him by the failure to perform the contract or the improper performance of the contract unless the failure or the improper performance is due neither to any fault of that other party nor to that of another supplier of services, because–

    (a) the failures which occur in the performance of the contract are attributable to the consumer;

    (b) such failures are attributable to a third party unconnected with the provision of the services contracted for, and are unforeseeable or unavoidable; or

    (c) such failures are due to–

        (i) unusual and unforeseeable circumstances beyond the control of the party by whom this exception is pleaded, the consequences of which could not have been avoided even if all due care had been exercised; or

        (ii) an event which the other party to the contract or the supplier of services, even with all due care, could not foresee or forestall.

(3) In the case of damage arising from the non-performance or improper performance of the services involved in the package, the contract may provide for compensation to be limited in accordance with the international conventions which govern such services.

(4) In the case of damage other than personal injury resulting from the non-performance or improper performance of the services involved in the package, the contract may include a term limiting the amount of compensation which will be paid to the consumer, provided that the limitation is not unreasonable.

(5) Without prejudice to paragraph (3) and paragraph (4) above, liability under paragraphs (1) and (2) above cannot be excluded by any contractual term.

(6) The terms set out in paragraphs (7) and (8) below are implied in every contract.

(7) In the circumstances described in paragraph (2)(b) and (c) of this regulation, the other party to the contract will give prompt assistance to a consumer in difficulty.

(8) If the consumer complains about a defect in the performance of the contract, the other party to the contract, or his local representative, if there is one, will make prompt efforts to find appropriate solutions.

(9) The contract must clearly and explicitly oblige the consumer to communicate at the earliest opportunity, in writing or any other appropriate form, to the supplier of the services concerned and to the other party to the contract any failure which he perceives at the place where the services concerned are supplied.

Paragraph numbers marked with a "+" can be found online and on CD.

"Proper performance of the contract"

3H–865   Regulation 15 does not impose strict liability in all cases. Whether there has been proper performance "can only be determined by reference to the terms of the contract. There may be absolute obligations, e.g. as to the existence of a swimming-pool or any other matter, but, in the absence of the assumption of an absolute obligation, the implication will be that reasonable skill and care will be used in the rendering of the relevant service. There will thus be no improper performance of the air carriage unless there is an absence of reasonable skill and care in the provision of that service": per Longmore L.J. in *Hone v Going Places Leisure Travel Ltd* [2001] EWCA Civ 947 at para.15.

The duty of reasonable care and skill requires, in the case of a hotel abroad, that the hotel complies with local safety regulations rather than British safety standards; compliance with local safety standards does not, however, preclude other possible breaches of the duty of care: *Codd v Thomson Tour Operators Ltd* [2000] CA transcripts 1470/2000, cited in *Evans v Kosmar Villa Holidays* [2007] EWCA Civ 1003; [2008] 1 W.L.R. 297. It was held in the latter case, applying *Tomlinson v Congelton* [2003] UKHL 47; [2004] 1 A.C. 46, that there was no duty to give a holiday maker, who was of full capacity and able to make an informed decision, a warning about the risks of diving into the shallow end of a small swimming pool at his holiday apartment complex.

The "other party to the contract"

3H–866   Regulation 15 ensures that the other party to the contract (usually the tour operator) is responsible for the proper performance of the contract by those supplying the relevant service, whether transport, accommodation or another service, irrespective of whoever it is that actually performs that service. In the conventional package holiday situation, the tour operator will be the other party to the contract. Query whether reg.15 imposes liability on a travel agent who, in addition to selling a tour operator's conventional package holiday and as part of that same transaction, himself arranges transport to the hotel or the airport. In that situation there are two "organisers", the tour operator and the agent, but arguably only the tour operator is the other party to the contract—see the commentary to reg.2 above. Where the travel agent has held himself out as principal (i.e. as the tour operator), he will on ordinary principles of the law of agency be liable as if he were the other party to the contract: see the High Court decision in *Hone v Going Places Leisure Travel Ltd* (QBD, November 16, 2000, Manchester District Registry, No.MA993390, confirmed on appeal at [2001] EWCA Civ 947). In *Hone*, the consumer had viewed the defendant travel agent's teletext advertisement, which had failed to make clear that the travel agent was merely an agent for the tour operator, and had then booked the package by phone to the defendant travel agent.

"Damage"

3H–867   It is thought that nothing hangs on the use of the different words "loss" and "damage" in regs 4 and 15 respectively. The latter certainly includes more than personal injuries (see reg.14(4)) and would appear to include any type of loss for which damages can be awarded for breach of contract. On assessment, see the General Note at the start of these regulations.

Exclusion clauses

3H–868   An exclusion clause is not effective except to the extent allowed under paras (3) and (4). The international conventions referred to in para.(3) include, but are not limited to: the Warsaw Convention on Carriage by Air; the Berne Convention on Carriage by Rail; the Athens Convention on Carriage by Sea; the Paris Convention on Liability of Hotel Keepers. Paragraph (4) allows a limitation (except in relation to personal injuries) which "is not unreasonable". This appears to involve a test similar to the requirement of reasonableness in s.11 of the Unfair Contract Terms Act 1977.

Unfair Contract Terms

3H–869   Regulation 15 (apart from para.(9)) deals with the contractual liability of the other party to the contract (usually the tour operator) and not with that of the consumer. The regulations are silent as regards contractual obligations which can be said to be unfair to the consumer, e.g. a clause imposing unreasonably high cancellation charges.

Paragraph numbers marked with a "+" can be found online and on CD.

Such obligations are, however, challengeable under the Unfair Terms in Consumer Contracts Regulations 1999, see below.

Regulations 16-26

[Regulations 16-22 require arrangements to be in place to cover the risk of the tour operator becoming insolvent, so that there is security for the refund of money paid over and for the repatriation of the consumer. **3H–870**

Regulations 23-26 (and also Schs 1 and 3) contain provisions relating to the criminal offences created by the regulations.]

* * * *

Saving for civil consequences

27. No contract shall be void or unenforceable, and no right of action in civil proceedings in respect of any loss shall arise, by reason only of the commission of an offence under regulations 5, 7, 8, 16 or 22 of these Regulations. **3H–871**

Terms implied in contract

28. Where it is provided in these Regulations that a term (whether so described or whether described as a condition or warranty) is implied in the contract it is so implied irrespective of the law which governs the contract. **3H–872**

* * * *

REGULATION 9   SCHEDULE 2

ELEMENTS TO BE INCLUDED IN THE CONTRACT IF RELEVANT TO THE PARTICULAR PACKAGE

1. The travel destination(s) and, where periods of stay are involved, the relevant periods, with dates. **3H–873**

2. [Repealed by the Enterprise Act 2002 (Part 8 Notice to OFT of Intended Prosecution Specified Enactments, Revocation and Transitional Provision) Order (SI 2003 No. 1376), art.3.]

3. Where the package includes accommodation, its location, its tourist category or degree of comfort, its main features and, where the accommodation is to be provided in a member State, its compliance with the rules of that member State.

4. The meals which are included in the package.

5. Whether a minimum number of persons is required for the package to take place and, if so, the deadline for informing the consumer in the event of cancellation.

6. The itinerary.

7. Visits, excursions or other services which are included in the total price agreed for the package.

8. The name and address of the organiser, the retailer and, where appropriate, the insurer.

9. The price of the package, if the price may be revised in accordance with the term which may be included in the contract under regulation 11, an indication of the possibility of such price revisions, and an indication of any dues, taxes or fees chargeable for certain services (landing, embarkation or disembarkation fees at ports and airports and tourist taxes) where such costs are not included in the package.

10. The payment schedule and method of payment.

11. Special requirements which the consumer has communicated to the organiser or retailer when making the booking and which both have accepted.

Paragraph numbers marked with a "+" can be found online and on CD.

12. The periods within which the consumer must make any complaint about the failure to perform or the inadequate performance of the contract.

Contracts (Rights of Third Parties) Act 1999

3H–874

1999 c.31

ARRANGEMENT OF SECTIONS

Paragraph numbers marked with a "+" denote content that is available on White Book on Westlaw UK or the Civil Procedure CD.

Unfair Terms in Consumer Contracts Regulations 1999

3H–886

(S.I. 1999 No. 2083)

ARRANGEMENT OF SECTIONS

General note

3H–887 The European Directive on Unfair Terms in Consumer Contracts (93/13) was first implemented in the UK by the Unfair Terms in Consumer Contracts Regulations 1994, which came into effect on July 1, 1995. Those regulations therefore apply to contracts entered on or after that date and before October 1, 1999 when the present regulations came into force. The present regulations replicate most of what was in the 1994 regulations with some relatively minor modifications to reflect more closely the wording of the Directive.

Contracts affected

3H–888 The regulations apply to contracts concluded between on the one hand a seller or supplier who is acting for purposes related to his trade, business or profession (whether publicly or private owned) and on the other a consumer who is a natural person (not a corporate body) acting for purposes which are outside his trade business or profession (whether publicly or private owned) and on the other a consumer who is a natural person (not a corporate body) acting for purposes which are outside his trade business

Paragraph numbers marked with a "+" can be found online and on CD.

or profession. In *Evans v Cherry Tree Finance Ltd* [2008] EWCA Civ 331; [2008] C.C.L.R. 5, the defendant owned premises used largely for the purposes of his business. He took out a loan, secured on those premises, in order (as the loan application made clear) to provide finance to pay off his divorce settlement. He was acting in the capacity of a consumer, i.e. for purposes outside his trade business or profession. Accordingly the terms of the agreement were assessable for fairness under the regulations. Similarly, where a wealthy professional couple, who did not earn their living from the investment industry, entered into foreign exchange contracts in the hope of making profitable use of their disposable income, these contracts were (despite the large amounts invested) made for purposes outside their trade, business or profession: *Standard Bank London Ltd v Apostolakis* [2002] C.L.C. 933 (High Ct).

The regulations overlap with other enactments, including particularly the Consumer Credit Act 1974 and the Unfair Contract Terms Act 1977. A term of a regulated consumer credit agreement could, for example, form the basis of a claim (under s.140B of the 1974 Act) that there was an unfair relationship between the creditor and the debtor and could also be rendered ineffective by the regulations. The range of contracts subject to the regulations is, in one respect, wider and, in another respect, narrower than those regulated by the Consumer Credit Act. It is wider in that it includes contracts involving all sorts of subject matter, and not just credit and hire agreements. It is narrower in that it does not cover contracts where the customer is making the contract for the purposes of his trade or profession. The scope of the two is the same in one respect, namely neither applies where the customer is a corporate body.

The overlap with the Unfair Contract Terms Act is that an exclusion clause could be rendered ineffective by either, or both of the regulations and the 1977 Act. Unlike the Act, the regulations do not apply (e.g. to standard form exclusion clauses) where both parties are acting for business purposes. On the other hand, where the regulations do apply to a contract, they apply, not just to exclusion clauses but also to other terms that may be unfair.

Effect of the regulations

3H–889

- All written terms are required to be in plain and intelligible language; if there is a doubt, the interpretation most favourable to the consumer applies (reg.7).
- Any terms which (a) are not core terms, (b) have not been individually negotiated and, (c) are unfair, are not binding on the consumer (reg.8). The validity of the rest of the contract is not affected, provided it is capable of continuing in existence without the unfair term. The test of unfairness is stated in reg.5 and a non-exhaustive indicative list of unfair terms is given in Sch.2.
- In so far as they are in plain and intelligible language, the core terms of the contract (i.e. those relating to the definition of the main subject matter of the contract or the adequacy of the price or remuneration) are not subject to the requirement to be fair (reg.6).

3H–890

Regulations 10 to 15 and Sch.1 which are not reproduced here, deal with the powers and duties of the Director General of Fair Trading (now the Office of Fair Trading) and other bodies under the regulations. Under the 1994 Regulations the Director General was given a duty to consider any complaint that a contract term drawn up for general use was unfair and was given a power to ask the court for an injunction to prohibit its use. The 1999 Regulations re-enact those provisions and extend the power to seek an injunction to a range of other regulatory bodies and to trading standards departments. They also extend the power to seek an injunction to the Consumers' Association. Pursuant to the 1994 and the 1999 Regulations, the Office of Fair Trading periodically publishes bulletins giving information on complaints received and undertakings taken from traders to change or abandon the use of particular clauses.

Case law

3H–891

The regulations have no express exclusion for land transactions and thus do apply to tenancy agreements between tenants and a local authority: *Khatun v Newham LBC* [2005] Q.B. 37; [2004] 3 W.L.R. 417. The protection provided for consumers by the Directive (which the regulations implement) entails the court being able of its own motion to determine whether a term of a contract (which is before the court) is unfair, when making its preliminary assessment as to whether to allow a claim to proceed,

Paragraph numbers marked with a "+" can be found online and on CD.

C–240/98 *Oceano Grupo Editorial SA v Rocio Murciano Qunitero*, June 27, 2000, ECJ. That case involved a number of contracts by a company which had its principal place of business in Barcelona, each such contract being a contract to sell, on instalment credit terms, an encyclopedia to a consumer domiciled in another part of Spain. Each contract contained a clause, not individually negotiated, giving exclusive jurisdiction to the Barcelona courts, which is where the seller commenced proceedings against consumers who had defaulted on their repayments. It was held that the Barcelona court should of its own motion (a) determine whether the jurisdiction clause was fair and (b) it being unfair, decline the jurisdiction it conferred.

For an example of a successful challenge under the 1994 Regulations to the terms of a mortgage loan agreement, see *Falco Finance Ltd v Gough* [1999] C.C.L.R. 16, noted in the commentary to the Consumer Credit Act 1974 s.138 (at para.3H–320, above). In *Director General of Fair Trading v First National Bank Plc* [2002] 1 A.C. 48; [2003] C.C.L.R. 8, HL, the Director General sought an injunction (under the 1994 Regulations) in respect of a clause in the standard form loan agreement used by the defendant Bank. The contractual rate of interest was stated and was variable in accordance with changes in the Bank's Base Lending rate. Clause 3 of the agreement provided that that rate of interest was to be charged on a day to day basis on the outstanding balance and debited to the account in arrears. Clause 8 provided that the same rate of interest would be charged on arrears until payment. It further provided that interest would continue to be charged at the same rate after judgment, until the debt was paid. Clause 3 and the other contract provisions which fixed the contractual rate of interest were core terms (concerned with the adequacy of the remuneration) which could not be challenged as unfair under the regulations (see now reg.6 of the 1999 Regulations). Clause 8, however was assessable for fairness. It was part of the Director General's case that not infrequently a borrower, against whom the Bank had brought proceedings to recover the outstanding balance, would agree to a consent order being made, such judgment being for the balance to be payable by instalments over an extended period. The effects of clause 8 were: (i) to reverse the common law rule that the right to interest merged with the judgment debt and thus evaporated after judgment; (ii) to oust the application of the County Court (Interest on Judgments) Order 1991 (under which no interest is payable on judgments for money due under regulated consumer credit agreements). The House of Lords held that clause 8 was not unfair within the 1994 Regulations. The problems for consumers (debtors) arose from the fact that debtors were unaware of the reliefs which the court could give them at the default stage. Those reliefs included: (i) re-opening an extortionate agreement (under s.139 of the Consumer Credit Act 1974); and (ii) reducing the rate of interest (under s.136 when granting a time order under s.128 of the 1974 Act). It was, however, not customary (nor was it a statutory requirement) that the debtor be given notice of those possible reliefs when the contract was made. Clause 8 was not rendered unfair by the absence of procedural safeguards for the debtor at the default stage. Such procedural safeguards, subsequently introduced by the Consumer Credit Act 2006, are now to be found in ss.86A to 86F of the Consumer Credit Act 1974. Section 86F prevents more than simple interest being payable on "default sums". *Cf. Bairstow Eves London Central v Smith* [2004] EWHC 263; [2004] E.G. 118, (QB), where the contract provided for an estate agent to be paid commission of 1.5 per cent of the purchase price. A clause entitling the estate agent to claim commission at 3 per cent if the commission was not paid in full within 10 days of completion of the sale, was held, (a) not to fall within reg.6(2) and thus to be assessable for fairness and, (b) to be unfair.

Arbitration agreements

3H–892   A term of an agreement which amounts to an arbitration agreement is unfair within the meaning of the regulations in so far as it relates to a claim for a pecuniary remedy which does not exceed £5000: Arbitration Act 1996 s.91(1)—see para.2E–324+. This provision can be seen as a more precise statement of a more vaguely worded provision in para.(q) of Schedule 2 to the Regulations. Also it applies even where the "consumer" is a legal person as well as when he is a natural person: Arbitration Act, s.90.

Citation and commencement

3H–893   **1.** These Regulations may be cited as the Unfair Terms in Consumer Contracts Regulations 1999 and shall come into force on 1st October 1999.

Paragraph numbers marked with a "+" can be found online and on CD.

Revocation

2. The Unfair Terms in Consumer Contracts Regulations 1994 are hereby revoked.

3H–894

Interpretation

3.—(1) In these Regulations—

3H–895

"the Community" means the European Community;

"consumer" means any natural person who, in contracts covered by these Regulations, is acting for purposes which are outside his trade, business or profession;

"court" in relation to England and Wales and Northern Ireland means a county court or the High Court, and in relation to Scotland, the Sheriff or the Court of Session;

"Director" means the Director General of Fair Trading;

"EEA Agreement" means the Agreement on the European Economic Area signed at Oporto on 2nd May 1992 as adjusted by the protocol signed at Brussels on 17th March 1993;

"Member State" means a State which is a contracting party to the EEA Agreement;

"notified" means notified in writing;

"qualifying body" means a person specified in Schedule 1;

"seller or supplier" means any natural or legal person who, in contracts covered by these Regulations, is acting for purposes relating to his trade, business or profession, whether publicly owned or privately owned;

"unfair terms" means the contractual terms referred to in regulation 5.

(1A) The references—

(a) in regulation 4(1) to a seller or a supplier, and

(b) in regulation 8(1) to a seller or supplier,

include references to a distance supplier and to an intermediary.

(1B) In paragraph (1A) and regulation 5(6) "distance supplier" means—

(a) a supplier under a distance contract within the meaning of the Financial Services (Distance Marketing) Regulations 2004, or

(b) a supplier of unsolicited financial services within regulation 15 of those Regulations; and

"intermediary" has the same meaning as in those Regulations.

(2) In the application of these Regulations to Scotland for references to an "injunction" or an "interim injunction" there shall be substituted references to an "interdict" or "interim interdict" respectively.

Note —Paragraphs (1A) and (1B) were added by the Financial Services (Distance Marketing) Regulations 2004 (SI 2004/2095). "Consumer"—In *Evans v Cherry Tree Finance Ltd* [2008] EWCA Civ 331; [2008] C.C.L.R. 5, the debtor who had applied for a loan stating the purpose to be "to pay equity to divorced wife and pay off existing mortgage" was held to have been acting for purposes outside his trade business or profession. For other cases on the meaning of "consumer", see *Benincasa v Dentalkit* [1997] E.C.R. I-3767 and *Standard Bank London Ltd v Apostolakis* [2002] C.L.C. 933.

3H–896

Paragraph numbers marked with a "+" can be found online and on CD.

CONSUMER

Terms to which these Regulations apply

3H–897   **4.**—(1) These Regulations apply in relation to unfair terms in contracts concluded between a seller or a supplier and a consumer.

(2) These Regulations do not apply to contractual terms which reflect—

(a) mandatory statutory or regulatory provisions (including such provisions under the law of any Member State or in Community legislation having effect in the United Kingdom without further enactment);

(b) the provisions or principles of international conventions to which the Member States or the Community are party.

Unfair Terms

3H–898   **5.**—(1) A contractual term which has not been individually negotiated shall be regarded as unfair if, contrary to the requirement of good faith, it causes a significant imbalance in the parties' rights and obligations arising under the contract, to the detriment of the consumer.

(2) A term shall always be regarded as not having been individually negotiated where it has been drafted in advance and the consumer has therefore not been able to influence the substance of the term.

(3) Notwithstanding that a specific term or certain aspects of its in a contract has been individually negotiated, these Regulations shall apply to the rest of a contract if an overall assessment of it indicates that it is a pre-formulated standard contract.

(4) It shall be for any seller or supplier who claims that a term was individually negotiated to show that it was.

(5) Schedule 2 to these Regulations contains an indicative and non-exhaustive list of the terms which may be regarded as unfair.

(6) Any contractual term providing that a consumer bears the burden of proof in respect of showing whether a distance supplier or an intermediary complied with any or all of the obligations placed upon him resulting from the Directive and any rule or enactment implementing it shall always be regarded as unfair.

(7) In paragraph (6)—

"the Directive" means Directive 2002/65/EC of the European Parliament and of the Council of 23 September 2002 concerning the distance marketing of consumer financial services and amending Council Directive 90/619/EEC and Directives 97/7/EC and 98/27/EC; and

"rule" means a rule made by the Financial Services Authority under the Financial Services and Markets Act 2000 or by a designated professional body within the meaning of section 326(2) of that Act.

3H–899   *Note* —Paragraphs (6) and (7) were added by the Financial Services (Distance Marketing) Regulations 2004 (SI 2004/2095). See, generally, case law mentioned in the general note at the start of these Regulations.

Assessment of unfair terms

3H–900   **6.**—(1) Without prejudice to regulation 12, the unfairness of a

Paragraph numbers marked with a "+" can be found online and on CD.

(a) Paragraph 1(g) is without hindrance to terms by which a supplier of financial services reserves the right to terminate unilaterally a contract of indeterminate duration without notice where there is a valid reason, provided that the supplier is required to inform the other contracting party or parties thereof immediately.

(b) Paragraph 1(j) is without hindrance to terms under which a supplier of financial services reserves the right to alter the rate of interest payable by the consumer or due to the latter, or the amount of other charges for financial services without notice where there is a valid reason, provided that the supplier is required to inform the other contracting party or parties thereof at the earliest opportunity and that the latter are free to dissolve the contract immediately.

Paragraph 1(j) is also without hindrance to terms under which a seller or supplier reserves the right to alter unilaterally the conditions of a contract of indeterminate duration, provided that he is required to inform the consumer with reasonable notice and that the consumer is free to dissolve the contract.

(c) Paragraphs 1(g), (j) and (l) do not apply to:
  – transactions in transferable securities, financial instruments and other products or services where the price is linked to fluctuations in a stock exchange quotation or index or a financial market rate that the seller or supplier does not control;
  – contracts for the purchase or sale of foreign currency, traveller's cheques or international money orders denominated in foreign currency.

(d) Paragraph 1(l) is without hindrance to price indexation clauses, where lawful, provided that the method by which prices vary is explicitly described.

The Consumer Protection (Distance Selling) Regulations 2000

(S.I. 2000 No. 2344)

3H–906

ARRANGEMENT OF REGULATIONS

Paragraph numbers marked with a "+" can be found online and on CD.

CONSUMER

Paragraphs numbers marked with a "+" denote content that is available on White Book on Westlaw UK or the Civil Procedure CD.

Sale and Supply of Goods to Consumers Regulations 2002

3H–954

(S.I. 2002 No. 3045)

ARRANGEMENT OF REGULATIONS

REG.

General note

3H–955 These regulations implemented the Directive on Certain Aspects of Sale of Goods and Consumer Guarantees (1999/44/EC). They made the seller liable for public statements made by the seller, the producer or his representative; they extended the range of remedies available to a consumer in the case of goods which fail to comply with statutory implied terms; they provide, in regulation 15, that a consumer guarantee takes effect as a contractual obligation. Regs 2 and 15 are the only free-standing provisions in the regulations. The other provisions all operate by making amendments to existing Acts, namely: Supply of Goods (Implied Terms) Act 1973; Supply of Goods and Services Act 1982; Unfair Contract Terms Act 1977; Sale of Goods Act 1979. See commentaries to ss.14(2D) and 48A of the Sale of Goods Act 1979 above.

Interpretation

3H–956 **2.** In these Regulations—

"consumer" means any natural person who, in the contracts covered by these Regulations, is acting for purposes which are outside his trade, business or profession;

"consumer guarantee" means any undertaking to a consumer by a person acting in the course of his business, given without extra charge, to reimburse the price paid or to replace, repair or handle consumer goods in any way if they do not meet the specifications set out in the guarantee statement or in the relevant advertising;

"court" in relation to England and Wales and Northern Ireland means a county court or the High Court, and in relation to Scotland, the sheriff or the Court of Session;

"enforcement authority" means the Director General of Fair Trading, every local weights and measures authority in Great Britain and the Department of Enterprise, Trade and Investment for Northern

Paragraph numbers marked with a "+" can be found online and on CD.

> Ireland; "goods" has the same meaning as in section 61 of the Sale of Goods Act 1979;
>
> "guarantor" means a person who offers a consumer guarantee to a consumer; and
>
> "supply" includes supply by way of sale, lease, hire or hire-purchase.

* * * *

Consumer guarantees

15.—(1) Where goods are sold or otherwise supplied to a consumer which are offered with a consumer guarantee, the consumer guarantee takes effect at the time the goods are delivered as a contractual obligation owed by the guarantor under the conditions set out in the guarantee statement and the associated advertising. **3H–957**

(2) The guarantor shall ensure that the guarantee sets out in plain intelligible language the contents of the guarantee and the essential particulars necessary for making claims under the guarantee, notably the duration and territorial scope of the guarantee as well as the name and address of the guarantor.

(2A) The guarantor shall also ensure that the guarantee contains a statement that the consumer has statutory rights in relation to the goods which are sold or supplied and that those rights are not affected by the guarantee.

(3) On request by the consumer to a person to whom paragraph (4) applies, the guarantee shall within a reasonable time be made available in writing or in another durable medium available and accessible to him.

(4) This paragraph applies to the guarantor and any other person who offers to consumers the goods which are the subject of the guarantee for sale or supply.

(5) Where consumer goods are offered with a consumer guarantee, and where those goods are offered within the territory of the United Kingdom, then the guarantor shall ensure that the consumer guarantee is written in English.

(6) If the guarantor fails to comply with the provisions of paragraphs (2) or (5) above, or a person to whom paragraph (4) applies fails to comply with paragraph (3) then the enforcement authority may apply for an injunction or (in Scotland) an order of specific implement against that person requiring him to comply.

(7) The court on application under this Regulation may grant an injunction or (in Scotland) an order of specific implement on such terms as it thinks fit.

Note —Amended by SI 2008/1277. **3H–957.1**

Extended warranties on electrical goods

In addition to the protection given under reg.15 above, a consumer who buys an extended guarantee (usually one lasting more than a year) relating to an electrical product may have further protection by virtue of the Supply of Extended Warranties on Domestic Electrical Goods Order 2005 (SI 2005/37). The 2005 Order does not apply to a warranty unless the consumer gives a monetary consideration for it and thus does not apply where a warranty or guarantee comes free with the goods. Nor does it **3H–958**

Paragraph numbers marked with a "+" can be found online and on CD.

apply to extended warranties that are distance contracts. It is designed to deal with the situation where a consumer buys an electrical item (usually making the purchase in-store) and also (for an additional amount) buys an extended warranty (usually one lasting more than one year after purchase of the goods). The Order requires, where an extended warranty is available for purchase at the same time as electrical goods are bought, that in-store (or in-catalogue) information be displayed, close to where the goods are displayed (or advertised) clearly indicating that purchase of the extended guarantee is optional and stating its duration and price. The Order makes it unlawful for the trader to supply the consumer with an extended warranty lasting more than a year unless the consumer is allowed certain cancellation and termination rights. As regards cancellation, the consumer must be allowed, for 45 days after purchasing the warranty (and provided no claim has been made under it), to give notice, either written or oral, to cancel it and to obtain a complete refund of the price of it. As regards termination, the consumer must be allowed, regardless of whether a claim has been made under the warranty, to give oral or written notice to terminate it after the 45 day period and to obtain a pro-rata refund. Where the price of the warranty exceeds £20, the supplier must give the consumer written notice of the consumer's rights of cancellation and termination.

Paragraph numbers marked with a "+" can be found online and on CD.

3I DISCRIMINATION

PRACTICE DIRECTION—PROCEEDINGS UNDER ENACTMENTS RELATING TO DISCRIMINATION

3I–1

Scope and Interpretation

1.1 This Practice Direction applies to certain county court proceedings under the enactments defined in paragraph 1.2.

1.2 In this Practice Direction—

(1) 'the 1975 Act' means the Sex Discrimination Act 1975[1];

(2) 'the 1976 Act' means the Race Relations Act 1976[2];

(3) 'the 1995 Act' means the Disability Discrimination Act 1995[3];

(4) 'the 2006 Act' means the Equality Act 2006[4]

(5) 'the Religion or Belief Regulations' means the Employment Equality (Religion or Belief) Regulations 2003[5];

(6) 'the Sexual Orientation Regulations 2003' means the Employment Equality (Sexual Orientation) Regulations 2003[6];

(7) 'the Age Regulations' means the Employment Equality (Age) Regulations 2006[7];

(8) 'the Sexual Orientation Regulations 2007' means the Equality Act (Sexual Orientation) Regulations 2007[8].

1.3 In this Practice Direction—

(a) a reference to 'the Commission', in relation to proceedings under a particular enactment is a reference to the Commission for Equality and Human Rights;

(b) where it applies to proceedings under the 1976 Act, 'court' means a designated county court under section 67(1) of that Act.

Commission to be given notice of claims

2.1 This paragraph applies to claims under—

3I–2

(a) section 66 of the 1975 Act;

(b) section 57 of the 1976 Act;

(c) section 25 of the 1995 Act;

(d) section 66 of the 2006 Act;

(e) regulation 39 of the Age Regulations;

(f) regulation 31 of the Religion or Belief Regulations;

(g) regulation 31 of the Sexual Orientation Regulations 2003; or

---

[1] 1975 c.65.
[2] 1976 c.74.
[3] 1995 c.50.
[4] 2006 c.3.
[5] S.I. 2003/1660.
[6] S.I. 2003/1661.
[7] S.I. 2006/1031
[8] S.I. 2007/1263.

Paragraph numbers marked with a "+" can be found online and on CD.

    (h)   regulation 20 of the Sexual Orientation Regulations 2007.

2.2 When a claim to which this paragraph applies is commenced, the claimant must—

    (a)   give notice of the commencement of the proceedings to the Commission;

    (b)   file a copy of that notice.

Assessors

3I–3   **3.** Rule 35.15 has effect in relation to an assessor who is to be appointed in proceedings under section 66 (1) of the 1975 Act.

Admissibility of Evidence

3I–4   **4.1** This paragraph applies where a claimant in a claim alleging discrimination has questioned the defendant under—

    (a)   section 74 of the 1975 Act;

    (b)   section 65 of the 1976 Act;

    (c)   section 56 of the 1995 Act;

    (d)   regulation 41 of the Age Regulations;

    (e)   regulation 33 of the Religion or Belief Regulations; or

    (f)   regulation 33 of the Sexual Orientation Employment Regulations 2003.

    (g)   section 70 of the 2006 Act; or

    (h)   regulation 24 of the Sexual Orientation Regulations 2007.

4.2 Either party may apply to the court to determine whether the question or any reply is admissible under that section.

(Part 23 contains general rules about making applications).

4.3 Rule 3.4 (power to strike out a statement of case) applies to the question and any answer as it applies to a statement of case.

Exclusion of persons from certain proceedings

3I–5   **5.1** In a claim—

    (1)   brought under section 66(1) of the 1975 Act;

    (2)   brought under section 57(1) of the 1976 Act;

    (3)   alleging discrimination under the 1995 Act;

    (4)   brought under section 66 of the 2006 Act; or

    (5)   brought under regulation 20 of the Sexual Orientation Regulations 2007,

the court may, where it considers it expedient in the interests of national security —

    (a)   exclude from all or part of the proceedings—

      (i) the claimant;

      (ii) the claimant's representatives; or

      (iii) any assessors

      (Section 67(4) of the 1976 Act allows an assessor to be appointed in proceedings under that Act);

    (b)   permit a claimant or representative to make a statement to the court before the start of the proceedings (or the part of the proceedings) from which he is excluded; or

Paragraph numbers marked with a "+" can be found online and on CD.

(c)   take steps to keep secret all or part of the reasons for its decision in the claim.

5.2 In this paragraph, a 'special advocate' means a person appointed under—

(1)   section 66B(2) of the 1975 Act;

(2)   section 67A(2) of the 1976 Act;

(3)   section 59A(2) of the 1995 Act;

(4)   section 71(2) of the 2006 Act; or

(5)   regulation 25(2) of the Sexual Orientation Regulations 2007.

5.3 In proceedings to which this paragraph refers, where the claimant or his representatives have been excluded from all or part of the proceedings—

(a)   the court will inform the Attorney General of the proceedings; and

(b)   the Attorney General may appoint a special advocate to represent the claimant in respect of those parts of the proceedings from which he or his representative have been excluded.

5.4 In exercise of its powers under paragraph 5.1(c), the court may order the special advocate not to communicate (directly or indirectly) with any persons (including the excluded claimant)—

(a)   on any matter discussed or referred to; or

(b)   with regard to any material disclosed,

during or with reference to any part of the proceedings from which the claimant or his representative are excluded.

5.5 Where the court makes an order referred to in paragraph 5.4 (or any similar order), the special advocate may apply to the court for directions enabling him to seek instructions from, or otherwise to communicate with an excluded person.

Expenses of Commission

6.1 This paragraph applies where the Commission has, in respect **3I–6** of a claim, provided a claimant with assistance under section 28 of the 2006 Act.

6.2 If the Commission claims a charge for expenses incurred by it in providing such assistance, it must give notice of the claim to—

(a)   the court; and

(b)   the claimant

within 14 days of determination of the proceedings.

6.3 If notice is given to the court under paragraph 6.2—

(a)   money paid into court for the benefit of the claimant that relates to costs and expenses must not be paid out unless this is permitted by an order of the court; and

(b)   the court may order the expenses incurred by the Commission to be assessed as if they were costs payable by the claimant to his own solicitor for work done in connection with the proceedings.

6.4 The court may either—

(a)   make a summary assessment of the expenses; or

Paragraph numbers marked with a "+" can be found online and on CD.

(b) order detailed assessment of the expenses by a costs officer.

Editorial note

3I-7   Proceedings for unlawful sex and race discrimination may be brought under the Sex Discrimination Act 1975 and the Race Relations Act 1976. Part VII of the former Act and Part VIII of the latter contain provisions dealing with (amongst other things) the bringing of civil proceedings for discrimination. Those provisions are set out below (see paras. 3I–9 *et seq.* to 3I–27). Extended commentary on these Parts then follows (see para.3I–41 *et seq.*). Proceedings for discrimination may also be brought under the Disability Discrimination Act 1995, the Employment Equality (Religion or Belief) Regulations 2003 (SI 2003/1660) and the Employment Equality (Sexual Orientation) Regulations 2003 (SI 2003/1661). Selected provisions relating to the bringing of proceedings under the Disability Discrimination Act 1995 are set out in paras 3I–47 *et seq.*, followed by commentary (para.3I–50). Part 2 of the Equality Act 2006 has also introduced provisions addressing religion and belief discrimination comparable to that made in the Sex Discrimination Act 1975 and the Race Relations Act 1976, including in relation to enforcement (ss.65–71). These provisions came into force on April 30, 2007. Selected provisions are set out in paras 3I–26 *et seq.* Part 3 of the Equality Act gives the Secretary of State power to introduce regulations "about discrimination or harassment on grounds of sexual orientation" and "in particular make provision of a kind similar to Part 2" of the Equality Act 2006 (s.81). Regulations have been made and brought into force with effect from April 30, 2007 (Equality Act (Sexual Orientation) Regulations 2007 (SI 2007/1263)). These Regulations contain measures prohibiting discrimination on grounds of sexual orientation in the provision of goods, facilities and services, education, the use and disposal of premises and the exercise of public functions. Their enforcement provisions mirror those provided for in the other anti discrimination enactments. Part 1 of the Equality Act 2006 establishes the Equality and Human Rights Commission ("EHRC"). From October 1, 2007, the EHRC has taken over the functions of the Commission for Racial Equality, the Equal Opportunities Commission and the Disability Rights Commission. The relevant provisions of the Equality Act are referred to in the notes below. As is indicated in the commentary, rules of court relating to proceedings under the legislation referred to above are found in CPR, Sch.2 CCR O.49, r.17 (see Vol.1, para.cc49.17).

Sex Discrimination Act 1975

3I-8   (1975 c.65)

ARRANGEMENT OF SECTIONS

PART VII

ENFORCEMENT

GENERAL

Paragraph numbers marked with a "+" can be found online and on CD.

PART VII

ENFORCEMENT

GENERAL

Restriction of proceedings for breach of Act

62.—(1) Except as provided by this Act no proceedings, whether   **3I–9**
civil or criminal, shall lie against any person in respect of an act by
reason that the act is unlawful by virtue of a provision of this Act.

(2) Subsection (1) does not preclude the making of an order of
certiorari, mandamus or prohibition.

(3) [...]

* * * *

ENFORCEMENT OF PART III

Claims under Part III

66.—(1) A claim by any person ("the claimant") that another   **3I–10**
person ("the respondent")—

    (a) has committed an act of discrimination or harassment
        against the claimant which is unlawful by virtue of Part
        III other than section 35A or 35B, or

    (b) is by virtue of section 41 or 42 to be treated as having
        committed such an act of discrimination or harassment
        against the claimant,

may be made the subject of civil proceedings in like manner as
any other claim in tort or (in Scotland) in reparation for breach of
statutory duty.

(2) Proceedings under subsection (1)—

    (a) shall be brought in England and Wales only in a county
        court, and

    (b) shall be brought in Scotland only in a sheriff court,

but all such remedies shall be obtainable in such proceedings as,
apart from this subsection and section 62(1), would be obtainable in
the High Court or the Court of Session, as the case may be.

(3) As respects an unlawful act of discrimination falling within
section 1(1)(b) ... no award of damages shall be made if the respondent proves that the requirement or condition in question was not
applied with the intention of treating the claimant unfavourably on
the ground of his sex.

(3A) Subsection (3) does not affect the award of damages in respect of an unlawful act of discrimination falling within section
1(2)(b).

(4) For the avoidance of doubt it is hereby declared that damages
in respect of an unlawful act of discrimination or harassment may

Paragraph numbers marked with a "+" can be found online and on CD.

include compensation for injury to feelings whether or not they include compensation under any other head.

(5) Civil proceedings in respect of a claim by any person that he has been discriminated against, or subjected to harassment, in contravention of section 22 or 23 by a body to which section 25(1) applies shall not be instituted unless the claimant has given notice of the claim to the Secretary of State and either the Secretary of State has by notice informed the claimant that the Secretary of State does not require further time to consider the matter, or the period of two months has elapsed since the claimant gave notice to the Secretary of State; but nothing in this subsection applies to a counterclaim.

(6) For the purposes of proceedings under subsection (1)—

    (a) section 63(1) (assessors) of the County Courts Act 1984 shall apply with the omission of the words "on the application of any party", and

    (b) [...]

(7) [...]

(8) A county court or sheriff court shall have jurisdiction to entertain proceedings under subsection (1) with respect to an act done on a ship, aircraft or hovercraft outside its district, including such an act done outside Great Britain.

3I–11   *Note* —Amended by SI 2005/2467.

Burden of proof: county and sheriff courts

3I–12   **66A.**—(1) This section applies to any claim brought under section 66(1) in a county court in England and Wales or a sheriff court in Scotland.

(2) Where, on the hearing of the claim, the claimant proves facts from which the court could, apart from this section, conclude in the absence of an adequate explanation that the respondent—

    (a) has committed an act of discrimination or harassment against the claimant which is unlawful by virtue of—

        (i) section 29, 30 or 31, or

        (ii) any other provision of Part 3 so far as it applies to vocational training, or

    (b) is by virtue of section 41 or 42 to be treated as having committed such an act of discrimination [or harassment] against the claimant,

the court shall uphold the claim unless the respondent proves that he did not commit, or, as the case may be, is not to be treated as having committed, that act.]

3I–13   *Note* —Amended by SI 2005/2467 and SI 2008/963.

National security

3I–14   **66B.**—(1) Rules of court may make provision for enabling a county court or sheriff court in which a claim is brought under section 66(1), where the court considers it expedient in the interests of national security—

Paragraph numbers marked with a "+" can be found online and on CD.

(a) to exclude from all or part of the proceedings—

    (i) the claimant;

    (ii) the claimant's representatives;

    (iii) any assessors;

(b) to permit a claimant or representative who has been excluded to make a statement to the court before the commencement of the proceedings, or the part of the proceedings, from which he is excluded;

(c) to take steps to keep secret all or part of the reasons for the court's decision in the proceedings.

(2) The Attorney General or, in Scotland, the Advocate General for Scotland, may appoint a person to represent the interests of a claimant in, or in any part of, proceedings from which the claimant or his representatives are excluded by virtue of subsection (1).

(3) A person may be appointed under subsection (2) only—

(a) in relation to proceedings in England and Wales, if he has a general qualification (within the meaning of section 71 of the Courts and Legal Services Act 1990 (c. 41)), or

(b) in relation to proceedings in Scotland, if he is—

    (i) an advocate, or

    (ii) qualified to practice as a solicitor in Scotland.

(4) A person appointed under subsection (2) shall not be responsible to the person whose interests he is appointed to represent.

Note —Inserted by the Equality Act 2006 s.87, with effect from April 18, 2006 (SI **3I–15** 2006/1082).

*   *   *   *

HELP FOR PERSONS SUFFERING DISCRIMINATION

Help for aggrieved persons in obtaining information etc

74.—(1) With a view to helping a person ("the person aggrieved") **3I–16** who considers he may have been discriminated against or subjected to harassment in contravention of this Act to decide whether to institute proceedings and, if he does so, to formulate and present his case in the most effective manner, the Minister shall by order prescribe—

(a) forms by which the person aggrieved may question the respondent on his reasons for doing any relevant act, or on any other matter which is or may be relevant;

(b) forms by which the respondent may if he so wishes reply to any questions.

(2) Where the person aggrieved questions the respondent (whether in accordance with an order under subsection (1) or not)—

(a) the question, and any reply by the respondent (whether in accordance with such an order or not) shall, subject to

Paragraph numbers marked with a "+" can be found online and on CD.

the following provisions of this section, be admissible as evidence in the proceedings;

(b) if it appears to the court or tribunal that the respondent deliberately, and without reasonable excuse, omitted to reply within the period applicable under subsection (2A) or that his reply is evasive or equivocal, the court or tribunal may draw any inference from that fact that it considers it just and equitable to draw, including an inference that he committed an unlawful act.

(2A) The period applicable for the purposes of subsection (2)(b) is—

(a) eight weeks beginning with the day when the question was served on the respondent, if the question relates to discrimination under—

(i) any provision of Part 2,

(ia) section 29, 30 or 31, except in so far as it relates to an excluded matter,

(ii) section 35A or 35B, or

(iii) any other provision of Part 3, so far as it applies to vocational training;

(b) a reasonable period, as regards any other question.

(3) The Minister may by order—

(a) prescribe the period within which questions must be duly served in order to be admissible under subsection (2)(a), and

(b) prescribe the manner in which a question, and any reply by the respondent, may be duly served.

(4) Rules may enable the court entertaining a claim under section 66 to determine, before the date fixed for the hearing of the claim, whether a question or reply is admissible under this section or not.

(5) This section is without prejudice to any other enactment or rule of law regulating interlocutory and preliminary matters in proceedings before a county court, sheriff court or employment tribunal, and has effect subject to any enactment or rule of law regulating the admissibility of evidence in such proceedings.

(6) In this section "respondent" includes a prospective respondent and "rules"—

(a) in relation to county court proceedings, means county court rules;

(b) in relation to sheriff court proceedings, means sheriff court rules.

3I–17   *Note* —Amended by SI 2005/2467, SI 2007/2914 and SI 2008/963.

* * * *

PERIOD WITHIN WHICH PROCEEDINGS TO BE BROUGHT

Period within which proceedings to be brought

3I–18   76.—(1) [...]

Paragraph numbers marked with a "+" can be found online and on CD.

(2) A county court or a sheriff court shall not consider a claim under section 66 unless proceedings in respect of the claim are instituted before the end of

    (a) the period of six months beginning when the act complained of was done; or

    (b) in a case to which section 66(5) applies, the period of eight months so beginning.

(2A) Where in England and Wales—

    (a) proceedings or prospective proceedings under section 66 relate to the act or omission of a qualifying institution, and

    (b) the dispute concerned is referred as a complaint under the student complaints scheme before the end of the period of six months mentioned in subsection (2)(a),

the period allowed by subsection (2)(a) shall be extended by three months.

(2B) In subsection (2A)—

"qualifying institution" has the meaning given by section 11 of the Higher Education Act 2004;

"the student complaints scheme" means a scheme for the review of qualifying complaints, as defined by section 12 of that Act, that is provided by the designated operator, as defined by section 13(5)(b) of that Act.

(2C) The period allowed by subsection (2)(a) or (b) shall be extended by three months in the case of a dispute which is referred for conciliation in pursuance of arrangements under section 27 of the Equality Act 2006 (unless the period is extended under subsection (2A)).

(3) [...]

(4) [...]

(5) A court or tribunal may nevertheless consider any such complaint or claim which is out of time if, in all the circumstances of the case, it considers that it is just and equitable to do so.

(6) For the purposes of this section—

    (a) where the inclusion of any term in a contract renders the making of the contract an unlawful act that act shall be treated as extending throughout the duration of the contract, and

    (b) any act extending over a period shall be treated as done at the end of that period, and

    (c) a deliberate omission shall be treated as done when the person in question decided upon it,

and in the absence of evidence establishing the contrary a person shall be taken for the purposes of this section to decide upon an omission when he does an act inconsistent with doing the omitted act or, if he has done no such inconsistent act, when the period expires within which he might reasonably have been expected to do the omitted act if it was to be done.

Note —Amended by the Higher Education Act 2004 s.19(1). Subsection (2A) was **3I–19**

Paragraph numbers marked with a "+" can be found online and on CD.

amended so as to extend the period from two months to three months, by the Equality Act 2006 s.40, Sch.3, paras 6, 14(1), (2) from October 1, 2007 (the Equality Act 2006 (Commencement No.3 and Savings) Order 2007 SI 2007/2603). Subsection (2C), providing for an extension of time where a complaint has been referred for conciliation pursuant to arrangements made under s.27 of the Equality Act 2006, was inserted by the Equality Act 2006 s.40, Sch.3, paras 6, 14(1), (3) from October 1, 2007 (the Equality Act 2006 (Commencement No.3 and Savings) Order 2007 SI 2007/2603. Subsection (3) is repealed by the Equality Act 2006 s.40, Sch.3, paras 6, 14(1), (4), Sch.4 from October 1, 2007 (the Equality Act 2006 (Commencement No.3 and Savings) Order 2007 SI 2007/2603. In subsection (5) the words "complaint, claim or application" were repealed and replaced with replaced with the words "complaint or claim" by the Equality Act 2006 s.40, Sch.3, paras 6, 14(1), (5), from October 1, 2007 (the Equality Act 2006 (Commencement No.3 and Savings) Order 2007 SI 2007/2603.

Public authorities: general statutory duty

31–20   **76A.**—(1) A public authority shall in carrying out its functions have due regard to the need—

     (a) to eliminate unlawful discrimination and harassment, and

     (b) to promote equality of opportunity between men and women.

   (2) In subsection (1)—

     (a) "public authority" includes any person who has functions of a public nature (subject to subsections (3) and (4)),

     (b) "functions" means functions of a public nature, and

     (c) the reference to unlawful discrimination shall be treated as including a reference to contravention of terms of contracts having effect in accordance with an equality clause within the meaning of section 1 of the Equal Pay Act 1970 (c. 41).

   (3) The duty in subsection (1) shall not apply to—

     (a) the House of Commons,

     (b) the House of Lords,

     (c) the Scottish Parliament,

   (ca) the National Assembly for Wales,

     (d) the General Synod of the Church of England,

     (e) the Security Service,

     (f) the Secret Intelligence Service,

     (g) the Government Communications Headquarters,

     (h) a part of the armed forces of the Crown which is, in accordance with a requirement of the Secretary of State, assisting the Government Communications Headquarters, or

     (i) a person specified for the purpose of this paragraph by order of the Minister (and a person may be specified generally or only in respect of specified functions).

   (4) The duty in subsection (1) shall not apply to the exercise of—

     (a) a function in connection with proceedings in the House of Commons or the House of Lords,

Paragraph numbers marked with a "+" can be found online and on CD.

   (b) a function in connection with proceedings in the Scottish Parliament (other than a function of the Scottish Parliamentary Corporate Body),

  (ba) a function in connection with proceedings in the National Assembly for Wales (other than a function of the National Assembly for Wales Commission),

   (c) a judicial function (whether in connection with a court or a tribunal),

   (d) a function exercised on behalf of or on the instructions of a person exercising a judicial function (whether in connection with a court or a tribunal), or

   (e) a function specified for the purpose of this paragraph by order of the Minister.

(5) Subsection (1)(b) is without prejudice to the effect of any exception to or limitation of the law about sex discrimination.

(6) A failure in respect of performance of the duty under subsection (1) does not confer a cause of action at private law.

Note —Inserted by the Equality Act 2006 s.84, with effect from April 18, 2006 (for **3I–21** certain purposes) and April 6, 2007 (for remaining purposes) (see SI 2006/1082); amended by SI 2007/1388 and SI 2007/2914.

Specific duties

76B.—(1) The Minister may by order impose on a person to **3I–22** whom the duty in section 76A(1) applies, or in so far as that duty applies to a person, a duty which the Minister thinks will ensure better performance of the duty under section 76A(1).

(2) Before making an order under subsection (1) the Minister shall consult the Commission.

(3) The Minister—

   (a) must consult the Welsh Ministers before making an order under subsection (1) in respect of a person exercising functions in relation to Wales, and

   (b) may not, without the consent of the Welsh Ministers, make an order under subsection (1) in respect of a person all of whose functions are public functions in relation to Wales.

(4) A failure in respect of performance of a duty imposed under subsection (1) does not confer a cause of action at private law.

Note —Inserted by the Equality Act 2006 s.85, with effect from April 18, 2006 (for **3I–23** certain purposes) and April 6, 2007 (for remaining purposes) (see SI 2006/1082); amended by SI 2007/1388 and SI 2007/2914. For subordinate legislation see, Sex Discrimination Act 1975 (Public Authorities) (Statutory Duties) Order 2006 (SI 2006/2930) (made under subs.(1)).

Specific duties: Scotland

76C.—(1) Section 76B(1) shall not apply in relation to a person **3I–24** who is a relevant Scottish authority or a cross-border authority.

(2) The Minister may by order impose on a cross-border authority to whom the duty under section 76A(1) applies, or in so far as

Paragraph numbers marked with a "+" can be found online and on CD.

that duty applies to the cross-border authority, a duty which the Minister thinks will ensure better performance of the duty under section 76A(1), to the extent that the cross-border authority's functions are not Scottish functions.

(3) The Scottish Ministers may by order impose on a relevant Scottish authority to whom the duty under section 76A(1) applies, or in so far as that duty applies to the relevant Scottish authority, a duty which the Scottish Ministers think will ensure better performance of the duty under section 76A(1).

(4) The Scottish Ministers may by order impose on a cross-border authority to whom the duty under section 76A(1) applies, or in so far as that duty applies to the cross-border authority, a duty which the Scottish Ministers think will ensure better performance of the duty under section 76A(1), to the extent that the cross-border authority's functions are Scottish functions.

(5) Before making an order under any of subsections (2) to (4) the person making the order shall consult the Commission.

(6) Before making an order under subsection (2) the Minister shall consult the Scottish Ministers.

(7) Before making an order under subsection (4) the Scottish Ministers shall consult the Minister.

(8) A failure in respect of performance of a duty imposed under this section does not confer a cause of action at private law.

(9) In this section—
"relevant Scottish authority" means—
(a) a member of the Scottish executive or a junior Scottish Minister;
(b) the Registrar General of Births, Deaths and Marriages for Scotland, the Keeper of the Registers of Scotland or the Keeper of the Records of Scotland;
(c) any office of a description specified in an Order in Council under section 126(8)(b) of the Scotland Act 1998 (other non-ministerial office in the Scottish Administration); or
(d) a public body, public office or holder of a public office—
(i) which (or who) is not a cross-border authority or the Scottish Parliamentary Corporate Body;
(ii) whose functions are exercisable only in or as regards Scotland; and
(iii) some at least of whose functions do not (within the meaning of the Scotland Act 1998) relate to reserved matters;
"cross-border authority" means a cross-border public authority within the meaning given by section 88(5) of the Scotland Act 1998;
"Scottish functions" means functions which are exercisable in or as regards Scotland and which do not (within the meaning of the Scotland Act 1998) relate to reserved matters;

31–25 Note —Inserted by the Equality Act 2006, s.85, with effect from April 18, 2006 (for

Paragraph numbers marked with a "+" can be found online and on CD.

certain purposes) and April 6, 2007 (for remaining purposes) (see SI 2006/1082); amended by SI 2007/2914. For subordinate legislation see, (for the UK) Sex Discrimination Act 1975 (Public Authorities) (Statutory Duties) Order 2006 (SI 2006/2930) (made under subs.(2)) and (for Scotland) the Sex Discrimination (Public Authorities) (Statutory Duties) (Scotland) Order 2007 (SSI 2007/32) (made under subs.(3)). For enforcement of the duties by the CEHR, see ss.31 and 32 of the Equality Act 2006 (repealing earlier provision in the Sex Discrimination Act 1975; see the Equality Act 2006 ss.40, 91, Sch.3, paras 6, 16 and Sch.4 as from October 1, 2007).

Race Relations Act 1976

(1976 c.74)

ARRANGEMENT OF SECTIONS

PART VIII

ENFORCEMENT

3I–26

PART VIII

ENFORCEMENT

Restriction of proceedings for breach of Act

53.—(1) Except as provided by this Act or the Special Immigration Appeals Commission Act 1997 or Part 5 of the Nationality, Immigration and Asylum Act 2002 no proceedings, whether civil or criminal, shall lie against any person in respect of an act by reason that the act is unlawful by virtue of a provision of this Act.

(2) Subsection (1) does not preclude the making of an order of certiorari, mandamus or prohibition.

(3) [...]

(4) Subsections (2) and (3) do not, except so far as provided by section 76, apply to any act which is unlawful by virtue of section 76(5) or (9) or by virtue of section 76(10)(b), (11) and (11B).

3I–27

* * * *

Claims under Part III etc

57.—(1) A claim by any person ("the claimant") that another person ("the respondent")—

   (a) has committed an act against the claimant which is unlawful by virtue of Part III other than, in relation to

3I–28

Paragraph numbers marked with a "+" can be found online and on CD.

discrimination on grounds of race or ethnic or national origins, or harassment, section 26A or 26B; or

(b) is by virtue of section 32 or 33 to be treated as having committed such an act against the claimant,

may be made the subject of civil proceedings in like manner as any other claim in tort or (in Scotland) in reparation for breach of statutory duty.

(2) Proceedings under subsection (1)—

(a) shall, in England and Wales, be brought only in a designated county court; and

(b) [...]

but all such remedies shall be obtainable in such proceedings as, apart from this subsection and section 53(1), would be obtainable in the High Court or the Court of Session, as the case may be.

(3) As respects an unlawful act of discrimination falling within section 1(1)(b), no award of damages shall be made if the respondent proves that the requirement or condition in question was not applied with the intention of treating the claimant unfavourably on racial grounds.

(4) For the avoidance of doubt it is hereby declared that damages in respect of an unlawful act of discrimination may include compensation for injury to feelings whether or not they include compensation under any other head.

(4A) As respects an act which is done, or by virtue of section 32 or 33 is treated as done, by a person in carrying out public investigator functions or functions as a public prosecutor and which is unlawful by virtue of section 19B, no remedy other than—

(a) damages; or

(b) a declaration or, in Scotland, a declarator;

shall be obtainable unless the court is satisfied that the remedy concerned would not prejudice a criminal investigation, a decision to institute criminal proceedings or any criminal proceedings.

(4B) In this section—

"criminal investigation" means —

(a) any investigation which a person in carrying out functions to which section 19B applies has a duty to conduct with a view to it being ascertained whether a person should be charged with, or in Scotland prosecuted for, an offence, or whether a person charged with or prosecuted for an offence is guilty of it;

(b) any investigation which is conducted by a person in carrying out functions to which section 19B applies and which in the circumstances may lead to a decision by that person to institute criminal proceedings which the person has power to conduct; or

(c) any investigation which is conducted by a person in carrying out functions to which section 19B applies and which in the circumstances may lead to a decision by that person to make a report to the procurator fiscal for the purpose of enabling him to determine whether criminal proceedings should be instituted; and

"public investigator functions" means functions of conducting criminal investigations or charging offenders;

and in this subsection "offence" includes any offence under the Army Act 1955, the Air Force Act 1955 or the Naval Discipline Act 1957 (and "offender" shall be construed accordingly).

(4C) Subsection (4D) applies where a party to proceedings under subsection (1) which have arisen by virtue of section 19B has applied for a stay or sist of those proceedings on the grounds of prejudice to—

    (a) particular criminal proceedings;

    (b) a criminal investigation; or

    (c) a decision to institute criminal proceedings.

(4D) The court shall grant the stay or sist unless it is satisfied that the continuance of the proceedings under subsection (1) would not result in the prejudice alleged.

(5) Civil proceedings in respect of a claim by any person that he has been discriminated against in contravention of section 17 or 18 by a body to which subsection (5A) applies shall not be instituted unless the claimant has given notice of the claim to the Secretary of State.

(5A) This subsection applies to—

    (a) local education authorities in England and Wales;

    (b) [...]

    (c) any body which is a responsible body in relation to an establishment falling within paragraph 3, 3B or 7B of the table in section 17.

(6) [...]

(7) This section has effect subject to section 57A.

Burden of proof: County and Sheriff Courts

57ZA.—(1) This section applies where a claim is brought under section 57 and the claim is that the respondent—   **3I–29**

    (a) has committed an act of discrimination, on grounds of race or ethnic or national origins, which is unlawful by virtue of any provision referred to in section 1(1B)(b) to (d), or Part IV in its application to those provisions, or

    (b) has committed an act of harassment.

(2) Where, on the hearing of the claim, the claimant proves facts from which the court could, apart from this section, conclude in the absence of an adequate explanation that the respondent—

    (a) has committed such an act of discrimination or harassment against the claimant, or

    (b) is by virtue of section 32 or 33 to be treated as having committed such an act of discrimination or harassment against the claimant,

Paragraph numbers marked with a "+" can be found online and on CD.

the court shall uphold the claim unless the respondent proves that he did not commit or, as the case may be, is not to be treated as having committed, that act.

* * * *

Help for persons suffering discrimination

Help for aggrieved persons in obtaining information etc

31–30   **65.**—(1) With a view to helping a person ("the person aggrieved") who considers he may have been discriminated against or subjected to harassment in contravention of this Act to decide whether to institute proceedings and, if he does so, to formulate and present his case in the most effective manner, the Minister shall by order prescribe—

(a) forms by which the person aggrieved may question the respondent on his reasons for doing any relevant act, or on any other matter which is or may be relevant; and

(b) forms by which the respondent may if he so wishes reply to any questions.

(2) Where the person aggrieved questions the respondent (whether in accordance with an order under subsection (1) or not)—

(a) the question, and any reply by the respondent (whether in accordance with such an order or not) shall, subject to the following provisions of this section, be admissible as evidence in the proceedings;

(b) if it appears to the court or tribunal that the respondent deliberately, and without reasonable excuse, omitted to reply within a reasonable period or, where the question relates to discrimination on grounds of race or ethnic or national origins, or to harassment, the period of eight weeks beginning with the day on which the question was served on him or that his reply is evasive or equivocal, the court or tribunal may draw any inference from that fact that it considers it just and equitable to draw, including an inference that he committed an unlawful act.

(3) The Minister may by order—

(a) prescribe the period within which questions must be duly served in order to be admissible under subsection (2)(a); and

(b) prescribe the manner in which a question, and any reply by the respondent, may be duly served.

(4) Rules may enable the court entertaining a claim under section 57 to determine, before the date fixed for the hearing of the claim, whether a question or reply is admissible under this section or not.

(4A) In section 19B proceedings, subsection (2)(b) does not apply in relation to a failure to reply, or a particular reply, if the conditions specified in subsection (4B) are satisfied.

Paragraph numbers marked with a "+" can be found online and on CD.

(4B) Those conditions are that—

    (a) at the time of doing any relevant act, the respondent was carrying out public investigator functions or was a public prosecutor; and

    (b) he reasonably believes that a reply or (as the case may be) a different reply would be likely to prejudice any criminal investigation, any decision to institute criminal proceedings or any criminal proceedings or would reveal the reasons behind a decision not to institute, or a decision not to continue, criminal proceedings.

(4C) For the purposes of subsections (4A) and (4B)—

    "public investigator functions" has the same meaning as in section 57;

    "section 19B proceedings" means proceedings in respect of a claim under section 57 which has arisen by virtue of section 19B.

(5) This section is without prejudice to any other enactment or rule of law regulating interlocutory and preliminary matters in proceedings before a county court, sheriff court or employment tribunal, and has effect subject to any enactment or rule of law regulating the admissibility of evidence in such proceedings.

(6) In this section "respondent" includes a prospective respondent and "rules"

    (a) in relation to county court proceedings, means county court rules;

    (b) [...]

(7) This section does not apply in relation to any proceedings under—

    (a) the Special Immigration Appeals Commission Act 1997; or

    (b) Part 5 of the Nationality, Immigration and Asylum Act 2002.

Note —Amended by SI 2007/2914.   **3I–30.1**

* * * * *

Period within which proceedings to be brought

68.—(1) [...]   **3I–31**

(2) Subject to subsection (2A) a county court or a sheriff court shall not consider a claim under section 57 unless proceedings in respect of the claim are instituted before the end of—

    (a) the period of six months beginning when the act complained of was done;

    (b) [...]

(2A) In relation to an immigration claim within the meaning of section 57A, the period of six months mentioned in subsection (2)(a) begins on the expiry of the period during which, by virtue of section 57A(1)(a), no proceedings may be brought under section 57(1) in respect of the claim.

Paragraph numbers marked with a "+" can be found online and on CD.

(3) [...]

(3A) Where in England and Wales—

    (a) proceedings or prospective proceedings by way of a claim under section 57 relate to the act or omission of a qualifying institution,

    (b) the dispute concerned is referred as a complaint under the student complaints scheme before the end of the period of six months mentioned in subsection (2), and

    (c) subsection (3) does not apply,

the period allowed by subsection (2) for instituting proceedings in respect of the claim shall be extended by two months.

(3B) In subsection (3A)—

    "qualifying institution" has the meaning given by section 11 of the Higher Education Act 2004;

    "the student complaints scheme" means a scheme for the review of qualifying complaints, as defined by section 12 of that Act, that is provided by the designated operator, as defined by section 13(5)(b) of that Act.

(4) An employment tribunal, county court or sheriff court shall not consider an application under section 63(2)(a) unless it is made before the end of the period of six months beginning when the act to which it relates was done; and a county court or sheriff court shall not consider an application under section 63(4) unless it is made before the end of the period of five years so beginning.

(5) An employment tribunal shall not consider a complaint under section 64(1) unless it is presented to the tribunal before the end of the period of six months beginning when the act complained of was done.

(6) A court or tribunal may nevertheless consider any such complaint, claim or application which is out of time if, in all the circumstances of the case, it considers that it is just and equitable to do so.

(7) For the purposes of this section—

    (a) when the inclusion of any term in a contract renders the making of the contract an unlawful act, that act shall be treated as extending throughout the duration of the contract; and

    (b) any act extending over a period shall be treated as done at the end of that period; and

    (c) a deliberate omission shall be treated as done when the person in question decided upon it;

and in the absence of evidence establishing the contrary a person shall be taken for the purposes of this section to decide upon an omission when he does an act inconsistent with doing the omitted act or, if he has done no such inconsistent act, when the period expires within which he might reasonably have been expected to do the omitted act if it was to be done.

3I–32   *Note* — Subsection (3) has been repealed by the Equality Act 2006 ss.40, 91, Sch.3, paras 21, 29(1), (2) and Sch.4 from October 1, 2007. Subsection (3A)(c) has been repealed by the Equality Act 2006 ss.40, 91, Sch.3, paras 21, 29(1), (3A) and Sch.4 from

Paragraph numbers marked with a "+" can be found online and on CD.

October 1, 2007 (the Equality Act 2006 (Commencement No.3 and Savings) Order 2007 SI 2007/2603. Subsection (3A) is amended so as to extend the period from two months to three months, by the Equality Act 2006 s.40, Sch.3, paras 21, 29(1) and (3)(b) from October 1, 2007 (the Equality Act 2006 (Commencement No.3 and Savings) Order 2007 SI 2007/2603. Subsection (3C), providing for an extension of time where a complaint has been referred for conciliation pursuant to arrangements made under s.27 of the Equality Act 2006, was inserted by the Equality Act 2006 s.40, Sch.3, paras 21, 29(1) and (4) from October 1, 2007 (the Equality Act 2006 (Commencement No.3 and Savings) Order 2007 SI 2007/2603. Subsection (4) and (5) have been repealed by the Equality Act 2006 ss.40, 91, Sch.3, paras 21, 29(1), (5), Sch.4 from October 1, 2007 (the Equality Act 2006 (Commencement No.3 and Savings) Order 2007 SI 2007/2603. In subs.(6) the words "complaint, claim or application" have been repealed and replaced with the words "complaint or claim" by the Equality Act 2006 s.40, Sch.3, paras 21, 29(1) and (6), from October 1, 2007 (the Equality Act 2006 (Commencement No.3 and Savings) Order 2007 SI 2007/2603.

* * * *

Specified authorities: general statutory duty

71.—(1) Every body or other person specified in Schedule 1A or **3I–33** of a description falling within that Schedule shall, in carrying out its functions, have due regard to the need—

> (a) to eliminate unlawful racial discrimination; and
>
> (b) to promote equality of opportunity and good relations between persons of different racial groups.

(2) The Minister may by order impose, on such persons falling within Schedule 1A as he considers appropriate, such duties as he considers appropriate for the purpose of ensuring the better performance by those persons of their duties under subsection (1).

(3) An order under subsection (2)—

> (a) may be made in relation to a particular person falling within Schedule 1A, any description of persons falling within that Schedule or every person falling within that Schedule;
>
> (b) may make different provision for different purposes.

(4) Before making an order under subsection (2), the Minister shall consult the Commission.

(5) The Minister may by order amend Schedule 1A; but no such order may extend the application of this section unless the Secretary of State considers that the extension relates to a person who exercises functions of a public nature.

(6) An order under subsection (2) or (5) may contain such incidental, supplementary or consequential provision as the Minister considers appropriate (including provision amending or repealing provision made by or under this Act or any other enactment).

(7) This section is subject to section 71A and 71B and is without prejudice to the obligation of any person to comply with any other provision of this Act.

Note—Substituted, together with ss.71A–71E for original s.71 by the Race Relations **3I–34** (Amendment) Act 2000 s.2(1), with effect from April 2, 2001 (SI 2001/566); amended by SI 2007/2914. For subordinate legislation made under subss.(2), (3)) see, (for the UK) Race Relations Act 1976 (Statutory Duties) Order 2001 (SI 2001/3458); Race Re-

Paragraph numbers marked with a "+" can be found online and on CD.

lations Act 1976 (Statutory Duties) Order 2003 (SI 2003/3006); Race Relations Act 1976 (Statutory Duties) Order 2004 (SI 2004/3125); Race Relations Act 1976 (Statutory Duties) Order 2006 (SI 2006/2471) and (for Scotland) Race Relations Act 1976 (Statutory Duties) (Scotland) Order 2002 (SSI 2002/62); Race Relations Act 1976 (Statutory Duties) (Scotland) Amendment Order 2003 (SSI 2003/566); Race Relations Act 1976 (Statutory Duties) (Scotland) Amendment Order 2004 (SSI 2004/521); Race Relations Act 1976 (Statutory Duties) (Scotland) Amendment Order 2006 (SSI 2006/467).

General statutory duty: special cases

3I–35   **71A.**—(1) In relation to the carrying out of immigration and nationality functions (within the meaning of section 19D(1)), section 71(1)(b) has effect with the omission of the words "equality of opportunity and".

(2) Where an entry in Schedule 1A is limited to a person in a particular capacity, section 71(1) does not apply to that person in any other capacity.

(3) Where an entry in Schedule 1A is limited to particular functions of a person, section 71(1) does not apply to that person in relation to any other functions.

3I–36   *Note*—Substituted, together with ss.71, 71B–71E for original s.71 by the Race Relations (Amendment) Act 2000 s.2(1), with effect from April 2, 2001 (SI 2001/566).

General statutory duty: Scotland and Wales

3I–37   **71B.**—(1) For the purposes of the Scotland Act 1998, subsections (2) to (4) of section 71 (and sections 71(6) and 74 so far as they apply to the power conferred by subsection (2) of section 71) shall be taken to be pre-commencement enactments within the meaning of that Act.

(2) Before making an order under section 71(2) in relation to functions exercisable in relation to Wales by a person who is not a Welsh public authority, the Secretary of State shall consult the Welsh Ministers.

(3) The Secretary of State shall not make an order under section 71(2) in relation to functions of a Welsh public authority except with the consent of the Welsh Ministers.

(4) In this section "Welsh public authority" means any person whose functions are exercisable only in relation to Wales and includes—

     (a) the National Assembly for Wales Commission;

     (b) the Welsh Ministers, the First Minister for Wales and the Counsel General to the Welsh Assembly Government.

3I–38   *Note*—Substituted, together with ss.71, 71A, 71C–71E for original s.71 by the Race Relations (Amendment) Act 2000 s.2(1), with effect from April 2, 2001 (SI 2001/566); amended by SI 2007/1388, with effect from May 25, 2007.

General statutory duty: codes of practice

3I–39   **71C.** [...]

3I–40   *Note*—Substituted, together with ss.71, 71A, 71B, 71D, 71E for original s.71 by the Race Relations (Amendment) Act 2000, s.2(1), with effect from April 2, 2001 (SI 2001/

Paragraph numbers marked with a "+" can be found online and on CD.

566); repealed by the Equality Act 2006 s.40, s.91, Sch.3, paras 21, 31 and Sch.4 with effect from October 1, 2007. For enforcement of the duties by the CEHR, see ss.31 and 32 of the Equality Act 2006.

Notes on Part VII of the Sex Discrimination Act 1975 and Part VIII the Race Relations Act 1976

Part VII of the Sex Discrimination Act 1975 (SDA) and Part VIII of the Race Relations Act 1976 (RRA) address enforcement and the evidential and procedural issues peculiar to the SDA and RRA. **3I–41**

Rules of court (CPR Sch.2, CCR O.49, r.17)

When the 1975 Act and the 1976 Act came into effect the County Court Rules 1984 were amended by the addition of r.17 to O.49 for the purpose of providing necessary rules of court. When the CPR came into effect, those provisions were carried forward into Sch.2 (see Vol.1, para.cc49.17). That rule has been amended from time to time, principally for the purpose of taking account of changes in primary legislation. The practice direction relating to discrimination proceedings (Practice Direction—Proceedings Under Enactments Relating To Discrimination) is at para.3I–1. **3I–42**

Jurisdiction and Proceedings

Proceedings in respect of the unlawful acts created by the SDA and RRA may be brought only in the way provided for by the Acts themselves (SDA s.62; RRA s.53). Nothing in the SDA or RRA prevents an application being made in judicial review (SDA s.62; RRA s.53; see *Secretary of State for Defence v Elias* [2006] EWCA Civ 1293). However (outside the employment and related fields), jurisdiction is in the main exclusively conferred on the county courts. Where appropriate, proceedings may be brought by way of a defence and/or counter claim (e.g. in defence of a possession action, see *Manchester City Council v Romano* [2004] EWCA Civ 834, June 29, 2004, unrep., CA, paras 63–64 ; *Lewisham LBC v Malcolm (Equality and Human Rights Commission intervening)* [2008] 1 A.C. 1399). In England and Wales proceedings under Pt III of the RRA (alone) may only be brought in a "designated" County Court (RRA s.57(2), as to which see RRA s.67; see too, s.57A for claims arising in certain immigration cases). In addition, by s.67(4) of the RRA, the judge hearing such a claim "shall, unless with the consent of the parties he sits without assessors, be assisted by two assessors". Assessors have a wide role (*Ahmed v Governing Body of the University of Oxford* [2002] EWCA Civ 1907; [2003] 1 W.L.R. 995, CA). They assist the judge in the broadest sense of helping him or her "evaluate the evidence in the area of race relations". They may therefore be involved in fact finding though the judge remains responsible for actually deciding the facts and the "ultimate decision has to be for the judge" (*ibid*. para.32). The fact that the assessors' primary role is in the decision making process, "militates against any general obligation of disclosure prior to judgment" but there may be circumstances where disclosure will be necessary, "for example where a point arises as a result of the assistance of the assessors which the parties clearly did not have in mind and which they should be entitled to address". Furthermore assessors, despite their primary role, may provide a piece of information akin to expert evidence, and here, once again, disclosure should be made (*ibid*., para.34). The judge must ensure that it is apparent from his or her judgment that s.67(4) has been complied with and the assistance of his assessors has been used in reaching conclusions on issues relating to possible racism (*ibid*., para.35). Where the judge accepts the evaluation of the assessors it will normally form part of the reasoning for the conclusion ultimately reached and this aspect should be recorded in the judgment (*ibid*., para.36). Disagreement between the judge and the assessors on issues relating to racism should be rare, at least if the assessors themselves are agreed (*ibid*., para.37). Where there is disagreement between the judge and the assessors as to an important matter, this should be recorded in the judgment with the judge explaining his reasons for taking a different view or, where the assessors are not agreed, preferring the advice of one assessor rather than the other (*ibid*., paras 38–39). In addition, the SDA makes specific provision allowing for the appointment of assessors under s.63 of the County Courts Act 1984 (SDA s.66(6)). Certain claims (but not counter claims) under the education provisions of the SDA and RRA may only be instituted after the Claimant has given notice of the claim to the Secretary of State (SDA s.66(5) and RRA s.57(5)–(5A)) and, in the case of claims under the **3I–43**

Paragraph numbers marked with a "+" can be found online and on CD.

SDA, two months has elapsed since notice has been given or the Secretary of State has indicated that no further time is required (the same requirement in the RRA was removed by the Race Relations (Amendment) Act 2000). Where proceedings are brought under RRA, s.19B (public authorities) and a party has applied for a stay of the proceedings on the grounds of prejudice to, particular criminal proceedings; a criminal investigation or a decision to institute criminal proceedings then the stay must be granted unless the court is satisfied that the continuance of the proceedings would not result in the prejudice alleged (RRA s.57(4C) and (4D)). The SDA makes comparable provision in respect of proceedings under s.21A (public authorities) (SDA s.21A(6)).

The SDA has been recently amended by the Employment Equality (Sex Discrimination) Regulations 2005 SI 2005/2467 so as to, amongst other things, introduce a statutory tort of harassment into certain parts of the SDA (already found in the RRA and Disability Discrimination Act 1995) and to move the unlawful acts applicable to the treatment of barristers, pupils and advocates from the jurisdiction of the County Court to the Employment Tribunals. These changes took effect from October 1, 2005 though the jurisdictional changes do not apply to proceedings where the act complained of took place before that date (see transitional provisions in regs 1(1) and 2(1)). The effect of these Regulations has been modified by the Sex Discrimination Act 1975 (Amendment) Regulations 2008 SI 2008/656, following *Equal Opportunities Commission v Secretary of State for Trade and Industry* [2007] I.R.L.R. 327 in which it was held that they were in part defective. The SDA has been further amended by the Sex Discrimination (Amendment of Legislation) Regulations 2008 SI 2008/963 to give effect to Council Directive 2004/113 EC ("the Gender Goods and Services Directive") so as to, amongst other things, extend the new meaning of discrimination, including harassment, to the unlawful acts outside the employment field.

Further, the SDA, the RRA and the DDA contain general duties upon public authorities to, amongst other things, have due regard to the need to eliminate unlawful discrimination and promote equality of opportunity (SDA s.76A; RRA s.71 and DDA s.49A) and pursuant to subordinate legislation made under the Acts, specific duties are imposed on certain public authorities. The duties may be enforced by way of judicial review (see *Secretary of State for Defence v Elias (CRE Intervening)* [2005] EWHC 1435 (Admin); [2006] EWCA Civ 1293; *R (on the application of C (A Minor, by his litigation friend MS)) v Secretary of State for Justice* [2008] EWCA Civ 882) and by the CEHR (EA s.32).

The Equality Act 2006 made a number of changes to the enforcement provisions of the SDA and RRA (s.40 and Sch.3, s.91 and Sch.4). These changes came into force on October 1, 2007 and give the CEHR power to "assess" the extent to which or manner in which a public authority has complied with a general or specific equality duty under the SDA, RRA (Equality Act 2006 s.31 and Sch.2) and the CEHR has power to issue compliance notices in respect of a breach of the general statutory duties (but only after an "assessment" has been carried out and only where the notice relates to the results of the "assessment") as well as the specific statutory duties (Equality Act 2006 s.32).

Time limits

3I–44 Proceedings under Pts III of the SDA and RRA must be instituted within six months of when the act complained was done (SDA s.76(2)(a); RRA s.68(2), and see s.68(2A) for a modification in relation to certain immigration claims under RRA s.19B). In cases falling under ss.22 and 23 of the SDA (education) proceedings must be instituted within eight months of when the act complained of was done (SDA s.76(2)(b)). In cases where the dispute involves a higher education institution and the complaint has been referred as a complaint under the "student complaints scheme" the time limit for instituting proceedings is extended by three months (SDA s.76(2A); RRA s.68(3A). As to when time begins to run, see SDA s.76(6); s.68(7) RRA.The circumstances in which an act might be said to "extend over a period" (usually described as a "continuing act") for the purposes of the time limits have proved problematic and controversial. A policy, rule or practice, in accordance with which decisions are taken from time to time, might constitute a "continuing act" for these purposes, even where such policy is unwritten and informal (*Owusu v London Fire and Civil Defence Authority* [1995] I.R.L.R. 574, EAT; *Cast v Croydon College* [1998] I.C.R. 500, CA). Likewise a continuing state of affairs may constitute a continuing act for these purposes (*Hendricks v MPC* [2003]

Paragraph numbers marked with a "+" can be found online and on CD.

I.R.L.R. 96, even where the individual acts relied upon are done by different persons and are done at different places). In addition, in each case, a claim may be considered notwithstanding that it has been instituted outside of the time limit where it would be "just and equitable" to do so (SDA s.76(5); RRA s.68(6)); as to the factors which are likely to be relevant, see *Anderson v Rover Group* (1999) 1426/99, EAT; *British Coal Corporation v Keeble* [1997] I.R.L.R. 336, EAT, at 338, and *London Borough of Southwark v Afolabi* [2003] I.R.L.R. 220, presented nearly nine years after the expiry of the statutory time limit). Each case is likely to turn very much on its own facts.

Enforcement and Remedies

The unlawful acts created by the SDA and RRA are statutory torts and in general **3I–45** terms the Courts have addressed their enforcement and remedies in relation to them in much the same way as with any other statutory tort. Thus, where an award of compensation is made in respect of joint tortfeasors, the award will be distributed according to what is just and equitable having regard to the extent of that person's responsibility for the damage in question (Civil Liability (Contribution) Act 1978; see *Prison Service v Johnson* [1997] I.C.R. 275). Further, where a person has a cause of action under the SDA and RRA that cause of action survives his or her death for the benefit of his estate (Law Reform (Miscellaneous Provisions) Act 1934; *Lewisham and Guys Mental Health NHS Trust v Harris* [2000] I.C.R. 707, CA). As to remedies under the SDA and RRA the county courts may make any order as would be available in the High Court (in England and Wales) and the Court of Session (in Scotland) and in particular awards of compensation, including an award for injury to feelings (*Vento v Chief Constable of West Yorkshire Police* [2002] EWCA Civ 1871; [2003] I.C.R. 318), and declarations may be made (SDA s.66(1)–(2) and (4) and RRA s.57(1)–(2) and (4)). In determining whether any particular losses are recoverable the test to be applied is whether such losses are caused by (or arise naturally and directly from) the discrimination found proved. There is no requirement of foreseeabilty (*Essa v Laing Ltd* [2004] EWCA Civ 2; [2004] I.C.R. 746, CA). In relation to many claims of indirect sex discrimination outside the employment field and certain claims of indirect race discrimination outside the employment field, no award of damages may be made if the defendant proves that the requirement or condition in question was not applied with the intention of treating the claimant unfavourably (SDA s.66(3); RRA s.57(3)) but a court may infer that a defendant had the requisite intention where he knew when he applied the offending requirement or condition that the discriminatory consequences would follow (*London Underground Limited v Edwards* [1995] IRLR 355, EAT; *JH Walker Ltd v Hussain* [1996] ICR 291, EAT).

The Equality Act 2006 gives the CEHR power to make arrangements for the provision of conciliation services for disputes in respect of which proceedings have been or could be brought under the SDA or RRA (Equality Act 2006 s.27). By s.27(3), information communicated to a person providing conciliation services in accordance with such arrangements may not be adduced in legal proceedings without the consent of the person who communicated the information. Certain persons are excluded from participating in the provision of such conciliation services (including CEHR Commissioners and staff; see s.27(6) of the Equality Act 2006).

Proving discrimination and the burden of proof

There is much guidance from the appellate courts on proving the different forms of **3I–46** discrimination provided for under the SDA and RRA (see, for example, *Anya v University of Oxford* [2001] EWCA Civ 405; [2001] I.C.R. 847, CA, at pp 851–855, *per* Sedley L.J.; *Qureshi v Victoria University of Manchester* [2001] I.C.R. 863, EAT, for the very helpful guidance of Mummery L.J.; *Shamoon v Chief Constable of the Royal Ulster Constabulary* [2003] UKHL 11; [2003] ICR 337, HL; *Chief Constable of the West Yorkshire Police v Khan* [2001] UKHL 48; [2001] I.C.R. 1065, HL). In addition, the SDA and RRA now make specific provision shifting the burden of proof in certain circumstances. Where a claimant proves facts from which a court could conclude in the absence of an adequate explanation that the defendant has committed an unlawful act, a court must uphold the complaint unless the defendant proves that he did not so act (SDA s.63A and s.66A; RRA s.54A and s.57ZA). This shift applies only in relation to certain of the unlawful acts created by the SDA and RRA, as the provisions themselves make clear. As to the impact of these provisions, see *Igen Ltd (formerly Leeds Careers Guidance) v.*

Paragraph numbers marked with a "+" can be found online and on CD.

Wong [2005] EWCA Civ 142; [2005] I.C.R. 931 ; *EB v BA* [2006] EWCA Civ 132; [2006] I.R.L.R. 471 and *Madarassy v Nomura International Plc* [2007] I.R.L.R 246. The SDA and RRA also make provision for the service of "questionnaires" (SDA s.74 and RRA s.65; see too, Sex Discrimination (Questions and Replies) Order 1975 (SI 1975/2048); Race Relations (Questions and Replies) Order 1977 (SI 1977/842)). Time limits are prescribed for the purposes of serving and replying to such questionnaires and provision is made allowing for adverse inferences to be drawn in cases where a questionnaire is not replied to or not replied to within the time limit prescribed for so doing (SDA s.74 and RRA s.65). Carefully crafted questions can assist a complainant in properly identifying his complaints and in proving them, as can be seen from the guidance in *Igen*, above(and see *West Midlands Passenger Transport Executive v Singh* [1988] I.R.L.R. 186, CA). The statutory Codes of Practice also provide valuable guidance as to the proving of discrimination.

Disability Discrimination Act 1995

3I–47

(1995 c.50)

ARRANGEMENT OF SECTIONS

PART IV

EDUCATION

PART IV

EDUCATION

Enforcement, remedies and procedure

3I–48 28V.—(1) A claim by a person—

(a) that a responsible body has discriminated against him, or subjected him to harassment in a way which is unlawful under this Chapter,

(b) that a responsible body is by virtue of section 57 or 58 to be treated as having done so, or

(c) that a person is by virtue of section 57 to be treated as having done so,

may be made the subject of civil proceedings in the same way as any other claim in tort or (in Scotland) in reparation for breach of statutory duty.

(1A) Where—

(a) a claim is brought under subsection (1), and

(b) the claimant (or pursuer, in Scotland) proves facts from which the court could, apart from this subsection, conclude in the absence of an adequate explanation that

Paragraph numbers marked with a "+" can be found online and on CD.

the defendant (or defender, in Scotland) has acted in a way which is unlawful under this Chapter,

the court shall uphold the claim unless the defendant (or defender, in Scotland) proves that he did not so act.

(2) For the avoidance of doubt it is hereby declared that damages in respect of discrimination in a way which is unlawful under this Chapter may include compensation for injury to feelings whether or not they include compensation under any other head.

(3) Proceedings in England and Wales may be brought only in a county court.

(4) Proceedings in Scotland may be brought only in a sheriff court.

(5) The remedies available in such proceedings are those which are available in the High Court or (as the case may be) the Court of Session.

(6) The fact that a person who brings proceedings under this Part against a responsible body may also be entitled to bring proceedings against that body under Part 2 is not to affect the proceedings under this Part.

(7) Part 4 of Schedule 3 makes further provision about the enforcement of this Part and about procedure.

Note —Amended by SI 2006/1721.

3I–49

Notes on Part IV of the Disability Discrimination Act 1995

When the 1995 Act came into effect the CCR O.49, r.17 was amended for the purpose of providing necessary rules of court; see now Sch. 2 CCR O.49, r.17 (Vol.1, para.cc49.17). In 2004, that rule was amended to take account of the coming into effect of the Disability Rights Commission Act 1999.

3I–50

Part IV, Chapters 1 and 2, of the Disability Discrimination Act 1995 (DDA) was inserted by the Special Educational Needs and Disability Act 2001 and it creates a number of unlawful acts in relation to schools and local education authorities in relation to pupils (ss.28A–C and 28F); in relation to further and higher education (s.28R to s.28T) and in relation to certain providers of statutory youth and community services including adult education in relation to students (s.28U and Sch.4C DDA). The provisions addressing discrimination by further and higher education institutions have recently been amended by the Disability Discrimination Act 1995 (Amendment) (Further and Higher Education) Regulations 2006 (SI 2006/1721) which create certain new unlawful acts, including by outlawing harassment. Claims under Part IV, Chapter 1 (discrimination in relation to pupils) are heard in Special Educational Need and Disability Tribunals (s.28I). Claims under Part IV Chapter 2 (discrimination in relation to students) are heard in the county courts (s.28V).

There are many similarities between the DDA, on the one hand, and the SDA and RRA on the other, but significant differences also. However, the DDA addresses remedies and enforcement in a similar way in respect of those unlawful acts it creates and, in particular, in respect of those justiciable in the county courts under Part III and IV DDA (Sch.3, paras. 2(1)–(2), 5(1)–(2), 9(1)–(2) and 12(1)–(2); ss.25(1), (2), (5) and 28V(1)–(5)). In addition the DDA provides for a shift in the burden of proof in respect of certain of the unlawful acts (s.17A(1C), s.25(7)–(9) and 28V(1A)); provides for a questionnaire procedure (s.56 DDA and Disability Discrimination (Questions and Replies) Order 2004 (SI 2004/1168)); addresses vicarious and secondary liability (ss.57–58 and s.64A DDA) and time limits (Sch. 3, paras. 6 and 13) and the guidance provided by the courts on these matters in relation to the SDA and the RRA should be taken as applying equally to proceedings under the DDA. The Equality Act 2006 gives the CEHR power to make arrangements for the provision of conciliation services for disputes in respect of which proceedings have been or could be brought under the DDA (s.27 of the Equality Act 2006). By s.27(3), information communicated to a person providing conciliation services in accordance with such arrangements may not

Paragraph numbers marked with a "+" can be found online and on CD.

be adduced in legal proceedings without the consent of the person who communicated the information. Certain persons are excluded from participating in the provision of such conciliation services (including CEHR Commissioners and staff; see s.27(6) of the Equality Act 2006).

* * * *

PART 5A

PUBLIC AUTHORITIES

General Duty

3I–51   **49A.**—(1) Every public authority shall in carrying out its functions have due regard to—

(a) the need to eliminate discrimination that is unlawful under this Act;

(b) the need to eliminate harassment of disabled persons that is related to their disabilities;

(c) the need to promote equality of opportunity between disabled persons and other persons;

(d) the need to take steps to take account of disabled persons' disabilities, even where that involves treating disabled persons more favourably than other persons;

(e) the need to promote positive attitudes towards disabled persons; and

(f) the need to encourage participation by disabled persons in public life.

(2) Subsection (1) is without prejudice to any obligation of a public authority to comply with any other provision of this Act.

3I–52   *Note* —Inserted by the Disability Discrimination Act 2005 s.3, with effect from December 5, 2005 (subs.(1), for the purpose only of regulations under s. 49D) and December 4, 2006 (subs.(1) remaining purposes, subs.(2)); see SI 2005/2774.

Meaning of "public authority" in Part 5A

3I–53   **49B.**—(1) In this Part "public authority"—

(a) includes any person certain of whose functions are functions of a public nature; but

(b) does not include—

(i) any person mentioned in section 21B(3);

(ii) the Scottish Parliament;

(iii) a person, other than the Scottish Parliamentary Corporate Body, exercising functions in connection with proceedings in the Scottish Parliament.

(iv) the National Assembly for Wales; or

(v) a person, other than the National Assembly for Wales Commission, exercising functions in connection with proceedings in the National Assembly for Wales.

Paragraph numbers marked with a "+" can be found online and on CD.

2966); Disability Discrimination (Public Authorities) (Statutory Duties) (Amendment) Regulations 2007 (SI 2007/618) and (for Scotland) Disability Discrimination (Public Authorities) (Scotland) Regulations 2005 (SSI 2005/565); (Disability Discrimination (Public Authorities) (Statutory Duties) (Scotland) Amendment Regulations 2007 (SSI 2007/195). For enforcement of the duties by the CEHR, see ss.31 and 32 of the Equality Act 2006 (repealing earlier provision in the Disability Discrimination Act 1995; see the Equality Act 2006 ss.40, 91, Sch.3, paras 41, 49, Sch.4 as from October 1, 2007).

Equality Act 2006

(2006 c.3)   3I–59

ARRANGEMENT OF SECTIONS

PART 2

DISCRIMINATION ON GROUNDS OF RELIGION OR BELIEF

ENFORCEMENT

PART 2

DISCRIMINATION ON GROUNDS OF RELIGION OR BELIEF

ENFORCEMENT

Restriction of proceedings

65.—(1) Except as provided by this Act, no proceedings, whether **3I–60** criminal or civil, may be brought against a person on the grounds that an act is unlawful by virtue of this Part.

(2) But subsection (1) does not prevent—

(a) an application for judicial review,

(b) proceedings under the Immigration Acts,

(c) proceedings under the Special Immigration Appeals Commission Act 1997 (c. 68), or

(d) in Scotland, the exercise of the jurisdiction of the Court of Session to entertain an application for reduction or suspension of an order or determination or otherwise to consider the validity of an order or determination, or to require reasons for an order or determination to be stated.

Claim of unlawful action

66.—(1) A claim that a person has done anything that is unlawful **3I–61** by virtue of this Part may be brought in a county court (in England

Paragraph numbers marked with a "+" can be found online and on CD.

and Wales) or in the sheriff court (in Scotland) by way of proceedings in tort (or reparation) for breach of statutory duty.

(2) Proceedings in England and Wales alleging that any of the following bodies has acted unlawfully by virtue of section 49 or 51 may not be brought unless the claimant has given written notice to the Secretary of State; and those bodies are—

(a) a local education authority, and

(b) the responsible body of an educational establishment listed in the Table in section 49.

(3) Proceedings in Scotland alleging that any of the following bodies has acted unlawfully by virtue of section 49 or 51 may not be brought unless the pursuer has given written notice to the Scottish Ministers; and those bodies are—

(a) an education authority, and

(b) the responsible body of an educational establishment listed in the Table in section 49.

(4) In subsection (1) the reference to a claim that a person has done an unlawful act includes a reference to a claim that a person is to be treated by virtue of this Part as having done an unlawful act.

(5) In proceedings under this section, if the claimant (or pursuer) proves facts from which the court could conclude, in the absence of a reasonable alternative explanation, that an act which is unlawful by virtue of this Part has been committed, the court shall assume that the act was unlawful unless the respondent (or defender) proves that it was not.

Immigration

3I–62   **67.**—(1) Proceedings may not be brought under section 66 alleging that a person has acted unlawfully by virtue of section 52 if the question of the lawfulness of the act could be raised (and has not been raised) in immigration proceedings (disregarding the possibility of proceedings brought out of time with permission).

(2) If in immigration proceedings a court or tribunal has found that an act was unlawful by virtue of section 52, a court hearing proceedings under section 66 shall accept that finding.

(3) In this section "immigration proceedings" means proceedings under or by virtue of—

(a) the Immigration Acts, or

(b) the Special Immigration Appeals Commission Act 1997 (c. 68).

Remedies

3I–63   **68.**—(1) This section applies to proceedings under section 66.

(2) A court may, in addition to any remedy available to it in proceedings for tort, grant any remedy that the High Court could grant in proceedings for judicial review.

(3) A court may not award damages in proceedings in respect of an act that is unlawful by virtue of section 45(3) if the respondent proves that there was no intention to treat the claimant unfavourably on grounds of religion or belief.

Paragraph numbers marked with a "+" can be found online and on CD.

(4) A court may award damages by way of compensation for injury to feelings (whether or not other damages are also awarded).

(5) In the application of this section to proceedings in Scotland—

    (a) a reference to the High Court shall be taken as a reference to the Court of Session,

    (b) a reference to tort shall be taken as a reference to reparation,

    (c) a reference to the respondent shall be taken as a reference to the defender, and

    (d) a reference to the claimant shall be taken as a reference to the pursuer.

(6) This section is subject to section 52(5).

Timing

69.—(1) Proceedings under section 66 may be brought only—   **3I–64**

    (a) within the period of six months beginning with the date of the act (or last act) to which the proceedings relate, or

    (b) with the permission of the court in which the proceedings are brought.

(2) In relation to immigration proceedings within the meaning of section 67, the period specified in subsection (1)(a) above shall begin with the first date on which proceedings under section 66 may be brought.

Information

70.—(1) In this section—   **3I–65**

    (a) a reference to a claimant is a reference to a person who has brought proceedings under this Part,

    (b) reference to a potential claimant is a reference to a person who—

        (i) thinks he may have been the subject of an act that is unlawful by virtue of this Part, and

        (ii) wishes to consider whether to bring proceedings under this Part, and

    (c) a person questioned by a potential claimant for the purpose of considering whether to bring proceedings is referred to as a potential respondent.

(2) The Minister shall by order prescribe—

    (a) forms by which a claimant or potential claimant may question the respondent or a potential respondent about the reasons for an action or about any matter that is or may be relevant, and

    (b) forms by which a respondent or potential respondent may reply (if he wishes).

(3) A claimant's or potential claimant's questions, and a respondent or potential respondent's replies, (in each case whether or not put by a prescribed form) shall be admissible as evidence in proceedings in respect of the act to which the questions relate if (and only if) the questions are put—

Paragraph numbers marked with a "+" can be found online and on CD.

(a) within the period of six months beginning with the date of the act (or last act) to which they relate, and

(b) in such manner as the Minister may prescribe by order.

(4) A court may draw an inference from—

(a) a failure to reply to a claimant's or potential claimant's questions (whether or not put by a prescribed form) within the period of eight weeks beginning with the date of receipt, or

(b) an evasive or equivocal reply to a claimant's or potential claimant's questions (whether or not put by a prescribed form).

(5) The Minister may by order amend subsection (3)(a) so as to substitute a new period for that specified.

(6) In the application of this section to Scotland—

(a) a reference to a claimant or potential claimant shall be taken as a reference to a pursuer or potential pursuer, and

(b) a reference to a respondent or potential respondent shall be taken as a reference to a defender or potential defender.

(7) An order under this section—

(a) shall be made by statutory instrument, and

(b) shall be subject to annulment in pursuance of a resolution of either House of Parliament.

(8) This section is subject to section 52(6).

3I–65.1   *Note*—Amended by SI 2007/2914.

National security

3I–66   **71.**—(1) Rules of court may make provision for enabling a county court or sheriff court in which a claim is brought under section 66, where the court considers it expedient in the interests of national security—

(a) to exclude from all or part of the proceedings

(i) the claimant;

(ii) the claimant's representatives;

(iii) any assessors;

(b) to permit a claimant or representative who has been excluded to make a statement to the court before the commencement of the proceedings, or the part of the proceedings, from which he is excluded;

(c) to take steps to keep secret all or part of the reasons for the court's decision in the proceedings.

(2) The Attorney General or, in Scotland, the Advocate General for Scotland, may appoint a person to represent the interests of a claimant in, or in any part of, proceedings from which the claimant or his representatives are excluded by virtue of subsection (1).

(3) A person may be appointed under subsection (2) only—

Paragraph numbers marked with a "+" can be found online and on CD.

(a) in relation to proceedings in England and Wales, if he has a general qualification (within the meaning of section 71 of the Courts and Legal Services Act 1990 (c. 41)), or

(b) in relation to proceedings in Scotland, if he is—

(i) an advocate, or

(ii) qualified to practice as a solicitor in Scotland.

(4) A person appointed under subsection (2) shall not be responsible to the person whose interests he is appointed to represent.

The Equality Act (Sexual Orientation) Regulations 2007

(S.I. 2007 No. 1263)   **3I–67**

ARRANGEMENT OF REGULATIONS

Restriction of proceedings

19.—(1) Except as provided by these Regulations, no proceedings,   **3I–68** whether criminal or civil, may be brought against a person on the grounds that an act is unlawful by virtue of these Regulations.

(2) But paragraph (1) does not preclude—

(a) proceedings by the Commission under Part 1 of the 2006 Act,

(b) an application for judicial review,

(c) proceedings under the Immigration Acts,

(d) proceedings under the Special Immigration Appeals Commission Act 1997, or

(e) in Scotland, the exercise of the jurisdiction of the Court of Session to entertain an application for reduction or suspension of an order or determination or otherwise to consider the validity of an order or determination, or to require reasons for an order or determination to be stated.

Claims of unlawful action

20.—(1) A claim that a person has done anything that is unlawful   **3I–69** by virtue of these Regulations may be brought—

(a) in England and Wales, in a county court, by way of proceedings in tort, or

(b) in Scotland, in the sheriff court, by way of proceedings in reparation,

for breach of statutory duty.

(2) Proceedings in England and Wales alleging that a local educa-

Paragraph numbers marked with a "+" can be found online and on CD.

tion authority or the responsible body of an educational establishment listed in Schedule 3 has acted unlawfully by virtue of regulation 7 or 8 may not be brought unless the claimant has given written notice to the Secretary of State.

(3) Proceedings in Scotland alleging that an education authority or the responsible body of an educational establishment listed in Schedule 3 has acted unlawfully by virtue of regulation 7 or 8 may not be brought unless the pursuer has given written notice to the Scottish Ministers.

(4) In paragraph (1) the reference to a claim that a person has done an unlawful act includes a reference to a claim that a person is to be treated by virtue of these Regulations as having done an unlawful act.

(5) In proceedings under this regulation, if the claimant (or pursuer) proves facts from which the court could conclude, in the absence of a reasonable alternative explanation, that an act which is unlawful by virtue of these Regulations has been committed, the court shall assume that the act was unlawful unless the respondent (or defender) proves that it was not.

Claims of unlawful action: immigration cases

3I–70   **21.**—(1) Proceedings may not be brought under regulation 20 alleging that a person has acted unlawfully by virtue of regulation 8 if the question of the lawfulness of the act could be raised (and has not been raised) in immigration proceedings (disregarding the possibility of proceedings brought out of time with permission).

(2) If in immigration proceedings a court or tribunal has found that an act was unlawful by virtue of regulation 8, a court hearing proceedings under regulation 20 shall accept that finding.

(3) In this regulation "immigration proceedings" means proceedings under or by virtue of—

> (a) the Immigration Acts, or
> (b) the Special Immigration Appeals Commission Act 1997.

Remedies for unlawful action

3I–71   **22.**—(1) In proceedings under regulation 20, the court (subject to paragraph (2))—

> (a) (in addition to granting any remedy available to it in proceedings for tort) may grant any remedy that the High Court could grant in proceedings for judicial review,
> (b) may award damages by way of compensation for injury to feelings (whether or not other damages are also awarded),
> (c) may not award damages in proceedings in respect of an act that is unlawful by virtue of regulation 3(5) if the respondent proves that there was no intention to treat the claimant unfavourably on grounds of sexual orientation,

(2) In respect of a contravention of regulation 8, the court—

> (a) shall not grant an injunction unless satisfied that it will

Paragraph numbers marked with a "+" can be found online and on CD.

not prejudice criminal proceedings or a criminal investigation, and

(b) shall grant any application to stay the proceedings under regulation 20 on the grounds of prejudice to criminal proceedings or to a criminal investigation, unless satisfied that the proceedings or investigation will not be prejudiced.

(3) In the application of this regulation to Scotland—

(a) a reference to the court shall be taken as a reference to the sheriff,

(b) a reference to the High Court shall be taken as a reference to the Court of Session,

(c) a reference to tort shall be taken as a reference to reparation,

(d) a reference to the claimant shall be taken as a reference to the pursuer,

(e) a reference to the respondent shall be taken as a reference to the defender,

(f) a reference to an injunction shall be taken as a reference to an interdict, and

(g) a reference to staying proceedings shall be taken as a reference to sisting proceedings.

Claims of unlawful action: timing

23.—(1) Proceedings under regulation 20 may be brought only— **3I–72**

(a) within the period of six months beginning with the date of the act (or the last act) to which the proceedings relate, or

(b) with the permission of the court in which the proceedings are brought.

(2) In relation to immigration proceedings (as defined in regulation 21) the period specified in paragraph (1)(a) shall begin with the first date on which proceedings under regulation 20 may be brought.

Claims of unlawful action: information

24.—(1) A claimant or a potential claimant may question a respon- **3I–73**
dent or a potential respondent about the reasons for an action or about any matter that is or may be relevant and may do so—

(a) in the form set out in Part 1 of Schedule 2, or

(b) in a form to the like effect with such variation as the circumstances require.

(2) A respondent or potential respondent may reply (if he so wishes) to questions served under paragraph (1)—

(a) in the form set out in Part 2 of Schedule 2, or

(b) in a form to the like effect with such variation as the circumstances require.

(3) A claimant's or potential claimant's questions (whether or not put in a form mentioned in paragraph (1)), and a respondent or potential respondent's replies shall be admissible as evidence in

Paragraph numbers marked with a "+" can be found online and on CD.

proceedings in respect of the action or about any matter that is or may be relevant, to which the questions relate if (and only if) the questions are served—

    (a) within the period of six months beginning with the date of the action (or last action) to which they relate, and

    (b) in accordance with paragraph (4).

(4) A question may be served on a respondent or potential respondent and a reply may be served on a claimant or potential claimant—

    (a) by delivering it to him,

    (b) by sending it by post to him at his usual or last known residence or place of business,

    (c) where the person to be served is acting by a solicitor, by delivering it at, or by sending it by post to, the solicitor's address for service,

    (d) where the person to be served is a claimant or potential claimant, by delivering the reply, or sending it by post, to him at his address for reply as stated by him in the document containing the questions, or if no address is so stated, at his usual or last known residence, or

    (e) where the person to be served is a body corporate or is a trade union or employers' association within the meaning of the Trade Union and Labour Relations (Consolidation) Act 1992, by delivering it to the secretary or clerk of the body, union or association at its registered or principal office, or by sending it by post to the secretary or clerk at that office.

(5) A court may draw an inference from—

    (a) a failure to reply to a claimant's or potential claimant's questions within the period of eight weeks beginning with the date the questions were served, or

    (b) an evasive or equivocal reply to such questions (whether or not put in a form mentioned in paragraph (1)).

(6) In this regulation—

    (a) "claimant" means a person who has brought proceedings under these Regulations,

    (b) "potential claimant" means a person who—

        (i) thinks he may have been the subject of an act that is unlawful by virtue of these Regulations, and

        (ii) wishes to consider whether to bring proceedings under these Regulations,

    (c) "potential respondent" means a person questioned by a potential claimant for the purpose of considering whether to bring proceedings under these Regulations

(7) In the application of this regulation to Scotland—

    (a) a reference to a claimant or potential claimant shall be taken as a reference to a pursuer or potential pursuer, and

Paragraph numbers marked with a "+" can be found online and on CD.

(b) a reference to a respondent or potential respondent shall be taken as a reference to a defender or potential defender.

(8) Paragraph (5) does not apply in relation to a reply, or a failure to reply, to a question—

    (a) if the respondent or potential respondent reasonably asserts that to have replied differently or at all might have prejudiced criminal proceedings or a criminal investigation,

    (b) if the respondent or potential respondent reasonably asserts that to have replied differently or at all would have revealed the reason for not instituting or not continuing criminal proceedings, or

    (c) if the respondent or potential respondent reasonably asserts that to have replied differently or at all would have frustrated the purpose of national security.

National security

25.—(1) Rules of court may make provision for enabling a county **3l–74** court or sheriff court in which a claim is brought under regulation 20, where the court considers it expedient in the interests of national security—

    (a) to exclude from all or part of the proceedings—

        (i) the claimant,

        (ii) the claimant's representatives, or

        (iii) any assessors,

    (b) to permit a claimant or representative who has been excluded to make a statement to the court before the commencement of the proceedings, or the part of the proceedings, from which he is excluded;

    (c) to take steps to keep secret all or part of the reasons for the court's decision in the proceedings.

(2) The Attorney General or, in Scotland, the Advocate General for Scotland, may appoint a person to represent the interests of a claimant in, or in any part of, proceedings from which the claimant or his representatives are excluded by virtue of paragraph (1).

(3) A person may be appointed under paragraph (2) only—

    (a) in relation to proceedings in England and Wales, if he has a general qualification (within the meaning of section 71 of the Courts and Legal Services Act 1990), or

    (b) in relation to proceedings in Scotland, if he is—

        (i) an advocate, or

        (ii) qualified to practise as a solicitor in Scotland.

(4) A person appointed under paragraph (2) shall not be responsible to the person whose interests he is appointed to represent.

Paragraph numbers marked with a "+" can be found online and on CD.

Note

3I–75 Part 2 of the Equality Act 2006 and the Equality Act (Sexual Orientation) Regulations 2007 (SI 2007/1263) (made under Pt.3 of the Equality Act 2006) outlaw discrimination connected to religion and belief and sexual orientation, respectively. Sections 65–71 of the Equality Act 2006 and regs 19–25 of the Equality Act (Sexual Orientation) Regulations 2007 (SI 2007/1263) address enforcement of the unlawful acts. In the main they reflect the enforcement provisions found in the SDA, RRA and DDA and the differences do not appear to have been intended to be material.

The Equality Act 2006 gives the CEHR power to make arrangements for the provision of conciliation services for disputes in respect of which proceedings have been or could be brought under the Equality Act and the Equality Act (Sexual Orientation) Regulation 2007 (s.27 of the Equality Act 2006). By s.27(3), information communicated to a person providing conciliation services in accordance with such arrangements may not be adduced in legal proceedings without the consent of the person who communicated the information. Certain persons are excluded from participating in the provision of such conciliation services (including CEHR Commissioners and staff: see s.27(6) of the Equality Act 2006). For the lawfulness of certain of the analogue Regulations enacted for Northern Ireland (Equality Act (Sexual Orientation) Regulation (Northern Ireland) 2006) addressing sexual orientation discrimination, see *The Christian Institute v Office of the First Minister and Deputy First Minister* [2007] NIQB 66.

Paragraph numbers marked with a "+" can be found online and on CD.

3J DIRECTORS DISQUALIFICATION PROCEEDINGS

PRACTICE DIRECTION—DIRECTORS DISQUALIFICATION PROCEEDINGS

3J–1

Editorial note

Purposes of the Company Directors Disqualification Act 1986 ("the Act")

The Directors Disqualification Proceedings Practice Direction ("the Practice Direction") needs to be interpreted and applied in the context of the underlying legislation. The Act was introduced as part of the substantial re-casting of the insolvency legislation in the mid-1980s, and came into force on December 29, 1986. Its main provisions were originally introduced under the Insolvency Act 1985, which was brought into force on April 28, 1986. Although earlier insolvency legislation also made provision for disqualification of directors in certain circumstances, the 1986 changes were such that earlier case law is largely (though not entirely) redundant. The court's approach to Parliament's intention in introducing the Act is summarised in the judgment of Henry L.J. in *Re Grayan Building Services Ltd* [1995] Ch. 241, at 257:

3J–2

> "The concept of limited liability and the sophistication of our corporate law offers great privileges and great opportunities for those who wish to trade under that regime. But the corporate environment carries with it the discipline that those who avail themselves of those privileges must accept the standards laid down and abide by the regulatory rules and disciplines in place to protect creditors and shareholders. ... The parliamentary intention to improve managerial safeguards and standards for the long term good of employees, creditors and investors is clear."

See also Sir Donald Nicholls V.-C. in *Re Swift 736 Ltd* [1993] B.C.C. 312 at 315:

> "Limited liability is a valuable tool in the promotion of trade and business, but it must not be misused. Those who make use of limited liability must do so with a proper sense of responsibility. The directors' disqualification procedure is an important sanction introduced by Parliament to raise standards in this regard."

On a closely related point, it has been frequently said that the primary purpose of the Act is to protect the public. This phrase is used in both a narrow and a wide sense. Even where the director no longer needs to be kept "off the road", the "wider interests of protecting the public" in making a disqualification order include a deterrent element in relation to both the director himself and as far as other directors are concerned: see the comments of Lord Woolf M.R. in *Re Westmid Packing Services Ltd* [1998] 2 All E.R. 124, at 131–2.

The court has also made clear that the disqualification jurisdiction is intended to be a summary jurisdiction, and has deprecated over-elaboration in the preparation and hearing of cases, and a technical approach to admissibility of evidence. "What is required and what the court should confine the parties to is sufficient evidence to enable the court to adopt a broad brush approach.": see Lord Woolf M.R. in *Westmid*, at 134–5. That is consistent with the "jury question" at the heart of most cases under s.6 of the Act (under which the vast majority of applications for disqualification orders are made), namely whether the person concerned is "unfit to be concerned in the management of a company" (s.6(1)(b) of the Act). Nevertheless, the summary approach is tempered by the fact that the court also recognises that in practice a disqualification order can represent "a serious interference with the freedom of an individual" (see Sir Donald Nicholls V.-C. in *Re Rex Williams Leisure Plc* [1994] Ch. 1, at 14. Further, breach of a disqualification order or undertaking can lead to criminal sanctions, of up to two years in prison and a fine (see s.11 of the Act).

Application of the CPR

In a number of places the Practice Direction makes specific provision that a certain aspect of the CPR shall or shall not apply. This can be a trap for the unwary. It should

3J–3

Paragraph numbers marked with a "+" can be found online and on CD.

be emphasised that the rules which primarily govern disqualification proceedings are the Insolvent Companies (Disqualification of Unfit Directors) Rules 1987 (as amended by the Insolvent Companies (Disqualification of Unfit Directors) Proceedings (Amendment) Rules 1999) and by the Insolvent Companies (Disqualification of Unfit Directors Proceedings (Amendment) Rules 2001) (as amended, "the Disqualification Rules"), which were made under the rule-making power contained in s.21 of the Act and s.411 of the Insolvency Act 1986. By r.2(1), the CPR and any relevant practice directions are applied to disqualification proceedings, "except where these Rules make provision to inconsistent effect". This is equivalent to the position in relation to proceedings under the Insolvency Act 1986: see r.7.51 of the Insolvency Rules 1986. Thus, for example, service out of the jurisdiction under r.5(2) of the Disqualification Rules is not subject to the regime set out in Pt 6 of the CPR (though the court may in its discretion apply parts of it by analogy): see *Re Seagull Manufacturing Co Ltd (No.2)* [1994] Ch. 91.

Companies Court Practice

3J–4   The large bulk of disqualification proceedings are brought in the Companies Court, part of the Chancery Division of the High Court in London, and practice elsewhere tends to reflect Companies Court practice. The notes to the Practice Direction make reference, where appropriate, to the practice of the Companies Court.

Part I

1. Application and interpretation

1.1 In this practice direction: 3J–5

(1)   "the Act" means the Company Directors Disqualification Act 1986 (as amended);

(2)   "the Disqualification Rules" means the rules for the time being in force made under section 411 of the Insolvency Act 1986 in relation to disqualification proceedings.[1]

(3)   "the Insolvency Rules" means the rules for the time being in force made under sections 411 and 412 of the Insolvency Act 1986 in relation to insolvency proceedings;

(4)   "CPR" means the Civil Procedure Rules 1998 and "CPR" followed by "Part" or "Rule" and a number means the part or Rule with that number in those Rules;

(5)   "disqualification proceedings" has the meaning set out in paragraph 1.3 below;

(6)   "a disqualification application" is an application under the Act for the making of a disqualification order;

(7)   "registrar" means any judge of the High Court or the county court who is a registrar within the meaning of the Insolvency Rules;

(8)   "companies court registrar" means any judge of the High Court sitting in the Royal Courts of Justice in London who is a registrar within the meaning of the Insolvency Rules.

(9)   except where the context otherwise requires references to;

   (a) "company" or "companies" shall include references to "partnership" or "partnerships" and to "limited liability partnership" and to "limited liability partnerships";

   (b) "director" shall include references to an "officer" of a partnership and to a "member" of a limited liability partnership;

   (c) "shadow director" shall include references to a "shadow member" of a limited liability partnership and in appropriate cases, the forms annexed to this practice direction shall be varied accordingly;

(10)   "disqualification order" has the meaning set out in section 1 of the Act and "disqualification undertaking" has the meaning set out in section 1A or section 9B of the Act (as the context requires);"; and

(11)   a " section 8A application"is an application under section 8A

---

[1] The current rules are the Insolvent Companies (Disqualification of Unfit Directors) Proceedings Rules 1987. For convenience relevant references to the Insolvent Companies (Disqualification of Unfit Directors) Proceedings Rules 1987, which apply to disqualification applications under ss.7, 8 and 9A of the Act (see rule 1(3)), are set out in footnotes to this Practice Direction. This Practice Direction applies certain provisions contained in the Insolvent Companies (Disqualification of Unfit Directors) Proceedings Rules 1987 to disqualification proceedings other than applications under ss.7, 8 and 9A of the Act.

Paragraph numbers marked with a "+" can be found online and on CD.

of the Act to reduce the period for which a disqualification undertaking is in force or to provide for it to cease to be in force;

(12) "specified regulator" has the meaning set out in section 9E(2) of the Act".

1.2 This practice direction shall come into effect on April 26, 1999 and shall replace all previous practice directions relating to disqualification proceedings.

1.3 This practice direction applies to the following proceedings ("disqualification proceedings"):

(1) disqualification applications made:

(a) under section 2(2)(a) of the Act (after the person's conviction of an indictable offence in connection with the affairs of a company);

(b) under section 3 of the Act (on the ground of persistent breaches of provisions of companies legislation);

(c) under section 4 of the Act (on the ground of fraud etc);

(d) by the Secretary of State or the official receiver under section 7(1) of the Act (on the ground that the person is or has been a director of a company which has at any time become insolvent and his conduct makes him unfit to be concerned in the management of a company);

(e) by the Secretary of State under section 8 of the Act (on it appearing to the Secretary of State from investigative material that it is expedient in the public interest that a disqualification order should be made); or

(f) by the Office of Fair Trading or a specified regulator under section 9A of the Act (on the ground of breach of competition law by an undertaking and unfitness to be concerned in the management of a company);

(2) any application made under sections 7(2) or 7(4) of the Act;

(3) any application for permission to act made under section 17 of the Act for the purposes of any of sections 1(1)(a), 1A(1)(a) or 9B(4), or made under section 12(2) of the Act;

(4) any application for a court order made under CPR Part 23 in the course of any of the proceedings set out in sub-paragraphs (1) to (3) above.

(5) any application under the Act to the extent provided for by subordinate legislation[1];

(6) any section 8A application.

Definition of "Director"

3J–6 Paragraph 1.1(9)(b) has been inserted to make it clear how the Practice Direction is to be interpreted where proceedings are brought arising out of the affairs of insolvent

---

[1] Current subordinate legislation includes the Insolvent Partnerships Order 1994 and the Limited Liability Partnerships Regulations 2001.

Paragraph numbers marked with a "+" can be found online and on CD.

partnerships and limited liability partnerships. The statutory definition of director is found in s.22(4) of the Act, which states that director "includes any person occupying the position of director, by whatever name called". Broadly speaking, directors within the meaning of the Act fall into three categories: (a) properly appointed (or "*de jure*") directors, who will normally be registered at Companies House; (b) "de facto" directors (i.e. those who, as a matter of fact after all the circumstances are considered, are treated as directors by the court); and (c) "shadow directors", namely persons in accordance with whose directions or instructions the directors of the company are accustomed to act (see s.22(5) of the Act).

[THE NEXT PARAGRAPH IS 3J–8.]

Restrictions imposed by Disqualification Orders and Disqualification Undertakings

A disqualification order is an order that, for a specified period, the specified person **3J–8** (a) "shall not be a director of a company, act as a receiver of a company's property or in any way, whether directly or indirectly, be concerned or take part in the promotion, formation or management of a company unless (in each case) he has the leave of the court", and (b) "shall not act as an insolvency practitioner" (see s.1 of the Act).

A disqualification undertaking is an undertaking, offered by a person and accepted by the Secretary of State for Business, Enterprise and Regulatory Reform (formerly the Secretary of State for Trade and Industry), in effect to be subject for a specified period to the restrictions found in a Disqualification Order. The Act originally contained no mechanism whereby the parties to proceedings could compromise, because a finding of unfitness could only be made by the court, and accordingly the statutory consequences of an order would not flow from any private agreement between the parties. This led to (a) the court developing the *Carecraft* procedure (see the notes after para.13 of the Practice Direction below), and (with the particular encouragement of Sir Richard Scott V.-C. (see for example Practice Note [1996] 1 All E.R. 442)) (b) the amendments to the Act introduced in the Insolvency Act 2000 (in force since April 2, 2001) which created the statutory undertakings regime.

Date of commencement of proceedings

The limitation period for the bringing of s.6 cases is found in s.7(2), which provides: **3J–9** "Except with the leave of the court, an application for the making under that section of a disqualification order against any person shall not be made after the end of the period of two years beginning with the day on which the company of which that person is or has been a director became insolvent". Although the general rule is that proceedings are started on the date of issue entered on a claim form by the court (see CPR r.7.2(1)–(2), which apply as set out in para.3J–3 above), that position is displaced where the provision at issue is a limitation provision, in which case proceedings are "brought" on the date on which the form is stamped as received at the court (see para.7PD.5.1.2). Thus, where a draft claim form was stamped as received on April 26, 2004, the two year limitation period expired on May 7, 2004, and the claim form was issued on May 17, 2004, it was held that proceedings had been brought in time: *Secretary of State v Vohora* [2007] EWHC 2656 (Ch); *The Times*, December 10, 2007.

2. Multi-track

2.1 All disqualification proceedings are allocated to the multi-track. **3J–10** The CPR relating to allocation questionnaires and track allocation shall not apply.

3. Rights of audience

3.1 Official receivers and deputy official receivers have right of **3J–11** audience in any proceedings to which this Practice Direction applies, including cases where a disqualification application is made by the

Paragraph numbers marked with a "+" can be found online and on CD.

Secretary of State or by the official receiver at his direction, and whether made in the High Court or a county court.[1]

Rights of audience

3J–12   It is occasionally assumed that because official receivers and deputy official receivers have rights of audience, the court will take a more flexible approach to directors being represented by accountants or insolvency advisers. This assumption is incorrect, and the general practice of the Companies Court is to require strict observance of the relevant statutory provisions as to rights of audience.

Part II

Disqualification applications

4. Commencement

3J–13   **4.1** Sections 2(2)(a), 3(4), 4(2), 6(3), 8(3) and 9E(3) of the Act identify the civil courts which have jurisdiction to deal with disqualification applications.

4.1A A disqualification application must be commenced by a claim form issued:

(1)   in the case of a disqualification application under section 9A of the Act, in the High Court out of the office of the companies court registrar at the Royal Courts of Justice;

(2)   in any other case,

(a) in the High Court out of the office of the companies court registrar or a chancery district registry; and

(b) in the county court, out of a county court office.

4.2 Disqualification applications shall be made by the issue of a claim form in the form annexed hereto and the use of the procedure set out in CPR Part 8,[2] as modified by this practice direction and (where the application is made under sections 7, 8 or 9A of the Act) the Disqualification Rules.[3] CPR, rule 8.1(3) (power of the Court to order the application to continue as if the claimant had not used the Part 8 Procedure) shall not apply.

4.3 When the claim form is issued, the claimant will be given a date for the first hearing of the disqualification application. This date is to be not less than eight weeks from the date of issue of the claim form.[4] The first hearing will be before a registrar.

Use of Pt 8 procedure

3J–14   The use of the Pt 8 procedure (and prior to 1999 the originating summons procedure under the RSC) is in some respects not entirely satisfactory, particularly in cases where a substantial amount of the factual evidence is disputed (a point indirectly al-

---

[1] Rule 10 of the Insolvent Companies (Disqualification of Unfit Directors) Proceedings Rules 1987.

[2] Rule 2(2) of the Insolvent Companies (Disqualification of Unfit Directors) Proceedings Rules 1987 as amended.

[3] For convenience, relevant references to the Insolvent Companies (Disqualification of Unfit Directors) Proceedings Rules 1987, which apply to disqualification applications under ss.7 and 8 of the Act (see rule 1(3)(a) and (b)) are set out in footnotes to this Practice Direction.

[4] Rule 7(1) of the Insolvent Companies (Disqualification of Unfit Directors) Proceedings Rules 1987.

Paragraph numbers marked with a "+" can be found online and on CD.

luded to by Sir Donald Nicholls V.-C. in *Re Rex Williams Leisure Plc* [1994] Ch. 1, at 9). However, use of the Pt 7 procedure with statements of case would be even less satisfactory, as the claimant's case (based on his conclusion that it is "expedient in the public interest that a disqualification order should be made") is not a cause of action which easily lends itself to being pleaded in the orthodox way (though the courts have recognised that the evidence in support of the application "has of necessity something of the character of a pleading": Laddie J, in *Re Finelist* [2003] EWHC 1780 (Ch); [2004] B.C.C 877 at [14]. The intention is that all the evidence deemed relevant by the parties can be put before the court, normally without the need for disclosure, so that (in the case of ss.6 to 9 of the Act) the court can decide the question of unfitness. Thus, although applications are occasionally made for an order that disqualification proceedings should proceed by way of statements of case, it is suggested that it will only be in the most exceptional circumstances that the court would consider it appropriate to make such an order.

County Court Proceedings

Most disqualification cases are issued in the High Court. By s.6(3) of the Act the only County Court which may make a disqualification order in relation to a director of a given lead company is the County Court which wound up the company, or had jurisdiction to do so. It has been held that the court has no jurisdiction to transfer a case from that County Court to a different one: see *Secretary of State v Shakespeare* [2005] B.C.C. 891. However, it should be noted that if proceedings are commenced in the wrong court they are not invalid, and they may be retained in that court: see s.6(3B) of the Act.

3J–15

5. Headings

5.1 Every claim form by which an application under the Act is begun and all affidavits, notices and other documents in the proceedings must be entitled in the matter of the company or companies in question and in the matter of the Act. In the case of any disqualification application under section 7 or 9A of the Act it is not necessary to mention in the heading any company other than that referred to in section 6(1)(a) or 9A(2) of the Act (as the case may be).

3J–16

6. The claim form

6.1 CPR, rule 8.2 does not apply. The claim form must state:

(1)   that CPR Part 8 (as modified by this practice direction) applies, and (if the application is made under sections 7, 8 or 9A of the Act) that the disqualification application is made in accordance with the Disqualification Rules[1];

(2)   that the claimant seeks a disqualification order, and the section of the Act pursuant to which the disqualification application is made;

(3)   the period for which, in accordance with the Act, the court has power to impose a disqualification period.

The periods are as follows:—

(a)   where the application is under section 2 of the Act, for a period of up to 15 years;

(b)   where the application is under section 3 of the Act, for a period of up to 5 years;

(c)   where the application is under section 4 of the Act, for a period of up to 15 years;

3J–17

---

[1] Rule 4(a) of the Insolvent Companies (Disqualification of Unfit Directors) Proceedings Rules 1987.

Paragraph numbers marked with a "+" can be found online and on CD.

      (d) where the application is under section 7 of the Act, for a period of not less than 2, and up to 15, years[1];

      (e) where the application is under section 8 or 9A of the Act, for a period of up to 15 years.[2]

    (4) in cases where the disqualification application is made under sections 7, 8 or 9A of the Act, that on the first hearing of the application, the court may hear and determine it summarily, without further or other notice to the defendant, and that, if the application is so determined, the court may impose a period of disqualification of up to 5 years but that if at the hearing of the application the court, on the evidence then before it, is minded to impose, in the case of any defendant, disqualification for any period longer than 5 years, it will not make a disqualification order on that occasion but will adjourn the application to be heard (with further evidence, if any) at a later date that will be notified to the defendant[3];

    (5) that any evidence which the defendant wishes the court to take into consideration must be filed in court in accordance with the time limits set out in paragraph 9 below (which time limits shall be set out in the notes to the Claim Form).[4]

7. Service of the claim form

3J–18   **7.1** Service of claim forms in disqualification proceedings will be the responsibility of the parties and will not be undertaken by the court.

7.2 The claim form shall be served by the claimant on the defendant. It may be served by sending it by first class post to his last known address; and the date of service shall, unless the contrary is shown, be deemed to be the 7th day following that on which the claim form was posted.[5] CPR, r.6.7(1) shall be modified accordingly. Otherwise Sections I and II of CPR Part 6 apply.[6]

7.3 Where any claim form or order of the court or other document is required under any disqualification proceedings to be served on any person who is not in England and Wales, the court may order service on him to be effected within such time and in such manner as it thinks fit,[7] and may give such directions as to acknowledgment of service as it thinks fit. Section III of CPR Part 6 shall not apply.

7.4 The claim form served on the defendant shall be accompanied by an acknowledgement of service.

---

[1] Rule 4(b)(i) of the Insolvent Companies (Disqualification of Unfit Directors) Proceedings Rules 1987.

[2] Rule 4(b)(ii) of the Insolvent Companies (Disqualification of Unfit Directors) Proceedings Rules 1987.

[3] Rule 4(c) and (d) of the Insolvent Companies (Disqualification of Unfit Directors) Proceedings Rules 1987.

[4] Rule 4(e) of the Insolvent Companies (Disqualification of Unfit Directors) Proceedings Rules 1987.

[5] Rule 5(1) of the Insolvent Companies (Disqualification of Unfit Directors) Proceedings Rules 1987.

[6] Attention is drawn to CPR, r.6.14(2) regarding a certificate of service of the claim form.

[7] Rule 5(2) of the Insolvent Companies (Disqualification of Unfit Directors) Proceedings Rules 1987.

Paragraph numbers marked with a "+" can be found online and on CD.

Service to be by the claimant

One of the more substantial changes effected by the CPR to High Court practice **3J–19**
was the provision (since October 1, 2008 to be found in CPR r.6.4) that service by the
Court is the general rule. Rule 7.1 of the Disqualification Rules preserves the pre-1999
High Court practice for disqualification proceedings. There is a great deal of sense in
this approach, in particular because of the very tight limitation period of two years following insolvency which applies in relation to applications under s.6 of the Act.
Investigations into the conduct of directors can be very time-consuming, and many applications are only issued towards the end of the two year period. It is clearly appropriate that the burden of complying with the time limits should in such circumstances be the particular responsibility of the claimants, and not the court.

Service should always comprise service of the claim form, the evidence in support,
and the acknowledgment of service.

NB—the reference in footnote to r.30.6, CPRr.6.14(2) is now obsolete. The provisions as to certificates of service are now found in CPR r.6.17.

Service to be at last known address

It should be noted that the wording of para.7.2 is more flexible than r.5(1) of the **3J–20**
Disqualification Rules (which states that "The claim form shall be served on the defendant by sending it by first class post to his last known address"). In the light of *Cran-
field v Bridgegrove Ltd* [2003] EWCA Civ 656; [2003] 1 W.L.R. 2441 (*inter alia* dealing
with the former CPR, r.6.5(6)), service at the last known address is good service, even
when the claimant knows or believes the defendant no longer resides there.

Deemed service

The phrase "unless the contrary is shown" contained in para.7.2 (and r.5(1) of the **3J–21**
Disqualification Rules) means that deemed service in this context was significantly different to the deemed service provision found until October 1, 2008 in CPR r.6.7(1)
(where the phrase was absent). The position on deemed service in general civil litigation reached as a result of *Anderton v Clwyd CC (No.2)* [2002] EWCA Civ 933; [2002] 1
W.L.R. 3174 therefore did not apply. The general provisions as to service were
substantially recast with effect from October 1, 2008.

Service out of the jurisdiction

As indicated above (see 3J–3, Application of the CPR), service out of the jurisdiction **3J–22**
is governed by the discretion given to the court under r.5(2) of the Disqualification
Rules (repeated as para.7.3 of the Practice Direction), rather than the provisions now
found in CPR, Pt 6.

8. Acknowledgment of service

8.1 The form of acknowledgment of service is annexed to this **3J–23**
practice direction. CPR, rule 8.3(2) and 8.3(3)(a) do not apply to
disqualification applications.

8.2 In cases brought under section 7, 8 or 9A of the Act, the form
of acknowledgment of service shall state that the defendant should
indicate[1]:

(1)   whether he contests the application on the grounds that, in
the case of any particular company:—

    (a) he was not a director or shadow director of that
company at a time when conduct of his, or of other
persons, in relation to that company is in question;

    (b) his conduct as director or shadow director of that
company was not as alleged in support of the application for a disqualification order;

---

[1] Rule 5(4) of the Insolvent Companies (Disqualification of Unfit Directors) Proceedings Rules 1987.

Paragraph numbers marked with a "+" can be found online and on CD.

> > (c) in the case of an application made under section 7 of the Act, the company has at no time become insolvent within the meaning of section 6; or
> >
> > (d) in the case of an application under section 9A of the Act, the undertaking which is a company did not commit a breach of competition law within the meaning of that section.
>
> (2) whether, in the case of any conduct of his, he disputes the allegation that such conduct makes him unfit to be concerned in the management of a company; and
>
> (3) whether he, while not resisting the application for a disqualification order, intends to adduce mitigating factors with a view to reducing the period of disqualification.

8.3 The defendant shall:

> (1) (subject to any directions to the contrary given under paragraph 7.3 above) file an acknowledgment of service in the prescribed form not more than 14 days after service of the claim form; and
>
> (2) serve the acknowledgment of service on the claimant and any other party.

8.4 Where the defendant has failed to file an acknowledgment of service and the time period for doing so has expired, the defendant may attend the hearing of the application but may not take part in the hearing unless the court gives permission.

Filing and service of acknowledgments of service

3J–24   Prior to 1999, there was simply a provision that the respondent (as the defendant was then called) had to file an acknowledgment of service with the court. Paragraph 8.3(2) of the Practice Direction has introduced the requirement that the defendant should also serve the acknowledgment on the claimant and other defendants. This has not worked entirely smoothly, as defendants and their advisers who intend to defend proceedings normally manage to file an acknowledgment at court, but not infrequently fail to serve a copy on the claimant or the other defendants. If finding out the stance of a particular defendant from whom an acknowledgment has not been received is important to any of the other parties, the only prudent course is to enquire of the court shortly before the first hearing date fixed for the claim.

Short of serious and deliberate flouting of court rules, it is difficult to imagine circumstances where at a first hearing the court will exercise the discretion given by para.8.4 against hearing a defendant who has attended at court without having filed and served his acknowledgment. However, it should be noted that it is increasingly the practice of the Companies Court in such circumstances to order the filing of the acknowledgment of service as a condition of being permitted to file evidence.

9. Evidence

3J–25   **9.1** Evidence in disqualification applications shall be by affidavit, except where the official receiver is a party, in which case his evidence may be in the form of a written report (with or without affidavits by other persons) which shall be treated as if it had been verified by affidavit by him and shall be prima facie evidence of any matter contained in it.[1]

9.2 In the affidavits or (as the case may be) the official receiver's report in support of the application, there shall be included:

---

[1] Rule 3(2) of the Insolvent Companies (Disqualification of Unfit Directors) Proceed-

Paragraph numbers marked with a "+" can be found online and on CD.

(1)   a statement of the matters by reference to which it is alleged that a disqualification order should be made against the defendant; and[1]

(2)   a statement of the steps taken to comply with any requirements imposed by sections 16(1) and 9C(4) of the Act.

9.3 When the claim form is issued:

(1)   the affidavit or report in support of the disqualification application must be filed in court;

(2)   exhibits must be lodged with the court where they shall be retained until the conclusion of the proceedings; and

(3)   copies of the affidavit/report and exhibits shall be served with the claim form on the defendant.[2]

9.4 The defendant shall, within 28 days from the date of service of the claim form[3]:

(1)   file in court any affidavit evidence in opposition to the disqualification application that he or she wishes the court to take into consideration; and

(2)   lodge the exhibits with the court where they shall be retained until the conclusion of the proceedings; and

(3)   at the same time, serve upon the claimant a copy of the affidavits and exhibits.

9.5 In cases where there is more than one defendant, each defendant is required to serve his evidence on the other defendant unless the court otherwise orders.

9.6 The claimant shall, within 14 days from receiving the copy of the defendant's evidence[4]:

(1)   file in court any further affidavit or report in reply he wishes the court to take into consideration; and

(2)   lodge the exhibits with the court where they shall be retained until the conclusion of the proceedings; and

(3)   at the same time serve a copy of the affidavits/reports and exhibits upon the defendant.

9.7 Prior to the first hearing of the disqualification application, the time for serving evidence may be extended by written agreement between the parties. After the first hearing, the extension of time for serving evidence is governed by CPR rules 2.11 and 29.5.

9.8 So far as is possible all evidence should be filed before the first hearing of the disqualification application.

---

ings Rules 1987. Section 441 of the Companies Act 1985 makes provision for the admissibility in legal proceedings of a certified copy of a report of inspectors appointed under Part XIV of the Companies Act 1985. Note that the requirements of paragraph 8.1(2)(c) and (d) of this practice direction are additional to the provisions in the said rule 5(4).

[1] Rule 3(3) of the Insolvent Companies (Disqualification of Unfit Directors) Proceedings Rules 1987.

[2] Rule 3(1) of the Insolvent Companies (Disqualification of Unfit Directors) Proceedings Rules 1987.

[3] Rule 6(1) of the Insolvent Companies (Disqualification of Unfit Directors) Proceedings Rules 1987.

[4] Rule 6(2) of the Insolvent Companies (Disqualification of Unfit Directors) Proceedings Rules 1987.

Paragraph numbers marked with a "+" can be found online and on CD.

Affidavits

3J–26   Arguably one of the anomalous features of the disqualification jurisdiction is the continued requirement for affidavits by parties other than the official receiver. Advisers who are less familiar with the jurisdiction will often file and serve witness statements on behalf of their clients, and find their clients ordered by the court to re-file and re-serve the evidence in affidavit form. However, it should only be in rare circumstances that this procedural default should have substantial consequences for a defendant (aside from on the question of costs): in the ordinary case, where a litigant appears at trial to be cross-examined on his evidence, it should make no practical difference that the evidence in the court bundle (and to be adopted in the witness box) is in witness statement rather than affidavit form.

Notwithstanding that it might be thought that the wording of the last clause of para.9.1 of the Practice Direction implies that affidavit evidence must be first hand, it is conclusively established on the case law that there is an implied hearsay exception available to the claimant allowing affidavit evidence for use at trial to include hearsay: see, e.g. *Re Rex Williams Leisure Plc* [1994] Ch. 350, CA, and *Secretary of State v Ashcroft* [1998] Ch. 71, CA. Moreover, the Court of Appeal has held (*Secretary of State v Aaron* [2008] EWCA Civ 1146) that the exception applies not only to the use of hearsay, but also to findings of fact and opinion when contained in investigatory material, i.e. reports or materials obtained under statutory powers—in *Aaron* the relevant report was an FSA report. By contrast, the Court of Appeal also held that there was no implied exception to the normal rules of evidence in respect of hearsay and conclusions of fact or opinion contained in other material on which the Secretary of State sought to rely which was not analogous to investigatory material (in that case, a decision of the Financial Ombudsman Service)—however, on the facts it was decided that the inadmissible material need not be excised, as the trial judge would simply be able to ignore it. Aside from the implied exception to the general rules of evidence, both claimants and defendants also take the benefit of the Civil Evidence Act 1995. The weight to be attached to hearsay evidence will of course be a matter for the court.

The claimant's evidence must include a statement of the matters by reference to which the defendant is alleged to be unfit (r.3(3) of the Disqualification Rules). The Vice-Chancellor confirmed (in *Secretary of State v Andrews*, January 27, 2005, unrep.) that this does not mean that the claimant is required to put all its evidence in support of the claim: i.e., if the claimant adds to the evidence in on an allegation in evidence in reply which is filed after expiry of the two-year limitation period, that will not be a good ground to have the additional evidence excluded. Depending on the facts, though, it may be appropriate for the defendant to have the opportunity to file evidence in rejoinder (see further 3J–32 below).

If the Secretary of State decides not to proceed with an allegation, all he need do is to send a letter to that effect. The CPR notice of discontinuance procedure is not apt for this situation: see *Secretary of State v Blunt* [2006] B.C.C. 112 .

Exhibits

3J–27   Notwithstanding the words of para.9.3(1), the Companies Court will often not require the lodging of the exhibits, because of pressures on court storage. If in doubt as to the practice, contact should be made with the court concerned.

Evidence timetable

3J–28   Rule 6 of the Disqualification Rules provides, in apparently mandatory terms, for a strict timetable for evidence in answer from the defendant, and evidence in reply from the claimant, subject only to the power in r.7(5) to make directions for further evidence if he adjourns the case for further consideration. Paragraph 9.8 of the Practice Direction recognises by implication that in practice this timetable will be hard to achieve.

It is entirely proper and understandable that the court should not wish to give encouragement to either claimants or defendants to think that the timetable contained in the rules should be ignored. Further, as the jurisdiction is intended to be a summary one, indulgent timetables for evidence would not be appropriate. However, as against that, the court is aware that disqualification proceedings are important regulatory proceedings, and fairness to the defendant, and to the public interest, may require extensions of time for evidence on both sides. Nevertheless, this flexibility is

Paragraph numbers marked with a "+" can be found online and on CD.

not intended to undermine the scheme of the rules, as confirmed by the Court of Appeal in *Rex Williams*, which is to advance the provision of evidence to well before trial. Thus, a party wishing to adduce affidavit evidence which should have been provided earlier will need to make a formal application to the court. In considering such an application, especially where it may lead to the delaying of a trial, it is suggested that the court will not only bear in mind the principles taken into account in late applications to amend statements of case under CPR, Pt 17 (see para.17.3.5 above), but also (1) the particular public interest in dealing with disqualification cases expeditiously, (2) the scheme of the Disqualification Rules, and (3) the explanation proffered as to why the evidence was not provided earlier.

Further, where an earlier order has been breached, any application for relief from sanction will have to address the criteria in CPR r.3.9 in the normal way.

The parties will frequently agree, subject to the court, what directions are appropriate, and the court will normally be content to make the directions in the form agreed. The court will pay particular regard when considering the appropriate timetable to the need (which often arises) for defendants and their advisors to inspect company documents held by a liquidator.

10. The first hearing of the disqualification application

10.1 The date fixed for the hearing of the disqualification applica-   **3J–29** tion shall not be less than 8 weeks from the date of issue of the claim form.[1]

10.2 The hearing shall in the first instance be before the registrar.[2]

10.3 The registrar shall either determine the case on the date fixed or give directions and adjourn it.[3]

10.4 All interim directions should insofar as possible be sought at the first hearing of the disqualification application so that the disqualification application can be determined at the earliest possible date. The parties should take all such steps as they respectively can to avoid successive directions hearings.

10.5 In the case of a disqualification application made under sections 7, 8 or 9A of the Act, the registrar shall adjourn the case for further consideration if:—

   (1)   he forms the provisional opinion that a disqualification order ought to be made, and that a period of disqualification longer than 5 years is appropriate,[4] or

   (2)   he is of opinion that questions of law or fact arise which are not suitable for summary determination.[5]

10.6 If the registrar adjourns the application for further consideration he shall—

   (1)   direct whether the application is to be heard by a registrar or by a judge.[6] This direction may at any time be varied by

---

[1] Rule 7(1) of the Insolvent Companies (Disqualification of Unfit Directors) Proceedings Rules 1987.
[2] Rule 7(2) of the Insolvent Companies (Disqualification of Unfit Directors) Proceedings Rules 1987.
[3] Rule 7(3) of the Insolvent Companies (Disqualification of Unfit Directors) Proceedings Rules 1987.
[4] Rule 7(4)(a) of the Insolvent Companies (Disqualification of Unfit Directors) Proceedings Rules 1987.
[5] Rule 7(4)(b) of the Insolvent Companies (Disqualification of Unfit Directors) Proceedings Rules 1987.
[6] Rule 7(5)(a) of the Insolvent Companies (Disqualification of Unfit Directors) Proceedings Rules 1987.

Paragraph numbers marked with a "+" can be found online and on CD.

the court either on application or of its own initiative. If the court varies the direction in the absence of any of the parties, notice will be given to the parties;

(2)   consider whether or not to adjourn the application to a judge so that the judge can give further directions;

(3)   consider whether or not to make any direction with regard to fixing the trial date or a trial window;

(4)   state the reasons for the adjournment.[1]

The first hearing date
3J–30   The timetable for the first hearing date is fixed to allow the parties to comply with the evidence timetable in the Disqualification Rules. For the reasons given above, it is very rarely the case that both evidence in answer and evidence in reply will have been filed and served before the first hearing, and in the majority of cases evidence in answer will not have been served or filed.

The hearing shall be before the registrar
3J–31   Surprisingly, para.10.2 omits reference to one of the procedural traps for those not familiar with the jurisdiction, as r.7(2) of the Disqualification Rules provides that the first hearing is before the registrar "in open court" (and therefore counsel and solicitors should be robed). The open court requirement had a practical consequence in terms of costs under the RSC, as chambers hearings would have had to have been certified fit for the attendance of counsel (a requirement which is not carried forward into the CPR). The principal residual significance of the rule is that the Companies Court general directions lists (in which all disqualification claims are listed for first hearing) normally include some cases which are to be disposed of by uncontested trial, and consistent with the continued general practice of the civil courts, these ought to be dealt with robed. The general lists are normally on a Monday, and it is not unusual to have 30 or more cases listed for directions or disposal.

Directions as to evidence
3J–32   In most cases where the defendant has indicated an intention to contest, the first hearing is used as a directions hearing. If the defendant has not already filed and served his evidence in answer, the court will direct that the evidence is to be filed and served by a certain date. Depending on the circumstances, it is possible that the court will give the directions on "unless" terms, but this is unusual at a first hearing. However, if by the date fixed for the second hearing the evidence still has not been provided, the court will normally only (absent special circumstances) grant a further extension of time on "unless" terms. The court takes a similar approach where claimants are concerned (though, consistent with the timetable set out in para.9 of the Practice Direction, claimants are normally allowed less time for evidence in reply than defendants are allowed for evidence in answer).

Although para.10.4 provides that all interim directions should as far as possible be dealt with at the first hearing, the court has found that a more flexible approach is required. Thus, in certain simple cases it will give fairly full directions at the first hearing, whereas in more complex cases it will normally only make provision for evidence in answer and evidence in reply and then direct that the matter come back for a second directions hearing.

In more complex cases, further rounds of evidence after evidence in reply are required, typically where the claimant has, as a result of further investigations, or as a result of the evidence in answer, decided to put forward further matters determining unfitness. One of the consequences of use of the Pt 8 procedure is that it is not realistic or sensible to order the claimant to amend his original evidence in support. Instead, any new matters by virtue of which it is alleged that the defendant is unfit (colloquially, "allegations") must be stated in the claimant's evidence in reply. Assuming no

[1] Rule 7(5)(b) of the Insolvent Companies (Disqualification of Unfit Directors) Proceedings Rules 1987.

Paragraph numbers marked with a "+" can be found online and on CD.

objection is taken to new matters being raised, the court will order a further evidential timetable so that the defendant can respond to the new allegations made. However, the court will normally be concerned to ensure that any directions given are not used as a cloak by either side to put in evidence which should have been provided before. Directions given by the Companies Court in these circumstances resort to the terminology used by the Court of Chancery to make this point explicit. Evidence from a defendant in response to new allegations is called evidence in rejoinder, and the claimant's response is called evidence in surrejoinder. Very occasionally new allegations are added by the claimant in surrejoinder, in which case the further two rounds of evidence are evidence in rebutter and evidence in surrebutter.

Cross-examination

It will be noted that no specific reference is made to cross-examination of deponents to affidavits and reports. It is possible that when the Act and Disqualification Rules were in their formative stages it was envisaged that proceedings might in certain cases be dealt with by way of trials on paper (subject to the power of the court under the RSC to order cross-examination on affidavit). It has however long been the settled practice to order cross-examination in all contested cases. However, the form of the cross-examination direction has a number of aspects peculiar to the jurisdiction. First, the court may dispense with any attendance by the deponent of a purely formal affidavit, such as a Secretary of State's affidavit which lists the allegations and states that the view has been reached that it is expedient in the public interest that proceedings should be brought, but does no more. Secondly, in cases brought by the official receiver, the court may direct that "the official receiver, or his successor in office" attend. The rationale for this is that an official receiver normally has no first hand knowledge of the matters referred to in his report, and another official receiver will be just as well placed to speak to the evidence. If, however, the official receiver is making an allegation based on matters within his own knowledge (for instance, non-cooperation) then this approach may not be appropriate.

It should be noted that the court's power to control cross-examination can be invoked. This power is part of the court's inherent jurisdiction, as well as being set out in CPR, r.32.1(3). See *Secretary of State for Trade and Industry v Gill* [2004] EWHC 175 (Ch); [2005] B.C.C. 24 where, after refusing an application by the Secretary of State for permission to amend an allegation shortly before trial, Blackburne J. that cross-examination of the defendants' witnesses "must be properly confined to the complaint as it presently stands".

Subject to the above points, the standard cross-examination direction in the Companies Court is "All deponents to affidavits and reports to attend for cross-examination on 21 days' written notice, in default evidence not to be read without the permission of the court". It is sometimes not appreciated that this direction means that, unless the opposing party writes more than 21 days prior to the hearing requiring the attendance of a particular witness at trial for cross-examination, then that witness's evidence will be treated as unchallenged, and he will not need to go into the witness box (unless of course (a) an application is successfully made to the court for cross examination notwithstanding late notice, or (b) the other party waives the late notice and produces the witness for cross examination). The confusion may in part arise because the practice outside London has not always been consistent, with some courts using the Companies Court formulation, and others ordering witnesses to attend unless the opposing party indicates that no cross-examination is required.

Adjournment for further consideration

Paragraph 10.5(1) (which is taken from r.7 of the Disqualification Rules) occasionally throws up practical difficulties. The clear intention behind the five year rule is that it should operate to protect defendants. However, if a defendant has indicated an intention not to contest the proceedings, this might lead to unnecessary cost being incurred if the claimant, knowing the matter clearly required a disqualification period of more than five years, was required in all circumstances to present the case in full with a view to having the matter adjourned for uncontested hearing on another date. The Companies Court has accordingly developed the following settled practice: (1) the requirement that a provisional view be formed that a disqualification order ought to be made, and that a period of longer than five years is appropriate, is treated as only

3J–33

3J–34

Paragraph numbers marked with a "+" can be found online and on CD.

being applicable to a first hearing. Accordingly, (2) if the court does not form that pre-liminary view on the first hearing, but at the second hearing decides that a period of longer than five years is appropriate, the court is not precluded from making a disqualification order for longer than five years at that second hearing. Nevertheless, (3) the court will normally (if there is time) invite the claimant briefly to outline those first hearing cases where there is the possibility that an order of longer than five years will be appropriate, so that (if it thinks fit) a provisional opinion can be formed and re-corded in the order for an adjournment (which will be served on the defendant). The court will also normally direct in such circumstances that the claimant send a letter to the defendant informing him in particular of the provisional opinion formed by the court.

Adjournment to the Judge

3J–35   It is comparatively rare for disqualification cases to be adjourned to be heard by a Judge. Although there is no specific guidance in the Practice Direction, in *Secretary of State for Trade and Industry v Lewis* [2003] B.C.C. 567, Neuberger J. made certain observations when rejecting an application that a trial be heard by a High Court Judge rather than a registrar. He pointed to four particular relevant factors:

(1) The likely length of the hearing, a long hearing being probably more ap-propriate for a judge.

(2) Complex issues of fact or law would probably be another factor favouring a hearing before a judge.

(3) High profile, in the sense of public interest, would probably favour a hearing before a judge.

(4) The court should also take into account the likely hearing date, working on the principle that the earlier the hearing date, the better.

He also indicated that a case might have other special factors to be considered. However, he recorded his acceptance of the Secretary of State's submission that the fact that the consequence of disqualification may be serious for the director concerned was not in itself a relevant factor, as on that basis every disqualification application could or should be heard by a judge.

11. Case management

3J–36   **11.1** On the first or any subsequent hearing of the disqualification application, the registrar may also give directions as to the following matters:

(1)   the filing in court and the service of further evidence (if any) by the parties[1];

(2)   the time-table for the steps to be taken between the giving of directions and the hearing of the application;

(3)   such other matters as the registrar thinks necessary or expe-dient with a view to an expeditious disposal of the applica-tion or the management of it generally[2];

(4)   the time and place of the adjourned hearing[3]; and

(5)   the manner in which and the time within which notice of the adjournment and the reasons for it are to be given to the parties.[4]

11.2 Where a case is adjourned other than to a judge, it may be

---

[1] Rule 7(5)(c)(ii) of the Insolvent Companies (Disqualification of Unfit Directors) Proceedings Rules 1987.

[2] Rule 7(5)(c)(iii) of the Insolvent Companies (Disqualification of Unfit Directors) Proceedings Rules 1987.

[3] Rule 7(5)(c)(iv) of the Insolvent Companies (Disqualification of Unfit Directors) Proceedings Rules 1987.

[4] Rule 7(5)(c)(i) of the Insolvent Companies (Disqualification of Unfit Directors) Proceedings Rules 1987.

Paragraph numbers marked with a "+" can be found online and on CD.

heard by the registrar who originally dealt with the case or by another registrar.[1]

11.3 If the companies court registrar adjourns the application to a judge, all directions having been complied with and the evidence being complete, the application will be referred to the Listing Office and any practice direction relating to listing shall apply accordingly.

11.4 In all disqualification applications, the Court may direct a pre-trial review ('PTR'), a case management conference or pre-trial check lists (listing questionnaires) (in the form annexed to this practice direction) and will fix a trial date or trial period in accordance with the provisions of CPR Part 29: the Multi Track as modified by any relevant practice direction made thereunder.

11.5 At the hearing of the PTR, the registrar may give any further directions as appropriate and, where the application is to be heard in the Royal Courts of Justice in London, unless the trial date has already been fixed, may direct the parties (by Counsel's clerks if applicable), to attend the Registrar at a specified time and place in order solely to fix a trial date. The court will give notice of the date fixed for the trial to the parties.

11.6 In all cases, the parties must inform the court immediately of any material change to the information provided in a pre–trial checklist.

Case Management Directions

One of the matters of greatest concern to the court over the years has been the **3J–37** number of disqualification cases set down for trial where a settlement (usually either by way of the acceptance of an undertaking or the *Carecraft* procedure) took place shortly before the date fixed for a hearing. Late settlement has historically caused significant wastage of judicial time. Partly with this in mind, and acknowledging that cost remained a significant factor cited as to why settlement took place, one of the directions until recently standard adopted and adapted s.4 of the Costs Practice Direction: prior to any PTR, the parties were ordered to serve on each other (a) a schedule of costs incurred to date, and (b) a schedule of likely costs up to and including trial. The intention was that if this was a factor of importance, it could be given early informed consideration by the respective clients. As the court now normally dispenses with PTRs (see 3J–39 below) these directions in relation to costs accordingly now rarely get made.

Pre–trial checklist (listing questionnaire)

Now that PTRs are normally dispensed with, pre-trial checklists are no longer, as a **3J–38** rule, sent out.

Listing directions

It will now normally be the case that Counsel's clerks will be ordered to attend **3J–39** before the Companies Court listing officer (or occasionally a Registrar) (with counsel's and witnesses' dates to avoid) on a fixed date to fix the trial date. This order was in the past normally given at the PTR, but is now generally given at the last direction hearing (i.e. the directions hearing at which the court is satisfied that there is no need for any further drections hearings). It should be noted that this procedure only applies if the trial is to be listed before a Registrar. If the case has been adjourned to the Judge for trial, then normal Chancery Division listing procedure should be followed.

---

[1] Rule 7(6) of the Insolvent Companies (Disqualification of Unfit Directors) Proceedings Rules 1987.

Paragraph numbers marked with a "+" can be found online and on CD.

PTRs

3J–40   It was normally standard when the Practice Direction was first introduced for all disqualification cases in the Companies Court being listed for trial to be adjourned, after the directions hearings had been completed, to a day set aside for dealing exclusively with PTRs. After the introduction of undertakings, far fewer cases needed to be listed for trial, with the result that PTRs tended to be dealt with in the general Monday directions list. Recently, the court has moved to dispensing with PTRs in most cases, and this should now be regarded as a reserve provision, only to be used in complex or otherwise unusual cases.

12. The trial

3J–41   **12.1** Trial bundles containing copies of:—

    (1)   the claim form;

    (2)   the acknowledgment of service;

    (3)   all evidence filed by or on behalf of each of the parties to the proceedings, together with the exhibits thereto;

    (4)   all relevant correspondence; and

    (5)   such other documents as the parties consider necessary;

shall be lodged with the court.

12.2 Skeleton arguments should be prepared by all the parties in all but the simplest cases whether the case is to be heard by a registrar or a judge. They should comply with all relevant guidelines.

12.3 The advocate for the claimant should also in all but the simplest cases provide: (a) a chronology; (b) a dramatis personae; (c) in respect of each defendant, a list of references to the relevant evidence.

12.4 The documents mentioned in paragraph 12.1–12.3 above must be delivered to the court in accordance with any order of the court and/or any relevant practice direction.[1]

    (1)   If the case is to be heard by a judge sitting in the Royal Courts of Justice, London, but the name of the judge is not known, or the judge is a deputy judge, these documents must be delivered to the Clerk of the Lists. If the name of the judge (other than a deputy judge) is known, these documents must be delivered to the judge's clerk;

    (2)   If the case is to be heard by a companies court registrar, these documents must be delivered to Room 409, Thomas More Building, Royal Courts of Justice. Copies must be provided to the other party so far as possible when they are delivered to the court;

    (3)   If the case is to be heard in the Chancery district registries in Birmingham, Bristol, Caernarfon, Cardiff, Leeds, Liverpool, Manchester, Mold, Newcastle upon Tyne or Preston, the addresses for delivery are set out in Annex 1;

    (4)   If the case is to be heard in a county court, the documents should be delivered to the relevant county court office.

---

[1] Attention is drawn to the provisions of the Chancery Guide. Chapter 7 of that Guide dated September 2000 provides guidance on the preparation of trial bundles and skeleton arguments. Unless the Court otherwise orders, para.7.16 of the Chancery Guide requires that the trial bundles be delivered to the Court seven days before trial and para.7.21 requires that skeleton arguments be delivered to the Court not less than two clear days before trial.

Paragraph numbers marked with a "+" can be found online and on CD.

12.5 Copies of documents delivered to the court must, so far as possible, be provided to each of the other parties to the disqualification application.

12.6 The provisions in paragraphs 12.1 to 12.5 above are subject to any order of the court making different provision.

Judgment

The Companies Court Registrar may occasionally be in a position to give an *ex tempore* judgment after trial, but a reserved judgment will be normal. It will often be the case that, if unfitness is found, further submissions on the appropriate period of disqualification will be invited at the hand-down hearing if they have not been made at the conclusion of the trial.　**3J–42**

13. Summary procedure

13.1 If the parties decide to invite the court to deal with the application under the procedure adopted in *Re Carecraft Construction Co Ltd* [1994] 1 W.L.R. 172, they should inform the court immediately and obtain a date for the hearing of the application.　**3J–43**

13.2 Whenever the *Carecraft* procedure is adopted, the claimant must:

(1) except where the court otherwise directs, submit a written statement containing in respect of each defendant any material facts which (for the purposes of the application) are either agreed or not opposed (by either party); and

(2) specify in writing the period of disqualification which the parties accept that the agreed or unopposed facts justify or the band of years (e.g. 4 to 6 years) or bracket (i.e. 2 to 5 years; 6 to 10 years; 11 to 15 years) into which they will submit the case falls.

13.3 Paragraph 12.4 of the above applies to the documents mentioned in paragraph 13.2 above unless the court otherwise directs.

13.4 Unless the Court otherwise orders, a hearing under the *Carecraft* procedure will be held in private.

13.5 If the Court is minded to make a disqualification order having heard the parties' representations, it will usually give judgment and make the disqualification order in public. Unless the Court otherwise orders, the written statement referred to in paragraph 13.2 shall be annexed to the disqualification order.

13.6 If the Court refuses to make the disqualification order under the *Carecraft* procedure, the Court shall give further directions for the hearing of the application.

Carecraft

At the time of the introduction of the Practice Direction, the *Carecraft* procedure (named after the case in which its use was first approved) was in effect the only means by which proceedings could be compromised. The procedure was developed so that the parties could put before the court a series of facts on which they were not in dispute, a statement by the defendant that certain matters determining unfitness alleged by the claimant were undisputed, and an agreement based on the undisputed facts and allegations either as to what the appropriate period of disqualification might be, or within which range of years the court might consider it to lie. It was normal to include in the *Carecraft* statement a list of matters of mitigation which had been taken　**3J–44**

Paragraph numbers marked with a "+" can be found online and on CD.

into account by the parties in reaching their suggestion as to the period of disqualification. The important factor to remember is that it remained for the court to decide, based on the *Carecraft* statement, whether (a) the defendant was unfit, and (b) if he was, what the court in its discretion believed the correct period of disqualification was. The first question was very rarely a difficulty, but it was not unknown that the court was unwilling to accept the parties' suggestion as to disqualification period.

Since the introduction of disqualification undertakings, the use of the *Carecraft* procedure has largely dropped away, principally because undertakings have advantages in terms of reduced expense. However, it remains open for the parties to use, and certain defendants have preferred it, in particular because the opportunity to include matters of mitigation is not (as a matter of the Secretary of State's policy) available in respect of disqualification undertakings, but (at least as matters currently stand) is available in the *Carecraft* procedure.

The Secretary of State's discretion as to the form in which an undertaking will be accepted (i.e. with or without mitigation; with or without a schedule of unfit conduct) is unfettered: *Re Blackspur Group (No.4)* [2001] EWCA Civ 1595; [2004] B.C.C. 839.

14. Making and setting aside of disqualification order

3J–45   **14.1** The court may make a disqualification order against the defendant, whether or not the latter appears, and whether or not he has completed and returned the acknowledgment of service of the claim form, or filed evidence.[1]

14.2 Any disqualification order made in the absence of the defendant may be set aside or varied by the court on such terms as it thinks just.[2]

Making a disqualification order in the absence of a defendant

3J–46   In a large number of cases, no contact is received from the defendant. In such circumstances the claimant simply has to provide the court with a certificate of service confirming that the proceedings were served on the defendant at his last known address in accordance with r.5(1) of the Disqualification Rules, and the court will, if there is sufficient time, proceed to hear the claimant's case uncontested. It is normal for a short judgment to be given, setting out the salient matters which have caused the registrar to come to his conclusion, in particular on the questions of whether the defendant is unfit, and, if so, of what the appropriate period of disqualification is. If the defendant is disqualified, the claimant's costs will normally be summarily assessed.

There is no reported authority under the Disqualification Rules as to the circumstances in which the court would set aside or vary a disqualification order made in the absence of a defendant. Rule 8(2) (from which para.14.2 is taken) is similar in form to RSC O.35, r.2(1) which provided that "any judgment, order or verdict obtained where one party does not appear at the trial may be set aside by the Court, on the application of that party, on such terms as it thinks just". RSC O.35, r.2(2) provided that such an application had to be made within seven days after trial. RSC O.35, r.2 clearly dealt principally with the situation where a defendant had been involved in all steps up to trial, but had failed to attend the hearing: case law (see Supreme Court Practice 1999) built up on this footing. Although r.8(2) is wide enough to cover that situation, it is suggested that the principal concern underlying r.8(2) was the potential for injustice caused by the deemed service provisions in r.5(1) (for instance in circumstances where a defendant had moved abroad accidently leaving an incorrect forwarding address). That interpretation is consistent with no time limit for an application under r.8(2) being found in the Disqualification Rules: it might be months or years after the making of a disqualification order before such a defendant became aware of the proceedings, and it would be unjust if he were subject to a disqualification order which he had no opportunity to challenge. However, notwithstanding the substantial number of

---

[1] Rule 8(1) of the Insolvent Companies (Disqualification of Unfit Directors) Proceedings Rules 1987.
[2] Rule 8(2) of the Insolvent Companies (Disqualification of Unfit Directors) Proceedings Rules 1987.

Paragraph numbers marked with a "+" can be found online and on CD.

23. Service[1]

23.1 Where a disqualification application has been made under **3J–55** section 9A of the Act or a disqualification undertaking has been accepted under section 9B of the Act, the claim form or application notice (as appropriate), together with the evidence in support thereof, must be served on the Office of Fair Trading or specified regulator which made the relevant disqualification application or accepted the disqualification undertaking (as the case may be).

23.2 In all other cases, the claim form or application notice (as appropriate), together with the evidence in support thereof, must be served on the Secretary of State.

Applications for permission to act

Paragraph 23 is broad enough to cover free-standing applications for permission to **3J–56** act, but it should be emphasised that the preferable course is that applications should be heard by the tribunal which deals with the trial of the disqualification proceedings. "It is in everyone's interest that if [an application to act] is envisaged before the disqualification application comes on for hearing, and if the director has advice it will have been envisaged, then it should be heard at the same time because, from the point of view of the director, it is desirable that if he or she is going to be allowed to continue as director of that company there should be no time passing before the leave is granted": Dillon L.J. in *Re Dicetrade* [1994] B.C.C. 371, at 373.

The court has expressed the view that where the original disqualification was made as a result of the *Carecraft* procedure, the parties should normally be confined to the facts contained in the *Carecraft* statement as to the basis of the original disqualification, unless those facts need to be clarified: *Re TLL Realisations* [2000] B.C.C. 998.

Part V

Applications

24. Form of application

24.1 CPR, Part 23 and the Part 23 practice direction (General **3J–57** Rules about Applications for Court Orders) shall apply in relation to applications governed by this practice direction (see paragraph 1.3(4) above) save as modified below.

Evidence in support of applications

The only point to be noted is that evidence in applications made within disqualifica- **3J–58** tion proceedings (other than applications for permission to act) will normally be expected to be in witness statement form, in accordance with the normal practice under CPR Pt 23.

25. Headings

25.1 Every notice and all witness statements and witness statements **3J–59** and affidavits in relation thereto must be entitled in the same manner as the Claim Form in the proceedings in which the application is made.

26. Service

26.1 Service of application notices in disqualification proceedings **3J–60** will be the responsibility of the parties and will not be undertaken by the court.

---

[1] Addresses for service on government departments are set out in the List of Authorised Government Departments issued by the Cabinet Office under section 17 of the Crown Proceedings Act 1947, which is annexed to the Practice Direction supplementing Part 66.

Paragraph numbers marked with a "+" can be found online and on CD.

26.2 Where any application notice or order of the court or other document is required in any application to be served on any person who is not in England and Wales, the court may order service on him to be effected within such time and in such manner as it thinks fit, and may also require such proof of service as it thinks fit. Section III of CPR Part 6 does not apply.

Part VI

Disqualification proceedings other than in the Royal Courts of Justice

3J–61   **27.1** Where a disqualification application or a section 8A application is made by a claim form issued other than in the Royal Courts of Justice this practice direction shall apply with the following modifications:

(1)   Upon the issue of the claim form the court shall endorse it with the date and time for the first hearing before a district judge. The powers exercisable by a registrar under this practice direction shall be exercised by a district judge.

(2)   If the district judge (either at the first hearing or at any adjourned hearing before him) directs that the disqualification claim or a section 8A application is to be heard by a High Court judge or by an authorised circuit judge he will direct that the case be entered forthwith in the list for hearing by that judge and the court will allocate (i) a date for the hearing of the trial by that judge and (ii) unless the district judge directs otherwise a date for the hearing of a PTR by the trial judge.

Part VII

Disqualification undertakings

28. Costs

3J–62   **28.1** The general rule is that the court will order the defendant to pay—

(1)   the costs of the Secretary of State (and, in the case of a disqualification application made under section 7(1)(b) of the Act, the costs of the official receiver) if:

(a) a disqualification application under section 7 or 8 of the Act has been commenced; and

(b) that application is discontinued because the Secretary of State has accepted a disqualification undertaking under section 1A of the Act;

(2)   the costs of the Office of Fair Trading or a specified regulator if:

(a) a disqualification application under section 9A of the Act has been commenced; and

(b) that application is discontinued because the Office of Fair Trading or specified regulator (as the case may be) has accepted a disqualification undertaking under section 9B of the Act.

Paragraph numbers marked with a "+" can be found online and on CD.

28.2 The general rule will not apply where the court considers that the circumstances are such that it should make another order.

Costs where disqualification undertakings are given

Paragraph 28.1 is introduced to make it clear that the normal rule on discontinu-   **3J–63** ance (that the claimant should pay the costs: see CPR, r.38.6 and r.44.12) is reversed where the claimant discontinues following acceptance of an undertaking.

Disqualification undertakings generally

It will be noted that there is very little in the Practice Direction in relation to   **3J–64** disqualification undertakings. This is because they are a matter between the claimant and the defendant, and (unlike the *Carecraft* procedure) do not require judicial sanction. Where proceedings are discontinued on the acceptance of an undertaking, it will not be normal for the undertaking to go on the court file.

The Court of Appeal has given consideration to the undertakings provisions in *Re Blackspur Group (No.4)* [2001] EWCA Civ 1595; [2004] B.C.C. 839, and has held that the Secretary of State has an unfettered discretion as to whether to accept an undertaking which has been offered, and is entitled to decide it would be inexpedient in the public interest to accept it without a schedule of unfit conduct.

Applications under section 8A of the act to reduce the period for which a disqualification undertaking is in force or to provide for it to cease to be in force

29. Headings

29.1 Every claim form by which a section 8A application is begun   **3J–65** and all affidavits, notices and other documents in the proceedings must be entitled in the matter of a disqualification undertaking and its date and in the matter of the Act.

Applications under section 8A of the Act

This procedure in effect mirrors the format of proceedings brought by the Secre-   **3J–66** tary of State or the Official Receiver for a disqualification order, though with the important difference that the starting point should be (except in unusual circumstances) that the claimant accepts that he was properly disqualified pursuant to his undertaking. It is envisaged that making a successful application under s.8A may in practice prove very difficult for a disqualified director.

In *Re INS Realisations* [2006] EWHC 135 (Ch); [2006] 1 W.L.R. 3433, Hart J. expressed the view that the jurisdiction should only be sparingly exercised where the application was (e.g.) based on an assertion that the defendant had given the undertaking because he could not afford legal advice and assistance, or on the fact that at a subsequent trial other defendants received lesser periods of disqualification for the same misconduct. On the facts, the judge allowed an application that the undertaking should cease to be in force: he particularly took into account the fact that the undertaking had been given in relation to the director's omissions in relation to matters complained of, and the fact that proceedings against the director alleged to have caused those matters were subsequently discontinued.

It should be noted that an application cannot be made under s.8A where the period of disqualification has already expired: *Eastaway v Secretary of State* [2006] EWHC 299 (Ch); [2006] 2 B.C.L.C. 489 (the decision was appealed, but not on this point: *Eastaway v Secretary of State* [2007] EWCA Civ 425; [2007] B.C.C. 550).

Much of the commentary in the notes on paras 4 to 12 of the Practice Direction is also relevant to paras 29 to 34 of the Practice Direction. Reference should be made to those notes as appropriate.

30. Commencement: the claim form

30.1 Section 8A(3) of the Act identifies the courts which have juris-   **3J–67** diction to deal with section 8A applications.

Paragraph numbers marked with a "+" can be found online and on CD.

30.1A A section 8A application must be commenced by a claim form issued:

    (1)   in the case of a disqualification undertaking given under section 9B of the Act, in the High Court out of the office of the companies court registrar at the Royal Courts of Justice;

    (2)   in any other case,

        (a) in the High Court out of the office of the companies court registrar or a chancery district registry; and

        (b) in the county court, out of a county court office.

30.2 A section 8A application shall be made by the issue of a Part 8 claim form, in the form annexed hereto and the use of the procedure set out in CPR Part 8, as modified by this practice direction. CPR rule 8.1(3)(power of the Court to order the application to continue as if the claimant had not used the Part 8 procedure) shall not apply.

30.3 When the claim form is issued, the claimant will be given a date for the first hearing of the section 8A application. This date is to be not less than eight weeks from the date of the issue of the claim form. The first hearing will be before the registrar.

30.4 CPR Rule 8.2 does not apply. The claim form must state:

    (1)   that CPR Part 8 (as modified by this practice direction) applies;

    (2)   the form of order the claimant seeks.

30.5 In the case of a disqualification undertaking given under section 9B of the Act, the defendant to the section 8A application shall be the Office of Fair Trading or specified regulator which accepted the undertaking. In all other cases, the Secretary of State shall be made the defendant to the section 8A application.

30.6 Service of claim forms in section 8A applications will be the responsibility of the claimant and will not be undertaken by the court. The claim form may be served by sending it by first class post and the date of service shall, unless the contrary is shown, be deemed to be the seventh day following that on which the claim form was posted. CPR r.6.7(1) shall be modified accordingly. Otherwise Sections I and II of CPR Part 6 apply.[1]

30.7 Where any order of the court or other document is required to be served on any person who is not in England and Wales, the court may order service on him to be effected within such time and in such manner as it thinks fit and may require such proof of service as it thinks fit. Section III of CPR Part 6 shall not apply.

30.8 The claim form served on the defendant shall be accompanied by an acknowledgement of service in the form annexed hereto.

Service

3J–67.1   Since October 1, 2008, the reference in footnote 50 has been obsolete. The provisions as certificates of service are now found in CPR r.6.17.

---

[1] Attention is drawn to CPR, r.6.14(2) regarding a certificate of service of the claim form.

Paragraph numbers marked with a "+" can be found online and on CD.

31. Acknowledgement of service

31.1 The defendant shall: **3J–68**

(1)   file an acknowledgement of service in the relevant practice form not more than 14 days after service of the claim form; and

(2)   serve a copy of the acknowledgement of service on the claimant and any other party.

31.2 Where the defendant has failed to file an acknowledgement of service and the time period for doing so has expired, the defendant may nevertheless attend the hearing of the application and take part in the hearing as provided for by section 8A(2) or (2A) of the Act. However, this is without prejudice to the Court's case management powers and its powers to make costs orders.

32. Evidence

32.1 Evidence in section 8A applications shall be by affidavit. The **3J–69** undertaking (or a copy) shall be exhibited to the affidavit.

32.2 When the claim form is issued:

(1)   the affidavit in support of the section 8A application must be filed in court; and

(2)   exhibits must be lodged with the court where thay shall be retained until the conclusion of the proceedings; and

(3)   copies of the affidavit and exhibits shall be served with the claim form on the defendant.

32.3 The defendant shall, within 28 days from the date of service of the claim form:

(1)   file in court any affidavit evidence that he wishes the court to take into consideration on the application; and

(2)   lodge the exhibits with the court where they shall be retained until the conclusion of the proceedings; and

(3)   at the same time, serve upon the claimant a copy of the affidavits and exhibits.

32.4 The claimant shall, within 14 days from receiving the copy of the defendant's evidence:

(1)   file in court any further affidavit evidence in reply he wishes the court to take into consideration; and

(2)   lodge the exhibits with the court where they shall be retained until the conclusion of the proceedings; and

(3)   at the same time serve upon the claimant a copy of the affidavits and exhibits upon the defendant.

32.5 Prior to the first hearing of the section 8(2) application, the time for serving evidence may be extended by written agreement between the parties. After the first hearing, the extension of time for serving evidence is governed by CPR, rules 2.11 and 29.5.

32.6 So far as is possible all evidence should be filed before the first hearing of the section 8A application.

Evidence in section 8A applications

In *Re INS Realisations* [2006] EWHC 135 (Ch); [2006] 1 W.L.R. 3433, Hart J. said **3J–70** that the agreement not to dispute certain facts embodied in the undertaking should be treated as binding in a s.8A application "unless either some ground is shown which

Paragraph numbers marked with a "+" can be found online and on CD.

would be sufficient to discharge a private law contract or some ground of public interest is shown which outweighs the importance of holding a party to his agreement". That evidential burden on the applicant is much heavier than (for instance) the burden associated with raising matters which have arisen since the undertaking was given.

33. Hearings and case management

3J–71   **33.1** The date fixed for the first hearing of the section 8A application shall be not less than 8 weeks from the date of issue of the claim form.

33.2 The hearing shall in the first instance be before the registrar.

33.3 The registrar shall either determine the case on the date fixed or give directions and adjourn it.

33.4 All interim directions should insofar as possible be sought at the first hearing of the section 8A applications so that the section 8A application can be determined at the earliest possible date. The parties should take all such steps as they respectively can to avoid successive directions hearings.

33.5 If the registrar adjourns the application for further considerations he shall:-

(1)   direct whether the application is to be heard by a registrar or a judge. This direction may at any time be varied by the court either on application or of its own initiative. If the court varies the direction in the absence of any of the parties, notice will be given to the parties;

(2)   consider whether or not to adjourn the application to a judge so that the judge can give further directions;

(3)   consider whether or not to make any direction with regard to fixing the trial date or a trial window.

33.6 On the first or any subsequent hearing of the section 8A application, the registrar may also give directions as to the following matters:

(1)   the filing in court and the service of further evidence (if any) by the parties;

(2)   the time-table for the steps to be taken between the giving of directions and the hearing of the section 8A application;

(3)   such other matters as the registrar thinks necessary or expedient with a view to an expeditious disposal of the section 8A application or the management of it generally;

(4)   the time and place of the adjourned hearing.

33.7 Where a case is adjourned other than to a judge, it may be heard by the registrar who originally dealt with the case or by another registrar.

33.8 If the companies court registrar adjourns the application to a judge, all directions having been compiled with and the evidence being complete, the application will be referred to the Listing Office and any practice direction relating to listing shall apply accordingly.

33.9 In all section 8A applications, the Court may direct a pre-trial review ('PTR'), a case management conference or pre-trial check lists (listing questionnaires) (in the form annexed to this practice direc-

Paragraph numbers marked with a "+" can be found online and on CD.

However, the position has changed by virtue of the amendments to para.17 of the Insolvency Proceedings Practice Direction effective from October 2, 2006. Insolvency proceedings (and by extension disqualification proceedings) are brought into line with general civil litigation, with the imposition of a requirement for permission to make a first appeal (para.17.6 of the Insolvency Proceedings Practice Direction, as substituted). The time limit for appeal is, as of October 2, 2006, 21 days (para.17.11(2)(b) of the Insolvency Proceedings Practice Direction, as amended).

Annex 1

Birmingham: The Chancery Listing Officer, The District Registry of **3J–76** the Chancery Division of the High Court, 33 Bull Street, Birmingham B4 6DS.

Bristol: The Chancery Listing Officer, The District Registry of the Chancery Division of the High Court, 3rd Floor, Greyfriars, Lewins Mead, Bristol BS1 2NR.

Caernarfon: The Chancery Listing Officer, The District Registry of the Chancery Division of the High Court, 1st Floor, Llanberis Road, Caernarfon, LL55 2DF.

Cardiff: The Chancery Listing Officer, The District Registry of the Chancery Division of the High Court, 1st Floor, 2 Park Street, Cardiff CF10 1ET.

Leeds: The Chancery Listing Officer, The District Registry of the Chancery Division of the High Court, Leeds Combined Court Centre, The Court House, 1 Oxford Row, Leeds LS1 3BG.

Liverpool and Manchester: The Chancery Listing Officer, The District Registry of the Chancery Division of the High Court, Manchester Courts of Justice, Crown Square, Manchester M60 9DJ.

Mold: The Chancery Listing Officer, The District Registry of the Chancery Division of the High Court, Law Courts, Civic Centre, Mold, CH7 1AE.

Newcastle upon Tyne: The Chancery Listing Officer, The District Registry of the Chancery Division of the High Court, The Law Courts, Quayside, Newcastle upon Tyne NE1 3LA.

*Preston:*The Chancery Listing Officer, The District Registry of the Chancery Division of the High Court, The Combined Court Centre, Ringway, Preston PR1 2LL.

Editorial note

The following forms which are annexed to this Practice Direction can be found in **3J–77** the *Civil Procedure Forms Volume*:

- **N500**
- **N500A**
- **N500B**
- **N501**
- **N501A**
- **N501B**
- **N502**
- **N503**
- **N504**

Paragraph numbers marked with a "+" can be found online and on CD.

3K   CIVIL RECOVERY PROCEEDINGS

PRACTICE DIRECTION—CIVIL RECOVERY PROCEEDINGS

3K-1 This Practice Direction was published in HMSO CPR Update 30, February 2003. It does not supplement any particular Part of the CPR, or Schedule rule, but is a consequence of the Proceeds of Crime Act 2002. See further para.sc115.0.2.1 above.

Editorial note

3K-2 The Practice Direction is concerned with powers under the Proceeds of Crime Act 2002 ("the 2002 Act") for the High Court to forfeit the proceeds of crime on application of certain government agencies.

On April 1, 2008, s.74 and Sch.8 of the Serious Crime Act 2007 ("the 2007 Act") came into force. These provisions abolished the Assets Recovery Agency and the office of the Director of the Assets Recovery Agency. The litigation functions of the Director under Pt 5 of the Proceeds of Crime Act 2002 were transferred to the Serious and Organised Crime Agency ("SOCA"). Consequently, all civil recovery proceedings in train as of April 1, 2008, were taken over by SOCA on that date.

Additionally, the 2007 Act conferred, for the first time, the power to bring civil recovery proceedings on the principal prosecuting authorities, namely the Director of Public Prosecutions (who is head of the Crown Prosecution Service), the Director of the Serious Fraud Office and the Director of the Revenue and Customs Prosecutions Office (the 2007 Act Sch.8, Pt 2, para.91).

Part 5 powers—power to make a recovery order

3K-3 The power in Pt 5 is for the High Court to make a "recovery order" against property if satisfied that the property is the proceeds of crime (see s.266(1) combined with ss.241, 242 and 304(1) of the 2002 Act). A recovery order is an order which forfeits the interests in the property to the State by vesting the property rights in a "trustee for civil recovery", a creature of the 2002 Act (see ss.266(2) and 267). Property may be traced and recovered from persons who did not carry out the crime, but there are various defences set out in Pt 5, the principal one of which is that the holder of the property is a good faith purchaser for value without notice of the unlawful origin of the property (s.308(1)). In domestic and European Convention of Human Rights law, civil recovery proceedings are civil proceedings, not criminal (*Charrington v Director of the Assets Recovery Agency* [2005] EWCA Civ 334; *Director of the Assets Recovery Agency v Ashton* [2006] EWHC 1064 (Admin)). The claimant does have to specify which *type* of crime generated the proceeds but does not have to identify a *particular* crime (*Director of Assets Recovery Agency v Green* [2005] EWHC 3168 (Admin)). In *Director of the Assets Recovery Agency v Olupitan* [2008] EWCA Civ 104 the Court of Appeal explained that to comply with the requirements identified in *Green* it was not necessary for the claimant to plead the facts in the same manner as in a civil case alleging fraud. All that was necessary was for the type of crime to be identified in the most general terms.

The nature of the claim is neither proprietary nor in personam, but sui generis (*Director of the Assets Recovery Agency v Creaven* [2006] 1 W.L.R. 622).

The 2002 Act inserts s.27A into the Limitation Act 1980 providing for a limitation period of 12 years from when the recoverable property was first obtained. In *Director of the Assets Recovery Agency v Szepietowski* [2007] EWCA Civ 766 the Court of Appeal had to grapple with the applicability of s.32(1) of the Limitation Act 1980 to civil recovery cases. Section 32 has, so far as civil recovery case are concerned, two limbs. The first limb, s.32(1)(a), extends the period of time within which proceedings must be brought in causes of action based on fraud to begin when the fraud is, or should have been, discovered by the claimant. Moore-Bick L.J. took the view that this applied to civil recovery cases, Waller L.J. thought not and Wall L.J. was undecided. However, all the members of the court thought that s.32(1)(b) did apply. This subsection provides that where a defendant conceals facts necessary for a claim from the claimant, time does not begin to run until those facts are, or should have been, discovered. Thus concealment of facts, including the incidence of fraud (on the facts of *Szepietowski*) from the claimant resulted in the limitation period starting when those facts were, or should have been, discovered.

Paragraph numbers marked with a "+" can be found online and on CD.

Part 5 powers—procedure on application for a recovery order

3K-4   The Practice Direction sets out how the claimant should make a claim for a recovery order (para.4). This must be read with the requirements in the Act. The claimant may bring proceedings against any person that they "think" holds recoverable property (s.243(1) of the 2002 Act). For the definition of "property" and holding property see s.316 of the 2002 Act. Such a person is called a "respondent" by the 2002 Act and the claim form must be served on that person (s.243(2) combined with s.316(1)). The claim form should also be served upon any person holding associated property, unless the court dispenses with service (s.243(2)). Associated property is property which is not itself recoverable property, but is another interest in recoverable property. (s.245). The claim form should therefore be served on all persons with an interest in the property (*Director of the Assets Recovery Agency v Charrington* [2004] EWHC 2345 (Admin)). The proceedings "must be made using the Part 8 procedure" (PD para.4.1). This is a curious choice made by the draftsman of the Practice Direction as civil recovery proceedings almost always involve substantial disputes of fact. They are better suited to the Pt 7 procedure. This is recognised by the court which will order a case to proceed under Pt 7 where appropriate (*Director of the Assets Recovery Agency v Creaven* [2006] 1 W.L.R. 622; *Director of the Assets Recovery Agency v Szepietowski* [2007] EWCA Civ 766).

Part 5 powers—making a recovery order

3K-5   If the court makes a recovery order, then the court must appoint a trustee for civil recovery who will act under the direction and instructions of the claimant ss.266– 267 of the 2002 Act). There are provisions in Pt 5 designed to protect the interests of innocent third parties, yet at the same time give effect to the intention to forfeit criminally obtained property to the State (see in particular ss.271 and 272). Express statutory provision is made for the parties to agree that the innocent person should retain the property on payment to the trustee for civil recovery of a sum relating to the criminally derived interest (s.271). The 2002 Act also permits the parties to enter into an order staying the proceedings on terms which the court thinks appropriate (s.276). These provisions do not represent the limit of the powers to settle proceedings. The CPR plainly applies to civil recovery proceedings as it does to any other statutory cause of action in the High Court and the parties may obviously enter into any consent order the court is prepared to endorse, pursuant to CPRPt 40.6.

The court has power to enter summary judgment against the respondent pursuant to Pt 24, but Pt 24 must be applied properly taking care not to act merely on suspicion or on the basis of a reverse burden of proof (*Director of the Assets Recovery Agency v Woodstock* [2006] EWCA Civ 741).

Part 5 powers—interim powers to preserve assets

3K-6   In order to preserve the asset, Pt 5 of the 2002 Act enables the High Court to make "a property freezing order", similar to a CPR Pt 25 freezing order (see s.245A of the 2002 Act, introduced by s.98 of the Serious Organised Crime and Police Act 2005). On January 1, 2006, the Practice Direction was amended to take into account this power.

Further, the High Court has power to make an "interim receiving order" (see s.245 of the 2002 Act). This is an order for detention, custody or preservation of the asset and for the appointment of a receiver. Such a receiver will be an officer of the court (as to which, in a different context, see *Re Andrews* [1999] 1 W.L.R. 1236). Unlike a conventional court appointed receiver in civil proceedings or a receiver appointed to manage assets in anticipation of, or to enforce, a criminal confiscation order, an interim receiver has a statutory investigative function in relation to the source of the asset. The court must confer certain powers on the receiver to report to it and to the parties on his findings in relation to the status of the property (see ss.247, 252 and 255 of the 2002 Act).

These specific statutory interim powers are not the limit of the court's powers. The CPR applies and so any of the interim remedies in Pt 25 are available to the court (and see s.243(5) of the 2002 Act, inserted by Sch.6 of the Serious Organised Crime and Police Act 2005). The court may therefore make a freezing order pursuant to Pt 25 as an alternative to the statutory freezing powers in the 2002 Act (*Director of the Assets Recovery Agency v Creaven* [2006] 1 W.L.R. 622).

Whether an application is made for a property freezing order or for the appoint-

Paragraph numbers marked with a "+" can be found online and on CD.

ment of an interim receiver, the threshold that the claimant must meet is the same. The claimant must show "a good arguable case" that the property is either recoverable property or "associated property" (ss.245A(5)/246(6) of the 2002 Act). Associated property is property which is not, itself, recoverable property, but is some other interest in property which is recoverable (s.245 of the 2002 Act). In *Director of the Assets Recovery Agency v Szepietowski* [2007] EWCA Civ 766 Moore Bick L.J. took the view that, in a case involving serious impropriety (as virtually all civil recovery cases will be), a good arguable case meant a case which was beyond merely speculative, but one which stood a good prospect of succeeding at trial. The claimant must also show that proceedings "may" be brought for the recovery of the property (ss.245A/246 of the 2002 Act); and an order may be discharged on application by a respondent or other party adversely affected by demonstrating that the claimant does not have a good arguable case (*Director and the Assets Recovery Agency v Kean* [2007] EWHC 112 (Admin)). The use of the word "may" heavily suggests that the claimant need not have taken a final decision to commence such proceedings and does not have to give an undertaking to commence such proceedings within a particular time. So far, without the matter being tested, the court has not required the claimant to give such an undertaking as a condition of the grant of such an order and it is thought that this approach is correct. An application for a property freezing order or interim receiving order may be made without notice if the giving of notice would "prejudice any right" of the claimant to obtain a recovery order (ss.245A(3)/246(3)).

The 2002 Act permits the court to exclude property from its ambit, in particular for living expenses and to permit businesses to trade provided the right of the claimant to recover the property is not thereby "unduly prejudiced" (s.252 of the 2002 Act).

However, as originally enacted, the 2002 Act did not permit property to be excepted to pay legal costs (s.252(4)). Instead, the respondent was required to use other property or obtain community funding from the Legal Services Commission. However the Serious Organised Crime and Police Act 2005 by Sch.6, para.14 amended s.252 of the 2002 Act by permitting legal expenses to be paid in accordance with regulations made by subordinate legislation. Such regulations have been made and came into force on the January 1, 2006. The Act and these Regulations, the Proceeds of Crime Act 2002 (Legal Expenses in Civil Recovery Proceedings) Regulations 2005, permit property to be excepted from a property freezing order or an interim receiving order to pay legal costs under strict conditions (see para.9B–1246). The 2002 Act and these Regulations must be read with paras 5B, 7A and 7B of the Practice Direction.

These provisions are dauntingly complex but their effect is as follows. If the court makes an interim receiving order or a property freezing order, it should normally exclude a sum not exceeding £3,000 to enable the respondent to take advice about the order, prepare a statement of assets for release of further sums to pay legal expenses and to apply to vary or set aside the order (PD, para.5B). The court has power to exclude further sums but the exclusion must be limited to sums that are reasonably incurred (s.245C(5)/s.252(4)(a)), such an exclusion must specify the stage or stages in the proceedings to which it relates (reg.4(a)), the court must specify a maximum sum to be released for each stage (s.245C(5)/s.252(4)(b); reg.4B), an application by the respondent must be supported by a witness statement setting out his assets (PD, para.7A.2 and 7A.3) and the court will not make an exclusion if the respondent has assets other than those subject to the interim receiving order or property freezing order from which he may meet legal costs (PD, para.7A.4). The respondent's evidence for this exclusion must contain details of the stage or stages to which the costs apply, include an estimate of the costs incurred or to be incurred in the same form as Precedent H in the costs practice direction in CPR Pt 48 and, where the court has previously made an exclusion in relation to the stage concerned, an explanation of why the costs have exceeded the amount previously allowed and state whether the costs are agreed by the claimant (PD, para.7.3).

Where the court makes an exclusion for legal costs, then in order for an excluded sum to actually be applied in satisfaction of legal costs, the respondent must comply with Pt 3 of the Regulations. These require the respondent to supply certain details of the work done to the claimant including evidence in support (reg.(8(1)). The respondent can only make one such request every two months and it must relate to work which has been carried out (reg.8(2)). If the claimant agrees the amount claimed, that amount may be applied in satisfaction of the costs (reg.10). In deciding whether to

Paragraph numbers marked with a "+" can be found online and on CD.

agree to the amount claimed the claimant must have regard to the hourly rates in the table in reg.17 (reg.9(3)). The table has sliding scales of rates from £75 to £270 per hour for solicitors and £100 to £330 per hour for counsel. If the amount is not agreed, then only 65 per cent of the amount claimed may be paid and the whole amount is later subject to assessment in the event that a recovery order is made (regs 10, 11 and 13). On an assessment of the respondent's legal costs (if there is one) post the making of a recovery order, the respondent's own client costs are assessed by application in accordance with CPR Pt 47. The application must be commenced within two months of the recovery order and the solicitor must file a request for a detailed assessment hearing within two months of the detailed assessment proceedings (reg.13(2)(a)). The costs are assessed on a standard basis in accordance with CPR Pt 44, but on the hourly rates set out in the table in reg.17 (regs 13 and 16).

The 2002 Act contains specific provisions empowering affected persons to apply to vary or set aside a property freezing order or an interim receiving order (ss.245B /251). In respect of an application for discharge of an interim receiver, if there is a receiver, the court should not normally accede to such an application on the basis that the property to which the application relates is not recoverable or associated property, until the receiver produces the report envisaged by the Act (*Director of Assets Recovery Agency v He and Chen* [2004] EWHC 3021 (Admin)). The receiver, any party or any person affected by action taken or proposed to be taken by the receiver may apply to the court for directions (s.251(1) of the 2002 Act). Before giving directions, all affected persons must be given an opportunity to be heard (s.252(2)). The Practice Direction sets out how such an application should be made (para.6) and by para.4 of the Practice Direction, Pt 69 of the CPR is applied. Consequently the receiver may apply for directions on uncontentious matters by letter (CPR Pt 69.8).

Scope and Interpretation

3K–7   **1.1** Section I of this practice direction contains general provisions about proceedings in the High Court under Parts 5 and 8 of the Proceeds of Crime Act 2002 and Part 5 of the Proceeds of Crime Act 2002 (External Requests and Orders) Order 2005.

1.2 Section II contains provisions about applications to the High Court under Part 5 of the Act and Part 5 of the Order in Council for—

(a)   a recovery order;

(b)   a property freezing order;

(c)   an interim receiving order;

(d)   a management receiving order; and

(e)   the register of external orders.

1.3 Section III contains provisions about applications to the High Court under Part 8 of the Act for any of the following types of order or warrant in connection with a civil recovery investigation or a detained cash investigation—

(a)   a production order;

(b)   a search and seizure warrant;

(c)   a disclosure order;

(d)   a customer information order; and

(e)   an account monitoring order.

1.4 Section IV of this practice direction contains further provisions about applications for each of the specific types of order and warrant listed in paragraph 1.3 above.

1.5 In this practice direction—

Paragraph numbers marked with a "+" can be found online and on CD.

(1) 'the Act' means the Proceeds of Crime Act 2002[1];

(1A) 'appropriate officer' has the meaning set out in section 378 of the Act;

(2) 'enforcement authority' has the meaning set out in section 316 of the Act;

(3) 'the Order in Council' means the Proceeds of Crime Act 2002 (External Requests and Orders) Order 2005;

(4) 'civil recovery proceedings' means proceedings under Part 5 of the Act or Part 5 of the Order in Council (as appropriate);

(4A) 'interim receiving order' has the meaning set out in section 246 of the Act;

(4B) 'management receiving order' means an order to appoint a receiver under section 245E of the Act;

(4C) 'property freezing order' has the meaning set out in section 245A of the Act;

(5) 'the Regulations' means the Proceeds of Crime Act 2002 (Legal Expenses in Civil Recovery Proceedings) Regulations 2005;

(5A) 'relevant Director' has the meaning set out in section 352(5A) of the Act;

(5B) 'CPR' means the Civil Procedure Rules 1998; and

(6) other expressions used have the same meaning as in the Act or the Order in Council (as appropriate).

Section I—General Provisions

Venue

2.1 A claim or application to the High Court under Part 5 or Part **3K–8** 8 of the Act or Part 5 of the Order in Council must be started in the Administrative Court.

2.2 The Administrative Court may transfer the claim or application to the Queen's Bench Division Central Office or Chancery Chambers.

Use of pseudonyms by staff

3.1 If a member of the staff of the relevant Director gives written **3K–9** or oral evidence in any proceedings using a pseudonym in accordance with section 449 or section 449A of the Act—

(1) the court must be informed that the witness is using a pseudonym; and

(2) a certificate under section 449(3) or 449A(3) (as appropriate) of the Act must be filed or produced.

Section II—Civil Recovery Proceedings under Part 5 of the Act or Part 5 of the Order in Council

Claim for a recovery order

4.1 A claim by the enforcement authority for a recovery order **3K–10** must be made using the CPR Part 8 procedure.

---

[1] 2002 c. 29.

Paragraph numbers marked with a "+" can be found online and on CD.

4.2 In a claim for a recovery order based on an external order, the claim must include an application to register the external order.

4.3 The claim form must—

(1) identify the property in relation to which a recovery order is sought;

(2) state, in relation to each item or description of property—

(a) whether the property is alleged to be recoverable property or associated property; and

(b) either—

(i) who is alleged to hold the property; or

(ii) where the enforcement authority is unable to identify who holds the property, the steps that have been taken to try to establish their identity;

(3) set out the matters relied upon in support of the claim;

(4) give details of the person nominated by the enforcement authority to act as trustee for civil recovery in accordance with section 267 of the Act or article 178 of the Order in Council; and

(5) in a claim which includes an application to register an external order, be accompanied by a copy of the external order.

4.4 The evidence in support of the claim must include the signed, written consent of the person nominated by the enforcement authority to act as trustee for civil recovery if appointed by the court.

4.5 In a claim which includes an application to register an external order, where—

(1) the sum specified in the external order is expressed in a currency other than sterling; and

(2) there are not funds held in the United Kingdom in the currency in which the sum specified is expressed sufficient to satisfy the external order,

the claim form, or particulars of claim if served subsequently, must state the sterling equivalent of the sum specified.

(Article 145(2) of the Order in Council provides that the sterling equivalent is to be calculated in accordance with the exchange rate prevailing at end of the day on which the external order is made.)

Applications

3K–11   **5.1** An application for a property freezing order, an interim receiving order or a management receiving order must be made—

(1) to a High Court judge; and

(2) in accordance with CPR Part 23.

5.2 CPR rule 23.10(2) and Section I of CPR Part 25 do not apply to applications for property freezing orders, interim receiving orders and management receiving orders.

5.3 The application may be made without notice in the circumstances set out in—

(1) section 245A(3) of the Act and article 147(3) of the Order in

Paragraph numbers marked with a "+" can be found online and on CD.

Council (in the case of an application for a property freezing order);

(2) section 246(3) of the Act and article 151(3) of the Order in Council (in the case of an application for an interim receiving order);

(3) section 245(E) of the Act and the Order in Council (in the case of an application for a management receiving order).

5.4 An application for a property freezing order must be supported by written evidence which must—

(1) set out the grounds on which the order is sought; and

(2) give details of each item or description of property in respect of which the order is sought, including—

(a) an estimate of the value of the property; and

(b) the additional information referred to in paragraph 5.5(2).

5.5 CPR Part 69 (court's power to appoint a receiver) and its practice direction apply to an application for an interim receiving order with the following modifications—

(1) paragraph 2.1 of the practice direction supplementing CPR Part 69 does not apply;

(2) the enforcement authority's written evidence must, in addition to the matters required by paragraph 4.1 of that practice direction, also state in relation to each item or description of property in respect of which the order is sought—

(a) whether the property is alleged to be—

(i) recoverable property; or

(ii) associated property,

and the facts relied upon in support of that allegation; and

(b) in the case of any associated property—

(i) who is believed to hold the property; or

(ii) if the enforcement authority is unable to establish who holds the property, the steps that have been taken to establish their identity; and

(3) the enforcement authority's written evidence must always identify a nominee and include the information in paragraph 4.2 of that practice direction.

5.5A Paragraph 2.1 of the PD supplementing CPR Part 69 does not apply to an application for a management receiving order.

5.6 Where an application is made for an interim receiving order or management receiving order, a draft of the order which is sought must be filed with the application notice. This should if possible also be supplied to the court in an electronic form compatible with the word processing software used by the court.

Property freezing order or interim receiving order made before commencement of claim for recovery order

5A. A property freezing order or interim receiving order which is made before a claim for a recovery order has been commenced will— **3K–12**

Paragraph numbers marked with a "+" can be found online and on CD.

(1) specify a period within which the enforcement authority must either start the claim or apply for the continuation of the order while he carries out his investigation; and

(2) provide that the order shall be set aside if the enforcement authority does not start the claim or apply for its continuation before the end of that period.

Exclusions when making property freezing order or interim receiving order

3K–13 **5B.1** When the court makes a property freezing order or interim receiving order on an application without notice, it will normally make an initial exclusion from the order for the purpose of enabling the respondent to meet his reasonable legal costs so that he may—

(1) take advice in relation to the order;

(2) prepare a statement of assets in accordance with paragraph 7A.3; and

(3) if so advised, apply for the order to be varied or set aside.

The total amount specified in the initial exclusion will not normally exceed £3,000.

5B.2 When it makes a property freezing order or interim receiving order before a claim for a recovery order has been commenced, the court may also make an exclusion to enable the respondent to meet his reasonable legal costs so that (for example) when the claim is commenced—

(1) he may file an acknowledgment of service and any written evidence on which he intends to rely; or

(2) he may apply for a further exclusion for the purpose of enabling him to meet his reasonable costs of the proceedings.

5B.3 Paragraph 7A contains general provisions about exclusions made for the purpose of enabling a person to meet his reasonable legal costs.

Interim receiving order or management receiving order or management receiving order: application for directions

3K–14 **6.1** An application for directions as to the exercise of the functions of —

(1) the interim receiver under section 251 of the Act or article 156 of the Order in Council, or

(2) the management receiver under section 245G of the Act or under the Order in Council,

may be made at any time by—

(a) the interim receiver or management receiver, as appropriate;

(b) any party to the proceedings; and

(c) any person affected by any action taken, or proposed to be taken, by the interim receiver or management receiver.

6.2 The application must always be made by application notice, which must be served on—

Paragraph numbers marked with a "+" can be found online and on CD.

(1)   the interim receiver or management receiver as appropriate (unless he is the applicant);

(2)   every party to the proceedings; and

(3)   any other person who may be interested in the application.

Application to vary or set aside an order

7.1 An application to vary or set aside a property freezing order, **3K–15** an interim receiving order or a management receiving order (including an application for, or relating to, an exclusion from the order) may be made at any time by—

(1)   the enforcement authority; or

(2)   any person affected by the order.

7.2 Unless the court otherwise directs or exceptional circumstances apply, a copy of the application notice must be served on—

(1)   every party to the proceedings;

(2)   in the case of an application to vary or set aside an interim receiving order or management receiving order, the interim receiver or management receiver (as appropriate); and

(3)   any other person who may be affected by the court's decision.

7.3 The evidence in support of an application for an exclusion from a property freezing order or interim receiving order for the purpose of enabling a person to meet his reasonable legal costs must—

(1)   contain full details of the stage or stages in civil recovery proceedings in respect of which the costs in question have been or will be incurred;

(2)   include an estimate of the costs which the person has incurred and will incur in relation to each stage to which the application relates, substantially in the form illustrated in Precedent H in the Schedule of Costs Precedents annexed to the Practice Direction supplementing CPR Parts 43–48 Costs;

(3)   include a statement of assets containing the information set out in paragraph 7A.3 (unless the person has previously filed such a statement in the same civil recovery proceedings and there has been no material change in the facts set out in that statement);

(4)   where the court has previously made an exclusion in respect of any stage to which the application relates, explain why the person's costs will exceed the amount specified in the exclusion for that stage; and

(5)   state whether the terms of the exclusion have been agreed with the enforcement authority.

Exclusions for the purpose of meeting legal costs: general provisions

7A.1 Subject to paragraph 7A.2, when the court makes an order or **3K–16** gives directions in civil recovery proceedings it will at the same time

Paragraph numbers marked with a "+" can be found online and on CD.

consider whether it is appropriate to make or vary an exclusion for the purpose of enabling any person affected by the order or directions to meet his reasonable legal costs.

7A.2 The court will not make an exclusion for the purpose of enabling a person to meet his reasonable legal costs, other than an exclusion to meet the costs of taking any of the steps referred to in paragraph 5B.1, unless that person has made and filed a statement of assets.

7A.3 A statement of assets is a witness statement which sets out all the property which the maker of the statement owns, holds or controls, or in which he has an interest, giving the value, location and details of all such property. Information given in a statement of assets under this practice direction will be used only for the purpose of the civil recovery proceedings.

7A.4 The court—

(1)   will not make an exclusion for the purpose of enabling a person to meet his reasonable legal costs (including an initial exclusion under paragraph 5B.1); and

(2)   may set aside any exclusion which it has made for that purpose or reduce any amount specified in such an exclusion,

if it is satisfied that the person has property to which the property freezing order or interim receiving order does not apply from which he may meet those costs.

7A.5 The court will normally refer to a costs judge any question relating to the amount which an exclusion should allow for reasonable legal costs in respect of proceedings or a stage in proceedings.

7A.6 Attention is drawn to section 245C of the Act and article 149 of the Order in Council (in relation to exclusions from property freezing orders) and to section 252 of the Act and article 157 of the Order in Council (in relation to exclusions from interim receiving orders). An exclusion for the purpose of enabling a person to meet his reasonable legal costs must be made subject to the 'required conditions' specified in Part 2 of the Regulations.

7A.7 An exclusion made for the purpose of enabling a person to meet his reasonable legal costs will specify—

(1)   the stage or stages in civil recovery proceedings to which it relates;

(2)   the maximum amount which may be released in respect of legal costs for each specified stage; and

(3)   the total amount which may be released in respect of legal costs pursuant to the exclusion.

7A.8 A person who becomes aware that his legal costs—

(1)   in relation to any stage in civil recovery proceedings have exceeded or will exceed the maximum amount specified in the exclusion for that stage; or

(2)   in relation to all the stages to which the exclusion relates have exceeded or will exceed the total amount that may be released pursuant to the exclusion,

Paragraph numbers marked with a "+" can be found online and on CD.

should apply for a further exclusion or a variation of the existing exclusion as soon as reasonably practicable.

Assessment of costs where recovery order is made

7B.1 Where the court—   **3K–17**

(1)   makes a recovery order in respect of property which was the subject of a property freezing order or interim receiving order; and

(2)   had made an exclusion from the property freezing order or interim receiving order for the purpose of enabling a person to meet his reasonable legal costs,

the recovery order will make provision under section 266(8A) of the Act or article 177(10) of the Order in Council (as appropriate) for the payment of those costs.

7B.2 Where the court makes a recovery order which provides for the payment of a person's reasonable legal costs in respect of civil recovery proceedings, it will at the same time order the detailed assessment of those costs. Parts 4 and 5 of the Regulations, CPR Part 47 and Section 49A of the Practice Direction supplementing CPR Parts 43–48 (Costs) apply to a detailed assessment pursuant to such an order.

Registers

7C. There will be kept in the Central Office of the Supreme Court **3K–18** at the Royal Courts of Justice, under the direction of the Senior Master, a register of external orders which the High Court has ordered to be registered.

Section III—Applications under Part 8 of the Act in respect of Civil Recovery Investigations and Detained Cash Investigations

How to apply for an order or warrant

8.1 An application for an order or warrant under Part 8 of the Act **3K–19** in connection with a civil recovery investigation or (where applicable) a detained cash investigation must be made—

(1)   to a High Court judge;

(2)   by filing an application notice.

8.2 The application may be made without notice.

Confidentiality of court documents

9.1 CPR rules 5.4, 5.4B and 5.4C do not apply to an application **3K–20** under Part 8 of the Act, and paragraphs 9.2 and 9.3 below have effect in its place.

9.2 When an application is issued, the court file will be marked 'Not for disclosure' and, unless a High Court judge grants permission, the court records relating to the application (including the application notice, documents filed in support, and any order or warrant that is made) will not be made available by the court for any person to inspect or copy, either before or after the hearing of the application.

Paragraph numbers marked with a "+" can be found online and on CD.

CIVIL RECOVERY

9.3 An application for permission under paragraph 9.2 must be made on notice to the appropriate officer in accordance with CPR Part 23.

(CPR rule 23.7(1) requires a copy of the application notice to be served as soon as practicable after it is filed, and in any event at least 3 days before the court is to deal with the application.)

Application notice and evidence

3K–21
10.1 The application must be supported by written evidence, which must be filed with the application notice.

10.2 The evidence must set out all the matters on which the appropriate officer relies in support of the application, including any matters required to be stated by the relevant sections of the Act, and all material facts of which the court should be made aware.

10.3 There must also be filed with the application notice a draft of the order sought. This should if possible also be supplied to the court on disk in a form compatible with the word processing software used by the court.

Hearing of the application

3K–22
11.1 The application will be heard and determined in private, unless the judge hearing it directs otherwise.

Variation or discharge of order or warrant

3K–23
12.1 An application to vary or discharge an order or warrant may be made by—

    (1)   the appropriate officer; or

    (2)   any person affected by the order or warrant.

12.2 An application under paragraph 12.1 to stop an order or warrant from being executed must be made immediately upon it being served.

12.3 A person applying to vary or discharge a warrant must first inform the appropriate officer that he is making the application.

12.4 The application should be made to the judge who made the order or issued the warrant or, if he is not available, to another High Court judge.

Section IV—Further Provisions About Specific Applications Under Part 8 Of The Act

Production order

3K–24
13.1 The application notice must name as a respondent the person believed to be in possession or control of the material in relation to which a production order is sought.

13.2 The application notice must specify—

    (1)   whether the application is for an order under paragraph (a) or (b) of section 345(4) of the Act;

    (2)   the material, or description of material, in relation to which the order is sought; and

    (3)   the person who is believed to be in possession or control of the material.

Paragraph numbers marked with a "+" can be found online and on CD.

SECTION 4

HOUSE OF LORDS APPEALS

4A   CIVIL APPEALS

Practice Directions Applicable to Civil Appeals

(with effect from 8 October 2007)

Part I—Directions on Petitions for Leave to Appeal

1.

PERMISSION TO APPEAL

Introduction

1.1 Subject to certain conditions, appeals in civil matters may be brought to the **4A–1** House of Lords from the Court of Appeal in England and Wales and in Northern Ireland, from the High Court in England and Wales and in Northern Ireland under the "leapfrog" procedure, and from the Court of Session in Scotland.[1] The judicial procedures of the House are regulated by statute, by standing orders of the House and by practice directions.[2] Copies of these and other documents may be obtained free of charge from the Judicial Office of the House of Lords or downloaded from *http://www.parliament.uk* [Accessed November 29, 2007].

Terminology

1.2 The Appellate Jurisdiction Act 1876 is the basic Act governing the judicial **4A–2** function of the House of Lords. This booklet uses the terminology of that Act. The term "leave to appeal" means permission to appeal. A "petition for leave to appeal" is an application for permission to appeal.

Right of appeal

1.3 The right of appeal to the House of Lords is regulated by statute and subject to **4A–3** statutory restrictions. The relevant statutes for civil appeals are: the Administration of Justice (Appeals) Act 1934; the Administration of Justice Act 1960; the Administration of Justice Act 1969; the Judicature (Northern Ireland) Act 1978; the Court of Session Act 1988; and the Access to Justice Act 1999. Every applicant for leave to appeal must comply with the statutory requirements before the application can be considered by the House. The Human Rights Act 1998 applies to the House in its judicial capacity. But that Act does not confer any general right of appeal to the House, or any right of appeal in addition to or superseding any right of appeal provided for in Acts passed before the coming into force of the Human Rights Act 1998.

Stay of execution

1.4 See direction 43.

4A–4

Appeals from (i) the Court of Appeal in England & Wales; and (ii) the Court of Appeal in Northern Ireland

1.5 An appeal to the House of Lords from any order or judgment of the Court of **4A–5** Appeal in England and Wales or in Northern Ireland may only be brought with the leave of the Court of Appeal or of the House of Lords.[3]

1.6 An application for leave to appeal must be made first to the Court of Appeal and

---

[1] For appeals "in a criminal cause or matter", see paras 4B–1+ to 4B–101+.
[2] The orders are made pursuant to the Appellate Jurisdiction Act 1876 s 11.
[3] Administration of Justice (Appeals) Act 1934, s 1(1); Judicature (Northern Ireland) Act 1978, s 42.

Paragraph numbers marked with a "+" can be found online and on CD.

only after that Court refuses leave may application be made to the House of Lords itself.[1] Application is made by presenting a petition for leave to appeal.[2]

Appeals from the Court of Session in Scotland

4A-6 1.7 Leave to appeal is not required in appeals to which directions 1.8 and 1.9 apply. Leave to appeal is required for appeals to which directions 1.10 and 1.11 apply.

1.8 As a general rule, leave to appeal is not required from an interlocutor of the Inner House of the Court of Session on the whole merits of the cause[3]. Standing Orders I and IV govern such appeals. The petition of appeal must be lodged within 3 months of the date of the interlocutor appealed from; and the petition of appeal must be signed by two Scottish counsel who must also certify that the appeal is reasonable[4].

1.9 As a general rule, leave to appeal is not required from an interlocutory judgment of the Court of Session where there is a difference of opinion among the judges or where the interlocutory judgment is one sustaining a dilatory defence and dismissing the action[5]. Standing Orders I and IV apply: the petition of appeal must be lodged within 3 months of the date of the interlocutor appealed from; and the petition of appeal must be signed by two Scottish counsel who must also certify that the appeal is reasonable.

1.10 Leave to appeal is required for an appeal to the House of Lords against any interlocutory judgment of the Court of Session that does not fall within direction 1.9, and only the Inner House of the Court of Session may grant such leave to appeal[6]. In all such cases a refusal of the Court of Session to grant leave to appeal is final and no petition for leave to appeal may then be presented to the House of Lords.

1.11 Leave to appeal from the Court of Session is also required for an appeal to the House of Lords under the provisions of certain Acts of Parliament, and such leave may be granted either by the Court of Session or, if refused by the Court of Session, by the House of Lords. When leave to appeal is granted pursuant to direction 1.10 or this direction, it is not necessary for two Scottish counsel to certify that the appeal is reasonable.

Appeals from (i) High Court of Justice in England & Wales; and (ii) High Court of Justice in Northern Ireland

4A-7 1.12 In certain cases, and subject to certain conditions, an appeal lies direct from the High Court in England and Wales or in Northern Ireland to the House of Lords. A certificate of the High Court must first be obtained and the leave of the House of Lords then sought and given before the appeal may proceed (see direction 6).[7] No application may be made to the House of Lords without the certificate of the High Court.

Civil contempt of court cases

4A-8 1.13 In cases involving civil contempt of court, an appeal may be brought under s 13 of the Administration of Justice Act 1960.[8] Leave to appeal is required and an

---

[1] This does not apply to applications for leave to cross-appeal where an Appeal Committee has given leave to appeal in the original appeal: direction 30.1.
[2] For form of petition, see Appendix A, Form 1.
[3] Court of Session Act 1988 s 40(1)(a). The right of appeal may however be restricted or excluded by statute e.g. Transport Act 1985 s 117, Sch 4, para 14(1).
[4] For the purposes of Standing Order IV the word "counsel" includes any enrolled solicitor having a right of audience in the House of Lords.
[5] Court of Session Act 1988 s 40(1)(a).
[6] Court of Session Act 1988 s 40(1)(b).
[7] Administration of Justice Act 1969, ss 12–15.
[8] Or, in Northern Ireland, under Judicature (Northern Ireland) Act 1978, s 44. Ap-

Paragraph numbers marked with a "+" can be found online and on CD.

application for such leave must first be made to the court below. If that application is refused, a petition for leave to appeal may then be presented to the House of Lords. Where the decision of the court below is a decision on appeal under the same section of the same Act, leave to appeal to the House of Lords is only granted if the court below certifies that a point of law of general public importance is involved in that decision and if it appears to that court or to the House, as the case may be, that the point is one that ought to be considered by the House. Where the court below refuses to grant the certificate required, a petition for leave to appeal is not accepted for presentation to the House.

Admissibility of petitions

1.14 Leave to appeal to the House of Lords is subject to statutory restrictions. The **4A–9** following types of petition are excluded by statute from the House's jurisdiction:

   (a) petitions for leave to appeal from a refusal by the Court of Appeal to grant leave to appeal to that court from a judgment or order of a lower court, or from any other preliminary decision of the Court of Appeal in respect of a case in which leave to appeal to the Court of Appeal was not granted [1];

   (b) petitions for leave to appeal brought by a petitioner in respect of whom the High Court has made an order under s 42 of the Supreme Court Act 1981 (restriction of vexatious legal proceedings), except a petition for leave to appeal against the s 42 order itself;

   (c) petitions for leave to appeal from a decision of the Court of Appeal on any appeal from a county court in any probate proceedings;

   (d) petitions for leave to appeal from a decision of the Court of Appeal on an appeal from a decision of the High Court on a question of law under Part III of the Representation of the People Act 1983 (legal proceedings).

1.15 The Judicial Office will not accept for lodgment any petition for leave to appeal that:

   (a) falls under direction 1.14(a); and

   (b) seeks leave to appeal against an order of the Court of Appeal which that Court has certified by virtue of section 54(4) of the Access to Justice Act 1999 may not be appealed to the House.

1.16 No petition for leave to appeal will be considered by an Appeal Committee unless:

   (a) the petition is properly served on the respondents (see direction 3.12);

   (b) all the required documents are supplied to the Judicial Office (see directions 3.13 and 4.2); and

   (c) the prescribed fee is paid or a form of waiver lodged (see directions 3.16-3.17).

1.17 When a petition for leave to appeal falls within directions 1.14 and 1.15, the Judicial Office informs the petitioner in writing that the House of Lords has no jurisdiction in the matter. The European Court of Human Rights accepts this letter as setting out the jurisdiction of the House in the litigation, for the purpose of determining whether the petitioner has satisfied the requirement, laid down by Article 35 of the European Convention on Human Rights, that all domestic remedies must be exhausted before an appeal can be made to the Strasbourg Court.

peals involving criminal contempt of court are subject to the *Practice directions applicable to Criminal Appeals* (January 2006 ed).

   [1] See the decisions of the House in *Lane v Esdaile* [1891] A.C. 210; also *R. v Secretary of State for Trade and Industry Ex p. Eastaway* [2000] 1 WLR 2222; Access to Justice Act 1999 s 54, and Pt.52 Civil Procedure Rules (as amended). S 54 of the Access to Justice Act 1999 does not extend to Northern Ireland and the Civil Procedure Rules do not apply there, but otherwise direction 1.14(a) and the rule in *Lane v Esdaile* apply to Northern Ireland. No appeal lies to the House from incidental decisions of the Court of Appeal which may be called into question by rules of court: Supreme Court Act 1981 s 58 (as amended by Access to Justice Act 1999 s 60).

Paragraph numbers marked with a "+" can be found online and on CD.

HL CIVIL

1.18 Under the rule in *Taylor v Lawrence*[1] the Court of Appeal can in exceptional circumstances reopen an appeal or application for permission to appeal after it has given a final judgment. If the Court of Appeal refuses an application to reopen a previously concluded appeal or application for permission to appeal, no application may be made to the House of Lords for permission to appeal against that refusal[2].

Judicial review: civil matters

4A–10 1.19 An application for permission to apply for judicial review is made to the Administrative Court (part of the Queen's Bench Division of the High Court). If the judge of the Administrative Court refuses the application without a hearing, an application can be made for the decision to be reconsidered at a hearing. Where permission to apply for judicial review has been refused by the Administrative Court after consideration of the papers and after reconsideration at an oral hearing, the applicant may appeal against the refusal of permission. Such an appeal must be lodged in the Court of Appeal within 7 days. For such an appeal to be successful, the applicant needs to be granted both i) permission to appeal against the Administrative Court's determination; and ii) permission to apply for judicial review.

1.20 If the Court of Appeal refuses permission to appeal to it against the decision of the Administrative Court refusing permission to apply for judicial review, there is no appeal to the House of Lords. The House of Lords has no jurisdiction to receive such an appeal[3]. However, if the Court of Appeal (a) grants permission to appeal to it against the Administrative Court's refusal of permission to apply for judicial review, but then (b) itself refuses permission to apply for judicial review, the House of Lords does have jurisdiction to hear an appeal against that refusal[4].

Cross-appeals

4A–11 1.21 See direction 30.

Public funding/legal aid

4A–12 1.22 See direction 41.

Counsel

4A–13 1.23 Petitioners and respondents to a petition for leave to appeal may instruct leading or junior counsel. However, on taxations (assessment of bills of costs) the general rule is that a single fee is allowed for one junior counsel only for preparing a petition for leave to appeal. Rarely, if ever, are fees allowed for two counsel, but a fee may be allowed for a Queens Counsel instead of junior counsel if this is held to be necessary because of the difficulty or complexity of the case or other good reason.[5] The House expects public funding authorities to limit funding certificates for petitions for leave to appeal to one counsel only, but this may be leading counsel or junior counsel depending on circumstances as set out above.

2.

TIME LIMITS

4A–14 2.1

    (a) Except for applications under direction 2.4, a petition for leave to appeal to the House of Lords should be lodged at the Judicial Office within one month

---

[1] [2002] EWCA Civ 90.
[2] Civil Procedure Rules, r.52.17.
[3] The House's decision in *R v Secretary of State for Trade and Industry, ex parte Eastaway* [2000] 1 WLR 2222 applying the principle in *Lane v Esdaile* [1891] AC 10.
[4] The House's decision in *R v Hammersmith and Fulham LBC, ex parte Burkett* [2002] 1WLR 1593.
[5] As to "necessary", see Lord Woolf C.J., *Home Office v Lownds* [2002] EWCA Civ 365.

Paragraph numbers marked with a "+" can be found online and on CD.

from the date of the order appealed from. The one month period runs from the date of the substantive order appealed from, not from the date on which the order is sealed or the date of any subsequent procedural order (e.g. an order refusing permission to appeal).

(b) If a petitioner has applied for public funding, the above period is extended to one month after the decision whether funding should be granted, including any appeals. The Judicial Office must be informed in writing within the original one month period that public funding has been applied for (direction 41).

(c) Petitions for leave to appeal out of time are admissible.

Petitions out of time

2.2 A petition for leave to appeal lodged outside the one month period is accepted by the Judicial Office for presentation to the House provided that: **4A–15**

(a) it has been drafted in the style required for such petitions and seeks leave to appeal out of time[1]; and

(b) it sets out in the first paragraph the reason(s) why it was not lodged within the time limit; and

(c) it is in order in all other respects

The reason(s) should not normally exceed one paragraph in length.

2.3 In considering a petition for leave to appeal out of time, the Appeal Committee may reject it solely on the ground that it is out of time; but the Appeal Committee may grant an extension of time and decide the application for leave on the merits.

Contempt of court

2.4 A petition for leave to appeal in a case involving civil contempt of court must be lodged in the Judicial Office within 14 days (not one month), beginning with the date of the refusal of leave by the court below (not the following day).[2] **4A–16**

3.
LODGMENT OF PETITION

Form of petition

3.1 A petition for leave to appeal should be produced on A4 paper, securely bound on the left, using both sides of the paper. The petition should set out briefly the facts and points of law; and conclude with a summary of the reasons why leave should be granted.[3] Petitions which are not legible or which are not produced in the required form are not accepted. A petition should not contain annexes or appendices. Parties may consult the Judicial Office at any stage of preparation of the petition, and may submit petitions in draft for approval. **4A–17**

3.2 Supporting documents other than those set out in direction 4.2 are not normally accepted.

3.3 Amendments to petitions and the lodging of supplementary petitions are allowed only in exceptional circumstances. The Head of the Judicial Office may allow amendments to petitions and the lodging of supplementary petitions if he is satisfied that this will assist the Appeal Committee and will not unfairly prejudice the respondents or cause undue delay. Any such amendments and supplementary petitions must be served on the respondents (see direction 3.12).

HL CIVIL

---

[1] For style see Appendix A, Form 3.
[2] Administration of Justice Act 1960, s 13 as amended.
[3] For style see Appendix A, Forms 1, 2.

Paragraph numbers marked with a "+" can be found online and on CD.

3.4 If a petition for leave to appeal

    (a) asks the House to depart from one of its own decisions;

    (b) raises issues relating to the Human Rights Act 1998; or

    (c) seeks a reference to the Court of Justice of the European Communities,

the point should be stated clearly in the petition.

3.5 A petition for leave to appeal must be signed by the petitioners or their agents

3.6 On the back of the petition for leave, underneath the certificate of service, there should be inserted the neutral citation of the judgment petitioned against, the references of any law report in the courts below, and subject matter catchwords for indexing (whether or not the case has been reported).

Case title

4A–18 3.7 Petitions for leave to appeal to the House of Lords carry the same title as in the court below, except that the parties are described as petitioner(s) and respondent(s). For reference purposes, the names of parties to the original action who are not parties to the appeal should nevertheless be included in the title: their names should be enclosed in square brackets. The names of all parties should be given in the same sequence as in the title used in the court below.

3.8 Petitions in which trustees, executors etc. are parties are titled in the short form, for example *Trustees of John Black's Charity (Respondents) v. White (Petitioner)*.

3.9 In any petition concerning minors or where in the court below the title used has been such as to conceal the identity of one or more parties to the action, this fact should be clearly drawn to the attention of the Judicial Office at the time the petition is lodged, so that the title adopted in the House of Lords can take account of the need for anonymity. Petitions involving minors are normally given a title in the form *In re B* (see also direction 9.9).

3.10 In case titles involving the Crown, the abbreviation "R" meaning "Regina" is used. "R" is always given first. So case titles using this abbreviation take the form *R v Jones (Petitioner)* or *R v Jones (Respondent)* (as the case may be) or *R (on the application of Jones) (Petitioner) v Secretary of State for the Home Department (Respondent)*.

3.11 Apart from the above, Latin is not used in case titles.

Service

4A–19 3.12 A copy of the petition must be served on the respondents or their agents, either by delivery in person or by first class post, before it is lodged in the Judicial Office. A certificate of such service (noting the full name and address of the respondents or their agents) must be endorsed on the back of the original petition and signed.[1]

Lodgment

4A–20 3.13 Two original copies of the original petition must be lodged in the Judicial Office, together with a copy of the order appealed from and, if separate, a copy of the order of the court below refusing leave to appeal. If the substantive order appealed against is not immediately available, the petition should nevertheless be lodged within the required time limits, and the order lodged as soon as possible thereafter.

3.14 An agent who attends the Judicial Office to lodge a petition for leave to appeal or accompanying papers must be familiar with the subject matter of the petition.

3.15 A petition for leave to appeal is presented to the House and recorded in the House of Lords Business on the day it is lodged or on the next sitting day of the House.

---

[1] For style see Appendix A, Form 2.

Paragraph numbers marked with a "+" can be found online and on CD.

Waiver of fees

3.16 Standing Order XIII provides that a fee is payable when a petition for leave to appeal is lodged. For the present level of fees, see Appendix C. **4A–21**

3.17 In circumstances where a petitioner would suffer financial hardship by the payment of fees to the House, the requirement to pay fees may be waived. Application should be made to the Judicial Office. In order to provide an objective test for determining financial hardship, and to keep in step with the courts below, the Judicial Office applies the provisions of the Civil Proceedings Fees Order 2004[1] to determine financial hardship for the purposes of Standing Order XIII. Waivers of fees are also granted to petitioners who have been granted a remission of fees in the court below.

The fee paid by a petitioner on a petition for leave to appeal is not refunded, even if the Appeal Committee dismisses the petition as inadmissible.

Appearance for respondents

3.18 Respondents or their agents enter appearance to a petition for leave as soon as they have received service. The respondents or their agents enter appearance by informing the Judicial Office by post of their name and address or that of their firm and paying the prescribed fee. The fee is refunded if the petition is dismissed as inadmissible. **4A–22**

3.19 Respondents who do not intend to take part in the proceedings do not need to enter appearance, but the Judicial Office sends communications concerning a petition for leave to appeal only to those who have entered appearance.

3.20 An order for costs will not be made in favour of a respondent who has not entered an appearance.

Interventions in petitions for leave to appeal

3.21 Save in exceptional circumstances, no application may be made to intervene in support of a petition for leave to appeal[2]. **4A–23**

Communications by fax/e-mail

3.22 See direction 26.2. **4A–24**

4.

APPEAL COMMITTEE

4.1 Petitions for leave to appeal to the House of Lords are considered by an Appeal Committee consisting of three Lords of Appeal. Petitions are generally decided on the papers alone, without a hearing. **4A–25**

Additional papers

4.2 The following additional papers for use by the Appeal Committee must be accepted within seven days of lodgment of the petition: **4A–26**
  (a) four copies of the petition;
  (b) four copies of the order appealed against;
  (c) if separate from the order at (b) above, four copies of the order of the court below refusing leave to appeal to the House of Lords;
  (d) four copies of the official transcript of the judgment of the court below;

---

[1] SI 2004/3121.
[2] For interventions in appeals, see direction 37.

Paragraph numbers marked with a "+" can be found online and on CD.

HL CIVIL

(e) four copies of the final order(s) of all other courts below;

(f) four copies of the official transcript of the final judgment(s) of all other courts below;

(g) four copies of any unreported judgment(s) cited in the petition or judgment of a court below.

No other papers are required, and documents other than those listed above are not accepted unless requested by the Appeal Committee.

4.3 Papers lodged in accordance with direction 4.2 above should be lodged as individual documents, double-sided, single stapled and not inserted into ring binders. Documents which are not clearly legible or which are not in the required style or form (see direction 3.1) are not accepted.

4.4 Where the required papers are not lodged within three months of presentation of the petition and no good reason is given, the petition may at the direction of the Head of the Judicial Office be referred to an Appeal Committee without the required accompanying papers.

Consideration on the papers

4A–27 4.5 The Appeal Committee decides first whether a petition for leave to appeal is admissible. The rules on admissibility are set out in direction 1.14. If the Appeal Committee determines that a petition is inadmissible, it may refuse leave on that ground alone and not consider the content of the petition. The Appeal Committee gives a reason for its decision that the petition is inadmissible.

4.6 If the Appeal Committee decides that a petition is admissible, the Committee may then:

(a) refuse leave (see direction 4.8);

(b) give leave outright (see direction 4.9);

(c) invite the respondents to lodge objections to the petition (see directions 4.10–4.14);

(d) give leave on terms (see direction 4.15);

(e) refer the petition for an oral hearing (see direction 4.16–4.21).

4.7 Leave to appeal is granted to petitions that, in the opinion of the Appeal Committee, raise an arguable point of law of general public importance which ought to be considered by the House at this time, bearing in mind that the matter will already have been the subject of judicial decision and may have already been reviewed on appeal. A petition which in the opinion of the Appeal Committee does not raise such a point of law is refused on that ground. The Appeal Committee gives brief reasons for refusing leave to appeal[1] but does not otherwise explain its decisions.[2]

Leave refused

4A–28 4.8 If the Appeal Committee is unanimous that a petition should be refused, the parties are notified that the petition is dismissed.

Leave given outright

4A–29 4.9 If the Appeal Committee is unanimous that a petition should be allowed without further proceedings, the House grants leave outright (without inviting respondents' objections).

---

[1] See also directions 34.2 and 34.3 for practice where a point of European Community law is raised on a petition for leave to appeal.
[2] See Appeal Committee, 38th Report (2002–03): *Petitions for leave to appeal: reasons for the refusal of leave* (HL Paper 89).

Paragraph numbers marked with a "+" can be found online and on CD.

Respondents' objections

4.10 Respondents may submit written objections giving their reasons why leave to appeal should be refused. They may do this:
  (a) within 14 days of the date of service on them of the petition for leave to appeal; or
  (b) within 14 days of any invitation by the Appeal Committee to do so; or
  (c) within 14 days of a petition for leave to appeal being referred for an oral hearing.

4A–30

4.11 Respondents' objections set out briefly the reasons why the petition should be refused or make submissions as to the terms upon which leave should be granted (for example, on costs). One master plus four copies of the respondents' written objections must be lodged at the Judicial Office. The objections must be produced on durable quality A4 paper, securely fastened, using both sides of the paper.

4.12 A copy of the respondents' objections should be sent to the agents for the other parties. In certain circumstances the Appeal Committee may invite further submissions from the petitioners in the light of the respondents' objections, but petitioners do not have a right to comment on respondents' objections. Where the Appeal Committee does not require further submissions, and provided the Committee is unanimous in its decision to grant or refuse leave, it reports its decision to the House and the parties are informed. Where the Appeal Committee proposes terms for granting leave, direction 4.15 applies.

4.13 Respondents' objections are subject to any order for costs made by the Appeal Committee or, if leave to appeal is granted, become costs in the appeal (see direction 5).

4.14 Respondents unable to meet the deadlines set out in direction 4.10 must write to the Head of the Judicial Office requesting an extension of time for lodging their written objections.

Leave given on terms

4.15 If the Appeal Committee decides that leave to appeal should be given on terms:
  (a) the Committee proposes the terms and the parties have the right to make submissions on the proposed terms within 14 days of the date of the Committee's decision to give leave to appeal;
  (b) prospective appellants who are granted leave to appeal subject to terms that they are unwilling to accept may decline to pursue the appeal;
  (c) in an application for leave to appeal under the "leapfrog"procedure (see direction 6), prospective appellants who decline to proceed on the basis of the terms proposed by the Appeal Committee may instead pursue an appeal to the Court of Appeal in the usual way.[1]

4A–31

Petition referred for oral hearing

4.16 In all cases where the members of the Appeal Committee are not unanimous, or where further argument is required, a petition for leave to appeal is referred for an oral hearing.

4A–32

4.17 If the respondents have not already lodged written objections, they may do so awithin 14 days of being informed that the petition has been referred for a hearing (direction 4.10(c)).

4.18 When a petition is referred for an oral hearing, the petitioners and all respondents who have entered appearance are notified of the date of the hearing before the Appeal Committee.

HL CIVIL

---

[1] *Ceredigion County Council v Jones* [2007] UKHL 24.

Paragraph numbers marked with a "+" can be found online and on CD.

4.19 Parties may be heard before the Appeal Committee by counsel, by agent, or in person, but one only may be heard on each side.

4.20 If counsel is briefed, agents should ensure that the Judicial Office is notified of their name.

4.21 Authorities are not normally cited before the Appeal Committee or provided for the Committee's use at the hearing.

Lodgment of petition of appeal

4A–33 4.22 If leave to appeal is given, the petition of appeal (direction 9) must be lodged with the prescribed fee within two weeks of the date of the Appeal Committee's decision. Failure to meet this deadline results in the petition of appeal being lodged out of time and referred to an Appeal Committee pursuant to direction 7.3.

Order of the House

4A–34 4.23 Copies of the House of Lords Business recording the report of the Appeal Committee and the order of the House are sent to all parties who have entered appearance.

4.24 A formal order of the Appeal Committee is not normally issued but will be issued on written request and on payment of a fee. A formal order is not required for taxation of costs arising from the application for leave to appeal.

Expedition

4A–35 4.25 Once the required papers are lodged in the Judicial Office (direction 4.2), the procedure described above is normally completed within eight sitting weeks (excluding any oral hearing). However, in cases involving liberty of the subject, urgent medical intervention or the well-being of children (see direction 4.26), application for expedition may be made in writing to the Judicial Office.

Expeditious hearing of proceedings under the Hague Convention etc

4A–36 4.26 The *Convention on the Civil Aspects of International Child Abduction* (the Hague Convention) deals with the wrongful removal and retention of children from their habitual country of residence. The Revised Brussels II Regulation also deals with these matters[1]. In the House of Lords an expedited timetable applies. The parties must therefore inform the Judicial Office that the proceedings fall under the Convention or Regulation. The House normally gives judgment within 6 weeks of the commencement of proceedings in the House. This can only be achieved with the fullest co-operation of the parties.

4.27 The following timetable may be taken as a general guideline[2]:

(a) an application for leave to appeal is decided by an Appeal Committee within 7 days of being lodged;

(b) an appeal is heard within 21 days of a decision to give leave to appeal;

(c) the result of the appeal is given immediately after the end of the hearing with reasons given later or, if judgment is reserved, the result of the appeal and the reasons are given within 2 weeks of the end of the hearing.

4.28 In order to achieve the timetable in direction 4.27 the House makes dispensing orders to set aside or vary the practice directions that normally apply to applications and appeals to the House.

4.29 Abridged procedures and special rules for the production of documents are

---

[1] Council Regulation (EC) No 2201/2003.
[2] *In re M* [2007] UKHL 57.

Paragraph numbers marked with a "+" can be found online and on CD.

applied to meet the circumstances of each application and appeal. The following timetable for the production of documents is therefore indicative only:

(a) the Statement of facts and issues is lodged within 7 days of the decision to give leave to appeal;

(b) the appellant's case is lodged within 10 days of the decision to give leave to appeal (or, if the relevant day falls on a Saturday or Sunday, the following Monday);

(c) the respondent's case is lodged within 14 days of the decision to give leave to appeal;

(d) the Bound Volumes (if required) and the authorities' volumes are lodged within 17 days of the decision to give leave to appeal (or, if the relevant day falls on a Saturday or Sunday, the following Monday).

5.

COSTS

5.1 Where a petition for leave to appeal is determined without an oral hearing, costs **4A–37** may be awarded as follows:

(a) to a publicly funded or legally aided petitioner, reasonable costs incurred in preparing papers for the Appeal Committee[1];

(b) to a publicly funded or legally aided respondent, only those costs necessarily incurred in attending the client, attending the petitioner's agents, perusing the petition, entering appearance and, where applicable, preparing respondent's objections to the petition[2];

(c) to an unassisted respondent where the petitioner is publicly funded or legally aided, payment out of the Community Legal Service Fund (pursuant to s 11 of the Access to Justice Act 1999[3]) of costs as specified at (b) above;

(d) to a respondent where neither party is publicly funded or legally aided, costs as specified at (b) above.

Where costs are sought under (c) or (d) above, the application may be made by letter addressed to the Judicial Office or may be included in a bill of costs lodged in the Judicial Office conditional upon the application being granted.

5.2 Where a petition for leave to appeal is referred for an oral hearing and is dismissed, application for costs must be made by the respondent at the end of the hearing. No order for costs is made unless requested at that time.

5.3 Where a petition for leave to appeal is allowed, costs of the petition become costs in the appeal.

5.4 Bills of costs for taxation must be lodged within three months from the date of the decision of the Appeal Committee or the date on which a petition for leave is withdrawn in accordance with direction 45.1. If an extension of the three month period is desired, application must be made in writing to the Taxing Officer and copies of all such correspondence sent to all interested parties In deciding whether to grant an application for an extension of time made after the expiry of the three month period the Taxing Officer takes into account the circumstances set out in the practice directions applicable to judicial taxations.

5.5 The practice directions relating to judicial taxations and forms of bills of costs are

---

[1] See *Practice directions applicable to judicial taxations in the House of Lords and forms of bills of costs*, available on request from the Judicial Office.
[2] *ibid.*
[3] Also pursuant to r.5(2) Community Legal Service (Cost Protection) Regulations 2000 and in accordance with the procedural requirements of rr.9, 10 Community Legal Service (Costs) Regulations 2000 as amended; or Legal Aid Act 1988, s 18; or in Scotland pursuant to Legal Aid (Scotland) Act 1986, s 19; or in Northern Ireland pursuant to Legal Aid Advice and Assistance (N.I.) Order 1981, Art.16.

Paragraph numbers marked with a "+" can be found online and on CD.

available from the Judicial Office and on the internet at www.parliament.uk. Fees are payable on taxation of a bill of costs.

Withdrawal of petitions for leave to appeal

4A–38 5.6 See direction 45.1.

6.

PETITIONS BROUGHT DIRECT FROM THE HIGH COURT

4A–39 6.1 In certain cases an appeal lies direct from the High Court in England and Wales or in Northern Ireland to the House of Lords. A certificate of the High Court must first be obtained and the leave of the House of Lords then given before the appeal may proceed.[1] Such appeals are known as "leapfrog" appeals.

Judge's certificate

4A–40 6.2 An application for a certificate may be made by any of the parties to any civil proceedings in the High Court before a single judge or before a Divisional Court. The application should be made immediately after the trial judge gives judgment in the proceedings or, if no such application is made, within 14 days from the date on which judgment was given.

6.3 The judge may grant a certificate under s 12 of the Administration of Justice Act 1969 if he is satisfied (a) that the relevant conditions are fulfilled; (b) that a sufficient case has been made to justify taking to the House of Lords an application for leave; and (c) that all the parties to the proceedings consent to the grant of a certificate.

6.4 The relevant conditions are that a point of law of general public importance is involved in the judge's decision, and that that point of law either (a) relates wholly or mainly to the construction of an enactment or of a statutory instrument and has been fully argued in the proceedings and fully considered in the judgment of the judge in the proceedings,[2] or (b) is one in respect of which the judge is bound by a decision of the Court of Appeal or House of Lords in previous proceedings and was fully considered in the judgments of the Court of Appeal or House of Lords in those previous proceedings.[3]

6.5 The judge may not grant a certificate in cases where no appeal would lie (with or without leave) from the judge's decision to the Court of Appeal, apart from the provisions of the Administration of Justice Act 1969. Similarly, a certificate may not be granted where no appeal would lie (with or without leave) from the Court of Appeal on an appeal from the judge's decision. Where no appeal would lie from the judge's decision to the Court of Appeal except with the leave of the judge or the Court of Appeal, no certificate may be granted unless it appears to the judge that it would be a proper case for granting such leave.

6.6 No certificate may be given where the judge's decision concerns punishment for contempt of court.

6.7 No appeal lies against the grant or refusal of a certificate, but if a certificate is refused the applicant may appeal to the Court of Appeal from the High Court's decision in the normal way, once the time for applying for a certificate has expired.

Petition for leave to appeal direct from High Court

4A–41 6.8 At any time within one month from the date on which the judge grants the

---

[1] Administration of Justice Act 1969. ss 12–15.
[2] Administration of Justice Act 1969, s 12(3)(a).
[3] Administration of Justice Act 1969, s 12(3)(b).

Paragraph numbers marked with a "+" can be found online and on CD.

certificate, or such extended time as the House of Lords may allow,[1] any of the parties may apply to the House of Lords for leave to appeal.[2] Application is made by petition. If any party to the action in the High Court is not a party to the petition, the petition must be endorsed with a certificate of service on that party.

6.9 One copy of the judge's certificate must be lodged with the petition. The petition should indicate whether the judge's certificate was granted under s 12(3)(a) or s 12(3)(b) of the Administration of Justice Act 1969.

6.10 The following additional papers for use by the Appeal Committee must be lodged within one week of the lodgment of the petition:
   (a) four additional copies of the petition;
   (b) four copies of order of High Court;
   (c) four additional copies of the High Court's certificate, if not contained in the order; and
   (d) four copies of the transcript of the judgment of the High Court.[3]

No other papers are required, and documents other than those listed above are not normally received.

6.11 Petitions for leave are determined by an Appeal Committee without a hearing.

6.12 In petitions where the certificate has been granted by the judge under s 12(3)(a) of the 1969 Act, the House only grants leave to appeal where:
   (a) there is an urgent need to obtain an authoritative interpretation by the House of Lords;
   (b) the case is one in which leave to appeal to the House of Lords would have been granted if it had not been brought direct to the House and the judgment had been that of the Court of Appeal; and
   (c) it does not appear likely that any additional assistance could be derived from a judgment of the Court of Appeal.

Similarly, where the certificate has been granted under s 12(3)(b) of the 1969 Act, the House only grants leave where:
   (i) the case is not distinguishable from the case that was the subject of the previous decision;
   (ii) the previous case was fully considered in previous judgment after argument that appears to have been adequate; and
   (iii) the case is one in which leave to appeal to the House of Lords would have been granted if it had not been brought direct to the House and the judgment had been that of the Court of Appeal.

6.13 The Judicial Office notifies the parties of the Appeal Committee's decision.

Extensions of time

6.14 If an applicant cannot lodge the petition within one month from the date on **4A–42** which the judge's certificate was granted, the applicant must within the one month period lodge in the Judicial Office:
   (i) a request for an extension of time, giving reasons why an extension is needed; and
   (ii) three copies of the transcript of the High Court's judgment.

The request is referred to an Appeal Committee and determined without a hearing. The Judicial Office notifies the applicant of the Appeal Committee's decision.

HL Civil

---

[1] For applications to extend time see direction 6.14.
[2] Administration of Justice Act 1969, s 13(1).
[3] If the judgment has been published in a report which is ordinarily received in court, copies of the report may be lodged in lieu of transcripts. Transcripts of judgments marked as in draft are not acceptable without certification by the relevant court that the copy is the final version of the judgment.

Paragraph numbers marked with a "+" can be found online and on CD.

Proceedings after leave to appeal is granted or refused

4A–43   6.15 If the House grants leave to appeal without terms (see direction 4.15), no appeal from the decision of the judge lies to the Court of Appeal but only to the House of Lords. The appeal is brought by petition and the usual requirements apply. However, an appeal does lie to the Court of Appeal from the judge's decision (i) where no application is made to the House of Lords within the one month period after the judge has granted the certificate; or (ii) where leave to appeal direct to the House has been refused by the House of Lords.

Prospective appellants who decline to proceed on the basis of the terms proposed by the Appeal Committee may instead pursue an appeal to the Court of Appeal in the usual way (see direction 4.15).[1]

Habeas corpus

4A–44   6.16 Proceedings for a writ of habeas corpus are subject to the procedures governing criminal appeals to the House of Lords. These are set out at paras 4B–1+ to 4B–101+ in the criminal practice directions. In proceedings for a writ of habeas corpus, an appeal lies from the Queen's Bench Divisional Court to the House of Lords at the instance of the defendant or prosecutor with the leave either of the Divisional Court or the House of Lords. No certificate stating a point of law of general public importance is required.

Such a petition is considered by an Appeal Committee without an oral hearing. Parties are notified of the Committee's decision.

6.17 Such a petition is considered by an Appeal Committee without an oral hearing. Parties are notified of the Committee's decision.

Part II – Directions Applying in All Appeals

7.

Time Limits

4A–45   7.1 A petition of appeal must be lodged in the Judicial Office within three months of the date on which the order appealed against was made[2].

7.2 However, this time limit may be varied by an order of the House when granting leave or by an order of the court below. The order appealed against is the substantive order complained of.

Out of time appeals

4A–46   7.3 Where a petition of appeal is not lodged within the time allowed, a petition for leave to present the appeal out of time may be lodged[3]. This petition is referred to an Appeal Committee.

Fees

4A–47   7.4 A fee is payable on a petition of appeal and on a petition for leave to present a petition of appeal out of time (see Appendix C).

8.

London Agents

4A–48   8.1 Solicitors outside London may appoint London agents. Those who decide not to

---

[1] *Ceredigion County Council v Jones* [2007] UKHL 24.
[2] Standing Order I. The court below may reduce but may not extend the three month period. For extensions of time in publicly funded/legal aid cases, see direction 41.3–41.4.
[3] Adapt Appendix A, Form 4 using Form 3 as a model.

Paragraph numbers marked with a "+" can be found online and on CD.

do so should note that any additional costs incurred as a result of that decision may be disallowed on taxation (assessment of costs).

9.
LODGMENT OF APPEAL
Form of petition of appeal

9.1 Petitions of appeal must be produced on A4 paper, bound on the left, using both sides of the paper[1]. **4A–49**

9.2 Where leave to appeal has been obtained, it is enough for the petition of appeal to be signed by the appellants or their agents. In appeals where leave to appeal is not required (for example, in most Scottish appeals) the petition of appeal must be certified as reasonable by two counsel from the relevant jurisdiction and signed by them.[2] In Scottish appeals a certificate of difference of opinion must also be included where appropriate.[3]

9.3 On the back page of the petition, below the certificate of service, there should be inserted the neutral citation of the judgment appealed against, the references of any law report of the case in the courts below and subject matter catchwords for indexing (whether or not the case has been reported).

Case title

9.4 Petitions of appeal to the House of Lords carry the same title as in the court **4A–50** below, except that the parties are described as appellant(s) and respondent(s). For reference purposes, the names of parties to the original action who are not parties to the appeal should nevertheless be included in the title: their names should be enclosed in square brackets. The names of all parties should be given in the same sequence as in the title used in the court below.

9.5 Petitions in which trustees, executors, etc. are parties are titled in the short form, for example *Trustees of John Black's Charity (Respondents) v. White (Appellant)*.

9.6 In any petition concerning minors or where in the court below the title used has been such as to conceal the identity of one or more parties to the action, this fact should be clearly drawn to the attention of the Judicial Office at the time the petition is lodged, so that the title adopted in the House of Lords can take account of the need for anonymity. Petitions involving minors are normally given a title in the form *In re B* (see also direction 9.9).

9.7 In case titles involving the Crown, the abbreviation "R" meaning "Regina" is used. "R" is always given first. Case titles using this abbreviation take the form *R v Jones (Appellant)* or *R v Jones (Respondent)* (as the case may be) or *R (on the application of Jones) (Appellant) v Secretary of State for the Home Department (Respondent)*.

9.8 Apart from the above, Latin is not used in case titles.

Anonymity and reporting restrictions

9.9 In any appeal concerning children, the parties, in addition to considering the case **4A–51** title to be used, should also consider whether it would be appropriate for the House

---

[1] see Appendix A, Form 4 for style of petition and direction 24 for preparation of documents.
[2] Standing Order IV. In such cases, counsel's signatures are required even if the appellants propose to conduct the appeal in person. For the purposes of the Standing Order, "counsel" includes any solicitor who has obtained a Higher Courts Qualification in respect of civil proceedings.
[3] See Standing Order XI.

Paragraph numbers marked with a "+" can be found online and on CD.

to make an order under s.39 of the Children and Young Persons Act 1933. The parties should always inform the Judicial Office if such an order has been made by a court below. A request for such an order to be made by the House should be made in writing, preferably on behalf of all parties to the appeal, as soon as possible after the appeal has been presented and not later than 14 days before the start of the hearing.

9.10 Direction 9.9 also applies to a request for an order under s 4 of the Contempt of Court Act 1981.

Human Rights Act 1998

4A–52 9.11 Appellants must notify the Judicial Office in writing when:
  (a) the House is to be asked to consider whether to make, uphold or reverse a declaration that a provision of primary or subordinate legislation is incompatible with a European Human Rights Convention right[1], or is to be asked to consider any issue which may lead the House to make such a declaration, or where such an issue is or may be raised in respect of a judicial act;
  (b) a party seeks to challenge an act of a public authority under the Human Rights Act 1998; or
  (c) a party relies in whole or in part on the provisions of the Human Rights Act 1998.

Appellants should indicate whether notification is made under (a), (b) or (c) above (see direction 33.1). They should set out briefly the arguments involved; and state whether the point was taken in the courts below. In appeals in which (a) above is an issue, the Crown has a right to be joined as a party to the appeal (see direction 33.2).

Service

4A–53 9.12 A copy of the petition of appeal must be served on the respondents or their agents, either by delivery in person or by first class post, before lodgment in the Judicial Office. A certificate of such service noting the full name and address of the respondents or their agents must be endorsed on the back of the original petition and signed by the appellants or their agents.[2]

Lodgment

4A–54 9.13 The petition of appeal together with seven copies must be lodged in the Judicial Office with the prescribed fee. If leave to appeal was granted by the court below, a copy of the order appealed from must also be lodged and, if separate, a copy of the order granting leave to appeal to the House of Lords. If the order is not immediately available, the petition should be lodged in time and the order lodged as soon as possible thereafter.

9.14 Once the petition of appeal has been lodged, it is presented to the House and recorded in the House of Lords Business. A copy of the House of Lords Business (the record of the Houses's proceedings) is sent to all parties who have entered appearance (direction 9.10).

Appearance for respondents

4A–55 9.15 Respondents or their agents should enter appearance to an appeal as soon as they have received service of the petition of appeal by informing the Judicial Office by post of their name and address or that of their firm, and paying the prescribed fee.

9.16 Respondents who do not intend to take part in the proceedings do not need to enter appearance, but the Judicial Office sends communications concerning the

---

[1] Human Rights Act 1998, which gives further effect in domestic law to much of the Convention for the Protection of Human Rights and Fundamental Freedoms agreed by the Council of Europe at Rome on 4 November 1950.
[2] For style see Appendix A, Form 5.

Paragraph numbers marked with a "+" can be found online and on CD.

appeal only to those who have entered appearance. An order for costs will not be made in favour of a respondent who has not entered appearance.

10.
SECURITY FOR COSTS

10.1 Within seven days of the presentation of an appeal, appellants must give security **4A–56** for costs by paying into the House of Lords Security Fund Account the sum fixed by the House[1]. The sum fixed is stated in Appendix C.. Failure to do so results in the appeal being dismissed by default (unless public funding or legal aid has been applied for: see direction 41.3).

10.2 Payment is normally made by banker's draft or cheque made payable to 'House of Lords Security Fund Account'. If an appellant wishes to pay in cash, the Judicial Office may only accept cash up to £10,000, in order to comply with money laundering regulations. No interest is payable on security money.

Waiver of security

10.3 Provided that all the respondents agree that security for costs should be waived, **4A–57** the appellants may lodge a consent form asking the House to release the appellants from the obligation to pay security for costs. The consent must be signed by all the respondents and lodged with the prescribed fee within one week of the presentation of the appeal. An order is then made absolving the appellants from giving security. A copy of the form of consent is available from the Judicial Office.

10.4 The following are not required to give security for costs and no waiver is necessary:

(a) an appellant who has been granted a certificate of public funding/legal aid;
(b) an appellant in an appeal under the Child Abduction and Custody Act 1985;
(c) a Minister or Government department.[2]

10.5 No security for costs or waiver is required in cross-appeals.

10.6 The House has the power to vary or dispense with the requirement to give security for costs when the respondents do not agree to a waiver, but uses this power rarely, and only after an Appeal Committee has recommended that the requirement for security should be waived.[3] The Appeal Committee normally takes this decision on the papers alone, without an oral hearing.

11.
STATEMENT OF FACTS AND ISSUES

11.1 It is the appellants' responsibility to lodge a Statement of the facts and issues **4A–58** (with an Appendix (see direction 12)). The Statement should be a succinct account of the main facts of the case, including an account of judicial proceedings up to that point and an account of the issues raised by the appeal. The appellants are responsible for drawing up the Statement in draft and they must submit it to the respondents for discussion and agreement. The Statement must be a single document agreed between the parties. In the event of disagreement, disputed material should be removed from the draft Statement and included instead in each party's case (see direction 15). The Statement must be signed on behalf of each party by at least one counsel who appeared in the court below or who will appear at the hearing before the House.

Form of Statement of facts and issues

11.2 The Statement of facts and issues should be produced on durable quality A4 **4A–59** paper and incorporate:

---

[1] Standing Order V(1).
[2] Standing Order V(2).
[3] See speech of Lord Chancellor Irvine of Lairg, HL Deb 26 July 1999, col 1292.

Paragraph numbers marked with a "+" can be found online and on CD.

HL CIVIL

(a) pages printed on both sides of the paper;

(b) capital letters down the inside margins;

(c) references on the outside margins to relevant pages of the Appendix;

(d) on the front cover, the reference of every law report of the case in the courts below, together with the catchword summary of one of the reports;

(e) on the front cover, a headnote summary, whether or not the case has been reported;

(f) on the front cover, a statement of the time occupied in the courts below;

(g) on the front cover, addresses of parties at foot of page; and

(h) at the end, the signatures of counsel for both parties above their printed names.

12.

APPENDIX

4A–60 12.1 It is the appellants' responsibility in consultation with the respondents to prepare and lodge an Appendix of documents considered necessary for the appeal. These documents include all the documents used in evidence or recording proceedings in the courts below.

12.2 The appellants bear the cost of preparing the Appendix, although these costs are ultimately subject to the decision of the House as to the costs of the appeal.

Contents of Appendix

4A–61 12.3 The Appendix contains only documents or extracts from documents that are necessary to support and understand the argument when the appeal is heard by the Appellate Committee. No document which was not used in evidence or does not record proceedings relevant to the action in the courts below may be included. Transcripts of arguments in the courts below may not be included unless remarks by a judge are relied on by any party or the arguments refer to facts which are admitted by all parties and as to which no evidence was called.

12.4 The Appendix consists of one or more parts. Part 1 must contain:

(a) formal originating documents;

(b) case stated (if any);

(c) judgments and orders relating to the decisions at first instance and on appeal;

(d) relevant legislative provisions including delegated legislation; and

(e) any relevant document on which the action is founded (such as a will, contract, map, plan etc.) or an extract from such document.

Published documents under (b), (c) and (d) above may so far as is practicable be placed in a pocket attached to the inside of the back cover of the Appendix.

12.5 For judgments that have been published, unbound parts of the relevant Law Reports or the Weekly Law Reports should be used if available; otherwise the All England Reports, Tax Cases, Simons' Tax Cases, Reports of Patent Cases and Lloyd's List Reports may be used. In Scottish appeals, Session Cases should be used where available; otherwise, Scots Law Times and Scottish Civil Case Reports may be used. Where, at the time of preparation of the Appendix, a judgment of a court below has not been published, a transcript must be included, which may later be replaced by the published version. In such circumstances, 15 copies of the published version should be submitted to the Judicial Office. Judgments in draft are not accepted. For legislation, if the printed Act or set of Regulations is conveniently small; it should be used; if the provisions are bulky or numerous, the relevant provisions should be copied. Halsbury's statutes may be used.

12.6 Other documents should be included in Part 2 of the Appendix and, if the bulk of the documents makes it necessary, in Parts 3, 4 etc. The Appendix volume should only be numbered Part 1 if there is more than one Part.

Paragraph numbers marked with a "+" can be found online and on CD.

Form of Appendix

12.7 The Appendix takes the following form: 4A–62

    (a) it must be A4 size bound with a plastic comb binding and blue card covers (blue indicating a civil appeal);

    (b) documents must be printed on both sides of the paper;

    (c) documents must be numbered;

    (d) original documents smaller than A4 may be enlarged to A4 size with a broad outside margin;

    (e) the Appendix must contain an index; and if there is more than one Part, Part 1 of the Appendix must also contain an index to all the other Parts;

    (f) in addition to the requirement at (e) above, if the Appendix has more than one Part, each Part must contain a list of its own contents;

    (g) documents of an unsuitable size or form for binding (for example, booklets or charts) should be included in a pocket attached to the inside back cover of the appropriate Appendix volume;

    (h) no tabs should be included in the Appendix.

Examination of Appendix

12.8 The Appendix is for the use of all parties and the contents of the Appendix   4A–63
must be agreed by appellants and respondents. Disputed documents (see direction 12.9) should not be included in the Appendix. As soon as proofs of the Appendix are available they should be examined against the originals by all parties, if possible at one joint examination. As soon as practicable after the examination, a final proof of the Appendix should be provided to each party.

Documents in readiness at hearing

12.9 Disputed documents and any document not included in the Appendix which   4A–64
may be required at the hearing should be held in readiness and, subject to leave being given by the Appellate Committee, may be introduced at an appropriate moment. Fifteen copies are required. All such documents are subject to previous examination by the other parties. Where the appellants refuse to include in the Appendix any documents that the respondents consider necessary, the respondents must prepare and reproduce the documents at their own expense, subject to the final order on costs.

Scottish Record

12.10 In all Scottish appeals the appellants are required to include in Part 1 of the   4A–65
Appendix:

    (1) a copy of the Record as authenticated by the Deputy Principal Clerk of Session or a Clerk of Session delegated by him;

    (2) a supplement containing an account, without argument or statement of other facts, of the further steps which have been taken in the appeal since the Record was completed; and

    (3) copies of the interlocutors (or parts of interlocutors) complained of.[1]

13.

LODGMENT OF STATEMENT AND APPENDIX

Time limits

13.1 The Statement and Appendix must be lodged by the appellants within six weeks   4A–66

---

[1] Standing Order VI(2).

Paragraph numbers marked with a "+" can be found online and on CD.

of the presentation of the appeal, or within such longer period as may be allowed on petition (see direction 13.3)[1].

13.2 If this time limit expires during a parliamentary recess, it is automatically extended to the third next sitting day of the House of Lords[2]; and if any party has applied for public funding/legal aid, the time limit is automatically extended to six weeks after the notification of the result of the funding decision, provided that the Judicial Office has been informed of the application.[3]

Petitions for extension of time—first extension

4A–67 13.3 Appellants who are unable to complete preparation of the Statement and Appendix within the initial six weeks' period may apply by petition for an extension of that time.[4] The petition takes the form common to all formal documents of the House. It should explain briefly the reason(s) why an extension is needed. Application may be made for an extension of up to six weeks from the original expiry date, and the petition must specify the date to which the extension is requested. If that date seems likely to fall in a parliamentary recess, the petition may request extension until '[specify date] or the third sitting day of the next ensuing meeting of the House'.[5]

13.4 A petition for extension of time must be signed by the appellants. It must be submitted to those respondents who have entered appearance for the endorsement of their consent, and it must bear their signature. One master of the petition plus one copy and prescribed fee must be lodged before the expiry of the six weeks initially allowed for lodging the Statement and Appendix.

Petitions for extension of time—second and subsequent extensions

4A–68 13.5 Up to three extensions of time are normally granted, provided that they do not prejudice the preparation for the hearing or its proposed date. A petition for a fourth extension of time, and any subsequent petitions, may, at the discretion of the Head of the Judicial Office, be referred to an Appeal Committee.

Respondents' consent

4A–69 13.6 Respondents are expected not to withhold unreasonably their consent to a petition for extension of time. If consent is refused the petition must be endorsed with a certificate that it has been served on the respondents. The petition is then referred to an Appeal Committee. In that event, eight copies of the petition must be lodged, together with the prescribed fee.

Lodgment

4A–70 13.7 When the Statement and Appendix are ready, one master plus seven copies of the Statement, eight copies of Part 1 of the Appendix and 15 copies of Parts 2 etc. (if any) must be lodged in the Judicial Office with the prescribed fee. The appellants must at the same time apply to set down the appeal for hearing.

---

[1] Standing Order VI(1). For extensions of time in publicly funded/legally aided cases, see direction 41.
[2] Standing Order VIII.
[3] See direction 41.3–41.4.
[4] For style see Appendix A, Form 6.
[5] As the "third sitting day" depends on future sittings of the House, the date of expiry is not fixed. The appellants should contact the Judicial Office from time to time to discover how sittings of the House affect this date.

Paragraph numbers marked with a "+" can be found online and on CD.

14.

SETTING DOWN FOR HEARING

14.1 An appeal is set down for hearing at the same time as the appellants lodge the **4A–71**
Statement and Appendix.[1]

14.2 Once an appeal has been set down for hearing, it may be called on at any time.
Certain directions, for example directions 15.13–15.14, may be dispensed with to
enable an appeal to be called on at short notice.

Estimates of length of time needed for hearing of appeal

14.3 Within seven days of the setting down of an appeal, each party must notify the **4A–72**
Judicial Office of the number of hours that their counsel estimate to be necessary for
each of them to address the Appellate Committee. Subject to any directions by the
Appellate Committee before or at the hearing, counsel are expected to confine their
submissions to the time indicated in these estimates. The Judicial Office should be
informed at once of any alteration to the original estimate.

14.4 The average length of appeals before the Appellate Committee is two days, and
appeals are listed for hearing on this basis. Estimates of more than two days must be
explained in writing to the Head of the Judicial Office and may be referred to the
Law Lords.

15.

APPELLANTS' AND RESPONDENTS' CASES

15.1 The case is the statement of a party's argument in the appeal.   **4A–73**

15.2 The case should be confined to the heads of argument that counsel propose to
submit at the hearing and omit material contained in the Statement of facts and
issues[2]. The members of the Appeal Committee who gave leave to appeal may not be
sitting on the Appellate Committee; and so it cannot be assumed that the members of
the Appellate Committee will be familiar with the arguments set out in the petition
for leave to appeal.

15.3 Page 1 of the case should set out the title of the party on whose behalf it is
lodged.

15.4 If either party is abandoning any point taken in the courts below, this should be
made plain in their case. If they intend to apply in the course of the hearing for leave
to introduce a new point not taken below, this should also be indicated in their case
and the Judicial Office informed. If such a point involves the introduction of fresh
evidence, application for leave must be made either in the case or by lodging a
petition for leave to adduce the fresh evidence.

15.5 If a party intends to invite the House to depart from one of its own decisions,
this intention must be clearly stated in a separate paragraph of their case, to which
special attention must be drawn. A respondent who wishes to contend that a decision
of the court below should be affirmed on grounds other than those relied on by that
court must set out the grounds for that contention in their case.

15.6 Transcripts of unreported judgments should only be cited when they contain an
authoritative statement of a relevant principle of law not to be found in a reported
case or when are necessary for the understanding of some other authority.

15.7 All cases must conclude with a numbered summary of the reasons upon which
the argument is founded, and must bear the signature of at least one counsel for

---

[1] For form of application for setting down, see Appendix A, Form 13.
[2] See Lord Diplock's speech in *MV Yorke Motors v. Edwards*, [1982] 1 W.L.R. 444.

Paragraph numbers marked with a "+" can be found online and on CD.

HL Civil

each party to the appeal who has appeared in the court below or who will be briefed for the hearing before the House.

15.8 The lodgment of a case carries the right to be heard by two counsel, one of whom may be leading counsel. The fees of two counsel only for any party are allowed on taxation unless the Appellate Committee orders otherwise on application at the hearing.

Separate cases

4A–74 15.9 All the appellants must join in one case. All the respondents must also join in one case, unless it can be shown that the interests of one or more of the respondents are distinct from those of the rest. If the respondents' interests are distinct, the agents who first lodge their case must certify in a letter to the Judicial Office as follows:

(a) 'We, as agents for the respondent(s) [*name particular parties*], certify that opportunity has been offered by us for joining in one case to the respondent(s) [*name particular parties*] whose interests are, in our opinion, similar to those set out in the case lodged by us.'; or

(b) 'We, as agents for the respondent(s) [*name particular parties*], certify that the interests represented in the case lodged by us are, in our opinion, distinct from those of the remaining respondent(s).'

15.10 When one of the foregoing certificates has been given, all remaining respondents wishing to lodge a case must respectively petition to do so in respect of each of their separate cases. Such petitions (which must be lodged with the prescribed fee) must be consented to by the appellants, and must set out the reasons for separate lodgment.

15.11 Parties whose interests in the appeal are passive (for example, stakeholders, trustees, executors, etc.) are not required to lodge a separate case but should ensure that their position is explained in one of the cases lodged.

Joint case

4A–75 15.12 The lodgment of a joint case on behalf of both appellants and respondents may be permitted in certain circumstances.

Lodgment and exchange of cases

4A–76 15.13 No later than five weeks before the proposed date of the hearing, the appellants must lodge in the Judicial Office one master plus seven copies of their case and serve it on the respondents.

15.14 No later than three weeks before the proposed date of the hearing, the respondents must serve on the appellants a copy of their case in response and lodge at the Judicial Office one master plus seven copies of their case in response, as must any other party lodging a case (for example, an intervener or advocate to the court).

15.15 The number of copies of cases exchanged should be enough to meet the requirements of counsel and agents and should not usually exceed eight. To enable the appellants to lodge the bound volumes, the respondents and any other party who has lodged a case must also provide the appellants with 15 further copies of their case.

15.16 Following the exchange of cases, further arguments by either side may not without leave be submitted in advance of the hearing.

Form of cases

4A–77 15.17 Cases must be produced on A4 paper, securely bound on the left, with:

(a) numbered paragraphs;
(b) capital letters down the inside margins;

Paragraph numbers marked with a "+" can be found online and on CD.

(c) references to Appendix and authorities on the outside margins; and

(d) signatures of counsel at the end, above their printed names.

Scottish cases

15.18 Each party must include in their case to the House a copy of the case **4A–78** presented by them to the Court of Session, with a short summary of any additional reasons on which they propose to insist. If no case was presented to the Court of Session, each party must set forth in their case as shortly and succinctly as possible the reasons upon which they found their argument[1].

16.

BOUND VOLUMES

16.1 As soon as all cases have been exchanged, and no later than 14 days before the **4A–79** proposed date of the hearing, the appellants must lodge (in addition to the documents already lodged on setting down) 15 bound volumes, each containing:

(a) petition(s) of appeal;

(b) petition(s) of cross-appeal (if any);

(c) Statement of facts and issues;

(d) appellants' and respondents' cases, with cross-references on the outside margins to the Appendix and authorities volume(s);

(e) case of the advocate to the court or intervener, if any;

(f) Part 1 of the Appendix; and

(g) index to the authorities volume(s).

Form of bound volumes

16.2 The bound volumes: **4A–80**

(a) should be bound in the same manner as the Appendix, with plastic comb binding and blue card covers;

(b) must include cut-out tabs for each of the documents set out in direction 16.1, with the name of the document on the tab;

(c) must show on the front cover a list of the contents and the names and addresses of the agents for all parties;

(d) must indicate on a sticker attached to the plastic spine the volume number and the short title of the appeal; and

(e) should include a few blank pages at either end.

Provision of documents

16.3 To enable the appellants to produce the bound volumes, the respondents must **4A–81** provide the appellants' agents with a further 15 copies of the respondents' case in addition to the cases already exchanged.

16.4 Respondents should arrange with the appellants' agents for the delivery to them of such bound volumes as the respondents' counsel and agents require.

17.

AUTHORITIES

17.1 Ten copies of all authorities that may be needed during the hearing must be **4A–82** lodged at the same time as the bound volumes. The authorities should be collected together into one or more volumes. The appellants are responsible for producing the authorities' volumes and lodging them in the Judicial Office. To enable the appellants to lodge the volumes, the respondents must provide the appellants with ten copies of

---

[1] Standing Order VI(2).

Paragraph numbers marked with a "+" can be found online and on CD.

any authorities which the respondents require but which the appellants do not, or arrange with the appellants for their photocopying. Respondents should arrange with the appellants for the delivery to them of such authorities' volumes as the respondents' counsel and agents require.

Form and content of authorities' volumes

4A–83   17.2 The authorities' volumes should:

    (a) be A4 size, comb bound with green card covers;

    (b) have flexible covers;

    (c) separate each authority in the volume by numbered dividers;

    (d) contain an index to that volume; the first volume must also contain an index to all the volumes;

    (e) be numbered consecutively on the cover and spine with numerals at least point 72 in size for swift identification of different volumes during the hearing;

    (f) have printed clearly on the front cover the title of the appeal and the names of the agents for all parties;

    (g) have affixed to the plastic spine a sticker indicating clearly the volume number and short title of the appeal;

    (h) include a few blank pages at either end;

    (i) not be more than 2½cm (1 inch) thick.

17.3 The first volume(s) should contain citations from the C and L series of the Official Journal of the European Union; the Law Reports; the All England Reports; the Weekly Law Reports; Session Cases; the Scots Law Times; and the current edition of Halsbury's Laws Subsequent volumes should contain all other material. In an appeal where there is a large number of authorities' volumes, it is helpful to produce an index of indexes, separate from the index contained in the first authorities volume.

17.4 The authorities' volumes should be lodged in the Judicial Office in separate containers from the Bound Volumes.

17.5 Where a case is not reported in the Law Reports or Session Cases, references to other recognised reports may be given (see direction 15.6). In Revenue appeals, Tax Cases may be cited but, wherever possible, references to the case in the Law Reports or Session Cases should also be given.

17.6 In order to produce the authorities' volumes, parties may download text from electronic sources; but the authorities' volumes may only be lodged in paper form.

17.7 In certain circumstances (e.g. when during the hearing before the Appellate Committee it becomes apparent that a particular authority is needed but is not in the authorities volume), the House of Lords Library can arrange for copies of authorities to be made available at the hearing[1]. Parties must themselves provide ten copies of any other authority or of unreported cases. They must similarly provide copies of any authority of which notice has not been given.

17.8 The cost of preparing the authorities' volumes falls to the appellants, but is ultimately subject to the decision of the House as to the costs of the appeal.

18.

Notice of Hearing

4A–84   18.1 Once an appeal has been set down, it may be called on at any time, possibly at short notice. However, the Judicial Office lists appeals to meet the convenience of all the parties.

---

[1] See Appendix B for a list of authorities held by the House of Lords Library.

Paragraph numbers marked with a "+" can be found online and on CD.

18.2 The Judicial Office agrees provisional dates with the parties well in advance of the hearing and makes every effort to keep to these dates Counsel, agents and parties are however advised to hold themselves in readiness during the week before and the week following the provisional date given. Agents receive formal notification shortly before the hearing.

18.3 Parties should inform the Judicial Office as early as possible of the names of counsel they have briefed.

18.4 Appellate Committees usually hear appeals on Mondays from 11am–1pm and from 2–4pm, and on Tuesdays to Thursdays from 10.30am–1pm and 2–4pm. Hearings take place in Committee Rooms 1 and 2 on the Committee Corridor of the Palace of Westminster.

19.

Costs

19.1 If counsel seek an order other than that costs should be awarded to the **4A–85** successful party, they should make submissions on costs at the conclusion of the argument before the Appellate Committee. Oral submissions should be followed up by written submissions within 14 days. If there have been no oral submissions, written submissions on costs may be made within 14 days of the conclusion of the hearing. One master plus seven copies of the written submissions must be lodged at the Judicial Office

Conditional fee agreements

19.2 Conditional fee agreements may properly be made by parties to appeals before **4A–86** the House of Lords[1]. It is open to the Taxing Officer to reduce the percentage uplift recoverable under a conditional fee agreement if he considers it to be excessive. The Taxing Officer decides questions of percentage uplift in accordance with the principles set out in *Designers Guild Limited v Russell Williams (Textiles) Limited (trading as Washington DC)* [2003] 2 Costs L.R. 204. If a party appearing before the House seeks a ruling that the percentage uplift provided for in a conditional fee agreement should be wholly disallowed on legal grounds, such a ruling should (unless otherwise ordered) be expressly sought from the House before the end of the hearing[2].

Submissions at judgment

19.3 If submissions on costs have not been made pursuant to direction 19.1, it may **4A–87** be appropriate for submissions on costs to be made in the light of the result of the appeal. In such cases the House postpones making an order for costs in order to allow the parties to make written submissions, usually within 14 days of the date on which judgment is given. One master plus seven copies of the submissions must be lodged at the Judicial Office, and copies sent to the other parties to the appeal.

19.4 The costs submissions are considered on the papers alone. **4A–88**

20.

Judgment

Place and time of judgment

20.1 Judgments are given in the Chamber of the House of Lords, usually on **4A–89**

---

[1] Conditional fee agreements are sanctioned by the Courts and Legal Services Act 1990, as amended by the Access to Justice Act 1999.
[2] See Appeal Committee, 58th Report (2001–02): *Conditional Fee Agreements* (HL Paper 78).

Paragraph numbers marked with a "+" can be found online and on CD.

Wednesdays at 9.45am. Agents are notified of the date. One week's notice is normally given.

Attendance of counsel

4A-90 20.2 One junior of counsel for each party or group of parties who have lodged a case is required to attend at the Bar of the House when judgment is delivered. Queen's Counsel may attend instead, but only a junior's fee is allowed on taxation. It is the convention that Queen's Counsel wear full-bottomed wigs when appearing at the Bar of the House. Counsel instructed to attend judgment must be familiar with the subject matter of the appeal and with the options for its disposal.

Conditions under which judgments are released in advance

4A-91 20.3 The opinions of the Law Lords who sat on the Appellate Committee and the questions to be put to the House to dispose of the appeal are available to certain persons before judgment is given. When judgment is given on a Wednesday morning, these documents are made available to counsel from 10.30 am on the previous Friday morning. They may be collected from the Judicial Office. In releasing these documents, the House gives permission for their contents to be disclosed to counsel, agents (including solicitors outside London who have appointed London agents) and in-house legal advisers in a client Government department. The contents of the documents and the result of the appeal must not be disclosed to the client parties themselves until judgment is given in the House.

20.4 It is the duty of counsel to check that the questions to be put to the House dispose of the appeal in accordance with the opinions of the members of the Appellate Committee. In the case of apparent error or ambiguity in the opinions, counsel are requested to inform the Judicial Office as soon as possible. This can be done at any time by e-mail to lawlords@parliament.uk, if possible no later than 4pm on the Monday before judgment.

20.5 Accredited members of the media may also be supplied in advance of judgment with the Appellate Committee's opinions and the questions to be put to the House to dispose of the appeal. The contents of these documents are subject to a strict embargo, and are not for publication, broadcast or use on club tapes before judgment has been delivered. The documents are issued in advance on the strict understanding that no approach is made to any person or organisation about their contents before judgment is given.

21.
ORDER OF THE HOUSE

Draft order

4A-92 21.1 After the House has given judgment, drafts of the order of the House are sent to all parties who lodged a case. The drafts must be returned to the Judicial Office within seven days of the date of receipt (unless otherwise directed), either approved or with suggested amendments. If amendments are proposed, they must be submitted to the agents for the other parties, who should indicate their approval or disagreement both to the agents submitting the proposals and to the Judicial Office. Where the amendments proposed are contrary to the questions put to and agreed by the House, a petition must be lodged.

Final order

4A-93 21.2 The final order is sent free of charge to the agents for the successful parties.

21.3 Prints of the final order are sent free of charge to the agents for all parties who have entered appearance.

Paragraph numbers marked with a "+" can be found online and on CD.

22.

BILLS OF COSTS

22.1 Bills of costs for taxation (assessment of costs) should be lodged within three **4A–94** months from the date of judgment[1] or the date on which a petition of appeal is withdrawn (see direction 45).

22.2 The practice directions relating to judicial taxations and forms of bills of costs are available from the Judicial Office and at *http://www.parliament.uk*. [Accessed: November 1, 2007].

23.

DISPOSAL OF SECURITY MONEY

23.1 When the appellants are ordered to pay the costs of the appeal, the respondents' **4A–95** costs are met in whole or in part by direct payment to the respondents of the money deposited in the Security Fund (see direction 10), unless the parties have come to some other arrangement.

23.2 If the total amount of the respondents' costs can be met from the money paid into the Security Fund, any balance is repaid to the party who paid it in.

23.3 If the respondents' costs are only partly met by such payment, any certificate of taxation which is forwarded to the respondents takes account of the amount so paid.

23.4 In appeals where more than one bill of respondents' costs is to be paid by the appellants, and the money deposited as security is not enough to meet all the bills, the money is divided between the bills in proportion to their amounts as allowed on taxation or in proportion to the amounts agreed by the respondents.

23.5 If the appellants are not ordered to pay the costs of the appeal, money paid into the Security Fund is returned to them when the final judgment order has been issued.

23.6 If an appeal is withdrawn before setting down or is dismissed for want of prosecution, or if the respondent fails to lodge a bill of costs or an application for extension of time within three months of the date of judgment (see direction 22), the appellants may apply in writing to the Judicial Office for the return to them of the money deposited in the Security Fund. The application must be accompanied by the written consent of all the respondents who have entered appearance. If any respondent refuses consent, the appellants may send them a written demand to lodge a bill of costs within four weeks from the date of notice. If the Clerk of the Parliaments is satisfied that such a demand was duly sent and if the respondent fails to lodge a bill of costs within the time specified, the money in the Security Fund is returned to the appellants.

24.

PREPARATION OF DOCUMENTS

General

24.1 All formal documents to the House of Lords must be produced on A4 paper, **4A–96** securely bound on the left, using both sides of the paper.

24.2 Documents which are not legible or which are not produced in the authorised form or which are unsatisfactory for some other similar reason are not accepted.

---

[1] This period is not affected by suspended orders made under Legal Aid (Scotland) Act 1986, s.19 or Legal Aid Advice and Assistance (N.I.) Order 1981 Article 16.

Paragraph numbers marked with a "+" can be found online and on CD.

24.3 Parties may consult the Judicial Office at all stages of preparation of documents and may submit proofs for approval where appropriate.

Number of documents required

4A–97 24.4 The following table shows the numbers of documents usually required for the hearing of an appeal. The numbers shown are the minimum prescribed in the directions. Actual requirements must be subject to agreement and depend on the number of parties, counsel and agents concerned, and on the special circumstances of each appeal. Copies for the use of the party originating the documents are not included in the numbers indicated.

The appellants must provide:

Document	For Judicial Office	For other side
Petition of appeal	Original and seven copies on lodgment	Two on service
Statement of facts and issues	Original and seven copies on setting down	As arranged
Appendix Part 1	Eight on setting down	One in advance otherwise as arranged
Appendix Part 2 and any subsequent Parts	15 on setting down	One in advance otherwise as arranged
Case	Original and seven copies no later than five weeks before the hearing	As arranged on exchange
Bound volumes	15 no later than two weeks before the hearing	As arranged
Authorities volumes	Ten no later than two weeks before the hearing	As arranged
Documents held in readiness at hearing (if any)	15 held at the Bar	At least three

The respondents (and any interveners) must provide:

Document	For Judicial Office	For other side
Case	Original and seven copies no later than three weeks before the hearing	As arranged on exchange; 15 for bound volumes
Respondents' additional documents (if any)	15 held at the Bar	As arranged

Form of documents

4A–98 24.5 Statement of facts and issues: See direction 11.2.

24.6 Appendix: see direction 12.7.

24.7 Cases: see direction 15.18.

24.8 Bound volumes: see direction 16.2.

24.9 Authorities volumes: see direction 17.2.

Paragraph numbers marked with a "+" can be found online and on CD.

25.

DISPOSAL OF DOCUMENTS

25.1 All petitions and supporting documents lodged become the property of the **4A–99** House. No documents submitted in connection with an application for leave to appeal can be returned. Certain documents submitted in connection with an appeal may be returned, on application to the Judicial Office within 14 days of judgment in the appeal. Master documents are retained in the parliamentary archives.

25.2 Documents lodged for the use of the Appellate Committee may with the permission of the Committee be inspected by persons who are not a party to the appeal. Such persons must comply with any anonymity orders and data protection requirements.

26.

LODGMENT

26.1 'Lodgment' and 'lodging' mean delivery to the Judicial Office or to a member of **4A–100** the Judicial Office staff by post or in person during opening hours. Where the time for lodging a document expires on a Saturday, Sunday, bank holiday, or any other day on which the Judicial Office is closed, the document will be received by the Judicial Office if it is lodged on the first day on which the Office is next open.

26.2 Communications with the Judicial Office may be transmitted by fax or e-mail only in urgent circumstances and by previous arrangement with the Office.

26.3 The Judicial Office will not receive by fax or e-mail any document which is to be presented to the House or on which a fee is payable.

26.4 Any agent attending the Judicial Office to lodge papers must be familiar with the subject matter to be dealt with.

27.

WAIVER OF FEES

27.1 In circumstances where a party to an appeal would suffer financial hardship by **4A–101** the payment of fees to the House, the requirement to pay the fee may be waived. Direction 3.17 applies.

Part III – Directions Applying in Certain Appeals Only

28.

BANKRUPTCY

28.1 If a party to an appeal is adjudicated bankrupt, their agent must give immediate **4A–102** notice in writing to the other parties and to the Judicial Office, who must also be provided with a certified copy of the bankruptcy order (Standing Order X). The bankrupt party must lodge a petition to render the appeal effective and the appeal cannot proceed until the petition has been agreed to by the House.

28.2 A petition to render the appeal effective must be lodged within three months of the date of the notice.

28.3 The form of petition and the procedure for any supplemental case follows that for abatement by death[1].

---

[1] Standing Order X; direction 31. For style of petition, adapt Appendix A, Form 8.

Paragraph numbers marked with a "+" can be found online and on CD.

HL CIVIL

29.

CONSOLIDATION AND CONJOINDER

4A–103 29.1 Where the issues in two or more appeals are similar, it may be appropriate for them to be consolidated or conjoined.

29.2 Consolidation results in the appeals being conducted as a single cause with one set of counsel and one case only on each side and with a single Appendix of documents

29.3 Conjoinder is a looser linking of two or more appeals, and a number of variations is possible. Commons forms of conjoinder are where: the appellants lodge separate cases with a separate junior for each appellant but a single leader; or the appellants lodge a single case with a single set of counsel but the respondents lodge separate cases and are separately represented.

29.4 The Judicial Office should be consulted on whether consolidation or some form of conjoinder is likely to be appropriate. A principal consideration should be to avoid wherever possible separate representation by counsel, or any duplication in the submissions made or in documents produced for the hearing.

29.5 Applications to consolidate or to conjoin appeals are made by petition[1]. The petition must be signed by the agents for all petitioners and must be submitted to the agents for all the other parties who have entered appearance for the endorsement of their consent. If consent is refused, the petition must be endorsed with a certificate that it has been served on the agents in question.

29.6 If all parties consent to or join in the petition, one master plus one copy of the petition should be lodged, together with the prescribed fee.

29.7 If any party refuses their consent, one master plus five copies of the petition should be lodged, together with the prescribed fee. The petition is then referred to an Appeal Committee and may be determined after a hearing.

30.

CROSS-APPEALS

4A–104 30.1 The presentation of an appeal does not entitle a respondent to an appeal to present a cross-appeal. Leave to cross-appeal is required. If leave to appeal has been given to the appellants by an Appeal Committee of the House, application for leave to cross-appeal may be made by the respondents directly to the Appeal Committee. If leave to appeal has been given by the Court of Appeal, then the respondents must first apply to the Court of Appeal for leave to cross-appeal and, if leave is refused, then to apply to the House.

30.2 A petition for leave to cross-appeal may only be lodged after leave to appeal has been granted to the original petitioner for leave to appeal. One master plus five copies of the petition for leave to cross-appeal must be lodged.

If leave to cross-appeal is granted, the petition of cross-appeal must be lodged with the prescribed fee within six weeks of the presentation of the original appeal [2]. One master plus seven copies of the petition of cross-appeal must be lodged. In a petition of cross-appeal, the original appellant in the House of Lords is designated as original-appellant/cross-respondent and the original respondent is designated as original-respondent/cross-appellant.

A cross-appeal may be presented out of time in accordance with direction 7.3.

---

[1] For style, see Appendix A, Form 7.
[2] Standing Order VII. For style of petition, see Appendix A, Form 4.

Paragraph numbers marked with a "+" can be found online and on CD.

30.3 No security for costs is required in cross-appeals (direction 10.5).

30.4 Argument in respect of a cross-appeal must be included by each party in their case in the original appeal. Such an inclusive case must clearly state that it is lodged in respect of both the original and cross-appeals.

30.5 In a cross-appeal, the cases on the original appeal must be lodged in accordance with direction 15.13, i.e. five weeks before the hearing. The cross-appellants' case for the cross-appeal must be lodged in accordance with direction 15.14, i.e. three weeks before the hearing as part of their reply to the original appellants' case. The original appellants/cross-respondents may reply to the case for the cross-appeal in their case lodged in the bound volumes.

30.6 There is only one Appendix for the original appeal and cross-appeal, and documents in respect of the appeal and cross-appeal must be included in the same Appendix. The original-appellants/cross-respondents are responsible for lodging the Statement and Appendix and setting the appeal and cross-appeal down for hearing (including payment of the fee).

31.

DEATH OF A PARTY

31.1 If a party to an appeal dies before the hearing, the appeal abates from the date **4A–105** of death (Standing Order X). Immediate notice of the death must be given in writing to the Judicial Office and to the other parties. The addition of a new party to represent the deceased person's interest cannot proceed until a petition for reviving the appeal has been agreed to by the House.

31.2 The petition for revivor must be lodged with the prescribed fee within three months of the date of notice of death[1]. It must be accompanied by an affidavit explaining the circumstances in which it is being lodged. It must be endorsed with a certificate of service on the respondents.

31.3 If abatement takes place after the case for the deceased person has been lodged but before the appeal has been heard, the appellants must lodge a supplemental case setting out the orders of the House on reviving the appeal and information about the newly-added parties.

32.

DISPUTE BETWEEN PARTIES SETTLED

32.1 It is the duty of counsel and solicitors in any pending appeal, if an event occurs **4A–106** which arguably disposes of the dispute between the parties, either to ensure that the appeal is withdrawn by consent or, if there is no agreement on that course, to bring the facts promptly to the attention of the House, and to seek directions.

33.

EUROPEAN CONVENTION ON HUMAN RIGHTS

Appeals notified under direction 9.11(a), (b) or (c)

33.1 Where an appeal involves a point notified under direction 9.11(a), 9.6(b) or **4A–107** 9.6(c), the petition of appeal must include the words 'in accordance with the Human Rights Act 1998 ' at the appropriate place in the prayer of the petition[2]. Details of the Convention right[3] which it is alleged has been infringed and of the infringement

---

[1] Standing Order X. For style of petition, adapt Appendix A, Form 8.
[2] See Appendix A, Form 4.
[3] See Human Rights Act 1998, which gives further effect in domestic law to much of

Paragraph numbers marked with a "+" can be found online and on CD.

must be set out in the Statement of facts and issues and dealt with in a separate paragraph of the cases of all parties to the appeal.

Appeals notified under direction 9.11(a)

4A–108 33.2 The Crown has the right to be joined as a party in any appeal where the House is considering whether to declare that a provision of primary or subordinate legislation is incompatible with a Convention right[1]. In any appeal where the House is considering, or is being asked to consider, whether to make, uphold or reverse such a declaration, whether or not the Crown[2] is already a party to the appeal, the Head of the Judicial Office notifies the appropriate Law Officer(s)[3].

33.3 Where such an issue is raised in respect of a judicial act[4], the Head of the Judicial Office notifies the Crown through the Treasury Solicitor as agent for the Lord Chancellor[5].

33.4 The person notified under direction 33.2 or 33.3 must within 21 days of receiving such notice, or such extended period as the Head of the Judicial Office may allow, serve on the parties and lodge in the Judicial Office a notice stating whether or not the Crown intends to intervene in the appeal; and the identity of the Minister or other person who is to be joined as a party to the appeal[6].

33.5 If a Minister or other person has already been joined to proceedings in the court below in accordance with the provisions of s 5 of the Human Rights Act 1998, the leave of the House is not required for the continued intervention of the Crown.

33.6 Once joined to the appeal, the case for the Minister or other person must be lodged in accordance with direction 15.

33.7 The House may order the postponement or adjournment of the hearing of the appeal for the purpose of giving effect to the provisions of this direction or the requirements of the Act.

Appeals notified under direction 9.11(b) or (c)

4A–109 33.8 Except as prescribed in direction 33.1, no special steps are required for appeals notified under direction 9.11(b) or 9.11(c).

34.

EUROPEAN COURT OF JUSTICE

4A–110 34.1 Article 234 of the Treaty establishing the European Community provides:

  1. The Court of Justice shall have jurisdiction to give preliminary rulings concerning:

    (a) the interpretation of this Treaty;

---

the Convention for the Protection of Human Rights and Fundamental Freedoms agreed by the Council of Europe at Rome on 4 November 1950.
  [1] Human Rights Act 1998, ss 4, 5.
  [2] Through a Minister, governmental body or other person defined in Human Rights Act 1998, s 5(2).
  [3] The Head of the Judicial Office notifies: (i) in appeals from England, the Attorney-General; (ii) in appeals from Scotland, the Advocate General for Scotland and the Lord Advocate; (iii) in appeals from Wales, if appropriate, the Counsel General of the National Assembly for Wales; (iv) in appeals from Northern Ireland, the Attorney General for Northern Ireland.
  [4] Human Rights Act 1998, ss 7, 9(3) and 9(4).
  [5] In appeals from Scotland, the Head of the Judicial Office notifies the Solicitor to the Scottish Executive; in appeals from Northern Ireland, he notifies the Crown Solicitor and the Departmental Solicitor.
  [6] Human Rights Act 1998, ss 5(2) and 9(5).

Paragraph numbers marked with a "+" can be found online and on CD.

     (b) the validity and interpretation of acts of the institutions of the Community and of the European Central Bank;

     (c) the interpretation of the statutes of bodies established by an act of the Council, where those statutes so provide.

2. Where such a question is raised before any court or tribunal of a Member State, that court or tribunal may, if it considers that a decision on the question is necessary to enable it to give judgment, request the Court of Justice to give a ruling thereon.

3. Where any such question is raised in a case pending before a court or tribunal of a Member State against whose decisions there is no judicial remedy under national law, that court or tribunal shall bring the matter before the Court of Justice.

34.2 When the House refuses leave to appeal to a petition which includes a contention that a question of Community law is involved, the House gives additional reasons for its decision not to grant leave to appeal (see direction 4.7). These reasons reflect the decision of the Court of Justice in *CILFIT v Ministry of Health* (Case C-283/81) which laid down the categories of case where the Court of Justice considered that no reference should be made to it, namely (a) where the question raised is irrelevant; (b) where the Community provision in question has already been interpreted by the Court of Justice; (c) where the question raised is materially identical with a question which has already been the subject of a preliminary ruling in a similar case; and (d) where the correct application of Community law is so obvious as to leave no scope for any reasonable doubt[1].

34.3 The House may order a reference to the Court of Justice before determining whether to grant leave to appeal. In such circumstances proceedings on the petition for leave to appeal are stayed until the answer is received. The directions below apply as appropriate [2].

34.4 When the House intends to make a reference, the hearing is adjourned and the parties are invited to submit an agreed draft of the question(s) to be referred. A further Statement of facts and issues, for the use of the Court of Justice, may also be appropriate. The House then makes the reference, with or without opinions. At this stage the appeal may also be disposed of in part.

34.5 Within one month of the judgment of the Court of Justice, the parties must make written submissions on whether a further hearing before the Appellate Committee is necessary or on how the appeal is to be disposed of.

Further proceedings in the House of Lords

34.6 If a further hearing is required, the parties may seek leave to lodge **4A–111** supplemental cases.

34.7 If supplemental cases are lodged, then:

     (a) no later than five weeks before the expected date of the further hearing, the appellants must lodge in the Judicial Office one master and seven copies of their supplemental case and also serve it on the respondents;

     (b) no later than three weeks before the expected date of the further hearing, the respondents must lodge in the Judicial Office one master and seven copies of their supplemental case and also serve it on the appellants;

     (c) no later than three weeks before the expected date of the further hearing, any other party lodging a case (e.g. an intervener or advocate to the court) must lodge in the Judicial Office one master and seven copies of their supplemental case, and also provide copies to the appellants and respondents.

---

[1] Appeal Committee, 38th Report (2002–03): *Petitions for leave to appeal: reasons for the refusal of leave* (HL Paper 89).
[2] Ibid.

Paragraph numbers marked with a "+" can be found online and on CD.

34.8 As soon as all the supplemental cases have been exchanged, and no later than two weeks before the date of the expected hearing, the appellants must lodge 15 additional sets of bound volumes[1] containing:

    (a) appellants' and respondents' cases;

    (b) cases of interveners etc, if any;

    (c) judgment of the European Court of Justice;

    (d) any additional authorities relied on that are not included in the original green authorities' volumes.

34.9 The Judicial Office supplies the Appellate Committee with the original bound volumes, appendices and authorities' volumes.

Costs

4A–112 34.10 The Court of Justice does not make orders for costs. The costs of the reference are included in the order of the House disposing of the appeal; and, if necessary, are taxed by the House's Taxing Officer.

35.
EXHIBITS

4A–113 35.1 Parties who require exhibits (such as machines in a patent action) to be available for inspection at the hearing must apply to the Judicial Office for permission for the exhibits to be brought to the House before the hearing.

36.
FEES AND SECURITY FOR COSTS

4A–114 36.1 Payments of fees and deposits of security money may be made in cash or by banker's draft or cheque. If an appellant wishes to pay in cash, the Judicial Office may only accept cash up to £10,000, in order to comply with money laundering regulations. Drafts and cheques for fees must be made payable to 'House of Lords Account'. Drafts and cheques for security money must be made payable to 'House of Lords Security Fund Account'.

37.
INTERVENERS

4A–115 37.1 A person who is not a party to an appeal may petition the House for permission to intervene[2].

37.2 The petition for leave to intervene[3], with the prescribed fee, may only be lodged after the petition of appeal has been presented to the House. One master plus seven copies of the petition for leave to intervene must be lodged. The petition must indicate whether leave is sought for oral and written interventions or for written intervention only. The petition should be certified with the consent of the parties in the case. If their consent is refused, the petition must be endorsed with a certificate of service on them with a brief explanation of the reasons for the refusal. All petitions for leave to intervene, whether or not opposed by the parties, are referred to an Appeal Committee.

---

[1] See direction 16.2.

[2] Article 15 of Council Regulation (EC) No 1/2003 of 16 December 2002 empowers the competition authorities in EU member states, acting on their own initiative, to submit written observations to the national courts of their member state on issues relating to the application of Articles 81 or 82 of the Treaty. With the permission of the court in question, they may also submit oral observations to the national courts of their member states.

[3] See Appendix A, Form 8.

Paragraph numbers marked with a "+" can be found online and on CD.

37.3 Persons who intervened in a court below are also required to petition, if they wish to intervene in an appeal to the House.

37.4 Petitions for permission to intervene orally or in writing or both must be lodged with the Judicial Office at least six weeks before the date of hearing of the appeal. If leave is given, written submissions must be lodged with the Judicial Office and also given to the appellants and respondents for incorporation into the bound volume at least three weeks before the hearing. Failure to meet these deadlines increases the burden on the parties in preparing their cases and the bound volumes, and may delay the hearing of the appeal.

37.5 All counsel instructed on behalf of an intervener with leave to address the House should attend the hearing unless specifically excused. But the House does not expect their continued attendance after such address has been made.

37.6 Subject to the discretion of the House, interveners bear their own costs.

37.7 Subject to the discretion of the House, any additional costs to the appellants and respondents resulting from an intervention are costs in the appeal.

37.8 If the Crown has been joined to proceedings in the court below in accordance with the provisions of s 5 of the Human Rights Act 1998, the leave of the House is not necessary for the continued intervention of the Crown (direction 33.5).

37.9 For intervention in petitions for leave to appeal, see direction 3.21.

38.

NEW SUBMISSIONS

38.1 If, after the conclusion of the argument on an appeal, a party wishes to bring to the notice of the House new circumstances which have arisen and which might affect the decision or order of the House, application must be made without delay (by letter to the Head of the Judicial Office) for leave to make new submissions. The application should indicate the circumstances and the submissions it is desired to make, and a copy must be sent to the agents for the other parties to the appeal. **4A–116**

39.

OPPOSED INCIDENTAL PETITIONS

39.1 Unless the Head of the Judicial Office directs otherwise, opposed incidental petitions (including any interlocutory petition which relates to any petition of appeal) are referred to an Appeal Committee and may be decided after an oral hearing. **4A–117**

39.2 One master plus seven copies of the petition must be lodged, with the prescribed fee. The original petition must bear a certificate of service on the other parties and must clearly indicate whether the other parties consent or refuse to consent to the prayer of the petition.

39.3 If the Appeal Committee orders an oral hearing, the parties may apply at that time to hand in affidavits and such other documents as they may wish. Eight copies are required. Copies of such documents must be served on the other parties before the oral hearing. Authorities are not normally cited before the Appeal Committee.

40.

PATENTS

40.1 This direction applies to any appeal direct from the High Court under ss 12 and 13 of the Administration of Justice Act 1969, from an order for the revocation of a patent made under s 32 or 61 of the Patents Act 1949 or under s 72 of the Patents Act 1977. **4A–118**

Paragraph numbers marked with a "+" can be found online and on CD.

40.2 Notice of intention to present an appeal, with a copy of the petition of appeal, must be served on the Comptroller-General of Patents, Designs and Trade Marks, as well as on the respondents.

40.3 If at any time before the appeal comes on for hearing the respondents decide not to appear on the appeal or not to oppose it, they must without delay serve notice of their decision on the Comptroller and on the appellants. Any such notice served on the Comptroller must be accompanied by a copy of the petition under s 32 of the 1949 Act or of the pleadings in the action and the affidavits filed therein.

40.4 The Comptroller must, within 14 days of receiving notice of the respondents' decision, serve on the appellant and lodge in the Judicial Office a notice stating whether or not he intends to enter appearance.

40.5 The Comptroller may appear and be heard in opposition to the appeal:
    (a) in any case where he has given notice of his intention to appear, and
    (b) in any other case (including in particular a case where the respondents withdraw opposition to the appeal during the hearing) if the House so directs or allows.

40.6 The House makes such orders for the postponement or adjournment of the hearing of the appeal as may appear necessary for the purpose of giving effect to the provisions of this direction.

41.

PUBLIC FUNDING AND LEGAL AID

4A–119 41.1 The House of Lords does not provide public funding or legal aid. Application for public funding must be made in England and Wales to the Legal Services Commission, in Scotland to the Scottish Legal Aid Board, and in Northern Ireland to the Legal Aid Committee.

41.2 A party to whom a public funding or legal aid certificate has been issued must lodge a copy in the Judicial Office as soon as possible thereafter. Any emergency certificate and subsequent amendments and the authority for leading counsel must also be lodged.

Effect of application by appellant for public funding/legal aid

4A–120 41.3 Provided the Judicial Office and the other parties have been notified in writing, an application by a petitioner or appellant for public funding or legal aid suspends proceedings in the House of Lords. Previously applicable time limits are set aside (including that for the deposit of security for costs).

41.4 Notification must be given far enough before the expiry of the original time limits to allow the Judicial Office to take the necessary steps to keep the petition or the appeal (as the case may be) from being dismissed as being out of time. A copy of the order appealed from must be submitted by the applicant with the notification. The original time limits are automatically extended to a date one month after the final decision is taken on the funding application (including any appeals against a refusal of funding)[1].

Effect of application by respondent for public funding/legal aid

4A–121 41.5 Where a respondent to an appeal has applied for public funding or legal aid, the Judicial Office should be informed within the original time limit for lodging the Statement and Appendix[2]. The period for lodging the Statement and Appendix is

---

[1] Standing Order IX.
[2] See direction 13.

Paragraph numbers marked with a "+" can be found online and on CD.

then extended to six weeks from the final determination of the funding or legal aid application (including any appeals against a refusal of funding).

Issuing of public funding/legal aid certificate

41.6 Where a public funding or legal aid certificate is granted, the relevant date for the purpose of calculation of time limits under directions 41.4 and 41.5 is the date of issue of the certificate. **4A–122**

42.

SPECIALIST ADVISERS

42.1 Any party to an appeal may apply in writing to the Judicial Office for Specialist Advisers to attend the hearing[1]. Such advisers provide assistance to the Appellate Committee and are strictly independent of the parties to the appeal. **4A–123**

43.

STAY OF EXECUTION

43.1 Presentation of a petition of appeal or a petition for leave to appeal does not in itself place a stay of execution on any order appealed from. A party seeking such a stay must apply to the court appealed from, not to the House of Lords. The House cannot stay an interlocutor of the Court of Session[2]. **4A–124**

44.

TRANSCRIPTION

44.1 Transcriptions are not made of hearings before the Appellate Committee. Any party may seek permission to arrange for its own transcription of a hearing, by writing to the Head of the Judicial Office. Permission is usually given. The service arranged must be silent. A single copy of the transcript should be lodged in the Judicial Office. **4A–125**

45.

WITHDRAWAL OF PETITIONS

Petitions for leave to appeal

45.1 A petition for leave to appeal may be withdrawn by writing to the Head of the Judicial Office, stating that the parties to the petition have agreed how the costs should be settled. The respondents should notify the Judicial Office of their agreement. **4A–126**

Petitions of appeal

45.2 An appeal that has not been set down for hearing may be withdrawn by writing to the Head of the Judicial Office, stating that the parties to the appeal have agreed the costs of the appeal. The nature of the agreement should be indicated. Where appropriate, the letter should also indicate how the money paid into the security fund (if any) should be disposed of. Written notification must also be given to the respondents who must notify the Judicial Office of their agreement to the withdrawal of the appeal and who must confirm that the costs have been agreed. **4A–127**

45.3 An appeal that has been set down for hearing may only be withdrawn by order

---

[1] Standing Order XIV. For Nautical Assessors, see also Supreme Court of Judicature Act 1891 s 3.
[2] Court of Session Act 1988, s 41(2).

Paragraph numbers marked with a "+" can be found online and on CD.

of the House on petition[1]. Such a petition should include submissions on costs and, where appropriate, indicate how the security money should be disposed of. The petition must be submitted for their consent to those respondents who have entered appearance. The petition should be lodged with the prescribed fee.

Statements to the House

JUDICIAL PRECEDENT

4A–128 **26 July 1966—BY THE LORD CHANCELLOR (LORD GARDINER)**

'Before judgments are delivered today, I wish to make the following statement on behalf of myself and the Lords of Appeal in Ordinary:

"Their Lordships regard the use of precedent as an indispensable foundation upon which to decide what is the law and its application to individual cases It provides at least some degree of certainty upon which individuals can rely in the conduct of their affairs, as well as a basis for orderly development of legal rules.

"Their Lordships nevertheless recognise that too rigid adherence to precedent may lead to injustice in a particular case and also unduly restrict the proper development of the law. They propose therefore to modify their present practice and, while treating former decisions of this House as normally binding, to depart from a previous decision when it appears right to do so.

"In this connection they will bear in mind the danger of disturbing retrospectively the basis on which contracts, settlements of property and fiscal arrangements have been entered into and also the especial need for certainty as to the criminal law.

"This announcement is not intended to affect the use of precedent elsewhere than in this House."'

PRINCIPLES FOR PARTICIPATION

4A–129 **22 June 2000—BY THE SENIOR LORD OF APPEAL IN ORDINARY (LORD BINGHAM OF CORNHILL)**

'My Lords, with the leave of the House, before the reports from the Appellate Committees are considered, I should like to make a statement on Recommendation 59 of the Royal Commission on the Reform of the House of Lords That recommendation is that "The Lords of Appeal should set out in writing and publish a statement of the principles which they intend to observe when participating in debates and votes in the second chamber and when considering their eligibility to sit on related cases."

'I should tell the House that my noble and learned friends have considered this recommendation and have agreed on the terms of a statement to give effect to it. I will now read the statement which has been agreed by all the Lords of Appeal in Ordinary:

General Principles

"As full members of the House of Lords the Lords of Appeal in Ordinary have a right to participate in the business of the House. However, mindful of their judicial role they consider themselves bound by two general principles when deciding whether to participate in a particular matter, or to vote: first, the Lords of Appeal in Ordinary do not think it appropriate to engage in matters where there is a strong element of party political controversy; and secondly the Lords of Appeal in Ordinary bear in mind that they may render themselves ineligible to sit judicially if they were to express an opinion on a matter which might later be relevant to an appeal to the House.

---

[1] For style of petition, adapt Appendix A, Form 16.

Paragraph numbers marked with a "+" can be found online and on CD.

"The Lords of Appeal in Ordinary will continue to be guided by these broad principles They stress that it is impossible to frame rules which cover every eventuality. In the end it must be for the judgment of each individual Lord of Appeal to decide how to conduct himself in any particular situation.

Eligibility

"In deciding who is eligible to sit on an appeal, the Lords of Appeal agree to be guided by the same principles as apply to all judges These principles were restated by the Court of Appeal in the case of *Locabail (UK) Ltd v Bayfield Properties Ltd and others and four other actions* [2000] 1 All E.R. 65 (CA)]."

'My Lords, that concludes the statement.'

46. Standing Orders

STANDING ORDER NO. 17 OF THE HOUSE OF LORDS RELATING TO PUBLIC BUSINESS

Recall of the House. 20 May 1970.

4A–130

(1) If, during any adjournment of the House, the Lord Speaker, after consultation with Her Majesty's Government,is satisfied that the public interest requires that the House should meet at a time earlier than that appointed, he may signify that he is so satisfied and notice shall be given and thereupon the House shall meet at the time stated in the notice, as if it had been duly adjourned to that time.

(2) If the Lord Chancellor is unable to act for the purposes of this Standing Order, the Chairman of Committees, after consultation with Her Majesty's Government, may act in his stead.

(3) Notwithstanding any adjournment of the House, the House may meet for judicial business at a time earlier than that appointed if the senior Lord of Appeal in Ordinaryis satisfied that it should do so and has signified that he is so satisfied and has given notice to such Lords as he thinks fit.

STANDING ORDER NO. 87 OF THE HOUSE OF LORDS RELATING TO PUBLIC BUSINESS

Appellate and Appeal Committees. 20 May 1970. 28 January 1984.

4A–131

(1) For the purposes of its appellate jurisdiction, the House shall have Appellate and Appeal Committees, of which all Lords qualified under the Appellate Jurisdiction Acts 1876 and 1887 shall be members.

(2) These Committees shall be:

(a) two Appellate Committees, which shall hear any cause or matter referred to them and shall report thereon to the House;

(b) two Appeal Committees, which shall consider any Petition or application for leave to appeal that may be referred to them and any matter relating thereto, or to causes depending, or formerly depending, in this House, and shall report thereon to the House.

(3) In any criminal matter, or in any matter concerning extradition, an Appeal Committee may take decisions and give directions on behalf of the House.

(4) In any Appellate or Appeal Committee the Chair shall be taken by the Lord Chancellor or, in his absence, by the senior Lord of Appeal in Ordinary present, such seniority being determined in accordance with the Commission for the time being appointing Speakers for the purpose of the hearing and determination of Appeals.

(5) For the purposes of section 8 of the Appellate Jurisdiction Act 1876, any Appellate Committee may sit and act while Parliament is prorogued.

HL CIVIL

Paragraph numbers marked with a "+" can be found online and on CD.

STANDING ORDERS OF THE HOUSE OF LORDS REGULATING JUDICIAL BUSINESS, MADE IN PURSUANCE OF THE APPELLATE JURISDICTION ACT 1876 AND SUBSEQUENT ENACTMENT

4A–132   The dates (round bracketed) are those of the original standing orders prior to 1876. The dates [square bracketed] are those of the original standing orders made in pursuance of the Appellate Jurisdiction Act 1876 The dates without brackets are those of subsequent amendments.

Time limit for presenting Appeals

4A–133   I. ORDERED, that no Petition of Appeal be received by this House unless the same be lodged in the Parliament Office for presentation to the House within the period of three months from the date of the last Order or Interlocutor appealed from.

(13 December 1661)

[14 August 1876]

26 February 1959

25 March 1964

Leave to Appeal from the Courts of Appeal

4A–134   II. ORDERED, that, in all Appeals from the Court of Appeal, the Court of Appeal in Northern Ireland or the Court of Session in Scotland in which the leave of the House is required under the provisions of any Act of Parliament, a Petition for Leave to Appeal be lodged in the Parliament Office within one month from the date of the last Order or Judgment appealed from, and that such Petition be referred to an Appeal Committee to consider whether such leave should be granted.

[24 October 1935]

3 March 1966

3 December 1969

Leave to Appeal from the High Court

4A–135   III. ORDERED, that, in all cases where application is made for leave for an Appeal to be brought direct to the House from the High Court of Justice in England and Wales or from the High Court of Justice in Northern Ireland—

(a) a Petition for such leave, together with the certificate granted by the High Court under section 12 of the Administration of Justice Act 1969, be lodged in the Parliament Office within one month from the date of the grant of such certificate or within such extended time as in any particular case the House may allow;

(b) any such Petition, and any application for extension of time or other incidental matter, be referred to an Appeal Committee for their consideration and report.

15 December 1969

Appeals to be signed and certified by counsel

4A–136   IV. ORDERED, that, except in cases where leave to appeal has been granted under the provisions of any Act of Parliament, all Petitions of Appeal be signed, and the reasonableness thereof certified, by two counsel.

(3 March 1697)

[14 August 1876]

3 March 1966

Security for costs

4A–137   V. (1) ORDERED, that, unless otherwise ordered by the House, in all Appeals the Appellants do give security for costs by paying into the House of Lords Security Fund Account within one week of the presentation of the Appeal such sum as shall be authorised from time to time by the House, to be subject to the Order of the House with regard to the costs of the Appeal.

On default by the Appellants in complying with the above conditions, the Appeal to stand dismissed.

(20 November 1680)

[14 August 1876]

7 August 1877

Paragraph numbers marked with a "+" can be found online and on CD.

think fit as Taxing Officer, and in all cases in which this House shall make any order for payment of costs by any party or parties in any cause, the amount thereof to be certified by the Clerk of the Parliaments, the Taxing Officer shall tax the Bill of Costs so ordered to be paid, and ascertain the amount thereof, and report the same to the Clerk of the Parliaments or Clerk Assistant: And it is further Ordered, that the same fees shall be demanded from and paid by the party applying for such taxation for and in respect thereof as are now charged or shall be authorised from time to time by the House; and such fees shall be added at the foot of the said Bill of Costs as taxed. And the Clerk of the Parliaments or Clerk Assistant may give a certificate of such costs, expressing the amount so reported to him as aforesaid, and in his certificate, as well as in the Taxing Officer's report, regard shall be had to any sum that has been paid in to the Security Fund Account of the House, as directed by Standing Order No. V; and the amount in money certified by him in such certificate shall be the sum to be demanded and paid under or by virtue of such order as aforesaid for payment of costs.

(3 April 1835)
[14 August 1876]
7 August 1877
2 June 1959
9 March 1977
27 June 1984

Fees

XIII. ORDERED, that fees be taken in this House on the documents specified in **4A–149** the Schedule hereto, that the fees to be charged shall be such as shall be authorised from time to time by the House, and that none of the said documents be issued from or received at the Parliament Office unless it shall have been endorsed with the date of lodgment and the amount of fee paid.

If the Clerk of the Parliaments is satisfied that a litigant who has been refused public funding or legal aid would suffer financial hardship by the payment of fees to this House, he shall report the circumstances to the Appeal Committee. The Appeal Committee shall have power to waive, modify or suspend such fees, either wholly or in part, and shall report thereon to the House.

[10 March 1902]
26 March 1970
27 April 1976
9 March 1977
21 July 1988
17 December 1991
19 May 1994
17 October 1995
10 October 2000

SCHEDULE

Petition for Leave to Appeal. **4A–150**
Interlocutory Petitions referred to an Appeal Committee (including the Report thereon).
Petition of Appeal.
Notice of Appearance.
Waiver of Security for costs.
Petition not referred to Appeal Committee.
Application to set down for hearing.
Petition to withdraw Appeal after setting down.

Specialist advisers

XIV. (1) ORDERED, that the Lord Chancellor or the Lord Speaker may direct that **4A–151** one or more Specialist Advisers shall attend the hearing of any Appeal in which they consider the House would benefit from such attendance.

(2) ORDERED, that the parties or either party to an Appeal may apply by letter to

Paragraph numbers marked with a "+" can be found online and on CD.

the Clerk of the Parliaments requesting, upon grounds stated in the letter, the attendance of Specialist Advisers Such an application shall be referred to and determined by the Lord Chancellor or Lord Speaker.

(3) ORDERED, that in any Appeal concerning nautical matters in which the attendance of Specialist Advisers is required, Nautical Assessors may be appointed of whom one shall be an Officer, active or retired, of Her Majesty's Navy, and the other an Elder Brother of the Corporation of Trinity House.

(4) ORDERED, that the fees and expenses paid to each Specialist Adviser shall be such as shall have been agreed between the parties and the Advisers and approved by the Lord Chancellor or Lord Speaker, or, failing such agreement, such sum as shall be authorised by the Lord Chancellor or Lord Speaker.

(5) ORDERED, that unless the House otherwise directs, the fees referred to in paragraph (4) shall be paid by the party against whom the House awards costs.

23 November 1995

APPENDIX A

STANDARD FORMS OF KEY DOCUMENTS

4A–152

FORM 1

PETITION for leave to appeal

(HL direction 3)

IN THE HOUSE OF LORDS

ON APPEAL FROM HER MAJESTY'S COURT OF APPEAL (CIVIL DIVISION) (ENGLAND)
(or relevant court)

Court of Appeal Ref: (eg, B3/2003/0038)
Neutral citation of judgment appealed against: (eg, [2003] EWCA Civ 1575)

BETWEEN

AB (Respondent)
and
CD (Petitioners)
[and]
[(2) EF]
[and]
[(3) GH]

PETITION FOR LEAVE TO APPEAL

TO THE RIGHT HONOURABLE THE HOUSE OF LORDS

THE HUMBLE PETITION OF *(set out full name(s) and address(es) of petitioners)*
PRAYING FOR LEAVE TO APPEAL SHOWS—

1.   That ....*[set out briefly in numbered paragraphs such facts and arguments as may be necessary to enable the Appeal Committee to decide whether leave to appeal should be given]*.
2.   ....
3.   ....etc.

[Note: it is usually appropriate for petitions for leave to appeal to deal with some or all of the following:

1. Narrative of the facts;
2. Statutory framework (*if any*);
3. Chronology of proceedings;
4. Orders made in the courts below;
5. Issues before Court of Appeal (*or court appealed from*);
6. Treatment of the issues by Court of Appeal (*or court appealed from*);
7. Issues in the petition for leave to appeal.]

HL Civil

Paragraph numbers marked with a "+" can be found online and on CD.

[At end of numbered paragraphs insert]

YOUR PETITIONER(S) HUMBLY SUBMIT(S) that leave to appeal to Your Lordships' House should be granted for the following among other

REASONS

[list here numbered reasons summarising the arguments]

(1) ....
(2) ....
(3) ....etc.

AND YOUR PETITIONER(S) WILL EVER PRAY

Signed

....
Signature of petitioner(s) or agent(s) for the petitioner(s)

[Note: for leapfrog petitions (direction 6) the prayer of the petition uses the words:

THE HUMBLE PETITION OF *[set out full name(s) and address(es) of petitioners]* PRAYING FOR LEAVE FOR AN APPEAL TO BE BROUGHT DIRECT FROM THE HIGH COURT OF JUSTICE IN ACCORDANCE WITH PART II OF THE ADMINISTRATION OF JUSTICE ACT 1969 SHOWS—]

[Use Form 2 for certificate of service to be endorsed on back of last page of petition for leave to appeal]

FORM 2

BACK OF PETITION for leave to appeal showing certificate of service to be endorsed on back of last page of original petition

[I *or* We], [(Messrs) (*name*), of (*address*),(agents for)] the petitioner(s) within-named, hereby certify that on (*date*) [I *or* we] served [(Messrs) (*name*) of (*address*) (agents for)] (*name(s) of respondent(s)*), the within-named respondent(s), with a correct copy of the petition for leave to appeal and with notice that the petition would be presented to the House of Lords on behalf of the petitioner(s) as soon as conveniently may be.	IN THE HOUSE OF LORDS ON APPEAL FROM (*name court*) BETWEEN: (*set out title of cause*)
(*signature of petitioner(s) or their agents*)	
	PETITION FOR LEAVE TO APPEAL
(*neutral citation of judgment petitioned against*) (*references to law reports*) (*indexing catchwords*) (*head-note summary*)	(*set out full name, address, telephone number, and reference (if any) of petitioner(s) or their agents*)

HL Civil

Paragraph numbers marked with a "+" can be found online and on CD.

FORM 3
PETITION for leave to appeal out of time
(HL directions 2 and 3)

IN THE HOUSE OF LORDS

ON APPEAL FROM HER MAJESTY'S COURT OF APPEAL CIVIL DIVISION (ENGLAND)
(or relevant court)]

Court of Appeal Ref: (eg, B3/2004/0039)
Neutral citation of judgment appealed against: (eg, [2004] EWCA Civ 3847)

BETWEEN
AB (Respondent)
and
CD (Petitioners)
[and]
[(2) EF]
[and]
[(3) GH]

PETITION FOR LEAVE TO APPEAL

TO THE RIGHT HONOURABLE THE HOUSE OF LORDS

THE HUMBLE PETITION OF *(set out full name(s) and address(es) of petitioners)*
PRAYING FOR LEAVE TO APPEAL NOTWITHSTANDING THAT THE TIME LIMITED BY
STANDING ORDER NUMBER II HAS EXPIRED SHOWS -

1. That *(set out briefly the reason(s) why the petition was not lodged in time)*.
2. That ......*(continue as in Form 1, setting out briefly in numbered paragraphs such facts
   and arguments as may be necessary to enable the Appeal Committee to decide whether
   to give leave to appeal out of time]*.
3. ....
1. ....etc.

*Note: it is usually appropriate for petitions for leave to appeal to deal with some or all of the
following:*

1. Narrative of the facts;
2. Statutory framework *(if any)*;
3. Chronology of proceedings;
4. Orders made in the courts below;
5. Issues before Court of Appeal *(or court appealed from)*;
6. Treatment of the issues by Court of Appeal *(or court appealed from)*;
7. Issues in the petition for leave to appeal.

Paragraph numbers marked with a "+" can be found online and on CD.

[*At end of numbered paragraphs insert*]

YOUR PETITIONER(S) HUMBLY SUBMIT(S) that leave to appeal out of time to Your Lordships' House should be granted for the following among other

REASONS

[*list here numbered reasons summarising the arguments*]

(1) ....
(2) ....
(3) ....etc.

AND YOUR PETITIONER(S) WILL EVER PRAY

Signed

....
Signature of petitioner or agent(s) for the petitioner

[*Use Form 2 for certificate of service to be endorsed on back of last page of petition for leave to appeal out of time*]

FORM 4

PETITION of appeal [or cross-appeal]

(HL direction 9)

IN THE HOUSE OF LORDS

ON APPEAL FROM HER MAJESTY'S COURT OF APPEAL (ENGLAND) *(or relevant court)*

BETWEEN:

AB (Respondents)

and

CD (Appellants)

[and]

[(2) EF]

[and]

[(3) GH]

(in a petition of cross appeal the original respondent lodging the cross appeal is designated as cross-appellant/original respondent and the original appellant is designated as original appellant/cross-respondent)

PETITION OF APPEAL

TO THE RIGHT HONOURABLE THE HOUSE OF LORDS

THE HUMBLE PETITION AND [CROSS-] APPEAL OF *(set out the full name(s) and address(es) of the appellant(s)).*

YOUR PETITIONER(S) humbly pray(s) that the matter of the Order(s)/Interlocutor(s) set forth in the Schedule hereto *[if Order is partly appealed against, insert the words: so far as therein stated to be appealed against]* may be reviewed before Her Majesty the Queen, in Her Court of Parliament, and that the said Order(s)/Interlocutor(s) *[if Order is partly appealed against, insert the words: so far as aforesaid]* may be reversed, varied or altered *[if appropriate, insert the words: in accordance with the Human Rights Act 1998]*, *[if specific relief is asked for, it should be so stated, prefaced by the words: and that]* or that the petitioner(s) may have such other relief in the premises as to Her Majesty the Queen, in Her Court of Parliament, may seem meet.

[signature(s) of appellant(s) or their agents or counsel, as appropriate].

Paragraph numbers marked with a "+" can be found online and on CD.

THE SCHEDULE REFERRED TO ABOVE
FROM HER MAJESTY'S COURT OF APPEAL (CIVIL DIVISION) (ENGLAND) (*or relevant court*)

In a certain cause [*or other matter*] wherein (*insert name(s)*) was/were claimant(s) [*or other designation*] and (*insert name(s)*) was/were defendant(s) [*or other designation*]. (*The names of all parties to the action, whether originally in the cause or added by subsequent order, must be given.*)

The Order(s)/Interlocutor(s) of (*state court*) of (*date*) appealed from is/are in the words following, [*add, if appropriate, the words*: the portion(s) complained of being underlined]: (*The whole of each Order/Interlocutor, including the recital, must be set out. All and only those parts of the Order/Interlocutor appealed from must be underlined. The recital should not be underlined. Where an Order/Interlocutor includes leave to appeal to the House of Lords, that part should not be underlined. Where leave to appeal has been granted by a subsequent Order of the court, that Order must also be set out but should not be underlined.*)

[*Where leave to appeal has been granted by order of the House, the following words are added:*

And your Lordships gave leave to appeal to your Lordships' House on (*date*)]

[*Where leave to appeal is not required under the provisions of any Act of Parliament (see direction 9.2), the following must be added and signed as indicated:*

We humbly conceive this to be a proper case to be heard before your Lordships by way of appeal.]

(*signatures and names of two counsel*)]

[*The special certificate required by HL Standing Order XI in certain Scottish appeals is added here if necessary*]

HL Civil

Paragraph numbers marked with a "+" can be found online and on CD.

FORM 5

BACK OF PETITION OF [CROSS-] APPEAL, showing certificate of service to be endorsed on original petition

[I *or* We], [(Messrs) (*name*), of (*address*),(agents for)] the [*cross-*] appellant(s) within-named, hereby certify that on (*date*) [I *or* we] served [(Messrs) (*name*) of (*address*) (agents for)] (*name(s)* of [*cross-*] *respondent(s)*), the within-named [cross-] respondent(s), with a correct copy of the petition of [cross-] appeal and with notice that the petition would be presented to the House of Lords on behalf of the petitioner(s) as soon as conveniently may be. (*signature of petitioner(s) or their agents*)	IN THE HOUSE OF LORDS ON APPEAL FROM (*name court*) BETWEEN: (*set out title of cause*) _____ PETITION OF [CROSS-] APPEAL _____
(*neutral citation of judgment petitioned against*) (*references to law reports*) (*indexing catchwords*) (*head-note summary*)	(*set out full name, address, telephone number, and reference (if any) of [cross-] appellant(s) or their agents*)

Paragraph numbers marked with a "+" can be found online and on CD.

FORM 6   4A–157

PETITION for extension of time to lodge Statement and Appendix

(HL direction 13)

IN THE HOUSE OF LORDS

ON APPEAL FROM HER MAJESTY'S COURT OF APPEAL (ENGLAND) (*or relevant court)*)

BETWEEN:

(set out title of appeal)

TO THE RIGHT HONOURABLE THE HOUSE OF LORDS

THE HUMBLE PETITION OF (*set out full name(s) of appellant(s)*) shows -

That your petitioner(s) presented a petition of appeal on (*date*) complaining of an Order of the (*state court*) dated (*date*).

That the time allowed by Standing Order VI for the appellant(s) to lodge the statement and appendix and to set down the cause for hearing [will expire *or* originally expired] on (*date*).

[That the House, pursuant to a petition from the appellant(s), granted an extension of time in which to lodge the statement and the appendix and set down the cause for hearing to (*date*).]

[That the House, pursuant to a further petition from the appellant(s), granted a second extension of time until (*date*).]

That the petitioner(s) will be unable to lodge the statement and appendix by the said date for the following reasons:

(set out brief reasons)

THEREFORE YOUR PETITIONER(S) HUMBLY PRAY(S)

That Your Lordships will be pleased to grant an extension of time until (*date*) to lodge the statement and appendix and set down the cause for hearing.

And your petitioner(s) will ever pray.

(signature of appellant(s) or their agents)

[Agents for the] Appellant(s) *(set out here name and address of appellant(s) or their agents)*

[I *or* We] consent to the prayer of the above petition.

(signature of respondent(s) or their agents)
[Agents for the] respondent(s) *(set out here name and address of respondent(s) or their agents)*

Paragraph numbers marked with a "+" can be found online and on CD.

FORM 7

PETITION for Consolidation or Conjoinder

(HL direction 29)

IN THE HOUSE OF LORDS

ON APPEAL FROM HER MAJESTY'S COURT OF APPEAL (ENGLAND)

(set out title of first appeal)

AND

(set out title of second, third etc appeals)

TO THE RIGHT HONOURABLE THE HOUSE OF LORDS

THE HUMBLE PETITION OF *(set out full name(s) of appellant(s)* SHOWS—

That your petitioner(s) presented [a] petition(s) of appeal on *(date)* complaining of (an) Order(s) of the *(name relevant court below)* dated *(date)*.

That your petitioner(s) *(name appellant(s) in other appeal(s), if different)* presented [a] petition(s) of appeal on *(date)* complaining of [an] Order(s) of the *(name relevant court below)* dated *(date)*.

That the same matters of law are raised in each of the appeals [and that the appeals of *(name relevant parties)* to *(name relevant court below)* were heard and argued together and one Judgment was delivered in respect of the [two] appeals].

That it is expedient that your petitioners' said appeals be [consolidated *or* conjoined].

YOUR PETITIONERS THEREFORE HUMBLY PRAY

[Consolidation:

> That the said appeals may be consolidated and that they be allowed to lodge one statement, one case and one appendix and be jointly represented in respect of the *(insert relevant number)* appeals and that the respondents have leave to lodge one case in respect of the appeals.]

[Conjoinder:

> That the said appeals may be conjoined and that they be allowed to lodge separate statements and cases and one appendix in respect of the *(insert relevant number)* appeals and that the respondents have leave to lodge separate cases in respect of the appeals and be separately represented or that such other Order may be made with a view to the convenient conduct of the said appeals as to your Lordships may seem meet *(or such variation as is required)*.]

Paragraph numbers marked with a "+" can be found online and on CD.

And your petitioner(s) will ever pray.

> *(signature of appellant(s) to first appeal or their agents)*
>
> [Agents for the] Appellant(s) *(set out here name and address of appellant(s) or their agents)*
>
> *(signature of appellant(s) to other appeal(s) or their agents)*
>
> [Agents for the] Appellant(s)/co-petitioners *(set out here name and address of appellant(s)/co-petitioners or their agents)*

[I *or* We] consent to the prayer of the above petition.

> *(signature of respondent(s)to first appeal or their agents)*
>
> [Agents for the] Respondent(s) *to first appeal (set out here name and address of respondent(s) or their agents)*
>
> *(signature of respondent(s) to other appeal(s) or their agents)*
>
> [Agents for the] Respondent(s) *to other appeal(s) (set out here name and address of respondent(s) or their agents) etc*

4A-159

FORM 8

PETITION for leave to intervene

(HL direction 37)

IN THE HOUSE OF LORDS

ON APPEAL FROM HER MAJESTY'S COURT OF APPEAL (ENGLAND) *(or relevant court))*

BETWEEN:

(set out title of appeal)

TO THE RIGHT HONOURABLE THE HOUSE OF LORDS

THE HUMBLE PETITION OF *(set out full name(s) of prospective intervener(s))* PRAYING FOR LEAVE TO INTERVENE SHOWS—

1. That on *(date)* *(set out full name(s) of appellant(s))* presented a petition of appeal to your Lordships' House, complaining of an Order of the *(state court)* dated *(date)*.

2. That your petitioner(s) seek(s) your Lordships' leave to present written [*add, if appropriate, the words:* and oral] submissions in intervention in the said appeal.

3. That *(set out briefly in numbered paragraphs such facts and arguments as may be necessary to enable the Appeal Committee to report to the House whether leave to intervene should be granted).*

YOUR PETITIONER(S) HUMBLY SUBMIT(S) that leave to intervene in the said appeal should be granted for the following among other

REASONS
(give numbered reasons summarising the arguments)

And your petitioner(s) will ever pray.

> *(signature of petitioner(s) or their agents)*
>
> *[Agents for the] Petitioner(s) (set out here name and address of petitioner(s) or their agents)*

[I *or* We] consent to the prayer of the above petition.

> *(signature of appellant(s) or their agents)*
>
> *[Agents for the] Appellant(s) (set out here name and address of appellant(s) or their agents)*

[I *or* We] consent to the prayer of the above petition.

> *(signature of respondent(s) or their agents)*
>
> *[Agents for the] Respondent(s) (set out here name and address of respondent(s) or their agents)*

Paragraph numbers marked with a "+" can be found online and on CD.

FORM 9

BACK OF PETITION for leave to intervene, showing certificate of service to be endorsed on original petition

[I *or* We], [(Messrs) (*name*), of (*address*),(agents for)] the petitioner(s) within-named, hereby certify that on (*date*) [I *or* we] served [(Messrs) (*name*) of (*address*) (agents for)] (*name(s) of appellant(s)*), the within-named appellant(s),and [*if different date, insert the words: on (date)*] [(Messrs) (*name*) of (*address*) (agents for)] (*name(s) of respondent(s)*), the within-named respondent(s),with a correct copy of the petition for leave to intervene and with notice that the petition would be presented to the House of Lords on behalf of the petitioner(s) as soon as conveniently may be.	IN THE HOUSE OF LORDS ON APPEAL FROM (*name court*) BETWEEN: (*set out title of cause*) _____ PETITION FOR LEAVE TO INTERVENE _____
(*signature of petitioner(s) or their agents*)	(*set out full name, address, telephone number, and reference (if any) of petitioner(s) or their agents*)

Paragraph numbers marked with a "+" can be found online and on CD.

4A–161

FORM 10

PETITION for restoration of appeal when time for lodging Statement has expired

(HL direction 13)

IN THE HOUSE OF LORDS

ON APPEAL FROM HER MAJESTY'S COURT OF APPEAL (ENGLAND)

BETWEEN: AB (Appellant(s))

                                                        and

                                                 CD (Respondent(s))

TO THE RIGHT HONOURABLE THE HOUSE OF LORDS

THE HUMBLE PETITION OF AB SHOWS –

That your petitioner(s) presented a Petition of Appeal on *(date)* complaining of an Order of the [Court of Appeal *or relevant court*] dated *(date)*.

That the time allowed by Standing Order VI for the appellant(s) to lodge the Statement of facts and issues and the Appendix and to set down the cause for hearing expired on the *(date)*.

That your petitioner(s) has/have been unable to lodge their Statement and the Appendix by the said date for the following reasons:

(set out reasons).

YOUR PETITIONER(S) THEREFORE HUMBLY PRAY(S) that your Lordships will be pleased to order that their appeal be restored and to grant them an extension of time until *(date)* to lodge the Statement and the Appendix and to set down the cause for hearing.

And your petitioner(s) will ever pray.

                                        (signature of appellant(s) or their agents)

                                        [Agents for the] Appellant(s) *(set out here name and address of appellant(s) or their agents)*

[I *or* We] consent to the prayer of the above petition.

                                        (signature of respondent(s) or their agents)
                                        [Agents for the] respondent(s) *(set out here name and address of respondent(s) or their agents)*

Paragraph numbers marked with a "+" can be found online and on CD.

FORM 11

RESPONDENTS' CONSENT to incidental petition

(HL direction 13.6)

(The consent is endorsed on the petition)

We consent to the prayer of the above petition.

(signature)

Respondent(s)/Agents for the respondent(s)

FORM 12

CONSENT to waiver of security for costs

(HL direction 10.3)

(Letter to be sent by respondent(s) or their agent(s) to the Judicial Office)

(date)

Dear Sirs,

AB v CD

[I or We], [as agents for] the Respondent(s) in the above appeal, consent to the appellant(s) being allowed to prosecute the appeal without giving the security for costs required by Standing Order V(1) regulating judicial business.

(signature)

Respondent(s)/Agents for
the respondent(s)

HL Civil

Paragraph numbers marked with a "+" can be found online and on CD.

FORM 13

APPLICATION to set down cause for hearing

(HL direction 14)

IN THE HOUSE OF LORDS

ON APPEAL FROM HER MAJESTY'S COURT OF APPEAL (ENGLAND) *(or relevant court)*

BETWEEN: AB   Appellant(s)

                                                         and

                                                  CD   Respondent(s)

The appellant(s) having lodged a Statement of facts and issues and the Appendix thereto pursuant to order of the House,

My Lords,

Please to move, That this cause be set down for hearing after those causes already appointed.

(signature of appellant(s) or their agents)

Appellant/Agents for the appellant

(set out name and address of appellant(s) or their agent)

Paragraph numbers marked with a "+" can be found online and on CD.

FORM 15

FORM OF COVER for authorities volume *(on green card)*

IN THE HOUSE OF LORDS

ON APPEAL FROM HER MAJESTY'S COURT OF APPEAL (ENGLAND) *(or relevant court))*

BETWEEN:

(set out title of appeal)

Sticker on spine:

[Set out short title of cause]

A 1

AUTHORITIES VOLUME

1

(The authorities volume is only numbered if there is more than one volume)

(Name and address of agents for appellant(s))

(Name and address of agents for respondent(s))

Paragraph numbers marked with a "+" can be found online and on CD.

4A–168

FORM 16

PETITION for withdrawal of appeal

(HL direction 45.2 - 45.3)

IN THE HOUSE OF LORDS

ON APPEAL FROM HER MAJESTY'S COURT OF APPEAL (ENGLAND)

BETWEEN: AB   Appellant(s)

                      and

                CD   Respondent(s)

TO THE RIGHT HONOURABLE THE HOUSE OF LORDS

THE HUMBLE PETITION OF the Appellant(s) shows –

That your petitioner(s) presented a Petition of Appeal on *(date)* complaining of an Order of the Court of Appeal *(or relevant court)* dated *(date)*.

That as security for the costs of their appeal your petitioner(s) paid [£25,000] into the Security Fund Account.

That your petitioner'(s)(s') appeal was set down for hearing before your Lordships' House on *(date)*.

That your petitioner(s) and the respondent(s) have agreed to terms of settlement of all matters in dispute between them, as follows:

1. That your petitioner(s) and the respondent(s) should join in making an application to your Lordships' House for leave that your petitioner'(s)(s') appeal might be withdrawn; and

2. That *(set out terms of agreement)*.

YOUR PETITIONER(S) THEREFORE HUMBLY PRAY(S) that your Lordships will be pleased to order that:

(1) your petitioner'(s)(s') appeal be withdrawn;

(2) *(state costs order sought, to dispose of appeal)*

And your petitioner(s) will ever pray.

                                        (signature)

                                        Agents for the appellant(s)

Paragraph numbers marked with a "+" can be found online and on CD.

APPENDIX B

LIST OF AUTHORITIES KEPT IN HOUSE OF LORDS LIBRARY

(see direction 17.5)

4A–169

The House of Lords Library keeps the following authorities:

All England Reports
Anglo American Law Review
British Yearbook of International Law
Cambrian Law Review
Cambridge Law Journal
Canadian Rights Reporter
Common Market Law Reports
Common Market Law Review
Cox's Criminal Law Cases (1843–49)
Criminal Appeal Reports
Criminal Appeal Reports (Sentencing)
Criminal Law Forum
Criminal Law Review
Crown Office Digest
English Reports
Estates Gazette Law Reports (1985—)
European Court Reports
European Human Rights Reports
European Law Digest
European Law Review
European Public Law
Family Law Reports
Financial Law Reports
Fleet Street Reports
Halsbury's Laws and Statutes
Housing Law Reports
Human Rights Law Journal
Immigration Appeal Reports
Industrial Cases Reports
Industrial Law Journal
Industrial Relations Law Reports
Industrial Tribunal Reports (1971–78)
International and Comparative Law Quarterly
International Litigation Procedure
Irish Jurist (1848–1866, 1935–1965)
Irish Jurist Reports
Irish Law Reports
Journal of Legal History
Journal of Legislative Studies
Journal of Planning and Environment Law
Journal of Social Welfare Law
Jurist—Reports of Cases in Law and Equity (1837–1866)
Justice of the Peace Reports
Law Journal Reports
Law Quarterly Review
Law Reports (1866—)
Law Times Reports
Legislative Studies Quarterly
Lloyd's Law Reports
Local Government Review Reports
Modern Law Review

Paragraph numbers marked with a "+" can be found online and on CD.

New Law Journal
Northern Ireland Law Reports
Northern Ireland Legal Quarterly (Vol 34 (1983)—)
Northern Ireland Statutes
Oxford Journal of Legal Studies
Planning and Compensation Reports (1963–67)
Property and Compensation Reports (1968—)
Public Law (British Journal of Administrative Law)
Reports of Patent Cases
Road Traffic Reports
Rydes Rating Cases (1956–1979)
Scots Law Times
Scottish Civil Law Reports
Scottish Criminal Case Reports (1983—)
Scottish Jurist (1829–1873)
Scottish Law Reporter (1865–1924)
Scottish Planning Law and Practice
Session Cases
Simons Tax Cases (1981—)
Solicitors Journal
Statute Law Review
Statutes
Tax Cases
Times Law Reports
Weekly Law Reports
Weekly Notes (1866–1952)
Weekly Reporter (1852–1906)

APPENDIX C

FEES AND SECURITY MONEY

4A–170   ### JUDICIAL FEES

The following fees are payable at the time of lodgment or collection of documents:

Petitions for leave to appeal—mandatory fees

Presentation	£570
Entering appearance	£115

Petitions of appeal—mandatory fees

Presentation (following successful petition for leave to appeal)	£570
Presentation (not following petition for leave)	£1,140
Entering appearance	£230
Lodging Statement and Appendix and setting down	£3,420

Petitions of appeal—occasional fees

Waiver of security	£115
First petition for extension of time	£230
Second petition for extension	£340
Third petition for extension	£570
Fourth or subsequent petition for extension	£1,000
Petition for leave to intervene	£570
Other interlocutory petition, if agreed	£230
Any interlocutory petition, if opposed	£570

Paragraph numbers marked with a "+" can be found online and on CD.

Appeal Committee Order or other certified document
(except Judgment Order, for which there is no fee)   £12

In respect of a joint petition, only one fee is payable. Fees for presenting petitions in respect of a cross-appeal are the same as fees for petitions in respect of an appeal.

(27th July 2000 [1])

Drafts and cheques for judicial fees are payable to 'House of Lords Account'.

TAXING FEES

The fees payable upon the sums allowed by the Taxing Officer are as follows:

(a) where the amount allowed does not exceed £500, a flat rate of £50;

(b) where the amount allowed exceeds £500, for every £1 or fraction of £1, an amount of 5p.

The fees payable on the withdrawal of a bill of costs (subject to written confirmation of the withdrawal from both parties to the taxation) are as follows:

(a) in respect of bills withdrawn within 21 days of the date appointed for taxation, 1 per cent. of the agreed sum or £50, whichever is the larger;

(b) in respect of bills withdrawn within 7 days of the date appointed for taxation, 2 per cent. of the agreed sum or £50, whichever is the larger.

(27th July 2000[2])

Drafts and cheques for taxing fees are payable to 'House of Lords Account'.

SECURITY MONEY

Security for costs, to be paid by the appellant(s)   £25,000

(27th July 2000 [3])

Drafts and cheques for security money are payable to
'House of Lords Security Fund Account'.

---

[1] House of Lords Offices Committee, 6th Report (1999–2000), HL Paper 97.
[2] ibid.
[3] ibid.

Paragraph numbers marked with a "+" can be found online and on CD.

4B   CRIMINAL APPEALS

4B–0

For "Practice Directions Applicable to Criminal Appeals" plus any related commentary see paragraphs 4B–1+ to 4B–143+ on White Book on Westlaw UK or the Civil Procedure CD.

HL CRIMINAL

Paragraph numbers marked with a "+" can be found online and on CD.

Paragraph numbers marked with a + can be found online and on CD.

1584

SECTION 5

EUROPEAN JURISDICTION

5 EUROPEAN JURISDICTION

GENERAL

The Brussels Convention

When the EEC Treaty (now called the EC Treaty (as a result of the Treaty of Maas- **5-1** tricht on European Union) and also referred to as the Treaty of Rome) was signed in 1957, the six original Member States agreed by art.220 that they would enter into negotiations with each other:

> "with a view to securing for the benefit of their nationals ... the simplification of formalities governing the reciprocal recognition and enforcement of judgments of courts or tribunals and of arbitration awards".

Subsequently, the Convention on Jurisdiction and Enforcement of Judgments in Civil and Commercial Matters was signed at Brussels on September 23, 1968 on behalf of these States (the Brussels Convention).

This Convention went beyond art.220 in that it was not confined to the recognition and enforcement of judgments, but also contained rules of jurisdiction applicable in all States. No provision was, however, made for the recognition of arbitration awards. In 1971 the Member States concluded a Protocol on the Interpretation of the 1968 Convention by the European Court of Justice (the 1971 Protocol). This provides for references for preliminary rulings on questions of interpretation of the Convention to be made to the Court by appellate courts of the Contracting States (see text of 1971 Protocol at para.5–140+ below).

The object of the Conventions is not to unify the rules of substantive law and of procedure of the different contracting states, but to determine which courts have jurisdiction in disputes relating to civil and commercial matters in relations between the contracting states and to facilitate enforcements of judgments (Case C–68/93 *Shevill v Presse Alliance* [1995] I.L.Pr. 267). However, the Conventions establish an enforcement procedure which constitutes an autonomous and complete system independent of the legal systems of the contracting states (*Société d'Informatique Realisation Organisation v Ampersand Software B.V.* [1995] All E.R. (EC) 783).

Accession of United Kingdom

When the United Kingdom, together with Denmark and Ireland, joined the **5-2** European Community, it undertook to accede to any Conventions provided for by art.220 of the Treaty of Rome and "to enter into negotiations with the original Member States in order to make the necessary adjustments thereto". The result was a Convention signed on October 9, 1978 amending the Brussels Convention and the 1971 Protocol and providing for the accession to them of the United Kingdom, Denmark and Ireland. In this instance, the amendments went well beyond mere "necessary adjustments".

Civil Jurisdiction and Judgments Act 1982

This Act has as its main purpose the implementation of the Brussels Convention as **5-3** amended by the 1978 Accession Convention and the 1971 Protocol. The Act gives the Conventions the force of law in the United Kingdom and requires judicial notice to be taken of them. They are set out, as s.2 states, for "convenience of reference" in the Act. Thus, the English text of the Brussels Convention (as it was at that time) is found in Sch.1, the 1971 Protocol in Sch.2 and the relevant provisions of the Accession Convention are in Sch.3. It is open to the UK islands and territories to ask that the Brussels Convention should be extended to them (see in this respect the Civil Jurisdiction and Judgments Act 1982 (Gibraltar) Order 1997) at para.5–164 below).

The Civil Jurisdiction and Judgments Act 1982 also contains rules of jurisdiction and rules for the enforcement of judgments as between the constituent parts of the United Kingdom, England and Wales, Scotland, and Northern Ireland. To this end, the Act sets out in Sch.4 a modified version of the jurisdictional rules found in the Brussels Convention and in addition contains a number of special provisions dealing with recognition and enforcement of judgments. It should be noted that the provisions of the 1982 Act, including the Brussels Convention and the 1971 Protocol (amended as explained below), contained in this Section of *Civil Procedure*, are confined

Paragraph numbers marked with a "+" can be found online and on CD.

to those dealing with the allocation of jurisdiction among the courts of the EC Member States. Schedule 4 of the 1982 Act contains provisions modelled on the Convention for the allocation business between the three separate jurisdictions within the UK. Its interpretation is a matter solely within the jurisdiction of the United Kingdom national courts (Case C–346/93 *Kleinwort Benson Ltd v City of Glasgow District Council, The Times,* April 17, 1995).

The Civil Procedure Rules and the relevant Practice Directions give procedural effect to the provisions of the Act and the Conventions. The principal rules are CPR r.6.19 (service of Claim Form where the permission of the Court is not required), and PD 6B paras 1.1 to 1.3 (form of certificates on claim form when service abroad is to be effected without permission). See also Sch.1 and RSC O.71 (reciprocal enforcement of judgments under the Conventions) and the Practice Direction supplementing O.71. For applications under RSC O.71 the appropriate Practice Forms should be used: see **PF 157QB** to **PF 165QB**.

Accession of Other States

5–4   Section 14(1) of the 1982 Act provides that the Act (including the texts of the Conventions in the Schedules) may be amended by Order in Council. The Civil Jurisdiction and Judgments Act 1982 (Amendment) Order 1989 (SI 1989/1346) modified the Act in consequence of a revision of the Brussels Convention and the 1971 Protocol occasioned by the accession to them of Greece by a Convention signed in Luxemburg on October 25, 1982. The Civil Jurisdiction and Judgments Act 1982 (Amendment) Order 1990 (SI 1990/2591) brought into effect in the UK revisions occasioned by the accession of Spain and Portugal as a result of the San Sebastian Convention signed on May 28, 1989 (as to ratification elsewhere, see para.5–6 below). The revisions made to the Brussels Convention on these occasions have not always been confined to what could be called "necessary adjustments" to cope with the accessions of new jurisdictions but in addition have included some changes thought necessary in the light of problems encountered in operating the provisions of the Convention over the years within the Member States.

EC and EFTA—The Lugano Convention

5–5   The Lugano Convention on Jurisdiction and the Enforcement of Judgments in Civil Matters was made between the Member States of the EC and those of the European Free Trade Association (EFTA). This Convention is very closely modelled on the Brussels Convention although there is no provision for references on interpretation to be made to the European Court. The Civil Jurisdiction and Judgments Act 1991 (brought into effect on May 1, 1992) gives the Lugano Convention the force of law in the UK and amends the 1982 Act so as to incorporate references in it to this Convention (as to ratification elsewhere, see para.5–6 below). By this statute the English text of the Convention is inserted in the 1982 Act as Sch.3C. Differences between the two Conventions are noted, except in relation to Titles VI and VII where the differences are more substantial.

Ratification

5–6   The San Sebastian Convention has been ratified by all Member States. (The UK ratified the San Sebastian Convention on September 13, 1991, with entry into force on December 1, 1991.) The Lugano Convention has been ratified by all EC and EFTA Member States. (The UK ratified the Lugano Convention on February 5, 1992, with entry into force on May 1, 1992).

Up-to-date information as to the progress of ratification by EFTA Member States acceding to the Brussels Convention may be obtained from the Lord Chancellor's Department, International Division, 28 Old Queen Street, London SW1H 9HP, or from the International Litigation Procedure Reports. The information contained therein is updated monthly.

Paragraph numbers marked with a "+" can be found online and on CD.

Civil Jurisdiction and Judgments Act 1982

(1982 c.27)

5–7

ARRANGEMENT OF SECTIONS

PART I

IMPLEMENTATION OF THE CONVENTIONS

MAIN IMPLEMENTING PROVISIONS

PART IV

MISCELLANEOUS PROVISIONS

PROVISIONS RELATING TO JURISDICTION

PART V

SUPPLEMENTARY AND GENERAL PROVISIONS

Introductory note

This Act incorporates into United Kingdom law the EC Convention on Jurisdiction **5–8** and Enforcement of Judgments in Civil and Commercial Matters of 1968, known as the "Brussels Convention". As stated in s.2(2), "for convenience of reference" the English text of this Convention is set out in Sch.1 to the Act. For the Articles of the Convention relating to jurisdiction, see paras 5–24 *et seq.*

Paragraph numbers marked with a "+" can be found online and on CD.

PART I

IMPLEMENTATION OF THE CONVENTIONS

MAIN IMPLEMENTING PROVISIONS

Interpretation of references to the Conventions and Contracting States

5–9   **1.**—(1) In this Act—

"the 1968 Convention" means the Convention on jurisdiction and the enforcement of judgments in civil and commercial matters (including the Protocol annexed to that Convention), signed at Brussels on 27th September 1968;

"the 1971 Protocol" means the Protocol on the interpretation of the 1968 Convention by the European Court, signed at Luxembourg on 3rd June 1971;

"the Accession Convention" means the Convention on the accession to the 1968 Convention and the 1971 Protocol of Denmark, the Republic of Ireland and the United Kingdom, signed at Luxembourg on 9th October 1978;

"the 1982 Accession Convention" means the Convention on the accession of the Hellenic Republic to the 1968 Convention and the 1971 Protocol, with the adjustments made to them by the Accession Convention, signed at Luxembourg on 25th October 1982;

"the 1989 Accession Convention" means the Convention on the accession of the Kingdom of Spain and the Portuguese Republic to the 1968 Convention and the 1971 Protocol, with the adjustments made to them by the Accession Convention and the 1982 Accession Convention, signed at Donostia—San Sebastián on 26th May 1989;

"the Brussels Conventions" means the 1968 Convention, the 1971 Protocol, the Accession Convention, the 1982 Accession Convention and the 1989 Accession Convention;

"the Lugano Convention" means the Convention on jurisdiction and the enforcement of judgments in civil and commercial matters (including the Protocols annexed to that Convention) opened for signature at Lugano on 16th September 1988 and signed by the United Kingdom on 18th September 1989.

"the Regulation" means Council Regulation (EC) No. 44/2001 of 22nd December 2000 on jurisdiction and the recognition and enforcement of judgments in civil and commercial matters, as amended from time to time and as applied by the Agreement made on 19th October 2005 between the European Community and the Kingdom of Denmark on jurisdiction and the recognition and enforcement of judgments in civil and commercial matters (OJ No. L 299 16.11.2005 at p62).

(2) In this Act, unless the context otherwise requires—

Paragraph numbers marked with a "+" can be found online and on CD.

(a) references to, or to any provision of, the 1968 Convention or the 1971 Protocol are references to the Convention, Protocol or provision as amended by the Accession Convention, the 1982 Accession Convention and the 1989 Accession Convention; and

(b) any reference to a numbered Article without more is a reference—

    (i) to the Article so numbered of the 1968 Convention, in so far as the provision applies in relation to that Convention, and

    (ii) to the Article so numbered of the Lugano Convention, in so far as the provision applies in relation to that Convention,

and any reference to a sub-division of a numbered Article shall be construed accordingly.

(3) In this Act—

"Contracting State", without more, in any provision means—

    (a) in the application of the provision in relation to the Brussels Conventions, a Brussels Contracting State; and

    (b) in the application of the provision in relation to the Lugano Convention, a Lugano Contracting State;

"Brussels Contracting State" means a state which is one of the original parties to the 1968 Convention or one of the parties acceding to that Convention under the Accession Convention, or under the 1982 Accession Convention, or under the 1989 Accession Convention, but only with respect to any territory—

    (a) to which the Brussels Conventions apply; and

    (b) which is excluded from the scope of the Regulation pursuant to Article 299 of the Treaty establishing the European Community;

"Lugano Contracting State" means one of the original parties to the Lugano Convention, that is to say—

Austria, Belgium, Denmark, Finland, France, the Federal Republic of Germany, the Hellenic Republic, Iceland, the Republic of Ireland, Italy, Luxembourg, the Netherlands, Norway, Portugal, Spain, Sweden, Switzerland and the United Kingdom, being a State in relation to which that Convention has taken effect in accordance with paragraph 3 or 4 of Article 61.

"Regulation State" in any provision, in the application of that provision in relation to the Regulation, means a Member State.

(4) Any question arising as to whether it is the Regulation, any of the Brussels Conventions, or the Lugano Convention which applies in the circumstances of a particular case shall be determined as follows—

    (a) in accordance with Article 54B of the Lugano Convention (which determines the relationship between the Brussels Convention and the Lugano Convention); and

    (b) in accordance with Article 68 of the Regulation (which

Paragraph numbers marked with a "+" can be found online and on CD.

determines the relationship between the Brussels Convention and the Regulation).

5-10 *Note* —Amended by the Civil Jurisdiction and Judgments Act 1982 (Amendment) Order 1989 (SI 1989/1346); the Civil Jurisdiction and Judgments Act 1982 (Amendment) Order 1990 (SI 1990/2591); the Civil Jurisdiction and Judgments Act 1991 s.2; the Civil Jurisdiction and Judgments Order 2001 (SI 2001/3929), Sch.2, para.1(c) and the Civil Jurisdiction and Judgments Regulations 2007 (SI 2007/1655).

The Conventions to have the force of law

5-11 **2.**—(1) The Brussels Conventions shall have the force of law in the United Kingdom, and judicial notice shall be taken of them.

(2) For convenience of reference there are set out in Schedules 1, 2, 3, 3A and 3B respectively the English texts of—

(a) the 1968 Convention as amended by Titles II and III of the Accession Convention, by Titles II and III of the 1982 Accession Convention and by Titles II and III of, and Annex I(d) to, the 1989 Accession Convention;

(b) the 1971 Protocol as amended by Title IV of the Accession Convention, by Title IV of the 1982 Accession Convention and by Title IV of the 1989 Accession Convention;

(c) Titles V and VI of the Accession Convention (transitional and final provisions) as amended by Title V of the 1989 Accession Convention;

(d) Titles V and VI of the 1982 Accession Convention (transitional and final provisions); and

(e) Titles VI and VII of the 1989 Accession Convention (transitional and final provisions),

(f) Titles V and VI of the 1996 Accession Convention (transitional and final provisions),

being texts prepared from the authentic English texts referred to in Articles 37 and 41 of the Accession Convention, in Article 17 of the 1982 Accession Convention and in Article 34 of the 1989 Accession Convention.

5-12 *Note* —Amended by the Civil Jurisdiction and Judgments Act 1982 (Amendment) Order 1989 (SI 1989/1346); the Civil Jurisdiction and Judgments Act 1982 (Amendment) Order 1990 (SI 1990/2591); the Civil Jurisdiction and Judgments Act 1991 s.3, Sch.2, para.1; and by the Civil Jurisdiction and Judgments Act 1982 (Amendment) Order 2000 (SI 2000/1824), art.6(e).

"1968 Convention ... 1971 Protocol"

5-13 This Convention, i.e. the Brussels Convention, and the attached 1971 Protocol are set out in, respectively, Sch.1 and 2 of the Act.

Interpretation of the Conventions

5-14 **3.**—(1) Any question as to the meaning or effect of any provision of the Brussels Convention shall, if not referred to the European Court in accordance with the 1971 Protocol, be determined in accordance with the principles laid down by and any relevant decision of the European Court.

Paragraph numbers marked with a "+" can be found online and on CD.

(2) Judicial notice shall be taken of any decision of, or expression of opinion by, the European Court on any such question.

(3) Without prejudice to the generality of subsection (1), the following reports (which are reproduced in the Official Journal of the Communities), namely—

    (a) the reports by Mr P. Jenard on the 1968 Convention and the 1971 Protocol; and

    (b) the report by Professor Peter Schlosser on the Accession Convention; and

    (c) the report by Professor Demetrios I. Evrigenis and Professor K. D. Kerameus on the 1982 Accession Convention; and

    (d) the report by Mr. Martino de Almeida Cruz, Mr. Manuel Desantes Real and Mr P. Jenard on the 1989 Accession Convention,

may be considered in ascertaining the meaning or effect of any provision of the Conventions and shall be given such weight as is appropriate in the circumstances.

Note—Amended by the Civil Jurisdiction and Judgments Act 1982 (Amendment) Order 1989 (SI 1989/1346); the Civil Jurisdiction and Judgments Act 1982 (Amendment) Order 1990 (SI 1990/2591); and the Civil Jurisdiction and Judgments Act 1991 s.3, Sch.2, para.1.   **5–15**

The Lugano Convention to have the force of law

3A.—(1) The Lugano Convention shall have the force of law in the United Kingdom and judicial notice shall be taken of it.   **5–16**

(2) For convenience of reference there is set out in Schedule 3C the English text of the Lugano Convention as amended on the accession of Poland to that Convention.

Note—Added by the Civil Jurisdiction and Judgments Act 1991 s.I(1). Amended by the Civil Jurisdiction and Judgments Act 1982 (Amendment) Order (SI 2000/1824), art.11.   **5–17**

"Lugano Convention"

The text of this Convention is set out in Sch.3C of the Act as amended; it is not included in this Section of *The Supreme Court Practice*. The Lugano Convention is made between the Member States of the EC and those of the European Free Trade Association (EFTA). It is very closely modelled on the Brussels Convention. The amendments to the 1982 Act required to accommodate the Lugano Convention were introduced by the Civil Jurisdiction and Judgments Act 1991. See further, para.5–194 below.   **5–18**

Interpretation of the Lugano Convention

3B.—(1) In determining any question as to the meaning or effect of a provision of the Lugano Convention, a court in the United Kingdom shall, in accordance with Protocol No.2 to that Convention, take account of any principles laid down in any relevant decision delivered by a court of any other Lugano Contracting State concerning provisions of the Convention.   **5–19**

(2) Without prejudice to any practice of the courts as to the matters which may be considered apart from this section, the report of the Lugano Convention by Mr P. Jenard and Mr G. Möller (which is

Paragraph numbers marked with a "+" can be found online and on CD.

reproduced in the Official Journal of the Communities of 28th July 1990) may be considered in ascertaining the meaning or effect of any provision of the Convention and shall be given such weight as is appropriate in the circumstances.

5–20 *Note* —Added by the Civil Jurisdiction and Judgments Act 1991 s.1(1). For Jenard and Möller report, see [1990] O.J. C189/07.

* * * *

OTHER SUPPLEMENTARY PROVISIONS

Allocation within UK of jurisdiction with respect to trusts and consumer contracts

5–21 **10.**—(1) The provisions of this section have effect for the purpose of allocating within the United Kingdom jurisdiction in certain proceedings in respect of which the 1968 Convention or the Lugano Convention confers jurisdiction on the courts of the United Kingdom generally and to which section 16 does not apply.

(2) Any proceedings which by virtue of Article 5(6) (trusts) are brought in the United Kingdom shall be brought in the courts of the part of the United Kingdom in which the trust is domiciled.

(3) Any proceedings which by virtue of the first paragraph of Article 14 (consumer contracts) are brought in the United Kingdom by a consumer on the ground that he is himself domiciled there shall be brought in the courts of the part of the United Kingdom in which he is domiciled.

5–22 *Note* —Amended by the Civil Jurisdiction and Judgments Act 1991 s.3, Sch.2.

"To which section 16 does not apply"

5–23 Section 16 deals with the allocation within the UK of jurisdiction in certain civil proceedings. The provisions set out in Sch.4 to the Act (which contains a modified version of Title II of the Brussels Convention) have effect for determining, for each part of the UK, whether the courts of law of that part have jurisdiction.

* * * *

PART IV

MISCELLANEOUS PROVISIONS

PROVISIONS RELATING TO JURISDICTION

Interim relief and protective measures in cases of doubtful jurisdiction

5–24 **24.**—(1) Any power of a court in England and Wales or Northern Ireland to grant interim relief pending trial or pending the determination of an appeal shall extend to a case where—

(a) the issue to be tried, or which is the subject of the ap-

Paragraph numbers marked with a "+" can be found online and on CD.

peal, relates to the jurisdiction of the court to entertain the proceedings;

    (b) the proceedings involve the reference of any matter to the European Court under the 1971 Protocol or

    (c) the proceedings involve a reference of any matter relating to the Regulation to the European Court under Article 68 of the Treaty establishing the European Community.

(2) [*Applies to Scotland*]

(3) Subsections (1) and (2) shall not be construed as restricting any power to grant interim relief or protective measures which a court may have apart from this section.

5–25

Note —Subsection (1)(c) was added by the Civil Jurisdiction and Judgments Order 2001 (SI 2001/3929), Sch.2, para.9(b).

"The issue to be tried ... relates to the jurisdiction of the court"

5–26

For example, where the issue is whether the court, or a court in a Contracting State, has jurisdiction under the Brussels Convention. See also art.24 of the Brussels Convention.

Interim relief in England and Wales and Northern Ireland in the absence of substantive proceedings

25.—(1) The High Court in England and Wales or Northern Ireland shall have power to grant interim relief where—

5–27

    (a) proceedings have been or are to be commenced in a Brussels or Lugano Contracting State or a Regulation State other than the United Kingdom or in a part of the United Kingdom other than that in which the High Court in question exercises jurisdiction; and

    (b) they are or will be proceedings whose subject-matter is within the scope of the Regulation as determined by Article 1 of the Regulation (whether or not the Regulation has effect in relation to the proceedings).

(2) On an application for any interim relief under subsection (1) the court may refuse to grant that relief if, in the opinion of the court, the fact that the court has no jurisdiction apart from this section in relation to the subject- matter of the proceedings in question makes it inexpedient for the court to grant it.

(3) Her Majesty may by Order in Council extend the power to grant interim relief conferred by subsection (1) so as to make it exercisable in relation to proceedings of any of the following descriptions, namely—

    (a) proceedings commenced or to be commenced otherwise than in a Brussels or Lugano Contracting State or Regulation State;

    (b) proceedings whose subject-matter is not within the scope of the Regulation as determined by Article 1 of the Regulation;

    (c) [...]

(4) An Order in Council under subsection (3)—

Paragraph numbers marked with a "+" can be found online and on CD.

(a) may confer power to grant only specified descriptions of interim relief;

(b) may make different provision for different classes of proceedings, for proceedings pending in different countries or courts outside the United Kingdom or in different parts of the United Kingdom, and for other different circumstances; and

(c) may impose conditions or restrictions on the exercise of any power conferred by the order.

(5) [...]

(6) Any Order in Council under subsection (3) shall be subject to annulment in pursuance of a resolution of either House of Parliament.

(7) In this section "interim relief", in relation to the High Court in England and Wales or Northern Ireland, means interim relief of any kind which that court has power to grant in proceedings relating to matters within its jurisdiction, other than—

(a) a warrant for the arrest of property; or

(b) provision for obtaining evidence.

5–28   *Note* — Subsections (1)(a) and (3)(a) amended by the Civil Jurisdiction and Judgments Act 1991 s.3, Sch.2, para.12(a); subs.(1)(b) amended by para.12. Subss.(3)(c) and (5) repealed by the Arbitration Act 1996. The power to grant interim relief under subs.(1) has been extended by the Civil Jurisdiction and Judgments Act 1982 (Interim Relief) Order 1997 (see para.5–161 below). Subsections (1)(a), (b) and (3)(b) were further amended and by the Civil Jurisdiction and Judgments Order (SI 2001/3929), Sch.2, para.10(b)(ii).

Security in Admiralty proceedings in England and Wales or Northern Ireland in case of stay, etc.

5–29   **26.**—(1) Where in England and Wales or Northern Ireland a court stays or dismisses Admiralty proceedings on the ground that the dispute in question should be submitted to the determination of the courts of another part of the United Kingdom or of an overseas country, the court may, if in those proceedings property has been arrested or bail or other security has been given to prevent or obtain release from arrest—

(a) order that the property arrested be retained as security for the satisfaction of any award or judgment which—

(i) is given in respect of the dispute in the legal proceedings in favour of which those proceedings are stayed or dismissed; and

(ii) is enforceable in England and Wales or, as the case may be, in Northern Ireland, or

(b) order that the stay or dismissal of those proceedings be conditional on the provision of equivalent security for the satisfaction of any such award or judgment.

(2) Where the court makes an order under subsection (1), it may attach such conditions to the order as it thinks fit, in particular conditions with respect to the institution or prosecution of the relevant legal proceedings.

Paragraph numbers marked with a "+" can be found online and on CD.

(3) Subject to any provision made by rules of court and to any necessary modifications, the same law and practice shall apply in relation to property retained in pursuance of an order made by a court under subsection (1) as would apply if it were held for the purposes of proceedings in that court.

Note —Amended by the Arbitration Act 1996.　　　　　　　　**5–30**

* * * * *

DOMICILE

Proceedings in England and Wales or Northern Ireland for torts to immovable property

30.—(1) The jurisdiction of any court in England and Wales or **5–31** Northern Ireland to entertain proceedings for trespass to, or any other tort affecting, immovable property shall extend to cases in which the property in question is situated outside that part of the United Kingdom unless the proceedings are principally concerned with a question of the title, or the right to possession of, that property.

(2) Subsection (1) has effect subject to the 1968 Convention and the Lugano Convention and the Regulation and to the provisions set out in Schedule 4.

Note —Amended by the Civil Jurisdiction and Judgments Act 1991 s.3, Sch.2, **5–32** para.13; and by the Civil Jurisdiction and Judgments Order (SI 2001/3929), Sch.2, para.13.

* * * *

PART V

SUPPLEMENTARY AND GENERAL PROVISIONS

Note —Under the Brussels Convention, domicile rather than presence (or national- **5–33** ity), is the key to the allocation of jurisdiction among the courts of the Contracting States, see Arts 2 and 52, paras 5–50 and 5–122, below. Consequently, this Part of the Act, *inter alia*, enacts particular rules governing domicile.

Domicile of individuals

41.—(1) Subject to Article 52 (which contains provisions for **5–34** determining whether a party is domiciled in a Contracting State), the following provisions of this section determine, for the purposes of the 1968 Convention the Lugano Convention and this Act, whether an individual is domiciled in the United Kingdom or in a particular part of, or place in, the United Kingdom or in a state other than a Contracting State.

(2) An individual is domiciled in the United Kingdom if and only if—

　(a) he is resident in the United Kingdom; and

　(b) the nature and circumstances of his residence indicate

Paragraph numbers marked with a "+" can be found online and on CD.

that he has a substantial connection with the United
Kingdom.

(3) Subject to subsection (5), an individual is domiciled in a particular part of the United Kingdom if and only if—

(a) he is resident in that part; and

(b) the nature and circumstances of his residence indicate
that he has a substantial connection with that part.

(4) An individual is domiciled in a particular place in the United
Kingdom if and only if he—

(a) is domiciled in the part of the United Kingdom in which
that place is situated; and

(b) is resident in that place.

(5) An individual who is domiciled in the United Kingdom but in
whose case the requirements of subsection (3)(b) are not satisfied in
relation to any particular part of the United Kingdom shall be treated
as domiciled in the part of the United Kingdom in which he is
resident.

(6) In the case of an individual who—

(a) is resident in the United Kingdom, or in a particular
part of the United Kingdom; and

(b) has been so resident for the last three months or more,
the requirements of subsection (2)(b) or, as the case may
be, subsection (3)(b) shall be presumed to be fulfilled unless the contrary is proved.

(7) An individual is domiciled in a state other than a Contracting
State if and only if—

(a) he is resident in that state; and

(b) the nature and circumstances of his residence indicate
that he has a substantial connection with that state.

5-35 *Note* — Subsection(1) amended by the Civil Jurisdiction and Judgments Act 1991
s.3, Sch.2, para.16.

Domicile and seat of corporation or association

5-36 **42.**—(1) For the purposes of this Act the seat of a corporation or
association (as determined by this section) shall be treated as its
domicile.

(2) The following provisions of this section determine where a
corporation or association has its seat—

(a) for the purpose of Article 53 (which for the purposes of
the 1968 Convention or, as the case may be, the Lugano
Convention equates the domicile of such a body with its
seat); and

(b) for the purposes of this Act other than the provisions
mentioned in section 43(1)(b) and (c).

(3) A corporation or association has its seat in the United
Kingdom if and only if—

(a) it was incorporated or formed under the law of a part of
the United Kingdom and has its registered office or some
other official address in the United Kingdom; or

Paragraph numbers marked with a "+" can be found online and on CD.

(b) its central management and control is exercised in the United Kingdom.

(4) A corporation or association has its seat in a particular part of the United Kingdom if and only if it has its seat in the United Kingdom and—

(a) it has its registered office or some other official address in that part; or

(b) its central management and control is exercised in that part; or

(c) it has a place of business in that part.

(5) A corporation or association has its seat in a particular place in the United Kingdom if and only if it has its seat in the part of the United Kingdom in which that place is situated and—

(a) it has its registered office or some other official address in that place; or

(b) its central management and control is exercised in that place; or

(c) it has a place of business in that place.

(6) Subject to subsection (7), a corporation or association has its seat in a state other than the United Kingdom if and only if—

(a) it was incorporated or formed under the law of that state and has its registered office or some other official address there; or

(b) its central management and control is exercised in that state.

(7) A corporation or association shall not be regarded as having its seat in a Contracting State other than the United Kingdom if it is shown that the courts of that state would not regard it as having its seat there.

(8) In this section—

"business" includes any activity carried on by a corporation or association, and "place of business" shall be construed accordingly; "official address", in relation to a corporation or association, means an address which it is required by law to register, notify or maintain for the purpose of receiving notices or other communications.

Note — Subsection(2)(a) amended by the Civil Jurisdiction and Judgments Act 1991 **5–37** s.3 and Sch.2, para.17.

Seat of corporation or association for purposes of Article 16(2) and related provisions

43.—(1) The following provisions of this section determine where a **5–38** corporation or association has its seat for the purposes of—

(a) Article 16(2) of the 1968 Convention or of the Lugano Convention (which confers exclusive jurisdiction over proceedings relating to the formation or dissolution of such bodies, or to the decisions of their organs);

(b) Articles 5A and 16(2); in Schedule 4 and

(c) and Rules 2(12), 4(1)(b) in Schedule 8.

Paragraph numbers marked with a "+" can be found online and on CD.

EUROPE

(2) A corporation or association has its seat in the United Kingdom if and only if—

    (a) it was incorporated or formed under the law of a part of the United Kingdom; or

    (b) its central management and control is exercised in the United Kingdom.

(3) A corporation or association has its seat in a particular part of the United Kingdom if and only if it has its seat in the United Kingdom and—

    (a) subject to subsection (5), it was incorporated or formed under the law of that part; or

    (b) being incorporated or formed under the law of a state other than the United Kingdom, its central management and control is exercised in that part.

(4) A corporation or association has its seat in a particular place in Scotland if and only if it has its seat in Scotland and—

    (a) it has its registered office or some other official address in that place; or

    (b) it has no registered office or other official address in Scotland, but its central management and control is exercised in that place.

(5) A corporation or association incorporated or formed under—

    (a) an enactment forming part of the law of more than one part of the United Kingdom; or

    (b) an instrument having effect in the domestic law of more than one part of the United Kingdom,

shall, if it has a registered office, be taken to have its seat in the part of the United Kingdom in which that office is situated, and not in any other part of the United Kingdom.

(6) Subject to subsection (7), a corporation or association has its seat in a Contracting State other than the United Kingdom if and only if—

    (a) it was incorporated or formed under the law of that state; or

    (b) its central management and control is exercised in that state.

(7) A corporation or association shall not be regarded as having its seat in a Contracting State other than the United Kingdom if—

    (a) it has its seat in the United Kingdom by virtue of subsection 2(a); or

    (b) it is shown that the courts of that other state would not regard it for the purposes of Article 16(2) as having its seat there.

(8) In this section "official address" has the same meaning as in section 42.

5–39   *Note* — Subsection(1)(a) amended by the Civil Jurisdiction and Judgments Act 1991 s.3 and Sch.2, para.18.

Persons deemed to be domiciled in the United Kingdom for certain purposes

5–40   44.—(1) This section applies to—

Paragraph numbers marked with a "+" can be found online and on CD.

(a) proceedings within Section 3 of Title II of the 1968 Convention or Section 3 of Title II of the Lugano Convention (insurance contracts), and

(b) proceedings within Section 4 of Title II of either of those Conventions (consumer contracts).

(2) A person who, for the purposes of proceedings to which this section applies arising out of the operations of a branch, agency or other establishment in the United Kingdom, is deemed for the purposes of the 1968 Convention or, as the case may be, of the Lugano Convention to be domiciled in the United Kingdom by virtue of—

(a) Article 8, second paragraph (insurers); or

(b) Article 13, second paragraph (suppliers of goods, services or credit to consumers),

shall, for the purposes of those proceedings, be treated for the purposes of this Act as so domiciled and as domiciled in the part of the United Kingdom in which the branch, agency or establishment in question is situated.

Note — Subsection(1) amended by the Civil Jurisdiction and Judgments Act 1991 s.3 and Sch.2, para.19. **5–41**

Domicile of trusts

45.—(1) The following provisions of this section determine, for the purposes of the 1968 Convention the Lugano Convention and this Act, where a trust is domiciled. **5–42**

(2) A trust is domiciled in the United Kingdom if and only if it is by virtue of subsection (3) domiciled in a part of the United Kingdom.

(3) A trust is domiciled in a part of the United Kingdom if and only if the system of law of that part is the system of law with which the trust has its closest and most real connection.

Note — Subsection (1) amended by the Civil Jurisdiction and Judgments Act 1991 s.3 and Sch.2, para.20. **5–43**

Domicile and seat of the Crown

46.—(1) For the purposes of this Act the seat of the Crown (as determined by this section) shall be treated as its domicile. **5–44**

(2) The following provisions of this section determine where the Crown has its seat—

(a) for the purposes of the 1968 Convention and the Lugano Convention (in each of which Article 53 equates the domicile of a legal person with its seat); and

(b) for the purposes of this Act.

(3) Subject to the provisions of any Order in Council for the time being in force under subsection (4)—

(a) the Crown in right of Her Majesty's government in the United Kingdom has its seat in every part of, and every place in, the United Kingdom; and

(aa) the Crown in right of the Scottish Administration has its seat in, and in every place in, Scotland; and

Paragraph numbers marked with a "+" can be found online and on CD.

(b) the Crown in right of Her Majesty's government in Northern Ireland has its seat in, and in every place in, Northern Ireland.

(4) Her Majesty may by Order in Council provide that, in the case of proceedings of any specified description against the Crown in right of Her Majesty's government in the United Kingdom, the Crown shall be treated for the purposes of the 1968 Convention the Lugano Convention and this Act as having its seat in, and in every place in, a specified part of the United Kingdom and not in any other part of the United Kingdom.

(5) An Order in Council under subsection (4) may frame a description proceedings in any way, and in particular may do so by reference to the government department or officer of the Crown against which or against whom they fall to be instituted.

(6) Any Order in Council made under this section shall be subject to annulment in pursuance of a resolution of either House of Parliament.

(7) Nothing in this section applies to the Crown otherwise than in right of Her Majesty's government in the United Kingdom, the Scottish Administration or Her Majesty's government in Northern Ireland.

5–45   *Note* — Subsections (2)(a) & (4) amended by the Civil Jurisdiction and Judgments Act 1991 s.3 and Sch.2, para.21. Subsections (3) and (7) are amended by the Scotland Act 1998 (c.46) s.125, Sch.8, para.18.

* * * *

Saving for powers to stay, sist, strike out or dismiss proceedings

5–46   **49.** Nothing in this Act shall prevent any court in the United Kingdom from staying, sisting, striking out or dismissing any proceedings before it, on the ground of forum non conveniens or otherwise, where to do so is not inconsistent with the 1968 Convention or, as the case may be, the Lugano Convention.

5–47   *Note* —Amended by the Civil Jurisdiction and Judgments Act 1991 s.3, Sch.2, para.24.

"Staying ... any proceedings"

5–48   This section should be read in conjunction with the Supreme Court Act 1981 s.49(3), see paras 9A–168, 9A–176, 9A–177.

🖰   **For Schs 1, 2 and 4 to the Civil Jurisdiction and Judgments Act 1982 (see Arrangement) plus any related commentary see paragraphs 5–49+ to 5–160+ on White Book on Westlaw UK or the Civil Procedure CD.**

Civil Jurisdiction and Judgments Act 1982 (Interim Relief) Order 1997

(S.I. 1997 No. 302)

5–161   **1.** This Order may be cited as the Civil Jurisdiction and Judgments Act 1982 (Interim Relief) Order 1997 and shall come into force on 1st April 1997.

Paragraph numbers marked with a "+" can be found online and on CD.

2. The High Court in England and Wales or Northern Ireland **5–162** shall have power to grant interim relief under section 25(1) of the Civil Jurisdiction and Judgments Act 1982 in relation to proceedings of the following descriptions, namely—

(a) proceedings commenced or to be commenced otherwise than in a Brussels or Lugano Contracting State or Regulation State;

(b) proceedings whose subject-matter is not within the scope of the Regulation as determined by Article 1 of the Regulation.

Civil Jurisdiction and Judgments Act 1982 (Gibraltar) Order 1997

(S.I. 1997 No. 2602)

1. This Order may be cited as the Civil Jurisdiction and Judgments **5–163** Act 1982 (Gibraltar) Order 1997 and shall come into force on 1st February 1998.

2.

(a) Provision corresponding to that made by the provisions of the 1968 Convention specified in paragraph (b) shall apply, so far as relevant, for the purpose of regulating, as between the United Kingdom and Gibraltar, the jurisdiction of courts and the recognition and enforcement of judgments.

(b) Those provisions are—

(i) Titles I–V;

(ii) Articles 54 and 57; and

(iii) Article 65 and the Protocol referred to therein.

3. For the purpose stated in Article 2 above the United Kingdom and Gibraltar shall be treated as if each were a separate Contracting State and the relevant provisions of the 1968 Convention and the 1982 Act shall be construed accordingly.

4. In determining any question as to the meaning or effect of the provision (or any part of the provision) made by Article 2 above—

(a) regard shall be had to any relevant principles laid down by the European Court in connection with Title II of the 1968 Convention and to any relevant decision of that court as to the meaning or effect of any provision of that Title; and

(b) without prejudice to the generality of paragraph (a), the reports mentioned in section 3(3) of the 1982 Act may be considered and shall, so far as relevant, be given such weight as is appropriate in the circumstances.

5. A judgment shall not be recognised under this Order if, had it been given in another Contracting State, recognition would be refused by virtue of an agreement to which Article 59 of the 1968 Convention applies.

6. This Order extends to Northern Ireland.

[THE NEXT PARAGRAPH IS 5–165.]

Paragraph numbers marked with a "+" can be found online and on CD.

Civil Jurisdiction and Judgments Act 1991

5–165   (1991 c.12)

ARRANGEMENT OF SECTIONS

Implementation and interpretation of the Lugano Convention

5–166   **1.**—(1) The Civil Jurisdiction and Judgments Act 1982 (in this Act referred to as "the 1982 Act") shall have effect with the insertion of the following after section 3—

The Lugano Convention to have the force of law

"**3A.**—(1) The Lugano Convention shall have the force of law in the United Kingdom, and judicial notice shall be taken of it.

(2) For convenience of reference there is set out in Schedule 3C the English text of the Lugano Convention.

Interpretation of the Lugano Convention

3B.—(1) In determining any question as to the meaning or effect of a provision of the Lugano Convention, a court in the United Kingdom shall, in accordance with Protocol No. 2 to that Convention, take account of any principles laid down in any relevant decision delivered by a court of any other Lugano Contracting State concerning provisions of the Convention.

(2) Without prejudice to any practice of the courts as to the matters which may be considered apart from this section, the report on the Lugano Convention by Mr P. Jenard and Mr G. Möller (which is reproduced in the Official Journal of the Communities of 28th July 1990) may be considered in ascertaining the meaning or effect of any provision of the Convention and shall be given such weight as is appropriate in the circumstances."

(2) In section 9 of that Act, after subsection (1) (which, as amended, will govern the relationship between other conventions and the 1968 and Lugano Conventions) there shall be inserted—

"(1A) Any question arising as to whether it is the Lugano Convention or any of the Brussels Conventions which applies in the circumstances of a particular case falls to be determined in accordance with the provisions of Article 54B of the Lugano Convention."

(3) After Schedule 3B to that Act there shall be inserted the Schedule 3C set out in Schedule 1 to this Act.

Interpretation of the 1982 Act

5–167   **2.**—(1) Section 1 of the 1982 Act (interpretation of references to the Conventions and Contracting States) shall be amended in accordance with the following provisions of this section.

(2) In subsection (1), in the definition of "the Conventions", for

Paragraph numbers marked with a "+" can be found online and on CD.

the words "the Conventions" there shall be substituted the words "the Brussels Conventions".

(3) At the end of that subsection there shall be added—

"the Lugano Convention" means the Convention on jurisdiction and the enforcement of judgments in civil and commercial matters (including the Protocols annexed to that Convention) opened for signature at Lugano on 16th September 1988 and signed by the United Kingdom on 18th September 1989."

(4) In subsection (2), for paragraph (b) (citation of Articles) there shall be substituted—

"(b) any reference in any provision to a numbered Article without more is a reference—

(i) to the Article so numbered of the 1968 Convention, in so far as the provision applies in relation to that Convention, and

(ii) to the Article so numbered of the Lugano Convention, in so far as the provision applies in relation to that Convention,

and any reference to a sub-division of a numbered Article shall be construed accordingly."

(5) In subsection (3) (definition of "Contracting State") for the words "In this Act "Contracting State" means—" there shall be substituted the words—

"In this Act—

"Contracting State", without more, in any provision means—

(a) in the application of the provision in relation to the Brussels Conventions, a Brussels Contracting State; and

(b) in the application of the provision in relation to the Lugano Convention, a Lugano Contracting State;

"Brussels Contracting State" means—".

(6) At the end of that subsection there shall be added—

""Lugano Contracting State" means one of the original parties to the Lugano Convention, that is to say—Austria, Belgium, Denmark, Finland, France, the Republic of Germany, the Hellenic Republic, Iceland, the Republic of Ireland, Italy, Luxembourg, the Netherlands, Norway, Portugal, Spain, Sweden, Switzerland and the United Kingdom, being a State in relation to which the Convention has taken effect in accordance with paragraph 3 or 4 of Article 61."

Other amendments of the 1982 Act

3. The 1982 Act shall have effect with the amendments specified in **5–168** Schedule 2 to this Act, which are either consequential on the amendments made by sections 1 and 2 above or otherwise for the purpose of implementing the Lugano Convention.

Application to the Crown

4. The amendments of the 1982 Act made by this Act bind the **5–169** Crown in accordance with the provisions of section 51 of that Act.

Paragraph numbers marked with a "+" can be found online and on CD.

Short title, interpretation, commencement and extent

5–170   **5.**—(1) This Act may be cited as the Civil Jurisdiction and Judgments Act 1991.

(2) In this Act—

"the 1982 Act" means the Civil Juridiction and Judgments Act 1982;

"the Lugano Convention" has the same meaning as it has in the 1982 Act by virtue of section 2(3) above.

(3) This Act shall come into force on such day as the Lord Chancellor and the Lord Advocate may apopint in an order made by statutory instrument.

(4) This Act extends to Northern Ireland.

For Schs 1 and 2 to the Civil Jurisdiction and Judgments Act 1991 (see Arrangement) plus any related commentary see paragraphs 5–171+ to 5–193+ on White Book on Westlaw UK or the Civil Procedure CD.

The Civil Jurisdiction and Judgments (Authentic Instruments and Court Settlements) Order 2001

(S.I. 2001 No. 3928)

5–194   **1.**—(1) This Order may be cited as the Civil Jurisdiction and Judgments (Authentic Instruments and Court Settlements) Order 2001 and shall come into force on 1st March 2002.

(2) In this Order—

"the Act" means the Civil Jurisdiction and Judgments Act 1982[1];

"the Regulation" means Council Regulation (EC) No. 44/2001 of 22nd December 2000 on jurisdiction and the recognition and enforcement of judgments in civil and commercial matters, as amended from time to time and as applied by the Agreement made on 19th October 2005 between the European Community and the Kingdom of Denmark on jurisdiction and the recognition and enforcement of judgments in civil and commercial matters;

"Regulation State", in any provision, in the application of that provision in relation to the Regulation, means a Member State;

"the 2001 Order" means the Civil Jurisdiction and Judgments Order 2001.

(3) In this Order—

(a) references to authentic instruments and court settlements are references to those instruments and settlements referred to in Chapter IV of the Regulation; and

(b) references to judgments and maintenance orders are references to judgments and maintenance orders to which the Regulation applies.

5–195   *Note* — Amended by the Civil Jurisdiction and Judgments Regulations 2007 (SI 2007/1655).

---

[1] As amended by the Civil Jurisdiction and Judgments Act 1991 (c.12) and by SI 1989/1346, SI 1990/2591, SI 1993/603 and SI 2000/1824.

Paragraph numbers marked with a "+" can be found online and on CD.

Article 2

2.—(1) Subject to the modifications specified in paragraphs (2) **5–196**
and (3), paragraphs 1 to 6 of Schedule 1 to the 2001 Order shall
apply, as appropriate, to authentic instruments and court settlements which—

> (a) do not concern maintenance as if they were judgments,
> (b) concern maintenance as if they were maintenance orders.

(2) In the application of paragraph 2(2) of Schedule 1 to the 2001
Order to authentic instruments and court settlements, for the words
"as if the judgment had been originally given" there shall be
substituted "as if it was a judgment which had been originally given".

(3) In the application of paragraph 3(3) of Schedule 1 to the 2001
Order to authentic instruments and court settlements, for the words
"as if the order had been originally made" there shall be substituted
the words "as if it was an order which had been originally made".

(4) Paragraph 8 of Schedule 1 to the 2001 Order shall apply to
authentic instruments as if they were judgments and in its application—

> (a) for sub-paragraph (1)(b) there shall be substituted the
> following—
>
> "(b) a certificate obtained in accordance with Article 57
> and Annex VI shall be evidence, and in Scotland suf-
> ficient evidence, that the authentic instrument is en-
> forceable in the Regulation State of origin."

; and

> (b) for sub-paragraph (2) there shall be substituted the fol-
> lowing—

"(2) A document purporting to be a copy of an authentic instrument drawn up or registered, and enforceable, in a Regulation
State other than the United Kingdom is duly authenticated for
the purposes of this paragraph if it purports to be certified to be a
true copy of such an instrument by a person duly authorised in
that Regulation State to do so.".

(5) Paragraph 8 of Schedule 1 to the 2001 Order shall apply to
court settlements as if they were judgments and in its application for
"Article 54" there shall be substituted "Article 58".

3. The disapplication of section 18 of the Act (enforcement of **5–197**
United Kingdom judgments in other parts of the United Kingdom)
by section 18(7) will extend to authentic instruments and court
settlements enforceable in a Regulation State outside the United
Kingdom which will fall to be treated for the purposes of their
enforcement as judgments of a court of law in the United Kingdom
by virtue of registration under the Regulation.

4. Section 48[1] of the Act (matters for which rules of court may **5–198**
provide) will apply to authentic instruments and court settlements as
if they were judgments or maintenance orders, as appropriate, to
which the Regulation applies.

[THE NEXT PARAGRAPH IS 5–201.]

---

[1] Section 48 was amended by para.23 of Sch.2 to the Civil Jurisdiction and Judgments Act 1991 (c.12) and para.17 of Sch.2 of the Civil Jurisdiction and Judgments
Order 2001 (SI 2001/3929).

Paragraph numbers marked with a "+" can be found online and on CD.

The Civil Jurisdiction and Judgments Order 2001

(S.I. 2001 No. 3929)

Citation and commencement

5–201   **1.** This Order may be cited as the Civil Jurisdiction and Judgments Order 2001 and shall come into force—

(a) as to articles 1 and 2, paragraphs 1(a), 1(b)(ii) and 17 of Schedule 2 and, so far as it relates to those paragraphs, article 4, on 25th January 2002; and

(b) as to the remainder of this Order, on 1st March 2002.

Interpretation

5–202   **2.**—(1) In this Order—

"the Act" means the Civil Jurisdiction and Judgments Act 1982;

"the 2005 Agreement" means means the Agreement made on 19th October 2005 between the European Community and the Kingdom of Denmark on jurisdiction and the recognition and enforcement of judgments in civil and commercial matters;

"the Regulation" means Council Regulation (EC) No. 44/2001 of 22nd December 2000 on jurisdiction and the recognition and enforcement of judgments in civil and commercial matters, as amended from time to time and as applied by the 2005 Agreement;

"Regulation State" in any provision, in the application of that provision in relation to the Regulation, means a Member State.

(2) In Schedule 2 to this Order, a section, Part, Schedule or paragraph referred to by number alone is a reference to the section, Part, Schedule or paragraph so numbered in the Act.

5–203   *Note* —Amended by the Civil Jurisdiction and Judgments Regulations 2007 (SI 2007/1655) reg.3.

The Regulation

5–204   **3.** Schedule 1 to this Order (which applies certain provisions of the Act with modifications for the purposes of the Regulation) shall have effect.

The 2005 Agreement

5–205   **3A.** The Regulation shall have effect as regards Denmark in accordance with the 2005 Agreement.

5–206   *Note* —Inserted by the Civil Jurisdiction and Judgments Regulations 2007 (SI 2007/1655) reg.3.

Amendments to the Civil Jurisdiction and Judgments Act 1982

5–207   **4.** Schedule 2 to this Order (which makes amendments to the Act) shall have effect.

Consequential amendments

5–208   **5.** Schedule 3 to this Order (which makes consequential amendments) shall have effect.

Paragraph numbers marked with a "+" can be found online and on CD.

1682

Transitional provisions

6.—(1) Where proceedings are begun before 1st March 2002 in any part of the United Kingdom on the basis of jurisdiction determined in accordance with section 16 of, and Schedule 4 to, the Act, the proceedings may be continued as if the amendments made by paragraphs 3 and 4 of Schedule 2 to this Order had not been made and those amendments shall not apply in respect of any proceedings begun before that date.

5–209

(2) Where proceedings are begun before 1st March 2002 in any court in Scotland on the basis of jurisdiction determined in accordance with section 20 of, and Schedule 8 to, the Act, the proceedings may be continued as if the amendments made by paragraphs 6 and 7 of Schedule 2 to this Order had not been made and those amendments shall not apply in respect of any proceedings begun before that date.

For Sch.1 to the Civil Jurisdiction and Judgments Order 2001 plus any related commentary see paragraphs 5–210+ to 5–221+ on White Book on Westlaw UK or the Civil Procedure CD.

COUNCIL REGULATIONS

Council Regulation (EC) No.1393/2007 of 13 November 2007 on the service in the Member States of judicial and extrajudicial documents in civil or commercial matters (service of documents), and repealing Council Regulation (EC) No.1348/2000

Editorial note

The Council adopted the initial Regulation on the service in the Member States of judicial and extra-judicial documents in civil or commercial matters on May 29, 2000 ("the Service Regulation"). The Regulation was passed with the aim of improving efficiency and speed in judicial procedures in civil matters by providing for the transmission of judicial and extra-judicial documents by direct and rapid means by local bodies designated by Member States. The Regulation entered into force on May 31, 2001 and applies in civil and commercial matters where a judicial or extra-judicial document has to be transmitted from one Member State to another for service there (art.1(1)).

5–222

The Regulation has two aims. First, it seeks to establish an efficient system for service of proceedings through agencies to be designated by each of the Member States, although there is also provision for service through diplomatic and consular channels and also by post, subject to the consent of and/or conditions imposed by the receiving state. Secondly, the Regulation tries to achieve consistency in the determination of the effective date of service, by identifying the system of law which governs that question. Generally, the law of the sending state is effective where under that system, the proceedings have to be served within a particular time. Otherwise, the law of the receiving state governs.

Each Member State shall designate the public officers, authorities or other persons competent for the transmission of judicial or extra-judicial documents to be served in another Member State ("transmitting agencies") (art.2(1)) and shall designate the public offices, authorities or other persons competent for the receipt of such documents (art.2(2)) ("receiving agencies"). Each Member State shall also designate a central body responsible for the following: supplying information to the transmitting agencies; seeking solutions to any difficulties which may arise during transmission of documents for service; and forwarding requests for service to the competent receiving agency (art.3). Article 4(1) provides that documents shall be transmitted "as soon as possible".

As to service, the receiving agency shall itself serve the document or have it served, either in accordance with the law of the Member State addressed, or by a particular

Paragraph numbers marked with a "+" can be found online and on CD.

form requested by the transmitting agency, unless such a method is incompatible with the law of that Member State (art.7(1)). Article 8 lays down certain circumstances in which the receiving agency may refuse to accept the document to be served. Notwithstanding the provisions of the Service Regulation, each Member State is free to effect service of judicial documents directly by post to persons residing in another Member State, and may specify the conditions under which it will accept such service (art.14).

There are particular provisions stipulating that where a document has been transmitted for the purpose of service and a defendant has not appeared, judgment shall not be given until certain conditions have been established (art.19).

According to art.23 of the service Regulation, the Member States shall communicate to the European Commission information referred to in certain of the Articles. This information (with the exception of the information referred to in art.17(a)) has been published in the Official Journal (O.J. C151 p.4.) and to date two updates have been published (O.J. C202, p.10 and O.J. C282 p.2).

A manual which contains the information provided by Member States concerning the names and addresses of the receiving agencies, the geographical areas in which they have jurisdiction, the means of receipt of documents available to them and the languages that may be used for the completion of the standard form has been compiled and published by the European Commission. A glossary which lists the documents in all the official languages of the European Union which may be served under the service Regulation has also been compiled and published. Both of these documents are updated regularly and may be found at: *http://ec.europa.eu* [Accessed March 28, 2007].

The operation of the Service Regulation is complicated by the fact that individual Member States are able to opt out of the Regulation for a transitional and potentially renewable period of up to fiveyears, the need to designate particular agencies, and the need to establish whether the receiving state allows service by post. Nevertheless, the service Regulation is important because of its impact on the date when proceedings are effectively commenced, which in some instances can be dispositive in determining which state has jurisdiction in a particular case.

Given the uncertainty surrounding this present state of implementation of the Regulation in Member States, it would generally be prudent to check a proposed method of service in the manual and with local lawyers in the receiving state.

CHAPTER 1—GENERAL PROVISIONS

ARTICLE 1

Scope

5–223   1. This Regulation shall apply in civil and commercial matters where a judicial or extrajudicial document has to be transmitted from one Member State to another for service there. It shall not extend in particular to revenue, customs or administrative matters or to liability of the State for actions or omissions in the exercise of state authority (*acta iure imperii*).

2. This Regulation shall not apply where the address of the person to be served with the document is not known.

3. In this Regulation, the term 'Member State' shall mean the Member States with the exception of Denmark.

ARTICLE 2

Transmitting and receiving agencies

5–224   1. Each Member State shall designate the public officers, authorities or other persons, hereinafter referred to as 'transmitting agencies', competent for the transmission of judicial or extrajudicial documents to be served in another Member State.

Paragraph numbers marked with a "+" can be found online and on CD.

2. Each Member State shall designate the public officers, authorities or other persons, hereinafter referred to as 'receiving agencies', competent for the receipt of judicial or extrajudicial documents from another Member State.

3. A Member State may designate one transmitting agency and one receiving agency, or one agency to perform both functions. A federal State, a State in which several legal systems apply or a State with autonomous territorial units shall be free to designate more than one such agency. The designation shall have effect for a period of five years and may be renewed at five-year intervals.

4. Each Member State shall provide the Commission with the following information:

(a) the names and addresses of the receiving agencies referred to in paragraphs 2 and 3;

(b) the geographical areas in which they have jurisdiction;

(c) the means of receipt of documents available to them; and

(d) the languages that may be used for the completion of the standard form set out in Annex I.

Member States shall notify the Commission of any subsequent modification of such information.

ARTICLE 3

Central body

1. Each Member State shall designate a central body responsible **5–225** for:

(a) supplying information to the transmitting agencies;

(b) seeking solutions to any difficulties which may arise during transmission of documents for service;

(c) forwarding, in exceptional cases, at the request of a transmitting agency, a request for service to the competent receiving agency.

A federal State, a State in which several legal systems apply or a State with autonomous territorial units shall be free to designate more than one central body.

CHAPTER II—JUDICIAL DOCUMENTS

SECTION 1—TRANSMISSION AND SERVICE OF JUDICIAL DOCUMENTS

Article 4

Transmission of documents

1. Judicial documents shall be transmitted directly and as soon as **5–226** possible between the agencies designated pursuant to Article 2.

2. The transmission of documents, requests, confirmations, receipts, certificates and any other papers between transmitting agencies and receiving agencies may be carried out by any appropriate means, provided that the content of the document received is true and faithful to that of the document forwarded and that all information in it is easily legible.

3. The document to be transmitted shall be accompanied by a

Paragraph numbers marked with a "+" can be found online and on CD.

request drawn up using the standard form set out in Annex I. The form shall be completed in the official language of the Member State addressed or, if there are several official languages in that Member State, the official language or one of the official languages of the place where service is to be effected, or in another language which that Member State has indicated it can accept. Each Member State shall indicate the official language or languages of the institutions of the European Union other than its own which is or are acceptable to it for completion of the form.

4. The documents and all papers that are transmitted shall be exempted from legalisation or any equivalent formality.

5. When the transmitting agency wishes a copy of the document to be returned together with the certificate referred to in Article 10, it shall send the document in duplicate.

Article 5

Translation of documents

5–227   1. The applicant shall be advised by the transmitting agency to which he forwards the document for transmission that the addressee may refuse to accept it if it is not in one of the languages provided for in Article 8.

2. The applicant shall bear any costs of translation prior to the transmission of the document, without prejudice to any possible subsequent decision by the court or competent authority on liability for such costs.

Article 6

Receipt of documents by receiving agency

5–228   1. On receipt of a document, a receiving agency shall, as soon as possible and in any event within seven days of receipt, send a receipt to the transmitting agency by the swiftest possible means of transmission using the standard form set out in Annex I.

2. Where the request for service cannot be fulfilled on the basis of the information or documents transmitted, the receiving agency shall contact the transmitting agency by the swiftest possible means in order to secure the missing information or documents.

3. If the request for service is manifestly outside the scope of this Regulation or if non-compliance with the formal conditions required makes service impossible, the request and the documents transmitted shall be returned, on receipt, to the transmitting agency, together with the notice of return using the standard form set out in Annex I.

4. A receiving agency receiving a document for service but not having territorial jurisdiction to serve it shall forward it, as well as the request, to the receiving agency having territorial jurisdiction in the same Member State if the request complies with the conditions laid down in Article 4(3) and shall inform the transmitting agency accordingly using the standard form set out in Annex I. That receiving agency shall inform the transmitting agency when it receives the document, in the manner provided for in paragraph 1.

Paragraph numbers marked with a "+" can be found online and on CD.

Article 7

Service of documents

1. The receiving agency shall itself serve the document or have it **5–229**
served, either in accordance with the law of the Member State addressed or by a particular method requested by the transmitting
agency, unless that method is incompatible with the law of that
Member State.

2. The receiving agency shall take all necessary steps to effect the
service of the document as soon as possible, and in any event within
one month of receipt. If it has not been possible to effect service
within one month of receipt, the receiving agency shall:

(a) immediately inform the transmitting agency by means of the
certificate in the standard form set out in Annex I, which shall be
drawn up under the conditions referred to in Article 10(2); and

(b) continue to take all necessary steps to effect the service of the
document, unless indicated otherwise by the transmitting agency,
where service seems to be possible within a reasonable period of
time.

Article 8

Refusal to accept a document

1. The receiving agency shall inform the addressee, using the stan- **5–230**
dard form set out in Annex II, that he may refuse to accept the document to be served at the time of service or by returning the document to the receiving agency within one week if it is not written in,
or accompanied by a translation into, either of the following languages:

(a) a language which the addressee understands;
or

(b) the official language of the Member State addressed or, if
there are several official languages in that Member State, the official
language or one of the official languages of the place where service is
to be effected.

2. Where the receiving agency is informed that the addressee refuses to accept the document in accordance with paragraph 1, it shall
immediately inform the transmitting agency by means of the certificate provided for in Article 10 and return the request and the documents of which a translation is requested.

3. If the addressee has refused to accept the document pursuant to
paragraph 1, the service of the document can be remedied through
the service on the addressee in accordance with the provisions of this
Regulation of the document accompanied by a translation into a
language provided for in paragraph 1. In that case, the date of service of the document shall be the date on which the document accompanied by the translation is served in accordance with the law of
the Member State addressed. However, where according to the law
of a Member State, a document has to be served within a particular
period, the date to be taken into account with respect to the applicant shall be the date of the service of the initial document
determined pursuant to Article 9(2).

Paragraph numbers marked with a "+" can be found online and on CD.

4. Paragraphs 1, 2 and 3 shall also apply to the means of transmission and service of judicial documents provided for in Section 2.

5. For the purposes of paragraph 1, the diplomatic or consular agents, where service is effected in accordance with Article 13, or the authority or person, where service is effected in accordance with Article 14, shall inform the addressee that he may refuse to accept the document and that any document refused must be sent to those agents or to that authority or person respectively.

Article 9

Date of service

5–231   1. Without prejudice to Article 8, the date of service of a document pursuant to Article 7 shall be the date on which it is served in accordance with the law of the Member State addressed.

2. However, where according to the law of a Member State a document has to be served within a particular period, the date to be taken into account with respect to the applicant shall be that determined by the law of that Member State.

3. Paragraphs 1 and 2 shall also apply to the means of transmission and service of judicial documents provided for in Section 2.

Article 10

Certificate of service and copy of the document served

5–232   1. When the formalities concerning the service of the document have been completed, a certificate of completion of those formalities shall be drawn up in the standard form set out in Annex I and addressed to the transmitting agency, together with, where Article 4(5) applies, a copy of the document served.

2. The certificate shall be completed in the official language or one of the official languages of the Member State of origin or in another language which the Member State of origin has indicated that it can accept. Each Member State shall indicate the official language or languages of the institutions of the European Union other than its own which is or are acceptable to it for completion of the form.

Article 11

Costs of service

5–233   1. The service of judicial documents coming from a Member State shall not give rise to any payment or reimbursement of taxes or costs for services rendered by the Member State addressed.

2. However, the applicant shall pay or reimburse the costs occasioned by:

(a) recourse to a judicial officer or to a person competent under the law of the Member State addressed;

(b) the use of a particular method of service.

Costs occasioned by recourse to a judicial officer or to a person competent under the law of the Member State addressed shall correspond to a single fixed fee laid down by that Member State in advance which respects the principles of proportionality and nondiscrimination. Member States shall communicate such fixed fees to the Commission.

SECTION 2—OTHER MEANS OF TRANSMISSION AND SERVICE OF JUDICIAL DOCUMENTS

Article 12

Transmission by consular or diplomatic channels

Each Member State shall be free, in exceptional circumstances, **5–234** to use consular or diplomatic channels to forward judicial documents, for the purpose of service, to those agencies of another Member State which are designated pursuant to Articles 2 or 3.

Article 13

Service by diplomatic or consular agents

1. Each Member State shall be free to effect service of judicial **5–235** documents on persons residing in another Member State, without application of any compulsion, directly through its diplomatic or consular agents.

2. Any Member State may make it known, in accordance with Article 23(1), that it is opposed to such service within its territory, unless the documents are to be served on nationals of the Member State in which the documents originate.

Article 14

Service by postal services

Each Member State shall be free to effect service of judicial **5–236** documents directly by postal services on persons residing in another Member State by registered letter with acknowledgement of receipt or equivalent.

Article 15

Direct service

Any person interested in a judicial proceeding may effect service **5–237** of judicial documents directly through the judicial officers, officials or other competent persons of the Member State addressed, where such direct service is permitted under the law of that Member State.

CHAPTER III—EXTRAJUDICIAL DOCUMENTS

Article 16

Transmission

Extrajudicial documents may be transmitted for service in an- **5–238** other Member State in accordance with the provisions of this Regulation.

CHAPTER IV—FINAL PROVISIONS

Article 17

Implementing rules

Measures designed to amend non-essential elements of this **5–239** Regulation relating to the updating or to the making of technical

Paragraph numbers marked with a "+" can be found online and on CD.

amendments to the standard forms set out in Annexes I and II shall be adopted in accordance with the regulatory procedure with scrutiny referred to in Article 18(2).

Article 18

Committee
5–240   1. The Commission shall be assisted by a committee.

2. Where reference is made to this paragraph, Article 5a(1) to (4), and Article 7 of Decision 1999/468/EC shall apply, having regard to the provisions of Article 8 thereof.

Article 19

Defendant not entering an appearance
5–241   1. Where a writ of summons or an equivalent document has had to be transmitted to another Member State for the purpose of service under the provisions of this Regulation and the defendant has not appeared, judgment shall not be given until it is established that:

(a) the document was served by a method prescribed by the internal law of the Member State addressed for the service of documents in domestic actions upon persons who are within its territory; or

(b) the document was actually delivered to the defendant or to his residence by another method provided for by this Regulation;

and that in either of these cases the service or the delivery was effected in sufficient time to enable the defendant to defend.

2. Each Member State may make it known, in accordance with Article 23(1), that the judge, notwithstanding the provisions of paragraph 1, may give judgment even if no certificate of service or delivery has been received, if all the following conditions are fulfilled:

(a) the document was transmitted by one of the methods provided for in this Regulation;

(b) a period of time of not less than six months, considered adequate by the judge in the particular case, has elapsed since the date of the transmission of the document;

(c) no certificate of any kind has been received, even though every reasonable effort has been made to obtain it through the competent authorities or bodies of the Member State addressed.

3. Notwithstanding paragraphs 1 and 2, the judge may order, in case of urgency, any provisional or protective measures.

4. When a writ of summons or an equivalent document has had to be transmitted to another Member State for the purpose of service under the provisions of this Regulation and a judgment has been entered against a defendant who has not appeared, the judge shall have the power to relieve the defendant from the effects of the expiry of the time for appeal from the judgment if the following conditions are fulfilled:

(a) the defendant, without any fault on his part, did not have knowledge of the document in sufficient time to defend, or knowledge of the judgment in sufficient time to appeal; and

Paragraph numbers marked with a "+" can be found online and on CD.

(b) the defendant has disclosed a prima facie defence to the action on the merits.

An application for relief may be filed only within a reasonable time after the defendant has knowledge of the judgment.

Each Member State may make it known, in accordance with Article 23(1), that such application will not be entertained if it is filed after the expiry of a time to be stated by it in that communication, but which shall in no case be less than one year following the date of the judgment.

5. Paragraph 4 shall not apply to judgments concerning the status or capacity of persons.

Article 20

Relationship with agreements or arrangements to which Member States are party

1. This Regulation shall, in relation to matters to which it applies, **5–242** prevail over other provisions contained in bilateral or multilateral agreements or arrangements concluded by the Member States, and in particular Article IV of the Protocol to the Brussels Convention of 1968 and the Hague Convention of 15 November 1965.

2. This Regulation shall not preclude individual Member States from maintaining or concluding agreements or arrangements to expedite further or simplify the transmission of documents, provided that they are compatible with this Regulation.

3. Member States shall send to the Commission:

(a) a copy of the agreements or arrangements referred to in paragraph 2 concluded between the Member States as well as drafts of such agreements or arrangements which they intend to adopt; and

(b) any denunciation of, or amendments to, these agreements or arrangements.

Article 21

Legal aid

This Regulation shall not affect the application of Article 23 of **5–243** the Convention on civil procedure of 17 July 1905, Article 24 of the Convention on civil procedure of 1 March 1954 or Article 13 of the Convention on international access to justice of 25 October 1980 between the Member States party to those Conventions.

Article 22

Protection of information transmitted

1. Information, including in particular personal data, transmitted **5–244** under this Regulation shall be used by the receiving agency only for the purpose for which it was transmitted.

2. Receiving agencies shall ensure the confidentiality of such information, in accordance with their national law.

3. Paragraphs 1 and 2 shall not affect national laws enabling data subjects to be informed of the use made of information transmitted under this Regulation.

Paragraph numbers marked with a "+" can be found online and on CD.

4. This Regulation shall be without prejudice to Directives 95/46/EC and 2002/58/EC.

Article 23

Communication and publication

5–245   1. Member States shall communicate to the Commission the information referred to in Articles 2, 3, 4, 10, 11, 13, 15 and 19. Member States shall communicate to the Commission if, according to their law, a document has to be served within a particular period as referred to in Articles 8(3) and 9(2).

2. The Commission shall publish the information communicated in accordance with paragraph 1 in the Official Journal of the European Union with the exception of the addresses and other contact details of the agencies and of the central bodies and the geographical areas in which they have jurisdiction.

3. The Commission shall draw up and update regularly a manual containing the information referred to in paragraph 1, which shall be available electronically, in particular through the European Judicial Network in Civil and Commercial Matters.

Article 24

Review

5–246   No later than 1 June 2011, and every five years thereafter, the Commission shall present to the European Parliament, the Council and the European Economic and Social Committee a report on the application of this Regulation, paying special attention to the effectiveness of the agencies designated pursuant to Article 2 and to the practical application of Article 3(c) and Article 9. The report shall be accompanied if need be by proposals for adaptations of this Regulation in line with the evolution of notification systems.

Article 25

Repeal

5–246.1   1. Regulation (EC) No 1348/2000 shall be repealed as from the date of application of this Regulation.

2. References made to the repealed Regulation shall be construed as being made to this Regulation and should be read in accordance with the correlation table in Annex III.

Article 26

Entry into force

5–247

This Regulation shall enter into force on the 20th day following its publication in the Official Journal of the European Union.

It shall apply from 13 November 2008 with the exception of Article 23 which shall apply from 13 August 2008.

This Regulation shall be binding in its entirety and directly applicable in the Member States in accordance with the Treaty establishing the European Community.

Paragraph numbers marked with a "+" can be found online and on CD.

Done at Strasbourg, 13 November 2007.

For the European Parliament
The President
H.-G. PÖTTERING

For the Council
The President
M. LOBO ANTUNES

For Annex I to Council Regulation (EC) No.1393/2007 see paragraph 5–248+ on White Book on Westlaw UK or the Civil Procedure CD.

Council Regulation (EC) No.44/2001 of 22 December 2000 on jurisdiction and the recognition and enforcement of judgements in civil and commercial matters

CHAPTER I—SCOPE

Article 1

1. This Regulation shall apply in civil and commercial matters **5–249** whatever the nature of the court or tribunal. It shall not extend, in particular, to revenue, customs or administrative matters.

2. The Regulation shall not apply to:

(a) the status or legal capacity of natural persons, rights in property arising out of a matrimonial relationship, wills and succession;

(b) bankruptcy, proceedings relating to the winding-up of insolvent companies or other legal persons, judicial arrangements, compositions and analogous proceedings;

(c) social security;

(d) arbitration.

3. In this Regulation, the term "Member State" shall mean Member States with the exception of Denmark.

CHAPTER II—JURISDICTION

SECTION 1—GENERAL PROVISIONS

Article 2

1. Subject to this Regulation, persons domiciled in a Member State **5–250** shall, whatever their nationality, be sued in the courts of that Member State.

2. Persons who are not nationals of the Member State in which they are domiciled shall be governed by the rules of jurisdiction applicable to nationals of that State.

Article 3

1. Persons domiciled in a Member State may be sued in the courts **5–251** of another Member State only by virtue of the rules set out in Sections 2 to 7 of this Chapter.

2. In particular the rules of national jurisdiction set out in Annex I shall not be applicable as against them.

Paragraph numbers marked with a "+" can be found online and on CD.

Article 4

5–252   1. If the defendant is not domiciled in a Member State, the jurisdiction of the courts of each Member State shall, subject to Articles 22 and 23, be determined by the law of that Member State.

2. As against such a defendant, any person domiciled in a Member State may, whatever his nationality, avail himself in that State of the rules of jurisdiction there in force, and in particular those specified in Annex I, in the same way as the nationals of that State.

SECTION 2—SPECIAL JURISDICTION

Article 5

5–253   A person domiciled in a Member State may, in another Member State, be sued:

1.—(a) in matters relating to a contract, in the courts for the place of performance of the obligation in question;

(b) for the purpose of this provision and unless otherwise agreed, the place of performance of the obligation in question shall be:

    – in the case of the sale of goods, the place in a Member State where, under the contract, the goods were delivered or should have been delivered,

    – in the case of the provision of services, the place in a Member State where, under the contract, the services were provided or should have been provided,

(c) if subparagraph (b) does not apply then subparagraph (a) applies;

2. in matters relating to maintenance, in the courts for the place where the maintenance creditor is domiciled or habitually resident or, if the matter is ancillary to proceedings concerning the status of a person, in the court which, according to its own law, has jurisdiction to entertain those proceedings, unless that jurisdiction is based solely on the nationality of one of the parties;

3. in matters relating to tort, delict or quasi-delict, in the courts for the place where the harmful event occurred or may occur;

4. as regards a civil claim for damages or restitution which is based on an act giving rise to criminal proceedings, in the court seised of those proceedings, to the extent that that court has jurisdiction under its own law to entertain civil proceedings;

5. as regards a dispute arising out of the operations of a branch, agency or other establishment, in the courts for the place in which the branch, agency or other establishment is situated;

6. as settlor, trustee or beneficiary of a trust created by the operation of a statute, or by a written instrument, or created orally and evidenced in writing, in the courts of the Member State in which the trust is domiciled;

7. as regards a dispute concerning the payment of remuneration claimed in respect of the salvage of a cargo or freight, in the court under the authority of which the cargo or freight in question:

(a) has been arrested to secure such payment, or

(b) could have been so arrested, but bail or other security has been given;

Paragraph numbers marked with a "+" can be found online and on CD.

provided that this provision shall apply only if it is claimed that the defendant has an interest in the cargo or freight or had such an interest at the time of salvage.

Article 6

A person domiciled in a Member State may also be sued:　　**5–254**

1. where he is one of a number of defendants, in the courts for the place where any one of them is domiciled, provided the claims are so closely connected that it is expedient to hear and determine them together to avoid the risk of irreconcilable judgments resulting from separate proceedings;

2. as a third party in an action on a warranty or guarantee or in any other third party proceedings, in the court seised of the original proceedings, unless these were instituted solely with the object of removing him from the jurisdiction of the court which would be competent in his case;

3. on a counter-claim arising from the same contract or facts on which the original claim was based, in the court in which the original claim is pending;

4. in matters relating to a contract, if the action may be combined with an action against the same defendant in matters relating to rights in rem in immovable property, in the court of the Member State in which the property is situated.

Article 7

Where by virtue of this Regulation a court of a Member State has **5–255** jurisdiction in actions relating to liability from the use or operation of a ship, that court, or any other court substituted for this purpose by the internal law of that Member State, shall also have jurisdiction over claims for limitation of such liability.

SECTION 3—JURISDICTION IN MATTERS RELATING TO INSURANCE

Article 8

In matters relating to insurance, jurisdiction shall be determined **5–256** by this Section, without prejudice to Article 4 and point 5 of Article 5.

Article 9

1. An insurer domiciled in a Member State may be sued:　　**5–257**

(a) in the courts of the Member State where he is domiciled, or

(b) in another Member State, in the case of actions brought by the policyholder, the insured or a beneficiary, in the courts for the place where the plaintiff is domiciled,

(c) if he is a co-insurer, in the courts of a Member State in which proceedings are brought against the leading insurer.

2. An insurer who is not domiciled in a Member State but has a branch, agency or other establishment in one of the Member States shall, in disputes arising out of the operations of the branch, agency or establishment, be deemed to be domiciled in that Member State.

Article 10

In respect of liability insurance or insurance of immovable prop- **5–258**

Paragraph numbers marked with a "+" can be found online and on CD.

erty, the insurer may in addition be sued in the courts for the place where the harmful event occurred. The same applies if movable and immovable property are covered by the same insurance policy and both are adversely affected by the same contingency.

Article 11

5–259 1. In respect of liability insurance, the insurer may also, if the law of the court permits it, be joined in proceedings which the injured party has brought against the insured.

2. Articles 8, 9 and 10 shall apply to actions brought by the injured party directly against the insurer, where such direct actions are permitted.

3. If the law governing such direct actions provides that the policyholder or the insured may be joined as a party to the action, the same court shall have jurisdiction over them.

Article 12

5–260 1. Without prejudice to Article 11(3), an insurer may bring proceedings only in the courts of the Member State in which the defendant is domiciled, irrespective of whether he is the policyholder, the insured or a beneficiary.

2. The provisions of this Section shall not affect the right to bring a counter-claim in the court in which, in accordance with this Section, the original claim is pending.

Article 13

5–261 The provisions of this Section may be departed from only by an agreement:

1. which is entered into after the dispute has arisen, or

2. which allows the policyholder, the insured or a beneficiary to bring proceedings in courts other than those indicated in this Section, or

3. which is concluded between a policyholder and an insurer, both of whom are at the time of conclusion of the contract domiciled or habitually resident in the same Member State, and which has the effect of conferring jurisdiction on the courts of that State even if the harmful event were to occur abroad, provided that such an agreement is not contrary to the law of that State, or

4. which is concluded with a policyholder who is not domiciled in a Member State, except in so far as the insurance is compulsory or relates to immovable property in a Member State, or

5. which relates to a contract of insurance in so far as it covers one or more of the risks set out in Article 14.

Article 14

5–262 The following are the risks referred to in Article 13(5):

1. any loss of or damage to:

(a) seagoing ships, installations situated offshore or on the high seas, or aircraft, arising from perils which relate to their use for commercial purposes;

(b) goods in transit other than passengers' baggage where the transit consists of or includes carriage by such ships or aircraft;

Paragraph numbers marked with a "+" can be found online and on CD.

2. any liability, other than for bodily injury to passengers or loss of or damage to their baggage:

(a) arising out of the use or operation of ships, installations or aircraft as referred to in point 1(a) in so far as, in respect of the latter, the law of the Member State in which such aircraft are registered does not prohibit agreements on jurisdiction regarding insurance of such risks;

(b) for loss or damage caused by goods in transit as described in point 1(b);

3. any financial loss connected with the use or operation of ships, installations or aircraft as referred to in point 1(a), in particular loss of freight or charter-hire;

4. which is concluded with a policyholder who is not domiciled in a Member State, except in so far as the insurance is compulsory or relates to immovable property in a Member State, or

5. notwithstanding points 1 to 4, all "large risks" as defined in Council Directive 73/239/EEC, as amended by Council Directives 88/357/EEC and 90/618/EEC, as they may be amended.

SECTION 4—JURISDICTION OVER CONSUMER CONTRACTS

Article 15

1. In matters relating to a contract concluded by a person, the **5–263** consumer, for a purpose which can be regarded as being outside his trade or profession, jurisdiction shall be determined by this Section, without prejudice to Article 4 and point 5 of Article 5, if:

(a) it is a contract for the sale of goods on instalment credit terms; or

(b) it is a contract for a loan repayable by instalments, or for any other form of credit, made to finance the sale of goods; or

(c) in all other cases, the contract has been concluded with a person who pursues commercial or professional activities in the Member State of the consumer's domicile or, by any means, directs such activities to that Member State or to several States including that Member State, and the contract falls within the scope of such activities.

2. Where a consumer enters into a contract with a party who is not domiciled in the Member State but has a branch, agency or other establishment in one of the Member States, that party shall, in disputes arising out of the operations of the branch, agency or establishment, be deemed to be domiciled in that State.

3. This Section shall not apply to a contract of transport other than a contract which, for an inclusive price, provides for a combination of travel and accommodation.

Article 16

1. A consumer may bring proceedings against the other party to a **5–264** contract either in the courts of the Member State in which that party is domiciled or in the courts for the place where the consumer is domiciled.

2. Proceedings may be brought against a consumer by the other

Paragraph numbers marked with a "+" can be found online and on CD.

party to the contract only in the courts of the Member State in which the consumer is domiciled.

3. This Article shall not affect the right to bring a counter-claim in the court in which, in accordance with this Section, the original claim is pending.

Article 17

5–265   The provisions of this Section may be departed from only by an agreement:

1. which is entered into after the dispute has arisen; or

2. which allows the consumer to bring proceedings in courts other than those indicated in this Section; or

3. which is entered into by the consumer and the other party to the contract, both of whom are at the time of conclusion of the contract domiciled or habitually resident in the same Member State, and which confers jurisdiction on the courts of that Member State, provided that such an agreement is not contrary to the law of that Member State.

SECTION 5—JURISDICTION OVER INDIVIDUAL CONTRACTS OF EMPLOYMENT

Article 18

5–266   1. In matters relating to individual contracts of employment, jurisdiction shall be determined by this Section, without prejudice to Article 4 and point 5 of Article 5.

2. Where an employee enters into an individual contract of employment with an employer who is not domiciled in a Member State but has a branch, agency or other establishment in one of the Member States, the employer shall, in disputes arising out of the operations of the branch, agency or establishment, be deemed to be domiciled in that Member State.

Article 19

5–267   An employer domiciled in a Member State may be sued:

1. in the courts of the Member State where he is domiciled; or

2. in another Member State:

(a) in the courts for the place where the employee habitually carries out his work or in the courts for the last place where he did so, or

(b) if the employee does not or did not habitually carry out his work in any one country, in the courts for the place where the business which engaged the employee is or was situated.

Article 20

5–268   1. An employer may bring proceedings only in the courts of the Member State in which the employee is domiciled.

2. The provisions of this Section shall not affect the right to bring a counter-claim in the court in which, in accordance with this Section, the original claim is pending.

Article 21

5–269   The provisions of this Section may be departed from only be an agreement on jurisdiction:

Paragraph numbers marked with a "+" can be found online and on CD.

1. which is entered into after the dispute has arisen; or

2. which allows the employee to bring proceedings in courts other than those indicated in this Section.

SECTION 6—EXCLUSIVE JURISDICTION

Article 22

The following courts shall have exclusive jurisdiction, regardless of **5–270** domicile:

1. in proceedings which have as their object rights in rem in immovable property or tenancies of immovable property, the courts of the Member State in which the property is situated. However, in proceedings which have as their object tenancies of immovable property concluded for temporary private use for a maximum period of six consecutive months, the courts of the Member State in which the defendant is domiciled shall also have jurisdiction, provided that the tenant is a natural person and that the landlord and the tenant are domiciled in the same Member State;

2. in proceedings which have as their object the validity of the constitution, the nullity or the dissolution of companies or other legal persons or associations of natural or legal persons, or of the validity of the decisions of their organs, the courts of the Member State in which the company, legal person or association has its seat. In order to determine that seat, the court shall apply its rules of private international law;

3. in proceedings which have as their object the validity of entries in public registers, the courts of the Member State in which the register is kept;

4. in proceedings concerned with the registration or validity of patents, trade marks, designs, or other similar rights required to be deposited or registered, the courts of the Member State in which the deposit or registration has been applied for, has taken place or is under the terms of a Community instrument or an international convention deemed to have taken place. Without prejudice to the jurisdiction of the European Patent Office under the Convention on the Grant of European Patents, signed at Munich on 5 October 1973, the courts of each Member State shall have exclusive jurisdiction, regardless of domicile, in proceedings concerned with the registration or validity of any European patent granted for that State;

5. in proceedings concerned with the enforcement of judgments, the courts of the Member State in which the judgment has been or is to be enforced.

SECTION 7—PROROGATION OF JURISDICTION

Article 23

1. If the parties, one or more of whom is domiciled in a Member **5–271** State, have agreed that a court or the courts of a Member State are to have jurisdiction to settle any disputes which have arisen or which may arise in connection with a particular legal relationship, that court or those courts shall have jurisdiction. Such jurisdiction shall be

Paragraph numbers marked with a "+" can be found online and on CD.

exclusive unless the parties have agreed otherwise. Such an agreement conferring jurisdiction shall be either:

(a) in writing or evidenced in writing; or

(b) in a form which accords with practices which the parties have established between themselves; or

(c) in international trade or commerce, in a form which accords with a usage of which the parties are or ought to have been aware and which in such trade or commerce is widely known to, and regularly observed by, parties to contracts of the type involved in the particular trade or commerce concerned.

2. Any communication by electronic means which provides a durable record of the agreement shall be equivalent to "writing".

3. Where such an agreement is concluded by parties, none of whom is domiciled in a Member State, the courts of other Member States shall have no jurisdiction over their disputes unless the court or courts chosen have declined jurisdiction.

4. The court or courts of a Member State on which a trust instrument has conferred jurisdiction shall have exclusive jurisdiction in any proceedings brought against a settlor, trustee or beneficiary, if relations between these persons or their rights or obligations under the trust are involved.

5. Agreements or provisions of a trust instrument conferring jurisdiction shall have no legal force if they are contrary to Articles 13, 17 or 21, or if the courts whose jurisdiction they purport to exclude have exclusive jurisdiction by virtue of Article 22.

Article 24

5–272 Apart from jurisdiction derived from other provisions of this Regulation, a court of a Member State before which a defendant enters an appearance shall have jurisdiction. This rule shall not apply where appearance was entered to contest the jurisdiction, or where another court has exclusive jurisdiction by virtue of Article 22.

SECTION 8—EXAMINATION AS TO JURISDICTION AND ADMISSIBILITY

Article 25

5–273 Where a court of a Member State is seised of a claim which is principally concerned with a matter over which the courts of another Member State have exclusive jurisdiction by virtue of Article 22, it shall declare of its own motion that it has no jurisdiction.

Article 26

5–274 1. Where a defendant domiciled in one Member State is sued in a court of another Member State and does not enter an appearance, the court shall declare of its own motion that it has no jurisdiction unless its jurisdiction is derived from the provisions of this Regulation.

2. The court shall stay the proceedings so long as it is not shown that the defendant has been able to receive the document instituting the proceedings or an equivalent document in sufficient time to enable him to arrange for his defence, or that all necessary steps have been taken to this end.

Paragraph numbers marked with a "+" can be found online and on CD.

3. Article 19 of Council Regulation (EC) No 1348/2000 of 29 May 2000 on the service in the Member States of judicial and extrajudicial documents in civil or commercial matters shall apply instead of the provisions of paragraph 2 if the document instituting the proceedings or an equivalent document had to be transmitted from one Member State to another pursuant to this Regulation.

4. Where the provisions of Regulation (EC) No 1348/2000 are not applicable, Article 15 of the Hague Convention of 15 November 1965 on the Service Abroad of Judicial and Extrajudicial Documents in Civil or Commercial Matters shall apply if the document instituting the proceedings or an equivalent document had to be transmitted pursuant to that Convention.

SECTION 9—LIS PENDENS—RELATED ACTIONS

Article 27

1. Where proceedings involving the same cause of action and be- **5–275** tween the same parties are brought in the courts of different Member States, any court other than the court first seised shall of its own motion stay its proceedings until such time as the jurisdiction of the court first seised is established.

2. Where the jurisdiction of the court first seised is established, any court other than the court first seised shall decline jurisdiction in favour of that court.

Article 28

1. Where related actions are pending in the courts of different **5–276** Member States, any court other than the court first seised may stay its proceedings.

2. Where these actions are pending at first instance, any court other than the court first seised may also, on the application of one of the parties, decline jurisdiction if the court first seised has jurisdiction over the actions in question and its law permits the consolidation thereof.

3. For the purposes of this Article, actions are deemed to be related where they are so closely connected that it is expedient to hear and determine them together to avoid the risk of irreconcilable judgments resulting from separate proceedings.

Article 29

Where actions come within the exclusive jurisdiction of several **5–277** courts, any court other than the court first seised shall decline jurisdiction in favour of that court.

Article 30

For the purposes of this Section, a court shall be deemed to be **5–278** seised:

1. at the time when the document instituting the proceedings or an equivalent document is lodged with the court, provided that the plaintiff has not subsequently failed to take the steps he was required to take to have service effected on the defendant, or.

2. if the document has to be served before being lodged with the

Paragraph numbers marked with a "+" can be found online and on CD.

court, at the time when it is received by the authority responsible for service, provided that the plaintiff has not subsequently failed to take the steps he was required to take to have the document lodged with the court.

SECTION 10—PROVISIONAL, INCLUDING PROTECTIVE, MEASURES

Article 31

5–279   Application may be made to the courts of a Member State for such provisional, including protective, measures as may be available under the law of that State, even if, under this Regulation, the courts of another Member State have jurisdiction as to the substance of the matter.

CHAPTER III—RECOGNITION AND ENFORCEMENT

Article 32

5–280   For the purposes of this Regulation, "judgment" means any judgment given by a court or tribunal of a Member State, whatever the judgment may be called, including a decree, order, decision or writ of execution, as well as the determination of costs or expenses by an officer of the court.

SECTION 1—RECOGNITION

Article 33

5–281   1. A judgment given in a Member State shall be recognised in the other Member States without any special procedure being required.

2. Any interested party who raises the recognition of a judgment as the principal issue in a dispute may, in accordance with the procedures provided for in Sections 2 and 3 of this Chapter, apply for a decision that the judgment be recognised.

3. If the outcome of proceedings in a court of a Member State depends on the determination of an incidental question of recognition that court shall have jurisdiction over that question.

Article 34

5–282   A judgment shall not be recognised:

1. if such recognition is manifestly contrary to public policy in the Member State in which recognition is sought;

2. where it was given in default of appearance, if the defendant was not served with the document which instituted the proceedings or with an equivalent document in sufficient time and in such a way as to enable him to arrange for his defence, unless the defendant failed to commence proceedings to challenge the judgment when it was possible for him to do so;

3. if it is irreconcilable with a judgment given in a dispute between the same parties in the Member State in which recognition is sought;

4. if it is irreconcilable with an earlier judgment given in another Member State or in a third State involving the same cause of action and between the same parties, provided that the earlier judgment fulfils the conditions necessary for its recognition in the Member State addressed.

Paragraph numbers marked with a "+" can be found online and on CD.

EUROPE

Article 35

1. Moreover, a judgment shall not be recognised if it conflicts with **5–283** Sections 3, 4 or 6 of Chapter II, or in a case provided for in Article 72.

2. In its examination of the grounds of jurisdiction referred to in the foregoing paragraph, the court or authority applied to shall be bound by the findings of fact on which the court of the Member State of origin based its jurisdiction.

3. Subject to the paragraph 1, the jurisdiction of the court of the Member State of origin may not be reviewed. The test of public policy referred to in point 1 of Article 34 may not be applied to the rules relating to jurisdiction.

Article 36

Under no circumstances may a foreign judgment be reviewed as to **5–284** its substance.

Article 37

1. A court of a Member State in which recognition is sought of a **5–285** judgment given in another Member State may stay the proceedings if an ordinary appeal against the judgment has been lodged.

2. A court of a Member State in which recognition is sought of a judgment given in Ireland or the United Kingdom may stay the proceedings if enforcement is suspended in the State of origin, by reason of an appeal.

SECTION 2—ENFORCEMENT

Article 38

1. A judgment given in a Member State and enforceable in that **5–286** State shall be enforced in another Member State when, on the application of any interested party, it has been declared enforceable there.

2. However, in the United Kingdom, such a judgment shall be enforced in England and Wales, in Scotland, or in Northern Ireland when, on the application of any interested party, it has been registered for enforcement in that part of the United Kingdom.

Article 39

1. The application shall be submitted to the court or competent **5–287** authority indicated in the list in Annex II.

2. The local jurisdiction shall be determined by reference to the place of domicile of the party against whom enforcement is sought, or to the place of enforcement.

Article 40

1. The procedure for making the application shall be governed by **5–288** the law of the Member State in which enforcement is sought.

2. The applicant must give an address for service of process within the area of jurisdiction of the court applied to. However, if the law of the Member State in which enforcement is sought does not provide for the furnishing of such an address, the applicant shall appoint a representative ad litem.

Paragraph numbers marked with a "+" can be found online and on CD.

3. The documents referred to in Article 53 shall be attached to the application.

Article 41

5–289 The judgment shall be declared enforceable immediately on completion of the formalities in Article 53 without any review under Articles 34 and 35. The party against whom enforcement is sought shall not at this stage of the proceedings be entitled to make any submissions on the application.

Article 42

5–290 1. The decision on the application for a declaration of enforceability shall forthwith be brought to the notice of the applicant in accordance with the procedure laid down by the law of the Member State in which enforcement is sought.

2. The declaration of enforceability shall be served on the party against whom enforcement is sought, accompanied by the judgment, if not already served on that party.

Article 43

5–291 1. The decision on the application for a declaration of enforceability may be appealed against by either party.

2. The appeal is to be lodged with the court indicated in the list in Annex III.

3. The appeal shall be dealt with in accordance with the rules governing procedure in contradictory matters.

4. If the party against whom enforcement is sought fails to appear before the appellate court in proceedings concerning an appeal brought by the applicant, Article 26(2) to (4) shall apply even where the party against whom enforcement is sought is not domiciled in any of the Member States.

5. An appeal against the declaration of enforceability is to be lodged within one month of service thereof. If the party against whom enforcement is sought is domiciled in a Member State other than that in which the declaration of enforceability was given, the time for appealing shall be two months and shall run from the date of service, either on him in person or at his residence. No extension of time may be granted on account of distance.

Article 44

5–292 The judgment given on the appeal may be contested only by the appeal referred to in Annex IV.

Article 45

5–293 1. The court with which an appeal is lodged under Article 43 or Article 44 shall refuse or revoke a declaration of enforceability only on one of the grounds specified in Articles 34 and 35. It shall give its decision without delay.

2. Under no circumstances may the foreign judgment be reviewed as to its substance.

Article 46

5–294 1. The court with which an appeal is lodged under Article 43 or

Paragraph numbers marked with a "+" can be found online and on CD.

Article 44 may, on the application of the party against whom enforcement is sought, stay the proceedings if an ordinary appeal has been lodged against the judgment in the Member State of origin or if the time for such an appeal has not yet expired; in the latter case, the court may specify the time within which such an appeal is to be lodged.

2. Where the judgment was given in Ireland or the United Kingdom, any form of appeal available in the Member State of origin shall be treated as an ordinary appeal for the purposes of paragraph 1.

3. The court may also make enforcement conditional on the provision of such security as it shall determine.

Article 47

5–295 1. When a judgment must be recognised in accordance with this Regulation, nothing shall prevent the applicant from availing himself of provisional, including protective, measures in accordance with the law of the Member State requested without a declaration of enforceability under Article 41 being required.

2. The declaration of enforceability shall carry with it the power to proceed to any protective measures.

3. During the time specified for an appeal pursuant to Article 43(5) against the declaration of enforceability and until any such appeal has been determined, no measures of enforcement may be taken other than protective measures against the property of the party against whom enforcement is sought.

Article 48

5–296 1. Where a foreign judgment has been given in respect of several matters and the declaration of enforceability cannot be given for all of them, the court or competent authority shall give it for one or more of them.

2. An applicant may request a declaration of enforceability limited to parts of a judgment.

Article 49

5–297 A foreign judgment which orders a periodic payment by way of a penalty shall be enforceable in the Member State in which enforcement is sought only if the amount of the payment has been finally determined by the courts of the Member State of origin.

Article 50

5–298 An applicant who, in the Member State of origin has benefited from complete or partial legal aid or exemption from costs or expenses, shall be entitled, in the procedure provided for in this Section, to benefit from the most favourable legal aid or the most extensive exemption from costs or expenses provided for by the law of the Member State addressed.

Article 51

5–299 No security, bond or deposit, however described, shall be required of a party who in one Member State applies for enforcement of a

Paragraph numbers marked with a "+" can be found online and on CD.

judgment given in another Member State on the ground that he is a foreign national or that he is not domiciled or resident in the State in which enforcement is sought.

Article 52

5–300   In proceedings for the issue of a declaration of enforceability, no charge, duty or fee calculated by reference to the value of the matter at issue may be levied in the Member State in which enforcement is sought.

SECTION 3—COMMON PROVISIONS

Article 53

5–301   1. A party seeking recognition or applying for a declaration of enforceability shall produce a copy of the judgment which satisfies the conditions necessary to establish its authenticity.

2. A party applying for a declaration of enforceability shall also produce the certificate referred to in Article 54, without prejudice to Article 55.

Article 54

5–302   The court or competent authority of a Member State where a judgment was given shall issue, at the request of any interested party, a certificate using the standard form in Annex V to this Regulation.

Article 55

5–303   1. If the certificate referred to in Article 54 is not produced, the court or competent authority may specify a time for its production or accept an equivalent document or, if it considers that it has sufficient information before it, dispense with its production.

2. If the court or competent authority so requires, a translation of the documents shall be produced. The translation shall be certified by a person qualified to do so in one of the Member States.

Article 56

5–304   No legalisation or other similar formality shall be required in respect of the documents referred to in Article 53 or Article 55(2), or in respect of a document appointing a representative ad litem.

CHAPTER IV—AUTHENTIC INSTRUMENTS AND COURT SETTLEMENTS

Article 57

5–305   1. A document which has been formally drawn up or registered as an authentic instrument and is enforceable in one Member State shall, in another Member State, be declared enforceable there, on application made in accordance with the procedures provided for in Articles 38, et seq. The court with which an appeal is lodged under Article 43 or Article 44 shall refuse or revoke a declaration of enforceability only if enforcement of the instrument is manifestly contrary to public policy in the Member State addressed.

2. A document which has been formally drawn up or registered as an authentic instrument and is enforceable in one Member State shall, in another Member State, be declared enforceable there, on ap-

Paragraph numbers marked with a "+" can be found online and on CD.

plication made in accordance with the procedures provided for in Articles 38, *et seq.* The court with which an appeal is lodged under Article 43 or Article 44 shall refuse or revoke a declaration of enforceability only if enforcement of the instrument is manifestly contrary to public policy in the Member State addressed.

3. The instrument produced must satisfy the conditions necessary to establish its authenticity in the Member State of origin.

4. Section 3 of Chapter III shall apply as appropriate. The competent authority of a Member State where an authentic instrument was drawn up or registered shall issue, at the request of any interested party, a certificate using the standard form in Annex VI to this Regulation.

Article 58

A settlement which has been approved by a court in the course of **5–306** proceedings and is enforceable in the Member State in which it was concluded shall be enforceable in the State addressed under the same conditions as authentic instruments. The court or competent authority of a Member State where a court settlement was approved shall issue, at the request of any interested party, a certificate using the standard form in Annex V to this Regulation.

CHAPTER V—GENERAL PROVISIONS

Article 59

1. In order to determine whether a party is domiciled in the **5–307** Member State whose courts are seised of a matter, the court shall apply its internal law.

2. If a party is not domiciled in the Member State whose courts are seised of the matter, then, in order to determine whether the party is domiciled in another Member State, the court shall apply the law of that Member State.

Article 60

1. For the purposes of this Regulation, a company or other legal **5–308** person or association of natural or legal persons is domiciled at the place where it has its:

(a) statutory seat, or

(b) central administration, or

(c) principal place of business.

2. For the purposes of the United Kingdom and Ireland "statutory seat" means the registered office or, where there is no such office anywhere, the place of incorporation or, where there is no such place anywhere, the place under the law of which the formation took place.

3. In order to determine whether a trust is domiciled in the Member State whose courts are seised of the matter, the court shall apply its rules of private international law.

Article 61

Without prejudice to any more favourable provisions of national **5–309** laws, persons domiciled in a Member State who are being prosecuted

Paragraph numbers marked with a "+" can be found online and on CD.

in the criminal courts of another Member State of which they are not nationals for an offence which was not intentionally committed may be defended by persons qualified to do so, even if they do not appear in person. However, the court seised of the matter may order appearance in person; in the case of failure to appear, a judgment given in the civil action without the person concerned having had the opportunity to arrange for his defence need not be recognised or enforced in the other Member States.

Article 62

5–310   In Sweden, in summary proceedings concerning orders to pay (betalningsföreläggande) and assistance (handräckning), the expression "court" includes the "Swedish enforcement service" (kronofogdemyndighet).

Article 63

5–311   1. A person domiciled in the territory of the Grand Duchy of Luxembourg and sued in the court of another Member State pursuant to Article 5(1) may refuse to submit to the jurisdiction of that court if the final place of delivery of the goods or provision of the services is in Luxembourg.

2. Where, under paragraph 1, the final place of delivery of the goods or provision of the services is in Luxembourg, any agreement conferring jurisdiction must, in order to be valid, be accepted in writing or evidenced in writing within the meaning of Article 23(1)(a).

3. The provisions of this Article shall not apply to contracts for the provision of financial services.

4. The provisions of this Article shall apply for a period of six years from entry into force of this Regulation.

Article 64

5–312   1. In proceedings involving a dispute between the master and a member of the crew of a seagoing ship registered in Greece or in Portugal, concerning remuneration or other conditions of service, a court in a Member State shall establish whether the diplomatic or consular officer responsible for the ship has been notified of the dispute. It may act as soon as that officer has been notified.

2. The provisions of this Article shall apply for a period of six years from entry into force of this Regulation.

Article 65

5–313   1. The jurisdiction specified in Article 6(2), and Article 11 in actions on a warranty of guarantee or in any other third party proceedings may not be resorted to in Germany, Austria and Hungary. Any person domiciled in another Member State may be sued in the courts:

(a) of Germany, pursuant to Articles 68 and 72 to 74 of the Code of Civil Procedure (Zivilprozessordnung) concerning third-party notices,

(b) of Austria, pursuant to Article 21 of the Code of Civil Procedure (Zivilprozessordnung) concerning third-party notices.

(c) of Hungary, pursuant to Articles 58 to 60 of the Code of Civil Procedure (Polgári perrendtartás) concerning third-party notices.

Paragraph numbers marked with a "+" can be found online and on CD.

2. Judgments given in other Member States by virtue of Article 6(2), or Article 11 shall be recognised and enforced in Germany, Austria and Hungary in accordance with Chapter III. Any effects which judgments given in these States may have on third parties by application of the provisions in paragraph 1 shall also be recognised in the other Member States.

CHAPTER VI—TRANSITIONAL PROVISIONS

Article 66

1. This Regulation shall apply only to legal proceedings instituted **5–314** and to documents formally drawn up or registered as authentic instruments after the entry into force thereof.

2. However, if the proceedings in the Member State of origin were instituted before the entry into force of this Regulation, judgments given after that date shall be recognised and enforced in accordance with Chapter III,

(a) if the proceedings in the Member State of origin were instituted after the entry into force of the Brussels or the Lugano Convention both in the Member State or origin and in the Member State addressed;

(b) in all other cases, if jurisdiction was founded upon rules which accorded with those provided for either in Chapter II or in a convention concluded between the Member State of origin and the Member State addressed which was in force when the proceedings were instituted.

CHAPTER VII—RELATIONS WITH OTHER INSTRUMENTS

Article 67

This Regulation shall not prejudice the application of provisions **5–315** governing jurisdiction and the recognition and enforcement of judgments in specific matters which are contained in Community instruments or in national legislation harmonised pursuant to such instruments.

Article 68

1. This Regulation shall, as between the Member States, supersede **5–316** the Brussels Convention, except as regards the territories of the Member States which fall within the territorial scope of that Convention and which are excluded from this Regulation pursuant to Article 299 of the Treaty.

2. In so far as this Regulation replaces the provisions of the Brussels Convention between Member States, any reference to the Convention shall be understood as a reference to this Regulation.

Article 69

Subject to Article 66(2) and Article 70, this Regulation shall, as be- **5–317** tween Member States, supersede the following conventions and treaty concluded between two or more of them:

– the Convention between Belgium and France on Jurisdiction and the Validity and Enforcement of Judgments, Arbitration Awards and Authentic Instruments, signed at Paris on 8 July 1899,

Paragraph numbers marked with a "+" can be found online and on CD.

– the Convention between Belgium and the Netherlands on Jurisdiction, Bankruptcy, and the Validity and Enforcement of Judgments, Arbitration Awards and Authentic Instruments, signed at Brussels on 28 March 1925,

– the Convention between France and Italy on the Enforcement of Judgments in Civil and Commercial Matters, signed at Rome on 3 June 1930,

– the Convention between the United Kingdom and the French Republic providing for the reciprocal enforcement of judgments in civil and commercial matters, with Protocol, signed at Paris on 18 January 1934,

– the Convention between the United Kingdom and the Kingdom of Belgium providing for the reciprocal enforcement of judgments in civil and commercial matters, with Protocol, signed at Brussels on 2 May 1934,

– the Convention between Germany and Italy on the Recognition and Enforcement of Judgments in Civil and Commercial Matters, signed at Rome on 9 March 1936,

– the Convention between Belgium and Austria on the Reciprocal Recognition and Enforcement of Judgments and Authentic Instruments relating to Maintenance Obligations, signed at Vienna on 25 October 1957,

– the Convention between Germany and Belgium on the Mutual Recognition and Enforcement of Judgments, Arbitration Awards and Authentic Instruments in Civil and Commercial Matters, signed at Bonn on 30 June 1958,

– the Convention between the Netherlands and Italy on the Recognition and Enforcement of Judgments in Civil and Commercial Matters, signed at Rome on 17 April 1959,

– the Convention between Germany and Austria on the Reciprocal Recognition and Enforcement of Judgments, Settlements and Authentic Instruments in Civil and Commercial Matters, signed at Vienna on 6 June 1959,

– the Convention between Belgium and Austria on the Reciprocal Recognition and Enforcement of Judgments, Arbitral Awards and Authentic Instruments in Civil and Commercial Matters, signed at Vienna on 16 June 1959,

– the Convention between the United Kingdom and the Federal Republic of Germany for the reciprocal recognition and enforcement of judgments in civil and commercial matters, signed at Bonn on 14 July 1960,

– the Convention between the United Kingdom and the Austria providing for the reciprocal recognition and enforcement of judgments in civil and commercial matters, signed at Vienna on 14 July 1961, with amending Protocol signed at London on 6 March 1970,

– the Convention between Greece and Germany for the Reciprocal Recognition and Enforcement of Judgments, Settlements and Authentic Instruments in Civil and Commercial Matters, signed in Athens on 4 November 1961,

– the Convention between Belgium and Italy on the Recognition

Paragraph numbers marked with a "+" can be found online and on CD.

1710

and Enforcement of Judgments and other Enforceable Instruments in Civil and Commercial Matters, signed at Rome on 6 April 1962,

– the Convention between the Netherlands and Germany on the Mutual Recognition and Enforcement of Judgments and Other Enforceable Instruments in Civil and Commercial Matters, signed at The Hague on 30 August 1962,

– the Convention between the Netherlands and Austria on the Reciprocal Recognition and Enforcement of Judgments and Authentic Instruments in Civil and Commercial Matters, signed at The Hague on 6 February 1963,

– the Convention between the United Kingdom and the Republic of Italy for the reciprocal recognition and enforcement of judgments in civil and commercial matters, signed at Rome on 7 February 1964, with amending Protocol signed at Rome on 14 July 1970,

– the Convention between France and Austria on the Recognition and Enforcement of Judgments and Authentic Instruments in Civil and Commercial Matters, signed at Vienna on 15 July 1966,

– the Convention between the United Kingdom and the Kingdom of the Netherlands providing for the reciprocal recognition and enforcement of judgments in civil matters, signed at The Hague on 17 November 1967,

– the Convention between Spain and France on the Recognition and Enforcement of Judgment Arbitration Awards in Civil and Commercial Matters, signed at Paris on 28 May 1969,

– the Convention between Luxembourg and Austria on the Recognition and Enforcement of Judgments and Authentic Instruments in Civil and Commercial Matters, signed at Luxembourg on 29 July 1971,

– the Convention between Italy and Austria on the Recognition and Enforcement of Judgments in Civil and Commercial Matters, of Judicial Settlements and of Authentic Instruments, signed at Rome on 16 November 1971,

– the Convention between Spain and Italy regarding Legal Aid and the Recognition and Enforcement of Judgments in Civil and Commercial Matters, signed at Madrid on 22 May 1973,

– the Convention between Finland, Iceland, Norway, Sweden and Denmark on the Recognition and Enforcement of Judgments in Civil Matters, signed at Copenhagen on 11 October 1977,

– the Convention between Austria and Sweden on the Recognition and Enforcement of Judgments in Civil Matters, signed at Stockholm on 16 September 1982,

– the Convention between Spain and the Federal Republic of Germany on the Recognition and Enforcement of Judgments, Settlements and Enforceable Authentic Instruments in Civil and Commercial Matters, signed at Bonn on 14 November 1983,

– the Convention between Austria and Spain on the Recognition and Enforcement of Judgments, Settlements and Enforceable Authentic Instruments in Civil and Commercial Matters, signed at Vienna on 17 February 1984,

– the Convention between Finland and Austria on the Recognition

Paragraph numbers marked with a "+" can be found online and on CD.

and Enforcement of Judgments in Civil Matters, signed at Vienna on 17 November 1986, and

– the Treaty between Belgium, the Netherlands and Luxembourg in Jurisdiction, Bankruptcy, and the Validity and Enforcement of Judgments, Arbitration Awards and Authentic Instruments, signed at Brussels on 24 November 1961, in so far as it is in force.

– the Convention between the Czechoslovak Republic and Portugal on the Recognition and Enforcement of Court Decisions, signed at Lisbon on 23 November 1927, still in force between the Czech Republic and Portugal,

– the Convention between the Federative People's Republic of Yugoslavia and the Republic of Austria on Mutual Judicial Cooperation, signed at Vienna on 16 December 1954,

– the Convention between the Polish People's Republic and the Hungarian People's Republic on the Legal Assistance in Civil, Family and Criminal Matters, signed at Budapest on 6 March 1959,

– the Convention between the Federative People's Republic of Yugoslavia and the Kingdom of Greece on the Mutual Recognition and Enforcement of Judgments, signed at Athens on 18 June 1959,

– the Convention between the Polish People's Republic and the Federative People's Republic of Yugoslavia on the Legal Assistance in Civil and Criminal Matters, signed at Warsaw on 6 February 1960, now in force between Poland and Slovenia,

– the Agreement between the Federative People's Republic of Yugoslavia and the Republic of Austria on the Mutual Recognition and Enforcement of Arbitral Awards and Arbitral Settlements in Commercial Matters, signed at Belgrade on 18 March 1960,

– the Agreement between the Federative People's Republic of Yugoslavia and the Republic of Austria on the Mutual Recognition and Enforcement of Decisions in Alimony Matters, signed at Vienna on 10 October 1961,

– the Convention between Poland and Austria on Mutual Relations in Civil Matters and on Documents, signed at Vienna on 11 December 1963,

– the Treaty between the Czechoslovak Socialist Republic and the Socialist Federative Republic of Yugoslavia on Settlement of Legal Relations in Civil, Family and Criminal Matters, signed at Belgrade on 20 January 1964, still in force between the Czech Republic, Slovakia and Slovenia,

– the Convention between Poland and France on Applicable Law, Jurisdiction and the Enforcement of Judgments in the Field of Personal and Family Law, concluded in Warsaw on 5 April 1967,

– the Convention between the Governments of Yugoslavia and France on the Recognition and Enforcement of Judgments in Civil and Commercial Matters, signed at Paris on 18 May 1971,

– the Convention between the Federative Socialist Republic of Yugoslavia and the Kingdom of Belgium on the Recognition and Enforcement of Court Decisions in Alimony Matters, signed at Belgrade on 12 December 1973,

– the Convention between Hungary and Greece on Legal Assis-

Paragraph numbers marked with a "+" can be found online and on CD.

tance in Civil and Criminal Matters, signed at Budapest on 8 October 1979,

– the Convention between Poland and Greece on Legal Assistance in Civil and Criminal Matters, signed at Athens on 24 October 1979,

– the Convention between Hungary and France on Legal Assistance in Civil and Family Law, on the Recognition and Enforcement of Decisions and on Legal Assistance in Criminal Matters and on Extradition, signed at Budapest on 31 July 1980,

– the Treaty between the Czechoslovak Socialist Republic and the Hellenic Republic on Legal Aid in Civil and Criminal Matters, signed at Athens on 22 October 1980, still in force between the Czech Republic, Slovakia and Greece,

– the Convention between the Republic of Cyprus and the Hungarian People's Republic on Legal Assistance in Civil and Criminal Matters, signed at Nicosia on 30 November 1981,

– the Treaty between the Czechoslovak Socialistic Republic and the Republic of Cyprus on Legal Aid in Civil and Criminal Matters, signed at Nicosia on 23 April 1982, still in force between the Czech Republic, Slovakia and Cyprus,

– the Agreement between the Republic of Cyprus and the Republic of Greece on Legal Cooperation in Matters of Civil, Family, Commercial and Criminal Law, signed at Nicosia on 5 March 1984,

– the Treaty between the Government of the Czechoslovak Socialist Republic and the Government of the Republic of France on Legal Aid and the Recognition and Enforcement of Judgments in Civil, Family and Commercial Matters, signed at Paris on 10 May 1984, still in force between the Czech Republic, Slovakia and France,

– the Agreement between the Republic of Cyprus and the Socialist Federal Republic of Yugoslavia on Legal Assistance in Civil and Criminal Matters, signed at Nicosia on 19 September 1984, now in force between Cyprus and Slovenia,

– the Treaty between the Czechoslovak Socialist Republic and the Italian Republic on Legal Aid in Civil and Criminal Matters, signed at Prague on 6 December 1985, still in force between the Czech Republic, Slovakia and Italy,

– the Treaty between the Czechoslovak Socialist Republic and the Kingdom of Spain on Legal Aid, Recognition and Enforcement of Court Decisions in Civil Matters, signed at Madrid on 4 May 1987, still in force between the Czech Republic, Slovakia and Spain,

– the Treaty between the Czechoslovak Socialist Republic and the Polish People's Republic on Legal Aid and Settlement of Legal Relations in Civil, Family, Labour and Criminal Matters, signed at Warsaw on 21 December 1987, still in force between the Czech Republic, Slovakia and Poland,

– the Treaty between the Czechoslovak Socialist Republic and the Hungarian People's Republic on Legal Aid and Settlement of Legal Relations in Civil, Family and Criminal Matters, signed at Bratislava on 28 March 1989, still in force between the Czech Republic, Slovakia and Hungary,

– the Convention between Poland and Italy on Judicial Assistance

Paragraph numbers marked with a "+" can be found online and on CD.

and the Recognition and Enforcement of Judgments in Civil Matters, signed at Warsaw on 28 April 1989,

– the Treaty between the Czech Republic and the Slovak Republic on Legal Aid provided by Judicial Bodies and on Settlements of Certain Legal Relations in Civil and Criminal Matters, signed at Prague on 29 October 1992,

– the Agreement between the Republic of Latvia, the Republic of Estonia and the Republic of Lithuania on Legal Assistance and Legal Relationships, signed at Tallinn on 11 November 1992,

– the Agreement between the Republic of Poland and the Republic of Lithuania on Legal Assistance and Legal Relations in Civil, Family, Labour and Criminal Matters, signed in Warsaw on 26 January 1993,

– the Agreement between the Republic of Latvia and the Republic of Poland on Legal Assistance and Legal Relationships in Civil, Family, Labour and Criminal Matters, signed at Riga on 23 February 1994,

– the Agreement between the Republic of Cyprus and the Republic of Poland on Legal Cooperation in Civil and Criminal Matters, signed at Nicosia on 14 November 1996, and

– the Agreement between Estonia and Poland on Granting Legal Assistance and Legal Relations on Civil, Labour and Criminal Matters, signed at Tallinn on 27 November 1998,

– the Convention between Bulgaria and Belgium on certain Judicial Matters, signed at Sofia on 2 July 1930,

– the Agreement between the People's Republic of Bulgaria and the Federative People's Republic of Yugoslavia on Mutual Legal Assistance, signed at Sofia on 23 March 1956, still in force between Bulgaria and Slovenia,

– the Treaty between the People's Republic of Romania and the People's Republic of Hungary on Legal Assistance in Civil, Family and Criminal Matters, signed at Bucharest on 7 October 1958,

– the Treaty between the People's Republic of Romania and the Czechoslovak Republic on Legal Assistance in Civil, Family and Criminal Matters, signed at Prague on 25 October 1958, still in force between Romania and Slovakia,

– the Agreement between the People's Republic of Bulgaria and the Romanian People's Republic on Legal Assistance in Civil, Family and Criminal Matters, signed at Sofia on 3 December 1958,

– the Treaty between the People's Republic of Romania and the Federal People's Republic of Yugoslavia on Legal Assistance, signed at Belgrade on 18 October 1960 and its Protocol, still in force between Romania and Slovenia,

– the Agreement between the People's Republic of Bulgaria and the Polish People's Republic on Legal Assistance and Legal Relations in Civil, Family and Criminal Matters, signed at Warsaw on 4 December 1961,

– the Convention between the Socialist Republic of Romania and the Republic of Austria on Legal Assistance in Civil and Family law and the Validity and Service of Documents and its annexed Protocol, signed at Vienna on 17 November 1965,

Paragraph numbers marked with a "+" can be found online and on CD.

– the Agreement between the People's Republic of Bulgaria and the Hungarian People's Republic on Legal Assistance in Civil, Family and Criminal Matters, signed at Sofia on 16 May 1966,

– the Convention between the Socialist Republic of Romania and the Hellenic Republic on Legal Assistance in Civil and Criminal Matters and its Protocol, signed at Bucharest on 19 October 1972,

– the Convention between the Socialist Republic of Romania and the Italian Republic on Judicial Assistance in Civil and Criminal Matters, signed at Bucharest on 11 November 1972,

– the Convention between the Socialist Republic of Romania and the French Republic on Legal Assistance in Civil and Commercial Matters, signed at Paris on 5 November 1974,

– the Convention between the Socialist Republic of Romania and the Kingdom of Belgium on Legal Assistance in Civil and Commercial Matters, signed at Bucharest on 30 October 1975,

– the Agreement between the People's Republic of Bulgaria and the Hellenic Republic on Legal Assistance in Civil and Criminal Matters, signed at Athens on 10 April 1976,

– the Agreement between the People's Republic of Bulgaria and the Czechoslovak Socialist Republic on Legal Assistance and Settlement of Relations in Civil, Family and Criminal Matters, signed at Sofia on 25 November 1976,

– the Convention between the Socialist Republic of Romania and the United Kingdom of Great Britain and Northern Ireland on Legal Assistance in Civil and Commercial Matters, signed at London on 15 June 1978,

– the Additional Protocol to the Convention between the Socialist Republic of Romania and the Kingdom of Belgium on Legal Assistance Civil and Commercial Matters, signed at Bucharest on 30 October 1979,

– the Convention between the Socialist Republic of Romania and the Kingdom of Belgium on Recognition and Enforcement of Decisions in Alimony Obligations, signed at Bucharest on 30 October 1979,

– the Convention between the Socialist Republic of Romania and the Kingdom of Belgium on Recognition and Enforcement of Divorce Decisions, signed at Bucharest on 6 November 1980,

– the Agreement between the People's Republic of Bulgaria and the Republic of Cyprus on Legal Assistance in Civil and Criminal Matters, signed at Nicosia on 29 April 1983,

– the Agreement between the Government of the People's Republic of Bulgaria and the Government of the French Republic on Mutual Legal Assistance in Civil Matters, signed at Sofia on 18 January 1989,

– the Agreement between the People's Republic of Bulgaria and the Italian Republic on Legal Assistance and Enforcement of Decisions in Civil Matters, signed at Rome on 18 May 1990,

– the Agreement between the Republic of Bulgaria and the Kingdom of Spain on Mutual Legal Assistance in Civil Matters, signed at Sofia on 23 May 1993,

Paragraph numbers marked with a "+" can be found online and on CD.

– the Treaty between Romania and the Czech Republic on Judicial Assistance in Civil Matters, signed at Bucharest on 11 July 1994,

– the Convention between Romania and the Kingdom of Spain on Jurisdiction, Recognition and Enforcement of Decisions in Civil and Commercial Matters, signed at Bucharest on 17 November 1997,

– the Convention between Romania and the Kingdom of Spain — complementary to the Hague Convention relating to civil procedure law (Hague, 1 March 1954), signed at Bucharest on 17 November 1997,

– the Treaty between Romania and the Republic of Poland on Legal Assistance and Legal Relations in Civil Cases, signed at Bucharest on 15 May 1999.

Article 70

5–318 1. The Treaty and the Conventions referred to in Article 69 shall continue to have effect in relation to matters to which this Regulation does not apply.

2. They shall continue to have effect in respect of judgments given and documents formally drawn up or registered as authentic instruments before the entry into force of this Regulation.

Article 71

5–319 1. This Regulation shall not affect any conventions to which the Member States are parties and which in relation to particular matters, govern jurisdiction or the recognition or enforcement of judgments.

2. With a view to its uniform interpretation, paragraph 1 shall be applied in the following manner:

(a) this Regulation shall not prevent a court of a Member State, which is a party to a convention on a particular matter, from assuming jurisdiction in accordance with that convention, even where the defendant is domiciled in another Member State which is not a party to that convention. The court hearing the action shall, in any event, apply Article 26 of this Regulation;

(b) judgments given in a Member State by a court in the exercise of jurisdiction provided for in a convention on a particular matter shall be recognised and enforced in the other Member States in accordance with this Regulation.

Where a convention on a particular matter to which both the Member State of origin and the Member State addressed are parties lays down conditions for the recognition or enforcement of judgments, those conditions shall apply. In any event, the provisions of this Regulation which concern the procedure for recognition and enforcement of judgments may be applied.

Article 72

5–320 This Regulation shall not affect agreements by which Member States undertook, prior to the entry into force of this Regulation pursuant to Article 59 of the Brussels Convention, not to recognise judgments given, in particular in other Contracting States to that Convention, against defendants domiciled or habitually resident in a third

Paragraph numbers marked with a "+" can be found online and on CD.

country where, in cases provided for in Article 4 of that Convention, the judgment could only be founded on a ground of jurisdiction specified in the second paragraph of Article 3 of that Convention.

CHAPTER VIII—FINAL PROVISIONS

Article 73

No later than five years after the entry into force of this Regula- **5–321** tion, the Commission shall present to the European Parliament, the Council and the Economic and Social Committee a report on the application of this Regulation. The report shall be accompanied, if need be, by proposals for adaptations to this Regulation.

Article 74

1. The Member States shall notify the Commission of the texts **5–322** amending the lists set out in Annexes I to IV. The Commission shall adapt the Annexes concerned accordingly.

2. The updating or technical adjustment of the forms, specimens of which appear in Annexes V and VI, shall be adopted in accordance with the advisory procedure referred to in Article 75(2).

Article 75

1. The Commission shall be assisted by a committee. **5–323**

2. Where reference is made to this paragraph, Articles 3 and 7 of Decision 1999/468/EC shall apply.

3. The Committee shall adopt its rules of procedure.

Article 76

This Regulation shall enter into force on 1 March 2002. **5–324**

This Regulation is binding in its entirety and directly applicable in the Member States in accordance with the Treaty establishing the European Community.

Done at Brussels, 22 December 2000.

For the Council

The President

C. Pierret

Annex I

[*Text omitted*] **5–325**

Annex II

[*Text omitted*] **5–326**

Annex III

[*Text omitted*] **5–327**

Annex IV

[*Text omitted*] **5–328**

Annex V

**Certificate referred to in Articles 54 and 58 of the Regulation on 5–329
judgments and court settlements**

(English, inglés, anglais, ingleses, ...)

Paragraph numbers marked with a "+" can be found online and on CD.

1. Member State of origin
2. Court or competent authority issuing the certificate
    2.1. Name
    2.2. Address
    2.3. Tel./fax/email
3. Court which delivered the judgment/approved the court settlement (*)
    3.1. Type of court
    3.2. Place of court
4. Judgment/court settlement (*)
    4.1. Date
    4.2. Reference number
    4.3. The parties to the judgment/court settlement (*)
        4.3.1. Name(s) of plaintiff(s)
        4.3.2. Name(s) of defendant(s)
        4.3.3. Name(s) of other party(ies), if any
    4.4. Date of service of the document instituting the proceedings where judgment was given in default of appearance
    4.5. Text of the judgment/court settlement (*) as annexed to this certificate
5. Names of parties to whom legal aid has been granted

The judgment.court settlement (*) is enforceable in the Member State of origin (Articles 38 and 58 of the Regulation) against:

Name:

Done at .... date ....

Signature and/or stamp ....
(*) Delete as appropriate

Annex VI

5–330   **Certificate referred to in Article 57(4) of the Regulation on authentic instruments**
(English, inglés, anglais, ingleses, ...)

1. Member State of origin
2. Competent authority issuing the certificate
    2.1. Name
    2.2. Address
    2.3. Tel./fax/email
3. Authority which has given authenticity to the instrument
    3.1. Authority involved in the drawing up of the authentic instrument (if applicable)
        3.1.1. Name and designation of authority
        3.1.2. Place of authority
    3.2. Authority which has registered the authentic instrument (if applicable)
        3.2.1. Type of authority
        3.2.2. Place of authority
4. Authentic instrument
    4.1. Description of the instrument
    4.2. Date
        4.2.1. on which the instrument was drawn up
        4.2.2. if different: on which the instrument was registered

Paragraph numbers marked with a "+" can be found online and on CD.

4.3. Reference number

4.4. Parties to the instrument

    4.4.1. Name of the creditor

    4.4.2. Name of the debtor

5. Text of the enforceable obligation as annexed to this certificate

The authentic instrument is enforceable against the debtor in the Member State of origin (Article 57(1) of the Regulation)

Done at .... date ....

Signature and/or stamp ....

Council Regulation (EC) No.1206/2001 of 28 May 2001 on cooperation between the courts of the Member States in the taking of evidence in civil or commercial matters

CHAPTER 1—GENERAL PROVISIONS

Article 1

Scope

1. This Regulation shall apply in civil or commercial matters where **5–331** the court of a Member State, in accordance with the provisions of the law of that State, requests:

(a) the competent court of another Member State to take evidence; or

(b) to take evidence directly in another Member State.

2. A request shall not be made to obtain evidence which is not intended for use in judicial proceedings, commenced or contemplated.

3. In this Regulation, the term "Member State" shall mean Member States with the exception of Denmark.

Article 2

Direct transmission between the courts

1. Requests pursuant to Article 1(1)(a), hereinafter referred to as **5–332** "requests", shall be transmitted by the court before which the proceedings are commenced or contemplated, hereinafter referred to as the "requesting court", directly to the competent court of another Member State, hereinafter referred to as the "requested court", for the performance of the taking of evidence.

2. Each Member State shall draw up a list of the courts competent for the performance of taking of evidence according to this Regulation. The list shall also indicate the territorial and, where appropriate, the special jurisdiction of those courts.

Article 3

Central body

1. Each Member State shall designate a central body responsible **5–333** for:

(a) supplying information to the courts;

Paragraph numbers marked with a "+" can be found online and on CD.

(b) seeking solutions to any difficulties which may arise in respect of a request;

(c) forwarding, in exceptional cases, at the request of a requesting court, a request to the competent court.

2. A federal State, a State in which several legal systems apply or a State with autonomous territorial entities shall be free to designate more than one central body.

3. Each Member State shall also designate the central body referred to in paragraph 1 or one or several competent authority(ies) to be responsible for taking decisions on requests pursuant to Article 17.

CHAPTER II—TRANSMISSION AND EXECUTION OF REQUESTS

SECTION 1—TRANSMISSION OF THE REQUEST

Article 4

Form and content of the request

5–334   1. The request shall be made using form A or, where appropriate, form I in the Annex. It shall contain the following details:

(a) the requesting and, where appropriate, the requested court;

(b) the names and addresses of the parties to the proceedings and their representatives, if any;

(c) the nature and subject matter of the case and a brief statement of the facts;

(d) a description of the taking of evidence to be performed;

(e) where the request is for the examination of a person:
- the name(s) and address(es) of the person(s) to be examined,
- the questions to be put to the person(s) to be examined or a statement of the facts about which he is (they are) to be examined,
- where appropriate, a reference to a right to refuse to testify under the law of the Member State of the requesting court,
- any requirement that the examination is to be carried out under oath or affirmation in lieu thereof, and any special form to be used,
- where appropriate, any other information that the requesting court deems necessary;

(f) where the request is for any other form of taking of evidence, the documents or other objects to be inspected;

(g) where appropriate, any request pursuant to Article 10(3) and (4), and Articles 11 and 12 and any information necessary for the application thereof.

2. The request and all documents accompanying the request shall be exempted from authentication or any equivalent formality.

3. Documents which the requesting court deems it necessary to enclose for the execution of the request shall be accompanied by a translation into the language in which the request was written.

Paragraph numbers marked with a "+" can be found online and on CD.

Article 5

Language

The request and communications pursuant to this Regulation **5–335** shall be drawn up in the official language of the requested Member State or, if there are several official languages in that Member State, in the official language or one of the official languages of the place where the requested taking of evidence is to be performed, or in another language which the requested Member State has indicated it can accept. Each Member State shall indicate the official language or languages of the institutions of the European Community other than its own which is or are acceptable to it for completion of the forms.

Article 6

Transmission of requests and other communications

Requests and communications pursuant to this Regulation shall **5–336** be transmitted by the swiftest possible means, which the requested Member State has indicated it can accept. The transmission may be carried out by any appropriate means, provided that the document received accurately reflects the content of the document forwarded and that all information in it is legible.

SECTION 2—RECEIPT OF REQUEST

Article 7

Receipt of request

1. Within seven days of receipt of the request, the requested **5–337** competent court shall send an acknowledgement of receipt to the requesting court using form B in the Annex. Where the request does not comply with the conditions laid down in Articles 5 and 6, the requested court shall enter a note to that effect in the acknowledgement of receipt.

2. Where the execution of a request made using form A in the Annex, which complies with the conditions laid down in Article 5, does not fall within the jurisdiction of the court to which it was transmitted, the latter shall forward the request to the competent court of its Member State and shall inform the requesting court thereof using form A in the Annex.

Article 8

Incomplete request

1. If a request cannot be executed because it does not contain all of **5–338** the necessary information pursuant to Article 4, the requested court shall inform the requesting court thereof without delay and, at the latest, within 30 days of receipt of the request using form C in the Annex, and shall request it to send the missing information, which should be indicated as precisely as possible.

2. If a request cannot be executed because a deposit or advance is necessary in accordance with Article 18(3), the requested court shall inform the requesting court thereof without delay and, at the latest,

Paragraph numbers marked with a "+" can be found online and on CD.

within 30 days of receipt of the request using form C in the Annex and inform the requesting court how the deposit or advance should be made. The requested Court shall acknowledge receipt of the deposit or advance without delay, at the latest within 10 days of receipt of the deposit or the advance using form D.

Article 9

Completion of the request

5–339   1. If the requested court has noted on the acknowledgement of receipt pursuant to Article 7(1) that the request does not comply with the conditions laid down in Articles 5 and 6 or has informed the requesting court pursuant to Article 8 that the request cannot be executed because it does not contain all of the necessary information pursuant to Article 4, the time limit pursuant to Article 10 shall begin to run when the requested court received the request duly completed.

2. Where the requested court has asked for a deposit or advance in accordance with Article 18(3), this time limit shall begin to run when the deposit or the advance is made.

Section 3—Taking of evidence by the requested court

Article 10

General provisions on the execution of the request

5–340   1. The requested court shall execute the request without delay and, at the latest, within 90 days of receipt of the request.

2. The requested court shall execute the request in accordance with the law of its Member State.

3. The requesting court may call for the request to be executed in accordance with a special procedure provided for by the law of its Member State, using form A in the Annex. The requested court shall comply with such a requirement unless this procedure is incompatible with the law of the Member State of the requested court or by reason of major practical difficulties. If the requested court does not comply with the requirement for one of these reasons it shall inform the requesting court using form E in the Annex.

4. The requesting court may ask the requested court to use communications technology at the performance of the taking of evidence, in particular by using videoconference and teleconference. The requested court shall comply with such a requirement unless this is incompatible with the law of the Member State of the requested court or by reason of major practical difficulties. If the requested court does not comply with the requirement for one of these reasons, it shall inform the requesting court, using form E in the Annex. If there is no access to the technical means referred to above in the requesting or in the requested court, such means may be made available by the courts by mutual agreement.

Article 11

Performance with the presence and participation of the parties

5–341   1. If it is provided for by the law of the Member State of the requesting court, the parties and, if any, their representatives, have

Paragraph numbers marked with a "+" can be found online and on CD.

the right to be present at the performance of the taking of evidence by the requested court.

2. The requesting court shall, in its request, inform the requested court that the parties and, if any, their representatives, will be present and, where appropriate, that their participation is requested, using form A in the Annex. This information may also be given at any other appropriate time.

3. If the participation of the parties and, if any, their representatives, is requested at the performance of the taking of evidence, the requested court shall determine, in accordance with Article 10, the conditions under which they may participate.

4. The requested court shall notify the parties and, if any, their representatives, of the time when, the place where, the proceedings will take place, and, where appropriate, the conditions under which they may participate, using form F in the Annex.

5. Paragraphs 1 to 4 shall not affect the possibility for the requested court of asking the parties and, if any their representatives, to be present at or to participate in the performance of the taking of evidence if that possibility is provided for by the law of its Member State.

Article 12

Performance with the presence and participation of representatives of the requesting court

1. If it is compatible with the law of the Member State of the **5–342** requesting court, representatives of the requesting court have the right to be present in the performance of the taking of evidence by the requested court.

2. For the purpose of this Article, the term "representative" shall include members of the judicial personnel designated by the requesting court, in accordance with the law of its Member State. The requesting court may also designate, in accordance with the law of its Member State, any other person, such as an expert.

3. The requesting court shall, in its request, inform the requested court that its representatives will be present and, where appropriate, that their participation is requested, using form A in the Annex. This information may also be given at any other appropriate time.

4. If the participation of the representatives of the requesting court is requested in the performance of the taking of evidence, the requested court shall determine, in accordance with Article 10, the conditions under which they may participate.

5. The requested court shall notify the requesting court, of the time when, and the place where, the proceedings will take place, and, where appropriate, the conditions under which the representatives may participate, using form F in the Annex.

Article 13

Coercive measures

Where necessary, in executing a request the requested court **5–343** shall apply the appropriate coercive measures in the instances and to

Paragraph numbers marked with a "+" can be found online and on CD.

the extent as are provided for by the law of the Member State of the requested court for the execution of a request made for the same purpose by its national authorities or one of the parties concerned.

Article 14

Refusal to execute

5–344   1. A request for the hearing of a person shall not be executed when the person concerned claims the right to refuse to give evidence or to be prohibited from giving evidence,

(a) under the law of the Member State of the requested court; or

(b) under the law of the Member State of the requesting court, and such right has been specified in the request, or, if need be, at the instance of the requested court, has been confirmed by the requesting court.

2. In addition to the grounds referred to in paragraph 1, the execution of a request may be refused only if:

(a) the request does not fall within the scope of this Regulation as set out in Article 1; or

(b) the execution of the request under the law of the Member State of the requested court does not fall within the functions of the judiciary; or

(c) the requesting court does not comply with the request of the requested court to complete the request pursuant to Article 8 within 30 days after the requested court asked it to do so; or

(d) a deposit or advance asked for in accordance with Article 18(3) is not made within 60 days after the requested court asked for such a deposit or advance.

3. Execution may not be refused by the requested court solely on the ground that under the law of its Member State a court of that Member State has exclusive jurisdiction over the subject matter of the action or that the law of that Member State would not admit the right of action on it.

4. If execution of the request is refused on one of the grounds referred to in paragraph 2, the requested court shall notify the requesting court thereof within 60 days of receipt of the request by the requested court using form H in the Annex.

Article 15

Notification of delay

5–345   If the requested court is not in a position to execute the request within 90 days of receipt, it shall inform the requesting court thereof, using form G in the Annex. When it does so, the grounds for the delay shall be given as well as the estimated time that the requested court expects it will need to execute the request.

Article 16

Procedure after execution of the request

5–346   The requested court shall send without delay to the requesting court the documents establishing the execution of the request and,

Paragraph numbers marked with a "+" can be found online and on CD.

where appropriate, return the documents received from the requesting court. The documents shall be accompanied by a confirmation of execution using form H in the Annex.

SECTION 4—DIRECT TAKING OF EVIDENCE BY THE REQUESTING COURT

Article 17

Direct taking of evidence by the requesting court Article 17

1. Where a court requests to take evidence directly in another **5–347** Member State, it shall submit a request to the central body or the competent authority referred to in Article 3(3) in that State, using form I in the Annex.

2. Direct taking of evidence may only take place if it can be performed on a voluntary basis without the need for coercive measures. Where the direct taking of evidence implies that a person shall be heard, the requesting court shall inform that person that the performance shall take place on a voluntary basis.

3. The taking of evidence shall be performed by a member of the judicial personnel or by any other person such as an expert, who will be designated, in accordance with the law of the Member State of the requesting court.

4. Within 30 days of receiving the request, the central body or the competent authority of the requested Member State shall inform the requesting court if the request is accepted and, if necessary, under what conditions according to the law of its Member State such performance is to be carried out, using form J. In particular, the central body or the competent authority may assign a court of its Member State to take part in the performance of the taking of evidence in order to ensure the proper application of this Article and the conditions that have been set out. The central body or the competent authority shall encourage the use of communications technology, such as videoconferences and teleconferences.

5. The central body or the competent authority may refuse direct taking of evidence only if:

(a) the request does not fall within the scope of this Regulation as set out in Article 1;

(b) the request does not contain all of the necessary information pursuant to Article 4; or

(c) the direct taking of evidence requested is contrary to fundamental principles of law in its Member State.

6. Without prejudice to the conditions laid down in accordance with paragraph 4, the requesting court shall execute the request in accordance with the law of its Member State.

SECTION 5—COSTS

Article 18

1. The execution of the request, in accordance with Article 10, **5–348** shall not give rise to a claim for any reimbursement of taxes or costs.

2. Nevertheless, if the requested court so requires, the requesting court shall ensure the reimbursement, without delay, of:

Paragraph numbers marked with a "+" can be found online and on CD.

– the fees paid to experts and interpreters, and

– the costs occasioned by the application of Article 10(3) and(4).

The duty for the parties to bear these fees or costs shall be governed by the law of the Member State of the requesting court.

3. Where the opinion of an expert is required, the requested court may, before executing the request, ask the requesting court for an adequate deposit or advance towards the requested costs. In all other cases, a deposit or advance shall not be a condition for the execution of a request. The deposit or advance shall be made by the parties if that is provided for by the law of the Member State of the requesting court.

CHAPTER III—FINAL PROVISIONS

Article 19

Implementing rules

5–349   1. The Commission shall draw up and regularly update a manual, which shall also be available electronically, containing the information provided by the Member States in accordance with Article 22 and the agreements or arrangements in force, according to Article 21.

2. The updating or making of technical amendments to the standard forms set out in the Annex shall be carried out in accordance with the advisory procedure set out in Article 20(2).

Article 20

Committee

5–350   1. The Commission shall be assisted by a Committee.

2. Where reference is made to this paragraph, Articles 3 and 7 of Decision 1999/468/EC shall apply.

3. The Committee shall adopt its Rules of Procedure.

Article 21

Relationship with existing or future agreements or arrangements between Member States

5–351   1. This Regulation shall, in relation to matters to which it applies, prevail over other provisions contained in bilateral or multilateral agreements or arrangements concluded by the Member States and in particular the Hague Convention of 1 March 1954 on Civil Procedure and the Hague Convention of 18 March 1970 on the Taking of Evidence Abroad in Civil or Commercial Matters, in relations between the Member States party thereto.

2. This Regulation shall not preclude Member States from maintaining or concluding agreements or arrangements between two or more of them to further facilitate the taking of evidence, provided that they are compatible with this Regulation.

3. Member States shall send to the Commission:

(a) by 1 July 2003, a copy of the agreements or arrangements maintained between the Member States referred to in paragraph 2;

Paragraph numbers marked with a "+" can be found online and on CD.

(b) a copy of the agreements or arrangements concluded between the Member States referred to in paragraph 2 as well as drafts of such agreements or arrangements which they intend to adopt; and

(c) any denunciation of, or amendments to, these agreements or arrangements

Article 22

Communication

By 1 July 2003 each Member State shall communicate to the Commission the following: **5–352**

(a) the list pursuant to Article 2(2) indicating the territorial and, where appropriate, the special jurisdiction of the courts;

(b) the names and addresses of the central bodies and competent authorities pursuant to Article 3, indicating their territorial jurisdiction;

(c) the technical means for the receipt of requests available to the courts on the list pursuant to Article 2(2);

(d) the languages accepted for the requests as referred to in Article 5.

Member States shall inform the Commission of any subsequent changes to this information.

Article 23

Review

No later than 1 January 2007, and every five years thereafter, the Commission shall present to the European Parliament, the Council and the Economic and Social Committee a report on the application of this Regulation, paying special attention to the practical application of Article 3(1)(c) and 3, and Articles 17 and 18. **5–353**

Article 24

Entry into force

1. This Regulation shall enter into force on 1 July 2001. **5–354**

2. This Regulation shall apply from 1 January 2004, except for Articles 19, 21 and 22, which shall apply from 1 July 2001.

This Regulation shall be binding in its entirety and directly applicable in the Member States in accordance with the Treaty establishing the European Community. Done at Brussels, 28 May 2001.   For the Council The President T. Bodström

Paragraph numbers marked with a "+" can be found online and on CD.

ANNEX

FORM A

Request for the taking of evidence

(Article 4 of Council Regulation (EC) No 1206/2001 of 28 May 2001 on cooperation between the courts of the Member States in the taking of evidence in civil or commercial matters (OJ L 174, 27.6.2001, p. 1))

---

1. Reference of the requesting court:

2. Reference of the requested court:

3. Requesting court:

    3.1.   Name:

    3.2.   Address:

           3.2.1.   Street and No/PO box:

           3.2.2.   Place and postcode:

           3.2.3.   Country:

    3.3.   Tel.

    3.4.   Fax

    3.5.   E-mail:

4. Requested court:

    4.1.   Name:

    4.2.   Address:

           4.2.1.   Street and No/PO box:

           4.2.2.   Place and postcode:

           4.2.3.   Country:

    4.3.   Tel.

    4.4.   Fax

    4.5.   E-mail:

5. In the case brought by the claimant/petitioner:

    5.1.   Name:

    5.2.   Address:

           5.2.1.   Street and No/PO box:

           5.2.2.   Place and postcode:

           5.2.3.   Country:

Paragraph numbers marked with a "+" can be found online and on CD.

5.3.   Tel.

5.4.   Fax

5.5.   E-mail:

6.   Representatives of the claimant/petitioner:

   6.1.   Name:

   6.2.   Address:

      6.2.1.   Street and No/PO box:

      6.2.2.   Place and postcode:

      6.2.3.   Country:

   6.3.   Tel.

   6.4.   Fax

   6.5.   E-mail:

7.   Against the defendant/respondent:

   7.1.   Name:

   7.2.   Address:

      7.2.1.   Street and No/PO box:

      7.2.2.   Place and postcode:

      7.2.3.   Country:

   7.3.   Tel.

   7.4.   Fax

   7.5.   E-mail:

8.   Representatives of defendant/respondent:

   8.1.   Name:

   8.2.   Address:

      8.2.1.   Street and No/PO box:

      8.2.2.   Place and postcode:

      8.2.3.   Country:

   8.3.   Tel:

   8.4.   Fax:

   8.5.   E-mail:

Paragraph numbers marked with a "+" can be found online and on CD.

9. Presence and participation of the parties:

    9.1. Parties and, if any, their representatives will be present at the taking of evidence: ☐

    9.2. Participation of the parties and, if any, their representatives is requested: ☐

10. Presence and participation of the representatives of the requesting court:

    10.1. Representatives will be present at the taking of evidence: ☐

    10.2. Participation of the representatives is requested: ☐

        10.2.1. Name:

        10.2.2. Title:

        10.2.3. Function:

        10.2.4. Task:

11. Nature and subject matter of the case and a brief statement of the facts (in annex, where appropriate):

12. Taking of evidence to be performed

    12.1. Description of the taking of evidence to be performed (in annex, where appropriate):

    12.2. Examination of witnesses:

        12.2.1. Name and surname:

        12.2.2. Address:

        12.2.3. Tel.

        12.2.4. Fax

        12.2.5. E-mail:

        12.2.6. Questions to be put to the witness or a statement of the facts about which they are to be examined (in annex, where appropriate):

        12.2.7. Right to refuse to testify under the law of the Member State of the requesting court (in annex, where appropriate):

        12.2.8. Please examine the witness:

            12.2.8.1. under oath: ☐

            12.2.8.2. on affirmation: ☐

        12.2.9. Any other information that the requesting court deems necessary (in annex, where appropriate):

    12.3. Other taking of evidence:

        12.3.1. Documents to be inspected and a description of the requested taking of evidence (in annex, where appropriate):

        12.3.2. Objects to be inspected and a description of the requested taking of evidence (in annex, where appropriate):

Paragraph numbers marked with a "+" can be found online and on CD.

13. Please execute the request

    13.1.   In accordance with a special procedure (Article 10(3)) provided for by the law of the Member State of the requesting court and/or by the use of communications technology (Article 10(4)) described in annex:

    13.2.   Following information is necessary for the application thereof:

Done at:

Date:

Notification of forwarding the request

Article 7(2) of Council Regulation (EC) No 1206/2001 of 28 May 2001 on cooperation between the courts of the Member States in the taking of evidence in civil or commercial matters (OJ L 174, 27.6.2001, p. 1).

---

14. The request does not fall within the jurisdiction of the court indicated in point 4 above and was forwarded to

    14.1.   Name of the competent court:

    14.2.   Address:

        14.2.1.   Street and No/PO box:

        14.2.2.   Place and postcode:

        14.2.3.   Country:

    14.3.   Tel.

    14.4.   Fax

    14.5.   E-mail:

Done at:

Date:

Paragraph numbers marked with a "+" can be found online and on CD.

FORM B

Acknowledgement of receipt of a request for the taking of evidence

(Article 7(1) of Council Regulation (EC) No 1206/2001 of 28 May 2001 on cooperation between the courts of the Member States in the taking of evidence in civil or commercial matters (OJ L 174, 27.6.2001, p. 1))

1. Reference of the requesting court:

2. Reference of the requested court:

3. Name of the requesting court:

4. Requested court:

    4.1. Name:

    4.2. Address:

        4.2.1. Street and No/PO box:

        4.2.2. Place and postcode:

        4.2.3. Country:

    4.3. Tel.

    4.4. Fax

    4.5. E-mail:

5. The request was received on … (date of receipt) by the court indicated in point 4 above.

6. The request cannot be dealt with because:

    6.1. The language used to complete the form is not acceptable (Article 5): ☐

        6.1.1. Please use one the following languages:

    6.2. The document is not legible (Article 6): ☐

Done at:

Date:

Paragraph numbers marked with a "+" can be found online and on CD.

FORM E

Notification concerning the request for special procedures and/or for the use of communications technologies

(Article 10(3) and (4) of Council Regulation (EC) No 1206/2001 of 28 May 2001 on cooperation between the courts of the Member States in the taking of evidence in civil or commercial matters (OJ L 174, 27.6.2001, p. 1))

EUROPE

1. Reference of the requested court:

2. Reference of the requesting court:

3. Name of the requesting court:

4. Name of the requested court:

5. The requirement for execution of the request according to the special procedure indicated in point 13.1 of the request (Form A) could not be complied with because:

    5.1.   the required procedure is incompatible with the law of the Member State of the requested court: ☐

    5.2.   the performance of the requested procedure is not possible by reason of major practical difficulties: ☐

6. The requirement for execution of the request for the use of communications technologies indicated in point 13.1 of the request (Form A) could not be complied with because:

    6.1.   The use of communications technology is incompatible with the law of the Member State of the requested court ☐

    6.2.   The use of the communications technology is not possible by reason of major practical difficulties ☐

Done at:

Date:

Paragraph numbers marked with a "+" can be found online and on CD.

FORM F

Notification of the date, time, place of performance of the taking of evidence and the conditions for participation

(Articles 11(4) and 12(5) of Council Regulation (EC) No 1206/2001 of 28 May 2001 on cooperation between the courts of the Member States in the taking of evidence in civil or commercial matters (OJ L 174, 27.6.2001, p. 1))

---

1.   Reference of the requesting court:

2.   Reference of the requested court:

3.   Requesting court

    3.1.   Name:

    3.2.   Address:

        3.2.1.   Street and No/PO box:

        3.2.2.   Place and postcode:

        3.2.3.   Country:

    3.3.   Tel.

    3.4.   Fax

    3.5.   E-mail:

4.   Requested court

    4.1.   Name:

    4.2.   Address:

        4.2.1.   Street and No/PO box:

        4.2.2.   Place and postcode:

        4.2.3.   Country:

    4.3.   Tel.

    4.4.   Fax

    4.5.   E-mail:

5.   Date and time of the performance of the taking of evidence:

6.   Place of the performance of the taking of evidence, if different from that referred to in point 4 above:

7.   Where appropriate, conditions under which the parties and, if any, their representatives may participate:

Paragraph numbers marked with a "+" can be found online and on CD.

8.   Where appropriate, conditions under which the representatives of the requesting court may participate:

Done at:

Date:

FORM G

Notification of delay

(Article 15 of Council Regulation (EC) No 1206/2001 of 28 May 2001 on cooperation between the courts of the Member States in the taking of evidence in civil or commercial matters (OJ L 174, 27.6.2001, p. 1))

---

1. Reference of the requested court:

2. Reference of the requesting court:

3. Name of the requesting court:

4. Name of the requested court:

5. The request can not be executed within 90 days of receipt for the following reasons:

6. It is estimated that the request will be executed by ... (indicate an estimated date)

Done at:

Date:

Paragraph numbers marked with a "+" can be found online and on CD.

FORM H

Information on the outcome of the request

(Articles 14 and 16 of Council Regulation (EC) No 1206/2001 of 28 May 2001 on cooperation between the courts of the Member States in the taking of evidence in civil or commercial matters (OJ L 174, 27.6.2001, p. 1))

---

1. Reference of the requested court:

2. Reference of the requesting court:

3. Name of the requesting court:

4. Name of the requested court:

5. The request has been executed. ☐

   The documents establishing execution of the request are attached:

6. Execution of the request has been refused because:

   6.1. the person to be examined has claimed the right to refuse to give evidence or has claimed to be prohibited from giving evidence:

      6.1.1. under the law of the Member State of the requested court: ☐

      6.1.2. under the law of the Member State of the requesting court: ☐

   6.2. The request does not fall within the scope of this Regulation ☐

   6.3. Under the law of the Member State of the requested court, the execution of the request does not fall within the functions of the judiciary: ☐

   6.4. The requesting court has not complied with the request for additional information from the requested court dated ... (date of the request): ☐

   6.5. A deposit or advance asked for in accordance with Article 18(3) has not been made: ☐

Done at:

Date:

Paragraph numbers marked with a "+" can be found online and on CD.

FORM I

Request for direct taking of evidence

(Article 17 of Council Regulation (EC) No 1206/2001 of 28 May 2001 on cooperation between the courts of the Member States in the taking of evidence in civil or commercial matters (OJ L 174, 27.6.2001, p. 1))

1. Reference of the requesting court:

2. Reference of the central body/competent authority:

3. Requesting court:

   3.1. Name:

   3.2. Address:

      3.2.1. Street and No/PO box:

      3.2.2. Place and postcode:

      3.2.3. Country:

   3.3. Tel.

   3.4. Fax

   3.5. E-mail:

4. Central body/competent authority of the requested State:

   4.1. Name:

   4.2. Address:

      4.2.1. Street and No/PO box:

      4.2.2. Place and postcode:

      4.2.3. Country:

   4.3. Tel.

   4.4. Fax

   4.5. E-mail:

5. In the case brought by the claimant/petitioner:

   5.1. Name:

   5.2. Address:

      5.2.1. Street and No/PO box:

      5.2.2. Place and postcode:

      5.2.3. Country:

Paragraph numbers marked with a "+" can be found online and on CD.

FORM J

Information from the central body/competent authority

(Article 17 of Council Regulation (EC) No 1206/2001 of 28 May 2001 on cooperation between the courts of the Member States in the taking of evidence in civil or commercial matters (OJ L 174, 27.6.2001, p. 1))

1. Reference of the requesting court:

2. Reference of the central body/competent authority:

3. Name of the requesting court:

4. Central body/competent authority:

    4.1. Name:

    4.2. Address:

        4.2.1. Street and No/PO box:

        4.2.2. Place and postcode:

        4.2.3. Country:

    4.3. Tel.

    4.4. Fax

    4.5. E-mail:

5. Information from the central body/competent authority:

    5.1. Direct taking of evidence in accordance with the request is accepted: ☐

    5.2. Direct taking of evidence in accordance with the request is accepted under the following conditions (in annex, where appropriate): ☐

    5.3. Direct taking of evidence in accordance with the request is refused for the following reasons:

        5.3.1. The request does not fall within the scope of this Regulation: ☐

        5.3.2. The request does not contain all of the necessary information pursuant to Article 4: ☐

        5.3.3. The direct taking of evidence requested for is contrary to fundamental principles of law of the Member State of the central body/competent authority: ☐

Done at:

Date:

_____

Paragraph numbers marked with a "+" can be found online and on CD.

Regulation (EC) No.805/2004 of the European Parliament and of the Council of 21 April 2004 creating a European Enforcement Order for uncontested claims

5–356

For Regulation (EC) No.805/2004 see paragraphs 5–357+ to 5–390+ on White Book on Westlaw UK or the Civil Procedure CD.

Paragraph numbers marked with a "+" can be found online and on CD.

6A   COURT FUNDS

Supreme Court Act 1981

(1981 c.54)

Accountant General of the Supreme Court

97.—(1) There shall continue to be an Accountant General of, and **6A-1**
an accounting department for, the Supreme Court.

(2) The Lord Chancellor shall appoint such person as he thinks
fit to the office in the Supreme Court of Accountant General of the
Supreme Court, and the person so appointed shall hold and vacate
office in accordance with the terms of his appointment.

(3) The Accountant General shall be paid such salary or fees as
the Lord Chancellor determines with the consent of the Treasury.

(4) If one person holds office both as the Accountant General and
as the Public Trustee then, if he ceases to be the Public Trustee, he
shall also cease to be the Accountant General unless the Lord
Chancellor otherwise directs.

(5) If a vacancy occurs in the office of Accountant General or the
person appointed to hold the office is for any reason unable to act for
any period such person as the Lord Chancellor appoints as deputy in
that office shall, during the vacancy or that period, perform the functions of that office (and any property vested in the Accountant General may accordingly be dealt with by the deputy in all respects as if
it were vested in him instead).

Note —Amended by the Public Trustee and Administration of Funds Act 1986 **6A-2**
Sch.3, para.5.

Court Funds Office

The name of this office has replaced the former name of the Supreme Court Pay **6A-3**
Office (see the Supreme Court Funds Rules 1975 r.3, paras 6A–26)This office is the office of the Accountant General of the Supreme Court (SCA 1981 s.97). The machinery
of this office is governed by the Court Funds Rules 1987 made by the Lord Chancellor, with the concurrence of the Treasury, under the powers conferred by AJA 1982
s.38(2) and (7). Pt VI of the AJA 1982 was brought into force by the Public Trustee
and Administration of Funds Act 1986.

Administration of Justice Act 1982

(1982 c.53)   **6A-4**

ARRANGEMENT OF SECTIONS

PART VI

FUNDS IN COURT

Paragraph numbers marked with a "+" can be found online and on CD.

PART VI

FUNDS IN COURT

Management and investment of funds in court

6A–5   **38.**—(1) Subject to rules made under subsection (7) below, all sums of money, securities and effects paid and deposited in, or under the custody of—

    (a) the High Court;

    (b) a county court; or

    (c) such other courts and tribunals as the Lord Chancellor may by rules made under that subsection prescribe,

shall be vested in the Accountant General.

(2) One or more accounts shall be opened and kept in the name of the Accountant General at such bank or banks as may be designated by the Lord Chancellor with the concurrence of the Treasury.

(3) Money and securities held by the Accountant General shall vest in his successor in office without any assignment or transfer.

(4) A sum of money paid and deposited in court may[...] be invested and reinvested by the Accountant General in any manner authorised by rules made under subsection (7) below.

(5) [...]

(6) The Accountant General may, in such cases as the Lord Chancellor may by rules made under subsection (7) below prescribe, apply to the court for an order for directions as to the manner in which a particular fund in court is to be dealt with.

(7) The Lord Chancellor, with the concurrence of the Treasury, may make provision as to the payment of interest on funds in court and may make rules as to the administration and management of funds in court including the deposit, payment, delivery and transfer in, into and out of any court of funds in court and regulating the evidence of such deposit, payment, delivery or transfer.

(8) Rules made under subsection (7) above may—

    (a) provide for the discharge of the functions of the Accountant General under the rules by a person or persons appointed by him;

    (b) provide for the transfer of money in court to and from the Commissioners;

    (c) provide for money paid and deposited in a county court to be vested in, and accounted for by, a person other than the Accountant General;

    (d) prescribe cases in which interest is to be paid on funds in court;

Paragraph numbers marked with a "+" can be found online and on CD.